American Casebook Series
Hornbook Series and Basic Legal Texts
Nutshell Series

of

WEST PUBLISHING COMPANY

St. Paul, Minnesota 55102

January, 1976

ACCOUNTING

Fiflis and Kripke's Cases on Accounting for Business Lawyers, 687 pages, 1971.

ADMINISTRATIVE LAW

Davis' Basic Text on Administrative Law 3rd Ed., 617 pages, 1972.

Davis' Cases, Text and Problems on Administrative Law, 5th Ed., 650 pages, 1973.

Davis' Police Discretion, 176 pages, 1975.

Gellhorn's Administrative Law in a Nutshell, 336 pages, 1972.

Mashaw and Merrill's Cases and Materials on Introduction to the American Public Law System, 1095 pages, 1975.

Robinson and Gellhorn's Teaching Materials on The Administrative Process, 928 pages, 1974.

ADMIRALTY

Healy and Sharpe's Cases on Admiralty, 2nd Ed., 875 pages, 1974.

AGENCY

Seavey and Hall's Cases on Agency, 431 pages, 1956.

Seavey's Text on Agency, 329 pages, 1964.

See Agency-Partnership.

AGENCY-PARTNERSHIP

Henn's Cases on Agency, Partnership and Other Unincorporated Business Enterprises, 396 pages, 1972.

Seavey, Reuschlein & Hall's Cases on Agency and Partnership, 599 pages, 1962.

AGENCY-PARTNERSHIP—Continued

Steffen's Cases on Agency and Partnership, 3rd Ed., 733 pages, 1969.

ANTITRUST LAW

Gellhorn's Antitrust Law and Economics in a Nutshell, about 420 pages, 1976.

Morgan's Cases on Economic Regulation of Business, 830 pages, 1976.

Oppenheim's Cases on Robinson-Patman Act, Pamphlet, 258 pages, 1967.

Oppenheim and Weston's Cases on Antitrust, 3rd Ed., 952 pages, 1968.

Oppenheim and Weston's Supplement, 1975.

Posner's Cases on Antitrust, 885 pages, 1974.

BANKRUPTCY

MacLachlan's Text on Bankruptcy, 500 pages, 1956.

Selected Bankruptcy Statutes, 486 pages, 1974.

Selected Commercial Statutes, 1016 pages, 1973.

See Creditors' Rights.

BUSINESS ORGANIZATIONS

See Agency-Partnership.

See Corporations.

BUSINESS PLANNING

Painter's Problems and Materials in Business Planning, 791 pages, 1975.

Painter's Problems and Materials in Business Planning, 1975 Supplement.

CIVIL PROCEDURE

See Pleading and Procedure.

LAW SCHOOL PUBLICATIONS — Continued

CLINICAL TEACHING

Cooper, Rabb and Rubin's Fair Employment Litigation—Text and Materials for Student and Practitioner, 590 pages, 1975.

Freeman and Weihofen's Cases on Clinical Law Training—Interviewing and Counseling, 506 pages, 1972.

See Office Practice.

COMMERCIAL PAPER

See Commercial Transactions.
See Negotiable Instruments.

COMMERCIAL TRANSACTIONS

Murray's Problems and Materials on Commercial Law, 366 pages, 1975.

Speidel, Summers and White's Teaching Materials on Commercial and Consumer Law, 2nd Ed., 1475 pages, 1974.

Stone's Uniform Commercial Code in a Nutshell, 507 pages, 1975.

White and Summers Text on the Uniform Commercial Code, 1054 pages, 1972.

Selected Commercial Statutes, 1016 pages, 1973.

Uniform Commercial Code, Official Text With Comments, 816 pages, 1972.

See Negotiable Instruments.
See Sales.

COMMON LAW PLEADING

Koffler and Reppy's Text on Common Law Pleading, 663 pages, 1969.

McBaine's Cases, Introduction to Civil Procedure, 399 pages, 1950.

Shipman's Text on Common Law Pleading, 3rd Ed., 644 pages, 1923.

COMMUNITY PROPERTY

Burby's Cases on Community Property, 4th Ed., 342 pages, 1955.

Huie's Texas Cases on Marital Property Rights, 681 pages, 1966.

Verrall and Sammis' Cases on California Community Property, 2nd Ed., 398 pages, 1971.

CONFLICT OF LAWS

Cramton, Currie and Kay's Cases—Comments—Questions on Conflicts, 2nd Ed., 1021 pages, 1975.

Ehrenzweig's Text on Conflicts, 824 pages, 1962.

Ehrenzweig's Conflicts in a Nutshell, 3rd Ed., 432 pages, 1973.

Ehrenzweig and Louisell's Jurisdiction in a Nutshell, 3rd Ed., 291 pages, 1973.

Goodriche and Scoles' Text on Conflict of Laws, 4th Ed., 483 pages, 1964.

CONFLICT OF LAWS—Continued

Scoles and Weintraub's Cases on Conflict of Laws, 2nd Ed., 966 pages, 1972.

CONSTITUTIONAL LAW

Engdahl's Constitutional Power in a Nutshell, 411 pages, 1974.

Ginsburg's Cases on Constitutional Aspects of Sex Based Discrimination, 129 pages, 1974.

Lockhart, Kamisar and Choper's Cases — Comments — Questions on Constitutional Law, 4th Ed., 1664 pages, plus Appendix, 1975.

Lockhart, Kamisar and Choper's Cases on The American Constitution, 4th Ed., 1249 pages, plus Appendix, 1975.

Lockhart, Kamisar and Choper's Annual Supplement.

See Constitutional Rights and Liberties.

CONSTITUTIONAL RIGHTS & LIBERTIES

Lockhart, Kamisar and Choper's Cases on Constitutional Rights and Liberties, 4th Ed., 1244 pages, plus Appendix, 1975.

Lockhart, Kamisar and Choper's Annual Supplement.

CONSUMER CREDIT

Kripke's Cases on Consumer Credit, 454 pages, 1970.

Uniform Consumer Credit Code, Official Text With Comments, 218 pages, 1974.

CONSUMER PROTECTION

Epstein's Consumer Protection in a Nutshell, about 330 pages, 1976.

Schrag's Cases on Consumer Protection, 2nd Ed., Pamphlet reprint from Cooper, et al. Law and Poverty, 2nd Ed., 197 pages, 1973.

CONTRACTS

Calamari & Perillo's Text on Contracts, 621 pages, 1970.

Corbin's Cases on Contracts, 3rd Ed., 1381 pages, 1947. 1953 Supplement, 36 pages.

Corbin's Text on Contracts, Student Edition, 1224 pages, 1952.

Freedman's Cases on Contracts, 658 pages, 1973.

Fuller and Eisenberg's Cases on Contracts, 1043 pages, 1972.

Jackson's Cases on Contract Law in a Modern Society, 1404 pages, 1973.

Reitz' Cases and Materials on Contracts as Basic Commercial Law, 763 pages, 1975.

r7202—2q

II

CONTRACTS—Continued

Schaber and Rohwer's Contracts in a Nutshell, 307 pages, 1975.

Selected Commercial Statutes, 1016 pages, 1973.

Simpson's Cases on Contracts, 592 pages, 1956.

Simpson's Text on Contracts, 2nd Ed., 510 pages, 1965.

White and Summer's Text on the Uniform Commercial Code, 1054 pages, 1972.

COPYRIGHT

Nimmer's Cases on Copyright and Other Aspects of Law Pertaining to Literary, Musical and Artistic Works, 828 pages, 1971.

Nimmer's 1974 Supplement.

CORPORATIONS

Henn's Text on Corporations, 2nd Ed., 956 pages, 1970.

Henn's Cases on Corporations, 1279 pages, 1974.

Henn's Statutory Supplement to Cases on Corporations, 1974.

CORRECTIONS

Krantz' Cases on the Law of Corrections and Prisoners' Rights, 1130 pages, 1973.

Krantz' 1974 Supplement.

Krantz' The Law of Corrections and Prisoners' Rights in a Nutshell, about 350 pages, 1976.

Model Rules and Regulations on Prisoners Rights and Responsibilities, 212 pages, 1973.

CREDIT TRANSACTIONS

See Mortgages.

CREDITORS' RIGHTS

Epstein's Teaching Materials on Debtor-Creditor Relations, 525 pages, 1973.

Epstein's Debtor-Creditor Relations in a Nutshell, 309 pages, 1973.

Riesenfeld's Cases and Materials on Creditors' Remedies and Debtors' Protection, 2nd Ed., 808 pages, 1975.

Riesenfeld's Statutory Supplement, 1975.

Selected Bankruptcy Statutes, 486 pages, 1974.

CRIMINAL LAW AND PROCEDURE

Cohen and Gobert's Problems in Criminal Law, about 300 pages, 1976.

Davis' Police Discretion, 176 pages, 1975.

CRIMINAL LAW AND PROCEDURE—C't'd

Dix and Sharlot's Cases on Criminal Law, 1360 pages, 1973.

Federal Rules of Civil-Appellate-Criminal Procedure, Law School Edition, 346 pages, 1975.

Grano's Problems in Criminal Procedure, 171 pages, 1973.

Heyman and Kenety's A Homicide in the Family, 340 pages, 1975.

Israel's and LaFave's Criminal Procedure in a Nutshell, 2nd Ed., 404 pages, 1975.

Johnson's Cases, Materials and Text on the Substantive Criminal Law in its Procedural Context, 878 pages, 1975.

Kamisar, LaFave and Israel's Cases on Modern Criminal Procedure, 4th Ed., 1572 pages, plus Appendix, 1974.

Kamisar, LaFave and Israel's Cases on Basic Criminal Procedure, 4th Ed., 767 pages, plus Appendix, 1974.

Kamisar, LaFave, and Israel's Annual Criminal Procedure Supplement.

LaFave and Scott's Text on Criminal Law, 763 pages, 1972.

Loewy's Criminal Law in a Nutshell, 282 pages, 1975.

Miller's Text on Criminal Law, 649 pages, 1934.

Stumberg's Texas Cases on Criminal Law, 505 pages, 1954.

Stumberg and Maloney's Texas Cases Supplement, 117 pages, 1965.

Uviller's Cases on The Processes of Criminal Justice-Adjudication, 991 pages, 1975.

Uviller's Cases on The Processes of Criminal Justice-Investigation, 744 pages, 1974.

Vorenberg's Cases and Materials on Criminal Law and Procedure, 1044 pages, 1975.

DAMAGES

Crane's Cases on Damages, 3rd Ed., 337 pages, 1955.

McCormick's Text on Damages, 811 pages, 1935.

See Remedies.

DECEDENTS ESTATES

Mennell's California Cases, 566 pages, 1973.

See Wills, Intestate Succession, Trusts, Gifts and Future Interests.

DICTIONARIES

Black's, one volume.

Bouvier's, two volumes.

DOMESTIC RELATIONS

Clark's Cases on Domestic Relations, 2nd Ed., 918 pages, 1974.

Clark's Text on Domestic Relations, 754 pages, 1968.

Kay's Cases on Sex Based Discrimination in Family Law, 305 pages, 1974.

Paulsen's Cases on Family Law and Poverty, 2nd Ed., Pamphlet reprint from Cooper, et al. Law and Poverty, 2nd Ed., 200 pages, 1973.

See Juvenile Courts.

DRUG ABUSE

Uelman and Haddox Cases on Drug Abuse Law, 564 pages, 1974.

EDUCATION LAW

Morris' Cases on the Constitution and American Education, 833 pages, 1974.

ENVIRONMENTAL LAW

Currie's Cases and Materials on Pollution, 715 pages, 1975.

Federal Environmental Law, 1600 pages, 1974.

Hanks, Tarlock and Hanks Cases on Environmental Law and Policy, 1242 pages, 1974.

EQUITY

Cook's Cases on Equity, 4th Ed., 1192 pages, 1948.

Dobbyn's Injunctions in a Nutshell, 264 pages, 1974.

McClintock's Text on Equity, 2nd Ed., 643 pages, 1948.

Van Hecke, Leavell and Nelson's Cases on Equitable Remedies and Restitution, 2nd Ed., 717 pages, 1973.

See Remedies.

ESTATE PLANNING

Lynn's Text on Introduction to Estate Planning, 274 pages, 1975.

EVIDENCE

Broun and Meisenholder's Problems in Evidence, 130 pages, 1973.

Cleary and Strong's Cases on Evidence, 2nd Ed., 1124 pages, 1975.

Federal Rules of Evidence for United States District Courts and Magistrates, 323 pages, 1975.

McCormick, Elliott & Sutton's Cases on Evidence, 4th Ed., 1088 pages, 1971.

McCormick, Cleary, et al., Text on Evidence, 2nd Ed., 938 pages, 1972.

Rothstein's Evidence in a Nutshell, 406 pages, 1970.

FEDERAL ESTATE AND GIFT TAXATION

See Taxation.

FEDERAL INCOME TAXATION

See Taxation.

FEDERAL JURISDICTION AND PROCEDURE

Currie's Cases on Federal Courts, 2nd, 1040 pages, 1975.

Ehrenzweig and Louisell's Jurisdiction in a Nutshell, 3rd Ed., 291 pages, 1973.

Forrester, Currier and Moye's Cases on Federal Jurisdiction and Procedure, 2nd Ed., 933 pages, 1970.

Forrester, Currier and Moye's Supplement, 1973.

Merrill and Vetri's Problems in Federal Courts and Procedure, 460 pages, 1974.

Wright's Text on Federal Courts, 2nd Ed., 745 pages, 1970.

Wright's Supplement, 1972.

FUTURE INTERESTS

Gulliver's Cases on Future Interests, 624 pages, 1959.

Gulliver's Introduction to the Law of Future Interests, Pamphlet reprint from Gulliver's Cases, 87 pages, 1959.

Powell's Cases on Future Interests, 3rd Ed., 621 pages, 1961.

Simes' Text on Future Interests, 2nd Ed., 355 pages, 1966.

See Wills, Intestate Succession, Trusts, Gifts and Future Interests.

GRATUITOUS TRANSFERS

See Wills, Intestate Succession, Trusts, Gifts and Future Interests.

HOUSING AND URBAN DEVELOPMENT

Berger's Cases on Housing, 2nd Ed., Pamphlet reprint from Cooper, et al. Law and Poverty, 2nd Ed., 254 pages, 1973.

Krasnowiecki's Cases on Housing and Urban Development, 697 pages, 1969.

Krasnowiecki's Statutory Supplement 1969.

See Land Use.

INSURANCE

Keeton's Cases on Basic Insurance Law, 655 pages, 1960.

Keeton's Basic Text on Insurance Law, 712 pages, 1971.

Keeton's Case Supplement to Keeton's Basic Text, 398 pages, 1971.

LAW SCHOOL PUBLICATIONS — Continued

INSURANCE—Continued

Keeton's Programmed Problems in Insurance Law, 243 pages, 1972.

Keeton & Keeton's Compensation Systems, Pamphlet reprint from Keeton & Keeton's Cases on Torts, 85 pages, 1971.

Vance's Text on Insurance, 3rd Ed., 1290 pages, 1951.

INTERNATIONAL LAW

Friedmann, Lissitzyn and Pugh's Cases on International Law, 1,205 pages, 1969.

Friedmann, Lissitzyn and Pugh's Supplement, 1972.

INTRODUCTION TO LAW

Dobbyn's So You Want To Go To Law School, 204 pages, 1976.

Fryer and Orentlicher's Cases on Legal Method and Legal System, 1,043 pages, 1967.

Kempin's Historical Introduction to Anglo-American Law in a Nutshell, 2nd Ed., 280 pages, 1973.

Kimball's Historical Introduction to Legal System, 610 pages, 1966.

Kinyon's Introduction to Law Study and Law Examinations in a Nutshell, 389 pages, 1971.

Mashaw and Merrill's Cases and Materials on Introduction to the American Public Law System, 1095 pages, 1975.

Rombauer's Legal Problem Solving, 2nd Ed., 212 pages, 1973.

Smith's Cases on Development of Legal Institutions, 757 pages, 1965.

See Legal Method.

JUDICIAL ADMINISTRATION

Nelson's Cases on Judicial Administration and the Administration of Justice 1032 pages, 1974.

JUDICIAL PROCESS

Aldisert's Readings, Materials and Cases in the Judicial Process, about 880 pages, 1976.

JURISPRUDENCE

Christie's Text and Readings on Jurisprudence—The Philosophy of Law, 1056 pages, 1973.

JUVENILE JUSTICE

Fox's Cases on Modern Juvenile Justice, 1012 pages, 1972.

Fox's The Law of Juvenile Courts in a Nutshell, 286 pages, 1971.

LABOR LAW

Federal Labor Laws, 642 pages, 1974.

Oberer and Hanslowe's Cases on Labor Law, 1091 pages, 1972.

Oberer and Hanslowe's Statutory Supplement, 1972.

Oberer and Hanslowe's 1975 Case Supplement.

Sovern's Cases on Racial Discrimination in Employment, 2nd Ed., Pamphlet reprint from Cooper et al. Law and Poverty, 2nd Ed., 167 pages, 1973.

See Workmen's Compensation.

LAND USE

Beuscher and Wright's Cases on Land Use, 788 pages, 1969.

Hagman's Cases on Public Planning and Control of Urban and Land Development, 1208 pages, 1973.

Hagman's Text on Urban Planning and Land Development Control Law, 559 pages, 1971.

LEGAL BIBLIOGRAPHY

Cohen's Legal Research in a Nutshell, 2nd Ed., 259 pages, 1971.

How To Find The Law, with Special Chapters on Legal Writing, 6th Ed., 313 pages, 1965.

How To Find The Law Student Problem Book.

Rombauer's Legal Problem Solving, 2nd Ed., 212 pages, 1973.

LEGAL ETHICS

Mellinkoff's Text on The Conscience of a Lawyer, 304 pages, 1973.

Pirsig's Cases on Professional Responsibility, 2nd Ed., 447 pages, 1970.

Pirsig's 1974 Supplement.

LEGAL HISTORY

Kempin's Historical Introduction to Anglo-American Law in a Nutshell, 2nd Ed., 280 pages, 1973.

Kimball's Historical Introduction to Legal System, 610 pages, 1966.

Smith's Cases on Development of Legal Institutions, 757 pages, 1965.

LEGAL INTERVIEWING AND COUNSELING

See Clinical Teaching.

LEGAL METHOD—LEGAL SYSTEM

Fryer and Orentlicher's Cases on Legal Method and Legal System, 1043 pages, 1966.

See Introduction to Law.

LEGAL PROCESS

See Legal Method.

LEGAL PROFESSION

See Legal Ethics.

LEGAL WRITING STYLE

Weihofen's Text on Legal Writing Style, 323 pages, 1961.
See Legal Bibliography.

LEGISLATION

Davies' Legislative Law and Process in a Nutshell, 279 pages, 1975.
Nutting, Elliott and Dickerson's Cases on Legislation, 4th Ed., 631 pages, 1969.

LOCAL GOVERNMENT LAW

McCarthy's Local Government Law in a Nutshell, 386 pages, 1975.
Michelman and Sandalow's Cases on Government in Urban Areas, 1216 pages, 1970.
Michelman and Sandalow's 1972 Supplement.
Stason and Kauper's Cases on Municipal Corporations, 3rd Ed., 692 pages, 1959.
Valente's Cases on Local Government Law, 914 pages, 1975.
See Land Use.

MASS COMMUNICATION LAW

Gillmor and Barron's Cases on Mass Communication Law, 2nd Ed., 1007 pages, 1974.

MORTGAGES

Maxwell, Riesenfeld, Hetland and Warren's California Cases on Security Transactions in Land, 2nd Ed., 584 pages, 1975.
Nelson and Whitman's Cases and Materials on Real Estate Finance and Development, 1064 pages, 1976.
Osborne's Cases on Secured Transactions, 559 pages, 1967.
Osborne's Text on Mortgages, 2nd Ed., 805 pages, 1970.

MUNICIPAL CORPORATIONS

See Local Government Law.

NATURAL RESOURCES

Trelease, Bloomenthal and Geraud's Cases on Natural Resources, 1131 pages, 1965.

NEGOTIABLE INSTRUMENTS

Nordstrom and Clovis' Problems on Commercial Paper, 458 pages, 1972.
Selected Commercial Statutes, 1016 pages, 1973.
Weber's Commercial Paper in a Nutshell, 2nd Ed., 361 pages, 1975.
See Commercial Transactions.

OFFICE PRACTICE

Strong and Clark's Law Office Management, 424 pages, 1974.
See Clinical Teaching.

OIL AND GAS

Hemingway's Text on Oil and Gas, 486 pages, 1971.
Huie, Woodward and Smith's Cases on Oil and Gas, 2nd Ed., 955 pages, 1972.
See Natural Resources.

PARTNERSHIP

Crane and Bromberg's Text on Partnership, 695 pages, 1968.
See Agency-Partnership.

PATENTS

Choate's Cases on Patents, 1060 pages, 1973.

PERSONAL PROPERTY

Aigler, Smith and Tefft's Cases on Property, 2 Vols., 1339 pages, 1960.
Bigelow's Cases on Personal Property, 3rd Ed., 507 pages, 1942.
Fryer's Readings on Personal Property, 3rd Ed., 1184 pages, 1938.

PLEADING AND PROCEDURE

Cound, Friedenthal and Miller's Cases on Civil Procedure, 2nd Ed., 1186 pages, 1974.
Cound, Friedenthal and Miller's Cases on Pleading, Discovery and Joinder, 643 pages, 1968.
Cound, Friedenthal and Miller's Civil Procedure Supplement, 1976.
Ehrenzweig and Louisell's Jurisdiction in a Nutshell, 3rd Ed., 291 pages, 1973.
Federal Rules of Civil-Appellate-Criminal Procedure, Law School Edition, 346 pages, 1975.
Hodges, Jones and Elliott's Cases on Texas Trial and Appellate Procedure, 2d Ed., 623 pages, 1974.
Hodges, Jones, Elliott and Thode's Cases on Texas Judicial Process Prior to Trial, 935 pages, 1966.

PLEADING AND PROCEDURE—Cont'd

Karlen, Meisenholder, Stevens and Vestal's Cases on Civil Procedure, 923 pages, 1975.

Karlen and Joiner's Cases on Trials and Appeals, 536 pages, 1971.

Karlen's Procedure Before Trial in a Nutshell, 258 pages, 1972.

McBaine's Cases on Introduction to Civil Procedure, 399 pages, 1950.

McCoid's Cases on Civil Procedure, 823 pages, 1974.

McElhaney's Trials, Problems and Materials on Effective Litigation, 457 pages, 1974.

POVERTY LAW

Cooper, Dodyk, Berger, Paulsen, Schrag and Sovern's Cases on Law and Poverty, 2nd Ed., 1208 pages, 1973.

Cooper and Dodyk's Cases on Income Maintenance, 2nd Ed., Pamphlet reprint from Cooper, et al. Law and Poverty, 2nd Ed., 449 pages, 1973.

LaFrance, Schroeder, Bennett and Boyd's Text on Law and the Poor, 558 pages, 1973.

REAL PROPERTY

Aigler, Smith & Tefft's Cases on Property, 2 Vols., 1339 pages, 1960.

Bernhardt's Real Property in a Nutshell, 425 pages, 1975.

Browder, Cunningham & Julin's Cases on Basic Property Law, 2d Ed., 1397 pages, 1973.

Burby's Text on Real Property, 3rd Ed., 490 pages, 1965.

Donahue, Kauper and Martin's Cases on Property, 1501 pages, 1974.

Moynihan's Introduction to Real Property, 254 pages, 1962.

Phipps' Titles in a Nutshell—The Calculus of Interests, 277 pages, 1968.

Smith and Boyer's Survey of the Law of Property, 2nd Ed., 510 pages, 1971.

Uniform Eminent Domain Code, Official Text With Comments, 160 pages, 1975.

See Housing and Urban Development.

REMEDIES

Cribbet's Cases on Judicial Remedies, 762 pages, 1954.

Dobbs' Text, on Remedies, 1067 pages, 1973.

Dobbs' Problems in Remedies, 137 pages, 1974.

Dobbyn's Injunctions in a Nutshell, 264 pages, 1974.

REMEDIES—Continued

Van Hecke, Leavell and Nelson's Cases on Equitable Remedies and Restitution, 2nd Ed., 717 pages, 1973.

Wright's Cases on Remedies, 498 pages, 1955.

York and Bauman's Cases on Remedies, 2nd Ed., 1381 pages, 1973.

See Equity.

RESTITUTION

See Equity.

See Remedies.

REVIEW MATERIALS

Ballantine's Problems.

Burby's Law Refreshers.

Smith Reviews.

SALES

Nordstrom's Text on Sales, 600 pages, 1970.

Nordstrom and Lattin's Problems on Sales and Secured Transactions, 809 pages, 1968.

Selected Commercial Statutes, 1016 pages, 1973.

See Commercial Transactions.

SECURED TRANSACTIONS

Henson's Text on Secured Transactions, 364 pages, 1973.

See Commercial Transactions.

See Sales.

SECURITIES REGULATIONS

Ratner's Materials on Securities Regulations, 893 pages, 1975.

Ratner's Statutory Supplement.

SEX BASED DISCRIMINATION

See Women and the Law.

SOCIAL LEGISLATION

See Workmen's Compensation.

SURETYSHIP AND GUARANTY

Osborne's Cases on Suretyship, 221 pages, 1966.

Simpson's Text on Suretyship, 569 pages, 1950.

TAXATION

Chommie's Text on Federal Income Taxation, 2nd Ed., 1051 pages, 1973.

Chommie's Review of Federal Income Taxation, 90 pages, 1973.

TAXATION—Continued

Hellerstein's Cases on State and Local Taxation, 3rd Ed., 741 pages, 1969.

Kragen & McNulty's Cases on Federal Income Taxation, 2nd Ed., 1107 pages, 1974.

Kramer and McCord's Problems for Federal Estate and Gift Taxes, 206 pages, 1976.

Lowndes, Kramer and McCord's Text on Federal Estate and Gift Taxes, 3rd Ed., 1099 pages, 1974.

McNulty's Federal Estate and Gift Taxation in a Nutshell, 343 pages, 1973.

McNulty's Federal Income Taxation in a Nutshell, 322 pages, 1972.

Rice's Problems in Federal Estate & Gift Taxation, 2nd Ed., 496 pages, 1972.

Rice's Problems in Federal Income Taxation, 2nd Ed., 589 pages, 1971.

Selected Federal Taxation Statutes and Regulations, 1133 pages, 1975.

TORTS

Green, Pedrick, Rahl, Thode, Hawkins and Smith's Cases on Torts, 1311 pages, 1968.

Green, Pedrick, Rahl, Thode, Hawkins and Smith's Cases on Injuries to Relations, 466 pages, 1968.

Keeton and Keeton's Cases on Torts, 1193 pages, 1971.

Keeton and Keeton's 1974 Supplement.

Noel and Phillips' Cases on Products Liability, about 850 pages, 1976.

Noel and Phillips' Products Liability in a Nutshell, 365 pages, 1974.

Prosser's Text on Torts, 4th Ed., 1208 pages, 1971.

Shapo's Cases on Tort and Compensation Law: Legal Response to Misfortune, about 1250 pages, 1976.

TRADE REGULATION

See Anti-Trust Law.
See Unfair Trade Practices.

TRIAL AND APPELLATE PRACTICE

Jeans' Handbook on Trial Advocacy, Student Edition, 473 pages, 1975.
See Pleading and Procedure.

TRUSTS

Bogert's Text on Trusts, 5th Ed., 726 pages, 1973.

Powell's Cases on Trusts and Wills, 639 pages, 1960.

See Wills, Intestate Succession, Trusts, Gifts and Future Interests.

UNFAIR TRADE PRACTICES

Oppenheim's Cases on Unfair Trade Practices, 3rd Ed., 1071 pages, 1974.

Oppenheim's Robinson-Patman Act Pamphlet, 258 pages, 1974.

WATER LAW

Trelease's Cases on Water Law, 2nd Ed., 863 pages, 1974.

WILLS

Atkinson's Text on Wills, 2nd Ed., 975 pages, 1953.

Mennell's Cases on California Decedents' Estates, 566 pages, 1973.

Turrentine's Cases on Wills, 2nd Ed., 483 pages, 1962.

See Wills, Intestate Succession, Trusts, Gifts and Future Interests.

WILLS, INTESTATE SUCCESSION, TRUSTS, GIFTS AND FUTURE INTERESTS

Gulliver, Clark, Lusky and Murphy's Cases on Gratuitous Transfers: Wills, Intestate Succession, Trusts, Gifts and Future Interests, 1017 pages, 1967.

Uniform Probate Code, Official Text With Comments, 278 pages, 1974.

WOMEN AND THE LAW

Davidson, Ginsburg and Kay's Cases on Sex Based Discrimination, 1031 pages, 1974.

Davidson, Ginsburg and Kay's 1975 Supplement.

WORKMEN'S COMPENSATION

Malone, Plant and Little's Cases on the Employment Relation, 1055 pages, 1974.

*

HANDBOOK
ON THE LAW OF
MORTGAGES

By

GEORGE E. OSBORNE
Professor of Law, University of California,
Hastings College of the Law

SECOND EDITION

HORNBOOK SERIES

ST. PAUL, MINN.
WEST PUBLISHING CO.
1970

Osborne Law of Mortgages 2d Ed. HB
2nd Reprint—1976

To the memory of my sister, Wenona

PREFACE

In the almost twenty years since the original of this text on Mortgages was written there have been a very large number of minor changes in the law both by decision and by statute. In most states there have been later compilations of statute law than those to which the innumerable citations throughout the volume referred. An attempt was made, not invariably successful for a variety of reasons, to update them.

Additionally there have been major developments and alterations in important areas. Among them are the greatly increased use of and changing doctrines in regard to subordination clauses; a further closing of the gap between mortgage law and contract of sale law in the use of the latter as a security device, especially in California; a necessary recast of thinking and practice, at least in California, with respect to the negative pledge clause; the change in character of problems since 1940 of the circuity of lien problem; the continuing difficult problem of fixture security under the Uniform Commercial Code; the increase in recent years of the importance of federal tax liens and the state of the law governing their priority before 1966 and the changes made by the 1966 amendment; and recent decisions and articles dealing with the rationales and applicability of anti-deficiency legislation, again especially in California.

Most of the text on the Statute of Frauds in Chapter 3 has been omitted. So detailed a consideration of it in the narrow field of its application to mortgage law seemed unwarranted. However, the blackface headnotes have been retained for two reasons. One, a mechanical one, was that keeping them would keep the same section numbers for the rest of the book, a matter of considerable importance because of the many cross references throughout. Also, it seemed worthwhile to retain the general treatment contained in the headnotes.

There is one unintentional omission. That is the effect of the enactment of the Uniform Commercial Code which by § 3–606 makes problems discussed in § 271 of the text unimportant.

The author is profoundly indebted to Myrl Jorgensen Northway not only for the compilation of a bibliography of legal periodical material published in the intervening years as well as abstracting most of it, but also for the checking of citations, typing the manuscript, and proof reading of galley and page proof. Without that dedicated help it is not too much to say that the task of this revision could not have been accomplished.

GEORGE E. OSBORNE

University of California
Hastings College of the Law
May 1970

SUMMARY OF CONTENTS

TABLE OF CONTENTS

CHAPTER 1. HISTORICAL DEVELOPMENT AND INTRODUCTION

A. EARLY FORMS

B. THE CLASSICAL COMMON LAW MORTGAGE

C. THE INTERVENTION OF EQUITY

D. AMERICAN DEVELOPMENTS

E. VARIANTS FROM THE NORM

CHAPTER 2. EQUITABLE MORTGAGES

CHAPTER 2.   EQUITABLE MORTGAGES—Continued

CHAPTER 3.   THE STATUTE OF FRAUDS

TABLE OF CONTENTS

CHAPTER 3. THE STATUTES OF FRAUDS—Continued

CHAPTER 4. RESTRICTIONS ON THE RIGHT TO REDEEM

A. THE ABSOLUTE DEED

B. CONDITIONAL SALE

C. TRIPARTITE TRANSACTIONS

CHAPTER 4. RESTRICTIONS ON THE RIGHT TO REDEEM—Continued

D. CLOGGING

E. SUBSEQUENT TRANSACTIONS

CHAPTER 5. THE OBLIGATION

A. NECESSITY AND NATURE OF OBLIGATION

B. DEFENSES TO OBLIGATION

C. FUTURE ADVANCES

TABLE OF CONTENTS

CHAPTER 6. RIGHTS AND DUTIES BEFORE FORECLOSURE

A. RIGHT TO POSSESSION

B. TORTIOUS INJURY TO LAND BY MORTGAGOR OR THIRD PERSONS

C. RIGHTS IN PRODUCT OF THE RES

D. RIGHT TO RENTS

E. RECEIVERSHIP

CHAPTER 6. RIGHTS AND DUTIES BEFORE FORECLOSURE—Continued

TABLE OF CONTENTS

CHAPTER 7. PRIORITIES—Continued

B. AS AFFECTED BY STATUTE

CHAPTER 8. TRANSFER BY THE MORTGAGEE

CHAPTER 9. TRANSFER BY THE MORTGAGOR

TABLE OF CONTENTS

CHAPTER 9. TRANSFER BY THE MORTGAGOR—
Continued

CHAPTER 10. SUBROGATION, CONTRIBUTION, AND EXONERATION—MARSHALLING ASSETS

A. SUBROGATION, CONTRIBUTION, AND EXONERATION

B. MARSHALLING

CHAPTER 11. DISCHARGE OF A MORTGAGE

CHAPTER 12. REDEMPTION

A. FROM THE MORTGAGE

B. FROM FORECLOSURE SALE

CHAPTER 13. FORECLOSURE

A. STRICT FORECLOSURE

B. FORECLOSURE BY STATUTORY SELF HELP AND ACTIONS AT LAW

TABLE OF CONTENTS

CHAPTER 13.   FORECLOSURE—Continued

C.   BY JUDICIAL SALE

D.   POWER OF SALE

†

HANDBOOK
ON THE
LAW OF MORTGAGES

CHAPTER 1
HISTORICAL DEVELOPMENT AND INTRODUCTION

A. EARLY FORMS

Sec.
1. The Glanvillian Gage.
2. Statutes Merchant and Staple.
3. The Jewish Gage of Land.
4. The Bractonian Mortgage.

B. THE CLASSICAL COMMON LAW MORTGAGE

5. Early Development of Common Law Mortgage.

C. THE INTERVENTION OF EQUITY

6. Mortgagor's Equity of Redemption.
7. Equity of Redemption as Equitable Estate.
8. Statutory Right to Redeem.
9. Position of Mortgagee.
10. Foreclosure.
11. Second Mortgages.
12. Modern English Mortgage.

D. AMERICAN DEVELOPMENTS

13. Principal American Theories.
14. Title and Intermediate Theories.
15. Lien Theory.
16. Critique of Theories.

E. VARIANTS FROM THE NORM

A. EARLY FORMS

THE GLANVILLIAN GAGE

1. The earliest form of property security in English law of which we have fairly detailed knowledge is the gage of Glanville's time. It was a transfer of possession to the creditor which was inadequately protected. It did have both a right of foreclosure in the creditor and a legal right of redemption in the debtor. If the creditor in possession had to apply the rents and profits to the debt it was a *vivum vadium* or live pledge; if he kept them it was a *mortgage* or dead pledge. The mortgage was considered usurious and was not satisfactory to either creditor or debtor.

Although transfers of property as security were undoubtedly used in early Anglo-Saxon times and survived the Conquest,[1] it is not until the twelfth century that we have much detailed knowledge of the form and incidents of the transaction. "It has been conjectured that in its oldest form the gage * * * was payment, subject only to the option of the purchaser to substitute at a later time payment in a different kind. Under this arrangement the handing over of the gage settled the debt; the creditor could not demand the substitution of a different kind of payment, and the debtor had no way of recovering any excess value in the gage over the price which he could substitute later."[2] By Glanville's time, however, there existed a transfer of possession[3] in pledge which gave the credi-

tor a sort of seizin, a seizin *ut de vadio*[4] as it was called, an interest difficult to define with precision although its incidents have been fairly well documented.

In describing the Glanvillian gage one writer, Coote, says the creditor got " * * * determinable or base fees, with a right of reverter in the feoffor or his heirs, on the payment of a given sum."[5] Such a classification is difficult to support. The truth seems to be that it was *sui generis*, describable only

prevent subsequent and fraudulent transfers of the same land; * * *. And the frauds which have arisen since the exchange of these public and notorious conveyances for more private and secret bargains, have well evinced the wisdom of our ancient law." 2 Blackstone, c. 10, § III.

It was an old statutory crime for a man to borrow twice on the same land without informing the second lender that his loan necessarily must be on second mortgage. Brace v. Duchess of Marlborough, 1728, 2 P.Wms. 491.

There is an intimation in Glanville, X, 6, that the debtor might remain in possession. For the view that the gage with possession in the debtor may be found in both Glanville and Bracton, see 2 Phillips, Eng. Reichsund Rechtsgeschichte, 239, 240; 2 Glasson, Histoire du droit et des institutions de l'Angleterre 313–316. See also, Stone, The Equitable Mortgage in New York, 1920, 20 Col.L.Rev. 519. This conflicts with Glanville, X, 8, and is flatly contrary to Sir William Blackstone who states that "In Glanville's time * * * no gage or pledge of lands was good, unless possession was also delivered to the creditor." 2 Bl.Com. 159. Agreements to pledge or mortgage not completed by delivery of possession were left to be dealt with by the ecclesiastical courts if they desired. See Turner, The Equity of Redemption, 17. These courts continued to claim jurisdiction over matters involving breach of faith concurrently with the Court of Chancery as late at Edward IV. See Turner, ibid., citing Y. B. 8 Ed. IV, 4.

1. 2 P. & M. 118. Wigmore, The Pledge Idea, 1897, 10 Harv.L.Rev. 321.

2. Plucknett, Concise History of the Common Law, 2d Ed., 540.
See Huebner, History of Germanic Private Law, 376.

3. Glanville, Beames, Beale's Ed., X, 8. 3 Holdsworth, History of English Law, 128; 2 P. & M. 120. "* * * for which the reason given is, to

4. 2 P. & M. 120; Hazeltine, The Gage of Land in Medieval England, 1904, 17 Harv.L.Rev. 549, 555; Chaplin, The Story of Mortgage Law, 1890, 4 Harv.L.Rev. 1, 6–7.

5. Coote, Mortgages, 9th Ed. 1. See also 1 Jones, Mortgages, 8th Ed. 5.

in terms of analogy to familiar interests in property. Coote may have confused the interest of the gagee with that of grantee of the fee on condition subsequent.[6]

In contrast Glanville's gage was on condition precedent, i. e., non-payment by the debtor was a condition precedent to the creditor's keeping by virtue of either an express clause of forfeiture, or in its absence, court action.[7]

The gagee received no protection against either the debtor or third persons. If the debtor ousted the creditor, the latter could sue the former only for his debt. If a third person cast out the creditor, only " * * * the debtor may have an Assise of Novel Disseisin".[8] It was too early for trespass q. c. f. to be available to the creditor for injuries to the land not amounting to an ouster.[9] Although Glanville's explanation is that the creditor's right is only to the debt, not the land itself,[10] the real reason seems to be the uncertainty of the king's justices as to the scope of the new possessory actions. "They are not quite sure whether the gagee really and truly has a *seisina* that calls for protection. Influenced perhaps by theories of the Italian glossators as to possessory protection, they end in refusing the gagee a remedy."[11]

The gagee took the rents and profits, and either applied them in reduction of the demand for which the pledge was given or kept them. If he did the former, it was called a *vif gage* or *vivum vadium* (live pledge); if the latter, it was a *mort gage* or *mortuum vadium* (dead pledge).[12] This explanation

of the term mortgage given by Glanville was quite accurate and descriptive of the security device with which he was familiar. Littleton, however, although retaining the same names, dropped the idea that the gage was dead when the rents and profits did not work off the debt. He said "that the cause why it is called mortgage is, for that it is doubtful whether the feoffor will pay at the day limited * * * ; and if he doth not pay, then the land * * * is taken from him for ever, and so dead (to him * * *. And if he doth pay the money, then the pledge is dead) as to the tenant, etc."[13] The difference in definition is due to the fact that the earlier system, under which the mortgagee took an interest which was ineffective although called seisin, had become obsolete. In Littleton's time it had been replaced by the entirely distinct common law mortgage in which the mortgagee at once got the estate which was to become absolute on non-payment at the time named whether it be a fee simple, fee tail, for life, or for a term of years.[14] Under this latter system, although he had the right to do so, the mortgagee normally did not go into possession and the old reasons therefore did not apply. So Littleton invented a new one. Coke, in his comment on this attempts to reconcile the two views by saying that the mortgage is so called to differentiate it from the *vivum vadium*. This he defines in Glanville's sense, and then sticks to Littleton's conception by saying that if the creditor's estate is granted only until he has received his debt out "of the issues and profits of the land, * * * neither money nor land dieth, or is lost, (whereof Littleton hath spoken * * *)".[15]

---

6. See infra, The Classical Common Law Mortgage, note 61.

7. See Hazeltine, Early English Equity in Vinogradoff, Essays in Legal History, 265.

8. Glanville, X, 11.

9. See Ames, Lectures on Legal History, 244 et seq.

10. Glanville, X, 11, XIII, 28–30.

11. Hazeltine, op. cit. supra note 4, at 555. See 2 P. & M. 120, 121. See also Chaplin, op. cit. supra note 4, at 6; Jenks, Short History of English Law, 125.

12. See Glanville X, 6 for this distinction which is agreed to by Hazeltine, op. cit. supra note 4, at

552; Chaplin, op. cit. supra note 4, at 8; 3 Holdsworth, op. cit. supra note 3, at 128; 2 P. & M. 119; and Turner, op. cit. supra note 3, at 17. See also Huebner, op. cit. supra note 2, at 378.

13. Littleton, Tenures (Wambaugh) Bk. III, C. V, § 332.

14. Litt. § 333.

15. Coke, Litt. § 332. See Fenwick v. Reed, 1816, 1 Mer. 124; Fisher and Lightwood, Mortgages, 7th

The *vivum vadium* was comparable to the *antichresis* of the Roman Law [16] and the similar security under the Code Napoleon [17] and is substantially the same as an ordinary mortgagee in possession under the later English law who must account in equity for the rents and profits. At a later day there is a variant of the Welsh mortgage in which the mortgagee takes the rents and profits in payment of the principal and interest as in the Glanvillian *vif gage,* but that is the only resemblance between them. In the Welsh mortgage proper, the rents and profits are in lieu of interest.[18]

The mortgage was looked upon as an unfair bargain and usurious. Usury itself, "though viewed in a criminal light, was not expressly prohibited. Nor was it punished, if the party amended; but, if he died in the crime, the act had reached the point of criminality—the offense was complete, and the punishment followed." [19]

In the *vivum vadium,* the creditor in possession depends upon the rents and profits for the payment of his loan. Consequently, even though he charges interest, he is looked upon as taking a business risk and the interest is only fair compensation for that risk. In the mortgage, however, the creditor has the obligation of the borrower to pay the loan and in addition takes the income without accountability. It is easy to understand,

therefore, why the *mort gage* was considered a "species of usury" and consequently governed by the same ideas applicable to usury proper.[20] Hence, although not prohibited [21] to Christians, if the mortgagee "die having such pledge * * * his property shall be disposed of no otherwise than as the effects of a usurer", i. e., his chattels were forfeited to the king.[22] Apparently this was no great deterrent, and the mortgage was the common contract for both Christians and Jews.[23] The gagee was absolutely liable for any injury to the property, and if he did not make satisfaction would lose his debt.[24] An effective agreement could be made ending all rights of the debtor in the property on non-payment; [25] and even without such an agreement the gagee had a court remedy quite analogous to the later equity foreclosure. The court ordered the debtor to pay within a reasonable time, and, if he did not, the gagee could "do whatever he choos-

---

ed., 8 n. a; Falconbridge, Mortgages, 3d ed., 1 et seq.

16. Dig. XX, 1, 11, 1; XIII, 33; XX, 1, 1, 3. See Melville, Roman Law, 354 note 5.

17. Sections 2085–2091.

18. See Coote, Mortgages, 9th Ed., C. III. The Welsh mortgage has long been obsolete. See 4 Kent, Comm., 137; Turner, op. cit. supra note 3, at 91; Talbot v. Braddil, 1686, 1 Vern. 394; Cassidy v. Cassidy, 1889, 24 L.R.Ir. 577, 578. See also 21 Halsbury, Laws of England, 87; Fisher and Lightwood, Mortgages, 7th ed., 8 n. (b), for additional features of the Welsh mortgage; Glanville, X, 8; ibid., VII, 16. See Hazeltine, op. cit. supra note 4, at 552.

19. Glanville, Beames, Beale's ed., p. 209 n. 1; ibid., VI, 16.

20. See Glenn, Morts. 2.

21. Glanville, X, 8. But see Regiam Majestatem, L. III, C. 5, which indicates it was prohibited. Usury was forbidden by the Mosaic Law, but the injunction against it could be and was circumvented. See Wigmore, The Pledge Idea, 1897, 10 Harv.L.Rev. 389, 405 n. 4, for the early Jewish law on the subject of usury. For a brief statement of the treatment of usury by the Romans, under the Norman code, and the severe law of Edward the Confessor, see Glanville, Beames, Beale's ed., VII, 16, p. 151 n. 1.

Regardless of whether there was or was not a legal prohibition against it, the Medieval Church did not permit Christians to charge interest on a loan of money. The Mosaic Law permitted Jews to charge interest on loans to Gentiles. See Fratcher, Restraints upon Alienation of Equitable Interests in Michigan Property, 1953, 51 Mich.L.Rev. 509, 538.

22. Glanville X, 8. See Hazeltine, op. cit. supra note 4, at 552.

23. Because the medieval courts of law "had been sharply limited in the exercise of any discretion over mortgages, whether the litigation related to *vif gage* or *mort gage*; the creditor might be tempted into the sin of usury, yet take his illicit gains scot free, without let or hindrance." Williams, Clogging the Equity of Redemption, 1933, 40 W.Va.L.Q. 31, 34.

24. Glanville, X, 8.

25. Glanville, X, 6; Hazeltine, op. cit. supra note 4, at 554.

es with" the property.[26] If the debtor paid, or even tendered, the right of the gagee to hold the property ended, and the debtor had an action to recover it.[27] Even though the debtor failed to pay on the day set by the agreement of gage, the debtor was given another chance to redeem, this second opportunity amounting to an early rudimentary legal counterpart of the later equity of redemption.[28] However, by the time of Edward the First, the law courts came to the position that a mortgagor who allowed the day set for payment to pass without performance would not be helped.[29] With this doctrine established, it was left to the equity court of a later time to reintroduce the "equity of redemption" into the law of mortgages in the form known in the modern law and by "failing thus to retain the equity of redemption as a working principle of their system of justice the common law courts lost for all subsequent ages jurisdiction over a highly important branch of English law." [30]

Such a mortgage was unsatisfactory to the debtor, not only because it might be harshly usurious, but also because he lost possession of his property.[31] It was unsatisfactory to the creditor because of the lack of protection given his possession.[32] It is rather natural, therefore, that the peculiar interest of the mortgagee as it existed according to Glanville should die out and be replaced by more definitely recognized and protected interests in the property, i. e., a term for years or a freehold estate for life or in fee. There also developed, first for Jewish creditors and then for merchant creditors generally, a security device in which the debtor kept possession.

STATUTES MERCHANT AND STAPLE

2. Following the Norman Conquest new forms of security created by formal acknowledgment of debts before designated officers or judges were provided for by statute. The most important of these were the Statutes Merchant and Staple. Under them the debtor was left in possession until default at which time the creditor was entitled to possession of all of the debtor's lands to hold until the claim was paid out of the rents and profits. They no longer exist.

In the era of commerce and industry which followed the Norman Conquest, new remedies and rights of creditors were created by statutes and recognized by the courts and administrative agencies. The Statute of Westminister the Second created the writ of *elegit* by which a creditor could seize through the sheriff half of the lands of his debtor to hold as tenant in elegit until his debt was satisfied. "Statutes", now obsolete,[33] were introduced by the statute *De Mercatoribus* [34] and the statute of the Staple.[35] These "statutes merchant" and "statutes staple" were acknowledgments of debts before a judge or

---

26. Glanville, X, 8; Chaplin op. cit. supra note 4, at 7–8; Hazeltine, op. cit. supra note 4, at 554; Walsh, Mortgages, § 1.

27. Glanville, X, 6, 8–10, XIII, 26–30; Hazeltine, op. cit. supra note 4, at 555.

28. Glanville, X, 8.

See Hazeltine, The Early History of English Equity, Essays in Legal History, 261, 267.

The right of redemption had been declared as a moral tenet at the Council of Lateran not many years before Glanville wrote. See Matthew Paris, Historia Major, 1684, 114–115; Williams, Clogging the Equity of Redemption, 1933, 40 W.Va.L.Q. 31, 33.

29. Britton, Book III, c. XV 6 (Nichols' ed. ii. 128).

See 2 Holdsworth, History of English Law, 249.

30. Hazeltine, op. cit. supra note 4.

31. "* * * no mortgagee or mortgagor ever yet made a contract, upon which the possession was to change immediately, unless it were the veriest grinding bargain that could be driven with a distressed man, who had no way to turn." Ruffin, J., in Poindexter v. McCannon, 1830, 16 N.C. 373, 377, 18 Am.Dec. 591.

32. See note 4, supra. The piecemeal repayment of the debt, most creditors then, as now, wanting a lump sum at one time, was an additional objection to the vif gage; probably it was never much used.

33. They were repealed in 1863. Williams, Real Property, 1901, 226 n. e.

34. 13 Ed. I, stat. 3.

35. 23 Ed. III, c. 9.

Recognizances in the nature of statutes staple were sanctioned by the statute of 23 Hen. VIII, c. 6.

other officer designated by statute, the acknowledgment thereupon becoming, by force of the statute, matters of record and deriving their efficacy from that fact under the statute, just as a bond derived its efficacy from being sealed and delivered by the debtor.[36]

Under the enactments creating these "statutes," an enrolled "statute" accompanied by a sealed instrument would bind all the lands owned by the debtor at the time and, according to the later law, lands subsequently acquired.[37] The debtor retained possession until default when the creditor might obtain the land from the debtor or his heir or transferee and hold it until the claim was paid out of the rents and profits.[38] The remedies of the merchant creditor under "statutes" different from those under an *elegit* in two respects: he must get the debtor to execute the "statute" or recognizance whereas the writ of elegit was available to creditors generally without regard to any action or consent of the debtor. On the other hand, unlike the writ of elegit which until modern times would reach only half of the lands of the debtor, he could take all the real property belonging to his obligor.[39]

THE JEWISH GAGE OF LAND

3. In the twelfth and thirteenth centuries there developed a separate type of security interest in property confined to Jewish creditors.

Along with retention of possession by the debtor it had a system of registration, methods of enforcement between the parties and more effective protection against third parties. It became obsolete with the expulsion of the Jews from England in 1290.

Quite separate from the statutory security interests just discussed, there developed in the twelfth and thirteenth centuries a gage of lands and tenements confined exclusively to Jewish creditors. In these also the creditor did not take possession. The Exchequer of the Jews [40] was set up as a branch of the Great Exchequer and it worked out and recognized a system of registration of written contracts under seal hypothecating the lands of the debtor as security for debts owed to Jews. The registration of the sealed instrument before public officials at the Jewish Exchequer in certain towns provided the necessary publicity and an effective recording scheme,[41] and by thus fulfilling the chief objectives of livery of seizin very successfully broke in on the requirements of the feudal system.

It was possible for the debtor to give a mortgage of either specific lands or all of the debtor's property. The latter, at least so far as lands were concerned, would bind the property in the hands of transferees.[42] On default the Jewish mortgagee or his assignee could obtain *seizina* [43] by court action and, unlike the interest of the Glanvillian

---

36. See Langdell, Brief Survey of Equity Jurisdiction, 141; 2 P. & M. 124; 3 Holdsworth, History of English Law, 131; Hazeltine, The Exchequer of the Jews, 1902, 18 L.Q.Rev. 308; II Blackstone, C. II, § IX on Stats. Staple and Merchant.

37. See Hazeltine, The Gage of Land in Medieval England, 1904, 18 Harv.L.Rev. 36, 47.

38. Hazeltine, op. cit. supra note 37.

"The Roman notion of lien by conventional hypotheca found its way into English law in the form of the Admiralty lien and in the statutory form of recognizances in the nature of statute staple, and the elegit which was the forerunner of the modern judgment lien bore some resemblance to it." Stone, The Equitable Mortgage in New York, 1920, 20 Col. L.Rev. 520.

See Black., Comm., 160.

39. Hazeltine, op. cit. supra note 37.

40. See Hazeltine, The Exchequer of the Jews, 1902, 18 L.Q.Rev. 305; Rigg, Jewish Exchequer, 15 Seld. Soc., IX–LXII; 1 Holdsworth, op. cit. supra note 3, at 45–46; 1 P. & M. 468–475; Hazeltine, The Gage of Land in Medieval England, 1904, 18 Harv.L.Rev. 36, 43 et seq.; Plucknett, op. cit. supra note 2, at 542; Carter, History of English Courts, c. XXIV; Jacobs, Jews of Angevin England; Gross, Exchequer of the Jews, 1 Publications of Anglo-Jewish Hist. Exhibition; Rabinowitz, The Story of Mortgage Law Retold, 1945, 94 U. of Pa.L.Rev. 94; Kamberg, Commercial Law According to the Talmud, 1933, 38 Commercial L.Jour. 239.

41. See 2 P. & M. 123; 3 Holdsworth, op. cit. supra note 3, at 131. See, also, Chaplin, op. cit. supra note 4, at 6 n.

42. Hazeltine, op. cit. supra note 40, at 45.

43. Ibid.

gagee, this seizin was protected by the courts.[44] After a year and a day redemption period, he could realize on his security either by holding the lands until the rents and profits satisfied his claim or by selling it. If he pursued the former course he was in effect the holder of a *vivum vadium* and subject to a duty to account which was not susceptible of being ended by any lapse of time. What the effect of the sale was has not yet been established by research in the unprinted records of the Jewish Exchequer; it is quite possible that there was a duty to account for any surplus after satisfying the claim.[45]

This Jewish mortgage possibly had some influence in the legislative creation of the writ of *elegit* and the tenancies under the statutes Merchant and Staple, but otherwise had no direct connection with the later development of English mortgage law, and itself ceased with the expulsion of the Jews in 1290.[46] It has been conjectured that our law of mortgages would have developed more easily and would have been simpler and less clumsy had they been permitted to stay and their security device allowed its normal growth.

THE BRACTONIAN MORTGAGE

4. **The Bractonian mortgage gave to the creditor a term for years which on default swelled into a fee. The mortgagee had possession and the better remedies of a termor. There were variants of this which persisted to the time of Littleton. These security interests were distinct from the "beneficial lease."**

With the innovations of the Jewish mortgage bearing no fruit and the lack of protection accorded the peculiar interest of the Glanvillian gagee a serious drawback, the next step in the evolution of land security was to give to the creditor one of the recognized interests in real property. This came in Bracton's time [47] when we find the gagee ordinarily being given a term for years and with it the better remedies of a termor.[48] The Bractonian mortgage, aside from this greater protection to the mortgagee, seems to be the same in theory and incidents as the earlier one. In both the mortgagee had possession and acquired the fee upon the failure of the mortgagor to pay,[49] a somewhat striking instance of a springing fee which the later law of Littleton's time would have thought impossible.[50]

"The enlargement of a term of years into a fee, characteristic of the Bractonian gage, raised no difficulties for the lawyers of that age; as yet the *forma donationis,* wide and flexible, had not been fettered by strict rules as to the difference between *possessio* and *seisina* and by fine distinctions between the term for years and the freehold." [51]

Variants of this consisted in demises of a term of years to the mortgagee followed by a redemise to the mortgagor at a fixed rent; or there might be a lease for a long term of years with a stipulation that the mortgagor was to have possession until default, and that, on payment, the lease should be void.[52]

---

44. See Bracton's Note Book, pl. 301, 1825; Plac. Abb., Rec.Com. 64, 82, 175; Jacobs, op. cit. supra note 40, 191, 234.

45. Hazeltine, op. cit. supra note 40, at 46.
See Rigg, Jewish Exchequer, 15 Seld.Soc. XIII; 3 Holdsworth, op. cit. supra note 3, at 131.

46. That the Jewish mortgage had more influence upon the common law mortgage than is generally believed, see Rabinowitz, The Story of the Mortgage Retold, 1945, 94 U.Pa.L.Rev. 94; Rabinowitz, The Common Law Mortgage and the Conditional Bond, 1943, 92 U.Pa.L.Rev. 179.

47. Bracton, F. 20, 268–9; 3 Britton, XV, §§ 2–7; Bracton's Notebook, pl. 889; 2 P. & M. 25, 122; Hazeltine, op. cit. supra note 4, at 556; Turner, op. cit. supra note 3, at 18; Chaplin, op. cit. supra note 4, at 8; Plucknett, op. cit. supra note 2, at 541.
See also Fratcher, Restraints upon Alienation of Equitable Interests in Michigan Property, 1953, 51 Mich.L.Rev. 509, 539. Cf. Durfee, Cases on Security, 1951, 9.

48. For the termor's remedies, see 2 P. & M. 107 et seq.

49. See authorities cited in note 47, supra.

50. See Co.Litt., 216–18.

51. Hazeltine, Preface to Turner, The Equity of Redemption, XXXV.

52. 7 Holdsworth, History of English Law, 375.

Mortgages of this sort continued to be employed even in Littleton's time.

Analogous to, but to be distinguished from, the foregoing mortgages was the so-called "beneficial lease". This was an outright purchase for cash of a lease for years. It provided the lessor with money and the lessee with an investment which might yield him a return on his money in the form of profits out of the land. There was no debt, and hence there could be no usury; further, the investor had a termor's protection of possession. With these advantages it is easy to see why such arrangements were popular outlets for capital.[53]

B. THE CLASSICAL COMMON LAW MORTGAGE

EARLY DEVELOPMENT OF COMMON LAW MORTGAGE

5. In the fourteenth century the conveyance of the fee upon condition subsequent emerged as the dominant form of mortgage and has lasted down to the present, modified as will be seen. Under it the mortgagee, having legal title, got the incidents of that title, including the right to immediate possession. For various reasons the practice developed of leaving the mortgagor in possession. When this was done without agreement his status caused courts much difficulty, the tendency being to classify him as a tenant of some sort. This tendency caused trouble in cases involving the defense of the Statute of Limitations.

The form of condition with provision for re-entry was gradually displaced by a proviso for reconveyance.

A conveyance of the fee on condition subsequent had existed as a security device alongside the Glanvillian gage, but not until the fourteenth century does it become the mortgage in common use.[54] It is frequently stated that the stricter ideas of the later real property law which found it legally impossible to swell a term into a fee [55] was the chief reason for the obsolescence of the older form and the growth of the new; but practical considerations of various sorts probably played a potent role.

In addition to objections already mentioned was the difficulty the gagee might encounter in actions involving the validity of his title. He always had the burden of proving his debt. Giving the creditor an absolute title at the inception which could not be defeated except by affirmative proof of payment "according to the strict letter of the deed * * * would throw the burden of proof upon the borrower, the pledgor, in any contest which might arise".[56]

Probably the prohibition against charging interest played an important role. By taking title and immediate possession the lender got the rents and profits. Although in theory he was supposed to apply them to the debt, almost certainly he made a surreptitious profit. The ability thus to circumvent the mandate against taking interest doubtless was a potent factor in the popularity of this form of security.[56a]

Whatever the reasons, it is thoroughly established by the time of Littleton and, though modified not only by equity but by the law courts, continues, with its imperfections, to plague the legal profession to the present day.[57] This clumsy device was listed as a part of the law of real property on es-

53. Hazeltine, op. cit. supra note 4, at 552. See also 3 Holdsworth, op. cit. supra note 3, at 129; 2 P. & M. 121–2.

54. Turner, The Equity of Redemption, XXXV; Hazeltine, The Gage of Land in Medieval England,

1904, 17 Harv.L.Rev. 549, 557; Plucknett, Concise History of the Common Law, 2d Ed., 543–4.

55. 3 Holdsworth, History of English Law, 130; 2 P. & M. 122; Litt., Tenures, §§ 349, 350; Co.Litt., 216–218; Walsh, Mortgages, 3; Hazeltine, op. cit. supra note 53, at 556.

56. Chaplin, The Story of Mortgage Law, 1890, 4 Harv.L.Rev. 1, 9.

56a. See Fratcher, Restraints upon Alienation of Equitable Interests in Michigan Property, 1953, 51 Mich.L.Rev. 509, 539, 541.

57. Pomeroy, Eq.Juris., 4th Ed., § 1179; 3 Holdsworth, op. cit. supra note 55, at 130; Turner, The Equity of Redemption, 19.

tates on condition, and reserved to the grantor a right of entry for condition broken [58] (or, more accurately, performed). Nowhere in the transaction was it directly and explicitly stated that the sole purpose of the transfer was security. A vigorous criticism of it says, "That is the worst of our mortgage deed * * *, it is one long *suppressio veri* and *suggestio falsi*. It does not in the least explain the rights of the parties; it suggests that they are other than really they are." [59] Nevertheless it did accomplish its purpose, although not as satisfactorily as could be desired. If the mortgagor performed he got back his estate.

Although a reentry or its equivalent by the feoffor seems to be necessary by the time of Littleton and later,[60] it appears that in its earlier use the feoffee got what was essentially a determinable fee, and performance ipso facto ended his estate.[61] If the mortgagor is in possession, performance alone ends the estate of the mortgagee.[62] This may account for statements that reentry is unnecessary. The technical rule really is immaterial, because as a practical matter the mortgagor has to get back possession by entry or ejectment, and cannot convey or enjoy the property until he does so.[63] If the mortgagor failed to perform, title was absolute in the grantee and the mortgagor had finally and irrevocably lost his land.[64] This harsh strictness was matched to some extent by a similar attitude toward the mortgagee. If the mortgagor tendered at the proper date, even though the mortgagee refused to accept it, that tender not only revested the estate in the mortgagor but ended any remedy of the mortgagee to collect his money. The reasons given were "because it shall be accounted to his own folly that he refused the money" and the more legalistic one that "the money is collateral to the land." [65]

Perhaps the most striking and important feature of this mortgage is that the grantee, having legal title from the outset, got the incidents of that title even though unnecessary or even antagonistic to the sole purpose of the conveyance, namely, security for the performance of an act by the grantor. Thus the wife got dower [66] until 1678 when Lord Nottingham overturned the rule; [67] the Rule in Shelley's case applied; [68] on the death of the mortgagee the property went to his

---

58. Litt., Tenures, §§ 332, 337; Co.Litt., 205 a; Lloyd, Genesis of the Lien Theory, 1923, 32 Yale L. J. 233; Chaplin, op. cit. supra, note 56, at 2; 3 Pomeroy, loc. cit. supra note 57; Coote, Mortgages, 9th Ed., C.I.; Durfee, The Lien or Equitable Theory of the Mortgage—Some Generalizations, 1912, 10 Mich.L.Rev. 587, 592.

Littleton, although he uses the term "mortgage" treats of it under the head of Estates upon condition without showing any differentiation in the law applicable to it. See Litt., supra.

See also Cowell, Interpretation of History Antiquities and Laws, 1607, s. v. Mortgage; Rastall, Termes de la Ley, s. v. Mortgage, Preface to 10 Co.Rep., circa 1550, cited in Glenn., Morts. 8 ns. 17, 18.

59. Maitland, Equity, 269. See Salt v. Marquess of Northampton, 1892, A.C. 1, 18–19. See also Chaplin, op. cit. supra note 56, at 2–4. "* * * it is to be expected that, with the passage of time, the crude conception of an estate on condition in the mortgagee will entirely disappear." 3 Tiffany, Real Prop., 2d Ed., § 600.

60. Hargrave and Butler's note to Co.Litt., § 332.

61. Hazeltine, General Preface to Turner, The Equity of Redemption, XXXVIII. See also McMillan v. Richards, 1858, 9 Cal. 365, 411, 70 Am.Dec. 655; Stevens v. Turlington, 1923, 186 N.C. 191, 194, 119 S.E. 210, 211, 32 A.L.R. 870.

62. Kales, Future Interests, 2d Ed., § 217.

63. Walsh, Mortgages, 5.

64. See authorities in note 58, supra. As was pointed out it was because of this that Littleton called it a mortgage. Litt., Tenures, § 332.

65. Litt., Tenures, § 335; Co.Litt. 207a.

66. Nash v. Preston, 1632, Cro.Car. 190. This led to the practice of giving mortgages of long terms of years. Co.Litt., § 332 n.; 2 Blackstone, 158; Turner, op. cit. supra note 54, at 50. One advantage of these was that on the death of the mortgagee the term vested in the personal representatives instead of the heir. A disadvantage was that on default by the mortgagor the mortgagee did not get the fee.

67. Noel v. Jevon, 1678, 2 Freem. 43.

68. Simes, Future Interests, 2d Ed., § 20 et seq.

heirs [69] or devisees; [70] creditors of the grantee could seize the property itself; [71] the mortgagee was entitled to all accretions to the property, [72] to compensation if the land was taken by eminent domain, [73] and to the title deeds; [74] he could bring actions against third parties and defend actions brought by them; [75] he might get the personal privilege of voting if he took possession; [76] his title would escheat; [77] and, most vital of all, he had the right to immediate possession. [78]

Possession in the mortgagee was, as has been seen, the rule in the pre-Littletonian mortgage, and under the form that emerged and became the dominant and lasting common law land security, the conveyance of the fee on condition, since it had to be by livery of seizin or other present transfer, necessitated a delivery of possession to the creditor. Further, the mortgagee desired possession in order to get a return on his loan in the form of rents and profits because taking interest was usury. Therefore, both for practical reasons and because of legal requirements, it was natural for the mortgagee to take and hold possession.

Possession by the debtor until default was provided for in the Jewish mortgages and, also, as has been seen, characterized the statutory security which was available under writs of elegit and the statutes Merchant and Staple. [79] Although it has been argued that the modern practice of leaving the mortgagor in possession is directly traceable to the latter devices or the history of judicial execution, [80] it is more likely that it was connected with the creation of the equity of redemption. Certainly it is true that the practice of leaving the mortgagor in possession coincided with the development of the equity of redemption, but was not thoroughly established until the middle of the seventeenth century. [81] With the fuller recognition of the mortgagor's equitable ownership and the strict accounting of a mortgagee who took possession, [82] the right to possession was exercised only in extreme cases as a last resort. [83]

When the mortgagor was left in possession without any agreement between the parties his position caused the courts and writers much difficulty. Some recognized him for what he so obviously was, a mortgagor in

---

69. Ex parte Morgan, 1804, 10 Ves. 101; see 2 Coote, Mortgages, 9th Ed., 863; Turner, op. cit. supra note 54, at 160. By statute the legal estate of a deceased mortgagor now vests in his personal representatives. 44 & 45 Vict. c. 41, § 30. See Coote, ibid., 867.

70. A general devise of lands, unless a contrary intention appears, passes the legal interest of the mortgagee. Co.Litt., 205a n.; Turner, loc. cit. supra note 69; Coote, loc. cit. supra note 69. However, see Littleton's Case, 1681, 1 Vern. 3.

71. Turner, op. cit. supra note 54, at 52.

72. Doe v. Pott, 1781, 2 Doug. 710; Coote, op. cit. supra note 69, at 816.

73. Ranken v. East and West India Docks Co., etc., 1849, 12 Beav. 298.

74. 2 Coote, op. cit. supra note 69, at 835.

75. 2 Coote, op. cit. supra note 69, at 817; Turner, op. cit. supra note 54, at 123–124; Pomeroy, Eq. Juris. § 1182.

76. 2 & 3 Will. IV c. 45, § 23; 6 & 7 Vict. c. 18, § 74.

77. Semble, Y.B. 5 Ed. IV, 18 pl., 7 b. See Turner, op. cit. supra note 54, at 55.

78. A thorough discussion of all the cases may be found in Turner, op. cit. supra note 54, at 88 et seq.

79. See § 2, supra.

80. Hazeltine, The Gage of Land in Medieval England, 1904, 18 Harv.L.Rev. 36. Cf. Wigmore, The Pledge Idea, 1897, 10 Harv.L.Rev. 321, 341.

81. Turner, op. cit. supra note 54, at 89–91.

Relaxation by both Church and State in their attitude against the charging of interest quite certainly was a dominant motivation in the changed practice. The permission to charge interest, given by statute in 1623 (Stat. 21 Jas. I, c. 17, § 2, made permanent, 3 Car. I, c. 4, § 5, 1627) enabled a mortgagee to make a reasonable return on his investment without taking possession. See Fratcher, Restraints upon Alienation of Equitable Interests in Michigan Property, 1953, 51 Mich.L.Rev. 509, 540–541.

82. See Dobson v. Land, 1850, 8 Hare 216, 220; Poindexter v. McCannon, 1830, 16 N.C. 373, 376, 18 Am.Dec. 591.

83. See Maitland, Equity, 274; Walsh, Mortgages, 15.

possession.[84] However, the inclination to reason by analogy, reinforced by resistance to the creation of new categories of interests in real property, tended to impose "an obsolete feudal classification on an interest which originally grew up by tacit agreement without any regard to the law of tenure"; [85] and so we find other courts styling him either a tenant at will or at sufferance. Since he could be ousted without notice and was not entitled to the emblements,[86] he could not be the former; and, since he did not hold over wrongfully, he was not, technically, the latter.[87] If the mortgagee covenanted that the mortgagor should remain in possession for a definite period, the mortgagor got a tenancy for a term; but a covenant that the mortgagor keep possession until default, or any other consent, express or implied in fact, that the mortgagor have possession, gave only a tenancy at will.[88]

The concept that the mortgagor in possession was a tenant of some sort also caused difficulty in cases involving the defense of the Statute of Limitations. It was first decided that twenty years' possession by the mortgagor after default did not bar the mortgagee; [89] and then it was held that it did.[90]

"The true ground of any equitable bar to the mortgagee's right to possession was not adverse possession, * * * but was a presumption of the satisfaction of the mortgage debt after twenty years' possession of the

mortgagor without any acknowledgment of the debt, on the principle that equity follows the law." [91] Mere retention of possession by the mortgagor does not make him a disseizor; there must be affirmative proof of some act incompatible with his position as mortgagor.[92]

The rights of the mortgagor and mortgagee against third parties,[93] the effect of the mortgage upon the duty to pay taxes, the processes which creditors might employ against the parties to the mortgage, and the right to the franchise [94] were other questions which came before the courts.

The condition with provision for reentry was gradually displaced by a proviso for reconveyance [95] which had a double operation. It was effective at law as a condition,[96] and

---

84. Turner, op. cit. supra note 54, at 102.

85. Turner, op. cit. supra note 54, at 104.

86. Coventry suggests that the mortgagee gets the emblements "because the crop, as well as the land, is a security for the debt." Powell, Mortgages, 208 n. B.

87. Tiffany, Real Prop. (2d Ed.) § 68; Turner, op. cit. supra note 54, at 101. Cf. Turner, ibid. 103.

88. Turner, op. cit. supra note 54 at 93, 108.

89. Leman v. Newnham, 1747, 1 Ves.Sen. 51; Toplis v. Baker, 1787, 2 Cox, 119; Trash v. White, 1791, 3 Bro.C.C. 289, contra. See discussion by Turner, op. cit. supra note 54, at 97, 99.

90. Christophers v. Sparke, 1820, 2 Jac. & W. 223; Cholmondeley v. Clinton, 1820, 2 Jac. & W. 1.

91. Turner, op. cit. supra note 54, at 98. See also Walsh, Mortgages, 18.

92. Hall v. Doe d. Surtees, 1822, 5 B. & Ald. 687; Turner, op. cit. supra note 54, at 101. See also Kales, Future Interests, §§ 17–20.

93. Turner, op. cit. supra note 54, at 99, 103; Walsh, Mortgages, 19.

94. Possession of an estate of a certain annual value determined the franchise right under the English statutes; hence either the mortgagor or mortgagee might have it. The amount of the mortgage was reckoned as reducing the annual value of the property. See 2 & 3 Will. IV c. 45, § 23; 6 & 7 Vict. c. 18, § 7. For a discussion of the cases and statutes, see Turner, op. cit. supra note 54, at 183–5.

95. Maitland, Equity, 266; Hazeltine, op. cit. supra note 60, at XXXII.

See also Rabinowitz, The Common Law Mortgage and the Conditional Bond, 1943, 92 U.Pa.L.Rev. 179; Distinction between Covenant and Condition in a Mortgage, 1940, 45 Dickinson L.Rev. 82.

96. Hazeltine criticizes (Hazeltine, op. cit. supra note 61, at XLIII citing Cromwell's Case, 1601, 2 Co. 69b) Turner's statement that the proviso "was not properly a condition but a covenant in the nature of a condition"; but later he states (ibid. XLVI) that "when the proviso for reconveyance was used due payment by the mortgagor did not, as in the case of the clause of defeasance, either ipso facto defeat the mortgagee's estate or give the mortgagor the right to defeat it by entry; it had the effect, however, of transforming the 'estate on condition' into a species of trust estate". That in the modern English law there has to be a reconveyance, see Coote, op. cit. supra note 58, at 5, citing In re Ethel and Mitchells and Butlers' Contract [1901] 1 Ch. 945.

also was a promise which equity would enforce specifically. Its development apparently coincided with that of the equity of redemption, and its popularity was based upon the practical advantages of getting back by a reconveyance, instead of by reentry, the interest conveyed to the mortgagee.[97] Regardless of which form was used, if the mortgagor failed to perform on the day set, the mortgagee's estate became absolute.[98]

C. THE INTERVENTION OF EQUITY

MORTGAGOR'S EQUITY OF REDEMPTION

6. Equity profoundly modified the unsatisfactory common law conveyance on condition subsequent by creating the equity of redemption. At first, equity aided a mortgagor who had not performed only on a special showing of some familiar ground of equitable jurisdiction. Quite suddenly, however, in the early part of the 17th Century relief was given as a matter of course subject to two qualifications:

(1) The mortgagor had to tender the principal and interest within a reasonable time after forfeiture;

(2) The mortgagee could go to court and obtain a decree ordering the debtor to pay by a fixed day or be forever barred.

This right of the mortgagor to get back his land was called an equity of redemption. Various explanations have been suggested for this development.

When legal machinery fashioned to do one job is used for another for which it is ill adapted, the work is badly done, and sooner or later alterations in the machine must be

made. So it was with the conveyance on condition or proviso intended as security for a debt. Equity first profoundly modified the workings of the device, and then the law courts either followed the lead of equity in greater or less degree or developed variations of their own.

The first interferences by chancery on behalf of mortgagors were on analogy to relief against a satisfied but outstanding bond[99] in cases where the mortgagor had performed.[1] In both cases equity was merely preventing forfeiture and penalty where the terms of the bargain had been fulfilled, and it would be an unconscionable breach of faith to exact a double payment in the one instance or to retain property in addition to the payment in the other.[2]

In the case of the satisfied mortgage there was the remedy of reentry available at law to prevent forfeiture. Equity's intervention really was to prevent the property being withheld in breach of good faith by the creditor. And it was a breach of good faith because the purpose of the transaction was security.[3]

Aid to the mortgagor to get back his property where he had not performed the condition at the time set and where, therefore, the mortgagee's title was absolute at law

---

97. Turner, op. cit. supra note 54, at 18–19; Hazeltine, op. cit. supra note 61, at XL et seq. Hazeltine suggests two bases for the proviso of reconveyance: one, the early attempts to cast the mortgage transaction into the form of a sale with an option or contract to repurchase which were treated by equity as mortgages if such in fact was the real intention (see Chaplin, op. cit. supra note 56, at 11); the other, the early chancery practice of compelling reconveyance if the debt was paid at the day set. The latter especially suggested to conveyancers the desirability of putting into the mortgage deed a covenant for reconveyance. Hazeltine, ibid. XLIV–XLV.

98. Hazeltine, op. cit. supra note 61, at XLVI.

99. Ames, Specialty Contracts and Equitable Defenses, 1895, 9 Harv.L.Rev. 49, 54; Barbour, History of Contract in English Equity, 4 Oxford Studies in Social and Legal History, 89; Turner, The Equity of Redemption, 22.

1. Bodenham v. Halle, 1456, 10 Seld.Soc.Pub. 137; 1470, Y.B. 9 Ed. IV, 25, 34. See 5 Holdsworth, Hist.Eng.Law, 293; Turner, op. cit. supra note 99, at 21–23; 1 Spence, The Equitable Jurisdiction of Chancery, 610; note, 1939, 25 Va.L.Rev. 947.

2. Turner, op. cit. supra note 99, at 23. See Storke, Introduction to Security, 1943, 16 Rocky Mt.L.Rev. 27, 37–39, pointing out that the mortgagor's right of redemption is really threefold: the common law right of redemption which can only be exercised on the law day; the equitable right of redemption which commences on default and continues for an indefinite period until it is cut off by foreclosure; and the statutory right of redemption, which commences at the date of the foreclosure sale and lasts for a fixed period set by statute.

3. Walsh, Mortgages, 7.

under the terms of the conveyance went considerably beyond this. At first it was done only in individual cases on a special showing of fraud, accident, oppression, or some similar familiar ground of general equity jurisdiction.

Here, also relief against forfeited bonds and penalty provisions seemed to be the precedents followed. Later the law courts recaptured their jurisdiction over forfeited bonds but did not do so as to mortgages. Coke suggests that this was because the bond agreement was still executory, whereas in the case of the mortgage it was executed, i. e., the mortgagee had title.[4] Quite suddenly, however, in the early part of the seventeenth century we find relief being given as a matter of course and right.[5] This right was subject to two conditions: one, the mortgagor must tender the principal and interest within a reasonable time after forfeiture; two, the mortgagee could go to court and obtain a decree ordering the debtor to pay by a fixed day or be forever barred.[6] The right thus given was called an equity of redemption.

The phrase "equity of redemption" had become common by 1700; the first case in which it appears, Duchess of Hamilton v. Countess of Dirlton was decided in 1654 but not published until 1693.[7]

The suggested explanations of this development have been various. The most exhaustive exploration of the question ends in the general conclusion that it was based upon a desire of chancery, possibly of one particular chancellor, to extend the scope of equity action so as to increase business at the expense of the law courts.[8] Certainly it is true that this development came at about the same time that the equity courts were established in power over the law courts.[9] This same discussion discounts the custom of relieving sureties against a default of the principal as a basis for extending relief to the mortgagor.[10] It also dismisses as anachronistic the doctrine that time is not of the essence in contracts for the payment of money. However, although denying it as a formulated principle, it does recognize, as an obviously present fact influencing the chancellor, that time in such case is not of sufficient importance to justify sacrificing property.[11] Finally it doubts what to a modern mind would seem a perfectly good and obvious reason, namely, that the mortgagee's right was only to the payment of his debt and the property was merely security for that purpose; and, since that was so, it would be a forfeiture to allow the mortgagee to keep it absolutely if the mortgagor was willing to pay even though the payment was somewhat belated.[12].

---

4. Co.Litt., § 334. See Turner, op. cit. supra note 99, at 33.

See Glenn, Morts., 13, ascribing the development of the equity of redemption to the bond analogy, equity having to intervene in the mortgage situation because the simple relief of refusing recovery for any sum other than that justly due which was available in the law courts was insufficient in the mortgage situation. The mortgagor wanted to get back his land and only equity could get him that by forcing the mortgagee to reconvey. Glenn, incidentally, regards the equity of redemption as a "natural right", Ibid., § 4.

5. Emanuel College v. Evans, 1625, 1 Ch.Rep. 18. But cf. Durfee, Cases on Security (1951) 16–20.

6. See Turner, op. cit. supra note 99, at 27.

7. 1 Ch.R. 165. See Turner, op. cit. supra note 99, at 56.

8. Turner, op. cit. supra note 99, at 30, 32, 35, 42.

9. See Betts, Power of Sale Without Notice, 1895, 15 Can.L.T. 1, 6.

10. Ibid. 34.

11. Ibid. 41.

12. See Lord Haldane's opinion in Kreglinger v. New Patagonia, etc., Co. [1914] A.C. 25, 35. Cf. note, 1939, 25 Va.L.Rev. 947, 948: "The latter [mortgagee] * * * could later [i. e., after strict foreclosure] sue at law upon the bond only upon the condition that the foreclosure be opened and the mortgagor permitted to redeem." By contrast it is somewhat startling to find in modern times the anachronism of a judge who believes that both our law of mortgages and the character of the people would have been better if the harsh rule of forfeiture by nonpayment on the very day set had not been abrogated by the development of the equity of redemption. See Lord Bramwell, in Salt v. Marquess of Northampton, 1892, A.C. 1, 18–19.

The notion that payment on the very day set is not vital to the debtor's ability to get back his property by payment later is not even a modern one.[13] It was an idea accepted in the courts of law in Glanville's time, as we have seen, as well as by the Council of Lateran in 1178,[14] and was a thoroughly established doctrine in the Roman Law by the time of Constantine which survived in the later codes.[15] That there was a clearly recognized forfeiture both in legal theory and in fact if the mortgagor is not permitted to redeem by a later payment has been frequently pointed out.

"While the mortgagor has lost his right to the land, the mortgage debt demains wholly unpaid; and consequently the mortgagee can at law keep the land, and yet compel the mortgagor to pay the mortgage debt. In a word the mortgagor loses (i. e., forfeits) his land merely by way of penalty for not performing the condition." [16]

The value of the property almost invariably greatly exceeded the amount of the debt, so that there was a striking actual forfeiture and penalty even though the debt itself was never enforced.[17] One writer lays it down flatly that equity's intervention in the case of mortgages was merely a specific exercise of the general jurisdiction to prevent penalties and forfeitures when they can be compensated for by an award of money.[18]

One thing not sufficiently stressed in this connection was the general dislike of courts, both common law and equity, of conditions. Relief against them in the guise of license, waiver, and estoppel became well recognized at law.[19] And equity helped out even where the condition was for the payment of money so that the damages, i. e., interest, could be said to be adequate.[20] The distinction between conditions for the preservation of an estate, of which the mortgage condition is one, was distinctly seen.[21]

It may be that these reasons were not expressly advanced at the time, and so, in that sense, are anachronistic. However, they seem implicit in any clear recognition that the conveyance on condition is for security purposes only. And that even the law courts did explicitly recognize this, before any action by equity, is admitted. Nothing could be clearer on the point than the words of a law judge speaking in 1314. "When a man pledges tenements his intention is not to grant an estate of inheritance, but to give security for the repayment of the money he has borrowed and to redeem the tenements; and in such case, if he repay the money he can enter." [22] To argue that the chancellor did not equally appreciate the true situation is to belittle his intelligence and knowledge.[23]

13. § 1, supra.

14. See Glenn, Morts., 6, 12. The erudite writer states in a footnote, idem, n. 9, that the canon is mentioned in Flowers of History, by Roger of Wendover. He also notes that in Spence, Equity, 1846, vol. 1, p. 628, it is attributed to Matthew Paris, but that this is error is shown by an 1852 edition (Bohn, London, Trans. by Giles) of the latter which indicates that the authentic work of Matthew Paris begins in 1235, and an appended Chronicle of earlier events was the work of Roger of Wendover.

15. See Sherman, Roman Law in the Modern World, 2d ed., 1922, §§ 614–621.

16. Langdell, Equity Jurisdiction.

17. See 3 Tiffany, Real Prop., § 599.

18. Pomeroy, Eq.Juris., 4th Ed., § 1180. See generally Loyd, Penalties and Forfeitures, 1915, 29 Harv. L.Rev. 117.

19. See Kales, Future Interests, §§ 278–282.

20. Kales, ibid.; Turner, op. cit. supra note 99, at 40. See also 5 Holdsworth, op. cit. supra note 1, at 330, quoting from Cary: " * * * the like favor is extendable against them that will take advantage upon any strict condition, for undoing the estate of another in lands, upon a small or trifling default."

21. Co.Litt., 206 a; Turner, op. cit. supra note 99, at LIX, 20. Simes, Future Interests, 2nd Ed. § 14; Coote, Mortgages, 9th Ed., 4; Robbins, Mortgages, 1, 4.

22. 3 Holdsworth, op. cit. supra note 1, at 130 n., quoting Spigurnel, J., in Anon. v. Anon., 1314, 3 Eyre of Kent, 29 Seld.Soc., 85. See Litt., Tenures, § 339 for a similar recognition. See also 2 Holdsworth, op. cit. supra note 1, at 579; Turner, op. cit. supra note 99, at 37, 39; Plucknett, Concise History of the Common Law, 2d Ed., 542.

23. See Walsh, Mortgages, 11 n. 30.

Of course, it is possible that the "automatic foreclosure, at a day fixed, of a security by conditional deed may have seemed to our ancestors no more harsh than the abrupt and final cutting off of an equity of redemption after the end of a fixed period allowed after entry, seems to us".[24] However, there is a vast difference, and one which has played an important part in mortgage law, between cutting off an interest in property by an agreement entered into at the time the loan is made and as a condition to getting it, and ending it later after a period fixed by the court of equity as reasonable and fair at the time the question is raised.

What part was played by the traditional view that mortgagors are necessitous men likely to be imposed upon by harsh conditions which would result in their losing their property, it is impossible to determine; probably quite a substantial one. The ideas and feelings which were responsible for the doctrines against clogging, improving the mortgagor out of his property, and collateral advantage, and the decisions receiving extrinsic evidence to show that a deed absolute on its face was meant to be a mortgage seem to be the same as those which brought the equity of redemption into existence in the first place; and here, certainly, tenderness for the mortgagor due to a belief in his weak economic status, plus, perhaps, some animus against the money lending class, was an important factor.

Legislative permission to charge interest coupled with a relaxation of the Church's opposition to it was another effective factor influencing the chancellor. The interest which the mortgagee could now collect was considered adequate compensation to the mortgagee, for delayed payment.[24a]

24. Chaplin, The Story of Mortgage Law, 1890, 4 Harv.L.Rev. 1, 10. See also Gavit, Under the Lien Theory of Mortgages Is the Mortgage Only a Power of Sale? 1931, 15 Minn.L.Rev. 147, 151.

24a. See Fratcher, Restraints upon Alienation of Equitable Interests in Michigan Property, 1953, 51 Mich.L.Rev. 509, 540, 541.

EQUITY OF REDEMPTION AS EQUITABLE ESTATE

7. Accepting the view that the mortgage was a security transaction, the equitable theory of the nature of the mortgagor's interest evolved from the original concept of a purely in personam right to that of an equitable estate. In certain respects this equitable ownership idea was departed from or not necessarily involved. It existed from the instant the mortgage was given, and therefore might have been differentiated from the equity of redemption as originally conceived which arose only on default. No such distinction was stressed and the term came to be applied indiscriminately to the mortgagor's interest both before and after default.

Whatever the original reasons for the chancellor's interventions, clearly the later equity view was that the property was only security and intercession needed no other justification than to limit and protect it for that purpose. It strains credulity to believe, even without the evidence to the contrary, that the law courts did not recognize just as clearly as did the courts of equity that the parties intended the transaction to be one for security purposes only. The difficulty was that, although they saw it, they felt powerless to alter the design of the legal device chosen by the parties to achieve their purpose. So far as the law courts were concerned, since the parties had seen fit to have the entire legal title given as security (not absolutely, since the mortgagor could get it back by paying on a certain day), that was that. There were, however, no such limitations felt by the courts of equity, and consequently, they could superimpose upon the legal device various restrictions or additions so as to give to the mortgagee only that protection in regard to the property which it thought necessary or desirable that he should have for the purpose of security. What this protection should be inevitably would be a compound of conflicting economic interests, contradictory social ideals, business expediency, feelings of "fairness" in the particular case, and attempts, justifiable or otherwise, at logical consistency with other legal rules plus other miscellaneous considerations. And, of course, these factors were not static, nor were they regardless of time and place.

In developing this view of the mortgage as a security transaction the equitable theory of the nature and incidents of the mortgagor's interest in the property before default underwent considerable change. For one thing, the term, equity of redemption, which had previously and appropriately been applied to the mortgagor's right to get back his property after default was applied somewhat inappropriately to this entirely distinct equitable ownership before default.[25] This, however, is merely a matter of nomenclature. But the analytical nature of the interest itself was the subject of serious and important inquiry and decision. Although the differences are many and fundamental, there is a certain analogy, which courts and writers frequently noted, to the equitable interest of a cestui que trust.[26]

At first the mortgagor's interest was looked upon as a purely in personam right[27] against the mortgagee, soon was perceived to be in rem, and finally was regarded as an equitable estate,[28] a conception conforming to both popular and legal notions. Thus it may be cut into lesser estates;[29] it must be conveyed by a formal conveyance with formal

limitations;[30] it will descend to the heirs of the mortgagor;[31] it may be devised,[32] mortgaged, or entailed;[33] it will prevail against heirs, purchasers, and other successors of the mortgagee;[34] on the mortgagor's death it is entitled to exoneration against the personal estate of the mortgagor;[35] and the mortgagor has an equitable seizin so that the husband is entitled to curtesy.[36] In some other respects the ownership idea was departed from or not necessarily involved. Thus, anomalously dower was denied on analogy to the rule in trusts;[37] but this was changed by statute which, however, gave the husband a power of disposition over it.[38] Again, the

25. See 3 Tiffany, Real Prop., 2d Ed., § 599.

26. See Turner, op. cit. supra note 99, at 157 et seq.; see also Glenn, Morts., § 6; Hargrove & Butlers notes, 3 Co. Litt., # 96, for a comparison of the equity of redemption and a trust.

27. Roscarrick v. Barton, 1672, 1 Ch.Ca. 217, held that being a mere right it was not an estate of inheritance capable of being entailed under the statute De Donis. See Pomeroy, op. cit. supra note 18, at § 1180; Coote, Mortgages, 9th Ed., 650; 3 Tiffany, Real Prop., 2d Ed., § 599; Turner, op. cit. supra note 99, at 65 et seq.

28. Co.Litt., 205a n.; Turner, op. cit. supra note 99, at 65 et seq.; Maitland, Equity, 281. See also Fratcher, Restraints upon Alienation of Equitable Interests in Michigan Property, 1953, 51 Mich.L. Rev. 509, 542.

29. Pomeroy, loc. cit. supra note 18; Turner, op. cit. supra note 99, at 80.

30. Maitland, loc. cit. supra note 28; 1 Prest., Abst., 146; 1 Coote, op. cit. supra note 27, at 650. Of course, the legal interest of the mortgagor before default was inalienable until made alienable by statute.

31. How v. Vigures, 1629, 1 Ch.R. 32. See 1 Coote, op. cit. supra note 27, at 668; Maitland, loc. cit. supra note 28.

32. Porter v. Emery, 1637, 1 Ch.R. 97. See Maitland, loc. cit. supra note 28.

33. See Coote, op. cit. supra note 27, at 656, 660; Pomeroy, loc. cit. supra note 18; Maitland, op. cit. supra note 28, at 282.

34. Hanmer v. Lochard, 1612, Tot. 132; Bacon v. Bacon, 1640, Tot. 133. See Pawlett v. A.–G., 1667, Hard. 465, 469. See, also, 6 Holdsworth, op. cit. supra note 1, at 664; Turner, op. cit. supra note 99, at 50, 54–55. Cf. Co.Litt., 205a n. The early rule was that the dower right of the mortgagee's wife took precedence over the equity of redemption. Nash v. Preston, 1632, Cro.Car. 190. This was changed by Noel v. Jevon, 1678, 2 Freem. 43.

35. Cope v. Cope, 2 Salk. 449; Pockley v. Pockley, 1681, 1 Vern. 36. See Holdsworth, loc. cit. supra note 34; Turner, op. cit. supra note 1, at 63–64. This rule was changed by Locke King's Act, 17 & 18 Vict. c. 113, and later acts. 30 & 31 Vict. c. 69; 40 & 41 Vict. c. 34. See Coote, op. cit. supra note 27, at 790.

36. Casborne v. Scarfe, 1738, 2 Jac. & W. 194. See Turner, op. cit. supra note 99, at 66–67; Coote, op. cit. supra note 27, at 667; Pomeroy, loc. cit. supra note 18; Walsh, Mortgages, 13.

37. In the United States the wife did get dower and the husband got curtesy in the redemption. See Glenn, Mortgages, §§ 38, 301; A.–G. v. Scott, 1735, Cases, t. Talb. 138, and cases in note. See Coote, op. cit. supra note 21, at 688. See generally Haskins, Dower in Mortgaged Property, 1951, 5 Miami L.Rev. 187.

38. 3 & 4 Will. IV c. 105. 15 Geo. V c. 23, § 56 repealed the Dower Act of 1833 as obsolete under the

trust analogy was followed to deny escheat.[39] Although the mortgagor was accorded personal rights and privileges of voting, holding court, settlements under poor laws,[40] and nominating to benefices,[41] these, with the exception of the last, turned upon possession rather than ownership of the property.[42] The redemption interest became assets which could be reached by creditors.[43]

STATUTORY RIGHT TO REDEEM

8. The statutory right to redeem from foreclosure sale is distinct from the mortgagor's equity of redemption. It arises only after the latter has been foreclosed by sale. Although created for the benefit of the mortgagor, it has been criticized. During the depression years of the thirties it proved inadequate to accomplish its primary purposes. A wave of additional legislation and judicial decisions followed for the purpose of correcting the defects.

The equity of redemption and equitable estate of the mortgagor must be carefully dis-

changes made in the land law in 1925. See Coote, loc. cit. supra note 37.

39. The beneficial interest was held to be vested in the trustee on the death of the cestui que trust intestate and without an heir. Burgess v. Wheate, 1757, 1 Eden, 177. This led Lord Eldon to believe that in the analogous case of the mortgagor dying intestate and without an heir no one could redeem from the mortgagee. Gordon v. Gordon, 1821, 3 Swans. 400, 470. Later, the equity of redemption being assets for the payment of debts, the mortgagor's personal representative might redeem. Beale v. Symonds, 1853, 16 Beav. 406. See Turner, op. cit. supra note 99, at 73.

40. Coote, op. cit. supra note 21, at 651; Turner, op. cit. supra note 99, at 80, 183.

41. Mackensie v. Robinson, 1747, 3 Atk. 559.

42. 7 & 8 Will. III c. 25, § 7; 7 & 8 Geo. V., c. 64. Cf. note 70d under The Classical Common Law Mortgage, ante.

43. A creditor of the mortgagor was allowed to redeem the property from the mortgagee. Mole v. Franklin, 1673, Rep.Temp.Finch, 51; Greswold v. Marsham, 1685, 2 Ch.Ca. 170. However, to levy on the equity of redemption the aid of equity had to be asked. Lyster v. Dolland, 1792, 3 Bro.C.C. 478; Forth v. Duke of Norfolk, 1820, 4 Mad. 503. See Turner, op. cit. supra note 99, at 60, 160 et seq.; Pomeroy, Eq.Juris., 4th Ed., § 1180.

For an excellent long note covering all aspects of the problem, see The Statutory Right of Redemption in California, 1964, 52 Cal.L.Rev. 846.

tinguished from a statutory right to redeem from the purchaser on a foreclosure sale. The latter right does not come into existence until the former is extinguished.[44] In order to extinguish the former, the chief requirement is performance of the obligation for which the mortgage is given.[45] The basic factor in redemption from foreclosure sale is payment of the sale price, but to this statutes add different amounts,[46] one of the most important under some statutes being the amount of the lien, other than the one under which the property was sold, held by a prior redemptioner who bought the property at the sale.[47] Further, the effects of redemption are quite different. On redemption from the mortgage the mortgagor has back his interest in the property as it existed at the time of the mortgage freed from the mortgage incumbrance.[48] The effect of statutory redemption cannot be stated simply. Different statutes provide for different results, and the consequences vary according to the persons who exercise the right. The matter is discussed more fully later,[49] and it may suffice to state here that the effect of statutory redemption always differs from that of redemption from a mortgage.

The statutory right of redemption was created, in part to give the mortgagor or other

44. See Powers v. Andrews, 1887, 84 Ala. 289, 291, 4 So. 263, 264; Viceman v. Finch, 1881, 79 Ind. 511; Higgs v. McDuffie, 1916, 81 Or. 256, 158 P. 953.

The whole purpose of foreclosure is to end the right to redeem from the mortgage. However, as has been pointed out (Durfee & Doddridge, 1925, 23 Mich.L.Rev. 825, 837 n. 40) and as will be seen later (Chapter 12A, post), the exact moment when the right to redeem from the mortgage ceases to exist is not always easy to determine. This is true not only of strict foreclosure (Chapter 13A, post), but of foreclosure by sale (Chapter 13, Subdivision C, infra, and Durfee & Doddridge, supra). See Storke, Introduction to Security, 1943, 16 Rocky Mt.L.Rev. 27, 38.

45. See § 303, infra.

46. See § 307, infra.

47. E. g., Iowa Code, § 4049; Cal.Code Civ.Proc. § 702.

48. See § 302, infra.

49. See Chapter 12, Subdivision B, **infra.**

person entitled to exercise the right additional time to refinance and save his property, but mainly to put pressure on the mortgage creditor (usually the chief if not the only bidder) to bid for the property on foreclosure sale its value, at least up to the amount of the mortgage debt.[50]

A subsidiary purpose seems to be to allow, as a sort of exemption, an additional period of occupancy to a hard-pressed mortgagor.[51] Ordinarily it can be exercised not only by the mortgagor and his successors, but by junior encumbrancers and judgment creditors.[52]

Usually there is a provision that if one of the latter redeem, other lienors, usually those junior to him, or to the lien under which the property was sold, may in turn redeem by paying both the foreclosure sale price and the amount of the encumbrance held by the prior redemptioner, if senior to him, plus certain other charges.

The effects of redemption by different persons who are given the right to redeem are not the same and are often a source of conflict. Redemption by a judgment debtor or his successor in interest ends the redemption period and unsatisfied junior liens reattach to the property. Redemption by a "redemptioner" operated as a transfer of the interest of the purchaser on foreclosure sale. Recently in California this distinction has been made uncertain.[52a]

Objections are several. The right is rarely exercised.[53] Relying on the right to the additional time period, mortgagors are inclined to become careless in keeping up their payments.[54] In order to redeem, the entire amount must be paid in cash; but there seldom would be a foreclosure if the mortgagor could pay even a substantial part of his debt in cash.[55] It prevents a speedy realization by the mortgagee and gives an opportunity to a hopeless mortgagor to milk the property. To

---

50. See Durfee and Doddridge, Redemption from Foreclosure Sale—The Uniform Mortgage Act, 1925, 23 Mich.L.Rev. 825; see note, 1937, 4 U. of Chi.L. Rev. 675, 676, summarizing the purposes for which the right was created as follows: "(1) to protect debtors from high personal obligations arising from high deficiency judgments; (2) to enable defaulting debtors to regain their properties; (3) to protect unsecured creditors from having to share in unencumbered assets with the holders of an oversized deficiency judgment; (4) to allow creditors to take advantage of an increase in value of foreclosed property."

"It seems clear that the first redemption period established by legislatures came as a consequence of early depressions, at a time when the courts had just abandoned their practice of granting the right to redeem after sale. This type of legislation may be traced back to 1820, when the country was sharing in the international economic disturbance following the Napoleonic Wars—in our country evidenced by the collapse of a land boom." Skilton, Government and the Mortgage Debtor, 19.

But cf. Glenn, Morts., § 229.

For a resume of the arguments for and against the statutory right of redemption see The Statutory Right of Redemption in California, 1964, 52 Cal.L. Rev. 846, 848 and 875.

51. "The purpose of the statutes appears to be to afford the mortgagor at least one crop year after default to recoup his losses and possibly achieve financial solvency." Skilton, Proposed Uniform Mortgage Legislation, 1942, 9 Am.L.School Rev. 1128, 1131.

See note, 1926, 26 Col.L.Rev. 363.

But most mortgages now contain assignments or pledges of rents and profits; and even in the absence of a pledge, a receiver may be appointed. See Tefft, The Myth of Strict Foreclosure, 1937, 4 U. of Chi.L.Rev. 575.

52. As to the right to execute on a statutory right of redemption, see notes, 1926, 26 Col.L.Rev. 363; 1926, 10 Minn.L.Rev. 440.

Look also at Higgs v. McDuffie, 1916, 81 Or. 256, 158 P. 953; Sayre v. Vander Voort, 1925, 200 Iowa 990, 205 N.W. 760, 42 A.L.R. 880.

The latter persons are called redemptioners. See West's Ann.Cal.Code Civ.Proc. § 701.

As to who can redeem, how much must be paid to redeem, to whom it may be paid, see The Statutory Right of Redemption in California, 1964, 52 Cal.L. Rev. 846, 853–862, 863–868, 866–872.

52a. Call v. Thunderbird Mortgage Co., 1962, 58 Cal. 2d 542, 25 Cal.Rptr. 265, 375 P.2d 169. See The Statutory Right of Redemption in California, 1964, 52 Cal.L.Rev. 846, 872–875.

53. Cf. note, 1938, 5 U. of Chi.L.Rev. 625, 627: " * * * the statute, if successful, was intended to operate only as a threat. It was not desired that redemption actually take place, but that the mortgagee bid adequately at the first sale. In fact, if redemption did actually occur in a given case, it was a sign that the statute had failed to work."

54. 1922, Handbook of Com. on Un.St.Laws, 260.

55. Russell, Foreclosures (Address before the U.S. Bldg. & Loan League, Oct. 7, 1937).

prevent this a receiver is usually appointed, and this generally results in less competent management and increased costs in fees to the receiver's attorney. Further, outsiders will not bid freely for property to which they cannot obtain an indefeasible title. As a result the system, under certain circumstances at least, works to the injury of the mortgagor in making his borrowing more difficult and expensive and "reducing the amount which the property will bring on the sale, making more doubtful the securing of any surplus over and above the mortgage debt".[56]

The experience of the depression years in the nineteen-thirties revealed that in periods of acute and prolonged deflation it is inadequate to accomplish its primary purposes. To fill in the deficiencies a wave of legislation followed, supplemented by decisions. Moratoria were granted.[57] Deficiency judgments were abolished or limited by using the fair value of the property rather than the proceeds of the foreclosure sale as basis for determining the amount of the deficiency.[58] Power to fix upset prices was given. Procedures for relief under the federal bankruptcy law were provided.[59]

POSITION OF MORTGAGEE

9. Having legal title the mortgagee had most, if not all, of the incidents that go with it. Equity did not interfere with the exercise of these legal incidents except to insist that he should reap the benefits of them for himself only insofar as it thought them necessary or desirable for his protection as a secured creditor.

The mortgagee's position at law caused little difficulty. He had the legal title and with it most, if not all, of the incidents that ordinarily go with it.[60] And equity did not prevent him from exercising those legal incidents, only insisting that he should reap the benefits of them for himself only insofar as, for one reason or another, it thought them necessary and desirable for his protection as a secured creditor. Thus he might exercise his legal rights to take possession and get the rents and profits, but he must account for them strictly in equity.[61] On his death title went to his heir or devisee, but it must be held for the one entitled to the performance

56. Walsh, Morts., 337.

In addition to references in the preceding footnotes, for discussions of the subject see, Carey, Brabner-Smith, and Sullivan, Studies in Foreclosures in Cook County: II. Foreclosure Methods and Redemption, 1933, 27 Ill.L.Rev. 595, 615; Kidd, Trust Deeds and Mortgages in California, 1915, 3 Calif.L. Rev. 381, 401; Becker and Harbert, Redemptions from Judicial Sales under the Laws of Illinois, May, 1929, Chicago-Kent Rev.; Harbert, Recent Problems Concerning Redemption from Judicial Sales by Judgment Creditors, 1938, 3 John Marshall L.Q. 335; note, 1938, 5 U. of Chi.L.Rev. 625; 1927, Handbook of Com.Un.St.Laws, 691; Special Report No. 1 on Social and Economic Effects of Existing Foreclosure Procedure Submitted to the Central Housing Committee, C.H.C. 52870 L & L of 6; Russell, Survey of Foreclosure Operations (H.O.L. C.Publ., Aug. 27, 1939). See also the foreclosure provisions of the proposed Uniform Real Estate Mortgage and Foreclosure Act as prepared by the Sub-Committee on Law and Legislation of the Central Housing Committee, Aug. 28, 1936; Wheeler and Durfee, Evasion of Mortgage Moratoria by Prosecution of Personal Remedy, 1935, 33 Mich.L. Rev. 1196, 1202–1209; Blum, Statutory Redemption After Mortgage Foreclosure, 1949, 35 Iowa L.Rev. 72; Reeve, The New Proposal for a Uniform Mortgage Act, 1938, 5 Law & Contemp.Prob. 564, 576; 2 Reeve, Illinois Law of Mortgages and Foreclosures, C. 35 (1932); Rothschild, The Proposed Illinois Mortgage Act, Annual Report of the Illinois State Bar Association, 1937, 138; MacChesney and Leesman, The Mortgage Foreclosure Problem—Its Evolution in Reorganizations and Bankruptcy Act Amendments, 1937, 23 A.B.A.J. 41, 47; 1941, 27 Va. L.Rev. 926, 934; 1938, 86 U. of Pa.L.Rev. 517, 522; 1927, 27 Col.L.Rev. 861, 867; 1930, 17 Va.L.Rev. 179, 185; 1932, Calif.State Bar, 231, 252; 1917, 16 Mich.L.Rev. 112; 1942, 28 Va.L.Rev. 651; 1941, 35 Ill.L.Rev. 485.

57. See § 331, infra.

58. See § 335, infra.

59. See § 330, n. 47, infra.

60. See, supra, The Classical Common Law Mortgage B.

61. Holman v. Vaux (about 13 Jac.) Tot. 133; Fulthrope v. Foster, 1687, 1 Vern. 476. See 6 Holdsworth, Hist.Eng.Law, 664; 5 Holdsworth, ibid. 332; Coote, Morts., 9th Ed., 821; Maitland, Equity, 274. "The situation of a mortgagee in possession is far from an eligible one." 2 Davidson's Precedents, 4th Ed., II, 90. See, supra, Subdivision B. The Classical Common Law Mortgage, note 82. See also Tefft, The Myth of Strict Foreclosure, 1937, 4 U. of Chi.L.Rev. 575, 582.

of the mortgagor.[62] He might have the legal right to the presentment of an advowson, but he must follow the mortgagor's wishes in making it.[63] And, on the mortgagor redeeming in equity after the death of the mortgagee, not his heirs but his personal representatives were entitled to the money.[64]

FORECLOSURE

10. To enable the mortgagee to be freed sometime of the threat of redemption by the mortgagor, equity invented the strict foreclosure proceeding. This operated to bar the mortgagor from redeeming unless he exercised his right within a specified time. In the United States strict foreclosure has been supplanted generally by foreclosure by sale. This takes two forms. One is by judicial sale; the other is by exercising a power of sale conferred upon the mortgagee. Other methods of foreclosure are found in a few states.

The creation of the mortgagor's equity of redemption required the development of additional rights in the mortgagee. To hold that the mortgagor's right to redeem would last forever would be to recreate the disadvantages of the old vif gage [65] with the added hazards of strict accounting. The mortgagee needed to be freed sometime of the threat of having the property redeemed, and this equity accomplished by foreclosure proceedings. At the request of the mortgagee, who would set forth the default of the mortgagor, the equity court would order the mortgagor to pay the debt, interest, and costs within a reasonable time (originally a definite time was set for each individual case; later the same time was fixed for all cases)

or be forever barred from redeeming.[66] The effect of such a proceeding was to leave the mortgagee at last with a title complete both at law and in equity. This proceeding was and is known as a strict foreclosure. Since, except in unusual cases, a lender does not advance nearly the value of the property, the strict foreclosure worked a forfeiture just as did the strict condition at law.[67] This statement does not take into account the possibility of reopening a foreclosure in England, for which no general rules were laid down, each individual case resting on its own merits.[68]

"If the mortgaged property was far more valuable than the mortgage debt, if it had for the mortgagor a *pretium affectionis* being an old family estate, if the mortgagor was prevented from redeeming by some accident, if he has come speedily—these all are circumstances in favour of permitting him to redeem, though an absolute order for foreclosure has been made against him." [69]

On the other hand, in the exceptional case where the property was inadequate security it might work to the disadvantage of the mortgagee if the debt were extinguished by the foreclosure.[70]

Although strict foreclosure continued in England and is found in many of the United

---

62. See Note to Casborne v. Scarfe, 1737, 1 Atk. 603. See also supra, Subdivision B. The Classical Common Law Mortgage, note 70.

63. See note 41, supra. See also 2 Coote, Morts., 9th Ed., 817.

64. Thornborough v. Baker, 1676, 3 Swans. 628. See Turner, The Equity of Redemption, 52, 58–59; Pomeroy, Eq.Juris, 4th Ed., § 1182. Cf. Co.Litt., §§ 334, 339.

65. See, supra, Subdivision A. Early Forms, note 32.

66. How v. Vigures, supra note 31. See 5 Holdsworth, op. cit. supra note 61, at 331; Maitland, op. cit. supra note 61, at 270 et seq.; 2 Coote, op. cit. supra note 61, at 1025.

67. See § 6, supra. See also §§ 311, 312, infra.

68. 2 Coote, Morts., 9th Ed., 1086. See § 311, infra.

69. Maitland, Equity, 272. See Campbell v. Holyland, 1877, 7 Ch.D. 166, 170. See also 2 Wiltsie, Mortgage Foreclosure, 4th Ed., § 910. For discussions of the workings of strict foreclosure in England and in this country, look at Turner, The English Mortgage of Land as Security, 1934. 20 Va.L. Rev. 729; Tefft, The Myth of Strict Foreclosure, 1937, 4 U. of Chi.L.Rev. 575; Glenn, A Study on Strict Foreclosure, 1943, 29 Va.L.Rev. 519; Thomas, Strict Foreclosure in Illinois, 1910, 4 Ill.L.Rev. 572; note, 1929, 27 Mich.L.Rev. 797; note, 1903, 47 Sol.J. 564; McDougal, Rev. of Walsh, Mortgages, 1935, 44 Yale L.J. 1278; note, 1939, 25 Va.L.Rev. 947.

See also §§ 311, 312, infra.

70. See § 6, supra. See also 2 Wiltsie, Mortgage Foreclosure, 4th Ed., § 909.

States,[71] it has been supplanted in large measure, by foreclosure by sale,[72] which takes two forms: one by court action; the other by a power of sale conferred on the mortgagee by the mortgagor. In both the fundamentals are the same. The mortgaged property is sold, under certain safeguards to secure its fair conduct, and the proceeds are used to pay the expenses of the proceedings and the claim of the mortgagee, with any surplus going to the mortgagor. If the property doesn't bring enough to pay the mortgage claim, the mortgagee may get a judgment for the deficiency.

Originally equity could not give the mortgagee a judgment on the mortgagor's covenant. If a mortgagee wanted such a judgment, he would have to bring a separate action in a court of law. Since the Judicature Act all relief can be given in the one action. This is also true generally today in the United States.[73]

Other methods of foreclosure in the United States are discussed later.[74]

SECOND MORTGAGES

11. Mortgages subsequent to the first could only be, under the system thus developed, equitable ones. There is authority in some American title states that such later mortgages are legal ones.

Second and succeeding mortgages under the scheme of mortgage law thus developed could only be equitable ones.[75] This made possible

71. See §§ 311, 312, infra.

72. See Maitland, Equity, 275; Turner, The Equity of Redemption, 120, 121. Today by statute every mortgage in England has in it a power of sale. Maitland, supra, 276; Walsh, Morts., 342 n. 8.

73. See Maitland, Equity, 272; 2 Wiltsie, Mortgage Foreclosure, 4th Ed., § 909; Note, 1929, 27 Mich.L. Rev. 797.

74. See Chapter 13, infra.

75. See Goodman v. White, 1857, 26 Conn. 317; Pomeroy, Eq.Juris., 4th Ed., § 1185; Maitland, Equity, 283.
Cf. Chamberlain v. Thompson, 1834, 10 Conn. 243, 26 Am.Dec. 390; Bates v. Coe, 1834, 10 Conn. 280;

the English doctrine of tacking,[76] whereby a third mortgagee by getting in the legal title of the first mortgagee could squeeze out the second mortgagee. Paradoxically, in the United States, the courts took the view even in "title" states that, although the mortgage passed a legal title to the mortgagee, that title was for the purpose of security and the general ownership, at law as well as in equity, remains in the mortgagor. If this is so, it followed that there remained in the mortgagor an interest capable of raising additional legal security interests in second and subsequent mortgagees.[77]

MODERN ENGLISH MORTGAGE

12. The 1925 Law of Property Act created a new system of mortgages in England. It provided for registered, indestructible legal interests of terms for years or by way of charge in the mortgagee. The mortgagee forecloses by either judicial or non-judicial sale which vests the fee in a purchaser. It is thus analogous to the mortgage of Bracton's day. Strict foreclosure is also possible. The equitable mortgage by deposit of title deeds was expressly preserved.

Since the 1925 Law of Property Act in England [78] the mortgagee of a freehold gets

Town of Clinton v. Town of Westbrook, 1871, 38 Conn. 9.

76. See Ames, Lectures on Legal History, 267; 2 Coote, Mortgages, 8th Ed., 1248 et seq.; Jenks, Short History of English Law, 219; Maitland, Equity, 286; Rollison, Priorities in the Law of Mortgages, 1932, 8 Not.D.Law, 28, 39; note, 1862, 2 Am. L.Reg., N.S., 1, 13. The doctrine was abolished in England in 1925. 2 Coote supra 1245; Maitland, Equity, Brunyate's Ed., 207.

77. Sanders v. Reed, 1842, 12 N.H. 558; Gooding v. Shea, 1869, 103 Mass. 360, 4 Am.Rep. 563.
See also Pomeroy, Equity Juris, 5th Ed., § 1233 n. 19. But see Jackson v. Turrell (1877) 39 N.J.L. 329, 333: "A second mortgagee is, in law, as in equity, a mere lien-holder * * * The reasons which support the claim of the first mortgagee defeat the claim of every other one to be regarded as the legal owner of the fee."

78. See Johnson, The Reform of Real Property Law in England, 1925, 25 Col.L.Rev. 609, 619 et seq.; Schnebly, The English Land Legislation of 1925, 1925, 40 Harv.L.Rev. 248, 284.

either a long term lease,[79] 3000 years unless otherwise specified, or a legal charge [80] which seems to be similar to the American "lien," the mortgagor retaining the full legal reversion expectant upon the determination of the mortgage term or of the charge. A second mortgagee obtains a similar term of years longer by one day than, but subject to, the first mortgage term.[81] Leaseholds may be mortgaged in a similar fashion by giving in mortgage a sublease for a term ten days less than that vested in the mortgagor, subsequent mortgagees taking a term one day longer than that of the immediately prior mortgagee.[82] The legal incidents of the term and the charge are the same and there seems no good reason for providing for two methods of accomplishing the same thing.[83]

The holder of an equitable mortgage by deposit of title deeds [84] is expressly protected in his security by the new legislation.[85] The continuance of this type of mortgage seems, on its face, inconsistent with the new scheme of mortgages which provides for registered, indestructible legal interests in the mortgagee. However, possession of the title deeds by the mortgagee is a substantial equivalent of registration. The equitable interest can be defeated only by a conveyance of the legal

title to a purchaser without notice, an event which could rarely happen since the purchaser must ask for the deeds to escape being defeated by a charge of negligence on his part.[86]

All mortgages not secured by deposit of title deeds must be registered.[87] The mortgagee may realize his claim on default either by court foreclosure and decree followed by sale or by the exercise by the mortgagee himself of a statutory power of sale and the sale in both cases will vest the fee simple in the purchaser subject to any prior legal mortgage.[88] There may also be a strict foreclosure which will vest title in the mortgagee.[89]

This modern English mortgage of a term for years which will expand into a fee upon foreclosure harks back to the Bractonian mortgage previously discussed, a similarity which has not gone unremarked.[90] It is worth noting, however, that it took a statutory provision to make possible this transformation of a term into a fee in present-day England, a tribute to the continuing rigidity of the conceptions of real property which had developed by the fifteenth century, whereas in Bracton's time the looser notions of seizin then prevailing found no difficulty in doing the same thing.[91]

79. Law of Prop. Act, 1925, 15 Geo. V, c. 20, § 85.

80. Ibid., § 87. See Steyning and Littlehampton Bldg. Soc. v. Wilson, [1951] Ch.D., 2 All E.R. 452.

81. Ibid., § 85(2).

82. Ibid., § 87.

83. See Topham, Law of Property Acts, 1925, 70 Sol. J. 135, "I rather think that if the idea of enabling people to create a legal mortgage by that somewhat short and simple form [i. e., a legal charge] that occurred to the draughtsmen before they brought in this system of mortgaging by demise, that might have taken the place of it; but it had gone so far that it could not very well be put in entirely in its place, so it was put in as an alternative form."

84. See § 34, infra.

85. L.P.A. § 13; ibid. § 2(3) (i); Settled Land Act, § 21(2) (i). This in spite of the fact that such a

mortgage need not, in fact could not by reason of its very nature, be registered. Land Charges Act, § 10(I) Class C(i). See Topham, Law of Property Acts, 1925, 70 Sol.J. 28, 61.

86. See § 34, infra. See also Schnebly, The English Land Legislation of 1925, 1925, 40 Harv.L.Rev. 248, 284.

87. Land Charges Act, §§ 10(I) Class C(i), 13(2).

88. L.P.A., §§ 88, 116.

89. L.P.A., § 88(2).

90. Note, Mortgages in Legal History, 1935, 180 L.T. (Jour.) 179.

91. See § 4, ante. On the question of priorities between non-registered legal mortgages and equitable puisne mortgages or equitable mortgages by deposit of title deeds, see Schnebly, English Land Legislation of 1925, 40 Harv.L.Rev. 248, 287.

D. AMERICAN DEVELOPMENTS

PRINCIPAL AMERICAN THEORIES

13. **America inherited the English law of mortgages but radically modified it. The three main streams into which it has divided are generally described as:**

(1) **The common law, title, or estate theory;**

(2) **The intermediate or hybrid theory;**

(3) **The lien theory.**

In all legal systems there seems to be in the law of mortgages an evolution from a forfeit-idea in which the res is given as conditional satisfaction of some act for which there is no personal duty (at least not one for which there is a direct action) to a security idea.[92] Although it is not a necessary consequence of this development, there goes along with it a change from creditor-possession of the res to debtor-possession.[93] As already noted there did exist at an early period in the common law, in the Jewish mortgage and the statutory registered agreements under seal, instances of security with debtor-possession.[94] These however died out, and the later progression from one to the other in the common law has been complicated and obscured by the dual system of law and equity. In England the two systems, so far as the law of mortgages is concerned, were kept fairly separate and distinct both as to procedure and substance up to 1875.[95] To the lawyer who has become accustomed to the unnatural duality, this has made for greater simplicity of legal theory. At law, with comparatively minor modifications (such as dower in the wife, attachments and levies by creditors, etc.), the rigid rules of the law of real property were adhered to; the language of the conveyance was taken at its literal face. In equity, on the other hand, the security idea was fully developed, and logically and symmetrically worked out. Equity, however, never directly touched the matter of the right to possession. It most effectively discouraged its exercise by insisting upon a rigidly strict accounting which at the same time gave to the mortgagor a substantial equivalent of his own enjoyment and use of the property. But the legal right to possession was always in the mortgagee, and he could use it if he chose.

America inherited this whole English law of mortgages, but has departed from it radically even in states which in form cling to it. The methods, kinds, and degrees of departure, although they should be fundamentally easy to understand, have been so complex and diverse as to cause bewilderment to anyone who looks at them unrelated to their historical background. There are actually only two methods which have been employed. However, because on one point a result has been reached so different from that arrived at by others using the same technique, an attempt has been made to create a third category. These three methods usually are described as, one, the common law, title or estate theory; two, the intermediate or hybrid[96] theory; and three, the lien theory. Accepting this traditional tripartite division as that generally encountered in common usage and as being, as will be argued later, useful even if not necessary or fundamental, a brief examination of it is in order.

---

92. Wigmore, The Pledge Idea, 1897, 10 Harv.L.Rev. 321, 389 and note, 1897, 11 Harv.L.Rev. 18; Turner, The Equity of Redemption, Preface, VIII.

93. See Hazeltine, General Preface, VIII, in Turner, The Equity of Redemption.

94. See supra, §§ 3, 4.

95. See Turner, The Equity of Redemption, 122 et seq.; Maitland, Equity, 272. It is true that mortgages with the mortgagor in possession were known in the time of Blackstone. See Glenn, Morts., § 2.

This did not alter the fact that, unless he agreed to the contrary, the mortgagee had the legal right to possession.

96. Campbell, Cas. on Morts., c. I, § 2; c. XIII, § II n. 1; Durfee, The Lien or Equitable Theory of Mortgages—Some Generalizations, 1911, 10 Mich.L. Rev. 579, n. 3. See also Note, Rights of Junior Lienholders in Wisconsin, 1959, 43 Marq.L.Rev. 89, 90.

TITLE AND INTERMEDIATE THEORIES

14. Title theory states retain the form of the common law mortgage but have whittled away many incidents of legal title considered unnecessary for security purposes. They do, however, leave the mortgagee the right to possession. This distinguishes them from the intermediate states where the mortgagee cannot get possession until default.

The first method has been to retain the form and language of the common law conveyance in fee on condition or proviso, but to whittle away at law incident after incident of the legal title which courts thought were unnecessary to the security of the mortgagee in the enforcement of his claim. In its very nature such a process is confusing because it is, in its essence, a contradiction. It says one thing, but does another. It takes Mr. Dooley literally, and says, "It manes what it manes and not what it says." Inevitably the paring down process will be different in different states, and will be uneven and contradictory in any one state. However, all of these states have one thing in common. When they came to the legal incident of possession, they kept hands off; that is, all except a few which kept hands off only until default by the mortgagor. These latter are the so-called "intermediate" or "hybrid" states; the others, the straight "title", or "estate", or "common law" theory states. In these "title" theory states (which is as convenient and descriptive a label as is necessary for any lawyer with a knowledge of the historical origin of our mortgage), the mortgagee has the right to possession, as he does in England; in the "hybrid" or "intermediate" states (again the need of some single word to designate them seems sufficiently answered by either term), the mortgagee has no right to possession until default or later. In all of them, theoretically and in form, the dual system is maintained, but, because of the infiltration into the legal conception of the equitable concept of the conveyance as security [97] only, the need for the equitable doctrine and help is dispensed with in large part. At law the mortgagor has the legal incidents which ordinarily go with title, not only as to third persons, but as to the mortgagee, except insofar as those incidents are thought necessary or desirable (sometimes, be it noted, desirable only in that particular case) to the mortgagee as part of his security,[98] according to some interpretation of the intention of the parties, or as a fair and desirable feature of such a transaction regardless of the intention of the parties, actual or presumed. And the only guiding generalization through the morass which can be ventured safely is that the necessity and desirability of according to the mortgagee various legal incidents of title for security purposes [99] will consciously or unconsciously influence the court in deciding whether the mortgagee has them or not. It is one of the evils of the fiction method of growth in the law that many judges will take fiction as gospel truth; or, perhaps the evil is that they are literal fundamentalists part of the time and for the rest are hypocritical atheists, believing not but giving lip service to the word. The confusion arises from the fact that they are not consistently one or the other.

97. See Subdivision C. The Intervention of Equity, supra.

98. See Johnson, C.J., in Martin v. Alter, 1884, 42 Ohio St. 94; Shaw, C.J., in Ewer v. Hobbs, 1842, 5 Metc., (Mass.) 1; Cartwright, J., in Lightcap v. Bradley, 1900, 186 Ill. 510, 58 N.E. 221.

99. See § 15, infra.

"Therefore it will be at once apparent that, when an inquiry arises whether a given incident belongs to such an estate, we can apply for assistance only in a secondary way to the rules of the common law; for the initial step in such an investigation, plainly, must be a solution of the question whether the incident so claimed is one reasonably necessary to give to the mortgagee that security for his mortgage that was intended." Devlin v. Collier, 1891, 53 N. J.L. 422, 426, 22 A. 201, 202.

LIEN THEORY

15. In lien theory states the mortgagor is regarded as retaining legal title until foreclosure; the mortgagee has no right to possession either before or after default. His right to realization out of the mortgaged property ahead of other claimants is, however, recognized and protected. His security interest is called a lien.

In the "lien" states the situation is clearer. Most of the difficulty in understanding it has been caused through trying to describe it by saying it is the "equitable theory" worked out at law. After all, in broad outlines, the "equitable theory" was nothing but the security idea in a high stage of development which left the mortgagee's right to possession untouched and had both the advantages and disadvantages of purely equitable recognition. The lien theory really came into existence when that most important incident of legal title, the right to possession, was denied to the mortgagee at any time whatsoever and his interest in the land was limited to a power to realize by sale. When this was done it was clear, and was consequently recognized by courts, that the mortgagor had practically every ordinary incident of legal title, and, therefore, should be recognized as being the legal owner; yet the mortgagee had an interest in the property which had to be called something, and was called a "lien".[1] Neither the label nor the conception of the transaction (as distinguished from all the worked out rules and principles) cause laymen or lawyers in "lien" states any great difficulty. They know that the mortgagee cannot get possession[2] of the land without first selling it, and that his power of realizing his claim out of specific property ahead of other claimants will be protected (i. e., he has rights in rem in his power). That is sufficient for them. Theoretically, it comes fairly close to the ideal type of security, i. e., one "which combines the most efficient protection of the creditor, the least interference with the rights of the debtor, and the security of third parties against fraud."[3]

CRITIQUE OF THEORIES

16. Treating title, lien or intermediate theories as fundamental and their concepts as necessarily controlling decisions has been vigorously criticised. While there is truth in the contention, and, for the lawyer it is of vital importance to determine what reasons influence the courts in adhering to or departing from these categories, nevertheless they do have utility and unquestionably have played an important part in molding the law of mortgages.

Any attempt to select either the title theory or the lien theory (or the intermediate theory) as fundamental has been trenchantly criticised.[4] And along the same line there is an elaborate exposition of the futility of using any one of these concepts as the sole, or in many instances, even an important, factor in reaching decisions in cases.[5] Although the writers of these critiques quite properly stress the importance of non-conceptual considerations in determining whether to grant or deny to the mortgagor or mortgagee various legal rights in particular cases or particular types of cases, regardless of whether courts say that the state is a "lien", "title", or "intermediate" jurisdiction, nevertheless neither would nor could deny that in a great many instances the result in a case squarely rests upon nothing more than the court's desire for consistency with what it considers the

---

1. See Gavit, Under the Lien Theory of Mortgages is the Mortgage Only a Power of Sale?, 1931, 15 Minn. L.Rev. 147.

2. See McDougal, 1935, 44 Yale L.J. 1278. See also §§ 127, 149, infra.

3. Turner, The Equity of Redemption, 118. See also Kidd, Trust Deeds and Mortgages in California, 1915, 3 Calif.L.Rev. 381. See, too, People v. Nogarr, 1958, 164 Cal.App.2d 591, 330 P.2d 858, discussed in 1957, 8 Hastings L.J. 29, 296–298; 1959, 47 Ky.L. J. 565; 1959, 11 Stan.L.Rev. 574; Million, Amandes, Lesar and Martz, 1960 Annual Survey of American Law: Real and Personal Property, 1960, 36 N.Y.U.L.Rev. 357, 382.

4. See McDougal, 1935, 44 Yale L.J. 1278.
See also Storke, Introduction to Security, 1943, 16 Rocky Mt.L.Rev. 27, 39–44.

5. Sturges and Clark, Legal Theory and Real Property Mortgages, 1928, 37 Yale L.J. 691.

"fundamental" nature of the mortgage theory obtaining in that state.

An even stronger statement might be argued. In respect to certain problems, at least, the patterns of the concepts are fairly well defined and adhered to, certainly in any one state. When the courts of a state adopt one concept, they usually treat it, at any rate when such problems are in issue, more or less as a unit. To be sure it is a quite flexible unit with indefinite boundaries and contours. Nevertheless, there is a large technical core of each which is implied in the mere use of the word, and the tendency of the courts is to say that you take the entire pattern or none, and that freedom of experiment in deviation to meet some particular needs shall meet some resistance. And in a surprisingly large number of the problems of the law of mortgages, especially those in which the law has crystallized and the developed rules (frequently for non-conceptual reasons) have become an integral part of the pattern itself, the concept (with its whole content, inherent and acquired) will be applied rather mechanically to reach the result; or at any rate it will be a potent force to be reckoned with.

Also, for the purpose of classifying many results, "lien", "title", and "intermediate" theories are convenient, if not necessary, labels, and have the advantage of traditional and general judicial and professional acceptance. Hence there is some utility in centering a certain amount of attention on the "nature" of these concepts.

Nevertheless, granting that this is true in whole or in part, the reasons why one pattern is chosen, or why, although followed ordinarily, is modified or departed from in certain instances and why certain unsightly lines and apparent excrescences are a part of it are, of course, for the lawyer, the vitals of the matter.

E. VARIANTS FROM THE NORM

TRUST DEED MORTGAGE

17. Trust machinery is frequently used for security purposes. Conveyance of the property by the debtor to a trustee as security for performance of the debtor's obligation often produces different results than an ordinary mortgage although the tendency is to abolish the distinction at least where the mortgagor is a natural person.

Trust deed mortgages must be distinguished from assignments in trust for the benefit of creditors.

In addition to the regular mortgage there is in common use in many states, both in lien and title, a device called a Trust Deed Mortgage.[6] It consists of a conveyance to a person (who usually is a third person but may be the creditor) on trust to hold the property as security for the payment of a debt to the

---

6. The use of a conveyance in trust for security purposes was recognized in the later 17th century in England. Benham v. Newcomb, 1684, 1 Vern. 232. It was well known in America from the early 19th century. Conway v. Alexander, 1812, 11 U.S. (7 Cranch) 218; Shilkaber v. Robinson, 1877, 97 U.S. 68, 24 L.Ed. 967; Hopkins v. Ward, 1817, 20 Va. (6 Munf.) 38; Koch v. Briggs, 1859, 14 Cal. 256, 73 Am.Dec. 651; Martin v. Alter, 1884, 42 Ohio St. 94; Camden v. Alkire, 1884, 24 W.Va. 674.

It is the prevailing or a commonly used form in several states. As already noted, it was employed at an early date in Virginia and in that state and West Virginia there is statutory recognition and regulation. Va.Code of 1950, §§ 55–58 to 55–60; W.Va.Code of 1966, 38–1–1a to 38–1–8. Although the straight form mortgage exists in California, the trust deed mortgage is the one ordinarily selected. See Cormack and Irsfeld, Distinctions between Mortgages and Trust Deeds in California, 1938, 26 Cal.L. Rev. 206; Trust Deed Foreclosure, etc., 1940, 27 Cal. L.Rev. 66; Comparison of California Mortgages, Trust Deeds and Land Sale Contracts, 1960, 7 U.C. L.A.L.Rev. 83–102; Arizona, see Barringer v. Lilley, 1938, 96 F.2d 607; Illinois, see White v. Macqueen, 1935, 360 Ill. 236, 195 N.E. 832, 98 A.L.R. 1115; North Carolina, Ownbey v. Parkway Properties, Inc., 1942, 222 N.C. 54, 21 S.E.2d 900, discussed 1943, 21 N.C.L.Rev. 223; Mortgages and Deeds of Trust, 1963, 41 N.C.L.Rev. 440; Oregon, see 1965, 44 Or.L.R. 149–157; Utah, see Trust Deed Security in Utah, 1962–1963, 8 Utah L.Rev. 125–140, are other states in which it is to be found.

For additional states, see Hanna, supra.

See Storke, Introduction to Security, 1943, 16 Rocky Mt.L.Rev. 27, 45–47.

lender. Both the debtor and the creditor are, technically, cestuis que trust. Essentially the purpose of the transaction is the same as a mortgage, but because of the different legal form used there are, in many particulars, different results. And, just as the American courts modified at law the legal incidents of the legal estate conveyed by an ordinary form mortgage, so, also, have they refused to follow here the usual trust doctrines, and have evolved a new thing which can be described only as a "trust deed mortgage", and which varies from state to state in its outlines and structure. Again, as in the mortgage in "title" states, it can be generalized that the courts recognize in varying degree its true function as a security device, and accord to it only those incidents which, for various reasons they think are necessary and desirable for security purposes, regardless of consistency with its language in other cases or in the very case it is deciding.[7] For example (and only as a sample), in a lien state the trustee may be *said* by the courts to get title (although, in others, he may be said to get only a lien as in a straight mortgage), yet he will be denied those incidents of title (notably the right to possession) which the courts in that state have decided should not be given to the mortgagee for his protection in collecting his debt. Perhaps the greatest difference both in theory and in practice lies in the method of enforcement. The theory is that the trustee is merely carrying out the terms of the trust; the practice is that the creditor is freed both from the requirements of ordinary foreclosure, frequently getting a speedier and more efficient method, and from the ordinary statutory right of redemption from foreclosure sale. Other important differences are in the methods of transferring the creditor's rights and in the application to them of statutory provisions which in terms apply either to mortgages or to trusts only.[8] There is a tendency for legislatures and courts to abolish the differences between them and ordinary form mortgages, at least so far as they are used by individual mortgagors.

Instead of attempting to deal with the trust deed mortgage separately in one place, it will be treated incidentally throughout this work in connection with the various problems taken up. Insofar as the law governing it differs from that regulating the ordinary form of mortgage the difference will be noted.[9]

The trust mortgage must be distinguished from the assignment in trust for the benefit of creditors. The latter is for the purpose of paying rather than securing the grantor's debts. It involves a complete divestiture of the debtor-grantor's interest in the property transferred apart from a resulting trust of any surplus remaining after the debts are paid. The transferor retains no right to redeem by paying off the debt out of other property. The trust deed mortgage on the other hand is merely for security and, like any other mortgage, leaves the grantor the general ownership of the property and the right to redeem by discharging the secured obligation.

TRUST DEED CORPORATE MORTGAGE

18. The trust deed corporate mortgage is largely sui generis. Although it will be dealt with in certain portions of this text no attempt will be made to give it complete treatment.

The modern trust deed corporate mortgage is in many respects sui generis. One of

---

7. For an early example of this attitude, see Marshall, C.J., in Conway v. Alexander, 1812, 11 U.S. (7 Cranch) 218, "That the conveyance is made to trustees is not a circumstance of much weight. It manifests an intention of the drawer of the instrument to avoid the usual forms of a mortgage * * *. This intention, however, would have no influence on the case, if the instrument was really a security for money advanced and to be repaid."

8. See § 338, infra.

9. See Hanna, Cases Security, re-edited, 2d Ed., 571–573, 895, for list of states using the trust deed mortgage.

See supra, note 6, for materials on trust deed mortgages.

See also Tiffany, Real Prop., 3d Ed., § 1400, for a brief summary of the trust deed form of mortgage.

the most important differences between it and other mortgages lies in the relationship between the trustee under such a mortgage and his cestuis que trust, as contrasted with that existing between an ordinary form mortgagee and his mortgagor, or, for that matter, between the trustee and his cestuis in a small, simple trust deed mortgage where the mortgagor is a natural person. The nature of this relationship and its legal consequences are dealt with chiefly in the chapters on Rights and Duties Before Foreclosure, and on Foreclosure. It may be observed that many of the problems of the corporate mortgage arise in connection with the reorganization of the corporation, especially in regard to the protection of minority bondholders. Reorganizations have been linked up with the bond foreclosure; sometimes worked out in lieu of foreclosure. To treat this matter adequately would overtax the limits of this book and trench too much upon subjects better considered in a course on Corporations, Business Organizations, Bankruptcy, or a separate course in Corporate Reorganization. However, a student of mortgage law who is not given at least a glimpse into this complex field, and some idea of its problems and their relation to the foreclosure simpliciter and the simpler mortgage law of real property, would have an incomplete picture of the subject. There has been an attempt to include materials on the matter in dealing with the subjects of receiverships, confirmation of foreclosure sales, the fixing of upset prices, trustee purchase (and other duties of the trustee), the statutory redemption right, and deficiency judgment.[10]

EXPRESS VENDOR'S LIEN

19. Where a seller of land expressly reserves a lien on it as security for the purchase price, technically only an equitable mortgage is created. Where such liens are given by statute they should be treated as legal mortgages unless the statute is construed as reserving legal title in the seller. In this latter case it is pos-sible to treat this transaction as a land sale contract.

Where the vendor of land has conveyed the title to his vendee there arises, by the weight of authority in the United States, an equitable lien or mortgage in favor of the seller called a "grantor's" lien.[11] Various explanations have been given as to its basis, some going on the theory that it rests upon an implied in fact agreement, others saying that it is law-created.[12] Where, however, the vendor inserts into the deed itself an express reservation of a lien or charge upon the land conveyed as security for the purchase price the security interest which ensues unquestionably stems from the written stipulation. In the absence of statute, what is created would seem to be an equitable mortgage grounded either upon principles of specific performance of an executory promise or on the theory that equity is giving specific effect to the intention of the parties in the same way it does in the analogous case of a declaration of a trust. This is discussed in the next chapter and will be left for analysis and elaboration at that place. In either

10. See Draper, A Historical Introduction to the Corporate Mortgage, 1930, 2 Rocky Mt.L.Rev. 71.

11. See Pomeroy, Eq.Juris., 5th Ed., 1941, § 1249. Cf. MacIntyre, Modern Consequences of Earlier Confusion Between a Vendor's Lien and the Interest of a *Cestui Que Trust*, 1952, 30 Can.B.Rev. 1016.

12. See, e. g., the opinion in Ahrend v. Odiorne, 1875, 118 Mass. 261, 19 Am.Rep. 449, for a survey of the chief rationales.

In some states the term "vendor's lien" is applied to three distinct transactions: (1) Where title has been conveyed without any express reservation to secure the payment of the purchase price; (2) where title has been expressly reserved as security for payment of the purchase price; (3) where there is a reservation in the deed of conveyance of a lien for the payment of the purchase price. See Boyer and Evans, The Vendor's Lien in Florida, 1966, 20 U. of Miami L.Rev. 767–795.

In Texas only the first two of these transactions are in common use. The first one is recognized as creating an equitable lien for the purchase money upon the legal title which has passed to the vendee. This lien is recognized as having a non-contractual basis. Where the vendor's lien is expressly reserved, the vendor is held to have kept legal title. See James R. Norvell, The Vendor's Lien and Reservation of the Paramount Legal Title—The Rights of Vendors, Vendees, and Subvendees, 1966, 44 Tex. L.Rev. 22–34.

event the security interest would seem not to be, technically, a legal mortgage. However, this seems a purely theoretical distinction because the deed can be recorded, thus giving notice and so affording protection against third parties as well as enforcement against the debtor. There is authority recognizing that it is in substance a legal mortgage.[13]

However, in some states, such liens are sanctioned by statute.[14] There is some disagreement as to whether this fact alters their nature and makes them legal mortgages.[15] The preferable view would be to hold that it does do so.[16] This statement must be subject to the reservation that the statute be construed as reserving only a security lien [17] and not title. Where the latter is the case the door is opened to treating the transaction as governed by the law of land sale contracts rather than of the law of mortgages,[18] a distinction which is dealt with in the next section.

LAND CONTRACTS

20. The long term land sale contract in which the buyer is given possession and the seller retains title is frequently used instead of purchase money mortgages. Although a security device it is governed by the body of law embedded in the doctrines of equity applying to specific performance of contracts rather than those dealing with mortgages. **These doctrines while parallel in some respects are strikingly dissimilar in others.**

The device which is the most serious rival of the mortgage in cases where the obligation is an agreement to pay the purchase price is the long term land sale contract in which the vendor has not conveyed title but the vendee, ordinarily, has been given possession. The similarity is obvious: the vendor under the land contract is the analogue of the mortgagee under a purchase-money mortgage; the vendee occupies the same relative position as does the mortgagor. The rules governing the two sorts of transactions, while parallel in some respects, are strikingly dissimilar in others.

It is outside the scope of this text on mortgages to explore in detail the law governing these executory contracts, that law being embedded in the doctrines of equity applying to the subject of specific performance of contracts and strongly influenced by ideas of "freedom of contract" and the inviolability of obligations based upon agreement.[19] The most important difference is that the vendor in a land contract, on default by the vendee, by summary proceedings analogous to strict foreclosure, may keep the land, all installments paid, and sue for installments due, if the contract so provides, with the vendee having no right of redemption [20]—a situation

13. Dingley v. Bank of Ventura, 1881, 57 Cal. 467; Markoe v. Andras, 1873, 67 Ill. 34; Hall v. Mobile, etc., Ry., 1877, 58 Ala. 10; See Pomeroy, Eq.Juris., 5th Ed., §§ 1255–1259. See Cunningham and Tischler, Equitable Real Estate Mortgages, 1963, 17 Rutgers L.Rev. 679, 700. See also Norvell, op cit. supra, note 12. See further § 48, infra.

14. See, e. g., W.Va.Code, 38–1–1; Va.Code 1950, § 55–53.

15. See Gordon v. Rixey, 1882, 76 Va. 694.

16. See Glenn, Mortgages, § 14.1.
See Cunningham and Tischler, op. cit., supra, note 13.

17. See Penn v. Hearon, 1897, 94 Va. 773, 27 S.E. 599; W.Va.Code, 38–1–1.

18. Bound v. Dillard, Tex.Civ.App.1940, 140 S.W.2d 520; Sheehan v. McKinstry, 1922, 105 Or. 473, 210 P. 167, 34 A.L.R. 1315; Hare v. Henderson, C.C.A. 5th, 1940, 113 F.2d 277, certiorari denied 311 U.S. 697, 61 S.Ct. 135, 85 L.Ed. 451.

19. For an excellent, brief summary of the nature and incidents of the land contract, stressing its security aspects, and comparing and differentiating it from a mortgage, see Land Contracts in Real Estate Sales Program, 1941, 7 Fed.Home Loan Bank Rev. 112. See Storke, Introduction to Security, 1943, 16 Rocky Mt.L.Rev. 27, 47–49. See also Land Sale Contracts in California: Compared with Mortgages and Trust Deeds, 1959, 7 U.C.L.A.L.Rev. 95–102.
For more recent discussions of the remedies of the parties for breach of land sale contracts, see Lee, Remedies for Breach of the Installment Land Contract, 1965, 19 Univ. of Miami L.Rev. 550, and references cited in note 20, infra.

20. Heckard v. Sayre, 1864, 34 Ill. 142 is probably the leading case holding that a land sale contract with a time of the essence clause prevented a vendee who defaulted from later getting specific performance of the contract. In a contract for the

completely repugnant to mortgage law ever since the original creation of the redemption right. Because of this advantageous treatment accorded the vendor, increasing numbers of sellers prefer to use the land contract, and by the same token, a purchaser prefers the mortgage as security for the payment of purchase money.[21]

While the foregoing is still true in the majority of states, radical changes have been made both by court decisions and by legislation. Three states, California, Connecticut and Utah have protected the vendee chiefly by judicial decisions.[22]

In several states there is legislation which is designed to protect the defaulting purchaser under a land contract.[23] One type, enacted in, e.g., Arizona, Iowa, Minnesota, North Dakota and South Dakota, grants the purchaser a period of grace to cure the default. In California code sections dealing with relief in cases of forfeiture [24] were seized on by the courts. The same type of statutes are found also in Montana, North Dakota and South Dakota. Maryland, although still following the general majority rule, in 1951 enacted a statute to protect certain purchasers from the rigors of that rule.[25]

As a consequence of the changes in California law that drastically changed the rights of the parties in installment land sale contracts it was stated in 1960 that "the land contract

---

sale of land in which there was a provision that time was of the essence, a defaulting buyer was denied recovery of his payments at law. Bryson v. Crawford, 1873, 68 Ill. 362; Glock v. Howard & Wilson Colony Co., 1898, 123 Cal. 1, 55 P. 713, 43 L.R.A. 199, 69 Am.St.Rep. 17. The doctrines of the above cases represent the clear weight of authority.

For the extent to which this state of the law has been changed by statute see 1938, 52 Harv.L.Rev. 129; N.Y.Law Revision Commission, Act, Recommendation and Study Relating to Installment Land Contracts, 1937, N.Y.Legis.Doc. No. 65(M). See, additionally, text and notes infra this section.

For discussions of the position in equity of a vendee under a long term contract for the sale of land, especially in cases where there is a clause making time of the essence or one providing for forfeiture of part payments on default, see III Am.L.Prop. § 11.78; Glenn, Mortgages, secs. 15, 15.1. See also Chafee and Simpson, Cases on Equity, 1224–1258; Chafee and Re, Cases on Equity, 5th Ed. 595–620; Durfee and Duffy, Foreclosure of Land Contracts in Michigan, 7 Mich.St.Bar.Jour. 166, 221; Vanneman, Strict Foreclosure on Land Contracts, 1930, 14 Minn.L.Rev. 342; Corbin, Rights of a Defaulting Vendee to the Restitution of Instalments Paid, 1931, 40 Yale L.Jour. 1013; Ballantine, Forfeiture for Breach of Contract, 1921, 5 Minn.L.Rev. 329; Equitable Relief Against Forfeiture in Land Sales, 1922, 32 Yale L.Jour. 65; Lee, Defaulting Purchaser's Right to Restitution Under the Installment Land Contract, 1965, 20 U. of Miami L.Rev. 1; Peterson, Purchase Agreements and Installment Contracts for Sale of Real Estate, 1960, 40 Neb.L.Rev. 271; Land Contracts—Waiver of Time Is of the Essence Clauses, 1964, 18 Ark.L.Rev. 175; Forfeiture and the Iowa Installment Land Contract, 1961, 46 Iowa L.Rev. 786–801; 1961 Wis.L.Rev. 324; 1964 Wis.L.Rev. 167.

See, additionally, note 22 et seq., infra, and text.

21. See Skilton, Government and the Mortgage Debtor, 37.

22. There have been a number of notes and articles considering the development of the law in California, the most important of which is Hetland, The

California Land Contract, 1960, 48 Cal.L.Rev. 729. Other references are: 1930, 18 Cal.L.Rev. 681; 1932, 20 Cal.L.Rev. 194; 1939, 27 Cal.L.Rev. 383; 1949, 37 Cal.L.Rev. 704; 1952, 40 Cal.L.Rev. 593; 1956, 3 U.C.L.A.L.Rev. 264; Flowers, Enforcement of Forefeiture Provisions in Land Sale Contracts, 1962, 14 Hastings L.J. 44; Warren, California Installment Land Sales Contracts: A Time for Reform, 1962, 9 U.C.L.A.L.Rev. 608. See also Hetland, Real Property and Real Property Security: The Well-Being of the Law, 1965, 53 Cal.L.Rev. 151, 152–159; 1958, 10 Stanford L.Rev. 355.

See Lee, Defaulting Purchaser's Right to Restitution Under the Installment Land Contract, 1965, 20 Univ. of Miami L.Rev. 1, 7–17.

23. See III Am.L.Prop. § 11.78.

24. West's Ann.Cal.Civ.Code §§ 3275 and 3369.

25. Md.Code 1957, art. 21, §§ 110–116 (Code Supp. art. 21, §§ 112, 114). For a discussion of the Maryland statute and a proposed statutory solution to the problems raised by the installment land contract, see Lee, Defaulting Purchaser's Right to Restitution Under the Installment Land Contract, 1965, 20 Univ. of Miami L.Rev. 1, 17–24.

For discussion of the results under various statutes see Installment Contracts: Legislative Protection of Defaulting Purchasers, 1938, 52 Harv.L.Rev. 129. And see: 1916, 26 Yale L.J. 405; 1921, 5 Minn.L. Rev. 466; 1927, 11 Minn.L.Rev. 458; 1924, 10 Iowa L.Bull. 85; 1927, 13 Iowa L.Rev. 93; 1931, 3 Dak. L.Rev. 376; Note, Is a Contract for the Sale of Land a Mortgage?, 1962, 16 U. of Miami L.Rev. 493, discussing Mid-State Inv. Corp. v. O'Steen, Fla.App.1961, 133 So.2d 455, certiorari denied, Fla. 1962, 136 So.2d 349. See also citations in note 20, supra.

is legally obsolete as a security device in California." [26]

"Paradoxically, the use of this mode of financing home purchases has expanded in recent years, and the early sixties find this device enjoying its greatest popularity." [27] This continued use probably cannot be explained on the ground that its shortcomings with respect to the vendor's remedies are overbalanced by other advantages to the vendor. Instead, it seems probable that "the vendor contrives to use the installment sale contract because he is willing to gamble that the vendee's rights under this device will never be asserted and his own contractual advantages will not be challenged." [28]

"A 'land contract' often is a security device in lieu of a mortgage or deed of trust. * * * But a 'land contract' also is an earnest money contract, or deposit receipt, or occasionally

mutual escrow instructions; in other words it is often the basic buy-sell agreement rather than a security device. And if this is what 'land contract' means, the security debtor's protection should not interfere with the vendor's action for damages, his retention of liquidated damages, or his action for specific performance." [29] A reasonable liquidated damage clause in a land contract may be enforceable.[30]

OTHER DEVICES

21. In addition to the foregoing, there are miscellaneous other devices used for security purposes.

There are other devices frequently employed. One is the lease for sale in which the rent reserved is in reality installments of the purchase price. Title is reserved by the lessor-seller as security, and there is usually a provision that time is of the essence in making payments, and, upon default, the seller may reenter and keep all past payments. This is, of course, only the land contract for sale in a thin disguise. Another takes the form of a sale and conveyance with a contract to resell at a higher price. The stated purchase price is actually a loan, and the resale price includes the interest charged. There is usually a time limit on the right to repurchase. Still another, one which has been employed from early times, is the deed absolute in form but with a collateral oral agreement that it is to be security only. The chief purpose of all these is to evade the requirement of formal foreclosure and other protections given to the mortgage when cast in its usual form. How far the purpose is achieved depends on whether the courts see what the substance of the transaction is, and how far, even so, they may be influenced by the form in which it is cast.

26. Hetland, The California Land Contract, 1960, 48 Cal.L.Rev. 729, 775.

27. Warren, California Land Sales Contracts: A Time for Reform, 1962, 9 U.C.L.A.Law Rev. 608, 633.

28. Ibid.
"Two factors—first land contracts can be executed in such a way that they are difficult to record, and second, they are frequently used to market low cost housing to people who are often financially incapable of asserting their legal rights—combine to give sellers using this device one enormously important advantage: If, as is usually the case, the buyer can be pursuaded to leave, no legal action need be taken to clear the title before resale. This is in contrast to the trust deed, where foreclosure either by sale or by action must occur in every case. Then too, the form contract bristles with provisions purporting to grant every conceivable advantage to the vendor. The buyer, when forcefully reminded by the authoritative-sounding voice of some member of the seller's organization that he has signed the agreement and is bound by every term of it, is in no position to doubt this; in fact, lawyers are hard put to know how enforceable some clauses of the form contract are." Ibid. For articles dealing with other aspects of the sale of land subject to security financing in California, see Gillies, Scarcity of Capital for Mortgage Lending in California: An Economic or Legal Problem?, 1962, 9 U.C.L.A.L. Rev. 545; Mayer, Protection of the Investor in Real Estate and Real Property Securities in California, 1962, 9 U.C.L.A.L.Rev. 643.

29. Hetland, The California Land Contract, 1960, 48 Cal.L.Rev. 729. See ibid., 736–745. See also Lee, Defaulting Purchaser's Right to Restitution Under the Installment Land Contract, 1965, 20 Univ. of Miami L.Rev. 1; Hetland, Real Property and Real Property Security: The Well-Being of the Law, 1965, 55 Cal.L.Rev. 151, 157–158.

30. Look at Caplan v. Schroeder, 1961, 56 Cal.2d 515, 15 Cal.Rptr. 145, 364 P.2d 321. See also Hetland, Real Property and Real Property Security: The Well-Being of the Law, 1965, 53 Cal.L.Rev. 151, 152–159; Hetland, The California Land Contract, 1960, 48 Cal.L.Rev. 729, 736–745.

CHAPTER 2

EQUITABLE MORTGAGES

INTRODUCTION

22. **Although the term equitable mortgage is frequently used in a broader sense it is employed here to cover only transactions which, although not satisfying the requirements of legal mortgages, result in the creditor acquiring only an equitable interest in the property for security purposes.**

Equitable mortgages are usually defined as security transactions which fail to satisfy the requirements of legal mortgages but nevertheless are treated as mortgages in equity.[1] Stated thus broadly they include cases in which the interest in the property in the hands of the creditor is the full legal ownership and the aid of equity is necessary to cut it down to a security interest and to establish the rights of the debtor as a mortgagor.[2] The problem dealt with here is the one in which the only interest acquired by the creditor in the property for security purposes is an equitable one. The doctrines of marshalling, subrogation and equitable reinstatement also create purely equitable interests as se-

---

1. See, e. g., 3 Tiffany, Real Prop., 2d Ed., § 603; Fisher and Lightwood's Law of Mortgages, 7th Ed., 16; Falconbridge, Mortgages. 3d Ed., §§ 41, 42. See also the discussion in London County and Westminster Bank v. Tompkins, [1918] 1 K.B. 514, 529. And see Cunningham and Tischler, Equitable Real Estate Mortgages, 1963, 17 Rutgers L.Rev. 679–683.

2. The problems of deeds absolute intended as mortgages, conditional sales, etc., discussed in Chapter 4, infra, are of this sort. So also would be the reservation in a deed of a vendor's lien for the purchase price, Pomeroy, Eq.Juris., 5th Ed., § 1255; Glenn, Mortgages, § 14, and cases of specific performance of contracts for the sale of land. Glenn, Mortgages, § 15.
See §§ 19, 20, supra.

curity, but they do so only in connection with mortgages already validly created. Further, they are in part, at least, non-consensual and so outside of the scope of the inquiry here.

REQUIREMENTS OF LEGAL MORTGAGE

23. Although there is little direct authority, the minimum requirement for the creation of a legal mortgage is a delivered written instrument describing the property so that it can be identified, stating the character of the transfer, and naming the parties. Some courts, especially in title states, indicate that compliance with the ordinary rules of conveyancing is necessary.

Whether or not the only interest acquired by the mortgagee is an equitable one requires, as a preliminary, an examination into what is essential to create a legal mortgage.[3] This is rather difficult because the matter is relatively unimportant for two reasons and, as a result, direct authority is scarce. One reason is that in most cases, mortgages are drawn by lawyers who carefully, even slavishly, follow established and more or less stereotyped forms.[4] Even when the mortgage is drawn by a layman he usually buys and uses a printed form so that the same result is achieved. The other is that where forms are departed from the security claimant generally relies upon the theory that the transaction is an equitable mortgage and it usually is unnecessary to decide whether it might be a legal mortgage.[5] Nevertheless, there are

cases indicating that in those states which profess to follow the title theory of mortgages the mortgage deed, to be effective, must comply with the ordinary rules of conveyances even to the extent of requiring words of inheritance if more than a life interest in the property is to pass in mortgage.[6]

In the lien and intermediate jurisdictions the picture is not so clear. In practice the forms used commonly follow the formal requirements of conveyancing deeds and it has been urged that this is necessary. Thus one writer argues that "the legal mortgage to which equity gave effect as security by the development of the mortgagor's equity of redemption and the mortgagee's right of foreclosure necessarily involved a conveyance of the legal title to the mortgagee, and when in the lien states the law courts adopted the equity view as the rule at law * * * the transactions to which this new law was applied were necessarily limited to legal mortgages. * * * It follows, therefore, that legal mortgage liens which are not subject to defeat by the application of that doctrine can arise only when created by instrument of conveyance which is sufficient to transfer an interest at law."[7]

The reasoning is open to criticism.[8] To say that the lien theory is merely the adoption by the law courts of the existing equitable theory of mortgages is an oversimplified and misleading generalization, especially when, as here, it is taken as the sole criterion and

---

3. While the question has been mooted as to whether in a lien jurisdiction the interest of the mortgagee is not always an equitable one, it seems so thoroughly settled that it is legal as to require no examination other than that given in Chapter 1, supra. See Durfee, The Lien or Equitable Theory of the Mortgage, 1912, 10 Mich.L.Rev. 587; Gavit, Under the Lien Theory of Mortgages is the Mortgage only a Power of Sale, 1931, 15 Minn.L.Rev. 147; Fogelman, The Deed Absolute as a Mortgage in New York, 1963, 32 Fordham L.Rev. 299. See also Cunningham and Tischler, 1963, 17 Rutgers L.Rev. 679, 694–699, for a discussion of the same problem.

4. See Durfee, Cas.Morts., 37 n. 1.

5. Ibid.

6. Sedgwick v. Laflin, 1865, 92 Mass.(10 Allen) 430; Allendorff v. Gaugengigl, 1888, 146 Mass. 542, 16 N. E. 283; Smith v. Haskins, 1900, 22 R.I. 6, 45 A. 741.

See also problem cases, Campbell, Cas.Morts., 2d Ed., 6, 7.

Statutes modifying the ordinary rules of conveyancing, e. g., Mass.Acts of 1912, c. 502, § 19, Mass.G.L. A. c. 183 § 13, would apply, presumably, to mortgages.

7. Walsh, Mortgages, 53, 72.

8. For other criticisms of the same type of reasoning involved in the quotation, see McDougal, 1935, 44 Yale L.J. 1278; Sturgis and Clark, Legal Theory and Real Property Mortgages, 1928, 37 Yale L.J. 691.

foundation of the lien theory. When all incidents of legal ownership are stripped away from the mortgagee, including any right to possession, as happened in the lien states, a law court naturally would conclude that such a transaction, even though it purported to transfer legal title would not do so but would give only a security interest which ought not to be described as legal title. To deduce from this, however, that a purported formal conveyance of title is the only kind of transfer that would accomplish the result of creating such a legal mortgage lien is a complete nonsequitur. When the different nature and incidents of the mortgage in the lien jurisdictions is recognized and established there is no reason why it should be "necessarily limited" in its creation by the law courts or the equity courts to the formal conveyance case. The opposite inference is far more reasonable. Indeed it is a little difficult to understand any court saying, in effect, "Now that we have come to the conclusion that a mortgagee does not get title even though the mortgage deed purports to give it to him, we must require, before we can hold that he does not get title but only a lien, that the mortgagor go through all the formalities necessary to give him the title he does not get."

To insist upon the former conveyancing requirements which applied to the title mortgage is no more necessary here than the retention of any other forms of allegations which once had substance but no longer serve any vital function. The solution should not rest upon any such formalistic reasoning based upon erroneous assumptions. Rather, it should depend upon an evaluation of how far it is desirable and essential that this particular interest in real property, recognizing its limited character both in regard to the transfer of incidents usually going with full ownership and the purposes for which they are given, can be created by expressions of intent less technical and formal than those required in an outright transfer of ownership or one in which more legal incidents are

given for security purposes. The answer might be the same in both instances, but the latter approach more accurately states what is involved in the decision.

On the other hand the view has been expressed that any written expression of intention, however informal, that properly described property be security for an obligation is sufficient.[9]

Statutory simple mortgage forms amounting in substance to a brief statement that M mortgages specifically described property to E to secure a described debt are common [10] but are permissive, not mandatory. The minimum requirements for a legal mortgage in any jurisdiction would seem to be a written instrument [11] describing the property with sufficient particularity that it may be identified,[12] stating the character of the transfer and the parties to it, and made operative by

---

9. Bredenberg v. Landrum, 1890, 32 S.C. 215, 10 S.E. 956.

There is authority that "heirs" is not necessary to pass the entire estate as security in an intermediate jurisdiction. Brown v. National Bank, 1886, 44 Ohio St. 269, 6 N.E. 648.

See 3 Tiffany, Real Prop., 2d Ed., 2743 where the author indicates that most written instruments which express an intention that certain property be security would create a legal mortgage and that the term "equitable mortgage" properly would apply only to instruments indicating an intention to create a lien in the future. "The courts of these states, however, appear to use the expression 'equitable mortgage' with considerable freedom, as applicable to all instruments intended for purposes of security, which assume an unusual form."

In a survey of what will constitute a defective formal mortgage, the result is to indicate what is essential to create a legal mortgage. For such a thorough survey, see Cunningham v. Tischler, Equitable Real Estate Mortgages, 1963, 17 Rutgers L.Rev. 679, 694–701.

10. E. g., West's Ann.Cal.Civ.Code, § 2948.

For statutory clarification of the short-form mortgage in New York, see Curtiss, The Commission and the Law of Real Property, 1955, 40 Cornell L.Q. 735, 741.

11. See Chapter 3, The Statute of Frauds. Regardless of whether the Statute of Frauds applies to the creation of equitable mortgages, it seems clear that a writing is necessary to create a legal mortgage even in lien jurisdictions.

12. See Description of the Property, § 39, infra.

delivery.[13] While a nominal or recited consideration might be insisted upon in jurisdictions in which conveyances operate under a Statute of Uses, it is quite clear that a legal mortgage can be executed to secure an existing obligation without any new or substantially valuable consideration just as effectually as can a gift conveyance of the whole title.[14]

CONSENSUAL EQUITABLE MORTGAGES

24. There are three basic kinds of consensual mortgages: (1) Specifically enforceable promises to give a legal mortgage or hold certain property as security; (2) Agreements intended to create a security interest but ineffective under conveyancing rules; (3) Agreements, in the form of promises or executed transactions, in which the subject matter of the security itself is equitable.

The broad division into consensual and non-consensual equitable mortgages or liens is fundamental although there is a border area between them in which classification of particular cases is difficult and the precise line of demarcation cannot always be traced with exactness. An example is found in conveyances to grantees who agree to support the grantor.[15] Since most non-consensual liens are imposed to prevent unfairness, and since in many instances where such unfairness would result that very fact is rather persuasive evidence of an implied in fact intention by the parties coextensive with the right awarded, it is understandable that consensual and non-consensual obligations frequently overlap. And, because ordinarily the result would be the same in either case, it is not surprising that the distinction is slurred over in border cases. With the non-consensual liens we have here no concern except by way

of analogy and differentiation. They are remedial devices covering an area which has been described appropriately as "intensely undefined." [16] It encompasses, roughly, the subject matter usually grouped formerly under the heading of quasi-contracts or constructive trusts and more recently under the more descriptive designation of restitution. In spite of the difficulties involved, attempts have been made to define the bases of non-consensual liens. Thus they have been said to rest "on a broad and somewhat indefinite principle that one who has parted with money or property expecting a specified return should be assured either that return or the redelivery of what he parted with." [17] Again, it is stated that "where there is a hardship which equity regards as deserving of alleviation, and which results from a transaction peculiarly involving some particular property, a lien may be imposed on that property, or property of which it has become a part, to secure the payment of money, if it will not unfairly affect other interests." [18] Examples of such transactions are loans for the improvement of land, enabling money loans (i. e., for the acquisition of land), conveyances for the support of the aged, and agreements for payment out of a certain fund or its proceeds. Whether or not the examples given are correctly classified, the list is suggestive and also illustrates the difficulty of exact cataloguing.[19]

16. Erle., J., in Brunsdon v. Allard, 1859, 2 El. & El. 19, 27. See Storke, An Introduction to Security, 1943, 16 Rocky Mt.L.Rev. 27, 44.

17. Williston, Transfers of After-Acquired Personal Property, 1906, 19 Harv.L.Rev. 557, 561.

18. See 1931, 31 Col.L.Rev. 1335.

19. See also Restatement of Restitution, § 161; Stone, The "Equitable Mortgage" in New York, 1920, 20 Col.L.Rev. 519, 521 (the "equitable mortgage or lien which is quasi-contractual in its origin * * * is based on the duty and power of equity to compel restitution where the property of one is improved or added to by another, induced by fraud or mistake under such circumstances as to entitle him to equitable relief"); 1933, 32 Mich.L. Rev. 685.

For an argument that the decisions in the cases are arrived at "on delicate appraisals of facts and upon

13. See 3 Tiffany, Real Prop., 2d Ed., pp. 2373, 2743. Further, see Sterling, Validity of "Myself" Notes and Deeds of Trust, 1958, 30 Rocky Mt.L.Rev. 195, 196–198.

14. See Chapter 5, infra.

15. See infra, § 47.

The consensual transactions which result in equitable mortgages are of three basic patterns: one, specifically enforceable promises by the obligor either to give a legal mortgage on or to hold certain property as security; two, agreements intended by the parties to transfer to, or create in, the obligee a present security interest in definite property but which are ineffectual under the conveyancing rules of the jurisdiction to create or transfer any legal interest; and, three, agreements in the form of promises or of executed transactions, in which the subject matter of the security is itself equitable.

PROMISE TO GIVE A MORTGAGE

25. A promise to give a mortgage creates an equitable mortgage if equity will specifically enforce the promise.

In the first group the equitable mortgage arises as a result of equity granting specific performance [20] of the promise and is co-extensive with the right to have it. Consequently, the requirements insisted upon by the ordinary doctrines of equity for the specific enforcement of promises are, in general, necessary and sufficient here. Inadequacy of the legal remedy, a present, valuable consideration for the promise, an agreement sufficiently definite for the court to order it to be performed, and, insofar as the Statute of Frauds is held to be applicable,[21] a written

instrument complying with its provisions are the most important of these.[22] Of course it does not follow that what will satisfy these tests in a security transaction are necessarily the same as in other transactions such as, for example, contracts for the sale of land.[23] Perhaps the two most important places where it may be urged that this is true are those in which the question is whether an antecedent debt is sufficient consideration and whether the Statute of Frauds applies to require a writing where the performance of the claimant consists in making a loan of money.

PROMISE TO GIVE A MORTGAGE— NECESSITY OF PERFORMANCE BY OBLIGEE

26. Where the obligee's promise has not yet been performed no equitable mortgage arises. A variety of explanations have been offered as to why this is so. The rule is in contrast to the accepted view as to specific performance of executory contracts for the sale of land.

Where the obligee has performed equity grants specific performance of promises to give security because damages, since they are so conjectural, would be inadequate. The extent to which the obligee must have performed is not entirely certain.

Where the obligee's own performance is still in the executory state, specific performance of a contract to make or to accept a loan to be secured by a mortgage will not be specifically enforced.[24] It follows that no equita-

---

the deciding authority's sense of justice" in both consensual and non-consensual transactions, see Britton, Equitable Liens—A Tentative Analysis of the Problem, 1930, 8 N.Car.L.Rev. 388 (dealing chiefly with personal property problems).

20. A possible qualification to this statement, so far as promises to hold the property as security are concerned, is considered in § 28, infra.

See Cunningham and Tischler, Equitable Real Estate Mortgages, 1963, 17 Rutgers L.Rev. 679, 701–711.

In Rex v. Warner, 1958, 183 Kan. 763, 332 P.2d 572, the running of the statute of limitations on a promise to give a mortgage preventing an action for specific performance barred an equitable mortgage. But see Note, Equitable Mortgages in Iowa, 1959, 44 Iowa L.Rev. 716, 726.

21. See §§ 49–51, infra.

See Chapter 3, Osborne, Mortgages, 1951, for a discussion of the Statute of Frauds in connection with equitable mortgages.

22. See Pomeroy, Equity Juris., 5th Ed., §§ 1402, 1405; See also Fogelman, The Deed Absolute as a Mortgage in New York, 1963, 32 Fordham L.Rev. 299.

Comment, Enforcement in Equity of Oral Promise to Give Security in Realty for Loan, 1952, 9 Wash. & Lee L.Rev. 269.

Holibaugh v. Stokes, 1961, 192 Cal.App.2d 564, 13 Cal.Rptr. 528, is authority for the proposition that a creditor who advanced money for the purchase of property in the debtor's name on an oral agreement by the debtor to execute a note and trust deed mortgage to creditor created an equitable mortgage in the creditor.

23. See Walsh, Mortgages, 48.

See § 20, supra.

24. Rogers v. Challis, 1859, 27 Beav. 175 (refusal to compel borrowing and giving of mortgage); Conklin v. People's Bldg. & Loan Ass'n, 1886, 41 N.J.Eq. 20,

lender → spec perf → borrower (handwritten annotation)

ble mortgage arises in such a case. A variety of explanations have been offered to explain this result.

Borrower → spec perf → Lender (handwritten annotation)

Where the would be borrower-mortgagor sues to compel the giving of the loan and accepting the mortgage, if the money could be borrowed elsewhere and the difference in cost recovered as damages the legal remedy would be adequate.[25] Where he cannot, "while the damages for breach of such a contract may be inadequate, the inadequacy is almost directly proportionate to the probability that the loan may not be repaid at maturity. Equity therefore in this as in many other cases refuses its relief because greater injustice may result from the exercise of its jurisdiction than would result from leaving the parties to their rights at law." [26] Occasionally, where the borrower could not obtain the loan elsewhere and the offered security is clearly adequate to guarantee repayment, specific performance has been given against the lender.[27]

The denial of specific performance by a lender against a borrower rests on scant authority and the reasons for it are not clearly enunciated. Usually the money market is such that the lender can lend just as advantageously elsewhere; or, if not, his remedy at law is adequate in that the amount of damage he suffers by not being able to put out his money on as good terms can be readily estimated. Further, policy considerations play a part. The courts are reluctant to compel a man to become a debtor and risk losing his property put up as security should he be unable to repay. And, finally, fuzzy notions about the necessity of mutuality of remedy no doubt exercise an influence.

Another, more technical explanation may be given. A legal mortgage will be security only for the obligation intended to be secured by it. So, too, an agreement that a mortgage will be given or that property be, or be held as, security will not create an equitable mortgage unless or until there is in existence the obligation which the property is intended to secure. And even where the obligation is in existence or arises, it will create an equitable mortgage only to the extent and size of the obligation.[28] In an executory contract by E to lend or perform in some other way and to receive security in return for M's promise to borrow and repay or pay, the property is intended to be security for the obligation to repay or pay and only to the extent of such a duty. Until the loan is made or the other stipulated performance is given, no duty to repay or pay arises. Since it was this duty which was intended to be secured no equitable mortgage will arise until E makes the agreed upon performance.[29] E's perform-

2 A. 615 (refusal to compel lending). See Glenn, The "Equitable Pledge", 1939, 25 Va.L.Rev. 422, 425; Pound, The Progess of Equity, 1920, 33 Harv. L.Rev. 420, 432; Falconbridge, Mortgages, 3d Ed., 77; note, 1931, 18 Va.L.Rev. 76; note, 1918, 18 Col. L.Rev. 491.

Cf. Columbus Club v. Simons, 1925, 110 Okl. 48, 236 P. 12, 41 A.L.R. 350.

That there must be present valuable consideration for the promise to execute a mortgage and that a preexisting indebtedness is insufficient, see Note, Equitable Mortgages in Iowa, 1959, 44 Iowa L.Rev. 710, 728.

See Cunningham and Tischler, op. cit. supra § 25, note 20, 705–707.

25. Gideon v. Putnam Development Corp., 1932, 113 W.Va. 200, 167 S.E. 140; Norwood v. Crowder, 1919, 177 N.Car. 469, 99 S.E. 345.

See McClintock, Equity 96; Falconbridge, Mortgages, 3d Ed. 77.

26. Stone, The "Equitable Mortgage" in New York, 1920, 20 Col.L.Rev. 519, 521.

27. Caplin v. Pennsylvania Mut. Life Ins. Co., 1918, 182 App.Div. 269, 169 N.Y.S. 756, affirmed 229 N.Y. 545, 129 N.E. 908; Columbus Club v. Simons, 1923, 110 Okl. 48, 236 P. 12, 41 A.L.R. 350, noted 24 Mich.L.Rev. 195; Jacobson v. First Nat. Bank, etc., 1941, 129 N.J.Eq. 440, 20 A.2d 19, 130 N.J.Eq. 604, 23 A.2d 409, noted 40 Mich.L.Rev. 303.

28. See Chapter 5, infra; Restatement, Security, § 10, comment b, semble.

" * * * a mortgage, whatever the amount of indebtedness which it purports to secure, operates to secure only the actual amount of the indebtedness." 3 Tiffany, Real Prop., 2d Ed., 2569.

29. Federal Land Bank v. Monroe Co., 1932, 165 Tenn. 364, 54 S.W.2d 716, rehearing denied 165 Tenn. 624, 57 S.W.2d 553; Fred T. Ley & Co. v.

ance is a condition precedent either to specific performance of a promise to give a mortgage or to giving effect to an agreement that property be held, or operate presently, as security.[30] This explanation, obviously, differentiates contracts for the sale of land in which specific performance by the vendor will be ordered even though the agreed performance by the vendee is entirely executory. One writer,[31] while correctly differentiating contracts for mortgages and contracts for the sale of land, seems to confuse the requirements of a court of equity for giving the extraordinary relief of specific performance with the question of what factors in a case will induce a court of equity to dispense with the necessity of a writing even though the agreement falls within the Statute of Frauds.[32] Further, on this latter point, while very usefully pointing out that the things which should and would be considered as sufficient in land sale contracts ought not to be the test in contracts for mortgage, it is erroneously stated that "the Statute of Frauds is not involved since the equitable mortgage arises because of the right to the security as a specific thing in reliance upon which the creditor has performed, not because of an enforceable legal contract to execute a formal mortgage." [33] This treats an equitable mortgage founded upon an express agreement that a legal mortgage shall be given, or that the property shall be security, or that it is presently pledged as security, as arising by operation of law out of the obligee's performance rather than as a consequence of the doctrine of specific performance of the obligor's promise, or an analogous doctrine,[34] with the performance by the obligee of a condition precedent to the relief. The difference between the two is more than formal: One ignores the fundamental distinction between consensual and non-consensual rights; the other follows it.[35]

Where the loan or other performance has been executed by the obligee, none of the objections urged against specific performance are present and equity will grant it on the ground that damages for breach of a promise to give security are inadequate. The measure of such damages would be the difference in value between a secured and an unsecured claim. This is dependent upon the present and future value of the security, the ability of the obligor to perform or of the obligee to collect at the time the obligation matures or is sued upon, factors obviously too speculative and indeterminate to make the legal remedy an adequate one.[36]

---

34. See, infra, § 28.

35. See Pound, Progress of the Law, 1918–1919, 1920, 33 Harv.L.Rev. 929, 936 where, in vigorously refuting the idea that courts of equity were enforcing law created "equities" instead of the contract where there has been part performance of an oral contract, it was stated: "The courts have not enforced and do not enforce the equitable claims of the plaintiff arising from fraud or part performance as such, but rather the contract itself, * * *."

A similar divergence of view as to the rationale of equitable mortgages of after-acquired property is discussed later. See infra, § 37. For another and somewhat astonishing misapprehension of the basis of specific performance of contracts to give security see Glenn, Mortgages, § 412. The nature of the property promised, contrary to the statement of that ordinarily accurate writer, is immaterial. It is because legal damages from failure to get *security* would be "speculative depending upon the future ability of the debtor to pay and the future need and value of the security." Stone, The "Equitable Mortgage" in New York, 1920, 20 Col.L.Rev. 519, 521.

Wheat, C.C.A.Fla.1933, 64 F.2d 257; Iowa Loan & Trust Co. v. Plewe, 1926, 202 Iowa 79, 209 N.W. 399.

30. See Restatement, Security, § 10, Comment b. Regardless of whether there must be as a rule of law, a personal obligation for the property to secure in the kind of transactions involved here, certainly where a loan is involved there is no *intention* that there shall be any security until the loan is made; and then only to the extent of the loan. In other words, until the loan is made the obligation *intended* to be secured is not in existence. See Walsh, Mortgages, 43.

31. Walsh, Mortgages, 48.

32. The question of the Statute of Frauds is discussed elsewhere. See Chapter 3, infra.

33. Walsh, Mortgages, 47.

36. Herman v. Hodges, 1873, L.R. 16 Eq. 18; Hicks v. Turck, 1888, 72 Mich. 311, 40 N.W. 339; Dean v. Anderson, 1881, 34 N.J.Eq. 496; Hale v. Omaha

Whether the lender's performance must be entirely executed and, if not, to what extent it must be, is not entirely clear. Sleeth v. Sampson,[37] usually cited as leading authority on what will constitute part performance under the Statute of Frauds, is explained on the ground that, although "some money was advanced to the debtor", the performance by the plaintiff was still so far executory as to fall under the rule governing unperformed promises to lend.[38] If only a small part of the loan has been advanced this distinction seems a sound one. On the other hand, it seems unlikely that the very last dollar of the loan must have been advanced. There is authority, however, that an agreement to give security will be specifically enforced and the property will stand as security for the amount actually loaned where only a small portion, £1,000 of a £30,000 loan, had been paid over.[39]

PROMISE TO GIVE A MORTGAGE— NON-CONSENSUAL THEORY

27. It has been asserted that the equitable mortgages in this first group, as well as all other equitable mortgages, rest, not upon principles of specific performance of promises, but upon non-consensual bases. There are strong objections to this view and it is not supported by the authorities.

One eminent writer explicitly rejects specific performance as a rationale of equitable mortgages even in cases where there is a promise to execute a legal mortgage, saying that "the principle of unjust enrichment is the guide";[40] that the "remedy is not specific performance, as that term is commonly understood"; and that the "rule, then, is 'transfer the security or give back the money' —in other words, the decree brings about 'restitution for unjust enrichment.'"[41] For

40. 1 Glenn, Mortgages, § 17.

41. 1 Glenn, Mortgages, § 17.1.
Semble, and cited by Glenn, op. cit., § 17.2 n. 6, is Schram v. Burt, C.C.A.Mich., 1940, 111 F.2d 557, in which the court said that the equitable lien is "controlled by the same equitable principles as that of the vendor of real estate for unpaid purchase money * * *. In one case a party receives the title to real property without paying for it, with or without an agreement that his vendor shall be secured by a lien upon it by way of mortgage or otherwise. In the other case, the party advances money under an agreement that its payment shall be secured by mortgage upon specific real estate, which agreement remains imperfect. The right of the vendor and the person advancing the money upon such an agreement is essentially the same * * *." The decision awarded an equitable lien for the amount of the loan used in paying taxes and insurance and for improvements on the property. If the court intended its reasoning to apply only to the facts of the particular case the analogy it invokes is perhaps not too inapposite. It is giving relief only to the extent to which it can trace the money with which the claimant parted into the land claimed. Therefore, the equitable lien could be classified correctly as non-consensual, as is the vendor's lien. But if the statement was intended to state the basis of all equitable liens, both consensual and non-consensual, it must be rejected. There is considerable controversy over the rationale of the vendor's lien but very clearly it is non-consensual in nature. See Ahrend v. Odiorne, 1875, 118 Mass. 261, 19 Am.Rep. 449; 4 Pomeroy, Eq. Juris., 5th Ed., § 1250. Further, none of the plausible explanations for its creation would apply to cases where the loan cannot be traced into the property on which the equitable lien is fastened. Even in cases where it can be, they apply only by analogy and extension.
In Walsh, Mortgages, 47, the author first draws a clear distinction between promises to execute legal mortgages, which are put, correctly upon principles of specific performance of contracts, and agree-

Nat. Bank, 1872, 49 N.Y. 626; Irvine v. Armstrong, 1883, 31 Minn. 216, 17 N.W. 343; Blum v. Planters' Bank & Trust Co., 1931, 161 Miss. 226, 135 So. 353; Sir Simon Stewart's Case, 1805, 2 Sch. & Lef. 381; Owens v. Continental Supply Co., C.C.A.Okl.1934, 71 F.2d 862; Bosch Magneto Co. v. Rushmore, 1915, 85 N.J.Eq. 93, 95 A. 614. See Durfee, Cases on Security, 1959, 439.

See Daggett v. Rankin, 1866, 31 Cal. 321. See also Williston, Transfers of After-Acquired Personal Property, 1906, 19 Harv.L.Rev. 557, 561; Stone, The "Equitable Mortgage" in New York, 1920, 20 Col.L.Rev. 519, 521; Walsh, Mortgages, 43; Tiffany, Real. Prop., 2d Ed., 2746; Fry, Specific Performance, 6th Ed., § 54; note, 1920, 33 Harv.L.Rev. 456. But see Brown v. E. Van Winkle Gin & Machine Works, 1904, 141 Ala. 580, 39 So. 243, 6 L.R.A.,N.S., 585. The court refused to enforce a contract to execute a mortgage where the debt was already due and there was no showing defendant was insolvent.

Kidwell v. Henderson, 1928, 150 Va. 829, 143 S.E. 336 held that a written agreement to give a trust deed mortgage created an equitable mortgage in the proposed beneficiary.

On the effect of insolvency on contracts to give security, see note, 1937, 51 Harv.L.Rev. 135.

37. 1923, 237 N.Y. 69, 142 N.E. 355, 30 A.L.R. 1400.

38. See Walsh, Mortgages, 48 note 30.

39. Hunter v. Lord Langdon, 1828, 2 Molloy, Ir.Ch., 272. See Falconbridge, Mortgages, 3d ed. 78.

this thesis the writer cites two groups of cases. The first of these are authority only for the proposition that not all equitable mortgages are dependent upon specific performance [42]—a perfectly sound statement the truth [43] of and the important consequences flowing from which are discussed in following sections. The other cases relied upon to establish the "rule" are ones in which the debt was due. Consequently, the alternative to specific performance, namely payment of the debt, would be rather obvious and desirable but would not establish any principle that the equitable mortgage itself rested on a nonconsensual foundation. The alternative, it should be emphasized, is not restitution but payment of the agreed upon amount. Indeed, in only two of the cases cited was it clearly the decision that the obligor was ac-

corded even this privilege.[44] Also, when the debt is due, it is unnecessary to force the formal execution of the promised legal mortgage since the plaintiff is permitted to foreclose the equitable mortgage at once without this formality.[45] Further, neither the "rule" nor the basic rationale on which it is said to rest are applied in the cases in which the debt is not due. In them the court forces the execution of the legal mortgage which the obligor promised to give.[46]

Entirely apart from the question of specific authorities there are strong objections to the doctrine enunciated. It would treat the granting to a plaintiff by a court of equity, because of the inadequacy of the legal remedy, of the very interest in property promised to him by the defendant as resting upon not the specific enforcement of the intent of the parties in a consensual transaction but the

---

ments that property shall be security, in which specific performance, at least in the sense of compelling the execution of a legal mortgage, is not necessary to the creation of the equitable security interest. Then, by implication rather than by a clear and explicit statement, he seems to place all equitable mortgages on a non-censensual basis. He says, ibid., 47, "His equity arises out of his performance relying on the promise or pledge of security, not on the technical right to specific performance of a written contract to give a mortgage." Again, ibid., 52, he states, "Where the legal title is not transferred to the creditor, but the intent is expressed that the property shall be security for a loan made or credit actually extended (as distinguished from being merely promised) in reliance upon such security, an equitable mortgage arises because as a matter of equity and justice the creditor should have the specific property pledged or promised, and in reliance upon which he made the loan or extended the credit." See, also, ibid., 51 n. 33, 56. If these statements mean, as they seem to, that equitable mortgages invariably arise by operation of law because of a performance by the obligee in reliance upon having specified security rather than as a reason for granting specific performance of the obligor's promise or giving effect to his intention that certain property be given as security or immediately be security, the criticisms, supra, and in the text are applicable. See also the criticisms § 26, supra; 37, infra. A similar problem arises in Chapter 3.

42. Metcalfe v. Archbishop of York, 1836, 1 Myl. & Cr. 547; Bridgeport Electric & Ice, etc., Co. v. Meador, C.C.A.Ala., 1895, 72 F. 115, 18 C.C.A. 451.

43. See also Walsh, Mortgages, 43; Jacob, Protection of Debenture Holders, 1938, 52 Harv.L.Rev. 77, 92 et seq.

44. Herman v. Hodges, 1873, L.R. 16 Eq. 18; Irvine v. Armstrong, 1883, 31 Minn. 216, 17 N.W. 343. In the latter case the court said that the trial court had permitted payment, rather than forcing the execution of a mortgage, apparently as a favor or indulgence and not as a "matter of right". It said that because the plaintiff had not taken an appeal the court did not have to inquire whether the defendants were entitled to this alternative or "whether the plaintiffs were not * * * entitled to a decree absolute for the execution of a mortgage."

In Bridgeport Electric & Ice, etc., Co. v. Meador, C.C. A.Ala., 1895, 72 F. 115, 13 C.C.A. 451, Sprague v. Cochran, 1894, 144 N.Y. 104, 38 N.E. 1000, and Dean v. Anderson, 1881, 34 N.J.Eq. 496, there is nothing to indicate that there would be any alternative to compelling the execution of the mortgage because the plaintiff was entitled to specific performance.

The English decisions that an equitable mortgagee by deposit of title deeds is entitled to the execution of a legal mortgage are also at variance with this view. See infra § 34.

45. See Sprague v. Cochran, 1894, 144 N.Y. 104, 38 N.E. 1000; Williston, Transfers of After-Acquired Personal Property, 1906, 19 Harv.L.Rev. 556, 560.

46. E. g., Hicks v. Turck, 1888, 72 Mich. 311, 40 N. W. 339. See also authorities cited in note 44, supra.

Ashton v. Corrigan, 1871, L.R. 13 Eq. 76 granted specific performance even though the debt was already due and the agreement to give the legal mortgage had been made after it was due.

See also the authorities holding that an equitable mortgagee by deposit of title deeds has a right to have a legal mortgage, executed, note 44, supra.

non-consensual principle of restitution to prevent unjust enrichment. This would obliterate the thoroughly settled and recognized distinction between rights created to effectuate the intention of the parties and rights created without regard for or contrary to their intention. To do so seems undesirable and, in this instance at least, entirely unnecessary. Further, it may be granted that the Restatement of Restitution does not purport to cover all instances of unjust enrichment.[47] Nevertheless it is a most unusual and, again in the cases involved here, unnecessary proposition that one is entitled on principles of restitution to get an interest in property belonging to another in which the claimant previously had never had an interest, into which he cannot trace any property which had ever previously belonged to him,[48] and which he had not been prevented from acquiring by fraud, tort, breach of a fiduciary relationship by the defendant or a third party, or some similar wrong.[49] Since this non-consensual theory of the basis of all equitable mortgages is involved in the problem of whether the Statute of Frauds requires a writing for the creation of an equitable mortgage, further discussion of it is postponed until that subject is treated. It may not be amiss to state in anticipation that the whole conception seems to be derived from one explanation of the "part performance" doctrine of taking a transaction out of the operation of the Statute of Frauds.[50]

PROMISE TO HOLD AS SECURITY

28. An agreement to hold or treat the property as security gives rise to an equitable mortgage according to the very terms of the expressed intention and the obligor will never be compelled to execute a legal mortgage. Such an agreement is susceptible of two constructions:

47. See Glenn, Morts., § 17.

48. See Restatement of Restitution, § 215.

49. See Restatement of Restitution, c. 9, Topic 1. See also Scott, Trusts, c. 13.

50. See Chapter 3, infra.

(1) that it is a promise as to future conduct and therefore rests on the doctrine of specific performance, or, as some courts prefer to say, principles analogous to it; (2) that it is intended to be a present transfer of a security interest in which case specific performance is not the basis. Although this distinction is fundamental few cases clearly draw it, but they usually reach the correct result.

Where the defendant's promise is merely to hold or treat the property as security, as distinguished from a promise to execute a legal mortgage specific performance seems applicable [51] and has been recognized as the correct explanation of the equitable mortgage in such cases.[52] However, there are many statements that the equitable mortgage arising from this second type of promise is not based, technically, upon specific performance but upon other grounds analogous to it.[53] If the term specific perform-

51. See Fry, Specific Performance, 6th Ed., § 38, "By specific performance is usually understood that peculiar and, as it is called, extraordinary jurisdiction, which that Court exercised in respect of executory contracts as contrasted with executed contracts." See also ibid., § 39.

52. "Equity will thus compel performance of the agreement to give security regardless of its particular form. The agreement may be to give a formal mortgage of specific property or that particular land or property will be held by the borrower as security to the lender * * *." Stone, the "Equitable Mortgage" in New York, 1920, 20 Col.L.Rev. 519, 521.
"That the lien is based on contract is necessarily involved in dicta or decisions that the transaction must be supported by a valuable consideration as well as in decisions that it must be evidenced by an instrument in writing which satisfies the fourth section of the Statute of Frauds." Tiffany, Real Prop., 2d Ed., 2747. Whether the statement about the Statute of Frauds is correct, see Chapter 4, infra. See Fogelman, The Deed Absolute as a Mortgage in New York, 1963, 32 Fordham L.Rev. 299.

53. See 3 Tiffany, Real Prop., 2d Ed., 2747, "principles analogous to those underlying the doctrine of specific performance."; Fry Specific Performance, 6th Ed., § 38, "other grounds of equitable relief approximate to specific performance", and § 42, "A contract for a legal or equitable charge, when the consideration has passed, itself creates an equitable charge independently of the doctrine of specific performance, but may in addition create a right to have a legal charge"; Matter of Lind, [1915] 2 Ch. 345, "It was then said for the defendants, that all equitable charges rest upon specific performance. * * * This is by no means so." The validity

ance is used to cover all cases of enforcement of executory [54] contracts the former seems correct. This is an orthodox if not an exclusive or necessary meaning of the words. On the other hand, if it is thought undesirable to use the term "where nothing remains to be done to define the rights of the parties but the court is merely asked to protect rights completely defined as between the parties to the contract" [55] then the latter expression is preferable. In any event the divergence of views points up a distinction between the two kinds of promises which should be noted.

Where the promise is to give a legal mortgage, the equitable mortgage arises when the promise becomes legally binding or enforceable.[56] This is not because there was, necessarily, an intention that there should be any security interest before the mortgage is executed. It is because of the equitable doctrine that an equitable interest comes into existence as a consequence of the right to specific performance, equity, as the usual expression of this conception goes, regarding that as done which it will compel to be done, or, less accurately, which ought to be done.[57]

In this case, however, the court is creating an equitable mortgage according to the very terms of the expressed intention that the property shall be held by the defendant as security; and it is important to remember that no legal mortgage will ever be ordered. It is possible that this latter feature of the transaction is the reason for opinions that specific performance does not apply or, at least, is not the sole rationale in such cases.[58] However, it is believed that the explanation of such expressed views may lie elsewhere.

Although the distinction between a promise as to future conduct and a present transfer as a fundamental one,[59] it is usually slurred over in these cases for two reasons. One is the difficulty in most of them of determining the question of fact as to which was actually intended. Indeed, if the property is

---

of a mortgage of an expectancy was under consideration; Walsh, Mortgages, 45, 52.

See also Higgins v. Manson, 1899, 126 Cal. 467, 469, 58 P. 907, 908, 77 Am.St.Rep. 192; Tailby v. Official Receiver, 1888, 13 App.Cas. 523, 547.

It is not at all certain that Walsh, supra, has in mind a *promise* that the property shall be security. The cases he relies upon for the statement he makes he treats as involving present pledges of the land as security. See Walsh, op. cit., 44, 45.

54. "The truth is that if a promisor must act *to keep his promise* the transaction is executory. The fact that, if the promisor does not act, the same result can be achieved by legal proceedings and thus damage to the promisee avoided is immaterial". Foley and Pogue After-Acquired Property under Conflicting Corporate Mortgage Indentures, 1929, 13 Minn.L.Rev. 81, 84.

See Fry, op. cit., supra, n. 53.

55. Tailby v. Official Receiver, 1888, 13 App.Cas. 523, 547.

56. See, §§ 42, 43, infra, for the problem of conditions precedent to the performance of a binding promise to give a mortgage.

57. See, e. g., Owens v. Continental Supply Co., C.C. A.Okl., 1934, 71 F.2d 862; Daggett v. Rankin, 1866,

31 Cal. 321, 327; Bridgeport Electric & Ice Co. v. Meador, C.C.A.Ala.1895, 72 F. 115, 18 C.C.A. 451.

Contrast: White v. Barnard, C.C.A.Mass., 1928, 29 F. 2d 510, certiorari denied 49 S.Ct. 346, 279 U.S. 848, 73 L.Ed. 992, in which there was an oral agreement to execute a deed as security for future advances. The advances were made and, later, the deed was executed within four months of bankruptcy. The majority of the court held that since there was no intent that the property should be security for the advances as they were made, no equitable mortgage ever arose prior to the execution of the deed. Even if the court was correct on its finding of fact as to intent, it would seem that an equitable mortgage should have been held to arise either at once or when the advances were made because the promise to give the deed was specifically enforceable. The promise was oral but the decision wasn't placed on this ground, apparently, because the court said that if there had been an intent that the property be security at the time of the advances, an equitable mortgage would have arisen then. Whether the court thought that this equitable mortgage would have arisen on the basis of a promise that it be security at that time, or on the basis that the agreement operated as an executed transaction at that time is not clear. Since the generally accepted doctrine is that transfers in futuro cannot be made operative by a present agreement, it would seem to be the former.

58. It has also been said not to be the sole rationale where the promise was to give a legal mortgage. See Fry, Specific Performance, § 42. In both cases there is a *promise* by the mortgagor *to do* something, i. e., the transaction is an executory one. In one case he is to execute a legal mortgage; in the other to hold the property as security.

59. See Fry, Specific Performance, 6th Ed., § 39.

then in existence and owned by the obligor, both intentions doubtless would be present.[60] The other reason is that it is only occasionally, as, for example, when the question of securing an existing debt is involved,[61] that the difference is of importance as a matter of law. Consequently, while specific performance is properly applicable only to promises to do something, and the equitable mortgage which arises out of giving effect to an intention that there be an immediate security interest could not rest upon that doctrine, it is not surprising that there should be some confusion or carelessness in statement, if not in decision.[62] Yet there are some cases which state the distinction with clarity. For example, in the leading case [63] for the proposition that specific performance of a promise to execute a legal mortgage is the sole basis for creating an equitable mortgage, the transaction was intended by the parties to be a completed one, i. e., that the property *be* security. The court quite properly reasoned that "there is no room for the doctrine of specific performance because there is nothing unperformed." [64] The court's decision that, consequently, there could be no equitable mortgage seems clearly wrong and contrary

to the authorities generally.[65] So, too, does its declaration that only agreements to give legal mortgages which give rise to the right of specific performance will create equitable mortgages.[66] However, its statement in respect to specific performance is accurate.

INTENT TO CREATE PRESENT SECURITY INTEREST

29. Equitable mortgages arising out of agreements in the second category depend for their validity upon invoking analogies and rules that go back into the law of conveyancing and the creation of trusts rather than into the law of contracts and specific performance of contracts. They are executed, not executory transactions. When this distinction is important the courts usually reach the correct result, even though they do not state the distinction as explicitly as could be wished.

The second group of consensual equitable mortgages differs from the first in that it is intended to be a completely executed transaction, not an executory one. The transaction in In re Snyder [67] is typical. The writing in that case referred to specific property which, it said, "is pledged." In holding that this created an equitable mortgage the court quoted with approval language from other cases stating that "any words would be sufficient which serve to show a transfer of the mortgaged property as security for the debt," and "every express agreement in writing, whereby the party clearly indicates an intention to make some particular property therein described as security for a debt, cre-

---

60. It is also true that an agreement to execute a legal mortgage in the future is not inconsistent with the existence of an agreement that the property be treated as security in the meantime. See Fry, Specific Performance, § 42. And see, especially, Jacob, Protection of Debenture Holders, 1938, 52 Harv.L. Rev. 77, 95. See, semble, Scott, Trusts, § 30. Nor, for that matter, are either or both of such agreements incompatible with an intention that it be security at once. Defective conveyances in mortgage are illustrative of this fact although it is not invariably recognized.

61. See § 30, infra.
It also becomes of importance in cases of conditional agreements to mortgage and conditional negative covenants are involved. See infra §§ 42, 43. See Jacob, note 60, supra.

62. As is pointed out later, where the distinction has legal importance the courts for the most part reach what the writer considers proper results. See § 30, infra.

63. Stoddard v. Hart, 1861, 23 N.Y. 556.

64. See Fry, Specific Performance, 6th Ed., § 38, accord.

---

65. See the following sections. But see Glenn, Mortgages, § 17.2, praising the decision as a commendable rebuke to laxness of thinking and practice.

66. See Walsh, Mortgages, 43, 45; Jacob, note 60 supra, 92.
Compare the extreme position of the court in Stoddard v. Hart in insisting upon specific performance of a promise to give a legal mortgage with the failure of the court in White v. Barnard, note 57, supra, to recognize specific performance of a contract to make a conveyance as security as creating an equitable mortgage.

67. 1908, 138 Iowa 553, 114 N.W. 615, 19 L.R.A.,N.S., 206. See § 24.

ates an equitable lien upon the property." [68] It resembles the second type of promise in the first group in that no legal mortgage is contemplated.[69] It differs from it, however, in being intended to be "conveyancesory" instead of promissory. It is, though not technically a trust,[70] at least a half-brother to one, and the analogies and rules to be invoked in determining its validity go back into the law of conveyancing and the creation of uses and trusts rather than into the law of contracts

and specific performance of promises.[71] As was pointed out previously,[72] the distinction between the two kinds of transactions, for understandable reasons, is not always recognized in the cases as explicitly as might be wished. However, when the difference is of importance, as when it is a question of whether present valuable consideration is necessary or whether a preexisting debt is sufficient, cases which otherwise might cause difficulty are reconcilable or comprehensible.[73] Also, the authorities which state that equitable mortgages may arise from a doctrine other than specific performance,[74] insofar as they refer to this second group of transactions, seem clearly correct.[75] Since these basic rationales of the equitable mortgage will be considered again in the following sections dealing with specific problems concerning them and the several varieties of them, the foregoing discussion at this time seems sufficient.

CONSIDERATION—SIGNIFICANCE OF PRE-EXISTING DEBT

30. (1) Where the equitable mortgage arises because equity will grant specific performance of a promise, there must be a legally binding promise and, in addition, the kind of consider-

---

68. Other cases include Jones v. Hill, 1934, 167 Okl. 552, 31 P.2d 145 ("I hereby list and give a lien"); Hackett v. Watts, 1896, 138 Mo. 502, 40 S.W. 113 (written statement of intent to mortgage together with the deposit of a contract for purchase held to create an equitable mortgage); Owens v. Continental Supply Co., C.C.A.Okl., 1934, 71 F.2d 862, 863 ("Payment * * * is secured by a lien on my riverbed leases * * * such lien to be evidenced later by a regular form mortgage."); accord, Sporle v. Whayman, 1855, 20 Beav. 607 also seems in point. See Durfee, Cases on Security, 1951, 442. In Hill v. Hill, 185 Kan. 389, 345 P.2d 1015, 1959, the words "it is hereby agreed that the Holder of this note shall have $2500 interest in above described Property" created an equitable mortgage in the property.

See, contra, Stoddard v. Hart, 1861, 23 N.Y. 556, 561, "Now, a loan of money, with a mere understanding that the land of the borrower is a security for the debt, does not create a mortgage, legal or equitable. If it be specifically agreed to execute a legal mortgage, a very different question arises." (The court suggested that, if it were a title state, the case, which was one of extending the mortgage by oral agreement to cover a new advance, could be decided differently.)

69. As pointed out previously there may be, in addition, a promise to give security or a mortgage and such a promise would not be inconsistent with a coexistent intent that there be an immediate security interest. Defectively executed mortgages may well be either or both. A similar problem in the law of trusts seems relevant. While the contemplation by the settlor of a subsequent execution of a formal instrument does not necessarily negative the present creation of a trust, the fact that he does contemplate the subsequent execution of such an instrument is a strong indication that he does not intend to create a trust until the instrument is executed. Scott, Cas.Trusts, 3d Ed., 111 n. 1.

70. See 4 Pomeroy, Eq.Juris., 5th Ed., § 1234, pointing out that in a true trust there are two estates in the same property: the legal estate in the trustee and the equitable estate in the beneficiary; whereas in an equitable lien, while the legal estate and possession are in one person and an equitable right over the property in another, this equitable right is quite different from the interest of a cestui que trust. It doesn't, as in the case of a trust, entitle

the holder to a conveyance of the property or to its use but is merely a right of realization by means of which the personal obligation "may be more effectively enforced than by a mere pecuniary recovery at law" and, therefore, "it is more accurate to describe these liens as *analogous* to trusts * * *."

71. Holder v. Williams, 1959, 167 Cal.App.2d 313, 334 P.2d 291, apparently recognized such a basis for the equitable mortgage.

Stoddard v. Hart, § 26, supra, is, of course, contra.

72. See § 26.

73. The leading authorities are cited in notes § 30, infra.

74. Glenn, as was noted supra, puts them all on the doctrine of unjust enrichment; and Walsh espouses another theory of non-consensual creation. The cases themselves are, as has been stated, not explicit. See § 26.

75. As has been pointed out elsewhere, § 25, supra, those authorities do not appear to have this distinction in mind. Tiffany and Stone place all equitable mortgages on the doctrine of specific performance. See § 30, infra.

ation required to induce a court of equity to act. Generally this is a present, valuable one. Hence, promises to give property as security for pre-existing debts should not create an equitable mortgage. Some cases hold that they do.

(2) Where the equitable mortgage *Present Transfer* is created by way of present transfer there is no reason why the transfer could not be entirely gratuitous, as in the case of a legal mortgage or a trust. Thus, the properly expressed intent that property be security for an antecedent debt should be sufficient. The existence of the debt has no significance as consideration. Most of the decisions are in accord; some cases and writers take a contrary view.

If the distinction between executory and executed equitable mortgages is borne in mind, the controversy over the necessity of a present valuable consideration for the creation of a consensual equitable mortgage may be resolved. Where the security agreement sounds in promise and the equitable mortgage arises because equity will grant specific performance of that promise—whether it be to give a legal mortgage or to hold or treat the property as security—the consideration requirements of the law of contracts and specific performance should be sufficient and probably necessary. Certainly there must be a legally binding promise. But granted this, there must be the sort of consideration that will induce a court of equity to act.[76] Generally this is held to be a present, valuable one.[77] But if it rests in present transfer there seems no more reason to require present valuable consideration here than in the effective declaration of a modern trust of real property.[78] It has been suggested that the minority of common-law decisions and the few statutes[79] requiring consideration in order to create a trust are "to some extent based on the misconception that a trust is a species of contract. To some extent they may reflect a survival of the old law of uses. They may also represent an unconscious revolt against the great ease with which gifts can be effected through trust declarations."[80]

None of these reasons would apply to the declaration that specific property be security. It is intended as a completed transfer as much as is a declaration of trust. The old doctrines of uses should be given no weight here any more than in the modern law of trusts. And, although there might be something said in trust cases in favor of the third explanation it should have no influence here. To throw a safeguard around claimed gifts is one thing; to apply the same reasoning to a situation in which the claimant would be able to reach the property in question on preliminary, or at least final, process in an action at law to enforce the obligation held by him is quite another. Giving effect to the declared intention that the property be security has only these results: it gives the claimant different methods of realizing his claim out of the property than those to which he is remitted if he is confined to his legal position as an unsecured creditor; it enables him to reach it in the hands of transferees of his obligors;[81]

76. See Pomeroy, Eq.Juris., 5th Ed., §§ 1293, 1405; Langdell, Brief Survey of Equity Jurisdiction 52; Pound, Consideration in Equity, 1918, 13 Ill.L.Rev. 667; "no court of conscience will enforce *donum gratuitum*, tho' the intent appear never so clearly, where it is not executed or sufficiently passed by law;". Bacon, Reading upon the Statute of Uses, 13, 14.

77. Pomeroy, Equity Juris., 4th Ed., § 1405. See Stone, The Equitable Mortgage in New York, 1920, 20 Col.L.Rev., 519, 523; Walsh, Mortgages, 52; Tiffany, Real Prop., 2d Ed., 2747; Restatement, Security, § 10, b. But see Pound, Consideration in Equity, 1919, 13 Ill.L.Rev. 667, questioning the validity as a true principle that equity will not execute a voluntary contract.

78. Although a nominal or recited consideration was necessary to create a use by bargain and sale, "in the law of trusts, which is the outgrowth of the old law of uses, the necessity for consideration has passed." Bogert, Trusts and Trustees, §§ 201, 202. See Scott, Trusts, § 28.1. There must be present valuable consideration for a promise to create a trust. Scott, Trusts, § 30; Bogert, Trusts and Trustees, § 203.

79. E. g., Cal.Civ.Code § 2222, discussed in McWilliams, Consideration and the Law of Trusts, 1926, 14 Cal.L.Rev. 188.

80. Bogert, op. cit., supra, note 78, § 202, n. 24.

81. Storke, An Introduction to Security, 1943, 16 Rocky Mt.L.Rev. 27. Of course a bona fide purchase or the operation of recording acts to which it might be subject would free the property in the

and it gives him priority over other creditor claimants. These effects date from the time the intent is operative. None of these consequences, it is submitted, would be sufficient reason to justify refusing to give effect to the declared intention of the parties.

Consequently, the properly expressed intention that property be security for an antecedent debt clearly should be valid. The existence of the debt should be necessary only if and to the extent that a personal obligation to be secured is an indispensable requisite of a mortgage.[82] The antecedent debt is frequently spoken of as "consideration" but there appears no good reason why the transfer should not be entirely gratuitous here as it clearly may be in the case of a *legal* mortgage to secure a pre-existing debt.[83] The role the existing debt plays is not to act as "consideration" but merely to provide the obligation necessary by law, or by the intention of the parties, in these cases before there can be a mortgage.[84] There is ample authority to support the views here expressed.[85] The numerous cases in which defective mortgage deeds given to secure antecedent debts have been upheld as creating equitable mortgages support these views.[86] The same distinction

is recognized where the mortgage subject matter is equitable, equity giving effect to a completed transfer without requiring present consideration but making it a requisite where the assignment is incomplete or rests upon contract.[87]

The much cited New York case of Stoddard v. Hart,[88] although it rejected an agreement that property be security as capable of creating an equitable mortgage, did so on the ground that they can be created only on the basis of specific performance of a promise to give a legal mortgage, a view which is against the overwhelming weight of authority and against good sense. There was in that case a present valuable consideration for the agreement that the property be security. In the case most frequently cited for the proposition that present consideration is necessary, the written promise involved was "to give" security and the court, although placing its decision on the ground that a subsequent legal mortgage was given, said that it thought the statement of the court below, which had directed judgment against the plaintiff on the ground that "a present valuable consideration, as distinguished from a past indebtedness, is essential to support an agreement to give a mortgage so as to make the specific enforcement of such an agreement enforcible in a court of equity"[89] was correct. And the only authority relied upon by the court in this case also was one in which there was a promise to give a mortgage which had in fact been executed and the court found there was present consideration for the promise although there was a strong intima-

hands of transferees in a position to assert such protection.

82. See Chapter 5, infra.

83. E. g., Spring v. Short, 1882, 90 N.Y. 538. See Chapter 5, infra.

84. See Chapter 5, infra.

85. McGuigan v. Rix, 1919, 140 Ark. 418, 215 S.W. 611; Farmers' State Bank v. St. Aubyn, 1926, 120 Kan. 66, 242 P. 466, are square authorities for the creation of an equitable mortgage to secure, presently, an antecedent debt. The cases cited in a following footnote in which an antecedent debt was held sufficient even where there was only a promise to give a mortgage or security would be, a fortiori, authority for the same proposition.

86. Among them are Duncan v. Miller, 1884, 64 Iowa 223, 20 N.W. 161; Abbott v. Godfroy's Heirs, 1849, 1 Mich. 178; Lee State Bank v. McElheny, 1924, 227 Mich. 322, 198 N.W. 928; Rea v. Wilson, 1900, 112 Iowa 517, 84 N.W. 539; Rhodes v. Outcalt, 1871, 48 Mo. 367; Hoyt v. Oliver, 1875, 59 Mo. 188; Sullivan v. Corn Exchange Bank, 1912, 154 App. Div. 292, 139 N.Y.S. 97 (alternative ground of deci-

sion); Comstock v. Coon, 1893, 135 Ind. 640, 35 N. E. 909; Citizens Nat. Bank of Attica v. Judy, 1896, 146 Ind. 322, 43 N.E. 259; Burns v. Peters, 1936, 5 Cal.2d 619, 55 P.2d 1182 (trust deed mortgage); Burn v. Burn, 1797, 3 Ves. 573. See 1928, 28 Col.L. Rev. 209, 214. See, semble, note, 1935, 15 Boston U.L.Rev. 165.

87. Fisher and Lightwood, Law of Mortgages, 16.

88. 1861, 23 N.Y. 556.

89. Dempsey v. McKenna, 1897, 18 App.Div. 200, 203, 45 N.Y.S. 973.

tion that the antecedent debt would have been sufficient.[90] The only jurisdiction which holds invalid an attempt to make property secure an antecedent debt presently as contrasted with a promise to give security is New Jersey.[91]

Indeed some of the cases go even farther and hold that a promise to give a legal mortgage to secure a pre-existing debt creates an equitable mortgage.[92] Cases of defective mortgage deeds given to secure antecedent debts might, on one theory as to why they are upheld, also be authority that an executory promise to give a mortgage to secure an antecedent debt creates an equitable mortgage. That theory is that "underlying the defective instrument of transfer is the agreement that some specific property shall be mortgaged and it is this agreement which equity specifically enforces." [93]

90. National Bank of Norwalk v. Lanier, 1876, 7 Hun (N.Y.) 623. Other cases in which present consideration was present or insisted upon and the defendants' agreement consisted of a promise to give a mortgage or security are Blum v. Planters' Bank & Trust Co., 1931, 161 Miss. 226, 135 So. 353; Baltimore & Ohio R. Co. v. Berkeley Springs & P. R. Co., C.C.A.W.Va., 1909, 168 F. 770; Carter v. Sapulpa & I. R. Co., 1915, 49 Okl. 471, 153 P. 853; Sprague v. Cochran, 1894, 144 N.Y. 104, 38 N.E. 1000. In Day & Barclift v. Stewart, 1918, 202 Ala. 229, 80 So. 289, the agreement might have been either a promise or a present transfer, but, there being present consideration, it would be immaterial which it was. White v. Barnard, C.C.A.Mass., 1928, 29 F.2d 510, certiorari denied 49 S.Ct. 346, 278 U.S. 484, 73 L.Ed. 992, as is pointed out elsewhere, refused, erroneously it is believed, to hold that there was an equitable mortgage created where there was present consideration for the promise to give a deed in the future, insisting upon an actual intent that the property be security. This is at the opposite extreme from Stoddard v. Hart, supra. None of these cases, obviously, is authority for requiring more than an antecedent debt where the transaction purports to establish a security interest forthwith in the property without any further action by the debtor. Some of them, in fact, go no farther than making present consideration sufficient for a promise to give security and do not negative the possibility that it is not necessary even when there is not an express suggestion that this is so. See e. g., National Bank of Norwalk v. Lanier, supra.

91. Wheeler v. Kirtland, 1873, 24 N.J.Eq. 552; Lovejoy v. Lovejoy, 1879, 31 N.J.Eq. 55 (defective dictum only); Miller v. Savage, 1901, 62 N.J.Eq. 746, 48 A. 1004. See Martin v. Bowen, 1893, 51 N.J.Eq. 452, 26 A. 823 (agreement that property be security for a prior indorsement created an equitable mortgage but the court distinguished it from the other New Jersey cases on the ground that there was full consideration at the time of the creation of the equitable mortgage). See also Restatement, Security, § 10, b.

See, however, Cunningham and Tischler, Equitable Real Estate Mortgages, 1963, 17 Rutgers L.Rev. 679, 697–99, especially 698 n. 95, where, after reviewing the New Jersey cases, it is stated that the assertion in the text is not supported by the New Jersey cases.

92. Stewart v. Tichborne, unreported but stated in Card v. Jaffray, [Ir.Ch., 1805] 2 Sch. & Lef. 374, 381; Ashton v. Corrigan, 1871, L.R. 13 Eq. 76; Atlantic Trust Co. v. Holdsworth, 1900, 50 App.Div. 623, affirmed, 1901, 167 N.Y. 532, 60 N.E. 1106; Payne v. Wilson, 1878, 74 N.Y. 348; Kidwell v. Henderson, 1928, 150 Va. 829, 143 S.E. 336.

See, semble, Tiffany, Real Property, 2d Ed., 2748, "It would seem to follow [from the statement that the lien is based on contract] that, except in jurisdictions where a past consideration is effectual to support a contract [for a lien] such an instrument by which it is sought to secure an indebtedness will not be given effect as an equitable lien or mortgage unless the indebtedness is created at the time of the delivery of the instrument, or some other valuable consideration passes at that time. The cases however make no suggestion to that effect, and presumably such a lien has occasionally been recognized as valid and effective although created merely to secure a past indebtedness without any new consideration."; Note 1928, 28 Col.L.Rev. 215, "As between the original mortgagor or his heirs or donee and the informal mortgagee whose instrument was founded on a past indebtedness there seems to be no reason why the mortgage should not be enforced. * * * the courts commonly apply the rule that a judgment creditor is subject to the same rights and liabilities as the debtor and, since there is no reason for not enforcing these agreements against the mortgagor, they should be enforced against the judgment creditors."; Ibid., 213, 215. In the first quotation, the author was speaking of agreements for liens which were not express promises to execute a legal mortgage, and treated them all as promises needing consideration. In the second quotation the writer not only did not segregate promises to give security from agreements that property be security, but also included in his remarks, promises to execute legal mortgages.

93. Stone, the "Equitable Mortgage" in New York, 1920, 20 Col.L.Rev. 519, 522. Look also at the defective mortgage cases cited in the preceding footnotes. In Goodman v. Randall, 1877, 44 Conn. 321, a defectively executed trust deed mortgage was held not to create an equitable mortgage, the court saying that the principle upon which such cases rest is "that there is a valid contract lying back of the deed which courts of equity will lay hold of and through it give relief". This interpretation, exclud-

One writer [94] who believes that present consideration is always necessary explains one case which has been cited for the opposite view [95] on the supposition that there was a present consideration in the form of an executed extension of time or other change of position which was probably overlooked. And this in spite of the fact that the court quoting it said that the point seemed so clear that it was not mentioned in the decision. The other authorities are brushed aside on the ground that there was no discussion of the basic principle on which the right of the equitable mortgagee rests and, therefore, are entitled to little weight.[96]

The authorities cited for the statement that mere pre-existing indebtedness is not sufficient to support a contract to give a mortgage or "security", which is stated to be the weight of actual authority, are three New Jersey cases, a dictum in Dempsey v. McKenna,[97] cases in which there was present consideration and which are construed as holding, "by implication", that a past indebtedness would be insufficient, a quotation from an article [98] which relied on the dictum in Dempsey v. McKenna, and two New York cases [99] neither of which is in point. Even the New Jersey cases intimate that an equitable mortgage might arise as between the parties. And the reasoning why it should not prevail against a subsequent judgment creditor, while expressing one view, is far from conclusive. Nowhere is there a clear differentiation between promises to give security and presently executed transfers. Additional cases cited by the writer to support his thesis that an antecedent debt is insufficient ever to create an equitable mortgage are ones in which the defect was that the mortgagee had merely promised to make the loan. They fall, therefore, under the well settled doctrine examined earlier, that a promise to lend, unlike the promise to pay the purchase price in a land contract of sale, although it is just as much a present consideration, is insufficient to induce a court of equity to grant specific performance of a promise to give a mortgage or security [1] and, possibly, also insufficient for it to hold that an intention that property be security presently will be given effect. No cases on this last point have been found. This detailed analysis of this one author's treatment of the problem and the authorities is given because it is rather typical of views expressed on this matter.

Even in the cases where the promise is to give security an argument might be made that, since this creditor has been vigilant and "more persistent than the other creditors and has cajoled at least evidence of an intention to mortgage out of the debtor" he ought to have his security even against other creditors. Certainly he should against the mortgagor and those who succeed to his rights.[2] Nevertheless these cases do conflict with the general requirement of equity in specific performance of promises and must be regarded as deviations. For the general requirement and distinction seem sound. To compel the debtor to do something in fulfill-

ing the treatment of the deed as an expression of present intention rather than a promise as to the future on which the equitable mortgage must rest, represents an attitude similar to that of the court in Stoddard v. Hart, supra. Like it, it does not represent the authorities generally.

94. Walsh, Mortgages, 49 n. 31.

95. Stewart v. Tichborne, supra, note 92.

96. The two cases referred to, incidentally, were ones in which the agreements were that the property be security, not promises to give security. They are McGuigan v. Rix, 1919, 140 Ark. 418, 215 S.W. 611; Farmers' State Bank v. St. Aubyn, 1926, 120 Kan. 66, 242 P. 466, both cited in the preceding footnote.

97. 1897, 18 App.Div. 200, 45 N.Y.S. 973.

98. Stone, supra, note 93.

99. Ladd v. Stevenson, 1889, 112 N.Y. 325, 19 N.E. 842; Roberge v. Winne, 1893, 71 Hun (N.Y.) 172, 54 St.R. 193, 24 N.Y.S. 562, affirmed 1895, 144 N.Y. 709, 39 N.E. 631, 71 St.R. 284.

1. The cases cited are Fred T. Ley Co. v. Wheat, C. C.A.Fla., 1933, 64 F.2d 257; Iowa Loan & T. Co. v. Plewe, 1926, 202 Iowa 79, 209 N.W. 399; Federal Land Bank v. Monroe, 1932, 165 Tenn. 364, 54 S.W. 2d 716.

2. 1928, 28 Col.L.Rev. 209, 215.

ment of a promise is quite a different matter from protecting rights created by that debtor's previous act. In the former it may be desirable even in mortgage cases to require present consideration. In the latter case there seems no more reason why an existing debt should not be sufficient than in the case of a legal mortgage. Even writers who insist, against the authorities, upon a present consideration in all equitable mortgage cases, recognize the difference in the case of a legal mortgage. Thus one said, "the distinction appears to be that between the executed gift which equity protects when it is once vested in the donee and the executory obligation which equity does not generally create unless consideration be given for it."[3] And another, in criticising cases upholding defective mortgages to secure antecedent debts, explained them as "possibly a confusion with the fact that a legal mortgage would need no greater consideration than an antecedent debt while ignoring the further point that a legal mortgage in fact can be purely gratuitous."[4] It is submitted that the cases are right and what is overlooked by the critic is that, provided that be the intention, a gratuitous equitable mortgage can be created presently without any requirement other than the existence of the debt meant to be secured just as a trust, which is an outright gift of the entire beneficial interest, a vastly more serious matter, can be created gratuitously. Further, whatever might be said about the desirability of distribution among all creditors, it should not prevent such a secured creditor from having priority over other creditors. And, it is believed that the authorities so hold.[5]

MORTGAGES OF EQUITABLE INTERESTS

31. If the subject matter of the mortgage is an equitable interest, such as that of the bene- ficiary of a trust, the mortgage is necessarily only an equitable one.

Under the title theory of mortgages in England all mortgages after the first are equitable. This has been changed by statute in England. In the United States, even in title theory states, second and succeeding mortgagees have been held, somewhat illogically, to get legal security interests.

A mortgage of an equitable interest in property cannot, of course, create a legal mortgage, even in title theory states.[6] Ordinary examples of such mortgages are those by a cestui que trust or a vendee under a contract for the purchase of land.[7] So, also, where the title theory of mortgages prevails and is carried out strictly, a second mortgage logically can give only an equitable interest since that is all the mortgagor had left to transfer.[8] Of course, before default on the first mortgage the mortgagor, in addition to his equitable estate, had a legal right of entry. This, however, was not transferable at common law and on default disappeared and was replaced by an equitable right of redemption. This was the view of the English courts.[9] However, as was noted earlier, the Law of Property Act of 1925 changed the

3.   Stone, op. cit., supra, note 93.

4.   1928, 28 Col.L.Rev. 209, 215n.

5.   Cf. 1928, 28 Col.L.Rev. 209, 215.

6.   Graves v. Arizona Central Bank, 1928, 205 Cal. 715, 272 P. 1063; Chapman v. Great Western Gypsum Co., 1932, 216 Cal. 420, 14 P.2d 758, 85 A.L.R. 917 (option to purchase); see Fisher and Lightwood's Law of Mortgages, 7th Ed., 16; Falconbridge, Mortgages, 3d Ed., § 43.

7.   Whitney v. Foster, 1898, 117 Mich. 643, 76 N.W. 114; Brockwag v. Wells, 1828, 1 Paige (N.Y.) 617 (lien state); Standorf v. Shockley, 1907, 16 N.D. 73, 111 N.W. 622, 11 L.R.A.,N.S., 869, 14 Ann.Cas. 1099. See Campbell, Cas. on Mortgages, 2d Ed., 43, Q. 2-28. In Matter of Plymouth Glass Co., E.D.Mich. 1957, 171 F.Supp. 650, although the assignment by a vendee in possession under a contract for purchase to a lender gave an equitable mortgage to the latter it was invalid as against a perfected execution lien because the assignment was unrecorded.

8.   Goodman v. White, 1857, 26 Conn. 317. Semble; Turrell v. Jackson, 1877, 39 N.J.L. 329. See 1 Coote, Mortgages, 9th Ed., 72 et seq.; Falconbridge, Mortgages, 3d Ed., § 43.

9.   Cave v. Cave, 1880, 15 Ch.D. 639. See Durfee, Cas. on Mortgages, 73 n. 20; 4 Pomeroy, Equity Juris., 5th Ed., 691 n. 19; Falconbridge, Mortgages, 3d Ed. § 43; Fisher and Lightwood's Law of Mortgages, 7th Ed., 16 n. e.

old rule and a second mortgagee of a freehold gets a legal term of years longer by one day than the first mortgage but subject to it with a similar rule applying to mortgages of a term of years.[10] On this point, as on many others, the American cases have departed from logic and hold without the aid of statute that second mortgagees do get legal interests for the purpose of security.[11] In lien jurisdictions all mortgagees, whether senior or junior, get legal liens which are alike aside from questions of priority.[12]

Whether present valuable consideration is necessary where the subject matter of the mortgage is equitable depends, as in other cases of equitable mortgages, on whether the transaction is an executed transfer or is an executory promise to transfer.[13]

DEFECTIVE LEGAL MORTGAGES

32. Defectively executed legal mortgages or trust deed mortgages create equitable mortgages. Some authorities regard them as resting upon the rationale of an executed transaction. Others treat them as executory agreements to execute a valid legal mortgage with the equitable mortgage arising by virtue of the doctrine of specific performance. The first

The theory that the second mortgagee got only an equitable mortgage made possible the doctrine of tacking by which a third or later mortgagee could be elevated to priority over intervening ones by acquiring the first mortgage or by the first mortgagee getting in the later mortgage. See 2 Coote, Mortgages, 9th Ed., 1244 et seq.; Ames, Lectures on Legal History, 267; Chapter 7, infra.

10. See 4 Pomeroy, Equity Juris., 5th Ed., 691 n. 19. See also § 11, supra.

11. Sanders v. Reed, 1842, 12 N.H. 558; Gooding v. Shea, 1869, 103 Mass. 360, 4 Am.Rep. 563. See 4 Pomeroy, Equity Juris., 5th Ed. § 1233 n. 19. See also § 10, supra.

In America the presence or absence of legal title, has, in general, little effect upon the substantive rights of the mortgagee either against the mortgagor or third persons, because of the prevalence of recording systems. See 3 Tiffany, Real Prop., 2d Ed., 2371; Durfee, Cas. on Mortgages, 73 n. 20.

12. See Durfee, The Lien or Equitable Theory of the Mortgage—Some Generalizations, 1912, 10 Mich.L. Rev. 587; Durfee, Cas. on Mortgages, 73 n. 20.

13. See Fisher and Lightwood's Law of Mortgages, 7th Ed., 16. See also § 28, supra.

view seems preferable although usually either rationale will explain the result. Where the obligation secured is a pre-existing one the first explanation should be mandatory.

By the very great weight of authority,[14] ranging from cases so early that the attempted conveyance was by feoffment and failed because there was no livery of seizin [15] down to the present, the courts have held consistently that a defectively executed mortgage [16] or trust deed mortgage,[17] although it fails to create a legal mortgage will be given effect as an equitable mortgage. As indicated by the cases cited in the footnotes, there is a wide variety of reasons which may make the in-

14. The authorities cited in the succeeding footnotes are representative of the decisions. See also Campbell, Cas. on Mortgages, 45 Defective Mortgages, Problem Cases Q. 2–31 to Q. 2–43A for additional cases.

15. Burgh v. Francis, Ch. 1673, Cases Temp.Finch, 28.

16. Welton v. Tizzard, 1864, 15 Iowa 495 (misdescription of property); Love v. Sierra Nevada Lake Water & Mining Co., 1867, 32 Cal. 639, 91 Am.Dec. 602 (agent executed mortgage in his own instead of principal's name); Courtner v. Etheredge, 1907, 149 Ala. 78, 43 So. 368 (not attested or acknowledged); Lebanon Savings Bank v. Hallenbeck, 1882, 29 Minn. 322, 13 N.W. 145 (no seal); Ward v. Stark Bros., 1909, 91 Ark. 268, 121 S.W. 382 (no words of grant); Stelts v. Martin, 1911, 90 S.C. 14, 72 S.E. 550 (second witness not present at execution); Hamilton Trust Co. v. Clemes, 1900, 163 N.Y. 423, 57 N.E. 614; Holmes v. Dunning, 1931, 101 Fla. 55, 133 So. 557 (fictitious person as mortgagee); Harney v. Montgomery, 1923, 29 Wyo. 362, 213 P. 378 (defective acknowledgment). See note, 1935, 15 Boston U.L.Rev. 165.

See Fogelman, The Deed Absolute as a Mortgage in New York, 1963, 32 Fordham L.Rev. 299, 300. See also Cunningham and Tischler, Equitable Real Estate Mortgages, 1963, 17 Rutgers L.Rev. 679, 694 et seq.

17. Atkinson v. Miller, 1890, 34 W.Va. 115, 11 S.E. 1007, 9 L.R.A. 544; Burns v. Peters, 1936, 5 Cal.2d 619, 55 P.2d 1182 (trustee refused to accept); Title Ins. & Trust Co. v. California Development Co., 1915, 171 Cal. 173, 200, 152 P. 542 (invalid because not registered as required under the law of Mexico which governed); Earle v. Sunnyside Land Co., 1907, 150 Cal. 214, 88 P. 920 (trust for unauthorized purpose); McQuie v. Peay, 1874, 58 Mo. 56 (name of trustee omitted); Martin v. Nixon, 1887, 92 Mo. 26, 4 S.W. 503 (trust deed mortgage witnessed, acknowledged, and recorded but not signed by the grantor)—accord. Contra, Goodman v. Randall, 1877, 44 Conn. 321 (grantor's name omitted although acknowledged and recorded).

strument ineffective to create the security at law.[18]

The very fact that the parties clearly tried to give a present legal mortgage would seem sufficient without more to establish the intent of the parties that the property be security from that time and, therefore, that the equitable mortgage in these cases could rest upon the rationale of an executed transaction. There are cases explicitly placing their decisions on this reasoning.[19] Other cases, especially those which hold that defectively executed mortgages are valid to secure antecedent debts, although not so definite in their language, could, and perhaps should, rest upon the same rationale.[20] There are, however,

See Sterling, Validity of "Myself" Notes and Deeds of Trust, 1958, 30 Rocky Mt.L.Rev. 195, 196–198.

18. Among the most frequent causes is misdescription of the property. See, e. g., Welton v. Tizzard, note 16 supra.

For a discussion of equitable mortgages arising where there has been a defective legal mortgage, see Cunningham and Tischler, Equitable Real Estate Mortgages, 1963, 17 Rutgers L.Rev. 679, 694–701.

19. Abbott v. Godfroy's Heirs, 1849, 1 Mich. 178, 182 (mortgage deed invalid to create legal mortgage because it was not witnessed. In holding it to be a good equitable mortgage the court said, "* * * the intention of the parties is most manifest. The contract is not to be performed, but is executed. The meaning and intention was to create a lien on the land, to secure the payment of a preexisting debt."); Rea v. Wilson, 1900, 112 Iowa 517, 521, 84 N.W. 539, 540 (legal mortgage invalid because of misdescription of the property held, valid equitable mortgage, having priority over subsequent attachment lien. The court said, "When Wilson and wife executed the mortgage with the intention of giving plaintiff a lien on their land as security for money [previously] advanced, they created an equitable right or title in plaintiffs, although the property was not fully described;"); Rhodes v. Outcalt, 1871, 48 Mo. 367, 372 (no legal mortgage because of misdescription but the defective deed created an equitable mortgage good, even though it was given to secure an antecedent debt, against a judgment creditor who purchased with notice at his own execution sale. The court quoted, as in all respects applicable, the following from the opinion in another case: "* * * he [the mortgagor] agreed and undertook, though defectively in the case of a court of law, to bind these lands of his—to set them apart, specifically to appropriate them to the plaintiffs. Now, in equity he did thus bind, appropriate and set them apart.").

20. See § 28, supra.

authorities which just as clearly treat the transaction as an application of the general rule that "defective deeds, signed by the parties, purporting to convey the legal title, but because of some defect not doing so, are treated in equity as agreements to convey; and specific execution of them will be decreed by providing for the execution of a formal and effectual conveyance."[21] Where there is present valuable consideration for the faulty mortgage it is ordinarily immaterial which view is followed. Where, however, the obligation secured is a pre-existing one, to accept the first theory is more in harmony with general doctrines and seems, in fact, the basis on which the courts go.[22]

REISSUE AGREEMENTS

33. A discharged mortgage cannot be reissued. An attempt to do so, however, may create an equitable mortgage for a new and different obligation if such is the intent of the parties.

It is familiar and sound law that a discharged mortgage cannot be reissued even for a new consideration.[23] The reason is that the original mortgage secured the old debt. If that is discharged and gone it cannot be recreated, and neither, therefore, can the mortgage securing it.[24] A new mortgage in iden-

21. Atkinson v. Miller, note 17, supra (trust deed mortgage); Love v. Sierra Nevada etc., Co. 1867, 32 Cal. 639, 91 Am.Dec. 602 (straight mortgage); Payne v. Wilson, 1878, 74 N.Y. 348. See Stone, The "Equitable Mortgage" in New York, 1920, 20 Col.L.Rev. 519, 522.

22. See cases cited in note 18, supra. See also § 28, supra. And see Note, Equitable Mortgages in Iowa, 1959, 44 Iowa L.Rev. 716, 720.

23. Bogert v. Bliss, 1896, 148 N.Y.194, 42 N.E. 582, 51 Am.St.Rep. 684; New Orleans Nat. Banking Ass'n v. Adams, 1883, 109 U.S. 211, 3 S.Ct. 161, 27 L.Ed. 910.

See Cunningham and Tischler, Equitable Real Estate Mortgages, 1963, 17 Rutgers L.Rev. 679, 724.

24. "In order to save expense in the way of recording fees and mortgage tax, parties may be tempted to use an old mortgage, still alive so far as the record goes, but actually discharged by payment or release of the debt by other methods. Now, that simply cannot be done." Glenn, Mortgages, § 50.4.

tical terms with the old as security for a new or different debt could be raised on the land, but ordinarily this is not the intention. However, where it is, there is no difficulty in giving effect to it. In such a case the transaction stands substantially on the same footing as any defective mortgage.[25] In a leading case the court reasoned that "there is no question as to the intention of the parties to revive the mortgage; and such an intention necessarily includes an assent that the land should be holden for the payment of the money to be secured by such revival. The agreement may not be operative in the way in which the parties intended that it should operate; but it expresses their intention so that we can give effect to it in another way consistently with the rules of law." [26]

TITLE DEEDS—ENGLAND

34. **In England delivery of title deeds to land as security for the payment of a money debt creates an equitable mortgage on the property represented by the deeds.[27] The subject of controversy and criticism, such mortgages have been justified as resting upon the presumed actual intention of the parties, as necessary to the creditor's protection, and in accord with commercial necessity.**

Whether the rule rests on the doctrine of specific performance of a presumed promise to execute a legal mortgage or on the theory of giving effect to an intent to create an immediate equitable security interest is not clear. The latter is more likely the actual intent of the parties.

Since the delivery of the deeds plus the loan do, in themselves, warrant the inference that a security interest in the land was intended presently, this would be sufficient to satisfy the Statute of Frauds.

Since 1783 [28] it has been a settled doctrine of English equity, unchanged by the Property Act or Land Charges Act of 1925,[29] that the delivery of title deeds to land [30] as security for the payment of a money debt creates an equitable mortgage on the property of the debtor of which the deeds constitute the title.[31] Nevertheless there has been considerable controversy over the rationale, the wisdom, and the scope of the rule.

As originally laid down by Lord Thurlow, evidence of an advance of the money by the creditor and the finding of the title deeds of the borrower in the hands of the lender is sufficient without more [32] to establish a re-

25. See preceding section.
In re Snyder, 1908, 138 Iowa 553, 114 N.W. 615, 19 L. R.A.,N.S., 206, which rests upon the same fundamental basis, also seems applicable.

26. Peckham v. Haddock, 1864, 36 Ill. 38, 49; Turner v. Givens, 1936, 176 Miss. 214, 166 So. 367, accord.
On the problem of equitable revival or reissued mortgages, see Cunningham and Tischler, Equitable Real Estate Mortgages, 1963, 17 Rutgers L.Rev. 679, 724.

27. For discussions of the doctrine of equitable mortgages by deposit of title deeds, see W. D. Rollison, The English Doctrine of Equitable Mortgages by Deposit of Title Deeds or other Muniments of Title, 1931, 6 Not.D.Law. 341; Rollison, The American Doctrine of Equitable Mortgages by Deposit of Title Deeds, 1944, 20 Not.D.Law. 11; notes, 1914, 14 Col.L.Rev. 672; 1882, 14 Cent.L.J. 426; 1882, 15 Cent.L.J. 46; 1904, 24 Can.L.T. 134; 1882, 16 Ir.L.T. 185, 197, 209; 1924, 33 Yale L.J. 785; Pomeroy, Equity Juris., 5th Ed., §§ 1264 et seq.
See also Note, Equitable Mortgages—A Wavering Doctrine in New York, 1952, 27 St. John's L.Rev. 78.
For a more recent review of the English law of equitable mortgages by deposit of title deeds, see Cunningham and Tischler, Equitable Real Estate Mortgages, 1963, 17 Rutgers L.Rev. 679, 711–713.

28. Russel v. Russel, 1783, 1 Bro.C.C. 269 is the case which definitely established the rule.

29. See Coote, Mortgages, 9th Ed., c. VII § 4(i), (v); Rollison, The English Doctrine of Equitable Mortgages by Deposit of Title Deeds or Other Muniments of Title, 1930, 6 Not.D.Law. 341, 351, 360. See also chapter 1, § 11, supra.

30. The doctrine does not apply to personal property. Carter v. Wake, 1877, L.R. 4 Ch.D. 605.

31. A deposit of deeds is incapable of creating an equitable mortgage on property to which they do not relate. Jones v. Williams, 1857, 24 Beav. 47. Cf. Daw v. Terrell, 1863, 33 Beav. 218, questioned in Ex parte Broderick, 1886, 18 Q.B.D. 380, 385. Prima facie the equitable mortgage covers all the property comprised in the deeds deposited. Ashton v. Dalton, 1846, 2 Coll. 565. Apparently it is not necessary to deposit all of the deeds constituting the chain of title. Dixon v. Muckleston, 1873, 21 W.R. 178. See note, 1879, 17 Sol.J. 477, 531.
See Fogelman, The Deed Absolute as a Mortgage in New York, 1963, 32 Fordham L.Rev. 299, 300.

32. "It has long been settled that a mere deposit of title deeds upon an advance of money, without a

buttable presumption [33] that there was a completely executed [34] agreement between the parties for a security interest in the land itself which could be realized on by foreclosure [35] rather than a purely defensive pledge of the deeds themselves. Rationalizations of the doctrine stress the factual and legal background in which it developed including the role played by title deeds in England as contrasted with America where the universal adoption of recording systems has made possession of the deeds to real property, once they have been recorded, of no real importance except in rare instances. In England, "the possession of the title deeds is evidence of ownership, as no one is supposed to have a right to retain them without having an estate or interest in the land they convey. They pass to the purchaser upon a sale, and are examined by the solicitor of the parties much as abstracts of title are examined in this country. This is for the rea-

son that, until the recent partial adoption of the Torrens system, save in some counties, there were no registries, where a search could be made to ascertain the title to lands, other than copy held titles which are recorded in the manor courts. The only proof which the purchaser seems to have for the validity of the title in his grantor is the exhibition of the deeds which establish it. So, after a deposit of his evidence of title with his creditor as security, the debtor cannot well dispose of his land without first satisfying the indebtedness secured, for, until this is done, he is not in a situation to obtain possession of his title papers either at law or in equity." [36] The extension of the creditor's security beyond this possessory defensive lien on the deeds themselves, has been vigorously criticised as perniciously violating the Statute of Frauds,[37] as being an unwarranted inference as to the intention of the parties,[38] and as existing solely by virtue of precedent.[39] Nevertheless, it was squarely rested, by the views that prevailed, upon the presumed actual intention of the parties,[40] and justified as essential to effectuate the object of the parties to give the creditor full security protection. This he would not have by mere possession of the deeds in cases where the value of the

word passing, gives an equitable lien ;" Lord Eldon in Ex parte Langston, 1810, 17 Ves. 230, 231.

Rockwell v. Hobby, 1844, N.Y., 2 Sandf.Ch. 9, 12 ; 1904, 24 Can.L.T. 134, 136, accord. But see Ebling Brewing Co. v. Gennaro, 1919, 189 App.Div. 782, 785, 179 N.Y.S. 384, 387. Mere possession of the deeds without evidence of the contract upon which the possession originated is not sufficient. See Dixon v. Muckleston, 1872, L.R., Ch.App. 155, 162. See also Bozon v. Williams, 1829, 3 Y. & J. 150, 161 ; Chapman v. Chapman, 1819, 13 Beav. 311 ; Williams v. Medlicot, 1819, 6 Price 495.

33. The presumption may be rebutted by written or parol evidence. See Shaw v. Foster, 1879, L.R. 5 H.L. 340 (terms of written document accompanying deposit will control) ; Ex parte Mountford, 1808, 14 Ves. 606 ("it was never decided that if the person with whom the deposit was made came forward himself and stated the terms upon which it was made, the Court would not examine the terms. The mischief of all these cases is that we are deciding upon parol evidence with regard to an interest in land within the Statute of Frauds") ; Ex parte Haigh, 1805, 11 Ves. 403 ; Norris v. Wilkinson, 1806, 12 Ves. 196.

34. "The contract is not to be performed, but is executed." Russel v. Russel, 1783, 1 Bro.C.C. 269.

Cf. 1952, 27 St. John's L.Rev. 78, 80–81.

35. Pryce v. Bury, 1854, L.R. 16 Eq. 153, note ; James v. James, 1873, L.R. 16 Eq. 153 ; Carter v. Wake, 1875, L.R. 4 Ch.D. 605 ; Backhouse v. Charlton, 1878, L.R. 8 Ch.D. 444. See 1904, 24 Can.L.T. 134, 147.

36. In re Snyder, 1908, 138 Iowa 553, 555, 114 N.W. 615, 19 L.R.A.,N.S., 206, 209.

37. See Ex parte Hooper, 1815, 19 Ves.Jun. 477, 478, 34 Eng.Rep. 593 ; Norris v. Wilkinson, 1806, 12 Ves.Jr. 192 ; Bozon v. Williams, 1829, 3 Y. & J. 150, 161. See also Chapter 3, infra, for a consideration of this objection.

See additionally Note, Equitable Mortgages—A Wavering Doctrine in New York, 1952, 27 St. John's L. Rev. 78, 81.

38. See, e. g., Lord Eldon in Ex parte Whitbread, 1812, 19 Vesey, Jun. 209, for a typical expression of such views. On the latter point he said, "Lord Thurlow's first decision went no further than an inference from the mere deposit that it was to give an interest in the land ; collecting that inference by asking, what other purpose could the deposit have? My answer would have been, to give an interest in the title deeds."

39. Lacon v. Allen, 1856, 3 Drew. 579, 582.

40. See Parker v. Housefield, 1834, 2 My. & K. 419, 420 ; M'Kay v. M'Nally, 1879, 13 Ir.L.T. 130, 135 ; Pryce v. Bury, 1853, 2 Drew. 41, 42.

land decreases so as to leave little margin over the debt, where the debtor is unable to pay, or possibly merely indifferent to doing so. It was defended, also as a recognition of commercial necessity, a convenient and customary method of handling small, short term loans.[41]

Since the judges responsible for the creation of this type of equitable mortgage did rest it upon a presumed intention of the parties, a closer examination of what that intention is, or is held to be, must be made to discover just how this particular variety of equitable mortgages should be classified under the general analysis already made. As was noted in the preceding paragraph, the correctness of inferring in fact an intent by the parties that the land should be charged in addition to the creditor holding possession of the deeds was vigorously if unsuccessfully challenged.[42] But beyond this is the question whether it could be inferred further that the intent was to convey legal title as security, i. e., to give a legal mortgage. Such an intent would be at variance with the apologia of convenience and custom which was offered to justify the informality of such arrangements and clearly is contrary to the conception of the doctrine as being an executed transaction, not one to be performed, as laid down by Lord Loughborough in the pioneer case.[43] Nevertheless, although there are statements to the contrary,[44] most authorities say that such is the intent.[45]

41. See Keys v. Williams, 1838, 3 Y. & C. 55, 60, 61; Gardner v. McClure, 1861, 6 Minn. 250, Gil. 167. Cf. the language of Sir William Grant in Norris v. Wilkinson, 1806, 12 Ves.Jun. 192, 197, stating that there was no case "* * * where a man is willing to part with his title deeds, in which he would not also be ready to sign a memorandum of two lines; specifying the purpose, for which he had parted with them."

42. See n. 36, supra.

43. Russel v. Russel, 1783, 1 Bro.C.C. 269.

44. In re Lind, [1915] 2 Ch. 345, 358; Metcalfe v. Archbishop of York, 1836, 1 My. & Cr. 547, 557; Matthews v. Goodday, 1861, 8 Jur.N.S. 90.

45. Jessel, M.R., in Carter v. Wake, 1877, L.R. 4 Ch. D. 605 is the most important exponent of this view.

If this is true and if, further, this is the *only* intent which creates the security interest, the equitable mortgage here would rest squarely upon the doctrine of specific performance. Several things would follow. If such an inferred actual intent does not violate the Statute of Frauds, it would seem that neither would an oral agreement to give a legal mortgage accompanying the deposit. The latter would be merely corroborative of the inference of fact drawn by the courts anyway and would have no other or different operation than unrequired corroboration. Or if it is held that the doctrine does violate the Statute of Frauds but is taken out of its operation by the part performances of making the loan and depositing the deeds, such part performances would be equally efficacious in the case of the oral promise.[46] Also, it would raise here, as in other cases of promises to give security, the question whether a deposit

See accord: Reporter's note to Russel v. Russel, 1783, 1 Bro.C.C. 269; In re Kerr's Policy, 1869, L. R. 8 Eq. 331; Pryce v. Bury, 1853, 2 Drew. 41; Ex parte Wright, 1812, 19 Vesey, 255; Birch v. Ellames, 1814, 2 Anst. 427, 431; Parker v. Housefield, 1834, 2 My. & K. 419, 420; James v. James, 1873, L. R. 16 Eq. 153; M'Kay v. M'Nally, 1879, 13 Ir.L.T. 130, 135; Harrold v. Plenty, [1901], 2 Ch. 314; Stubbs v. Slater, [1910], 1 Ch. 632, 639; London County & Westchester Bank v. Tompkins, [1918], 1 K.B., 515, 529; Falconbridge, Mortgages, 3d Ed., 78; Pomeroy, Equity Juris., 5th Ed., §§ 1264, 1267 n. 20.

A mere deposit for the purpose of preparing a legal mortgage has been held to create a present equitable mortgage "upon the ground that an express purpose of preparing a legal mortgage is stronger than the implied intention." Ex parte Bruce, 1813, 1 Rose's Bank.Cas. 374; Keys v. Williams, 1838, 3 Y. & C. 55, 62. See cases in Reporter's note to Norris v. Wilkinson, 1806, 12 Ves.Jun. 192, which held the other way. If the loan has been made at the time the deeds are deposited, the intention of the parties that there be a present security interest in the property is not contradicted by the delivery of the deeds for the expressed purpose of having a legal mortgage prepared. Further, in such a case it would be difficult to believe there was not a promise to execute the legal mortgage. If the loan has not been made, the whole transaction is executory, and under the principle looked at in the first part of this chapter no equitable mortgage would arise.

46. A written promise for a legal mortgage would be good, of course, regardless of the deposit of the deeds, on principles previously discussed. See Pomeroy, Equity Juris., 5th Ed. 782; note, 1904, 24 Can.L.T. 140.

as security for an antecedent debt would be effective. That it seems to be may be some ground for believing that specific performance of a promise is not the correct, or at any rate the only, basis on which the doctrine rests.[47]

An alternative explanation is that the parties intended that there be at once a security interest in the property, i. e., an executed transaction. Such an intent would not, as has been noted elsewhere, be inconsistent with an intent that there should be a legal mortgage given later on. However, such latter agreement would be a distinctly different one and would face, on its own, the questions whether: (a) there was sufficient basis in the transaction to warrant inferring its existence as a fact; (b) such implied in fact agreement, if warranted, would be violative of the Statute of Frauds; and (c) whether, if no such agreement could be implied in fact and there was an oral agreement for the legal mortgage, the presence of the acts of delivering the title deeds plus the making of the loan would be sufficient to dispense with the necessity of a writing. The Statute of Frauds point needs to be, and will be, discussed later in its general setting. However, it seems appropriate to state here that the most reasonable inference of actual intent in these title deeds cases in England, both in single isolated cases and against the background of the actual uses made of this method of giving security, is that the parties intended the security to consist of, first of all, the possession of the deeds and, in addition, an immediate interest in the property itself. Except in the cases where there is independent evidence to indicate that a legal mortgage was to be prepared, it is improbable that it was intended to have one executed. Since the delivery of the deeds plus the loan do, in themselves, warrant an inference that a security interest in the land was intended presently, this would seem sufficient to satisfy the Statute of Frauds so far as creating an equitable mortgage on this rationale is concerned. But since the inference of fact raised by the delivery and loan is that that interest is a present security interest, and not one to be given by legal mortgage in the future, any agreement for the latter would have to rest upon other, or at least additional, evidence as to its existence. If that other evidence is an oral agreement, it is difficult to see how these two acts are so connected with it that they could be urged as a part performance sufficient to satisfy the Statute of Frauds. Rarely, however, it is submitted, would it be necessary to deal with this problem, since the other rationale is sufficient to protect the claimant and account for the actual decisions.

TITLE DEEDS—UNITED STATES

35. With the exception of one or two states the English doctrine of equitable mortgage by deposit of title deeds is rejected in the United States. The usual reasons given are that it is out of harmony with our recording system and violates the Statute of Frauds. The first reason is questionable. However, it is true that the American recording system practically eliminated the conditions which formed the basis for the English doctrine.

47. Daw v. Terrell, 1863, 33 Beav. 218, although questioned by one judge on a different point in Ex parte Broderick, 1886, 18 Q.B.D. 380, 385, seems a square authority that a deposit of title deeds to secure an antecedent debt will create an equitable mortgage. In that case the title deeds actually handed over, together with an order to the holder of the deeds of the property sought to be charged, were of other property but the court held that this was sufficient part performance to permit the property to be held as security. "If it were necessary to decide the specific point, I should say that an agreement to grant a mortgage for money already advanced, and a deposit of deeds for the purpose of preparing a mortgage, is in itself an equitable mortgage by deposit;" Keys v. Williams, 1838, 3 Y. & C. Ex. 58, 60. The court held there was a present consideration. "* * * it is now settled in England (and some American states), that if the debtor deposits his title deeds to an estate with a creditor, as security for an antecedent debt, or upon a fresh loan of money, it is a valid agreement for a mortgage between the parties, and is not within the operation of the Statute of Frauds." 2 Story, Eq.Jur., § 1020. Cf. Hutzler Bros. v. Phillips, 1886, 26 S.C. 136, 147, 1 S.E. 502, 4 Am.St.Rep. 687; Probasco v. Johnson, 1858, 2 Disn. 96, 100, 13 Ohio Dec. 60.

Although there was some early acceptance of the English doctrine in the United States,[48] today, apart from New Jersey [49] and perhaps New York and Colorado,[50] it is generally rejected as not being in harmony with the recording or registry laws or as being in violation of the Statute of Frauds, or both.[51]

The first of these objections is extremely dubious. With only a few exceptions,[52] the recording acts do not either by explicit provision [53] or by their policy [54] make recordation a condition precedent to the creation or transfer of an interest in real property. Instead they effectuate their policy through the mechanics of putting certain persons in a position to divest unrecorded interests and giving to recordation the effect of notice so as to prevent the destruction of interests which, without it, might be wiped out.[55] There are a considerable number of interests in land, both legal and equitable, which are outside of the operation of the recording systems.[56] Most of them arise by events or transactions other than the execution of written instruments and could not have been cast into a form which would be recordable and still have precisely the same operative effect.[57] Whether interests created in such ways shall be stricken down as violative of the purpose of the acts or merely left to the operation of ordinary rules as being outside of and

48. See Rockwell v. Hobby, 1844, 2 Sandf.Ch., (N.Y.,) 9; Hutzler Bros. v. Phillips, 1886, 26 S.C. 136, 1 S. E. 502.

49. Bullowa v. Orgo, 1898, 57 N.J.Eq. 428, 41 A. 494. See Gale's Executors v. Morris, 1878, 29 N.J.Eq. 222.

The most recent examination of the doctrine in both England and the United States concludes that New Jersey would not recognize the doctrine today. Cunningham v. Tischler, op. cit. supra §§ 34, n. 27, 711, 713–715.

50. Strong doubt was cast upon the early New York decision of Rockwell v. Hobby, note 48, supra, by the court in Ebling Brewing Co. v. Gennaro, 1919, 189 App.Div. 782, 785, 179 N.Y.S. 384, and an alternative ground for its decision was suggested in Bloomfield State Bank v. Miller, 1898, 55 Neb. 243, 251, 75 N.W. 569, 572, 44 L.R.A. 387, 70 Am.St.Rep. 381. Nevertheless Judge Cardozo, in Sleeth v. Sampson, 1923, 237 N.Y. 69, 74, 142 N.E. 355, 30 A. L.R. 1400 said: "To what extent, if at all, this form of equitable mortgage is permitted in New York, is involved in some obscurity."

See Note, Equitable Mortgages—A Wavering Doctrine in New York, 1952, 27 St. John's L.Rev. 78, 87–91.

In Colorado Valley State Bank v. Dean, 1935, 97 Colo. 151, 47 P.2d 924, discussed in Storke, Priority Between Equitable Interests, 1935, 8 Rocky Mt. L.Rev. 1, there was delivery by the beneficiary of title deeds running to a resulting trustee. There was also, the court found, a clear intention on the part of the resulting beneficiary to charge his interest in the property with his debt to the plaintiff lender.

51. Typical is In re Snyder, 1908, 138 Iowa 553, 556, 114 N.W. 615, 616, 19 L.R.A.,N.S., 206, 210 which said: "As it is conceded by the English authorities to be in violation of the statute of frauds, and supported by precedent only, and is said to have occasioned much injustice, we are not inclined to adopt it, but rather to follow the authorities of this country to the effect that the doctrine has no applicability because of our registry laws." For a collection and analysis of the American cases disapproving the doctrine, see Rollison, The American Doctrine of Equitable Mortgages by Deposit of the Title Deeds, 1944, 20 Not.D.Law, 11, 13.

See also Durfee, Cases on Security, 1951, 443; Note, Equitable Mortgages—A Wavering Doctrine in New York, 1952, 27 St. John's L.Rev. 78, 85–87. But see Note, Equitable Mortgages in Iowa, 1959, 44 Iowa L.Rev. 716, 725, for authority that an oral agreement plus delivery of title deeds will create an equitable mortgage in Iowa.

52. See, e. g., Code Pub.Gen.Laws Md.1911, § 1, art. 21.

53. The ordinary language of the acts is either that "every conveyance" shall be "void as against" or "no conveyance" shall be "valid as against" certain specifically designated persons, none of whom are the grantee or grantor. See, e. g., West's Ann.Cal. Civ.Code § 1214; Conn.G.S.A. § 47–10.

54. The object of "our system of conveyancing and registry is to afford security to titles by a public record which parties dealing with land may, and for their own protection must, examine, and on which they may rely. Secret transfers and liens are sought to be prevented thereby." In re Snyder, note 49, supra.

55. See Aigler, op. cit. infra, note 55.

See §§ 195, 196, infra.

56. For a long list of interests in property not covered by recording systems and therefore outside of their operation, see Haymond, Title Insurance Risks of Which the Public Records Give No Notice, 1928, 1 So.Calif.L.Rev. 422; 1929, 2 id. 139.

See § 211, infra.

57. The language of recording or registry acts expressly covers only written instruments. See Aigler, Operation of the Recording Acts, 1924, 22 Mich.L.Rev. 405, 415, 420. Insofar as they affect other transactions it is only by invocation of the policy of the statutes.

untouched by them is always a question of the relative strengths of competing policies. The deposit of title deeds, if it creates an equitable mortgage, is, of course, unrecordable. However, it may be distinguished from most unrecordable transactions in that it could easily have been cast in a recordable form without altering its character.[58] Since this is so, there is more reason to hold that it should be subject to the policy of recording acts than is the case as to other sorts of unrecordable interests. Even so, it is difficult to see why the *policy* of the system should invalidate an interest which is unrecordable, regardless of whether it could have been put in a recordable form, to a greater or different extent than the statute in any particular jurisdiction affects recordable but unrecorded interests, i. e., those specifically covered by its *express* provisions. If it does not, even assuming the policy of the acts does apply, a deposit of title deeds, at least so far as any objection stemming from recording statutes is concerned, could create an equitable security interest in real property valid between the parties and in general as to third parties other than bona fide purchasers,[59] who would prevail anyway on general equitable principles entirely apart from the recording acts. And in some half of the states, it would be good as to creditors of various descriptions.[60]

However, it is true that our recording system has practically eliminated in this country the conditions which formed the basis of the English doctrine. As one court expressed it, "Under our system of registry, possession of title deeds is of no real importance to the owner of the estate. He can convey the land without them. They are not necessary in order to ascertain the condition of the title. For all practicable purposes, certified copies of the record copies will serve as well as the originals." [61] Consequently, at least where the deeds are recorded, possession of them is ineffective either as a defensive lien or to put persons dealing with the debtor on inquiry or notice. This, however, seems a drawback to their use rather than a statement of policy which would forbid them.

Similarly there is lacking the factual foundation on which inferences as to the intent of the parties rests in England and which in that country made surmountable the objection that the Statute of Frauds was violated. In the absence of commercial necessity, and none has been suggested, the foregoing, especially as it relates to the difficulty with the Statute of Frauds,[62] seem the real reasons why the American courts have reached their results and probably is what is meant by being out of harmony with our recording systems. And, although it has been argued that even though the deeds are of slight importance their transfer does mean something and should be operative at least between the parties,[63] or even as against third parties with notice and as to creditors,[64] the attitude of the American courts seems sound so far as recorded deeds are concerned. The objection of the Statute of Frauds is too weighty to be overcome by acts of such little practical importance and significance.[65] In the case of

---

58. See the statement of Sir William Grant that there is no case " * * * where a man is willing to part with his title deeds, in which he would not also be ready to sign a memorandum of two lines, specifying the purpose, for which he had parted with them," 1806, Norris v. Wilkinson, 12 Ves.Jr. 192, 197.

59. Bona fide purchasers, which term includes mortgagees, are universally named as persons in whose favor the recording acts operate.

60. In only about half of the states are creditors of any variety protected against unrecorded interests in real property. See § 210, infra. Apart from recording acts, the general rule is that equitable mortgages prevail over general creditors or even those with judgment liens. Welton v. Tizzard, 1864, 15 Iowa 495. See § 189, infra.

61. In re Snyder, note 51, supra.

62. See § 34. See also Chapter 3, infra.

63. 4 Pomeroy, Eq.Juris., 5th Ed. § 1266.

64. See Rollison, The American Doctrine of Equitable Mortgages by Deposit of Title of Deeds, 1944, 20 Not.D.Law. 11, 17, 30; Note, 1914, 14 Col.L.Rev. 672.

65. See the strong opinion of Flandrau, J., in Gardner v. McClure, 1861, 6 Minn. (Gil. 167) 250, condemning the doctrine on this ground.

unrecorded deeds, and possibly other instruments whose possession is important in dealing with the real property with which they are concerned, where there is a closer approximation to the significance of the English title deeds, the rule might well be different, and there is some indication that it is.[66]

EXPECTANCIES

36. Expectancies usually are not regarded as presently existing interests. Hence a mortgage of one is only effective if it rests on an enforceable contract or on the intent that the mortgage shall be created upon acquisition of the property without any further act by the mortgagor. The theory that an expectancy is a present equitable interest capable of immediate transfer is reasonable but little accepted by courts.

Expectancies of an heir or devisee under the will of a living person are non-transferable at law. The reason ordinarily given is that they are not presently existing interests in property.[67] Other considerations, however, have exerted influence, the chief ones being the strong policy in England, especially at an earlier day when feudal ties were still powerful, of preserving the family property intact; the later paternalistic protection of the expectant heir who was regarded as young, incompetent, and necessitous; the feeling that the transaction was a wagering one against public interest; the idea that it was a fraud on the ancestor or testator; and, to some extent, a belief that such transfers were in violation of statutes of wills and intestate succession.[68] In equity expectancies are generally [69] held to be assignable. To this rule there are ordinarily attached qualifications which stem from the forces responsible for the original rule at law,[70] the most common of which is that the bargain must be on fair consideration.

There has been some controversy as to what is meant by being "assignable in equity." One view is that since the expectancy has no present existence there can be no present transfer of it in equity any more than at law; that the phrase merely means that the expectant owner may bind himself by contract to transfer it if and when he should thereafter acquire it and equity will grant

---

66. Jennings v. Augir, D.C.Wash., 1914, 215 F. 658. Cf. Grames v. Con. Timber Co., D.C.Or.1914, 215 F. 785. In Gardner v. McClure, 1861, 6 Minn. (Gil. 167) 250, the unrecorded deed was accompanied by a writing stating that the deed itself was intended to be held as security. The court held, quite correctly, that no intention to create any interest in the property was present and therefore no equitable mortgage arose. The opinion went further, however, and strongly condemned the whole doctrine as in violation of the Statute of Frauds. It has been held that the deposit of School Land Certificates, which pass title by assignment, creates an equitable mortgage. Mowry v. Wood, 1860, 12 Wis. 413; Jarvis v. Dutcher, 1862, 16 Wis. 307.

Cf. People v. Glass, 1960, 181 Cal.App.2d 549, 5 Cal. Rptr. 289, holding that a reconveyance by the trustee of a recorded trust deed mortgage which was unauthorized by the creditor-beneficiary and which deprived the latter of his security constituted grand theft.

67. See, e. g., Restatement, Second, Trusts § 86 accepting this view as the reason why an expectancy cannot be transferred in trust.

68. See Evans, Certain Evasive and Protective Devices Affecting Succession to Decedents' Estates, 1933, 32 Mich.L.Rev. 478, 488; 1925, 25 Col.L.Rev. 215.

69. In some states, e. g., Kentucky, the courts are adamant in opposition to the assignability of an heir's expectancy. Look at Hunt v. Smith, 1921, 191 Ky. 443, 230 S.W. 936, 17 A.L.R. 588. Maryland also is opposed. Aged Women's & Aged Men's Home v. Pierce, 1905, 100 Md. 520, 60 A. 277, 70 L. R.A. 485, 10 Am.St.Rep. 450. New Jersey by statute prohibits the assignability of real property expectancies. N.J.Comp.Stat., 1910, p. 1539, § 19. On the other hand, in California code provisions declaring that a mere possibility is not an interest of any kind and cannot be assigned are said to be merely statements of common law rules and do not affect equity rules. Bridge v. Kedon, 1912, 163 Cal. 493, 126 P. 149, 43 L.R.A.,N.S., 404. See further 1933, 32 Mich.L.Rev. 478, 490 n. 53. See note, 1926, 44 A.L. R. 1465.

Considering the problem of a mortgage of expectancies, with special attention to New Jersey law, see Cunningham v. Tischler, Equitable Real Estate Mortgages, 1963, 17 Rutgers L.Rev. 679, 722–723.

70. E. g., the requirement that the ancestor must consent flows from the idea of fraud on him; that the bargain must be fair springs from a paternalistic solicitude for the heir which has been carried in some cases to ridiculous extremes. See Tynte v. Hodge, 1864, 2 Hem. & Mill. 287, 296 where a forty-seven year old man, quite competent in handling his affairs, was regarded as an "unprotected heir."

specific performance [71] of such a contract as in any other case if the legal remedy is inadequate, plus, perhaps, additional requirements rooted in these particular agreements.[72] Another view is that the equitable interest arises in accordance with " 'the real meaning of the agreement between the parties' * * * directly it is acquired—automatically on the happening of the event, and without any further act on the part of the assignor—and does not merely rest in, and amount to, a right in contract giving rise to an action." [73] Both of these rationales treat the expectancy as no different from any other sort of future acquired property and both of them postulate the giving of a present valuable consideration by the assignee. If the transaction is looked upon as a contract the requirement of valuable consideration is understandable as a prerequisite to specific performance.[74] The reason for its requirement under the second explanation probably lies in the insistence by the law of greater guarantees of the intention of the party or parties to a future transfer of property than is the case in a present transfer.[75] A third theory is that the expectancy is an existing equitable interest in property which is capable of present transfer.[76] This last conception is reasonable enough: the analytical distinction which treats a conditional limitation, executory devise, or contingent remainder as existing property interests although their enjoyment hinges upon exceedingly improbable events which may be within the control of the creator, and yet regards the expectancy of an heir or devisee under the will of a living person as non-existent is too fine for either logical or practical justification. If accepted it would follow that a present transfer of an expectancy in mortgage to secure an antecedent debt would be effective whereas, if the transaction, regardless of the form in which it is cast,[77] can take effect only as a contract to transfer, the antecedent debt will not be regarded as sufficient consideration.

Cases squarely holding that the assignee in such cases gets nothing [78] indicate that, regardless of the language used in cases where there was a present fair consideration,[79] the courts do not accept this third theory.[80]

---

71. This is the view taken by the Restatement, Second, Trusts § 86, Comment b, in the analogous problem of a transfer of an expectancy in trust. See also, § 74 Comment b.

72. E. g., the necessity of "fair" as contrasted with "valuable" consideration.

73. In re Lind, [1915] 2 Ch. 345, 360.

74. See, semble, Restatement, Second, Trusts § 26, Comment m and § 86, Comment b.

75. "A person can dispose of what he has more easily and with less formality than he can create a personal obligation to do something in the future." Restatement, Second, Trusts, § 74 Comment a. The same would hold true for a present attempt to transfer property in the future which is held to be operative otherwise than by the creation presently of a personal obligation to make the transfer in the future.

76. "In the case of a loan, according to these principles, there is created by the assignment a present equitable charge on the property, which equity recognizes as vested, although it is neither vested nor valid at law, and which, when the descent is cast at once ripens into a lien upon the property for the security of the money loaned." Bridge v. Kedon, 1912, 163 Cal. 493, 500, 126 P. 149, 151, 43 L.R.A.,N. S., 404. See Pomeroy, Equity, 5th Ed. §§ 1287, 1288a.

77. See Restatement, Second, Trusts § 86, Comment b, semble. Probably the same would be true on the second of the three rationales.

78. Bayler v. Commonwealth, 1861, 40 Pa. 37, 80 Am.Dec. 551, 10 Am.L.Reg. 444; Avon State Bank v. Commercial & Savings Bank of Sioux Falls, 1926, 49 S.D. 575, 207 N.W. 654, 44 A.L.R. 1462, discussed 1927, 27 Col.L.Rev. 227.

79. See note 67, supra.

80. It would seem that a proper manifestation of intent that the property be security, made at the time that the expectancy is realized or any time thereafter, would be sufficient to make it so even though the debt is an antecedent one. See §§ 27, 28, supra. See, semble, Restatement, Second, Trusts § 26, Comments j, k, l. The problem of what would be such a subsequent manifestation of intent is different in the case of real property than in personal property because of the difference in formalities necessary for the transfer of the two sorts of property. In the case of real property the question would be whether all the formalities necessary for the creation or transfer of an equitable interest in the property must be fulfilled at the later time to make

Bankruptcy cases in which the creditor's claim was secured by the mortgage of an expectancy which is realized after the debtor's discharge hold that the intervening discharge does not deprive the creditor of his lien upon the property.[81] Although to regard the expectancy itself as presently existing security at the time of bankruptcy would provide an easy explanation of such decisions, the one actually given, i. e., that the transaction was a contract for a mortgage of future property which had a present operative existence as security for the debt with the same status for bankruptcy purposes as a mortgage would have,[82] is a satisfactory enough explanation.[83]

AFTER-ACQUIRED PROPERTY

37.   There are four theories as to the creation of equitable mortgages of after-acquired property:

the manifestation of intention at that time effective.

81. In re Lind, [1915], 2 Ch. 345; Hall v. Glass, 1899, 123 Cal. 500, 56 P. 336, 69 Am.St.Rep. 77, semble, accord.   A, owning land, mortgaged crops thereon to B.   Held, a discharge in bankruptcy intervening between the delivery of the mortgage and the planting of the crops did not deprive B of his lien upon the crops.

82. " * * * the mortgagees under the [mortgage] deeds * * * elected to rely upon their security, and not to prove, and therefore as mortgagees they stand outside the bankruptcy; and * * * any contract contained in those deeds for vesting the future property in the mortgagees was ancillary not to the debt, but to the mortgage by which the debt was secured, in like manner as a covenant not to revoke a will which had appointed a sum of money to a mortgagee * * *" In re Lind, [1915] 2 Ch. 345, 360.

83. Cf. Glenn, Mortgages, § 412 where it is argued that if the lien depended upon specific performance of a contract the contract right would be a provable claim which would be discharged.   No explanation is offered as to what the security was at the time of bankruptcy if it was not an existing contract right.   The statement that it was an "equitable lien", meaning that it was grounded upon unjust enrichment, would give it no existence prior to the realization of the expectancy, which was after the discharge in bankruptcy.   Yet obviously the court considered the debt to be secured at the time of bankruptcy, and therefore the mortgagees "stand outside of bankruptcy."

1.   Specific performance of the mortgagor's agreement that his future property shall be mortgaged—this is the most common view;

2.   Presently manifested intent to transfer or create an interest in property is operative in equity as soon as the property is acquired, by analogy to present transfer of property or creation of trust.

3.   The mortgage is an equitable assignment of the present possibility; it becomes an assignment of the equitable ownership as soon as the property is acquired.

4.   "[A] broad and somewhat indefinite principle that one who has parted with money or property expecting a specified return should be assured either that return or the redelivery of what he has parted with." [84]

Expectancies are generally regarded as one species of after-acquired property and consequently pose the basic problem of rationale of mortgages of such interests.   Nevertheless, because they involve special considerations not universally applicable they are usually regarded as unsafe guides for wider generalizations.   Other sorts of after-acquired property are commonly lumped together and in respect to mortgages of them certain generalizations may be and are indulged in.   But here, too, it is necessary to utter the caution that no clear understanding can be reached without differentiating among the several varieties of property dealt with.[85]   The rules governing mortgages and sales or assignments of after-acquired tangible personal property or book accounts and other choses in action provide no reliable map for similar mortgages of real property.[86]   Since it is

84. Williston, Transfers of After-Acquired Personal Property, 1906, 19 Harv.L.Rev. 557.

85. See Cohen and Gerber, The After-Acquired Property Clause, 1939, 87 U. of Pa.L.Rev. 635; Glenn, Mortgages, § 409; Durfee, Cases on Security, 1951, 457–459.

86. See Williston, Transfers of After-Acquired Personal Property, 1906, 19 Harv.L.Rev. 556, 558.   To emphasize the point it is sufficient to mention the salient differences between the two as to the significance and importance and varying rules in respect to such matters as retention of possession, the theory and operation of recording statutes, the diverse provisions of the statutes of frauds, and the formalities necessary to transfer title.

with the latter we are concerned the former [87] ordinarily would be ignored. There are, however, reasons for spilling over into the other domain. For one thing, the after-acquired property clause in mortgages commonly lumps together both realty and personalty and segregation is impossible. Again there is a fringe area in which the property in question has both a factual and legal connection with the real property. Perhaps a more accurate statement is that because of the factual connection the property is treated somewhat different legally than is other like property where the nexus is absent. Fixtures and crops are the readiest examples; but there are other types of property used in or having some reasonable connection with the business property other than for resale which, although not falling within the classification of fixtures, yet may have different rules applied to them than to similar kinds of personalty which do not have the required relationship.[88] Mortgages of stocks of merchandise and of accounts receivable, however, are controlled by considerations having so little bearing upon our problems here that they will be entirely excluded from the discussion even when they include after-acquired clauses.[89] Durable things acquired by the mortgagor for use, typically machinery, are another story and one which we need to notice.[90]

Generalizations. Dealing first only with generalizations and leaving necessary qualifications, differentiations and particular problems for later sections, we find in the cases and writings four more or less clearly stated theories as to the creation of equitable mortgages of after-acquired property.[91] They are the same ones discussed earlier when the rationales of equitable mortgages in general were under examination;[92] but here the fact that there is no property owned by the mortgagor at the time of the transaction throws into sharp relief the differences between them and the consequences flowing from

buys for use and not resale. * * * The difference is important, and it runs through our entire law." Glenn, Mortgages, § 409.

91. In Massachusetts and a few other states an after-acquired property clause will not create an equitable mortgage on the subsequent acquisition of personal property by the mortgagor. Moody v. Wright, 1847, 54 Mass. (13 Metc.) 17, 46 Am.Dec. 706. In a few other states there are miscellaneous limitations on the operation of such a clause. See Cohen and Gerber, The After-Acquired Property Clause, 1939, 87 U. of Pa.L.Rev. 635, 639–642. In the great majority of jurisdictions, however, they do create equitable mortgages and the questions which are important are the theories of their creation and the extent of their validity as between the parties and as to third parties.

As to whether an equitable interest under a land contract gives a right to after-acquired property, see Note, 1954, 23 U. of Cin.L.Rev. 508, discussing Bank of Ohio v. Lawrence, 1954, 161 Ohio St. 543, 120 N. E.2d 88.

For discussions of the laws of some particular jurisdictions see Francis, Mortgages of After-Acquired Property in Kentucky, 1947, 35 Ky.L.J. 320; Ethridge, The After-Acquired Property Doctrine and Its Application in Mississippi, 1945, 17 Miss.L.J. 153; After-Acquired Property Clauses—La., 1941, 51 Tulane L.Rev. 314.

For some other authorities and comments on after-acquired property clauses in mortgages, look at the following: Note, Mortgages—After-Acquired Property Clause in Mortgage Is Valid, 1956, 28 Rocky Mt. L.Rev. 432, commenting on United States v. Westmoreland Manganese Corp., E.D.Ark.1955, 134 F. Supp. 898; Note, After-Acquired Property and the Title Search, 1955, 24 Ford.L.Rev. 412, commenting on Fries v. Clearview Gardens Sixth Corp., 2d Dept. 1955, 285 App.Div. 568, 139 N.Y.S.2d 573. See also Arnold, 1959, After-Acquired Property as Mortgage Security in Maryland, 19 Md.L.Rev. 294.

For a thorough examination of the problem of after-acquired property clauses in mortgages, see Cunningham and Tischler, Equitable Real Estate Mortgages, 1963, 17 Rutgers L.Rev. 679, 715–723.

92. See §§ 24–29, supra.

---

87. For a collection of cases and citations to authorities on mortgages of after-acquired personal property, see Osborne, Cases on Property Security, 2d ed., 1954, 543–585.

88. See the *in praesenti* rule, § 39 infra.

Statutory recognition of the desirability of lumping together after-acquired property clauses covering both realty and personal property is found in the liberalization, in 1954, of the New York Lien Law, c. 754, 29 N.Y.U.L.Rev. 1019.

The increasing use, in recent years, of the "package mortgage" in the financing of sales of homes has emphasized the importance of the mortgage covering not only the realty and fixtures but a variety of appliances, usually desired by a home owner. See The Package Mortgage, 1957, 6 Kan.L.Rev. 66–77.

89. For a collection of cases and authorities on security interests in fluctuating stocks of merchandise, see Osborne, Cases on Property Security, 2d ed., 566–585.

90. " * * * we must draw the line between mercantile goods and those which the mortgagor

each, and makes a reexamination of them worth while even at the expense of some repetition.

The most generally accepted view starts with the venerable legal dogma that "A man cannot grant or charge that which he hath not," [93] and concludes from this, with an aura of inevitable logic,[94] that they rest upon an "application of the principles of specific performance, and * * * that what is actually done is to enforce the mortgagor's agreement that his future property shall be mortgaged or stand as security. The occasional denial that the case is one of specific performance is due partly to the fact that the mortgagor often uses no words of promise but purports to transfer presently, and partly to the fact that the court does not order the execution of any mortgage." [95] "But, in the nature of the case, since a present transfer is impossible, this can mean nothing more than a promise to mortgage, while justice and the presumable intention of the

parties requires that it should mean as much as a promise" [96] and " * * * the court does not order the execution of a mortgage only because it is unnecessary." [97] The foregoing explanation has not gone uncriticised. It is urged that in almost all of the cases there is no agreement express or implied to execute a mortgage after the property is acquired, and "to say that is an implied promise to mortgage at the later time, and that the courts do not actually require that such mortgage be made because it is unnecessary, is merely to add one fiction to another." [98] Again it is said that specific performance will not do for two reasons: a. because "while the after-acquired property may be land (in

93. Perkins, Profitable Book *15. The work first appeared in 1532. In Hickson Lumber Co. et al. v. Gay Lumber Co., 1909, 150 N.C. 282, 286, 63 S.E. 1045, 1047, 21 L.R.A.,N.S., 843, 845, one of the leading cases on mortgages of after-acquired property, the court stated its reasoning thus, "It is well understood that at common law nothing can be mortgaged that is not in existence and does not at the time belong to the mortgagor, for a person cannot convey that which he does not own; but it is now well settled that equity will give effect to a contract to convey future-acquired property, whether real or personal. Equity considers that done which the mortgagor has agreed to do, and treats the mortgage as already attaching to the newly acquired property as it comes into the mortgagor's hands."

94. Whether the conclusion is inevitable in this particular problem depends upon whether a. the assumption in these cases that the mortgagor has no interest presently in after-acquired property is correct, and b. even admitting no interest does exist presently in the mortgagor whether the security interest in the future when the property is acquired may arise merely by virtue of the previously manifested intention that it should arise then or only by virtue of specific performance of a *contract* right to have the mortgage given or to have it stand as security. See Pennock v. Coe, 1859, 64 U.S. (23 How. 117), 128, 16 L.Ed. 436.

95. Williston, Transfers of After-Acquired Personal Property, 1906, 19 Harv.L.Rev. 556, 560.

96. Id. 558.

97. Id. 560. Among the most prominent authorities accepting specific performance as the basis for the equitable mortgage in after-acquired property cases are Grape Creek Coal Co. v. Farmers' Loan & Trust Co., Ill., 1894, 63 F. 891, 896, 12 C.C.A. 350, affirmed 65 F. 717, 13 C.C.A. 87; Borden v. Croak, 1889, 131 Ill. 68, 22 N.E. 793, 19 Am.St.Rep. 23; Guaranty Trust Co. v. N. Y. & Queens Co. Ry. Co., 1930, 253 N.Y. 190, 199, 170 N.E. 887, reargument denied 254 N.Y. 126, 172 N.E. 264, appeal dismissed 282 U.S. 803, 51 S.Ct. 86, 75 L.Ed. 722; Trust Co. of America v. Rhinelander, C.C.Wis., 1910, 182 F. 64, 69; Holroyd v. Marshall, 1862, 10 H.L.Cas. 191, 211; Kribbs v. Alford, 1890, 120 N.Y. 519, 524, 24 N.E. 811, 813; Stone, The "Equitable Mortgage" in New York, 1920, 20 Col.L.Rev. 519, 524; Foley and Pogue, After-Acquired Property under Conflicting Corporate Mortgage Indentures, 1929, 13 Minn.L. Rev. 81, 82–84; Cohen and Gerber, The After-Acquired Property Clause, 1939, 87 U. of Pa.L.Rev. 635, 646; 3 Tiffany, Real Prop., 2d Ed., 2747; Note, Equitable Assignee's Right to Future Refund as Against Those of Judgment Lienor: City of New York v. Bedford Bar & Grill, Inc., 1958, [2 N.Y.2d 429, 161 N.Y.S.2d 67, 141 N.E.2d 575], 43 Cornell L. Q. 289. For other discussions of the same case, see 1957, 26 Fordham L.Rev. 552; 1957, 7 Buffalo L. Rev. 104.

In Mitchell v. Winslow, C.C.Me., 1843, Fed.Cas.No. 9673, 6 Law Rep. 347, the pioneer American case which antedated Holroyd v. Marshall, Story pretty obviously was thinking in terms of specific performance of a contract although certain passages of his opinion, especially the most quoted, when taken out of their setting could be interpreted as indicating a belief that the lien arose either as the result 1. of equity recognizing the present transfer of an existing possibility as a property interest, or 2. of equity effectuating the presently expressed intention that the security interest should arise in the future.

98. Walsh, Mortgages, 56.

which case specific performance can be invoked as a matter of course) then again it may * * * be of the most commonplace variety" in which "case the remedy of specific performance would be denied"; b. because, if the mortgagee's right is contractual it would be provable, and hence dischargeable, in bankruptcy.[99] The first of these last two reasons reveals a curious misapprehension as to the basis for specific performance of contracts to mortgage. It is not the character of the property which is the vital ingredient here but the purely speculative amount of damages which results from not getting *security,* it being practically impossible to determine in terms of money the difference in value between a secured and an unsecured obligation regardless of the character of the property promised for this purpose.[1] The case [2] relied upon for the second of them does not stand for any such conclusion. Even if it did, provability and dischargeability under the terms of any particular bankruptcy statute [3] should not be decisive of the nature of such mortgages. A more valid objection is that, although specific performance is a proper and adequate explanation in many cases, it would confine the scope of the rule too narrowly to restrict it to cases in which there could be found a real promise, whether express or implied in

fact, that the mortgagor would act in giving security when the property is acquired, and that in fact the cases do not so confine it.[4]

This brings us to another of the four rationales. This second view proceeds upon the assumption that, regardless of the rule in the courts of law, there is no reason in the nature of things why, in equity, a present manifestation of intention to transfer or create an interest in property immediately upon acquisition of that property in the future cannot be operative to do so on the happening of that event in the same way that a similar manifestation of intent to grant at once an interest in existing and then owned property is effective to do so.[5] "The inquiry here is, not whether a person can grant *in praesenti* property not belonging to him and not in existence, but whether the law will permit the grant or conveyance to take effect upon the property when it is brought into existence and belongs to the grantor, in fulfillment of an express agreement, founded upon a good and valuable consideration." [6] The analogy invoked is that of trust or conveyance rather than of contract, of actual transfer or creation instead of a promise to transfer or create. The language used is significant:—"The assignor, having received the consideration, becomes in equity, on the happening of the event, trustee for the assignee of the property devolving upon or acquired by him, and which he had previously sold and been paid for." [7] In some states there are statutes

---

99. Glenn, Mortgages of Real Property, § 412.

1. See Stone, supra note 97, 521; Williston, Transfers of After-Acquired Personal Property, 1906, 19 Harv.L.Rev. 557, 585. See also supra § 26.

2. In re Lind [1915] 2 Ch. 345. See § 36.

3. The mortgage or pledge of property to be acquired subsequently has caused considerable difficulty under the federal bankruptcy law in determining whether the mortgagee has received a preference, or, even if not, whether he will lose to the trustee in bankruptcy under some other provision in the act. The solution of these questions requires a determination of the legal position of such a mortgagee or pledgee under the proper state law, and then the application to it of the provisions of the bankruptcy act. See Walsh, Mortgages of Property to be Subsequently Acquired, 1933, 10 N.Y.Univ.L.Q. Rev. 311, 323; notes, 1928, 12 Minn.L.Rev. 378; 1939, 26 Va.L.Rev. 219; 1928, 28 Col.L.Rev. 943; 1924, 24 Col.L.Rev. 68; 1922, 31 Yale L.J. 662; 1916, 14 Mich.L.Rev. 339; 1905, 18 Harv.L.Rev. 606.

4. See Tailby v. Official Receiver, 1888, 13 A.C. 523, 546–547, "It is difficult to suppose that * * * considerations applicable to cases of specific performance, properly so-called, where the contract is executory are to be applied to every case of equitable assignment dealing with future property."

5. See Campbell, Cas.Mortgages, 2d ed., 50, n. 1, 38 n. 2.

6. Pennock v. Coe, 1859, 64 U.S. (23 How.) 117, 128, 16 L.Ed. 436. See further, §§ 24–29, 36.

7. In re Lind, 1915, 2 Ch. 345, 360. See Tailby v. Official Receiver, 1888, 13 A.C. 523, 543, 547; Morrill v. Noyes, 1863, 56 Me. 458, 472, 96 Am.Dec. 486 ("it can be enforced in equity as a case of trust"). See also Blair, The Allocation of After-Acquired Mortgaged Property Among Rival Claimants, 1926,

which, on their face, seem to create legal mortgages when the property is acquired later. Thus it is provided that "An agreement may be made to create a lien upon property not yet acquired by the party agreeing to give the lien, or not yet in existence. In such case the lien agreed for attaches from the time when the party agreeing to give it acquires an interest in the thing, to the extent of such interest." [8] Under a similarly worded statute, it has been held that "the original contract, *ipso facto,* immediately upon the acquirement or creation of such property, awakens and brings into life the lien agreed upon." [9] And under the quoted statute, the mortgagee of a street railway company was held to have obtained through it a legal mortgage upon subsequently acquired real property under a clause in the mortgage covering such property. [10]

Although this second explanation is a happier one in that it frees the doctrine from the objected to narrowness of the first, it faces some difficulties of its own. For one thing, it is no easier to find from the language of present giving in mortgage an intention that it should be operative only at a later time than to imply a promise to transfer in the future from the same language. [11] For an-

other, if it really is a conveyance or trust created *in futuro* it necessitates giving some explanation as to why a valuable consideration *in praesenti* is insisted upon. Of course, it can be answered that this is so because it is not a present transfer and, as was noted before, greater guarantees are insisted upon in such cases whether it be a matter of specific performance or of trust arising in the future. [12] But if this is true it merely amounts to saying that the difference between the two conceptions amounts to tweedledum and tweedledee. Further, and most difficult to meet, is that the trust analogy relied upon flies directly in the face of the considered conclusion of the Restatement of Trusts in the similar situation. [13] In the case of after-acquired property no trust is created by either a present declaration or transfer or even an express declaration of intention to be trustee of property from and after a future date without something more. [14] There must be either a new manifestation of intent when the property is acquired [15] or the trustor must have bound himself by a contract which equity will specifically enforce. [16]

In trusts, since no formalities are required to create trusts of personal property with the

40 Harv.L.Rev. 222, 226; Ashburner, Principles of Equity, Browne ed. 1933, 245–247; note, 1900, 13 Harv.L.Rev. 598.

8. West's Ann.Cal.Civ.Code § 2883.

9. Grand Forks Nat. Bank v. Minneapolis & N. Elevator Co., 1889, 6 Dak. 357, 43 N.W. 806.

10. California Title Ins. and Trust Co. v. Pauly, 1896, 111 Cal. 122, 43 P. 586. Look at Mason v. Citizens' Nat. Trust and Savings Bank, C.C.A.Cal.1934, 71 F.2d 246; In re Los Angeles Mfg. Co., D.C.Cal. 1933, 7 F.Supp. 567. See notes, 1935, 23 Cal.L.Rev. 628; 1935, 8 So.Cal.L.Rev. 358.

Cal.Civ.Code § 2930 and similar provisions may have an effect in these cases. It provides that "Title acquired by the mortgagor subsequent to the execution of the mortgage, inures to the mortgagee as security for the debt in like manner as if acquired before execution." Probably, however, it applies merely to cases within the doctrine of estoppel by deed. See Cohen and Gerber, The After-Acquired Property Clause, 1939, 87 U. of Pa.L.Rev. 635, 643.

11. See Foley and Pogue, After-Acquired Property Under Conflicting Corporate Mortgage Indentures,

1929, 13 Minn.L.Rev. 81, 83, criticising this theory as resting upon a loose and incorrect conception of what constitutes an executory as contrasted with an executed transaction.

12. See § 36, supra.

13. See Restatement, Second, Trusts §§ 26, Comments a, j, k; 74 Comment a; 75, Comments a, c; 86, Comments b, c.

14. See Restatement, Second, Trusts § 26, Comment j for this last, extreme case. This is true even though the property was then owned by the trustor. A fortiori it would be true as to property not then owned by him. See citations in preceding note.

15. Restatement, Second, Trusts §§ 26, Comments j, k; 76, Comment c; 76, Comment g; 86, Comment c.

16. Restatement, Second, Trusts §§ 74, Comment a; 26, Comment m; 75, Comments a, b; 76, Comment f; 86, Comment b. See also Brainard v. Commissioner of Internal Revenue, C.C.A.7th, 1937, 91 F.2d 880, 883, certiorari granted 58 S.Ct. 480, 302 U.S. 682, 82 L.Ed. 525, certiorari dismissed 58 S.Ct. 748, 303 U.S. 665, 82 L.Ed. 1122.

result that today enormous amounts of wealth can be so disposed of without the safeguard of a writing, the requirement of valuable present consideration as a desirable guarantee of intention seems justified.

Although it has already been pointed out [17] that mortgages, because they create or transfer a security interest only as contrasted with the full beneficial interest in the case of trusts, are a fortiori cases for giving as great an effect to an intention that they should spring into existence as is done in the case of trusts, it is difficult to find any sufficient reason for going beyond the law of trusts in this case. Indeed, it seems desirable that some limitation be put on the tying up of future ability to borrow without getting a new loan in exchange. The analogy to the justification for the *in praesenti* rule is apt. Of course, it is also desirable that a mortgagor be able to get credit on future property, but not as security for past debts or on all of his property. A stronger statement is warranted. The most important objective sought and achieved by mortgages of after-acquired property is the acquisition of new capital for present use in other enterprises or expansion of existing ones on the security of future property. No such justification exists in ordinary trust law. Nor would a mortgage fulfill this function if future property could be added as security for already existing indebtedness.

In the third place, going to the other extreme from and neatly evading the apparently irrefutable logic of the first solution, it is stated that although the mortgage of after-acquired property "does not operate as an immediate alienation at law, it operates as an equitable assignment of the *present possibility,* which changes into an assignment of the *equitable ownership* as soon as the property is acquired by the vendor or mortgagor." [18] This conception of a bare possi-

bility of acquiring property in the future, extending in the case of personal property to things not even in existence, as a present property interest analogous to the present ownership of a contingent remainder is as was previously stated,[19] one that is perfectly reasonable.[20] If restricted to personal property [21] more headway might be made with it. When applied to real property it encounters the policy against creation or recognition of new or additional sorts of property interests.

The fourth explanation rests "on a broad and somewhat indefinite principle that one who has parted with money or property expecting a specified return should be assured either that return or the redelivery of what he has parted with." [22] This non-consensual basis was examined earlier and what was said

property, the reasoning applies equally to real property and the authority cited included real property cases, especially those of expectancies. See also Walsh, Mortgages, 60, with which compare the author's statement on page 56. The author not only seems to accept contradictory bases for the creation of equitable mortgages in these cases but carries the confusion over into the time they arise.
See also 1957, 7 Buffalo L.Rev. 104, 105, citing Capitol Distributor's Corp. v. 2131 Eighth Avenue, 1956, 1 N.Y.2d 842, 153 N.Y.S.2d 222, 135 N.E.2d 726.

19. See § 36.

20. Cf., Williston, Sales, 2d Ed., § 132 et seq.

21. In fact Pomeroy enunciates the doctrine in a section explanatory of the immediately preceding one which dealt solely with after-acquired personal property. However, he relies in part on cases of expectancies of an heir of devisee of real property. See Pomeroy, Equity Jurisdiction, 5th Ed., § 1288a.

22. Williston, Transfers of After-Acquired Personal Property, 1906, 19 Harv.L.Rev. 557. Accord are Glenn, Mortgages, §§ 17, 17.1, 421; Walsh, Mortgages, 52, 56.
The last named writer argues that the Statute of Frauds has no application to equitable mortgages (id. 47, 48 n. 30, 52) because the mortgagee's equity arises, not out of the enforceable agreement of the parties but "on the fact that he has advanced or given credit in reliance on the mortgagor's agreement", i. e. by operation of law. Nevertheless, when it is a question of relating the after-acquired property to the prior mortgage agreement to determine its date for preferential purposes under the bankruptcy act, he says that the mortgage in such a case arises "in accord with the obvious intention of the parties." Id. 60. He also intimates both that it really arose at the prior time and, also, that

17. See § 30, supra.

18. Pomeroy, Equity Juris., 5th Ed., § 588a. While the statement is made with respect to personal

there is applicable here.[23] Although like the first and probably the second of the bases it provides an explanation of the requirement of a valuable consideration, it runs into trouble in other directions. Unlike those first two, and also the third, its reasoning would require valuable consideration in the case of presently owned property as well.[24] But equitable mortgages to secure antecedent debts are recognized as has previously been pointed out.[25] Again if accepted it would take all equitable mortgages outside of the operation of the recording acts,[26] but this is not true.[27] Indeed there is authority, debatable as to its soundness, that recording acts not only apply to mortgages of after-acquired property but that recordation before acquisition is valid.[28] Further, it necessitates rejecting the applicability of the Statute of Frauds [29] even though the property be land, a matter which will be discussed lated.[30]

---

it could be validly recorded before the property was acquired. Id. At still another place he seems to accept the contract theory. Id. 55. In other words, without seeming to be aware of any inconsistency the author, at one place or another espouses all four rationales of the equitable mortgage.

23. See also Williston, Transfers of After-Acquired Personal Property, 1906, 19 Harv.L.Rev. 557, 586. See §§ 24, 27, supra.

24. See Glenn, Mortgages, § 17.1; Walsh, Mortgages, 49, 56.

25. See § 30, supra.

26. See Stone, The "Equitable Mortgage" in New York, 1920, 20 Col.L.Rev. 519, 529.

27. Id. 528. See § 199, infra.

28. Hickson Lumber Co. v. Gay Lumber Co., 1909, 150 N.C. 282, 63 S.E. 1045, 21 L.R.A.,N.S., 843; First Nat. Bank of Alexandria v. Turnbull & Co., 1880, 73 Va. (32 Grat.) 695, 34 Am.Rep. 791. For a collection of authorities and articles, see Osborne, Cases on Property Security, 2d Ed., 1954, p. 559 n. 9.

29. See Walsh, 47, "the Statute of Frauds is not involved since the equitable mortgage arises because of the right to the security as a specific thing in reliance upon which the creditor has performed,".

30. See Chapter 3, infra.

AFTER-ACQUIRED PROPERTY—DISTINGUISHED FROM OTHER DOCTRINES

38. Mortgages of after-acquired property must be distinguished from cases resting upon doctrines of estoppel, potential possession, and accession or the employment of the supplemental indenture.

Mortgages of after-acquired property simpliciter must be distinguished from cases resting upon estoppel, the doctrine of potential possession, or the principle of accession.

Estoppel. Although estoppel by deed, as in all other kinds of estoppel, requires both a misrepresentation of existing fact and a reliance upon that misrepresentation, a few courts have sustained mortgages of after-acquired property upon that doctrine.[31] The inapplicability of estoppel to cases in which there is no representation or warranty by the mortgagor that he owned the property at the time and, therefore, no reliance by the mortgagee seems too obvious to need elaboration.[32] As one court put it, "recitals, it is true, and covenants, may conclude parties and privies, and estop them from denying that the operation of the deed is what it professes to be. And when a deed purports to pass a present interest, recitals and covenants have, in many cases, been held efficacious to pass to the grantee an interest subsequently acquired by the grantor. But when the deed does not undertake to convey any existing estate, * * * it is difficult to conceive of it as anything more than a covenant for a future conveyance. In the very nature of things it must be executory." [33]

---

31. Galveston H. & H. R. Co. v. Cowdrey, 1870, 78 U.S. (11 Wall.) 459, 20 L.Ed. 199. See Susquehanna Trust & Safe Deposit Co. v. United Telephone & Telegraph Co., C.C.A., Pa.1925, 6 F.2d 179, 181. See 1948, 168 A.L.R. 1149.

32. See § 37.

33. Bayler v. Commonwealth, 1861, 40 Pa. 37, 42, 10 Am.L.Reg. 444, 80 Am.Dec. 551. See Cohen and Gerber, The After-Acquired Property Clause, 1937, 87 U. of Pa.L.Rev. 635, 643; Blair, The Allocation of After-Acquired Mortgaged Property Among Rival Claimants, 1926, 40 Harv.L.Rev. 222, 227; Tiffany, Real Prop., 2d Ed., § 545.

Statutes in some jurisdictions, probably enacted to enlarge the scope of the doctrine of estoppel by deed to include mortgages not containing express covenants or warranties of title,[34] were so broadly worded as to make them apply literally to after-acquired property clauses and create legal mortgages on acquisition by the mortgagor.[35] Although the interpretation which will be made of them is still in doubt, it is likely that they will be confined to cases where the mortgagor purported to own the specific property at the time of mortgage. A case holding that if the grantee has knowledge that the grantor did not have title at the time of the conveyance the statute does not apply points in this direction.[36] No words of the statute requires this, it being a limitation of the common law theory of estoppel.

Potential possession. Proceeding upon the theory that a person having a present ownership of the means of producing was the owner of the future product of that thing,[37] there was developed first in English cases [38] and later in America an exception at law to the rule that what was not in existence could not be transferred. This doctrine of "potential possession" or "potential existence" has been abolished by the Sale of Goods Act in England [39] and in the United States the Uniform Sales Act eliminates it as to sales of goods.[40] It still exists, however, in the law of mort-

gages although confined in its application to future crops [41] and the future young of animals.[42] In the case of crops it is frequently difficult, if not impossible, to tell whether the mortgage which arises on the future crop when it comes into existence is a legal one with an existence dating from the original mortgage agreement under the doctrine of potential possession, or an equitable one founded upon one of the rationales we have been considering.[43] Usually it does not make any difference. Clearly, however, the doctrine of potential possession has no operation in the case of mortgages of future acquired real property. Its chief significance for us lies in the fact that by recognizing, even though perhaps by a fiction, that even the law courts would treat the possibility of acquiring something in the future as capable of present transfer, it lends support to the third of the theories in regard to mortgages of after-acquired property.[44]

Accession. Insofar as property subsequently acquired by the mortgagor becomes an accession to the mortgaged property it feeds the mortgage unaided by any after-acquired property clause.[45] The difficulty with this statement of almost axiomatic law lies in the fact that what constitutes an accession, or more commonly, a fixture, is a variable concept—variable both as to time and the class of persons whose rights are affected.[46]

---

34. See Kline v. Ragland, 1886, 47 Ark. 111, 117, 14 S.W. 474, 476; 23 Cal.L.Rev. 628, 630, n. 10; 87 U. of Pa.L.Rev. 635, 644.

35. See Cal.Civ.Code § 2930; 23 Cal.L.Rev. 628.

36. Viele v. Van Steenberg, C.C.Iowa, 1887, 31 F. 249; 87 U. of Pa.L.Rev. 635, 644.

37. See Grand Forks Nat. Bank v. Minneapolis & Northern Elevator Co., 1889, 6 Dak. 357, 359, 43 N. W. 806, 807; Williston, Sales, 2d Ed., §§ 132 et seq. See also Osborne, Cases on Property Security, 2d Ed. 1954, 543–549.

38. Grantham v. Hawley, 1616, Hobart 132a, is the case most frequently cited as the parent of the doctrine. As to future crop reservations by land contract vendors, see 1948 Wis.L.Rev. 240.

39. S.G.A. § 5(3). See Williston, Sales, 2d Ed., § 134.

40. Uniform Sales Act § 75. See U.C.C. sec. 2–105.

41. Williston, Sales, 2d Ed., § 135. Most cases hold that the crop need not be planted at the time the mortgage is given. There are, however, either by statute or decision, some limitations on what future crops may be mortgaged.

42. Williston, supra, § 136.

43. Williston, Sales, 2d Ed., § 135.

44. "There seems no rational distinction between one class of future goods and another." Chalmers, Sale of Goods Act, 8th Ed., 27.

45. McFadden v. Allen, 1892, 134 N.Y. 489, 32 N.E. 21.

46. See Bingham, Some Suggestions Concerning the Law of Fixtures, 1907, 7 Col.L.Rev. 1; Cohen and Gerber, The After-Acquired Property Clause, 1939, 87 U. of Pa.L.Rev. 635, 645. For a collection of cases and references to authorities and discussions

For example, it has been stated that "the nature of railroad property will cause the principle of accession to be liberally applied, so that things not strictly fixtures and interests not strictly incorporeal hereditaments, may be brought within the principle as if they were fixtures or appurtenances under a narrow definition." [47] Because of the confusion in the cases and the uncertainties as to the exact boundaries of the law of fixtures, mortgagees have been unwilling to trust to its operation to give them the security of after-acquired property and tend to rely upon the insertion of a clause covering such property.[48] This practice has to some extent added to the confusion because courts often base on the clause a decision which would clearly fall within even an illiberal view of what constitutes a fixture.[49] As between the original parties to the mortgage it would seldom make much difference on which claim the mortgagee based his right. When the mortgagor transfers the property, or an original corporate mortgagor consolidates with another corporation, it becomes necessary to examine the question more closely.[50] It is sufficient here to note that if the principle of accession does apply the mortgagee will acquire at law under his mortgage a security interest in the subsequently acquired property and the after-acquired property clause is superfluous.

Supplemental indentures. Coupled with the after-acquired property clause in mortgages is commonly a covenant to convey to the mortgagee from time to time as acquired subsequent to the mortgage various parcels of property, land or chattels. When the mortgagor in fulfillment of such a covenant does execute a deed or bill of sale of the property, from that instant on as to that property the mortgagee has a legal mortgage. Consequently the after-acquired property clause ceases to operate on it and its only significance will be as to rights in the property between the time of acquisition and the giving of the supplemental indenture. In jurisdictions rejecting the doctrine of equitable mortgages arising by virtue of after-acquired property clauses it is customary to use periodic supplemental indentures to catch all property acquired by the mortgagor during the year.[51]

AFTER-ACQUIRED PROPERTY—LIMITATIONS AND SPECIAL CASES

39. Several limitations and special cases exist or are urged in the creation of mortgages of after-acquired property.

(1) The property must be described so as to identify it between the parties and put third parties on notice.

(2) The "in praesenti" rule requires that the future property be connected with property presently in existence.

(3) "Floating charges" exist in Great Britain. They are equitable charges on all assets for the time being of a going concern.

(4) Attempts have been made to base distinctions upon the character of the mortgagor.

(5) The nature of the property involved has been urged as a determining factor in the validity of such mortgages.

Description. Although it is sometimes laid down as gospel that a lien "must necessarily apply to some designated property, either *in*

on the law of fixtures with special reference to priority problems in the law of mortgages, see Osborne, Cases on Secured Transactions, 1967, 360–372. See also Chapter 7, infra.

47. Cardozo, J., in Guaranty Trust Co. of New York v. New York & Q. C. Ry. Co., 1930, 253 N.Y. 190, 206, 170 N.E. 887, 893, reargument denied 254 N.Y. 126, 172 N.E. 264, appeal dismissed 282 U.S. 803, 51 S.Ct. 86, 75 L.Ed. 722.

48. E. g., Manufacturer's Trust Co. v. Peck-Schwartz Realty Corp., 1938, 277 N.Y. 283, 14 N.E.2d 70, reargument and motion denied 278 N.Y. 482, 15 N.E.2d 72; Shelton Holding Corp. v. 150 East 48th St. Corp., 1934, 264 N.Y. 339, 191 N.E. 8, motion denied 265 N.Y. 502, 193 N.E. 291. See Friedman, The Scope of Mortgage Liens on Fixtures and Personal Property in New York, 1938, 7 Ford.L.Rev. 331, 341–353.

49. See, e. g., Mackall-Paine Veneer Co. v. Vancouver Plywood Co., 1934, 177 Wash. 503, 32 P.2d 530.

50. See § 41, infra.

51. See Cohen and Gerber, The After-Acquired Property Clause, 1939, 87 U. of Pa.L.Rev. 635, 661.

esse or expectancy, and this clearly and unmistakably",[52] such statements cannot be accepted without qualification. "As between the parties, a specific and particular description is not necessary; but to be effectual as against third persons, it must point out the subject matter so that such persons by it, together with such inquiries as the instrument suggests, may be able to identify the property intended to be covered." [53] Both branches of this statement are sound. Even as between the parties, however, a mere general promise to give property as security is ineffective [54] because it "puts the creditor in no better position than an agreement to pay money." [55] On the other hand, in spite of some statements to the contrary,[56] there is ample authority that a clause covering all after-acquired property is good.[57] So far as the decisions are genuinely concerned with the sufficiency of the description to identify the property between the parties or to put third parties on notice [58] it is difficult to see any ground for holding that "all" is not a sufficiently definite identification of the property covered.[59] If the clause so worded is inoperative to carry what it describes it must rest upon some other ground. One that has been suggested is that "a man might almost be able to sell himself into virtual slavery in that everything he has or ever will have can be encumbered before he even gets it".[60] Perhaps there is sufficient reality in the danger to justify applying the *in praesenti* rule, discussed below as a limitation in the case of mortgages given by in-

---

52. Seymour v. Canandaigua & Niagara Falls R. Co., 1857, 25 Barb. (N.Y.) 284, 304, 14 How.Pr. 531; Jones, Mortgages, 8th ed., 265; Glenn, Mortgages, § 413.

The description was held insufficient in Williams v. Lucas, 1789, 2 Cox, 160 ("to give a security by mortgage of lands when required"); Wood Mowing & Reaping Mach. Co. v. Minneapolis & N. E. Co., 1892, 48 Minn. 404, 51 N.W. 378 (forty acres of wheat to be grown on a specified quarter section); Wattles v. Cobb, 1900, 60 Neb. 403, 83 N.W. 195, 83 Am.St.Rep. 537 (340 acres of corn out of 425, the corn uneven in quality); Langley v. Vaughn, 1873, 57 Tenn. (10 Heisk.) 553 ("on real estate or my interest in same"). In Mitchell v. Abernathy, 1915, 194 Ala. 608, 69 So. 824, L.R.A.1917C, 6 (200 bushels of 1912 crop which crop produced less than 200 bushels); Payne v. Wilson, 1878, 74 N.Y. 348 (mortgage of one of thirteen houses then being built, a particular one later being agreed upon); Dunman v. Coleman, Mathis & Fulton, 1883, 59 Tex. 199 (1000 cattle in a herd of a larger number) the description was sufficient.

Sometimes the sufficiency of the description is held to be a jury question. Reeves & Co. v. Brown, 1909, 80 Kan. 292, 102 P. 840.

53. National Bank of Chelsea v. Fitts, 1895, 67 Vt. 57, 30 A. 697.

54. Fremoult v. Dedire, 1718, 1 P.Wms. 432.

55. Mechanics' & Metals Nat. Bank of City of New York v. Ernst, 1913, 231 U.S. 60, 67, 34 S.Ct. 22, 23, 58 L.Ed. 121.

56. See Re Kansas City Journal-Post Co., C.C.A.Mo., 1944, 144 F.2d 808, 810; Tadman v. D'Epineuil, 1881, 20 Ch.Div. 758; Reinig v. Johnson, 1927, 202 Iowa 1366, 212 N.W. 59, noted, 1927, 12 Iowa L.Rev. 421 ("all other personal property which I own or may own")—accord; Tailby v. Official Receiver, 1888, L.R. 13 App.Cas. 523; In re Kelcey [1899] 2 Ch.D. 530; note, 13 Harv.L.Rev. 598.

57. Hickson Lumber Co. v. Gay Lumber Co., 1909, 150 N.C. 282, 63 S.E. 1045, 21 L.R.A.,N.S., 843; Colonial Trust Co. v. Harmon Creek Coal Co., 1926, 287 Pa. 284, 135 A. 134; Cohen, and Gerber, The After-Acquired Property Clause, 1939, 87 U. of Pa. L.Rev. 635, 651; Note, 1953, 53 Col.L.Rev. 392, 394.

Granting that a corporation might mortgage all after-acquired property, it has been pointed out that the undesirability of such coverage has led courts to impose limitations on the operation of after-acquired property clauses in corporate mortgages. See Note, Limitations on the Scope of the After-Acquired Property Clause, 1953, 53 Col.L.Rev. 392.

58. See 1939, 87 U. of Pa.L.Rev. 635, 653.

59. An argument can be made that if the mortgage covers only "all property owned at the date of the mortgage" or "all property acquired after the date of the mortgage" the burden of ascertaining the date of acquisition, this being one item in the description, from non-record sources would make the description insufficiently definite for constructive notice to third persons. Where the coverage is of "all property now owned or hereafter acquired" this objection could not be raised. Similar objections can be urged where the locality in which the property is to be acquired is part of the description. As between the parties, however, any of these descriptions would seem to be sufficient to identify the property. Look at Tailby v. Official Receiver, 1888, 13 A.C. 523, holding that an individual may contract to assign all his future book account and that this is neither too vague nor indefinite.

60. Belding v. Read, 1865, 3 H. & C. 955; 1935, 23 Cal.L.Rev. 628, 631; Llewellyn, Cases and Materials on the Law of Sales, 1930, 577, accord. See Cohen and Gerber, supra note 51, 654.

dividuals.[61] Such a reason of course has no application, to a corporation. Nevertheless a completely unrestricted rule in the case of corporations presents the danger that it "would become a straitjacket upon future financing"[62] and thus defeat one of the chief functions of the clause, i.e., making future assets available for present credit.[63]

"In praesenti." "An after-acquired property clause will not be enforced in a particular case unless there exists 'something *in praesenti*, of which the thing *in futuro* is to be the product, or with which it is to be connected, as necessary for its use, or as incident to it, constituting a tangible, existing basis for the contract' ".[64]

This often cited statement has been paraphrased to read that "after-acquired property may not be mortgaged in gross, but only as an appurtenance to property in esse and owned by the mortgagor at the date of the mortgage."[65] As a rule of *inclusion* there would be much to be said for such a test. In corporate mortgages especially, "the value of the security * * * depends upon the mortgage embracing as an entirety the real and personal property of the corporation, so that in case of foreclosure the entire plant can be sold as a unit."[66] There is also another idea involved here, and a very practical one. When the mortgaged property is a business or manufacturing plant it is constantly deteriorating, wearing out or becoming obsolete and replacements are looked upon not as additional security but rather as a keeping up or restoration of the principal of the original security.[67] The same holds true of mortgages by individuals. And in their case the doctrine seems to make sense also as a rule of exclusion if regarded as merely bearing upon intention.[68] "For example, the private owner of a manufacturing plant mortgages the plant and 'all property hereafter acquired by the mortgagor'; subsequently he acquires a new residence. Most courts would probably find little difficulty in concluding that the lien of the mortgage does not embrace the mortgagor's personal home. But all property acquired by the mortgagor relating to the manufacturing plant would be included."[69] In the case of individuals the limitation also may have some connection with the policy against permitting a man to bargain himself into a position of "refined peonage."[70]

Nevertheless, the restriction has been vigorously criticised and probably would be rejected as a positive rule of law fettering a mortgagor's ability to borrow on the faith of future property without giving a mortgage presently on property with which the subsequently acquired property was connected.[71]

---

61. A mortgaged *all* his property thereafter to be acquired to secure a debt. Held, mortgage lien must be confined to property to be acquired for use in connection with a specified business. Ferguson v. Wilson, 1899, 122 Mich. 97, 80 N.W. 1006, 80 Am.St. Rep. 543, noted, 1900, 13 Harv.L.Rev. 598.

62. See 1935, 48 Harv.L.Rev. 474, 475; Note, 1953, 53 Col.L.Rev. 392, 394.

63. Vold, Sales, 2nd Ed., 241–243.

64. Morrill v. Noyes, 1863, 56 Me. 458, 467, 96 Am. Dec. 486. Ferguson v. Wilson, note 61, supra, is a similar authority.

65. Blair, The Allocation of After-Acquired Mortgaged Property Among Rival Claimants, 1926, 40 Harv.L.Rev. 222, 228. See Glenn, Mortgages, § 414.
See also Durfee, Cases on Security, 1951, 457; Note, 1953, 53 Col.L.Rev. 392, 394–398.

66. 1935, 23 Cal.L.Rev. 628, 631.

67. See Glenn, Mortgages, § 432; 1935, 23 Cal.L. Rev. 628, 631.

68. Cohen and Gerber, The After-Acquired Property Clause, 1939, 87 U. of Pa.L.Rev. 635, 652.

69. Cohen and Gerber, The After-Acquired Property Clause, 1939, 87 U. of Pa.L.Rev. 635, 653.

70. See, under Description, supra.

71. See Note, 1953, 53 Col.L.Rev. 392, 397; Cohen and Gerber, The After-Acquired Property Clause, 1939, 87 U. of Pa.L.Rev. 635, 647, 650; 1935, 23 Cal.L.Rev. 628, 630. Cf. Glenn, Mortgages, § 432.
"Property thereafter acquired by the mortgagor itself will be subject to the mortgage, if within the description of the covenant, however alien it may be in quality or function to the property presently subjected to the lien." Guaranty Trust Co. v. N. Y. & Q. R. Co., 1930, 253 N.Y. 190, 199, 170 N.E. 887, 895, reargument denied 254 N.Y. 126, 172 N.E. 264, dismissed 51 S.Ct. 86, 282 U.S. 803, 75 L.Ed. 722.

Floating charge. In Great Britain a device known as a floating charge is commonly used to secure corporate indebtedness. It amounts to an equitable charge upon all of the "assets for the time being of a going concern. It attaches to the subject charged in the varying condition it happens to be from time to time. It is of the essence of such a charge that it remains dormant until the undertaking charged ceases to be a going concern or until the person in whose favor the charge is created intervenes." [72] Its most important feature is "the power of the corporation to 'do business in due course' without interference from debenture holders, and without tying up with fixed charges large corporate assets which could be more productively applied to business uses." [73] The closest analogy to it in the United States is the chattel mortgage on stocks in trade with the mortgagor left in possession with a power of sale.[74] Since it does not exist in this country,[75] although its virtues have been expounded and arguments presented that there are no obstacles to a judicial adoption of it, it is mentioned here for two purposes only. One is to suggest by illustration how wide and indefinite may be the boundaries of the concept "equitable mortgage". The other is to differentiate this British device from the type of equitable mortgage here being dealt with.[76]

Character of the mortgagor: Railroad and other public utilities, private corporations, individuals. The character of the mortgagor has been suggested as a factor in determining both the validity of mortgages of after-acquired property and their coverage. This idea originated in early railroad bond mortgages and was extended to other types of public utilities and corporations. It poses the question whether there are sound reasons for accepting it as a basis for drawing distinctions.

The practical necessity of financing the development of the American railroad system in the nineteenth century drove the courts to a recognition of the after-acquired property clause in the case of railroad corporations. "As a practical proposition, it is well known that most, if not all, of the railroads of any length in the United States * * * have been constructed by issuing, in advance, bonds upon their entire lines, including the unbuilt portions as well as those already constructed, with mortgages to secure the bonds covering the whole." [77] A good many authorities attempt to treat the railroads as an exceptional separate class,[78] founding the distinction upon several grounds: First, "the necessity or public policy of preserving intact and holding together the whole of a railroad or system of railroads * * * " in continued operation.[79] Second, the statutory authority given to railroad companies to borrow money and mortgage

For some examples of what after-acquired property clauses are construed as intending to cover, see Foley and Pogue, after-acquired Property under Conflicting Corporate Mortgage Indentures, 1929, 13 Minn.L.Rev. 85 ; 1945, 32 Va.L.Rev. 177.

72. Government etc. Investment Co. v. Manila Rail Co., [1897] A.C. 81, 86. See Curtis, The Theory of the Floating Charge, 1941, 4 U. Toronto L.Rev. 131.

73. Note, 1928, 28 Col.L.Rev. 360. See Jacobs, The Effect of Provision for Ratable Protection of Debenture Holders in Case of Subsequent Mortgage, 1938, 52 Harv.L.Rev. 77, 88 et seq.

74. See Availability of the Floating Charge as a Security Device in the United States, 1928, 28 Col.L. Rev. 360.

75. See Howard v. Iron & Land Co., 1895, 62 Minn. 298, 301, 64 N.W. 896, 898.

76. See Glenn, Mortgages, § 426. See also the discussion of negative covenants and agreements to

pay out proceeds of the sale of property, infra §§ 44, 45.

77. Georgia Southern & Florida R. R. v. Mercantile Trust, etc. Co., 1894, 94 Ga. 306, 320, 21 S.E. 701, 706, 32 L.R.A. 208, 47 Am.St.Rep. 153. See Platt v. N. Y. & Sea Beach Ry., 1896, 9 App.Div. 87, 41 N. Y.S. 42, 72 St.R. 497, affirmed 1897, 153 N.Y. 670, 48 N.E. 1106; Philadelphia, Wilmington & Baltimore R. Co. v. Woelpper, 1870, 64 Pa. 366, 373; note, 1940, 26 Va.L.Rev. 104, 109; Machen, Modern Law of Corporations, 1502.

78. See Miss. Val. Co. v. Chicago, etc. R. Co., 1881, 58 Miss. 896, 904, 38 Am.Rep. 348.

79. See In re Adamant Plaster Co., D.C.N.Y.1905, 137 F. 251, 255, quoting from Cook, Corporations, § 857.

not only their property but their franchises to acquire property and operate the roads. This is viewed as carrying with it, as an incident of the franchises, future acquired property even though the rule in other cases might be that a mortgage of after-acquired property is ineffective.[80] Third, since the stations, tracks, engines, cars, and machinery are necessarily undergoing constant wear and deterioration, the mortgages would have little value if they did not extend to what took the place of such property.[81] Fourth, such corporations mortgage all their property so habitually that persons dealing with such corporations are not misled.[82] It was quickly realized that these reasons, even if valid, would apply to public service corporations generally and the rule was enlarged to cover them [83] and, today, in spite of some

opinion that the doctrine goes no further than this,[84] it is clear that it extends to private corporations.[85] While the first reason above might not apply to private corporations it provides only an additional and not the chief justification of the rule, i.e., the desirability of promoting productive enterprise by permitting the use of future acquisitions as security for credit expansion.[86] The second explanation has been vigorously criticised and, again, would merely add another basis for the rule.[87] The third reason applies as much to one type of corporation as another. While there is something in the fourth, it is doubtful whether such a line of demarcation could be drawn between the bonds of a big steel corporation and a small city traction company.

A recent scholarly and thorough survey of the development of (and limitations on) the priority for purchase-money security interests provided for by after-acquired property clauses, traces its application first in the railroad cases and then in the case of industrial, particularly the manufacturing corporation.[88] In the railroad cases, the "resolution of the priority problem was, apparently, satisfactory to all concerned and became the established pattern for railroad finance: the 'permanent structure' of the road was reserved as security for the bondholders; the rolling stock—'loose property'

---

80. See Seymour v. The Canandaigua Railroad Co., 1857, 25 Barb., N.Y., 284, 308, 14 How.Pr. 531; Platt v. New York & Sea Beach R. Co., 1896, 9 App.Div. 86, 41 N.Y.S. 42, 72 St.R. 497, affirmed 1897, 53 N.Y. 670, 48 N.E. 1106; Buck v. Seymour, 1878, 46 Conn. 156; Morrill v. Noyes, 1863, 56 Me. 458, 96 Am.Dec. 486; Pierce v. Emery, 1856, 32 N. H. 484; Pierce v. Milwaukee & St. P. R. R. Co., 1869, 24 Wis. 551, 1 Am.Rep. 203.

"A mortgage by a public utility corporation is valid in respect to after-acquired property necessary and appropriate for its physical operation under its franchise and the performance of its public duties." Ithaca Trust Co. v. Ithaca Traction Corp., 1928, 248 N.Y. 322, 328, 162 N.E. 93, 95. See, also, Glenn, Mortgages, § 423. Cf. Parker v. New Orleans, B. R. & V. R. Co., C.C.La., 1888, 33 F. 693, reversed 12 S.Ct. 364, 143 U.S. 42, 36 L.Ed. 66; Louisville Trust Co. v. Cincinnati Inclined-Plane Ry. Co., C.C.Ohio, 1897, 91 F. 699. "The right to mortgage after-acquired property is not necessarily dependent on the right to mortgage franchises." Compton v. Jesup, C.C.Ohio, 1895, 68 F. 263, 287, 15 C.C. 397, certified questions answered 17 S.Ct. 795, 167 U.S. 1, 42 L.Ed. 55. Butler v. Rahm, 1876, 46 Md. 541.

81. "Had the road even been fully equipped at the date of the mortgage, can it be doubted that the legislature meant that it should comprise everything subsequently acquired to replace old and worn-out materials, and to maintain and keep up the equipment." Philadelphia, Md. & Balt. R. Co. v. Woelpper, 1870, 64 Pa. 366, 373. See Shaw v. Bell, 1877, 95 U.S. 10, 15, 24 L.Ed. 333; Williston, Transfers of After-Acquired Personal Property, 1906, 19 Harv.L.Rev. 557, 576.

82. Williston, supra, note 81.

83. See Cook, Corporations, 7th ed., 1913, 3238.

84. See Hamilton, Future Property Clauses in Corporate Mortgages, 1930, 4 Temp.L.Q. 131; Cook, op. cit. supra, note 83. For a collection of a few authorities preserving the distinction between public service corporations and private corporations, see Cohen and Gerber, supra note 68, 649.

85. Hickson Lumber Co. v. Gay Lumber Co., 1909, 150 N.C. 282, 63 S.E. 1045, 21 L.R.A.,N.S. 843; Mason v. Citizen's Nat. Trust and Savings Bank of Los Angeles, C.C.A.Cal., 1934, 71 F.2d 246, 23 Cal.L. Rev. 628; Maxwell v. Wilmington Dental Mfg. Co., C.C.Del., 1896, 77 F. 938; Williston, supra note 81, 575. See also Note, 1953, 53 Col.L.Rev. 392.

86. Cohen and Gerber, supra note 68, 649.

87. Jones, Corporate Bonds & Mortgages, §§ 95, 97; Williston, supra note 81, 576.

88. Gilmore, Security Interests in Personal Property, §§ 28.1–28.3.

in Mr. Justice Bradley's phrase—came in subject to purchase-money priority under one or another variant of the railroad equipment trust." [89]

The judicially devised solution in the railroad cases could not with literal accuracy fit the pattern of the industrial, particularly the manufacturing corporation. In these corporations there is nothing that corresponds to the "loose property"—the rolling stock of the railroad. The machines and other fixed equipment were like part of the "permanent structure" of the railroads. Consequently it was agreed that the lien of a mortgage would cover later additions to the plant either under the doctrine of accession as fixtures or as falling under an after-acquired property clause or both. [90]

The problem of priority between the existing mortgage and the purchase-money security interest in the later affixed equipment presented the difficulty of reconciliation with the railroad cases. Under them, since the addition looked just like a part of the "permanent structure" the mortgage lien would prevail over the purchase-money security interest. Nevertheless by 1920, aside from a few minority or "Massachusetts rule" jurisdictions it was established that the prior mortgagee claiming under the doctrine of accession or an after-acquired property clause would be subordinated to the purchase-money security interest later furnished to the enterprise, even when the equipment was affixed to the realty. [91] This statement must be qualified by a consideration of the law dealing with the subject of retained security interests in chattels later annexed to realty both as developed by court decision and by statutory enactment. [92]

To differentiate between corporations and individuals offers a more defensible ground for distinction, certainly so far as imposing some limitations are concerned. Nevertheless, the foundation cases establishing the doctrine of equitable mortgages of after-acquired property were unincorporated manufacturers. [93] And it would be economically undesirable to deprive individuals entirely of this source of credit. [94] Courts generally refuse to do so [95] in spite of the fact that the dangers of peonage and greater likelihood of deception of third parties which exist in the case of individuals probably account for limitations that are found where they are involved.

Character of property. It has been argued persuasively that the nature of the property to be acquired in the future is one of the most important factors in determining the validity of mortgages of such assets. [96] Thus the recognition and the extent of protection accorded to such mortgages of stocks of goods held for resale would depend upon considerations inapplicable or applicable to a greatly different degree than to similar mortgages of future crops, of personalty used in business, and of land. Explicit judicial recognition of such a thesis is lacking. Such an analysis is nevertheless helpful in reconciling the actual decisions of cases in these varied groups. One clear thing on the authorities is that mortgages of land to be

---

89. Gilmore, supra note 88, p. 753.

90. Gilmore, op. cit. supra, note 88, § 283.

91. Gilmore, op. cit. supra note 88, § 28.4.

92. See §§ 217–220 infra.

93. Mitchell v. Winslow, C.C.Me., 1843, 17 Fed.Cas. No. 9673; Holroyd v. Marshall, 1862, 10 H.L.Cas. 191.

94. See Ginsburg, Mortgages of After-Acquired Personalty in Illinois, 1933, 11 Neb.L.Bull. 289, 290.

95. See Mississippi Valley Co. v. Chicago, St. Louis, and New Orleans R. Co., 1881, 58 Miss. 896, 904, 38 Am.Rep. 348. Cohen and Gerber, supra note 68, 650 n. 82. In the case of a corporation there would not ordinarily be as clear grounds for cutting down the scope of an all inclusive clause. But even in such cases there might be evidence that the coverage was intended to be limited to the property related to the type of business carried on at the time the mortgage was given. See Cohen and Gerber, supra note 68, 853.

96. Cohen and Gerber, supra note 71, 654–661; Williston, Transfers of After-Acquired Personal Property, 1906, 19 Harv.L.Rev. 557, 558.

acquired in the future will be upheld,[97] and probably for the reason that the dangers of peonage and of notice to third parties are at a minimum in them. The same reasoning would apply to all sorts of capital goods used in a business and provides an explanation, perhaps, of cases that are expressed in terms of description or the *in praesenti* doctrine.

AFTER-ACQUIRED PROPERTY— PRIORITY

40. **The principle determining the priority of mortgages of after-acquired property is that the lien arises only when the property is acquired, "and in the condition in which it is acquired, and subject to all existing liens."** [98]

Priority. Although the whole problem of priority is reserved for extensive treatment in a later chapter it is desirable to note briefly here that the equitable mortgage of after-acquired property when it attaches generally will prevail over creditors of the mortgagor[99] but will be postponed to subsequent bona fide purchasers[1] and take subject to existing equities.[2] The fundamental principle is that an after-acquired property clause "creates a lien upon property subse-

quently acquired only when it is acquired, and in the condition in which it is acquired, and subject to all existing liens."[3] The application of recording acts to equitable mortgages of after-acquired property will be discussed later.[4]

AFTER-ACQUIRED PROPERTY— TRANSFER OF PROPERTY

41. **Where property subject to a mortgage with an after-acquired property clause is transferred and the transferee subsequently acquires property falling within the terms of the clause, it does not become subject to the mortgage unless the clause most explicitly covers the property and**

(1) The clause purports to bind successors as to future property, the successor clearly assumes this obligation, and the property acquired is used in connection with the property originally mortgaged; or

(2) The successor assumes a covenant to maintain or replace the mortgaged property and acquires and uses property for such purposes; or

(3) The doctrine of accession applies, in which case the clause is immaterial.

In the absence of statute these principles apply to transfers by mortgagor-corporations by merger or consolidation. Statutes frequently subject successor corporations to the mortgage obligations, including after-acquired property clauses, of predecessors.

Where property bound by an after-acquired property clause is subsequently acquired by a successor to serve a consolidated property though some authority would prorate the security no dogmatic rule is possible. Similarly, when there is a conflict between after-acquired property clauses binding upon a successor and similar clauses in mortgages executed by the successor, the results cannot be stated with certainty.

"It is axiomatic that A cannot mortgage B's present property. A fortiori A cannot

---

97. Howard v. Iron & Land Co., 1895, 62 Minn. 298, 64 N.W. 896; Pere Marquette R. R. v. Graham, 1904, 136 Mich. 444, 99 N.W. 408; Blum v. Planters' Bank & Trust Co., 1931, 161 Miss. 226, 135 So. 353; Ehret v. Price, 1927, 122 Okl. 277, 254 P. 748; Lang v. Choctaw, O. & G. R. R., C.C.A.Ark., 1912, 198 F. 38, 117 C.C.A. 146, certiorari denied, 1913, 227 U.S. 680, 33 S.Ct. 463, 57 L.Ed. 701. See Glenn, Mortgages, §§ 412, 418, 419; 1941, 25 Minn.L.Rev. 514; Massachusetts Gasoline & Oil Co. v. Go-Gas Co., 1927, 259 Mass. 585, 593, 156 N.E. 871, 874; Maher v. Smead Heating & Ventilating Co., 1896, 11 Ohio C.C. 381, contra.

98. Central Trust Co. of New York v. Kneeland, 1891, 138 U.S. 414, 423, 11 S.Ct. 357, 359, 34 L.Ed. 1014.

99. Foley and Pogue, After-Acquired Property under Conflicting Corporate Mortgage Indentures, 1929, 13 Minn.L.Rev. 80, 84.

See Cunningham and Tischler, Equitable Real Estate Mortgages, 1963, 17 Rutgers L.Rev. 679, 720–721.

1. Hickson Lumber Co. v. Gay Lumber Co., 1909, 150 N.C. 282, 63 S.E. 1045, 21 L.R.A.,N.S., 843.

2. See Blair, supra note 65, 240 et seq.; Glenn, Mortgages, § 416.

3. Central Trust Co. of New York v. Kneeland, 1891, 138 U.S. 414, 423, 11 S.Ct. 357, 359, 34 L.Ed. 1014.

See Cunningham and Tischler, Equitable Real Estate Mortgages, 1963, 17 Rutgers L.Rev. 679, 721.

4. See Chapter 7, infra. See also Glenn, Morts., § 418.

mortgage B's future property. Any attempt to do so can have no effect upon B or upon B's property." [5] "To spread the lien of the mortgage to property acquired by [purchasers, and even at times, successors], there must be an independent ground of duty. This may have its origin in a statute or in a covenant of assumption or in principles of estoppel or accession, or in some other kindred equity." [6]

These staatements may be accepted but it is still necessary to examine both the catalogue and the operation of the independent grounds of duty in cases where the mortgaged property is transferred to a person other than the mortgagor.[7] Further, at the outset, it is desirable to differentiate between kinds of transfers. Transfer by ordinary purchase and conveyance is one class which may occur regardless of the nature of the mortgagor. In the case of corporate mortgagors, however, there is the additional possibility of transfer by merger, consolidation, or reorganization.[8] Regardless of how the transfer is effected there is a successor to the mortgagor who is a distinct and different person,[9] but in the second type of

transfer the governing statutory provisions have to be considered as a separate factor bearing upon the rights of the original mortgagee.[10]

To put our problem concretely, let us suppose that corporation A gives a mortgage containing in it an after-acquired property clause. After this we can assume that several things happen: 1. A acquires future property falling within the clause and then transfers the mortgaged property to corporation B either by a. ordinary sale and conveyance, or b. by merger, etc.[11] 2. B then acquires property which would have been subject to the clause had there been no transfer and the property had been obtained by A. 3. A then acquires some property which would have fallen under the clause had it retained the mortgaged property. In addition to these situations we can complicate the second by supposing that B, prior to the acquisition of A's mortgaged property, had executed a mortgage with an after-acquired property clause in it and that the property acquired later fell within the description of this clause as well as that in A's mortgage.[12] The question in all these cases is to what extent A's original mortgagee can reach the various parcels of after-acquired property

---

5.　Foley and Pogue, After-Acquired Property under Conflicting Mortgage Indentures, 1929, 13 Minn.L. Rev. 81, 87. See Trust Co. of America v. City of Rhinelander, Wis., C.C.Wis., 1910, 182 F. 64, 69; Metropolitan Trust Co. of City of N. Y. v. Chicago, etc., R. Co., C.C.A.Ill., 1919, 253 F. 868, certiorari denied 248 U.S. 586, 39 S.Ct. 184, 63 L.Ed. 434.

6.　Guaranty Trust Co. v. N. Y. & Q. C. Ry. Co., 1930, 253 N.Y. 190, 199, 170 N.E. 887, 890, reargument denied 254 N.Y. 126, 172 N.E. 264, dismissed 51 S.Ct. 86, 282 U.S. 803, 75 L.Ed. 722, per Cardozo, J.

7.　See Friedman, The Scope of Mortgage Liens, 1938, 7 Fordham L.Rev. 331, 360.

8.　See Ballantine, Corporations, §§ 237, 240, 248.

9.　The term "successor" as used in after-acquired property clauses has been construed to mean "those successor corporations that preserve or continue the corporate *persona*." Cardozo, J., in Guaranty Trust Co. v. N. Y. & Q. C. Ry. Co., 1930, 253 N.Y. 190, 200, 170 N.E. 887, 895, reargument denied 254 N.Y. 126, 172 N.E. 264, dismissed 282 U.S. 803, 51 S.Ct. 86, 75 L.Ed. 722. This is not, however, the general construction. The parties when using it ordinarily intend to include purchasing, merging, consolidating, and reorganization companies which might succeed

to the corporate business. Ballantine, Private Corporations, 744; 1930, 16 Va.L.Rev. 823.

10.　Apart from this factor no distinction is drawn between sales and mergers, etc. See 1939, 26 Va.L. Rev. 104, 105.

11.　In merger and consolidation of corporations the merged or consolidated corporations cease to exist. Whether one corporation, B, is the survivor of the operation, as is the case in merger, or whether an entirely new corporation, C, is created, as in consolidation, does not affect our problem and is disregarded in stating it. For the differences between merger, etc., see Ballantine, Private Corporations, C. XIX. See note, 1939, 26 Va.L.Rev. 104, 105.

12.　This was the problem raised by Guaranty Trust Co. of N. Y. v. Minneapolis & St. Louis R. R., C.C. A.Minn., 1929, 36 F.2d 747; C.C.A.Minn.1931, 52 F. 2d 418, discussed in 1932, 45 Harv.L.Rev. 1403; 1932, 41 Yale L.Jour. 466; 1932, 80 U. of Pa.L.Rev. 461. See list of notes and articles, Osborne, Prop. Security, 39 n. 12 especially Foley and Pogue, 1928, 13 Minn.L.Rev. 81, 97 et seq.

either by virtue of his after-acquired property clause or some independent ground.

The first case is an easy one to explain. When A acquired the property the equitable mortgage attached to it and follows it into the hands of any transferee save a bona fide purchaser for value and without notice.[13] Such a transferee is theoretically possible. As a practical matter, there scarcely would ever be a case in which he did not know of the terms of the after-acquired clause and also that the property in question was covered by it. This is peculiarly true in the case of corporate mortgages. Although this result has been expressed in terms of "estoppel to repudiate an equitable duty subsisting at the moment of transfer," [14] apparently nothing more than the foregoing simple and elementary proposition was involved. The use of the term in this connection is both inappropriate and unfortunate since none of the various doctrines grouped under it are properly applicable.[15]

The third case also may be disposed of without serious difficulty. When A transfers the mortgaged property to B, although A still remains liable to his mortgagee for the payment of the debt, it would be an extraordinary case in which the covenant in respect to after-acquired property would continue to bind him. To be sure there is no technical reason why it could not. However, to so construe the clause would run counter to the universally accepted view that when a mortgagor disposes of the property he gave as security his connection with it ceases. In the absence of the clearest expression of intention to the contrary, it would seem that

the mortgagee would be unsuccessful in establishing that property acquired by A after transferring the original mortgaged property, even though it fell within the description of the after-acquired clause,[16] would feed his mortgage by virtue of it. That B could not bring it within the mortgage is even clearer. B can no more subject A's future property than A could B's.[17]

Where the transferee, B, is the one who acquires the property subsequent to the transfer the problem is both more common and more difficult. Although our narrower concern here is with the ability of the after-acquired property clause in the original mortgage to create an equitable mortgage in this subsequent property, an excellent way of discovering the extent of that ability is to examine the other grounds upon which courts have purported to rest the rights of the mortgagee of the transferor.

Accession. If the property acquired by the transferee is an accretion to the original property of the transferor which constitutes an accession to it under the common law of fixtures the original mortgage will fasten on it under well settled doctrines.[18] As was noted earlier,[19] there is talk in some of the cases to the effect that, in certain instances at least, the principle of accession will be applied here very liberally,[20] although that was

---

13. See Glenn, Mortgages, §§ 427, 429.

14. Guaranty Trust Co. v. N. Y. & Q. C. Ry. Co., 1930, 253 N.Y. 190, 202, 170 N.E. 887, 891, reargument denied 254 N.Y. 126, 172 N.E. 264, appeal dismissed 282 U.S. 803, 51 S.Ct. 86, 75 L.Ed. 722, Galveston H. & H. R. Co. v. Cowdrey, 1870, 78 U.S. 459, 20 L.Ed. 199, gives a similar explanation.

15. Estoppel as an explanation of rights in property subsequently acquired by a transferee is even more clearly inapplicable than here. See text immediately following. See also text and notes, supra § 38.

16. The "in praesenti" rule as a rule of *intention* of the parties would be pertinent here. It would exclude future acquisitions by A which were unconnected with the business mortgaged just as it would exclude, as not falling within the intention of the parties, an after-acquired home when the mortgage covered a business plant and "all after-acquired property."

17. See Glenn, Mortgages, § 427.

18. Trust Co. of America v. City of Rhinelander, Wis., C.C.Wis., 1910, 182 F. 64; Mississippi Valley Trust Co. v. So. Trust Co., C.C.A.Ark., 1918, 261 F. 765, 781; Hinchman v. Point Defiance Ry. Co., 1896, 14 Wash. 349, 44 P. 867.

19. See supra, § 38.

20. Look at Phoenix Iron Works Co. v. New York Security & Trust Co., C.C.A.Ky.1897, 83 F. 757, 28 C.C.A. 76. For the so-called "institutional" or "functional" test of what will be considered a fix-

not necessary to the decisions. If accession is applicable, it is scarcely necessary to repeat that it is immaterial whether there was or was not an after-acquired property clause in the predecessor's mortgage. The accession would automatically feed the mortgage when it was so affixed to the mortgaged property for the doctrine to apply.

Estoppel. If the transferee has not assumed the mortgage obligations there is no ground whatsoever for finding a representation upon which to found any sort of an estoppel. Even where there is an assumption "the successor does not represent that its after-acquired property will feed the mortgage unless the after-acquired clause on a proper construction, includes property of a successor, in which case it is not necessary to invoke estoppel." [21] Clearly neither estoppel by deed or by estate has any proper application.

"Kindred equity." Another ground which cannot be neatly pigeon-holed but is illustrative of the sort of thing which may be embraced under the "kindred equity" from the statement quoted at the outset is that "the consolidation was effected so soon after the execution of the constituent company's mortgage as either to taint the transaction with fraud or to afford a basis for a presumption that the defeasance of the lien of such mortgage was not intended." [22]

Assumption. If the transferee assumes merely the mortgage "debts and liabilities" as contrasted with the "mortgage obligations" no contract obligation to subject after-acquired property can be spelled out.[23] Even though the latter are assumed, since mortgage obligations covering after-acquired property are ordinarily construed to apply only to property acquired by the mortgagor and not to include property acquired by a successor,[24] the assumption would not subject after-acquired property of a successor to the lien of the mortgage.[25] It is only where the assumed obligation in terms purports to bind successors as to future property acquired by them that property acquired by the assuming successor may be held to feed the original mortgage in spite of the transfer. Even here one important case, by construing "successor" to mean only those persons who continue the corporate persona or entity would narrowly confine the doctrine.[26] Generally, however, the word has been held to include purchasing, consolidating, and merging corporations which might succeed to the corporate business.[27] But even this interpretation would apply only to such of the business of the transferor as the successor continued to operate and to property which would pass under the terms of the after-acquired clause, if the predecessor was still operating that business.[28] And, finally, although within the limits above, the assump-

ture as between a mortgagee of the land and a conditional vendor of a chattel, see Osborne, Cases on Property Security, 378 n. 66. The conception of the courts in the cases under discussion seems to be somewhat similar.

21. Foley and Pogue, supra, note 12, 95, 96.

22. Blair, The Allocation of After-Acquired Mortgaged Property Among Rival Claimants, 1926, 40 Harv.L.Rev. 222, 237, citing Compton v. Jesup, C.C.A.Ohio, 1895, 68 F. 263, 15 C.C.A. 397, certified questions answered 17 S.Ct. 795, 167 U.S. 1, 42 L.Ed. 55. See also, 1939, 26 Va.L.Rev. 104, 108.

23. Irving Bank-Columbia Trust Co. v. N. Y. Rys. Co., D.C.N.Y., 1923, 292 F. 429, 433, affirmed C.C.A., 1923, 292 F. 440, certiorari denied 44 S.Ct. 38, 263 U.S. 713, 68 L.Ed. 520; Mississippi Valley Trust Co. v. Southern Trust Co., C.C.A.Ark.1919, 261 F. 765, 767; Susquehanna Trust & Safe Deposit Co. v. United Telephone & Telegraph Co., C.C.A.Pa.1925, 6 F.2d 179, 181.

24. New York Security and Trust Co. v. Louisville, E. & St. L. Consol. R. Co., 1900, 102 F. 382, 398. See Foley and Pogue, supra, note 5, 85.

25. Metropolitan Trust Co. of City of New York v. Chicago & E. I. R. Co., C.C.A.Ill., 1918, 253 F. 868, certiorari denied 39 S.Ct. 184, 248 U.S. 586, 63 L.Ed. 434; but see, In re Sentenne & Green Co., D.C.N.Y. 1903, 120 F. 436, 440.

26. Guaranty Trust Co. v. N. Y. & Q. C. Ry., 1930, 253 N.Y. 190, 200, 170 N.E. 887, 890, reargument denied 254 N.Y. 126, 172 N.E. 264, dismissed 51 S.Ct. 86, 282 U.S. 803, 75 L.Ed. 722. See note 9 supra.

27. Ballantine, Private Corporations, 744.

28. See 1930, 16 Va.L.Rev. 820, 824.

tion would provide a logical basis for spreading the clause to property acquired by the successor after the transfer, no case has adopted this reasoning as the basis of its decision and the only case [29] cited in support of it can be explained on other grounds.[30] It has been pointed out not only that there is no authority holding that any such covenant would run but it would be undesirable to achieve on such a dubious analogical extension a result which can be reached by inserting in the mortgage a clause that any successor must assume the covenant.[31]

Frequently the mortgage includes a covenant to maintain or replace the mortgaged property and if the successor assumes this covenant property acquired and used for such purposes would feed the mortgage of the predecessor.[32] A distinction between mandatory and permissive covenants of this sort has been urged along with an argument that the former would be a covenant running with the land binding successors regardless of assumption.[33]

The distinction between mandatory and permissive provisions, with one qualification, seems immaterial. The test is not whether the successor was bound to acquire the future property but whether the property actually so acquired was within the terms of a clause concerning it which was binding upon him,[34] and covered that property even though acquired by the successor instead of the predecessor.[35] The qualification applies to a case where the acts of the successor might be held to be tortious because they aid in causing a breach of an affirmative obligation of the predecessor to acquire property.[36] In such a case it is possible to argue that the doctrine of specific reparation may be invoked to subject to the mortgage the property added by the successor.[37]

One final observation. Today courts will not find an assumption of an after-acquired property clause by a successor unless it is very clear that the parties intended it. This represents a reversal of the attitude of the courts towards the coverage of these provisions that prevailed in the pioneering days of the nineteenth century. It has been argued plausibly that the change is due to the fact that in the earlier cases the contemplated security for the bond issues by which enterprises in a rapidly growing economy were financed, especially railroads and utilities, was the road or plant *to be built.* Consequently, since little existing property was conveyed courts would go to great lengths in preventing transfers of any sort from cutting off the mortgage lien from the after-acquired property which provided the bulk of the security for the loan by which the project was made possible. Today, however, the new property is chiefly for the purpose of extending and improving existing facilities and not for creating completely new construction. Consequently "the courts have correspondingly tended to be unfriendly toward the extension of after-acquired property clauses to

---

29. Compton v. Jesup, C.C.A.Ohio 1895, 68 F. 263, 15 C.C.A. 397, certified questions answered 167 U.S. 1, 17 S.Ct. 795, 42 L.Ed. 55.

30. See note, 1940, 26 Va.L.Rev. 104, 110, 111.

31. Foley & Pogue, supra, note 12, 93.

32. National Bank of W. & B. v. Wilmington, N. C. & S. R. Co., 1911, 9 Del.Ch. 258, 81 A. 70, 25 Harv. L.Rev. 294, semble. See In re Sentenne & Green Co., D.C.N.Y.1903, 120 F. 436. But see, Metropolitan Trust Co. of City of New York Co. v. Chicago & E. I. R. Co., C.C.A.Ill.1918, 253 F. 868, 878, certiorari denied 248 U.S. 586, 39 S.Ct. 184, 63 L.Ed. 434.

33. Blair, Allocation of After-Acquired Mortgaged Property, 1926, 40 Harv.L.Rev. 222, 234. See also 1948, 17 Fordham L.Rev. 132; Friedman, The Scope of Mortgage Liens, 1938, 7 Fordham L.Rev. 331, 360.

34. It might be binding upon him because he assumed it or because the statute governing merger, etc. so provided.

35. See Glenn, Mortgages, § 431.

36. See Foley & Pogue, supra, note 12, 95, citing and explaining Wade v. Chicago, Springfield and St. Louis R. Co., 1893, 149 U.S. 327, 13 S.Ct. 892, 37 L. Ed. 755, on this ground although the court itself did not mention any such theory.

37. But see, 1939, 26 Va.L.Rev. 104, 110.

plant additions and improvements not contemplated when the original bonds were issued, in the belief that after-acquired property clauses should not cover all subsequent acquisitions of a corporation, and that those who furnish capital for plant improvements and additions should have a first lien thereon." [38] This attitude of the courts is the same towards the construction of statutes governing merger or consolidation of statutes, which is discussed next, as in determining whether there has been an actual assumption by a successor to the mortgagor.[39]

Consolidation of corporate mortgagor. Some earlier type statutes either did not subject the successor corporation into which the corporate mortgagor is merged or consolidated to any of the obligations of the predecessor or else used language too narrow to cover the obligation of the mortgage as distinct from the debt.[40] In such cases the problem of the mortgagee in reaching after-acquired property must be resolved upon one or another of the bases previously discussed.[41] Most statutes, however, subject the successor corporation to all of the obligations of the predecessor including the after-acquired property clause. One such statute does so upon the construed intention that the successor be a continuation of predecessor's legal existence. Consequently any property acquired by it which would have fed the mortgage if it had been acquired by the original mortgagor will feed the mortgage notwithstanding the consolidation.[42] More generally however the statute merely imposes upon the successor the mortgage obligations of the predecessor.[43] Here, as in the case of a voluntary assumption, if the after-acquired property clause expressly covers future property acquired by successors (and the term covers this particular kind of successor) [44] then "property acquired by the successor which would have fed the constituent mortgage had it been acquired prior to consolidation will feed the constituent mortgage in spite of the consolidation." [45]

Assuming that through assumption, or by force of a governing statute in the case of

---

38. 1939, 26 Va.L.Rev. 104, 111, citing as examples Guaranty Trust Co. of New York v. Minneapolis & St. L. R. R., C.C.A.Minn.1931, 52 F.2d 418; Guaranty Trust Co. v. N. Y. & Q. C. Ry., 1930, 253 N.Y. 190, 170 N.E. 887, reargument denied 254 N.Y. 126, 172 N.E. 264, dismissed 51 S.Ct. 86, 282 U.S. 803, 75 L.Ed. 722. See also, 1935, 48 Harv.L.Rev. 474, 475.

39. The Citizens Savings & Trust Co. v. The Cincinnati & Dayton Traction Co., 1922, 106 Ohio St. 577, 599, 140 N.E. 380, 387.

40. Some earlier type statutes which imposed the "debts and liabilities" of the predecessor corporate mortgagor were construed as not embracing the after-acquired property clause in the mortgage. E. g., In re New York, S. & W. R. Co., C.C.A.N.J.1940, 109 F.2d 988, certiorari denied 310 U.S. 633, 60 S.Ct. 1075, 84 L.Ed. 1402. Look also at Irving Bank-Columbia Trust Co. v. N. Y. Rys. Co., C.C.A.N.Y.1923, 292 F. 429, affirmed, C.C.A., 292 F. 440, certiorari denied 44 S.Ct. 38, 263 U.S. 713, 68 L.Ed. 520; Irvine v. N. Y. Edison Co., 1913, 207 N.Y. 425, 101 N. E. 358; Guaranty Trust Co. v. N. Y. & Q. C. R. Co., 1930, 253 N.Y. 190, 170 N.E. 887, reargument denied 254 N.Y. 126, 172 N.E. 264, dismissed 51 S.Ct. 86, 282 U.S. 803, 75 L.Ed. 722.

41. A consolidation agreement that the after-acquired property clause shall extend to property acquired by the successor would seem to be, analytically in the same category as an assumption by a transferee in an ordinary sale of mortgaged property. Such provisions are to be found occasionally or may be implied. See Blair, note 22, supra, 236; 1939, 26 Va.L.Rev. 104, 108.

42. Citizens Savings & Trust Co. v. Cincinnati & D. Traction Co., 1922, 106 Ohio St. 577, 140 N.E. 380. See Marfield v. Cincinnati, D. & T. Traction Co., 1924, 111 Ohio St. 139, 144 N.E. 689, 40 A.L.R. 357. Some statutes are more precise in stating the extent to which the successor corporation will be bound, see C. C. C. § 361(7). "Upon the merger or consolidation, as provided herein, the separate existence of the constituent corporations shall cease, except that of the surviving corporation in case of merger, and the consolidated or surviving corporation shall succeed, without other transfer, to all the rights and property of each of the constituent corporations, and shall be subject to all the debts and liabilities of each, in the same manner as if the surviving or consolidated corporation had itself incurred them.

All rights of creditors and all liens upon the property of each of said former corporations shall be preserved unimpaired, limited in lien to the property affected by such liens immediately prior to the time of the consolidation or merger. * * *"

43. See Foley & Pogue, supra note 12, p. 88 n. 30.

44. See Foley and Pogue, supra, note 12, 85.

45. 1939, 26 Va.L.Rev. 104, 107.

merger or consolidation, the after-acquired property clause itself will spread the lien of the original mortgage to some at least of the future property acquired by a successor of the mortgagor, two questions of some difficulty remain. One is to just what property will it attach? The other is how will conflicts between two different after-acquired property clauses embodied in the separate mortgages of different constituent companies, or of the successor company, which cover the same property be resolved?

The answer to the first is clearer today than to the second. Even though, as noted before, courts are more reluctant today than formerly to extend the clause to future acquisitions of the successor, insofar as the later property falls within the terms of the clause and is obtained for use solely in connection with the property which the predecessor mortgaged originally the original mortgagee can claim it.[46] On the other hand if the property in issue contributed by the successor company is not used in connection with the predecessor's business, the authorities indicate that the clause will not spread to it,[47] at least in the absence of the most explicit expression of intent.[48] The words of a great judge, Cardozo, may serve as a guide here: "To the extent that improvements, though made upon newly-acquired lands through the use of the new loan, have been charged with a lien, declared with reasonable clarity, in favor of underlying mortgage bondholders, the court will give effect, through the remedy of specific performance, to the ensuing equitable right. On the other hand, the advantages incidental to merger and consolidation would be discouraged, and new loans would be precarious, if less than reasonable clarity were exacted as a condition of subordination and extension."[49] Where the new property serves the entire consolidated business, including that of the original mortgagor, there is some authority indicating that a pro-rated allocation of the property itself, a tenancy in common in it if it is not divisible, or of the proceeds of its sale may be made.[50] But the policy considerations in favor of restricting the operation of the clause and the practical difficulties in prorating which increase with the passage of time make reliance upon what authority there is dubious and prevent any dogmatic assurance as to what the rule ought to be.[51] There has been some excellent discussion[52] of possible solutions of our second

---

46. In re New York, S. & W. R. Co., C.C.A.N.J.1940, 109 F.2d 988, certiorari denied 310 U.S. 633, 60 S.Ct. 1075, 84 L.Ed. 1402; National Bank, etc. v. Wilmington, etc., Ry., 1911, 9 Del.Ch. 258, 81 A. 70 (replacement); Citizens Savings & Trust Co., Trustee v. The Cincinnati & Dayton Traction Co., 1922, 106 Ohio St. 577, 140 N.E. 380. See Guaranty Trust Co. v. N. Y. & Queens County Ry., 1930, 253 N.Y. 190, 212, 170 N.E. 887, 895, reargument denied 254 N.Y. 126, 172 N.E. 246, dismissed 51 S.Ct. 86, 282 U.S. 803, 75 L.Ed. 722; Hamlin v. Jerrard, 1859, 72 Me. 62, 80; 1930, 16 Va.L.Rev. 824; Foley and Pogue, supra note 12, 88.

47. Metropolitan Trust Co. v. Chicago, etc., R. R., C. C.A.Ill.1918, 253 F. 868, certiorari denied 1918, 248 U.S. 586, 39 S.Ct. 184, 64 L.Ed. 434.

48. Commercial Trust Co. v. Chattanooga Ry. & Light Co., D.C.Tenn.1921, 281 F. 856.

49. Guaranty Trust Co. v. N. Y. & Q. C. Ry. Co., 1930, 253 N.Y. 190, 212, 170 N.E. 887, 895, reargument denied 254 N.Y. 126, 172 N.E. 264, dismissed 51 S.Ct. 86, 282 U.S. 803, 75 L.Ed. 722.

50. Citizens Savings & Trust Co., Trustee v. Cincinnati & Dayton Traction Co., 1922, 106 Ohio St. 577, 609, 140 N.E. 380. See Ithaca Trust Co. v. Ithaca Traction Corp., 1928, 248 N.Y. 322, 162 N.E. 93. See also, 1930, 16 Va.L.Rev. 820, 824; Foley and Pogue, supra note 5, 90; 1932, 41 Yale L.Jour. 466.

51. Although neither an assumption by agreement nor by statutory imposition was involved in Guaranty Trust Co. v. N. Y. & Q. C. R. Co., supra, note 26, the refusal of the court to extend the mortgage lien of a constituent company upon any ground so as to bind even partially a power house serving the lines of all the consolidated companies is significant.

52. See Blair, The Allocation of After-Acquired Mortgaged Property Among Rival Claimants, 1926, 40 Harv.L.Rev. 222; Foley and Pogue, After-Acquired Property Under Conflicting Corporate Mortgage Indentures, 1929, 13 Minn.L.Rev. 81; Hamilton, Future Property Clause in Corporate Mortgages, 1930, 4 Temple L.Q. 131; Goodbar, Conflicting Corporate Mortgage Indentures and After-Acquired Property, 1931, 12 Boston U.L.Rev. 648; Klooster, Mortgages of After-Acquired Railroad Property, 1933, 27 Ill.L.Rev. 781; Ginsburg, Mortgages of After-Acquired Personalty, 1933, 11 Neb. L.Bull. 289; Cohen and Gerber, After-Acquired

problem. The most important direct authority [53] adopted the principle that the mortgage which was first in time would have priority under its after-acquired property clause as to all acquisitions after transfer. It has been so vigorously criticized as to render it somewhat suspect.[54] Since the problem is essentially one of priorities the principles governing which are reserved for extensive treatment later,[55] there the matter will be left for the present.

This rather broad survey has carried into areas outside that of our immediate concern, the equitable mortgage resulting from an after-acquired property clause. So far as that narrower problem is involved in cases of transfers of the sorts we have been discussing, we can summarize by stating that an after-acquired property clause, *as such,* will bind successors only if the successor has clearly assumed it or, in the case of merged or consolidated corporations, only if the statute governing the operation has the effect of imposing its terms upon the successor corporation, and those terms include the successor. Even in such cases the lien will surely attach only to that part of the property acquired in connection with the predecessor's business. And here it may come into conflict with similar clauses of other constituent corporations with results that cannot be stated dogmatically.[56] Insofar as the mortgagee is unwilling to accept these limitations upon the operation of his security clause affecting

after-acquired property and to rely upon the increased prospects of payment resulting from the amalgamation of two or more corporations or the additional claim against an assuming grantee, he should protect himself by express stipulations. He should require that any of the types of transfers here considered must provide that, at his option,[57] they should be considered events of default which accelerate the debt and permit him to foreclose at once.[58]

AFFIRMATIVE CONDITIONAL AGREEMENTS

42. Affirmative conditional agreements to mortgage create an equitable mortgage upon the happening of the condition. There is a sharp conflict whether they create a security interest in the property before the condition happens. The parties intend to create a limited form of security interest at once on the issuance of the debentures and there is no reason why this intent should not be given effect.

Agreements to give a mortgage upon the happening of some event in the future, although found now and then in the simpler dealings of individuals,[59] have their chief use and importance in corporate debentures.[60] The term debenture is not one with a precise legal or business content.[61] Debenture issues range from completely unse-

---

Property Clause, 1939, 87 U. of Pa.L.Rev. 635; Cabell, Effect of Consolidation, etc., upon After-Acquired Property Clause, 1939, 26 Va.L.Rev. 104; 1931, 44 Harv.L.Rev. 472; 1931, 45 Harv.L.Rev. 1403; 1932, 80 U. of Pa.L.Rev. 461; 1932, 41 Yale L.J. 466; 1935, 48 Harv.L.Rev. 474.

53. Guaranty Trust Co. v. Minneapolis & St. Louis R. R., C.C.A.Minn.1931, 52 F.2d 418.

54. See 1932, 80 Univ. of Pa.L.Rev. 461; 1932, 45 Harv.L.Rev. 1403; 1932, 41 Yale L.Jour. 466. See also Foley and Pogue, supra, note 5; Glenn, Mortgages, § 430.

55. See Chapter 7, infra.

56. See note 1930, 16 Va.L.Rev. 820, 823, 824.

57. Lisman v. Michigan Peninsular Car Co., 1900, 50 App.Div. 311, 63 N.Y.S. 999. See Chapter 12, infra.

58. See Glenn, Mortgages, §§ 430, 432.

59. Ely v. Norman, 1918, 175 N.C. 294, 95 S.E. 543; Cummings v. Jackson, 1896, 55 N.J.Eq. 805, 810, 38 A. 763, 765; Wickes v. Hynson, 1902, 95 Md. 511, 514, 52 A. 747, 748; Mathews v. Damainville, 1905, 100 App.Div. 311, 91 N.Y.S. 524, 15 N.Y.Anno.Cas. 436, are examples.

60. A study by Professor Saxon of Yale showed 845 debenture issues listed in a leading investment manual in the years 1929, 1930, 1931. Of these 577 contained some sort of restrictive covenant which seemed to assure to the purchaser greater safety than the general credit of the corporation afforded. See 1932, 46 Yale L.Jour. 97.

61. See Stetson in Some Legal Phases of Corporate Financing, etc., 14.

See Gilmore, Security Interests in Personal Property, § 38.2.

cured obligations to instruments containing provisions which, in the minds of the investing public at least, purport to give the holder security which will bring him in ahead of at least the general creditors. Typical of these provisions are the ones under consideration in this and the next section. Sometimes genuine mortgage bonds have been issued with the title of "debenture."[62]

One form of such agreements is an affirmative covenant that, should the obligor thereafter mortgage its property, "this debenture and the indebtedness evidenced thereby shall participate in the security of such mortgage on equal terms with all other indebtedness or evidences of indebtedness to be secured by such mortgage."[63] The property covered by such a promise might be that existing at the date of the debenture.[64] Or it might, and usually does, include after-acquired property as well.[65] Upon the happening of the condition there exists no doubt that an equitable mortgage would exist from that moment since the promise would then be specifically enforced.[66] But the real problem is whether an equitable security interest arose before

that time, dating from the issuance of the debenture. Upon this there has been some sharp conflict of opinion centering upon the narrow question of whether the doctrinal foundation of equitable mortgages would permit finding one in this type of agreement; whether the agreement contemplated in fact a present security; and whether considerations of policy favored one result as against another.[67]

The technical argument against the equitable mortgage arising before the happening of the condition is based upon the thesis that specific performance of a promise to give security is the sole foundation of equitable mortgages and, until the condition precedent is fulfilled there will be no right to specific performance.[68] This objection, as has been pointed out in the earlier part of this chapter, is untenable. Specific performance is one but not the exclusive basis for the creation of equitable mortgages.[69] A present intention that there be an existing security interest in property is sufficient not only in cases where no right to specific performance is involved or contemplated but also where specific performance is contemplated although subject to contingencies which have not yet occurred.[70] A subsidiary objection, that the subject matter of the mortgage cannot be known with certainty until identified by the happening of the condition, i.e., the giving of a mortgage, has little merit. The description in the debenture can be perfectly adequate to point out the property covered, and the contingency of giving a mortgage on all or any part of it is no part of that description. All that the happening of the contingency does is to end any power of the obligor to withdraw from the coverage of the debenture the part of the property falling within

---

62. See 1936, 22 Va.L.Rev. 440.

63. This clause, typical of the affirmative conditional mortgage provision, is taken from Connecticut Co. v. N. Y., N. H. & H. R. Co., 1919, 94 Conn. 13, 16, 107 A. 646, 647. The first extensive use of this form of promise was in the railroad and electric railroad financing of the nineties. See Jacob, The Effect of Provision for Ratable Protection of Debenture Holders in Case of Subsequent Mortgage, 1938, 52 Harv.L.Rev. 77, 78. The negative conditional pledge clause and the straight negative covenant were later evolutions. Id. 79.

See Gilmore, Security Interests in Personal Property, § 38.2 for consideration of the Connecticut Co. case.

64. Connecticut Co. v. N. Y., N. H. & H. R. R. Co., supra, note 63.

65. Chase Nat. Bank of New York v. Sweezy, 1931, 281 N.Y.S. 487, affirmed, 1933, 261 N.Y. 710, 185 N. E. 803, reargument denied 237 App.Div. 818, 260 N. Y.S. 983, although in form a negative conditional pledge, is an example.

See Gilmore, op. cit. supra, note 63 at pp. 1002–1004 for consideration of the Sweezy case.

66. All judges in the Connecticut Co. case, supra note 63, agreed upon this. See 1920, 33 Harv.L. Rev. 456; Jacob, note 63, supra.

67. Jacob, supra note, 63 is the fullest and most competent duscussion of these various issues.

68. 1920, 33 Harv.L.Rev. 456, 457; 1936, 49 Harv.L. Rev. 619, 626.

69. See §§ 24–30, supra.

70. Jacob, note 63, supra, 92, 95.

the terms of the mortgage. Further, the fact that there exists in the obligor power to free some or all of the property from the lien of the debenture, or to add other identifiable property to it up to the time of the happening of some prescribed event, does not mean that the description of the property is inadequate. There might be some policy objection to such an arrangement, but such security cannot be attacked on the ground it is impossible to tell what property is meant. If it could be, so would an option to purchase Blackacre or any part of it fail as against a transferee of Blackacre on the ground that, until the option is exercised, the agreement does not cover any identifiable property. Even where the clause covers after-acquired property, a description sufficient to identify the property to be included where there is no contingency provided for should be sufficient where there is. However, a covenant not to mortgage "any of its property" so long as the debenture in which the covenant appeared was outstanding unless "such mortgage shall provide that this debenture shall be secured equally" was held not to apply to any specific property.[71]

The most obvious analogy to invoke in cases of this sort is that of an option to purchase land, and it has been cited by both sides to the controversy.[72] Without attempting to settle the conflict in respect to the effect of option contracts, it suffices to note that in spite of the argument of one great scholar [73] that an option is merely a unilateral offer accepted only by performance with a collateral contract to keep the offer open, and that, consequently, it creates no equitable property in-

terest in the real property which is the subject of the option, there is excellent and probably preferable authority that the holder of an option does have an equitable property interest in the optioned land.[74] Certainly the

71. Kelly v. Central Hanover Bank & Trust Co., D. C.N.Y.1935, 11 F.Supp. 497, 508, case remanded, C. C.A., 85 F.2d 61.

See Gilmore, op. cit. supra note 63 for an exposition of the facts and holding by Judge Mack in the Kelly case together with an appraisal of reasoning.

72. See 1920, 33 Harv.L.Rev. 456; Jacob, supra, note 63, 95. For other analogies, see Jacob, supra, 97, 98. See also 1949, 10 Montana L.Rev. 70.

73. Langdell, Summary of Contracts, § 178. See McClintock, Equity, § 53, n. 30.

74. Horgan v. Russell, 1913, 24 N.D. 490, 499–501, 140 N.W. 99, 102–103, 43 L.R.A.,N.S., 1150. See, 1913, 26 Harv.L.Rev. 747. Cf. Ludy v. Zumwalt, 1927, 85 Cal.App. 119, 130, 259 P. 52. But in Chapman v. Great Western Gypsum Co., 1932, 216 Cal. 420, 428, 14 P.2d 758, 761, 85 A.L.R. 917, an option held by a lessee was held to be a covenant running with the land which bound any transferree with notice from the lessor. The court said, "The phrase 'interest in land' is meaningless unless the total of rights included therein is defined. It is true that a contract to purchase land is bilateral in the sense that it may be enforced by either party, while an option contract is enforceable only by the holder thereof, and an option holder cannot be compelled to buy. But in both cases the owner of the land has parted with one of the rights incidental to ownership—the right to convey the property to any but the vendee or optionee. Whether this constitutes bestowing on the optionee an 'interest' in the land we deem immaterial."

See 1933, 85 A.L.R. 927; 1927, 50 A.L.R. 1314. An option to purchase land is within the Statute of Frauds. Granger Real Estate Exch. v. Anderson, Tex.Civ.App., 1912, 145 S.W. 262. See Wiliston, Contracts, Rev.Ed., § 491. Knight v. Chamberlain, 1957, 6 Utah 2d 394, 315 P.2d 273, noted, 1957, 5 Utah L.Rev. 565, held, an option to purchase real estate was an interest in land subject to the Utah Statute of Frauds.

As to the doctrine of equitable conversion in option cases, see McClintock, Equity, § 103. The fact that on the death of the option holder the right to exercise the option and the right to receive the conveyance when the option is exercised goes to the personal representative may be argued to be evidence that there is no equitable interest in the land created by the option. However, equitable conversion in such cases depends upon factors not necessarily determinative of whether the contract creates an equitable property interest or not. The one who succeeds to the assets with which the price will be paid has a claim to get the property paid for regardless of its character.

An option to purchase land has been held to be within the meaning of acts requiring recordation of conveyances of interests in land. Chesbrough v. Vizard Investment Co., 1915, 156 Ky. 149, 160 S.W. 725; Fields & Comas v. Vizard Investment Co., 1916, 168 Ky. 744, 182 S.W. 934; Donnally v. Parker, 1872, 5 W.Va. 301. Cf. Ludy v. Zumwalt, supra. However, see Chapman v. Great Western Gypsum Co., 1932, 216 Cal. 420, 433, 14 P.2d 758, 85 A.L.R. 917 (lease with option to purchase contrasted with bare option). See 1927, 27 Col.L.Rev. 749, 751. For an extensive collection of authorities on whether an option contract creates an interest in the land optioned, see Chafee and Simpson, Cases on Equity, 901, n. 2. See also Ames, Cases on Equity, 491, n. 2. Although a conditional agreement to give a

authority is clear that anyone who buys or takes a mortgage on property which is subject to an option with notice of that option will take subject to the holder's right to specific performance should he later take it up.[75] Since this is so, "there does exist during the interim period an interest in X [the option holder] of such character that a purchaser from Y [the giver of the option] with notice cannot take clear of it. Whether this interest be called an equitable lien or whether, as Maitland might call it, it is a mere personal right valid against anyone taking the property with notice of it seems scarcely im-

portant."[76] On authority, therefore, the analogy does not preclude holding that there is an equitable mortgage here before the condition is fulfilled.

The matter of *intent* that a security interest exist prior to the happening of the condition is more arguable. The courts have not confined their inquiry to the bare words of the clause but have gone into the circumstances surrounding the issue of the debentures in order to determine what the parties intended.[77] There seems little doubt that, so far as the investing public is concerned, "when an investor buys a debenture he has the idea that he is somewhat or other of a secured creditor."[78] And in one of the most important cases, testimony of an official of the issuing company given before a legislative committee for the purpose of establishing the debentures as a legal investment for savings banks was relied upon to bind the company. The court said that while the "statements * * * of course do not make the contract, they are definite and forcible expositions of what the company, at the time debentures were issued, believed the contract to mean, and at any rate are what it wished the savings banks and other investors should believe that it meant."[79] On the oth-

---

mortgage has been held to be unrecordable, Mathews v. Damainville, 1905, 100 App.Div. 311, 91 N.Y.S. 524, the holding has been questioned, Stone, The "Equitable Mortgage" in New York, 1920, 20 Col.L.Rev. 519, 523, and there is authority the other way. Todd v. Eighmie, 1896, 4 App.Div. 9, 38 N.Y.S. 304, 73 St.R. 671. See Stone, supra, 523, n. 19.

75. "If A contracts to mortgage his horse to B if it rains next Thursday, and B advance the money, before Thursday B will have no property right. But if A before Thursday gives his horse to C, or C purchases it with notice of the agreement, and Thursday is rainy, B should be able to compel a mortgage of the horse from C. Such is the result in the case of an option to buy land. A donee or purchaser with notice from the vendor must convey to the option holder if the latter exercises his option. Ross v. Parks, 1890, 93 Ala. 153, 8 So. 368, 11 L.R.A. 148, 30 Am.St.Rep. 47; Calanchini v. Branstetter, 1890, 84 Cal. 249, 24 P. 149; Horgan v. Russell, 1913, 24 N.D. 490, 140 N.W. 99, 43 L.R.A., N.S., 1150; Faraday Coal & Coke Co. v. Owens, 1904, 80 S.W. 1171, 26 Ky.Law Rep. 243; Sizer v. Clark, 1903, 116 Wis. 534, 93 N.W. 539; Forney v. City of Birmingham, 1911, 173 Ala. 1, 55 So. 618. No better reason can be assigned for this rule than that it is unconscionable for C thus to prevent performance of a bargain of which he has knowledge. Dean Ames suggested unjust enrichment. See 'Specific Performance for and against Strangers to the Contract' [1904] 17 Harv.L.Rev. 174." 1920, 33 Harv.L.Rev. 456, 457 n. 9. The statement that "before Thursday B will have no property right" seems an unwarranted conclusion. Certainly B has some sort of right in respect to that horse before Thursday. See text.

"A gives B an option to purchase land. A then sells to C within the option period, C having notice. B can get the land. And I urge upon your consideration that he gets it, not by way of specific performance against C, with whom he never contracted, but by way of reparation by C, who interfered with his reasonable property expectancy based on contract." Jacob, note 63, supra, 114.

76. Jacob, note 63, supra, 96. See the discussion in the next two sections of the text.

77. See Connecticut Co. v. N. Y., N. H. & H. R. R. Co., 1919, 94 Conn. 13, 44, 107 A. 646, 656; Kelly v. Central Hanover Bank & Trust Co., D.C.N.Y.1935, 11 F.Supp. 497, 503, case remanded, C.C.A., 85 F.2d 61.

78. Jacob, note 63 supra, 80.

79. Connecticut Co. v. N. Y., N. H. & H. R. R. Co., 1919, 94 Conn. 13, 44, 107 A. 646, 656. See also 1936, 22 Va.L.Rev. 440, 453; Jacob, note 63, supra, 87, "If I read the corporate mind aright, the purpose was * * * to get as much money as possible, on as little security as possible, but with as great appearance of security as possible.
"* * * to obtain as much money as possible and yet leave specific assets as free as possible * * * it seems to give security, and yet provides only for the lesser of two evils in which security will be needed—provides for mortgage, does not provide for bankruptcy. * * * The investment mind * * * was looking to security; not to the security of a first mortgage bond, it is

er hand, the fact that the obligor can prevent,[80] and no doubt was intended to be able to prevent, the condition ever happening has been relied upon as indicating there was an intention that there be no hold upon any of the property before the condition occurred. In fact there is judicial opinion that such a power is necessarily inconsistent with the existence of any lien, regardless of intention.[81]

Both of these conclusions may be disputed. It is true that if the obligor transfers the property to any purchaser or if it is levied on and sold by some other creditor the debenture holder's interest in it will be cut off for good and all. As a matter of fact we may even grant that as against such persons the holder had no security interest in the property prior, at least, to the happening of the condition. However, it is just as clear that the holder was intended to get and would get a security interest from the outset in the property as against any subsequent mortgagee of the property with notice of the debenture claim. Ordinarily it is true that an equitable mortgage will give priority in the security against people generally except subsequent bona fide purchasers. But neither the fact that the security is good only against one

group of claimants nor that the obligor has power to free it from even this claim [82] necessarily precludes the idea of there being an equitable lien to this limited extent. It may well be that the term *mortgage* should be reserved for those security interests having the full and customary quota of security features. However, there seems no compelling reason why a lesser protection should not be included within a broader description such as equitable *security*. At any rate, regardless of what we call it that is what the parties intended here. And, unless there is some policy reason to forbid it, that is what the debenture holder should get, i .e., an interest in the property from the instant the debenture is issued, which will give him equal standing as to any of the property within the description of the debenture with any subsequent mortgagee with notice.[83] Perhaps, we should point out, also, that in addition to the interest in the property prior to the happening of the condition being available only against one limited group of possible claimants, one other feature of the ordinary concept of a mortgage is absent here, viz., the right to foreclose.[84] Not until the condition happens will that right accrue. The absence of this feature merely emphasizes that the structure of this hold on the property by the creditor is weaker than in the more usual type of secured claim which we call a mortgage. But, again, this should not prevent it being recognized as a security interest in the property. The common law possessory lien gave no right of realization except in a few instances. Yet the absence of such a right did not pre-

---

true, but to something better than guaranty security. This was not really what the corporate mind was looking at, but it was what the corporate mind intended the investment mind to look at."

80. The option to purchase case is distinguished by one writer on the ground that while a transferee before the option is exercised will be bound nevertheless, in our case "this situation can not arise, because, if the corporation sells any of its property, they cannot later mortgage it, and as to that property the contingency can never happen." 1920, 33 Harv.L.Rev. 457, n. 9.

81. See Kelly v. Central Hanover Bank & Trust Co., D.C.N.Y.1935, 11 F.Supp. 497, 507, case remanded, C.C.A., 85 F.2d 61, "Furthermore, the company at all times, whether before or after breach of the covenant, had the right while solvent to sell all of the stock in its portfolio to a purchaser with knowledge of the restrictive covenants and of their violation. That right, although not contradictory to the restrictive covenants, is inconsistent with a right to an equitable lien on the assets."

See also Kuppenheimer & Co. v. Mornin, C.C.A.Iowa 1935, 78 F.2d 261, 265.

82. Racouillat v. Sansevan, 1867, 32 Cal. 376 is an authority for the proposition that a power in the mortgagor to sell property free and clear of the secured creditor's claim in it does not prevent there being an equitable mortgage on the property in the meantime if so intended.

83. See Jacob, note 63, supra, 99, 100.

84. Priority over the claims of third persons and the ability to realize on specific property by foreclosure are generally regarded as the two fundamental features of security so far as the rights of the secured creditor is concerned. See Storke, An Introduction to Security, 1943, 16 Rocky Mt.L.Rev. 26, 31.

vent it being classed as an important type of security.[85] Similarly, the possession of mortgaged real property by the mortgagee after the mortgage has been extinguished through the running of the statute of limitations and the possession of title deeds in England provide other examples of security with defective methods of realization.

The matter of policy [86] may be quickly disposed of. Since the debenture will not prevent the company from dealing freely with its assets, with the one exception that it cannot mortgage the particular property subject to the debenture except by giving the debenture holder equality with the mortgagee, there seems scant objection to it as fettering the free conduct of business and uselessly tying up assets. Nor does likening it to the English floating charge condemn it. Although that English device is not accepted by American courts it is doubtful whether there is any strong policy objection to it.[87] Even if there were, our affirmative conditional mortgage is distinguished from it in that its charge is upon specifically designated property rather than upon the general assets of the undertaking. Further, it is available only against subsequent mortgagees as contrasted with the protection against creditors generally afforded by the English charge in case of bankruptcy. Obviously a policy founded upon deception of creditors by the retention of a power of disposition which may seem inconsistent with the existence of any lien has no application to a security interest that does not purport to be operative against creditors generally until the power of free disposition is ended by giving a mortgage.[88]

NEGATIVE PLEDGE CLAUSES

43. **Negative conditional pledge clauses raise two questions: One is whether they can be construed to be the equivalent of the affirma-**

tive conditional mortgage clause. **The other is whether, even so, the holder can be given adequate protection. Arguments in favor of an affirmative answer to both questions are the more persuasive. On the authorities both questions may be considered open.**

Instead of the affirmative conditional mortgage clause there appears frequently, if not usually, in debenture issues what is called a negative pledge clause. By it the issuer, instead of promising affirmatively that he will give the holder an equality of position with any later mortgagee, covenants that he will *not* mortgage *unless* the debenture holder should be ratably protected. Although the actual decided cases adjudicating such clauses are few [89] one at least,[90] involving the In-

---

85. See Brown, Personal Property, c. XIII.

86. See Jacob, note 63, supra, 99, 100.

87. See 1928, 28 Col.L.Rev. 360; Jacob, note 63, supra, 98.

88. 1936, 49 Harv.L.Rev 620, 626.

89. Chase National Bank v. Sweezy, 1931, 281 N.Y. Supp. 487, affirmed mem., 1932, 236 App.Div. 835, 259 N.Y.Supp. 1010, affirmed mem., 1933, 261 N.Y. 710, 185 N.E. 803 is most squarely in point. It has been suggested that the result could have been reached on the ground that there was a breach of trust by the debenture trustee, upon which basis Kaplan v. Chase Nat. Bank, 1934, 156 Misc. 471, 281 N.Y.Supp. 825, protected the debentures. Jacob, note 63, supra, 100 n. 50. Since the court considered the fact important only insofar as it indicated that the pledgee had actual notice of the terms of the debenture this would not distinguish the case from the Kelly case cited in the next footnote, 1936, 49 Harv.L.Rev. 620, 626.

90. Kelly v. Central Hanover Bank & Trust Co., D. C.N.Y.1935, 11 F.Supp. 497, reversed and sent back for further findings on the question, inter alia, whether the banks involved had knowledge of the restrictive covenants in the debentures, C.C.A.N.Y. 1936, 85 F.2d 61. The litigation was later compromised. The case is discussed in The Insull Case, 1936, 49 Harv.L.Rev. 620; Jacob, The Effect of Provision for Ratable Protection of Debenture Holders in Case of Subsequent Mortgage, 1938, 52 Harv.L.Rev. 77; Protection for Debenture Holders, 1936, 46 Yale L.J. 97; note, 1935, 30 Ill.L.Rev. 487; note 1936, 22 Va.L.Rev. 440; note, 1936, 36 Col.L.Rev. 319. The court decided that the negative pledge clause itself had not been violated as to some of the banks; that the acceleration clause gave an adequate legal remedy against all except one defendant because the issuer was solvent at the time of breach; and that as to the one defendant who violated the restrictive clauses when the issuer was insolvent, and against whom therefore an injunction might have issued, there was no claim. This was because the transaction was consummated, the court finding no equitable interest in the property pledged by reason of equitable pledge, equitable servitude, or by way of reparation for interfering with the debenture holders' contract rights or participat-

sull manipulations, is famous. Such clauses raise two questions. One is whether this negative expression can be construed to be the equivalent of the affirmative clause previously discussed. The other is whether, even so, there is any way to give the holder protection as adequate as that of the affirmative clause. Since the two cases most directly in point [91] reached opposite conclusions both questions may be considered open.[92]

One approach to the problem of construction is to read the clause to determine what the words say as a matter of English. Literally the only words of promise are negative that the obligor will not mortgage *except on the condition* that he equally secure the debentures. That negative promise can be enforced either by way of an action at law for damages, or by, possibly, specific performance, if the condition has been broken.[93] But what is wanted is to imply an affirmative promise into the conditional clause, i. e., that the obligor will equally secure the deben-

tures. But that simply cannot be done because it is not a promise but merely a conditional clause qualifying the only promise made, namely, not to mortgage.

In answer to this it has been argued as follows: "The promise to which * * * we have the defendant bound is 'we won't do X unless we do Y.' The promise to which (in the interest of the debenture holder) we are trying to see the defendant bound is 'we will do Y if we do X'." There is authority in point [94] holding that the defendant could not do X without the prior doing of Y. In other words, out of our original negative promise not to do X unless the promisor did Y, the defendant was in effect bound to the promise "we must do Y if we will do X" and the substance of this promise is "we will do Y if we do X". Thus we arrive at the affirmative promise we seek.[95]

Another approach is less technical and, without much analysis, concludes that the difference in the wording of the two clauses does not result in a difference in meaning; that upon the total transaction security is intended and therefore will be given.[96]

Upon the second question, whether as adequate protection can be given to the holder of a debenture containing a negative mortgage clause as one with an affirmative conditional clause, the decision in the Kelly case, sharply differentiating between a right in personam against the obligor which might be enforced in advance of breach by an injunction against the obligor or third parties with notice, and a right in rem in the property which would be necessary to upset a consummated breach of the promise not to mort-

---

ing in a breach of trust. This last ground was held inapplicable because the transferees had no actual knowledge of the terms of the covenants and the doctrine did not extend to negligent interferences.

For a discussion of some of the methods by which breach of restrictive covenants in debentures may be and are avoided, see 1936, 46 Yale L.Jour. 97.

91. The Kelly and Sweezy cases, supra notes 84, 85. The Kelly case attempted to distinguish the Sweezy case on the ground that the latter did not contain an acceleration clause but it has been pointed out that there was an acceleration clause in it. 1936, 49 Harv.L.Rev. 620, 624.

92. The best discussion is in an excellent article by Jacob, note 63, supra. The text rather inadequately, in spite of direct quotations, does little more than express salient points in it. For a resume of three cases to add to the Kelly and Sweezy cases see Gilmore, Security Interests in Personal Property, § 38.3. None of them supported the proposition that a purely negative covenant creates an interest in the property subject to the covenant. In § 38.4 Professor Gilmore reviewed case law analogies and jurisprudential doctrine and concluded "that the beneficiaries of negative covenants (apart from debenture holders) have had little success in asserting claims against third parties, either to the property subject to the covenant or to its proceeds."

93. Whether such a pure negative covenant standing alone will create an equitable mortgage is considered in the next section.

94. Manchester Ship Canal Co. v. Manchester Racecourse Co. [1901] 2 Ch. 37.

95. Jacob, note 63, supra, 106.

96. See 1936, 36 Col.L.Rev. 319, 320; 1936, 49 Harv. L.Rev. 620, 624. In the Sweezy case the court stressed the fact that the debenture holders could have obtained injunctive relief against a proposed violation of the covenant by the company. Sweezy case, supra note 89, 491.

gage [97] is rather strong authority in the negative. The argument in the affirmative rests upon the thesis that regardless of whether the clause is in form negative or affirmative, the debenture holder has an expectancy in his favor affecting the property resting not on the express or implied promises as such but "upon a reasonable anticipation that the undertaking would be fulfilled upon the contingency of mortgage." To protect this, reparation is "available against any person taking not for value or with notice, upon the happening of the contingency." [98] Therefore, before the happening of the contingency there exists a "negative equitable lien." And, finally, "There is not a fine line between equitable property interests on the one hand, and, on the other, contracts personal but affecting property as against persons with notice." [99]

PURELY NEGATIVE COVENANTS

44. Purely negative covenants not to mortgage certain property while the obligation of the owner remains unpaid do not, on the authorities, create any security interest in the property in the promisee. Even here it is arguable that, to a limited extent, it should do so. And an important recent case indicates it may do so.

The purely negative covenant not to mortgage certain property while the obligation of the owner remains unpaid seems, on the authorities,[1] pretty clearly not to create any security interest in the promisee. "The creation of a lien is an affirmative act, and the intention to do such an act cannot be implied from an express negative." [2] Yet it seems probable that under certain circumstances [3] the covenantor might be enjoined from violating his promise and third persons with notice could be prevented from taking a mortgage.[4] This right, however, has been said as we have seen, to rest upon the protection of a purely in personam contract right rather than upon an equitable lien.[5] To this may be given again the answer that "The fine line between an equitable interest in property, and a personal right affecting property and not subject to interference by persons taking not for value, and with notice, is simply the fine line which Maitland undertook to preserve by calling the interest of a *cestui que trust* a right in personam." [6]

In 1964 the case of Coast Bank v. Minderhout [7] made the foregoing pretty much obso-

---

97. In the Kelly case the court drew a distinction between enjoining acts which would interfere with the performance of a promise to which the plaintiff was entitled and the overturning of a consummated transaction made contrary to that same promise and with full knowledge of the breach. The latter would not be ordered unless the plaintiff had an equitable interest in the property transferred in violation of the promise. See the Kelly case, supra note 90, 513; 1936, 49 Harv.L.Rev. 620, 628.

98. "A nuisance lien, like the repairman's lien or the landlord's distress at common law, but none the less a lien on that account." Jacob, note 63, supra, 116.

99. Jacob, note 63, supra, 115, 116.
For a discussion of the rights of the holder of a debenture containing affirmative or negative mortgage clauses when the issuing company becomes bankrupt, see Jacob, note 63, supra, 117–126.

1. Knott v. Shepherdstown Mfg. Co., 1888, 30 W.Va. 790, 5 S.E. 266; Western States Finance Co. v. Ruff, 1923, 108 Or. 442, 215 P. 501, modified and rehearing denied 108 Or. 455, 216 P. 1020. See Kuppenheimer & Co. v. Mornin, C.C.A.Iowa 1935, 78 F. 2d 261, 101 A.L.R. 75; Kelly v. Central Hanover Bank & Trust Co., supra note 90, 507, semble.

2. Knott v. Shepherdstown Manufacturing Co., supra note 1, 796.

3. E.g., insolvency or threatened insolvency of the obligor. Kelly v. Central Hanover Bank & Trust Co., supra, note 85, 512. See 1936, 49 Harv.L.Rev. 620, 627. Insolvency at time of suit rather than insolvency at time of breach seems the preferable test. See 1936, 36 Col.L.Rev. 319, 320. On the other hand, in the Kelly case an acceleration clause effective on breach was held to make the remedy at law adequate, the obligor being solvent at the time Kelly case, note 90, supra, 510. See 1936, 49 Harv. L.Rev. 620, 623; 1936, 22 Va.L.Rev. 440, 448. Cf. 1935, 30 Ill.L.Rev. 487, 490; 1936, 46 Yale L.Jour. 97, 605.

4. See id. See also the Kelly case, supra note 1, 512.

5. See § 43.

6. Jacob, note 63 supra, 116.

7. Supreme Court of Calif., 1964, 61 Cal.2d 311, 38 Cal.Rptr. 505, 392 P.2d 265.
The case is discussed in a note in 1965, 12 U.C.L.A.L. Rev. 951. On the Negative Covenant aspect of the case, see, ibid., 962, 963; IV Am.L.Prop. § 16.38.

lete, at least in California. Primarily in older cases in which a disguised or masked security transaction came before the courts the only important consequences of holding one way or the other was whether there was created an equity of redemption and, reciprocally, the right and duty to foreclose.

In *Coast Bank,* however, there was "imported all the deficiency, acceleration, reinstatement, form of action, redemption and recordation changes of the last fifty years." [8]

The agreement in *Coast Bank* was executed by the borrower along with a note covering some small loans and some contemplated future advances. The agreement provided that the borrower would not sell or encumber certain described real property until he had repaid all present and future advances. It provided also for acceleration of all indebtedness on default in payment or on breach of the property agreement. It gave permission to the bank lender to record the agreement at such time as the bank might choose. It did not state whether or not it was a lien on the property to secure the indebtedness.[9]

The bank did record; the borrower while still indebted conveyed the property; there was a default; the bank accelerated the due date and then brought an action to foreclose the equitable mortgage that it claimed the agreement created. The defendant demurred generally and failed to answer the plaintiff's

allegation that the parties intended to create a security interest in the property. The lower court decreed foreclosure and, on appeal, the judgment was affirmed.

Although technically the holding only went so far as to hold that the pleaded meaning, to which defendant demurred, was "reasonably susceptible" to that interpretation,[10] it seems clear that the same result would have been reached if the question had been "what meaning appears from the face of the instrument alone." " * * * proof that the transaction is secured will be, in almost every case, overwhelmingly clear. To start with, the bank drew the agreement. The agreement describes specific real property and prevents the sale or encumbrance thereof until a certain indebtedness is paid. The indebtedness is subject to acceleration either upon default in payments on the concurrent promissory note, or for breach of the agreement through sale, additional encumbrance, or even failure to pay taxes on specifically described property. The whole thing is recordable. Simply to describe it is to describe a mortgage. * * * The creditor would have difficulty in trying to explain what it is if it is not a mortgage." [11]

Once established that it is a mortgage the borrower gets all the protection of a mortgagor. He may reinstate the loan without acceleration at any time before final judgment in the foreclosure action which is the only action the lender may bring. If the property is sold on foreclosure sale the buyer is subject to the statutory period of redemption from foreclosure sale and the lender is faced with the restrictions on deficiency judgments should the property sell for less than his claim.[12]

For an analysis of and an evaluation of the case see Hetland, Real Property and Real Property Security: The Well-Being of the Law, 1965, 53 Cal.L. Rev. 151, 165–171.

See also Gilmore, Security Interests in Personal Property, § 38.3, pp. 1010–1013.

On an analogous question as to the validity of Debtor-Selection provisions in trust deed mortgages, see Note, 1962, 35 So.Cal.L.Rev. 475. Such provisions stipulate that if title passes from the original trustor without the written consent of the beneficiary, the transfer constitutes a default and the entire principal balance becomes immediately payable at the instance of the beneficiary.

8. Hetland, Real Property and Real Property Security: The Well-Being of the Law, 1965, 53 Cal.L.Rev. 151, 166.

9. See Hetland, op. cit., supra note 8, 165.

10. See Note, 1965, 12 U.C.L.A.L.Rev. 951, 963.

11. Hetland, op. cit. supra note 7, 168.

But see Coogan, Kripke and Weiss, The Outer Fringes of Article 9. Subordination Agreements, * * *, Negative Pledge Clauses, * * *, 1965, 79 Harv.L. Rev. 229, 263–266.

12. See Hetland, op. cit. supra note 7, 169.

Another question in the *Coast Bank* case was whether the restrictions on conveyance or encumbering the property was not invalid as a restraint upon alienation. Without deciding whether the promise "would be directly enforceable by injunction, specific performance or an action for damages." [13] The court held that it was not unreasonable for the lender, to condition its continued extension of credit * * * on their [the borrower] retaining their interest that stood as security for the debt. Accordingly, plaintiff validly provided that it might accelerate the due date if the Enrights [borrowers] encumbered or transferred the property."

This last holding presents the lender with another problem. The restraint is valid only as a reasonable provision of the mortgage. Should the bank, after recording the agreement, allege that "the document does not encumber the real property but is, instead, simply an invalid contractual restraint upon alienation, its recordation clouds the title with a false claim of an encumbrance so that the bank pleads itself into a clear case of disparagement." [14]

The California Financial Code [15] prohibits savings banks and trust companies from securing their loans by taking second liens. So, should such an institution use the agreement in Coast Bank and assert that it did create an equitable mortgage it would be directly within the prohibition of the Financial Code if the property was already encumbered. [16]

When the negative covenant is to refrain from doing other acts unconnected with specific property, such as refraining from creating additional indebtedness so as to make its

total indebtedness exceed a certain percent of the value of its assets as of a certain time [17] there is less foundation for finding an intention that property of the promisor be security for the payment of the obligation. [18]

Commenting on the Minderhout case, an eminent authority stated that, until that decision, "it was possible to say that all the case law there was supported the proposition that a purely negative covenant creates no interest in the property subject to the covenant. We now have a current case, unanimously decided by an influential court, buttressed with a scholarly opinion by a distinguished jurist, which takes the opposite tack. No doubt there will be a good deal more litigation about such covenants in the future than there has been in the past and no doubt the Minderhout case will be a weighty counter in the argument."

Parting company with Justice Traynor's opinion in the Minderhout case, he expresses vigorous objection. "Negative covenants should not, it is submitted, be allowed to operate as informal or inchoate security arrangements, even against third parties with notice. If a creditor wants security, let him take a security in some recognized form: mortgage, pledge Article [9] security interest or what not. If he wants protection against third parties, let him take possession of the collateral or file. Nothing is to be gained by giving a shadowy effectiveness to informal arrangements which conform to no recognized pattern. The debtor's covenant not to encumber property, * * * should be treated, as on the whole the case law has done, as a covenant "merely personal"—good enough to give rights against the covenantor for breach, to bring an acceleration clause into play, to constitute an "event of default" under a loan agreement but not good enough to give

---

13. See Hetland, op. cit. supra note 7, 167; Note 1965, 12 U.C.L.A.L.Rev. 954, 965.

14. Hetland, op. cit. supra note 7, 169.

15. §§ 1413, 1542. Even without this prohibition banks and savings institutions do not, as a matter of sound policy make loans on junior mortgages.

16. See Note, 1965, 12 U.C.L.A.L.Rev. 954, 964.

17. This was one of the two restrictive covenants in the Kelly case, supra note 90.

18. For one thing, such a clause does not speak of any specific property. Kelly case, 513.

rights, whether they be called legal or equitable in property." [19]

AGREEMENT TO PAY DEBT FROM PROCEEDS OF SALE

45. A promise to pay debt out of the proceeds of the sale of specified real property creates an equitable mortgage upon the property before sale if there is a binding agreement, express or implied in fact, that the property will be sold. The equitable security interest on the land in such a case will follow it into the proceeds.

If there is no obligation to sell, no equitable lien will be created as to the property before sale. It is arguable that a limited security interest might be recognized in such cases, but on the whole the line of demarcation excluding it seems properly drawn.

The proceeds of the sale of the property has a prima facie similarity to standard cases of mortgages of after-acquired property. There are differences, however, which justify the courts in refusing to treat it as such, at least where sale of the property is optional.

The authority is almost unanimous that a promise to pay a debt out of the sale of some specific property if sold does not create an equitable mortgage upon either the property before the sale occurs or upon the proceeds of the sale.[20] On the other hand, there is authority that if there is an agreement, even though implied in fact from the whole transaction, that the property is to be sold and payment made out of the sale money an equitable mortgage will attach to the property before sale.[21] And, of course if this is true, it will attach to the proceeds of the sale as long as it can be certainly identified and has not passed into the hands of a bona fide purchaser.[22]

The question of an equitable mortgage on the proceeds, as distinct from the land which produces them, merits separate consideration. At first blush, regardless of whether the sale of the land was mandatory or not, the case looks as though it might be assimilated to the category of ordinary mortgages of after-acquired property. There are, however, several elements that differentiate it. In the first place there is difficulty finding any security intent. The promise is to use the very proceeds themselves to *pay* the obligation, not to have them held as security for the payment.[23] But even if this difficulty is not conclusive there are others. An equitable mortgage will arise only if there is ground for the intervention of equity. If security is intended or promised, ordinarily the intervention of equity is as nearly *de cursu* as anything equity does and the nature of the property is

19. Gilmore, Security Interests in Personal Property, § 38.3 at p. 1013 and § 38.4 at p. 1017. In § 38.5 Professor Gilmore concludes that under U.C.C. § 9 the negative covenant does not create an interest in property.

20. Kuppenheimer & Co. v. Mornin, C.C.A.Iowa, 1935, 78 F.2d 261, 101 A.L.R. 75; Vaniman v. Gardner, 1901, 99 Ill.App. 345; Hibernian Banking Association v. Chicago Title & Trust Co., 1920, 217 Ill.App. 36, affirmed 295 Ill. 537, 129 N.E. 540; Hibernian Banking Association v. Davis, 1920, 295 Ill. 537, 129 N.E. 540; Finn v. Donahoe, 1890, 83 Mich. 165, 47 N.W. 125, reversed 87 Mich. 292, 49 N.W. 632; Hossack v. Graham, 1898, 20 Wash. 184, 55 P. 36; Britt v. Harrell, 1890, 105 N.C. 10, 10 S.E. 902. See Pomeroy, Equity Juris., 5th ed., § 1283a; 1931, 31 Col.L.Rev. 1335, 1340. On the analogous question in trusts involving the Statute of Frauds where there has been a sale of lands in pursuance of an oral agreement to sell and pay over the proceeds, see Scott, Trusts, § 52.1 See also Williston, Contracts, § 429; Gilmore, Security Interests in Personal Property, § 38.4.

21. Johnson v. Johnson, 1874, 40 Md. 189, Brown v. Brown, 1885, 103 Ind. 23, 2 N.E. 233, and Blackburn v. Tweedie, 1875, 60 Mo. 505 (possession of the land given to the creditor to be held until the land was sold), semble. See Earle v. Sunnyside Land Co., 150 Cal. 214, 88 P. 920 (agreement to pay only out of sale by land company of lots at a fixed minimum price per lot held not to prevent creditor having lien upon the lots).

See Cunningham and Tischler, Equitable Real Estate Mortgages, 1963, 17 Rutgers L.Rev. 689, 725.

22. Racouillat v. Sansevain, 1867, 32 Cal. 376, 390. See Pomeroy, Equity Juris., 5th ed., § 1280. Dodd v. Cantzwell, 1960, 179 Cal.App.2d 727, 4 Cal.Rptr. 113, held that a promise to pay employees their wages out of the proceeds of land, when sold, created an equitable mortgage on the land as against a donee of it.

23. See State Central Sav. Bank v. Hemmy, C.C.A. Iowa 1935, 77 F.2d 458, 460.

immaterial.[24] However, if that property is money, especially money which is to be used to pay the obligation, the courts are likely to feel that the legal remedy is as adequate as the equitable one and therefore decline to intervene.[25] Another court stressed a policy factor in words which, though applied to the facts of the particular case, were intended to be a generalization: "business and commerce will be greatly harmed, hamstrung, and impeded if every agreement of an Iowa farmer to pay a debt out of a crop of corn, when he shall have sold the corn, is to be held to be an equitable assignment of the proceeds of such corn."[26] Along with this might be suggested the practical difficulties of any notice being given to third parties.[27] But most influential of all is the thoroughly settled distinction between an order and a promise to pay out of a fund.[28] The distinction is sound enough. However, stating it and, too frequently, applying it as though it were a mechanical, self-operating rule is not. What is involved is nothing more than the fundamental difference between a transaction which is intended to and capable of transferring or creating a property interest in some specific property and one which is merely a promise of a sort which will not give rise, because specific performance of it will not be granted, to an equitable property interest either presently or in the future. The particular property involved here is the proceeds of the sale of land. In other words, future property. Modified by the considerations just mentioned, there are involved no principles here other than those previously explored in connection with the general discussion of mortgages of after-acquired property.[29] One *caveat* may be entered to this statement. In the cases here dealt with, the after-acquired funds are the product of the sale of presently owned property which is mentioned in the

---

24. Jacob, Protection of Debenture Holders, 1938, 52 Harv.L.Rev. 77, 100, 116.

25. See Hossack v. Graham, 1898, 20 Wash. 184, 191, 55 P. 36; Cushing v. Chapman, C.C.Mo.1902, 115 F. 237, 242; Jamison Coal & Coke Co. v. Goltra, C.C. A.Mo.1944, 143 F.2d 889, 893, 154 A.L.R. 1191, certiorari denied 65 S.Ct. 122, 323 U.S. 769, 89 L.Ed. 615; Union Trust Co. of Md. v. Townshend, 1939, 101 F.2d 903, 911, certiorari denied 59 S.Ct. 1044, 307 U.S. 646, 83 L.Ed. 1526, "The reason at the basis of the rule that a mere agreement to pay a debt out of a fund creates no lien on the fund is that, where there is no appropriation of a part of the fund to the payment of the debt, the whole remains under the unfettered dominion of the debtor, and the failure on his part to carry out the agreement is a mere breach of the contract, no different in character from his failure to pay the debt."

26. Kuppenheimer & Co. v. Mornin, C.C.A.Iowa 1935, 78 F.2d 261, 265, 101 A.L.R. 75. It is not entirely clear just what this business inconvenience would be. So far as the debtor himself is concerned, of course it might be inconvenient to have to set aside this very sum of money to pay this particular debt. After all that is what he agreed to do and there is difficulty in seeing enough objection from his point of view to raise it to a matter sufficient to outweigh that agreement. As to third parties being inconvenienced by having to take subject to an equitable lien, it may be pointed out that any purchaser without notice will take free and clear of it. It does, however, hamper the free currency of the money in that donees and, possibly, creditors, could not safely take it free of the encumbrance.

27. The court in the Kuppenheimer case was impressed by this factor as having importance in cases which recognize a lien where collateral is pledged.

28. "There is, of course, a vast difference in law between an order to pay a debt out of a particular fund and a promise to pay out of such fund. That the former, when accepted, is binding, is almost, if not quite, hornbook law. That the latter is not binding is well-nigh as well settled. Rufe v. Commercial Bank, C.C.A.Va.1938, 99 F. 650, 40 C.C.A. 27; Long v. Farmers' State Bank, C.C.A.Iowa 1906, 147 F. 360, 363, 77 C.C.A. 538, 9 L.R.A.,N.S., 585; Trist v. Child, 1874, 21 Wall. 441, 22 L.Ed. 623; Dillon v. Barnard, 1874, 21 Wall. 430, 22 L.Ed. 673; East Side Packing Co. v. Fahy Market, C.C.A.N.Y. 1928, 24 F.2d 644; Smedley v. Speckman, C.C.A.Pa. 1908, 157 F. 815, 819, 85 C.C.A. 179; Cogan v. Conover Mfg. Co., 69 N.J.Eq. 358, 60 A. 408, 411, reversed 69 N.J.Eq. 809, 64 A. 973, 115 Am.St.Rep. 629; Cushing v. Chapman, C.C.Mo.1902, 115 F. 237, 239; State Central Savings Bank v. Hemmy, C.C.A.Iowa 1935, 77 F.2d 458, decided by this court recently." Kuppenheimer & Co. v. Mornin, C.C.A. Iowa 1935, 78 F.2d 261, 264, 101 A.L.R. 75. See Pomeroy Equity Juris., 5th ed., §§ 1280, 1283, 1283a.

Even the English courts now seem to subscribe to this distinction after having at one time held that a promise to pay out of a fund constituted an equitable assignment of the fund. Palmer v. Carey, [1926] A.C. 703. See 1936, 36 Col.L.Rev. 329 criticizing the doctrine, especially as applied in the Kuppenheimer case.

29. See § 37, supra. The analogy of the creation of a trust of the proceeds of the sale of land is pertinent here. See Scott, note 20, supra.

agreement and which constitute part of the identifying description of those funds. This being so, it is possible to argue that the very promise to pay out of the proceeds from specific property is itself "patently probative of an intention to add to the ordinary liability of the promisor, the security of the proceeds of a specific fund." [30] In this case the fund is the land. If the promisor was bound by his promise to sell the land that would provide an additional factor indicative of an intention to have the proceeds a genuine security fund.[31]

The more important question, however, is whether there is an equitable security interest in the property before any sale takes place regardless of whether there is a duty to sell. Fundamentally, as practically all of the courts state, this depends upon whether the parties intended that the property should be security.[32] Possibly the fact that many of the leading cases shaping the doctrine were cases in which the property to be sold consisted of promissory notes,[33] insurance policies,[34] and similar sorts of mercantile instruments [35] in respect to which there would be a fairly strong antagonism to creating equitable interests that would be difficult to ascertain, likely to be deceptive to creditors, and to some extent tend to impair their commercial utility may account for the answer generally being in the negative. However that may be,

there are present here some of the features we encountered in the cases of conditional agreements to mortgage. For one thing there is the power, or even the duty, in the obligor to sell the property. And the dual argument is raised that such ability to cut off all of the creditor's rights in the property he claims as security for his debt is, on the one hand, inconsistent with the existence of a security interest, and, on the other, is indicative of an intent that there be no such fetter on the property. The answer to the first is that it is perfectly possible to have a mortgage with the mortgagor being given a power to sell the property free and clear of the mortgage, at least if substitution is mutually contemplated.[36] As a matter of fact there is in every equitable mortgage the power to destroy the mortgage by the mortgagor selling to a bona fide purchaser but no one has ever thought to argue that therefore there could not be such a mortgage because this power existed. So here the power given by the mortgagee to sell free and clear to anyone should not be a foundation for such a contention. Nor does it show there was no *intent* to have the property be security. The obligee would still be protected against donees and other creditors, including mortgagees who took with notice of his rights. That is the chief protection he is seeking. The sale by the mortgagor merely relieves him of the job of having the property sold through foreclosure proceedings.[37] The fact that where there is a *duty* to sell the court will find an equitable mortgage [38] seems conclusive on these points. The case for an equitable mortgage here, so far as these factors are concerned, is stronger than in the case of the affirmative conditional pledge clause in debentures which protects only against subsequent mortgagees with notice and only ratably as

30. 1936, 36 Col.L.Rev. 331, criticizing the decision in the Kuppenheimer case, supra note 26.

31. See Pomeroy, Equity Juris., 5th ed., § 1283, "The fund need not be actually in being, if it exists potentially,—that is, if it will in due course of things arise from a contract or arrangement already made or entered into when the order is given,—the order will operate as an equitable assignment of such fund as soon as it is acquired. * * *"

32. See, e.g., the Kuppenheimer case, note 26 supra.

33. Christmas v. Russell, 1871, 81 U.S. 69, 20 L.Ed. 762, a leading case in the United States.

34. Long v. Farmers' State Bank, C.C.A.Iowa 1906, 147 F. 360, 77 C.C.A. 538, 9 L.R.A.,N.S., 585; State Central Sav. Bank v. Hemmy, C.C.A.Iowa 1935, 77 F.2d 458.

35. Cushing v. Chapman, C.C.Mo.1902, 115 F. 237, bonds.

36. Racouillat v. Sansevain, 1867, 32 Cal. 376, 390. See Jacob, Protection of Debenture Holders, 1938, 52 Harv.L.Rev. 77, 85.

37. Johnson v. Johnson, supra note 21.

38. Idem.

to them. Consequently, even where there is no promise to sell but merely a promise to pay out of the proceeds of the property *if* sold, it would seem that promise might well be held to create an equitable interest in the property protecting the creditor to this extent at least: that there should be no dealings with the property which would prevent there being proceeds. In other words, that it won't be given away, or mortgaged, and will be protected against being levied on by creditors. Where there is the express promise to sell, this is the result.[39] However, where there is no such promise, unless there are other factors in the whole transaction to indicate an intention to bind the property, it would be difficult to imply an intention that there would be proceeds. So perhaps the line is properly drawn there.[40]

MISCELLANEOUS TRANSACTIONS

46. Several other transactions create equitable mortgages on the basis of the parties' intent that the property involved be security.

(1) Giving an irrevocable power to sell and apply proceeds to payment of a debt.

(2) Giving power to take possession and apply rents and profits to debt.

(3) Giving possession and use of the property, with the proceeds of its sale to be used to pay the debt.

(4) Handling over possession until debt is paid with use of land in lieu of interest.

Closely related to the preceding cases are a group of miscellaneous transactions in which the central problem facing the courts is whether there is an intention that the property be security. One such case is where an irrevocable power to sell certain property and apply the proceeds to the payment of the debt is given. The foundation American case[41] was one in which there clearly was an intention to have certain property, two ships, be security for an obligation. However, the power of attorney to sell was deliberately given as the security. Marshall, declaring that powers coupled with an "interest" in the property subject to the power would survive, found there was no "interest" in the property and therefore the power was ended by the death of the obligor. Nevertheless he "revived" it on equitable grounds. The net result of the decision, disregarding Marshall's theory which has been criticized,[42] was to make the power survive and permit the creditor to realize on the property. Even without the explicit finding of intent to charge the property, it would seem abundantly clear that "where there is not only an interest in the proceeds, but also an irrevocable power of sale so that proceeds shall be assured, to say that there is not an interest in the thing itself is to make a distinction of no practical value."[43] Whether it is a sufficient "interest" to permit the power to survive the death of the obligor depends on theories of agency powers, but the answer should be in the affirmative.[44]

In England a power to take possession and collect and apply the rents and profits until the debt was paid has been held to create an equitable charge upon the freehold which would survive the death of the debtor.[45] The fact that the words of the power itself more clearly indicated an intention that the property should be security seems insufficient to differentiate it from the preceding cases.

39. Note 21, supra.

40. It may be noted that where land is the property to be sold any argument about business inconvenience, etc., accounting for the result has little force. See ante for a discussion of this factor in connection with raising an equitable lien on the proceeds.

41. Hunt v. Rousmanier's Administrators, 1823, 21 U.S. (8 Wheat.) 174, 5 L.Ed. 589; 1828, 26 U.S. (1 Pet.) 1, 7 L.Ed. 27. See Durfee, 1951, Cases on Security, 444; Ferson, Irrevocable Powers: Cognovit Notes, 1961, Duke L.J. 216, 223. See also Cunningham and Tischler, Equitable Real Estate Mortgages, 1963, 17 Rutgers L.Rev. 679, 726.

42. Seavey, Proprietary Powers of Attorney, 1922, 31 Yale L.Jour. 283.

43. Seavey, supra note 42, 290.

44. Seavey, supra, note 42, 294. The cases, however, seem to require a legal lien. Id. 297 n. 70.

45. Spooner v. Sandilands, 1842, 1 Y & C.C.C. 390.

There is American authority that giving possession and use of the property with the proceeds of a sale of the property to be used to pay the debt is sufficient to create an equitable mortgage in the land.[46] So, too, where possession of the land is given until the debt is paid with the use of the land to be in lieu of interest.[47]

CONVEYANCE IN CONSIDERATION OF PROMISE TO SUPPORT

47. Considerable authority protects the grantor of a conveyance conditioned on support by giving him an equitable lien on the property transferred. Some courts require an intent, express or implied, that the property be security. But probably most courts would accept a law-created lien, where the consensual basis is lacking, as "an intermediate ground between affirmative specific performance and complete rescission."[48]

Courts have tended to treat conveyances of land expressed to be in consideration of the grantee's promise to support the grantor, or conditioned on such support, as in a class by themselves.[49] It is held with substantial unanimity that, on breach of the promise or condition, equity will grant relief. However, there is great disagreement as to the grounds and form of the relief.[50]

Our concern is with relief through the creation and enforcement of an equitable lien. That such relief will be granted is supported by a very considerable body of authority.[51] However, even this one form of relief has been founded upon a variety of grounds. Some courts hold that an express intent to charge the land is necessary.[52] Others re-

ent jurisdictions, deeds given to secure the grantor's support have been annulled on general grounds of equity, without much attempt to refer the relief to any specific rule. Peck v. Hoyt, 39 Conn. 9; Penfield v. Penfield, 41 Conn. 474; Jenkins v. Jenkins, 19 (3 T.B.Mon.) Ky. 327; Reeder v. Reeder, 89 Ky. 529, 12 S.W. 1063, 11 Ky.Law Rep. 731; Patterson v. Patterson, 81 Iowa 626, 47 N.W. 768; Dodge v. Dodge, 92 Mich. 109, 52 N.W. 296; Rexford v. Schofield, 101 Mich. 480, 59 N.W. 837; Wilfong v. Johnson, 41 W.Va. 283, 23 S.E. 730. See 1948, 9 U. of Pitt. 206. In Illinois the court rescinds the transaction, presuming if necessary to the relief, that the conveyance was obtained with fraudulent intent. Frazier v. Miller, 16 Ill. 48; Oard v. Oard, 59 Ill. 46; Cooper v. Gum, 152 Ill. 471, 39 N.E. 267. In Oregon it is considered that rescission is not permissible, and the grantor's support is secured by making it a charge upon the property. Watson v. Smith, 7 Or. 448; Patton v. Nixon, 33 Or. 159, 52 P. 1048. In Rhode Island a reconveyance is decreed, upon the theory that the deed creates a continuing obligation in the nature of a trust, and that the failure to support is a renunciation of the trust. Grant v. Bell, 26 R.I. 288, 58 A. 951. In Indiana the agreement to support is considered a condition subsequent, the breach of which entitles the grantor to re-enter and maintain a suit to quiet the title. Richter v. Richter, 111 Ind. 456, 12 N.E. 698; Cree v. Sherfy, 138 Ind. 354, 37 N.E. 787. In Wisconsin it was formerly considered that this ground of relief was not tenable, but this view is repudiated in the recent case of Glocke v. Glocke, 113 Wis. 303, 89 N.W. 118, 57 L.R.A. 458. It is said in that case that the property conveyed is held on condition subsequent; that upon a breach of the condition the title will revert, at the election of the grantor, without judicial aid; and that the grantor can have in equity "such appropriate relief as may be necessary to judicially establish his status as regards the property and quiet his title thereto."

See also Dowdle, Judicial Interpretation of Conveyances in Consideration of Support, 1946, 21 Wash.L. Rev. 229; 1947 Wis.L.Rev. 125; 1944, 32 Cal.L.Rev. 191; 1941, 19 Ky.L.J. 235; 1931, 31 Col.L.Rev. 1335, 1339; 1939, 8 Fordham L.Rev. 126.

46. Brown v. Brown, 1885, 103 Ind. 23, 2 N.E. 233. In Charpie v. Stout, 1912, 88 Kan. 318, 128 P. 396, rehearing denied 88 Kan. 682, 129 P. 1166, an oral agreement for security coupled with transfer of possession to the creditor who improved, cultivated, rented, and managed it openly for eighteen years was held to give an equitable mortgage to secure an existing debt.

47. Blackburn v. Tweedie, 1875, 60 Mo. 505.

48. 1934, 32 Mich.L.Rev. 685, 686.

49. See Bruer v. Bruer, 1909, 109 Minn. 260, 262, 123 N.W. 813, 814, 28 L.R.A.,N.S., 608; 1939, 8 Fordham L.Rev. 126.

50. See a rather complete note on the various types of relief open to the grantor in, 1912, 43 L.R.A.,N. S., 916. While the catalogue is not complete, the following summary by the court in Abbott v. Sanders, 1907, 80 Vt. 179, 180, 66 A. 1032, 13 L.R.A.,N.S., 725, 726, 130 Am.St.Rep. 974, 975, 12 Ann.Cas. 898 is sufficient to reveal how varied are the remedies accorded in these cases: "In many cases in differ-

51. See collections of authorities in 1908, 13 L.R.A., N.S., 725; 1910, 28 L.R.A.,N.S., 607; 1913, 43 L.R. A.,N.S., 916, 929; 1930, 64 A.L.R. 1250. See also 1934, 32 Mich.L.Rev. 685; 1939, 8 Fordham L.Rev. 126.

52. Loar v. Poling, 1929, 107 W.Va. 280, 148 S.E. 114, 64 A.L.R. 1246; Whipp v. Whipp, 1931, 110 W.Va. 361, 158 S.E. 382.

quire an intent that the property shall be security for the performance by the grantee but will infer that intent not only from language [53] referring to the land in terms reasonably indicative of such intent but also from the mere presence in the deed of conveyance of the condition [54] or promise [55] of support. Sometimes the reasoning of the court is spelled out. Thus the Vermont court reasoned that a conditional deed should be and was treated as a mortgage in equity because it "could not see wherein this differed from the ordinary case of the conveyance of an absolute title with a mortgage back to secure a payment of purchase money, saying that here the defeasance was inserted in the deed of conveyance, while in the ordinary case of conveyance and mortgage the defeasance is inserted in the latter, but that in such a case both instruments are construed together as one and the same contract, effectuating the conveyance of a defeasible title to the purchaser." [56] On the other hand the result is reached by some courts with no reliable clue as to rationale.[57]

In spite of the possibility of explaining many of the cases as orthodox consensual equitable mortgages, it seems probable that even were such a foundation lacking [58] a law

created equitable lien would be accepted by the courts as "an intermediate ground between affirmative specific performance and complete rescission." It would be regarded "primarily as a remedial device used to secure the most workable and flexible relief in difficult situations." [59]

VENDOR'S RESERVATION OF SECURITY INTEREST

48. An equitable mortgage to secure the payment of the purchase price of land may be created by an express reservation in the deed of conveyance of a lien upon the property. Such a consensual equitable mortgage has several advantages over the law created grantor's lien.

The equitable lien of a grantor of real property upon the property for the unpaid purchase price is common and familiar.[60] It is, however, generally agreed that it arises by operation of law,[61] although there is very considerable divergence of opinion as to its origin and rationale.[62] Consequently it is outside the scope of this treatment which con-

53. Bonebrake v. Summers, 193 Pa. 22, 44 A. 330, "the support of A, during his life is a part of the consideration and therefore the grantee's title shall not become clear of incumbrance until A's death." Loar v. Poling, supra, "said maintenance to be on the land." Quite explicit is the language in Chase v. Peck, 1860, 21 N.Y. 581, "pledged the entire produce of the farm for such support and, if the produce be insufficient, then the entire fee shall be appropriated for such purpose."

54. Doescher v. Spratt, 1895, 61 Minn. 326, 63 N.W. 736.

55. Childs v. Rue, 1901, 84 Minn. 323, 87 N.W. 918.

56. Abbott v. Sanders, supra note 50.

57. E.g., Webster v. Cadwallader, 1909, 133 Ky. 500, 505, 118 S.W. 327, 328, 134 Am.St.Rep. 470; Stephens v. Daly, 1919, 266 F. 1009, 49 App.D.C. 389.

58. It is true, however, that some courts have refused to grant a vendor's lien in support cases on the ground that the amount is unliquidated. Burroughs v. Burroughs, 1909, 164 Ala. 329, 50 So. 1025, 28 L.R.A.,N.S., 607, 137 Am.St.Rep. 59, 20

Ann.Cas. 926; Peters v. Tunell, 1890, 43 Minn. 473, 45 N.W. 867, 19 Am.St.Rep. 252. But contrast, Doescher v. Spratt, note 54 supra; Childs v. Rue, note 55 supra.

59. 1934, 32 Mich.L.Rev. 685, 686. It can be used to obtain specific performance indirectly where a direct order would be inadvisable because of the domestic difficulties involved. Or, if there were no such difficulties it could supplement the injunction. Further, in cases where rescission for failure of consideration by the grantee might work injustice because of improvements made by him, the lien affords the fairest solution. See 1931, 31 Col.L.Rev. 1335, 1339.

60. See Pomeroy, Equity Juris., § 1250, for a catalogue of the states accepting or rejecting the doctrine. See also Patterson, Annual Survey of Georgia Law, 1957, 7 Mercer L.Rev. 151, 153.

61. "The implication that there is an intention to reserve a lien for the purchase money in all cases in which the parties do not by express acts evince a contrary intention, is in almost every case inconsistent with the truth of the fact, and in all instances without exception, in contradiction of the express terms of the contract, which purport to be a conveyance of everything that can pass." Kauffelt v. Bower, 7 Serg. & R., Pa., 64, 76, 77, 10 Am. Dec. 428. See Ahrend v. Odiorne, 1875, 118 Mass. 266.

62. Pomeroy, supra note 60.

cerns itself with security created by the intention of the parties. However, the grantor may expressly reserve in the deed of conveyance a lien upon the property to secure the payment of the purchase price. In such a case there will be a consensual equitable mortgage no different fundamentally either in character or the basis of its creation than any other created in existing property in accordance with an expressed intention that that property be security.[63]

This consensual equitable mortgage by reservation has several advantages over the law created grantor's lien. Since the intention to burden the property with the payment of the purchase money appears in the deed which is recorded, notice of it will be given to all who claim under the deed.[64] Again, the assignment of the debt will carry the security.[65] And, although, of course, the grantor may waive his equitable lien either expressly or by acts directly inconsistent with its existence and evidencing a clear intention to waive,[66] the mere acceptance of distinct independent security for the purchase price does not discharge the lien[67] as it does in the analogous grantor's lien.[68] It is also

treated as a mortgage when it comes to enforcement by foreclosure and similar relief.[69]

takes a security upon the land sold for the whole or a part of that money, the equitable lien is waived, unless there is an express agreement that it be kept alive; Fish v. Howland, 1 Paige, 20. I understand the effect of this rule to be this: That if the vendor of lands chooses to convey, and to take back no security upon them or other lands, nor any security independent of the personal liability of the vendee to respond for the consideration-money, he may rely upon an implied lien which equity gives him upon the lands conveyed, subject to some infirmities which such a lien suffers. But if he takes such security as is just above indicated, he thereby waives that implied lien, that equitable lien, upon the lands. This rule does not go to the extent, that if an equitable lien has once arisen, the subsequent taking of a legal and perfected lien, to the same extent and upon the same property, extinguishes it, by waiver or merger: Stafford v. Van Rensselaer, N.Y., 1827, 9 Cow. 316. The equitable lien has had, in the case in hand, an existence. There has been no express waiver of it. The law is not anxious to imply a waiver. Whether it has ceased to exist, depends upon the rules of equity, which determine whether a merger has taken place. It is a general rule, that where an equitable and legal estate meet and vest in the same ownership, the former is merged in the latter. But the doctrine of merger, as applied to mortgages, is founded upon equitable principles, and is only applied where equity requires that it should be. Where the owner of the legal and equitable titles has an interest in keeping those titles distinct, as where there is an intervening incumbrance, he has a right so to keep them, and the equitable title will not be merged and thereby extinguished; Millspaugh v. McBride, 1839, 7 Paige, 509, 34 Am.Dec. 360; McKinstry v. Merwin, 3 J.C.R., 466." Payne v. Wilson, 1878, 74 N.Y. 348, 353.

See Wells v. Harter, 1880, 56 Cal. 342; Avery v. Clark, 1890, 87 Cal. 619, 25 P. 919, 22 Am.St.Rep. 272; Finnell v. Finnell, 1909, 156 Cal. 589, 105 P. 740, 134 Am.St.Rep. 143.

63. Dingley v. Bank of Ventura, 1881, 57 Cal. 467. See Pomeroy, supra note 60. Provided that the intention is clear, no particular form is necessary.

Express Vendor's Lien, § 19, supra. See Cunningham and Tischler, Equitable Real Estate Mortgages, 1963, 17 Rutgers L.Rev. 679, 700.

64. Dingley v. Bank of Ventura, supra, note 63; Carter v. Thompson, 1925, 167 Ark. 272, 267 S.W. 790, 38 A.L.R. 1053 (deed lost and not of record but purchaser claimed through it). See 1933, 91 A.L.R. 150, 151.

65. Dingley v. Bank of Ventura, supra, 472. Cf.Cal. Civ.Code § 3047, providing that the absolute transfer by the seller of the contract for the purchase price waives the grantor's lien.

66. Beard v. Payne, 1917, 64 Ind.App. 324, 115 N.E. 782; Frazier v. Hendren, 1885, 80 Va. 265.

67. See Dingley v. Bank of Ventura, supra note 64, 471; Beard v. Payne, supra note 65.

68. "It is a rule, that where a vendor of land might have an equitable lien for the purchase-money, yet

69. Markoe v. Andras, 1873, 67 Ill. 34; Gaston v. White, 1870, 46 Mo. 486. But contrast Priddy & Chambers v. Smith, 1912, 106 Ark. 79, 152 S.W. 1028, 44 L.R.A.,N.S., 285 (no right of redemption from foreclosure sale). Like a legal purchase money mortgage it will have priority over dower of the vendee's wife and outstanding judgment liens. Holland Jones Co. v. Smith, 1929, 152 Va. 707, 148 S.E. 581.

On the distinction between reserving a lien and reserving the title itself until the price is paid, look at Bound v. Dillard, Tex.Civ.App., 1940, 140 S.W.2d 520; Sheehan v. McKinstry, 1922, 105 Or. 473, 210 P. 167, 34 A.L.R. 1315.

CHAPTER 3
THE STATUTE OF FRAUDS

Any discussion of the Statute of Frauds as applicable to mortgages necessarily involves its application to other transactions. Since this is so it seems appropriate to omit any intensive treatment of the subject in this work.

It has seemed desirable, however, to retain the black letter headnotes of the first edition so that the topics considered will be stated and, in most instances, the holdings of the authorities and their rationales. If more detailed information is wanted reference can be made to the text of the sections in the first edition.

An exception has been made to the foregoing in the case of two sections that have both an important practical application to security transactions today and also involve matters of legal theory worth attention by the student of mortgage law.

INTRODUCTION

49. The relevant section of the statute of frauds provides that no action shall be brought upon any contract or sale of lands, or any interest in or concerning them.[1]

APPLICATION TO LEGAL MORTGAGES

50. A legal mortgage must fulfill the requirements of the Statute of Frauds.

APPLICATION TO CONSENSUAL MORTGAGES

51. The Statute of Frauds only applies to consensual transactions. Hence it can apply only to the creation of those equitable mortgages with such a foundation; it has no application to equitable mortgages arising by operation of law.

1. See Cunningham and Tischler, Equitable Real Estate Mortgages, 1963, 17 Rutgers L.Rev. 679, 681–683.

THE DOCTRINE OF PART PERFORMANCE IN GENERAL

52. Under the equitable doctrine of part performance certain conduct by the plaintiff is sufficient to take the case out of the Statute of Frauds. In the event of such conduct equity in effect specifically enforces the agreement, although it has been argued that it really enforces "independent equities" created by the part performance.

There is much disagreement as to what will constitute part performance. The two basic requirements, aside from the "possession" cases which may have an independent foundation, probably are

(1) Evidentiary conduct corroborating the agreement sufficiently to satisfy the policy of the statute; and

(2) Substantial change of position by the plaintiff in reliance on the agreement.[2]

As the hardship increases there is a relaxation of the evidentiary requirement and vice versa. The trend is to be liberal in taking cases out of the statute, especially in the case of mortgages as compared to sales of land.

PART PERFORMANCE AND EQUITABLE MORTGAGES

53. Three groups of cases will be considered:

(1) Where money is loaned for purposes other than the purchase of land or its improvement.

(2) Where money is loaned to pay for land to be mortgaged.

(3) Where money is loaned to improve the land promised to be given in mortgage.

GROUP 1—PART PERFORMANCE BY THE LENDING OF MONEY

54. The mere lending of money does not remove the case from the Statute of Frauds.[3] The soundness of this rule depends on

(1) Whether there is a distinction between the loan as essential to create an equitable mortgage and as sufficient part performance;

2. See Cunningham and Tischler, Equitable Real Estate Mortgages, 1963, 17 Rutgers L.Rev. 679, 706–710.

3. See Cunningham and Tischler, op. cit. supra, §§ 49, 52.

(2) Whether a loan is sufficient to take equitable mortgages in general out of the statute.

CREATION OF EQUITABLE INTEREST DISTINGUISHED FROM PART PERFORMANCE

55. Since in purchase-of-land cases a written contract creates an equitable interest but an oral agreement is not enforced without part performance, the acts of part performance have significance apart from (and cannot be the reason for) the creation of a consensual equitable interest.

CREATION OF EQUITABLE INTEREST DISTINGUISHED FROM PART PERFORMANCE—FUNCTION OF LOAN

56. No equitable mortgage arises until the loan is made. If the loan is also relied on as part performance the problem of creating the mortgage and of removing the case from the statute could be identical. Whether this is sound depends on whether the reasons for recognition of the mortgage and for removal from the statute are identical.

NON-CONSENSUAL THEORY OF EQUITABLE MORTGAGES

57. An equitable mortgage may arise, analogously to a vendee's lien, by operation of law to secure the lender's quasi-contractual right to recover the value of his performance. This does not negative the existence of consensual equitable mortgages as the normal basis of his rights.

COMPARISON OF NON-CONSENSUAL EQUITABLE MORTGAGE AND PART PERFORMANCE

58. The non-consensual rationale of equitable mortgages resembles the "independent equity" view of part performance in that equity intervenes in both to grant restitution where the legal remedy is inadequate. But the two theories are distinct since—

(1) Payment is not sufficient part performance, although it is sufficient to create a mortgage and

(2) "Equitable fraud" is required for part performance but not to give rise to a mortgage.

COMPARISON OF CONSENSUAL EQUITABLE MORTGAGE AND PART PERFORMANCE

59. The consensual theory of equitable mortgages is markedly different from the doctrine of part performance.

PAYMENT OF MONEY AS PART PERFORMANCE

60. As in vendor-vendee cases, payment of money is not sufficient part performance. This rule is sound.[3a]

PART PERFORMANCE BY ACTS OTHER THAN LENDING MONEY

61. Additional conduct by plaintiff, such as taking possession or giving up a mortgage on other land may be sufficient part performance.

TITLE DEEDS AND PART PERFORMANCE

62. Delivery of title deeds by the mortgagor is not sufficient part performance in the United States.[4] It is in England.[5]

GROUP 2—MONEY LOANED FOR PURCHASE OF LAND WHICH IS TO BE MORTGAGED

63. A loan to be used for the purchase of land which the borrower orally promises to mortgage as security for the repayment of the loan gives rise to an equitable mortgage on that land if the money is applied according to the agreement.

The second group of cases generally hold that one who lends money to be used by the borrower to pay for specific land which the latter orally promises to mortgage as security for the repayment of the loan gets an equitable mortgage on that land if the money is applied according to the agreement.[6] There are some authorities contra and the reasons given in any one opinion seldom expresses with precision the exact basis or bases of the result regardless of which way it went.[7] Further, in the cases taken collectively, not one but several lines of thought have been advanced both for and against the lien. Although it is this group which is chiefly relied upon for broad statements that the stat-

---

3a. See Cunningham and Tischler, Equitable Real Estate Mortgages, 1963, 17 Rutgers L.Rev. 679, 704.

4. See Cunningham and Tischler, 1963, 17 Rutgers L.Rev. 679, 714–715.

5. See Cunningham and Tischler, op. cit. supra, note 4, 711–713.

6. Craven v. Hartley, 1931, 102 Fla. 282, 135 So. 899, is typical.

There is a considerable body of authority allowing, for one reason or another, an equitable security interest in cases like Craven v. Hartley. Foster Lumber Co. v. Harlan County Bank, 1905, 71 Kan. 158, 80 P. 49, 114 Am.St.Rep. 470, 6 Ann.Cas. 44; Hughes v. Mullaney, 1904, 92 Minn. 485, 100 N.W. 217; Baker v. Baker, 1891, 2 S.D. 261, 49 N.W. 1064, 39 Am.St.Rep. 776 (loan to pay off a mortgage with an oral agreement to execute a new mortgage to the lender. The Statute of Frauds referred specifically to the creation of mortgages. Another statutory provision stated as an exception to the general Statute of Frauds that equity had the power to compel specific performance of contracts for the sale of real property in cases of part performance.); Cole v. Cole, 1874, 41 Md. 301 (the defendant did not rely on the Statute of Frauds but the court says he would have failed if he had because it cannot be used as an instrument of fraud); Krost v. Kleg, Mo.1932, 46 S.W.2d 866 (loan to pay off part of a first mortgage); Dean v. Anderson, 1881, 34 N.J.Eq. 496 (the consideration given by the plaintiff was land conveyed to a third party who in turn conveyed the property involved in the oral promise to the defendant).

See also Bagley v. Pollock, Tex.Civ.App.1929, 19 S.W. 2d 193, discussed in 1930, 8 Tex.L.Rev. 312.

See too Cunningham and Tischler, 1963, 17 Rutgers L.Rev. 679, 709–711.

7. There are a number of cases refusing relief where the agreement for security was oral. The most carefully reasoned opinion is in Newman v. Newman, 1921, 103 Ohio St. 230, 133 N.E. 70, 18 A.L.R. 1089. Relief was denied the lender because (1) the contract was oral; (2) since the money was loaned to the vendee there could be no resulting trust; (3) since there was no evidence of fraud there could be no constructive trust; (4) having derived no interest from the vendor, and not having been a party to the sale, the plaintiff could not be accorded a vendor's lien. Other cases are Whaley v. Whaley, 1881, 71 Ala. 159; Wooldridge v. Scott, 1879, 69 Mo. 669; Marquat v. Marquat, 1853, 7 How.Pr. (N.Y.) 417 reversed 12 N.Y. 336; Frank Clothing Co. v. Deegan, Tex.Civ.App.1918, 204 S.W. 471. See The Statute of Frauds and Oral Agreements to Mortgage Land, 1930, 44 Harv.L.Rev. 269. See also 1922, 18 A.L.R. 1098.

ute of frauds does not apply to any oral agreement for a mortgage [8] because they arise by operation of law or that the payment of the loan is a sufficient part performance to take any oral agreement for a mortgage of land out of the statute of frauds, they properly stand only for a much narrower proposition. Indeed both the decisions which deny any equitable intervention in the first group and those which award it in this second one seem correct and reconcilable. The latter may be supported on either of two courses of thought: first, that the equitable lien in this type of case does arise by operation of law upon principles of restitution; second, that the policy of the Statute of Frauds is saved in this sort of transaction and, although the argument of irreparable hardship on the plaintiff is not of the strongest even though sufficient on the decisions to warrant intervention on the first line of reasoning, nevertheless it is sufficient to justify dispensing with the requirement of a writing and enforcing the agreement itself. To understand and support these conclusions requires an analysis of various solutions in the cases. In some of these it becomes important to distinguish the cases according to whether the loan was made before or after the contract of purchase or prior mortgage had been entered into by the borrower, or after conveyance to him from the third person but before payment of the purchase price, or contemporaneously with the conveyance to the borrower from the third person with the loaned money being at the same time paid to the seller.

Four theories have been advanced to explain why the plaintiff's equitable lien should be held to arise by operation of law in these cases. The first is that it is in the nature of a resulting trust. But proof that the money was loaned at once destroys this explanation.[9] A second one is that it rests upon

subrogation to the rights of the original grantor or vendor, invoking the analogy of cases which give subrogation to the rights of a former encumbrancer when money is loaned on the faith of a defective mortgage for the purpose of discharging prior encumbrances.[10] This solution would work where the borrower had a contract for purchase with legal title still in the vendor and also in those jurisdictions which accord a grantor's lien to a seller who conveys before getting paid the purchase price. But it would fail in jurisdictions where there is no such grantor's lien or where it is personal to the grantor and also in those cases in which the loan precedes even the existence of the contract for purchase and the money loaned is paid in exchange for the conveyance, since there never would be a security interest at any time to which subrogation could be given under these circumstances. A third possibility in these last cases is to extend the doctrine giving an unpaid grantor an equitable lien to one who is not the grantor but who advances the purchase price as a loan.[11] Such an extension

8. See Walsh, Mortgages, 45ff. and cases in footnotes, especially notes 27, 33.

9. See Newman v. Newman, note 7, supra.

10. In Warford v. Hankins, 1898, 150 Ind. 489, 50 N. E. 468, the loan was given to pay off a note and mortgage with an oral agreement that the note was to be kept alive for the lender, and he was to get the lien securing it. The court held the lender was entitled to subrogation. In Otis v. Gregory, 1887, 111 Ind. 504, 13 N.E. 39, where the oral agreement was to give a mortgage on land to be bought by the borrower, a married woman, subrogation was given the lender to the vendor's equitable lien. Chapman v. Abrahams, 1878, 61 Ala. 108 and Durant v. Davis, 1873, 57 Tenn. (10 Heisk) 522, contra. In Allen v. Caylor, 1897, 120 Ala. 251, 24 So. 512, 74 Am.St.Rep. 31, subrogation was allowed on an allegation that the plaintiff had paid the vendor at the borrower's request with an oral agreement that he should have a lien on the land for the amount paid. The court distinguished Chapman v. Abrahams, supra, on the ground that the lender there had relied entirely on getting the mortgage and had not expected substitution.
See 1930, 44 Harv.L.Rev. 27, note 12.

11. In Floyd v. Hammond, Tex.Com.App.1925, 268 S. W. 146 and Bagley v. Pollock, Tex.Civ.App.1929, 19 S.W.2d 193, discussed in note, 1930, 8 Tex.L.Rev. 311, while the court said the oral agreement to give a mortgage on property to be bought with the loan could not create an equitable mortgage, it would be treated as a vendor's lien or purchase money mortgage to prevent "fraud" on the lender.

seems questionable; [12] certainly it goes beyond the original doctrine itself which only protected those who parted with their lands on credit. The fourth explanation, and one which would apply regardless of the time when the loan was made, invokes the principle of restitution in specie of performance by a plaintiff when the defendant prevents the enforcement of the agreement between them by setting up the Statute of Frauds; the failure to restore is treated as a wrong which entitles the plaintiff to follow his res into any product of it, in this case the land purchased with it, for the purpose of securing the repayment of the amount of the plaintiff's performance.[13]

Although one or another of the foregoing theories is sufficient to explain the decisions in this second group another suggestion may

In Carey v. Boyle, 1881, 53 Wis. 574, 11 N.W. 47, E bought land from X and had the conveyance made to M who repaid E part of the purchase price and gave him his note for the balance. M went into possession. E had possession of the deed. There was no evidence of any oral agreement. The court held that E had an equitable vendor's lien. The court said "It must be understood that the extension of this equity to a third person is strictly confined to those who furnish or advance the purchase money to the purchaser in such manner that they can be said either to have paid it to the vendor, personally, or caused it to be paid, on behalf or for the benefit of the purchaser; and to this extent they become parties to the transaction. It must not be a general loan, to be used by the purchaser to pay the consideration of the purchase or to be used for any other purpose at his pleasure. In such case, the simple fact that the money can be traced into the land as having been paid by the purchaser to the vendor as the whole or part of the purchase money, gives the person who loaned it no such right." Soukup v. Wenisch, 1925, 163 Minn. 365, 204 N.W. 35, accord.

12. "The doctrine is anomalous, and probably should not be so extended. It is usually held that in the absence of an agreement that A is to have a security interest, he has no such lien. If, however, an oral agreement is made between A and B that A is to have a lien, while the oral agreement is unenforceable yet A can be put in *statu quo* only by giving him a lien; and accordingly, it has been held that he is entitled to a lien." Scott, Resulting Trusts Arising Upon the Purchase of Land, 1927, 40 Harv.L.Rev. 669, 681. See Pomeroy, Eq.Juris., 5th ed., § 1250.

13. See Scott, supra, note 12; note, 1930, 44 Harv.L. Rev. 262, 269.

be made. They may be differentiated from the cases in the first group in that there are circumstances in all of them which go far in satisfying the policy of the statute. The statute does not bar showing the whole agreement. The fact of the loan, the agreement as to what the money was to be used for, and that the money was so used may be proved. The third party from whom the property came and who received the money usually will be in a position to corroborate much of the plaintiff's story by his testimony and relate the plaintiff's money to the specific property. The transaction is no longer a two-party money lending but a three-party dealing in which new property is being acquired as well as money loaned. Granting some hardship on the plaintiff such as possible loss of priority over other creditors, even though not sufficiently great as to be able to invoke the doctrine of part performance in the first group type of case where this corroborative element is not present, this factor, which can be called upon to obtain subrogation or an equitable lien for restitution purposes on the doctrine which permits following the res, may be regarded as sufficient, where the policy of the statute is not offended, to justify enforcing the agreement itself. Added to this may be the fact that the defendant is not hurt because the payment will be enforced by the lien on land which he did not have before and was able to acquire only by the use of the plaintiff's money.

GROUP 3—MONEY LOANED FOR IMPROVING THE LAND WHICH IS TO BE MORTGAGED

64. Where money is loaned to pay for improvement of specific land in return for the borrower's oral promise to mortgage that land as security, authorities are divided whether an equitable mortgage arises if the money is used as agreed.

In the third group of cases also the doctrine of putting the plaintiff in *statu quo* by following the res into the improvements by giving a lien upon the land seems justified.[14] Further, although there is no third party whose part in the transaction can be relied upon to corroborate the plaintiff's story and to be a substantial guarantee against perjury by him, yet the fact that the money was agreed to be used and actually was used for improvements on the land, none of which evidence is barred by the statute, is sufficient to satisfy the purpose of the statute. There are, however, authorities both ways.[15]

14. Logically, perhaps, if this rationale is applied the lien should attach only to the improvement, not the land. No such distinction appears.

See Cunningham and Tischler, Equitable Real Estate Mortgages, 1963, 17 Rutgers L.Rev. 679, 710.

15. Smith v. Smith, 1891, 125 N.Y. 224, 26 N.E. 259; Poole v. Tannis, 1908, 137 Wis. 363, 118 N.W. 188, 864; Perry v. Board of Missions, 1886, 102 N.Y. 99, 6 N.E. 116; Schram v. Burt, C.C.A.Mich.1940, 111 F.2d 557, 562 (invoking the analogy of vendor's lien) sustain the lien. Spencer v. Williams, 1933, 113 W.Va. 687, 170 S.E. 179, 89 A.L.R. 1451; Slack v. Collins, 1896, 145 Ind. 569, 42 N.E. 910, semble— contra.

E, a mortgagee of land, told P that if P loaned to M, the mortgagor, for the purpose of building on the mortgaged land that P would be protected by a lien on the improvements, and he, E, would look only to the bare land. The court held that the Statute of Frauds did not prevent P from showing the agree-

CONTRACTS TO ASSIGN MORTGAGES

65. By the prevailing and preferable American view the Statute of Frauds does **not** apply to assignments of mortgages.

RELEASE OF THE MORTGAGE

66. Release of the mortgagor's personal liability is not within the Statute of Frauds. But an agreement to relinquish the property securing the obligation is, by the better view, within the statute.

TRANSFER OF THE MORTGAGOR'S INTEREST

67. The transfer of a mortgagor's interest is within the Statute of Frauds.

OTHER MORTGAGE TRANSACTIONS

68. The following transactions are not within the Statute: extension of maturity date or of redemption period, subordination agreements.

Agreements to extend a mortgage to cover other loans, to substitute other land, to revive a satisfied mortgage, or to modify a contract to give a mortgage are within the Statute.

ment. Godeffroy v. Caldwell, 1852, 2 Cal. 489, 56 Am.Dec. 360. See Sumner, The Doctrine of Estoppel Applied to the Statute of Frauds, 1931, 79 U. of Pa.L.Rev. 440; note, 1934, 89 A.L.R. 1455.

CHAPTER 4

RESTRICTIONS ON THE RIGHT TO REDEEM

A. THE ABSOLUTE DEED

Sec.
69. Deed Absolute with Separate Instrument of Defeasance.
70. Straight Mortgage vs. Trust Deed Mortgage.
71. Reasons for Prevalent Use.
72. Parol Evidence, Authorities.
73. Parol Evidence at Law.
74. Proof.
75. Deed Absolute as Trust Deed Mortgage.
76. Factors Establishing Absolute Conveyance as a Mortgage.
77. Effect of Deed Absolute Between the Parties.
78. Grantee's Title.
79. Rights of Grantor on Sale by Grantee.
80. Creditors of Grantee.
81. Deed Absolute Mortgages as Fraudulent Conveyances.
82. Recordation.
83. Objections to Parol Evidence.
84. Parol Evidence Rule.
85. The Statute of Frauds.
86. Parol Mortgage vs. Parol Trust or Parol Condition Subsequent to a Written Contract.

B. CONDITIONAL SALE

87. Nature of Transaction.
88. Extrinsic Evidence.
89. Factors Establishing Conditional Sale as Mortgage.

C. TRIPARTITE TRANSACTIONS

90. Purchase Money Resulting Trusts.
91. —— Security Agreements.
92. Statute of Frauds in Tripartite Cases.
93. Continuing Equitable Ownership in the Borrower.
94. Effect of Abolition of Purchase Money Resulting Trusts.
95. Contract or Option to Purchase.

D. CLOGGING

E. SUBSEQUENT TRANSACTIONS

A. THE ABSOLUTE DEED

DEED ABSOLUTE WITH SEPARATE INSTRUMENT OF DEFEASANCE

69. The common law mortgage takes the form of a deed absolute with a condition of defeasance. That condition may be expressed in a separate instrument to take effect at the same time as the deed. Law, but not equity, requires the instrument to be of equal formality with the original conveyance. Parol evidence is admissible to show that the two instruments constituted one transaction. A condition of defeasance must be distinguished from an option or contract to repurchase.

The common law mortgage takes the form of a "deed conveying lands conditioned to be void upon the payment of a sum of money, or the doing of some other act." [1] This condition of defeasance was ordinarily tacked onto the end of what otherwise read as an ordinary straight deed of absolute conveyance. Although there are statutory forms of mortgages in many jurisdictions the language of the traditional deed of conveyance is still commonly used even in lien theory jurisdictions. When it is all put into one document no doubts are raised as to the effectiveness of the instrument to accomplish the intended result. Equity added onto the express terms of the transaction, for reasons which were examined earlier,[2] a right in the grantor to redeem even though the terms of the defeasance were not fulfilled and title had vested absolutely in the grantee, and gave a corresponding right in the grantee to foreclose that right of redemption—neither of which rights were founded on any expression of intention of the parties either explicit or implied in fact, and one of them at least, the redemption right, in flat contradiction to the stated terms of the instrument. Sometimes, however, the defeasance is expressed in a separate instrument and the question arises whether the two can be read together so as to make out a legal mortgage. The practice has not gone uncriticised, one chancellor in the time of George II stating with vigor that "it will always appear with a face of fraud: for, the defeasance may be lost; and then an absolute conveyance is set up. I would discourage the practice as much as possible." [3] Nevertheless the well settled rule is that "the condition may be * * * by a separate deed, executed, or at least taking effect, at the same time [as the deed of conveyance], so as to be part of one and the same transaction. It must be by deed, and cannot be by parole or instrument in writing not under seal. It must take effect at the time the deed of conveyance takes effect, and not at a subsequent time." [4] There is some author-

1.   Lund v. Lund, 1817, 1 N.H. 39, 41, 8 Am.Dec. 29, 30.

2.   See Chapter I, Subdivision C, supra.

3.   Cottrell v. Purchase, 1732, Cas.Temp.Talbot, 61, 64.

4.   Lund v. Lund, 1817, 1 N.H. 39, 41, 8 Am.Dec. 29, 30; Sears v. Dixon, 1867, 33 Cal. 326, agreement for reconveyance executed, in accordance with terms of original agreement, after the absolute conveyance. "If the defeasance forms a part of the original transaction, it is not material that it be executed at the same time as the deed."; Cosby v. Buchanan, 1886, 81 Ala. 574, 1 So. 898, agreement

ity that where the instruments are separate the result is not a legal mortgage but an "equitable" mortgage only. "Equitable" mortgage in this connection is used to mean that the *mortgagor* has only an equitable interest which these courts seem to regard, even in title jurisdiction, as different from the redemption right of a mortgage executed as one document, a view that seems illogical and undesirable even though the consequences are of little importance.[5]

The substitution of the proviso for reconveyance for the defeasance clause in the debtor's deed did not alter the fundamental character of the common-law mortgage. The proviso was given a double construction; it operated as a condition subsequent to the grant, and it also was specifically enforceable as a promise.[6] If, instead of one instrument being used, the transaction consisted of a deed of the land, absolute in form, given by the debtor to the creditor concurrently with the execution by the creditor of a bond of defeasance or a sealed promise to reconvey on payment of the debt, the two instruments were construed together and held to create a legal mortgage.[7] Although the requirement

that the contemporaneous writing had to be of equal dignity and formality with the original conveyance, i. e., under seal if the deed were so executed, was the rule of the law courts,[8] in equity it was not necessary for the separate instrument to be of an equal dignity with the original conveyance.[9]

Oral evidence can always be introduced to establish the fact that the two instruments really constituted one transaction; the parol evidence rule cannot be invoked to bar its admission since it is "not introduced to contradict or vary the writings, but as showing that the papers constituted one arrangement agreed upon at one and the same time." [10] Indeed, it has been held that, where the separate deed and the qualifying defeasance are one single transaction, parol evidence is inadmissible to show that the transaction was intended as a sale or a conditional sale.[11] And, of course, the Statute of Frauds is inapplicable since the defeasance is in writing.

The foregoing statements of law presuppose that the character of the separate in-

---

subsequent to deed but made in performance of the original agreement by which the deed was executed; Erskine v. Townsend, 1807, 2 Mass. 493, 3 Am. Dec. 71; Waters v. Crabtree, 1887, 105 N.C. 394, 11 S.E. 240, agreement of defeasance made at time of deed but reduced to writing at subsequent time; Van Oehsen v. Brown, 1912, 148 Wis. 236, 134 N.W. 377; Teal v. Walker, 1884, 111 U.S. 242, 4 S.Ct. 420, 28 L.Ed. 415.

5. Williams v. Williams, 1915, 270 Ill. 552, 110 N.E. 876; Ferguson v. Boyd, 1907, 169 Ind. 537, 81 N.E. 71, rehearing denied 169 Ind. 537, 82 N.E. 1064. See note, 1928, 23 Ill.L.Rev. 80.

6. See Turner, The Equity of Redemption, General Preface, XXXII, XL–XLIV.

7. Sears v. Dixon, 1867, 33 Cal. 326; Ives v. Stone, 1883, 51 Conn. 446; Erskine v. Townsend, 1807, 2 Mass. 493, 3 Am.Dec. 71; Mills v. Darling, 1857, 43 Me. 565. See Williams v. Williams, 1915, 270 Ill. 552, 110 N.E. 876. Equity courts reached the same result. Edrington v. Harper, Ky.1830, 3 J.J.Marsh. 353, 20 Am.Dec. 145; Hill v. Edwards, 1866, 11 Minn. 22, Gil. 5; Froidevaux v. Jordan, 1908, 64 W.Va. 388, 62 S.E. 686, 131 Am.St.Rep. 911; Williams v. Williams, supra, note 5. Semble, Brown v. Bement, N.Y.1811, 8 Johns. 96; Dickinson v. Oliver,

1909, 195 N.Y. 238, 88 N.E. 44. See Holmes v. Grant, N.Y.1840, 8 Paige 243. See also Turner, loc. cit. supra note 6. Here, also, some of the cases say that the transaction is technically not a legal mortgage. Furguson v. Boyd, supra note 5; Williams v. Williams, supra note 5.

8. Warren v. Lovis, 1866, 53 Me. 463; Kelleran v. Brown, 1808, 4 Mass. 443; Lund v. Lund, 1817, 1 N.H. 39, 8 Am.Dec. 29; Fitch v. Miller, 1902, 200 Ill. 170, 179, 65 N.E. 650, 653. See Illinois Trust Co. of Paris v. Bibo, 1928, 328 Ill. 252, 257, 159 N.E. 254, 256.

9. See Kelleran v. Brown, 1808, 4 Mass. 443. Cf. Emerson v. Murray, 1827, 4 N.H. 171, 17 Am.Dec. 407; Whitfield v. Parfitt, 1851, 4 De G. & Sm. 240 (a written defeasance on the back of the deed of conveyance, if there when the instrument was executed, will constitute a mortgage at law).

10. Reitenbaugh v. Ludwick, 1858, 31 Pa.St. 131, 138, 15 L.I. 101; Sears v. Dixon, 1867, 33 Cal. 326; First Nat. Bank of Florida v. Ashmead, 1887, 23 Fla. 379, 2 So. 657; Cosby v. Buchanan, 1886, 81 Ala. 574, 1 So. 898, accord.

11. Woods v. Wallace, 1853, 22 Pa. 171, 1 P.L.J. 130, 2 Am.L.Reg. 186; Snyder v. Griswold, 1865, 37 Ill. 216. See Haines v. Thomson, 1872, 70 Pa. 434, 440. But see Gassert v. Bogk, 1888, 7 Mont. 585, 19 P. 281, 1 L.R.A. 240, affirmed 149 U.S. 17, 13 S.Ct. 738, 37 L.Ed. 631.

strument, whether it be in the form of a condition subsequent or a proviso for reconveyance as a clause of defeasance on the performance of a secured obligation is clear.[12] In such cases the only problem is to show that the two instruments constitute one transaction and are to be construed together. When, however, the separate instrument is cast in the form of a written option or contract to repurchase the issue is not merely whether the two instruments should be treated as though they had been embodied in one document and to be construed accordingly, but whether what has been stated as, for example, a resale agreement is in actual fact intended by the parties to be quite a different thing, namely, a defeasance clause in a mortgage. A later section deals with this and it suffices here to differentiate it from the simple question whether extrinsic evidence can be used to establish the unity in transaction of the two physically separate writings.

STRAIGHT MORTGAGE vs. TRUST DEED MORTGAGE

70. If there is doubt whether the instrument is a trust deed mortgage or a straight mortgage, it will be construed as the latter. A defeasance clause is almost conclusive evidence that the instrument is a straight mortgage.

As noted earlier, the trust device can be utilized for security purposes and when so used is generally referred to as a trust deed mortgage.[13] Even when there is no doubt that the instrument executed is a true trust deed mortgage, for a great many purposes it has been regarded as having the incidents of a mortgage rather than a trust and as being governed by the rules of mortgage law rather than trust law—[14] a development analogous to the similar molding of the device of conveying title subject to a defeasance clause for purposes of security into our modern mortgage. Frequently the question at issue is whether the document in question constitutes a trust deed mortgage or an ordinary mortgage. A defeasance clause making the conveyance in trust void has been held to be practically conclusive that the instrument was a mortgage,[15] while the absence of such a clause indicates the reverse.[16] Although there is authority that if the creditor is named as trustee it must be a mortgage,[17] the better view is that this is not a material factor.[18] Nor is it decisive that it cannot be a mortgage that it runs to a third party rather than the creditor.[19] Where there is doubt as to whether the instrument is a trust deed mortgage or a straight

---

12. Where there is a conveyance by deed and a condition of defeasance in a collateral paper, any doubt whether the transaction is a mortgage will be resolved in favor of its character as a mortgage. Hennessey v. Rafferty, 1945, 326 Ill.App. 259, 61 N. E.2d 409. McKinney's New York Real Prop. Law, L.1909, c. 52, § 320: "A deed conveying real property, which by any other written instrument, appears to be intended only as a security in the nature of a mortgage, although an absolute conveyance in terms, must be considered a mortgage; and the person for whose benefit such deed is made, derives no advantage from the recording thereof unless every writing, operating as a defeasance of the same, or explanatory of its being desired to have the effect only of a mortgage, or conditional deed, is also recorded therewith, and at the same time." Maryland, Nebraska, New Jersey, North Dakota, and South Dakota have statutes similarly worded. See Stinson, Am.Stat.Law, 1886–1892, § 1860. If the defeasance is oral such statutes have been held not applicable. Livesay v. Brown, 1892, 35 Neb. 111, 52 N.W. 838; Kline v. McGuckin, 1874, 24 N.J.Eq. 411.

13. See Chapter I, Subdivision E.

14. See 5 Tiffany, Real Prop., 3d ed., § 1400.

15. Turner v. Watkins, 1877, 31 Ark. 429, stressing also the fact that the trustee was given a power of sale; De Wolf v. A. & W. Sprague Mfg. Co., 1881, 49 Conn. 282; Martin v. Alter, 1884, 42 Ohio St. 94; Union Co. v. Sprague, 1884, 14 R.I. 452; Wisconsin Cent. R. Co. v. Wisconsin River Land Co., 1888, 71 Wis. 94, 36 N.W. 837.

16. Lance, Appeal of, 1886, 112 Pa.St. 456, 4 A. 375, stressing the presence of a power of sale in the transferee.

17. Eaton v. Whiting, 1826, 20 Mass. (3 Pick.) 484; Chowning v. Cox, 1823, 22 Va. (1 Rand.) 306, 10 Am.Dec. 528.

18. More v. Calkins, 1892, 95 Cal. 435, 30 P. 583, 29 Am.St.Rep. 128.

19. Anglo-Californian Bank v. Cerf, 1905, 147 Cal. 384, 81 P. 1077. Marvin v. Titsworth, 10 Wis. 320, contra, in Merrill v. Hurley, 1895, 6 S.D. 592, 62 N.W. 958, 55 Am.St.Rep. 859, it was held a mortgage but the court stressed as conclusive that the creditor had the option to foreclose. There was, however, a similar option in the Wisconsin case.

mortgage, it has been held that it will be construed to be the latter.[20]

REASONS FOR PREVALENT USE

71. An absolute deed coupled with an oral understanding that the property should be held only as security is very common. Creditors hope to gain certain advantages by this device, especially avoidance of time-consuming and expensive foreclosure proceedings. The net benefits to the grantee are dubious.

Judging from the large number of adjudicated cases involving the question, the practice of a debtor executing an absolute deed of conveyance to his creditor with only an oral understanding with him that the latter should hold it as security only and reconvey it to the grantor when the obligation has been satisfied must be extremely common. The reasons for this prevalence must be, to some extent, speculative. However, there is, in the cases, sufficient evidence as to what motivated the parties to warrant some reliable conclusions. For the most part these reasons center around the avoidance of foreclosure and its attendant costs and delays,[21] the right to rents and profits in lien jurisdictions, and other features.[22] Recent studies[23] have emphasized how time-consuming and expensive our foreclosure proceedings

are, especially if looked at in the light of the law relating to statutory redemption periods. They tend to justify efforts to avoid the strict requirements of mortgage law or at least make such efforts understandable. In addition, the grantee frequently desires to obtain some advantages that he expects to flow from having the deed convey legal title to him in jurisdictions following the lien theory of mortgages. As will be seen in the discussion that follows, the advantages that are sought and thought to be secured frequently are not obtained. And, on the contrary, it is to be observed that there are certain dangers and disadvantages lurking in the arrangement which are unexpected. To mention some of the most frequent objectives and disadvantages which do or may attend their attempted achievement may make the foregoing statements somewhat more definite.[24]

Avoidance of the slowness and costs of regular foreclosure has already been mentioned as one purpose. But the grantee runs the risk of a suit to establish that a mortgage was what the dealings really constituted and if it succeeds, on top of it will come the foreclosure difficulties he sought to avoid. Further, since the agreement is not in regular mortgage form, there is always the chance that some step in the foreclosure proceedings may encounter judicial disapproval, as well as the hazard of what the mortgagor may swear to, and the trier of fact believe, as to the terms of the oral mortgage agreement. Along with the proceeding there is often the hope of a more informal release of the mortgagor's interest; again, a hope that cannot be relied upon unless the matter has been settled judicially. Further this is offset to a degree by the necessity of a formal reconveyance by the grantee should the grantor redeem. And, too, the difficulties of recording in many states—should it go with the mort-

---

20. Godfrey v. Monroe, 1894, 101 Cal. 224, 35 P. 761, "the intervention of a trustee is not always, but is generally, a serious inconvenience and expense."; Banta v. Wise, 1901, 135 Cal. 277, 67 P. 129; First Federal Trust Co. v. Sanders, 1923, 192 Cal. 194, 219 P. 440, discussed, 1923, 12 Cal.L.Rev. 307.

21. E.g., Brinkman v. Jones, 1878, 44 Wis. 498, 503, "he told Jones [mortgagor] * * * that old contract might be considered a mortgage, and it would subject him to a foreclosure and a year's redemption." Miller v. Thomas, 1853, 14 Ill. 428, "if he took a mortgage it would take as long as it would to sue the note. He then said he would buy the land, but in such a way that he could sell it at a certain day, for he would not have his money out of his hands, beyond his control."

22. See Osborne, Cas.Prop.Security, 779, 780 and footnotes for a statement of observations on needed reforms in mortgage law.

23. See preceding footnote.

24. See an excellent résumé in a note, Hanna, Cases and Materials on Security, 3d ed., 733.

gages? or with the deeds? or neither?—raise a spectre of doubt to haunt title.

The ease of conveying the property to a purchaser if the mortgagor acquiesces in the sale and the capacity for informal enlargement of the mortgage to cover future advances are additional advantages that may be thought to accrue.

As to the first, the advantage over more usual methods is not great; and as to the second, the law of future advances seems sufficiently simple and efficient as it stands in most jurisdictions to accomplish legitimate activities.

Some of the advantages sought for hinge upon the deed operating to transfer legal title. One is the right to possession in the grantee in lien states before default. As will be seen, the grantee may find the courts holding that he acquired neither title nor the right to possession. And even if he does get possession, it will not be free from the onerous duty to account in equity—a duty which usually is a considerable deterrent to exercising the right in title jurisdictions where the mortgagee would get it in a straight mortgage. Another is the maintenance of the mortgagee's rights to chattels severed from the realty. And still a third is a hoped for different effect from the running of the statute of limitations on the debt. When all these matters are weighed it seems dubious whether there are really any substantial benefits to be obtained to the grantee-mortgagee in having the transaction framed in this fashion.[25] Yet creditors in large numbers undoubtedly think so. And because they do, we must look at the law which governs when they act upon their beliefs.

25. Although the objectives of the grantee are usually dominant, and, as will be seen, the assumption that it is the grantee who forces the grantor to consent to this form has an important bearing on the law, it should be observed that the deed absolute form may serve a deservedly frowned upon purpose of the grantor, i.e., to hide away this asset from his other creditors.

PAROL EVIDENCE, AUTHORITIES

72. Parol evidence is admissible in equity to show that a deed absolute on its face was intended as a mortgage. In some states this is so by statute. A small minority require proof that the defeasance was omitted by fraud, mistake or some similar general equitable ground for relief. Also a few states have placed statutory restrictions on the doctrine.

Where the only written instrument in the transaction consists of a deed absolute on its face but nevertheless it was the intention of the parties that it should be operative as a mortgage, the state of the law on the admissibility of parol evidence to establish such intention, although voluminous and somewhat complicated in parts, nevertheless can be set forth rather readily. In the first place the cases deciding that parol evidence is admissible in equity to show that a deed absolute on its face was intended as a mortgage even though it was knowingly cast in that form and its execution was not affected in any way by fraud, mistake, ignorance, duress or undue influence are so numerous and constitute so great a weight of authority that any extensive documentation of authorities is unnecessary.[26] In several states by direct statutory sanction it may be proved that a transfer was a mortgage even though the fact does not appear by the terms of the instrument.[27] And in other states a similar result is reached under statutory definitions of a mortgage.[28] There are, however, a few

26. In Pierce v. Robinson, 1859, 13 Cal. 116, 125, a leading and typical case, the court said, "I consider parol evidence admissible in equity, to show that a deed absolute upon its face was intended as a mortgage, and that the restriction of the evidence to cases of fraud, accident, or mistake, in the creation of the instrument, is unsound in principle and unsupported by authority."

For an extensive collection of authorities, see L.R.A. 1916B, 1, 46, 76 et seq. Parol evidence is also admissible to show that an absolute transfer of chattels was intended as a mortgage. Butts v. Privett, 1887, 36 Kan. 711, 14 P. 247; Jones v. Rahilly, 1871, 16 Minn. 320, Gil. 283; Newton v. Fay, 1865, 92 Mass. [10 Allen] 505.

27. E.g., West's Ann.Cal.Civ.Code § 2925.

28. E.g., see 46 Okl.St.Ann. § 1.

states that require that the plaintiff, in order to introduce evidence of the real purpose of the transfer, must allege and prove that the defeasance clause was omitted by reason of "ignorance, mistake, fraud, or undue advantage" or some similar ground which would make out a case for reformation in equity.[29] This narrower view is merely a special application of a general doctrine of equity jurisdiction and does not represent any view peculiar to the law of mortgages.[30] Also, in some states there are statutory restrictions on the doctrine. Thus it is provided in Georgia that if the deed is absolute and accompanied by possession of the property, a circumstance which is both very infrequent in mortgages of land because ordinarily the reason for mortgaging instead of selling is that the mortgagor wants the use of the property and also extremely misleading, only "fraud in the procurement" will permit the deed to be proved to be a mortgage by parol evidence at the instance of the parties.[31] New Hampshire goes even further and provides flatly that for an instrument to operate as a mortgage the agreement to that effect must be "inserted in the condition of the conveyance and made a part thereof", thus striking down even a separate written defeasance. This seems far too drastic even

if it be conceded that there are objections [32] to the usual doctrine.[33]

PAROL EVIDENCE AT LAW

73. **Authorities are divided whether parol evidence to show that an absolute deed was intended as mortgage is admissible in a legal action. The correct and more modern view holds it is admissible.**

There are a considerable number of cases, mostly older ones although sporadically more recent ones can be found,[34] maintaining the distinction that the admissibility of parol evidence to establish a deed absolute as a mortgage is exclusively an equitable doctrine, and that if the action be a legal one the evidence will be barred.[35] There are, however, other authorities permitting the evidence to be used in actions at law.[36] It his been sug-

---

29. Newton v. Clark, 1917, 174 N.C. 393, 93 S.E. 951; Williamson v. Rabon, 1919, 177 N.C. 302, 98 S.E. 830; Waddell v. Aycock, 1928, 195 N.C. 268, 142 S. E. 10. See L.R.A.1916B, 18, 41 et seq. Where the conveyance comes to the creditor from a third person North Carolina seems to dispense with any special showing of fraud, etc. Sandling v. Kearney, 1911, 154 N.C. 596, 70 S.E. 942; Lutz v. Hoyle, 1914, 167 N.C. 632, 83 S.E. 749.

See Fogelman, The Deed Absolute as a Mortgage in New York, 1963, 32 Fordham L.Rev. 299, 302.

30. "Fraud, accident, and mistake, are special grounds of equity jurisdiction, and may be shown by any satisfactory evidence, written or verbal, with reference not merely to mortgages, but to all written instruments." Pierce v. Robinson, 1859, 13 Cal. 116, 127.

31. Georgia Code §§ 67–104. Rights of creditors of the mortgagor as against the mortgagee are not affected by the statute. Miss.Code 1942, § 272, accord.

32. N.H.Rev.Stats.Ann., 1968, ch. 479:1 and 479:2. Pennsylvania follows New Hampshire with the exception that a separate defeasance "made at the time the deed is made and—in writing, signed and delivered by the grantee in the deed to the grantor" will be given effect although it must be acknowledged and recorded to be effective against any subsequent grantee or mortgagee for value. 21 Pa.S. § 951.

33. See notes, 1914, 2 Cal.L.Rev. 147; 1920, 8 Cal.L. Rev. 259; 1926, 20 Ill.L.Rev. 732; 1930, 15 Iowa L. Rev. 192; 1913, 23 Yale L.J. 185.

34. E.g., Carleton & Hovey Co. v. Burns, 1934, 285 Mass. 479, 189 N.E. 612, mortgagee under a deed absolute cannot foreclose by a legal writ of entry but must bring suit in equity. Zaff v. Brown, 1928, 265 Mass. 598, 164 N.E. 476; Carlson v. Chicago Title, etc., Co., 1940, 375 Ill. 125, 30 N.E.2d 632, grantor under deed absolute intended as mortgage does not have a freehold estate but only the right to acquire it by redemption in equity from the grantee. Y.B., 1470, 9 Edw. IV, 25, 34, is the earliest case in which the law court stated that relief would be granted in equity. See also Maxwell v. Montacute, 1719, Prec.Ch. 526.

35. Jones v. Trawick, 1857, 31 Ala. 253; Inhabitants of Reading v. Weston, 1830, 8 Conn. 117, 20 Am. Dec. 97; Finlon v. Clark, 1886, 118 Ill. 32, 7 N.E. 475; Reilly v. Cullen, 1900, 159 Mo. 322, 60 S.W. 126; Abbott v. Hanson, 1853, 24 N.J.L. 493; Billingsley v. Stutler, 1903, 52 W.Va. 92, 43 S.E. 96.

36. Jackson v. Lodge, 1868, 36 Cal. 28, plaintiff in an action of ejectment allowed to show by parol evidence that an older deed, absolute on its face, is a mortgage; Walls v. Endel, 1883, 20 Fla. 86, grantee denied ejectment at law; McAnnulty v. Seick, 1882, 59 Iowa, 586, 13 N.W. 743, replevin by a holder of

gested that cases like the above are explainable on the ground that the jurisdictions allowing the evidence at law are code states in which law and equity have been merged into a single system as to courts, procedure, and substantive law.[37] While this may be true of some of the cases,[38] it is certainly not the basis of decision in others.[39] Also, in some

an absolute bill of sale of personal property defeated by admission of parol evidence that it was a mortgage, the issue being one for the jury on the preponderance of the evidence as contrasted with the requirement of clear and convincing proof when the issue is an equitable one. Maytag v. Morgan, 1929, 208 Iowa 658, 226 N.W. 93, real property, forcible entry and detainer, parol evidence admissible but must establish mortgage intent beyond reasonable doubt. Fuller v. Parrish, 1854, 3 Mich. 211; Despard v. Walbridge, 1857, 15 N.Y. 374; Snyder v. Parker, 1898, 19 Wash. 276, 53 P. 59, 67 Am.St.Rep. 726; Kent v. Agard, 1869, 24 Wis. 378, plaintiff permitted to show that defendants, although grantees under a deed absolute, were really mortgagees under a satisfied mortgage. Dobbs v. Kellogg, 1881, 53 Wis. 448, 10 N.W. 623, although equitable issues had to be set up by counterclaim and tried by the court, the defense to an action of ejectment that a deed-absolute was a mortgage could be pleaded at law and decided by a jury.

See, in addition cases such as the following: The creditor of a grantor of a deed absolute intended as a mortgage was held entitled to levy execution upon the land without invoking the aid of equity. Flynn v. Holmes, 1906, 145 Mich. 606, 108 N.W. 685, 11 L.R.A.,N.S., 209. Security Savings & Trust Co. v. Loewenberg, 1900, 38 Or. 159, 62 P. 647, accord. Cf. Virginia-Carolina Chemical Co. v. Williams, 1917, 146 Ga. 482, 91 S.E. 543. The grantor under a deed absolute intended as security brought an action of conversion against B who bought timber cut by a trespasser on the land. Neither B nor the trespasser claimed any interest in the property through the grantee. Held, the grantor could show that he was a mortgagor. Jones v. Bradley Timber & Ry. Supply Co., 1911, 114 Minn. 415, 131 N.W. 494. Similarly a grantor was permitted to maintain ejectment against a third party. Hulsman v. Deal, 1913, 90 Kan. 716, 136 P. 220; Cunningham v. Hawkins, 1865, 27 Cal. 603 (against lien claimant). Cf. German Ins. Co. v. Gibe, 1896, 162 Ill. 251, 44 N.E. 490, evidence admissible at law when the title is not directly in issue.

See also Fogelman, The Deed Absolute as a Mortgage in New York, 1963, 32 Fordham L.Rev. 299, 301–303.

37. Walsh, Mortgages, 35 n. 3, 37, 38 n. 8. See also L.R.A.1916B, 77 and the dissenting opinion in Pratt v. Pratt, 1922, 121 Wash. 298, 209 P. 535, 28 A.L.R. 548.

38. E.g., Jackson v. Lodge, Walls v. Endel, Despard v. Walbridge cited in note 36, supra.

39. E.g., Dobbs v. Kellogg, 1881, 53 Wis. 448, 10 N.W. 623.

of the cases holding that the only relief was in equity when the deed was absolute on its face the same result would have been reached had the deeds been inscribed in the proper mortgage form.[40] Further, there seems scant place for any such procedural distinction in the modern law. Even in 1881 one court pointed out that "it is now too well established to be questioned, that a deed absolute on its face may be shown, even by parol, to be in fact a mortgage. * * * As a fact, then, why may it not be as well shown before a jury under the instruction of the court, and be found by them, as before the court sitting in equity * * * ?"[41] The answer seems clear. Granting that the basis of the enforcement of the mortgage in such cases began as a purely equitable doctrine, precisely the same thing could be and was said when equity interfered in the first place with the workings of the strict rules of real property law and the expressed intention of the parties to create the equity of redemption. And, although the idea persisted for a long time that the mortgage incidents of the transaction were superimposed solely by equity upon the legal situation, today the mortgage conception is thoroughly accepted as a legal doctrine not merely in lien states but in large measure in states retaining the title theory. And in lien states the law courts would never think of holding that a mortgage executed in the traditional form of a conveyance of title with a clause of defeasance created anything other than a legal lien in the grantee. Since that is so, it seems splitting hairs to say that the deed alone without the defeasance cannot be shown to be a mortgage in a court of law although it can be in equity.

40. E.g., Finlon v. Clark, 1886, 118 Ill. 32, 7 N.E. 475. Abbott v. Hanson, 1853, 24 N.J.L. 493 apparently is another case of this sort since the mortgage was executed after the lease and therefore would carry with it the right to rents, which was what the plaintiff was entitled to as grantee under a deed absolute.

41. Dobbs v. Kellogg, 1881, 53 Wis. 448, 453, 10 N.W. 623, 624.

It has been argued that the lien theory itself was the result of the merger of law and equity in one procedure,[42] just as it is here urged that only the code merger permits law courts to receive evidence that the deed absolute was a mortgage. One answer to this is that the lien theory was developed in New York, a pioneer state, before code merger. Further, if code merger of law and equity were the cause of eliminating the title of the mortgagee it would seem that it should likewise have destroyed the title of a trustee, which, of course, it has not. To explain this inconsistency it is urged that the "trust is a great and useful instrument of modern life, and the merger of law and equity results in no change in trusts because * * * the separate legal title of the trustee * * * is just as essential to the institution as is the equitable title of the beneficiary." On the other hand, "the legal title of the mortgagee is simply an unnecessary appendage left over from an earlier time as a remnant from a crude legal instrumentality long since outgrown, demanding excision as the vermiform appendix of the modern English law." [43] The distinction between the trust and mortgage has some merit. But the real reason for the adoption of the lien theory by law courts in the mortgage case was not the merger of law and equity in one proceeding, although that would facilitate the development, but the cumbersome, outworn machinery of the title mortgage as it had come down to us. What really needs to be excised is the continuing conception that, regardless of whether lien or title theory is accepted, a court of law should be barred from establishing that the transaction is a mortgage so as to grant any relief which it could grant had the transaction been expressed in ordinary mortgage form.

PROOF

74. The party seeking to establish the conveyance as a mortgage has the burden of proof. The proof must be clear and convincing, not by a mere preponderance of the evidence.

The burden of proof, of course, is upon the party seeking to establish that a deed absolute is a mortgage.[44] But when it comes to the proof necessary to make out the plaintiff's case, although a few decisions seem to be satisfied with a mere preponderance of the evidence,[45] most courts demand that it be

---

42. See Walsh, Mortgages, § 6.
But see Fogelman, The Deed Absolute as a Mortgage in New York, 1963, 32 Fordham L.Rev. 299, 303.

43. Idem.

---

44. Kellogg v. Northrup, 1897, 115 Mich. 327, 73 N. W. 230. The same degree of proof is required whether the grantor or grantee seeks to have the deed declared a mortgage. Holman v. Mason City Auto Co., 1919, 186 Iowa 704, 171 N.W. 12.
See Fogelman, The Deed Absolute as a Mortgage in New York, 1963, 32 Fordham L.Rev. 299, 303.
Additional cases attesting the heavy burden upon a claimant in establishing a mortgage transaction by clear and convincing evidence are noted by Updike, Mortgages, in 1956 Annual Survey of American Law, 1957, 32 N.Y.U.L.Rev. 789. See also Karesh, Security Transactions, in Survey of South Carolina Law, 1955, 8 S.C.L.Q. 122; Note, The Equitable Mortgage in Kansas, 1956, 5 U. of Kan. L.Rev. 114, 116; Young, Parol Evidence and Texas Deeds: Some Current Problems, 1956, 34 Texas L.Rev. 351, 360. See Stolk v. Lucas, 1956, 146 Cal.App.2d 417, 304 P.2d 33, and Evans v. Evans, 1955, 226 S.C. 451, 85 S.E.2d 726, which are in accord. So also are Howard v. Steen, 1956, 230 S.C. 351, 95 S.E.2d 613, noted in Karesh, Security Transactions, in Survey of South Carolina Law, 1957, 10 S.C.L.Q. 114, 115; Kohler v. Gilbert, 1959, 216 Or. 483, 339 P.2d 1102; Child v. Child, 1958, 8 Utah 2d 261, 332 P.2d 981.

That parol evidence is not admissible to show that a mortgage in form was intended as a conditional sale or outright conveyance, see Young supra, at 362. But cf. Atkins v. Wallace, 1955, 6 Ill.App.2d 362, 127 N.E.2d 500, commented on in Survey of Illinois Law, 1954–1955, 1956, 34 Chi.-Kent L.Rev. 78, holding that a deed which recited that it was security for repayment of an advance and future advances was only an option to repurchase on proof that the grantor was not obligated to make repayment. See Updike supra, at 790.

45. Welch v. Thomas, 1936, 102 Mont. 591, 61 P.2d 404. See Campbell, Cas.Morts., 2d ed., 83 n. 1 for a collection of cases. Some of the decisions are not very clear and others are not in harmony with other authorities in the same jurisdiction, e.g., Schmidt v. Barclay, 1910, 161 Mich. 1, 125 N.W. 729, 20 Ann.Cas. 1194, preponderance of evidence is sufficient; Polokoff v. Vebb, 1924, 226 Mich. 541, 198 N.W. 194, "clear, irrefragable and most convincing proof."

clear and convincing. In its absence the presumption that the conveyance is what it purports to be must prevail.[46] In a few cases it even has been held that the grantor must establish his case beyond a reasonable doubt.[47] The reason for such strictness is not hard to understand. The general interest in the security of transactions and acquisitions, especially important in real estate dealings which have been committed to writing, would counsel extreme caution in opening the door to false swearing by an unscrupulous grantor who regretted his bargain and seeks to avoid it by "redeeming" the property. The greater stringency of the restricted rule requiring fraud, etc., by the grantee is, so far as this factor is concerned, a salutary one. So, too, the prevailing rule lends encouragement to debtors who wish to conceal their equity in the property from creditors by putting the apparently complete title in the name of the mortgagee, another evil which the narrower doctrine minimizes. And, also, there is the hard fact that, although, deeds absolute intended as mortgages are frequent, the great bulk of such transactions are exactly what they purport to be, final and complete transfers. Consequently, the requirement of greater proof than is usually required in civil cases seems justified.

When the question comes before an appellate court for review in a jurisdiction demanding that the mortgage intent be established for the trier of fact by clear and convincing evidence, it has been held that this "does not mean that the evidence in the record on appeal must be entirely plain and convincing to an appellate court. * * * while the appellate court will consider the question as to the sufficiency of the evidence in the light of that rule, it will not disturb the finding of the trial court * * * where there is substantial evidence warranting a clear and satisfactory conviction to that effect." [48]

DEED ABSOLUTE AS TRUST DEED MORTGAGE

75. Parol evidence that a deed absolute was intended as a trust deed mortgage is admissible in jurisdictions permitting parol trusts. The same should be true in states not recognizing parol trusts.

The question remains whether when the deed executed is absolute on its face parol evidence can be admitted to show that it was intended by the parties to be a trust deed mortgage rather than a regular mortgage. In a jurisdiction permitting parol trusts there would be no more objection to showing this than there would be to establishing it as an ordinary mortgage. But in jurisdictions in which an oral trust cannot be shown where there has been a conveyance by deed absolute will the rule in respect to parol mortgages be applied to allow in the evidence of intent to create a trust deed mortgage? It has been said that this cannot be done.[49] Whether the rule admitting parol evidence to prove that a deed absolute was intended as a mortgage is reconcilable with the rule that similar evidence cannot be introduced to establish a trust is considered later. Regardless of the answer to that question generally, when a trust deed mortgage is involved, since in spite of the different legal

46. Coyle v. Davis, 1885, 116 U.S. 108, 6 S.Ct. 314, 29 L.Ed. 583; Rodgers v. Burt, 1908, 157 Ala. 91, 47 So. 226; Mahoney v. Bostwick, 1892, 96 Cal. 53, 30 P. 1020, 31 Am.St.Rep. 175; Beeler v. American Trust Co., Cal.App.1942, 129 P.2d 13, dictum, the court excluding oral testimony of the grantor that a mortgage was intended as contradicting a sworn written statement by the grantor accompanying the deed that it was an absolute conveyance.

47. Rinkel v. Lubke, 1912, 246 Mo. 377, 152 S.W. 81. Cf. the strength of evidence required for the reformation of writings. See Southard v. Curley, 1892, 134 N.Y. 148, 151, 155, 31 N.E. 330, 331, 332, 16 L. R.A. 561, 30 Am.St.Rep. 642, rejecting the test of proof beyond a reasonable doubt.

48. Wadleigh v. Phelps, 1906, 149 Cal. 627, 637, 87 P. 93, 98. Look also at Welch v. Thomas, 1936, 102 Mont. 591, 61 P.2d 404; Buck v. Jewett, 1959, 170 Cal.App.2d 115, 338 P.2d 507.

49. Hodgkins v. Wright, 1900, 127 Cal. 688, 60 P. 431. Cf. Renton v. Gibson, 1906, 148 Cal. 650, 84 P. 186. See note, 1924, 12 Cal.L.Rev. 307.

mechanism used it is in substance a straight mortgage, the soundness of excluding parol evidence to establish it on the ground that it is technically a trust in form may be queried. This would be especially true if to exclude the agreement on the ground it was a trust would let the deed absolute stand. On the other hand, if the evidence of intent for security, even though for a particular form which would not be enforced, were allowed in to create a mortgage, in view of the court's preference for it over the trust deed mechanism, no serious objection could be urged.

FACTORS ESTABLISHING ABSOLUTE CONVEYANCE AS A MORTGAGE

76. The most important facts evidencing an intent that a deed absolute be a mortgage are:

(1) Indebtedness by grantor to grantee;

(2) Value of property considerably exceeds amount purportedly paid for it;

(3) Retention of possession by grantor.

A wide variety of other facts are also relied upon by the courts to establish the mortgage intent.

In determining whether an absolute conveyance is a mortgage, by far the most important fact is whether there is an indebtedness on the part of the grantor to the grantee, left unaffected by the conveyance. The debt may either have existed prior to the conveyance or have arisen from a loan made at the time of the conveyance. The existence of such an indebtedness is considered as almost conclusive that the transaction was a mortgage.[50] Whether or not the existence

of a personal obligation is an essential ingredient in the existence of a mortgage is canvassed at some length at another place.[51] If it is, of course the absence of a debt would preclude there being a mortgage. However, even if it is legally possible to have a mortgage without a personal debt, its absence raises such a strong natural inference in this sort of a case that the transaction was a sale that it practically establishes the point. This is especially true if a pre-existing debt was treated as extinguished or satisfied by the conveyance, the surrender or cancellation of the written evidences of the original indebtedness being very important evidence of this.[52]

Another strong evidential fact is adequacy or inadequacy of the amount paid by the grantee in purported consideration for the transfer to him. If the value of the property is very considerably greater than the amount advanced by the transferee this is strong evidence that what was paid was a loan rather than purchase price and the inference is that the transaction was a mortgage.[53] On the

---

50. Todd v. Todd, 1912, 164 Cal. 255, 128 P. 413; Anglo-Calif. Bank Ltd. v. Cerf, 1905, 147 Cal. 384, 81 P. 1077, future advances as well as existing indebtedness; Holmberg v. Hardee, 1926, 90 Fla. 787, 108 So. 211; Holman v. Mason City Auto Co., 1919, 186 Iowa 704, 171 N.W. 12, retention in grantee's possession, without cancellation, of written evidence of debt raises strong presumption of mortgage; Thomas v. Klemm, 1945, 185 Md. 136, 43 A.2d 193; Dean v. Smith, 1924, 53 N.D. 123, 204 N.W. 987; Corey v. Roberts, 1933, 82 Utah 445, 25 P.2d 940; Hunter v. Bane, 1929, 153 Va. 165, 149 S.E. 467, "a mortgage without debt to support it is a legal solecism"; Hofmeister v. Hunter, 1939, 230 Wis. 81, 283 N.W.

330, 121 A.L.R. 444. See Fogelman, The Deed Absolute as a Mortgage in New York, 1963, 32 Fordham L.Rev. 299, 305, 306.

See also When Is an Absolute Conveyance a Mortgage, 1955, 8 U. of Fla.L.Rev. 132, discussing Rosenthall v. LeMay, Fla.1954, 72 So.2d 289.

51. Chapter 5, infra.

52. McKinley v. State, 1933, 188 Minn. 325, 247 N.W. 389; American Nat. Bank v. Groft, 1930, 56 S.D. 460, 229 N.W. 376; Ditto v. Bank of Gillette, 1928, 38 Wyo. 120, 264 P. 1013.

53. See Horn v. Ketaltas, 1871, 46 N.Y. 605, 42 How. Pr. 138. The authorities to this effect are numerous. For collections of authorities, see, 1934, 90 A. L.R. 1504; 1940, 129 A.L.R. 1504. See also Fogelman, The Deed Absolute as a Mortgage in New York, 1963, 32 Fordham L.Rev. 299, 307. So too, the negotiations and conduct of the parties which lead to the "deed" are significant in reaching a conclusion as to the character of the transaction. Ibid.

The absence of disproportion between the value of the land and the expressed consideration is evidence that the transaction is not a mortgage. Howard v. Steen, 1956, 230 S.C. 531, 95 S.E.2d 613, noted in Karesh, Security Transactions in Survey of South Carolina Law, 1957, 10 S.C.L.Q. 114, 115.

other hand, if there is no great disparity between the value of the land and the amount paid, this tends to show that the transfer was a sale.[54] Among other factors which have been held to be evidence that the transaction was a mortgage are the following: the transferee was a money lender by occupation;[55] the transferee was not in the business of buying and selling property of the description conveyed;[56] the fact that the transferor was in financial difficulties at the time of the execution of the conveyance, although this might indicate a forced sale just as well as a mortgage if it stood by itself;[57] prior negotiations for a loan from the grantee of approximately the amount paid;[58] payment of taxes by the grantor subsequent to the deed;[59] and the continued possession of the grantor, collection of rents, making improvements and the like.[60]

EFFECT OF DEED ABSOLUTE BETWEEN THE PARTIES

77. A deed absolute established as a mortgage will be treated as a regular mortgage between the parties. Thus the grantor may redeem and a grantee in possession must account. The grantee may foreclose the redemption right but not by strict foreclosure or by exercise of a power of sale.

Whenever a deed absolute on its face is established as a mortgage, the general rule is that as between the parties it will be treated as though it were a mortgage executed in regular form. "All the rights and obligations incident to that relation attach to the parties. * * * "[61] Thus the grantor may maintain an action to redeem.[62] And even though the grantee obtains possession he will be treated as a mortgagee in possession and must account as such.[63] So, too, the transferee may maintain an action to foreclose the grantor's redemption right.[64] This flows from the general doctrine that the right to foreclose, like

---

54. Conway v. Alexander, 1812, 11 U.S. 218, 3 L.Ed. 321. So, too, if the grantor made a highly advantageous disposition of his interest by the transaction this indicates that the deed was intended to be absolute. Vinquist v. Siegert, 1929, 58 N.D. 820, 227 N.W. 556.

55. Haggerty v. Brower, 1898, 105 Iowa 395, 75 N.W. 321.

56. Desloge v. Ranger, 1842, 7 Mo. 327.

57. Lewis v. Wells, D.C.Alaska, 1898, 85 F. 896; Smith v. Berry, 1913, 155 Ky. 686, 160 S.W. 247.

58. Couts v. Winston, 1908, 153 Cal. 686, 96 P. 357; Evans v. Thompson, 1903, 89 Minn. 202, 94 N.W. 692; Macauley v. Smith, 1892, 132 N.Y. 524, 30 N.E. 997.

59. King v. Crone, 1914, 114 Ark. 121, 169 S.W. 238; Hart v. Randolph, 1892, 142 Ill. 521, 32 N.E. 517. See Karesh, Security Transactions, in Survey of South Carolina Law, 1957, 10 S.C.L.Q. 114, 115.

60. Parks v. Parks, 1880, 66 Ala. 326; Kohler v. Gilbert, 1959, 216 Or. 483, 339 P.2d 1102, considers several factors that are evidence that the transaction was intended as a mortgage. See Fogelman, The Deed Absolute as a Mortgage in New York, 1963, 32 Fordham L.Rev. 299, 308, discussing the significance of retention of possession by the "grantor" and miscellaneous factors in the transaction.

Cf. Hopper v. Smyser, 1900, 90 Md. 363, 45 A. 206, in which payment of taxes by the grantee together with transfer of possession to him, making improvements by him and no accounting of any income or recognition of any debt or payment of interest proved that no mortgage existed. Possession in the grantor may be explained by his having tak-

en a lease back. Pancake v. Cauffman, 1886, 114 Pa.St. 113, 7 A. 67; Brickle v. Leach, 1899, 55 S.C. 510, 33 S.E. 720; Edwards v. Wall, 1884, 79 Va. 321. On the other hand, a lease back to the grantor is not conclusive that the conveyance is not a mortgage. See Rogers v. Davis, 1894, 91 Iowa 730, 59 N.W. 265; Brickle v. Leach, supra; Bearss v. Ford, 1883, 108 Ill. 16.

61. Carr v. Carr, 1873, 52 N.Y. 251, 258. As to differences between a mortgage by deed absolute and a straight form mortgage, see 1949, 28 Neb.L.Rev. 481.

62. Campbell v. Dearborn, 1872, 109 Mass. 130, 12 Am.Rep. 671. A large proportion of the cases brought to establish that the absolute deed was intended as a mortgage are cases of this sort and will be found in other footnotes.

63. Husheon v. Husheon, 1886, 71 Cal. 407, 12 P. 410; Murdock v. Clark, 1891, 90 Cal. 427, 27 P. 275; Miller v. Peter, 1909, 158 Mich. 336, 122 N.W. 780; Pratt v. Pratt, 1922, 121 Wash. 298, 209 P. 535, 28 A.L.R. 548, deed absolute from a third party. Cf., however, Barnard v. Jennison, 1873, 27 Mich. 230, the duty to account is not so stringent as in the case of the ordinary mortgagee in possession.

64. Shadman v. O'Brien, 1932, 278 Mass. 579, 180 N.E. 532; Hughes v. Edwards, 1824, 22 U.S. (9 Wheat.) 489, 495, 6 L.Ed. 142.
For other cases holding that a deed absolute intended as security may be foreclosed in equity as a mortgage, see, 1909, 22 L.R.A.,N.S., 572.

the right to redeem [65] or to compel an accounting, does not depend upon any provision in the mortgage but is one of the legal consequences flowing from the existence of the mortgage relation.[66] This general doctrine, however, does not apply to permit a strict foreclosure of a deed absolute mortgage.[67] Further, since foreclosure by the exercise of a power of sale is permitted only when such a power has been expressly granted in the mortgage itself,[68] and since a mortgage by deed absolute of course does not contain such a power this method of foreclosure is not available.[69]

65. "The right to redeem is an essential part of a mortgage, read in by the law if not inserted by the parties." Mooney v. Byrne, 1900, 163 N.Y. 86, 92, 57 N.E. 163, 165.

66. See Scheibe v. Kennedy, 1885, 64 Wis. 564, 568, 25 N.W. 646, 647, "In order to give a court of equity the right to maintain an action to foreclose a mortgage it is not necessary that the mortgage itself should provide for such a foreclosure. * * * This must be so; otherwise the many decisions of this court which hold that an absolute deed, given in security * * * may and must be foreclosed as a mortgage, should be overruled."

67. Libel v. Pierce, 1934, 147 Or. 132, 31 P.2d 1106. But cf. Northwestern State Bank of Hay Springs v. Hanks, 1932, 122 Neb. 262, 240 N.W. 281; and see § 313, infra.

In Hermann v. Churchill, 1963, 235 Or. 327, 385 P.2d 190, in a suit to have a deed absolute declared a mortgage, the court decreed strict foreclosure in spite of 1963 ORS 88.010 providing that liens upon real property shall be foreclosed and the property sold by judicial sale. In Note, 1964, 43 Or.L.Rev. 350–356, the decision was criticised on these grounds: Strict foreclosure is not a proper remedy unless legal title is in the mortgagee. In Oregon, the grantee of a deed-absolute mortgage in a bipartite transaction acquires only a lien, not legal title. In a tripartite transaction with a purchase-money resulting trust, title is in the mortgagee. Analysis of mortgage history, legislative policy, and case law would indicate that, in Oregon, statutory provisions have replaced the judicial remedy of strict foreclosure in mortgage-default cases, whether the action is framed as a suit to redeem or a suit to foreclose.

68. See Very v. Russell, 1874, 65 N.H. 646, 23 A. 522; Gunn v. Brantley, 1852, 21 Ala. 633; Goodenow v. Ewer, 1860, 16 Cal. 461, 468, 76 Am.Dec. 540. Cf. Kornegay v. Spicer, 1877, 76 N.C. 95; Mowry v. Sanborn, 1877, 68 N.Y. 153. In England every mortgage, by statute, has a power of sale. See Osborne, Cases, Secured Transactions, p. 530. This applies, however, only to regular mortagages.

69. The ability of the grantee under a deed absolute mortgage to cut off the rights of the mortgagor by

GRANTEE'S TITLE

78. **In title states the deed absolute grantee gets title. In lien states by the better view he only gets a lien.**

Another point upon which there has been a difference of opinion and one which has sometimes been involved in the question whether parol evidence is admissible at law is whether the grantee under a deed absolute intended as a mortgage gets an interest in the property different from that received when the regular mortgage form is used. In title theory states the mortgagee gets legal title when the deed is in the form of a conveyance with a defeasance clause and a fortiori would get a like interest where the defeasance clause is omitted but nevertheless the conveyance is for security purposes.[70] Parenthetically it may be observed that in such jurisdictions ordinarily where an action at law is brought by the holder of the legal title it is immaterial to the solution of the controversy whether that legal title was held for security only or absolutely. This irrelevance may explain many rulings on the admissibility of oral evidence to establish the fact of mortgage in actions at law as compared with equitable proceedings. On the other hand, if the jurisdiction follows the lien theory, it makes a difference in several directions whether the deed absolute grantee gets title with the mortgagor having only an equitable interest or whether the result is precisely the same as though the conventional form of mortgage was employed. There is good authority for what, it is submitted, is the preferable view that the grantee under a deed absolute intended as a mortgage gets only a lien with the grantor retaining title.[71]

a sale to a bona fide purchaser is discussed, infra. It is not, however, foreclosure for the grantor still has rights against the proceeds or, if the purchaser is not bona fide, against the property in his hands.

70. Finlon v. Clark, 1886, 118 Ill. 32, 7 N.E. 475.

71. Jackson v. Lodge, 1868, 36 Cal. 28, later overruled by cases cited in the next footnote which

Nevertheless, there are decisions to the effect that the mortgagee under a deed absolute in a lien jurisdiction does get title.[72]

were then overturned by the enactment of the California Civil Code which in §§ 2888, 2924, 2925, and 2927 restored the rule of Jackson v. Lodge, Locke v. Moulton, 1892, 96 Cal. 21, 30 P. 957; Brandt v. Thompson, 1891, 91 Cal. 458, 27 P. 763; Shirey v. All Night and Day Bank, 1913, 166 Cal. 50, 134 P. 1001; Hulsman v. Deal, 1913, 90 Kan. 716, 136 P. 220; Flynn v. Holmes, 1906, 145 Mich. 606, 108 N. W. 685, 11 L.R.A.,N.S., 209; Shattuck v. Bascom, 1887, 105 N.Y. 39, 12 N.E. 283; Snyder v. Parker, 1898, 19 Wash. 276, 53 P. 59, 67 Am.St.Rep. 726; Clambey v. Copeland, 1909, 52 Wash. 580, 100 P. 1031; Pratt v. Pratt, 1922, 121 Wash. 298, 209 P. 535, 28 A.L.R. 548, deed absolute from a third party to creditor; Dobbs v. Kellogg, 1881, 53 Wis. 448, 10 N.W. 623. A deed absolute mortgage is not an alienation of the title within the meaning of fire insurance policies. Barry v. Hamburg-Bremen Fire Ins. Co., 1888, 110 N.Y. 1, 17 N.E. 405. Cf. Modlin v. Atlantic Fire Ins. Co., 1909, 151 N.C. 35, 65 S.E. 605. See note, 1906, 11 L.R.A.,N.S., 209 for a collection of additional cases as well as cases holding that the grantee gets legal title. See also 1924, 28 A.L.R. 554; Herron v. Millers National Ins. Co., 185 F.Supp. 851 (D.C.Or.1960); See Fogelman, The Deed Absolute as a Mortgage in New York, 1963, 32 Fordham L.Rev. 299, 310, on the effect of a deed absolute as creating only a lien in New York.

Note, 1964, 43 Or.L.Rev. 350, 353.

72. Hughes v. Davis, 1870, 40 Cal. 117 and De Espinosa v. Gregory, 1870, 40 Cal. 58, which were later overturned, preceding footnote; Woodson v. Veal, 1878, 60 Ga. 562; Gibson v. Hough, 1878, 60 Ga. 588; Shumate v. McLendon, 120 Ga. 396, 48 S.E. 10; Ferguson v. Boyd, 1907, 169 Ind. 537, 81 N.E. 71, rehearing denied 196 Ind. 537, 82 N.E. 1064; Burdick v. Wentworth, 1876, 42 Iowa 440; Baxter v. Pritchard, 122 Iowa 590, 98 N.W. 372, 101 Am.St. Rep. 282, mortgagor's interest being purely equitable may be surrendered by parol; Lindberg v. Thomas, 1908, 137 Iowa 48, 114 N.W. 562; Williams v. Williams, 1915, 270 Ill. 552, 110 N.E. 876, deed absolute with separate written agreement to reconvey, grantor's interest only equitable and therefore transferable without a deed. Illinois, however, is a hybrid state; First Nat. Bank of Plattsmouth v. Tighe, 1896, 49 Neb. 299, 68 N.W. 490, mortgagor's interest being equitable a judgment lien does not attach to it; First Nat. Bank of David City v. Spelts, 1913, 94 Neb. 387, 143 N.W. 218; Northwestern State Bank v. Hanks, 1932, 122 Neb. 262, 240 N.W. 281, mortgagee entitled to strict foreclosure since he had title; Hall v. O'Connell, 1908, 52 Or. 164, 95 A. 717, 96 P. 1070, modified on rehearing 52 Or. 164, 96 P. 1070; dissenting opinion, Pratt v. Pratt, 1922, 121 Wash. 298, 209 P. 535, 28 A.L.R. 548, conveyance from third party and therefore, if grantee got only a lien, it was argued that the third party would still have title, and the mortgagor would have an anomalous right; Beebe v. Wis-

Turning to a consideration of the merits of the question, it would seem that the parties should not be able to alter the legal character and incidents of the mortgage as developed in a lien jurisdiction by the simple expedient of leaving out the defeasance clause. When the defeasance clause remains in, the deed purports to pass the title but the courts, as we have seen, will not permit such an operation to it. And the same result should follow, regardless of the desires of the parties, once it is established that the intent was to mortgage. To hold otherwise would permit the parties to reinstitute the title theory of the mortgage in a lien jurisdiction by merely buying and using a different form. On the other hand a deed absolute intended as a mortgage and a regular mortgage should not be treated alike, at least in some instances. The latter sets forth the real nature of the transaction; it reveals on its face that there is a property interest—the redemption right —left in the transferor. The former falsely depicts the actual transaction, leaving the true situation to be revealed by oral testimony. They are therefore sufficiently different, certainly as to third parties and to some extent between the parties, to justify the application of different rules.[73] The

consin Mortgage Loan Co., 1903, 117 Wis. 328, 93 N.W. 1103.

See Note, 1964, 43 Or.L.Rev. 350, 354.

In Howell v. Wieas, 1925, 232 Mich. 227, 205 N.W. 55, discussed in note, 1926, 10 Minn.L.Rev. 353, the court held that a grantee under a deed absolute intended as security had legal title so that on a conveyance by him to the grantor and his wife a tenancy by the entireties was created.

73. As an instance of the desirability of treating the deed absolute mortgage differently from the orindary mortgage, see Report of the Committee on a Uniform Real Estate Mortgage Act, Handbook of the National Conference of Commissioners on Uniform State Laws and Proceedings of the Thirty-Seventh Annual Meeting, 1927, 680. In drafting a statute of limitations to bar the lien of a mortgage it was expressly provided that the sections should not apply to deeds absolute mortgages "unless such deed and the separate instrument operating as a defeasance are both recorded at least one year prior to the time when the period of limitation would expire if it applied."

straightforward way of dealing with the problem would be to face squarely the question as to what extent and in whose favor the usual rights created by a mortgage should be modified by reason of the deceptive form in which this type of mortgage has been cast. Instead the courts have been somewhat inclined to adopt a mechanical attitude and let the solution flow from a determination of whether the grantee got "title" rather than a "lien," or whether the parol evidence would be admissible at law or only in equity. Since in most cases, it is believed, a desirable result will be reached on this type of reasoning, or at least one not particularly undesirable, about the only criticism that can be leveled at the cases which concern themselves with or decide rights on the basis of whether a deed absolute intended as a mortgage conveys the legal title to the grantee is the mode of reasoning by which they reach their results.

The cases in which the courts have raised the question of title include actions for possession by the grantee-lender, assertion of rights in severed crops, timber or fixtures against third parties, the ability of creditors to reach the interest of the grantor by legal process, the formalities necessary for the transfer or surrender of the grantor's interest, and whether the running of the statute of limitations on the debt will prevent foreclosure of the property as a mortgage.[74] In a case of the last sort the question was complicated by the fact that the deed absolute came to the creditor from a third party thus presenting the difficulty in a lien state of getting title into the borrower-mortgagor who does not appear in the deed or on the record at all.[75] A separate section is devoted to this tripartite type of transaction [76] and the question of whether the running of the statute of limitations on the obligation secured should affect the mortgage is considered later and therefore will not occupy us here.[77] However it may be stated here that the question of whether the running of the statute of limitations on the debt should bar the enforcement of the mortgage ought not to depend upon any legalistic distinction as to whether the mortgagee got a lien or a title by his regular form mortgage, and, even less, upon whether, in a lien jurisdiction a deed absolute intended as a mortgage gave the creditor a lien or title as security, but rather upon an examination of the desirability of permitting the enforcement of the security to survive the barring of a direct action to enforce the obligation secured. Upon this there may be, and are, different views.[78] And, further, since the security here rests in oral understanding, the remedy to enforce it, regardless of the effect upon it of the debt being barred, properly may be governed by a different statutory period than where it is in writing.[79]

RIGHTS OF GRANTOR ON SALE BY GRANTEE

79. A bona fide purchaser from the grantee prevails over the grantor in both lien and title states. The grantor has a redemption action against the grantee for the value of the land or, at his election, the proceeds of the sale.

Even courts in lien jurisdictions which, in other connections, say that a grantor under a deed absolute intended as security retains legal title with the grantee getting only a lien, agree that a bona fide purchaser from the

74. See cases cited in the preceding footnotes.

75. Pratt v. Pratt, 1922, 121 Wash. 298, 209 P. 535. See notes, 1923, 8 Cornell L.Q. 172; 1923, 71 U. of Pa.L.Rev. 284; 1923, 32 Yale L.J. 611. See also 1924, 28 A.L.R. 554; 1908, 11 L.R.A.,N.S., 209, 825. See also Coutts, Does a Mortgagee under Deed Absolute in Form Gain Rights Not Incident to an Ordinary Mortgage? 1901, 52 Cent.L.J. 360.

76. Subdvision C, infra.

77. See Chapter 11, infra.

78. See preceding footnote.

79. Although there is some authority to the contrary, the general rule is that the equitable rule as to laches may bar the grantor from establishing that the deed absolute was a mortgage even though the delay on his part was short of the statute of limitations period. See 28 A.L.R. 554.

grantee will prevail over the grantor.[80] A fortiori, in a jurisdiction following the title theory a purchaser from the grantee for a valuable consideration and without notice that the property has been conveyed for security will hold the land free from any equity of the grantor to redeem.[81]   This result, apart from statute, has been explained as resting upon the doctrine of a bona fide purchase of the legal title cutting off equitable rights.   Since this is the rationale invoked, the cases preferring the bona fide purchaser are usually cited as establishing that the deed absolute intended as a mortgage gives to the grantee the full legal title and leaves only an equitable interest in the grantor.[82] Estoppel in pais by reason of the grantor having vested apparently complete title in the transferee by a deed of conveyance would seem an equally valid basis for the conclusion that the purchaser prevails and would not require holding that the grantee actually acquired title rather than a lien.   In many states statutes provide that the bona fide purchaser shall prevail unless a separate defeasance has been recorded.[83]

Even though the mortgagor's rights in the land may have been cut off by the sale to a bona fide purchaser, he "is not prevented by that wrongful act from any form of redemption now practicable. * * * In order to prevent him [the grantee] from making a profit out of his wrong, the law raises the presumption that he now has the full value of the land as a separate fund in his hands, and, treating it as land, allows the plaintiff to redeem. * * *[84] The value of the land which he is permitted to recover has been held to be that at the time of the redemption action,[85] at the time of tender of payment,[86] and at the time of sale.[87] Of course he is always entitled, at his election, to take the proceeds realized by the sale.[88] However, the action, it should be noted again, even though it will bring only money to the plaintiff, is an action to redeem land from a mortgage and not to recover money and, consequently the statute of limitations fixing the time within which to bring an action to redeem governs.

CREDITORS OF GRANTEE

80. **The grantor prevails over the grantee's creditors.**

Apart from statutory recording requirements affecting the problem, it would seem that the grantor would prevail over creditors of the grantee, the courts following the general rule that creditors merely stand in the

---

80. Mooney v. Byrne, 1900, 163 N.Y. 86, 57 N.E. 163. See, 1911, 32 L.R.A.,N.S., 1046; L.R.A.1916B, 584. Macauley v. Smith, 1892, 132 N.Y. 524, 30 N.E. 997; Meehan v. Forrester, 1873, 52 N.Y. 277; Pancake v. Cauffman, 1886, 114 Pa. 113, 7 A. 67; Harrington v. Butte & Superior Copper Co., 1916, 52 Mont. 263, 157 P. 181. The grantor's rights continue against a grantee with notice. Graham v. Graham, 1876, 55 Ind. 23; Hadley v. Stewart, 1886, 65 Wis. 481, 27 N.W. 340.

Where the grantor under a deed absolute intended as a mortgage remains in possession, he may prove his equity by parol evidence against the grantee and also against a purchaser for value from him who had no actual notice of the occupant-grantor's equity and made no inquiry of him. Williamson v. Floyd C. Wildlife Ass'n, Inc., 1960, 215 Ga. 789, 113 S.E.2d 626, noted by Smith, Security Transactions, 1960, 12 Mercer L.Rev. 182, 188.

81. Hogan v. Jacques, 1868, 19 N.J.Eq. 123, 97 Am. Dec. 644.

82. See Walsh, Mortgages, 37; 5 Pomeroy, Equity Juris., 5th ed., 587.

83. See, e. g., West's Ann.Cal.Civ.Code, § 2950; Carpenter v. Lewis, 1898, 119 Cal. 18, 50 P. 925; Payne v. Morey, 1904, 144 Cal. 130, 77 P. 83. See also Jones, Mortgages, 8th Ed., §§ 304, 631. For authorities as to where a deed absolute may or must be

recorded and the effect of recordation statutes dealing with deeds absolute with separate defeasance clauses, either written or oral, see Chapter 7, infra.

84. Mooney v. Byrne, 1900, 163 N.Y. 86, 95, 57 N.E. 163, 166.

85. Mooney v. Byrne, supra note 84; Boothe v. Feist, 1891, 80 Tex. 141, 15 S.W. 799.

86. Clark v. Morris, 1913, 88 Kan. 752, 129 P. 1195. See note, 1913, 13 Col.L.Rev. 442.

87. Staples v. Barret, 1926, 214 Ala. 680, 108 So. 742, 46 A.L.R. 1084; Brimie v. Benson, 1920, 216 Ill. App. 474.

88. Staples v. Barret, supra, note 87; Shillaber v. Robinson, 1877, 97 U.S. 68, 24 L.Ed. 967; Meehan v. Forrester, 1873, 52 N.Y. 277.

shoes of their debtors.[89] And even where there is a statute requiring recordation of a defeasance when the mortgage is by deed absolute, in the absence of an express provision that non-compliance will defeat the grantor as against creditors of the grantee the statute will not be construed to so operate.[90]

DEED ABSOLUTE MORTGAGES AS FRAUDULENT CONVEYANCES

81. Many courts hold deed absolute mortgages constructively fraudulent and void as to the grantor's creditors. Others consider them presumptively fraudulent. Some will not so consider them unless actual fraudulent intent is established.

Use of the deed absolute as a means of fraudulent concealment of an insolvent debtor's property from his creditors is a matter which has engaged the attention of the courts. It is true, of course, that a regular form mortgage may be made the vehicle of defrauding creditors and the fact that the value of the mortgaged property is greatly disproportionate to the amount of the debt invites throwing out the mortgage as fraudulent.[91] But when the mortgage is used cooperation by the mortgagee in fabricating fictitious debts is usually necessary to accomplish the purpose and this ordinarily will present difficulties. The mortgage by itself is not inherently deceptive. On the other hand, the creditor very frequently prefers a deed absolute without any collusion with the debtor in respect to the latter's creditors, while the form it takes automatically operates to conceal an asset. Consequently many courts treat deed absolute mortgages as constructively fraudulent and, as a matter of law, void even as security, not only as to subsequent but as to prior creditors.[92]

As one of these courts said, "The law will not tolerate such a transaction; for if it did, an insolvent debtor could easily arrange with a favored creditor to become the absolute owner of his effects, thus securing them, by the absolute nature of the transfer or conveyance, from liability to his other debts, while at the same time, he could avail himself of the effects as secured in trust: could speculate upon his equity of redemption, or pocket the residuum should a sale take place, or use the transfers as a cover for future advances. It requires neither argument nor illustration to show with what ease such transfers could be converted to the worst of purposes. * * *

"There is no hardship in requiring those who seek to gain a preference over other creditors of an insolvent debtor, to make the written evidence of the contract substantially conform to the truth. The propriety of such a course is obvious to every ingenuous mind. By doing so, the other less fortunate creditors of the insolvent party will not be deluded by false appearances, the registration laws will not be defeated in securing the object which led to their enactment, and the unfortunate debtor himself will be cut off from temptations to fraud and circumvention in creating secret trusts for his benefit. * * * * "[93]

Others hold the transaction cast in this form to be a "badge of fraud," not conclusive but capable of rebuttal by proof of the actual good faith of the parties.[94] Other de-

---

89. Vallely v. First Nat. Bank of Grafton, 1905, 14 N.D. 580, 106 N.W. 127, 5 L.R.A.,N.S., 387, 116 Am. St.Rep. 700. On the question of priorities of an equitable mortgagee against creditors of the mortgagor, an analogous problem, see Welton v. Tizzard, 1864, 15 Iowa 495.

90. See preceding footnote.

91. Butts v. Peacock, 1868, 23 Wis. 359; Jones v. Third Nat. Bank of Sedalia, C.C.A.Mo.1926, 13 F.2d 86.

92. Bryant v. Young, 1852, 21 Ala. 264. See Fogelman, The Deed Absolute as a Mortgage in New York, 1963, 32 Fordham L.Rev. 299, 312.

93. Bryant v. Young, 1852, 21 Ala. 264, 269.

94. McClure v. Smith, 1890, 14 Colo. 297, 23 P. 786 and Hanneman v. Olson, 1928, 209 Iowa 372, 222 N. W. 566 (badge of fraud but not conclusive).

cisions require actual fraudulent intent to be established as a fact.[95]

A grantee who is a party to an actual fraudulent design in giving and taking a deed absolute not only loses the property to creditors of the grantor but has no right to reimbursement for the amount loaned when the conveyance is set aside.[96] If the grantor had an actual fraudulent intent he is not entitled to relief against the grantee.[97]

RECORDATION

82. **There is diverse opinion as to whether and where a deed absolute mortgage may be recorded effectively.**

The question of whether and where a deed absolute intended as a mortgage may be recorded effectively so as to preserve priorities or give notice has produced considerable divergence of opinion. It has been held that it is unrecordable as either a deed or a mortgage and consequently is invalid against creditors of the grantor.[98] There are some authorities, however, which hold it may be recorded as a deed; others that it may or must be recorded as a mortgage. Under statutes providing for the recordation of a separate defeasance for the deed to be valid against third parties a distinction has been drawn between oral and written defeasances, the statute applying to the latter only.[99]

OBJECTIONS TO PAROL EVIDENCE

83. **The two main objections to the admission of oral evidence for the purpose of establishing a deed absolute as a mortgage have been the Statute of Frauds and the parol evidence rule.**

In spite of the overwhelming weight of authority admitting, on one condition or another, parol evidence to establish that a deed absolute on its face was intended as a mortgage, there are two objections raised to the introduction of such evidence which need to be considered. One is the parol evidence rule; the other is the Statute of Frauds. The explanations offered as to why the evidence should not be barred by one or the other of these two rules have been various and reconciliation with the results in analogous cases, particularly those in which there is a conveyance on oral trust, while possible, is not free from difficulty. Although in many cases there is no clear segregation of the parol evidence rule from the Statute of Frauds, they will be considered separately here even though some of the reasons urged as to why there is either no violation of the rule or Statute or, even if there is, why there should be an exception made are applicable to both. For, in spite of the fact that at least some of the same arguments may be valid to justify the admission of the evidence in the face of both, the two are quite independent of each other in their operation and theory.[1] The parol evidence rule bars extrinsic agreements which would vary the terms of the single written instrument or group of instruments

95. Capital Lumber Co. v. Saunders, 1914, 26 Idaho 408, 143 P. 1178; Hutchison v. Page, 1910, 246 Ill. 71, 92 N.E. 571. See note, 1862, 2 Am.L.Reg.,N.S., 1, 11. See also L.R.A.1916B, 576–580. See Glenn, Fraudulent Conveyances, rev. ed., § 299a.

96. Svalina v. Saravana, 1930, 341 Ill. 236, 173 N.E. 281, 87 A.L.R. 821.

97. Baldwin v. Cawthorne, 1812, 19 Ves.Jun. 166. See 3 Williston, Contracts, rev. ed., 1828.

98. Gulley v. Macy, 1881, 84 N.C. 434.

99. Livesey v. Brown, 1892, 35 Neb. 111, 52 N.W. 838. The following are a few representative authorities on the questions suggested above. Ives v. Stone, 1883, 51 Conn. 446 (agreement to reconvey construed as a defeasance); Clemons v. Elder, 1859, 9 Iowa 272; Marston v. Williams, 1890, 45 Minn. 116, 47 N.W. 644, 22 Am.St.Rep. 719; Kline v. McGuckin, 1874, 24 N.J.Eq. 411; Dey v. Dunham, N.

Y.1816, 2 Johns.Ch. 182, reversed 15 Johns. 555, 8 Am.Dec. 282, affirmed 16 Johns. 367, 8 Am.Dec. 323; In re Mechanics' Bank, 1913, 156 App.Div. 343, 141 N.Y.S. 473, affirmed 209 N.Y. 526, 102 N.E. 1106; Security Savings & Trust Co. v. Loewenberg, 1900, 38 Or. 159, 62 P. 647. See L.R.A.1916B, 600; 1 Jones, Mortgages, 8th Ed.1928, §§ 304, 631. See also White v. Moore, N.Y.1829, 1 Paige 551. See Fogelman, The Deed Absolute as a Mortgage in New York, 1963, 32 Fordham L.Rev. 299, 311.

1. See Andrews v. New Britain National Bank, 1931, 113 Conn. 467, 473, 155 A. 838, emphasizing the distinction between the requirements of the parol evidence rule and the Statute of Frauds.

which the parties have executed with the intention that it or they be the complete expression and embodiment of their entire agreement in respect to the transaction in question.[2] The Statute of Frauds, on the other hand, is a statutory requirement that certain agreements must be expressed in writing.[3]

PAROL EVIDENCE RULE

84. The parol evidence rule does not block the showing of a deed absolute mortgage because the parties did not intend to embody their whole agreement in the deed.

Many cases say the rule does apply but allow in the oral evidence on the ground that

(a) There are independent equities superior to the written agreement; or

(b) An exception to the rule is warranted to prevent fraud or unjust enrichment—an erroneous view. The sound basis for exception lies in the strong policy in favor of the mortgagor's redemption interest.

Let us, then, turn first to the parol evidence rule. The simplest explanation of the admission of parol evidence so far as the parol evidence rule is concerned is that the deed absolute did not embody, and was not intended by the parties to embody, their whole agreement. The oral agreement merely supplements the deed with respect to a matter on which the instrument is silent and with which it does not purport to deal. As stated by Wigmore, "the act of transfer and the user of the property transferred are distinct legal ideas; or, put still differently, the kind of estate—according to the categories of fee simple, life estate, and the like—is a different thing from the quality of the estate, i. e., trust or security. The simple

question is, then, whether the parties, under all the circumstances, appear to have intended the document to cover merely the kind of estate transferred, or to cover all possible aspects of the transfer, including that of the quality of the estate, i. e., its subjection to an equity of redemption; in the latter case, no extrinsic agreement can be considered." [4] A few cases have taken this latter view in these deed absolute cases, and if a court does conclude that the parties intended the document to cover the entire scope of the transaction it is difficult to see how parol evidence of a mortgage intent can be received, as one such court said, "without contradicting the instrument, for the reason, that the instrument and the parol testimony both assume to state the transaction; and as they differ, they must naturally be in contradiction. They both historically relate the same transaction, and the one says it was an absolute sale—the other, it was not such, but a mere mortgage, and is not this a plain contradiction? * * * " [5] That court also felt that logic in the matter was reinforced by sound policy. It said, " * * * The general rule, that parol shall not be received to contradict written evidence, is founded in true policy, and in good sense. Why should parties state, in solemn instruments, that which is not true? These instruments assume to state the truth, and the whole truth; and if parties will state that which is untrue, should they not justly suffer the consequences? Is not the rule that parties must be held to mean what they say, the plain, honest, simple, and correct rule at last?" And the same court found a further logical difficulty in another direction. " 'A formal conveyance may certainly be shown to be a mortgage by extrinsic proof, while a formal mortgage may not be shown to be a conditional sale

---

2. The parol evidence rule "only applies where the parties to an agreement reduce it to writing, and agree or intend that that writing shall be their agreement." Pollock, C. B., in Harris v. Rickett, 1859, 4 H. & N. 1, 7. See Wigmore, Evidence, § 2425. Williston, Contracts, rev. ed., §§ 632, 633.

3. For the historical connection between the parol evidence rule and the Statute of Frauds, see IX Wigmore, Evidence, 3d ed., § 2426.

4. IX Wigmore, Evidence, 3d ed., § 2437. See also Scott, Trusts, § 38; I Bogert, Trusts, 2d ed. 410–412; Smedley and Blunk, Oral Understandings at Variance with Absolute Deeds, 1939, 34 Ill.L.Rev. 189, 198.

5. Lee v. Evans, 1857, 8 Cal. 424, 432.

by the same means. * * * ' But here, again, I must confess I cannot see the reason of the distinction. To say that a deed absolute is a mere mortgage, is no contradiction—while, to say a mortgage cannot be made a conditional sale, without a contradiction, is making a distinction without a difference." To this last an answer may be given that while a deed absolute can be argued to be silent as to the purpose for which title was conveyed and, therefore, the oral evidence merely supplements and does not contradict, when the instrument expressly states that it is a mortgage it clearly would contradict terms clearly embodied in the agreement as written to put in evidence that it was intended to be a conditional sale. It would be much the same as attempting to show that a deed containing a written trust was not intended to create a trust but to operate as a sale with an option in the grantor to repurchase. In addition it could be urged that there is a technical difficulty at least, in lien jurisdictions certainly, in swelling a mortgage lien interest which was given on the face of the instrument into a fee in the grantee which he would have if it were construed to be a conditional sale. Furthermore, a policy factor which plays an important, in fact, it is believed, a decisive role in permitting the oral agreement in to establish a mortgage, is not present when the question is one of transforming a mortgage into something else. That policy factor is the traditional solicitude of the courts toward a mortgagor's redemption right a matter which has been stressed earlier and will be mentioned again, and which is a basic consideration in the problems considered in this chapter.

On the other hand, if the former view is taken, there is no objection to proof of an extrinsic agreement so far as the parol evidence rule is concerned.[6] It would seem a proper interpretation of the holding of the cases which freely admit parol evidence in this situation is that they do so on the ground that it was not the intention of the parties that the deed itself tell the entire story and that, consequently, the evidence comes in in accordance with the parol evidence rule itself.

In spite of this rather obvious conclusion, the opinions of many of the cases seem to assume that the rule is applicable to bar the agreement; that is, that the deed did contain and was intended to contain the parties' entire agreement, and then, because the evidence of the oral agreement for the mortgage is nevertheless let in, feel compelled to advance reasons why this can be done. These reasons can be boiled down to two sorts: those that seek to allow it in on the ground that there are present factors which will create an independent equity superior to the written agreement;[7] and those that seem to proceed upon the notion that the evidence comes in as an exception to the parol evidence rule. The first proceeds upon the theory that the written instrument can only be considered to be contradicted when the oral agreement is allowed in to enforce it according to its terms, and if it is allowed in to establish an equity arising by operation of law in the property, such use of the oral agreement is not in conflict with the other words used by the parties and put into the writing even though they intended that writing to be the sole repository and expression of their intention. The latter goes upon the conception that the oral words are admitted to enforce them, that they do contradict or add to the document, but that this is permitted by a flat exception to the rule making

6. This same reasoning applies equally to a deed absolute with an oral agreement by the grantee to hold in trust. It has been suggested that the cases barring the oral trust do not do so because of the proper interpretation of the holding of the cases which freely admit parol evidence in this situation is that they do so on the ground that it was not the intention of the

parol evidence rule but because of the Statute of Frauds covering trusts. See Wigmore, supra, preceding note. This seems correct.

7. See, e. g., Pierce v. Robinson, 1859, 13 Cal. 116, 131, "The parol evidence is admitted * * * not for the purpose of contradicting or varying the written instrument, but to show facts *dehors* the instrument creating an equity superior to its terms."

it inoperative where certain factors are present.

One of these explanations, which we may consider as possibly applying to explain why the parol evidence rule will not exclude the agreement, although it is usually advanced in connection with the Statute of Frauds objection, is that it is a virtual fraud upon the grantor for the grantee subsequently to refuse to perform his promise to treat the conveyance as security.[8] And this fraudulent conduct by the grantee justifies making an exception to the parol evidence rule, or the Statute of Frauds, even if admission of the agreement does contradict the deed. Or, in the alternative it may be argued that the fraud warrants the imposition upon the grantee of a constructive trust founded upon the fraud itself, that the terms of the oral agreement are not being enforced, and, consequently, the parol evidence rule which would bar the oral agreement for the purpose of enforcing it, is not involved at all. It has been pointed out in criticism of this explanation that in effect the court is lifting itself by its own bootstraps. For there is no fraud to justify the admission of the parol agreement unless there has been a breach of the parol agreement. And yet the parol agreement is first admitted in order to show a breach of it which will establish the fraud that justifies admitting it.[9] Or, to put the matter in a little different way, the fraud which will justify the admission of the parol evidence, if it is admitted for that reason, must occur when the transaction is entered into. The alleged fraud here consists in later insisting that it was intended as a sale when actually it was intended as a mortgage. The very question at issue before the court, therefore, is whether it was intended to be a mortgage or a sale. Until the court decides

that it was intended to be a mortgage there would be no justification in saying that the defendant was fraudulent in insisting that it was a sale. What the court does is to admit the parol evidence to discover what the intention really was, and then, having already admitted the evidence and determined the question in issue, it says that this determination makes the defendant's conduct fraudulent and consequently parol evidence is admissible to decide the question it had already decided, namely, that a mortgage was intended.[10] Another objection to this line of reasoning is that it treats the later breach of the agreement as establishing fraud in the entering into the agreement in the first place. Logically this amounts to converting a subsequent breach of contract into fraud in the inception of the contract, a generalization which should be summarily rejected. But the basic objection, so far as the argument concerns the parol evidence rule, although not when it is directed at the Statute of Frauds, is a fundamental fallacy in the reasoning. The assumption is that the parol evidence rule does operate to exclude the oral agreement that the property was to be held as security and returned on payment of the debt. If this assumption is true, it means that the court has concluded that the deed itself was intended by the parties to constitute the entire and complete transaction between the parties and consequently the oral agreement was not intended to have any legally operative effect and therefore, for this reason, is excluded from considera-

8. Strong v. Stewart, 1819, 4 Johns.Ch. 167; Taylor v. Luther, C.C.R.I., 1835, 2 Sumn. 228, Fed.Cas.No. 13,796; Jenkins v. Eldredge, 1845, 3 Story 299, Fed.Cas.No.7,267. See Newton v. Fay, 1865, 92 Mass. 505; 4 Pomeroy, Eq.Juris., 5th ed., § 1196.

9. See Smedley and Blunk, supra note 4, 197.

10. A similar criticism was voiced in a leading case where the analogous question of allowing in a parol trust in the face of the Statute of Frauds was involved. The court said, "But it seems apparent to my mind to say, in such a case, it shall be admitted to establish the fraud, is equally a violation of the Statute. Because the fraud consists only in the refusal to execute the trust. The court, therefore, cannot say that there is a fraud, without first saying that there is a trust. And the parol evidence, if admitted, must be admitted to establish the trust, in order that the court may charge the party with fraud in setting up his claim against it." Administrators of Rasdall's Adm'rs v. Rasdall, 1859, 9 Wis. 379.

tion. If this is so, it seems nonsense to predicate fraud upon the violation of an agreement which, by hypothesis, was barred from consideration initially on the ground that it was not intended by the parties to be a legally binding part of their agreement in the matter. If it was not intended to be legally binding the grantee or grantor should be perfectly free to disregard it. It is nonsense to talk of the refusal of the party to perform such an agreement as fraud justifying its admission in order to enforce it in the face of the parol evidence rule which excluded it only because the parties did not intend it to be a part of their bargain; and, for the same reason, it is equally nonsense to argue that non-performance of such an agreement is a fraud justifying the imposition of a constructive trust. Since it was barred because the court believed the parties did not intend it to be legally binding it should continue to be regarded as without legally operative significance for any purpose whatsoever. Actual fraud in the procurement of a deed absolute intended as a mortgage is, it is true, a perfectly good ground for allowing in evidence of a parol agreement for a mortgage which was omitted by reason of the fraud. But the rule which permits parol evidence of the fraud demands that it establish "some independent fact or representation, some fraud in the procurement of the instrument or some breach of confidence concerning its use," and not simply and solely an agreement directly at variance with the terms of the writing.[11] And yet, as we have seen, in most jurisdictions the parol evidence is admitted merely upon a claim, and proof, of an oral agreement that it be treated as security. In such cases, the only oral proof of the so-called fraud would consist solely in the oral agreement itself. And, to repeat, it is the

court's initial assumption that that oral agreement is excluded on the ground that the parties had not intended that it be any part of their final, legally operative agreement; that the writing, and the writing alone, contained all of their agreement that they intended to be binding upon them. If this reasoning is correct, the above explanation cannot be valid. On the other hand, if the assumption is incorrect, the explanation is not needed. The oral agreement would come in as fulfilling the test of the parol evidence rule. If it is barred, it is by reason of the Statute of Frauds.

Quite similar to the foregoing, but differing from it in that there is no attempt to make out a case of fraudulent conduct by the transferee, is the explanation that, even in the absence of fraud or undue influence, it is permissible to show an oral trust or contract for the purpose of preventing unjust enrichment. Here the transferee would be unjustly enriched if he were allowed to keep the property, and this unjust enrichment should be prevented by compelling the transferee to return the property on payment of the debt by the transferor.[12] But here also, if it is assumed that the parol evidence rule would bar the parol agreement because the parties did not intend that it should be any binding part of their transaction, it balks the intelligence to understand why the non-performance of such an agreement should be considered as establishing unjust enrichment and therefore justify

11. Bank of America, etc., Ass'n v. Pendergrass, 1935, 4 Cal.2d 258, 263, 48 P.2d 659, 661. See semble, Newton v. Clark, 1917, 174 N.C. 393, 394, 93 S. E. 951, "the intention must be established, not merely by proof of declarations, but by proof of facts and circumstances, dehors the deed, inconsistent with the idea of an absolute purchase."

12. See Scott, Conveyances upon Trusts Not Properly Declared, 1923, 37 Harv.L.Rev. 663. See also Stone, Resulting Trusts and the Statute of Frauds, 1906, 6 Col.L.Rev. 326, 339. "The substanbasis of the jurisdiction is the inequitable conduct of the grantee in receiving property for one purpose, and using it for another, and equity, consequently, imposes upon the grantee, an equitable obligation to restore the property to the grantor upon payment of the mortgage indebtedness. The inequitable conduct of the grantee in retaining the property for his own purposes is sufficient to give equity jurisdiction to declare the deed a mortgage, despite the parol evidence rule, and the provisions of the Statute of Frauds." Ames, Constructive Trusts Based upon the Breach of an Express Oral Trust of Land, 1907, 20 Harv.L.Rev. 549, 553.

the admission of it in evidence either for the purpose of enforcing it according to its terms or founding upon it a constructive trust or mortgage. And, here, again, if the parol evidence rule does not bar it, there is no need to talk unjust enrichment in connection with its admission unless the Statute of Frauds is urged as an obstacle. If the Statute is set up as a defense the argument seems sound. The only difficulty is that it would be just as applicable to an oral trust. But, as we shall see, the American authorities generally do not accept it in the latter case.

A third explanation, and one which is believed to be the true one, certainly the one which best distinguishes the oral mortgage from the oral trust case, is one rooted in the history of and policy of the courts toward the mortgagor's equity of redemption. As was pointed out by Field, J., in the leading case of Pierce v. Robinson,[13] which gives one of the best statements of this rationale, "The entire doctrine of equity, in respect to mortgages, has its origin in considerations independent of the terms in which the instruments are drawn. In form, a mortgage in fee is a conveyance of a conditional estate, which, by the strict rules of the common law, became absolute upon breach of its conditions. But, from an early period in the history of English jurisprudence, Courts of Equity interposed to prevent a forfeiture of the estate and gave to the mortgagor a right to redeem, upon payment within a reasonable time, of the principal sum secured, interest and costs. * * * And when the right to redeem had been once established, to prevent its evasion, the rule was laid down and has ever since been inflexibly adhered to, that the right is inseparably connected with the mortgage, and cannot be abandoned or waived by any stipulations entered into between the parties at the time, whether inserted in the instrument or not. * * * It is against the policy of the law to allow irredeemable

mortgages, just as it is against the policy of the law to allow the creation of inalienable estates. Under no circumstances will equity permit this end to be effected, either by express stipulation, or the absolute form of the instrument. * * *" In creating the redemption right the courts clearly recognized that they were defeating the expressed intention of the parties as contained in the instrument. In other words, it involved as much or more of a departure from the terms of the instrument than the conveyance of an absolute conveyance executed as security. "The conveyance upon condition, by its terms, purports to vest the entire estate upon the breach of the condition, just as the absolute conveyance does in the first instance. The equity arises and is asserted, in both cases, upon exactly the same principles, and is enforced without reference to the agreement of the parties, but from the nature of the transaction to which the right attaches, from the policy of the law, as an inseparable incident. * * * Unless parol evidence can be admitted, the policy of the law will be constantly evaded. Debtors, under the force of pressing necessities, will submit to almost any exactions for loans of a trifling amount, compared with the value of the property, and the equity of redemption will elude the grasp of the Court, and rest in the simple good faith of the creditor."[14] This last point particularly, the notion that the mortgagor is in a weak economic position as compared with the mortgagee, a continual object of oppression and therefore the subject of special solicitude and protection of the chancellor, has been stressed over and over again and is a dominant consideration in mortgage law. Typical of this attitude is the much quoted statement of Lord Northington in Vernon v. Bethell that "necessitous men are not, truly speaking, free men; but, to answer a present emergency, will submit to any terms that

---

13. 1859, 13 Cal. 116.

14. Pierce v. Robinson, supra note 7, at 126. See also Glenn, Mortgages, 55; Walsh, Mortgages, 35.

the crafty may impose upon them." [15] This strong policy in favor of the mortgagor's redemption interest is sufficient to account for the letting in of parol evidence to establish it even if both the parol evidence rule and the Statute of Frauds logically applied to exclude it. It is also sufficient to outweigh any policy objections against countenancing the deed absolute form of mortgage on the ground that it opens an easy way to debtors to conceal their assets from their creditors, a possibility which, we have noted previously, has been inveighed against and given as a bolstering reason for excluding the oral agreement.[16]

It is worth noting again that the redemption right, as was stated by Field, was created by the court of equity, for reasons of policy, in flat violation of the expressly stated intentions of the parties in the mortgage and for the purpose of defeating those intentions. In the deed absolute case, however, at least when the oral agreement is excluded by the Statute of Frauds, the problem is one of showing the true intention of the parties in spite of a positive rule of law that would prohibit it. Just as the strong policy of equity overrode the express terms of the agreement in the mortgage in the form of a deed with a defeasance, so it may override the

positive statutory rule of the Statute of Frauds forbidding the showing of the actual intent when it is expressed orally. So far as the parol evidence rule is concerned, even if the court should find that under its application the parol agreement could not be considered because the parties intended the deed to be the complete expression of the whole transaction, it would do no more violence to either the intention of the parties or the positive rule of law which bars the oral proof in such a case, for the courts to say that they should both be disregarded when a claim of mortgage is made, than the original creation of the equity did to the expressed intention of the parties and the strict workings of real property law.

A final suggestion may be made as to why the evidence is let in. It may be that it is so common an occurrence for parties to enter into transactions of this sort that the courts, recognizing this fact, have established a positive rule of law as a square exception to the parol evidence rule, that when a claim of mortgage is made the issue of whether the claim is borne out by the evidence shall go directly to the trier of fact without any preliminary inquiry by the court into whether the parties intended the written deed to constitute their entire agreement. The courts may well feel that such an exception is sufficiently safeguarded by the usual rule requiring exceptionally strong evidence to establish the claim.

THE STATUTE OF FRAUDS

85. **The Statute of Frauds does not prevent the showing of a deed absolute mortgage. The best view is that the statute is inapplicable because evidence deals with the retention, and not the transfer, of an interest.**

The Statute of Frauds is considerably more of an obstacle to the introduction of the parol agreement of defeasance than is the parol evidence rule. In the latter case, the easiest and soundest view is, as we saw, that the application of the rule does not operate to

---

15. 1762, 2 Ed. 110, 113. See also Russell v. Southard, 1851, 53 U.S. (12 How.) 139, 13 L.Ed. 927; Marshall, C. J., in Conway's Ex'rs v. Alexander, 1812, 11 U.S. (7 Cranch) 218, 3 L.Ed. 321, 328, "lenders of money are less under the pressure of circumstances which control the perfect and free exercise of the judgment than borrowers", and they frequently make the effort "to avail themselves of the advantage of this superiority in order to obtain inequitable advantages."; Lord Chancellor Hardwicke in Toomes v. Conset, 1745, 3 Atk. 261; Thomas v. Klemm, 1945, 185 Md. 136, 43 A.2d 193.

Protection of the mortgagor against agreements made at the time of the mortgage are found in the Roman law. An edict of Constantine made void express agreements that the property pledged should pass to the creditor without sale or appraisement or that the debtor should forfeit his right of redemption if he did not pay at the date specified. Mackeldey, Civil Law, 2d Am. ed. 1849, § 349, and fn. See also Longwith v. Butler, 1845, 8 Ill. 32, 36.

16. Lee v. Evans, 1857, 8 Cal. 424, 432. See text, §§ 67, 77, supra.

exclude the evidence. Further, upon the assumption that it did exclude the showing of the agreement, we looked at various justifications for admission in spite of the rule. Three of them have been advanced as reasons for avoiding the prohibition of the Statute of Frauds.[17] The second and third clearly are theories that afford rational grounds for admitting the evidence in spite of the Statute. Although the final stricture on the first explanation would be inapplicable where the Statute of Frauds is the obstacle, the other criticisms of it seem appropriate. Another reason closely connected with this first explanation is most frequently expressed by saying that rules of law designed to prevent fraud must not be used so as to produce fraud, and "that it would be a virtual fraud for the grantee to insist upon the deed as an absolute conveyance of the title, which had been intentionally given to him, and which he had knowingly accepted, merely as security, and therefore in reality as a mortgage."[18] But perhaps the best reason advanced as to why the Statute of Frauds has not prevented showing that the transaction was a mortgage is that it is not violated.[19]

"It is frequently and correctly stated that the statute of frauds has no application to parol proof of an equitable mortgage, but this is for the obvious reason that such proof by establishing an equitable mortgage does not transfer to the mortgagor an interest in land. The oral proof simply limits the effect of a conveyance absolute in form to the agreed effect—a transfer as security."[20]

17. I. e., fraud upon the grantor, unjust enrichment of the grantee, and policy in favor of protecting the redemption interest. See preceding section for a full discussion of them.

18. See Smith v. Smith, 1907, 153 Ala. 504, 508, 45 So. 168, 169; Pomeroy, Eq.Juris., 5th ed., § 1196. See also 1929, 15 Iowa L.Rev. 193.

19. De Bartlett v. De Wilson, 1906, 52 Fla. 497, 42 So. 189, 11 Ann.Cas. 311. See L.R.A.1916B, 71, 73.

20. Bennett v. Harrison, 1911, 115 Minn. 342, 355, 132 N.W. 309, 314, 37 L.R.A.,N.S., 521.

In other words, the parol evidence merely shows that the grantor *retained* a part interest in the property, namely the beneficial ownership of the property; and parol evidence showing that a person never even purported to part with the beneficial ownership of property does not constitute a transfer or creation of an interest in property.[21]

PAROL MORTGAGE vs. PAROL TRUST OR PAROL CONDITION SUBSEQUENT TO A WRITTEN CONTRACT

86. The Statute of Frauds blocks evidence of an oral trust to vary an absolute deed. The parol mortgage cases are distinguishable because of the tenderness of the law toward the mortgagor due to his weak economic position; the difference in the statutory provisions and other factors.

The analogy between a parol mortgage and a parol condition subsequent to a written contract is obviously invalid.

The great weight of authority in the United States holds that an oral express trust agreement by the grantee under a deed absolute cannot be shown to enforce it or to impose a constructive trust in favor of the intended beneficiary, the grantor.[22] The question arises whether an oral agreement to hold

21. See Smedley and Blunk, Oral Understandings at Variance With Absolute Deeds, 1940, 34 Ill.L.Rev. 189, 198, where the argument was made that such an agreement did not, for this reason, violate either the parol evidence rule or the trust provision of the Statute of Frauds. However, even where there is a special statute, rather than § 4 of the English Statute of Frauds or a paraphrase of it, expressly requiring "mortgages" to be "created, renewed, or extended" by an instrument in writing, it has been held that it would be no bar to the admission of oral evidence that a deed absolute was intended as a mortgage. Anglo-Californian Bank v. Cerf, 1905, 147 Cal. 384, 81 P. 1077. See Fogelman, The Deed Absolute as a Mortgage in New York, 1963, 32 Fordham L.Rev. 299, 303.

22. See Scott, Conveyances Upon Trusts Not Properly Declared, 1924, 37 Harv.L.Rev. 653; Ames, Constructive Trusts Based upon the Breach of an Express Oral Trust of Land, 1907, 20 Harv.L.Rev. 549; Costigan, Trusts Based on Oral Promises to Hold in Trust, to Convey, or to Devise Made by Voluntary Grantees, 1914, 12 Mich.L.Rev. 427, 515; Stone, Resulting Trusts and the Statute of Frauds, 1906, 6 Col.L.Rev. 326.

an absolute conveyance as mortgage should be treated differently from an oral agreement to hold as trustee so far as either the parol evidence rule or the Statute of Frauds is concerned.[23] In respect to the parol evidence rule no plausible distinction between the two types of cases has been offered. And, indeed, in spite of some respectable authorities [24] that imply, at least, that the parol evidence rule would bar it if there were not some basis for an exception to it, the clearly preferable view, and, it is believed, the one accepted by most cases, is that the rule raises no barrier to the introduction of the oral agreement in either case. The real hurdle is the Statute of Frauds.[25]

At the outset one reconciliation of the two groups of cases so far as the Statute of Frauds is concerned may be suggested. It is that trusts are specifically covered by two sections of the English Statute of Frauds, seven and eight,[26] whereas there are no sections specifically dealing with mortgages and, if they are covered, it is because the general language of section one or four is construed to apply. But there is authority for the view that establishing the mortgage only shows a reservation of an interest in the grantor and

the Statute doesn't prevent doing this.[27] This distinction, however, has seldom been pointed out [28] and, although some courts simply dismiss the apparent inconsistency by saying, without giving any reasons, that the oral mortgage cases are distinguishable from the oral trust cases,[29] more important authorities have stated flatly that they "can see no distinction between an express trust and a parol agreement making a deed a mortgage," [30] so far as the Statute is concerned. But, even assuming that both trusts and mortgages are governed by the requirements of the Statute of Frauds, there are several grounds upon which to reconcile the two lines of cases.

One reconciliation, although that seems scarcely an appropriate term for it, is to say that the problem in the two cases is identical, that the mortgage cases are correct, and that in the oral trust cases the evidence should be let in also, not for the purpose of enforcing it, but to show unjust enrichment of the grantee and forfeiture of the grantor's interest in order to impose a constructive trust; that the policy of the Statute against false claims and any other policy against permitting a transaction which permits the concealment of assets is outweighed by the policy against permitting one person to be enriched at the expense of another plus the general desirability of permitting the intention of the parties to a transaction to be enforced.[31] It

---

23. For a thorough discussion of the whole problem, see Smedley and Blunk, Oral Understandings at Variance with Absolute Deeds, 1939, 34 Ill.L.Rev. 189.

24. E. g., Pierce v. Robinson, supra note 7.

25. See IX, Wigmore, Evidence, 3d ed., § 2437; Scott, Trusts, § 38; Bogert, Trusts and Trustees, 2d Ed., § 51.

26. In some states in the United States there is no provision in the Statute of Frauds applying to trusts. In these jurisdictions an additional reason exists why the parol evidence rule should not bar the oral trust, because if it did the courts "would be faced with the uncomfortable problem of having a valid oral trust with a destruction of the only means whereby the trust can be enforced. This would be in effect to add a trust provision to the Statute of Frauds by force of judicial decision." Smedley and Blunk, Oral Understandings at Variance with Absolute Deeds, 1939, 34 Ill.L.Rev. 189, 197. The same argument would apply to an oral mortgage to which the Statute of Frauds did not apply.

27. See preceding section. But cf. Anglo-Californian Bank v. Cerf, 1905, 147 Cal. 384, 81 P. 1077, holding that a Statute of Frauds explicitly referring to mortgages would not prevent showing the oral mortgage.

28. See, however, Smedley and Blunk, Oral Understandings at Variance With Absolute Deeds, 1939, 34 Ill.L.Rev. 189, 204.

29. E. g., Sturtevant v. Sturtevant, 1859, 20 N.Y. 39, 40, 75 Am.Dec. 371; Patton v. Beecher, 1872, 68 Ala. 579.

30. Rasdall's Adm'rs v. Rasdall, 1859, 9 Wis. 379, a leading case. See Stone, Resulting Trusts and the Statute of Frauds, 1906, 6 Col.L.Rev. 326, 341.

31. See Scott, Trusts, § 44; Stone, Resulting Trusts and the Statute of Frauds, 1906, 6 Col.L.Rev. 326, 339; Ames, Oral Trusts of Lands, 1906, 20 Harv.L. Rev. 549, 553.

has even been urged that the forfeiture in the trust case is greater than in the mortgage case and thus presents an even stronger basis for relief because in the latter "the party would get it for the money he had loaned, while in the latter he would get it for nothing." [32] This seems an error. The establishment and collection of the debt by the grantee would not be affected by the Statute of Frauds or the parol evidence rule; and there is no reason to assume that if the court refused to admit the oral evidence of the mortgage that it would, because of this, prevent the collection of the debt. If so the amount of forfeiture would be the same in both cases.

The most important difference between the two cases is the one which best explains why courts, even though there may be strong objections in the mortgage case to letting in the evidence, nevertheless do allow it. That is the notion which has played such a part in the protection of the mortgagor's redemption interest, namely, that the mortgagor is an economic weakling who must be protected against his own agreements because he makes them under the pressure of necessity. The mortgagee has money and the mortgagor needs it. The mortgagee has a leverage on the mortgagor and can virtually club him into giving a deed absolute with the mortgagor having to rely on the oral agreement. And this strong policy in favor of the mortgagor's redemption right overbalances, as we have suggested, counter policies against both fraudulent claims and possible [33] fraudulent concealment of assets. In the case of the oral trust there is no similar reason to excuse the grantor. And the forfeiture

and unjust enrichment, which exists in the mortgage case also, is not sufficient to overcome the opposing considerations.

It may be remarked in passing that this tenderness of the law toward the mortgagor, if it is based upon the assumption that the owner of money is in a strong position, is not altogether logical. A owns Blackacre and is in dire need of money. B has money. A can get money from B either by mortgaging Blackacre to B or selling it to him. If A gives to B a deed absolute, the courts will allow A to show it is a mortgage and get back his property. But if it is a sale A cannot rescind the sale and get back the property on the ground that B drove a hard bargain when A was necessitous. Of course it can be answered that in the mortgage case equity is granting the relief to effectuate the executory intention of the parties as expressed orally while in the sale case it would be defeating an executed intention. Yet this seems only verbally to distinguish the cases for, in pursuance of its solicitude for the mortgagor, as, for example, in the original creation of the redemption right, equity did not hesitate to defeat a completely executed intention of both parties that title should be absolute in the mortgagee if the debt was not paid. Possibly the difference is psychological. In the mortgage case the mortgagee plays not merely upon the *necessities* of A but upon his *hopes* of getting the land back and his hopes lead him to make foolish bargains. In the case of the sale, however, the buyer plays only upon the needs of the other.

There are other distinctions between the mortgage and the trust cases which may play some part in causing the divergent results. For one thing there are no rules of law which prevent proving the existence of a debt which existed before or arose at the time of the conveyance and continued to exist after the conveyance. This observable and independent circumstance gives corroboration to the grantor's story that the conveyance was for security. There is no similar external guar-

---

32. Rasdall's Adm'rs v. Rasdall, 1859, 9 Wis. 379. See also Scott, Abridgment of the Law of Trusts, § 44.3: "Indeed, the unjust enrichment is greater in the case of an oral trust than in the case of an oral mortgage; for if no relief is given in the former case the whole of the property is lost, while in the latter case only the value above the amount of the debt is lost."

33. See Scott, Conveyances upon Trusts Not Properly Declared, 1924, 37 Harv.L.Rev. 653, 663; Scott, Abridgment of the Law of Trusts, § 44.3.

antees for the grantor who claims an oral trust. Again, there were historical precedents permitting the oral mortgage to be shown before the enactment of the Statute of Frauds whereas there was no similar power found in the case of oral trusts. Although it might not have more sanction than the influence of precedent, the courts may well have coupled the express provisions in the newly enacted Statute covering trusts, the lack of any such explicit coverage of mortgages, and the older mortgages cases to arrive at the conclusion that the oral trust was prohibited but the oral mortgage not.[34]

It has also been suggested that the cases allowing the oral mortgage to be shown are inconsistent with the well settled rule that an obligor upon a written contract or a negotiable instrument cannot prove an extrinsic condition subsequent. It has been answered that the "distinction must rest on the assumption that A may very likely give an actual conveyance of Blackacre in absolute form when it is agreed that the transfer shall operate merely as a security, but that he is not so likely to make a written contract promising to transfer Blackacre in absolute form when the understanding of the parties is, as before, that the transaction shall be defeasible upon a certain contingency."[35] An acute observation, this, which requires no addition.

B. CONDITIONAL SALE

NATURE OF TRANSACTION

87. **Conveyances by deed absolute coupled with a separate written contract or option to repurchase are called conditional sales. Just as in deed absolute cases, the question arises whether such transactions are what they purport to be or are, instead, intended to be mortgages.**

Where there is a conveyance by deed absolute on its face and, in addition, executed

as part of the same transaction, a separate written agreement, there is no difficulty in construing the two instruments together. If the separate agreement provides by its terms that the deed is to be void on the payment of a debt which was part of the transaction, or that the grantee should reconvey on the same event, the whole transaction is clearly a mortgage. This we have already discussed.[36] But the written agreement may not disclose unambiguously that the property is to go back to the grantor on the payment of a debt, and likewise it may not clearly purport to be a contract or option for a resale of the property to the grantor. In such cases there is a question as to whether the separate writing was a mortgage defeasance or a contract of sale of some sort.[37] To answer this question there exists no doubt but that extrinsic evidence can be admitted to ascertain the true character of the writing.[38] But there are a large number of cases in which the separate instrument without any ambiguity at all professes expressly to be a contract or option to resell to the grantor the property conveyed by the deed.[39] In some instances, indeed, in addition to spelling out the transaction, the parties may insert quite explicit statements negativing the existence of a debt as the foundation of a mortgage or affirming the character of the undertaking as a contract.[40] When this is done the question of

34. See Smedley and Blunk, supra, 202–204.

35. 3 Williston, Contracts, rev. ed., § 635.

36. Chapter 4, § 69, supra.

37. There is authority that if the instrument leaves it doubtful, it will be construed a mortgage. Graham v. Mullins, 1936, 286 Ill.App. 393, 3 N.E.2d 723. See Smith v. Swendsen, 1937, 57 Idaho 715, 69 P.2d 131, 111 A.L.R. 441.

38. Keithley v. Wood, 1894, 151 Ill. 466, 38 N.E. 149, 42 Am.St.Rep. 265; Chase Nat. Bank v. Tover, 1935, 245 App.Div. 615, 283 N.Y.S. 832, affirmed without opinion, 1936, 271 N.Y. 518, 2 N.E.2d 674. See note, 1937, 111 A.L.R. 448, 455.

39. See cases cited in the following footnotes. For a collection of cases, see 1932, 79 A.L.R. 937; 1945, 155 A.L.R. 1104.

40. People ex rel. Ford v. Irvin, 1861, 18 Cal. 117. McMurry v. Mercer, Tex.Civ.App.1934, 73 S.W.2d 1087, discussed in note, 1935, 13 Tex.L.Rev. 241: X and Y executed deeds, absolute in form, to Z, reciting a

determining whether, nevertheless, the transaction is a mortgage presents more difficulty and is the subject of our present inquiry.

This type of transaction goes back into the early history of mortgage law and probably has its origin in rather primitive communities in which there was great sensitivity to the social humiliation attached to being forced to mortgage the family estates and to resort to money lenders to do so. "The transaction, then, which will raise the needed money, will leave the way open for a winning back of the family inheritance when its fortunes have been regained, and will at the same time avoid the stigma of being forced by a pecuniary need, is the transaction which will commend itself as the desirable one, * * *. Such a transaction is the sale for repurchase." [41] Such considerations may still play some part but probably other reasons are more important. There are a wide variety of them, but the desire to avoid the rules of mortgage law, especially the necessity of foreclosure, is one of the most usual.[42]

There are many types of these undertakings which affirmatively indicate a transaction different from either an absolute conveyance of the property or a mortgage of it.

The most frequent of them are "(1) a sale and conveyance of the land by R to E with option in R to repurchase it; (2) the same as (1) with the addition of a deed of reconveyance deposited in escrow * * *; (3) a sale and conveyance by R to E and a lease by E to R with option in R to repurchase; (4) a sale and conveyance by R to E with an unconditional contract by E to resell and by R to repurchase the land, that is, the creation of the relation of vendor and purchaser, rather than that of mortgagor and mortgagee, attended with a different right of foreclosure * * *; (5) the same as (4), with the addition of a deed of reconveyance deposited in escrow * * *; (6) a sale and conveyance by R to E with a written agreement that in the event of further sale the proceeds over and above a certain sum should be paid in whole or part to R * * *; (7) a sale and conveyance made by one already a mortgagor to the mortgagee, with a provision that the former should have the same privilege of redemption as would be given by statute in that state after a foreclosure sale." [43] The term conditional sale has been loosely applied to all such arrangements although frequently this description has been restricted to a sale with merely an option to repurchase.[44]

cash payment and promissory notes from Z for the purchase price. Z executed to each of the grantors an option to repurchase, defeasance to be made on payment of a smaller sum than the purchase price named in the deeds from X and Y to Z. Grantors X and Y sought to introduce parol evidence that the deeds were intended as mortgages to secure their debt to Z. Held, where the consideration for the conveyance is contractual in nature and the writings are unambiguous, parol evidence is inadmissible to show that the transaction is a mortgage. See Smith v. Swendsen, 1937, 57 Idaho 715, 69 P.2d 131; note 1937, 111 A.L.R. 441, 451.

41. Wigmore, The Pledge-Idea, 1897, 10 Harv.L.Rev. 389, 393.

42. See Miller v. Thomas, 1853, 14 Ill. 428. The cases as reported seldom go into the reasons why the parties used the form they did. In one case, Nitkey v. Ward, 1937, 199 Minn. 334, 271 N.W. 873, certiorari denied 302 U.S. 706, 58 S.Ct. 25, 82 L.Ed. 545, rehearing denied 302 U.S. 775, 58 S.Ct. 134, 82 L.Ed. 600, a tax problem figured. See also the reasons for using the straight deed absolute. § 71, supra.

43. See Campbell, Cases on Mortgages, 2d ed., 109 n. 3. The list of type examples in the text is taken from this note with the citation of authorities contained therein omitted.

See also Updike, Mortgages, in 1956 Annual Survey of American Law, 1957, 32 N.Y.U.L.Rev. 789, 790 (1957); Note, The Equitable Mortgage in Kansas, 1956, 5 U. Kan.L.Rev. 114, 117; Note, Validity, construction and effect of contract, option, or provision for repurchase by vendor, 1955, 44 A.L.R. 2d 342; Note, Is a Contract for the Sale of Land a Mortgage?, 1962, 16 U. of Miami L.Rev. 493, discussing Mid-State Inv. Corp. v. O'Steen, Fla.App.1961, 133 So.2d 455 certiorari denied, Fla. 1962, 136 So.2d 349.

44. See Campbell, Cases on Mortgages, 2d ed. 97 n. 1.

See also Sargent v. Hamblin, 1953, 57 N.M. 559, 564, 260 P.2d 919, 926; When Is an Absolute Conveyance a Mortgage?, 1955, 8 U. of Fla.L.Rev. 132, Discussing Rosenthal v. Le May, Fla.1954, 72 So.2d 289.

EXTRINSIC EVIDENCE

88. Extrinsic evidence is admissible to show whether a transaction is a conditional sale or a mortgage. Courts tend to require less proof to establish the mortgage in these cases than in the deed absolute cases.

In all of these situations the question again arises whether extrinsic evidence can be introduced to show that the transactions, notwithstanding the terms of the agreements, are mortgages. And, again, in spite of some cases holding to the contrary,[45] the authorities in general answer yes.[46] But there is one striking difference here from the case where the only written instrument is the deed absolute. Here the extrinsic evidence establishing the fact that the parties intended the transaction to be a mortgage collides head on with the written agreement integrated with the deed as the full statement of the parties' agreement. It squarely contradicts it. There can be no explanation here that the oral agreement merely fills out a part of the transaction not covered, and intended not to be covered, by the part which was written. And yet, as was just said, the evidence comes in. Also, although there are many authorities requiring the mortgage intent to be established by clear and convincing evidence,[47] as in the deed absolute cases, others hold that a preponderance of evidence will suf-

fice.[48] Further, in doubtful cases the courts will construe the arrangement as a mortgage[49] and in one state the rule is that if there is any agreement executed contemporaneously with an absolute deed whereby the grantor may, within a limited time, demand a reconveyance the transaction is conclusively a mortgage.[50] In other words the task of establishing the transaction to be a mortgage is distinctly easier than in the straight deed absolute case in spite of an apparently clear encroachment on the parol evidence rule, certainly clearer than in the deed absolute case. At first sight this seems

---

45. Thomas v. Ogden State Bank, 1932, 80 Utah 138, 147, 13 P.2d 636, 639; Carter v. Simpson Estate Co., 1922, 103 Or. 383, 388, 391, 193 P. 913, 203 P. 580, 581, 582 (alternative decision); McMurry v. Mercer, Tex.Civ.App.1934, 73 S.W.2d 1087, 1089, criticised, 1934, 13 Tex.L.Rev. 241.

46. See cases cited, Campbell, Cases on Mortgages 2d ed., 110 n. 3; Orlando v. Berns, 1957, 154 Cal.App. 2d 753, 316 P.2d 705; McKinley v. Hinnant, 1955, 242 N.C. 245, 87 S.E.2d 568, noted in Third Annual Survey of North Carolina Case Law: Credit Transactions, 1955, 34 N.C.L. Rev. 35; Cowles v. Zlaket, 1959, 167 Cal.App.2d 20, 334 P.2d 55.

47. Parks v. Mulledy, 1930, 49 Idaho 546, 290 P. 205, 79 A.L.R. 934; Nitkey v. Ward, 1937, 199 Minn. 334, 271 N.W. 873, certiorari denied 302 U.S. 706, 58 S.Ct. 25, 82 L.Ed. 545, rehearing denied 302 U.S. 775, 58 S.Ct. 134, 82 L.Ed. 600; Sargent v. Hamblin, 1953, 57 N.M. 559, 260 P.2d 919; Cowles v. Zlaket, 1959, 167 Cal.App.2d 20, 334 P.2d 55.

48. Westberg v. Wilson, 1932, 185 Minn. 307, 309, 241 N.W. 315, 316. See Campbell, Cases on Mortgages, 2d ed., 110 n. 3.

For recent cases on the quantum of proof, see Updike, Mortgages, in 1953 Annual Survey of American Law, 1954, 29 N.Y.U.L.Rev. 829, 830.

49. "In all doubtful cases a contract will be construed to be a mortgage rather than a conditional sale, because in the case of a mortgage the mortgagor, although he has not strictly complied with the terms of the mortgage, still has his right of redemption; while in the case of a conditional sale, without strict compliance, the rights of the conditional purchaser are forfeited." Matthews v. Sheehan, 1877, 69 N.Y. 585, 590. See, Russell v. Southard, 1851, 53 U.S. (12 How.) 139, 13 L.Ed. 927.

"A matter of intention is entirely one of fact to be determined by the trial court and a finding by it in this regard will not be set aside unless it is clearly or manifestly against the weight of the evidence." Nitkey v. Ward, 1937, 199 Minn. 334, 340, 271 N.W. 873, 876, certiorari denied 302 U.S. 706, 58 S.Ct. 25, 82 L.Ed. 545, rehearing denied 302 U.S. 775, 58 S.Ct. 134, 82 L.Ed. 600.

See Campbell, Cases on Mortgages, 2d ed., 106 n. 2.

See also Fogelman, The Deed Absolute as a Mortgage in New York, 1963, 32 Fordham L.Rev. 299, 307 on the significance of the existence of a written defeasance.

50. Kerr v. Gilmore, Pa.1837, 6 Watts 405; Brown v. Nickle, 1847, 6 Pa. 390. Only slightly weaker than this is the attitude of a Canadian court expressed in Hawke v. Milliken, 1866, 12 Grant Ch. 236, 238, "when an obligation to purchase and pay the money is exacted from the grantor, that is sufficient to show the real character of the transaction to be a mortgage, though the form of it is a sale."

It has been held that a grantee may establish that the transaction was a mortgage if he meets the requirements of proof which would be required of the grantor. Holman v. Mason City Auto Co., 1919, 186 Iowa 704, 171 N.W. 12; Goodbar & Co. v. Bloom, 1906, 43 Tex.Civ.App. 434, 96 S.W. 657; Baldwin v. McDonald, 1916, 24 Wyo. 108, 156 P. 27 (semble).

curious and an apparent aberration. As one court said, " * * * it seems illogical to hold that clear and convincing evidence is required to establish that the transaction is a mortgage, where the deed is absolute and there is no collateral writing, but that where there is a contemporaneous agreement to sell the property, less evidence is required * * *." [51] Yet the explanation is not hard to find. The same solicitude for the redemption right is just as existent here to prevent the summary ending of the grantor's right which would occur if he is held to be merely an optionee or vendee of a contract of purchase and to preserve to him the benefits of the mortgagor's right of redemption. This idea was stressed in a leading case the court saying "it is not to be forgotten, that the same language which truly describes a real sale, may also be employed to cut off the right of redemption, in case of a loan on security; that it is the duty of the court to watch vigilantly these exercises of skill, lest they should be effectual to accomplish what equity forbids; and that, in doubtful cases, the court leans to the conclusion that the reality was a mortgage, and not a sale. * * * It is true [the mortgagor] must have given his assent to this form of the memorandum; but the distress for money under which he then was, places him in the same condition as other borrowers, in numerous cases reported in the books, who have submitted to the dictation of the lender under the pressure of their wants; and a court of equity does not consider a consent, thus obtained, to be sufficient to fix the rights of the parties." [52]

In addition, since by the evidence the grantor does have a written claim to get the property from the grantee and the only controversy is whether it is to be by virtue of a contract of purchase or by a right to redeem as mortgagor, there is not nearly the violence of alteration of the situation of the parties as there is where the grantor is allowed to take away property from the person who, by the only written evidence, has an absolute and indefeasible title to it. This also cuts in another direction. There is a policy objection in the deed absolute cases both against permitting the grantor to conceal his assets by making a conveyance which does not reveal by a writing that there is a string to it by which the property can be pulled back, and, also, in favor of the grantee, against the possibility of false swearing to do him out of his property. Here the written agreement minimizes both such policies. There is not only a written clue to the grantor's continued interest in the conveyed property for his creditors to follow up, but also no great hardship is going to fall on the grantee if the amount the grantor is to pay is held to be a debt rather than a contract purchase price and his right, consequently, to be one of redemption instead of one upon the grantee's promise to reconvey. The chief injury the grantee suffers is in being deprived of his ability to end the grantor's right on default by means other than foreclosure; and it would be difficult to argue that this is of great seriousness; or, if it is, or might be, substantial, that it is not outweighed by the greater possible hardship on the grantor of the opposite result.

FACTORS ESTABLISHING CONDITIONAL SALE AS MORTGAGE

89. The intent of the parties controls whether a conditional sale is a mortgage. Many factors enter into the determination of this question of fact. Two of the most important ones indicating that a mortgage was intended are the existence of a debt and the disparity between the value of the land and the purported resale price.

---

51. Johnson v. National Bank of Commerce, 1911, 65 Wash. 261, 275, 118 P. 21, 25, L.R.A.1916B, 4.

52. Russell v. Southard, 1851, 53 U.S. (12 How.) 139, 151, 13 L.Ed. 927.

"It may be premised that where upon the face of the transaction it is doubtful whether the parties intended to make a mortgage or conditional sale, courts of equity will always incline to consider it a mortgage, because by means of conditional sales oppression is frequently exercised over the needy, and they are too often made the vehicle of extortion." Earp v. Boothe, 1874, 24 Gratt. (Va.) 368, 375.

In determining whether the transaction is a mortgage, or an absolute or conditional sale, the problem is substantially the same as in the straight deed absolute case. It is the intention of the parties at the time the transaction is entered into, as gathered from the writings themselves and from relevant extrinsic evidence, which governs.[53] Many factors enter into the determination of this question of fact. A good summary of some of the essential elements to be considered as laid down by the authorities includes, "whether or not there is a continuing obligation on the part of the grantor to pay the debt or meet the obligation which it is claimed the deed was made to secure; the question of relative values; the contemporaneous and subsequent acts; the declarations and admissions of the parties; the form of the written evidences of the transactions; the nature and character of the testimony relied upon; the various business, social and other relationship of the parties; and the apparent aims and purposes to be accomplished." [54]

A couple of these are worth an additional glance. One is the question whether, when the agreement gives the grantor only an option of repurchase and it is clear that there is no duty upon him to pay the sum specified as "purchase" money, the transaction can be a mortgage. The argument against it is that a mortgage requires a binding personal obligation for its existence. Whether this is so is considered at some length at another place and will not here be gone into in detail.[55] Of course if there can be no mortgage without a binding legal obligation to secure there would be no mortgage where the grantor is not bound to pay the grantee anything.[56] But even if the mortgage conception does not demand this, a personal debt is so unusual that its lack is the strongest sort of evidence to indicate that the parties did not intend a mortgage.[57] On the other hand, evidence of the existence of a debt is strongly persuasive of a mortgage intent.[58]

Another matter of great significance is great disparity between the value of the land and the purported resale price.[59] The basic

---

53. Both parties must intend a mortgage. Douglass v. Moody, 1885, 80 Ala. 61, 69; Nitkey v. Ward, 1937, 199 Minn. 334, 271 N.W. 873, certiorari denied 302 U.S. 706, 58 S.Ct. 25, 82 L.Ed. 545, rehearing denied 302 U.S. 775, 58 S.Ct. 134, 82 L.Ed. 600.

54. Corey v. Roberts, 1933, 82 Utah 445, 452, 25 P.2d 940, 942. Another excellent summary of the evidence indicating the factors going into the finding is in Morton v. Allen, 1912, 180 Ala. 279, 286, 60 So. 866, 868, L.R.A.1916B, 11. See also Gray v. Frazer, 1942, 63 Idaho 552, 123 P.2d 711; Nitkey v. Ward, 1937, 199 Minn. 334, 271 N.W. 873, certiorari denied 302 U.S. 706, 58 S.Ct. 25, 82 L.Ed. 545, rehearing denied 302 U.S. 775, 58 S.Ct. 134, 82 L.Ed. 600; O'Briant v. Lee, 1939, 214 N.C. 723, 200 S.E. 865; Dean v. Smith, 1925, 53 N.D. 123, 204 N.W. 987, discussed in note, 1926, 20 Ill.L.Rev. 732; Selik v. Goldman Realty Co., 1927, 240 Mich. 612, 216 N.W. 422, discussed, 1928, 26 Mich.L.Rev. 821; notes, 1938, 16 N.Car.L.Rev. 416, 418.

Both Orlando v. Berns, 1957, 154 Cal.App.2d 753, 316 P.2d 705, and McKinley v. Hinnant, 1955, 242 N.C. 245, 87 S.E.2d 568, noted in Third Annual Survey of North Carolina Case Law: Credit Transactions, 1955, 34 N.C.L.Rev. 35, relied chiefly upon the wide difference between the value of the property conveyed and the amount of consideration paid to find that the transaction was a mortgage. See also Updike, Mortgages, in 1956 Annual Survey of American Law, 1957, 32 N.Y.U.L.Rev. 789.

55. See Chapter 5, infra.

56. See Henley v. Soper, 1871, 41 Cal. 22, 28.

57. "Neither that fund nor the option imposed any obligation to repurchase. It was entirely a matter of choice with the lessee. * * * That is a strong circumstance tending to prove that the conveyance was what it purported to be (see Dixon v. Wright, 175 Miss. 191, 166 So. 374), * * *." Nitkey v. Ward, 1937, 199 Minn. 334, 341, 271 N.W. 873, 877; Goodman v. Grierson, 1813, 2 Ball. & B. 274 (Ir.Ch.).

58. O'Briant v. Lee, 1939, 214 N.C. 723, 733, 200 S.E. 865, 871, "If there was a debt, either antecedent or presently created, the instrument must be construed to constitute a mortgage, unless a contrary intent clearly appears upon the face of the instrument." See Hawke v. Milliken, 1866, 12 Grant.Ch., Upper Can., 236. See note, 1926, 20 Ill.L.Rev. 732, 733.

In Investors' Mortgage Security Co. v. Hamilton, 1931, 51 Idaho 113, 4 P.2d 347, discussed in note, 1932, 2 Idaho L.J. 151, the fact that the grantee, who took a conveyance of mortgaged property in purported satisfaction of the grantor's mortgage debt to him, retained the original evidence of indebtedness was thought to be convincing evidence that the conveyance and option to repurchase constituted a mortgage.

59. See, however, Bogk v. Gassert, 1893, 149 U.S. 17, 13 S.Ct. 738, 37 L.Ed. 631, where very great inade-

reason for this has been pointed out by a great scholar.

"A primary reason for relief in equity from the strict terms of a mortgage is that the mortgagor must pay the debt in any event, where the mortgaged property is insufficient for the purpose. On the other hand, in a sale with option to repurchase, the parties are taking a business chance which may or may not turn out favorably to the purchaser. If the land diminishes in value, the seller will not exercise his option to repurchase, and the purchaser must bear the loss. This it is conceived balances the chance that the purchaser may get an advantage if the land exceeds in value the price fixed for its repurchase, and the seller nevertheless fails by negligence or misfortune to exercise his option.

"It is obvious, however, that as a practical matter this distinction amounts to nothing if the price paid for the granted property is much below its value. In such a case the grantee is amply protected without any right of action for the recovery of a debt. All that

he can desire is to be left in undisturbed possession of the property.

"A ready means is thus provided for nullifying the rules which equity had gradually built up in regard to mortgages. To be sure, in cases of doubt, a transaction is construed as a mortgage, and inadequacy of the price is a strong circumstance tending to show that a conveyance was intended merely to secure a debt. In this way hard cases are generally taken care of; but unless it is observed that the ultimate distinction on any principle of justice depends not on the form of the transaction, whether that of a mortgage or of a sale with option to repurchase, but on gross inequality between the amount received and the value of the property, the law is likely to be confused and the chance of injustice unnecessarily great." [60]

C. TRIPARTITE TRANSACTIONS

PURCHASE MONEY RESULTING TRUSTS

90. When, in a purchase of land, the money paid by the party taking the title is advanced by him as a loan to another, a resulting trust arises in favor of the latter. Oral evidence is admissible to establish the loan. The burden of establishing such a resulting trust is on the party asserting it.

"The rule is familiar that when, upon a purchase of real property, the purchase money is paid by one person, and the conveyance is made to another, a resulting trust immediately arises against the person to whom the land is conveyed, in favor of the one by whom the purchase money is paid. The real purchaser of the property is considered as the owner, with the right to control the title in the hands of the grantee, and to demand a conveyance from him at any time." [61] Precisely "the same rule prevails

---

quacy was not thought sufficient to upset a jury's verdict that the transaction was a conditional sale.

Courts generally treat inadequacy of price as one of the important facts in determining whether a mortgage was intended. See Glass v. Hieronymus Bros., 1899, 125 Ala. 140, 28 So. 71, 82 Am.St.Rep. 225; Rogers v. Davis, 1894, 91 Iowa 730, 59 N.W. 265; Daniels v. Johnson, 1872, 24 Mich. 430; Lawrence v. DuBois, 1880, 16 W.Va. 443; Carpenter & Carpenter v. Kingman, 1941, 56 Wyo. 314, 109 P.2d 463. See 1945, 155 A.L.R. 1109; 1934, 90 A.L.R. 953, for additional authorities.

In Osipowicz v. Furland, 1935, 218 Wis. 568, 260 N.W. 482, discussed in note, 1935, 11 Wis.L.Rev. 118, the court was strongly influenced to hold the transaction a mortgage because the repurchase price was exactly the amount owed by the grantors to the grantee at the time of the conveyance. Lipe v. Beechnut Packing Co., 1935, 243 App.Div. 433, 277 N.Y.S. 832, took a similar view.

Warren, Regulation of California Housing Financing: A Forgotten Consumer, 1961, 8 U.C.L.A.L.Rev. 555, 577, cites Cowles v. Zlaket, 1959, 167 Cal.App.2d 20, 334 P.2d 55, as a classic example of the use of the sale with an option to repurchase to cloak usury. And he cites Orlando v. Berns, 1957, 154 Cal.App. 2d 753, 316 P.2d 705, as a case in which the court, in holding the transaction to be a loan, gave considerable weight to the fact that the value of the property conveyed greatly exceeded both the purchase and repurchase price.

60. Williston, Some Modern Tendencies in the Law, 43 et seq. See also Weaver v. Lapsley, 1868, 42 Ala. 601, 613, 94 Am.Dec. 671.

61. Campbell v. Freeman, 1893, 99 Cal. 546, 34 P. 113. See Scott, Trusts, § 440; Bogert, Trusts and

if the money paid by the party taking the title is advanced by him as a loan to the other." [62] In all cases the burden of establishing the resulting trust is on the party asserting it. In the first type of case the alleged real purchaser "must prove not only that the consideration for the conveyance was paid by him or out of his funds, but also that the money was paid as the purchase price and not as a loan" to the grantee.[63] In the second case the fact of loan by the grantee must be clearly proved.[64] In both cases, however, when A establishes the fact that it was his money that paid for the land, regardless of whether it was his before the transaction or borrowed from B, the grantee, to consummate it, the burden of proof is met because, without further evidence, the inference is drawn that B does not take the beneficial interest and, therefore, that B holds on resulting trust for A. B may rebut this inference, but the burden of proof is upon him to do so.[65] Furthermore, in both cases, it is thoroughly settled that Statutes of Frauds do not prevent such trusts arising. It is frequently stated that this is so because the trust arises by operation of law and therefore is within an express exception of the Statute of Frauds.[66] A better reason, given by an authority in the field, is that although such resulting trusts "arise out of the intention of the parties, that intention is evidenced by the circumstances of the transaction rather than by the language of the parties. There is not, therefore, as a practical matter the same danger of perjured testimony as in cases where the only evidence of intention is the oral language of the parties." [67] Quite obviously the parol evidence rule has no application: the only writing is the deed from the third party and it would not control as the sole memorial of the agreed upon rights between the grantee and the alleged purchaser.[68]

PURCHASE MONEY RESULTING TRUSTS —SECURITY AGREEMENTS

91. A grantee-lender under a purchase money resulting trust who stipulates that the land shall be security for the loan is both a resulting trustee of the title and a mortgagee.

Where the grantee of title under a purchase-money resulting trust has loaned the money, it is usual for him to stipulate that the land shall be security for the loan, and such an agreement, even though oral, is recognized.[69] As one court stated, "In such a case the grantee holds a double relation to the real purchaser,—he is his trustee of the legal title to the land, and his mortgagee for the money advanced for its purchase, and, as in the case of any other mortgage which is evidenced by an absolute deed, is entitled to retain the title until the payment of the claim for which it is held as security; and he may also enforce his lien by an action of foreclosure. The conveyance is nonetheless a mortgage because it was conveyed to him directly by a third party, to secure his loan to the purchaser for the amount of the purchase money, than if the conveyance had

Trustees, 2d Ed., § 454. In some states statutes restate the common law purchase money resulting trust principle. E. g., West's Ann.Cal.Civ.Code § 853.

62. Campbell v. Freeman, supra, note 61. See also Scott, Trusts, § 440; Bogert, Trusts and Trustees, 2d Ed., § 454.

Accord: Kohler v. Gilbert, 1959, 216 Or. 483, 339 P. 2d 1102.

63. Phillips v. Phillips, 1913, 81 N.J.Eq. 459, 461, 86 A. 949, 950, affirmed 83 N.J.Eq. 345, 91 A. 1070. See Scott, Cases on Trusts, 2d Ed., § 440 et seq. for a collection of authorities on purchase money resulting trusts. See also 1926, 42 A.L.R. 10, 21.

64. McDonough v. O'Niel, 1873, 113 Mass. 92.

65. See Scott, supra note 63; Bogert, supra note 62, § 455.

66. Anonymous, 1683, 2 Vent. 361.

67. Scott, Trusts, p. 2242.

"This resulting trust is a form of trust dependent for its existence on the actual intent of the creator, expressed in acts other than writing or talking". Bogert, Trusts and Trustees, 2d Ed., § 454.

68. See Williston, Contracts, Rev.Ed., § 647.

69. Miller v. Miller, 1905, 101 Md. 600, 61 A. 210. See Note, Equitable Mortgages in Iowa, 1959, 44 Iowa L.Rev. 716, 721–723.

been made directly to the purchaser in the first instance, and the purchaser had then made a conveyance to him, as a security for the money that he had previously borrowed with which to make the purchase." [70]   It should be noted in this connection that, although the burden of establishing the resulting trust is on the alleged purchaser, including the proof that the money paid by the grantee was in fact a loan, the burden of establishing the mortgage agreement is a separate and distinct question and is on the one asserting its existence. Usually this is the purchaser and when it is the courts do not clearly differentiate between the tasks of establishing the resulting trust and the mortgage, saying that both must be proved by strong evidence. Since one element in the security agreement is the loan by the grantee, which must be proved to make out the resulting trust, it is easy to understand why the two problems are not segregated. [71] When the grantee is seeking to foreclose on the property there is a similar overlapping. His main task is to prove the fact of loan as an element in the mortgage; but when he does this he has made out the resulting trust. The additional part of his case, the agreement that the property be security for the

payment of the loan, is treated either as controlled by the rules governing the creation of the trust, or as involving precisely the same problem raised in the case of a straight deed absolute from the borrower to the lender. [72]   So far as burden and standard of proof are concerned there is no objection to this approach. However, this tripartite situation is different from the two-party one with respect to the possible application to it of the Statute of Frauds. [73]

STATUTE OF FRAUDS IN TRI-PARTITE CASES

92. The Statute of Frauds does not bar an oral agreement that the grantee-trustee-lender under a purchase money resulting trust is to hold his title as security for the loan.

Although the Statute of Frauds is no objection to the creation of the resulting trust interest in the purchaser in these cases, it is not so clear that the oral agreement between the parties that the grantee-trustee shall hold his title as security for his loan does not fall within its prohibition, and hence some analysis of the matter is in order. It would seem clear that where T is an existing trustee under an express written trust and makes a loan to C, the beneficiary, with an oral agreement that T is to hold title to the trust property as security for repayment of the loan, the Statute of Frauds applies to prevent enforcement of the mortgage agreement by T. The same is true where T holds property as trustee for C under a purchase money resulting trust and later T loans money to C under an oral agreement that the property shall be security. [74]   Whether in these cases the Statute would bar T from showing the agreement in case C brought an action to compel a con-

70. Campbell v. Freeman, 1893, 99 Cal. 546, 548, 34 P. 113.

Accord: Hicks v. Bridges, 1957, 152 Cal.App.2d 146, 313 P.2d 15.

See Note, 1965, 13 Kan.L.Rev. 585, discussing Duncan v. Essary, 1964, 193 Kan. 241, 392 P.2d 877, in which the court held that equitable mortgages were created by a warranty deed from the defendant of property owned by it and also on property conveyed to the plaintiff from a third party grantor which had been bought by defendant with money loaned by plaintiff for that purpose. The note writer's thesis was that in the tripartite transaction it would be possible, and in some instances advantageous to either creditor or debtor, to choose between advancing the theory that the transaction was a purchase money resulting trust or an equitable mortgage. The Kansas statutes in respect to the existence in Kansas of purchase money resulting trusts was blamed by the writer for what he considered was confusion in the Kansas law on the tripartite problem.

71. Hall v. O'Connell, 1908, 52 Or. 164, 167, 95 P. 717; Jackson v. Maxwell, 1915, 113 Me. 366, 94 A. 116, Ann.Cas.1917C, 966, 970.

72. See Campbell v. Freeman, supra, note 70.

73. The same is true as to the parol evidence rule but, as was pointed out supra, it so clearly has no bearing here that discussion of it may be omitted. The Statute of Frauds is dealt with in § 92.

74. See Warner v. Tullis, 1928, 206 Iowa, 680, 218 N.W. 575; Pierce v. Parrish, 1900, 111 Ga. 725, 37 S.E. 79, semble.

veyance seems to depend upon the purpose and use of the loan. If the borrowed money went into improvements or the clearing off of other liens, the court will invoke the principle that C must do equity in order to get the aid of the court of equity. As one court said in a case of this sort, "for equity to actively interpose its decree * * * denying to plaintiff all compensation for expenditures in improving and preserving the property is abhorrent, not only to a sense of natural justice, but to those fundamental principles upon which equity grants or withholds its peculiar remedies." [75] On the other hand, where the loan is made for purposes having no relation to the land, C may get the property from T without paying, the Statute of Frauds preventing T from showing the oral agreement. [76]

If the Statute of Frauds applies in the two cases just discussed, it is pertinent to inquire why it does not apply also to the case where T loans C the money with which to buy property from X, taking title in a direct deed absolute from X, but with an oral agreement at the time with C that T is to hold the property as security for the repayment of the loan. One answer is that the agreement is used only to rebut pro tanto the creation of the resulting trust. [77] Parol evidence of the intention of C that T should have the beneficial interest for the limited purpose of security violates neither the Statute of Frauds nor the parol evidence rule. If resulting trusts arise because it is presumed from the facts that the payor of the money intended that the grantee should not have the beneficial

interest, if it is shown that he intended that the grantee should have the complete or a limited beneficial interest, the foundation for raising the resulting trust does not exist. [78] Or, if the language of courts holding that purchase money resulting trusts are not under the Statute of Frauds because they arise by "operation of law" is taken at face value, the same result follows. If it arises by "operation of law," it is an interest independent of the intention of the parties and the parol evidence of what the payor's intention actually was is let in, not for the purpose of vitiating rights effectuating anyone's intention, but for the purpose of establishing by this proof that the law, for reasons other than effectuating intent, ought not to operate to create the right, or to create it only to a limited extent. Whichever of these views is accepted, there seems no reason why, on this rationale, the security agreement should not extend not only to the purchase money loan itself but to additional loans. [79]

Another explanation invokes the "do-equity" rationale mentioned before. The idea is that the loan has paid for the property under an agreement that it be so used and, therefore, before the borrower should be allowed to obtain it from the lender under the resulting trust he should pay the loan just as he should have to pay off loans obtained for and used to make improvements. [80] This explanation would confine the enforceable security agreements to those covering loans of purchase money.

A contributing influence, no matter what theory is followed, undoubtedly is the fact that in this sort of transaction there are normally present factors, e. g., the fact of loan, the dealings involving the third party

75. Warner v. Tullis, supra note 74, 206 Iowa at 692, 218 N.W. at 580.

76. Pierce v. Parrish, 1900, 111 Ga. 725, 37 S.E. 79; Warner v. Tullis, supra, note 74, loan for funeral expenses not included in debts which must be paid as condition to compelling conveyance.

77. "No doubt the resulting trust might be rebutted by parol evidence of the fact of a debt, and that the conveyance was made by way of security for that debt." Card v. Jaffray, 1805, Ir.Ch. 2 Sch. & Lef. 381.

78. Scott, Trusts, § 441.1.

79. In a leading case the security agreement was recognized for enforcement by the grantee-mortgagee not only for the original purchase-money loan but for agreed upon subsequent advances. Campbell v. Freeman, 1893, 99 Cal. 546, 34 P. 113.

80. See Warner v. Tullis, note 74, supra.

with his story available, the borrower-payor frequently being let into possession and paying taxes, which minimize the evils at which the Statute aims.[81] On the other hand, it should be noted that it differs from the straight deed absolute cases, in which it is clear that traditional solicitude for the hard pressed borrower who has to put up his property at risk of losing it in order to get the money he needs plays a part. Here the borrower is expanding his operations, acquiring new property, not risking old, and pledging as security only the property he never had before and for the money which enabled him to get it. Certainly no very convincing argument can be made for any special tenderness to the mortgagor in cases of this sort.

CONTINUING EQUITABLE OWNERSHIP IN THE BORROWER

93. The borrower may have a continuing equitable interest in the land because of a prior contract or option to buy. This does not prevent the grantee-lender from showing the oral security agreement.

In many cases the borrower-payor, instead of acquiring an interest in the property by way of resulting trust arising for the first time out of the transaction, had a prior equitable ownership.

Instances of this are contracts [82] or options [83] to purchase the property entered into by the borrower before the loan was made or the property conveyed to the lender by the contract vendor. On the question of showing the oral agreement for mortgage in such cases analogy to the two-party deed absolute cases can be invoked here, the prior equitable interest in the borrower giving to him a standing comparable to that of the legal owner-grantor; and the fact that the conveyance is from a third party, but at the direction of the borrower, is insufficient to change the substance of the transaction. Indeed the argument in favor of allowing the oral agreement is stronger here because the borrowed money was used to complete the payments necessary for the borrower to acquire the land. But apart from this, it would seem that the reasoning in the purchase money resulting trust with oral security agreement cases is also applicable here. In both cases it is the borrower's money that pays for the property conveyed to the lender; it should be immaterial to the creation of a resulting trust by reason of this fact that the buyer had a prior equitable interest in the property because of an executory contract for its purchase and that the grantee, not being a bona fide purchaser, would take subject to it.

A still different approach may be suggested. As previously pointed out the Statute of Frauds presents no obstacle where an oral agreement for a mortgage is made by one who borrows the money for the purpose of paying the vendor under a contract of purchase, if the money is so used and the conveyance made to the borrower.[84] It would be only a slight extension to apply this to the case we have here in which the conveyance is made to the lender in accordance with the intention of the borrower. If this reasoning is accepted, the grantee-lender would be able to enforce an equitable security interest in the property to which he holds legal title. And, of course the borrower would have to do equity by paying the debt

---

81. A good illustration is Miller v. Miller, 1905, 101 Md. 600, 61 A. 210, in which M, the borrower-purchaser, went into possession, made improvements, paid taxes, and not only paid interest on his loan from E, the grantee, but also the interest on the loan owed by E to T, the grantor.

82. McConnell v. Gentry, 1907, 30 Ky.L.Rep. 548, 99 S.W. 278; Grout v. Stewart, 1905, 96 Minn. 230, 104 N.W. 966; but see Anderson v. Anderson, 1900, 81 Minn. 329, 84 N.W. 112. See also Logue's Appeal, 1883, 104 Pa. 136, 40 L.I. 485, 31 P.L.J. 116, in which A purchased land at a judicial sale and having borrowed from B the money with which to pay the sheriff, had conveyance made to B under an oral agreement for security. See note, 1926, 42 A.L.R. 10, 25.

83. Stitt v. Rat Portage Lumber Co., 1905, 96 Minn. 27, 104 N.W. 561.

84. This is either on the doctrine of subrogation or of rescission and imposition of a lien by constructive trust upon a traced res. See Chapter 2, supra.

before he would be entitled to a conveyance in enforcement of either his preexisting equitable interest or his interest as beneficiary under a purchase money resulting trust.

EFFECT OF ABOLITION OF PURCHASE MONEY RESULTING TRUSTS

94. In states where purchase money resulting trusts are abolished by statute oral security agreements are generally unenforceable because the alleged mortgagor has no mortgageable interest. The New York rule is contra.

"It is elementary * * * that some estate or interest capable of being mortgaged, held by the mortgagor, is essential to the existence of a mortgage. When a transaction constitutes a mortgage, therefore, there must be, either, independently of the transaction, some interest in the mortgagor capable of being mortgaged, or through the transaction itself such interest must be acquired by the mortgagor. Courts of equity have long been concerned with preserving from forfeiture this interest in the mortgagor. * * *

"The nature or extent of the interest in the premises, or the manner in which it is evidenced, is unimportant; but under the rule as stated there must be some interest in the claimed mortgagor which, but for the protection of a court of equity, would be surrendered and lost through the transaction." [85]

Where there is either a prior legal or equitable interest in the alleged mortgagor or where, by virtue of a purchase money resulting trust, one arises out of the transaction which, it is asserted, creates the mortgage, the foregoing rule is satisfied. But in several states purchase money resulting trusts are abolished by statute.[86] In such states, unless there are present circumstances which either create an exception to the statutory abolition

in that jurisdiction,[87] or else provide some other basis for the result, an oral agreement for mortgage in these tripartite cases will be invalid under the Statute of Frauds. This is so because, apart from the specific enforcement of the oral agreement, the alleged mortgagor has no interest whatsoever in the property either beforehand or arising out of the transaction, and to permit the purely executory oral agreement to create an interest would squarely contravene the Statute of Frauds.[88]

Some courts stick more closely than others to the language of the statutes barring resulting trusts. Thus Minnesota has refused to permit the trust and, consequently, the mortgage, in cases where there is an oral agreement that the grantee shall hold the title as security for the purchase money loan and, subject thereto, for the benefit of the borrower.[89] In a similar situation, New York holds that the resulting trust arises and the oral mortgage is good, the reasoning being twofold: (1) that the statute bars resulting trusts which would arise *solely* from the payment of the purchase money and have no other foundation. It therefore is inapplicable because there is another foundation

---

85. In re Bennett, 1911, 115 Minn. 342, 350, 132 N.W. 309, 312, 37 L.R.A.,N.S., 521.

86. See Campbell, Cases on Mortgages, 2d ed., 124 n. for references to these statutes.

87. The statutes exempt from the abolition of the rule the cases where the grantee either "1. takes the property as an absolute conveyance, in his own name, without the consent or knowledge of the person paying the consideration; or 2. in violation of some trust, purchases the property so conveyed with money or property belonging to another." New York (McKinney's General Obligations Law, § 5–703; EPTL 7–1.3), Michigan (M.C.L.A. §§ 555.7–555.9, 566.106, 55.107), Minnesota (M.S.A. §§ 501.06–501.09, 513.04) Kentucky (KRS 381.170), and Wisconsin (W. S.A. §§ 231.07–231.09, 240.07, 240.06, 243.01) have similar statutory provisions. Two states, Kansas (K.S.A. 33–105, 58–2401 to 58–2408) and Indiana (Burns' Ann.St. §§ 56–601, 56–606 to 56–608) also except the case where the grantee agrees, without fraudulent intent, to hold the land or some interest therein in trust for the party paying the purchase money or some part thereof.

88. In re Bennett, supra, note 85.

89. Anderson v. Anderson, 1900, 81 Minn. 329, 84 N.W. 112, approved in Nelson v. Nelson, 1921, 149 Minn. 285, 288, 183 N.W. 354, 355; contra, alternative decision, Stitt v. Rat Portage Lumber Co., 1905, 96 Minn. 27, 36, 104 N.W. 561, 565.

in the oral agreement and the lending transaction. (2) That the transaction was purely one of oral mortgage.[90] The latter ground was justified in the New York decision enunciating it on the basis that the title had been taken by the grantee "upon paying a balance due upon a contract of purchase" previously entered into by the borrower with the grantor;[91] in other words it was a case of a previously existing interest in the borrower claimant.

In many cases, even though no resulting trust can be established as an exception to the statutes prohibiting them, the borrower can work out a constructive trust in his favor which will bring him within the requirement of an interest in the property before or at the time of the mortgage transaction as effectively as would the resulting trust. An oral promise by the lender-grantee to hold it for the borrower should be sufficient to accomplish this.[92] Where there is an oral agreement with the borrower to bid in property about to be sold at foreclosure, execution, tax, partition or other judicial sale, coupled with forbearance on the part of the borrower, in reliance upon the agreement, to take steps to protect his interest, the courts have no difficulty in giving relief in spite of the fact the agreement was oral.[93] As one court put it, "where one of the parties to a

contract, void by the statute of frauds, avails himself of its invalidity, but unconscientiously appropriates what he has acquired under it, equity will compel restitution; and it constitutes no objection to the claim, that the opposite party may happen to secure the same practical benefit, through the process of restitution, which would have resulted from the observance of the void agreement."[94] The same doctrine has been applied to oral agreements to redeem land for the owner after forced sale on foreclosure or execution.[95] Similarly, if the purchase was made by one standing in a confidential relation to the borrower,[96] or if the purchase was in breach of a fiduciary duty[97] a constructive trust will be imposed.

A preliminary inquiry in all of these cases is whether the arrangement between the parties was for a loan by the grantee to the claimant or whether it was for the grantee to buy the property and then resell it to the claimant. The latter clearly falls within the prohibition of the Statute of Frauds even in jurisdictions where purchase money resulting trusts are not abolished. Since this is so, it is not surprising that where the agreement is for a loan and security, but because of the abolition of purchase money resulting trusts the borrower gets no interest in the property, the courts should say that this is bad because the Statute of Frauds prevents the enforcement of the oral agreement. In other words they treat it the same way that they treat an oral agreement for purchase. This seems sound, for in both cases the claimant can acquire an interest in the property for the first time only by the enforcement of the executory oral agreement. And yet one cannot es-

---

90. Carr v. Carr, 1873, 52 N.Y. 251 (there was a prior oral contract of purchase between the borrower and the grantor as well as part payment of the purchase price and taking of possession by the borrower contemporaneously with the conveyance); Widmayer v. Warner, 1920, 192 App.Div. 499, 182 N.Y.S. 629 (alternative decision). See Bogert, Trusts and Trustees, 2d Ed., § 467; Scott, Trusts, § 440.2.

91. Carr v. Carr, supra note 90.

92. See Scott, Trusts, § 440.2.

93. Ryan v. Dox, 1866, 34 N.Y. 307, 90 Am.Dec. 696; Congregation Kehal Adath Jeshurun M'Yassy v. Universal Bldg. & Const. Co., 1909, 134 App.Div. 368, 119 N.Y.S. 72; Widmayer v. Warner, 1920, 192 App.Div. 499, 182 N.Y.S. 629, alternative decision. If the borrower did not refrain from taking steps to protect himself no constructive trust will arise. Wheeler v. Reynolds, 1876, 66 N.Y. 227, 232; Southwick v. Spevak, 1925, 252 Mass. 354, 357, 147 N.E. 885, 886. See note, 1926, 42 A.L.R. 10, 78.

94. Ryan v. Dox, supra, note 83, at 319.

95. Wood v. Rabe, 1884, 96 N.Y. 414, 425, 427, 48 Am.Rep. 640. See note, 1926, 42 A.L.R. 10, 118; 54 id. 1207.

96. Foreman v. Foreman, 1929, 251 N.Y. 237, 241, 167 N.E. 428, is a leading case.

97. Peppard Realty Co., Inc. v. Emdon, 1925, 213 App.Div. 824, 209 N.Y.S. 5, affirmed 241 N.Y. 588, 150 N.E. 566. See note 1926, 42 A.L.R. 10, 28.

cape an uneasy feeling that the result may rest more upon adherence to what the courts consider the basic theory of a mortgage than concern with the Statute of Frauds. The usual mortgage involves a prior property interest in the mortgagor which is put up by him as collateral to obtain money and which will be lost if the mortgage is valid and is foreclosed. Starting with this as the norm, it is not difficult to see that courts might establish as an indispensable part of the mortgage concept that there must be property interest in the mortgagor. Where the property interest in the mortgagor is acquired for the first time in and through the transaction which results in the mortgage, the concept still could be held to be satisfied even though the hazard the borrower runs in such a case is only that of losing what he acquired by the use of the loan. But where there exists only an executory right to get an interest in the property the mortgage concept will not stretch and the courts assimilate the case to that of a contract to sell.

CONTRACT OR OPTION TO PURCHASE

95. The agreement between the grantee and the alleged mortgagor may take the form of a written contract or option to purchase. Extrinsic evidence is admissible to prove the transaction a mortgage, but the burden of proof is heavier than in similar two-party cases.

We saw in the two-party deed absolute case that the agreement between the parties may in form be one for an option or a contract to purchase, rather than an oral agreement that the property is to be security. The same may be true here where the deed comes to the grantee from a third person.[98] Sometimes, indeed, the parties use the utmost care to adopt the form of a sale and purchase and not of a loan and mortgage.[99] When this

is done the problem is similar to the two-party cases previously considered in which the deed absolute transaction was accompanied by an agreement or option to resell. In both the question is whether the transaction is what it purports to be or whether it actually is a mortgage. And in both there is no legal prohibition against resolving that question by any relevant evidence that is admissible. Plainly, in these tripartite cases he who would transform the expressed contract for sale into a different one which is supposed to be hidden by it carries a heavy burden.[1] And the proponent of such a proposition cannot meet it by pointing to the elements which are common both to a contract of sale and to a mortgage.

"Such common elements are: First, each is accompanied by a defeasance; in the mortgage contract this may be expressly stated or may be implied even from oral proofs; in the sale contract it is the essence of the document; in each case, upon the performance of the conditions, the title, legal or equitable, passes to the one who has performed. Second, each is a security; one for the debt for money borrowed and the other for the purchase price debt. Third, in each there is an absolute, unconditional debt; the origin of one is the money which has been loaned; the origin of the other is the agreed purchase price; in neither case is the payor's promise optional, nor can he escape personal liability for a deficiency or its equivalent. * * * The presence of one, or two, or three of these always common elements cannot be controlling in deciding whether a given transaction is a sale or is a loan; to suggest all or any one of them as of decisive effect is to suggest this plain fallacy; and such decisions as seem to make any one of these—e.g., absolute liability—alone a sufficient criterion cannot, we

---

98. See Pollak v. Millsap, 1929, 219 Ala. 273, 278, 122 So. 16, 20, 65 A.L.R. 110, semble.

99. E.g., Stark v. Bauer Cooperage Co., C.C.A.Ohio 1925, 3 F.2d 214, certiorari denied 45 S.Ct. 464, 267 U.S. 604, 69 L.Ed. 809.

1. Idem. 215. But cf. the following statement: "all doubts are resolved in favor of it being a mortgage, and not a conditional sale." Pollak v. Millsap, 1929, 219 Ala. 273, 278, 122 So. 16, 21, 65 A.L.R. 110.

think, have been well considered."[2] Further, even though it is true that in a very broad sense there is an equivalency between a sale contract of property and loan secured by a mortgage upon that same property, nevertheless it "cannot be said that the legal title held by the grantee in a deed subject to a sale contract for $1,000 is the same as the equitable title held by a $1,000 mortgagee. There are differences in tax and other public obligations, in matters of possession and control, of foreclosure, of the extent and nature of the equity, of waste, of future statutory regulation and of other things, depending upon the laws of the particular state. When the parties have deliberately adopted one code to govern their relations, the law will not lightly subject them to a different code, even though similar in many respects."[3] Granting this, it still remains true, just as in the two-party cases, that by meeting the burden of proof and by proper evidence, the transaction can be proved to be a mortgage. And the factors which guide the courts in the two-party deals are much the same ones that will influence their decisions here.[4] However there is one vitally important point to stress again here: that to find a mortgage there must be in the mortgagor, either prior to, or arising through, the transaction otherwise than by the terms of the agreement that he should get it, an interest in the mortgaged property. As was stated in a penetrating opinion, "So far as we can find, every case in which the existence of an absolute promise by an ostensible vendee to pay the sum involved has been thought to indicate that the transaction was merely a loan instead of having the character in which it was made to appear, is a case where the contract vendee had parted with his recent title and was ar-

ranging to get it back again. In no case was the contract one for the purchase of property which he had never before owned."[5] Further, while in the two-party cases the tendency to find the transaction to be a mortgage was observed, the contrary is the general rule in this type of transaction. And the reason for this stems from the fact that in this sort of business deal the hazard is not of losing what the obligor had owned before, but only of failing to get for the first time what he had bargained for.

D. CLOGGING

PRINCIPAL DOCTRINES

96. **To effectuate the purposes of the equity of redemption, equity developed three doctrines:**

(1) **"Once a mortgage, always a mortgage";**

(2) **The mortgagee shall have no "collateral advantage";**

(3) **There must be no stipulation in the mortgage which will "fetter" the property on redemption.**

When the courts of equity created the equity of redemption, they did direct violence to the explicit intention of the parties. They did this by allowing the mortgagor to get back his property by performing the secured obligation after the legal title to the property had vested absolutely in the mortgagee—vested according to the express language of the parties in the mortgage deed and according to the effect the law courts gave to that language. The reasons which motivated equity in this action have been briefly surveyed earlier[6] and will be referred to again in the succeeding sections. Following its original invention equity developed three doctrines which stem directly from it, all three of which may be grouped under the generic heading of clogging the equity of redemp-

---

2. Idem, 216.

3. Idem, 217. For a good short discussion of the chief differences between a contract for the sale of land and a loan and mortgage arrangement, see Glenn, Mortgages, §§ 15, 15.1.

4. See supra, § 89.

5. Stark v. Bauer Cooperage Co., supra note 99, at 216.

6. See Chapter 1, Subdivision C.

tion [7] and may be classified by the labels: (1) "Once a mortgage, always a mortgage"; (2) the mortgagee shall not have a "collateral advantage"; and (3) there must be no stipulation in the mortgage which will "fetter" the property on redemption.[8] Although all three did stem from the original creation of the equity of redemption their separate histories have been influenced not only in different degrees by the various reasons for it but, also, in the course of the years by distinct considerations. They will therefore be discussed separately even at the cost of some overlapping. However it should be observed at the outset that originally the entire doctrine began as a flexible administrative standard to accomplish the purposes behind the establishment of the equity of redemption; that it was carried to extremes and to a large extent was crystallized into a hard and fast rule of property against which modern equity courts inveighed; and, due in chief measure to the opinion of Lord Haldane in Kreglinger v. New Patagonia Meat Co.[9] has today, at least as to the second and third phases of the doctrine, been restored to reasonableness and elasticity in accordance with modern ideas. Further, it should be observed that only the first of the rules has ever played any important role in the United States although there always exists the danger that the other two, especially the third one, might be imported.

"ONCE A MORTGAGE * * *"

97. The doctrine of "once a mortgage, always a mortgage" voids any provision in the original mortgage agreement limiting or nullifying the right of redemption. Neither it, nor any analogous rule, nor the Rule Against Perpetuities prohibits long term mortgages.

The first of these doctrines, expressed by the familiar maxim "Once a mortgage, always a mortgage" is clear law not only in England but in the United States. As was said, "it is only another way of saying that a mortgage cannot be made irredeemable."[10] It was merely a corollary of the original creation of the equity of redemption and was born of the necessity of preventing evasion of it by ingenious and determined mortgagees through a wide variety of clauses

---

7. The first use of the term clog is in Bacon v. Bacon, 1639, Tot. 133–4: "Where the mortgagee will suddenly bestow unnecessary costs upon the mortgaged lands, of purposes to clogg the lands, to prevent the mortgagor's redemption."

See Williams, Clogging the Equity of Redemption, 1933, 40 W.Va.L.Q. 31, 33 for various theories as to the origin and historical development of the doctrine against clogging. For other discussions of the problem or some aspects of it, see Wyman, The Clog on the Equity of Redemption, 1908, 21 Harv. L.Rev. 459; Coutts, Once a Mortgage Always a Mortgage—Stipulations in the Mortgage, 1900, 50 Cent.L.J. 464; Coughlin, Clogging Redemption Rights in Illinois, 1937, 3 John Marshall L.Q. 11; Falconbridge, Legal Mortgages in Equity, 1918, 54 Can.L.J.N.S., 1; Turner, The Equity of Redemption, 175–183; E.N.D., The Basis of Relief from Penalties and Forfeitures, 1922, 20 Mich.L.Rev. 646. For a concise résumé of English decisions, see note, 1913, 136 L.T. 137. For an incorporation of the doctrine in a statutory enactment, see West's Ann. Cal.Civ.Code § 2889. For a recent statement of the doctrine see Fratcher, Restraints upon Alienation of Equitable Interests in Michigan Property, 1953, 51 Mich.L.Rev. 509, 542.

There are cases both affirming and denying that the mortgagor's statutory right of redemption from a foreclosure sale may be waived. Nippel v. Hammond, 1878, 4 Colo. 211; King v. King, 1905, 215 Ill. 100, 74 N.E. 89 hold that it may; Parmer v. Parmer, 1883, 74 Ala. 285; Lambright v. Bales, 1919, 139 Ark. 48, 213 S.W. 2, contra. See Skilton, Government and the Mortgage Debtor, 23.

8. See Lord Davey in Noakes v. Rice, [1902] A.C. 24 and Lord Haldane in Kreglinger v. New Patagonia Meat Co., [1914] A.C. 25 for excellent statements of this threefold division.

9. [1914] A.C. 25.

10. Lord Davey in Noakes v. Rice, [1902] A.C. 24, 32. See Fogelman, The Deed Absolute as a Mortgage in New York, 1963, 32 Fordham L.Rev. 299, 301.

This doctrine of mortgage law is in striking contrast to the attitude of courts of equity toward provisions making time of the essence in contracts for the sale of land. See III Am.L.Prop. §§ 11.45, 11.46, 11.75, 11.76; Osborne, Cases on Secured Transactions, 1967, Note p. 246 and Note p. 251; Note, Minnesota Land Contract Law in Installment Land Contracts, 1953, 26 Rocky Mt.L.Rev. 107, discussing Self v. Watt, 1953, 128 Colo. 61, 259 P.2d 1074; Rudolph, The Installment Land Contract as a Junior Security, 1956, 54 Mich.L.Rev. 953; Van Zile, Land Contracts: Summary Proceedings for Forfeiture, 1956, 34 U. of Detroit L.Rev. 209; Note, Installment Land Contracts: Termination of Vendee's Rights after Default, 1956, 3 U.C.L.A.L.Rev. 264. See also § 20, supra.

which, while recognizing the existence of the equity, in practical effect nullified or restricted its operation. One of the earliest and crudest of these attempts was by the insertion of clauses limiting redemption to a certain time after the law day.[11] Equity struck them down out of hand. So, too, when the same attempt took the form of a warranty by the mortgagor not to redeem after the law day [12] or a provision making time of the essence.[13] Similarly provisions that only the mortgagor himself, as distinct from his executor or heir,[14] or that only the mortgagor and the heirs male of the body [15] might redeem were held invalid, a restriction upon the persons who may exercise the right to redeem being as offensive as a time limit within which it may be exercised. By a parity of reasoning, an agreement allowing the mortgagee to keep any part of the mortgaged property, redemption being limited to the balance, fails.[16] Nor is the mortgagee allowed at the time of the loan to enter into an option or contract for the purchase of the mortgaged property. This rule was established early and still continues to be the law.[17] So strong was the policy behind these

various decisions and so jealous was equity of any devices that might cut off the right to redeem that at one time the menace to it in an express power of sale given to the mortgagee in the mortgage deed was thought doubtful as an attempt to defeat the rule.[18] And when an escrow arrangement was attempted in which the mortgagor executed a deed at the time the loan and mortgage was given and deposited it in escrow to be delivered to the mortgagee in payment of the debt in case of default the court held that the mortgagor still retained his right to redeem, that the arrangement violated the ancient doctrine and must fall.[19] Not quite so clear a case was a stipulation providing for a jump in the interest rate on nonpayment on a fixed law day.[20] The difficulty was that

Wilson v. Fisher, 1908, 148 N.C. 535, 62 S.E. 622; Hyndman v. Hyndman, 1845, 19 Vt. 9, 46 Am.Dec. 171. Cf. Smith v. Smith, 1926, 82 N.H. 399, 135 A. 25. See note, 1920, 20 Col.L.Rev. 920.

In Hamud v. Hawthorne, Cal.App.1958, 332 P.2d 727, reversed 1959, 52 Cal.2d 78, 338 P.2d 387, an agreement made at the time a third deed of trust was executed to deliver a quitclaim deed in escrow, in satisfaction of the mortgage debt and with a provision that the mortgagor-trustor could not redeem when it was carried out was held void but the mortgagor-trustor was held barred by laches.

See Boyer, Real Property Law, 1967, 22 U. of Miami L.Rev. 278, 308 noting MacArthur v. North Palm Beach Utilities, Inc., Fla. 4th Dist., 1966, 187 So. 2d 681, quashed, Sup.1967, 202 So.2d 181.

18.   Turner, The Equity of Redemption, 179. See Galt, Power of Sale Without Notice, 1893, 13 Can. L.T. 36; Betts, Powers of Sale Without Notice, 1895, 15 Can.L.T. 1–20, 40–49; Durfee, Cases on Mortgages, 263n. Look at Mooney v. Byrne, 1900, 163 N.Y. 86, 57 N.E. 163 (power to sell at private sale, invalid).

See also Tefft, The Myth of Strict Foreclosure, 1937, 4 U.Chi.L.Rev. 575, 581; 1 Powell, Mortgages, 13ff (4th ed. 1799). The validity of such powers of sale was established in the early nineteenth century and had become a customary part of an English mortgage by the middle of that century. See 1 Coote, Morts., 128 (1st ed. 1821); Clark v. Royal Panopticon, 1857, 4 Drew. 26, 30. See also note 16, supra.

19.   Plummer v. Ilse, 1905, 41 Wash. 5, 82 P. 1009, 2 L.R.A.,N.S., 627. Also see Pollak v. Millsap, 1928, 219 Ala. 273, 122 So. 16, 65 A.L.R. 110.

20.   Holles v. Wyse, 1693, 2 Vern. 289; Strode v. Parker, 1694, 2 Vern. 316. See Salt v. Marquess of Northampton, [1892] A.C. 1, 19; Firth, Freedom of Contract in Mortgages, 1895, 11 L.Q.Rev. 144, 153. See also Goodyear Shoe Mach. Co. v. Selz, Schwab & Co., 1895, 157 Ill. 186, 41 N.E. 625.

---

11.   Bradbury v. Davenport, 1896, 114 Cal. 593, 46 P. 1062, 55 Am.St.Rep. 92 (four months); Heirs of Stover v. Heirs of Bounds, 1853, 1 Ohio St. 107 (before a fixed date); Frazer v. Couthy Land Co., 1929, 17 Del.Ch. 68, 149 A. 428 (three years); Price v. Perrie, 1702, Freem.Ch. 258 and Floyer v. Lavington, 1714, 1 P.Wms. 268 (life of the mortgagor); Jason v. Eyres, 1681, Freem.Ch. 69 (three years "if the mortgagor so long lives"); Salt v. Marquess of Northampton [1892] A.C. 1 (mortgagor dying in lifetime of his father). But compare Newcomb v. Bonham, 1681, 1 Vern. 7. See Toomes v. Conset, 1745, 3 Atkyns 261.

12.   East India Co. v. Atkyns, 1740, 1 Comyns 347; Cowley v. Shields, 1913, 180 Ala. 48, 60 So. 267.

13.   Jackson v. Lynch, 1889, 129 Ill. 72, 21 N.E. 580, rehearing denied 129 Ill. 72, 22 N.E. 246. See note 10, supra.

14.   Newcomb v. Bascomb, 1681, 1 Vern. 7.

15.   Howard v. Harris, 1681, 1 Vern. 33.

16.   Salt v. Marquess of Northampton, [1892] A.C. 1.

17.   Willett v. Winnell, 1687, 1 Vern. 488; Orby v. Trigg, 1722, 9 Mod. 2; In re Edwards' Estate, 1861, 11 Ir.Ch. 367; Linnell v. Lyford, 1881, 72 Me. 280;

if the higher rate was stipulated for at the outset with a reduction for punctual payment the agreement is valid. Yet in both cases precisely the same amounts of money would be payable at exactly the same times.[21] Of course a case could be imagined where the jump in interest rate would be so enormous, or the provision for the payment of a bonus on default so huge, that as a practical matter the mortgagor would be unable to pay it. This clearly would be recognized as merely a device to make the mortgage irredeemable and therefore bad. But quite apart from anything of this sort, and with a jump in interest rate which is relatively mild, although any jump does, of course, make it more difficult to redeem, nevertheless, the decisions seem correct upon a principle which underlies relief from all penalties and forfeitures.[22] That principle is that relief will be granted where there has been a misreliance upon the "mirage of hope." Ordinarily the courts have talked in terms of granting relief because of solicitude for the "impecunious landowner" [23] or "necessitous men [who] are not, truly speaking, free men." [24] But another most important factor is in the mortgagee playing upon the optimism to which all mankind is prone, the "over-confidence in ones own capacities and faith in a special providence [which] leads us to over-sanguine commitments." [25] Equity takes this human failing into account. So where the bargain is expressed in terms of a future jump in the amount due, which the mortgagor never expects to become liable for, rather than a firm commitment to the higher rate at the very outset which he knows he has bound himself to pay but may reduce by future effort, the bargain is bad. The same applies to a bonus to be paid to the mortgagee on redemption under certain conditions.[26] And a stipulation that unpaid interest should be capitalized and interest paid on it has been held void.[27]

Provisions that the mortgagor shall pay the mortgagee's expenses in collecting the secured debt and that the mortgage shall secure this additional item have been upheld by some courts and disallowed by others.[28] The former seem preferable as the additional amount is merely fair compensation for extra trouble and expense by the mortgagee. Of course if an excessive sum is provided for, the effect of which is to interfere with the mortgagor's right to redeem, it will be disallowed and cut to a reasonable amount.[29]

If instead of attempting in some way to cut off, limit, or make more difficult the exercise of the right to redeem when it arises, the parties agree that it shall not arise until a long time in the future, although when it does arise it shall be completely free of restriction, quite a different problem is presented. It has been observed that "there should be no objection to such a stipulation; since until the law day arrives, there is no right in equity to redeem, and therefore

---

21. See the dubious *quaere* in Strode v. Parker, supra note 20.

22. See note, 1922, 20 Mich.L.Rev. 646.
Finger v. McCaughey, 1896, 114 Cal. 64, 45 P. 1004, held valid a jump in the interest rate on a mortgage if not paid, from ten percent to twelve percent.

23. "Impecunious landowner in the toils of a crafty money lender." Samuel v. Jarrah Timber & W. P. Corp., Ltd., [1904] A.C. 52, 55.

24. Vernon v. Bethel, 1761, 2 Eden 113.

25. 1922, 20 Mich.L.Rev. 646, 647.

26. Chapple v. Mahon, 1870, Ir.R. 5 Eq. 225.

27. Chambers v. Goldwin, 1804, 9 Ves.Jun. 254, 271.

28. Valid: Clawson v. Munson, 1870, 55 Ill. 394; Baker v. Jacobson, 1899, 183 Ill. 171, 55 N.E. 724; Weatherby v. Smith, 1870, 30 Iowa 131, 6 Am.Rep. 663; Tholen v. Duffy, 1871, 7 Kan. 405 (but see Foote v. Sprague, 1874, 13 Kan. 155); Gaither v. Tolson, 1897, 84 Md. 637, 36 A. 449; Pierce v. Kneeland, 1863, 16 Wis. 672, 84 Am.Dec. 726. See Voechting v. Grau, 1882, 55 Wis. 312, 13 N.W. 230. Invalid: Thomasson v. Townsend, Ky.1873, 10 Bush 114; Kittermaster v. Brossard, 1895, 105 Mich. 219, 63 N.W. 75, 55 Am.St.Rep. 437; Northwestern M. L. Ins. Co. v. Butler, 1899, 57 Neb. 198, 77 N.W. 667; Turner v. Boger, 1900, 126 N.C. 300, 35 S.E. 592, 49 L.R.A. 590; Miller v. Kyle, 1911, 85 Ohio St. 186, 97 N.E. 372; Daly v. Maitland, 1879, 88 Pa. 384, 32 Am. Rep. 457, 11 Lanc.Bar 9.

29. Daly v. Maitland, 1879, 88 Pa. 384, 32 Am.Dec. 457, 11 Lanc.Bar 9.

nothing for chancery to protect." [30]   Certainly in the United States there has been no objections to long term mortgages by either individuals or corporations although an attempt to create a perpetual mortgage would not succeed.[31] In England, however, it has been thought until recently that there was a rule, analogous to or a corollary of the "once a mortgage, always a mortgage" doctrine, prohibiting the postponement of the mortgagor's contractual right to redeem for more than a reasonable period, though the length of the supposed period was in doubt.[32] The case of Knightsbridge Estates Trust, Ltd. v. Byrne,[33] seems to indicate that there is no such rule although the point was made in the Court of Appeal and not passed upon by the House of Lords [34] when it was carried up. The Court of Appeal said that "equity does not reform mortgage transactions because they are unreasonable. It is concerned to see two things—one, that the essential requirements of a mortgage transaction are observed, and the other that oppressive or unconscionable terms are not enforced. * * * and in deciding whether or not a particular transaction falls within this category the length of time for which the contractual

right to redeem is postponed may well be an important consideration." However, when the agreement is a commercial one, "entered into by business people negotiating at arms length" it would be difficult to find the "features of an oppressive bargain where the borrower is at the mercy of an unscrupulous lender." [35] Since the decision in the House of Lords was placed on the narrow ground that the mortgage was an authorized "debenture" within the meaning of the Companies Act, 1929, the conclusive establishment that long term mortgages are *per se* unobjectionable in England must be left for the future.

The Knightsbridge case did give a definitive answer to the question of whether long term mortgages might be invalid under the Rule against Perpetuities, the trial court,[36] the Court of Appeals,[37] and the House of Lords [38] being in agreement that they constituted a well settled exception to it.[39] The point was raised by counsel because the reason frequently advanced for exempting them was "that a condition in a mortgage precluding redemption for over 21 years would be void in equity." [40] Since the Court of Appeals repudiated any such rule in equity and the House of Lords ignored it, the reason given by the Court of Appeals, that "such transactions do not produce the mischief which the rule was intended to prevent" must be accepted as the reason for exempting them. In addition it was pointed out in the Court of Appeals that long term mort-

30. Note, 1912, 12 Col.L.Rev. 627.

31. Taylor v. Philadelphia, etc., R. R. Co., C.C.Pa. 1881, 7 F. 386.

32. See Talbot v. Braddill, 1683, 1 Vern. 183; Cowdry v. Day, 1859, 1 Giff. 316; Teevan v. Smith, 1882, 20 Ch.Div. 724, 729 (dictum by Sir George Jessel); Biggs v. Hoddinott, [1898] 2 Ch. 307; Bradley v. Carritt, [1903] A.C. 253; Williams v. Morgan, [1906] 1 Ch. 804; Morgan v. Jeffreys, [1910] 1 Ch. 620; Davis v. Symons, [1934] 1 Ch. 442; In re Fortescues' Estate, [1916] 1 Ir. 268. See also notes, 1912, 12 Col. L.Rev. 627; 1934, 78 Sol.J. 330. Cf. Abbe v. Goodwin, 1829, 7 Conn. 377.

33. [1939] 1 Ch. 441. The decision of Luxmoore, J., of the trial court, in which judgment was given in favor of the mortgagor entitling him to redeem at any time, instead of waiting the specified forty year period the loan was agreed to run, was extensively discussed. See notes, 1939, 6 U. of Chi.L.Rev. 323; 1939, 52 Harv.L.Rev. 1020; 1939, 25 Va.L.Rev. 373; 1939, 3 The Modern L.Rev. 72; 1939, 7 Camb.L.J. 146.

34. 1940, 56 T.L.R. 652, discussed in 1940, 56 L.Quar. Rev. 304.

35. [1939] 1 Ch. 441, 455. See Williams, The Doctrine of Repugnancy, 1944, 60 L.Q.Rev. 190, 192.

36. [1938] Ch. 757–763.

37. [1939] Ch. 463, 464.

38. 56 T.L.R. 652, 656.

39. This view fulfilled the hope of Gray who desired the courts to declare such mortgages valid by way of an exception to the Rule, and "not, by attempting to reconcile them with the Rule, bring confusion into the Rule itself." Gray, Perpetuities, 3d ed., § 570. See Berg, Jr., Long-Term Options and the Rule Against Perpetuities, 1949, 37 Calif.L.Rev. 1, 29.

40. 56 T.L.R. 652, 656.

gages have been rcognized in the power to mortgage given to local authorities by various acts of Parliament; and by the House of Lords, that since the Law of Property Act, 1925, it would be very difficult to invoke the Rule.

COLLATERAL ADVANTAGE

98. **An old English doctrine holds that the mortgagee may have no collateral advantage. Its origins are not clear and various theories have been advanced to explain it. Today a collateral advantage, even if it outlasts redemption, will be relieved against only on general doctrines of oppression and unconscionable advantage.**

That aspect of the general clogging doctrine classified under the heading of "collateral advantage" can be traced directly to a loose statement in the case of Jennings v. Ward.[41] The mortgagee had bargained for the purchase of ground rents at twenty years with the mortgagor being permitted to redeem sooner and having done so. The court struck down the agreement for purchase and in doing so uttered the statement which plagued English courts from then down to recent times that "A man shall not have interest for his money and a collateral advantage besides for the loan of it, or clog the redemption with any by-agreement."

As originally interpreted the ban on collateral advantages had a two-fold operation: first, the collateral advantage perhaps was bad per se; second, it was certainly bad if it outlasted redemption. The latter sort, while ordinarily a part of a collateral advantage, nevertheless acquired a separate test, and a more mechanical one until recent times, which will be discussed under the next section dealing with "fetters" upon the redemption interest. Both parts had their roots in the same considerations which led to the creation of the equity of redemption itself and the clear corollary of it examined in the preceding section. In addition some explana-

tions have been advanced which have peculiar application to the collateral advantage. One that applies generally to the whole clogging problem traces it back through the influence of the Church on the learning and attitudes of the early chancellors to the Council of Lateran in 1179[42] and thence back into the Roman law.[43] The proof of such an origin rests largely on assumption and, more likely, the idea had an independent and indigenous origin.[44] The more usual and better documented belief is that the collateral advantage rule itself rested upon the usury legislation beginning with the Tudors, strengthened by various acts down to the reign of Anne, and finally, under the influence of freedom of contract ideas, repealed in 1854.[45] The equity courts, influenced probably by their general tenderness to the mortgagor for other reasons, took the usury statutes to be expressive of a general policy not limited to their express restrictions and struck down in mortgage cases as a "clog" any agreement that tended to be usurious.[46] With the repeal of the usury laws and the accentuation of the ancient distinction between payment for the use of money and compensation for ventured risk[47] and other

---

41. 1705, 2 Vern. 520.

42. This council established the principle that the debtor was entitled to have back his pledged property if the creditor had been paid his debt and expenses out of the profits. Matthew Paris, Historia Major, 1684, 114–115.

43. Spence, Equitable Jurisdiction, 599; Coughlin, Clogging Redemption Rights in Illinois, 1937, 3 J. Marshall L.Q. 10.

44. See Williams, Clogging the Equity of Redemption, 1933, 40 W.Va.L.Q. 30, 34; Turner, The Equity of Redemption, 176.

45. 17 & 18 Vict. c. 90. For a brief résumé of the earlier legislation see Williams, supra note 44. See also Glenn, Oppressive Bargains, 1933, 19 Va.L.Rev. 594, 602 et seq.; Wyman, The Clog on the Equity of Redemption, 1907, 21 Harv.L.Rev. 459, 468–470.

46. See Firth, Freedom of Contract in Mortgages, 1895, 11 L.Q.Rev. 144 (dealing chiefly with the influence of usury laws upon the doctrine of collateral advantages).

47. See Noakes and Co., Ltd. v. Rice, [1902], A.C. 24, opinion of Lord Davey. See also Glenn, Oppressive Bargains, 1933, 19 Va.L.Rev. 594, 597, "these laws [usury] were judicially interpreted as not applying

factors, while the older attitudes tended to persist it was natural for them gradually to die out.[48] A third view rejects the usury basis and believes that the collateral advantage rule, just like other phases of the clogging doctrine, was just an incident of the unique jurisdiction which equity had established over mortgages when it created the equity of redemption and constituted merely another manifestation of the Chancellor's vigilance in seeing that the "mortgagor was not unduly pressed, and did not directly or indirectly contract out of his equity of redemption." [49] And in the first examination of the whole problem by an American scholar, the conclusion was reached that all of the various clogging rules were examples of "the great truth that the ethical standard of our law is often higher than the average morality of the business community." [50]

Still another theory is that the entire "clogging" rule is "based simply on the original policy of equity toward hard bargains," i. e., it was not a separate and independent doctrine but merely one application of a general jurisdiction that equity had exercised from the earliest times.[51] The truth probably is that each one of these played some part, with the exact role of any one not only being difficult if not impossible to assess but varying at different stages. Certainly it is true that some of the rules definitely crystallized at one stage into inflexible rules of property; but it seems equally true that perhaps in its origin even the equity of redemption was looked upon as merely one important and frequent instance of relieving in the particular case against oppressive bar-

gains; and at the present time it is quite clear that in the absence of usury statutes being violated,[52] a collateral advantage, even though it outlasts redemption, will be relieved against only on general doctrines of oppression and unconscionable advantage.[53]

FETTERING

99. The doctrine of fettering was formerly a rigid English rule that invalidated any bargain binding the mortgaged property beyond the redemption period. There were some exceptions to the rule. It is not applied today where the provision under attack is part of, or connected with, an independent legitimate business agreement. The doctrine has not been applied in the United States.

The third doctrine has been summed up as meaning "that the mortgagee shall not make any stipulation which will prevent a mortgagor, who has paid principal, interest, and costs, from getting back his mortgaged property in the condition in which he parted with it." [54]

Such a stipulation was a collateral advantage and therefore subject to the same objections. But it was regarded as standing upon separate footing because it affected the mortgaged property itself. Consequently any bargain which, as part of the original mortgage, bound the mortgaged property beyond redemption was regarded as a fetter upon the right to redeem and hence bad. Where the agreement would not last beyond redemption it was not difficult to hold that it did not offend as a fetter, the only possible

to a lender who shared in the hazards of the borrower".

48. See Wyman, supra note 45. Kreglinger v. New Patagonia Meat & Cold Storage Co., [1914], A.C. 25, opinion of Haldane, L.C.

49. Turner, The Equity of Redemption, 118, 176.

50. Wyman, The Clog on the Equity of Redemption, 1908, 21 Harv.L.Rev. 459, 475. Cf. Williams, supra note 44, p. 36.

51. Williams, supra note 44, p. 36 et seq.

52. See Vilas v. McBride, 1891, 62 Hun 324, 17 N.Y. S. 171, affirmed 1892, 136 N.Y. 634, 32 N.E. 1014.

53. Kreglinger v. New Patagonia Meat & Cold Storage Co., [1914] A.C. 25, "a collateral advantage may now be stipulated for by the mortgagee provided that he has not acted unfairly or oppressively". See Biggs v. Hoddinott, 1898, 2 Ch.D. 307. See also Williams, Clogging the Equity of Redemption, 1933, 40 W.Va.L.Q. 31, 49, for instances in which English, Irish, and Dominion courts have upheld collateral advantages.

For an estimate of the American cases, see Wyman, supra note 50, p. 469; Williams, supra note 44.

54. Opinion of Lord Davey, Noakes and Co., Ltd. v. Rice, [1902] A.C. 24, 33.

objection to it being that it was invalid as a collateral advantage.[55] Where it extended beyond the law day, however, this rule tended to become mechanical and to solidify into a rigid rule of property invalidating perfectly fair bargains between men of business dealing at arm's length on the ground that they were "repugnant" to the equitable right to redeem.[56] In Bradley v. Carritt,[57] this was carried to the extreme of holding void a proviso in a mortgage that the mortgagor of most of the shares in a tea company would use his best endeavors to induce the company "always thereafter" to employ the mortgagee as exclusive broker of all of the company's teas, and to pay him damages equal to the commission he would have earned in case teas were sold otherwise. Here the agreement did not bind the business directly but only the mortgagor personally. It is similar to an agreement by a mortgagor that if he transfers his business he will pay a sum of money to the mortgagee. That would not bind the business itself; the mortgagor could still go ahead and sell the business. But it does act as a strong deterrent and binds the business indirectly. Nevertheless the agreement seems only an ordinary, fair commercial bargain and the view of the court of King's Bench seems preferable that, there being no evidence of undue influence or pressure and the stipulations being reasonable, they should be upheld because they are "emi-

nently of a kind as to which business men in such a position may well be left to decide for themselves."[58]

Even in the heyday of rigorous treatment of the doctrine as a machine-like rule of real property mortgage law there were cases which were treated as exceptions. For one, if it was in reality a family settlement arrangement equity would not interfere.[59] A far more important exception was made when it was decided that mortgagees of West India plantations could provide that they be consignees of all produce of the plantations.[60] This was especially important both as a legal recognition of a long existing business practice and also as the basis for a generalization that if the loan is only a subordinate part of another essentially different and clearly defined business transaction, it could be upheld.[61] But most important of all was the view that the mortgage agreement and another bargain, even though entered into at the same time and as part of the same transaction, could nevertheless be regarded as separate and independent in substance. At first the rather artificial fact that the two agreements were kept physically separate and a short period of time was allowed to intervene between their executions was seized upon to justify segregating the two in the face of the patently clear intention of the parties that both actually constituted one entire agreement.[62] So factitious a distinction was undesirable and in the Kreglinger case,[63] Lord Haldane obliterated it. He established

---

55. Biggs v. Hoddinott, [1898] 2 Ch.D. 307, covenant for the mortgagor to buy from the mortgagee during the period of the mortgage all malt liquor sold on the mortgaged premises. See preceding section.

56. See opinion of Lord Davey in Noakes v. Rice, [1902] A.C. 24; opinion of Lord Parker in the Kreglinger case, supra, note 48. See also Williams, The Doctrine of Repugnancy—III: "Clogging the Equity", 1944, 60 L.Q.Rev. 190.

57. [1903] A.C. 253. The court overruled Santly v. Wilde, [1899] 2 Ch. 474, in which case A mortgaged a leasehold to secure a debt to B. A agreed that B should receive as further consideration for the loan profits that might be derived from a theater operated upon the mortgaged premises. The profits were payable during a period beyond the maturity of the debt, and the mortgage secured the performance of A's collateral obligation. Held, mortgage valid security for both of A's obligations.

58. Carritt v. Bradley, [1901] 2 K.B. 550, 560.

59. See Howard v. Harris, 1683, 1 Vern. 190; Kreglinger v. New Patagonia etc. Co., [1914] A.C. 25, 36; Stapilton v. Stapilton, 1739, 1 Atk. 2; Falconbridge, Legal Mortgages in Equity, 1918, 54 Can.L. J.,N.S., 1, 5; Williams, supra note 44, p. 38.

60. Bunbury v. Winter, 1820, 1 Jac. & W. 255. See opinion of Lindley in Biggs v. Hoddinott, [1898] 2 Ch. 307.

61. See Williams, supra note 44, pp. 39, 40.

62. Reeve v. Lisle, [1902] 1 Ch. 53; [1902] A.C. 461. Cf. Maxwell v. Tipping, 1903, 1 Ir. 498.

63. [1914] A.C. 25.

the principle that, in spite of the fact that the mortgagors on redemption "will not get back their business as free from obligation as it was before the date of the security", if "outside the security and consistently with its terms there was a contemporaneous but collateral contract, contained in the same document as constituted the security, but in substance independent of it" such contract would be good, provided that "if there had been no mortgage such a contract as the one in question would have been an ordinary incident in such a business." [64]   In other words the test today seems to be whether the objected to provision is a part of, or connected with, an independent legitimate business agreement.   This is true even though that agreement is conditioned upon the giving of a mortgage at the same time it is entered into if the provision itself is reasonable and fair. Such a general standard has reintroduced flexibility into the law on the point, gives considerable latitude to courts in applying it in the prevention of unconscionable bargains; and, although still preserving it,[65] nevertheless provides an effective curb on a doctrine which Lord Mersey likened to "an unruly dog, which, if not securely chained to its own kennel, is prone to wander into places where it ought not to be." [66]

The rule against fetters has been involved in only a few cases in the United States and in those the objected to provisions were upheld.[67]   Its chief importance lies in the possibility that some of the decisions applying the rule with blind rigidity might "even at this late date be received over into American law, and serve to fasten down an archaic theory in the decadence of equity." [68]   For this reason, it has been urged that the whole doctrine as a separate one be given up and remit all relief to the ordinary supervision of equity over oppression.[69]

E. SUBSEQUENT TRANSACTIONS

SALE OF EQUITY OF REDEMPTION

100. The equity of redemption may be sold to the mortgagee subsequent to the execution of the mortgage. But the transaction will be scrutinized to see that it is free of fraud or oppression and on adequate new consideration.

An executory contract, entered into subsequent to the mortgage, that if the mortgagor does not pay his debt within a certain time he shall forfeit all right to the property, is invalid.

The rules that the mortgagor's equity of redemption cannot be affected by any agreement contemporaneous with the mortgage are inapplicable, for the most part, to transactions subsequent to its creation. But the jealous eye with which equity guards the mortgagor has also been cast upon such dealings. The equity of redemption should be treated like any other asset. Its outright sale and conveyance to the mortgagee should be permitted with no restrictions that would not be imposed if the bargain was with any third party dealing with the mortgagor at arm's length. However, the courts generally have not so treated it. An extreme position was stated in a much quoted dictum in which it was said that "Principles almost as stern are applied as those which govern where a sale by a cestui que trust to his trustee is drawn in question. To give validity to such a sale by a mortgagor it must be shown that the conduct of the mortgagee was, in all

---

64. See Gleason's Administratrix v. Burke, 1869, 20 N.J.Eq. 300; Bonham v. Newcomb, 1683, 1 Vern. 232.   In De Beers Consol. Mines v. Brit. So. Africa Co. [1912] App.Cas. 52 (floating charge to secure debentures, with collateral advantage extending beyond maturity of debt), the decision was rested on the ground that the stipulation in question was not part of the mortgage transaction.

65. That the doctrine would still be applied is evidenced by Mehrban Khan v. Makhna, 1930, L.R 57 Ind.App. 168, a case decided by the Privy Council. See also Williams, Clogging the Equity of Redemption, 1933, 40 W.Va.L.Q. 30, at p. 52, n. 135.

66. Kreglinger case, supra note 59, at 46.

67. Cleveland & Sandusky Brewing Co. v. Demko, 1907, 29 Ohio Cir.Ct.Rep. 102; Cleveland & Sandus-

ky Brewing Co. v. Kraval, 1908, 36 Ohio Cir.Ct.Rep. 557—contra. See note, 1908, 2 Ill.L.Rev. 402.

68. Williams, supra note 65, at p. 52.

69. Williams, supra note 65.

things fair and frank, and that he paid for the property what it was worth. He must hold out no delusive hopes; he must exert no undue influence; he must take no advantage of the fears or poverty of the other party. Any indirection or obliquity of conduct is fatal to his title. Every doubt will be resolved against him." [70] Under the rigorous common law mortgage, at least after default when title was absolute in the mortgagee, and in which possession or the right to take possession was held by mortgagee, the view that the relationship was so close to a trust as to warrant applying fiduciary tests to it may have made sense.

In modern lien states, or for that matter in title states today, unless the mortgagee has some power or control over the estate before foreclosure there seems no justification for such a criterion, and there is authority to that effect.[71] Today the majority of courts adopt a middle course and, although they permit the mortgagee to purchase the equity of redemption from the mortgagor, they will scrutinize the transaction to make sure that it is free from fraud or oppression on the part of the mortgagee and is on an adequate new consideration, the burden of establishing these requirements being on the mortgagee.[72]

As a matter of fact, although the courts state the rule in traditional terms of fraud and oppression, what the courts really examine the transaction for is to be sure that it is actually subsequent to the mortgage and not merely a disguised part of the original arrangement.[73] There is still, however, a minority view that the relationship in which the mortgagee stands to the mortgagor is such that from its existence "where a mortgagee buys the equity of redemption of his mortgagor, the law presumes fraud and the burden is upon the mortgagee to show the *bona fides* of the transaction." [74] And the general suspicion with which the courts view all dealings between mortgagor and mortgagee even after the relation is entered into keeps cropping up in various ways.[75] Where a "trust deed mortgage" is employed in such a minority state with title vested in a third party, the rule is held to have no application

70. Villa v. Rodriguez, 1870, 79 U.S. (12 Wall.) 323, 339, 20 L.Ed. 406.

71. De Martin v. Phelan, 1897, 115 Cal. 538, 47 P. 356, 56 Am.St.Rep. 115.

72. Gould v. McKillip, 1940, 55 Wyo. 251, 99 P.2d 67, 129 A.L.R. 1427 and cases there cited; Earle's Adm'r v. Blanchard, 1911, 85 Vt. 288, 81 A. 913. Cf. Ferris v. Wilcox, 1883, 51 Mich. 105, 16 N.W. 252, 47 Am.Rep. 551 (mortgagor to be given the benefit of any doubt); Odell v. Montross, 1877, 68 N.Y. 499. But see Bailey v. St. Louis Union Trust Co., 1905, 188 Mo. 483, 87 S.W. 1003. Cf. Trull v. Skinner, 1835, 34 Mass. (17 Pick.) 213; Stone v. Jenks, 1886, 142 Mass. 19, 8 N.E. 403 (gift by mortgagor to mortgagee). If the price paid is inadequate, the sale will be set aside. Peugh v. Davis, 1877, 96 U. S. 332, 24 L.Ed. 755. If the mortgagee buys on an execution sale under a judgment recovered by a third person, or upon a judgment recovered by the mortgagee on a debt other than that which is secured by the mortgage, the same rule of scrutiny is not applied. This is "for the very good reason that, at this public sale conducted by an officer of the court, the mortgagee has no opportunity to ov-

erreach the mortgagor and take undue advantage of his economic weakness. *Per contra*, to permit to purchase on the same terms as any stranger adds one (and a most important one) to the potential market for the land, to the advantage of the mortgagor as well as the mortgagee." Wheeler and Durfee, Evasion of Mortgage Moratoria by Prosecution of Personal Remedies, 1935, 33 Mich.L.Rev. 1196, 1198. See § 279, infra, as to levy and purchase under a judgment on the mortgage debt.

Farmers Union Trading Co. v. Wiggins, 1954, 127 Mont. 481, 267 P.2d 117, noted in Updike, Mortgages, in 1954 Annual Survey of American Law, 1955, 30 N.Y.U.L.Rev. 805, 806, is a recent case upholding the deed where the consideration is fair and the debt is discharged.

73. See Glenn, Mortgages, § 45.

74. Massengill v. Oliver, 1942, 221 N.C. 132, 134, 19 S.E.2d 253, 254. See notes, 1928, 6 N.Car.L.Rev. 340; 1935, 13 N.Car.L.Rev. 334.

75. In McAllister v. Drapeau, 1939, 14 Cal.2d 102, 92 P.2d 911, 125 A.L.R. 800, commented on in, 1940, 25 Cornell L.Q. 304; 1939, 13 So.Cal.L.Rev. 162, the first mortgagee, as a secret condition to agreeing with the mortgagor to accept H.O.L.C. bonds in exchange for a release of its mortgage, insisted upon the mortgagor giving a note and second mortgage on the property equal to the difference between the face value of the first mortgage and the bonds it was to receive from the H.O.L.C. In an action by the mortgagor to cancel this note and second mortgage, held, for the mortgagor. See Bridewell, Validity of Second Mortgages Taken by Former Mortgagees in H.O.L.C. Refinancing Operations, 1940, 5 John Marshall L.Q. 373; Payne,

where the conveyance is to the lender of the money, not to the trustee.[76]

Subsequent executory contract for sale of redemption. The rule, just examined, that the mortgagor may release to the mortgagee his equity of redemption has been held to mean "merely that the mortgagor may at any time after the execution of the mortgage sell to the mortgagee outright all his interest in the property, by a conveyance operating at once, and in that sense release his right to redeem. But he cannot, even after the mortgage has been made, bind himself by an agreement that, if he does not pay his debt by a certain time in the future, he will forfeit all right to the property." [77] This distinction between subsequent executed and executory transactions has been criticized on the ground that a man should be able to contract to sell what he could dispose of at once. Nevertheless, it may be defended. The bases for the policy back of the rule are the necessity of the borrower to obtain the loan coupled with an optimistic overconfidence in his capacities to surmount future difficulties. The two combine to lead to over-sanguine commitments. Both are present at the time the mortgage is entered into originally. When the transaction is subsequent to the mortgage and is consummated at once, neither exerts any influence. However, if it is a subsequent agreement for *future* forfeiture, the "mirage of hope" is sufficiently strong to bring it under the general ban against forfeitures due to "misreliance upon airy hope." [78] If this reasoning is valid, executory contracts to waive statutory rights of redemption from foreclosure sale should be unenforceable. There are, however, authorities holding such agreements good.[79] It has been suggested that the test should be whether the parties actually intended a sale agreement or whether it was merely an arrangement for additional security for the loan on different terms, one of which involved cutting off by the agreement, the new equity of redemption which arose out of the new or modified mortgage agreement.[80] Since the real question is why such an agreement, whether it is to sell in futuro the redemption interest or to release it in satisfaction of the debt when it comes due and unpaid, should not be valid when it is not a part of the original mortgage, such a suggestion has little merit.

Enforceability of Agreements Between Mortgagors of the H.O.L.C. and Third Parties, 1939, 45 W.Va. L.Q. 332.

76. Simpson v. Fry, 1927, 194 N.C. 623, 140 S.E. 295; Murphy v. Taylor, 1938, 214 N.C. 393, 199 S.E. 382, commented on in, 1939, 17 N.C.L.Rev. 295.

77. Holden Land & Livestock Co. v. Inter-State Trading Co., 1912, 87 Kan. 221, 227, 123 P. 733, 736, L.R.A. 1915B, 492, appeal dismissed 233 U.S. 536, 34 S.Ct. 61, 58 L.Ed. 1083. Batty v. Snook, 1858, 5 Mich. 231; Tennery v. Nicholson, 1877, 87 Ill. 464; Cohn v. Bridgeport Plumbing Supply Co., 1921, 96 Conn. 696, 115 A. 328, 24 A.L.R. 808, accord.

See notes, 1913, 13 Col.L.Rev. 170; 1931, 29 Mich.L. Rev. 757; 1937, 36 Mich.L.Rev. 111; 1909, 22 Harv. L.Rev. 295; 1933, 19 Va.L.Rev. 302. See also 1897, 55 Am.St.Rep. 100; 1906, 2 L.R.A.,N.S., 628; 1930, 65 A.L.R. 120, for discussions of and collections of cases on the problem presented in the principal case and some analogous situations. Bradbury v. Davenport, 1898, 120 Cal. 152, 52 P. 301, is usually cited as the leading case contra to the Holden case. See also Ravnaas v. Andrich, 1932, 60 S.D. 281, 244 N.W. 361, noted 19 Va.L.Rev. 302; Brockington v. Lynch, 1922, 119 S.C. 273, 112 S.E. 94.

See additionally Durfee, Cases on Security, 1951, 167.

See Lisle v. Reeve, 1902, 1 Ch. 53, affirmed L.R.1902, A.C. 461; note, 1913, 13 Col.L.Rev. 171. See also Glenn, Mortgages, § 45, dismissing the rule as unsound in principle and contrary to more recent and better authority.

78. See note, 1922, 20 Mich.L.Rev. 646, 648, arguing that such misreliance is a basis for relief against forfeitures generally with the mortgage cases only one illustration.

79. Nippel v. Hammond, 1878, 4 Colo. 211; Cook v. McFarland, 1889, 78 Iowa 528, 43 N.W. 519; King v. King, 1905, 215 Ill. 100, 74 N.E. 89; U. S. Bldg. & Loan Ass'n v. Stevens, 1932, 93 Mont. 11, 17 P. 2d 62 (clause in mortgage waiving right to possession during redemption period valid) semble. On the other hand there is authority that a waiver of such a right contained in the mortgage itself is invalid. Parmer v. Parmer, 1883, 74 Ala. 285; Lambright v. Bales, 1919, 139 Ark. 48, 213 S.W. 2.

80. See note, 1913, 13 Col.L.Rev. 171.

DEED IN LIEU OF FORECLOSURE

101. The mortgagee may take a deed from the mortgagor in satisfaction of the debt. For the former it avoids the expense of a foreclosure action, for the latter it avoids a deficiency judgment. Hazards of the transaction include failure to cut off encumbrances subsequent to the mortgage and danger that the mortgagor's creditors or a non-assuming grantee may be able to set the deed aside.

We have seen that an outright conveyance of the redemption interest is valid if on new consideration and free of fraud or oppression.[81] Relying on that rule the mortgagee often takes a deed from the mortgagor in satisfaction of the mortgage debt. He does so, ordinarily, to avoid the further expense of a foreclosure action in which, even though he gets it, a deficiency judgment will probably not be worth the candle. The mortgagor on his part is quite frequently glad to give the deed in order to avoid, in states not having anti-deficiency judgment statutes, a possible personal judgment against him which might cause him trouble in the future even though at present it was uncollectable. Also, some mortgagors are actuated either by a genuine desire to aid the mortgagor, an aversion to the publicity and trouble of a court action against him, or both. Nevertheless, the transaction holds certain hazards [82] entirely apart from those inherent in the rules of close scrutiny for fraud or oppression as between the parties which have already been noted. For one thing any encumbrances subsequent to the mortgage will not be cut off as they would be by foreclosure proceedings. Consequently a thorough search for them is necessary before a deed may be taken safely. Also there exists the possibility that because of insolvency of the mortgagor or an actual intent on his part to defraud his creditors the conveyance may be subject to avoidance at the suit of creditors outside of bankruptcy or under the bankruptcy laws should the mortgagor go or be forced into bankruptcy. If the deed is not by the mortgagor but by a non-assuming grantee of the mortgagor, a release of the debt, since there was no personal liability, would be no consideration for the conveyance to the mortgagee and subject it to being set aside. Then, too, there is always the hazard that later the mortgagor will claim that the intent of the parties was to continue the security transaction and not finally to clear up the deal by an absolute conveyance. And, finally, there is the danger, especially in periods of inflation which may follow a depression, that the courts or legislatures may make title unmarketable by retroactive decisions or legislation uttered or enacted to lend aid to what, as a matter of hindsight, may seem to have been an oppressed debtor class.

---

81. See § 100, supra.

For recent cases, see Updike, Mortgages, in 1953 Survey of American Law, 1954, 29 N.Y.U.L.Rev. 829, 830; Updike, Mortgages, in 1954 Annual Survey of American Law, 1955, 30 N.Y.U.L.Rev. 805, 806.

82. For a thorough survey of these pitfalls, see note, 1937, 36 Mich.L.Rev. 111. The text merely summarizes the content of the note which is comprehensive.

Johnson v. Hapke, 1960, 183 Cal.App.2d 255, 6 Cal. Rptr. 603, held that a transfer of title to the beneficiary or mortgagee of real property encumbered by a trust deed mortgage or mortgage for the purpose of avoiding foreclosure proceedings and deficiency judgments is valid where the transactions are fair, honest, free from improper influence and based on adequate consideration. Accord: Cavanaugh v. High, 1960, 182 Cal.App.2d 714, 6 Cal.Rptr. 525. See Brodky, Current Changes in Illinois Real Property Law, 1960, 10 DePaul L.Rev. 566, 580 (statute permits mortgagor, after institution of foreclosure, to file consent to a decree vesting absolute title in the mortgagee and declaring the debt satisfied).

See Note, 1966, 31 Mo.L.Rev. 312, 314–315, for a discussion of the inherent dangers in using an absolute deed in lieu of, or in conjunction with, foreclosure, concluding that it serves no useful purpose, creates the possibility of litigation which will make title unmarketable and may be very expensive in time and money.

CHAPTER 5

THE OBLIGATION

A. NECESSITY AND NATURE OF OBLIGATION

B. DEFENSES TO OBLIGATION

C. FUTURE ADVANCES

A. NECESSITY AND NATURE OF OBLIGATION

COMMON LAW

102. **A mortgage is security for the performance of an act by some person. A personal obligation to perform the act was essential to the classical common law mortgage.**

The conception of a mortgage as security for the performance of an act [1] is so universally accepted that it requires no citation of authority. The question whether there must be an obligation by someone to perform the act is not so easily disposed of.

1. See, e.g., West's Ann.Cal.Civ.Code §§ 2872, 2909.

In its oldest form the gage was a transfer of property in provisional payment subject to an option in the gagor to redeem.[2] There was no debt or personal obligation of the gagor for the simple reason that in primitive stages of society the institution of credit is unknown and all such transactions are what we would call cash or present transfers.[3] The historical development of the security idea in practically all systems of law has been a progression from such a conception and practice to one in which the property is collateral security for an independent obligation.[4] It is conjectured that this same progression occurred in the English law and that the original gage form once existed;[5] but as early as the time of Glanville in the twelfth century the gage was so clearly regarded as security only for a debt that he explains the failure to protect the gagee's seizin against the gagor by saying that what the gagee is really entitled to is the debt and not the land; and if he comes into court he must ask for that to which he is entitled.[6] It has been pointed out [7] that this explanation is rather surprising in view of the feeble enforcement available for debt judgments. An answer may be that the possessory remedies in regard to land were dubious so far as the mortgagee was concerned. In the classical common law mortgage the requirement of an obligation was so strong that, when the usual covenant for payment was omitted in favor of the later form of the "Proviso, that if the Mortgagor pay the Money at the Day,

that the Mortgage shall be void", Hale, after some hesitation, held that nevertheless there was a duty on the mortgagor to pay which would support an action of debt.[8] And, even in the now obsolete Welsh mortgage, in which no direct action against the mortgagor personally would lie in the absence of an express covenant,[9] the existence of a debt was implied for the purpose of adjusting such equities as might exist between the real and personal estates of the mortgagor.[10]

MODERN LAW

103. There is still much authority holding there can be no mortgage without an obligation. However, the obligation may be that of someone other than the mortgagor, it may be unenforceable by direct action, and there is some reputable authority that it need not exist at all.

The question remains whether today in the common law a mortgage can exist without an obligation which it secures. There is impressive authority holding and saying that it cannot.[11] Some of the cases which

2. Wigmore, The Pledge Idea, 1897, 10 Harv.L.Rev. 321; Hazeltine, The Gage of Land in Medieval England, 1904, 17 Harv.L.Rev. 549; Huebner, History of Germanic Private Law, 375.

3. Wigmore, op. cit. supra note 2, 322.

4. Wigmore, op. cit. supra note 2, 321, 388 and 1897, 11 Harv.L.Rev. 18; Hazeltine, op. cit. supra note 2.

5. Plucknett, Concise History of Common Law, 2d Ed., 540; Hazeltine, op. cit. supra note 2.

6. Glanville, X, 11, XIII, 28–30; 2 Pollock & Maitland, 121; Turner, The Equity of Redemption, 17; Hazeltine, op. cit. supra note 2, 555, 556.

7. 2 Pollock & Maitland, 121.

8. Holmes v. Chandler, 2 Levinz 116. In the Roman Law *fiducia cum creditore*, which occupied in that system a place similar to the common law classical mortgage and resembled it in many respects, the creditor, in addition to his proprietary rights in the *res* had a personal claim against the debtor for the repayment of the loan. Dernberg, Pfandrecht, 1, 18, 19.

9. Cassidy v. Cassidy, 24 L.R.Ir. 577. See Falconbridge, Mortgages, 3d Ed., 4; Fisher & Lightwood, Mortgages, 7th Ed., 8 n.

10. King v. King, 1735, 3 P.Wms. 358. The court said, "that every mortgage implies a loan, and every loan implies a debt; and that though there were no covenant nor bond, yet the personal estate of the borrower of course remains liable to pay off the mortgage."

11. Coon v. Shry, 1930, 209 Cal. 612, 289 P. 815 (note and mortgage, without consideration and intended as gift, held void in spite of West's Ann.Cal.Civ.Code §§ 2872, 2884, 2890, 2909, and 2928 defining liens as security for an act); Kuhne v. Gau, 1917, 134 Minn. 34, 163 N.W. 982 (mortgage securing note without consideration); Tyler v. Wright, 1923, 122 Me. 558, 119 A. 583 (instruction in action by mortgagee against mortgagor that "a conveyance cannot be a mortgage unless given to secure the performance of an obligation" upheld); Cotten, Trustee v. Graham, 1887, 84 Ky. 672, 2 S.W. 647, 8 Ky.Law Rep. 658 (note without consideration); Burr v. Beckler, 1914, 264 Ill. 230, 106 N.E. 206 (mortgage on Illinois

hold the mortgage unenforceable because the obligation is invalid for lack of consideration may be explained on the ground that the intention was that the mortgage should secure a certain note or obligation and, consequently, would not be enforceable if that note or obligation failed for want of consideration.[12] The giving of a note or bond along

land to secure note of married woman, void under law of place of making); Beck v. Sheldon, 1932, 259 N.Y. 208, 181 N.E. 360 (bond and mortgage executed without consideration); Baird v. Baird, 1895, 145 N.Y. 659, 40 N.E. 222, 28 L.R.A. 375 (no debt intended and, probably, no mortgage either); Weich v. Graham, 1910, 124 N.Y.S. 945, affirmed, 1911, 148 App.Div. 900, 132 N.Y.S. 1150, and 1914, 210 N.Y. 637, 105 N.E. 1102, without further opinions (mortgage to secure bond executed without consideration, intended as gift, and with no intention that maker should pay anything during his lifetime. The action was during maker's lifetime and could have been decided on that ground, although lack of consideration was the one that was stressed.); McCourt v. Peppard, 1905, 126 Wis. 326, 105 N.W. 809 (note without consideration and also intended as a testamentary disposition); Bernheim v. Pessou, 1917, 143 La. 609, 79 So. 23 (release of mortgagor from debt with attempted reservation of rights in the mortgaged property; the court said, "[the mortgagor] was released from all obligation on the $11,000 note. If so, the mortgage securing this note ceased to exist, since a mortgage is a mere secondary obligation, and a secondary obligation cannot in the nature of things, exist in the absence of a primary."). See Perkins v. Trinity Realty Co., 1905, 69 N.J.Eq. 723, 727, 61 A. 167, affirmed 71 N.J.Eq. 304, 71 A. 1135.

See also Smith v. Haertel, 1952, 125 Colo. 348, 353, 244 P.2d 377, 379. Cf. Standard Fire Ins. Co. v. Fuller, 1952, 90 U.S.App.D.C. 300, 195 F.2d 782, noted, 1952, 101 U. of Pa.L.Rev. 286, no mortgage interest under the "Standard Mortgage Clause" where note secured is invalid. And see Validity of a Mortgage Intended as a Gift, 1953, 39 Iowa L.Rev. 195, discussing De Penning v. Bedell, 1950, 242 Iowa 102, 44 N.W.2d 385. Look also at Sterling, Validity of "Myself" Notes and Deeds of Trust, 1958, 30 Rocky Mt.L.Rev. 195; Karesh, Security Transactions in Survey of South Carolina Law, 1957, 10 S.C.L.Rev. 114, 124, noting Johnston v. Farmers and Merchants Bank, 1956, 229 S.C. 603, 93 S.E.2d 916.

In 1956, the Supreme Court of Indiana, in Egbert v. Egbert, 1956, 235 Ind. 405, 132 N.E.2d 910, criticized by Updike, Mortgages, in 1956 Annual Survey of American Law, 1957, 32 N.Y.U.L.Rev. 789, 791, held that, since a mortgage cannot exist without an obligation to be secured, a deed-in-lieu-of-foreclosure, which operated as an accord and satisfaction of the debt, wiped out the mortgage.

That there must be debt as basis of an equitable mortgage under Kansas law, see Note, 1965, 13 Kan.L. Rev. 585, 587, 588.

12. See Walsh, Mortgages, 89, 90 n. 50.

with the mortgage, especially if coupled with the usual recital in the mortgage that it secures the note, or a similar recital in the note that it is secured by the mortgage is, in itself, an indication that this was the intention of the parties.[13]

Cases in which the mortgage is in the form of a deed absolute constitute another group in which the existence of a debt has been held vital.[14] In these cases, since the central question is whether a mortgage is intended in spite of the transaction being cast in the form of an absolute transfer or a transfer with a resale agreement, optional or absolute, there are considerations not present when the transaction takes the regular mortgage form.[15] In them the courts might well insist more rigidly upon a debt as a guarantee of mortgage *intent*. In the latter case, as between the parties, the intent in regard to the nature of the transaction is clear and the questions to decide are whether there can be a mortgage without a personal obligation, or whether, even if there can be, the parties intended this particular mortgage to be binding regardless of the validity of the personal duty. Both of these questions have been obscured in the cases by the entirely distinct one of whether, as between the

13. Among such cases are Hannan v. Hannan, 1877, 123 Mass. 441, 25 Am.Rep. 121; Saunders v. Dunn, 1900, 175 Mass. 164, 55 N.E. 893; Anderson v. Lee, 1898, 73 Minn. 397, 76 N.W. 24; Brooks v. Owen, 1892, 112 Mo. 251, 19 S.W. 723, reversed on rehearing 112 Mo. 315, 20 N.W. 492; Cawley v. Kelly, 1884, 60 Wis. 315, 19 N.W. 65.

14. Conway v. Alexander, U.S.1812, 7 Cr. 218, 3 L. Ed. 321 (in holding the transaction a conditional sale rather than a mortgage Marshall, C.J., said: "It is * * * a necessary ingredient in a mortgage, that the mortgagee should have a remedy against the person of the debtor"); Henley v. Hotaling, 1871, 41 Cal. 22 (option to repurchase insufficient); Caraway v. Sly, 1906, 222 Ill. 203, 78 N.E. 588 (option to repurchase insufficient); Holmberg v. Hardee, 1925, 90 Fla. 787, 108 So. 211; Holmes v. Warren, 1904, 145 Cal. 457, 78 P. 954; 1 Jones, Mortgages (8th ed.) §§ 309, 311, 316; 3 Pomeroy, Equity Juris. (4th ed.) §§ 1195, 1192, 1196. See 1926, 20 Ill.L.Rev. 732.

See Fogelman, The Deed Absolute as a Mortgage in New York, 1963, 37 Fordham L.Rev. 299, 306.

15. See Chapter 4, supra.

parties, a mortgage requires consideration, and this, in turn, is confused with problems of precedence and validity against third parties, i. e., matters of priority, actual and constructively fraudulent conveyances, estoppel, and the doctrine of *bona fide* purchase. There is also a failure to segregate the necessity of consideration for the transfer or creation of the security interest in the property from the necessity of consideration for the creation of the obligation secured.[16]

Another group of authorities relied upon holds executed and recorded mortgages to secure optional future advances void until the advances are made as against a subsequent purchaser from the grantor on the ground that a debt is essential to a mortgage.[17] Support for requiring an obligation is also found in the definition of a pledge as an interest created "for the purpose of securing the payment of a debt or the performance of some other duty." [18] Text writers also can be cited in favor of the contention.[19] And in both the French and German civil law a debt is indispensable to the existence of a mortgage (hypothec) of real property.[20]

Turning to the opposite view, arguments and lines of authority can be mustered in defense of the thesis that no personal obligation is vital to the existence of a mortgage. "Thus, a mortgage to secure the debt of a third person, the mortgagor being subject to no obligation, is clearly valid." [21] It is also thoroughly settled that an express provision in the mortgage that there shall be no personal liability for the debt or claim on the mort-

---

16. See infra, § 107.

17. Ladue v. Detroit & Milwaukee R. Co., 1865, 13 Mich. 380, 87 Am.Dec. 759 (" * * * the mortgage instrument, without any present debt, liability or obligation secured by it, can have no present legal effect as a mortgage * * * and it can make no difference in the result whether there has once been a debt or liability which has been satisfied, or whether the debt or liability to be served has not yet been created * * * as in this case. * * * "). See Freutel v. Schmitz, 1921, 299 Ill. 320, 323, 132 N.E. 534, 535 ("A mortgage is security for a debt, and, without a debt, it has no effect as a lien. * * * If there is no mortgage debt in existence, there is nothing for the mortgage to operate on, and the lien begins only when money is advanced or the contemplated debt comes into existence in the course of dealing between the parties.").

However, cf. West's Ann.Cal.Civ.Code § 2884 (A lien may be created by contract to take immediate effect, as security for the performance of obligations not then in existence). Cases like Ackerman v. Hunsicker, 1881, 85 N.Y. 43, 39 Am.R. 621, upholding a recorded mortgage for optional advances to the amount of advances made as against subsequent claims in the property acquired before the advances, are not necessarily opposed. The court in that case admitted that no mortgage existed as a charge upon the land until the optional future obligation arose but, for other reasons postponed it to judgment liens arising after recordation but before the option was exercised. See infra, § 118. As will be pointed out later, the true situation in these mortgages for future advances is that the obligation secured exists in practically every case, prior to any advances and regardless of whether the advances are optional or obligatory. It is the present binding promise to repay the advances made in the future. If there were no consideration for this

promise there would, of course, be no obligation. Seldom, if ever, would this be the case even where the future advances are optional. See infra, §§ 108, 114, 115.

18. Restatement, Security, Chapter 1, § 1.

19. Holland, Jurisprudence, 223. See, Jones and Pomeroy, supra note 14. See also 3 Tiffany, Real Prop., 3d ed., § 606; Falconbridge, Mortgages, 3d ed., 6; Pingrey, Mortgages, § 61; Hazeltine, Preface to Turner, Equity of Redemption, XLIII; Barnes, Consideration in Mortgages, 1931, 19 Ky. L.J. 146, 151.

20. French Civil Code (Cachard) § 2114; 2 Planiol & Ripert, Droit Civil, § 2650; German Civil Code (Chung Hui Wang) §§ 1113, 1163. The German civil code also provides, § 1191, for a "land charge" in which a specified sum of money is to be paid out of the land. This is distinguished from the hypothec by not presupposing an obligation, but is governed otherwise by the same rules. § 1192. See Huebner, History of Germanic Private Law, 391, 392.

That there can be no mortgage without a debt under the civil law of Louisiana, see Dainow, Work of Louisiana Supreme Court for 1957–1958 Term: Security Devices, 1959, 19 La.L.Rev. 327, noting Baton Rouge Production Credit Ass'n v. Alford, 1958, 235 La. 117, 102 So.2d 866.

21. Halderman v. Woodward, 1879, 22 Kan. 734; Garretson Inv. Co. v. Arndt, 1904, 144 Cal. 64, 77 P. 770; Theodore v. Mozie, 1956, 230 S.C. 216, 95 S.E.2d 173, 1957, 10 S.C.L.Rev. 114, 123.

Even though the notes of a third party for which the mortgage was given as security are void because they are in violation of the Bankruptcy Act, the mortgage has been held valid. Amherst Factors, Inc. v. Kochenburger, 1958, 4 N.Y.2d 203, 173 N.Y.S. 570, 149 N.E.2d 863, discussed in, 1958, 8 Buffalo L.Rev. 102.

gagor or any other person, the creditor limiting his rights to enforcing his interest in the land under the mortgage, is valid and effective.[22] In these cases, although it is possible to conceive of the agreement as merely limiting the remedy of collection to certain property or, perhaps, to regard it as creating a duty of imperfect obligation,[23] it is also possible to construe it as negativing the existence of any independent obligation except insofar as the land itself can be looked upon as owing a "real" obligation.[24] Further, barring an action to enforce the personal liability of the mortgagor by the statute of limitations does not affect, in most states, the validity of the mortgage.[25] The same is true of a discharge from personal obligation by bankruptcy proceedings.[26] Nor does the avoidance of the note by alteration have any effect upon the mortgage.[27] There also is

22. Seieroe v. First Nat. Bank of Kearney, 1897, 50 Neb. 612, 70 N.W. 220; Weikel v. Davis, 1919, 109 Wash. 97, 186 P. 323; Wells v. Flynn, 1921, 191 Iowa 1322, 184 N.W. 389, 17 A.L.R. 710; Rice v. Rice, 1826, 21 Mass. (4 Pick.) 349, are typical. See 1922, 17 A.L.R. 717; Parks, Cas. on Mort., 96 n. 1. McKinney's Real Property Law of N.Y. § 249, provides that "A mortgage of real property does not imply a covenant for the payment of the sum intended to be secured; and where such covenant is not expressed in the mortgage, or a bond or other separate instrument to secure such payment has not been given, the remedies of the mortgagee are confined to the property mentioned in the mortgage." West's Ann.Cal.Civ.Code § 2928, is similar. See Van Brunt v. Mismer, 1863, 8 Minn. 232, Gil. 202; Demond v. Crary, C.C.N.Y.1882, 9 F. 750, 752. See also Restatement, Security, § 1(b). A mortgage to secure the obligation of a trustee limited to his liability *qua* trustee is good. In re Robinson's Settlement, 1912, 81 L.J.Ch.Div. 393. See Coote, Mortgages, 9th Ed., 11. In 1956 the Illinois Court of Appeals, in Bedian v. Cohn, 1956, 10 Ill.App.2d 116, 134 N.E. 2d 532, commented on by Updike, Mortgages in 1956 Annual Survey of American Law, 32 N.Y.U.L.Rev. 789, 790 (1956), held that documents may effectively provide that the mortgagor shall not be personally liable without affecting the validity of the mortgage.

23. See Williston, and Thompson, Contracts, Rev.Ed., § 16; Restatement, Contracts, § 14. Similar cases of personal substantive obligations recognized as existing but with remedies curtailed or unavailable are (1) mortgages in states with valid "no deficiency" statutes, (2) quasi in rem actions against absent defendants who have property in the jurisdiction, (3) broad exemption statutes covering all of the debtor's property within the jurisdiction, (4) a non-assuming grantee of mortgaged property in the state with the mortgagor-transferor out of the state or with the remedy against him barred by statute of limitations, etc.

24. See 3 Tiffany, Real Property, 2d Ed. § 607 ("the debt being in such case regarded as due by the land itself"); Walsh, Mortgages, § 16 ("a mortgage * * * may create a real obligation in a business transaction with an express provision excluding any personal obligation on which the mortgagor may be held liable."); Durfee, Lien or Equitable Theory

of Mortgage, 1912, 10 Mich.L.Rev. 589, n. 16. Matthews v. Sheehan, Rice v. Rice, Mooney v. Byrne, and Niggeler v. Maurin, infra note 32, may be regarded as illustrations of such "real" debts. See Langdell, Brief Survey of Equity Jurisdiction, 192, 199. "A real obligation is undoubtedly a legal fiction, i. e., a fiction invented by the law for the promotion of convenience and the advancement of justice. The invention consists primarily in personifying an inanimate thing, and giving it, so far as practicable, the legal qualities of a human being. The invention was originally made by the Romans, and it has been borrowed from them by the nations which have succeeded them. * * * by the Roman law, when a personal obligation was broken the obligee or creditor originally had no legal means of procuring satisfaction from the debtor's property; he could compel satisfaction out of the debtor's property only indirectly, namely, by exerting his legal power over the debtor's body. It is plain, however, that the interests of debtors and creditors alike required that a debtor should be able to give a creditor the same rights against the debtor's property, or some portion of it, that a personal obligation gave him against the debtor's body; and no better or more obvious mode of accomplishing this object could be adopted than that of enabling a debtor to impose upon his property an obligation in favor of his creditor, in analogy to the obligation which he imposed upon his person, and accordingly real obligations were invented and came into use, * * * (p. 199) A real obligation may, however, itself create a debt and so be a principal obligation; and, in that case, if there be also a personal obligation on the part of the owner of the property to pay the debt, the latter will be merely accessory to the real obligation. There are in English law two real obligations in particular which are always principal obligations, namely, rent and predial tithe."

See also Walsh, Mortgages, 90 n. 50. See Tiffany, Real Property, § 414 as to rent as a "real" obligation.

25. See Chapter 11, infra. These cases also may be explained, as may the bankruptcy discharge cases, as duties of imperfect obligation, the substantive right remaining unaffected even though remedies have been prohibited.

26. Bush v. Cooper, 1853, 26 Miss. 599, 59 Am.Dec. 270, affirmed 59 U.S. 82, 15 L.Ed. 273; Brown v. Hoover, 1877, 77 N.C. 40; Wilson v. Russell, 1859, 13 Md. 494, 71 Am.Dec. 645.

27. Cheek v. Nall, 1893, 112 N.C. 370, 17 S.E. 80; Smith v. Smith, 1887, 27 S.C. 166, 3 S.E. 78, 13 Am.

authority that a mortgage given to secure the note of a married woman, void because of the maker's coverture, can be foreclosed although there could be no personal judgment against the maker.[28] However, with the development of the doctrine that a married woman could charge her separate estate for certain debts for which she would not be personally liable, it seems difficult to understand why, if the debt could be regarded as existent, or unnecessary, for the purpose of charging the separate estate in equity, it could not also be regarded as similarly existent, or unnecessary, to support a mortgage of her separate property. The mystery of such a position is accentuated by cases holding that the mortgage would be sufficient to establish that the debt had been incurred with reference to the separate property covered by the mortgage and therefore, although the mortgage was invalid, the debt could be charged upon the property in equity.[29] It may be added that the ability to charge separate property with the payment of money is sufficient collateral legal recognition to warrant classification of the claim as a substantive duty of imperfect obligation capable of

supporting a mortgage.[30] Where the mortgage of a married woman secures the debt of another in addition to her own no doubts of the validity of the mortgage seems to exist.[31] And, finally, there is authority that a mortgage is valid by way of gift where, because of lack of consideration, no personal obligation ever arose or where, for some other reason, it is clear there is in existence no independent obligation for the mortgage to secure.[32] One standard text writer argues that, regardless of theory and authorities, the existence of a personal obligation in most

---

1859, 9 Wis. 516. Gregory v. Van Voorst, supra note 28, may be explained as rejecting this inconsistency.

30. See footnotes 23, 25, supra.

31. First Nat. Bank of Salisbury v. Fries, 1897, 121 N.C. 241, 28 S.E. 350, 61 Am.St.Rep. 663; Russ v. Wingate, 1855, 30 Miss. 440; Johnson's Adm'r v. Ward, 1887, 82 Ala. 486, 2 So. 524; Cook v. Landrum, 1904, 26 Ky.L.Rep. 813, 82 S.W. 585.

32. Goethe v. Gmelin, 1931, 256 Mich. 112, 239 N.W. 347 (note and mortgage intended as gift, note void for want of consideration. The court placed the decision on the ground that no consideration is necessary for a mortgage and did not discuss the lack of an obligation to be secured). Cf. Cooklin v. Cooklin, 260 Mich. 69, 244 N.W. 232, in which the court said that "it is not necessary that a mortgage be accompanied by a note provided the mortgage itself contains a promise to pay" and treated the Goethe case, inferentially, as not involving any question other than the necessity of consideration for the mortgage which secures the debt. Other cases more clearly holding no obligation necessary are Cook v. Johnson, 1896, 165 Mass. 245, 43 N.E. 96 (instruction that transaction was a mortgage not inconsistent with verdict that no debt existed because conveyance extinguished the personal obligation); Matthews v. Sheehan, 1877, 69 N.Y. 585 (deed absolute with only an option to repurchase); Rice v. Rice, 1826, 21 Mass. (4 Pick.) 349 (deed absolute, no personal duty to pay); Mooney v. Byrne, 1900, 163 N.Y. 86, 57 N.E. 163 (deed absolute, no covenant to pay and agreement for no deficiency, but court said there was a debt); Niggeler v. Maurin, 1885, 34 Minn. 118, 24 N.W. 369 (deed absolute, no covenant for payment). See Pearson v. Mulloney, 1935, 289 Mass. 508, 194 N.E. 458 (dictum only, second mortgage "subject to" first mortgage estopped to deny validity of first mortgage); Campbell v. Tompkins, 1880, 32 N.J.Eq. 170 (dictum, want of consideration for bond secured held closed to inquiry); Fisk v. Stewart, 1877, 24 Minn. 97 (dictum, debt existed); Campbell v. Dearborn, 1872, 109 Mass. 130, 12 Am. Rep. 671 (dictum in deed absolute case; debt existed); In re Robinson's Settlement, 1912, 81 L.J. Ch. 393 (dictum, note and mortgage both being illegal, that covenant "as trustee" bound the cove-

---

St.Rep. 633. In such cases, however, it may be said that the mortgage secures not the note but the money obligation behind the note. This same problem is involved, of course, in the cases of renewal and substituted notes; and a similar one arises where the original obligation secured has been merged in the judgment obtained in an action upon it against the mortgagor. See infra, § 105. That an improper and voluntary alteration of both bond and mortgage by the mortgagee would prevent foreclosure by him or his assignees in a lien jurisdiction, see Waring v. Smyth, 1847, 2 Barb.Ch. 119, 47 Am. Dec. 299.

28. Gregory v. Van Voorst, 1882, 85 Ind. 108. In United States Savings Fund & Investment Co. v. Harris, 1895, 142 Ind. 226, 40 N.E. 1072, rehearing denied 142 Ind. 226, 41 N.E. 451, a mortgage given to secure a note which was disaffirmed by the maker, an infant feme-covert, without returning the consideration, was held enforceable even though there was no personal liability. Cf., however, Burr v. Beckler, note 11, supra, and Hodges v. Price, 1881, 18 Fla. 342; Heburn v. Warner, 1873, 112 Mass. 271, 17 Am.Rep. 86, (criticised in 10 Am.L. Rev. 371), contra.

29. Heburn v. Warner, supra note 28; Patton v. Kinsman, 1864, 17 Iowa 428; Heath v. Van Cott,

modern mortgages is of no practical importance and not only should be but is ignored.[33]

NECESSITY OF OBLIGATION—THEORY

104. There is no reason why a mortgage without a personal obligation should not be permitted. This is important in several types of cases, e. g., where the personal duty is restricted, where the obligation has been released with rights in the mortgaged property reserved by agreement, and where the transaction is intended as a gift.

It is possible to distinguish between (1) the cases where the mortgage was attempted as a gift and no personal obligation ever arose because of lack of consideration, and (2) those cases in which a debt or other obligation is created with the property as security for it but there is (a) a limitation on the enforcement of the personal duty, by agreement or by rules of law, or (b) a release of the personal obligation with rights in the mortgaged property reserved by agreement, (e. g., (i) the mortgagee releases the mortgagor in the usual two party agreement, (ii) the mortgagee releases the mortgagor after the latter has conveyed to a non-assuming grantee, but by agreement with both mortgagor and grantee reserves all rights against the mortgaged property, (iii) the mortgagee releases the debtor from personal liability in a case in which the property was given in mortgage by a third party, but by agreement with the mortgagor the release of the debt is not to affect the rights of the mortgaged land).

In the gift cases, a suggested test of validity is whether the parties *intended* the mortgage to secure a debt or other personal obligation.[34] Almost universally that is the intent, and in such cases if the obligation does

not arise the mortgage should not because that is the intention. The court would never reach the question whether there *could* be a mortgage without a personal obligation. Further, since only a sporadic case could not be decided on this reasoning, the ultimate question in this type of case may be regarded as of theoretical rather than practical importance.

In the second group, the parties' intention usually is express and entirely clear. They mean the mortgage to remain valid in spite of restrictions upon the enforcement or even the complete extinction of the personal obligation which existed at the outset and which the property without question was intended to secure. Whether effect can be given to the intention in this last, extreme case is of more than academic interest. Since there is no guesswork about intention, since the agreement is entered into subsequent to the creation of the mortgage and therefore the most valid reasons for scrutinizing or restricting agreements is absent, and since the problem is clearly presented so that all arguments will be faced squarely, it would seem that only the most rigid, mechanical conceptualism would defeat the agreement.[35]

There should be no objection to giving effect to the intention of parties entering into any one of the following transactions: (1) a transfer of property as security for an act for whose performance some person is under an obligation recognized as substantively existing; (2) a transfer of property subject to the payment of money to a third person but without personal obligation on the transferee to make payment; (3) a transfer of an undivided interest in property equal in value to a stated amount of money; (4) a transfer of property subject to an option in the transferor to get it back on the performance of an act for which no one is personally bound; (5) the creation, by the transfer in mortgage of property or an interest in it, of a "real" obligation in favor of the

nantor only with respect to trust funds). See also Walsh, Mortgages, 75 n. 2; Coote, Mortgages, 9th Ed., 11; 1922, 2 Wis.L.Rev. 60; 1936, 14 Tex.L.Rev. 560; 1932, 31 Mich.L.Rev. 102, 105; 58 N.J.L.J. 1; 1930, 4 St. John's L.Rev. 276.

33. See Wiltsie, Mortgage Foreclosure, 5th ed., § 1.

34. Walsh, Mortgages, §§ 16, 17d; note 11, 12, supra.

35. Cf. Berheim v. Pessou, note 11, supra.

transferee for the performance of an act, the property mortgaged being the sole obligor in addition to being security for the doing of the act. The only questions should be ones of terminology and category.

It is important to add that there is no intent to depreciate the last mentioned matters. In every established category or concept there is a well defined pattern of rules and principles which the courts tend to accept as a unit and then apply rather mechanically to all cases within the category. Some of the unique and most important doctrines of the law of mortgages, e. g., those dealing with restrictions on the right to redeem, are predicated upon the existence of a necessitous, landowning borrower.[36] To have the category mortgage include situations in which this factor is entirely absent, and therefore the reason for a considerable body of mortgage law non-existent, may well be questioned as tending to lead to undesirable results through an undiscriminating application of all mortgage law. Granting this we may examine our five transactions.

The first is the one which is ordinarily called a mortgage and to which the fairly well recognized and bounded body of law covered by that label is customarily applied and, it is arguable, should be confined.[37] The second is the familiar equitable charge with its own established and defined sphere.[38] The third obviously is not a security transaction of any sort but an attempt to convey an absolute although undivided interest in real property with the size of that interest measured in terms of money. Historically the fourth type has existed alongside the currently standard security in its different stages of development and been differentiated from it and resorted to by parties for reasons which changed from period to period.[39] The

situation of the parties in and the purposes of the regular mortgage are sufficiently different today from this sale-option to repurchase to warrant its continued segregation.[40] The last one is a security transaction and no strong reason for excluding it from the mortgage category suggests itself.[41] Whether it is capable of being created as a gift without consideration is quite another matter.[42] The nature of the "real" obligation is not precisely defined [43] but it would seem to be just as executory as a personal promise by the donor. If so, it is puzzling to understand why there is not as much necessity for consideration in the creation of a "real" executory obligation as a personal one.[44] It is arguable that the giving of a mortgage to secure any kind of executory agreement, otherwise invalid because without consideration and intended as a gift, should be sufficient to make that agreement binding. That it does not in the case of a personal promise [45] suggests that

cessitous landowner and, later, the money owner preferred this kind of bargain.

40. See Williston, Some Modern Tendencies in the Law, 43; Chapter 4, Subdivision B, supra.

41. The German law, however, gives the separate label of "land charge" to this sort of arrangement but, apart from the absence of personal obligation, applies to it all the law governing the hypothec. See note 20, supra. Another example of establishing a separate category and name for a security transaction in which there is no personal obligation is the "antichresis" of the French law. Unlike the "land charge," however, it differs from the hypothec in other respects. French Civ.Code (Cachard) Art. 2072.

The risk that the courts might not recognize a new category and therefore defeat the parties' intention by not sustaining it except as a mortgage is a make-weight factor.

42. See § 107, infra.

43. See Langdell, Brief Survey of Equitable Jurisdiction, 192, quoted note 24, supra.

44. Courts have consistently refused to convert an executory personal promise to give into a valid trust. Scott, Trusts, §§ 3, 74–88; Bogert, Trusts and Trustees, 2d Ed., §§ 19–24; Restatement, Second, Trusts §§ 74–88.

45. In re James, 1895, 146 N.Y. 78, 40 N.E. 876, 48 Am.St.Rep. 774; Nesson v. Millen, 1910, 205 Mass. 515, 91 N.E. 995.

The executory personal promise is unlimited in the value which may be covered whereas the executory

36. See Chapter 4.

37. See note 20, supra.

38. See 1 Scott, Trusts, § 10.

39. See Wigmore, the Pledge Idea, 1897, 10 Harv.L. Rev. 389, for explanations as to why, first, the ne-

a "real" obligation cannot be created gratuitously. That the property alone is involved perhaps obscures the fact that it is playing a double role, i. e., that of a personified "real" obligor and that of property securing the performance of the obligation which it owes.[46] One eminent authority suggests that the parly-perfected intended gift should be completed on the theory that an impasse in which neither party can utilize the property is undesirable and the courts should not help an "Indian giver" to get a release or reconveyance of the security interest from the intended beneficiary.[47] This result may be desirable but it ignores the fact that the intention was not to give the property itself but some other performance with the property meant merely as security for that other intended benefit.

NATURE OF OBLIGATION

105. Any obligation capable of reduction to a money equivalent may be secured by a mortgage.

Where the obligation is one of support, not all of the ordinary rules of mortgage law are

"real" obligation can bind only the res itself. This difference in the amount of wealth involved may be justification for distinguishing them in regard to enforceability without consideration.

46. If the mortgage is executed under seal, as is customary in many jurisdictions, or with such other formalities which, by the law of the jurisdiction, would be sufficient to make a promise enforceable without consideration, this would seem to be sufficient to uphold the executory "real" obligation and the mortgage itself. No case or writer has suggested this possibility. Cf. Anderson v. Lee, 1898, 73 Minn. 397, 76 N.W. 24 (mortgage under seal invalid where given to secure note void for want of consideration).

47. See Glenn, Mortgages, 34, citing Herbert v. Simson, 1915, 220 Mass. 480, 180 N.E. 265, L.R.A.1915D 733; Farrell v. Passaic Water Co., 1913, 82 N.J.Eq. 97, 88 A. 627; Miller v. Silverman, 1928, 247 N.Y. 447, 160 N.E. 910. In all of these cases the donor's intention was to give the property itself and the transaction carrying out the intent had gone far enough to vest some interest in the property in the donee. In the case under consideration the *security* part of the transaction has been completed and the only question is whether the promised performance of something else can be enforced out of the property security.

applicable and it has been doubted whether the transaction should be classified as a mortgage.

The mortgage secures the indebtedness itself, not the written evidence of it. Hence changes in the form of the obligation do not affect the mortgage.

Certainty of amount. Any obligation capable of being reduced to a money value may be secured by a mortgage.[48] Thus unliquidated debts such as open book accounts and even contingent obligations that are also uncertain in amount, e. g., indemnity bonds, may be secured by mortgages.[49]

Whether an obligation which is impossible of reduction to a money equivalent can be secured by a mortgage is somewhat doubtful.[50] The objection to such mortgages as between the parties is that, because foreclosure is customarily by sale, there would be difficulty in allocating the proceeds.[51] Creditors of the mortgagor would face the same perplexity in realizing on the mortgaged property; the mortgagee would find difficulty in assign-

48. Stub v. Belmont, 1942, 20 Cal.2d 208, 124 P.2d 826 (consignment contract); Cook v. Bartholomew, 1891, 60 Conn. 24, 22 A. 444, 13 L.R.A. 452 (promise to support during life); Dover Lumber Co. v. Case, 1918, 31 Idaho 276, 170 P. 108 (faithful performance of a contract to cut and deliver timber). See West's Ann.Cal.Civ.Code § 2920. Contra, Bethlehem v. Annis, 1860, 40 N.H. 34, 77 Am.Dec. 700 ("Wherever the condition, when broken, gives rise to no claim for damages whatever, or to a claim for unliquidated damages, the deed is not to be regarded as a mortgage in equity * * *"). Cf. French Civil Code §§ 2132, 2148–4, 2153–3, 2163, 2165 (if the claim secured is conditional as to its existence or unsettled as to amount, the creditor must record an expressly stated maximum estimate of value).

49. Merills v. Swift, 1847, 18 Conn. 257, 46 Am.Dec. 315; Emerson v. Knight, 1908, 130 Ga. 100, 60 S.E. 255; McDaniels v. Colvin, 1844, 16 Vt. 300, 42 Am. Dec. 512; Fidelity and Deposit Co. v. Oliver, 1910, 57 Wash. 31, 106 P. 483.

50. Bethlehem v. Annis, note 48, supra. For example, would a mortgage of Whiteacre given by T to secure his legally binding promise to E to give a mortgage of Blackacre to secure M's unmatured debt to E be a valid mortgage?

51. This objection would not apply to strict foreclosure except in those American jurisdictions which permit, after foreclosure, an action on the debt with the value of the property deducted. See Sears Roebuck & Co. v. Camp, 1938, 124 N.J.Eq. 403, 1 A.2d 425, 118 A.L.R. 762.

ing; and, most serious of all, the mortgagor's ability to sell or to obtain second mortgages from other lenders would be impaired by the impossibility of determining the value of the redemption interest.

Mortgages for support. Two peculiarities of the normal agreement for support secured by a mortgage of land, i. e., that performance is to be by the mortgagor personally and out of the use of the property, make it inadvisable to apply to it all of the ordinary rules of mortgage law and have even caused some doubt as to whether it should be classified as a mortgage at all.[52] Thus, if default is unintentional and causes no irreparable harm the mortgagor will not be permitted to redeem.[53] Although the mortgagee may obtain or accept damages in lieu of the promised support, he cannot be forced to take them.[54] The

mortgagee cannot assign the mortgage,[55] and not only is the mortgagor unable to transfer the property without the mortgagee's consent[56] but creditors of the mortgagor cannot reach it except subject to possession being retained by the mortgagor until the purpose of the mortgage has been fulfilled.[57]

Form. Because of the primary importance of the obligation, it is natural to find many questions raised as to its form, the effect of changes in its form, and the sufficiency and controlling character of descriptions in the mortgage deed. In England it was customary for a long time to take a bond for the payment of the secured debt. This was due to the advantages a specialty creditor had in enforcing a deficiency against the assets of a deceased mortgagor.[58] Modern statutes make practically all assets of a decedent liable for his debts without preference to specialty debts.[59] As a result this custom has died out in England and most of the United States[60] so far as mortgages to secure the debts of individuals are concerned.[61] However, it is still the usual practice to have the debt separately expressed and, ordinarily, this is done by a signed note or series of instalment notes falling due at different dates, or, less often, by bonds.[62]

---

52. See Bethlehem v. Annis, 1861, 40 N.H. 34, 77 Am. Dec. 700; Soper v. Guernsey, 1872, 71 Pa. 219, 221.

Typically the agreement is an intra-family one with the mortgagee elderly or feeble. And, since to permit the mortgagee to take possession would deprive the mortgagor of the means by which it was contemplated he was to carry out his obligation, the mortgagor is held to have the right to possession. Flanders v. Lamphear, 1838, 9 N.H. 201; Rhoades v. Parker, 1839, 10 N.H. 83; Colman v. Packard, 1819, 16 Mass. 39, contra.

The problem presented by these factors is also faced in cases where the consideration for an absolute conveyance is a promise to support which in many cases is oral. The majority of courts allow rescission by the grantor for failure of the grantee to perform. In such cases "courts are not so much concerned as to the proper theory upon which such contracts may be avoided, as they are that they must be set aside in order to prevent grave injustice and the imposition upon aged people, by unscrupulous persons, who pretend love, devotion, and friendship, where no one of such elements exists." Anderson v. Reed, 1915, 20 N.M. 202, 215, 148 P. 502, 506, L.R. A.1916B, 862; Sweeny v. Patton, 1922, 134 Va. 117, 113 S.E. 715. Contra: Conley v. Sharpe, 1943, 58 Cal.App.2d 145, 136 P.2d 376, discussed in note, 1944, 32 Cal.L.Rev. 191; Spangler v. Yarborough, 1909, 23 Okl. 806, 101 P. 1107, 138 Am.St.Rep. 856; Drake v. Drake, 1928, 148 S.C. 147, 14 S.E. 705.

53. Bryant v. Erskine, 1867, 55 Me. 153, 157; Henry v. Tupper, 1857, 29 Vt. 358; Dunklee v. Adams, 1848, 20 Vt. 415, 50 Am.Dec. 44; Rowell v. Jewett, 1879, 69 Me. 293, 301.

54. Cook v. Bartholomew, 1891, 60 Conn. 24, 22 A. 444, 13 L.R.A. 452; Ridley v. Ridley, 1895, 87 Me. 445, 32 A. 1005; Tuttle v. Burgett's Admr., 1895, 53 Ohio St. 498, 42 N.E. 427, 30 L.R.A. 214, 53 Am.St.

Rep. 649; Austin v. Austin, 1837, 9 Vt. 420; Joslyn v. Parlin, 1881, 54 Vt. 670, contra.

55. Bryant v. Erskine, 1867, 55 Me. 153.

56. Bethlehem v. Annis, 1860, 40 N.H. 34, 77 Am.Dec. 700; Bryant v. Erskine, 1867, 55 Me. 153; Eastman v. Batchelder, 1858, 36 N.H. 141, 72 Am.Dec. 295; Flanders v. Lamphear, 1838, 9 N.H. 201.

57. Bodwell Granite Co. v. Lane, 1891, 83 Me. 168, 21 A. 829; Greenleaf v. Grounder, 1894, 86 Me. 298, 29 A. 1082.

58. Langdell, Brief Survey of Equity Jurisdiction, 140, 145–146.

59. Tiffany, Real Property, 2d Ed., § 552.

60. New York, Pennsylvania and some other states continue the practice. 3 Tiffany, Real Property, 2d Ed., 2409.

61. In corporate mortgages, of course, the obligation takes the form of a bond issue.

62. See Tiffany, Real Property, § 513.

Where there is a separately executed note or bond it frequently is necessary to decide whether the mortgage secures the instrument itself or the debt underlying it with the writing either merely evidence [63] or "collateral security." [64] Quite uniformly the cases hold, both where the instrument is executed contemporaneously with the creation of the debt and where it is given subsequently, that it is the debt that is secured.[65] As a corollary to this, changes in the form of the obligation such as the substitution of new notes bearing a different maturity date and altering various incidents of the obligation do not affect the mortgage so long as, or beyond the extent that the secured debt itself is not destroyed.[66] This tendency is so strong that it is followed even in states where a negotiable note given for a preexisting unsecured debt is presumed to be payment of it.[67] In order to protect the mortgagee against intervening liens or dower interests or to preserve the priority of the original mortgage as one securing the purchase money, the courts have gone to great lengths in holding that even the execution of a new mortgage does not affect either the original mortgage or the debt it secures.[68] In order to protect the

63. "Equity, which regards the substance of things, holds the debt as the thing actually intended to be secured, and regards the note as merely the evidence of the debt." Dumell v. Terstegge, 1864, 23 Ind. 397, 398, 85 Am.Dec. 466.

64. "The common law deems it collateral security." Shaw, C. J., in Fowler v. Bush, 1838, 38 Mass. (21 Pick.) 230; 3 Tiffany, Real Property, 2d Ed., 2410.

65. See Williston, Contracts, Rev.Ed., § 1875F; Montgomery v. Wade, 1944, 195 Okl. 60, 154 P.2d 943. In Lierman v. O'Hara, 1913, 153 Wis. 140, 140 N.W. 1057, 44 L.R.A.,N.S., 1153, although the mortgage expressly stated that it secured a note which was invalid because unsigned the court held the mortgage valid as securing the indebtedness, not the note. But cf. Leader Pub. Co. v. Grant Trust & Sav. Co., 1909, 174 Ind. 192, 91 N.E. 498, and cases in notes 11, 12, supra.

The rule that the mortgage secures the debt and not the written instrument aids in preventing extortion of excessive amounts by writing those amounts into the note. See 3 Tiffany, Real Property, 2d Ed., 2410.

66. Whether the substitution of a new note is taken as a mere change in form or as payment of the debt depends fundamentally upon the intention of the parties. That intention may be found in express statements or in the circumstances of the transaction. However, in the absence of definite evidence of intent that the debt shall be discharged all but a few courts refuse to treat the new note as extinguishing the original indebtedness or mortgage securing it. See Tolman v. Smith, 1898, 85 Cal. 280, 287, 24 P. 743, 745, ("in the absence of an agreement to that effect, the payment of one note by another is only conditional and not absolute payment. It extends the time for payment until the maturity of the new note, or, as it is said, 'suspends' the remedy upon the old note, but does not extinguish it."). London & San Francisco Bank v. Bandmann, 1898, 120 Cal. 220, 52 P. 583. 65 Am.St.Rep. 179; Bonestell v. Bowie, 1900, 128 Cal. 511, 61 P. 78 (marking sur-

rendered old note "paid" is not conclusive evidence of the extinguishment of the debt which the mortgage secures); Bunker v. Barron, 1887, 79 Me. 62, 8 A. 253, 1 Am.St.Rep. 282, accord; Fowler v. Bush, 1838, 38 Mass. (21 Pick.) 230, contra. See Britton, Bills and Notes, § 263. The same is true even though the new note is given by a third party (purchaser from the mortgagor) or to an assignee of the mortgage. Foster v. Paine, 1884, 63 Iowa 85, 18 N.W. 699 (Hadlock v. Bulfinch, 1850, 31 Me. 246, contra); Moody v. Stubbs, 1915, 94 Kan. 250, 146 P. 346. So, also, where there is a part payment with a new note for the balance, where there have been additions, changes in interest rates, in sureties, and other incidents of the debt. Lippold v. Held, 1874, 58 Mo. 213; Bosheimer v. Gunn, 1871, 24 Mich. 372; Darst v. Bates, 1869, 51 Ill. 439, 1880; Moore v. Thompson, 1896, 100 Ky. 231, 37 S.W. 1042, 18 Ky. Law Rep. 681; Buck v. Wood, 1892, 85 Me. 204, 27 A. 103. See 3 Tiffany, Real Property, 2d Ed., § 640 (h). The same is true where the original debt was not evidenced by any note. Gravlee v. Lamkin, 1898, 120 Ala. 210, 24 So. 756; Shipman v. Lord, 1900, 60 N.J.Eq. 484, 46 A. 1101.

Even the substitution of instruments of entirely different character does not alter the rule. Whittaker v. Dick, 1840, 5 How. (Miss.) 296, 35 Am.Dec. 436, (recognizance for note); Cover v. Black, 1845, 1 Pa. 493 (judgment note for single bill); Maryland N. Y. Coal & Iron Co. v. Wingert, 1849, 8 Gill. (Md.) 170 (note for bond).

See also McGuire v. Van Pelt, 1876, 55 Ala. 344; Copp v. Millen, 1938, 11 Cal.2d 122, 77 P.2d 1093; Darst v. Bates, 1880, 95 Ill. 493; Port v. Robbins, 1872, 35 Iowa 208; Lee v. Fletcher, 1891, 46 Minn. 49, 48 N. W. 456, 12 L.R.A. 171; Hutchinson v. Swartsweller, 1879, 31 N.J.Eq. 205. See also 1912, 35 L.R.A.,N.S., 86. Cf. Daly v. Proetz, 1874, 20 Minn. 411, Gil. 363. See notes, 1920, 4 Minn.L.Rev. 372; 1929, 13 Minn.L. Rev. 157; 1930, 6 Not.D.Law. 132; 1862, 2 Am.L. Reg.,N.S., 1, 7. See also Postponement of Maturity Dates under Trust Indentures, 1937, 46 Yale L.J. 1041.

67. See Lovell v. Williams, 1878, 125 Mass. 439, 441.

68. Higman v. Humes, 1900, 127 Ala. 404, 30 So. 733; Birrell v. Schie, 1858, 9 Cal. 104 (surrender of old note and cancellation of mortgage of record with new note and mortgage for larger amount is not evidence of payment); White v. Stevenson, 1904, 144 Cal. 104, 77 P. 828; Packard v. Kingman, 1860, 11

mortgagee against intervening liens courts hold that the recovery of a personal judgment on the secured debt, although it merges [69] the original claim into the judgment so as to prevent any later action on it, nevertheless has no effect upon the enforcement of the mortgage.[70] Other important corollaries of the fundamental proposition that the mortgage secures the indebtedness itself rather than any written evidence of it are found in the rules that a covenant to pay need not, and usually does not, appear in the mortgage deed;[71] that permit showing a deed absolute is a mortgage,[72] and that the amount of the debt was misstated.[73]

DESCRIPTION

106. The obligation need not be described or mentioned in the mortgage.

Notwithstanding the central importance of the obligation, there is, as between the parties, no reason why the law should require that it be described or even mentioned in the mortgage itself.[74] Self interest of the parties, however, ordinarily dictates rather accurate statements of essential elements of the secured obligation (amount, date, maturity, form, etc.). The mortgagee will want this evidence, for example, to facilitate transfers of the claim and security and foreclosures or to preserve priorities. To the mortgagor it is important when seeking new financing or selling. When others than the parties are involved, whether, and the extent to which, a description of the secured claim is obligatory is of concern to the law as is, also, the interpretation and application of any description required or used. On these last matters, however, there is considerable confusion in the cases.

Iowa 219 (chattel mortgage); Jones v. Davis, 1899, 121 Ala. 348, 25 So. 789; Hassell v. Hassell, 1901, 129 Ala. 326, 29 So. 695; Austin v. Underwood, 1865, 37 Ill. 438, 87 Am.Dec. 254; Gray v. Kappos, 1936, 90 Utah 300, 61 P.2d 613 (chattel mortgage). See 3 Tiffany, Real Property, 2d Ed., § 641.

69. See Pirsig, Merger by Judgment, 1944, 28 Minn.L. Rev. 419, for a criticism of the lack of analysis and discrimination in the use of the doctrine of merger in judgments.

70. Nagle v. Macy, 1858, 9 Cal. 426; Freeburg v. Eksell, 1904, 123 Iowa 464, 99 N.W. 118; Economic Life Assur. Soc. v. Usborne, [1902] A.C. 147. See, 1910, 24 L.R.A.,N.S., 1095; notes, 1923, 18 Ill.L.Rev. 206; 1881, 20 Am.L.Reg.,N.S., 681.

71. See Hickox v. Lowe, 1858, 10 Cal. 197; § 1 note 12, supra; West's Ann.Cal.Civ.Code § 2928, which expressly provides that a mortgage will not bind the mortgagor personally to perform the act for which it is security unless there is an express covenant therein, does not prevent binding the mortgagor personally by obligations dehors the mortgage. Jones v. Gardner, 1881, 57 Cal. 641.

Recitals in the condition that payment of the debt is the event upon which the conveyance is to be avoided do not warrant implying a promise. See semble, West's Ann.Cal.Civ.Code § 2890 (no promise implied from the creation of a lien). But cf. Eugley v. Sproul, 1916, 115 Me. 463, 99 A. 443.

72. See Chapter 4, supra.

73. See infra, § 108.

74. "A mortgage given to secure a debt existent at the making of the mortgage, or contemporaneous therewith, is valid, even as against subsequent purchasers and creditors, although it does not explicitly state the amount of such debt or liability, provided there are means of ascertaining such amount. And extrinsic evidence is admissible for the purpose of showing the debt which the mortgage was intended to secure." Durfee, Cas. on Mortgages, 41.

The deed absolute cases are striking testimony to the truth of this. See Chapter 4, Subdivision A, supra.

Cf. French Civ.Code, Cachard, Rev.Ed., § 2136. "A conventional mortgage is only valid if the amount for which it is granted is fixed and determined by the deed."

There is authority that the maturity date of the obligation is such a vital part of the mortgage that its omission makes the mortgage unenforcible under the statute of frauds. Sullivan v. Laddon, 1924, 101 Conn. 166, 125 A. 250, noted 71 N.Y.L.Jour. 1712. This seems entirely inconsistent with the deed absolute cases and has been criticized. See 1 Glenn, Mortgages, § 23. It has been suggested that showing the true amount of the loan is on the same footing as evidence to show that the actual consideration for a deed is different from that expressed in the instrument. See Nazro v. Ware, 1888, 38 Minn. 443, 38 N.W. 359. The analogy is invalid. Consideration in a deed may be either nominal or recited, if it is required at all, for the reason that no substantially valuable consideration is necessary to make the deed legally operative. See 2 Tiffany, Real Property, 2d Ed., § 438; 4 Wigmore, Evidence, § 2425 et seq. But in a mortgage to secure a debt the existence and amount of the debt is vital, and determines the validity and extent of the mortgage. The real explanation seems rather that it is either an exception to the parol evidence rule and Statute of Frauds or outside of their operation. See Chapter 4, Subdivision A, supra.

NECESSITY OF CONSIDERATION

107. A legal mortgage does not require consideration, despite many statements to the contrary. To the extent that there must be an obligation for the mortgage to secure, the validity of the mortgage depends indirectly on consideration for the obligation.

The legal mortgage itself is an executed conveyance and no more requires consideration than any other executed transfer of property.[75] This is obviously true of the common law mortgage conveying legal title, for if an owner may convey the whole title by deed of gift he surely may convey the lesser, security interest in the form of title subject to a condition subsequent.[76] No different rule should apply where the mortgage gives a lien, for, regardless of any controversy over the precise nature of the lien,[77] the transaction is executed. That a mortgage is valid without consideration is evidenced by mortgages given to secure the debts of third persons.[78] Other proof is in the almost universal rule that mortgages may be given to secure preexisting debts.[79] Nevertheless the cases are full of statements that consideration is an essential ingredient of a mortgage.[80] There are several explanations of such statements. Perhaps the most frequent source of confusion is the failure to differentiate between the mortgage and the obligation it secures.[81] "The mortgage itself is an executed conveyance, defeasible upon the carrying out of an executory contract. This executory contract is subject to all the laws applicable to contracts, and must, of course, be supported by consideration."[82] One reason for this failure to distinguish between the two disparate ingredients is the inveterate habit of using the word mortgage to refer indiscriminately to the debt, the property security, or the composite unit of the

75. "Consideration has to do with contracts not executed conveyances." National City Bank of Chicago v. Wagner, C.C.A.Ill.1914, 216 F. 473, 132 C.C.A. 533, certiorari denied 235 U.S. 698, 35 S.Ct. 199, 59 L. Ed. 431.
Perry v. Miller, 1953, 330 Mass. 261, 112 N.E.2d 805, commented on by Updike, Mortgages, in 1953 Annual Survey of American Law, 1954, 29 N.Y.U.L. Rev. 829, 830, is a recent case.

76. "There need not be proven, and there need not exist, as I understand it, any consideration between the mortgagor and the mortgagee for the defeasible conveyance manifested by the mortgage itself." Perkins v. Trinity Realty Co., 1905, 69 N.J.Eq. 723, 726, 61 A. 167, 168, affirmed 71 N.J.Eq. 304, 71 A. 1135. Actually, of course, mortgages of this sort existed prior to the development of any doctrine of consideration.

77. See Gavit, Under the Lien Theory of Mortgages is the Mortgage Only a Power of Sale? 15 Minn.L. Rev. 147; Durfee, Lien or Equitable Theory of Mortgage, 1912, 10 Mich.L.Rev. 587; Chapter 1, D, supra. See also 1922, 2 Wis.L.Rev. 59; 1933, 8 Wis.L.Rev. 184; 1931, 19 Ky.L.J. 146, 155.

78. Garretson Inv. Co. v. Arndt, 1904, 144 Cal. 64, 77 P. 770; Herron v. Stevenson, 1918, 259 Pa. 354, 102 A. 1049. It is immaterial that the debt of the third party is a pre-existing one. Buck v. Axt, 1882, 85 Ind. 512; Lee State Bank v. McElheny, 1924, 227 Mich. 322, 198 N.W. 928; Lee v. Kirkpatrick, 1862, 14 N.J.Eq. 264 (given in payment of debt of third party); Moore v. Fuller, 1877, 6 Or. 272; Nat. City

Bank of Chi. v. Wagner, C.C.A.Ill.1914, 216 F. 473, 132 C.C.A. 553, certiorari denied 235 U.S. 698, 35 S. Ct. 199, 59 L.Ed. 431; Bynum Mercantile Co. v. First Nat. Bank of Anniston, 1914, 187 Ala. 281, 65 So. 815; Bell v. Bell, 1908, 133 Mo.App. 570, 113 S. W. 667; Kansas Mfg. Co. v. Gandy, 1881, 11 Nev. 448, 9 N.W. 569, 38 Am.Rep. 370; Ray v. Hollenbeck, C.C.N.Y.1890, 42 F. 381 (dictum), contra.

79. Bray v. Comer, 1877, 82 Ala. 183, 1 So. 77; Usina v. Wilder, 1877, 58 Ga. 178; Hewitt v. Powers, 1882, 84 Ind. 295; Rea v. Wilson, 1900, 112 Iowa 517, 84 N.W. 539 (valid against subsequent attaching creditor); Barrett v. Weber, 1890, 125 N.Y. 18, 25 N.E. 1068; Lehrenkrauss v. Bonnell, 1910, 199 N.Y. 240, 92 N.E. 637 (valid against creditors even though given while insolvent and with intent to defeat other creditors provided mortgagee not chargeable with notice of such intent); Reeves & Co. v. Dyer, 1915, 52 Okl. 750, 153 P. 850; Richeson v. Richeson, 1846, 43 Va. (2 Grat.) 497 (valid against creditor). See Jones, Mortgages, 8th Ed., § 757; Tiffany, Real Property, 2d Ed. § 606; Walsh, Mortgages, § 14. Accord: Campbell v. Bagley, C.A.La.1960, 276 F.2d 28.

80. See Tiffany, Real Property, 2d Ed., § 606, n. 65 for a collection of cases so stating. See also 1932, 31 Mich.L.Rev. 102.

81. "Such confusion as exists with respect to the right to plead and prove no consideration arises, I think, out of the failure to distinguish between the mortgage and the debt which the mortgage is given to secure." Perkins v. Trinity Realty Co., 1905, 69 N.J.Eq. 723, 726, 61 A. 167, 169, affirmed 71 N.J.Eq. 304, 71 A. 1135. For an example of such confusion, see Barnes, Consideration in Mortgages, 1931, 19 Ky.L.J. 146, 148–151.

82. Perkins v. Trinity Realty Co., note 81 supra, at 727, 61 A. at 168. This statement is not, of course,

two.[83] More influential is the requirement that, either because it is the parties' intention or a positive rule of law demands it, there must be an obligation for the mortgage to secure. This makes the validity of the mortgage depend indirectly upon consideration, not for the mortgage itself, but for the obligation upon which it ordinarily depends.[84] In some cases, flowing also from the conception of a mortgage requiring an obligation, the doctrine that a mortgage can be enforced only to the amount of the debt due regardless of the face of the bond, etc., seems to be what the court means by its requirement of consideration.[85] Many other cases which say consideration is necessary are dealing with the validity of the mortgage as against third parties, not as between the mortgagor and mortgagee. In some of these cases the problem of "consideration" really is one of "value" in the doctrine of bona fide purchase.[86] In others the kind and amount of consideration involves doctrines of the law

of fraudulent conveyances in determining intent and whether the taker is a volunteer.[87] Even where there is no personal obligation to secure and the question is the creation of a "real" obligation, the problem of consideration vel non should be, analytically, of consequence only in determining whether such executory "real" obligation is subject to the same rules as the corresponding personal obligation.[88]

Whether consideration is essential to the creation of an equitable mortgage is considered elsewhere.[89]

AMOUNT OF DEBT

108. By the majority view the amount of the debt need not be stated precisely; there need only be sufficient description to make identification reasonably possible.

Misstatement of the amount does not make the mortgage void in absence of an intent to deceive.

Failure to state the maturity date makes the debt payable on demand.

precisely accurate because it does not take into account the effect of a seal or other circumstances (e. g., facts creating a promissory estoppel) which would make a promise enforceable without consideration.

83. A striking example of this is the conclusion of the court in Perkins v. Trinity Realty Co., note 81, supra, at 729, 61 A. at 169, that "there was consideration for the mortgage", i. e., the debt.

84. Chesser v. Chesser, 1914, 67 Fla. 6, 64 So. 357; Hall v. Davis, 1884, 73 Ga. 101; Conwell v. Clifford, 1873, 45 Ind. 392; Hannan v. Hannan, 1877, 123 Mass. 441; Saunders v. Dunn, 1900, 175 Mass. 164, 55 N.E. 893; Anderson v. Lee, 1898, 73 Minn. 397, 76 N.W. 24; Brooks v. Owen, 1892, 112 Mo. 251; 19 S.W. 723, reversed on rehearing 112 Mo. 251, 20 S.W. 492; Hughes v. Thweatt, 1879, 57 Miss. 376; Bradshaw v. Farnsworth, 1909, 65 W.Va. 28, 63 S.E. 755; Cawley v. Kelley, 1884, 60 Wis. 315, 19 N.W. 65.

85. E. g., Laylin v. Knox, 1879, 41 Mich. 40, 1 N.W. 913. See Barbour, History of Contract in Early English Equity, 4 Oxford Studies 89; 3 Tiffany, Real Property, 2d Ed. § 606.

86. For example, a legal mortgage given to secure an existing debt is perfectly valid between the parties (note 79, supra) but the taker could not qualify, in most jurisdictions, as a bona fide purchaser for value under the equitable doctrine or under the requirements in recording acts. See 1927, 36 Yale L.J. 564; 1913, 23 Yale L.J. 186.

87. Lehrenkrauss v. Bonnell, note 79 supra, (mortgage to secure existing debt, given by mortgagor while insolvent, is not voidable as fraudulent conveyance); Brigham v. Brown, 1880, 44 Mich. 59, 6 N.W. 97 (unrecorded mortgage given to secure either a non-existent debt or an existing debt already amply secured held invalid against a subsequent recorded mortgage taken for value and without notice. The court uttered this dictum: "a man may give a voluntary mortgage * * * and it is fraudulent only as to those who are or would be defrauded by it."); Rea v. Wilson, note 79, supra ("a mortgage given for a pre-existing debt is founded on a valid consideration and, is not voluntary" as against subsequent attaching creditors); Brooks v. Dalrymple, 1866, 94 Mass. (12 Allen) 102 (note and mortgage executed by M to his daughter, C, in consideration of his wife joining in a conveyance of other property to T held not a fraudulent conveyance as to subsequent creditors of M); even though both note and the mortgage securing it are executed without consideration, where the transaction was entered into with actual intent to defraud another the mortgage is binding between the mortgagor and mortgagee. Fitzgerald v. Forristal, 1868, 48 Ill. 228.

88. See § 98, supra. See also Clapp, Consideration is not Necessary for a Mortgage, 58 N.J.L.J. 1; Schaffer, Validity of Mortgage Created as a Gift, 1930, 4 St. Johns L.Rev. 276; A Mortgage as a Gift, 1947, 37 Ky.L.J. 121.

89. See Chapter 2, § 30, supra.

Cases involving the amount of the debt may be divided into two classes: those in which the amount is omitted entirely, or is expressed in general terms, or by way of reference; and those in which although specified, it is either overstated or understated.[90] The objections to the validity of the first group are the possibilities afforded for the substitution of fictitious claims [91] and the burden of investigations dehors the mortgage to discover what could easily have been inserted in it. Nevertheless, most courts uphold them,[92] although there is a minority view requiring the amount of the debt to be stated as accurately as its nature permits on pain of having the mortgage held void as to third parties.[93] The divergence in the decisions reflects the courts' attempts to balance the interests. The mortgagee wants to be protected as long as the description of the obligation is adequate to warn a person looking at it and to enable discovery of the truth by inquiry. The searcher of records, on the other hand, wants to be able to rely on them; he does not want to make any more inquiries outside the record than absolutely necessary. Even in the majority jurisdictions the claim must be described and defined with such accuracy as to make identification reasonably possible and certain.[94] And, of course, in all jurisdictions the mortgage will operate as security for only those obligations which are covered by the agreement of the parties and identified by it. The problem of extending it to secure other existing or subsequently created debts or claims is dealt with in connection with mortgages to secure future advances, consolidation of mortgages, and the rule requiring, as a condition to redemption, the repayment of unsecured debts owing to the mortgagee.[95]

Where there is an untruthful statement of the amount it can be urged that actual deception, or the danger of it, should invalidate the mortgage as to creditors and some other third parties. If the amount is overstated there is, in effect, a concealment of an asset to the extent of the overage; and an understatement may be misleading as to the debtor's affluence. In the absence of an actual intent to deceive, however, such mortgages are not void.[96] One reason for this is that the original amount stated, even though correct at the time, is seldom the amount actually due on the mortgage. Usually there will have been payments on the principal or accumulations of unpaid interest, instalments,

90. Where the amount of the debt is stated falsely it can be argued that the parol evidence rule prevents the true sum being shown even between the parties. Where the amount is omitted or stated generally or by reference to other data there is no contradiction of the mortgage statement. In this case, however, the extrinsic evidence does contradict the parties' written statement of the amount embodied in the mortgage. That the cases do not forbid this contradiction is another illustration of the paramount importance of the debt and the accessory character of the mortgage.

91. "The incumbrance on the property must be so defined, as to prevent the substitution of everything which a fraudulent grantor may devise to shield himself from the demands of his creditors." Pettibone v. Griswold, 1822, 4 Conn. 158, 10 Am.Dec. 106.

92. Equitable Bldg. & Loan Ass'n v. King, 1904, 48 Fla. 252, 37 So. 181; Hurd v. Robinson, 1860, 11 Ohio St. 232; Goff v. Price, 1896, 42 W.Va. 384, 26 S.E. 287. See Robinson v. Williams, 1860, 22 N.Y. 380. See also 1943, 145 A.L.R. 375.

93. Pearce v. Hall, 1876, 75 Ky. (12 Bush) 209; Hart v. Chalker, 1840, 14 Conn. 77; Bullock v. Battenhousen, 1883, 108 Ill. 28. As to the description of an unliquidated debt, see Stoughton v. Pasco, 1825, 5 Conn. 442, 13 Am.Dec. 72. A statute may require that the exact amount of the debt be stated. Linton v. Purdon, 1845, 9 Rob. (La.) 482. See German Civil Code, Wang, § 1115.

94. See Harper v. Edwards, 1894, 115 N.C. 246, 20 S.E. 392. See also 1943, 145 A.L.R. 385; 1896, 49 Am.St.Rep. 207. See additionally Smith v. Haertel, 1952, 125 Colo. 348, 353, 244 P.2d 377, 379.

95. See §§ 113–124, infra.

96. Nazro v. Ware, 1888, 38 Minn. 443, 38 N.W. 359. See Shirras v. Caig, 1812, 11 U.S. (7 Cranch) 34, 3 L.Ed. 260; Burnett v. Wright, 1892, 135 N.Y. 543, 32 N.E. 253. Cf., contra, Stearns v. Porter, 1878, 46 Conn. 313. See also Thompson, What Description of the Debt is Sufficient in a Recorded Mortgage, 1897, 44 Cent.L.J. 490; Redfield, The Necessity of Describing the Security upon the Registry, 1862, 2 Am.L.Reg.,N.S., 1.

If the debt is overstated with the intention of defrauding the mortgagor's creditors, the transaction will not be sustained. Holt v. Creamer, 1881, 34 N.J.Eq. 181. See Tully v. Harloe, 1868, 35 Cal. 302, 95 Am.Dec. 102.

or taxes; and third parties, whether creditors or subsequent purchasers or encumbrancers would be unjustified in relying on the original statement.[97] Although this is true and although it is customary for purchasers from the mortgagor and subsequent encumbrancers to ascertain the exact amount of the prior mortgage, there seems little reason why they should not be entitled to depend on the expressly stated amount as the correct original indebtedness if there has been actual reliance and if an alteration would be disadvantageous to them. Ordinarily, of course, it will not harm purchasers or subsequent mortgagees to cut down the amount of an overstatement to the actual debt.[98] General creditors, however, may have been harmed through inactivity by them [99] caused by the concealed value of the redemption interest; and the extent of this injury may be difficult to measure and not necessarily cured by revelation of the truth. The problem of an overstatement which is intended to cover future advances involves much the same considerations but, because of certain differences, will be mentioned again later.[1] Where the amount is understated it cannot, of course, be enforced beyond the stated sum as against subsequent purchasers and encumbrancers, and, presumably, any creditors who actually rely on the incorrect amount.[2]

The date of maturity is of importance to transferees or creditors of both the mortgagor or mortgagee in order that they may know when a default may occur, and therefore it should be set forth in the mortgage. A failure to do so will not, however, ordinarily invalidate the mortgage but instead will be construed as merely making the debt payable on demand.[3]

Agreements, made subsequent to the original mortgage for the extension of the mortgage to claims not included in the original agreement, if for consideration, are enforcible between the parties provided Statutes of Frauds requirements are met.[4] The effect of the agreement is to create an equitable mortgage and its validity against the claims of third parties is no different than that of other equitable mortgages.[5]

The functional purpose of the mortgage as security for an obligation which is normally expressed separately and customarily referred to by recitals in the mortgage as so operating leads to the rule that in case of conflict between statements in the mortgage and those in the separate instrument of indebtedness on any material item of the secured claim (amount, maturity, etc.) the mortgage recital must give way.[6]

---

97. See Bell v. Fleming's Ex'rs, 1858, 12 N.J.Eq. 13, 18, affirmed 12 N.J.Eq. 490.

98. See Chapter 9, infra, for the problem which arises when the mortgage debt has been recited as being a certain amount "subject to" which the subsequent transferee from the mortgagor takes.

99. "He [the creditor] finds an encumbrance on record for as much as the debtor's property is worth, and thinks it useless to take legal means to secure his debt; whereas, if the mortgage had truly expressed the debt actually due, the creditor might have secured his debt." Griffin v. New Jersey Oil Co., 1855, 11 N.J.Eq. 49, 53.

1. See § 116, infra.

2. Gilchrist v. Gough, 1878, 63 Ind. 576, 30 Am.Rep. 250; Burriss v. Owen, 1907, 76 S.C. 481, 57 S.E. 542. Look at Johns v. Church, 1832, 29 Mass. (12 Pick.)

557, 23 Am.Dec. 651 (personal property, actual amount enforcible against creditors).

3. Green v. Richards, 1872, 23 N.J.Eq. 32, affirmed 23 N.J.Eq. 536; Cavanna v. Brooks, 1925, 97 N.J. Eq. 329, 127 A. 247, 37 A.L.R. 361; Ansorge v. Kane, 1927, 244 N.Y. 395, 155 N.E. 683, reargument denied 245 N.Y. 530, 157 N.E. 845; N. E. D. Holding Co. v. McKinley, 1927, 246 N.Y. 40, 157 N.E. 923, semble, accord. See 1927, 12 Cornell L.Q. 367.

On the question whether the omission of the maturity date makes the mortgage unenforceable under the Statute of Frauds, see § 68, supra.

4. Riess v. Old Kent Bank, 1931, 253 Mich. 557, 235 N.W. 252, 76 A.L.R. 571. See, 1932, 76 A.L.R. 574; 3 Tiffany, Real Prop., 2d Ed., p. 2417. See also Chapter 3, supra.

5. See Chapter 2, supra, and Chapter 7, infra.

6. E. g., Adler v. Berkowitz, 1930, 254 N.Y. 433, 173 N.E. 574. See note, 1931, 31 Col.L.Rev. 328; Chapter 13, infra.

B. DEFENSES TO OBLIGATION

IN GENERAL

109. **To the extent that the secured obligation is invalid or subject to a defense, so too, in general, is the mortgage securing it.**

Although the question of whether a personal obligation is a vital ingredient in the existence of a mortgage is an engaging one which has been explored in previous sections, as a practical matter it recedes in importance because of the fact that virtually all mortgages are given with the intention that they be security for a personal duty and not with any intent of creating only a real obligation. When we have this usual situation the dependence of the mortgage upon the debt as an accessory to it is strikingly illustrated in cases where the obligation is affected by illegality, usury, fraud, mistake, duress, and failure of consideration. The bar of the statute of limitations or a discharge in bankruptcy are excluded from consideration at this juncture both because it is the commonly accepted view that they only affect the remedy on the debt and do not go to the substance, and also because they have to do with subsequent events ending the rights or remedies of the parties and therefore can be more conveniently dealt with in connection with the discharge of the mortgage.[7]

In considering the effect of these various factors no attempt will be made to examine the law as to them generally, a matter belonging elsewhere and plainly outside the scope of this work. Nor, since we are here concerned with the mortgage obligation and how it affects the mortgage, will we stop to examine the play of those same factors when they concern the mortgage alone.[8] With our subject so described we may lay it down as a general proposition that to the same ex-

tent that the secured obligation is invalid or subject to a defense, so too is the mortgage securing it. In general the rights and remedies of the parties, both defensive and offensive, as to the obligation will determine those as to the mortgage. This flows logically from the conception of the mortgage as security only. However, since the mortgage has given to the creditor either an actual or an apparent interest in the debtor's property which he may wish to get back or have removed as a cloud on his title, there is an element in the mortgage phase of the transaction which has led some courts to arrive at questionable results at variance with the treatment accorded the debt itself. Consequently it is worth while making a brief examination of these various causes of invalidity or defense.

(1) ILLEGALITY

110. **Illegality that renders the obligation unenforceable also makes the mortgage unenforceable. Some title states erroneously let the mortgagee bring an action of ejectment.**

If the obligation is partly legal and divisible, the mortgage is usually valid to secure the legal part.

A mortgage given to secure a promise unenforceable because of illegality cannot be enforced by the mortgagee by court action either at law or in equity.[9] Such, at least, is the general rule. Instances in which the doctrine has been invoked include promises to suppress a criminal prosecution,[10] transactions whose purpose was to defraud cred-

---

7. See Chapter 11, infra.

8. The effect upon the negotiability of the obligation of provisions in the mortgage is considered in Chapter 8, infra.

9. It is well settled that all defenses (except the statute of limitations) that can be made against the notes, can also be made against the mortgage. Atwood v. Fiske, 1869, 101 Mass. 363, 100 Am.Dec. 124.

10. Small v. Williams, 1891, 87 Ga. 681, 13 S.E. 589; Peed v. McKee, 1876, 42 Iowa 689, 20 Am.Rep. 631; Owens v. Green, 1898, 103 Ky. 342, 45 S.W. 84, 20 Ky.Law Rep. 44; Atwood v. Fiske, 1869, 101 Mass. 363, 100 Am.Dec. 124; Pearce v. Wilson, 1885, 111 Pa. 14, 2 A. 99, 56 Am.Rep. 243, 17 W.N.C. 67, 43 L.I. 216, 33 P.L.J. 290. See Williston, Contracts, Rev. ed. 1936, §§ 1612–1614.

itors,[11] to pay the price of future illicit cohabitation,[12] or a note given in payment of a fine or penalty.[13] Other examples are mortgages to secure debts for liquor sold in violation of the law,[14] or gambling debts,[15] promissory notes illegally issued by a bank in violation of a statute,[16] and a loan of confederate money.[17]

Of course it may be that the illegality is only on the part of the mortgagor and the mortgagee may be completely free of it, in which case he will not be barred.[18] Nor will the assignee of a valid debt secured by a mortgage be prevented from enforcing it because the consideration for the assignment was illegal.[19] However, in the general run of cases both parties are tarred with the illegality and the position the courts take is that nothing will be done to give either party affirmative relief and, as a corollary, that either can set up the illegality as a defense to a court action against him. The purpose of the law is to leave the parties where it finds them.[20] This means, in the mortgage case, that although the mortgagor can defeat a foreclosure action[21] he cannot get the mortgage cancelled and it remains a cloud upon his title.[22] There would not be any objection or difficulty in applying this general principle and practice to the case of a mortgage were it not for the fact that here is an instance where ideas about the nature of the mortgagee's security interest as "title" have caused trouble. In "title" states the mortgagee cannot get the aid of equity to foreclose any more than he can in a lien state.[23] But in some of these "title" states the courts have been unduly influenced (1) by the general doctrine that a conveyance, no matter how directly connected with and founded upon illegality, nevertheless does give the grantee title,[24] and (2) by the decisions according to the mortgagee, as incident to the "title," the right to possession.[25]

This has led them to the view that as far as the mortgagee is concerned the transaction is an executed rather than an executory one, and therefore despite the illegality the mortgagee can maintain an action of ejectment. So, also, if the mortgagee enters and retains possession until the right of redemption is ended, a method of foreclosure permitted in Massachusetts, he can hold his title.[26] Such results ignore the reality of the fact that regardless of whether the mortgagee gets title or lien his interest in the prop-

11. Weeden v. Hawes, 1833, 10 Conn. 50; Scott v. Magloughlin, 1890, 133 Ill. 33, 24 N.E. 1030; McQuade v. Rosecrans, 1881, 36 Ohio St. 442; Norris v. Norris' Adm'rs, 1840, 39 Ky. (9 Dana) 317.

12. W——— v. B———, 1863, 32 Beav. 574.

13. Kelley v. Tillamook Co., 1923, 107 Or. 607, 215 P. 176, 29 A.L.R. 4. See 1923, 29 A.L.R. 7.

14. Brigham v. Potter, 1860, 80 Mass. (14 Gray) 522; McLaughlin v. Cosgrove, 1868, 99 Mass. 4; Ressegieu v. Van Waganan, 1889, 77 Iowa 351, 42 N.W. 318.

15. Ellsworth v. Mitchell, 1850, 31 Me. 247; Barnard v. Backhaus, 1881, 52 Wis. 593, 6 N.W. 252; Luetchford v. Lord, 1892, 132 N.Y. 465, 30 N.E. 859; Hudson v. Moon, 1913, 42 Utah 377, 130 P. 774.

16. Leavitt v. Palmer, 1849, 3 N.Y. 19, 51 Am.Dec. 333.

17. Stillman v. Looney, 1866, 43 Tenn. (3 Cold.) 20; Scheible v. Bacho, 1868, 41 Ala. 423, contra.

18. Krake v. Alexander, 1889, 86 Va. 206, 9 S.E. 991; Lefebvre v. Dutruit, 1881, 51 Wis. 326, 8 N.W. 149, 37 Am.Rep. 833.

19. Berridge v. Gaylord, 1920, 108 Kan. 105, 193 P. 1066, 21 A.L.R. 393 (assignment to evade income tax); Reed v. Bond, 1893, 96 Mich. 134, 55 N.W. 619 (assignment in discharge of gambling debt).

20. Union Exch. Bank v. Joseph, 1921, 231 N.Y. 250, 131 N.E. 905, 17 A.L.R. 323, per Cardozo, J.

21. Patterson v. Donner, 1874, 48 Cal. 369.

22. Albertson v. Laughlin, 1896, 173 Pa. 525, 529, 34 A. 216, 51 Am.St.Rep. 777.

23. W——— v. B———, 1863, 32 Beav. 574. But cf. Whaley v. Norton, 1687, 1 Vern. 483. Jones v. Dannenberg Co., 1900, 112 Ga. 426, 37 S.E. 729, 52 L.R.A. 271; McQuade v. Rosecrans, 1881, 36 Ohio St. 442; Atwood v. Fiske, 1869, 101 Mass. 363, 100 Am.Dec. 124.

24. Packman's Case, 1585, 6 Co.Rep. 18b. A statute may alter the rule and prevent title from passing. Southern Express Co. v. Duffey, 1873, 48 Ga. 358.

25. Raguet v. Roll, 1836, 7 Ohio 70; Williams v. Engelbrecht, 1881, 37 Ohio 383; Pearce v. Wilson, 1885, 111 Pa. 14, 2 A. 99, 56 Am.Rep. 243, contra.

26. McLaughlin v. Cosgrove, 1868, 99 Mass. 4.

erty is only security for the payment of the debt and the transaction is no more executed in one type of state than in another. To permit the mortgagee to go forward in enforcing any of the incidents of his security is inconsistent with the general hands-off policy of the law in illegality cases. In substance it gives him aid in satisfying his illegal contract claim. The predicament in which a jurisdiction finds itself when it permits ejectment by the mortgagee of an illegal debt led one court to try to escape from it by permitting the mortgagor to redeem the property by paying the illegal debt![27] Having aided the mortgagee to get the land by entertaining the ejectment suit, the court could hardly set that aside in effect by permitting the mortgagor to regain the land and to stand discharged of the condition because of its illegality, nor to give the land to the mortgagee outright free of the equity of redemption.[28] A better solution, and one in accord with the reality of the fact that the land is security only and that the same result should be reached regardless of whether the jurisdiction is a title or lien state, would be to permit the mortgagor to defeat all attempts by the mortgagee to realize upon his security or to better his position in respect to it by interposing in every case the defense that the interest held by the mortgagee in the land was security for an illegal obligation and therefore no incident of it could be enforced affirmatively. At least one old English case, and a leading one, went so far as to order cancellation of the mortgage instrument as the best way of effectuating the policy of the law against illegality in the circumstances before it, coming to the conclusion that that would prevent the agreement from being carried out.[29]

If the mortgage secures the payment of an obligation part of which is illegal and part legal, if the good can be separated from the bad, the mortgage is usually permitted to stand as security for the valid part.[30] Since the legal items are enforceable by actions at law it would seem proper to hold the mortgage enforceable to the extent that it secures the legal portions. Where the mortgage debt is represented by a single note although the amount of the note is made up of several items, some legal and others illegal, there are a few decisions holding that the mortgage is totally invalid.[31] While the single note may be some evidence that the total amount constitutes an indivisible obligation, it is more likely that the courts are influenced by the notion that the mortgage secures the note rather than the debt or debts behind it, an idea normally rejected and, it is believed, quite unsound.[32] The test should be whether the separate items going into the whole could be recovered by separate action.[33] Of course, if the debt is not actually divisible into separate and independent items, illegality as to any part will vitiate the whole.[34] So, too, where there are two elements of considerations for the payment of a single sum, one legal and the other illegal, the courts will not segregate the evil consideration from the good but will strike down the whole agreement. Such is the case where a mortgage is given to secure a promise to repay em-

---

27. Cowles v. Raguet, 1846, 14 Ohio 38.

28. Walsh, Mortgages, 83, n. 83.

29. W——— v. B———, 1863, 32 Beav. 574. But cf. Whaley v. Norton, 1687, 1 Vern. 483. See also Breathwit v. Rogers, 1878, 32 Ark. 758.

30. See Feldman v. Gamble, 1875, 26 N.J.Eq. 494; Shaw v. Carpenter, 1881, 54 Vt. 155, 41 Am.Rep. 837; Judd v. Flint, 1855, 70 Mass. (4 Gray) 557; Morris v. Way, 1847, 16 Ohio 469; Sheehy v. Sheehy, L.R., 1901, 1 Ir. 239.

31. Brigham v. Potter, 1859, 80 Mass. (14 Gray) 522; Bick v. Seal, 1892, 45 Mo.App. 475.

32. Barbour, History of Contract in Early English Equity, 4 Oxford Studies 89. See § 105, supra.

33. Shaw v. Carpenter, 1881, 54 Vt. 155, 41 Am.Rep. 837.

34. In McQuade v. Rosecrans, 1880, 36 Ohio St. 442, there was only one real debt but the notes were given for double the amount owed for the purpose of defrauding creditors. The court held the entire transaction illegal.

bezzled money in return for a promise not to prosecute.[35] A mortgage securing the promise to repair the wrong done would be good, standing by itself. But here the deal is made to depend also on the illegal promise not to prosecute. This links the illegal aspect of the consideration inextricably with the whole and the bargain fails *in toto*.

(2) USURY

111. If the debt secured by the mortgage is usurious, the mortgage is either unenforceable or enforceable only to the amount of the debt plus lawful interest, depending on the statutes of the jurisdiction. To get the mortgage cancelled the mortgagor must pay the debt plus legal interest.

Usury [36] is one form of illegality but it differs from other kinds in that it invariably depends upon statute and, what is more important, the parties are not regarded as *in pari delicto*. The consequence is that the policy of refusing to grant affirmative relief to either party is not present. Most states have usury laws [37] but their provisions and their construction varies considerably. It would be impossible to make any extended examination of the many problems raised under these acts as to what constitutes usury [38] and the detailed consequences of such bargains. Some generalizations can be made, however, and the effect upon a mortgage to secure a usurious agreement can be examined. Here, of course, as elsewhere, the mort-

gage is an incident of the debt and stands or falls with it.[39]

Usury statutes are of two kinds: one provides that the entire usurious obligation is void so that the creditor cannot recover any part of it; [40] the other forfeits all interest in excess of the legal rate. This latter type follows the old English statutes on usury. Under the first type of statute, since the debt itself is void and there can be no recovery by the creditor upon either an express contract or quasi-contractual duty to pay any part of the sum loaned or interest on it, neither can there be any enforcement whatsoever by the creditor of the mortgage given to secure it.[41] However, if the mortgagor comes into equity asking affirmative relief to have the mortgage cancelled, the weight of authority requires him to pay the amount of the principal and interest at the legal rate as a condition to granting relief.[42] In a few states relief is granted on condition that the mortgagor pay or tender the principal only without any interest.[43] In New York, the original usury statute making the obligation void was held to have the effect just described, i. e., that the mortgagee could have no remedy to foreclose but that the mortgagor must pay debt and legal interest as a condition of cancellation.[44] This general rule was later altered by an unusually severe statute which pro-

---

35. See cases cited in note 10, supra.

36. See Ryan, Usury and Usury Laws; Collins, Evasion and Avoidance of Usury Laws, 1941, 8 Law and Contemp.Problems, 54, 386.

37. See Ryan, op. cit. supra note 36, pp. 28–31. Only five were listed as being without some sort of usury statute in 1921.

38. Usury strikes only at an excessive charge for the use of money. Most of the problems involving the question of whether a particular payment constitutes usury boil down to whether it was for the use of the money no matter how it might be concealed as compensation for other things or whether it actually was a legitimate recompense for something other than the use of the borrowed money.

39. Weaver Hardware Co. v. Solomovitz, 1923, 253 N.Y. 321, 139 N.E. 353, reargument denied 236 N.Y. 591, 142 N.E. 296.

40. Typical of this type is N.Y.Gen.Business Law, §§ 373, 377. See Williams v. Fitzhugh, 1868, 37 N.Y. 444. See also discussing similar statutes, Scott v. Austin, 1887, 36 Minn. 460, 32 N.W. 89, reversed 36 Minn. 460, 32 N.W. 864; Draper v. Emerson, 1867, 22 Wis. 147.

41. See cases in next note.

42. Moncrief v. Palmer, 1921, 44 R.I. 37, 114 A. 181, 17 A.L.R. 119. See note, 1921, 17 A.L.R. 123 for a collection of cases.

43. E. g., Morrison v. Miller, 1877, 46 Iowa 84; First Nat. Bank of Abbeville v. Clark, 1909, 161 Ala. 497, 49 So. 807. For additional cases, see 1921, 17 A.L.R. 126.

44. Fanning v. Dunham, N.Y.1821, 5 Johns.Ch. 122, 9 Am.Dec. 283.

vided that no court should require or compel the payment or deposit of the principal sum or interest, or any portion thereof, as a condition of granting relief to the borrower in any case of usurious loans forbidden, etc.[45] The statute has been construed strictly by stressing the fact that it applies only to the "borrower" [46] and, consequently that it does not apply to the original mortgagor's heir or devisee,[47] grantee,[48] trustee in bankruptcy,[49] or to the borrower himself if he later purchases the property from the trustee in bankruptcy [50] and any of these have to pay the principal and legal rate of interest in order to get cancellation. It was held also that if a mortgage was given to secure several loans, of which some are usurious and others not, the mortgagor cannot have a cancellation without paying off the debts unaffected by usury and if the mortgagor refuses to do this, although the usurious notes will be ordered cancelled, the other notes will be left outstanding in the mortgagee with the mortgage securing them.[51]

In states that have the second type of statute the situation is fairly simple. The courts are influenced by the belief that there is a moral obligation on the debtor to pay his debts and that it is equitable to make him do so. They are further influenced by the theory that the lender incurs no penalty un-less he actually takes usury.[52] As a result they generally hold that the mortgagor can get the mortgage cancelled only on condition that he pay the debt together with interest at the legal rate. This was the rule in England under the old usury laws [53] and was followed again after 1900 when another statute forbidding usury was passed.[54] It is also the general rule in the United States.[55] The rule seems eminently sensible for to permit the mortgagor to defeat the foreclosure suit would still leave him under the necessity of bringing an action to have the mortgage cancelled, and in that action he would have to pay the debt and lawful interest.[56]

When the mortgagor attempts to use the statute as a defense in an action of foreclosure by the mortgagee, instead of it being a bar causing a dismissal of the action, it will merely result in cutting down the mortgagee's decree to the amount of the debt plus lawful interest, with any excess interest previously paid being deducted as a set-off.[57] And,

---

45. 19 McKinney, Consol.Laws, c. 25, § 377. In 1964 this section was repealed and substantially the same provision covered by 23a McKinney's Consol.Laws of New York General Obligations Law § 5–515.

46. See, similarly, cases in note 40, supra, especially Scott v. Austin, 1887, 36 Minn. 460, 32 N.W. 89, reversed 36 Minn. 460, 32 N.W. 864; Draper v. Emerson, 1867, 22 Wis. 147.

47. Buckingham v. Corning, 1883, 91 N.Y. 525. See also cases in note 40, supra.

48. Bissell v. Kellogg, 1875, 65 N.Y. 432.

49. Wheelock v. Lee, 1876, 64 N.Y. 242.

50. Schermerhorn v. Talman, 1856, 14 N.Y. 93.

51. Williams v. Fitzhugh, 1868, 37 N.Y. 444. This result should be compared with the cases involving the same problem where illegality of a different sort tainted some but not all of the various items making up the total sum secured. See preceding section.

52. See Welch v. Wadsworth, 1861, 30 Conn. 149, 79 Am.Dec. 239.

53. Berney v. Pitt, 1686, 2 Vern. 14; Taylor v. Bell, 1686, 2 Vern. 171. Ex parte Skip, 1752, 2 Ves.Sr. 489 (distinguishing between the rule in equity and in bankruptcy; in the latter no tender need be made). See also Scott v. Nesbit, 1788, 2 Bro.C.C. 641.

54. Lodge v. National Union Ins. Co., [1907] 1 Ch. 300. Cf. Chapman v. Michaelson, [1909] 1 Ch. 238.

55. Moncrief v. Palmer, 1921, 44 R.I. 37, 114 A. 181, 17 A.L.R. 119. For additional cases, see note, 1921, 17 A.L.R. 123.

56. The same rule applies to the mortgagor's request to enjoin the mortgagee from foreclosing by exercising his power of sale. C. D. Kenny Co. v. Hinton Hotel Co., 1935, 208 N.C. 295, 180 S.E. 697; Lindsay v. U. S. Savings & Loan Co., 1900, 127 Ala. 366, 28 So. 717, 51 L.R.A. 393; Powell v. Hopkins, 1872, 38 Md. 1.

57. Pond v. Causdell, 1872, 23 N.J.Eq. 181; Ward v. Sharp, 1843, 15 Vt. 115; Harbison v. Houghton, 1866, 41 Ill. 522. Cf. Holm v. First Nat. Bank of Clark, 1901, 15 S.D. 75, 87 N.W. 526, allowing the foreclosure action to be defeated. The crediting of excess interest goes back into the English cases. Bosanquett v. Dashwood, 1735, Cas.Temp.Talb. 38. Whether a grantee who takes subject to the mortgage debt or assumes it, the face amount being deducted from the purchase price, will be entitled to set up the defense of usury against the mortgagor is dealt with in Chapter 9, infra.

further, if the defense is not set up in the foreclosure action and the property has been sold under court decree, the defense is gone even if the purchaser on the foreclosure sale is the mortgagee.[58] The same would be true of a sale to purchaser without notice at a power of sale foreclosure.[59]

(3) FRAUD, DURESS, MISTAKE

112. Fraud, duress, or mistake constituting a defense to an action on the debt is also a defense to an action on the mortgage. To get cancellation, the mortgagor must do equity.

We have seen [60] the general rule that "in an action brought by a mortgagee against his mortgagor on a mortgage given to secure payment of a note, the defendant may show the same matters in defence * * * which he might show in defence of an action on the note" [61]. This applies to obligations obtained by fraud or duress or entered into by mistake just as in the case of obligations tainted by illegality or usury. In the illegality cases, however, we saw that there was an objection to giving affirmative relief to the mortgagor as well as the mortgagee, and in the usury cases there was the problem of differing statutory provisions and of statutory construction influenced by policy considerations.[62] In these present defences there is no

objection to affirmative relief and in general the law is to be found in court decisions. What that law is cannot be gone into here in any detail.[63] It will suffice for our purposes to point out a few elementary principles which govern when a mortgage secures a debt which admittedly was obtained by the mortgagee [64] through what is legally recognized as fraud, duress or mistake of the sort which will vitiate the contract. There is a fundamental difference, of course, and one which runs through all three defences, between a course of conduct which, because of the nature of the fraud, duress, or mistake involved, fails to create any legal obligation at all, and one which creates an obligation but an obligation which can be avoided or whose enforcement can be defeated.[65] However, all that this means in the law of mortgages securing such obligations, or purported obligations, is that the mortgage is good or bad to the same extent as is the secured obligation.

That the mortgagor can set up fraud, duress or mistake as to the obligation to prevent foreclosure of the mortgage is too clear to warrant much more than the statement.[66] Also, even though the debt secured is perfectly valid, fraud and duress in obtaining the giving of the mortgage to secure it will give

---

As to the right of a subsequent mortgagee to raise the question of usury in a prior mortgage transaction, see notes, 1939, 87 U. of Pa.L.Rev. 881; 1939, 24 Minn.L.Rev. 124.

58. Jones v. Meriwether, 1919, 203 Ala. 155, 82 So. 185, commented on, 1919, 19 Col.L.Rev. 419; Tyler v. Massachusetts Mut. Ins. Co., 1883, 108 Ill. 58. Whether a mortgagee who purchased at his own power of sale foreclosure would have to give up the property to the mortgagor on payment of the principal and legal rate of interest is not clear.

59. Tyler v. Massachusetts Mut. Ins. Co., 1883, 108 Ill. 58; Jackson v. Henry, N.Y.1813, 10 Johns. 185, 6 Am.Dec. 328; Weaver Hardware Co. v. Solomovitz, 1923, 235 N.Y. 321, 139 N.E. 353, reargument denied 236 N.Y. 591, 142 N.E. 296, purchaser of note without notice takes free of the defense of usury.

60. See § 109, supra.

61. Vinton v. King, 1862, 86 Mass. (4 Allen) 562, 564.

62. See two preceding sections.

63. For a general discussion of the law of the effect of fraud, duress, and mistake upon contractual obligations, see 5 Williston and Thompson, Contracts, rev. ed., Chapters XLV–XLVII.

64. If the mortgagee is not a party to the duress and has no knowledge of it the mortgagor has no defence to its enforcement. Marston v. Brittenham, 1875, 76 Ill. 611; Gardner v. Case, 1887, 111 Ind. 494, 13 N.E. 36; Robinson, Norton & Co. v. Randall, 1912, 147 Ky. 45, 143 S.W. 769.

65. See 5 Williston and Thompson, Contracts, rev. ed., §§ 1488 (fraud), 1624 and 1626 (duress), 1538 (mistake) for the distinction between transactions being void or voidable as the result of different sorts of fraud, duress, and mistake.

66. Vinton v. King, supra, note 61 (duress and fraud); Melendy v. Keen, 1878, 89 Ill. 395 (fraud); Fairchild v. McMahon, 1893, 139 N.Y. 290, 34 N.E. 779, 36 Am.St.Rep. 701 (fraud); Lomerson v. Johnston, 1890, 47 N.J.Eq. 312, 20 A. 675, 24 Am.St.Rep. 410 (fraud); First, etc. Bank of Nevada v. Bryan, 1883, 62 Iowa 42, 17 N.W. 165 (duress).

a defense to the enforcement of the mortgage.[67] On the other hand, if the mortgagor seeks the affirmative relief of cancellation, as a condition to obtaining it he must "restore the one against whom relief is sought, as far as possible to that which shall be a just situation as respects the rights he held antecedently to the transaction",[68] i. e., in the traditional language, he who seeks equity must do equity. However, where duress and fraud are involved it frequently happens that the debt and mortgage are obtained from the mortgagor without his having received anything in return. In such cases he may get cancellation or redemption without condition.[69]

C. FUTURE ADVANCES

IN GENERAL

113. A mortgage securing future obligations is a common business device. It is used to finance, among others, construction loans and bond issues. It has distinct advantages for both parties.

67. Winfield Nat. Bank v. Croco, 1891, 46 Kan. 620, 26 P. 939; First, etc., Bank of Nevada v. Bryan, 1883, 62 Iowa 42, 17 N.W. 165 (duress in obtaining both the note and mortgage from wife to pay husband's obligation); Lomerson v. Johnston, 1889, 44 N.J.Eq. 93, 13 A. 8; McCandless v. Engle, 1865, 51 Pa. 309.

68. Carlton v. Hulett, 1892, 49 Minn. 308, 320, 51 N.W. 1053.

69. Fisher v. Bishop, 1888, 108 N.Y. 25, 15 N.E. 331, 2 Am.St.Rep. 357, note and mortgage to secure debt of son obtained by undue influence and pressure on the part of a fiduciary; cancellation granted without payment of the debt secured; coveney v. Pattullo, 1902, 130 Mich. 275, 89 N.W. 968, cancellation without payment of note and mortgage for unconscionable fee of attorney for prisoner; Nourse v. Jennings, 1902, 180 Mass. 592, 62 N.E. 974, fraud and mistake in mortgage securing a forged note, redemption permitted without payment. Bond St. Bank v. Vaughn, 1931, 241 Ky. 524, 44 S.W.2d 527, seems to go beyond the preceding cases. In none of them was there any obligation owed by the mortgagor to the mortgagee, which ought to pay. In this case, however, the mortgagee by wrongfully threatening prosecution of the mortgagor for overdrawing his account with the mortgagee, overdrawing not being illegal, extorted a note and mortgage to pay for the overdrawn amount. The court annulled the note and mortgage without compelling payment of the debt it was given for and which, so far as appeared, was still owed by the mortgagor.

There are many transactions in which business desirability is heavily on the side of a mortgage securing not only a presently created or preexisting debt but future obligations as well.[70] Typical of such dealings are construction or improvement loans with instalments to be advanced as the work progresses; [71] mortgages by way of indemnity for prospective indorsements, guarantees, and accommodations of commercial paper to be

70. See Jones, Mortgages Securing Future Advances, 1930, 8 Tex.L.Rev. 371. See Stealey, The Mortgage for Future Advances in West Virginia, 1954, 56 W. Va.L.Rev. 107.

Some states accord statutory recognition to such mortgages. See, e. g., West's Ann.Cal.Civ.Code § 2884. The German Civil Code provides for them. See German Civ.Code, Wang, §§ 1113, 1163, 1190. In France, also, they are possible provided they are inscribed or recorded. French Civ.Code, Cachard, Rev.Ed., §§ 2132, 2148(4).

See also Note, Mortgages to Secure Future Advances, 1953, 81 N.C.L.Rev. 504; McSween, Mortgages to Secure Future Advances, 1954, 23 Tenn.L.Rev. 195–211; Stealey, The Mortgage for Future Advances in West Virginia, 1954, 56 W.Va.L.Rev. 107–119; Comment, The Extent of Debts Secured by a Mortgage in Arkansas, Winter, 1954–1955, 9 Ark.L.Rev. 45; Note, Advance Money Provisions, 1954, 29 N.Y. U.L.Rev. 733.

71. New Baltimore Loan & Savings Ass'n v. Tracey, 1923, 142 Md. 211, 120 A. 441; Whelan v. Exchange Trust Co., 1913, 214 Mass. 121, 100 N.E. 1095.

For recent cases and discussions of the use of the open-end mortgage in financing home building, repairs, and major household appliances, see Updike, Mortgages in 1953 Annual Survey of American Law, 1954, 29 N.Y.U.L.Rev. 829, 832; Updike, Mortgages, in 1954 Annual Survey of American Law, 1955, 30 N.Y.U.L.Rev. 805, 807; Blackburn, Mortgages to Secure Future Advances, 1956, 21 Mo.L. Rev. 209; Note, The Open-End Mortgage in Ohio, 1956, 25 U. of Cin.L.Rev. 82 (including discussion of priorities under existing case law and proposed legislation); Note, The Open-End Mortgage—Future Advances: A Survey, 1955, 5 DePaul L.Rev. 76; Updike, Mortgages, in 1956 Annual Survey of American Law, 1957, 32 N.Y.U.L.Rev. 789, 791; Note, Refinements in Additional Advance Financing: The "Open End" Mortgage, 1954, 38 Minn.L.Rev. 507; Note, Federal Tax Liens—Priority of Advances Under "Open End" Mortgages, 1956, 24 Geo.Wash.L. Rev. 725.

Vidalia Production Credit Ass'n v. Durrence, 1956, 94 Ga.App. 368, 94 S.E.2d 609, commented on in 1957, 14 Wash. & Lee L.Rev. 273, held that an "open end" clause in a mortgage to *E*, "his successors, heirs, executors, administrators and assigns" covered the independent debt claim of an assignee of *E* which he had acquired prior to the mortgage assignment, and that it took priority over intervening junior

issued by the mortgagor; [72] fluctuating current balances under lines of credit established with the mortgagee; [73] and an security for a bond issue, or a series of issues.[74] The advantages of such arrangements in which the borrower wants only a fraction of the loan to begin with but will need more in the future are numerous and substantial. The mortgagor saves interest on the surplus until ready to use it and escapes the burden of proper investment of it for the interim. He also avoids the expense and inconvenience of refinancing the mortgage so as to include the additional needed sum, or, in the alternative, of executing second and later mortgages for each new advance with attendant higher interest rates and financing charges. In the case of corporate bond issues it is especially advantageous to have all the bonds ranked as first mortgage bonds; they are more marketable and at lower interest rates; they participate in the added value of the security accretions and after-acquired property clauses; and they can be sold without expense, delay, and inconvenience in getting stockholders' approval, etc., involved in a new flotation. The mortgagee, on his part, minimizes the bother and costs of frequent financing (which even though not borne by him tend to discourage borrowing). Further, he has the ability, especially important in building loans, to pay out the money piecemeal as the value of the property is increased by construction rather than handing over the full amount of the loan at once, when the unimproved property is insufficient security, and relying on the honesty and continued

solvency of the mortgagor until the proceeds are applied to the agreed improvements.[75] And, although we shall see that this result is not always attained, he attempts to, and to some extent does, avoid the necessity of new title examinations before each advance.[76]

IN GENERAL—OBLIGATION SECURED

114. The obligation secured by a mortgage for future advances is a single promise, made when the transaction is first entered into, to repay all specified future advances. Making the advances is a condition precedent to performance of the promise; it is not necessary to its existence.

Simple and clear as the matter is, or should be, it is not always realized that the obligation secured by a mortgage for future advances is the legally binding, single promise of the mortgagor, made when the transaction is first entered into, to repay all of those advances within the scope of the agreement which repay all of those advances within the scope of the agreement which actually are made then and later. The obligation secured does not consist of a series of separate and independent promises by the mortgagor, each one requiring its own consideration, but of one promise covering the entire group of specified present and subsequent transactions. So, also, the conveyance of the interest in the property, made when the transaction is first entered into, is not a piecemeal affair but is intended to stand as security from the outset for the entire performance by the mortgagor of this one promise. And this is true irrespective of whether the nature of the interest transferred or cre-

---

liens even though acquired with knowledge of them and the advance was optional.

72. E. g., Ackerman v. Hunsicker, 1881, 85 N.Y. 43, 39 Am.Rep. 621; Robinson v. Williams, 1860, 22 N. Y. 380.

73. McDaniels v. Colvin, 1844, 16 Vt. 300, 42 Am.Dec. 512.

74. Reed's Appeal, 1888, 122 Pa. 565, 16 A. 100; Claflin v. South Carolina R. Co., C.C.S.C.1880, 8 F. 118, 4 Hughes 12; In re Sunflower State Refining Co., D.C.Kan.1911, 183 F. 834, 11 Col.L.Rev. 459. See infra § 123.

75. See Kuhn v. Southern Ohio Loan & Trust Co., 1919, 12 Ohio App. 184, 186, 29 O.C.A. 577, 579, affirmed 101 Ohio St. 34, 126 N.E. 820; Watkins, Maryland Mortgages for Future Advances, 1940, 4 Md.L.Rev. 111, 127, 127 n. 46. See Mortgages for Future Advances: The Need for Legislation in Wisconsin, 1965 Wis.L.Rev. 175, 176, for a summary of the advantages of the mortgage for future advances.

76. §§ 117–121. See Tapia v. Demartini, 1888, 77 Cal. 383, 19 P. 641, 11 Am.St.Rep. 288.

ated be regarded as the legal estate, a legal lien, or an equitable mortgage.

The mortgage for future advances is sometimes compared with mortgages of after-acquired property.[77] In these latter cases it is impossible for any security interest in the property to arise before the property is acquired by the mortgagor, and even after acquisition there can be no legal mortgage without the aid of a statute[78] until a proper instrument of transfer has been executed although, of course, there may be an equitable mortgage from the time the mortgagor gets it. If the mortgage, when it arises, is held to relate back to the date of the original agreement for any purpose, that relation back is by fiction or rule of law. And, of course, the validity of recordation before acquisition of the property is logically and practically difficult to uphold. In the mortgage to secure future advances, however, the property mortgaged is owned at the time and a present legal security interest is transferred by a validly executed and recordable conveyance. In a "title" theory state it would be difficult indeed to say that the conveyance was inoperative entirely or conveyed only a piecemeal title even if the erroneous view were taken that the obligation secured did not arise until the later advances were made and then arose piecemeal. And to draw a distinction in this respect today between "title" and "lien" states would seem so unjustifiable that even the most legalistically conceptual of courts should balk at doing so.[79]

Also, to get back on our main track again, just as in the case where a present lump sum loan repayable by instalments is split up into a number of notes having different maturity dates, there is a single promise to repay all future advances even though each advance is evidenced by a new note. Further, regardless of whether the advances are optional or obligatory, this one promise is binding as between the parties in practically all cases from the time it is made. If the advances are obligatory this would seem beyond argument.[80] If the mortgagee has promised to make the advances his promise is by itself, regardless of anything else, consideration for the mortgagor's promise to repay, and therefore the latter is binding at once although its performance, of course, is subject to the condition precedent of the advance being made by the mortgagee.[81] But even where the advances are non-obligatory, there is almost invariably present consideration in the form of a concurrent advance, forbearance to sue, or other conduct by the mortgagee sufficient to make the mortgagor's promise immediately binding. If, for consideration, M gives E an option to buy Blackacre, promising to convey if E takes up the option, and then M executes a mortgage of Whiteacre to E as security for the conditional promise to convey, there is at once a valid mortgage of Whiteacre with the exercise of the option a condition precedent to the *performance* of the obligation to convey but not to its existence. The same is true here. Even in the exceptional case where for lack of consideration the promise to repay all the advances, made when the mortgage is executed, is not binding, the very first advance made would be sufficient to sustain the creation of the entire obligation at that time. Since this is so, it would be an extremely rare case in which the obligatory or non-obligatory character of the advances would have any bearing on the

77. See Chapter 2, supra. See also Glenn, Mortgages, § 407.

78. E. g., West's Ann.Cal.Civ.Code § 2930.

79. Cf., however, the views of some courts as to the effect of a deed of conveyance by a mortgagee unaccompanied by an assignment of the debt. Chapter 8, infra.

80. "As the mortgagee is bound from the date of his agreement to make the advance, the obligation to repay him, from his point of view, arises at that time." Rowley, Obligatory and Non-Obligatory Advances in Ohio, 1927, 1 Cin.L.Rev. 351, 355.

81. In Brinkmeyer v. Browneller, 1876, 55 Ind. 487, the mortgage was held to be consideration for the promise to make advances. The reverse would be true as to the mortgagor's promise to repay the advances.

question of when the entire mortgage obligation arose or of its enforceability between the parties as of the date of its execution. In both kinds of advances repayment by the mortgagor is subject to the condition precedent that the mortgagee make the advances. And in both the promise to pay, if the condition is performed, is equally enforceable although in no case, of course, beyond the amount actually advanced. That all this is so has been obscured, perhaps, by the distinction drawn in the cases between the two sorts of advances in determining priority over other encumbrances,[82] and the explanation given in some of them that, in the optional advance cases, no mortgage can arise until the advance is made because before then there exists no debt to secure.[83] Of course in an occasional case where there is no consideration until the later advance is made this view would be correct. But in such a case the obligation and the mortgage logically should become effective together at that later time for all purposes and not be held to "relate back" so as to have priority from the date of the agreement, or recording, for any purpose.[84]

The soundness of the foregoing analysis is supported by a writer whose opinions are entitled to great respect. In criticism of the view that no mortgage arises except as an advance is made, he said "The fundamental error of this view * * * consists * * * in regarding the lien as arising at and from the *act of making the advance,* instead of from the previous *executory agreement* by which the land was bound as security for future advances."[85] Possibly a failure to have it in mind may account for not very illuminating discussion of the basis of the mortgage securing future advances in a leading text.[86]

One consequence of the foregoing general proposition is that the original mortgage agreement must provide for the future advances. If it does not, attempts to make it cover later advances will be treated as separate and distinct transactions subject to independent tests as to their validity and will not partake of the priority of the original mortgage.[87] The importance of this point will be elaborated later.[88]

---

82. See infra § 116.

83. Ladue v. Detroit & Milwaukee R. Co., 1865, 13 Mich. 380, 87 Am.Dec. 759, is probably the leading authority for this view. See also Ter-Hoven v. Kerns, 1845, 2 Pa. 96 ("Every future advancement is, in reality, a new debt * * *"); Walsh, Mortgages, 77 ("Mortgages given to secure advances to be made in the future create no lien either at law or in equity until such advances are made. As money is advanced under a mortgage of this kind of lien at law arises thereunder to the extent of the advance actually made. This lien relates back in equity to the original date of the mortgage * * *"); 4 Pomeroy, Eq.Juris, 594. Bank of Montgomery County's Appeal, 1860, 36 Pa. 170, 3 Grant 300; Alexandria Sav. Inst. v. Thomas, 1877, 70 Va. (29 Gratt.) 483 are to be the same effect. See also 1911, 11 Col.L.Rev. 459.

Similarly, Second Nat. Bank of Warren v. Boyle, 1951, 155 Ohio St. 482, 99 N.E.2d 474, noted, 1952, 13 U. of Pitt.L.Rev. 431, took the position that a mortgage for optional future advances was only an offer to provide security if and when such advances were made. Further, such advances must be made in reliance upon the mortgage.

84. But cf., infra § 121.

85. 4 Pomeroy, Eq.Juris., 595, n. 17. See also Tapia v. Demartini, 1888, 77 Cal. 383, 19 P. 641, 11 Am.St. Rep. 288. Accord: Sparrenberger v. National City Bank of Evansville, Indiana, C.A.Ind.1959, 272 F.2d 696.

86. See 3 Glenn, Mortgages, § 399.

87. "If the original bargain did not look to future advances, no subsequent advance can be a charge, unless the subsequent transaction is equivalent to the original charge." Ex parte Whitbread, 1812, 19 Vesey, Jun. 209.

See supra, note 75. See also § 124, infra.

The looseness permitted in the description of the particular future obligations secured, the rule that a stated flat total sum may be shown by oral evidence to be not presently owing or advanced but is to be loaned in the future, and the doctrine that a deed absolute may be established as a mortgage for future advances do not, of course, contradict this principle. They have to do with certainty of description and the evidence usable to establish the fact that the agreement does include the subsequent obligations. Pacific Fruit Exchange v. Duke, 1930, 103 Cal.App. 340, 284 P. 729; Adler v. Berkowitz, 1930, 254 N.Y. 433, 173 N.E. 574, noted, 1931, 31 Col. L.Rev. 328; 17 Va.L.Rev. 80; Kennedy v. Gibson, 1904, 68 Kan. 612, 7 P. 1044 (acceleration provision in the note was optional; in the mortgage it was absolute). Cf. Bell v. Engvolsen, 1911, 64 Wash. 33, 116 P. 456, 35 L.R.A.,N.S., 577. See 1913, 46 L.R.A., N.S., 477; 1943, 143 A.L.R. 587.

88. See infra § 124.

DISTINGUISHED FROM ESCROW LOAN

115. The test in distinguishing future advances from an escrow loan is whether the mortgagee has put it out of his power to withhold payments in the future.

In at least one jurisdiction there has been litigation to distinguish between an escrow loan and a mortgage to secure future advances. The problem arises because the full amount of the mortgage loan may be segregated and either placed in the hands of a third person under an escrow or trust agreement or retained by the mortgagee to be distributed in the future, in either case to the mortgagor or at his order in accordance with a definite agreement.[89] In such cases the fact that the mortgagor does not receive the money until later does not prevent the mortgage being considered as given for a present loan of the entire amount rather than for future advances. The test is whether the mortgagee has put it out of his power to withhold the payments in the future. Where the proceeds are put in the control of an independent third person the courts have no difficulty in finding this to be the case.[90] Even when retained by a financial institution-mortgagee and the loan is either credited on the books of the mortgagee or handed over to the mortgagor and then deposited by him in the lending institution subject to agreements as to withdrawals, it has been held to be a fully present loan.[91] That the same result would be reached in the case of an individual mortgagee seems improbable.[92]

89. See Watkins, Maryland Mortgages for Future Advances, 1940, 4 Md.L.Rev. 111, 127.

90. Neeb v. Atlantic Mill & Lumber Realty Co., 1939, 176 Md. 297, 5 A.2d 283; Manhattan Land Corp. v. New Baltimore Loan & Sav. Ass'n, 1921, 138 Md. 529, 114 A. 469; Western Nat. Bank v. Jenkins, 1917, 131 Md. 239, 252, 101 A. 671, 1 A.L.R. 1577; White Eagle Polish American Bldg. & Loan Ass'n v. Hart Miller Islands Co., 1934, 168 Md. 199, 204, 178 A. 214, 215.

91. Edelhoff v. Horner-Miller Straw-Goods Mfg. Co., 1898, 86 Md. 595, 39 A. 314; New Baltimore Loan & Savings Ass'n v. Tracey, 1923, 142 Md. 211, 120 A. 441; White Eagle Bldg. & Loan Ass'n v. Hart

FORMS OF MORTGAGE

116. The mortgage for future advances may assume one of two forms: A total sum stated as a present advance or the total amount left unstated but providing expressly for the advances. The former is a deceptive overstatement of the obligation but is generally upheld. The latter is held sufficiently definite not to invalidate the mortgage.

The mortgage for future advances may be cast into one or the other of two forms. (1) It may name a certain total sum as a present loan although in truth that amount, by extrinsic agreement which may be oral, includes advances to be made later on. Or (2) it may state that it secures advances to be made in the future but leave the amounts, and sometimes their character, indefinite. When the first course is followed there is a false representation of fact which is in itself, on well established rules, some evidence of actual fraud.[93] Disregarding this possible fraud, which ordinarily would be hard to establish, the transaction is like the overstated present obligation already mentioned[94] but with two differences. One is that there exists the possibility of increasing the indebtedness up to the amount stated as now owing and doing so in strict accordance with the parties' agreement. The other is that this overstatement ordinarily is deliberate. The second, at least, of these two

Miller Islands Co., Co.1934, 168 Md. 199, 204, 178 A. 214, 215.

92. See Groh v. Cohen, 1930, 158 Md. 638, 643, 149 A. 459, 461.

Similarly an elaborate and ingenious attempt to cast a mortgage for future advances under a construction loan into the form of an indemnity mortgage given by a straw man to the mortgagor was balked by the Maryland court. High Grade Brick Co. v. Amos, 1902, 95 Md. 571, 52 A. 582.

93. Tully v. Harloe, 1868, 35 Cal. 302, 95 Am.Dec. 102. See Glenn, Fraudulent Conveyances and References, rev. ed., § 299b. See also note 83, supra.

See also Mortgages for Future Advances: The Need for Legislation in Wisconsin, 1965 Wis.L.Rev. 175, 177; Stealey, The Mortgage for Future Advances in West Virginia, 1954, 56 W.Va.L.Rev. 107, 108, for a résumé of the forms the mortgage for future advances may take.

94. See supra § 108.

factors accentuates the objections urged to the overstatement simpliciter which were discussed previously.[95] One state has found the transaction thus expressed sufficiently objectionable to be constructively fraudulent against subsequent encumbrancers except for the amount of the present advance.[96] And other states have enacted legislation affecting the practice.[97] Nevertheless the mortgage is perfectly good not only between the parties [98] but, by the great weight of authority, as against creditors and subsequent encumbrancers.[99] However, even courts accepting the doctrine [1] occasionally object to it and vigorously inveigh against a dishonesty for which there seems scant justification in business necessity or expediency,

the dangers of injurious deception of at least some creditors, and the difficulties facing third parties who may want to deal with the mortgagor.[2] While recognizing that there is force in such strictures, most courts feel that the fixing of a definite outside limit gives sufficient certainty for third parties [3] and that the deception of creditors and encumbrancers can be overlooked because they do or should expect to reach the mortgaged property only after the expressed maximum claim is satisfied. When they find out the truth, i. e., that there is more of the property unencumbered than they thought, they are just that much better off than they expected to be and should have no complaint.[4] This reasoning is valid as to subsequent creditors and encumbrancers but it does not answer the point made in respect to existing creditors.[5] And, it may be remarked, after credit has been extended by the subsequent lender, he is thenceforward an existing creditor as to anything transpiring after that and his conduct from then on may be adversely influenced by the false statement lulling him into inactivity. He may fail to obtain security by legal process or, under the rules to be noted later, he may neglect to do acts which would end the priorities of the first mortgagee as to later advances. But apart from other considerations the business advantages of such a useful device outweigh any possible dangers and objections involved in its employment.

The practice of stating the total amount of present and future loans as a single amount already owing sometimes results in a different sort of problem. The mortgagee may sell the obligation and mortgage to a transferee who buys without knowledge that future advances were involved and that some or all of them had not been made. Whether the mortgagor has any defense against such

---

95. See supra § 108.

96. Matz v. Arick, 1904, 76 Conn. 388, 56 A. 630. See 1928, 2 Conn.B.Jour. 237.

97. See infra § 122.

98. See 4 Pomeroy, Eq.Juris., 5th ed., § 1197.

99. Shirras v. Caig, 11 U.S. (7 Cranch) 34, 3 L.Ed. 260; Griffin v. New Jersey Oil Co., 1855, 11 N.J.Eq. 49; Whelan v. Exchange Trust Co., 1913, 214 Mass. 121, 100 N.E. 1095; Witczinski v. Everman, 1876, 51 Miss. 841; Kramer v. Trustees of Farmers' & Mechanics' Bank of Steubenville, 1846, 15 Ohio 253; Savings & Loan Society v. Burnett, 1895, 106 Cal. 514, 39 P. 922 (trust deed); Tully v. Harloe, 1868, 35 Cal. 302, 95 Am.Dec. 102; Tapia v. Demartini, 1888, 77 Cal. 383, 19 P. 641, 11 Am.St.Rep. 288; Straeffer v. Rodman, 1911, 146 Ky. 1, 141 S.W. 742, Ann.Cas. 1913C, 549; Merchants' State Bank of Fargo v. Tufts, 1905, 14 N.D. 238, 103 N.W. 760, 116 Am.St. Rep. 682—accord. Cf. Youngs v. Wilson, 1863, 27 N.Y. 351; Winchell v. Coney, 1886, 54 Conn. 24, 5 A. 354—contra.

See also Thomson, Titles as Affected by Liens: Open-End Mortgages and Mortgages to Secure Future Advances, 1961, 28 Tenn.L.Rev. 354.

Even when the recorded debt was stated to be a presently owed fixed sum but actually was for a standing credit of that amount covering future advances, so that although payments were made which normally would diminish the amount of the mortgage these were offset by subsequent advances, the mortgage was upheld against a judgment lien. Wardman v. Iseman, 1930, 99 Pa.Super. 551, 79 U. of Pa.L.Rev. 647.

The German Civil Code permits a hypotheca with only the maximum amount stated. German Civ.Code, Wang, § 1190.

1. See e. g., Griffin v. New Jersey Oil Co., 1855, 11 N.J.Eq. 49.

2. Griffin v. New Jersey Oil Co., supra.

3. See Tapia v. Demartini, supra note 99, 386.

4. See 3 Glenn, Mortgages, § 397.

5. Supra § 108 note 99.

a transferee is dealt with in a subsequent chapter.[6]

Where the parties employ the second pattern, expressly stating that it is for future advances [7] but leaving the amount indefinite or unlimited, the only question is whether this uncertainty as to the ultimate debt should invalidate the mortgage. In answering this in the negative, the court in a leading case said, "If it were practicable, it might be desirable, that, in all cases, the true situation of real estate, and the extent of all incumbrances upon it, should be definite and certain, and appear on the record. The effect of this, however, would be to limit the beneficial effect of mortgage securities, and confine them to cases where the extent of the incumbrance could be ascertained and rendered certain at the time of executing the mortgage, and be made to appear in the condition; this would exclude all mortgages of indemnity, all mortgages to secure against official neglects and delinquencies, and all mortgages to secure future advances. All this class of mortgages must necessarily be to secure sums indefinite and uncertain at the time the mortgage is executed. Thus to limit the power of mortgaging is not called for by considerations of expediency, and is opposed to authority. * * * Nor can we consider it either void, or inoperative as against subsequent attaching creditors, purchasers, or mortgagees, inasmuch as all such have notice by the record of the incumbrance, and of what it is intended to secure; and, furthermore, it is in the power of such creditors, &c., by giving the requisite notice, to limit the amount of such further advances, so far as they are interested so to do." [8] Practically all authority is in accord with this statement,[9] only a few decisions [10] and some states by statute [11] require more definiteness.

---

6. See Chapter 9, infra.

7. The courts are liberal in construing the parties' agreement as including future advances. See McDaniels v. Colvin, 1844, 16 Vt. 300, 42 Am.Dec. 512; Citizens' Sav. Bank v. Kock, 1898, 117 Mich. 225, 75 N.W. 458; Huntington v. Kneeland, 1905, 102 App.Div. 284, 92 N.Y.S. 944, affirmed, 1907, 187 N.Y. 563, 80 N.E. 1111; Blackmar v. Sharp, 1901, 23 R. I. 412, 50 A. 852; Lamoille County Sav. Bank & Trust Co. v. Belden, 1916, 90 Vt. 535, 98 A. 1002. Cf. Hendricks v. Webster, C.C.A.Iowa, 1908, 159 F. 927, 87 C.C.A. 107; First Nat. Bank of Auburn v. Manser, 1908, 104 Me. 70, 71 A. 134. See also 1919, 1 A. L.R. 1586. Parol evidence may be used to show that future advances are included. Langerman v. Puritan Dining Room Co., 1913, 21 Cal.App. 637, 132 P. 617.

See Mortgages for Future Advances: The Need for Legislation in Wisconsin, 1965 Wis.L.Rev. 175, 179.

A mortgaged property to B to secure future advances. B made an advance, which A subsequently paid. Still later B made a further advance. Held, mortgage secured B's second advance to A. Courier-Journal Job-Printing Co. v. Schaefer-Meyer Brewing Co., C.C.A.Ky.1900, 101 F. 699, 41 C.C.A. 614. See Louisville Banking Co. v. Leonard, 1890, 90 Ky. 106, 13 S.W. 521. Cf. Moran v. Gardemeyer, 1889, 82 Cal. 96, 23 P. 6; Doyle v. White, 1846, 26 Me. 341, 45 Am.Dec. 110.

8. McDaniels v. Colvin, 1844, 16 Vt. 300, 42 Am.Dec. 512.

9. The pioneer English case of Gordon v. Graham, 1716, 7 Vin.Abr. 52, 2 Eq.Cas.Ab. 598, pl. 16, was a case of this sort and, although possibly overruled on one point, would still be followed in this respect. Among the American cases in accord are: Frank H. Buck Co. v. Buck, 1912, 162 Cal. 300, 122 P. 466; Robinson v. Williams, 1860, 22 N.Y. 380; Michigan Ins. Co. of Detroit v. Brown, 1863, 11 Mich. 265; Batten v. Jurist, 1932, 306 Pa. 64, 158 A. 557, 81 A.L.R. 625; James v. Lawson, 1927, 103 W.Va. 165, 136 S.E. 851. See D. M. Field, Security Transactions—Survey of Georgia Law, 1951–1952, 1952, 4 Mercer L.Rev. 153; Comment, The Extent of Debts Secured by a Mortgage in Arkansas, Winter 1954–1955, 9 Ark.L.Rev. 45, stating that a "general description of the debt will be sufficient so long as it will place a person examining the record upon inquiry and direct him to the proper source for more minute and particular information of the amount of the incumbrance." See also Thomson, Titles as Affected by Liens: Open-End Mortgages and Mortgages to Secure Future Advances, 1961, 28 Tenn.L. Rev. 354.

As to the validity of unlimited future advances, see 1932, 81 A.L.R. 631.

It is thoroughly settled that a deed absolute in form may be shown to be intended as a mortgage to secure future advances and is valid for that purpose. Anglo-Californian Bank v. Cerf, 1905, 147 Cal. 384, 81 P. 1077; Stitt v. Rat Portage Lumber Co., 1905, 96 Minn. 27, 104 N.W. 561; Merchants' State Bank of Fargo v. Tufts, 1905, 14 N.D. 238, 103 N.W. 760, 116 Am.St.Rep. 682; Rhines v. Baird, 1861, 41 Pa. 256; McClure v. Smith, 1902, 115 Ga. 709, 42 S.E. 53 (semble). Of course the deed absolute cases are grounded in considerations having nothing to do with future advances, Chapter 4, Subdivision A, supra, but the extension of the doctrine to such obligations is illustrative of the indulgence with which they are regarded.

10. Pettibone v. Griswold. 1822, 4 Conn. 158, 10 Am. Dec. 106; Matz v. Arick, note 96, supra; Balch v.

11. See Note 11 on page 185.

LIMITATIONS ON PRIORITIES: RATIONALES

117. **The validity and priority of mortgages for future advances is subject to restrictions. Several rationales for such limitations have been advanced.**

(1) Mechanical in nature, bases the limitations on the theory, in optional advance cases, that no mortgage arises until the advance is made. This explanation is unsound and encounters numerous difficulties.

We have seen that there are sufficiently persuasive reasons to uphold mortgages for future advances despite either false statements that the total amount is a present loan or vagueness as to what future obligations are covered.[12] However, most courts agree that there should be some limitation to their validity and priority over the claims of the mortgagor's creditors and other third parties. Several reasons are given for such restriction and the reasons tend to define its scope.[13]

Some courts rest the limitation on the ideas (1) that there can be no mortgage unless there is an obligation to secure, and (2) that in optional advance cases the existence of the obligation depends on the actual making of the advance—a belief that has been criticized earlier.[14] This view treats the mortgage for optional future advances as a series of separate mortgages arising at different times but all bound together by the original agreement which, when each advance is made, creates an equitable relation back[15] to the time of that original agreement unless an intervening claimant has cut it off by acts or a transaction which will make him prevail over this equity.

The nature of this mortgage regarded as arising when the advance is made is not entirely clear. Is it a legal one with an equitable relation back? Or does the equity arise at the time of the original agreement? If so, does it remain equitable until the making of the advance transforms it into a legal interest? Or does it, perhaps, attach to a legal mortgage which somehow springs into existence at that time? Thus, for example, one text[16] in successive sentences says: "As money is advanced * * * a lien at law arises * * *. This lien relates back in equity to the original date of the mortgage * * *. By contract the land is regarded as security for any and all such advances as of the date when the mortgage was given * * *" Later in the same section it is stated explicitly that both the legal and equitable mortgages arise at the time of the subsequent advance with an equitable relation back. No attempt is made to explain what effect the original conveyance in mortgage

Chaffee, 1900, 73 Conn. 318, 47 A. 327, 84 Am.St.Rep. 155; Youngs v. Wilson, 1857, 24 Barb. (N.Y.) 510, reversed 27 N.Y. 351. Chancellor Kent urged that not only the fact that a mortgage is for future advances but the limits of the advances or liabilities should appear on its face. 4 Kent, Comm. 176.

Where the language in the trust deed purported broadly to cover future advances as well as a specific antecedent debt, it was held not to cover future advances which bore no significant relation to the antecedent debts. National Bank of Eastern Ark. v. General Mills, Inc., C.A.Ark.1960, 283 F.2d 574.

11. See infra, § 118.

12. See supra § 116.

13. Occasionally attempts are made to explain the development and present basis of mortgages for future advances in terms of "legal title," "lien," or equitable theories of the nature of the security interest created. See 1911, 11 Col.L.Rev. 459; 3 Glenn, Mortgages, § 399. Whatever merit there may be in such efforts, it is difficult to discern any, they shed little light on the problem considered here.

One writer argues vigorously that "a duly recorded mortgage or deed of trust for future advances, optional or not, which states with sufficient clarity the amount and character of future advances which it is intended to secure, should take priority as to future advances over subsequent encumbrancers and purchasers, whatever the nature of the encumbrance and regardless of actual notice or knowledge of the subsequent lien." Stealey, The Mortgage fir Future Advances in West Virginia, 1954, 56 W.Va. L.Rev. 107, 117.

14. See supra § 114.

15. West's Ann.Cal.Civ.Code § 2884, seems to make the security effective from the date of the original agreement even in the unusual case where the obligation secured actually does not arise until later. See City of Santa Monica v. Los Angeles Co., 1911, 15 Cal.App. 710, 115 P. 945.

16. Walsh, Mortgages, § 407.

had or just how the later advance could create, *ipso facto,* a legal mortgage at that time. While it may be true that without a debt there can be no mortgage, the consequences of such a view would seem to be either that the conveyance was completely nugatory or else that it passed a legal interest other than that of a mortgage, something perfectly possible in a title state at least. If the first theory is adopted, it is rather curious to have a legal mortgage arise even in a lien theory state by the unilateral act of the mortgagee making a later advance of money without the execution by the mortgagor of a new mortgage instrument. Such a theory does even greater and unnecessary violence to traditional concepts in title states. It is more consistent with property and mortgage law ideas generally to say that not only the mortgage which arises subsequently but also its relation back are purely equitable. Further, if there is no interest, legal or equitable, until the later advance is made, it is somewhat extraordinary that recordation should have any effect in giving constructive notice of such possible subsequent mortgages to intervening encumbrancers.[17] As was previously pointed out, the foundation of this theory is at variance with the truth of the matter in regard to what obligation is secured and when it arises.[18]

But even if this basic error is ignored, the doctrine still presents difficulties. Taking literally the premise that the first mortgage is non-existent as to each advance until that advance is made, it would seem to follow logically that when any new third party lien attaches it is automatically prior to the subsequently arising series of new mortgages created by the later advances. As a consequence, each of these new mortgages arising by the subsequent advances would be junior to any intervening encumbrances and the problem would then become one of displacing the priority of that intervening encumbrance. To say that, by the mortgagee advancing the money later, the prior agreement would displace it by "equitable relation back" unless there was actual notice of the intervening encumbrance merely states a conclusion of law at variance with ordinary rules governing priorities without explaining why this should be true. Of course good reasons can be adduced for the result, but only by departing from this sort of mechanical reasoning and taking into account relative desirabilities of the possible solutions looked at as including factors other than fairness between the parties.

Even if the subsequently arising mortgage is looked upon as tied up to a present equity created by the original agreement for future advances, either at once or by "relation back" when the advance is made, there is still a departure from usual results. On general principles of equitable rights between parties, knowledge of a prior equitable claim by one subsequent in time will prevent displacement of the prior one.[19] This rule would seem to apply here if the equitable right of the first mortgagee is looked upon as existing by virtue of and from the time of the original agreement, or even if it merely "relates back" by force of it. If it does apply it would be logical to accept the conclusion that the mortgage to secure future advances has an absolute preference over in-

17. See also the statement of differences between agreements for the addition of after-acquired property and these cases of enlargement of the obligation secured, supra, § 114.

18. See supra § 114. The ability of subsequent encumbrancers to prevail, under certain circumstances, over advances made after they come into existence rests upon various considerations of desirability and policy and not because they intervene before a new mortgage arises by reason of the advance being made. This statement is, of course, at variance with the reasoning of the courts who advocate the rationale here considered and those who use it also to justify treating recordation of the subsequent mortgage as constructive notice to the prior mortgagee. There may be very good reasons why the results reached by those courts should be favored but this particular one seems fallacious. Further, its acceptance has the positive demerit of preventing the focusing of attention upon the real considerations upon which the solution should turn.

19. See infra Chapter 7.

tervening encumbrancers with notice.[20] The preference should extend even to optional advances made after receipt of actual notice of such encumbrancers. Yet where the priority of optional future advances is involved, most American courts hold that, in spite of knowledge by the later encumbrancer, the existing equity or "equitable relation-back" priority of advances made subsequent to this latter interest can be prevented through notice to the prior claimant.[21]

Again, if the first mortgage is treated either as non-existent until the advance is made or as having an equitable life of some sort from the date of the mortgage, trouble is encountered in another direction. It is simple law that if a subsequent legal interest is acquired for value and without notice of the prior equity it takes precedence as of the time it is acquired over the prior unknown equity and does so without regard to any notice of its existence by the holder of the prior equitable interest.[22] Yet in these optional advances cases, until the prior mortgagee is charged with notice of the later encumbrance, the advances made by him subsequent to its creation for value will continue to acquire priorities over it in spite of the fact that it was taken in ignorance of such potentialities and, consequently, also without knowledge of any ability to prevent the accrual and piling up of the priorities of these later advances.[23] Even where the ignorance is due to an intentional [24] overstatement of the present amount of the first mortgage so as to include in it optional future advances without mentioning this fact, it is true that a second encumbrancer should nevertheless only expect to get a lien good after the amount named in the first mortgage is taken out, and it is on this reasoning that such prior mortgages are justified as

---

20. This was the conclusion reached by Gordon v. Graham, 1716, 7 Vin.Abr. 52, 2 Eq.Cas.Abr. 598, pl. 16. The case has had some recognition in this country. See 4 Pomeroy, Eq.Juris., 5th ed., 596 n. 20; Witczinski v. Everman, 1876, 51 Miss. 841. But see 1961, 32 Miss.L.J. 325, citing North v. J. W. McClintock, Inc., 1950, 208 Miss. 289, 44 So.2d 412, as bringing Mississippi into the majority.

Gordon v. Graham, after standing as law for a century and a half, was overruled by Hopkinson v. Rolt, 1861, 9 H. of L. 514, 34 L.J.Ch. 468, 11 Eng.Rep. 829. Although in his decision in this case Lord Chancellor Campbell severely criticized the doctrine of Gordon v. Graham and expressly stated that it was unsound and overruled, he also pointed out that the case was distinguishable because actually there had been no notice to the first mortgagee of the attaching of the subsequent encumbrance. It may be noted further that the doctrine of that case was limited to second encumbrancers taking with notice of the first one. See 1862, 2 Am.L.Reg.N.S., 1, 17.

The reasoning of Lord Campbell in Hopkinson v. Rolt, supra, was that the first mortgagee, being secure as to advances made and having actual knowledge of the intervening encumbrance, could refuse additional advances unless he thought the property sufficient security for all claims. Also, though the effect would be to reduce the first mortgagee to the position of a third mortgagee as to the later advances, there was no objection to this. There is no fraud chargeable to the second mortgagee since the first mortgagee has the option, with knowledge of the situation, to make or refuse further advances. And the mortgagor is "entitled to do what he pleases with his own." Cavins v. Planters Bank & Trust Co., C.A.Miss.1951, 187 F.2d 906, is accord the North case, supra, note 20. But see Blackburn, Mortgages to Secure Future Advances, 1956, 21 Mo.L. Rev. 220 n. 5, listing Alabama, Florida and Texas as following the earlier Mississippi rule.

Since Hopkinson v. Rolt it has been English law that actual notice to the mortgagee will cut off his priority as to all optional advances thereafter made. See notes, 2 Am.L.Reg.,N.S., 1, 16 et seq. (1862); 77 Sol.J. 844, 877 (1933).

21. As to whether this notice must be actual or may be constructive through recordation and whether something more than notice is essential, see infra § 119.

22. Authority for this elementary proposition is scarcely necessary. But see Pomeroy, Eq.Juris., 4th Ed., §§ 737 et seq.; 2 Tiffany, Real Prop., 2d Ed., 2172.

23. Tapia v. Demartini, 1888, 77 Cal. 383, 19 P. 641, 11 Am.St.Rep. 288, is an example of this. Ignorance of the existence of the nature of the prior encumbrance may be due, as has been pointed out, supra § 116, to its concealment behind a false statement that it was for a present flat sum, or to language so vague and ambiguous that only resort to extrinsic evidence would reveal it as covering future advances, or even the extreme case of a deed absolute in which the fundamental fact of the mortgage itself is hidden as well as that it was for future advances.

24. Where the overstatement is negligent the argument is not so strong but, even so, since the fault is that of the first mortgagee the same results should ensue.

valid.[25] But, pursuing this same reasoning, it can be argued further that the later one should be no better off just because that full amount had not been advanced at the time he acquired his later security interest. Indeed, this "unjustified windfall" argument could support the conclusion that even after the second claimant discovers the true nature of the first mortgage and gives notice, or after the first mortgagee finds out about the existence of the second, the optional future advances could be continued with priority for them up to the full outside limit stated in the mortgage. This would seem to go even beyond the original English doctrine, for that was limited to cases where the junior encumbrancer knew that the prior mortgage was for future advances. And, of course, this is not permitted by the great weight of American authority.

On the other hand, an argument can be made that the priority of the future advances in cases where the fact of future advances is concealed by stating the mortgage debt is presently owing should be limited to those made prior to the existence of the later lien.[26] The argument is that, had the first mortgage revealed that part of it was for future advances, the second would have had the ability, and would have known that he had the ability, by giving notice, to prevent advances subsequent to his own having priority over it. Of course when he makes loans on this known status, his action is based upon the calculable and understood lesser risk he is running due to this ability at that time; and, consequently, in such a case, if he exercises his power he is not getting the unexpected windfall that accrues if he is permitted to obtain priority from the date of

his own mortgage where he thinks the entire amount of the first mortgage already has precedence. But even where it is by chance that he discovers the true nature of the transaction and notifies the prior mortgagee, or, apparently, if the prior mortgagee gets knowledge of a subsequent judgment lien, the second one prevails from the time of notice.[27] Clearly in this last case there is an "unexpected windfall" to the later lienor and, quite obviously, there is no reason why the courts should object to his getting it. Quite as obviously, where from the record he thinks the first mortgagee already has priority for the full amount stated, he probably will not exercise the power he has to get this windfall. Consequently it may be urged that this concealment by the first mortgagee is sufficiently reprehensible and unjustified that the later one should be given the greatest priority which might have been acquired by him had the truth been stated; or, to put it in another way, that the first mortgagee should not be able to get a chance for additional priority by masking the transaction. This would give the later lienor priority over all advances subsequent to his own.

Finally, if the resolution of the priorities of the claimants depends on weighing their individual equities, it is "very difficult to perceive on what equitable principle concerning priorities the rights of the second encumbrancer can at all depend upon the fact of the advances being either optional or obligatory. The equities of the second encumbrancer must arise from *his own position,* his own relations with the subject matter and with the prior parties; it does not seem to be in accordance with settled doctrines of equity that the parties to the prior mortgage should be able to alter the equities of the second encumbrancer by any independent agreement or arrangement between themselves to which he was not a party and of which he might be completely

---

25. See supra § 116.

26. In Griffin v. New Jersey Oil Co., 1855, 11 N.J. Eq. 49, although there was actual knowledge by the first mortgagee of the later judgment lien, the rule was stated without qualification that "a judgment or mortgage subsequent to a mortgage given to secure future advances, has priority over all advances made subsequent to the existence of such liens."

27. Griffin v. New Jersey Oil Co., supra, note 26.

ignorant." [28] And yet the distinction between obligatory and non-obligatory advances is all but universal in the American cases.[29]

LIMITATIONS ON PRIORITIES: RATIONALES

117a. Continued.

(2) Another theory rests the limitations upon a broad principle that a debtor's property should be available to his creditors as it stands when they acquire their liens and a prior mortgagee who has no duty to loan additional sums should not be able to prejudice them by increasing voluntarily the amount of his encumbrance.

(3) A third justifies it as necessary to prevent the device from being used as a vehicle of fraudulent or at least preferential arrangements.

(4) The soundest explanation for restricting the first mortgagee's priority lies in a desire to keep the mortgagor's title free for additional mortgages by others, or for sale.

A second explanation says the doctrine "should rest, on the broad and essential principle, that the property of a debtor must be subject, at all times, to appropriation for the security or payment of his debts, and a junior encumbrancer for an existing debt, and an attaching creditor, acquire a lien upon the property *as it then is;* and, as it is not *neces-*

sary to the rights of the prior mortgagee that he should advance further, he can not be permitted to prejudice their rights or destroy their lien knowingly, by adding voluntarily to his encumbrance." [30]

A third rationale is that it is necessary in order to prevent the device from being used as a vehicle of fraudulent or at least preferential arrangements.[31] The reality of such an abuse apparently was one factor leading to the original statute in Maryland placing restrictions upon such mortgages.[32] If this were the reason for the doctrine it would seem that the concealed and the extremely broad and highly indefinite mortgages for future advances should be invalidated completely rather than merely ending their priortiy as to later advances.[33]

The so-called "dragnet" clause is an example of the kind of provisions for future advances that courts find objectionable as oppressive if not a device for outright fraud on an impoverished mortgagor.[34] "What often happens in dragnet cases is that a mortgagee who holds a mortgage given to secure a small claim on an otherwise impoverished debtor's one valuable piece of property—which may be his homestead—buys up, no doubt at a large discount, other claims against the mortgagor and adds these to the mortgage debt. A variant is that the mortgagee, after his debt has been largely paid, will assign the mortgage to another creditor, who asserts that his previously unsecured claim is now, by virtue of the drag-

---

28. Pomeroy, Eq.Juris., 5th Ed., 595 n. 19. He could easily be completely ignorant of the obligatory character of the advances because it might be oral. See infra § 120 note 55.

29. See infra § 120.

Contrast the following argument: "Where the mortgagee is obligated to make certain definite future advances to the mortgagor, the question of notice, either actual or constructive, is generally held to be unimportant. Being bound to make the advances, he can not avoid doing so, and it cannot longer be urged that it is inequitable for him to advance after knowledge of the intervening claim. To say that he would have a defense to an action on his contract to advance would be to beg the question. It is clear that the only possible defense he could have would be that the mortgagor gave an encumbrance which takes priority over his own." Rowley, Obligatory and Non-Obligatory Advances in Ohio, 1927, 1 Cin.L.Rev. 348, 350.

See Kuhn v. Southern Ohio Loan & Trust Co., 1920, 101 Ohio St. 34, 126 N.E. 820.

30. Butler, J., dissenting, in Boswell v. Goodwin, 1862, 31 Conn. 74, 81 Am.Dec. 169. See Spader v. Lawler, 1848, 17 Ohio 371, 49 Am.Dec. 461.

31. Cole v. Albers & Runge, 1843, 1 Gill, Md., 412, 424. See 1929, 8 Tex.L.Rev. 371, 382; Watkins, Maryland Mortgages for Future Advances, 1940, 4 Md.L.Rev. 111, 112.

32. Md.Laws, 1825, ch. 50. See Albers v. Cole & Runge, supra, note 31.

33. This is the result of the Maryland legislation. See infra § 122.

34. See Gilmore, Security Interests in Personal Property, § 35.2 (1965).

net clause, the debt secured." [35] Courts, although reluctant to protect a mortgagor by invoking the doctrine of unconscionability have put judicial limitations on the unrestricted use of the clause by flexible interpretation. "No matter how all embracing the clause may be, the mortgagee who seeks to assert a claim under it will find himself restricted by a rule of reason and good faith." [36]

A fourth interpretation attributes the rule permitting the ending of the first mortgagee's priority as to later advances to a concern over the marketability of the mortgagor's title either for the purpose of additional mortgages by others or of sale.[37] This concern is compounded of the traditional solicitude of the courts for the mortgagor as a person who needs unusual protection,[38] the deepseated policy in favor of free alienability of land,[39] and, most of all, of a desire to make the device an effective one in securing the various economic and business advantages for which it was invented. This rationale, particularly the last ingredient, supplemented or modified by the preceding ones in some instances, provides the most satisfactory explanation of the decisions. It makes understandable the latitude allowed to these transactions in spite of features quite likely to work disadvantageously as to some creditors.[40] It permits treating the mortgage as

legal from the outset and as securing the promise made then to repay all advances because the restrictions are imposed for policy reasons and not technical or legalistic ones.[41] Because there is ample room for difference of opinion as to how much weight should be accorded various factors of policy, the operation of settled general rules of law, and arguments of relative merits of the opposing parties, the divergence of view in the cases as to just where the line should be drawn in ending priorities and the resort to artificial and conflicting explanations of the results is natural. And, finally, the distinction drawn by most American courts between obligatory and non-obligatory advances is made sensible. On this last matter, it is pointed out that if optional advances had an absolute preference, the mortgagor, although having no right to demand the contemplated additional demands, would be unable to obtain financing elsewhere for no one else would lend on a security which could be cut down by subsequent action by the first mortgagee. And, for like reason, the mortgagor would be unable to sell the property. It is true that even if the advances are obligatory he may find himself with a claim which is quite empty practically.[42] Nevertheless he does have a legal right to performance by the mortgagee and as great, or probably a far greater actual probability of getting it from his mortgagee than he would from another lender even though this other were given power to end the priorities of the first. So long as the mortgagor and his property constitute a good risk, the mortgagee will fulfill his contract; when the risk becomes

35. Gilmore, op. cit. supra, note 34, p. 918.

36. Ibid., 920.
In Akamine & Sons, Ltd. v. American Security Bank, 1968, 50 Hawaii 304, 440 P.2d 262, it was held that the statute authorizing mortgages to secure future advances permits a mortgage containing a dragnet clause to secure debts not specifically mentioned only if they relate to the same transaction or series of transactions described in the mortgage.

37. See 2 Tiffany, Real Prop., 2d Ed., § 637; Jones, Mortgages Securing Future Advances, 1929, 8 Tex. L.Rev. 371, 381.

38. See supra Chapters 1, 4.

39. The Rule Against Perpetuities and the judicial doctrine against restraints on alienation are other manifestations of this same policy.

40. See e. g., supra § 116.

41. As a matter of fact, since the limitations are set because of practical considerations, what the analytical situation is as to the nature of the security interest, whether it is legal or equitable and when it arises, ceases to have much importance.

42. Agreements to lend money are not specifically enforceable. Conklin v. People's Bldg. & Loan Ass'n, 1886, 41 N.J.Eq. 20, 2 A. 615. See also Blackburn, Mortgages to Secure Future Advances, 1956, 21 Mo.L.Rev. 209, 215 n. 26, listing Georgia and New Hampshire in addition to Maryland as having such statutes.

so bad that the mortgagee refuses to continue, the chance of successful financing elsewhere would be remote.

LIMITATIONS ON PRIORITIES: AUTHORITIES

118. Most courts uphold mortgages for future advances against later encumbrances to the extent of advances made before those encumbrances attached and before notice of the intervening encumbrance. A lien for optional advances will only prevail for advances made up to that time.

So far as the authorities are concerned, practically all courts uphold these mortgages, subject to the operation of recording laws,[43] against subsequent encumbrances to the extent of the advances made prior to the time the later encumbrances attached.[44] In addition, most courts hold that the lien for optional advances made after notice by the first mortgagee of an intervening encumbrance will be postponed to that encumbrance [45] although the former will prevail for all advances made up to that time.[46] One court went beyond this and stated that mere knowledge by the mortgagee of the existence of the subsequent interest was insufficient; that the later claimant must give notice and "an intimation, at least, that no further advances are to be made on the security of the mortgage as against them".[47] This view probably would not be followed today by the court uttering it.[48]

Payments made by a mortgagee to preserve the value of the security, even though he has no "legally binding" commitment to make them, have been held to take priority from the date of the mortgage. Such expenditures include taxes, assessments, insurance premiums, mechanics' liens, perhaps even essential repairs. It has been asserted both that such expenditures are "truly obligatory," [49] and also that being so closely re-

---

43. See infra Chapter 7.

See Note, Priority of the Real Estate Mortgage for Present and Optional Future Advances, 1968, 21 Okla.L.Rev. 79, covering the law generally including a résumé of rationales for divergent views. Oklahoma recognizes the validity of mortgages to secure optional future advances but has no statutory or decision authority on the question of limitation of the priority of optional future advances by notice of an intervening lien either through recording it or by actual notice. A federal case applying Oklahoma law held that actual notice of the subsequent encumbrancer's interest would prevent the mortgagee having priority as to advances made after such notice. Continental Supply Co. v. Marshall, D.C. Okl.1943, 52 F.Supp. 717, reversed on other grounds, C.C.A.Okl.1945, 152 F.2d 300 (10th Cir.), certiorari denied Federal Nat. Bank of Shawnee, Okl. v. Continental Supply Co., 1946, 327 U.S. 803, 66 S.Ct. 962, 90 L.Ed. 1028. See note 20 supra.

44. Thomas v. Blair, 1922, 208 Ala. 48, 93 So. 704; State Bank v. Tinker, 1930, 131 Kan. 525, 292 P. 748; note 1932, 81 A.L.R. 631; National Bank of Eastern Arkansas v. Blankenship, D.C.Ark.1959, 177 F.Supp. 667, affirmed, C.A.Ark.1960, 283 F.2d 574.

In 1958 the California Law Revision Commission recommended that the California law, which followed the majority of jurisdictions in respect to its rules governing mortgages of real property to secure future advances should not be revised by statute. It did recommend certain changes with respect to the similar law covering mortgages of personal property. See Stanton, Law Revision: 1959 Report, 1959, 34 J.S.B.Cal. 84, 92.

45. Boswell v. Goodwin, 1862, 31 Conn. 74, 81 Am. Dec. 169.

46. Ackerman v. Hunsicker, 1881, 85 N.Y. 46, 39 Am. R. 621, is probably the leading case for the proposition that optional advances subsequent to the later encumbrance but made before actual notice of it will have priority over it. See also Shirras v. Caig, 1812, 11 U.S. (7 Cranch) 34, 3 L.Ed. 260.

The majority view is in accord with this statement of the law. See 1 Jones, Mortgages, 8th Ed., § 452. See also notes, 1863, 3 Am.L.Reg.,N.S., 91; 1872, 11 Am.L.Reg.,N.S., 273; 1927, 1 U. of Cin.L.Rev. 348; 1920, 8 Calif.L.Rev. 260; 1930, 14 Minn.L.Rev. 695; Jones, Mortgages Securing Future Advances, 1930, 8 Tex.L.Rev. 371.

Where the first mortgagee had actual knowledge of the existence of a second mortgage which also was for optional future advances, the majority opinion in one case seemed to place them on a precise equality with each one required to make inquiry of the other concerning the state of the debts before making further advances. Boswell v. Goodwin, 1862, 31 Conn. 74, 81 Am.Dec. 169. There was a vigorous dissent in the case which was approved by a learned commentator. See Judge Redfield, 1863, 3 Am.L.Reg.,N.S., 93. In such a case the burden of watching the state of the dealings should be thrown upon the junior encumbrancer.

47. McDaniels v. Colvin, 1844, 16 Vt. 300, 42 Am.Dec. 512.

48. See 1862, 2 Am.L.Reg.,N.S., 1, 20.

49. See Blackburn, Mortgages to Secure Future Advances, 1956, 21 Mo.L.Rev. 209, 220–221 (1956).

lated to the security, are not really future advances at all.[50]

A "purchase-money security interest will take priority even over existing mortgages for advances already made; it will, a fortiori, take priority over the mortgagee's subsequent advances." [51] Whether recent legislation, whose draftsmen seem to have intended to put the "open end" and "package" mortgages on a secure legal footing [52] automatically determined all priority disputes in favor of the open-end mortgage remains to be seen.[53]

"If the holder of the intervening encumbrance is the United States, with a lien for taxes or a priority under § 3466 of the Revised Statutes, the future advance lender may as well give up hope. It has become too plain for argument that the federal lien or priority will, as a matter of federal law, prevail over all advances subsequently made. State law * * * yields to the federal rule * * *." [54]

PRIORITIES—NOTICE

119. The weight of authority requires actual notice by the junior encumbrancer.

By the weight of authority the notice necessary must be actual [55] but there is a

minority holding that constructive notice through recordation of the junior lien will postpone to it later optional advances by the first mortgagee.[56] The arguments for the majority view are that the operation of the recording laws are prospective, not retrospective, and therefore should constitute no notice to the first mortgagee who should not

50. See Gilmore, Security Interests in Personal Property 929 (1965).

51. Gilmore, op. cit. supra note 50, at p. 931. See § 213 infra.

52. Gilmore op. cit. supra note 50, p. 923.

53. Gilmore, op. cit. supra note 50, p. 931.

54. Gilmore, op. cit. supra note 50, p. 931. See § 221A. Of course this statement was made before the 1966 amendments of the Federal General Tax Lien. See § 221A, infra.

55. Shirras v. Caig, 1812, 11 U.S. (7 Cranch) 34, 3 L. Ed. 260; Tapia v. Demartini, 1888, 77 Cal. 383, 19 P. 641, 11 Am.St.Rep. 288; Schmidt v. Zahrndt, 1897, 148 Ind. 447, 47 N.E. 335; Everist v. Carter, 1926, 202 Iowa 498, 210 N.W. 559; Nelson's Heirs v. Boyce, 1832, 7 J.J.Marsh. (30 Ky.) 401; Ward v. Cooke, 1861, 17 N.J.Eq. 93; Williams v. Gilbert, 1883, 37 N.J.Eq. 84; Ackerman v. Hunsicker, 1881, 85 N.Y. 46, 39 Am.R. 21; National Bank of Eastern Arkansas v. Blankenship, E.D.Ark.1959, 177 F.Supp.

667, affirmed, C.A.1960, 283 F.2d 574. See Thomson, Titles as Affected by Liens: Open-End Mortgages or Mortgages to Secure Future Advances, 1961, 28 Tenn.L.Rev. 354. A federal tax lien filed against property mortgaged for a present loan and optional future advances has priority over the subsequent advances. Bank of America Nat. Trust & Sav. Ass'n v. Embry, 1961, 188 Cal.App.2d 425, 10 Cal.Rptr. 602. See Note, Priority of Real Estate Mortgage for Present and Optional Future Advances, 1968, 21 Okla.L.Rev. 79, 80, 82, covering the law generally and that of Oklahoma specifically. See Mortgages for Future Advances: The Need for Legislation in Wisconsin, 1965 Wis.L.Rev. 175, 179–182, for a discussion of the relative desirability of actual as opposed to constructive notice. See also Stealey, The Mortgage for Future Advances in West Virginia, 1954, 56 W.Va.L.Rev. 107, 111, 116. For a resume of the "actual knowledge" rule, see Gilmore, Security Interests in Personal Property 1965, 928.

56. Frye v. President, etc., of Bank of Ill., 1849, 11 Ill. 367; Ladue v. Detroit & Milwaukee R. Co., 1865, 13 Mich. 380, 87 Am.Dec. 759; Stone v. Welling, 1866, 14 Mich. 514; McMasters v. Campbell, 1879, 41 Mich. 513, 2 N.W. 836; Spader v. Lawler, 1848, 17 Ohio, 371, 49 Am.Dec. 461; Ter-Hoven v. Kerns, 1845, 2 Pa. 96. At one time eminent commentators expected this minority view to prevail. See Judge Redfield in, 1863, 3 Am.L.Reg.,N.S., 92; 1 Washburn, Real Prop., 1st Ed. 542.

This was the Ohio rule with respect to optional future advances until legislation in 1965 provided that the lien of the original mortgagee shall be prior in right to that of a subsequent intervening lienor, unless the original mortgagee had received *written* notice of the intervening lien prior to making the subsequent advances. See Note, Mortgages to Secure Future Advances, 1966, 17 Western Reserve L.Rev. 1429, 1431. If such written notice is given the Ohio Revised Code § 5301.23 provides that the intervening encumbrancer shall prevail. Where the intervening encumbrance is made expressly subject, by the terms of the contract, there is a conflict between the contract terms and section 5301.23. One case, Boswell v. Goodwin, 1862, 31 Conn. 74, held that the statute rule governed and the intervening lien took priority in spite of the terms of the contract. See 17 Western Reserve L.Rev. 1429, 1432. See Gilmore, op. cit. supra, note 55, for a summary of the "constructive notice" rule.

A different problem is raised when neither the mortgagee making optional future advances nor the intervening lienor records his interest in the manner required by statute. See ibid., supra.

have to keep on examining the records after he has satisfied all of the law's requirements as to his own mortgage; [57] that it is unjust for a man to lose his security by the mere registration of a subsequent lien, i. e., by no act of his own; that as a practical matter the majority rule is better calculated to subserve the business convenience which called the practice into being; [58] that this is especially true where continuous dealings with frequent advances are contemplated; that the hardship on the first mortgagee through having to make new examinations of title before each later advance, added to these considerations, more than balance any hardship on the later encumbrancer through having to give actual notice; that so far as inconvenience to the later claimant is concerned, since ordinarily he has to make an investigation before acquiring his interest, it would seldom be much additional trouble to give the required actual notice; and that if the first mortgagee is so inaccessible as to make it a real hardship to give actual notice "it would be equally inconvenient, in such a case, for the mortgagor to obtain further advances" and therefore little danger would arise from the requirement. [59]

The chief argument for the minority is based on the premise that each optional advance is the equivalent of a new mortgage. Therefore, the argument runs, when the first mortgagee makes it he is in the position of a subsequent and not a prior party. Consequently he is on notice of the record just as much "as if he were about to make an advancement to, or create a liability with, the party for the first time." [60] A variant of this is that under the recording acts the record of the first mortgage gives notice only to the extent of advances already made and therefore the second lien prevails under the act through lack of notice of the later advances. [61] As a practical matter it is also urged that the first mortgagee can always find out the state of the title without much difficulty by searching the record. Hence, it is fairer to put this burden on him rather than require "that every junior encumbrancer shall be bound to run after [him], and give him personal notice." "In some instances it may be almost, if not wholly, impracticable for the junior encumbrancer to do so;" a requirement of actual notice in such cases "would most likely put it out of the power of the party whose estate is so encumbered to borrow or obtain money upon it and his ruin would be produced in consequence of it. [62] Obviously there is substantial merit in

---

57. See 1914, 62 U. of Pa.L.Rev. 556, 558.

58. Union Nat. Bank of Oshkosh v. Milbourn & Stoddard Co., 1897, 7 N.D. 201, 73 N.W. 527.

59. McDaniels v. Colvin, 1844, 16 Vt. 300, 42 Am.Dec. 512. See notes, 1920, 6 Va.L.Rev. 280; 1914, 62 U. of Pa.L.Rev. 556; 1927, 1 Cin.L.Rev. 348, 350; 1863, 2 Am.L.Reg.,N.S., 12, 19; 1872, 11 Am.L.Reg., N.S., 273.

60. Ter-Hoven v. Kerns, 1845, 2 Pa. 96, 99, "Every future advancement or responsibility created, is, in

reality, a new debt, and such responsibility is created by a new contract, having a reference merely to the prior encumbrance, for the purpose of making it a lien upon the debtor's real estate; so that with respect to those who have acquired liens upon the real estate of the debtor, in the meantime, there is no ground or just reason whatever, why such future advances or responsibilities should not be looked on and considered as having no connection with the prior encumbrance under which they may have been made." See Alexandria Sav. Inst. v. Thomas, Va.1877, 29 Grat. 483. Cf. Home Savings & Loan Ass'n v. Burton, 1899, 20 Wash. 688, 698, 56 P. 940.

61. Micklin v. Nelson, 1884, 11 Or. 406, 5 P. 51, 50 Am.Rep. 477; Ketcham v. Wood, 1880, 22 Hun (N. Y.) 64. See 1920, 6 Val.L.Rev. 280, 284.

62. Ter-Hoven v. Kerns, supra, note 56, at 99.

See Ladue v. Detroit & Milwaukee R. Co., 1865, 13 Mich. 380, 87 Am.Dec. 759; Spader v. Lawler, 1848, 17 Ohio, 371, 49 Am.Dec. 461, accord. See also notes, 1914, 62 U. of Pa.L.Rev. 556; 1919, 6 Va.L.Rev. 280. See Atkinson v. Foote, 1919, 44 Cal.App. 149, 163, 186 P. 831, 837, discussed in note, 1920, 8 Cal.L.Rev. 260, suggesting that the purchaser on foreclosure sale under a second mortgage who records will prevail over future advances by the first mortgagee even though the second mortgagee himself would have had to give an actual notice. The mortgages were in the form of trust deeds but the ordinary law of future advances applies to such instruments. No reason for such a distinction commends itself and the dictum is an unfortunate one.

" * * * the problem of the effect of an assignment of the mortgage is presented. Will the assignee be affected by constructive notice of the at-

at least some of the arguments on each side with no heavy balance on either one.

PRIORITIES—OBLIGATORY ADVANCES

120. Legally obligatory advances enjoy priority over later liens regardless of notice.

Where the later advances are legally obligatory, most American cases follow the rule that all of them enjoy priority over later liens regardless of any notice.[63] This is true

even though the agreement to make the advances is oral.[64]

The English cases draw no distinction between obligatory and non-obligatory advances, postponing the first mortgagee with actual knowledge of the intervening second mortgagee in both cases. However, the first mortgagee may refuse to make advances in such a case.[65] And at least one American court, also rejecting the distinction, went to the opposite extreme and permitted the mortgagee to continue making optional advances which would rank as of the date of the mortgage even after full knowledge of an

taching of a subsequent interest by virtue of the fact that he gets an interest after recordation of the junior claim? Will he be affected by actual notice to himself? Will actual notice to the original mortgagee prior to the assignment affect his rights, or will actual notice have to be brought home to each successive assignee of the mortgage? These questions have apparently never been raised in the cases." Jones, 1930, 8 Tex.L.Rev. 371, 376.

63. Whelan v. Exchange Trust Co., 1913, 214 Mass. 121, 100 N.E. 1095; Waverley Co-op Bank v. Haner, 1930, 273 Mass. 477, 173 N.E. 699; Hill v. Aldrich, 1892, 48 Minn. 73, 50 N.W. 1020; Landers-Morrison-Christenson Co. v. Ambassador Holding Co., 1927, 171 Minn. 445, 214 N.W. 503, 53 A.L.R. 573; Platt v. Griffith, 1876, 27 N.J.Eq. 207; Hyman v. Hauff, 1893, 138 N.Y. 48, 33 N.E. 735, 51 St.R. 731; Kuhn v. Southern Ohio Loan & Trust Co., 1920, 101 Ohio St. 34, 126 N.E. 820; Kingsport Brick Corp. v. Bostwick, 1921, 145 Tenn. 19, 235 S.W. 70; Anglo-American Sav. & Loan Ass'n v. Campbell, 1898, 13 App.D.C. 581, 43 L.R.A. 622. See Note, Mortgages to Secure Future Advances, 1966, 17 Western Reserve L.Rev. 1429, 1431; Mortgages for Future Advances: The Need for Legislation in Wisconsin, 1965 Wis.L.Rev. 175, 178.

Even Connecticut, see § 116 note 10, supra, follows this rule. Weissman v. Volino, 1911, 84 Conn. 326, 80 A. 81. See law review notes, § 119 supra, note 59.

If the mortgagor is in default so that the mortgagee in an obligatory contract for future advances need not continue to make them, nevertheless advances made by him will not be treated as optional. Landers-Morrison-Christenson Co. v. Ambassador Holding Co., supra. See note, 1930, 14 Minn.L.Rev. 695.

Even though there is no contractual obligation to make further advances, advances which are necessary to prevent the mortgagee suffering loss through the bankruptcy of the mortgagor or to preserve the first mortgagee's security will be assimilated to the category of "obligatory" advances. Rowan v. Sharp's Rifle Mfg. Co., 1860, 29 Conn. 282. See Citizens' Sav. Bank v. Mack, 1919, 180 Cal. 246, 180 P. 618.

In Simpson v. Simpson, Fla.App.1960, 123 So.2d 289, commented on in 1961, 32 Miss.L.Rev. 325, after recordation of a mortgage for legally obligatory future advances, a declaration of homestead was filed. Later, with knowledge of the homestead, an advance was made. The court held that the subse-

quent advance prevailed over the homestead. See Note, Mortgages to Secure Future Advances, 1966, 17 Western Reserve L.Rev. 1429, 1432.

To what extent would a mortgage for obligatory future advances be prior to an unrecorded mortgage executed prior to it but discovered before all of the advances had been made? Durst v. Daugherty, 1891, 81 Tex. 650, 17 S.W. 388, semble.

On the confusion as to what constitutes an "obligatory" advance, see 1954, 29 N.Y.U.L.Rev. 733, 734 n. 8.

See Stealey, The Mortgage for Future Advances in West Virginia, 1954, 56 W.Va.L.Rev. 107, 113.

64. Whelan v. Exchange Trust Co. note 63; Lumber & Builders Supply Co. v. Ritz, 1933, 134 Cal.App. 607, 25 P.2d 1002, discussed in note, 1934, 22 Cal.L. Rev. 705. See City of Santa Monica v. Los Angeles Co., 1911, 15 Cal.App. 710, 712, 115 P. 945, 946; note, 1931, 79 U. of Pa.L.Rev. 647.

Such a result would be difficult to understand if the second rationale of the limitation on these mortgages, i. e., that it is to curtail fraudulent practices, is accepted; however it does not conflict with the third explanation.

65. West v. Williams, 1899, 1 Ch. 132; note, 1899, 43 Sol.J. 364. See note, 1911, 11 Col.L.Rev. 459.

For the present English law as to future advances, see Cheshire, Real Property, 7th ed., p. 620; 1925 L.P.A. secs. 198(1), 94(1). The 1925 Law of Property Act retained as part of the law of tacking, generally abolished, that a mortgagee may tack his future advances to his original mortgage when he has no notice of the intermediate mortgage. Where future advances are not expressly provided for in the prior mortgage, registration of the intermediate mortgage constitutes notice to the prior mortgage and gives priority to the intermediate mortgage. Where future advances are expressly provided for in the mortgage, for the later mortgagee to get priority over subsequent advances there must be actual notice. If the prior mortgagee's advances are obligatory, there is an immediate charge for both present and future advances and neither actual nor record notice will affect it. L.P.A. secs. 198(1) and 94(1).

intervening encumbrance.[66] The case has since been discredited.[67] However, an amendment in 1963, was held by Silver-Waters Corp v. Murphy [68] to have abolished in Florida the generally recognized distinction between obligatory and optional advances and consequently optional advances after an intervening second mortgage were given priority over it.

Stressing the point that a contract to lend money will never be enforced,[69] an eminent authority emphatically states that "it is nonsense, at least on the conceptual level, to make a distinction between obligatory and voluntary advances: A lender, although he is committed to the hilt, is as free as air; if he makes an advance he makes it voluntarily." [70]

In spite of this severe stricture he finds a possible virtue or utility in the distinction. "* * * the consensually nonsensical distinction between 'obligatory' and 'voluntary' has had a result (which is not in the least nonsensical) of preserving (or creating) a wide area of judicial discretion. There are few, if any, future advance clauses which an astute judge cannot, at will, classify on one side or the other of the line between obligatory and voluntary. When he has picked his label, he has also picked his priority rule. The distinction amounts to an absence of rule; the judges are invited to pick and choose, case by case, ad hoc or ad hominem. This is a recurrent phenomenon in a common law system when the arguments for and against a given position balance each other exactly. * * *" There is, then, much to be said for having no rule at all, or only a make-believe rule, and for letting the judge decide: judges are not necessarily wiser than other people, but they are paid to decide things." [71]

He makes an additional suggestion. "The cases offer almost no discussion of the character of the intervening encumbrance. It may be that a painstaking analysis of the cases would reveal that the character of the encumbrance does have an effect, subterranean and hidden, on the court's choice of a priority rule." [72]

PRIORITIES—TIME OF ATTACHMENT

121. The priority of a mortgage for advances ordinarily dates from the time the original agreement becomes binding, subject to the operation of the recording laws.

Since, as has been pointed out,[73] the mortgage for future advances secures the promise to repay them made at the time the transaction is entered into, it follows that priority dates from the day that promise became binding.[74] This day, ordinarily, is the day the agreement was entered into. In the sporadic case where this is not so, it would be binding from the time of the first advance. But such a mortgage is no more exempt from the operation of the recording acts and the rules governing bona fide purchase for value and without notice than any other mortgage. Consequently, in most instances, unless the later encumbrancer has actual notice of it, its priority will date only from recordation.[75] Although most cases do

---

66. Witczinski v. Everman, 1876, 51 Miss. 841. The advances were obligatory in this case but the decision was not placed on that ground. This was, as noted previously, the original English view.

67. See § 117 note 20, supra.

68. D.C.Fla.1965, 177 So.2d 897, noted in Boyer, Real Property, 1967, 22 U. of Miami L.Rev. 278, 308.

69. See § 26 supra. See also Gilmore, Security Interests in Personal Property (1965), 926.

70. Gilmore, op. cit. supra note 69. Professor Gilmore admits that his statement may not do justice to psychological and economic factors that exert pressures upon bankers to honor their commitments. Ibid. note 4.

71. Gilmore, op. cit., supra, note 69, at pp. 929, 930.

72. Ibid.

73. See § 114, supra.

74. Tapia v. Demartini, 1888, 77 Cal. 383, 19 P. 641, 11 Am.St.Rep. 288. Accord: Simpson v. Simpson, Fla.App.1960, 123 So.2d 289 (obligatory advances given priority over homestead arising between agreement and advance).

75. See Chapter 7, infra.

not differentiate subsequent mechanics' liens and judgment liens from other subsequent encumbrances, the provisions of recording acts and other statutes, especially mechanics' liens laws, sometimes specifically deal with the matters of priority in these cases.[76]

STATUTORY RESTRICTIONS

122. A few states have statutory restrictions on mortgages for future advances. Maryland's are the most stringent. They provide that the mortgage becomes a lien only from the time the advance is made.

Statutory restrictions on mortgages for future advances are imposed in some states. Georgia requires that the mortgage "specify the debt".[77] This has been liberally construed to mean that, although the mortgagor's duty must be specified the duty need not be specific, and not only are future advances permitted but their amount may be indefinite if the means of finding it out is plain.[78] The New Hampshire act requires that the mortgage, in order to be valid, shall state the nature of the future obligations, the amount of the present advances, and the "limitations, if any, with respect to the total or maximum amount." [79] The Maryland statute was originally enacted in 1825 [80] apparently because of serious abuses of the device adversely affecting creditors. It was aimed at preventing prejudice to them through concealment of the real nature of the transaction and through provisions so broad as to cover debts owed to third parties and bought up by the mortgagee at depreciated prices.[81] There have been additions to and changes of this original legislation.[82] At the present time, with certain exceptions, mortgages for future advances are a lien only from the time the advance is made and the amounts and times of such advances must be specifically stated and, if they are not, the mortgage is completely void.[83] This legislation, at least the consequences attached to non-conformity with it, seems dubiously drastic in the light of the generally recognized policy favoring

---

76. See 4 Pomeroy, Equity Juris., 5th Ed., §§ 1199a, 1199b; note, 1920, 5 A.L.R. 398; note, 1928, 53 A. L.R. 580. Look at Home Savings & Loan Ass'n v. Sullivan, 1929, 140 Okl. 300, 284 P. 30, noted, 1929, 14 Minn.L.Rev. 695.

It has been pointed out that the rule ending the priority of future advances on actual notice of a later encumbrance may cause difficulties in construction loan mortgages if applied to mechanics' liens. It would probably subordinate the mortgage lender's future advances to the mechanics' liens "as almost every such lender has actual notice of the pendency of construction and of the fact that work is being done and materials furnished, although whether actual notice existed of any particular mechanic's or materialmen's claim would, in each case, be a question of fact." Stealey, The Mortgage for Future Advances in West Virginia, 1954, 56 W.Va. L.Rev. 107, 112. See also Note, The Doctrine of Future Advances, 1966, 68 W.Va.L.Rev. 419, stressing the difficulty of applying the rule of actual notice in cases of corporate lenders. Stealey, op. cit. supra, 117, makes the same point.

77. Ga.Ann.Code, Park, 1914, § 3257.

For a state-by-state analysis of statutes covering future advances, see Russell and Prather, The Open End Mortgage, 1952, 19 U.S.Sav. and Loan League Legal Bull. 180. See also Note, Advance Money Provisions, 1954, 29 N.Y.U.L.Rev. 733.

78. Allen v. Lathrop, 1872, 46 Ga. 133.

79. N.H.Rev.Laws, 1942, c. 261, §§ 3, 4 (RSA 479:3, 479:4); Mica Products Co. v. Heath, 1925, 81 N.H. 470, 128 A. 805. The mortgage may be invalid as to the subsequent advance but valid as to the present debt. Johnson v. Richardson, 1859, 38 N.H. 353; New Hampshire Bank v. Willard, 1839, 10 N.H. 210.

See also § 3A inserted in N.H.Rev.Laws, c. 261 by c. 72 of Acts of 1945, giving subsequent advances for repairs and improvements up to a certain amount the same priority and security as the original indebtedness so long as the total does not exceed the amount originally secured.

The 1965 amendments in Ohio require, for its provisions to apply, that the contract must state, in substance or effect, that the parties intend it to secure unpaid balances arising from loan advances made by the mortgagee at the request of the mortgagor. In addition provision must be made to limit the total amount of indebtedness to be secured. See Note, Mortgages to Secure Future Advances, 1966, 17 W.Res.L.Rev. 1429.

80. Md.Laws, 1825, c. 50. The present law, Md.Code, 1957, art. 66, §§ 2, 3, is substantially a reenactment of the original provisions.

81. See Cole v. Albers & Runge, 1843, 1 Gill, 412, 414; Watkins, Maryland Mortgages for Future Advances, 1940, 4 Md.L.Rev. 110, 111. Cf. § 116, note 7, supra.

82. See Watkins op. cit., supra note 81, 121 et seq.

83. High Grade Brick Co. v. Amos, 1902, 95 Md. 571, 52 A. 582; 53 A. 148; In re Shapiro, 1940, 34 F. Supp. 737.

such mortgages.[84] Such an extreme hazard unnecessarily discourages the employment of a useful device.

CORPORATE BOND ISSUES

123. Priority restrictions on mortgages for future advances are not applied to corporate bonds. Unless the entire issue is treated equally it would be unmarketable.

Corporate bond issues are, analytically, just one variety of mortgage for future advances although one of the most important and useful of them. This is true whether the entire issue consists of one series with the bonds marketed at different times or whether it consists of several different series with separate dates of issue for each series. Statements are sometimes made that the single series bond offering, in spite of variance in the dates of actual issue of the bonds comprising it, is a single debt and not a mortgage for future advances.[85] Obviously such statements are incorrect. The truth is, and this is what is really meant by such denial, that the rules limiting and restricting the priority of subsequent optional advances in the simpler form of such mortgages executed by natural persons is rejected here for very excellent reasons that are pointed out by the courts.[86] Financial operations of great mag-

nitude necessary to the business and economic welfare of the community and the country at large are effected through the widespread marketing of these bonds to large numbers of the public who normally buy them in the open market. To carry out these operations successfully the bonds are ordinarily in negotiable form and expressly intended to be equally secured. Unless all bonds of the whole issue are accorded the intended equality of security interest and priority, the marketability of this class of instruments would be seriously impaired and the object of their employment largely defeated.[87] Not only are the mechanics, magnitude, and importance of this particular type of security for future borrowings sufficient to justify distinguishing it from the ordinary mortgage by a natural person for similar purposes, but the practices concerning them are so well known and understood in the commercial world that arguments of injustice to junior claimants are minimized.[88] Consequently the authorities quite uniformly treat the entire issue of such bonds, even though there is no obligation to put them out as dating from the same time without regard to the time when they are actually sold or contracted for.[89] That common date is the day on

---

84. Cf. note, 22 Cal.L.Rev. 705, 707, where the severity of the penalty imposed by the Maryland law for a defectively executed mortgage for future advances does not seem to have been realized.

In Maryland a mortgage for present advances, so defectively executed as to be non-recordable and therefore void under the Maryland recording law which makes recordation a condition precedent to the validity of mortgages, Md.Ann.Code, 1939, Flack, Art. 21, §§ 14, 16 (now Md.Code 1957, art. 21, §§ 10, 12), is nevertheless upheld against creditors as an equitable mortgage. Re Shapiro, supra; Jackson v. County Trust Co. of Maryland, 1939, 176 Md. 505, 6 A.2d 380. And compare the curious Maryland rule recognizing the lien for future advances under a confessed judgment as relating to the date of the judgment. Robinson v. Consolidated Real Estate & Fire Ins. Co., 1880, 55 Md. 105.

85. See, e. g., 3 Glenn, Mortgages, § 405.

86. See e. g., Reed's Appeal, 1888, 122 Pa. 565, 573, 16 A. 100; Claflin v. South Carolina R. Co., C.C.S. C.1880, 8 F. 118, 125, 126; Central Trust Co. v.

Continental Iron Works, 1894, 51 N.J.Eq. 605, 28 A. 595, 40 Am.St.Rep. 539; Westinghouse Electric, etc., Co. v. Brooklyn Rapid Transit Co., 1922, D.C.N.Y., 291 F. 863.

See Stealey, The Mortgage for Future Advances in West Virginia, 1954, 56 W.Va.L.Rev. 106, 113–14.

87. See Reed's Appeal, supra note 86; Claflin v. South Carolina R. Co., supra note 86.

88. See Claflin v. South Carolina Railroad Co., supra note 86, at 126.

89. In addition to the cases in note 86, supra the following cases are among those accepting this view: Central Trust Co. of New York v. Bodwell Water Power Co., C.C.Me.1910, 181 F. 735; Re Sunflower State Refining Co., D.C.Kan., 1911, 183 F. 834, commented on 1911, 11 Col.L.Rev. 459; U. S. Fidelity, etc., Co. v. U. S. etc., Trust Co., C.C.A.Kan.1916, 234 F. 238, 148 C.C.A. 140, L.R.A.1916F, 1067; Lanz v. First Mortgage Corp., 1932, 121 Cal.App. 587, 9 P.2d 316; Landers-Morrison-Christenson Co. v. Ambassador Holding Co., 1927, 171 Minn. 445, 214 N.W. 503, 53 A.L.R. 573; Integrity Trust Co. v. Club Atlantic, 1932, 111 N.J.Eq. 295, 162 A. 241, affirmed, 1933,

which the mortgage is executed subject, however, to the operation of recording acts.[90]

Where more than one series of bonds is expressly provided for by the mortgage, it is arguable that no sufficiently urgent reasons prevent treating each separate series as a future advance subject to the ordinary rules governing them. If a contract with a third party requires the issuance of the additional series, this factor would be sufficient here, as it generally is in the ordinary future advances case, to give priority to the bonds of such series even though issued after an intervening lien.[91] But where the issuance of a new series is optional, an intervening lien of which there is notice should have priority.[92]

ENLARGEMENT OF THE MORTGAGE DEBT

124. Certain rules have the effect of making mortgaged property security for obligations other than those for which it was pledged.

114 N.J.Eq. 80, 168 A. 379; Kelly v. Wellsburg, etc., Co., 1914, 74 W.Va. 130, 81 S.E. 712.

"It would be hard to imagine how an issue could be marketed under any other rule; the odd thing is that the future advance rules have come into the discussion at all, even if only to be distinguished away." Gilmore, Security Interests in Personal Property (1965), 929.

90. Since prior, perfected liens prevail over unrecorded mortgages, in actual practice the date of recordation of the mortgage rather than of its execution fixes the priority of the bonds. A few cases have preferred mechanic's liens which attached after execution and recording but before any of the bonds were actually issued or contracted for. Reynolds v. Manhattan Trust Co., C.C.A.Neb.1897, 83 F. 593, 27 C.C.A. 620; Sanders v. Southern Traction Co., D.C.Ill.1918, 253 F. 511; Allis-Chalmers v. Central Trust Co., C.C.A.Me.1911, 190 F. 700, 111 C.C.A. 428, 39 L.R.A.,N.S., 84. Such a rule introduces an unfortunate element of uncertainty adversely affecting the free marketability and negotiability of such bonds which is counter to the policy ordinarily followed in these cases.

91. Allis-Chalmers Co. v. Central Trust Co., supra note 90.

92. International Trust Co. v. Davis, etc., Mfg. Co., 1899, 70 N.H. 118, 46 A. 1054, seems an a fortiori authority for this proposition since there was no express provision for separate series and yet the intervening lien prevailed. See also Glenn, Mortgages, § 406.2.

(1) **The English doctrine of consolidation and the rule that if there is, subsequent to the mortgage debt, a loan upon bond, payment of both debts is necessary for redemption, has been largely rejected.**

(2) **Agreements to extend the mortgage to new obligations not within the contemplation of the original mortgage are generally valid, at least to the extent that the mortgagor must pay off both loans to get back his property free of either encumbrance.**

The fundamental principle that the mortgage secures only the obligation intended by the parties at the time it was created has been noted before.[93] This basic doctrine necessitates discussing and differentiating certain rules of law which have the effect, in spite of it, of making the mortgaged property a modified sort of security for the performance of obligations other than those for which it was pledged.

The first of these is the English doctrine of "consolidation" of mortgages.[94] This rule is "that if two or more distinct mortgages be made of different estates between the same parties, or if a sum of money be advanced on one estate, and other estates be afterwards made a security for the sum already advanced, and also for further advances, although without any agreement that the first estate shall be charged with the further advances, nevertheless, neither the mortgagor nor any one claiming under him the equity of redemption of one of the estates, although without notice of the other mortgage or charge, shall be permitted to redeem one mortgage with-

93. See, supra, §§ 114, 123.

94. "The doctrine of consolidation of securities is often treated as if it were a branch of the doctrine of tacking, but it in fact rests on different principles.

"Tacking is the union of several debts upon one estate; consolidation is the union of several debts, respectively charged upon several estates. Consolidation does not depend, like tacking, upon the possession of the legal estate. In tacking notice is material, in consolidation it is not. The object of tacking is to oust a mesne encumbrancer, but the effect of consolidation may be to enable a puisne mortgagee to throw his debt onto another estate." Coote, Mortgages, 9th Ed., 882. Tacking will be considered further, Chapter 7, infra.

out redeeming both." [95] The English courts rested the requirement on the "do equity" principle and developed a considerable body of law governing its operation [96] before it was abolished by statute in 1881. [97] The American courts never accepted the principle [98] and, consequently, detailed consideration of it is unnecessary.

In America the term "consolidation" has several usages none of which have any connection with the English one here considered. Most frequently it refers to the merging of two or more corporate mortgagors into a single one, either directly under procedures set up to accomplish this result or by the creation of a new corporation to which the assets of the others are transferred on their dissolution. [99] Occasionally it describes the supplanting of two or more mortgages on the same property, or on different parcels, by one new mortgage. [1] Also, it sometimes is used to denote the doctrine of "merger" which operates when the redemption interest is united with the debt and the security interest in the same hands. [2] As is noted in the next paragraph, a few American courts, apparently unmindful of the separate genealogy of the "consolidation" cases and the idea of tacking to the mortgage unsecured claims held by the mortgagee against the mortgagor, applied the reasoning of the English courts in the former to the latter situation to arrive at a result quite at variance with either.

The second of these rules of law was that "where the mortgagee lends more money upon bond to the mortgagor he shall not redeem till he pays the bond-debt as well as the money due upon the mortgage." [3] This doctrine was distinct in origin from the "consolidation" theory just dealt with and the reason for it is obscure. It was quickly modified in England to apply only to the heir of the mortgagor [4] and, so limited, was based upon the sound and understandable rationale of preventing circuity of action which would otherwise result in the administration of the mortgagor's estate when the encumbered land went to the heir. [5] And in no case was the mortgagee permitted to tack his unsecured bond onto the mortgage so as to prevail over other creditors. [6] A few early American cases, apparently overlooking the restricted scope and reason of the English rule and not perceiving the difference between it and the "consolidation" principle, held that because of the "do equity" condition of obtaining the aid of equity, the mortgagor, in order to redeem, must pay all other debts, though unsecured, that he owed to the mortgagee. [7]

However, most American courts reject this view and "the general rule is that the mortgagee cannot require as a condition of redemption the payment of any other debt not

95.   Coote, op. cit., supra note 94. See also Maitland, Equity, Brunyate's Ed., 200.

96.   See Coote, op. cit., supra c. XLIII.

97.   Conveyancing Act of 1881, § 17, reenacted in 1925, 15 Geo. V., C. 20, § 93. See, Coote, op. cit., supra note 94, 892. Under the statute it still is possible to reserve the right by express provision in at least one of the mortgages.

98.   See, e. g., Bech v. Ruggles, 1879, 6 Abb.N.Cas. (N.Y.) 69.

99.   See Chapter 2, supra.

1.   See Chapter 10, infra.

2.   See Chapter 9, infra.

3.   Anon. 1702, 3 Salk. 84, pl. 7. The first case so holding seems to have been Baxter v. Manning, 1684, 1 Vern. 244.

4.   Shuttleworth v. Laycock, 1684, 1 Vern. 245, and cases cited in 3 Salk. 84, pl. 7, note.

5.   See note to Shuttleworth v. Laycock, supra, note 4; Langdell, Brief Survey of Eq.Juris., 145 et seq.

6.   See note to Anon., supra note 3.

7.   Anthony v. Anthony, 1861, 23 Ark. 479; Scripture v. Johnson, 1819, 3 Conn. 211; Walling v. Aiken, 1840, McMull.Eq. (S.Car.) 1; Lake v. Shumate, 1883, 20 S.C. 23. Even in these states the rule does not apply to redemption by anyone other than the mortgagor. Cohn v. Hoffman, 1892, 56 Ark. 119, 19 S.W. 233 (judgment lienholder); Hays v. Cretin, 1906, 102 Md. 695, 62 A. 1028, 4 L.R.A.,N.S., 1039 (dower claimant).

Further, it is confined to redemption and does not govern in foreclosure actions by the mortgagee. Anthony v. Anthony, supra.

a lien on the land and the "do equity" maxim has no application to situations "where the demand of the defendant is based upon a contract separate and distinct from that which forms the subject of the plaintiff's action." [8]

The third rule involves the effect of agreements to extend [9] the mortgage to obligations not within the contemplation of the original mortgage. A sharp distinction must be drawn between such agreements, oral or written, and the admission of oral or other evidence to establish just what the secured obligation actually is. This latter is quite liberally permitted and does not violate either the Statute of Frauds or the parol evidence rule.[10] The former has been mentioned before but is of especial importance in connection with subsequently arising obligations which might have partaken of the protection afforded by the doctrine [11] of mortgages securing future advances had they been included, which they were not, in the original mortgage. They are in substance and effect separate and independent agreements for a new mortgage and, subject to the exception to be mentioned, are treated as such.[12]

Whether and the extent to which they may or may not be upheld and enforced depends upon the construction of the applicable Statute of Frauds,[13] how far they fall within the doctrines and rules of equitable mortgages and, if they do, the amount of protection they will receive.[14] In cases involving priority with other encumbrances they must stand on their own footing precisely as though there was no other mortgage in existence to which they might have been tied and in whose priorities they might have shared to some extent if they had been framed as part of an original mortgage for future advances.[15] Nevertheless, as between the parties, the situation seems a much clearer case for the application of the "do equity" doctrine than either of the two preceding instances. The express agreement of the mortgagor, even though only oral, that the property should secure both the old and the new obligations, on the faith of which he obtained the latter, seems amply sufficient to compel him to pay off both loans in order to get back his property free from either encumbrance. For the sole and limited purpose of redemption many

---

8. Mahoney v. Bostwick, 1892, 96 Cal. 53, 30 P. 1020, 31 Am.St.Rep. 175. See also Mackenna v. Fidelity Trust Co., 1906, 184 N.Y. 411, 77 N.E. 721, 3 L.R.A., N.S., 1068, 112 Am.St.Rep. 620, 6 Ann.Cas. 471; Brooks v. Brooks, 1897, 169 Mass. 38, 47 N.E. 448; Presbyterian Corp. v. Wallace, 1831, 3 Rawle (Pa.) 109.

9. The phrase, extension of the mortgage, is used to designate three different transactions: postponement of the time for performance of the secured obligation; adding other property to that already standing as security for the one debt; and making the same property security for additional obligations. It is the last usage which is under consideration here.

10. See supra §§ 105, 106, 108.

11. Supra § 114.

12. Riess v. Old Kent Bank, 1931, 253 Mich. 557, 235 N.W. 252, 76 A.L.R. 571. See 1932, 76 A.L.R. 574; note, 1933, 11 N.Car.L.Rev. 174; 1906, 1 L.R.A.,N.S., 405 (semble).

An indebtedness owing by a third person to the mortgagor under an open-end clause in a mortgage which had been transferred by the mortgagor to an assignee of the mortgagee is not an obligation of

the mortgagor within the meaning of an open-end clause. Milikin v. Murphy, 1958, 214 Ga. 130, 103 S.E.2d 549, noted in 1958, 10 Mercer L.Rev. 161.

13. Ex parte Hooper, 1815, 19 Ves.Jun. 477 (a legal mortgage cannot be extended by a later oral agreement to cover additional loans); Stoddard v. Hart, 1861, 23 N.Y. 556, 561; Johnson v. Anderson, 1875, 30 Ark. 745; Briggs v. Steele, 1909, 91 Ark. 458, 121 S.W. 754; Hester v. Gairdner, 1907, 128 Ga. 531, 58 S.E. 165; Leger v. Leger, 1907, 118 La. 322, 42 So. 951; Hayhurst v. Morin, 1908, 104 Me. 169, 71 A. 707.

See West's Ann.Cal.Civ.Code, § 2922; London & San Francisco Bank v. Bandman, 1898, 120 Cal. 220, 223, 52 P. 583, 584, 65 Am.St.Rep. 179 ("extended" in § 2922 "refers to a broadening of the security to cover additional advances"). A legal mortgage can be extended by a written agreement. See Butts v. Broughton, 1882, 72 Ala. 294 (the agreement creates an equitable mortgage). An equitable mortgage by deposit of title deeds can be enlarged orally. Ex parte Kensington, 1813, 2 V. & B. 79. See dictum in Ex parte Hooper, 1815, 19 Ves.Jun. 477, 479, accord.

14. See Chapter 2, supra, and Chapter 7, infra.

15. Keese v. Beardsley, 1923, 190 Cal. 465, 213 P. 500, 26 A.L.R. 1538; Crooks v. Jenkins, 1904, 124 Iowa 317, 100 N.W. 82, 104 Am.St.Rep. 326; Joslyn v. Wy-

cases so hold [16] although a few deny it even this narrow operation, at least if it is not in writing.[17]   The mortgagee, of course, can- not avail himself of both mortgages as one in a foreclosure action.[18]

man, 1862, 5 Allen (87 Mass.) 62; Brown v. Hard- castle, 1885, 63 Md. 484; Norwood v. Norwood, 1892, 36 S.C. 331, 15 S.E. 382, 31 Am.St.Rep. 875.

16. Carpenter v. Plagge, 1901, 192 Ill. 82, 61 N.E. 530; Upton v. Nat. Bank of So. Reading, 1876, 120 Mass. 153; Riess v. Old Kent Bank, supra, note 12; Tierney v. Citizens Bank, 1931, 51 R.I. 329, 154 A. 653; Ellis v. Sullivan, 1922, 241 Mass. 60, 134 N.E. 695.

17. Loe v. Brown, 1923, 155 Ga. 24, 116 S.E. 309 (oral agreement); Maus v. McKillip, 1873, 38 Md. 231 (statute); Stoddard v. Hart, 1861, 23 N.Y. 556 (oral agreement).   There is authority that the subsequent agreement cannot be related to the original mort- gage even against the mortgagor's creditors.   Whit- ney v. Metallic, etc. Co., 1905, 187 Mass. 557, 73 N.E. 663; Barry v. General Mortg. & Loan Corp., 1926, 254 Mass. 282, 150 N.E. 293.   See Upton v. Nat. Bank of So. Reading, 1876, 120 Mass. 153, 155.

18. Hayhurst v. Morin, 1908, 104 Me. 169, 71 A. 707. See Upton v. Nat. Bank of So. Reading, supra note 16.   Cf. Kapalczinsky v. Sitniski, 1920, 91 N.J.Eq. 524, 111 A. 24.

CHAPTER 6

RIGHTS AND DUTIES BEFORE FORECLOSURE

A. RIGHT TO POSSESSION

Sec.
125. Title States.
126. Intermediate States.
127. Lien Theory.

B. TORTIOUS INJURY TO LAND BY MORTGAGOR OR THIRD PERSONS

128. Tortious Injury by Mortgagor.
129. Injury by Third Persons.
130. Severed Property—Mortgagee's Rights.
131. Injunction Against Removal of Severed Property.
132. Injury by Third Persons—Mortgagor's Rights.
133. Relation of Rights of Mortgagor and Mortgagee Against Third Parties.
134. Equitable Relief Against Mortgagor.
135. Mortgagee's Duty to Enjoin Waste.

C. RIGHTS IN PRODUCT OF THE RES

136. Eminent Domain.
137. Insurance—Separate Policies.
138. Agreement to Insure.
139. Types of Policies.
140. Restoration of Premises.

D. RIGHT TO RENTS

141. In General.
142. Lease Before Mortgage—Title States.
143. —— Advance Payment.
144. Mortgage Before Lease—Title States.
145. —— Advance Payment.
146. Lien States.

A. RIGHT TO POSSESSION

TITLE STATES

125. In title states the mortgagee theoretically still has a legal right to possession. It is almost never asserted because of burdensome duties to account. Agreements permitting the mortgagor to stay on the property are usual, and courts are quick to imply them. Law courts attempt to fit him into a category of tenant.

As has been seen,[1] the very early method of giving land as security was by a transfer of possession to the creditor—the gage of land in the twelfth and thirteenth centuries. It is true that the Jewish mortgage and the forms of security provided by Statutes Merchant and Staple left the debtor in posses-

1. Chapter 1, subdivision A.

sion, but these devices did not form a part of the main current of mortgage law and left little or no direct imprint on it.[2] When the basic mortgage transaction became the conveyance of the fee on condition subsequent —defeasance being performance on the law day by the mortgagor—possession passed to the mortgagee upon execution of the mortgage. There were two reasons for this. (1) Livery of seizin was necessary to the conveyance. (2) Possession by the mortgagee was in accord with the practice of the times and the theory of the legal rights conferred upon the creditor by the transaction. As late as the beginning of the seventeenth century it was unusual for the mortgagor to be left in possession and it is not until about the time of the Restoration that it became the general rule to do so. It is likely that the practice was connected with the creation of the equity of redemption; certainly it coincided with it.[3] And this was natural, for with the fuller recognition of the mortgagor as equitable owner of the property, there was, of course, the corresponding understanding that the sole interest of the mortgagee in the property, regardless of his technical legal rights, was that of security. With the acceptance of this view the mortgagee who exercised his right to possession was held to strict accountability to the mortgagor. The onerous duties of accounting became an effective deterrent: the right was resorted to infrequently and only in extreme cases.[4] Nevertheless, although seldom exercised, the right to possession was, as it still is, a fundamental incident of the mortgagee's legal security title. He could maintain ejectment

against the mortgagor, or, if he entered by self-help, he could not be sued by the mortgagor in trespass. This was true not only in England but in the United States. We adopted at the outset the title theory as developed in the mother country.[5] However, because possession is of little value to the mortgagee as a remedy, realization by foreclosure being the substance of his right; and, further, because possession by the mortgagor is normally essential in order for him to have a real chance to redeem, it was natural, if not inevitable, that the mortgagor be allowed to stay in possession. When this occurred, in the eyes of equity the mortgagor was looked upon as owner in possession. But the law courts, because the mortgagee had the legal title, tried to fit the mortgagor into an established category and find that he was a tenant of some sort. When there was no agreement about possession, express or implied, between the parties, there was some attempt to assimilate the mortgagor to the status of a tenant at will. This was apparently based on the language of Mansfield in Keech d.

2. Ibid.

3. Turner, The Equity of Redemption, 89–91.

4. See Maitland, Equity, 274.

In England, since 1936, actions by mortgagees for possession must be brought in Chancery. In such actions the judge, through the exercise of a discretionary power, not clearly defined, of adjourning the case, may afford a defaulting mortgagor an opportunity to delay or defeat the mortgagee. Robertson v. Cilia, 1956, 1 W.L.R. 1502, commented on in 1957, 73 L.Q.Rev. 17. See also id. at 300.

5. Trannon v. Towles, 1917, 200 Ala. 82, 75 So. 458; Brown v. Cram, 1818, 1 N.H. 169; Gilman v. Wills, 1877, 66 Me. 273 (trespass denied to mortgagor against mortgagee who took possession before default); Doe ex dem. Roby v. Maisey, 1828, 8 Barn. & C. 767 (ejectment by mortgagee against mortgagor); Jamieson v. Bruce, 1834, 6 Gill & J. 72, 26 Am.Dec. 557 (personal property; trespass denied to mortgagor against mortgagee who took possession before default). See Brown v. Loeb, 1912, 177 Ala. 106, 58 So. 330; Green v. Kemp, 1816, 13 Mass. 515, 7 Am.Dec. 169.

See also Collins, Rights of a Mortgagee to Immediate Possession, 1929, 3 Temple L.Q. 196; 1893, 18 L.R.A. 781, 788; Betts, The Right to Emblements Upon Foreclosure of Mortgages on Real Estate, 1885, 19 Am.L.Rev. 24. For a critical estimate of the value to the mortgagee of his right to get possession, see Tefft, The Myth of Strict Foreclosure, 1937, 4 U. of Chi.L.Rev. 575, 583. Second mortgagees, having only an equitable interest, do not have a right to possession by virtue of their mortgage alone. See Willoughby, The Rights of Second Mortgagees Regarding Possession, 1908, 24 L.Q.Rev. 297; Coote, Mortgages, 9th Ed., 823; note, 1930, 170 L.T. 137. Equitable mortgagees who have the right to call for a legal mortgage also have the right to take possession. Re Gordon, 1889, 61 L.T.Rep. 299; General Finance, Mortgage & Discount Co. v. Liberator Permanent Benefit Building Society, 1878, 10 Ch.D. 15, 24. See the apparently conflicting statutory provi-

Warne v. Hall.[6] But it was soon pointed out that since "he may be turned out of possession without notice, and is not entitled to emblements" [7] this classification was incorrect. A closer approximation was to consider him a tenant at sufferance, or at least "no more than a tenant at sufferance," for against the mortgagee his rights in the property were just those.[8] But to look upon the person, who in equity and in common law regard was considered as the owner and who was left in possession with the consent of the mortgagee, as being on the same basis as a tenant who was holding over wrongfully [9] is unsatisfactory, even if not "fantastic" as one comment put it.[10] The best solution would seem to be to reject the concept that he is a tenant of any sort and conclude with Parke, B., that "he can be described merely by saying that he is a mortgagor." [11] Normally, however, there is an express agreement permitting the mortgagor to stay on the property. If the covenant is that he shall have possession until some specified date, a tenancy for

a term is said to be established.[12] On the other hand, if the agreement is that the mortgagor may enjoy the property until default or without specifying any terminal date, a tenancy at will is the result.[13] And even without an express stipulation, the courts are quick to find an implied in fact agreement for the mortgagor to remain in possession from provisions in the mortgage or the nature and circumstances of the loan, e. g., that the mortgagor "should deliver * * * one half of all the yearly produce" of the mortgaged premises [14] or that the premises had been conveyed to the mortgagor for the support of the mortgagee with the mortgage given as security for performance.[15] All of this can be justified on a narrow technical basis. Nevertheless even in cases where there is an express agreement between the parties it would seem that the mortgagor in possession should be recognized in modern law as something more than a tenant of the mortgagee at will, at sufferance, or even for a set term. And that he is in fact recognized as more than any of these is evidenced in various rights accorded him by decision or by statutory enactment which came from the "endeavor of the Legislature to complete the

---

sions in Massachusetts as to the mortgagee's right to take possession. Rev.Stat.1836, c. 107, § 9, Mass. Gen.Laws Ann. c. 244 § 9; Acts of 1912, c. 502, § 23, Mass.Gen.Laws Ann. c. 183 § 26. The latter section appears to be paramount. Harlow Realty Co. v. Cotter, 1933, 284 Mass. 68, 187 N.E. 118.

For a scholarly argument in support of the right to possession of an equitable mortgagee, see Wade, An Equitable Mortgagee's Right to Possession, 1955, 71 L.Q.Rev. 204. See § 148, infra.

6. "When the mortgagor is left in possession, the true inference to be drawn, is an agreement that he shall possess the premises at will in the strictest sense * * *". 1778, 1 Doug. 21, 22.

7. Christophers v. Sparke, 1820, 2 J. & W. 234. See Turner, The Equity of Redemption, c. V, for a detailed discussion of the controversy over the position of the mortgagor left in possession.

8. Thunder v. Belcher, 1803, 3 East 449; Doe d. Roby v. Maisey, 1828, 8 B. & C. 767. See Turner, The Equity of Redemption, 103.

9. Walsh and Simpson, Cas. Morts., 25.

10. Idem.

11. Litchfield v. Ready, 1850, 20 L.J.,N.S., Ex. 51. See also Wilton v. Dunn, 1851, 17 Q.B. 299; Tripe v. Marcy, 1859, 39 N.H. 439, 444; note, 1932, 32 Col. L.Rev. 124. See Turner, op. cit. supra, note 8, 104. The law of Property Act, 1925, does not change the problem in England, Idem. 105.

It has been repeatedly held that no tenancy exists between a mortgagee and the mortgagor in possession as will entitle a mortgagee seeking to gain possession after default to use summary process of ejectment provided by landlord and tenant acts. Willis v. Eastern Trust & Banking Co., App.D.C.1898, 169 U.S. 295, 18 S.Ct. 347, 42 L.Ed. 752; Hastings v. Pratt, 1851, 62 Mass. (8 Cush.) 121; McCombs v. Wallace, 1872, 66 N.C. 481; Ballow v. Motheral, 1875, 64 Tenn. (5 Baxt.) 600.

See note, 1933, 8 Notre Dame Law 253.

12. Gibbs v. Cruikshank, 1873, L.R., 8 C.P. 461; Doe d. Parsley v. Day, 2 Q.B. 147.

13. Smartle v. Williams, 1695, Holt 478; Andrew Newport's Case, 1695, Skin. 423, Turner, op. cit. supra note 8, 93.

14. Hartshorn v. Hubbard, 1822, 2 N.H. 453.

15. Wales v. Mellen, 1854, 67 Mass. (1 Gray) 512; Rhoades v. Parker, 1839, 10 N.H. 83. See Keech v. Hall, 1778, 1 Doug. 21; Brown v. Loev, 1912, 177 Ala. 106, 58 So. 330; Flagg v. Flagg, 1831, 28 Mass. (11 Pick.) 475. Cf. Davis v. Poland, 1904, 99 Me. 345, 59 A. 520. See 1 Tiffany, Landlord and Tenant, § 45.

work begun by Equity of making the mortgagor more nearly owner of the land." [16] Perhaps the most important of these is the doctrine that, except as between the mortgagor and the mortgagee, or one claiming under him, the mortgagor is to be regarded as owner.[17]

INTERMEDIATE STATES

126. In intermediate states the mortgagee's right to possession accrues either on default or when the condition of the mortgage has been broken.

Under the title theory we saw that the mortgagee technically has the right to possession from the time the mortgage is given.[18] Under the lien view he never gets that right qua mortgagee.[19] Several states have adopted a compromise between the two and hold that the right accrues on default. To explain why this is so courts have talked in terms of legal title being in the mortgagor until default and then, "after condition has been broken, the legal title is in the mortgagee." [20] Other courts have been more cautious and merely hold that the mortgagee's right to possession has been limited to cases where the condition of the mortgage has been broken; [21] and in some states statutory provisions establish that rule.[22] A vigorous attack upon the rule has been made based upon the thesis that the only correct and desirable view of the mortgage relation is that the mortgagor, not the mortgagee, is the legal owner and therefore is alone entitled to possession; and, further, that it is completely indefensible to treat the mortgagor as owner before default and the mortgagee as owner after default since this would be combining two utterly inconsistent theories. Further it is stated flatly that the lien theory, in which the mortgagee has no right to possession, fully protects the creditor whose only interest should be recognized to be one of security.[23] In criticism of such an unqualified condemnation it may be suggested that the real issue is not whether title is in the mortgagor or mortgagee but whether it is desirable or undesirable to accord to a mortgagee as a part of his security interest in the property the right to take possession at some time or other. If posed in this fashion there is something to be said in favor of permitting a mortgagee to take possession after his debtor has defaulted. Certainly it is difficult to argue that under no circumstances should the mortgagee be permitted to take possession. And to reach this result upon the concept that the mortgagor has legal title is to reason as mechanically as do the courts which allow the mortgagee to have possession because he has title. In addition, the large

16.   Turner, The Equity of Redemption, 103.

17.   Orr v. Hadley, 1858, 36 N.H. 575; Huckins v. Straw, 1852, 34 Me. 166; Cotton v. Carlisle, 1887, 85 Ala. 175, 4 So. 670, 7 Am.St.Rep. 29; Seaman v. Bisbee, 1896, 163 Ill. 91, 45 N.E. 208—accord. See Woods v. Hilderbrand, 1870, 46 Mo. 284, 2 Am.Rep. 513, affirmed 49 Mo. 124. See note, Campbell, Cases Mortgages, 13 n. 2.

Cf. Parker and Others v. Brathwaite and Another, Ch. D. [1952] 2 All E.R. 837; Church of England Building Soc. v. Piskor [1954] 2 W.L.R. 952, discussed in 1954, Camb.L.J. 192, involved the problem whether a lease made before the formal completion of the purchase by a purchase money mortgagor who went into possession was binding upon the mortgagee.

18.   See § 125, supra.

19.   See § 127, infra.

20.   Bradfield v. Hale, 1902, 67 Ohio St. 316, 65 N.E. 1008. See also Taylor v. Quinn, 1941, 68 Ohio App. 164, 39 N.E.2d 627.

21.   Kransz v. Uedelhofen, 1901, 193 Ill. 477, 62 N.E. 239.

22.   E. g., 12 V.S.A. (Vt.) § 4772. "Every mortgagor shall, until condition broken, have, as against the mortgagee, the legal right to possession to the mortgaged premises, unless it is otherwise stipulated in the mortgage deed." Crahan v. Chittenden, 1909, 82 Vt. 410, 74 A. 86.

Other authorities to the effect that the mortgagee has no right to possession until default are Walcop v. McKinney's Heirs, 1846, 10 Mo. 229; Wilson v. Reed, 1917, 270 Mo. 400, 193 S.W. 819; Miss.Code 1942, § 849. See also Dickerson v. Bridges, 1898, 147 Mo. 235, 48 S.W. 825; Sanderson v. Price, 1846, 21 N.J. L. 637, 646; Shields v. Lozear, 1869, 34 N.J.L. 496, 3 Am.St.Rep. 256; Cohn v. Plass, 1915, 85 N.J.Eq. 153, 95 A. 1011; Mershon v. Castree, 1895, 57 N.J.L. 484, 31 A. 602; Stewart v. Fairchild-Baldwin Co., 1919, 91 N.J.Eq. 86, 108 A. 301; Steinberg v. Kloster Steel Corp., 1932, 266 Ill.App. 60.

23.   Walsh, Mortgages, 93.

number of instances in which the mortgagee may obtain possession, or the fruits of possession, would indicate that, on the merits, a rule permitting him possession cannot be dismissed as completely bad and outmoded. As one writer pointed out, "To establish his thesis that nature's livery of seisin pending foreclosure sale is to the mortgagor, the author [Walsh] must struggle not only with the ejectment cases that begot the 'title' and 'intermediate' theories but also with four other varieties of hostile decision. There are the cases that allow the mortgagee (a) to collect rent from tenants of the mortgagor, (b) merely by adding a few words to the mortgage agreement to obtain possession any time he wants it, (c) to come into possession by means of a receiver, and (d) if he has obtained possession peaceably, but without valid foreclosure, to stay in until he is paid. Of these decisions at least the (b), (c), and (d) varieties are indigenous to so-called 'lien' jurisdictions."[24] To this may be added the observation that at least one state has restored by statute the title theory, at the option of the parties,[25] and, this statutory form, although only one variety available, has been selected as the type meant by the parties when they have employed a deed absolute and it is established that a mortgage was intended.[26] Such vitality seems inconsistent with a thesis that the title theory is moribund or the only desirable theory.[27]

LIEN THEORY

127. In a majority of states the mortgagee has no right to possession before foreclosure. The mortgagor has the legal title; the mortgagee has only a security interest which is termed a lien.

24. McDougal, Review of Walsh, Mortgages, 1935, 44 Yale L.J. 1278, 1280.

25. Ga.Code § 67–1301. Oliver v. Slack, 1941, 192 Ga. 7, 14 S.E.2d 593.

26. Holt v. Tate, 1941, 193 Ga. 256, 18 S.E.2d 12.

27. See Glenn, Mortgages, § 30.

Even in states avowedly following the title theory, the equitable idea that the grantee holds his title only for security purposes was generally accepted by the law courts. As a consequence, incident after incident of legal title was whittled away although to varying extents in different jurisdictions and sometimes not consistently in the same jurisdiction. In many states the whittling-away process cut down title so far that it was called a chattel interest or even a chose in action.[28] There was one right, however, which was not eliminated, and it is the presence or absence of it that marks the dividing line between lien and title theory. That right was the right to possession before foreclosure. When that right was denied to the mortgagee, as it has been in a majority of the states of the United States,[29] so that at no time before foreclosure could he, *qua* mortgagee, take possession as of right, it became obvious that the mortgagee could no longer be said to have legal title, that ownership was in the mortgagor not only in equity but at law, and the interest of the mortgagee was only a security interest which was

28. A good example of this, together with a résumé in the opinion of many of the normal incidents of legal title which are not accorded to the mortgagee's interest in states following the title theory, is Stevens v. Turlington, 1923, 186 N.C. 191, 119 S.E. 210, 32 A.L.R. 870.

In People v. Nogarr, 1958, 164 Cal.App.2d 591, 330 P.2d 858, criticized in 1959, 11 Stanford L.Rev. 574, it was held that a mortgage given by one joint tenant created merely a lien which did not sever the estate and was void against rights of the surviving joint tenant.

Compare In re Keil's Estate, 1958, 51 Del. (1 Storey) 351, 145 A.2d 563, discussed in 1959, 58 Mich.L.Rev. 137, 73 Harv.L.Rev. 425, holding that where husband and wife, tenants by the entirety, borrowed and gave a mortgage to secure the loan which was used to improve the property and then the husband died, the wife was entitled to contribution from the husband's estate.

29. See Pomeroy, Eq.Juris., 5th ed., § 1188, listing Arizona, California, Colorado, Florida, Georgia, Idaho, Indiana, Iowa, Kansas, Kentucky, Louisiana (Civil Law), Michigan, Minnesota, Montana, Nebraska, Nevada, New Mexico, New York, North Dakota, Oklahoma, Oregon, South Carolina, South Dakota, Texas, Utah, Washington, Wisconsin, and Wyoming as lien states.

called a lien.[30] For the most part this achievement was the result of statutory enactments [31] the earliest of which was in South Carolina.[32] This act provided not only that the mortgagee should not be entitled to maintain any possessory action for the mortgaged real estate even after default but explicitly said that the "mortgagor shall be still deemed to be owner of the land." [33] Other statutes variously phrased, accomplish the same thing. Some state that the mortgage shall not be deemed a conveyance so to enable the mortgagee to recover possession without foreclosure and sale.[34] Others provide that a mortgage does not entitle the mortgagee to possession unless there is an express provision to that effect; some are combinations of these two.[35] Still others say that the mortgagee shall not be able to maintain an action of ejectment against the mortgagor, or that the mortgagor shall have the right to possession "regardless of the terms of the instrument." [36]

It was a provision denying the mortgagee the right to bring ejectment [37] that transformed New York into a lien state. The history of the conversion is interesting and important, especially so since New York is not only a representative but influential exponent of the lien theory. An early decision limited the effect of the enactment by holding that the mortgagor could not oust the mortgagee who got possession peaceably after default because "he is still considered as having the legal estate after condition broken." [38] It took two later developments to establish without question that all that the mortgagee ever got at any time was a legal lien and that the mortgagor at all times before foreclosure remained the legal owner. One was a change in the decisions as to the circumstances under, and theory upon, which a mortgagee would be considered a "mortgagee in possession" entitled to hold as against the mortgagor, a matter which will be dealt with later.[39] The other was a holding,[40] under the

---

30. For a discussion of the nature of the lien thus created see Durfee, The Lien Theory of the Mortgage—Two Crucial Problems, 1913, 11 Mich.L.Rev. 495. For an elaborate argument that the mortgagee in a lien theory state gets a power of sale as that term is employed and understood in the law of real property, see Gavit, Under the Lien Theory is Mortgage Only a Power of Sale, 1931, 15 Minn.L.Rev. 147. And see People v. Nogarr, 1958, 164 Cal.App. 2d 591, 330 P.2d 858, criticized in 1959, 11 Stan.L. Rev. 574. See also Durfee, Cas. on Security, 1951, 43–55 for origin, development and nature of the lien theory.

31. The lien theory has also been established, inadvertently perhaps, by judicial decision. Franklin Plant Farm Co. v. Nash, 1915, 118 Va. 98, 86 S.E. 836; Gravatt v. Lane, 1917, 121 Va. 44, 92 S.E. 912. See note, 1921, 8 Va.L.Rev. 224.

32. See Lloyd, Mortgages—The Genesis of the Lien Theory, 1922, 32 Yale L.Jour. 233, 241.

33. S.Car., Laws of 1791, pp. 32 and 33; Code 1962, § 45–51; Bredenberg v. Landrum, 1890, 32 S.C. 215, 10 S.E. 956.

34. West's Ann.Cal.Code Civ.Proc., § 744; Minn.Stat. Ann. § 559.17; Or.Rev.Stat. 86.010; Rev.Code Wash. Ann. § 7.28.230.

35. West's Ann.Cal.Civ.Code, § 2927; Burns' Ann.Ind. Stats., § 56–701; cf. Ind.Rev.Stats., 1843, p. 459. See also 3 Tiffany, Real Prop., 2d Ed., 2427; Uniform Mortgage Act § 2.

36. Colo.Code Civ.Proc., 1921, § 281. For a collection of citations of statutes embodying the various

types of provisions mentioned in the text, see 1933, 43 Yale L.Jour. 111.

37. Revised Stat. of N.Y. (1828) Part 3, Ch. V, § 57: "No action of ejectment shall hereafter be maintained by a mortgagee, or his assigns, or representatives, for the recovery of the possession of the mortgaged premises."

N.Y.Civ.Prac.Act, Action to Recover Real Prop., § 991: "A mortgagee, or his assignee or other representative, cannot maintain such an action to recover the mortgaged premises." Cf. Harlem Savings Bank v. Cooper, 1950, 199 Misc. 1110, 101 N.Y.S.2d 641, discussed in 1952, 52 Col.L.Rev. 150, holding that a mortgagor in possession was not a "tenant" entitled to protection against eviction under emergency rent laws as against purchaser at foreclosure sale. Since 1963, this provision in slightly different form is in Real Prop.Actions and Proc.Law, Art. 6, § 611, in 49½ McKinney's Consol.Laws of New York, Ann.

38. Phyfe v. Riley, 1836, 15 Wend. 248, 256, 30 Am. Dec. 55. See also Mickles v. Townsend, 1859, 18 N.Y. 575, 584; Packer v. Rochester etc., R. R. Co., 1858, 17 N.Y. 283, 287. And in holding that the right to redeem was limited by the section of the Code governing equitable actions generally, reasoning from the same decision on the mortgagee's right to defeat ejectment by the mortgagor after the mortgagee has possession, it was said that it can "hardly be said that such a mortgagee has no legal title." Hubbell v. Sibley, 1872, 50 N.Y. 468, 472.

39. See infra, § 129.

40. Trimm v. Marsh, 1874, 54 N.Y. 599, 13 Am.Rep. 623. Rev.Stats.N.Y., 1828, vol. 2, p. 368, §§ 31, 32;

then New York statute which permitted levy of execution upon legal but not equitable interests in land, that a mortgagee who recovers a judgment against his mortgagor on a cause of action other than the mortgage debt,[41] levies execution upon, sells, and buys in the mortgaged property gets the full title thereto which is not subject to redemption by the mortgagor. The reasoning of the court was that, since under the New York statutes the mortgagee had no right to possession therefore the mortgage "gives the mortgagee no title or estate whatever", that "the mere right, when he goes into possession by the consent of the mortgagor,[42] to retain possession, is not an attribute of title" and since the mortgagee does not get legal title it must therefore remain in the mortgagor because it must be somewhere.[43]

In contrast to the doubts and difficulties attending the establishment of the lien theory in New York, in many other states which had enacted statutes similar to the New York legislation, the courts adopted the lien theory without question, Michigan being a typical example.[44] Similarly under the California

legislation, in a leading case, Field, J., said that, "This section takes from the [mortgage] instrument its common law character, and restricts it to the purposes of security. It does not, it is true, in terms, change the estates at law of the mortgagor and mortgagee, but, by disabling the owner from entering for condition broken, and restricting his remedy to a foreclosure and sale, it gives full effect to the equitable doctrine, upon a consideration of which the section was evidently drawn. An instrument which confers no right of either present or future possession, possesses little of the character of a conveyance, and can hardly be deemed to pass any estate in the land." [45]

In states where the lien theory is established the courts apply it even though the parties do not use the ordinary mortgage form. Thus, under a trust deed mortgage in a lien jurisdiction the grantor-trustor has the right to possession until the trustee realizes on the security by sale.[46] And the

Co., 1865, 13 Mich. 380, 87 Am.Dec. 759; Hogsett v. Ellis, 1868, 17 Mich. 351, 363; Newton v. McKay, 1874, 30 Mich. 380.

45.   McMillan v. Richards, 1858, 9 Cal. 365, 409, 70 Am.Dec. 655, 661.

46.   Tyler v. Granger, 1874, 48 Cal. 259 (ejectment by the trustee against the grantor-trustor denied); Wisconsin Cent. R. Co. v. Wisconsin River Land Co., 1888, 71 Wis. 94, 36 N.W. 837 (ejectment by grantor-trustor against third party allowed). See Sacramento Bank v. Alcorn, 1898, 121 Cal. 379, 384, 53 P. 813, 814: " * * * it would seem that, while we must say that title passes, none of the incidents of ownership attach, except that the trustees are deemed to have such estate as will enable them to convey." Although the California courts constantly state as fundamental that in a mortgage there is only a lien created while in a trust deed legal title actually passes (see, e. g., Bayer v. Hoagland, 1925, 95 Cal.App. 403, 273 P. 58) nevertheless they also have repeatedly come to the conclusion stated in the extract from Sacramento Bank v. Alcorn. Bostwick v. McEvoy, 1882, 62 Cal. 496; McLeod v. Moran, 1908, 153 Cal. 97, 100, 94 P. 604 ("it is practically and substantially only a mortgage with power of sale"); Hollywood Lumber Co. v. Love, 1909, 155 Cal. 270, 100 P. 198; Curtin v. Krohn, 1906, 4 Cal. App. 131, 135, 87 P. 243; Wyser v. Truitt, 1928, 95 Cal.App. 727, 273 P. 147; Wasco Creamery & Const. Co. v. Coffee, 1931, 117 Cal.App. 298, 3 P.2d 588; Wilson v. McLaughlin, 1937, 20 Cal.App.2d 608, 67 P. 2d 710; Pacific States Sav. & Loan Co. v. North

N.Y. Civil Pract.Act, Laws 1920, c. 925, §§ 710, 711, provided that the interest of the mortgagor, his heirs or assigns, should not be sold on execution levied thereon by virtue of a judgment recovered on the mortgage debt. It was recognized that this statute would be applicable in Trimm v. Marsh, 1874, 3 Lans. 509, 511, affirmed 54 N.Y. 599, 13 Am. Rep. 623. The statute was applied in Delaplaine v. Hitchcock, 1843, 6 Hill (N.Y.) 14, and a similar one in Linville v. Bell, 1874, 47 Ind. 547. In the absence of such legislation the authorities are in conflict upon the power to and effect of a levy by the mortgagee upon the interest of the mortgagor. See infra, Chapter 11.

41.   Trimm v. Marsh, note 40, supra.

42.   Under the later New York rule, as contrasted with the earlier view, consent of the mortgagor was essential to the mortgagee's right to hold possession. See infra, § 160.

43.   Phyfe v. Riley, supra note 38.

44.   The 1843 Act in Michigan was substantially the same as the 1828 statute in New York. For the development of the law in that state see the following cases collected in Campbell, Cases Mortgages, 2d ed., 22, n. 3; Stevens v. Brown, 1842, Walk.Ch. 41; Mundy v. Monroe, 1848, 1 Mich. 68; Crippen v. Morrison, 1864, 13 Mich. 23; Ladue v. Detroit etc.

same is true of deeds absolute intended as mortgages.[47]

In a few states adopting the lien theory it has been held that there is a statutory policy against possession in the mortgagee that invalidates agreements in the mortgage permitting him to enter.[48] In most of them, however, an agreement between the parties, giving the mortgagee the right to possession of the mortgaged premises, is valid.[49] Indeed in one of the most frequently enacted types

American Bond & Mortg. Co., 1940, 37 Cal.App.2d 307, 99 P.2d 355; C. A. Warren Co. v. All Persons, 1908, 153 Cal. 771, 96 P. 807 (the trustor has an estate of inheritance which may pass by devise or descent against all persons except the trustee); Aitchison v. Bank of Am. Assn., 1936, 8 Cal.2d 400, 65 P.2d 890 (trustor has a legal estate which he may convey subject to the trust deed).

There is some authority drawing a distinction between trust deed mortgages containing a condition subsequent in the conveyance that it was to be void on payment by the trustor and those providing only that the trustee have power to sell on default; the former being construed to leave legal title in the trustor until sale and the latter to reserve only an equitable interest. Martin v. Alter, 1884, 42 Ohio St. 94; National Bank v. Tennessee etc., Co., 1900, 62 Ohio St. 564, 585, 588, 57 N.E. 450, 453, 454; City of Chicago v. Sullivan Machinery Co., 1915, 269 Ill. 58, 69, 109 N.E. 696, 700, all containing defeasance clauses. Morris v. Way, 1847, 16 Ohio 469, 479 (no condition subsequent).

47. A granted land to B by absolute deed to secure a debt. Held, B, as such grantee, not entitled to possession. Yingling v. Redwine, 1902, 12 Okl. 64, 69 P. 810. See also Hall v. Savill, Iowa, 1851, 3 G. Greene 37, 54 Am.Dec. 485; Flynn v. Holmes, 1906, 145 Mich. 606, 108 N.W. 685, 11 L.R.A.,N.S., 209.

48. Teal v. Walker, 1884, 111 U.S. 242, 252, 4 S.Ct. 420, 28 L.Ed. 415; Hall v. Hall, 1893, 41 S.C. 163, 167, 19 S.E. 305, 44 Am.St.Rep. 696; Orr v. Bennett, 1917, 135 Minn. 443, 161 N.W. 165, 4 A.L.R. 1396; State ex rel. Gwinn, Inc. v. Superior Court, 1932, 170 Wash. 463, 16 P.2d 831, following Western Loan & Bldg. Co. v. Mifflin, 1931, 162 Wash. 33, 297 P. 743; Rives v. Mincks Hotel Co., 1934, 167 Okl. 500, 30 P.2d 911. By statute in 1927, the Oregon policy was modified in certain instances. ORS 86.010. See a full discussion in Investors Syndicate v. Smith, C.C.A.Or.1939, 105 F.2d 611.

49. Mich. Trust Co. v. Lansing Lumber Co., 1894, 103 Mich. 392, 61 N.W. 668; Rice v. St. Paul & Pac. R. R., 1878, 24 Minn. 464; Kelly v. Roberts, 1932, 93 Mont. 106, 17 P.2d 65. See Geraldson, Clauses Increasing the Possessory Rights of Mortgagees, 1935, 10 Wis.L.Rev. 492. As to whether, in a lien jurisdiction, a mortgagee can obtain the rents and profits of the mortgaged property through the appointment of a receiver, see infra, § 149.

of statute such agreements are expressly contemplated.[50] And, as will be seen more in detail later,[51] if the mortgagee actually goes into possession with the consent of the mortgagor, or even, in many jurisdictions, without such consent but peaceably, or under color of legal right, he may hold onto possession until his debt is paid. The courts differentiate between an executory agreement for such possession and the executed transaction.[52] But in the absence of such an agreement, wherever the lien theory of a mortgage prevails, a mortgagor, prior to foreclosure, may sue the mortgagee for any illegal interference with his possession of the mortgaged premises as freely as any owner of land, under similar circumstances, may sue a wrongdoer.[53]

The lien theory of a mortgage, even in those jurisdictions where it prevails as to real estate mortgages, has not always been extended to chattel mortgages. In some of such states it is held that a chattel mortgagee, at least upon the mortgagor's default, if not prior thereto, has title to the mortgaged property.[54]

B. TORTIOUS INJURY TO LAND BY MORTGAGOR OR THIRD PERSONS [55]

TORTIOUS INJURY BY MORTGAGOR

128. A mortgagor in possession may do such acts on the land as are proper in course of

50. E. g., West's Ann.Cal.Civ.Code § 2927.

51. See infra, § 160 et seq.

52. See Rundle, Mortgages, 1933, 9 Wis.L.Rev. 40, 42, 43; Tiffany, Real Prop., 3d ed., § 1416.

53. Mills v. Heaton, 1879, 52 Iowa, 215, 2 N.W. 1112; Humphrey v. Hurd, 1874, 29 Mich. 44.

54. See Demers v. Graham, 1907, 36 Mont. 402, 93 P. 268, 14 L.R.A.,N.S., 431, 122 Am.St.Rep. 384, 13 Ann.Cas. 97.

55. See, generally, on the mortgagee's rights against the mortgagor or third parties for injuries to the mortgaged property, note, 1931, 10 Tex.L.Rev. 475; note, 1939, 17 N.Car.L.Rev. 291; Stocke, Rights of a Mortgagee and Creditors under Missouri Law When Mortgagor Retains Possession, 1925, 11 St. Louis L.Rev. 42; Denton, Right of a Mortgagee to

good husbandry. **Excess of permissible use gives the mortgagee a right to damages. The title theory measures the recovery by injury to the property; the lien theory by injury to the security interest. The latter is determined in some states by the value of the property before and after the injury, in others by the reduction of its value below the amount of the debt. Any recovery is limited to the balance due on the mortgage debt and must be applied to it.**

The mortgagor of land in possession may do such acts on the mortgaged property as constitute user of it in the same manner as such property is ordinarily used, or, in the common phrase, are "usual and proper in the course of good husbandry." He may do them even though they involve severance of fixtures or parts of the realty and result in a diminution of the value of the property.[56] In a lien state the ownership and possession being in the mortgagor would be sufficient justification of the rule, technically at least. In title states it has been thought necessary to rest it upon the terms of a license. The license may be either express or implied from the relations of the parties and the consent of the mortgagee to the mortgagor's retention of possession.[57]

When the limits of permissible use have been exceeded the mortgagee has a right to recover damages for the injury he has suffered by the mortgagor's acts. There are, however, different theories as to the basis of the mortgagee's right and as to the proper measure of damages that he may recover.

One view is that the mortgagor's conduct constitutes legal waste, or a tort in the nature of waste, the mortgagor in possession being treated as a tenant of the mortgagee.[58] "The right of action in such case is based upon the plaintiff's interest in the property; and the damages are measured by the extent of injury to that property. * * * It does not depend upon, and the damages are not to be measured by, proof of insufficiency of the remaining security."[59] Such a solution finds its logical grounding in the title theory of the mortgage but it also provides a simpler and more practical answer to the problem than do the decisions stemming from the lien theory. The mortgagor is protected, for of course any recovery by the mortgagee is ap-

Recover Damages from a Third Party for Injury to Mortgaged Property in Ohio, 1939, 3 Ohio St.L.J. 161; Train, Mr. Tutt's Casebook, 224; Walsh, Mortgages, §§ 22, 23; 3 Tiffany, Real Prop., 2d ed., § 618.

56. Searle v. Sawyer, 1879, 127 Mass. 491, 34 Am. Dec. 425.

Cf. Ingell v. Fay, 1873, 112 Mass. 451. See Walsh, Mortgages, 113 and cf. McDougal, 1935, 44 Yale L.J. 1278, 1281 n. 15.

A, a mortgagor, while in possession of the mortgaged premises, cut a reasonable quantity of wood. B, the mortgagee, thereafter evicted A. Held, A, upon quitting the land, was privileged to remove the wood for use elsewhere. Judkins v. Woodman, 1889, 81 Me. 351, 17 A. 298, 3 L.R.A. 607.

On the exploitation of oil or gas resources of land by the mortgagor, or purchaser, or lessee subsequent to the mortgage as waste as against the mortgagee, see note, 1935, 9 Tulane L.Rev. 283. See also 1935, 95 A.L.R. 957.

57. Smith v. Moore, 1840, 11 N.H. 55; Page v. Robinson, 1852, 64 Mass. (10 Cush.) 99; Searle v. Sawyer, 1879, 127 Mass. 491, 34 Am.Dec. 425.

58. Delano v. Smith, 1910, 206 Mass. 365, 92 N.E. 500, 30 L.R.A.,N.S., 474. Since common law waste is limited to acts by tenants for life or years, unless the mortgagor were left in possession under a tenancy for years his conduct would not accurately be waste but a tort in the nature of waste for which either the action of trespass or case might be brought. Anon., 1589, Savile, 84; West v. Treude, 1630, 3 Croke, 187; Langdon v. Paul, 1850, 22 Vt. 205. Camden Trust Co. v. Handle, 1942, 132 N.J.Eq. 97, 26 A.2d 865, 154 A.L.R. 602, noted, 1942, 27 Minn. L.Rev. 407, allowed recovery for voluntary "waste" but denied it for permissive "waste" against a transferee of the mortgagor who did not assume payment of the mortgage debt.

59. Byrom v. Chapin, 1873, 113 Mass. 308, 311. See also First Nat. Bank of Gadsden v. Sproull, 1894, 105 Ala. 275, 16 So. 879; Scaling v. First Nat. Bank, 1905, 39 Tex.Civ.App. 154, 87 S.W. 715. Cf. Ellis v. Glover & Hobson, Ltd. [1908] 1 K.B. 388, 399.

"Whether the mortgagee is in possession of the mortgaged premises or not, or whether his right to possession begins only with the breach of condition and there has been no breach, nevertheless he has such an interest in the property and its preservation as enables him to maintain an action in his own name for injury to it. Such right of action is founded not upon the right to present possession, but on title to the estate. He may maintain such an action, although his is a junior mortgage and although the security remains ample for his protection. He has a right to his security unimpaired." Delano v. Smith, 1910, 206 Mass. 365, 369, 92 N.E. 500, 501, 30 L.R.A.,N.S., 474.

plied on the debt or accounted for; and the mortgagee is fully protected in being assured the full benefit of the value of the entire mortgaged property, the very security he bargained for.[60] Other cases, allowing the same recovery, have permitted the mortgagee to sue the mortgagor in trespass [61] for such acts as the removal of buildings although one court found it "difficult to see upon what principle, trespass, an action appropriate only to an injury to the possession of the plaintiff, can be maintained by a mortgagee who has never had possession of the mortgaged property against a mortgagor who is in possession of it, upon the ground that the former, by the cutting of the timber or the like, is exceeding his power over the mortgaged property." * * * [62] It has been suggested that waste committed by a tenant at will is regarded as ending the tenancy and making him liable as a trespasser.[63]

Other cases base the mortgagee's right to recover upon the impairment of his security interest, not upon the damage to the property itself.[64] They represent the lien theory view that the mortgagee, not having title, possession, or the right to possession, cannot maintain an action of trespass against a mortgagor who is guilty of acts of waste but can only recover in an action on the case for the damage to his security interest. It follows that the mortgagee's damages "would be limited to the amount of the injury to the mortgage, however great the injury to the land may be." [65]

Since that is the test, the chief problem is what constitutes an impairment of the security. One rule is the difference in value of the property before and after the wrongful acts.[66] Under this the measure of damages is almost identical with that in title states.[67] Another rule requires that the impairment of the security must go to the extent of reducing the value of the remaining mortgaged property below the amount of the debt secured.[68] This seems objectionable as unfair to the mortgagee. The interest rate and the discount rate of the debt and mortgage on transfer are both determined in large measure by the amount of property securing the obligation and varies in proportion to the ratio between the debt and the value of the security. If a low rate of interest has been charged because ample security has been given, the mortgagee is forced to bear a risk he did not bargain for if part of the security can be taken away even though what is left still equals the debt.[69] And, also, the sale value of his debt and mortgage similarly will be reduced. It may be pointed out, further, that if the value of the remaining security is to be considered, so too should the solvency or insolvency of the mortgagor. Although one early case,[70] later

60. The claim "when recovered applies in payment *pro tanto* of the mortgage debt, and thus, ultimately for the benefit of the mortgagor if he redeem." Gooding v. Shea, 1869, 103 Mass. 360, 4 Am.Rep. 563. See note, 1932, 10 Tex.L.Rev. 475, 476.

61. Stowell v. Pike, 1823, 2 Me. 387; Page v. Robinson, 1852, 64 Mass. (10 Cush.) 99; Pettengill v. Evans, 1829, 5 N.H. 54; Smith v. Moore, 1840, 11 N.H. 55; cf. Stevens v. Smathers, 1899, 124 N.C. 571, 32 S.E. 959; Hoskin v. Woodward, 1863, 45 Pa. 42, 3 Leg. & Ins.Rep. 27.

62. Waterman v. Matteson, 1857, 4 R.I. 539, 543.

63. Walsh, Property, 2d ed., 78.

64. Heath v. Haile, 1896, 45 S.C. 642, 24 S.E. 300.

65. Van Pelt v. McGraw, 1850, 4 N.Y. 110.

66. President & Directors of Manhattan Co. v. Mosler Safe Co., 1935, 264 App.Div. 785, 284 N.Y.S. 145; Atlantic etc., R. Co. v. Rutledge, 1935, 122 Fla. 154, 165 So. 563; Ogden Lumber Co. v. Busse, 1904, 92 App.Div. 143, 86 N.Y.S. 1098.

67. Under the title theory the mortgagee may recover in trespass or trover the value of the severed property, e. g., gravel, which may either exceed or be less than the diminution in value to the land caused by its removal. Consequently the two measures are not always the same. Bates v. Humboldt County, 1938, 224 Iowa 841, 277 N.W. 715.

68. "The action must rest upon proof that, before the alleged injury, the mortgaged premises were of sufficient value to pay the plaintiff's mortgage, or a part of it, and that, by reason of such injury, they became inadequate for that purpose." Schalk v. Kingsley, 1880, 42 N.J.L. 32, 33.
Carroll v. Edmondson, Tex.Com.App.1931, 41 S.W.2d 64, commented on, 1932, 10 Tex.L.Rev. 475; Lieberman, etc., v. Knight, 1925, 153 Tenn. 268, 283 S.W. 450; Turrell v. Jackson, 1877, 39 N.J.L. 329.

69. Note, 1932, 10 Tex.L.Rev. 475, 478.

70. Gardner v. Heartt, 1846, 3 Denio (N.Y.) 232.

repudiated, so held, this clearly is a factor which should not determine the extent to which the mortgagee has been injured by wrongful reduction of the value of the property taken in mortgage.[71] A further limitation imposed, whichever rule of damages is followed, is that in no event can the mortgagee recover an amount in excess of his mortgage debt and expenses, or any balance due upon it.[72] Most of the cases have arisen after maturity in connection with foreclosure proceedings [73] but there is authority, on the theory that the creditor is not injured until the foreclosure sale fails to raise enough money to pay his debt, that the mortgagee must first obtain a deficiency judgment.[74] When this is the case there is no difficulty in both limiting the mortgagee's recovery to an amount not to exceed his deficiency and in compelling him to apply it to his claim. However, this restriction even more than the rule taking into account the value of the remaining property at the time of the wrong, deprives the mortgagee of the benefit of the security he bargained for, and substitutes for it not merely only so much of it as a court may consider adequate, but what the remaining property may bring at a foreclosure sale in the future.[75] Further, a judgment for damages against the mortgagor for taking or injuring the mortgaged property which cannot be brought before default is of no benefit to the mortgagee because he is then able to get a judgment for the entire debt or a deficiency after foreclosing on the remaining property. A second judgment at that time equal to a part or all of the mortgage debt or deficiency would be a completely useless duplication. The clearly preferable view, for which there is ample authority, is that the mortgagee may sue before default or foreclosure and recovery of a deficiency.[76] Although it is urged in such a case that the amount of damage to the security could not be ascertained without difficulty, and that it would be unfair to give it to the mortgagee before his debt is due neither objection has great weight. On any rule of damages, except the one requiring a foreclosure first, the amount can be ascertained. And, although the mortgagee could not be compelled to accept payment before maturity, or the mortgagor to pay, the mortgagee should be permitted to take payment if he wishes and the mortgagor, who has committed a wrong in injuring the security, ought not to be heard to object. Practically, the mortgagor will have little cause to complain for his debt will

71. Ogden Lumber Co. v. Busse, 1904, 92 App.Div. 143, 86 N.Y.S. 1098; Toledo v. Brown, 1936, 130 Ohio St. 513. See Denton, Right of a Mortgagee to Recover Damages from a Third Party, 1936, 3 Ohio L.J. 161, 164.

"It certainly is not just, and cannot be lawful, to leave a mortgagee without redress for the destruction of that substantial security upon the strength of which he loaned his money, because he is unable to show the present insufficiency of that wavering staff, the solvency of his debtor, upon which he never expected to rely". Turrell v. Jackson, 1877, 39 N.J.L. 329, 332.

72. Lavenson v. Standard Soap Co., 1889, 80 Cal. 245, 22 P. 184, 13 Am.St.Rep. 147; Heath v. Haile, 1896, 45 S.C. 642, 24 S.E. 300; Cottle v. Wright, 1931, 140 Misc. 373, 251 N.Y.S. 699; Bowden v. Bridgman, Tex.Civ.App. 1911, 141 S.W. 1043; Edler v. Hasche, 1887, 67 Wis. 653, 31 N.W. 57.

73. E. g., Cottle v. Wright, 1931, 140 Misc. 373, 251 N.Y.S. 699, discussed 1932, 32 Col.L.Rev. 146; Heath v. Haile, 1896, 45 S.C. 642, 24 S.E. 300.

In Cottle v. Wright, supra, note 73, the court said: "The bringing of a separate action at law by a mortgagee for waste presents two difficulties. The basis of his action limits him to damages representing the impairment of his security at the time of the commission of the waste. Yet he is further limited in that he cannot receive more than his mortgage debt and expenses, which can only be determined upon a sale in foreclosure. On the other hand, the amount realized upon the foreclosure sale in no way determines the impairment of his security at the time of the commission of waste for later intervening extraneous conditions such as insolvency of mortgagor or market depression may materially affect the foreclosure sale price."

74. Taylor v. McConnell, 1884, 53 Mich. 587, 19 N.W. 196.

75. See 1932, 10 Tex.L.Rev. 479; 1939, 17 N.C.L.Rev. 291, 294.

76. President & Directors of Manhattan Co. v. Mosler Safe Co., 1935, 246 App.Div. 785, 284 N.Y.S. 145; Hummer v. R. C. Huffman Const. Co., C.C.A.Ill. 1933, 63 F.2d 372; Toledo v. Brown, 1936, 130 Ohio St. 513, 200 N.E. 750; Arnold v. Broad, 1900, 15 Colo.App. 389, 62 P. 577. Cf., however, Aggs v. Shackleford County, 1892, 85 Tex. 145, 19 S.W. 1085.

be reduced and along with it the amount of interest payments, and it is doubtful whether he could have used the amount he will have to pay to much better advantage. Even if he could, it should be no answer to the mortgagee's claim to redress for the mortgagor's tort.

Other rules of damages for the impairment of the mortgagee's security are the reasonable cost of restoring the land to its former condition when this is less than the diminution in market value of the whole property by reason of the injury; as a minimum, the amount [77] received from the sale of wrongfully severed fixtures or part of the realty; [78] and "such an amount to be applied on the mortgage debt as will make the debt after this application bear the same ratio to the mortgaged estate after the injury as the original debt bore to the mortgaged property before the injury."

INJURY BY THIRD PERSONS

129. A third person who damages mortgaged property is liable to the mortgagee (1) for the injury to the property in a title state, or (2) for the injury to the security in a lien state. In lien states there is authority that the third person is only liable if he had notice of the mortgage and knew that his act would impair the security. Such notice and knowledge should be immaterial.

Where the action for injuries to the mortgaged property is against a third party, the authorities and theories follow substantially the same pattern as in the cases against the mortgagor. Thus in title states the mortgagee is allowed to bring trespass for injuries done to the land [79] and actions of re-

plevin [80] or trover [81] to recover severed fixtures or parts of the realty or their value. In jurisdictions where the mortgagee can hold the mortgagor only for impairment of the security, he is similarly restricted against third parties.[82] There are, however, some problems and considerations involved when the action is against third parties that are not present when the action is against the mortgagor. For one thing, an action for damages against the mortgagor is a useless remedy if it is not or cannot be brought until after default or foreclosure and a deficiency judgment. But against a third party it can be very valuable. Again, in lien jurisdictions before the mortgagee can recover for injury to his security he must show that such injury was intentional. Indeed, there was an early view expressed in New York [83] that not only must there be knowledge of the fact of mortgage but an actual fraudulent design to injure the mortgagee.

In spite of language to the same effect in later cases,[84] the present rule is based upon the principle that a man must be deemed to

of Columbia v. Jones, 1937, 211 N.C. 317, 190 S.E. 479 (after default by mortgagor); Jeffers v. Pease, 1902, 74 Vt. 215, 52 A. 422 (after condition broken); Harris v. Haynes, 1861, 34 Vt. 220 (after condition broken only).

80. Dorr v. Dudderar, 1878, 88 Ill. 107.

81. Searle v. Sawyer, 1879, 127 Mass. 491, 34 Am. St.Rep. 425. In Houle v. Guilbeault, 1944, 70 R.I. 421, 40 A.2d 438, noted, 1945, 25 Boston Univ.L.Rev. 149, a junior mortgagee in a title state was held unable to bring an action on the case against a third party for removal of fixtures without joining the first mortgagee.

82. Bates v. Humboldt County, 1938, 224 Iowa 841, 277 N.W. 715; Carroll v. Edmondson, Tex.Com.App. 1931, 41 S.W.2d 64, discussed, 1932, 10 Tex.L.Rev. 475; Federal Land Bank of Columbia v. St. Clair Lumber Co., 1938, 58 Ga.App. 532, 199 S.E. 337 (Ga. App.), discussed, 1939, 17 N.C.L.Rev. 291. The same conclusion has been reached in some title states on the ground that title is in the mortgagee only for security purposes and in relation to the mortgagor. McKelvey v. Creevey, 1900, 72 Conn. 464, 45 A. 4, 77 Am.St.Rep. 321; Verner v. Betz, 1890, 46 N.J.Eq. 256, 19 A. 206, 7 L.R.A. 630, 19 Am.St.Rep. 387; Cooper v. Davis, 1843, 15 Conn. 556.

83. Gardner v. Heartt, 1846, 3 Denio (N.Y.) 232.

84. Wilson v. Maltby, 1874, 59 N.Y. 126.

77. Hartshorn v. Chaddock, 1892, 135 N.Y. 116, 31 N.E. 997, 17 L.R.A. 426; Cedar Ave. Bldg. etc. v. McLaughlin, 1918, 69 Pa.Super. 73. See Ogden Lumber Co. v. Busse, 1904, 92 App.Div. 143, 86 N.Y.S. 1098.

78. See Cottle v. Wright, 1931, 140 Misc. 373, 251 N.Y. S. 699. Note, 1932, 10 Tex.L.Rev. 475, 482.

79. Smith v. Goodwin, 1822, 2 Greenl., Me., 173; Frothingham v. McKusick, 1844, 24 Me. 403; Sanders v. Reed, 1842, 12 N.H. 558; Federal Land Bank

intend the necessary consequences of his voluntary acts. It holds that he is liable if he
can be charged with knowledge of the mortgage and that his act would impair the mortgagee's security.[85] In a leading case this
has been reduced to knowledge of the existence of the mortgage which need not even be
actual but constructive from the prior registration of the mortgage.[86] This last rule
seems preferable. In fact there seems no
good reason why a third person who negligently injures mortgaged property should
not be liable to the mortgagee for the amount
of damage to the security regardless of
knowledge or notice of the existence of the
mortgage; and the same should be true
where the act is one for which there is absolute liability without regard to intention
or fault.[87] But if the requirement of notice
is adhered to, especially if it is extended to
the fact of impairment of the security, it
marks a distinct practical difference between
the mortgagor and a third party who does
the wrongful act. There is seldom much
difficulty in establishing the requisite elements as to the mortgagor for he not only
knows of the mortgage, having executed it,
but can scarcely escape knowing both the
value of the property and the effect of his
acts upon it. But charging a third party
presents real difficulties. A sensible suggestion [88] is that if the third person's acts
arose out of dealings with the mortgagor involving the purchase of a house, for example, in which the nature of the chattel
would strongly suggest its relation to realty,
as contrasted with petty articles, or, perhaps, even timber or other severed parts of
the land, he should be charged with examining title and thus with knowledge of the mortgage and the ensuing impairment of the se-

curity consequent upon the removal of his
purchase.[89]

SEVERED PROPERTY—MORTGAGEE'S RIGHTS

**130. Under the title theory the mortgagee
can follow and recover property separated from
the mortgaged land. Under the lien theory he
cannot. The best and probable majority view
lets him assert his security interest as against
all but bona fide purchasers.**

Still another problem, and one closely related to that just considered, is how far the
mortgagee can follow and reclaim or subject to his mortgage fixtures, buildings or
other things severed from the mortgaged real
property. Here again title and lien theories
have affected the opinions of the courts.
Thus in Betz v. Verner,[90] the court summarized the two lines of reasoning as follows:
"It seems that where the mortgage is regarded as a conveyance of the legal title
to the property, giving the mortgagee the
right of possession, his legal ownership, and
actual or constructive possession, give him
the right to follow and recover the property
severed. The principle applied is that property severed from the realty, so as to become
a chattel, belongs to the legal owner of the
land; but where the mortgage is regarded
merely as a lien for security, and the mortgagor has the right of possession until ejectment or foreclosure, there the mortgagee has
merely the right to restrain the removal of
the property by injunction, to protect his
lien, or, after the removal, only a right to
recover damages for the wrongful diminution of his security." Following this reasoning in title states, since the mortgagee has

---

85. Van Pelt v. McGraw, 1850, 4 N.Y. 110; Jackson
     v. Brandon Realty Co., 1906, 100 N.Y.S. 1005.

86. Turrell v. Jackson, 1877, 39 N.J.L. 329.

87. See Denton, Right of a Mortgagee to Recover
     Damages from a Third Party, 1936, 3 Ohio St.L.J.
     161, 165.

88. Glenn, Mortgages, § 34.2.

89. Such is the effect of Turrell v. Jackson, supra.
     So, also, although the question was not one of dam-
     ages but the continuance of the lien upon the sev-
     ered articles, in Johnson v. Bratton, 1897, 112 Mich.
     319, 70 N.W. 1021; Hoskin v. Woodward, 1863, 45
     Pa. 42, 3 Leg. & Ins.Rep. 27. Contrast Betz v. Ver-
     ner, 1890, 46 N.J.Eq. 256, 19 A. 206, 7 L.R.A. 630, 19
     Am.St.Rep. 387; Tomlinson v. Thompson, 1882, 27
     Kan. 70.

90. 1890, 46 N.J.Eq. 256, 19 A. 206, 7 L.R.A. 630, 19
     Am.St.Rep. 387.

"legal ownership and right of possession, he may follow things severed from the mortgage lands without his consent wherever he can find them," [91] and recover them by an action of replevin or through the appointment of a receiver, or, in the alternative, recover their value in trover.[92] On the other hand, the lien view has been followed to deny to the mortgagee any rights in things severed.[93] However, in a few title jurisdictions, the courts have decided that, because title was for the limited purpose of security, severance would divest the title so that no rights could be asserted in the severed article.[94]

On the other hand there are several lien states that hold that the lien will continue after severance. It can be enforced even though in the hands of a third party provided he took with notice of the mortgagee's lien or acted in collusion with the mortgagor; [95] it will be cut off by a bona fide purchase.[96] Some of the cases allowing foreclosure on the severed part have been made conditional on the remaining property being insufficient to pay the debt but others have ignored this requirement.[97] Here, as elsewhere, the rights of the parties ought not to be fixed upon any legalistic reasoning from the concepts of title or lien but upon considerations of how far a secured creditor should have protection. It is believed that the rule allowing him to assert his security interest in the severed property as against all but bona fide purchasers is the preferable view in all jurisdictions, and that the test of how far con-

---

91. Betz v. Verner, 46 N.J.Eq. 256, 19 A. 206, 7 L. R.A. 630, 19 Am.St.Rep. 387.

92. Dorr v. Dudderar, 1878, 88 Ill. 107 (replevin); Burley v. Pike, 1882, 62 N.H. 495 (replevin); Waterman v. Matteson, 1856, 4 R.I. 539 (replevin against the mortgagor); First National Bank & Trust Co. v. Hagar Oil Co., 1929, 105 N.J.Eq. 62, 146 A. 878, noted 1929, 78 U. of Pa.L.Rev. 269 (receiver); Langdon v. Paul, 1850, 22 Vt. 205 (trover); Searle v. Sawyer, 1879, 127 Mass. 491, 34 Am.St.Rep. 425.

93. In Buckout v. Swift, 1865, 27 Cal. 433, 437, 87 Am.Dec. 90, the defendant, who purchased the house, was not a bona fide purchaser. "But we consider that by removal from the land the house was effectually removed from the operation of the mortgage lien. * * * A building, severed and removed from mortgaged lands, of which lands it formed a part when the mortgage was given, is disencumbered of the lien, * * *."
Other cases denying the mortgagee a right to recover the severed chattel in actions at law are Vanderslice v. Knapp, 1878, 20 Kan. 647 (replevin denied against a purchaser from the mortgagor); Moore v. Moran, 1902, 64 Neb. 84, 89 N.W. 629 (replevin denied against a third party). Odell v. Buck, 3d Dept.1958, 5 A. D.2d 732, 168 N.Y.S.2d 756, noted in 1958, 24 Brooklyn L.Rev. 372. An equitable lien on a leasehold does not extend to oil converted to personal property by severance. Onyx Refining Co. v. Evans Production Corp., N.D.Tex.1960, 182 F.Supp. 253.

94. "If the mortgagee have the legal ownership and right of possession, he may follow things severed and removed from the mortgage lands without his consent wherever he can find them. If he holds title under the mortgage only as security for his lien, then the remedies appointed for preserving the security, and compensating for any loss sustained by its diminution, are such, only, as the mortgagee may use. The theory in the latter case is that, as to innocent third parties, the mortgagor is the owner of the property, and may sever and sell until restrained by injunction, or ejected by entry, or barred by foreclosure." Betz v. Verner, supra, note 91, at 267, 19 A. at 208; Cooper v. Davis, 1843, 15 Conn. 556; McKelvey v. Creevey, 1900, 72 Conn. 464,

45 A. 4, 77 Am.St.Rep. 321; Kircher v. Schalk, 1877, 39 N.J.L. 335 (replevin denied, his remedy being limited to an action for damages).

95. A mortgagor moved a house off the mortgaged premises onto other lands. Held, a decree of foreclosure sale, giving the purchaser leave to remove the house, proper. Turner v. Mebane, 1892, 110 N.C. 413, 14 S.E. 974, 28 Am.St.Rep. 697; Federal Land Bank v. Davis, 1934, 228 Ala. 85, 152 So. 226 (foreclosure), accord; Dakota Loan & Trust Co. v. Parmalee, 1894, 5 S.D. 341, 58 N.W. 811, Campbell, Cas. Morts., 153 n. 5; Hamlin v. Parsons, 1882, 12 Gil. (Minn. 108) 59, 90 Am.Dec. 284 (foreclosure on house on land of a third person who took with notice); Mills v. Pope, 1931, 90 Mont. 569, 4 P.2d 485 (foreclosure permitted); Johnson v. Bratton, 1897, 112 Mich. 319, 70 N.W. 1021; Partridge v. Hemenway, 1891, 89 Mich. 454, 50 N.W. 1084, 28 Am.St.Rep. 322.

96. "So long as the mortgagor continues in possession, or when the property severed passes into the possession of a person in collusion with him to defeat the lien and security of the mortgage, whether upon or off the mortgaged premises, it would seem that the rights of the mortgagee would be unaffected. But when the property is severed, and sold to an innocent purchaser, the lien in equity is gone, and the remedy of the mortgagee is an action at law against the mortgagor, and those who act with him to impair or defeat the security of the mortgage." Betz v. Verner, supra, note 90 at 268, 14 A. at 208. In New Jersey, the court, although saying that the mortgagee has title, limits it to security purposes and, on the point involved here, follows the rule of lien jurisdictions.

97. See 1932, Tex.L.Rev. 481.

structive notice should be invoked to prevent there being such a claimant ought to depend, as previously suggested, upon the character of the severed property. And, indeed, this seems to be the result of a majority of the cases, regardless of the reasoning by which they arrived there.

INJUNCTION AGAINST REMOVAL OF SEVERED PROPERTY

131. Under the better view the mortgagor may be enjoined from removing severed property if removal would not leave adequate security. However, there is authority in both title and lien states that no injunction will normally be granted.

Some authorities, influenced by the title theory, say that a mortgagor who wrongfully severs fixtures, buildings, or part of the land itself is liable for conversion. The reason is found in the view of the mortgagee as having title to the severed product.[98] In these states equity courts hold further that normally the mortgagee cannot have an injunction against the mortgagor to restrain the asportation or other conversion of the severed portion. An injunction will lie only if the mortgagor is insolvent or money damages would be inadequate.[99] In the states in which severance from mortgaged land frees the severed part from the lien of the mortgage so that the mortgagee has no right to sue at law for it, it follows that the mortgagee would have no claim to an injunction to prevent the removal of the severed product. In these latter states even the insolvency of the mortgagor would not be sufficient to warrant an injunction.[1] The result is that in all states the mortgagee's only reliable

remedy is to prevent the commission of waste in the first place.[2]

It is submitted that both lines of cases are wrong. Regardless of whether the state is of lien or title theory persuasion, severance should not shake off the mortgagee's security interest in the severed article. Further, the criterion for issuing an injunction against a mortgagor should not be whether the subject matter of the mortgage is real or personal property, but whether if it is disposed of there will be sufficient property left still subject to the mortgage to leave the plaintiff adequate security.[3]

INJURY BY THIRD PERSONS— MORTGAGOR'S RIGHTS

132. In both title and lien states the mortgagor in possession is treated as owner as to third persons. Therefore he may recover from them the full amount of damage.

A mortgagor in possession, even in title states, is treated as owner of the mortgaged property as to all persons other than the mortgagee or one claiming under the mortgagee, and this is *a fortiori* true in lien states.[4] It follows that he may recover from a third person for injuries done to the premises the full amount of damage done just as though the property were not subject to a mortgage.[5] This view, it has been argued

---

98. See supra, § 130.

99. See, McClintock, Equity, 2d ed., §§ 45, 47.

1. Ames, Cas.Eq., 484 n. However, see American Trust Co. v. North Belleville Quarry Co., 1879, 31 N.J.Eq. 89; Chanango Bank v. Cox, 1875, 26 N.J. Eq. 452; Ennis v. Smith et al., 1911, Del.Ch., 80 A. 636.

2. Watson v. Hunter, 1821, 5 Johns.Ch. 169, 9 Am. Dec. 295.

See Cooper v. Davis, 1843, 15 Conn. 556; Vanderslice v. Knapp, 1878, 20 Kan. 647; Tomlinson v. Thomson, 1882, 27 Kan. 70. See note, 1911, 60 U. of Pa. L.Rev. 135.

3. Ensign v. Colburn, 1845, 11 Paige (N.Y.) 503; Hutchins v. King, 1862, 68 U.S. (1 Wall.) 53, 17 L. Ed. 544. As to tests of adequacy of security, see § 134.

4. Huckins v. Straw, 1852, 34 Me. 166, Campbell, Cases Mortgages, 2d Ed., 13; Cotton v. Carlisle, 1887, 85 Ala. 175, 4 So. 670, 7 Am.St.Rep. 29; Orr v. Hadley, 1858, 36 N.H. 575; Seaman v. Bisbee, 1896, 163 Ill. 91, 45 N.E. 208; Huckins v. Straw, 1852, 34 Me. 166.

5. Hamilton v. Griffin, 1898, 123 Ala. 600, 26 So. 243; Craig v. W. P. Carmichael Co., 1917, 271 Mo. 516, 197 S.W. 141; Watkins v. Kaolin Mfg. Co., 1902, 131 N.C. 536, 42 S.E. 983, 60 L.R.A. 617; Van Dyke v.

with vigor, is completely inconsistent with the title theory of mortgages and, most especially is it incompatible with the rule in title states that the mortgagee may recover severed parts of the realty or their value from third parties in actions of replevin or trover.[6] If this thesis were carried to its logical conclusion, the mortgagee would be denied any remedy against a third party. But he can always recover to the extent that his security has been impaired even in lien jurisdictions.

There seems little more objection to allowing the mortgagee to recover entire damages without regard to the measure of his own security, or the severed portion itself, and then crediting his recovery on the debt or accounting for it than there is in allowing a partial recovery limited to the extent his security interest is impaired and applying or accounting for it. Further, to restrict any relief of the mortgagee to holding the mortgagor and giving to the mortgagor the sole rights against third parties would pose practical difficulties in forcing the mortgagor to sue. In addition, such a view ought to permit settlements [7] between the mortgagor and the third party to preclude any recovery by the mortgagee, and, carried to a logical absurdity, deny relief to the mortgagee where the third party has acted to injure the property with the connivance of the mortgagor so that the latter has no action of his own.[8] Such considerations should not merely refute any argument that the sole desirable solution is to vest the right to full recovery against third parties exclusively in the mortgagor, but to lend support to the view that, as a practical solution, permitting the mortgagee not only the right to sue but to recover full damages has considerable mer-

it. And, indeed, the vitality of such a view is evidenced by legislation in a number of states altering the rule that restricts him to recovery of the diminution of his security interest.[9]

RELATION OF RIGHTS OF MORTGAGOR AND MORTGAGEE AGAINST THIRD PARTIES

133. (1) If the mortgagor sues first he may recover the full amount. The mortgagee is barred but he gets a lien on the judgment.

(2) If the mortgagor settled with the tortfeasor without suit, the mortgagee is not barred.

(3) If the mortgagee sues first, the mortgagor may recover the difference between the total amount of damage and the mortgagee's recovery.

There is another difficulty that arises because of the fact that courts have recognized rights by both the mortgagor and the mortgagee against third parties who have injured the property. In states [10] where the mortgagee can have no action unless the remaining property is less than the debt, if the injury has not reduced the security below that mark the mortgagor is the only one injured, and therefore he can recover for the entire damage done. The question of whether there must be two suits, one by the mortgagor and one by the mortgagee, or whether there may be a full recovery in one action by either party, is raised in two situations. (1) Where the injury has impaired the value of the remaining property to such an extent that it is insufficient to pay the debt. (2) In jurisdic-

Grand Trunk R. Co., 1910, 84 Vt. 212, 78 A. 958, Ann.Cas.1913A, 640.

6. Walsh, Mortgages, § 23.

7. See cases cited Campbell, Cases Mortgages, 2d Ed., 152, n. 4.

8. See Sanders v. Reed, 1842, 12 N.H. 558.

9. E. g., Ga.Code Ann. (Park, Supp.1939) § 105–1412. See 1939, 53 Harv.L.Rev. 503.

In Rome Kraft Co. v. Davis, 1958, 213 Ga. 899, 102 S.E. 2d 571, conformed to 97 Ga.App. 347, 103 S.E.2d 168, noted in 1958, 10 Mercer L.Rev. 162, it was held that plaintiff, a transferee of the mortgagor and assignee of the security deed "together with all the rights, remedies and powers contained therein" could not maintain trespass for timber cut on the mortgaged property before the transfer and assignment, even though the mortgagor had a right of action and so did the mortgagee.

10. See Garrow v. Brooks, 1938, 123 N.J.Eq. 138, 196 A. 460.

tions which permit the mortgagee to recover for the injury to the property itself.[11] In a jurisdiction in which the mortgagee's right to recover is a limited one, the mortgagor who sued first was allowed a complete recovery. The court said that the defendant would be protected against an action by the mortgagee because such recovery would be a legal bar to further recovery by either.[12] Further, the judgment recovered by the mortgagor would be subjected to the lien of the mortgage as substitute collateral "to the extent that it may be found the proceeds of the judgment represent the amount of damage sustained by the complainant under the rule as to the measure thereof",[13] i. e., the diminution in value of the security. In a title jurisdiction, the mortgagor's recovery would be subject, on a parity of reasoning, to a lien for the entire amount of the mortgagee's debt claim.

On the other hand, if there has been a settlement without suit between the mortgagor and the third person, the mortgagee will not be barred from recovering against the tortfeasor.[14]

"When the mortgagee has instituted the prior suit, and recovered his damages, as he may, there is no difficulty about the rule. The owner may still maintain an action for the injury, and the trespasser can protect himself by giving in evidence the recovery by the mortgagee in mitigation of damages. The owner has suffered damage to the full extent of the injury, but his claim has been satisfied pro tanto by payment to the mortgagee for his loss."[15] Of course, if the mortgagee had been permitted to recover the entire amount of damage done, this should be a complete bar to the mortgagor's action.

EQUITABLE RELIEF AGAINST MORTGAGOR

134. The mortgagee may enjoin threatened waste by the mortgagor if the injury would bring the value of the security dangerously close to inadequacy. If an injunction is not sufficient, equity may appoint a receiver.

It is thoroughly settled that a mortgagee may have an injunction against a mortgagor in possession to prevent him from injuring the mortgaged property under certain circumstances. The only question is what those circumstances are. This is true even though the mortgagee has the right to take possession of the mortgaged premises. The severe rules of accounting, theory to the contrary notwithstanding, make this such an inadequate remedy that it will not prevent the granting of equitable relief in appropriate cases.[16] There is some authority that equity will act to prevent the mortgagor doing any serious injury to the property over and above the normal use of it in the course of good husbandry, as by cutting down an undue amount of timber or the removal of buildings or fixtures.[17] And there is much sense in such a view. If five acres of land have been given in mortgage the mortgagor could not sell off, free and clear of the mortgage, one acre even though what is left is more than ample

11. See Turner Coal Co. v. Glover, 1892, 101 Ala. 289, 13 So. 478; Paine v. Woods, 1871, 108 Mass. 160. See also Ann.Cas.1913A, 652. Cf. Gooding v. Shea, 1869, 103 Mass. 360, 4 Am.Rep. 563; Jenks v. Hart Cedar & Lumber Co., 1906, 143 Mich. 449, 106 N.W. 1119, 114 Am.St.Rep. 673; Sanders v. Reed, 1842, 12 N.H. 558.

12. Delaware etc., Telephone Co. v. Elvins, 1899, 63 N.J.L. 243, 43 A. 903, 76 Am.St.Rep. 217; Garrow v. Brooks, supra note 10.

13. Garrow v. Brooks, 1938, 123 N.J.Eq. 138, 141, 196 A. 460, 462. "The mortgagee was entitled to the building as part of her security and is now entitled to look to the fund in the hands of the sheriff as converted into its original form." Idem.

14. Taylor v. Federal Land Bank, 1932, 162 Miss. 653, 657, 138 So. 596, 597; Guaranty Savings & Loan Ass'n v. Springfield, Mo.App. 1938, 113 S.W.2d 147, 154; Federal Land Bank of Columbia v. Jones, 1937, 211 N.C. 317, 190 S.E. 479.

15. Delaware, etc., Telephone Co. v. Elvins, 1899, 63 N.J.L. 243, 245, 43 A. 903, 76 Am.St.Rep. 217.

16. See Glenn, Morts., § 211. Cf. the attitude of courts in England and in title states in America toward the appointment of a receiver of rents and profits in a foreclosure action. §§ 147, 148, infra.

17. Nelson v. Pinegar, 1863, 30 Ill. 473; Williams v. Chicago Exhibition Co., 1900, 188 Ill. 19, 58 N.E. 611.

to secure the debt. The mortgagee took the entire five acres and he is entitled to keep all of it. He is not compelled to run the risk that though now the property that is left is ample, it might not be later when the debt is due. And so here. He bargained for the greater amount of security and he should not have to accept anyone else's judgment on whether it, or what is left of it after the mortgagor does an act reducing its value, is adequate.

Most courts, however, follow the rule that the threatened injury must be one that will bring the value of the security down to a point where it is in the danger zone so that it might not be ample.[18] In one of the early and leading cases, the test was put this way: "It is rather a question of prudence than of actual value. I think the question which must be tried is whether the property the mortgagee takes as a security, is sufficient in this sense, that the security is worth so much more than the money advanced that the act is not to be considered as substantially impairing the value, which was the basis of the contract between the parties at the time it was entered into."[19] What is the danger zone will depend on the nature of the property in part. A bigger margin of security must be left if the property is subject to wide and frequent fluctuations in value than if it is of stable value, but probably in no case would the security have been considered adequate security by a prudent lender unless it was worth one-third more than the amount of the money lent at the time of the mortgage.[20] In no case would it be sufficient that

the value of the property was barely equal to the mortgage debt.[21] And, quite properly, the insolvency of the mortgagor is immaterial on this question. The mortgagee demanded the mortgage before making the loan so that he would not have to rely upon the general pecuniary condition of the mortgagor and it would be inequitable to take into account in granting relief a factor which the mortgagee took care to guard against by seeing to it that he was a secured and not a general creditor.[22]

Waste of the property through the mortgagor's failure to make necessary repairs was taken care of at common law by the ability of the mortgagee to take possession and do the job himself.[23] There is a clear implication in a case decided by Chancellor Kent, that in a proper case, equity would grant relief against permissive waste and neglect by the mortgagor.[24]

The ability of the court of equity to protect the mortgagee from the commission of waste is not limited to the issuance of injunctions. Although "it is true that in general a receivership is ancillary or incidental to the main purpose of the bill, it does not follow that where a case is presented which demands the relief which can be best given by a receivership, such relief must be refused, because the time has not arrived when other substantial relief can be asked. For example, although as a rule, a mortgagee cannot ask for relief until his mortgage debt has become

---

18. King v. Smith, 1843, 2 Hare, 239; Fairbank v. Cudworth, 1873, 33 Wis. 358; Fidelity Trust Co. v. Hoboken etc. R. Co., 1906, 71 N.J.Eq. 14, 63 A. 273; Coker v. Whitlock, 1875, 54 Ala. 180; Collins v. Rea, 1901, 127 Mich. 273, 86 N.W. 811; Hastings v. Perry, 1848, 20 Vt. 272; Brady v. Waldron, 1816, 2 Johns.Ch. (N.Y.) 148. For a collection of cases in accord, see Ames, Cas.Eq., 483n.

19. King v. Smith, supra, at 243.

20. King v. Smith, supra note 18; Moriarty v. Ashworth, 1890, 43 Minn. 1, 3, 44 N.W. 531, 532; 19 Am. St.Rep. 203. "If the debt is not yet mature it is to

be considered whether, during the time which may elapse before maturity, the present value of the property may not become depreciated from causes not now known."

21. Moriarty v. Ashworth, supra note 20; Beaver Flume and Lumber Co. v. Eccles, 1903, 43 Or. 400, 73 P. 201, 99 Am.St.Rep. 759.

22. Fairbank v. Cudworth, supra note 18; Core v. Bell, 1882, 20 W.Va. 169.

23. See infra, § 160 ff.

24. See Campbell v. Macomb, 1820, 4 Johns.Ch., N.Y., 534, 541, "How far the court could or ought to interfere in a case of negligent or permissive waste, rapidly impairing the security, is a question which need not now be discussed."

due, he can go into a court of equity before that time has arrived and ask for an injunction and a receiver to prevent the subject-matter of his mortgage from being impaired and wasted."[25] Nevertheless "the appointment of a receiver and authorizing him to take possession of property is the exercise of a higher and more far reaching power than the granting of an injunction, and should not be resorted to where an injunction will as well serve the purpose of the judicial proceedings, and to the same extent protect the rights of the complainant."[26] This attitude of the courts toward the appointment of a receiver, it should be stressed, leaves out of account the appointment of a receiver at the request of a mortgagee who has begun foreclosure. That is considered separately later.

MORTGAGEE'S DUTY TO ENJOIN WASTE

135. Where the mortgagor is a surety—e. g., has conveyed subject to the mortgage—it has been argued that the mortgagee must enjoin waste by the mortgagor's grantee if he wants to preserve his right to collect the debt from the mortgagor. The better view does not require this.

If a mortgagee has knowledge of the commission of waste by the mortgagor's assuming grantee may he, nevertheless, obtain a deficiency judgment against the mortgagor? Put in other terms, the question is whether a mortgagee may, at his option, fail to pursue his equitable remedy to enjoin waste and still have his legal remedies intact to collect the debt against the mortgagor where the mortgagor stands in the position of a surety. In one case squarely raising the question an affirmative answer was given.[27] The decision, however, has been criticized, although the validity of the stricture is questionable.[28]

It would seem clear that as between the mortgagee and the party who is committing the waste the mortgagee, if he chooses, may allow the injury to the security to be done and seek his redress in an action at law or not at all. When the mortgagor conveys to a purchaser who assumes the mortgage debt, or who takes "subject to" it, the mortgagor stands in the position of surety with the mortgaged land and the assuming grantee as principals.[29] And when the mortgagee acquires a surety, the restrictive rules of suretyship came into operation and affect his freedom of conduct in several ways, one of which is to impose upon him the duty of preserving his rights against the principal debtor for the benefit of the surety. More particularly, he must take reasonable steps to preserve and to protect any security he holds for the same debt the surety is bound to pay to him, at least if "the creditor is the only person who can conveniently take the appropriate action."[30] "This is especially true prior to the maturity of the creditor's claim."[31] After maturity the mortgagor-surety may protect himself by paying off the mortgagee and, by subrogation to his rights, bring the injunction suit himself, and so in such a case

25. Brassey v. New York & N. E. R. Co., C.C.Conn. 1884, 19 F. 663, 669. Long Dock Co. v. Mallery, 1858, 12 N.J.Eq. 431, 448: "The power of the court to preserve the pledge from destruction and to answer to the exigency of the mortgage, is undoubted. * * * If the bill shows a case for an injunction and a receiver, the exercise of the power is called for, although the time of payment, set in the mortgage, has not come unless the equity of the bill is met by the answer."

See also Farmers' Loan & Trust Co. v. Meridian Waterworks Co., C.C.Miss.1905, 139 F. 661; Davis v. Alton, Jacksonville & P. Ry. Co., 1913, 180 Ill.App. 1. Cf. American Loan & Trust Co. v. Toledo, C. & S. Ry. Co., C.C.Ohio 1886, 29 F. 416. But see, contra, Houston & B. V. Ry. Co. v. Hughes, Tex.Civ.App. 1916, 182 S.W. 23 (appointment of a receiver must be ancillary to foreclosure, and will not be made where the mortgagor has not defaulted in performance of obligation secured).

26. Schack v. McKey, 1901, 97 Ill.App. 460, 465. See also Original Vienna Bakery Co. v. Heissler, 1893, 50 Ill.App. 406, 413; Clark, Receivers, § 59.

27. Damiano v. Bergen County Land Co., 1935, 118 N.J.Eq. 535, 180 A. 489.

28. Glenn, Morts., § 197. See note, 1936, 36 Col.L. Rev. 328.

29. See Chapter 9, infra.

30. Restatement, Security, § 132, cf. Schroeppel v. Shaw, 1850, 3 N.Y. 446. See Arant, Suretyship, 174.

31. Restatement, Security, § 132, c, Comment.

the mortgagee-creditor should retain his option to enjoin or not as he pleases without affecting his rights against the mortgagor-surety. Even before maturity it may be that the mortgagor-surety would have a direct right of his own against the principal debtor to enjoin the commission of waste, and if so, the mortgagee-creditor need not act.[32]

But even if it is before maturity and the mortgagor-surety has no ability to prevent the waste on an independent right, it is doubtful whether the mortgagee-creditor should have to act at peril of losing his rights to any extent against the mortgagor. The duty on him to preserve the security is only that he use "ordinary business prudence" and "the creditor should not be required to make financial outlay, assume risk or perform acts that are very burdensome."[33] Indeed a majority of the courts hold that the creditor owes no duty to the surety to act affirmatively to protect the security.[34] This seems wrong and the minority cases[35] holding that he must do such acts as recording an instrument, docketing a deficiency judgment so that its lien would bind other property of the mortgagor,[36] taking out insurance on the mortgaged property when he is authorized to do so, revive a lien,[37] pay taxes so as to prevent the loss of the mortgage security,[38] or

even to foreclose[39] seem the preferable view. To compel the mortgagee to bring an action to enjoin waste would seem to be over the line as imposing upon him a more onerous duty of affirmative action than the general test of "ordinary business prudence" would justify. Even if such a duty does exist, it should be noted that it should, of course, be imposed only where the mortgagee had actual knowledge or notice of the threatened waste, and the mortgagor should be released only to the extent that the security is lost by reason of the failure to act.[40]

C. RIGHTS IN PRODUCT OF THE RES

EMINENT DOMAIN

136. Where part of the mortgaged land is taken by eminent domain the mortgagee, by the preferable one of three views, is entitled to the whole award up to the amount of the debt. Where all of the land is taken the same rule should apply.

Authorities are divided whether a mortgagee is a necessary party to a condemnation proceeding.

Where mortgaged land is taken by eminent domain the mortgagee's rights in the land follow the award and attach to it.[41] In this way the condemnor is insured a title free from the encumbrance and the benefit of his security is saved to the mortgagee. "The underlying theory of the right of a mortgagee to part or all of the award is that, as the parties are powerless to prevent the taking of the property by the public and the mortgagee loses his lien on the part taken, the award equitably stands in the place of the land taken; and, as the mortgage does

32. 1936, 36 Col.L.Rev. 329. That the mortgagor has a right to a receiver against a grantee to protect himself against a deficiency, look at 1929, 248 Mich. 76, 226 N.W. 892. See notes, 1932, 78 A.L.R. 872; 1930, 43 Harv.L.Rev. 1162.

33. Arant, Suretyship, § 63.
See Simpson, Suretyship, § 75.

34. Arant, Suretyship, 240.

35. Seymour v. Bank of Thomasville, 1923, 159 Ga. 99, 121 S.E. 578; Sullivan v. State, 1894, 59 Ark. 47, 26 S.W. 194.

36. Schroeppel v. Shaw, 1850, 3 N.Y. 446.

37. Willard v. Welch, 1904, 94 App.Div. 179, 88 N.Y.S. 173, affirmed 186 N.Y. 564, 79 N.E. 1118; Appeal of Kindt, 1883, 102 Pa. 441, 40 L.I. 261, 13 W.N.C. 137, 30 P.L.J. 499; Campbell v. Sherman, 1892, 151 Pa. 70, 25 A. 35, 31 Am.St.Rep. 735, 31 Wkly.Notes Cas. 22.

38. Wasson v. Hodshire, 1886, 108 Ind. 26, 8 N.E. 621.

39. See 1930, 34 Dick.L.Rev. 119.

40. Arant, Suretyship, § 48. The rule laid down is in case of failure to act to perfect security but it would apply to failure to prevent destruction.
See Simpson, Suretyship, § 75.

41. Calumet River Co. v. Brown, 1891, 136 Ill. 322, 26 N.E. 501, 12 L.R.A. 84. See also cases in succeeding notes. See further, as to the rights of the mortgagee where property has been taken in condemnation proceedings, 1947, 22 N.Y.Univ.L.Q.Rev. 730.

not cover the award in law, it is held to operate as an equitable lien thereon. This results in two separate encumbrances, the legal mortgage on the remainder of the land and the equitable lien on the award."[42] Where the entire property subject to the mortgage is taken, the mortgagee is entitled to the entire award, or so much of it as is necessary to satisfy his mortgage debt.[43] Where only part of mortgaged land is condemned there are three different views in the cases as to the mortgagee's rights. One view gives the mortgagee the entire amount of the award without distinction as to whether or not the mortgage has been foreclosed or even as to whether or not it has matured.[44] This is sound because it is in accord with the theory that a mortgage is a lien on every portion of the land to the full amount of the secured obligation. Another view requires the mortgagee first to foreclose on the part not taken and then, but only then, to reach the proceeds of the partial condemnation to satisfy the deficiency.[45] The objection to this is that it involves expense and delay which seems unnecessary and involves impounding the fund until the condition is met. A third suggestion is that the court should allocate to the mortgagee a portion of the award measured by the ratio which the mortgage debt bears to the whole mortgaged land, thus preserving the ratio of debt to security.[46]

Whether or not the mortgagee is a necessary party in a condemnation suit is for the most part governed by statute and there is a divergence of view on the matter.[47] Where a mortgagee of record has not been joined, one line of cases has held that the condemnor secures good title upon paying the damages to the mortgagor.[48] Curiously enough these decisions are from title jurisdictions in which it might have been expected that the mortgagee's interest would be accorded paramount importance. The mortgagee is remitted to recovering the award from the condemnor before it is paid to the mortgagor or from the mortgagor if it has already been handed over.[49] Such a result, at least if the

42. Petition of Dillman, 1936, 276 Mich. 252, 258, 267 N.W. 623, 625, Campbell, Cases Mortgages, 2d Ed., 176.

43. Calumet River Ry. v. Brown, 1891, 136 Ill. 322, 26 N.E. 501, 12 L.R.A. 84; Chicago v. Gage, 1915, 268 Ill. 232, 109 N.E. 28; Connell v. Kakauna etc., Co., 1916, 164 Wis. 471, 159 N.W. 927, Ann.Cas.1918A 247, rehearing denied 164 Wis. 471, 160 N.W. 1035. It is immaterial whether the mortgage debt is or is not due. Morgan v. Willman, 1927, 318 Mo. 151, 1 S.W.2d 193, 58 A.L.R. 1518; Federal Trust Co. v. East Hartford Fire Dist., C.C.A.Conn.1922, 283 F. 95. See Teague, Condemnation of Mortgaged Property, 1966, 44 Tex.L.Rev. 1535, 1537–1939.

44. In re Forman, 1930, 138 Misc. 501, 240 N.Y.S. 718, noted 1931, 44 Harv.L.Rev. 1142; In re Public Park, 1918, 184 App.Div. 509, 172 N.Y.S. 50, dismissed, 1918, 224 N.Y. 697, 121 N.E. 356. If not mature, a rebate of interest on the debt must be given. See Teague, Condemnation of Mortgaged Property, 44 Tex.L.Rev. 1535, 1539.

45. Woolf v. Leicester Realty Co., 1909, 134 App.Div. 484, 119 N.Y.S. 288; Gray v. Case, 1893, 51 N.J.Eq. 426, 26 A. 805; Rose v. Conlin, 1921, 52 Cal.App. 225, 198 P. 653, certiorari denied 1921, 257 U.S. 647, 42 S. Ct. 56, 66 L.Ed. 415.

See Teague, Condemnation of Mortgaged Property, 1966, 44 Tex.L.Rev. 1535, 1540, where the second view is stated to be that when there is a partial taking the mortgagee is entitled to receive only an amount from the condemnation award that will compensate him for the extent of the impairment of his security.

46. Trustees of Schools v. Harshman, 1914, 262 Ill. 72, 104 N.E. 235. See Teague, Condemnation of Mortgaged Property, 1966, 44 Tex.L.Rev. 1535, 1543. See idem., 1543–1547 for the law in Texas. Idem., 1547–1548 sets forth as the most desirable rule that the mortgagee should receive that proportion of the condemnation award that the mortgage debt bears to the value of the entire mortgage estate; thus preserving the ratio between the debt and the security.

47. See 2 Lewis, Eminent Domain, 3d ed., 947, § 523. See also Teague, Condemnation of Mortgaged Property, 1966, 44 Tex.L.Rev. 1535–1537.

48. As to the rights against the condemnor of a mortgagee of record who was not made a party to the condemnation proceedings, see notes, 1933, 11 Tex. L.Rev. 387; 1932, 32 Col.L.Rev. 1240; 1932, 17 Minn.L.Rev. 92; 1935, 14 Or.L.Rev. 483. See also Hill, Mortgages on Property Taken by Eminent Domain, 1938, 3 John Marshall Law Q. 391.

49. Whiting v. New Haven, 1877, 45 Conn. 303; Parish v. Gilmanton, 1840, 11 N.H. 293; Read v. Cambridge, 1879, 126 Mass. 427; Goodrich v. Com'rs of Atchison Co., 1891, 47 Kan. 355, 27 P. 1006, 18 L.R. A. 113; Thompson v. Chicago etc., Ry. Co., 1892, 110 Mo. 147, 19 S.W. 77.

mortgagee has not been given notice, would seem to be unconstitutional.[50] In any event, it seems undesirable in that it deprives the mortgagee of his bargained for security and leaves him with inadequate protection for, after the money has been paid over to the mortgagor, he is in the same position he would have been in had he never bargained for and obtained security.

Another line of authorities protect the unjoined mortgagee although they do so in different ways. Some of them hold that the land condemned is still subject to his mortgage and the mortgagee can foreclose on it.[51] If the original award has not been paid to the mortgagor, the mortgagee may seek and obtain a revaluation and new award and have this paid to him in amount sufficient to satisfy his mortgage claim.[52] Others hold that even though the full award has been made and paid to the mortgagor, the mortgagee is entitled as against the condemnor to so much of the original award as is necessary to compensate him for his interest in the property taken[53] or to have a new valuation of the property taken and be satisfied out of it.[54]

Although there have not been many cases involving allocation between mortgagor and mortgagee of funds awarded for the damaging of mortgaged property the solutions offered range from giving the mortgagee nothing to allowing him the full amount awarded as damages to the extent of the mortgage debt.[55]

Other questions that have arisen in condemnation cases and have been given diverse answers either by legislation or decision are: 1. the mortgagee's right to recover from the condemnor when the condemnor pays condemnation proceeds to the wrong person;[56] or 2. when the mortgagor has suffered no harm.[57] Whether a mortgagee should be compensated for the interest he would have received had there not been a taking of the property is arguable.[58] The rights of the mortgagee in condemnation proceeds as against other claimants in general are exactly the same as they were with regard to the mortgaged property, the condemnation award being regarded as a substitute for it.[59]

INSURANCE—(1) SEPARATE POLICIES

137. Since insurance is a personal contract of indemnity, neither the mortgagor nor the mortgagee has any interest in the proceeds of a separate policy held by the other. The mortgagee cannot recover both on the policy and the debt: his insurer becomes subrogated to his right against the mortgagor on payment of loss.

Both the mortgagor and the mortgagee of real property have an insurable interest in the mortgaged property. Hence each may protect himself against loss by his own con-

50. 2 Lewis, Em.Dom., 3d ed., ch. 13, § 523, p. 947.

51. Grigsby v. Miller, 1933, 144 Or. 551, 25 P.2d 908, giving, however, a reasonable time to the condemnor to secure the property by new condemnation or purchase. See also Wilson v. European & N. A. R. Co., 1877, 67 Me. 358; Michigan Air Line Ry. Co. v. Barnes, 1879, 40 Mich. 383; Morgan v. Willman, 1927, 318 Mo. 151, 1 S.W.2d 193, 58 A.L.R. 1518; Wade v. Hennessy, 1882, 55 Vt. 207; Stamnes v. Milwaukee etc., Ry. Co., 1907, 131 Wis. 85, 109 N. W. 100, rehearing granted 131 Wis. 85, 109 N.W. 925, opinion modified 131 Wis. 85, 111 N.W. 62; North Coast Ry. Co. v. Hess, 1909, 56 Wash. 335, 105 P. 853.

52. Seaboard All-Florida Ry. Co. v. Leavitt, 1932, 105 Fla. 600, 141 So. 886, noted, 1932, 32 Col.L.Rev. 1240; Calumet River Ry. Co. v. Brown, 1891, 136 Ill. 322, 26 N.E. 501, 12 L.R.A. 84; Stamnes v. Milwaukee etc. Co., 1907, 131 Wis. 85, 109 N.W. 100.

53. Stemper v. Houston County, 1932, 187 Minn. 135, 244 N.W. 690, noted, 1932, 17 Minn.L.Rev. 92; South Park Com'rs v. Todd, 1884, 112 Ill. 379; Sherwood v. City of Lafayette, 1886, 109 Ind. 411, 10 N.E. 89, 58 Am.St.Rep. 414; note, 58 A.L.R. 1534, 1539.

54. South Park Com'rs v. Todd, 1884, 112 Ill. 379; Gray v. Case, 1893, 51 N.J.Eq. 426, 431, 26 A. 805, 807.

55. See Teague, Condemnation of Mortgaged Property, 1966, 44 Tex.L.Rev. 1535, 1549–1552.

56. See Teague, Condemnation of Mortgaged Property, 1966, 44 Tex.L.Rev. 1535, 1552–1555.

57. See Teague, op. cit. supra note 56, 1555–1558.

58. See Teague, op. cit. supra note 56, 1558–1562.

59. See Teague, op. cit. supra note 56, 1562.

tract of insurance.[60] The insurable interest of the mortgagor is the full value of the property[61] while that of the mortgagee is limited to the amount of the mortgage itself, i. e., the amount of the debt secured.[62] Traditionally courts have insisted that insurance is a purely personal contract of indemnity against diminution in the value of the property;[63] the proceeds of the contract are not regarded as a substitute res for the destroyed property.[64] As a result, if the mortgagor insures his interest in the property and there is a loss, he alone is entitled to payment. The mortgagee has no interest whatsoever in the proceeds in the absence of an agreement to insure for his benefit.[65]

So, too, on the same idea that the contract is a purely personal one of indemnity, a mortgagee who insures his interest at his own expense and with no understanding with the mortgagor, is entitled to recover even though the property remaining undestroyed is fully ample to cover his debt,[66] and the money paid

belongs to him alone, the mortgagor being a stranger to the contract and entitled to no benefit under it. Consequently, in such a case, the payment to the mortgagee does not reduce the mortgage debt; but in order to prevent the mortgagee from getting double payment, the insurer, on payment of the loss becomes subrogated *pro tanto* to the mortgage debt.[67] The only result, so far as the mortgagor is concerned, is that his creditor is changed.[68]

(2) AGREEMENT TO INSURE

138. A common mortgage clause provides for the insurance of both parties' interests in one policy. If the mortgagor violates the agreement and insures only his interest the mortgagee gets a lien on the amount due him under the policy.

Normally, instead of both mortgagor and mortgagee taking out separate policies, there

55 N.Y. 343, 14 Am.Rep. 271; Aetna Ins. Co. of Hartford, Conn. v. Baker, 1880, 71 Ind. 102; Meader v. Farmers' etc. Ass'n, 1931, 137 Or. 111, 1 P.2d 138.

67. Excelsior Fire Ins. Co. v. Royal Ins. Co., 1873, 55 N.Y. 343, 14 Am.Rep. 271; Foster v. Van Reed, 1877, 70 N.Y. 19, 26 Am.Rep. 544; Honore v. Lamar Ins. Co., 1851, 51 Ill. 409; Norwich Fire Ins. Co. v. Boomer, 1869, 52 Ill. 442, 4 Am.Rep. 618; Gould v. Maine Farmers Mut. Fire Ins. Co., 1916, 114 Me. 416, 96 A. 732, L.R.A.1917A, 604; Leyden v. Lawrence, 1911, 79 N.J.Eq. 113, 81 A. 121, affirmed 80 N.J.Eq. 550, 85 A. 1134; Gainesville Nat. Bank v. Martin, 1937, 187 Ga. 559, 1 S.E.2d 636; Le Doux v. Dettmering, 1942, 316 Ill.App. 98, 43 N.E.2d 862. Cf. King v. State Mutual Fire Ins. Co., 1851, 61 Mass. 1, 54 Am.Dec. 683.

The result is that the insurance company that charged a premium to assume the risk of loss of the property in effect takes only the risk of the mortgagor's insolvency or that the remaining property will not be worth the amount it pays out under the policy. This, although recognized, is said to be immaterial. Le Doux v. Dettmering, supra. In effect the rule makes the insurance contract one of suretyship. See Milwaukee Mechanics Ins. Co. v. Ramsey, 1915, 76 Or. 570, 149 P. 542, 543, L.R.A.1916A, 556, Ann.Cas. 1917B, 1132. Suffolk Fire Ins. Co. v. Boyden, 1864, 91 Mass. 123 goes to the opposite extreme. Not only does it deny subrogation to the insurer but permits the mortgagee, in addition to getting the insurance, to collect his debt from the mortgagor, i. e., to collect twice. But see 1928, 28 Col.L.Rev. 202 for later change in Massachusetts law. See also Kirk v. Fletcher, 1932, 123 Neb. 634, 243 N.W. 855.

68. See Gainesville Nat. Bank v. Martin, 1937, 187 Ga. 559, 1 S.E.2d 636.

60. Connecticut Mut. Life Ins. Co. v. Scammon, Ill. 1885, 117 U.S. 634, 6 S.Ct. 889, 29 L.Ed. 1007. See Honore v. Lamar Fire Ins. Co., 1851, 51 Ill. 409.

61. Florea v. Iowa State Ins. Co., 1930, 225 Mo.App. 49, 32 S.W.2d 111; Strong v. Mfg. Ins. Co., 1830, 27 Mass. 40, 20 Am.Dec. 507.

62. Lockett v. Western Assur. Co., 1935, 190 Ark. 1135, 83 S.W.2d 65; Foster v. Van Reed, 1877, 70 N.Y. 19, 26 Am.Rep. 544; Grevemeyer v. Southern Mut. Fire Ins. Co., 1869, 62 Pa. 340, 1 Am.Rep. 420; Excelsior Ins. Co. v. Royal Ins. Co., 1873, 55 N.Y. 343, 14 Am. Rep. 271; Savarese v. Ohio Farmers' Insurance Co., 1932, 260 N.Y. 45, 182 N.E. 665, 91 A.L.R. 1341; Thompson v. National Fire Ins. Co., 1925, 48 S.Dak. 224, 203 N.W. 464.

63. See 1 May, Insurance, 4th ed. § 6.

64. There is occasional judicial recognition of the idea that insurance takes the place of the property destroyed. See Gordon v. Ware Savings Bank, 1874, 115 Mass. 588, 591. See note, 1933, 19 Va.L.Rev. 508 advocating the rule that insurance proceeds are a "new form of the old res." See, also, Gilligan, Insurance on Mortgaged Property, 1940, 88 U. of Pa. L.Rev. 347; Glenn, Mortgages, § 27.4.

65. See Walsh & Simpson, Cas.Security Transactions, 184 Note (1) citing, Niagara Fire Ins. Co. v. Scammon, 1891, 144 Ill. 490, 28 N.E. 919, affirmed 144 Ill. 490, 32 N.E. 914, 19 L.R.A. 114; Ryan v. Adamson, 1881, 57 Iowa 30, 10 N.W. 287.

66. Kernochan v. New York etc. Co., 1858, 17 N.Y. 428; Excelsior Fire Ins. Co. v. Royal Ins. Co., 1873,

is an agreement in the mortgage that only one policy shall be taken out but that it shall insure the respective interests of both parties. Usually it is the mortgagor who is bound to take out the policy. If in violation of the agreement the mortgagor only insures his separate interest, the mortgagee may impress an equitable lien on the amount due him under the policy. The extent of the lien is the mortgagee's interest in the mortgaged property covered by the agreement to insure.[69] This equitable lien, it has been pointed out, arises as a consequence of the mortgagee's right to specific performance because of the inadequacy of money damages at law for breach of the contract to insure.[70] The amount realized by the mortgagee upon the lien must be applied in *pro tanto* satisfaction of the mortgage debt. Consequently, the insurer is not entitled to be subrogated to any rights that the mortgagee had against the mortgagor.[71] On the other hand, even though the insurance is taken out by the mortgagee in his own name, if "it has been effected at the request or by the authority of the mortgagor, or under circumstances that would make him chargeable with the premium, the mortgagor, in case of loss, is entitled to have the proceeds of the insurance applied in liquidation of the mortgage debt pro tanto." [72] The consequence again is that

subrogation will be denied to the insurer.[73] The same applies where the mortgagor takes out the insurance for the benefit of the mortgagee. The mortgagee is compelled to apply the proceeds insofar as the debt is due, and if he fails to do so, the law will make the application.[74]

(3) TYPES OF POLICIES

139. Under the older loss-payable policy the mortgagee's right to collect insurance hinged on the right of the mortgagor against the insurer. Under the New York standard mortgage policy his interest is insured as fully as if he had taken out a separate policy. As long as the policy has not been forfeited to the mortgagor payments of loss to the mortgagee must be applied to the debt and the insurance company is not subrogated to the rights of the mortgagee.

Loss-payable policy

Usually the agreement that one policy shall be taken out expressly insuring the interests of both parties is carried out. The older form of insurance obtained was a policy

---

69. Nichols v. Baxter, 1858, 5 R.I. 491, Walsh & Simpson, Cas.Security Transactions, 180; Wheeler v. Factors' & Traders' Ins. Co., 1879, 101 U.S. 439, 25 L.Ed. 1055; Grange Mill Co. v. Western Assur. Co., 1886, 118 Ill. 396, 9 N.E. 274, apply the same rule to a vendee. Where insurance had been taken out before the agreement but the mortgagor neglected to have it transferred, the same rule applies. See Walsh & Simpson, Cas. Security Transactions, 184 Note (2), citing Ames v. Richardson, 1882, 29 Minn. 330, 13 N.W. 137; Nordyke, etc. Co. v. Gery, 1887, 112 Ind. 535, 13 N.E. 683, 2 Am.St.Rep. 219.

70. Walsh, Mortgages, § 25.

71. See Glenn, Mortgages § 27.5.

72. Le Doux v. Dettmering, 1942, 316 Ill.App. 98, 109, 43 N.E.2d 862, 867; Elliott v. Pendleton, 1887, 67 Mich. 496, 35 N.W. 97; see Honore v. Lamar Ins. Co., 1851, 51 Ill. 409, 413.

73. Waring v. Loder, 1873, 53 N.Y. 581, true although insurer took assignment; Kernochan v. New York Bowery Fire Ins. Co., 1858, 17 N.Y. 428, 441. See Pendleton v. Elliott, 1887, 67 Mich. 496, 498, 35 N.W. 97. There is authority that in a case of this sort, by agreement with the mortgagee, the insurer can reserve a right of subrogation. Foster v. Van Reed, 1877, 70 N.Y. 19, 26 Am.Rep. 544. As was succinctly observed, "This, however, does not make sense." 1 Glenn, Mortgages, 187, fn. 6. Imperial Fire Ins. Co. v. Bull, 1889, 18 Can.S.C. 697, denied subrogation in spite of a stipulation for it unknown to the mortgagor.

74. Thorp v. Croto, 1905, 79 Vt. 390, 65 A. 562, 10 L.R. A.,N.S., 1166, 118 Am.St.Rep. 961, 9 Ann.Cas. 58; Gordon v. Ware Savings Bank, 1874, 115 Mass. 588. By statute in New York, the mortgagee may either hold the insurance and apply it to payment of the debt as it matures, or pay it over to the mortgagor for the purpose of rebuilding, McKinney's, N.Y.Real Prop.Law § 254(4). And this may be the common law rule without the aid of statute, although the mortgagee does not have to pay over the fund upon a mere promise of the mortgagor to rebuild. Fergus v. Wilmarth, 1886, 117 Ill. 542, 7 N.E. 508. If the debt is not yet due, unless the mortgagor consents, the mortgagee cannot apply the insurance money to the debt nor can he be forced to do so. Thorp v. Croto, supra; Naquin v. Texas Sav. & Real Estate Inv. Ass'n, 1902, 95 Tex. 313, 67 S.W. 85, vendee case. See 1920, 11 A.L.R. 1295, 1301.

issued to the mortgagor with a clause providing that the loss, if any, should be payable to him and to the mortgagee as his interest may appear. Under such a policy the courts were virtually unanimous in holding that the mortgagee is a mere appointee of the mortgagor to receive payment. Therefore his right to recover is completely dependent upon the right of the mortgagor, so that a breach of the conditions of the policy by the mortgagor, which would prevent a recovery by him, bars recovery by the mortgagee.[75] After loss, it has been held that the interest of the mortgagee becomes independent and is not affected by a breach of the policy by the mortgagor subsequent to the loss.[76] And the weight of authority clearly is that the mortgagee is not bound by any settlement of the loss or appraisal agreed upon between the mortgagor and the insurer to which he was not a party and did not consent.[77] However, since the mortgagee is only the appointee to receive what the mortgagor is entitled to under the policy, it follows that on receipt it goes in reduction of what the mortgagor owes on the mortgage debt just as though the mortgagor had paid him directly.[78] Consequently, even though there was a clause in the policy providing for subrogation of the insurer, it would be un-

availing. The mortgagee would have no rights to which to subrogate him.[79] Or, to put it in another way, to permit subrogation would nullify the mortgagor's insurance by preventing the payment of the insurance money from discharging his debt. If, however, the mortgagor's rights have been forfeited, but the policy is continued as to the mortgagee, since the only interest now insured is that of the mortgagee, a clause providing for subrogation of the insurer in case of payment to the mortgagee when no liability existed to the mortgagor will be honored.[80] The same has been held where there was no stipulation for subrogation in the policy.[81]

New York standard mortgage policy

To have the mortgagee's right to collect insurance dependent upon the right of the mortgagor against the insurer, as it was under the older simple loss-payable policy, was unsatisfactory. So to it was added another clause: "and this insurance, as to the interest of the mortgagee only therein, shall not be invalidated by any act or neglect of the mortgagor." This is the standard New York mortgage insurance clause which is now in wide-spread use. The effect of the provision is to insure the mortgagee's interest as fully and to the same extent as if he had taken out a separate policy directly from the insurer free from the conditions imposed upon the mortgagor, at least to the extent that no act or neglect of the mortgagor which occurs subsequent to the issuance of

---

75. Hill v. International Indemnity Co., 1924, 116 Kan. 109, 225 P. 1056, 38 A.L.R. 362; Inland Finance Co. v. Home Ins. Co., 1925, 134 Wash. 485, 236 P. 73, 48 A.L.R. 121; St. Paul Fire & Marine Ins. Co. v. Ruddy, C.C.A.Neb.1924, 299 F. 189. See 1931, 17 Cornell L.Q. 151. See also 1927, 48 A.L.R. 124; 1925, 38 A.L.R. 367 for collections of cases.

76. McDowell v. St. Paul Fire & Marine Ins. Co., 1913, 207 N.Y. 482, 101 N.E. 457.

77. First Nat. Bank of Duluth v. National etc. Co. of Am., 1923, 156 Minn. 1, 194 N.W. 6, 38 A.L.R. 380. See 1925, 38 A.L.R. 383, for a collection of cases. Officer v. American etc. Co., 1932, 175 La. 581, 143 So. 500, noted, 1933, 7 Tulane L.Rev. 449, holding the mortgagee bound by an appraisal of which he had no knowledge represents a minority view. Of course if he does know and consent, he is bound. Scania Ins. Co. v. Johnson, 1896, 22 Colo. 476, 45 P. 431.

78. Sisk v. Rapuano, 1920, 94 Conn. 294, 108 A. 858, 11 A.L.R. 1291. See 1921, 11 A.L.R. 1296, for a collection of cases.

79. Imperial Fire Ins. Co. v. Bull, 1889, 18 Can.S.C. 697; Burton-Lingo Co. v. Patton, 1910, 15 N.M. 304, 107 P. 679, 27 L.R.A.,N.S., 420; Milwaukee Mech. Ins. Co. v. Ramsey, 1915, 76 Or. 570, 149 P. 542, L.R. A.1916A, 556, Ann.Cas.1917B, 1132; see Atlantic etc. Bk. v. Farmers' etc. Ass'n, 1932, 203 N.C. 669, 166 S.E. 789. Foster v. Van Reed, 1877, 70 N.Y. 19, 26 Am.Rep. 544, is contra, but as observed before, seems indefensible.

80. Ins. Co. of N. Am. v. Martin, 1898, 151 Ind. 209, 51 N.E. 361; Washington Fire Ins. Co. v. Cobb, Tex. Civ.App., 1914, 163 S.W. 608.

81. First Nat. Bank v. Springfield etc. Co., 1919, 104 Kan. 278, 178 P. 413, standard clause.

the policy will defeat the mortgagee's right.[82] As to misconduct of the mortgagor at the time the policy is issued there is a split, but the weight of authority protects the mortgagee even here.[83] This is in spite of the argument that, on agency principles, the insurance company should have a defense against the mortgagee, and, although in general it is abhorrent that the mortgagee should be at the mercy of the mortgagor as to whether his insurance is good, there would be no great burden upon him to make the mortgagee check on the mortgagor's conduct at the inception of the contract to make sure

that it is valid.[84] The insurance being for the benefit of both the mortgagor and the mortgagee,[85] so long as the insurer remains liable to the mortgagor, any payments for loss made to the mortgagee under the policy must go in reduction of the mortgage debt as being in substance a payment from the mortgagor.[86] This seems an indirect admission that in this situation, at least, the proceeds do take the place of the destroyed property.[87]

If, on the other hand, the policy has been forfeited as to the mortgagor, by reason of the violation of some provision not affecting the mortgagee, the mortgagor, since he is not entitled to recover under the policy, therefore is not entitled to have money paid to the mortgagee under the policy applied in satisfaction of his debt, but rather the insurance company is entitled to be subrogated to the rights of the mortgagee against the

82. Savarese v. Ohio Farmers' Ins. Co., 260 N.Y. 45, 182 N.E. 665; Magoun v. Fireman's Fund Ins. Co., 1902, 86 Minn. 486, 91 N.W. 5, 91 Am.St.Rep. 370; Beaver Falls etc. Ass'n v. Allemania Fire Ins. Co., 1931, 305 Pa. 290, 157 A. 616, noted 1932, 16 Minn.L. Rev. 597; American Building & Loan Ass'n v. Farmers Ins. Co., 1895, 11 Wash. 619, 40 P. 125. See note, 1926, 11 Corn.L.Q. 553, 555. That it is not an independent contract between the insurer and the mortgagee but that it is a contract between the mortgagor and the insurer with the mortgagee as third party beneficiary, see Walker v. Queen Ins. Co., 1926, 136 S.C. 144, 134 S.E. 263, 270; see also Davis v. German-American Ins. Co., 1883, 135 Mass. 251, 256; Union Central Life Ins. Co. v. Codington County Farmers Fire & Lightning Mut. Ins. Co., 1939, 66 S.D. 561, 287 N.W. 46, 124 A.L.R. 1027, creditor beneficiary. This last idea seems incorrect for, if accepted, it would make the mortgagee subject to defenses of the insurance company against the mortgagor, the very thing the standard clause outlaws. Erie Brewing Co. v. Ohio Farmers Ins. Co., 1909, 81 Ohio St. 1, 89 N.E. 1065, 25 L.R.A.,N.S., 740, 135 Am. St.Rep. 735, 18 Ann.Cas. 265, seems to stand alone in holding that the mortgagee's rights under such a policy are derivative through the mortgagor.

Since the standard clause only protects the mortgagee against the mortgagor interfering with the mortgagee's rights in the policy, it is possible for the insurer to reserve a power to cancel the policy and, it has been held, to exercise that power in furtherance of an agreement, between the insurer and mortgagor, to cancel on a certain contingency. B. X. Corp. v. Aetna Ins. Co., 1946, 187 Misc. 806, 63 N.Y. S.2d 14, commented on, 1947, 47 Col.L.Rev. 153. The right of the mortgagee to the unearned premiums on cancellation, it was determined under a statute, going to the mortgagor.

83. Goldstein v. National Liberty Ins. Co. of Am., 1931, 256 N.Y. 26, 175 N.E. 359, discussed, 1931, 17 Cornell L.Q. 151, settled the law in New York after a period of doubt. See 1931, 17 Cornell L.Q. 151, 152, n. 2, for a collection of cases in accord. The earlier New York case for the proposition is Hastings v. Westchester Fire Ins. Co., 1878, 73 N.Y. 141.

84. In Canada and a minority of states in the United States the mortgagee is protected in such cases. See 1919, 55 Can.L.J. 151; 1931, 17 Cornell L.Q. 151, 153 n. 4. Graham v. Fireman's Ins. Co., 1881, 87 N.Y. 69, 41 Am.Rep. 349, is the leading American case.

85. "The insurance was for indemnity to the mortgagor as well as to the mortgagee." Gordon v. Ware Sav. Bank, 1874, 115 Mass. 588, 591. For an argument that one clause of such a standard policy, that providing for payment of premiums by the mortgagee in case of default by the mortgagor, is construed too favorably to the mortgagee, see Hartnett & Thornton, Is the Mortgagee a Free Rider, 1949, 1949 Wis.L.Rev. 714.

86. See Tarrant Land Co. v. Palmetto Fire Ins. Co., 1930, 220 Ala. 428, 125 So. 807.

"Reason also points to the conclusion that when a fire occurs the insurance company must pay the loss to the mortgagee in accordance with its contract with him. The mortgagor benefits by such payment as the insurance money reduces the amount of the mortgage debt. Waring v. Loder, 53 N.Y. 581. The value taken out of the property by the fire is taken off the mortgage by the payment of the insurance money, and the parties remain in the same relative position after as before the fire." Savarese v. Ohio Farmers' Ins. Co., 1932, 260 N.Y. 45, 53, 182 N.E. 665, 667.

87. See 1932, 19 Va.L.Rev. 508, 511. As pointed out by the writer of this note, the New York statute, McKinney's, N.Y.Real Prop.Law, § 254, permitting the mortgagee either to apply the insurance pro-

mortgagor.[88] This is true not only where the policy contains a stipulation for subrogation,[89] but also where there is no such agreement.[90] Where there is more than one mortgage on the property and the insurance includes only the first in the mortgage clause, the insurer, if not liable to the mortgagor, is entitled to subrogation not only to the rights of the first mortgagee against the mortgagor but to his priority over the subsequent mortgagee.[91] But when the second mortgagee also is included in the mortgage clause in the policy, the insurer's rights by subrogation are postponed to the second mortgagee's rights.[92] This is right because if the insurer were permitted, through subrogation, to enforce the first mortgage against the property left after the destruction it would result in making the property satisfy the first mortgage twice—once by the destruction of enough of it to justify the insurer in paying off the first mortgage, and again by enforcement of the assigned first mortgage on the property left—before the second mortgagee could enforce his claim. This would impair the second mortgagee's ability to collect his claim and thus violate the provision in a standard mortgage clause that the insurer's subrogation shall not impair the right of the mortgagee to recover the full amount of his claim.[93]

(4) RESTORATION OF PREMISES

140. In England and New York the mortgagee has the option of having insurance proceeds applied toward restoration of the premises or reduction of the debt.

Where the mortgagor rebuilds, the mortgagee's rights to the proceeds under the standard mortgage clause depend, by the best view, on whether the loss occurred before or after maturity of the debt. In the former case the mortgagor should be able to have the insurance applied to the repairs.

Under the older law in England, when the mortgagor insured his property, although the mortgagee could not claim the proceeds when there was a loss, he had the right under an act in the time of George III, to require that they be used to reinstate the property to its former condition.[94] The Law of Property Act gives the mortgagee the option of having the money applied to rebuilding of the property or in reduction of the mortgage debt.[95]

In the United States, insurance policies generally give the insurer an option to repair the damaged premises instead of paying the loss in money to the insured. By statute in New York the mortgagee has the option of holding the proceeds and paying the debt as

---

ceeds to the payment of his debts or turn them over to the mortgagor to rebuild also reaches the same result. Similarly, in England, under the Law of Property Act of 1925. 1925, 15 Geo. V, c. 20.

88. See cases in next two footnotes.

89. To permit the application of the proceeds of the policy to payment of the mortgagor's debt when the mortgagor has forfeited his rights to any benefit under the policy would render the insurer's declaration of non-liability to the mortgagor futile. The effect of the payment to the mortgagee is not to pay the mortgagor's debt but to give the insurer an equitable proportionate interest in the mortgage as a subsisting obligation. Grangers' Mut. Fire Ins. Co. v. Farmers Nat. Bank, 1933, 164 Md. 441, 165 A. 185; Springfield Fire & Marine Ins. Co. v. Allen, 1871, 43 N.Y. 389, 3 Am.Rep. 711. See note, 1928, 52 A.L.R. 278. In one state, the mortgagor is required by statute to include a stipulation for subrogation in the standard mortgage clause which the statute demands shall be attached to the policy. Miss.Code, Hemingway, 1927, § 5854. The 1942 Mississippi Code does not have this provision in it and has no reference to when it was deleted. See 1932, 19 Va.L.Rev. 508, 512.

90. First Nat. Bk. v. Springfield Fire & Marine Ins. Co., 1919, 104 Kan. 278, 178 P. 413; Hastings v. Westchester Fire Ins. Co., 1878, 73 N.Y. 141; see Tarrant Land Co. v. Palmetto Fire Ins. Co., 1930, 220 Ala. 428, 430, 125 So. 807. But see 1932, 19 Va.L.Rev. 508, 510.

91. Hare v. Headley, 1896, 54 N.J.Eq. 545, 35 A. 445; Tarrant Land Co. v. Palmetto Fire Ins. Co., 1930, 220 Ala. 428, 125 So. 807.

92. Mutual Fire Ins. Co. v. Dilworth, 1934, 167 Md. 232, 173 A. 22, discussed 1934, 19 Minn.L.Rev. 125, 1934, 83 U. of Pa.L.Rev. 273; Perretta v. St. Paul Fire & Marine Ins. Co., 1919, 106 Misc. 91, 174 N.Y.S. 131, affirmed 1919, 188 App.Div. 983, 177 N.Y.S. 923.

93. See 1934, 83 U. of Pa.L.Rev. 273, 274.

94. 1774, 14 Geo. 3, c. 78, § 83. See Sinnott v. Bowden, [1912] 2 Ch. 414.

95. [1925] 15 Geo. 5, c. 20.

it falls due [96] or of paying it over to the mortgagor to restore the property to its former condition.[97] Possibly the mortgagee has this same choice at common law.[98]

What effect does rebuilding by the mortgagor have upon the mortgagee's rights to the insurance proceeds? The question has not been heavily litigated. Of obvious relevancy on this point is the recognized rule that the mortgagee's right to recover on an insurance policy protecting his interest does not depend upon the destruction impairing his security in the sense that it is no longer adequate. He may recover the full amount of damage done to the property, up to the amount of his debt, even though the portion of the premises remaining is greater in value than his debt.[99]

On the direct point under consideration here, the older cases were of two kinds. In one the insurance was on the mortgagee's separate interest only.[1] In this case restoration by the mortgagor does not prevent recovery by the mortgagee.[2] The other kind contained loss-payable clauses. These, since they are construed as making the mortgagee

a mere appointee of the mortgagor with his rights purely derivative through the mortgagor,[3] afforded a basis for permitting the mortgagor by his act of restoration to defeat the right of the mortgagee to collect.[4]

In 1932, the issue was decided under a standard mortgage clause in a case where the mortgagor had rebuilt after the maturity of the debt but before the expiration of the period which had to elapse after loss before the mortgagee could bring an action to recover from the insurer. The court held that the mortgagee's right was unaffected by the rebuilding.[5]

In part the decision rested upon the New York statute giving the mortgagee an option to apply the money to the debt or turn it over to the mortgagor to use for repairs. "Such a right is single by nature; it cannot exist in both the mortgagor and the mortgagee, otherwise the former might decide for repairs and the other for payment, and nothing would result. No; the choice is with the mortgagee alone and in this case he asks for payment of the insurance money and does not consent that it be applied to repairs." [6]

---

96. Before the debt falls due the money is regarded as a substituted *res* for the destroyed security and cannot be applied by the mortgagee to the debt without the mortgagor's consent. Gordon v. Ware Savings Bank, 1874, 115 Mass. 588.

97. McKinney's, New York Real Prop.Law, § 254.

98. Fergus v. Wilmarth, 1886, 117 Ill. 547, 7 N.E. 508. See Glenn, Morts., § 27.4.

99. Thompson v. National Fire Ins. Co., 1925, 48 S.D. 224, 203 N.W. 464; Meader v. Farmers' Mut. Fire Relief Ass'n, 1931, 137 Or. 111, 1 P.2d 138, loss-payable clause; Excelsior Fire Ins. Co. v. Royal Ins. Co., 1873, 55 N.Y. 343, 14 Am.Rep. 271; Uhlfelder v. Palatine Ins. Co., 1904, 44 Misc. 153, 89 N.Y.S. 792, loss-payable clause; Kent v. Aetna Ins. Co., 1903, 84 App.Div. 428, 82 N.Y.S. 817. It has been pointed out that such a view is not consistent, theoretically, with principles of strict indemnity. See Gilligan, Insurance of Mortgaged Property, 1940, 88 U.Pa.L.Rev. 347, 352.

1. Foster v. Equitable etc. Co., 1854, 68 Mass. 216, in which the policy had been assigned to the mortgagee by the mortgagor, thus giving, in effect, insurance on the mortgagee's separate interest. Aetna Ins. Co. of Hartford, Conn. v. Baker, 1880, 71 Ind. 102.

2. See note, 1940, 88 U.Pa.L.Rev. 347, 354.

3. See § 139, supra.

4. Friemansdorf v. Watertown Ins. Co., C.C.Ill.1879, 1 F. 68, stressed this distinction; Huey v. Ewell, 1900, 22 Tex.Civ.App. 638, 55 S.W. 606.

5. Savarese v. Ohio Farmers' Ins. Co., 1932, 260 N.Y. 45, 182 N.E. 665, 91 A.L.R. 1341.

For comments on the case, see notes, 1933, 42 Yale L.J. 788; 1933, 17 Minn.L.Rev. 448; 1933, 81 U. of Pa.L.Rev. 481; 1933, 18 Cornell L.Q. 601; 1933, 7 U. of Cin.L.Rev. 190; 1933, 13 Boston U.L.Rev. 150; Gilligson, Insurance of Mortgaged Property, 1940, 88 U.Pa.L.Rev. 347, 352. See also 1934, 91 A.L.R. 1354.

6. Savarese v. Ohio Farmers' Ins. Co., 1932, 260 N.Y. 45, 55, 182 N.E. 665, 668, 91 A.L.R. 1341. It might be argued that the insurer's option to repair excluded a similar option in the mortgagor. Also that the statutory option of the mortgagee, if it applied during the period during which the insurer's option was available, would be inconsistent with it and therefore nullify it. This conclusion could be avoided by construing the statutory option in the mortgage as available against the mortgagor but not the insurer. Further, since the statute in terms gave the option to the mortgagee as to the proceeds when *received*, it could have been held that the statute did not apply in the principal case where the repairs were made before receipt and the question

However, the same result was reached in a later Michigan case where there was no similar statute.[7]

There was another ground, though, that was stressed in the New York case. It argued that the mortgagee's right under the standard mortgage clause was an independent contract right of indemnity [8] which became vested at the time the loss occurred and could not be defeated by subsequent acts of third parties, including the mortgagor, in replacing the security when under no obligation to do so. The dissent reasoned that the cause of action by the mortgagee would not arise until he could sue and by that time the premises had been restored with the consequence that no cause of action ever accrued.

Although it would seem possible to decide either way on this point, the majority view that the insurer's option was a condition subsequent rather than a condition precedent to the mortgagee's cause of action seems more persuasive.[9] However, practical considerations also enter into the question whether the decision is a good one. To permit the mortgagor to defeat the mortgagee's right by rebuilding would force the mortgagee to litigate the extent and sufficiency of the repairs.[10] On the other hand, although it is true that the mortgagor benefits by having the property free from the mortgage by the extent of the loss, in most cases he probably cannot afford to rebuild except with the aid of insurance money and the result of the decision would be to force him to take out separate insurance.[11] In general it would seem that if the loss occurred after the maturity of the mortgage debt the balance of desirability is in favor of letting the mortgagee have the money and remitting the mortgagor to other means of financing his rebuilding.[12] On the other hand, if the loss occurs before maturity, it would be better in most cases to permit the mortgagor to rebuild and have the insurance applied to that purpose. There is authority for such a result, the mortgagor being allowed to have the insurance money applied to the cost of repairs even though it had already been paid over to the mortgagee.[13] And, it may be observed in conclusion, that as between a theory of insurance in these cases being a matter of contractual indemnity and the concept that the insurance proceeds are a "new form of the old *res*" the latter is preferable and, regardless of the express reasoning in the opinions of courts, provide a satisfactory explanation of most decisions.

D.   RIGHT TO RENTS

IN GENERAL

141.   Rights to rents of mortgaged property largely depend on whether the lease precedes

---

was whether the mortgagee could obtain receipt of the insurance. See 1933, 42 Yale L.Jour. 788, 789; 1933, 18 Cornell L.Q. 601, 603.

7. Pink v. Smith, 1937, 281 Mich. 107, 274 N.W. 727.

8. "While payment of the insurance to the mortgagee, of course, discharges the mortgage debt *pro tanto*, the mortgagee has the same security for the remainder of the debt that he formerly had for the entire obligation. The decision is consequently at some variance with the established doctrine that a contract for insurance of property is a contract of indemnity only." 1933, 42 Yale L.Jour. 788. But no more so than the general rule, noticed supra, that the mortgagee is entitled to recover the full amount of the loss regardless of the adequacy of the remaining property to secure his debt.

9. See 1932, 81 U.Pa.L.Rev. 481. This note also pointed out that the mortgagor should not be given any relief by subrogation to the mortgagee's rights because he was a mere volunteer and to do so would, in effect, force the mortgagee to rebuild and thus contravene the statute which gave the mortgagee the sole disposition of the insurance. But see 1933, 18 Cornell L.Q. 601, 603.

10. "Must the mortgagee litigate the extent and sufficiency of the repairs, or, if partially repaired, is his insurance to be reduced in proportion?" Savarese v. Ohio Farmers' Insurance Co., supra note 5, at 55, 182 N.E. at 668.

11. See 1933, 42 Yale L.Jour. 788, 789.

12. In addition to taking out separate insurance on his interest, a matter of foresight now in view of the decision in the Savarese case, the mortgagor could negotiate a new mortgage loan.

13. Cottman Co. v. Continental Trust Co., 1936, 169 Md. 595, 182 A. 551. The statute in New York giving to the mortgagee the option of holding the in-

or follows the giving of the mortgage and whether the lien or title theory is applied.

The rights to rents of mortgaged property are largely determined by (1) whether the lease precedes or follows the giving of the mortgage and, (2) as a matter of legal right, whether the particular jurisdiction follows the title or lien theory. The importance of this latter factor is minimized in actual practice, as will be seen later, (a) by agreements which are ordinarily entered into by the parties respecting possession, either permitting the mortgagor to remain in possession in title states [14] or the mortgagee to take possession in lien states; (b) by clauses assigning or pledging the rents; (c) by the appointment of receivers; (d) by the practical inefficacy of remedies by which a mortgagee may enforce his rights to possession against a noncooperative mortgagor or his tenant; and (e) by the burdens and strictness of the accounting to which a mortgagee in possession is subjected. This last is a reality which makes the exercise of the right to possession a matter of last and undesirable resort. Leaving these matters aside for the present, when the lease precedes the mortgage it is clear in all jurisdictions that the tenant's term cannot be affected by the later mortgage.[15] In both title and lien jurisdictions the only interest the mortgagor had to give in security was the reversion. And the difference between the two kinds of mortgages of it is that title to the reversion passes in one case and in the other the mortgagee gets only a lien upon it.[16] This difference is vital, however, on the matter of the legal right to rents.

LEASE BEFORE MORTGAGE—TITLE STATES

142. **Where the lease precedes the mortgage, the mortgagee in title and intermediate jurisdictions is entitled to all rents becoming due and payable after execution of the mortgage. The right is rarely exercised before default.**

In a title jurisdiction the transfer of the reversion carries the right to rent with it and creates a privity of estate between the mortgagee and the tenant of the mortgagor.[17] In the early law, due to the personal nature of the relation between landlord and tenant, there had to be consent by the tenant to be the tenant of the transferee before the relationship arose.[18] However, this requirement of attornment was dispensed with by the Statute of Anne [19] in England. The same result was reached in this country either by similar statutes or by decision.[20] The tenant, by a saving provision, is always protected as to rents paid to his original landlord before notice to him of the transfer. Today, therefore, in title jurisdictions, the law is that the "mortgagee has by force of the conveyance a right, which he may exercise or not at his pleasure, to demand and recover all rent which becomes due and payable subsequently to the conveyance. To this end he may give notice, whenever he chooses to

surance proceeds or paying it over to the mortgagor for rebuilding would prevent such a result in that state.

14. See Tefft, The Myth of Strict Foreclosure, 1937, 4 U. of Chi.L.Rev. 574, 582.

15. American Freehold Land Mortgage Co. v. Turner, 1891, 95 Ala. 272, 11 So. 211. 1 Tiffany, Landlord and Tenant, § 146e. See Anderson, The Mortgagee Looks at the Ground Lease, 1957, 10 U. of Fla.L. Rev. 1; Boshkoff, Financing Construction on Long Term Leasehold Estates, 1956, 5 Buffalo L.Rev. 257. That a mortgagee in possession of the mortgaged premises of a lessee in a lien state is not an assignee of the lease and therefore not liable on a covenant for rent was held in Amco Trust, Inc. v. Naylor, 1958, 159 Tex. 146, 317 S.W.2d 47, discussed in 1959, 58 Mich.L.Rev. 140.

16. Burden v. Thayer, 1841, 44 Mass. (3 Metc.) 76, 37 Am.Dec. 117, title state; Metropolitan Life Ins. Co. v. Childs Co., 1921, 230 N.Y. 285, 130 N.E. 295, 14 A.L.R. 658, reargument denied 231 N.Y. 551, 132 N.E. 885, lien state: "if a lease is prior to a mortgage, a sale under the latter is but a sale of the reversion."
See II Am.L.Prop. § 9.45.

17. Moss v. Gallimore, 1779, 1 Doug. 279, a decision by Lord Mansfield is the leading authority.

18. See Litt. § 551; Co.Litt. 309a; 2 Sheppard's Touchstone, c. 13, 253–266.

19. 34 Anne, c. 16, §§ 9, 10.

20. 1 Tiffany, Landlord and Tenant, § 146.

do so, of this right to the lessee, who will thereupon become bound to pay the rent to him. This liability however is limited to rent becoming due after execution of the deed of conveyance, and does not extend to that which was then already due, or to that which before notice of the conveyance has been paid to the lessor. For rent which is due and payable at the time when the conveyance is made is a mere chose in action; a debt which the lessee owes to the lessor, and which being disconnected from the reversion does not pass to the grantee by a conveyance of it." [21]

As to rents which become due but unpaid after the mortgage but before notice by the mortgagee, it has been argued that the mortgagee should be entitled to them only if he asserts his right to them in connection with a foreclosure action,[22] in which case the mortgagor is in no moral position to object. Otherwise the mortgagee should be entitled only to rents which are current or of later maturity than the notice.

The rule is otherwise,[23] however, and both technically and substantially it seems correct. The mortgagee became entitled as transferee of the reversion to all rents accruing after the mortgage, although if paid to the mortgagor the tenant would be protected and the mortgagor would clearly be entitled to keep them. However, if they have not been paid over there seems no reason why the mortgagee should not be able to assert his right to them even though past due and, if the tenant pays the mortgagor thereafter, he should be liable again, for he is outside the protection afforded him by the statute.[24]

The mortgagee's right to collect the rents before enforcement of the mortgage for default has been criticized as in "direct violation of the essence of the transaction which is to give the mortgagee security and security only." [25] But there seems no reason why, if he is entitled to the rents, that right should not extend to unpaid but accrued rent to which he succeeds as mortgagee of the reversion. In addition, although it is arguable that all jurisdictions should adopt the lien view giving to the mortgagor prior to foreclosure all rights in the property including possession and the fruits of possession, the latter covering rents as well as emblements and profits, such is not the law in a good many states. In these states a mortgagee lends in reliance upon being able to reach the lease and rents as part of his security and should be fully protected in reaching the rents to apply to his debt if he wishes to do so, including accrued rents unpaid [26] at the time he asserts his right.

Further, it would be agreed generally that before default the mortgagor ought to have

21. Coffey v. Hunt, 1883, 75 Ala. 236; Baldwin v. Walker, 1851, 21 Conn. 168; Noble v. Brooks, 1916, 224 Mass. 288, 112 N.E. 649—accord. But see St. Louis Nat. Bank v. Field, 1900, 156 Mo. 306, 56 S.W. 1095. See also 1921, 14 A.L.R. 640; Russell v. Allen, 1861, 84 Mass. (2 Allen) 42; King v. Housatonic R. R. Co., 1877, 45 Conn. 226; Burden v. Thayer, 1841, 44 Mass. (3 Metc.) 76. 37 Am.Dec. 117—accord.

22. Glenn, Mortgages, § 33.4, citing N. Y. Life Ins. Co. v. Fulton Development Co., 1934, 265 N.Y. 348, 193 N.E. 169, a receivership case in a lien state in which the court said the receiver might collect rents already accrued but not paid to the mortgagor.

23. King v. Housatonic Ry., 1877, 45 Conn. 226, 234, "he [the mortgagee] becomes entitled to all rents accruing after the execution of the mortgage and in arrear and unpaid at the time of the notice, as well as to those which accrue afterwards. But the rents in arrear at the time the mortgage was executed belong to the mortgagor." But cf., New Order Bldg. & Loan Ass'n v. 222 Chancellor Ave., 1930, 106 N.J.Eq. 1, 149 A. 525, receivership case; Stewart v. Fairchild etc., Co., 1919, 91 N.J.Eq. 86, 108 A. 301, receivership case.

24. Ex parte Wilson, 1813, 2 V. & B. 252, 253: "the mortgagor does not receive the rents for the mortgagee." Payment of rent to record senior mortgagee at a time when he no longer had title to the mortgage is not a defense to the claim of a second mortgagee in possession. Lamson & Co. v. Abrams, 1940, 305 Mass. 238, 25 N.E.2d 374, noted, 1940, 53 Harv.L.Rev. 1402; 1940, 26 Va.L.Rev. 1070. This would be true regardless of whether the lease preceded or followed the first mortgage. However, the decision emphasizes the dilemma of a tenant who must at his peril determine which party to the mortgage transaction he must pay in spite of possibly unascertainable facts and intricate questions of law.

25. Walsh, Mortgages, 95.

26. See Note, 1941, 50 Yale L.J. 1424, 1434.

possession and all income from his property; security for the mortgagee's payment of his money claim does not warrant depriving the mortgagor of any use or fruit of his property before then. Indeed the mortgagee before default rarely wants the rent; what he wants is the interest on his debt. He does not want the trouble of collecting the rents and then being subjected to the strict and burdensome rules of accounting for them. Consequently the usual practice in title states is to permit the mortgagor to stay in possession and to take and keep for himself the rents. Not until default does the picture change and the mortgagee, in spite of the drawbacks, want to reach the rent.[27]

When default is made and the picture does change there is merit in the idea that the mortgagee should be able to take over the property and its income.[28] The experience of mortgagees in the last depression when the capital value of the security asset practically vanished emphasized the importance to mortgagees of having the ability to reach the rents as well as the corpus of the property as part of their security and to be able, on default, to impound it. The title and intermediate theories accord such a right to mortgagees without any stipulation for it. Even in lien jurisdictions it can be and is bargained for with varying success or achieved by means of a foreclosure receivership as we shall see.[29] Since this is so, the difference between the different types of jurisdictions is narrowed to such an extent that, on this point, there seems scant warrant for an all-out assault upon the title theory result. If any criticism of it is to be made, it should be aimed only at the right of the mortgagee to take over before default. But, since in practice this right is seldom exercised, either being bargained away or not exercised because of its burdensome disadvantages to the mortgagee, the objection even here is largely academic.

LEASE BEFORE MORTGAGE— ADVANCE PAYMENT

143. **Where the lease precedes the mortgage, a lessee who pays his rent in advance is only protected if he paid in accord with the lease terms or if the mortgagee had notice of the payment when he gave the mortgage.**

The tenant of the mortgagor, where the lease precedes the mortgage, is protected in paying his rent to the mortgagor before notice of the mortgagee's claim to it provided he pays in accordance with the provisions of the lease.[30] But he is not protected when he pays his rent in advance when it is not called for by the lease contract even though he did not know of the mortgage at the time.[31] His privilege to pay, and of the mortgagor to receive, rents is only to do so as they fall due. A fortiori it would be no defense to the tenant if he makes payment in advance of the date due after notice of the mortgage but before demand upon him by the mortgagee.

Entirely apart from the operation of technical rules of real property, the rule is fair. The tenant could bargain for the payment of his rent to be made in any way he wished at the time he made the lease. Prepayment of the entire rent may be a stipulation of the lease and, if so, the later mortgagee cannot complain. A mortgage cannot affect a prior lease except to make the lessee pay to the mortgagee rent accruing under the lease after the mortgage is given if the mortgagee demands it. Further, if a prepayment has

---

27. Note, 1931, 80 U. of Pa.L.Rev. 270, 272.

28. "The fairness of the claim to sequester the rents is generally conceded when default has rendered it imperative to take possession." Note, 1932, 45 Harv. L.Rev. 901, 903.

29. See Note, 1941, 50 Yale L.Jour. 1424. See also infra § 146.

30. Baltimore Markets v. R. E. etc. Co., 1935, 120 Pa.Super. 40, 181 A. 850.

31. De Nichols v. Saunders, 1870, L.R. 5 C.P. 599.
For legislation in New York enacted to prevent mortgagors from "milking" the mortgaged premises by manipulating the terms of the lease and by prepayment of rent, see Norvell, 1959, Annual Survey of New York Law: Property, 1960, 35 N.Y.U.L.Rev. 1495, 1507.

been made, not in accordance with the terms of the lease, before the mortgage is taken and the mortgagee can be charged with notice of this deviation, the payment should be good against the mortgagee because he has gone ahead and made the loan on that basis. However, in the absence of notice it is reasonable to charge the tenant with knowledge that the property might later be mortgaged, that the rent provisions of the lease would be relied on in part to determine whether the loan should be made, and consequently that a change would prejudice the mortgagee and should not be permitted.[32]

MORTGAGE BEFORE LEASE— TITLE STATES

144. Where the lease is made after the mortgage, the lessee has no better rights than the mortgagor. Thus he may be ousted from possession. But there is no privity between the mortgagee and the lessee, so the mortgagee cannot simply by giving notice compel payment of rent to him. New agreements between mortgagee and lessee, called attornments, are common.

Where the mortgage precedes the lease the lessee's rights can rise no higher than those of his landlord, the mortgagor. "The mortgagor has no power, express or implied, to let leases, not subject to every circumstance of the mortgage. * * * The tenant stands exactly in the situation of the mortgagor."[33] It follows that if the mortgagee could take possession against the mortgagor, as he can in title states at any time in the absence of agreement to the contrary and in intermediate states after default, he has the same right against a tenant of the mortgagor. And if such a right is exercised the mortgagee can repudiate the lease and treat the tenant as a trespasser subject to eviction by an action of ejectment.[34] Also, like all interests in the

mortgaged property attaching to it subsequent to the mortgage, the lease can be wiped out by foreclosure in all jurisdictions, title or lien.[35] However, a mortgage transfers no reversion against subsequent tenants and therefore there is no privity of estate or contract between the mortgagee and the mortgagor's tenant. Consequently the mortgagee "cannot, by mere notice, compel the tenant to pay rent to him,"[36] nor exercise any of the remedies of a landlord against the tenant.[37] "Until there has been an actual entry, or some act equivalent thereto has occurred, the mortgagee can maintain no action against him for the recovery of rent, except upon an express promise to pay it."[38]

However, having the right to oust the mortgagor and his tenant, he may assert the right and compel the tenant to agree to pay the rent to him in order to avoid eviction. Such an agreement is commonly referred to as an "attornment" by the lessee.[39] Actually, however, it is the creation of an entirely new lease between the mortgagee and ten-

N.E. 462; City of Hagerstown v. Groh, 1905, 101 Md. 560, 61 A. 467; Brown to Use of Par Bond & Mortgage Co., v. Aiken, 1938, 329 Pa. 566, 198 A. 441. See note, 1939, 4 U. of Newark L.Rev. 183.

35. In lien states the lessee should be joined to defeat his interest but in title states it would not seem necessary to join him. See 1942, 17 Wash.L.Rev. 3741. The point is considered infra in connection with the right of receivers were the lease is subordinate to the mortgage.

36. Kimball v. Lockwood, 1859, 6 R.I. 138, 139; Long v. Wade, 1879, 70 Me. 358; Winnisimmet Trust, Inc. v. Libby, 1920, 234 Mass. 407, 125 N.E. 599, 14 A.L.R. 638; Trask v. Kelleher, 1919, 93 Vt. 371, 107 A. 486.

37. Burke v. Willard, 1923, 243 Mass. 547, 137 N.E. 744. See Teal v. Walker, 1884, 111 U.S. 242, 248, 4 S.Ct. 420, 28 L.Ed. 415.

38. Russell v. Allen, 1861, 84 Mass. (2 Allen) 42, 44; Peoples-Pittsburgh Trust Co. v. Henshaw, 1940, 141 Pa.Super. 585, 15 A.2d 711; noted, 1941, 89 U. of Pa.L.Rev. 679.

39. E. g., "the tenant of the mortgagor may attorn to the mortgagee, and by thus placing him in possession of the mortgaged premises, entitle him to the rents thereof." Kimball v. Lockwood, 1859, 6 R.I. 138, 139. See Anderson v. Robbins, 1890, 82 Me. 422, 19 A. 910, 8 L.R.A. 568.

32. See Berick, The Mortgagee's Right to Rents, 1934, 8 Cin.L.Rev. 250, 263.

33. Keech v. Hall, 1778, 1 Doug. 21, 22; Zimmern v. People's Bank, 1919, 203 Ala. 21, 81 So. 811.

34. Keech v. Hall, 1778, 1 Doug. 21; West Side Trust & Savings Bank v. Lopoten, 1934, 358 Ill. 631, 193

ant.[40] Such new lease, or "attornment," is "no violation of the principle which estops a lessee from denying his lessor's title" for "by promising to pay the mortgagee upon the latter's rightful entry, the tenant saved the trouble and expense of eviction, which he could not lawfully prevent," [41] and "only recognizes a title which his landlord has granted".[42]

Whether the new lease between the mortgagee and the tenant is for the balance of the original one upon the same terms as were contained in it would seem to be a question of fact in each case.[43] In most cases the parties would have in mind the terms of the original lease. Further, talking of the new lease in terms of attornment by the lessee, although technically incorrect, nevertheless probably is a faithful enough portrayal of the attitude of the parties toward the relationship they are entering into. Yet there is authority that the mere payment and acceptance of rent, without more, creates only a tenancy from year to year.[44]

When the mortgagee takes over possession of the property in the middle of the term of a lease, several questions arise. If the tenant stays on under an agreement with the mortgagee, that agreement usually is

called an attornment and normally will provide for paying to the mortgagee rent for the entire term, including that portion of it prior to the mortgagee's entry. Since the lease really is a new one beginning when the mortgagee enters, it would seem that it covers a period of time over which the mortgagee had no rights. The mortgagor, it is arguable, should have a right to hold the tenant for the use and occupation during that portion of the term prior to entry by the mortgagee and this right should not be affected by the new agreement by the tenant with the mortgagee. That is not, however, the law. The new agreement, if it covers the entire term, will bar any recovery by the mortgagor.[45]

But the lessee may refuse to make any agreement with the mortgagee and in such case the mortgagee cannot hold him for rent as such for any period.[46] Rent falling due and paid to the mortgagor prior to taking possession may be kept by the mortgagor.[47] So, too, rent due but not paid to the mortgagor before the mortgagee takes possession belongs to the mortgagor.[48] But there is the portion of the term before the mortgagee entered during which the tenant was in occupation. The mortgagor cannot collect on the lease for this portion because rent is not

40. See Berick, The Mortgagee's Right to Rents, 1934, 8 Cin.L.Rev. 250, 266.

41. Anderson v. Robbins, 1890, 82 Me. 422, 426, 19 A. 910, 911, 8 L.R.A. 568; Magill v. Hinsdale, 1827, 6 Conn. 464a, 16 Am.Dec. 70; Smith v. Shepard, 1833, 32 Mass. (15 Pick.) 147, 25 Am.Dec. 432—accord. See Towerson v. Jackson [1891] 2 Q.B. 484; Reed v. Bartlett, 1881, 9 Ill.App. 267; note, 1887, 1 Harv.L. Rev. 255; note, 1918, 18 Col.L.Rev. 91; note, 1932, 80 U. of Pa.L.Rev. 602. See 1921, 14 A.L.R. 640; 1936, 105 A.L.R. 744; note, 1926, 70 Sol.J. 972. See also McDougal, Review of Walsh, Mortgages, 1935, 44 Yale L.J. 1278, 1280.

42. Kimball v. Lockwood, 1889, 6 R.I. 138, 139.

43. See Taylor, Landlord & Tenant, § 120; note, 1935, 1 J.Marshall L.Quar. 161, 168.

44. Gartside v. Outley, 1871, 58 Ill. 210, 11 Am.Rep. 59; West Side, etc., Bank v. Lopoten, 1934, 358 Ill. 631, 193 N.E. 462. By statute in Missouri the new tenancy runs from month to month. V.A.M.S. § 441.060; Roosevelt Hotel Corp. v. Williams, 1933, 227 Mo.App. 1063, 56 S.W.2d 801.

45. The cases uniformly hold that the tenant does not have to pay twice. Bulger v. Wilderman, 1931, 101 Pa.Super. 168; Magill v. Hinsdale, 1827, 6 Conn. 464a, 16 Am.Dec. 70; Hinck v. Cohn, 1914, 86 N.J.L. 615, 92 A. 378 are cases so holding in addition to Kimball v. Lockwood, supra note 42, and Anderson v. Robbins, supra note 41.

46. The mortgagee, in the absence of an "attornment" by the lessee, cannot enforce any of the terms of the lease against him. Evans v. Elliot (1838) 9 A. & E. 342; Trask v. Kelleher, 1919, 93 Vt. 371, 107 A. 486; Moran v. Pittsburgh, C. & St. L. Ry. Co., C. C.Ohio 1887, 32 F. 878; Bessemer Inv. Co. v. Fell, C.C.A.Pa.1915, 225 F. 13, 140 C.C.A. 473, discussed in note 1916, 16 Col.L.Rev. 76; Mack v. Beeland Bros. Mercantile Co., 1925, 21 Ala.App. 97, 105 So. 722, certiorari denied 213 Ala. 554, 105 So. 725.

47. Kimball v. Lockwood, 1889, 6 R.I. 138.

48. Clarke v. Curtis, 1844, 1 Gratt. 289.

apportionable.[49] The mortgagee has no claim to payment for it because his rights accrue only on entry and here he gets no payment for it by agreement with the tenant.[50] If the mortgagor brings a quasi-contractual action for use and occupation there are difficulties in allowing recovery. If the mortgagor had deliberately brought on the entry by his actions, or had not apprized the tenant of the possibility of such an entry, recovery should be denied. On the other hand, if the mortgagor did inform the tenant of the mortgage and the possibility of entry and did not do things to bring on the entry and it occurred prior to default, it would seem the mortgagor ought to be able to recover.

If the mortgagee enters because of default by the mortgagor the question is closer. Here the lease has been ended by the mortgagee because of the mortgagor's failure to pay and the lessee in such a case can escape any liability to his landlord, the mortgagor, because the mortgagor was responsible for the loss of the lease.[51] In title states where the mortgagee could have entered prior to default and the tenant knew it, to let the tenant acquire such a windfall at the expense of the defaulting mortgagor seems undesirable, at least in cases where the mortgagee was willing to permit the lessee to stay on under the terms of the old lease, as is usually the case.

But the tenant may stay on after the mortgagee takes over, at the same time refusing to come to any agreement with him. The mortgagee may bring ejectment, which is slow and cumbersome,[52] or an action to foreclose, which is also time consuming. Equity would not help him to get possession,[53] the legal remedy being considered adequate, although that adequacy has been described as "Pickwickian", and probably was so considered because equity did not want the mortgagor to be ousted from his property prior to foreclosure.[54] As a result, a recalcitrant tenant might well occupy the property for a considerable period of time without any agreement to pay rent. In such a case the mortgagee should be able to hold him for use and occupation of the premises from the time the mortgagee entered until the tenant departs and collect the fair rental value regardless of the rent reserved in the original lease.[55]

It is worth observing here that the doctrine that a mortgagee who takes possession cannot affirm the leases made by his mortgagor subsequent to the mortgage because

---

49. Anderson v. Robbins, 1890, 82 Me. 422, 19 A. 910, 8 L.R.A. 568.

50. "The lessee becomes liable to the mortgagee for rent accruing due after the latter's entry and the lessee's promise to pay, but not for rent due before such entry and promise, as prior thereto there would be no privity between them." Anderson v. Robbins, 1890, 82 Me. 422, 424, 19 A. 910, 911.

51. Where a receiver disaffirms a lease and demands payment of the value of the use and occupation, this constitutes a breach of the covenant of quiet enjoyment in a lease, releasing the tenant from liability under the lease. In re O'Donnell, 1925, 240 N.Y. 99, 147 N.E. 541; Casassa v. Smith, 1910, 206 Mass. 69, 91 N.E. 891. The tenant can also sue the mortgagor for breach of covenant of quiet enjoyment. Ganz v. Clark, 1929, 252 N.Y. 92, 169 N.E. 100, lease ended by foreclosure.

52. See Tefft, The Myth of Strict Foreclosure, 1937, 4 U. of Chi.L.Rev. 575, 583, n. 43, for authority that eight to eleven months would elapse before the plaintiff would be in possession in an ejectment action.

53. Seton, Decrees, 140, 143. This was true both before and after a foreclosure decree. After decree an order for possession is now obtainable. Keith v. Day, 1888, L.R. 39 Ch.D. 452.

54. See Tefft, op. cit. supra, note 52, 582. See also notes, 1931, 80 U. of Pa.L.Rev. 269, 274; 1941, 50 Yale L.J. 1424, 1436.

55. Lucier v. Marsales, 1882, 133 Mass. 454. See 1 Tiffany, Landlord & Tenant, § 73a. On the other hand in Burke v. Willard, 1923, 243 Mass. 547, 137 N.E. 744, the mortgagee was denied recovery on the ground that the tenant was holding adversely to the mortgagee under the lease from the mortgagor.
Most of the authorities allowing recovery are receivership cases, but the principle is the same. Rohrer v. Deatherage, 1929, 336 Ill. 450, 168 N.E. 266, fair rental value; Monro-King, etc., Corp. v. Ninth Ave., etc., Corp., 1931, 233 App.Div. 401, 253 N.Y.S. 303, 32 Col.L.Rev. 144. A similar right was given to a purchaser on foreclosure sale in Harris v. Foster, 1893, 97 Cal. 292, 32 P. 246.

of lack of privity between him and the lessee is a most dubious one. The mortgagee, although he comes in by paramount title as a technical matter is quite unlike the ordinary third party who enters. This is because in fact and in law the mortgagor still continues to be the substantial owner of the property and the mortgagee has only asserted an additional security right that he had, the right to possession which carries with it the income. Whatever the merits of the rule permitting tenants to disaffirm leases in the ordinary case where his landlord's interest has been completely ended, to permit him to do so here works an impairment not only of the mortgagee's security interest but of the mortgagor's substantial interest.[56] It has been pointed out that the doctrine was extended to the mortgage cases only after considerable controversy and in the face of a line of cases that had held that the mortgagee by giving notice might affirm the mortgagor's leases.[57] A possible justification of the rule, apart from the argument that it is desirable to let the general real property rule as to privity operate mechanically in all cases to achieve the merit of certainty as to rights, is that it would be an additional deterrent to mortgagees' asserting their legal rights to possession and thus bolster the mortgagor's protection. This last reason would be inapplicable to receivership cases in which the same question arises and will be discussed later. In England there is little left of the rule as the result of statute.[58]

---

56. See Tefft, Receivers and Leases Subordinate to the Mortgage, 1934, 2 U.Chi.L.Rev. 33, 41. See also note, 1942, 17 Wash.L.Rev. 37, 46.

57. See Tefft, supra note 56, 42 n. 35, citing Pope v. Biggs, K.B.1829, 9 B. & C. 245; Waddilove v. Barnett, K.B.1835, 4 Dowl. 347; Brown v. Storey, C.P. 1840, 1 Man. & G. 117; Underhay v. Read, 1887, 20 Q.B.D. 209, 1 Harv.L.Rev. 255. Cf. Evans v. Elliot, K.B.1838, 9 Ad. & El. 342; Towerson v. Jackson, 1891, 2 Q.B. 484; 1 Tiffany, Landlord & Tenant, § 73a(6).

58. 44 & 45 Vict. c. 41, § 18, supplanted by 15 Geo. V, c. 20, § 99.

MORTGAGE BEFORE LEASE— ADVANCE PAYMENT

145. Where the mortgage precedes the lease the tenant can never improve his position by paying his rent in advance.

Where a mortgage precedes the lease even if the tenant pays his rent in advance according to the terms of his lease he may nevertheless be ousted by the mortgagee who enters. And, if he stays on in possession, he must either come to terms with the mortgagee or be liable for the fair rental value from the time of the mortgagee's entry.[59]

LIEN STATES

146. In lien states the mortgagee has no right to rents at least until foreclosure.

Under the lien theory of mortgages the mortgagor remains the full legal and beneficial owner of the mortgaged property until his rights are ended by foreclosure sale. The mortgagee, having no right to possession prior to foreclosure except where he acquires the status of a "mortgagee in possession", a matter discussed later, is not entitled to rents from the mortgagor's tenants regardless of whether the leases preceded or followed the giving of the mortgage.[60] If he has leased the property before giving the mortgage, the lien acquired on the reversion gives the mort-

---

59. See note, 1932, 46 Harv.L.Rev. 491, 493. See also Berick, The Mortgagee's Right to Rents, 1934, 8 Cin.L.Rev. 250, 271. The last three cases in the preceding footnote are ones in which the tenant paid in advance to the mortgagor and yet when their leases were ended were held liable for occupational use. The problem as presented in receivership cases, which raises the question of the powers of a receiver to disaffirm leases subsequent to the mortgage even in lien states, is discussed in connection with foreclosure receiverships in following sections.

60. Wagar v. Stone, 1877, 36 Mich. 364.

On the problem of a mortgagee's security interest in crops, with especial reference to California law, see Smith, Security Interests in Crops, 1958, 10 Hastings L.J. 23, 156.

Woolley v. Holt, 1879, 77 Ky. (14 Bush) 788, in which the mortgagor, who leased the property before mortgaging it, transferred the lease to X. Held, on foreclosure, X took free and clear of the mortgage lien.

gagee no right to the rents accruing under the lease. If a mortgagor leases the mortgaged premises subsequently to giving the mortgage, he is entitled to the rents until title passes under a decree of foreclosure.[61]

Foreclosure of the mortgage in lien states creates problems similar to those in title jurisdictions when the mortgagee before foreclosure asserts his right to possession against the mortgagor and seeks to reach the rents. If the lease preceded the mortgage and the latter was taken with actual or constructive notice of it, only the lessor's interest can be sold on foreclosure and the tenant's rights under the lease cannot be extinguished.[62] However the purchaser on foreclosure sale has rights analogous to those of a mortgagee in a title state who takes a mortgage on leased property. Where the mortgage precedes the lease, since title remains in the mortgagor until foreclosure, the lease by the mortgagor cannot be affected until foreclosure. Since it depends upon the mortgagor's interest it may, however, be foreclosed along with it if the tenant is properly joined in those proceedings.[63] The purchaser on foreclosure sale acquires rights to rents and in respect to the lease that the mortgagee did not possess.[64]

If the mortgagor puts the mortgagee into possession with authority to collect the rents this will not affect the leases apart from altering the person to whom the rents are to be paid by the lessee. Although the leases are subject to the mortgage, the mortgagee cannot end them except by foreclosure unless the tenant consents or breaks some condition in the lease.[65] A foreclosure receivership in lien jurisdictions will also alter the simple general rule that the mortgagor is entitled to the rents before foreclosure.[66]

E. RECEIVERSHIP

BASIS FOR APPOINTMENT—ENGLAND

147. **In England by statute the mortgagee may appoint a receiver to take possession whenever he may exercise the power of sale. The receiver is considered the agent of the mortgagor and thus the difficulties of accounting are avoided.**

The original English rule was that, since a legal mortgagee could take possession if he wished, the equity court would not help him out by appointing a receiver to do so.[67] The legal remedy of self help if the mortgagor did not object, or ejectment in case he did, was considered adequate. On the other hand if he were a second or other subsequent mortgagee, or an equitable mortgagee only of any sort, since he had no ability to take possession himself equity did appoint a receiver on his petition.[68] Because a legal

---

61. See Mills v. Hamilton, 1878, 49 Iowa 105; Mills v. Heaton, 1879, 52 Iowa 215, 2 N.W. 1112; Orr v. Broad, 1897, 52 Neb. 490, 72 N.W. 850; Mason v. Lenderoth, 1903, 88 App.Div. 38, 84 N.Y.S. 740. The mortgagee of a lessee in possession in a lien state is not an assignee of the lease and thus is not liable on the covenant for rent. Note, 1959, 58 Mich.L. Rev. 140.

62. Possession by the tenant or recordation of the lease will give notice of it. Taylor v. Bell, 1900, 129 Ala. 464, 29 S.W. 572; Tropical Inv. Co. v. Brown, 1920, 45 Cal.App. 205, 187 P. 133; Heaton v. Grand Lodge No. 335, IOOF, 1913, 55 Ind.App. 100, 103 N.E. 488.

63. For the effect of non-joinder in foreclosure proceedings, see infra, Chapter 13.

64. E. g., a purchaser at a foreclosure sale may eject the mortgagor's tenant, or make a new lease. McDermott v. Burke, 1860, 16 Cal. 580. See 1907, 8 L.R.A.,N.S., 404; 1921, 14 A.L.R. 664.

65. Fidelity Bond and Mortgage Co. v. Paul, 1931, 90 Colo. 94, 6 P.2d 462.

66. The effect of foreclosure, of receiverships on foreclosure, and of agreements in respect to rents and possession in lien jurisdictions upon leases and the right to rents in those jurisdictions is dealt with in the sections upon those topics.

67. Clark, Receivers, 2d ed., 1929, § 49.

68. The leading English case is Berney v. Sewell, 1820, 1 Jac. & W. 648. Lord Eldon's opinion stated: "If a man has a legal mortgage, he cannot have a receiver appointed; he has nothing to do but take possession. If he has only an equitable mortgage, that is, if there is a prior mortgage, then, if the prior mortgagee is not in possession, the other may have a receiver, without prejudice to his taking possession;". Aberdeen v. Chitty, 1838, 3 Y. & C. 379. See Perry v. Oriental Hotel Co., 1870, L.R. 5 Ch.App. 420.

mortgagee was reluctant to exercise his right to take possession due to the burdens of strict accountability imposed upon him if he did so,[69] the English practice took a turn here which has no counterpart in this country. It is somewhat misleading because the terminology is the same but with a different content. A provision would be inserted in the mortgage calling for the appointment of a "receiver" out of court. Originally the mortgagor appointed him but later the power was given to the mortgagee to do so. This practice was finally sanctioned by statute and, in the absence of an expressed intention to the contrary, a power to appoint a "receiver", exercisable whenever the mortgagee is entitled to exercise the statutory power of sale conferred by the same statute, is implied in every mortgage.[70] Under both the statutory power and the express agreement the "receiver" is deemed the agent of the mortgagor and not of the mortgagee. Thus the latter is not considered in possession and avoids the difficulties of accounting.[71] But though this is the theory, the receiver so appointed can make the mortgagor in possession pay occupational rent or have him evicted on court order. Such out of court "receiver," appointed on written order by the mortgagee, is obviously very different from one appointed by a court. It was not until the Judicature Act of 1873 [72] that a legal mortgagee could get a court receiver appointed, and then only when the court thinks it "just or convenient to do so", a conclusion the English courts do not come to lightly.[73]

BASIS FOR APPOINTMENT IN UNITED STATES—TITLE JURISDICTIONS

148. In title states the situation necessary for obtaining a receiver is a strong danger that the mortgage security will be inadequate without the rents and profits. The mortgagee must show that his legal remedies are inadequate.

In the United States, unless the right to a receiver is based on statute—as it is in a large number of states [74]—the mortgagee must establish (1) a right to the property to be taken over by the receiver, and (2) a reason strong enough to make equity intervene and embark on the formidable task of caretaking and management involved when property is taken over by a court receiver. In states following the title theory, and in the intermediate states on default, no question arises as to the right of the mortgagee to take possession and with it the fruits of possession, the rents and profits of the land. Both the corpus and the income from it are part of his security by the creation of the mortgage, and no additional agreements are necessary either to give him the right to possession or the rents of the land that go with it.[75] Earlier we saw that equity, al-

69. See 1935, 35 Col.L.Rev. 1248; 1938, 47 Yale L. Jour. 1000.

70. Lord Cranworth's Act of 1860 and the Conveyancing and Law of Property Act of 1881, c. 41, § 19 (iii). See Gaskell v. Goshing, 1896, L.R. 1 Q.B.D. 669, 691, for an account of this development. The Act of 1881 has now been superseded by Law of Property Act, 1925, 15 & 16 Geo. V, c. 20, § 101(i), (iii). See also Carey and Brabner-Smith, Studies in Realty Mortgage Foreclosures: III. Receiverships, 1933, 27 Ill.L.Rev. 717, 730; Turner, Economic Aspects of the Deficiency Judgment, 1933, 20 Va.L.Rev. 719, 730.

71. Tefft, The Myth of Strict Foreclosure, 1937, 4 U. of Chi.L.Rev. 575, 585; Davidson, Precedents and Forms in Conveyancing, pt. II, 642 (3d ed. 1868).

72. § 27(8). See Clark, Receivers, 2d ed. 1929, §§ 930, 934.

73. See Prytherch v. Williams, 1889, L.R. 42 Ch.D. 590, 600, 61 L.T. 799.

74. Statutes in many states provide for the appointment of receivers at the discretion of a court in foreclosure actions where it is shown that waste is being committed or that the value of the property is insufficient to cover the debt. For a collection of such statutes see 1933, 43 Yale L.Jour. 111 n. 27. The states listed are Arkansas, California, Georgia, Idaho, Indiana, Iowa, Kansas, Nebraska, Nevada, North Dakota, Ohio, Oklahoma, Oregon, South Carolina, South Dakota, Texas, Utah, Washington, Wisconsin, and Wyoming. Practically all of them, it will be noted, are those classified as lien states. See, e. g., West's Ann.Cal.Code Civ.Proc. § 564. The California statute is fairly typical. West's Ann. Cal.Code Civ.Proc. §§ 564, 568. See 12 Los Angeles Bar Ass'n Jour. 174.

75. "In England, and in some of the States of the Union, the right of a mortgagee to a receivership of the rents and profits of the mortgaged premises

though it would enjoin acts by the mortgagor that would imperil the adequacy of the mortgagee's security before foreclosure and in extreme cases might appoint a receiver, nevertheless took this latter step with the greatest reluctance. In general the court of equity took the position that either the legal remedy of obtaining possession or equitable remedies [76] restraining harmful conduct by the mortgagor were sufficient protection to the mortgagee.[77]

The filing of a bill to foreclose did not alter the situation. The mortgagee still could exercise his legal right to enter by self help or ejectment and the equity court would still enjoin acts of waste by the mortgagor. There was one difference, of course. The foreclosure action having been brought, the mortgagee was now in an equity court and in that action incidental relief might be granted. But there had to be a strong reason for the incidental relief of the appointment of a receiver instead of remitting the mortgagee to going into possession and protecting himself or obtaining an injunction.

The early American cases followed the English decisions. Even in foreclosure actions receivership was denied. The mortgagee was left to his remedies at law. The courts insisted they were adequate despite the facts (1) that ejectment was so far from expeditious that the foreclosure action might well be concluded first, (2) that when pursued it had the unfortunate consequence of destroying leases subordinate to the mortgage and saddling the mortgagee with the hazard and burden of making new agree-

ments for keeping the premises productive of income, and (3) that it subjected the mortgagee to an intentionally severe and strict accounting.[78]

What then will induce a court in a title jurisdiction to appoint a receiver of rents and profits in a foreclosure action? It is believed that the clue to the solution may be found in the reason invoked in lien jurisdictions to give to the mortgagee a claim to the rents and profits prior to the sale on foreclosure.[79] That reasoning has been expressed by an able court thus: "There can be no doubt, that in a proper case where a bill was filed for specific performance of a contract to convey land, the court might appoint a receiver of the rents accruing during the pendency of the action, for equity treats that as done which ought to be done, and, therefore, considers a conveyance as made at the time when it ought to have been made, and the rents as belonging in equity, to the vendee from the time when he became entitled to the conveyance. On the same principle it may deem the foreclosure of a mortgage completed as of the time when the mortgagee becomes entitled to it. The legal right to the rents, as well as to the possession, continues in the mortgagor until foreclosure and sale, as it does in a vendor until conveyance. But when default has been made in the condition of the mortgage, the mortgagee at once becomes entitled to a foreclosure of the mortgage and a sale of the mortgaged premises. *This process requires time,* and on general principles of equity, the court may make the decree, when obtained, relate back to the time of the commencement of the action, *and where necessary for the security of the mortgage debt,* may appoint a receiver of the

has sometimes been placed upon his legal right to the possession of the premises, and consequently to the rents thereof." Hollenbeck v. Donell, 1884, 94 N.Y. 342, 346.

76. See § 134, supra.

77. That the chancellor would not appoint a receiver to sequestrate rents and profits preceding foreclosure, Cortelyeu v. Hathaway, 1855, 11 N.J.Eq. 39, 64 Am.Dec. 478; Williams v. Robinson, 1844, 16 Conn. 517; Morrison v. Buckner, C.C.Ark.1843, Fed. Cas. 9,844. Cf. the early New York rule. Bank of Ogdensburgh v. Arnold, 1835, 5 Paige (N.Y.) 38.

78. See § 147, supra. See also Tefft, The Myth of Strict Foreclosure, 1937, 4 U. of Chi.L.Rev. 575, 582, 591; Carey & Brabner-Smith, op. cit. supra, n. 75, 730.

79. Since the lien theory leaves the mortgagor in possession until foreclosure sale, it prima facie negatives such a claim in the absence of an agreement between the parties.

rents and profits accruing in the meantime, thus anticipating the decree and sale."[80]

That sort of reasoning, of course, would be applicable in a title jurisdiction just as much as in a lien jurisdiction provided it were needed, or as an additional ground even if it is not needed. And, in fact, that reasoning is not necessary in title jurisdictions to establish a substantive right in the mortgagee to the rents and profits for he has that right as part of his security from the outset, as was previously noted. But entirely apart from the question of substantive right to the income the property produces as distinct from the property itself, it nevertheless has pertinency on the point of getting the aid of equity in reaching all the property he is entitled to reach, and of getting it in the foreclosure action itself, i. e., on whether his legal remedy is adequate. It should be as true in a title state as in a lien state that, on default and the beginning of a foreclosure action, the mortgagee is entitled to have applied to his claim as of the date of the beginning of his action all of the property to which he has a right as security, regardless of how that right originated, provided that property is *necessary* to the satisfaction of his claim. If the corpus of the property is adequate without the rents and profits, the court of

equity will not ordinarily undertake the management of the property in order that the rents and profits as well as the corpus may be available for payment of the debt. To get the aid of equity in the form of a receivership the mortgagee must show that there is a genuine danger that his security will be inadequate without the rents and profits. When he does make such a showing this will be sufficient to make the court undertake the preservation of the entire security through a receivership.[81] When there is a real need for equity's aid all talk of the courts about the mortgagee's remedies at law being adequate are either forgotten or recognized as patently untrue. Further, when the mortgagor is in default and the mortgagee has actually started his realization on the mortgage, the policy which is operative in favor of leaving the mortgagor in possession of the property and enjoyment of the rents and profits, a policy that finds expression in title states in holding the remedies of the mortgagee adequate when the contrary is true, and in deterring the exercise of the right by imposing burdensome duties of accountability, is largely vitiated. Striking testimony to this is found in the reasoning just examined as the foundation of the right of the mortgagee to the incidents of the corpus, the rents and profits, as of the date the foreclosure action is begun in lien states where the policy in favor of leaving the mortgagor undisturbed reaches its greatest and frankly stated protection.[82]

This view, that it is the inadequacy of the mortgage security which induces equity to appoint the receiver, also finds corroboration in the test laid down in cases where equity did appoint receivers even before default, namely, in equitable mortgages.[83] The receivership was granted in such cases on the

---

80. Hollenbeck v. Donell, 1884, 94 N.Y. 342, 347, opinion by Rapallo, J. The order of the quotation has been altered. The italics are the author's. Bank of Ogdensburgh v. Arnold, 1838, 5 Paige (N.Y.) 38, was the earlier New York case relied upon. To the same effect is the opinion of Groner, J., in Totten v. Harlowe, 1937, 67 App.D.C. 132, 90 F.2d 377, 111 A.L.R. 726, certiorari denied 301 U.S. 711, 57 S.Ct. 945, 81 L.Ed. 1364. See also Glenn, Mortgages, 917, where the same idea is expressed. " * * * so long as the debtor has not defaulted, he should retain possession. * * * But when default comes * * * if he does not pay, he cannot object to the loss of his security through foreclosure. But that process takes time, and to whom meanwhile should intervening income go, the debtor who has defaulted or the creditor who presses his right to apply security to the debt? The answer clearly is in favor of the debtor. Hence the equity court, whose process has been invoked on the main point that the security should be applied to payment of the defaulted debt, dispenses incidental justice by capturing the income."

81. See Tefft, Receivers and Leases Subordinate to the Mortgage, 1934, 2 U. of Chi.L.Rev. 33.

82. See quotation from Glenn, supra note 80.

83. See supra, § 147, in the discussion of receiverships in England.

ground that the mortgagee had no legal remedy to recover possession. "But, as equity would give effect to a mortgage only so far as to afford protection to the mortgagee, he could not enforce his right to the rents and profits in equity, unless he could show that the property itself was inadequate security."[84] So here, where the legal remedy to take possession is normally said to be adequate for the purpose of getting at the additional part of the security consisting of rents and profits, it is the inadequacy of the security itself to cover the debt that moves the court to act.

On the foregoing analysis, inadequacy of the security without the rents and profits emerges as a sufficient reason for the appointment of a receiver in a title jurisdiction. However, it has been stated that "the prevailing rule is that inadequacy of security and insolvency of the mortgagor are not in themselves regarded as sufficient grounds to justify the appointment of a receiver in foreclosure proceedings. There must be shown some additional, distinct, equitable ground, such as danger of loss, waste, destruction, or serious impairment of the property, to warrant the appointment."[85] Are these additional requirements necessary or would they be sufficient of themselves?

So far as insolvency is concerned it ought to be completely immaterial and, it is believed that it is, for a reason previously mentioned.[86] The creditor who takes security is entitled to rely upon it exclusively for the payment of the entire debt without resorting to other assets of the mortgagor, if he so wishes, because that is why he took it in the first place. It is quite true that a solvent mortgagor will pay the debt to save the property if it is worth more than the mortgage debt. And it is equally true that a solvent mortgagor usually will pay the debt even though the property is worth less than the mortgage debt, for in this latter case he would have to pay the difference anyway through a deficiency judgment against him with the property normally bringing, on a forced foreclosure sale, less than the mortgagor could dispose of it for should he redeem.[87] Consequently it would be an extraordinary case in which the question of receivership would arise unless the mortgagor was insolvent. Nonetheless it ought to be no part of the mortgagee's case to have to establish insolvency as a condition to his relief. And when the courts do not balk at appointing a receiver when there is, in addition to the mortgaged property, a solvent surety for the payment of the debt, the requirement of insolvency cannot in reality have much force.[88]

But how about waste as an additional requirement?[89] Where the acts constituting waste will impair the adequacy of the security no new test is in fact added.[90] Of course, it may be that if the inadequacy is caused or threatened by acts that are tortious a court might be more willing to grant

---

84. Grether v. Nick, 1927, 193 Wis. 503, 213 N.W. 304, 55 A.L.R. 525, affirmed 193 Wis. 503, 215 N.W. 571, 55 A.L.R. 525.

85. Grether v. Nick, supra note 84 at 508, 213 N.W. at 306. Although the quotation is from a decision in a lien state, it states correctly the requirements which are usually expressed to be essential in all jurisdictions. First National Bank of Joliet v. Illinois Steel Co., 1898, 174 Ill. 140, 51 N.E. 200; Cortelyeu v. Hathaway, 1855, 11 N.J.Eq. 39 (inadequacy and insolvency not sufficient); Broad etc., Bank v. Larsen, 1917, 88 N.J.Eq. 245, 102 A. 265; Totten v. Harlowe, 1937, 67 App.D.C. 132, 90 F.2d 377, 111 A.L.R. 726, are other cases laying down requirements beyond inadequacy of the security.

86. See section on equitable relief, supra, § 134.

87. Where the deficiency can only be the excess over the "fair value" of the property, as has been enacted in many states by statute, the pressure on a solvent mortgagor to redeem to prevent sacrifice sale of the property is diminished.

88. Cohn v. Bartlett, 1918, 182 App.Div. 245, 169 N.Y.S. 604; Buck v. Stuben, 1901, 63 Neb. 273, 88 N.W. 483.

89. "The appointment of a receiver can be justified only for the purpose of preventing waste." Grether v. Nick, supra note 84 at 509, 213 N.W. at 307.

90. See supra, for the position in some title states that any serious injury to the property itself is waste.

the relief. But, fundamentally, it is the inadequacy of the security without the rents and profits that is the point. If it were not, an injunction might serve the purpose sufficiently, even though it is true, as has been observed, that regardless of the adequacy or inadequacy of the security, it is "not the mortgagor's privilege to reduce its value by his own acts or omissions." [91] If this is the case, where the waste consists of some serious damage to the property but nevertheless leaves it quite adequate to pay the debt, there would seem to be no reason why a receiver to reach rents and profits should be appointed.

There is another point worth mentioning. It is quite true that the commission of the waste as a tortious act may have a bearing in lien jurisdictions upon the question of the mortgagee's right to claim the rents and profits before foreclosure sale as part of his security and to have it impounded. If the mortgagor has wrongfully damaged the capital asset, or is threatening to do so, this fact, when coupled with the justice of allowing to the mortgagee the corpus and its incidents of rents and profits as of the time he starts his action to realize on his security, is a strong factor in the conclusion that the mortgagee should have a right to that additional property to replace what has been destroyed or threatened with destruction.[92] This argument is weakened somewhat by regarding as waste the failure to pay delinquent taxes and interest or insurance or even by mere neglect which will allow the property to deteriorate rapidly.[93] But, as has

been pointed out, in title jurisdictions there is no difficulty about the mortgagee's rights to get the rents and profits; the difficulty lies in overcoming the dogma that his legal remedies to capture them are adequate. And while the commission of waste might highlight the real reason for action by equity, inadequacy of amount of security alone should be a sufficient reason.[94]

BASIS FOR APPOINTMENT— LIEN STATES

149. In lien states the basis for receivership is not wholly clear. The best explanation is that it will be granted where the security is inadequate in the time between the start of the foreclosure action and its completion. Many jurisdictions stress waste as a basis.

In jurisdictions following the lien theory the main obstacle to the appointment of a receiver is the mortgagor's right to possession until foreclosure. We have seen that this right is founded upon a policy so strong that a few states even strike down agreements permitting the mortgagee to have possession.[95] On the other hand, the principal difficulty encountered in title states is not present here. That is the objection that the mortgagee has a remedy to get possession which is normally considered adequate. The mortgagee in lien jurisdictions had no rem-

91. See Glenn, Mortgages, 923.

92. McBride v. Comley, 1927, 204 Iowa 622, 215 N.W. 613; Nielsen v. Heald, 1922, 151 Minn. 181, 186 N.W. 299, 26 A.L.R. 29. Grether v. Nick, supra, n. 84, while insisting upon waste as the sole reason for the appointment of a receiver in foreclosure, did not justify the taking of the rents and profits by the receiver on the ground that waste had been committed but merely accepted it as a consequence of the receivership on thoroughly established practice which the court did not attempt to vindicate.

93. Grether v. Nick, supra note 84; Shepherd v. Pepper, 1890, 133 U.S. 626, 10 S.Ct. 438, 33 L.Ed.

706; Title Insurance & Trust Co. v. California Development Co., 1912, 164 Cal. 58, 127 P. 502; Larson v. Orfield, 1923, 155 Minn. 282, 193 N.W. 453.

94. That the full significance of the policy difference between the common law mortgage and the American lien theory mortgage has not been taken into account in these receivership cases has been given judicial recognition. The Minnesota court in referring to decisions in which the receiver was appointed and applied the income to the mortgage debt said "Doubtless some of them have been influenced by preconceived ideas derived from the common law, while others, which hold that a receiver of rents and profits may still be appointed, have failed fully to appreciate the limitations upon the right resulting from the change in the law of mortgages." Marshall and Ilsley Bank v. Cady, 1899, 76 Minn. 112, 78 N.W. 978. Cf. Glenn, Mortgages, § 172.

95. See Geraldson, Clauses Increasing the Possessory Rights of Mortgagees, 1935, 10 Wis.L.Rev. 492.

edy to get possession. In this respect he is the counterpart of the equitable mortgagee in England, who was given a receiver on the ground that he had no legal right to possession.[96] But there is a significant difference between the two that should not be overlooked. In England there was no strong policy, at least not one that was explicitly recognized, against taking possession from the mortgagor. The legal mortgagee had the right to do so and a remedy to enforce it except when he voluntarily relinquished it. It was only natural, therefore, for equity to attempt to place the equitable mortgagee on a substantial equality with the legal mortgagee, preserving the latter's priority, in respect to getting possession and its benefits, and a receivership was the answer. But in lien states in this country no mortgagee has the right to get possession by virtue of his mortgage, and the reason he has not is the clearly recognized and strong policy in favor of letting the mortgagor stay in possession until foreclosure sale. This fact must be taken into account in evaluating the relevancy as precedents of receivership cases in equitable mortgages in England.

The first problem, therefore, is to find any basis of right in the mortgagee to have the rents and profits of the land, the fruits of possession. This basis must be found in the face of the conflicting right, founded on strong policy, of the mortgagor to have them until foreclosure sale. In the preceding discussion of the situation in title states there was set forth, incidentally, the theories on which such a right is grounded. As was seen, the common and best explanation is the time lag between the commencement of his action to realize on the security to which he is entitled on default and his ultimate success in that action. We also saw that another basis was offered, either as a supplement or a substitute. It stresses wrongful conduct by the mortgagor in impairing the

res to which the mortgagee is entitled, or threatening to do so by active misconduct or neglect. Such wrongdoing, it is argued, makes it reasonable to give the mortgagee the yield of the res as a sort of compensatory substitute.[97]

The question arises as to why, if it is admitted that the mortgagee has a right on one or the other or both of these lines of reasoning, the lack of a legal remedy to enforce the right—a lack which clearly exists— should not be sufficient to invoke the desired aid of equity. Normally if there is a right but no remedy at law, equity will supply the deficiency. But here something more is required. Generally, just as in title states, the courts in lien states find that additional something in inadequacy of the security in relation to the debt.[98] And the

---

96. Berney v. Sewell, 1820, 1 Jac. & W. 648. See § 147, supra.

97. This reasoning affords both another explanation of the mortgagee's right to the rents and profits and a reason, over and beyond that of lack of remedy at law to enforce the right, why equity should give effect to the right by granting a receivership.

98. See Title Insurance Co. v. California Development Co., 1912, 164 Cal. 58, 127 P. 502.

In California a mortgagee claiming under an instrument without a rents and profits clause is not entitled to the appointment of a receiver on an allegation that the land is insufficient to pay the debt. This is true even though West's Ann.Cal.Code Civ. Proc. § 564(2) empowers a court to appoint a receiver in an action to foreclose "where it appears that the mortgaged property is in danger of being lost, removed or materially injured, or that the conditions of the mortgage have not been performed, and that the property is probably insufficient to discharge the mortgage debt." Reasoning that to allow appointment of a receiver under this section to create a right to rents and profits would be to convert a remedial section into a device for giving the mortgagee something more than that for which he bargained the court held that this would not be permitted. Locke v. Klunker, 1898, 123 Cal. 231, 55 P. 993.

Although the mere taking of possession or the appointment of a receiver, even though valid, does not expand the mortgagee's security interest in the land to cover rents and profits, yet where possession is taken after condition broken, with the consent of the mortgagor, it will be presumed that the mortgagee is to receive the rents and profits to apply to the debt, unless there is strong evidence to the contrary. Smith, Security Interests in Crops, 1958, 10 Hastings L.Jour. 156, 162.

Even though the mortgagee has the right to apply the rents and profits to the debt he may do so only

reason is not hard to find. Not only does the receivership fly in the face of policy favoring the mortgagor but it imposes a heavy administrative burden upon chancery which it undertakes reluctantly.[99] Furthermore, receiverships are more costly than if the mortgagor managed the property himself.[1] This is true even if competent receivers are appointed, something which is more than dubious. Consequently it is understandable that equity will not grant the relief unless it is *necessary* to the mortgagee's payment, i. e., unless there is actual or threatened inadequacy of security to meet the debt.

Here, as in the title states, there must be faced also the question whether insolvency of the mortgagor or waste are not also necessary. The first need not detain us. All that was said about insolvency as a factor in title states is equally applicable where the lien theory prevails. The matter of waste requires some attention, however, because there are a few lien states that insist upon it even to the extent of arguing that it is the sole basis upon which a receiver should be appointed. Waste in lien jurisdictions means conduct that impairs the mortgagee's

security interest and so, looked at from this angle, the requirement adds nothing to the argument. However waste, quite separate and apart from the reasoning looked at above, which found in it a justification for according to the mortgagee a right to the rents and profits and a receivership to effectuate that right, is an independent ground in some instances for the appointment of a receiver to preserve the security *res* against wrongful conduct by the mortgagor. But on this view the *res* to be preserved is just the property itself and not its yield. The waste, or threatened waste, does not justify giving the mortgagee any additional security but only sanctions the preservation of that security which the mortgagee took originally. It would follow logically from this that the receiver in taking over the *res* should allocate the rents and profits, not to the mortgagee, but to the mortgagor and his general creditors.[2]

There is authority that follows the above line of thought and concludes that in a lien jurisdiction the prevention of waste as thus outlined is the sole ground upon which a receiver should be and is appointed.[3] As stated by the court in the leading case supporting this view "there is no warrant or authority for the appointment of a receiver in foreclosure proceedings merely because the security is inadequate or the mortgagor irresponsible. The mortgagee has seen fit to loan money upon the security of the prem-

subject to an accounting to the mortgagor. See secs. 165, 164, 167, 166, infra, for a more detailed consideration of the account process. And see IV Am.L.Prop. §§ 16.96–16.106.

99. Both of these reasons are operative also in title states. Today, of course, even in title states there does exist a policy in favor of leaving the mortgagor in possession even though it stops short of giving him the legal right to do so. And the administrative burden, also, would be the same in a title jurisdiction.

1. For an example of the difference of cost of administering the property by a receiver as contrasted, for example, with a mortgagee in possession, see Wolkenstein v. Slonim, 1934, 355 Ill. 306, 189 N.E. 312. See also Folk v. U. S., C.C.A.Okl.1916, 233 F. 177, 147 C.C.A. 183; 50 Yale L.Jour. 1424, 1447; Carey and Brabner-Smith, Studies in Realty Mortgage Foreclosures: III. Receiverships, 1933, 27 Ill. L.Rev. 717, 753. In 1935, 44 Yale L.Jour. 701, 705, is an excellent summary of the arguments against both the doctrine that, even on default and the commencement of foreclosure proceedings, the rents and profits should form any part of the mortgagee's security, and that a receiver should be appointed to collect them.

2. Wagar v. Stone, 1877, 36 Mich. 364. See Rundell, Work of the Wisconsin Supreme Court: Mortgages, 1933, 9 Wis.L.Rev. 40, 43.

3. "The appointment of the receiver in the first instance can be justified only for the purpose of preventing waste in the exercise of the well-established jurisdiction of courts of equity for that purpose. It may be that this requirement is occasionally overlooked by the courts and may be misunderstood by the bar. But a review of the cases in this court fails to reveal any case where a receiver has been appointed in foreclosure proceedings in the absence of circumstances amounting to waste." Grether v. Nick, 1927, 193 Wis. 503, 213 N.W. 304, 55 A.L.R. 525, affirmed 193 Wis. 503, 215 N.W. 571, 55 A.L.R. 525; Crosby v. Keilman, 1931, 206 Wis. 252, 239 N.W. 431, accord.

ises. The statutes relating to the foreclosure of mortgages provide the manner in which he may realize from the security upon which he was content to rely. There is no principle which in morals justifies a court in adding to the security which the mortgagee accepted at the time of making the loan. The mortgagee is, however, entitled to have that security preserved and protected from waste and dissipation. Where the premises become the subject of waste, the well-known jurisdiction of a court of equity to prevent waste is aroused, and under certain circumstances a court of equity may interfere to prevent waste, to the end that the security may be preserved in its original value. This a court of equity does by the well-established practice of the appointment of a receiver to take possession and manage the mortgaged premises." [4] As was pointed out above, the logical conclusion from this reasoning would exclude the receiver from applying the rents and profits to the mortgage debt. The court recognized this but found the law to be contrary, a finding which it accepted only as based on established precedent. [5]

A very few other lien jurisdictions did, however, accept the full implications of the lien theory policy and carried it to its logical conclusion. One of the clearest expressions of this view is found in a much cited Michigan case in which the question in issue was whether the mortgagee could reach the income of the mortgaged property through a foreclosure receivership. In denying the right the court said, "The rents and profits of land do not enter into or form any part of the security. At the time of giving the security both parties understand that the mortgagor will and the mortgagee will not, be entitled to the rents, issues or profits of the mortgaged premises, until the title shall have become absolute upon a foreclosure of the mortgage. * * * It would be a novel doctrine to hold that the mortgagee had a right incident to ownership, and yet that he had neither a legal title or right to possession. The legislature, in depriving him of the means of enforcing possession, intended thereby also to cut off and deprive him of all rights which he could have acquired, in case he obtained possession before acquiring an absolute title. To deprive him of this particular remedy, and yet allow him in some other proceeding to, in effect, arrive at the same result, * * * would not be securing to the mortgagor those substantial rights which it was the evident intent he should have." [6] It was only a step beyond this to hold that an executory agreement to deliver possession in the future is void as against public policy. [7] And, although it anticipates

---

4. Grether v. Nick, supra note 3 at 508, 213 N.W. at 306.

5. "When the receiver so takes possession, whether there is any foundation for it in principle, it is well established that the rents and profits so collected by the receiver may be applied upon the mortgage indebtedness, even though such rents and profits have not been pledged as security for the mortgage debt by the terms of the contract between the parties. We do not attempt to vindicate this practice, but simply accept it as a thoroughly established principle of equity jurisprudence." Grether v. Nick, supra note 3, at 509, 213 N.W. at 306. See also Rundell, op. cit. supra, note 2.

6. Wagar v. Stone, 1877, 36 Mich. 364, 366. In accord with this view, look at Teal v. Walker, 1884, 111 U.S. 242, 4 S.Ct. 420, 28 L.Ed. 415, applying Oregon law; Investors' Syndicate v. Smith, C.C.A.Or.1939, 105 F.2d 611, reviewing and applying Oregon law; American Investment Co. v. Farrar, 1893, 87 Iowa 437, 54 N.W. 361; Moncrieff v. Hare, 1906, 38 Colo. 221, 87 P. 1082, 7 L.R.A.,N.S., 1001.

On a similar line of reasoning, the statutory right of redemption from foreclosure sale, which gives the mortgagor a period after foreclosure in which to redeem from the purchaser at foreclosure sale and in the meantime to remain in possession has been held to bar appointment of a receiver of rents and profits during foreclosure. Farm Mortgage Co. v. Pettet, 1924, 51 N.D. 491, 200 N.W. 497, 36 A.L.R. 598. See also Lich v. Strohm, 1925, 134 Wash. 490, 236 P. 88. The answer to these decisions, as has been pointed out, is that the possession guaranteed to the mortgagor under such statutes is the possession after foreclosure, whereas the possession of the mortgage receiver ousts the mortgagor only prior to the completion of foreclosure. Glenn, Mortgages, § 171.

7. See Hazeltine v. Granger, 1880, 44 Mich. 503, 505, 7 N.W. 74, 76; Teal v. Walker, supra note 6; Investors' Syndicate v. Smith, supra, note 6. See also Geraldson, op. cit. supra, note 95. Contrast Mon-

in part a subject to be discussed next, it is implicit in such a doctrine that rents and profits, which are an incident of possession, are not subject to mortgage and a purported express pledge of them will be nugatory.[8]

In criticism of these minority decisions, it has been urged that the mortgage receivership really does not violate the statutory prohibition against the mortgagee taking possession because it is "an 'equitable remedy,' it is of a temporary character only; and it is granted * * * in support of the mortgagee's security during the process of foreclosure only."[9] What this really amounts to saying is that the arguments accepted in most lien states as sufficient to justify the appointment of a foreclosure receiver outweigh the policy considerations in favor of leaving the mortgagor in undisturbed possession. However, the point is minimized in importance in these few states by statutory enactments which modify the rule against foreclosure receiverships. In Michigan they may be appointed in trust deed mortgages;[10] in Oregon by virtue of an amendment which was construed to permit the mortgage or pledge of rents and profits of real property it was held that a court

might appoint a receiver to collect them;[11] and in Iowa the qualification "in the absence of stipulations to the contrary" covers what is called a "receivership clause" which is more accurately a "pledge of rents and profits."[12]

Although the foregoing seems a sound analysis and delineation of the main lines of authorities and their rationales, an incorrect picture might be given unless it were cautioned in conclusion that not only is there confusion in the cases as to the circumstances which will justify a court of equity in appointing a receiver of rents and profits at the request of a mortgagee, but the practice has not always conformed to the theory expressed in the decisions.[13]

---

crieff v. Hare, supra note 6, in which a pledge of the rents and profits was held valid.

8.   Orr v. Bennett, 1917, 135 Minn. 443, 161 N.W. 165, 4 A.L.R. 1396; Smith v. Grilk, 1933, 64 N.Dak. 163, 250 N.W. 787; Uniform Real Estate Mortgage Act, § 2(1): "The mortgage gives no right to possession or to the rents and profits of the mortgaged premises to the mortgagee or purchaser at the foreclosure sale until it is foreclosed and the period of redemption has expired, even though the mortgage contains a conveyance, or agreement for possession by the mortgagee, or pledge of the rents and profits, or other provision to the contrary."; note, 1917, 4 A.L.R. 1396, 1400, 1408. See Rundell, op. cit. supra note 2, 44.

9.   Glenn, Mortgages, 912, citing Lowell v. Doe, 1890, 44 Minn. 144, 46 N.W. 297; Hollenbeck v. Donell, 1884, 94 N.Y. 342.

10.   M.C.L.A. (Mich.) § 600.2932. See note, 1933, 31 Mich.L.Rev. 1124.

11.   ORS 86.010; Investors' Syndicate v. Smith, C. C.A.Or.1939, 105 F.2d 611.

12.   Iowa Code of 1939, § 10053 (now I.C.A. § 557.14). See note, 1942, 27 Iowa L.Rev. 626. See also Wis. Laws 1933, c. 11, § 1. See Rundell, Work of the Wisconsin Supreme Court: Mortgages, 1933, 9 Wis. L.Rev. 40, 44; Geraldson, Clauses Increasing Rights of Mortgagees, 1935, 10 Wis.L.Rev. 492. See also 1952, Storke and Sears, Colorado Security Law, 135–145.

13.   For discussions of the problem, see Carey and Brabner-Smith, Studies in Realty Mortgage Foreclosures: III. Receiverships, 1933, 27 Ill.L.Rev. 717; Leesman, Corporate Trusteeship and Receivership, 1933, 28 Ill.L.Rev. 238; Allen, Appointment of Receivers in Mortgage Foreclosure Actions, 1932, 16 Marq.L.Rev. 168; Glenn, Foreclosure Receiverships in Kentucky, 1936, 25 Ky.L.Rev. 26; Rundell, Mortgage Receiverships, 1933, 9 Wis.L.Rev. 40; note, 1932, 45 Harv.L.Rev. 901; note 1933, 46 Harv.L.Rev. 491; note, 1936, 14 Neb.L.Bull. 272; note, 1926, 11 Iowa L.Rev. 174; note, 1926, 11 Iowa L.Rev. 283; note, 1933, 18 Iowa L.Rev. 251; note 1883, 16 Cent. L.J. 85; Berick, The Mortgagee's Right to Rents, 1934, 8 U. of Cin.L.Rev. 250, 278; 1923, 26 A.L.R. 33; 1925, 36 A.L.R. 609; 1928, 55 A.L.R. 533; 1933, 87 A.L.R. 1008. For the English law, see Turner, The English Mortgage of Land as a Security, 1934, 20 Va.L.Rev. 729, 731; Tefft, The Myth of Strict Foreclosure, 1937, 4 U. of Chi.L.Rev. 575, 585. Storke and Sears, Colorado Security Law 135–145 (1952); Note, The Statutory Right of Redemption in California: Value of Use of Property During Redemption Period, 52 Cal.L.Rev. 846, 865–869; Smith, Security Interests in Crops, 1958, 10 Hastings L.J. 156, 159–169.

AGREEMENTS FOR RENTS, PROFITS, AND RECEIVERSHIP

150. Common mortgage clauses pledge rents and profits and provide for appointment of a receiver on default. A few states hold the pledge invalid; some hold it a valid present transfer effective on default; in most states it creates a security interest in the rents which the mortgagee can only realize by taking possession or getting a receiver. Receivership clauses do not bind the courts but, combined with the pledge clause, generally make it easier to get an appointment.

To add to the mortgagee's rights, it has become a common practice to include in the mortgage two types of clauses.[14] One in terms conveys, pledges, or assigns the rents and profits of the mortgaged land and empowers the mortgagee on default to take possession and collect them.[15] The other provides for the appointment of a receiver on default to collect rents and profits and apply them to the secured debt.[16]

These clauses have two purposes. One is to give the mortgagee a right to the rents and profits as part of his security, distinct from the capital asset, the land. The other is to provide an additional basis for the appointment of a receiver to capture them, or, in the alternative, the privilege of taking possession to achieve the same end. The mortgagee wants this right not only to be able to reach and apply the rents and profits of the land to his debt as against the mortgagor but, also, in priority to other mortgagees and general creditors. And he normally wants the right to exist either completely independent of taking possession,—or at least giving him a right anterior to any dealing with possession—together with the right to enforce it on default by acquiring possession either by his own act or through a receivership.[17]

It is clear that the parties cannot by their own stipulations either confer upon a court jurisdiction to appoint a receiver,[18] or to compel a court to exercise a jurisdiction it has. Therefore the second clause, insofar as it deals only with the matter of receivership, which it seldom does since its only purpose is

---

14. "In the absence of statutory definition the phrase 'rents and profits' offers difficulty, courts and text writers use the terms with an easy familiarity, but clear-cut decisions regarding its meaning are few." 1935, 31 Mich.L.Rev. 1124, 1129. See Detroit Trust Co. v. Detroit City Service Co., 1933, 262 Mich. 14, 43, 247 N.W. 76: "Under the common law, the word 'profits' when used in connection with rents, meant usually the usufruct of the land."

15. See May, The Effect and Operation of a Pledge of the Rents and Profits of Real Estate, 1946, 21 N.Dame L. 225.

16. See 1941, 50 Yale L.Jour. 1424, 1426 n. 10; 1932, 45 Harv.L.Rev. 902, n. 9.

17. The following is typical of the wording of such clauses: "This covenant shall become effective immediately after the happening of any such default, regardless of whether or not an action has been brought to foreclose this mortgage, or whether or not possession has been taken of the mortgaged premises by the mortgagee, or whether or not a receiver has been appointed." Prudential Insurance Co. of America v. Liberdar Holding Corp., C.C.A. N.Y.1934, 74 F.2d 50, 52. In spite of this explicit and clear language, the court held at p. 52 that there was no indication in the applicable law, New York, "that an assignment of rents upon a default entitles the mortgagee to the rents and profits without taking further steps to protect his rights."

18. "Where a court has no authority under the law to appoint a receiver, such authority cannot be conferred by consent or stipulation of the parties." Baker v. Varney, 1900, 129 Cal. 564, 565, 62 P. 100, 79 Am.St.Rep. 140; Hubbell v. Avenue Inv. Co., 1896, 97 Iowa 135, 66 N.W. 85; Hazeltine v. Granger, 1880, 44 Mich. 503, 7 N.W. 74; Aetna Life Ins. Co. v. Broecker, 1906, 166 Ind. 576, 77 N.E. 1092. Cf. Moncrieff v. Hare, 1906, 38 Colo. 221, 87 P. 1082, 7 L.R.A.,N.S., 1001. Under McKinney's N.Y.Real Property Law, § 254(10), where the mortgage so provides, the mortgagee may have a receiver appointed on default as a matter of right. In Michigan the statute authorizing the appointment of a receiver applies only to trust deed mortgages. Mich. Comp.Laws, 1929, § 14956 (now M.C.L.A. § 600.2932); see note, 1933, 31 Mich.L.Rev. 1124. For discussion of Iowa Code, 1939, § 10053 (now I.C.A. § 557.14), see 1942, 27 Iowa L.Rev. 626; Oregon Code, 1930, §§ 5–112 (now ORS 86.010) is considered at some length in Investors' Syndicate v. Smith, C.C.A.Or. 1939, 105 F.2d 611. For the Colorado law, see Storke and Sears, Colorado Security Law 135–145 (1952). California law is discussed by Smith, Security Interests in Crops, 1958, 10 Hastings L.J. 156, 159–169; Note, The Statutory Right of Redemption in California: Value of Use of Property During Redemption Period, 1964, 52 Cal.L.Rev. 856, 865–869; Osborne, Cases Secured Transactions, 1967, Notes pp. 308, 309 and Note pp. 314, 315.

to reach the rents and profits, has no effect except as the fact that the mortgagor consents to the receivership may be a factor entering into the court's conclusion that a receivership is warranted. The courts are frequently influenced by this,[19] especially if the agreement is subsequent to the original mortgage.[20] However, the real purpose of this clause is the same as of the others: to give the mortgagee the rents and profits as part of his security. It differs only in the method which may be used to effectuate that purpose.[21] Consequently it has received little separate consideration [22] and it is not surprising to find that a statute recognizing the validity of such clauses lumps the two together in providing a short form clause covering the subject.[23]

The first of the two clauses has received varying interpretations and consequences but they boil down to three.[24] One of these, previously mentioned,[25] outlaws them on the ground that they violate a fundamental policy of the law of the state as expressed in statutes banning ejectment, confirming pos-

---

19. The decisions, examined in the preceding section, appointing a receiver of rents and profits in a foreclosure proceeding upon equitable grounds, "had accustomed courts of equity to appointing a receiver * * *. It was thus an easy step to hold that that remedy might be contracted for." Israels & Kramer, The Significance of the Income Clause in a Corporate Mortgage, 1930, 30 Col.L.Rev. 489, 492.

20. In some states statutes specifically state that agreements as to the possession of the mortgaged property may be made subsequent to the date of the mortgage. West's Ann.Cal.Civ.Code, § 2927; N. Dak. Century Code 35–02–13; Rev.Code Mont.1947, § 52–107; Ariz.Rev.Stat. § 33–703. See 1941, 50 Yale L.Jour. 1424, 1429: "Some courts hold that a subsequent agreement respecting possession or rents will be enforced according to its terms, even though controverting the general statutory policy of maintaining the mortgagor in possession until foreclosure sale." Illustrative of this distinction are State ex rel. Gwinn v. Superior Court for King County, 1932, 170 Wash. 463, 16 P.2d 831, clause in mortgage covering rents and profits invalid as amounting to agreement for possession prior to foreclosure sale in violation of statute; Debentures, Inc. v. Zech, 1937, 192 Wash. 339, 73 P.2d 1314, assignment of rents by separate contract three years after execution of mortgage, valid. This distinction between stipulations in the original mortgage agreement and those entered into subsequently seems to be an extension of the familiar view that protects to the utmost the mortgagor's redemption interest against any bargain entered into as a part of the mortgage at the time of its creation. See Chapter 4, supra.

21. "It would seem that whenever there is a stipulation for a receiver the court should find an implied in fact pledge of the rents and profits." 1942, 27 Iowa L.Rev. 626, 627. See also 1925, 11 Iowa L. Rev. 175; ibid. 283.

22. See Geraldson, Clauses Increasing the Possessory Rights of Mortgagees, 1935, 10 Wis.L.Rev. 492, 506, for a discussion of cases involving receivership clauses.

In California, where the parties to a mortgage or deed of trust expressly agree that the mortgagee or trustee should have the right on default to take possession and collect the rents and profits of the mortgaged land to be applied to the indebtedness equity will grant specific performance of the agreement and under West's Ann.Cal.Code Civ.Proc. § 564(7), will appoint a receiver to execute their agreement. Section 564(7) authorizes the appointment of a receiver "in all other cases where receivers have heretofore been appointed by the usages of courts of equity." Mines v. Superior Court in and for Los Angeles County, 1932, 216 Cal. 776, 16 P.2d 732.

Where the lending parties or their trustees are expressly given the right to enter and take possession of the property and collect and apply the rents and income to the discharge of the indebtedness, they have the option to take such possession personally or to file a petition to have a receiver appointed to take possession. Snyder v. Western Loan & Bldg. Co., 1934, 1 Cal.2d 697, 37 P.2d 86.

23. McKinney's N.Y. Real Prop. Law, § 254, subd. 10, as amended in 1930.

24. Decisions holding that the inclusion of the words "together with the rents, issues and profits thereof" in the description of the property mortgaged does no more than describe the lands should, perhaps, be put into a still different category. Myers v. Brown, 1921, 92 N.J.Eq. 348, 112 A. 844, affirmed 93 N.J.Eq. 196, 115 A. 926; In re Foster, D.C.N.Y.1872, Fed. Cas.No.4,963, 6 Ben. 268, 10 N.R.B. 523, affirmed C.C.N.Y., Fed.Cas.No.4,981, 10 N.R.B. 523.

25. See minority view, preceding section, and authorities there cited. Rundell, Work of the Wisconsin Supreme Court: Mortgages, 1934, 9 Wis.L.Rev. 40, 44, "It is implicit in a holding that an executory agreement to deliver the possession of the mortgaged premises to the mortgagee is contrary to the policy of the jurisdiction that rents and profits are not subject to mortgage. A provision in the mortgage pledging the rents and profits as a part of the mortgage security therefore adds nothing to the security. Equally, it would seem to follow that an agreement contained in a mortgage providing for a receivership would have no effect in such a jurisdiction in adding to the security." State ex rel. Gwinn, Inc., v. Superior Court for King County, 1932, 170 Wash. 463, 16 P.2d 831, 87 A.L.R. 620, accord.

session in the mortgagor, or declaring mortgages to be liens.[26]

At the opposite extreme are those cases that treat such clauses as transferring the legal right to the rents of the land in *prœsenti* subject to a condition precedent that it shall become effective upon default by the mortgagor.[27] "Rent that has accrued may be assigned like any other chose in action, and rent to accrue may be assigned at common law independent of the reversion so as to enable the assignee to recover thereon when due." [28] Although this is never questioned, the courts have been extremely slow to find that there was in actuality any such assignment.[29] Some courts stress the language used and differentiate between an "assignment" and a "pledge" to arrive at the result. As the court in a leading case said " * * * an examination of the cases cited as authority for the statement that the mortgagor [sic] is not entitled to the rents until he takes possession, or until a receiver is appointed, convinces me that the word 'pledge' was there used as distinguished from the word 'assigned.' There is a marked difference between a pledge and an assignment. Ordinarily a pledge is considered as a bailment, and delivery of possession, actual or constructive, is essential, but transfer of title is not. On the other hand, by assignment, title is transferred although possession need not be. There may, of course, be pledges accompanied by an assignment where both possession and title are transferred to the pledgee; and there may also be a qualified assignment where neither possession nor complete title passes." [30] As has been point-

---

26. See, especially, Smith v. Grilk, 1933, 64 N.D. 163, 250 N.W. 787. See also Geraldson, Clauses Increasing the Possessory Rights of Mortgagees, 1935, 10 Wis.L.Rev. 492; note, 1941, 50 Yale L.Jour. 1424, 1426, 1427; Israels & Kramer, The Significance of the Income Clause in a Corporate Mortgage, 1930, 30 Col.L.Rev. 488, 493.

On the policy of the lien theory statute, see Storke and Sears, 1952, Colorado Security Law 137.

27. "The agreement of the parties * * * may provide that in the event of default, the rents are assigned absolutely to the mortgagee. It has been held that such a provision, rather than pledging the rents as additional security, operates to transfer to the mortgagee the mortgagor's right to the rentals upon the happening of the specified condition." Kinnison, v. Guaranty Liquidating Corp., 1941, 18 Cal.2d 256, 261, 115 P.2d 450, 453; Granniss-Blair Audit Co. v. Maddux, 1934, 167 Tenn. 297, 69 S.W.2d 238; New Jersey Nat. Bank & Trust Co. v. Morris, 1931, 9 N.J.Misc. 444, 155 A. 782. Such assignments may be made either by a clause in the mortgage contract or by a separate instrument. Paramount Building & Loan Ass'n v. Sacks, 1930, 107 N.J.Eq. 328, 152 A. 457, clause in mortgage; Harris v. Taylor, 1898, 35 App.Div. 462, 54 N.Y.S. 864, separate clause. That such a clause when it appears in the granting clause of the mortgage is ineffective, being only an extended description of the land, Myers v. Brown, 1921, 92 N.J.Eq. 348, 112 A. 844, affirmed 93 N.J.Eq. 196, 115 A. 926. That it does operate to transfer a right, see Randal v. Jersey Mortgage Inv. Co., 1932, 306 Pa. 1, 158 A. 865.

Where the rent assignment is executed either at the time of the mortgage, or subsequently but before default, the doctrine of equitable mortgage on after-acquired property could be invoked to make the agreement self-executing. Simon v. State Mutual Life Ins. Co., 1939, 126 S.W.2d 682. See 1941, 50 Yale L.Jour. 1424, 1429. Contra: Re Berdick, D.C. N.Y.1931, 56 F.2d 288. See 1938, 47 Yale L.Jour. 1000, 1001. Separate lease assignments both of existing leases and leases to be made have proved effective. Franzen v. G. R. Kinney Co., Inc., 1935, 218 Wis. 53, 259 N.W. 850, 105 A.L.R. 740, commented on, 1935, 19 Marq.L.Rev. 262; Fargo Building & Loan Ass'n v. Rice, 1935, 66 N.D. 100, 262 N.W. 345. Some courts have relied upon statutes validating the assignment of rents and profits to hold that an assignment clause transfers title. Security Trust Co. v. Sloman, 1930, 252 Mich. 266, 233 N.W. 216; Abrin v. Equitable Trust Co., 1935, 271 Mich. 535, 261 N.W. 85. See 1933, 31 Mich.L.Rev. 1124. A clause assigning rents solely for the payment of taxes, insurance premiums, and repairs has been held operative on default because the mortgagor's failure to pay them was waste. Fidelity-Philadelphia Trust Co. v. West, 1929, 178 Minn. 150, 226 N.W. 406; Mut. Benefit Life Ins. Co. v. Canby Inv. Co., 1933, 190 Minn. 144, 251 N.W. 129.

28. Sullivan v. Rosson, 1918, 223 N.Y. 217, 222, 119 N.E. 405, 407, 4 A.L.R. 1400. There are a variety of opinions expressed in the cases that the assignment operates automatically. "Agreements made after default are generally effective as assignments *in presenti* on the theory that title to the rents passes at the time the instrument is executed." 1941, 50 Yale L.Jour. 1424, 1429.

29. Fisher v. Norman Apartments, 1937, 101 Colo. 173, 72 P.2d 1092, is a good example.

30. Paramount B. & L. Ass'n v. Sacks, 1930, 107 N. J.Eq. 328, 331, 152 A. 457, 458. For other discussions of the effect of an assignment or pledge of rents and profits to the mortgagee or third persons, see note, 1933, 43 Yale L.J. 107; note, 1938, 47 **Yale**

ed out, to achieve such a great difference in result upon such a distinction seems "to place an inordinately high premium upon the phraseology of the instrument. If the rents are available in one case without the requirement of obtaining possession, no policy ground is perceivable for denying them in the other." [31]

Others rely "upon the theory that the mortgagee can acquire the rights flowing from possession only in the manner provided by statute." [32] A fear, also, has been expressed that if the clause operated automatically to transfer the right to rents, logically the mortgagor would be held subject to the imposition of a constructive trust upon all rents collected and expended by him after default, a result which would "impose unworkable restrictions upon industry." [33] Additionally it has been urged that, since the clause imposes no duty upon the mortgagee to collect rents, to permit these clauses to give automatic accrual would both deprive the mortgagor of his rights to the rents and use of them and give him no assurance that the mortgagee would collect them and apply them to the debt.[34] Even if this were true,

as a practical matter the mortgagor would not have to worry that a mortgagee, after default by the mortgagor, would fail to collect any rents if they were available and apply them in payment.[35] But it is not true, as was pointed out by a court in giving one of the best reasons for construing the agreement as stopping short of an assignment. The court said, "the question before us is not dependent upon the power of the parties to the mortgage to contract as to the rents and profits of the mortgaged property, but upon the intention of the parties as expressed by them in the mortgage instrument. We do not think that the parties * * * intended * * * to make an absolute and unqualified assignment of the rent of the mortgaged property * * *. If so, the mortgagee should be charged with the amount of the rents accruing after default, at least if they could have been collected with reasonable diligence." [36] Probably most important of all is the policy of protecting the mortgagor's possession prior to foreclosure sale. But the validity of even this reason has been challenged. A defaulting mortgagor is usually insolvent and beset by creditors. Therefore, it has been pointed out, the most likely result of the policy is to deny the mortgagee priority on this contracted for asset—priority to which he should be entitled against general creditors by virtue of his foresight in demanding it.[37]

Unquestionably the great bulk of the cases are in between the foregoing extremes and hold that the clause creates in the mortgagee only a security interest in the rents and profits and one which requires some further positive action by the mortgagee before he can harvest the subject matter of his bargain. One explanation of the need for further ac-

---

L.J. 1000; Israels and Kramer, The Significance of the Income Clause in a Corporate Mortgage, 1930, 30 Col.L.Rev. 488; Abelow, An Historical Analysis of Assignment of Rents in New York, 1936, 6 Brooklyn L.Rev. 25, 52; note, 1933, 31 Mich.L.Rev. 1124 (discussion of Michigan statute permitting the assignment of rents and profits to a trustee under a trust deed mortgage); note, 1933, 18 Iowa L.Rev. 251; note, 1936, 21 Iowa L.Rev. 646; note, 1937, 50 Harv.L.Rev. 1322; note, 1941, 50 Yale L.Jour. 1424; note, 1941, 21 Notre Dame Law. 225; Berick, The Mortgagee's Right to Rents, 1934, 8 U. of Cin.L. Rev. 250, 283; Leesman, Corporate Trusteeship and Receivership, 1933, 28 Ill.L.Rev. 238, 239; 1919, 4 A.L.R. 1405; 1928, 55 A.L.R. 1020; 1933, 87 A.L.R. 625; 1934, 91 A.L.R. 1217.

31. 1941, 50 Yale L.Jour. 1424, 1428.

32. Kinnison v. Guaranty Liquidating Corp., 1941, 18 Cal.2d 256, 261, 115 P.2d 450, 453, citing Rives v. Mincks Hotel Co., 1934, 167 Okl. 500, 30 P.2d 911; Western Loan & Bldg. Co. v. Mifflin, 1931, 162 Wash. 33, 297 P. 743.

33. Prudential Ins. Co. of America, v. Liberdar Holding Corp., C.C.A.N.Y.1934, 74 F.2d 50.

34. Kidd's Estate, Re, 1936, 161 Misc. 631, 292 N.Y.S. 888.

35. See 1941, 50 Yale L.Jour. 1424, 1427.

36. Sullivan v. Rosson, 1918, 223 N.Y. 217, 223, 119 N.E. 405, 407.

37. 1941, 50 Yale L.Jour. 1424, 1427. See Smith, op. cit. supra note 18; Storke and Sears, op. cit. supra note 18.

tion is that the clause amounts to an inchoate or executory pledge,[38] thus invoking the analogy of pledges or mortgages of after-acquired chattels.[39] Another one is that the security interest the mortgagee acquires in the rents and profits is of like character as that of the mortgage [40] of the real property with the consequence in a lien jurisdiction that no right to possess them vests in the mortgagee prior to foreclosure sale. Coupled with this is the idea that the collection of rents and profits, in the absence of a severance of them from the reversion by a valid transfer of title to them by assignment, is inseparable from the possession of the land. This latter notion is as applicable to a title state as a lien state, the only difference between them being in respect to the right of the mortgagee to obtain possession of the land and, through it, the rents and profits.[41] And they all lead to the same answer as to just what positive

action is required of the mortgagee: he must either take possession of the property himself or get a receiver appointed.[42] This seems definite enough but an examination of the cases where the mortgagee attempted to take possession without the appointment of a receiver makes it "apparent that possession is an elusive quality and that there is no uniform method which is certain to accomplish the desired end." [43] Apparently a physical entry either by self-help or court help such as would be necessary were there no pledge clause is usually required.[44] Consent of the mortgagor to entry has been insisted upon by a New York decision in which there was only

38. See quotation from Paramount B. & L. Ass'n v. Sacks, supra, in text, preceding note-call 30. See Restatement of Security, §§ 1, 10.

39. See Conn. Mut. Life Ins. Co. v. Shelly Seed Corp., 1933, 46 Ohio App. 548, 189 N.E. 654, rent clause referred to as an equitable chattel mortgage of after-acquired chattels; Lincoln Joint Stock Land Bank v. Barlow, 1933, 217 Iowa 323, 251 N.W. 501, mortgage with pledge of rents and profits recorded as both a real estate and chattel mortgage. See Kinnison v. Guaranty Liquidating Co., 1941, 18 Cal.2d 256, 261, 115 P.2d 450, 453. See also Simpson v. Ferguson, 1895, 112 Cal. 180, 40 P. 104, 53 Am.St.Rep. 201; Modesto Bank v. Owens, 1898, 121 Cal. 223, 53 P. 552.

40. "The mortgage as it relates to the real property * * * is * * * but a pledge of property as security for the debt. It would appear that the assignment of rent in this case is of the like character as the conveyance of real property and not intended as an absolute transfer thereof." Sullivan v. Rosson, 1918, 223 N.Y. 217, 224, 119 N.E. 405, 407. See Smith, Security Interests in Crops, 1958, 10 Hastings L.J. 156, 161–164.

41. "In jurisdictions where the mortgagor retains the legal title and right of possession, as here, it follows that the right to collect rents and profits remains in the mortgagor until he is deprived of possession in the manner provided by law, and this notwithstanding the fact that the mortgagee may pledge the rents and profits." Grether v. Nick, 193 Wis. 503, 512, 215 N.W. 571, 572, 55 A.L.R. 525. The same result is reached in a title jurisdiction. Rohrer v. Deatherage, 1929, 336 Ill. 450, 168 N.E. 266.

42. " * * * even where the income is expressly pledged as security for the mortgage debt, with the right in the mortgagee to take possession upon the failure of the mortgagor to perform the conditions of the mortgage, the general rule is that the mortgagee is not entitled to the rents and profits of the mortgaged premises until he takes actual possession, or until possession is taken, in his behalf, by a receiver." Freedman's Savings & Trust Co. v. Shepherd, 1887, 127 U.S. 494, 502, 8 S.Ct. 1250, 32 L.Ed. 163.

"To a great extent the rights of the receiver and of the mortgagee personally in possession will be identical * * *.

Generally speaking, the receiver is entitled to collect all rents accruing after his appointment. This right does not extend to rents which became payable to the mortgagor prior to appointment of the receiver, even though the mortgagor had not yet collected them. It appears, however, that there is no apportionment to be made, so that if the receiver is appointed on the day before the rent for the past year falls due, he is entitled to the full amount thereof. That the date of appointment controls the right to receive rents appears settled * * *.

It appears that the right to collect rents and profits continues until the time of sale, * * * At any rate, it is clear that the rents and profits accruing between the time of appointment * * * and the time of sale of the property may be collected by the receiver to be applied to the debt." Smith, Security Interests in Crops, 1958, 10 Hastings L.Jour. 156, 163.

43. 1933, 43 Yale L.Jour. 107, 112 and cases cited.

44. "All of the authorities agree that a pledge of rents and profits does not create any lien upon the rents and profits until the mortgagee acquires possession * * *." Grether v. Nick, 1927, 193 Wis. 503, 513, 215 N.W. 571, 572, 55 A.L.R. 525; Paramount Building & Loan v. Sacks, 1930, 107 N. J.Eq. 328, 331, 152 A. 457, 458.

Storke and Sears, Colorado Security Law, 141–143 (1952).

an assignment of the rents.[45] But there is authority that if the clause, in addition to pledging the rents and profits, gives the mortgagee the right to possession, a demand and refusal of possession will enable the mortgagee to collect in spite of an antagonistic mortgagor.[46] It has been suggested that a provision in the pledge agreement carefully stating that the collection of rents would constitute a taking of possession would be advisable as giving a definite test.[47]

The effect of the pledge clause upon the mortgagee's ability to get a receiver appointed has not been uniform either in theory or in practice.[48] There are cases holding that the pledge of rents and profits is sufficient by itself, without showing inadequacy or waste of the security or insolvency of the mortgagor, to entitle the mortgagee to a receiver.[49] The better view, however, is that apart from giving to the mortgagee a clear right to the rents and profits as part of his security,[50] thus clearing the hurdle that faced lien theory states where there was no clause covering them, the same considerations should govern the appointment of the receiver where there is a pledge agreement as where there is none.[51] In other words, if the mortgagee's security including in that the right to rents and profits which his agreement gave to him, is adequate, equity should not grant a receivership even though his bargain also expressly purported to give him a right to one. But although it is recognized that a mortgagee can claim no absolute right to a receiver and cannot bind a court by stipulations in the mortgage or separate agreement for the appointment of one,[52] nevertheless, the presence of rent assignment or pledge and receivership clauses in the mortgage increases the chances of a receiver being appointed.[53]

EFFECT OF RECEIVERSHIP ON RENTS— (1) IN GENERAL

151. There are a number of problems concerning the receiver's rights to rents and profits. They include the effect of prior and subsequent leases, problems arising from the mortgagor's possession and priority questions.

When a receiver has been appointed in a foreclosure action many questions arise as to his rights to rents and profits. One is as to what rents the receiver is entitled to collect. Another is whether he may disaffirm leases and, accompanying this, how far a tenant may be bound on his lease when a receiver has been appointed, or be held liable upon any other basis. Although the most difficult problems have arisen in respect to leases made subsequent to the mortgage, there is also the question of the right of the

---

45. Dime Savings Bank v. Altman, 1936, 249 App. Div. 174, 291 N.Y.S. 417, affirmed 1937, 275 N.Y. 62, 9 N.E.2d 788, 50 Harv.L.Rev. 1322, 7 Brooklyn L. Rev. 115. Entry by the mortgagee with the mortgagor's consent would be good. 148th Street Realty Co., Inc. v. Conrad, 1925, 125 Misc. 142, 145, 210 N. Y.S. 400.

46. Long Island Bond etc., Co. v. Broson, 1939, 171 Misc. 15, 11 N.Y.S.2d 793; Freedman's Saving and Trust Co. v. Shepherd, 1888, 127 U.S. 494, 503, 8 S. Ct. 1250, 32 L.Ed. 163. See 1941, 50 Yale L.Jour. 1424, 1430.

47. See 1933, 43 Yale L.Jour. 107, 113.

48. See Israels & Kramer, The Income Clause in a Corporate Mortgage, 1930, 30 Col.L.Rev. 488, 492; 1941, 50 Yale L.Jour. 1424, 1439.

49. Howard v. Burns, 1916, 201 Ill.App. 579, affirmed 279 Ill. 256, 116 N.E. 703; Ohio Mut. Savings & Loan Co. v. Public Construction Co., 1926, 26 Ohio N.P.,N.S., 371; see Rhinelander v. Richards, 1918, 184 App.Div. 67, 70, 171 N.Y.S. 436, 437; Berick, The Mortgagee's Right to Rents, 1934, 8 Cin.L.Rev. 250, 290; 1932, 45 Harv.L.Rev. 902 n. 10; 1933, 27 Iowa L.Rev. 627; 1933, 43 Yale L.Jour. 112.

50. "All authorities agree that a pledge of rents and profits vests in the mortgagee a right thereto which equity will recognize and enforce in a proper manner." Grether v. Nick, supra note 44.

51. See § 149, supra. Aetna Life Ins. Co. v. Broecker, 1906, 166 Ind. 576, 77 N.E. 1092; Althausen v. Kohn, 1921, 222 Ill.App. 324.

52. See supra n. 17.

53. Martorano v. Spicola, 1933, 110 Fla. 55, 148 So. 585; Pizer v. Herzig, 1907, 121 App.Div. 609, 106 N.Y.S. 370. This statement, of course, does not take into account those jurisdictions which hold void an executory agreement pledging or assigning rents and profits.

receiver to rents of leases prior to the mortgage. Still a different matter is involved when the mortgagor himself is in possession and the receiver seeks to hold him for income actually earned or for an occupational rental. Indeed, this goes back to the question of whether a receiver is justified at all in such a case, a point which was not covered in the earlier discussion of the basis for receiverships. Priorities on rents and profits between various mortgagees and other creditors form still another area of controversy. Conduct of the mortgagor, generally classified as "milking" the mortgaged property, also becomes important especially in times of depression. And in all of these cases there is the inquiry as to whether title and lien theories as well as rents and profits and receivership clauses affect the solutions.

EFFECT OF RECEIVERSHIP ON RENTS —(2) LEASES PRIOR TO MORTGAGE

152. A receiver cannot disaffirm leases made before the mortgage. All rents accruing after his appointment belong to him. The same should be true of rents accrued at the time of appointment, but some authorities make it depend on clauses pledging rents and profits.

Where the lease is entered into prior to the mortgage both theory and practice are fairly clear. As was seen earlier,[54] such leases are superior to the mortgage and will not be affected by foreclosure. The purchaser on foreclosure sale is bound by them. "It is entirely clear that if a lease is prior to a mortgage a sale under the latter is but a sale of the reversion." [55] It follows that the receiver has no power to disaffirm such leases; all that he can do is to collect the rents from the tenants. The only question is as to what rent he is entitled, and even this narrows down to rent which had accrued but was unpaid at the time of his appointment, since it is clear that rent accruing between the

date of his appointment and the date of sale belongs to him.[56] It is worth noticing here that the receiver's claim is generally held to vest at the time of his appointment.[57] But there is authority that it relates back to the commencement of the foreclosure action if a receiver is then requested; and if not, to the time in the action when a petition for one is made.[58] This latter rule has the sound merit of not penalizing the mortgagee by delays in appointment beyond his control after he has done all that he can to make his claim to the rents and profits operative.[59]

Where there are no rent clauses in the mortgage, in title jurisdictions the mortgagee may assert his right to possession even before default and the rule gives to the mortgagee accrued and unpaid rent on the date that the mortgagee asserts his right.[60] The receiver, it is true, does not take possession or collect rents under the rights of the mortgagee but as an officer of the court.[61] However, he stands in a stronger position than the mortgagee because he is not appointed until the mortgagor is in default and the mortgagee has started to realize upon his security, which in title states by virtue of the mortgage itself includes not merely the legal title to the reversion carrying the rents but the right to collect them, absent an agreement to the contrary, at any time. The defaulting mortgagor has no standing to in-

---

54. See § 144, supra.

55. Metropolitan Life Ins. Co. v. Childs Co., 1921, 230 N.Y. 285, 290, 130 N.E. 295, 297, 14 A.L.R. 658.

56. This right is conceded in all cases and is usually expressly conferred in the order appointing the receiver. Argall v. Pitts, 1879, 78 N.Y. 239; Johnston v. Riddle, 1881, 70 Ala. 219; Noyes v. Rich, 1862, 52 Me. 115; Stewart v. Fairchild-Baldwin Co., 1919, 90 N.J.Eq. 139, 106 A. 406, affirmed 1919, 91 N.J.Eq. 139, 106 A. 406.

57. Rankin-Whitham State Bank v. Mulcahey, 1931, 344 Ill. 99, 176 N.E. 366; Rohrer v. Deatherage, 1929, 336 Ill. 450, 168 N.E. 266; Greenwich Sav. Bank v. Samotas, 1940, 17 N.Y.S.2d 772.

58. Kooistra v. Gibford, 1926, 201 Iowa 275, 207 N. W. 399.

59. See 1942, 27 Iowa L.Rev. 626, 635.

60. See § 142, supra.

61. See First National Bank of Chicago v. Gordon, 1936, 287 Ill.App. 83, 4 N.E.2d 504.

sist that he be allowed to collect and keep any part of the property which was subject to the mortgagee's security claim.[62]

And the same result should follow in a lien jurisdiction. In them, the right to collect the rents and profits, as was seen, does not come from the mortgage even though leases prior to the mortgage, being attached to the mortgaged reversion, are under the mortgagee's security in the sense that they will be subject to foreclosure sale in the same way that the land itself is. Nevertheless, on equitable considerations previously examined,[63] receivers are appointed to collect rents and profits which otherwise belong to the mortgagor up to foreclosure sale or even to the end of the period of redemption from sale. Those equitable considerations apply as much to accrued but unpaid income from the property as to that which accrues after appointment. A clause pledging rents and profits should not alter the situation because such a pledge gives no rights to collect rents prior to the receivership.[64] Whether an assignment of the rents and profits would affect the question depends upon what rents were covered by the assignment. If it covered rents accruing prior to the receivership, even payment to the mortgagor, if with notice of the assignment, would not save the tenant from having to pay again to the mortgagee; and consequently, insofar as the rents have not been paid over to the mortgagee,[65] the receiver should be able to collect them from the tenant dating from the time the assignment transferred the right to them to the mortgagee. On the other hand, if the assign-

ment by its terms were to be operative on the appointment of the receiver, it would confer upon the receiver no rights to rents accruing before that date whether paid or unpaid.[66]

The authorities on the point are not so clear as the above analysis would indicate they should be.[67] While there are cases to the effect that the receiver will be entitled, without the aid of rents and profits clauses, to rent accrued but unpaid prior to his appointment,[68] other cases stress the presence of rent clauses in giving the receiver the right to such rent as against the mortgagor [69] and junior mortgagees [70], and there is still another authority that, in the absence of a clause pledging or assigning the rents, he would have no such right.[71] There is, also, authority that prior attaching creditors of the mortgagor will prevail over the receiver as to back rent.[72]

---

62. "Being in default upon the obligation which his mortgage secures, the debtor who starts a quarrel over this point is met by the answer, 'Well, if you pay up, of course you can have the rent. But since you refuse to do that, you are not in a position to demand the rent.'" Glenn, Mortgages, § 181.

63. See § 149, supra.

64. See Paramount Building & Loan Ass'n v. Sacks, 1930, 107 N.J.Eq. 328, 331, 152 A. 457. See § 150, supra.

65. See §§ 146, 149, 150, supra.

66. Paramount Building & Loan Ass'n v. Sacks, 1930, 107 N.J.Eq. 328, 152 A. 457.

67. See 1933, 33 Col.L.Rev. 1211, 1216; 1941, 50 Yale L.Jour. 1424, 1440.

68. Codrington v. Johnstone, 1838, 1 Beav. 520; Russell v. Russell, 1853, 2 Ir.Ch.R. 574; Palmieri v. N. Y. Prep. School, 1931, 248 N.Y.S. 934; see Wychoff v. Scofield, 1885, 98 N.Y. 475, 477; New Way Bldg. Co. v. Mortimer Taft Bldg. Corp., 1927, 129 Misc. 170, 171, 220 N.Y.S. 665, 666; Lofsky v. Maujer, 1845, 3 Sandf.Ch. 76, 78.

69. Touroff v. Weeks, 1935, 155 Misc. 577, 278 N.Y.S. 867; cf. Watts' Adm'r v. Smith, 1933, 250 Ky. 617, 63 S.W.2d 796, 91 A.L.R. 1206.

70. New York Life Ins. Co. v. Fulton Development Corporation, 1934, 265 N.Y. 348, 352, 193 N.E. 169, 171, "When the senior mortgagee has a receiver appointed, the lien of the senior mortgagee immediately attaches not only to future rents but also to past rents due and uncollected. As between the equitable liens of the senior and junior mortgagees, that of the senior is superior."; Paramount Building & Loan Ass'n v. Sacks, 1930, 107 N.J.Eq. 328, 152 A. 457, prior mortgagee holding an assignment clause may have receiver appointed who will be entitled to unpaid rent as against junior mortgagee in possession.

71. New Order Bldg. & Loan Ass'n v. 222 Chancellor Ave., 1930, 106 N.J.Eq. 1, 149 A. 525. See also Paramount Building & Loan Ass'n v. Sacks, 1930, 107 N.J.Eq. 328, 152 A. 457, indicating that a pledge of rents would be insufficient.

72. Peoples Trust Co. of Binghamton v. Goodell, 1929, 134 Misc. 692, 236 N.Y.S. 549; In re Barbizon

EFFECT OF RECEIVERSHIP ON RENTS
—(3) LEASES SUBSEQUENT TO MORT-
GAGE—IN GENERAL

153. In determining the receiver's rights to affirm or disaffirm leases made after execution of the mortgage, the chief question is whether the particular rents and profits are part of the mortgagee's security. Title and lien concepts have influenced the court's answers.

A receiver in foreclosure is appointed in order to conserve and prevent injury to property in which the mortgagee has a security interest. Consequently, in determining the rights of a receiver to rents and profits, there is always the question whether the particular rents and profits constitute a part of the security of the mortgagee which he is entitled to have preserved and protected from injury. Where the lease is subsequent to the mortgage title and lien theories have played a part in the reasoning of the courts in answering this question. In such a lease the tenant's rights are dependent upon those of his landlord, the mortgagor, as against the mortgagee, and this marks the starting point in both types of states. In title states the mortgagee, at least on default, gets the right to possession and with it all of the rents and profits of the land as part of his security. However, while he can assert his right by evicting the mortgagor or his tenant, he does not acquire the mortgagor's rights under the lease against the tenant because, as it is said, he is not in privity with him. His only rights against the tenant in such cases is either to come to a new agreement with him or, failing that, to hold him for the occupational use of the property as to such period as the tenant stays on after the mortgagee asserts his rights. And, reciprocal to the right of the mortgagee to oust the tenant, is the tenant's privilege of vacating the property, treating the mortgagee's assertion of rights as an eviction justifying his action and, also, giving him a right to sue the mortgagor for breach of covenant of quiet enjoyment.

Should the mortgage contain an assignment of the rents and profits, this can operate as an automatic transfer in equity of the future leases made by the mortgagor. It gives them to the mortgagee according to the terms of the assignment, usually upon default by the mortgagor, quite independent of rights in the capital asset or flowing from them.

Clauses purporting to transfer rents and profits usually are construed to operate as agreements to pledge and are inoperative to give any rights in them until either the mortgagee takes possession or a receiver is appointed. When such an event occurs the agreement can be regarded as giving to the mortgagee at that moment an independent right to the mortgagor's rights against the lessee. It would be the same as though at the time the mortgagee determined to take over he had made an arrangement with the mortgagor whereby the mortgagor then assigned his leases to the mortgagee. Only the most artificial and mechanical sort of reasoning would hold in such an event that the mortgagee's entry into possession necessarily destroyed the interest of the mortgagor in the property and, along with it, the leases dependent upon it so that they could not be preserved to the mortgagee by agreement.[73] The mortgagee really occupied a dual position: (1) he is an assignee of the mortgagor's reversionary interest;[74] (2) he is a mortgagee who has taken possession. He

---

73. There is good authority that the mortgagee will succeed to the mortgagor's lease rights against the tenant on this reasoning in spite of claiming the rents "as mortgagee." International Paper Co. v. Priscilla Co., 1932, 281 Mass. 22, 183 N.E. 58. Chicago City Bank & Trust Co. v. Walgreen Co., 1933, 272 Ill.App. 434, also gave the mortgagee the right to collect rents from the mortgagor's tenant on the ground that he was a transferee of those rights and claiming them did not constitute an eviction ending the lease.

74. See note, 1942, 17 Wash.L.Rev. 37, 41.

Plaza, D.C.N.Y.1933, 3 F.Supp. 415. Contra: Donlon & Miller Mfg. Co. v. Cannella, 1895, 89 Hun 21, 69 St.R. 8, 34 N.Y.S. 1065.

should have his option as to which set of rights he will assert.[75]

All of the foregoing we have looked at before.[76] What concerns us now is the effect of these principles upon the rights of a receiver when he is appointed. The chief difficulty in title states will be in giving the receiver a right to affirm leases in spite of the lessee's desire to disaffirm them; and, on the other hand, there will be no trouble in permitting the receiver to disaffirm leases regardless of the wishes of the tenant. In lien states, as we shall see, the chief problem is whether the receiver can disaffirm leases by the mortgagor subsequent to the mortgage.[77]

EFFECT OF RECEIVERSHIP ON RENTS—(4) LEASES SUBSEQUENT TO MORTGAGE—TITLE STATES

154. **In title jurisdictions the receiver may disaffirm leases subsequent to the mortgage. The sound view also gives him the option to affirm them; the objections that there is no privity of estate between him and the tenant and that this would be unfair to the tenant are without merit.**

Turning first to title states, there is no doubt that the receiver may disaffirm all leases subsequent to the mortgage and collect from the tenant the reasonable rental value of the premises for occupancy after the receiver's appointment.[78] This is a con-

servation measure where the reserved rent is less than occupational rental and the mortgagee's security interest is endangered by the lower yield. Ordinarily, however, the lease rental is higher than either an occupational rental or the rent that can be obtained under a new lease negotiated by the receiver, and the receiver consequently wants to hold the tenant to the existing lease.[79] Two difficulties confront the receiver in such a case if the tenant on his part wants to escape from the lease, as he usually will when he is paying under his agreement more than the fair rental value of the property. One is that there is no privity of estate between the receiver and the tenant any more than there is between the mortgagee who takes possession and the tenant, the receiver being the equivalent of a mortgagee in possession.[80] The other is that since the receiver is not bound by the mortgagor's leases and may hold the tenant for occupational rent if that

75. Only the last point has not been discussed before.

76. See §§ 144, 145, 150, supra. See Boteler v. Leber, 1933, 112 N.J.Eq. 441, 442, 164 A. 572, et seq.

77. See § 155, infra.

78. Rohrer v. Deatherage, 1929, 336 Ill. 450, 456, 168 N.E. 266, 268, "Since he [the lessee] and the receiver failed to make any agreement, his liability was for the reasonable cash value of the use and occupation of the premises from the time of the appointment of the receiver until his occupation ceased. It is said that he did not attorn to the receiver, but this was not necessary. His occupation, which before the appointment of the receiver was under his valid lease from Deatherage [mortgagor], had no basis, after the appointment of the receiver, except the order of the court, which permitted him to remain in possession as the receiver's tenant."; Ran-

kin-Whitham Bank v. Mulcahey, 1931, 344 Ill. 99, 176 N.E. 366; Henshaw, Ward & Co. v. Wells, 1848, 28 Tenn. 568; Lord Mansfield v. Hamilton, 1804, 2 Sch. & Lef. 28.

79. "Not only will the foreclosure ordinarily be commenced when real estate values are depressed, but the receiver's leases will of necessity be forced transactions negotiated under most unfavorable circumstances." Tefft, Receivers and Leases Subordinate to the Mortgage, 1934, 2 Chi.L.Rev. 33, 37.

80. See First National Bank of Chicago v. Gordon, 1936, 287 Ill.App. 83, 4 N.E.2d 504, noted, 1936, 4 Chi.L.Rev. 151, 504. Walgreen Co. v. Moore, 1934, 116 N.J.Eq. 348, 349, 173 A. 587, 588, "It is argued that possession by the receiver is possession by the mortgagee; that that possession terminated the mortgagor's possession and title; and that, since the subsequent lessee's interest is derived from the mortgagor, the interest of the lessee is also terminated."

On this reasoning it is inaccurate to talk of the receiver "disaffirming" the lease. He can only enter into a new lease or hold the tenant upon quasi-contractual principles, for there exists no landlord-tenant relation between the receiver and the mortgagor's lessee and, consequently, nothing that the receiver can disaffirm. And the receiver's ouster of the tenant cannot operate as a disaffirmance of the lease agreement between the mortgagor and the tenant although it does, of course, prevent it from being carried out. If it could disaffirm it the tenant could not, it would seem, sue the mortgagor for breach of covenant of quiet enjoyment. And yet he may do so. See note, 1942, 17 Wash.L.Rev. 37, 50. Ganz v. Clark, 1929, 252 N.Y. 92, 169 N.E. 100.

be higher than the amount reserved in the lease, it is only just that the tenant have a reciprocal power to disavow the lease and either vacate the premises or, if he stays on without a new agreement, be liable only for the fair value of the use and occupation.[81]

A short answer to the first argument is that it is inconsistent with the fundamental nature of receiverships in mortgage foreclosure cases. Rent receivers are appointed as officers of the court to preserve the security interest of the mortgagee in the property subject to his mortgage.[82] And, in the fulfillment of this purpose, the court has the power to direct the receiver to disaffirm the mortgagor's leases in cases where the mortgagee's margin of security cannot be preserved adequately without avoiding them. If the mortgagee's margin of security can be preserved without cancelling the mortgagee's leases, they should continue until wiped out by foreclosure sale.[83] The theory that the appointment of the receiver is the equivalent of entry by the mortgagee, amounting therefore to an eviction of the tenant of the mortgagor and for this reason ending the lease, is so foreign to the true basis of the receivership and the ground on which leases are avoided or affirmed under them that it has been characterized as "both novel and startling." [84] As the same court pointed out, "if that argument were sound no mortgagee would ever take possession of mortgaged premises under the clause giving him a right to do so, nor would any receiver of rents ever be appointed in foreclosure proceedings, as upon such appointment the rental income would cease. But while the possession of a rent receiver has been likened to that of a mortgagee in possession, it is the possession of the court and not of the mortgagee. Such possession does not *terminate* the rights of any party to the proceeding, much less those of one not a party. They are merely held in abeyance and preserved pendente lite. And, moreover, the title of the mortgagor is not 'terminated' until final decree and sale." [85] Furthermore the contention that the appointment of the receiver is really the equivalent of the entry by the mortgagee into possession is not only at variance with an imposing array of decisions dealing with the appointment of receivers,[86] but is also most disadvantageous to the mortgagor and his assigns.[87] Consequently it may be concluded with confidence that this objection to the receiver holding tenants of the mortgagor on their leases is unsound.

The other argument has more plausibility but convincing answers have been made to it. For one, the lessee's plight is the consequence of a risk he voluntarily assumed and could have guarded against. A lessee who takes a lease when there is a prior mortgage on the land knows that his lease may be wiped out by a foreclosure of the mortgage, or, in title states, before that by entry by the mortgagee. And such a lessee can find out whether there is such a mortgage by examining his lessor's title, the most ordinary of precautions. If he failed to investigate he

---

81. See Holmes v. Gravenhorst, 1933, 263 N.Y. 148, 157, 188 N.E. 285, 288, 91 A.L.R. 1230. Crouch, J., dissenting.

82. Desiderio v. Iadonisi, 1932, 115 Conn. 652, 163 A. 254, 88 A.L.R. 1349; Chicago Title & Trust Co. v. McDowell, 1931, 257 Ill.App. 492.

83. See Tefft, Receivers and Leases Subordinate to the Mortgage, 1934, 2 Chi.L.Rev. 33, 35, citing, In re Newdigate Colliery, Ltd., 1912, 1 Ch. 468; In re Great Cobar, Ltd., 1915, 1 Ch. 682; Stamer v. Nisbitt, 1846, 9 Ir.Eq.R. 96; Murtin v. Walker, 1837, Sau. & Sc. 139; American Brake Shoe & Foundry Co., v. N. Y. R. Co., D.C.N.Y.1922, 278 F. 842.

84. Walgreen v. Moore, 1934, 116 N.J.Eq. 348, 350, 173 A. 587, 588. Quoted with approval in First Nat. Bank of Chicago v. Gordon, 1936, 287 Ill.App. 83, 4 N.E.2d 504. See comment, 1935, 2 Chi.L.Rev. 487.

85. Id.

86. See Tefft, Receivers and Leases Subordinate to the Mortgage, 1934, 2 Chi.L.Rev. 33, 38–42.

87. The mortgagor is damaged not only because he loses a valuable lease, but also because he will be liable for breach of covenant to the tenant who is evicted. Mack v. Patchin, 1870, 42 N.Y. 167, 1 Am. Rep. 506; Ganz v. Clark, 1929, 252 N.Y. 92, 169 N.E. 100; B. F. Avery & Sons Plow Co. v. Kennerly, Tex.Com.App.1929, 12 S.W.2d 140.

must be regarded as willing to take a blind chance without protecting himself by providing for a covenant against encumbrances with a clause making breach a ground for ending the lease. On the other hand, if he knew of the mortgage, at the time he made the lease he could have insisted that the mortgagee become a party to the lease; [88] or have asked the mortgagee to agree, as part of the consideration for the lease, not to evict him in case of foreclosure; or he might even have got an agreement subordinating the mortgage to the lease. Further, even if the receiver does reject the lease, the hardship on the lessee is mitigated by the rule that the receiver must decide promptly; [89] and, if he does renounce it, the tenant is then free to vacate [90] without liability other than for occupational rent during the period he has stayed on.[91]

In the second place, if the receiver is allowed to preserve the lease, the tenant's position is in no way jeopardized or made more burdensome than was his hope when he entered into it. His rights and obligations are the same as they would have been had there been no default by his landlord, the mortgagor, and no resulting foreclosure action. The fact that the risk he voluntarily took has been realized would seem no sufficient reason to give him the option of avoiding his bargain.

In the third place, the tenant's argument of fairness is inconsistent with other rules of law denying the tenant a privilege of disaffirmance when the mortgagee has an option

of adopting or rejecting the lease.[92] One is the rule in foreclosure sales that the mortgagee, at his option, may have the property sold subject to the lease or free and clear of it. In a lien jurisdiction the mortgagee exercises this option by joining or not joining the tenant in the foreclosure action.[93] If the tenant is not joined his lease is unaffected by the foreclosure sale and the purchaser may enforce the lease as a transferee of the reversion.[94] If he is joined, the purchaser takes the property title as it existed at the time the mortgage was entered into, i. e., free of the subsequent lease, and may therefore evict the tenant.[95] In a title jurisdiction it would

88. Flynn v. Lowrance, 1924, 110 Okl. 150, 236 P. 594.

89. Central Republic Trust Co. v. 33 So. Wabash Bldg. Corp., 1934, 273 Ill.App. 380.

90. "It would be manifestly unjust to permit a receiver to disaffirm the lease and put new obligations on the tenant without giving the tenant the reciprocal privilege to treat these demands as an interference with his title and equivalent to a constructive eviction." Monro-King & Gremmels Realty Corp. v. 9 Ave.-31 St. Corp., 1931, 233 App.Div. 401, 404, 253 N.Y.S. 303, 307.

91. Sager v. Rebdor Realty Corp., 1930, 230 App. Div. 106, 243 N.Y.S. 314.

92. See, semble, 1 Tiffany, Landlord and Tenant, § 78, for an analogous doctrine in which the tenant is subject to having his lease abrogated and yet has no reciprocal right of avoidance. Closer to the problem at hand is the ability of a trustee in bankruptcy or the receiver of an insolvent corporation do adopt or reject the leases of bankrupt or the insolvent corporation without any reciprocal right of disaffirmance in the lessee. See Clark, Foley, and Shaw, Adoption and Rejection of Contracts and Leases by Receivers, 1933, 46 Harv.L.Rev. 1111; note, 1931, 31 Col.L.Rev. 297.

93. See notes, 1921, 14 A.L.R. 664; Ann.Cas.1915A, 397; 1928, 42 Harv.L.Rev. 280; 1913, 13 Col.L.Rev. 553; 1937, 21 Minn.L.Rev. 610; 1942, 42 Wash.L. Rev. 37.

94. See Metropolitan Life Ins. Co. v. Childs Co., 1921, 230 N.Y. 285, 130 N.E. 295, 14 A.L.R. 658, reargument denied 231 N.Y. 551, 132 N.E. 885, "If * * * he [the tenant] is not a party to the action, his rights are not affected. There is never an eviction. Until the sale he must pay his landlord. Afterwards the purchaser. As to the latter there is no necessity of attornment." The foreclosure sale "was a grant of what interest the mortgagor had in the property at the time the mortgage was given, less the leased estate—the grant of what was left after the leased estate was subtracted. It is precisely the same so far as the estate granted was concerned as if the lease had been prior to the mortgage."

Commonwealth Mort. Co. v. De Waltoff, 1909, 135 App. Div. 33, 119 N.Y.S. 781; Dundee Naval Stores v. McDowell, 1913, 65 Fla. 15, 61 So. 108; Markantonis v. Madlan Realty Corp., 1933, 262 N.Y. 354, 186 N.E. 862. Contra: McDermott v. Burke, 1860, 16 Cal. 580; really a dictum since the lease was after suit was started and therefore subject to the decree under the doctrine of lis pendens; Dolese v. Bellows-Claude Neon Co., 1932, 261 Mich. 57, 245 N.W. 569, discussed in 1933, 32 Mich.L.Rev. 119. See 1942, 17 Wash.L.Rev. 37, 41 et seq.

95. The tenant, as a holder of an interest in the property subject to destruction by foreclosure sale, would

seem that it is not necessary to join a tenant in order to give the purchaser on foreclosure sale a title free and clear of the lease.[96] However, in such a state, the same option of preserving the lease may be exercised through the insertion or omission of an order of the court that the property shall be sold subject to the lease.[97]

The other rule is that which permits the mortgagee to acquire the option of adopting or rejecting the mortgagor's leases by becoming the assignee of the mortgagor's rights under them. When the mortgagor leases the land he divides into two parts the interest in the land which remained in him after he executed the mortgage: one part goes to the tenant in possession; the other remains in the mortgagor as a reversion expectant upon the leasehold.[98] Both parts remain subject to the mortgage and can be foreclosed. Further, the reversionary part left in the mortgagor can be assigned or pledged to the mortgagee either before or after default and will carry with it the right to enforce the lease without [99] affecting the rights of the mortgagee *qua* mortgage. If this is done the mortgagee then has his choice: he can assert his rights *qua* mortgagee and be free of the lease; or he can elect to enforce his rights as assignee of the lease.

EFFECT OF RECEIVERSHIP ON RENTS— (5) LEASES SUBSEQUENT TO MORTGAGE—LIEN STATES

155. In lien jurisdictions the receiver generally cannot disaffirm leases. But he should be able to if continuance of the leases would

render the margin of security inadequate; if he cannot the purpose of the receivership is nullified to that extent.

In lien states the mortgagor remains the owner and is entitled to possession, hence to rents and profits, until foreclosure. Therefore, any leases subsequent to the mortgage are also binding as against the mortgagee until then. The logical consequence of this is that the rents and profits of the land where they are subsequent to the execution of the mortgage form no part of the mortgagee's security by virtue of the mortgage alone. Clauses assigning or pledging the rents and profits can, as we have seen, operate to bring them under the security of the mortgage, although if it is the latter, not without the mortgagee taking possession or getting a receiver appointed.[1] Further, even without any agreement in respect to them, by an equity extrinsic to the mortgage terms, the mortgage terms, the mortgagee under proper conditions is generally held to be entitled to have them collected by a receiver appointed in foreclosure suit even though the mortgagee himself would not have been entitled to them. Also, as was just seen, the mortgagee has the option to determine whether the lease shall survive foreclosure or not, the tenant being powerless in the matter apart from being able to prevent the sale by redeeming the property. If the mortgagee omits the tenant from the foreclosure action, the lease remains in full force in the hands of the purchaser on the foreclosure sale who buys the reversionary interest carrying it.[2] From the foregoing it is apparent that, in contrast to title states, the chief problem in lien states is not whether the receiver can affirm these leases. Rather it is whether he can disaffirm them and hold the tenant for the reasonable value of the use and occupation of the property, where that is higher than the reserved rental, in the

have the privilege of redeeming from the mortgage and being subrogated to the mortgagee's rights. In this way he is able to protect his interest from destruction. See Glenn, Mortgages, § 181.1.

96. See note, 1942, 17 Wash.L.Rev. 37, 41.

97. See Western Union Tel. Co. v. Brown & Randolph Co., 1932, 154 Ga. 229, 114 S.E. 36.

98. See quotation from Metropolitan etc. Co. v. Childs Co., supra note 94.

99. International Paper Co. v. Priscilla Co., 1932, 281 Mass. 22, 183 N.E. 58; Chicago City Bank & Trust Co. v. Walgreen Co., 1933, 272 Ill.App. 434.

1. See § 150, supra.

2. See § 154, supra. Metropolitan etc. Co. v. Childs Co., 1921, 230 N.Y. 285, 130 N.E. 295, 14 A.L.R. 658, reargument denied 231 N.Y. 551, 132 N.E. 885.

face of the lessee's usual right to have them valid up to the time of the foreclosure sale. It should be scarcely necessary to say that if the mortgagee, or his receiver, cannot repudiate the mortgagor's leases prior to foreclosure sale, the tenant will not be able to do so. And the same is true, even though there might be a power in the mortgagee to reject the lease, if he has acted to preserve it by omitting the tenant from the foreclosure action.[3] In such cases, all the receiver can do is to collect the rents reserved in the leases.

The mortgagee may elect, however, to sell the property free and clear of the subsequent lease by joining the tenant in the foreclosure suit. If he does, the question arises whether the receiver, for the period from his appointment to the foreclosure sale, is entitled only to the rent reserved in the lease or whether he may disaffirm it and either make a new lease with the tenant or hold him for the fair value of the use and occupation. In New York, where the question received rather thorough consideration,[4] there were at first holdings by lower courts that he could do the latter, although if he did, the tenant would have a reciprocal right to vacate.[5] The theory of these decisions was that the mortgagee is equitably entitled to the property and all it will produce from the time of the mortgagor's default and the commencement of the mortgagee's action to realize on

his security by foreclosure. Equity, it was reasoned, through the appointment of a receiver, will collect and impound such product of the mortgaged property for the benefit of the mortgagee if the property itself is inadequate to secure payment of his debt.[6] The tenant entered into his lease with the mortgagor with knowledge of these rights of the mortgagee on default. Therefore, he could be compelled to prevent any loss to the mortgagee by paying the difference between the rent reserved in the lease and a reasonable rent for the use and occupation of the premises which the property might have produced.[7] The possible opportunities which might otherwise exist for mortgagors and their tenants to defraud the mortgagee by reduced rentals or advance payments was also an influencing factor.[8]

In 1932, however, these lower court decisions were overruled by the Court of Appeals and the doctrine was established that, barring the presence of fraud and collusion, the receiver on foreclosure sale could not disaffirm the leases entered into by the mortgagor subsequent to the mortgage, but could collect only the rent reserved in the lease itself.[9] The court said that "Though, during the pendency of the action, a court of equity has power to issue interlocutory orders for the protection of an asserted lien, such orders must be auxiliary to the right to foreclose the

---

3. Metropolitan etc. Co. v. Childs Co., supra note 2; Hewen Co. v. Malter, 1932, 145 Misc. 635, 260 N.Y.S. 624; Markantonis v. Madlan Realty Corp., 1933, 262 N.Y. 354, 186 N.E. 862; Knickerbocker Oil Corp. v. Richfield Oil Corp., 1931, 234 App.Div. 199, 254 N.Y.S. 506, affirmed 259 N.Y. 657, 182 N.E. 222; Lynch v. Harrer, 1933, 146 Misc. 493, 261 N.Y.S. 565.

4. See note, 1933, 33 Col.L.Rev. 1211, and cases there cited.

5. Monro-King & Gremmels Realty Corp. v. 9 Ave.-31 St. Corp., 1931, 233 App.Div. 401, 253 N.Y.S. 303, noted, 1932, 32 Col.L.Rev. 145. The exercise of this latter right was unsatisfactory, however, because even though the tenant was joined in the suit originally, the action against him might be discontinued, in which case the lease would be held to be still in effect. Metropolitan etc. Co. v. Childs Co., supra note 2. See 1933, 33 Col.L.Rev. 1211, 1213; 1941, 50 Yale L.Jour. 1424, 1441.

6. Fletcher v. McKeon, 1902, 71 App.Div. 278, 75 N.Y. S. 817.

7. State ex rel. Coker v. District Court of Tulsa County, 1932, 159 Okl. 10, 11 P.2d 495.

8. "To hold that such right existed would open the door for successful fraud in every case of rent-productive mortgaged premises, where the security is inadequate for the payment of the mortgage debt." Fletcher v. McKeon, 1902, 71 App.Div. 278, 281, 75 N.Y.S. 817, 818.

9. Prudence Co. v. 160 W. 73 St. Corp., 1932, 260 N.Y. 205, 183 N.E. 365, 86 A.L.R. 361, Hanna, Cas. Security, 963, 86 A.L.R. 361, noted 1933, 33 Col.L.Rev. 1211, 1933, 3 Brooklyn L.Quar. 248, 1933, 10 N.Y.U.L. Quar.Rev. 248; see Smith v. Cushatt, 1925, 199 N. W. 690, 202 N.W. 548; Ottman v. Cheney, 1931, 204 Wis. 56, 234 N.W. 325; First Trust Joint-Stock Land Bank v. Cuthbert, 1933, 215 Iowa 718, 246 N.W. 810.

lien, and cannot deprive any part of a title or a right, which, though subordinate to the lien of the mortgage, survive and are valid until the lien is foreclosed by a sale under a judgment of foreclosure. * * * Until the lien of the mortgage is foreclosed, the mortgagee has no paramount title which would justify eviction of the occupants or abrogation of the agreements. The order of the court directing the occupants to vacate the premises or pay to the receiver the reasonable value of the use and occupancy deprives the occupants of a right which they have obtained by agreement. It does more than protect the security of the mortgage debt. It gives to the mortgagee a security beyond the stipulations of the mortgage and deprives the occupants of their enjoyment of rights secured by contract." [10]

The logic of the lien theory, and probably its policy also, supports the view which prevailed.[11] Under that theory only the foreclosure sale itself should ever cancel the lease because it is only the sale which will affect the interest of the landlord, the mortgagor. Nevertheless, looking at the problem broadly, there seems no justification for arriving at different results on the basis of title or lien theories. The receivership is granted in any state to preserve the property and to prevent injury to the mortgagee's security. If the rents and profits do not constitute any part of the mortgagee's security, then clearly the receiver should not be able either to collect the reserved rent for the mortgagee or to cancel any of the mortgagor's leases. On the other hand, if they do constitute a part of the mortgagee's security, whether that be by reason of his position *qua* mortgagee, by virtue of clauses assigning or pledging the rents and profits to him, or because the court of equity feels that he should have the produce of the property as of the time he starts to realize on the property itself in which he had his security interest, then, whether or not the receiver should be permitted, or rather, directed, to avoid the mortgagor's leases ought to depend, as has been urged, "upon the answer to a simple question: can the mortgagee's margin of security be preserved adequately without avoiding" [12] them. If the continuance of the leases will render the margin inadequate, the receiver should be directed to avoid them.

The argument that this runs counter to the lien theory is not insurmountable. The appointment of a receiver in a lien state also does violence to the theory by taking possession away from the mortgagor before foreclosure sale. It does so especially when combined with allocation to the mortgagee of the rents and profits that arise and are collected by the receiver before sale. On the lien doctrine these belong to the mortgagor until sale in the absence of an agreement to the contrary. It is true that to allow the receiver, in addition, to disaffirm leases by the mortgagor subsequent to the mortgage would be going beyond this, and, the New York court believed, a step too far. However it really comes down to a question of degree, of how far the court thinks it is desirable to go in contravention of the view that the mortgagor and those claiming under him should be left in undisturbed enjoyment of the property, up to foreclosure sale, on the terms agreed upon between them. The encroachments on the mortgagor's rights under the lien theory which the courts have permitted have been justified on the ground that the protection of the mortgagee's security interest through a receivership was paramount.

10. Prudence Co. v. 160 W. 73 St. Corp., 1932, 260 N.Y. 205, 211, 183 N.E. 365, 366, 86 A.L.R. 361. The court was also moved by the unfortunate situation of the tenants under the decisions in New York, pointing out "that, if they vacate they not only lose the rights acquired under their agreements, but remain subject to its obligations, at least until there is a sale under a judgment of foreclosure, and even after that date, if the plaintiff should decide to discontinue the action as to them; if they do not vacate, they can be put out, unless they pay more than they agreed to pay."

11. See Glenn, Mortgages, § 181.1.

12. Tefft, Receivers and Leases Subordinate to the Mortgage, 1934, 2 Chi.L.Rev. 33, 35.

That same justification would extend to permitting the receiver to nullify any act by the mortgagor subsequent to the execution of the mortgage that operated to impair the adequacy of the mortgagee's security. Leases which fail to bring in the fair value of the use and occupation of the property, when the total security including the rents and profits is inadequate, do operate to impair the mortgagee's interest, and, therefore, if permitted to stand nullify pro tanto the purpose of the receivership. Consequently it boils down to whether it is more desirable to achieve completely the purpose for which the receiver was appointed, a purpose which in the very appointment of the receiver was considered sufficiently important to override the policy and rule in lien jurisdictions that the mortgagor not be ousted before foreclosure sale, or whether it will stop short of that on a combination of reasoning about the lien theory and solicitude for the plight of a tenant [13] who, after all, can be considered to have acted voluntarily at his peril.[14] It is submitted that the former is the better view and that the receiver should have the power to disaffirm leases subsequent to the mortgage on the test suggested and not be confined merely to collecting the rents stipulated for in the leases.

EFFECT OF RECEIVERSHIP ON RENTS— (6) MORTGAGOR IN POSSESSION

156. Where the defaulting mortgagor is in possession the better view permits the appointment of a receiver who may collect an occupational rental if necessary to the adequacy of the security.

Closely related to the foregoing is the question whether a receiver may be appointed when the mortgagor remains in possession of the mortgaged property and uses it as a home or for other non-income producing purpose. Although the cases are not numerous, there

13. See supra note 9.

14. State ex rel. Coker v. District Court of Tulsa Co., 1932, 159 Okl. 10, 11 P.2d 495.

is authority not only that a receiver may be appointed to take over such property but that the mortgagor can be compelled by the receiver to pay an occupational rental.[15] This was also the law in New York until the case of *Holmes v. Gravenhorst* [16] was decided. This case was foreshadowed by the *Prudence* [17] case, which made it seem illogical to allow the receiver more power over the owner, by collecting an occupational rent from him, than over tenants whose interests are carved out of his.[18] However, although relying upon the *Prudence* case, in the *Holmes* case the

15. Yorkshire Bank v. Mullan, 1887, 35 Ch.D. 125; Pratchett v. Drew, 1924, 1 Ch. 280; Astor v. Turner, 1848, 3 How.Pr. (N.Y.) 225; Public Bank v. London, 1913, 159 App.Div. 484, 144 N.Y.S. 561. In New Jersey if the premises are in the possession of the mortgagor, especially if they are occupied by him as a home, the court will be most reluctant to appoint a receiver; and, in such a case will demand a clearer showing of the existence of the reasons for which receivers are appointed. See Rehberger v. Wegener, 1930, 107 N.J.Eq. 391, 152 A. 700, for a review of early and unofficially reported cases on the point. There was no showing that there was any possibility of a deficiency in the foreclosure suit and the receivership was denied. However, it was indicated that in a proper case one would be appointed and the mortgagor ordered to pay occupational rent or vacate. See 1934, 91 A.L.R. 1236, for a collection of cases.

16. 1933, 263 N.Y. 148, 188 N.E. 285, 91 A.L.R. 1230, expressly overruling Citizens Savings Bank v. Wilder, 1896, 11 App.Div. 63, 42 N.Y.S. 481.
The case is discussed in Abelow, The Doctrine of Holmes v. Gravenhorst, 1934, 3 Brooklyn L.Rev. 212; note, 1934, 11 N.Y.Univ.L.Q.Rev. 480; note, 1935, 20 Cornell L.Q. 366; note, 1934, 8 U. of Cin.L.Rev. 213; note, 1933, 33 Col.L.Rev. 1211 (a general discussion of the receiver of rents and profits in New York, covering the situation after the decision in the Prudence case and the Appellate Division decision in the principal case); 1934, 91 A.L.R. 1236.

17. Prudence Co. v. 160 W. 73d St. Corp., 1932, 260 N.Y. 205, 183 N.E. 365, 86 A.L.R. 361, discussed § 146, supra.

18. In spite of this, before the Court of Appeals had reversed the Appellate Division decision, 238 App. Div. 313, 263 N.Y.S. 738, which had held that the mortgagor was bound to pay occupational rent, it had been predicted that the result would be upheld because "to compel the owner of the equity to pay an occupational rent does not entail the hardships incident to the receiver's power to disregard a lease" and "the contrary rule would effect too great an impairment of the mortgagee's security." 1933, 33 Col.L.Rev. 1211, 1215. The reasoning was good but the prophesy bad.

court heavily stressed the fact that the receiver was appointed under a receivership clause covering rents and profits, and not under the general equity jurisdiction of the court, and the additional fact that there were no rents and profits for the receiver to take under the terms of the contract. Even regarding the decision as only one of interpreting the terms of the agreement, it may be questioned. The dissenting opinion's view that "rents and profits" includes the personal occupancy by the mortgagor because that occupancy gives him a "benefit in all respects equivalent to rents and profits" is clearly a reasonable one.[19] However the distinction stressed by the court makes it possible to distinguish the *Holmes* case from one in which the receiver is appointed on general equity principles. Where the receiver is appointed by virtue of the receivership clause alone without regard to the adequacy of the security there is no necessity for compelling the mortgagor to furnish additional security by way of rent. If the security is not shown to be inadequate, the result normally will be that any rents that the mortgagor is forced to pay as additional security will eventually be returned to him after the foreclosure sale. The imposition of the duty upon him to make payments under such circumstances is unwarranted. Where, however, the receiver is appointed under the general equity jurisdiction of the court because of the inadequacy of the security, the rent exacted from the mortgagor will go in payment or be a guaranty against a threatened deficiency. In such a case the justification for imposing the duty on the mortgagor is the same as that dis-

cussed in the preceding section in connection with tenants of the mortgagor. So long as the mortgagor is not in default he is privileged to keep the mortgaged property without regard to whether it produces any income of any sort. When he defaults, however, the mortgagee is entitled to enforce his security and, through the appointment of a receiver, have it produce income from the time he starts to realize on it, provided the security is inadequate without that income. Consequently the mortgagor, if he stays on, should have to pay rent. If he does not wish to do so, he should vacate the premises and allow the receiver to obtain income by renting to someone else or utilizing the premises in some other profitable way. The result of the decision, unless the suggested distinction is followed, is, as has been pointed out, to create a new exemption for debtors by judicial decision rather than by statute.[20] Whether its effects can be avoided by adding to the receivership clause a waiver of the exemption in the form of a provision that the mortgagor will pay the receiver a reasonable rent if the premises continue to be occupied by him must be regarded as doubtful unless the clause also grants the receiver the right of possession.[21]

19. "In effect, the mortgagor-occupant charges himself with the value of the space occupied as rent and credits himself with this amount as income. With the appointment of a receiver, the income credit—like the income from any other tenant—goes to the receiver. He continues to charge himself with rent, but he pays it to the receiver instead of to himself. He loses nothing since the rent goes to the receiver's fund to carry the property (a duty resting on him), and thereafter to meet a deficiency, if there be one, otherwise to himself." Crouch, J., dissenting, in Holmes v. Gravenhorst, supra note 16, at 158, 188 N. E. at 288.

20. See Glenn, Mortgages, § 184. A mortgagor who remains in possession during the redemption period after foreclosure but does not redeem has been held not liable to the purchaser for the use and occupation of the premises under a statute providing that "the purchaser from the time of sale until a redemption * * * is entitled to receive from the tenant in possession the rents of the property sold or the value of the use and occupation thereof." Local Realty Co. v. Lindquist, 1938, 96 Utah, 297, 85 P.2d 770, discussed in note, 1939, 52 Harv.L.Rev. 843. But other courts have interpreted the words "tenant in possession" in similar statutes to include the mortgagor. Walker v. McCusker, 1887, 71 Cal. 594, 12 P. 723; Clifford & Co. v. Henry, 1918, 40 N. D. 604, 169 N.W. 508. It has been suggested that the first interpretation is the result of a judicial desire to allow hard-pressed mortgagors with little hope for redemption to remain in possession as long and as inexpensively as possible. See 1939, 52 Harv.L.Rev. 843, 844.

21. In Carlin Trading Corp. v. Bennett, 1st Dep't 1965, 24 A.D.2d 91, 264 N.Y.S.2d 43, discussed in Note, 1966, 17 Syracuse L.Rev. 774, a mortgage pro-

EFFECT OF RECEIVERSHIP ON RENTS— (7) MORTGAGOR CONDUCTING BUSINESS

157. Where the mortgagor in possession conducts a business, the appointment of a receiver of rents and profits depends on the type of business. The cases are not in agreement, but in general a receiver will only be appointed if the rent factor in the business is predominant, e. g., in the case of apartment houses and, perhaps, hotels.

Where the mortgagor conducts a business on the mortgaged premises instead of renting them or occupying them as a home the first problem is whether the business is subject to the mortgage either by virtue of its being a product of the land or of an express inclusion under the terms of the mortgage.[22] This is so because it is clear that a mortgage foreclosure receiver cannot take into his possession or control property not covered by the mortgage, and a "mortgage covers the land and building—not the business enterprise housed".[23] The type of business ought to and does make a difference. Where the mortgagor has rented the property—a clear case for receivership—it is nevertheless true that the mortgagor, as landlord, engages in activities that come under the description of business, such as repairs, taking out insurance, paying taxes, getting tenants and executing leases with them and then collecting the rents, or, ousting them if they violate the conditons of the lease.[24] Notwithstanding the contribution to the income from these activities, the entire amount of the rent is regarded as issuing out of the land itself and there is no attempt to allocate the share of the total due to the work and abilities of the landlord-mortgagor. When a mortgagor conducts a business of any sort on his own land, the rental value of that land, whether explicitly recognized or not, is one of the elements comprising the gross income of the business, along with other factors such as price of materials, management, and interest on capital. Attempts to segregate from gross income that portion earned by the mortgaged real property can be little more than an arbitrary estimate in most cases.[25] It is not surprising, therefore, to find the courts appointing receivers in cases where the rent element clearly predominates and the services of the mortgagor are essentially the same in kind as those of any landlord, even though accentuated in degree, and the contribution to the income of other conveniences furnished is

vided that, upon default, the mortgagor would pay reasonable occupational rent to any receiver appointed. A receiver was appointed but the mortgagor failed to pay the rent fixed by the court. In a foreclosure action the court held that the mortgage provision could not be enforced unless the mortgage specifically grants the receiver the right of possession. The note writer, recognizing that the court would permit eviction where the mortgage clearly and expressly permits the receiver to take possession, thought it advisable for New York to refuse to enforce any mortgage clause which disturbs the mortgagor's possession before foreclosure unless absolutely necessary to protect the mortgagee's security interest. Prior to the Bennett case it had been thought that the granting to the receiver of the right of possession was unnecessary. See 2 Wiltsie, Mortgage Foreclosure, 5th ed., 1009, n. 23. In Guaranty Trust Co. v. Bisjo Realty Corporation, 1934, 152 Misc. 522, 272 N.Y.S. 155, the trust indenture gave to the trustee the right to immediate possession of the mortgaged premises on default, and further provided that any receiver appointed should have the rights conferred upon the trustee. Held, the receiver appointed was entitled to possession although the mortgagor himself was in possession. Cf. In re Aville Realty Corporation, 1932, 57 F.2d 882, discussed in notes, 1932, 32 Col.L.Rev. 1249; 1933, 8 Not.D.Law. 253, holding that an agreement by the mortgagor with the third mortgagee, that on default the latter should have the right to enter and the mortgagor would pay a reasonable rental from the time of default with a right in the mortgagee or a receiver appointed by him to dispossess the mortgagor on failure to pay such rental, did not create any landlord and tenant relationship between them which would entitle the mortgagee to collect the agreed upon rent.

22. "We have, therefore, in the first instance, to ask, before appointing a manager to manage a business, whether the business is included in the security." Whitley v. Challis [1892] 1 Ch. 64, 70.

23. Abelow, The Doctrine of Holmes v. Gravenhorst, 1933, 3 Brook.L.Rev. 212; Scott v. Farmers' etc. Co., C.C.A.N.D.1895, 69 F. 17, 16 C.C.A. 358; Smith v. McCullough, 1881, 104 U.S. 25, 26 L.Ed. 637; Thomas v. Armstrong, 1915, 51 Okl. 203, 151 P. 689, L.R.A.1916B, 1182. See 14 St.Louis L.Rev. 315.

24. Glenn, Mortgages, § 185.

25. See 1941, 50 Yale L.Jour. 1427, 1440; 1935, 44 Yale L.Jour. 701, 704.

small.[26] This would cover apartment houses and, probably, a garage or parking lot.[27] Where, in addition to the land and buildings, the business utilizes considerable amounts of chattels, good will is a substantial factor and the part that management plays is large, the propriety of permitting the mortgagee to take over the business through a receiver is dubious. Of course, if the chattels and good will are also given in mortgage, the receivership has more justification.[28] But even without such inclusion, receivers have been appointed for hotels,[29] although there is some authority to the contrary,[30] and one case limited the receivership to that portion of the revenues derived from rent actually paid for rooms occupied.[31] On the other hand a receiver of mortgaged premises on which the mortgagor conducted a dance hall, restaurant and ice cream parlor was denied on the ground that there were no rents and profits within the meaning of the *Holmes* case.[32] Nor is it surprising to find a receiver appointed

of property on which the mortgagor has a tree nursery, the trees being treated as part of the realty.[33] Whether or not when the premises are used for a mixed purpose, e. g., a doctor using part of his home as an office, a receiver could compel the payment of some rent has been mooted but not answered by the courts.[34]

The cases reflect a conflict between penalizing the mortgagor for conducting a business on his property by taking from him the entire profits instead of just that part which represents the share properly allocable to rents, an allocation that cannot be made, as was pointed out, except by arbitrary estimate, and penalizing the mortgagee who, if the property were rented, would be entitled to collect the rents. The policy of the court toward protecting one or the other, as well as its attitude in regard to the desirability or undesirability of receiverships as a remedy are factors that help explain the decisions.[35]

MILKING [36]

158. Milking agreements between the mortgagor and his lessee—such as prepayment not in accord with the lease and lease cancellations or rent reductions for cash payments—may be avoided by the mortgagee if the tenant had notice of the mortgage.

When a mortgagor's condition becomes hopeless or shaky, or where the deflation of real estate prices has wiped out the entire value of his redemption interest, the mortgagor, resigned to the loss of his property, fre-

26. See 1935, 44 Yale L.Jour. 701, 703.

27. Garage: Fairchild v. Gray, 1930, 136 Misc. 704, 242 N.Y.S. 192; Title etc. Co. Belgrave Motor Sales Co., Inc., N.Y.L.J., Jan. 27, 1934, at 932, col. 4. Parking lot: City Bank Farmers Trust Co. v. Mishol Realty Co., N.Y.L.J., Jan. 27, 1934, at 441, col. 5.

28. See Cake v. Mohun, 1896, 164 U.S. 311, 17 S.Ct. 100, 41 L.Ed. 447, "furniture, equipment and other personal property" of hotel; Knickerbocker v. Mc-Kindley Coal & Mining Co., 1898, 172 Ill. 535, 50 N.E. 330, 64 Am.St.Rep. 54; Pacific N. W. Packing Co. v. Allen, C.C.A.Wash.1901, 109 F. 515, 48 C.C.A. 521, tools, stock, and "outfit" of cannery. See 1935, 44 Yale L.Jour. 701, 702.

29. Lowell v. Doe, 1890, 44 Minn. 144, 46 N.W. 297; Warwick v. Hammell, 1880, 32 N.J.Eq. 427; Fidelity Trust Co. v. Saginaw Hotels, Inc., 1932, 259 Mich. 254, 242 N.W. 906; see Makeel v. Hotchkiss, 1901, 190 Ill. 311, 60 N.E. 524, 83 Am.St.Rep. 780.

30. Chatham-Phoenix Bank v. Hotel Park-Central, 1931, 146 Misc. 208, 261 N.Y.S. 490, receiver denied, not because the property was a hotel, but because the court thought a receivership could not accomplish the purpose of conservation and preservation any better than well advanced reorganization plans; Whitley v. Challis [1892] 1 Ch. 64.

31. Stadtmuller v. Schorr, N.Y.L.J., Nov. 3, 1934, at 1633, col. 4.

32. Bartels v. Fowler, 1936, 160 Misc. 584, 290 N.Y.S. 908.

33. Heller v. Amawalk Nursery, Inc., 1938, 253 App. Div. 380, 2 N.Y.S.2d 196, affirmed 278 N.Y. 514, 15 N.E.2d 671, noted, 1938, 23 Cornell L.Quar. 614.

34. See Abelow, The Doctrine of Holmes v. Gravenhorst, 1934, 3 Brook.L.Rev. 212, 223.

35. See, 1935, 44 Yale L.Jour. 701, 704–705.

36. Although the problem dealt with here arises in other than receivership cases, it is chiefly encountered in them and is so intimately connected with the matters just discussed that it seemed desirable to consider it at this point even though the subject matter is broader than the topic under which it is placed.

quently attempts to squeeze out of it as much money as he can before surrendering it. The chief devices by which such mortgagors attempt to "milk" the property are leases which require payment in advance for the entire term, the execution of a lease at an inadequate rental in return for a present cash consideration, the assignment of future rents to a third person, and the cancellation of a long term lease favorable to the lessor in exchange for a cash payment to the mortgagor.[37] The problem of preventing such undesirable practices necessitates reconciliation of three conflicting interests: safeguarding the mortgagee's security against impairment; protecting a tenant who made a lease in good faith from hardship; and preserving to the mortgagor the benefits of ownership.[38] It is, of course, bound up with the question whether the mortgagee or his receiver may affirm or disaffirm leases made by the mortgagor.[39]

Where the lease is executed prior to the mortgage, if it provides for prepayment, then prepayment in accordance with the terms of the lease is binding on the mortgagee for the simple reason that he took his mortgage subject to that very provision.[40] However, prepayments not in accordance with the terms of the lease, if made with notice of the mortgage, will not be binding on the mortgagee or receiver even in the absence of proof of an actual fraudulent intent by the mortgagor or participation in it by the lessee.[41] This is true even though put in the form of an agreement altering the terms of the original lease.[42] Indeed such cases in most instances might well rest upon a theory generally more difficult to establish factually, that of setting aside a collusive agreement to defraud the mortgagee. As has been pointed out, any arrangement for prepayment of the rent for the whole term or a large portion of it is abnormal and, if made after a mortgage has attached to the property, indicates clearly a design to defeat the mortgagee's assertion of claim to it on default and foreclosure.[43] Since this is so, the tenant who agrees to such an arrangement must be charged with collusive acquaintance with the scheme[44] and, on this ground, the courts are justified in giving no validity to the prepayment, provided, of course, the tenant knew of the existence of the mortgage at the time.[45]

The cancellation of a favorable lease antedating the mortgage, or a reduction in the rent of such leases for a cash payment to the mortgagor might also be treated as fraudulent conveyances, if, in fact, such was the case.[46] Here, however, there is not present the abnormality of the transaction to charge

---

37. See Remedies Against "Milking" of Property by Mortgagors, 1933, 46 Harv.L.Rev. 491; Cancellation of Leases by Mortgagor as Affecting Mortgagee, 1935, 12 N.Y.Univ.L.Q.Rev. 501; Murray, Milking Time, 1932, 159 Atl.Monthly, 419. There are other ways in which the mortgagor can milk the property. He may collect the rents and use them at the same time failing to pay taxes, keep up insurance, make repairs, etc.

38. See 1941, 50 Yale L.Jour. 1427, 1437.

39. See §§ 154, 155, supra.

40. If the prepayment agreement in the lease was inserted for the purpose of preventing the mortgagee having the benefit of any rent as part of his security, and the tenant participated in this design, although such an agreement should be invalid against a mortgagee who had no notice of it, it is difficult to see why it should not be valid against a mortgagee who was aware of it, even though the scheme might possibly be characterized as fraudulent. If the mortgagee went ahead with his eyes open, there is no reason to invalidate the agreement and give him more than he voluntarily bargained for.

41. See § 143, supra. Boteler v. Leber, 1933, 112 N.J. Eq. 441, 164 A. 572.

42. Colter Realty Co. v. Primer Realty Co., 1941, 262 App.Div. 77, 27 N.Y.S.2d 850.

43. See Glenn, Mortgages, § 183.1.

44. See Glenn, Fraudulent Conveyances and Preferences, rev. ed., §§ 299–299b.

45. "The court will take care of a sharper, as landlord, who leases premises for a long term, with rent payable in advance, and lets the mortgagee take the 'empty shell.'" Nerwal Realty Corp. v. 9th Ave.-31st St. Corp., 1935, 154 Misc. 565, 278 N.Y.S. 766. But where the lease was untainted by dishonesty payment in advance will be valid and the lease will stand. S. C. See 1947, 22 N.Y.Univ.L.Q.Rev. 731.

46. Sager v. Redbor Realty Corp., 1930, 230 App.Div. 106, 243 N.Y.S. 314.

the tenant with collusion as in the prepayment case, and difficulties of proof would make it an ineffective remedy. However, such acts do constitute a clear injury to the mortgagee's security because they deprive the mortgagee or his receiver of the rents they would be able to collect on entry into possession or on appointment. It is an injury which, looking at the mortgagor's responsibility, may be considered as waste insofar as it threatens to impair the security.[47] However, the mortgagee's remedies against the mortgagee's remedies against the mortgagor for such a wrong would not be very satisfactory. An action for damages against him, even if allowed and pursued, would probably be worthless since he is likely to be insolvent.[48] An injunction should be allowed, but only against a particular threatened cancellation, and consequently constant vigilance and a series of suits by the mortgagee might be necessary.[49] To be able to hold the tenant on his original lease would give the mortgagee what he really wants. Notice to the tenant of the existence of the mortgage on the reversion should be sufficient to restrict his ability to enter into agreements with the mortgagor that will reduce the value of the security. Proof of actual fraud is unnecessary.[50]

Where the lease is subsequent to the mortgage, in those jurisdictions, chiefly title states, in which the mortgagee or a receiver in foreclosure may disaffirm the mortgagor's leases, neither a prepayment of the rental, even if in accordance with the terms of the lease, nor a lease calling for an inadequate rental will be binding. In the event that it is disregarded, other questions arise. One is whether the tenant may be held to pay a reasonable rental for the period of his use and occupation from the time that the mortgagee or the receiver takes over rather than being allowed to assert the terms of his agreement with the mortgagor as setting the bounds of his liability.[51] Another is whether, if the prepayment of inadequate rent was by an agreement changing the terms of a previous lease, also subsequent to the mortgage, the tenant could be held to the higher terms of the original lease or whether he could treat the entrance by the mortgagee or appointment of the receiver as an eviction releasing him from his lease.[52]

Where the mortgagee or receiver seeks to take advantage of such a favorable lease by voiding the cancellation of it he is met by arguments that he cannot do so. Lack of privity of title between the mortgagee and tenant together with the notion of eviction of the tenant by superior title are relied upon to block such action. This ground has already been considered, and will not be retraversed except to say that if the cancellation or other agreement altering unfavorably the terms of such a lease can be established to have been effected in anticipation of foreclosure with the intent of defrauding the mortgagee it generally will be set aside. But, as was noted above, proof of this is ordinarily too difficult to make the rule of practical benefit. If the latter is the case, relief from milking operations of this sort may be illu-

47. See 1933, 46 Harv.L.Rev. 491, 494; 1941, 50 Yale L.Jour. 1427, 1438. See §§ 148, 149, 152. Also see §§ 128, 134.

48. See § 128, supra.

49. See 1941, 50 Yale L.Jour. 1424, 1438; 1933, 46 Harv.L.Rev. 494.

50. Bank of Manhattan Trust Co. v. 571 Park Ave. Corp., 1933, 263 N.Y. 57, 188 N.E. 156, noted, 1934, 11 N.Y.Univ.L.Q.Rev. 480. Cf. Colter Realty, Inc., v. Primer Realty Corp., 1941, 262 App.Div. 77, 27 N.Y.S.2d 850. Both cases involved leases subsequent to the mortgage with clauses making the rents and profits security for the debt. In holding that agreements lessening the yield of the property were invalid the court did so on the ground that, even short of fraud and collusion, the mortgagor and his tenant could not impair the mortgagee's security, with notice of the mortgagee's rights, even though the agreement was made before those rights had become operative. The case of a lease antedating the mortgage would be an *a fortiori* one.

51. Rohrer v. Deatherage, 1929, 336 Ill. 450, 168 N.E. 266.

52. First National Bank of Chicago v. Gordon, 1936, 287 Ill.App. 83, 4 N.E.2d 504. See supra, §§ 153, 154.

sory. If the tenant is unwilling to come to terms on a new lease, at most he can be held only for use and occupation of the premises from the time the rights of the mortgagee or receiver accrue until he moves out, and then a new tenant must be found.

In lien states which hold that the mortgagee or a receiver in foreclosure is bound by the terms of the mortgagor's subsequent leases and cannot disaffirm them, an exception was expressly indicated to the effect that an order appointing a receiver "may [not] be frustrated by a collusive or fraudulent lease for an inadequate rental or advance payment of rent in anticipation of a foreclosure action." [53] Further, since the mortgagee may preserve favorable leases subsequent to the mortgage and have them sold as part of his security on foreclosure sale, cancellation of such leases can be regarded as an impairment of the mortgagee's security on the same reasoning as in the case of a lease prior to a mortgage, and the same consequences should attend it. In other words, notice of the mortgagee's rights should suffice to prevent a valid agreement being made even though no fraudulent design to defeat his claim can be adduced. This clearly ought to be, and apparently is, true where the milking agreement surrendering or changing the subsequent lease occurs after the date when an assignment or pledge of such rents has become operative.[54] It is also true where it is made after an action for the foreclosure of the property and appointment of a receiver has

been begun and notice of *lis pendens* has been filed although the receiver is not appointed until after the agreement and prepayment.[55] It should further be true of agreements made before that time but with notice that under certain contingencies the mortgagee would become entitled to the rent stipulated for in the lease with the mortgagor.

This has been held to be so in New York where the mortgage contained a pledge of rents and profits, the operative contingency in such a case being the appointment of a receiver. The court, while still affirming its ruling that a "receiver could not require a tenant in occupation under a lease to pay any sum for use and occupation beyond the sum which the lease called for," pointed out that it had not intended by its earlier decision [56] to hold that the mortgagor's agreement was conclusive upon the mortgagee where such agreements were in contravention of the express covenants and the necessary implications of a recorded mortgage prior in lien. The court held that where a mortgagor's agreement is made surrendering the right to receive rent for the mortgaged premises, or for the assignment of rents collectible therefrom, it was an impairment of the lien of the mortgage upon the rent. "The court also held that it was not necessary to find collusion in the making of such an arrangement; that it was beyond the power of the parties to appropriate the pledged rents to a different indebtedness, or defeat the pledge by leasing the premises rent free." [57] The result of such a decision

53. Prudence Co. v. 160 W. 73d St. Corp., 1932, 260 N.Y. 205, 213, 183 N.E. 365, 367, 86 A.L.R. 361, Hanna, Cas.Security, 983. Webber v. King, 1928, 205 Iowa 612, 218 N.W. 282, Gaynor v. Blewett, 1892, 82 Wis. 313, 52 N.W. 313, 33 Am.St.Rep. 47, might be explained on this same ground although the intent to defraud would have to be based on constructive notice of *lis pendens* of the suit to foreclose.

54. "After the mortgagors' release to the mortgagee of their right to rents under the lease became operative, the landlord had no right to modify the lease or enter into any agreement of modification that would bind the mortgagee without the latter's consent or approval." Franzen v. G. R. Kinney Co., 1935, 218 Wis. 53, 57, 259 N.W. 850, 852, 105 A.L.R. 740.

55. Gaynor v. Blewett, 1892, 82 Wis. 313, 52 N.W. 313.

56. Prudence Co. v. 160 W. 73d St. Corp., 1932, 260 N.Y. 205, 183 N.E. 365, 86 A.L.R. 361.

57. Colter Realty, Inc., v. Primer Realty Co., 1941, 262 App.Div. 77, 80, 27 N.Y.S.2d 850, 852, summarizing Bank, etc. Co. v. 571 Park Ave. Corp., 1933, 263 N.Y. 57, 188 N.E. 156, and holding that the same reasoning invalidated a prepayment arrangement under a lease subsequent to the mortgage in which there was a pledge of the rents, the prepayment occurring before the receiver was appointed and, therefore, before the pledge became operative. See § 150, supra.

is the recognition of an equitable lien on the rents and profits at least sufficient to prevent arrangements between the mortgagor and the tenant with notice, made prior to the date when the pledge would become operative by the appointment of a receiver, which would impair the mortgagee's security.

On the other hand, in Grether v. Nick,[58] the Wisconsin court, in spite of the presence of a valid pledge of the rents and profits, held that a prepayment of rent by a subsequent lessee was valid against the receiver in foreclosure and the tenant could not be made to pay again. The case, however, can be distinguished from the New York cases even though in its opinion the court emphasized the rule that a pledge of rents and profits does not create any rights in them until a receiver is appointed or the mortgagee takes possession. The right of a receiver to collect rents and profits rests upon the theory that they form part of his security either by express agreement or by an equity extrinsic to the mortgage stipulations.[59] Further, the power of a receiver to disregard various sorts of milking arrangements, or, more broadly, to affirm or disaffirm leases of his mortgagor, rests upon the idea that his action is justified to prevent the security to which the mortgagee is entitled from being impaired. Applying this to the case of prepaid rents, if the mortgagor used them to improve the mortgaged property instead of diverting them to his own pockets, then "the mortgagee enjoys the full benefit of the advanced payment, and * * * a court of equity should not work oppression by requiring its payment a second time." This was the express rationale of Grether v. Nick, the prepaid rent having been used to complete a building on the mortgaged premises.[60]

The question remains whether it is one of the "implications of a prior recorded mortgage" without a rent pledge that the right of a mortgagee to obtain a receiver to collect rents and profits when the mortgagor defaults creates before that time an equitable interest in them as effective, as against anyone charged with notice of the mortgage, as that generated by a pledge clause? If so, then contracts by the mortgagor impairing that interest by surrendering his right to receive the rents, collecting them in advance, or assigning them should be invalid as against the receiver in foreclosure.

It ought to be immaterial whether the contingency which would make operative the right of the mortgagee or a receiver to collect the rents under the lease is one provided for and made effective by an assignment or pledge of the rents and profits [61] or one which by a rule of equity is conferred upon a receiver appointed in foreclosure after default by the mortgagor. In either case, while the terms of the lease might be altered for the period up to the time when the rights of the mortgagee or receiver became operative, from that time on the rights on the lease as originally written should be enforced. Nevertheless, in a prior decision in Grether v. Nick,[62] in which the court mistakenly assumed there was no rent pledge, it was held that, although a receiver of rents and profits was appointed, the prepayment of rents by the subsequent lessee before that time was

---

travention of the rights of the mortgagee to them. Gaynor v. Blewett, 1892, 82 Wis. 313, 52 N.W. 313, was distinguished on this ground.

61. "These rents were expressly made security for the mortgage indebtedness in the event of default, and the scope of the contracts the mortgagor or its successors might make was necessarily limited to that extent. The pledge of these rents could not subsequently be rendered worthless either by another assignment of rents to be received, or by contracting away the right to collect any rent." Bank of Man. Tr. Co. v. 571 Park Ave. Corp., 1933, 263 N.Y. 57, 63, 188 N.E. 156, 158.

---

58. 1927, 193 Wis. 503, 215 N.W. 571, 55 A.L.R. 525.

59. See § 147 et seq., supra.

60. See Glenn, Mortgages, § 183.1. Grether v. Nick was also differentiated from the sort of case in which prepayments of rent were made to enable the mortgagor to appropriate them in fraudulent con-

62. 1927, 193 Wis. 503, 213 N.W. 304, 215 N.W. 571, 55 A.L.R. 525.

binding on the receiver.[63] The court reasoned that the rent paid in advance bought a leasehold interest in the property which, though subordinate to the mortgage in the sense that it can be ended when the mortgagor's title is divested by foreclosure sale, nevertheless is valid against a receiver of the mortgagor who is entitled only to those rents and profits which become due after his appointment. Further, in Wisconsin, a receiver was appointed only on the ground of prevention of waste, not inadequacy of the security, and this fact made the court reluctant to grant any greater rights to the rents and profits than precedent required. The answer to this is twofold. First, the ground on which the case was put when it was found that there was a pledge of rents and profits, although not mentioned in the first decision, is equally applicable to it. Second, if valid, it would open too wide a door to almost any sort of "milking" by the mortgagor.[64] Certainly a fraudulent prepayment should not be valid [65] and the broader rule of the New York cases hitting agreements that impair the mortgagee's security when made with notice is a desirable one.

PRIORITIES BETWEEN MORTGAGEES AS TO RENTS

159. A junior mortgagee who obtains a receiver is, by the prevailing view, entitled to the rents and profits until the senior mortgagee asserts his rights. This is so regardless of clauses pledging the rents unless there is an assignment of them to the senior mortgagee.

63. See Berick, The Mortgagee's Right to Rents, 1934, 8 Cin.L.Rev. 250, 274. See also Allen, Appointment of Receivers in Mortgage Foreclosure Cases, 1932, 16 Marquette L.Rev. 168.

64. See Glenn, Mortgages, § 183.1.

65. Webber v. King, 1928, 205 Iowa 612, 218 N.W. 282.
"Even this court [Grether v. Nick], however, would not protect a tenant who pays his rent in advance after the foreclosure is begun. And all the courts in the same group indicate that if an assignment of rent or the prepayment of rent or the execution of a lease upon an inadequate rental, are the result of a deliberate fraud and collusion to defeat the mortgagee, the transaction will not be permitted to prejudice the mortgagee." Berick, The Mortgagee's Right to Rents, 1934, 8 Cin.L.Rev. 250, 275.

Frequently there is a race between different mortgagees to obtain for themselves the rents and profits of the mortgaged property through the appointment of a receiver. When this happens how are the priorities to be determined? Most courts hold that a junior mortgagee who obtains a receiver is entitled to all rents and profits collected by the receiver prior to the assertion of the rights of a senior mortgagee through the extension of the receivership to him,[66] the appointment of a new receiver at his petition, or the getting of possession.[67] This is a reward to the junior mortgagee for his diligence, for had it not been for his action, the rents up to the time the senior mortgagee asserted his rights, would have gone to the mortgagor-landlord. Or, to put the matter in a different way, in spite of superiority of lien through seniority, a mortgagee who has done nothing to capture the rents should be in no better position than he would have been in had the mortgagor continued in possession.[68]

There is, however, minority authority that even though the junior mortgagee obtains a receiver first, if the senior mortgagee inter-

66. See Yoelin v. Kudla, 1941, 302 Ill.App. 413, 24 N.E.2d 67.

67. Detroit Properties Corp. v. Detroit Hotel Co., 1913, 258 Mich. 156, 242 N.W. 213; Post v. Dorr, 1845, 4 Edw.Ch. (N.Y.) 412; Sullivan v. Rosson, 1918, 223 N.Y. 217, 119 N.E. 405, 4 A.L.R. 1400, noted, 1918, 27 Yale L.Jour. 1085; N.Y.Life Ins. Co. v. Fulton Development Corp., 1934, 265 N.Y. 348, 193 N.E. 169; Goddard v. Clarke, 1908, 81 Neb. 373, 116 N.W. 41; Longdock Mills & Elevator Co. v. Alpen, 1913, 82 N.J.Eq. 190, 88 A. 623; Bermes v. Kelley, 1931, 108 N.J.Eq. 289, 154 A. 860; Re Metr.Amal.Ests., 1912, 2 Ch. 497; Re Belbridge Prop. Trust, 1941, 165 L.T. Rep. 170. See 1945 50 Yale L.Jour. 1424 1442; 1933, 43 Yale L.Jour. 107 108; 1935, 95 A.L.R. 1050.

68. "His [the senior mortgagee's] failure to take any action would, or might have been as serious to him if the receiver had never been appointed as he now claims it will be if the money in the hands of the receiver is not paid to him as mortgagee. He is not now entitled to appropriate the proceeds of the diligence of a junior mortgagee." Sullivan v. Rosson, 1918, 223 N.Y. 217, 225, 119 N.E. 405, 408. See Tefft, Receivers and Leases Subordinate to the Mortgage, 1934, 2 U.Chi.L.Rev. 33, 41; 1933, 33 Col.L.Rev. 1211, 1218.

venes, all of the rents and profits collected by the receiver will be allocated in the order of the priorities of the mortgages, thus depriving the junior mortgagee of his advantage as to the part already collected.[69]

The general rule is equally clear that a first mortgagee, even without a rents and profits clause, who obtains a receiver or takes possession, will prevail as to all rents thereafter [70] to the exclusion of any other claimant whether junior mortgagee,[71] judgment creditor [72] or general creditor.[73] This includes accruing and uncollected back rents.

69. Bergin v. Robbins, 1929, 109 Conn. 329, 146 A. 724; Wolkenstein v. Slonim, 1934, 355 Ill. 306, 189 N.E. 312, noted 2 Chi.L.Rev. 149, possibly is susceptible to the same interpretation because the receiver was ordered to pay over to the first mortgagee all of the rents and profits collected by the receiver appointed in the foreclosure action by the second mortgagee. However, the first mortgagee, although he did not know at the time of the prior action by the second mortgagee, began his own foreclosure action on the day that the receiver was appointed in the prior suit and there is nothing in the facts to indicate that any rents had been collected by the receiver before the first mortgagee petitioned to have the receiver turn over to him all of the rents and profits. See, also, N. J. Title & Guarantee Co. v. Cone & Co., 1902, 64 N.J.Eq. 45, 53 A. 97, in which the first mortgagee, who began his foreclosure before the second mortgagee began his and obtained a receiver, was held entitled to all rents and profits, the second mortgagee being denied any priority as to them by securing the appointment of the receiver.

70. Both as to income earned prior to default and after default, "it is usually stated as an elementary proposition of law that the mortgagee or trustee [in a trust deed mortgage] has no right to income unless and until he either makes a demand for possession of the mortgaged premises, applies to the court for the appointment of a receiver, or intervenes in a proceeding brought by a junior mortgagee or a general creditor." Israels & Kramer, Income Clause in a Corporate Mortgage, 1930, 30 Col.L.Rev. 488, 498.

71. Last v. Winkel, 1916, 86 N.J.Eq. 356, 97 A. 961, affirmed 86 N.J.Eq. 431, 99 A. 1070; Metropolitan Life Ins. Co. v. Tash-Lap Realty Corp., 1930, 138 Misc. 68, 245 N.Y.S. 281.

72. Central Trust Co. v. Chattanooga R. & C. R. R., C.C.A.Ga., 1899, 94 F. 275, 36 C.C.A. 241.

73. Hayes v. Dickenson, 1876, 9 Hun (N.Y.) 277. See Israels & Kramer, Income Clause in Corporate Mortgages, 1930, 30 Col.L.Rev. 488, 503.

The mortgagee's ability to obtain the rents of mortgaged property after bankruptcy of the mortgagor is considered in note, 1932, 45 Harv.L.Rev. 901;

The effect upon these general rules of clauses assigning or pledging the rents and profits has not been definitively settled.[74] Since the first mortgagee without a rents and profits clause will generally prevail as to rents and profits uncollected and accruing from the time he intervenes to assert his rights, *a fortiori* the same would be true if it contained such a clause.[75] It would seem clear, also, that if the first mortgage contained an assignment of rents and profits which operated to give rights to the mortgagee prior to the appointment of a receiver or taking possession, the first mortgagee should be entitled as against a receiver appointed on the application of a second mortgagee to all rents accruing after the date the assignment became effective even though collected by the receiver prior to intervention by the first mortgagee.[76] On the other hand,

1941, 50 Yale L.Jour, 1424, 1445; 1918, 18 Col.L. Rev. 91; Berick, The Mortgagee's Right to Rents, 1934, 8 Cin.L.Rev. 250, 292; 1942, 56 Harv.L.Rev. 305; 1931, 75 A.L.R. 1526. Cf. In re Hotel St. James Co., C.C.A.Cal., 1933, 65 F.2d 82. For his right to rents and profits during an agricultural composition proceeding, see note, 1938, 11 Rocky Mt.L.Rev. 65.

74. See 1933, 43 Yale L.J. 107.

75. Sullivan v. Rosson, 1918, 223 N.Y. 217, 119 N.E. 405, 4 A.L.R. 1400 noted, 1918, 27 Yale L.Jour. 1085, as against junior mortgagee; Atlantic Trust Co. v. Dana, C.C.A.Kan.1903, 128 F. 209, 62 C.C.A. 657, as against judgment creditor; Newport etc. Co. v. Douglas, 1877, 75 Ky. (12 Bush.) 673, as against judgment creditor; Re Banner, D.C.N.Y.1907, 149 F. 936, as against general creditor; First Savings, etc., v. Stuppi, C.C.A.N.M.1924, 2 F.2d 822, as against general creditors.

76. Harris v. Taylor, 1898, 35 App.D. 462, 54 N.Y.S. 864, assignment by separate instrument; John McMenamy Investment & Real Estate Co. v. Dawley, 1914, 183 Mo.App. 1, 165 S.W. 829; Paramount Building & Loan Ass'n v. Sacks, 1930, 107 N.J.Eq. 328, 152 A. 457, clause in mortgage. A prior assignee of rents as security will prevail as to all rents accruing after the assignment as against a later first mortgage of the land with a clause pledging the rents on default and a subsequent assignment of the rents to the mortgagee who entered with permission of the mortgagor and collected the rents. Conley v. Fine, 1918, 181 App.Div. 675, 169 N.Y.S. 162. In New Orleans Bank & Trust Co. v. Hart, C. C.A.La.1929, 32 F.2d 721, certiorari denied 280 U.S. 576, 50 S.Ct. 30, 74 L.Ed. 627, the first mortgage contained a clause covering the rents and profits

if the clause is construed to be only a pledge of the rents and profits any inchoate equitable lien which may be raised by it before being made effective through affirmative action by the mortgagee [77] is insufficient to give him any claim to rents and profits collected by the receiver of a later mortgagee prior to that affirmative action.[78]

The effect upon the rights of a prior mortgagee of rents and profits clauses in a subsequent mortgage has been involved in some of the cases. Where the first mortgage contains no clause and the later one contains a pledge clause, the general rule that the prior one will prevail as to rents and profits from the time of intervention has been followed.[79]

The same has been true where there was an assignment of rents and profits in the later mortgage.[80] It would follow that if the prior mortgage contained a pledge of rents and profits the same result would be reached. Where both the earlier and the later mortgages contain clauses that are construed to be pledges only of the income, although the first mortgagee will be entitled to priority as to rents and profits from the time he effectively asserts his rights by having the receivership extended to him, a junior mortgagee who previously obtains a receiver is entitled to all rents collected up to the time of the first mortgagee's intervention.[81] In Iowa there were cases that in such a situation the mortgagee first getting a receiver appointed is entitled to all of the rents and profits up to the date of his foreclosure sale in priority to the earlier mortgagee even though the latter intervenes.[82] This rule put it in the power of the mortgagor, by contesting one suit and not the other, to prefer either mortgagee he desired.[83] The rule was changed by statute [84] in cases where both earlier and later mortgages contained rents and profits clauses to give priority as to

---

but permitted the mortgagor to collect them before default. The rents and profits were later pledged to a second mortgagee, who, on default by the mortgagor obtained a foreclosure receiver. In an action by the receiver to determine to whom rents collected should be paid, it was held that the first mortgagee had priority as to all rents after default on the first mortgage. However, if the prior assignee of rents and profits acquiesces for too long a time in the collection of rents and profits by the receiver of a later mortgagee he will be held to have lost his priority of right as to them. Berman v. 145 Belmont Ave. Corp., 1931, 109 N.J.Eq. 256, 156 A. 830, affirmed 112 N.J.Eq. 171, 163 A. 893.

77. See § 150, supra. Normally this action consists in asking for a receiver, or for the extension of an existing receivership.

78. Sullivan v. Rosson, supra note 75; N. Y. Life Ins. Co. v. Fulton, supra, n. 67; Abrahams v. Berkovitz, 1911, 146 App.Div. 563, 131 N.Y.S. 257; Prudential Ins. Co. v. Liberdar Holding Co., C.C.A. N.Y.1934, 74 F.2d 50, clause "assigning" rents and profits on default gave no rights against prior equity receiver for benefit of creditors as to rents collected by the receiver prior to the appointment of the mortgagee's receiver in foreclosure. That a "rents, issues, and profits" clause combined with a receivership clause gives to the mortgagee an inchoate lien valid in Kentucky against general creditors but not against subsequent assignees or specific liens, see Francis, Mortgages on After-Acquired Property in Kentucky, 1947, 35 Ky.L.J. 320, 327. See 1941, 50 Yale L.Jour. 1427, 1443; 1930, 30 Col. L.Rev. 488, 503; 1934, 43 Yale L.Jour. 107, 108.

79. Fidelity Mort. Co. v. Mahon, 1929, 31 Ohio App. 151, 166 N.E. 207. In McBride v. Comley, 1927, 204 Iowa 622, 215 N.W. 613, where both a prior and subsequent mortgagee applied for a receiver, the junior mortgagee was given the prior right to the rents and profits on the ground that it contained a receivership clause while the earlier one did not but based its right to a receiver solely on the ground

that the security was inadequate and the mortgagor was insolvent. The court's reasoning was that a receiver appointed on the latter grounds had no power to use the rents to pay the debt of the mortgagee. If the prior mortgagee had obtained a receiver on the ground of waste or impairment of the security, this would carry the right to have the rents applied to the debt, and the court intimates the prior mortgagee would then prevail over the later one with a clause in it calling for a receiver or pledging the rents.

80. Wiggins v. Freeman, 1916, 174 App.Div. 304, 160 N.Y.S. 448.

81. Sullivan v. Rosson, supra note 75.

82. Lynch v. Donahoe, 1927, 205 Iowa 537, 215 N.W. 736, commented on, rehearing denied 205 Iowa 537, 218 N.W. 144, 1927, 13 Iowa L.Rev. 356, 1928, 41 Harv.L.Rev. 539. The first mortgagee could protect himself by executing a chattel mortgage on the rents and profits and recording both real estate and chattel mortgages. Iowa Code, 1927, § 10032 (now I.C.A. § 556.21).

83. See Israels & Kramer, Income Clause in a Corporate Mortgage, 1930, 30 Col.L.Rev. 488, 503.

84. Iowa Laws, 1935, c. 181, § 1; I.C.A. § 654.13.

them according to the priority of the respective mortgages on the real estate, thus giving a senior mortgagee the rents and profits pledged to him even though the junior mortgagee first files his petition for foreclosure and appointment of a receiver.[85]

RIGHT TO RENTS AND PROFITS AFTER FORECLOSURE SALE

159A. The provision for statutory redemption in about half the states raises questions as to who is entitled to the rents and profits during the redemption period when, usually, the mortgagor is entitled to possession. Because the statutes on redemption differ in phraseology and a multitude of details only the law of one state, California, is looked at, and it but briefly.

On foreclosure sale title to the mortgaged property ordinarily vests in the purchaser. In about half the states statutes provide for redemption by specified persons from the purchaser or from one who has previously redeemed from him. The statutory periods for such redemption vary from six months to two years. Although it is usually immaterial whether the sale took place under a power of sale or in a judicial proceeding, in some states, e. g., California, the statutory redemption does not apply to sales under a power of sale. In most of the states having such redemption statutes the mortgagor is entitled to possession during the redemption period. There have arisen, therefore, questions as to who is entitled to the rents and profits during the redemption period. Although the general subject of statutory redemption is dealt with later, in Chapter 12, Subdivision B, infra, some consideration of the rents and profits problem seems appropriate at this point. However, the statutes on redemption have widely varying phrase-

ology and differ in a multitude of details. Hence only the law of one state, California, will be looked at, and it but briefly.[86]

California Law. It is clear that during the redemption period the mortgagor is entitled to possession. However, by West's Ann.Cal. Code Civ.Proc. § 707, the purchaser or redemptioner is entitled to the rents of the property, or the value of its use and occupation, from the tenant in possession [87] from the time such purchaser or redemptioner acquires his interest until he is in turn redeemed from. Three situations must be considered: (1) The mortgagor remains in possession personally; (2) The mortgagor may have leased the property after the mortgage and his lessee is in possession; (3) The mortgagor may have leased the property before the mortgage and his lessee is in possession.

Where the mortgagor remains in possession, it is settled that he is a "tenant in possession" within the meaning of the statute and is liable for use and occupation.[88]

In the third case, where a tenant of the mortgagor is in possession under a lease preceding the mortgage, "The interest which is mortgaged does not include the right to possession of the land for the term of the mortgage; it is rather the mortgagor's re-

---

85. See 1942, 27 Iowa L.Rev. 626, 634. An earlier case in Iowa, Oviatt v. Read, 1933, 215 Iowa 700, 246 N.W. 779 gave priority according to the date of execution of agreements for a mortgage of profits of land, the liens under the agreements actually attaching later at the same time when the crops came into existence.

86. For a discussion of the origin, nature and main features of statutory redemption from foreclosure sale generally see § 8, supra and §§ 307–310, infra; IV Am.L.Prop. §§ 16.8, 16.174–177. For a survey of the California law, see The Statutory Right of Redemption in California, 1964, 52 Cal.L.Rev. 846; Statutory Right of Redemption from Execution and Foreclosure Sales in California, 1957, 45 Cal.L.Rev. 19. On the narrow question of rents and profits during the statutory redemption period in California, see Smith, Security Interests in Crops, 1958, 10 Hastings L.J. 156, 164–169; The Statutory Right of Redemption in California, 1964, 52 Cal.L.Rev. 846, 865–869.

87. "The word *tenant* as used in section 707 is not used in the specific sense, as referring to the relation of landlord and tenant, but is employed in its generic sense, indicating one who holds possession of land by any kind of title." Bessinger v. Grotz, 1944, 66 Cal.App.2d 947, 949, 153 P.2d 369, 370.

88. Carpenter v. Hamilton, 1944, 24 Cal.2d 95, 147 P. 2d 563, 133 A.L.R. 733.

version and his right to the rents under the lease when they become due which are given as security. Hence, if the mortgage is foreclosed and the mortgaged interest is sold prior to the payment of the rent under such a lease, the *entire* rental payment belongs to the purchaser." [89]

In the second situation, where the mortgagor leased subsequent to the mortgage, the tenant does not become the tenant of the purchaser by virtue of the sale, but remains the tenant of the mortgagor-lessor.[90] Yet he is liable to the purchaser for rent. The right of the purchaser to rents being a statutory one, it is not subject to the normal rules denying apportionment of rent between successive owners of land. The purchaser is entitled to rents from the time he receives the sheriff's certificate until he receives the deed. Hence a rental payment not due until after the sale which covers a period including time both before and after the sale must be apportioned between the mortgagor-lessor and the purchaser at the sale.[91] So, too, a tenant of the mortgagor who has prepaid the rent for a period extending into the redemption period is nonetheless liable to the purchaser for the statutory rents.[92] However, where the tenant in possession had no actual or constructive notice of the sale and paid rents to the mortgagor-lessor after the sale he will be held harmless and the lessor alone would be liable for the rents received.[93] Thus prepayment by a tenant before sale, when there is no way of knowing that it will take place does not exonerate the tenant, but payment after the sale will exonerate, if there had been no notice.

The view that, although the purchaser is entitled to the rents, the tenant in possession is still the tenant of the mortgagor, has created problems. In First National Trust and Sav. Bank v. Staley,[94] the purchaser sought to enjoin the mortgagor from interfering with his collecting rents from tenants in the apartment building which he had purchased at foreclosure sale. The injunction was denied on the grounds that to do so would be the equivalent of appointing a receiver for collection of rents. This, under a prior decision could not be done.[95] In order to protect the tenant, who in the absence of interpleader is liable to two persons for the same rent, Section 564(4), West's Ann.Cal.Code Civ. Proc., was amended in 1941 to allow for the appointment of a receiver to collect the rents and to disburse them as directed by the court.

"While the availability of a receiver eased the situation where a lease is involved, the purchaser still cannot get a receiver to collect the profits, or to preserve the value of the use by the mortgagor. Although provision is made for the enjoining of waste, there may be use of the land by the person in possession not amounting to waste which nevertheless should be restrained, or at least made subject to a receiver in order to protect the interests of the purchaser. Courts should be allowed to exercise discretion in determining whether an injunction or a receiver is merited by the facts of the individual case. While the policy of allowing the mortgagor to retain and use the land should be preserved, such use should not be permitted to work to the detriment of the purchaser, who is entitled by law to the beneficial interest in the land from the time of his purchase." [96]

---

89. The Statutory Right of Redemption in California, 1964, 52 Cal.L.Rev. 846, 865, citing, cf. Fowler v. Lane Mortgage Co., 1922, 58 Cal.App. 66, 207 P. 919.

90. McClintock v. Powley, 1930, 210 Cal. 333, 291 P. 833.

91. Becker v. Munkelt, 1938, 27 Cal.App.2d 761, 81 P.2d 1041; Clarke v. Cobb, 1898, 121 Cal. 595, 54 P. 74.

92. Harris v. Foster, 1893, 97 Cal. 292, 32 P. 246; Webster v. Cook, 1869, 38 Cal. 423.

93. Title Ins. & Trust Co. v. Pfenninghausen, 1922, 57 Cal.App. 655, 207 P. 927.

94. 1933, 219 Cal. 225, 25 P.2d 982.

95. Boyd v. Benneyan, 1928, 204 Cal. 23, 266 P. 278.

96. 1964, The Statutory Right of Redemption in California, 1964, 52 Cal.L.Rev. 846, 867.

Further problems. Two problems remain and without square authority on them. The first is the exact nature of the liability of a tenant in possession (other than the mortgagor) claiming under a lease subject to the mortgage.[97]

The other problem concerns receivers appointed during the foreclosure action. The purchaser on foreclosure sale is held not to be entitled to a receiver to take rents and profits during the redemption period although he is entitled to them. There are recurring dicta that a mortgagee may obtain appointment of a receiver to take rents and profits during the redemption period to satisfy a deficiency judgment. Although usually the mortgagee is also the purchaser on a foreclosure sale he may be a third party. In such a case there would be a conflict between a mortgagee, claiming through a receiver in possession to apply rents and profits to his deficiency, and a purchaser claiming them in satisfaction of his statutory claim. It has been urged that the dicta suggesting that the mortgagee could obtain these rents and profits through a receiver to apply to a deficiency judgment are extremely dubious.[98]

F. MORTGAGEE IN POSSESSION

"MORTGAGEE-IN-POSSESSION" RULE

160. A mortgagee who lawfully acquires possession in his status as a mortgagee may stay in possession until redemption or foreclosure. Lien states generally accept the same doctrine although in them there is divergence as to what will constitute lawful possession making it operative.

The mortgagee may lawfully acquire possession while the mortgage is still subsisting. The courts have developed the doctrine that if he does his security interest as mortgagee in possession entitles him to hold the premises until either the mortgagor redeems or the property is foreclosed.[99]

As we have already seen,[1] in jurisdictions following the title theory of mortgages, the mortgagee, in the absence of an agreement or a statutory provision to the contrary, is entitled as a matter of right to possession before or after default.[2] In the "intermediate" jurisdictions the same is true after default.[3] In both types of states, when the mortgagee

---

97. See Smith, Security Interests in Crops, 1958, 10 Hastings L.J. 156, 167.

98. See Smith, op. cit. supra note 97, 167–169.

99. While this general statement is true, he may be ousted for gross mismanagement, by the extinction of the mortgage through tender, merger, or sale of the property by the mortgagee to a purchaser without notice, or by the assertion of a prior mortgage interest. For cases, see 1935, 35 Col.L.Rev. 1248, 1253 notes 31, 33, 34.

The doctrine that a mortgagee in possession cannot be dispossessed by the mortgagor without payment of the mortgage debt applies although an action on the debt or the right to foreclose the mortgage is barred by the statute of limitations. Jasper State Bank v. Braswell, 1938, 130 Tex. 549, 111 S.W.2d 1079, 115 A.L.R. 329; Spect v. Spect, 1891, 88 Cal. 437, 26 P. 203, 13 L.R.A. 137, 22 Am.St.Rep. 314; Bulson v. Moffatt, 1916, 173 Cal. 685, 161 P. 259, noted in 5 Cal.L.Rev. 258; Kelso v. Norton, 1902, 65 Kan. 778, 70 P. 896, 93 Am.St.Rep. 308. Knight v. Hilton, 1954, 224 S.C. 452, 79 S.E.2d 871, noted by 1954, Karesh, Survey of South Carolina Law: Security Transactions, 7 S.C.L.Q. 171. See Burns v. Hiatt, 1906, 149 Cal. 617, 87 P. 196, 117 Am.St.Rep. 157. Nor does a hostile reentry on the land by the mortgagor divest the rights of the mortgagee as mortgagee in possession. Finley v. Erickson, 1913, 122 Minn. 235, 142 N.W. 198; Cory v. Santa Ynez Land, etc. Co., 1907, 151 Cal. 778, 91 P. 647. On the ability of a mortgagee in possession to acquire title by adverse possession, see 1922, 6 Minn.L.Rev. 510, and Cory v. Santa Ynez Land Co., supra.

Knight v. Hilton, supra. That a mortgagor out of possession does not have an absolute right to exercise his equity of redemption, and the court of equity must consider such defenses as laches, estoppel, fraud and lack of equity, see 1959, Harbel Oil Co. v. Superior Court of Maricopa Co., 86 Ariz. 303, 345 P.2d 427.

One who enters property as a "statutory" tenant under the Rent Restrictions Act in England has been held not to be a mortgagee in possession by acquisition of the mortgage if he continues to pay rent. Silsby v. Holliman [1955] 2 All E.R. 373.

1. See § 125, supra.

2. Cook v. Curtis, 1925, 125 Me. 114, 131 A. 204; Weathersbee v. Goodwin, 1918, 175 N.C. 234, 95 S.E. 491; Brown v. Loeb, 1912, 177 Ala. 106, 58 So. 330.

3. Wilson v. Reed, 1917, 270 Mo. 400, 193 S.W. 819; Wells v. Kemme, 1916, 145 Ga. 17, 88 S.E. 562; Cohn v. Plass, 1915, 85 N.J.Eq. 153, 95 A. 1011.

exercises his right to enter, his possession is clearly lawful within the scope of the doctrine and he becomes a mortgagee in possession.

In lien states the mortgagor has the right to possession of the mortgaged premises both before and after default until foreclosure and the expiration of the period of redemption from foreclosure.[4] Consequently, on first impression, it would seem that the doctrine of mortgagee in possession would have no place in them. Nevertheless, it has generally been accepted although there is a divergence of view especially as to what will constitute lawful possession making the doctrine operative. One group of states, of which New York [5] is the most important, could reconcile it with the lien concept only upon the basis of consent, express or implied in fact, on the part of the mortgagor that the mortgagee be in possession of the mortgaged premises. As one of the leading cases expressed it, "it would seem to follow that when the legislature deprived the mortgagee of the only legal method by which he could get possession of the mortgaged premises without the mortgagor's consent, prior to foreclosure, there was no way left by which the mortgagee could acquire such possession except by the mortgagor's consent." [6] Further, the consent in New York must be to an entry by the mortgagee "under or by virtue of the mortgage," or, at least, "for purposes, or under circumstances not inconsistent with their relative legal rights under the mortgage." [7] Thus when the mortgagee gets possession in a capacity other than that of mortgagee, e. g., as a tenant of the mortgagor, he cannot, during, or after the expiration of his term as lessee, assert a right of possession as mortgagee, without the express or implied consent of the mortgagor.[8] So, too, if he enters as the agent of the mortgagor, he will not be a mortgagee in possession, only an agent with the liabilities of that relation.[9] And, of course, if he acquired possession as the result of a void foreclosure sale he would not be permitted to hold it.[10] However, even though the mortgagee entered wrongfully,

---

4.   See § 127, supra.

5.   For a discussion of the development of the problem of lawful possession after default by a mortgagee in New York, where the doctrine originated, see note, 1908, 8 Col.L.Rev. 486. See also E.N.D., The Mortgagee in Possession in New York and in Michigan, 1916, 15 Mich.L.Rev. 58; note, 1928, 7 Tex.L. Rev. 170 (discussing Majors v. Strickland, Tex.Civ. App.1928, 6 S.W.2d 133, in which a grantee under a deed absolute intended as a mortgage, put into possession by the grantor-mortgagor, was held entitled to hold onto possession until his debt was fully discharged); note, 1898, 46 Cent.L.J. 407; note, 1922, 22 Col.L.Rev. 451, 454.

6.   Barson v. Mulligan, 1908, 191 N.Y. 306, 315, 84 N. E. 75, 78, 16 L.R.A.,N.S., 151. McClory v. Ricks, 1902, 11 N.Dak. 38, 88 N.W. 1042, accord: 1908, 8 Col.L.Rev. 486; note by E.N.D., 1916, 15 Mich.L. Rev. 58. A few lien jurisdictions, it is true, invalidate executory agreements for the mortgagee to take possession. See Geraldson, Clauses Increasing the Possessory Rights of Mortgagees, 1935, 10 Wis.

L.Rev. 492; Tiffany, Real Prop., 3d ed., § 1416. This result, however, can be regarded as "an extension of the familiar view early developed in equity that the mortgagor shall not be permitted to bargain away his right to redemption as a part of his mortgage contract," Rundle, Work of the Wisconsin Supreme Court—Mortgages, 1933. 9 Wis. 33, 40, and thus distinguished from cases holding that a later actual entry with consent is valid. See Chapter 4, subdivisions D, E. Even if this distinction is not accepted, these decisions are out of harmony with other cases involving the same point, see § 119, supra, and, of course, opposed to the commonly accepted doctrine of mortgagee in possession not only in those jurisdictions which limit it to entry with the mortgagor's consent, see Walsh, Morts., § 18 n. 16, but even more strikingly, those that recognize it where there is no consent.

7.   Barson v. Mulligan, supra note 6, at 322, 84 N.E. at 81. See 1882, 26 Albany L.Jour. 526; 1883, 27 Albany L.Jour. 6.

8.   Barson v. Mulligan, supra n. 6; Robinson v. Smith, 1939, Tex.Com.App., 128 S.W.2d 27, discussed, 1939, 24 Minn.L.Rev. 434; Russell v. Ely, 1862, 67 U.S. (2 Black.) 575, 17 L.Ed. 258, a mortgagee who obtains possession from the tenant of the mortgagor after his lease had expired is not lawfully in possession. See 1908, 8 Col.L.Rev. 486.

9.   Realty Inv. & Sec. Corp. v. H. L. Rust Co., 1939, 71 App.D.C. 213, 109 F.2d 456; Ireland v. U. S., etc. Co., 1902, 72 App.Div. 95, 76 N.Y.S. 177, affirmed 1903, 175 N.Y. 491, 67 N.E. 1083; Whitley v. Barnett, 1911, 151 Iowa 487, 131 N.W. 704.

10.   Herrmann v. Cabinet Land Co., 1916, 217 N.Y. 526, 112 N.E. 476; Howell v. Leavitt, 1884, 95 N.Y. 617, can rest upon the ground of entry by force. See 1908, 8 Col.L.Rev. 486, 487.

the mortgagor can waive the wrong. He can sue for redemption and account by the mortgagee as mortgagee in possession; the mortgagee is in no position to claim otherwise.[11]

Another line of reasoning has sometimes been advanced. It has been asserted that "the possession of the land is a special security for the debt, distinct and separate from the mortgage, which has been conferred by an act of the debtor, and the right to retain the same is independent of and distinct from any right springing from the mortgage."[12]

Possession is not an incident of the mortgage in a lien jurisdiction and "the *fact* of possession is entirely distinct from the *contract* of hypothecation.[13] When, therefore, * * * the debtor gives to his creditor the possession of the mortgaged premises, he thereby, in addition to the mortgage which he has executed, also pledges the land to him as security for the debt, and confers on him such rights as are incident to a pledge."[14] The conception of a pledge of the land itself goes back to Glanville so there is historical warrant for its use.[15] Further, in certain problems it provides a useful technical explanation for the result which is, or should be, reached.[16]

However, there are some objections to such an analysis. It would limit the doctrine to consensual transactions between the mortgagor and mortgagee. Logically, also, it would dispense with the necessity of the existence at any time of a mortgage; and, in place of the requirement that the mortgagee should be in possession as mortgagee, demand that he be in possession as pledgee. This last test, however, is never suggested. This may be because there is no difference between the two But if this is so it minimizes the utility of the distinction drawn.

The doctrine of mortgagee in possession in lien jurisdictions is not confined, however, to cases where the mortgagee entered with the consent of the mortgagor.[17] In some states a peaceable entry, in good faith, and under color of right, e. g., under a void foreclosure sale, is sufficient to make the possession lawful without any consent whatsoever by the mortgagor.[18] And in others it is enough that the entry was peaceable.[19] But in all such

11. Reich v. Cockran, 1915, 213 N.Y. 416, 107 N.E. 1029, remittitur amended 214 N.Y. 629, 108 N.E. 1106.

12. The quotation is from Spect v. Spect, citation in note 14 infra.

13. The court uses the term "hypothecation" in the Roman Law and modern Civil Law sense of a security interest in property which gives no possessory rights to it, i. e., the equivalent of the lien theory.

The quotation is from Spect v. Spect, citation in note 14, infra.

14. Spect v. Spect, 1891, 88 Cal. 437, 441, 26 P. 203, 13 L.R.A. 137, 22 Am.St.Rep. 314. See Kortright v. Cady, 1860, 21 N.Y. 343, 78 Am.Dec. 145; Brinkman v. Jones, 1878, 44 Wis. 498, 512.

15. See Chapter 1, subdivision A. But cf. Tiffany, Real Prop., 3d ed., § 1415, criticizing this view on the ground that a pledge of land, separate from any estate or tenancy in it, is unknown although he cites, in a footnote, Hazeltine, Gage of Land in Medieval England, 1903, 17 Harv.L.Rev. 549, 1904, 18 id. 36.

16. E. g., in jurisdictions where the mortgage itself is extinguished by the running of the statute of limitations, e. g., West's Ann.Cal.Civ.Code, § 2911, to segregate the possession from the mortgage gives an easier explanation of why the mortgagee can still hold onto possession. So, too, when courts are influenced by legalistic reasoning in regard to title, as in the question whether a mortgagee is liable on or can take advantage of covenants running with the land, or whether the mortgagor has an interest subject to legal execution under a judgment against him by the mortgagee, such a different conceptual basis for the doctrine can be helpful.

17. See 1928, 7 Tex.L.Rev. 170; 1939, 18 N.Car.L. Rev. 61.

18. Jasper State Bank v. Braswell, 1938, 130 Tex. 549, 111 S.W.2d 1079, 115 A.L.R. 329; Raggio v. Palmtag, 1909, 155 Cal. 797, 103 P. 312; Cameron v. Ah Quong, 1917, 175 Cal. 377, 165 P. 961; Pettit v. Louis, 1911, 88 Neb. 496, 129 N.W. 1005, 34 L.R.A., N.S., 356; Caro v. Wollenberg, 1913, 68 Or. 420, 136 P. 866. In such states, a mortgagee who entered into possession under an agreement with his mortgagor that he should do so as additional security would be given, a fortiori, the status of a mortgagee in possession. Spect v. Spect, 1891, 88 Cal. 437, 26 P. 203, 13 L.R.A. 137, 22 Am.St.Rep. 314.

19. Stouffer v. Harlan, 1903, 68 Kan. 135, 74 P. 610, 64 L.R.A. 320, 104 Am.St.Rep. 396 same case, 1911,

states, in order for the occupation of the premises to entitle him to the status of mortgagee in possession, he must assert his claim to have and to hold them under and by virtue of his lien, i. e., *qua* mortgagee.[20] If he enters as the result of a defective foreclosure sale, the most usual case, this satisfies the requirement.[21] But suppose that, although a mortgagee at the time, he enters peaceably in a capacity other than mortgagee and later claims to hold possession as mortgagee. Or, that he takes possession peaceably under an invalid claim derived from a third party and later, while in possession he thus acquires a subsisting mortgage and then claims as mortgagee in possession. It has been suggested that possession so acquired might be regarded as having been obtained by fraud and thus as illegal as though obtained by force.[22] However, the mortgagee's claim probably will be sustained.[23] Whether or not it should be ought to depend on whether the case falls within the reason of the rule in preventing useless litigation.[24]

JUSTIFICATION FOR RULE IN LIEN STATES

161. In lien states that accept a non-consensual basis for the doctrine, the rule probably originated as an anachronistic survival of the title theory. The justification for its continuance lies in the mortgagee's strong interest in possession after default, and to avoid multiplicity of actions.

Where the mortgagee in possession is there with the consent of the mortgagor the doctrine of according him rights as such is not inconsistent with lien theory.[25] When, however, consent by the mortgagor to the mortgagee's entry is dispensed with as a nec-

---

84 Kan. 307, 114 P. 385; Burns v. Hiatt, 1906, 149 Cal. 617, 87 P. 196, 117 Am.St.Rep. 157; West v. Middlesex Banking Co., 1914, 33 S.D. 465, 146 N.W. 598; Pierce v. Grimley, 1889, 77 Mich. 273, 43 N.W. 932 (power of sale illegally exercised); Jaggar v. Plunkett, 1910, 81 Kan. 565, 106 P. 280, 25 L.R.A., N.S., 935. But see State ex rel. Montgomery v. Superior Court, 1899, 21 Wash. 564, 58 P. 1065; Herrmann v. Cabinet Land Co., 1916, 217 N.Y. 526, 112 N.E. 476 (mortgagor not served with process in foreclosure action).

20. Daniel v. Coker, 1881, 70 Ala. 260; Anglo-Calif. Bank v. Field, 1908, 154 Cal. 513, 98 P. 267, in possession under deed of redemption right of mortgagor; Armistead v. Bishop, 1913, 110 Ark. 172, 161 S.W. 182, in possession as tenant; Compton v. Jesup, 1895, 68 F. 263, 15 C.C.A. 397. A mortgagee who, without the consent of the mortgagor, acquires possession after the mortgage lien has become extinguished cannot assert the rights of a mortgagee in possession. Faxon v. All Persons, 1913, 166 Cal. 707, 137 P. 919. See Tiffany, Real Prop., 3d ed., § 1419; Pomeroy, Eq.Juris., 5th ed., § 1215.

21. See supra note 18. Even though the purchaser under a defective foreclosure sale taking possession under such sale is not the mortgagee himself, he succeeds to the rights of the mortgagee although the sale under foreclosure is void, and he is treated, therefore, as a mortgagee in possession. Bryan v. Brasius, 1892, 3 Ariz. 433, 31 P. 519, affirmed 162 U.S. 415, 16 S.Ct. 803, 40 L.Ed. 1022; Kaylor v. Kelsey, 1912, 91 Neb. 404, 136 N.W. 54, 40 L.R.A.,N. S., 839. See note, 1912, 40 L.R.A.,N.S., 839.

22. See E.N.D., 1916, 15 Mich.L.Rev. 58, 60. See also 1939, 24 Minn.L.Rev. 434, 436; Jaggar v. Plunkett, 1910, 81 Kan. 565, 568, 106 P. 280, 281, 25 L.R.A.,N.

S., 935, "Good faith * * * [requires] a surrender of the possession acquired under the lease before asserting a hostile and inconsistent right."; Robinson v. Smith, 1939, Tex.Com.App., 128 S.W.2d 27, 32.

23. A purchased mortgaged premises under a void tax sale and went into possession. Later A acquired by assignment the mortgage and the debt secured, continuing in possession with no further consent from the mortgagor. Held, A was entitled to the rights of a mortgagee in possession. Jaggar v. Plunkett, 1910, 81 Kan. 565, 106 P. 280, 25 L.R.A., N.S., 935.

A mortgagor sought to evict his tenant. Held, tenant, having acquired, by assignment, the mortgage and debt secured, could not be ousted. Niles v. Ransford, 1849, 1 Mich. 338, 51 Am.Dec. 95. Accord: Pearce v. Dunn, 1923, 122 S.C. 441, 115 S.E. 621, discussed in note, 1923, 32 Yale L.J. 739. Cf. Barson v. Mulligan, 1910, 198 N.Y. 23, 90 N.E. 1127. See 1908, 16 L.R.A.,N.S., 151. Robinson v. Smith, Tex.Com.App.1939, 128 S.W.2d 27, commented on in, 1940, 24 Minn.L.Rev. 434, held that a mortgagee who had possession as a tenant of the mortgagor could not change his relation to that of a mortgagee in possession without first obtaining the consent of his mortgagor-landlord.

24. See next section. Pearce v. Dunn, 1922, 122 S.C. 441, 115 S.E. 621, noted, 1923, 32 Yale L.Jour. 759. A foreclosure action had been brought by the mortgagee and the court indicated that its decision was on the ground of avoidance of useless litigation; and delay; Plunkett v. Jaggar, 1910, 81 Kan. 565, 106 P. 280, 25 L.R.A.,N.S., 935. See 1939, 24 Minn. L.Rev. 434, 436.

25. See Glenn, Mortgages, § 31.1, p. 203.

essary ingredient in the doctrine of mortgagee in possession, it becomes more difficult to reconcile it with lien dogma.[26] One explanation of the extension is that "the old rule, existing when a mortgage actually passed the title to the property, kept its hold upon the later opinions when the reason which led to it was gone." [27] In other words, it is just an anachronistic survival of the title view of mortgages. While this may have been, and probably was, the origin of the rule,[28] its vitality and wide acceptance demands a better rationalization. The one most commonly accepted is that the mortgagee's "right to retain possession does not depend upon an estate held by him. His possession is protected by his lien. It is certainly more simple and just that the mortgagee should be left in possession, and the mortgagor forced to redeem, than that the mortgagor should be permitted to recover the possession by an action at law, and be immediately liable to the consequences of a foreclosure suit in equity brought by the mortgagee." [29]

Both the doctrine itself and this last justification of it have been criticized on the ground that, under the lien theory, the right

to possession before foreclosure "admittedly belongs to the mortgagor and his suit in ejectment by which he enforces it can hardly be called useless or unnecessary," and that the doctrine gives "the mortgagee a right to possession in fact though acquired without right, and forces the mortgagor to redeem long before he is required to do so under the general principles of equity applying to the action to redeem." The cases following it are called "anomalous, without explanation other than an undefined equity or feeling of abstract justice is the basis of it." [30]

Several answers may be made. One is that, in the face of this strong judicial authority recognizing the right of the mortgagee to hold onto possession, it is difficult to say that "admittedly" possession belongs to the mortgagor under all circumstances before foreclosure is complete.[31] These decisions are square holdings to the contrary, creating an exception to the general rule, and the only question ought to be whether the result is a good one, taking into account not only a mechanical concept of the lien theory, but the practical situation involved in the particular problem. The interest of the mortgagor in having possession after default must be balanced against the mortgagee's interest in continuing in possession of the property he took as security. Before default, it is generally agreed that the mortgagor's interest outweighs any claim the mortgagee may assert. But when the mortgagee has acquired the right, through the default of the mortgagor, to realize on his security, his interest in having possession of the property and getting its proceeds to apply on the debt become very strong. As we have seen, he can take possession away from the mortgagor by getting a receiver appoint-

26. The extension of the doctrine beyond cases of consent by the mortgagor has been vigorously criticized. See Walsh, Mortgages, § 19, which in turn is criticized by McDougal, 1935, 44 Yale L.Jour. 1278, 1281; E.N.D., 1916, 15 Mich.L.Rev. 58; Tiffany, Real Prop., 3d ed., § 1415.

27. Stouffer v. Harlan, 1903, 68 Kan. 135, 74 P. 610, 64 L.R.A. 320, 104 Am.St.Rep. 396, attributing it to Howell v. Leavitt, 1884, 95 N.Y. 617. This basis is, however, older and was expressed in Phyfe v. Riley, 1836, 15 Wend. 248. See E.N.D., 1916, 15 Mich.L. Rev. 58.

28. Pomeroy accepts this view as to the origin of the doctrine in lien jurisdictions, Pomeroy, Eq.Juris., 5th Ed., § 1189.

29. Pomeroy, Eq.Juris., 5th ed., § 1189, quoted and adopted by the court in Stouffer v. Harlan, supra note 8, as its *ratio decidendi*. This reasoning also is to be found in Phyfe v. Riley, 1836, 15 Wend. 248. See E.N.D., 1916, 15 Mich.L.Rev. 58. See also 1922, 32 Yale L.Jour. 739; 1928, 7 Tex.L.Rev. 170; 1939, 24 Minn.L.Rev. 434; Brinkman v. Jones, 1878, 44 Wis. 498, 512; Glenn, Mortgages, § 33.1; Walsh, Mortgages, § 19.

30. Walsh, Mortgages, 100. See also ibid., 100 n. 24

31. See also McDougal, Rev. of Walsh, Mortgages, 1935, 44 Yale L.Jour. 1278, pointing out other lines of authority inconsistent with the thesis that possession by the mortgagor is a fundamental and inevitable feature of the lien theory. See § 125, supra.

ed and, although inadequacy of the security or waste are, in theory, essential requirements for this, in actual practice receivers are appointed pretty much as a matter of course.[32] The mortgagee in possession has advantages in keeping down costs and, under the lash of strict accountability, of producing better management than a receivership affords.[33] Further, when the mortgagor's action for possession can be immediately nullified by an action to foreclose by the mortgagee, it can properly be regarded as "useless or unnecessary" unless justified by substantial reasons.[34]

One of the chief arguments for allowing the mortgagor to have possession is that it is the source of his ability to get income with which to pay off the mortgage debt. However, the mortgagee in possession must account for all rents and profits, which will be applied to payment of the mortgage debt, thus accomplishing the same result and benefiting the mortgagor. There exists, of course, the possibility that the mortgagor could have made more out of the property had he been in possession, and thus, it should be assumed, have paid off more of the mortgage debt.[35] No doubt there is some substance to this, but it overlooks the reality that the benefit the mortgagor will receive by any increased earnings will not be by virtue of their reducing the amount of the mortgage debt but by the mortgagor having all of the income from the property to use for other purposes, leaving the debt unpaid except insofar as the sale on foreclosure of the property will do so. The reason for this is plain. The doctrine is seldom invoked except in cases where the

mortgagor is in at least a precarious,[36] if not hopeless, condition, for it is applicable in lien jurisdictions only after default, and, practically, occurs most frequently, when consent to entry is not obtained, after a defective foreclosure has taken place. The dangers to the mortgagee, under such conditions, that the mortgagor will resort to "milking" the property if he regains possession, or at least attempt to maintain it at a minimum expense with the result that the property would become run down, are great and the ability of the mortgagee to protect himself is unsatisfactory.[37] To allow the mortgagor to get back possession of the property under these circumstances would amount, in effect, to a judicial exemption founded upon mechanical application of the lien theory and tenderness to mortgagors at the expense of mortgagees. Such considerations amount to more than an "undefined equity [38] or feeling of abstract justice" and, it is suggested, serve both to explain and support the desirability of the strong current of decisions accepting the doctrine of mortgagee in possession even in cases where there is no consensual basis for it.

WHAT CONSTITUTES POSSESSION

162. To be a mortgagee-in-possession the mortgagee must exercise dominion and control over the property by virtue of his mortgage. Otherwise his conduct is tortious.

In any jurisdiction, in order for a mortgagee to become a mortgagee in possession

---

32. See Carey & Brabner-Smith, Studies in Realty Mortgage Foreclosures: Receiverships, 1933, 27 Ill. L.Rev. 717; §§ 147–149, supra.

33. See 1935, 35 Col.L.Rev. 1248, 1260.

34. American Trust Co. v. England, C.C.A.Cal.1936, 84 F.2d 352, where the mortgagee is in possession after a breach of the conditions in a mortgage, the mortgagor must show affirmatively that his possession is not lawful.

35. See 1928, 7 Tex.L.Rev. 170.

36. "The paucity of redemption cases points to the probability that possession is merely a prelude to foreclosure. In that event, continuation of possession in a mortgagee may be socially desirable, since it gives him control over his security without resort to receivership." 1935, 35 Col.L.Rev. 1247, 1254

37. See § 158, supra.

38. "Should not this 'undefined equity' be investigated? It might prove more compelling than the logic of the lien. Might not a simple and efficacious remedy for the mortgagee be of advantage to all parties? Why deprive the mortgagee of one remedy only to give him another more expensive to both him and the mortgagor?" McDougal, Rev. of Walsh, Mortgages, 1935, 44 Yale L.Jour. 1278, 1282.

he must have possession of the premises *qua* mortgagee.[39] What constitutes such occupation *qua* mortgagee varies with the nature and condition of the property.[40] Indeed both the words "possession" and "occupation" are somewhat misleading because a mortgagee can be a mortgagee in possession without actually occupying the premises.[41] Consequently "exercise of dominion and control" over the property as mortgagee is more descriptive.[42]

If a mortgagee, without the consent of the mortgagor, invades the mortgaged property except under and by virtue of his mortgage, even though in a jurisdiction where his mortgage gives him a right of entry, his action will be tortious. The mortgagor may maintain an action for damages against him,[43] and, if the acts are repeated or otherwise warrant the interference of equity to grant relief, they will be enjoined.[44]

LIABILITY OF MORTGAGEE IN POSSESSION TO THIRD PARTIES

163. The mortgagee in possession is liable to third parties if he fails to perform the legal duties of a landowner and for services furnished him during his occupancy. He is liable on covenants to pay rent, but, by the better view, not on other covenants running with the land.

When a mortgagee goes into possession questions as to his personal liability arising out of his relations with third persons arise. Since he is the person in possession of the premises he is personally liable in tort for injuries resulting either through his actionable fault in utilizing the property or by reason of his failure to perform duties imposed by law upon the owner of land.[45] Even more clearly he is liable for goods and services furnished to him during his occupancy.[46] His liability on covenants running with the land presents a more dubious case. Insofar as there are covenants running with the land restricting its use, a mortgagee taking possession should be bound by them. So, too, if

---

39. See § 160, supra.

40. See 1935, 35 Col.L.Rev. 1248, 1250; 1899, 106 L. Times 407.

41. E. g., urban property occupied by tenants and vacant rural land might not be occupied in fact by the mortgagee. The job of management and collection of rents in one case and paying taxes, securing tenants, making repairs in the other may constitute sufficient possession. See cases in 1935, 35 Col.L. Rev. 1248, 1250, notes, 14, 15, 16. Gandrud v. Hansen, 1941, 210 Minn. 125, 297 N.W. 730, discussed, 1942, 26 Minn.L.Rev. 880, 887 et seq. How far a mortgagee can get lawful possession by inducing the mortgagor's tenant in a lien jurisdiction to attorn to him is in some doubt. See 1908, 8 Col.L. Rev. 486.

42. Zisman v. City of Duquesne, 1941, 143 Pa.Sup. 263, 18 A.2d 95, noted, 1941, 7 Pitts.L.Rev. 345. Collection of rents is not a decisive criterion of possession. Bank of America Nat. Trust & Sav. Ass'n v. Bank of Amador Co., 1933, 135 Cal.App. 714, 28 P.2d 86; Stephens Invest. Co. v. Berry Schools, 1939, 188 Ga. 132, 3 S.E.2d 68; management and control are the important tests. Ireland v. United States Mortgage & Trust Co., 1902, 72 App.Div. 95, 76 N.Y.S. 177, affirmed 175 N.Y. 491, 67 N.E. 1083; cf. Whitley v. Barnett, 1911, 151 Iowa 487, 131 N. W. 704. See 1935, 35 Col.L.Rev. 1248, 1250; 1941, 50 Yale L.Jour. 1427, 1431 n. 42.

43. A mortgagee, not in possession of the mortgaged premises, although entitled thereto under the mortgage, caused sawdust to be deposited upon the land. Held, the mortgagor could recover damages for the injury thus caused in an action on the case. Morse, Adm'x v. Whitcher, 1888, 64 N.H. 591, 15 A. 207.

44. Morse v. Whitcher, 1888, 64 N.H. 590, 15 A. 217.

45. See Restatement, Second, Torts, § 329, comments a, c. Zisman v. City of Duquesne, 1941, 143 Pa.Sup. 263, 18 A.2d 95, noted, 1941, 7 Pitts.L.Rev. 345; Daniels v. Hart, 1875, 118 Mass. 543; Rogers v. Wheeler, 1870, 2 Lans. (N.Y.) 486, affirmed 43 N.Y. 598; Barter v. Wheeler, 1869, 49 N.H. 9, 6 Am.Rep. 434; Sprague v. Smith, 1857, 29 Vt. 421, 70 Am.Dec. 424. The liability is probably exclusive. See Sabiston's Adm'r v. Otis Elevator Co., 1933, 251 Ky. 222, 229, 64 S.W.2d 588, 591. Exceptions to this may be based upon an agency relationship between the mortgagor and the mortgagee in possession as to third persons, Grand Tower Mfg. & Transp. Co. v. Ullman, 1878, 89 Ill. 244, or in the case of a known dangerous condition existing at the time of transfer of possession to the mortgagee, at least if the transfer was consented to. Restatement, Second, Torts §§ 353, 354.

46. Baumgard v. Bowman, 1928, 31 Ohio App. 266, 167 N.E. 166; First National Bank v. Matlock, 1934, 99 Okl. 150, 226 P. 328, 36 A.L.R. 1088. He probably can avoid such liability, as can a foreclosure receiver, by express stipulation in the contract with the third person. Cf. Knickerbocker Ice Co. v. Benson, 1935, 155 Misc. 738, 741, 279 N.Y.S. 86.

an intent to assume them can be established, he should be liable upon them—and taking possession may be sufficient to justify an inference that such was the intent. Probably that would be the case where the mortgaged property was a leasehold and the issue was liability for rent. In England, in spite of Lord Mansfield's earlier opinion to the contrary,[47] a mortgagee was held to be bound by the covenant to pay rent in a mortgaged leasehold even without entry on the theory that he got the legal title to it and the covenant ran with the title.[48] The English rule was followed a few years later in New Hampshire, but probably it would find no favor in any other jurisdiction.[49] Where the mortgagee goes into possession in a title state, even Lord Mansfield[50] intimated that he would then be liable on covenants to pay rent, and this view has support in title jurisdictions in this country as well as in England.[51] In lien jurisdictions very clearly the mortgagee, before entry, would not be liable upon covenants running with the mortgaged property.[52] There are New York cases holding that he will be bound after entry, upon the theory that then the mortgagee acquired title, a proposition which had, as was noted, an important[53] influence in establishing the doctrine of mortgagee in possession in that state.[54] However, there are other, and preferable cases holding that the mortgagee never becomes liable even though he has taken possession. This result has been reached on the ground that the "mere act of the parties of going into possession, and consenting to or acquiescing in it can [not] have the effect to pass the mortgagor's estate to the mortgagee" and, therefore, just as he could not sue on a covenant running with the land "because he is not the owner of the land with which such covenants run" so he is not liable on them.[55] A preferable basis, and one that should apply in title states as well, would have been that, whether technically the mortgagee has legal title or lien, his interest is only for security purposes and liabilities that are founded upon full ownership should not attach to it. However, if they are rested upon the legalistic concept that liability *vel non* depends on the mortgagee in possession being regarded as having acquired the mortgagor's title, then it would follow that New York should no longer follow its earlier decisions. For in Trimm v. Marsh,[56]

---

47. Eaton v. Jaques, 1780, 2 Doug. 455.

48. Williams v. Bosanquet, 1819, 1 Brod. & Bing. 238. The effect of the rule could be avoided by a careful draftsman by making the mortgage of a leasehold consist of a portion of the term only, e. g., for one day less than the entire term. See Eaton v. Jaques, 1780, 2 Doug. 455, 459. This, however, would not give as complete security to the mortgagee. See Jones, Mortgages, 8th ed., § 990.

49. McMurphey v. Minot, 1827, 4 N.H. 251.

50. Eaton v. Jaques, 1780, 2 Doug. 455.

51. See 1914, 52 L.R.A.,N.S., 987. Cf. Olcese v. Val Blatz Brewing Co., 1908, 144 Ill.App. 597; Gibbs v. Didier, 1915, 125 Md. 486, 94 A. 100, Ann.Cas.1916E, 833; Purchase v. Lichfield Brew. Co. [1915] 1 K.B. 184.

52. Cargill v. Thompson, 1894, 57 Minn. 534, 59 N.W. 638.

53. Astor v. Hoyt, 1830, 5 Wend. (N.Y.) 603, 617, "When the mortgagee takes possession, he then has all the right, title and interest of the mortgagor";

Moffatt v. Smith, 1850, 4 N.Y. 126. Cockrell v. Houston Packing Co., 1912, 105 Tex. 283, 147 S.W. 1145, accord.

54. See § 162, supra.

55. Cargill v. Thompson, 1894, 57 Minn. 534, 543, 59 N.W. 638, 640; Johnson v. Sherman, 1860, 15 Cal. 287, 76 Am.Dec. 481. "We suspect the courts of New York would hesitate to hold that as soon as he gets possession he may sue upon or may release such covenants, which he certainly can do, if he has an estate that makes him the owner of the land." Cargill v. Thompson, supra note 33, at 544, 59 N.W. at 640. The mortgagee in possession under an arrangement with the mortgagor to manage the mortgaged leasehold was held not liable to the landlord on the ground that he was acting as agent of the mortgagor in holding possession. Cleveland v. Detroit Trust Co., 1933, 264 Mich. 253, 249 N.W. 842, commented on in 1934, 32 Mich.L.Rev. 864.

56. 1874, 54 N.Y. 599, 13 Am.Rep. 623. A mortgagee's interest in lands is not subject to seizure under execution or attachment. McLaughlin v. Shepherd, 1850, 32 Me. 143, 52 Am.Dec. 646; Columbia Bank v. Jacobs, 1862, 10 Mich. 349, 81 Am. Dec. 792. See also Eaton v. Whiting, 1826, 20 Mass. (3 Pick.) 484.

in determining whether, after a mortgagee in possession after default got a judgment against his mortgagor, an interest remained in the latter that could be seized and sold on execution, it was held that it did. The court said, "Before taking possession the mortgagee had a mere lien upon the real estate pledged for the security of his debt. After possession he has in his possession the property pledged as his security, the title remaining as it was before. The mortgagor's title is still a legal one, with all the incidents of a legal title subject to the pledge, and the mortgagee's interest is still a mere debt secured by the pledge. * * *

"The notion that a mortgagee's possession, whether before or after default, enlarges his estate, or in any respect changes the simple relation of debtor and creditor between him and his mortgagor, rests upon no foundation." [57]

G. ACCOUNTING

IN GENERAL

164. Stringent rules of accounting govern a mortgagee in possession. They are stringent in order to discourage exercise of the right to possession.

Once the character of mortgagee in possession is assumed a number of legal consequences follow.[58] The mortgagee becomes entitled to the income of the property on the one side and on the other he becomes subject to certain duties in respect to management of the property. Also he is permitted to do some things, for the cost of which he can get reimbursement, even though they are outside the scope of those activities he is bound to perform or be charged for failure to do so. Although these rights, duties, and privileges are non-consensual, law-created ones attending the status he occupies as mortgagee in possession, two things must be noted. One is that the court of equity, in supervising the mortgagee's account, may vary them in particular cases to avoid hardship.[59] The other, and more important, is that practically everyone of these legal incidents can be altered by agreement between the parties. Thus, although the severity of the rules governing the mortgagee's stewardship while in possession have justified, probably, the much quoted statement that "the situation of a mortgagee in possession is far from an eligible one" [60] and caused mortgagees to assume it only in extreme cases as a last resort.[61] All this can be ameliorated by provisions in the contract.

These matters apart, it should not be forgotten that the rules of accounting for a mortgagee in possession are harsh.[62] But there are reasons for this harshness. As was seen in examining the development of the lien theory and in other connections, there is a strong policy in favor of leaving the mortgagor in possession which is furthered by

---

57. Trimm v. Marsh, supra note 56, at 606. See Duval's Heirs v. P. & M. Bank, 1846, 10 Ala. 636; Harrison v. Roberts, 1856, 6 Fla. 711; Sturdevant v. Mather, 1866, 20 Wis. 576.

58. One of the legal consequences is that a mortgagee in possession has both a right and a duty to an account. Knight v. Hilton, 1954, 224 S.C. 452, 79 S.E.2d 871, noted by Karesh, Survey of South Carolina Law: Security Transactions, 1954, 7 S.C.L.Q. 171.
Once a mortgagee has acquired the status of mortgagee in possession, so far as his accounting is concerned, the same rules are applied indifferently whether the jurisdiction be title or lien. See 1939, 18 N.Car.L.Rev. 61; Walsh, Mortgages, § 20.

59. See 1935, 35 Col.L.Rev. 1248, 1251, citing as examples, Madison Ave. Baptist Church v. Baptist Church in Oliver St., 1878, 73 N.Y. 82; Walter v. Calhoun, 1913, 88 Kan. 801, 129 P. 1176.

60. Davidson's Precedents, 4th ed., 90, quoted in Maitland, Equity, 1936 ed., 187; Glenn, Morts., § 211.

61. See Maitland, Equity, 274.

62. American judges have not been as strict in the standards for accounting by a mortgagee in possession as the English chancellors. See Tefft, The Myth of Strict Foreclosure, 1937, 4 U.Ch.L.Rev. 575, 592. Nevertheless, a foremost scholar of mortgage law warned against the risks incident to taking possession as a mortgagee. "Upon the whole, the rules regarding the accounting of the mortgagee in possession are so severe that mortgagees who are well advised will seldom take possession." Durfee, Cas.Morts., 382.

stringent rules discouraging mortgagees from taking over even when they have the legal right to do so. Realization by sale of the capital asset is the essence of the mortgagee's right. To take possession from the mortgagor is justified by the danger of "milking" by a hard pressed mortgagor, and the idea that the mortgagee is entitled not only to the capital asset itself but all it yields in the form of income from the time his right to realize accrues and he starts to exercise it; the time lag between starting and final realization should not defeat his rights. But on both counts possession is purely in the mortgagee's interest and deprives the mortgagor of a source of income and sometimes the means by which he has the best chance of saving his property. Further, the mortgagee in possession holding the property as security has it in his power to prolong the period of his responsibility or to shorten it by foreclosure proceedings. And, since the income of the property must be applied to the payment of the mortgage debt, the mortgagee who takes control of the source of that income should answer pretty strictly for any conduct that prevents income arising.[63]

NATURE OF ACCOUNTING

165. An account is a determination on equitable principles of how much of the income received by a mortgagee in possession is to be applied to the debt. It can only be demanded in a foreclosure action or when the mortgagor seeks to pay the debt.

The mortgagee's possession, carrying with it the yield of the property, is for precisely the same purpose as his mortgage interest in the land itself, security for the payment of the mortgage debt. There is, however, a semi-fiduciary character to the relationship he thus assumes that finds expression in the cases in labeling him as having the *"quasi* character of trustee or bailiff"* [64] or of being a "trustee",[65] a "constructive trustee"[66] or a "pledgee in possession".[67] Actually the mortgagee in possession is not a trustee and he is not truly a fiduciary, and invoking these designations is chiefly by way of analogy and for the purpose of ascribing to him certain rights and duties. It would have been better to have recognized that his position was *sui generis* and then determined what legal incidents should attach to it. However the other method is an inveterate one in the legal profession, and so long as it is recognized, as it usually is, there is no harm in using inaccurate labels.[68] Whatever the tag, the mortgagee in possession has a duty of conduct in respect to the mortgaged property which is substantially that of a provident owner—"to manage the property in a reasonably prudent and careful manner so as to keep it in a good state of preservation and productivity" and to use the yield of the property for no other purpose than to credit it upon the mortgagee's claim by way of equitable set-off. However, the mortgagee in possession in the course of his management of the property, in addition to re-

bailiff of the mortgagor. * * * They are applied in equity as an equitable set-off to the amount due on the mortgage debt." Hubbell v. Moulson, 1873, 53 N.Y. 225, 228, 13 Am.Rep. 519.

65. "In courts of equity, the theory of a mortgage is, that until foreclosure it is a mere security for a debt, the mortgagor continuing the real owner of the fee. From this theory results the general principle, that a mortgagee in possession, before or after default in the payment of the mortgage debt, and before foreclosure, is a trustee of the rents and profits for the mortgagor, and bound to apply them in extinguishment of the mortgage debt." Toomer v. Randolph, 1877, 60 Ala. 356, 360; Anglo-Calif. Bank v. Field, 1908, 154 Cal. 513, 98 P. 267.

66. Real Estate-Land, Title & Trust Co. v. Homer Building & Loan Ass'n, 1940, 138 Pa.Super. 563, 10 A.2d 786; Travis v. Schonwald, 1939, Tex.Civ.App., 131 S.W.2d 827.

67. Spect v. Spect, 1891, 88 Cal. 437, 26 P. 203, 13 L.R.A. 137, 22 Am.St.Rep. 314.

68. See Cholmondeley v. Lord Clinton, 1820, 2 Jac. & Walk. 7, 183, "It is only in a secondary point of view and under certain circumstances, and for a particular purpose that the character of a trustee constructively belongs to a mortgagee."; Ten Eyck v. Craig, 1875, 62 N.Y. 406, 422.

63. See Glenn, Mortgages, § 211.

64. "The mortgagee in possession takes the rents and profits and the *quasi* character of trustee or

ceiving income, will have incurred various expenses for which he is entitled to be reimbursed, or by his affirmative conduct or neglect have subjected himself to charges other than income actually received which will be assessed against him. It is only the balance, after these charges and debits have been cast up and set off against each other, that goes in satisfaction of the debt. But in determining this balance "in many cases complicated equities must be determined and adjusted before it can be ascertained what part, if any, of the rents and profits received is to be applied upon the mortgage debt." [69] From the foregoing two things are apparent. One is that before it can be known how much of the income is to be applied to the mortgage debt there must be an accounting which can be made only in accordance with equitable theory and practice regardless of whether the jurisdiction is title or lien.[70] The other is that the application in the accounting of the balance when ascertained is in the nature of an equitable set-off when the debt is being paid. This being so,[71] it must be made

in a proceeding or transaction directly involving the satisfaction of the mortgage debt.[72] Consequently an account can be called for only when the mortgagee enforces his debt by foreclosure or when the mortgagor seeks to pay it, either by voluntary agreement with the mortgagee or else in an action in equity to redeem.[73] Therefore, questions as to the accountability of the mortgagee in possession cannot be raised in actions at law for possession by the mortgagor [74] or by action and garnishment by a junior encumbrancer or any similar action not putting the payment of the mortgage debt directly in issue.[75]

PERSONS ENTITLED TO ACCOUNTING

166. The mortgagor, junior mortgagees, and assignees of the redemption interest may have an accounting from the mortgagee in possession. A senior mortgagee may not have an accounting from a junior encumbrancer in possession or a transferee from the mortgagor.

It is elementary that the mortgagor is entitled to an accounting from any mortgagee in possession. So, too, may junior encumbrancers,[76] because they derive their interest

69. Hubbell v. Moulson, 1873, 53 N.Y. 225, 13 Am. Rep. 519. See Toomer v. Randolph, 1877, 60 Ala. 356, 360.

70. "It is easy to see that where the English doctrine prevails, the mortgage conveys a legal title to the mortgaged premises, the right of a mortgagor to an account of the rents and profits of the land received by the mortgagee is purely and exclusively of equitable cognizance. * * * But the necessity to resort to an accounting in equity, in order to have the rents and profits applied to the satisfaction of the mortgage is not obviated by the fact that here the mortgagor retains the legal title." Hubbell v. Moulson, 1873, 53 N.Y. 225, 13 Am.Rep. 519.

"All reasonable expenditures for taxes, necessary repairs, and other necessary expenses incurred on account of the estate, the mortgagee is allowed to retain from the rents and profits; and it is the balance only which may be applied in extinguishment of the mortgage debt. * * * An accounting is necessary to the ascertainment of the balance." Toomer v. Randolph, 1877, 60 Ala. 356, 360.

71. "The law does not apply the balance of the rents and profits to the mortgage debt; * * * It is in equity only the application is made, in the nature of an equitable set-off,". Toomer v. Randolph, 1877, 60 Ala. 356, 360.

See Hubbell v. Moulson, 1873, 53 N.Y. 225, 13 Am.Rep. 519, "It depends upon the result of an accounting

upon equitable principles whether any part of the rents and profits so received shall be so applied."

72. "In the absence of an agreement between the parties there is no legal satisfaction of the mortgage by the receipt of rents and profits by a mortgagee in possession to an amount sufficient to satisfy it, and his character as mortgagee in possession is not divested, until they are applied by a judgment of the court in satisfaction of the mortgage." Hubbell v. Moulson, 1873, 53 N.Y. 225, 13 Am.Rep. 519.

73. See 1910, 23 Harv.L.Rev. 301. As has been pointed out, although the procedure is somewhat different, due to local rules, in Pennsylvania and Massachusetts, even there the substance of the statement is true. Glenn, Mortgages, § 206.

74. Hubbell v. Moulson, 1873, 53 N.Y. 225, 13 Am. Rep. 519; Green v. Thornton, 1908, 8 Cal.App. 160, 96 P. 382.

75. Toomer v. Randolph, 1877, 60 Ala. 356. See note, 1909, 23 Harv.L.Rev. 301.

76. Gaskell v. Viquesney, 1890, 122 Ind. 244, 23 N.E. 791, 17 Am.St.Rep. 364; Hirsch v. Northwestern Mut. Life Ins. Co., 1941, 191 Ga. 524, 13 S.E.2d 165; Mallalieu v. Wickham, 1886, 42 N.J.Eq. 297, 10 A.

from and participate in the mortgagor's right to redeem. And the same is true of transferees of the mortgagor's redemption interest.[77] Similarly, an assignee of the mortgagee in possession will be bound to render an accounting.[78] On the other hand, a senior mortgagee has no right to an accounting from either a junior mortgagee in possession [79] or a transferee of the mortgagor. This follows from the fact that they stand in the same position as the mortgagor and the mortgagee has no right to compel an accounting from the mortgagor in possession.[80]

DUTY TO ACCOUNT FOR RENTS

167. If the mortgagee in possession rents the property he must account for rents actually received. If he does not use reasonable diligence he is liable for the fair rental value. If he keeps possession himself he is usually charged with the reasonable rental value. If he entered under an honestly mistaken belief that he was the owner he need only account for actual receipts.

When a mortgagee takes possession of the mortgaged property he may either rent it or occupy it himself. In either case he "assumes the duty of treating the property as a provident owner would treat it, and of using the same diligence to make it productive that a

provident owner would use." [81] Applied to the case where the property is rented the mortgagee must account for the rents and profits actually received.[82] This is the minimum, although, if the mortgagee has lived up to the standard of diligence and prudence demanded of him, it will be also the maximum.[83] Yet it must not be forgotten that he is a fiduciary to the extent that he is bound to observe a certain standard of conduct and if he falls below it he will be charged with what he might otherwise have realized out of the property, i. e., the reasonable rental value. The standard to which he was held by the older law was what he might have made but for his willful default or gross negligence,[84] and this phrasing is repeated by later authorities.[85] That is too strong and

81. Shaeffer v. Chambers, 1847, 6 N.J.Eq. 548, 47 Am.Dec. 211. See Gerrish v. Black, 1870, 104 Mass. 400.

82. Gerrish v. Black, 1870, 104 Mass. 400.

83. Denham v. Lack, 1940, 200 Ark. 455, 139 S.W.2d 243; Benham v. Rowe, 1852, 2 Cal. 387, 56 Am.Dec. 342, in the absence of negligence in leasing, the mortgagee is chargeable only with the actual rents received, not with what he might have received if he had leased differently; Williams Realty & Loan Co. v. Simmons, 1939, 188 Ga. 184, 3 S.E.2d 580; Gerrish v. Black, 1870, 104 Mass. 400; Pollard v. American Freehold Land Mortgage Co., 1903, 139 Ala. 183, 35 So. 767; White v. Atlas Lumber Co., 1896, 49 Neb. 82, 68 N.W. 359. Cf. Carroll v. Tomlinson, 1901, 192 Ill. 398, 61 N.E. 484, 85 Am.St.Rep. 344; Whitley v. Barnett, 1911, 151 Iowa, 487, 131 N.W. 704. See note, 1934, 32 Mich.L.Rev. 864.

84. Anon., 1682, 1 Vern. 45. This still seems to be the English rule. See Coote, Morts., 9th ed., 1927, 1223.

85. Moshier v. Norton, 1881, 100 Ill. 63.
"In the same paragraph in which Chancellor Kent defines the duty of a mortgagee in possession to be that of a provident owner, he also says he will be accountable for the actual receipts of the net rents and profits, and nothing more, unless they were reduced or lost by his wilful default or gross negligence. 4 Kent, Com., 6th Ed., 166. And it is said a mortgagee will not be obliged to account according to the value of the lands; he will not be bound by any proof that the land was worth so much, unless it can likewise be proved that he actually made that sum of it, or might have made it had he not been guilty of fraud or wilful deceit, as, if he turned out a sufficient tenant, &c.; for it is the laches of the mortgagor that he lets the land lapse

880, holder of judgment lien. Thus it has been held that a mortgagee in possession is under a duty to a junior encumbrancer to refrain from permitting the mortgagor to receive the rents. Gandrud v. Hansen, 1941, 210 Minn. 125, 297 N.W. 730, discussed at length in note, 1942, 26 Minn.L.Rev. 880.

77. Dicken v. Simpson, 1915, 117 Ark. 304, 174 S.W. 1154; Ruckman v. Astor, 1842, 9 Paige (N.Y.) 517; Elliott v. Brady, 1916, 172 N. Car. 828, 90 S.E. 951.

78. Strang v. Allen, 1867, 44 Ill. 428; Ackerman v. Lodi Branch R. Co., 1879, 31 N.J.Eq. 42.

79. Leeds v. Gifford, 1888, 41 N.J.Eq. 464, 5 A. 795, affirmed 45 N.J.Eq. 245, 19 A. 621.

80. A corollary of this is that if a mortgagee goes into possession under a title derived from the mortgagor in possession, he is then under no duty to account to a junior encumbrancer. See Williams v. Marmor, 1926, 321 Ill. 283, 287, 151 N.E. 880, 46 A. L.R. 132.

the modern view substitutes merely due care and reasonable diligence, putting the burden of establishing it upon the mortgagee.[86] Thus if he remits to a tenant part of the rent which he could have collected with reasonable diligence he will be charged for it.[87] Even under the older test of willful default or gross negligence he would be liable for the difference in rental he might have received if he had not put restrictions in the lease on the use of the property which were not only unnecessary but yielded a personal profit to the mortgagee.[88] However, the standard itself predicates a certain amount of flexibility in bargaining with tenants as to amount of rent, extension of time for payment and length of lease and other similar matters[89] and he will

not be liable if the standard of provident owner is adhered to.[90] Even occasional vacancies will not be charged to him if he has used reasonable diligence to obtain tenants.[91]

When a mortgagee occupies the premises himself instead of leasing them several questions arise. One is whether there is any duty upon him to work or operate it in case he has tried with due diligence to rent it and failed. The answer should be yes and there is authority so holding, at least in the case of a farm.[92] If the mortgagee retains possession when he finds that he cannot rent the property, he should have to work it or, if he does not, he should be held for the fair rental value. Business property would present a more difficult case and it would seem undesirable to force a mortgagee to start a new business on it[93] although there should be a duty to carry on an existing business.[94]

---

into the hands of the mortgagee by the nonpayment of the money. 3 Powell on Mortgages, 949." Gerrish v. Black, 1870, 104 Mass. 400, 405.

86. Shaeffer v. Chambers, 1847, 6 N.J.Eq. 548, 47 Am.Dec. 211.

"A mortgagee in possession is only bound to account for what he receives or might receive from the mortgaged premises by the use of fair, reasonable diligence and prudence, and if the premises are rented, and rents lost by the failure of a tenant, without fault of the mortgagee, he is not held liable to account." Sanders v. Wilson, 1861, 34 Vt. 318, 321.

Johns v. Moore, 1959, 168 Cal.App.2d 709, 336 P.2d 579.

87. Carroll v. Tomlinson, 1901, 192 Ill. 398, 61 N.E. 484, 85 Am.St.Rep. 344; Miller v. Lincoln, 1856, 72 Mass. (6 Gray) 556, allowing "notoriously insolvent" tenant to remain in possession eighteen months made mortgagee chargeable for the lost rent.

88. White v. City of London Brewery, 1889, 42 Ch. Div. 237. The mortgagee restricted his tenant on the mortgaged property to buying all beer sold in his tavern from the mortgagee. The mortgagee was held accountable for the amount of rent the premises would have brought without the restriction. The mortgagee was not liable, however, for the profit made out of the sale of the beer. He made this profit *qua* brewer, not *qua* mortgagee. Or at any rate, he should not be liable for both the difference in rental value and the profit from the beer sale. In Curtiss v. Sheldon, 1892, 91 Mich. 390, 51 N.W. 1057, the restriction in the lease prevented the operation of a bar on the premises, thus reducing the possible rent.

89. Chapman v. Cooney, 1904, 25 R.I. 657, 57 A. 928, 11% reduction to retain tenant who could not afford former rental; Wilmarth v. Johnson, 1905, 124 Wis. 320, 102 N.W. 562, rent remission to tenant

"probably insolvent" when "times were hard" and mortgagor had consented; Eldridge v. Hoefer, 1908, 52 Or. 241, 93 P. 246, modified 52 Or. 257, 94 P. 563, motion to recall mandate denied 52 Or. 241, 96 P. 1105, ten year lease; Hays v. Christensen, 1926, 114 Neb. 764, 209 N.W. 609, five year lease; Brown v. So. Boston Savings Bank, 1889, 148 Mass. 300, 19 N.E. 382, rent below value stated by expert testimony.

90. The mortgagee's conduct of his own affairs will influence the judgment as to whether the standard has been met. Cf. First Nat. Bk. v. Currie, 1924, 105 Okl. 175, 232 P. 94. "The reasonableness of the mortgagee's action must be tested in light of general economic conditions, the character of the premises, the likely duration of his possession, and the extent of the mortgagor's residual interest." 1941, 50 Yale L.Jour. 1424, 1432.

91. Whitley v. Barnett, 1911, 151 Iowa 487, 131 N.W. 704, recognizing that vacancies might occur despite "the very best management obtainable"; Chapman v. Cooney, 1904, 25 R.I. 657, 57 A. 928; cf. McDonald v. Lingle, 1930, 199 N.C. 219, 220, 153 S.E. 848. *Contra*: Humrich v. Dalzell, 1933, 113 N.J.Eq. 310, 166 A. 511.

92. "But at all events, if the farm and buildings are not rented he ought to cause the farm to be tilled, and that in a husbandlike manner." Shaeffer v. Chambers, 1847, 6 N.J.Eq. 548, 47 Am.Dec. 211.

93. Cf. Moore v. Cable, 1815, 1 Johns.Ch. 385, wild lands need not be converted into paying property when capital expenditure by the mortgagee would be necessary.

94. Baumgard v. Bowman, 1928, 31 Ohio App. 266, 167 N.E. 166, mortgagee in possession must operate

But when the mortgagee does operate it for how much should he be held accountable? The prevailing view is to charge him with the fair rental value no matter what he makes, letting him keep any excess and bear the loss if he makes less. In support of this it is argued that "The rule is founded in sound policy, for the reason that the particular items of expenditure, in labor or otherwise, as well as the profits received, are wholly within the knowledge of the mortgagee, and if he is not disposed to render a full and honest account, it would be impossible for the mortgagor to show them, or to establish errors in the mortgagee's account."[95] Another possibility is to allow the mortgagor to hold the mortgagee for the fair rental value as a minimum but, in the alternative, the actual net rents and profits.[96] This would be fair enough in case

it were established that the mortgagee had intentionally falsified his accounts. It seems unduly harsh upon the hard luck mortgagee to make him liable for all he makes when successful but to hold him for a fair rental even when unsuccessful. The only possible justification for it would be a very strong policy of discouragement to mortgagees taking possession.

Where the mortgagee has entered believing that he is owner and not mortgagee, although in fact the latter is his status, he will be charged only with the rents actually received. The reason is the obvious unfairness of holding a man to a standard of responsibility based upon a conscious occupation of the property of another when no knowledge of the situation on which the liability is founded exists.[97] On the other hand if possession is taken wrongfully and with knowledge of the wrongfulness the least the mortgagee will be charged with is the rental value.[98]

MAINTENANCE

168. The mortgagee in possession must make necessary repairs other than those due to ordinary wear and tear. He need not spend more than the rents and profits he receives. He is entitled to credit for maintenance expenditures. His privilege to make repairs is broader than his duty.

The duty of the mortgagee in possession to maintain the physical condition of the property reflects the fact that, however precarious his financial condition may be, the mortgagor is the beneficial owner of the premises and, as such, is entitled to protection against depletion of its value. Clearly any acts of destruction of the corpus of the property by the mortgagee will be waste for

oil wells. But see Engleman Transp. Co. v. Longwell, C.C.Mich.1880, 48 F. 129, "Mrs. Longwell, as mortgagee in possession of the undivided one-half of the mill property, would not be accountable for rent if she had been unable to lease the property * * *."

A mortgaged land to B. B was in constructive, but not actual, possession of the premises. Held, possession of the land in its then condition being valueless, B could not be charged therefor. Peugh v. Davis, 1885, 113 U.S. 542, 5 S.Ct. 622, 28 L.Ed. 1127. The problem of whether the mortgage would cover any business started on the premises by the mortgagee or, indeed, whether it covered a going enterprise already there would play a decisive role in excluding any duty on the mortgagee if the enterprise fell outside of his lien. If his lien did cover it, then what is said in the text would apply.

95. Sanders v. Wilson, 1861, 34 Vt. 318, 321; Barnett v. Nelson, 1880, 54 Iowa, 41, 6 N.W. 49, 37 Am.Rep. 183; Walter v. Calhoun, 1913, 88 Kan. 801, 129 P. 1176; Miller v. Peter, 1915, 184 Mich. 142, 150 N.W. 554; Liskey v. Snyder, 1909, 66 W.Va. 149, 66 S.E. 702—accord. See 1927, 46 A.L.R. 138, 153; 1887, 4 Am.St.Rep. 69. See also Shaeffer v. Chambers, 1847, 6 N.J.Eq. 548, 47 Am.Dec. 211, and Moshier v. Norton, 1881, 100 Ill. 63, 69, contra: "Here are the actual receipts, and what is the reason why the well-established rule of actual receipts should be discarded, and the complainant be charged the reasonable rental value of the lands, according to the conjectural estimate of various witnesses as to the probable rental value; their opinions differing in amount from $1 and less per acre to $5 per acre?"

96. This seems to be what was done in Engleman Transportation Co. v. Longwell, C.C.Mich.1880, 48 F. 129, for after an accounting for net rents and profits, of which there were none, the mortgagee was held for fair rental.

97. Parkinson v. Hanbury, 1867, L.R. 2 H.L. 1. Anglo-Cal. Bank v. Field, 1908, 154 Cal. 513, 98 P. 267; Morris v. Budlong, 1879, 78 N.Y. 543. The problem involved here is also considered in connection with allowances to the mortgagee for permanent improvements. Infra § 169.

98. Sedlak v. Duda, 1944, 144 Neb. 567, 13 N.W.2d 892, 154 A.L.R. 490.

which he will be accountable.[99] Mismanagement of the property is treated as akin to impairment of the property itself and the mortgagee will be charged with damage resulting from it.[1] But the mortgagee's duty goes beyond refraining from actively harming the property. He "is bound to use reasonable means to preserve the estate from loss and injury." [2] He must, therefore, conserve its value by making necessary repairs,[3] and this duty is recognized on the one hand by charging him for any loss that flows from his failure to act[4] and, on the other, by allowing him credit for expenditures in carrying it out.[5] There are, however, limitations on this. One is that he is not bound to dig into his own pocket and so need not expend more than the rents and profits he receives.[6] Another is that he does not have to make good or prevent the depreciation caused by ordinary wear and tear—"the silent effect of waste and decay from time." [7] Indeed, in casting

99. American Freehold Land Mortgage Co. v. Pollard, 1902, 132 Ala. 155, 32 So. 630, timber removed; Smith v. Stringer, 1934, 228 Ala. 630; 155 So. 85, grapevines destroyed; Whiting v. Adams, 1894, 66 Vt. 679, 30 A. 32, 25 L.R.A. 598, 44 Am.St.Rep. 875, timber removed; Sandon v. Hooper, 1843, 6 Beav. 246, cottages torn down; Hansom v. Derby, 1700, 2 Vern. 398, wainscoting destroyed; Brown v. Daniel, 1941, 219 N.C. 349, 13 S.E.2d 623, timber removed. The measure of damages will be the diminution in the value of the estate caused by the destruction, Smith v. Stringer, supra; or, in case there is a severance and sale, either the proceeds or market value of the severed portion, Brown v. Daniel, supra. In addition to the right to an accounting, the mortgagor may have an injunction against the commission of waste, Lord Hardwicke, in Farrant v. Lovel, 1750, 3 Atk. 723, or, in an aggravated case of wanton destruction, even the return of the property although he is a pauper, Hansom v. Derby, supra.

1. Baumgard v. Bowman, 1928, 31 Ohio App. 266, 167 N.E. 166. The mortgagee's irresponsibility or mismanagement may also be relieved against by the appointment of a receiver. Harding v. Garber, 1907, 20 Okl. 11, 93 P. 539; Brayton & Lawbaugh v. Monarch Lumber Co., 1917, 87 Or. 365, 169 P. 528, rehearing denied 87 Or. 365, 170 P. 717; Gibson v. Hamilton & Rourke Co., 1899, 21 Wash. 365, 58 P. 217.

2. Barnard v. Paterson, 1904, 137 Mich. 633, 634, 100 N.W. 893; McCarron v. Cassidy, 1856, 18 Ark. 34; Woodward v. Phillips, 1859, 80 Mass. (14 Gray) 132; Eggensperger v. Lanpher, 1904, 92 Minn. 503, 100 N.W. 372—accord. See Barthell v. Syverson, 1880, 54 Iowa 160, 6 N.W. 178; 1914, 49 L.R.A.,N.S., 122. Cf. Williams v. Rouse, 1899, 124 Ala. 160, 27 So. 16 (statute); Halbert v. Turner, 1908, 233 Ill. 531, 84 N.E. 704.

3. Shaeffer v. Chambers, 1847, 6 N.J.Eq. 548, 47 Am. Dec. 211, "a mortgagee in possession is not at liberty to permit the property to go to waste, but is bound to keep it in good ordinary repair; and if it be a farm he is bound to good ordinary husbandry." Scherer v. Bang, 1925, 97 N.J.Eq. 497, 500, 128 A. 258, 259, "such repair as is absolutely necessary for the protection of the estate"; Hirsh v. Arnold, 1925, 318 Ill. 28, 148 N.E. 882.

4. "The rule holds the mortgagee in possession should make necessary repairs and improvements to prevent the property from waste, and, if he neglects so to do, upon the redemption of the mortgage he may be charged with waste, and for the rents and profits that, with the exercise of reasonable care and attention, he would have received from the mortgaged premises." Miller v. Ward, 1913, 111 Me. 134, 138, 88 A. 400, 402, 49 L.R.A.,N.S., 122; see S.P. Wragge v. Denham, 1836, 2 Younge & C. 117, 121; Hughes v. Williams, 1806, 12 Ves. 493; Dexter v. Arnold, 1834, 7 Fed.Cas. 597, 604. As to the liability of a receiver of rents and profits for failure to make authorized repairs, see note, 1935, 4 Fordham L.Rev. 136.

5. Burns v. Williams, 1921, 147 Ark. 608, 228 S.W. 726; Hidden v. Jordan, 1865, 28 Cal. 301; Buettel v. Harmount, 1891, 46 Minn. 481, 49 N.W. 250; Mosier v. Norton, 1876, 83 Ill. 519; Miller v. Curry, 1889, 124 Ind. 48, 24 N.E. 219, rehearing denied 124 Ind. 48, 24 N.E. 374; Wise v. Layman, 1925, 197 Ind. 393, 150 N.E. 368; Gordon v. Krellman, 1924, 207 App. Div. 773, 202 N.Y.S. 682; Lynch v. Ryan, 1908, 137 Wis. 13, 118 N.W. 174, 129 Am.St.Rep. 1040. "He will not only be allowed for repairs, but he will be also allowed for doing that which is essential for the protection of the title of the mortgagor." Sandon v. Hooper, 1843, 6 Beav. 246, 248; Godfrey v. Watson, 1747, 3 Atk. 517. See Campbell, Cases on Mortgages, 2d ed., 338 n. 3, for a collection of cases. See also, Walsh & Simpson, Cas.Security Transactions, 148 Note (2).

6. Fidelity Trust Co. v. Saginaw Hotels Co., 1932, 259 Mich. 254, 242 N.W. 906; Carter v. McMillan, 1922, 68 Dom.L.R. 653. See Dexter v. Arnold, 1834, 7 Fed.Cas. 597, 604.

7. Dexter v. Arnold, 1834, 2 Sumn. 108, Fed.Cas.No. 3,858, Story, J.; Brown v. So. Boston Savings Bank, 1889, 148 Mass. 300, 19 N.E. 382. See also Russell v. Smithies, 1792, 1 Austr. 96; S. P. Wragge v. Denham, 1836, 2 Younge & C. 117, 121. It has been pointed out that the mortgagee's duty in this respect is different from that of a true trustee who may be bound to provide for such depreciation. In the mortgage situation, such long range impairment properly should be looked after by the owner, the mortgagor, not the mortgagee who is in only for a temporary purpose and one which is largely selfish but which must take into account and safeguard, up to a point, the interests of the debtor-owner. But that point does not go beyond ordinary maintenance. See Glenn, Mortgages, § 215.

upon him this duty of affirmative conduct the standard for its invocation is "willful default",[8] "gross negligence", or "recklessness and improvidence", a rather low standard of responsibility whose mildness is explained by the fact that the mortgagor, the owner, also should look after the upkeep of his own property. And, fairly enough, his liability is based upon the condition of the property as of the time he took over.[9]

When it is a question, not of duty to make repairs, but of privilege of doing so, there seems to be considerably more latitude in determining what will constitute necessary repairs than when it is a matter of duty to do so.[10]

8. "But where a mortgagee is guilty of wilful default or gross neglect as to repairs, he is properly responsible for the loss and damage occasioned thereby. * * * And there is the stronger reason for this doctrine because it is also the default of the mortgagor himself, if he does not take care to have suitable repairs made to preserve his own property." Dexter v. Norton, 1834, 7 Fed.Cas. 597, 604. Toole v. Weirick, 1909, 39 Mont. 359, 102 P. 590, 133 Am.St.Rep. 567, mortgagee accountable for depreciation resulting from "the reckless or improvident management of the property." See Parkinson v. Hanbury, L.R. 2 H.L. 1, 14.

Other cases laying down the test of "wilful default or gross negligence" include: Dozier v. Mitchell, 1880, 65 Ala. 511; Fidelity Trust Co. v. Saginaw Hotels Co., 1932, 259 Mich. 254, 242 N.W. 906; Mosier v. Norton, 1876, 83 Ill. 519. But in Burnett v. Nelson, 1880, 54 Iowa 41, 6 N.W. 49, 37 Am.Rep. 183, the court said the standard the mortgagee must use in keeping up the premises was ordinary care and he is not exonerated because not guilty of fraud or gross carelessness.

9. Barnard v. Paterson, 1904, 137 Mich. 633, 100 N. W. 893, the mortgagee must conserve the estate in as good condition as that in which he received it. See Glenn, Mortgages, § 214.1.

10. Gordon v. Krellman, 1924, 207 App.Div. 773, 202 N.Y.S. 682, in which new stoves and other items of a permanent nature put in to obtain tenants on advantageous terms was allowed as repairs. On the other hand, in Fletcher v. Bass River Sav. Bank, 1902, 182 Mass. 5, 64 N.E. 207, 94 Am.St.Rep. 632, repairs made for the purpose of enhancing the sale price but not necessary to preserve it from deterioration for the short period it would be occupied by the mortgagee, although of such a nature as ordinarily would be credited to a mortgagee in possession, were disallowed. Today in Massachusetts, by statute, the mortgagee will be permitted to make "reasonable repairs and improvements." Mass.Gen. LawsAnn. c. 244, § 20; McFarlane v. Thompson, 1922, 241 Mass. 486, 135 N.E. 869.

A mortgagee who obtains possession wrongfully is not entitled to an allowance for repairs.[11]

IMPROVEMENTS

169. In the absence of statute a mortgagee in possession gets no credit for improvements except:

(1) Those made with the express or implied consent of the mortgagor; or

(2) Those that are either reasonably undertaken for the maintenance or productivity of the property, or improvements made in the good faith belief that the mortgagee is the owner.

It is old and well settled mortgage doctrine that a mortgagee in possession shall not be allowed to make improvements on the property and to charge them on the mortgagor in his account, a rule which is in sharp contrast with that governing repairs.[12] The reason for it is simple and sound. It "is a rule to protect the interests of the mortgagor, and to prevent the mortgagee from rendering it more difficult for the mortgagor to redeem the premises".[13] The idea is trenchantly expressed by the statement that to permit it might enable the mortgagee "to improve the mortgagor out his estate." [14] But the line of

11. Malone v. Roy, 1895, 107 Cal. 518, 40 P. 1040. See Roberts v. Fleming, 1870, 53 Ill. 196.

12. Sandon v. Hooper, 1843, 6 Beav. 246; Schuetz v. Schuetz, 1941, 237 Wis. 1, 296 N.W. 70, discussed, 1941, 40 Mich.L.Rev. 133. See also authorities cited in following footnotes.

13. Miller v. Ward, 1913, 111 Me. 134, 138, 88 A. 400, 402, 49 L.R.A.,N.S., 122.

14. "He [mortgagee] has no right to lay out money in what he calls increasing the value of the property, which may be done in such a way as to make it utterly impossible for the mortgagor, with his means, ever to redeem: this is what has been termed improving a mortgagor out of his estate—an expression which has been used both in this argument and on former occasions." Sandon v. Hooper, 1843, 6 Beav. 246, 248; Burns v. Williams, 1921, 147 Ark. 608, 228 S.W. 726; Kinkead v. Peet, 1911, 153 Iowa 199, 132 N.W. 1095; Cook v. Ottawa University, 1875, 14 Kan. 548; Moore v. Cable, N.Y. 1815, 1 Johns.Ch. 385—accord.

See Bacon v. Bacon, 1639, Toth. 133, the mortgagee "may not bestow unnecessary costs upon the land of purposes to clog the land, to prevent the mortgagor's redemption."

demarcation between repairs and improvements is wavering and blurred if not, as has been suggested in criticism of the distinction, fictional.[15] Certain it is that the rule against improvements is not inflexible.[16]

Although it would be going too far, perhaps, to discard it altogether and substitute for it as a test "the reasonableness of the mortgagee's action in the light of economic conditions, the probable duration of his possession, and the nature of the property and the mortgagor's interest," there are exceptions to it, or at least cases to which it does not apply.[17] For one thing, if the improvements were made in pursuance of an agreement with the mortgagor or with his consent, either express or implied in fact, there can be no question but that the cost is an allowable item.[18] This will carry a long way but it is a mistake to try to make it an all-solving touchstone.[19] Credit will be given to a mortgagee who completes an unfinished building in order to make it tenantable, something most beneficial to the mortgagor and some-

thing he ought to want to have the mortgagee do.[20] However, the charge is justified, not on the ground of the mortgagor's acquiescence, but because the improvement was necessary to prevent deterioration on the one hand and to make it productive of income on the other, both essential to the protection of the interest of the mortgagor and for that reason chargeable to him as a matter of justice and equity.[21] Similarly, the mortgagee may make reasonable improvements which are fairly and competently undertaken for the maintenance or increased income yield of the property.[22] But the character of the property cannot be altered. It cannot be made into a new and different thing rather than a better and more productive version of the premises taken over. Still another group of cases in which the mortgagee is allowed credit for improvements is where he is in possession believing in good faith that he is the owner or at least free from the possibility of redemption by the mortgagor whereas in truth all he has is his security interest and therefore has, even though he does not know

---

15. See 1935, 35 Col.L.Rev. 1248, 1258.

16. "This rule [against improvements] is not inflexible, for the allowance may be regulated by the justice and equity arising out of the circumstances of each particular case." Wells v. Van Dyke, 1885, 109 Pa. 330, 42 L.I. 345, 16 W.N.C. 151.

17. 1935, 35 Col.L.Rev. 1248, 1259.
"The rule forbidding an allowance for permanent improvements is not an inflexible one, but is suspended in exceptional cases, if justice and the equity of the case require it. 4 Kent.Com. 167, and note." Morgan v. Walbridge, 1883, 56 Vt. 405, 409.

18. Shellnutt v. Shellnutt, 1939, 188 Ga. 306, 3 S.E.2d 900; Fort v. Colby, 1913, 165 Iowa 95, 144 N.W. 393; McGuire v. Halloran, 1917, 182 Iowa 209, 160 N.W. 363, rehearing denied 182 Iowa 209, 165 N.W. 405; Lynch v. Ryan, 1908, 137 Wis. 13, 118 N.W. 174, 129 Am.St.Rep. 1040. See 1913, 49 L.R.A.,N.S., 122, 128.

19. See Glenn, Mortgages, § 219, where implied consent of the mortgagor, based upon the condition of the premises, is pushed to the extreme of attributing consent to the mortgagor in all cases where the improvement is an "immediate necessity" and the result is beneficial, for if the latter is the case, the "mortgagor cannot complain." Both factors justify the result regardless of any finding of fact of consent as an inference from them and the courts approach the question from the point of view of fair result rather than the intent of the mortgagor.

20. Miller v. Ward, 1913, 111 Me. 134, 88 A. 400, 49 L.R.A.,N.S., 122; Gilpin v. Brooks, 1917, 226 Mass. 322, 115 N.E. 421.

21. "It was the duty of the defendant [mortgagee], having taken possession of the mortgaged property, with a house nearly finished but untenantable, and left in that condition by the mortgagor, to protect the interests of the mortgagor, and that the finishing of the house, * * * and thereby changing it from unproductive property to income-producing property, was proper management of the mortgaged premises, and that such repairs and improvements were beneficial to the estate." Miller v. Ward, supra note 1.

22. Hays v. Christiansen, 1921, 105 Neb. 586, 181 N.W. 379, new boiler; Gordon v. Krellman, 1924, 207 App.Div. 773, 202 N.Y.S. 682, new ranges and other items of permanent nature to keep tenants and attract new ones, the court classifying them as "repairs"; Wells v. Van Dyke, 1885, 109 Pa. 330, 42 L.I. 345, 16 W.N.C. 151, new improved machinery to enable mill to compete successfully with other mills; McFarlane v. Thompson, 1922, 241 Mass. 486, 135 N.E. 869, new cesspool, but statute covered case; Shepard v. Jones, 1882, 21 Ch.D. 469, deepening of well increase sale value although purchaser did not use water supply, mortgagee allowed for increased value.

it, only the rights of a mortgagee in possession.[23]

These cases, in addition to pointing to the good faith[24] by the mortgagee, the beneficial character of the improvements and their reasonableness, stress the fact that the mortgagor stood by in silence without asserting his rights while the improvements were being made. This makes the injustice of permit-

ting him to redeem without paying anything for the value added to his property so clear that the ordinary rule against allowances for improvements will not be followed.[25] This conduct by the mortgagor, it should be observed, is the foundation for imposing a non-consensual[26] obligation upon him to prevent

23. Such cases include those in which the mortgagee purchased at a defective foreclosure sale. McSorley v. Larissa, 1868, 100 Mass. 270; Hicklin v. Marco, C.C.Or.1891, 46 F. 424, affirmed 56 F. 549, 6 C.C.A. 10; Bradley v. Snyder, 1853, 14 Ill. 263, 58 Am.Dec. 564; Poole v. Johnson, 1883, 62 Iowa 611, 17 N.W. 900. See Martin v. Ratcliff, 1890, 101 Mo. 254, 13 S.W. 1051, 20 Am.St.Rep. 605 (defective exercise of power of sale); Freichnecht v. Meyer, 1885, 39 N.J. Eq. 551; Green v. Dixon, 1859, 9 Wis. 532 (statute). Cf. McCumber v. Gilman, 1854, 15 Ill. 381. Also those in which he was a grantee under a deed absolute given as security, so that by the form of the transaction he has reason to believe he is owner. Gillis v. Martin, 1833, 17 N.C. 470, 25 Am.Dec. 729; Harper's Appeal, 1870, 64 Pa. 315; Liskey v. Snyder, 1909, 66 W.Va. 149, 161, 66 S.E. 702, 708. Miller v. Curry, 1889, 124 Ind. 48, 24 N.E. 219, 374, contra, in spite of good faith by the mortgagee. Cf. Wilson v. Fisher, 1908, 148 N.C. 535, 541, 62 S.E. 622, 624–5, in which it was held that the appreciation was merely deductible from the charge for rents and profits.

The inchoate dowager of a mortgagor, who was omitted from the foreclosure proceedings and therefore was entitled to redeem from the purchaser on foreclosure sale, was given the right to elect between a release of her dower right from the lien of the mortgage under which the defendant, purchaser on foreclosure sale who had improved the property, took title, or the payment to her of the value thereof, with the right to full redemption if the defendant does neither. McKenna v. Fidelity Trust Co., 1906, 184 N.Y. 411, 77 N.E. 721, 3 L.R.A.,N.S., 1068, 112 Am.St.Rep. 620, 6 Ann.Cas. 471.

24. Where the mortgagee takes possession wrongfully, claiming to be owner although he knows of the mortgagor's claim, there is an absence of good faith and no allowance will be made. Mahoney v. Bostwick, 1892, 96 Cal. 53, 30 P. 1020, 31 Am.St.Rep. 175; Malone v. Roy, 1895, 107 Cal. 518, 40 P. 1040; Bradley v. Merrill, 1896, 88 Me. 319, 34 A. 160; Dougherty v. McColgan, Md., 1834, 6 Gill & J. 275; Sedlak v. Duda, 1944, 144 Neb. 567, 13 N.W.2d 892, 154 A.L.R. 490; Shelley v. Cody, 1907, 187 N.Y. 166, 79 N.E. 994; Cookes v. Culbertson, 1874, 9 Nev. 199; Witt v. Trustees of Grand Grove of United Ancient Order of Druids, 1884, 55 Wis. 376, 13 N.W. 261. By the weight of authority, constructive notice from a record of the existence of a paramount title or interest does not prevent an occupant from being an improver in good faith. See 1930, 68 A.L. R. 288.

25. Hadley v. Stewart, 1886, 65 Wis. 481, 27 N.W. 340; Morgan v. Walbridge, 1883, 56 Vt. 405; Mickles v. Dillaye, 1858, 17 N.Y. 80. Also, basing the allowance on the fact that the mortgagor had permitted a long period to elapse without asserting his rights, see Roberts v. Fleming, 1870, 53 Ill. 196; Montgomery v. Chadwick, 1858, 7 Iowa 114; Miner v. Beekman, 1872, 50 N.Y. 337. See also Morris v. Budlong, 1879, 78 N.Y. 543. There are, however, some cases that require only that the mortgagee believe that he is the owner and make beneficial improvements in good faith. Hicklin v. Marco, C.C. Or.1891, 46 F. 424, affirmed 56 F. 549, 6 C.C.A. 10; Ensign v. Batterson, 1896, 68 Conn. 298, 36 A. 51; Liskey v. Snyder, 1909, 66 W.Va. 149, 162, 66 S.E. 702, 708; Green v. Dixon, 1859, 9 Wis. 532.

26. The whole approach to the question, as revealed in the language of the courts, is one of doing equity and justice, not enforcing an implied in fact intention of the mortgagor. Thus in Morgan v. Walbridge, supra note 25, at 410, after stating that exceptions will be made to the rule forbidding allowance for permanent improvements "if justice and the equity of the case require it", decides that, "When the mortgagee has been lulled into the belief that the right of redemption has been barred or abandoned, and the mortgagor, knowing, or having reason to believe, that the mortgagee supposes that he is the absolute owner stands by and sees the mortgagee make lasting improvements upon the land, in kind and character, such as the land in its condition and wants clearly requires, and which are obviously sanctioned by the usages of good husbandry and faithful stewardship, then the right to redeem will be burdened with the expense of such improvements."

And in Mickles v. Dillaye, supra note 25, at 92, after stressing the fact that the mortgagor had acquiesced for a long time in the mortgagee's adverse possession, thus contributing to the mistake under which the mortgagee acted in making the improvements said, "Under such circumstances, he should not be allowed in a court of equity, to enrich himself at the expense of one who has acted innocently. The improvements are a substantial benefit to the property, and if he would redeem, he ought, *ex aequo et bono*, to pay for them to the extent of such benefit." So, too, in Hadley v. Stewart, supra note 25 at 486, 27 N.W. at 342, where the court, after recounting the situation, said that, "Under such circumstances, it would be inequitable on the part of the plaintiff [mortgagor] to claim the improvements. * * * In adjusting the equities, the court should allow the defendant, [mortgagee] such sum for his improvements as they have enhanced the value of the plaintiff's property."

unjust enrichment rather than the basis for inferring an implied in fact contract to pay for the improvement.[27] Indeed, in an extreme case, the mortgagor's continued passivity over a long time may be so reprehensible in view of the mortgagee's reliance upon it as to estop the mortgagor altogether from redeeming.[28] And, finally, in some states there are statutory provisions making changes in the rule. Thus in Massachusetts improvements which are "reasonable" may be made and charged to the mortgagor.[29] And in Alabama there was a statute permitting the mortgagee to charge for improvements up to the amount of rents charged against him.[30]

Where the property after improvement has been sold, even though the case does not fall under any of the exceptional situations discussed, since the great objection to allowing the mortgagee to charge for improvements, that it will make redemption more difficult, is not present, there is no reason why there should not be allocated to the mortgagee from the proceeds of the sale the amount the property brings in the market because of the improvement over what it would have sold for without it, and it has been so held.[31]

AMOUNT ALLOWED FOR IMPROVEMENTS

170. If improvements are made with consent of the mortgagor or to increase productivity, the mortgagee is credited with reasonable expenditures. If the mortgagee acted in the mistaken belief that he was the owner, he is credited with the value added to the property up to the actual amount expended.

The amount to be allowed to the mortgagee for improvements depends upon the basis for allowing them at all. Where they are allowed because of consent by the mortgagor[32] or in order to make or keep the property tenantable or productive, the amount reasonably expended is the criterion. Just as in the analogous case of necessary or authorized repairs.[33] However, where the mortgagee acted under an honest belief that he was the owner, or that the redemption interest was barred or would never be exercised—a belief to which the mortgagor's conduct usually contributes—an entirely different principle is operative. Its purpose is the prevention of unjust enrichment due to justifiable misreliance because of mistake. Consequently the value added to the property by the improvement, not to exceed its actual cost is the proper measure of recovery and the one recognized by the courts in such cases.[34] Inci-

27. See, however, Glenn, Mortgages, § 220.

28. Ferguson v. Boyd, 1907, 169 Ind. 537, 81 N.E. 71, rehearing denied 169 Ind. 537, 82 N.E. 1064; Purcell v. Thornton, 1915, 128 Minn. 255, 150 N.W. 899. That mere silence by the mortgagor should not work an estoppel, see Glenn, Mortgages, § 220.1, criticizing Purcell v. Thornton, supra. The estoppel in cases of this sort is against showing that the right of redemption exists, either because the foreclosure was defective or because the transaction, although not in form a mortgage, was so intended by the parties, and not against asserting a redemption right already established. It does not, therefore, violate, technically at least, the rule safeguarding the exercise of the equity of redemption once it has been shown to exist. See Glenn, Mortgages, § 220.1.

29. Mass.Gen.Laws Ann., c. 244 § 20; McFarlane v. Thompson, 1922, 241 Mass. 486, 135 N.E. 869.

30. Dozier v. Mitchell, 1880, 65 Ala. 511. For the statutory rule requiring payment for improvements by a redemptioner from a foreclosure sale, Ala.Code 1940, Tit. 7, §§ 732, 740; Rudisill v. Buckner, 1944, 244 Ala. 653, 15 So.2d 333. "Bettermen" statutes have been enacted in many states protecting the improver in good faith of another's property. See Woodward, Quasi-Contracts, 301. See 1930, 30 Col. L.Rev. 575, 576, on the requirement of good faith under "betterment" statutes.

31. Halbert v. Turner, 1908, 233 Ill. 531, 84 N.E. 704.

32. Lynch v. Ryan, 1908, 137 Wis. 13, 19, 118 N.W. 174, 176, 129 Am.St.Rep. 1040, "where the making of the improvements was authorized or consented to * * * the legitimate basis is the reasonable cost, the same as in repairs. * * *".

33. E. g., Miller v. Ward, 1913, 111 Me. 134, 139, 88 A. 400, 402, 49 L.R.A.,N.S., 122, "the money expended * * * was a proper charge"; Hays v. Christiansen, 1921, 105 Neb. 586, 181 N.W. 379; Gordon v. Krellman, 1924, 207 App.Div. 773, 202 N. Y.S. 682.

34. Hadley v. Stewart, 1886, 65 Wis. 481, 485, 27 N. W. 340, 342, "the sum the improvements enhanced the value of the whole premises, and not their cost, in case the cost exceeds the value which they have added to the premises."; Mickles v. Dillaye, 1858, 17 N.Y. 80, 93, "he should be required to make equi-

dentally, it may be remarked, that the quasi-contractual measure of recovery recognized in these cases is additional proof that the relief is non-consensual and not based upon any theory of implied in fact agreement by the mortgagor to pay for them.

Where the mortgagee is not allowed any charge for improvements, since the mortgagee is going to lose his capital investment, it seems unfair to charge him for any rent other than for the property without the improvement, and this has been held to be the rule.[35] Or, reaching a somewhat similar result when the mortgagee was charged with the full rental value of the property as improved, as an offset, he was held to be entitled to interest upon the cost of the improvement.[36] Indeed, going beyond this, there is authority that, although the full value of the improvement cannot be allowed, the mortgagee will be able to recoup so much of its value as will be covered by the net income of the property for which he is chargeable.[37]

Where the mortgagee is permitted to charge for the improvements the rule has been laid down that "no interest should be allowed the [mortgagee] appellant on the value of his improvements, as he has had the use of them, and, under the rule of estimating the rent * * * he will not be charged any rent for the use of his improvements."[38]

COMPENSATION FOR SERVICES

171. A mortgagee in possession may employ such persons as are reasonably necessary to manage the property. But by the prevailing view he cannot charge for services he himself performs. A better minority allows him a fair commission or leaves the matter of compensation to the discretion of the court.

It is quite clear that, if, the circumstances are such that an owner would be reasonable[39] in employing someone to take care of the premises and do such things as collecting the rents, the mortgagee in possession may hire it done and charge the expense up to the mortgagor.[40] However, the English cases[41] and the majority of American authorities hold that, even though the situation is such that the mortgagee could have hired someone else, he cannot do the job himself and charge the mortgagor compensation or com-

table compensation for the benefits he will receive from the improvements."; see quotation, s. c., supra, § 169 note 26. Merriam v. Goss, 1885, 139 Mass. 77, 28 N.E. 449; Halbert v. Turner, 1908, 233 Ill. 531, 84 N.E. 704; Moore's Guardian v. Williamson's Ex'r, 1923, 201 Ky. 561, 257 S.W. 711; Howard v. Clark, 1900, 72 Vt. 429, 48 A. 656; see 49 L.R.A.,N.S., 122, 129.

Warwick v. Harvey, 1930, 158 Md. 457, 148 A. 592, 68 A.L.R. 284, discussed in note, 1930, 30 Col.L.Rev. 575. T, the purchaser of mortgaged premises, had been induced to believe by a fraudulent agent through whom he bought the property, that the mortgage had been released. Acting under this erroneous belief, T erected a house on the property. On default the mortgagee foreclosed and bought in the property for less than its improved value. In an action against T by the mortgagee to obtain possession, the court held that he should be required to pay T the increased value of the land due to the improvements, or, at the plaintiff's option, to convey to T on payment by him of the value of the land without such improvements at the date of the foreclosure. See note, 1930, 4 Tulane L.Rev. 633.

35. Bradley v. Merrill, 1898, 91 Me. 340, 40 A. 132; Gresham v. Ware, 1885, 79 Ala. 192; see 49 L.R.A., N.S., 122, 130.

36. Lynch v. Ryan, 1908, 137 Wis. 13, 118 N.W. 174, 129 Am.St.Rep. 1040.

37. Dozier v. Mitchell, 1880, 65 Ala. 511; Montgomery v. Chadwick, 1858, 7 Iowa 114, 7 Clarke 114; Wilson v. Fisher, 1908, 148 N.C. 535, 62 S.E. 622.

38. Hadley v. Stewart, 1886, 65 Wis. 481, 27 N.W. 340; Howard v. Clark, 1900, 72 Vt. 429, 48 A. 656; Poole v. Johnson, 1883, 62 Iowa 611, 17 N.W. 900; see Lynch v. Ryan, supra note 36; 49 L.R.A.,N.S., 122, 130.

39. The mortgagee in possession cannot, however, obtain a court's opinion as to the reasonableness of contemplated expenditures, a matter of some uncertainty. Colonial Life Ins. Co. v. Anson Realty Co., 1932, 111 N.J.Eq. 267, 162 A. 111.

40. Godfrey v. Watson, 1747, 3 Atk. 517; Turner v. Johnson, 1888, 95 Mo. 431, 7 S.W. 570, 6 Am.St.Rep. 62; Johnson v. Hosford, 1887, 110 Ind. 572, 10 N.E. 407, rehearing denied 110 Ind. 572, 12 N.E. 522; see Harper v. Ely, 1873, 70 Ill. 581. But in American Freehold Land Mort. Co. v. Pollard, 1902, 132 Ala. 155, 32 So. 630, although the mortgagor had voluntarily given possession to a non-resident corporation mortgagee, the court refused to recognize that fact of non-residence as sufficient reason to allow payment of agents to collect the rents.

41. French v. Baron, 1740, 2 Atk. 120; Godfrey v. Watson, 1747, 3 Atk. 517.

missions for so doing.[42] One reason advanced is that the mortgagee in possession is comparable to a trustee,[43] and the courts do not want the fiduciary relation which exists under such circumstances to be permitted with the mortgagee having a selfish interest adverse to that of the mortgagor. The interest of the mortgagor is in having the work done for as little as possible; the interest of the employee, is in getting paid as much as possible. The rule as to trustees, however, has been changed either by statute or decision, and, since admittedly the mortgagee situation is a weaker one for imposing the restriction, it should be abandoned there also.[44] Another reason given for denying the mortgagee compensation is that he is in possession solely for his benefit and consequently there is no foundation for implying in fact any agreement to charge or to impose a quasi-contractual obligation on the mortgagor.[45] But an answer to this is that the care and management of the premises is also necessary to preserve the value of the mortgagor's redemption interest.[46] There are two minority views in the United States permitting compensation to the mortgagee. Massachusetts and a few other states allow the mortgagee a reasonable commission for his services.[47] The other rule leaves the setting of compensation to the discretion of the court.[48]

When there is an express contract for compensation there still is opposition to permitting it to be enforced. The English courts frowned on it for the same reasons they struck down other agreements which tended to make redemption by the mortgagor more onerous, as tending to usury and oppression.[49] The safeguard of reasonableness of the services and charges should be sufficient safeguard against the first concern, and it should not be given great weight when the agreement is not part of the original mortgage but only at the time possession is taken. Since the services are completely separate from the debt and the charges for them can be related to them, the agreement not only is not usurious but does not lend itself easily to a cover for usury. Consequently, even though the compensation is fixed at a percentage on the amount of the debt, which prima facie makes the transaction appear usurious, if the result of the computation by this method is a reasonable compensation for the services performed, the contract should be and has been held to be valid.[50]

---

42. Barnard v. Paterson, 1904, 137 Mich. 633, 100 N. W. 893; Lynch v. Ryan, 1908, 137 Wis. 13, 118 N. W. 174; Wadleigh v. Phelps, 1906, 149 Cal. 627, 87 P. 93; Shaw v. G. B. Beaumont Co., 1917, 88 N.J. Eq. 333, 102 A. 151, 2 A.L.R. 122; Moore v. Cable, 1815, 1 Johns.Ch. (N.Y.) 385. His own out of pocket expenses incurred in management and collection do not fall under the ban. Harper v. Ely, 1873, 70 Ill. 581; Turk v. Page, 1917, 64 Okl. 251, 167 P. 462. See 170 A.L.R. 181.

43. Bonithron v. Hockmore, 1685, 1 Vern. 316. See Green v. Lamb, 1881, 24 Hun (N.Y.) 87, 89, "the mortgagee in possession is classed with a trustee; and it is said that neither was entitled to commissions. Plainly the law is changed as to a trustee."

44. In re Hemphill's Estate 1914, 157 Wis. 331, 147 N.W. 1089; see Green v. Lamb, note 43, supra; Scott, Trusts, § 242.

45. Benham v. Rowe, 1852, 2 Cal. 387, 408, 56 Am. Dec. 342, "his care and trouble are bestowed for the furtherance and protection of his own interests."; Barnard v. Paterson, 1904, 137 Mich. 633, 100 N.W. 893.

46. See 1924, 24 Col.L.Rev. 318, 319.

47. Van Vronker v. Eastman, 1843, 48 Mass. (7 Met.) 157; Barry v. Dow, 1922, 240 Mass. 419, 134 N.E. 367; Barry v. Harlowe, 1922, 242 Mass. 159, 136 N. E. 105, possession by consent does not alter the rule; Waterman v. Curtis, 1857, 26 Conn. 241; Bradley v. Merrill, 1898, 91 Me. 340, 40 A. 132.

48. Walter v. Calhoun, 1913, 88 Kan. 801, 129 P. 1176. Green v. Lamb, 1881, 24 Hun (N.Y.) 87, held the same way but five years later the court swung to the majority rule where there was no contract. Blunt v. Syms, 1886, 40 Hun (N.Y.) 566. However, a more modern case reverted, without comment, to the earlier view. Massari v. Girardi, 1922, 119 Misc. 607, 197 N.Y.S. 751.

49. Bonithron v. Hockmore, 1685, 1 Vern. 316; French v. Baron, 1740, 2 Atk. 120; Eyre v. Hughes, 1876, 2 Ch.D. 148. Cf. Snow v. Warwick Inst. for Savings, 1890, 17 R.I. 66, 67, 20 A. 94; Hupart, Rights and Liabilities of a Mortgagee in Possession in New Jersey, 1935, 1 N.J.L.Rev. 140, 146. See 1935, 35 Col.L.Rev. 1248, 1259, n. 85.

50. Gordon v. Krellman, 1924, 207 App.Div. 773, 202 N.Y.S. 682, noted, 1924, 24 Col.L.Rev. 318; cf. Tholen v. Duffy, 1871, 7 Kan. 405; Johns v. Moore, 1959, 168 Cal.App.2d 709, 336 P.2d 579.

REIMBURSEMENT FOR INSURANCE

172. In the absence of an agreement a mortgagee in possession may not charge the mortgagor for insurance on the premises. A strong argument can be made, however, that a mortgagee in possession, like a trustee, should have a duty to keep the property insured.

Today the usual mortgage contains a clause requiring the mortgagor to keep the premises insured for the benefit of the mortgagee, or, more commonly, as their interest shall appear. In case there is such a contractual duty and the mortgagor fails to insure, the mortgagee is privileged to do it and charge the expense thereof to the mortgagor as an addition to the mortgage debt.[51] It has been laid down as law that, in the absence of such agreement or an authorization by the mortgagor, a mortgagee may not insure the mortgaged premises and charge the mortgagor.[52] It has been pointed out, however, that some of these authorities are older

cases, representing an attitude toward insurance out of harmony with present day notions, while others are those in which the mortgagee insured only his own interest.[53] Trustees today have a duty to keep trust property insured and are surcharged in their accounts if they do not do so and a loss occurs.[54] The same duty should apply to a mortgagee in possession. As was pointed out in a leading case, "in the light of modern ideas in respect to the reasonable care of property by one in possession thereof in the nature of trustee for another, having a duty or authority to preserve the same, reasonable expenditures for insurance are as legitimate as such expenditures for repairs and to prevent loss by decay or destruction otherwise.[55] Indeed it has been urged by a foremost authority that the duty or privilege of insuring should extend beyond that against the hazard of fire to any kind that a reasonable man,[56] in charge of his own property, would take out. This certainly is in advance of the cases at present, but it makes good sense.

TAXES

173. A mortgagee in possession is under a duty to pay taxes. He is entitled to credit for such payment, but he can only enforce his claim as part of the mortgage debt, except where he paid after foreclosure or after the debt claim was barred by the statute of limitations or in other situations of hardship.

A mortgagor in possession has the duty of paying all taxes on the mortgaged property.[57]

51. Baker v. Aalberg, 1899, 183 Ill. 258, 55 N.E. 672; Jehle v. Brooks, 1897, 112 Mich. 131, 70 N.W. 440; Sanford v. Litchenberger, 1901, 62 Neb. 501, 57 N. W. 305; Hays v. Christiansen, 1926, 114 Neb. 764, 209 N.W. 609. See 1945, 20 St. John's L.Rev. 59, for a review of the clarifying provisions in N.Y. Real Prop. Law, §§ 258, Sched.M.N., cov. 2, and § 254, subdiv. 4, spelling out the mortgagor's covenant to keep insured.

See also Note, 1953 Western Reserve L.Rev. 164; Note, 1952, 32 Or.L.Rev. 78; Report of Committee on Real Property: Rights of Mortgagees to Retain Fire Insurance Proceeds, 1953, 8 Record of Ass'n of Bar, City of N.Y. 42; The Mortgagee and Insurance Appraisals, 1951, 3 Stan.L.Rev. 352; King, Subrogation Under Contracts Insuring Property, 1951, 30 Tex.L.Rev. 62; Note, 1950, 9 A.L.R.2d 299, 301–309; Note, Application of Proceeds of Fire Insurance Policy During Redemption Period, 1957, 36 Or.L.Rev. 182, discussing Haskin v. Greene, 1955, 205 Or. 140, 286 P.2d 128.

In Equitable Life Assur. Soc. of the United States v. Bennion, 1959, 81 Idaho 445, 346 P.2d 1053, on the mortgagee paying delinquent premiums, the mortgaged property became security for the reimbursement of such payments but this obligation to repay was separate and apart from the original mortgage debt.

52. Curtis v. Curtis, 1912, 180 Ala. 70, 60 So. 165; Barnett v. Nelson, 1880, 54 Iowa 41, 6 N.W. 49, 37 Am.Rep. 183; Saunders v. Frost, 1827, 22 Mass. (5 Pick.) 259, 16 Am.Dec. 394; Faure v. Winans, N.Y., 1824, 1 Hopk.Ch. 283, 14 Am.Dec. 545; see United States Trust Co. v. Miller, 1927, 116 Neb. 25, 29, 215 N.W. 462, 469.

53. See Glenn, Mortgages, § 213. Miller v. Ward, 1913, 111 Me. 134, 88 A. 400, 49 L.R.A.,N.S., 122, policy in mortgagee's own name; Wise v. Layman, 1926, 197 Ind. 393, 150 N.E. 368, no showing that payment would be other than to mortgagee's personal favor.

54. Restatement, Second, Trusts § 176; Scott, Trusts, § 176.

55. Lynch v. Ryan, 1908, 137 Wis. 13, 23, 118 N.W. 174, 178, 129 Am.St.Rep. 1040. Cf. Land Finance Corp. v. Giorgio, 1935, 280 N.Y.S. 924.

56. Glenn, Mortgages, § 213.

57. Dayton v. Rice, 1877, 47 Iowa 429; Pines v. Novick, 1915, 168 App.Div. 155, 153 N.Y.S. 891. Under local tax laws the mortgagor may continue liable

If he fails to do so the law is well settled that the mortgagee may pay them to protect his security interest in the land. If the property has been sold for taxes, the mortgagee may redeem it from the tax sale. In either event he may add the amounts so expended to the mortgage debt.[58] If the mortgagee is in possession, there is a duty upon him, at least to the extent of rents and profits received, to pay taxes.[59] But, since the pay-

ment nevertheless enures to the benefit of the mortgagor, the beneficial owner of the property, he can in such cases also demand credit for the payment and add it to his claim.[60] Consequently, whether the payment is made by a mortgagee in possession or out of possession the right clearly is one for reimbursement on quasi-contractual principles because of the benefit conferred upon the mortgagor in relieving his property of the charge upon it for taxes.[61] However, it is a right which inures to him only in his capacity as mortgagee, for, were it not for the mortgage relationship, the rule would apply that "the payment of the taxes of one man by another without some request, express or implied, would be such a voluntary payment as would not support an action."[62]

Although this is true, it would be in accord with ordinary rules of restitution to permit the right to be enforced either by subrogation to the rights of the taxing power [63] or by a direct independent action, as well as by doing the same thing, in effect, by adding the amount onto the sum of the mortgage debt and treating the mortgage as securing

---

for taxes in spite of possession in the mortgagee. Cf. Hood ex rel. Planters', etc., Co. v. McGill, 1934, 206 N.C. 83, 173 S.E. 20; Provident Trust Co. of Philadelphia v. Judicial, etc., Ass'n, 1934, 112 Pa. Super. 352, 171 A. 287.

58. Horrigan v. Wellmuth, 1883, 77 Mo. 542; Sidenberg v. Ely, 1882, 90 N.Y. 257, 43 Am.St.Rep. 163, rule applies to redemption from tax sale as well as taxes paid; Farmers' Security Bank of Park River v. Martin, 1915, 29 N.D. 269, 150 N.W. 572, L.R.A., 1915D, 432, tax invalid but mortgagee paid without actual notice; Sharp v. Thompson, 1881, 100 Ill. 447, 39 Am.Rep. 61; Williams v. Hilton, 1853, 35 Me. 547, 58 Am.Dec. 729; Hopkins v. Sanders, 1912, 172 Mich. 227, 137 N.W. 709—accord. The rule includes taxes paid after foreclosure judgment but before sale. Wyoming Building & Loan Ass'n v. Mills Construction Co., 1928, 38 Wyo. 515, 269 P. 45, 60 A.L.R. 418; see collection of cases, 1929, 60 A.L.R. 425.

For collections of cases, see 1933, 84 A.L.R. 1366; 1939, 123 A.L.R. 1248. The rule extends to cases where taxes were paid in the mistaken belief, bona fide, that the payor held a mortgage on the land. Central Wisconsin Tr. Co. v. Swenson, 1936, 222 Wis. 331, 267 N.W. 307, 106 A.L.R. 1207; see 1933, 84 A.L.R. 1366, 1371, 1372; 1939, 123 A.L.R. 1248, 1250, 1252, 1253. A first mortgagee who pays taxes can add the amount paid to his debt in priority to a second mortgage. Wiggin v. Lowell Five Cent Sav. Bank, 1938, 299 Mass. 518, 13 N.E.2d 433.

Additional authorities include Redic v. Mechanics & Farmers Bank, 1954, 241 N.C. 152, 84 S.E.2d 542, discussed in Third Annual Survey of North Carolina Case Law: Credit Transactions, 1955, 34 N.C.L. Rev. 36; Crofts v. Johnson, 1957, 6 Utah 2d 350, 313 P.2d 808. Although the mortgaged property becomes security for the right to reimbursement for delinquent taxes paid by the mortgagee, this right of repayment is separate and apart from the original mortgage debt. Equitable Life Assurance Soc. of the United States v. Bennion, 1959, 81 Idaho 445, 346 P.2d 1053. See note 51, supra.

59. Brown v. Simons, 1863, 44 N.H. 475; Shoemaker v. Commonwealth Bank, 1881, 15 Phila. (Pa.) 297, 11 W.N.C. 284, 39 L.I. 81; see Ten Eyck v. Craig, 1875, 62 N.Y. 406.

Neither an express provision in a trust deed mortgage authorizing the trustee to enter on default, collect rents and apply them to taxes, nor a statutory provision giving him a right to enter and pay taxes

and creating a lien for such payment, imposes a duty on the trustee to pay taxes. Redic v. Mechanics & Farmers Bank, 1954, 241 N.C. 152, 84 S.E.2d 542, discussed in Third Annual Survey of North Carolina Case Law: Credit Transactions, 1955, 34 N.C.L.Rev. 36.

60. Hays v. Christiansen, 1926, 114 Neb. 764, 209 N. W. 609; see Wise v. Layman, 1926, 197 Ind. 393, 399, 150 N.E. 368, 371; Brown v. Berry, 1918, 89 N. J.Eq. 230, 236, 108 A. 51, 54; Johns v. Moore, 1959, 168 Cal.App.2d 709, 336 P.2d 579; United States v. Bond, E.D.Va.1959, 172 F.Supp. 759 reversed, C.A. 1960, 279 F.2d 837, certiorari denied 364 U.S. 895, 81 S.Ct. 220, 5 L.Ed.2d 189. The latter case resulted in circuity of lien where the real estate mortgage was superior to the federal lien for income taxes but inferior to county real estate taxes. The mortgagee, on paying the county taxes to maintain the integrity of its lien was entitled to priority over the government lien for the amount so paid.

61. See 1941, 90 U.Pa.L.Rev. 90.

62. Horrigan v. Wellmuth, 1883, 77 Mo. 542, 545.

63. For general collections of cases on the right of subrogation to the right of the taxing power by one who pays taxes, see 1929, 61 A.L.R. 587, 601, payment by mortgagees; 1937, 106 A.L.R. 1212, 1217, payment by mortgagees.

the enlarged sum. Nevertheless, it is also the clear weight of authority that "this claim must be enforced as a part of the mortgage debt, and cannot be made the basis of an independent action against the mortgagor, as for money paid to his use, * * * or * * * by virtue of the law of subrogation." [64] In other words, the mortgagor is limited to reimbursement as part of the action of foreclosure or redemption. The explanation given for this rule is that the amount due for taxes, together with the amount due on the mortgage, constitutes a single, indivisible debt, and "could become a lien only in connection with and because of the mortgage, and could not exist independent of it" and consequently, mortgagees "could not at pleasure split up their demand and make the parts the subjects of separate suits." [65] The plain answer to this is that the debt claim itself is a contract claim and the mortgage securing it is the result of a consensual transaction, while the claim for reimbursement for taxes paid is clearly non-consensual as is the lien on the property to secure it. It is true that the mortgage must exist, or be honestly thought to exist, at the time of payment in order for the mortgagee not to be classed as a volunteer and denied recovery altogether. But the existence of the mortgage as a necessary condition to the creation of the non-censensual right to restitution obviously does not make the right so created an integral part of his mortgage debt claim. Rather the rule would seem to rest upon the practical ground that it is so intimately, if not indissolubly, connected with the mortgage debt that the whole matter should be, as a matter of expediency and fairness to the mortgagor, settled in the one suit in which the mortgage debt is enforced; the mortgagee should not be permitted inexcusable tardiness in not presenting his demand at the time the entire transaction was in issue.

So viewed, the rule seems a sound one, certainly as to all taxes paid before the foreclosure decree. If this is the proper basis it should not be applied mechanically. Independent recovery should be and has been permitted where payment is made (1) after entry of a foreclosure decree; [66] (2) after the debt claim has been barred by a statute of limitations or non-claim; [67] or (3) in other situations where hardship on the mortgagee justifies departure from the rule.[68] Where

---

64. Horrigan v. Wellmuth, supra note 62, at 545; Northern Finance Corp. v. Byrnes, C.C.A.Mo.1922, 5 F.2d 11; Home Owners' Loan Corp. v. Joseph, 1940, 306 Ill.App. 244, 28 N.E.2d 330; Criswell v. McKnight, 1930, 120 Neb. 317, 232 N.W. 586, 84 A.L.R. 1361; The Praetorians v. State, Tex.Civ.App., 1932, 53 S.W.2d 334; Vincent v. Moore, 1883, 51 Mich. 618, 17 N.W. 81; Eblen v. Major's Admr., 1912, 147 Ky. 44, 143 S.W. 748; Stone v. Tilley, 1907, 100 Tex. 487, 101 S.W. 201, 10 L.R.A.,N.S., 678, 123 Am. St.Rep. 819, 15 Ann.Cas. 524. See 1907, 10 L.R.A., N.S. 679. But see Childs v. Smith, 1909, 51 Wash. 457, 99 P. 304, 130 Am.St.Rep. 1107. Cf. Hill v. Townley, 1891, 45 Minn. 167, 47 N.W. 653. See 1933, 84 A.L.R. 1366, 1387; 1939, 123 A.L.R. 1248, 1256, for collections of cases. And, it has been reasoned, that since the mortgagee cannot have an independent action against the mortgagor, even more clearly he should be denied independent relief against a non-assuming grantee of the mortgagor. Citizens Sav. Bank v. Guar. Loan Co., 1939, 62 R.I. 448, 6 A.2d 688, 123 A.L.R. 1236; cf. Conaty v. Guar. Loan Co., 1939, 62 R.I. 470, 6 A.2d 698, noted and criticized, 1939, 53 Harv.L.Rev. 144.

65. Vincent v. Moore, 1883, 51 Mich. 618, 17 N.W. 81.

66. Hogg v. Longstreth, 1881, 97 Pa. 255, 10 W.N.C. 95; New Haven Sav. Bank v. Atwater, 1883, 51 Conn. 429; Mut. Life Ins. Co. v. Newell, 1894, 78 Hun 293, 28 N.Y.S. 913, affirmed without opinion, 1894, 144 N.Y. 627, 39 N.E. 494. See 1941, 90 U.Pa. L.Rev. 90, 93.

67. Federal Land Bank of Columbia v. Brooks, 1939, 139 Fla. 506, 190 So. 737, noted with approval, 1939, 17 N.Y.Univ.L.Q.Rev. 295, subrogation to lien of state for taxes paid; Catlin v. Mills, 1926, 140 Wash. 1, 247 P. 1013, 47 A.L.R. 545, quasi-contractual recovery; Hill v. Townley, 1891, 45 Minn. 167, 47 N.W. 653, contra.
It has been held that the mortgagee may maintain an action against the mortgagor for taxes paid on the latter's covenant to pay them. Gilmour v. First Nat. Bank, 1912, 21 Colo.App. 301, 121 P. 767; British Col. etc. Agency v. Robinson, 1922, 32 B.C. 375, 1923, 4 D.L.R. 416. But see Hitchcock v. Merrick, 1864, 18 Wis. 357.

68. There is both older and more recent authority allowing recovery in these situations. White v. First Nat. Bank, D.C.Pa.1938, 24 F.Supp. 290; Dunlop v. James, 1903, 174 N.Y. 411, 67 N.E. 60. See cases in two preceding footnotes. See also 1939, 123 A.L.R. 1248, 1256; 1939, 17 N.Y.Univ.L.Q.Rev. 295, 297 notes 16, 17; Restatement, Restitution, 1937, § 104, comment a, illustration 3.

the mortgage debt will not be due for a considerable period after the taxes fall due, the mortgagor by defaulting can compel a forced additional loan by the mortgagee which, under the majority rule, cannot be collected until the mortgage debt matures. To guard against such hardship, most mortgages contain acceleration clauses, making defaults in payment of taxes ground for foreclosure at once, in addition to the privilege of paying them and adding them to the mortgage debt.[69] Where no such clause has been written into the mortgage, it would seem desirable to permit an independent action at once, either directly at law for reimbursement or by equitable subrogation to the right of the taxing power. A possible solution, indeed, would be to treat defaulted taxes paid by the mortgagee as on the same footing as defaulted interest or a defaulted installment of payment of the principal.[70]

ANNUAL RESTS

174. In taking an account annual rests are ordered when the net income in any year exceeds the interest accruing in that year. The excess is deducted from the principal.

Rents received by a mortgagee in possession are not automatically applied on the mortgage debt or the interest on it. Before any of the income received by him is appropriated to such a purpose there must be, as was seen, an accounting in which the mortgagee's allowable expenses and charges are first set-off against what he has taken in, and such an accounting is had only when there is either an action to foreclosure or to redeem.[71] Consequently the mortgagor cannot omit payments of interest or installments of principal on the ground that the mortgagee has in his hands income from the property more than sufficient to cover them.[72] However, an accounting is a matter of equitable set-off. So when it is taken there is no inherent difficulty in balancing off as of a prior date, if that be desirable, the net rents as they would have been at that time in payment or reduction of principal and income. And, quite obviously, there would be injustice to the mortgagor if, in any one year, the mortgagee has in his hands a surplus of income over outgo which might be used to pay interest and also to reduce part of the principal debt so that the interest on it for the ensuing year would be less, and it were not so credited. One way of handling such a situation would be to compute on the one side, interest on the debt for the entire period without annual rests together with interest on the various items of expenses allowed to the mortgagee as they accrued, while on the other he would be charged interest on the rents and profits as and when received down to the date of the accounting.[73] Most courts, however, when an account is taken, meet the problem by ordering annual [74] rests in all cases where the net income is in excess of the annual interest. An unsurpassed and frequently quoted state-

---

69. E. g., in Laventall v. Pomerantz, 1933, 263 N.Y. 110, 188 N.E. 271; see Security First Nat. Bank v. Lamb, 1931, 212 Cal. 64, 297 P. 550, 74 A.L.R. 502. Mere default by the mortgagor in the payment of taxes, absent a clause making it a breach of the condition of the mortgage permitting foreclosure, will not operate to give the mortgagee the right to foreclose. Williams v. Townsend, 1865, 31 N.Y. 411.

70. See Glenn, Mortgages, § 91.

71. "A mortgagee in possession first deducts expenses, and then what remains goes against principal and interest; but till an account is taken there is no set-off, there is no appropriation of the rents." Cockburn v. Edwards, 1881, 18 Ch.D. 449, 456, per Jessel, M.R. See § 165, supra.

72. See cases in preceding note. This is contrary to an earlier expression. Brocklehorst v. Jessop, 1835, 7 Sim. 438.

73. Keeline v. Clark, 1906, 132 Iowa 360, 106 N.W. 257; Morrow v. Turney's Adm'r, 1859, 35 Ala. 131; Walter v. Calhoun, 1913, 88 Kan. 801, 129 P. 1176; cf. Green v. Westcott, 1861, 13 Wis. 606, net rents applied to interest but the surplus over this not applied on the principal yet interest allowed on this surplus "to keep pace with the interest on the debt" —an equivalent, of course, to an application on the debt.

74. Occasionally, when justice demands it, semi-annual rests may be ordered. Gibson v. Crehore, 1827, 20 Mass. (5 Pick.) 146, rents and profits considerable and the interest on the debt payable semi-annually; Adams v. Sayre, 1884, 76 Ala. 509.

ment of this method is that of the great Shaw, C. J., who said, "1. State the gross rents received by the defendant to the end of the first year. 2. State the sums paid by him for repairs, taxes, and a commission for collecting the rents,[75] and deduct the same from the gross rents, and the balance will show the net rents to the end of the year. 3. Compute the interest on the note for one year and add it to the principal, and the aggregate will show the amount due thereon at the end of the year. 4. If the net annual rent exceeds the year's interest on the note, deduct that rent from the amount due, and the balance will show the amount remaining due at the end of the year. 5. At the end of the second year go through the same process, taking the amount due at the beginning of the year as the new capital to compute the year's interest upon. So to the time of judgment."[76]

RESTS—CONSTRUCTION OF CLAUSES

175. Where the mortgage provides for a reduction of interest if paid within a certain time, the mortgagor must actually pay to avail himself of the benefit. But if the proviso is for acceleration or capitalization of interest upon default, the mortgagor is entitled to annual rests.

A similar question has arisen in the construction of provisos calling for (1) acceleration and foreclosure if payments of interest shall be in arrears,[77] or (2) for capitalization of the interest if it should be in arrears for

a certain time,[78] or (3) for a reduction in the rate of interest if it is paid within a stipulated time.[79] In the last case the court decided that actual payment by the mortgagor was contemplated, not the receipt by the mortgagee of rents and profits sufficient for the payment was intended, something which could not be determined without an accounting. In the second one, though, the court pointed out that the question was not one of actual payment but whether, within the meaning of the proviso, interest was in arrears so as to allow the mortgagee to treat it as an accession to the principal debt and have it bear interest. In concluding that it was not, the court said that "one's mind revolts somewhat against a construction which will give the mortgagee a right to interest upon interest—for that is the meaning of capitalization when he has in his pocket money of the mortgagor available for payment of the interest, and which the mortgagee could use for that purpose, if he thought fit to do so. We ought not to put such a construction upon such a proviso unless we arrive at the conclusion that this must have been the intention of the parties. * * * if the mortgagee has in his hands such an amount of rents as, after deducting all proper outgoings, exceeds or is equal to the interest due, he is not entitled to say that the interest is in arrear."[80] The principle underlying the decision, in the language of another court faced with the same sort of problem, is "that the burden shall be made as light upon the debtor as is consistent with giving to the creditor all that the debtor has bound himself to pay. If the creditor, by any application that may be made for him, can receive all for which the debtor is under an obligation to him, it is but equity that it

---

75. In Massachusetts commissions are allowed. See supra, § 158. Of course where not allowed this item would not be deducted. Similarly, as to insurance, for example, there might or might not be a deductible item, § 172, supra.

76. Van Vronker v. Eastman, 1843, 48 Mass. (7 Metc.) 157, 163. Gladding v. Warner, 1863, 36 Vt. 54; Adams v. Sayre, 1884, 76 Ala. 509; Powell v. Williams, 1848, 14 Ala. 476, 48 Am.Dec. 105; McConnel v. Holobush, 1849, 11 Ill. 61; Shaeffer v. Chambers, 1847, 6 N.J.Eq. 548, 47 Am.Dec. 211; Snavely v. Pickle, 1877, 70 Va. (29 Grat.) 27—accord. See also Lynch v. Ryan, 1908, 137 Wis. 13, 118 N.W. 174, 129 Am.St.Rep. 1040.

77. See Cockburn v. Edwards, 1881, 18 Ch.D. 449.

78. Wrigley v. Gill, [1906] 1 Ch. 165; Murdock v. Clarke, 1890, 3 Cal.Unrep.Cas. 265, 24 P. 272.

79. Bright v. Campbell, 1889, 41 Ch.Div. 388; see note, 1931, 171 L.T. 6. See also 1910, 23 Harv.L. Rev. 301.

80. Vaughan Williams, L. J., in Wrigley v. Gill, [1906,] 1 Ch. 165, 173.

should be applied in such a mode as will be least onerous to the debtor. On the other hand, when the interest of the debtor cannot be promoted by any particular application of the payment, or when it is a matter of indifference to him in which mode the application is made, the law raises a presumption that the payment was actually received in the way that was of most advantage to the creditor. If the application can be made so as to discharge all the obligations of the debtor without increasing his burden, it will be deemed indifferent to him upon which obligation the payment shall be applied."[81]

Applied to a proviso "which, in the event of the default of the mortgagor in paying the interest, gives the mortgagee a right to something beyond that to which he would otherwise be entitled under the mortgage deed" it would seem sound to decide, as the court did, that "the mortgagee could not, within the meaning of this proviso, say that interest was in arrear which would cease to be in arrear the moment he chose without any further act by the mortgagor." [82] On the other hand, when the proviso would give to the mortgagor a benefit, relieving him of an obligation he had contracted to perform, the court felt it would not be consistent with giving to the creditor all that he had contracted for to construe receipt of rents and profits to be a payment of the interest justifying a diminished interest rate from the mortgagor.

RESTS—LIMITATIONS

176. No annual rests are ordered

(1) Where the interest in any year exceeds the net rents; a rest would result in undesirable interest on interest; or

(2) By the better view: where interest was in arrears when the mortgagee took possession, until net rents exceed the combined amount of interest in arrears and current interest.

There is a strong policy in the law, entirely apart from usury, against giving a creditor interest upon interest.

"There should be no rest resulting in a compounding of interest nor any other than such as equity requires." [83] Consequently, if the income taken in by the mortgagee in any year is exceeded by the interest accrued, no rest will be taken for there would then be a surplus of interest due to be added onto the capital amount and start drawing of interest. Instead simple interest continues on the original principal until net income received equals or exceeds the interest due.

Where there is interest in arrear at the date of the mortgagee's entry, the English view, supported by some American cases and the authority of distinguished writers, is that the arrears should be added to the interest accruing after entry to determine whether there was an excess of income over interest and, consequently, whether or not there should be a rest with a reduction of the principal.[84] There is, however, authority for the view that the old arrear should be disregarded for the purpose of determining whether there should be annual rests, only the current interest being set off against the income received after entry and any surplus

81. Murdock v. Clarke, 1891, 88 Cal. 384, 390, 26 P. 601, 603.

82. Wrigley v. Gill, supra note 80, at 173

83. Lynch v. Ryan, 1908, 137 Wis. 13, 21, 118 N.W. 174, 177, 129 Am.St.Rep. 1040. See also Reed v. Reed, 1830, 27 Mass. (10 Pick.) 398; Thorneycroft v. Crockett, 1848, 2 H.L.C. 239. Cf. Vanderhaise v. Hugues, 1861, 13 N.J.Eq. 410.

Income should be applied in the first place to the payment of interest due and the surplus to the principal; subsequent interest is to be calculated on the balance of the principal. If payment is less than the interest, the surplus interest is not to be added to the principal. See Karesh, Security Transactions, in Survey of South Carolina Law, 1957, 10 S.C.L.Q. 114, 116.

On the burden of proof in priority problems, see 1958, 10 Baylor L.Rev. 42.

84. Horlock v. Smith, 1844, 1 Coll.Ch. 287; Patch v. Wild, 1861, 30 Beav. 99; Vanderhaise v. Hugues, 1861, 13 N.J.Eq. 410; Bennett v. Cook, N.Y. 1874, 2 Hun 526; Shepherd v. Elliott, 1819, 4 Madd. 254; 2 Story, Eq., § 1016a; Glenn, Mortgages, § 224.1.

over such interest going in reduction of the principal.[85] The former view seems preferable. In the absence of directions by a debtor as to which of several debts shall be paid out of money of the debtor paid to the creditor, the creditor is privileged to apply it to his greatest advantage.[86] The arrearage may be considered a separate debt and one which caused the mortgagee to enter. The mortgagee may, if he wishes, and he would so desire because it is to his advantage, apply the first income to the arrearage.

H. ACQUISITION OF TITLE IN BREACH OF DUTY

ACQUISITION BY MORTGAGOR

177. A mortgagor or his assuming grantee cannot acquire title free of the mortgage at a foreclosure or tax sale. His breach of duty to pay the obligation or the taxes led to the sale and he may not benefit from such a breach. Authorities are divided whether he can get clear title from a bona fide purchaser.

A mortgagor is under a duty to the mortgagee to discharge the secured obligation. Hence he cannot fail to do so, buy the property in on foreclosure, and hold it free of the mortgage. He can do this neither directly nor through intermediaries.

Thus, where there are covenants of title and to defend by the mortgagor in a second mortgage, he cannot acquire title on the foreclosure sale of a defaulted first mortgage so as to cut off a second mortgage by direct [87] purchase or through collusion with another.[88]

The same has been held to be true even though the second mortgage was expressly subject to the first mortgage, such a clause being construed as mere identification of a lien already existing and superior from the standpoint of priority on foreclosure but in no way affecting the covenant between the parties.[89] The same rule has been applied to a grantee from the mortgagor who assumed the payment of the mortgage debt,[90] but not

---

wrong of failing to perform one's duty. See Dorff v. Bornstein, 1938, 277 N.Y. 236, 242, 14 N.E.2d 51, motion granted 278 N.Y. 566, 16 N.E.2d 105; Wood & Oberreich, Revival of a Second or Subsequent Mortgage upon Reacquisition of Title by the Original Mortgagor after Foreclosure of a First Mortgage, 1936, 11 Ind.L.J. 429. See White, Revival of Mortgages, 1936, 10 U. of Cin.L.Rev. 217, for a state by state review of the authorities followed by a critical discussion of them; 1930, 44 Harv.L.Rev. 128. The doctrine of estoppel has been invoked in behalf of a foreclosing first mortgagee to refasten the lien of his mortgage upon a title obtained by the mortgagor from a third party when the original mortgage given by him was defective. Yerkes v. Hadley, 1888, 5 Dak. 324, 40 N.W. 340, 2 L.R.A. 363. So, too, where a mortgage contained a warranty of title, but before the execution of the mortgage the property, unknown to the mortgagor, had been sold for taxes, a reacquisition by the mortgagor of the title from the state will inure to the benefit of the mortgagee. Jacobsen v. Nieboer, 1941, 299 Mich. 116, 299 N.W. 830, noted, 1941, 26 Va.L.Rev. 101. The doctrine has been held inapplicable in such a situation where the mortgage is given to the vendor for the purchase money. The mortgagee in such a case having first conveyed the defective title to his mortgagor has no standing to invoke the rule. Florida Land Investment Co. v. Williams, 1922, 84 Fla. 157, 92 So. 876, 26 A.L.R. 171. Butterfield v. Lane, 1915, 114 Me. 333, 96 A. 233, accord. But see Clark v. Baker, 1860, 14 Cal. 612, 76 Am.Dec. 449; Toms v. Boyes, 1883, 50 Mich. 352, 15 N.W. 506. See 1923, 26 A.L.R. 173.

See Note, 1953, 29 N.Dak.L.R. 50, reviewing the different theories on which the courts hold that junior liens revive.

89. Martin v. Raleigh State Bank, 1927, 146 Miss. 1, 111 So. 448, 51 A.L.R. 442. See 1927, 51 A.L.R. 445; 1937, 111 A.L.R. 1285; Merchants National Bank of Fargo v. Miller, 1930, 59 N.D. 273, 229 N. W. 357. Contrast Huzzey v. Heffernan, 1887, 143 Mass. 232, 9 N.E. 570; Sandwich Mfg. Co. v. Zellmer, 1892, 48 Minn. 408, 51 N.W. 379; Chamberlain v. Forbes, 1901, 126 Mich. 86, 85 N.W. 253. Federal Farm Mort. Corp. v. Larson, 1938, 227 Wis. 221, 278 N.W. 421, prior mortgage excepted in covenant of warranty; Zandri v. Tendler, 1937, 123 Conn. 117, 193 A. 598, 111 A.L.R. 1280.

90. Beitel v. Dobbin, Tex.Civ.App.1898, 44 S.W. 299.

---

85. Moshier v. Norton, 1881, 100 Ill. 63.

86. See Glenn, Mortgages, § 224.1 and cases there cited.

87. Home Owners Loan Corp. v. Guaranty Title Trust Co., 1934, 168 Tenn. 118, 76 S.W.2d 109; Hilton v. Bissell, N.Y. 1844, 1 Sandf. Ch. 407.

88. Stiger v. Mahone, 1874, 24 N.J.Eq. 426, no covenant. The result is reached by holding that the purchase was payment of the prior mortgage, that the covenant operated either as an estoppel or a contract which would be given specific effect, or by saying that a title cannot be founded upon the

to one who merely[91] took "subject to" it. The distinction is that in the latter case there is no duty on the non-assuming grantee to pay off the mortgage. Whether a mortgagor who reacquires title after foreclosure and sale to an independent third party takes it discharged of a later mortgage is the subject of some difference of opinion. Some courts hold that the mortgagor, on reacquisition, is still subject to the lien of the subsequent mortgage.[92] Others hold that he will take free and clear in the absence of any contract duty or fraudulent conduct by the mortgagor toward the second mortgagee.[93] The protection of the bona fide purchaser in his disposition of the property, he having bought upon the assumption he could sell and convey a title free from subsequent encumbrances to the one foreclosed to anyone, including the mortgagor, seems to be a factor in this result.[94]

Purchase of the mortgaged premises by the mortgagor at a tax sale provides another illustration of the general doctrine. "If a tax deed always conveyed title clear of all past encumbrances, it would be possible for delinquent owners to extinguish outstanding encumbrances by a repurchase of their property at a tax sale."[95] To prevent such manipulation, it is the rule that one who owes to another the duty of paying taxes cannot, as to that other at least, default in his duty and then better his title by purchase on the tax sale resulting from his breach of duty.[96] The mortgagor in possession, being bound to pay the taxes as between himself and the mortgagee cannot, therefore, default in his obligation, allow the property to be sold for taxes, which constitute a paramount lien, and then buy in at the tax sale free and clear of the mortgage.[97] He cannot base a title on the violation of his duty[98] and his purchase, so far as the mortgagee is concerned, will be considered a payment of the taxes.[99] The doctrine extends even to the case where the sale is held after the foreclosure of the mortgage,[1] for, even though at the time of purchase the mortgagor-mortgagee relation no longer existed, his title would still be based upon a failure of duty during the time it did exist and one that caused the land on foreclosure to be sold subject to the tax lien rather than free of it, thus reducing the avails from the security

91. Searles v. Kelley, 1906, 88 Miss. 228, 40 So. 484, 8 L.R.A.,N.S., 491.

92. Federal Land Bank of Columbia v. Bank of Lenox, 1941, 192 Ga. 543, 16 S.E.2d 9, discussed, 1942, 27 Iowa L.Rev. 482; Kerr v. Erickson, Tex.Com. App., 1930, 24 S.W.2d 21, noted, 1930, 30 Col.L.Rev. 742; Jensen v. Duke, 1921, 71 Cal.App. 210, 234 P. 876, statute; Johnson v. Clark, 1936, 7 Cal.2d 529, 61 P.2d 767, statute; Jones v. Kingsey, 1856, 55 N. C. 463; Martin v. Raleigh State Bank, 1927, 146 Miss. 1, 111 So. 448, with aid of statute; Merchants National Bank of Fargo v. Miller, 1930, 59 N.D. 273, 229 N.W. 357; Baird v. Chamberlain, 1931, 60 N.D. 784, 236 N.W. 724. See Wood & Oberreich, Revival of a Second or Subsequent Mortgage upon Reacquisition of Title by the Original Mortgagor after Foreclosure of a First Mortgage, 1936, 11 Ind.L.J. 429; but a mortgage given to secure the loan with which to pay the purchase price will be given priority over the revived second mortgage, Bank of Columbia v. Bank of Lenox, supra.

93. Zandri v. Tendler, 1937, 123 Conn. 117, 193 A. 598, 111 A.L.R. 1280; Dorff v. Bornstein, 1938, 277 N.Y. 236, 14 N.E.2d 51, noted, 13 St. John's L.Rev. 182; cf. Schultz v. Cities Service Oil Co., 1939, 149 Kan. 148, 86 P.2d 533, noted, 1939, 52 Harv.L.Rev. 1176. Cf. also McDonald v. Duckworth, 1946, 197 Okl. 576, 173 P.2d 436, criticized 1947, 60 Harv.L. Rev. 658. See also 1944, 30 Va.L.Rev. 496.

94. See 1938, 13 St. John's L.Rev. 182, 183.

95. 1936, 46 Yale L.J. 334.

96. 3 Cooley, Taxation, § 1437. It has been pointed out that, since it seems inequitable to permit one to profit by buying in a tax title after neglecting the duty to pay them, regardless of to whom the duty ran, a broader statement is desirable. See 1936, 46 Yale L.J. 334, n. 2.

97. Dayton v. Rice, 1877, 47 Iowa 429; Woodbury v. Swan, 1879, 59 N.H. 22. Cf. Allison v. Armstrong, 1881, 28 Minn. 276, 9 N.W. 806, 41 Am.Rep. 281. See 1908, 16 L.R.A.,N.S., 121.

98. Pines v. Novick, 1915, 168 App.Div. 155, 153 N.Y. S. 891.

99. Waring v. Nat. Sav. & Trust Co., 1921, 138 Md. 367, 114 A. 57; Allison v. Armstrong, 1881, 28 Minn. 276, 9 N.W. 806, 41 Am.Rep. 281. See 1941, 90 U.Pa.L.Rev. 90, 94.

1. Adams v. Sims, 1928, 177 Ark. 652, 9 S.W.2d 329, noted, 1929, 42 Harv.L.Rev. 583. See also 1914, 52 L.R.A.,N.S., 877, 878.

accruing to the mortgagee.[2] Further, the great weight of authority holds that a transferee of the mortgagor, whether he assumes the payment of the mortgage debt or merely takes subject to it cannot defeat the lien of the mortgagee any more than could the mortgagor.[3]

ACQUISITION OF TAX TITLE
BY MORTGAGEE

178. A mortgagee in possession and, by the weight of authority, one not in possession cannot by acquisition of the premises at a tax sale cut off the mortgagor's right of redemption or the interests of prior mortgagees.

A mortgagee in possession of the mortgaged premises has the duty of keeping up the taxes and he cannot, therefore, after failing to pay them purchase the property on a tax sale brought about by his default and hold the property free of the mortgagor's claim to redeem.[4] Where the mortgagee is not in possession there is a split in the authorities.[5] Some let him buy in the title on

2. Barnard v. Wilson, 1888, 74 Cal. 512, 16 P. 307.

3. See 1908, 16 L.R.A.,N.S., 121, 124; 1914, L.R.A.,N. S., 877, 878, for collections of cases. See also 1941, 90 U.Pa.L.Rev. 90, 95. Zuege v. Nebraska Mort. Co., 1914, 92 Kan. 272, 140 P. 855, 52 L.R.A.,N.S., 877, is against the great weight of authority in holding that a purchaser from the mortgagor subject to the mortgage debt may buy a tax title free of the mortgage and seems incorrect. Ownership of the redemption interest, not personal obligation to pay the mortgage debt, is the criterion of duty to pay taxes. And it is the failure of the duty to pay the taxes that prevents the founding of a title on the tax sale purchase.

4. Schenck v. Kelley, 1882, 88 Ind. 444; Dusenbery v. Bidwell, 1912, 86 Kan. 666, 121 P. 1098; Howze v. Dew, 1889, 90 Ala. 178, 7 So. 239, 24 Am.St.Rep. 783; Brown v. Simons, 1863, 44 N.H. 475; Hall v. Westcott, 1886, 15 R.I. 373, 5 A. 629. See also Moore v. Titman, 1867, 44 Ill. 367. Cf. Beckwith v. Seborn, 1888, 31 W.Va. 1, 5 S.E. 453; Ten Eyck v. Craig, 1875, 62 N.Y. 406, 422. See 1941, 140 A.L.R. 294, 318, for a collection of cases. A mortgagee in possession under an invalid foreclosure sale purchase has been held to be barred from acquiring a valid tax title as against the mortgagor. Nat. Surety Co. v. Walker, 1910, 148 Iowa 157, 125 N.W. 338, 38 L.R.A.,N.S., 333.

5. See 1941, 90 U.Pa.L.Rev. 90, 95.

a tax sale and cut off the rights of the mortgagor in the premises. They argue that the mortgagee had no duty to pay the taxes and stood in no fiduciary relation to the mortgagor. A denial of the privilege would let the mortgagor—who did have the duty to pay taxes—force the mortgagee still to hold only as a security claimant. This would allow the mortgagor to take advantage of his own default.[6] Further, the rule does not operate harshly against the mortgagor since, under tax statutes, he can redeem from the tax sale.[7] And, possibly most important, the incentive to the mortgagor and other mortgagees to pay taxes promptly and to purchase at the tax sale would be increased.[8] The clear weight of authority, however, will not permit the mortgagee thus to shake off the claim of the mortgagor.[9] When it comes

6. Jones v. Black, 1907, 18 Okl. 344, 88 P. 1052, 11 Ann.Cas. 753; Price v. Salisbury, 1914, 41 Okl. 416, 138 P. 1024, L.R.A.,1917D, 520; Williams v. Townsend, 1865, 31 N.Y. 411, 415, "A mortgage is a mere security for a debt; and there is no such relation of trust or confidence between the maker and holder of a mortgage as prevents the latter from acquiring title to its subject matter, either under his own or any other valid lien. The defendant [mortgagee] had no duty to perform to the plaintiff, or toward the mortgaged premises, that precluded her from buying at the tax sale; she was under no obligation to pay the taxes."; McLaughlin v. Acom, 1898, 58 Kan. 514, 50 P. 441, noted 1898, 11 Harv.L. Rev. 343; Reimer v. Newel, 1891, 47 Minn. 237, 49 N.W. 865. Cf. First Nat. Bank of Rapid City v. McCarthy, 1904, 18 S.D. 218, 100 N.W. 14; see Waterson v. Devoe, 1877, 18 Kan. 223; Beckwith v. Seborn, 1888, 31 W.Va. 1, 5 S.E. 453. See also 1941, 140 A.L.R. 294, 311.

7. 4 Cooley, Taxation, 4th ed. 1924, § 1565.

8. See Baird v. Fischer, 1928, 57 N.D. 167, 185, 220 N.W. 892, 899, Christianson, J., dissenting.

9. Koch v. Kiron State Bank, 1941, 230 Iowa 206, 297 N.W. 450, 140 A.L.R. 273; Hadlock v. Benjamin Drainage Dist., 1936, 89 Utah 94, 53 P.2d 1156, 106 A.L.R. 876, discussed, 1936, 46 Yale L.J. 334; Eck v. Swennenson, 1887, 73 Iowa 423, 35 N.W. 503, 5 Am.St.Rep. 690; Porter v. Corbin, 1900, 124 Mich. 201, 82 N.W. 818. See Shepard v. Vincent, 1905, 38 Wash. 493, 80 P. 777; Burchard v. Roberts, 1887, 70 Wis. 111, 35 N.W. 286, 5 Am.St.Rep. 148; note, 1936, 46 Yale L.J. 334. See also 1909, 11 Ann.Cas. 750; 1912, 38 L.R.A.,N.S., 333; L.R.A.,1917D, 522; 1941, 140 A.L.R. 294, 302. In Maxfield v. Willey, 1881, 46 Mich. 252, 9 N.W. 271, Cooley, J., permitted the mortgagor the option of treating the tax title acquired by the mortgagee as valid or not, on the

to the ability of a mortgagee to acquire a tax title which will cut off the rights of a prior mortgagee, although there is authority that he may,[10] most cases hold that a junior mortgagee cannot procure and assert a tax title against a senior mortgage where both mortgages are outstanding.[11] Several reasons have been advanced for denying to a mortgagee the ability to acquire a new and independent title to the mortgaged property good against the mortgagor and other mortgagees. Occasionally it is said that the mortgagee is like a trustee and therefore is debarred from founding a title on the tax sale in opposition to the mortgagor or other mortgagees.[12] But the mortgagee may buy in at even his own court foreclosure sale and, consequently, even if it were true that he is a trustee, which it is not,[13] it is difficult to see why purchase

at a tax sale would be in breach of any fiduciary obligation owed to the mortgagor, and, even more so, to other mortgagees. Sometimes the analogy of joint tenants is invoked.[14] But each joint tenant has a duty to pay the taxes and therefore as to them the general principle applies that one cannot profit by failing to do his duty. There is no duty on a mortgagee not in possession, in the absence of an express contract, running either to the mortgagor or to another mortgagee to pay the taxes and, therefore, that reason fails.[15] Still other courts stress the community of interest of the parties in preserving the estate by the payment of taxes, drawing the conclusion therefrom that it would be inequitable conduct to acquire and assert a tax title against the others, or that presumably it is paid for the common protection.[16] The last is probably contrary to fact; just why it is inequitable when there is neither a contractual duty or one arising out of their relationship to pay the taxes is not explained; and the common derivation of their interests in the land does not create a common interest but rather antagonistic interests, certainly as between two mortgagees. The courts may be disturbed by the possibility that one who had merely a lien upon the property might obtain a tax deed for a small sum and by it destroy the liens of other

---

principle that "neither party to a mortgage can, against the will of the other, buy at a tax sale and cut off the interest of the other."

10. Security Mortgage Co. v. Herron, 1927, 174 Ark. 729, 296 S.W. 363; see 1941, 140 A.L.R. 294, 329. Security Mortgage Co. v. Harrison, 1928, 176 Ark. 423, 3 S.W.2d 59.

11. Connecticut Mut. Life Ins. Co. v. Bulte, 1881, 45 Mich. 113, 7 N.W. 707; Chrisman v. Hough, 1898, 146 Mo. 102, 47 S.W. 941; Oregon Mortgage Co. v. Leavenworth Sec. Corp., 1938, 197 Wash. 436, 86 P. 2d 206, noted 1939, 14 Wash.L.Rev. 231; Baird v. Fischer, 1928, 57 N.D. 167, 220 N.W. 892, noted, 1929, 13 Minn.L.Rev. 623; 1928, 38 Yale L.J. 263; 1929, 29 Col.L.Rev. 93. See notes, 1939, 14 Wash.L. Rev. 231; 1897, 11 Harv.L.Rev. 343. See also 1909, 11 Ann.Cas. 759; L.R.A.1917D, 522; 1941, 140 A.L. R. 294, 322; 1941, 90 U. of Pa.L.Rev. 90, 96. That a prior mortgagee cannot cut off a subsequent mortgagee, Anson v. Anson, 1866, 20 Iowa 55, 89 Am.Dec. 514. The junior mortgagee obtains his position in this respect as holder of a security interest in the redemption right of the mortgagor. There is a difference of opinion as to whether the fact that the title had become absolute and irredeemable in the hands of a third person when the mortgagee acquires it alters the result. Safe Deposit and Trust Co. v. Wickhem, 1896, 9 S.D. 341, 69 N.W. 14, 62 Am.St.Rep. 873, rehearing denied 9 S.Dak. 515, 70 N.W. 654. Contra: Chrisman v. Hough, 1898, 146 Mo. 102, 47 S.W. 941.

12. See, e. g., Finlayson v. Peterson, 1902, 11 N.D. 45, 89 N.W. 855; Ten Eyck v. Craig, 1875, 62 N.Y. 406, 422, mortgagee in possession: "A mortgagee is often called a trustee, and in a very limited sense this character may be attributed to him."

13. See Cholmondeley v. Clinton, 1820, 2 Jac. & W. 1, 183; Ten Eyck v. Craig, supra note 12, at 419 et

seq. See also supra, § 161. This is most clearly true as between successive mortgagees.

14. E. g. Connecticut Mut. Life Ins. Co. v. Bulte, 1881, 45 Mich. 113, 122, 7 N.W. 707, 710, "It is as just and as politic here as it is in the case of tenants in common, to hold that the purchase is only a payment of the tax."

15. "It certainly cannot be said that the second mortgagee owes any duty to the first mortgagee to protect his lien against tax sale. Neither, on the other hand, does the first mortgagee owe any such duty to the second mortgagee, or to the owner. To the state each one of the three may be said to owe the duty to pay the taxes; and the state will sell the interest of all if none of the three shall pay." Connecticut Mut. Life Ins. Co. v. Bulte, 1881, 45 Mich. 113, 121, 7 N.W. 707, 710.

16. Fair v. Brown, 1875, 40 Iowa 209; Woodbury v. Swan, 1879, 59 N.H. 22; Hall v. Westcott, 1886, 15 R.I. 373, 5 A. 629.

mortgagees and the mortgagor; if the payment were viewed as a redemption, "the mortgagee, acquiring a prior lien on the property to the amount expended in that redemption would be placed in a position no worse than that which he occupied prior to the delinquency, while at the same time the other lienors would be materially benefitted." [17] Another suggestion is expressed legalistically by arguing that the rule preventing tax title purchase by one who owes a duty to another person to pay them should be broadened out to include all who owe a duty to the public to pay taxes. Such a duty is then found in the fact that the mortgagee, if he does not pay them, will lose his entire interest in the property.[18] Probably the same idea, but more broadly based, is expressed by saying that it is against public policy to allow the mortgagee to purchase at the tax sale and gain an advantage by so doing in that it would encourage him to fail to take advantage of his privilege to pay taxes. It is to the interest of the state that taxes be paid promptly, and since the mortgagee is fully protected by his privilege of paying when they are due, he should not be encouraged to fail to take advantage of that privilege.[19] But this is an argument that cuts both ways [20] and the incentive in any event is speculative and dubious.

17.   1936, 46 Yale L.J. 334, 338.

18.   1936, 46 Yale L.J. 334, 337. See quotation from Connecticut Mut. Life Ins. Co. v. Bulte, 1881, 45 Mich. 113, 7 N.W. 707, supra note 15. But judgment creditors, who also have a security interest in the property, are not subject to the rule. Wilson v. Jamison, 1886, 36 Minn. 59, 29 N.W. 887, 1 Am.St. Rep. 635. "The recognition of a disability to purchase an unencumbered tax title, an issue of policy and not of legal rules, depends on a balancing of social interests that are far from clear; certainly there is no basis for a blanket disqualification of all such lienors." 1936, 46 Yale L.J. 334, 337.

19.   See 3 Tiffany, Real Prop., § 616; Baird v. Fischer, 1928, 57 N.D. 167, 185, 220 N.W. 892, 899, Christianson, J., dissenting.

20.   See supra, text, where the possibility that one mortgagee might acquire a clear tax title is cited as an incentive to other mortgagees and the mortgagor to see to it that taxes are paid.

TAX PAYMENT BY SUBSEQUENT MORT-GAGEE—EFFECT ON PRIOR MORTGAGEE

179.   **Authorities are divided whether a junior mortgagee who pays off the paramount tax lien of the taxing authority is subrogated to that lien as against a prior mortgagee.**

If a second mortgagee pays off the paramount tax lien of the taxing authority, it is quite clear that he can add that amount to his own mortgage debt or be subrogated to the lien of the taxing power as against the mortgagor.[21] Whether he can be subrogated to that paramount lien as against a prior mortgagee is a more difficult question. In Laventall v. Pomerantz,[22] the first mortgage contained a clause accelerating the right to foreclosure on nonpayment of taxes. The New York Court of Appeals held that payment of the taxes by a holder of a subordinate mortgage would give him no right to be subrogated to the priority of the tax lien over the first mortgage. There are, however, cases giving subrogation to the second mortgagee, some of them even where there is an acceleration clause permitting foreclosure on default by the mortgagor in paying taxes, although most of them do not mention whether or not the mortgagor had such a right.[23] In these latter cases there may have been no such right; or it is possible that there was one but it had been so neglected that it could not be and was not seriously urged.[24] In a few jurisdictions the

21.   See supra, § 173.

22.   1933, 263 N.Y. 110, 188 N.E. 271, discussed in notes, 1934, 19 Cornell L.Q. 487; 1934, 11 N.Y.Univ. L.Q.Rev. 655; 1934, 1 U. of Chi.L.Rev. 813; 1934, 29 Ill.L.Rev. 123; 1934, 20 Va.L.Rev. 914. See also notes, 1933, 46 Harv.L.Rev. 1036; 1933, 42 Yale L.J. 971; 1937, 17 Tex.L.Rev. 352.

23.   Marks v. Baum Bldg. Co., 1918, 73 Okl. 264, 175 P. 818, acceleration clause; Noeker v. Howry, 1899, 119 Mich. 626, 78 N.W. 669, "usual tax clause"; Ringo v. Woodruff, 1884, 43 Ark. 469; Fiacre v. Chapman, 1880, 32 N.J.Eq. 463. For collections of cases holding both ways, see 1933, 84 A.L.R. 1366, 1393; 1939, 123 A.L.R. 1248, 1261.

24.   See 1934, 29 Ill.L.Rev. 123.

taxpaying junior encumbrancer is given a prior lien by statute.[25]

Where there is an acceleration clause in the first mortgage allowing foreclosure on non-payment of taxes by the mortgagee, the strongest argument against giving subrogation to the paramount lien for taxes as against the first mortgagee is that such payment destroys a most valuable right of the first mortgagee.[26] The right to foreclose on tax default is a valuable one because it is an effective means of forcing the mortgagor to pay the taxes and, also, because it provides a remedy at the first signs of financial irresponsibility of the mortgagor.[27] Consequently a junior mortgagee who destroys that recourse to the detriment of the earlier mortgagee should have no claim to be elevated to priority over the first mortgagee but should be remitted to adding the amount paid to his own mortgage debt,[28] at least in the absence of unreasonable refusal or delay of the prior mortgagee to act for the protection of his own interest.[29] But other reasons have been advanced. It is said that the first mortgagee is not unjustly enriched because he merely got a benefit to which he was entitled, and to grant subrogation would deprive him of a part of the security upon which he based his original loan.[30] The tax lien is the obligation of the mortgagor and if paid by someone else it should not detract from the mortgagee's security any more than if paid by the mortgagor himself.[31] Furthermore, the payment should be considered voluntary because it is made for the purpose of keeping the senior mortgagee from foreclosing, not for the purpose of relieving the estate of any tax liens,[32] and the *quid pro quo* he received was the extinguishment of the prior mortgagee's power to foreclose.[33] Also, where the mortgagor is liable, subrogation cannot be given as against another mortgagee because subrogation cannot be invoked against a third party not liable for the indebtedness discharged.[34] And in any event,

No rule of law or dictate of justice, equity, or good conscience would justify a court of equity in regarding as still existent the lien of the taxes in priority to the plaintiffs' mortgage. The price that the defendants expected and received for their payment was the extinguishment of the plaintiffs' right to foreclose for the owner's default in paying the taxes. They may not repudiate the legal effect of their act after they have received the price." Laventall v. Pomerantz, 1933, 263 N.Y. 110, 115, 88 N.E. 271, 273.

25. Ky.Rev.Stat. 134.080; La.Rev.Stat.—Civ.Code art. 2161; see Timken v. Wisner Estates, 1923, 153 La. 262, 95 So. 711.

26. Laventall v. Pomerantz, supra note 22.

27. See 1934, 29 Ill. L.Rev. 123.

28. Sidenberg v. Ely, 1882, 90 N.Y. 257, 43 Am.Rep. 163, 11 Abb.N.C. 354.

29. "The right to foreclose upon default in payment of taxes was intended as a means to compel the payment of such taxes, or to provide a remedy, in case of nonpayment, for consequent diminution in the plaintiffs' security. When the defendants paid the taxes, they met an obligation which the owner owed both to the prior mortgagees and to the city. Because the obligation had been met, there was no longer room for invoking the plaintiffs' stipulated remedy against default. The defendants, having knowingly produced that result, may not thereafter claim that equity should still regard the lien of the taxes as existent and the owners' obligation towards the prior mortgage still unperformed. The payment of taxes must be given effect according to the stipulations of the mortgages, and the intentions of the parties. It discharged the lien of the city and discharged at the same time the obligation of the owner towards the prior mortgage. The defendants are entitled to add the amount of the payment to their mortgage debt. They are not entitled to any relief at the expense of the prior mortgagee.

30. See 1932, 42 Yale L.J. 972.

31. 1933, 20 Va.L.Rev. 914.

32. Pearmain v. Massachusetts Hospital Life Ins. Co., 1910, 206 Mass. 377, 92 N.E. 497; Fiacre v. Chapman, 1880, 32 N.J.Eq. 463, contra. For a brief discussion of the subrogation of a volunteer, see 1941, 40 Mich.L.Rev. 133. See also Osborne, Cas. Prop.Security, 523 n. 6, 529 n. 8.

33. Laventall v. Pomerantz, supra n. 22.

34. Lawyers' Title & Guaranty Co. v. Claren, 1932, 237 App.Div. 188, 260 N.Y.S. 847. But see 1933, 46 Harv.L.Rev. 1036; 1934, 1 U.Chi.L.Rev. 813, 814; 1932, 42 Yale L.J. 972.

Under the Georgia statute delinquent taxes become a prior lien on all of the taxpayer's real estate. M owned three separate parcels of real estate, each one mortgaged to a different mortgage. M became insolvent and was unable to pay the taxes upon any of his property, whereupon the county levied execution on one of the three parcels for the taxes due on all three and sold it for the aggregate sum

a subordinate mortgagee stands in the mortgagor's shoes and gets no better rights than does the mortgagor his rights being thus limited by reason of his position as mortgagee of the redemption interest. Since it was the mortgagor's duty, owed to all mortgagees, to pay the taxes, although he can add the tax to his claim against the mortgagor, he has no more power to be subrogated to a lien prior to that of the senior mortgagee than would his mortgagor.[35] Moreover, payment of the taxes legally destroys the lien so that there is nothing to which the paying mortgagee can be subrogated.[36] And to grant subrogation would encroach upon the privileges of sovereignty by according to a private individual the privilege of the taxing body's methods of collection.[37]

The chief arguments advanced in favor of permitting subrogation, either made affirmatively or in rebuttal of arguments for the opposite result, are that it would encourage payment of taxes,[38] a socially desirable result;[39] prevent the conferring of an unjust enrichment on the prior mortgagee because the second mortgagee, by discharging the tax lien has to that extent increased the proceeds available to the prior mortgagee; the first mortgagee is not injured because other-

wise he would be subordinate to the lien of the taxing authority[40]; and not only is the prior mortgagee not injured but he is benefited positively by the prevention of accrual of tax penalties and a sale of the land for taxes[41] and this benefit offsets the value to the prior mortgagee of the right to foreclose under an acceleration clause.[42] Further, there is some doubt whether payment by anyone other than the mortgagor would prevent the acceleration clause from becoming operative.[43] Additionally it is pointed out that subrogation to the lien of the taxing power can be *pro tanto* for the purpose of priority only and need not include granting the states methods of collection which might be considered a delegation to a private individual of functions reserved to the public government.[44] The absence of personal liability of the prior mortgagee is no bar for the subrogation is to the lien, and not to a right *in personam* against a third party; and further, it is arguable that there is a[45] duty on all mortgagees to pay taxes and the subsequent one therefore is performing that duty.[46] Although the tax lien may be destroyed legally by payment, it is a well settled doctrine that equity can preserve or recreate legal rights that have ceased to exist where it is necessary to prevent unfairness.[47] And finally, the motive of the junior encumbranc-

---

of the taxes. The mortgagee who had thus lost his security recovered in personam judgments against the other two mortgagees for contribution of proportionate shares of the tax liens discharged. The appellate court reversed the decrees on the ground that there was "no joint or common liability as between [the plaintiff] and the other creditors, to be discharged by him in behalf of all." Snyder v. Elkan, 1938, 187 Ga. 164, 199 S.E. 891, discussed in note, 1939, 48 Yale L.J. 1293.

35. Glenn, Mortgages, § 39.2.

36. 1934, 11 N.Y.Univ.L.Q.Rev. 655, 656.

37. Sperry v. Butler, 1903, 75 Conn. 369, 53 A. 899.

38. But it should not go unnoticed that one of the purposes of an acceleration clause is to compel the mortgagor to pay taxes, and encouragement of other mortgagee to pay lessens the pressure on the mortgagor.

39. See 1933, 46 Harv.L.Rev. 1037; 1934, 11 N.Y. Univ.L.Q.Rev. 655; 1934, 19 Cornell L.Q. 487. See also preceding section.

40. See 1932, 46 Harv.L.Rev. 1037; 1934, 19 Cornell L.Q. 487.

41. 1934, 11 N.Y.Univ.L.Q.Rev. 655.

42. See Noeker v. Howry, 1899, 119 Mich. 626, 78 N. W. 669; Fiacre v. Chapman, 1880, 32 N.J.Eq. 463; 1934, 1 U.Chi.L.Rev. 813, 814; 1934, 29 Ill.L.Rev. 123.

43. See 1932, 46 Harv.L.Rev. 1037; 1934, 1 U.Chi. L.Rev. 813, 814.

44. 1932, 42 Yale L.J. 971, 972; 1934, 1 U.Chi.L.Rev. 813, 814.

45. 1932, 42 Yale L.J. 972; 1934, 19 Cornell L.Q. 487.

46. See Connecticut Mut. Life Ins. Co. v. Bulte, 1881, 45 Mich. 113, 7 N.W. 707; 1936, 46 Yale L.J. 334, 337.

47. Title Guaranty & Trust Co. v. Haven, 1909, 196 N.Y. 487, 89 N.E. 1082, 25 L.R.A.,N.S., 1308, 17 Ann.Cas. 1131. See 1934, 11 N.Y.Univ.L.Q.Rev. 655; 1932, 42 Yale L.J. 971, 972.

er in paying to avoid foreclosure by the first mortgagee rather than of the tax lien ought not to be the test for granting subrogation; even if the primary purpose were to avoid such foreclosure, that is not sufficient cause for conferring so great a benefit on the prior mortgagee at the expense of the subordinate one.[48]

48. See 1932, 46 Harv.L.Rev. 1037; 11 N.Y.Univ.L. Q.Rev. 655.

CHAPTER 7

PRIORITIES

INTRODUCTION

180. A brief and elementary statement of the general rules of priority of rights in property, legal and equitable, is essential to an understanding of the problems of priorities in the law of mortgages.

A statement of the general rules governing priority of rights in real property, apart from statutory modifications, is essential to an understanding of the problems of priorities in the law of mortgages. That statement, however, will be brief and elementary, for the same general rules apply to other than mortgage transactions and it is beyond the possible or proper scope of this work either to examine these rules in any great detail or to scrutinize them critically. Further, since they are so fundamental and so well known, citation of much authority in support of them seems superfluous. What authorities are cited will be chiefly those concerned with mortgage applications of the general doctrines. Since, however, in some instances the mortgage problem involved presents unique features, as for example in the case of tacking, or is of some especial importance, a more intensive treatment will be made of them in their proper place.

What has just been said about priorities apart from statutes, applies also to the subject of priorities as affected by statute. No attempt will be made there to discuss the great variety of detailed variations in the different statutes in all the states. A classification of the various types of statutes, the theories they embody, and their general structure and typical provisions with their interpretations is, however, necessary to any adequate picture of the law of priorities as to mortgages in America today. Further, certain problems concerning mortgages present unique aspects under the recording acts and they will be accorded a more detailed consideration. The difference in treatment between matters which are simply application in a mortgage case of principles and rules that apply generally and those which are of first importance, or present difficulties peculiar to mortgage law are sufficiently differentiated by the method of presentation as to need no additional labeling.

A. ASIDE FROM STATUTES

GENERAL RULE

181. In both title and lien states a prior legal mortgage prevails over a subsequent legal mortgage. A fortiori it prevails over a subsequent equitable mortgage.

The elementary proposition has been stated frequently that as between successive transfers of legal interests in the same tract of land the one first in time prevails. Notice or lack of notice and even the absence of a valuable consideration in the earlier conveyance are immaterial. The reason advanced for the rule is that O, having transferred to A all or part of his legal property interest, can transfer only what he has left to B. If he has previously transferred his entire estate he, of course, has nothing to give a later grantee. This rationale, obviously, applies [1]

---

1. See Pomeroy, Eq.Juris., 4th Ed., §§ 679, 735; Aigler, Operation of the Recording Acts, 1924, 22 Mich.L.Rev. 405. Under statutes declaring conveyances made for the purpose of defrauding subsequent purchasers void (e. g., 27 Eliz. c. 4), a conveyance made without valuable consideration had been held voidable.

See Storke and Sears, The Perennial Problem of Security; Priority and Recordation, 1952, 24 Rocky Mt.L.Rev. 180.

See also, examining especially New Jersey law, Cunningham and Tischler, Equitable Real Estate Mort-

as between first and second mortgages in title states.[2] The first mortgagee got the legal title and the second mortgagee could receive from the mortgagor only an interest in the equitable right of redemption, that being the only disposable interest left in him.[3] Does it, however, apply to mortgages in lien theory states in which the legal title remains in the mortgagor and each successive mortgagee acquires as security a legal lien? Since, in the United States, priority is largely determined by recording acts, it is difficult to find precise authority. In Neslin v. Wells, the court said: "Under this provision [Utah statute establishing the lien theory] all mortgages, without respect to their relative dates, are legal liens, and priority cannot attach to the earlier in date by reason of the superior dignity of the estate conveyed. The rule, therefore, that gives preference to the legal title has no application, and the priority among them must be determined by purely equitable considerations."[4] In other words, the rule applicable to successive equitable mortgages should be used. The truth of this last statement may be tested by two cases in lien theory states in which, for one reason or another, the solution is not affected by the recording acts.

1. O gives a legal mortgage on Blackacre to E, and later conveys the full legal title to P, a purchaser for valuable consideration without notice of the prior mortgage to E.

2. O gives an equitable mortgage on Blackacre to E–1, and later gives a legal mortgage to E–2 who made the loan and took the mortgage without knowledge of the prior equitable mortgage to E–1.

The authorities are not numerous,[5] but they indicate that E wins in the first case[6] and E–2 in the second.[7] Although in both cases O is regarded as retaining the legal ownership of the property, nevertheless, in the first case he has invested E with a legal interest in the land that cannot be affected by the application of the doctrine of bona fide purchaser for value without notice; and in the second case the legal mortgage to E–2 gives him a sufficient legal interest in the property for him to be able to assert the same doctrine in his favor so as to cut off the prior equitable interest in E–1. In both cases, if the lien mortgage were treated as creating only an equitable interest in the mortgagee opposite results would have been reached: P would have won in the first, while E–1 would have prevailed in the second.

---

gages, II. Priority of Equitable Mortgages, 1963, 17 Rutgers L.Rev. 679, 688–694.

2. "Ordinarily the priority between incumbrances is determined by their quality, as each successive conveyance passes only what title remains after satisfying those which precede it. The first mortgage conveys the legal estate; the second, merely an equity of redemption; and as equity follows the law, and the owner of the legal title, by means of it, has a legal right, after condition broken, to the possession and a remedy at law for acquiring it, he is entitled to possession." Neslin v. Wells, F. & Co., 1881, 104 U.S. 428, 440, 26 L.Ed. 802.

3. This accounts, of course, for the rule that all mortgages subsequent to the first are equitable and rank among themselves according to the rules governing successively created equitable interests.

4. Neslin v. Wells, F. & Co., 1881, 104 U.S. 428, 440, 26 L.Ed. 802.

5. For a thorough discussion and collection of authorities supporting the conclusion that successive mortgages in lien jurisdictions create legal interest in the property which rank *inter sese* in the order in which they are created, see Durfee, The Lien Theory of the Mortgage—Two Crucial Problems, 1913, 11 Mich.L.Rev. 495.

6. Fallass v. Pierce, 1872, 30 Wis. 443, prior unrecorded mortgage in lien state prevails over subsequent bona fide purchaser for value without notice who did not record. Ely v. Scofield, N.Y.1861, 35 Barb. 330, accord.

7. A subsequent mortgagee in a lien state taking in good faith, for value and without notice, will prevail over prior equitable interests without the aid of recording acts: Parker v. Barnesville Sav. Bank, 1899, 107 Ga. 650, 34 S.E. 365; Fisk v. Potter, 1864, 41 N.Y. (2 Keyes) 64; Austin v. Pulschen, 1896, 112 Cal. 528, 44 P. 788; Gaar v. Milliken, 1879, 68 Ind. 208; Parsons v. Crocker, 1905, 128 Iowa 641, 105 N.W. 162; Yancey v. Blackmore, 1897, 95 Va. 263, 28 S.E. 336; Murphy's Hotel Co. v. Benet, 1916, 119 Va. 157, 159, 89 S.E. 104, second deed of trust; Bader v. Johnson, 1914, 78 Wash. 350, 139 P. 32.

If a prior legal mortgage prevails over a subsequent legal mortgage, a fortiori it prevails over a subsequent equitable mortgage.[8]

EARLIER EQUITABLE MORTGAGE

182. Where the earlier mortgage is equitable its priority over subsequent mortgages depends upon two rules:

1. As between persons whose equities are otherwise equal, the one whose equity is prior in time shall prevail.

2. As between persons whose equities are equal except as to priority in time, the one having the legal right shall prevail.

Priorities between an equitable mortgage followed by another equitable mortgage or by a later legal mortgage are governed by two general rules. One is that as between persons having equitable interests in the same property, otherwise equal, the one whose interest is prior in time shall prevail.[9] The other is that as between persons whose equitable interests in the same property are equal except as to priority in time, the one who has the legal right to the property shall prevail.[10]

The first of these rules has been disparaged as largely one of convenience,[11] as being "the ground of preference last resorted to." [12] Also, it has been urged against it that, in spite of a surface appearance of ease and certainty in application, there are frequently cases in which there is difficulty in determining which equity is prior in time, and divergent results are reached according to whether the equity is regarded as purely *in personam* or *in rem*.[13] On the other hand, it has been defended as "a principle founded on solid reason. The older title cannot, in the nature of things, be aware of the later: the converse is by no means true. The longer a man has enjoyed a right, either in possession or anticipation, the keener will be his suffering if it is taken away." [14] There is a further ground suggested for the rule. It is said that a court of equity will not assist a claimant to enforce an equitable right to property if in so assisting him the court would have to compel the defendant to commit a breach of a specifically enforceable duty.[15]

In the case where the second rule applies the subsequent claimant is allowed to keep what he has already acquired for value and without notice of the prior claim. In follow-

---

8. For the general rules as to priorities in land in England in the three situations, (a) legal followed by equitable, (b) equitable followed by equitable, (c) equitable followed by legal, see Hanbury, Modern Equity, 4th ed., 416–428. For the provisions and effects of the legislation of 1925 on priorities, see idem, 434–444.

See Storke and Sears, The Perennial Problem of Security, Priority and Recordation, 1952, 24 Colo.L. Rev. 180, 181–183.

See also IV Am.L.Prop. §§ 17.1–17.3.

9. Rice v. Rice, 1853, 2 Drew. 73, 77, per Sir R. T. Kindersley, V.-C.

"As between successive equitable mortgages, although priority will ordinarily be determined by the rule 'first in time, first in right,' it seems that an equitable mortgagee for value and without notice may prevail over an earlier equitable mortgagee who did not give value [in New Jersey]." Cunningham and Tischler, Equitable Real Estate Mortgages, 1963, 17 Rutgers L.Rev. 679, 688. See also Storke and Sears, The Perennial Problem of Security, Priority and Recordation, 1952, 24 Colo.L.Rev. 180, 182.

10. For a criticism of both rules and the suggestion "that as between the holder of an equity and a subsequent purchaser for value, the general rule should be that neither priority in time nor the fact that the purchaser has happened to receive, or has

failed to receive, the legal title shall be a determining factor, and that whenever, in consequence, the equity judge shall find himself unable to give preference to either of the parties, he should divide the loss between them." See Costigan, The Theory of Chancery in Protecting Against the Cestui Que Trust One Who Purchases from a Trustee for Value and Without Notice, 1923, 12 Cal.L.Rev. 356.

On the doctrine of bona fide purchase prevailing over a prior equitable claimant, see also Cunningham and Tischler, op. cit. supra note 1, 684.

See also Storke and Sears, op. cit. supra note 9.

11. Costigan, op. cit. supra note 10, 364.

12. Rice v. Rice, 1854, 2 Drew. 73, 78. Also Ross, J., in In the Matter of etc. Bobbett, [1904] 1 Ir.Rep. 461, 472, "But priority in point of time is of no great weight as against other equities."

13. See Costigan, op. cit. supra note 10, for a number of instances of this sort.

14. Jenks, The Legal Estate, 1908, 24 Law Q.Rev. 147, 155.

15. See Scott, Trusts, § 286.

ing the rule the court refuses to upset a completed breach of duty. This must be distinguished from the situation of two successive equitable interests. There the prior claimant has only an executory claim to get the legal interest at the time he receives notice of the prior claim. Hence, if the court did not apply the first rule it would compel the transferor to complete a breach of duty to the prior transferee by completing the transfer to the later claimant. The former falls within the basic policy favoring commercial transactions by protecting persons who have bought property in good faith, a matter which will be elaborated in a moment in connection with the *bona fide* purchase of an equitable interest in property. But since this means sacrificing the prior equitable interest of another claimant, the favoritism is extended only to a completed transaction, to one in which the purchaser has paid the price and received title to the property before he gets notice of the prior equity. One is encouraged to enter into dealings to the extent that he can be sure of keeping what he has actually acquired for value before notice; but not to the extent of being aided to get what he has only an equitable right to get when that right is no better than a similar one held by a prior claimant of which he receives notice before getting in title.[16]

In the law of mortgages, this first rule governed priorities between second and later mortgages under the common law title theory of mortgages. It also has importance where there is no legal mortgage at all, but only an equitable mortgage preceded or followed by either another equitable mortgage or some other sort of equitable interest. However, in America today, the prevalence of the lien theory, under which all mortgages are legal, and the universality of the recording systems have minimized its importance in the field of mortgage law.

BONA FIDE PURCHASER OF EQUITABLE INTEREST

183. A bona fide purchaser of an equitable interest will not prevail over a prior equitable right to it.

In the last section we spoke of the policy of protecting good faith buyers. This policy raises a question of considerable significance in connection with the rule that as between equal equities the earlier prevails. The question has a significance in the field of legal theory concerning the nature of an equitable interest that transcends its practical importance. It raises the problem whether, when the subject matter against which the equity runs is itself an equitable interest, the rule that the prior equitable claim to it will prevail must be qualified by holding that a *bona fide* purchaser for value and without notice of the equitable interest will take it discharged of the prior equitable claim to it in precisely the same way that the *bona fide* purchaser for value of a legal title takes it free of equities in it which are prior in time to that of the purchaser. In such a case, just as where the legal title is involved, the transaction is complete. The buyer has got in the actual subject matter of his bargain before notice of the prior claim and after paying value. Why therefore should he not be allowed to keep it?

It was urged that he should be by one of the great legal scholars, Ames.[17] His argu-

---

16. In criticism of this line of demarcation it may be pointed out that, "Whether, at the time the misconduct of the trustee or other wrongdoer is discovered, the purchaser has or has not obtained the legal title is purely a matter of chance, and, despite their general sporting dispositions, the English dislike to have a decision turn on anything so fortuitous where neither party knowingly took a chance." Costigan, Protecting Purchasers for Value, 1923, 12 Cal.L.Rev. 356, 363.

17. Ames, Purchase for Value Without Notice, Lectures on Legal History, 253, 261, "the rule [that, as between adverse equitable claimants, he who is prior in time is stronger in law] requires, at least in point of principle, an important qualification, namely, that the equities of the adverse claimant must be immediate equities against the same person. * * * But the rule as to conflicting equities, it is conceived, may be expressed more comprehensively. Just as an honest purchaser of a legal title from one who holds it subject to an equity acquires the legal title discharged of the equity, so

ment was concerned with and based upon an *in personam* view of the nature of an equitable right to property and much of the discussion of the rationale of the doctrine of *bona fide* purchase in general has been concerned with the controversy over whether equitable rights are purely *in personam, in rem,* or both.[18] While the last view seems correct on this technical point, later discussions of the doctrine of *bona fide* purchase give a more enlightening and satisfying explanation of it. This later explanation regards it as a rule based upon the social policy of encouraging transactions in, and the free circulation of, certain classes of property in which there is particular business utility in "preventing property from stagnating." As previously stated, the rule accomplishes this result by "protecting the *bona fide* purchaser even at the expense of the property rights of the previous owner." Not only is the rule operative in equity but also at law, e. g., in the doctrine of sale in market overt, in the rule applicable to the sale of money and negotiable instruments, in the law which prefers a second honest purchaser of goods left in the possession of the seller by a prior purchaser, as well as many statutory extensions of the same principle expressed in recording acts, Factors' Acts, and legislation increasing the application of the doctrine of negotiability to bills of lading, warehouse receipts, and stock certificates.

The special classes of property in which the social interest in promoting trade and commerce outweighs the interest in the security of existing acquisitions tends to increase "as a nation becomes more industrial and commercial in its economy, but they are

as yet exceptional." If a man has completely acquired the legal title to the property, the policy justifies the rule that it will cut off purely equitable claims to it which are prior in time, provided of course, he qualifies as a *bona fide* purchaser. However, equitable interests in property "are at present not regarded as of the special sort as to which the encouragement of free exchange is of prime social importance."[19] At least that is the way the authorities stand today. "Only an occasional case can be regarded as in any way supporting Professor Ames, if indeed any case can, and there are well reasoned cases against him."[20] It would seem that

19. The argument and the quotations in the text are from Huston, Enforcement of Decrees in Equity, 127–131. See Scott, Trusts, § 285, "The real question is whether equitable interests, like legal interests, are not such usual subjects of commerce that commercial transactions with respect to them deserve protection." See also Costigan, Protecting Purchasers for Value, 356, 361.

20. Costigan, Protecting Purchasers for Value, note 18, supra, 356, 369.

"* * * every equitable title is incomplete on its face. It is, in truth, nothing more than a title to go into chancery, to have the legal estate conveyed; and therefore, every purchaser of a mere equity takes it subject to every clog that may lie on it, whether he has had notice of it or not." Chew v. Barnet, Pa.1824, 11 Serg. & R. 389, 392. See also Webb, Record of Title, § 203.

See, however, Restatement, Second, Trusts § 285; Scott, Trusts, § 285, "The tendency of the law has been more and more to protect persons who in good faith enter into business transactions rather than those who simply seek to retain what they already have. If it is a sound policy, and not a mere matter of technique, which underlies the protection given to purchasers of trust property who pay value and have no notice that the trustee is committing a breach of trust, it would seem that the same protection should be given to purchasers of equitable interests."; Chafee and Re, Cases on Equity, 5th Ed., 327, 328. For a collection of cases, see Ann.Cas. 1918C, 462. For other discussions of Ames' suggestion and the doctrine of bona fide purchase generally, see Huston, Enforcement of Decrees in Equity, 144, 116 et seq.; Kenneson, Purchase for Value Without Notice, 1914, 23 Yale L.J. 193, 205; note, 1911, 24 Harv.L.Rev. 490; Maitland, Equity, Rev. Ed. by Brunyate, 126; Ballantine, Purchaser for Value and Estoppel, 1922, 6 Minn.L.Rev. 87; Jenks, The Legal Estate, 1908, 24 Law Q.Rev. 147; Willoughby, The Legal Estate, Ch. II; Pomeroy, Equity Juris., 5th ed., §§ 737 et seq.; Sugden, Vendors & Purchasers, 14th ed., 791, 798; 1912, 12 Col.L.Rev. 156, 158; 1925, 39 Harv.L.Rev. 271, 272.

also the purchaser of an equitable title from one who holds it subject to an equity takes the equitable title discharged of the equity. In all other cases the rule of priority governs, unless modified by the principle of estoppel."

See also Cunningham and Tischler, Equitable Real Estate Mortgages, 1963, 17 Rutgers L.Rev. 679, 686.

18. See, e. g., Costigan, Protecting Purchasers for Value, 1923, 12 Cal.L.Rev. 356, 371 et seq.; Scott, Trusts, § 285.

under the common law title theory of mortgages the equitable right of redemption left in the mortgagor after giving the first mortgage[21] should be regarded as one equitable property interest which is such a usual subject of commerce that a completed sale of it should be protected in the same way as the sale of a legal interest.[22] Indeed there was English authority for this view[23] but it was overruled.[24] In the United States, however, the doctrine of the overruling case is of dubious acceptance and our recording system effectively does away with it.[25]

Going beyond Ames' view that a completed transfer of an equitable interest in land for value, *bona fide* and without notice of a prior equity in the interest should take free of it is Valley State Bank v. Dean.[26] In this case, S was the owner of the entire beneficial interest in certain land by reason of a purchase money resulting trust. S borrowed money from P, a bank, and created an equitable lien on the beneficial interest to secure it. S then contracted to sell the same interest to B who paid value without notice of the bank's prior equitable lien. Holding that B acquired an equitable right, which he could enforce by a suit for specific performance, the court decided that P could not enforce its equitable lien as against B. It granted specific performance of B's contract right to have a conveyance from S and decreed that title should be quieted in him.

Professor Storke in an article[27] discussed the problem raised in Valley State Bank v.

21. See §§ 6, 31, supra.

22. Scott, Trusts, § 285.

23. Penny v. Watts, 1848, 2 DeG. & Sm. 501; Lane v. Jackson, 1855, 20 Beav. 535.

24. Cave v. Cave, 1880, 15 Ch.D. 535.

25. Scott, Trusts, § 285. See Glenn, Mortgages, § 32, n. 2, and § 324.1; Restatement, Second, Trusts § 285. See also § 229, infra.

26. Supreme Court of Colorado, 1935, 97 Colo. 151, 47 P.2d 924.

27. Storke, Priority Between Equitable Interests, 1935, 8 Rocky Mt.L.Rev. 1.

Dean. After quoting from Pomeroy the orthodox rule that "where the equities of two or more conflicting claimants to the same subject matter, are equal in all respects, the one which is prior in point of time shall prevail" Professor Storke considers Pomeroy's proposition "that the junior claimant may be preferred when his equity is superior." He notes that "most of the cases which are cited by Pomeroy are those in which the preference is given to the junior claimant results from fraud, estoppel, or negligence operating against the senior claimant. That writer [Pomeroy], however, thinks that some equities have an intrinsic superiority over others regardless of such facts."

Professor Storke then suggests, "Why not accept the idea that equities are rarely equal, and that a more careful fact-finding process and a closer legal analysis will almost always disclose a basis for preferring one to the other regardless of the order of time. He then refers to an earlier analysis he had made of the *Dean Case* as an example of the technique courts might follow in discriminating between equities. In that analysis "Attention was paid to the factor of possession and the extent of compliance with normal business practice. It was also suggested that a contract vendee should usually prevail over the holder of an irregular form of security. The analysis could be carried further by considering what weight should be given to the fact that the transactions between the Deans were designed to evade the claims of Sam Dean's creditors. We might also inquire whether the bank, as a business institution, should not be held to a higher degree of compliance with business standards than could be expected of two farmers engaged in a family transaction."

He concludes, "It may well be that this decision, erroneous as it is from the standpoint of orthodox legal theory, is merely one more step in the long process by which courts of equity have blurred the once sharply drawn distinction between executory contract and conveyance, and have conferred upon the holder of a mere equity more and more of the rights of actual ownership. Even more deeply, it shows the tendency of a commercial age to prefer the social interest in the security of transactions to the interest in the security of ownership."

In criticism of Professor Storke's thesis it may be suggested that one of the most important objectives in the field of real property is certainty of title. To employ the technique advocated by him might result in better justice between the individual parties in each case, but it does so at the expense of stability of property rights. It would promote litigation because decisions would rest on unpredictable findings on questions and matters on which there is no adequate factual research or unanimity of opinion. And thus it would impair the very thing that it purports, in part, to promote, i. e, mobility of property and freer transferability of it. Since even Ames' more mechanical proposal has found only small minority acceptance, it seems unlikely that courts will go beyond it.

"MERE EQUITY" AND EQUITABLE ESTATE

184. No distinction is or should be drawn in respect to priorities between an equitable interest and a "mere equity" in property.

One other point in connection with the preceding problem should be mentioned. There is some authority, going back to a distinction first laid down by Lord Westbury in Phillips v. Phillips,[28] that where the prior claimant has a mere "equity"[29] while the later one has an "equitable estate" the subsequent equitable claimant prevails. The distinction has

been criticized as one "between convertible terms. Every equity attaching to property is an equitable estate. The equity of a defrauded vendor is no less an equitable estate than the interest of *cestui que trust*."[30] Even Lord Westbury[31] failed to observe it later and there are other authorities to the same effect.[32] Thus the later taker of an equitable mortgage would not prevail over the equity of the prior defrauded vendor of the same property to recover it from the mortgagor.

BONA FIDE PURCHASE OF LEGAL INTEREST

185. A purchaser of the legal interest will prevail over prior equitable claimants (1) if he paid value, (2) without notice of the prior equities, (3) in a transaction untainted by fraud or inequitable conduct.

1068. Apparently constructive trusts created by law to prevent unjust enrichment were the mere "equities" as contrasted with those resting on a consensual basis.

See also Gray, Equitable Priorities and the Matrimonial Domicile, 1955, 18 Mod.L.Rev. 596, criticizing Westminster Bank Ltd. v. Lee [1955] 3 W.L.R. 397, [1955] 2 All E.R. 883, which held that a later equitable mortgagee for value and without notice prevails over what the court termed the "mere equity" of a deserted wife's equitable right to occupy the matrimonial home; Note, Deserted Wife's Right to Matrimonial Home—Equitable Interests and "Mere Equities," Nov. 1955, Camb.L.J. 158, noting Street v. Denham, [1955] 3 W.L.R. 376, which held that the deserted wife's equity to occupy the matrimonial home loses against a subsequent equitable mortgage given for value and without notice, and saying, "The dividing line between equitable interests and mere equities is perhaps the discretionary character of the latter. Equitable claims to set aside deeds, or to secure their rectification, or to reopen a foreclosure, are at the discretion of the court in a way which does not apply to equitable titles such as those of beneficiaries under a trust or a mortgagor's equity of redemption. It is natural that the court should be unwilling to exercise its discretion to the detriment of an innocent purchaser even though he lacks the armour of the legal estate."

30. Ames, Purchase for Value Without Notice, Lectures on Legal History, 253, 254.

31. Eyre v. Burmester, 1862, 10 H.L.C. 90, in which a prior defrauded vendor prevailed over a later holder of a contract of purchase.

32. Cave v. Cave, 1880, 15 Ch.D. 639; Wasserman v. Metzger, 1906, 105 Va. 744, 54 S.E. 893, 7 L.R.A.,N. S., 1019.

28. 1861, 4 DeG. F. & J. 208. This case involved an equity of redemption on which an annuity had been charged. The annuity was held to be prior to a subsequent conveyance of the equity of redemption under a marriage settlement without notice. But see Lane v. Jackson, 1855, 30 Beav. 535, holding a judgment lien on an equity of redemption subordinate to a subsequent grantee thereof for value and without notice.

29. Scott v. Scott, [1924] 1 I.R. 141; Luckel v. Phillips Petroleum Co., Tex.Com.App.1922, 243 S.W.

The second of the two rules[33] is of considerably greater practical importance than the first. The basic policy underlying it has been sufficiently stated in discussing the question whether or not it should be applied to *bona fide* purchases of equitable interests.[34] However, to rationalize the doctrine in terms of basic policy does not tell the whole story.

For one thing it fails to disclose its historical origin in the division of jurisdiction between the courts of law and equity which allowed the holder of the legal title to prevail.[35] Although one writer in examining the effect of this dichotomy on the rule finds an explanation of it in the "superiority admitted, even in courts of equity, to the legal title" together "with the respect the latter [courts of equity], more or less perforce, paid to the former [courts of law]",[36] this may be doubted.[37] As has been pointed out, "equity seems never to have regarded the legal title as superior to the equitable, but quite the reverse." The true explanation is that "where the parties were of equal merit as to the matter involved, the chancellor simply let the law courts dispose of the matter and in consequence the legal title prevailed." [38]

For another thing, the exposition of that policy has not brought out, perhaps, as clearly as it should, that not only the rule itself but the rather mechanical character of the doctrine and its operation affords a present practical explanation and justification of it "in its serviceability as a definite means of arriving at certainty as to ownership." And this is true even though it has been predicted that "the possibility of injustice which lurks in" that same mechanical character "forbodes its ultimate disappearance." [39]

But the most important omission is that which views the rule as one of ethical conduct between the parties; and it is this explanation that best accounts for the particular requirements of the rule. In other words, granting that the basic policy of encouraging commercial dealings applies to this particular sort of property, there still remains the inquiry: what are the particular circumstances that must be present before the participant in the transaction will be protected at the expense of the prior claimant? One of the best statements of the rationale which serves to delimit the requirements of the rule is that of Ames, who stated that the rule "is simply an application of that comprehensive principle which lies at the foundation of constructive trusts and other equitable obligations created by operation of law * * * namely, that a court of equity will compel the surrender of an advantage by a defendant whenever, but only whenever, upon grounds of obvious justice, it is unconscientious for him to retain it at another's expense. * * * If he acquired the title with notice of another's equity his acquisition was dishonest, and he must, of course, surrender it. If he gave no value, though his acquisition was honest, his retention of the title, after knowledge of the equity, is plainly dishonest. If he gave value, and had no notice of the equity, it is eminently just for him to keep what he has got." [40]

Viewed in this light, the subsequent claimant must have paid value, done so before notice of the prior equity, and have got in the legal interest. The words *bona fide* which are an almost invariable part of the rule are

33. See § 182, supra.

34. See § 183, supra.

35. See Scott, Trusts, § 284, for an excellant brief history of the development of the doctrine.

36. Huston, The Enforcement of Decrees in Equity, 135.

37. See Cook, Cas.Equity, 3d ed., 1 vol., 55–58.

38. Costigan, Protecting Purchasers for Value, 1923, 12 Cal.L.Rev. 356, 364 n. 23. See also Pomeroy, Eq.Juris., 5th ed., § 743.

39. Huston, The Enforcement of Decrees in Equity, 135.

40. Ames, Purchase for Value Without Notice, Lectures on Legal History, 253, 255. See also Pomeroy, Eq.Juris., 5th ed., §§ 737–743; Scott, Trusts, § 284. See also Cunningham and Tischler, Equitable Real Estate Mortgages, 1963, 17 Rutgers L.Rev. 679, 684, 686–688.

in part redundant for they frequently mean substantially the same thing as being without notice. But, in addition, they require that the transaction not be tainted by fraud directed either at the vendor by the purchaser, or against creditors of the vendor in collusion with him, or that the transfer be obtained through other kinds of inequitable conduct which, though stopping short of fraud, are of a sort that equity refuses to countenance.[41] The first and third of these requisites will be covered briefly in the following sections. Just what constitutes notice will be taken up in connection with the same problem under the recording acts. Whether, in certain instances, the purchaser may gain priority in spite of notice will be taken up along with the doctrine of *tabula in naufragio,* or tacking, and the case where title is acquired subsequent to the creation of the equity.

VALUE—IN GENERAL

186. **The test of value in the doctrine of bona fide purchase is, in general, the same where a mortgagee claims its protection as in the case of an outright purchase.**

"Value" is a term which has different meanings depending upon the purpose for which it is required. Thus the test of what constitutes value in the law of fraudulent conveyances is determined by one set of criteria while it is delimited by different requirements when the doctrine of *bona fide* purchase is involved. We are here concerned with its meaning in the latter connection. Further, our interest is centered on the test of value in mortgage transactions. While the test of what will be value is no different where a mortgagee claims the benefit of the doctrine than where an outright purchaser does so, the sorts of things a mortgagee could, or normally would, have done or given, that would raise any real question are relatively few. In contrast, when someone other than a mortgagee claims the benefit of the

bona fide purchase rule, the range of things that can be given or done and be value within the meaning of the rule is very extensive. The latter question is too large to cover in detail in his work, and, further, seems a needless task since it has been done competently in available standard works.[42] Consequently, a brief résumé at this point of the more important things that will constitute value, leaving aside until later those that cause difficulty or occur frequently in the law of mortgages, should be sufficient.

Normally the value given is in the form of a present transfer of money or property of some sort. Thus in a mortgage the usual exchange is the giving of money as a loan in return for the property as security. Both will be regarded as present value, making the mortgagor a purchaser for value of the money, and the mortgagee a purchaser for value of a security interest in the land. The property may consist of land, chattels, or a chose in action against a third person. The interest in property need not be legal, the parting with an equitable interest being sufficient.[43] Performance of services and marriage are other kinds of present value that are recognized. A promise to pay in the future is not value even if it is in the form of a negotiable instrument, although in the latter case it will be if it has been negotiated by the seller to a holder in due course even though notice is given before payment.[44] And the same is

---

41. See Pomeroy, Equity Juris., 5th ed., § 762.

42. See, e. g., Pomeroy, Equity Juris., 5th ed., §§ 747–751; Scott, Trusts, §§ 297A–309.1.

43. See Westbrook v. Gleason, 1879, 79 N.Y. 23.

44. The Uniform Sales Act, § 76, provides that " 'Value' is any consideration sufficient to support a simple promise * * *" This would make a promise to pay "value". Under § 24, however, the rule of *bona fide* purchase cutting off equities applies only where the seller had a voidable title. Consequently, the Act would seem inapplicable to a prior equitable mortgage or to a trust since in neither case is the equity held one which will avoid the legal title of the seller.

There is also authority that a promise in the form of a note or check will be value when the property bought is itself a negotiable instrument. Goodale v. Thorn, 1926, 199 Cal. 307, 249 P. 11, is an example.

true of other promises on which the promisor would still be liable even though he were deprived of the property purchased, as in the case where his promise runs to a third party.[45] A change of position by the transferee before notice, such that it would be inequitable to deprive him of the property, will give him the same standing as would have the payment of recognized value. This qualification is especially important where the consideration given is a promise and notice is acquired before payment but after a change of position. Inadequacy of the consideration given will not make the transfer one not for value, although great inadequacy is evidence that the purchaser was on notice of the defect in the title; or, if bad faith is negatived, that it was really a gift instead of a sale.[46] The value may be paid either before or after the transfer of the property provided it is done before notice.

The taking of property in satisfaction of or as security for an antecedent debt are so bound together that, although only the latter is of great importance in the law of mortgages, a more detailed treatment of the former as well is necessary, and separate following sections will be devoted to each. Before proceeding to them, however, it is worth while pointing out that, while an antecedent debt may not be value so as to make a mortgagee able to cut off prior equities as a *bona fide* purchaser when the problem is turned around and the question is whether a *prior* mortgage given to secure a pre-existing debt will prevail over a subsequent equity or a subsequent transfer, the answer is that it is immaterial whether the consideration for the prior mortgage was present or past.[47]

VALUE—SATISFACTION OF ANTECEDENT DEBT

187. Under the majority view extinguishment of a pre-existing debt is not value, except if:

(1) The property transferred is a negotiable instrument or money; or

(2) The transferee releases security he held for the debt in addition to extinguishing it; or

(3) A revival of the debt would not restore the transferee to his prior position; or

(4) The transferee is a judgment creditor purchasing at his own execution sale, by the better view.

In many states statutes confirm or add to the exceptions. Where only part of the consideration is the extinguishment of an antecedent debt, the rest of it being present value, the whole is treated as value.

The cases generally hold that extinguishment of an antecedent debt in exchange for property does not constitute value.[48] The common explanation of this result is that if the property is taken away from the transferee the debt will revive and the transferee will be no worse off than he was before. Further, when the fact of satisfaction is not evidenced by any act of the creditor, but depends upon mere parol evidence, the door is opened wide for the easy admission of fraud. The rights of third persons are given little protection since they will depend upon the testimony of those whose interest it is to destroy them.[49] In criticism it has been ar-

---

See U.C.C. § 1–201(44) for the definition of "value" under that Code.

45. E. g., Citizens' Bank of Parker v. Shaw, 1900, 14 S.D. 197, 84 N.W. 779.

46. Merely nominal consideration will not be value. Cf. Ten Eyck v. Witbeck, 1892, 135 N.Y. 40, 31 N.E. 994, 31 Am.St.Rep. 809; but contrast Strong v. Whybark, 1907, 204 Mo. 341, 102 S.W. 968, 12 L.R. A.,N.S., 240, 120 Am.St.Rep. 710.

47. Young v. Guy, 1882, 87 N.Y. 457. See Glenn, Mortgages, 1560. But contrast Wheeler v. Kirtland, 1873, 24 N.J.Eq. 552, equitable mortgage to secure an antecedent debt postponed to a later equitable mortgage for a new consideration.

48. The American Law Institute accepts this as a correct statement of the law. Restatement, Second, Trusts § 304; Restatement, Restitution, § 173.

49. See Sutton v. Ford, 1916, 144 Ga. 587, 596, 87 S. E. 799, L.R.A.1918D, 561, Ann.Cas.1918A, 106; Pomeroy, Equity Juris., 5th ed., § 479a; 1926, 36 Yale L.J. 564, 567.

gued that the giving up of the debt clearly surrenders something of value as much as the payment over of money; that reviving the debt when the property is taken away amounts merely to restoring the value given, and "there is no recognized principle that a purchaser for value shall not be allowed to hold property transferred to him if the value which he has given can be restored to him";[50] that revival of the debt does not constitute a complete restoration for it does not take into account the possible difference in ability to collect the debt on revival as compared with the earlier date or the prejudicial effect upon the rights and remedies of the creditor by having been lulled into inaction through taking the property and releasing the claim.[51] The preceding point is emphasized by the rule that an extension of time by the creditor will be value.[52] The creditor, by accepting payment, "places himself in a worse condition than he would have done by a definite forbearance of the debt."[53]

Not only are there minority cases holding that the satisfaction of an antecedent debt by a transfer of land[54] or chattels[55] will con-

stitute value so as to make the transferee a *bona fide* purchaser, but there are also well established exceptions to the general rule. Thus where the property transferred is a negotiable instrument[56] or money,[57] cancellation of an antecedent debt constitutes value in exchange for them. This rule as to negotiable instruments has been codified in the N.I.L.[58] The social interest in their free marketability applies in both cases to override the interest of prior third party claimants. Further, if the owner of the pre-existing debt held security for it and, in addition to discharging the debt in consideration of the transfer to him, released the security, this will be regarded as value; and the fact that the security is worth less than the property transferred seems immaterial,[59] provided, of course, it is of more than nominal value. A third exception to the general rule is where, owing to a change of circumstances, the transferee could not be restored to his former position by the revival of the debt, as, for example, where the debtor has received a bankruptcy discharge, the Statute of Limitations has run on the debts, sureties for the debt have been discharged, or the debt has

50. Williston, Sales, 2d ed., § 620. See Scott, Trusts, § 298.5.

51. See State Bank of St. Louis v. Frame, 1892, 112 Mo. 502, 512, 20 S.W. 620, 623; Sutton v. Ford, 1916, 144 Ga. 587, 595, 87 S.E. 799, L.R.A.1918D, 561, Ann.Cas.1918A, 106.

52. Tripler v. McDonald Lumber Co., 1916, 173 Cal. 144, 159 P. 591; De Mey v. Defer, 1894, 103 Mich. 239, 61 N.W. 524, error dismissed 168 U.S. 703, 18 S.Ct. 941, 42 L.Ed. 1211; O'Brien v. Fleckenstein, 1905, 180 N.Y. 350, 73 N.E. 30, 105 Am.St.Rep. 768; cf. Davis v. Lutkiewiez, 1887, 72 Iowa 254, 33 N.W. 670, under recording acts.

53. State Bank of St. Louis v. Frame, 1892, 112 Mo. 502, 512, 20 S.W. 620, 623.

54. E. g., Riley v. Martinelli, 1893, 97 Cal. 575, 32 P. 579, 21 L.R.A. 33, 33 Am.St.Rep. 209, judgment creditor purchaser at own execution sale; Alstin's Ex'r v. Cundiff, 1880, 52 Tex. 453; Sutton v. Ford, 1916, 144 Ga. 587, 87 S.E. 799, L.R.A.1918D, 561, Ann. Cas.1918A, 106; Adams v. Vanderbeck, 1897, 148 Ind. 92, 45 N.E. 645, 62 Am.St.Rep. 497, rehearing denied 148 Ind. 92, 47 N.E. 24, 62 Am.St.Rep. 497; Pugh v. Highley, 1898, 152 Ind. 252, 53 N.E. 171, 44 L.R.A. 392, 71 Am.St.Rep. 327, judgment creditor buying in on own sale under judgment; cf. Schluter v. Harvey, 1884, 65 Cal. 158, 3 P. 659, within

meaning of recording act; State Bank of St. Louis v. Frame, 1892, 112 Mo. 502, 20 S.W. 620, under recording acts. But see Glenn, Mortgages, 1565, casting doubt upon the rule in Indiana and Missouri, citing Soders v. Jackson, 1942, 112 Ind.App. 179, 44 N.E.2d 310; Straus v. Hirsch, 1895, 63 Mo. App. 95; Kemper Dry Goods Co. v. Kidder Savings Bank, 1899, 81 Mo.App. 280

55. Butters v. Haughwout, 1866, 42 Ill. 18, 89 Am. Dec. 401; Bughman v. Central Bank, 1893, 159 Pa. 94, 28 A. 209.

56. National City Bank of N. Y. v. Waggoner, 1934, 243 App.Div. 305, 276 N.Y.S. 449, affirmed, 1936, 270 N.Y. 592, 1 N.E.2d 345; Perry & Sons v. Mand, 1932, 110 N.J.Eq. 111, 158 A. 378, 80 A.L.R. 392, negotiable instrument secured by mortgage taken in satisfaction of pre-existing debt; N.J.L. § 25; see Brannan Negotiable Instruments Law, 6th ed., 391.

57. Stephens v. Board of Education, 1879, 79 N.Y. 183, 187, 35 Am.Rep. 511.

58. § 27. See also U.C.C. § 1–201(44).

59. Grand Rapids Nat. Bank v. Ford, 1906, 143 Mich. 402, 107 N.W. 76, 114 Am.St.Rep. 668, 8 Ann.Cas. 102; McCleerey v. Wakefield, 1889, 76 Iowa 529, 41 N.W. 210, 2 L.R.A. 529.

become uncollectible because of the debtor's altered finances.[60]

The judgment creditor purchasing at his own execution sale and paying the price by satisfying or partially satisfying the judgment debt, although paying a form of consideration usually not regarded as value, i. e., the extinguishment of a pre-existing debt, has been held to be a taker for value.[61] One reason for this is a matter of policy, of encouraging bidding at judicial sales. The judgment creditor is one of the chief bidders at an execution sale and, if he is to be willing and able to bid, he should be on a parity with others. If he is held to take subject to prior equities while his competitors take free of them, he is at such a disadvantage that his bidding will be discouraged with the result that the price fetched on a judicial sale, which is a forced one always, would bring even less than it normally would. But another reason is the injustice to the judgment creditor lying in the fact that if he loses the property he cannot be put back in *statu quo*. By the sale, as was pointed out in a leading case, the judgment creditor loses both his execution lien and his judgment lien on all property of his debtor to which they attached. Even though his rights were subsequently revived, he could not be put back into the same position he occupied prior to the satisfaction of the judgment.[62] There are, however, many courts that hold such a purchasing judgment creditor not within the protection of *the bona fide* purchase rule on the ground that he gives no new consideration since he merely credits his bid on his

debt, which is past consideration, or that he is on constructive notice.[63]

In addition to minority cases and well recognized exceptions to the general rule that satisfaction of an antecedent debt is not value, there are statutory provisions modifying the rule. In addition the previously noted provision of the N.I.L., other uniform acts dealing with commercial documents of title [64] have made the satisfaction of an antecedent debt value, and the same is true of the Uniform Sales Act.[65] Also recording acts in many states include creditors as well as purchasers among those who will be protected against persons claiming a prior interest in the land under an unrecorded instrument.

Where part only of the consideration consists in the extinguishment of a pre-existing debt and the balance is new consideration, the transferee has been held to be a purchaser for value.[66]

VALUE—TRANSFER TO SECURE ANTECEDENT DEBT

188. A transfer of property to secure a pre-existing debt is not for value in most states, subject to the exceptions noted in § 187. A

60. Dunlap v. Green, C.C.A.Tex.1894, 60 F. 242, 8 C. C.A. 600; Payne v. Allen, 1936, 178 Okl. 328, 62 P. 2d 1227; Restatement, Second, Trusts § 304(2) (c), comment.

61. Riley v. Martinelli, 1893, 97 Cal. 575, 32 P. 579, 21 L.R.A. 33 33 Am.St.Rep. 209; cf. Cady v. Purser, 1901, 131 Cal. 552, 63 P. 844, 82 Am.St.Rep. 391, under recording acts; Pugh v. Highley, 1899, 152 Ind. 252, 53 N.E. 171, 44 L.R.A. 392; Gower v. Doheny, 1871, 33 Iowa 36; Adams v. Buchanan, 1871, 49 Mo. 64. See Restatement, Second, Trusts § 309.

62. See Restatement, Second, Trusts § 309, Comment b.

63. Harrison v. Caddo Valley Bank, 1917, 128 Ark. 462, 194 S.W. 854; Ettenheimer v. Northgraves, 1888, 75 Iowa 28, 39 N.W. 120; McCalla v. Knight Inv. Co., 1908, 77 Kans. 770, 94 P. 126, 14 L.R.A.,N. S., 1258; Stauffacher v. Great Falls Pub. Service Co., 1935, 99 Mont. 324, 43 P.2d 647. See 1890, 10 L.R.A. 411; 1892, 16 L.R.A. 668; L.R.A.1918A, 1089; 1919, 4 A.L.R. 434; 1911, 21 Ann.Cas. 864. See also note, 1913, 13 Col.L.Rev. 539; Pomeroy, Equity Juris., 5th ed., § 724.

64. Uniform Bills of Lading Act, § 53; Uniform Warehouse Receipts Act, § 58. See also Uniform Stock Transfer Act, § 22. So too under U.C.C. § 1–201(44).

65. Uniform Sales Act, § 76.

66. Glidden v. Hunt, 1836, 41 Mass. (24 Pick.) 221; Noe v. Smith, 1917, 67 Okl. 211, 169 P. 1108, L.R.A. 1918C, 435; Swenson v. Seale, Tex.Civ.App., 1894, 28 S.W. 143. The consideration must be more than nominal. Victoria Paper Mills v. N. Y. & Pa. Co., 1899, 28 Misc. 123, 58 N.Y.S. 1070. Also, in some cases it has been held that the transferee is entitled to protection only to the extent of the new money paid, such protection being afforded by giving a lien for the amount upon the property. Weaver v. Barden, 1872, 49 N.Y. 286. See Ann.Cas.1918A, 115.

transfer in accord with a promise made at the creation of the debt is for value. A binding extension of time by the creditor has been held value. There is authority that a creditor taking a mortgage to secure both an old debt and a new loan holds for value as to the combined amounts. The preferable rule would make him a taker for value only to the extent of the new consideration.

One of the important problems of value in the law of mortgages is whether the securing of an antecedent debt is value within the meaning of the judicial doctrine of *bona fide* purchase. The great weight of authority is that it is not.[67] This would follow *a fortiori* from the general rule that extinguishment of an antecedent debt is not for value. However, even here it can be argued that it should be treated as value on the ground of change of position. As was urged by a great scholar, "though one who takes as security in fact gives no value, his subsequent conduct is almost sure to be affected by the possession of the security. Even though forbearance is not expressly bargained for, the effect of conveying security is almost inevitably to cause the creditor to forbear or diminish his efforts to obtain satisfaction of his claim from other sources."[68] Further, it is arguable that the probability of change of position and the difficulty of proof are sufficient reason to establish taking of property to secure an antecedent debt as value regardless of whether there was proved to be a change of position in a particular case or not. These views did not prevail in the case of ordinary real or personal property.

Nevertheless, there are the same exceptions to the general rule as exist in the case of extinguishment of a pre-existing claim. Although there was a split on the point, even before the N.I.L. the majority view was that taking a negotiable instrument as security for an old debt was for value and, though § 25 of the N.I.L. was not explicit on the point, it has been interpreted to cover securing as well as satisfying pre-existing debts.[69] The

---

67. "The transfer * * * was a simple collateral security, * * * for the old indebtment and liability of the parties to the notes described in the instrument of transfer. * * * But the protection is not given by the rules of law to a party in such a predicament merely. He must not only have had no notice, but he must have paid a consideration at the time of the transfer, either in money, or other property, or by a surrender of existing debts or securities, held for the debts and liabilities. * * * But here the bank has merely possessed itself of the property transferred, as auxiliary security for the old debts and liabilities. It has paid or given no new consideration upon the faith of it. It is, therefore, in truth no purchaser for value in the sense of the rule." Morse v. Godfrey (1844) 17 Fed.Cas. 856, 863, 3 Story, 364. People's Sav. Bank v. Bates (1886) 120 U.S. 556, 7 S.Ct. 679, 30 L.Ed. 754; First Nat. Bank of Martinsville v. Conn. Mut. Life Ins. Co. (1891) 129 Ind. 241, 28 N.E. 695; Met. Bank v. Godfrey (1860) 23 Ill. 579; Boxheimer v. Gunn (1872) 24 Mich. 372; Pancoast v. Duval (1875) 26 N.J.Eq. 445; Young v. Guy, 1882, 87 N.Y. 457, accord. See 1927, 36 Yale L.J. 564, 565 n. 6. The same is true under recording acts. McDonald & Co. v. Johns, 1911, 62 Wash. 521, 114 P. 175, 33 L.R.A.,N.S., 57. But, in contrast, is an old English case. M, owner of Blackacre, gave an equitable mortgage to E–1 to secure an antecedent debt. He later gave a legal mortgage to E–2 to secure an antecedent debt. E–2 had no knowledge or notice of E–1. Which prevails? In Plumb v. Fluitt, 1791, 2 Anst. 432, the court preferred E–2 but said, "I wish I saw, in a Court of Equity, some solid distinction established between a consideration which is an old debt, and a sum advanced *de novo*; there certainly is a great difference: in the one case the creditor jumps at any security he can get; * * * but till such a distinction is established, it is difficult to apply the reasoning which would belong to it."

And in a few states even the securing a pre-existing debt is held to be a valuable consideration. Connecticut Life Ins. Co. v. McCormick, 1872, 45 Cal. 580; Smitton v. McCullough, 1920, 182 Cal. 530; 189 P. 686, pledge of stock; Gilbert Bros. & Co. v. Lawrence Bros., 1905, 56 W.Va. 281, 49 S.E. 155. In California it has been held to be for value so as to prevail over a prior grantor's lien. Schut v. Doyle, 1959, 168 Cal.App.2d 698, 336 P.2d 567; noted 1960, 11 Hastings L.J. 345. So, too, it is held to be for a "valuable consideration" under West's Ann.Cal.Civ.Code, § 1214. Frey v. Clifford, 1872, 44 Cal. 335. Dorr v. Meyer, 1897, 51 Neb. 94, 70 N.W. 543, accord under recording act. Valley Vista Land Co. v. Nipomo Water & Sewer Co., 1968, 266 Cal. App.2d 331, 72 Cal.Rptr. 181, accord Schut v. Doyle, supra.

68. Williston, Sales, 2d ed., § 620.

69. Railroad Co. v. National Bank, 1880, 102 U.S. 14, 26 L.Ed. 61; Culver v. Benedict, 1859, 79 Mass. (13 Gray) 7. See 1923, 33 Yale L.J. 628. The same is true of money. Spaulding v. Kendrick, 1898, 172 Mass. 71, 51 N.E. 453. The Restatement, Second, Trusts § 305(2) a, accepts this rule as law. The Uniform Sales Act § 76, the Uniform Warehouse Receipts Act § 58, the Uniform Bills of Lading Act, § 53, and the Uniform Stock Transfer Act, § 22, all

justification is commercial expediency to encourage the credit and circulation of negotiable paper. The rule enables the creditor to give prolonged credit and forbear enforcement of his legal rights while it also permits the debtor to use his negotiable securities as the equivalent of cash.[70] Consequently, if the debtor executes a negotiable note for the amount of the old debt and secures it by a mortgage and then assigns the note and mortgage before maturity as security to the creditor for the old debt, this will make the creditor a holder for value of the note and mortgage.[71] Two other exceptions, paralleling those where the old claim is given up, are the surrender of other security[72] and a change of position.[73] In addition, there are cases holding that if the creditor gives a binding extension of time he will be considered as having given value.[74] As was previously pointed out, if an extension of time constitutes the equivalent of value, it would seem that a complete relinquishment of the debt should be.[75]

If, at the time of the creation of the debt or obligation the mortgagor promised to execute a mortgage in the future to secure it, the later giving of the mortgage in fulfillment of that promise is regarded as for value.[76] The mortgage is looked upon as part of the agreed equivalent for the original loan rather than a subsequent, separate act securing a preexisting debt.[77]

Where a mortgage is given to secure both a preexisting debt and a new loan, there is authority that the creditor is a holder for value as to the combined amounts.[78] There are, however, other cases holding that he will be a holder for value only as to the amount of the loan made at the time of the transfer.[79] The latter seems the better view.[80]

VALUE—CREDITORS

189. The following are not purchasers for value and will be postponed to prior equitable mortgagees: attaching, levying, or judgment lien creditors, assignees for the benefit of creditors, trustees in bankruptcy, and receivers. Estoppel is occasionally invoked to let a creditor prevail over prior security interests, but the

---

expressly provide that securing an antecedent debt or other claim constitutes a transfer for value. So too under U.C.C. § 1–201(44).

70. See Story, J., in Swift v. Tyson, 1842, 41 U.S. (16 Pet.) 1, 10 L.Ed. 865; 1926, 36 Yale L.J. 564, 568.

71. Freeman v. Davenport Peters Co., 1930, 272 Mass. 321, 172 N.E. 234, assignment of negotiable note and mortgage to secure a pre-existing debt makes assignee a holder in due course.

72. Richardson v. Wren, 1908, 11 Ariz. 395, 95 P. 124, 16 L.R.A.,N.S., 190, giving up equitable mortgage on other property; McCleerey v. Wakefield, 1889, 76 Iowa 529, 41 N.W. 210, 2 L.R.A. 529; see Restatement, Second, Trusts § 305(2) b.

73. Dunlap v. Green, C.C.A.Tex.1894, 60 F. 242, 8 C. C.A. 600; Tobin v. Benson, Tex.Civ.App.1913, 152 S.W. 642; see Restatement, Second, Trusts § 305(2) c.

74. Tripler v. McDonald Lumber Co., 1916, 173 Cal. 144, 159 P. 591; O'Brien v. Fleckenstein, 1905, 180 N.Y. 350, 73 N.E. 30, 105 Am.St.Rep. 768; De Mey v. Defer, 1894, 103 Mich. 239, 61 N.W. 524, error dismissed 168 U.S. 703, 18 S.Ct. 941, 42 L.Ed. 1211; Davis v. Lutkiewiez, 1887, 72 Iowa 254, 33 N.W. 670, under recording act. See 1926, 36 Yale L.J. 564, 567. See also, 1913, 23 Yale L.J. 186.

75. See preceding section.

76. Gibson v. Lenhart, 1882, 101 Pa. 522. The security given was a note but at the time Pennsylvania held that taking a negotiable note as security for a previous debt was not value, therefore the decision rested upon the ground it had been bargained for. See 1926, 36 Yale L.J. 564, 568; Restatement, Second, Trusts § 305(3).

77. The same is true even though the agreement does not specify the property which is to be given. Miller & Co. v. Boykin, 1881, 70 Ala. 469; see Restatement, Second, Trusts § 305(3) comment h. But see 1926, 36 Yale L.J. 564, 568.

78. Williams v. Oconee County Bank, 1926, 162 Ga. 615, 134 S.E. 478; Merchants' Bank of Greene v. Soesbe, 1908, 138 Iowa 354, 116 N.W. 123, chattel mortgage; Gurley v. Reed, 1906, 190 Mass. 509, 77 N.E. 642, pledge of stock; Hees v. Carr, 1898, 115 Mich. 654, 74 N.W. 181; Branch v. Griffin, 1888, 99 N.C. 173, 5 S.E. 393; Commercial Bank of Independence, Kan. v. Pirie, C.C.A.Kan.1897, 82 F. 799, 27 C.C.A. 171, chattel mortgage.

79. Wells v. Morrow, 1861, 38 Ala. 125; Lawshe v. Trenton Banking Co., 1916, 87 N.J.Eq. 56, 99 A. 617, reversed 88 N.J.Eq. 347, 102 A. 633, assignment of mortgage; National Safe Deposit, Savings & Trust Co. v. Gray, 1898, 12 App.D.C. 276.

80. See 1926, 36 Yale L.J. 564, 569.

circumstances of its application cannot be defined with precision. In states where a judgment or creditor's lien relates back to some prior time it may prevail over intervening encumbrances.

A general creditor, prior to taking action by way of attachment, levy of execution, or obtaining a judgment and docketing or recording it as the law in the particular jurisdiction may require, is commonly said not to have any *in rem* interest in his debtor's property.[81] On this narrow ground it is argued that he cannot prevail over a prior equitable mortgage on his debtor's property. A better ground is that, though in a sense the general creditor has paid a consideration in the advancement of credit or the non-enforcement of his rights, he has not done so on the security of specific land, and consequently is not disappointed in the same sense that a subsequent mortgagee for value would be if he were to take subject to prior equities of which he had no notice.[82] Is he helped by acquiring a specific lien on definite items of the debtor's property by attachment or execution? Or by a recorded or docketed judgment giving him a general lien on all of the debtor's realty within the jurisdiction? No; even then he is postponed on the ground that he has given no new value and therefore is not entitled to the protection of the *bona fide* purchase rule. He merely steps into the shoes of his debtor even as to such assets as negotiable instruments or money. We have seen that if the debtor gives negotiable paper, documents of title made negotiable by statute or decision, or even ordinary chattels to secure an antecedent debt, the creditor is a holder for value.[83] Behind those decisions

and statutes is a policy of encouraging sales and security transactions in types of property where the commercial interest in free marketability is great. This policy does not apply to a creditor who seizes his debtor's property under legal process or acquires a judgment lien on it.[84] Consequently, not only will levying and attaching creditors [85] take subject to prior equities of third persons in the debtor's property, but the same is true of judgment lien creditors.[86] A distinction between judgment lien creditors on the one hand and execution or attachment lien creditors on the other, on the ground that the latter, because they have actually seized particular property, can be said to have acted in reliance upon its being unencumbered, has been rejected.[87] And the holder of the

81. This statement is true so far as our present problem of priorities is concerned. That general creditors may be considered to have an *in rem* interest in their debtors' property when the question arises under the law of fraudulent conveyances is another matter.

82. Finch v. Winchelsea, 1715 1 P.Wms. 277; Burgh v. Francis, 1670, 1 Eq.Cas.Abr. 320, pl. 1; Whitworth v. Gaugain, 1844, 3 Hare 416; 1846, 1 Phil. 728.

83. See preceding section.

84. See Restatement, Second, Trusts § 308 Comment a.

85. Fitzgerald v. Fitzgerald, 1916, 97 Kan. 408, 155 P. 791; Houghton v. Davenport, 1883, 74 Me. 590; Westervelt v. Hagge, 1901, 61 Neb. 647, 85 N.W. 852, 54 L.R.A. 333; Carroll v. Ryder, 1912, 34 R.I. 383, 83 A. 845.

86. Welton v. Tizzard, 1864, 15 Iowa 495; Atkinson v. Miller, 1890, 34 W.Va. 115, 11 S.E. 1007, 9 L.R.A. 544; McGuigan v. Rix, 1919, 140 Ark. 418, 215 S.W. 611. See Webb, Record of Title, § 192; Pomeroy, Eq.Juris., 4th Ed., §§ 721, 722. Sullivan v. Corn Exchange Bank, 1912, 154 App.Div. 292, 296, 139 N.Y. S. 97, 101, "An equitable mortgage takes precedence over a lien, whether general or special, which only attaches, as does a judgment, to such right, title, or interest as the debtor has in real property."

In Dwight v. Newell, 1849, 3 N.Y. 185, where the judgment lien of A and the equitable mortgage to B to secure an antecedent debt were assumed by the court to have attached to after-acquired real property at the same instant, the court said A had priority. (An alternative ground of the decision was that B's security interest did not arise until later.)

In New Jersey, if a prior equitable mortgage was not given for value and the creditor obtains his judgment without notice of the mortgagee's prior equity, the judgment lien is apparently superior to the equitable mortgage. See Cunningham and Tischler, op. cit. supra note 1, 687.

87. Cf. Shear Co. v. Currie, C.C.A.Tex., 1923, 295 F. 841, 843, in which the court in repudiating the distinction said, "An attachment creates only an inchoate lien, which ripens into a perfect lien, only upon the rendition of the judgment. It is inconceivable that a creditor who reduces his claim to judgment, and his attachment lien to a judgment lien, thereby loses the superiority he obtained through the levy

prior equity wins even though the creditor had contracted, in effect, for a confessed judgment, in which case it is closer to a voluntary transfer. In such a case, the contract is merely for the creditor to be given what he would get by such a judgment, not more, and "that gives him nothing more than a right to that which belongs to his debtor." [88] The same rule applies to assignees for the benefit of creditors,[89] trustees in bankruptcy,[90] and receivers.[91]

If the creditor had actually relied upon the property being unencumbered, either in extending the credit, or in failing to take steps to protect himself in the collection of an existing loan, there is a possibility that he may prevail as against an equitable interest in the property whose holder might be considered negligent in permitting the false appearance of full ownership to exist. One case preferred such a judgment creditor over the holder of a vendor's equitable lien.[92] The theory was that the lien is "a secret, invisible trust, known only to the vendor and vendee, and to those to whom it may be communicated in fact." Its holder should reduce it to a mortgage to give notice of it to the world. Failure to do so makes the vendor "in some degree accessory to the fraud committed on the

public by an act which exhibits the vendee as the complete owner of an estate in which he claims a secret lien." The creditor who relies on the appearance of unencumbered title is to be "regarded as a *quasi* purchaser for a valuable consideration, without notice."

Such a doctrine would be applied with caution to types of transactions in which the prior equity holder could legitimately be charged with negligence in leaving the transaction in a misleading form and where the judgment creditor clearly had acted on the deceptive appearance in becoming a creditor, or otherwise to his actual detriment.[93] The exact scope of the application of this principle of estoppel is impossible to define with any precision.[94]

Under the earlier English law the lien of a judgment related back to the first day of the term, and in some American jurisdictions there is a similar relating back to a time prior to rendition. Under such a rule even a legal mortgage given in the intervening period would be displaced by the relating back of the subsequent judgment lien. A similar problem would be presented in the case of execution liens in those jurisdictions in which an execution lien attaches when the writ is issued or delivered to the sheriff and there is a mortgage given before seizure.[95]

of his attachment." This reasoning would not apply to the levy of execution.

88. Whitworth v. Gaugain, 1844, 3 Hare, 416, 428; 1846, 1 Phil. 728.

89. In Martin v. Bowen, 1893, 51 N.J.Eq. 452, 26 A. 823, the court held that an equitable mortgage to secure an antecedent debt prevailed over a later assignment for the benefit of creditors. Commercial & Farmers Bank v. Scotland Neck Bank, 1912, 158 N.C. 238, 73 S.E. 157; Stainback v. Junk Bros. Lumber & Manufacturing Co., 1897, 98 Tenn. 306, 39 S.W. 530; see, accord, Restatement, Second, **Trusts § 306.**

90. See National Bankruptcy Act, §§ 70a(5), 70c (11 U.S.C.A. § 110). See Restatement, Second, Trusts § 307.

91. Bailey v. State, 1919, 72 Okl. 203, 179 P. 615; Peurifoy v. Boswell, 1931, 162 S.C. 107, 160 S.E. **156,** modified 161 S.E. 927; Andresen v. Kaercher, C.C.A.Minn.1930, 38 F.2d 462.

92. Hulett v. Whipple, N.Y., 1870, 58 Barb. 224. See 2 Tiffany, Real Prop., 2d Ed., 2176.

93. Cf. Spring v. Short, 1882, 90 N.Y. 538.

94. For a further consideration of the same problem, see § 210, infra.

95. See Norfolk State Bank v. Murphy, 1894, 40 Neb. 735, 59 N.W. 706, 38 L.R.A. 243. See 2 Tiffany, Real Prop., 2d Ed., §§ 670, 672. Coutts v. Walker, 1830, 2 Leigh, (Va.) 268. Although a creditor secured by a deed of trust on the debtor's property is a purchaser for value and his lien is superior to the lien of an unrecorded judgment of which he had no notice at the time the deed of trust was taken and recorded, the case of Cooper v. Cooper, 1957, 142 W.Va. 847, 98 S.E.2d 769, criticised in Note, 1957, 60 W.Va.L.Rev. 102, held that, under the doctrine of relation back of the judgment lien, the judgment lien would have priority in cases where the taker of the note and trust deed is, at the time of taking them, "fully aware and has actual notice of a suit which resulted in a judgment."

"Statutes now usually determine whether and when a judgment becomes a lien upon real estate. In most states it becomes a lien upon docketing or other

The attitude of courts towards creditors who come in conflict with prior equitable mortgages and other equitable interests is in some contrast with that of legislatures as revealed by those they protect in enacting recording acts. In roughly half of the states creditors of some sort are included among the persons who are protected against unrecorded conveyances under the recording statutes.[96] Further, the general reluctance of the courts to give creditors rights beyond those of their debtors is reflected in the construction of such enactments, the tendency being to adopt a restricted interpretation which narrows the rights of the creditors where the language of the law will permit.[97]

ACQUISITION OF LEGAL TITLE BY SUBSEQUENT EQUITABLE CLAIMANT

190. If the holder of a subsequent equitable mortgage for value and without notice gets legal title to the property while without notice of the earlier equity, he acquires priority. If he had notice, only a minority of courts and the now abolished English doctrine of tacking give him priority. Under the majority view he only gets priority if the act of transfer is so far complete that it can be finished without any breach of duty to the earlier claimant. By some authority, a "best right" without acquisition of legal title prefers the later equity.

As has been seen, where there exists an equitable interest in property, a subsequent equitable mortgage given for value and without notice of the prior equity will be postponed to it because of its priority in time.[98] But, suppose, as occasionally happens, that the subsequent equitable mortgagee obtains the legal title either from the mortgagor, or from another mortgagee who had taken legal title, i. e., a common law legal mortgagee. He may have got in such legal title either before or after receiving notice of the prior equitable interest. Will he, in such an event now be able to assert priority over the equity which otherwise would have prevailed? In the case where he obtained his legal interest before notice of the prior equity the answer is yes.[99] Where, however, title is not acquired until after notice of the earlier equity there is not only a divergence among the cases [1] but some difference of opinion among scholarly commentators.

In the English law there existed until 1925 a much criticized doctrine known as *tabula in naufragio*,[2] or tacking, in which the subsequent equitable mortgagee, providing he had no notice of intervening equitable mortgages at the time he loaned his money,[3] could buy in the first legal mortgage later with full

---

96. See Patton, Titles, 2d Ed., § 17.

97. See Patton Titles, 2d Ed., § 17.

98. See supra § 182.

record; in some states, on rendition." Campbell, Cases on Mortgages, 2d ed., 490 n. 2.

"In England and a majority of states, statutes provide that judgments shall be liens on equitable, in the same manner as on legal, interests in real estate, but the rule is generally otherwise in the absence of statute." Idem, 481 n. 3.

See additional authorities, Campbell, Cases on Mortgages, 2d ed., 490 n. 2.

---

99. See 5 Tiffany, 3d ed., § 1261; 1927, 37 Yale L.J. 790, 791, listing fifteen states confining the doctrine to where there is no notice before legal title is acquired; Restatement, Second, Trusts § 299, Comment a.

See also Cunningham and Tischler, op. cit. supra, 684 n. 1.

Of course he must have paid value. See § 185, supra. Generally, the securing of antecedent debts by giving a mortgage is not for value. §§ 188, supra. However, in a few states, including Schut v. Doyle, 1959, 168 Cal.App.2d 698, 336 P.2d 567, noted in 1960, 11 Hastings L.J. 345, a trust deed mortgage to secure an antecedent debt is a bona fide purchaser for value and so prevails over a prior grantor's lien.

1. See 1927, 37 Yale L.J. 790, 791, listing a minority of American states, including Illinois, Iowa, North Carolina, and Ohio as protecting a purchaser even though he obtained his legal title after notice. The weight of authority clearly is contra.

See Cunningham and Tischler, op. cit. supra, 685 n. 1.

E. g., Grimstone v. Carter, N.Y., 1832, 3 Paige 421, 436, 24 Am.Dec. 230.

2. The figure of speech was first used by Chief Baron Hale in Marsh v. Lee, 1671, 2 Vent. 337, and has since been used constantly.

3. "It is essential to the existence of this equity * * * that the advance, in respect to which the equity is claimed, shall have been made expressly or presumptively on the credit of the estate without notice of the mesne equity." Adams, Equity, 5th Am.Ed., 333.

knowledge of the intervening equitable mortgages and gain priority over them by tacking his later equitable mortgage to the prior legal one.[4] The idea was that in the financial shipwreck of the mortgagor the two equitable claimants to the particular property are equally meritorious and consequently he who lawfully seizes the plank of legal title to the property is entitled to save himself with it notwithstanding the fact that the other's equity was older.[5]

This doctrine of tacking was criticized in England [6] and by both courts and writers in this country.[7] As Ames put it, "Even if a third mortgagee should buy up the first mortgage, being still in ignorance of the second, he would not, upon principle, be entitled to priority over the second mortgagee. For, as he gave his money solely for the first mortgage, if he should be allowed to get anything more than that he would get it for nothing, and could not, therefore, honestly keep it at the expense of the second mortgagee." [8]

Pomeroy, on the other hand, insists that "The only conclusions consistent with settled principles are the following: It is only where a party has acquired an equitable *estate* by means of a conveyance which purported to convey the land itself, and has received the instrument and paid the consideration without notice of a prior claim, that he can, after notice, procure the legal title and with it the protection of a *bona fide* purchaser. Where a party has acquired only an equitable lien or interest, not by conveyance, and has advanced the consideration without notice, he cannot, after notice, get in the legal estate, and thus obtain precedence over a prior equity." [9] "The most common example [of the former] is that of a subsequent mortgage of land, through a mortgage in the ordinary form of a legal conveyance, where his estate is necessarily equitable, since the legal estate has been conveyed to and is outstanding in the first mortgagee." [10] In addition, Pomeroy differentiates between the acquisition of a *priority* over an earlier equity

---

4. The leading case on tacking in England is Marsh v. Lee, 1671, 2 Vent. 337. In Brace v. Duchess of Marlborough, 1728, 2 P.Wms. 491, is an exposition of the various rules of the doctrine. Taylor v. Russell, 1891, 1 Ch. 8. See generally, 2 Coote, Mortgages, 9th Ed., 1244 et seq.; Turner, English Mortgage of Land as a Security, 1934, 20 Va.L.Rev. 729, 739; Willoughby, The Legal Estate, Ch. III; Jenks, Short History of English Law, 219.

5. "But the Court of Chancery's respect for legal right may best be seen in the rules relating to the tacking of mortgages. * * * Now one might have thought that equity would have shown its respect for legal rights sufficiently if it held that the person who took a legal estate without notice of an equitable right was protected against that right, and that no advantage should have been attainable by taking a conveyance of a legal right with notice of an equitable right. And indeed if courts of equity could begin again perhaps they would not carry the doctrine to this extreme. But the view taken seems to be that suggested by the phrase, *tabula in naufragio*, applied in some of these cases to the legal estate. Y and Z are both equally honest men, one of them must lose his money—here is a shipwreck—he who can lawfully come by a legal plank may save himself; the fact that Y's equitable right is older than Z's is not a sufficient reason for depriving Z of what he has obtained by his own diligence and the law of the land, namely, a true proprietary right." Maitland, Equity, Rev.Ed. by Brunyate, 129. A corollary was that the first legal mortgagee could get in a third mortgage without notice of a mesne equitable incumbrance, and squeeze it out. The English courts also regarded the precedence of subsequent advances by a first mortgagee upon the faith of his original mortgage but not provided for in the original bargain, and without notice of intervening equitable mortgages, as having the same rule apply to them. However, a creditor by judgment cannot, by getting in the first mortgage, gain anything from the doctrine because he has not advanced money on the faith of the security. See Campbell, Cases on Mortgages, 2d ed., 486 n. 1.

6. Jennings v. Jordan, 1881, 6 A.C. 698, 714.

7. See Siter, Price, & Co. v. McClanachan, 1845, 43 Va. 280; Osborn v. Carr, 1837, 12 Conn. 195, 208; 4 Kent, Comm. 178, 179.

8. Ames, Lectures on Legal History, 268. "But the English doctrine, which permits tacking by the third mortgagee, even when he has notice of the second mortgage * * * seems * * * indefensible * * *. Such a case is hardly to be distinguished from the cases where the holder of a bill collects it with knowledge that it is forged, or drawn without funds, and that the drawer is acting under a mistake." Ames, op. cit. supra, 283 n. 2.

9. Pomeroy, Equity Juris., 5th ed., § 756.

10. 3 Pomeroy, Equity Juris., 5th ed., 67.

and completely cutting it off by a *bona fide* purchase.[11] As to the former, he says that "The very object of the rule [that where equities are equal he who has the legal interest prevails] is, that a person who has in good faith become holder of an equitable lien or interest, on discovering his danger of being postponed to an outstanding equity already in the hands of another, may protect himself and secure his priority by procuring the legal title. * * * The decisions and dicta which conflict with this conclusion will be found, upon examination, to be dealing with the alleged rights of a *bona fide* purchaser for value, and not with a mere question of priority." [12]

As to Pomeroy's first point, it may be observed that if it rests upon an attempted differentiation between an equitable estate and a mere equity, it is unsound.[13] The distinction drawn, however, seems to be between a completed transfer of an equitable interest in the property and an executory equitable right to get the legal title. Of course, if the doctrine of *bona fide* purchase applies to the sale and transfer of equitable interests in property as well as legal interests the thesis could be sustained; [14] for having bought and had conveyed to him the equitable interest in the property, the prior equitable interest would already be cut off and, therefore, the later one could properly acquire the legal title even after getting notice of the earlier

equity. But, the cases have not accepted this view.[15]

The second distinction also is open to objection. Unless the property to which the claims attach is sufficient to satisfy all of them, priority of satisfaction out of it necessarily entails a destruction *pro tanto,* or *in toto* of the postponed liens. Consequently, it seems dubious to permit a later encumbrancer to prevail over an earlier one by his getting in legal title after notice on the theory that he is not defeating the earlier but only getting paid first out of the property.

If the doctrine that the later holder of an equity can prevail over a prior equity by getting in legal title after notice were limited to cases of tacking it would be of practically no importance today. It was abolished in England, except in certain situations, by the Law of Property Act,[16] and it never obtained acceptance in the United States. Even if the American courts had accepted the doctrine, it would have had little or no significance for two reasons. One is our universal adoption of recording or registry systems under many of which it is possible to give constructive notice of some of the most common equitable interests.[17] The other is that in lien jurisdictions, the doctrine could have no application because all mortgagees have legal liens; and even in title states second and subsequent mortgagees are regarded as acquiring more than an equitable interest in the property so as to preclude the doctrine.[18]

---

11. "In a case of priorities merely, the court in a proper proceeding awards the subject matter to the various claimants in the order of precedence; in the other case it refuses any relief to the plaintiff attempting to establish his title or claim against the *bona fide* purchaser." Pomeroy, Equity Juris., 5th ed., § 729, n. 20. See also idem, § 727, n. 13.

12. Pomeroy, Equity Juris, 5th ed., § 729.

13. See § 184, supra, especially note 29.

14. "It is a probable explanation of the minority rule that it arose out of the influence of Sugden, who argued strenuously for protecting the bona fide purchaser of an equitable title, and whose ideas were widely disseminated in this country during the early nineteenth century." 1927, 37 Yale L.J. 790, 796.

15. See supra, § 183. See also 3 Pomeroy, Equity Juris., 5th ed., 70.

16. 1925, 15 & 16 Geo. V, c. 20, § 94(3). In addition to abolishing the doctrine expressly, the act made the mortgagor the owner of the legal reversion with every mortgagee getting a legal term of years, and priority going first of all to the mortgagee with the title deeds, and thereafter in order of registration. See Pomeroy, Equity Juris., 5th ed., § 768. See also 1927, 37 Yale L.J. 790, 794.

17. See Osborn v. Carr, 1837, 12 Conn. 195, 208; Siter, Price & Co. v. McClanachan, 1845, 43 Va. 280. As to the application of the recording acts to equitable interests on land, see § 211, infra.

18. Sanders v. Reed, 1842, 12 N.H. 558; Gooding v. Shea, 1869, 103 Mass. 360, 4 Am.Rep. 563; see Pom-

However, the doctrine has been stated more broadly so as to apply in favor of all equitable owners and encumbrancers for value without notice of prior equitable interests who get in the legal estate from persons who commit no breach of trust or other duty in parting with it to them, even though at the time of getting it in the transferee had received notice of the earlier equitable claim.[19] An equitable encumbrancer who gets in the legal title from a trustee or mortgagor who commits a breach of trust or other duty to a prior equitable claimant by conveying it to him, clearly if such breach of trust or duty is known to him [20] and, in the opinion of some able judges, even if it were not,[21] will not prevail. This broader statement also covers the narrow *tabula in naufragio,* or tacking, case because there the legal mortgagee in transferring his legal mortgage to a later equitable mortgagee, who thus gets squeezed out, is violating no duty to anyone.[22] In addition, it applies to certain transfers of legal title after notice, even those coming from the mortgagor, where business-like practice does not involve the completion of the transfer at the time the value is paid,[23] and where the additional acts transferring title do not involve any breach of duty to the holder of the prior equity.[24] Thus if the mortgage deed has been delivered in escrow before notice, the delivery after notice will not prevent the acquisition of legal title by virtue of the delivery from the one who holds the deed in escrow.[25] So, too, if the mortgagor has executed and delivered a mortgage deed before notice, and the transfer is incomplete because the officer who took the acknowledgment of the deed failed to sign his name, the transfer can be completed after notice by having the officer sign, he owing no duty not to do so.[26] And also where the *bona fide* purchaser has been given an express and irrevocable power to transfer the title of the property but has not exercised it at the time he receives notice.[27]

Even though the legal title has never been acquired, some courts have preferred the holder of the subsequent equity, having acquired it for value and without notice, on the ground that he has the "best right" to call for the legal title.[28] Just what will give such a "best right" is not entirely clear.[29] One

eroy, Equity Juris., 5th ed., § 1233 n. 19; Rollison, Priorities in the Law of Mortgages, 1932, 8 Notre Dame Law. 28, 43.

19. See Bailey v. Barnes [1894] 1 Ch. 25, 37; Bates v. Johnson, 1859, Johns. 304; Restatement, Second, Trusts §§ 310, 311, 312. See also Scott, Trusts, § 311.1.

20. Frequently it is stated, as an exception, that the right of a *bona fide* purchaser later to get in legal title must not involve a breach of trust upon the part of the person from whom legal title is obtained. See, e. g., Pomeroy, Equity Juris., 5th ed., § 729. There are many cases so holding. Saunders v. Dehew, 1692, 2 Vern. 270; Allen v. Knight, 1846, 5 Hare 272; Sharples v. Adams, 1863, 32 Beav. 213; Mumford v. Stohwasser, 1874, L.R. 18 Eq. 556; Taylor v. London & County Banking Co., [1901] 2 Ch. 231. But the doctrine is broad enough to cover any breach of duty. See Scott, Trusts, § 311.1; Restatement, Second, Trusts § 311. Other cases and authorities include Fash v. Revesies, 1858, 32 Ala. 451; Gallion v. M'Caslin, Ind.1820, 1 Blackf. 91, 12 Am.Dec. 208; Campbell v. Brackenridge, Ind.1847, 8 Blackf. 471. See 2 Tiffany, Real Prop., 2d Ed., 2173; Maitland, Equity, Rev.Ed. by Brunyate, 130.

21. See Mumford v. Stohwasser, L.R.1874, 18 Eq. 556; Carter v. Carter, 1857, 3 K. & J. 617; Bailey v. Barnes, 1894, 1 Ch. 25, 37; Pomeroy, Equity Juris., 5th ed., § 728.

22. See Bailey v. Barnes, 1894, 1 Ch. 25, 37.

23. Chafee and Re, Cases on Equity, 326.

24. See Ames, Lectures on Legal History, 257; Campbell v. Brackenridge, Ind.1847, 8 Blackf. 471; Carroll v. Johnston, 1854, 55 N.C. 120.

25. Fuller v. Peabody, C.C.A.Ky.1924, 1 F.2d 965. Cf. Restatement, Second, Trusts § 312, Comment a.

26. Hume v. Dixon, 1881, 37 Ohio St. 66. Cf. Restatement, Second, Trusts § 312, Comment (a).

27. Dodds v. Hills, 1865, 2 H. & M. 424. See Ames, Lectures on Legal History, 257.

28. See Dueber Watch Case Mfg. Co. v. Daugherty, 1900, 62 Ohio St. 589, 596, 57 N.E. 455; see Rollison, Priorities in the Law of Mortgages, 1932, 8 Not.D.Law. 28, 39; Pomeroy, Equity Juris., 5th ed., 769; Tiffany, Real Prop., 3d ed., § 1261.

29. See 5 Tiffany, Real Prop., 3d ed., § 1261.
In Assaf v. Fuwa, 1954, 3 W.L.R. 552, the court stated that the "Better Right to Legal Estate" doctrine was applicable "only where there has been some transaction between the [later] claimant and the

case invoking it is where, instead of taking title himself, the subsequent claimant has it conveyed to a trustee to hold on trust for him.[30] This seems only an extension of the rule in the cases just considered. Where the purchaser merely gets the holder of the legal title to declare himself trustee of it,[31] or to contract to sell it,[32] the foundation for a "best right" is difficult to see.

Where, in ignorance of a second mortgage, a lender advances money that is to be used in part to buy in a first mortgage, which is assigned to him as security, the balance to be used for other purposes, the lender will prevail over the second mortgagee to the full extent of his loan.[33] The result does not depend, however, upon any doctrine of tacking or *tabula in naufragio*. Rather, as Ames pointed out, since the mortgagee advanced all of his money on the faith of the legal title at that time conveyed to him, his rights should be the same as if the first mortgagee

> owner of the legal estate, so that in equity the claimant can be regarded as a direct assignee. The legal estate, furthermore, must be outstanding in some third person who at the time of the special transaction had no notice of the earlier, competing equity; for otherwise the equity created by the assignment would be subject to the earlier equity, the legal estate already being held in trust for the earlier incumbrancer."

30. Stokes v. Riley, 1887, 121 Ill. 166, 11 N.E. 877. Cf. also Buck v. Winn, Ky.1850, 50 Ky. 320, purchaser at sheriff's sale has such an "inchoate legal title" even before getting deed as to be considered a *bona fide* purchaser.

31. See Stirling, L.J., in Taylor v. London etc. Co., [1901] 2 Ch. 231, 261.

32. Preston's Adm'r v. Nash, 1881, 76 Va. 1. Although the court did not mention the point as governing the decision, the fact that the prior claimant had neglected to record his deed may have influenced the court. The question arose under the recording act. The language of the doctrine has also been applied by courts which determine priority between successive assignees of a chose in action or of an equitable interest by the rule that he prevails who first gives notice to the debtor or trustee of legal title. See Peacock v. Burt, 1834, 4 L.J.Ch., N.S., 33; Campbell, Cases on Mortgages, 2d ed., 484.

33. Peacock v. Burt, 1834, 4 L.J.Ch.,N.S., 33. See Crosbie-Hill v. Sayer [1908] 1 Ch. 866, 877. See also infra, Chapter 10, Subrogation.

had reconveyed to the mortgagor and the latter had in turn conveyed it to the lender.[34]

FRAUDULENT OR NEGLIGENT CONDUCT BY PRIOR CLAIMANT

191. The priority of a legal or equitable mortgage may be lost by fraudulent or negligent conduct on the part of the mortgagee entitled to priority apart from such conduct.

An exception to the general rule that a legal mortgage will prevail over subsequent encumbrances, legal or equitable, occurs where the holder of the legal mortgage has actively assisted in or connived at the fraud[35] by which a subsequent mortgage has been obtained by the mortgagor through misleading the taker of it into believing that he is to be first in line.[36] And, similarly, another case in which the legal mortgagee will be postponed is that in which he has made "the mortgagor his agent with authority to raise money and the security given for raising such money has by misconduct of the agent been represented as the first estate."[37] Although as late as 1884[38] in England, it had been considered that nothing short of fraud, or such gross negligence as would be evidence of fraud,[39] would suffice to displace the priority of a legal mortgage, today it is pretty definitely settled in both England[40] and the United States[41] that in cases of active misleading mere negligence will suffice. Where the misrepresentation is by passivity, however, fraud or bad faith is an essential

34. Ames, Lectures on Legal History, 268 n. 3.

35. Northern etc. Co. v. Whipp, 1884, 26 Ch.D. 482.

36. Idem.

37. Maitland, Equity, Rev.Ed. by Brunyate, 128.

38. Northern etc. Co. v. Whipp, 1884, 26 Ch.D. 482.

39. For a trenchant criticism of the alternative test, "evidence of fraud", which dispenses with the existence of actual fraud, see Ewart, Estoppel, 259 et seq.

40. Walker v. Linom [1907] 2 Ch. 104; see Maitland, Equity, Rev.Ed. by Brunyate, 137.

41. See Pomeroy, Equity Juris., 5th ed., § 731.

element in the postponement.[42] **The false representation upon which the later encumbrancer acts, whether made fraudulently or negligently by the prior legal mortgagee, is sufficient basis to move an equity court to protect the subsequent mortgagee if he acquired only an equitable mortgage,[43] and to raise an estoppel in favor of a later legal mortgagee.[44]**

Not only will fraud or negligence postpone an earlier legal mortgage to a later encumbrance but negligence, and, *a fortiori*, fraud, on the part of a later legal mortgagee will prevent him from acquiring a priority over an earlier equitable mortgage which otherwise would have accrued to him. Thus where title deeds to land in England were in the hands of an equitable mortgagee and the mortgagor sold and conveyed legal title to the land to a purchaser who had no actual knowledge of the prior mortgage but did not require an abstract of the title or production of the title deeds, the court held in favor of the equitable mortgagee.[45] And the opinion of Lindley, M. R., put the decision on the ground that, apart from any question of constructive notice to him, the purchaser had been guilty of such negligence that he ought to be postponed to the equitable mortgagee.[46]

There is some authority that fraud is necessary in all cases to postpone a prior legal mortgagee of land, the reason given being that this would be a transfer of land, in effect, which would have to be in writing under the Statute of Frauds.[47] There are several answers to this. One is that the only effect is to change the order of precedence of interests in the land that are not otherwise affected, and this is no more a transaction falling within the Statute of Frauds than is an express subordination[48] agreement. Again, even if it amounts to a transfer of an interest in land, it is one by operation of law. And, by one view, although an estoppel is in practical operation just as good as a transfer of title it is not so as a matter of legal theory.[49]

Negligence of a prior equitable mortgagee that results in misleading a later one to lend on what he justifiably believes is an unencumbered security will result in the later one prevailing. The general rule that the equity prior in time prevails is inapplicable because the prior equity here, due to the careless conduct of its possessor, is not equal but inferior to the later one and so it wins.[50] This was exemplified in a case where A loaned money to B, a solicitor, on the security of title deeds which were delivered to him. A subsequently loaned the title deeds to B on a fraudulent representation by him that he desired to prepare an abstract of title and conditions of sale in order to sell and pay off the debt. B then borrowed a further sum from C, depositing the deeds with him as security—and soon after absconded. The property would only suffice to pay A or C. C was preferred.[51] The explanation of the

---

42. Ewart, Estoppel, 97.

43. See Pomeroy, Eq.Juris., 5th ed., §§ 686, 731, 732.

44. See 2 Tiffany, Real Prop., 2d ed., § 546.

45. Oliver v. Hinton [1899] 2 Ch. 264.

46. Cf. Hewitt v. Loosemore, 1851, 9 Hare, 449. The subsequent grantee had asked for the deeds and was given a reasonable excuse for their nonproduction. Look also at Berwick & Co. v. Price [1905] 1 Ch. 632. As to the signifance of title deeds as notice to a subsequent transferee, see Pomeroy, Eq. Juris., 4th Ed., § 718; Rollison, Priorities in the Law of Mortgages, 1932, 8 Notre Dame Law. 28, 54.

47. See Pomeroy, Eq.Juris., 5th ed., § 807.

48. Loewen v. Forsee, Mo.Sup.1896, 35 S.W. 1138; see note, 1927, 12 Iowa L.Rev. 201; cf. Gillig v. Maass, 1863, 28 N.Y. 191, subordination agreement not an "instrument in writing by which an estate or interest in real property is created, aliened, mortgaged or assigned or by which the title to real estate may be affected in law or in equity" within the provisions of a recording act. Cf. Pomeroy, Equity Juris., 5th ed. § 728.

49. See 2 Tiffany, Real Property, 2d ed., 2138.

50. Rice v. Rice, 1853, 2 Drew. 73.

51. Where the deeds have been returned to the mortgagor for the purpose of borrowing upon the security of them, but with the expectation that the mortgagor would disclose the existence of the prior mortgage, the first mortgagee has been postponed to the second mortgagee. Briggs v. Jones, 1870, L.R. 10, Eq.Cas. 92.

decision is that "He [the mortgagee] ought not, (as a matter of prudence), to let deeds get into the mortgagor's hands on any pretence—even though the pretext is such as a man might well believe to be true. * * * a prudent mortgagee does not let deeds get into the hands of the mortgagor. We cannot say that a suspicion of fraud ought to have been aroused, but we can say that it is careless to part with the deeds." [52] Another possible explanation is that the possession of the title deeds with C gave him a legal pledge interest in them and therefore the second rule is invoked, that where equities are equal the one with the legal right in the property prevails.[53] However, the first view is sufficient, for clearly C's equity is a superior one and would prevail without reliance upon any legal interest. So, too, in a case where M borrowed from E–1 and agreed to give him a legal mortgage (thus creating an equitable mortgage in E–1). E–1 made on inquiries for the title deeds and did not demand or obtain a legal mortgage. M borrowed money from E–2 and as security delivered the title deeds. E–2 had no notice of E–1. Pretty clearly E–2 wins.[54] E–1's negligence makes his equity inferior to that of E–2.[55] But suppose either that (1) the first mortgagee made inquiry for them and received a reasonable excuse for their nondelivery; or (2) he received a part of the deeds in the reasonable belief that he was receiving all of them. In neither of these cases will the ordinary rule of priority in time be upset, for

the holder of the prior equitable mortgage is innocent of fault in the misleading of the later one and therefore his equity is equal to that of the later mortgagee and so priority according to time determines the rights of the parties.[56]

It will not have escaped notice that many of the cases cited in the foregoing discussion and in other places in this chapter have involved equitable mortgages arising out of title deeds transactions which are, of course, foreign to the experience and, frequently, the knowledge of an American lawyer.[57] Nevertheless the reasoning of the decisions in them can be relied upon as establishing general principles of priority with respect to negligent misleading or notice which are valuable precedents for him by way of analogy even though most of his problems arise under the operation of recording acts.

RECEIVERSHIPS—SIX MONTHS' RULE

192. In the case of railroads and public utilities, claims for labor and supplies arising shortly before the appointment of a receiver are given priority over existing liens if the claims arose in reliance that they would be paid out of current income. Under the prevailing view this priority attaches only to income received by the receiver as long as no income is diverted to the benefit of the mortgagees. There are, however, two other views.

When a receiver is appointed, the ordinary priority of a mortgage lien may be postponed by the operation of judge made rules giving precedence to the payment of some claims.

---

52. Maitland, Equity, Rev.Ed. by Brunyate, 127. Cf. Martinez v. Cooper, 1826, 2 Russ. 196.

53. See Ewart, Estoppel, 276 et seq.

54. Farrand v. Yorkshire Banking Co., 1888, L.R., 40 Ch.Div. 182.

55. "* * * the equity of a vendor's lien has occasionally been postponed to the subsequent equity of one who purchased in ignorance of the lien, the conduct of the lienor in failing to take a mortgage to secure his claim, or otherwise to make the existence of the lien a matter of record, being regarded as involving an element of negligence, and as consequently making his equity inferior to that of the subsequent purchaser." 2 Tiffany, Real Prop., 2d Ed., 2176.

56. See Rollison, Priorities in the Law of Mortgages, 1932, 8 Not.D.Law. 28, 33. See also Mills v. Rossiter, Eureka Oil Burner & Manufacturing Co., 1909, 156 Cal. 167, 103 P. 896; Frost v. Wolf, 1890, 77 Tex. 455, 14 S.W. 440, 19 Am.St.Rep. 761; Wasserman v. Metzger, 1906, 105 Va. 744, 54 S.E. 893, 7 L. R.A.,N.S., 1019; In re Castell & Brown, Ltd. [1898] 1 Ch.Div. 315; Pomeroy, Eq.Juris., 4th Ed., §§ 686, 687; note, 1882, 16 Ir.L.T. 185, 197, 209; note, 1907, 51 Sol.J. 585. Cf. Berrisford v. Milward, 1740, 2 Atk. 49; Garland v. Harrison, 1852, 17 Mo. 282.

57. For a tabulation of cases involving the significance of the possession of the title deeds in determining priorities between A. legal and equitable mortgages, and B. successive equitable mortgages, see Ewart, Estoppel, 279 et seq.

This precedence may be given either by permitting the claims to be paid first out of certain assets of the debtor; or it may be accomplished by selling receivership certificates and using the proceeds to make payments and then giving the holder of the certificates priority over other claimants.[58] In either event, the basis for and extent of the priority involves the six months' rule [59] and statutes enacted in some jurisdictions embodying, to a greater or lesser degree, its ideas.[60]

The six months' rule, first enunciated in the famous case of Fosdick v. Schall in 1878,[61] is that various claims for labor and supplies which are a current expense of ordinary operation and maintenance and have arisen within a short period, usually set at six months, prior to the appointment of a receiver [62] shall have priority not only over all general claims, but also under certain circumstances, over existing liens.[63] It must appear, expressly or impliedly, that the current debt arose on the faith that it would be paid out of current income rather than in reliance upon the general credit of the debtor.[64] The doctrine originated in the case of a railroad receivership,[65] and, although extended by the lower federal courts to public utility corporations generally,[66] has never been applied to any other kind of enterprise by the highest federal court.[67] Some state courts have held that it also is applicable to private corporations; [68] but the preponderance of state authority [69] and the decisions of the lower federal courts [70] are the other way.

There are three views [71] as to what assets priority of payment under the doctrine will attach. One of these limits the priority of

---

58. See 1909, 9 Col.L.Rev. 172. Cf., note, 1947, 56 Yale L.J. 1258.

59. See also FitzGibbon, The Present Status of the Six Months' Rule, 1934, 34 Col.L.Rev. 230; Fordham, Preferences of Prereceivership Claims in Equity Receiverships, 1931, 15 Minn.L.Rev. 261; Wham, Preference in Railroad Receiverships, 1928, 23 Ill.L.Rev. 141. See notes, 1931, 79 U. of Pa.L. Rev. 788; 1917, 17 Col.L.Rev. 69; 1909, 7 Mich.L. Rev. 239; 1909, 22 Harv.L.Rev. 373; 1909, 9 Col.L. Rev. 172; 1926, 40 A.L.R. 244; 1931, 31 Col.L.Rev. 170; 1934, 34 Col.L.Rev. 1558; 1934, 19 Minn.L.Rev. 253; 1935, 44 Yale L.Jour. 1107; 1940, 19 N.Car.L. Rev. 89; 1941, 50 Yale L.J. 490.

60. For a survey of such statutes, see Fordham, Preferences of Prereceivership Claims in Equity Receiverships, 1930, 15 Minn.L.Rev. 260, 285; Kauper, Insolvency Statutes Preferring Wages Due Employees, 1932, 30 Mich.L.Rev. 504.

61. 99 U.S. 235, 25 L.Ed. 339.

62. "By long established practice, the doctrine has been applied only to unpaid expenses incurred within six months prior to the appointment of the receivers." St. Louis & S. F. R. Co. v. Spiller, 1927, 273 U.S. 680, 47 S.Ct. 111, 71 L.Ed. 837. As to a longer period, see Pettibone-Mulliken Co. v. Guaranty Trust Co., C.C.A.Minn.1928, 25 F.2d 948.

63. See FitzGibbon, The Present Status of the Six Months' Rule, 1934, 34 Col.L.Rev. 230, 235.

64. Birmingham Trust & Savings Co. v. Atlanta etc. Co., D.C.Ga.1924, 300 F. 173; Virginia & Alabama Coal Co. v. Central etc., Co., 1898, 170 U.S. 355, 365, 18 S.Ct. 657, 661, 42 L.Ed. 1068, 1071; Southern Ry. Co. v. Carnegie Steel Co., 1900, 176 U.S. 257, 285, 20 S.Ct. 347, 358, 44 L.Ed. 458, 471; Dictaphone Sales Corp. v. Powell, C.C.A.Va.1935, 77 F.2d 795.

65. Fosdick v. Schall, 1878, 99 U.S. 235, 25 L.Ed. 339.

66. See, e. g., Virginia Passenger & Power Co. v. Lane Bros., C.C.A.Va.1909, 174 F. 513, 98 C.C.A. 295, certiorari denied 215 U.S. 610, 30 S.Ct. 411, 54 L.Ed. 348; 1940, 19 N.Car.L.Rev. 88, 90.

67. See Fordham, Preferences of Prereceivership Claims in Equity Receiverships, 1931, 15 Minn.L. Rev. 261, 281.

68. E. g., Lunsky v. Criterion Construction Co., (N.J.) 1930, 151 A. 490, commented on 1931, 31 Col.L.Rev. 490. See 1931, 79 U. of Pa.L.Rev. 788; 1940, 19 N. Car.L.Rev. 89. See infra note 76 for additional authorities.

69. First National Bank of Grand Junction v. Wyman, 1901, 16 Colo.App. 468, 66 P. 456; Standley v. Hendrie & Bolthoff Mfg. Co., 1900, 27 Colo. 331, 61 P. 600; Merriam v. Victory Mining Co., 1900, 37 Or. 321, 60 P. 997; Oldroyd v. McCrea, 1925, 65 Utah 142, 235 P. 580, 40 A.L.R. 230; see 1 Clark, Receiverships, 2d ed., § 470(b).

70. E. g., Spencer v. Taylor Creek Ditch Co., Alaska 1912, 194 F. 635, 114 C.C.A. 407; see note, 1926, 40 A.L.R. 244, 247.

71. A fourth theory, called the "special equities", is sometimes advanced. Gregg v. Metropolitan Trust Co., 1905, 197 U.S. 183, 25 S.Ct. 415, 49 L.Ed. 717; see Wham, Preference in Railroad Receiverships, 1928, 23 Ill.L.Rev. 141, 147. Rather than expressing a different rule as to what assets it applies, it seems to be one explanation of the doctrine itself, although, as such, it would have, of course, an influence upon the scope of its application.

the claims to "net profits made by the receiver, and does not displace the lien of the mortgages on the corpus." An exception is made if the current operating income subject to the preference was "diverted to pay the mortgagees of the corpus, or to permanently increase or improve the mortgaged corpus." [72] In that case the priority will extend to the corpus to the extent of the diversion.[73] A second view, which rests the doctrine on the "necessity of *payment*" of certain claims in order, as a business requirement, to continue operations, allows preference against corpus after exhaustion of income without regard to whether there has been any diversion of income to the benefit of the mortgagees.[74] A third view also would subject the corpus to the priority of the specified claims regardless of any diversion of income on the ground that the business involved "from its nature and public responsibilities, must be kept a going concern. * * * It cannot depend upon diversion of income or upon existence of income. * * * And there is no infringement of the rights of the mortgagees. Their interests are served, as those of the public are, by keeping [in this case] the railroad in operation." [75] The first of these three views is the dominant one and,

under it, mortgages, unless they covered income [76] as well as corpus, would be seldom affected and then only to the extent income had been paid to them which should have gone to the claimants. Under the other two, however, mortgagees of the corpus may be postponed.

The granting of priority in these cases has been justified on various grounds.[77] One is that there is an implied agreement by the mortgagees that the mortgage shall not apply to the gross income but only to the net income after payment of current operating expenses. This, of course, is a pure fiction in most, if not all, cases. Another reason is that the claims are for labor and supplies which inure directly to the benefit of the mortgage security and therefore it is fair to impress it with an equitable lien in favor of the claimants.[78] A third explanation is that wage earners and small supply men who are especially dependent on daily earnings and prompt payment of their claims for their livelihood and who have, normally, no means of discovering or protecting themselves against impending insolvency of the debtor corporation should be given this advantage.[79] Most courts, however, found the rule on the public concern in the continued operation of the business and, for this reason, confine its application to railroad corporations and to public utilities. There is, of course, some public concern in the continuation of business of private corporations, but it would seem to be insufficient to justify the postponement of secured creditors to current claimants in order to achieve that purpose. Those cases that include private corporations restrict the rule to the preservation of the property during liquidation and rule out

72. Birmingham Trust & Savings Co. v. Atlanta etc. Co., D.C.Ga.1924, 300 F. 173, 177. See Fordham, Preferences of Prereceivership Claims in Equity Receiverships, 1931, 15 Minn.L.Rev. 264, 265, 283, 285; Wham, Preference in Railroad Receiverships, 1928, 23 Ill.L.Rev. 140, 144.

73. Union Trust Co. v. Souther, 1883, 107 U.S. 591, 2 S.Ct. 295, 27 L.Ed. 488. See 15 Minn.L.Rev. 261, 280.

74. "The ground of such allowance as was made was not merely that the supplies were necessary for the preservation of the road, but that the *payment* was necessary to the business of the road—a very different proposition." Gregg v. Metropolitan Trust Co., 1905, 197 U.S. 183, 187, 25 S.Ct. 415, 416, 49 L.Ed. 717, majority opinion. See also Moore v. Donahoo, 1914, 217 F. 177, 133 C.C.A. 171, certiorari denied 235 U.S. 706, 35 S.Ct. 283, 59 L.Ed. 434. Chicago etc. Co. v. U. S. & Mexican Trust Co., C.C.A. Kan.1915, 225 F. 940, 945, 141 C.C.A. 64.

75. Gregg v. Metropolitan Trust Co., 1905, 197 U.S. 183, 196, 25 S.Ct. 415, 420, 49 L.Ed. 717, dissenting opinion. See 1931, 15 Minn.L.Rev. 261, 267, 281; 1928, 23 Ill.L.Rev. 141, 146, 151.

76. See Campbell, Cases Mortgages, 2d ed., 492 n. 1. Railroad mortgages almost universally embrace income as well as corpus.

77. See 1935, 44 Yale L.Jour. 1107, 1108.

78. See St. Louis Trust Co. v. Riley, C.C.A.Ark.1895, 70 F. 32, 36, 16 C.C.A. 610, 30 L.R.A. 456.

79. See Finance Co of Penn. v. Charleston etc. Co., C.C.S.C.1892, 49 F. 693, 694.

expenses of continued operation except where that is necessary to preserve the property.[80] Possibly public interest plays some part here also, but a belief that the services and supplies rendered benefit the security and that the producers of the benefit should have first claim for payment out of the property benefited, together with the special equity inherent in the nature of the claimants, as explained in the third reason above, afford a better explanation of the decisions.

B. AS AFFECTED BY STATUTE

RECORDING STATUTES IN ENGLAND

193. In England there are registration acts in some counties and a national act covering certain types of mortgages. The latter provides for priority according to date of registration. Most priorities are not governed by statute.

Priorities among mortgages, in addition to being governed by the principles discussed

in the first part of this chapter, are also controlled by statutes, the most important of which, in the United States, are recording acts. In England this has not been true. The statute of uses [81] resulted in new methods of conveyances which avoided the publicity inherent in the old form of transfer by livery of seisin. In an effort to prevent clandestine conveyances, parliament prescribed a substitute method of publicity in the Statute of Enrolments.[82] Since it applied only to bargains and sales of freehold estates, it was a simple matter to evade its application by resort to a method of transfer by "lease and release", neither of which was within the terms of the act.[83] The Statute of Enrolments, although copied in colonial Virginia,[84] had no important influence in this country,[85] nor did it play any part in the modern English law.

Today in England there are land registry acts in the counties of Middlesex [86] and York,[87] a Torrens law in the city and county

80. Sockport Felt Co. v. United Box Board & Paper Co., 1908, 74 N.J.Eq. 686, 70 A. 980, commented on, 1908, 7 Mich.L.Rev. 239; 1909, 9 Col.L.Rev. 173; 1909, 22 Harv.L.Rev. 373. See notes 1931, 79 U. of Pa.L.Rev. 788, 790; 1940, 19 N.Car.L.Rev. 89. On whether preservation covers anything beyond preventing destruction or deterioration of the physical property, see 1931, 79 U. of Pa.L.Rev. 788, 791, 794 et seq.; 1909, 22 Harv.L.Rev. 373, 374. Sometimes, of course, as in the case of oil wells or mines, preservation demands continued operation. See Rhode Island Hosp. Tr. Co. v. S. H. Greene & Sons Corp., 1929, 50 R.I. 305, 310, 146 A. 765, reargument denied 147 A. 425; see 1931, 79 U. of Pa.L.Rev. 788, 799. So, too, the completion of construction of an apartment house has been held to be necessary to preserve the assets. Lunsky v. Criterion Construction Co., (N.J.) 1930, 151 A. 490, commented on 1931, 31 Col.L.Rev. 490. North Carolina apparently sanctions an operating receivership with receivership expenses payable before secured claims if it benefit the secured creditors by making liquidation of the assets more successful. Bank of Pinehurst v. Mid-Pines Country Club, Inc., 1935, 208 N.C. 239, 179 S. E. 882; Wood v. Woodbury & Pace, Inc., 1940, 217 N.C. 356, 8 S.E.2d 240, commented on 1940, 19 N. Car.L.Rev. 89. Other occasional cases go beyond preservation and cover continued operation. Drennen v. Mercantile Trust Co., 1897, 115 Ala. 592, 23 So. 164, 39 L.R.A. 623, 67 Am.St.Rep. 72, commented on by Fordham, Preferences of Prereceivership Claims in Equity Receiverships, 1930, 15 Minn.L. Rev. 261, 281; Bowen v. Hockley, C.C.A.Md. 1934, 71 F.2d 781, 94 A.L.R. 856, noted, 1934, 34 Col.L. Rev. 1558, 19 Minn.L.Rev. 253, 44 Yale L.Jour. 1107.

Both cases involved wage claims. See also 1935, 44 Yale L.Jour. 1107, 1109; 1931, 79 U. of Pa.L.Rev. 788, 799.

81. 27 Hen. VIII, c. 10 (1535).

82. 27 Hen. VIII, c. 6, (1536). Under the statute a bargain and sale deed had to be enrolled within six months after its execution on penalty of being void as to creditors, heirs, and purchasers. The enrollment had to be in one of the courts of record at Westminster, or in other specified offices.

83. This clumsy device involving the execution of two instruments persisted until 1841 when the necessity for the fictitious lease was abolished followed, in 1845, by legislation making a simple deed sufficient to transfer all estates. 8 & 9 Vict. c. 106, § 2; Williams, Real Prop., 24th ed., 232.

84. See 2 Minor, Real Prop., 2d ed., Ribble, § 1296, n. 1.

85. The Statute of Enrolments was not considered to be in force in this country without specific enactment. See Givan v. Doe, ex dem. Tout, 1844, 7 Blackf. (Ind.) 210; 3 Gray, Cas.Prop., 2d ed., 193. See also Beale, The Origin of the System of Recording Deeds in America, 1907, 19 Green Bag 335.

86. 7 Anne, c. 20 (1708).

87. 5 Anne, c. 18 (1705); 6 Anne, c. 35 (1706); 18 Geo. II, c. 6 (1735). A similar registry law was enacted for Ireland. 6 Anne, c. 2 (1707). See Hanna,

of London,[88] and under the Land Charges Act of 1925, a nation-wide registration act applicable to "puisne mortgages" [89] and equitable mortgages other than those created by deposit of title deeds which rank according to their dates of registration.[90]

It will be noticed that the last of these laws explicitly provides for priority in accordance with registration. The earlier registry acts mentioned above did not in terms deal with priority. What they did was to provide that conveyances should be "adjudged fraudulent and void against any subsequent purchaser or mortgagee for valuable consideration, unless such memorial thereof be registered as by the act is directed, before the registering of the memorial of the deed or conveyance under which the subsequent purchaser or mortgagee shall claim. * * * " [91] Under this legislation the law courts would give preference to a subsequent purchaser for value who first recorded regardless of notice by him at the time he took his conveyance of a prior unrecorded deed.[92] The English equity courts, however, accorded priority to the earlier conveyance if the later taker had notice of it, holding that "the design of those Acts [was] only to give parties notice, who might otherwise, without such registry, be in danger of being imposed on by a prior purchase or mortgage, which they are in no danger of when they have notice thereof in any manner, though not by the registry." [93] Equity refused, however, to give the effect of notice to the registration itself, holding that registration gave "no greater efficacy to deeds * * * than they had before." [94] The doctrine of constructive notice from registration therefore had no place in England under this statute, a result in sharp contrast to the effect of recordation under American statutes.

Apart from these laws, proof of title in England is by possession of the land and exhibition of the original title deeds, and priorities are determined on non-statutory rules and principles based upon this system.[95]

RECORDING STATUTES IN THE UNITED STATES

194. Despite differences in phraseology, particular provisions, and theory as well as mechanics of operation, all states except Louisiana have essentially similar recording systems. The Torrens System of land registration provides an optional alternative in many states but is little used.

The recording system as it exists in America,[96] while probably deriving the provision

---

The Extension of Public Recordation, 1931, 31 Col. L.Rev. 617, 618.

88. See Williams, Real Prop., 24th ed., 244–247, 767–813.

89. I. e., mortgages not accompanied by immediate entry by the mortgagee or delivery to him of the title deeds.

90. Law of Prop. Act, 1925, § 97. See Cheshire, Modern Real Prop.Law, 4th ed., 1937, 623 et seq.

91. Stat. 7 Anne, c. 20 (1709).

92. Doe dem. Robinson v. Allsop, 1821, 5 B. & Ald. 142.

93. Blades v. Blades, 1727, 1 Eq.Cas.Abr. 358, pl. 2. See also Le Neve v. Le Neve, 1747, Ambl. 436.

It has been pointed out that, apart from its significance on the matter of statutory priority by registration, this legislation vivifies the fact that equitable mortgages by deposit of title deeds are still important in modern English law and that a mortgagee can still take possession of the property at the time the mortgage is given. It also is worthy of note that the legislation expressly includes ordinary equitable mortgages within its operation. See Glenn, Mortgages, § 365.

94. Bedford v. Backhouse, 1730, 2 Eq.Cas.Abr. 615 pl. 12.

95. See In re Snyder, 1908, 138 Iowa 553, 114 N.W. 615, 19 L.R.A.,N.S., 206.

For a recent survey of the systems of title registration in Scotland and recent developments in England, see Fiflis, Security and Economy in Land Transactions: Some Suggestions from Scotland and England, 1968, 20 Hastings L.J. 171.

96. For discussions of the recording system in the United States, see Beale, The Origin of the System of Recording Deeds in America, 1907, 19 Green Bag, 335; Bordwell, Recording Instruments Affecting Land, 1916, 2 Iowa L.Bull. 51, 109, 169 and, 1917, 3 Iowa L.Bull. 25; Aigler, The Operation of the Recording Acts, 1924, 22 Mich.L.Rev. 405; Bailey, Recording of Mortgages—"He Who First Records," 1935, 15 Or.L.Rev. 66; Logan, New York Mortgages and the Recording Act, 1906, 6 Col.L.Rev. 547; Rol-

for acknowledgment from English borough or manorial custom which was adopted in Plymouth colony,[97] had its origin in an ordinance of 1640 in the colony of Massachu-

setts.[98] There were other colonial statutes but the Massachusetts one, which may have been patterned on the English Statute of Enrollments [99] but more likely was of indigenous creation,[1] was the most influential. The Massachusetts statutory scheme was separate and distinct from a procedure designed only to prevent fraudulent conveyances and contained the essential features of a modern recording act: acknowledgment before a public official; recordation of the whole deed; passage of title at the time of the conveyance and not at the time of recording; and assurance of priority of right to the first of several grantees who promptly recorded his deed.[2] Today all states of the United States with the exception of Louisiana [3] have recording systems which are

lison, Priority in the Law of Mortgages, 1932, 8 Not.D.Law. 215; McCormack, Possible Improvements in the Recording Acts, 1925, 31 W.Va.L.Q. 79; Sewards, Proposed Plan for the Improvement of the Present System of Recording, 1872, 1 So. L.Rev. 476; Rood, Registration of Land Titles, 1914, 12 Mich.L.Rev. 379; Rundell, Recording of Deeds in Wisconsin, 1922, 1 Wis.L.Rev. 340; Hackman, Changes in Washington Land Record Title Law, 1927, 2 Wash.L.Rev. 211; Haskins, The Beginnings of the Recording System in Massachusetts, 1941, 21 Boston U.L.Rev. 281; Howe, The Recording of Deeds in the Colony of Massachusetts Bay, 1948, 28 Boston U.L.Rev. 1; Chaplin, Record Title to Land, 1893, 6 Harv.L.Rev. 312; Leesman, Operation of the Illinois Recording Act, 1944, 38 Ill.L. Rev. 396; Philbrick, Limits of Record Search and Therefore of Notice, 1944, 93 U. of Pa.L.Rev. 125, 259, 391; Title Examination Standards, 1941, 20 Neb.L.Rev. 346; Patton on Titles, 2 Tiffany, Real Prop., 2d Ed., §§ 567 et seq.; 2 Pomeroy, Eq.Juris., 4th Ed., §§ 645 et seq. (especially valuable for a digest of the American statutes). For a discussion and elaborate digest of recording acts dealing with personal property transactions, see Hanna, Extensions of Public Recordation, 1931, 31 Col.L.Rev. 617. For an excellent discussion together with an extended bibliography on the Torrens System, see Hanna, Cases on Security, 657. For other recent discussions of the Torrens System, see Powell, Registration of the Title to New York, reviewed in 1939, 23 Minn.L.Rev. 874, and 1939, 16 N.Y.Univ.L. Q.R. 510 as well as criticized by Fairchild and Springer, 1939, 24 Corn.L.Q. 557; McDougal and Brabner-Smith, Land Title Transfer: A Regression, 1939, 48 Yale L.J. 1125; Bordwell, The Resurrection of Registration of Title, 1940, 7 Univ. of Chi. L.Rev. 470; McDougal, Title Registration and Land Law Reform: A Reply, 1940, 8 Univ. of Chi.L.Rev. 63; 1946, 21 Notre Dame Law. 344.

The term "recordation": covers four methods of giving public notice: "Recording," which means copying the original instrument in full in a permanent book preserved in the record office; "Registration," the method used where the Torrens system is in effect; "Instrument filing," which means that the original document is not copied but is left permanently in the record office; "Notice filing," which means that a statement is filed in the record office that the debtor has given a security interest in his property or intends to do so. Storke and Sears, The Perennial Problem of Security Priority and Registration, 1952, 24 Colo.L.Rev. 180, 185. Only the first method is considered in this text.

97. The Dutch system may have been a source of the practice of acknowledgment adopted at Plymouth. See Haskins, The Beginnings of the Recording System in Massachusetts, 1941, 21 Boston U.L. Rev. 281, 291, 303.

98. See Beale, The Origin of the System of Recording Deeds in America, 1907, 19 Green Bag 335; Hassam, Land Transfer Reform, 1890, 4 Harv.L. Rev. 271. There were earlier enactments, but it was the 1640 ordinance that gave definitive shape to the law.

99. See Patton on Titles, 2d Ed., § 8. But, to the contrary, see Haskins, The Beginnings of the Recording System in Massachusetts, 1941, 21 Boston U.L.Rev. 281, 293.

1. See Beale, The Origin of the System of Recording Deeds in America, 1907, 19 Green Bag 335. But see Haskins, The Beginnings of the Recording System in Massachusetts, 1941, 21 Boston U.L.Rev. 281, 303.

2. See articles in preceding note. Amendments in 1648 to the Massachusetts act required recording only if the grantor remained in possession, thus making it similar to the provision in the Virginia statute, a point not noticed by Beale. Probably this was altered in 1652 to require all deeds of conveyance to be recorded. See Howe, The Recording of Deeds in the Colony of Massachusetts Bay, 1948, 28 Boston U.L.Rev. 1.

3. The law of registration in Louisiana is governed by legislation going back to the Civil Code of 1808 and is based upon earlier French statutes and customs with the exception of mortgages, the provision for registration of them being taken from the Code Napoleon. Patton, Titles, 2d Ed., § 6. See also Redmann, The Louisiana Law of Recordation: Some Principles and Some Problems, 1965, 39 Tulane L.Rev. 491–512; Dainow, Mortgages—Public Records Doctrine, 1967, 27 Louisiana L.Rev. 492, discussing Lacour v. Ford Investment Corp., La. App. 4th Cir. 1966, 183 So.2d 463, application dismissed, 1967, 250 La. 459, 196 So.2d 275.

fundamentally similar. This is true even though the phraseology of the acts in the different states varies widely and the points of divergence in their provisions are many and striking. Among them are: (a) the time allowed for recording and the effect of recording within or after the time set (fully two-thirds of the acts contain no time limitation); (b) what persons and under what circumstances persons other than purchasers will be protected (purchasers, which term includes mortgagees, are always named); (c) what interests in property and what sorts of transactions (release? assignment? etc.) in respect to them are covered; (d) whether, either by the language of the statute or the construction of it by the courts, the law (1) allots priority among purchasers strictly according to priority of record, (2) invalidates or postpones an unrecorded conveyance as against a subsequent *bona fide* purchaser regardless of recordation by him, or (3) requires, in order for the subsequent purchaser to prevail over a prior unrecorded conveyance that he not only have bought for value, in good faith and without notice, but that his conveyance be recorded first.

In addition to the variation in their detailed provisions, there is some divergence of view as to the general theories upon which they are framed and the mechanics of their operation. In spite of this, either in the express language of the acts or construed as inherent in them, are certain main features common to practically all. Further, in the United States, there is substantial unanimity as to their main objectives.[4] This last statement is so even though the criticism has been made that some of the objectives are contradictory of or tend to vitiate others.[5]

The Torrens System of land registration originated in Australia in 1858 on analogy to ship registration and later was adopted in England and her other dependencies as well as in modified form by the most important nations of western Europe and a large number of states of the United States.[6] It was devised to remedy the defects of the ordinary recording systems adopted in England and in the United States as well as the English system of preservation, production, and transfer of title deeds. In the United States where enacted it has not supplanted the existing system of recordation but only provides an optional alternative. Its chief distinctive feature is that it registers and determines title to land so as to amount to practically a government patent to each purchaser, rather than merely recording instruments as evidence of title.[7] Although its more enthusiastic advocates claim great advantages for the system, practice with it has revealed some serious disadvantages and, regardless of any merits it possesses as an improvement over the common system of recordation in the United States, it has not been used to any appreciable extent where it has been enacted.[8] No further consideration, therefore, will be given to its operation.[9]

5. For an intensive elaboration of this last thesis, with especial reference to the doctrine of inquiry notice, see Philbrick, Limits of Record Search and Therefore of Notice, 1945, 93 U. of Pa.L.Rev. 125, 259, 391.

4. Patton, Titles 2d Edition, §§ 9, 19; Webb, Record of Title, §§ 6, 7, 10, 12, and c. 2; Aigler, The Operation of the Recording Acts, 1924, 22 Mich.L.Rev. 405; Philbrick, Limits of Record Search and Therefore of Notice, 1945, 93 U. of Pa.L.Rev. 125, 146.

6. See Peyser, A Note on the Torrens System printed in 1933, Handler, Cases and Materials on the Law of Vendor and Purchaser, reprinted, 1940, Hanna, Cas.Security, 715. The European nations listed are Norway, Sweden, Denmark, France, Germany, Austria, and Switzerland. Nineteen American states were listed: California, Colorado, Illinois, Massachusetts, Minnesota, Mississippi, Nebraska, New York, North Carolina, North Dakota, Ohio, Oregon, South Carolina, South Dakota, Tennessee, Utah, Virginia, Washington.

7. See Peyser, op. cit. supra note 6.

8. See 1923, 16 Lawyer & Banker 37, quoted in Peyser, op. cit. supra note 6.

9. For a comprehensive discussion of the Torrens System, see Powell, Registration of the Title to Land in New York (1938). For an extensive bibliography on it, see Hanna, Cas.Security, 715, n. 1. See also McDougal and Brabner-Smith, Land Title Transfer: A Regression, 1939, 48 Yale L.J. 1125; Fairchild and Springer, A Criticism of Powell's Book, 1939, 24 Corn.L.Q. 557; Bordwell, The Resur-

FEATURES COMMON TO AMERICAN STATUTES

195. Some features common to most recording acts in the United States are that recordation is not essential to the passage of title, recordation gives constructive notice, non-record notice to a purchaser will exclude him from the protection of the statutes, and recordation consists in copying the instrument into books kept for the purpose.

Before considering the basic objectives of the acts some of the important features common to most of them should be noted. For one thing, recordation is not essential to the passage of title, the deed itself being operative for that purpose prior to its recording.[10] This is true in spite of the argument that, as a means of forcing all titles documents to be recorded for the purpose of showing a complete history of title, "no instrument operating *inter vivos* and ostensibly affecting title should have any *validity* unless and until recorded." [11] Again, apart from the few jurisdictions in which priority under the statutes is determined strictly in accordance with priority of recordation with notice being immaterial,[12] recordation operates as constructive notice to subsequent claimants of an interest in the property in cases in which notice is a material factor in determin-

ing the rights of the parties under the recognized doctrines of law and equity apart from any operation of the recording acts themselves.[13] Also, in spite of expressed views that the acts operate as legislative extensions or adoption of estoppel [14] or the principle that as between two persons one of whom must suffer by reason of the act of a third party the one whose default made it possible should bear the loss,[15] it seems quite clear that the "effect of the statute really is that the person claiming under the instrument in question by his failure to observe the direction of the statute confers upon the party who executed the instrument, the moving party, a statutory power to displace the interest vested by the execution of the instrument. This power may be effectively exercised only by those specified in the statute * * *." [16] The last statement must be qualified. Although the English statutes did not in terms exclude a subsequent purchaser with knowledge of an unrecorded conveyance from the protection of the statute, the English equity courts, apparently first upon a theory of real fraud on the part of a subsequent purchaser who takes a conveyance when he has actual knowledge of a prior one, engrafted by judicial decision the doctrine that any one who has notice from any source of the existence of the prior unrecorded conveyance cannot claim the assistance of the act.[17] The same question as to non-record no-

---

rection of Registration of Title, 1940, 7 U. of Chi. L.Rev. 470; McDougals, Title Registration and Land Law Reform: A Reply, 1940, 8 U. of Chi.L. Rev. 63; Bade, Review of Powell, 1939, 23 Minn.L. Rev. 874; Walsh, Review of Powell, 1939, 16 N.Y. U.L.Q. 510; Priority of Liens under the Torrens System of Land Registration, 1946, 21 Notre Dame Law. 344.

10. Philbrick, Limits of Record Search and Therefore of Notice, 1945, 93 U. of Pa.L.Rev. 125, 142. In this respect the ordinary recording act differs from Torrens laws.

11. See Philbrick, Limits of Record Search and Therefore of Notice, 1944, 93 U. of Pa.L.Rev. 125, 127. Yet only a couple of states, and those not completely, so provide. Md.Code 1957, art. 21, §§ 1, 109; N.Car.G.S. § 47–18. Philbrick, op. cit. supra, 140 ff.

12. See Patton, Titles, 2d Edition § 8, citing North Carolina, and, as to mortgages, Arkansas, Ohio, and perhaps Pennsylvania apart from the thirty day protection given to purchase-money mortgages without recordation.

13. See Aigler, The Operation of the Recording Acts, 1924, 22 Mich.L.Rev. 405, 414, 420.

14. Boynton v. Haggart, C.C.A.Ark.1903, 120 F. 819, 57 C.C.A. 301, certiorari denied 191 U.S. 573, 24 S. Ct. 845, 48 L.Ed. 307.

15. Smith's Heirs v. Branch Bank of Mobile, 1852, 21 Ala. 125. See Patton, Titles, 2d Ed., § 19.

16. Aigler, Operation of the Recording Acts, 1924, 22 Mich.L.Rev. 405, 415. The embodiment of this consequence into the statutes made recording something more than a means of preserving evidence; it made them operate to determine priority between conveyances. See Van Cortlandt v. Tozer, N.Y.1837, 17 Wend. 338, 344–5, affirmed 20 Wend. 423; Philbrick, Limits of Record Search and Therefore of Notice, 1945, 93 U. of Pa.L.Rev. 125, 146.

17. See Baart v. Martin, 1906, 99 Minn. 197, 212, 108 N.W. 945, 116 Am.St.Rep. 394, for a review of the

tice first arose in this country in Massachusetts and the court there, in spite of the fact that the 1640 Act which governed did not in terms exclude purchasers with notice, held that they were outside its protection.[18] The statute was later amended to accord with the court's enlargement of it,[19] and today most of the American states expressly incorporate the doctrine that a taker with notice is outside the statutory operation. A few states whose statutes have not covered the point have been construed to include it in the same way that the English and Massachusetts tribunals accomplished that result, by judicial legislation.[20] In only a few states, as noted above, is non-record notice to the subsequent purchaser immaterial.

Other features are that the deed must be acknowledged before a public official, and that the whole deed, not merely a memorandum of its contents shall be copied into books kept for that purpose.[21]

PURPOSES AND OPERATION OF RECORDING STATUTES

196. Recording systems were established to provide an element of publicity in realty transactions. Prompt recording is induced by (1) loss of priority of unrecorded transfers to a later grantee; (2) preservation of priority through recordation which gives constructive notice. There has been criticism of the rule which protects a later buyer only if (1) he has no notice of the unrecorded conveyance and (2) he records first. The best statutes give priority strictly according to priority of recording. Early statutes permitted a varying period of time within which to record but only a few states now have such a provision.

There is no doubt that recording systems were established to provide a substitute for the publicital element of livery of seizin and the protection it afforded to subsequent purchasers.[22] The achievement of this general objective involved the provision and preservation of a history of the title available to the public by which a purchaser might, in considerable degree at least, determine the risk he ran in taking a title.[23] This is basic in all American recording systems. To accomplish this fundamental purpose the immediate end was to force prompt recordation of each successive conveyance.[24] One means of accomplishing this result would have been to give no force or efficacy at all to any conveyance unless and until it has been recorded. This method, as has been seen, was not adopted in most jurisdictions.[25] Instead, the device of divesting an unrecorded conveyance in favor of a subsequent purchaser was utilized for that purpose.[26] In addition to this incentive in the form of a stick, a carrot was held out to those grantees whose interests were of a sort that might be divested by a sale to a *bona fide* purchaser: proper recordation was made constructive notice to all

English decisions. See also Philbrick, Limits of Record Search and Therefore of Notice, 1945, 93 U. of Pa.L.Rev. 125, 128, 143 ff., 269 ff.; Patton, Titles, 2d Ed., §§ 8, 9, 19.

18. Reading of Judge Trowbridge, 1807, 3 Mass. 573, 575; Marshall v. Fisk, 1809, 6 Mass. 24, 4 Am.Dec. 76.

19. Rev.St.1836, c. 59, § 28; Gen.St.1860, c. 89, § 3; M.G.L.A., c. 183, § 4.

20. See Patton, Titles, 2d Ed., §§ 8, 9, 19; Philbrick, Limits of Record Search and Therefore of Notice, 1945, 93 U. of Pa.L.Rev. 125, 269.

21. See Beale, The Origin of the System of Recording Deeds in America, 1907, 19 Green Bag 335; Notice: The Unacknowledged Instrument, 1967, 20 Okl.L.Rev. 83.

22. Neslin v. Wells, 1881, 104 U.S. 428, 26 L.Ed. 802. See Losey v. Simpson, 1856, 11 N.J.Eq. 246, 249; Patton, Titles, 2d Ed., § 19; Philbrick, Limits of Record Search and Therefore of Notice, 1945, 93 U. of Pa.L.Rev. 125, 137.

See Storke and Sears, the Perennial Problem of Security Priority and Recordation, 1952, 24 Colo.L.Rev. 180, 188.

23. See Aigler, Operation of the Recording Acts, 1924, 22 Mich.L.Rev. 405, 416.

24. See Patton, Titles, 2d Ed., § 6.

25. See § 195, supra.

26. See Philbrick, Limit of Record Search and Therefore of Notice, 1945, 93 U. of Pa.L.Rev. 125, 146 ff., listing seven purposes that have been suggested as being served by the recording acts. In addition to those covered in the text are the protection of those who might succeed to the rights of the recording grantee; the saving from improvident

subsequent takers.[27] This latter effect of recordation has been regarded by many American authorities[28] as the chief purpose of recording but this view has been criticized.[29]

Realization of the purposes of the recording acts clearly involves the principle that a prior non-recording grantee should not be aided in any way. However, another doctrine, incorporated into the acts or engrafted on them by judicial decision, injects a cross-purpose. That is the rule depriving a subsequent purchaser with non-record notice of the benefit of the statutes. This substantially impairs the basic policy of the acts; at least it has diminished the pressure for prompt recordation.[30] Originally actual knowledge by the subsequent grantee was required.[31] There is something to be said in favor of preventing a fraudulent grantee from prevailing over a prior unrecorded deed

even at the expense of weakening the recording system. However, when the vaguer test of inquiry notice is substituted for actual knowledge, and with it dislike for an unethical taker is diminished, the desirability of effectuating the dominant policy of the acts in forcing prompt recordation becomes more important. Nevertheless, an estimated two-thirds of the states accept the requirement of no notice as a requisite to invoking the act.[32]

About half of the states require, in addition to the subsequent purchaser being without notice of a prior unrecorded conveyance, that he record his conveyance before the earlier one is recorded.[33] As has been pointed out, such acts engraft "the doctrine of actual notice onto the principle of priority on the record, at the same time qualifying the protection to innocent purchasers with the requirement of first recording." [34] In support of the provision it has been stated that it has the virtue of stimulating early recording and so effectuating the policy of the recording statutes.[35] It has also been

investments those subsequent purchasers who searched the records; the broader one of saving those who search the records and also make due inquiry when put on notice dehors the record; the giving of constructive notice. Probably all of these were to some extent present but the analysis in the text seems to cover the basis rationale of the acts.

See Storke and Sears, op. cit. note 22, supra.

27. See Aigler, Operation of the Recording Acts, 1924, 22 Mich.L.Rev. 405, 412. Recordation under the English Acts does not give notice. Ibid.
See Storke and Sears, op. cit. note 22, supra.

28. See 2 Tiffany, Real Prop., 2d ed., § 567; note, 1934, 33 Mich.L.Rev. 454.

29. "The question as to who may be charged with notice by recording, while ordinarily not difficult, may yet give rise to perplexing problems and differences of opinion. But where notice entirely aside from the Recording Acts would not be a vital circumstance in determining priorities, there would seem to be no occasion to discuss it in a case arising under the Acts, for by these statutes notice in its operation and effect is left just where it was." Aigler, Operation of the Recording Acts, 1924, 22 Mich.L.Rev. 405, 420.

30. This is a major and sound thesis of the series of articles by Professor Philbrick which have been cited in preceding footnotes.

31. The idea was that if the subsequent taker actually knew of the prior conveyance he could not be other than dishonest. See Patton, Titles, 2d Ed., § 8; Brinkman v. Jones, 1878, 44 Wis. 498.

32. See Patton, Titles, 2d Ed., § 9. See also Philbrick, Limits of Record Search and Therefore Notice, 1945, 93 U. of Pa.L.Rev. 125, 161, 416 ff.

33. See Patton, Titles, 2d Ed., § 10.

34. "He Who First Records" Provision, 1935, 15 Or. L.Rev. 66, 71.

35. See Philbrick, Limits of Record Search and Therefore of Notice, 1945, 93 U. of Pa.L.Rev. 125, 128; Tiffany, Real Prop., 3d ed., § 1276. This, however, has also been denied. "The 'he who first records' clause does not even fulfill its chief mission, an added incentive for early filing. Let us assume that X conveys to A and then to B, with both instruments unrecorded. A's only incentive to record is to cut off subsequent parties, yet such incentive is as strong under one statute as under the other. The fact that A can still prevail by first recording after conveyance to second party would tend to cause delinquency and not stimulate action. As for B, he must record to protect himself against bona fide purchasers subsequent to himself, even in absence of the clause under consideration. In most cases, he remains unaware of A's conveyance, with little reason for believing that such contesting rights exist. It is only when A and B obtain actual notice of each other's claims that the race to the registry begins, and then at the expense of certaintly of property titles as revealed by public record." 1935, 15 Or.L.Rev. 66, 71. See also Webb, Record of Title. §§ 13–15; Hanna, Cases on Security, 2d ed., 774; note, 1924, 37 Harv.L.Rev. 1141.

criticized as embodying two completely inconsistent theories [36] that, in some situations, lead to disconcerting results. An example is where B takes a mortgage from O, the record owner, without actual notice or knowledge that O had previously given a mortgage to A who had not recorded at the time of B's *bona fide* purchase.[37] Apart from the recording acts, if A's mortgage is a legal one, he has priority over B. But under recording acts that do not adhere to strict priority of record regardless of notice, and do not have the requirement of first recording in addition to lack of notice, B would prevail if neither mortgagee recorded,[38] or even if A should be the one first to record after B's acquisition. However, under a statute requiring earlier recordation in addition to lack of notice by the later mortgagee, A gains priority over B if he beats B to the recording office.[39] This cannot be, of course, on the ground that recording gives constructive notice, for such notice is no more effective than would be actual knowledge. If B later learned of A it would not affect the equities between the parties, for actual notice after B has completed his purchase comes too late. There is authority that the result in such a case would be different if the first mortgage to A, first recorded but after the giving of the subsequent one to the *bona fide* mortgagee, B, were an equitable one.[40] In such a case, apart from the recording acts, B would have acquired priority over A.[41] Under the recording acts B would retain that priority if he recorded before A did. The question, therefore, is whether A's act of recording first divested B's priority. On the language of the typical statute the answer would be no. In terms the statutes avoid a *first* conveyance against a *subsequent* one under certain conditions, the pertinent one here being that the latter record first. They do not say that the *subsequent* one is voided if the prior one records first. It is true that courts frequently pay little attention to exact language in statutes if a result at variance with it is demanded by the policy of the legislation. There appears to be here, however,

See Cunningham and Tischler, Equitable Real Estate Mortgages, 1963, 17 Rutgers L.Rev. 679, 693: "The 'record first' requirement * * * does encourage prompt recording and undoubtedly tends to make the county land records more reliable, for, whenever the instrument which was executed first is also recorded first, it is clearly entitled to priority. This would not be true under a statute which simply made prior unrecorded deeds and mortgages void as against any subsequent bona fide purchasers and mortgages, without any requirement that the latter record first."

36. But in defense of the first recording requirement, see Tiffany, Real Prop., 3d ed., § 1276, arguing that there is no "particular injustice in confining the benefits of the recording acts to those subsequent purchasers who act promptly" to record.

37. See Patton, Titles, § 19 n. 238; Fallass v. Pierce, 1872, 30 Wis. 443.

38. Randall v. Hamilton, 1923, 156 Ga. 661, 119 S.E. 595, 32 A.L.R. 342; Craig v. Osborn, 1923, 131 Miss. 323, 98 So. 598. But see Miss.Acts of 1924, c. 239, enacting a first recording provision. See Patton, Titles, 2d Ed., § 9. See also notes, 1924, 37 Harv.L. Rev. 1141; 1935, 33 Mich.L.Rev. 454; 1934, 9 Wash.L.Rev. 175; Rollison, Priorities in the Law of Mortgages, 1933, 8 Notre Dame Law. 215, 235; 1924, 32 A.L.R. 344; Ann.Cas.1912A, 194.

39. "It is impossible to reconcile the determination of priority on record with the protection of bona fide purchasers. If a prior unrecorded conveyance is fraudulent as to subsequent parties at the same time the bona fide purchaser takes conveyance, it remains fraudulent irrespective of the order in which the two instruments are recorded. The bona fide purchaser either does or does not have notice, actual or constructive, when he takes his conveyance; and his rights should be determined accordingly as of that date. If the prior party is permitted to record and prevail, after the bona fide purchaser has taken his conveyance, this confers greater efficacy on constructive notice than that given to actual notice; because actual notice acquired by the second party after he took title would not cause him to lose preference. Finally, such an arrangement violates the rule that recording is constructive notice only to subsequent parties, because in this case the notice is made to operate backward and affect the rights of a prior party." 1935, 15 Or.L. Rev. 66, 71; Zimmer v. Sundell, 1941, 237 Wis. 270, 296 N.W. 589, 133 A.L.R. 882, noted, 1942, Wis.L. Rev. 127, 1943, Wis.L.Rev. 86, 1945 Wis.L.Rev. 1945.

40 Rathbone v. Groh, 1904, 137 Mich. 373, 100 N.W. 588, commented on by Aigler, 1924, 22 Mich.L.Rev. 405, 412 n. 17.

41. This is in contrast to the case considered supra, where A's mortgage is legal, in which even A prevails over B apart from the recording statute, and the question is whether that priority is divested by the statute.

no sufficiently strong and clearly accepted policy to justify a different result. If the mortgages are legal ones and neither is recorded, the prior one, A, would come in first.[42] An explanation is that the statutory requirement of A's postponement, the only grounds for preferring B, has not been satisfied. And it seems to be true that if the later mortgagee, B, recorded first but learned of the prior encumbrance between the time of receiving and recording his own mortgage, he would nevertheless prevail over A.[43]

The few states that give priority strictly upon the basis of priority of record quite obviously come closest to fulfilling the purposes of the recording acts as thus outlined, and in so doing tend to secure certainty as to titles by an early recording of all conveyances.[44] In such states, even though a later mortgage be taken with actual notice or knowledge of the earlier one, it will have precedence over it if recorded first.[45]

The English Statute of Enrollments allowed six months for enrollment and the earlier American statutes allowed varying periods up to one year for the recordation of instruments.[46] Such a provision presents great practical difficulties in present times when real estate transactions are numerous with one deal closely following another, and today such provisions are in force [47] in only a few states.[48] Where they are in effect, if the mortgage is recorded at any time within the statutory period it relates back to its date of execution and takes precedence over any transfer executed between the date of its execution and the date of recording even though the second transfer was recorded first.[49] Where the conveyance is recorded after the time specified it will generally be regarded as validly recorded from the time of recording for the purpose of giving constructive notice, to preserve a position of advantage or to determine whether it had been first recorded.[50] Where neither mortgage is recorded within the statutory period, priority would be determined just as if no period of time had been prescribed.[51]

CHAIN OF TITLE

197. Only instruments that are recorded so as to be in the chain of title are validly recorded. The fundamental test of whether they are in the chain of title is whether they could have been discovered by reasonable search. Thus a recorded deed from a grantee under an unrecorded deed is invalid against a subsequent mortgagee from the grantor.

It is a clear general rule that only instruments so recorded as to be in the chain of title are validly recorded. The fundamental test of whether an instrument is in the chain of title is whether it could have been discovered by reasonably diligent search.[52] In spite

---

42. See Ely v. Scofield, N.Y. 1861, 35 Barb. 330; Durfee, The Lien Theory of a Mortgage, 1913, 11 Mich.L.Rev. 495.

43. See note, 1926, 14 Cal.L.Rev. 480.

44. See Patton, Titles, 2d Ed., §§ 8, 19.

45. Lynch v. Johnson, 1915, 170 N.C. 110, 86 S.E. 995, rehearing denied 171 N.C. 611, 89 S.E. 61; Quinnerly v. Quinnerly, 1894, 114 N.C. 145, 19 S.E. 99. See Webb, Record of Title, § 217; Rollison, Priorities in the Law of Mortgages, 1933, 8 Notre Dame Law. 215, 234.

46. E. g., see Dixie Grain Co. v. Quinn, 1913, 181 Ala. 208, 61 So. 886; Ky.Gen.Stat.1873, p. 257, § 14.

47. Hackman, Time for Recording Title Instruments, 1926, 19 Lawyer & Banker 20.

48. For example South Carolina which had such a term provision, Civ.Code S.C.1922, § 5312, eliminat-

ed it by amendments in 1925 and 1927. Code Supp. 1936, § 8875. Patton, Titles, 2d Ed., § 18, n. 72, lists only six states retaining such provisions in any cases.

49. Betz v. Mullin, 1878, 62 Ala. 365.

50. Adair v. Davis, 1883, 71 Ga. 769 (after record of first outside of time limit, second one executed and recorded within time limit: first one prevails); Harding v. Allen, 1889, 70 Md. 395, 17 A. 377 (second mortgage executed and recorded within time limit before the recordation of the one which was first executed: second prevails).

51. See Fleschner v. Sumpter, 1885, 12 Or. 161, 6 P. 506. See also Rollison, Priorities in the Law of Mortgages, 1933, 8 Notre Dame Law. 215, 246. See generally, Webb, Record of Title, § 131 et seq.

52. See Philbrick, Limits of Record Search and Therefore of Notice, 1945, 93 U. of Pa.L.Rev. 125, 164; idem, 178; idem, 180, "search is required only

of the superior merits of keeping records of conveyances by means of a plat system, most states provide only grantor and grantee indexes.[53] Because of this, only instruments that are recorded so as to be traceable through such indexes are regarded as being in the chain of title. And they are so traceable only when they run back to a common grantor. Thus a recorded deed from a grantee in an unrecorded deed is ineffective as against a subsequent mortgagee from the grantor.[54] In such a case the giver of the prior recorded deed appears nowhere on the record as owner and his conveyance, even though recorded, could be discovered only by a search of every instrument filed for record, an obviously unreasonable, if not impossible, task. The same rule governs even as to a recorded purchase money mortgage given by the vendee under a recorded deed,[55] for the statutes do not require search to be made for deeds given to former record owners, only for deeds given by them.[56]

RESTRICTIVE COVENANTS

198. Although there are minority cases to the contrary, the weight of authority and better view is that restrictive covenants in recorded conveyances binding land retained by the grantor are in the chain of title of subse- quent mortgagees or other purchasers of the land so retained.

An owner of land may convey part of his property by a deed containing restrictive covenants binding some or all of the portion retained by him. This is frequently the case in real estate subdivisions. When he later mortgages or transfers the land so retained to persons who pay value and take without actual notice of the restriction, the question arises as to whether the prior conveyance, if recorded, is notice to such takers under the recording acts. On the ground that such acts apply only to subsequent purchasers of the same *land*, not to subsequent purchasers from the same *grantor*, it has been held that, since the restriction appears only in a deed conveying other land, it is not in the chain of title of mortgagees or purchasers of the retained land and therefore they take free of it.[57] The weight of authority is the other way and it is immaterial whether the burden created on the land is legal or equitable, or whether it is by a separate instrument or in the deed conveying other property of the mortgagor or grantor.[58] Since such restrictions can be discovered without an unreasonably burdensome search the majority view seems preferable.[59]

RECORDED CONVEYANCE BEFORE ACQUISITION OF TITLE

199. If a grantor conveys and records before he has record title, the conveyance is not in the chain of title as against a subsequent mortgage given by him after he becomes record owner.

when it must reveal the hostile claim without subjecting the purchaser to an unreasonable burden"; 1904, 17 Harv.L.Rev. 482; Tiffany, Real Prop., 3d ed., § 1265; Storke and Sears, op. cit. ante, § 196, note 22, 193–196.

53. See Patton, Titles 2d Ed., § 125.

54. Losey v. Simpson, 1856, 11 N.J.Eq. 246. Kerfoot v. Cronin, 1882, 105 Ill. 609; Burke v. Beveridge, 1870, 15 Minn. 205, Gil. 160; Truitt v. Grandy, 1894, 115 N.C. 54, 20 S.E. 293—accord. See also Gross v. Watts, 1907, 206 Mo. 373, 104 S.W. 30, 121 Am.St.Rep. 662; Collins v. Aaron, 1894, 162 Pa. 539, 29 A. 724. Cf. Van Diviere v. Mitchell, 1895, 45 S.C. 127, 22 S.E. 759; Balch v. Arnold, 1899, 9 Wyo. 17, 59 P. 434 (plat system of recordation).

55. Dobbins v. Economic Gas Co., 1920, 182 Cal. 616, 189 P. 1073.

56. Pyles v. Brown, 1899, 189 Pa. 164, 42 A. 11, 69 Am.St.Rep. 794. See Philbrick, Limits of Record Search and Therefore of Notice, 1945, 93 U. of Pa. L.Rev. 125, 170 n. 146.

57. Glorieux v. Lighthipe, 1915, 88 N.J.L. 199, 96 A. 94, Ann.Cas.1917E, 484; Hancock v. Gumm, 1921, 151 Ga. 667, 107 S.E. 872, 16 A.L.R. 1003.

58. Lowes v. Carter, 1914, 124 Md. 678, 93 A. 216; McQuade v. Wilcox, 1921, 215 Mich. 302, 183 N.W. 771, 16 A.L.R. 997; King v. St. Louis Union Trust Co., 1909, 226 Mo. 351, 126 S.W. 415; Holt v. Fleischman, 1902, 75 App.Div. 593, 78 N.Y.S. 647; Jones v. Berg, 1915, 105 Wash. 69, 177 P. 712.

59. See Tiffany, Real Prop., 2d ed., 2188, cited with approval in McQuade v. Wilcox, 1921, 215 Mich. 302, 183 N.W. 771, 16 A.L.R. 997.

Where instead of a deed from one who is not a record owner because he cannot be found as a grantee, there is a deed from one who is on the list of record owners but the deed is given and recorded *before* he became such, the question of whether such a deed is in the chain of title is more debatable. In the former case, the later mortgagee is without any clue to guide him in his search; in the latter it is only a question of whether he should be forced to search the record for possible conveyances by each successive grantor prior to the time that such grantor appeared on the record as owner. The majority and better view is that the record of such a prior deed should not be regarded as validly recorded because it would involve too burdensome a search to discover it.[60] There are, however, cases holding the other way.[61] In jurisdictions where a plat system of recording title is operative, the recordation should be valid in this sort of case and also in the type of case discussed in the preceding section.[62]

Interwoven with the question of the operation of the recording acts in this situation is that of the passing to a grantee by estoppel of a title subsequently acquired by a grantor.[63] If it were not for this doctrine, the deed given by the grantor before he acquired title could be regarded as a nullity and subsequent mortgagees or purchasers from the grantor after acquisition of title would prevail on this ground and there would be no question of the recording statute having any application.[64] However, the doctrine is general that on later acquisition of title by the grantor the grantee either automatically gets legal title or has an equitable right to have it.[65] If he gets legal title, the subsequent taker from the grantor theoretically should not be able to displace him without invoking the aid of the recording acts on the claim that the deed recorded prior to the acquisition of title is not validly recorded and, consequently, in the absence of actual notice, the title obtained by estoppel is divested by the statutory power. On the other hand, if only an equitable interest arises, a subsequent *bona fide* mortgagee or purchaser would prevail over it on familiar principles unless the prior recordation was valid so as to give constructive notice. Thus stated, the recording acts by their own operation have a direct effect upon the rights of the parties. But it may also be urged that the existence of the recording system and its policies should prefer the later purchaser over the grantee claiming by estoppel upon a different theory. This theory is that such grantee was guilty

---

60. Bingham v. Kirkland, 1881, 34 N.J.Eq. 229. See Philbrick, Limits of Record Search and Therefore of Notice, 1945, 93 U. of Pa.L.Rev. 125, 176 ff; Stevens, Effect of Recording a Mortgage before Mortgagor's Deed is Recorded, 1945 Wis.L.Rev. 630; Rawle, Covenants for Title, 5th ed., 406. See also on the effect of recording a mortgage containing an after-acquired property clause, § 42, ante. See, also, Storke and Sears, op. cit. § 196 note 22 supra, 198.

61. E. g., Tefft v. Munson, 1875, 57 N.Y. 97; White v. Patten, 1837, 41 Mass. (24 Pick.) 324; Campbell, Cases on Mortgages, 2d ed. 509. See also Campbell, op. cit. supra, 512 n. 2, for a collection of authorities.

62. Balch v. Arnold, 1899, 9 Wyo. 17, 59 P. 434. See Patton, Titles, 2d Ed., §§ 69–71.

63. For discussions of the doctrine of estoppel by deed in relation to recording acts, see notes, 1928, 16 Cal.L.Rev. 341; 1904, 17 Harv.L.Rev. 482; 1916, 29 ibid. 457; 1927, 40 ibid. 499; 1924, 22 Mich.L.

Rev. 405, 415; 1922, 1 N.Car.L.Rev. 56; 1933, 8 Not.D.Law. 215, 228; 2 Tiffany, Real Prop., 2d Ed., § 545e. See, 1894, 23 L.R.A. 565; L.R.A.1918C, 792; Ann.Cas.1914A, 1288; 1923, 25 A.L.R. 83; 1923, 26 A.L.R. 173.

64. See Philbrick, Limits of Record Search and Therefore of Notice, 1945, 93 U. of Pa.L.Rev. 125, 181.

65. See Tiffany, Real Property, 3d ed., §§ 1231 et seq.; Rawle, Covenants for Title, 5th ed., §§ 245–6, 255; Patton, Titles, 2d Ed., §§ 70, 71. See also references in the three preceding footnotes. The most satisfactory theory of the doctrine treats the original, worthless deed, as a contract to convey which equity will specifically enforce and the grantee's equitable right flows from this. Cf. §§ 25, 32, 37, supra. The doctrine is generally held to be inapplicable to purchase money mortgages. Nelson v. Dwiggins, 1933, 111 Fla. 298, 149 So. 613; Florida Land Invest. Co. v. Williams, 1922, 84 Fla. 157, 92 So. 876, 26 A.L.R. 171, 173. But cf. Jackson v. Holt, 1942, 192 Miss. 702, 6 So.2d 915, commented on in 1942, 91 U. of Pa.L.Rev. 161.

of such culpable negligence in first, purchasing from one who had no record title, and second, failing to record *after* he acquired title, that he should be postponed on equitable considerations to a subsequent purchaser without actual notice.[66]

DEEDS PRIOR TO RECORDED DEED

200. **Instruments executed before but recorded after the execution and recordation of a later deed by the same grantor are validly recorded as to purchasers from the second grantee subsequent to the recordation of the first deed.**

Where A, the record owner, gives a deed to B but before B records A makes a second conveyance to C who promptly records, apart from the effect upon their rights of the recording acts, B prevails over C for the simple reason that B had legal title and A had nothing left to give to C.[67] Whether C prevails over B under the recording acts depends on whether he gave value and had no notice of B's prior conveyance, it being clear in the case put that C recorded first.[68] Of course, if C is a *bona fide* purchaser, any subsequent purchaser, E, from him will prevail over B. Does E have the burden of proving that C was a *bona fide* purchaser? Or must B prove that C was not one? This should depend on who has the burden between C and B. E can assert no more rights than C has. For he claims his title derives from C and depends on the validity of C's right rather than on an independent right of his own against B. The cases generally put the burden on C although the basic policy of the acts would seem to indicate that it should be [69] on B.[70]

In justification of the majority view it may be said that the task of establishing these facts would ordinarily be far easier for C, within whose area of activity and knowledge they lie, than for B.

Even though C is a donee or took with notice of the prior conveyance, if before B records E takes a mortgage from C for value and without actual notice of B, E will prevail over B under the recording acts, although if priority of record is necessary under the particular statute, he may have to record his mortgage before B records his deed. Here E claims not on the basis of a better right derived from C but, in spite of such title not being better, in his own right arising under the operation of the recording acts as a *bona fide* purchaser who is entitled to prevail over a prior unrecorded deed of which he has no notice. But if B records his prior conveyance after the recordation by C but before the mortgage to E, the majority of courts hold that this is a valid recordation so far as E is concerned, with the result that B prevails over E as to any claim based upon his own, independent right as a *bona fide* purchaser.[71]

66. See Philbrick, Limits of Record Search and Therefore of Notice, 1945, 93 U. of Pa.L.Rev. 125, 184.

67. See Woods v. Garnett, 1894, 72 Miss. 78, 16 So. 390, 392.

68. See Fallass v. Pierce, 1872, 30 Wis. 443, 474; Parrish v. Mahany, 1897, 10 S.D. 276, 73 N.W. 97, 66 Am.St.Rep. 715; § 195, supra.

69. E. g., Bell v. Pleasant, 1904, 145 Cal. 410, 78 P. 957, 104 Am.St.Rep. 61. There are, however, cases

contra. E. g., Lowden v. Wilson, 1908, 233 Ill. 340, 84 N.E. 245. A few cases follow a compromise rule that the subsequent purchaser has the burden of proving that he paid value, but if he does so, the burden of proving that he had notice is on the prior party seeking to defeat him on that ground. Walter v. Brown, 1902, 115 Iowa 360, 88 N.W. 832. For a collection of authorities, see, 1912, 36 L.R.A., N.S., 1124.

70. To fulfill the fundamental policies of the recording acts it is urged that the subsequent purchaser should be protected to the utmost possible extent in relying upon the record, "and the burden of proof in litigation between him and the negligent nonrecorder of the prior deed should invariably be upon the latter;". Philbrick, Limits of Record Search and Therefore of Notice, 1945, 93 U. of Pa.L.Rev. 125, 127.

71. Woods v. Garnett, 1894, 72 Miss. 78, 16 So. 390; Mahoney v. Middleton, 1871, 41 Cal. 41; Parrish v. Mahany, supra, note 68; Fallass v. Pierce, supra, note 68; Morse v. Curtis, 1885, 140 Mass. 11, 2 N.E. 929, 54 Am.St.Rep. 456, contra. If it is a valid recording it would be sufficient to preserve a position of advantage which B would have apart from the acts, to prevent, by giving constructive notice, any subsequent purchaser from acquiring a priority he would otherwise acquire in the absence of actual

This holding means that in order to protect himself a purchaser must search forward in the record under the name of each prior grantor through whom he traces his title to see that there are no conveyances executed by such grantor prior, but recorded subsequently, to the one through which he claims title.[72] This seems a pretty heavy burden of search to put upon a purchaser, especially if there is no time limit set within which deeds may validly be recorded.[73] Indeed, professional title searchers probably do not make such a search as the rule requires.[74] Further, it is somewhat inconsistent with the rule that conveyances executed *after* the grantor has parted with record title cannot be validly recorded. That is, if A makes a voidable conveyance to B who records, and then A later sells and conveys to C who records, as to a subsequent purchaser from B the conveyance to C is not validly recorded so as to put him on notice of C's right to upset B's title.[75] Yet as a practical matter,

since he must search for possible conveyances made *prior* to the deed to B but recorded after its making and recordation, there would be no additional burden placed upon him and he would discover the later deed to C.[76]

If E seeks to prevail on a derivative title through C, the case seems a clearer one for imposing the burden on him of establishing that C was a *bona fide* purchaser than where B had never recorded. There is a deed to B of which he is on constructive notice and one which could be found by search and which when found would warn him of the possibility that C might have been subordinate to it. In any event, since he claims to stand in C's shoes he should stand in them for the purpose of burden of proof.[77]

But see Philbrick, Limits of Record Search and Therefore of Notice, 1945, 93 U. of Pa.L.Rev. 125, 297 et seq., arguing that *any* conveyance by a grantor made after a recorded prior conveyance by him is a complete nullity and, therefore, for *this* reason is ineffective against subsequent purchasers from the grantee under the prior recorded conveyance. Further, that the taker of a conveyance from a grantor whose prior deed is on record cannot have any equity against the grantee under that prior recorded deed because he is on notice of it. Consequently the conclusion is reached that the result in the case would never be affected by any operation of the recording acts.

In answer it may be pointed out that a recorded deed absolute from A to B does not preclude the possibility that A may have an equitable right to avoid the conveyance and A could transfer that right to C. If a purchaser from B has notice of such a right, he will take subject to it. If he has actual notice of a subsequent conveyance from A to C that should be sufficient to put him on inquiry notice as to the validity of A's conveyance to B. It does not follow, of course, that if record of the conveyance by A to C operated as constructive notice of its existence that the same result would be reached. Indeed, it has been forcefully said that it should not. See White v. McGregor, supra. Nevertheless, the possibility is not so remote that it can be completely excluded. And if it is not excluded whether such a record is within the scope of the recording acts would, in such a case, play a part in the result.

notice, and to fulfill the requirement of first recording so as to defeat a later claimant who, under the particular statute, has the duty to record his deed first as a condition to getting priority. For a critical discussion of the rule followed by a collection and analysis of the cases, see Philbrick, Limits of Record Search and Therefore of Notice, 1945, 93 U. of Pa.L.Rev. 125, 391 et seq., 416 et seq. Professor Philbrick's analysis of the authorities finds that the majority view is supported by "eleven decisions in seven (of clear decisions, by nine in five) jurisdictions, in addition to two *dicta* from other jurisdictions." On the other hand, five decisions in two jurisdictions and a dubious dictum in each of two other states form a minority group of authorities. Philbrick, op. cit. supra, 430.

72. See 1924, 23 Cal.L.Rev. 108, 109.

73. Some jurisdictions expressly set a definite time limit within which conveyances may be validly recorded. E. g., S.C.Code 1962, §§ 60–101, 60–156; 21 P.S. (Pa.) § 444. See Webb, Record of Title, § 7.

74. See Philbrick, Limits of Record Search and Therefore of Notice, 1945, 93 U. of Pa.L.Rev. 125, 415, 440.

75. Hooker v. Pierce, N.Y.1842, 2 Hill. 650; White v. McGregor, 1899, 92 Tex. 556, 50 S.W. 564, 71 Am. St.Rep. 875. See 1934, 23 Cal.L.Rev. 108, 110. If such a purchaser had actual notice of the conveyance to C, he should be put upon inquiry of the validity of the conveyance to B under whom he claims. See Tiffany, Real Prop., 2d ed., § 567(f).

76. Cf. 1934, 34 Cal.L.Rev. 108, 110. See Tiffany, Real Property, 2d ed., § 567(g). But see the criticism by Philbrick, Limits of Record Search and Therefore of Notice, 1945, 93 U. of Pa.L.Rev. 125, 391, 411.

77. E. g., Parrish v. Mahany, 1899, 12 S.D. 278, 81 N.W. 295, 76 Am.St.Rep. 604, reversing S.C., 1897, 10 S.D 276, 73 N.W. 97, 66 Am.St.Rep. 715, which had held the other way. The court expressly

ANCESTOR'S UNRECORDED CONVEYANCE

201. Unrecorded conveyances from an ancestor are invalid under the recording acts as against subsequent bona fide mortgagees for value and without notice from the heir.

According to most cases, under the recording acts a *bona fide* mortgagee or other purchaser for value and without notice from an heir acquires good title as against a prior unrecorded deed or mortgage from the ancestor, of which he did not have notice.[78] A minority view reasoned that the heir got no title at common law since the ancestor had conveyed it away. Nor did he acquire any title by virtue of the recording acts for they either explicitly say that the unrecorded conveyance is good as against him or fail to include him in the class of persons protected by the acts. Since the heir acquired no title, he could convey none under the acts.[79] In criticism it has been pointed out, first, that the argument proved too much in that it would apply equally to any subsequent conveyance by the grantor; and, second, that the grantor had a statutory power to defeat the prior

refused to express an opinion as to where the burden of proof should lie where there has been no recordation at all by B. In such a case there would be nothing that could be found on the records by E to warn him that C might not be a *bona fide* purchaser. Unless E had actual notice of B, in which case the lack of record would be immaterial, E could prevail on his own right and need not rely on a derivative title. Day v. Clark, 1853, 25 Vt. 397, prefers E on the ground that, although the record of B's conveyance is constructive notice to him of the existence of that conveyance, nevertheless E does not have actual notice that C, his grantor, was not a *bona fide* purchaser. See Rollison, Priorities in the Law of Mortgages, 1933, 8 N.D.Law, 214, 238. Cf. Ross v. Title Guarantee & Trust Co., 1934, 136 Cal.App. 393, 29 P.2d 236, commented on, 1934, 23 Cal.L.Rev. 108. In a jurisdiction in which C does not have the burden of proof, it would seem that E should not have it.

78. Hallett v. Alexander, 1911, 50 Colo. 37, 114 P. 490, 34 L.R.A.,N.S., 328, Ann.Cas.1912B, 1277; see Crosson v. Kartowitz, 1919, 43 N.D. 466, 175 N.W. 868; note, 1929, 65 A.L.R. 365; Storke and Sears, op. cit. supra § 196, note 22, 196–197.

79. Hill v. Meeker, 1855, 24 Conn. 211; Wright v. Black, 1929, 159 Tenn. 254, 17 S.W.2d 917, 65 A.L.R. 357.

unrecorded deed and the heir would succeed to it.[80] In addition, in favor of the majority view is the fact that it furthers the purposes and policies of the recording system.

SIMULTANEOUS EXECUTION OR RECORDATION

202. Simultaneously executed mortgages, apart from agreement, rank equally except in the few states determining priority solely by priority of record. In those they rank equally only if recorded at the same time, but regardless of the time of execution. In all other states a mortgage executed before another one has priority regardless of simultaneous recording. Some states deal with these situations by statute.

When two or more mortgages are executed simultaneously without any agreement, express or implied,[81] as to priority between them, they will rank equally apart from any operation of a recording act.[82] Since most recording acts become applicable only when one of the parties is a *subsequent* taker,[83] the only type of recording statute that will alter this result is one which makes priority of record the sole criterion of priority of right.[84] And even under this sort of statute, if the instruments are recorded simultaneously it becomes impossible to hold that one is prior to the other.[85] Where one mortgage is executed subsequent to another but both are recorded simultaneously, in jurisdictions where priority of recordation is the only test there will be equality between them. Under other types of recording acts, priority will

80. See Aigler, The Operation of the Recording Acts, 1924, 22 Mich.L.Rev. 405, 416.

81. If an agreement between the parties as to priority can be established, it will control. Trompczynski v. Struck, 1900, 105 Wis. 437, 81 N.W. 650. See 3 Tiffany, Real Prop., 2d Ed., § 634; Gillig v. Maass, 1863, 28 N.Y. 191.

82. Dahlstrom v. Ablieter, 1912, 156 Iowa 187, 135 N.W. 567, 39 L.R.A.,N.S., 524.

83. Greene v. Warnick, 1876, 64 N.Y. 220. See Pomeroy, Equity Juris., 5th ed., § 719.

84. See § 196, supra.

85. Chatten v. Knoxville Trust Co., 1926, 154 Tenn. 345, 289 S.W. 536, 50 A.L.R. 537, semble.

not be affected by the recordation.[86] There has not been a first recording by either under those that have such a requirement in addition to lack of notice; and under the more common type, recordation by either or both after the execution of the subsequent mortgage is immaterial. In some states there are specific statutory provisions that apply in some or all of the cases of the sort here considered.[87] As solutions they provide for priority to the mortgage having the earlier filing notation,[88] the lower filing number,[89] the earlier date of execution,[90] or for no priority.[91]

ERRORS IN RECORDING

203. The better, majority view places the responsibility for correct copying on the recording owner of the instrument. The same applies to incorrect indexing where indexing is part of the record, and to copying of the instrument into the wrong set of books.

Under most statutes, recordation of a mortgage is complete so as to give notice [92] when it is deposited with the recording officer. The instrument itself stands in lieu of the record until transcription and then the copied record takes its place.[93] Where there has been an error in transcription a minority of courts hold that the risk falls upon the subsequent purchaser because the one who offered the instrument had completed his full duty when he handed it to the public officer.[94] This conclusion is generally predicated upon a literal reading of statutory language stating that an instrument shall be effectively recorded from the time it is filed or deposited. Such a view, it has been pointed out, offends the policy of the recording acts in that, instead of being able to rely upon the record as a correct history of title "no person could be safe in his purchase without hunting out and inspecting the original mortgage." [95] Probably a majority of courts hold that if the mortgage is incorrectly copied by the recorder, it will not be validly recorded so as to give constructive notice of the correct contents [96] unless the existence of error is apparent on the face of the record.[97] This serves the policy of the act in making the

86. Naylor v. Throckmorton, Va.1836, 7 Leigh, 98, 30 Am.Dec. 492; Noakes v. Martin, 1853, 15 Ill. 118. Glenn, Mortgages, § 373.

87. See note, 1933, 17 Minn.L.Rev. 554; Webb, Record of Title, §§ 168, 169. See also Howard v. Chase, 1870, 104 Mass. 249; Pomeroy v. Latting, 1860, 81 Mass. (15 Gray) 435; Van Aken v. Gleason, 1876, 34 Mich. 477. Cf. Clark v. Brown, 1862, 85 Mass. (3 Allen) 509. As to priority between a judgment entered and a mortgage recorded on the same day, see 1925, 37 A.L.R. 268.

88. Virginia, Code 1950, § 55–101.

89. Minn.Stat.Ann. § 386.31. Priority of numbering, however, creates only a *prima facie* presumption of order of recordation which can be rebutted. Dear v. Remington, 1929, 176 Minn. 559, 223 N.W. 925; Fender v. Appel, 1932, 187 Minn. 281, 245 N.W. 148.

90. 25 Del.Code § 2107; Doe ex dem. Hammond v. Roe, 1832, Dud. 177.

91. Louisiana S.A.–Civ.Code § 3358.

92. E. g. Mutual Life Ins. Co. v. Dake, 1881, 87 N.Y. 257; Lewis v. Hinman, 1888, 56 Conn. 55, 13 A. 143.

93. Pringle v. Dunn, 1875, 37 Wis. 449, 19 Am.Rep. 772. See White v. Himmelberger-Harrison Lumber Co., 1911, 240 Mo. 13, 25, 139 S.W. 553, 42 L.R.A.,N. S., 151. If the deed is withdrawn before copying there is no valid recordation as against persons whose rights are acquired during its absence. Turman v. Bell, 1891, 54 Ark. 273, 15 S.W. 886.

94. Chapman v. Johnson, 1904, 142 Ala. 633, 38 So. 797, 4 Ann.Cas. 559; Gillespie v. Rogers, 1888, 146 Mass. 610, 16 N.E. 711; Tucker v. Shaw, 1895, 158 Ill. 326, 41 N.E. 914; see Mangold v. Barlow, 1884, 61 Miss. 593, 48 Am.Rep. 84.

Storke and Sears, op. cit., supra § 196, note 22, finds Colorado accord.

95. Frost v. Beekman, N.Y.1814, 1 Johns.Ch. 288, 298, reversed on another point, 18 Johns. 544; see Miller v. Bradford, 1861, 12 Iowa 14; Bordwell, Recording of Instruments, 1917, 3 Iowa L.Bull. 24, 29. On the impracticability of examining the original instruments, see Terrell v. Andrew Co., 1869, 44 Mo. 309.

96. St. Paul Electric Co. v. Baldwin Engrg. Co., 1924, 159 Minn. 221, 199 N.W. 9; White v. Himmelberger-Harrison Lumber Co., 1911, 240 Mo. 13, 139 S. W. 553, 42 L.R.A.,N.S., 151; New York Life Ins. Co. v. White, 1858, 17 N.Y. 469; Prouty v. Marshall, 1909, 225 Pa. 570, 74 A. 550, 25 L.R.A.,N.S., 1211 and note; see 1944, 38 Ill.L.Rev. 396, 398. See note, 1931, 70 A.L.R. 603, for collection of cases.

97. Teague v. Sowder, 1908, 121 Tenn. 132, 114 S.W. 484.

record a reliable history of title and finds additional justification in placing the duty of having the instrument correctly recorded upon the one who, having the instrument in his possession and offering it for record, has it in his power to compare the transcription with the original and correct any errors. The statement in some cases that the owner of the instrument is responsible for mistakes in copying because the recording officer is his agent is a fiction evoked, probably, by the foregoing considerations.[98] The same may be said of the distinction that recordation is not complete until there is a correct transcription when notice is the purpose of record whereas for other purposes it is complete when the instrument is deposited.[99]

In some states proper indexing is a part of the record and in them errors in indexing follow the same rules as do errors of transcription.[1] There are, however, cases holding that indexing is not a part of the record with the result that incorrect indexing, or even failure to index at all would not affect the validity of the record.[2]

Where the recording error consists in copying the mortgage into the wrong set of books in states whose statutes provide that mortgages shall be recorded in separate books kept for that purpose rather than in the books of deeds, different considerations enter.[3] Normally anyone intending to take a mortgage or conveyance would search the records not only to discover whether there was a prior outstanding mortgage but also whether the full title had previously been transferred by a deed. Consequently he

---

98. See Cady v. Purser, 1901, 131 Cal. 552, 63 P. 844, 82 Am.St.Rep. 391.

99. "For the purpose of complying with a statutory requirement, as in the case of official bonds or certificates of marriage, where the evident purpose of the statute is to make the instrument a matter of public record, or when the recording of an instrument is an essential step in perfecting some right or completing some act of the party, as in the case of a declaration of homestead, or an assignment for the benefit of creditors, the depositing of the instrument in the recorder's office is sufficient; but, when merely making a record of the instrument is not the ultimate purpose of the party, but the recording of the instrument is the means by which his ultimate purpose is to be carried into effect,—as when his purpose is to give notice of his interest in real estate," recordation is not complete until it has been correctly transcribed into the proper books. Cady v. Purser, 1901, 131 Cal. 552, 557, 63 P. 844, 845, 82 Am.St.Rep. 391.

See Edwards v. Grand, 1898, 121 Cal. 254, 53 P. 796 (mortgage deposited in recorder's office after office hours; declaration of homestead by mortgagor's wife handed to recorder on his way to the office the next morning).

As to the effect of a subsequent alteration of the record (e. g., entry of a release), unauthorized by the mortgagee, but actually relied upon by a subsequent encumbrancer, see Commercial Building & Loan Co. v. Foley, 1927, 25 Ohio App. 402, 158 N.E. 236; notes, 1928, 2 U. of Cin.L.Rev. 92; 1928, 76 U. of Pa.L.Rev. 464; 1928, 26 Mich.L.Rev. 581. Here the subsequent purchaser properly takes the risk since nothing short of continued constant watchfulness on the part of the prior mortgagee could prevent a subsequent alteration of the record.

See also 1910, 23 L.R.A.,N.S., 127; 2 Tiffany, Real Prop., 2d Ed., § 567j.

For other cases where a mortgage has been duly delivered to the proper official for recording, and

thereafter improperly recorded by such official, see Seibold v. Rogers, 1895, 110 Ala. 438, 18 So. 312; Craig v. Dimock, 1868, 47 Ill. 308, 319; Terrell v. Andrew County, 1869, 44 Mo. 309; Prouty v. Marshall, 1909, 225 Pa. 570, 74 A. 550, 25 L.R.A.,N.S., 1211, and note; 1902, 96 Am.St.Rep. 397; Ann.Cas. 1913B, 69; 1921, 5 Minn.L.Rev. 143 (recording in realty records of mortgage covering both realty and personalty); Dorman v. Goodman, 1938, 213 N.C. 406, 196 S.E. 352, commented on in, 1938, 52 Harv. L.Rev. 170 (incorrect indexing of grantor's middle initial held fatal.)
See also Improper Indexing of Deeds of Trust and Liens, 1962, 40 N.Car.L.Rev. 515.

1. Dougery v. Bettencourt, 1931, 214 Cal. 455, 6 P.2d 499; Rice v. Taylor, 1934, 220 Cal. 629, 32 P.2d 381; Parry v. Reinertson, 1929, 208 Iowa 739, 224 N.W. 489, 63 A.L.R. 1051; Rev.Code Wash.Ann. 65.04.050, Wis.Stat.Ann. 59.52.

See notes, 1934, 23 Cal.L.Rev. 107; 2 Tiffany, Real Prop., 2d Ed., § 567k. See also 1929, 63 A.L.R. 1056. Look at Ritchie v. Griffiths and Metcalfe, 1890, 1 Wash. 429, 25 P. 341, 12 L.R.A. 384, 22 Am. St.Rep. 155; Notes, 1920, 6 Iowa L.Bull. 246; 1928, 14 Va.L.Rev. 318, 324; 1877, 4 Cent.L.J. 340.

2. Scott v. Thomas, 1924, 211 Ala. 420, 100 So. 778; Lincoln Bldg. & Sav. Ass'n v. Hass, 1880, 10 Neb. 581, 7 N.W. 327; Mutual Life Ins. Co. v. Dake, 1881, 87 N.Y. 257; Terrell v. Scott, 1928, 129 Okl. 78, 262 P. 1071, certiorari denied sub nom. Means v. Bell, 277 U.S. 596, 48 S.Ct. 559, 72 L.Ed. 1006; Board of Com'rs for Sale of School Land v. Babcock, 1875, 5 Or. 472. See Patton, Titles, 2d Ed., §§ 67, 68.

3. Some sixteen states have such statutory provisions. See note, 1941, 40 Mich.L.Rev. 315, 316 n. 7.

would discover the mortgage even though it was copied erroneously into the book of deeds. Nevertheless the general rule is that such a mistake prevents the record being notice.[4] Of course if the statute is merely directory as to where the mortgage should be recorded, then copying into the deed book would be sufficient.[5] And in jurisdictions holding that the recordation is valid from date of deposit in spite of errors in transcription by the recorder, the recording mortgagee would be protected.[6]

RECORDING OF DEED ABSOLUTE MORTGAGES

204. Authorities are divided whether a deed absolute mortgage may be recorded validly as a deed or as a mortgage.

Where a deed absolute on its face but intended to be a mortgage is given the problem of valid recordation is complicated by the question of whether it can be validly recorded at all, and, if it can be, whether it is to be recorded with mortgages or with deeds.[7]

4. Cady v. Purser, 1901, 131 Cal. 552, 63 P. 844, 82 Am.St.Rep. 391; Sinclair v. Gunzenhauzer, 1913, 179 Ind. 78, 133, 98 N.E. 37, modified and rehearing denied 179 Ind. 78, 100 N.E. 376; Gordon v. Constantine Hydraulic Co., 1898, 117 Mich. 620, 76 N.W. 142; Hadfield v. Hadfield, 1941, 128 N.J.Eq. 510, 17 A.2d 169, commented on in 1941, 40 Mich.L.Rev. 315 (mortgagee had directed that mortgage be recorded as deed and it was so recorded).

5. Smith v. Smith, 1862, 13 Ohio St. 532. Though copied into the book of deeds it was indexed as a mortgage but little weight was given to this fact. But see Nevada Rev.Stat. 247.160, copying in wrong book immaterial if properly indexed. So too where no statute requires that separate sets of books be kept. Ivey v. Dawley, 1905, 50 Fla. 537, 39 So. 498, 7 Ann.Cas. 354; Cawthon v. Stearns Culver Lumber Co., 1910, 60 Fla. 313, 53 So. 738.

6. Farabee v. McKerrihan, 1896, 172 Pa. 234, 33 A. 583, 51 Am.St.Rep. 734; Lignoski v. Crooker, 1893, 86 Tex. 324, 24 S.W. 278, 788.

7. See note, 1941, 40 Mich.L.Rev. 315, 317. As to whether chattel mortgage recording acts apply to a bill of sale of personal property, absolute in form but intended as security. See Glenn, The Chattel Mortgage as a Statutory Security, 1939, 25 Va.L.Rev. 316, 329. See also Corning v. Records, 1898, 69 N.H. 390, 46 A. 462, 76 Am.St.Rep. 178. Cf. the earlier Massachusetts case of Coggan v. Ward, 1913, 215 Mass. 13, 102 N.E. 336.

There are well considered cases which hold that recordation as a deed is sufficient to protect the grantee by giving notice of his actual interest.[8] There are two parts to the reasoning by which this result is reached. In the first place, it is argued that "One seeking to acquire title to land, or lien on it to secure a debt, and having a due regard for his own interest, would not content himself with an examination to ascertain whether there was a mortgage on the property, but would further inquire whether the person who proposed to sell or mortgage the land was its owner. This would or ought to induce an examination of the records showing absolute conveyances, as well as those showing mortgages or other liens. * * *"[9] In the second place, one should know that a deed appearing to convey an absolute title might in fact convey a lesser interest and, therefore, should be charged with knowing or finding out what actual interest was conveyed.[10] It may be added to this, that even if he did not find out that an interest less than a fee had been conveyed he still would have no cause for complaint. On the face of the record he should not have expected to get anything and, consequently, he cannot be hurt by permitting an apparent absolute interest

8. Ruggles v. Williams, Tenn.1858, 1 Head, 141. Livesey v. Brown, 1892, 35 Neb. 111, 52 N.W. 838; Kennard v. Mabry, 1892, 78 Tex. 151, 14 S.W. 272; Kent v. Williams, 1905, 146 Cal. 3, 79 P. 527.

9. Kennard v. Mabry, 1890, 78 Tex. 151, 156, 14 S.W. 272, 273.

10. "Every person is presumed to know that a deed absolute on its face may have been intended by the parties to it only as a mortgage, and that the courts will so hold it to be if executed only for the purpose of securing a debt. So knowing, every person ought to be held to be affected with notice of every right less than absolute ownership the person holding under a deed so recorded has. If the record shows an absolute conveyance, it gives notice of the fact that the vendor has parted with all interest he had in the land; and such notice ought to be binding on a subsequent purchaser or mortgagee, who must know that, as between the parties, on proof of the fact that it was executed to secure a debt, the courts will hold it to be only a mortgage." Kennard v. Mabry, 1890, 78 Tex. 151, 156, 14 S.W. 272, 273 Livesey v. Brown, 1892, 35 Neb. 111, 52 N.W. 838, accord.

to be cut down to a mere security claim. Further, any argument that such a recordation should be ineffective because it adversely affects creditors may be answered that in a large number of states creditors are not included among the classes protected by the recording acts and, therefore, the manner of recordation or even nonrecordation would be immaterial as to them. In addition, if the transaction is a fraudulent conveyance as to them, recordation of it as a deed, even if such a recordation is authorized, will not validate the conveyance.[11] On the other hand, however, if it were recorded as a mortgage, which it really is, it would seem that this fact would be sufficient to suggest to a searcher that the instrument was, in spite of its form, a mortgage.[12] On balance, however, it would seem that the policy of the recording acts in having full title spread upon the records is violated, and it is dubious whether there is sufficient utility in protecting such transactions to justify it. Certainly to some searchers it would make a difference and upon them it puts the burden both of knowing the fact that such deeds are frequently used as mortgages and the law that they are permitted to be thus used, as well as the task of finding out in particular cases that they were so employed. There are authorities that hold such an instrument void when recorded only in the books of deeds.[13] In some states the recordation of a written defeasance is made by statute the condition upon which the mortgagee shall derive any benefit from the record of the deed.[14] But it has been held that such statutes are inapplicable where the defeasance is oral.[15] While the first part, as a practical matter, seems sensible and would impose no undue hardship of search, the latter may be questioned. So far as the policy of the statutes is concerned such a distinction is difficult to justify, but since the language specifically refers to *written* defeasances, the criticism is aimed at the legislature.[16]

INVALID DEEDS AND INVALID RECORDATION

205. (1) The record of an invalid deed is not constructive notice. If it is seen it is not actual notice of anything except the fact of nullity.

(2) An invalid recordation—e. g., of an unacknowledged mortgage—is not constructive notice, but if seen it imparts actual notice.

Nat. Bank v. Ford, 1906, 143 Mich. 402, 107 N.W. 76, 114 Am.St.Rep. 668, 8 Ann.Cas. 102; Johnson v. Cook, 1914, 179 Mich. 117, 146 N.W. 343; Ives v. Stone, 1883, 51 Conn. 446 (absolute deed recorded not notice to attaching creditors when defeasance not recorded); Matter of Mechanics' Bank, 1913, 156 App.Div. 343, 347–348, 141 N.Y.S. 473, 476, affirmed 209 N.Y. 526, 102 N.E. 1106.

"The fact that an instrument purporting to be an absolute grant is subject to a defeasance, or may be shown to be a mortgage, does not authorize it to be recorded among mortgages. Only such instruments as are mortgages by their terms are to be so recorded." Kent v. Williams, 1905, 146 Cal. 3, 10, 79 P. 527, 530. But see Jones, Mortgages, 8th Ed., § 629.

See Fogelman, The Deed Absolute as a Mortgage in New York, 1963, 32 Fordham L.Rev. 299, 311 for a consideration of the New York law as to the recordation of a deed absolute intended as a mortgage.

11. See § 205, infra.

12. See quotation in next footnote.

13. "There can be no hardship or injustice in such a construction; but on the contrary, it will more effectually carry into effect the intention of the legislature, and prevent fraudulent conveyances, and secret trust. If a conveyance is intended only as a mortgage, there can be no good reason why the terms on which it is to be defeasible should not appear on its face. If through inadvertence, it is taken as an absolute deed, the holder may comply with the terms of the statute, by making a written defeasance, specifying the conditions on which it was intended to be given, and recording both together in the book of mortgages. If he does this before the rights of any third party have intervened, he will be protected. And if he neglects it, he will only be in the same situation of every other mortgagee who neglects to have his security recorded." White v. Moore, N.Y.1829, 1 Paige 551, 554; Grand Rapids

14. Art. 66, § 1, Code 1957; McKinney's New York Real Prop.Law, § 320; Nebraska, North Dakota, and South Dakota have similarly worded statutes. See Hanna, Cases on Security, 2d ed., 654 n. 4. Cf. Ing v. Brown, 1850, 3 Md.Ch. 521; Owens v. Miller, 1868, 29 Md. 144, 159; Snowden v. Pitcher, 1876, 45 Md. 260.

15. See L.R.A.1916B, 69, 600. See also Jones, Mortgages, 8th Ed., §§ 631, 304.

16. See Kline v. McGuckin, 1874, 24 N.J.Eq. 411.

Void deeds are not rendered valid by recording them. The deed may be a nullity for a reason that is apparent on its face, as in the case where the name of the grantor or grantee is omitted or the description of the land is left out.[17] On the other hand it may be void because of a defect discoverable only by inquiry outside the record, e. g., lack of delivery. Any such deed in the grantee's direct line of title is fatal notwithstanding the complete absence of anything to put him on notice.[18] If an invalid deed of either variety has been executed to a third person by a grantor in the chain of title, such a record does not constitute constructive notice.[19] Nor, even if it is actually seen, should such a recorded instrument have the effect of putting a subsequent purchaser on inquiry.[20] Even if the inquiry were pursued it would only result in the discovery of a nullity which would not affect his rights.[21]

Where a mortgage, valid between the parties at least, has been invalidly recorded because statutory requirements such as acknowledgment have not been met, the record is regarded as incapable of giving constructive notice.[22] In some jurisdictions it is provided by statute that if a defectively acknowledged instrument is actually recorded, after the lapse of a certain length of time, it shall operate to give constructive notice.[23] Whether such an invalidly recorded instrument when actually seen will be regarded as imparting actual notice is more debatable, although the weight of authority is that it will.[24]

NON-RECORD NOTICE—IN GENERAL

206. Under most recording acts non-record notice of a prior unrecorded transfer prevents a subsequent grantee from acquiring priority. Justifications for the doctrine are open to criticism and it introduces an uncertainty into recorded titles violative of the policy of the acts. There is controversy as to what constitutes such notice.

As previously seen, in most states it is held that even though a conveyance of an interest in land has not been recorded, if a subsequent mortgagee or other purchaser has non-record notice or knowledge of its existence, he cannot obtain priority over it under the recording acts by virtue of the fact that it is unrecorded.[25] The original justification for this

17. See Bordwell, Recording of Instruments, 1917, 3 Iowa L.Bull. 24; idem 26, for discussion and cases of variance in names and misdescription of property.

18. See Haymond, Title Insurance Risks of Which the Public Records Give No Notice, 1928, 1 So.Cal. L.Rev. 422, 429; see Bordwell, Recording of Instruments, 1916, 2 Iowa L.Bull. 169, 185, on the effect of recordation creating a presumption of delivery; Rood, Registration of Land Titles, 1913, 12 Mich.L. Rev. 379. Forgery, disability of the grantor, the relationship of husband and wife, the after-born child and pretermitted heir are among other common risks.

19. Marx & Sons v. Jordan, 1904, 84 Miss. 334, 36 So. 386, 105 Am.St.Rep. 456; Disque v. Wright, 1878, 49 Iowa 538; Gardner v. Cole, 1866, 21 Iowa 205; Loomis v. Brush, 1877, 36 Mich. 40, 46–7; see Sherod v. Ewell, 1897, 104 Iowa 253, 73 N.W. 493. Some courts seem to hold that the recorded nullity does give constructive notice but only of the existence of the instrument *as* a nullity. See Gardner v. Cole, 1866, 21 Iowa 205, 214–15; see Bolton v. Johns, 1847, 5 Pa. 145, 149, 47 Am.Dec. 404; Pearson v. Creed, 1899, 78 Cal. 144, 147–8, 20 P. 302, 303; People, for Use of Esper, v. Burns, 1910, 161 Mich. 169, 125 N.W. 740.

20. See Stiles v. Japhet, 1892, 84 Tex. 91, 97–8, 19 S. W. 450, 452–3, a not too clear case dealing with inquiry notice from reading the deed.

21. See Philbrick, Limits of Record Search and Therefore of Notice, 1945, 93 U. of Pa.L.Rev. 257, 278. See cases, supra note 17.

22. Jacoway v. Gault, 1859, 20 Ark. 190, 73 Am.Dec. 494; Woods v. Garnett, 1894, 72 Miss. 78, 16 So. 390. See notes, 1912, 38 L.R.A.,N.S., 400; 1921, 19 A.L.R. 1080; 1931, 72 A.L.R. 1039. See also Graves v. Graves, 1856, 72 Mass. (6 Gray) 391; Cockey v. Milne's Lessee, 1860, 16 Md. 200; 2 Tiffany, Real Prop., 2d Ed., § 567c. Cf. Nordman v. Rau, 1911, 86 Kan. 19, 119 P. 351, 38 L.R.A.,N.S., 400, Ann.Cas. 1913B, 1068; Hastings v. Cutler, 1852, 24 N.H. 481; Simpson v. Hillis, 1911, 30 Okl. 561, 120 P. 572, Ann.Cas.1913C, 227. See Musick v. Barney, 1872, 49 Mo. 458.

23. See, e. g., West's Ann.Cal.Civ.Code, § 1207.

24. See § 206 for a further consideration of this matter.

25. See § 196, supra. "The statutes almost invariably, however, without reference to the particular language used, have received the same construction,

result was that the recording acts "were intended to protect only those who purchase in good faith, and not those who purchase in fraud of the party holding the real title." [26] Two criticisms of this theory are pertinent. One is that it is inconsistent with the statutes in North Carolina, Ohio, Arkansas and Louisiana under which a later mortgagee with full knowledge of the prior conveyance may nevertheless prevail.[27] Another is that while a subsequent mortgagee who has actual knowledge of the prior interest may be legitimately regarded as fraudulent and deprived of the benefits of the statute for that reason, when the doctrine is extended, as it has been, to inquiry notice such a basis loses force.[28]

Another rationale of the doctrine that actual notice is equivalent to recording is that it effectuates the purpose of the recording acts, viz., to provide a source of information by means of which title to land can be fully ascertained.[29] It has been suggested that such a theory is difficult to support with respect to (a) statutes allowing a definite time to record regardless of a conveyance to a bona fide purchaser in the interim; (b) statutes upholding the validity of an unrecorded mortgage as against a subsequent bona fide purchaser who does not record.[30] Furthermore, titles dependent on the sort of proof permitted to establish non-record notice are more uncertain than in a system where the record alone controls. This is so even if the requisite knowledge is equivalent to what might have been obtained from properly recorded instruments. In addition the doctrine reduces the necessity of prompt recordation. Thus it violates the policy of the statute in two ways.[31]

When it comes to determining what constitutes notice there has been great confusion and disagreement both as to analysis and terminology of the subject.[32] There is, it is true, rather general concurrence in characterizing as "constructive notice" the knowledge with which one is charged by reason of the fact that a mortgage or other instrument has been validly recorded. In such a case the formal act of recordation creates a conclusive legal presumption of knowledge of the recorded instrument, not because the person so charged knows anything about it nor because he ought to have known about it, but simply because the law, to achieve the purposes of the statute, attaches that legal consequence to the act. In other words, it is a rule of substantive statutory law that when the act of recording is done, subsequent mortgagees and other purchasers will be treated just as though they had knowledge of the instrument recorded. While this doctrine

as affording protection to a subsequent purchaser only when he is without notice of the unrecorded conveyance." 2 Tiffany, Real Prop., 2d ed., § 568. See Walsh, Mortgages, § 33.

26. Brinkman v. Jones, 1878, 44 Wis. 498, 520; see Patton, Titles, 2d Ed., § 8.

27. Priority in these states is determined strictly in accordance with priority of record. See § 187, supra; Patton on Titles, 2d Ed., § 8.

28. See Chancellor Kent in Dey v. Dunham, N.Y. 1816, 2 Johns.Ch. 182, 190. See also Pomeroy, Equity Juris., 5th ed., § 592, pointing out the distinction between notice as a reason for affecting the priority of a right and notice or knowledge as an ingredient making a transaction fraudulent.

29. See Philbrick, Limits of Record Search and Therefore of Notice, 1945, 93 U. of Pa.L.Rev. 259, 270.

30. See Hanna, Cases on Security, 3d ed., 869.

In Georgia, curiously enough, a mortgage not recorded within the time set by the statute will be valid as to subsequent liens created by contract and taken with notice, but invalid as to subsequent liens arising by operation of law, regardless of notice. See Central Union Trust Co. v. Appalachian Corporation, D.C.1924, 300 F. 397, affirmed 2 F.2d 581.

31. See Philbrick, Limits of Record Search and Therefore of Notice, 1945, 93 U. of Pa.L.Rev. 125, 128, 268 et seq. Even the argument that greater justice between the parties results from the doctrine may be questioned. Idem, 131.

32. See Story, Equity Juris., 13th ed., § 399; Pomeroy, Equity Juris., 5th ed., §§ 592 et seq.; Bispham, Equity, 9th ed., 458; Webb, Record of Title, § 221; Wade, Notice, §§ 5, 8; Glenn, Mortgages, § 386; Rollison, Priorities in the Law of Mortgages, 1932, 8 Notre Dame Law, 28, 45; 2 Tiffany, Real Prop., 2d ed., § 573; note, 1880, 10 Cent.L.J. 313. See also Merrill, The Anatomy of Notice, 1936, 3 U. of Chi. L.Rev. 417; Philbrick, Limits of Record Search and Therefore of Notice, 1945, 93 U. of Pa.L.Rev. 259.

is quite clear it is worth noting that the *knowledge* with which the person is charged is expressed in terms of *notice*. At the other extreme, if there is, without further inquiry, full, actual knowledge of the ultimate fact of a hostile conveyance, there is no difficulty found in the cases as to the effect of such knowledge as satisfying the rule that one who has it cannot prevail over the prior holder of the hostile interest in the property even though it be unrecorded. Here, again, however, such *knowledge* is frequently spoken of as actual *notice*.[33] Apart from these two extremes lie the cases in which knowledge will be attributed to a person[34] because he has a duty to make inquiry and the inquiry, if made, would have revealed the facts, knowledge of which will affect his rights. Thus "one who does not know a fact affecting his legal position may nevertheless be conscious of other facts so strongly indicating the existence of the ultimate fact that a man of ordinary prudence would inquire concerning it or conduct his business as though it existed."[35] It has been suggested that the term "inquiry notice" be used to cover these cases, the other two situations being non-inquiry ones.[36] While such a terminology has merit, recording and other statutes[37] that employ the phrases "actual notice," "no-tice" and "constructive notice" require a classification according to these terms.[38] Some courts when faced with this question have held that actual notice and actual knowledge mean the same thing.[39] Others have extended it to include what *should* be known, either because a reasonable man would draw the inference that it did exist by logical deduction or from general human experience or from knowledge of other facts in his possession, or else, as a man of ordinary prudence, he would find out by additional inquiry or conduct his affairs on the assumption that it existed.[40] It should be observed that while in such a case the knowledge of the facts upon which the duty of inquiry is based must actually be brought home, the knowledge of the ultimate fact is then attributed to him on a reasonable man standard of ratiocination and prudent conduct regardless of whether the particular individual actually so thought or would have acted.[41] In other words, when knowledge of certain facts would have been established the person will be treated, by a rule of substantive law, as though he had knowledge of the ultimate fact that affects his rights regardless of whether in fact he did or did not have such knowledge. Since, however, actual

33. E. g., West's Ann.Cal.Civ.Code § 18(1). See Pomeroy, Equity Juris., 5th ed., § 592 distinguishing between knowledge and notice.

34. A more accurate way of stating this would be to say that the person will be subjected to the same legal consequences that would follow had he actual knowledge regardless of the fact that he did not have it. In other words, actual knowledge of the ultimate fact is immaterial. However, the way it is stated is so usual and so commonly understood to mean the more correct statement that no need is felt to spell out the truth of the matter.

35. Merrill, The Anatomy of Notice, 1936, 3 U. of Chi.L.Rev. 417, 419; Brinkman v. Jones, 1878, 44 Wis. 498.

36. See Philbrick, Limits of Record Search and Therefore of Notice, 1945, 93 U. of Pa.L.Rev. 259, 266.

37. E. g., West's Ann.Cal.Civ.Code, § 19 defining "constructive notice"; §§ 1217. 2925, "notice"; § 2950, "actual notice".

38. See Brinkman v. Jones, 1878, 44 Wis. 498, 521, "We recognize the obligation to give some effect to the term 'actual notice' as distinguished from mere 'notice,' * * *."

39. E. g., Myhra v. Rustad, 1929, 58 N.D. 258, 262, 225 N.W. 796, 797 "'Actual notice' * * * consists in express information of a fact,"; Lamb v. Pierce, 1873, 113 Mass. 72; see Brinkman v. Jones, 1878, 44 Wis. 498, West's Ann.Cal.Civ.Code, § 18(1).

40. "We think the true rule is, that notice must be held to be actual when the subsequent purchaser has actual knowledge of such facts as would 'put a prudent man upon inquiry, which, if prosecuted with ordinary diligence, would lead to actual notice of the right or title in conflict with that which he is about to purchase.'" Brinkman v. Jones, 1873, 44 Wis. 498, 519, Cooper v. Flesner, 1909, 24 Okl. 47, 103 P. 1016, 23 L.R.A.,N.S., 1180, 20 Ann.Cas. 29.

41. Of course if the inquiry is shown to have been made and failed to have disclosed the ultimate fact, the legal consequences of knowledge of that ultimate fact do not attach. Williamson v. Brown, 1857, 15 N.Y. 354.

knowledge of the inquiry stimulating facts must be brought home, there is justification for classifying such notice as actual even though the ultimate knowledge is ascribed to him by operation of a rule of substantive law. Still others, however, have called notice of this sort "constructive." [42] If, in addition, knowledge of the facts upon which the duty is grounded is attributed to the individual because he as a reasonable person would, or should, have discovered them, without proof that in fact he had done so, it would be straining the natural meaning of the term "actual notice" to say it covered such a case. Here the legal consequences of actual knowledge of the ultimate fact become operative upon establishing certain facts without showing that the person whose rights are affected actually knew either the facts established or the ultimate facts.[43] Indeed there seems no real analytical difference between this last case, except in the way the result is reached, and constructive notice by recordation. In one the statute by fiat charges the person with knowledge by reason of an act done by another person. In the other, the law, by applying an artificial, reasonable man standard, first says that he is charged with knowing the existence of certain facts regardless of whether he does or does not know them; and then, by applying the same standard charges him with further knowledge which he ought to have acquired in consequence of his attributed knowledge of the first facts. Such a situation certainly should not be classed as "actual notice". In addition to the fact that it would be a somewhat strained use of the term "actual notice", to so classify a

result which follows from the establishment of certain facts regardless of any actual notice contravenes the policy of the recording act which dictate that the terms of the statute embodying the doctrine should not be interpreted liberally.

NON-RECORD NOTICE—APPLICATIONS

207. The general principles of the preceding section have found chief application in the following instances: (a) where the property taken in mortgage was in possession of someone other than the mortgagor; (b) where an effective prior instrument affecting title to the property was invalidly recorded but actually seen by the mortgagee; (c) where the mortgage was given by quit claim deed; (d) and, in England, where the title deeds of the property were in the possession of a third party when the mortgagee took his mortgage.

The problem of non-record notice discussed in general terms in the preceding section is chiefly exemplified in cases where such notice is based upon (a) possession, (b) actual knowledge of an invalidly recorded instrument, (c) a quitclaim deed, and (d) in England, outstanding title deeds.

(a) Possession

Possession of land in some person who is not the mortgagor or other grantor, if it be open, notorious, visible and exclusive, will operate as notice to a mortgagee or other purchaser of the property of the hostile claim of the party in possession.[44] Some authorities take the extreme view that such possession by itself, even though unknown to the subsequent taker, will operate to charge him with notice by operation of a rule of law in the same way that recording the claim would have done.[45] Other cases, however, give a

---

42. E. g., West's Ann.Cal.Civ.Code, § 19; Ponder v. Scott, 1870, 44 Ala. 241; Wilkerson v. Thorp, 1900, 128 Cal. 221, 60 P. 679; Shell v. Guthrie, 1930, 129 Kan. 632, 284 P. 420.

43. The case here supposed must not be confused with one in which the facts established are such as would be evidence that the person actually knew them, either strong enough for the court to direct a jury that he must have known them or sufficient to justify a finding that he did. See, e. g., Sensenderfer v. Kemp, 1884, 83 No. 581. Such a case would be no different from the immediately preceding one.

44. See Rollison, Priorities in the Law of Mortgages, 1932, 8 Notre Dame Law. 28, 56 et seq.; 1908, 13 L.R.A.,N.S., 49–140.

45. Van Baalen v. Cotney, 1897, 113 Mich. 202, 71 N. W. 491; Tate v. Pensacola, G. L. & D. Co., 1896, 37 Fla. 439, 20 So. 542, 53 Am.St.Rep. 251; Bowman v. Anderson, 1891, 82 Iowa 210, 47 N.W. 1087, 31 Am. St.Rep. 473; Galley v. Ward, 1880, 60 N.H. 331; see Pomeroy, Equity Juris., 5th ed., § 615. But see, 1907, 13 L.R.A.,N.S., 58, 61.

less sweeping effect to the fact of possession. What seems [46] to be the weight of authority requires that the subsequent taker either have or be charged with knowledge of the possession before he will be held to have notice of the hostile title. Such knowledge may be actual, and some cases regard possession as having probative value in establishing the fact of actual knowledge in the taker.[47] The more common view is that it creates a presumption of such knowledge which can be rebutted by showing either that prudently diligent inquiry did not discover or would not have discovered the possession.[48] It should be noted that, after the establishment of knowledge of the possession in one or the other of the two foregoing ways, there is a second step taken. It consists in the finding in, or charging to, the subsequent taker knowledge of the ultimate matter at issue, the hostile claim of the one holding the unrecorded interest in the property to which it is urged the subsequent taker is subject because he took with notice. In taking this second step the process noted above is repeated. The fact of possession plus knowledge of it by the taker is either the basis for a warranted or, in certain cases in which the facts point so indubitably to knowledge that no other conclusion could be reached reasonably, a compelled finding of the fact of knowledge of the hostile title, or else it raises a rebuttable presumption of such knowledge. Under statutes requiring actual notice there is authority that actual possession, actually known is not sufficient to constitute such notice.[49] Unless notice is synonymous with knowledge these cases go too far.[50] But there is other authority that actual knowledge of the fact of possession which creates a rebuttable, not an absolute, presumption of knowledge of the hostile conveyance will suffice.[51] Whether a rebuttable presumption of knowledge of the hostile conveyance founded upon a rebuttable presumption of knowledge of possession based upon the proved fact of possession would satisfy a statutory requirement of actual notice is not clear. In a couple of states statutes have eliminated possession as operating to give notice.[52]

Most of the cases involving possession as notice are ones in which a prior deed has been given to a mortgagee or purchaser who goes into possession, and the question is whether

---

46. For the difficulties in determining precisely just what the cases actually hold, see Pomeroy, Equity Juris., 5th ed., § 623. To what is said there may be added the great obscurity and confusion that exists in the decisions generally when presumptions, burden of proof, and burden of going forward with the evidence are involved. In a great many of the mortgage cases involving notice the action is in equity with the entire decision, both law and fact, by the court. The result is to make it more difficult to determine whether possession is regarded as a probative fact and knowledge of it is found to exist actually; or whether, when its existence is established, knowledge of it then is imputed as a conclusion of law. And the same is true as to the ultimate fact of hostile title.

47. E. g., Vaughn v. Tracy, 1856, 22 Mo. 415.

48. "It is well settled that the possession must exist when the subsequent purchase is made; must be actual and open; the inconsistency between it and the record title must be reasonably apparent; the purchaser is put on inquiry only if a person of ordinary prudence would be led by the facts known to investigate further; and, finally, if the purchase be actually made, a court will not retrospectively hold it lacking in good faith provided an inquiry was made of reasonable scope and persistence, even though it did not bring home to the purchaser knowledge of a superior title actually outstanding." Philbrick, Limits of Record Search and Therefore of Notice, 1945, 93 U. of Pa.L.Rev. 259, 272. As to the effect of reputation in the community as to title as charging with notice, see 1937, 109 A.L.R. 746.

49. Mara v. Pierce, 1857, 75 Mass. (9 Gray) 306; see, 1907, 13 L.R.A.,N.S., 58, 62.

50. See Pomeroy, Equity Juris, 5th Ed., § 592.

51. Brinkman v. Jones, 1878, 44 Wis. 498; see 1907, 13 L.R.A.,N.S., 58, 63. A fortiori, actual possession shown to be known in fact would be sufficient.

52. S.Car.Code, 1962, § 60–109; Va.Code, 1950, § 55–96. See Foster v. Bailey, 1909, 82 S.C. 378, 64 S.E. 423; Payne v. Buena Vista Extract Co., 1919, 124 Va. 296, 98 S.E. 34. Such statutes apply only to possession and not to other inquiry stimulating facts. See Glenn, Mortgages, § 388.1. But look at Gray v. Harvey, 1908, 17 N.D. 1, 113 N.W. 1034, holding possession by the grantor under a deed absolute intended as a mortgage is not "actual notice" under a statute providing that such a grant is not defeated against persons other than those with actual notice unless a defeasance is recorded.

that possession [53] is notice to a second mortgagee who relies upon record title in the mortgagor.[54] But there are other cases in which
the mortgagor's grantor remained in possession, and there is a split of authority as to
whether the mortgagee is put on notice by
such possession.[55] Some courts hold the
mortgagee may safely rely upon the clear
record title in the mortgagor and assume,
even if he knows of the possession by the
mortgagor's grantor, that it was at sufferance of the record owner.[56] On the other
hand a large number of courts treat such
possession as no different from possession by
any other third party.[57] The first view has
the merit of furthering the policy of the recording acts by emphasizing the reliance that
may be placed upon the records; while the
latter, if the doctrine of notice from posses-

sion is accepted, seems more logically consistent with other cases.[58]

Where the land is in the possession of a
tenant the authorities are conclusive that his
possession gives notice of his rights as tenant [59] and, by the English cases [60] and a
majority of the American cases,[61] any additional interest he may have in the property
independent of his tenancy. However, the
English courts and a few American decisions
confine the notice from the tenant's possession to the tenant's title only and hold that it
gives no notice of his landlord's title.[62] But
the majority American view is that the prospective mortgagee is charged in that event
not only with notice of the lease itself but
also of the identity of the lessor and the
character of his title.[63] Which view is preferable depends on whether it is desirable to
give a restricted or a broad scope to the doctrine of non-record notice, a matter which
has been commented on before [64] and will be
mentioned again.

(b) Defectively recorded instrument as notice

If a mortgage or other instrument of conveyance is validly recorded it operates to give
constructive notice to a subsequent mortgagee not only of all material recitals in it but

53. E. g., Mackenzie v. Augimeri, 1924, 210 App.Div.
156, 205 N.Y.S. 462.

54. There is at least one case that holds that the
possession of a mortgagee of record who had taken
a conveyance of the redemption interest but had
not recorded it is not notice to a subsequent purchaser from the mortgagor of the latter conveyance; the possession is regarded as consistent with
the equitable title of record being in the mortgagor.
Plumer v. Robertson, Pa.1820, 6 Serg. & R. 179.
Possession by the mortgagee, certainly in lien jurisdictions where he is not legally entitled to possession and also in title jurisdictions where the right
to possession exists but is seldom exercised, should
operate as notice of an interest in the property by
him other than the mortgage interest. See 1937, 23
Va.L.Rev. 717.

55. That the occupation of the grantor must be inconsistent with the rights of the grantee in such a
case for it to operate as notice, see notes, 1927, 25
Mich.L.Rev. 812; 1927, 12 Iowa L.Rev. 311; 1932, 8
Not.D.Law. 28, 59; 2 Tiffany, Real Prop., 2d ed., §
571c.

56. McKinley v. Crawford, 1932, 58 F.2d 528, 61
App.D.C. 123; Wicklein v. Kidd, 1926, 149 Md. 412,
131 A. 780; see Strong v. Strong, 1936, 128 Tex.
470, 98 S.W.2d 346, 109 A.L.R. 739; 1936, 105 A.L.
R. 845, 849. Pomeroy, Equity Juris, 5th ed., § 617.
As to notice from possession consistent with the
record see 1927, 25 Mich.L.Rev. 812.

57. Chandler v. Georgia Chemical Works, 1936, 182
Ga. 419, 185 S.E. 787, 105 A.L.R. 837; see Turman
v. Bell, 1890, 54 Ark. 273, 15 S.W. 886, 26 Am.St.
Rep. 35; Groff v. State Bank of Minneapolis, 1892,
50 Minn. 234, 52 N.W. 651, 36 Am.St.Rep. 640; Teal
v. Scandinavian-American Bank, 1911, 114 Minn.
435, 131 N.W. 486; 1936, 105 A.L.R. 846, 882. See

also Gray v. Harvey, 1908, 17 N.D. 1, 113 N.W.
1034.

58. See Tiffany, Real Prop., 2d ed., § 571g.

59. See 1907, 13 L.R.A.,N.S., 96.

60. Daniels v. Davison, 1809, 16 Ves.Jr. 249.

61. Coari v. Olsen, 1878, 91 Ill. 273; Crooks v. Jenkins, 1904, 124 Iowa 317, 100 N.W. 82, 104 Am.St.
Rep. 326.

62. Hunt v. Luck, 1901, L.R. 1 Ch. 45; 1902, L.R. 1
Ch. 428. See 1912, 12 Col.L.Rev. 449 criticizing the
English rule. See also Rollison, Priorities in the
Law of Mortgages, 1932, 8 N.D.Law. 28, 60. Beatie
v. Butler, 1855, 21 Mo. 313, 64 Am.Dec. 234.

63. Wood v. Price, 1911, 79 N.J.Eq. 620, 81 A. 983, 38
L.R.A.,N.S., 772, Ann.Cas.1913A, 1210. See 1907, 13
L.R.A.,N.S., 100. For an extreme application, Pen-
rose v. Cooper, 1912, 86 Kan. 597, 121 P. 1103, re-
versed 88 Kan. 210, 128 P. 362, criticized, 1912, 12
Col.L.Rev. 549, 551.

64. § 206.

of the existence and contents of all other instruments to which reference is made in it which may affect his title.[65] This is true even though such instruments be unrecorded,[66] provided, of course, that it would be reasonably possible for him to acquire knowledge of them.[67] Further, even though an instrument be unrecorded and is not referred to by any instrument of which the subsequent mortgage is on constructive notice, if it is an essential link in his chain of title "he is conclusively presumed to know all the recitals and matters contained therein affecting the title or the estate." [68]

Where, however, an instrument which is not an essential link in the mortgagee's chain of title is actually spread upon the record but, because of a defective acknowledgment or other reason it is invalidly recorded, it clearly does not operate as constructive notice to a subsequent mortgagee.[69] If the defect is not apparent on the face of the record, although there is authority that the same is true, the weight of authority holds to the contrary.[70]

The question remains whether the invalid record if actually discovered should operate to give notice. There is authority that it does not,[71] and it has been argued with vigor that it should not.[72] As one scholar has pointed out, "—thinking only of equities, and ignoring recording policies—one might say that at least the negligent non-recorder has tried to record. But the recording policy should not be ignored. All forms of inquiry notice excuse the non-recording of prior title, but this particular type of inquiry notice destroys the policy of the recording acts by a perversion of the record itself. The recorded paper does not satisfy their formal requirements; it flouts their policy; under them there is admittedly no record. Yet this ostensible record is made the substantive equivalent of a perfect and lawful record. And, as regards procedure, an instrument which admittedly is not itself evidence of its own existence and contents is nevertheless * * recognized as evidence of secondary character; and, which is worse, although only in this restricted sense evidence at all in a court, is unrestrictedly made 'evidence' to the purchaser who is held to be put upon inquiry

65 Union & Planters' Bank & Trust Co. v. Simmons 1924, 166 Ark. 285, 265 S.W. 953; see Loomis v. Cobb, Tex.Civ.App.1913, 159 S.W. 305, 307; Guerin v. Sunburst Oil & Gas Co., 1923, 68 Mont. 365, 218 P. 949; Costigan, Protecting Purchasers for Value, 1924, 12 Cal.L.Rev. 356, 385.

66. Taylor v. Mitchell, 1897, 58 Kan. 194, 48 P. 859; Croasdale v. Hill, 1908, 78 Kan. 140, 96 P. 37; Baker v. Mather, 1872, 25 Mich. 51; Sweet v. Henry, 1903, 175 N.Y. 268, 67 N.E. 574; see 1942, 10 J.B.A.Kan. 282.

67. Spellman v. McKeen, 1911, 96 Miss. 693, 51 So. 914; Acer v. Westcott, 1871, 46 N.Y. 384, 7 Am.Rep. 355; In re Nisbet & Potts' Contract, [1905] 1 Ch. 391.

68. Green v. Maddox, 1911, 97 Ark. 397, 403, 134 S. W. 931, 933; Stees v. Kranz, 1884, 32 Minn. 313, 20 N.W. 241, accord.

69. First Nat. Bank of Casselton v. Casselton Realty Co., 1919, 44 N.D. 353, 175 N.W. 720, 29 A.L.R. 911; First Nat. Bk. v. Gage, 1914, 71 Or. 373, 142 P. 539; See Ebling Brewing Co. v. Gennaro, 1919, 189 App. Div. 782, 179 N.Y.S. 384; note 19 A.L.R. 1074. There are curative acts in some states. See 1922, 19 A.L.R. 1074, 1081; 1931, 72 A.L.R. 1039, 1042; Patton, Titles, 2d Ed., §§ 83, 84, 543 for their operation and effect.

70. Woolridge v. Lacrosse Lumber Co., 1921, 291 Mo. 239, 236 S.W. 294, 19 A.L.R. 1068; Mutual Life Ins.

Co. v. Corey, 1892, 135 N.Y. 326, 31 N.E. 1095; note 1922, 19 A.L.R. 1074.

71. Kerns v. Swope, Pa.1833, 2 Watts 75; Choteau v. Jones, 1849, 11 Ill. 300, 318, 50 Am.Dec. 460; see 1922, 19 A.L.R. 1074; 1931, 72 A.L.R. 1039. In states where recordation is essential to the passage of title between the parties any actual knowledge of the record or of the deed itself would be immaterial. E. g., Cumberland B. & L. Ass'n v. Sparks, 1901, 111 F. 647, 49 C.C.A. 510, following Main v. Alexander, 1848, 9 Ark. 112, 47 Am.Dec. 732.

72. "This court is of the opinion (not shared by the writer) that one who has seen the record of an unacknowledged instrument is not deemed, because of that fact to have actual notice of the instrument itself, upon these grounds: To charge him with such notice is to require him to assume, without proof and without competent evidence, that a valid conveyance is in existence, corresponding to the unauthorized copy. If he is required to give any attention to the matter at all, he may, with equal or greater reason, suppose the parties to have abandoned whatever intention they may have had to execute such a conveyance from the fact that they failed to have a certificate of acknowledgment attached. To charge him with actual notice of the existence of a conveyance, because he had seen a

by it." [73] Nevertheless either by actual decision,[74] by dicta, or by legislation [75] there is a formidable body of authority for the view that one who sees the invalid record is on notice of the instrument itself. There is, however, no presumption from the existence of the invalid record alone that it had been seen.[76]

(c) Quitclaim deeds

There is a division of authority as to the priority between a mortgagee who holds under an instrument in the form of a quitclaim conveyance of the security interest and a prior grantee from the mortgagor claiming under an unrecorded conveyance. The weight of authority is that the mortgagee in a quitclaim mortgage deed occupies the same position under the recording acts as the grantee in any other form of conveyance.[77] The minority view is that the subsequent claimant under a quitclaim deed cannot prevail under the recording acts in such a case [78] for one or the other of two reasons: one, that since a quitclaim deed purports to convey only the interest of the grantor it can have no operation after he has parted with his interest and, this being so, lack of notice to his grantee is immaterial; two, that the restricted language of the deed should put the taker of it on inquiry.[79] Although the first reason would be valid if such were the effect of the deed, and of course it could be if the intent was made clear,[80] the ordinary interpretation of a deed in this form is that is a conveyance of the property as such, not just whatever interest in it the grantor had.[81] The second reason is without force since there are many reasons other than lack of title why a grantor does not wish to use a conveyance with covenants in it.[82] Further, the acceptance of such a deed indicates confi-

---

copy of it which, without legal authority, has been written in a book of public records, is essentially to give such copy the force of a valid record. To hold that the record of an unacknowledged conveyance, if known to a prospective buyer, amounts to actual notice of the instrument, is to compel him to give it force as evidence, which the court itself would refuse." Nordman v. Rau, 1911, 86 Kan. 19, 22, 119 P. 351, 353, 38 L.R.A.,N.S., 400, 402, Ann.Cas.1913B, 1068, 1069.

73. Philbrick, Limits of Record Search and Therefore of Notice, 1945, 93 U. of Pa.L.Rev. 259, 306. See also idem, 289. But see, 1942, 10 J.B.A.Kan. 282, 283, "If the adverse interest had been brought to the attention of the subsequent taker by word from its holder or by word from other parties in a manner which some courts would call 'hearsay,' if it were presented in court, then he would be deemed to have had 'actual notice.' Why is not an actual view of the defective record the same type of notice even though it is incompetent as evidence in court?" See aso Pomeroy, Equity Juris., 5th ed., §§ 626, 652, 600.

74. E. g., Hastings v. Cutler, 1852, 24 N.H. 481; Woods v. Garnett, 1894, 72 Miss. 78, 16 So. 390; Morrill v. Morrill, 1880, 53 Vt. 74, 38 Am.Rep. 659; Parkside Realty Co. v. McDonald, 1913, 166 Cal. 426, 137 P. 21.

75. See Philbrick, Limits of Record Search and Therefore of Notice, 1945, 93 U. of Pa.L.Rev. 259, 289 n. 308, 290 n. 310 for collections of cases and statutes. Some statutes provide that instruments which because of formal defects fail to create intended legal interests but do create equitable interests in the property may be recorded and this shall operate as record notice of the equitable interest so created. Conn.Gen.Stats.Ann. § 47.17; see Philbrick, supra, 283.

76. See James v. Morey, N.Y.1823, 2 Cow. 246, 288, 14 Am.Dec. 475; Bradley v. Walker, 1893, 138 N.Y.

291, 33 N.E. 1079, 52 Am.St.Rep. 365; St. John v. Conger, 1866, 40 Ill. 535, 537; Philbrick, Limits of Record Search and Therefore of Notice, 1945, 93 U. of Pa.L.Rev. 259, 290.

77. McDougall v. Murray, 1910, 57 Wash. 76, 106 P. 490, 26 L.R.A.,N.S., 159; Phoenix Title & Trust Co. v. Old Dominion Co., 1927, 31 Ariz. 324, 253 P. 435, 59 A.L.R. 625; Staggs v. Joseph, 1923, 158 Ark. 133, 249 S.W. 566; Graff v. Middleton, 1872, 43 Cal. 341; Moelle v. Sherwood, 1892, 148 U.S. 21, 13 S.Ct. 426, 37 L.Ed. 350; 1929, 18 Cal.L.Rev. 202; 1910, 10 Col.L.Rev. 371; 1895, 29 L.R.A. 33; 1910, 26 L.R.A.,N.S., 159; 1908, 12 L.R.A.,N.S., 240; 1927, 59 A.L.R. 632.

78. Messenger v. Peter, 1901, 129 Mich. 93, 88 N.W. 209; Ridings v. Hamilton Sav. Bk., 1920, 281 Mo. 288, 219 S.W. 585; Fowler v. Will, 1905, 19 S.D. 131, 102 N.W. 598, 117 Am.St.Rep. 938, 8 Ann.Cas. 1093; see notes and collections of cases cited in preceding section.

79. See McDougall v. Murray, 1910, 57 Wash. 76, 106 P. 490, 26 L.R.A.,N.S., 159.

80. Fitzgerald v. Libby, 1886, 142 Mass. 235, 7 N.E. 917.

81. See Tiffany, Real Prop., 2d ed. § 567m.

82. See Moelle v. Sherwood, 1892, 148 U.S. 21, 13 S. Ct. 426, 37 L.Ed. 350.

dence in the title rather than the reverse on the part of the grantee and an insistence on covenants would indicate a lack of confidence.[83] Even in those jurisdictions that follow the minority rule as to the grantee of a quitclaim deed and one claiming under the immediate grantor, if the quitclaim deed is back in the chain of title a purchaser for value without any other notice than would be given by the form of the antecedent conveyance is entitled to the protection of the acts.[84] Although the interest in marketable titles makes such a result desirable, it is nevertheless inconsistent with the minority decisions and the reasons given for them.

(d) Possession of title deeds

Due to the prevalence of the recording system in the United States notice of a prior equitable mortgage by possession in the mortgagee of the title deeds is of slight importance as such. It does loom large in England, however, and also, as analogous to the possession of the property itself, has interest for the American lawyer. Going upon the theory that it is culpable negligence on the part of a subsequent grantee not to require the production of the title deeds or to make inquiry as to why they are not produced, the English courts hold that he is charged with notice of the facts he might have learned by due inquiry.[85] If he is informed of the possession by the third party, the same result should follow, certainly if he intentionally refrains from making inquiry,[86] and even without any showing that the neglect to do

so was due either to intention or wilfulness.[87] On the other hand, if he makes inquiry and is given a reasonable excuse for the absence of the title deeds,[88] or if received a part of the deeds in the reasonable belief that he was receiving all of them when in fact part of them were in the hands of a third party, he will prevail.[89]

BURDEN OF PROOF

208. Under the recording acts authorities are divided on who has the ultimate burden of persuading the trier of fact on the issue of bona fide purchase by the subsequent claimant. The policy of the recording acts makes it preferable to put the burden on the holder of the prior unrecorded instrument.

Where the equitable *bona-fide* purchase doctrine as it exists apart from statute is involved, authorities are not unanimous on the burden of proof.[90] The prevailing view puts it on the purchaser. It is regarded as an affirmative defense to an asserted equity. It has to be pleaded as such by the purchaser and then established by a preponderance of the evidence.[91] This rule has a practical

83. See Rawle, Covenants for Title, § 29. The rule as to quitclaim deeds depends mostly on the local acceptance of such deeds as the normal form of conveyance.

84. Hannan v. Seidentopf, 1901, 113 Iowa 658, 86 N. W. 44; Rabinowitz v. Keefer, 1930, 100 Fla. 1723, 132 So. 297; see 1910, 25 L.R.A.,N.S., 1035. Cf. Houston Oil Co. v. Niles, Tex.Civ.App. 1923, 255 S. W. 604.

85. Oliver v. Hinton, 1899, 2 Ch. 264; Wormald v. Maitland, 1866, 35 L.J.Ch.,N.S., 69. The court in this latter case called the notice so charged "constructive". See § 191, supra.

86. Birch v. Ellames, 1776, 2 Anstr. 427.

87. Maxfield v. Burton, 1873, L.R. 17 Eq. 15, 18; Kellogg v. Smith, 1863, 26 N.Y. 18, 23, semble.

88. Hewitt v. Loosemore, 1851, 9 Hare, 449. See also Berwick & Co. v. Price, [1905] 1 Ch. 632.

89. Dixon v. Muckleston, 1873, 21 W.R. 178; see 1873, 17 Sol.J. 477, 531.

90. See, e. g., cases holding both ways in the case of trust property cited in Bogert, Trusts and Trustees, 2d Ed., § 881.

91. More v. Mayhow, 1663, 1 Ch.Cas. 34; Harris v. Ingledew, 1730, 3 P.Wms. 91; Jewett v. Palmer, N. Y.1823, 7 Johns.Ch. 65; Independent Coal Co. v. U. S., 1927, 274 U.S. 640, 47 S.Ct. 714, 71 L.Ed. 1270; see Rouskulp v. Kershner, 1878, 49 Md. 516. See also Pomeroy, Equity Juris., 5th ed. § 785. But see Langdell, Summary of Equity Pleading, 90, 91, arguing that the burden should be on the plaintiff asserting the equity to allege and prove that the defendant had notice or did not pay value. And see also Bell v. Pleasant, 1904, 145 Cal. 410, 415, 78 P. 957, 959, 104 Am.St.Rep. 61. "The underlying reason for this rule is, that as the debtor or the trustee, as the case may be, holds the legal title at the time of the conveyance, the legal effect of his deed is to convey that title to his grantee, and thus there is established a legal condition which enures to the benefit of the grantee and cannot be changed

reasonableness: the essential elements of the defense are for the most part peculiarly within the knowledge of the purchaser.[92]

In most jurisdictions the same sort of problem arises under the recording acts [93] due to the rule that, in order to prevail over a prior unrecorded deed a subsequent mortgagee or purchaser must have paid value, *bona fide* and without notice. Analysis of the cases is not always easy [94] due to the fact that the phrase is frequently used without explicit differentiation to mean two quite distinct things: one, the ultimate burden of persuasion of the trier of fact; two, the burden of going forward with the evidence.[95] This second burden may shift back and forth during the progress of the case regardless of which one on the whole case has the burden of persuasion. Thus proof of payment of value may raise a *prima facie* case of good faith and lack of notice on the part of a mortgagee and shift to the other party the duty of producing evidence to show that there was notice or lack of *bona fides*,[96] leaving, however, the ultimate burden of establishing the

essential facts by a preponderance of the evidence wherever it had been placed originally.[97] When the term is confined to the first usage, there is a decided divergence of authority as to which party bears it where the question in issue is that of *bona fide* purchase under the statutes.[98] By some courts it is placed upon the subsequent mortgagee.[99] The reasoning is that the prior conveyance, although unrecorded, does give to the grantee a valid legal title which can be displaced by a *bona fide* purchase only by virtue of the fact that the statute so provides; and therefore only those who establish affirmatively that they qualify under the terms of the statute will prevail over it.[1] It has seemed logical to some courts accepting this general rule to hold that where the prior interest is an equitable one, and consequently would be subject to being cut off under the equitable doctrine of *bona fide* purchase quite apart from the operation of the recording acts, the burden or proof should be placed upon the prior equitable claimant, at least where his

---

in equity, except by proof of circumstances to show a superior equity in the party who disputes it. Equity follows the law, and a legal condition or *status* being once established, the burden of proof of facts necessary in equity to change the *status* is upon him who asserts the equitable right."

Also on the burden of proof in priority problems, see 1958, 10 Baylor L.R. 42.

92. See Shotwell v. Harrison, 1871, 22 Mich. 410.

93. See § 196, supra.

94. This is especially true where the court determines questions of both fact and law without any clear segregation and the sharper test of an instruction to the jury is not available to determine what guide for passing on the evidence was being laid down.

95. See 4 Wigmore, Evidence, § 2485 et seq.; Thayer, Preliminary Treatise on Evidence, 353–389. See also Hood v. Webster, 1936, 271 N.Y. 57, 2 N.E.2d 43, 107 A.L.R. 497, where the difference between the two is clearly pointed out and used to distinguish earlier New York cases that had been regarded as placing the burden of proof in the first sense upon the holder of the prior unrecorded conveyance. See note, 1937, 107 A.L.R. 502, 528.

96. See Kruse v. Conklin, 1910, 82 Kan. 358, 108 P. 856, 36 L.R.A.,N.S., 1124; note, 1937, 107 A.L.R.

502, 523. Cf. White v. Hughes, Mo.App. 1935, 88 S.W.2d 268, "presumed" to be innocent purchasers "without evidence to the contrary"; Federman v. Van Antwerp, 1936, 276 Mich. 344, 267 N.W. 856, recordation of later instrument raises a presumption of good faith throwing the burden of overcoming it by showing notice onto the other party.

97. See Tiffany, Real Prop., 2d ed., 2266; Pomeroy, Equity Juris., 5th ed., § 785d.

98. A very full collection of authorities may be found in 1937, 107 A.L.R. 502.

99. Bell v. Pleasant, 1904, 145 Cal. 410, 78 P. 957, 104 Am.St.Rep. 61.

1. "A subsequent deed by the grantor to another person does not of its own force convey any title, for the grantor, having previously parted with his title, has left in himself nothing to convey and his deed alone can therefore convey nothing. It can only be effective, as against the first grantee, when supplemented by proof that it was first recorded, and that the grantee therein named purchased for value and without notice of the prior deed, or of the rights of the first grantee. This, also, is an attempt to change a legal condition; the necessary facts cannot be presumed in favor of the second grantee, and hence the burden is on him to make the supplementary proof." Bell v. Pleasant, 1904, 145 Cal. 410, 415, 78 P. 957, 959, 104 Am.St.Rep. 61.

claim arose by operation of law as contrasted with an agreement for it.[2]

The other line of authority argues that the holder of a prior unrecorded mortgage or other deed, because he has failed to comply with the statute, should and does have the burden of showing that his title has not been divested or postponed by someone who has satisfied the statutory requirements for doing so.[3]

What should be the rule as to burden of proof of *bona fide* purchase? Where the equitable, non-statutory doctrine is in question, loss very properly may be made to depend upon considerations of relative fault of the parties, or of ease or difficulty of proof of different elements by one or the other of the claimants, or of a policy in favor of free transferability of property interest, which may be stronger or weaker according to the kind of property involved.[4] Even the mechanical attitude that one who has only an equitable interest must sustain the burden as against one who has acquired a legal interest,

provided that otherwise the justice of their claims is good and therefore one "equity" cannot be considered better than the other, may be defended. But when the question arises under recording acts, the strong policy of these statutes is in favor of the subsequent taker, especially if he himself has complied with the requirement of recordation. This policy should outweigh the considerations of fairness or expediencey between particular claimants, or the nature of the competing interests as legal or equitable. It should place the burden squarely in all cases on the holder of the prior unrecorded instrument.[5]

CIRCUITY OF LIEN

209. Circuity of lien is the dilemma in which the first claimant has priority over the second, the second over the third and the third over the first. Numerous methods for apportioning the available funds among the claimants have been proposed. None are completely satisfactory. The Dixon formula is probably the best where one party is responsible for the circuity; the Benson rule is theoretically preferable where no one was at fault. If the circuity exists because a subsequent encumbrancer is subrogated to a prior claimant's superiority over an intervening one still a third formula is applicable.

The problem of circuity of lien, aptly termed "a first-rate legal puzzle",[6] has been before the courts for over two and one-half centuries [7] with a remarkable variety of solutions and, in the last fifty-odd years, has been repeatedly examined by legal scholars who have suggested additional answers.[8]

---

2. Commonwealth B. & L. Ass'n v. Howard, Tex.Civ. App.1933, 61 S.W.2d 546, affirmed 1936, 127 Tex. 365, 94 S.W.2d 144; Wittenbrock v. Parker, 1894, 102 Cal. 93, 36 P. 374, 24 L.R.A. 197, 41 Am.St.Rep. 17; Hawke v. California Realty Co., 1915, 28 Cal. App. 377, 152 P. 959; see Bell v. Pleasant, 1904, 145 Cal. 410, 415, 78 P. 957, 104 Am.St.Rep. 61. Although these cases state the rule broadly, they may be distinguished on the ground that they dealt with prior equitable interests arising by operation of law and hence unrecordable. Consequently, the decisions do not involve the doctrine of *bona fide* purchase under the recording acts.

3. Cessna v. Hulce, 1926, 322 Ill. 589, 153 N.E. 679; Butler v. Stevens, 1847, 26 Me. 484; McGrath v. Norcross, 1911, 78 N.J.Eq. 120, 79 A. 85, affirmed 82 N.J.Eq. 367, 91 A. 1069. Some cases put the burden of establishing notice on the holder of the prior, unrecorded instrument, but compel the purchaser to establish the payment of value on the ground that "the consideration which a party has himself paid for his own deed, is a fact peculiarly within his own knowledge, a fact affirmative in its nature, and which must, therefore, be presumed to be much more easy of proof than the negative fact of its non-payment could be to the opposite party." Shotwell v. Harrison, 1871, 22 Mich. 410, 419. Steinman v. Clinchfield Coal Co., 1917, 121 Va. 611, 93 S.E. 684.

4. See §§ 183, 185, 191.

5. See § 196, supra.

6. By Professor Albert Kocourek in 1935, 29 Ill.L. Rev. 952.

7. Greswold v. Marsham, 1685, 2 Ch.Cas. 170, is a pioneer case. Ingram v. Pelham, 1752, 1 Ambl. 153, 27 Eng.Rep. 102 and Jones v. Jones, Ch.1838, 8 Sim. 633 are other earlier English cases grappling with the problem.

8. The most important discussions are Benson, Circuity of Lien—A Problem in Priorities, 1935, 19 Minn.L.Rev. 139; Campbell, Protection Against Indirect Attack, Harvard Legal Essays, 1934, 3, 16, 20; Circuity of Liens—A Proposed Solution, 1938,

38 Col.L.Rev. 1267; Kocourek, A First Rate Legal Puzzle—A Problem in Priorities, 1935, 29 Ill.L.Rev. 952 (incidentally throwing out the suggestion that the admiralty rule of general average might be applied to the problem); White, A Problem in Priorities, 1926, 25 Ohio L.Bull. & Rep. 116; Tucker, The Deeds of Trust Puzzle, 1895, 1 Va.L.Reg. 4; Moon, The Deeds of Trust Puzzle—A Reply, 1895, 1 Va.L. Reg. 254; Kellogg, Priorities Puzzle Under Ship Mortgage Act, 1927, 2 Wash.L.Rev. 117; note, 1922, 8 Va.L.Rev. 550; note, 1928, 15 Va.L.Rev. 90, 94; note, 1926, 36 Yale L.J. 129, 134.

There have been several more recent considerations of the problem. One of these is Gilmore, Security Interests in Personal Property, 1965, C. 39. This is the most thorough and thoughtful of all the published material whether in judicial decisions or by legal scholars. He first points out, in § 39.1, the three types of situations out of which circular systems may arise. They are the same three set forth in this text following note-call 9, infra. He next discusses proposed solutions which are the seven outlined in this text following note-call 12 infra. In doing so, in a footnote, p. 1030 n. 21, he gives a formula that might be used in the seventh solution in the text. See supra. He brings out that, although most pre-1940 litigation and discussion arose out of the operation of the recording (or filing) systems, since then provisions of the statutory priority for United States tax liens perfected under Internal Revenue Code §§ 6321–6323 (26 U.S.C.A.) and of the Federal Bankruptcy Act § 67(c) (1) and § 64, (11 U. S.C.A. §§ 107, 104) in conflict with bodies of state law have provided the focus of litigation. Because there were important amendments to both statutes in 1966, a year after his book was published, their possible effects are not considered. In § 39.4, summarizing his survey in § 39.3 of post-1940 litigation, he finds that in the last two types of litigation, aside from the decisions in the Third Circuit, distribution has been according to the method stated in this text as the third one, following note-call 14 and classified as the third type in the text following note-call 9. Uniformly, the solutions proposed by legal scholars have been ignored. Professor Gilmore concludes: "As is not infrequently the case, the courts have been doing a good deal better than their critics."

Patton, in IV Am.L.Prop. § 17.33, after a survey of the various solutions found in the cases and writings concludes that the rule as expressed in the Mississippi case of Goodbar & Co. v. Dunn, 1884, 61 Miss. 618 best resolves the factors that should be considered in cases of circuity arising under the recording acts by the failure of one party to record. See text at note-call 20 and note 20, infra.

A note on Circular Priority in Mortgages, 1964, 17 Okl.L.Rev. 223, surveys the sources of the circularity problem and the various answers given by courts and writers. It ends with a look at the unresolved law in Oklahoma and an expressed hope that the courts not bind themselves to any one formula but apply "the rule most consistent with the type of circularity presented. * * *"

The Bankruptcy Act § 67c (11 U.S.C.A. § 107(c)) was amended in 1966 to invalidate and postpone many statutory liens and to clarify priorities among liens

As has been pointed out,[9] there are really three different types of cases in which circuity occurs. One is where the circuity results from the fault or neglect of one party to do some act which would have prevented it, normally by charging subsequent lien claimants with notice. The usual example of such a case is that of three mortgages: E–1, the first mortgagee fails to record; E–2, the second mortgagee records promptly but takes with actual notice of E–1; E–3, the third mortgagee takes without any knowledge or notice of E–1, is charged with record notice of E–2, and records promptly. The second category consists of cases in which the circuity arises by reason of the operation of certain rules of law independent of any element of fault or neglect by any one of the parties. Thus E–1 may have an unrecordable equitable vendor's lien which is prior to E–2's subsequent judgment lien that, in turn, is prior to a later recorded mortgage held by E–3, the last being prior to E–1's lien under the equitable doctrine of *bona fide* purchase.[10] The third type consists of cases in which by waiver or other agreement or by rule of law E–3 is entitled to be subrogated

in bankruptcy. In an excellent note covering deficiencies in the prior law, the invalidation and postponement of certain statutory liens, and finally, the problem of circularity under the amendment, the writer concludes that the circularity problem should no longer exist in bankruptcy. Statute Note, 1966, 45 Texas L.Rev. 374.

Dainow, Vicious Circles in the Louisiana Law of Privileges, 1964, XXV Louisiana L.Rev. 1, rather briefly outlines a variety of ways in which the problem of circularity could arise under Louisiana law.

9. 1938, 38 Col.L.Rev. 1267, 1268.

10. E. g., Campbell v. Sidwell, 1899, 61 Ohio St. 179, 55 N.E. 609. Another example is Wilcocks v. Waln, Pa.1824, 10 S. & R. 380, in which E–1 had a judgment under which execution had not been levied, the judgment being prior to E–2's mortgage, E–2's mortgage was prior to E–3's tax lien. E–3, in this case was the United States and its tax lien, on commission of an act of bankruptcy by the owner of the property, became superior to E–1's judgment lien. In some cases like these it may be possible to argue that there really is fault in that E–1 has neglected to cast his security interest in a recordable form; or, in the Wilcocks v. Waln situation, is at fault in not being more diligent in levying execution under his judgment. See Campbell, Protection

to E–1's rights in priority to E–2.[11] In choosing among the various solutions offered the group to which the particular case belongs must be taken into account because, obviously, they differ in most important respects. For example, the third category presents no real difficulty and is appropriately solved by the third method considered below. The other two, although frequently undifferentiated, present problems for which no uncriticized solutions have been given.

Turning to the answers given to the problem by courts and writers[12] the chief ones meriting consideration may be briefly summarized. One method is first to pay E–1, then E–2, and finally E–3. The reasoning is simple. "The creditors subsequent to the second mortgage could not come in until it was satisfied, and it cannot be until the first mortgage is." E–2 cannot complain,[13] but E–3 is treated unfairly and E–1 given an unjustified advantage by disregarding E–3's priority over E–1.

A second method, and a popular one, is to pay E–2 first, then E–3, and then E–1. The reasoning is that E–2 is clearly prior to E–3 and that because E–3, through E–1's fault, is prior to E–1,[14] E–2 also is prior to E–1 to the full extent of E–2's debt claim. This gives E–2 an unwarranted windfall by disregarding E–1's priority over him. E–1's fault may have postponed him to E–3 but neither it nor the action of E–3, a third party, should

affect the previously existing relationship between E–1 and E–2.[15]

A third method is first to segregate from the fund available for distribution the amount of E–1's debt claim. The balance left is all that E–2 is entitled to because he is junior to E–1's full claim. However he is entitled to it ahead of E–3 and therefore it should be paid over to him. The segregated amount is then paid first to E–3 and then to E–1. If these payments do not exhaust the entire fund, any surplus would be paid to E–3 and then to E–1.[16] The theory is to keep E–2 in his original position as junior to E–1 and senior to E–3, but to prefer E–3 over E–1 to the extent that E–1 had priority over E–2. E–1 is postponed to E–2 only to the extent that his priority over E–2 is exhausted by E–3 taking it. In criticism it has been pointed out that the underlying concept is that, because of non-recordation or other neglect by E–1, the share that otherwise would go to E–1 should pass to E–3. While such a result would be correct if there were an agreement between E–1 and E–3 that E–3 should stand in E–1's shoes, i. e., in the third category of cases, it is inapplicable where there is no agreement. Recording acts do not provide that the benefit of an unrecorded first mortgage shall accrue to E–3 but that it shall be void as to him.[17] And any other rule that defeats E–1 as to E–3 but does not affect his position *vis a vis* E–2 should result only in elevating E–3 to the position of a second encumbrancer instead of a third. It should not put E–3 ahead of E–2 into the shoes of E–1 as would an express agreement. Al-

Against Indirect Attack, Harvard Legal Essays, 1, 34 n. 56.

11. Walbridge v. Barrett, Ohio 1921, 11 O.C.D. 634, 21 Ohio C.C. 522; cf. White, A Problem in Priorities, 1926, 25 Ohio L.Bull. & Rep. 116.

12. See Osborne, Cases Property 2d Ed. Security, 330, for a résumé of various solutions.

13. See Loucheim Brothers' Appeal, 1870, 67 Pa. 49, 53.

14. Ferris v. Chic-Mint Gum Co., 1924, 14 Del.Ch. 232, 124 A. 577; Clement v. Kaighn, 1862, 15 N.J. 47; Andrus v. Burke, 1901, 61 N.J.Eq. 297, 48 A. 228; Hill v. Rixey, Va., 1872, 26 Grat. 72, 81; Renick v. Ludington, 1878, 14 W.Va. 367; McClaskey v. O'Brien, 1879, 16 W.Va. 791; Ingram v. Pelham, 1752, 1 Ambl. 153, 27 Eng.Rep. 102.

15. See, 1922, 8 Va.L.Rev. 550; Tucker, The Deeds of Trust Puzzle, 1895, 1 Va.L.Reg. 4; The Deeds of Trust Puzzle—A Reply by J. B. Moon, 1895, 1 Va.L. Reg. 254; 1888, 12 Va.L.Jour. 424.

16. Bacon v. Van Schoonhoven, 1879, 19 Hun 158, 87 N.Y. 446; Hoag v. Sayre, 1881, 33 N.J.Eq. 552. See White, A Problem in Priorities, 1926, Ohio L.Bull. & Rep. 116; note, 1922, 8 Va.L.Rev. 550. In re Weniger's policy, 1910, 2 Ch. 291 reached practically the same result.

17. See Dixon, J., dissenting, Hoag v. Sayre, 1881, 33 N.J.Eq. 552.

though E–2 is not injured, E–1 is dealt with unjustly in that in most cases he will be postponed to the claims of both E–2 and E–3. And E–3 gets an unwarranted advantage, putting him in a better position than he would have been in had E–1's claim not existed.[18]

Apart from an objection to be discussed later, the most satisfactory method of distribution in cases of the first category is that laid down by Dixon J., dissenting, in Hoag v. Sayre.[19] His proposal is first, deduct from the *whole fund* the amount of E–2's lien, and apply the balance to pay E–3, this being his share as junior encumbrancer to E–2; next deduct from the *whole fund* the amount of E–1's lien, the balance being the sum that E–2 should receive as junior to E–1; and finally apply any balance to E–1's lien after these two payments have been made out of the whole fund.[20] This disposition is based upon treating E–2 and E–3 as junior encumbrancers and paying to each his reasonable expectation as such, at the same time that E–1 is deprived of his priority because of his fault insofar as it is necessary to protect the other claimants. It has been criticized on the ground that, although the result is proper so far as E–2 and E–3 is concerned, it does injustice to E–1 in that it overlooks the priority of his full claim over E–2.[21] It has been justified, however, on the ground that it is necessary, and, because E–1's culpable conduct is responsible for the circuity, entirely proper to protect E–3 in his priority over E–1 against indirect attack by the latter. For if E–1 can reach ahead of E–2 that part of the fund which has been segregated for him in preference over E–3, then E–2, whose lien actually rests on the entire fund ahead of E–3, would be driven to asserting his priority on the part that had been allocated for payment to E–3.[22] It has been suggested also that this subordination of E–1 to E–2 might be sustained, in cases where E–1 knows of E–2, on the reasoning that "(1) E–2 is a surety, since his second mortgage lien is exposed to the risk of non-payment of the first mortgage debt, and (2) that E–1 owes to him as 'real' surety, as a creditor would owe to a surety personally bound * * *, the duty of recording the first mortgage so as to preserve its priority and thereby safeguard the equity of subrogation of E–2 therein."[23] A more serious objection is the startling result that E–1 would receive the entire fund under some circumstances although the circuity was due to his fault.[24] Recognizing the

---

18. See Benson, Circuity of Lien—A Problem in Priorities, 1935, 19 Minn.L.Rev. 139, 143; note, 1938, 38 Col.L.Rev. 1267, 1269; Campbell, Protection Against Indirect Attack, Harvard Legal Essays, 3, 17.

19. 1881, 33 N.J.Eq. 552.
"The Dixon formula is accurate, clear, easily understood, and quickly applicable, in form to any three-party situation involving so-called circuity of lien. Moreover, this formula must be regarded as a construct of formidable ingenuity, of great subtility, and remarkable esthetic beauty." Kocourek, A First-Rate Legal Puzzle, 1935, 29 Ill.L.Rev. 952.

20. The same rule was employed in Day v. Munson, 1863, 14 Ohio St. 488, 493; but see White, A Problem in Priorities, 1926, 25 Ohio L.Bull. & Rep. 116. See also Goodbar & Co. v. Dunn, 1884, 61 Miss. 618, analyzed in Campbell, Protection Against Indirect Attack, Harvard Legal Essays, 34 n. 56; Campbell, id., 17. The formulas set forth in the last three authorities are not identical but their results are.

21. Benson, Circuity of Lien—A Problem in Priorities, 1935, 19 Minn.L.Rev. 139, 145.

22. Campbell, Protection Against Indirect Attack, Harvard Legal Series, 3, 18.

23. Id., 34 n. 57.

24. E. g., If the fund is $5,000 and the claims of E–1, E–2, and E–3 are each $5,000, under the Dixon formula neither E–2 nor E–3 would be entitled to anything and E–1 would take all. See White, A Problem in Priorities, 1926, 25 Ohio L.Bull. & Rep. 116, characterizing such a result as "absurd".
The additional objection, that it doesn't make sense for E–1's share to decrease as the fund increases has been answered by saying that "the result is not only required by the true interpretation of the Recording Act [where the circuity has been caused by E–1's failure to record] but also works no injustice to E–1; for, admittedly, * * * the share of E–2 increases *pari passu* with the net proceeds, thereby exhausting the increment therein; and the share of E–3 should likewise increase, inasmuch as the amount necessary to meet his just expectations becomes so much the greater." Campbell, Protection Against Indirect Attack, Harvard Legal Series, 3, 35 n. 58.

validity of the criticism, it has been suggested that the Dixon formula be kept as a general rule but that it be supplemented by a provision that in such cases the fund should be distributed equally.[25]

A fifth method is first, deduct from the fund the amount of E–2's claim and pay the balance to E–3; second, apply the deducted amount to the payment of E–1's full claim and then to E–2's claim.[26] This works injustice to E–2 in that in most cases it will postpone him not only to E–1 but also to E–3. It gives protection against indirect attack by E–1 at the expense of E–2 rather than E–1, the party at fault. E–2's priority upon the *whole fund* should have been preserved ahead of E–3 unless the priority of E–1 over E–2 is cut down by the amount paid to E–3. But if this is done we have the Dixon solution.

A sixth proposal, advanced by Professor Benson, is to treat each one as a junior lienholder and pay to each that part of the fund remaining after an amount equal to the sum of the claims prior to his has been set aside. Under this solution difficulties arise where (a) the fund is so small that no claimant is entitled to any of it as a junior lienholder; (b) the fund is more than sufficient to pay the amounts to which the claimants are entitled as junior lienholders; (c) the fund is not sufficient to pay all the amounts to which the claimants are entitled as junior lienholders.[27] In (a) and (b), the fund or the surplus left will be divided equally or in some other arbitrary manner on the ground that it is a windfall. In (c) the largest lesser amount that the fund could have been without being exceeded by the junior lienholder's claims is to be ascertained and a portion of the fund equal to this amount distributed as though it were the whole fund. The remainder is then divided equally among those whose actual claims as junior lienholders have not been completely satisfied by the first operation.

This sixth method draws no distinction between cases where the fault or neglect of one person has caused the circuity and where it arises without blame attaching to anyone. The fundamental proposition upon which it rests is that each and every claimant stands in the position of a junior lienholder. In criticism, it has been said that it is equally as correct to state that each claimant stands in the position of a senior lienholder and that either proposition is a logical impossibility.[28] Moreover the formula is so intricate and complex that it probably would present administrative difficulties in application as well as almost certainly resulting in bewilderment to most clients, many lawyers, and some judges.[29] Also, in most cases a part of the fund will have to be distributed in a purely arbitrary way, and in the interests of simplicity it may be urged that entire fund be disposed of the same way in all cases. Nevertheless, in cases of circuity without fault it seems clearly fair to each one to say that the amount of the claim he is entitled to have satisfied out of the fund is not his full debt claim but the actual value of his *lien* claim, i. e., the amount of the fund after the sum of the claims prior to his has been set aside, and the fund should be distributed as nearly as possible in accordance with these

25. See Kocourek, A First-Rate Legal Puzzle, 1935, 29 Ill.L.Rev. 952, 957. Although the reasoning is different and in such a case no one would have been entitled to any of the fund, under the Benson theory a similar rule of equality of distribution is reached.

26. Dyson v. Simmons, 1877, 48 Md. 207. Benson erroneously cited Goodbar & Co. v. Dunn, 1855, 61 Miss. 618 as employing this method, overlooking the fact that in that case the amount paid to E–3 should first be subtracted from E–1's claim before he was paid out of the sum equal to E–2's claim that had previously been deducted from the fund. See Benson, Circuity of Lien—A Problem in Priorities, 1935, 19 Minn.L.Rev. 139, 144.

27. See Benson, Circuity of Liens—A Problem in Priorities, 1935, 19 Minn.L.Rev. 139; note, 1938, 38 Col.L.Rev. 1267.

28. "If one person cannot be junior to himself, neither can three persons be junior to each other, in the same reference." Kocourek, A First-Rate Legal Puzzle, 1935, 29 Ill.L.Rev. 952, 953.

29. The adjectives may be misplaced.

junior lienholder's claims. Consequently, if it were not for its intricacy and another objection to be considered it would seem to be the best solution, at least in non-fault cases, just as the Dixon formula is most satisfactory in cases where there is fault.

There is one defect, previously suggested but not yet discussed, common to both the Dixon and Benson methods of distribution. Under them it is possible for a claimant to receive less if the fund is large than he would if it were smaller.[30] Because of this, there is an inducement to the other two claimants to act in concert to bid up the property to an amount which would cause the share of the third to shrink and their own portions to increase. This third claimant might protect himself partially by making an agreement with one of the other two to give him part of the share subject to shrinkage in return for not combining to boost the price. Or he might be protected either by being given the power to compel valuation of the property or by being given a right to the largest share he could have received had the fund been smaller if he can establish that there had in fact been collusion between the other two to raise the price artificially. None of these are satisfactory.[31] The first merely demonstrates that there are additional possibilities of collusive action in the realization of the fund with the result that each one of the three parties has chances, by combining with one of the others, to get one-half of that part of share subject to shrinkage. The second would normally be impractical because of difficulties of proof. And to invoke the last the claimant would face the task of establishing the amount the property would have brought at a forced sale free from collusion—a novel standard of value presenting obviously troublesome problems. Consequently, although these rules may be regarded with favor for a first decision in any jurisdiction, after they have been once established their future operation may be objectionable.

With the foregoing critique of the Dixon and Benson rules in mind, a seventh solution has been offered. Where the circuity arises without fault, labeled "true circuity," the premise is accepted that, since all the parties are similarly situated, the aim should be to distribute the fund according to a method that will most nearly give to each one the amount of his claim as a junior lienholder. At the same time the method should be one that would make the share of no claimant less at a larger fund than at a smaller one. Further, those claimants who are junior lienholders to the smallest claim should receive some preference on the ground that their junior lienholder's claims are first to arise. However, the larger the fund, the less important should be this element because, as the fund comes closer and closer to being sufficient to satisfy all claims in full, the more nearly should the amount each one is paid correspond to the size of his claim. And, finally, the formula should exhaust the whole fund exactly without leaving either a surplus or deficit to allocate by some other rule. The formula meeting these conditions is stated as follows:

"Ascertain what the junior lienholders' claims would be if the fund were of such size that the sum of the junior lienholders' claims were equal to what the fund is in fact. Pay these amounts to the respective claimants.

"What this amounts to is paying the party who is subsequent to the smallest lien first, and paying him the amount he expects to get before any one else expects to get anything (this *may* mean treating two people alike in time of paying, for if two claims are of the same size, two junior lienholders' claims will arise at the same time). Then

---

30. See White, A Problem in Priorities, 1926, Ohio L.Bull. & Rep. 116; Kocourek, A First Rate Legal Puzzle, 1935, 29 Ill.L.Rev. 952, for tables illustrating this difficulty under the Dixon formula. The same may occur to a lesser degree under the Benson method. See 1938, 38 Col.L.Rev. 1267, 1273. But see note 24, supra, in answer.

31. See 1938, 38 Col.L.Rev. 1267, 1272.

he and the party whose junior lienholder's claim arises next are paid increments equally until each has received the amount he expected to get before the third party expected to get anything. Then all three are paid the increments equally. If before exhaustion of the fund a party is paid off the remaining parties divide the increments." [32]

Where the circuity is caused by the fault of E–1, to obviate the difficulty of E–1's share diminishing as the size of the fund increases, a different system under which a *minimal share* which E–1 would receive independent of the size of the fund was devised. [33] And, to round out the whole, the situation where two of the three claims are concurrent was considered, both where no one is at fault and where one party is guilty of fault. [34]

This last solution has unquestionable merit as a matter of theory, but it suffers from the fact that it is more difficult to understand and, probably, to administer, than the Benson method, as well as introducing some questionably arbitrary methods of allocation to achieve what it considers desirable ends. Further, while the spectacle of a party's share diminishing as the size of the fund increases is undesirable, it certainly can be born with equanimity where the share that diminishes is that of the one whose fault is responsible for the circuity. In such a case the result that is really objectionable and which can be corrected more simply is for the one at fault to receive the entire fund. [35] Also, the dangers of collusion under the Dixon and Benson methods in bidding the property to an artificially high price, while undeniably present, seem exaggerated and the possible remedies unduly minimized. At least the dangers and faults seem scarcely

sufficient to justify the erection of still another and complex system, however pleasurable and enticing the project might have been.

Professor Grant Gilmore, in his study of the problem, [36] found that "Since 1940 or thereabouts all the cases which have been discovered, except two, involve circularities which arise from contradictory systems of priorities established by state and federal law, either under 67(c) (1) of the Bankruptcy Act [37] [which gives priority to administration expenses and wage claims over statutory liens and landlord's liens; these liens by state law, have priority over consensual security interests; and the security interests, if perfected, have priority over the unsecured administration expenses and wage claims] or under the Supreme Court's doctrine relating to tax liens and other federal claims [under this doctrine state, county, and municipal tax claims have been subordinated to subsequent claims of the United States; the claims so subordinated by federal law, however, typically have priority by state law over both antecedent and subsequent security interests; the security interests although thus postponed to local tax claims continue by federal law to have priority over subsequently accruing or perfected claims of the United States]. * * * These are, then, cases of the type which have been called 'true circularities'; the circularity arises by operation of law, none of the claimants being chargeable with fault." [38]

Professor Gilmore also found that "The most popular solution has been to apply the rule used in cases of apparent circularity re-

---

32. 1938, 38 Col.L.Rev. 1267, 1273.

33. Id., 1275.

34. Id., 1276. This was true in Hoag v. Sayre, 1881, 33 N.J.Eq. 552.

35. See text, supra, discussing the Dixon formula.

36. Gilmore, Security Interests in Personal Property, 1965, C. 39, § 39.3, briefly outlined note 8, supra.

37. The 1966 Amendments to § 67c of the Bankruptcy Act make Professor Gilmore's exposition of circularity under that Act subject to revision. See Statute Note, 1966, 45 Texas L.Rev. 374, which concludes that circularity problems under the Act should no longer exist. See infra, text at note-call 41.

38. Op. cit. supra note 36.

sulting from a subordination agreement. In the subordination case A, B and C have liens which rank in that order; A then subordinates his claim to C's. The solution is to set aside from the fund the amount of A's claim; pay that to C and the balance, if any, to A; pay B from the remainder of the fund, the balance, if any, going to C and A in that order. In a true subordination case, it is assumed that there is no difficulty in establishing the normal order of priority which would have settled the distribution (A first, then B, then C) except for A's subordination to C. The real difficulty in applying the subordination rule to cases of true circularity is that there is no 'normal' order to start from. * * * Which of the three claimants is A, which B, which C? Until we know, there is no way in which we can distribute the fund according to the subordination rule. * * * the courts appear to have been guided in making this crucial allocation more by instinct than by reason." [39]

"The principal confusion which has arisen in applying the subordination rule to true circularity cases has been the allocation of claimants to the A, B and C Slots. In failure-to-file cases the allocation presents no particular difficulty * * * But in the no-fault cases, arising from the conflict of inconsistent federal and state priority systems, the allocation becomes tricky. In the nonbankruptcy cases, which do not involve § 67(c)(1), there is a federal lien or claim in competition with two non-federal interests, which depend for their validity and rank on state law: the trouble comes from the fact that, by Supreme Court doctrine the federal claim is superior to the interest which is senior by state law but inferior to the interest which is junior by state law. In this situation the courts which have applied the subordination rule have without exception called the federal claim B, the senior interest by state law C, the junior interest A; that

is, in the typical case of a mechanic's lien, a mortgage (or other security interest) and a federal tax lien, the court orders the amount of the mortgage (A) to be set aside, the mechanic's lien (C) to be paid from this amount and the federal lien (B) to be paid from the balance remaining after the setting aside." [40]

In the bankruptcy cases the 1966 Amendment to the Bankruptcy Act adopted an order of distribution based on a theory of subordination. That order has been described as follows: "The statutory lien is subordinated to the unsecured claims, but otherwise the nonbankruptcy order is retained. Specifically,

1. A sum equal to the amount due under the postponed statutory lien is set aside and applied in order to

    (a) administration expenses and wage claims,

    (b) the statutory lien.

2. The indefeasible lien is paid in full.

3. The remaining balance is first used to satisfy any possible unpaid balance of administration expenses and wage claims, and then to satisfy the statutory lien as far as possible." [41]

This discussion may end appropriately with quotations from Professor Kocourek and Professor Gilmore, followed by reference to further consideration later of the changes effected by legislation in 1966. "Any reader not already familiar with the problem will wish to * * * find the solution for himself, at least if he is an independent thinker. We warrant he will find it an interesting intellectual task and that no matter what his solution, if it has in it the smallest germ of coherence and rationality, it probably will

---

39.   Gilmore, op. cit. supra note 36, p. 1032.

40.   Gilmore, op. cit. supra note 36, p. 1044.

41.   Statute Note, 1966, 45 Texas L.Rev. 374, 382. For a description of this distribution, see Jordan v. Hamlett, 5th Cir. 1963, 312 F.2d 121, 124.

Further consideration of the 1966 amendments of the Bankruptcy Act will be found in § 221A, infra.

find verifiable support somewhere in case law." [42]

"Experience, as Justice Holmes might have told us, solves more problems than logic. With respect to circular priorities, the logicians had their turns at bat but, if we go by the case-law boxscore, struck out. In the cases decided since 1950, the courts, however motivated, have been deciding circularity cases with an impressive record of consistency which has been marred only by the Third Circuit's fall from grace in *Quaker City*.[43] Textbook and law review discussions of the circularity problem have usually emphasized the extraordinary number of "solutions" which have been proposed and leave the reader with the impression that the courts have picked now one, now another, in a completely random fashion. According to the recent returns, however, there is only one solution which is regularly followed, and that is distribution in the same way that would be ordered if the circularity had arisen from a contractual subordination. * * * As is not infrequently the case, the courts have been doing a good deal better than their critics." [44]

The circularity problem arising because of the operation of federal tax liens and Bankruptcy Act provisions and the solution of it in the authorities discussed in this section most importantly by Professor Gilmore, have been drastically affected by legislation passed in 1966. The effect of this legislation on priorities of security interests in real property considered in this text will be dealt with in a later section.[45]

CREDITORS

210. In many states recording acts do not in terms provide protection to creditors. In those that do, the language is extremely varied, ranging from the quite explicit to the very general "all creditors" or "creditors." The non-explicit statutes are generally construed to include only subsequent creditors who have fastened an attachment, judgment, or execution lien upon the property without notice, before the lien is acquired, of the prior interest. The doctrine of estoppel is available to creditors, within undefined boundaries, as a supplement to the recording acts.

In many states the recording acts require recordation as a condition to validity only as against subsequent purchasers or mortgagees for value and without notice.[46] In such states, either on the ground that creditors, whether general, attaching, levying, or having a judgment lien, are not purchasers,[47] or, because of the general common-law rule which governs in the absence of express statutory change, that creditors' liens attach only to such interest in the land as the debt-

---

42. A First-Rate Legal Puzzle, 1935, 29 Ill.L.Rev. 952. Professor Kocourek threw out in passing the suggestion that the admiralty rule of general average, although never applied to the problem, might be preferable to, for example, the first method considered in the text.

43. In re Quaker City Uniform Co., 3d Cir. 1956, 238 F.2d 155, certiorari denied, 1957, 352 U.S. 1030, 77 S.Ct. 595, 1 L.Ed.2d 599 and Veloric v. College Hall Fashions & Synthetic Specialists, Inc., 352 U.S. 1030, 77 S.Ct. 596, 1 L.Ed.2d 599, discussed Gilmore, op. cit, supra n. 36, pp. 1038–1043.

44. Gilmore, op. cit. supra note 36, pp. 1045–1046.

45. See § 221A, infra.

46. See, e. g., West's Ann.Cal.Civ.Code § 1214; Patton, Titles, 2d Ed., § 17. See § 189, supra for a discussion of the rights of creditors apart from recording acts.

47. Vallely v. Grafton First Nat. Bank, 1905, 14 N.D. 580, 106 N.W. 127, Hanna, Cas. Security, 3d ed., 766, 5 L.R.A.,N.S., 387, 116 Am.St.Rep. 700, general creditors; Shear Co. v. Currie, C.C.A.Tex.1923, 295 F. 841, Hanna, Cas. Security 3d ed. 790, attaching creditors; Sullivan v. Corn Exchange Bank, 1912, 154 App.Div. 292, 139 N.Y.S. 97, Campbell, Cases Mortgages, 2d ed., 476, judgment creditors; Wilcoxon & Farris v. Miller, 1867, 49 Cal. 193; Bank of Ukiah v. Petaluma Sav. Bk., 1893, 100 Cal. 590, 35 P. 170.

Under the Massachusetts recording act a subsequent attaching creditor without notice has been held to be a purchaser for value and therefore entitled to prevail over prior unrecorded mortgages, a result strikingly at variance with most authorities. McMechan v. Griffing, 1830, 26 Mass. (3 Pick.) 537; Woodward v. Sartwell, 1880, 129 Mass. 210; Cowley v. McLaughlin, 1886, 141 Mass. 181, 4 N.E. 821. The same protection is not accorded to a non-attaching creditor. Stoneham Five Cents Sav. Bk. v. Johnson, 1936, 295 Mass. 390, 3 N.E.2d 730, 106 A.

or actually has,[48] the acts do not affect the priority of prior unrecorded mortgages or security interests of any sort against creditors.[49]

In those jurisdictions which do seek to protect creditors against unrecorded conveyances[50] the language in the statutes is extremely varied. Sometimes it is fairly explicit, e. g., "subsequent creditors (whether lien creditors or simple contract creditors)";[51] "creditors of the party making such deed, who may trust such party after the date of the said deed";[52] "existing or subsequent creditors,";[53] "any creditor * * * obtaining a judgment or decree, which by law may be a lien";[54] "subsequent judgment creditors".[55] More generally the language is either "all creditors" or "creditors" without limitation.

Where the statutory language is not so explicit as to be decisive, strikingly exemplified by acts of the last type, there is considerable latitude for interpretation. The controversies center about the following problems: (1) Should antecedent as well as subsequent creditors be protected? (2) Must the creditor have obtained a lien of some sort before recordation? And is there a difference between judgment liens which attach to all property of the debtor in a designated area and execution or attachment liens which arise only when action is taken by the creditor with respect to specifically designated property? (3) Must the creditor be ignorant of the prior mortgage at the time he became a creditor? At the time he obtained his lien by legal proceedings?

On the first point there is authority that only creditors who become such subsequent to the execution of the deed are within the operation of the act but there is also authority the other way.[56] The choice seems to be between taking the language of the statute at its face, a course indicated by the fact that the same requirements, as a matter of grammar at least, are not attached to creditors as they are to purchasers, or holding that the purpose of requiring recording is the same as to both purchasers and creditors and therefore putting the latter on the same basis as the former regardless of the difference in terms describing the two classes.[57]

On the second question raised there is good authority that the creditor must have

L.R. 1333. Compare, also, Weinberg v. Brother, 1928, 263 Mass. 61, 160 N.E. 403, and O'Gaspian v. Danielson, 1933, 284 Mass. 27, 187 N.E. 107, 89 A.L.R. 1159.

As to whether the creditor who purchases at his own execution sale is a purchaser for value, see § 187, supra.

48. Dyson v. Simmons, 1877, 48 Md. 207; Holden v. Garrett, 1879, 23 Kan. 98, construing Kan.Stat. Ann. 58–2223, 67–223.

49. See Shear Co. v. Currie, C.C.A.Tex.1923, 295 F. 841.

50. For an excellent analysis and digest of recording statutes applicable to personal property transactions and a critique of the reasons for invoking the sanction of recording acts in favor of creditors, see Hanna, Extension of Public Recordation, 1931, 31 Col.L.Rev. 617.

51. So.Car.Code 1962, §§ 60–101, 60–156.

52. Dyson v. Simmons, 1877, 48 Md. 207.

53. Code of Tenn. (M. & V., 1884) § 2890.

54. Ark.Dig., 1874, c. 29, § 860.

55. Rev.Laws N.J., 1877, 155, § 14.

See Cunningham and Tischler, Equitable Real Estate Mortgages, 1963, 17 Rutgers L.Rev. 679, 691: "Judgment creditors without notice are given substantially the same status as bona fide purchasers and mortgagees for valuable consideration * * *."

See Storke and Sears, op. cit. supra, § 196 note 22, 189 pointing out that the language of Colo.St.Ann. c. 40, § 114 (1935), "any class of persons with any kind of rights," is unique. It probably will not be taken literally but would seem to include "judgment creditors."

56. In re Watson, D.C.Ky.1912, 201 F. 962, affirmed 216 F. 483, 132 C.C.A. 543, commented on, 1913, 13 Col.L.Rev. 539. But contra is Price v. Wall's Exrs., 1899, 97 Va. 334, 33 S.E. 599, 75 Am.St.Rep. 788; Reichert v. McClure, 1860, 23 Ill. 516, 517; Thorpe v. Helmer, 1916, 275 Ill. 86, 113 N.E. 954. And compare the reasoning in Griffin v. New Jersey Oil Co., 1855, 11 N.J.Eq. 49; Barrett v. Barrett's Adm'r, 1868, 31 Tex. 344; See In re Shirley, 1901, 112 F. 301, 50 C.C.A. 252, chattel mortgage.

57. "But registry acts furnish striking instances of the interpretation of statutes according to the general intention of the legislature, rather than according to the strict language." Lamberton v. Merchants' Nat. Bk., 1877, 24 Minn. 281, 283.

acquired a lien of some sort before recordation of the prior encumbrance; [58] but any distinction between judgment liens on the one hand and attachment or execution liens on the other is rejected.[59]

Whether the creditor must be without notice is expressly covered by statute in many jurisdictions, most of them making it a requirement[60] although under a few of them it is immaterial.[61] Where the statute does not make specific provision on the point, there are many decisions that the rule applicable to purchasers under the acts will be extended by analogy to creditors.[62]

But the question still remains: notice at what time? Quite clearly notice that does not come until after the creditor has fastened his lien, judgment or other, upon the property comes too late. So it has been held that the holder of an unrecorded legal mortgage, by giving notice of its existence at a sheriff's sale upon a judgment, could not bind the

mortgaged estate in the hands of the purchaser at such a sale, where the judgment creditor had no notice of the mortgage when his judgment was entered.[63] Quite as clearly notice given before the creditor has extended his credit will be effective.[64] But how about the notice that comes before the creditor has fastened his lien upon the property by judgment or otherwise but after the claimant has become a creditor, i. e., in cases where the creditor may have extended his credit while in ignorance of the fact that, though his debtor has record title, in fact he had previously encumbered it by an unrecorded mortgage of which he is informed only just before he obtains judgment. The authority seems to be that such notice is sufficient.[65] It is logical enough to say that a notice is sufficient which reaches a person at any time before he qualifies as one of the class singled out for protection. Yet the result in these cases is curious and may be questioned on the ground that it does not serve the policy purposes of the acts to force prompt recordation[66] and to afford knowledge of the state of the title to people who take risks on the

---

58. In re Watson, 1912, 201 F. 962, affirmed 216 F. 483, 132 C.C.A. 543, discussed in 1913, 13 Col.L.Rev. 539; Daniel v. Sorrells, 1846, 9 Ala. 436; Loughridge v. Bowland, 1876, 52 Miss. 546; Dulaney v. Willis, 1898, 95 Va. 606, 29 S.E. 324, 64 Am.St.Rep. 815.

59. See § 189, supra.
Butterwick v. Fuller & Johnson Mfg. Co., 1918, 140 Minn. 327, 168 N.W. 18, no protection is given to a judgment creditor when the judgment is not against the record owner.

60. E. g., Ala. Code 1940, Tit. 47, § 120; New Jersey Rev.Stat.Ann. § 46:22–1. See Patton, Titles 2d Ed., § 17, n. 58, for a list of such states.
In Nebraska the judgment creditor without notice is refused priority over an earlier unrecorded mortgage because the statute protecting "all creditors" added the words "whose deeds, mortgages or other instruments shall be first recorded." Galway, Semple & Co. v. Malchow, 1878, 7 Neb. 285; Omaha Loan & Bldg. Assn. v. Turk, 1946, 146 Neb. 859, 21 N.W.2d 865, noted, 1946, 32 Va.L.Rev. 654.

61. E. g., Ark.Stats. § 51–1002.

62. E. g., Lamberton v. Merchants' Nat. Bank, 1877, 24 Minn. 281. See Patton, Titles, 2d Ed., § 17, n. 60, for a collection of cases. But reaching the conclusion that when the statute is silent on the subject that notice is immaterial, Guerrant v. Anderson, 1826, 4 Randolph, Va., 208; Neff's Adm'r v. Newman, 1928, 150 Va. 203, 142 S.E. 389; Lillard v. Ruckers, 1863, 9 Yerg. (17 Tenn.) 64.

63. Uhler v. Hutchinson, 1854, 23 Pa. 110, 113. The court said, "The priority of judgment liens can only be made effective by permitting the estate charged with their payment to be sold free from encumbrances which have no existence as against the judgments. We do not wish to be understood as admitting that the result would have been different if notice of the existence of the mortgage had been given to the judgment creditor before the lien of his judgment had attached." See Guerrant v. Anderson, 1826, 25 Va. 208, 4 Rand. 208; Abney v. Ohio Lumber & Min. Co., 1898, 45 W.Va. 446, 32 S. E. 256. See also Massey v. Westcott, 1866, 40 Ill. 160; Guiteau v. Wisely, 1868, 47 Ill. 433, 436.
In Gawrillow v. Rutkowski, 1929, 104 N.J.Eq. 329, 145 A. 544, where the statutory language was "subsequent judgment creditor without notice", it was held that a tortfeasor who obtained judgment without notice was entitled to priority over a prior unrecorded mortgage.

64. Britton's Appeal, 1863, 45 Pa. 172.

65. Lamberton v. Merchants' Nat. Bank, 1877, 24 Minn. 281; Priest v. Rice, 1822, 18 Mass. 164, 11 Am.Dec. 156; Van Gundy v. Tandy, 1916, 272 Ill. 319, 11 N.E. 1020; Morris v. White, 1882, 36 N.J. Eq., 324.

66. See §§ 196, 206, supra.

faith of it. Possibly the courts are influenced in their construction by their belief that even though given the protection of the acts the creditor's claim is not too strong a one because he has not advanced his money on the faith of a specific pledge of property.[67]

In jurisdictions where the recording acts do not in terms protect creditors from the hazards of an unrecorded mortgage or other conveyance by their debtor who remains the record owner, or who deny them protection under the acts if actual notice reaches them before they fix a lien upon the property, it is possible for the creditor to prevail over the prior unrecorded instrument by invoking the doctrine of estoppel. Quite clearly the enactment of recording acts does not preempt the entire field of possible protection to parties. The doctrine of estoppel may exist along side the recording acts and fill in gaps left by them. Not only that, but "the recording acts have themselves become operative facts which taken in connection with the general methods of transacting business which have grown up under the influence of such acts, enable one to make a representation in a way unknown to the English law as we inherited it",[68] i. e., by record title to stand in the name of one who is not the owner.[69] The boundaries of the doctrine are vague and undefined not only as to what acts

of reliance by the creditor are necessary,[70] but also as to what conduct and culpability is essential on the part of the person estopped and other factors which may or should be taken into account.[71] Nevertheless it has been recognized and invoked in a sufficiently large number of instances as to make it a live and important doctrine.[72]

APPLICABILITY OF RECORDING ACTS TO VARIOUS INTERESTS

211. The recording acts are inapplicable, or of doubtful applicability, to a variety of legal and equitable interests.

(1) Interests created without writing generally need not be recorded to be protected against subsequent transfers, unless the transaction could readily have been cast in a recordable form.

(2) Acquirers of legal interests which need not be recorded under (1) are generally held not to be within the class of persons protected by the statutes against prior unrecorded interests. The preferable rule includes takers of equitable mortgages in such class, especially if the statute includes mortgagees without limitation.

There are a variety of interests in land that raise problems regarding the application of the recording acts to them.[73] The problems may be caused by the nature of interests themselves or by the fact that they arise by operation of law. The operative facts that create the interests may not be written or

67. See Britton's Appeal, 1863, 45 Pa. 172, 176, 3 Luz.L.O. 233, 4 Leg. & Ins.Rep. 82.

68. W.W.C., Estoppel by Misrepresentation and the Recording Acts, 1919, 28 Yale L.J. 685, 689. See Carey & Cilella, Protection of Creditors by Estoppel, 1935, 29 Ill.L.Rev. 1000; Leesman, Operation of the Illinois Recording Act, 1944, 38 Ill.L.Rev. 396, 403.

69. Bergin v. Blackwood, 1919, 141 Minn. 325, 170 N. W. 508; Marling v. Milwaukee Realty Co., 1906, 127 Wis. 363, 106 N.W. 844, 5 L.R.A.,N.S., 412, 115 Am.St.Rep. 1017, 7 Ann.Cas. 364. In re Oswegatchie Chemical Products Corp., C.C.A.N.Y., 1922, 279 F. 547, certiorari denied 259 U.S. 580, 42 S.Ct. 464, 66 L.Ed. 1073; Bryant v. Klatt, D.C.N.Y.1924, 2 F.2d 167, semble; Goldberg v. Parker, 1913, 87 Conn. 99, 87 A. 555, 46 L.R.A.,N.S., 1097, (a husband and wife case, which seems to be viewed in a different light than others, probably with reason); note, 1913, 46 L.R.A.,N.S., 1097.

70. Compare Hart v. Casterton, 1925, 56 N.D. 581, 218 N.W. 644 with Greer v. Mitchell, 1896, 42 W.Va. 494, 26 S.E. 302.

71. See § 189, supra.

72. See authorities and articles cited in preceding notes.

73. For an enumeration and discussion of a variety of defects in title which will not be apparent of record see Rood, Registration of Land Titles, 1914, 12 Mich.L.Rev. 379, 389; Chaplin, Record Title to Land, 1893, 6 Harv.L.Rev. 302; Chaplin, The Element of Chance in Land Titles, 1898, 12 Harv.L. Rev. 24; Haymond, Title Insurance Risks of Which the Public Records Give No Notice, 1928, 1 So.Cal. L.Rev. 422; 2 id. 139; Ferrier, The Recording Acts and Titles by Adverse Possession and Prescription, 1926, 14 Cal.L.Rev. 287: note, 1913, 26 Harv.L.Rev. 762. See also § 193, supra.

they may not be susceptible to spreading on the pages of a record book. The form in which the parties express their agreement may be unorthodox.[74]

One question is whether the transaction in question qualifies as a conveyance or transfer within the statutory language so that it either may or must be recorded. Another is whether it falls within one of the protected classes under the act so that it will prevail over a prior unrecorded mortgage or other conveyance. In a state that has a first recording provision this second question overlaps the first.

Legal interests

It can be laid down as a general rule that interests in property of any character that are created or transferred without a writing are outside of the requirement in the recording acts that they must be recorded at peril of being cut off or postponed to other designated claimants. The reason is simple: there is nothing to record.[75] This principle clearly should, and in general does, apply where not only is the interest created or transferred without a writing but also is not the sort of transaction that could just as readily have been cast by the parties in a recordable form. Title by adverse possession is one example of this sort.[76] Dower rights and community property interests is another.[77] It would

seem that, logically, easements by prescription would be another,[78] and yet there is some authority that "in the absence of a record or other means of putting a purchaser upon notice" the easement, although a legal one, will be cut off.[79] The reason given for this is that easements by prescription are based on the fiction of a "lost grant"; [80] the fiction is extended to holding that the presumed grant should have been recorded before it was lost. This explanation has merit only to the extent that the policy of the recording acts justifies invalidation of secret legal interests even though they are unrecordable and could not readily be made recordable—a step that seems entirely too drastic.[81] Whether a prior easement arising by implied grant or reservation is sufficiently different from an easement by prescription as to be held to be cut off under the recording acts by a subsequent sale or mortgage for value and without notice would seem to be dubious, yet there is rather recent authority that it will be.[82] Such easements arise by virtue of an unrecordable physical situation existing at the time the deed conveying the dominant estate is ex-

---

74. The problem of whether a deed or mortgage that is defective for some reason but nevertheless has been recorded is validly recorded or otherwise operative has been considered. See § 205, supra.

75. See Walsh and Simpson, Cas. Security Transactions, 199 note.

76. Faloon v. Simshauser, 1889, 130 Ill. 649, 22 N.E. 835; Ridgeway v. Holliday, 1875, 59 Mo. 444; Schall v. Williams Valley R. Co., 1860, 35 Pa. 191. Winters v. Powell, 1912, 180 Ala. 425, 61 So. 96, discussed 1913, 26 Harv.L.Rev. 762, 1925, 14 Cal.L.Rev. 287, 288, extends the hazards of a title by adverse possession by holding that it applies to a grantee under an unrecorded deed, a decision that, regardless of its soundness on the question of what constitutes adverse possession, runs counter to the policy of the recording acts.

77. See Haymond, Title Insurance Risks, 1928, So. Cal.L.Rev. 422, 433.

78. Shaughnessey v. Leary, 1894, 162 Mass. 108, 112, 38 N.E. 197.

79. Schwartz v. Atlantic Bldg. Co., 1913, 41 App.D.C. 108, 111. Other cases, by holding that the subsequent purchaser takes subject to the easement *because* of notice, imply that notice, either actual or by record, is essential. Schmidt v. Brown, 1907, 226 Ill. 590, 80 N.E. 1071, 11 L.R.A.,N.S., 457, 117 Am.St.Rep. 261; St. Cecelia Society v. Universal, etc., Co., 1921, 213 Mich. 569, 182 N.W. 161.

80. Angus v. Dalton, 1877, L.R. 3 Q.B.Div. 85; S.C., 1878, 1878 L.R. 4 Q.B.Div. 162; S.C., 1881, 6 App. Cas. 740; see Smith v. Hawkins, 1895, 110 Cal. 122, 126, 42 P. 453, 454. The prescriptive easement case can be distinguished on this ground from the title by adverse possession which does not rest upon any supposition of grant. People v. Banning, 1914, 167 Cal. 643, 649, 140 P. 587.

81. See Ferrier, The Recording Acts and Title by Adverse Possession and Prescription, 1925, 14 Cal. L.Rev. 287, 291.

82. Backhausen v. Mayer, 1931, 204 Wis. 286, 234 N. W. 904, 74 A.L.R. 1245, criticized, Walsh, Mortgages, 141; Hawley v. McCabe, 1933, 117 Conn. 558, 169 A. 192, commented on in 1934, 14 Boston Univ. L.Rev. 432.

ecuted which creates it as an implied term of the deed, and that deed is duly recorded. Consequently there is nothing to record here any more than in the prescriptive easement case. In rebuttal it may be argued that here certainly it would have been possible for the parties to have put the reservation of the easement in a recordable form and the situation is sufficiently close to an easement arising by oral grant, which would be invalid as against a *bona fide* purchaser, to warrant holding that the policy of the recording acts covers such a case so as to invalidate the easement under them as against protected classes.[83]

None of these interests seem to fall within any of the classes named in recording acts as against which a prior unrecorded mortgage will be void.

Equitable interests

Equitable interests arising other than by written instrument, e. g., the right of reinstatement of a mortgage discharged by reason of the fraud of the mortgagor,[84] rights of reformation of an instrument, and constructive and resulting trusts are outside of the operation of the recording acts because their existence depends upon matters incapable of recordation. Since there is nothing to record, the right to assert such claims is unaffected by the fact that they do not appear of record. Whether other parties take free of them depends upon principles previously discussed.[85] On the other hand the creation or transfer of certain kinds of equitable security or other interests in property may fall under the recording statutes. Insofar as an equitable encumbrance on the property may be recorded, its recordation will "give to it an intrinsic superiority, under the statute,

over one which is not recorded." [86] The result would be to give to a recorded equity as secure a status as the common law gives to a legal interest. And, if they not only may but must be recorded, failure to record will postpone them to persons, e. g., judgment creditors, over whom they normally would prevail.[87] There is authority that equitable mortgages arising by agreement of the parties not only may [88] but must [89] be recorded. No question arises as to the correctness of these decisions when applied to instruments creating an equitable security interest in presently owned legal property, or instruments transferring or mortgaging presently owned equitable interests. As to other types of possible equitable mortgages this is not true. For example, mortgages of expectancies or other forms of after-acquired property may create an equitable mortgage, at least when the expectancy falls in or the

---

86. Pomeroy, Eq.Juris., 4th Ed., § 683 n. 2. See Aigler, Operation of the Recording Acts, 1924, 22 Mich.L.Rev. 405, 412.

See Storke and Sears, op. cit. infra, note 90, 182. See also Cunningham and Tischler, Equitable Real Estate Mortgages, 1963, 17 Rutgers L.Rev. 679, 691. And see id. at 694, for an argument that the New Jersey statute, if followed literally, would give an unrecorded equitable interest a position potentially superior to that which it would have in the absence of a recording act. The argument is that, under the language of the statute, an unrecorded deed or mortgage creating an equitable interest would be "valid and operative" even against a subsequent bona fide purchaser or mortgagee who acquired a legal interest thereby so long as the subsequent claimant did not satisfy the "record first" requirement. The holder of the equitable interest could still establish an indefeasible statutory priority by recording *after* the subsequent purchaser or mortgagee paid value but *before* he recorded.

87. See §§ 189, 210, supra.

88. O'Neal v. Seixas, 1888, 85 Ala. 80, 4 So. 745; Weston & Co. v. Dunlap, 1878, 50 Iowa 183; Edwards v. McKernan, 1885, 55 Mich. 520, 22 N.W. 20; Wilder v. Brooks, 1865, 10 Minn. 50, Gil. 32, 88 Am.Dec. 49; Digman v. McCollum, 1871, 47 Mo. 372; Wooton v. Seltzer, 1914, 83 N.J.Eq. 163, 90 A. 701, affirmed 84 N.J.Eq. 207, 93 A. 1087; Atkinson v. Miller, 1890, 34 W.Va. 115, 11 S.E. 1007, 9 L.R.A. 544, alternative ground.

89. General Ins. Co. v. U. S. Ins. Co., 1857, 10 Md. 517, 69 Am.Dec. 174; Russell's Appeal, 1850, 15 Pa. 319; Batts & Dean v. Scott, 1872, 37 Tex. 59; see Patton, Titles, 2d Ed., § 7, n. 86.

---

83. See Ferrier, The Recording Acts and Titles by Adverse Possession and Prescription, 1925, 14 Cal. L.Rev. 287, 295.

84. But see Powers, J., dissenting in Island Pond Nat. Bank v. Lacroix, 1932, 104 Vt. 282, 303, 158 A. 684, noted, 1932, 46 Harv.L.Rev. 160.

85. See §§ 181, 192, 210.

property is acquired, but the mortgage agreement may be recorded before that time, a matter previously considered. The objection to holding such recordation valid is the greatly increased burden on any prospective mortgagee of the property. He would have to search the records for mortgages that might have been made and recorded prior to the acquisition of the property by the mortgagor.[90] The equitable mortgage by deposit of title deeds, we have already seen, fails of recognition in the United States generally, partly at least, on the ground that to permit such security interests which could easily have been expressed in written, recordable form violates the policy of the recording system in this country.[91] Conditional agreements to mortgage also have caused trouble.[92] Insofar as the agreement can be held to create by the time of recordation a security interest in presently owned specific property it would seem properly to fall under most recording acts.[93] The same should be true of pure negative covenants[94] and agreements to pay out of the proceeds of the sale of property.[95]

The equitable lien for the purchase price of a grantor of real property arises by operation of law[96] and therefore the recording acts logically do not affect them. They are, however, at variance with the policy of our system of recording land titles and have been looked upon with disfavor in many jurisdictions.[97] There are, indeed, statutes to be found making the lien ineffective except as it is made a matter of record,[98] a requirement emphasizing the fact that the parties can make written provision for it in recordable form. When the lien is expressly reserved in a conveyance it creates an equitable lien to which the recording acts apply.[99]

We have seen previously that the judicial doctrine of *bona fide* purchase does not, by the great weight of authority, extend to the taker of equitable interests in land.[1] Whether the similar question under the recording acts should be decided the same way is questionable. The policy of the recording acts would seem applicable to takers of equitable mortgages or other interests as well as to legal ones, and there is some authority supporting such a view.[2] Statutes that specifi-

90. See §§ 36, 37, 38, 199, supra.
See Storke and Sears, The Perennial Problem of Security, Priority and Recordation, 1952, 24 Colo.L. Rev. 180, 198–200, stating that such recordation should not be effective.
91. In re Snyder, 1908, 138 Iowa, 553, 114 N.W. 615, 19 L.R.A.,N.S., 206, see § 33, supra.
92. Mathews v. Damainville, 1905, 100 App.Div. 311, 91 N.Y.S. 524, not recordable, two judges dissenting. Todd v. Eighmie, 1896, 4 App.Div. 9, 38 N.Y.S. 304, recordable. See Stone, The "Equitable Mortgage" in New York, 1920, 20 Col.L.Rev. 519, 523.
93. See §§ 42, 43, supra.
94. See § 44, supra.
95. See § 45, supra.
96. See § 48, supra.

97. See Shove v. Burkholder Lumber Co., 1922, 154 Minn. 137, 191 N.W. 397; Wilson v. Lyon, 1869, 51 Ill. 166; 1919, 33 Harv.L.Rev. 485.
98. Iowa Code Ann. §§ 557.18, 557.19; Ohio R.C. § 5301.26.
99. E. g., Dingley v. Ventura Bank, 1881, 57 Cal. 467.
1. See § 183, supra.
2. "* * * we think the true rule to be that, where a person purchases an equitable title, without notice, he takes it, as he would a legal title, divested of all liens thereon of that character that constructive notice of them may be given by record." Weston & Co. v. Dunlap, 1878, 50 Iowa, 183, 185. General Ins. Co. v. United States Ins. Co., 1857, 10 Md. 517, 69 Am.Dec. 174; Batts & Dean v. Scott, 1872, 37 Tex. 59.
In Buck v. McNab, Fla.1962, 139 So.2d 734, certiorari denied 146 So.2d 374, criticised by Boyer and Ross, Real Property Law, 1964, 18 Univ. of Miami L.Rev. 799, 810, a vendee under a contract to purchase parcels of real property was classified as a purchaser entitled to the protection of the recordings acts so as to prevail over prior unrecorded conveyances of the legal title.
See Cunningham and Tischler, Equitable Real Estate Mortgages, 1963, 17 Rutgers L.Rev. 679 pointing out that under New Jersey R.S. 46:22–1 (Supp.1940) if a bona fide purchaser or mortgagee for value obtains and records a deed or mortgage which is duly acknowledged or proved (and thus entitled to be recorded), he should be protected against claims based on prior unrecorded instruments, whether the interest conveyed to him is legal or equitable. To this extent the definition of purchaser under the New Jersey provision seems broader than it is un-

cally designate subsequent mortgagees without limitation in addition to purchasers can be construed even more readily as covering equitable as well as legal mortgages.[3] If the statute requires a first recording, the subsequent equitable interest would have to be capable of recordation. Further, if the prior interest, even though an equitable one such as a right to have a mortgage reinstated because released by reason of fraud, is by its nature unrecordable, it would seem that it should not be cut off by a subsequent equitable interest even though it qualified under the statutory test of *bona fide* purchase and was recordable and recorded. Much less should this be true of an unrecordable equitable pledge.[4] But even in this last case it has been argued that the policy of the recording acts should apply to invalidate the prior unrecorded and unrecordable equity.[5]

---

der the equitable doctrine of bona fide purchase, which requires (under the prevailing view) that the subsequent purchaser must have acquired a legal interest for value and without notice.

But there is authority the other way. "The titles, if any, acquired by the parties * * * are equitable and not legal, consequently section 2788 of the code (recording statute) has no application, for the reason that 'purchasers for a valuable consideration without notice' therein referred to are purchasers of the legal title or estate, and not purchasers of a mere equitable title or estate." Dedeaux v. Cuevas, 1914, 107 Miss. 7, 9, 64 So. 844, 845; Wailes v. Cooper, 1852, 24 Miss. 208; Combs v. Nelson, 1883, 91 Ind. 123.

3. The term "purchaser" is construed as covering mortgagees and assignees of mortgagees, but in many states the statute in terms adds the category "mortgagee." E. g., West's Ann.Cal.Civ.Code, § 1214.

4. Island Pond Nat. Bank v. Lacroix, 1932, 104 Vt. 282, 158 A. 684, noted, 1932, 46 Harv.L.Rev. 160.

5. See dissent in Island Pond Nat. Bank v. Lacroix, 1932, 104 Vt. 282, 158 A. 684; note, 1932, 46 Harv. L.Rev. 160.

In some states equitable claims that are unrecordable *per se* may be the foundation of an action which may be recorded as pending litigation. See Mass. Gen.Laws Ann. c. 184 § 15. Where this possibility exists, if the later taker of an equitable interest would qualify under the recording acts as a *bona fide* purchaser, it is a stronger case for contending that the failure to bring the action will cause him to be postponed on the ground that the policy of the recording acts should extend to defeating such interests.

SUBORDINATION AGREEMENTS

212. Subordination agreements alter the priorities between mortgagees. Their enforceability against subsequent transferees of the subordinating mortgagee depends, by the better view, on whether assignees take subject to the latent equities of third parties in the particular jurisdiction. Subordination rights based on estoppel are not recordable; those based on agreement should be. They are generally not enforceable against the prior assignee of the subordinator's mortgage, even though the transfer was not recorded.

The subordinator takes the risk that the purpose of the agreement may be frustrated through unauthorized use by the mortgagor of money loaned by the mortgagee who was given priority.

Although the trustee under a trust deed mortgage has no power to subordinate the mortgage without the consent of the mortgagee bondholders, yet if the subsequent mortgagee forecloses the issue of priority will be conclusive on the bondholders even though they were not made parties and were unaware of the action.

It is well established that two or more mortgagees whose mortgages are executed at the same time on the same property may by agreement determine their relative priority in the mortgaged property.[6] Likewise a senior mortgage can be subordinated to a junior mortgage by agreement between the parties affected.[7] And it has also been held that a second mortgagee may take advantage of such an arrangement without being a party to it.[8] The enforceability of the sub-

6. Trompczynski v. Struck, 1900, 105 Wis. 437, 81 N.W. 650, Parks, Cas.Morts., 180; State Finance Co. v. Halstenston, et al., 1908, 17 N.D. 145, 153, 114 N.W. 724, 728.

7. McCaslin v. Advance Mfg. Co., 1900, 155 Ind. 298, 58 N.E. 67; James v. Allen, 1928, 205 Iowa 962, 218 N.W. 916; Brown v. Barber, 1912, 244 Mo. 138, 148 S.W. 892.

8. Londner v. Perlman, 1908, 129 App.Div. 93, 113 N. Y.S. 420, affirmed 198 N.Y. 629, 92 N.E. 1090; Mitchell v. West End Park Co., 1930, 171 Ga. 878, 156 S.E. 888; Liebers v. Plainfield Spanish Homes Bldg. Co., 1931, 108 N.J.Eq. 391, 155 A. 270. See Dunlop v. Teagle, 1931, 101 Fla. 721, 135 So. 132. As to effect of foreclosure of subsequent mortgage as prior lien under subordination agreement of which bondholders had no knowledge, see 1941, 39 Mich.L.Rev. 503.

ordination agreement may rest upon either one of two grounds: that it is a contract upon valuable consideration which equity will specifically enforce;[9] or that it is an application of the theory of estoppel to statements of intention of the one encumbrancer relied upon by the other in changing his position.[10] In either case, the right under the agreement is an equitable one.[11]

Clearly this equitable right is an *in personam* one against the subordinating mortgagee himself. Does it also create an equitable right in respect to the mortgage debt and the security interest in the mortgaged property held by the mortgagee? The question becomes important in two directions: (1) will the one who has the right to be elevated to priority be able to enforce it against subsequent transferees or other claimants of in-

terest for value and without notice either a. apart from the recording acts, or b. under them; (2) will the acquirer of such a subordination right from a mortgagee who previously had transferred his mortgage to one who did not record the transfer be able to enforce it, a. entirely apart from any question of the application of the recording acts, b. as one who falls under the protection of those acts as against prior unrecorded interests in the property?

Taking up the first question and looking at it apart from any question of the recording acts, it would seem that the right to subordination, regardless of its basis, constitutes an equitable claim not only against the other mortgagee but against him in an important respect in regard to his property, namely, his debt and the mortgage interest in land securing it. Quite clearly the burdens of the agreement run with the subordinated mortgage to those taking with notice and notice appears to be broadly construed.[12] Since this is so, the right would constitute an equitable property interest rather than a purely personal right against the subordinating mortgagee.[13] So far as claimants under the sub-

---

In spite of a recorded agreement with the mortgagor, M, by a purchase money mortgagee, E–1, to subordinate his mortgage to any new construction mortgage to be created on the property, E–1 was permitted to sell the property on foreclosure free and clear of a later construction mortgage by E–2. E–2's mortgage was subject to an intervening judgment lien by C. The ground of decision was that, under the general rule in Pennsylvania, a sheriff's sale discharges all prior and subsequent liens unless the sale is made expressly subject to prior liens and the statutory saving exception where a mortgage lien is "prior to all other liens" did not apply because C's judgment lien was prior to E–2's mortgage. Liss v. Medary Homes, Inc., 1957, 388 Pa. 139, 130 A.2d 137, discussed in Plowman, in 1956–1957 Survey of Pennsylvania Law. Mortgages and Security Transactions, 1958, 19 U. of Pitt.L. Rev. 292, 294.

9. "That the owner of the mortgage may contract to do this is plain; and if the contract be in good faith, and founded on a valuable consideration, a court of equity would adjust the parties accordingly." Gillig v. Maass, 1863, 28 N.Y. 191, 213.

10. See Londner v. Perlman, 1908, 129 App.Div. 93, 113 N.Y.S. 420, affirmed 198 N.Y. 629, 92 N.E. 1090, non-consensual case, estoppel in equity; Mitchell v. West End Park Co., 1930, 171 Ga. 878, 156 S.E. 888. It has also been suggested that the transaction is a valid third party beneficiary contract. Rose v. Provident Savings, Loan & Investment Ass'n, 1901, 28 Ind.App. 25, 62 N.E. 293. While this is possible it is unlikely that the facts in most cases would support such a conclusion.

11. See cases in preceding and subsequent notes.

For a thorough discussion of subordination agreements, their theories and uses, see Calligar, Subordination Agreements, 1961, 70 Yale L.J. 367.

12. Bank for Savings v. Frank, 1878, 45 N.Y. (56 How.Pr.) 403; Trompczynski v. Struck, 1900, 105 Wis. 437, 81 N.W. 650.

"Both mortgages were recorded at the same time. * * * Their having been so recorded did not preclude either mortgagee from asserting a priority, or from having such priority established by extrinsic evidence. * * * The fact that they were recorded at the same time was sufficient notice to put Mrs. Hodgson or any purchaser at the sale (a foreclosure sale) on inquiry as to priority. The record was notice * * * that either mortgagee might have a superior lien." State Finance Co. v. Halstenson, 1908, 17 N.D. 145, 152, 114 N.W. 724, 727.

13. "There is not a fine line between equitable property interests on the one hand, and, on the other, contracts personal but affecting property as against persons with notice." Jacobs, The Effect of Provision for Ratable Protection of Debenture Holders in Case of Subsequent Mortgage, 1938, 52 Harv.L. Rev. 77, 116. See § 43, See Coogan, Kripke and Weiss, The Outer Fringes of Article 9: Subordination Agreements, * * *, 1965, 79 Harv.L.Rev. 229, 233–261, especially A. Does Subordination Create a Security Interest, pp. 237–242.

ordinating mortgagee are concerned it is a latent equity in favor of a third person, and whether it would be enforceable against them if they took for value and without notice of it should depend upon the attitude the courts in the particular jurisdiction take on that question.[14]

The problem remains whether the right to subordination is one that may or must be recorded. The answer to that question should depend in part, at least, on the basis of the right. If it is founded upon an estoppel it would seem to fall within the class of transactions creating interests in property by circumstances which are unrecordable. On the other hand, if it rests upon an agreement of the parties this objection is not present. Although the language in the particular statute designating what sorts of interests are to be recorded must be looked at, they are so uniformly broad and general, both by phraseology and by construction, that it would appear perfectly proper, at least, to hold that they cover subordination agreements.[15] And by express statutory pro-

vision in some states a subordination agreement is recordable.[16] Even in a jurisdiction holding them incapable of being recorded and also enforceable against assignees of the other mortgagee for value and without notice, the recording acts may operate to defeat them. If the mortgage in whose favor the right runs is unrecorded and the other mortgage is recorded, an assignee of the latter, being classed under the recording acts as a subsequent purchaser for value, will take free and clear both of the unrecorded mortgage and, incidental to that, any right to subordination belonging to it.[17]

The second part of the question presents different difficulties. Ignoring for the time being the existence of recording acts, it is essential to distinguish between rights based upon estoppel and rights based upon agreement. For the former to prevail the estoppel would have to reach not only the mortgagee who made the representation but the person to whom the mortgagee had assigned his interest prior to making the representation.[18] Whether the latter would take free of the prior mortgage assignee would seem to depend on whether he qualifies under the doctrine of *bona fide* purchase. Assuming the payment of value and absence of notice we get back to the earlier question of whether the right is purely *in personam* or is an interest in property. If the former, the inquiry ends. If the latter, there are still some

14. See note, 1932, 30 Mich.L.Rev. 1342; Restatement, Contracts, § 174; Chapter 8, § 229, infra. Thus, in New York where assignees take subject to latent equities, in the absence of an estoppel, the subordination agreement would bind even *bona fide* transferees for value and without notice from the subordinating mortgagee. See Greene v. Warnick, 1876, 64 N.Y. 220; Decker v. Boice, 1880, 83 N.Y. 215. But see Riddle v. George, 1856, 58 N.H. 25, where there were two mortgages executed and recorded simultaneously, with an oral agreement that one was to have priority, the court said: "The right of priority, as between the original mortgages, was an equitable, not a legal, right. A purchaser of property for a valuable consideration, without notice, actual or constructive, of an equitable right, will hold the property discharged of the right." See, also, Vredenburgh v. Burnet, 1879, 31 N.J.Eq. 229.

15. Clason and Steever v. Shepherd, 1859, 6 Wis. 369. Even recordation of two mortgages at the same time has been held to give notice that there might be an agreement as to priority between them. State Finance Co. v. Halstenson, 1908, 17 N.D. 145, 114 N.W. 724. But see the reasoning in Gillig v. Maass, 1863, 28 N.Y. 191, 212, "It cannot be pretended that any interest was, or was intended to be, conveyed in the mortgaged premises, or in the security as such. It is in substance a stipulation * * * not as regards any thing entering into or af-

fecting the debt or the security—for both the debt and the lien of the mortgage were to remain, but in relation to priority simply." See also Bank for Savings v. Frank, 1878, 45 N.Y. (56 How.Pr.) 403.

16. See, e. g., West's Ann.Cal.Civ.Code, § 2934, permissive, not mandatory. See also the present New York statute, McKinney's Real Prop.Law, § 290(3).

17. Decker v. Boice, 1880, 83 N.Y. 215.

18. See the discussion, § 210, supra, of the application of the doctrine of estoppel to creditors. See also § 191, ante. The reliance factor is clearer here but the task of finding culpability sufficient to estop the prior assignee is not an easy one. Where recording acts enter and the assignee leaves the record title in the mortgagee, it would seem that the possibility of success is increased. See, 1919, 28 Yale L.J. 685, 689.

obstacles. The judicial doctrine of *bona fide* purchase does not generally apply to one who buys only an equitable interest;[19] and even its advocates distinguish between transferees of equitable interests and the acquisition of an equitable interest in property retained by the seller.[20] The right to subordination being of the latter sort at most, it would follow that it would not qualify under the doctrine.

When we turn to the recording acts most of what has just been said is applicable to give us our answers. Insofar as the right is based upon estoppel it does not fall within any of the usual categories of protected transactions. And, in jurisdictions with a "first recorded" requirement it would be unable to qualify because it is unrecordable. Where it rests upon agreement, although the factor of statutory policy alters the problem and makes it possible to reach a different conclusion from that where the judicial doctrine is involved, to do so would constitute a substantial departure.[21] Nevertheless there is some authority classifying it as a subsequent *bona fide* purchase so as to make it enforceable against the assignee of the mortgagee giving it who, although taking his assignment before the subordination agreement was executed by assignor-mortgagee, failed to record it.[22]

In recent years the use of and problems arising from subordination agreements have increased enormously both in volume of transactions employing them and amount of capital involved.[23]

His act is based upon the expectation that the increased value of the property from the improvements will result in a better security position in spite of his now junior ranking.[24] This expectation may fail of realization for several reasons. The improved property may not increase in value sufficiently even though the construction loan is properly used as originally planned. The subordinator, of course, takes this risk. However the mortgagor, after obtaining the building loan may divert it to other purposes or employ it in construction substantially different and less valuable than contemplated when the first mortgagee gave up his preferred position to the lender for improvement purposes. Will such a subsequent frustration of the purpose of the subordination agreement through the failure of the lender to see that his loan was applied as contemplated enable the first mortgagee to resume his original position of priority? In the absence of collusion with the mortgagor in diverting the money from its purpose, unless the subordinator has exacted an express promise to see to the proper application of the sums advanced, there are cases, none of them of recent date, that hold this is a risk that the subordinator has to run.[25]

---

19. See § 183, supra.

20. See Ames, Purchase for Value Without Notice, Lectures on Legal History, 253, 261.

21. E. g., securing an antecedent debt by a mortgage of land held for value under the recording acts. Frey v. Clifford, 1872, 44 Cal. 335. See also the question of other types of equitable interests being the subject of protection under the statutory test of *bona fide* purchase. § 211, supra.

22. Squire Co. v. Hedges, 1925, 200 Iowa 877, 205 N. W. 525. But vigorously *contra* is Gillig v. Maass, 1863, 28 N.Y. 191.

23. For a thorough and practically helpful survey of the financing aspect of this phenomenon, see Storke

and Sears, Subdivision Financing, 1956, 28 Colo.L. Rev. 549. The authors point out that the ones usually involved are the following: (1) the original owner-vendor; (2) subdivider; (3) financer; (4) home-owner; (5) contractor; (6) supplier, (mechanic or materialman); (7) realtor; (8) guarantor of payment or performance. They then discuss: Land acquisition financing; construction financing; home-owner financing. They end with a summary and critique, one of the purposes of which is to alert homeowners and lawyers of possible pitfalls and ways to guard against them.

See also Fry, Subordination Provisions in Land Purchase Agreements, 1962, 37 Cal.St.Bar J. 381–390.

24. As to the reasons why the seller is willing to subordinate, see Note, The Subordination of Purchase-Money Security, 1964, 52 Cal.L.Rev. 157. Doubtless he receives additional consideration, usually in the form of a higher purchase price.

25. Brooklyn Trust Co. v. Fairfield Gardens, Inc., 1932, 260 N.Y. 16, 182 N.E. 231, reversed 235 App. Div. 768, 256 N.Y.S. 719; Iowa Loan & Trust Co. v. Plewe, 1926, 202 Iowa 79, 209 N.W. 399, noted, 1927, 12 Iowa L.Rev. 201. See note, 1933, 42 Yale L. Jour. 980. As to effect of modifications of first

Of course the self-interest of the building loan owner in the value of his own security is a practical sanction in inducing him to see to it that the proceeds of the loan are properly used.

Much of the controversy in recent years has centered upon the extent to which the seller of property, his purchase money security interest in which is to be subordinated, can protect himself by the terms of the subordination agreement.[26] The validity and effectiveness of these agreements[27] have been challenged at two points in the transaction: 1. While the agreement is still executory; and 2. after the development loan and mortgage have been made and a contest develops

over priority between the seller and the development lender when one foreclosed.[28]

When the first problem is raised the critical question to determine is whether the requisite specificity for enforcement of the subordination agreement exists or whether some other test of its enforceability may govern.[29] This question can arise in two ways. In the first, the transfer of the property to the buyer has been completed, and the seller's deed of trust has been recorded along with an agreement to subordinate the lien thereby created to the lien of a future loan. In the second situation, the seller has agreed as part of his executory contract of sale to accept a note for the unpaid balance of the purchase price, to be secured by a lien which shall be junior to the first lien of a construction loan to be obtained by the buyer.[30]

In order for a court to order specific performance of the seller's promise, it is important that the terms of the construction loan be set forth with exceptional certainty.[31]

---

mortgage upon rights of second mortgagee under subordination agreement, see 1947, 22 N.Y.Univ.L.Q. Rev. 731.

26. "The agreement altering priority may be contained in a separate writing or it may be set forth in the recorded security instrument. In either case the provisions of the subordination agreement are regulated, in part, by statute, and it must be recorded in order to impart constructive notice of its contents. By the terms of the 'automatic' subordination agreement the seller's lien is recorded with an agreement that the lien of a subsequent lender will automatically be senior to the seller's lien without further acts on his part. By the terms of the other common form, the seller promises to execute a subsequent instrument which will subordinate his lien to that of the lender. However, even under the 'automatic' subordination agreement, a title company will usually require the seller to execute another document at the time the new lien is recorded, in order specifically to subordinate the seller's lien to the new lien." Miller, Starr and Regalia, Subordination Agreements in California, 1966, 13 U.C.L.A.L.Rev. 1298, 1299.

27. "Another problem, sometimes loosely called a "subordination" problem, should be distinguished. It occurs when the seller agrees in the deposit receipt or other contract of sale, or in escrow instructions, that the buyer can obtain a construction loan which shall be recorded as a first deed of trust at the time the buyer receives his title. Immediately after the recordation of the deed to the buyer and the lender's deed of trust, the seller receives a deed of trust which will be junior by virtue of the time of its recordation. The problem of the resulting priorities does not involve alteration of lien priority; that is, it does not involve the subordination of an earlier lien to a later lien, because by the execution of the purchase transaction the priorities are determined by the initial creation and recordation of the liens. Since the seller at no time has a "prior" lien, he is not "subordinating" his lien but

merely agreeing to accept junior security. The problem, therefore, is primarily one of contract law between the buyer and the seller and not one of lien law between the seller and the lender." Miller, Starr and Regalia, Subordination Agreements in California, 1966, 13 U.C.L.A.L.Rev. 1298 at 1301. See also, ibid., 1306–1312.

28. Note, Subordination of Purchase Money Security, 1964, 52 Cal.L.Rev. 157, 158.

29. Note, Subordination of Purchase Money Security, 1964, 52 Cal.L.Rev. 157, 160–164; Miller, Starr and Regalia, op. cit. supra note 27, 1302–1306. The California Supreme Court 1966–1967: X. Secured Transactions, A. Subordination Agreements, 1967, 55 Cal.L.Rev. 1184–1187.

30. Miller, Starr and Regalia, op. cit. supra note 27, 1302.

31. See Miller, Starr and Regalia, op. cit. supra note 27, 1302–1306; Note, Subordination of Purchase Money Security, 1964, 52 Cal.L.Rev. 157, 160–164. "When the seller subordinates to other purchase money security, a less complete and detailed subordination agreement is justified by the substantially smaller risk involved. In such a case the seller receives the principal of the subordinating loan as a cash payment on the purchase price. The lender therefore has presumptively loaned for less than the market value of the property, and the sum of the two liens should not exceed the purchase price.

"The subordination agreement should specify at least the maximum principal, interest rate, and term, and mode of repayment of the new loan." [32] It was suggested that the true test of the enforceability of an executory subordination agreement is the fairness and reasonableness of the obligation imposed upon the seller.[33] And in Handy v. Gordon,[34] the first case on the problem to be decided in California by the Supreme Court, the court held that whether or not the terms of the contract were too indefinite, the contract was nevertheless unenforceable, since it was not "just and reasonable" from the seller's viewpoint. The court found two major defects in the subordination agreement: It did not require the buyer to use the loan for construction and refinancing; and it did not set a maximum for the loan.[35]

The second point of challenge is when the subordination agreement has been executed by the seller and it provides that the money from the subordinating lender shall be used for certain specified purposes, usually restricting those purposes to construction on the property. The questions that arise are what is the effect upon priorities (1) if the buyer obtains a loan that does not conform to the specified terms, or (2) if the buyer uses the funds for purposes not designated in the agreement. This problem was discussed before in this section on the basis of earlier authorities.[36] Recent discussions [37] of these questions have found no conclusive answers. It may be that non-compliance with either type of restriction has no effect on priority. The subordination is effective and the seller's only remedy is an action for damages against the buyer. An alternative is that the specified terms are conditions of subordination, and subordination occurs only upon fulfillment. On the more recent authorities, the conclusion is warranted that if the terms of the construction loan deviate substantially from those prescribed by the seller, the subordination will not occur.[38] Whether the same is true when the non-compliance is with use requirements designated in the construction loan is more doubtful. The basic conflict is whether the terms of the subordination agreement are to be regarded as conditions to subordination and extend to the use of the funds loaned. Or whether the issue is one of privity of contract between the seller and the lender. There seems no reason why the seller cannot condition subordination of his prior lien upon a specified use of the funds as well as upon the term, interest rate and amount of the new loan.[39]

* * * Conversely, in the construction loan situation, until the value of the improvements have substantially increased the market value, the property is overencumbered. The substantially smaller risk in the purchase-money situation justifies a less complete subordination agreement." Note, Subordination of Purchase Money Security, 1964, 52 Cal.L. Rev. 157, 161. See also Note, 1969, 26 A.L.R.3d 855, on requisite definiteness of provision in contract for sale or lease of land that vendor or landlord will subordinate his interest to permit other party to obtain financing. And see Lawrence v. Shutt, 1969, 269 Cal.App.2d 749, 75 Cal.Rptr. 533, for what terms of clause subordinating trust deed of vendors may include.

See Annotation, Requisite Definiteness of Provision in Contract for Sale or Lease of Land, that Vendor or Landlord Will Subordinate His Interest to Permit Other Party to Obtain Financing, 1969, 26 A.L. R.3d 855.

32. Miller, Starr and Regalia, op. cit. supra note 27, 1302. There are innumerable other provisions of the new loan that might be specified, for example, the minimum term. Id. 1303–1306. See also Note, Subordination of Purchase Money Security, 1964, 52 Cal.L.Rev. 157, 160–164.

And see Lawrence v. Shutt, note 31, supra.

33. See 1964, 52 Cal.L.Rev. 157, 161.

34. 1967, 65 Cal.2d 578, 55 Cal.Rptr. 769, 422 P.2d 329, discussed 1967, 55 Cal.L.Rev. 1184.

35. 1967, 55 Cal.L.Rev. 1184, 1186.

36. See text this section at note 25.

37. Note, Subordination of Purchase Money Security, 1964, 52 Cal.L.Rev. 157, 164–170; Miller, Starr and Regalia, Subordination Agreements in California, 1966, 13 U.C.L.A.L.Rev. 1298, 1306–1309.

38. See Note, Subordination of Purchase Money Security, 1964, 52 Cal.L.Rev. 157, 166–168; Miller, Starr and Regalia, op. cit. supra note 37, 1306.

39. See Miller, Starr and Regalia, Subordination Agreements in California, 1966, 13 U.C.L.A.L.Rev. 1298, 1308. See also Note, Subordination of Purchase Money Security, 1964, 52 Cal.L.Rev. 157, 168–170.

In 1963, California enacted an amendment[40] to provide that subordination clauses or separate subordination agreements, where the secured loan to be subordinated is $25,000 or less, must contain a prominent warning on the instrument that the clause or agreement may subordinate the holder of the security to another lien which otherwise would have a lower priority. Failure to do this permits the person whose interest is subordinated, or his successor, to avoid the agreement, but only if he had no actual knowledge of it. The election to void must be made within two years after the execution of the lien receiving priority by the agreement, and is made by recording notice.[41] Frequently the subordination problems arise in purchases of large tracts of land for subdivision. Typically the purchaser needs long term credit for both the purchase and the development of the property. For the former he gives a purchase money mortgage to the seller. For the latter he turns to an institutional lender (bank, savings and loan association, and trust company). By law such institutions may lend only on the security of a first lien on the property. To obtain this improvement loan, it is customary to include in the sale and purchase money mortgage a provision that the seller's purchase money mortgage will be subordinated to the later mortgage for development purposes.

The trustee under a trust deed mortgage has no power to subordinate it without consent of the mortgage bondholders unless the trust instrument so provides.[42] If the trustee improperly subordinates the trust deed mortgage to another without the knowledge and consent of some of the bondholders, and the subsequent mortgagee then forecloses under the agreement as a prior lienor, the trustee not defending although served and authoriz-

ed by the trust indenture to represent the bondholders in all actions, and the bondholder having no knowledge of the suit, nevertheless the judgment is conclusive against all bondholders on the issue of priority.[43] The harshness of such a holding is probably justified by the business desirability of using the trust mortgage arrangement in large scale borrowings with great numbers of lenders participating and the practical impossibility of forcing anyone dealing with such a mortgage to contact directly the possibly thousands of scattered bondholders at peril of having his agreement nullified.[44]

PURCHASE MONEY MORTGAGES

213. Purchase money mortgages in favor of a vendor or third party lender of the price have priority over all earlier claims arising through the mortgagor against the vendee attaching to the property before or upon acquisition. A vendor's purchase money mortgage has priority over that of a lender.

Purchase money mortgages must be recorded to be protected against subsequent transfers.

The vendor of land may have security in the property for the payment of the purchase price in a variety of ways. He may frame the transaction in the form of an installment contract for the sale of the land, retaining the legal title in himself.[45] At the opposite extreme, he may have conveyed the property before receiving payment without any agreement for security, in which case he nevertheless is given an equitable grantor's lien.[46] Or, in this second sort of transaction, he may

40. West's Ann.Cal.Civ.Code, §§ 2953.1–2953.5.

41. See Fry, Subordination Provisions in Land Purchase Agreements, 1962, Cal.St.Bar.J. 381–390.

42. See Belknap Sav. Bank v. Lamar Land & Canal Co., 1901, 28 Colo. 326, 64 P. 212.

43. King v. Franmor Equity Corp., 1940, 260 App. Div. 303, 20 N.Y.S.2d 909, affirmed 285 N.Y. 563, 33 N.E.2d 244, noted, 1940, 39 Mich.L.Rev. 503.

44. See 1940, 39 Mich.L.Rev. 503.

45. "[A] vendor who sells on credit, retaining the title as security for the purchase money, sustains the same relation to the vendee, so far as the question of security is concerned, as does the mortgagee to the mortgagor." Moses Bros. v. Johnson, 1889, 88 Ala. 517, 521, 7 So. 146, 147, 16 Am.St.Rep. 58. See Ames, Cas. Equity, 1904, 240 n; § 20, supra.

46. See § 48, supra; West's Ann.Cal.Civ. Code, § 3046. Contra, Ahrend v. Odiorne, 1875, 118 Mass. 261, 19 Am.St.Rep. 449; 1934, 91 A.L.R. 148.

have reserved to himself a security interest which will give to him a consensual equitable mortgage.[47] Finally, he may, either in pursuance of a prior contract or without one, convey title to the buyer, receive at the time part of the purchase money and receive back as part of the same transaction a mortgage upon the property to secure the balance of the purchase money. This last is the ordinary purchase money mortgage and it merits attention because of the special priority accorded it.[48]

It is familiar learning that a purchase money mortgage, executed at the same time with the deed of purchase of land, or in pursuance of agreement as part of one continuous transaction, takes precedence over any other claim or lien attaching to the property through the vendee-mortgagor. This is so even though the claim antedates the execution of the mortgage to the seller.[49] It will also have priority if it is in favor of a third person who advanced the purchase money paid to the vendor,[50] provided the money was loaned for this purpose only. The mortgagee has the burden of establishing such facts.[51]

In some states the priority of the purchase money mortgage is provided for by statute.[52] These apply, of course, to the mortgage executed to the grantor and there is a little authority construing them as limiting priority to such mortgages,[53] but the better view and authority extends them to the third party lender of the price.[54] Thus the purchase money mortgage will prevail over a claim of dower,[55] community property,[56] or homestead.[57]

---

47. See §§ 48, 211, supra. On the effect of expressly reserving a lien or taking a purchase money mortgage as waiving the equitable grantor's lien, see Payne v. Wilson, 1878, 74 N.Y. 343, 348.

48. Holbrook v. Finney, 1808, 4 Mass. 569, 3 Am.Dec. 243, and Stow v. Tift, 1818, 15 Johns. (N.Y.) 458, 8 Am.Dec. 266, are early cases in this country. This priority is frequently postponed to later mortgages for construction purposes under subordination agreements. See preceding section.

49. See 1943, 29 Va.L.Rev. 491.

50. Stewart v. Smith, 1886, 36 Minn. 82, 30 N.W. 430, 1 Am.St.Rep. 624; Protestant Episcopal Church of the Diocese of Ga. v. E. E. Lowe, 1908, 131 Ga. 666, 63 S.E. 136, 127 Am.St.Rep. 243; Laidley v. Aikin, 1890, 80 Iowa 112, 45 N.W. 384, 20 Am.St.Rep. 408; Hill v. Hill, 1959, 185 Kan. 389, 345 P.2d 1015.

51. Van Loben Sels v. Bunnell, 1898, 120 Cal. 680, 53 P. 266; Lorenz Co. v. Gray, 1931, 136 Or. 605, 298 P. 222, rehearing denied and adhered to 136 Or. 605, 300 P. 949; Carey v. Boyle, 1881, 53 Wis. 574, 11 N.W. 47; Soukup v. Wenisch, 1925, 163 Minn. 365, 204 N.W. 35, semble.

As to the priority of a mortgage given to E to secure money advanced to M to purchase property at the foreclosure sale on a first mortgage on M's property, over an existing second mortgage on the same

property, see note, 1921, 35 Harv.L.Rev. 91. Cf. Nicholson v. Aney, 1905, 127 Iowa 278, 103 N.W. 201, mortgage given to secure loan for purpose of paying off a prior loan that had been used to purchase land is not a purchase money mortgage.

A mortgage, given by a grantee to his grantor or to a third party at the same time he received his conveyance, but to secure, not the purchase price or a loan for the payment of it, but another debt, will not take priority over an earlier judgment against the grantee. Weil v. Casey, 1899, 125 N.C. 356, 34 S.E. 506, 74 Am.St.Rep. 644; Ray v. Adams, 1875, 4 Hun (N.Y.) 332.

52. E. g., West's Ann.Cal.Civ.Code, § 2898; D.C. Code Encyclopedia § 15–104.

53. Heuisler v. Nickum, 1873, 38 Md. 270, and Stansell v. Roberts, 1844, 13 Ohio, 148, 42 Am.Dec. 193, where the court relied upon the statutory definition of purchase money mortgages to give the judgment priority. But see, 1897, Mut. Aid Building & Loan Co. v. Gashe, 56 Ohio St. 273, 46 N.E. 985; Ward v. Carey, 1883, 39 Ohio St. 361.

54. Hopler v. Cutler, N.J.Ch.1896, 34 A. 746; Bradley v. Bryan, 1887, 43 N.J.Eq. 396, 13 A. 806, semble; Home Owners Loan Corp. v. Humphrey, 1938, 148 Kan. 779, 85 P.2d 7; Kneen v. Halin, 1899, 6 Idaho 621, 59 P. 14; Jackson v. Austin, 1818, 15 Johns., N.Y., 477. See 1948, 36 Georgetown L.J. 676.

In Mercantile Collection Bureau v. Roach, 1961, 195 Cal.App.2d 355, 15 Cal.Rptr. 710, a third party who loaned money to a judgment debtor to purchase real estate, took title in his own name and then conveyed it to the judgment debtor, taking back a trust deed mortgage, was held to be a purchase money mortgagee whose mortgage was superior to the lien of the judgment creditor, though the latter was prior in time.

55. Stow v. Tift, 1818, 15 Johns. (N.Y.) 458, 8 Am. Dec. 266; Clark v. Munroe, 1817, 14 Mass. 351; Gilliam v. Moore, 1832, 4 Leigh (Va.) 30, 24 Am.Dec. 704; McKinney's N.Y.Real Prop.Law, § 193. In all but two states, Georgia and Kentucky, the former by statute, this is the rule. See Note, 1915, 52 L.R.A.,N.S., 541.

56. Kneen v. Halin, 1899, 6 Idaho 621, 59 P. 14; Davidson v. Click, 1926, 31 N.M. 543, 249 P. 100, 47 A.L.R. 1016.

57. Lassen v. Vance, 1857, 8 Cal. 271, 68 Am.Dec. 322; Foster Lumber Co. v. Harlan County Bank,

One of the frequent and important instances of its superiority is over liens arising under judgments against the grantee-mortgagor under a judgment obtained and docketed or recorded before the purchase money mortgage is executed.[58] It is given preference also over other mortgages which have been executed prior to or simultaneously with the purchase money mortgage and fasten upon the property when it is acquired by the mortgagor. Thus it wins over after-acquired property clauses in previously executed mortgages that would cover the subject matter of the purchase money mortgage.[59] This is clear enough because such clauses operate only to create equitable mortgages and consequently cover only the property as it lies in the hands of the mort-

gagor.[60] The same is true of mortgages that accrue by way of estoppel under mortgages executed and recorded by the vendee-mortgagor before he received title and executed the purchase money mortgage.[61] Even more clearly this is true if such a mortgage was taken with knowledge that the grantee-mortgagor did not yet have title.[62] Where the contest is between a purchase money mortgage to a third person who advances part of the purchase price and a purchase money mortgage to the vendor for the balance, the latter is given preference [63] even if he had notice of the former.[64] As to the mortgages or liens that may attach to the property subsequent to the deed to the grantee-mortgagor the purchase money mortgage would seem to stand on the same footing as any other mortgage. If the purchase money mortgage has also been executed before the other mortgage or lien comes into existence, we have the situation of a prior legal mortgage, which ordinarily prevails.[65] If the other mortgage or lien

1905, 71 Kan. 158, 80 P. 49, 114 Am.St.Rep. 470, 6 Ann.Cas. 44; Powers v. Pense, 1912, 20 Wyo. 327, 123 P. 925, 40 L.R.A.,N.S., 785. But see Eyster v. Hathaway, 1864, 50 Ill. 521, 99 Am.Dec. 537, with which compare Jones v. Parker, 1881, 51 Wis. 218, 8 N.W. 124; 1943, 29 Va.L.Rev. 491, 495.

As to whether a lease made before the formal completion of the purchase by a purchase money mortgagor who obtained possession is binding upon the mortgagee, see Church of England Building Soc. v. Piskor, 1954, 2 W.L.R. 952, discussed in 1954, Camb.L.J. 192.

Under Alaskan statutes a tax lien on cannery operations was given priority over a purchase money mortgage. Schlothan v. Territory of Alaska, C.A. 9th, 1960, 276 F.2d 806, certiorari denied 362 U.S. 990, 80 S.Ct. 1079, 4 L.Ed.2d 1022.

58. The cases are numerous. Among them are Scott, Carhart & Co. v. Warren, 1857, 21 Ga. 408; Stewart v. Smith, 1886, 36 Minn. 82, 30 N.W. 430, 1 Am. St.Rep. 624; Joseph v. Donovan, 1934, 118 Conn. 80, 171 A. 24; Holland Jones Co. v. Smith, 1929, 152 Va. 707, 148 S.E. 581.

59. U. S. v. New Orleans R. R., 1870, 12 U.S. (12 Wall.) 362, 20 L.Ed. 434; Faulkner County Bk. & Trust Co. v. Vail, 1927, 173 Ark. 406, 293 S.W. 40; see Chase Nat. Bk. v. Sweezy, 1931, 281 N.Y.S. 487, affirmed, 1933, 261 N.Y. 710, 185 N.E. 803; § 40, supra. Louisiana holds the other way. Equitable Securities Co. v. Talbert, 1897, 49 La.Ann. 1393, 22 So. 762.

See Storke and Sears, op. cit. § 211, note 90, supra, 200.

As to the priority of a purchase money mortgage subordinated by its terms to a later construction loan mortgagee, see Housing Mortgage Corp. v. Allied Construction, Inc., 1953, 374 Pa. 312, 97 A.2d 82, discussed in Updike, Mortgages, in 1953 Annual

Survey of American Law, 1954, 29 N.Y.U.L.Rev. 829, 831.

60. See § 37, supra.

61. Ellsberry v. Duval-Percival Trust Co., 1926, 220 Mo.App. 239, 282 S.W. 1054, noted, 1926, 40 Harv.L. Rev. 500; Dusenbury v. Hulbert, 1875, 59 N.Y. 541. See §§ 38, 199, supra.

62. Fecteau v. Fries, 1931, 253 Mich. 51, 234 N.W. 113, comment, 1931, 17 Iowa L.Rev. 99, Hanna, Cas.Security, 3d ed., 867; Hoffman v. Kleinjan, 1929, 54 S.D. 634, 224 N.W. 187, matter of notice in doubt. See § 37, supra.

63. Schoch v. Birdsall, 1892, 48 Minn. 441, 51 N.W. 382; Brower v. Witmeyer, 1889, 121 Ind. 83, 22 N. E. 975; Turk v. Funk, 1878, 68 Mo. 18, 13 Am.Rep. 771; Protection Bldg. & Loan Ass'n v. Knowles, 1896, 54 N.J.Eq. 519, 34 A. 1083, affirmed 55 N.J.Eq. 822, 41 A. 1116.

64. Rogers v. Tucker, 1888, 94 Mo. 346, 7 S.W. 414; Truesdale v. Brennan, 1900, 153 Mo. 600, 55 S.W. 147; Boies v. Benham, 1891, 127 N.Y. 620, 28 N.E. 657, 14 L.R.A. 55. There is not much direct authority. See Tiffany, Real Prop., 3d ed., § 1462.

65. See § 181, supra.

That a prior purchase money mortgagee with an after-acquired property clause who bought in on foreclosure sale prevails over a later conditional vendor of a fixture, see Note, Fixtures in Tennessee, 1956, 24 Tenn.L.Rev. 372.

arose intermediate the execution of the deed and the giving of the purchase money legal mortgage, there would be in the purchase money mortgagee at that time only an equitable security interest and whether it would be defeated would depend on the nature of the intervening interest and the rules governing the cutting off of such equitable interests.[66] This is, of course, apart from the effect of recording acts, a matter that will be reverted to presently. The extent of superiority over mechanics' liens will be considered in the following section.

Several rationales have been advanced for this favoritism of the law for the purchase money mortgagee. The most venerable and frequently stated explanation is that of transitory seizin. The idea is that title shot into the grantee and out of him again into the purchase money mortgagee so fleetingly—*quasi uno flattu,* in one breath, as it were—that no other interest had time to fasten itself to it: the grantee-mortgagor must be regarded as a mere conduit.[67] Such a theory breaks down in lien states where the fee remains permanently in the grantee-mortgagor. It also is inconsistent with the cases of quite common occurrence in which some considerable time elapses between the conveyance to the mortgagor and the execution of the mortgage. If the reason were to be taken literally it would require the execution of the deed of purchase and the execution of the

mortgage to be practically simultaneous, something that is ordinarily not feasible and not required by the cases. As was said by an able judge in a leading case, "An examination of the cases will show that the real test is not whether the deed and mortgage were in fact executed at the same instant, or even on the same day, but whether they were parts of one continuous transaction, and so intended to be, so that the two instruments should be given contemporaneous operation in order to promote the intent of the parties."[68] Again, if the theory has validity, it would seem it should apply to any case where the grantee mortgaged the property the instant he got the conveyance rather than confining it to mortgages for the purchase price in favor of the vendor or a third party lender.[69] And, further, some theory other than transitory seizin would seem necessary to explain the priority of the vendor's purchase money mortgage over that of the third party lender of part of the purchase money insofar, at least, as the latter's priority is

---

66. See § 182, et seq., supra.

67. The principle is stated in Nash v. Preston, 1631, 3 Cro.Car. 190 and is found in Coke, Litt. § 31a who is cited as authority in early and leading American cases. Stow v. Tift, 1918, 15 Johns. (N.Y.) 458, 8 Am.Dec. 266; Scott, Carhart & Co. v. Warren, 1857, 21 Ga. 408. Other important cases accepting the doctrine are Holbrook v. Finney, 1808, 4 Mass. 566, 3 Am.Dec. 243; Adams v. Hill, 1854, 29 N.H. 202; Wheatley's Heirs v. Calhoun, 1841, 39 Va. (12 Leigh) 264, 37 Am.Dec. 654; see Kent, Com., 5th ed., 173, 174. The theory of transitory seizin is also used as an explanation of the priority of the mortgage to a third party lender of the purchase money. Protestant Episcopal Church of the Diocese of Ga. v. E. E. Lowe, 1908, 131 Ga. 666, 63 S.E. 136, 127 Am.St.Rep. 243; Marin v. Knox, 1912, 117 Minn. 428, 136 N.W. 15, 40 L.R.A.,N.S., 272.

68. Mitchell, J., in Stewart v. Smith, 1886, 36 Minn. 82, 84, 30 N.W. 430, 431, 1 Am.St.Rep. 624.

In Wheatley's Heirs v. Calhoun, Va.1841, 12 Leigh 264, 37 Am.Dec. 654, a purchase money mortgage to the vendor, executed ten months after the conveyance, was held to have priority over the dower rights of the widow of the grantee.

In Ray v. Adams, N.Y., 1875, 4 Hun 332, about a year elapsed after the vendee received title before he executed the previously agreed upon mortgage to secure E, who had loaned part of the purchase price; nevertheless E prevailed over a judgment obtained against the vendee before he obtained title. See, also, Demeter v. Wilcox, 1893, 115 Mo. 634, 22 S.W. 613, 37 Am.St.Rep. 422.

69. "If the grantor should convey to the grantee, in satisfaction of a prior debt due from the grantor to the grantee, would the grantee be permitted to mortgage to a third person with such effect that his mortgage would be allowed to prevail over the widow's dower and the claims of prior judgment and lien creditors? If so, on what principle? Simply because he mortgaged the instant he got the conveyance, and not some appreciable period of time, be it a minute or an hour, afterwards?" N. J. Bldg., Loan & Inv. Co. v. Bachelor, 1896, 54 N.J. Eq. 600, 603, 35 A. 745, 747. The answer is that such a mortgage would not prevail. See text, supra, and note 46, supra.

said to rest upon the same doctrine.[70] For when this last is the case, the title could just as readily shoot through the grantee-mortgagor as a conduit into the third party as to double back on its course and return to the vendor.

A better statement of the reason for the rule is that the title comes to the purchaser already charged with the encumbrance in favor of the grantor-mortgagor; that regardless of the form all that the transaction ever transfers is the redemption right.[71] While such a conclusion would square with the decisions where the purchase money mortgage goes to the vendor, it is more difficult to apply it to the mortgage going to a third party lender of the purchase price, although it has been advanced in such a case.[72] Furthermore, it would seem that the opposite conclusion could have been reached just as easily. Indeed it would have been easier to do so, since in form there is a transfer of the full title without reservation, and the grantee then by a separate mortgage instrument creates the charge on it. So, unless the matter is dug into more deeply, one is left unsatisfied as to why this one of two perfectly possible conclusions has been chosen. A little delving, though, does give more illuminating answers. One is somewhat technical and legalistic, the other more satisfactorily deals with it as a matter of intrinsic fairness based upon the just expectations on the part of the purchase money mortgagee. The first answer suggests that the purchase money mortgage always takes the place of an equitable interest in the property that precedes any lien or interest of any kind attaching to the purchaser's estate at the time of acquiring title.[73] Where there is a prior contract of sale this equitable interest consists of a specifically enforceable contract right to have the purchase money mortgage given on taking title and the equitable estate under the purchase contract is subject to this right. Where there is no prior contract the vendor has left in him on conveying title without receiving payment an equitable vendor's lien. When the purchase money mortgage is given it merely replaces and takes the priority of one or the other of these prior equities, and this is so whether it is given at once or subsequently, provided it is part of the same transaction. The prevalence of the third party lender of the purchase money is an extension of this. He is said to be in the position of an assignee of prior equitable rights of the vendor,[74] a theory similar to one advanced when the question was as to the applicability of the Statute of Frauds to a promise to give a mortgage on lands to be acquired with money loaned for the purpose by the promisee.[75]

The other answer justifies the doctrine on the equity and justice of protecting one who has parted with his property on the faith of having a security interest in it until the money for which he was exchanging it is received as against persons who, for different reasons, have inferior claims.[76] Certainly the vendor should prevail over claimants of dower, curtesy, community property or home-

70. And there are cases stating that it does so rest. Moring v. Dickerson, 1881, 85 N.C. 466; Demeter v. Wilcox, 1893, 115 Mo. 634, 22 S.W. 613, 37 Am.St. Rep. 422.

71. See N. J. Bldg., Loan & Inv. Co. v. Bachelor, 1896, 54 N.J.Eq. 600, 603, 35 A. 745, 747.

72. "One who executes a purchase-money mortgage is not regarded as obtaining the title and then placing an incumbrance on it. He is deemed to take the title charged with the incumbrance, which has priority over preexisting claims. And a mortgage given to a third person to obtain the money used in buying the property is entitled to the same preference." Warren Mortgage Co. v. Winters, 1915, 94 Kan. 615, 619, 146 P. 1012, 1013, Ann.Cas.1916C, 956.

73. See Boorum v. Tucker, 1893, 51 N.J.Eq. 135, 26 A. 456, affirmed 52 N.J.Eq. 587, 33 A. 50; Davidson v. Click, 1926, 31 N.M. 543, 249 P. 100, 47 A.L.R. 1016; Walsh, Mortgages, 168.

74. Protestant Episcopal Church of the Diocese of Ga. v. E. E. Lowe Co., 1908, 131 Ga. 666, 63 S.E. 136, 127 Am.St.Rep. 243; Laidley v. Aikin, 1890, 80 Iowa 112, 45 N.W. 384, 20 Am.St.Rep. 408.

75. See § 63, supra.

76. See Tiffany, Real Prop., 3d ed., § 1462.

stead rights, for any of these would be acquiring a pure windfall for which he paid nothing and would be getting it out of the unpaid for property of the vendor.[77] As against judgment lien creditors he should win because they have not extended their credit in reliance on the right to be repaid out of *any* specific property, much less out of property previously owned by another and coming to the debtor unpaid for, with the seller of it relying upon that very property he has parted with for his payment. Furthermore, their judgments are obtained before their debtor receives the property to which it attaches on acquisition so they could not have relied upon it in getting their judgment lien. In such a case the general rule that such creditors' rights should rise no higher than their debtors' seems clearly appropriate. As against other mortgagee claimants to the property, especially those who have made their loan for the purpose of paying part of the purchase price, the question is closer; for these, unlike the others, have relied upon getting paid out of the same specific property and have parted with value on that reliance. Even so, the vendor has the edge because the property he is relying on for payment was previously his up to the time of sale and mortgage back; there was never an instant when he relinquished a hold on it; and he would never have parted with it at all except upon the belief and faith that if his buyer defaulted he could either recapture his property or get paid out of it. And this is normally so even though he may know that his buyer is going to finance the deal in part by borrowing some of the purchase money from another and give him a mortgage on the property. Other mortgagees, on the other hand, even including lenders of purchase money, parted only with money in which they retained no interest whatsoever, and placed their reliance for repayment of their debts on getting a security interest in other property not only never previously owned by them but not even owned by the mortgagor at the time the money was loaned, even though they might not have known that fact.[78] This difference in attitude toward the hazard of losing property previously owned and that of not getting an interest in property which had never before belonged to the claimant is an old and important one as has been seen previously in other connections.[79] Here it justifies preferring the vendor purchase money mortgagee over even the third party lender of the purchase money as well as the mortgagee under an after-acquired property clause or one who became a mortgagee by estoppel under a mortgage by the grantee-mortgagor executed before he got title from the vendor. Much the same reasoning applies to the money-lending purchase money mortgagee to give him priority over all but the vendor who comes into competition with him. He relied upon getting security upon this very property and his money went into the payment of it. Without his advance of money, the mortgagor would never have received the property. It is this last feature that serves to bring him in ahead of other mortgagees whose loans were not limited in their use to the acquisition of the property which was to be security for repayment. *A fortiori* he prevails over the other types of claimants.

The priority of the purchase money mortgage is subject to the operation of the recording acts. Consequently if, after conveying title and taking his mortgage, the mortgagee fails to record it, he will be postponed to subsequent takers who qualify as members of protected classes under the recording stat-

---

77. See Davidson v. Click, 1926, 31 N.M. 543, 249 P. 100, 47 A.L.R. 1016.

78. Of course if the vendor was in collusion with the mortgagor in representing to the lender that the mortgagor owned the property with any claims of the vendor on it for payment to be subordinate to the money lender's mortgage the latter would be able to argue estoppel or an implied subordination agreement. See text later this section. See also §§ 191, 210, 212.

79. See §§ 94, 95, supra.

utes.[80] Where, however, the other mortgage or lien, even though it is for a loan of part of the purchase money, arises before or contemporaneously with the deed to the grantee-mortgagor, it will gain no priority over the purchase money mortgage by virtue of the recording acts even though it is recorded before the recordation of the purchase money mortgage.[81] This is for the simple reason that only conveyances *subsequent* to the unrecorded mortgage are within the protection of most recording acts.[82] Where the other mortgage is recorded prior to the deed to the grantee-mortgagor, an additional reason is added: that the vendor should not be bound to take account of encumbrances placed upon property and recorded while it was still his own.[83] Where the vendor actually learns of the purchase money loan and the mortgage given to secure it, it is possible to find an implied agreement to subordinate his mortgage

---

80. See, 1923, 26 A.L.R. 171, 173, semble. Cf. Donovan v. Twist, 1905, 105 App.Div. 171, 93 N.Y.S. 990.

V conveyed to M and took back a mortgage for the purchase price. The deed was recorded but the mortgage was not. M then borrowed from E and gave him a mortgage on the premises as security. E had no actual notice of the mortgage to V. E prevails. Jackson v. Reid, 1883, 30 Kan. 10, 1 P. 308. See also Plumb v. Bay, 1877, 18 Kan. 415.

If V, in the above case, had recorded his mortgage but did so prior to the recordation of his deed to M, whether that would be a valid recordation depends upon matters previously considered. See §§ 199, 200. It should not be. And see Protection Bldg. & Loan Ass'n v. Knowles, 1896, 54 N.J.Eq. 519, 34 A. 1083, purchase money to lender preferred over purchase money to vendor as to amounts loaned after execution of deed to grantee-mortgagor and before registry of vendor's mortgage. See 1942, 137 A.L.R. 571; 1948, 168 A.L.R. 1164. So too a judgment obtained subsequent to the giving of a purchase money mortgage and prior to its recording where the act protects judgment creditors. Thorpe v. Helmer, 1916, 275 Ill. 86, 113 N.E. 954; see Leesman, Operation of the Illinois Recording Act, 1944, 38 Ill.L. Rev. 396, 403.

In Savings Bank & Trust Co. v. Brock, 1928, 196 N.C. 24, 144 S.E. 365, criticized in note, 1928, 7 N.Car.L. Rev. 95, V gave a deed of certain property to M who thereupon executed a mortgage on it to E as security for the loan of the purchase price. Later M gave a mortgage to V to secure a previous indebtedness. V recorded this latter mortgage before E recorded his mortgage. The original deed from V to M was not recorded until after both mortgages had been recorded. Under North Carolina law, a later grantee or mortgagee who records his grant or mortgage before a prior one will prevail over it even if he had knowledge of the earlier one. Held, E has priority over V.

81. Dusenbury v. Hullbert, 1875, 59 N.Y. 541, Osborne, Cases Property Security, 2d Ed., 348, mortgage to lender of purchase money executed either before or contemporaneously with the execution of deed to grantee-mortgagor and giving of purchase money mortgage to vendor but recorded before the latter although not until the deed had passed title to the mortgagor. Held, for the vendor.

See Storke and Sears, op. cit. § 211, note 90 supra, 198.

In Schoch v. Birdsall, 1892, 48 Minn. 441, 51 N.W. 382, part of the purchase money was loaned and a

mortgage given to and recorded by E before M, the mortgagor, obtained title from V. M, when he did obtain title from V, gave back a mortgage for the balance of the price. Held, V has priority over E. See also note, 1927, 40 Harv.L.Rev. 499; Turk v. Funk, 1878, 68 Mo. 18, 30 Am.Rep. 771, accord.

In Fecteau v. Fries, 1931, 253 Mich. 51, 234 N.W. 113, commented on in, 1931, 17 Iowa L.Rev. 99, the lender of part of the purchase money made his loan and was given a mortgage before the acquisition of title from and giving back of a mortgage for the balance of the price to the vendor. Later both mortgages were recorded on the same day but that to the lender was recorded first. At the time of the loan and mortgage to the lender he knew of the intended mortgage in favor of the vendor. Still later the lender assigned his mortgage to one who had no actual notice of the vendor's security. Held, the vendor has priority. The fact that the records showed a deed to the vendee and a mortgage back to the vendor was sufficient to put the assignee of the lender's mortgage on inquiry of a purchase money mortgage. Look also at Brower v. Witmeyer, 1889, 121 Ind. 83, 22 N.E. 975; Smith v. McCarty, 1876, 119 Mass. 519.

In Higgins v. Dennis, 1898, 104 Iowa 605, 74 N.W. 9, the mortgage to the lender was not executed until *after* the execution of the deed to the grantee-mortgagor and was recorded before that deed was recorded and before the vendor's mortgage was recorded. Both mortgages were executed on the same day but in what order did not appear. It was held that the vendor was on notice of the other mortgage by reason of the prior mortgage. See also cases cited in preceding notes.

82. See § 202, supra. This rule may be altered in states which go by strict rules of priority of recording. See §§ 194–196, supra. The decision in Savings Bank & Trust Co. v. Brock, 1928, 196 N.C. 24, 144 S.E. 365 was in such a jurisdiction but it seems dubious even so, as well as undesirable, if the statute does not compel it. See 1928, 7 N.Car.L.Rev. 95.

83. See Schoch v. Birdsall, 1892, 48 Minn. 441, 51 N. W. 382; 1943, 29 Va.L.Rev. 491, 495.

to it,[84] and there are decisions so holding. This is a question of fact, and in view of the normal equities favoring the vendor, such an implied agreement should be clearly established.[85]

MECHANICS' LIENS—IN GENERAL

214. Mechanics' liens are created by statute to give persons in the construction industry security for their claims. Statutes and their construction differ greatly. The prevalent type protects subcontractors only to the amount owing under the main contract; the Pennsylvania type gives them an independent status. In many states the liens attach when the construction starts; in others when each lienor begins his performance or when the claim is filed. The lien attaches to the structure itself, to the contracting owner's interest in the land, and sometimes to the interest of the non-contracting owner.

The most common, probably the most important, and quite certainly the most complicated of the liens created by statute with which the lender who takes a real property mortgage comes into competition is the mechanics' lien. Although the legal scholar can find authority that a form of it existed in the Roman law,[86] was well developed in the civil law[87] and incorporated in the Code Napoleon,[88] it was unknown in England, either at common law or in equity[89] and, so far as our present laws are concerned, is of native origin in the United States, dating back to the Maryland statute of 1791.[90] Today in every state in the Union such legislation exists,[91] but because the liens are wholly statutory, because the laws creating them have been and are extremely varied both in their provisions and in the courts' construction of them, and because legislatures have been prolific with amendments, generalizations are extremely difficult and always must be checked against local enactments.[92] Fur-

84. See § 212. Ex parte Johnson, 1928, 147 S.C. 259, 145 S.E. 113; Walter v. Kressman, 1917, 25 Wyo. 292, 169 P. 3.

85. See Truesdale v. Brennan, 1899, 153 Mo. 600, 55 S.W. 147; Boies v. Benham, 1891, 127 N.Y. 620, 28 N.E. 657, 14 L.R.A. 55.

86. Mackeldy, Handbook of the Roman Law, Dropsie's Translation, 274.

87. See Canal Co. v. Gordon, 1867, 73 U.S. (6 Wall.) 561, 571, 18 L.Ed. 894. Jones v. Great So. Fireproof Hotel Co., C.C.A. 6, 1898, 86 F. 370, 386, 30 C.C.A. 108, reversed 177 U.S. 449, 20 S.Ct. 690, 44 L.Ed. 842; 1 Domat, Civil Law, 1861 ed., 681—4, arts. 1736, 1741—5.

88. Code Napoleon, Privileges and Mortgages, § 2 (2103).

89. See Canal Co. v. Gordon, 1867, 73 U.S. (6 Wall.) 561, 571, 18 L.Ed. 894; Van Stone v. Stillwell & Bierce Mfg. Co., 1891, 142 U.S. 128, 136, 12 S.Ct. 181, 183, 35 L.Ed. 961. "Mechanic's liens on build-ings and land, though recognized and favored by the civilians, had no place in the common law, which, from its feudal character, was reluctant to subject realty to the payment of any claims other than feudal." Durling v. Gould, 1890, 83 Me. 134, 137, 21 A. 833.

90. Acts of General Assembly of Maryland, 1791, c. 45, § 10. "The origin of such laws, in America, arose from the desire to establish and improve, as readily as possible, the city of Washington. In 1791, at a meeting of the commissioners appointed for such purpose, both Thomas Jefferson and James Madison were present, and a memorial was adopted urging the General Assembly of Maryland to pass an act securing to *master-builders*, a lien, on houses erected, and land occupied. The requested law was enacted December 19, 1791." Moore-Mansfield Const. Co. v. Indianapolis N. C. & T. R. Co., 1913, 179 Ind. 356, 369, 101 N.E. 296, 44 L.R.A., N.S. 816, Ann.Cas.1915D, 917. The next statute was in Pennsylvania in 1803. Act of April 1, 1803, P.L. 791; see Cushman, Proposed Mechanics' Lien Law, 1932, 80 U.Pa.L.Rev. 1083 n. 3.

91. See Armour & Co. v. Western Construction Co., 1905, 36 Wash. 529, 78 P. 1106. In at least one state mechanics' liens are provided for in its constitution. Cal. Const. Art. XX, § 15.

92. See Eastin, Priorities Between Mortgages and Mechanics' Liens, 1935, 36 U.Mo.Bull. No. 1. Law Ser. 48; 1926, 36 Yale L.J. 129. The point is made vivid by even a cursory examination of the digest made by the Commissioners on Uniform State Laws of state legislative provisions governing the persons to whom mechanics' liens are accorded, the interests in the property to which they attach, and the limitations on the amount of the liens. See, 1928, Handbook of Comm. on Un.St.Laws, 473 et seq., 497 et seq. There have been several analyses of the mechanics' lien laws in individual states, some of them quite comprehensive, others dealing with only certain aspects. Among them are California, 1934, 22 Cal.L.Rev. 312; Iowa, 1932, 17 Iowa L.Rev. 516; Michigan, 1933, 3 Detroit L.Rev. 211, 212; New York, 1929, 29 Col.L.Rev. 996, covering the 1929 revision; Pennsylvania, in Cushman, The Proposed Uniform Mechanics' Lien Law, 1932, 80 U.Pa.L.Rev. 1083, 1099; Wisconsin, 1943, Wis.L. Rev. 277; Virginia, 1942, 29 Va.L.Rev. 121.

thermore, case law is unreliable in the field because the decisions are meaningless except with reference to the particular statute under which each arose and the precise language of the act at that time. This variability has been justified on the ground that the problems involved are dissimilar in different parts of the country,[93] even perhaps from state to state. It has been urged that this would not be true, or at least so true, as to make it impracticable to draft a special, uniform act applicable only to home con-

In addition to the citations supra, there have been published a great many articles and notes in legal periodicals upon all aspects of mechanics' liens. A quite full citation of these will be found in the footnotes to IV Am.L.Prop. § 16.106F, including biennial supplements to 1962. Among the materials published since then, most of them dealing with the laws of particular states, are the following: California Mechanics' Liens, 1963, 51 Cal.L.Rev. 331; California Mechanics' Liens: A Symposium, 1964, 16 Hastings L.J. 155–229, consisting of four articles and a long note; Mechanics' Liens in Indiana—The Extent of the Property and Property Interests Subject to the Lien, 1921, 36 Indiana L.J. 526; Owner's Liability to Subcontractors Under the Iowa Mechanics' Lien Law, 1961, 47 Iowa L.Rev. 144; Davis, Mechanics' Liens—Shifting Responsibility for Building Contractor's Debts, 1963, 48 Iowa L.Rev. 794; Mangum, Mechanics' Liens in North Carolina, 1963, 41 N.Car.L.R. 173; Sell, The Pennsylvania Mechanics' Lien Law, 1963, 35 U. of Pittsburgh L. R. 265; Florey, Priority of Mechanics and Materialmen's Liens in Texas, 1962, 40 Texas L.Rev. 872; The Mechanics' Lien in Virginia, 1960, 17 Wash. and Lee L.Rev. 307.

Other published materials include the following: Townsend, The Mechanics' Lien in Arizona: Is It a Practical Remedy?, 1966, 7 Ariz.L.Rev. 296–307; Goulden and Dent, More On Mechanics' Liens, Stop Notices and the Like, 1966, 54 Cal.L.Rev. 179–210; Note, General Mechanics' Lien Laws in Colorado: 1965 Amendments, 1966, 39 Univ.Colo.L.Rev. 105–125; Seawell, Problems of Buying a House Which is to be Constructed, 1965, 37 Univ.Colo.L.Rev. 457, 459–464; Davis, Mechanics' Liens and Construction Financing—Consistent Priorities?, 1966, 51 Iowa L.Rev. 862–881; Brown, Mechanics' Liens: Mississippi Notice Requirements, 1966, 37 Miss.L.J. 385–395; Note, The Right to a Mechanic's Lien in Ohio: A Survey, 1966, 18 Western Reserve L.Rev. 297–320; Sell, Secured Transactions, 1966, 27 Univ. Pittsburgh L.Rev. 359, 364–368; Hite, The Utah Law of Mechanics' Liens, 1966, Utah L.Rev. 181–194; Moss, Mechanic's Liens and Related Remedies, 1968, 43 Jour. State Bar of Cal., 930–944, a survey of California law.

93. See Glenn, Mortgages, § 351.

struction.[94] But a proposed general Uniform Mechanics Lien Law, originally drafted in 1932 after eight years of work, was adopted by only one state [95] in eleven years, and was withdrawn in 1943 for the stated reason that varied conditions made uniformity impossible.[96] Even if the task were less formidable, any extensive consideration of the law of mechanics' liens generally falls outside of the scope of this work. Nevertheless, it is possible and highly important, to outline by groups, with sufficient definiteness to be helpful, certain common features and structures of these acts [97] which are relevant to determining and understanding the areas of collision between them and mortgages, and to discover types of adjustments or proposed solutions of the conflicting claims of security priority.

The basic idea of the mechanic's lien is that it gives security for the payment of the claims of those who enhance the value of the land to which it attaches by services or materials in construction or improvement.

94. See Stalling, The Need for Special Simplified Mechanics' Lien Acts Applicable to Home Construction, 1938, 5 Law & Contemp.Probs. 592.

95. Florida, in 1935, with modifications.

96. See 1943, Handbook of Comm. on Uniform State Laws, 150. There were features of the act, e. g., the requirements of filing notice of intention to claim a lien, § 4, and the time limit for filing claims of lien, § 17, that aroused opposition and criticism which may have been instrumental in its failure to obtain legislative approval. However, it seems more probable that the controversy over its content reflected sufficient regional opposition, as contrasted with antagonistic interests of different groups affected by the statute, to account for its lack of success.

There were several critical discussions of the act and they constitute, in addition to their comments on its provision, valuable surveys of the whole field of mechanics' lien law, particularly with reference to similarities and diversities among the various states. Among the best of these are 1931, Note, Sixth Tentative Draft of a Uniform Mechanics' Lien Statute, 41 Yale L.J. 271; 1932, 19 Va.L.Rev. 406; Cushman, The Proposed Uniform Mechanics' Lien Law, 1932, 80 U.Pa.L.Rev. 1083; Imlay, Problems in Uniform Mechanics' Lien Act, 1933, 19 A.B. A.J. 116; 1933, 3 Detroit L.Rev. 211.

97. Particularly helpful in this task are the various notes and articles cited in the preceding footnotes.

Beginning with the original Maryland statute "These laws grew, and their validity became established, as the courts held that the building business did not have the protection inherent in the widespread distribution of credit risk common to other businesses, and therefore needed this broader and special protection. Contractors, subcontractors, materialmen, and other building groups were frequently obliged to extend credit in larger amounts, and for longer time, than other businesses. Such parties might have their entire capital, or a substantial part of it, tied up in one or two, or ten or twenty, projects under construction." [98]

To begin with only master-builders were given protection under the acts.[99] But by a process of amendment and enlargement of the similar acts that were passed in other states, today "practically every segment composing the construction industry—including contractors, subcontractors, material dealers, laborers, artisans, architects, landscape architects, engineers, surveyors—is granted liens of varying extent under varying conditions for the labor, services, or materials furnished or contracted to be furnished for the particular improvement." [1]

If the mechanics' lien were limited to those with whom the owner dealt with directly little question would arise as to the amount of the lien upon the property—it would be for the unpaid amount still owing under the contract. When the acts extended the coverage to persons who had no direct dealings with the owner, the statutes divided into two main classes. One, generally designated the "Pennsylvania" type, gives the subcontractor or materialman a direct right of his own regardless of the existence of any indebtedness between the owner and general contractor [2] and measured by the value of his contribution. Conceivably,[3] under such statutes the claims of the ancillary contractors could exceed the contract price or would still exist even though the owner had paid the general contractor in full, nevertheless they are generally upheld when attacked as unconstitutional.[4] The other, and by far the most prev-

98. Stalling, Mechanics' Lien Laws As They Exist Today, 1938, 4 F.H.L.B.Rev. 232.

99. Acts of General Assembly of Maryland, 1791, c. 45, § 10.

1. Stalling, op. cit. supra note 98.
"It has long been the theory justifying the granting of a mechanics' lien that the labor, services, or materials of the lien claimant have so gone into the structure created on the land as to make it impossible for him to secure the return thereof in case of non-payment and, except for a suit for the contract price, the lien claimant would be destitute of remedy unless some form of statutory lien be authorized in his behalf. If, by reason of a contract, the claimant would be entitled to recapture the improvement made, the theoretical basis for the lien would then be removed. Hence, it has been held that no statutory mechanic's lien may be claimed where personal property has been sold on conditional sale basis, even though the personal property has become incorporated into the realty or in the improvements made thereon." Survey of Illinois Law, 1951–1952: Mechanics Liens—Fixtures, 1952, 31 Chi.-Kent L.Rev. 71. As to the right to mechanic's lien as for "labor" or "work" in case of preparato-

ry or fabricating work done on materials intended for use and used in particular building or structure, see, 1952, 25 A.L.R.2d 1370. In Nolte v. Smith, 1961, 189 Cal.App.2d 140, 11 Cal.Rptr. 261, a civil engineer who surveyed, planned and prepared a subdivision map for recording and erected permanent markers and monuments on the property was held to be entitled to a mechanic's lien. However a surveyor who had cut brush to get to site lines, staked road, established location for a channel and constructed iron pipe monuments at lot corners in connection with subdivision of land into saleable lots was not entitled to a mechanic's lien against a partnership and subsequent purchasers under Minnesota's lien law. The Supreme Court of Minnesota, opinion by Justice Frank T. Gallagher, stated that the surveyor's recovery must be on the basis of a personal judgment against the partners by whom he had been employed. Anderson v. Breezy Point Estates, 1969, 283 Minn. 490, 168 N.W.2d 693.

2. Cf. Baldwin Locomotive Works v. Edward Hines Lumber Co., 1919, 189 Ind. 189, 125 N.E. 400, holding that an express stipulation between owner and general contractor could negative a direct lien.

3. Statutes usually fix the contract price as the uppermost limit for such claims. See Prince v. Neal-Millard Co., 1906, 124 Ga. 884, 53 S.E. 761, 4 Ann. Cas. 615.

4. E. g., Jones v. Great Southern Fireproof Hotel Co., 1898, 86 F. 370, 30 C.C.A. 108, certiorari granted 173 U.S. 704, 19 S.Ct. 885, reversed 177 U.S. 449, 20 S.Ct. 690, 44 L.Ed. 842; Hightower v. Bailey, 1900, 108 Ky. 198, 56 S.W. 147, 22 Ky.Law Rep. 88, 49 L.R.A. 255, 94 Am.St.Rep. 350; Becker v. Hop-

alent type, usually referred to as the "New York" system, measures the liability of the owner's property by the price stated in the original contract with the general contractor less payments properly made to the contractor.[5] The theory of these statutes is that all lien rights are based directly or derivatively upon the contract between the owner and general contractor.[6]

Of more important concern to a competing mortgagee is the time when mechanics' liens fasten onto the property.[7] In about half of the states they attach at the commencement of building.[8] In theory there would seem no objection to a rule that the commencement of the lien is to be fixed by something that can be discovered by viewing the land itself. As a practical matter, though, just what constitutes the commencement of building within the rule is frequently a difficult question [9] and acts, such as piling lumber on the property, which are sufficient in one,[10] are not enough in another state.[11] The second most popular time is the date each lienor begins his service or furnishing of materials.[12] The difficulties under such statutes, of determining such commencement of services or supplies are considerably greater than those of being sure when the whole building opera-

---

per, 1914, 22 Wyo. 237, 138 P. 179, Ann.Cas.1916D, 1041, affirmed on rehearing 23 Wyo. 209, 147 P. 1085, Ann.Cas.1918B, 35. But, contra, Selma Sash, Door & Blind Factory v. Stoddard, 1897, 116 Ala. 251, 22 So. 555. Raising a somewhat analogous problem, some states, notably California, West's Ann.Code Civ.Proc. § 1183.1, and Minnesota, 1945, M.S.A. § 514.06, subject the interest of the non-contracting owner of property to the lien of the mechanic under certain circumstances unless he posts or records notice of non-responsibility in a specified manner. These provisions have been held constitutional by the state courts insofar as they have been passed upon, but the soundness of these decisions has been questioned. See Myhre, Fiction, Fallacy and Facts in Relation to "Implied Consent" Provisions of Certain Mechanics' Lien Statutes, 1948, 32 Minn.L.Rev. 559.

5. See N.Y.Cons.Laws, Cahill, 1930, c. 34, §§ 4, 14 (now McKinney's Lien Law, §§ 4, 14).

6. See Lurton, J., in Jones v. Great So. Fireproof Hotel Co., C.C.A. 6th 1898, 86 F. 370, 379, 30 C.C.A. 108, certiorari granted 173 U.S. 704, 19 S.Ct. 885, reversed 177 U.S. 449, 20 S.Ct. 690, 44 L.Ed. 842. Commonly there are additional provisions making it the duty of the owner, on notification to him of unpaid obligations by the contractor to subcontractors, to withold payments to the contractor for the benefit of the notifying lien claimant. Other statutes make it the duty of the owner, on making payments under the contract, to require a statement under oath from the contractor of the sums owed to subcontractors and then to withhold those sums. See 1931, 41 Yale L.J. 271; 1932, 80 U. of Pa.L.Rev. 1083, 1084. See additional statutes in 1931, 41 Yale L.J. 271, fns. 3–8.

Arrows Builders Supply Corp. v. Hudson Terrace Apts., 1954, 15 N.J. 418, 105 A.2d 387, discussed in 1955, 9 Rutgers L.Rev. 586, deals with the New Jersey law on this question.

7. See, 1942, 29 Va.L.Rev. 121, 127; 1926, 36 Yale L. J. 129; Eastin, Priorities Between Mortgages and Mechanics' Liens, 1935, 36 U.Mo.Bull. No. 1, Law Ser. 48, p. 6; 1932, 5 So.Cal.L.Rev. 312; 1930, 18 Cal.L.Rev. 704.

Most mechanics' lien laws require that, in order to perfect a lien, the lien claimant file notice of completion of the work and, within a specified short period of time thereafter, begin action to enforce the lien. Or when a building is deemed complete for the purpose of giving such notice, see Hartman, Creditors' Rights and Security Transactions—1955 Tennessee Survey, 1955, 8 Vand.L.Rev. 989, discussing Dealers Supply Co. v. First Christian Church, 1954, 38 Tenn.App. 568, 276 S.W.2d 769. See Storke and Sears, Highlights of 1955 Colorado Legislative Session: Security Transactions, 1956, 28 Rocky Mt. L.Rev. 76, for an amendment of the Colorado law.

8. The 1928 Handbook of the Commissioners on Uniform State Laws, 495, cited the statutes of twenty-four states as embodying this provision. They were Ala., Ark., Colo., D. C., Ga., Iowa, Kans., La., Md., Mich., Minn., Mo., Mont., N. J., N. D., Ohio, Okl., Or., Pa., R. I., S. D., Tex., Wis., Wyo.

9. E. g., the question whether a change in the design and specifications during the progress of the work so materially alters the plan as to make the whole a different building from that originally started with the construction of the altered structure dating from the changed plans. Haxtun Steam-Heater Co. v. Gordon, 1891, 2 N.D. 246, 50 N.W. 708, 33 Am.St.Rep. 776. See note, Ann.Cas.1916B, 634.

See also Silverstein, Florida Mechanics Lien Law—Visible Commencement, 1953, 7 Miami L.Q. 477; Note, Acquisition and Priorities, 1951, 29 N.C.L. Rev. 480.

10. See James v. Van Horn, 1877, 39 N.J.L. 353, 363.

11. Kansas Mort. Co. v. Weyerhaeuser, 1892, 48 Kan. 335, 29 P. 153. See also 1926, 36 Yale L.J. 129, 131; Sides v. Tidwell, 1939, 216 N.C. 480, 5 S.E.2d 316.

12. 1928 Handbook, note 8, supra, lists Ariz., Cal., Conn., Del., Ind., Ky., Ida., Neb., Nev., N. H., N. M., N. C., Tenn., Va., Wash., W. Va.

See Geiser v. Permacrete, Inc., Fla. 1956, 90 So.2d 610, 612.

tion started. There is also the possibility of an intervening mortgage dividing the lien claimants into prior and subsequent groups creating a problem of concern where the mechanics' lien statute provides that all lien claimants shall, as among themselves, be on a parity.[13] In third place come some half dozen jurisdictions that make the lien attach from the time of filing the claim.[14] In a few states the liens attach at the date of the general contract,[15] of the lienor's contract,[16] or when notice of contract is recorded.[17] In some states the liens attach at different times depending upon various factors involved.[18]

Closely allied to the foregoing is the question as to what property interests they attach. In general, the interest of the contracting owner in the property, whatever it may be at the time the liens arise, are subjected to them.[19] In addition, the liens extend to the improvement, at least if it consists of a structure of some sort capable of removal.[20] And in some states this is true under express terms of the statute even though the contracting party has no interest in the land.[21] Beyond this there are a considerable number of states that provide for subjecting the interests in the property of owners who are not parties to the contract [22] under certain circumstances, usually knowledge of the improvement and failure to post or file notice of non-responsiblity,[23] or upon a presumed consent or agency when the contracting party is the husband or wife of the

---

derson, the Mortgagee Looks at the Ground Lease, 1957, 10 U. of Fla.L.Rev. 1, 10.

20. See, e. g., West's Ann.Cal.Code Civ.Proc. §§ 1181, 1182; which are the basic lien provisions in California. See also 1932, 22 Cal.L.Rev. 312, 314.

21. See 1928 Handbook, supra note 8, 509, listing Ill., Me., Mich., Ohio, Okl., Penn., Wash., and Wis. as having such laws.

22. For a critique of the rationales of such provisions and objection to them on the grounds they are vague and unsound, arbitrary, and oppressive, unreasonable, and unjust to such an extent that they should be held unconstitutional, see Myhre, Fiction, Fallacy and Facts in Relation to "Implied Consent" Provisions of Certain Mechanics' Lien Statutes, 1948, 32 Minn.L.Rev. 559.

23. E. g., West's Ann.Cal.Code Civ.Proc. § 1183.1; Minn.Stat.Ann. § 514.06; see 1928 Handbook, n. 8, supra, 509, for additional statutes. Materialman seeking mechanic's lien against owner must give written notice under statute relating to notice, an oral notice being insufficient. Windsor Mills v. Richard B. Smith, Inc., 1969, —— Cal.App.2d ——, 77 Cal.Rptr. 300.

In 1959, Calif.Code of Civil Procedure § 1193 was added to the California mechanics' lien laws. It requires all lien claimants, except those under direct contract with the property owner or those performing labor for wages on the premises to serve a preliminary notice on the property owner within 20 days after commencement of work on or furnishing of materials to such property. In Halspar, Inc. v. LaBarthe, 1965, 238 Cal.App.2d 897, 48 Cal.Rptr. 293, the lien claimant failed to comply with this requirement and the property owner failed to post notice of nonresponsibility within 10 days after knowledge that such work was being done as required by California Code of Civil Procedure § 1183.1 (b) (formerly § 1192). For a discussion of the relationship between these two code sections in the light of the above decision, see Note by James A. Rundel, 1969, 21 Hastings L.J. 216–234.

13. Pacific States Sav., Loan & Building Co. v. Dubois, 1905, 11 Idaho, 319, 83 P. 513; Ward v. Yarnelle, 1910, 173 Ind. 535, 91 N.E. 7; Henry & Coatsworth Co. v. Fisherdick, Adm'r, 1893, 37 Neb. 207, 55 N.W. 643, and Meister v. J. Meister, Inc., 1928, 103 N.J.Eq. 78, 142 A. 312, permit the intervening encumbrance to create two different classes of mechanics' liens. See, accord, Conn.Pub.Acts, 1925, 3905–6, (now Conn.G.S.A. § 49–33). Gardner v. Leck, 1893, 52 Minn. 522, 54 N.W. 746, preferred all the lien claimants to the mortgagee. Cf. Finlayson v. Crooks, 1891, 47 Minn. 74, 49 N.W. 398, 645, rehearing denied 47 Minn. 74, 49 N.W. 645.

14. 1928 Handbook, note 8, supra, giving Fla., Ga., N. Y., S. C., Vt., N. J., Pa., the last two as to repairs only. Some jurisdictions in the first two categories have the lien relate back from the time of filing, e. g., Del., Ind., Ky.

15. Id., Ill., Miss., S. C., Tex.

16. Id., Me.

17. Id., Mass.

18. E. g., in Tex., under verbal contracts the time is the commencement of building; under written contracts, the date of the contract. Id., 496.

19. For the provisions of most of the state statutes, which, in spite of the differing language embodying the rule, so stipulate, see Id. 497.
See also Note, Mechanics Liens and Homestead, 1955, 7 Baylor L.Rev. 433; Note, Estoppel to Deny Mechanic's Lien on Homestead, 1956, 8 id. 59; Boshkoff, Financing Construction on Long Term Leasehold Estates, 1956, 5 Buffalo L.Rev. 257, 266; An-

non-contracting owner.[24] Lessors and vendors of land under an executory contract of sale have been held to fall within such a category, but mortgagees and trust deed mortgagees have been placed outside of it.[25]

MECHANICS' LIENS—PRIORITIES— ORDINARY MORTGAGES

215. **Mechanics' liens attaching first will prevail over subsequent mortgages and vice versa. Unrecorded mortgages will be postponed to later mechanics' liens arising without notice Some statutes give a later mechanics' lien priority on buildings and improvements constructed subsequent to the mortgage. Statutes purporting to displace an existing mortgage on the land or building are probably valid as to prospective, invalid as to retrospective, operation. Statutes giving mechanics' lien priority as to building or improvement encounter difficulties of enforcement.**

Mechanic lien prior in time

Turning to the problem of priority between mortgages and mechanics' liens, the rules applicable to ordinary mortgages will be considered first. It is well-settled in probably every jurisdiction that if the mechanics' lien has attached to the property first it prevails over a subsequent mortgage on it. This applies to both the land and the improvement.[26]

Here, of course, we have to refer back to the rules determining when mechanics' liens attach and to note again that the mortgagee who takes a mortgage in most jurisdictions cannot rely upon an examination of the records but must make investigation outside of them to discover and determine factual matters on tests that not infrequently are far from definite.[27]

Mortgage before mechanics' lien

Equally true as a general rule, so far as the land itself as distinct from the improvement is concerned, is that a mortgage that is promptly recorded will prevail over any subsequent mechanics' lien that may arise. If the prior mortgage is unrecorded the later mechanics' lien cannot displace it as a *bona fide* purchaser under the recording acts for he is not so considered.[28] However, statutes requiring recordation as against creditors seem to include mechanics' lien claimants.[29]

24. E. g., N.J.S.A. 2A:44–69, Wyoming, Comp.Stats., Wyo.Stat.1957, § 29–3.

25. See note, 1933, 22 Cal.L.Rev. 312, 317, 319, 320.

See also Note, 1952, Wash.U.L.Q., 453; Foreclosing a Mechanic's Lien on an Equitable Interest, 1954, 38 Marq.L.Rev. 46; Boyer, Real Property Law, in Survey of Florida Law: 1953–1955, 10 Miami L. Rev. 389, commenting on Tremont Co. v. H. A. Paasche, Fla.1955, 81 So.2d 489, holding that a vendor's interest is subject to a mechanic's lien when the vendor requires as a condition of the sale the construction of improvements by the vendee.

26. See 1928, Handbook, Comm.Un.State Laws, 518–522 for a summary of state laws. See also 1942, 29 Va.L.Rev. 121, 127; 1927, 36 Yale L.J. 129, 131.

See Million, Lesar, Martz, 1959 Annual Survey of American Law: Real and Personal Property, 1960, 35 N.Y.U.L.Rev. 427, 449. However, the commencement of a mechanic's lien foreclosure against only the owner of property and not also against the trustee or the subsequent holder of a trust deed is not effective to preserve the lien and to prevail over the rights of interested persons not named, as

parties within the statutory period of the foreclosure of the lien. Riley v. Peters, 1961, 194 Cal. App.2d 296, 15 Cal.Rptr. 41.

27. See preceding section. "It may be that the person who takes a mortgage upon realty whereon a building is in process of erection assumes some risks that he cannot accurately measure. But so the law is written. Nor is there any great hardship in it. The mechanic or materialman is entitled to no lien until he has augmented the value of the property, and then only to the amount, theoretically and presumptively, of such augmented value. This increased value of his security is directly beneficial to the mortgagee. It is true that to save his mortgage lien he may be required to make an increased investment in the security, but the increased investment is measured by the increased value. One lien or the other must be superior, and the legislature, in its wisdom, has seen proper to require that the mortgagee should take care of the mechanic's lien —usually insignificant in amount as compared with the mortgage—rather than that the mechanic, often a day laborer, should take care of the mortgage of the capitalist." Haxtun Steam-Heater Co. v. Gordon, 1891, 2 N.D. 246, 254, 50 N.W. 708, 710, 33 Am. St.Rep. 776, Parks, Cas.Morts., 189. See also Hanna, Cas.Security, 3d ed., 804.

28. Fletcher v. Kelly, 1893, 88 Iowa, 475, 55 N.W. 474, 21 L.R.A. 347; Mathwig v. Mann, 1897, 96 Wis. 213, 71 N.W. 105, 65 Am.St.Rep. 47. Cf. Maine v. Waterloo Sav. Bank, 1924, 198 Iowa, 16, 199 N.W. 414.

29. McLaughlin v. Green, 1873, 48 Miss. 175; Thielman v. Carr, 1874, 75 Ill. 385; Gause v. Venango Construction Co., 1914, 188 Ill.App. 130; Landreth

And mechanics' lien laws themselves specifically provide for the lien to have priority over unrecorded mortgages of which the claimant had no notice.[30] In addition, of course, the prior mortgagee may be postponed because of a subordination agreement[31] or by an estoppel[32] but these are general principles.

Statutory priority of mechanics' liens over prior mortgages

Statutory attempts to make the subsequent mechanics' lien prior as to the property covered by a mortgage already existing at the time the statute was enacted would pretty clearly be invalid.[33] And this has been held to be true even where the work was done by the state and was a proper exercise of the police power so far as the mortgagor-owner of the property was concerned.[34] When the statute is to operate merely prospectively to prefer mechanics' liens over existing mortgages not only as to the improvement or the additional value of the property[35] resulting from the improvement, but as to the land and existing buildings, it would seem that the same result should be reached.[36]

When it comes to allocating priority as to the building or improvement we face quite a different situation and two lines of authority. It is familiar learning previously noted[37] that all accessions to the mortgaged land such as new buildings, additions to old ones, or other permanent improvements of the land "feed" the mortgage. Following this line of strict property law reasoning, one view is that a prior mortgage on the land before the mechanics' lien attaches will be prior not only as to the land itself but also the improvement added by the work and materials of the mechanics' lien claimants.[38] This result seems an unjustifiable enrichment of the prior encumbrancer of the land.[39]

Machinery Co. v. Roney, Adm'r, 1914, 185 Mo.App. 474, 171 S.W. 681 (conditional sales recording act).

30. See, e. g., West's Ann.Cal.Code Civ.Proc. § 1188.1. A similar provision was inserted in the Uniform Mech.Lien Act, § 21. See also 1928 Handbook, supra note 8.

31. See § 212, supra.

32. Ash v. Honig, C.C.A.N.Y.1933, 62 F.2d 793, certiorari denied 288 U.S. 614, 53 S.Ct. 405, 77 L.Ed. 988, see §§ 191, 210, 211, supra.

33. Meyer v. Berlandi, 1888, 39 Minn. 438, 40 N.W. 513, 1 L.R.A. 777, 12 Am.St.Rep. 663. See 1939, 39 Col.L.Rev. 889, 890; cf. § 205, infra in respect to tax liens.

34. Central Savings Bank v. City of N. Y., 1939, 279 N.Y. 266, 18 N.E.2d 151, 121 A.L.R. 607, noted in 1939, 39 Col.L.Rev. 889; 1939, 8 Fordham L.Rev. 384, holding unconstitutional a New York statute providing that when a multiple dwelling fell into such disrepair as to menace life or health, and the owner or mortgagee refused to make repairs, the State might do so, and file a mechanics' lien for the expense, which should be prior to any existing mortgage.

35. Wimberly v. Mayberry, 1891, 94 Ala. 240, 10 So. 157, 14 L.R.A. 305; see 1931, 121 A.L.R. 616.

36. "Mechanics' liens are not peculiar in any way so that they may claim exemption from the general rule that existing priority of lien cannot in the face of the contract clause be displaced by statute." 1939, 39 Col.L.Rev. 889, 892. See Meyer v. Berlandi, 1888, 39 Minn. 438, 444, 40 N.W. 513, 1 L.R.A. 777, 12 Am.St.Rep. 663. Priority of Repair Liens over Existing Mortgages—Proposed Legislation, 1939, 39 Col.L.Rev. 889; 1939, 121 A.L.R. 616. But contra, Gleissner v. Hughes, 1923, 153 La. 133, 95 So. 529; see Eastin, Priorities Between Mortgages and Mechanics' Liens, 1935, 36 U.Mo.Bull.Law Ser. 48, pp. 10, 23. The matter is however, largely academic because few states have statutes which purport to have such an operation and it is doubtful whether the courts would so construe them. Id.

37. See IV Am.L.Prop. § 16.38.

38. In California, it was held in English v. Olympic Auditorium, Inc., 1933, 217 Cal. 631, 20 P.2d 946, 87 A.L.R. 1281, commented on in, 1934, 22 Cal.L.Rev. 312, that mechanics' lien claimants had priority as to the improvement by virtue of a provision in the state constitution, over a lessor who had authorized the construction of the building but had posted notice of non-responsibility and had expressly stipulated that the expense was to be borne by the lessee, that the improvement was not removable by the lessee, and that mechanics' liens should not affect the rights of the lessor in the building. Nevertheless, it was later held that liens of a prior recorded mortgage and deed of trust of land were superior to mechanics' liens both as to the land and the building erected upon it. San Pedro Lumber Co. v. Wilson, 1935, 4 Cal.App.2d 41, 40 P.2d 605 (Supreme Court hearing denied March 21, 1935), noted, 1935, 23 Cal.L.Rev. 636. See note, 1939, 8 Ford.L.Rev. 384.

39. See 1925, 39 Harv.L.Rev. 384; 1926, 36 Yale L.J. 129.

The other line of statutes, while it preserves the earlier mortgagee's priority on the land gives the preference on the building or improvement to the mechanics' lien claimant. The general theory behind these enactments is that since the lienor created this value by his work or materials he should have the first claim to repayment out of what he has created; and that the prior mortgagee of the land cannot, in justice, complain at being deprived of priority in a windfall for which he paid nothing since he is just as well off as he would have been if the addition had never been made. Such statutes have been uniformly held valid not only as to mortgages taken after the statute was enacted,[40] but even as to a mortgage antedating the statute.[41] The only questions that arise are as to enforcement.

The improvement may consist of an entirely new addition, or it may consist merely in alterations or additions to existing structures or other improvements, in which latter case the possibility of severance of the new from the old in any practicable manner is almost certain to be out of the question, and, equally, no apportionment of value could be made on any very acceptable basis. Further, the improvement itself, although wholly new, may be a building or other structure possible of severance and removal without important damage to the realty, or it may consist of a sidewalk, a road, a well, a ditch, or something else which is either incapable of being removed at all or, if so, only by acts such as breaking up a concrete sidewalk which will destroy the improvement and may damage the land itself so as to reduce its value below what it was before the improvement was made. In view of these problems it is not remarkable that there should be a variety of solutions to the question of how the mechanics' lien claimant should enforce his priority on the improvement. One of these methods is by a separate sale and removal of the improvement, a result which is satisfactory enough when severance is both feasible and will not result in a considerable diminution in value of the building or improvement. But where severance is impossible, to insist upon removal as the only remedy available is merely to wipe out the priority altogether, a result reached by courts under some statutes where enforcement in this way is the only one for which provision is made.[42] Even where severance is physically feasible but will cause a serious impairment of value, to so limit the remedy will result in an undesirable and unnecessary destruction of property.[43] Recognizing this, some courts under such circumstances may order a sale of the entire prop-

---

40. Wimberly v. Mayberry, 1891, 94 Ala. 240, 10 So. 157, 14 L.R.A. 305; see 1939, 121 A.L.R. 616, 618.

First Nat. Bank of Anchorage v. Vasey, 1953, 14 Alaska 414, 114 F.Supp. 913 (mechanics' lien on improvement to existing building prior to existing recorded mortgage where no assertion that enforcement would diminish security of the mortgage). Drake Lumber Co. v. Paget Mortgage Co., 1954, 203 Or. 66, 274 P.2d 804. In Samms v. Chicago Title & Trust Co., 1953, 349 Ill.App. 413, 111 N.E.2d 172, commented on in Survey of Illinois Law, 1952–1953, 32 Chi.-Kent L.Rev. 78, there was a government lien for taxes between a recorded prior mortgage and the mechanics lien, so that it involved a question of circuity. On the problem of the circuity of a lien see IV Am.L.Prop. § 17.33.

41. Dunham Lumber Co. v. Gresz, 1942, 71 N.D. 491, 2 N.W.2d 175, 141 A.L.R. 60.

42. Johnson v. Puritan Min. & Mill Co., 1896, 19 Mont. 30, 47 P. 337; Fleming-Gilchrist Constr. Co. v. McGonigle, 1935, 338 Mo. 56, 89 S.W.2d 15, 107 A.L.R. 1003; see Eastin, Priorities Between Mortgages and Mechanics' Liens, 1935, 36 U.Mo.Bull. No. 1, 48 Law Ser. 5, 24; 1937, 107 A.L.R. 1012, 1013. But the same result has been reached where a sale of the entire property was permissible. The court construed the priority of the lien on the improvement to apply only where it was removable without waste, and in a series of decisions the court generally found that such removal was impossible. See, 1932, 17 Iowa L.Rev. 516, 519; 1926, 15 Geo.L.J. 477.

43. E. g., Grand Opera House Co. v. McGuire, 1894, 14 Mont. 558, 37 P. 607. In Bitter v. Mouat Lumber Co., 1897, 10 Colo.App. 307, 51 P. 519, affirmed 27 Colo. 120, 59 P. 403, where the loss that would be caused by removal was not clearly brought out, it was held that there must be sale and removal of the improvements. And Ecker Bros. v. Jones, 1960, 186 Cal.App.2d 775, 9 Cal.Rptr. 335, held that a landowner could compel sale and removal within twenty days after the sale of a building subject to a mechanic's lien which did not extend to the land despite the statute's giving a creditor ten years to enforce his judgment.

erty and then apportion the fund.[44] In other states the lienor's only method is this last one.[45] When it is employed, the usual measure of apportionment is first to ascertain the value of the land without the improvements and then determine the extent to which the improvements have enhanced the value of the property, this enhancement in value,[46] not the original cost of services or materials or the value of the improvement considered apart from the land,[47] being the value of the improvement. The property is then sold and the proceeds "apportioned to what shall be designated a building and lot fund, in the proportion which the value of the improvements and the lots, as found by the court, bear to each other. These funds shall be applied upon the respective claims in the order or priority they have been decreed liens upon the property from which such funds have been realized."[48] Another method of apportionment is to deduct from the proceeds of the sale the estimated value of the land without the improvement and pay that to the mortgagee, with the residue of the sale proceeds going to the lien claimants.[49] One objection to either of these two last methods is that the senior encumbrancer may be forced to foreclose even though his debt is not yet due,[50] and it should be subject to the limitation that his objection could prevent it. A second defect is the difficulty of making the valuations demanded by the rule as the basis of apportionment.[51] A still different method is followed in Virginia. Under the statute there [52] the mortgage is a first encumbrance on the land and a second one on the improvement, which, as frequently is provided, includes sufficient of the land for its necessary use and enjoyment.[53] The mechanics' lien is first on the improvement but second on the rest of the property. The mortgagee cannot be forced to foreclose or accept payment of less than the amount of his mortgage debt.[54] On the other hand, the mechanics' lien claimant is not barred from foreclosing and selling the entire property. But unless the mortgagee joins in the foreclosure, the buyer on foreclosure sale takes it subject to the mortgage.[55]

---

44. Atkinson v. Colorado Title & Trust Co., 1915, 59 Colo. 528, 151 P. 457; Joralmon v. McPhee, 1903, 31 Colo. 26, 71 P. 419, semble. In Morrison v. State Trust Co., Tex.Civ.App.1925, 274 S.W. 341, discussed in note, 1926, 39 Harv.L.Rev. 384, under a statute providing for sale and removal of encumbrances by mechanics' lien claimants but with a stipulation that any prior encumbrance on the land be not affected thereby, the Texas court ordered the entire property sold and the proceeds prorated in a case where the improvement (a pavement) could not be separated from the land without destroying it and damaging the freehold. Cf. Fleming-Gilchrist Construction Co. v. McGonigle, 1935, 338 Mo. 56, 89 S. W.2d 15, 107 A.L.R. 1003.

Under a statute giving the mechanics' lien claimant priority on the improvement over existing liens on the land, and providing for separate sale and removal of the improvement, an Oregon decision reversed a decree giving the lien priority in the proceeds of the sale of the land but gave no directions as to allocation of the proceeds in case the building had no takers at the sale. Drake Lumber Co. v. Paget Mortgage Co., 1954, 203 Or. 66, 274 P.2d 804 commented on in Updike, Mortgages, in 1954 Annual Survey of American Law, 1955, 30 N.Y.U.L. Rev. 805, 807.

45. Some statutes specifically so provide. Ill.Rev. Stat.1967, c. 82, § 16; Bradley v. Simpson, 1879, 93 Ill. 93.

46. Wimberly v. Mayberry & Co., 1891, 94 Ala. 240, 10 So. 157, 14 L.R.A. 305; Bradley v. Simpson, 1879, 93 Ill. 93.

47. Cf. Joralmon v. McPhee, 1903, 31 Colo. 26, 71 P. 419.

48. Id. at 39, 71 P. at 423.

49. Fidelity Loan & Trust Co. v. Dennis, 1896, 93 Va. 504, 25 S.E. 546.

50. Smith v. Shaffer, 1877, 46 Md. 573. See Joralmon v. McPhee, supra note 47. The objecting mortgagee here was a junior mortgagee but the senior mortgagee wished to foreclose. The court said that if it were not for this fact the objection would have merit.

51. See, 1925, 39 Harv.L.Rev. 384, 385.

52. Va.Code of 1950, §§ 43-1 to 43-3, 43-20, 43-21.

53. See n. 52 supra.

54. In which case there would be apportionment of the proceeds.

55. Federal Land Bank of Baltimore v. Clinchfield Lumber & Supply Co., 1939, 171 Va. 118, 198 S.E. 437.

Most of the existing statutes make no specific provision for the repair situation[56] and the courts in interpreting them hold that the statutes in speaking of buildings and improvements mean a new separate and distinct building or erection, not merely improvements or repairs of existing structures, when it is a question of giving the lien priority over an earlier mortgage on the property.[57] In some states, however, repairs are specifically included.[58] Where the priority of the mechanics' lien extends to repairs, there is some authority allowing a severance where that is possible,[59] and if not, a sale and apportionment.[60] The objections to this method are especially strong in cases of repairs,[61] and in some states, even in the face of an express statutory provision specifically including repairs in the priority rule, incapability of severance of the improvement has been held to destroy the priority of the mechanics' lien.[62]

MECHANICS' LIENS—PURCHASE MONEY AND BUILDING LOAN MORTGAGES

216. Purchase money mortgages prevail over mechanics' liens, except, in some states, if the vendee is bound to build by contract with the mortgagee, or builds with his consent or knowledge. Building loan mortgages have priority if given before attachment of the lien and if advances are obligatory. Their priority is often extended by statute.

Purchase money mortgages vs. mechanics' liens

As a general rule purchase money mortgages, whether in favor of the grantor[63] or a third party,[64] prevail over mechanics' liens even though these arose under contracts that antedated the mortgage. The reasons ordinarily advanced for the primacy of the mortgage for the purchase price[65] are sometimes supplemented here by construing the me-

---

56. See, 1931, 41 Yale L.J. 271, 277.

57. E. g., Equitable Life Ins. Co. v. Slye, 1877, 45 Iowa 615. See Eastin, Priorities Between Mortgages and Mechanics' Liens, 1935, 36 U.Mo.Bull. No. 1, 48 Law Ser. 5, 24; 1932, 17 Iowa L.Rev. 516, 519.

58. See, e. g., Ill.Rev.Stat.1967 (Smith-Hurd), c. 82, § 2; 1928, Handbook, Comm.Un.State Laws, 473 et seq., 518–522.

59. Cameron v. Truehart, Tex.Civ.App.1914, 165 S.W. 58.

60. Wimberly v. Mayberry & Co., 1891, 94 Ala. 240, 10 So. 157, 14 L.R.A. 305; Morrison v. State Trust Co., Tex.Civ.App.1925, 274 S.W. 341.

61. See 1926, 36 Yale L.J. 129, 131.

62. "The statute intended that such priority of liens should cover such structures, additions, or repairs as may be detached from the land or the permanent buildings thereon without diminishing the value they had at the time a prior mortgage was recorded. This appears to be a reasonable and equitable construction to be placed upon the statute." Bratzel v. Stafford, 1932, 140 Or. 661, 664, 14 P.2d 454, 455, rehearing denied 140 Or. 661, 16 P.2d 991, commented on, 1933, 12 Or.L.Rev. 352; Johnson v. Puritan Mining Co., 1896, 19 Mont. 30, 47 P. 337.

"The **argument** that a materialman who builds a chicken house, coal bin, or digs a cistern or well equipped with pump, and windmill upon a valuable city homestead, which is already incumbered, is entitled to have the homestead sold and the proceeds prorated, because his improvement is entire and separate, while another lienholder, who adds a story or puts a new roof on the same house, is to be

postponed to the prior lien because his work and material do not constitute a separate betterment, does not strike us as being sound." Morrison v. State Trust Co., Tex.Civ.App.1925, 274 S.W. 341, 345.

63. Green v. Saxton, 1923, 196 Iowa, 1086, 196 N.W. 27, and cases cited in succeeding footnotes. See Eastin, Priorities Between Mortgages and Mechanics' Liens, 1935, 48 Law Ser.Mo.Bull. 5, 17; notes, 1930, 9 Or.L.Rev. 520; 1926, 36 Yale L.J. 129, 133; 1928, 2 Cin.L.Rev. 205; 1943, 29 Va.L.Rev. 491, 497. See also 1931, 72 A.L.R. 1516; 1929, 58 A.L.R. 911; 1936, 102 A.L.R. 233. Georgia, due to a peculiar statute, Ga.Code, Michie, 1926, §§ 3352–3 (see Ga. Code, §§ 67–2001, 67–2002), is at variance with the law generally and gives the mechanics' lien priority over purchase money mortgages. Tanner v. Bell, 1878, 61 Ga. 584; Bradley v. Cassells, 1903, 117 Ga. 517, 43 S.E. 857; Baisden & Co. v. Holmes-Hartsfield Co., 1908, 4 Ga.App. 122, 60 S.E. 1031. A similar result is reached in the case of a grantor's lien. E. g., Kuschel v. Hunter, 1897, 5 Cal.Unrep. 793, 50 P. 397.

See Washington Case Law—1959: Security Transactions, 1960, 35 Wash.L.Rev. 232, 233, commenting on Nelson v. Bailey, 1959, 154 Wash. 153, 33 P.2d 757, holding that the purchase money mortgagee prevails if the lien claimant has had notice.

64. New Jersey Bldg. Loan & Ins. Co. v. Bachelor, 1896, 54 N.J.Eq. 600, 35 A. 745; Bond v. Westine, 1929, 128 Kan. 370, 278 P. 12. Cf. note, 1917, 30 Harv.L.Rev. 293 (purchase money mortgage to person other than grantor).

65. Malmgren v. Phinney, 1892, 50 Minn. 457, 52 N. W. 915, 18 L.R.A. 753; Neil v. Kinney, 1860, 11 Ohio St. 58. See § 213, supra.

chanics' lien statute as not including a contracting vendee in possession within the meaning of "owner" of an interest in the property to which the lien could attach.[66] There is a divergence in the authorities on the effect of contracts between the vendor and purchaser requiring the latter to build,[67] some holding that the purchase money mortgage still prevails,[68] others deciding in favor of the mechanics' lien[69] on rather dubious theories of agency, implied subordination, or estoppel. Some of the cases go further[70] and prefer the mechanics' lien if the vendor has consented to the construction work,[71] and a few do so even if he merely has knowledge that the vendee is building on the land.[72] A compromise solution gives the mechanics' lien priority to the extent of the value added by the work.[73] And, in a few states, if the vendor has knowledge of the work and fails to post and/or record a notice of non-responsibility, his interest under the contract of sale and the purchase money mortgage that is later taken will be subjected to the priority of the mechanics' lien.[74]

An agreement by the purchase money mortgagee to subordinate his mortgage to that of one given to a lender of money for construction does not, in addition, subordinate it to mechanics' liens that should have been paid out of the construction loan.[75]

Building loan mortgages vs. mechanics' liens

Mortgages given under building loan contracts by which the mortgagor-owner receives his loans in installments are common and come into frequent collision with mechanics' liens.[76] Apart from qualifications to be noted, they are one of the important va-

66. E. g., Saunders v. Bennett, 1893, 160 Mass. 48, 49, 35 N.E. 111, 39 Am.St.Rep. 456, "[The vendee in possession under a contract of purchase] cannot be regarded as the owner, within the meaning of the statute, before the moment of the conveyance to him, notwithstanding his subsequent acquisition of title." See Wilson v. Lubke, 1903, 176 Mo. 210, 75 S.W. 602, 603, 98 Am.St.Rep. 503. Russell v. Grant, 1894, 122 Mo. 161, 26 S.W. 958, 43 Am.St.Rep. 563; Getto v. Friend, 1891, 46 Kan. 24, 26 P. 473; Hillhouse v. Pratt, 1901, 74 Conn. 113, 49 A. 905. A *fortiori* the same is true if the contracting party is not yet in possession and has only an option to purchase, Hayward Lumber & Inv. Co. v. Starley, 1932, 124 Cal.App. 283, 12 P.2d 66, or is only negotiating for the purchase of the property. Rochford v. Rochford, 1905, 188 Mass. 108, 74 N.E. 299, 108 Am. St.Rep. 465. See 1931, 72 A.L.R. 1516, 1525.

But Sontag v. Abbott, 1959, 140 Colo. 351, 344 P.2d 961, commented on in 1960, 58 Mich.L.Rev. 1072, held that the mechanic's lien for materials ordered by an option holder was prior to a subsequently issued purchase money mortgage executed the same day as the conveyance by the vendor to the optionee, the court saying that an optionee is "owner" within the meaning of the statute and that a purchase money mortgage is not excepted.

67. See, 1943, 29 Va.L.Rev. 491, 497; 1926, 36 Yale L.J. 129, 134; 1929, 58 A.L.R. 911 et seq.; 1936, 102 A.L.R. 233 et seq. See, semble, in case of improvements by a lessee, 1929, 28 Mich.L.Rev. 321; 1933, 22 Cal.L.Rev. 312.

68. Franklin Soc. for Home Building & Savings v. Thornton, 1916, 85 N.J.Eq. 525, 96 A. 921; Fish v. Anstey Constr. Co., 1911, 71 Misc. 2, 130 N.Y.S. 927; Chicago Lumber Co. v. Schweiter, 1891, 45 Kan. 207, 25 P. 592.

69. Jones v. Osborne, 1899, 108 Iowa, 409, 79 N.W. 143; Carew v. Stubbs, 1892, 155 Mass. 549, 30 N.E. 219.

See Lacey, Creditors' Rights and Security Transactions—1960 Tennessee Survey, 1960, 13 Vand.L.Rev. 1055, commenting on Rowland v. Lowe, 1959, 46 Tenn.App. 60, 326 S.W.2d 681, holding that a mechanic's lien prevailed over a prior vendor's lien even though the contract requiring the purchaser to make improvements also provided that there should never be any mechanic's lien on the property sold.

70. See 1931, 72 A.L.R. 1516, 1520, 1523.

71. Hill v. Gill, 1889, 40 Minn. 441, 42 N.W. 294; White v. Kincade, 1915, 95 Kan. 466, 148 P. 607, Ann.Cas.1916B, 667.

72. Buckstaff v. Dunbar, 1883, 15 Neb. 114, 17 N.W. 345; cf. Allen v. Rowe, 1890, 19 Or. 188, 23 P. 901.

73. Braden Co. v. Lancaster Lumber Co., 1934, 170 Okl. 30, 38 P.2d 575, 102 A.L.R. 230; City Realty & Mortgage Co. v. Tallapoosa Lumber Co., 1935, 231 Ala. 238, 164 So. 55.

74. West's Ann.Cal.Code Civ.Proc. § 1183.1; Minn. Stat.Ann. § 514.06; Avery v. Clark, 1891, 87 Cal. 619, 25 P. 919, 22 Am.St.Rep. 272. See Myrhe, Fiction, Fallacy and Facts in Relation to "Implied Consent" Provisions of Certain Mechanics' Lien Statutes, 1948, 32 Minn.L.Rev. 559; 1933, 22 Cal.L.Rev. 312, 319; 1929, 58 A.L.R. 911, 944; 1936, 102 A.L.R. 233, 240.

75. Community Lumber Co. v. Chute, Cal.1930, 292 P. 1069; Hoagland v. Lowe, 1894, 39 Neb. 397, 58 N.W. 197; Watson Land etc., Co. v. Salyers, 1916, 247 Pa. 454, 93 A. 495, Ann.Cas.1916B, 672.

76. See Hanna, Cases on Security, 3d ed., 804.

rieties of mortgages to secure future advances and are governed by the rules of such mortgages, a matter previously discussed at some length.[77] Broadly speaking, if the mortgage is for obligatory advances and is prior to the attachment of the mechanics' lien, it will prevail over it as to all advances. If the advances are optional, it will be prior only as to advances made up to the time of notice of the attachment of the lien.[78] Also, if it were treated like an ordinary mortgage, even though it were earlier than the mechanics' lien, it would be postponed to it in some jurisdictions so far as the building or improvement is concerned. So, too, it would be inferior to the mechanics' lien, regardless of whether the advances were obligatory or optional, as to the entire mortgage if the lien attached before the mortgage had its inception. By statute or decision, however, the building construction mortgage wins out over the mechanics' lien under certain circumstances where, if ordinary rules were followed, it would be postponed to it. Thus it has been held in a jurisdiction where by statute a subsequent mechanics' lien has a superior claim on the building, that the construction loan mortgage is prior as to both the land and the building with respect to the money actually used to pay for construction.[79] Statutes have also given complete priority to the building loan mortgage,[80] or only to the extent of advances made prior to the filing of the lien.[81] But the more desirable type of statutes gives priority to the building loan mortgage but makes that priority depend on the rightful application of the building loan installments.[82]

CONDITIONAL SALES OF CHATTELS ANNEXED TO REALTY—INTRODUCTION

217. The vendor of a chattel which is subsequently annexed to realty frequently retains a security interest in it. As a result questions of priority between it and mortgages of the land arise. In such cases, because of the confusion in the cases and the difficulties of applying them to extremely varied fact-patterns, prediction of outcome in particular cases is not easy.

Related to the problem of mechanics' liens[83] is that of chattels sold by a vendor who retains security interest in them for the purchase price although they are subsequently annexed to realty which is, or after becomes,

---

77. See §§ 113–122, supra.

78. See note, 1930, 14 Minn.L.Rev. 695; 1920, 5 A.L.R. 398; 1928, 53 A.L.R. 580; 1932, 76 A.L.R. 1402. See also Eastin, Priorities Between Mortgages and Mechanics' Liens, 1935, 48 Law Ser.Mo.Bull. 5, 21.

79. Joralman v. McPhee, 1903, 31 Colo. 26, 71 P. 419. Chauncey v. Dyke Bros., C.C.A.Ark.1902, 119 F. 1, 55 C.C.A. 579. "The theory is that the building loan mortgagee is performing a service in the construction of the building just as much as the mechanics who perform labor or furnish materials. It is submitted a more equitable arrangement would be to equalize the claims of the building loan mortgagee and the mechanic lien claimant as to the building rather than to prefer the mortgagee." 1926, 36 Yale L.J. 129, 133.

80. See Ark.Stats. § 51–605.

81. D.C.Code, Encyclopedia § 38–109.

82. N.Y.Const.Laws, Cahill, 1930, c. 34, § 13(3) (now McKinney's Lien Law, § 13(3)); N.J.Stat.Ann. 2A:44–89; Lincoln Materials Co., Inc. v. Goodwin Const. Co., et al., 1930, 106 N.J.Eq. 326, 150 A. 829, commented on in 1931, 8 N.Y.U.L.Q.R. 333; Ohio R.C. § 1311.14; Knollman Lumber Co. v. Hillenbrand, 1940, 64 Ohio App. 549, 29 N.E.2d 61; see Magrish, Disbursment of Ohio Construction Mortgage Loans, 1938, 12 U.Cin.L.Rev. 1. See also, 1931, 41 Yale L.J. 271, 278. For a discussion of the New York statute, see 1929, 29 Col.L.Rev. 996, 999; 41 Col.L.Rev. 1269, discussing Cassino v. Yacewich, 1941, 261 App.Div. 685, 27 N.Y.S.2d 95; Cushman, The Proposed Uniform Mechanics'. Lien Law, 1932, 80 U.Pa.L.Rev. 1083, 1095; Kyser v. MacAdam, C. C.A.N.Y.1941, 117 F.2d 232.

The Oregon mechanics' lien statute has been construed to give the mechanics' lien priority on the improvement over all prior mortgages including building loan mortgages for future advances. Drake Lumber Co. v. Paget Mortgage Co., 1954, 203 Or. 66, 274 P.2d 804.

83. The conditional vendor of a fixture ordinarily will be able to qualify as the claimant of a mechanics' lien. But the filing of a mechanics' lien is such an election as to bar the right to repossess under the conditional sale. Heating & Plumbing Finance Corp. v. Friedman, 1934, 264 N.Y. 285, 190 N. E. 641; Kirk v. Crystal, 1908, 118 App.Div. 32, 103 N.Y.S. 17, aff'd, 193 N.Y. 622, 86 N.E. 1126. Further the mechanics' lien is an unsatisfactory remedy to the seller of chattels. See 1937, 22 Cornell L.Q. 421.

subject to a mortgage. Before the general enactment of the Uniform Commercial Code,[84] the vendor of the chattel sold it on conditional sale or with a chattel mortgage taken for the purchase price.[85] In dealing with this problem the law as it existed prior to the enactment of statutory solutions will be considered first. Then the provisions of the Uniform Conditional Sales Act will be looked at. And finally the solutions in the Uniform Commercial Code will be covered.

There is an astonishing amount of litigation in the reports and discussion in legal periodicals on this question,[86] but, apart from the strong likelihood of having to resort to legal action in order to enforce his rights, it is of less concern to the mortgagee of the realty than are mechanics' liens. One reason is that, with exceptions to be noted, the governing rules either favor the land mortgagee or do not prejudice his legitimate interests to any great extent. For example, there is in no case any danger here of an earlier security interest of the land mortgagee in the land itself or a structure on it being displaced by any claim of the subsequent seller of the annexed chattel. Further the subject matter involved, even though frequently consisting of articles of very considerable size and value, does not often equal in importance, number of claims, and amounts those with which a mortgagee has to reckon in the case of mechanics' liens. Even so minimized the matter still looms rather large, partly because the clashes are so frequent, and a brief treatment of it is desirable. It might be added that a short statement presents difficulty because,

added to some complexity in the problems themselves, there is much confusion and diversity in the cases; and even when the applicable rule, principle, or standard is clear, there is practical difficulty in predicting its outcome when applied to an extremely varied set of fact-patterns. A major source of this difficulty and confusion is the necessity the courts have felt of determining as a prior question whether or not the annexed article has become a fixture.[87] This interjects a subject which, despite illuminating analyses by judges [88] and scholars,[89] is not inappropriately characterized as a morass. Into it we cannot venture even though the question whether an erstwhile chattel, for the purpose of adjusting the rights of disputing parties, should be treated as part of the land, or as a distinct object of property,[90] is a matter of frequent controversy in the law of mortgages.[91] Stand-

---

84. See § 220A, infra.

85. For the sake of simplicity of statement the term conditional sale will be used to cover both security devices except where it is necessary to differentiate between the two.

86. See not only the numerous references to notes and articles in legal periodicals cited in the following footnotes, but the great number of authorities listed and discussed by them. See also, notes and articles in Fryer, Readings on Personal Property, 3d ed., 970–1088, especially covering conditional sales of fixtures, 1024–1055.

87. "The books are full of decided cases upon the subject of fixtures, from the yearbooks down to the present time, and, strange to say, after all the ability that has been displayed upon this subject, no rule can be found that clearly defines the line where an article loses its legal quality as a chattel and assumes that of real estate." Capen v. Peckham, 1868, 35 Conn. 88, 92. See Teaff v. Hewitt, 1853, 1 Ohio St. 511, 524, 59 Am.Dec. 634.

88. E. g., the powerfully influential opinion of Bartly, C. J., in Teaff v. Hewitt, 1853, 1 Ohio St. 511, 59 Am.Dec. 634.

89. One of the most helpful is Bingham, Some Suggestions Concerning the Law of Fixtures, 1907, 7 Col.L.Rev. 1. See, also, Niles, The Intention Test in the Law of Fixtures (1934) 12 N.Y.Univ.L.Q.Rev. 66; Niles, The Rationale of the Law of Fixtures: English Cases, 1934, 11 N.Y.Univ.L.Q.Rev. 560; Luther, The Law of Fixtures as Affected by the Relationship of the Litigants, 1939, 23 Marq.L.Rev. 136; notes, 1920, 18 Mich.L.Rev. 405; 1935, 15 Boston U.L.Rev. 410 (Massachusetts law); 1913, 13 Col.L.Rev. 247; 1937, 21 Minn.L.Rev. 855; 1940, 19 Or.L.Rev. 152; 1947, 1 Ark.L.Rev. 300; 1940, 24 Marq.L.Rev. 166.
See also Kratovil, Fixtures and the Real Estate Mortgagee, 1948, 97 U. of Pa.L.Rev. 180 (taking, as one writer expressed it, "an unenthusiastic view of the achievements of Bingham").

90. This way of stating the problem seems better than discussing it in terms of fixture *vel non*. See Bingham, op. cit. supra at p. 5.

91. In the Uniform Conditional Sales Act, § 7, an attempt to state in more particular terms just what situation was being covered so as not to introduce

ing on the edge, however, we can see plainly enough a broad threefold grouping,[92] although the boundaries between them are blurred, and it is easy to observe that most of the trouble centers in the middle one.[93] On one side are those objects which by reason of their physical incorporation into the land or some improvement on it have so completely lost their identity as separate objects of property as to have become necessarily a part of the land, e. g., the brick, stone and plaster placed in the walls of a building.[94] This class seldom causes much difficulty. Clear on the opposite side is the group of certain chattels which by reason of their nature cannot be held to have become part of the land without doing violence to commonly prevailing conceptions.[95] It would seem that

here again we should be upon firm footing with a bright sharp boundary to guide us. Nevertheless, as we shall see later, New York, at least, has decided certain objects are in this area that would seem more properly[96] to fall in the middle ground, the majority of the court using what a vigorous dissent characterized as the "employment of an old-fashioned mold to give" to the objects in question "the outworn shape of movable chattels." [97] "Between the two classes of chattels, those which, after annexation, due to the inherent nature of the subject or the mode of annexation, remain personalty, and those which, due to the mode and purposes of annexation, conclusively become real estate, there was, at common law, a large class of movables which, after attachment, continued to be personal property, or became real estate, accordingly as the owner of the chattels and the owner of the real estate might have agreed." [98] This is the trouble zone. It is from this group that cases most frequently find their way into court. However, having made this quick survey of the territory, we shall assume that the chattel annexed to the land has been properly determined under the law of real property to be part of the realty or not part of it for the purpose in hand, and confine ourselves to the narrower question of the law of mortgages with which we are now immediately concerned.

Previously we have seen that when anything owned by the mortgagor is so annexed to the realty that under the law of real property it would be treated as part of the land it became a part of the mortgagee's security.[99] Here our inquiry is how far the re-

the whole question of whether the object was or was not a fixture, has not been marked by success. See Kleps, Uniformity *versus* Uniform Legislation: Conditional Sale of Fixtures, 1939, 24 Cornell L.Q. 394.

92. See Chasnov v. Marlane Holding Co., Inc., 1930, 137 Misc. 332, 244 N.Y.S. 455. See Storke and Sears, The Perennial Problem of Security Priority and Recordation, 1952, 24 Colo.L.Rev. 180, 204.

93. See §§ 38, 215, supra, and text, infra, this section.

94. Even here there may be occasional troublesome cases. How about a modern sky-scraper taken as a whole? See Bingham, op. cit. supra note 89 at p. 12, n. 1. "Professor Bogert, in section 66 of volume 2A, refers to certain cases dealing with goods so closely incorporated or united to land as to lose their legal existence or identity, and then states: 'The common law has long recognized that goods may be so closely united to land or so closely attached to it that no one will be allowed to assert that they any longer have any legal existence separate and distinct from the land. They are swallowed up or drowned in the realty.'" People's Savings & Trust Co. v. Munsert, 1933, 212 Wis. 449, 457, 249 N.W. 527, 531, 88 A.L.R. 1306, rehearing denied 212 Wis. 449, 250 N.W. 385, 88 A.L.R. 1306. See Madfes v. Beverly Devel. Corp., 1929, 251 N.Y. 12, 166 N.E. 787

95. "We can conceive of no circumstances under which chairs, tables, movable desks, stoves, tools, and ordinary vehicles could be classed as fixtures at all." Scudder v. Anderson, 1884, 54 Mich. 122, 125, 19 N.Y. 775. "Certain chattels have such a determinate character as movables that they remain personal property, after their annexation to real estate, independently of any agreement between the owner of the chattels and the owner of the realty

which so provides." Madfes v. Beverly Devel. Corp., supra, note 22 at 15, 166 N.E. at 788.

96. See text, infra.

97. Madfes v. Beverly Devel. Corp., supra note 94, 251 N.Y. at 18, 166 N.E. at 789.

98. Madfes v. Beverly Devel. Corp., supra note 94, 251 N.Y. at 15, 166 N.E. at 788.

99. "No one ever doubted that a mortgage of land bound a house subsequently built upon it, nor that

tention of a security interest in the annexed chattel by its vendor will be successful in preserving to him his claim to it in priority to the land mortgagee. On this, the cases fall naturally into two classes which will be considered separately: first, those in which the land mortgage precedes the conditional sale; second, those in which the conditional sale is the first transaction.

CONDITIONAL SALES OF CHATTELS ANNEXED TO REALTY—LAND MORTGAGE PRIOR TO CONDITIONAL SALE

218. Where the mortgage precedes the conditional sale of the fixture, the conditional vendor prevails by the weight of authority if removal of the chattel will not substantially injure the premises. Courts differ as to what constitutes damage. Under the Massachusetts rule the mortgagee always prevails—in theory. The results in decided cases are not substantially different from those in "majority jurisdictions." Construction mortgages, although not clearly formulated as a distinct basis for priority over the later conditional seller, seem to be one.

Massachusetts Rule. We turn first, then, to the question of title to chattels between the mortgagee of real estate and the vendor of chattels sold to the mortgagor under a conditional sale; the sale being subsequent to the real estate mortgage and the chattels having been affixed to the realty. There are two well-defined doctrines on the subject; one being directly opposed to the other.[1]

it bound anything originally personal which became afterwards part of the land." Hoyle v. Plattsburg & M. R. Co., 1873, 54 N.Y. 314, 323. See Winslow v. Merchants Ins. Co., 1842, 45 Mass. (4 Metc.) 306.

1. A vendor of realty under a contract of sale is treated like a prior mortgagee so far as his priority over a subsequent seller of chattels on conditional sale is concerned. See notes, 1934, 18 Minn.L.Rev. 812, 832; 1935, 19 Minn.L.Rev. 342; 1927, 11 Minn. L.Rev. 667, 1928, 13 Iowa L.Rev. 350, and 1927, 16 Geo.L.J. 120 (commenting on Des Moines Imp. Co. v. Holland Furnace Co., 1927, 204 Iowa, 274, 212 N. W. 551, in which the land vendor was preferred); 1936, 14 Tenn.L.Rev. 120. So also is a lessor of the land, whether claiming a lien or forfeiture. National Bank of Republic v. Wells-Jackson Corporation, 1934, 358 Ill. 356, 193 N.E. 215, 98 A.L.R. 618, commented on in notes, 1936, 34 Mich.L.Rev. 426;

One of these, law only in a few jurisdictions, is known as the Massachusetts rule.[2] The

1935, 9 U. of Cin.L.Rev. 197; 1935, 21 Va.L.Rev. 703; 1935, 1 John Marshall L.Q. 64; 1935, 98 A.L. R. 628. See notes, 1935, 48 Harv.L.Rev. 857; 1931, 3 Dak.L.Rev. 272. See also 1926, 45 A.L.R. 967. Cf. Francis H. Leggett & Co. v. Orangeburg Piggly Wiggly Co., 1935, 176 S.C. 449, 180 S.E. 483, commented on in, 1936, 45 Yale L.J. 523; 1935, 49 Harv.L.Rev. 144; 1936, 20 Minn.L.Rev. 436; 1940, 26 Va.L.Rev. 379; 1941, 25 Marq.L.Rev. 103. On the right of a tenant to remove fixtures as against a prior mortgagee, look at Standard Oil Co. v. La Crosse Super Auto Service, Inc., 1935, 217 Wis. 237, 258 N.W. 791, 99 A.L.R. 60, discussed in notes, 1935, 20 Iowa L.Rev. 849; 1936, 9 So.Cal.L.Rev. 416.

As to the right of the mortgagee of the land against a subsequent purchaser or chattel mortgagee of a fixture which was subject to the land mortgage, see notes, 1929, 78 U. of Pa.L.Rev. 269; 1934, 18 Marq. L.Rev. 263.

See § 220A, infra.

2. Clary v. Owen, 1860, 81 Mass. (15 Gray) 522; Waverley Co-op. Bank v. Haner, 1930, 273 Mass. 477, 173 N.E. 699; General Heat & Appliance Co. v. Goodwin, 1944, 316 Mass. 3, 54 N.E.2d 676; Gaunt v. Allen-Lane Co., 1929, 128 Me. 41, 145 A. 255, 73 A.L.R. 738, noted, 1929, 29 Col.L.Rev. 836. For collections of cases on this and the other problems of priorities between conditional vendors of fixtures and mortgagees of land, prior and subsequent, see notes in 1921, 13 A.L.R. 448; 1923, 23 A.L.R. 806; 1931, 73 A.L.R. 748; 1933, 111 A.L.R. 380; 1942, 141 A. L.R. 1290. The Federal courts also have followed it in cases involving railroads. Porter v. Pittsburg Steel Co., 1886, 122 U.S. 267, 7 S.Ct. 1206, 30 L.Ed. 1210; Phoenix Iron-Works Co. v. N. Y. Security & Trust Co., C.C.A.Ky.1897, 83 F. 757, 28 C.C.A. 76. These cases, because they make the test whether through annexation the chattel has become an integral part of the realty, have sometimes been regarded as a distinct category of cases which should be classed as an exception, analogous to the "institutional" test in New Jersey and the Pennsylvania "industrial plant" doctrine, to the general rule permitting removability if no material injury will result. See 1934, 18 Minn.L.Rev. 812, 825 n. 52, 828. The same result is reached in England, where, because of the absence of a recording system, the result is even more severe than in this country. Reynolds v. Ashby, 1903, 72 L.J.K.B.D. 51, affirmed [1904] A.C. 466; cf. Gough v. Wood & Co., [1894] 1 Q.B. 713, 10 Times L.R. 318.

For an excellent treatment of the railroad cases and the priority of their mortgages on after-acquired property and the limitations on that priority developed in the federal courts, see Gilmore, Security Interests in Personal Property, 1965, §§ 28.1–28.3. See also § 39, supra.

For discussion of the English law of priority between mortgagees of land and sellers of chattels, see Hollond, Equitable Liens Under Hire-Purchase Agreements, 1928, 3 Camb.L.J. 173; Niles, Rationale of

doctrine was originally based on the severely legalistic ground that the mortgagee got legal title and consequently acquired all additions which became a part of the realty,[3] the mortgagor having no power "by any agreement made with a third person after the execution of the mortgage, to give to such person the right to hold anything to be attached to the freehold, which as between mortgagor and mortgagee would become a part of the realty."[4] Logically, such a rationalization would restrict the doctrine to title states,[5] yet the same result was reached in a lien theory jurisdiction.[6] It has been limited in Massachusetts to cases in which the mortgage was recorded.[7] The question of injury

to the mortgaged premises by removal, however, has had no significance in determining the rights of the parties.[8] The rule is a harsh one, giving to the mortgagee when strictly applied some very handsome windfalls.[9] It is not surprising, therefore, to find triers of fact, in avoiding its rigors, going to extremes in declaring heavy and firmly affixed objects not to be fixtures at all.[10] The decisions may have done justice in the individual cases but the resulting precedents are very confusing and, consequently, predictability is low.

A trenchant comment on the Massachusetts rule has been made by an outstanding scholar. "The existence of a 'minority rule' under which the truth of a proposition which is apparent to most courts is stubbornly denied by a few is always a matter of interest: Not infrequently an investigation * * *

the Law Fixtures: English Cases, 1934, 11 N.Y. Univ.L.Q.Rev. 560, 584; notes, 1905, 39 Ir.L.T. 131; 1903, 16 Harv.L.Rev. 531.

3. "The lien of the mortgage covers not only the fixtures installed at the inception of the mortgage but those subsequently installed. After-acquired fixtures are deemed to feed the mortgage by accession." Friedman, The Scope of Mortgage Liens on Fixtures and Personal Property in New York, 1938, 7 Ford.L.Rev. 331, 340. See § 38, supra.

4. Clary v. Owen, 1860, 81 Mass. (15 Gray) 522, 525. See Niles, The Intention Test in the Law of Fixtures, 1934, 12 N.Y.U.L.Q.R. 66, 73, 91.

5. See Merchants' Nat. Bank of Crookston v. Stanton, 1893, 55 Minn. 211, 220, 56 N.W. 521, 43 Am.St. Rep. 491.

6. Fuller-Warren Co. v. Harter, 1901, 110 Wis. 80, 85 N.W. 698, 53 L.R.A. 603, 84 Am.St.Rep. 867. The adoption in Wisconsin of the U.C.S.A. altered the law on this point. People's Sav. & Trust Co. v. Munsert, 1933, 212 Wis. 449, 249 N.W. 527, 88 A.L. R. 1306, rehearing denied 212 Wis. 449, 250 N.W. 385, 88 A.L.R. 1306.

7. Security Coop. Bank v. Holland Furnace Co., 1931, 274 Mass. 389, 174 N.E. 721.

Mass.Laws (1912) c. 271, § 1, providing that "no conditional sale * * * shall be valid as against any mortgage * * * unless * * * recorded * * *," has been held inapplicable to prior recorded mortgages of realty. Therefore, the ordinary rule preferring such a mortgagee over a subsequent conditional vendor of a chattel annexed to the land governs even though the chattel could be removed without substantial damage and the sales contract was recorded. Waverley Co-Operative Bank v. Haner, 1930, 273 Mass. 477, 173 N.E. 699, discussed in note, 1931, 29 Mich.L.Rev. 1086. Cf. Medford Trust Co. v. Priggen Steel Garage Co., 1930, 273 Mass. 349, 174 N.E. 126, noted, 1931, 5 So. Cal.L.Rev. 71 (holding that a portable steel garage,

although not within the terms of the Massachusetts act, remained personal property, and therefore the subsequent vendor prevailed over the prior mortgagee of the realty. Cf. also People's Savings & Trust Co. v. Munsert, supra, note 6, p. 369.

See note, 1932, Boston U.L.Rev. 694 for a general discussion of the operation of the Massachusetts act, which is limited to certain types of annexed chattels. See, 1947, 27 Bost.U.L.Rev. 317 for a general discussion of the Massachusetts law on the priority between realty mortgagees and conditional vendors of fixtures.

8. Greene v. Lampert, 1931, 274 Mass. 386, 174 N.E. 669; Gaunt v. Allen-Lane Co., 1929, 128 Me. 41, 145 A. 255, 73 A.L.R. 738 and note 748; Fuller-Warren Co. v. Harter, 1901, 110 Wis. 80, 85 N.W. 698, 53 L. R.A. 603, 84 Am.St.Rep. 867 and note 877.

9. Bankers' & Merchants' Credit Co. v. Harlem etc., Ass'n, 1931, 160 Md. 230, 153 A. 64, metal garages; Gaunt v. Allen-Lane Co., 1929, 128 Me. 41, 145 A. 255, 73 A.L.R. 738, woolen mill machinery; General Heat & Appliance Co. v. Goodwin, 1944, 316 Mass. 3, 54 N.E.2d 676, central heating plant.

10. Carpenter v. Walker, 1886, 140 Mass. 416, 5 N.E. 160, engine and boiler weighing 5600 pounds, and heavy planing and joining machinery fastened to the floor and connected with a central power shaft; Commercial Credit Corp. v. Gould, 1931, 275 Mass. 48, 175 N.E. 264, frigidaire system in apartment building, including compressor in basement with pipes to units in each apartment; Medford Trust Co. v. Priggen Steel Garage Co., 1930, 273 Mass. 349, 174 N.E. 126, sheet metal garages on cement pillars, one with cement floor; part of mortgage money even expressly advanced to pay for garages.

will reveal that the so-called minority rule does not exist at all (in holding as distinguished from dictum) or that the minority cases all involve a factual variant which is not present in the majority cases or that accident rather than design has led some courts to accept a deviant formulation of a rule. It is not surprising that the state of law in a minority jurisdiction is apt to appear confused and inconsistent: the courts in such a jurisdiction find themselves in the position of saying one thing while they are doing the opposite, of paying lip service to a rule which exists only to be avoided, of building up artificial distinctions and legal fictions." [11]

The Massachusetts rule is usually traced back to Clary v. Owen [12] which categorically denied priority to the purchase-money security interest in water wheels and machinery installed in a mill which was already subject to a mortgage. Nevertheless, although making obeisance to the rule in that case the results in the decided cases were not substantially different from those arrived at in "majority rule" states. "The principal difference was that Massachusetts had more priority litigation of this type than did most other states. * * * The volume of Massachusetts litigation made one thing abundantly clear: The rule of Clary v. Owen did little or nothing to discourage purchase-money financing of equipment installed in mortgaged property." [13]

MAJORITY RULE—LATER PURCHASE-MONEY SECURITY PREVAILS

Contrary to the Massachusetts rule, the great weight of authority is to the effect that where the removal of the attached object will not materially injure the premises, the conditional vendor's rights are superior to those of the prior mortgagee of the land.[14] The courts following this rule base it upon one or the other of two theories. One, which may be labeled the legal doctrine, puts it upon the ground that the conditional sales contract is as clear an indication of the chattel vendor's intention that the object should remain personalty as would be an express agreement between him and the mortgagor.[15] If, as some courts say,[16] such an agreement is effective to prevent the object from becoming a part of the realty, it could follow that it never became part of the property in which the land mortgagee had an interest.[17] Even if, as other courts contend,[18] agreements of this sort cannot prevent the object from becoming a part of the land but merely give a right to remove it, there is no reason why such a right of removal should not be as effective against the prior mort-

---

11. Gilmore, Security Interests in Personal Property, 1965, 759.

12. 1860, 81 Mass. (15 Gray) 522.

13. Gilmore, Security Interests in Personal Property, 1965, 762.

14. See Storke and Sears, The Perennial Problem of Security Priority and Recordation, 1952, 24 Colo.L. Rev. 180, 203–205.

15. "The conditional sales contracts expressly stipulate that they were to remain the property of the appellant until they were fully paid for. This is wholly inconsistent with any idea that they were intended to become part of the realty. We entertain no doubt that the parties designed and purposed that they were to be, and remain, articles of personalty until paid for, and by their attachment to the building were not to lose their character as such." Sears Roebuck & Co. v. Piasa B. & L. Ass'n, 1934, 276 Ill.App. 389, 394. The leading case is Tifft v. Horton, 1873, 53 N.Y. 377, 13 Am.Rep. 537. See also Detroit Steel Cooperage Co. v. Sistersville Brewing Co., 1914, 233 U.S. 712, 34 S.Ct. 753, 58 L. Ed. 1166; Cochran v. Flint, 1877, 57 N.H. 514.

16. Tifft v. Horton, 1873, 53 N.Y. 377, 13 Am.Rep. 537; Powers v. Harris, 1880, 68 Ala. 409; Sowden & Co. v. Craig, 1868, 26 Iowa 156, 96 Am.Dec. 125; Gill v. De Armant, 1892, 90 Mich. 425, 51 N.W. 527.

17. Wurlitzer Co. v. Cohen, 1929, 156 Md. 368, 144 A. 641, 62 A.L.R. 358, where mortgagor never acquires title, mortgagee cannot have lien on thing affixed to realty. See Niles, The Intention Test in the Law of Fixtures, 1934, 12 N.Y.U.L.Q.R. 66, 93.

18. Prescott v. Wells, Fargo & Co. 1867, 3 Nev. 82; Havens v. Germania F. Ins. Co., 1894, 123 Mo. 403, 27 S.W. 718, 26 L.R.A. 107, affirmed 135 Mo. 649, 37 S.W. 497; Ginners' Mut. Underwriters of San Angelo, Tex. v. Wiley & House, Tex.Civ.App.1912, 147 S.W. 629.

gagee as the other agreement.[19] In either case it boils down to whether an agreement to which the mortgagee is not a party can prevent him from getting any, or only a limited, interest in the attached object. Since it would do no violence to logic to hold either way on that point, the second rationale, set forth in the leading New Jersey case of Campbell v. Roddy,[20] and sometimes termed the equitable doctrine, is more satisfying. It rests upon the sensible and fair view that where the original security upon which the prior land mortgagee relied in making his loan is not diminished by allowing the conditional vendor to take back the annexed article, it would be unjust not to permit him to do so.[21]

Courts following the majority view generally limit the doctrine to cases where removal will not cause substantial damage to the premises. But there is a divergence of opinion as to what will constitute such damage. Most courts require physical injury to the realty or the chattel.[22] Just how much injury there must be is not easy to state except in terms of a standard—material or substantial.[23] If the removal would cause some damage, but not sufficient to prevent removal entirely, then "the depreciation must first be made whole to the real estate mortgagee before the right of the chattel mortgagee can be recognized."[24]

An entirely different test of removability, and one that has been subjected to strong criticism,[25] is whether, even though the an-

19. Of course it could be argued that the right to remove is only *in personam*, but there seems no reason why it could not be classed just as easily as at least an equitable right in the property itself analogous to a right to emblements or an equitable lien. See, 1926, 36 Yale L.J. 713; Town of Camden v. Fairbanks, Morse & Co. 1920, 204 Ala. 112, 86 So. 8.

20. 1888, 44 N.J.Eq. 244, 14 A. 279.

21. "[I]t is difficult to perceive any equitable ground upon which the property of another, which the mortgagor annexes to the mortgaged premises, should inure to the benefit of a prior mortgagee of the realty. The real estate mortgagee had no assurance at the time he took his mortgage that there would be any accession to the mortgaged property. He may have believed that there would be such an accession, but he obtained no right, by the terms of his mortgage, to a lien upon anything but the property as it was conditioned at the time of its execution. He could not compel the mortgagor to add anything to it. So long therefore as he is secured the full amount of the indemnity which he took, he has no ground for complaint. There is therefore no inequity towards the prior real estate mortgagee, and there is equity toward the mortgagee of the chattels, in protecting the lien of the latter to its full extent so far as it will not diminish the original security of the former." Campbell v. Roddy, 1888, 44 N.J.Eq. 244, 251, 14 A. 279, 283, 6 Am.St. Rep. 889. For other cases, see 1921, 13 A.L.R. 448, 460; 1923, 23 A.L.R. 805, 806; 1931, 73 A.L.R. 748, 755; 1937, 111 A.L.R. 373; 1942, 141 A.L.R. 1288. For comments on other cases preferring the conditional vendor of the chattel to the prior mortgagee of the realty, see 1935, 7 Miss.L.J. 438; 1914, 9 Ill.L. Rev. 197; Hunter, Priority as to Fixtures in Missouri, 1944, 19 N.D.Law. 273.

22. E. g., General Motors Acceptance Corporation v. Farm & Home Savings & Loan Ass'n, 1933, 227 Mo. App. 832, 58 S.W.2d 338; Evans v. Argentina Building & Loan Ass'n, 1920, 180 Ark. 654, 22 S.W.2d 377; German Sav. & Loan Soc. v. Weber, 1896, 16 Wash. 95, 47 P. 224, 38 L.R.A. 267.

23. E. g., held *not* material: removing a brick wall enclosing a tank, Detroit Steel Cooperage Co. v. Sistersville Brewing Co., 1914, 233 U.S. 712, 34 S.Ct. 753, 58 L.Ed. 1166; breaking cement base to remove fountain, Metropolitan Stone Works, Inc. v. Probel Holding Corp., 1928, 131 Misc. 519, 227 N.Y. S. 414; injury to masonry supporting the machine to be removed, Binkley v. Forkner, 1888, 117 Ind. 176, 19 N.E. 753, 3 L.R.A. 33; screw-holes in wall and floor, Evans v. Argenta B. & L. Ass'n, 1929, 180 Ark. 654, 22 S.W.2d 377. In this last case, however, excavation of water pipes from the ground and removal of pipes from the walls were said to be material injury.

24. Campbell v. Roddy, 1888, 42 N.J.Eq. 244, 252, 14 A. 279, 6 Am.St.Rep. 889. See Binkley v. Forkner, 1889, 117 Ind. 176, 19 N.E. 753, 3 L.R.A. 33; Hurxthal's Ex'rs. v. Hurxthal's Heirs, 1898, 45 W.Va. 584, 32 S.E. 237. In Pennsylvania by statute, 69 Pa.Stat., § 404, the conditional seller who has filed properly can always remove as against a prior mortgagee by posting bond for the making of immediate repairs of any physical damage done. See 1941, 90 U.Pa.L.Rev. 77, 82 et seq. For an account of the law in Pennsylvania prior to the enactment in 1954 of the U.C.C., see Gilmore, Security Interests in Personal Property, 1965, § 28.6.

25. "The question is not whether they were attached to the soil, but we repeat, whether the fact that they were necessary to the working of the brewery gives a preference to the mortgagee. We see no sufficient reason for that result. The class of need to use property belonging to another is not yet recognized by the law as a sufficient ground for authority to appropriate it." Detroit Steel Cooperage Co. v. Sistersville Brewing Co., 1914, 233 U.S. 712,

nexed chattels could be taken out with no appreciable physical injury to land or building, they are essential to the functioning of a plant or building as an institution.[26] Under the New Jersey equitable reasoning the test is impairment of the mortgagee's security as it stood originally before the annexation.[27] But if the holder of a prior mortgage makes advances after the annexation of the articles, without knowledge of the conditional character of the sale, he is entitled to priority over the conditional seller, at least to the extent of such subsequent advances.[28] So, too, a prior mortgagee who has clearly relied upon the chattels to be installed as part of his security without knowledge of the fact they were to be purchased on conditional sale will be protected as against the conditional vendor.[29]

In California, the early New Jersey rule requiring the removal not to diminish the mortgagee's *original* security was expanded, in a case involving a construction loan prior mortgage, to include *any* substantial damage or injury to the security of the prior encumbrancer, using the "institutional" test as the criterion.[30] Although an after-acquired

---

717, 34 S.Ct. 753, 58 L.Ed. 1166, per Holmes, J. See People's Sav. & Trust Co. v. Munsert, 1933, 212 Wis. 449, 249 N.W. 527, 88 A.L.R. 1306, reviewing the decisions; note, 1936, 22 Corn.L.Q. 421; Bodine, J., dissenting, in Russ Distributing Corp. v. Lichtman, 1933, 111 N.J.L. 21, 166 A. 513; 1932, 30 Mich.L.Rev. 469; 1933, 13 Bost.U.L.Rev. 739. But cf., In re Brownsville Brewing Co., C.C.A.Pa., 1941, 117 F.2d 463; 83 U.Pa.L.Rev. 916.

26. Dauch v. Ginsburg, 1931, 214 Cal. 540, 6 P.2d 952, discussed in 1932, 20 Cal.L.Rev. 567; see Future Building & Loan Ass'n v. Mazzocchi, 1931, 107 N.J.Eq. 422, 152 A. 776. For discussions of the New Jersey "institutional" test of "material injury to the freehold", see notes, 1939, 37 Mich.L.Rev. 490 (conditional sale to contractor); 1938, 23 Cornell L.Q. 324; 1937, 22 Cornell L.Q. 421 (applied as against a subsequent mortgagee of the land); 1936, 16 Boston U.L.Rev. 977 (as against subsequent transferee of the lessee who bought on conditional sale); 1933, 13 Boston U.L.Rev. 759; 1935, 48 Harv.L.Rev. 857 (as against the lessor of the conditional vendee). Pennsylvania also adopted the doctrine in preferring a prior mortgagee of the land. Central Lithograph Co. v. Eatmor Chocolate Co., 1934, 316 Pa. 300, 175 A. 697, discussed in notes, 1935, 12 N.Y.Univ.L.Q.Rev. 517 (1935) 83 U. of Pa. L.Rev. 916. Pennsylvania, by amending U.C.S.A. § 7 in 1935 (69 Pa.Stat.Ann., Purdon, 1936 Supp. § 404), later avoided the theory by providing that, upon proper filing, the conditional vendor may always remove his goods, but he is liable to a prior mortgagee or owner for the *physical* damage done to the structure. See 1941, 90 U.Pa.L.Rev. 79, 82, for a discussion of the Pennsylvania statute and cases. Apparently where the annexed chattel is subject to a chattel mortgage instead of a conditional sale, the test in New Jersey was one of material *physical* injury. Kramer v. Yocum, 1929, 104 N.J.Eq. 79, 144 A. 188. See Gilmore, op.cit. supra note 24 for both the New Jersey and Pennsylvania doctrines.

27. Campbell v. Roddy, 1888, 42 N.J.Eq. 252, 14 A. 279, 6 Am.St.Rep. 889; see Binkley v. Forkner, 1889, 117 Ind. 176, 184, 19 N.E. 753, 3 L.R.A. 33; North West Mut. Life Ins. Co. v. George, 1899, 77 Minn. 319, 325, 79 N.W. 1028, 1064, rehearing denied 77 Minn. 319, 79 N.W. 1064.

28. Chasnov v. Marlane Holding Co., Inc., 1930, 137 Misc. 332, 244 N.Y.S. 455; Mississippi Valley Trust Co. v. Cosmopolitan Club, 1932, 111 N.J.Eq. 277, 162 A. 396, commented on in, 1933, 81 U. of Pa.L.Rev. 465; Swift Lumber & Fuel Co. v. Elwanger, 1934, 127 Neb. 740, 256 N.W. 875, commented on in, 1935, 19 Minn.L.Rev. 342; Central Chandelier Co. v. Irving Trust Co., 1932, 259 N.Y. 343, 182 N.E. 10, reargument denied 260 N.Y. 564, 184 N.E. 94, commented on in, 1938, 13 St.John's L.Rev. 1, 16.

If the advances are obligatory, payment after notice of the conditional sale will not prevent the mortgagee having priority. See Waverley Co-Operative Bank v. Haner, 1930, 273 Mass. 477, 481, 173 N.E. 699, 701; Greene v. Lampert, 1931, 274 Mass. 386, 389, 174 N.E. 669, 670.

In Kommel v. Herb-Gner Const. Co., 1931, 256 N.Y. 333, 176 N.E. 413, commented on in, 1931, 31 Col.L. Rev. 1191, the court held that an instrument purporting to secure the repayment of advances has no inception as a mortgage until the advances have been made and therefore may rank as a subsequent mortgage. See §§ 113–123, supra, on future advances generally.

29. Dauch v. Ginsburg, 1931, 214 Cal. 540, 6 P.2d 952; McCrillis v. Cole, 1903, 25 R.I. 156, 55 A. 196; King v. Title Trust Co., 1920, 111 Wash. 508, 191 P. 748, discussed, 30 Yale L.J. 307, advances substantially contemporaneous with installation; Great Western Mfg. Co. v. Bathgate, 1905, 15 Okl. 87, 79 P. 903.

30. Dauch v. Ginsburg, 1931, 214 Cal. 540, 6 P.2d 952, noted, 1932, 20 Cal.L.Rev. 567, 568; Hammel Radiator Corporation v. Mortgage Guarantee Co., 1933, 29 Cal.App. 468, 18 P.2d 993, noted, 1934, 19 Iowa L.Rev. 378. See 1937, 22 Corn.L.Q. 421, 425. Morrow Mfg. Co. v. Race Creek Coal Co., 1928, 222 Ky. 807, 2 S.W.2d 662, seems to reach a similar result in the case of an ordinary prior mortgage. This case may rest upon the ground of physical damage to the annexed object by removal.

In answer to the argument that the prior mortgagee, "having advanced nothing in reliance on the value

property clause [31] in the prior real-estate mortgage does not operate to give the mortgagee [32] priority under the majority rule, it seems to have influence in establishing such reliance.[33] So, too, does the fact that the prior mortgage was for construction of the improvement to which the chattel was annexed.[34]

of the subsequently annexed fixtures, should not be permitted to enhance his original security as against the expression of a contrary intention by the parties installing the chattels" it has been said that "this argument * * * assumes that the mortgagor-mortgagee relationship contemplates the restriction of the security to the property in its physical condition as of the time it was pledged—a dubious assumption in cases where the security is an industrial concern whose chief value is its attribute as a business institution. The equity of permitting the mortgagee to take advantage of normal improvements is even more forceful when it is realized that he, almost alone, bears the loss of depreciation and unfavorable market fluctuations. Nor is the conditional sale vendor left without protection, as is frequently supposed, since he may adequately secure himself by obtaining the readily procured assent of the mortgagee to his reservation of title." In re Brownsville Brewing Co., C.C.A.Pa. 1941, 117 F.2d 463, 468, quoting with approval from note, 83 U.Pa.L.Rev. 916, 917.

31. See §§ 37–41, supra.

32. Hachmeister v. Power Mfg. Co., 1924, 165 Ark. 469, 264 S.W. 976; Wood v. Holly Mfg. Co., 1893, 100 Ala. 326, 13 So. 948, 46 Am.St.Rep. 56; Davis v. Bliss, 1907, 187 N.Y. 77, 79 N.E. 851. Also as to the effect of an "after-acquired property" clause in a prior mortgage of the realty upon property subsequently sold under a conditional sale and annexed to the realty, see Whitney, Conditional Vendors and Prior Realty Mortgagees, 1938, 13 St. John's L.Rev. 1, 11; notes, 1939, 17 N.Car.L.Rev. 442; 1938, 13 St. John's L.Rev. 184; 1929, 4 Ala.L.J. 333; 1934, 18 Minn.L.Rev. 812, 830; Friedman, The Scope of Mortgage Liens on Fixtures and Personal Property in New York, 1938, 7 Ford.L.Rev. 331, 343 et seq. Even if the real estate mortgage had expressly covered fixtures the result would not give priority to the mortgagee. See Hanna, Cases on Security, 2d ed., 702 n. 1. See notes, 1921, 13 A.L.R. 448, 466; 1931, 73 A.L.R. 748, 761; 1937, 111 A.L.R. 362, 380; 1942, 142 A.L.R. 1283, 1290.

33. Dauch v. Ginsburg, 1931, 214 Cal. 540, 6 P.2d 952; Swift Lumber & Fuel Co. v. Elwanger, 1934, 127 Neb. 740, 256 N.W. 875, noted, 1934, 19 Minn.L. Rev. 342. See Friedman, The Scope of Mortgage Liens on Fixtures and Personal Property in New York, 1938, 7 Ford.L.Rev. 331, 346 et seq.

34. See cases in preceding footnote.

CONSTRUCTION MORTGAGES

The idea that the construction mortgage should prevail over purchase-money claims which accrue in the course of construction has persisted in a wide variety of cases and in different jurisdictions. Perhaps Dauch v. Ginsburg,[35] the California case referred to above, is the leading case. The rationale of that decision was explained in a later California intermediate court of appeals [36] case. The fact that the loan was made for the specific purpose of constructing a hotel which was to be security for the loan and was known to be for this purpose by the conditional seller of equipment, who also knew that the hotel could not be operated if the equipment were removed was decisive in giving the mortgagee priority.

In commenting upon the phenomenon of the construction mortgagee's recurring priority, a highly qualified scholar made these observations: "There has never been a clear formulation in the cases of the policy which may underlie the persistent tendency of courts in various jurisdictions under a great variety of theories to prefer the construction mortgagee. There seems to have been an uneasy feeling that to subordinate the mortgagee would be somehow to work a fraud on him, but exactly why this should be so was never pursued. By hypothesis the mortgagee advanced his funds in the expectation that they would be used to finance the construction and that the completed structure (apartment house, hotel, factory or whatnot), free of paramount liens, would be his security. However, the owner-builder-mortgagor, in violation of his agreement, brought in some or all of the equipment subject to purchase-money claims. The mortgagee is naturally disappointed, but it remains true that the purchase-money man supplied the equipment and remains unpaid.

35. 1931, 214 Cal. 540, 6 P.2d 952.

36. Grupp v. Margolis, 1957, 153 Cal.App.2d 500, 504, 314 P.2d 820, 823.

Why should the mortgagee be made whole at his expense? Should not the mortgagee, instead of trusting the mortgagor to disburse the funds properly, have seen to it that the purchase-money men were paid? It may be that the cases obscurely reflect the thought that, as between the typical mortgagee (or typical bondholder) and the typical purchase-money man, the latter is in the better position to prevent the fraud. At all events, the consistency of result in cases of this type, no matter what doctrine the court swears its allegiance to, argues for the soundness of some underlying, albeit, inarticulate policy" [37]

Although it is possible that some of the cases under UCSA § 7 may have involved prior construction mortgages and the later conditional sale of a fixture which unquestionably could have been removed without damage to the property, none of them mentioned the possibility of an exception in such a case of the priority accorded the purchase-money seller.

REPLACEMENTS

Finally, some decisions mention the fact that the fixture replaced another article which was part of the realty when the prior land mortgage was given, but the courts are at variance as to the effect to be given to it. To the extent that the removal of the old fixture diminished the value of the mortgagee's security at the time of removal it would seem that the prior mortgagee should have a claim against the vendor of the fixture or upon the new fixture in priority to him to the amount of the diminution.[38] Apart

from this, it is difficult to see why the case should not be dealt with like any other case of fixture subsequent to the mortgage.[39]

CONDITIONAL SALES OF CHATTELS ANNEXED TO REALTY—LAND MORTGAGE SUBSEQUENT TO CONDITIONAL SALE

219. **Where the land mortgage is subsequent to the conditional sale of the chattel, the mortgagee prevails, by the weight of authority, if he has no notice of the conditional sale and if he could reasonably believe that the objects in question were included in the mortgage. Courts disagree on what constitutes notice.**

Where the land mortgage is subsequent to the conditional sale of the fixture, if the mortgagee has notice of the reservation of title, he will be in no better position than the original buyer.[40] However, it has been suggested by several courts that where the annexed chattels have become so merged with the realty as to lose their separate identity or to be incapable of separation without great damage they pass to the subsequent mortgagee with the land even though there is notice.[41] Where the mortgagee has no notice, the great weight of authority prefers him to the vendor if, using an objective standard, it was reasonable to believe from all of the circumstances that the object in question was included in the mortgage that was being giv-

37. Gilmore, Security Interests in Personal Property, 1965, 775. See id. at 830–832.
For a discussion of the importance and mechanics of construction loan financing, see Storke and Sears, Subdivision Financing, 1956, 28 Rocky Mt.L.Rev. 549, 555–562.

38. See Holland Furnace Co. v. Bird, 1933, 45 Wyo. 471, 21 P.2d 825. See Gilmore, Security Interests in Personal Property, 1965, 773, 774. See also id. at 836; Kripke, Fixtures Under the Uniform Commercial Code, 1964, 64 Col.L.Rev. 44, 78.

39. Comly v. Lehmann, 1934, 218 Iowa 644, 253 N.W. 501, reasoned that since the new fixture was merely a substitution for part of the original security a removal of it necessarily would diminish the original security. But contrast Fred. Wolf Co. v. Hermann Sav. Bank, 1912, 168 Mo.App. 549, 153 S.W. 1094. See 1941, 90 U.Pa.L.Rev. 77, 80; Friedman, The Scope of Mortgage Liens on Fixtures and Personal Property in New York, 1938, 7 Ford.L.Rev. 331, 358; 1934, 18 Minn.L.Rev. 812, 830.

40. Moller, Inc. v. Mainker, 1934, 314 Pa. 314, 171 A. 476; Freiermuth v. Faustino, 1932, 120 Cal.App. 136, 7 P.2d 370; Workman v. Henrie, 1928, 71 Utah 400, 266 P. 1033, 58 A.L.R. 1346.

41. Hachmeister v. Power Mfg. Co., 1924, 165 Ark. 469, 264 S.W. 976; Ford v. Cobb, 1854, 20 N.Y. 344; see Detroit Steel Cooperage Co. v. Sistersville Brewing Co., 1914, 233 U.S. 712, 34 S.Ct. 753, 85 L. Ed. 1166.

en.[42] One explanation that has been given is purely mechanical: that the object has be-

come real property and no agreement between the conditional vendor and the mortgagor-vendee can alter this [43] as to a subsequent purchaser without notice. Others say the rule is fair because the conditional vendor must have known the chattel would be put on the land and relied on by the later mortgagee as part of the security he expected to get for his loan.[44] A third line of reasoning maintains that to hold otherwise would violate the policy of the recording acts of having all interests in land matters of record.[45]

42. "The exact question has often arisen in other states, and the overwhelming weight of authority is to the effect that the title of the seller of personal property of this character, which title is to be held by him until the price thereof is paid, and which is afterwards affixed to land of the vendee, so as to become part of the realty, is subject to the lien of a subsequent mortgagee in good faith without notice of the reserved title. This is fully shown in the elaborate note of Mr. Freeman to Fuller-Warren Co. v. Harter, 110 Wis. 80, 85 N.W. 698, 53 L.R.A. 603, in 84 Am.St.Rep. at pages 892 and 893, and also in the notes to Muir v. Jones, 23 Or. 332, 31 P. 646, in 19 L.R.A. 444, and Lawton, etc., Co. v. Ross-Kellar, etc., Co., 33 Okl. 59, 124 P. 43, in 49 L R.A.,N.S., at page 396, to which we refer for a list of the cases." Oakland Bank of Savings v. California Pressed Brick Co., 1920, 183 Cal. 295, 302, 191 P. 524, 527, commented on, 1920, 8 Cal.L.Rev. 442; Alf Holding Corp. v. American Stove Co., 1930, 253 N.Y. 450, 171 N.E. 703, noted 5 St. John's L.Rev. 120, semble. See notes, 1935, 23 Geo.L.J. 563; 1931, 1 Idaho L.J. 199; 1930, 16 Iowa L.Rev. 116; 1927, 21 Ill.L.Rev. 517; 1926, 10 Minn.L.Rev. 348; 1919, 32 Harv.L.Rev. 732.

The purchaser at a foreclosure sale under a prior mortgage of the realty, without notice of the conditional sale agreement, is classed as a subsequent purchaser of the property for value and without notice. Kohler Co. v. Brasun, 1928, 249 N.Y. 224, 164 N.E. 31, noted, 1929, 14 Cornell L.Q. 334, 337. See note, 1901, 15 Harv.L.Rev. 236. If the purchaser is the prior mortgagee who pays only a nominal amount beyond the amount of his mortgage debt, Industrial Bank of Richmond v. Holland Furnace Co., 1930, 109 W.Va. 176, 153 S.E. 309, or takes a deed from the mortgagor in satisfaction of the mortgage, Warren v. Liddell, 1895, 110 Ala. 232, 20 So. 89, he will not improve his position.

Some five states, including New York before 1904, held to the contrary view that the vendor would prevail. Adams Machine Co. v. Interstate Bldg. etc. Ass'n, 1893, 119 Ala. 97, 24 So. 859, 49 L.R.A.,N.S., 395; Carlin v. Gordy, 1880, 32 La.Ann. 1285; Baldwin v. Young, 1895, 47 La.Ann. 1466, 17 So. 883; Peaks v. Hutchinson, 1902, 96 Me. 530, 53 A. 38, 59 L.R.A. 279; Godard v. Gould & Strong, 1853, 14 Barb. (N.Y.) 662; Ford v. Cobb, 1859, 20 N.Y. 344; but cf. Kohler Co. v. Brasun, 1918, 249 N.Y. 224, 164 N.E. 31; Lawton Pressed Brick & Tile Co. v. Ross-Keller Tripple Pressure Brick Mach. Co., 1912, 33 Okl. 59, 124 P. 43, 49 L.R.A.,N.S., 395. See notes, 1934, 18 Minn.L.Rev. 812, 815; 1932, 6 Temple L.Q. 282; 1929, 29 Col.L.Rev. 1018.

Usually the conditional seller of the chattel intervened in the foreclosure proceedings before the sale took place so that a purchase without notice did not occur. E. G, People's Savings and Trust Co. v. Munsert, 1933, 212 Wis. 449, 249 N.W. 527, rehearing denied 212 Wis. 449, 250 N.W. 385. See Gilmore, Security Interests in Personal Property, 1965, 772, 773.

See Storke and Sears, the Perennial Problem of Security Priority and Recordation, 1952, 24 Colo.L.Rev. 180, 200–201. For a situation where the execution of a mortgage with an after-acquired property clause is substantially contemporaneous with the acquisition of the property by the debtor from the vendor-creditor in a purchase money transaction, see id. at 201.

43. See Massachusetts rule, supra where mortgage is prior.

44. "We think the proposition is in accordance with justice and reason. The seller of the personal property voluntarily placed it in the possession and control of his vendee, with knowledge that, if it was put to the use for which it was designed, it would be affixed to land. Its character was such that it could not ordinarily be used at all by the vendee, unless it was so affixed to the real estate comprising its plant. The seller, because of these facts, is presumed to have agreed that the personal property should be, or might be, converted into real property. By this transformation it was brought under the operation of the laws for recording contracts affecting realty and for the protection of innocent purchasers thereof, regardless of the conditions of the agreement of sale. * * * A person about to loan money on the security of a mortgage or trust deed on such real property, and having no information of the secret agreement as to the title, would be justified in believing that all the machinery would be hypothecated by such mortgage or deed and would have the right to rely on such belief and to make the loan accordingly. He is the innocent party in the transaction, and he should be protected, rather than he who caused the deceitful appearances." Oakland Bk. of Savings v. California Pressed Brick Co., 1920, 183 Cal. 295, 302, 191 P. 524, 527; Andover, Inhabitants of v. McAllister, 1920, 119 Me. 153, 109 A. 750, putting it upon estoppel.

45. See Union Bank & Trust Co. v. Fred W. Wolf Co., 1904, 114 Tenn. 255, 86 S.W. 310, 108 Am.St. Rep. 903, 4 Ann.Cas. 1070; Washburn v. Inter-Mountain Min. Co., 1910, 56 Or. 578, 109 P. 382, Ann.Cas.1912C, 357.

As to what will constitute notice there is the greatest diversity of opinion. The fact that fixtures of the type involved are ordinarily sold on conditional sale contract has been sufficient to justify holding that the subsequent mortgagee is under a duty to inquire about the title of the fixture.[46] There is a conflict in the authorities as to whether recordation under the ordinary conditional sale or chattel morgage recording act will operate to give notice to a subsequent purchaser or encumbrancer of the realty to which the conditionally sold or mortgaged property has been annexed. The weight of authority is that it will not.[47] In support of this view it is argued that it is unreasonable to compel a mortgage to search personal property records regarding every article of a building that might have been sold separately; and that as a matter of proper policy instruments affecting the title to real estate should appear in real estate records.[48] In

answer it is urged that the prospective mortgagee must search a variety of other records such as tax and judgment files [49] as well as take the risk of a variety of nonrecordable interests and it is no great additional hardship to make him search the personal property records; [50] the chattel recording acts insofar as they cover fixtures must be considered a part of the recording system containing the line of title of the land to which they are annexed.[51] And there is always the question of whether the court will decide that the particular chattel remains personal property, and so under the statute, or has become part of the realty.[52] The New York courts, in particular, have been prone to protect the conditional vendor by holding that articles such as gas ranges which today are normally considered a part of the realty are of such a determinate character as moveables that even without agreement they remain personal property and therefore validly recordable under conditional sales or chattel mortgage recording acts.[53] In one state, at least, recording has been regarded as sufficient to keep the articles personalty after annexation

46. Catlin v. C. E. Rosenbaum Mach. Co., 1929, 180 Ark. 739, 22 S.W.2d 906; Continental Gin Co. v. Clement, 1928, 176 Ark. 864, 4 S.W.2d 901; see Liddell v. Cork, 1922, 120 S.Car. 481, 113 S.E. 327, 23 A.L.R. 800.

47. Elliott v. Hudson, 1912, 18 Cal.App. 642, 124 P. 103, 108, rehearing denied 18 Cal.App. 642, 124 P. 108; Tibbetts v. Horne, 1889, 65 N.H. 242, 23 A. 145, 15 L.R.A. 56, 23 Am.St.Rep. 31; Brennan v. Whitaker, 1864, 15 Ohio St. 446; see Abramson v. Penn, 1928, 156 Md. 186, 194, 143 A. 795, 73 A.L.R. 742, commented on, 1929, 77 U.Pa.L.Rev. 1022. Contra: Liddell Co. v. Cork, 1922, 120 S.C. 481, 113 S. E. 327, 23 A.L.R. 800; Lasch v. Columbus Heating & Ventilating Co., 1932, 174 Ga. 618, 163 S.E. 486; North Shore Co. v. Broman, 1933, 188 Minn. 433, 247 N.W. 505; Monarch Laundry Co. v. Westbrook, 1909, 109 Va. 382, 63 S.E. 1070; see Sword v. Low, 1887, 122 Ill. 487, 503, 13 N.E. 826. See 1921, 13 A. L.R. 448, 484; 1931, 73 id. 748, 773; 1934, 88 id. 1318, 1344; 1937, 111 id. 362, 387; 1942, 141 id. 1283, 1295.

For discussions of the problem, see notes, 1938, 36 Mich.L.Rev. 1200 (conditional sale); 1938, 13 Wash. L.Rev. 46 (conditional sale); 1931, 19 Geo.L.J. 238 (conditional sale); 1932, 17 St.Louis L.Rev. 183 (chattel mortgage); 1931, 9 N.Car.L.Rev. 205 (conditional sale recorded as chattel mortgage); 1931, 15 Minn.L.Rev. 242 (chattel mortgage); 1939, 13 Tulane L.Rev. 600 (chattel mortgages on buildings on leased ground in Louisiana); Reid, Recording Chattel Mortgages on Fixtures, 1940, 15 Wash.L.Rev. 252.

48. 2A Uniform Laws Annotated, Bogert's Commentaries on Conditional Sales, § 65, quoted with ap-

proval in In re Brownsville Brewing Co., C.C.A.Pa. 1941, 117 F.2d 463, Bogert, Cas.Sales, 2d ed., 264. See cases and discussions in the preceding footnote.

49. See § 221, infra.

50. See Lasch v. Columbia Heating & Ventilating Co., 1932, 174 Ga. 618, 624, 163 S.E. 486; Sword v. Low, 1887, 122 Ill. 487, 503, 13 N.E. 826.

51. Liddell Co. v. Cork, 1922, 120 S.C. 481, 488, 113 S.E. 327, 23 A.L.R. 800. See 1940, 15 Wash.L.Rev. 252.

52. For a consideration of the perplexing problem of where to file a conditional sale contract of a chattel which is to be annexed to realty, see notes, 1933, 18 Cornell L.Q. 597; 1931, 9 Can.B.Rev. 381. As to when a conditional sale contract must be filed, see note, 1938, 13 St.John's L.Rev. 205.

53. Madfes v. Beverly Development Corp., 1929, 251 N.Y. 12, 166 N.E. 787, commented on in 1929, 29 Col.L.Rev. 1018; 1929, 7 N.Y.Univ.L.Q.Rev. 211; 1929, 4 St.John's L.Rev. 131; 1930, 4 Temple L.Q. 184. See notes, 1929, 14 Cornell L.Q. 334; 1928, 13 Cornell L.Q. 435; 1932, 18 Iowa L.Rev. 93; 1927, 36 Yale L.J. 713; Abrahamson v. Penn, 1928, 156 Md. 186, 143 A. 795, 73 A.L.R. 742, accord.

quite apart from any question of notice.[54] There is some authority that the conditional sales agreement might be recorded under the ordinary recording acts as affecting the title to realty if the conditional sale agreement specifies that the article is to be attached to the realty and the vendor's continuing title is then to be an interest in the land recordable as such and then properly describes the land.[55] And it is specifically so provided in the Uniform Conditional Sales Act and other similar legislation.[56]

CONDITIONAL SALES OF CHATTELS ANNEXED TO REALTY—UNIFORM CONDITIONAL SALES ACT

220. Under the uniform conditional sales act if the chattels can be severed without material injury the conditional vendor can maintain his priority against a later mortgagee by recording the sales agreement in the realty records. Objects not so severable cannot be removed without consent of the person who has not assented to the reservation of title by the vendor.

In an effort to afford greater certainty in the law where the conditional sale of a fixture was involved a few states enacted specific legislation,[57] dealing with the problem and these in turn formed the model on which, in 1918, § 7 of the Uniform Conditional Sales Act was drafted.[58] This act was adopted in only twelve states, in three of which it was enacted with modifications, before it was withdrawn in 1943 pending preparation of a Commercial Code.[59] In spite of the purpose to achieve uniformity it has had indifferent success in that direction, partly because the substantive problems of fixtures were, in general, left unaltered, and partly because of differing constructions placed upon governing provisions of the act itself, notably the requirement of removability only when it could be done "without material injury to the freehold." [60]

Section 7 of the act divides chattels sold on conditional sale which have been affixed to realty so as to become a part thereof into two classes: those that can and those that cannot be severed "wholly or in any portion without material injury to the freehold." If they fall into the first class, the reservation of title is void against subsequent purchasers, who include, of course, mortgagees of the land for value and without notice of the vendor's title, unless the sales agreement, describing briefly the realty and stating that

---

54. Standard Motors Finance Co. v. Weaver, 1930, 199 N.C. 178, 181, 153 S.E. 861, discussed in 1931, 9 N.Car.L.Rev. 205.

55. See Oakland Bank of Savings v. California Pressed Brick Co., 1920, 183 Cal. 295, 303, 191 P. 524, 527, "by this transformation [into a fixture] it was brought under the operation of the laws for recording contracts affecting realty. * * *."
See notes, 1903, 16 Harv.L.Rev. 531; 1920, 8 Cal.L. Rev. 442, 445; 1926, 36 Yale L.J. 713; Reid, Recording Chattel Mortgages on Fixtures, 1940, 15 Wash.L.Rev. 252. A conditional vendor of articles acquires no lien *per se*, against the realty. Re Master Knitting Corp., C.C.A.N.Y.1925, 7 F.2d 11; East N. Y. Electric Co. v. Petmaland Realty Corp., 1926, 243 N.Y. 477, 154 N.E. 530, 58 A.L.R. 1119.

56. U.C.S.A. § 7; M.G.L.A. c. 106 § 9–313; McKinney's N. Y. Uniform Commercial Code, § 9–313; Or.R.S. 79.3130, and see 1940, 19 Or.L.Rev. 152, 167; Pa.St., Tit. 12A, § 9–313.

See §§ 220 and 220A infra.

57. See last footnote, § 219, supra.

58. See Bogert, Cases on Sales, 2d ed., 268.

59. See 1945 Handbook, Commissioners on Uniform State Laws, 99. The nine jurisdictions adopting it: Alaska, Arizona, Delaware, New Hampshire, New Jersey, New York, South Dakota, West Virginia, Wisconsin. Adopting it with reservations: Hawaii, Indiana, Pennsylvania.

60. For a survey of the operation in New York, New Jersey, and Pennsylvania of the provisions of the U.C.S.A. § 7 on conditional sales of fixtures, see Kleps, Uniformity versus Uniform Legislation: Conditional Sale of Fixtures, 1939, 24 Cornell L.Q. 394.
For a recent and thorough study of the fixture provisions of the U.C.S.A., see Gilmore, Security Interests in Personal Property, 1965, §§ 28.5, 28.6 (dealing with the New Jersey "institutional doctrine" and the Pennsylvania "industrial plant mortgage doctrine"), and 28.7 covering fixture litigation after 1920. Especially careful scrutiny is devoted to the U.C.S.A. fixture filing and priority provisions. Id. at pp. 764–767. This is important because comparable Article 9 provisions of the U.C.C. were in large part modeled on them.

the goods are to be affixed to it, is recorded in the realty records before the purchase.[61] If they fall into the second class, they cannot be removed without the consent of any person who has not assented to the reservation, a category that includes prior mortgagees of the land and subsequent mortgagees with notice. Recordation by the conditional vendor is immaterial because in such cases the attempt to reserve title is itself ineffectual.[62] That the drafters of the act intended this test to be the equivalent of the first of the three groups of articles [63] into which the American courts generally divide chattels annexed to or used in connection with land is clear.[64] Nevertheless the distinction has been said to create a new, statutory test of what kind of fixtures are covered by it.[65] However, even accepting this view, in construing the statutory test courts have taken the opportunity to diverge both on what would constitute material injury and whether the injury must be physical or can be to the institution or industrial plant.[66] Also, although not intended to change the existing law as to priorities be-

tween a prior mortgagee of the land and the later conditional vendor, one of the minority courts used it as an excuse for departing from the Massachusetts view.[67]

Where the land mortgage is prior in time it is only when the object falls into the second class under the act that the mortgagee is affected by it.[68] In determining what constitutes injury to the freehold so that the assent of the prior mortgagee must be obtained, some courts have held that the injury must be a physical one,[69] while New Jersey decided that the institutional test should be applied.[70] Pennsylvania also followed its

---

61. In his notes on this provision of the Uniform Act (2–A Uniform Laws, Annotated, § 64), George G. Bogert says: "The theory of the Act is that a conditional seller of a fixture should be given protection and allowed to retain title as security for the payment of the price of the fixture, but that in order to retain such title he should be required to give notice adapted as nearly as possible to reaching dealers in real property." * * *

62. This, as is brought out in the text, post, is of especial importance where the New Jersey "institutional doctrine" or the Pennsylvania "industrial plant mortgage doctrine" is followed as the test of material injury.

63. See text, supra, at beginning of this section. For the three groups referred to see § 217, supra.

64. See Bogert, Conditional Sales, 2–A Un.L.Ann. § 66.

65. People's Savings & Trust Co. v. Munsert, 1933, 212 Wis. 449, 453, 249 N.W. 527, 529, 88 A.L.R. 1306, rehearing denied 212 Wis. 449, 250 N.W. 385, 88 A. L.R. 1306, "it is not ruled by the law of fixtures but by the law of conditional sales; and consequently the well established common law applicable to fixtures has, in our opinion, little to do with this controversy." Bank of Am. Nat. Ass'n v. Le Reine Hotel Corp., 1931, 108 N.J.Eq. 567, 156 A. 28.

66. See cases cited in succeeding footnotes.

67. People's Sav. & T. Co. v. Munsert, 1933, 212 Wis. 449, 453, 249 N.W. 527, 529, 88 A.L.R. 1306, rehearing denied 212 Wis. 449, 250 N.W. 385, 88 A.L.R. 1306. On the other hand, under the Massachusetts statute, it has been decided that the fact that the fixture conditionally sold can be removed without material injury does not preclude its passing to the prior mortgagee of the realty under the minority Massachusetts view. Furthermore, under the Massachusetts statute, her own rule persists even though the conditional vendor records, as required by statute, among the real estate records, provided the prior land mortgage was recorded. Waverley Co-op. Bank v. Haner, 1930, 273 Mass. 477, 173 N.E. 699, noted 29 Mich.L.Rev. 1086; Greene v. Lampert, 1931, 274 Mass. 386, 174 N.E. 669, 11 Bost.U.L.Rev. 209.

68. In New York, if the chattel is of the sort that is inherently personal property section 7 doesn't apply to it at all. Chasnov v. Marlane Holding Co., 1930, 137 Misc. 332, 244 N.Y.S. 455. See text, supra. If it is in the first class, the conditional vendor may prevail even though the conditional sale is unrecorded. American Laundry Mach. Co. v. Larson, 1934, 217 Wis. 208, 257 N.W. 608.

69. Harvard Financial Corp. v. Greenblatt Construction Co., Inc., 1933, 261 N.Y. 169, 184 N.E. 748, motion denied 261 N.Y. 694, 185 N.E. 796; Industrial Bank of Richmond v. Holland Furnace Co., 1930, 109 W.Va. 176, 153 S.E. 309; People's Sav. & T. Co. v. Munsert, 1933, 212 Wis. 449, 249 N.W. 527, discussed in notes, 1934, 18 Minn.L.Rev. 812 (a thorough note covering all phases of the rights against third persons of the conditional vendor of a chattel which is annexed to realty); 1934, 9 Wis.L.Rev. 198; 1934, 32 Mich.L.Rev. 555; 1934, 88 A.L.R. 1318. See Whitney, Conditional Vendors and Prior Realty Mortgagees, 1938, 13 St. John's L.Rev. 1; Ayer, Recent Legislation in Washington, Particularly Where Personalty is Attached to Buildings on Realty, 1938, 13 Wash.L.Rev. 46; Friedman, The Scope of Mortgage Liens on Fixtures and Personal Property in New York, 1938, 7 Ford.L.Rev. 331.

70. Domestic Electric Co., Inc. v. Mezzaluna, 1932, 109 N.J.L. 574, 162 A. 722, discussed, 10 N.Y.U.L.Q.

analogous "industrial plant" test [71] until statutory amendment in 1935 made it clear that the legislative intent was that damage done to the physical structure or improvement was the criterion; but the statute made recordation before annexation a requirement even as against the prior land mortgagee in order for the act to apply.[72] The institutional and industrial plant tests, of course, greatly expands the number of articles that cannot be removed without the assent of the prior mortgagee.

As to subsequent [73] mortgagees, if the annexed chattel is in the first class, those that

can be removed without material injury to the freehold, the conditional vendor will prevail if the contract is properly recorded in the realty books; but if it is not, the reservation of title is void if the subsequent mortgagee took without notice and for value.[74]

There are, however, two doctrines that militate against the effectiveness of this provision, one of them disadvantageous to the later land mortgagee, the other advantageous to him. One is the New York category of chattels that continue to be personalty regardless of attachment to the land, which means that as to them the conditional vendor will be protected without recording against subsequent mortgagees of the land for value and without notice.[75] On the other hand, where the definition of "material injury to

R. 388; Smyth Sales Corp. v. Norfolk Building & Loan Ass'n, 1936, 116 N.J.L. 293, 184 A. 204, 111 A.L.R. 357; Lumpkin v. Holland Furnace Co., 1935, 118 N.J.Eq. 313, 178 A. 788; see Future Building & Loan Ass'n v. Mazzocchi, 107 N.J.Eq. 422, 152 A. 776. The doctrine has been strongly criticized and also has been defended. Lower New Jersey courts had earlier said that the statute should be interpreted to mean physical injury. Bank of Am. Nat. Ass'n v. Le Reine Hotel Corp., 1931, 108 N.J.Eq. 567, 156 A. 28, discussed in notes, 1931, 80 U.Pa.L.Rev. 297, 1932, 30 Mich.L.Rev. 469; Reliable Building & Loan Ass'n of City of Newark v. Purifoy, 1933, 111 N.J.Eq. 575, 163 A. 151.

For a discussion of the New Jersey "institutional doctrine" and the Pennsylvania "industrial plant mortgage doctrine," see Gilmore, Security Interests in Personal Property, 1965, § 28.6. The New Jersey doctrine is dealt with on pp. 768, 769. For an analysis of the New Jersey cases prepared in a study for the New York Law Revision Commission see its 1942 Report, pp. 10–26. See note 60, supra.

71. Central Lithograph Co. v. Eatmore Choc. Co., 1935, 316 Pa. 300, 175 A. 697, noted, 83 U.Pa.L.Rev. 916; 14 N.Y.U.L.Q.Rev. 388.

72. Penn.Stats., Purdon 1940 Supp., tit. 69, § 404 (see now 12 A.P.S. §§ 2–107, 9–401, 9–313); see 1941, 90 U.Pa.L.Rev. 77, 84. The amendment provided that if the conditional sale was recorded prior to annexation the chattel should not be considered part of the realty or of any *operating plant* to which it is attached and shall be subject to removal against *any* mortgagee, provided that, as against a *prior* mortgagee the conditional vendor would have to post bond for any damage done to the *physical* structure or improvement.

For a careful history of the legislation and decisions in Pennsylvania involving the Pennsylvania Industrial Plant Mortgage Doctrine up to 1954, when the U.C.C. § 9 went into effect, see Gilmore, Security Interests in Personal Property, 1965, pp. 769–770. See note 60, supra.

73. In its decision denying a rehearing in People's Savings & Trust Co. v. Munsert, 1933, 212 Wis. 449,

464, 250 N.W. 385, 386, 88 A.L.R. 1306, the court said: "neither a mechanic's lien claimant, a judgment creditor, nor a purchaser of a bond subsequent to its original sale, is a subsequent purchaser as defined by the act. * * * Clearly, * * * an unfiled conditional sales contract is void only as to 'subsequent purchasers.' Had those who drafted this act intended that holders of mechanics' liens, judgment creditors, and purchasers of bonds subsequent to their original issue and sale, should be included in the definition of 'purchaser,' it is reasonable to conclude that they would have so provided."

74. American Laundry Mach. Co. v. Larson, 1934, 217 Wis. 208, 257 N.W. 608. See 1944, 19 N.D.Law. 254. As to subsequent mortgages under the Massachusetts act, look at Security Co-op. Bank of Brockton v. Holland Furnace Co., 1931, 274 Mass. 389, 174 N.E. 721.

75. Madfes v. Beverly Development Corp., 1929, 251 N.Y. 12, 166 N.E. 787; see text, supra. A clause in a subsequent realty mortgage stating that it covered "all articles of personal property now or hereafter attached to the land" has been held to make the realty mortgagee also a *bona fide* purchaser of the conditionally-sold articles as chattels. Cohen v. 1165 Fulton Ave. Corp., 1929, 251 N.Y. 24, 166 N.E. 792, reargument denied 252 N.Y. 576, 170 N.E. 149; Kommel v. Herb-Gner Const. Co., Inc., 1931, 256 N.Y. 333, 176 N.E. 413, Hanna, Cases on Security, 703. But cf. Lightolier Co. v. Del Mar Club Holding Co., 1933, 237 App.Div. 432, 262 N.Y.S. 32, affirmed 1934, 263 N.Y. 588, 189 N.E. 711 (electric light fixtures not inherent personalty); Voss v. Melrose Bond & Mort. Corp., 1936, 160 Misc. 30, 288 N.Y.S. 576 (refrigerating plant not determinate personalty). See Friedman, The Scope of Mortgage Liens on Fixtures and Personal Property in New York, 1938, 7 Ford.L.Rev. 331.

the freehold" is extended, as in New Jersey, to include the institution as a going concern, and in Pennsylvania as falling under the industrial plant mortgage doctrine, the subsequent mortgagee may prevail even though the conditional sale is recorded as required by the statute and no physical injury would result from removal on the ground that the case falls under the first sentence of the section requiring consent by the mortgagee.[76] The ease with which the New Jersey courts under the institutional test find that removal will cause material injury to the freehold within the meaning of the act is in striking contrast to New York where, in addition to eliminating many cases from the application of the act by its doctrine of inherent personalty,[77] it is difficult to find any decisions holding that removal, under the test of physical injury, would cause material damage.[78]

UNIFORM COMMERCIAL CODE—FIXTURES UNDER ARTICLE 9

220A. With the widespread adoption of the Uniform Commercial Code, there occurred an unforeseen and violent storm of criticism of the fixture provisions. As a result there have been new studies which have revealed both the many difficulties involved and also suggested solutions. A few states deleted or changed some of the Code provisions.

---

76. Smyth Sales Corp. v. Norfolk, Building & Loan Ass'n, 1936, 116 N.J.L. 293, 184 A. 204, 111 A.L.R. 357. See 1937, 22 Cornell L.Q. 421 suggesting that the impossibility of obtaining express assent of subsequent land mortgagees may force the abandonment of the conditional sale in merchandising these goods. See also 1938, 23 Cornell L.Q. 324.

77. Which, in turn, creates uncertainty as to where conditional sales of chattels to be annexed to realty should be recorded. See 1933, 18 Cornell L.Q. 597, 1931, 9 Can.B.Rev. 381.

78. See Kleps, Uniformity versus Uniform Legislation, 1938, 24 Cornell L.Q. 394, 404 n. 36, 406 n. 45. See also the Massachusetts cases holding objects not to be fixtures where the land mortgage is prior in time. Text supra, discussing the minority Massachusetts rule.

See, generally, note, 1950, 17 U. of Chi.L.Rev. 745, Policies Underlying the Adjustment of Creditors' Security Rights in Fixtures.

The Uniform Commercial Code by 1967 had been enacted in all but three states and two other American jurisdictions.[79] The draftsmen of the Code started with the assumption that, aside from the test set forth in it for determining the removability of fixtures, Section 7 of the Uniform Conditional Sales Act had worked well and should be the model for the treatment of the subject of security interests in fixtures in Article 9 of the Code. All that needed to be done was to remedy that one defect, redraft the solutions of the U.C.S.A. and integrate them into the Code.[80] The objected to test for determining removability of fixtures was whether it was "severable without material injury to the freehold." To eliminate it, removal of fixtures was permitted but payment of damages was required for physical injury to the real estate (but not for any diminution in value of the real estate caused by the absence of the goods removed or any necessity for replacing them).[81] "It was the thought of the draftsmen that coupling the right to remove with the duty to reimburse effectively limited the subsection (1) priority so that the competing chattel and real estate interests would come out about as they had

---

79. See Report No. 3 of the Permanent Editorial Board for the Uniform Commercial Code, IX, Dec. 15, 1966. The three states were Arizona, Idaho and Louisiana. The other two jurisdictions were Guam and Puerto Rico.

80. See Kripke, Fixtures Under the Uniform Commercial Code, 1964, 64 Col.L.Rev. 44, 46; Gilmore, Security Interests in Personal Property, 1965, §§ 30.1, 30.2; Comment, accompanying the text of § 9–313, prepared by American Law Institute.

81. U.C.C. § 9–313(5). See Kripke, Fixtures Under the Uniform Commercial Code, 1964, 64 Col.L.Rev. 44, 47; Gilmore, Security Interests in Personal Property, 1965, §§ 30.1, 30.2.

Permitting removal of the fixtures but requiring payment of damages for injury to the real estate had been tried earlier in Pennsylvania. Pa.Laws, 1935, No. 239, at 658; Pa.Laws 1923, No. 91, at 117; Pa. Laws 1915, No. 386, at 866.

For a similar provision added to West's Ann.Cal.Civ. Code § 1013.5 providing for a right of removal and payment of damages, a right which may defeat a subsequent bona fide purchaser or mortgagee of the land, see Work of the 1953 California Legislature, 1953, 27 S.Cal.L.Rev. 70, 89–91.

under pre-Code law in 'majority rule' states. That is to say, the requirement that all 'physical injury' be paid for would make the priority useless with what may be described as 'structural materials': if removal would destroy or disintegrate the structure, the remover would have to pay for rebuilding. Thus the priority and the right to remove would be worth having only for non-structural equipment."[82] The language used, it was thought, also would preclude any court from finding that either the pre-Code New Jersey "institutional" or Pennsylvania "industrial plant mortgage" doctrines was still tenable.[83] The party entitled to reimbursement was given the right to prevent removal until the secured party had furnished adequate security.[84] Like the U.C.S.A. § 7 requirement of filing "in the office where a deed of the realty would be recorded or filed," the Code provides for filing "in the office where a mortgage on the real estate concerned would be filed or recorded."[85] Under U.C.S.A. § 7 only "subsequent purchasers of the realty for value and without notice "would prevail over a prior conditional sale of a "severable fixture" unless the contract was filed before such purchase. The Code section 9–313 includes within the class of protected subsequent interests not only purchasers but lien creditors and prior lenders who, under certain circumstances, make subsequent advances against the real estate.[86]

In 1956 the original text of Code § 9–313 was revised "primarily for clarification" according to those who made the changes. Yet there are changes of substance. Subsection (3) of the revision validates a security interest "which attaches to goods after they become fixtures." This "post-affixation security interest" is, by subsection (4), given the same priority over subsequent real estate interests as the pre-affixation security interest. The post-affixation interest is subordinated by subsection (3) to all existing real estate interests except for contractual waivers and disclaimers.[87]

The most important change in 1956 was to subsection (1) of § 9–313. The final sentence, which is new ("This Act does not prevent creation of an encumbrance upon fixtures or real estate pursuant to the law applicable to real estate.") has been accurately characterized as being completely unnecessary although probably doing no harm.[88] The second sentence replaces the opening clause of the 1952 draft and seems to be a mere rephrasing of it. However, the change in language from "so affixed . . . as to be a part thereof" to the term "fixtures," although apparently not intended to have any significance, has resulted in some misunderstanding.[89]

The new first sentence of subsection (1) reads as follows: "The rules of this section do not apply to goods incorporated into a structure in the manner of lumber, bricks, tile, cement, glass, metal work and the like and no security interest in them exists under this Article unless the structure remains personal property under applicable law." The second part of the sentence is unclear but seems unimportant.[90] The first part of the sentence causes all of the trouble. As has been pointed out, it can be argued that, under revised §

82. Gilmore, Security Interests in Personal Property, 1965, 805.

83. Gilmore, op. cit. supra, 807, 816. But see Robinson, McGough and Scheinholtz, The Effect of the Uniform Commercial Code on Pennsylvania Industrial Plant Doctrine, 1955, 16 U. of Pitt.L.Rev. 86 (discussing the 1952 draft).

84. Gilmore, op. cit. supra, 805.

85. Kripke, Fixtures Under the Uniform Commercial Code, 1964, 64 Col.L.Rev. 44, 52.

86. U.C.C. § 9–313(4(a), (b), (c).

87. For a criticism of the addition made by subsection (3) see Gilmore, op. cit. supra note 82, at 810. But see Kripke, defending it as important under Pennsylvania law. Id. at 810 n. 6.

88. Gilmore, op. cit. supra note 82, at 811.

89. The term "fixture" in the 1956 revision was used not only in § 9–313(1) but in §§ 1–210(37); 9–102(1); 9–104(j); 9–401; 9–402. See Gilmore, op. cit. supra note 82, at 815, 819.

90. See Gilmore, op. cit. supra note 82 at 812.

9–313, courts must divide affixed goods into three classes: (1) "goods incorporated into a structure in the manner of lumber, bricks * * * and the like"; (2) goods which, although incorporated into the structure, are not incorporated "in the manner of lumber, bricks * * * and the like"; (3) goods which, although they have become fixtures under the non-Code law, still remain, so to say, unincorporated goods. Goods in class (1) could not be removed at all—indeed could not be the subject of a security interest. Goods in class (2) would be presumably the removable goods whose removal would cause "physical injury" to the structure for which the secured party would have to reimburse subordinate real estate interests. Goods in class (3) would be those whose removal would cause no "physical injury" and thus not lead to a reimbursement claim.[91]

With the widespread adoption of the Code, there occurred an unforeseen and violent storm of criticism of the fixture sections; they were asserted to be unworkable and even wrong as a matter of policy. As a result there were new and searching studies made of the entire problem and their published comments[92] have revealed both the

many difficulties involved and also suggested solutions. A few states either deleted or changed some of the Code provisions.[93]

See also Clark, U.C.C. Articles 9 and 10: Some Problems Solved and Some Problems Created, 1965, 38 U. of Colo.L.Rev. 99, 111; Stiller, the Maryland Law of Fixtures, 1965, 25 Maryland L.Rev. 21–40; Boyce, The Uniform Commercial Code in Utah, 1966 Utah L.Rev. 31, 60; Sachse, Security Rights in Movables Under the U.C.C. and Louisiana Law—A Transactional Comparison, 1966, 40 Tulane L.Rev. 747 (Fixtures: 809–830); Sachse, Report to the Louisiana Law Institute on Article Nine of the Uniform Commercial Code, 1967, 41 Tulane L.Rev. 504–554, 785–848 (Fixtures: 528–531; 824–826); Hamilton, Integration of the U.C.C. Fixture Filings with the Real Estate Recordation System—Recent Developments, 1967, 45 Tex.L.Rev. 1175–1198; Panel Discussion on Secured Transactions, 1968, 39 Miss.L.R. 217–260, Fixtures (by Coogan) 243–249.

93. California refused to adopt section 9–313 when it adopted the Code, although it did enact sections 9–102(1) and 9–102(1) (c). Cal.Laws 1963, ch. 819 (effective Jan. 1, 1965). The situation in California has been summarized as follows: "A transaction which is intended to create a security interest in goods which are or are later to become fixtures is within the scope of the Code, which governs the rights of the original parties and third parties not having an interest in the real property. The California version of the Code has deleted provisions concerning the conflicting interests in fixtures as between a secured party and third persons holding an interest in the real property. However, as between the secured party and the debtor, the interest will remain a security interest within the scope of the article so long as an interest in goods—i. e., personalty—was intended. The proposition that goods may be fixtures as between the secured party and third persons and yet remain personalty as between the secured party and the debtor if so intended, is consistent with numerous California cases." Project: California Chattel Security and Article Nine of the Uniform Commercial Code, 1961, 8 U.C. L.A.L.Rev. 812, 931. See also The Uniform Commercial Code: Special Report by the California State Bar Committee on the Commercial Code, 1962, 37 Cal.St.B.Jour. 119, 201; Shanker, Fixture Security Interests, 1964, 73 Yale L.Jour. 788, 790; Gilmore, Security Interest in Personal Property, 1965, 802, n. 2; Warren, Coverage of the Secured Transaction Decisions of the California Commercial Code, 1966, 13 U.C.L.A.L.Rev. 250–284, Fixtures, 269.

Ohio, after adopting section 9–313 substantially revised it after about a year. See Ohio Rev.Code tit. 13, § 1309.32, effective Oct. 8, 1963. See Shanker, Fixture Security Interests, 1964, 73 Yale L.Jour. 788, 789. The purpose of the revision was to give the prior real estate mortgagee priority over the security interest. See Hollander, Imperfections in Perfection of Ohio Fixture Liens, 1963, 14 W.Res. L.Rev. 783, 798; Gilmore, Security Interests in Personal Property, 1965, 802 n. 2; Holtman, Ohio **Lien** Priority Rules Affecting Mortgages, **Mechanics'**

---

91. Gilmore, op. cit. supra note 82 at 813.

92. The most important recent thorough discussions of the fixture provisions in Article 9 of the Uniform Commercial Code are Coogan, Security Interests in Fixtures Under the Uniform Commercial Code, 1962, 75 Harv.L.Rev. 1319; Gilmore, Purchase Money Priority, 1963, 76 Harv.L.Rev. 1333; Shanker, Fixture Security Interests, 1964, 73 Yale L.Jour. 788; Shanker, A Further Critique of the Fixture Section of the Uniform Commercial Code, 1964, VI Boston College Industrial and Commercial L.Rev. 61; Kripke, Fixtures Under the Uniform Commercial Code, 1964, 64 Col.L.Rev. 44; Coogan & Clovis, The Uniform Commercial Code and Real Estate Law, 1963, 38 Ind.L.J. 535; Coogan, Public Notice and Chattel Security Law, 1962, 47 Iowa L.Rev. 289, 326; Hollander, Imperfections in the Perfection of Ohio Fixture Liens, 1963, 14 W.Res.L.Rev. 633; Project: California Chattel Security and Article Nine of the Uniform Commercial Code, 1961, 8 U.C.L.A.L.Rev. 812, 931–942. For a list of earlier articles see Osborne, Cases on Property Security, 2d ed., p. 250 n. 8. Coogan in his article in 73 Harv. L.Rev. supra, at pp. 790–793 appraises the policy questions pro and con in the priority provisions of section 9–313.

There has been fairly complete agreement by writers on Article 9 of the Code as to the problems involved in the fixture sections although there is divergence among them as to many of the proposed remedies. The difficulties discussed have included the following subjects which will be described but not dealt with in detail.

One of the thorniest problems facing critics of the Code's solutions as to fixtures is what the filing requirements should be. Both U.C.S.A. § 7 and U.C.C. § 9-401 provided for recording with the real estate records. Although there are a few differences in formulation between the U.C.S.A. version and that of the U.C.C. they seem unsubstantial.[94] However, neither codification gave any explanation as to why the filing should be with the real estate records. Nor did either attempt to lay down any rules as to the mechanics of filing or recording, an obviously impossible task in view of the great diversity of recording systems among the states.[95]

Code section 9-401 does make real estate filing for fixtures exclusive. If they are not fixtures, then the chattel files are the only ones that can be used. However, whether they are or are not fixtures is a determination that few lawyers would venture to predict with confidence. As a result, when there is doubt, the usual case, the secured party, to be sure of protection must file both with the realty and the chattel records.[96] Although

twice disapproved in the Reports of the Permanent Editorial Board for the Uniform Commercial Code several states have added to the requirement of § 9-402 that the financing statement contain "a description of the real estate concerned" a further requirement that it contain "the name of the record owner thereof." [97]

The question of what "subsequent" real estate interests are protected against an unperfected fixture interest under § 9-313(1) has come in for attention. Not only purchasers, which covers mortgagees, are included as they were under U.C.S.A. § 7, and the ambiguity as to whether purchasers at a foreclosure sale held after default under a prior mortgage were "subsequent" was resolved in the affirmation in the final sentence of § 9-313(4). However, another ambiguity still exists: is a purchase made during the period after attachment and before affixation "subsequent" ? [98]

The priority over pre-existing security interests is extended under § 9-313(4) to creditors who have obtained a "lien by judicial proceedings * * * without knowledge of the security interest and before it is perfected." The result is anomalous. An unsecured creditor who reduces his claim to judgment and acquires a judicial lien against the real estate before perfection of the fixture interest wins over the fixture interest, while a mortgage of the realty loses to a subsequent fixture interest even if the latter is never perfected. And the same ambiguity noted in reference to "subsequent" in connec-

---

Liens and Fixture Security Interests, 1967, 18 W. Res.L.R. 1284, 1293.

In 1967 Florida amended Art. 9-313 to reverse the priority of the security interest in the goods over existing security interests in the realty. See Boyer, Survey of Florida Law: Real Property, 1967, 22 Univ. of Miami L.Rev. 303.

94. Section 7 of the U.C.S.A. read that the filing was to be made in the office "where a *deed* of the realty would be *recorded* or *registered*." U.C.C. § 9-401 specified "the office where a *mortgage* on the real estate concerned would be *filed* or recorded." Neither enactment required a full legal description.

95. See Gilmore, op. cit. supra note 82, pp. 817, 818.

96. See Shanker, op. cit. supra note 92, at 796 et seq., would impose a multiple filing requirement (one with the chattel records and an additional one

with the real estate records) as a matter of law. Kripke, op. cit. supra note 92, at 57 et seq. proposes that the only filing required should be with the chattel records. As a condition of priority of the holder of a security interest in fixtures against subsequent interests in the realty he would require real estate filing (or "notification" as he prefers to call it). Gilmore, op. cit. supra note 82, pp. 821, 834-836, agrees with Kripke but adds the suggestions that actual notification to certain prior or existing real estate interests should be an additional condition of priority in certain situations.

97. See Gilmore, op. cit. supra note 82 at 832.

98. See Gilmore, op. cit. supra note 82, § 30.6(3) (a).

tion with the "purchaser" provision recurs with respect to the judicial lien creditor.[99]

It has been suggested that "when the debtor in a fixture security transaction is a contractor who installs the fixture on land belonging to a third party, the landowner is substantially in the same position as the mortgagee who makes further advances." A further suggestion is that actual notification of the fixture security interest in a contractor must be given to "the present record owner of the land and any mortgagee whose mortgage has been recorded within the preceding three years."[1]

In U.C.S.A. § 7 provision was made for special treatment of the owner of land who is not the debtor in the fixture security transaction. There are two chief situations in which this may occur: One is the case of fixtures installed by a contractor who is building (or repairing) a structure on someone else's land; the other is the case of fixtures installed by a tenant. The former was dealt with in U.C.S.A. § 7 by requiring the conditional sale to be filed before affixation in order to be good against the landowner. The provision could apply to the tenant case, but was not actually so intended. And properly so, since the landowner does not normally rely on the fact that fixtures installed by a tenant will be unencumbered. Admittedly not a perfect solution, it would seem that some other and better answer can be developed.

The case of the construction mortgage, previously considered apart from any code treatment[2] has been mentioned with conflicting opinions.[3] The problem of waste or replacement of fixtures has also received comment but none with any firm conviction.[4]

Future advances by a prior mortgagee of the land are protected to a restricted extent under U.C.C. § 9–313(4), a provision awkwardly phrased and the requirement of which that it be "of record" meaningless. Further, the time reference of "prior" and "subsequent" have the same ambiguity here as in other paragraphs of the section previously criticised.[5] Whether or not, as a matter of policy, the prior mortgagee should be protected as to his subsequent advances seems substantially the same question previously mentioned as to the construction mortgagee and the landowner to whose property goods have been affixed by a third party who is the debtor.

There is an incongruity in two priority rules under the Code enacted in § 9–312(4) and § 9–313. "It results from the Code's insertion in the rules for ordinary chattels of a limitation on the apparently permanent common-law priority of purchase-money security over an after-acquired property clause in a prior mortgage; by this limitation the priority applies only to cases in which the purchase-money security is filed within ten days after delivery of possession to the debtor. But in the fixture provision, section 9–313, the Code preserved the common-law priority of the purchase-money security interest against the prior mortgage."[6]

---

99. Gilmore, op. cit. supra note, 82, § 30.6(3) (b).

1. Gilmore, op. cit. supra note 82, § 30.6(1), (5), (6); quotations, pp. 834, 835; see Kripke, op. cit. supra note 92, pp. 62–70.

2. See § 218 supra.

3. Contrast Gilmore, op. cit. supra note 82, 820–832 with Kripke, op. cit. supra note 92, 71–74.

4. Gilmore suggests that the duty could be imposed upon the fixture remover to account to the mortgagee of the land for the value of the goods wrongfully removed by analogy of the duty under § 9–313(5) of the fixture party's duty to reimburse the mortgagee for physical damage to the structure. Gilmore, op. cit. supra note 82, § 30.6(7). Kripke thinks it should be left for future judicial development. Kripke, op. cit. supra note 92, 78. See also § 218, supra.

5. See Gilmore, op. cit. supra note 82, § 30.6(3) (c). For a treatment of the general subject of future advances, see Chapter Subdivision C, §§ 117–122, supra. Professor Gilmore proposes some clarifying language in the wording of the section as well as considering the policy question mentioned in the text following the note call.

6. Kripke, op. cit. supra note 92, 74. See also Gilmore, op. cit. supra note 82, § 30.6(2). Kripke does

MISCELLANEOUS INTERESTS

221. There are a number of statutory interests taking precedence over subsequent, and sometimes over existing mortgages. Tax liens are the most important. Others are liens for wage claims, for supplies sold to transport companies, for certain tort claims against railroads, homestead claims and "year's support" claims.

There are a considerable number of miscellaneous liens or claims of interests in land which are created, or at least notice of which is provided for, by statute that constitute risks of which a mortgagee must take account. Foremost among these is the tax lien. The simplest of these is the lien imposed upon real property to secure the payment of taxes or assessments upon that specific property. Such liens customarily constitute a paramount claim upon the property, displacing mortgages already on it and, of course, coming in ahead of subsequent ones.[7] The hazards of such possible displacement constitute a normal risk that the mortgagee runs and enters into his calculations.[8] Stat-

utes providing that taxes on personalty shall give rise to a lien on the owner's real property constitute a greater danger. Some provide specifically that the lien on the real property shall be paramount to existing mortgages,[9] and such statutes have been held to be constitutional[10] although, criticized as unjust.[11] Where the language is not explicit in making such tax liens superior to existing mortgages, most courts hold them to be inferior to existing liens,[12] but a respectable minority has held the other way.[13] As a matter of desirable policy the lien of such taxes, and similar ones to be mentioned that are not levied directly upon the land but either on other property or activities of the mortgagor that have little or no relation to the land,[14] should be subordinate to existing

---

not believe the matter to be of sufficient practical importance to warrant any change in either section unless and until a complete reexamination of the Code's priority rules is made. He also thinks the problem would be automatically taken care of by requiring regular chattel filing for fixtures and an additional real estate notification for protection against real estate interests. See note 96, supra.

7. Delahunt v. Oklahoma Co., C.C.A.Okl.1915, 226 F. 31, 141 C.C.A. 139.

For cases dealing with the priority of a tax lien over that of a purchase-money mortgage, see Bodertha v. Spencer, 1872, 40 Ind. 353; Clifton v. Cincinnati, 1878, 5 Ohio Dec. 570. Cf. Sweeney v. Arrowsmith, 1910, 43 Pa.Super. 268. See also note, 1926, 74 U. of Pa.L.Rev. 511. The question of the priority of a special assessment over a mortgage has been decided and discussed frequently. Baldwin v. Moroney, 1910, 173 Ind. 574, 91 N.E. 3, 30 L.R.A.,N.S., 761; Morrow v. Dows, 1877, 28 N.J.Eq. 459; State v. Bank of Mineral Wells, Tex.Civ.App.1923, 251 S.W. 1107; Seattle v. Hill, 1896, 14 Wash. 487, 45 P. 17, 35 L.R.A. 372. See German Savings & Loan Ass'n v. Ramish, 1902, 138 Cal. 120, 124, 69 P. 89, 92, affirmed 138 Cal. 120, 70 P. 1067; Bowers, Special Assessment vs. Mortgage Lien—In Event of Conflict Which Holds Priority? 1923, 32 Yale L.J. 460.

8. It is immaterial as to such liens whether the displaced mortgage antedated the enactment of the

statute or not. Baldwin v. Moroney, 1910, 173 Ind. 574, 91 N.E. 3, 30 L.R.A.,N.S., 761.

9. Getchell v. Walker, 1929, 129 Or. 602, 278 P. 93; Union Central Life Ins. Co. v. Black, 1926, 67 Utah 268, 247 P. 486, 47 A.L.R. 372.

10. California Loan etc. Co. v. Weis, 1897, 118 Cal. 489, 50 P. 697. As to mortgages antedating the enactment of statutes creating paramount liens upon realty for personal property, franchise, and other taxes levied upon something other than the mortgaged property itself it would seem the statutes are unconstitutional although valid in their prospective operation. See note, 1940, 54 Harv.L.Rev. 112.

11. See Advance Thresher Co. v. Beck, 1910, 21 N.D. 55, 60, 128 N.W. 315, 317, Ann.Cas.1913B, 517.

12. Gifford v. Callaway, 1896, 8 Colo.App. 359, 46 P. 626; Scottish American Mort. Co. v. Minidoka Co., 1928, 47 Idaho 33, 272 P. 498, 65 A.L.R. 663, 1929, 42 Harv.L.Rev. 961, 3 So.Cal.L.Rev. 118; Miller v. Anderson, 1891, 1 S.D. 539, 47 N.W. 957, 11 L.R.A. 317.

13. Woodill & Hulse Electric Co. v. Young, 1919, 180 Cal. 667, 182 P. 422, 5 A.L.R. 1296; Guinn v. McReynolds, 1918, 177 Cal. 230, 170 P. 421; Bodertha v. Spencer, 1872, 40 Ind. 353; Albany Brewing Co. v. Meriden, 1880, 48 Conn. 243; New England Loan & Trust Co. v. Young, 1880, 81 Iowa 732, 39 N.W. 116, 10 L.R.A. 478; Dungan's Appeal, 1871, 68 Pa. 204, 8 Am.Rep. 169.

14. E. g., franchise taxes lien on corporate property, Ohio R.C. §§ 5727.52, 5733.18; gasoline taxes lien on realty and personalty of tax debtor, Mich.C.L.A. § 207.114; Tex.Civ.Stats., art. 7065a–7 (Repealed by Acts 1941, 47th Leg., p. 269, Ch. 184, Art. XVII, § 28); see State v. Wynne, 1939, 134 Tex. 455, 133 S.W.2d 951, commented on, 1940, 53 Harv.L.Rev 889; State v. Nix, 1939, 134 Tex. 476, 133 S.W.2d

mortgages, attaching themselves only to whatever interest the mortgagor had at the time. To subject the mortgagee's interest to them is to make "the mortgagee a surety for the mortgagor's wanderings at large, and such a fiscal policy would make the mortgage a very unstable security."[15] Nevertheless, franchise taxes[16] and taxes on the capital stock of corporations[17] have been made a first lien upon the taxpayer's realty, although legislatures have been known to change an established rule to that effect.[18] Other liens which have been given priority by statute over existing mortgages are those for claims of unpaid water rent,[19] hail indemnity,[20] industrial accident fees,[21] and, applica-

ble only to personal property, school, poll and dog taxes.[22] One limitation on the validity of such displacement may be that the lien result from a foreseeable use of the property to which it attaches.[23] And other liens have been held not entitled to priority under the statutes by finding that they do not fall within the meaning of the word taxes as employed in the acts[24] or the statutes themselves make it clear they are to take subject to existing mortgages.[25] But even when this last is the case, once they attach they are encumbrances that must be looked for by any prospective mortgagee, and, sometimes they arise without any written notice or record in any public office to which resort may be had for search.[26] And, further, under recording acts that protect creditors as against an unrecorded mortgage, the govern-

---

963; income taxes lien on realty and personalty of tax debtor, Okl.Supp. tit. 68, §§ 221, 223 (Repealed by Laws 1951, p. 206, § 3; inheritance taxes lien on property transmitted, W.Va.Code, 11–11–9; Unemployment Compensation payments lien on employer's realty, Ohio R.C. §§ 4141.27, 5721.10; Workmen's Compensation claims lien on realty where work done, Or.Rev.Stats. 656.560, 656.990.

15. Glenn, Mortgages, § 436.

16. In re Century Steel Co., Inc., C.C.A.N.Y.1927, 17 F.2d 78.

17. Harper v. Consolidated Rubber Co., 1925, 284 Pa. 444, 131 A. 356, noted 1925, 74 U.Pa.L.Rev. 511.

18. Thus in New York, a franchise tax that had been held to be paramount to existing mortgages on real property, N. Y. Terminal Co. v. Gaus, 1912, 204 N.Y. 512, 98 N.E. 11, reargument denied 205 N.Y. 588, 98 N.E. 1109, and In re Century Steel Co., Inc., C.C.A.N.Y.1927, 17 F.2d 78, was changed by amendment in 1925 so as to be subordinate to them. McKinney's N.Y.Tax Law, c. 60, § 197; People of State of New York v. Maclay, C.C.A.N.Y.1930, 37 F.2d 22, noted, 1930, 30 Col.L.Rev. 744.

19. Dunbar v. City of N. Y., 1920, 251 U.S. 516, 40 S.Ct. 250, 64 L.Ed. 384; Ford Motor Co. v. Town of Kearny, 1918, 91 N.J.L. 671, 103 A. 254, L.R.A. 1918D, 361; City of East Grand Forks v. Luck, 1906, 97 Minn. 373, 107 N.W. 393, 6 L.R.A.,N.S., 198, 7 Ann.Cas. 1015, including charges for light also; Provident Institution for Savings in Jersey City v. Jersey City, 1885, 113 U.S. 506, 5 S.Ct. 612, 28 L.Ed. 1102.

20. Federal Farm Mort. Corp. v. Falk, 1936, 67 N.D. 154, 270 N.W. 885, 113 A.L.R. 724, certiorari denied 302 U.S. 704, 58 S.Ct. 24, 82 L.Ed. 544.

21. Cf. State v. Johnson, 1926, 54 N.D. 184, 208 N.W. 966, holding hail insurance tax not a "tax" within the statute and, additionally, that the mortgage was unaffected because it arose before the statute was

effective to create the lien. See 1926, 11 Minn.L. Rev. 182.

22. Minneapolis Threshing Machine Co. v. Roberts County, 1914, 34 S.D. 498, 149 N.W. 163, L.R.A. 1915D, 886.

23. Federal Farm Mortgage v. Berzel, 1940, 69 N.D. 760, 291 N.W. 550, claim for workmen's compensation arising from operation of a bakery not from a normal foreseeable use of farm land on which mortgage existed; Ford Motor Co. v. Town of Kearny, 1918, 91 N.J.L. 671, 673, 103 A. 254, 255, L. R.A.1918D, 361; Bill White's Market v. Dixie Creek Gold Mining Co., 1938, 159 Or. 406, 80 P.2d 712. But this does not square with statutes making personal property taxes a prior lien on realty. See text, supra. And also, cf. Minneapolis Threshing Machine Co. v. Roberts County, 1914, 34 S.D. 498, 149 N.W. 163, L.R.A.1915D, 886.

24. Eccles v. Will, 1918, 23 N.M. 623, 170 P. 748, L. R.A.1918C, 1022, work not beneficial to property done in exercise of police power; State v. Johnson, 1926, 54 N.D. 184, 208 N.W. 966, hail insurance; Strand v. Marin, 1915, 30 N.D. 165, 152 N.W. 280, seed charge lien. Similarly, Central Savings Bank v. City of N. Y., 1938, 279 N.Y. 266, 18 N.E.2d 151, 121 A.L.R. 607, commented on, 1939, 39 Col.L.Rev. 889, 1939, 8 Fordham L.Rev. 384.

25. E. g., Ormsbee v. U. S., D.C.Fla.1928, 23 F.2d 926, federal income tax lien.

26. The federal estate tax becomes a lien upon the day of death without assessment, demand, or filing of notice. Detroit Bank v. U. S., 1943, 317 U.S. 329, 63 S.Ct. 297, 87 L.Ed. 304, affirming Paul v. U. S., C.C.A.Mich.1941, 127 F.2d 64.

mental unit holding a perfected tax lien [27] will prevail over a prior mortgagee who has failed to record.[28]

In addition to tax liens, there is a miscellany of other statutory encumbrances and interests in real property that a prospective mortgagee must take into account, some of which are of general enactment and others almost esoteric in their uniqueness. Some of these will be effective only as against subsequent mortgages, and as to them all that the mortgagee need worry about is whether they are in existence when he takes his security. Others will take precedence over his mortgage even though they arise later, and this is a risk that he must calculate when he lends. Statutes that go beyond mere priority of payment and give wage claimants a lien upon the property of their employer when certain procedure is complied with fall in the latter class in some states.[29] Related to the wage lien statutes, and also to the "six months rule" previously examined,[30] are statutes giving a prior lien to persons furnishing supplies necessary for the operation of any transportation company.[31] Pertinent at this point, since they are confined to liens on the property of railroads, are the statutes creating paramount liens in favor of tort claimants whose persons or whose animals have been injured by the railroad and who bring their actions or file their claims with a receiver within a certain specified time.[32]

An entirely different sort of statutory interest, but one which provides a familiar and common form of protection to debtors, is the homestead law.[33] Since each state has its own statutory variations generalizations are difficult. A typical statute,[34] however, provides that mortgages executed and recorded prior to recordation of the declaration of homestead shall prevail over it; that it can be subjected to a mortgage if the mortgage is executed and acknowledged by husband and wife or by an unmarried claimant; that it may be abandoned by declaration, but such a declaration is effectual only from the time of recordation; and that it will not be exempt from execution in satisfaction of judgments on debts secured by vendor's liens or mechanic's and materialmen's liens.[35] Another type of exemption statute is the "year's support" accorded out of the estate of a debtor for the support of his widow and minor children for varying periods. There are some dozen states having such statutes which operate as a shield against creditors as to the personal property of the deceased,[36] but at

---

27. Until the statutory tax lien is perfected by actual proceedings it is usually regarded as a mere debt claim which, although it may be entitled to priority over other like claims does not constitute a specific lien. U. S. v. State of Texas, 1941, 314 U. S. 480, 62 S.Ct. 350, 86 L.Ed. 356, noted, 1942, 28 Va.L.Rev. 552.

28. Underwood v. U. S., C.C.A.Tex.1941, 118 F.2d 760.

29. See Va.Code 1950, § 43-24. There are similar statutes in other states. Hess v. Jewell, 1897, 85 Md. 235, 36 A. 758; Graham v. Magann Fawke Lumber Co., 1904, 118 Ky. 192, 80 S.W. 799; Re Brannon, C.C.A.Tex.1933, 62 F.2d 959, certiorari denied 289 U.S. 742, 53 S.Ct. 692, 77 L.Ed. 1489. With the dropping from the Bankruptcy Act in 1938 of priorities granted under state laws, the lien aspect of various claims under state law which will assure them of getting paid out of the bankrupt's property ahead even of prior liens upon it assumes new importance.

30. See § 192, supra.

31. Va.Code 1950, § 43-24.

32. See Ark.Stats. §§ 73-737, 73-738, 73-739; N.Car. G.S. § 55-44; S.Car.Code 1962, § 58-744; Thompson v. Evans, C.C.A.Mo.1940, 113 F.2d 794, Arkansas law; St. Louis, I., M. & S. Ry. Co. v. Ingram, 1916, 124 Ark. 298, 187 S.W. 452, affirmed 244 U.S. 647, 37 S.Ct. 741, 61 L.Ed. 1370; Birmingham Trust & Savings Co. v. Atlanta, B. & A. Ry. Co., D.C.Ga. 1923, 287 F. 561, Georgia law.

33. See Note, 1953, 33 Texas L.Rev. 534; Swenson, The Utah Land Title Standards, I, 1954, 4 Utah L. Rev. 157. And see Harvey v. Thomas, 1960, 239 La. 510, 119 So.2d 446, noted by Dainow, Security Devices, 1961, 21 La.L.Rev. 305.

34. West's Ann.Cal.Civ.Code §§ 1237-1269.

35. West's Ann.Cal.Civ.Code, §§ 1241-1244.

36. See State of New York Legislative Document, 1930, No. 69.

Somewhat analogous are liens for alimony. See Periodic Support Payments in Divorce Decrees as Liens, 1954, 4 Drake L.Rev. 67; Swenson, The Utah Land Title Standard, I, 1954, 4 Utah L.Rev. 157, 170.

least one of them goes farther and allows the year's support, on application, to apply to the deceased's real property and to prevail over any outstanding mortgage on it,[37] except a purchase money mortgage,[38] so that the property may be subject to a year's free occupancy by the mortgagor's relict and his minor off-spring. Finally, mention may be made of one statute, unique to Georgia, which in spite of language broad enough to make it paramount to existing mortgages does not, apparently, do so. That is the peculiar lien for accountability of a tenant in common.[39]

FEDERAL TAX LIENS

221 A. Although of scant importance even in 1954 there was a tremendous number of decisions and a huge amount of legal periodical and other published material dealing with the Federal General Tax Lien in the period between that year and 1966. In 1966 comprehensive amendments to the Internal Revenue Code were effected which effected major changes in the pre-existing law of the Federal General Tax Lien. The law as it stood before 1966 as it

affected security problems considered herein will be discussed first followed by a treatment of the changes made by the 1966 legislation. There is also attention given to some remaining problems and suggestions for their solution.

When this text was first published in 1951 the Federal General Tax Lien merited and was given scant attention. Even in 1954, when a shortened and revised version was published as section 16 of the American Law of Property, little more was thought necessary. In the intervening years, however, there has been almost a tidal wave of decisions, legal periodical and other published material dealing with the problem.[40]

In 1966, comprehensive amendments to the Internal Revenue Code were enacted by Congress effective at once with minor exceptions, and operative even retroactively. This legislation effected major changes in the pre-existing law of the Federal General Tax Lien. There have been several excellent analyses and discussions of the new legislation as well as proposals for further changes.[41]

---

37. Ga.Code, 1933, § 113–1508. See Lunsford v. Kersey, 1941, 191 Ga. 738, 13 S.E.2d 803.

38. Ga.Code, 1933, §§ 113–1010, 113–1508(1). See House v. House, 1941, 191 Ga. 678, 13 S.E.2d 817.

39. See Ga.Code, 1933, § 85–1004; Collier v. Bank of Tupelo, 1940, 190 Ga. 598, 10 S.E.2d 62; Bank of Tupelo v. Collier, 1941, 191 Ga. 852, 14 S.E.2d 59.

Lenoir County v. Outlaw, 1954, 24 N.C. 97, 84 S.E.2d 330, noted in Third Annual Survey of North Carolina Case Law: Credit Transactions, 1955, 34 N.C.L. Rev. 37, 69, held that an old-age assistance lien became a lien from the date of filing as a general lien to the same extent as would a judgment when docketed.

Statutes making delinquent sales taxes a lien on all property of the delinquent have been generally enacted. See Note, The Unrecorded Sales Tax Lien, 1955, 5 Drake L.Rev. 51.

For other statutory liens, see Shattuck, Review of Washington Legislation—1955; Creditors' Rights, 1955, 30 Wash.L.Rev. 198, noting sprayers and dusters liens, seed liens, nurserymen's liens; Note, More Lien Trouble for Landowners and Conveyancers, 1953, 38 Mass.L.Q. No. 4, p. 10; Note, 1953, 38 Mass.L.Q. No. 5, p. 26. Old Age Assistance Liens. "One of the more distressing aspects of the haphazard proliferation of lien statutes is the legislature's assumption that the process can go on indefinitely." Shattuck supra at 198.

40. A compilation of references to this material covering the law before the legislation enacted in 1966 can be found in the biennial supplements from 1954 to 1962 of IV Am.L.Prop. § 16.106I. A more discriminating list is set forth by Professor Gilmore, Security Interests in Personal Property, 1965, § 40.2 n. 1. Gilmore's own treatment of the subject up to 1965 in Chapter 40 covers not only the Federal General Tax Lien but also federal priority for debts. And, since he is mainly concerned with personal property security he includes a section, 40.6, on Article 9 of the UCC and the inchoate and general lien. Additional references are to be found in the foregoing lists of references. Among the more important contributions to the literature are Plumb and Wright, Federal Tax Liens, 1961; Kennedy, The Relative Priority of the Federal Government: The Pernicious Career of the Inchoate and General Lien, 1954, 63 Yale L.J. 905; Anderson, Federal Tax Liens—Their Nature and Priority, 1953, 41 Cal.L.Rev. 241, 256–260, 260–271; Plumb, Federal Tax Collection and Lien Problems, 1958, 13 Tax.L. Rev. 247 and 459.

41. For a comprehensive coverage, see Plumb and Wright, Federal Tax Liens, 1967, a revision of the 1961 work. It is published by the American Law Institute. For shorter surveys see Plumb, The New Federal Tax Lien Law, 1967, 53 A.B.A.J. 66; Plumb, The New Federal Tax Lien Law, 1967, 22 Bus. Law. 271; Creedon, The Federal Tax Lien Act of 1966—An Historic Breakthrough, 1967, 4 Harv. J.Legis. 163. For a critical examination and ap-

Pre 1966 priority of the federal general tax lien. The federal general tax lien arises by force of section 6321 of the Internal Revenue Code (26 U.S.C.A.), unchanged by the 1966 Act. It reads as follows:

"If any person liable to pay any tax neglects or refuses to pay the same after demand, the amount * * * shall be a lien in favor of the United States upon all property and rights to property, whether real or personal, belonging to such person."

The lien so provided attaches from the date that the assessment list is received by the local director of Internal Revenue.[42] Since the assessment was a nonpublic administrative act, the existence of the lien might be known neither to the taxpayer nor to third persons.

In 1913 and again in 1939, Congress amended the lien statute to provide in section 6323(a) that the tax lien should not be valid against "any mortgagee, pledgee, purchaser, or judgment creditor, until notice thereof has been filed * * *"

The place for filing the notice of tax lien in order that it operate against the classes named in section 6323(a) can be, and has been determined, by state legislation. In the absence of such designation by state enactment, the proper place to file is with the clerk of the United States district in which the property is located. The congressional delegation of authorization goes only to the *place* of recording and nothing else; the states are not empowered to attach other conditions to the filing of notice, such as, that the instrument be acknowledged, that the instrument affecting real property contain a description thereof.[43]

Neither section 6321 nor section 6323(a) explicitly confers priority. Holding that this is a federal, not a state question, the basic formula laid down is that "first in time is first in right."[44] The determination of which is first in time is complicated by the federal doctrine that a lien must first have become "choate" before it can be "first in time." "That word 'choate,' an illegitimate back formation which was not in most dictionaries until the Supreme Court gave it currency, was not truly an antonym for 'inchoate.' A lien might be completed and perfected for every purpose of state law, and hence not 'inchoate' as we understand that term. Yet it would not be 'choate,' by federal judicial standards unless (1) the identity of the lienor, (2) the property subject to the lien, and (3) the amount payable were fixed beyond possibility of change."[45]

---

42. See Anderson, op. cit. supra note 40, pp. 241–3 for a description of the administrative procedure in the assessment process.

In addition to the general tax lien there are other types of federal liens. Special liens provided the government security for unpaid federal estate taxes, Int.Rev.Code of 1954, § 6324a; and federal gift taxes, Int.Rev.Code of 1954; § 6324(b), (26 U.S.C.A.). For a discussion of these special liens both before and after the 1966 amendments, see Plumb and Wright, Federal Tax Liens, 1967, Part II, Introduction and Chapters 1 and 2. For the pre 1966 situation as to them see Anderson, op. cit. supra note 40, pp. 272–276.

43. See Priority of Federal Tax Liens, 1963, 8 Utah L.Rev. 252, 253 n. 12; Anderson, op. cit. supra note 40, p. 257.

Most state statutes enacted pursuant to this federal authorization provide that notice of lien be filed with the local recorder of the county in which the property is located. Anderson, op. cit. supra note 40.

44. United States v. City of New Britain, 1954, 347 U.S. 81, 85, 74 S.Ct. 367, 370, 98 L.Ed. 520.

45. Plumb, Federal Liens and Priorities—Agenda for the Next Decade, 1967, 77 Yale L.J. 228, 230. The three requirements for "choateness" are enunciated by United States v. Pioneer American Ins. Co., 1963, 374 U.S. 84, 89, 83 S.Ct. 1651, 10 L.Ed.2d 770, conformed to 236 Ark. 897, 370 S.W.2d 445. Earlier

---

praisal, see Young, Priorty of the Federal Tax Lien, 1967, 34 Univ.Chi.L.Rev. 723. Coogan, The Effect of the Federal Tax Lien Act of 1966 upon Security Interests Created Under the Uniform Commercial Code, 1968, 81 Harv.L.Rev. 1369, prefaces his main topic with a treatment of the Law of Liens generally and Federal Tax Liens before the 1966 legislation.

After a summary of what the 1966 law has accomplished, a study of additional changes that should be considered is set forth in three installments of an article by Plumb which he titled Federal Liens and Priorities—Agenda for the Next Decade, 1967, 77 Yale L.J. 228, 605, 1104.

This text will confine itself to problems concerning consensual real property security interests and mechanics' liens with relation to the federal general tax lien. The first generally will fall under the term "mortgagee" in section 6323(a).[46]

Several questions arose as to the application of the theory of choateness to consensual security interests, e. g., mortgages under § 6323(a). In United States v. Pioneer American Insurance Co.[47] the Supreme Court apparently committed itself to the proposition that consensual security interests must meet the same standards of choateness as non-consensual liens. As Gilmore points out, "The trouble with the proposition is that the application of the strict choate lien theory for consensual security interests seems to strip § 6323(a) of the tax lien statute of any meaning. * * * the holder of a lien which

has become choate before notice of the federal tax lien is filed wins even if he is not a morgtagee, pledgee, purchaser, or judgment creditor * * *. Now, if, say, a mortgagee, in order to win his case, must prove not only that his mortgage antedated the filing of the tax lien but also that his mortgage met the *New Britain*[48] standard of choateness before the filing, then it became irrelevant whether he is a mortgagee or not. That is, he would win as the holder of a choate lien, no matter what sort of lien he held."[49]

One question never definitively resolved is whether a mortgage or trust deed mortgage *executed* before notice of tax lien has been filed but not recorded until after notice of the tax lien has been filed would be superior to the federal tax lien. The mortgage or trust deed mortgage does have a superior lien if it has been recorded before filing of the notice of tax lien even though not executed and recorded until after the assessment lien has arisen. And there is some authority[50] that a mortgagee who has not recorded before the tax lien filing will nevertheless prevail on what Gilmore calls a "curiously literal reading of the statutory language."[51]

---

formulation of the same three requirements of choateness were made by Justice Minton in United States v. City of New Britain, 1954, 347 U.S. 81, 86, 77 S.Ct. 367, 371, 98 L.Ed. 520, 526 and by Justice Rutledge in State of Illinois ex rel. Gordon v. Campbell, 1946, 329 U.S. 362, 375, 67 S.Ct. 340, 347, 91 L.Ed. 348, 357–358.

For other discussions of the doctrine of the "inchoate and general tax lien," see Gilmore, op. cit. supra note 40, §§ 40.3, 40.4 (application of the theory of the inchoate and general lien to consensual security interests: The Supreme Court Decisions); § 40.5 (the present state of the controversy; hypotheses and speculations); Kennedy, op. cit. supra note 40, pp. 905, 911–930; Coogan, op. cit. supra note 41, pp. 1373–1380; Plumb, op. cit. supra note 41, pp. 229–233.

46. Just exactly who is a "mortgagee, pledgee, purchaser, or judgment creditor" within the meaning of section 6323(a) was never definitively spelled out in the cases. The federal tax regulation, 2 Fed. Tax Regulations (1963) §§ 30.1, 6323(2)(ii) and case-law discussions indicate a fairly broad view of what types of security interests are covered. Certainly a conventional mortgage or trust deed mortgage would be. See Gilmore, Security Interests in Personal Property, 1965, pp. 1063–1068. The 1966 amendment substituted "holder of security interest" for "mortgagee" and "pledgee." And a "security interest" is broadly defined as "any interest in property acquired by contract for the purpose of securing payment or performance of an obligation or indemnifying against loss or liability." Int.Rev.Code § 6323(a) and (h)(1) (26 U.S.C.A.). Consequently the question is now unimportant.

47. 1963, 374 U.S. 84, 83 S.Ct. 1651, 10 L.Ed.2d 770, conformed to 236 Ark. 897, 370 S.W.2d 445.

48. United States v. City of New Britain, Conn., 1954, 347 U.S. 81, 74 S.Ct. 367, 98 L.Ed. 520, discussed in Gilmore, Security Interests in Personal Property, 1965, pp. 1053, 1054.

49. Gilmore, Security Interests in Personal Property, 1965, pp. 1065, 1066. Gilmore concludes that the only possible way of giving significance to the purported distinction of the classes of mortgagees and others singled out in § 6323(a) is to say that the standards of choateness they must meet are in some way that has not yet been worked out less rigorous than the standard which must be met apart from § 6323(a).

See also Priority of Federal Tax Liens, 1963, 8 Utah L.Rev. 252, 257.

50. Gauvey Rig & Trucking Co. v. United States, C. A.N.D. 1961, 291 F.2d 42.

51. Gilmore, Security Interests in Personal Property, 1965, p. 1068: "That is, § 6323 says 'any mortgagee'

There is, however, authority that a mortgagee is not entitled to priority over a federal tax lien unless in a state where recording by state statute is required to be valid as against subsequent purchasers without notice and existing creditors, he has recorded his mortgage.[52] This result may be justified on the application of the federal doctrine of choateness. Perfection under state law is a prerequisite of federal choateness. An interest that could be defeated by a bona fide purchaser or creditor under state law would be unperfected and consequently inchoate under federal law.[53]

Related to the question of recording is that of actual notice by a mortgagee of the existence of an assessment lien at the time he takes his mortgage. In United States v. Beaver Run Coal Co.,[54] the court held that good faith by a mortgagee was immaterial and therefore a mortgagee with actual notice of the taxes and assessment lien prevailed over the tax lien.

In view of the decisions in the actual notice cases, it is not surprising that present valuable consideration was not required in order for a mortgagee to prevail over the tax lien: an antecedent debt is sufficient.[55]

Future advances[56] and after-acquired property clauses[57] have encountered difficulties with the federal doctrine of choateness and the federal tax lien.[58] The Treasury Department had ruled that after a tax lien is filed it takes priority over optional advances made thereafter regardless of actual notice of it. And a later, but unpublished ruling, stated that obligatory advances on construction loans have priority over a federal tax lien which attached before the advance was made. However, United States v. R. F. Ball Construction Co.[59] held an obligatory advance made by an indemnitor subsequent to a tax lien to be inchoate. Consequently neither optional nor obligatory advances made after filing of a tax lien could be certain of priority over the tax lien. And, "if future advance arrangements are vulnerable," as Gilmore points out, "it is hard to suggest a plausible reason why after-acquired property interests should not receive the same treatment." Indeed "since certainty in amount at the time the federal lien or priority attaches, is said to be one of the requisites of choateness, the conclusion could be reached that the pre-lien as well as the post-lien advances should be subordinated. The same argument, leading to the same conclusion, could be made with respect to security agreements which contain an after-acquired property clause."[60]

The requirement of choateness that the amount of a competing lien be definite has

---

and a mortgagee who has not perfected his interest by filing is quite as much a mortgagee as one who has."

52. Mason City & C.L.R.R. v. Imperial Seed Co., N. D. Iowa 1957, 152 F.Supp. 145.

53. See Priority of Federal Tax Liens, 1963, 8 Utah L.Rev. 252, 258.

See also Anderson, op. cit. supra note 40, pp. 258, 259 for citation of authorities.

United States v. Dickerson, E.D.Mo.1951, 101 F.Supp. 262, held that if the taxpayer has only an unrecordable equitable interest in real property the federal tax lien does not attach to it.

54. 3d Cir. 1938, 99 F.2d 610. Schmitz v. Stockman, 1940, 151 Kan. 891, 101 P.2d 1962, applied the same rule more strikingly in a case where the trial court had found that the mortgage was given for the purpose of evading payment of the federal tax.

55. Ferris v. Chic-Mint Gum Co., 1924, 14 Del.Ch. 232, 124 A. 577.

56. For the law of future advances, see supra Chapter 5, Subdivision C. Future Advances, §§ 113–124, especially §§ 118–121 covering the problem of priorities.

57. For discussion of the law governing after-acquired property in mortgage law see §§ 37–42 supra.

58. See Gilmore, Security Interests in Personal Property, 1965, pp. 1068 et seq.; Priority of Federal Tax Liens, 1963, 8 Utah L.Rev. 252, 259, Anderson, op. cit. supra note 40, pp. 259, 260.

The after-acquired property question was not much litigated. See Gilmore, op. cit. supra, p. 1069 n. 20.

59. 1958, 355 U.S. 587, 78 S.Ct. 442, 2 L.Ed.2d 510. See additionally, Plumb and Wright, op. cit. supra note 41, p. 78 and cases in footnote 35.

60. Gilmore, op. cit. supra note 58, p. 1069.

postponed a variety of liens to that of the general tax lien. Thus in United States v. White Bear Brewing Co.,[61] a mechanic's lien, affixed by statute to specific property and perfected in the usual sense under state law was subordinated to the federal tax lien even though judicial proceedings to enforce it had been commenced before the federal tax lien was assessed. Apparently the holding was based on the fact that a final judgment had not yet been entered. Suffering the same fate as mechanic's liens are statutory liens of various sorts, e. g., local tax liens, which may have priority over land mortgages.[62] Similarly a mortgagee's payment of real estate taxes, assessments, water rates and attorney's fees, these being added to the debt secured by the mortgage, have been subordinated to the priority of the tax lien.[63]

As was pointed out in an earlier section,[64] in recent years the conflict of state and federal systems of priority frequently resulted in "circular priority" situations. "The conflict was resolved, not at the expense of the non-federal lien that failed the 'choateness' test, but at the expense of a mortgagee or other fully perfected and 'choate' interest which had, in all other respects, priority over the federal tax lien. Suppose, for example, that a $10,000 mortgage had priority under *federal* law over a $15,000 federal tax lien, which had priority under *federal* law over a $3,000 state or local tax lien (or a mechanic's lien, landlord's lien or attachment), which in turn had priority under *state* law over the mortgage. Upon foreclosure, suppose the property produced $24,000, which was insufficient to satisfy the $28,000 in liens. The solution adopted by the Supreme Court was first to set aside the amount of the prior mortgage ($10,000), leaving $14,000 to be applied on the federal claim, which under federal law was junior only to the mortgage. From the $10,000 which had been set aside, $3,000 would be applied on the lien which had priority over the mortgage under state law, leaving $7,000 for the mortgagee—who, were it not for the *junior* federal tax lien, would have been amply protected by equity cushion against any impairment of his interest by property tax delinquencies." [65]

The 1966 tax lien act. In 1966 Congress enacted comprehensive tax lien legislation and also made major changes in the position of federal taxes in bankruptcy.[66] Although most of the changes that had been urged were incorporated in the new law its provisions "satisfied no one completely, [it] achieved the unanimous support of the American Bar Association and some seventeen interested trade associations." [67] How-

61. 1956, 350 U.S. 1010, 76 S.Ct. 646, 100 L.Ed. 871 reversing 7th Cir., 1955, 227 F.2d 359, rehearing denied 351 U.S. 958, 76 S.Ct. 845, 100 L.Ed. 1480. See Priority of Federal Tax Liens, 1963, 8 Utah L.Rev. 253, 255; Plumb, The New Federal Tax Lien Law, 1967, 53 A.B.A.J. 68; Plumb, Federal Liens and Priorities—Agenda for the Next Decade, 1967, 77 Yale L.J. 228, 230 n. 24. Plumb thinks that the decision in this case, "appropriating the labor and materials of workmen to the tax delinquency of another," * * * "probably gave the greatest impetus to the reform movement which culminated in the 1966 Act."

See additional references on the question of priority of mechanics' liens and a federal general tax lien, Osborne, Cases Secured Transactions, 1968, p. 374, 2d col. ¶ 6.

62. See Note, 1960, 12 Syracuse L.Rev. 119; note, 1956, 25 Ford.L.Rev. 100; 957, 29 Rocky Mt.L.Rev. 436; Note, 1955, 27 Miss.L.J. 69. On circuity problems that arise out of such priorities look at Manchester Federal Savings & Loan Ass'n v. Emery-Waterhouse Co., 1959, 102 N.H. 233, 153 A.2d 918. See also Gilmore, Circular Priority Systems, 1961, 71 Yale L.J. 52–74; Anderson, Federal Tax Liens, 1953, 41 Cal.L.Rev. 241, 269–271. Cf. Notes, 1957, 66 Yale L.J. 784; 1957, 32 N.Y.U.L.Rev. 851. See also Osborne, Cases Secured Transactions, 1968, Chapter 19, § 2 at pp. 342–347.

63. See Notes, 1962, 38 Notre Dame Law. 89; 1961, 35 Tulane L.Rev. 248.

64. Section 209. Circuity of Lien.

65. Plumb, Federal Liens and Priorities—Agenda for the Next Decade, 1967, 77 Yale L.Jour. 228, 231.

66. The most complete coverage and analysis of the new legislation is by Plumb and Wright, Federal Tax Liens, published in 1967 by the Joint Committee on Continuing Legal Education of the American Law Institute and the American Bar Association. A short survey of the enactment is by Plumb, The New Federal Tax Lien Law, 1967, 53 A.B.A.J. 66–69. For additional discussions, see note 41, supra.

67. See Plumb, op. cit. supra note 66, p. 66.

ever, many problems remain to be dealt with [68] and objections to and difficulties have been pointed out in the provisions that were enacted.[69]

One change of language was to substitute "holder of a security interest" for "mortgagee" and "pledgee," and to define "security interest" as "any interest in property acquired by contract for the purpose of securing payment or performance of an obligation or indemnifying against loss or liability." [70]

The rules governing security for future advances before 1966 have been termed "intolerable." [71] The 1966 changes, although not going as far as was desired by proponents of alteration have resulted in some amelioration.

So far as the effect of actual notice is concerned although not as yet authoritatively settled, it is probable that the former majority view [72] has been adopted by the 1966 law,[73] but with an exception to be noted with respect to future advances.

Under the 1966 Act a "security interest" exists as against a subsequently filed federal tax lien "to the extent that at such time the holder has parted with *money or money's*

worth" [74] and also that it has become so far protected under state law that it would be protected against a judgment lien arising as of the time notice of the tax lien is filed.[75] Even though the security interest came into existence after the tax lien notice filing the tax lien is not valid with respect to it if it falls under the terms of Int.Rev.Code § 6323 (c) (1) B and (d) (2), 26 U.S.C.A. The first of these provisions allows 45 days following the perfection of security under local law (i. e., the security interest would be protected against judgment liens arising out of a judgment arising out of an unsecured obligation, Int.Rev.Code § 6323d(2), at the time of the filing) during which the creditor may safely disburse the loan or other consideration without searching for a filed intervening federal tax lien. Should the creditor before the 45 days are up obtain *actual notice or knowledge* that a federal lien has been filed any further disbursement after then is subordinated to the tax lien.[76]

The foregoing exception applies only if the property subject to the security interest was property belonging to the taxpayer-debtor at the time of the tax filing, and also was covered as to the postfiling disbursement by a written agreement entered into before the tax lien filing.[77]

The application of this provision is very limited.[78] Obviously it will not be of any use

---

68. Plumb op. cit. supra note 65, 605, 670, 1104.

69. See Young, op. cit. supra note 41.

70. Int.Rev.Code § 6323(a) and (h), (i) (26 U.S.C.A.).

71. Plumb v. Wright, op. cit. supra note 66, p. 58.

72. See text and footnote at notecall 54, supra. This made actual knowledge immaterial if notice of the lien had not been filed.

73. Plumb and Wright, op. cit. supra note 66, p. 76, basing the belief on Int.Rev.Code of 1954, § 6323(d), which is noted later. This section deals with priority of disbursements made within 45 days after the filing of notice of the lien "or (if earlier) before the person making such disbursement had actual notice or knowledge of tax lien filing." It would be anomalous if security before filing were subordinated to known but unfiled liens while postfiling advances are protected unless not only the lien but the filing thereof is known.

See also Plumb, Federal Liens and Priorities—Agenda for the Next Decade II, 1968, 77 Yale L.J. 605, 654–6.

74. Int.Rev.Code, § 6323(h) (1) (B) (26 U.S.C.A.). See Plumb and Wright, op. cit. supra note 66, pp. 78–79.

75. Int.Rev.Code, § 6323(h) (9) (A) (26 U.S.C.A.). Under this provision if the lender takes the steps that local law requires for perfecting his security interest against subsequent judgment lien creditors, it will be protected against the tax lien. If local law does not require recording or filing in order to maintain the priority of a security interest as against intervening judgment lien creditors, this refiling will be necessary to protect the security against a federal tax lien. See Plumb and Wright, op. cit. supra note 66, pp. 97–98.

76. Plumb and Wright, op.cit. supra note 66, p. 79.

77. Int.Rev.Code § 6323(d) (1) (26 U.S.C.A.). Security in after-acquired property is discussed later.

78. Plumb and Wright, op. cit. supra note 66, p. 79, suggest it may be helpful in mortgage transactions

in a typical open-end mortgage where the future advances are spread over a long time.

A special exception of much greater importance is the one providing for the financing of construction or improvement of *real property* by cash advances either to the owner or the contractor.[79] For this exception to apply there must have been here also a written agreement to make the loans entered into before the tax lien was filed, and perfected as against judgment liens before this time.[80] However, there is no time limit on when the advances may thereafter be made, even after knowledge of the lien, and the advances need not be obligatory.[81] The protection is limited to cash disbursements and extends only to security consisting of the real property itself, in the case of advances to the owner, or the proceeds of the contract in case of advances to the contractor.[82] The priority accorded to real property construction loans may extend also to property acquired after the filing of a federal tax lien provided the security interest must have been intended to embrace such after-acquired property and must be protected under state laws as against judgment liens arising as of the time the tax lien is filed.[83]

Under the pre 1966 law many expenses the mortgagee might incur in enforcing his security were not protected against the federal tax lien even though the mortgage itself was. The 1966 amendments provide, however, that if the federal tax lien is not valid against a security interest, and if local law or valid agreement so provide, the priority of the security interest shall extend to the "reasonable" expenses of collecting or enforcing the obligation.[84] Subject to the same conditions, the priority extends to the "reasonable" charges and expenses of an indenture trustee or agent holding the security interest; to the "reasonable" costs of insuring, preserving, or repairing the property, and of insuring the payment of the obligation; and to amounts paid to satisfy a lien on the property, provided such lien itself had priority over the federal lien.[85]

Commercial transactions financing agreements, which are defined by § 6323(c)(2)(C)(iii) to include mortgages on real property, are given priority over a federal tax lien even though it came into existence after notice of the tax lien had been filed. All the conditions of the general exception to the priority of the federal tax lien must be met.[86] The principal feature that this commercial financing exception adds is the permission to add or substitute security not owned by the borrower at or before the tax lien is filed, but acquired by him within 45 days thereafter.[87] As previously stated, it was decided before 1966 that a mechanic's lien on the property improved was too "inchoate" to prevail over a federal tax lien unless the mechanic's lien was reduced to judgment be-

---

when there may be a delay between the search of title and actual disbursement. Also, perhaps, in corporate bond issues. See § 123 supra. They involve, technically, the making of optional advances by each original purchaser, at a date later than the search of title and execution of the mortgage.

79. Int.Rev.Code, § 6323(c)(3)(A)(i) and (ii) (26 U.S.C.A.).

80. Int.Rev.Code, § 6323(c)(1) (26 U.S.C.A.).

81. See Plumb and Wright, op. cit. supra note 66 p. 85, fn. 70.

82. See Plumb and Wright, op. cit. supra note 66, p. 86.

83. Plumb and Wright, op. cit. supra note 66, p. 90. Fixtures subsequently added to mortgaged realty, if they become a part thereof under local law, apparently would not be considered after-acquired property. Id. at p. 93.

84. Int.Rev.Code, § 6323(e)(3) (26 U.S.C.A.).

85. Int.Rev.Code, § 6323(e)(2), (4), (5) and (6) (26 U.S.C.A.). § 6323(e)(1) provides that the unpaid interest and carrying charges shall have the same priority as the debt.

86. See text at notecalls 75 and 77, ante. See also Plumb and Wright, op. cit. supra note 66, pp. 80–85.

87. Int.Rev.Code, § 6321(c)(2)(B) (26 U.S.C.A.). See also Plumb and Wright, op. cit. supra note 66, p. 81. For a discussion of the exception and criticism, id. at pp. 82–85. For coverage of the law as to after-acquired and substituted security under this exception, see id., pp. 89–96.

fore the federal tax lien was filed.[88] "Thus, the value that the mechanic's lienor added to the property was appropriated to pay the owner's taxes, whether the taxes were assessed before or after the work was done." [89]

The 1966 amendment, § 6323(a), extended to mechanic's lienors the same protection against subsequent and unfiled federal tax liens that it gave to holders of security interests. Int.Rev.Code § 623(h)(2) (26 U.S.C. A.) defines Mechanic's Lienor as "any person who under local law has a lien on real property (or on the proceeds of a contract relating to real property) for services, labor, or materials furnished in connection with the construction or improvement of such property." The mechanic's lienor still must perfect and maintain his lien under local law but he no longer is subordinated because all of these further steps were not taken before filing of the federal tax lien.

Under Int.Rev.Code § 6323(h)(2) (26 U.S. C.A.) the mechanic's lien's priority over the federal tax lien cannot date back before the particular lienor begins "to furnish the services, labor, or materials." That is true even though under local law his lien is good against other parties from the time the building project was started or from the date of the contract. The mechanic's lien thus perfected will take priority over federal tax liens filed after the earliest date at which it "becomes valid under local law against subsequent purchasers without actual notice." [90]

The almost universal rule of state law is that real property taxes are imposed upon the entire property, including all interests therein, and therefore are paramount to all such interests. The lien interest of the United States could not constitutionally be subjected to these burdens without the consent of Congress.[91]

In 1966 Congress provided by Int.Rev. Code § 6323(b)(6)(A) and (B) (26 U.S. C.A.) that preference should be given to a lien on real property securing payment of a tax of general application levied by any taxing authority based upon the value of this real property. An important proviso is that the real property tax lien be one that had priority under local law over preexisting security interests in the property. Special assessments levied directly on the realty to pay for public improvements were given the same preference on the same condition.

As a result of the pre 1966 law of priority, where state real property taxes or assessments came in competition with mortgages of realty and a general federal tax lien on that same property a problem of circularity arose. The mortgage had priority over a subsequently filed federal tax lien, which had priority over the state tax upon the realty; but the state property tax was superior to the mortgage under state law. A previous consideration of the matter pointed out the solution reached by the federal courts.[92]

88. See text and footnotes at notecalls 61 and 65, supra.

89. Plumb and Wright, op. cit. supra note 66, p. 127.

90. Int.Rev.Code, § 6323(h)(2) (26 U.S.C.A.).

In a few states the mechanic's lien dates from a time after the commencement of work or supplying materials, i.e., from the time of filing a claim of lien. See § 214, supra. As against the federal tax lien it will win over it only if that filing is before the federal tax lien filing.

As previously noted, § 215, supra, some statutes give a later mechanic's lien priority over buildings and improvements subsequent to a mortgage on the property. The new Act to a minor degree, and modified by a number of petty and difficult to justify requirements, gives limited protection to such

mechanic's lienors. See Plumb v. Wright, op. cit. supra note 66, pp. 129, 130.

For a survey of status of mechanics' liens under the 1966 legislation, see Plumb, op. cit. supra note 65, pp. 287, 676–680.

91. United States v. City of New Britain, Conn.1954, 347 U.S. 81, 74 S.Ct. 367, 98 L.Ed. 520; United States v. Allegheny County, Pa.1944, 322 U.S. 174, 64 S.Ct. 908, 88 L.Ed. 1209. See Plumb and Wright, op. cit. supra note 66, p. 152.

92. See text and notes at notecalls 64 and 65, supra. See also Plumb and Wright, op. cit. supra note 66, pp. 99–101.

This solution was to set aside from the proceeds of the property the amount of the prior mortgage and award to the federal tax lien the balance, or enough of it to satisfy it. State law was then free

In 1966 Congress by Int.Rev.Code § 6323 (b) (6) (26 U.S.C.A.) ended this major circularity problem in the matter of state real property taxes and assessments. It did so by according them priority over the federal tax lien. The result is that, after payment of the foregoing preferred local liens, the mortgagee will be paid in full before the federal general tax lien can claim anything.

The circuity problem may still arise with respect to other kinds of state liens that are prior to a real property mortgage under state law but are still postponed to the federal tax lien. Examples are other state taxes, mechanic's liens, attachments, and landlord's liens. Several methods of avoiding these remaining circuity problems have been suggested but none of them are completely satisfactory or free from difficulty.[93]

The methods of divesting a federal lien clearly are within the power of Congress to prescribe. In a decision involving two companion cases, the Supreme Court held that state law governing divestiture of federal tax liens was to be adopted as federal law, except to the extent that Congress might have entered the field; and that both in the case of a judicial sale under Pennsylvania

law and in the case of a sale by a trustee-mortgagee pursuant to powers of sale without institution of judicial proceedings in accordance with California law, a junior federal lien was effectively extinguished, though the United States was not, and was not required to be, a party to the proceedings under the state law.[94]

As a result of this decision Congress, in 1966, by Int.Rev.Code § 7425 (26 U.S.C.A.), superimposed certain protective requirements on the state procedures, which otherwise were left as they were before. The new protections are applicable only to tax liens. Consequently junior federal mortgages and nontax liens may still be cut off without notice, if state procedures permit.[95] It has been urged that the requirements of notice to the government and redemption from sale in mortgage foreclosures should apply to federal mortgages and nontax liens as well as to federal tax liens.[96]

LIS PENDENS

222. The doctrine of lis pendens, in spite of statutory modification, still constitutes a risk to the mortgagee.

The doctrine of lis pendens is another matter of which a mortgagee must take cognizance. Originating as a judicial doctrine

to divide the amount so set aside according to its own rules. This resulted in the state preferred lien for realty taxes, assessments, mechanic's liens and other charges being first satisfied and the mortgagee got only what was left of the amount set aside for him. In 1963 the Supreme Court refused to reconsider this solution. United States v. Buffalo Sav. Bank, 1963, 371 U.S. 228, 83 S.Ct. 314, 9 L.Ed. 2d 283.

For a recent case involving circuity, look at H. B. Agsten & Sons, Inc. v. Huntington Trust and Sav. Bank, 1967, 388 F.2d 156.

93. See Plumb and Wright, op. cit. supra note 66, pp. 102–105. The priority problems arising out of federal priority under section 3466 of the Revised Statute are dealt with, id., Chapter Six. See also Gilmore, Security Interests in Personal Property, 1965, pp. 1048–1054; Plumb, The New Federal Tax Lien Law, 1967, 53 A.B.A.J. 66, 69.

That real property taxes incurred during bankruptcy may still create the very circular priority problem that the 1966 legislation tried to end, see Plumb, Federal Liens and Priorities—Agenda for the Next Decade, 1967, 77 Yale L.J. 228, 286.

94. United States v. Brosnan and Bank of America Nat. Trust & Sav. Ass'n, 1960, 363 U.S. 237, 80 S.Ct. 1108, 4 L.Ed.2d 1192.

In United States v. John Hancock Mut. Life Ins. Co., 1960, 364 U.S. 1, 81 S.Ct. 1, 5 L.Ed.2d 1, discussed and criticised in Note, 1961, 10 Kan.L.Rev. 99, where the United States had been joined as a party in the proceeding, the United States could redeem within one year from the date of sale as provided in 28 U.S.C.A. § 2410(e), notwithstanding the conflicting state statute. See also § 307 note 36, infra.

95. See Plumb and Wright, op. cit. supra note 66, pp. 232–235 for an account of the new requirements and their effects. See also, Plumb, Federal Liens and Priorities—Agenda for the Next Decade, 1968, 77 Yale L.J. 1104, 1168–1188.

96. See Plumb, The New Federal Tax Lien Law, 1967, 53 A.B.A.J. 69. See also Plumb and Wright, op. cit. supra note 66, pp. 296–299.

in England,[97] it was received in the United States,[98] and today in most states is covered to a greater or lesser degree by statutes that generally are construed to be merely supplementary to and not in substitution of the original doctrine.[99] That doctrine concerns persons who acquire an interest in property [1] which is subject to litigation. If the property is specifically described and within the court's jurisdiction, it is taken subject to the final determination in the action; it is immaterial that the person acquiring it is not named as a party or that he has no actual knowledge of either the suit or the claim under litigation.[2] Some cases erroneously fail to differentiate the doctrine from that of actual notice of the plaintiff's rights,[3] which would bind a taker of the property regardless of pendency of litigation, the principle of privity of title which applies to alienees after judgment against a grantor,[4] and the rule that property in custody of the court cannot be alienated in derogation of the court's later order.[5] Courts frequently speak of the doctrine as resting upon constructive notice,[6] but its true basis is public policy, the necessity of having such a rule in order to give effect to the judgments of courts. Without such a rule, it would be possible to defeat the judgment by a conveyance to some stranger, and the plaintiff would be forced to commence a new action against him.[7]

The hardship of the judicial doctrine of lis pendens upon innocent purchasers of property who, as a practical matter, could not discover pending litigation affecting the property they bought, led to the enactment generally in the United States of statutes compelling litigants to file notice of the pendency of their suits in order for third parties to be bound by the doctrine.[8] Since few of the statutes [9] include the entire field of the judicial doctrine, and since the judicial doctrine is unaffected except to the extent that the statutes apply, there are many situations in which it still operates—a fact that might prove a pitfall to the unwary pur-

---

97. See Ord.No. 12 in Chancery, 15 Bacon's Works, 353; Co.Lit. 344b.

98. See Murray v. Ballou, 1815, 1 Johns.Ch., N.Y., 566, 577, opinion by Chancellor Kent.

99. See Note, Statutory Lis Pendens, 1935, 20 Iowa L.Rev. 476, for a list and analysis of statutes dealing with lis pendens. For the nature and operation of the doctrine of *lis pendens* in Louisiana, see Redmann, The Louisiana Law of Recordation: Principles and Some Problems, 1965, XXXIX Tulane L. Rev. 491, 509–511.

1. The doctrine applies to real property, and, in the United States, by majority rule, to some, although not all, kinds of personal property. See notes, 1934 47 Harv.L.Rev. 1023; 1932, 12 Or.L.Rev. 68; 1912, 12 Col.L.Rev. 361; 1916, 25 Yale L.J. 506.

2. See 1934, 47 Harv.L.Rev. 1023, 1024; 1937, 25 Cal.L.Rev. 480.

3. E. g., not observing the distinction between lis pendens and actual notice: Fogg v. Providence Lumber Co., 1885, 15 R.I. 15, 23 A. 31; Dent v. Pickens, 1906, 59 W.Va. 274, 53 S.E. 154. On the other hand, observing the difference: Dillard & Coffin Co. v. Smith, 1900, 105 Tenn. 372, 59 S.W. 1010; People's Bank of Wilkesbarre v. Columbia Collieries Co., 1914, 75 W.Va. 309, 84 S.E. 914.

4. Gale v. Tuolumne County Water Co., 1914, 169 Cal. 46, 145 P. 532; Hungate v. Hetzer, 1910, 83 Kan. 265, 111 P. 183; Comanche Ice & Fuel Co. v. Binder & Hillery, 1917, 70 Okl. 28, 172 P. 629.

5. E. g., where the property has been attached, sequestered or is in the hands of a receiver. Merchants' Nat. Bank of Omaha v. McDonald, 1901, 63 Neb. 363, 88 N.W. 492, rehearing denied 63 Neb. 363, 89 N.W. 770; Sherburne v. Strawn, 1883, 52 Kan. 39, 34 P. 405; Young v. Clapp, 1892, 147 Ill. 176, 32 N.E. 187, s. c., 1893, 35 N.E. 372.

6. E. g., "A *lis pendens* duly prosecuted is notice to a purchaser so as to effect and bind his interest." Jackson ex dem. Hendricks v. Andrews, 1831, 7 Wend. (N.Y.) 152, 156, 22 Am.Dec. 574.

7. See Newman v. Chapman, 1823, 23 Va. 93, 102, 14 Am.Dec. 766; Jarrett v. Holland, 1938, 213 N.C. 428, 196 S.E. 314; Brown v. Cohn, 1896, 95 Wis. 90, 69 N.W. 71, 60 Am.St.Rep. 83. "This necessity [of the rule] is so obvious, that there was no occasion to resort to the presumption that the purchaser really had or by inquiry might have had, notice of the pendency of the suit, to justify the existence of the rule. In fact, it applied in cases in which there was a physical impossibility that the purchaser, could know, with any possible diligence on his part, of the existence of the suit, * * *." Newman v. Chapman, supra, at 102.

8. E. g., West's Ann.Cal.Code Civ.Proc. § 409.

9. Only three statutes embrace all lis pendens. **Fla.** S.A. § 48.23; Mich.C.L.A. § 565.25; Va.Code 1950, §§ 8–142, 8–143.

chaser who relied solely upon an investigation of the records of notice.[10]

Even as to situations covered by the statutes there are problems as to their effect.[11] Clearly the recorded notice of lis pendens will bind all subsequent mortgagees of the property, but what is its effect upon prior unrecorded mortgages and other conveyances? There seems no doubt that if a party has actual knowledge of the unrecorded mortgage at the time of filing his notice, the mortgagee will not be bound by the judgment unless made a party to the action.[12] Where he learns of the unrecorded mortgage after recording notice and before judgment one jurisdiction [13] at least imposes upon him the affirmative duty of joining the holder of the mortgage, but several others merely permit the latter to intervene and, if he fails to do so, he is bound by the judgment.[14]

But, assuming that the filing of the notice of lis pendens will be binding upon the holder of the prior unrecorded mortgage, there is still the question of just what effect these statutes have upon his substantive rights. Two situations may be considered. In one the mortgagee or grantee who had taken his conveyance prior to the filing of lis pendens acquired an encumbrance or title inferior to that of the plaintiff who is claiming the benefit of the lis pendens. In the other, the prior mortgagee or grantee has a superior, although unrecorded interest and, if he had been made a party to the action, would have prevailed. The first situation is illustrated by an unrecorded second mortgage which is recorded after an action of foreclosure is

brought and notice of lis pendens is filed by the first mortgagee. The second may arise where a mortgagee for value and without notice that his mortgagor has obtained the property from the plaintiff by fraud fails to record before an action to recover the property from his mortgagor has been brought and lis pendens filed. Or, again, the plaintiff bringing the action and filing lis pendens against the mortgagor of the unrecorded mortgage may have the status of a creditor only who, both by judicial doctrine and under the recording acts would be inferior to the unrecorded mortgage, leaving aside the effect upon his rights of the lis pendens statute. The courts generally say that the lis pendens statutes have only a procedural operation and do not affect substantive rights. Applying this to the second type of case, there are authorities holding that, since the prior mortgagee or grantee with a superior right would have prevailed even if he had been made a party to the action, his interest will not be cut off by the filing of lis pendens.[15] On the other hand, since the holder of the inferior interest would have lost as against the plaintiff if he had been joined in the action, the filing of lis pendens will enable the plaintiff to prevail over him without joinder.[16] It will be noticed that when the court is asked to determine whether the filing of lis pendens will preclude the holder of the prior unrecorded interest from contesting

---

10. See 1934, 20 Iowa L.Rev. 476, 480–483.

11. In addition to the ones discussed in the text, see notes, 1942, 20 N.Car.L.Rev. 311; 1933, 23 Cal.L. Rev. 108; 1934, 22 Cal.L.Rev. 677, 681.

12. See Munger v. T. J. Beard & Bro., 1907, 79 Neb. 764, 113 N.W. 214, 126 Am.St.Rep. 688; Lamont v. Cheshire, 1875, 65 N.Y. 30.

13. Chaudoin v. Claypool, 1933, 174 Wash. 608, 25 P. 2d 1036, note, 1934, 8 Wash.L.Rev. 197.

14. Bristol Lumber Co. v. Dery, 1931, 114 Conn. 88, 157 A. 640; Ayrault v. Murphy, 1873, 54 N.Y. 203.

15. Justice v. Shaw, 1919, 103 Neb. 423, 172 N.W. 253; Nugent v. Foley, N.Y.Sup.Ct.1912, 137 N.Y.S. 705; Lamont v. Cheshire, 1875, 65 N.Y. 30, also on the grounds of notice at the time of filing notice; Tallyn v. Cowden, 1930, 158 Wash. 335, 290 P. 1005; Chaudoin v. Claypool, 1933, 174 Wash. 608, 25 P.2d 1036, also on ground of notice at time of filing lis pendens.

16. Moore v. Schneider, 1925, 196 Cal. 380, 238 P. 81; Bristol Lumber Co. v. Dery, 1931, 114 Conn. 88, 157 A. 640; Globe Const. Co. v. Yost, 1933, 173 Wash. 522, 23 P.2d 892; Bernard v. Baldwin, 1919, 106 Misc. 631, 175 N.Y.S. 138; Globe Const. Co. v. Yost, 1932, 169 Wash. 319, 13 P.2d 433. See Peoples Trust Co. v. Tonkonogy, 1911, 144 App.Div. 333, 128 N.Y.S. 1055. Such also is the effect of a statute dealing not with lis pendens but directly with foreclosure actions. West's Ann.Cal.Code of Civ.Proc. § 726.

the plaintiff's title, it decides at that time whether the latter would or would not have prevailed if the other had been made a party. But even in the second type of case there is authority that the filing of lis pendens has a substantive operation similar to that of the recording acts so that a prior conveyance or mortgage will be held to be void against subsequent judgments affecting title if it is not recorded prior to the filing of the notice of lis pendens. In one state the general recording act itself explicitly so provides.[17] This code section has been held not to cut off a prior unrecorded deed as against the purchaser on a tax sale who filed lis pendens in a quiet title action against the record holder, but it is not clear it would not apply to a donee grantee of the owner of record; the court suggested that the section was applicable to persons having a claim to the property based upon an affirmative act by a predecessor of the holder of the unrecorded conveyance.[18] In other states recording acts with no specific provision on lis pendens have been held to extend the doctrine of lis pendens so as to detetrmine substantive rights and cut off otherwise superior titles because they were unrecorded.[19] Perhaps the policy of the recording acts justifies protecting thus a *bona fide* claimant to land who undertakes the cost of litigation.[20]

17. West's Ann.Cal.Civ.Code § 1214, amendment of 1895.

18. Taylor v. Chapman, 1936, 17 Cal.App.2d 31, 61 P. 2d 476, discussed in note, 1937, 25 Cal.L.Rev. 480, reproduced in Osborne, Cases Property Security, 351.

19. Board of Commissioners of Atchison County v. Lips, 1904, 69 Kan. 252, 76 P. 851; Lind v. Goble, 1926, 117 Okl. 195, 246 P. 472; Smith v. Worster, 1898, 59 Kan. 640, 54 P. 675, 68 Am.St.Rep. 385.

20. See note, 1937, 25 Cal.L.Rev. 480, 485.

For a more recent discussion of the cases and the problem, see Gilmore, Security Interests in Personal Property, 1965, § 38.2.

CHAPTER 8

TRANSFER BY THE MORTGAGEE

MODES OF TRANSFER

223. Transfers of the mortgagee's interest are made in terms of (1) assignment of the obligation; (2) conveyance of the interest in the land itself; or (3) of an "assignment of the mortgage."

The mortgagee of real property has two things, the personal obligation [1] and the interest in the realty securing that obligation. This twofold character of the rights of the mortgagee must be kept in mind when transfers by the mortgagee are considered. For a transfer to be complete both the obligation and the security interest must pass to the same person. We have already considered the wide range of obligations that may be secured by a mortgage. [2] The rules governing their transfer are part of the law of subjects, chiefly contracts and negotiable instruments, which are outside the purview of this work. Although it will be necessary to state many of them, this will be done briefly and without much critical examination except in those instances in which the rules determining, and the consequences of their transfer are affected by the fact that the obligations are secured by real property mortgages. The extent and characteristics of the security interest in the property and the broad di-

---

1. See §§ 102–105, supra, on the question of the necessity of an obligation.

2. See Chapter 5, supra.

vision of American states into title, lien, and intermediate states has previously been examined in some detail.[3] As will be seen, these differing theories have some theoretical and practical consequences on the matter of transfer by the mortgagee. It is important, however, to emphasize that regardless of what general theory governs, or what incidents are accorded to this interest, its sole function is to serve as security for the performance of the obligation. The obligation is correctly regarded as the principal thing with the interest in the land attached to it in an extremely important, but subsidiary, capacity. This idea has been expressed variously by saying that the mortgage debt is the principal and the hold upon the land the incident,[4] the accessory;[5] or, resorting to figure of speech, the mere shadow of the substance,[6] which is the obligation. This notion is of fundamental importance. It means that the security is inseparable from the obligation and that whoever can establish his priority of claim to the obligation gets with it the security interest in the land provided it is still in existence. This is true even though it may be that, under the laws governing its ownership, title to it is in another.[7] This last qualification is a reminder

that, in spite of the dominance of the obligation, the mortgagee's rights are nevertheless dual in their nature. This duality makes it possible, in title jurisdictions at least, for the mortgagee to transfer his legal interest in the land to one person, or to keep title to it in himself, and to assign the secured debt to another.[8] Or, even more strikingly, since the debt is ordinarily in the form of a written instrument such as a bond or promissory note, there are instances where the mortgagee has conveyed the land to one, assigned the bond to a second, and delivered the deed in pledge to a third.[9] This same duality accounts for the fact that in transferring, or attempting to

3. §§ 13–18, 65, and Chapter 6, supra.

4. Morris v. Bacon, 1877, 123 Mass. 58, 25 Am.Rep. 17; Paige v. Chapman, 1878, 58 N.H. 333; Magie v. Reynolds, 1893, 51 N.J.Eq. 113, 26 A. 150. See Note, Transfer of the Mortgagee's Interest in Florida, 1961, 14 U. of Fla.L.Rev. 98.

5. Ladue v. Detroit & M. R. Co., 1865, 13 Mich. 380, 87 Am.Dec. 759.

6. Mead v. York, 1852, 6 N.Y. 449, 57 Am.Dec. 467.

7. Pomeroy, Eq.Juris., 5th ed., § 1210.
In Kernohan v. Manss, 1895, 53 Ohio St. 118, 41 N.E. 258, 29 L.R.A. 317, the mortgagee, before the maturity of a negotiable note secured by a mortgage, first forged a duplicate of the note and transferred it and the legal title of the mortgage to A, and then negotiated the genuine note to B who knew nothing of the prior transfer to A. The court held that A, although he got legal title to the mortgage and an equitable right to the note, lost to B, who, as a holder in due course, had the better right to the mortgage obligation. On the other hand, where the genuine note is transferred to B after its maturity

and B is held to take it subject to the prior equitable right in A to it, A will prevail over B as to both the debt and the mortgage. Kernohan v. Durham, 1891, 48 Ohio St. 1, 26 N.E. 982, 12 L.R.A. 41.

8. Stewart v. Crosby, 1863, 50 Me. 130. Another instance of separation of the title to the property and the debt secured occurred at common law when the mortgagee died. The title to the land went to the heirs but the debt went to the personal representative. Kinna v. Smith, 1834, 3 N.J.Eq. 14; Demarest v. Wyncoop, 1897, 3 Johns.Ch. (N.Y.) 129, 8 Am.Dec. 467, "Though the technical fee may descend to the heir, he takes it in trust for the personal representatives" of the mortgagee. The latter is the only one who can foreclose, Swinton v. Cuffman, 1919, 139 Ark. 121, 213 S.W. 409; Stribling v. Splint Coal Co., 1888, 31 W.Va. 82, 5 S.E. 321, and, although it would seem correct to join the heir as holder of the title, dry though it be, it has been held that he need not be made a part at all. See Kinna v. Smith, 1834, 3 N.J.Eq. 14, stating this last to be the general rule; Citizens Nat. Bank v. Dayton, 1886, 116 Ill. 257, 4 N.E. 492. He is also the one to whom payment must be made. Drake v. Cloonan, 1894, 99 Mich. 121, 57 N.W. 1098, 41 Am. St.Rep. 586. And he can transfer it to another person and the assignment will operate to give the assignee the security, certainly in equity. Kinna v. Smith, 1834, 3 N.J.Eq. 14. For such a transfer to be complete technically title would have to be conveyed by the heir to the transferee. Barrett v. Hinckley, 1888, 124 Ill. 32, 14 N.E. 863, 7 Am.St. Rep. 331; cf. McCausland v. Baltimore Humane Society, 1902, 95 Md. 741, 52 A. 918. Statutes frequently provide that the entire mortgage interest, the debt, and the interest in the land, shall go to the personal representative. Act 44 and 45 Vict. c. 41, § 30, (1881); Md., Ann.Code 1939 (Flack), tit. Morts., Art. 66, § 22; Nathan Miller & Sons v. Blinn, 1914, 219 Mass. 266, 106 N.E. 985. And, of course, in lien jurisdictions no such division would occur, all going to the personal representatives.

9. Merritt v. Bartholick, 1867, 36 N.Y. 44; Barrett v. Hinckley, 1888, 124 Ill. 32, 14 N.E. 863.

transfer, his interests, the mortgagee has resorted to three different methods or combinations of them. Thus he may deal solely in terms of assignment of the obligation, solely in terms of a conveyance of the interest in the land itself, or he may frame the transaction in terms of an "assignment of the mortgage." This last phrase could possibly comprise either one or both of the other two. Quite naturally therefore, it lends itself to some divergence of interpretation as to its meaning and effect.

TRANSFER OF THE DEBT [10]

224. A transfer of the debt carries with it the mortgage. This is invariably true in equity; in some jurisdictions it is not true, for certain purposes at least, at law.

From the fundamental principle just noted, that the one and only function of the mortgage is to be security for the obligation, it follows that the transfer of the obligation will carry with it the mortgage as an inseparable incident of it.[11] In lien states this may

be true both at law and in equity and without any formalities [12] other than are required for an effective assignment of the particular variety of obligation the mortgagee happens to have in the case in question. Since the mortgagee's lien is an interest in real property it would seem that the formalities necessary for the transfer of realty should be complied with before the transmission would be effective at law, and there is authority to that effect.[13] What is necessary and suffi-

---

10. The terms "assignment" and "transfer" are used interchangeably and without discrimination to designate any type of transaction by which the rights of the mortgagee in the obligation, as distinct from the security interest in the property, are passed on to another person, disregarding, except when specifically mentioned, any difference in theory as to whether such assignee or transferee gets legal title to the mortgagee's obligation right, or merely an equitable interest alone or coupled with a legal power to enforce it. For an excellent bibliography on the question of what happens when a debt, nonnegotiable in form, is assigned, see Glenn, The Assignment of Choses in Action; Rights of Bona Fide Purchaser, 1934, 20 Va.L.Rev. 621, n. 1. Professor Glenn's own discussion is a valuable addition to the literature on the subject. Also, the terms "debt", "chose in action," and "right in personam" are employed, as indeed they have been in much of this book, as equivalent to the broader "obligation," without spelling out all the problems involved in the question of the mortgage obligation that were considered when it was under direct scrutiny. See Chapter 5, supra. However, since the distinction is of vital importance in the discussions to follow, if the obligation involved is in the form of a negotiable instrument that fact will be noted.

11. See authorities cited in following notes.
" 'The assignment of a bond or note secured by deed of trust carries with it, as an incident of such assignment, the benefit of the lien of the deed of

trust, unless excluded expressly or by fair and reasonable implication.' * * * The assignment or endorsement of the note carried with it to the indorsee or assignee the benefit of the trust lien." Emmons v. Hawk, 1907, 62 W.Va. 526, 531, 59 S.E. 519, 521. Cf. Cooper v. Smith, 1889, 75 Mich. 247, 254, 42 N.W. 815. And see Note, Transfer of the Mortgagee's Interest in Florida, 1961, 14 U. of Fla. L.Rev. 98, 99.
See § 65, supra, on the question of the application of the statute of frauds.

12. In some states statutes explicitly enact the above rule, e. g., Cal.Civ.Code § 2936, "The assignment of a debt secured by a mortgage carries with it the security." Fryer v. Rockefeller, 1875, 63 N.Y. 268; Jones v. Titus, 1919, 208 Mich. 392, 175 N.W. 257. See Note, Transfer of the Mortgagee's Interest in Florida, 1961, 14 U. of Fla.L.Rev. 98, 99.

13. Morrison v. Mendenhall, 1881, 18 Minn. 232, relying, in part, upon a statute requiring recordation of the assignment of a mortgage as a condition precedent to foreclosure by the assignee. See Northern Cattle Co. v. Munro, 1901, 83 Minn. 37, 85 N.W. 919, 85 Am.St.Rep. 444. Look also at Trustees of Union College v. Wheeler, 1874, 61 N.Y. 88, 117, 118. The fact that assignments of mortgages are generally held to be within the terms of either permissive or mandatory recording acts, which would necessitate a written instrument acknowledged by the grantor, would indicate the desirability of such a requirement. See § 233, post. See, also, statutes requiring acknowledgment and recordation of assignments of mortgages before the assignee may foreclose by power of sale in the mortgage. "Where a power to sell real property is given to a mortgagee, or other incumbrancer, in an instrument intended to secure the payment of money, the power is to be deemed a part of the security, and vests in any person who, by assignment, becomes entitled to the money so secured to be paid, and may be executed by him whenever the assignment is duly acknowledged and recorded." West's Ann.Cal.Civ.Code § 858. McKinney's N.Y. EPTL 10–5.3; Mich.C.L.A. § 556.60; Wis.Stat.Ann. 232.56 —semble.
"The reason for this requirement [i. e., recordation] is to make certain that after foreclosure there will be a clear record title. Further, the mortgagor could not safely redeem from one whose interest in the property was not indicated by the record. These

cient to transfer the rights in different sorts of obligations is, as stated above, outside of our project, except to note that it may range from a purely oral assignment,[14] through delivery of the written instrument in which the obligation is expressed [15] or indorsement and delivery of it,[16] to formal or informal written transfers of the debt [17] or note or bond.[18] In title states, the transfer of the debt will carry with it in equity the security of the land.[19] It will not give to the transferee the

legal interest in the property. That will remain in the mortgagee.[20]

The lack of legal title will not prevent the assignee from bringing a bill in equity to foreclose.[21] It will prevent him from enforcing rights, such as bringing ejectment or a writ of entry at law,[22] a customary mode of foreclosure in some states, which are dependent upon having legal title to the land. Furthermore, since the benefit of the security goes to the one who buys the debt, it follows that he gets it even though he did not know at the time of his purchase that the debt was secured.[23] To hold otherwise would involve a separation of the debt and security. It would either leave the latter in the hands of the mortgagee who can do nothing with it since he no longer has the debt, or else would extinguish it because of the happenstance of the transferee's ignorance of its existence. This last result would confer an unjustified windfall upon the mortgagor.[24]

---

reasons are lacking in the case of a trust deed [mortgage] since no lien passes to the creditor, to be assigned by him, and legal title remains at all times in the trustee. Consequently, an assignee of the creditor can order the trustee to sell the property, without having had his assignment recorded [citing Stockwell v. Barnum, 1908, 7 Cal.App. 413, 94 P. 400]." Cormack & Irsfeld, Jr., Applications of the Distinctions Between Mortgages and Trust Deeds in California, 1938, 26 Calif.L.Rev. 206, 210. See also Note, Comparison of California Mortgages, Trust Deeds and Land Sale Contracts, 1960, 7 U.C. L.A.L.Rev. 83, 84.

14. Perkins v. Sterne, 1859, 23 Tex. 561, 76 Am.Dec. 72 (title state, dictum); see Runyan v. Mercereau, 1814, 11 Johns. (N.Y.) 534, 6 Am.Dec. 393, "The assignment of the debt, even by parol, draws the land after it as a consequence."; Pratt v. Bennington Bank, 1838, 10 Vt. 293, 33 Am.Dec. 201, (title state, bill to foreclose).

"As to the mode of transferring the debt, with the incidental right to the benefit of the mortgage lien, absolutely no formalities are required, a merely oral transfer of the debt being regarded as sufficient, as is, obviously, an express written transfer of the debt". 3 Tiffany, Real Prop., 2d Ed., 2525.

15. "A promissory note payable to order, but not indorsed, is the subject of a gift causa mortis," and such gift carries with it the mortgage which secures the obligation. Druke v. Heiken, 1882, 61 Cal. 346, 44 Am.Rep. 553; Kiff v. Weaver, 1886, 94 N.C. 274, 55 Am.Rep. 601.

16. See Kent, J., in Johnson v. Hart, 1802, 2 Johns. Cas. (N.Y.) 322, 329, "wherever the note goes, it will carry the charge upon the land along with it. The estate in the land is here the same thing as the money due upon the note."

17. Cortelyou v. Jones, 1901, 132 Cal. 131, 64 P. 119; Larned v. Donovan, 1894, 31 Abb.N.C. 308, 61 St.R. 337, 29 N.Y.S. 825, affirmed 84 Hun. 533, 32 N.Y.S. 731, 65 St.R. 852.

18. Miller v. Larned, 1862, 103 Ill. 562; Hewell v. Coulbourn, 1880, 54 Md. 59.

19. Jordon v. Cheney, 1883, 74 Me. 359. See other cases in following footnotes.

20. In some cases there seems to be a distinction drawn between the bare legal title to the land, which is real property, held by the mortgagee, and the "security" interest, consisting in the rights and powers to apply the property to the payment of the debt, which is regarded as personalty and an inseparable incident of the debt itself. See Lester v. Walker, 1911, 172 Ala. 104, 55 So. 619.

21. Lawrence v. Knap, 1791, 1 Root (Conn.) 248, 1 Am.Dec. 42; Pettus v. Gault, 1908, 81 Conn. 415, 71 A. 509; Kinna v. Smith, 1834, 3 N.J.Eq. 14; Rembert v. Ellis, 1941, 193 Ga. 60, 17 S.E.2d 165, 137 A. L.R. 479.

22. Adams v. Parker, 1858, 78 Mass. (12 Gray) 53, writ of entry; Bailey v. Winn, 1890, 101 Mo. 649, 12 S.W. 1045, ejectment. Nor will the power of sale contained in the mortgage go to an assignee of the obligation only. Dameron v. Eskridge, 1889, 104 N.C. 621, 10 S.E. 700; cf. Lester v. Walker, 1911, 172 Ala. 104, 55 So. 619; Strother v. Law, 1870, 54 Ill. 413. On the other hand, the mortgagee who has retained the dry legal title can enforce his legal right of entry by court action. Stanley v. Kempton, 1871, 59 Me. 472, writ of entry; see Bailey v. Winn, supra, ejectment. Cf. Barrett v. Hinckley, 1888, 124 Ill. 32, 14 N.E. 863, 7 Am.St. Rep. 331.

23. Betz v. Heebner, 1830, 1 Pen. & W. (Pa.) 280.

24. Of course to give it to the assignee who knew nothing of its results in a gift to him, a fact that weakens any argument based on fairness or justice. It is possible that the courts, faced with a choice between windfalls, let the decision flow from a me-

An even clearer case is where the debt obligation only is transferred to an assignee who knows of the mortgage. The legal title to the land security may remain in the mortgagee[25] or it may be transferred to a third party.[26] Except where the mortgage is in the form of a deed absolute[27] the fact of mortgage would be in the chain of title so that the third party could not be a bona fide purchaser.[28] In such cases the mortgagee or third person who holds the bare security title will hold it in trust[29] for the owner of the debt. If necessary he will be compelled to transfer it to him.[30] Since it is an interest in real property, and, in theory, the legal title however attenuated, it can be transferred only by an instrument that is sufficient by

chanical adherence to the general concept that the security is an incident of the debt and follows it. Further, since the debt is going to be collected from the mortgagor anyway, the only benefit he could reap would be by declaring a homestead in it. It seems doubtful whether the policy of the exemption statutes should extend to favor beating a creditor out of an asset that the debtor had previously subjected to the payment of a particular debt. Apart from this, the property could be seized on execution and the question is really whether the property should be subject to a priority in favor of the debt it was given to secure as against other claims. See Note, Transfer of the Mortgagee's Interest in Florida, 1961, 14 U. of Fla.L.Rev. 98, 99.

25. Jordan v. Cheney, 1883, 74 Me. 359; Barrett v. Hinckley, 1888, 124 Ill. 32, 14 N.E. 863, 7 Am.St. Rep. 331; Romberg v. McCormick, 1901, 194 Ill. 205, 62 N.E. 537; Commonwealth v. Globe Inv. Co., 1897, 168 Mass. 80, 46 N.E. 410.

26. Morris v. Bacon, 1877, 123 Mass. 58, 25 Am.Rep. 17, Osborne, Cases Property Security, 392; Welsh v. Phillips, 1875, 54 Ala. 309, 25 Am.Rep. 679; Averill v. Cone, 1930, 129 Me. 9, 149 A. 297.

27. See § 79, supra.

28. Jordan v. Cheney, 1883, 74 Me. 359; Lord v. Crowell, 1883, 75 Me. 399; see Hussey v. Fisher, 1900, 94 Me. 301, 47 A. 525.

29. Jordan v. Cheney, supra, "the mortgagee and all holding under him will hold the mortgaged property in trust for the holder of the notes."; Lord v. Crowell, supra; Barrett v. Hinckley, 1888, 124 Ill. 32, 14 N.E. 863, 7 Am.St.Rep. 331, "If the mortgagee conveys the land without assigning the debt to the grantee, the latter would hold the legal title as trustee for the holder of the mortgage debt."; Kinna v. Smith, 1834, 3 N.J.Eq. 14.

30. Morris v. Bacon, 1877, 123 Mass. 58, 25 Am.Rep. 17, Osborne, Cases Property Security, 392.

the laws of the jurisdiction in which the property is to pass a legal interest. And, in general, the same requirements will be insisted upon as are necessary where the grantor is the full owner of the legal interest held in mortgage.[31]

CONVEYANCE OF THE LAND

225. There are divergent views as to whether a conveyance by the mortgagee which purports to transfer the mortgaged land will operate also to assign the debt.

Where the mortgagee executes a deed or other instrument which in terms only purports to transfer the mortgaged land, there is considerable difference of opinion as to the effect of his action and, to a degree, title as contrasted with lien theories contribute to the divergent results. As previously noted, in title jurisdictions it is quite possible, provided the proper formalities of conveyance are observed, for the legal interest in the land to be transferred without the debt,[32] but it is not that with which we are here concerned. The present problem is whether such action by the mortgagee will operate not only to transfer the interest in the land but to carry the debt as well. Many

31. Adams v. Parker, 1858, 12 Gray (78 Mass.) 53. See Campbell, Cases Mortgages, 2d ed., 525 n. 1, for cases on the formal requirements necessary to transfer the security interest in the land at law in "title," "intermediate" and "lien" jurisdictions. "In title theory states requiring a deed of conveyance of the legal title to the assignee, all the rules as to form, delivery and acceptance of deeds conveying land in the usual cases between grantor and grantee apply, as to names of the parties, words of conveyance, use of the word 'heirs', recital of a consideration of value or proof by parol of a valuable consideration or a consideration of marriage to make the deed effective under the Statute of Uses, the use of a seal in states where seals are still required and other formal requirements of deeds." Walsh, Mortgages, 253. Cf. Barnes v. Boardman, 1889, 149 Mass. 106, 21 N.E. 308, 3 L.R.A. 785, holding that a deed of assignment of the note and mortgage would pass the fee simple title of the mortgagee in spite of the omission of the word "heirs". Lamson & Co. v. Abrams, 1940, 305 Mass. 238, 25 N.E.2d 374.

32. E. g., Averill v. Cone, 1930, 129 Me. 9, 149 A. 297. See text, supra, § 224.

courts hold that it does give to the grantee at least an equitable right to the secured indebtedness,[33] and this without regard for whether the deed is warranty or quitclaim. But other results have also been reached. In New Hampshire and Maine the deed has this effect only if the mortgagee is in possession at the time; otherwise it is inoperative.[34] This conclusion is based upon the reasoning that before entry by the mortgagee his sole interest, including his right to take possession, is so exclusively for security purposes that it should not even be considered an interest in real property. Rather it is a chattel interest or chose in action inseparably attached to the debt. Consequently, any attempt to transfer it by itself without the debt is in operative.[35] It is, in effect although not admittedly, an adoption *pro tanto* of the lien theory. On the other hand, after entry, the mortgagee has acquired possession and rights going with it which are looked upon as an alienable interest in land even without the debt.[36] Since such an interest can be and is transferred, it apparently has seemed to these courts that it may take the right to the debt with it.[37] The true criterion should

be intent to assign the debt and, consequently, whether the deed does, or does not, have an operative effect to pass some interest in the land independent of the debt would not seem to be decisive on whether it would assign the debt as well. It has also been held that only the bare legal title passes.[38] Other cases hold that the deed is a nullity.[39]

In lien states, if the mortgagee attempts a conveyance in terms of the property or his interest in it, all authorities agree that the effort fails so far as the security interest in the land as a separate item is concerned.[40] Further, the courts ordinarily hold that the conveyance will not operate as an assignment of the debt which would carry the mortgage with it. Some of them talk as though this were a rule of law based either upon the mechanical reason that a conveyance of the incident cannot carry the principal, or else because it is desirable policy.[41] Other courts

---

33. Welsh v. Phillips, 1875, 54 Ala. 309, 25 Am.Rep. 679, warranty deed; Ruggles v. Barton, 1859, 79 Mass. (13 Gray) 506; Hinds v. Ballou, 1863, 44 N. H. 619, quitclaim. Even a release has been held to be sufficient. Welch v. Priest, 1864, 90 Mass. (8 Allen) 165.

34. Ellison v. Daniels, 1840, 11 N.H. 274; Furbush v. Goodwin, 1852, 25 N.H. 425, 456; Wyman v. Porter, 1911, 108 Me. 110, 79 A. 371; Farnsworth v. Kimball, 1914, 112 Me. 238, 243, 91 A. 954, 956.

35. "A conveyance of the land does not transfer the debt, because, so long as the mortgage is considered as an incident to the debt it cannot pass without a transfer of the principal." Smith v. Smith, 1844, 15 N.H. 55, 65. See Farnsworth v. Kimball, 1914, 112 Me. 238, 243, 91 A. 954, 956.

36. See Smith v. Smith, 1844, 15 N.H. 55, 66; "A mortgagee, especially after entry for foreclosure, is considered as having a legal estate, which may be alienated and transferred by any of the established modes of conveyance. * * *" Hunt v. Hunt, 1833, 31 Mass. (14 Pick.) 374, 380.

37. It would seem that similar reasoning should apply in lien states to a conveyance by a mortgagee in possession. See Rollison, Priorities in the Law

of Mortgages, 1933, 9 N.D.Law 50, 80. An answer may be that the basis is too mechanical a test of transfer of the debt.

38. Farrell v. Lewis, 1887, 56 Conn. 280, 14 A. 931; Island Pond Nat. Bank v. Lacroix, 1932, 104 Vt. 282, 158 A. 684. Where the mortgage has previously disposed of the debt to another this is the only operation the conveyance can have. Wolcott v. Winchester, 1860, 81 Mass. (15 Gray) 461; see Ruggles v. Barton, 1859, 79 Mass. (13 Gray) 506.

See Note, Effect of Assignment Without Assigning the Debt—Formalities Necessary to Transfer the Mortgagee's Title to the Mortgaged Property, 1958, 36 N.C.L.Rev. 225, discussing Gregg v. Williamson, 1957, 246 N.C. 356, 98 S.E.2d 481.

39. Devlin v. Collier, 1891, 53 N.J.L. 422, 22 A. 201; Delano v. Bennett, 1878, 90 Ill. 533.

For a general discussion of the effect of a conveyance of the mortgaged premises by the mortgagee, see Rollison, Priorities in the Law of Mortgages, 1933, 9 Notre Dame Law. 50.

40. "A transfer of the mortgage without the debt is a nullity, and no interest is acquired by it. The security cannot be separated from the debt and exist independently of it. This is the necessary legal conclusion, and recognized as the rule by a long course of judicial decisions." Merritt v. Bartholick, 1867, 36 N.Y. 44. See cases in following notes.

41. Peters v. Jamestown Bridge Co., 1855, 5 Cal. 334, 63 Am.Dec. 134; Carter v. Bennett, 1852, 4 Fla. 283, 347; Merritt v. Bartholick, 1867, 36 N.Y. 44; Johnson v. Cornett, 1867, 29 Ind. 59; Swan v. Yaple, 1872, 35 Iowa 248; see Devlin v. Collier, 1891,

treat it as a matter of intention but hold that the intention that the conveyance operate as an assignment of the debt must be shown affirmatively.[42] Where the mortgage is in the form of a deed absolute intended as security for a debt, both lien and title states agree that a deed of conveyance will operate to transfer the interest in the property and the debt it secures.[43] There seems no sufficient reason for treating the deeds absolute cases as different from others. In all cases, regardless of lien or title theory, the inquiry is, or should be directed to whether an assignment of the debt was intended and whether, if so, there is any reason why that intent should not be given effect. The more reasonable inference in the case of a conveyance by a mortgagee is that he intended it to be operative to transfer all of his interest in the property, including the debt. This interpretation certainly is preferable to the futility of a nullity. Consequently, unless there is definite evidence of a contrary intent, the finding should be that he did so intend and that intention should be given effect, at least in equity.

Where a purchaser buys at a void foreclosure sale and is given a conveyance in terms of the land, both the mortgage debt and the security are treated as having passed to him even though this was not the intent because it was supposed that full title to the property was being transferred.[44] Also if the

purchaser of the property on the void foreclosure sale then conveys it, his deed will operate at least as an equitable assignment of both the mortgage title and the mortgage debt.[45] The last two cases do not depend upon a contractual assignment of the mortgage debt but the result comes by operation of law through the doctrine of equitable subrogation.[46]

ASSIGNMENT OF THE "MORTGAGE"

226. An assignment in terms of the mortgage, by the better view, operates as an assignment of both the indebtedness and the security interest in the property. This is true regardless of the form of the indebtedness.

A formal written assignment of the "mortgage" is usual in order that it may be recorded under the recording acts either to give notice or to qualify as a beneficiary under those statutes that require first recording by a claimant. When this form of transfer is used several questions arise. One is what mode of execution is necessary for it to have the effect of transferring the mortgagee's interest in the property. Another is what is required for it to be recordable. The two questions are not identical,[47] although usually if the instrument satisfies the first it will also meet most, if not all, of the requirements of the second. The latter is, of course, determined by the statutory provisions on the subject in each jurisdiction. The first is usually a question of what the courts consider the nature of the mortgagee's interest in the property to be, and then what is re-

53 N.J.L. 422, 427, 22 A. 201, 203. Cf. Gottlieb v. City of New York, 1908, 128 App.Div. 148, 112 N.Y. S. 545; Hawley v. Levee, 1910, 66 Misc. 280, 123 N.Y.S. 4.

42. Noble v. Watkins, 1906, 48 Or. 518, 87 P. 771; Greve v. Coffin, 1869, 14 Minn. 345, Gil. 263, 269; Blessett v. Turcotte, 1910, 20 N.D. 151, 127 N.W. 505; McCammant v. Roberts, 1894, 87 Tex. 241, 27 S.W. 86.

43. Halsey v. Martin, 1863, 22 Cal. 645; Maginn v. Cashin, 1917, 196 Mich. 221, 162 N.W. 1009; Webb v. Crouch, 1912, 70 W.Va. 580, 74 S.E. 730, Ann. Cas.1914A, 728; Hawkins v. Elston, 1915, 58 Colo. 400, 146 P. 254. See §§ 79, 80, ante on the effect, generally of a conveyance by the grantee under a deed absolute intended as a mortgage.
44. Muir v. Berkshire, 1875, 52 Ind. 149; Dutcher v. Hobby, 1890, 86 Ga. 198, 12 S.E. 356, 10 L.R.A. 472,

22 Am.St.Rep. 444; see Parks, Cas. Mortgages, 291 n.; 1912, 40 L.R.A.,N.S., 389.

45. Cooper v. Harvey, 1907, 21 S.D. 471, 113 N.W. 717; Lawrence v. Murphy, 1915, 45 Utah 572, 147 P. 903; Lamprey v. Nudd, 1854, 29 N.H. 299.

46. See Rollison, Priorities in the Law of Mortgages, 1933, 9 Notre Dame Law. 50, 66.

47. E. g., acknowledgment may be a requirement for recordation but not for the transference of the mortgagee's interest in the property.

quired to transfer it at law and in equity, a matter that was considered above.[48]

A further question is whether an assignment in terms only of the mortgage will operate to transfer the mortgagee's interest in the property without the debt. A distinction should be noted between such a purported transfer and one by a deed expressed in terms of the land itself. In the latter case, there is authority in title states that the instrument will operate to convey the bare legal title to be held on a dry trust for the owner of the indebtedness.[49] But it is possible to differentiate between the legal title to the land, the mortgage security interest in the property, and the mortgage debt. That distinction has judicial recognition in cases holding that an assignment of the mortgage, although it may transfer the last two, will not convey the mortgagee's legal title in title jurisdictions.[50] If the distinction is accepted, the most that the instrument could do would be to pass the security interest. However, such an attempt, without the debt, would be regarded as a nullity by any court. Even if it is rejected and the interest in the property is regarded as a unit, instead of being split up into bare legal title and security interest, when the mortgagee expresses his intent in regard to his transfer of it in terms of its

mortgage function, the same result should follow. Without the debt, such an assignment would be without any meaning or use.[51] "The mortgage interest as distinct from the debt is not a fit subject of assignment. It has no determinate value." [52]

The last question is whether an assignment in terms of the mortgage, granting that it is nugatory unless the mortgage debt is transferred by, or with, it, should not operate to assign both the indebtedness and the security interest in the property; the latter at law if in proper form, and if not, in equity. Relying on the principle just referred to, that a transfer of the mortgage without the debt is a nullity, there are cases holding that an assignment in terms of the mortgage is insufficient to transfer the debt and, consequently, is completely ineffective.[53] Additionally there are cases where the debt was in the form of a bond or note which was neither delivered or referred to and this was the basis for holding that the assignment failed completely.[54] This is true although where there is no such separate instrument of indebtedness there is authority that the assignment transfers both debt and mortgage.[55] The theory of these cases apparently is that the failure either to deliver or refer to the separate bond or note indicates an intention not to transfer the debt. Also, it has been said that an assignment of the mortgage is

---

48. By statute in some jurisdictions, an assignment under seal of the mortgage and notes will convey the legal estate in the mortgaged land. Barnes v. Boardman, 1889, 149 Mass. 106, 21 N.E. 308, 3 L.R.A. 785; Lamson & Co. v. Abrams, 1940, 305 Mass. 238, 25 N.E.2d 374. See Smith v. Kelley, 1847, 27 Me. 237, 46 Am.Dec. 595. But cf. cases, post, where an assignment carrying the debt and security interest did not transfer legal title.

49. See text, supra.

50. Lester v. Walker, 1911, 172 Ala. 104, 55 So. 619; McCook v. Kennedy, 1917, 146 Ga. 93, 90 S.E. 713; Williams v. Teachey, 1881, 85 N.C. 402; Morton v. Blades Lumber Co., 1911, 154 N.C. 336, 70 S.E. 623. Look, again, at Northern Cattle Co. v. Munro, 1901, 83 Minn. 37, 85 N.W. 919, 85 Am.St.Rep. 444. Cf. H. Weil & Bros. v. Davis, 1915, 168 N.C. 298, 84 S.E. 395. See Note, Effect of Assignment Without Assigning the Debt—Formalities Necessary to Transfer the Mortgagee's Title to the Mortgaged Property, 1958, 36 N.C.L.Rev. 225, discussing Gregg v. Williamson, 1957, 246 N.C. 356, 98 S.E.2d 481.

51. Pope & Slocum v. Jacobus, 1859, 10 Iowa 262.

52. Id.

53. Hamilton v. Browning, 1883, 94 Ind. 242, semble; Pope & Slocum v. Jacobus, 1859, 10 Iowa 262; Miller v. Berry, 1905, 19 S.D. 625, 104 N.W. 311; see Merritt v. Bartholick, 1867, 36 N.Y. 44.

See Note, Transfer of the Mortgagee's Interest in Florida, 1961, 14 U. of Fla.L.Rev. 98.

54. "The bond represents the debt, while the mortgage is a mere security for the payment of such debt. One is the principal, the other is the mere accessory; and while the assignment of the principal carries with it the accessory, the assignment of the accessory does not carry with it the principal." Cleveland v. Cohrs, 1878, 10 S.C. 224.

55. See, 1873, Carpenter v. O'Dougherty, 1873, 67 Barb. (N.Y.) 397; Earll v. Stumpf, 1882, 56 Wis. 50, 13 N.W. 701.

equivocal and therefore affirmative evidence of intention to transfer the debt must be adduced.[56] The foregoing authorities have been vigorously criticized on the ground that "the expression 'assignment of the mortgage' is almost universally used, not only by the general public, but also by the legislature, the courts, and the legal profession, to describe the transfer of the totality of the mortgagee's rights, that is, his right to the debt as well as the lien securing it. And to hold, as these cases apparently do, that when one in terms assigns a mortgage, he intends, not an effective transfer of his rights as [secured] creditor against the land, but a transfer of his lien alone,[57] which is an absolute nullity, not only ignores the ordinary use of the term "mortgage", but also is in direct contravention of the well recognized rule [58] that an instrument shall, if possible, be construed so as to give it a legal operation."[59] The present writer heartily concurs in these views and there are cases that serve to support them.[60] In all cases, while the basic test should be the intention of the mortgagee, a formal written assignment of the mortgage should create an inference that an assignment was intended and this should be rebutted only by very definite proof of intention to the contrary. And this is true, also, where the debt is in the form of a note or bond.[61] The mortgage secures the debt itself,[62] not the note or bond, they being merely evidence of, or additional security for, the debt, and the mortgagee may intend to assign the debt without dealing with the instruments either by physical delivery or reference to them.[63] And, if it is possible for the intent of the mortgagee to operate to assign the debt without the instruments, or to transfer at least an equitable interest in them without delivery or written reference to them specifically, an assignment in terms of the mortgage should have that effect. For any inference of intent that the mortgagee did not mean to transfer his beneficial interest in the debt, or note, as well as his mortgage on the land securing it because he failed either to deliver the instrument or mention it separately is more than offset by improbability that he intended the utter futility of attempting to transfer his lien while keeping the debt for himself.[64]

NON-NEGOTIABLE DEBTS—EQUITIES OF THE MORTGAGOR

227. The assignee of a mortgage securing a non-negotiable debt takes subject to all equities of the mortgagor existing at the time of the creation of the mortgage and arising before notice to him of its assignment. The same is true as to equities arising after notice if the equity is based on a right of the mortgagor inherent in the terms of the assigned obligation.

A gift by will of a "mortgage" has been held to include the debt. Johnson v. Goss, 1880, 128 Mass. 433.

56. See Fletcher v. Carpenter, 1877, 37 Mich. 412.

57. "It is difficult to imagine a case of formal written assignment of the mortgage in which an unexpressed intent to reserve the debt could exist. It would be a merely futile act without reason or motive. Though the debt is the principal thing and the mortgage its incident, nevertheless the security which the mortgage gives to the creditor is the element of greatest importance and value in the secured debt as property, and an assignment of the mortgage, therefore, is universally regarded, by laymen and lawyers alike, as an assignment of both debt and mortgage." Walsh, Mortgages, 249.

58. Citing Foster v. Johnson, 1888, 39 Minn. 378, 40 N.W. 255; Hamilton v. Browning, 1883, 94 Ind. 242, contra.

59. 5 Tiffany, Real Prop., 3d ed., § 1451.

60. Buell v. Underwood, 1880, 65 Ala. 285; Seabury v. Henley, 1911, 174 Ala. 116, 56 So. 530; Andrews v. Townshend, 1888, 56 Super. 140, 16 St.R. 876, 1 N.Y.S. 421; id., 16 N.Y.St.Rep. 876; Loveridge v. Shurtz, 1897, 111 Mich. 618, 70 N.W. 132, semble; Foster v. Johnson, 1888, 39 Minn. 378, 40 N.W. 255, semble. See, also, Rollison, Priorities in the Law of Mortgages, 1933, 9 Notre Dame Law. 50, 86. See additionally, Note Effect of Assignment Without Assigning the Debt—Formalities Necessary to Transfer the Mortgagee's Title to the Mortgaged Property, 1958, 36 N.C.L.Rev. 225, discussing Gregg v. Williamson, 1957, 246 N.C. 356, 48 S.E.2d 481.

61. See Earll v. Stumpf, 1882, 56 Wis. 50, 13 N.W. 701.

62. See § 105, supra.

63. Campbell v. Birch, 1875, 60 N.Y. 214; Price v. Northern Bond & Mort. Co., 1931, 161 Wash. 690, 297 P. 786, note, under circumstances of the case, regarded as an incident of the mortgage lien.

64. See Tiffany, op. cit., supra note 59.

The fundamental general concept that the debt is the principal and the mortgage a mere incident of it is strikingly illustrated when the assignee of a mortgage securing a non-negotiable obligation, or of a negotiable instrument assigned in a manner other than would constitute the assignee a holder for value in due course, seeks to realize upon his security. In such a case the authorities uniformly follow the rule that he will be able to enforce the mortgage to the same extent, and to same extent only, that he can enforce the obligation.[65] Just precisely the extent to which he can do that is determined by the law governing the assignment of such choses in action, any detailed or critical study of which is, as was previously stated, beyond the scope of this inquiry. However, a brief survey of the main features of that field is desirable in order to have some idea of how the security rights of the assignee are affected by them, and to be able to examine the instances in which the rules may be different by reason of the security feature of the obligation. But leaving this latter point aside for the time being, the general rule is uniformly followed that all defenses to the obligation, legal or equitable,[66] that the mortgagor may have had against the assignor at the time of the assignment are available to the mortgagor when the assignee of the mortgage, even though he bought for value

and took without notice,[67] attempts to enforce it,[68] unless the mortgagor by the form of the instrument intrusted to the assignor or otherwise has estopped himself from setting up a defense.[69] Thus when he seeks to foreclose he may be met by the defense that the bond the mortgage was to secure was void for lack of consideration,[70] that it was partially or wholly paid,[71] or was obtained by mistake, fraud, or duress,[72] was tainted by illegality,[73] that there had been an accord and satisfaction, or was subject to set-offs[74] or counterclaims arising out of another trans-

---

65. The pioneer cases in England are Davies v. Austen, 1790, 1 Ves.Jr. 247, and Matthews v. Wallwyn, 1798, 4 Ves. 118. The latter is usually cited as originating the doctrine. The earliest cases in this country seem to be Norton v. Rose, 1796, 2 Wash. (Va.) 233, and Murray v. Lylburn, 1817, 2 Johns.Ch. (N.Y.) 441, the latter a decision by Chancellor Kent.

66. See § 109, supra, for a survey of these. They include not only the defenses based upon the theory that there is no legal obligation in existence either because it never arose or has been extinguished, e. g., forgery, fraud in the factum or full performance, but the defenses termed equitable because they were originally allowed in that court, such as fraud in the inducement and mistake, and, in addition, all allowable offsets and counterclaims existing at the time of the assignment that the mortgagor could assert against the mortgagee when sued by him.

67. Beck v. Sheldon, 1932, 259 N.Y. 208, 181 N.E. 360. See Williston and Thompson, Contracts, rev. ed., § 432. See Note, Transfer of Mortgagee's Interest in Florida, 1961, 14 U. of Fla.L.Rev. 98, 100.

68. "The rule is conceded that the assignee of the mortgage takes subject to the equities between the original parties, and has no greater rights than the original mortgagee." Rapps v. Gottlieb, 1894, 142 N.Y. 164, 36 N.E. 1052; Davis v. Bechstein, 1877, 69 N.Y. 440, 25 Am.Rep. 218. See also Karesh, Security Transactions, in Survey of South Carolina Law, 1957, 10 S.C.L.Q. 114, 120, discussing Carolina Housing & Mortgage Corp. v. Orange Hill A.M.E. Church, 1957, 230 S.C. 498, 97 S.E.2d 28.

69. See text, infra, § 228.

70. Rapps v. Gottlieb, 1894, 142 N.Y. 164, 36 N.E. 1052; Taylor v. Jones, 1913, 165 Cal. 108, 131 P. 114; Clanton v. Clanton, 1956, 229 S.C. 356, 92 S.E. 2d 878, noted in Karesh, Security Transactions, in Survey of South Carolina Law, 1957, 10 S.C.L.Q. 114, 117.

71. "Whatever the assignee pays he can claim nothing under the assignment but what is actually due between the mortgagor and mortgagee", Chambers v. Goldwin, 1804, 9 Ves. 254; Matthews v. Wallwyn, 1798, 4 Ves. 118; Adams v. Hopkins, 1904, 144 Cal. 19, 77 P. 712; Hellen v. City of Boston, 1907, 194 Mass. 579, 80 N.E. 603.

72. Kerby v. Wade, 1912, 101 Ark. 543, 142 S.W. 1121, fraud; Henry v. State Bank of Laurens, 1906, 131 Iowa 97, 107 N.W. 1034, duress; Hunter v. Chase, 1923, 144 Md. 13, 123 A. 393, fraud and lack of consideration; Paika v. Perry, 1917, 225 Mass. 563, 114 N.E. 830, fraud. See § 112, supra. Glaser v. Connell, 9th Cir. 1958, 266 F.2d 149, rehearing denied Feb. 24, 1959; Carolina Housing & Mortgage Corp. v. Orange Hill A.M.E. Church, 1957, 230 S.C. 498, 97 S.E.2d 28, discussed in Karesh, Security Transactions, in Survey of South Carolina Law, 1957, 10 S.C.L.Q. 114, 120.

73. See § 110, supra.

74. De Laval Separator Co. v. Sharpless, 1907, 134 Iowa 28, 111 N.W. 438, Hanna, Cas.Security, 3d ed., 900.

action or by reason of the mortgagee having been in possession.[75]

Indeed it may be that his rights in the security are subject not only to all of the imperfections of the debt obligation in his hands but, in addition, to those that may relate only to the mortgage itself, e. g., that the deed creating it was defective, or that it was obtained by fraud or in some other manner that would vitiate the mortgage but would not affect the right upon the debt it secured.[76] This is rather academic, however, because it is difficult to imagine an actual case where, as between the parties, the debt was entirely valid but the mortgage securing it subject to a defense.[77] If such a case arose, the argument would be strong that the ordinary rules governing bona fide purchase of real property should apply to determine the rights of the assignee.[78] If the mortgage created was a legal one, the assignment should cut off equitable rights in it of the mortgagor as well as of third parties, provided, of course, that the assignment was such as to transfer to him the legal interest in the property.[79] On the other hand, if it was an equitable mortgage, or if the mortgage was completely void, the assignee should take subject to the rights of the mortgagor.[80] The argument against such a conclusion is that when land is given as security for an obligation it should be treated as though it were property connected with not only the legal incidents of the obligation but governed also by other rules and practices governing the transaction. The divided interests in the property, security interest in the mortgagee and redemption interest in the mortgagor, are sufficiently analogous to the two party relationship between them as to the obligation, and so closely related to it, as to make properly applicable a rule that, as a matter of common prudence, the assignee should inquire of the mortgagor whether there was any defect in the security just as he should in respect to the obligation.

The mortgagor's defenses, furthermore, are not confined to those arising prior to the assignment, although there are some cases that would so limit it,[81] but extend to all that arise prior to knowledge of the assignment by the mortgagor even though after the assignment;[82] and, even beyond this, to defenses that arise after notice if they are based on a right of the defendant inherent in the terms of the assigned obligation.[83]

NON-NEGOTIABLE DEBTS—ESTOPPEL —ESTOPPEL CERTIFICATES

228. Assignees of non-negotiable obligations secured by mortgage usually demand an estoppel certificate, i. e., a written statement signed by the mortgagor, setting forth the amount due on the mortgage and whether it is subject to any defenses or offsets. Other affirmative representations of the mortgagor may also operate as an estoppel. The possibility and general practice of making inquiry of the mortgagor are

75. Matters of set-off and counterclaim are statutory and what claims can be utilized and to what extent they may be asserted against assignees is a matter of statutory language and construction in each jurisdiction. See Williston & Thompson, op. cit., supra note 67.

76. See Trustees of Union College v. Wheeler, 1874, 61 N.Y. 88, 115; Hunter v. Chase, 1923, 144 Md. 13, 123 A. 393, semble, fraud in obtaining mortgage.

77. Even in the defective deed case an equitable mortgage usually arises. See § 32, supra.

78. See § 180, supra.

79. Cf. Trustees of Union College v. Wheeler, 1874, 61 N.Y. 88, 117, 118. See § 185, supra and 229, infra.

80. See § 182, supra.

81. Marling v. Fitzgerald, 1909, 138 Wis. 93, 120 N. W. 388, 23 L.R.A.,N.S., 177, 131 Am.St.Rep. 1003; Bush v. Cushman, 1876, 27 N.J.Eq. 131, alternative ground; Merchants Bank of Buffalo v. Weill, 1900, 163 N.Y. 486, 57 N.E. 749, 79 Am.St.Rep. 605; id., 29 App.Div. 101, 52 N.Y.S. 37, explained in Rollison, Priorities in the Law of Mortgages, 9 Notre Dame Law. 215, 240, on the ground the defense was on a secret, collateral agreement concerning which the assignee had no duty to inquire.

82. See Restatement, Contracts, § 167(1).

83. E. g., where performance in the future by the mortgagee is stipulated for and there is a default in that performance after assignment and notice given of the assignment. See Williston & Thompson, Contracts, rev. ed., § 433.

important both in delimiting the boundaries of estoppel against the mortgagor and differentiating the similar problem in the case of latent equities.

Because of the danger of defenses or offsets by the mortgagor against the mortgagee to which an assignee of a mortgage securing a nonnegotiable obligation would take subject, it is a common and prudent practice [84] for an assignee to demand from the mortgagor an estoppel certificate. This is a written statement, signed by the mortgagor, setting forth the amount due on the mortgage and whether or not it is subject to any offsets, or legal or equitable defenses. The effect of such a certificate is to estop the mortgagor from setting up his defenses against not only the immediate assignee to whom it was made and who relied upon it, but to subsequent assignees claiming under him. [85]

While the formal estoppel certificate is the most certain way of estopping the mortgagor, it is not the only one. Any statements, oral or written, or other conduct by the mortgagor which amount to affirmative representations by the mortgagor that he has no defenses and which are reasonably relied upon by the assignee in taking the assignment for value are sufficient to prevent the mortgagor from using them. [86] Similarly, where A delivered a mortgage to B without consideration in order that B might raise money on it for A, and B assigned the mortgage to C for value but did not account to A, the mortgage is valid in C's hands. [87] Nevertheless, what may be sufficient in the way of misleading conduct or reasonable reliance to establish an estoppel in other situations, e. g., where latent equities are concerned, are not sufficient as against the mortgagor. The reasons are not difficult to understand. They flow from the duty of the assignee, imposed upon him by the uniform rule that the mortgagor's defenses are good against him, to make inquiry of the mortgagor before taking an assignment, [88] coupled with the practice which has grown out of that duty of demanding a formal estoppel certificate. This practice, since it is feasible, gives certainty, and is not unduly burdensome has become so general as to make failure to ask for one a cause of remark [89] and sharply differentiates

---

84. Long ago it was stated that though "in fact it does happen that assignments of mortgages are taken without calling upon the mortgagor;" to do so is regarded as "extremely unfit and very rash, and a very indifferent security" and "no conveyancer of established reputation would recommend" it "without making the mortgagor a party and being satisfied that the money was really due." Matthew v. Wallwyn, 1798, 4 Ves. 118, 127. The short form mortgage in New York, recognizing the practice, includes a covenant by the mortgagor that he will deliver, on request, a statement of the amount due.

85. Griffiths v. Sears, 1886, 112 Pa. 523, 4 A. 492; Nixon v. Haslett, 1908, 74 N.J.Eq. 789, 70 A. 987, affirmed 75 N.J.Eq. 302, 78 A. 1134; 1910, 23 L.R. A.,N.S., 177. See Smyth v. Munroe, 1881, 84 N.Y. 354 on the establishment of reliance by the assignee on the certificate. Weyh v. Boylan, 1881, 85 N.Y. 394, 39 Am.Rep. 669, second assignee may prevail even though first assignee had notice of defense, usury.

A first mortgagee may be estopped as against a junior mortgagee if he represents the amount of his mortgage to be less than it is. Garrett v. Wm. A. Cochrane Co., 1961, 189 Cal.App.2d 566, 11 Cal.Rptr. 345.

By two new sections added to West's Ann.Cal.Civ. Code §§ 2943 and 2954, statutory footing to "estoppel certificates" from the lender was established in 1961. As to instruments executed as mortgages or deeds of trust after its effective date, the lender or his assignee must furnish the borrower, his agent, or successor in interest, a statement showing unpaid balance, interest rate, periodic payments and due dates.

86. Bush v. Cushman, 1876, 27 N.J.Eq. 131, mortgagor affirmatively persuaded the assignee to take the assignment; see Melendy v. Keen, 1878, 89 Ill. 395; Rothschild v. Title Guar. & Trust Co., 1912, 204 N.Y. 458, 97 N.E. 879, 41 L.R.A.,N.S., 740, semble; Pomeroy, Equity Juris., 5th ed., § 704.

87. Bogart v. Stevens, 1905, 69 N.J.Eq. 800, 63 A. 246, 115 Am.St.Rep. 627.

88. "The ordinary duty incumbent upon the purchaser of a bond and mortgage, for his protection, is to estop the mortgagor, by his formal declarations as to the amount being justly due and owing, from thereafter questioning his liability." Merchants' Bank of Buffalo v. Weill, 1900, 163 N.Y. 486, 57 N.E. 749, 79 Am.St.Rep. 605.

Glaser v. Connell, C.A.Wash.1958, 266 F.2d 149, rehearing denied, Feb. 24, 1959.

89. "Plaintiff bought the mortgage when it was past due, at a discount, and without an estoppel certificate. It follows that the defense of no consideration has been sustained." Beck v. Sheldon, 1932, 259 N.Y. 208, 181 N.E. 360.

the case of the mortgagor's equities from the latent equities of third parties, where such a practice would be impossible. Thus the mere fact of executing a mortgage and leaving it in the hands of the mortgagee,[90] or even of recitals or statements in the mortgage itself that the amount of the loan has been received,[91] should not so operate to prevent, for example, the mortgagor from setting up the defense of lack of consideration. It is too common a practice for a mortgage for future advances to state that the entire flat sum has been loaned when none of it has been advanced and there is no intimation of the character of the transaction in the mortgage instrument,[92] and too frequently are the executed mortgage instruments placed in the hands of the mortgagee before receiving the expected money [93] to make reliance in such instances reasonable without something more, such as an executed receipt [94] or the usual estoppel certificate.

Where the note and mortgage never had any validity as between the original parties because of the non-performance of a condition precedent to their becoming binding, it has been suggested that the buyer, no matter how innocent, cannot prevail because his assignor never had any mortgage to give to him.[95] The explanation is not helpful. Even if the mortgage had come into existence but was subject to a defense in favor of the mortgagor, legal or equitable, we have just seen that the assignee would take subject to it, and the case put needs no new or different explanation than the one just stated in order to reach the same result. Further, the doctrine of estoppel can be invoked equally well, if the requisite elements of representation and reliance are present, to bar the mortgagor from setting up that no legal debt and mortgage ever came into existence as to deny him the ability to claim that he had either a legal or equitable defense or offset to a debt and mortgage that had come into existence.[96]

Whether this distinction has validity for the purpose of differentiating the estoppel

---

90.   Glenn, Mortgages, § 322.

91.   But if the mortgagor has given a separate receipt he will be estopped. Bickerton v. Walker, 1885, 31 Ch.D. 151, "there is no reason for giving a receipt until the money is actually received, unless it be to enable the person taking the receipt to produce faith by it. A deed is not always, perhaps rarely, understood by the parties to it, but a receipt is an instrument level with the ordinary intelligence of men and women who transact business * * *."

92.   See § 227, supra. On this ground, while the principle of estoppel was correctly stated it was erroneously applied in Marling v. Fitzgerald, 1909, 138 Wis. 93, 120 N.W. 388, 23 L.R.A.,N.S., 177, 131 Am.St.Rep. 1003. "A mortgage for future advances in good faith is not a representation that the money has been actually advanced any more than that the mortgage is free from fraud or any other defense." Walsh, Mortgages, 258 n. 33. But if the assignee, before assignment, has made inquiry of the mortgagor and was not informed that the advances were not already made but were to be in the future when the note on its face appeared to be a straight present loan of the full amount, the mortgagor will be estopped. Sherwood v. Robertson, 1920, 48 Cal.App. 208, 191 P. 972.

93.   E. g., Marling v. Fitzgerald, and Bogart v. Stevens, supra; Rapps v. Gottlieb, and Davis v. Bechstein, infra.

94.   Rapps v. Gottlieb, 1894, 142 N.Y. 164, 36 N.E. 1052; Davis v. Bechstein, 1877, 69 N.Y. 440, 25 Am.Rep. 218. See Bickerton v. Walker, 1885, 31 Ch.D. 151.

95.   See Glenn, Mortgages, 1304, explaining Rapps v. Gottlieb, 1894, 142 N.Y. 164, 36 N.E. 1052, on this ground; Davis v. Bechstein, 1877, 69 N.Y. 440, 25 Am.Rep. 218, is a similar case. "We take it that * * * the general rule that an assignee of a mortgage takes subject to the equities existing against the assignor, [is] postulated upon the prior existence of a mortgage or other chose in action then having legal vigor. An instrument purporting to secure the repayment of advances made according to the terms of a certain bond, in the hands of a mortgagee named, who has neither made advances nor caused them to be made, is not a legal instrument; it is not a mortgage; nor is its holder a mortgagee." Kommel v. Herb-Gner Const. Co., 1931, 256 N.Y. 333, 176 N.E. 413. Although the statement was made generally the problem was one of cutting off the rights of a third-party, conditional vendor of fixtures by the purchaser of the mortgage, not of defenses of the mortgagor by reason of the invalidity of the obligation.

96.   E. g., silence and payment of interest on a forged bond and mortgage by the purported mortgagor with knowledge of the facts will estop the mortgagor. Rothschild v. Title Guaranty & Trust Co., 1912, 204 N.Y. 458, 97 N.E. 879, 41 L.R.A.,N.S., 740. See Marling v. Fitzgerald, 1909, 138 Wis. 93, 120 N.W. 388, 23 L.R.A.,N.S., 177, 131 Am.St.Rep. 1003, "It [estoppel] is a rule of justice which, in its proper field, has a power of mastery over all other rules."

of a mortgagor from that of an assignee cutting off latent equities by estoppel under the doctrine of McNeil v. Tenth Nat. Bank [97] is another matter. Unless the obligation has existence there would be no property interest in which a third person, not a party to the obligation, could claim a latent equity, and, consequently, the possibility of a contest between the assignee over it would not, as a practical matter, occur. But apart from this, it is submitted that there is no need to invoke any technical doctrine based upon the one time existence of a legal right in order to distinguish the application of the principle of estoppel in the two kinds of cases. That doctrine, as invoked in these cases, involves, in addition to the difficult questions of fact as to whether the conduct of one was culpably responsible for creating a deceptive, or possibly deceptive appearance and whether the other justifiably relied upon that appearance to change his position, matters of commercial policy, expediency and business custom which may either justify permitting conduct that may deceive or tend to deceive others or may have a bearing, factually, upon whether it was deceptive or reasonably should have been relied upon. And between the case of the mortgagor's defenses and that of the latent equity there is a striking practical business difference of sufficient importance to illuminate the divergent attitudes of the courts toward them. It consists, as was pointed out above, in the practical possibility of inquiring of the mortgagor and the general custom of getting from him a statement which will estop him, courses which are wholly impractical in the case of latent equities.

NON-NEGOTIABLE DEBTS—LATENT EQUITIES—IN THE LAND

229. Latent equities reside in third persons not parties to the mortgage transaction. A bona fide assignee of the mortgage for value and without notice takes free of latent equities in the property.

In contrast to the well settled rule that an assignee of a mortgage securing a nonnegotiable obligation takes it subject to the defenses and offsets of the mortgagor, there is dispute as to how far he is subject to latent equities. "Latent equities * * * embrace those equities which are secret and undisclosed at the time of the assignment of the chose, residing either in some prior assignor, or in some third party, a stranger to the assignment." [98]

Latent equities in the land

Equities external to the mortgage may exist with respect to the land as distinct from the mortgage obligation and the security interest in the property. For example, the mortgaged property may have been acquired by the mortgagor in fraud of a former owner,[99] it may have been subject to a trust in favor of another person which was not of public record but known to the mortgagee,[1] or the mortgage itself may have been given to defraud the mortgagor's creditors.[2] In any

97. 1871, 46 N.Y. 325. See § 229 for a discussion of latent equities and the doctrine of the McNeil case.

98. George A. Lee, "Latent Equities," 68 Albany L.J. 290, 1906; 2 Pomeroy, Equity Jurisprudence, 4th ed., 1918. See Walsh & Simpson, Cas. Security Transactions, 390, Note. In the classification of equities in or against the debt and mortgage as "patent" or "latent," the former always includes the equities of the mortgagor. Equities of the mortgagee, who is always in the assignee's chain of title, or those of an intermediate assignor who is in the *known* chain of title should be included in the "patent" group. See Campbell, Cases on Mortgages, 2d ed., 528 n. 1; Stevenson Brewing Co. v. Iba, 1898, 155 N.Y. 224, 49 N.E. 677, "By third parties he refers to those outside of the original debtor and the subsequent transferees in the line of ownership of the chose in action." See also Bush v. Lathrop, 1860, 22 N.Y. 535, "He may inquire of all the persons in the chain of title, but their admissions will not affect a party in possession of an equitable right derived from them."

99. Humble v. Curtis, 1895, 160 Ill. 193, 43 N.E. 749; Simpson v. Del Hoyo, 1883, 94 N.Y. 189.

1. Mott v. Clark, 1848, 9 Pa.St. 399, 1 Am.L.J. 379, 49 Am.Dec. 566.

2. Moffett v. Parker, 1898, 71 Minn. 139, 73 N.W. 850, 70 Am.St.Rep. 319; Danbury v. Robinson, 1862, 14 N.J.Eq. 213, 82 Am.Dec. 244; McMurtry v. Bowers, 1920, 91 N.J.Eq. 317, 109 A. 361.

of these cases, if the mortgagee himself had taken for value and without notice, the third person's equity in the land would have been cut off under the doctrine of *bona fide* purchase. The mortgagee's interest in the land is a sufficient legal interest for that purpose not only in title but in lien jurisdictions.[3] This is true in spite of language by courts in the latter states referring to the interest as a personal one with ownership remaining in the mortgagor.[4]

Granting this, it should follow that any assignee of the mortgage, since he would be a purchaser of the identical kind of legal interest in the property that enabled the mortgagee to qualify as a *bona fide* purchaser, should also acquire that status so as to cut off at least latent equities in the land although in the hands of the mortgagee it was subject to them.[5] Further, as has been noted

before[6] and will be looked at again,[7] an assignee of a mortgage is held to be a bona fide purchaser within the provisions of recording acts so as to prevail over prior unrecorded mortgages of the land even though they are legal and not equitable ones.[8] Although the results under the recording acts do not necessarily control the equitable doctrine of bona fide purchase,[9] they are so closely allied as to indicate persuasively that a similar conclusion should be reached under the latter when the prior claim to be defeated is only equitable.

Such a conclusion is not only consistent with the legal conceptions involved in the doctrine of *bona fide* purchase but finds strong support in practical considerations. As was said in an important case holding in favor of the assignee in the leading jurisdiction for the proposition that an assignee takes subject to latent equities in the obligation, "it would lead to great inconvenience and great insecurity, if persons taking or purchasing mortgages were obliged to go back of the mortgagor who owned the land and had the record title thereto and at their peril ascertain whether any fraud had been perpetrated upon some prior owner of the land." [10] A further reason for reaching this result, and one strongly influencing the New York court just quoted, will be adverted to below in discussing the doctrine of McNeil v. Tenth National Bank.[11]

---

3. See § 180, supra. See also §§ 181, 183–185.
"It is contended that one cannot claim protection as a purchaser in respect of lands unless he holds the legal title. No support is found for this position in the adjudicated cases. The error has probably arisen from confusing the expression 'legal right,' often used in the cases on this subject, with that of legal title or estate. * * * When equities are equal, he that has the legal title will be preferred. The expression 'title,' as just used, in its broadest sense, includes all rights capable of being enjoyed and secured under the law. One holding a legal title to lands is certainly included, but rights amounting to less than the full legal title are equally included within it." Haynsworth v. Bischoff, 1874, 6 S.C. 159, 166, et seq. See Durfee, Lien Theory of the Mortgage, 1913, 11 Mich.L.Rev. 495. See also Webb, Record of Title, § 33.

4. "In this state the rules of law and equity in regard to mortgages have never differed in any degree; it being the doctrine of both systems that a mortgage is but a personal interest merely." Kortright v. Cady, 1860, 21 N.Y. 343, 363, 78 Am.Dec. 145.
"In this state the law is well settled that a mortgage is a mere security or pledge of the land covered by it for the money borrowed or owing, * * * and that the mortgagor remains the owner of the estate mortgaged. * * *" Id., 347.

5. Simpson v. Del Hoyo, 1883, 94 N.Y. 189. Cf. Trustees of Union College v. Wheeler, 1874, 61 N.Y. 88, 115, 117, 118. See § 227, supra, as to whether even equities of the mortgagor should not be cut off.

6. See §§ 194, 212.

7. See § 235, infra.

8. Decker v. Boice, 1880, 83 N.Y. 215.

9. E. g., Decker v. Boice, supra note 8.

10. Simpson v. Del Hoyo, supra note 5. Another ground in this case, that the defrauded grantor to the mortgagor should be estopped because she had clothed the latter, and through her, the mortgagee, with indicia of title seems untenable. A person whose actions have been induced by fraud, certainly in the absence of clear evidence of negligence in succumbing to the fraud, ought not to be the subject of an estoppel.

11. 1871, 46 N.Y. 325.

It would seem clear, therefore, that the assignee of a mortgage who pays value without actual notice of the equities of third parties in the land should take free of them. There is authority that such will be the result[12] unless he is put on inquiry through possession of the property by the owner of the equity[13] or because it is recorded.[14] In such cases he would be charged with notice. The doctrine, of course, cannot cut off legal rights of third persons in the land in the absence of estoppel or failure to record under an applicable recording statute.[15]

---

12. Simpson v. Del Hoyo, supra note 5 one of the most important of these authorities both because it is a New York case and because it is well reasoned; Robertson v. U. S. Livestock Co., 1914, 164 Iowa 230, 145 N.W. 535; Bloomer v. Henderson, 1860, 8 Mich. 395, 77 Am.Dec. 453; Moffett v. Parker, 1898, 71 Minn. 139, 73 N.W. 850, 70 Am.St.Rep. 319; McMurtry v. Bowers, 1920, 91 N.J.Eq. 317, 109 A. 361. A good many of the cases preferring the assignee have other or additional explanations. Thus Congregational Church Bldg. Soc. v. Scandinavian Free Church of Tacoma, 1901, 24 Wash. 433, 64 P. 750, could rest upon the ground that the latent equity in the land was unrecorded and therefore defeated by the operation of the recording acts; it was also in a jurisdiction rejecting the doctrine giving supremacy to latent equities in choses in action. Mott v. Clark, 1848, 9 Pa.St. 399, 1 Am.L.J. 379, 49 Am.Dec. 566, similarly relies upon the nonrecordation of the latent equitable interest in the land to defeat its owner on the ground of laches. In Humble v. Curtis, 160 Ill. 193, 43 N.E. 749, the land itself had been sold to a bona fide purchaser and the mortgage note, which was asked to be cancelled was a negotiable one in the hands of a holder in due course.

13. Seymour v. McKinstry, 1887, 106 N.Y. 230, 12 N. E. 348, 14 N.E. 94. An equitable vendor's lien, the vendor remaining in possession after conveyance, held to prevail over a bona fide assignee for value of the mortgage given by the vendee to one who had knowledge of the vendor's claim. The mortgage had been recorded but the continued possession of the vendor put the assignee upon notice of his interest. See Fisk v. Potter, 1865, 2 Keyes, N. Y., 64, 1865; cf. Bloomer v. Henderson, 1860, 8 Mich. 395, 77 Am.Dec. 453. See also, § 206, supra.

14. See Osborne, Cases Property Security, 2d Ed., 432 n. See also § 241, infra.

15. Lockwood v. Noble, 1897, 113 Mich. 418, 71 N.W. 856.

NON-NEGOTIABLE DEBTS—LATENT EQUITIES—IN THE SECURED OBLIGATION

230. The weight of authority, and preferable view, is that a bona fide assignee of the mortgage for value and without notice takes free of latent equities in the non-negotiable secured obligation.

Latent equities in the case of a debt and its accompanying mortgage exist most frequently in two types of cases. One is where it is the subject of an express trust. The other is where it was acquired by an assignor who was himself an assignee by means of fraud or under other circumstances which would make him hold it subject to an equity of rescission, constructive trust, or other equitable rights in favor of his assignor or some other party. The rule in England,[16] New York[17] and some other states[18] in the United States is that the holder of the prior latent equity in the mortgage obligation prevails.

The majority view probably,[19] and pretty

---

16. Davies v. Austen, 1790, 1 Ves.Jr. 247, "A purchaser of a chose in action must always abide by the case of the person from whom he buys."; Cockell v. Taylor, 1851, 15 Beav. 103; cf. Redfearn v. Somervail, 1813, 1 Dow. 50, coming from Scotland; see Central Trust Co. v. West India Imp. Co., 1901, 169 N.Y. 314, 323, 62 N.E. 387.

17. Bush v. Lathrop, 1860, 22 N.Y. 535, repudiating Kent's dictum in Murray v. Lylburn, 1817, 2 Johns. Ch., (N.Y.) 441; Trustees of Union College v. Wheeler, 1874, 61 N.Y. 88; Stevenson Brewing Co. v. Iba, 1898, 155 N.Y. 224, 49 N.E. 677; Central Trust Co. v. West India Imp. Co., 1901, 169 N.Y. 314, 62 N.E. 387.

18. Patterson v. Rabb, 1892, 38 S.C. 138, 17 S.E. 463, 19 L.R.A. 831; Kernohan v. Durham, 1891, 48 Ohio St. 1, 26 N.E. 982, 12 L.R.A. 41, semble; see Williston & Thompson, Contracts, rev. ed., § 438 for additional cases.

19. It is difficult to determine what the majority view is, not only as to choses in action *simpliciter*, but also as to those secured by a mortgage. For one reason the cases generally have drawn no distinction between the secured and the unsecured obligation, and writers in citing collections of cases have followed suit. As an example of the divergent opinions as to what the weight of authority is, the following state the majority rule to be that the prior latent equity will not be cut off: Pomeroy,

clearly the present tendency,[20] is to hold that a bona fide assignee for value and without no-

Equity Juris., 5th ed., § 708, but see critical comment in Keigwin, Cas.Morts., 387n; Campbell, Cas. Mortgages, 2d ed., 529n.; Glenn, Assignment of Choses in Action, 1934, 20 Va.L.Rev. 621, 626, 627, 646; Walsh & Simpson, Cas.Security Transactions, 390 Note, citing Campbell, supra, and Williston, infra; and Williston & Thompson, Contracts, rev. ed., § 438, this last not so clearly. See also Glenn, supra, 627, interpreting the American Law Institute's statement as to the weight of authority.

On the other hand, the following say the weight of authority is with those jurisdictions that permit the assignee to take free and clear of a latent equity: Walsh, Mortgages, § 62, in contrast to Walsh & Simpson, supra; Tiffany, Real Prop., 3d ed., § 1456; Glenn, Mortgages, § 324, in contrast to the statements in his article, supra; and Keigwin, Cas. Mortgages, 386. This last in a loose statement that, read literally, puts England in the group of cases that permit the assignee to take free and clear, citing only Redfearn v. Somervail, 1813, 1 Dow. 50, the Scotch case, as authority.

One possible explanation of these contradictory views may be that, with the exception of Campbell, relied on by Walsh & Simpson, the authorities in the first group are talking of the doctrine primarily with the rule as to choses in action *simpliciter* in mind, while those in the second group are primarily interested in the secured obligation. Campbell seems to have placed his reliance upon Williston, supra.

For a critique of the various views and authorities, see Note, Latent Equities, 1952, 20 U. of Chi.L.Rev. 692.

20. The Restatement of Contracts, § 174, states this to be the rule, partly, no doubt, in order to influence the courts in making it so. See Williston & Thompson, Contracts, rev.ed., § 438; Glenn, Assignment of Choses in Action, 1934, 20 Va.L.Rev. 621, 627.

"If an assignor's right against the obligor is voidable by someone other than the obligor or is held in trust for such a person, an assignee who purchases the assignment for value in good faith without notice of the right of such person cannot be deprived of the assigned right or its proceeds." Restatement, Contracts, § 174. Even Pomeroy, who opposed this view, admitted that the tendency was to extend the scope of the doctrine of *bona fide* purchaser cutting off equities so as to include "all species of things in action which are embodied in contracts or instruments in writing." Pomeroy, Equity Juris., 5th ed., § 711.

In Restatement of Contracts II, Tent. Draft No. 4, April 1968, § 175, latent equities in an obligor's right are defined and the rule set forth in § 174 of the original Restatement is followed. The comment to the rule states that it "is an application to contractual rights of the rules stated in Restatement of Trusts 2d §§ 284–285 and Restatement of Restitution § 172 as applying to property generally.

tice[21] of such latent equities takes free of them.

Several explanations of the minority view have been offered. One ground is that the doctrine of bona fide purchase cannot operate in his favor because it requires the acquisition of legal title[22] and the assignee gets only an equitable interest.[23] The argument that the assignee, because he gets a legal power of attorney, should be within it[24] is rejected. It is insisted that, under the decided cases this is an insufficient quality or quantity of the necessary legal interest.[25] Consequently the applicable rule is said to be that, as between two equities the prior in time here the latent one, prevails.[26] Also rejected as being against the authorities is the argument advanced by Ames, which could be applicable in many instances, that the sale of an equitable interest should be within the scope of the doctrine.[27] Further, it is said that "as long as the distinction between negotiable and non-

* * * But the rule does not apply to cases of successive assignments by the same assignor * * *"

21. Of course if the assignee is a donee or took with notice he will be subject to such equities and also equities of defense. Danbury v. Robinson, 1862, 14 N.J.Eq. 213, 82 Am.Dec. 244; McMurtry v. Bowers, 1920, 91 N.J.Eq. 317, 109 A. 361; County Bank of San Luis Obispo v. Fox, 1897, 119 Cal. 61, 51 P. 11; see Mott v. Clark, 1848, 9 Pa.St. 399, 1 Am.L.J. 379, 49 Am.Dec. 566.

22. See §§ 182, 185.

23. See Moore v. Metropolitan Nat. Bank, 1873, 55 N.Y. 41, 47, 14 Am.Rep. 173, "the assignee of a chose in action, not negotiable at law, obtained an equitable title only; and the equity of the former owner, being prior in time to that acquired by the purchaser, is superior thereto, the rule in equity being that, where the equities are equal, the first in time shall prevail." See also Williston & Thompson, Contracts, rev. ed., §§ 434, 447.

24. Ames, Purchase for Value Without Notice, 1887, 1 Harv.L.Rev. 1, 7, Lectures in Legal History, 252, 259.

25. See Williston & Thompson, Contracts, rev. ed., 1268.

26. Bush v. Lathrop, 1860, 22 N.Y. 535. See § 182, supra.

27. Ames, Lectures on Legal History, 252, 261. See § 183, supra.

negotiable obligations is preserved in our jurisprudence" [28] the doctrine must be regarded as correct, and no distinction should be drawn between latent and patent equities. To do so would make the nonnegotiable chose negotiable and thus wipe out the distinction between them.[29] In addition it is insisted that admitting the doctrine does restrict free alienability of this sort of property, it is a defect inherent in the nature of nonnegotiable rights of action[30] which should be changed, if at all by legislative action.[31] And change of the rule in any way is opposed on the ground of unfairness to the holder of the prior latent equity, it being urged that "the destruction of the actual equitable property rights of third persons in these cases is too high a price to pay for whatever public advantage may be gained from greater transferability of nonnegotiable choses in action." [32]

The proponents of the majority view have presented their arguments with vigor. In addition to the proposition that the doctrine should apply to the sale of purely equitable interests,[33] they stress the point that, even if the *bona fide* purchase rule is confined to legal interests the assignee qualifies under it.[34] The assignee has a legal interest in his power of attorney which should satisfy the requirement.[35] But beyond this the enactment of real party in interest[36] and similar statutes[37] operate today to give the assignee legal title.

Apart from these somewhat legalistic matters, it is urged that such choses in action actually are dealt with daily as articles of commerce and they should, as a matter of sound policy, be transferable according to the same rules that govern transfers of tangible property.[38] Moreover, to allow latent equities to be cut off would not affect the rule that defenses of the mortgagor cannot be. The two kinds of equities are so utterly different in their practical aspects as to make a distinction between them a matter of obvious common-sense. As stated by Kent, "the assignee can always go to the debtor and ascertain what claims he may have against the bond or other chose in action which he is about purchasing from the obligee; but he may not be able, with the utmost diligence, to ascertain the latent equity of third per-

28. Pomeroy, Equity Juris., 5th ed., § 708.

29. See Pomeroy, Equity Juris., 5th ed., § 711. Cf., semble, Moore v. Metropolitan Nat. Bank, 1873, 55 N.Y. 41, 48, "The counsel further insists that to apply the same rule to non-negotiable choses in action will, in effect, make them negotiable. Not at all. No one pretends but that the purchaser will take the former subject to all defenses, valid as to the original parties, nor that the mere possession is any more evidence of title in the possessor than is that of a horse. In both respects, the difference between these and negotiable instruments is vital and not at all affected by the application of the same rule as to chattels."

30. Walsh, Mortgages, 265.

31. "This quality certainly forms an impediment to the free negotiation and circulation of that class of choses in action. Whether sound policy requires that it should be removed, and the circulation of such securities promoted, is a question upon which men may differ. At one period in the history of the law it was thought highly impolitic to encourage their negotiation. * * *. If they are to be further assimilated to commercial paper, the legislature must so provide." Bush v. Lathrop, 1860, 22 N.Y. 535.

32. Walsh, Mortgages, 265.

33. See Glenn, Mortgages 1366 and § 52, invoking in this connection the analogy of the second mortgagee in title states as a transferee of the mortgagor's right of redemption which is an intangible chose in action and an equitable one at that. The argument is weakened by the fact that Cave v. Cave, 1880, 15 Ch.D. 639, held the second mortgagee took subject to latent equities. But see Scott, Trusts, § 285; Restatement, Second, Trusts, § 285. See also § 31, supra.

34. See Glenn, Assignment of Choses in Action, 1934, 20 Va.L.Rev. 621, 622, 644.

35. See text, supra, this section.

36. E. g., West's Ann.Cal.Code Civ.Proc. § 367. See Nat. Exch. Bank v. McLoon, 1882, 73 Me. 498, 40 Am.Rep. 388.

37. E. g., McKinney's General Obligations Law, §§ 1–203, 13–101, 13–103, 13–105, 13–107. Ga.Code, § 85–1803.

38. See Williston & Thompson, Contracts, rev. ed., 1270. This view was accepted by the American Law Institute in drafting the Restatement of Contracts, § 174.

son against the obligee. He has not any object to which he can direct his inquiries * * *." [39] As a consequence, while it would not destroy the transferability of a chose in action to hold it subject to the debtor's defenses, to allow latent equities to follow it into the hands of a bona fide purchase would do so. In the latter case no assignments could ever be taken with safety.[40] Consequently the destroyed transferability of this chose is not due, as claimed, to a defect inherent in a nonnegotiable obligation. Instead it is solely the result of a determined insistence that latent equities must prevail. And this in spite of a perfectly clear practical difference between the two kinds of equities [41] which would justify a distinction between them and which, if accepted, would not obliterate the division between negotiable and nonnegotiable choses because the assignee still would take subject to the debtor's equities in the latter.

So far as unfairness of sacrificing the holder of a prior latent equity to the interests of free transferability of property is concerned, it is difficult to see why he should be singled out for solicitude. The holder of prior equities in other common sorts of property, a horse, a plot of ground, and, of course, a negotiable instrument, is similarly sacrificed.[42] Even in the very kind of case with which we are concerned, the assignment of a nonnegotiable debt secured by a mortgage, a latent equity in the mortgaged property itself is, as was seen, held to be destroyed as against the assignee of the mortgage in the state[43] which is the citadel of the minority rule. As one learned writer in commenting on this said "if such a rule is commendable, as the New York court has said, in order to promote the security of those who deal in mortgages, why draw a distinction between latent equities that burden the mortgagor and those that burden the assignor of a mortgage? It is hard to conceive of a rational answer." [44]

Again, the doctrine, i. e., of protection of the latent equity, where adopted excludes a variety of nonnegotiable choses in action of the sort represented by indispensable or commercial documents.[45] In the case of one of them, the past due negotiable instrument, the transferee gets legal title, the instrument being both a chattel and a chose, and although the fact that it is past due suggests defenses by the obligor and puts on inquiry as to them, it remains otherwise negotiable so that getting legal title to it cuts off equities of third parties in it.[46] As to others, a rule first laid down in the New York case of McNeil v. Tenth National Bank[47] applies to cut off latent equities. The rule of this case "is some-

---

39. Murray v. Lylburn, 1817, 2 Johns.Ch. 441, 442. See also Kent's vigorous dissent in the earlier case of Bebee v. Bank of N. Y., 1806, 1 Johns. 529, when Kent was on the Supreme Court before he became Chancellor. See § 228, supra.

40. Lord Eldon, in Redfearn v. Somervail, 1813, 1 Dow. 50, quoted by Kent, in Murray v. Lylburn, supra. Lord Eldon added that "for so long as our Scotch neighbors retained any part of their characteristic shrewdness, they would never take an assignment if they were aware that, by means of latent equities, such assignments might give them nothing."

41. Not only is the difference a practical one but it is an analytical one as well. See Chafee, Rights in Overdue Paper, 1918, 31 Harv.L.Rev. 1104, 1111, discussing negotiable paper. But the same ideas hold true no matter what the chose in action so far as the distinction between equities of ownership in the obligee's right and the defenses the obligor may have against the obligee are concerned. Another statement in the article also seems pertinent: "Theory and practice are improperly opposed. If a proposition is bad in practice, then its theory is wrong." Id. 1146.

42. Simpson v. Del Hoyo, 1883, 94 N.Y. 189. See text supra and infra.

43. New York. See n. 17, supra.

44. Glenn, Mortgages, § 324.1.

45. See Fairbanks v. Sargent, 1887, 104 N.Y. 108, 9 N.E. 870, 6 L.R.A. 475, 58 Am.Rep. 490.

46. Wolf v. Am. Trust and Sav. Bank, C.C.A.Ill.1914, 214 F. 761, 132 C.C.A. 410; Frank v. Brown, 1931, 255 Mich. 415, 238 N.W. 237, comment, 1932, 30 Mich.L.Rev. 1342, reprinted, Osborne, Cases Property Security, 405. See Chafee, Rights in Overdue Paper, 1918, 31 Harv.L.Rev. 1104.

47. 1871, 46 N.Y. 325; Moore v. Metropolitan Nat. Bank, 1873, 55 N.Y. 41, 14 Am.Rep. 173; Williston & Thompson, Contracts, rev.ed., § 438.

times said to involve the doctrine of estoppel;[48] a more accurate statement is that, when a third person having an interest, say of ownership or lien, in a chose in action which is embodied in a formal document (e. g., a certificate of stock, a bond or note, even though nonnegotiable, or an insurance policy) delivers the document to another person who falls within its tenor, e. g., a mortgagor delivers a mortgage to a mortgagee,[49] an assignee of the latter, if he be a *bona fide* purchaser or incumbrancer for value and without notice, and if he receives delivery of the document is protected accordingly against such person. * * * In such situations the bona fide assignee for value is protected even though the prior equity was vested in one who was within the known chain of title." [50] The mortgage has not been included by the New York court in the list of instruments covered by the rule [51] but it is submitted that it should be.[52] The mortgage is an indispensable document.[53] In addition, if that is a requirement, it is so much the subject of commerce that there is no justification for not putting it on a par, so far as rules making for free transferability go, with the other instruments that are covered by the rule.[54]

MORTGAGES SECURING NEGOTIABLE INSTRUMENTS—EFFECT ON MORTGAGE

231. A mortgage securing a negotiable instrument has imparted to it the qualities of negotiability of the obligation it secures. However, the mortgage can be enforced only in accordance with the written terms of the mortgage. Further, a holder in due course of the note and assignee of the mortgage takes subject to prior legal defects and recorded interests and priorities in the fee.

Where the secured obligation is a negotiable instrument, the fundamental general conception that the mortgage is incidental to

48. But see Ames, Lectures on Legal History, 260, for a criticism of this theory as inappropriate.

49. "But what is it that brings the transferee within the tenor of the instrument? If it is the act of the former owner in conferring upon the assignor of the transferee the apparent *indicia* of absolute ownership, then the doctrine is to be rationalized on the basis of estoppel." Rollison, Priorities in the Law of Mortgages, 1934, 9 N.D.Law. 215, 238n.

50. Campbell, Cases on Mortgages., 2d ed., 529n. See Walsh & Simpson, Cas.Security Transactions, 407 n. 2. "For a similar reason, a second assignee, who is a *bona fide* purchaser or incumbrancer of such chose in action for value and without notice and receives delivery of the document, is protected as against a first assignee who left the document in, or returned it to, the possession of the assignor. Bridge v. Connecticut Life Ins. Co., 1890, 152 Mass. 343, 25 N.E. 612; Township of Washington v. First National Bank, 1907, 147 Mich. 571, 111 N.W. 349, 11 L.R.A.,N.S., 471." Id. "In the application of the doctrine of *estoppel* in this class of transactions there seems to be no reason for inquiring whether the assignee acquires a *legal* or an equitable interest. If the assignee acquires an *equitable* interest estoppel will prevent the assertion of the legal title by the former absolute owner of the chose in action. The same factual situation will *estop* one from asserting either a legal or an equitable title." Rollison, Priorities in the Law of Mortgages, 1934, 9 Notre Dame Law. 215, 237n.

51. Trustees of Union College v. Wheeler, 1874, 61 N.Y. 88; Owen v. Evans, 1892, 134 N.Y. 514, 31 N. E. 999.

52. Curiously enough the New York court in Simpson v. Del Hoyo, 1883, 94 N.Y. 189, in holding that a latent interest in the property would be cut off by the assignment of the mortgage relied upon both the McNeil v. Tenth Nat. Bank and Moore v. Metropolitan Nat. Bank cases along with Greene v. Warnick, 1876, 64 N.Y. 220.

53. Thus the mortgage may be the subject of a pledge, Security Restatement, § 1, comment e; it can be recovered in specie by the mortgagee if taken or withheld wrongfully, Pierce v. Lamson, 1862, 87 Mass. (5 Allen) 60, 81 Am.Dec. 732; and its production must be demanded when the mortgagor pays the principal amount of the mortgage debt. Assets Realization Co. v. Clark, 1912, 205 N.Y. 105, 98 N.E. 457, 41 L.R.A.,N.S., 462, Osborne, Cas., Property Security, 2d ed., 270, Walsh & Simpson, Cas.Security Transactions, 418, Campbell, Cases on Mortgages, 2d ed., 544, Hanna, Cas.Security, 3d ed., 927. See note, 1929, 29 Col.L.Rev. 61. Cf. Napieralski v. Simon, 1902, 198 Ill. 384, 64 N.E. 1042. See § 233, infra.

54. See Glenn, Mortgages, § 324.1; Williston & Thompson, Contracts, rev.ed., § 447. But see Baily v. Smith, 1863, 14 Ohio St. 396, 84 Am.Dec. 385, Osborne, Cases Property Security, 2d ed., 266, Campbell, Cases on Mortgages 2d ed., 532, Hanna, Cas.Security, 3d ed., 907, "Now mortgages are not necessities of commerce, they have none of the 'attributes of money,' they do not pass in currency in the ordinary course of business, nor do any of the prompt and decisive rules of the law merchant apply to them." See also Strong v. Jackson, 1877, 123 Mass. 60, 25 Am.Rep. 19, Osborne, Cases Property Security, 2d ed., 287, semble.

the debt it secures again comes into play. The great weight of authority is that a negotiation of the negotiable instrument to a holder who takes it in good faith, for value, and without notice before maturity, i. e., a holder in due course, to whom the mortgage is then formally assigned,[55] will take the mortgage as he takes the note, free from defenses and defensive defects that would have been available to the mortgagor against the mortgagee.[56] As might be expected from the dis-

cussion of latent equities in the case of nonnegotiable choses in action, the holder in due course of a negotiable instrument secured by a mortgage, "especially if he then receives a formal assignment of the mortgage, takes the mortgage as well as the note unaffected by prior equitable and legal interests of ownership or lien of third persons"[57] in the mortgage. The same would be true of prior equitable interests in the fee of the mortgaged property itself.[58] The chief explanation of the majority view is "that the debt is the principal thing, and the mortgage the mere incident, following the debt wherever it goes, and deriving its character from the instrument which evidences the debt. To which may be added the consideration * * * that, if a recovery may be had for the debt, the mortgagor can have no interest in withdrawing the mortgaged property from liability to satisfy it."[59] If he were permitted

55. The exact extent to which a taker of negotiable paper will hold it free of defenses properly belongs to treatises on negotiable instruments. It may be noted that certain defenses, "real defenses," such as forgery and non-delivery are not cut off. 2 Ames, Cas.Bills & Notes, 812.

56. Carpenter v. Longan, 1872, 83 U.S. (16 Wall.) 271, 21 L.Ed. 313, the leading case; American Savings Bank & Trust Co. v. Helgesen, 1911, 64 Wash. 54, 116 P. 837, Ann.Cas.1913A, 390. See Restatement, Security, § 34. Courts have said and held that the same is true even though there has not been an assignment or delivery of the mortgage. Hawley v. Bibb, 1881, 69 Ala. 52; see Morgan v. Farmington Coal & Coke Co., 1924, 97 W.Va. 83, 94, 124 S.E. 591, 596. And it has been held to be unnecessary for the mortgagor to be a party to the note. Gabbert v. Schwartz, 1880, 69 Ind. 450. Where the security takes the form of a trust deed mortgage with the conveyance in trust to a third party as trustee, the holder in due course of the note is held entitled to the security free from defenses. Mayes v. Robinson, 1887, 93 Mo. 114, 122, 5 S.W. 611, 613; Borgess Inv. Co. v. Vette, 1898, 142 Mo. 560, 573, 44 S.W. 754, 757, 64 Am.St.Rep. 567; Webb v. Hoselton, 1876, 4 Neb. 308, 19 Am.Rep. 638; Buehler v. McCormick, 1897, 169 Ill. 269, 48 N.E. 287. Although this seems to violate the rule that prior equities prevail, since all that the holder would get would be the equitable right against the trustee, there seems no reason why the rule should not operate to impart the negotiable qualities of the note to such an equitable interest as well as to the legal security interest in the land. Also where the holder in due course of the note received delivery, but not a formal assignment, of the mortgage. Preston, Kean & Co. v. Morris Case & Co., 1876, 42 Iowa 549, an extreme case because the note was not intended to be operative when delivered. However, in Carolina Housing and Mortgage Corp. v. Reynolds, 1957, 230 S.C. 491, 96 S.E.2d 485, criticized in Karesh, Security Transactions, in Survey of South Carolina Law, 1957, 10 S.C.L.Q. 114, 117, an assignee for value before maturity of a negotiable note, without actual knowledge of the defense of failure of consideration by the maker, took free of the defense on the note but, since the mortgage was defectively executed on its face the lower court held, and the holding was not appealed, that he could not enforce the mortgage. See also Note, Transfer of the Mortgagee's Interest

in Florida, 1961, 14 U. of Fla.L.Rev. 98, 100. In Gribble v. Mauerham, 1961, 188 Cal.App.2d 221, 10 Cal.Rptr. 296, the holder in due course of a negotiable note secured by a trust deed mortgage was held to take both the note and trust deed mortgage free of the defense of no consideration for the note.

57. Campbell, Cases Mortgages, 2d ed., 542 n. 1, citing, Holt v. Guaranty & Loan Co., 1931, 136 Or. 272, 282, 296 P. 852, 856; Gold Bros. Security Co. v. Fidelity Trust Co., 1923, 47 S.D. 31, 195 N.W. 830; Frystad v. Graff, 1929, 55 S.D. 523, 226 N.W. 745, accord. In addition look at Frank v. Brown, 1931, 255 Mich. 415, 418, 238 N.W. 237, 30 Mich.L.Rev. 1342.

58. Stock Growers' Finance Corp. v. Hildreth, 1926, 30 Ariz. 505, 249 P. 71. In the light of Simpson v. Del Hoyo, 1883, 94 N.Y. 189, this seems an a fortiori case. See preceding section. Pope v. Beauchamp, 1920, 110 Tex. 271, 219 S.W. 447, in spite of a lis pendens notice filed against the assignor to cancel the deeds to the property. Ross v. Title Guarantee & Trust Co., 1934, 136 Cal.App. 393, 29 P.2d 236, accord. The California court stressed the statutory language in determining the scope of lis pendens and concluded it did not apply to this situation. For a critical discussion of the case and the problem generally, see note, 1934, 22 Cal.L.Rev. 677, 678, 681, and 684. See also note, 1938, 16 Tex.L. Rev. 534.

59. Baily v. Smith, 1863, 14 Ohio St. 396. "There is no analogy between this case and one where a chose in action standing alone is sought to be enforced. * * * The mortgage can have no separate existence. * * * This dependent and incidental relation is the controlling consideration * * *." Carpenter v. Longan, supra note 56.

to do so, the mortgagee "could then sue at law, recover judgment, and sell the mortgaged premises under execution."[60]　Thus the net result would be the same except that (1) he might lose as against other creditors priorities he would have had in the property as mortgagee, and (2) the mortgagor will be given an opportunity to declare a homestead in the property which will defeat any claim against it under execution.　The minority view[61] is that the security is property and the fact that it is security for a negotiable instrument does not affect its character as property.　Nor is there any reason in policy why it should.　For "mortgages are not necessities of commerce, they have none of the 'attributes of money,' they do not pass in currency in the ordinary course of business, nor do any of the prompt and decisive rules of the law merchant apply to them. They are 'securities,' or 'documents for debts,' used for the purposes of investment, and unavoidably requiring from those who would take them with prudence and safety an inquiry into the value, condition, and title of the property upon which they rest; nor have we the least apprehension that commerce will be impeded by requiring the further inquiry of the mortgagor, whether he pretends to any defense, before a court will foreclose his right to defend against those which have been obtained by force or fraud.

"Against any amount of mere theory, advanced to sustain the position that commerce requires these instruments to be invested with negotiable qualities, may be successfully opposed the stubborn fact, that in the first commercial country of the world, as well as in the great commercial states of the American Union, they have never been used for such purposes or heard of in such a connection." [62]

Also contra to the view of the majority expressed above is the opinion that there are legitimate interests which should not be sacrificed.[63]　Other lienholders and creditors have such an interest in obtaining a priority in the property over the mortgagee.　So too does the mortgagor in defeating collection of the claim, even though it is perfectly valid against him, by putting the property from its reach through a declaration of homestead.　Further it is argued that to apply the same rule to a mortgagor who is a third party,[64] frequently the wife not subject to the obligation of the note, and thus enable the property, no matter by how gross and palpable a fraud it was obtained, to be reached in satisfaction of a debt for which the mortgagor was not personally liable would be obviously unjust.[65]　And finally it is noted as inconsistent with imparting the negotiability quality of the note to the mortgage the universal doctrine that guarantees indorsed upon the note itself are not similarly affected.[66]

In spite of the fact that from 1843, when the question first arose, to 1915 courts of last resort have passed upon it at least a hundred

---

60.　Baily v. Smith, supra note 59.

61.　Baily v. Smith, supra note 59, is the leading case.　See Note, Transfer of the Mortgagee's Interest in Florida, 1961, 14 U. of Fla.L.Rev. 98, 100.

62.　Baily v. Smith, supra note 59.　"The court's remarks * * * are typical of a persistent confusion, in court and out, between paper which really serves as a medium of exchange (bank notes, Federal Reserve notes, checks, and inter-city drafts) and paper which serves as a medium of *credit*, not of currency (notes, acceptances).　Here again another distinction passes too largely unnoted, between long term, or permanent, or investment credit, and short term or operating credit; to the former belong most mortgage notes, corporate (notable or registered) bonds (also typically secured by mortgage), and corporate stock.　Liquidity of credit-instruments has been found desirable, quite irrespective of whether those instruments serve as a substitute for money, i. e., as currency. * * * No discussion equals that of Moulton, Financial Organization of Society (2d ed. 1925)." Hanna, Cas.Security, 3d ed., 912 n. 3.

63.　Baily v. Smith, supra note 59.

64.　Gabbert v. Schwartz, 1880, 69 Ind. 450.

65.　Id.

66.　Id. The majority rule has also been criticized as compelling courts to treat the mortgage securing the negotiable note not merely as an incident of it but as having actually no existence. Pomeroy, Equity Juris., 5th ed., § 734e.

and fifty times,[67] it is still undecided in a remarkably large number of states. In 1937, a careful summary said that "The present status of the two rules is not well defined. Some twenty-five states and the federal courts are said to follow the majority rule, the tendency being to favor it and limit the minority rule. Of the three states which early adopted the minority rule, only Minnesota appears to have held to it unequivocally. Ohio, one of its early supporters, has on several occasions limited its application to cases where the defense that the mortgagee fraudulently procured the mortgage is urged against the assignee." [68] "Illinois, a minority jurisdiction, has alleviated the harshness of the rule by introducing three specific exceptions for negotiable railroad bonds, accommodation paper, and equities of a mortgagor arising out of transactions collateral to the mortgage. More important, it has adopted a general qualification permitting an assignee of a mortgage to foreclose free of latent equities of third persons of which he had no notice." [69]

Apart from Illinois, which more recently has apparently swung completely to the majority rule,[70] the statement is still substantially correct.[71]

One clear limitation on the majority doctrine is that the bona fide purchaser of the note and mortgage, or of the note alone, "can have no greater right respecting the land than the deed reserving [or creating] the lien confers by its terms properly interpreted, * * *. In seeking the benefit of the lien, the purchaser of the notes cannot deny notice of the provisions of the deed, the very instrument under which it claims." [72] Furthermore, subject to the operation of the recording acts, legal defects in the ownership of the property as it came into his hands,[73] or arising later by reason of the mortgagee's recorded release of it[74] cannot be overriden by the fact that the mortgage secures a negotiable note that has got into the hands of a holder in due course. And the same is true as to priorities that attach to the fee of the

---

67. Britton, Assignment of Mortgages, 1915, 10 Ill.L. Rev. 337.

68. With the consequence that, for practical purposes, the doctrine is overruled in the jurisdiction which decided the leading case for it. See Dennis v. Rotter, 1932, 43 Ohio App. 330, 183 N.E. 188. That the assignee will take free of latent equities in the mortgage as well as the debt in Ohio, First Nat. Bank v. Brotherton, 1908, 78 Ohio St. 162, 84 N.E. 794.

69. Note, 1937, 32 Ill.L.Rev. 120, 122.

70. Marks v. Pope, 1939, 370 Ill. 597, 19 N.E.2d 616, 127 A.L.R. 185.

71. See note, 1940, 127 A.L.R. 190 for a collection of cases.

There have been numerous discussions of the two rules. See Britton, Assignment of Mortgages, 1915, 10 Ill.L.Rev. 337; Dashiel, Negotiability of Deeds of Trust, 1916, 3 Va.L.Rev. 296; Martin, Negotiability of Mortgages Given to Secure Negotiable Instruments—Ohio Theories, 1934, 8 U. of Cin.L.Rev. 328; note, 1930, 3 So.Cal.L.Rev. 335, 352; note, 1927,

22 Ill.L.Rev. 214; note, 1938, 16 Tex.L.Rev. 534; note, 1933, 21 Cal.L.Rev. 287. See also Leeper v. Hunkin, 1926, 22 Ohio App. 204, 153 N.E. 519, commented on in 1927, 22 Ill.L.Rev. 214. Cf. Starck v. Goodman, 1937, 288 Ill.App. 347, 6 N.E.2d 503, commented on in 1937, 32 Ill.L.Rev. 120, 123.

For another discussion of the two rules and the effect of the Florida Assignment of Mortgage Statute, Fla.Stat.Ann. § 701.02, see Note, Transfer of the Mortgagee's Interest in Florida, 1961, 14 U. of Fla. L.Rev. 98, 100. The writer concludes that the implication of the Florida cases "is that the Florida * * * statute requires recordation of all mortgage assignments to protect them against creditors of and subsequent purchasers from the mortgagor, the mortgagee, or prior assignees. It logically follows that all prospective purchasers of the mortgaged land or prospective assignees of the mortgage should be bound by, and entitled to rely on the record. The limitation placed on negotiability of mortgage notes is justified by a uniform rule that reduces the possibility of fraudulent transfers to a minimum and lets the prospective purchaser know exactly where he stands. Application of the principal-incident rule should be used to let the character of the secured note determine the defenses that are valid against the assignee, but not to defeat a recorded assignment."

72. Shanabarger v. Phares, 1920, 86 W.Va. 64, 103 S. E. 349.

73. Murphy v. Williams, 1910, 103 Tex. 155, 124 S.W. 900. See 1938, 16 Tex.L.Rev. 539.

74. Wood v. Sparks, Tex.Com.App.1933, 59 S.W.2d 361, rehearing denied 63 S.W.2d 1109, rehearing denied mem., 63 S.W.2d 1109, commented on 1938, 16 Tex.L.Rev. 537.

property and fall under the protection of the recording acts.[75]

MORTGAGES SECURING NEGOTIABLE INSTRUMENTS—EFFECT ON INSTRUMENT SECURED

232. **An express incorporation of the terms of a mortgage into the note by language on the face of the note will destroy its negotiability. Apart from such incorporation by reference courts generally hold that the terms of a mortgage cannot be imported into the note for the purpose of varying or contradicting any of the terms of the note. A few cases have made an exception in the case of an acceleration clause in a mortgage, holding that it may be imported into the note for the purpose of obtaining a deficiency judgment at the time of foreclosure.**

The effect upon a mortgage of the fact that it secures a negotiable instrument has just been examined. Now the question is raised, what is the effect upon the negotiability of an instrument, otherwise negotiable, of (1) the fact that it is secured by a mortgage; (2) language in the instrument referring in various ways to the mortgage, or vice versa; and (3) the contemporaneous execution of the two documents? Properly this is a question for the law of negotiable instruments and can be discussed adequately only against a background of the rules and principles governing negotiability in general. However, it also concerns persons who are parties to mortgages and those dealing in them and mortgaged land, and so a short statement of elementary principles applying to the specific problem posed seems advisable.

It is well settled that neither the fact that a note is secured by a mortgage nor a recital on a note that it is so secured will render it

nonnegotiable.[76] Where the note and mortgage are executed as a part of the same transaction, there is an additional question as to whether they should, therefore, be construed together in such a manner that the provisions contained in the mortgage are imported into the note. In some jurisdictions, contemporaneously executed instruments are looked upon as though they were in fact one instrument.[77] Applied to notes secured by a mortgage, the logical conclusion from such a doctrine would be that, regardless of what might be in the mortgage, the note would be nonnegotiable.[78] No court, however, has so held. Unless there is in the mortgage some provision which, when read as a part of the note, would violate some requirement of negotiability, the note remains nego-

---

75. E. g., R gives a mortgage to E-1 who records. R then mortgages to E-2 to secure a negotiable promissory note which is then transferred by E-2 to a holder in due course, E-2 and the transferee both recording. Clearly E-1's recorded mortgage is not lost by reason of the fact that the mortgagor executed another mortgage to secure a negotiable note that got into the hands of a holder in due course. If E-1 had not recorded, he would lose. Johnson v. Masterson, 1917, Tex.Civ.App., 193 S.W. 201.

76. Shanabarger v. Phares, 1920, 86 W.Va. 64, 103 S. E. 349; Page v. Ford, 1913, 65 Or. 450, 131 P. 1013, 45 L.R.A.,N.S., 247, Ann.Cas. 1915A, 1048, See Britton, Bills and Notes, 65. Statutes sometimes provide that a recital on the note that it is secured by a mortgage will make it subject to defenses. Security Trust and Savings Bank v. Telford, 1918, 211 Ill.App. 149. Also some states have a statutory provision that no action can be maintained upon a note secured by a mortgage unless the mortgage has been foreclosed. Under such a rule (West's Ann.Cal.Code Civ.Proc. § 726) California held that all notes secured by a mortgage were non-negotiable. Meyer v. Weber, 1901, 133 Cal. 681, 65 P. 1110. See note, 1921, 9 Cal.L.Rev. 425. In 1923, Cal.Civ. Code § 3265 was amended to provide that "the negotiability of a promissory note otherwise negotiable in form, secured by a mortgage or deed of trust upon real or personal property shall not be affected or abridged by reason of a statement therein that it is so secured, nor by reason of the fact that said instrument is so secured nor by any conditions in the mortgage or deed of trust securing the same." As to the effect of this amendment see notes, 1930, 3 So.Calif.L.Rev. 335, 352; 1934, 22 Calif.L.Rev. 677, 679; 1933, 21 Calif.L.Rev. 287. Look at Minn. Laws 1927, c. 416 for a similar statute. See, also, Brannan, Negotiable Instruments Law, 5th Ed.1933, 6, 625. See also Mann v. Leasko, 1960, 179 Cal.App. 2d 692, 4 Cal.Rptr. 124.

77. Nebraska is such a jurisdiction. Garnett v. Meyers, 1902, 65 Neb. 280, 91 N.W. 400, 94 N.W. 803.

78. I. e., on the ground that the note by itself is incomplete. The rule of construction has exactly the same effect by virtue of a rule of law as would an express incorporation of the terms of the mortgage by words on the face of the instrument. See text, infra, this section.

tiable.[79] And most courts, even though there are such provisions in it, hold that the two instruments are separate and distinct, and the negotiability of the note is entirely unaffected by the contents of the contemporaneous mortgage securing it.[80] Generally, it is held that, to affect the negotiability of a note, there must be express incorporation by reference to the provisions in the mortgage which would make the note non-negotiable. "Time, labor, and ink without limit have been spent by both courts and writers in seeking to work out consistent rules with respect to the character of the language which will effect incorporation of an extrinsic writing and thereby render the purported note or bill subject to the terms and conditions of the other writing and hence non-negotiable." [81]

Where a note on its face incorporates by reference the terms of a mortgage securing it, that *ipso facto* makes it nonnegotiable regardless of whether there are, or are not, conditions or provisions in the mortgage which, if they were on the face of the note would make it nonnegotiable.[82] "In such a case nonnegotiability results from the direction to the prospective taker to look into the terms of some other writing and does not result from what he may find in the designated writing when and if he does look at it." [83]

Apart from incorporation by reference through provisions on the note, the courts, as a rule, hold that the terms of the mortgage cannot be imported into the note for the purpose of varying or contradicting any of the terms of the note even though language in the mortgage itself purported to do so.[84] By the decisions of a great many courts the same is held to be true of acceleration clauses in a mortgage even though in terms therein expressed to be applicable to the note, the clauses being limited to the acceleration of the mortgage foreclosure and the maturity

---

79. If there is in the mortgage a provision which, when read as a part of the note under this rule of construction, would violate some requirement of negotiability, the note will be non-negotiable. Brooke v. Struthers, 1896, 110 Mich. 562, 68 N.W. 272, 35 L.R.A. 536; see Roblee v. Union Stockyards Nat. Bank, 1903, 69 Neb. 180, 95 N.W. 61. If the note and mortgage are acquired together, or in any other way so that the taker has actual notice of the provision in the mortgage, he will take subject to its terms. Roblee v. Union Stockyards Nat. Bank, supra.

80. See Aigler, Conditions in Bills and Notes, 1928, 26 Mich.L.Rev. 471, 491–8; Bailey, Negotiable Instruments and Contemporaneously Executed Written Contracts 1935, 13 Tex.L.Rev. 278; 1936, 14 Tex.L.Rev. 307; Norton, Bills and Notes, 109–113; Britton, Bills and Notes, § 15. See also 1897, 35 L.R.A. 536; 1931, 75 A.L.R. 1210; 1911, 32 L.R.A.,N.S., 858.

81. Bailey, supra note 80, 413. In addition to the citations, supra note 80, see notes, 1933, 31 Mich.L. Rev. 984; 1930, 3 So.Cal.L.Rev. 335, 352; 1926, 26 Col.L.Rev. 622; 1928, 37 Yale L.J. 665; 1915, 3 Cal.L.Rev. 144; 1930, 4 U. of Cin.L.Rev. 234; 1928, 23 Ill.L.Rev. 183; Norton, Bills and Notes, 114. See also 1911, 32 L.R.A.,N.S., 858–866; 1926, 45 A. L.R. 1074, 1093.

Similar problems have arisen in connection with the negotiability of corporate bonds. See Effect of Deeds of Trust on the Negotiability of Corporate Bonds, 1928, 42 Harv.L.Rev. 115; note, 1935, 33 Mich.L.Rev. 604, 1082; note, 1927, 27 Col.L.Rev. 443, 447; note, 1929, 29 Col.L.Rev. 365; note, 1935, 83 U. of Pa.L.Rev. 679. As to the negotiability of the bonds of a Massachusetts trust, see note, 1935, 45 Yale L.J. 176.

There are many cases holding that in the case of corporate bonds which incorporate the terms of the mortgage securing them into the bond the negotiability of the bond is not affected. E. g., Pflueger v. Broadway Trust & Sav. Bank, 1932, 351 Ill. 170, 184 N.E. 318; Thomas v. De Moss, 1932, 202 N.C. 646, 163 S.E. 759; Pollard v. Tobin, 1933, 211 Wis. 405, 247 N.W. 453; Gerrish v. Atlantic Ice & Coal Co., C.C.A.Ga.1935, 80 F.2d 648. See Britton, Bills and Notes, § 17, for additional cases and also for others holding the same way when the terms of incorporation were not so sweeping. See Gen.Laws, Cal., § 860. "Bonds payable to bearer or holder shall be negotiable, notwithstanding any condition contained therein or in the mortgage, deed of trust or other instrument securing the same." Look at Siebenhauer v. Bank of California Nat. Ass'n, 1930, 211 Cal. 239, 294 P. 1062, which although involving a bond, not a note, relied on West's Ann.Cal.Civ.Code § 3265 instead of Gen.Laws, § 860.

82. Old Colony etc. v. Stumpel, 1926, 126 Misc. 375, 213 N.Y.S. 536; see 1928, 37 Yale L.Jour. 665; Steffen, Bills and Notes, 811, 266. Cf. Utah Lake Irrigation Co. v. Allen, 1924, 64 Utah 511, 231 P. 818, 37 A.L.R. 651.

83. Britton, Bills and Notes, 68.

84. See § 108, supra. See Britton, Bills and Notes, 68.

of the note not being affected by them.[85]
"Some courts, however, impressed by the incongruity of permitting foreclosure when the
accelerating event has occurred and of denying a right to a deficiency judgment until
the date of maturity specified in the note has
arrived, have held that the accelerating
clause is imported into the note." [86]   The
general policy against permitting negotiable
instruments being varied as to any of their
terms by any writing extrinsic to it makes
the first group of decisions preferable.   Going
further, it has been suggested that, in order
to be in harmony with the general doctrine
that the note imports its negotiability to the
mortgage, the maturity date in the note
should make inoperative the acceleration
clause in the mortgage even for foreclosure
purposes.[87]   But this would run counter to
the rule that the note, although it may cut
off defenses, cannot affect the terms of the
mortgage, and a holder in due course of the
note and mortgage must enforce the latter
according to the terms written into it.[88]

PAYMENT TO ASSIGNOR—NEGO-
TIABLE INSTRUMENTS

233.   The rules applicable to the negotiable
instrument it secures determines the discharge
of a mortgage by payment.   It follows that payment to an assignor will not discharge a mortgage if the note and mortgage had previously
been transferred to a bona fide holder for value
before maturity.

"Where a negotiable instrument is secured
by a mortgage, the latter will not be discharged by payment to the record holder if
as a matter of fact the note and mortgage
had already been transferred to a bona fide
holder for value before maturity, even though
no assignment has been recorded." [89]   Such
is the general rule by the very definite weight
of authority.[90]   This flows from the general
rule that in such cases the mortgage follows
the rules applicable to the negotiable instrument it secures.   One has a right to insist
upon the production and surrender of negotiable instruments, or upon being given an
indemnity bond in lieu thereof, as a condition
of payment,[91] and failure to enforce this right
is at peril of getting no defense if payment
is made to any one other than the holder.[92]
Nor will the result be different if the mortgagor asked for the note and was given a
plausible but false explanation for its non-
production.[93]   The risk is absolute.   And
the same is true of part payments.   For although surrender of the note cannot be de-

85.   Adler v. Berkowitz, 1930, 254 N.Y. 433, 173 N.E.
574, commented on, 1931, 31 Col.L.Rev. 328; Kennedy v. Gibson, 1904, 68 Kan. 612, 75 P. 1044; Waddell v. McComas, 1933, 113 W.Va. 344, 167 S.E. 866;
see Durham v. Rasco, 1924, 30 N.M. 16, 227 P. 599,
34 A.L.R. 838.   Cf. Bell v. Engvolsen, 1911, 64
Wash. 33, 116 P. 456, 35 L.R.A.,N.S., 577.

See Note, 1953, 39 Va.L.Rev. 371.

86.   Britton, Bills and Notes, 69; Durham v. Rasco,
1924, 30 N.M. 16, 227 P. 599, 34 A.L.R. 838.   See
notes, 1923, 7 Minn.L.Rev. 594; 1931, 9 N.Car.L.
Rev. 201; 1927, 27 Col.L.Rev. 579; 1949, 29 Or.L.
Rev. 46.   Look at Charleston Five Cents Sav. Bank
v. Zeff, 1931, 275 Mass. 408, 176 N.E. 191, noted,
1932, 12 Boston U.L.Rev. 108.   On whether, in a jurisdiction holding that an acceleration provision allows a foreclosure at a premature date but leaves
the note itself unmatured, the proceeds of the foreclosure sale should be applied at once among the
holders of the different notes or should be applied
only to the payment of such notes as on their face
have matured, look at Bank of Clinton v. Goldsboro
Sav. & T. Co., 1930, 199 N.C. 582, 155 S.E. 261, noted in 1931, 9 N.Car.L.Rev. 201, 204.

87.   See Britton, Bills and Notes, 70.

88.   See preceding section.

Osborne Law of Mortgages 2d Ed. HB—30

89.   Assets Realization Co. v. Clark, 1912, 205 N.Y.
105, 98 N.E. 457, 41 L.R.A.,N.S., 462.   The application of recording acts to assignments of mortgages,
both those securing negotiable and those securing
non-negotiable obligations, is considered later in §
216 ff.

90.   Smith v. First Nat. Bank of Cadiz, 1909, 23 Okl.
411, 104 P. 1080, 29 L.R.A.,N.S. 576 and note.   See
authorities in following footnotes.

91.   N.J.L. § 174.   See 1921, 11 A.L.R. 969, § 134;
1927, 50 A.L.R. 1200; 1935, 98 A.L.R. 1489.

92.   Smith v. Jarman, 1922, 61 Utah, 125, 211 P. 962.
See 1913, 41 L.R.A.N.S., 462; 1934, 89 A.L.R. 171,
193; 1936, 104 A.L.R. 1301, 1308.

93.   Kellogg v. Smith, 1862, 26 N.Y. 18.   But see Clinton Loan Ass'n v. Merritt, 1893, 112 N.C. 243, 17 S.
E. 296, semble.

manded in such case, its production can be, and partial payment endorsed upon it.[94] Also, although it has been urged that the rule should be different when a grantee of the mortgagor pays,[95] especially if he does not assume payment of the debt or if he bought only a part of the land and wants only a partial release, because in such a case the note is not to be surrendered to him, the rule seems to be otherwise, i. e., it is the same as in payment by the mortgagor.[96] Where the mortgage itself mentions the extraneous written evidence of the debt this seems correct. In such a case a transferee of the mortgagor should not be permitted to assume that the debt has not been assigned since he can demand inspection of the written evidence and thus determine who has title to the debt and whether it is in the person to whom he intends to make payment even though the surrender on payment is not to be to himself.[97] But mortgages secure open accounts and debts not evidenced by any written evidence. Since this is so, if the mortgage itself makes no mention of the written debt, it is plausible that a transferee of the mortgagor should be able to assume that there had been no assignment and pay the original mortgagee so as to free the land he bought from the mortgage lien even though it would not discharge the negotiable note in the hands of the assignee.[98] If the

assignee of the note held not only the note but the mortgage also, since payment should not be made without production of the mortgage itself, this should not be true. But if the assignee of the note left the mortgage with his assignor and its possession was relied on in making payment it is believed such a result has merit.[99] In a couple of the minority states, which hold to the view that the mortgage retains its independent character as land, although the mortgagor would still be liable on the note,[1] he can blindly pay the mortgagee without production of the note or inquiry about it and free his land from the mortgage lien; and in Minnesota this is true even though the assignee held not only the note and mortgage, but also a formal, recorded assignment of the mortgage.[2] In neither jurisdiction does this rule apply to transferees of the mortgagor.[3]

---

94. Baumgartner v. Peterson, 1895, 93 Iowa 572, 62 N.W. 27; Bartel v. Brown, 1899, 104 Wis. 493, 80 N.W. 801; see 1929, 29 Col.L.Rev. 61, 63. But see Assets Realization Co., supra n. 89.

95. See Ross, Double Hazard of a Note and Mortgage, 1931, 16 Minn.L.Rev. 123, 125.

96. Bautz v. Adams, 1907, 131 Wis. 152, 111 N.W. 69, 120 Am.St.Rep. 1030; Shoemaker v. Minkler, 1926, 202 Iowa 942, 211 N.W. 563. See § 237, infra.

97. There is statutory recognition of the significance of mention in the mortgage of the written instrument it secures. E. g., West's Ann.Cal.Civ.Code § 2935. See § 237, infra.

98. See, semble, Citizens Nat. Bank of Connellsville v. Harrison-Doddridge Coal & Coke Co., 1911, 39 W.Va. 659, 109 S.E. 892; Carlin, Release of Assigned Liens, 1938, 44 W.Va.L.Q. 175, 180. See also Pomeroy, Equity Juris., 5th ed., 994. In this re-

spect the assignee is unlike a mortgagor who, being a party to the original transaction, would know the form it took.

99. Whether in such an event the assignee could enforce the note against the mortgagor is a different question depending upon several additional circumstances: did the transferee ask the mortgagor about the character of the debt and was he told there was no note? In such a case the negligence of the assignee in not taking the mortgage along with the note would be offset by the misrepresentation of the mortgagor plus the act of the original assignor in fraudulently taking payment. Of course, if the mortgagor told the truth, the transferee would be on notice. Again, did the assignee know of the mortgage or was he ignorant of it? Also, if the transferee failed to inquire of the mortgagor, should this be regarded as a neglect which should affect his standing? Whether he inquired of the mortgagee-assignor whom he is paying would seem to be a useless act; such a one is fraudulent and any answer by him could scarcely be of additional significance. The authorities leave these questions in doubt.

1. Blumenthal v. Jassoy, 1882, 29 Minn. 177, 12 N.W. 517.

2. Redin v. Branhan, 1890, 43 Minn. 283, 45 N.W. 445; Johnson v. Howe, 1929, 176 Minn. 287, 223 N. W. 148. See note, 1929, 13 Minn.L.Rev. 622. The same is true in Illinois, at least if the assignment has not been recorded. Towner v. McClelland, 1884, 110 Ill. 542; Napieralski v. Simon, 1902, 198 Ill. 384, 64 N.E. 1042; Bartholf v. Bensley, 1908, 234 Ill. 336, 84 N.E. 928.

3. Johnson v. Howe, supra (transferee took "subject to" the mortgage; the assignment had been record-

Courts also sometimes protect the mortgagor by saying that the assignee is estopped to deny that the mortgagee was his agent to receive payment.[4]

PAYMENT TO ASSIGNOR—NON-NEGOTIABLE DEBTS

234. Payment may be made to the mortgagee at any time before actual or constructive notice of an assignment of a nonnegotiable obligation secured by a mortgage. If the obligation is in written form and the assignee has possession of it and the mortgage instrument, although the authorities are divided, the preferable rule is that payment to the assignor is not good.

When the mortgage is given to secure a non-negotiable note it has long been the accepted rule that the mortgagor may safely pay the original mortgagee at any time before actual or constructive[5] notice of an assignment of the debt by the mortgagee.[6] After notice to the debtor of the assignment, payment to the assignor will give no defense as against the assignee.[7] Where the non-negotiable debt is in the form of a bond or note and the assignee has taken possession of the written instrument evidencing the debt and also the mortgage there is a division of opinion as to whether payment may be made to the assignor. One view is that the general rule in the case of non-negotiable choses permitting the debtor to pay the assignor until he is given notice of the assignment should apply and the fact that the debt has

written form is immaterial since, unlike a negotiable instrument, there is no legal right to its production.[8] The preferable view is that "where a party makes what is treated as a final payment in satisfaction of a bond and mortgage without taking a satisfaction and without requiring production of the instruments, or receiving some sufficient excuse for their nonproduction, the payment is at his peril and not good as against an assignee for value under an unrecorded assignment. The reason for this rule lies outside of the recording act, and is found in the fact that on such final and full payment, at least if no formal satisfaction is taken, it is so far the ordinary rule to produce and deliver up the instruments which are being paid and satisfied that the failure to do this in the absence of sufficient explanation and excuse is a circumstance calculated to put the payer on inquiry and lead him to ascertain the true ownership of them. * * * "[9] If the mort-

8. See 1929, 29 Col.L.Rev. 61, 62, stating this to be the weight of authority, but citing only Jones v. Smith, 1870, 22 Mich. 360, and Fox v. Cipra, 1897, 5 Kan.App. 312, 48 P. 452. In the first of these cases there is nothing to show whether the assignee had the instruments or whether their production was demanded. The situation in Kansas is different from most states and the date of the case makes it unreliable as a precedent elsewhere. See Ward and Stewart, Mortgage Assignment and Payment Statutes, 1940, 8 Jour.B.A.Kan. 488; Seed, Mortgage "Payment" Statutes in Kansas and New Mexico, 1954, 3 U. of Kan.L.Rev. 87. Although the mortgagor cannot demand an indemnity bond if the non-negotiable bond is not forthcoming, the failure to produce it or account for its nonproduction has been held to be a condition of payment. Novoprutsky v. Morris Plan Co., 1935, 319 Pa. 97, 179 A. 218, 98 A.L.R. 1486; see 1935, 98 A.L.R. 1489.

Note, Mortgages: Effect of Failure to Record a Mortgage Assignment in Florida, 1954, 7 U. of Fla.L. Rev. 93, 94: "The existing authorities on this point * * * is to the effect that payments on a nonnegotiable note by the mortgagor to mortgagee, after an unrecorded assignment by the latter, will nevertheless discharge the mortgage."

9. Assets Realization Co. v. Clark, supra, § 233, note 89.

"As stated, the plain principle underlying and affirmed by all of these decisions is that when a party makes a payment, or completes a transaction intended like a merger to operate as a payment, in full discharge of a bond and mortgage, or **takes a** transfer thereof, the evidence of the debt **naturally** and ordinarily is produced and delivered, and **there-**

ed); Schultz v. Sroelowitz, 1901, 191 Ill. 249, 61 N. E. 92 (the transferee "assumed the payment" of the mortgage; the assignment had not been recorded). In the first case the facts do not disclose whether the mortgage mentioned the notes or whether the transferee knew of them. In the Illinois case the mortgage described the notes.

4. Erickson v. Kendall, 1920, 112 Wash. 26, 191 P. 842. See note, 1928, 26 Mich.L.Rev. 579.

5. Constructive notice from recording will be discussed in connection with the recordation of assignments later in the section.

6. Hand v. Kemp, 1922, 207 Ala. 309, 92 So. 897; O'Maley v. Pugliese, 1922, 272 Pa. 356, 116 A. 308, part payments. See 1929, 42 Harv.L.Rev. 1082.

7. See Williston, Contracts, Rev.Ed., 1253; Restatement, Contracts, § 170.

gage secures an obligation not evidenced by writing or if the only evidence of the debt is the promise to pay contained in the mortgage instrument itself, it has been suggested that the mortgage debtor has no way of finding out whether there has been an assignment of the debt and, consequently, if he pays the assignor before notice is given to him by the assignee he should be protected.[10] In answer it may be ventured that, at least in the case where the mortgage contained the written promise to pay, the mortgagor should have demanded the production of the mortgage itself before paying and a failure to do so should be sufficient warning to him that there might be an assignment of it.[11] Indeed prudent business practice would go beyond this and require that there be a demand for the production and surrender of the mortgage itself in every case of final payment. If a demand has been made for the non-negotiable instruments and a reasonable excuse for their non-appearance, contrary to the rigid rule in the case of the negotiable instruments, payment may be made effectively to the assignor.[12] Whether or not part payment made to the assignor after an assignment to one who took and held the note and mortgage would be valid against an assignee where

there was no other notice to the payor ought to depend upon whether there is or is not such a general business practice to do so as to make it reasonable for the assignee to rely upon his possession as safeguarding his rights.[13] Generally no such practice seems to exist.[14]

Payment by a transferee of the mortgagor to the assignor of a non-negotiable bond or note secured by a mortgage is not differentiated from a similar payment by the mortgagor.[15] Certainly it would seem that an assignee who, in addition to having possession of the non-negotiable note and mortgage, gave actual notice to the mortgagor should be protected against payment to the mortgagee by a transferee of the mortgagor. Certainly this should be true if the notification was before the purchase from the mortgagor. So too even if it were not until after such a transaction. Whether the transferee "as-

---

fore the failure to do this in the absence of sufficient explanation constitutes notice which makes the payment or transaction unavailing as against a prior assignment although unrecorded. * * *" Id.

Rosecky v. Tomaszewski, 1937, 225 Wis. 438, 442, 274 N.W. 259, 261, transfer of negotiable instrument without indorsement; only partial payment but this not relied on, semble. See Hanna, Cas.Security, 2d ed., Notes, 849–851 on the significance of the papers from both a legal and business viewpoint. See also Necessity for Demand of Production of the Documents on Payment of a Mortgage, 1929, 29 Col.L.Rev. 61; 1911, 29 L.R.A.,N.S., 577; 1913, 41 L.R.A.,N.S., 462.

10. See Carlin, Release of Assigned Liens, 1938, 44 W.Va.L.Q. 175, 180.

11. See McKinney's N.Y.Real Prop.Law § 324, requiring production of the mortgage before a release or satisfaction will be recorded.

12. See Brown v. Blydenburgh, 1852, 7 N.Y. 141, 146, 57 Am.Dec. 506; Clinton Loan Ass'n v. Merritt, 1893, 112 N.C. 243, 17 S.E. 296.

13. "We do not desire to be regarded as holding that the rule applied in this case to a final payment would necessarily be applicable to a partial payment of principal or a payment of interest, and that the payer in such latter cases would always be under obligation to call for the production of the bond. While that question is not here for decision, it is apparent that quite different reasoning might be applied to the case of full and final payment and to that of one which was only partial and did not entitle the payer to surrender of the instruments. Foster v. Beals, 21 N.Y. 247, 251, 252." Assets Realization Co. v. Clark, supra, § 233, note 89.

14. "Where part payment is made by the mortgagor there is no similar business practice [of demanding production of the non-negotiable instrument] and so in probably all jurisdictions the payment would be effectual to reduce the mortgagor's obligation on the mortgage." 1929, 29 Col.L.Rev. 61, 62. See Ward & Stewart, Mortgage Assignment and Payment Statutes, 1940, 8 Jour.B.A.Kan. 488, 489. Kellogg v. Smith, 1862, 26 N.Y. 18, 25. Cf. Baumgartner v. Peterson, 1895, 93 Iowa, 572, 62 N.W. 27.

15. "It is true that in the Brown Case the payment was by the mortgagor of his own obligation, and therefore the propriety of his taking it up was more pronounced than in a case like the present where payment was attempted of the obligation of another. I think, however, that this is a matter merely of degree, and that the principle is applicable in the latter case." Assets Realization Co. v. Clark, supra, § 233, note 89; Federal Land Bank v. Corinth Bank & Trust Co., 1926, 214 Ala. 146, 107 So. 88; Clinton Loan Ass'n v. Merritt, 1893, 112 N. C. 243, 17 S.E. 296. See note, 1932, 16 Minn.L.Rev. 123, 126.

sumed" the mortgage debt or merely took subject to it should be immaterial.[16] The obligee's duty of notification should extend no further than to his original obligor who still remains such regardless of who else may have become liable for the debt or interested in the property securing it. If that obligor is notified before payment, neither he nor anyone else should be able to discharge his debt by paying the original obligee rather than the assignee. A transferee of the mortgagor should both make inquiry of the mortgagor and, on payment, insist on production of the instruments. The result would be different if the recorded instrument itself did not reveal the existence of written evidences of the debt. The same would be true if it stated that payment might be made to the original mortgagee as trustee. Especially would this be so if, in addition, there was a recording act applicable to assignments of mortgages and the transferee relying on the record paid the record mortgagee and took and recorded a discharge.[17]

RECORDING ACTS—APPLICABILITY TO ASSIGNMENTS—GENERAL CONSIDERATIONS

235. Recording acts generally apply to the assignment of mortgages. The dual nature of mortgages, involving a conflict between desirable mobility of the debt on the one side and stability of ownership of land on the other, causes difficulty in the application of the statutes.

The problem of the application of recording acts to assignments of mortgages arises in several ways. One is between an assignee of the debt and mortgage and a mortgagor or transferee of the mortgagor who seeks to discharge the mortgage by payment or other agreement, a matter considered apart from the recording acts in the preceding section. Another is between an assignee of the debt

and mortgage and a later purchaser or mortgagee of the land itself. A third is between different assignees of the debt and mortgage. An additional situation in which the recording acts play a part is where there is a prior unrecorded mortgage or other interest in the land and a subsequent mortgage to a mortgagee who takes with notice of the earlier, unrecorded one, and therefore subject to it. An assignee of the latter mortgage is classed as a *bona fide* purchaser under the recording statutes so as to prevail over the prior unrecorded one.[18] This would be true regardless of recordation of the assignment except in those jurisdictions requiring a first recordation by the protected person in addition to qualifying as a bona fide purchaser for value without notice. In such states, unless the assignment of a mortgage is at least permitted, if not required, the later assignee could not qualify; but otherwise recordation of the assignment has no significance. These problems will be taken up in order, but as a preliminary some generalizations about the recording acts in these situations seem desirable.

The dual nature of the mortgage is the source of considerable difficulty in the application of recording acts to transactions involving one. This is especially true of an assignment of a mortgage. There are always two different interests involved—(1) the debt, and (2) the mortgage securing the debt. Although the two have to operate in harmony, nevertheless they are independent and even contradictory in their operational effects and the policies governing them.

---

16. But cf. Barry v. Stover, 1906, 20 S.D. 459, 463, 107 N.W. 672, 674, 129 Am.St.Rep. 941, semble.

17. This was the situation in Barry v. Stover, supra note 16.

18. See § 212, supra. Dulin v. Hunter, 1893, 98 Ala. 539, 13 So. 301; Jackson v. Reid, 1883, 30 Kan. 10, 1 P. 308; Smyth v. Knickerbocker Life Ins. Co., 1881, 84 N.Y. 589.
"It is a well-settled proposition that a subsequent mortgagee is a purchaser within the meaning of this statute. * * * If a mortgagee be a purchaser within the meaning of the statute, there is no reason for denying that character to the assignee of the mortgage." Central Trust Co. v. Stepanek, 1908, 138 Iowa 131, 115 N.W. 891, 15 L.R.A., N.S., 1025, 128 Am.St.Rep. 175, Osborne, Cases Property Security, 2d Ed., 437.

Commercial transactions demand that the debt, especially if it be in negotiable form, shall have free mobility. These notions of unhampered transferability often come into conflict with requirements of formality of transfer and stability and certainty of ownership involved when land, in which the interest in the security of acquisitions is a dominant consideration, is concerned. As has been pointed out, "While the efficacy of the debt is generally wholly independent of the lien, and the debt, simply as a debt, in its commercial peregrinations, may wander independently of the lien without losing its virtues; yet the lien, in order to serve its purpose, should in some way keep pace with the debt, an activity to which, from its nature, it is ill adapted." [19] Further, the mortgage itself reflects in its nature the duality of the composite. "It for some purposes being treated as an interest in land and subject to the rules governing the creation, transfer and extinguishment of such interests, and for some purposes being treated as merely an incident of the debt it is given to secure, and subject to the rules governing, if not the creation of debts, at least their assignment and discharge." [20] An illustration of this, and one out of which in no small measure many of the difficulties arise, is the principle previously noted that the mortgage lien may be assigned by either one of two main methods: (1) by an express assignment in terms of the mortgage lien itself,[21] or to some extent in terms of a conveyance of the land; [22] or (2) by operation of law through assignment of the debt which the lien secures.[23]

such assignment, in many instances being by most informal methods. The problem of enacting and applying the recording statute is one of trying to satisfy the demands of recordation required by the fact that the subject matter of the mortgage is land and, at the same time, not to interfere with the mobility of the debt or with the functioning of the security aspect of the mortgage which makes it a mere incident of the debt.[24] Since this is so, it is obvious that the rules governing the recording of other conveyances cannot be applied *in toto.* Further, the extent of their application will not be the same in all situations but will depend upon the particular kind of transaction in which their provisions are invoked. For example, as between two claimants, both of whom dealt with the mortgage merely as an incident of the same debt, e. g., successive assignees of the same mortgage, their respective rights must be decided almost entirely by the rules governing successive assignments of choses in action and the area for possible application of the recording acts is at a minimum. In other cases, however, they should and do have their ordinary operative effect. Just how far they apply in the different situations will be discussed when they are taken up for separate examination.

The purposes for which recordation may be required [25] are conditioned by the three

---

19. Carlin, Release of Assigned Liens, 1938, 44 W. Va.L.Q. 175, 176.

20. Rundell, Recording of Deeds in Wisconsin, 1922, 1 Wis.L.Rev. 340, 356.

21. See § 226, supra.

22. See § 225, supra.

23. See § 224, supra. In West Virginia for two years following 1921 the assignment of a note secured by a deed of trust or mortgage was void unless recorded. W.Va.Acts 1921, c. 61. This provision was repealed in 1923 on the ground that it had

been found to interfere too radically with the negotiation of promissory notes and banking activities. W.Va.Acts 1923, c. 61. However, in 1931, under the Revised Code, c. 38, art. 12, § 4, (now W.Va.Code, 1966, c. 38, art. 12, § 4) it appears that the assignment of *any debt,* whether or not evidenced by a writing, is recordable if it is secured by lien. See Carlin, Release of Assigned Liens, 1938, 44 W.Va.L. Q. 169, 184, 189.

24. "Regulations required for a proper functioning of the lien will be opposed to a proper functioning of the debt and *vice versa.* The best that can be attempted is to seek a medium, although it may not be altogether happy, designed to permit as much recordability as possible for purposes of the lien, but at the same time not to encroach too much upon the mobility of the debt." Carlin, Release of Assigned Liens, 1938, 44 W.Va.L.Q. 169, 190.

25. See Carlin, op. cit. supra note 24, 178.

generic situations stated above as those in which the problem arises. Looked at in that setting, one set of objectives is to provide a method by which the authority of anyone assuming to grant a release will appear on the record to the exclusion of others, or which will in some other way preclude possible competing claimants to the lien from disputing that the authority did exist at the time of the release. The first of these, and to some extent the second, could be accomplished by recordation at the time of the execution of the release. To achieve them statutes have provided either for recordation of the assignment, or chain of assignments back to the original mortgagee along with the release, or to require that the assignor join in the release.[26] A more important purpose, partially overlapping the second of the preceding one, is to preclude some other person, e. g., the original mortgagee or a prior assignee, from executing a valid release, or subsequent persons from taking either a valid assignment of the mortgage or a conveyance of the land itself either in fee or in mortgage. As is true of recording acts generally, prompt registration is necessary for this purpose to be successful.

The foregoing discussion should be kept in mind when it is stated that in most jurisdictions the recording statutes apply to require recordation of assignments of mortgages as it does other conveyances.[27] Some of the acts are general ones which by express statement or by construction apply to assignment of mortgages. Others are special recording acts dealing separately with the matter.[28] In some states it is held that in the absence of an express stipulation in the statute to that effect,[29] it is not necessary that an assignment be recorded in order for it to be valid, although its being placed upon record will give constructive notice to persons within the terms of the statute for that purpose.[30] Even in a jurisdiction where recordation is not mandatory but merely permissive with the resultant effect of giving notice, failure to record, although it does not invalidate the conveyance by force of the statute may be the basis of an estoppel on the part of one who exercised reasonable diligence to discover the truth, although the rationale of such a holding seems a dubious one.[31] In a very few jurisdictions it is the rule that the recording acts do not apply to assignments of mortgages either for the purpose of invalidation for non-recordation or to give notice if recorded.[32] These statements, however, still

26. Statutes governing the discharge of record of mortgages and deeds of trust might well require the releasor to submit evidence to the recording officer that he is at the time the owner of the mortgage. See, e. g., Mo.St.Ann. § 3078, p. 1909. Look at First National Bank v. Sauls, 1922, 183 N.C. 165, 110 S. E. 865 (production of the notes and mortgages required under certain circumstances but not when the mortgagee in person makes or authorizes the cancellation); Oregon & Washington Trust Co. v. Shaw, C.C.1877, 5 Sawy. 336, 340. See also Carlin, Release of Assigned Liens, 1938, 44 W.Va.L.Q. 175; Patterson, Marginal Releases of Trust Deeds, 1921, 7 Va.L.Reg.,N.S., 161.

27. See 1934, 89 A.L.R. 171; 1936, 104 A.L.R. 1301; 1907, 5 Ann.Cas. 339; note, 1940, 6 Pitts.L.Rev. 300, n. 2. See also Logan, New York Mortgages and the Recording Acts, 1906, 6 Col.L.Rev. 547.

28. "It is true we have no statute which in express terms requires the recording of assignments of mortgages either of real or personal property, but it has very frequently been held that as to the former an unrecorded assignment will be avoided in favor of subsequent purchasers and existing creditors without notice. * * * Some of the states, for instance, after providing a general law upon the subjects of mortgages and conveyances, expressly require assignments of mortgages to be recorded. Our law, by using general terms, well defined and understood, obviates the necessity of more specific legislation." Central Trust Co. v. Stepanek, 1908, 138 Iowa, 131, 115 N.W. 891, 15 L. R.A.,N.S., 1025, 128 Am.St.Rep. 175.

29. Adler v. Newell, 1895, 109 Cal. 42, 41 P. 799; Garrett v. Fernauld, 1912, 63 Fla. 434, 57 So. 671.

30. West's Ann.Cal.Civ.Code (1937) § 2934. Any assignment of a mortgage and any assignment of the beneficial interest under a deed of trust may be recorded, and from the time the same is filed for record operates as constructive notice of the contents thereof to all persons; * * *

31. Second Nat. Bank of New Haven v. Dyer, 1939, 126 Conn. 101, 9 A.2d 503, criticized in 1940, 6 Pitt. L.Rev. 301.

32. Williams & Co. v. Paysinger, 1880, 15 S.C. 171; Singleton v. Singleton, 1901, 60 S.C. 216, 38 S.E. 462; Watson v. Dundee Mortgage & Trust Co.,

leave open questions of how far, even though the recording acts apply to assignments of mortgages, their operation affects the problems in the three groups of cases enumerated above, and how far the character of the debt and the mode of assignment may enter into the matter.

RECORDING ACTS—PAYMENT BY THE MORTGAGOR

236. Recordation of an assignment does not, in most jurisdictions, give notice to the mortgagor so as to affect payment of the mortgage debt by him. Similarly, failure to record an assignment does not affect the assignee's rights against the mortgagor on the debt and mortgage.

The first question to scrutinize more closely is the effect of recording acts which apply to assignments of mortgages upon payments by the mortgagor.[33] Assume that the mortgage is recorded and so too the assignment of it, after which the mortgagor makes either a part or final payment to the mortgagee. Will the recorded assignment operate as constructive notice to the mortgagor? And, if the debt is in the form of an instrument to the holder of which payment must be made apart from any effect upon the rule by the recording acts,[34] will the mortgagor be safe in paying an assignee of record regardless of whether he has the instrument, at least if the recordation is notice to him of the fact of assignment? Generally speaking, the answer is no to both questions.[35]

So far as the first question is concerned, one reason for the result is that the mortgagor's interest antedates the assignment and the record of it, and notice from recordation is normally prospective and not retrospective.[36] Further, it is to the interest of the assignee, not his, that the assignment should be made effectual and, at least in the case of part payments, "it would be an intolerable hardship if, every time he may wish to make a payment and obtain a credit on his debt, he should be compelled to visit the recorder's office to ascertain whether or not his mortgage has been assigned." [37] Even in case of final payment, while the argument of hardship is not so strong, the other reasons are still present, and therefore the same result should follow.[38]

Statutes expressly stating that the record of the assignment is not notice so as to invalidate payments by the mortgagor to the

1885, 12 Or. 474, 8 P. 548; Bamberger v. Geiser, 1893, 24 Or. 203, 33 P. 609, but see later Oregon statute, Or.Laws 1895, p. 55, §§ 1, 2, discussed, Brown & Dougherty, Assignment of Realty Mortgages in Oregon, 1938, 17 Or.L.Rev. 83, 87; Hellweg v. Bush, 1934, 228 Mo.App. 876, 74 S.W.2d 89, trust deed mortgage, "The simple assignment of a note, or deed of trust securing same, is not required to be recorded, and the recording thereof cannot be regarded as constructive notice of the contents thereof."

33. See 1934, 89 A.L.R. 171, 191 ff.; 1936, 104 A.L.R. 1301, 1307 ff.

34. See § 233, supra.

35. See 1934, 89 A.L.R. 171, 193, "Where, from the record of the mortgage it appears that the instrument secured thereby is negotiable, the payor is charged with notice of the fact that the instrument may be in the hands of a bona fide purchaser, and payment must be made to the holder or some person authorized by him to receive payment in order to discharge the payor. This is a rule of negotiable instruments, and it is not affected by the recording laws. Consequently, in the absence of statute to the contrary, the assignee of a mortgage securing a negotiable instrument need not record his assignment in order to invalidate payments made by the mortgagor or others to the mortgagee, even though the recording laws provide for the recordation of assignments of mortgages; and in making payment the payor relies on the records at his peril." If the payor is the mortgagor he will know the form of the obligation and therefore the above applies even though the recorded mortgage does not disclose that the secured debt was a negotiable instrument.

36. See Ward and Stewart, Mortgage Assignment and Payment Statutes, 1940, 8 Jour.B.A.Kan. 488, 495.

37. Foster v. Carson, 1894, 159 Pa. 477, 28 A. 356, 39 Am.St.Rep. 696.

38. An extreme application of this was noted in § 233, supra, in the holding in states adhering to the minority view that the mortgage does not partake of the negotiable quality of the note which permits the mortgagor, although not a transferee from him, to discharge the mortgage, but not the note, by payment to the mortgagee or known assignee in spite of a formal, recorded assignment of another who also held the negotiable note and mortgage.

mortgagee are common.[39] Under similar laws in other states, e. g., California, this is true only if payment by the mortgagor is to the holder of the "promissory note, bond, or other instrument designated in the mortgage or deed of trust." [40] Under such a statute it has been held that record of the assignment would be notice to the mortgagor so as to invalidate any payment made by the mortgagor to the original mortgagee after he has ceased to be a holder of the documents.[41]

Occasionally statutes make the record of the assignment constructive notice to the mortgagor of the assignee's rights.[42] In Kansas, after earlier legislation had been held inapplicable to require recordation of assignments of mortgages securing negotiable instruments in order to prevent payment by the mortgagor to the mortgagee or last as-

signee of record being valid,[43] statutes embodying such a requirement were passed[44] These statutes, originally conceived as affording a means by which the mortgagor might protect himself, were construed as giving notice to the mortgagor of a recorded assignment, clearly so where the assigned mortgage secures a negotiable instrument, and possibly in the case of nonnegotiable instruments also.[45] Even though the assignments are recorded and operate as constructive notice to the mortgagor, they should not, and probably do not, preclude payment to the legal holder of the note.[46] And, although in Kansas the burden of giving notice to the

39. E. g., Consol.Laws of N.Y. (1909) c. 52, § 324, amended by L.1930, c. 476 (now in McKinney's Consol.Laws of N.Y., 1968, Book 49, Real Prop.Law § 324). The recording of an assignment of a mortgage is not in itself a notice of such assignment to a mortgagor, his heirs or personal representatives, or to an owner of the mortgaged premises, where such assignment is recorded subsequent to the recording of the conveyances of such premises to such owner, so as to invalidate a payment made by either of them to the mortgagee or to a prior assignee of the mortgage. See Williams v. Keyes, 1892, 90 Mich. 290, 51 N.W. 520, 30 Am.St.Rep. 438; Eggert v. Beyer, 1895, 43 Neb. 711, 62 N.W. 57; Ward & Stewart, op. cit. supra note 36, 494 n. 51, states that similar statutes exist in California, Idaho, Kansas, Michigan, Minnesota, Montana, Nebraska, Wisconsin, and Wyoming. See 1934, 89 A.L.R. 171, 197; 1936, 104 A.L.R. 1301, 1309.

40. West's Ann.Cal.Civ.Code, § 2935. When a mortgage or deed of trust is executed as security for money due or to become due, on a promissory note, bond, or other instrument designated in the mortgage or deed of trust, the record of the assignment of the mortgage or of the assignment of the beneficial interest under the deed of trust, is not of itself notice to the debtor, his heirs, or personal representatives, so as to invalidate any payment made by them, or any of them, to the person holding such note, bond, or other instrument.

41. Rodgers v. Peckham, 1898, 120 Cal. 238, 52 P. 483. Note that the rule includes non-negotiable instruments. See 1934, 22 Cal.L.Rev. 677, 680.

42. Cade v. Dukes, 1929, 157 Md. 45, 145 A. 222. See, note, 1929, 17 Georgetown L.J. 358. Look also at Mayer v. McLaughlin, 1912, 80 N.J.Eq. 342, 84 A. 1054.

43. Burhans v. Hutcheson, 1881, 25 Kan. 625, 37 Am.Rep. 274, "Section 3 speaks of the recording of the assignment of the mortgage, and does not by its terms refer to negotiable paper; and it seems to us a strained interpretation to hold its provisions applicable, where a debt is evidenced by a negotiable note, secured by mortgage upon real estate, when such mortgage is merely ancillary thereto, and follows the note wherever it goes, deriving its character from such instrument. A better interpretation, and one clearly more in accord with the law of mortgages in this state, is that such section has reference only to a mortgage standing alone, or one securing debts and notes of a nonnegotiable character. Under this interpretation, section 3 of the statute is not nugatory, but has ample room for operation."

44. Kan.Laws of 1899, c. 168, § 3, now G.S.1935, 67–321, and Laws of 1868, c. 68, § 3, now G.S. 1935, 67–304, as well as Laws of 1897, c. 160, § 5, which was repealed in 1899. See Moreau, Bills and Notes —Commercial Policy vs. Other Interests, 1934, 2 Jour.B.A.Kan. 214.

45. Detwilder v. Heckenlaible, 1901, 63 Kan. 627, 66 P. 653, dealing with the act of 1897 and holding it covered both negotiable and nonnegotiable notes; look at Allen v. Waddle, 1922, 111 Kan. 690, 208 P. 551, construing the act of 1899 and saying it applied to both negotiable and nonnegotiable debts; Walmer v. Redinger, 1924, 116 Kan. 580, 227 P. 329, holding that recording charged the mortgagor with constructive notice and not limiting its language to negotiable instruments. But see Ward and Stewart, Mortgage Assignment and Payment Statutes, 1940, 8 Jour.B.A.Kan. 488, 492 ff., arguing that under the present law, while the mortgagor is permitted to pay the mortgagee or last assignee of record in the case of nonnegotiable instruments, absent actual notice of another claimant to the debt and mortgage, recordation of an assignment of a mortgage is constructive notice only in the case of negotiable instruments.

46. See Ward and Stewart, op. cit. supra note 45, 498.

mortgagor is on the holder of the negotiable note if he has not recorded, contrary to the rule almost everywhere, the mortgagor, after actual notice of such unrecorded assignment, cannot pay to the mortgagee or last holder of record.[47]

Just as recordation does not in most jurisdictions give the mortgagor constructive notice of a recorded assignment of a mortgage so as to affect his payments of the debt, so also, failure to record an assignment does not affect the assignee's rights against the mortgagor on the debt and mortgage. This is clearly so under statutes which merely permit recordation with the result that the mortgagor cannot rely upon the state of the record when the debt is in the form of a negotiable instrument but must find and pay the holder of it.[48] Since recording under mandatory statutes as a rule does not give notice to a mortgagor, failure to record is likewise of no consequence. Nor do statutes expressly stating that recordation shall not give notice so as to invalidate payments to the mortgagee by the mortgagor have any application.[49] Under statutes like the Cali-

fornia one, if the assignee of a nonnegotiable or negotiable note, bond, or other instrument had possession of the instrument but did not record the assignment, a payment to the mortgagee by the mortgagor should be invalid as against the assignee.[50] In Kansas, however, the holder of even a negotiable "note and mortgage, who traditionally under the law merchant need give no notice of his interest and yet could enforce his claim free of all defenses of payment" is forced to record his assignment on penalty if he did not that "payment to the mortgagee or the last assignee of record would extinguish the debt and leave him solely to his remedy of assumpsit against the person paid by the mortgagor." [51]

From this survey it is apparent that, regardless of the fact that assignments of mortgages are within the terms of recording acts, neither recording nor failure to record has, as a general proposition, any effect upon the ordinary rules governing payment by the mortgagor apart from any operation of the recording act. Since the dealings here are basically with the debt itself such a conclusion seems sound and in harmony with the considerations and analysis set forth in the preceding section.

RECORDING ACTS—PAYMENT BY TRANSFEREE OF MORTGAGOR

237. Recordation of an assignment is constructive notice to others than the mortgagor desiring to pay the mortgage. Such persons cannot rely upon non-recordation of an assignment in making payment to the mortgagee or last assignee of record.

In flat contrast to the law governing payments made by a mortgagor, it must be regarded "as settled that in the case of another

---

47. Id.

48. See § 233, supra, quoting from Assets Realization Co. v. Clark, 1912, 205 N.Y. 105, 98 N.E. 457, 41 L. R.A.,N.S., 462.

49. "It was not intended to authorize the mortgagor to pay the mortgage to one not the holder of the note, but, if a payment be made to one who, by the possession of the evidence of debt, shows himself *prima facie* entitled to receive payment, or, in case of nonnegotiable security, if the payment be made to the original holder, the fact that an assignment has been placed of record will not, of itself, invalidate a payment made in good faith to such apparent owner. The statute means no more than that the mortgagor shall not be required to search the record before making payment to the one *prima facie* entitled to receive it. In case of negotiable securities, the holder alone is the one *prima facie* entitled to receive payment. Neither under the statute nor under the law-merchant can the maker of a negotiable note assume that it has not been transferred, and make payment thereof before maturity to the original holder, and thus defeat the right of a purchaser for value before maturity." Williams v. Keyes, 1892, 90 Mich. 290, 51 N.W. 520, 30 Am. St.Rep. 438.

See Restatement, Contracts, § 170(3), (4); Assets Realization Co. v. Clark, supra note 48; see notes, 1931, 26 Ill.L.Rev. 688, 1936, 31 Ill.L.Rev. 350.

50. Clinton Loan Ass'n & Dunn v. Merritt, 1893, 112 N.C. 243, 17 S.E. 296, semble (no recording act involved). Cf. Federal Land Bank v. Corinth Bank & Trust Co., 1926, 214 Ala. 146, 107 So. 88. See § 233, supra.

51. Ward and Stewart, Mortgage Assignment and Payment Statutes, 1940, 8 Jour.B.A.Kan. 488. See authorities there cited and supra, note 45.

than the mortgagor, as for instance the purchaser of the equity of redemption, a record of an assignment of a mortgage is constructive notice to one desiring to make a payment on the mortgage." [52] This is true for more than one reason. Perhaps the most important and basic is that the payments are made by the purchaser of the land from the mortgagor as part of the price under the terms of the contract of purchase and in order to free the land of an encumbrance upon it. He is not a debtor whose primary object is to discharge his own debt nor is he a buyer of a debt claim.[53] Instead, his interest as a vendee of the property is to get the title to the property cleared of encumbrances upon it, and to do this he has to make a search of the records in order to find out in whose name such liens may stand so as to be sure that he is dealing with the owner of them. A release, a discharge, or a satisfaction-piece is a conveyance within the meaning of recording acts,[54] and the purchaser of the land

should no more risk paying and taking one from a person who is not the record owner of the encumbrance he wishes to get off his land than he should hazard paying the purchase price to and taking a conveyance of the fee from one who does not have record title to it. Another reason is that the payment and taking of the discharge, release, or satisfaction constitutes a *subsequent* purchase so that the transaction properly falls within the prospective operation of notice by recordation. Statutes saying that record of an assignment shall not constitute notice so as to invalidate payment specify payments by mortgagors only,[55] and in their construction are held inapplicable to others not designated.

Turning to the effect of non-recordation of an assignment of a mortgage, we find the preponderance of authority to be that a purchaser from a mortgagor, who assumes or takes subject to the mortgage debt and later seeks to pay it off and take a discharge of the mortgage, cannot safely pay the mortgagee or last assignee of record relying on the fact that there is no other assignment recorded.[56] The issue in such a case is whether, as a corollary to the rule that record of

---

52. Assets Realization Co. v. Clark, 1912, 205 N.Y. 105, 98 N.E. 457, 41 L.R.A.,N.S., 462; Cornish v. Woolverton, 1905, 32 Mont. 456, 81 P. 4, 108 Am.St. Rep. 598; Viele v. Judson, 1880, 82 N.Y. 32. See Robbins v. Larson, 1897, 69 Minn. 436, 72 N.W. 456, 65 Am.St.Rep. 572.

If the assignee recorded his assignment after the purchase of the redemption interest but before the payment by the purchaser to the mortgagee, this would operate as notice so as to invalidate the payment as against the assignee. Brewster v. Carnes, 1886, 103 N.Y. 556, 9 N.E. 323.

53. See Bacon v. Van Schoonhoven, 1882, 87 N.Y. 446, Campbell, Cas.Mortgages, 2d ed., 551, Hanna, Cas. Security, 3d ed., 932, Walsh v. Simpson, Cas.Security Transactions, 413. This seems clear enough in all cases except where the grantee assumes the payment of the mortgage debt and then pays it off later. Even here, although he may have become directly liable to the mortgagee for the payment of the amount of the mortgage debt, his primary concern, both when he entered into the contract of purchase and, later, when he pays in accordance with the promises he made in that contract, is to free the land he bought from the burden of an encumbrance upon its title.

54. A "mortgage is a conveyance within the express terms of the act, and we think that the satisfaction-piece also comes within the statutory definition. * * * It is equivalent to a release of the mortgaged premises. Instruments creating liens by way of mortgage, being expressly declared to be embraced * * * in the term 'conveyance,' it

is difficult to conceive any reason why instruments discharging such liens should not be included * * *." Bacon v. Van Schoonhoven, 1882, 87 N.Y. 446.

In Merchant v. Woods, 1881, 27 Minn. 396, 7 N.W. 826, the court said that a release by a mortgagee of his interest in the mortgaged premises, whether by entry in the margin of the record, or by a certificate of discharge, or by decree of court is a conveyance which must be recorded in order not to be defeated by a subsequent bona fide purchase from the mortgagee; and that a payment of the mortgage debt, unaccompanied by any written release could have no greater efficacy.

55. New York Consol.Laws, 1909, c. 52, § 324, amended by L.1930, c. 476, is a notable exception, its language (retained in McKinney's Consol.Laws of N. Y.1968, Book 49, Real Prop.Law § 324.) clearly protecting grantees of the mortgagor as well as the mortgagor.

56. Porter v. Ourada, 1897, 51 Neb. 510, 71 N.W. 52, mortgage debt unmatured; Drew v. Anderson, Clayton & Co., 1926, 120 Okl. 250, 252 P. 64. The same is true even though the debt is matured. See § 233, supra.

an assignment will be constructive notice to him, he should be regarded, so far as satisfaction of the mortgage is concerned, solely as an innocent purchaser entitled to the protection of the recording act as against an unrecorded assignment of the mortgage, or whether, in addition, he should be looked upon as a debtor discharging a debt.[57] The answer is that the latter is the correct view,[58] the dual aspect of the mortgage again appearing and, for this particular purpose under these circumstances, the debt aspect being dominant. In such cases, whenever the purchaser knows, through statements in the mortgage or otherwise,[59] that there were written evidences of the debt which customarily are produced on payment, whether they be negotiable or not, he should insist upon getting them or a satisfactory excuse for their nonproduction before he pays,[60] instead of relying upon the record as establishing without further inquiry to whom he should or may pay. There is some authority to the contrary where the purchaser, upon paying, takes and records a satisfaction piece,[61] the argument being that this is a conveyance within the meaning of the recording acts[62] entitled to protection against prior unrecord-

---

57. Rundell, Recording of Deeds in Wisconsin, 1922, 1 Wis.L.Rev. 340, 359.

58. Bautz v. Adams, 1907, 131 Wis. 152, 111 N.W. 69, 120 Am.St.Rep. 1030. See § 233, supra. See also 1932, 26 Ill.L.Rev. 688 n. 2.

59. Chase v. Commerce Trust Co., 1924, 101 Okl. 182, 224 P. 148.

60. "If the lien instrument mentions no written evidence of the debt (for example, a promissory note or bond) which may be the subject of negotiation or assignment, a purchaser of the property, unless having notice to the contrary, may assume that there has been no assignment of the debt and that the original lienor had authority to execute a release. Apparently the hazards which the assignee of the debt assumes in such cases must seek justification in the fact that, when he takes an assignment of a debt so secured, he must understand that he is assuming the risk of being deprived of his lien by a release executed by the original lienor; the law permitting the purchaser of the property to indulge in his assumption because he has no practicable means for determining whether the debt has been assigned, or, if so, to whom. However, if the lien instrument mentions extraneous written evidence of the debt, a purchaser of the property is not permitted to assume that the debt has not been assigned, because he can demand inspection of the evidence of the debt (for example, the bond or the note) and thus determine who had title to the debt and whether it has been discharged. In such cases, the assignee of the debt, in the absence of conduct on his part amounting to an estoppel, will be protected against release of the lien by merely holding evidence of the debt." Carlin, Release of Assigned Liens, 1938, 44 W.Va.L.Q.

169, 180. Note, 1934, 89 A.L.R. 171, 193, accord. See Porter v. Ourada, 1897, 51 Neb. 510, 71 N.W. 52. See also § 233, supra. That the transferee, at least in the absence of actual notice that he is paying to the wrong person (and possession of the negotiable notes and mortgage plus a recorded assignment by the assignee is not such actual notice), may recover back his payment, Blair v. Haas, 1929, 127 Kan. 323, 273 P. 400, commented on, 1929, 42 Harv.L.Rev. 1082.

61. See text, supra, this section.

62. "Neither do we intend to determine that appellant would not have been protected as against the unrecorded assignment if when he made his payment he had taken a satisfaction piece of the bond and mortgage, although without production of the latter, and had placed the same on record before the assignment was recorded. While that question strictly is not here, and therefore cannot be decided, there are strong reasons for saying that in such case appellant would have been protected by the Recording Act. * * * [S]ince a 'conveyance' has been held to include a discharge of a mortgage, logically it should be held that one to whom a discharge is executed is a purchaser within the statute.

Furthermore, since a mortgage, even though somewhat incongruously in the light of its real nature as a mere security, is a conveyance for the purposes of the Recording Act of an estate or interest in the land mortgaged, it is no great stretch to regard a discharge of the mortgage as releasing and thereby conveying the mortgagee's interest and thus bringing it within the exact language defining a purchaser. Decker v. Boice, 83 N.Y. 215, 220, 221. If a discharge is a 'conveyance' and the person to whom it is executed a 'purchaser,' there would be no difficulty in concluding that payment of the amount due on the mortgage would make the purchaser one for value, and thus entitle him to the benefit of the Recording Acts." Assets Realization Co. v. Clark, 1912, 205 N.Y. 105, 98 N.E. 457, 41 L. R.A.,N.S., 462.

Barry v. Stover, 1906, 20 S.D. 459, 107 N.W. 672, 129 Am.St.Rep. 941. (A non-negotiable debt and mortgage was assigned but the assignment was not recorded. The transferee of the mortgagor, who took "subject to" the mortgage, paid the mortgagee without actual notice of the assignment, and took and recorded a discharge from the mortgagee. Held, the failure of the assignee to record his assignment invalidated it as against the transferee's recorded discharge.) Merrill v. Luce, 1894, 6 S.D. 354, 61 N.W. 43, 55 Am.St.Rep. 844, accord.

ed conveyances, in which category assignments of mortgages also fall.[63] The answer is that granting the discharge, release, or satisfaction piece is a conveyance within the meaning of the recording acts the failure of the purchaser to demand the production of the bond and mortgage before paying should charge him with notice and on this ground prevent him from qualifying under the act.[64]

There is no inconsistency from the point of view of either land law policy or that governing commercial instruments in holding, on the one hand, that if the assignee holder of a negotiable note and mortgage records his assignment it will be notice to a transferee of a mortgagor which cannot be ignored when the latter seeks to pay the mortgage debt and thus rid the land of an encumbrance; and, on the other hand, saying that, by virtue of the assignee holding possession of the same note and mortgage but without recording his assignment, the mortgagor's transferee will be put on inquiry over and above what the records show as to the ownership of the mortgage. The land policy demands that, to free the land from the encumbrance he must search the records. The commercial policy governing the note demands that he pay only its actual holder, not the person that the land records indicate is the present owner of it. It may be observed that giving effect to the latter policy here imposes no greater burden of search outside the records than is required in several other instances where non-record notice is recognized.[65]

RECORDING ACTS—ASSIGNEE vs. PURCHASER OF PROPERTY

238. A recorded assignment of a mortgage is in the chain of title of the land if the mortgage is recorded. If the assignment is not recorded and the mortgage has been discharged on the record **by its record owner, a bona fide purchaser of the property without notice of the assignment will prevail over it.**

If an assignee of the mortgage records his assignment that record will be in the chain of title of any person who later seeks to purchase an interest in the land itself.[66] Where the mortgage of which he is the assignee remains undischarged of record, it is not necessary that he record his assignment, for any subsequent purchaser or mortgagee of the same land will be on notice of the mortgage and will take subject to it, and it is a matter of indifference to such a taker whether it is held by the mortgagee or an assignee.[67] But there are situations in which the assignee fails to record, usually relying upon possession of the instruments of indebtedness and the mortgage to protect him, and later, made possible by the fact that another is, on the record, the owner of the property, a third person, bona fide and for value, purports to buy or take a mortgage upon the land after the existing assigned mortgage has been cleared from the records by the action of the person who was its apparent owner.[68] Here land policy, exemplified in the provisions and purposes of the recording acts, comes into conflict with mercantile notions applicable to negotiable instruments, and, to a more limited extent, to some nonnegotiable written evidences of the debt.[69] On balance, the desirability of giving effect to the former policy justifies sacrificing the latter. The holders of negotiable notes and mortgages, whether they have failed to take written assign-

63. See § 235, supra.

64. Chase v. Commerce Trust Co., 1924, 101 Okl. 182, 224 P. 148. See § 233, supra.

65. See §§ 206, 207, supra.

66. Larned v. Donovan, 1898, 155 N.Y. 341, 49 N.E. 942.

67. Zehner v. Johnston, 1899, 22 Ind.App. 452, 53 N. E. 1080; Wilson v. Campbell, 1896, 110 Mich. 580, 68 N.W. 278, 35 L.R.A. 544; Bridges v. Bidwell, 1886, 20 Neb. 185, 29 N.W. 302; Curtis v. Moore, 1897, 152 N.Y. 159, 46 N.E. 168, 57 Am.St.Rep. 506; Berger v. Baist, 1931, 165 Wash. 590, 6 P.2d 412, 89 A.L.R. 164.

68. See 1934, 89 A.L.R. 171, 184; 1936, 104 A.L.R. 1301, 1305.

69. See § 233, supra.

ments [70] or have taken but not recorded them,[71] will bear the loss. This result is justified "both upon principles of equity and under the [recording] statutes * * * for the reason that by not taking and recording an assignment of the mortgage they made the commission of the fraud possible." [72] This reasoning, as well as the basic land policy underlying part of it, applies not only to mandatory statutes,[73] which by their own terms and operation would reach this result insofar as the assignment was held to fall under it, but also to acts under which recording of assignments, although permitted, is not compulsory.[74] It does not apply, however, where an assignment cannot be recorded at all. In such jurisdictions the assignee holder of the negotiable note and mortgage apparently would be protected in spite of the strong land policy involved.[75]

In applying these principles, it is held that where the record holder of the mortgage executes and records a satisfaction-piece under circumstances that leave the debt still alive in the hands of the assignee who had failed to record his assignment, a vendee of the land who buys from the mortgagor later on, relying on the record and making no inquiries outside of it, will hold the land discharged from the mortgage.[76] A similar case is where, after an assignment of a negotiable note and the mortgage securing it, the assignment being unrecorded, the mortgagee of record by fraud obtains a renewal note and mortgage on the same property and then, after cancelling the original mortgage on the record, transfers the renewal note and mortgage to a bona fide purchaser for value and without notice. On the ground that an unrecorded assignment of a mortgage is a conveyance under the recording acts which is void as against subsequent purchasers, and the further ground that it is well settled that a subsequent mortgagee is a purchaser within the meaning of the act and consequently the same should be true of an assignee of the mortgage, the assignee of the renewal note and mortgage has been preferred.[77] Another case involving the same principles is where,

70. Henniges v. Paschke, 1900, 9 N.D. 489, 84 N.W. 350, 81 Am.St.Rep. 588; Merrill v. Hurley, 1895, 6 S.D. 592, 62 N.W. 958, 55 Am.St.Rep. 859.

71. Merrill v. Luce, 1894, 6 S.D. 354, 61 N.W. 43, 55 Am.St.Rep. 844.

72. Henniges v. Paschke, 1900, 9 N.D. 489, 84 N.W. 350; 81 Am.St.Rep. 588.

73. Id.

74. See id.; Marling v. Nommensen, 1906, 127 Wis. 363, 368, 106 N.W. 844, 845, 5 L.R.A.,N.S., 412, 115 Am.St.Rep. 1017, 7 Ann.Cas. 364, upon an estoppel theory. Cf. Northup v. Reese, 1914, 68 Fla. 451, 67 So. 136, L.R.A.1915F, 554; and see the Kansas cases, infra, this section.

75. Reeves v. Hayes, 1884, 95 Ind. 521; Lee v. Clark, 1886, 89 Mo. 553, 1 S.W. 142; Bamberger v. Geiser, 1893, 24 Or. 203, 33 P. 609; Williams & Co. v. Paysinger, 1880, 15 S.C. 171; Fischer v. Woodruff, 1901, 25 Wash. 67, 64 P. 923, 87 Am.St.Rep. 742. In some of the foregoing jurisdictions later enactments changed the law as to recordation of assignments and under them the unrecorded assignment loses. E. g., Conn. Mut. Ins. Co. v. Talbot, 1887, 113 Ind. 373, 14 N.E. 586, 3 Am.St.Rep. 655, protecting the later mortgagee of the property on the ground that a recording act applicable to assignments had been enacted subsequent to the transaction which had been litigated in the earlier decision; Willamette Coll. & Credit Service v. Gray, 1937, 157 Or. 77, 70 P.2d 39, commented on, 1938, 17 Or.L.Rev. 83, 87, 90, 1938, 5 U. of Chi.L.Rev. 151.

76. "The rule is well settled under recording acts that a bona fide purchaser of property from a mortgagor, who finds upon the record a satisfaction or release by the record mortgagee and relies thereupon, is given priority over one whose claim is based upon an unrecorded assignment from the mortgagee. The principle upon which this rule rests is that where one of two innocent parties must suffer a loss, he whose negligence caused the injury should bear it. The assignee may record his assignment and avert the loss, while there is nothing feasible the purchaser can do." Note, 1937, 5 U. of Chi.L.Rev. 151. Porter v. Ourada, 1897, 51 Neb. 510, 71 N.W. 52; Stetler v. Wineger, 1924, 75 Colo. 500, 226 P. 858; Hart v. Adler, 1895, 109 Ala. 467, 19 So. 894, semble; see Fallass v. Pierce, 1872, 30 Wis. 443. See also 1932, 16 Minn.L.Rev. 126 n. 19 for a collection of authorities.

77. Central Trust Co. v. Stepanek, 1908, 138 Iowa 131, 115 N.W. 891, 15 L.R.A.,N.S., 1025, 128 Am.St. Rep. 175; Jackson v. Stickney, 1882, 107 U.S. 478, 2 S.Ct. 814, 27 L.Ed. 529 (secured debt negotiable and in hands of holder in due course); Merrill v. Hurley, 1895, 6 S.D. 592, 62 N.W. 958, 55 Am.St.Rep. 859 (same facts as in preceding case)—accord. See also Havighorst v. Bowen, 1905, 214 Ill. 90, 73 N.E. 402; Torrey v. Deavitt, 1881, 53 Vt. 331. See note, 1932, 16 Minn.L.Rev. 123, 127. See also 1908, 15 L. R.A.,N.S., 1025; L.R.A.1915F, 554.

there being an unrecorded assignment, the mortgagee of record foreclosed by advertisement, bought in at the foreclosure sale, recorded the sheriff's certificate of purchase and, after the period of redemption from foreclosure sale had expired, sold the land to a purchaser who relied upon record title in his vendor.[78] Of course if the purchaser has actual notice that the record holder who released the mortgage or purported to foreclose it was not the real owner he will not be permitted to succeed on the ground that he was entitled to rely on the record. However, the fact that a release was executed before the maturity of the note secured by the mortgage should not be sufficient to warn subsequent purchasers that the release might be unauthorized, payments before maturity being not uncommon and it being the duty of mortgagees to give releases upon payment whenever it is accepted.[79]

There are decisions, chiefly older ones, e. g., in Kansas, in cases where the mortgage of record by its terms showed that it was security for a negotiable note, which hold that,

because a "bona fide holder of negotiable paper transferred to him by indorsement thereon before maturity, and secured by a real-estate mortgage, need not record the assignment of the mortgage"[80] a subsequent mortgagee or purchaser of the land has a "duty to inquire whether the release was executed before or after the assignment, and by persons having authority to do so"[81] and so protect the assignee holder of the note.[82] In Kansas, the statute was altered as to negotiable instruments secured by a mortgage so far as payment is concerned;[83] and it would seem that a purchaser from the mortgagor, relying upon a prior recorded release or discharge to him, should prevail today.[84]

A step removed from the case where the mortgage has already been discharged of record before the purchaser or mortgagee makes his bargain is that in which a prospective purchaser knows of the outstanding mortgage on the property but insists that, before he pays over his money, either it shall be discharged of record or that he shall receive, along with his conveyance from the mortgagor, an executed satisfaction piece from the holder of record of the mortgage. Many cases hold that the purchaser in such a case prevails over an unrecorded assignment even though the assignee holds the

78. Huitink v. Thompson, 1905, 95 Minn. 392, 104 N. W. 237, 111 Am.St.Rep. 476, 5 Ann.Cas. 338. The mortgagor, in such a case, will have a remedy against the mortgagee who foreclosed wrongfully. See 1939, 18 N.Car.L.Rev. 61, 65.

M mortgaged land to E to secure a negotiable note. The mortgage was recorded. E transferred the note and assigned the mortgage to A who did not record his assignment. Thereafter, M conveyed his interest in the mortgaged property to E, the deed being recorded. Thereupon, E conveyed in fee to P, a bona fide purchaser. Will P hold the land free of A's rights as assignee of the mortgage? And, if he will, may A, nevertheless, enforce the note against M? Since the problem involves the question of merger it is discussed in the next chapter although it also comes within the principles here being considered. See § 272 et seq., infra.

79. Kennell v. Herbert, 1931, 342 Ill. 464, 174 N.E. 558, rested its result partly upon this ground. See note, 1932, 26 Ill.L.Rev. 688, 691, criticizing such a distinction, and citing authorities to the contrary. The later Illinois case of Marsh v. Stover, 1936, 363 Ill. 490, 2 N.E.2d 559, discussed, 1936, 31 Ill.L.Rev. 350, held that a release executed on the very day of maturity would not put on inquiry-notice the later purchaser of the notes and mortgage which were executed the same day as a replacement of the released mortgage.

80. Mutual Ben. Life Ins. Co. v. Huntington, 1897, 57 Kan. 744, 48 P. 19, citing, Burhans v. Hutcheson, 1881, 25 Kan. 625, 37 Am.St.Rep. 274.

81. Id.

82. A fortiori the same would be true where the assignment is not under the recording acts at all. See Northup v. Reese, 1914, 68 Fla. 451, 67 So. 136, L.R.A.1915F, 554; Bamberger v. Geiser, 1893, 24 Or. 204, 33 P. 609; Lee v. Clark, 1886, 89 Mo. 553, 1 S.W. 142; Reeves v. Hayes, 1884, 95 Ind. 521. Cf. Connecticut Mut. Life Ins. Co. v. Talbot, 1887, 113 Ind. 373, 14 N.E. 586, 3 Am.St.Rep. 655; Willamette Collection & Credit Service v. Gray, 1937, 157 Or. 77, 70 P.2d 39. See note, 1937, 5 U. of Chi.L. Rev. 151.

83. See § 236, supra.

84. See Ward and Stewart, Mortgage Assignment and Payment Statutes, 1940, 8 Jour.B.A.Kan. 488, 499, 500. See also text, supra.

negotiable note and mortgage instrument and the mortgage referred to the note.[85] Even where the purchaser pays the amount of the mortgage as part of the purchase price and in the same transaction receives a conveyance of the land and a release of the mortgage procured by or through his vendor, the mortgagor, from the mortgagee as apparent owner of the lien by virtue of the record, the purchaser knowing that the money he pays over is to be and is applied in securing such discharge, there is authority that the same is true.[86] And at least one court has held the same way when the buyer himself paid the money directly to the holder of record of the mortgage.[87]

On the other hand, it has been urged "that a distinction should be drawn between the purchaser who relies upon the record as he *finds* it, and the one who relies upon the record as he *makes* it or *procures it to be made*.[88] * * * When the purchaser knows only that the encumbrance is released of record, a request that the releasor produce the note would be unavailing, for the instruments, shown by the record to be valueless, would have been destroyed. But in a case in which the purchaser procures the release it is only reasonable that a request for the valuable instruments be made."[89] This rea-

soning would apply where the purchaser, as part of the transaction, himself paid over the money directly and took the discharge rather than doing so through the mortgagor and would seem applicable to the latter situation also.[90] It would be possible to stretch it to the next preceding case above, thus forcing him to demand that his prospective vendor, the mortgagor, produce not merely a satisfaction piece but the cancelled instruments of indebtedness and mortgage themselves as well. However, reasonable business practice does not seem to go that far. The idea of "burning the mortgage" rather than preserving the discharged instruments as proof of payment is so thoroughly ingrained as to make such a requirement, if not too burdensome, at least one that would be regarded as demanding overly-cautious and suspicious conduct on the part of a purchaser.

Another question, and one on which there is scant authority,[91] is whether in a jurisdiction which would prefer the purchaser of the property from the mortgagor, following an unauthorized release by the mortgagee after he had transferred the negotiable note and the mortgage to A who did not record the assignment to him, A would be able to enforce the negotiable note against the mortgagor? Similarly, would an assignee of a note and mortgage who had lost the mortgaged property to a purchaser from the mortgagee of record who had foreclosed and bought in the

85.   Bacon v. Van Schoonhoven, 1882, 87 N.Y. 446. Chittick v. Thompson Hill Devel. Corp., 1930, 230 App.Div. 410, 245 N.Y.S. 71, affirmed 259 N.Y. 223, 181 N.E. 458, after reasonable excuse from non-production of documents had been given; Swasey v. Emerson, 1897, 168 Mass. 118, 46 N.E. 426, 60 Am. St.Rep. 368, (apparently); Heintz v. Klebba, 1904, 5 Neb.Unoff. 289, 98 N.W. 431, contra.

86.   Vann v. Marbury, 1893, 100 Ala. 438, 14 So. 273, 23 L.R.A. 325, 46 Am.St.Rep. 70; Lewis v. Kirk, 1882, 28 Kan. 497, 42 Am.Rep. 173; Marling v. Jones, 1909, 138 Wis. 82, 119 N.W. 931, 131 Am.St. Rep. 996; City Bank of Portage v. Plank, 1910, 141 Wis. 653, 124 N.W. 1000, 135 Am.St.Rep. 62, 18 Ann.Cas. 869; see 1929, 29 Col.L.Rev. 61, 63.

87.   Foss v. Dullam, 1910, 111 Minn. 220, 126 N.W. 820.

88.   Windle v. Bonebrake, C.C.Kan.1885, 23 F. 165.

89.   Note, 1937, 5 U. of Chi.L.Rev. 151; Metropolitan Life Ins. Co. v. Guy, 1931, 223 Ala. 285, 135 So. 434; Heintz v. Kebba, 1904, 5 Neb.Unoff. 289, 98

N.W. 431, seems to be in this category. See 1932, 16 Minn.L.Rev. 127, n. 21, for a collection of cases.

"Should the releasor produce a forged or fraudulently procured note or mortgage at the request of the purchaser, or should he give a written release in a jurisdiction where the first recorded instrument gains priority, the suggested rule should not be applied, for the purchaser would have done all that a reasonable search required." 1937, 5 U. of Chi.L. Rev. 151.

90.   Federal Land Bank v. Corinth Bank & Trust Co., 1926, 214 Ala. 146, 107 So. 88.

91.   The decisions "often leave this point obscure, because the mortgagor commonly defaults in the litigation and so his rights and obligations are not carefully considered." Ross, Double Hazard of Note and Mortgage, 1931, 16 Minn.L.Rev. 123, 131.

property on foreclosure sale [92] still be able to enforce his note against the mortgagor? If the purchaser of the note bought it without any notice that it was secured by a mortgage and therefore was completely unaware of the possibility of taking and recording an assignment, it is difficult to see how his rights as a holder in due course could be defeated.[93] If the assignee of the note knew it was secured, since it was his neglect of doing the simple act of taking and recording an assignment that made the loss possible, the obligor should have a defense except where he is in the position of a principal, not surety, so far as the land is concerned.[94] If recovery on the note is allowed, an action should lie by the payor against the wrongdoing holder of record of the mortgage whose actions made it possible for the property to get into the hands of a bona fide purchaser relying upon the state of the record.[95]

RECORDING ACTS—TRUST DEED MORTGAGES

239. **There are good reasons why the recording acts should not apply to assignments of the mortgage creditor's rights under a trust deed mortgage. Purchasers of the property after an unauthorized release by the trustee are protected.**

Trust deed mortgages involve considerations not present in ordinary form mortgages. As a rule, the only assignment of the security consists in the negotiation of the notes or, if the secured debt is in some other form, in whatever is necessary to assign that particular variety of obligation. The legal security title to the property is vested in and normally remains with the responsible party who has been chosen by the debtor and creditor to act as trustee for the purpose of receiving and holding it until the debt is discharged and then releasing it. These powers and duties in the trustee are so far discretionary and fiduciary in character that they are nondelegable.[96] Where the debt is in the form of a negotiable instrument, the holder of it, in addition to his right against the maker-obligor, is the beneficiary under the deed of trust. His interest in the security title held by the trustee is an equitable one which should be inseparable from the debt and therefore follow it into the hands of each holder.[97] Because of these features, especially that of security title always remaining in the original trustee to be released by him, it has been suggested by a learned writer, that the interest of the note holders in the security should be treated "as of the same character as the notes themselves, that is to say as personal property—not real estate." The consequence would be that the recording acts would not apply to their assignment.[98]

---

92. Huitink v. Thompson, 1905, 95 Minn. 392, 104 N. W. 237, 111 Am.St.Rep. 476, 5 Ann.Cas. 338.

93. In such a case it has been suggested that the purchaser of the land should lose. See 1931, 16 Minn.L.Rev. 123, 135.

94. See Chapter 9, infra. See also Ross, The Double Hazard of a Note and Mortgage, 1932, 16 Minn.L. Rev. 123, 133; Brown and Dougherty, Assignment of Realty Mortgages in Oregon, 1938, 17 Or.L.Rev. 83, 95; note, 1938, 16 Tex.L.Rev. 534, 536. Look at Hampe v. Manke, 1912, 28 S.D. 501, 134 N.W. 60 (semble). A similar question might be raised in connection with Central Trust Co. v. Stepanek, 1908, 138 Iowa, 131, 115 N.W. 891, 15 L.R.A.,N.S., 1025. This statement assumes that the actions of the mortgagor in getting the mortgage discharged on the record were innocent and free of negligence or other circumstances which would leave him liable on the note because he dealt with the wrong obligee and so shared the responsibility of getting the property into the hands of a purchaser who could keep it free from the claims of the holder of the note. E. g., Kennell v. Herbert, 1931, 342 Ill. 464, 174 N.E. 558, commented on, 1932, 26 Ill.L.Rev. 688.

95. See 1929, 42 Harv.L.Rev. 1082.

96. Of course a trustee may be replaced in the same way that any trustee may, and title to the property and the powers and duties of the trust would be transferred to the new trustee. The point is that in no event would the legal security interest, or the right to have it do so, follow the debt into the hands of its transferees.

97. See Campbell, Cases on Mortgages, 2d ed., 540 n.

98. Greeley, Note, 1931, 26 Ill.L.Rev. 688, 693. "The notion of a security as fluid as the notes themselves does not mix well with rules making recorded assignments constructive notice." Id. In California, Civ.Code § 2934, "any assignment of the beneficial interest under a deed of trust may be recorded, and from the time the same is filed for record

This would not mean that the mortgagor or a transferee of the mortgagor who seeks to pay off the debt should be relieved of the duty of finding and paying the holder of the note any more than in the case of an ordinary form mortgage securing such debts.[99] But it would deprive holders of "the notes of protection against a fraudulent release [by the trustee] which a record of the assignment would afford if permitted. * * * [But] as the parties have created a security fundamentally based upon the honesty, capacity, and good faith of the trustee they have selected, their security should, so far as necessary

operates as constructive notice of the contents thereof to all persons ;". However, although an assignee of an ordinary form mortgage cannot exercise a power of sale contained in the mortgage, although it passes to him as a part of the assigned security, unless the assignment has been duly acknowledged and recorded, West's Ann.Cal.Civ.Code § 858; N.Y.Real Prop.Law, § 146 (repealed EPTL 14–1.1, eff. Sept. 1, 1967); M.C.L.A. (Mich.) § 556.60 W.S.A. (Wis.) 235.525; Civ.Code Ala. (1907) § 4986, semble), the assignee of the beneficial interest under a trust deed mortgage has no similar need to record his assignment. "The reason for this requirement, [i. e., recordation] is to make certain that after foreclosure there will be a clear record title. Further, the mortgagor could not safely redeem from one whose interest in the property was not indicated by the record. These reasons are lacking in the case of a trust deed [mortgage] since no lien passes to the creditor, to be assigned by him, and legal title remains at all times in the trustee. Consequently, an assignee of the creditor can order the trustee to sell the property, without having had his assignment recorded [citing Stockwell v. Barnum, 1908, 7 Cal.App. 413, 94 P. 400].

"Under a deed of trust [mortgage], the creditor's assignee cannot himself sell the property, because his assignor did not have a power of sale to transfer. In the case of a mortgage, however, the assignee of the note which is secured can himself exercise the power of sale." Cormack and Irsfeld, Jr., Applications of the Distinctions Between Mortgages and Trust Deeds in California, 1938, 26 Cal.L.Rev. 206, 210.

However, in Domarad v. Fisher & Burke, Inc., 1969, —— Cal.App.2d ——, 76 Cal.Rptr. 529, the court held that a deed of trust is a mere incident of the debt it secures, having no existence apart from it and where assignment of notes and deeds of trust securing them was recorded, assignment operated as constructive notice of its contents to third persons.

99.　Kennell v. Herbert, 1931, 342 Ill. 464, 174 N.E. 558; see Marsh v. Stover, 1936, 363 Ill. 490, 492, 2 N.E.2d 559, 560. See also Greeley, Note, 1931, 26 Ill.L.Rev. 688; Leesman, Note, 1936, 31 Ill.L.Rev. 350. Look also at West's Ann.Cal.Civ.Code, § 2935.

to protect innocent third persons, be subject to be defeated by the wrongful release of the trustee." [1]

These arguments for doing away entirely with recordation of assignments in the case of trust deed mortgages apply with equal force to protect purchasers on the record after a discharge of record by the trustee in jurisdictions where the recording acts permit recordation of assignments of trust deed mortgages.[2] They apply a fortiori if recording is required. And, although the cases protecting the purchaser rely strongly upon the fact that a release was recorded, where the security is in the form of a trust deed and the trustee wrongfully executes a release but the release is not recorded, it is argued that nevertheless the purchaser should be protected. This is placed "on the principle which protects an innocent purchaser for value of a legal title as against merely equitable rights or interests of which he has no notice. The release deed even though wrongful revests or destroys the security title or interest,[3] leaving only equi-

1.　Greeley, Note, 1931, 26 Ill.L.Rev. 688, 693. See also Carlin, Release of Assigned Liens, 1938, 44 W. Va.L.Q. 175, 191. Cf. Bluefield Nat. Bank v. Bernard, 1930, 109 W.Va. 459, 155 S.E. 306, Maxwell, J., dissenting. Cf., also, the text and cases, supra, protecting the holder of the negotiable note in jurisdictions where an assignment of a mortgage cannot be recorded.

2.　Mann v. Jummel, 1900, 183 Ill. 523, 56 N.E. 161; Lennartz v. Quilty, 1901, 191 Ill. 174, 60 N.E. 913, 85 Am.St.Rep. 260; Vogel v. Troy, 1908, 232 Ill. 481, 83 N.E. 960, discussed in 1908, 3 Ill.L.Rev. 97; Marsh v. Stover, 1936, 363 Ill. 490, 2 N.E.2d 559; Williams v. Jackson, 1882, 107 U.S. 478, 2 S.Ct. 814, 27 L.Ed. 529. See Greeley, Note, 1931, 26 Ill.L.Rev. 688; Leesman, Note, 1936, 31 Ill.L.Rev. 352. See also W.Va.Rev.Code (1931) c. 38, art. 12, § 2, discussed by Carlin, Release of Assigned Liens, 1938, 44 W.Va.L.Q. 175, 191, extending the power of a trustee under a trust deed mortgage to execute a valid release regardless of authority in the deed of trust.

On the rights of a mortgagor not in default against a bona fide purchaser after a wrongful sale under the power of sale by the trustee in a trust deed mortgage, see note, 1939, 18 N.Car.L.Rev. 61.

3.　Connor v. Wahl, 1928, 330 Ill. 136, 142–145, 161 N.E. 306, and cases cited.

table rights in the note holders to set it aside and enforce the security." [4]

Some states permit a release not by the trustee only but by the "creditor", i. e., the holder of the note, by means, for example, of entry on the margin of the record. It has been held in such states that if the trust deed named a creditor, a fraudulent release by him after transferring the note would be valid as to a subsequent purchaser on the record.[5] But if the trust deed secured notes naming no payee so that the name of the creditor did not appear in the trust deed, a subsequent purchaser takes the risk of the release on the record having been executed by the owner of the note.[6] To remedy the hazard to the holder of the note in the first situation legislation has been enacted which requires that proof of ownership of the note be produced to the registrar before the discharge can be noted of record.[7] The protection to the holder of the note is not perfect,[8] but a purchaser of the property can safely buy on the record in such a case.[9]

4. Greeley, Note, 1931, 26 Ill.L.Rev. 688, 693.

5. Evans v. Roanoke Savings Bank, 1897, 95 Va. 294, 28 S.E. 323.

6. Brooking v. Nolde, decided by the Chancery Court of Richmond, Va., March 15, 1905, with appeal by Supreme Court denied without opinion. For a statement of the case, see Patterson, Marginal Releases of Trust Deeds, 1921, 7 Va.L.Reg.,N.S., 161, 167. See also 2 Va.L.Reg. 227.

7. Va.Code of 1950, §§ 43–67 to 43–69, 55–66.2 to 55–66.5, 55–66.7. See also Mo.Stat.Ann. § 3078; Oregon & Washington Trust Co. v. Shaw, C.C.1877, 5 Sawy. 336, 340; 1938, 5 U. of Chi.L.Rev. 151. First Nat. Bank v. Sauls, 1922, 183 N.C. 165, 110 S.E. 865, Hanna, Cas.Security, 3d ed., 935 (production of the notes and mortgages required under certain circumstances but not when the mortgagee in person makes or authorizes the cancellation).

8. "This is not entirely satisfactory, for it substitutes the judgment of an administrative officer for that of a court, but it is protection so far as it goes." Glenn, Mortgages, § 338.

9. Id. The legislation apparently leaves the second situation unaffected. See Patterson, Marginal Release of Trust Deeds, 1921, 7 Va.L.Reg.,N.S., 161.

SUCCESSIVE ASSIGNMENTS— GENERAL RULE

240. As between successive assignments of the debt and mortgage the prior in time prevails. There are exceptions to this rule.

If unaffected by recording act provisions, most American jurisdictions would determine priority between two successive assignments of the debt and mortgage by the mortgagee in accordance with the rule followed in a great many American courts and adopted by the Restatement of Contracts as the general rule where there have been successive assignments of the same right. This rule is that the assignee prior in point of time will be protected even though he has given no notice of his assignment to either the subsequent assignee or the debtor.[10] Where adopted this rule is subject to exceptions, applicable also to the competing rule discussed below.[11] If the subsequent assignee bought his assignment for value in good faith without notice of the prior assignment and obtains payment or satisfaction from the obligor, effects a novation with him, reduces his claim to judgment against him, or gets delivery of a tangible token or writing, surrender of which is required by the obligor's contract for its enforcement, he prevails over the first assignee.[12]

The foregoing rule does not take into account the doctrine of Dearle v. Hall [13] as later applied to assignments of choses in action, that a subsequent assignee, who paid value in good faith without notice of a prior assignment and who inquired of the debtor and gave him notice of his assignment, was entitled to priority over a prior assignee who

10. Restatement, Contracts, § 173(c). It was adopted as being the more widely known, if not the better, of the two rules found in the decisions. See Williston, Contracts, Rev. ed., § 435.

11. See Ames, Cas.Trusts, 2d ed., 328.

12. Restatement, Contracts, § 173(b). In addition, a subsequent assignee will prevail over a prior assignment which is revocable or voidable by the assignor. Id., 173(a).

13. 1823, 3 Russ., Ch., 1.

had failed to give such notice. The original requirement of inquiry was later dropped, and the subsequent assignee prevails if he first gives notice to the debtor, even though, after his assignment and before he gives notice to the debtor, he learns of the prior assignee; and, on the other hand, the prior assignee prevails if he gives notice at any time before the later assignee gives notice.[14]

The Dearle v. Hall rule, however, does not concern us. For one thing it does not apply to assignments of interests in land. And "although a mortgage debt is a chose in action, yet, where the subject of the security is land, the mortgagee is treated as having 'an interest in land,' and priorities are governed by the rules applicable to interests in land."[15] For another, since one of the chief purposes and foundations of the rule is to fulfill the function of a recording system,[16] the rule does not apply where recordation of assignments is provided for[17]—and that the recording acts in practically all states, at least permissively, do so provide has already been seen.[18]

SUCCESSIVE ASSIGNMENTS—EFFECT OF RECORDING ACTS—NON-NEGOTIABLE OBLIGATIONS

241. Recordation of a first assignment will protect it against subsequent assignees. Failure to record, if recordation is mandatory, will postpone a prior assignment to a subsequent assignee for value without notice; if recordation is not mandatory, it will not defeat the priority of the first assignment.

Where the mortgage debt is non-negotiable and the first assignee records his assignment, it is clear that a subsequent assignee will be charged with notice of it and consequently will be postponed to it.[19] The policy interest in the mobility of such debts is not so important as that in certainty of ownership in, or the power to affect, them and the security interest in land attached to them. Indeed the recordation in such instances merely preserves the rights the prior assignee would have in the absence of recording laws and seems to be chiefly important in preventing a possible argument of estoppel which otherwise might be presented.[20]

On the other hand, if there is a failure to record, a distinction must be drawn between statutes which require recordation of assignments of mortgages and those that merely permit it. Under the first type of statute the normal priority of the first assignee will

---

14. The Dearle v. Hall rule is followed in a large number of American jurisdictions. See Williston, Contracts, Rev.Ed., § 435 n. 7. For discussions, see notes, 1925, 13 Cal.L.Rev. 141; 1924, 24 Col.L.Rev. 501; 1924, 37 Harv.L.Rev. 1133; 1924, 33 Yale L.J. 767.

For a possible third rule, see note, 1939, 17 N.Car.L. Rev. 421. See Hanford, Modern Equity, 4th ed., 428–434, 440 et seq., for the discussion of the rule of Dearle v. Hall as it affects mortgages in England before 1926 and the effect of the 1925–1926 legislation upon it.

15. Taylor v. London and County Banking Co., [1901] 2 Ch. 231, 254. See Jones v. Gibbons, 9 Ves. 407, 410, 7 R.R. 247, 250; Jenkinson v. New York Fin. Co., 1911, 79 N.J.Eq. 247, 258, 266, 82 A. 36; State ex rel. Crane Co. v. Stokke, 1937, 65 S.D. 207, 218, 272 N.W. 811, 110 A.L.R. 761.

16. "The English [Dearle v. Hall] rule would have the same advantages in a lesser degree which a recording system for deeds and mortgages possesses." Williston and Thompson, Contracts, Rev. ed., § 435; "The English doctrine [Dearle v. Hall], as has been well said, made the obligor a registrar of conveyances." Glenn, Assignment of Choses in Action, 1934, 20 Va.L.Rev. 621, 652. See Huston, Enforcement of Equity Decrees, 146; Pomeroy, Equity Juris., 5th ed., §§ 693, 695.

17. See State ex rel. Crane Co. v. Stokke, 1937, 65 S.D. 207, 218, 272 N.W. 811, 110 A.L.R. 761; Pomeroy, Equity Juris., 5th ed., § 765; note, 1924, 33 Yale L.J. 767.

18. See § 235, et seq., supra.

19. Crane v. Turner, 1876, 67 N.Y. 437; Stein v. Sullivan, 1879, 31 N.J.Eq. 409, even where the bond and mortgage were obtained from the first assignee and sold to the second; Mott v. Newark German Hospital, 1897, 55 N.J.Eq. 722, 37 A. 757; Murphy v. Barnard, 1894, 162 Mass. 72, 38 N.E. 29, 44 Am. St.Rep. 340, negotiable note involved, redelivered to mortgagee after recorded assignment and then sold to a second assignee; Strong v. Jackson, 1877, 123 Mass. 60, 25 Am.St.Rep. 19.

20. Mott v. Newark German Hospital, 1897, 55 N.J. Eq. 722, 732, 736, 37 A. 757, 761, 762.

be defeated;[21] under the second it will not be.[22]

SUCCESSIVE ASSIGNMENTS—NEGOTIABLE INSTRUMENTS

242. **Recordation of a prior assignment has no effect, by the preferable view, upon a later transfer of a negotiable note secured by a mortgage. The assignee of a mortgage securing a negotiable note who gets and keeps possession of the note but does not record his assignment, by the better authority, prevails over a subsequent purchaser of the mortgage from its record owner.**

Where the mortgage debt is in the form of a negotiable instrument there is greater diversity of opinion as to the effect both of recordation and non-recordation of mortgage assignments. Where the first assignee not only records his assignment but gets and keeps possession of the mortgage documents there would be no question but that he would be protected against a later assignee. The controversy arises where, although the first assignment has been recorded, the negotiable note and mortgage has been left in the possession of the mortgagee, redelivered to him, or obtained by him from the assignee wrongfully through fraudulent representations or otherwise, and then sold to one, who, aside from any effect of the recording acts upon the situation, would be a holder in due course entitled to the note and mortgage as against the prior assignee.

On this question there are three views.[23] One is that a promissory note, by virtue of

being secured by a real estate mortgage does not lose its character as commercial paper and imparts its negotiable character to the mortgage, thus bringing them both within the purview of statutes dealing with commercial paper. The result is that recording the prior assignment has no effect upon the later transferee of the note and mortgage security. Any constructive notice from the recordation is insufficient to prevent him being a holder in due course of the note, actual notice is necessary for that. And the same is true as to the mortgage which is regarded as accompanying it as an inseparable incident of it.[24]

A second view, at the opposite extreme from the first, is that the later indorsee of the note takes no title to the note since his vendor in fact had none and the prior recorded assignment was notice to him of the infirmity so as to preclude him from being a holder in due course.[25] In reaching this conclusion the court in one of the leading cases distinguished a note secured by a realty mortgage from ordinary commercial paper in a business sense. It said, "It is quite clear that a note payable five years after date, with a memorandum upon it that it is secured by mortgage upon real estate,

---

21. Second Nat. Bank v. Dyer, 1936, 121 Conn. 263, 184 A. 386, 104 A.L.R. 1295; Price v. Northern Bond & Mort. Co., 1931, 161 Wash. 690, 297 P. 786; Morrow v. Stanley, 1913, 119 Md. 590, 87 A. 484, decided after amendment of earlier statute made title to the debt secured by a mortgage conclusively presumed to be in the person holding record title to the mortgage; Blunt v. Norris, 1877, 123 Mass. 55, 25 Am.Rep. 14; see 1934, 89 A.L.R. 171, 177; 1936, 104 A.L.R. 1303.

22. Byles v. Tome, 1873, 39 Md. 461, under earlier Maryland statute which has now been superseded.

23. For discussions of the problem, see notes, 1924, 8 Minn.L.Rev. 347; 1934, 22 Cal.L.Rev. 677, 681, 684;

1942, 10 Jour.B.A.Kan. 282, 284; Ross, Double Hazard of a Note and Mortgage, 1932, 16 Minn.L.Rev. 130; Brown and Daugherty, Assignment of Realty Mortgages, 1938, 17 Or.L.Rev. 83, 91–93. See semble, note 1929, 78 U. of Pa.L.Rev. 108; 1938, 16 Tex.L.Rev. 534, 535. Cf. the somewhat analogous problem of notice to the purchasers of a bond of the contents of a trust indenture securing it. Note, 1927, 27 Col.L.Rev. 443, 447–9. And see §§ 231, 232, 235, ante.

24. Foster v. Augustana College & Theological Seminary, 1923, 92 Okl. 96, 218 P. 335, 37 A.L.R. 854; U. S. Nat. Bank v. Holton, 1921, 99 Or. 419, 195 P. 823; Ross v. Title Guarantee & Trust Co., 1934, 136 Cal.App. 393, 29 P.2d 236, discussed 1934, 22 Cal.L. Rev. 677, 681, 684; 1934, 23 Cal.L.Rev. 108; Security Mortgage Co. v. Delfs, 1920, 47 Cal.App. 599, 191 P. 53, semble; prior assignment recorded first but not until after the second assignment. See 1925, 37 A.L.R. 860; 1940, 127 A.L.R. 201.

25. Murphy v. Barnard, 1894, 162 Mass. 72, 38 N.E. 29, 44 Am.St.Rep. 340; Strong v. Jackson, 1877, 123 Mass. 60, 25 Am.St.Rep. 19.

is not what by men of business is usually denominated commercial or business paper; and we think there is a material distinction between securities of this kind and strictly mercantile paper; and that such paper as this may be subject to equities, when strictly mercantile paper would not be; not that the rule of law is different, but what would attract no attention in relation to purely business paper should attract the attention in paper of this description. * * *

"The reference upon the note to the mortgage, under the circumstances, is of much significance; the mortgage describes the note; the note refers to the mortgage; and, in the condition of things at the time the First National Bank took the security, we think that the taker of either must take according to the true title of him who transfers it, as such title is apparent upon proper examination of it." [26]

The third view is that the transferee of the note is a holder in due course as to it; but since the element of negotiability is lacking in mortgages, he takes the mortgage with notice of the prior, recorded assignment and cannot foreclose in the collection of the note.[27] Apart from its holding as to the

note, this last solution has little to commend it. It infringes upon the basic principle that the assignment of a debt secured by a mortgage carries with it the right to the security.[28] Further, while giving the indorsee of the note the right to collect the debt, the prior holder's recorded interest as assignee of the mortgage is valueless because he has no right to collect the debt which is essential to its utilization.[29] "Thus, either the mortgage lien is extinguished because there is no one entitled to enforce the security, and the maker of the note gets a windfall[30] in having the premises freed of the lien of the mortgage or deed of trust; or the holder of the prior recorded right to the mortgage, through a power to assign the

instruments and their language, "Of which the bank had constructive notice, were sufficient to put the bank [holder of the note for $2,250 and complainant in the action in the case to foreclose a mortgage alleged to secure it on the same property for which a mortgage of $2,500 was claimed by a third party] upon inquiry * * * [which] would have informed the bank that the $2,500 mortgage was executed and acknowledged as a substitute for the $2,250 mortgage, and also that the $2,-500 mortgage was held by a third party for value, and without notice of the existence of the $2,250 mortgage that was offered by the original mortgagee to the bank. Under these circumstances the holder of the $2,250 mortgage cannot be regarded as a purchaser without notice of the $2,500 mortgage. * * *

The court further stated that "While the constructive record notice is * * * sufficient to put the bank upon inquiry in taking an assignment of the $2,250 mortgage, and such inquiry would have disclosed [its] invalidity * * * yet such record notice is not of such a nature as to make the action of the bank in taking the $2,250 note amount to *bad faith* * * *; and therefore the bank is, on this record, a holder for value of the negotiable note, as against Caro [the maker and purported mortgagor]."

26. Strong v. Jackson, supra note 25, at page 63. If the note had not referred to the mortgage and the later purchaser had bought it as a plain, unsecured note, he very clearly would be a holder in due course. And, if so, it would seem that he should be entitled to the security. The first assignee should not be entitled to it and there is no reason to give the mortgagor a windfall by treating it as released. See Ross, Double Hazard of Note and Mortgage, 1931, 16 Minn.L.Rev. 121, 131; § 207, supra; text, infra, this section.

27. Taylor v. American Nat. Bank, 1912, 64 Fla. 525, 60 So. 783; Wood v. Sparks, Tex.Com.App.1933, 59 S.W.2d 361, rehearing denied, 63 S.W.2d 1109, discussed in note, 1932, 10 Tex.L.Rev. 201; note, 1938, 16 Tex.L.Rev. 534, 537—accord. See § 231, supra.

See Note: Mortgages: Effect of Failure to Record a Mortgage Assignment in Florida, 1954, 7 U. of Fla. L.Rev. 93. The writer of the note states, p. 96 n. 2, that the Taylor case, cited supra, does not stand for the proposition for which it was cited because there were two mortgages involved. The case holds precisely what it was cited for. The second mortgage in the case was taken in substitution for the first one. The court held that the records of the

28. See § 223, supra.

29. See § 226, supra.

30. It has been suggested that in practice the result may be substantially the same under this view as under the first. If the holder of the note can enforce it by getting judgment on it he can then levy on the land. The prior assignee, having no debt claim, would not be able to defeat the execution. The holder of the note would, however, run the risk of intervening encumbrances, which he would have priority over if he got the mortgage with the note. See note, 1942, 10 Jour.B.A.Kan. 282, 284.

mortgage to the indorsee of the note, is in a position to use pressure to obtain from the indorsee the practical value of the security." [31]

As between the other two views, the first one, as indicated earlier, seems preferable.[32] Assignees of mortgages are engaged, dominantly, in buying a debt claim, and therefore the rules applying to that particular form of debt should govern its sale. If it is in the form of a negotiable instrument, just as its negotiability is not affected by the fact that it is secured by a mortgage,[33] neither should it be subject to the hazard of having to investigate real property records in order to be sure that he will be a holder in due course. And this is true even though, in good part, the value of the claim is high because it is secured, and even though title to the security may be investigated in determining whether to buy. If he does not wish to investigate he should not be under compulsion to do so on penalty of not getting the main thing he was bargaining for, the note. As was just pointed out, if he gets the note, he should get the mortgage with it.

Where the assignee of a mortgage securing a negotiable note fails to record his assignment but gets and keeps possession of the note he should, and by what is believed to be the better authority, does prevail over a subsequent purchaser of the mortgage from its record owner.[34] The reason is substantially the same one that should leave the purchaser of the secured negotiable note free to ignore prior recorded assignments of the mortgage, i. e., the principal thing that is being bought is the note itself, not its accessory, the mortgage. At least that is the controlling thought and should prevail in determining the rules governing the priorities of the parties who take successive assignments of it. Commercial policy in the free mobility of the debt is more important in a case of this sort than the land policy. It is true that the assignment transaction may be and is sometimes couched in terms which do not mention the debt as distinct from the security; and when this is the case the agreement nevertheless will carry at least an equitable right to the negotiable note or the bond as well as the security interest in the property.[35] Nevertheless, whenever a purchaser is apprized, whether from recitals in the mortgage or otherwise, that the obligation he is about to buy is expressed in the written form of a negotiable instrument,[36] the natural, and the only prudent, course is to ask for the docu-

31. 1934, 22 Cal.L.Rev. 677, 695.

32. See § 235, supra. See also Hanna, Rev. of Glenn, Mortgages, 1944, 53 Yale L.Jour. 590, 593. Cf. Walsh, Mortgages, § 63. It is believed that the last writer fails to take into account the complexity of the problem.

33. See § 232, supra.

34. Syracuse Sav. Bank v. Merrick, 1905, 182 N.Y. 387, 75 N.E. 232; Barringer v. Loder, 1905, 47 Or. 223, 81 P. 778; Richards Trust Co. v. Rhomberg, 1905, 19 S.D. 595, 104 N.W. 268; Miller Brewing Co. v. Manasse, 1898, 99 Wis. 99, 74 N.W. 535. Adler v. Newell, 1895, 109 Cal. 42, 41 P. 799 under a special recording statute making recordation of a mortgage assignment notice but not requiring recordation for validity as in the case of recording of conveyances. Guessing at the reason for the differ-

ence between the two types of recording acts the court said, "Probably the legislature did not intend to hamper too greatly the transfer and exchange of debts and obligations secured by mortgage, which are usually in the form of negotiable paper * * *."

"However, the apparent record owner of the mortgage is the only one having the power to do injury to his interest, and, if he chooses to rely upon the apparent owner's honesty and integrity, he is taking only such chances as may be involved in the dishonorable and fraudulent acts of the apparent record owner in executing a satisfaction of the mortgage. Such chances are further minimized by the fact that he has physical possession of the mortgage and, as against the actual holder of the mortgage, the debtor is not protected in paying it to one unable to surrender it and the note which it secures. Marling v. Jones, 138 Wis. 82, 119 N.W. 931, 131 Am.St.Rep. 996. In view of this rule, coupled with the probability that a subsequent bona fide purchaser will insist on the delivery of the note and mortgage, the risk assumed by an assignee of the mortgage in failing to record the assignment is not great." Thauer v. Smith, 1933, 213 Wis. 91, 250 N.W. 842.

35. See §§ 223, 226, supra.

36. As indicated previously, § 234, the doctrine may desirably go beyond strictly negotiable instruments.

ment, for that is what he wants.[37] Indeed he normally wants both the note and the mortgage. So far as he is concerned they are indispensable documents. If they are not forthcoming, he has adequate warning that something may be amiss. He cannot rely upon the records in such a case any more than can one who goes to pay the debt.[38] And it follows that an assignee who gets and holds onto the negotiable note and mortgage, although he runs some risks if he does not record his mortgage,[39] should not run the hazard of losing to a subsequent assignee from his assignor.

In spite of the foregoing there are several cases in which the failure of a prior assignee who held the negotiable note and mortgage to record his mortgage resulted in a subsequent assignee prevailing. It is possible to account for some of the results on the basis of the language of the statute involved,[40] or special facts justifying reliance upon appearances created by the wrongful conduct of the mortgagee for which, it is true, the assignee was not responsible but which were made possible by the assignee's failure to do the simple act of recordation.[41] And in one, the transaction was such that the mortgage, not the note, was what was being bought,

and therefore quite properly the failure to record was penalized.[42]

PARTIAL ASSIGNMENTS—EXPRESS PROVISIONS AS TO PRIORITY

243. Where parts of one debt secured by a single mortgage are transferred to different holders priority among them and the original mortgagee may be determined by express provisions in the mortgage or in the contracts of assignment.

In cases of mortgages of large amount mortgagees have reduced the amount of their own investment by selling fractional interests in it. Where the debt is in the form of a single, whole amount payable at one time, this can be done by ordinary partial assignments which will be governed by the rules applicable to partial assignments so far as the debt is concerned, and will make the partial assignee a "tenant in common" of the mortgage security.[43] More frequently, however, the mortgage secures a series of notes or bonds, each one for a fractional part of the debt, either representing an instalment of the principal, in which case they will have different maturity dates, or else just a proportionate part of the whole with all having the same maturity date.[44] The notes or

---

37. See Thauer v. Smith, 1933, 213 Wis. 91, 250 N.W. 842, semble.

38. See §§ 234, 235, 236, supra.

39. See § 238, supra. See also the analogous problem of conveyance by a mortgagee to a bona fide purchaser of the land after a conveyance to him by the mortgagor following an unrecorded assignment to a third party. Chapter 9, infra.

40. Morrow v. Stanley, 1913, 119 Md. 590, 87 A. 484, under a strongly worded statute making record ownership of the mortgage conclusive of ownership of the debt.

41. Blunt v. Norris, 1877, 123 Mass. 55, 25 Am.Rep. 14, a new, genuine note obtained by fraud by the mortgagee from the mortgagor and transferred together with an assignment of the mortgage; Second Nat. Bank v. Dyer, 1936, 121 Conn. 263, 184 A. 386, 104 A.L.R. 1295, criticized in note, 1940, 6 Pitt. L.Rev. 300, forged instruments transferred to the second assignee (cf. Morris v. Bacon, 1877, 123 Mass. 58, 25 Am.Rep. 17).

42. Price v. Northern Bond & Mort. Co., 1931, 161 Wash. 690, 297 P. 786, under the terms of the deed of trust, it was the *mortgage* that was regarded as the principal and the note merely an incident.

43. "It is recognized by all courts that the assignment of a part of the debt carries with it the assignment of at least a coparcenary interest in the security." Domeyer v. O'Connell, 1936, 364 Ill. 467, 4 N.E.2d 830, 108 A.L.R. 476. See 1934, 34 Col.L. Rev. 663, 675, 676 n. 51; Williston, Contracts, Rev. ed., §§ 441–444.

44. Such series are different from bond issues which are used for the purpose of obtaining future advances. See § 117, supra. Here the entire loan is made to the mortgagor at the outset and then the mortgagee disposes of fractional interests in it by marketing the already existing and binding notes and bonds. In this latter case the original mortgagee is the one who advances the whole amount and the purchasers are partial assignees from him. In the former case, each purchaser of a bond is himself an original co-mortgagee, the amount he pays being a part of the original total loan to the mortgagor.

bonds are then assigned for value either by way of indorsement or without recourse, a matter of significance in determining the rights of the parties as will be seen.[45] Also quite common is the practice of the mortgagee to keep the original debt and mortgage and to issue participation certificates which are then sold to investors. Sometimes payment of these participation certificates is guaranteed by a third person,[46] sometimes by the mortgagee seller,[47] and sometimes they are sold without guarantee.[48] Usually they contain rather extensive statements of the rights and duties of the seller and the holder of the certificate.[49] The first two methods of carrying out the transaction seem quite clearly to constitute partial assignments of a single debt rather than the transfer of a divisible portion of the obligation.[50] The third, while it would be possible to classify it, technically, as a trust with the mortgagee holding the debt and mortgage as trustee for the holders of the participating certificates, is, nevertheless, so patently just another method of making partial assignments [51] that the courts have treated it as governed by the same considerations.[52] They deny, at any rate, that there is a fiduciary relationship between the certificate holder and the seller.[53]

In any of the cases just outlined, but especially in the second and third types, difficult questions of priority have arisen as between the various partial assignees and as between the assignor and the assignees, and among the authorities there are conflicting views as to what the law is or should be.[54] These problems will be taken up in the succeeding sections, but before doing so it should be noted that most of the difficulties could be obviated by clear statements of intention of the parties on the points that cause trouble.[55] The most appropriate and most effective place for such a provision is in the mortgage itself, for it will be on record so that all can go and read it and can be charged with notice of it whether they read it or not. A provision in the mortgage, whether it be a simple one between individuals or a corporate mortgage securing a bond issue, that it shall equally and ratably secure all the notes or bonds without preference or priority of any one over another or

---

45. See § 245, infra.

46. E. g., Title Guar. & Trust Co. v. Mortgage Commission, 1937, 273 N.Y. 415, 7 N.E.2d 841.

47. E. g., Re Title & Mortgage Guaranty Co. of Sullivan County, 1937, 275 N.Y. 347, 9 N.E.2d 957, 115 A.L.R. 35; Pink v. Thomas, 1938, 282 N.Y. 10, 24 N.E. 724; Prudence Realization Corp.v. Geist, 1942, 316 U.S. 89, 62 S.Ct. 978, 86 L.Ed. 1293; Reconstruction Finance Co. v. Smith, Tex.Civ.App.1936, 96 S.W.2d 824.

48. See 1934, 34 Col.L.Rev. 706.

49. E. g., Title Guar. & Trust Co. v. Mortgage Commission, supra.

50. See Williston, Contracts, Rev.ed., § 441. But cf. the implication to the contrary in the pro tanto theories which are a part of the "order of assignment" and "order of maturity" rules discussed infra, § 244.

51. E. g., Title Guaranty & Trust Co. v. Mortgage Commission, 1937, 273 N.Y. 415, 7 N.E.2d 841, "* * * the certificate holders became tenants in common, each entitled to an aliquot share of the mortgage referred to in the certificate." See 1945, 32 Va.L.Rev. 176.

52. See 1934, 34 Col.L.Rev. 663, 675.

53. See Title Guarantee and Trust Co. v. Mortgage Commission, 1937, 273 N.Y. 415, 426, 7 N.E.2d 841, "Perhaps the trend of legal thought on the question may be indicated in the following statement from the Restatement of the Law of Trusts, * * * 'If a partial assignment of a chose in action is made, the assignor does not become trustee for the assignee * * *. There is a fiduciary relation between trustee and beneficiary. In the case of a partial assignment, as in the case of a total assignment, there is not a fiduciary relation between the assignor and the assignee.'" Cf. Glenn, Mortgages, § 317. But see, id., §§ 131.2, 317.2.

54. See Rollison, Priorities in The Law of Mortgages, 1934, 9 N.Dame Law 215, 220–230.

55. "All the authorities agree that the order in which several notes or instalments, secured by one mortgage, shall be paid out of the proceeds of the security, is entirely a matter of contract; that the parties, at the time of the execution of the mortgage, may contract for any order of payment they see fit; * * *." Wilson v. Eigenbrodt, 1882, 30 Minn. 4, 13 N.W. 907, Campbell, Cases on Mortgages, 2d ed., 584; People v. Mitchell, 1921, 223 Ill. App. 8; 1927, 50 A.L.R. 543, 576; 1937, 108 A.L.R. 485, 496.

others, or fixing their relative priority, as the case may be, is legally effective according to its terms and forestalls most of the questions we are about to consider. If no provision is made in the original contract as to order of payment, "the mortgagee, when he assigns the notes, may by contract fix any order of payment as between himself and his assignee, or between his several assignees, that they may agree upon." [56] Such an agreement between the assignor and assignee, if properly manifested, is legally effective not only against the assignor but subsequent assignees of the other notes or bonds with knowledge or notice thereof.[57] It has been observed, however, that recording acts do not apply to partial assignments of mortgages,[58] that they are couched in terms of total assignments.[59] Consequently

56. Wilson v. Eigenbrodt, 1882, 30 Minn. 4, 13 N.W. 907. "The parties have a right by their contract to create such liens as the see fit within the law. They have a right by mortgage to fix priorities as to payment of the debt or debts thereby secured; they have the right in the face of their negotiable promissory notes to do the same; they have even the right in the transfer of these papers to an assignee to limit their rights or to provide for priorities in so far as they may not prejudicially affect others." Conway v. Yadon, 1928, 132 Okl. 36, 269 P. 309; Walker v. Dement, 1866, 42 Ill. 272. See note, 1937, 25 Cal.L.Rev. 504.

57. Campbell, Cases on Mortgages, 2d ed., § 585 n. 2. See 1927, 50 A.L.R. 543, 575, 579; 1937, 108 A.L.R. 485, 496, 497. In states where an assignee takes subject to latent equities, a later transferee would take subject to such a stipulation without notice. Bank of England v. Tarleton, 1851, 23 Miss. 173.

58. See Glenn, Mortgages, § 317.

59. N.Y. Real Prop.Law, § 324; Rev.Stats.N.J., §§ 46:9–9, 18–3, 18–4, 22–3, 22–4; West's Ann.Cal.Civ. Code §§ 2934, 2935. While this may be true of statutes dealing expressly with assignments, it does not answer the question as to statutes where assignments of mortgages are construed to be within the meaning of broad provisions covering "conveyances" and "instruments affecting title," etc. If the partial assignment operates to make the assignee a "tenant-in-common" of the security interest in the land it would seem quite proper to hold that it falls under such acts. Morgan v. Kline, 1889, 77 Iowa 681, 42 N.W. 558. Look at Miami Oil Co. v. Florida Discount Corp., 1931, 102 Fla. 209, 135 So. 845, noted, 1932, 6 Cin.L.Rev. 247. However, to compel partial assignments to be recorded would seriously affect the commercial use of the device of participation certificates. See Glenn, Mortgages, § 317.1.

a partial assignee, as these transferees of participating certificates or notes representing parts of the whole debt are, although they become assignees of corresponding fragment interests in the mortgage security cannot record their assignments so as to give notice of its terms. Nor are they penalized for failure to do so. In a remarkable number of cases there is no express agreement settling the matter and the questions then are raised: what order shall the law adopt either because that *ought* to be the order in the particular transaction or particular type of transaction; or because, presumably, that was the unexpressed "intention" of the parties. The word "intention" is purposely put in quotes. Although the courts frequently talk as though they were basing their results upon an inquiry into the implied, but actual, intention of the parties, and sometimes that is true, in many instances they obviously rest upon no such foundation. In such cases it taxes the ability of the reader to determine just precisely what were the real reasons for the decisions. The applicability of this observation will be more apparent in connection with the discussion of the particular problems.

PARTIAL ASSIGNMENTS—PRIORITY AMONG ASSIGNEES IN ABSENCE OF AGREEMENT

244. Where a mortgage secures several notes which are assigned to different holders, in the absence of an express provision for priority, the weight of authority and preferable rule prorates the security among them. Other cases award priority according to the dates of assignment or the times of maturity of their notes.

Where there is a mortgage given to secure several notes and the notes are assigned to different holders and there is no express provision either in the mortgage or the contracts of assignments, as between the several assignees the cases fall into three general divisions.[60] One rule gives priority to the

60. See text and footnotes infra, this section.

various assignees according to the respective dates of their assignments.[61] Another line of cases holds that the notes are entitled to priority of payment in the order in which they mature.[62] The third class of decisions holds that all the notes or instalments secured by one mortgage should be paid pro rata out of the proceeds of the security, without regard to the dates of their assignment, or the times of their maturity. This last is not only the weight of authority but has generally been approved by courts and writers as the best rule of the three.[63]

The priority of assignment rule is based upon the theory that the assignment operates as between the assignor and assignee to give to the assignee so much [64] of the mortgage as is necessary to satisfy in full the notes assigned.[65] With this as a premise it is reasoned that the equity of the first transferee being fixed since an assignee gets no greater rights than his assignor,[66] second and succeeding assignees must take the remaining notes subject to priorities already created in favor of earlier assignees.[67] The basic objection to this theory is that, contrary to what is claimed to be the practically universal intention of the parties, it splits up what

---

61. Cullum v. Erwin, 1842, 4 Ala. 452. This was the earlier rule in Virginia but after a vigorous attack upon it by J. W. H. Pilson, 1933, 19 Va.L.Rev. 878, it was changed by statute. Va.Code 1950, § 55-60-1.

Look at Miami Oil Co. v. Florida Discount Corporation, 1931, 102 Fla. 209, 135 So. 845, commented on in, 1932, 6 U. of Cin.L.Rev. 247. See 1912, 42 L.R. A.,N.S., 183, 205; 1927, 50 A.L.R. 543, 574; 1937, 108 A.L.R. 485, 496.

62. Wilson v. Hayward, 1855, 6 Fla. 171; see 1912, 42 L.R.A.,N.S., 183, 199; 1927, 50 A.L.R. 543, 556; 1937, 108 A.L.R. 486, 490.

63. Phelan v. Olney, 1856, 6 Cal. 478; Conway v. Yadon, 1928, 132 Okl. 36, 269 P. 309, commented on in, 1928, 77 U. of Pa.L.Rev. 266; Donley v. Hays, 1828, 17 Serg. & R., Pa., 400.

"It may be said, however, that by the great weight of authority the courts of this country, whether adopting the so-called pro tanto or the pro rata rule, as between assignee and mortgagee, are agreed that as between assignees of notes bearing the same maturity date there is not, in the absence of contract, a preference or priority. Studebaker Bros., Mfg. Co. v. McCurgur, 20 Neb. 500, 30 N.W. 686; Adams v. Lear, 3 La.Ann. 144; Burhans v. Mitchell, 42 Mich. 417, 4 N.W. 178; Penzel v. Brookmire, 51 Ark. 105, 10 S.W. 15, 14 Am.St.Rep. 23; Smith v. Bowne, 60 Ga. 484; Campbell v. Johnston, 4 Dana, Ky., 177, 178; Dixon v. Clayville, 44 Md. 573; Wilson v. Eigenbrodt, 30 Minn. 4, 13 N.W. 907, 908; Bank of England v. Tarleton, 23 Miss. 173; Bridenbecker v. Lowell, 32 Barb., N.Y., 9; Andrews v. Hobgood, 1 Lea, Tenn., 693; Keyes v. Wood, 21 Vt. 331; First Nat. Bank v. Andrews, 7 Wash. 261, 34 P. 913, 38 Am.St.Rep. 885." Domeyer v. O'Connell, 1936, 364 Ill. 467, 4 N.E.2d 830, 108 A.L.R. 476.

See notes, 1933, 19 Va.L.Rev. 898 (urging the statutory enactment of the rule); 1886, 22 Cent.L.J. 130; 1919, 88 Cent.L.J. 446; 1913, 42 L.R.A.,N.S., 183; Ann.Cas.1914C, 143; 1927, 50 A.L.R. 543, 546; 1937, 108 A.L.R. 485, 487. See also note, 1936, 10 Tulane L.Rev. 303.

"But the principle has no application to money paid by the mortgagor to the mortgagee on the remaining note, when, so to speak, the money so paid never saw the mortgaged lands, was independent, and not the legitimate offspring of them. Such money could in no wise be imbued or infected with the mortgage lien security." Brewer v. Atkeison, 1899, 121 Ala. 410, 413, 25 So. 992, 993, 77 Am.St.Rep. 64. See Campbell, Cases on Mortgages, 2d ed., 586 n. 3, 587 n. 4, for departures from or qualifications of the general rules adopted by the courts in the same jurisdictions.

64. This is the "so-called pro tanto rule—that is, that upon assignment of a mortgage note the mortgagee assigned, pro tanto, sufficient of the mortgage to pay the note." Domeyer v. O'Connell, 1936, 364 Ill. 467, 4 N.E.2d 830, 108 A.L.R. 476.

65. "The cases adopting this rule usually place it upon the ground that, in the act of assigning a note secured by a mortgage, there is an implied agreement on the part of the assignor that his assignee shall have the benefit of the security to the extent necessary to pay the note assigned, and therefore that the assignment of the note operates as an assignment of the security pro tanto, and not merely pro rata." Wilson v. Eigenbrodt, 1882, 30 Minn. 4, 13 N.W. 907. See J. W. H. Pilson, 1933, 19 Va.L.Rev. 878, 880. The reasoning in back of this assumption is discussed in § 244, infra.

66. "Some States, Alabama (Cullum v. Erwin, 4 Ala. 452, 458); Virginia (McClintic v. Wise's Adm'rs, 25 Grat. 448, 18 Am.Rep. 694), and West Virginia (Jenkins v. Hawkins, 34 W.Va. 799, 12 S.E. 1090), for example, hold that the mortgage note first assigned takes priority over all notes later assigned, on the ground that the first assignment carries with it the mortgage, and the assignees of the notes later assigned take only what is left in the mortgagee." Domeyer v. O'Connell, 1936, 364 Ill. 467, 4 N.E.2d 830, 108 A.L.R. 476. The cases cited represent the law in Virginia before it was changed by statute. That later assignees would ordinarily be on notice from the terms of the mortgage that there were other parts of the debt, see text, infra, this section.

67. 1928, 77 U.Pa.L.Rev. 266, 268.

was executed as a single mortgage to secure a single debt represented by a series of notes [68] into a series of mortgages each securing a single note.[69] Although the rule makes it easier to dispose of the notes or bonds first assigned, by the same token, since later assignees are relegated to the position of second, third, or later mortgagees, it usually makes it from difficult to impossible to sell or borrow on the ones retained—a consequence which, if it were known, would scarcely ever be intended by either assignor or assignee.[70] Theoretically it is true that, because a transferee knows that he is getting only a part of the debt, since the recorded mortgage would contain information as to the amount and character of the debt, he should, in the exercise of ordinary prudence, make inquiry

and find out where the other parts are.[71] Nevertheless without a "search of safe-deposit boxes from Kamchatka to Key West", an obvious impracticability, it may be impossible to know who are now the assignees of the bonds or notes and, since frequently the transfer is by undated assignment, what the order of assignment is even when the holders are found.[72] The result is, contrary to desirable business practice and good commercial policy, that the rights of assignees are subject to such uncertainties as to impair seriously their marketability. In a state where the rule existed, one investigation disclosed that practically all business men and most bankers were ignorant of the rule and many lawyers were unaware of some of its consequences so that it constituted a "veritable trap for the unwary."[73]

The order of maturity rule, like that of the order of assignment is founded on the idea that the assignment of each note is an assignment pro tanto of a corresponding portion of the mortgage so that the different instalments represented by the several notes, "are to be regarded as so many *successive* mortgages, each having priority according to the time of maturity."[74] The fallacy here, as under the prior assignment rule, is that "the different instalments are not secured by different mortgages of different dates, but by one mortgage executed equally for the benefit of all the instalments."[75] If the doctrine were correct, then "it would follow that if separate mortgages were executed contemporaneously to different persons, to secure different debts maturing at different dates, the mortgagee whose debt first ma-

---

68. "Some authorities hold that in effect there are as many mortgages as there are notes to be secured; that the several notes are in some way protected by an assignment of so much of the mortgage as is necessary to protect the notes, and, therefore, that these several notes when assigned carry with them either pro tanto or pro rata assignments of the original mortgage. But it seems to us that, without any refinement of reasoning, the status of these notes may be arrived at by determining just what the intention of the parties was, and judging such intention by what they actually did in the premises. In more than 99 cases out of 100 a mortgage is given to secure a single debt. It may be for the difference in exchange of lands, or for the purchase of live stock or for the loan of money, or what not. It may be, and more often is, the fact that the debt is to be liquidated in partial payments. Sometimes this is for the benefit of the mortgagor; sometimes for the benefit of the mortgagee; then again it may be for the advantage of both that the amount of the original debt be split up into payments extending over a period. The mortgagor secures the additional time and the mortgagee secures the additional interest incident to the forbearance." Conway v. Yadon, 1928, 132 Okl. 36, 269 P. 309. The court was speaking specifically of the earlier maturity rule, but what it said is equally applicable to the prior assignment rule. "But, inasmuch as the mortgage stands equally as security for *all* the notes, we fail to see how the mere act of assigning one of them can raise any presumption that the parties intended that it should operate as an assignment of any more than its *pro rata* proportion of the security." Wilson v. Eigenbrodt, 1882, 30 Minn. 4, 13 N.W. 907. See J. W. H. Pilson, 1933, 19 Va.L.Rev. 878.

69. See 1928, 77 U.Pa.L.Rev. 266, 267, 268.

70. See J. W. H. Pilson, 1933, 19 Va.L.Rev. 878, 880.

71. See Tiffany, Real Prop., 3d ed., § 1458.

72. Id.

73. Id. The vigorous criticism leveled at the rule led to the enactment by statute of the rule of ratable distribution among assignees unless the instrument creating the lien clearly provides otherwise. Va.Code 1950, § 55–60–1.

74. Wilson v. Eigenbrodt, 1882, 30 Minn. 4, 13 N.W. 907.

75. Id.

tured would be entitled to precedence." [76] This, however, is not the case. [77] Another suggestion in favor of the rule is that the law of the remedy gives precedence to the note having the first maturity, for when it falls due it may be foreclosed and this right of action carries with it priority of payment out of the property. The objection to this is that it assumes that the right to foreclose on maturity carries with it a right to priority in the proceeds of the foreclosure. Of course this is not true. If it were a second mortgage whose note fell due before that of a first mortgagee could thereby gain priority over him. The rights of parties under the lien of the mortgage date from the date of the mortgage, and not from the time the cause of action accrues under it. Although there may be a foreclosure of a part of a debt when that part falls due, the owners of parts maturing later cannot be excluded from participation in the foreclosure. The latter may insist upon being parties and the sale must be made so as to safeguard the rights of the holders of the subsequent instalments. This may be done by ordering the property sold subject to a lien upon it for the instalments not yet due just as, in the similar case of foreclosure by a second mortgagee, the property is sold subject to the lien of the first mortgage. Or, if the property is sold free of the entire indebtedness, there should be an order as to the application of the proceeds that will

protect the holders of later maturing notes. [78] The treatment of later maturing notes as junior mortgages is especially weak in view of the growing use of acceleration clauses. [79] In some states such a clause is held to exclude the operation of the rule. [80] Effect has been given to the clauses by saying that the notes are due at maturity or as much sooner as there is default by any one. [81] Others, however, either on the ground that acceleration merely gives an earlier distribution to all but does not affect priorities which were fixed by the original maturity dates, or because to let it affect the priority would render the value of the notes uncertain and enable the mortgagor and mortgagee by collusion to destroy the priority of the earlier maturity notes, have refused to allow acceleration clauses to alter the operation of the rule. [82] Perhaps the chief difficulty with the whole prior maturity rule is to find in a mortgage that does not provide for maturity anything to indicate an intention that priorities nevertheless shall be given. To infer intention from the dates of the notes is unwarranted. Normally the mortgagor has no interest or intent in regard to priority, and, just as in the similar case of giving precedence in order of assignment, it is

---

76. Id.

77. "It is the well-settled law of this state that, if a mortgage be given to secure successive instalments of a debt, evidenced by promissory notes maturing at different times, and the notes pass into different hands, * * * the holders of the several notes have priority of lien in the order in which their respective demands become due. * * * It by no means follows, however, that a like priority shall prevail when a single mortgage is given to secure separate obligations to different parties, maturing at different times. Such a mortgage is in all essential respects equivalent to the simultaneous giving of separate mortgages to secure such obligations." Shaw v. Newsom, 1881, 78 Ind. 335, 337. Coons v. Clifford, 1898, 58 Ohio St. 480, 51 N.E. 39, accord. See 1928, 77 U.Pa.L.Rev. 266, 268.

78. See Leesman, The Effect of Foreclosure of Part Only of a Mortgage Debt, 1937, 31 Ill.L.Rev. 1056.

79. See 1937, 4 U.Chi.L.Rev. 502.

80. Whitehead v. Morrill, 1891, 108 N.C. 65, 12 S.E. 894, pro rate; Bushfield v. Meyer, 1859, 10 Ohio St. 334, pro rate; Pierce v. Shaw, 1881, 51 Wis. 316, 8 N.W. 209, pro rate.

81. Id.

82. Leavitt v. Reynolds, 1890, 79 Iowa 348, 44 N.W. 567, 7 L.R.A. 365; Horn v. Bennett, 1893, 135 Ind. 158, 34 N.E. 321, 24 L.R.A. 800, rehearing denied 135 Ind. 158, 34 N.E. 956, 24 L.R.A. 800. Koester v. Burke, 1876, 81 Ill. 436. Cf., semble, People's Saving Bank v. Finney, 1878, 63 Ind. 460, extension deprives of priority.

Look at Metelmann v. Buchanan, 1935, 101 Ind.App. 150, 198 N.E. 460, discussed in note, 1936, 22 Va.L. Rev. 592. See also Leesman, The Effect of Foreclosure of a Part Only of a Mortgage Debt, 1937, 31 Ill.L.Rev. 1056; note, 1939, 4 John Marshall L.Q. 434.

against the interest of the assigning mortgagee to have the earlier maturity notes preferred since such priorities make it doubly difficult to dispose of the later maturing ones.[83] Indeed, it is only by assuming the point at issue that priority can be given to the holders of the notes first due and the claims of the holders of other instalments to share equally in the security can be ignored.[84] In spite of these strictures the doctrine has been accepted in a considerable number of states.[85]

The pro rata rule has the positive merits of fulfilling the general principle that equality is equity and of being in accord with the well founded common-sense presumption[86] that the intention of the parties is that the mortgage shall secure one part of the debt to the same extent as any other part.[87] These virtues also enable it to escape the criticisms leveled at the other rules. They also account for the fact that it was adopted early[88] and is clearly the present weight of authority,[89] as well as that it is growing in favor as evidenced by its adoption through statutory enactment[90] and court decision[91] and its extension to mortgage participation certificates[92] and its application to pledges of personal property.[93]

PARTIAL ASSIGNMENTS—ASSIGNOR VS. ASSIGNEE

245. Express provisions stating the order of priority between assigned and retained notes secured by one mortgage will govern. In the absence of such provisions other than an indorsement without recourse, although there is considerable authority to the contrary, no agreement should be implied that the mortgage notes in the hands of an assignee shall take priority over those remaining in the hands of a mortgagee. Nor is there, in such cases, an equity in favor of the assignee independent of agreement.

Where the original mortgagee or an intervening assignor[94] assigns one or more of a series of notes secured by the same mortgage and retains others, express provisions in either the mortgage or the contract of assignment may state the order of priority between the payment of the assigned notes and those still retained in case there is insufficient proceeds from the sale of the property. Such

83.   1928, 77 U.Pa.L.Rev. 266. See text, supra, this section.

84.   See Tiffany, Real Prop., 3d ed., § 1458.

85.   In Conway v. Yadon, 1928, 132 Okl. 36, 269 P. 309, the court said that it was "more or less consistently followed in Alabama, Florida, Illinois, Indiana, Iowa, Kansas, Ohio, New Hampshire, and Wisconsin." For modifications of the order of maturity rule where accepted, see Campbell, Cases on Mortgages, 2d ed., 586 n. 3.

86.   Born out not only by reason of the fairness and certainty of the rule but by its past and growing popularity.

87.   "We adopt this rule as being not only the more equitable but also as sound in principle, because in accordance with the implied intention of the parties as inferable from the nature of the contract. The mortgage is as much security for one note as another. There is no priority of lien in favor of one as against another, for the mortgage is one; and the mortgage being a mere incident to the debt, an assignment of a part of a debt carries with it a *pro rata* proportion of the security. The different holders of the mortgage debt, therefore, stand *aequali jure*, and consequently are entitled to participate *pari passu* in the fund derived from the security." Wilson v. Eigenbrodt, 1882, 30 Minn. 4, 13 N.W. 907. See Conway v. Yadon, 1928, 132 Okl. 36, 269 P. 309.

88.   Donley v. Hays, Pa.1828, 17 Serg. & R. 400.

89.   "This doctrine is sustained by cases from the United States Supreme Court and from the Supreme Courts of the following states: Arkansas, California, Georgia, Connecticut, Louisiana, Maine, Maryland, Massachusetts, Michigan, Mississippi, Nebraska, New Jersey, New York, North Carolina, Pennsylvania, South Carolina, South Dakota, Tennessee, Texas, and Washington." Conway v. Yadon, 1928, 132 Okl. 36, 269 P. 309. See 1927, 50 A.L.R. 543, 546; 1937, 108 A.L.R. 485, 487.

90.   In Virginia, as previously mentioned.

91.   See Title Guarantee & Trust Co. v. Mortgage Commission, 1937, 273 N.Y. 415, 7 N.E.2d 841, reviewing the cases in New York.

92.   Id. And see cases cited § 242, supra.

93.   Jenkins & Co., Bankers v. Greene, 1927, 44 Idaho 306, 256 P. 950, 52 A.L.R. 1386; Reconstruction Fin. Corp. v. O'Keefe, C.C.A.N.J.1938, 98 F.2d 820, applying New Jersey law, noted, 1938, 25 Va.L.Rev. 375. It was adopted as the most satisfactory rule in the Restatement of Security, § 30, dealing with pledges.

94.   See 1927, 50 A.L.R. 563, 568.

express provisions will control.[95] The transfer may be made by indorsement with recourse or it may be accompanied by a guaranty of payment by the transferor or a third party. In such cases the question arises whether the contractual liability so created is purely a personal one against the indorser or guarantor or whether it carries with it a priority of payment out of the security. This question will be considered in the following section.[96]

Here the concern is with the question of priority between the assigned and retained notes when nothing appears in either the mortgage or the contract of assignment other than that in the latter the notes may be indorsed without recourse. In such cases the problem may be stated as follows: First, is there an implied agreement that mortgage notes in the hands of an assignee shall take priority over those remaining in the hands of the mortgagee and if not, then, second, is there an equity in favor of the assignee arising out of the mere act of assignment.[97] In spite of the fact that many courts say that there is such an implied agreement, the answer to the first of these inquiries should be no.[98] This would be true if the ordinary rules of construction of contracts are followed for there is nothing in the terms of such a bargain from which, justifiably, an implied

agreement can be discovered.[99] One writer has suggested that the answer "would seem properly to depend on whether, in that jurisdiction, the assignor of a chose in action is ordinarily to be regarded as impliedly warranting the payment of the claim. If he is so to be regarded there is a clear equity in favor of the assignee that the assignor shall not, by asserting a conflicting claim against a fund from which it is payable, interfere with its payment in full, while, on the other hand, if no warranty is to be implied it is somewhat difficult to perceive any ground for raising an equity in favor of the assignee as to the application of the mortgaged security, in the absence of language showing an agreement to give him priority."[1] Under such a test, although there may be some cases to the contrary,[2] under the common law, an assignment of a chose in action does not carry with it a warranty that it would be paid,[3] and the same is true of assignments

---

95. See § 243, supra.

96. § 246, infra.

97. Domeyer v. O'Connell, 1936, 364 Ill. 467, 4 N.E.2d 830, 108 A.L.R. 476. This case contains an elaborate discussion of the entire question together with a good collection of authorities. In large part its reasoning is followed in the text. For comments on it see notes, 1937, 4 U. of Chi.L.Rev. 502; 1937, 2 John Marshall L.Q. 422; 1936, 31 Ill.L.Rev. 111. See 1927, 50 A.L.R. 543; 1937, 108 A.L.R. 485; 1938, 115 A.L.R. 40. Look also at Title Guarantee & Trust Co. v. Mortgage Commission, 1937, 273 N.Y. 415, 7 N.E.2d 841, discussed in notes, 1937, 37 Col. L.Rev. 1010; 1937, 14 N.Y.Univ.L.Q.Rev. 259.

98. If the instrument of transfer in terms refers to the mortgage or the transferor's interest therein as well as to the debt this ordinarily would be sufficient to show an intention that the part of the debt transferred should have priority. Noyes v. White, 1872, 9 Kan. 640; Foley v. Rose, 1878, 123 Mass.

557; Solberg v. Wright, 1885, 33 Minn. 224, 22 N. W. 381; Langdon v. Keith, 1837, 9 Vt. 299; Miller v. Washington Sav. Bank, 1892, 5 Wash. 200, 31 P. 712; see Campbell, Cases on Mortgages, 2d ed., 585 n. 2. But see Henderson v. Herrod, Miss.1846, 10 Smedes & M. 631.

99. "Under no rule of construction can we say that an intention to give priority to assigned notes may be implied in the absence of stipulation or the use of language from which such intention necessarily arises. An implied intention is one necessarily arising from language used or a situation created by such language. If such intention does not necessarily arise, it cannot be implied. On the other hand, absence of a provision from a contract is evidence of an intention to exclude such provision. Certainly, the fact of such absence cannot, of itself, give rise to an implied intention to include it. * * * To hold otherwise would be to make a new contract for the parties." Domeyer v. O'Connell, supra, note 97.

1. Tiffany, Real Property, 3d ed., § 1458, and cited with approval in Domeyer v. O'Connell, supra, note 97.

2. See Tiffany, op.cit. supra; Williston, Contracts, rev. ed., § 445.

3. Domeyer v. O'Connell, supra note 97, "the assignor, at common law, warranted only his title to the chose in action and that it was genuine and not a forgery, otherwise the assignee was left to the ordinary legal remedies for the collection of the debt." See Restatement, Contracts, § 175.

of negotiable instruments by delivery or without recourse.[4] Further, as a matter of ordinary common sense, as a distinguished writer put it, when a mortgagee whose debt is expressed in several notes offers to sell one of them "it is incredible that he means to add, 'your note will be first lien, and my other[s] will now be second.' If ever such a lopsided bargain was ever in the minds of sensible men, then the mortgage debt would always be expressed in a single note or bond, because no mortgagee would dare split the debt for any purpose; nor would participation certificates ever have arisen as a form of investment." [5]

Most of the cases giving the assignee priority do not rely upon the ground of an implied agreement for priority or, what comes to the same thing, not to compete with the assignee for payment out of the mortgaged property. They put it upon the broad ground that, the transferee having paid value, it would be inequitable and contrary to good faith for the assignor to assert any claim which would interfere with payment of the assigned part of the debt to the assignee in priority to his own.[6] There are several explanations advanced as to just why this would be inequitable, no one of which is free from objection.

One suggestion [7] is that it reflects the influence of the early common law rule which gave to the mortgagee the right to immediate possession upon the execution of the mortgage.[8] "If the mortgagee assigned a part of the mortgage, he kept possession but had to account to the assignee for the latter's portion of the rents—thus he was in a position of a trustee for the benefit of the assignee, an equitable relationship. As trustee, it was felt that it was inequitable for him to take rents from the land at the expense of the assignee. It followed that an assignment of a note was held to be an assignment of so much of the mortgage as was necessary to pay off that note." [9] While this historical explanation is plausible, its actual influence seems dubious since the early cases place no reliance upon it.[10] Further, it would be inapplicable in lien jurisdictions, and even in title states a mortgagee today takes possession so infrequently that the rule should have no influence in determining the rights of parties in a problem such as the one under consideration.

Another idea advanced is that the doctrine of an equity arising in a grantee of part of land subject to a mortgage to have the land retained by the grantor sold first, or as it is usually stated, to have the mortgaged property sold in the inverse order of alienation of the parts, applies here.[11] The analogy is superficial and false. That doctrine, which

---

4. N.J.L., § 65.

5. Glenn, Mortgages, § 318.2.

6. The dissenting opinion of Gibson, C. J., in Donley v. Hays, Pa.1828, 10 Sergeant & R., 400, 405 is, apparently, the source of the pro tanto rule, it being relied upon in Cullum v. Erwin, 1842, 4 Ala. 452, 459. Yet Gibson conceded there was no implied contract but argued that there was a "moral obligation, which, although insufficient to raise a promise by implication, is a sufficient foundation for an equity * * *." Pomeroy, Equity Juris., 5th ed., § 1203, gave currency to this idea, citing Cullum v. Erwin, supra, and later cases, which in turn adopted the reasoning in that case. His statement of the reason was that "The mortgagee having transferred his note and received the consideration therefor, it would be inequitable in him to deprive the assignee of any part of its value by insisting upon a priority or even an equality of right in sharing the insufficient proceeds." French commentators recognized the same principle and Louisiana, following them, accepted the pro tanto theory as between the as-

signor and assignees. Salzman v. His Creditors, La.1842, 2 Rob. 241; see 1937, 11 Tulane L.Rev. 656.

7. See Domeyer v. O'Connell, supra note 97; 1937, 31 Ill.L.Rev. 1111, 1112; 1937, 2 J.Marshall L.Rev. 423.

8. See § 125, supra.

9. 1937, 31 Ill.L.Rev. 1111, 1112.

10. See dissent of Gibson, C. J., in Donley v. Hays, Pa.1828, 17 Serg. & R. 400, 406; Cullum v. Erwin, 1842, 4 Ala. 452; McClintic v. Wise's Admrs., Va. 1874, 25 Gratt. 448, 18 Am.Rep. 694; Lawson v. Warren, 1912, 34 Okl. 94, 124 P. 46, 42 L.R.A.,N.S., 183, Ann.Cas.1914C, 139.

11. McClintic v. Wise, Va.1874, 25 Gratt. 448, 456, 18 Am.Rep. 694. See Glenn, Mortgages, 1335.

seldom finds application in actual fact, is based upon payment of the full price for the land without deduction on account of the mortgage debt, "while in these cases the assignee pays only for that part of the debt assigned to him and is entitled to no priority in the absence of contract to that effect."[12]

A still different contention is that to permit the mortgagee to participate on a parity with the assignees would result, in case of insufficient security, in his securing a larger percentage of his claim than the assignees would get of theirs, and that this is not right.[13] As has been pointed out, "the argument seems based on curiously unsound logic. In the absence of guarantee by the mortgagee to the assignee, the latter has simply taken over one-half of the investment and put himself in the same position as to that half as is occupied by the mortgagee as to the other half; the two are in precisely the same situation as they would have been if they had each originally contributed one-half of the loan to the mortgagor and had taken equal shares in the bond and mort-

gage."[14] The fact that the assignee has given value to the assignor is balanced by the fact that the latter has also given value for it in his original loan to the mortgagor.[15] The fact that the assignee's interest may come to him through an intermediate assignment obviously makes no difference in the rights of the parties, granting the absence of a guaranty.[16]

In addition to criticizing the arguments advanced in favor of the pro tanto rule preferring the assignee over the assignor, it has been assailed as illogical. For one thing, it is pointed out that although a few courts hold that as against each other assignees rate priority in the order of their assignments,[17] yet "the great majority of courts, including courts adopting the pro tanto rule as against the mortgagee, hold that the assignees share pro rata as among themselves.[18] Certainly, this generally adopted rule of pro rata sharing among assignees without regard to the date of the assignment is at war with the logic of the so-called pro tanto rule as to the assignment of the mortgage debt. If A, as mortgagee, owns three notes, one of which he

---

12. Walsh & Simpson, Cas. Security Transactions, 431 Note (1).

13. See Lawson v. Warren, 1912, 34 Okl. 94, 100, 124 P. 46, 48, 42 L.R.A.,N.S., 183, Ann.Cas.1914C, 139: "When two notes are assigned to different persons they are both presumed to have paid value, and they must share equally in the proceeds of the mortgaged property in order to preserve the equality which is equity. But to apply the same rule between the mortgagee and a person to whom he had transferred one of the notes would lead to inequality. For illustration, say that the mortgagee holds two notes for $1,000 each. He assigns one of them for value. The property securing their payment only brings $1,000, or enough to pay one note. If the mortgagee shares in the proceeds, he will get out of the debt $1,500, the $1,000 he received for the first note and the $500 he receives from the proceeds of the mortgaged property, while the assignee for half the debt only receives $500. The mortgagee would thus receive more than if he had kept both notes. This is not right. The same illustration applies to the case of a person to whom all of a series of notes have been assigned, and who afterwards assigns one of a series." But if the assignee bought at a discount (say 50%), it would be possible for him under the pro tanto theory to realize $1000 on a $500 investment, leaving the mortgagee only $500 on a $2000 investment. See 1937, 31 Ill.L.Rev. 1111, 1113, n. 12.

14. Kelly v. Middlesex Title Guarantee & Trust Co., 1934, 115 N.J.Eq. 592, 598, 171 A. 823, affirmed, 1934, 116 N.J.Eq. 574, 174 A. 706. To the same effect, see Domeyer v. O'Connell, 1936, 364 Ill. 467, 4 N.E.2d 830, 108 A.L.R. 476.

15. See 1928, 77 U. of Pa.L.Rev. 266; 1937, 14 N.Y. Univ.L.Q.Rev. 259; Domeyer v. O'Connell, supra note 14.

16. Kelly v. Middlesex Title etc. Trust Co., supra note 14.

17. See § 243, supra.

18. Meriwether v. New Orleans Real Estate Board, 1935, 182 La. 649, 162 So. 208, commented on, 1936, 10 Tulane L.Rev. 304; see 1937, 31 Ill.L.Rev. 1111; 1937, 11 Tulane L.Rev. 656; text, infra, and authorities cited. See also, § 243, supra. There is also authority that although the mortgagee is subject to the pro tanto rule his creditors, like subsequent assignees, get the benefit of the pro rata rule. This, too, is illogical because the general rule, of course, is that creditors take subject to outstanding debts with exceptions which have no application here. Kelly v. Middlesex Title Guaranty & Trust Co., 1934, 115 N.J.Eq. 592, 171 A. 823, affirmed, 116 N.J.Eq. 574, 174 A. 706; Reconstruction Finance Co. v. O'Keefe, C.C.A.N.J.1938, 98 F.2d 820, noted, 1938, 25 Va.L.Rev. 375.

assigns to B and later assigns another to C, retaining one, then if the pro tanto rule is applied can be said to be logical, B, who took the first assignment, would, logically, be entitled to be first paid out of the insufficient security, and it would also logically follow that neither A, the mortgagee, nor C, the second assignee, could participate on an equal basis with B, yet most courts hold assignees participate pro rata." [19]

"The so-called pro tanto rule is illogical in another respect. Assuming, in the illustration just given, that the security is sufficient to pay but the note first assigned, then the other two notes are of no value if they remain in A's hands, yet if A assigns a second note it shares pro rata with the one first assigned. Thus A gives to it a value it did not theretofore have. That value is given against the interest of the first assignee, who must now share the security with such second assignee, though in all likelihood the second assignment is made without the knowledge of the first assignee. So, also, if A choose to assign the third note he will thereby give it a value that it does not have in his hands. * * * By what logic may it be said that by the mere transfer of one of these notes, in the example above given, its value may be enhanced to, as may be, absorb all of the security and later decreased to one-half its value by the assignment of a second note, or to one-third by the assignment of all of the notes? Certainly the so-called pro tanto rule, as applied, rests upon peculiarly grotesque logic." [20]

Relying both on the non-existence of any implied in fact contractual basis for the rule and the foregoing attacks upon it, the existence of any moral obligation in favor of the assignee against the assignor has been vigor-

ously denied.[21] And, finally because in operation the rule makes it difficult for an assignee to compute the value of his notes it has been condemned as violative of sound and desirable commercial policy.[22]

In spite of the strictures upon the pro tanto theory as between an assignor and assignee, a considerable body of authority follows it although there is a strong group of cases which adheres to the pro rata doctrine.[23]   Juris-

---

19. Domeyer v. O'Connell, 1936, 364 Ill. 467, 4 N.E.2d 830, 108 A.L.R. 476. The case contains a collection of authorities following the pro rata rule as among assignees.

20. Ibid. See 1937, 11 Tulane L.Rev. 656; 1937, 12 N.D.Law, 336.

21. "Is there, then, a moral obligation on the part of the mortgagee assignor to refrain from participating on a parity with his assignees in the insufficient proceeds of the security? If so, what is it? In the absence of a contract giving priority to the assignee, the latter simply takes over a part of the investment. He knows from the mortgage that he does not have it all. He also knows that other notes in the hands of the mortgagee may be assigned, and that he has no right to complain if they are. If the mortgagee has not done an act he has no right to perform, but in the further assignment of mortgage notes does but that which, as his assignee well knows, he has a right to do, from what does his moral obligation to his assignee arise? The argument leads to this: Though the mortgagee, if he choose, may dispose of all of the balance of the notes without any moral obligation on his part to refrain from so affecting the value of the notes first assigned, yet if, perchance, he retain one of the notes he may not urge its equal participation in the insufficient proceeds of the security because, forsooth, there is a moral obligation resting upon him, and this despite the knowledge by the assignee that he was taking but a part of the debt and that the security was given to secure all the notes. This argument seems curiously wanting in logic." Domeyer v. O'Connell, supra note 19. See 1937, 11 Tulane L.Rev. 656, 658.

22. "Mortgage notes have to-day become generally used as commercial paper. While it may be said to be prudent that the contract of the parties definitely provide for equality in participation or priority, as the parties choose, yet the requirements of present-day commercial business are such as to render it strongly advisable that a rule affecting the value of assigned mortgage notes, which will render as nearly certain as possible the means of determining that value, be announced. An illogical rule which leaves the investor uncertain as to his rights but causes them to depend upon whether he is the only assignee, or whether the mortgagee has assigned other or all of the mortgage notes, ought not be adopted." Ibid., n. 21. See 1937, 11 Tulane L. Rev. 656, 657; 1937, 31 Ill.L.Rev. 1111; 1937, 12 N. Dame Law. 336.

23. "Omitting those cases where the question was not directly passed upon or the statements in opinions touching the question were obiter dicta, the courts adopting the pro tanto rule, where the matter was directly involved, are, so far as our investi-

dictions which have adopted the order of maturity rule generally give priority to the assignee regardless of the dates of maturity.[24] Since the basis of the holding is that the assignment of the note carries the security pro tanto and not pro rata, this is true regardless of whether the transfer is by unqualified indorsement or without recourse.[25] There is, however, some authority that an earlier maturity note kept by the assignor will prevail over a later maturity one in the hands of an assignee in the absence of agreement or paramount equity and the mere transfer for value creates no such paramount equity.[26] And the same is true where the maturity dates are the same.[27]

PARTIAL ASSIGNMENTS—EFFECT OF GUARANTEE OR INDORSEMENT WITHOUT QUALIFICATION

246. Where some of the notes, bonds or participation certificates secured by a single mortgage are transferred by unqualified indorsement or with a guaranty of payment by the transferor, most cases hold that, as between transferor and transferee, the latter is entitled to priority of payment.

Where some of the notes, bonds, or participation certificates secured by a single mortgage are transferred by unqualified indorsement,[28] or with an accompanying guaranty of payment by the transferor,[29] most of the cases hold that the transferee is entitled to payment out of the security in preference to the transferor in case of insufficient assets to pay all. The result has sometimes been put upon the ground that a guaranty of payment to the transferee is tantamount to an agree-

---

gation has disclosed: Alabama (Cullum v. Erwin, supra); Georgia (statute); Indiana (Parkhurst v. Watertown Steam-Engine Co., 107 Ind. 594, 8 N.E. 635); Oklahoma (Lawson v. Warren, 34 Okl. 94, 124 P. 46, 48, 42 L.R.A.,N.S., 183, Ann.Cas.1914C, 139); Louisiana (Salzman v. His Creditors, 2 Rob. 241); and Ohio (Anderson v. Sharp, 44 Ohio St. 260, 6 N.E. 900). Those states adopting the pro rata rule when the question was definitely before the court are as follows: Pennsylvania (Donley v. Hays, 17 Serg. & R. 400, 403); Maryland (Dixon v. Clayville, 44 Md. 573); Mississippi (Pugh v. Holt, 27 Miss. 461); Tennessee (Andrews v. Hobgood, 69 Tenn. 693, 1 Lea. 693); New Jersey (Kelly v. Middlesex Title Guarantee & Trust Co., 115 N.J.Eq. 592, 171 A. 823, 826); Michigan (Jennings v. Moore, 83 Mich. 231, 47 N.W. 127, 21 Am.St.Rep. 601); and Texas (Salmon v. Downs, 55 Tex. 243). Many other opinions appear in the books in which the view of the court on this question is hinted at, but where it was not directly before the court." Domeyer v. O'Connell, supra note 19. To these should be added the Domeyer case itself. See, stating the pro tanto rule to be the majority and the pro rata the minority view, 1927, 50 A.L.R. 543, 564, 566; 1937, 108 A.L.R. 485, 492, 493.

24. Parkhurst v. Watertown Steam Eng. Co., 1886, 107 Ind. 594, 8 N.E. 635; Roberts v. Mansfield, 1861, 32 Ga. 228; Lawson v. Warren, 1912, 34 Okl. 94, 124 P. 46, 42 L.R.A.,N.S., 183, Ann.Cas.1914C, 139. See 1937, 4 U.Chi.L.Rev. 502; 1937, 12 N. Dame Law. 336; 1936, 22 Va.L.Rev. 592; 1927, 50 A.L.R. 543, 560. But see, 1937, 14 N.Y.Univ.L.Q. Rev. 259.

25. See 1937, 4 U.Chi.L.Rev. 502, 503.

26. Aultman-Taylor Co. v. McGeorge, 1884, 31 Kan. 329, 2 P. 778; Massie v. Sharpe, 1862, 13 Iowa 542; Hinds v. Mooers, 1860, 11 Iowa 211.

27. Domeyer v. O'Connell, 1936, 364 Ill. 467, 4 N.E.2d 830.

28. Anderson v. Sharp, 1886, 44 Ohio St. 260, 6 N.E. 900; Dixon v. Clayville, 1876, 44 Md. 573; Fourth Nat. Bank's Appeal, 1889, 123 Pa. 473, 16 A. 779, 10 Am.St.Rep. 538; Louisville Title Co.'s Receiver v. Crab Orchard Banking Co., 1933, 249 Ky. 736, 61 S. W.2d 615; Fidelity Trust Co. v. Orr, 1926, 154 Tenn. 538, 289 S.W. 500; Reconstruction Finance Corp. v. Smith, Tex.Civ.App.1936, 96 S.W.2d 824, noted, 1937, 15 Tex.L.Rev. 271; see 1937, 37 Col.L. Rev. 1010; 1937, 31 Ill.L.Rev. 1111, 1114; 1928, 77 U. of Pa.L.Rev. 266, 269.

29. Matter of Lawyers Mort. Co., 1934, 151 Misc. 744, 272 N.Y.S. 390; Matter of Lawyers Mort. Co., 1936, 157 Misc. 813, 284 N.Y.S. 740; In re Title and Mortgage Co., 1937, 275 N.Y. 347, 9 N.E.2d 957, 115 A.L.R. 35; Pink v. Thomas, 1939, 282 N.Y. 10, 24 N.E.2d 724, commented on, 1940, 26 Va.L.Rev. 825; Lawyers Title and Guar. Co., In re, 1942, 287 N.Y. 264, 39 N.E. 233, commented on 1942, 55 Harv.L. Rev. 882; Ferris v. Prudence Realization Corp., 1944, 292 N.Y. 210, 54 N.E.2d 367, affirmed on certiorari, Prudence Realization Co. v. Ferris, 1945, 323 U.S. 650, 65 S.Ct. 539, 89 L.Ed. 528; commented on, 1945, 32 Va.L.Rev. 176; In re 1934 Realty Corp., C. C.A.N.Y.1945, 150 F.2d 477, commented on, 1945, 32 Va.L.Rev. 176; In re Phillippi, 1938, 329 Pa. 581, 198 A. 16; Cannon v. McDaniel & Jackson, 1876, 46 Tex. 303. For a discussion of problems arising in connection with guaranteed mortgages, see 1934, 34 Col.L.Rev. 663. "The guarantor of a mortgage, who is also a part owner of it, is free to stipulate that he may share in a liquidation on an equal footing with other owners of the mortgage despite his default on his guaranty, and that effect will be given to such a stipulation." Prudence Realization Corp. v. Geist, 1942, 316 U.S. 89, 94, 62 S.Ct. 978, 86 L.Ed. 1293.

ment for priority.[30] More generally it is placed upon the equitable principle of non-competition, i. e., that it is not fair for a mortgagee who has bound himself to an assignee to see that the assigned debt is paid, and who is now insolvent, to compete with the latter in the distribution of the proceeds of foreclosure until that debt is paid.[31] The principle operates to give the assignee priority not only against the guarantor, but upon his insolvency, his unsecured creditors.[32] It has even been extended to subordinate a later pledgee of the guarantor, thus depriving him, except to the extent he ranks ahead of general creditors, of his collateral.[33] The cases so holding have been criticized[34] and there are authorities the other way.[35]

Contrary to the holding in most cases, there is some authority that a guaranty of payment by the transferor does not give priority to the transferee.[36] In support of this minority view it has been reasoned that, in jurisdictions where without a guaranty the assignor and assignees share pro rata, the addition of a guaranty alters the situation only to the extent that it gives the assignees an in personam, unsecured claim against the assignor which puts them, as to it, on a par with other unsecured creditors and carries with it no substantive equitable right of priority in the mortgaged property.[37] This being so, the sole logical basis for preventing the assignor from sharing in the proceeds of the security with the assignee is found in the theory of avoidance of circuity of action.[38] Priority of distribution to the assignee, in other words, is merely a procedural device for enforcing the obligation of the guarantor to make up to the assignee any deficiency to the assignee where his pro rata share of the mortgage is insufficient to pay him in full, and it applies where the assignor is able to perform his promise, i. e., where he is solvent.[39] If the transferor is in liquidation and the contest is between assignees and creditors of the assignor, the question ceases to be purely procedural and becomes

30. E. g., Reconstruction Fin. Corp. v. Smith, Tex. Civ.App.1936, 96 S.W.2d 824, noted, 1937, 15 Tex.L. Rev. 271; Pustejovsky v. K. J. Z. T. Lodge, 124 Tex. 504, 79 S.W.2d 1084; In re Title and Mortgage Guaranty Co. of Sullivan County, 1937, 275 N.Y. 347, 9 N.E.2d 957, 115 A.L.R. 35, affirming, s. c., 1937, 249 App.Div. 484, 293 N.Y.S. 4, commented on 1938, 47 Yale L. Jour. 480.

31. Campbell, Cases on Mortgages, 2d ed., 594 n. 1, where, in addition to citation of mortgage assignment cases it is pointed out that the principle of noncompetition extends beyond mortgage law.

32. See In re Title & Mortgage Guaranty Co. of Sullivan County, 1937, 275 N.Y. 347, 355, 9 N.E.2d 957, 960, 115 A.L.R. 35. But cf. the minority view, text and footnotes, infra, this section.

33. In re Lawyers Title etc. Co., 1942, 287 N.Y. 264, 39 N.E. 233, (5–2 decision), criticized, 1942, 55 Harv.L.Rev. 882; Kissimmee Everglades Land Co. v. Carr, 1924, 88 Fla. 387, 102 So. 335.

34. 1942, 55 Harv.L.Rev. 882.

35. Land Title Bank & Trust Co. v. Schenck, 1939, 335 Pa. 419, 6 A.2d 878; Waynesboro Nat. Bank v. Smith, 1928, 151 Va. 481, 145 S.E. 302.

36. Kelly v. Middlesex Title Guaranty & Trust Co., 1934, 115 N.J.Eq. 592, 171 A. 823, affirmed 116 N.J. Eq. 574, 174 A. 706; Prudence Realization Corp. v. Geist, 1942, 316 U.S. 89, 62 S.Ct. 978, 86 L.Ed. 1293. Look also at Hinds v. Mooers, 1860, 11 Iowa 211, rule of priority of maturity applied; Wilcox v. Allen, 1877, 36 Mich. 160, 172, pro rata rule applied.

37. "By that contract [of guaranty] the guarantor pledged only its personal obligation for the payment of the certificates. It gave to the certificate holders no lien upon, or other priority right in, its interest in the mortgage more than to its other assets." Prudence Realization Corp. v. Geist, 1942, 316 U.S. 89, 97, 62 S.Ct. 978, 86 L.Ed. 1293. See Kelly v. Middlesex Title etc. Co., supra note 36; 1940, 26 Va.L.Rev. 825, 826.

38. Kelly v. Middlesex Title etc. Co., supra note 36. Other cases relying upon circuity are Prudence Realization Corp. v. Geist, 1942, 316 U.S. 89, 62 S.Ct. 978, 86 L.Ed. 1293; Preston v. Morsman, 1905, 75 Neb. 358, 372, 106 N.W. 320. See 1940, 26 Va.L.Rev. 825; 1938, 47 Yale L.Jour. 480, 482; 1937, 37 Col. L.Rev. 1010, 1011; 1937, 31 Ill.L.Rev. 1111, 1113; 1928, 77 U.Pa.L.Rev. 266, 269.

39. "If the assignee's share is not sufficient to pay him in full, the assignor is bound by his guaranty to pay him the deficiency. Giving the assignee a preferred interest in the proceeds in such a case enforces the performance of the guaranty; it saves the assignee the delay, trouble and cost of a separate suit to enforce the guaranty and works no inequity to the guarantor or anyone else—if there is no other person having an interest in the security [i. e., if the assignor is solvent]." Kelly v. Middlesex Title Guaranty & Trust Co., 1934, 115 N.J.Eq. 592, 599, 171 A. 823, affirmed 116 N.J.Eq. 574, 174 A. 706. See 1938, 47 Yale L.Jour. 480, 482.

one of substantive rights. Under such circumstances, to grant to an assignee priority for which he has not contracted has the undesirable effect of giving the assignee a preference at the expense of the unsecured creditors.[40] Further, and more important in cases where the transferor is a company doing an extensive business in selling and guaranteeing participation certificates or notes or bonds secured by single mortgages, "since the amount of unsecured creditors' claims is usually comparatively small, the ruling has the effect of preferring the holders of certificates in a single bond and mortgage in which the company happened to hold a large share at the time of liquidation over holders of certificates in other bonds and mortgages in which the company had a smaller share." [41] The United States Supreme Court, although it recognizes the general rule of non-competition, says that it applies only to cases where the guarantor or surety attempts to compete with the guaranteed creditors by taking indemnity from his principal or by virtue of his right of subrogation.[42] Apart from this it seems to approve the reasoning of the minority view. Thus, if the transferor acquires "its interest in the mortgage as an original investment before it sold and guaranteed shares in the mortgage, [or acquires] * * * its own certificates independently of its obligation as a guarantor of the certificates" [43] it will not be barred from competing on an equality with the assignees. On the other hand, if it is in the position of a "subrogee," i. e., if "it acquired its claim to participate in the mortgage through performance of its guaranty," which may be done "by purchase, after default, of the certificates of participation which it had guaranteed", then the rule of non-competition applies.[44] Although the federal court in a bankruptcy proceeding may permit the question to be determined by "a court of competent jurisdiction," [45] there is some doubt as to whether the Supreme Court would hold that its previously expressed views on the matter might still be followed if the federal court itself decides the question.[46] Where the guaranty is by a third person there is no foundation for implying a contract for priority, for invoking the principle of non-competition, or the doctrine of avoidance of circuity of action against the assignor and, consequently, its presence will not affect the ordinary order of distribution rule in even New York, the leading jurisdiction for the majority view.[47]

---

40. "The claim of the assignees on the guaranty is a general, unsecured claim. To grant to them any greater right or interest in the bond and mortgage than that which was specifically assigned to them as security would be giving them, as such unsecured creditors, an unlawful and inequitable preference over the other unsecured creditors." Kelly v. Middlesex Title etc. Co., supra note 39; Prudence Realization Co. v. Geist, 1941, 316 U.S. 89, 97, 62 S. Ct. 978, 86 L.Ed. 1293.

41. 1938, 47 Yale L.Jour. 480, 482.

42. Under such circumstances "if the surety were allowed to prove his own claim before the creditor is paid, he would to that extent diminish the creditor's dividends upon his claim, and thus defeat the purpose for which he had given the indemnity." Prudence Realization Corp. v. Geist, 1942, 316 U.S. 89, 96, 62 S.Ct. 978, 86 L.Ed. 1293. "For like reasons equity requires the surety who holds security of the insolvent principal to give the benefit of it to the creditor for whom he is surety until the debt is paid." Idem

43. Prudence Realization Corp. v. Ferris, 1944, 323 U.S. 650, 657, 65 S.Ct. 539, 89 L.Ed. 528, concurring opinion of Stone, C. J.

44. Ibid.

45. Ferris v. Prudence Realization Corp., 1944, 292 N.Y. 210, 54 N.E.2d 367, affirmed on certiorari, Prudence Realization Corp. v. Ferris, 1945, 323 U.S. 650, 65 S.Ct. 539, 89 L.Ed. 528.

46. Prudence Realization Corp. v. Ferris, supra note 43; In re 1934 Realty Corp., C.C.A.N.Y.1945, 150 F. 2d 477. See 1945, 32 Va.L.Rev. 176.

47. Title Guarantee & Trust Co. v. Mortgage Commission, 1937, 273 N.Y. 415, 7 N.E.2d 841.

CHAPTER 9

TRANSFER BY THE MORTGAGOR

TRANSFERABILITY OF MORT-GAGOR'S INTEREST

247. The mortgagor has an interest in the mortgaged property that is alienable. He cannot transfer to another his duty to perform the obligation the property secures.

The mortgagor's position is the obverse of the mortgagee's and, like it, has two aspects. Just as the mortgagee has, normally, a personal right against the mortgagor to have performance of the secured obligation,[1] so,

necessarily, the mortgagor has the duty of performing that obligation. The mortgagee has an interest in the property as security; the mortgagor has the redemption interest, i. e., he is owner of the property subject to the security interest of the mortgagee.[2]

However, when it comes to transfer the problems of the mortgagor are radically different from those of the mortgagee. The

---

1. See §§ 102, 103, supra.

2. This statement disregards differences in the technical content of the two interests in the property due to varying theories of the nature of a mortgage. See, e. g., §§ 13–15, supra.

mortgagee can alienate his personam rights without limitations other than those inherent in its nature as a chose in action. He also can transfer his security interest in the property but the ability is restricted. This is because its character as security ties it to the debt as an incident of it.[3] The mortgagor, on the other hand, cannot ever transfer to another his duty of performance. He always remains subject to it unless it is discharged [4] according to the rules of contract governing the particular obligation by which he is bound. The rights of the mortgagee cannot be affected without his consent by any arrangement between the mortgagor and his assuming grantee.[5] As to his redemption interest in the land,[6] however, he is an owner of property and as such can transfer it freely by sale, mortgage, or otherwise.[7] In lien states he is the legal owner subject only to the legal lien of the mortgagee.[8] In title states, regardless of technical legal title being in the mortgagee, the mortgagor is recognized as the owner in substance.[9] And if the mortgage is equitable only, *a fortiori* the mortgagor is owner with full powers of trans-

fer. The transfer in all cases is made by a deed purporting to convey the property.

A transfer by the mortgagor will not, it is true, shake off the mortgage.[10] The mortgage, subject to two chief exceptions, will continue and attach to the property in the hands of whomsoever it comes. In this sense every transfer is made subject to the mortgage. The two exceptions are: (1) the mortgage is an equitable one and the property is acquired by a *bona fide* purchaser for value and without notice;[11] (2) the mortgage is cut off under an applicable recording statute because it is unrecorded.[12] But this does not any more affect the general proposition that the mortgagor's interest in the land is an alienable one of an owner of property than does the similar case of an easement following the land into the hands of a grantee.

SALES

248. The mortgagor may sell the mortgaged property. Terms on which the purchaser may buy are three: (1) he may take subject to the mortgage debt but assume no personal obligation to pay it; (2) he may assume the payment of it; or (3) he may pay the full value of the property to the mortgagor who agrees to pay off the mortgage.

Terms upon which a mortgagor may sell his interest in mortgaged property are three.

1. The purchaser may pay to the mortgagor only the agreed upon value of the redemption interest, i. e., the difference between the amount of the mortgage debt and the amount set by the parties in their sale agreement as the total value of the land.[12a] He may not, however, assume any personal liability for the payment of the mortgage

---

3. See Chapter 8, supra, especially §§ 223–226.

4. See Adair v. Carden, 1892, 29 L.R.Ir. 464, 481, the mortgagor "cannot get rid of his personal liability as between him and the mortgagee, where such liability exists, in the absence of anything amounting to a complete novation of the contract."

5. Hakes v. Frank, 1930, 210 Iowa 1169, 231 N.W. 1; Chatterly v. Safe Deposit & Trust Co., 1935, 168 Md. 656, 178 A. 854; Mellen, Administratrix v. Whipple, 1854, 67 Mass. 317; Lowry v. Hensal's Heirs, 1924, 281 Pa. 572, 127 A. 219. See Warm, Rights and Liabilities of Mortgagee, Mortgagor and Grantee, 1935, 10 Temple L.Q. 116, 124. An assuming grantee cannot relieve himself of personal liability for the indebtedness by transferring the property to another who assumes and agrees to pay the mortgage. McLeod v. Building & Loan Ass'n of Jackson, 1933, 168 Miss. 457, 151 So. 151; Corning v. Burton, 1894, 102 Mich. 86, 62 N.W. 1040.

6. That the Statute of Frauds applies to transfers of the mortgagor's interest, see § 67 supra.

7. E. g., by gift conveyance inter vivos or by will, should the mortgagor die intestate it will descend to his heir. See §§ 250, 251, infra.

8. See §§ 15, 127, supra.

9. See §§ 6, 14, 125, 126, supra.

10. See Adair v. Carden, 1892, 29 L.R.Ir. 469, 481; Glenn, Purchasing Subject to the Mortgage, 1941, 27 Va.L.Rev. 853, 854.

11. See § 188, supra.

12. See §§ 193–196, supra.

12a. This amount has been aptly termed the "basic bargain price." See Storke and Sears, Transfer of Mortgaged Property, 1953, 38 Corn.L.Q. 185, 187. The article contains an excellent critical survey of

debt.[13] He takes, as it is said, "subject" to the mortgage. The effect of such a transaction is considered later.[14]

2. The purchaser may pay to the mortgagor, as in the first transaction, only the value of the redemption interest. In addition the purchaser may promise the mortgagor to pay off the mortgage debt. Such promises are referred to as assumptions of the mortgage and ordinarily the language used says that the transferee "assumes" it.[15] The promises do not relieve the mortgagor of his duty of payment to the mortgagee.[16] In addition to giving the mortgagor a personal right against the transferee to have him instead of the mortgagor pay the mortgage debt, it also operates to make the land in the hands of the transferee "subject" to the mortgage debt as in the first case.[17] The promise of the transferee to pay necessarily eliminates any claim between the parties that the transferor should pay instead of having the debt satisfied out of the land. The rights such an assumption gives to the mortgagee

are considered in later sections.[18] So, too, in more detail, are the rights of the transferor against an assuming grantee.[19]

3. The purchaser may pay the full value of the land, as agreed upon, free from the incumbrance. The mortgagor in return agrees to pay off the mortgage debt when it comes due.[20] This transaction reverses the situation as it exists in the second situation. The land in the hands of the transferee is likened to a real surety with the mortgagor having the primary duty, as principal, to discharge the debt. If the mortgagor breaks his contract by failing to pay, the transferee has rights against him which will be looked at again.[21] The relationship between the mortgagor and the land in the hands of such a transferee will also affect possible subsequent action by the mortgagee, another matter for subsequent elaboration.[22]

Which one of these three transactions was the one actually entered into presents questions which are considered in the following sections.[23]

---

the modes and consequences of transfers of mortgaged property by the mortgagor.

13. A grantee of mortgaged property does not become personally obligated to pay the mortgage debt unless he expressly or impliedly agrees to pay it. Interstate Land & Investment Co. v. Logan, 1916, 196 Ala. 196, 72 So. 36; Rosenthal v. Heft, 1928, 155 Md. 410, 142 A. 598; Stebbins v. Hall, N.Y. 1859, 29 Barb. 524; Hulin v. Veatch, 1934, 148 Or. 119, 35 P.2d 253, 94 A.L.R. 1319. But cf., Glenn, Purchasing Subject to the Mortgage, 1941, 27 Va.L. Rev. 853, 865.

14. § 252, et seq.

15. The word "assumes" in a deed is usually held to be equivalent to "assumes and agrees to pay." Thomas v. Home Mut. Bldg. & Loan Ass'n, 1910, 243 Ill. 550, 90 N.E. 1081; Curry v. La Fon, 1908, 133 Mo.App. 163, 113 S.W. 246; cf. Adcock v. Home Mutual Building & Loan Ass'n, 1909, 148 Ill.App. 514; Greer v. Orchard, 1913, 175 Mo.App. 494, 161 S.W. 875.

16. See § 247, supra.

17. Johnson v. Zink, 1873, 51 N.Y. 333; Howard v. Robbins, 1902, 170 N.Y. 498, 63 N.E. 530.

18. §§ 260–265, infra.

19. See §§ 253, 258.

20. "Ordinarily, where the owner of lands subject to a mortgage to secure his debts conveys the mortgaged premises, or any part of the same, to a purchaser, without any express provision with reference to the mortgage debt, such purchaser takes the same subject, of course, to the mortgage, but so far as the rights of the mortgagor and his grantee are concerned with reference to such mortgage debt the mortgagor will be regarded as the principal in such debts, and the land conveyed standing as his surety therefor * * *." Kinney v. Heuring, 1909, 44 Ind.App. 590, 596, 87 N.E. 1053, 1055.

See also Van Valkenburg v. Jantz, 1915, 161 Wis. 336, 154 N.W. 373; Wadsworth v. Lyon, 1883, 93 N.Y. 201, 45 Am.Rep. 190; 3 Tiffany, Real Prop., 2d Ed., §§ 622, 624; 3 Pomeroy, Eq.Jur., 4th Ed., § 1205, note 6.

21. See Chapter 10, infra. They are substantially the same as those a mortgagor has against an assuming grantee.

22. See §§ 269–270, infra.

23. §§ 252–258, infra.

MORTGAGES OF THE MORT-GAGOR'S INTEREST

249. The mortgagor may mortgage his interest in the property.

The transfer by the mortgagor may be by way of security instead of outright sale. In such a case the lender ordinarily will expect that the mortgagor will protect him against the prior encumbrance.[24] His expectation is similar to that of the buyer who pays over the full amount of the purchase price to the mortgagor as in the third case above.

This normal situation may be varied by agreement.[25] Thus it could be agreed that, although the junior mortgagee does not bind himself to pay off the prior mortgagee, the mortgagor has no duty to do so for his benefit. Such an agreement would be analogous to a purchaser buying subject to the mortgage. Or the junior mortgagee might promise that he would pay off the earlier mortgage. This would be the analogue of an assumption of the mortgage debt by a purchaser. In effect, though, such a promise would be to make a loan in the future.[26]

INTER VIVOS GIFTS

250. A mortgagor may make a gift conveyance of his interest in the property.

The mortgagor may desire to make a gift of the mortgaged property and, of course, he may do so. An immediate question arises: did he intend to give merely the redemption interest subject to the mortgage? Or did he intend to make a present of the entire property free of the debt? The latter would involve not merely transferring presently the redemption interest in the property but binding himself to the donee to pay off the debt in the future when it comes due. Any promise to do this, made as part of the gift transaction, would lack consideration.[27] The result is that the donee has no right to demand that the mortgagor pay and, if the donee himself pays, he has no right to reimbursement against his donor.[28] And, of course, the attempt to create a right in the donee would negative any right in the would-be donor to have the donee pay.

If the mortgagor intends to give away only the redemption interest subject to the mortgage it is even clearer that the donee will have no right to compel payment of the debt by his donor by way of exoneration or reimbursement. If such a right does not arise when the donor intends it to be a part of his gift, it will not when his intent is to give only the land as it stands saddled with the payment of the debt. On the other hand the donor in such a case acquires no personal right against the donee that he shall pay. Such a right can be created only by contract and the notion of gift excludes the idea of a binding contract upon the transferee to pay.[29]

One question remains. Is the relationship between the donor-mortgagor and the land in the hands of the donee the same as where there is a sale subject to the mortgage? That is, if the mortgagor has to pay off the debt will he be entitled to reimbursement out of the land? Or to use the common terminology, is the mortgagor a surety only with the land the principal? The correct answer, it is believed, is that the mortgagor should be entitled to reimbursement if his gift was only of the redemption interest.[30] To hold other-

---

24. See Glenn, Purchasing Subject to Mortgage, 1941, 27 Va.L.Rev. 853, 855.

25. See Ross, Covenants of Title in Junior Mortgages, 1928, 12 Minn.L.Rev. 34, 39, for a situation in which a junior mortgage is made "subject to" a senior encumbrance.

26. See § 266, infra, for the effect of such an assumption.

27. There exists, of course, the possibility of binding himself by a promise under seal.

28. Fischer v. Union Trust Co., 1904, 138 Mich. 612, 101 N.W. 852, 68 L.R.A. 987, 110 Am.St.Rep. 329; Adee v. Hallett, 1896, 38 N.Y.S. 273, 3 App.Div. 308, 73 St.R. 754.

29. See Latimer v. Latimer, 1892, 38 S.C. 379, 385, 16 S.E. 995.

30. See Adair v. Carden, 1892, 29 L.R.Ir. 469, 482. The case on its merits seems analogous to that of a devise by a mortgagor. See § 251, post.

wise would enable the transferee to get the benefit of a forced donation never contemplated.[31] The opposite result might well be reached where the intent of the donor was that the grantee should have the entire property. The fact that no contract right arose to force the mortgagor to go ahead and finish his full intention should not prevent this result. His original donative intent should be given effect to the extent of treating the payment exacted by the mortgagee, or voluntarily paid, as the fulfillment of a promised gift which it is not unfair for the recipient to keep.

TRANSFERS AT DEATH

251. The heir or devisee of a mortgagor takes the mortgaged property with a right to compel payment out of the personal estate. The rule is undesirable and has been altered to some extent by statute and may be changed by expression of intention in the will. The rule does not apply to decedent non-assuming transferees, nor in England and some American states to decedent assuming transferees.

When a mortgagor died intestate the mortgaged property in England went to his heir. However it was the duty of his personal representative to pay off the debt and the heir could compel him to do so.[32] The reason for such a rule was that the personal estate had benefited from the loan and therefore should discharge it.[33] Another possible explanation for it may be found in the policy of protecting landed estates.[34] This same rule was extended to devisees.[35] The result in such cases

has been placed upon the presumed intention of the testator.[36]

Where the decedent was under no obligation to pay the mortgage debt it follows that there is no debt for his personal representative to pay. Consequently in such cases the heir has no right to call upon him to discharge the mortgage.[37] Similarly if the decedent was a transferee who had not assumed the payment of the mortgage debt.[38] If the decedent was a transferee who had assumed the mortgage debt the English cases reached the same result.[39] This was because of the English rule that the mortgagee cannot directly hold an assuming grantee for the payment of the debt. Some American cases follow the same reasoning and arrive at the same result.[40] Others, on the ground that the assumption makes the mortgage debt that of the assumer, have held that the heir or devisee may have exoneration.[41]

The rule enabling the heir to compel payment of the debt out of the personal estate is an unfair one.[42] There is no reason why he should get more than the value of the redemption interest that came to him by descent. The rule should be abolished and

---

31. But see Re Darby, [1907] 2 Ch. 465. Cf. 5 Tiffany, Real Prop., 3d ed., § 1446, notes 97, 99.

32. See Kent, J., in Cumberland v. Codrington, 1818, 3 Johns.Ch. 229, for a review of the English cases.

33. See Hoff's Appeal, 1855, 24 Pa. 200.

34. See Simpson, Equitable Conversion, 1935, 44 Yale L.J. 559, 565; Lumsden v. Fraser, 1841, 12 Sim. 263.

35. Hewes v. Dehon, Mass.1855, 3 Gray 205; Turner v. Laird, 1896, 68 Conn. 198, 35 A. 1124.

36. Id.

37. Evelyn v. Evelyn, 1732, 2 P.Wms. 659; Scott v. Beecher, 1820, 5 Madd. 96; Steiglitz v. Migatz, 1914, 182 Ind. 549, 105 N.E. 465.

38. But see the criticism of a holding that a devisee of a testator, not liable for the mortgage debt, impliedly assumed the payment of the mortgage when he accepted a devise with a clause in it to that effect. 1942, 90 U.Pa.L.Rev. 862, discussing Ryan v. Monast, 1942, 67 R.I. 377, 24 A. 615, 139 A.L.R. 703.

39. Tweddell v. Tweddell, 1786, 2 Bro.C.C. 101; Evelyn v. Evelyn, 1732, 2 P.Wms. 659.

40. Creesy v. Willis, 1893, 159 Mass. 249, 34 N.E. 265; Mount v. Van Ness, 1880, 33 N.J.Eq. 262; In re Hunt, 1895, 19 R.I. 139, 32 A. 204, 61 Am.St.Rep. 743.

41. Barlow v. Cain, 1920, 146 Ark. 160, 225 S.W. 228; Smith v. Kibbe, 1919, 104 Kan. 159, 178 P. 427, 5 A.L.R. 483; Hoff's Appeal, 1855, 24 Pa. 200; O'Connor v. O'Connor, 1889, 88 Tenn. 76, 12 S.W. 447, 7 L.R.A. 33.

42. See Glenn, Mortgages, § 303.

there is legislation in that direction.[43] In addition, since testamentary directions as to what property shall be used to pay the mortgage debt are binding and will be enforced in equity, the intention of the testator as found in the will can effectually alter the rule. If no intention can be found in the will, the rules of disposition outlined above will control.[44]

TRANSFER "SUBJECT" TO THE MORTGAGE

252. A transfer "subject" to the mortgage constitutes an agreement that, as between the transferee and the transferor, the debt is to be satisfied out of the land. The resulting relationship is commonly characterized as one of suretyship, the land being principal and the transferor surety.

As noted earlier,[45] the mortgagor may transfer his interest in the property "subject" to the mortgage. This language goes beyond its apparent meaning that the land in the hands of the transferee can be reached by the mortgagee on default in priority to any right of the former in it. This is always true regardless of any agreement by the parties.[46]   What it means in this connection is that the transferee agrees, as between him and his transferor, that the debt is to be satisfied out of the land.[47] Or, as it is frequently put, the land is the principal and the transferor is only in the position of a surety or one secondarily liable.[48] However, the grantee does not become personally liable, without more, to either the mortgagor or to the mortgagee.[49] Nor does it affect the

---

43. See 1927, 40 Harv.L.Rev. 630.

44. Fulenwider v. Birmingham Trust Co., 1930, 222 Ala. 95, 130 So. 801, 72 A.L.R. 702. In this respect the gift by will is unlike the gift of the property by conveyance *inter vivos*. In the latter case an expressed intent in the conveyance or otherwise that the donor bound himself to pay the debt would give no right in the donee to compel him to do so. See § 250, supra.

For a general discussion of the problem of liability on transfers by death and an analysis of the California law, see Note, 1952, 40 Cal.L.Rev. 457. See also In re Estate of Nawrocki, 1954, 200 Or. 660, 268 P.2d 363, considered in 1955, 34 Or.L.Rev. 211, where a specific devisee (the widow) of mortgaged property was held entitled to exoneration against the residuary legatee where the debt was the testator's own, there was sufficient residue, and a contrary intent did not appear.

45. See § 247, supra.

46. That the mortgagor cannot free the land from the lien of the mortgage by conveying it away, see § 247, supra.

47. Although such language may be construed as a condition subsequent to the estate permitting the grantor to recover it if the grantee does not pay, such operative effect is collateral only and not the main purpose of the clause. See Pike v. Brown, 1851, 61 Mass. 133, 135.

48. "When the grantee merely takes subject to the mortgage, while it is true that the grantee assumes no personal liability whatever, nevertheless the security in his hands is liable for the payment of the mortgage debt, which liability as between the grantee and the mortgagor is primary. Therefore, to the extent of the value of such security properly applicable to the mortgage debt, the original mortgagor and the grantee subject to the mortgage stand in a relation one to another, which, while not a true suretyship, is nevertheless equitably analogous thereto and subject to the operation of the same principles." Zastrow v. Knight, 1930, 56 S.D. 554, 229 N.W. 925, 72 A.L.R. 379. Accord: North End Sav. Bank v. Snow, 1908, 197 Mass. 339, 83 N. E. 1099, 125 Am.St.Rep. 368; Johnson v. Zink, 1873, 51 N.Y. 333; Howard v. Robbins, 1902, 170 N.Y. 498, 63 N.E. 530, Campbell, Cases on Mortgages, 2d ed., 407; King v. Whitely, 1843, 10 Paige 465; see Campbell, op. cit. supra, 417 n. 3, 4; Wright v. Anderson, 1934, 62 S.Dak. 444, 451, 253 N.W. 484, 487, 95 A.L.R. 81, L.R.A.1917C, 592, 593. If the land is sold "on execution against the mortgagor or under a second mortgage the purchaser acquires only the equity of redemption and the land becomes the primary source from which the mortgage must be satisfied, not the personal responsibility of the mortgagor." Howard v. Robbins, 1902, 170 N.Y. 498, 502, 63 N.E. 530, 531. The concept of a suretyship relation as between the mortgagor on the one side and the land and the transferee on the other is frequently invoked. Both the validity of the concept and its consequences will be considered in later sections, especially in those dealing with the effect of extensions of time and other actions by the mortgagee. See §§ 269–271, infra. It also is important on the question of subrogation and other rights. See Chapter 10, infra.

49. Wolfert v. Guadagno, 1933, 130 Cal.App. 661, 20 P.2d 360; Andrews v. Robertson, 1918, 177 Cal. 434, 170 P. 1129; First Trust Joint Stock Land Bank of Chicago v. Cuthbert, 1933, 215 Iowa 718, 246 N.W. 810; Chilton v. Brooks, 1890, 72 Md. 554, 20 A. 125; Flynn v. Kendrick, 1934, 285 Mass. 446, 189 N.E. 207; Winans v. Wilkie, 1879, 41 Mich. 264, 1 N.W. 1049; Malcolm v. Lavinson, 1933, 110 N.J.Eq. 63, 164 A. 318; Brewer v. Maurer, 1883, 38 Ohio St. 543, 43 Am.Rep. 436; Johnson v. Davis, 1930, 146 Okl. 170, 293 P. 197; Hylands' Estate v. Foote's Es-

obligation of the mortgagor to the mortgagee.[50] But the mortgagor has no obligation to the transferee to pay it for the purpose of relieving the land in the hands of the transferee. And, although he may not be able to compel the mortgagee to proceed first against the land before seeking payment from him,[51] he does have a right against the grantee that the land be first exhausted in payment of the debt.[52] Likewise, if the mortgagor pays, he will be entitled to reimbursement out of the land.[53]

The transferee on his part, although under no personal duty to pay the debt, has the privilege of doing so. If he fails to exercise this privilege he runs the risk of losing his land by having either the mortgagee or the mortgagor apply it to the indebtedness. If he does pay, the mortgage is extinguished and he will hold the land free and clear. He will not, however, be able to obtain any reimbursement from his grantor.[54]

There are cases in which the conveyance in terms is only "subject" to the mortgage where the courts have held that the grantee should be regarded as having assumed the payment of the mortgage debt. They will

be considered later in a section dealing with implied personal obligations.[55]

A clause in a subsequent mortgage that it is subject to a prior one would seem to have no effect other than showing notice of the earlier one.[56] Unlike a purchaser of the property "subject" to a mortgage, a later mortgagee taking "subject" to a prior one receives no consideration by reason of its existence. Hence it is not inequitable, as it would be for a purchaser who has received a consideration, ordinarily a reduction to the extent of the mortgage debt, for him to insist that the mortgagor and not the land should be primarily liable.[57]

ASSUMPTION OF THE MORTGAGE[58]—IN GENERAL

253. Whether there is an assumption of the mortgage debt by a transferee depends upon principles of contract law.

When a mortgagor sells the mortgaged property the sale transaction consists of an agreement, express or implied, as to the terms of the bargain and, in addition, a conveyance which passes to the purchaser the title to the property. Whether by the agreement there is an assumption of the mortgage, i. e., whether it creates a binding obligation on the purchaser to pay off the mortgage debt, depends upon principles of contract law. The contract need not be formal.[59] The agreement may be contained solely in the deed of conveyance.[60] On the other hand it

tate, 1933, 106 Vt. 1, 168 A. 925; Shepherd v. May, 1885, 115 U.S. 505, 6 S.Ct. 119, 29 L.Ed. 456; see J. H. Magill Lumber Co. v. Lane-White Lumber Co., 1909, 90 Ark. 426, 430, 119 S.W. 822, 823; Comstock v. Hitt, 1865, 37 Ill. 542, 548; Crawford v. Nimmons, 1899, 180 Ill. 143, 54 N.E. 209; Fourth Nat. Bank in Wichita v. Hill, 1957, 181 Kan. 683, 314 P. 2d 312.

50. Conway Savings Bank v. Vinick, 1934, 287 Mass. 448, 192 N.E. 81; Stevenson v. Black, 1831, 1 N.J. Eq. 338; Syracuse Trust Co. v. First Trust & Deposit Co., 1931, 141 Misc. 603, 252 N.Y.S. 850; In re May's Est., 1907, 218 Pa. 64, 67 A. 120.

51. See cases in note 50, supra. But see § 258, infra.

52. Syracuse Trust Co. v. First Trust & Deposit Co., 1931, 141 Misc.Rep. 603, 252 N.Y.S. 850.

53. Braun v. Crew, 1920, 183 Cal. 728, 192 P. 531; Harvey v. Lowry, 1932, 204 Ind. 93, 183 N.E. 309, discussed, 1933, 42 Yale L.J. 798; Johnson v. Zink, 1873, 51 N.Y. 333; Murray v. Marshall, 1884, 94 N. Y. 611; Marsh v. Pike, N.Y. 1844, 10 Paige 595.

54. See Wright v. Anderson, 1934, 62 S.Dak. 444, 450, 253 N.W. 484, 487, 95 A.L.R. 81.

55. See § 257, infra.

56. Such a clause in a second mortgage of part of the land under the first mortgage has been held to indicate an intention that the part should contribute pro rata to the payment of the prior mortgage. Savings Investment & Trust Co. v. United Realty & Mort. Co., 1916, 84 N.J.Eq. 472, 94 A. 588.

57. See Tiffany, Real Prop., 3d ed., § 1435.

58. Assuming the "mortgage" means assuming the mortgage debt. Tuttle v. Armstead, 1885, 53 Conn. 175, 22 A. 677; Schley v. Fryer, 1885, 100 N.Y. 71, 2 N.E. 280.

59. Howard v. Robbins, 1901, 67 App.Div. 245, 73 N. Y.S. 172, affirmed 1902, 170 N.Y. 498, 93 N.E. 530.

60. See § 253, infra.

"may be made orally or in a separate instrument; it may be implied from the transaction of the parties, or it may be shown by circumstances under which the purchase was made, as well as by the language used in the agreement." [61] It must, however, be established by clear and unequivocal proof.[62]

ASSUMPTION OF THE MORTGAGE—PROVISIONS IN THE DEED

254. Assent by a grantee to an assumption clause in a deed which he accepts is binding.

Most commonly the deed of conveyance contains an assumption clause. It usually recites the mortgage and declares that the grantee assumes and agrees to pay it as part of the consideration for the conveyance. The grantee does not have to sign such a deed for

---

61. Hopkins v. Warner, 1895, 109 Cal. 133, 138, 41 P. 868, 871.

The assumption of a mortgage debt is not within the general provisions of statutes of frauds. Some states have special statutes covering it. See § 255, infra.

For New York legislation broadening the requirement that the assumption of the mortgage indebtedness by a grantee of the mortgage must be in writing, see Curtiss, The Commission and the Law of Real Property, 1955, 40 Cornell L.Q. 735, 742. On the other hand, Rosenberg v. Rolling Inn, Inc., 1857, 212 Md. 552, 129 A.2d 924 noted in 1958, 18 Md.L. Rev. 138, held that the Statute of Frauds does not apply to an assuming promise. And Manget Foundation, Inc. v. White, 1960, 101 Ga.App. 239, 113 S. E.2d 235, noted by Smith, Security Transactions, 1960, 12 Mercer L.Rev. 182, 188, held that the Statute of Frauds does not prevent the showing of an oral assumption by a grantee who accepts a warranty deed reciting that the grantee agreed to pay the grantor's debt as part of the consideration.

An assumption by a grantee may be established by evidence extrinsic to a deed containing covenants of warranty or stating that it is "subject" to the mortgage. See § 256 infra.

In Barkhausen v. Continental Illinois Nat. Bank & Trust Co., 1954, 3 Ill.2d 254, 120 N.E.2d 649, rev'g 1953, 351 Ill.App. 388, 115 N.E.2d 640, noted in 1954, 33 Chi.-Kent L.Rev. 83, the beneficiaries of a trust were not liable upon an assumption of a pre-existing mortgage by a trustee as trustee, that being the intention of all parties to the transaction.

62. Perkins v. Brown, 1934, 179 Wash. 597, 38 P.2d 253, 101 A.L.R. 275. See note, 1934, 101 A.L.R. 281 as to what language amounts to an assumption.

---

him to be bound by the provision.[63] However, assent to the assumption clause must be established as a fact.[64] Consequently the plaintiff must show that the grantee accepted the deed, either with knowledge of the assumption clause in it [65] or under such circumstances as would raise a presumption of knowledge of its existence.[66]

A covenant in the mortgage that it shall bind all persons in whom title to the mortgaged property shall be vested is not a covenant running with the land so as to bind a grantee.[67]

The deed may not contain an assumption clause. It may be in the form of a quit claim deed [68] or it may contain covenants of warranty not only of title but against encum-

---

63. Thomas v. Home Mut. Bldg. Ass'n, 1910, 243 Ill. 550, 90 N.E. 1081; Jager v. Vollinger, 1899, 174 Mass. 521, 55 N.E. 458; Furnas v. Durgen, 1876, 119 Mass. 500, 20 Am.Rep. 341; Sparkman v. Gove, 1882, 44 N.J.Law 252; Schley v. Fryer, 1885, 100 N.Y. 71, 2 N.E. 280; S. Car. Ins. Co. v. Kohn, 1918, 108 S.C. 475, 95 S.E. 65; Thacker v. Hubbard & Applby, 1918, 122 Va. 379, 94 S.E. 929; Bishop v. Douglass, 1870, 25 Wis. 696; Keller v. Ashford, 1889, 133 U.S. 610, 10 S.Ct. 494, 33 L.Ed. 667. See note, Walsh & Simpson, Cas. Security Transactions, 309.

64. McFarland v. Melson, 1929, 323 Mo.App. 977, 20 S.W.2d 63; see Perkins v. Brown, 1934, 179 Wash. 597, 600, 38 P.2d 253, 256, 101 A.L.R. 275. See also 1936, 13 N.Y.Univ.L.Q.Rev. 486; 1934, 9 Wash.L. Rev. 118; Campbell, Cases on Mortgages, 2d ed., 415 n. 1. Acceptance of the conveyance without knowledge of the assumption clause does not bind the grantee who repudiates it on discovery of its presence in the deed. Blass v. Terry, 1898, 156 N.Y. 122, 50 N.E. 953, 6 N.Y.Ann.Cas. 79. See L.R.A. 1918A, 1003.

65. Hamilton Co. v. Rosen, 1933, 53 R.I. 346, 166 A. 691; Magallon v. Schreiner, 1917, 97 Wash. 15, 165 P. 1048.

66. Blass v. Terry, 1898, 156 N.Y. 122, 50 N.E. 953, 6 N.Y.Ann.Cas. 79.

67. Seventeenth and Locust Streets Corp. v. Montcalm Corp., C.C.A.Pa.1931, 54 F.2d 42.

A covenant by a grantee of an equity of redemption to discharge the mortgage debt does not run with the land. Clement v. Willett, 1908, 105 Minn. 267, 117 N.W. 491, 17 L.R.A.,N.S., 1094, 127 Am.St.Rep. 562, 15 Ann.Cas. 1053. But see Wilcox v. Campbell, 1887, 106 N.Y. 325, 12 N.E. 823.

68. E. g., Howard v. Robbins, note 48, supra.

brances.[69] It may also, whether in form a quit claim or warranty deed, contain a statement that it is conveyed "subject to" the mortgage.[70] In such cases whether there has been an assumption of the mortgage depends upon establishing the fact of an agreement for it by evidence extrinsic to the deed of conveyance. That evidence may consist of either a separate written or oral express agreement. Or it may consist of the circumstances accompanying the transaction, the most important of which is the amount paid by the grantee for the property. These situations present several questions. One is whether any or all of this kind of extrinsic evidence is barred by either the Statute of Frauds [71] or the parol evidence rule.[72] Another is, if the evidence is admitted, whether the language used or the facts proved establish that an assumption by the transferee was intended.[73]

ASSUMPTION OF THE MORTGAGE— STATUTE OF FRAUDS

255. The assumption of a mortgage debt is not within the general provisions of Statutes of Frauds. Some states have special statutes covering it.

The assumption of a mortgage debt is not within that provision of the Statute of Frauds covering promises to answer for the debt or default of another.[74] The reasons usually given are that the promise is to pay the transferee's own debt, or that the promise is not to the creditor, the mortgagee, but to the debtor, the mortgagor. Unless taken out by some doctrine of part performance, it would seem that such a promise would be under that section of the Statute of Frauds relating to contracts not to be performed within a year; [75] the cases, however, have given little consideration to the point. Additional but untenable explanations are that the acceptance of a deed with an assumption clause in it is equivalent to an execution of it by the grantee,[76] or that, by reason of such acceptance, the law imposes an "implied" obligation identical in scope with the provision in the deed.[77] Mere acceptance of the deed seems insufficient to invoke the doctrine of part performance; and the obligation on the transferee is contractual not non-consensual.

Although cases holding that contracts of assumption are not within the provisions of the ordinary Statutes of Frauds seem correct, there are good reasons why a writing should be required.[78] Such contracts are long term ones with several of them being created during the existence of a mortgage as the mortgaged land is sold to successive buyers. The question of whether there has been an assumption is frequently raised years after the alleged event at a time when recollection is uncertain and intermediate grantees [79] may well have lost their copies of the

---

69. E. g., Bolles v. Beach, 1850, 22 N.J.L. 680, 53 Am.Dec. 263.

70. If a deed contains a warranty covenant against incumbrances and also mentions any mortgage as a prior lien, either by stating that the conveyance is "subject to" it or that the grantee assumes payment of it, the additional language destroys the effect of the covenant as to that mortgage. King v. Whitely, N.Y.1843, 10 Paige 465.

71. See § 255, infra.

72. See § 256, infra.

73. See §§ 257, 258, infra.

74. White v. Schader, 1921, 185 Cal. 606, 198 P. 19, 21 A.L.R. 499; Herrin v. Abbe, 1908, 55 Fla. 769, 46 So. 183, 18 L.R.A.,N.S., 907; Lamb v. Tucker, 1875, 42 Iowa, 118; Neiswanger v. McClellan, 1890, 45 Kan. 599, 26 P. 18; Strohauer v. Voltz, 1880, 42 Mich. 444, 4 N.W. 161; Langan v. Iverson, 1899, 78 Minn.

299, 80 N.W. 1051; see Enos v. Anderson, 1907, 40 Colo. 395, 93 P. 475, 15 L.R.A.,N.S., 1087; 1908, 15 L.R.A.,N.S., 1087; 1910, 25 L.R.A.,N.S., 1202. Cf. Rooney v. Koenig, 1900, 80 Minn. 483, 83 N.W. 399.

75. See Tiffany, Real Prop., 3d ed., § 1437; Enos v. Anderson, 1907, 40 Colo. 395, 93 P. 475, 15 L.R.A., N.S., 1087.

76. Foster v. Atwater, 1875, 42 Conn. 244; Schmucker v. Sibert, 1877, 18 Kan. 104, 26 Am.Rep. 765; Baldwin v. Emery, 1896, 89 Me. 496, 36 A. 994.

77. Pike v. Brown, 1851, 61 Mass. (7 Cush.) 133; Urquhart v. Brayton, 1877, 12 R.I. 169. See 1934, 14 Bost.U.L.Rev. 692.

78. See Glenn, Mortgages, § 257.

79. The mortgagee may not only maintain an action against the mortgagor and his assuming grantee,

contracts and memoranda. Consequently it is not surprising to find a few statutes explicitly dealing with the matter. For example in California it is provided that the contract of assumption must be in writing signed by the transferee unless it is specifically provided for in the conveyance of the property.[80] There is a similar statutory provision in New York dating from 1938.[81]

ASSUMPTION OF THE MORTGAGE— PAROL EVIDENCE RULE

256. An assumption by a grantee may be established by evidence extrinsic to a deed containing covenants of warranty or stating that it is "subject" to the mortgage.

Where the conveyance from a mortgagor is by quit claim deed with a recital of a nominal consideration and no other evidence is presented, the presumption is that the land is to be charged primarily with the payment of the mortgage.[82] Since the presumption arises only where there is no other evidence as to intention, if there is a clearly expressed intention in a separate agreement it will control.[83] In such a case there is no ques-

tion of the extrinsic agreement varying the terms of the deed. The deed neither contained any part of the terms of the contract governing the sale nor was meant to cover the question whether the transferee did or did not assume the mortgage debt. The separate agreement is the sole expression of the contract and supplants the presumption which exists in the absence of affirmative evidence of intent.

However, the deed may contain covenants of warranty against incumbrances without any express provision in respect to the mortgage on the property and without any other evidence as to the parties' intent. In such a case the inference is that as between the grantor and grantee the former is to pay the debt to the exoneration of the land.[84] If, in addition to the covenant against incumbrances, the deed also contains a statement that the conveyance is "subject" to a certain mortgage or other explicit statement of intention that the covenant is not to apply to the mortgage specified, the covenant will be nullified as to it.[85] The terms of the deed dealing directly with the mortgage will govern as they would had there been no covenant against incumbrances in the instrument.

Where the deed contains only the covenant against incumbrances the question arises whether extrinsic evidence, in the form of a written or oral agreement or of accompanying circumstances,[86] may be introduced in spite of the covenant to show that the

but also against one or all of successive grantees who assume and agree to pay the mortgage. Baber v. Hanie, 1913, 163 N.C. 588, 80 S.E. 57; Wright v. Bank of Chattanooga, 1933, 166 Tenn. 4, 57 S.W.2d 800; Hofheimer v. Booker, 1935, 164 Va. 358, 180 S.E. 145. An assuming grantee cannot escape liability by transferring it to another. Central Life Ins. Co. v. Thompson, 1931, 182 Ark. 705, 33 S.W.2d 388; McLeod v. Building & Loan Ass'n of Jackson, 1933, 168 Miss. 457, 151 So. 151. But contra, Brinton v. Davidson, 1932, 308 Pa. 371, 162 A. 905.

80. West's Ann.Cal.Civ.Code § 1624(7). See note, 1937, 11 So.Cal.L.Rev. 109.

81. N.Y.Civ.Prac.Act, § 1083c, added by N.Y.Laws 1938, c. 502. See note, 1938, 13 St. John's L.Rev. 215. By construction the Pennsylvania statute has been largely emasculated. Pa.Stat.Ann. (Purdon 1930) tit. 21, §§ 655, 656, discussed in note, 1936, 84 U.Pa.L.Rev. 909. See further, § 258, infra.

82. See Howard v. Robbins, 1902, 170 N.Y. 498, 93 N.E. 530; Scribner v. Malinowski, 1907, 148 Mich. 447, 111 N.W. 1032, is to the same effect. See also 2 A.L.R. 242. Presumably, in such a case the purchase price is paid for the value of the mortgagor's actual interest in the property rather than the full unencumbered property. Walsh, Mortgages, 203.

83. Society of Friends v. Haines, 1890, 47 Ohio St. 423, 25 N.E. 119.

84. Maher v. Lanfrom, 1877, 86 Ill. 513; Wadsworth v. Williams, 1868, 100 Mass. 126; Hooper v. Henry, 1883, 31 Minn. 264, 17 N.W. 476; Barnes v. Mott, 1876, 64 N.Y. 397, 21 Am.Rep. 625.

85. King v. Whitely, N.Y.1843, 10 Paige 465; Drury v. Holden, 1887, 121 Ill. 130, 13 N.E. 547; Hopper v. Smyser, 1900, 90 Md. 363, 45 A. 206; Brown v. South Boston Sav. Bank, 1889, 148 Mass. 300, 19 N. E. 382; Fuller v. Devolld, 1910, 144 Mo.App. 93, 128 S.W. 1011; Belmont v. Coman, 1860, 22 N.Y. 438, 78 Am.Dec. 213; Gerdine v. Menage, 1889, 41 Minn. 417, 43 N.W. 91; Calkins v. Copley, 1882, 29 Minn. 471, 13 N.W. 904. See §§ 252, 254, as to the effect of such provisions in the deed.

86. E. g., the amount of the purchase price paid to the grantor.

grantee assumed the mortgage. Prima facie such a deed seems to cover exactly the subject with which the extrinsic evidence, if let in, also deals. And the provision in the deed apparently is directly varied and contradicted by the evidence.[87] Nevertheless the evidence is let in,[88] although the reasons advanced for doing so have not escaped criticism.[89] Some cases say it is admissible to show the consideration;[90] others feel that the

parol agreement is an independent contract neither at variance with the deed nor merged in it.[91] Still others admit the evidence when the mortgagee is plaintiff on the ground that the parol evidence rule is inapplicable to strangers to the deed.[92] The real reason for admission seems to be that if it is excluded the grantee would be unjustly enriched. Properly the evidence should be admitted, not to enforce the agreement to assume, but to recover the amount of enrichment which would otherwise accrue unfairly to the grantee.

A case of less difficulty is where the deed itself says that the conveyance is "subject" to the mortgage and extrinsic evidence is offered that the grantee assumed the mortgage.[93] The parol evidence rule clearly does not[94] and should not exclude this evidence. The term "subject" to the mortgage deals with and is meant to be limited to part only of the transaction, i. e., the relationship be-

87. In Simanovich v. Wood, 1887, 145 Mass. 180, 13 N.E. 391, parol evidence was excluded on this reasoning; Hicks v. Sullivan, 1921, 127 Miss. 148, 89 So. 811; Patterson v. Cappon, 1905, 125 Wis. 198, 102 N.W. 1083, accord.

88. Bolles v. Beach, 1850, 22 N.J.L. 680, 53 Am.Dec. 263; Hays v. Peck, 1886, 107 Ind. 389, 8 N.E. 274; Laudman v. Ingram, 1872, 49 Mo. 212; Deaver v. Deaver, 1904, 137 N.C. 240, 49 S.E. 113; Johnson v. Elmen, 1900, 94 Tex. 168, 59 S.W. 253, 52 L.R.A. 162. See also cases cited in following footnotes. However, insofar as parts of the contract other than the covenant against incumbrances are contained in the deed they cannot be contradicted by extrinsic evidence. Mott v. American Trust Co., 1916, 124 Ark. 70, 186 S.W. 631; Lamoille Bank v. Beldon, 1916, 90 Vt. 535, 98 A. 1002; see Johnson v. Walter, 1882, 60 Iowa 315, 320, 14 N.W. 325, 328; 25 L.R.A.,N.S., 1194, 1203; 50 A.L.R. 1220, 1222. Thus if the deed contains an assumption clause known to the grantee it cannot be contradicted by parol evidence of a different understanding when the grantor sues the grantee. Muhlig v. Fiske, 1881, 131 Mass. 110, 113; Clark v. Henderson, 1931, 62 N.D. 503, 244 N.W. 314, 84 A.L.R. 347. Where the mortgagee sues there is authority that it is admissible. Nissen v. Sabin, 1927, 202 Iowa 1362, 212 N.W. 125, 50 A.L.R. 1216; Stowers v. Stuck, 1936, 131 Neb. 409, 268 N.W. 310; Page v. Hinchee, 1935, 174 Okl. 537, 541, 51 P.2d 487, 491. For a criticism of the distinction, see 1937, 12 Wis.L.Rev. 405. The evidence must be clear and convincing. McFarland v. Melson, 1929, 323 Mo. 977, 985, 20 S.W.2d 63, 66. If the clause was inserted by fraud or mistake there may be relief. See 28 L.R.A.,N.S., 785, 819; L.R.A.1918A, 1003; 26 A.L.R. 528; 100 A.L.R. 911; 1935, 22 Va.L.Rev. 355.

89. See notes, 1937, 12 Wis.L.Rev. 405; 1929, 78 U. of Pa.L.Rev. 432.

90. Hays v. Peck, 1886, 107 Ind. 389, 8 N.E. 274; Bolles v. Beach, 1850, 22 N.J.L. 680, 53 Am.Dec. 263; Deaver v. Deaver, 1904, 137 N.C. 240, 49 S.E. 113; Johnson v. Elmen, 1900, 94 Tex. 168, 59 S.W. 253, 52 L.R.A. 162, 86 Am.St.Rep. 845. See 1927, 50 A.L.R. 1216, 1228; 1931, 84 A.L.R. 347, 358. The English doctrine of estoppel which has been applied to the consideration clause in a deed of conveyance is not, in general, followed in the United States. Instead the decisions are "in favor of free inquiry in regard to the fact of payment in actions for purchase money, etc." Bolles v. Beach, supra.

91. Laudman v. Ingram, 1872, 49 Mo. 212; Bolles v. Beach, supra note 90. See 1927, 50 A.L.R. 1216, 1229; 1931, 84 A.L.R. 347, 360.

The contract of assumption is so far a collateral undertaking, personal in its nature and not relating to the land, that the statute of limitations applicable is that governing contracts not under seal. Nutter v. Mroczka, 1939, 303 Mass. 343, 21 N.E.2d 979.

92. See cases note 88, supra. For cases, semble, see 1927, 50 A.L.R. 1216, 1226; 1931, 84 A.L.R. 347, 358.

93. Such a situation may arise where there are covenants against incumbrances with the additional statement that the conveyance is "subject" to the mortgage in question. See text, supra, this section.

94. White v. Schader, 1921, 185 Cal. 606, 198 P. 19, 21 A.L.R. 499; Herrin v. Abbe, 1908, 55 Fla. 769, 46 So. 183, 18 L.R.A.,N.S., 907; Strohauer v. Voltz, 1880, 42 Mich. 444, 4 N.W. 161; Lamb v. Tucker, 1875, 42 Iowa, 118; Langan v. Iverson, 1899, 78 Minn. 299, 80 N.W. 1051; Gustafson v. Koehler, 1929, 177 Minn. 115, 224 N.W. 699; Gilmer v. Powell, Mo.App.1923, 256 S.W. 124; Ordway v. Downey, 1898, 18 Wash. 412, 51 P. 1047, 63 Am.St.Rep. 892. See Warm, Rights and Liabilities of Mortgagee, Mortgagor and Grantee, 1935, 10 Temple L.Quar. 116, 121, 3 Mercer Beasley L.R. 113; 1930, 9 Tex. L.Rev. 453; 1910, 25 L.R.A.,N.S., 1202; 1927, 50 A. L.R. 1220, 1222; 1931, 84 A.L.R. 355, 356; Hood v. Young, 1928, 178 Ark. 439, 11 S.W.2d 767; Wayne International Building & Loan Ass'n v. Beckner, 1922, 191 Ind. 664, 134 N.E. 273, contra. See 1930, 78 U.Pa.L.Rev. 432, criticizing the grounds of admission.

tween the grantor and the land. The extrinsic agreement of assumption concerns an entirely separate and independent matter, the personal liability of the transferee to pay the mortgage debt.[95] It does not in any way vary or affect the terms of the instrument of conveyance. It merely creates a quite distinct contract obligation. Other grounds for admitting the evidence are those relied upon where there is only a covenant against incumbrances in the deed, i. e., that it may come in to show the consideration,[96] or, when the mortgagee is suing, that the exclusion rule does not apply to strangers to the deed.[97]

IMPLIED PERSONAL OBLIGATIONS

257. **In some states a conveyance subject to the mortgage, by itself or together with an expression that the consideration is the full value of the land with the amount of the mortgage deducted and the balance paid, implies a personal obligation to assume the mortgage or to indemnify the mortgagor.**

The general rule, as previously seen,[98] is that a conveyance "subject" to a mortgage creates no personal obligation upon the grantee. However, in Pennsylvania[99] in this country, and in England[1] and Canada,[2] one who buys property expressed to be subject to a mortgage becomes thereby bound to indemnify[3] the mortgagor although no promise in terms is made to do so. This implied obligation has been spoken of variously as "founded on principles of equity and fair dealing," as "purely contractual in nature", and as "impliedly contractual."[4] It runs in favor of the vendor[5] but the grantee incurs no liability to the mortgagee or his assignee.[6] The Pennsylvania doctrine has been explained as arising out of a misconstruction of early cases in that state in which the conveyance was subject not to the mortgage but to "the payment" of it, a form of expression which understandably could be construed as amounting to an assumption of payment.[7]

Orient Building & Loan Ass'n v. Freud, 1930, 298 Pa. 431, 435, 148 A. 841, 842, accord. See 1936, 84 U. Pa.L.Rev. 909.

1. See Waring v. Ward, 1802, 7 Ves. 332, 338; Mills v. United Counties Bank, [1912] 1 Ch. 231; Adair v. Carden, 1892, 29 L.R.Ir. 469.

2. See Falconbridge, Mortgages, 3d ed. 1942, § 134; 1937, 111 A.L.R. 1114, 1132. But cf. Esser v. Pritzker, 1926, 2 D.L.R. 645; 1926, 40 Harv.L.Rev. 503.

3. The obligation is one of indemnity and no recovery can be had without proof of loss, i. e., that the transferor had paid. Faulkner v. McHenry, note 99, supra. See Ann.Cas.1913D, 1152. See additionally, other cases in note 12, infra.

4. See Moschzisker, C. J., in Dobkin v. Landsberg, 1922, 273 Pa. 174, 180, 116 A. 814, 816. A like diversity of reasoning exists in England and Canada. See authorities cited, notes 1, 2, supra. see also note 16, infra.

5. Faulkner v. McHenry, 1912, 235 Pa. 298, 83 A. 827, Ann.Cas.1913D, 1151; Orient Building & Loan Ass'n v. Freud, 1930, 298 Pa. 431, 435 148 A. 841, 842.

6. Taylor v. Mayer, 1880, 93 Pa. 42, 44. The courts of Pennsylvania recognize that an express promise of assumption is more than one of indemnity against loss and hence hold that, the mortgagee being unpaid, an action may be brought against the assuming grantee by the mortgagor, preferably in the name of the mortgagor. Frey v. United Traction Co., 1935, 320 Pa. 196, 199, 181 A. 775, 776; Putnam v. United Traction Co., 1935, 320 Pa. 203, 181 A. 778; Fair Oaks Building & Loan Ass'n v. Kahler, 1935, 320 Pa. 245, 252, 181 A. 779, 781, 111 A.L.R. 1108; Ruzyc v. Brown, 1935, 320 Pa. 213, 181 A. 783. See 1936, 84 U.Pa.L.Rev. 909.

7. See Tiffany, Real Prop., 3d ed., § 1435.

---

95. Strohauer v. Voltz, 1880, 42 Mich. 444, 4 N.W. 161; McFarland v. Melson, Mo.App.1929, 323 Mo. 977, 20 S.W.2d 63; Ordway v. Downey, 1898. 18 Wash. 412, 51 P. 1047, 63 Am.St.Rep. 892.

96. White v. Schader, 1921, 185 Cal. 606, 198 P. 19, 21 A.L.R. 499; Brosseau v. Lowy, 1904, 209 Ill. 405, 70 N.E. 901; Swarthout v. Shields, 1915, 185 Mich. 427, 152 N.W. 202; Morgan v. South Milwaukee Lake View Co., 1897, 97 Wis. 275, 72 N.W. 872; Wayne International Building & Loan Ass'n v. Beckner, 1922, 191 Ind. 664, 134 N.E. 273, contra.

97. McFarland v. Melson, 1929, 323 Mo. 977, 20 S.W. 2d 63, noted, 1930, 78 U.Pa.L.Rev. 432, See 1937, 12 Wis.L.Rev. 405; L.R.A.1918A, 1003.

98. See § 252, supra.

99. Faulkner v. McHenry, 1912, 235 Pa. 298, 83 A. 827, Ann.Cas.1913D, 1151, "The words 'under and subject' in a conveyance, import that the grantee takes the land subject to an encumbrance, the amount of which has been deducted from the agreed price, and the covenant to be inferred from it is that of indemnity for the protection of the grantor."

The English doctrine may have been established to give the mortgagor protection at a time before the doctrine of subrogation had been sufficiently developed to do so.[8]

Where in addition to a conveyance subject to the mortgage the full value of the land is agreed on [9] as the purchase price and from it the purchaser has deducted the amount of the mortgage and has paid the balance, there are a good many cases holding that the purchaser has become personally liable.[10] This has been explained on the ground that "His [the grantee's] retention of the vendor's money for the payment of the mortgage, imposes upon him the duty of protecting the vendor against the mortgage debt. This must be so * * * for it would seem to be almost intolerably unjust to permit him to keep back the vendor's money with the understanding that he would pay the vendor's debt, and still be free of all liability for a fail-

ure to apply the money according to his promise." [11] The personal liability so created generally is held to be an assumption of the debt, but in some instances it is one of indemnity as in England, Canada, and Pennsylvania.[12] In end result there is little difference between a personal obligation to pay the debt and one to reimburse another person who has had to pay it.

These decisions have been vigorously and, it is believed, justly criticized.[13] It is a fair enough inference from the fact that the conveyance is subject to a mortgage that the purchaser paid only the value of the redemption interest.[14] And it is a further proper inference that the grantee in such a case, as between him and the grantor, assumes the debt as a charge upon the land he has acquired.[15] Thus far the English, Canadian and Pennsylvania cases are on sound footing. Such an interpretation exposes the grantee only to the risk of losing the property and to no additional loss should it prove to be inadequate security for the debt. But to impose upon such a grantee, whether on grounds of implication of fact or ideas of fairness,[16] a duty to recoup his vendor when he has had to pay the mortgage irrespective

8. Id.

9. This agreement frequently appears in the deed of conveyance. See cases in note 10, infra. It may, however, be established by admissible extrinsic evidence. E. g., Canfield v. Shear, 1882, 49 Mich. 313, 13 N.W. 605; Hawn v. Malone, 1920, 188 Iowa 439, 176 N.W. 393. See § 256 supra.

10. Townsend v. Ward, 1858, 27 Conn. 610; Drury v. Holden, 1887, 121 Ill. 130, 137, 13 N.E. 547, 548; Lamka v. Donnelly, 1913, 163 Iowa 255, 143 N.W. 869; Canfield v. Shear, 1882, 49 Mich. 313, 13 N.W. 605; Heid v. Vreeland, 1879, 30 N.J.Eq. 591, 594; Sanderson v. Turner, 1918, 73 Okl. 105, 174 P. 763, 2 A.L.R. 347; Parlette v. Equitable Farm Mort. Ass'n, 1933, 165 Okl. 155, 25 P.2d 300. Holding that no personal obligation is created; Belmont v. Coman, 1860, 22 N.Y. 438, 78 Am.Dec. 213; Equitable Life Assurance v. Bostwick, 1885, 100 N.Y. 628, 3 N.E. 296; Fiske v. Tolman, 1878, 124 Mass. 254, 26 Am.Rep. 659, (but otherwise if *payment* of the mortgage is stated to be part of the consideration, Jager v. Vollinger, 1899, 174 Mass. 521, 55 N.E. 458, and cf. Flynn v. Kenrick, 1934, 285 Mass. 446, 189 N.E. 207, noted 1934, 14 Bost.U.L.Rev. 692; yet see 101 A.L.R. 281, 283); McFarland v. Melson, 1929, 323 Mo. 977, 20 S.W.2d 63; Redhead v. Skidmore Land Credit Co., 1927, 194 Wis. 123, 215 N.W. 937. For discussions and additional authorities, see Warm, Rights and Liabilities of Mortgagee, Mortgagor, Grantee, 1935, 10 Temple L.Quar. 116, 119; Friedman, Creation and Effect of Personal Liability of Mortgage Debts in New York, 1940, 50 Yale L.J. 224, 226; Walsh, Mortgages 209, note 16; notes, 1920, 8 Cal.L.Rev. 447; 1931, 9 Tex.L.Rev. 453; 1934, 18 Minn.L.Rev. 481; 1934, 14 Boston U.L.Rev. 692; L.R.A.1917C, 592; 1937, 111 A.L.R. 1114.

11. Heid v. Vreeland, 1879, 30 N.J.Eq. 591, 593. See Dimmitt v. Johnson, 1913, 199 Iowa 966, 969, 203 N.W. 261, 263, for a similar statement of rationale.

12. Lamka v. Donnelly, 1913, 163 Iowa 255, 143 N.W. 869; Hawn v. Malone, 1920, 188 Iowa 439, 176 N. W. 393; Friedman v. Zuckerman, 1929, 104 N.J.Eq. 322, 145 A. 541; Britton v. Roth, 1933, 313 Pa. 352, 169 A. 146.

13. See Warm, op. cit. supra note 10; Walsh, op. cit. supra note 10; Tiffany, Real Prop., 3d ed., § 1435; Glenn, Mortgages § 256.

14. See Adair v. Carden, 1892, 29 L.R.Ir. 469, 482; Faulkner v. McHenry, note 99, supra; Orient Bldg. & Loan Assn. v. Freud, note 99, supra.

15. See Adair v. Carden, note 14, supra; Glenn, Mortgages, § 252. This is the result of the American cases generally. See § 252, supra.

16. That the obligation is not based upon an implication of fact as to the parties' intention, see Farwell, J., in Mills v. United Counties Bank, [1912] 1 Ch. 231, commented on in 1912, 28 L.Q.Rev. 122; Adair v. Carden, 1892, 29 L.R.Ir. 469, 482 et seq. See authorities in note 1, 2, 4, supra.

of the value of the land seems unwarranted.[17] Such a risk should not be imposed upon him in the absence of clear and explicit evidence of an intention to do so.[18] And the same criticism applies to the American cases which rest the result upon the terms of the agreement as to the purchase price which must be established in addition to the fact of taking subject to the mortgage.[19] As has been pointed out: "In actual fact there is not the slightest difference between a sale of the equity subject to the mortgage for a stated price to be paid for the equity and a sale of the same property by a contract which states the price at the full value of the property unencumbered and provides for payment to the amount of the mortgage by taking subject to the mortgage, the balance to be paid in cash. * * * To say that the purchaser has retained the vendor's money to pay the mortgage is simply contrary to the fact."[20]

17. Additionally, it has been suggested, that if the obligation is imposed at all it should be to pay the debt, not merely to recoup the transferor to the extent he has had to pay it. See Tiffany, Real Prop., 3d ed., § 1435. This may be correct if the obligation rests upon an implication of fact as to the parties' intention. If however, the basis is unjust enrichment at the expense of the transferor, limiting recovery to the amount of loss established by him can be defended.

18. See Warm, op. cit. supra note 10, 121; Glenn, op. cit. supra, note 15, § 256.

19. See note 10, supra.

20. Walsh, Mortgages, 209 note 16. See also, Warm, op. cit. supra note 10, 120, "What money has been deducted or retained? Why do the parties take this roundabout way of entering into an assumption agreement? For a court to draw such an inference is to make an arrangement for the parties which they never contemplated. It opens the door to fraud and uncertainty. It results in contracts made, for the most part, by the court whose findings as to what the parties meant is made in the light of what has since transpired." Cases in which the conveyance is subject to the mortgage and where the consideration is other property serve to illustrate the difficulty in application and weakness of the theory of assumption in these decisions. Id., 123. But see Adair v. Carden, 1892, 29 L.R.Ir. 469, 482, "It is, no doubt, reasonable to suppose that one who sells a property charged with a debt, and who therefore presumably receives for it just so much less money than he would otherwise have received, would regard himself as having got rid of the whole thing, liability as well as security."

RIGHTS OF TRANSFEROR— NON-ASSUMING GRANTEE

258. Where a grantee does not assume the mortgage, the grantor's rights, against the land only, are (1) to pay the debt and either (a) be subrogated to it and the mortgage lien, or (b) preferably have them assigned to him; (2) bring a suit for exoneration out of the land; (3) possibly invoke the doctrine of Pain v. Packard where it is recognized.

As against a non-assuming grantee the mortgagor or other transferor has no personal claim to have him pay off the debt.[21] However, the land in the hands of such a grantee becomes the principal fund for payment and the mortgagor stands in the position of a surety.[22] When the debt comes due the mortgagor may pay it and then be subrogated to the rights of the mortgagee in the mortgage.[23] There are difficulties in such a course due to the rule that, technically, payment of the mortgage debt discharges it and releases the mortgage.[24] Consequently, as an alternative, the mortgagor may ask that the mortgagee assign both the debt and the mortgage to a nominee of the mortgagor so that the lien clearly will be kept alive for his benefit. Since the mortgagee cannot be injured by such action and it is important to the mortgagor's protection, equity will grant specific performance of such a request.[25] The

See, also, Glenn, Puchasing Subject to the Mortgage, 1941, 27 Va.L.Rev. 853, 856. Contrast, id., 861–862.

21. See § 252, supra. Cf. Fitzgerald v. Flanagan, 1912, 155 Iowa, 217, 135 N.W. 738, Ann.Cas.1914C, 1104; Locke v. Homer, 1881, 131 Mass. 93, 41 Am.Rep. 199; Hall v. Morgan, 1883, 79 Mo. 47; Woodbury v. Swan, 1878, 58 N.H. 380; Hoy v. Bramhall, 1868, 19 N.J.Eq. 563, 569, 97 Am.Dec. 687; Faulkner v. McHenry, 1912, 235 Pa. 298, 83 A. 827, Ann.Cas. 1913D, 1151. But cf., Glenn, Purchasing Subject to the Mortgage, 1941, 27 Va.L.Rev. 853, 865.

22. § 252, supra.

23. University State Bank v. Steeves, 1915, 85 Wash. 55, 147 P. 645, 2 A.L.R. 237. See 1919, 2 A.L.R. 242, 243. See further, Chapter 10, infra; § 252, supra.

24. See Chapter 10, post. See also, § 252, ante.

25. E. g., Johnson v. Zink, 1873, 51 N.Y. 333; Howard v. Robbins, 1902, 170 N.Y. 498, 63 N.E. 530; see 1919, 2 A.L.R. 242. But see Lamb v. Montague, 1873, 112 Mass. 352. See further Chapter 10, infra.

mortgagor may then reach the land by using the mortgagee's rights to realize out of it by foreclosure. Since the grantee's duty is limited to having the land in his hands go to pay the debt, this remedy gives the mortgagor adequate relief.

Although it has been stated that this is the sole remedy of the mortgagor in the case of a non-assuming grantee,[26] two others are possible. One is to bring a suit for exoneration out of the land, i. e., to have the premises sold and the proceeds used for the payment of the debt. Such relief has been criticized when invoked against an assuming grantee,[27] but it is well established.[28] There seems no sufficient reason why, if available against an assuming grantee to compel him to pay or to reach the lands in his hands for that purpose, it should not be available to the latter limited extent against a non-assuming transferee.[29]

Another possibility, directed not at the grantee but at the mortgagee, is to invoke the doctrine of Pain v. Packard,[30] in those jurisdictions in which it is followed.[31] This would enable the mortgagor after maturity of the debt to demand of the mortgagee that he institute an action of foreclosure so that, to the extent of its value, it would be used to pay the debt. The mortgagor, then, would not have to do so. Failure to comply would result in a discharge to the extent of the loss thereafter sustained. There is considerable doubt as to whether the doctrine applies to a suretyship relation arising subsequent to the mortgage by virtue of the transfer of the property.[32] Nevertheless there is some authority applying it to the case of a non-assuming grantee.[33]

RIGHTS OF TRANSFEROR—ASSUMING GRANTEE

259. A mortgagor has the same rights against the land where the grantee assumes the mortgage as where he takes subject to it. In addition he may, against an assuming grantee, (1) pay the debt and obtain reimbursement directly or by way of subrogation or assignment; (2) by the weight of authority, without paying the debt, sue and recover its full amount if the grantee does not pay it on maturity; (3) obtain exoneration against the grantee. It is doubtful whether the mortgagor has any rights against an assuming grantee after a break in the chain of assumption; a non-assuming grantee should have none.

As against an assuming grantee, the mortgagor has the same rights in respect to reach-

---

26. Glenn, Purchasing Subject to Morgage, 1941, 27 Va.L.Rev. 853, 866.

27. See Glenn, op. cit. supra note 26, 868. The chief objection is that it should be exercised when all three parties, grantor, grantee and mortgagor, are before the court. This is to insure a conclusive determination of the debt. Where the only relief sought is against the land, it would seem that an action quasi in rem without personal jurisdiction over the grantee could be brought where the land is.

28. Marsh v. Pike, N.Y.1844, 10 Paige 595; Rubens v. Prindle, N.Y.1864, 44 Barb. 336; Marshall v. Davies, 1879, 78 N.Y. 414, 421, semble. See Friedman, Discharge of Mortgage Debts, 1943, 52 Yale L.J. 771, 795.

29. See cases in preceding note. These are cases where the grantee assumed the payment of the mortgage. So far as the right of exoneration against the land is concerned this would seem to be immaterial.

30. N.Y.1816, 13 Johns. 174.

31. The rule prevails in fifteen states by statute and in three more by decision. Restatement, Security, 1940, § 127; Arant, Suretyship, 1931, 312–317. See 1928, 37 Yale L.J. 971; L.R.A.1918C, 10, for surveys of the rule. See also Glenn, op. cit. supra, note 26, 869. See also Friedman, op. cit. supra note 28, 795.

32. See Friedman, op. cit. supra note 28, 796. Fish v. Glover, 1894, 154 Ill. 86, 39 N.E. 1081, rejects the doctrine in the case of mortgages on the ground it applies only to conventional suretyship.

33. Gottschalk v. Jungmann, N.Y.1903, 78 App.Div. 171, 79 N.Y.S. 551; 1903, 3 Col.L.Rev. 199; Nat. Sav. Bank of City of Albany v. Fermac Corp., 1934, 241 App.Div. 204, 271 N.Y.S. 836, affirmed 266 N.Y. 443, 195 N.E. 145; Osborne v. Heyward, N.Y.1899, 40 App.Div. 78, 57 N.Y.S. 542; see cases in Union Trust Co. v. Rogers, N.Y.1941, 261 App.Div. 882, 25 N.Y.S.2d 120. But see Marshall v. Davies, 1879, 78 N.Y. 414; Glenn, op. cit., supra note 26, 869. The Fermac case, supra, was affirmed solely on the ground that the mortgagor had made a tender. National Sav. Bank v. Fermac Corp., 1934, 266 N.Y. 443, 195 N.E. 145. Of course if the mortgagee complied with the request he might then go ahead and get a deficiency against the mortgagor, a contingency that could be, in certain instances, a substantial deterrent.

ing the property in his hands as in the case of a nonassuming grantee.[34] In addition, however, he has personal rights against the transferee. One of these is to pay the debt and then sue for reimbursement. It is self-evident that this right exists under any theory of the nature of the contract of assumption.[35] Furthermore it could rest upon a quasi-contractual basis, at least in those jurisdictions in which the assumption gives to the mortgagee a personal right against the assuming grantee.[36] In such a case the grantor would be benefiting the grantee by discharging the latter's obligation to pay. The grantor would be privileged to make the payment because he remained liable; the grantee is unjustly enriched because he had the primary duty of payment.

Some few jurisdictions have limited the right of the mortgagor to the foregoing relief, holding that the grantor may not sue until he has paid the debt.[37] The weight of

authority is that the assumption agreement calls for the payment of the debt when it falls due and consequently it is broken when, at the maturity of the debt, it is not paid.[38] The measure of damages for the breach is the face amount of the debt with interest.[39] The objection to the majority rule is that "a grantee might be subjected to two judgments for the same debt; one in favor of the grantor, and the other in favor of the mortgage. One

was so decided partly on the ground that the agreement of assumption, properly interpreted, was merely one of "indemnity," i. e., reimbursement. Other cases arrive at the same result for the reason that the right is not contractual but a surety's relational right to compensation against his principal. See note 36, supra.

38. White v. Schader, 1921, 185 Cal. 606, 198 P. 19, 21 A.L.R. 499; Locke v. Homer, 1881, 131 Mass. 93, 41 Am.Rep. 199; Gustafson v. Koehler, 1929, 177 Minn. 115, 224 N.W. 699, commented on, 1929, 13 Minn.L.Rev. 737; Kirk v. Welch, 1942, 212 Minn. 300, 3 N.W.2d 426; Sanderson v. Turner, 1918, 73 Okl. 105, 174 P. 763, 2 A.L.R. 347. "The weight of authority is that an action in favor of the grantor accrues when the mortgage debt assumed becomes due without being paid. It has been so held in California, Colorado, Connecticut, Kansas, Maine, Massachusetts, Michigan, Nebraska, New Jersey, Oklahoma, Oregon, South Dakota, and Vermont,", Gustafson v. Koehler, 1929, 177 Minn. 115, 118, 224 N. W. 699, 700.

See Corbin, Contracts for the Benefit of Third Persons, 1918, 27 Yale L.J. 1008, 1022; Williston, Contracts for the Benefit of a Third Person, 1902, 15 Harv.L.Rev. 767, 795; note, 1925, 38 Harv.L.Rev. 502. See also 1922, 21 A.L.R. 504; 1932, 76 A.L.R. 1191; 1935, 97 A.L.R. 1076; Restatement, Contracts, § 136(1).

34. That, as respects the land, an assuming grantee is in the same position as one who only takes subject to the mortgage, see § 247, supra. See also § 252.

35. Taintor v. Hemmingway, N.Y.1879, 18 Hun 458, affirmed 1880, 83 N.Y. 610; Comstock v. Drohan, 1877, 71 N.Y. 9; Evans v. Sperry, D.C.Ill.1926, 12 F.2d 438. See 1922, 21 A.L.R. 504, 520; 1935, 97 A. L.R. 1076, 1079; 1932, 76 A.L.R. 1191, 1196, for collections of cases. See Restatement, Contracts, § 141(2).

36. Graham v. Burnbaugh, 1919, 44 Cal.App. 482, 186 P. 798; Harvey v. Lowry, 1932, 204 Ind. 93, 183 N. E. 309, semble; Poe v. Dixon, 1899, 60 Ohio St. 124, 54 N.E. 86, 71 Am.St.Rep. 713; see Glenn, Morts., § 260. In some cases the right of reimbursement is regarded as merely a surety's relational right of reimbursement against his principal. See Hildrith v. Walker, Mo.App.1916, 187 S.W. 608, 610; Poe v. Dixon, supra, the relational right being looked upon as justified by reason of the conference of a benefit by the surety; John Deere Plow Co. of Moline v. Tuinstra, 1924, 47 S.D. 555, 200 N.W. 61.

37. See Gustafson v. Koehler, 1929, 177 Minn. 115, 224 N.W. 699, "Missouri, New York, Ohio and Pennsylvania courts holding that the grantor may not sue until he has paid the debt, and decisions in Texas and Washington are tending in the same direction." See also 1922, 21 A.L.R. 504, 514; 1932, 76 A.L.R. 1192, 1195; 1935, 97 A.L.R. 1076, 1078. This result is reached on different grounds. E. g., in Sloan v. Klein, 1911, 230 Pa. 132, 79 A. 403, and in Tritten's Estate, 1913, 238 Pa. 555, 86 A. 461, it

39. Gustafson v. Koehler and other cases cited in preceding footnote. See 3 Sutherland, Damages, 4th ed., § 766. See also Stout v. Folger, 1871, 34 Iowa 71, 11 Am.Rep. 138; Sparkman v. Gove, 1882, 44 N.J.L. 252. Recovery of substantial damages has been criticized as running counter to the general rule which denies compensation for merely probable loss. 2 Sedgwick, Damages, 9th ed., § 790. See Lathrop v. Atwood, 1851, 21 Conn. 117, 126, Waite, J., dissenting; 1925, 38 Harv.L.Rev. 502, 505, "There is no adequate answer to this argument against substantial damages. The contention that nominal damages will leave the promisee continuing under a liability which the promisor has promised to discharge, without an adequate remedy, is answered by the fact that, although the promisee-surety's rights upon the positive promise to pay are merged in his judgment for nominal damages, the promisee as surety may have specific performance in equity of a principal's obligation to exonerate his surety by paying the debt as it falls due." See also Campbell, Cases on Mortgages, 2d ed., 435 n. 3.

answer to this is that he has brought this upon himself by not carrying out his agreement. Had he paid the mortgage debt (which is in reality the balance of the purchase price) when it became due, as he agreed, he would not have been sued. And, if sued by the grantor, payment then of the mortgage would be a perfect defense."[40] Further, if the transferor-plaintiff does collect the debt he can be compelled to hold it as trustee for the payment of the mortgage debt.[41]

In addition to the courses previously discussed the mortgagor has open to him a suit in equity to compel an assuming grantee to exonerate him by paying the debt to the mortgagee.[42] In theory this is a completely satisfactory remedy but in practice it is not. The reason is that before the mortgage debt can be paid off by judicial process the amount of the debt then due must be ascertained. To do this requires an accounting to which the mortgagee must be a party.[43] Further if there are several successive grantees all are necessary parties, in addition to the mortgagee.[44] The absence from the state of either the mortgagee or an assuming grantee will make the remedy useless.[45]

The right of a mortgagor to compel the payment of the debt assumed by his grantee extends to a grantee or successive grantees of the first grantee who in their turn assume payment.[46] The fact that a grantee who has assumed the payment of a mortgage has subsequently sold the land to another is no defense to an action by the grantor for a breach of his contract of assumption.[47]

What rights, if any, does a mortgagor have against a subsequent grantee who in buying from a non-assuming grantee assumes the payment of the mortgage? If the mortgagor has paid off the debt he should be entitled to be subrogated to any rights its holder had not only against the land but against the

---

40. Gustafson v. Koehler, 1929, 177 Minn. 115, 118, 224 N.W. 699, 700. The danger of double payment would not exist in jurisdictions denying to the holder of the mortgage debt a direct right against the assuming grantee. See 1925, 38 Harv.L.Rev. 502, 506.

41. "If plaintiff now collects the judgment against defendant, she holds it as trustee for the owner of the mortgage debt, or the one who has sued her. It does not appear that the latter is within the jurisdiction of the court; but it is not to be apprehended that the court cannot provide against the danger of collecting twice of defendant for the debt he agreed to pay." Gustafson v. Koehler, note 38, supra. See Parke, B., in Loosemore v. Radford, 1842, 9 M. & W. 657. See also Heins v. Byers, 1928, 174 Minn. 350, 219 N.W. 287. For various suggested ways of relieving the grantee from risk of further payment see Williston, Contracts, Rev. ed., 1936, § 392; Wilson v. Stilwell, 1859, 9 Ohio St. 467, 75 Am.Dec. 477; Locke v. Homer, 1881, 131 Mass. 93, 108, 41 Am.Rep. 199; 1925, 38 Harv.L.Rev. 502, 505; 1929, 13 Minn. 737; Campbell, Cases on Mortgages, 2d ed., 435 n. 3; Williston, Contracts, Rev. ed., § 392; Restatement, Contracts, §§ 141(1), 136(1)c.

42. Marsh v. Pike, N.Y., 1844, 10 Paige 595; Mowry v. Mowry, 1904, 137 Mich. 277, 100 N.W. 388, semble; see 1943, 41 Mich.L.Rev. 975; Williston, Contracts, Rev. ed., § 392 n. 3; Restatement, Contracts, § 138. See also authorities notes 27, 28, supra.

43. See Chapters 12, 13, infra. Even where the amount is not in dispute as between the mortgagor and assuming grantee the mortgagee should be made a party so as to have a conclusive determination of the amount due as against him. Otherwise he could claim that more was due him than was ordered paid in the exoneration suit. See Glenn, Mortgages, 1166 n. 3. But see Arant, Suretyship, 320–321.

44. See Chapters 12, 13, infra.

45. Cf. n. 27, supra.

46. Robson v. O'Toole, 1923, 60 Cal.App. 710, 214 P. 278; Comstock v. Drohan, 1877, 71 N.Y. 9. See 1922, 21 A.L.R. 504, 507; 1932, 76 A.L.R. 1191, 1194; 1935, 97 A.L.R. 1076, 1077. Williston, Contracts, Rev. ed., § 386.
The problem of the rights of a mortgagor against an assuming grantee after a break in the chain is analyzed in Maxwell and Meyers, The Mortgagor's Rights Against Remote Assuming Grantees, 1952, 29 Tex.L.Rev. 869, 880. See also Storke and Sears, Transfer of Mortgaged Property, 1953, 38 Corn.L.Q. 185, 198.

47. Kollen v. Sooy, 1912, 172 Mich. 214, 137 N.W. 808; Reed v. Paul, 1881, 131 Mass. 129; Kirker v. Wylie, 1904, 207 Pa. 511, 56 A. 1074. The same is true of quasi-contractual liability. Reilly v. Lucraft, 1921, 34 Idaho 41, 198 P. 674, deficiency judgment already paid by grantor. See Williston, Contracts, Rev. ed., § 386. But see Penn.Act of June 12, 1878, P.L. 205 (21 P.S. 655, 656).

later assuming grantee.[48] To the extent that he has discharged any personal obligation of such a person or freed his land from the lien of the mortgage he has conferred a benefit upon that person for which he should be able to collect.[49] If the mortgagor has not paid it is doubtful whether he has any rights against such an assuming grantee.[50] It is true that the third party beneficiary doctrine has been held to permit a mortgagee to recover against an assuming grantee after a break in the chain of assumptions.[51] But to extend a similar right to a remote grantor whose immediate grantee did not personally assume the debt is a step beyond this and one which courts seem unlikely to take in the absence of special circumstances indicating that such grantor should be regarded as within the class of third persons who can sue as beneficiaries of a contract to which they are not parties.[52] A non-assuming grantee who in turn sells to one who assumes the payment of the debt has no interest in having the debt paid. He never became personally bound for the debt and he no longer owns land he might lose if the debt is not discharged. Technically he has a contract right against his grantee on which he might sue. Since he suffers no injury his damages should be nominal.[53] As against

grantees subsequent to the first one who also assume the mortgage whether or not the non-assuming grantor himself can recover depends upon whether in the particular jurisdiction the rule permitting third party beneficiaries to sue will be extended to such a person.[54]

MORTGAGEE vs. ASSUMING GRANTEE— THEORIES OF LIABILITY— IN GENERAL

260. In the United States a mortgagee may enforce in some way, either directly or derivatively through the rights of the mortgagor, the assumption promise of a grantee of the mortgagor. There is, however, diversity as to rationale and procedure. In England, Canada, and Ireland the mortgagee does not have this ability.

The mortgagee, where there has been a transfer by the mortgagor to an assuming grantee, continues to have his original right against the mortgagor and his security interest in the land follows it into the hands of the transferee.[55] The mortgagor, as has been seen, acquires personal rights against the grantee upon this undertaking. The question remains whether only the mortgagor can enforce the promise to assume the mortgage, or whether the mortgagee ac-

---

48. As to the rights of a mortgagee against one who assumes the mortgage after a break in the chain of assumptions, see § 265, infra.

49. Harvey v. Lowrey, 1932, 204 Ind. 93, 183 N.E. 309, discussed, 1933, 42 Yale L.J. 798, is to the contrary, but seems incorrect on this point.

50. Harvey v. Lowrey, supra note 49, holds that he does not have; Carter v. Holohan, 1883, 92 N.Y. 498, accord. Semble, McGinty v. Dennehy, Tex.Civ. App.1927, 2 S.W.2d 546, noted 1929, 7 Tex.L.Rev. 482. The court put the decision on the ground that the defendant's assumption had not been accepted by the mortgagee.

51. See § 265, infra. There is a division of authority on the point.

52. See 1933, 42 Yale L.J. 798, commenting on Harvey v. Lowrey, n. 49, supra.

53. No cases of this sort have been found. Probably the reason is that, as a practical matter, it would

accomplish no useful purpose. That he does have a contract right which is enforceable, Brenner v. Ebbets-McKeever Exhibition Co., 1939, 256 App.Div. 980, 10 N.Y.S.2d 323. The assumption was of the mortgage on an entire tract part of which was retained by the promisee who was a non-assuming grantee. Since the promise would benefit the portion left in the promisee's hands the damages here would be substantial.

54. At least one decision has allowed recovery. Calder v. Richardson, D.C.Fla.1935, 11 F.Supp. 498, commented on, 1936, 49 Harv.L.Rev. 652. Recovery should be limited, where allowed, to any actual damage the non-assuming grantor may be exposed to. Id.

For an excellent critique of the problem, stressing Texas law, see Maxwell and Meyers, The Mortgagor's Rights Against Remote Assuming Grantees, 1951, 29 Tex.L.Rev. 869, 860–879. See also Storke and Sears, Transfer of Mortgaged Property, 1953, 38 Corn.L.Q. 185, 198.

55. See § 247, supra.

quires a right to do so. England,[56] Canada,[57] and Ireland [58] deny the mortgagee any right to reach the assuming grantee.[59] In the United States, Massachusetts comes closest to the English doctrine in rejecting any such right in the mortgagee.[60] No other American jurisdiction has denied the right of a mortgagee the right to enforce, in some way, the promise of the assuming grantee. There is, however, diversity of view both as to the substantive basis of the right and the pro-

cedural method of enforcing it.[61] Since each view begets its own logical corollaries,[62] (which, however, to add to the confusion, are frequently modified by subsidiary or conflicting ideas), it is essential, for an intelligent consideration of a large number of mortgage problems,[63] that these various theories be understood.

As a generalized proposition the bases of recovery by the mortgagee against an assuming grantee are two: (1) by virtue of a direct and independent right of the mortgagee; (2) by virtue of enforcing the promise of the assuming grantee derivatively, i. e., through the right against him of the mortgagor or other transferor. Different reasons are assigned in different states for adopting one or the other of these solutions. Frequently identical results are reached regardless of purported theory.[64] Not only do the theory and rules governing a given rationale

56. Tweddell v. Tweddell, 1787, 2 Bro.Ch. 152; Oxford v. Rodney, 1807, 2 Ves. 417; Re Errington, [1894] 1 Q.B. 11. See note 59, infra.

57. See Falconbridge, Mortgages, 2d ed., 241–6. Where the mortgagor in consideration of a release assigns his right of indemnity against an assuming grantee the mortgagee may recover from the grantee. Esser v. Pritzker, [1926] 2 Dom.L.R. 645, noted 1927, 40 Harv.L.Rev. 503.

58. See Barry v. Harding, 1844, 1 Jones & Lat. 475, 485.

59. See Williston, Contracts, Rev.Ed., §§ 367, 383; note, 1933, 19 Va.L.Rev. 624, 626. See Corbin, Contracts for the Benefit of Third Persons, 1930, 46 Law Q.Rev. 12 for a review of the English cases, and Marsh, The Right of a Mortgagee to a Personal Order Against the Purchaser of the Mortgaged Property, 1882, 2 Can.L.Times 49, 109, 157, 217 for a somewhat old discussion of the Canadian law.

60. Mellen v. Whipple, 1854, 67 Mass. 317 is the leading case rejecting the doctrine of Lawrence v. Fox which would allow a direct legal right by the mortgagee against the assuming grantee. Prentice v. Brimhall, 1877, 123 Mass. 291; Coffin v. Adams, 1881, 131 Mass. 133, accord. The "suretyship" principle upon which the subrogation theory, discussed post in the text of this section, is based appears not to have been received. Nevertheless Professor Williston's "equitable assets" theory, q. v. post this section, seems to be definitely accepted by later decisions. See Forbes v. Thorpe, 1911, 209 Mass. 570, 582, 95 N.E. 955, 959 for the first recognition. It was also acknowledged as existing in Gillis v. Bonelli-Adams Co., 1933, 284 Mass. 176, 187 N.E. 535; Bloch v. Budish, 1932, 279 Mass. 102, 180 N.E. 729, discussed 1933, 19 Va.L.Rev. 624, 628, although holding the creditor could not recover because of the bankruptcy of the assuming grantee; Collins Mfg. Co. v. Wickwire Spencer Co., 1927, 14 F.2d 871, noted, 1927, 36 Yale L.J. 709, accepting this as the law of the state. See Corbin, Contracts for the Benefit of Third Persons, 1918, 27 Yale L.J. 1008, 1026. Consequently today the mortgagee may maintain a creditor's bill in which the mortgagor and the assuming grantee are joined, and have the promise enforced as an asset of the mortgagor with the proceeds applied to the mortgage debt. See Williston, Rev. ed., § 367.

61. Union Mut. Life Ins. Co. v. Hanford, 1891, 143 U.S. 187, 189, 12 S.Ct. 437, 438, 36 L.Ed. 118, "Few things have been the subject of more difference of opinion and conflict of decision than the nature and extent of the right of a mortgagee of real estate against a subsequent grantee who by the terms of the conveyance to him agrees to assume and pay the mortgage." See Campbell, Cases on Mortgages, 2d ed., 417 n. 3, 419, n. 2.

See also §§ 269–264 post; Storke and Sears, Transfer of Mortgaged Property, 1953, 38 Corn.L.Q. 185, 197; Ferson, Contracts in Favor of Third Parties, 1955, 6 Hastings L.J. 354, 365.

62. See Berick, Personal Liability for Deficiency in Mortgage Foreclosures, 1934, 8 U. of Cin.L.Rev. 103; 1933, 19 Va.L.Rev. 624; 1939, 25 Va.L.Rev. 993, 995.

63. These problems include not only the question of what affirmative rights the mortgagee acquires against an assuming grantee but also what rights and defenses may accrue to the mortgagor against the assuming grantee, see § 258, or the mortgagee, see §§ 269–271, infra.

64. See Corbin, Contracts for the Benefit of Third Persons in the Federal Courts, 1930, 39 Yale L.J. 601, 606, citing Keller v. Ashford, 1890, 133 U.S. 610, 10 S.Ct. 494, 33 L.Ed. 667, as an example; Friedman, Personal Liability on Mortgage Debts, 1940, 50 Yale L.J. 224, 234, using Vrooman v. Turner, 1877, 69 N.Y. 280, 25 Am.Rep. 195, as an illustration; cf. Aetna Life Ins. Co. of Hartford, Conn. v. Maxwell, C.C.A.W.Va.1937, 89 F.2d 988, 995.

vary from state to state,[65] but they change in the process of development in the same state.[66] Further, in single jurisdictions there has been a shift from one basis to another and sometimes more than one has been recognized simultaneously.[67] The result of such changes is that many of the decisions are outdated. Hence, any precise classification of jurisdictions is difficult, would be transient and not particularly helpful. Therefore it is not attempted here. The theories themselves are, however, illuminating. Consequently a brief survey is made at this point of the chief rationales of the mortgagee's rights advanced by courts and writers.

MORTGAGEE vs. ASSUMING GRANTEE— THIRD PARTY BENEFICIARY [68]

261. By a growing weight of authority, a mortgagee has a direct right as third party beneficiary of a contract against an assuming grantee of a mortgagor.

The first and most important view is that the mortgagee is allowed to sue the assuming grantee simply as a third party beneficiary of a contract.[69] The great weight of au-

---

65. E. g., contrast the test for permitting the mortgagee to sue an assuming grantee as laid down in Connecticut and in New York, both states accepting the view that the mortgagee may sue as a third party beneficiary. Schneider v. Ferrigno, 1929, 110 Conn. 86, 147 A. 303, intent to confer a right of action sufficient; Vrooman v. Turner, 1877, 69 N.Y. 280, 25 Am.Rep. 195, not only intent of promisee-grantor to benefit mortgagee but an obligation owing from former to latter. See 1940, 88 U.Pa.L.Rev. 611, 612.

66. E. g., see the evolution in Virginia, 1939, 25 Va.L.Rev. 993; Warm, Rights and Liabilities of Mortgagee, Mortgagor, Grantee, 1936, 10 Temple L. Q. 116, 130 n. 41. See 1936, 84 U. of Pa.L.Rev. 909 for the development in Pennsylvania. See also 1940, 88 U.Pa.L.Rev. 611, 612, giving as examples the experience in Minnesota and Rhode Island.

67. This seems to be the situation in New York, with some resulting uncertainty as to which rule is to be applied. Seaver v. Ransom, 1918, 224 N.Y. 233, 120 N.E. 639, 2 A.L.R. 1187. See Friedman, Personal Liability on Mortgage Debts in New York, 1940, 50 Yale L.J. 224, 231–236, 236 n. 90; 1940, 88 U. of Pa.L.Rev. 611, 612; see also 1939, 25 Va.L. Rev. 993, 996, for the law in Virginia. In California by statute, West's Ann.Cal.Civ.Code § 1559, a third party beneficiary may sue the promisor directly. See note, 1938, 26 Cal.L.Rev. 627. A mortgagee may sue an assuming grantee of the mortgagor under this statutory provision. Bank of Alameda County v. Hering, 1933, 134 Cal.App. 570, 25 P. 2d 1004; see Alvord v. Spring Valley Gold Co., 106 Cal. 547, 40 P. 27. Yet he also is able to reach such an assuming grantee from his mortgagor, not under the statute, but on the theory of "equitable subrogation." Hopkins v. Warner, 1895, 109 Cal. 133, 41 P. 868; see Williston, Contracts, Rev.ed., 1115 n. 3. In some states by statute in the enforcement of a debt secured by a mortgage the mortgage must be foreclosed before there can be any judgment for a deficiency. In such jurisdictions the liability of the assuming grantee is limited to the amount of the deficiency. E.g., Kenyon Inv. Co. v. Belmont St. Bank, 1923, 69 Mont. 282, 221 P. 286; Hopkins v. Warner, supra. See 1931, 17 Va.L.Rev. 844, 848.

68. "Where the performance of a promise in a contract will benefit a person other than the promisee, that person is classified as a * * * beneficiary." Aetna Life Ins. Co. v. Maxwell, C.C.A.W. Va.1937, 89 F.2d 988, 993. Beneficiaries who may recover are of two kinds, donee beneficiaries and creditor beneficiaries. Id. A person is classified as a creditor beneficiary when "the performance of the promise will satisfy an actual or supposed or asserted duty of the promisee to the beneficiary." Restatement, Contracts, § 133(1)b. See Aetna Life Ins. Co. v. Maxwell, supra. The leading American case permitting a creditor beneficiary a direct right against the promisor is Lawrence v. Fox, 1859, 20 N.Y. 268. He is a donee beneficiary "when the promise is in the nature of a gift or confers upon the beneficiary a right against a promisor to some performance which the promisee is under no obligation to render." Aetna Life Ins. Co. v. Maxwell, supra. See Restatement, Contracts, § 133(1)a which adds that there must not be a "supposed or asserted" obligation. In jurisdictions accepting the third party beneficiary rationale the mortgagee as a general proposition recovers, if at all, as a creditor beneficiary. However, see § 265, infra, discussing the case where the promisee-grantor is under no liability to the mortgagee. See, also, § 259, supra, as to rights of a transferor against an assuming grantee after a break in the chain of assumptions.

69. E.g., Burr v. Beers, 1861, 24 N.Y. 178, 80 Am.Dec. 327.

The two most enlightening discussions of the rights of third party beneficiaries, of which the mortgagee is one of the most important, are Williston, Contracts for the Benefit of a Third Person, 1902, 15 Harv.L.Rev. 767, and Corbin, Contracts for the Benefit of Third Persons, 1918, 27 Yale L.J. 1008. See also Whittier, Contract Beneficiaries, 1923, 32 Yale L.J. 790; Hening, History of the Beneficiary's Action in Assumpsit, 1909, 3 Select Essays in Anglo-American Legal History; Finlay, Contracts for the Benefit of Third Persons, 1939; 1940, 26 Va.L.Rev. 778. For other discussions, dealing primarily with the assuming grantee of a mortgagor, see Friedman, Personal Liability on Mortgage Debts in New York, 1940, 50 Yale L.J. 224; Mechem, Assumption of Mortgages, 1884, 18 Cent.L.J. 23; Tucker, Per-

thority accepts this view [70] but this fact does not free it from difficulty. The right of recovery depends upon theories and rules of general contract law [71] which are still in a

period of growth, not only varying from state to state but within a given jurisdiction.[72] Changes in the general law, both as to basic dogma and specific rule, will affect the rights of the mortgagee under mortgage law, the latter being merely specific applications of the broader doctrines. Since some courts do not clearly see that this last is true, the application of new ideas to mortgage law is frequently delayed and some confusion occurs.[73] Among the more important points on

sonal Liability of One Assuming Payment of a Deed of Trust, 1917, 4 Va.L.Rev. 464; Glassie, The Assuming Vendee, 1923, 9 Va.L.Rev. 196; Hand, Purchase of Incumbered Land—Rights and Liabilities of Parties, 1899, 48 Cent.L.J. 489; Warm, Some Aspects of the Rights and Liabilities of Mortgagee, Mortgagor, and Grantee, 1936, 10 Temple L.Q. 116; Berick, Personal Liability for Deficiency in Mortgage Foreclosures, 1934, 8 U. of Cin.L.Rev. 103; notes, 1939, 25 Va.L.Rev. 993 (Virginia law); 1938, 13 St. John's L.Rev. 215; 1923, 11 Cal.L.Rev. 139; 1923, 11 Cal.L.Rev. 429; 1938, 26 Cal.L.Rev. 627; 1910, 10 Col.L.Rev. 765; Note, The Third Party Beneficiary Concept: A Proposal, 1957, 57 Col.L. Rev. 406; 1919, 4 Cornell L.Q. 53; 1924, 9 Cornell L.Q. 213; 1936, 84 U. of Pa.L.Rev. 909; 1931, 17 Va.L.Rev. 844; 1933, 19 Va.L.Rev. 624; 1930, 39 Yale L.J. 746. See also 1922, 21 A.L.R. 439; 1927, 47 A.L.R. 339. As to the right of a mortgagee as creditor beneficiary in Pennsylvania under the statute in that state, see 1949, 10 U. of Pitt.L.Rev. 419. In addition, see authorities cited in preceding footnote this section. See also notes 50–54, supra, § 259.

70. See elaborate compilation of authorities in 1922, 21 A.L.R. 439, 454; 1927, 47 A.L.R. 339, 341. See also Williston, Contracts, Rev.ed., 1112, n. 13, listing thirty-six jurisdictions as permitting a mortgagee to sue at law an assuming granted of the mortgagor.

71. "There appears to be no good reason why the contract whereby a grantee assumes a mortgage should be treated differently from any other contract made for the benefit of a third person, notwithstanding historical precedent to the contrary." 1940, 88 U. of Pa.L.Rev. 611, 613. See Corbin, Contracts for the Benefit of Third Persons, 1918, 27 Yale L.J. 1008, 1016, accord. This statement is true as a matter of general principle. It is also true in most jurisdictions as a matter of actual development. However, historically to some extent, the right of the mortgagee was dealt with separately, possibly because the mortgagee tried to reach an assuming grantee in equity before creditors of other debts made similar attempts. See Williston, Contracts, Rev. ed., § 384. Further, in some states statutory provisions applicable only to mortgage assumption cases or to third party beneficiary cases other than mortgage assumptions have affected the **law.** E. g., M.C.L.A. (Mich.) § 619.26 limiting a mortgagee to a deficiency decree in foreclosure. Both the grantee and the mortgaged land must be within the jurisdiction. Kollen v. Sooy, 1912, 172 Mich. 214, 137 N.W. 808. See Grismore, Beneficiary Contracts in Michigan, 1938, 8 Detroit L.Rev. 1. Similarly statutory provisions in Pennsylvania have affected the mortgagee's right of recovery. Act of June 12, 1878, P.L. 205(2); 21 P.S. 655, 656. See 1936, 84 U.Pa.L.Rev. 909; and § 257, note 1, for Pennsylvania authorities as to the right of a mort-

gagee against an assuming grantee of the mortgagor, for the situation in Virginia and West Virginia, see 1939, 25 Va.L.Rev. 993; Warm, Rights and Liabilities of Mortgagor, Mortgagee, Grantee, 1936, 10 Temple L.Q. 116, 130 n. 41. Look also at Schneider v. Ferrigno, 1929, 110 Conn. 86, 147 A. 303. See generally, Williston, Contracts, Rev.ed., §§ 357, 383; Corbin, Contracts for the Benefit of Third Persons, 1918, 27 Yale L.J. 1008, 1028.

72. "The history of the third party beneficiary doctrine since *Lawrence v. Fox* has been a checkered one of sorties and retreats." Friedman, op. cit. supra note 64, 233. See id., 236; 1940, 88 U.Pa.L.Rev. 611, 612; Williston, Contracts, Rev.ed., § 383. In Berick, Personal Liability for Deficiency in Mortgage Foreclosures, 1934, 8 U. of Cin.L.Rev. 103, 112, the beneficiary cases are grouped into three classes. 1. Those permitting the third person to sue only if the promise was made for his sole and exclusive benefit. 2. Those requiring as prerequisites: (a) a clear intent to benefit the third person, and (b) an obligation owing by the promisee to the third person. These limitations were laid down by the New York courts "because of early efforts to find a justification for the doctrine." See other discussions of the New York cases in notes, 1919, 4 Cornell L. Q. 53; 1918, 27 Yale L.J. 1008, 1027; Friedman, op. cit. supra, this note. Those which do not concern themselves with justifying the rule but accept it as well established, and require only an intent to benefit, with the one limitation that incidental or indirect benefit to the third person is insufficient to confer rights upon him. See Aetna Life Ins. Co. v. Maxwell, C.C.A.W.Va.1937, 89 F.2d 988, 993. See also Restatement, Contracts, §§ 133–136, 147.

73. "There is confusion not only between the different courts, but confusion in the decisions in many jurisdictions in the same court." Tweeddale v. Tweeddale, 1903, 116 Wis. 517, 519, 93 N.W. 440, 442, 61 L.R.A. 509, 96 Am.St.Rep. 1003. A thorough survey of the general law and theory of third party beneficiaries is, of course, beyond the possible scope of this work. However, the importance of a knowledge of that law and theory and the danger of an inadequate understanding of it is exemplified in a criticism of cases allowing the mortgagee to sue an assuming grantee at law. See Warm, Rights and Liabilities of Mortgagee, Mortgagor, Grantee, 1936, 10 Temple L.Q. 116, 130. The author bases his strictures upon the notion that the parties must

which there is divergence are whether the promisee must be liable to the mortgagee; [74] when the right vests indefeasibly in him; [75] how far it may be affected by defenses between (a) the assuming grantee and his promisee and (b) the promisee and the mortgagee; [76] the effect of subsequent agreements between the promisor and promisee on the rights of the mortgagee, [77] and the consequences as to a mortgagee's other rights of binding extensions of time or releases by him to an assuming grantee. [78] Where the third party beneficiary doctrine is accepted as the foundation of the mortgagee's right, it is clearly an independent one enforceable by an action at law. [79]

MORTGAGEE vs. ASSUMING GRANTEE— "SURETYSHIP" SUBROGATION

262. Many jurisdictions, including some that recognize the direct right of the mortgagee, permit the mortgagee to reach an assuming grantee through equitable subrogation to the mortgagor's rights against him. This is on the theory that the mortgagor is a surety and

contract with an intention to benefit primarily the third party, in this case the mortgagee. Such an intent would be sufficient, but it is not so generally regarded as essential as to justify adopting it as the exclusive test in a confused and growing area of the law. See 1940, 26 Va.L.Rev. 778. See also Williston, Contracts, Rev.ed., § 357; Corbin, Contracts for the Benefit of Third Persons, 1918, 27 Yale L.J. 1008, 1015, 1017; Restatement, Contracts, § 133.

74. See § 265, infra.

75. See § 268, infra.

76. See § 267, infra.

77. See Restatement, Contracts, §§ 142, 143.

78. See §§ 269–271, infra.

79. "The promise creates a duty which the promisor must perform, and this duty, if not performed, may be made the basis of an action by the beneficiary against the promisor." Aetna Life Ins. Co. v. Maxwell, C.C.A.W.Va., 1937, 89 F.2d 988, 993. See Williston, Contracts, Rev.ed., §§ 357, 383; Restatement, Contracts, §§ 136(1)a; 135, 141(1).

In allowing the mortgagee to sue the assuming grantee in an action at law, the court in Rosenberg v. Rolling Inn, Inc., 1957, 212 Md. 552, 129 A.2d 924, noted in 1958, 18 Md.L.Rev. 138, seemed to recognize the mortgagee's right as that of a third party creditor-beneficiary.

the rights are security given to him by the grantee as principal, to which the mortgagee, as creditor is entitled.

A second group of cases, invoking a "suretyship" theory of solution invoke what is called the doctrine of equitable subrogation. [80] The principle of these cases is "that in equity the creditor is entitled to the benefit of all collateral obligations, for the payment of the debt, which a person standing in the situation of a surety for others has received for his indemnity, and to relieve him or his property from liability for such payment." [81] In order for the principle to apply

80. The use of the term subrogation in this sense has been criticized as suggesting "analogies which do not exist, with the position of a surety who has paid the debt." In such a case, and this is the one in which the word is most commonly employed, the surety-debtor is subrogated to the rights of the creditor he has paid. As used here it means that the mortgagee-creditor is enabled to reach a right in the hands of his debtor, the mortgagor, against a third party, the assuming grantee, on the theory that the mortgagor-debtor had become a surety-debtor. See Williston, Contracts for the Benefit of a Third Person, 1902, 15 Harv.L.Rev. 767, 789. See also Arant, Suretyship, 370 et seq. But see Warm, Rights and Liabilities of Mortgagee, Mortgagor, Grantee, 1936, 10 Temple L.Q. 116, 129.

81. King v. Whitely, N.Y.1843, 10 Paige 465. Earlier cases in New York are Curtis v. Tyler & Allen, N.Y.1842, 9 Paige 432; Halsey v. Reed, N.Y.1842, 9 Paige 446. See Jennings, Creditor's Rights in Surety's Securities, 1938, 22 Minn.L.Rev. 316; Restatement, Security, § 140(1). This "suretyship" theory of solution has been accepted in a good many jurisdictions: Hopkins v. Warner, 1895, 109 Cal. 133, 136, 41 P. 868; Crawford v. Edwards, 1876, 33 Mich. 354; Klapworth v. Dressler, 1860, 13 N.J.Eq. 62, 78 Am.Dec. 69; Crowell v. Hospital of St. Barnabas, 1876, 27 N.J.Eq. 650, 655; Willard v. Worsham, 1882, 76 Va. 392; Keller v. Ashford, 1890, 133 U.S. 610, 623, 10 S.Ct. 494, 497, 33 L.Ed. 667. See Warm, Rights and Liabilities of Mortgagee, Mortgagor, Grantee, 1936, 10 Temple L.Q. 116, 128; Friedman, Personal Liability on Mortgage Debts in New York, 1940, 50 Yale L.J. 224, 230; Glassie, The Assuming Vendee, 1923, 9 Va.L.Rev. 196, 199; notes, 1931, 17 Va.L.Rev. 844, 847; 1933, 19 Va.L. Rev. 624, 625; 1910, 10 Col.L.Rev. 765, 767; 1937, 4 U. of Chi.L.Rev. 469, 476; 1931, 25 Ill.L.Rev. 721, 723; 1938, 26 Cal.L.Rev. 627; 1939, 25 Va.L.Rev. 993, 996; 1922, 21 A.L.R. 439, 451; 1927, 47 A.L.R. 339, 341. It has been adversely criticized. See Corbin, Contracts for Benefit of Third Persons, 1918, 27 Yale L.J. 1008, 1015. The grantee has deposited with the grantor nothing except a promise to protect him against the enforcement of the mortgage debt. To treat this as security given to him is **at**

a "suretyship" situation must exist. A suretyship situation requires a triangle with the person at each foot of the triangle being bound to the creditor at the apex by their respective contracts.[82] Where there is only one person owing a single obligation to another person no suretyship situation can exist. For a person's duty to be that of a surety, in addition to his obligation to the creditor, there must be a separate one, the principal, for whose performance it stands surety. In a mortgage, to begin with, there is a personal obligation running between the mortgagor and the mortgagee. There is also, existing between the mortgagee and the land in the hands of the mortgagor, a relationship normally referred to as a security interest in the property. When the land is transferred by the mortgagor to a grantee, as between the continuing personal duty of the mortgagor to the mortgagee and the continuing relationship between the mortgagee and the land now in the hands of another, the situation may be treated with some verisimilitude as one of suretyship.[83] In such a case the mortgagee has two rights, one against the land, the other against the mortgagor. Which one is surety and which is principal depends upon the terms of the transfer.[84] If the mortgagor received the full value of the land and agreed to pay the debt he would be principal and the land would be surety. And *vice versa* if the transferee paid only the value of the redemption interest and took "subject" to the mortgage or assumed it.[85]

When the mortgagor transfers to an assuming grantee, the suretyship situation just described will exist as between the mortgagor, the land and the mortgagee.[86] But the suretyship situation to which the cases purport to apply the principle is a different and additional one in which the assuming grantee personally, not the land, is the principal. If the assumption creates a new direct right in the mortgagee against the assuming grantee, a suretyship situation results in which the new right is the principal obligation and the old right against the mortgagor becomes that of a surety. However, unless the mortgagee does acquire such a separate right against the assuming grantee in addition to his continuing personal right against the mortgagor no suretyship relation in the ordinary sense can exist.[87] If the assuming grantee is not personally a principal, i. e., obligated directly to the mortgagee, his promise to the mortgagor to pay the debt cannot be regarded as the collateral security given by him, as principal, to the mortgagor, as his surety, for indemnity against liability to the mortgagee. It follows that, if the situation is really one of suretyship, the courts actually are recognizing that the contract of assumption creates a new right in the mortgagee against the assuming grantee—a result in substance no different from that which recognizes openly that it does so under the doctrine that the beneficiary of a contract may enforce it.[88] In spite of this, the theory

---

variance with the ordinary understanding of the term. See Arant, Suretyship, 370 et seq.

82. See Glenn, Mortgages, § 268; 1937, 4 U. of Chi. L.Rev. 469, 476.

83. See 1937, 4 U. of Chi.L.Rev. 469, 479. But see Penfield v. Goodrich, N.Y.1877, 10 Hun 41, overruled by Murray v. Marshall, 1884, 94 N.Y. 611; Sheperd v. May, 1885, 115 U.S. 595, 6 S.Ct. 119, 29 L.Ed. 456; Friedman, Discharge of Mortgage Debts, 1943, 52 Yale L.J. 771, 777.

84. See §§ 247, 252, 253, supra.

85. Id.

86. See § 259, supra.

87. 1937, 4 U. of Chi.L.Rev. 469, 476. But see Friedman, Discharge of Mortgage Debts, 1943, 52 Yale L.J. 771, 796, "True, the conventional suretyship triangle is not present but similar logic might once have been urged against the creation of constructive and resulting trusts. * * * Furthermore, the right of subrogation, and the penalty for its impairment, appears in situations other than that of conventional suretyship."

88. "For the mortgagor to be a surety, it is necessary that the mortgagee have an independent right against the grantee. Yet for the mortgagee to get this 'direct' right by the above analogy [i. e., that of suretyship subrogation of the mortgagee to the rights of the mortgagor, it was necessary to assume that the mortgagor was a surety; thus assuming

on which the process of enforcement goes is that the mortgagee is enforcing his right against the mortgagor-surety and reaching the assuming grantee through the right which the mortgagor as surety has against him. Consequently the mortgagee's right on this theory must be classed as a derivative one.[89] A logical consequence is that, if the promisee-grantor is not bound to pay the debt he is not a surety, the doctrine is inapplicable, and the mortgagee cannot reach the assuming grantee.[90]

One other thing to note is that the doctrine is equitable.[91] Further, it would seem

that the mortgagor should always be joined as a party since it is his right that is being enforced.[92] However courts frequently permit the suit to be maintained without joinder of the mortgagor.[93]

MORTGAGEE vs. ASSUMING GRANTEE— EQUITABLE ASSETS

263. Some authorities allow the mortgagee to reach the assuming grantee's promise as an asset of the mortgagor of a sort that can be got at only with the aid of equity.

A third rationale, advanced by Professor Williston and known as the equitable assets theory,[94] has some following in the authorities.[95] Instead of looking at the assuming grantee's promise to the grantor-promisee as indemnity security in the latter's hands as surety, given to him by the principal obligor, it is regarded as an asset of the mortgagee's only debtor, the mortgagor, of a sort which can be reached only by the aid of equity.[96]

The theory has certain distinct merits. On the one hand it avoids both the difficulty of giving reasons why a person who is not privy to a contract may nevertheless maintain an action on it against the promisor and the practical objection to permitting it that the promisor may be exposed to possible

---

the conclusion." 1937, 4 U. of Chi.L.Rev. 469, 476. "The doctrine of subrogation has no doubt been very beneficial in spite of fiction and artificiality; but in this instance it has been used to confer new security and new rights upon a creditor, as a gift out of a clear sky. In suretyship it is used only as against one who is already legally indebted in order to secure the fulfillment of that legal duty. A doctrine whose purpose was the enforcement of a previously recognized duty cannot properly be given as the sole reason for creating an entirely new duty." Corbin, Contracts for the Benefit of Third Persons, 1918, 27 Yale L.J. 1008, 1015.

"The extension of the subrogation theory to cover this case, where the promisor was not indebted to the third party by reason of any operative fact other than his promise to the promisee, is merely a cumbrous intellectual expedient for holding that a contract between two parties can create an enforceable right in a third." Corbin, supra, at 1016, n. 32.

89. See cases, note 81, supra. See also Binns v. Baumgartner, 1929, 105 N.J.Eq. 58, 60, 146 A. 879, "The equity on which his relief depends is the right of the mortgagor against his vendee, to which right the mortgagee is permitted to succeed, by substituting himself in the place of the mortgagor." Duvall-Percival Trust Co. v. Jenkins, C.C.A.Kan.1926, 16 F.2d 223, 226.

90. See § 261, infra.

91. See Duvall-Percival Trust Co. v. Jenkins, C.C.A. Kan.1926, 16 F.2d 223, 226, Osborne, Cases Property Security, 2d Ed., 465; Rector v. Lyda, 1921, 180 N. C. 577, 105 S.E. 170, 21 A.L.R. 411. See also authorities, note 81, supra. However even where the beneficiary is allowed a direct right, the mortgagee may sue in equity for foreclosure of the mortgage and obtain a deficiency decree against the mortgagor and the assuming grantee. E. g., Scott v. Wharton, 1933, 226 Ala. 601, 148 So. 308; Elliott v. Cravens, 1930, 182 Ark. 893, 33 S.W.2d 373; Enns-Halbe Co. v. Templeton, 1931, 101 Fla. 609, 135 So. 135; Grimes v. Kelloway, 1927, 204 Iowa 1220, 216 N.W. 953; Walser v. Farmers' Trust Co., 1933, 126 Ohio St. 367, 185 N.E. 535; see Burr v. Beers, 1861,

24 N.Y. 178, 80 Am.Dec. 327; Walsh & Simpson, Cases Security Transactions, 309, Campbell, Cases on Mortgages, 2d ed. 418.

92. See Williston, Contracts, Rev.ed., § 385.

93. See, e. g., Keller v. Ashford, 1890, 133 U.S. 610, 626, 10 S.Ct. 494, 33 L.Ed. 667.

94. Williston, Contracts for the Benefit of a Third Person, 1902, 15 Harv.L.Rev. 766, 767.

95. See, e. g., cases note 60, supra; Restatement, Contracts, § 136, Comment d.

96. "Obviously a promise to pay a debt due a third person cannot be taken on an execution against the debtor, nor is it the subject of garnishment; for the promisor, if he is willing to perform his promise, cannot be compelled to do anything else, and as the promise is not to pay the promisee, the promisor cannot be charged as garnishee or trustee for him. The aid of equity is, therefore, necessary in order to compel the application of such property to the creditor's claim, and acting as it does by personal decree, equity can readily give the required relief." Williston, op. cit. supra note 94.

double liability on one promise.[97] On the other hand, it escapes the fictitious, or apparently contradictory,[98] aspects of the "suretyship" solution which seems to create, or at least recognize the existence of, a primary personal obligation of the assuming grantee running to the mortgagee and yet holds that the only way to realize on that obligation is by reaching, in equity, security in the form of a promise to indemnify given by the grantee-promisor as principal to his grantor-promisee as surety.[99]

There are, nevertheless, certain aspects of the theory that have aroused adverse comment. For one thing, the asset is a peculiar sort of one in that, unlike other assets, it is available only to one particular creditor, the mortgagee.[1] This is because the promisor cannot be required to do anything other than what he promised. This feature has caused one critic to assert that "[t]o apply the 'equitable asset' theory is merely to recognize the third party beneficiary's right under another and mis-descriptive name." [2] This is

not, of course, entirely true, for the right on this theory is purely derivative,[3] a fact that has important consequences.[4] Another possible criticism of the doctrine is that, by offering a good, if not perfect solution of the problem, it tends to retard the complete triumph of the third party beneficiary direct right rule.

MORTGAGEE vs. ASSUMING GRANTEE—MISCELLANEOUS

264. In some jurisdictions statutes give the mortgagee a right against the assuming grantee either expressly or by construction. In a few others the courts, predicating the relief upon the substantive rights of the mortgagee against the mortgagor and of the latter against his assuming grantee, permit the mortgagee to proceed directly against the grantee to avoid plurality of actions and harassment of the mortgagor.

A few authorities offer solutions which are procedural [5] in nature. One of these is that statutes providing that action shall be brought in the name of the real party in interest gives to the mortgagee a right to sue the assuming grantee.[6] The prior question

---

97. "In a bill against the indebted promisee and the promisor, the court can order the promisor to perform his promise by paying the plaintiff. As the promisee is a party to the litigation, his rights will be concluded by such a decree, and the promisor will not be subjected to the hardship of the possibility of two actions against him by virtue of a single promise. As in the case of garnishment, the payment to the plaintiff will discharge the obligation to the promisee." Williston, op. cit. supra note 94. See § 259, supra.

98. The logical corollary of the reasoning by which the mortgagee is given a right to reach the "security" in the hands of promisee-grantor as surety is that he has a direct right against the principal. To confine him to asserting his right against the mortgagor-surety only and reaching the principal solely through the promise made to him either negates the existence of the alleged suretyship situation or imposes on it unexplained restrictions.

99. See note 80, supra.

1. See note 96, supra. If the creditor collected out of other property of the debtor-promisee any creditor of the latter would then be able to reach the claim he would have against the promisor. See § 259, supra.

2. Corbin, Contracts for the Benefit of Third Persons, 1918, 27 Yale L.J. 1008, 1021. "By differentiating this particular creditor from other creditors and this particular 'asset' from other assets we are

merely recognizing that he has obtained a special right in personam as against the promisor, a right that is created by a contract to which he was not a party. He gains this special right because the contracting parties intended that he should have it, or at least that the performance should go direct to him." Idem. But see Friedman, Personal Liability on Mortgage Debts, 1940, 50 Yale L.J. 224, 230.

3. Williston, Contracts, Rev.ed., § 364.

4. E. g., on the ability of the promisee to release the promisor, on the availability of supervening defenses of the promisee against the mortgagee, the necessity of the promisee being obligated to the mortgagee, etc. See §§ 267, ff, infra.

5. The equitable assets theory also may be classed as such. Because of its stress upon the substantive rights which are the basis of the procedural method of reaching the assuming grantee as well as the argument that, in effect, it is simply a recognition of a substantive direct right by the mortgagee against the grantee it is not labeled as such.

6. Marianna Lime Products Co. v. McKay, 1933, 109 Fla. 275, 147 So. 264; Cooper v. Bane, 1923, 110 Neb. 74, 193 N.W. 97; see Ellis v. Harrison, 1891, 104 Mo. 270, 277, 16 S.W. 198; Hepburn, Cas. Code Pleading, 1901, 233.

is, of course, whether he is the real party in interest. And that goes back to the question of substantive law as to whether the promise of the assuming grantee creates any right against him in favor of the mortgagee.[7] Other statutes specifically state that a mortgagee may sue on the contract of assumption.[8]

It is not entirely clear whether, assuming the mortgagee may bring his action by virtue of a statute, the right he is enforcing is a direct one or a derivative one. It should depend upon whether the statute is interpreted to be merely procedural or whether it creates substantive rights.[9] If the latter, the right so created would seem to be direct. If the former, the substantive law apart from statute would determine.

Another small group of cases assert that the mortgagee is permitted to reach the assuming grantee to avoid plurality of actions and harassment of the mortgagor.[10] Here again, no new rationale of the substantive right itself is advanced. Rather the existence of the procedural relief is predicated upon the existence of a substantive right by the mortgagee against the mortgagor which in turn makes operative a right over by the

mortgagor against his assuming grantee.[11] In other words the right of the mortgagee here, as in the "suretyship" or equitable assets rationales, is derivative.

SUCCESSIVE PURCHASERS

265. **Where there are successive purchasers of the mortgaged property, each one assuming the mortgage, the mortgagee may charge any one of them on his promise; and he may do so even after the grantee has parted with the property. There is a division of authority as to whether assuming grantees subsequent to an intermediate non-liable grantee may be held by the mortgagee.**

It frequently happens that there is a series of sales of the mortgaged property with each grantee in turn agreeing with his immediate grantor to assume the mortgage. In such a case all of them become liable to the mortgage creditor who may successfully invoke as to each one in succession whichever doctrine enabled him to reach the first grantee of the mortgagor.[12] The same reasoning which justifies holding the first grantee by virtue of his promise to the mortgagee's debtor applies to charge the second grantee by reason of his promise to the first grantee and so on down to the last grantee. If the mortgagee reached the first grantee derivatively through the right of the mortgagor against him he can reach the second one derivatively through the right of the first grantee since the mortgagor, whose right he is using could have done so. If his right is a direct one as creditor beneficiary of the contract between his original debtor, the mortgagor, and the first grantee, so too his right will be a direct one against the second grantee as creditor beneficiary of the assumption contract between his new

7. See Corbin, Contracts for the Benefit of Third Persons, 1918, 27 Yale L.J. 1008, 1029; Williston, Contracts, Rev.ed., § 366.

8. E. g., Schneider v. Ferrigno, 1929, 110 Conn. 86, 147 A. 303.

9. See Warm, Rights and Liabilities of Mortgagee, Mortgagor, Grantee, 1936, 10 Temple L.Q. 130, n. 42, criticizing Schneider v. Ferrigno, supra note 8.

10. "Recovery * * * is adjudged in a court of equity to the mortgagee not in virtue of any original equity residing in him. He is allowed, by a mere rule of procedure, to go directly against the person ultimately liable, in order to avoid circuity of action, and save the mortgagor, as the intermediate party, from being harassed for the payment of the debt, and then driven to seek relief over against the person who has indemnified him, and upon whom the liability will ultimately fall." Crowell v. Hospital of St. Barnabas, 1876, 27 N.J.Eq. 650, 656. See Biddle v. Pugh, 1900, 59 N.J.Eq. 480, 481, 45 A. 626; Y. M. C. A. v. Crofts, 1898, 34 Or. 106, 114, 55 P. 439, 441, 75 Am.St.Rep. 568; Osborne v. Cabell, 1883, 77 Va. 462, 467.

11. "The equity on which his relief depends is the right of the mortgagor against his vendee, to which he is permitted to succeed by substituting himself in the place of the mortgagor." Crowell v. Hospital of St. Barnabas, 1876, 27 N.J.Eq. 650, 656. See Osborne v. Cabell, 1883, 77 Va. 462, 467.

12. Robson v. O'Toole, 1919, 45 Cal.App. 63, 187 P. 110; Carnahan v. Tousey, 1883, 93 Ind. 561; Corning v. Burton, 1894, 102 Mich. 86, 62 N.W. 1040; Hurst v. Merrifield, 1933, 144 Or. 78, 23 P.2d 124.

obligor, the first grantee, and the second grantee. Moreover all who have thus assumed the mortgage are liable regardless of having in turn parted with land to subsequent grantees and even though the later transferees assumed the mortgage.[13] Each one's own valid contract, which is the source of his liability, is not affected by his selling the premises. His protection, in case he is forced to pay, lies in his rights against his own and subsequent grantees and the land.[14]

Where one of the successive transferees takes title without promising his vendor to assume the mortgage he incurs no personal responsibility to anyone for the payment of the debt.[15] If such a purchaser in turn sells to a grantee who promises him to pay the debt, the question arises whether the second purchaser, thus bound to his vendor, is liable also to the mortgage creditor. On this point there is diversity of decision.[16] His liability depends upon the rationale under which the mortgagee is allowed to hold an assuming grantee in the particular jurisdiction and the rules governing liability under the rationale followed in that jurisdiction.

Insofar as the mortgagee's rights against an assuming grantee are derivative, i.e., rest upon the theory that he is allowed to apply the rights of his own debtor through subrogation or as an equitable asset the mortgagee cannot compel payment by any transferee who takes after the break in the chain of assumptions. The assuming vendees in such a case have promised a vendor against whom the mortgage creditor has no right and, consequently, to whose claim against the assuming vendee he can lay no claim. The same would be true of those cases which permit the mortgagee to proceed against the assuming grantee to prevent plurality of actions, for in order to have plurality of actions there must first be a right of action by the mortgage creditor against the promisee-grantor. Hence the rule in all these cases is that the mortgagee's right stops with the last grantee who assumed in direct succession.[17]

In those jurisdictions which give the mortgagee a direct right as third party beneficiary of a contract there is a conflict in the decisions as to whether or not recovery should be allowed. Whether or not he can recover ought to depend upon the requirements in each particular jurisdiction in order for the right to arise in a third party beneficiary. A good many decisions can be grouped in this manner with assurance. A considerable number of others are not sufficiently definite in their statement of rationale to make classification certain.

The mortgagee is usually regarded as a creditor beneficiary. Since he actually has no right against the promisee-grantor, those cases that insist that an obligation to pay

---

13. See cases preceding note. In Pennsylvania, by virtue of the terms of a statute, it is possible that a grantee who expressly assumed the mortgage would not continue liable unless there was express assumption of a continuing liability. Sloan v. Klein, 1910, 230 Pa. 132, 79 A. 403. See 1936, 84 U. of Pa.L.Rev. 909, 910. See, semble, § 259, n. 47, supra, as to right of the mortgagor against subsequent assuming grantees.

14. See §§ 258, 259, supra.

15. See §§ 247, 252, 258, supra.

16. See cases cited in succeeding footnotes. Also see notes, 1923, 11 Cal.L.Rev. 139; 1940, 88 U. of Pa.L. Rev. 611; 1932, 6 U. of Cin.L.Rev. 361; 1934, 8 U. of Cin.L.Rev. 103, 125; 1924, 9 Cornell L.Q. 213; 1931, 16 Minn.L.Rev. 114; 1927, 13 Va.L.Rev. 500; 1931, 17 Va.L.Rev. 844; 1930, 39 Yale L.J. 746; Restatement, Contracts, §§ 133, 144, Illustration 2; Williston, Contracts, Rev.Ed., § 386A. See also 1921, 12 A.L.R. 1528; L.R.A.1916D, 154.

Further, see § 259, semble, where the problem is one of the mortgagor, or other grantor, reaching an assuming grantee after a break in the chain of assumptions.

17. Ward v. De Oca, 1898, 120 Cal. 102, 52 P. 130; Morris v. Mix, 1896, 4 Kan.App. 654, 46 P. 58; Colorado Sav. Bk. v. Bales, 1917, 101 Kan. 100, 165 P. 843; Norwood v. De Hart, 1879, 30 N.J.Eq. 412; Eakin v. Shultz, 1900, 61 N.J.Eq. 156, 47 A. 274; Osborne v. Cabell, 1883, 77 Va. 462; see South Carolina Ins. Co. v. Kohn, 1917, 108 S.C. 475, 480, 95 S.E. 65. See also Berick, Deficiency in Mortgage Foreclosures, 1934, 8 U. of Cin.L.Rev. 103, 108.

Dail v. Campbell, 1961, 191 Cal.App. 416, 12 Cal.Rptr. 739, is in accord as to the remote grantee who assumed a purchase price mortgage where an intermediate grantee had not assumed the mortgage.

must exist in order for a creditor beneficiary to have rights against the assuming grantee would deny recovery to him as such.[18] Courts also deny recovery on the ground that there is no intent to benefit the mortgagee.[19] A broader test, adopted by the Restatement of Contracts classifies a person as a creditor beneficiary when the "performance of the promise will satisfy an actual or supposed or asserted duty of the promisee to the beneficiary."[20] If the stipulation was inserted intentionally,[21] it most likely was to guard against a supposed or possible liability of the promisee which did not in fact exist.[22] If so, it would fall under this test of a creditor beneficiary and it is possible to justify a good many decisions allowing recovery on this ground although the opinions in them do not explicitly adopt it.[23]

Some courts deny the mortgagee recovery as a creditor beneficiary and also as a donee beneficiary.[24] There are other courts that apparently recognize a right to recover as a donee beneficiary.[25] Some of them reason that since the non-assuming grantor is not personally liable to the mortgagee and is no longer owner of the premises he has no interest in the performance of the assumption promise. The only object of exacting such a stipulation is to confer a gratuitous benefit or right upon the mortgagee.[26] In others, the courts seem to assume the donative intent, treating it as a question of the power of the promisee to create such a right in the mortgagee. The reasoning on this is that, since the contract is enforceable by the promisee, he can direct that the performance go to whomsoever he wishes and the promisor cannot object.[27]

ASSUMPTION BY SECOND MORTGAGEE

266. A prior mortgagee cannot hold a subsequent mortgagee who agrees with the mortgagor to pay off the prior mortgage.

---

18. Vrooman v. Turner, 1877, 69 N.Y. 280, Walsh & Simpson, Cases Security Transactions, 312; Wager v. Link, 1892, 134 N.Y. 122, 31 N.E. 213; see Hinckley Estate Co. v. Gurry, 1935, 56 Idaho 38, 48 P.2d 1111; De Leon v. Rhines, 1934, 64 App.D.C. 73, 75, 74 F.2d 477, 479. See also 1923, 9 Cornell L.Q. 213; 1930, 39 Yale L.J. 746.

19. Case v. Egan, 1922, 57 Cal.App. 453, 207 P. 388; Y. M. C. A. v. Crofts, 1898, 34 Or. 106, 55 P. 439, 75 Am.St.Rep. 568; Fry v. Ausman, 1912, 29 S.D. 30, 135 N.W. 708, 39 L.R.A.,N.S., 150, Ann.Cas.1914C 842. See also cases in preceding note.

20. § 133(1) b. See also § 241, note 63, ante.

21. See Les Affreteurs Réunis v. Walford, [1919] A. C. 801, Lord Birkenhead, "In my experience important clauses do not 'find their way' into important contracts. They are on the contrary, the fruits of negotiation and consideration." While this may be true, and the sale of property is an important contract, nevertheless one may wonder whether in this country the inclusion of the clause may not have been due less to the "fruits of negotiation and consideration" than to a very prevalent habit of using printed forms in which they occur and failure to scrutinize them with care or else indifference to the inclusion of a clause that can do, so it may be thought, no harm. Of course if the inclusion was a mistake, the grantee could have reformation of the deed. Cushing v. Newbern, 1919, 75 Okl. 258, 183 P. 409; see 1940, 88 U. of Pa.L.Rev. 611, 614; cf., Restatement, Contracts, § 144.

22. See Williston, Contracts, Rev.ed., § 386 A; 1930, 39 Yale L.J. 746; 1923, 9 Cornell L.Q. 213.

23. Scott v. Wharton, 1933, 226 Ala. 601, 148 So. 308.

24. The cases in notes 18, 19, supra, may rest upon this ground. See 1930, 39 Yale L.J. 746; 1923, 9 Cornell L.Q. 213; 1940, 88 U.Pa.L.Rev. 611, 613.

25. Schneider v. Ferrigno, 1929, 110 Conn. 86, 147 A. 303, intent to confer right of action sufficient to make mortgagee a donee beneficiary; South Carolina Ins. Co. v. Kohn, 1917, 108 S.C. 475, 480, 95 S.E. 95. See 1931, 25 Ill.L.Rev. 723. Also cases in following footnotes.

26. Casselman's Adm'x v. Gordon & Lightfoot, 1916, 118 Va. 553, 88 S.E. 58; see 1939, 25 Va.L.Rev. 993, 997.

27. Dean v. Walker, 1883, 107 Ill. 540, 47 Am.Rep. 467; Marble Sav. Bank v. Mesarvey, 1897, 101 Iowa 285, 70 N.W. 198; Clement v. Willett, 1908, 105 Minn. 267, 117 N.W. 491, 17 L.R.A.,N.S., 1094; 127 Am.St.Rep. 562, 15 Ann.Cas. 1053; Crone v. Stinde, 1900, 156 Mo. 262, 55 S.W. 863; Hare v. Murphy, 1895, 45 Neb. 809, 64 N.W. 211, 29 L.R.A. 851; Brewer v. Maurer, 1882, 38 Ohio St. 543, 43 Am.Rep. 436; Mullin v. Claremont Realty Co., 1930, 39 Ohio App. 103, 177 N.E. 226; Walser v. Farmers' Trust Co., 1933, 126 Ohio St. 367, 185 N.E. 535; Merriman v. Moore, 1879, 90 Pa. 78, 7 W.N.C. 425; Title Guaranty etc. Co. v. Bushnell, 1921, 143 Tenn. 681, 228 S.W. 699, 12 A.L.R. 1512; Corkrell v. Poe, 1918, 100 Wash. 625, 171 P. 522, 12 A.L.R. 1524; Enos v. Sanger, 1897, 96 Wis. 150, 70 N.W. 1069, 37 L.R.A. 862, 65 Am.St.Rep. 38; Prudential Ins. Co. of America v. Clybourn Realty Co., 1934, 214 Wis. 409, 253 N.W. 397; Duvall-Percival Trust Co. v. Jenkins, C.C.A.Kan.1926, 16 F.2d 223, Osborne, Cases Property Security, 465 applying Missouri law.

When a mortgagor, instead of selling the property to a purchaser who assumes the mortgage, gives a second mortgage to one who agrees to pay off the first mortgage, the first mortgagee who seeks to recover on this contract is denied any right.[28] The second mortgagee, unlike a purchaser who has received property for which he must pay, as part of the price, the amount of the first mortgage, has received nothing from the mortgagor. In effect the second mortgagee's promise is to lend to the mortgagor the amount af the first mortgage by paying it to the first mortgagee.[29] Whether the mortgagor sued for breach of the promise or paid off the first mortgage and then sought reimbursement from the second mortgagee, his recovery, if permitted at all, would be for nominal damages. The only result of the breach is either that the mortgagor continues liable to the first mortgagee instead of becoming liable to the second mortgagee for the amount of the first mortgage, or else he has freed himself of his obligation to the first mortgagee without enriching the second mortgagee in any way. If the first mortgagee's ability to reach one who promises to pay off the mortgage is derivative it is clear that he would be reaching no right of the mortgagor that had any substantial value. If his right is being asserted as the direct right of a third party beneficiary, again the performance of the promise to him, even if he had a right to it, should give him no greater benefit than the promisee was entitled to. The cases, therefore, seem correctly decided.[30]

GRANTEE'S DEFENSES AGAINST MORTGAGEE

267. The defenses available to a transferee of a mortgagor against the mortgagee depend upon the terms of the transfer and the defenses he may assert against his transferor.

Whether or not the mortgagee can enforce the mortgage or the mortgage debt against a transferee of the mortgagor to a different extent than he could do so against the mortgagor had there been no transfer properly depends upon the terms of the transfer and the intention of the transferor.[31] If the transferee promises to take subject to or to assume a specific mortgage, the amount of which has been deducted from the agreed on purchase price of the property,[32] he becomes bound by contract to have the land in his hands subjected to payment of the full amount of the debt so agreed upon and, where he assumes its payment, to pay it. It is immaterial whether or not his promisee is actually indebted to that amount or not by an enforceable obligation.[33] By so including it and mak-

---

should agree with another, for a consideration moving from him, * * * to advance money to pay his debts, could be enforced by the parties whose claims were thus to be * * * paid." Garnsey v. Rogers, note 28, supra, 241.

31. See 1942, 141 A.L.R. 1184. Consequently, as has been pointed out, it becomes immaterial that a creditor beneficiary includes, as a rule of law, one to whom the promisor has promised to perform the promisee's duty though such duty is barred by the Statute of Limitations, or by a discharge in bankruptcy, or is unenforceable under the Statute of Frauds. See Williston, Contracts, Rev. ed., § 399, n. 2.

32. "In all the cases where it has been held that the grantee cannot question the validity of the mortgage, he has purchased the property on the basis of a clear title, at an agreed price, and has assumed to pay the mortgage debt as a part of the consideration, or the amount of such debt has been deducted from the purchase price of the land on the basis of such clear and complete title." Crawford v. Nimmons, 1899, 180 Ill. 143, 54 N.E. 209.

33. "If one assumes to pay a definite amount of the indebtedness of another, it is none of his concern whether the debt thus assumed is greater or less than the actual indebtedness." Oglesby v. South Georgia Grocery Co., 1917, 18 Ga.App. 401, 402, 89 S.E. 436.

---

28. Garnsey v. Rogers, 1872, 47 N.Y. 233, 7 Am.R. 440, Walsh & Simpson, Cases Security Transactions, 316; Savings Bank of Southern California v. Thornton, 1896, 112 Cal. 255, 44 P. 466. See Tiffany Real Prop., 3d ed., § 1441.

29. "Such an understanding is simply a promise to advance money to pay the debt of his grantor or mortgagor, which money, when advanced, the junior mortgagee can collect under his mortgage." Garnsey v. Rogers, note 28, supra, 240.

30. "If such a contract could be enforced by the creditor who would be incidentally benefited by its performance, every agreement by which one party

ing its payment binding on the land,[34] or the land and the transferee personally,[35] he has shown that he intends the obligation to be valid so far as his transferee is concerned,[36] and thus negatives any intention to confer a benefit upon him to the extent that the debt may be invalid or unenforceable. To permit the transferee under such circumstances to defeat the mortgagee on the ground that mortgagor was not liable in whole or in part would unjustly enrich the transferee [37] by enabling him to get the property for an amount less than he had agreed to pay for it, contrary to the intention of the transferor.[38] Where the grantee has assumed or taken subject to a specific mortgage most of the cases refuse to permit him to set up

usury [39] or other defenses [40] which would have been available to the mortgagor. A good many of the cases do so, however, on the ground either that the transferee is estopped [41] to deny the validity or extent of the mortgage or that the defense is personal to the mortgagor.[42] Neither doctrine is properly applicable. The amount of the debt is not a term of the mortgage to which estoppel

34. Crawford v. Nimmons, 1899, 180 Ill. 143, 54 N.E. 209; Freeman v. Auld, 1870, 44 N.Y. 50; Higbee v. Aetna Bldg. & Loan Ass'n, 1910, 26 Okl. 327, 109 P. 236, Ann.Cas.1912B, 223; see Scull v. Idler, 1911, 79 N.J.Eq. 466, 81 A. 746, 747.

35. Miller v. Thompson, 1876, 34 Mich. 10; Bogart v. Geo. K. Porter Co., 1924, 193 Cal. 197, 223 P. 959, 31 A.L.R. 1045; Burnett v. Young Men's B. & L. Ass'n, 1913, 155 Ky. 59, 159 S.W. 609, 48 L.R.A.,N. S., 840, see Hartley v. Harrison, 1861, 24 N.Y. 170, 172; 1942, 141 A.L.R. 1184, 1195.

36. If the grantee should resell to the mortgagor the latter will be able to set up, if he wishes, any defense available to him even though the grantee could not do so. Berk v. Isquith Productions, 1926, 98 N.J.Eq. 608, 131 A. 526.

37. See Campbell, Cases on Mortgages, 2d ed., n. 1; Crawford v. Nimmons, note 38, infra.

38. Where, for example, usury that could not be collected from the mortgagor formed part of the consideration for the purchase, it "would be permitting a fraud to allow the grantee to plead usury. If the mortgagor chooses to affirm his contract, and sets apart, out of the purchase price for the complete title, an amount sufficient to pay it, whether with an express agreement of the grantee to make such payment, or with an option to either pay or suffer foreclosure, the grantee cannot question the amount. If the usury has become a part of the consideration in the agreement between the mortgagor and his grantee, it is an affirmance of the debt by the mortgagor; and when the grantee contracts with a view to the payment of the incumbrance, equity demands that he shall pay it, or lose the property." Crawford v. Nimmons, 1899, 180 Ill. 143, 54 N.E. 209, Davis v. Davis, 1912, 19 Cal.App. 797, 127 P. 1051; Trusdell v. Dowden, 1890, 47 N.J.Eq. 396, 20 A. 972; U. S. Bond Co. v. Keahey, 1916, 53 Okl. 176, 155 P. 557, L.R.A.1917C, 829, accord.

39. Crawford v. Nimmons, 1899, 180 Ill. 143, 54 N.E. 209; Pinnell v. Boyd, 1880, 33 N.J.Eq. 190, reversed 33 N.J.Eq. 600; Central Holding Co. v. Bushman, 1927, 238 Mich. 261, 213 N.W. 120. See 1907, 8 L. R.A.,N.S., 814; 1914, 48 L.R.A.,N.S., 840; L.R.A. 1917C, 832. See also notes, 1933, 67 U.S.L.Rev. 163; 1936, 14 Tex.L.Rev. 559; 1935, 13 Tex.L.Rev. 375.

40. Freeman v. Auld, 1870, 44 N.Y. 50, failure of consideration; Davis v. Davis, 1912, 19 Cal.App. 797, 127 P. 1051 (statute of limitations); see Bogart v. Geo. K. Porter Co., 1924, 193 Cal. 197, 223 P. 959, 31 A.L.R. 1045, statute of limitations; Bennett v. Bates, 1884, 94 N.Y. 354, 370, invalidity of mortgage; Exchange Tr. Co. v. Ireton, 1923, 88 Okl. 262, 213 P. 309, forgery in creation of mortgage debt; see Roberts, The Defense of Jus Tertii in Mortgage Cases, 1936, 16 Bost.Univ.L.Rev. 644, for a survey of a large variety of defenses. In Bloch v. Budish, 1932, 279 Mass. 102, 180 N.E. 729, criticised in 1933, 19 Va.L.Rev. 624, an assuming grantee was given a defense against the mortgagee by reason of the mortgagor's bankruptcy. In Massachusetts a mortgagee's right against an assuming grantee is derivative. Most jurisdictions hold that the right of the mortgagor against the transferee does not pass into the general estate on bankruptcy of the mortgagor but remains available to the mortgagee. In such a case whether the defense of bankruptcy should be available to the grantee should depend on the same considerations as other defenses. The Massachusetts court, however, held that the mortgagor's right of indemnity did pass into his general estate on his bankruptcy and therefore the mortgagee could not reach the assuming grantee. What right the trustee in bankruptcy would have against the assuming grantee in such a case is not clear. Nor is it made definite how far the mortgagee may come in as a general creditor if the land is insufficient. Possibly the rule of the English cases would be followed. See 1933, 19 Va.L.Rev. 624, 629.

41. Key West Wharf & Coal Co. v. Porter, 1912, 63 Fla. 448, 58 So. 599; Freeman v. Auld, 1870, 44 N.Y. 50, Campbell, Cases on Mortgages, 2d ed., 427; see Bogart v. Geo. K. Porter Co., 1924, 193 Cal. 197, 223 P. 959, 31 A.L.R. 1045. See note, 1942, 141 A. L.R. 1184; Ann.Cas.1914A, 185.

42. Central Holding Co. v. Bushman, 1927, 238 Mich. 261, 213 N.W. 120; Higbee v. Aetna Bldg. & Loan Ass'n, 1910, 26 Okl. 327, 109 P. 236, Ann.Cas.1912B, 223; see Hartley v. Harrison, 1861, 24 N.Y. 170, 172. See 1940, 24 Minn.L.Rev. 124; 1939, 87 U. of Pa.L.Rev. 881; 1914, 48 L.R.A.,N.S., 840.

by deed applies and no showing of reliance by the mortgagee upon the terms of the promise, a requirement of estoppel generally, is insisted upon.[43] If the defense were really personal to the mortgagor it should be so in all cases. Yet in cases where the terms of the contract indicate that the transferee is binding himself only to be subject to or to pay the amount of the debt actually due or legally enforceable,[44] no objection is raised to his setting up defenses which have been at other times denied as personal to the mortgagor. The same is true if the conveyance is by way of gift.[45] In neither case would the grantee be getting any greater benefit than was intended by being allowed to cut down the mortgagee's recovery out of the land to the amount he could have collected had there been no transfer.

Where the grantee has not withheld any part of the purchase price, the grantee should be permitted to set up defenses to a foreclosure action which are available to the mortgagor.[46] And the same is true *a fortiori* if it is established that the full value of the land was paid with an agreement for the mortgagor to discharge the mortgage. It would be extraordinary to construe such a contract as intended to preclude the mortgagor from using his defenses if he wished to. The grantee is interested only in having the land free and clear of any incumbrance, not in having a portion of the money he has paid being earmarked for the full face of the mortgage debt to go to the mortgagee regardless of his right to it as against the mortgagor. Consequently, the grantee who is in the position of a surety with respect to the mortgagor should be entitled to have the mortgagor exonerate him only to the extent of the valid obligation of the mortgagor. So, too, if he paid the mortgagee, as he may, his right of reimbursement, whether enforced directly or by virtue of subrogation, should be no greater.[47] Since this is so, he should be entitled to discharge the debt by paying only what the mortgagor actually owed or, if the mortgagee sues to collect by foreclosure, limit the foreclosure recovery to the same amount.

A second mortgagee who takes his mortgage subject to a prior one should be permitted, in a foreclosure action by the first mortgagee, to set up defenses available to his mortgagor.[48] There is, however a diversity of view among the cases on the point. Those that deny the privilege do so on the ground that the defense is personal to the borrower and those in privity with him.[49] The cases allowing him to set up the defenses are clearly preferable.[50] The junior mortgagee has an interest in having the senior mortgage dis-

---

43. Of course, if the elements of estoppel are actually present and established a case could be decided upon this basis. The point is that the cases that deny a defense to the transferee on this rationale do not require that the elements of estoppel, as generally recognized, be present.

44. National Mut. Building & Loan Ass'n v. Retzman, 1903, 69 Neb. 667, 96 N.W. 204; Washington Nat. Building & Loan Ass'n v. Andrews, 1902, 95 Md. 696, 53 A. 573; National Loan & Ins. Co. of Detroit v. Stone, Tex.Civ.App.1898, 46 S.W. 67; Loder v. Hatfield, 1877, 71 N.Y. 92. A general assumption of all liens or debts would be given this interpretation. Purdy v. Coar, 1888, 109 N.Y. 448, 17 N.E. 352, 4 Am.St.Rep. 491; Crowe v. Malba Land Co., 1912, 76 Misc. 676, 135 N.Y.S. 454. See 1933, 67 U. S.L.Rev. 164.

45. First Nat. Bank v. Drew, 1907, 226 Ill. 622, 80 N. E. 1082, 10 L.R.A.,N.S., 857, 117 Am.St.Rep. 271.

46. Grove v. Great Northern Loan Co., 1908, 17 N.D. 352, 116 N.W. 345, 138 Am.St.Rep. 707; see Ford v. Washington Nat. Building & Loan Inv. Ass'n, 1904, 10 Idaho 30, 76 P. 1010, 109 Am.St.Rep. 192.

47. Cf., the reasoning, post, in the case of a junior mortgagee seeking to assert defenses of his mortgagor against a senior mortgagee.

48. As to the right of a subsequent mortgagee to raise the question of usury in a prior mortgage transaction, see notes, 1939, 87 U. of Pa.L.Rev. 881; 1939, 24 Minn.L.Rev. 124; 1930, 30 Col.L.Rev. 902.

49. Union Nat. Bank v. International Bank, 1888, 123 Ill. 510, 14 N.E. 859; Pritchett v. Mitchell, 1876, 17 Kan. 355, 22 Am.Rep. 287; Richardson v. Baker, 1872, 52 Vt. 617; Ready v. Huebner, 1879, 46 Wis. 692, 1 N.W. 344, 32 Am.Rep. 749. See 1940, 24 Minn.L.Rev. 124; 1939, 87 U. of Pa.L.Rev. 881.

50. Evans v. Faircloth-Byrd Merc. Co., 1910, 165 Ala. 176, 51 So. 785, 21 Ann.Cas. 1164; Pinnix v. Maryland Casualty Co., 1939, 214 N.C. 760, 200 S.E. 874, 121 A.L.R. 871. See 1940, 24 Minn.L.Rev. 124; 1939, 87 U. of Pa.L.Rev. 881.

charged at the least possible cost. Although he would be increasing the value of his security by thus cutting down the amount of the prior lien he would not be unjustly enriched by such a result. He has the right to collect the amount of his debt and will not get more than that in any event. Further, to deny such a right would confer an unwarranted benefit on the prior mortgagee at the expense of the junior encumbrancer. The junior mortgagee may pay off the senior mortgage to protect his own interest and then be subrogated to the senior mortgagee's rights against the mortgagor. The mortgagor could then limit recovery against him on the right to which he is subrogated to the amount that the senior mortgagee could have collected.[51]

A grantee of the mortgagor who assumes or takes subject to a specific mortgage is permitted to set up as against the mortgagee any defenses he could use against his transferor.[52] This clearly is correct where the mortgagee's rights are derived through the mortgagor.[53] But it is equally true where the rights are direct ones as a third party beneficiary.[54] The beneficiary of a contract should take his rights subject to any defects in them as against the promisee who created them in his behalf.

SUBSEQUENT DISCHARGE OR MODIFICATION OF RIGHTS BETWEEN GRANTOR AND GRANTEE

268. Stemming from variance in theory upon which the rights of a mortgagee are based, there is great diversity of authority as to whether, and under what circumstances, a contract of assumption may be ended or modified by a transaction between a grantor and an assuming grantee.

As to whether, and under what circumstances, a contract of assumption may be ended or modified by a transaction between a grantor and an assuming grantee so as to be legally operative as against the mortgagee there is great diversity of authority.[55] For the most part this variance stems from the differences in theory upon which the right of the mortgagee is rested.[56] If the security of the land is sufficient to pay the debt, the question is of no practical importance to the mortgagee, for no agreement between the mortgagor or later transferors and grantees can affect his mortgage on the land.[57] Where the mortgagee's right is held to be derivative, i. e., merely a right to avail himself of the benefit of the contract right of the transferor,[58] it is unquestioned that there can be no rescission or alteration after action has been brought by the mortgagee.[59] Indeed this is

51. 1939, 87 U. of Pa.L.Rev. 881.

52. Dunning v. Leavitt, 1881, 85 N.Y. 30, 39 Am.Rep. 617. On the right of an assuming grantee to set up, as against the mortgagee, defenses which he has against his grantor, see notes, 1934, 12 N.Car. L.Rev. 383; 1936, 22 Va.L.Rev. 355; 1938, 36 Mich. L.Rev. 847; Williston, Contracts, Rev.Ed., §§ 394, 395.

Any defense permitted to a second mortgagee who assumes the first mortgage should be set up in a foreclosure action by the first mortgagee.

53. Dunning v. Leavitt, note 52, supra; Waddell v. Roanoke Mut. Building & Loan Ass'n, 1935, 165 Va. 229, 181 S.E. 288, 100 A.L.R. 906, noted, 1936, 22 Va.L.Rev. 355.

54. Fulmer v. Goldfarb, 1937, 171 Tenn. 218, 101 S.W. 2d 1108, discussed, 1938, 36 Mich.L.Rev. 847.

55. For discussions and collections of authorities see Page, The Power of the Contracting Parties to Alter a Contract for Rendering Performance to a Third Person, 1937, 12 Wis.L.Rev. 141, 181; notes, 1927, 7 Boston U.L.Rev. 316; 1927, 13 Cornell L.Q. 123; 1910, 10 Col.L.Rev. 765; 1930, 24 Ill.L.Rev. 828; 1925, 9 Minn.L.Rev. 295; 1934, 8 U. of Cin.L. Rev. 103, 109, 122. See also 1922, 21 A.L.R. 439, 462; 1926, 41 A.L.R. 317; 1927, 47 A.L.R. 340, 342; 1936, 100 A.L.R. 911; Campbell, Cases on Mortgages, 2d Ed., 420 n.

56. See §§ 260–265, supra.

57. See § 247, supra.

58. See §§ 262–265, supra.

59. Wallace v. Hammonds, 1926, 170 Ark. 952, 281 S. W. 902; Field v. Thistle, 1899, 58 N.J.Eq. 339, 43 A. 1072, affirmed 60 N.J.Eq. 444, 46 A. 1099; Carnahan v. Tousey, 1883, 93 Ind. 561. See Restatement, Contracts, § 143. See also Morstain v. Kircher, 1933, 190 Minn. 78, 250 N.W. 727, discussed in note, 1934, 47 Harv.L.Rev. 1065, accord. The bringing of

the rule without dissent no matter what rationale is followed.[60] But short of bringing an action does the mortgagee have power to prevent the parties wiping out or changing this contract? One writer has argued that the mortgagee's right of subrogation vests as soon as the contract of assumption is made.[61] Most courts, however, would permit discharge or variation of the contract by the promisee at any time before suit by the mortgagee[62] with two limitations. 1. The mortgagee must not have materially changed his position in reliance on the assumption before he knows of the discharge or variation.[63] 2. The promisee's action is not in fraud of creditors.[64] These are the tests laid down in the Restatement of Contracts.[65] The general rule and first limitation are sound. The mortgagee has admittedly picked up an unexpected windfall in being able to reach the assuming grantee and there is no policy in favor of helping him[66] at the expense of free dealing between the grantee and grantor. If, however, the mortgagee can show material change of position in reliance on the promise, familiar principles would justify preventing the destruction or alteration of the asset.[67] The second limitation, except as to the amount the mortgage debt exceeds the value of the security, is on less firm ground. It has been criticized as invoking in favor of a secured creditor the doctrine of conveyances in fraud of creditors, which should be restricted to unsecured creditors.[68]

If the promisee is under no obligation to the mortgage creditor, he should be able to release the grantee at any time, even after action to foreclose is brought. Since the mortgagee's right to reach the assuming grantee depends upon his having an enforceable claim against the promisee-transferor, he has no ground to object to a release or alteration of the grantee's promise when that claim does not exist.[69]

---

the suit is effective to prevent alteration or discharge either on the ground that it constitutes a material change of position by the mortgagee in reliance upon the promise; or an assertion of dominion over it equivalent to the actual seizure of possession of a chattel by a pledgee or the fastening onto property of an attachment, execution or judgment lien. See Restatement, Contracts, § 143 for an expression of the first idea. See Glenn, Mortgages, §§ 180, 271, for a statement of the second.

60. Gifford v. Corrigan, 1889, 117 N.Y. 257, 22 N.E. 756, 6 L.R.A. 610, 15 Am.St.Rep. 508; New York Life Ins. Co. v. Aitkin, 1891, 125 N.Y. 660, 26 N.E. 732; Whiting v. Gearty, N.Y.1878, 14 Hun 498. See Friedman, Personal Liability on Mortgage Debts, 1940, 50 Yale L.Jour. 224, 238; note 1928, 13 Cornell L.Q. 123. This is on the theory that an acceptance makes the mortgagee's direct right indefeasible and the institution of an action is conclusive evidence of an acceptance. See also West's Ann.Cal.Civ.Code § 1559; Orloff v. Metropolitan Trust Co., 1940, 38 Cal.App.2d 688, 102 P.2d 562.

61. Pomeroy, Eq.Juris, § 1206, n. 3.

62. Biddel v. Brizzolara, 1883, 64 Cal. 354, 30 P. 609; Crowell v. Currier, 1876, 27 N.J.Eq. 152, affirmed 27 N.J.Eq. 650; see note, 1921, 12 A.L.R. 1528, 1529. But cf. Willard v. Worsham, 1882, 76 Va. 392; McCown v. Nicks, 1926, 171 Ark. 260, 284 S.W. 739, 47 A.L.R. 332.

63. See n. 59, supra.

64. See Youngs v. Trustees, 1879, 31 N.J.Eq. 290, 298–302. What would constitute fraud of creditors would depend upon the law of fraudulent conveyances in the particular jurisdiction. If the promisee is solvent, has no actual intent to defraud creditors, or, even if insolvent, gives the discharge bona fide for valuable consideration, it would not be in fraud of creditors. See Williston, Contracts, Rev. ed., § 397.

65. § 143.

66. See dissenting opinion, Douglass v. Wells, N.Y. 1879, 18 Hun 88, 98, 57 How.Pr. 378; note, 1919, 4 Corn.L.Q. 53, 55; Friedman, Personal Liability on Mortgage Debts, 50 Yale L.J. 224, 240.

67. See Gifford v. Corrigan, 1887, 105 N.Y. 223, 229, 11 N.E. 498, "to permit a change * * * while the creditor is relying upon it, would be grossly inequitable."

68. See Glenn, Mortgages, §§ 271, 5.1; Restatement, Security, § 140.

69. There are some decisions that apparently consider that "acceptance" by the mortgagee is necessary and sufficient. E. g., Hubard & Appleby v. Thacker, 1922, 132 Va. 33, 53, 110 S.E. 263, 21 A.L.R. 423. Such a requirement seems insupportable, except upon the dubious ground that "from that moment, certainly in equity, even more than at law, the mortgagee must be assumed to have acted or to have omitted to act in reliance upon it." Since the right is an unanticipated bonus, it would seem preferable to require that the mortgagee establish affirmatively that he had actually relied upon it be-

In jurisdictions that accept the third party beneficiary direct right rationale, the problem would seem to be one of what the basis for according the right is and, consequently, one of when it vests in the mortgagee.[70] A few such courts hold that the mortgagee's right becomes indefeasibly vested immediately upon the assumption.[71] If the argument that the relationship established is purely contractual, the contract being the offer, acceptance and consideration between the promisor and promisee,[72] such a conclusion would be logical.[73] That contract is complete on the making of the promise of assumption. The weight of authority, however, requires acceptance or adoption by the mortgagee before deeming the right vested.[74] There is divergence as to what will satisfy these requirements. Thus it has been held that acceptance will be presumed and therefore on this ground the right arises at the time the contract is made subject only to dis-

affirmance by the mortgagee.[75] On the other hand, there is authority that notice must be given by the mortgagee to the promisor.[76] Others seem to make the test of acceptance or adoption synonymous with material change of position that will make it inequitable to deprive the mortgagee of the right.[77] These last would seem perfectly sound. If the mortgagee's right is regarded as a contract right arising by conduct between the promisor and the beneficiary, the necessity of an "acceptance" is supportable. But if the analogy on which the right is given is to a trust or an insurance policy without right to change the beneficiary an opposite result would follow.[78] In any event it has been suggested "that no fetish should be made of the mortgagee's 'acceptance,' particularly in those communities where it is the general practice to let mortgages run past due if taxes and interest are paid."[79]

Many courts following the direct right theory have permitted recovery in spite of non-liability of the promisee-grantor to the mortgagee, but it is not altogether clear in all cases whether he does so as a donee or as a creditor beneficiary.[80] If he is classed as the former it does not necessarily follow that the rule generally followed in such cases[81] as to the indefeasibility of the beneficiary's right should apply to the mortgagee. The rule was established in cases in which there are present social considerations which do

fore giving him an indefeasible right to it. See note-call 66, supra.

70. "One difficulty in reaching a satisfactory conclusion is the paucity of judical analysis of the basis upon which *Lawrence v. Fox* rests. With questionable analysis which disregards the growth of the law, it has been regarded as a legal saltation that fails to fit snugly into any preexisting legal categories." Friedman, Personal Liability on Mortgage Debts, 50 Yale L.J. 224, 239. See also authorities cited in note 55, supra.

71. Bay v. Williams, 1884, 112 Ill. 91, 1 N.E. 340, 54 Am.Rep. 209; Starbird v. Cranston, 1897, 24 Colo. 20, 48 P.2d 652.

72. Corbin, Contracts for the Benefit of Third Persons, 1918, 27 Yale L.J. 1008, 1020.

73. See 1910, 10 Col.L.Rev. 765, 766; 1927, 13 Cornell L.Q. 123, 126. Friedman, Personal Liability on Mortgage Debts, 1940, 50 Yale L.J. 224, 239.

74. Gifford v. Corrigan, 1889, 117 N.Y. 257, 262, 22 N.E. 756, 757, 6 L.R.A. 610, 15 Am.St.Rep. 508; Smith v. Kibbe, 1919, 104 Kan. 159, 163, 178 P. 427, 429, 5 A.L.R. 483; New York Life Ins. Co. v. Aitkin, 1891, 125 N.Y. 660, 675, 26 N.E. 732; and Hill v. Hoeldtke, 1912, 104 Tex. 594, 142 S.W. 871, 40 L.R.A.,N.S., 672. That the assumption may be revoked any time before the mortgagee brings suit, knowledge or any acceptance or adoption not being shown, Ellis v. Kristoferson, 1927, 129 Misc. 443, 222 N.Y.S. 370, see Wheat v. Rice, 1884, 97 N.Y. 296, 302; 1925, 9 Minn.L.Rev. 295; 1934, 47 Harv.L. Rev. 1066, 1067.

75. Rogers v. Gosnell, 1875, 58 Mo. 589.

76. Berkshire Life Ins. Co. v. Hutchings, 1884, 100 Ind. 496; see Carnahan v. Tousey, 1883, 93 Ind. 561, 562, 564.

77. Morstain v. Kircher, 1933, 190 Minn. 78, 250 N.W. 727. This is the view of the Restatement of Contracts applicable in all cases regardless of the theoretical basis of the mortgagee's right. § 143.

78. See Friedman, op. cit. supra note 73.

79. Idem, citing Union Trust Co. v. Kaplan, 1936, 249 App.Div. 280, 284, 292 N.Y.S. 152, 159, judicial knowledge of custom.

80. See § 264, supra.

81. See Williston, Contracts, Rev. ed., § 396.

not exist in mortgage cases.[82] This is especially important because of the extremely dubious basis in fact of a donative intent on the part of either the promisee or promisor.[83] If he is regarded as a creditor beneficiary there seems no substantial reason for treating him, so far as this point is concerned, as in a different position than one to whom the promisee-grantor is liable.

EXTENSION AGREEMENTS—SURETYSHIP RULES

269. By suretyship rules, important in mortgage law because invoked in cases of transfers by the mortgagor, legally binding extensions of time by the creditor to the principal debtor discharges the surety. Four bases, all of them subjected to criticism, have been offered for the rule. The most important is that such an agreement impairs the surety's right of subrogation.

In spite of a conceptual difficulty in states following a derivative theory of the right of a mortgagee against an assuming grantee,[84] the courts are in general agreement that the relation created by a conveyance from a mortgagor to an assuming grantee is to be treated as one of suretyship. The mortgagor is looked upon as a surety while the land and the assuming grantee are regarded as principals.[85] Further, accepting the suretyship concept, they also in general follow the rules of suretyship in the particular jurisdiction as to the rights of the mortgagor-transferor to subrogation, reimbursement, exoneration, and, in minority jurisdictions, the doctrine of Pain v. Packard.[86] In addition, and this is the problem to which attention is now directed, for the most part they tend to follow uncritically[87] those rules of suretyship which give a defense to the surety, in whole or in part, as a consequence of extension agreements[88] or releases given by the creditor to the principal debtor.[89] Consequently it is desirable to make a brief survey of the bases of these defenses and to examine their application to mortgage transactions. In doing so the well-settled general rule that a binding extension of time given by the creditor to a principal debtor completely discharges a surety[90] will be first considered, followed by an examination of exceptions and minority views.

82. See note 1927, 13 Corn.L.Q. 123, 128; Friedman Personal Liability on Mortgage Debts, 50 Yale L.J. 224, 240. See, also, note-call 66, ante. It should be noted that the mortgagee, unlike the usual donee beneficiary, already has rights against the mortgagor, even if not the promisee-grantor, and the land. And he differs from most creditor beneficiaries in his security right in the land in the hands of the transferee-promisor in addition to his claim against the mortgagor or other transferor.

83. See § 265, supra.

84. See §§ 262, 263, supra. The difficulty is the possible absence of an independent right against the assuming grantee. See also 1937, 4 U. of Chi.L. Rev. 469, 479.

85. See §§ 260–264, supra. "When the grantee assumes the mortgage debt as between the grantee and the mortgagor, not only is the land a primary fund for the payment of the debt, but likewise the personal liability thus assumed by the grantee. On the other hand, when the grantee merely takes subject to the mortgage, while it is true that the grantee assumes no personal liability whatever, nevertheless the security in his hands is liable for the payment of the mortgage debt, which liability as between the grantee and the mortgagor is primary." Zastrow v. Knight, 1930, 56 S.D. 554, 229 N. W. 925, 72 A.L.R. 379.

86. N.Y.1816, 13 Johns. 174. See §§ 258, 259, supra. See also Chapter 10, post.

87. See § 270, infra. See also authorities cited in next footnote.

88. Restatement, Security, § 83, Comment on Clause (c). See note, 1937, 4 U. of Chi.L.Rev. 469 for a thorough exposition of the rationales, criticisms, and limitations of the suretyship rule that a binding extension of time to a principal by a creditor without the consent of the surety will release the latter, followed by a critical discussion of its application, by analogy, to mortgage cases. See also Cardozo, Nature of the Judicial Process, 152; Glassie, The Assuming Vendee, 1923, 9 Va.L.Rev. 196, 203; note, 1929, 15 Iowa L.Rev. 79 (discussing the Iowa view which gives the mortgagor no defense); note, 1931, 79 U. of Pa.L.Rev. 1151 (effect of mortgagee's ignorance of the grantee's assumption); 1926, 41 A.L.R. 277; 1926, 43 A.L.R. 89; 1931, 72 A.L.R. 389; 1932, 81 A.L.R. 1016; 112 A. L.R. 1324; Friedman, Discharge of Mortgage Debts, 1943, 52 Yale L.J. 771, 796. Warm, Rights and Liabilities of Mortgagee, Mortgagor, Grantee, 1936, 10 Temple L.Q. 116, 136.

89. See § 270, infra.

90. See Arant, Suretyship, § 68.

The general rule itself has been summarized[91] as follows: In order for the rule to operate the creditor's promise must be supported by legal consideration and be definite enough to be enforced. The surety is not discharged when the creditor reserves his remedies against the surety,[92] when the surety consents to the extension, when the creditor was unaware of the existence of the suretyship when he extended the time of payment,[93] or when the surety is indemnified.[94] There is a tendency to refuse discharge to compensated sureties unless they show that the extension agreement caused injury to them.

Four explanations have been advanced for the general rule of discharge of the surety by extension of time. Of these four, one of them, because it is not only the traditional view but remains most generally accepted today in spite of heavy criticism, must be regarded, as a practical matter, of primary importance. This is usually referred to as the impairment of rights theory. The other three may be labeled as the rescission, the increase-of-risk, and the intent to release theories.[95]

The rescission theory is that "the contract with reference to which surety promised is terminated by the creditor's agreement to extend the time of time of payment. The surety is not a party to the new agreement, and cannot be held liable on it merely because it is no more burdensome than the agreement terminated to which he was a party."[96] About the only merit of this explanation is that it affords a reason why the surety is discharged without any showing of even possible injury. It is difficult to regard a change in one term in the original agreement, the time of payment, as a termination of the entire original agreement.[97] Further the result ignores any argument as to the merits of the result, resting it purely upon a dubious legal technicality. And it would seem to have no application to mortgage assumption cases in any event. The mortgagor's contract with the mortgagee antedates any rights the mortgagee may acquire against an assuming grantee. Those rights arise, no matter what theory is used, as result of the later contract and conveyance between the mortgagor and the assuming grantee. The suretyship relation, insofar as it is recognized as arising, does so as a result of this later transaction. Hence it cannot be said with any reality that the mortgagor's original promise, which because of the later rights arising in the mortgagee is changed from that of principal to one of surety, was made with reference to the terms of the new right of the mortgagee.[98]

The notion that the creditor intended to release the surety, based on the reasoning that if he had not he would have reserved rights against him, is equally devoid of sub-

---

91. Arant, Suretyship, § 68, headnote.

92. This statement must be qualified when applied to mortgage transactions. See § 270, infra.

93. See § 270, as to the requirement of knowledge in mortgage cases.

94. See Arant, Suretyship, 297–298. Indemnity as used here means property security or the promise of someone other than the principal debtor. Although in mortgage cases courts invoke the analogy of "security" given to the mortgagor for his indemnity in order to allow the mortgagee to recover, the "security" actually is only the unsecured promise of the assuming grantee. Hence the exception to discharge on grounds of indemnity would not rule out a discharge in the mortgage cases.

95. For an exposition of the first two of these, see Arant, Suretyship, § 68. For the third, see 1937, 4 U. of Chi.L.Rev. 469, 473.

96. Arant, Suretyship, 286.

97. See Durfee, Book Review, 1932, 17 Cornell L.Q. 707, 709, n. 5.

98. In answer it may be argued that the mortgagor in creating the right of the mortgagee against the grantee by virtue of the assumption contract at that time created the suretyship by transforming his original obligation as principal into one of a surety. And, further, that it was his intention at that time that the rights which he, by his contract, gave to the mortgagee should not be changed without abrogating the right against him. Such an argument is not only strained factually, but would necessitate finding that the original terms of the mortgagor's debt to the mortgagee were changed without the consent of the mortgagee at the time of the assumption agreement and by virtue of it.

stance.[99] Insofar as it purports to rest upon an actual intention it is completely unfounded. Insofar as it is a fictional intent designed to release a surety, it should rest upon some substantial justification for invoking it. There may be such justification in the case of mortgages, at least to the extent of the value of the land or some lesser amount, but whatever it may be should be explicitly recognized and not concealed by either an unwarranted inference of genuine intent or an unexplained fiction.

The increase-of-risk theory has more to commend it.[1] However, its validity depends upon the correctness of the assumption of fact upon which it rests, i. e., that the parties contemplated that the creditor would not do things to increase the probability of the principal not paying and that an extension of time may so operate.[2] Not only may this be doubted,[3] but if based on this idea it is out of harmony with other cases denying discharge in analogous situations.[4]

The last, and as noted, the most important theory is that the creditor by his extension agreement has impaired the surety's rights. It is possible that occasionally a court may have in mind rights other than that of sub- rogation.[5] However, it is almost always confined to the right of subrogation,[6] the argument being that the creditor's agreement has deprived the surety of his right to pay and then to bring suit in the name of the creditor against the principal to obtain reimbursement.[7] There is some doubt as to whether the logical foundation of the rule, i. e., that the surety would be bound by the extension agreement, actually exists. The cases generally assume the point,[8] although there is a little authority that he would not be bound by it, upon the theory that the principal's right extends only to non-action by the creditor personally.[9] However, it is the merits of the rule that have been subjected to the severest criticism.

5. See, e. g., 1937, 4 U. of Chi.L.Rev. 469, 471. In the discussion immediately following in the text the effect of the extension agreement upon the rights to reimbursement, breach of contract, and exoneration is considered, incidentally, in evaluating them as the equivalent of subrogation.

6. See, e. g., Arant, Suretyship, 85.

7. See Arant, Suretyship, § 68; 1937, 4 U. of Chi.L. Rev. 469, 470. The idea is expressed in mortgage cases as follows: "Through the right of subrogation the vendor [mortgagor] could secure his safety, and that right could not be invaded with impunity. When the creditor extended the time of payment by a valid agreement with the grantee, he at once, for the time being, took away the vendor's original right of subrogation." Murray v. Marshall, 1884, 94 N.Y. 611.
"The fundamental reasons for granting an absolute discharge to the surety where the creditor without the consent of the surety extends time to the principal are twofold: First, that the risk of the surety is thereby increased; and, second, that the creditor has thereby limited the surety's right to pay at any time and proceed against the principal by way of subrogation." Zastrow v. Knight, 1930. 56 S.D. 554, 229 N.W. 925, 72 A.L.R. 379.

8. E. g., Calvo v. Davies, 1878, 73 N.Y. 211, 29 Am. Rep. 130; Murray v. Marshall, 1884, 94 N.Y. 611; Union Mut. Life Ins. Co. v. Hanford, 1892, 143 U.S. 187, 12 S.Ct. 437, 36 L.Ed. 118.

9. See Friedman, Discharge of Mortgage Debts, 1943, 52 Yale L.J. 771, 775, 797, citing, Joyce, to Use of Fidelity-Philadelphia Trust Co., v. Hawtof, 1939, 135 Pa.Super. 30, 4 A.2d 599, disapproved in 1939, 5 U. of Pitt.L.Rev. 286; Cacavalle v. Lombardi, 1927, 106 Conn. 339, 138 A. 155, reimbursement; and, semble, Excelsior Savings Bank v. Cohen, 1917, 176 App.Div. 740, 163 N.Y.S. 1017, affirmed 228 N.Y. 570, 127 N.E. 912. See also 1937, 4 U. of Chi.L.Rev.

99. See 1937, 4 U. of Chi.L.Rev. 469, 473.

1. For one thing, it is frequently given as a reason by the courts, at least when coupled with the suspension of the right of subrogation, as constituting the risk. E. g., Murray v. Marshall, 1884, 94 N.Y. 611, "He put upon the mortgagor a new risk not contemplated, and never consented to." See also note 7, infra.

2. See Arant, Suretyship, 287.

3. See Arant, Suretyship, 283, n. 83, "The writer has no data to support a contention that the fact assumption upon which the validity of this theory must depend is correct. The exactly opposite assumption may be the correct one, namely, that extension of time by the creditor is such a common practice that the surety impliedly assents to it when he contracts." See also Durfee, Book Review, 1932, 17 Corn.L.Q. 707 arguing that extension agreements, obviously not unusual, should always be a contemplated risk.

4. See 1937, 4 U. of Chi.L.Rev. 469, 474.

It is recognized that the rule is a just one in cases where the surety can show that actual damage resulted, although even here recovery should be confined to the extent of the damage.[10] And it is further conceded that it might be fair to apply the rule whenever the surety actually attempted to enforce, by tendering payment and demanding subrogation, the rights presumed to have been taken from him by the agreement.[11] But the rule gives a complete discharge without the necessity of proving either the slightest damage or any attempt to invoke the surety's rights.[12] That this is absurd and inconsistent with the "realities of business experience and the moralities of life" has been vigorously pointed out by a great judge.[13] Further, except where

the creditor is secured or has other priority rights, the surety's other rights give him a protection so nearly equivalent to that which he could obtain by using subrogation that even if he were deprived of it it should not be sufficient reason to grant a complete discharge.[14] Since he himself is liable for the debt he may pay it in spite of any extension to the principal and then maintain an action for money paid in order to obtain reimbursement.[15] Further, it would seem that if he had a contract of indemnity against liability,[16] as contrasted with one against loss, he should be able to sue for breach of the contract. The contract of extension between the creditor and the principal debtor should not destroy or postpone the right on a contract between the principal debtor and the surety.[17] The

---

469, 471; see Campbell, Protection Against Indirect Attack, Harvard Legal Essays, 3, 6.

10. Cardozo, Nature of the Judicial Process, 153. But see Durfee, Book Review, 1932, 17 Cornell L.Q. 707, 711 n. 9, "It would be inconvenient and, perhaps, unfair to surety to require proof (or, shifting the burden, to admit proof) of the relative financial condition of principal before and after the period of extension, though that issue is opened in connection with the rule of Pain v. Packard. * * * It would be even more questionable to make the defense depend upon balance of actual injury against actual benefit—for example where principal's financial condition has deteriorated but creditor obtained security upon the extension. It might be still worse to have the defense turn upon the degree of reasonableness, or unreasonableness, of creditor's action. This has been used as an argument to support the unconditional rule on extension of time, and it has much force." Professor Durfee, however, disapproves of the present rule of discharge without showing even any effort on the part of the surety to exercise his rights. Ibid., n. 10. A proposal by a revisory committee in New York (Report of New York Revis. Comm., 1937, 875 et seq.) that a surety would not be discharged by a change in the principal obligation except to the extent to which the surety is prejudiced thereby was rejected. See Friedman, Discharge of Mortgage Debts, 1943, 52 Yale L.J. 771, 798.

11. Cardozo, Nature of the Judicial Process, 153. "Perhaps the burden of disproving prejudice ought to be cast upon the creditor." Idem.

12. See Arant, Suretyship, § 68.

13. Cardozo, Nature of the Judicial Process, 155. "The law has shaped its judgments upon the fictitious assumption that a surety, who has probably lain awake at nights for fear that payment may some day be demanded, has in truth been smarting under the repressed desire to force an unwelcome

payment on a reluctant or capricious creditor. * * * Such rules are survivals of the days * * * when sureties were commonly generous friends whose confidence had been abused, and when the main effort of the courts seem to have been to find some plausible excuse for letting them out of their engagements." Idem, 154. See also 1937, 4 U. of Chi.L.Rev. 469, 472; Friedman, Discharge of Mortgage Debts, 1943, 52 Yale L.J. 771, 798.

14. See § 259, supra, and § 270, infra.

15. Williston, Contracts, Rev.Ed., § 386. It may be noted that the reasoning is circular. He may pay because liable, i. e., the extension did not discharge him. If he were not liable, he could not, of course, pay and recover. But this would merely assume the point, i. e., that the extension discharged him.

16. § 259, supra.

17. See 1937, 4 U. of Chi.L.Rev. 469, 471. If the contract of the principal is to prevent liability of the surety arising by paying the debt, his breach occurs when the debt falls due and is unpaid. The fact that he is not liable, because of extension, does not prevent the surety from being exposed to action, which was the event the principal promised he would prevent by paying when the debt fell due. No clear cases have arisen, probably because the surety usually is held to be discharged and therefore prefers to rely on this than to sue the principal for damages. In Finzer v. Peter, 1930, 120 Neb. 389, 232 N.W. 762, 73 A.L.R. 1170, the mortgagor, who was held not to be discharged by an extension of time given to a remote assuming grantee, successfully maintained an action against intermediate assuming grantees. And this was true notwithstanding the argument that the intervening grantees had been discharged from liability by the extension to the later grantee. See 1930, 15 Iowa L.Rev. 82, citing decisions from minority jurisdic-

surety, in spite of the extension agreement, also has his right of exoneration,[18] although this is not so clear.[19] But even without it, his rights are sufficient to protect him; giving him a right of subrogation would add nothing of value.

EXTENSION AGREEMENTS—MORT-GAGE APPLICATIONS

270. Although criticized, the great weight of authority, applying suretyship principles to mortgage transactions, is that if a mortgagee with knowledge of the conveyance and assumption gives a legally binding extension of time to an assuming grantee the mortgagor is completely discharged regardless of injury. A mortgagor whose grantee merely took subject to the mortgage rather than assuming it, by the weight of authority, is similarly discharged to the extent of the value of the mortgaged property at the time of extension. Releases follow corresponding patterns. Extensions or releases to mortgagors, they being treated as sureties, do not affect the mortgagee's rights against grantees who assume or take subject to the mortgage.

Suretyship rules of discharge are invoked in cases where mortgagees give binding extensions of time to grantees of the mortgagor. Transactions in which the grantee assumes the mortgage have to be differentiated from those in which he merely takes subject to it.[20] In the former, by the great weight of au-

thority, if the mortgagee with knowledge of the conveyance and assumption,[21] gives time to an assuming grantee by a binding agreement with him, the mortgagor is completely discharged regardless of any showing of injury.[22] The same is true as to any intermedi-

21. Since usually assumption terms will be in the conveyance, of which a mortgagee should be on notice, this requirement normally will be fulfilled in mortgage assumption cases. But see Blumenthal v. Serota, 1930, 129 Me. 187, 151 A. 138. Even if the grantee's deed is silent, it would be an extraordinary case in which the mortgagee has known enough about the grantee to give him an extension of time and yet be able to establish that he was unaware of the existence of the assumption agreement. See Murray v. Marshall, 1884, 94 N.Y. 611, "the fact that he dealt with the grantee for an extension of the mortgage shows that he knew of the conveyance, and that it left the land bound in the hands of the grantee. Knowing this he is chargeable with knowledge of the mortgagor's equitable rights, and meddled with them at his peril." But in some cases the mortgagor is held not to be discharged unless the mortgagee had knowledge that the relationship of principal and surety existed between the grantee and mortgagor. Pratt v. Conway, 1899, 148 Mo. 291, 49 S.W. 1028, 71 Am.St.Rep. 602, in which the agreement of assumption was not contained in the deed of conveyance; Wolfe v. Murphy, 1918, 47 App.D.C. 296, in which the mortgagee was not charged with knowledge although the agreement of assumption was in the deed of conveyance and it was recorded. That the mortgagor is not discharged if the mortgagee did not know of the assumption at the time of the execution of the extension agreement, De Lotto v. Zipper, 1934, 116 N.J.Eq. 344, 173 A. 588, affirmed 120 N.J.Eq. 339, 185 A. 54. See 1931, 79 U. of Pa.L.Rev. 1151; 1926, 41 A.L.R. 277, 302; 1931, 72 A.L.R. 389, 397; 1932, 81 A.L.R. 1016, 1023; 1938, 112 A.L.R. 1324, 1340.

22. Calvo v. Davies, 1878, 73 N.Y. 211, 29 Am.Rep. 130; Union Mut. Life Ins. Co. v. Hanford, 1892, 143 U.S. 187, 12 S.Ct. 437, 36 L.Ed. 118. See 1926, 41 A.L.R. 277; 1931, 72 A.L.R. 389; 1932, 81 A.L.R. 1016; 1938, 112 A.L.R. 1324.

In Germania Life Ins. Co. v. Casey, 1904, 98 App.Div. 88, 90 N.Y.S. 418, the mortgagor was completely discharged by the acceptance by the mortgagee from the assuming grantee of a payment of the interest for six months one day before it was due, thus extending the time of payment of the mortgage debt by one day.

The waiver of an acceleration clause is not an extension of time to a grantee so as to release the mortgagor, see notes, 1929, 7 N.Y.Univ.L.Q.Rev. 214; 1931, 31 Col.L.Rev. 328. See Friedman, Discharge of Mortgage Debts, 1943, 52 Yale L.J. 771, 782–787 for other agreements between mortgagee and grantees of the mortgagor that will discharge the mortgagor. As to the effect of a request by the mortgagor to the mortgagee to foreclose the property in the hands of a grantee who took it "subject

tions in which the mortgagor is not discharged. See also 1931, 73 A.L.R. 1177, citing, in addition to Finzer v. Peter, supra, Hyde v. Miller, 1899, 45 App.Div. 396, 60 N.Y.S. 974, affirmed 1901, 168 N.Y. 590, 60 N.E. 1113.

18. West Huntsville Cotton Mills v. Alter, 1910, 164 Ala. 305, 51 So. 338.

19. The possible defense to an action to compel the principal to pay the debt is that, payment being postponed, it is not yet due. Note to Nisbet v. Smith, 1789, 2 Bro.C.C. 578, 583. The answer is the same as in the case of an action for damages for breach of the contract of indemnity. The duty of the principal is to exonerate the surety from the surety's duty to pay; and it has not been extended by the extension to the principal. No agreement between the creditor and principal can affect the right of the surety against the principal. See 1937, 4 U. of Chi.L.Rev. 469, 472.

20. See § 269, note 88, for critiques of the doctrine.

ate grantees.[23] Even inclusion in the extension agreement of a reservation of rights against the mortgagor will not, as in ordinary cases of suretyship,[24] prevent the extension from operating as a discharge.[25] There is a little authority that an extension does not discharge the mortgagor, the theory being that the mortgagee is not bound by the suretyship relation between the mortgagor and the transferee but may treat both

as principals severally liable unless he assents to the arrangement.[26]

The prevailing view has been criticized. In those jurisdictions using subrogation to the mortgagor's rights or other derivative notions, on which to found the mortgagee's ability to proceed against the assuming grantee personally, impairment of the power to be subrogated to the mortgagee's rights is manifestly an untenable basis for granting a discharge beyond the value of the mortgaged property. "The only right the mortgagee has is to enforce the obligation of the grantee to the mortgagor, and no action of the mortgagee can deprive the mortgagor of this right. He does not need to be subrogated to the right; he has it without subrogation." [27] In jurisdictions where the mortgagee's right is recognized as direct, discharge of the mortgagor to an amount above the value of the mortgaged property has been attacked. It is argued that no possibility of injury exists beyond the value of the property since the extension does not affect his rights other than that of subrogation and they give him in every respect a practical equivalent of it. Any discharge as to this is purely technical.[28] In addition it is urged that, because the mortgagor does not assume

---

to" the mortgage, see §§ 258, 259, supra. See also note, 1935, 20 Cornell L.Q. 249; More, Failure of a Creditor to Sue the Principal at the Surety's Request, 1929, 1 Rocky Mt.L.Rev. 232; note, 1928, 37 Yale L.J. 971.

23. Phoenix Trust Co. v. Garner, 1933, 227 Mo.App. 929, 59 S.W.2d 779; Meldola v. Furlong, 1932, 142 Misc. 562, 255 N.Y.S. 48. Whether an extension to a grantee who assumes but whose grantor had not will discharge the mortgage completely depends on the local law as to whether such an assumption creates a personal liability. See § 265, supra.

In DeLeon v. Rhines, 1934, 64 U.S.App.D.C. 73, 74 F. 2d 477, an extension to the last grantee whose predecessors had not assumed gave no discharge. Even though the grantee incurred no personal liability the case should be governed by the rule of conveyances subject to the mortgage. See infra, this section.

24. See § 269, supra.

25. Calvo v. Davies, 1878, 73 N.Y. 211, 29 Am.Rep. 130, holding that such an agreement is only conditional on the consent to it of the surety; Metzger v. Nova Realty Co., 1915, 160 App.Div. 394, 145 N. Y.S. 549, affirmed 214 N.Y. 26, 107 N.E. 1027; Maier v. Thorman, Tex.Civ.App.1921, 234 S.W. 239; see 1926, 4 A.L.R. 277, 304; 1931, 72 A.L.R. 387, 398; 1932, 81 A.L.R. 1016, 1025; 1938, 112 A.L.R. 1325, 1342: Such a reservation does not give a grantee an unconditional extension but possibly a mere substitution of creditors. The effect is to leave the mortgagor an unconditional right to pay and enforce subrogation and therefore is without effect on either the rights or liabilities of the mortgagor. This result in mortgage cases is justified. See Glenn, Morts., § 276, "Here [in mortgage transfer cases] an extension may seriously alter the mortgagor's position, inasmuch as meanwhile the assuming grantee is in possession. * * * and so the rule cannot apply that, in other situations, will sanction 'reservation of recourse' in connection with extensions." If a reservation of rights against the mortgagor is written into the mortgage itself it is part of the security agreement and thus will permit the mortgagee to have recourse against the mortgagor regardless of any extension agreements he may make. Bailey v. Inman, 1932, 105 Fla. 1, 140 So. 783; Continental Nat. Bank & Trust Co. v. Reynolds, 1936, 286 Ill.App. 290, 3 N.E.2d 319; Kent v. Rhomberg, 1937, 288 Ill.App. 328, 6 N.E.2d 271; Mutual Life Ins. Co. v. Rothschild,

1916, 160 N.Y.S. 164, affirmed 1918, 226 N.Y. 599, 123 N.E. 880; Kohn v. Beggi, 1933, 147 Misc. 701, 264 N.Y.S. 274.

26. Bailey v. Inman, 1932, 105 Fla. 1, 140 So. 783; Blank v. Michael, 1929, 208 Iowa 402, 226 N.W. 12. See 1933, 81 U. of Pa.L.Rev. 641; 1929, 15 Iowa L. Rev. 79; 1935, 13 N.Car.L.Rev. 337; 1926, 41 A.L. R. 277, 285; 1931, 72 A.L.R. 383, 389; 1938, 112 A. L.R. 1324, 1331.

27. Williston, Contracts, Rev. ed. § 386. Restatement, Contracts, § 146, accord. Wolfe v. Murphy, 1918, 47 U.S.App.D.C. 296; see Keller v. Ashford, 1890, 133 U.S. 610, 625, 10 S.Ct. 494, 33 L.Ed. 667. But see note 40, infra. Courts which do not allow the mortgagee to sue the grantee at all, it may be assumed, would not release the mortgagor when there has been an extension of time to the grantee.

28. See Williston, Contracts, Rev. ed., § 386; cf. 1929, 15 Iowa L.Rev. 79. The criticism here is the same as that leveled at complete discharge of the surety without proof of injury previously looked at. See § 269, supra. See also Authorities, § 269, note 88, ante. But see § 269, note 10, supra.

his obligation gratuitously, having received a loan or other value and having usually been the principal debtor for some time, he resembles one of the more protected type of sureties commonly described as compensated.[29] Such sureties are not discharged by mere extension of time; they must show injury.[30]

The cases dealing with the effect on the liability of the original mortgagor of an extension given by a mortgagee to a grantee who took subject to, but without assuming, the mortgage have not been entirely unanimous.[31] It has been held that the rights of the mortgagee against the mortgagor are not in any manner affected thereby.[32] It has also been held that, under such circumstances, the mortgagor is released entirely.[33] Another rule of discharge is the amount which, due to the extension, the value of the property has depreciated below the mortgage debt.[34] The weight of authority, however, is that, under such circumstances, the mortgagor is released to the extent of the value of the security properly applicable to the mortgage debt in the hands of the grantee at the time the extension is granted.[35]

---

29. See Stevens, Extension Agreements in the "Subject-to" Mortgage Situation, 1941, 15 U. of Cin.L. Rev. 58, 73, "the 'mortgagor-surety' in such cases is not just compensated but has actually received the *quid pro quo.*" See also 1937, 4 U. of Chi.L.Rev. 469, 478; 1929, 42 Harv.L.Rev. 712; Tiffany, Real Prop., 3d ed., § 445, n. 54. But cf. 1916, 29 Harv.L. Rev. 314, 317.

30. See Arant, Suretyship, § 299; § 269, supra.

31. See Stevens, Extension Agreements in the "Subject-to" Mortgage Situation, 1941, 15 U. of Cin.L. Rev. 58, 70, for a critical analysis of the several rules. See also Campbell, Cases on Mortgages, 2d ed., 442, n. 4.

As to the effect of an extension agreement on the rights of junior mortgagees, see Meislin, Extension Agreements and the Rights of Junior Mortgagees, 1956, 42 Va.L.Rev. 939.

32. Chilton v. Brooks, 1890, 72 Md. 554, 20 A. 125; DeLeon v. Rhines, 1934, 64 U.S.App.D.C. 73, 74 F.2d 477; Pfeifer v. W. B. Worthen Co., 1934, 189 Ark. 469, 74 S.W.2d 220, accord. See notes, 1929, 15 Iowa L.Rev. 79; 1935, 13 N.Car.L.Rev. 337. In Maryland and in the federal courts it is held, however, that an extension granted to an assuming grantee will discharge the mortgagor. George v. Andrews, 1882, 60 Md. 26, 45 Am.Rep. 706; Asbell v. Marshall Building & Loan Ass'n, 1928, 156 Md. 106, 143 A. 715; Keller v. Ashford, 1890, 133 U.S. 610, 10 S.Ct. 494, 33 L.Ed. 667. The distinction has been explained as follows: "The argument is that an extension can have no effect unless there is privity between the three parties—mortgagee, mortgagor and grantee; and privity there cannot be unless all three are under contract, which is not the case unless the grantee assumes." Glenn, Morts., § 1201. The distinction is fallacious. The requirement of "privity" is artificial. Even if insisted upon, it can be argued that it is satisfied. "The theorem * * * starts with the land as common security, and this brings the parties into privity; the assumption is merely additional collateral, and

naturally the privity remains which always was in effect." Glenn, Mortgages, § 278.

33. Braun v. Crew, 1920, 183 Cal. 728, 192 P. 531, discussed in notes, 1921, 5 Minn.L.Rev. 150; 1921, 19 Mich.L.Rev. 351; 1934, 10 Not.D.Law. 83, 84. A provision in the California Civil Code influenced the decision. See also 1926, 41 A.L.R. 277, 292; 1938, 112 A.L.R. 1324, 1334. A later decision in California rejects this rule where the mortgage secures a negotiable note. Mortgage Guarantee Co. v. Chotiner, 1936, 8 Cal.2d 110, 64 P.2d 138, 108 A.L.R. 1080. See § 271, infra, on the effect of the N.I.L. on discharge in mortgage cases by reason of extensions.

34. North End Savings Bank v. Snow, 1908, 197 Mass. 339, 83 N.E. 1099, 125 Am.St.Rep. 368. This may be the New York rule. See Syracuse Trust Co. v. First Trust & Deposit Co., 1931, 141 Misc. 603, 252 N.Y.S. 850, commented on in, 1932, 9 N.Y. Univ.L.Q.Rev. 502; Feigenbaum v. Hizsnay, 1919, 187 App.Div. 126, 175 N.Y.S. 223.

35. "When the mortgagor in this case sold expressly subject to the mortgage, remaining liable upon his bond, he had a right as against his grantee to require that the land should first be exhausted in the payment of the debt. * * * When the creditor extended the time of payment by a valid agreement with the grantee, he at once, for the time being, took away the vendor's original right of subrogation. * * * But it does not follow that the vendor was thereby wholly discharged. The grantee stood in the quasi relation of principal debtor only in respect to the land as the primary fund, and to the extent of the value of the land. If that value was less than the mortgage debt, as to the balance he owed no duty or obligation whatever, and as to that the mortgagor stood to the end, as he was at the beginning, the sole principal debtor. From any such balance he was not discharged, and as to that no right of his was in any manner disturbed. The measure of his injury was his right of subrogation, and that necessarily was bounded by the value of the land." Murray v. Marshall, 1884, 94 N.Y. 611; Spencer v. Spencer, 1884, 95 N.Y. 353; Zastrow v. Knight, 1930, 56 S.D. 554, 229 N. W. 925, 72 A.L.R. 379.

See notes, 1936, 22 Va.L.Rev. 964 (discussing Commercial Casualty Ins. Co. v. Roman, 1936, 269 N.Y. 451, 199 N.E. 658 in which the mortgagor was held for a

As was noted earlier,[36] the right of subrogation of a surety to his creditor's rights gives him nothing of substantial value if the creditor has no security or other priority rights and if he himself has rights over against the principal debtor. The personal right of the creditor against the principal debtor is no better than his own personal rights. But if the creditor has security which the surety might reach by subrogation at the maturity of the debt, it is obvious that his risk has been increased by an extension which prevents him or the mortgagee from realizing on it until later.[37] Thus the cases that deny any discharge would seem to be wrong. But the maximum injury would be the value of the land at the time of the injury and therefore a complete release, unless the land exceeded the amount of the debt, would seem to be unjustified. The burden of proof to establish the elements of the defense in these cases is upon the mortgagor.[38] If it were a difficult and onerous task to establish the actual amount of injury suffered by the extension, the majority rule could be accepted without objection. However, it would seem practicable to prove the extent to which the property has depreciated below the mortgage debt during the extension. Further, whether this rule or discharge to the full value of the land at the date of extension is adopted, a presumption that the land was equal in value to the debt at the time the extension was granted seems justified as founded on normal practice and business common sense.[39]

Releases

Release by the mortgagee of the personal obligation of an assuming grantee operates, in jurisdictions following suretyship ideas, to discharge the mortgagor completely.[40] Even if the mortgagor and assuming grantee were regarded as co-principals, the same result would follow from the general rule that the

---

deficiency equal to the amount that the mortgage debt exceeded the value of the land at the time of the extension); 1937. 4 U. of Chi.L.Rev. 469, 478; 1934, 10 Not.D.Law. 83; 1916, 5 Br.Rul.Cas. 633. See also 1926, 41 A.L.R. 277, 292; 1931, 72 A.L.R. 389, 394; 1932, 81 A.L.R. 1016, 1021; 1938, 112 A.L.R. 1324, 1331. As was stated before, this amount was urged as the proper measure in both assumption and non-assumption cases. Williston, Contracts, Rev. ed., § 386. But see Glassie, The Assuming Vendee, 1923, 9 Va.L.Rev. 196, 205, n. 36, "With submission, this [discharge equal to value of land at time of extension] does not help in a practical sense. For it introduces the most gaseous of all questions of fact—the value of land at some time other than that of a sale." See also Stevens, Extension Agreements in the "Subject-to" Mortgage Situation, 1941, 15 U. of Cin.L.Rev. 58, 74.

36. § 269, supra.

37. See Zastrow v. Knight, 1930, 56 S.D. 554, 564, 229 N.W. 925, 930, 72 A.L.R. 379, quoted § 269, n. 7, supra.

38. Meldola v. Furlong, 1932, 142 Misc. 562, 255 N.Y. S. 48; Commercial Casualty Ins. Co. v. Roman, 1936, 269 N.Y. 451, 199 N.E. 658, amended 270 N.Y. 563, 200 N.E. 319; Mutual Ben. Life Ins. Co. v. Lindley, 1933, 97 Ind.App. 575, 183 N.E. 127, commented on in, 1933, 33 Col.L.Rev. 368, 1933, 81 U. of Pa.L.Rev. 641.

39. Murray v. Marshall, 1884, 94 N.Y. 611, treated, however, as a dictum and disregarded in Feigenbaum v. Hizsnay, 1919, 187 App.Div. 126, 175 N.Y.S. 223; Mutual Benefit Life Ins. Co. v. Lindley, 1932, 97 Ind.App. 575, 183 N.E. 127, noted 1933, 33 Col.L. Rev. 368, and, 1933, 81 U. of Pa.L.Rev. 641. "In fact, one cannot imagine a stronger presumption. Whoever heard of a man deliberately lending upon inadequate security, in the absence of a special reason." Glenn, Mortgages, § 277.

40. Gilliam v. McLemore, 1925, 141 Miss. 253, 106 So. 99, 43 A.L.R. 79; Merriam v. Miles, 1898, 54 Neb. 566, 74 N.W. 861, 69 Am.St.Rep. 731; Insley v. Webb, 1922, 122 Wash. 98, 209 P. 1093, 41 A.L.R. 274. The release from a deficiency judgment of a purchaser who assumed the mortgage discharges the mortgagor. Wagoner v. Brady, 1927, 221 App. Div. 405, 223 N.Y.S. 99, discussed in note, 1927, 41 Harv.L.Rev. 261; note, 1921, 93 Cent.L.J. 183. Getting a deficiency judgment against the mortgagor alone which, under a local statute, barred obtaining a similar judgment against the assuming grantee, is ground for setting aside the judgment. Tousey v. Barber, 1928, 132 Misc. 861, 231 N.Y.S. 133, discussed in note, 1929, 42 Harv.L.Rev. 583. See 1926, 41 A.L.R. 277, 311; 1931, 72 A.L.R. 389, 398, 399; 1932, 81 A.L.R. 1016, 1025; 1938, 112 A.L.R. 1324, 1343. See also, Arant, Suretyship, § 49. It might be expected that jurisdictions following the derivative theory of the mortgagee's personal rights against an assuming grantee would not discharge a mortgagor by reason of a purported release by the mortgagee of his rights against such a grantee since he would not have anything to release. See 1940, 88 U. of Pa.L.Rev. 611, 615. But there are cases to the contrary. Herd v. Tuohy, 1901, 133 Cal. 55, 65 P. 139; Codman v. Deland, 1918, 231 Mass. 344, 121 N.E. 14; Reeves v. Cordes, 1931, 108 N.J.Eq. 469, 155 A. 547.

release of one joint and several debtor discharges the others.[41]

The effect of the release of the mortgaged property in the hands of an assuming grantee or one who took it subject to the mortgage is not so clear cut. The general rule of suretyship law is that when a secured creditor surrenders to the debtor, negligently loses, or damages the security it discharges a surety to the extent of the value so lost.[42] This same reasoning has been applied to releases of the mortgaged property, completely or in part, in the hands of grantees who assumed or took subject to the mortgage.[43] Other courts, however, refusing to inquire into the extent of the injury caused by the giving up of security, give a complete discharge to the mortgagor even where there has been a release of only part of the mortgaged property.[44]

Extensions or releases to mortgagor—"Loaned Collateral"

Since a mortgagor who has conveyed to a grantee who assumes the mortgage is surety, neither an extension of time to or release of him from liability will affect the mortgagee's rights against the assuming vendee.[45] The same is true where the vendee has taken subject to the mortgage, for the land in his hands is the principal and the mortgagor, up to the value of the land, is surety only. Of course, if the mortgagor or his property had the duty of paying to exonerate the grantee or the land in the hands of the grantee the suretyship situation would be reversed, hence extensions and releases of the mortgagor would give defenses to the grantee.[46] In a case of "loaned collateral," i. e., the owner of the property gives a mortgage on it to secure the debt of another but does not become personally bound, since the obligor is the principal debtor in such a case and the land is surety only, an extension of time to the debtor will discharge the lien on the land.[47]

EXTENSION AGREEMENTS—EFFECT OF NEGOTIABLE INSTRUMENTS LAW

271. Following the general, although almost universally criticised, rule that the Negotiable Instrument Law abrogates all existing surety-

---

41. See Williston, Contracts, Rev. ed., § 334.

42. Security, Restatement, § 132. See Arant, Suretyship, §§ 62, 63.

43. Woodward v. Brown, 1897, 119 Cal. 283, 51 P. 2, 63 Am.St.Rep. 108, modified 119 Cal. 283, 51 P. 542, 63 Am.St.Rep. 108; Mann v. Bugbee, 1933, 113 N.J. Eq. 434, 167 A. 202; see 1926, 41 A.L.R. 277, 306; 1931, 72 A.L.R. 389; 1932, 81 A.L.R. 1016, 1025; 1938, 112 A.L.R. 1324, 1343. Similarly, a mortgagee who fails to record his mortgage and thus permits a grantee of the mortgagor to sell the full title to the property to a bona fide purchaser cannot enforce the mortgage debt against the mortgagor. Hampe v. Manke, 1912, 28 S.D. 501, 134 N.W. 60. However, a mortgagee has been held to have a right to a deficiency judgment against the mortgagor in spite of his knowledge of the commission of waste by the mortgagor's grantee. Damiano v. Bergen County Land Co., 1935, 118 N.J.Eq. 535, 180 A. 489, commented on in 1936, 36 Col.L.Rev. 328. But the mortgagor was discharged in Lynn Five Cents Bank v. Portnoy, 1940, 306 Mass. 436, 28 N.E.2d 418, where the mortgagee consented to the grantee making wasteful changes in the premises. An increase in the amount of the mortgage debt by an agreement between the mortgagee and the mortgagor's grantee discharges the mortgagor to the extent of the increase. Union Bank of Brooklyn v. Rubenstein, 1912, 78 Misc. 461, 138 N.Y.S. 644, commented on in note, 1913, 13 Col.L.Rev. 238.

44. The release of the mortgaged property in the hands of an assuming grantee on the grantee's paying the full market value of the land to the mortgagee was held to give a complete defense to the mortgagor in Farmers' & Merchants' State Bank v. Tasche, 1928, 53 S.D. 603, 222 N.W. 139, criticized

---

in note, 1929, 42 Harv.L.Rev. 712; Elsey v. People's Bank, 1915, 166 Ky. 386, 179 S.W. 392, noted, 1916, 16 Col.L.Rev. 165; In Re Hunter's Estate, 1917, 257 Pa. 32, 101 A. 79, mortgagee takes risk that unreleased portion is of sufficient value to secure his debt; Albright v. Aliday, Tex.Civ.App.1896, 37 S. W. 646, part only released; Brown v. Turner, 1932, 202 N.C. 227, 162 S.E. 608, discussed in note, 1932, 11 N.Car.L.Rev. 96, release of part of the mortgaged premises; Restatement, Contracts, § 146, accord. See Glenn, Mortgages, § 281, approving this result.

45. Keller v. Parrish, 1929, 196 N.C. 733, 147 S.E. 9, criticised, 1930, 24 Ill.L.Rev. 828, because the released mortgagor had reassumed the debt and was therefore principal, yet the assuming grantee was not discharged; Esser v. Pritzker, [1926] 2 D.L.R. 645, noted, 1927, 40 Harv.L.Rev. 503; see 1931, 29 Mich.L.Rev. 1091. See Arant, Suretyship, § 258.

46. See 1924, 24 Col.L.Rev. 804. See also Chapter 10, infra.

47. Metz v. Todd, 1877, 36 Mich. 473.

ship law with respect to negotiable instruments, the weight of authority is that a binding extension of time by a mortgagee to a grantee who assumes or takes subject to the mortgagee will not discharge a mortgagor where the mortgage secures a negotiable instrument executed by him. Such an extension discharges intermediate assuming grantees from liability to the mortgagee but the mortgagor may recover against them.

Where the mortgage secures a negotiable instrument, the weight of authority is that a binding extension of time to a grantee who assumes or takes subject to the mortgage does not discharge the maker-mortgagor.[48] The basis for this holding is the general, although almost universally criticized,[49] rule that suretyship defenses are not available to one who appears as primarily liable upon the face of a negotiable instrument, it being the legislative intent in adopting the Uniform Act to abrogate all existing suretyship law with reference to negotiable instruments in the interests of uniformity.[50] More especially, it is the ap-

plication of that general doctrine which refuses a discharge to an accommodation maker,[51] that is most influential, it being difficult to hold such a person liable and yet discharge a mortgagor, the *only* one who has signed and liable on the note, because, as the result of a later transaction of sale of the mortgaged property, he is treated by the courts generally as though he were a surety entitled to the benefit of suretyship defenses. This reason is especially prominent where the conveyance is only subject to the mortgage.[52]

1941, 50 Yale L.J. 387, 407; Roberts, Defenses of an Accommodation Maker, 1938, 23 Iowa L.Rev. 335, 338. The comment was as to the defenses of an accommodation maker, but since the rule there is relied on in mortgage case, it seems apt. The Chotiner case, supra note 48, also relies upon this, buttressed by the belief that this particular defense in question to which the decision was explicitly confined, i. e., extension of time to the principal, "is one of the more technical suretyship defenses, the injuries resulting to the surety by reason thereof being more likely to be theoretical than real."

51. See Hilpert, op.cit. supra note 50; Roberts, Defenses of an Accommodation Maker, 23 Iowa L.Rev. 335, 340; note, 1939, 25 Va.L.Rev. 1000; 1934, 18 Minn.L.Rev. 473; 1934, 43 Yale L.J. 1015; 1940, 53 Harv.L.Rev. 1390; 1927, 48 A.L.R. 715; 1930, 65 A. L.R. 1425; 1937, 108 A.L.R. 1088; 1949, 2 A.L.R.2d 260. The Chotiner case, note 48, supra, stresses this analogy as do other cases involving mortgages. It summarizes the reasoning that influences the courts following the majority rule as follows: "It is reasoned that section 119, which covers discharge of the instrument also covers discharge of the primary parties, the greater including the less, and that, together, these sections cover the whole field of who are parties primarily and secondarily liable and the manner in which they may be discharged from liability, the enumerated methods of discharge being exclusive. It is argued that the inclusion of some suretyship defenses in the methods of discharge of secondary parties in section 120 and the omission of any reference to such defenses from section 119 shows a clear intent to abrogate such defenses as to one who appears upon the face of the paper as primarily liable. An additional ground for their conclusion given by the later majority rule cases is that the act was adopted after this interpretation had been put upon it in the majority of jurisdictions considering the question and, further, the paramount purpose of uniformity was a compelling reason for following the majority rule."

48. Mortgage Guaranty Co. v. Chotiner, 1936, 8 Cal. 2d 110, 64 P.2d 138, 108 A.L.R. 1080, commented on, 1937, 10 So.Cal.L.Rev. 511; Continental Mutual Savings Bank v. Elliott, 1932, 166 Wash. 283, 6 P.2d 638, 81 A.L.R. 1005, commented on in, 1933, 19 Va. L.Rev. 618; 1932, 2 Idaho L.J. 143; 1933, 17 Minn. L.Rev. 220; Peter v. Finzer, 1928, 116 Neb. 380, 217 N.W. 612, 65 A.L.R. 1418, noted in 1928, 42 Harv.L. Rev. 136; 1928, 6 Neb.L.Bull. 417; 1928, 26 Mich. L.Rev. 929; 1928, 12 Minn.L.Rev. 668; Washer v. Tontar, 1934, 128 Ohio St. 111, 190 N.E. 231.

49. In Mortgage Guaranty Co. v. Chotiner, 1936, 8 Cal.2d 110, 64 P.2d 138, 108 A.L.R. 1080, the court, which made an exhaustive review of the authorities, states that only two writers, Daniel, Negotiable Instruments; 7th ed., § 1511 and Crawford, Negotiable Instruments Law, Rev. 4th ed., 201 champion the rule. "Other than these, the discussions examined unite in its condemnation as an unnecessarily strict interpretation of the Negotiable Instruments Law, while conceding that it is probably so well entrenched that an amendment would be required to effect a change."

50. Daniel, op.cit. supra note 49, supports the majority rule solely on this ground. But see Brannan, Some Necessary Amendments to the Negotiable Instruments Law, 1913, 26 Harv.L.Rev. 588, 595, pointing out that, in view of diverse decisions under the act, especially since Fullerton Lumber Co. v. Snouffer, 1908, 139 Iowa 176, 117 N.W. 50, this argument is of doubtful weight. See also Hilpert, Discharge of Latent Sureties on Negotiable Instruments Because of Release or Extension of Time,

52. See Stevens, Extension Agreements in the "Subject-to" Mortgage Situation, 1941, 15 U. of Cin.L. Rev. 58, 69–70, "the mortgagor remains, as he was before the sale of the land subject to the mortgage, the only person personally liable on the negotiable instrument, or otherwise. * * * an accommo-

There is, however, a minority that grants a discharge to the mortgagor in spite of the mortgage debt being in the form of a negotiable instrument governed by the Negotiable Instruments Law.[53] This result has met with approval by commentators. "Most writers are in agreement that the situation is either covered by subdivision (4) of section 119 (providing that the instrument is discharged "by any other act which will discharge a simple contract for the payment of money") or is an omitted case, being neither the discharge of the instrument (section 119) nor the discharge of a person secondarily liable (section 120) and, under section 196, is governed by the law merchant."[54] It may be remarked that the approval of the minority view goes only to the interpretation of the Negotiable Instruments Law as not excluding suretyship rules generally and does not go to the merits of the particular suretyship rule involved.

> dation maker cannot set up suretyship defenses under the Negotiable Instruments Law. * * * It would indeed be strange * * * that a mortgagor, who signed as principal, can make use of 'surety' defenses although an accommodation maker cannot do so."

53. Industrial Trust Co. v. Goldman, 1937, 59 R.I. 11, 193 A. 852, 112 A.L.R. 1313, assumption of the mortgage; Zastrow v. Knight, 1930, 56 S.D. 554, 229 N.W. 925, 72 A.L.R. 379, conveyance subject to the mortgage; Isaacs v. Van Hoose, 1931, 171 La. 676, 131 So. 845; Jefferson Co. Bank v. Erickson, 1933, 188 Minn. 354, 247 N.W. 245; Stapler v. Anderson, 1933, 177 Ga. 434, 170 S.E. 498.

54. Mortgage Guarantee Co. v. Chotiner, note 48, supra, at 121. "Additional criticisms of the deduction that the methods of discharge enumerated in sections 119 and 120 are exclusive are an elaboration of the argument that the Negotiable Instruments Law was not intended to cover the entire subject of suretyship and that it is erroneous to draw the conclusion that it was from the incomplete provisions respecting suretyship contained in section 120 (10 Ill.L.Rev. 277) and that at least three other sections (51, 122, and 124) deal with methods of discharge. * * *

Aside from the criticism that the statute itself does not compel the overruling of the existing suretyship law, the most cogent objection to the majority rule is that the rights of the surety do not depend upon the face of the paper but on outside equities, and a recognition thereof would not actually obstruct negotiability or impair circulation, since the rule only applies where the holder has knowledge of the prin-

As one court stated, there is "little room under the majority rule for logical distinctions between the various suretyship defenses (for reason surely demands that, if any existing suretyship defenses are held to be abrogated by means of interpreting sections 119 and 120 as exclusive, the Negotiable Instruments Law must be held to have superseded all such defenses not enumerated in those sections)."[55] Yet at least one court created some doubt as to whether distinctions nevertheless might not be drawn.[56]

Where there have been several successive conveyances and assumptions it would be pretty difficult to find that the Negotiable Instruments Law governed the rights and liabilities of those subsequent to the mortgagor. None of them are parties to the instrument in any way. Consequently an extension to

cipal and surety relation between the obligors and has acted in disregard of the equities arising from the contract of suretyship." Ibid. In addition to Brannon, Negotiable Instruments Law, 5th ed., 888, the court listed the following comments appearing in legal periodicals in support of these strictures, "30 Harv.L.Rev. 141; 19 Marq.L.Rev. 122. See also 42 Harv.L.Rev. 136; 12 Minn.L.Rev. 668; 6 Neb.L. Rev. 417; 26 Mich.L.Rev. 929; 28 Mich.L.Rev. 930; 31 Am.Bar Rep. 1164; 59 U. of Pa.L.Rev. 532; 13 St. Louis L.Rev. 69 and 215; 2 U. of Cin.L.Rev. 441; 22 Ky.L.Rev. 371; 11 Tenn.L.Rev. 285; 14 Or.L.Rev. 273; 10 Tul.L.Rev. 139; 17 Minn.L.Rev. 220; 2 Idaho L.Rev. 143." See also Raymond, Suretyship at "Law Merchant" 1916, 30 Harv.L. Rev. 141; Warm, Rights and Liabilities of Mortgagee, Mortgagor, Grantee, 1936, 10 Temple L.Q. 116, 139; 1933, 81 U. of Pa.L.Rev. 641; Glenn, Mortgages, § 275. A third method of achieving the result is to bring the maker within the meaning of that section providing for the discharge of parties secondarily liable. Grace v. Wilson, 1931, 139 Misc. 757, 250 N.Y.S. 212; see 1933, 19 Va.L.Rev. 618, 621, n. 27.

55. Mortgage Guarantee Co. v. Chotiner, note 54, supra.

56. By expressly limiting the scope of its decision to an extension case and stating that it was induced to hold that the act excluded that suretyship defense because of its technical character. Mortgage Guarantee Co. v. Chotiner, note 54, supra.

A mortgagor-maker of a note who pays the holder and takes an assignment has been held not to discharge it but is entitled to enforce it against an assuming grantee. Mueller v. Jagerson Fuel Co., 1930, 203 Wis. 453, 233 N.W. 633, 72 A.L.R. 1059, noted 1931, 15 Minn.L.Rev. 818; 1931, 5 U. of Cin. L.Rev. 369.

an ultimate assuming grantee should and apparently does discharge intermediate assuming grantees from their liability to the mortgagee.[57] However, this discharge may be illusory. It has been held that when the mortgagee proceeds against the mortgagor, who on the majority rule remains liable, he in turn then may sue and recover from his assuming grantee.[58] The result is desirable and provides an additional argument against the majority rule.[59]

MERGER—GENERAL INTRODUCTION

272. The doctrine of merger, although it may relate exclusively to the mortgaged property, generally applies to determine the enforceability of the debt, and with it the mortgage, in three types of cases which are discussed in following sections.

Where the security interest in mortgaged property, whether it be legal or equitable, lien or title, and the redemption interest, also regardless of its technical nature, vest in the same person a problem is created that is usually discussed in terms of merger *vel non* of the mortgage.[60] As in other instances, the use of the word mortgage may lead to confusion or erroneous ideas since it quite commonly is employed to mean, indifferently, the security interest in the land, the obligation secured, or both.[61] So here, the doctrine of merger is sometimes talked about as though it concerned only the interests in the land itself [62] or, less frequently, only the enforceability of the debt in whole or in part with the fate of the mortgage depending upon the decision as to the obligation.[63] Actually, either may be the case. Instances of the latter sort are not only the most common but are of paramount practical importance. Nevertheless it may be that, concededly, the debt is alive, and yet it may be possible for the problem to arise whether the two interests in the property in the hands of the one person will, notwithstanding, be kept, or at least treated as, separate and distinct, or will be allowed to merge into a single undivided unit of ownership in the holder. For example, the mortgagee may receive a gift conveyance of the redemption interest from one who bought it from the mortgagor under an agreement that the mortgagor, who received the full value of the property, would pay the

---

57. This seemed to be assumed to be true by the court in Finzer v. Peter, 1930, 120 Neb. 389, 232 N. W. 762, 73 A.L.R. 1170, commented on in, 1931, 8 N.Y.Univ.L.Q.Rev. 511; 1931, 44 Harv.L.Rev. 999; 1931, 29 Mich.L.Rev. 1090; 1931, 9 Neb.L.Bull. 453. See 1931, 73 A.L.R. 1177.

58. Finzer v. Peter, note 57, supra. The court said that "no act of the mortgagee which does not result in a release of *all* of the parties can affect the contract between the grantor and the grantee." Hyde v. Miller, 1899, 45 App.Div. 396, 60 N.Y.S. 974, affirmed 1901, 168 N.Y. 590, 60 N.E. 1113, accord. See 1931, 73 A.L.R. 1177.

59. See 1931, 44 Harv.L.Rev. 999. The enactment of the Uniform Commercial Code § 3–606 made problems under the N.I.L. unimportant.

60. The question involved may more properly be one of "payment, extinguishment or confusion." See 1935, 95 A.L.R. 89. "The doctrine of merger, properly speaking, is a common-law doctrine having to do with estates in or charges upon realty. * * * The question here involved has nothing to do with any estate in the land, but is a question of whether the personal liability of the maker has been extinguished. The applicable doctrine though sometimes discussed in the phraseology of merger, is more properly spoken of as 'extinguishment' or 'confusion of rights.' It goes back through the civil law to the Roman law doctrine of 'confusio' where-

by a concurrence in the same person at the same time of the characters of debtor and creditor with respect to the same debt extinguishes the debt." Wright v. Anderson, 1934, 62 S.D. 444, 253 N.W. 484, 95 A.L.R. 81. See also, Tiffany, Real Prop., 3d ed., § 1479.

61. See §§ 107, 226, 253.

62. E. g., Hines v. Ward, 1898, 121 Cal. 115, 118, 53 P. 427, 428; Shaw, C. J., in Hunt v. Hunt, 1883, 31 Mass. (14 Pick.) 374, 385, 25 Am.Dec. 400.

63. E. g., see Tiffany, Real Prop., 3d ed., § 1479, "As we have before seen, the debt is the principal thing, and the mortgage is merely an incident, and the question is, not whether the mortgage is merged, but whether the acquisition by one person of both the mortgaged land and the debt secured by the mortgage has the effect of extinguishing or merging the debt. If the debt is extinguished under such circumstances, the mortgage lien is necessarily also extinguished, while if the debt remains, the mortage lien also remains." It may be conceded that if the debt which the mortgage secures is extinguished the mortgage will go with it. The debt may remain however without the mortgage continuing to exist, as is brought out in the text following this note-call.

debt.[64] In such a case, assuming no intervening liens or other interest in favor of third persons, usually there is no reason why the mortgagee, who is now owner of all interests in the property as well as proprietor of the debt claim against the mortgagor, would wish to keep alive and separate a mortgage on his own land to secure his debt right. On the other hand there is no reason why he should not be able to do it if he so wishes. He may wish to transfer the debt as a secured one by way of gift or by sale, in the latter case having in mind a more ready market than he could find for an unsecured obligation. Whether there would be merger in such a case should depend upon the intent of the mortgage creditor in whom all interests in the property came together. In the absence of affirmative evidence of intention to keep the mortgage alive, it seems a reasonable presumption that he did not intend to do so.[65]

In lien states it would be impossible for the mortgage debt to be held by one person with the security interest in another.[66] Such a situation, however, although not usual, can occur in a title state. In such jurisdictions a mortgagee may convey legal title to the property at the same time keeping the debt; or he may transfer the debt without conveying the legal title to the property which he holds as security.[67] In either case, the one in whom the bare legal security title is vested will hold it in equity as a constructive trustee for the holder of the debt.[68] If, in either of these two events, the mortgagor should then convey his redemption interest to the holder of the legal security title a situa-tion would be created in which one person would have the entire legal interest and a different person would have the debt. In order for merger to occur, however, both interests in the land must be held in the same right.[69] Consequently, if the holder of the legal security title took the conveyance of the redemption interest, not to hold it as trustee for the owner of the debt, but in his own right, there would be no merger.[70] If he took it to hold for the debt owner, whether or not merger would result would depend upon whether that would be the effect if the legal interests as well as the equitable interests were in the hands of the owner of the debt. Similarly, if the legal owner of the security title should convey it to the mortgagor, it would not affect the right of the holder of the debt to enforce it and the mortgage on the land. Or, if the mortgagor conveyed his redemption interest to the holder of the debt, the fact that the legal security title was outstanding in the hands of a third person as trustee would not affect the question of merger vel non.[71]

Not only should the foregoing distinctions be borne in mind but so should the fact that the question of merger arises in quite distinct ways with different considerations determining the outcome in each category. Indeed there are instances in which merger quite properly is held to apply as between certain parties and yet as to others the debt and mortgage will be held to have continued or revived existence.[72] The ways in which the

64. That in such a transaction the mortgagor would be the principal debtor and the land in the hands of the purchaser merely a surety, see § 247, supra. A similar case would be for the mortgagee to transfer the debt and mortgage to a grantee from the mortgagor.

65. See § 273, infra. See also, § 275, infra.

66. See § 224, supra.

67. See §§ 224, 225, supra.

68. Ibid.

69. Hooper v. Goldstein, 1930, 336 Ill. 125, 168 N.E. 1, certiorari denied 281 U.S. 724, 50 S.Ct. 239, 74 L. Ed. 1141; Ingstad v. Farmers' State Bank, 1931, 61 N.D. 194, 237 N.W. 704. See Shaw, C. J., in Hunt v. Hunt, 1883, 31 Mass. (14 Pick.) 374, 385, 25 Am. Dec. 400.

70. Hough v. De Forest, 1839, 13 Conn. 472; Denzler v. O'Keefe, 1881, 34 N.J.Eq. 361; Swayze v. Schuyler. 1899, 59 N.J.Eq. 75, 45 A. 347; Angel v. Boner, N.Y.1862, 38 Barb. 425, semble.

71. Brown v. Bartee, Miss.1844, 10 Smedes & M. 268. See Hatz's Appeal, 1861, 40 Pa.St. 209.

72. "Where a mortgagee becomes owner of the legal title * * * if there are junior mortgages on the land, it will be necessary to keep the titles sep-

question of merger may be presented are as follows: (1) those cases in which the question arises between the holder of the mortgage debt plus both the security and redemption interests in the property and one who has the duty of paying the debt;[73] (2) those in which the controversy is between the holder of the debt together with the security and redemption interests and an intervening lien or claim of a third person;[74] and (3) those in which the question is whether a subsequent purchaser of the entire property from the person who was the record holder of all interests in the property and owner of the mortgage debt will prevail over the holder of a prior unrecorded assignment of the debt and mortgage.[75] The three problems will be taken up seriatim in the following sections.

MERGER—BETWEEN PARTIES TO THE MORTGAGE—GENERAL PRINCIPLES

273. Where the question of merger arises between the parties to the merger, the intention of the one in whom all interests unite generally is a factor in determining the result. Courts commonly state that his interest will be presumed in accordance with his best interests. While this might afford a basis for a factual inference in the absence of or along with other evidence, usually the presumption is a rule of law which operates regardless of actual intent. This is strikingly so when it is used to justify prevention of merger where there is a clear intention to extinguish the debt and mortgage. In some cases the debt and mortgage will be extinguished without regard to intent to keep them alive.

arate, so as to protect the mortgagee from such inferior liens. As between the mortgagor and mortgagee a merger would be proper, but not as between the holders of the different mortgage liens. Instances might be multiplied where merger would be unobjectionable as to some parties and injurious as to others." Graves, J., in Fort Scott Building & Loan Ass'n v. Palatine Ins. Co., 74 Kan. 272, 276, 86 P. 142. Cf. Metzen v. Shaeffer, 1884, 65 Cal. 81, 3 P. 92.

73. See § 273, infra.

74. See § 275, infra.

75. See § 276, infra.

The problem of merger as between the holder of the debt and mortgage plus the redemption interest and one who is liable for the payment of the debt may arise in four different ways: (1) The mortgage creditor may acquire the redemption interest from the mortgagor. (2) The mortgage creditor may acquire the redemption interest from a grantee of the mortgagor. (3) The mortgage creditor may transfer the debt and mortgage to the mortgagor. (4) Or the mortgage creditor may transfer his entire interest in the debt and land to a grantee of the mortgagor. The last two logically could have been treated under transfers by the mortgagee rather than in this chapter. However, since all four involve problems so similar it seemed best to treat them together. And, because certain of the principles of solution require a knowledge of the results of a transfer of the property by the mortgagor, treatment at this later point appeared desirable.

When the owner of the mortgage acquires the entire interest in the land, except as protection against known or possible intervening claims of third persons, ordinarily there is no point in his keeping the mortgage alive on his own land. This was noted before as well as the observation that, in the absence of affirmative evidence of intent or interest to the contrary, the reasonable presumption is that there is no intention to keep it on foot.[76] However, unless the mortgage debt is extinguished by the doctrine of merger there is no objection to his doing so. Whether or not it will be extinguished is usually said to depend upon the intention of the person in whom the

76. See § 272, supra.

"It is true that, under ordinary circumstances, where the holder of a mortgage acquires the estate of a mortgagor, the mortgage interest is merged in the fee and the mortgage is extinguished. This is the ordinary legal effect of the transaction, and ordinarily the intention is presumed to accord with the act accomplished." Anglo-California Bank v. Field, 1905, 146 Cal. 644, 653, 80 P. 1080, 1083. See also Tiffany, Real Prop., 3d ed., § 1480; Pomeroy, Equity Juris, 5th ed., § 790.

interests unite;[77] or, in the absence of any expression of intention, upon his best interests in the matter.[78] The latter factor, while of great importance where there are intervening claims to the property,[79] seldom is of consequence as between the parties to the mortgage, at least in cases where the mortgage debt is not extinguished, in which case there will be automatic merger or destruction of the mortgage.[80] For the former to govern it has been said that it is the intention that exists at the time the interests came together which determines,[81] but there are authorities holding that subsequently expressed intention will be given effect.[82] The correct rule would seem to be as follows: If there was no intention at the time of union, or if there was an effective intention against merger at that time, a subsequent intention to merge should control.[83] On the other hand, if an intention to merge existing at the time

of union has operative effect, a subsequent change of intention cannot recreate the destroyed interests, at least if the merger has wiped out the debt instead of merely resulting in the property interests coalescing.[84]

The intention as to merger or no may be manifested in various ways and is determined from all of the circumstances of the particular case.[85] Expressions of intention contained in the instruments of transfer of the land or of the mortgage will ordinarily be given effect,[86] as will also express agreement accompanying the transfers.[87] A release or satisfaction of the mortgage has been held to indicate an intention to merge[88] whereas an absence of such a release or satisfaction has been regarded as showing an opposite intent.[89] Later dealings with the property are also looked to in order to discover intention. Thus a later conveyance with covenants of title which cover the mortgage is regarded as showing an intention to merge.[90] On the other hand, a subsequent conveyance of the property subject to the mortgage[91] or a later assignment of the debt and mortgage[92] evidences an intention against merger.

77. See Woodside v. Lippold, 1901, 113 Ga. 877, 39 S. E. 400, 84 Am.St.Rep. 267, "It has been uniformly held, in the application of the equitable doctrine concerning merger, that the intention, when expressed, of the person in whom the two estates meet, must control."

In re B. F. Dewees, Inc., C.A.Pa.1968, 404 F.2d 519, held that, although when a mortgagee acquires the equity of redemption there is a presumption he intends to extinguish the mortgage interest by merging it in the estate in fee, the presumption is rebuttable and was rebutted in the principal case.

78. "He can, by expressly declaring his intention, either keep it alive or destroy it. If there is no reason for keeping it alive, then equity will, in the absence of any declaration of his intention, destroy it; but if there is any reason for keeping it alive, such as the existence of another encumbrance, equity will not destroy it." Sir George Jessel in Adams v. Angell, 1876, 5 Ch.D. 634. See § 272, supra.

79. See § 275, infra.

80. That there will be, in certain cases, an automatic extinguishment of the debt, in whole or in part, regardless of intention, see infra, this section.

81. McClain v. Weise, 1886, 22 Ill.App. 272; see 1934, 8 U. of Cin.L.Rev. 212; Pomeroy, Eq.Juris., 5th ed., § 792.

82. Goodwin v. Keney, 1880, 47 Conn. 486; Fort Scott Building & Loan Ass'n v. Palatine Ins. Co., 1906, 74 Kan. 272, 277, 86 P. 142; Nagle v. Conard, 1911, 79 N.J.Eq. 124, 81 A. 841, affirmed 80 N.J.Eq. 253, 86 A. 1103.

83. See cases in preceding note.

84. Cheffee v. Geageah, 1925, 253 Mass. 586, 149 N.E. 620; McCabe v. Farnsworth, 1873, 27 Mich. 52. See Tiffany, Real Prop., § 1480. If the debt is still alive, whether the security interest in the land can be recreated once it is gone depends upon whether that can be done merely by an expression of intent. See §§ 23, 30, 33, supra.

85. Dubbels v. Thompson, 1914, 49 Mont. 550, 143 P. 986; see Pomeroy, Equity Juris., 5th ed., § 792.

86. E. g., Anglo-California Bank v. Field, 1905, 146 Cal. 644, 80 P. 1080; see 1935, 95 A.L.R. 628, 649.

87. E. g., Gibbs v. Johnson, 1895, 104 Mich. 120, 62 N.W. 145; see 1935, 95 A.L.R. 628, 650.

88. E. g., Woodside v. Lippold, 1901, 113 Ga. 877, 39 S.E. 400, 84 Am.St.Rep. 267.

89. E. g., Davis v. Randall, 1897, 117 Cal. 12, 48 P. 906.

90. Pearson v. Bailey, 1902, 180 Mass. 229, 62 N.E. 265; see § 276, infra.

91. Saint v. Cornwall, 1903, 207 Pa. 270, 56 A. 440; see Clift v. White, 1855, 12 N.Y. 519.

92. Goodwin v. Keney, 1880, 47 Conn. 486; Security Title & Trust Co. v. Schlender, 1901, 190 Ill. 609, 60 N.E. 854; see 1910, 27 L.R.A.,N.S., 816.

Where there is no evidence as to intention in respect to merger, it is stated that equity will presume the intention to be in accordance with the best interests of the owner of both interests.[93] While in some instances such a presumption may be justified as an inference of fact, for the most part in such cases actual intent is immaterial. In reality the presumption of intent in such a case is a rule of law, the basis of which is examined in the next section.[94] Further, in the discussion immediately following, there will be instances in which the terms of the transaction will operate to prevent any enforcement of the debt as between the parties regardless of intent or self-interest which may keep it alive for certain purposes against others.[95]

MERGER—SPECIFIC PROBLEMS

274. Acquisition by the mortgage creditor of the interest of the mortgagor or his grantee may extinguish the mortgage because it was received in satisfaction of it by way of payment, substituted performance, or accord and satisfaction. If the mortgage creditor assumed payment of the mortgage there will be merger of the entire debt without regard to his intention. So too, up to the value of the land, if he took the property subject to the mortgage. In such a case, if he paid value, some authorities give a complete discharge. The same principles govern acquisitions from a grantee of the mortgagor. Nor, generally, do different principles govern when a junior and senior mortgage are in the same hands and the mortgagee buys in on foreclosure sale of one. The acquisition of the mortgage by one primarily bound to discharge it, whether he be mortgagor or assuming grantee extinguishes the mortgage. The same is true of one taking subject to the mortgage who buys it in. Where it was a gift to him he may be able to enforce the debt as to any excess over the value of the land.

1. *Acquisition from mortgagor by mortgage creditor.* Keeping the foregoing general considerations in mind, we can turn to an examination of the four types of transac-

tions enumerated at the beginning of the section. In the first of these, where the mortgage creditor acquires the redemption interest from the mortgagor, whether the acquisition will permit enforcement of the debt and mortgage according to the intention of acquisitor, or will preclude regardless of intention, will depend upon the terms of the transfer. If it was a gift conveyance by the mortgagor it is obvious that the debt claim of the mortgage creditor would be unaffected and whether there would be a merger of the interests in the land would depend, as previously noted, upon the intent of the mortgage creditor.[96] Quite as clearly, if the conveyance is made and accepted as payment of the mortgage debt no question of merger is possible. The debt is discharged by payment, or perhaps more accurately, by substituted performance or accord and satisfaction; but not by merger.[97] The creditor now has full title to the property with no debt in existence for it to secure. If the mortgage debt is extinguished, the mortgage itself is never kept alive. Consequently there is automatic merger of the two interests in the property and no intent on the part of the creditor can keep them separate.

There is a similar result for different reasons if the conveyance to the mortgagee is accompanied by an assumption of the mortgage. If the mortgagee were permitted to recover from the mortgagor the latter could turn around and sue him to get back the same amount. Or even more strikingly, when sued, the mortgagor might bring a bill in equity against the plaintiff mortgagee to make him exonerate the mortgagor by paying to himself the debt he is seeking to collect.[98] To prevent this circuity of action a

---

93. See, e. g., Pomeroy, Equity Juris., 5th ed., § 791.

94. See § 275, infra.

95. See note-call and note 80, supra; § 275, infra.

96. See note 76, supra; § 272, supra.

97. Dennis v. McIntyre Merc. Co., 1914, 187 Ala. 314, 65 So. 774; McCabe v. Farnsworth, 1873, 27 Mich. 52; see, 1935, 95 A.L.R. 89, 95. If the conveyance is accepted at or before maturity it operates by way of substituted performance; if after maturity, by accord and satisfaction.

98. See § 258, supra.

court of equity would give a complete defense to the mortgagor to any action on the debt. If there has been an assumption there is complete merger because there is complete circuity. No intent or self-interest on the part of the mortgage creditor could prevent this ending of the claim against the mortgagor and, with it, any mortgage interest in the property securing it.[99]

Where the conveyance to the mortgage creditor is subject to the mortgage, if the agreement is that it is to be accepted in satisfaction of the mortgage debt it will so operate.[1] If this is not the agreement there may be, technically, no extinguishment of the mortgage debt.[2] And, if there is an express agreement that it shall not operate to extinguish the mortgage, the agreement will be given effect.[3] Nevertheless, such a conveyance makes the land in the hands of the mortgage creditor the principal and the personal obligation of the mortgagor, up to the value of the land, surety only.[4] Consequently, up to the value of the land, the mortgagor has a defense to any enforcement of the debt against him regardless of whether it is technically alive by agreement or not.[5] And usually the courts treat the situation as one of merger with the debt discharged, as it clearly is in effect if the land equals the debt in value.[6] However, if there was no agree-

ment that the conveyance should be a discharge and the value of the land was less than the debt, the mortgage creditor can maintain an action for the excess of the debt over the land.[7] In such a case there is merger of the debt only up to the value of the land because there is circuity only to this extent.

2. *Acquisition from grantee of mortgagor by mortgage creditor.* The same principles govern where the redemption is obtained by the mortgage creditor from a grantee of the mortgagor, but the application of them becomes somewhat more complicated. There must first be an ascertainment of the terms on which the grantee held the property from

89, 93. Whenever a mortgagee buys the mortgaged property from the mortgagor subject to his own mortgage, whether it be on an execution sale or otherwise, in theory the price includes the amount of the mortgage. A court, therefore, would be strictly logical in taking the position that if he paid in present value anything, the land must be, at least in his opinion, worth the full amount of the debt plus whatever he was willing to pay to get the redemption interest. This would lead to the conclusion that any purchase of the land by the mortgagee subject to the mortgage must necessarily extinguish the mortgage debt. And there is authority to that effect. Biggins v. Brockman, 1872, 63 Ill. 316; Speer v. Whitfield, 1854, 10 N.J.Eq. 107; Schnell v. Schroder, S.C.1831, Bailey Eq. 334.

7. Contrary to the attitude of courts in the cases cited in the preceding footnotes, other courts take a realistic view and recognize that mortgagees quite commonly buy in redemption interests for small amounts, especially where the mortgagor is in insolvency proceedings, in order to avoid the expense of foreclosure or for other reasons and yet the land is worth less than the amount of the debt. They reach the conclusion that the debt, therefore, should be discharged only up to the actual value of the land at the time and do not preclude the mortgagee from establishing it. " 'The purchase of the equity of redemption by the mortgagee at a sale by the mortgagor's assignee in insolvency, or on execution is not at law a satisfaction of the mortgage debt, and the mortgagee is not estopped from claiming that the property is of less value than the amount of the debt.' " Clark v. Jackson, 1887, 64 N.H. 388, 391, 11 A. 59; Findlay v. Hosmer, 1817, 2 Conn. 350; Marston v. Marston, 1858, 45 Me. 412; Spencer v. Harford's Ex'rs, N.Y.1830, 4 Wend. 381. Cf. Miller v. Little, 1917, 37 N.D. 612, 164 N.W. 19; Ex parte Powell, 1904, 68 S.C. 324, 47 S.E. 440. See 1935, 8 U. of Cin.L.Rev. 213; 1902, 15 Harv.L.Rev. 740; 1935, 95 A.L.R. 89, 94. But see Glassie, The Assuming Vendee, 1923, 9 Va.L.Rev. 196, 205, n. 36, quoted § 250, n. 35, supra.

99. Forthman v. Deters, 1903, 206 Ill. 159, 69 N.E. 97, 99 Am.St.Rep. 145; Kneeland v. Moore, 1884, 138 Mass. 198; First State Bank v. Arneson, 1920, 109 Wash. 346, 186 P. 889; see 1935, 95 A.L.R. 89, 94. But see § 275, as to whether the mortgage may be kept alive as to third parties.

1. See supra, this section. See also Tiffany, Real Prop., 3d ed., § 1479.

2. Murphy v. Zuigaro, 1924, 72 Pa.Super.Ct. 511; Sheehan Building & Loan Ass'n v. Scanlon, 1933, 310 Pa. 6, 164 A. 722.

3. Sheehan Building & Loan Ass'n v. Scanlon, 1933, 310 Pa. 6, 164 A. 722.

4. See §§ 252, 258, supra.

5. E. g., Eagan v. Engeman, 1908, 125 App.Div. 743, 110 N.Y.S. 366.

6. Cock v. Bailey, 1892, 146 Pa. 328, 23 A. 370; see 1935, 8 U. of Cin.L.Rev. 212, 213; 1935, 95 A.L.R.

the grantor and the legal results of those terms in a particular jurisdiction. Then the terms of acquisition by the creditor from the grantee must be determined. For example, the case may be like the one previously explored.[8] The grantee may have bought from the mortgagor paying full value and with an agreement that the mortgagor was to pay the mortgage when it matured and then made a gift conveyance to the mortgage creditor. The result then would be the same as a gift conveyance directly from the mortgagor to the mortgagee. On the other hand conveyances in satisfaction of the mortgage debt, or with the mortgage creditor assuming or taking the property subject to the mortgage debt, will operate as would similar direct transactions between the mortgagor and mortgage creditor.[9] If the grantee has taken subject to the mortgage debt the mortgage creditor will also take it in the same way with an automatic merger, at least to the extent of the value of the land.[10] If the grantee has assumed the debt, again the land also would be principal and, if it is acquired by the mortgage creditor, bars the debt up to its value.[11] If, in addition, the mortgage creditor, in his turn, assumes the payment of the debt it will operate to preclude enforcement of any of the debt.

3. *Two mortgages in same hands—purchase on foreclosure of one.* Where the mortgage creditor holds not only a first mortgage but a second one questions have arisen as to the effect of purchase on foreclosure sale of one of the mortgages upon his rights under the other one. The general rule is that the purchase of mortgaged property by the hold-er of a junior mortgage at a sale on foreclosure of the senior mortgage, does not extinguish the debt secured by the junior mortgage.[12] And the same is true even though the foreclosed first mortgage also was owned by the purchasing second mortgagee.[13] However, if the holder of both a junior and senior mortgage forecloses the junior and buys it in on foreclosure sale it is generally held that, in the absence of an agreement to the contrary,[14] the mortgagor's personal liability for the debt secured by the first mortgage is extinguished.[15] The reason given is that on foreclosure sale under a junior mortgage the purchase is subject to the payment of the prior lien with the result that "the mortgagor has an equitable right to have the land pay the mortgage before his personal liability is called upon"[16] and the purchaser, if he owns or acquires the mortgage, will not be permitted to enforce it against the mortgagor personally. Nor will such a purchaser who has been willing to pay money for the redemption interest subject to the mortgage be permitted to say, as against the persons li-

8. See §§ 272, 274, supra.

9. E. g., Dickason v. Williams, 1880, 129 Mass. 182, 37 Am.Rep. 316; National Investment Co. v. Nordin, 1892, 50 Minn. 336, 52 N.W. 899, assuming grantees of mortgagor conveyed to mortgagee subject to the mortgage and thus extinguished it.

10. Lilly v. Palmer, 1869, 51 Ill. 331, see 1935, 95 A. L.R. 89, 95.

11. Russell v. Pistor, 1852, 7 N.Y. 171, 57 Am.Dec. 509; cases notes 9, 10, supra.

12. Ferry v. Fisk, 1921, 54 Cal.App. 763, 202 P. 964. Cf. Miller v. Little, 1917, 37 N.D. 612, 164 N.W. 19.

13. Blackwood v. Sakwinski, 1922, 221 Mich. 464, 191 N.W. 207, 29 A.L.R. 1314; Sautter v. Frick, 1930, 229 App.Div. 345, 242 N.Y.S. 369, affirmed 1931, 256 N.Y. 535, 177 N.E. 129, reversing, 1929, 133 Misc. 517, 232 N.Y.S. 529. Cf. Fischer v. Spierling, 1919, 93 N.J.L. 167, 107 A. 420. See 1924, 29 A.L.R. 1318; 1935, 95 A.L.R. 89, 103. After foreclosure and sale under a first mortgage, a conveyance by the first mortgagee, who bought it in, to the mortgagor will not revive the second mortgage on the land in his hands. See 1935, 12 N.Y.U.L.Q.Rev. 319.

14. Continental Title & Trust Co. v. Devlin, 1904, 209 Pa. 380, 58 A. 843; Toston v. Utah Mortgage Loan Co., C.C.A.Idaho 1940, 115 F.2d 560; Van Woerden v. Union Imp. Co., 1930, 156 Wash. 555, 287 P. 870.

15. Belleville Sav. Bank v. Reis, 1891, 136 Ill. 242, 26 N.E. 646; Maulding v. Sims, 1919, 213 Ill.App. 473; McDonald v. Magirl, 1896, 97 Iowa 677, 66 N.W. 904; Wright v. Anderson, 1934, 62 S.D. 444, 253 N. W. 484, 95 A.L.R. 81; see 1935, 95 A.L.R. 89, 104. It will not merge the first mortgage, however, as against intervening liens. Citizens State Bank v. Peterson, 1926, 114 Neb. 809, 210 N.W. 278; see Wright v. Anderson, 1934, 62 S.D. 444, 450, 253 N. W. 484, 487, 95 A.L.R. 81, 86.

16. See Wright v. Anderson, 1934, 62 S.D. 444, 450, 253 N.W. 484, 487, 95 A.L.R. 81, 86.

able on that mortgage, that the land he bought, the primary fund for the payment of the prior mortgage obligation, is not worth its amount.[17]

While this is true if the foreclosure sale under the junior mortgage has the same effect as a sale of the redemption interest on execution under the judgment of a third party creditor,[18] under some second mortgages this is not or should not be true. If the second mortgage is by warranty deed containing covenants covering the first mortgage, on foreclosure sale the covenants in the mortgage pass to the purchaser. He stands as though the mortgagor had conveyed the land to him by deed on the date of the second mortgage with the deed containing the covenants that actually were put in the mortgage.[19] Consequently, the mortgagor would continue to be the principal debtor and purchase by the first mortgagee should not affect his debt claim against the mortgagor.[20]

4. *Acquisition from mortgage creditor by mortgagor.* When the mortgage creditor transfers the debt claim and mortgage securing it to the mortgagor the inevitable result as between them is to extinguish both the debt and, along with it, the mortgage.[21] The same person cannot be both debtor and creditor.[22] This would be true regardless of whether the transfer was by way of gift or for value. In the latter case, especially if the value given was the amount of the mortgage debt, the transaction is likely to be intended to extinguish the debt by payment or an accord and satisfaction. If so, its demise should not be considered as occurring by reason of the doctrine of merger.[23]

5. *Acquisition from mortgage creditor by grantee of mortgagor.* A similar situation occurs where the mortgagor has conveyed to a grantee who assumes the mortgage and the mortgage creditor then assigns the debt and mortgage to him. He is the principal debtor in such a case and his acquisition of the claim against himself not only extinguishes it as to him [24] but also as to the mortgagor who stands in the position of a surety.[25] This would be true of a gift transfer to him and also if he paid value. The latter case parallels the one considered previously. Here as there, the debt may be regarded as extinguished by payment, substituted performance or accord and satisfaction rather than by merger. If the mortgagor was bound by agreement with the grantee to pay off the debt, an assignment of the debt and mortgage to the latter would not prevent him enforcing it against the principal debtor, the mortgagor.[26] Whether there would be merger as to the land would here again depend upon the intent or interest of the holder of it.

If the grantee had taken subject to the mortgage without assuming its payment the

---

17. Idem. But see cases, note 7, supra.

18. Murphy v. Elliott, Ind.1843, 6 Blackf. 482, "a mortgagee, by purchasing at a sheriff's sale on execution the equity of redemption, thereby extinguishes, to the extent of the value of the mortgaged premises, after deducting the sum paid for the equity of redemption, the mortgage debt."

19. Allis v. Foley, 1914, 126 Minn. 14, 147 N.W. 670; Knapp v. Foley, 1918, 140 Minn. 423, 426, 168 N.W. 183; see Ross, Covenants of Title in Mortgages, 1927, 12 Minn.L.Rev. 34, 41.

20. See Ross, Covenants of Title in Mortgages, 1927, 12 Minn.L.Rev. 34. See, semble, White, Revival of Mortgages, 1936, 10 U. of Cin.L.Rev. 217.

21. Hussey v. Hill, 1897, 120 N.C. 312, 26 S.E. 919, 58 Am.St.Rep. 789; Hill v. Hall, La.1843, 4 Rob. 416.

22. "The fundamental principle is that a man cannot be both debtor and creditor with respect to the same debt at the same time and when a situation arises where the hand that is obligated to pay the debt is the same hand that is entitled to receive it, the debt is extinguished and forever gone." Wright v. Anderson, 1934, 62 S.D. 444, 253 N.W. 484, 95 A.L.R. 81. See Coote, Mortgages, 9th ed., 1453. As to merger of the security interest and the redemption interest, see ibid., pp. 1439–1450.

23. See Tiffany, Real Prop., 3d ed., § 1482.

24. Russell v. Pistor, 1852, 7 N.Y. 171, 57 Am.Dec. 509; Barnett & Jackson v. McMillan, 1912, 176 Ala. 430, 58 So. 400; Fouche v. Delk, 1891, 83 Iowa 297, 48 N.W. 1078; Lydon v. Campbell, 1910, 204 Mass. 580, 91 N.E. 151, 134 Am.St.Rep. 702. See 1935, 95 A.L.R. 89, 111; 1927, 46 A.L.R. 329.

25. See §§ 269–271, supra.

26. Barnett & Jackson v. McMillan, 1912, 176 Ala. 430, 58 So. 400, as to the second mortgage.

only one personally liable is the mortgagor. Where such a grantee takes an assignment of the mortgage, as a general rule the debt secured by the mortgage is held to be extinguished and personal liability on it cannot be enforced.[27] Up to the value of the land there would seem no question as to the result. The mortgagor is surety only and the land principal with the result that, to prevent circuity the mortgagor could defeat any recovery up to that amount, and this is true regardless of whether the mortgage is acquired for value or as a gift. Where the debt exceeds the value of the land a question may arise as to the right of such a grantee-assignee to recover a deficiency.[28] If the grantee paid the amount of the debt for the assignment, the mortgagor should be able to insist that it constituted payment of the debt rather than purchase of it. The reason is that, although the grantee incurred no personal obligation to pay off the mortgage, nonetheless when he bought the land subject to it, his bargain included as a part of the price the amount of the mortgage debt. As a consequence, even though the mortgagor could not compel him to pay and the mortgage creditor has no right against him personally, yet it is so far his duty to discharge the debt that if he does so he should have no recourse against the mortgagor for reimbursement.[29] It would seem, therefore, that regardless of the value of the land, when a grantee subject to the mortgage buys in the mortgage, he cannot

enforce any right on it against the mortgagor.

It has been suggested, however, that if the mortgage creditor assigned the debt and mortgage to such a grantee by way of gift or for less than the amount of the debt it could be enforced by him as to any excess of the debt over the value of the land.[30] An argument can be made in favor of such a result along these lines. The mortgage creditor could have enforced the mortgage debt to the amount of its excess over the value of the land against the mortgagor without the latter having any recourse against the grantee who took subject to the mortgage. If he did so, after collecting it, the creditor could make a gift of those proceeds to anyone he wishes, including the grantee, free of any claim of the mortgagor to it. It would seem to follow that he has equal ability to make a gift of the right to collect the deficiency. Thus he might have given it to third person or to the mortgagor. If, instead, his donee is the mortgagor's grantee subject to the mortgage, it seems logical to say that the mortgagor cannot object to his enforcement of it.

MERGER—INTERVENING INTERESTS

275. Merger will be relieved against as to intervening liens and other interests except where (1) with knowledge of their existence the holder of both the mortgage and redemption intentionally extinguished the mortgage, and (2) where he assumed or took subject to them. The better view is that negligence in not discovering such liens or interests is immaterial. In certain cases, the acquisition of the redemption interest by the mortgagee will be given the same effect as a strict foreclosure as to junior interests.

As previously pointed out,[31] whether there is merger as between the mortgage creditor and the mortgagor or a grantee of the mortgagor is not decisive as to whether it also occurs as between the mortgage creditor and

---

27. Lilly v. Palmer, 1869, 51 Ill. 331; Atherton v. Toney, 1873, 43 Ind. 211; Price v. Rea, 1894, 92 Iowa 12, 60 N.W. 208; Wonderly v. Giessler, 1906, 118 Mo.App. 708, 93 S.W. 1130; see 1935, 95 A.L.R. 89, 107.

28. See notes 6, 7, supra, where the cognate question of the owner of the mortgage buying in the redemption interest is considered. In Southworth v. Scofield, 1873, 51 N.Y. 513, a purchaser on execution sale was permitted to recover a deficiency even though he took it subject to a mortgage which he later acquired.

29. For a further consideration of the same problem, see § 278, infra, on the point whether a grantee subject to the mortgage who pays off the mortgage debt is entitled to be subrogated to it.

30. See Tiffany, Real Prop., § 1482.

31. See § 272, note-call 72, supra.

holders of junior incumbrances[32] or other interests.[33] When the question arises in the latter situation it is generally said that merger is a question of intention and that intention will be presumed, in the absence of express manifestation, in accordance with the interests of the party in whom all interests in the debt and mortgaged property are united.[34] This statement, while it has certain merits, is an inadequate exposition of the principles governing the decisions. A more satisfactory explanation of the results of the cases requires an analysis of the proper role of actual intention, whether express or implied in fact, and the basis for "presuming" an intention in accordance with interest.

In the first place, in certain cases both intent and self interest will be immaterial. If the mortgage creditor in acquiring the land assumes not merely the first mortgage but also the payment of the junior incumbrance no expression of intent to keep the mortgage alive, or self interest in doing so, will avail as against the junior incumbrancer.[35] A plea of circuity of action by the later mortgagee will effectively preclude enforcement of the earlier mortgage in the hands of such a creditor.[36] The same would be true up to the value of the land if the property were acquired subject to the later mortgage.[37]

It is also clear that if the mortgage creditor knew of the intervening interest and nevertheless clearly indicated an intention that his prior mortgage should be discharged there will be merger and the junior encumbrance will be elevated to priority regardless of his best interests being to the contrary.[38]

Turning to cases in which the courts hold that the first mortgage will be preserved or reinstated as against intervening incumbrances or interests,[39] in some of them the mortgage creditor clearly indicated his intention to keep the first mortgage in existence as against such interests and the courts rest the result upon that ground.[40] This is true even though there may be an automatic merger of the first mortgage between the parties to it by reason of an assumption of or taking subject to it.[41] In a large number of cases in which there is no evidence of intention to keep the prior mortgage alive, other than that it would be to the interest of the mortgage creditor to do so, it is held that there is no merger.[42] But the courts go beyond this and hold, in spite of an undisputed

32. See 1909, 39 L.R.A.,N.S., 834; 1935, 95 A.L.R. 628, for collections of cases. See also Note, The Rights of a Junior Lienholder in Wisconsin, 1959, 42 Marq.L.Rev. 89, 94.

33. See 1927, 46 A.L.R. 322.

34. See, e. g., McCraney v. Morris, 1933, 170 S.C. 250, 170 S.E. 276, 95 A.L.R. 622; note, 1935, 95 A.L.R. 628, 629, General Rules.

35. Ernst v. McChesney, 1900, 186 Ill. 617, 58 N.E. 399; Kneeland v. Moore, 1884, 138 Mass. 198; Drew v. Anderson, Clayton & Co., 1927, 120 Okl. 250, 252 P. 64, noted, 27 Col.L.Rev. 609; Bolln v. La Prele Live Stock Co., 1921, 27 Wyo. 335, 196 P. 748; Brown v. Stead, 1832, 5 Sim. 535.

36. See § 273, supra. If there is an assumption of the second mortgage by the first mortgage creditor it will be extinguished on grounds of circuity even though there is no merger of the first mortgage as to the land or the mortgagor.

37. Id.

38. Townsend v. Provident Realty Co., 1905, 110 App.Div. 226, 96 N.Y.S. 1091; Beacham v. Gurney, 1894, 91 Iowa 621, 60 N.W. 187; Errett v. Wheeler, 1909, 109 Minn. 157, 123 N.W. 414, 26 L.R.A.,N.S., 816; Stantons v. Thompson, 1870, 49 N.H. 272; see 1910, 31 L.R.A.,N.S., 323. Cases of assumption of the later lien or taking subject to it might be placed upon this ground. However, circuity of action would apply to prevent any enforcement of the earlier mortgage in priority to the later lien regardless of intent in respect to discharge or merger of the first mortgage.

39. It hardly needs to be stated that the preservation of the mortgage is solely for foreclosure purposes and, even for that purpose, only as to the intervening liens or other interests. See Glenn, Mortgages, § 337.

40. Gibbs v. Johnson, 1895, 104 Mich. 120, 62 N.W. 145. See 1935, 95 A.L.R. 628, 649, 650.

41. Barnett & Jackson v. McMillan, 1912, 176 Ala. 430, 58 So. 400; Fouche v. Delk, 1891, 83 Iowa 297, 48 N.W. 1078; Senter v. Senter, 1913, 87 Ohio St. 377, 101 N.E. 272, subject to; Nebraska Central Building & Loan Ass'n v. H. J. Hughes & Co., 1931, 121 Neb. 266, 236 N.W. 699, semble. See 1935, 95 A.L.R. 628, 649, 650. But look at Clay v. Banks, 1883, 71 Ga. 363.

42. See 1918, 18 Col.L.Rev. 280. See also cases in following footnotes.

intent on the part of the mortgage creditor to discharge the first mortgage, that nevertheless he may use it for foreclosure purposes against junior interests.[43] This is the almost uniform result where the mortgage creditor was ignorant of the intervening lien.[44] Although there is some authority that his negligence in not discovering the existence of the later interest [45] or in mistakenly relying on its not being enforced [46] will prevent him using it against the subsequent claimant, other and, it is believed, better authority holds to the contrary.[47] Indeed the rule may be laid down broadly that, except for the two cases stated at the outset of this section, merger will not operate to permit a later incumbrance to be elevated to a position of priority over the first mortgage regardless of its fate as between the parties to that first mortgage.[48] Actual intent, where it exists, is an adequate basis for the result. The mortgage creditor has a legitimate interest to protect himself against the elevation of the later interest. By bringing a foreclosure action in which they were joined as parties defendant the property could have been sold free and clear of their interests and he could have bought it in that state. Acquisition of the redemption in any other way should not prejudice his position with respect to such junior interests if he did not intend it to do so and was not under a duty to do acts which would have that result. The owner of the junior interest, under such circumstances, cannot object to being kept or put back into his position in the rear because he never bargained for advancement that would come to him by destruction of the first mortgage. But more generally the decisions may be justified on grounds of unjust enrichment, a doctrine implicit in the rationale of fairness in giving effect to the mortgage creditor's intent when it appears. By the destruction of the prior mortgage, the later lien or interest is elevated to a priority for which its owner paid nothing and hence is, as to him, a pure windfall. And it is a windfall at the expense of the prior mortgagee. If the owner of the prior mortgage knew of the later interest and intended nevertheless to discharge or otherwise wipe out the first mortgage, there is, of course, no injustice to him in permitting the later claimant to take advantage of his unmerited advancement. Where the first mortgagee knew of the second man and intended to prevent him getting this benefit it would be unconscionable to permit him

43. Brooks v. Rice, 1880, 56 Cal. 428, conveyance by mortgagor to mortgagee in satisfaction of the mortgage held not to operate as a merger against an intervening mortgage; Richardson v. Hockenhull, 1877, 85 Ill. 124; Moffet v. Farwell, 1906, 222 Ill. 543, 78 N.E. 925; Sullivan v. Saunders, 1909, 66 W.Va. 350, 66 S.E. 497, 42 L.R.A.,N.S., 1010, 19 Ann.Cas. 480; Fitch v. Applegate, 1901, 24 Wash. 25, 64 P. 147; See 1912, 39 L.R.A.,N.S., 834; 1935, 95 A.L.R. 628, 643.

"On this point, I am of the opinion that upon such a state of facts, showing a title intervening between the mortgage and quitclaim deed, it is to be presumed, as a matter of law, that the parties did not intend to extinguish the mortgage. * * *" Stantons v. Thompson, 1870, 49 N.H. 272, 276. See also Wilson v. Vanstone, 1892, 112 Mo. 315, 20 S.W. 612; Grellet v. Heilshorn, 1869, 4 Nev. 526. See note, 1918, 18 Col.L.Rev. 280; note, 1934, 12 N.Y.Univ.L. Q.Rev. 317.

44. Silliman v. Gammage, 1881, 55 Tex. 365; Seiberling v. Tipton, 1893, 113 Mo. 373, 21 S.W. 4; Howard v. Clark and Teachout, 1899, 71 Vt. 424, 45 A. 1042, 76 Am.St.Rep. 782; see Woodhurst v. Cramer, 1902, 29 Wash. 40, 48, 69 P. 501, 503; 1935, 95 A.L. R. 628, 643; 1934, 40 W.Va.L.Q. 280; Frazee v. Inslee, 1839, 2 N.J.Eq. 239, contra. A fortiori, the same would be true where the discharge of the prior lien was obtained by fraud. See 1935, 95 A. L.R. 628, 647.

45. See Fort Dodge Building & Loan Ass'n v. Scott, 1892, 86 Iowa 431, 434, 53 N.W. 283, 284, semble. And see Rice v. Winters, 1895, 45 Neb. 517, 63 N.W. 830; Bohn Sash & Door Co. v. Case, 1894, 42 Neb. 281, 60 N.W. 576.

46. Woodside v. Lippold, 1901, 113 Ga. 877, 39 S.E. 400, 84 Am.St.Rep. 267; cf. Beacham v. Gurney, 1894, 91 Iowa, 621, 60 N.W. 187; Errett v. Wheeler, 1909, 109 Minn. 157, 123 N.W. 414, 26 L.R.A.,N.S., 816; Frazee v. Inslee, 1839, 2 N.J.Eq. 239; Gainey v. Anderson, 1910, 87 S.C. 47, 68 S.E. 888, 31 L.R.A., N.S., 323. See 1910, 27 L.R.A.,N.S., 816.
See also note, 1927, 27 Col.L.Rev. 609.

47. McCraney v. Morris, 1933, 170 S.C. 250, 170 S.E 276, 95 A.L.R. 622; Home Owners Loan Corporation v. Collins, 1936, 120 N.J.Eq. 266, 184 A. 621; semble; see 1927, 27 Col.L.Rev. 609.

48. See 1935, 95 A.L.R. 628, 629.

to have it. The same seems true of a case where a mortgagee gave up his mortgage in the mistaken belief that a later one would not be enforced. So, too, if he didn't know of the later interest and so didn't know that the result of his action with respect to the first mortgage would be to confer this advantage on it. That the ignorance or mistake was due to negligence on his part should make no difference. The only consequence of the negligence is to confer a benefit upon the later lienors or other claimants which, if taken away, would leave them in no worse position than they were before the occurrence. Since it does not put them at any disadvantage or cause them any loss, it should not prevent the first mortgagee from being restored to his position by reinstating his mortgage.[49] And, it is believed that this principle of restitution to prevent unjust enrichment can be justifiably extended to include all cases in which there is no actual intent with respect to the later interest. And there is no ground for automatic merger of it regardless of intent. Indeed, whether the courts clearly analyse it in this way or not, it would seem to be the best justification of their reiterated statements that in the absence of express intention on the part of the mortgagee his intention will be presumed in accordance with his interests.

Reinstating the lien of a prior mortgagee in cases where he has taken a conveyance in satisfaction of the mortgage is sufficient to protect him against junior incumbrances when the debt is equal to the value of the land when the latter's claim is asserted. It is inadequate where the claim is brought forward years later when, subsequent to the mortgagee's acquisition of title, the land is risen in value. In such cases, there is authority that the conveyance to the mortgagee will be treated as equivalent to a foreclosure cutting off the interests of junior lienors.[50]

MERGER—SUBSEQUENT PURCHASER

276. Where the record shows the mortgage title and redemption interest in the same person authorities divide as to whether a subsequent purchaser, relying upon a merger, will prevail over the holder of the note and mortgage under an unrecorded assignment executed before the union of the two interests apparently occurred. Depending upon the strength of the evidence of merger, the better view, although the question is a close one, is that he should.

In a previous chapter there was discussion of the rights of a subsequent purchaser of the land in reliance upon a discharge by the record mortgagee after making an assignment which the assignee failed to record.[51] A cognate problem, referred to at that time, arises when the mortgagee, after assigning the mortgage and delivering the mortgage and note to the assignee who does not record, then takes and records a conveyance from the mortgagor. A purchaser, relying upon the union of the entire title to the property in the holder of record of the mortgage, buys the property without demanding proof that the mortgage was in fact extinguished or determining that there was no outstanding assignment. Will he prevail over the assignee of the mortgage? There is a sharp division in the relatively few cases on the point and a similar divergence of opinion as to the proper rule.[52] The group of states that hold against the purchaser and in favor of the assignee [53] rely upon three

49. See McCraney v. Morris, 1933, 170 S.C. 250, 260, 170 S.E. 276, 280, 95 A.L.R. 622, 627.

50. Jaubert Bros. Inc. v. Walker, 1948, 203 Miss. 242, 33 So.2d 827. See 1948, 48 Col.L.Rev. 955.

51. Chapter 8, §§ 235, 237–239.

52. See cases and authorities cited in following footnotes. See also 1934, 89 A.L.R. 171, 180; 1936, 104 A.L.R. 1301, 1304.

53. Thauer v. Smith, 1933, 213 Wis. 91, 250 N.W. 842, commented on in 1934, 82 U. of Pa.L.Rev. 547; 1934, 29 Ill.L.Rev. 121; 1934, 9 Wis.L.Rev. 408; 1935, 10 Wis.L.Rev. 292; Merchants' Trust Co. v. Davis, 1930, 49 Idaho 494, 290 P. 383; Purdy v. Huntington, 1869, 42 N.Y. 334, 1 Am.Rep. 532; Curtis v. Moore, 1897, 152 N.Y. 159, 46 N.E. 168, 57 Am.St.Rep. 506, decided not only on the ground of constructive notice arising from non-production of the instruments, but also on the ground that the recording act did not require an assignment to be recorded to be effective against subsequent purchasers of the fee, a curious belief in view of Bacon v. Van Schoonhoven, 1882, 87 N.Y. 446; Zorn v. Van

distinct grounds: (1) that merger is not an automatic consequence of the union of the mortgage title and redemption interest in the mortgage creditor. Extraneous factors such as the intention of the creditor, whether it is to his interest to keep the estate separate and distinct, and the terms of acquisition with respect to payment of the mortgage affect the result. (2) A purchaser, therefore, cannot assume that there has been a merger discharging the mortgage unless it has been discharged of record or by the judgment of the court. (3) The purchaser will be treated, therefore, as a buyer, although in one transaction, of two separate and distinct interests: (a) the redemption interest, which is burdened by a mortgage standing in the name of the mortgagee; (b) the security interest which also stands in the name of the mortgagee. As purchaser of the redemption interest it is immaterial to him who the owner of the security interest may be. He can get nothing more than the redemption interest until the mortgage is discharged.[54] As purchaser of the mortgage, where it secures a negotiable note, he cannot rely upon the record ownership but must demand the instruments.[55] Failing to take that precaution he takes the risk of an assignment turning up to which his purchase of the redemption interest will be subject and which, in spite of non-recordation, will be prior to his assignment of the mortgage from the mortgagee of record.

Authorities that believe the purchaser should be protected,[56] at least where the record shows that the mortgagee of record had assumed the mortgage and that the conveyance to the purchaser was with covenants of title sufficient to protect against the mortgage, make several points. In the first place it is urged that the purchaser should be allowed to assume that a merger had occurred.[57] The assumption of the mortgage by the record mortgagee if he was owner of it at the time, results in an automatic destruction of the debt and merger of the mortgage interest in the property without regard to intention.[58] And the conveyance by warranty deeds would prevent the mortgagee denying that merger occurred.[59] And the absence of any junior interest of record prevents any presumption on the ground of interest that no merger was intended as to them.[60]

In the second place, it is suggested that the fact that the mortgage is undischarged of

Buskirk, 1925, 111 Okl. 211, 239 P. 151, emphasizing the absence of a recorded release; Howard v. Shaw, 1894, 10 Wash. 151, 38 P. 746, on the ground that assignments were not covered by the recording acts then in force.

54. "So far as the purchaser of the encumbered fee is concerned, he has no interest in the question of who the owner of the mortgage may be. His only interest is in the fact that the fee is encumbered by the outstanding mortgage." Thauer v. Smith, note 53, supra.

55. See § 242, supra. "He is charged with knowledge that a mortgage is a mere incident to the note which it secures, and title thereto passes along with title to the note." Thauer v. Smith, note 53, supra.

56. Gregory v. Savage, 1864, 32 Conn. 250; McCormick v. Bauer, 1887, 122 Ill. 573, 13 N.E. 852, in effect overruling Edgerton v. Young, 1867, 43 Ill. 464; Artz v. Yeager, 1903, 30 Ind.App. 677, 66 N.E. 917; Jenks v. Shaw, 1906, 99 Iowa 604, 48 N.W. 900, 61 Am.St.Rep. 256; Ames v. Miller, 1902, 65 Neb. 204, 91 N.W. 250; see Lands, To Use of Security Savings & Trust Co. v. Robacker, 1933, 313 Pa. 271, 273, 169 A. 891, 892.

57. See Brown & Dougherty, Assignment of Realty Mortgages in Oregon, 1938, 17 Or.L.Rev. 83, 99.

58. See § 273, supra; 1935, 29 Ill.L.Rev. 121, 122; Landis v. Robacker, 1933, 313 Pa. 271, 273, 169 A. 891, 892. However, it has been suggested that the peculiarity of a mortgagee's assumption of the mortgage debt might well be regarded as putting a purchaser who knew of it on notice that the mortgage had been assigned. See 1934, 82 U. of Pa.L. Rev. 547, 548; 1934, 9 Wis.L.Rev. 408, 411; see also, Mathews v. Jones, 1896, 47 Neb. 616, 624, 66 N.W. 622, 624; Ames v. Miller, 1902, 65 Neb. 204, 211, 91 N.W. 250, 253; Peterborough Sav. Bank v. Pierce, 1898, 54 Neb. 712, 716, 723, 75 N.W. 20, 21, 23. And, of course, unless the mortgagee had the mortgage at the time, there could be no merger.

59. Peterborough Sav. Bank v. Pierce, note 58, supra. See § 273, supra: A statement in the deed of conveyance that it was given in consideration of the satisfaction of the mortgage debt would seem to have a somewhat similar effect.

60. See § 275, supra.

record is a technicality without substance. Aside from a few jurisdictions which require proof of ownership,[61] the record holder of the mortgage may enter a satisfaction of the mortgage on the record. If the mortgagee of record is willing to execute a warranty deed to a purchaser when he knows he has previously transferred the mortgage he would not scruple at fraudulently executing a satisfaction piece and recording it—which apparently would have protected the purchaser.[62] Consequently no distinction should be drawn between a satisfaction of record and a conveyance by warranty deed.[63]

Finally, objection is taken to the requirement of inquiry by the purchaser for the note and mortgage.[64] Of whom shall the purchaser inquire? The original mortgagor has no necessary knowledge of the facts. The as-signee will be unknown and the record mortgagee who is willing to give a warranty deed may be expected to deny having made any assignment.[65] Also, if there has been a merger, it is reasonable to assume that the mortgagee would have destroyed documents which merely evidence the fact that he is his own debtor.[66]

Which of the two results is preferable depends in large measure on the weight accorded to two conflicting policies. One is the amount of burden that should be imposed upon an assignee of a note and mortgage; the other policy is that of certainty of land titles through the operation of the recording acts. The question is a close one. However, if the transactions spread on the record would, if the mortgagee were owner as he appears to be, result in an automatic merger regardless of intent or are conclusive of intent to merge so far as a purchaser is concerned, it would be better to give effect to the policy of the recording acts by imposing upon the assignee the duty of recording his assignment as the price of protection against the possible fraudulent conduct of his assignor.[67]

---

61. See § 239, supra.

62. But it may be answered that a purchaser may well rely upon the record as he finds it but if he procures it he must take the risk that the one he procured to make the record had the authority to do so. See § 238, supra; note, 1937, 5 U. of Chi.L. Rev. 151, 152. Consequently if the satisfaction had been placed on the record by the mortgagee before the purchaser sought to buy, he would be protected. If, however, it was executed at his request as a condition to the purchase, he would be bound to discover whether the mortgagee had any authority to do so.

63. "To all intents and purposes a warranty deed executed by one who appears of record as the mortgagee has the same practical effect as a satisfaction piece. In one case the mortgagee announces that the mortgage has been satisfied; in the other he warrants the property free and clear of incumbrances and since he appears of record as the person to enter the satisfaction piece, the mortgage must have been satisfied." 1934, 29 Ill.L.Rev. 121, 122.

64. See note 55, supra.

65. 1934, 9 Wis.L.Rev. 408, 411.

66. 1934, 29 Ill.L.Rev. 121, 123.

67. "To impose on the assignee of a mortgage the duty of recording the assignment in order that he may be protected and the possibilities of fraud be minimized is a still less objectionable burden [than putting upon the purchaser the not unreasonable task of demanding that his vendor enter a satisfaction of the mortgage before he can be treated as a purchaser without notice under the statute], and certainly one more in keeping with the policy underlying the recording acts." 1934, 82 U. of Pa.L. Rev. 547, 548. He now takes that risk in the cognate case referred to at the outset of this section.

CHAPTER 10

SUBROGATION, CONTRIBUTION, AND EXONERATION—MARSHALLING ASSETS

A. SUBROGATION, CONTRIBUTION, AND EXONERATION

B. MARSHALLING

A. SUBROGATION, CONTRIBUTION, AND EXONERATION

SUBROGATION—GENERAL PRINCIPLES

277. Subrogation is the substitution of one person to the position of another, an obligee, whose claim he has satisfied. A common division is into (a) legal, by operation of law, and (b) conventional, by reason of agreement between the parties. A preferable analysis is that all subrogation is non-consensual; that it is given where justice requires on the facts of particular cases. However there is a strong tendency to formulate rules and establish categories governing its application. The basic principles underlying subrogation are the same as those in constructive trusts, prevention of merger, and equitable liens, i. e., restitution to prevent forfeiture and unjust enrichment.

Subrogation is the substitution of one person to the position of an obligee whose claim he has satisfied.[1] The result of subrogation is that the person subrogated stands in the shoes of the one whose claim has been discharged by his performance and succeeds to all of the rights, priorities, liens and securities of the former obligee.[2] The statement is frequently made that it originated in and

---

1. Sheldon, Subrogation, 2d ed., § 1.

2. See Aetna Life Ins. Co. v. Town of Middleport, 1887, 124 U.S. 534, 548, 8 S.Ct. 625, 629, 31 L.Ed. 537, quoting from Sheldon, Subrogation, § 2; Page Trust Co. v. Godwin, 1925, 190 N.C. 512, 130 S.E. 323; United States F. & G. Co. v. Bramwell, 1923, 108 Or. 261, 217 P. 332, 32 A.L.R. 829; 1933, 31 Mich.L.Rev. 826, 830; Arant, Suretyship, § 79.

was borrowed from the Roman law.[3] Although the doctrine was known in that system,[4] the evidence of it is scattered [5] and it is not certain how much influence it exercised on Anglo-American developments.[6] It was, however, given currency in France in the eighteenth century,[7] and its modern development in common law countries apparently stems from or was stimulated by the civil law of that period.[8] However, it is a vigorous and still growing body of law with areas still not definitely worked out even in the field of mortgage law.[9] It is closely related to the constructive trust, the non-consensual equitable lien,[10] and the prevention of merger.[11] Indeed, the basic principles of suretyship, and restitution or reimbursement

to prevent forfeiture or unjustifiable benefit [12] are the key to an understanding of all three doctrines.

Many courts state that subrogation is not only wholly of equitable origin but depends upon principles of natural justice, fairness, and good conscience applied to the facts of each particular case.[13] However, it was originally rather narrowly confined in the English cases, being recognized chiefly where a surety paid the debt of his principal.[14] In this country there has been a persistent effort to establish categories of cases and lay down rules to guide the courts in the invocation of the doctrine. Thus, traditionally, subrogation has been separated into two kinds, legal and conventional.[15] Legal subrogation is said to be given by operation of law,[16] whereas conventional subrogation is regarded as resulting from an agreement between the subrogee and either the debtor or creditor.[17]

3 See Dixon, Subrogation, 1862, 7–20, setting forth Roman sources; Sheldon, Subrogation, 2d ed., § 1; 1 Story, Equity, 1836, § 635; 1938, 24 Va.L.Rev. 771.

4. Radin, Handbook of Roman Law, 1927, § 104.

5. E. g., Buckland, Equity in Roman Law, 1911, 45–55.

6. Comment, 1933, 31 Mich.L.Rev. 826, 829.

7. 1 Oeuvres de Pothier, tit. 20, sec. 5 (1845).

8. Hayes v. Ward, N.Y.1819, 4 Johns.Ch. 123, 130; Martin v. Hickenlooper, 1936, 90 Utah, 150, 154, 59 P.2d 1139, 1140, 107 A.L.R. 762, rehearing denied 90 Utah 185, 61 P.2d 307; Harris, Subrogation, 1889, § 1; 2 Story, Equity Juris., 14th ed., § 715. But see the use of subrogation in a suretyship case in England in 1637: Morgan v. Seymour, 1637, 1 Ch.Rep. 120. See also 1938, 24 Va.L.Rev. 771.

9. See, e. g., the survey of the doctrine in fairly recent cases; Martin v. Hickenlooper, 1936, 90 Utah 150, 59 P.2d 1139, 107 A.L.R. 762, rehearing denied 90 Utah 185, 61 P.2d 307, discussed in notes, 1937, 36 Mich.L.Rev. 151; 1937, 6 Fordham L.Rev. 138; 1937, 107 A.L.R. 785; Burgoon v. Lavezzo, 1937, 68 App.D.C. 20, 92 F.2d 726, 113 A.L.R. 944, commented on, 1939, 48 Yale L.J. 683; Home Owners' Loan Corp. v. Collins, 1936, 120 N.J.Eq. 266, 184 A. 621. Look also at notes, 1929, 42 Harv.L.Rev. 962; 1921, 21 Col.L.Rev. 470; 1933, 31 Mich.L.Rev. 826, 833; 1932, 9 N.Y.Univ.L.Q.Rev. 378; 1913, 26 Harv.L. Rev. 261; 1931, 70 A.L.R. 1396; 1938, 113 A.L.R. 958. And see, additionally, the cases and other authorities cited in the footnotes in this and following sections. See also Storke and Sears, Transfer of Mortgaged Property, 1953, 38 Corn.L.Q. 185, 193, 194, 196.

10. See 1938, 24 Va.L.Rev. 771, 774; 1933, 31 Mich. L.Rev. 826, 829; §§ 24, 27, supra.

11. See §§ 272–275, supra.

12. "Equitable substitution is invoked * * * simply as an appropriate means of preventing unjust enrichment." 1913, 26 Harv.L.Rev. 261, 262. See Restatement, Restitution, § 162, treating subrogation as a method of restitution for unjust enrichment.

13. See, e. g., Arlington, State Bank v. Paulsen, 1899, 57 Neb. 717, 747, 78 N.W. 303, reversed 59 Neb. 94, 80 N.W. 263; Martin v. Hickenlooper, 1936, 90 Utah, 150, 154–155, 59 P.2d 1139, 1141, 107 A.L.R. 762, rehearing denied 90 Utah 185, 61 P.2d 307; Burgoon v. Lavezzo, 1937, 68 App.D.C. 20, 24, 92 F. 2d 726, 729, 13 A.L.R. 944. It is, however, recognized by courts of law. See Dunlop v. James, 1903, 174 N.Y. 411, 415, 67 N.E. 60.

14. Idem. See n. 8, supra. A minority of courts in this country still deny that subrogation is a benevolent doctrine and refuse to adopt the "liberal" attitude toward it. Citizens Merc. Co. v. Easom, 1924, 158 Ga. 604, 611, 123 S.E. 883, 886, 37 A.L.R. 378, commented on, 1924, 38 Harv.L.Rev. 265. See 1939, 48 Yale L.J. 683, 684.

15. See First Nat. Bank v. Thompson, 1901, 61 N.J. Eq. 188, 193, 48 A. 333; Martin v. Hickenlooper, 1936, 90 Utah, 150, 156, 59 P.2d 1139, 1141, 107 A.L. R. 762, rehearing denied 90 Utah 185, 61 P.2d 307; 1938, 24 Va.L.Rev. 771, 773.

16. Western Union Tel. Co. v. Smith, 1935, 50 Ga. App. 585, 178 S.E. 472.
See note 15, supra.

17. See First Nat. Bank v. Thompson, 1901, 61 N.J. Eq. 188, 193, 48 A. 333; Erwin v. Brooke, 1925, 159 Ga. 683, 126 S.E. 777. See also note 15, supra.

The foregoing dichotomy has been criticised and quite properly so.[18] The notion that conventional subrogation is contractual in nature is clearly erroneous.[19] "Under no theory, * * * can one say that by virtue of an agreement between the debtor and the one claiming to be subrogated, the rights of the creditor are transferred to the latter." On the other hand, "if the agreement be made with the creditor, it is plain that the result is nothing more than an assignment, or an agreement to assign enforceable in equity, of either a legal or an equitable *chose in action*"—conceptions which are, of course, valid and recognized, but quite certainly not intended to be included under the designation subrogation.[20] The "confusion of thought" arises, as has been pointed out, "from the fact that in some cases the presence of an agreement may be a circumstance which equity will take into consideration in determining whether or not it will allow subrogation."[21] In other words, in all cases, subrogation arises by operation of law.

PAYMENT AS SURETY

278. **A person who is obligated to pay the debt but only as a surety is entitled to subrogation; a primary obligor who pays is not.**

The question remains, what are the circumstances that warrant the granting of subrogation. All courts agree that if the one who pays is himself obligated, but only as a surety, he is entitled to be subrogated to the rights of the creditor against the principal obligor. Thus in the law of mortgages, a mortgagor who has sold the property to an assuming grantee and then has had to pay is entitled to be subrogated to all rights of the mortgage creditor, both against the assuming grantee personally and in the mortgaged property in his hands.[22] Similarly, if the sale is subject to the mortgage and the mortgagor is forced to pay, he gets subrogation to the creditor's security interest in the property now owned by the grantee, it being regarded as the principal and the mortgagor, as to it, surety.[23] Or, if the pur-

---

18. See 1921, 21 Col.L.Rev. 470.
"But back of legal and conventional subrogation are principles more nearly ultimate. The first is founded on the principle that one cannot enrich himself at the expense of another by getting free of a debt by letting another, not so fundamentally or primarily bound, pay it. * * * it is a matter of comparative equities. Where one is more fundamentally or primarily liable for a debt which another is compelled or obligated to pay, or the equities lean more toward his paying it than they do toward the other paying it, such person shall not enrich himself by escaping his obligation. If both are equally liable, contribution but not subrogation may be applicable. In the case of *conventional* subrogation, equity says: Where the lender of money did it with the intention and understanding that he was to be placed in the position of the creditor whose debt he paid, but without taking an assignment of the credit, equity, where no innocent parties will suffer or no right has intervened, will treat the matter as if an assignment had been executed." Martin v. Hickenlooper, 1936, 90 Utah, 150, 157, 59 P.2d 1139, 1141, 107 A.L.R. 762, rehearing denied 90 Utah 185, 61 P.2d 307.

19. "Even when there is an agreement to subrogate, the so-called right of subrogation is not one inherent in the contract, but arises in equity and can therefore be withheld or applied as in equity seems meet according to sound judicial discretion, which is another way of saying, according to the dictates of justice. The doctrine of subrogation has its roots in the soil of justice and equity, and not in contract." Martin v. Hickenlooper, 1936, 90 Utah, 150, 161, 59 P.2d 1139, 1143, 107 A.L.R. 762, rehearing denied 90 Utah 185, 61 P.2d 307.

20. The difference between subrogation and assignment is illustrated by the question discussed, § 284, infra, as to whether one who is entitled to subrogation may compel an assignment.

"But the right to subrogation arises by operation of law only when there has been a judgment and extinguishment of the mortgage by one entitled to redeem. An assignment implies the continued existence of the debt and the equitable right does not arise." Lamb v. Montague, 1873, 112 Mass. 352, 353.

21. All quotations from Note, 1921, 21 Col.L.Rev. 470, 471. See also note, 1937, 36 Mich.L.Rev. 151, 153.

22. Howard v. Burns, 1917, 279 Ill. 256, 116 N.E. 703; Begein v. Brehm, 1889, 123 Ind. 160, 23 N.E. 496; Minnesota Loan & Trust Co. v. Peteler Car. Co., 1916, 132 Minn. 277, 156 N.W. 255; Orrick v. Durham, 1883, 79 Mo. 174; see Hampe v. Manke, 1912, 28 S.D. 501, 134 N.W. 60.
See Storke and Sears, Transfer of Mortgaged Property, 1953, 38 Corn.L.Q. 185, 192 et seq. For a discussion of the problem where there are fractional sales and assumptions, see id. 199–201.

23. "This relation between the mortgagor and his grantee does not deprive the obligee from enforcing

chaser has paid the full value of the property with the mortgagor bound to pay, the suretyship relation runs the other way. Consequently if the grantee pays, he is entitled to subrogation to the mortgage debt claim against the mortgagor.[24]

It is equally clear that a principal obligor who pays is not entitled to subrogation as against a party to the same obligation who occupies the position of a surety.[25] Such a payment would be merely the performance of his own duty. So an assuming grantee,[26] or a mortgagor who was bound to protect his grantee against the mortgage [27] are not entitled to subrogation against the transferor, in the first case, or the grantee, in the second, if they pay the mortgage. A grantee subject to the mortgage who pays cannot have subrogation as against the mortgagor

unless the amount of payment exceeds the value of the land, for up to that extent, clearly, he is paying on behalf of the principal, the land.[28] Whether he may have subrogation as to the excess of the debt he pays over the value of the land would seem to be governed by the same principles previously discussed in connection with merger.[29] It is believed he should not. The amount of the debt was figured in on the original purchase price of the land. Even though the agreement imposed no personal duty to pay, nevertheless the payment of the mortgage was a condition to his retention of the land and he should not be able, by paying it, to recover any portion of it from his vendor, the mortgagor, through the agency of subrogation or otherwise. The fact that at the time the mortgage has to be paid the land is no longer equal in value to the amount of the debt [30] would not justify him being able to recover from his seller, in the face of his original bargain, any excess paid over its then value.[31]

Where the debt is in the form of a negotiable instrument there are occasional cases in which the question arises whether the enactment of the Negotiable Instruments Law excludes subrogation as an equitable doctrine in cases where it would otherwise be available.[32] The authorities probably will

the bond against the obligor. He is entitled to his debt, and has a right to avail himself of all his securities. Equity however requires that the obligor, on the payment of the debt out of his own funds, should be subrogated to the rights of the obligee, so that he can reimburse himself by a recourse to the mortgaged premises for that purpose. This cannot prejudice the creditor, and it is clearly equitable as between the debtor and the owner of the land. He clearly has no right or color of right, justice or equity to claim that he, notwithstanding the conveyance of the property subject to the mortgage, and thus entitling him only to its value over and above it, should in fact enjoy and hold it discharged of the incumbrance, without any contribution toward its discharge and satisfaction from the land. This equitable principle is * * * so consistent with right and justice as to require no authorities to sustain it." Johnson v. Zink, 1873, 51 N.Y. 333; Howard v. Burns, 1917, 279 Ill. 256, 116 N.E. 703; Woodbury v. Swan, 1878, 58 N.H. 380; University State Bank v. Steeves, 1915, 85 Wash. 55, 147 P. 645, 2 A.L.R. 237, accord.

24. Simpson v. Ennis, 1901, 114 Ga. 202, 39 S.E. 853; Hazle v. Bondy, 1898, 173 Ill. 302, 50 N.E. 671; Wadsworth v. Lyon, 1883, 93 N.Y. 201, 45 Am.R. 190; Hudson v. Dismukes, 77 Va. 242.

25. Sheldon, Subrogation, 2d ed., § 46.

26. Dodds v. Spring, 1917, 174 Cal. 412, 163 P. 351; Drury v. Holden, 1887, 121 Ill. 130, 13 N.E. 547; Lydon v. Campbell, 1910, 204 Mass. 580, 91 N.E. 151, 134 Am.St.Rep. 702; cf., Lackawanna Trust & Safe Deposit Co. v. Gomeringer, 1912, 236 Pa. 179, 84 A. 757. See 1915, 15 Col.L.Rev. 171.

27. Wadsworth v. Williams, 1868, 100 Mass. 126; Byles v. Kellogg, 1887, 67 Mich. 318, 34 N.W. 671; Hooper v. Henry, 1883, 31 Minn. 264, 17 N.W. 476.

28. Drury v. Holden, 1887, 121 Ill. 130, 13 N.E. 547; Northwestern Nat. Bank v. Stone, 1896, 97 Iowa 183, 66 N.W. 91; In re Wisner's Estate, 1870, 20 Mich. 442; Guernsey v. Kendall, 1880, 55 Vt. 201.

29. See § 274(4) (5), supra.

30. Although the value at the time the subject-to grantee must pay or lose the land may be less than the debt, he may yet elect to save his property by paying off the mortgage. Sentimental considerations or a belief that eventually the value in an unforced sale will yield a profit may be motivations for such an act.

31. But recovery was allowed in Southworth v. Scofield, 1873, 51 N.Y. 513. And see Tiffany, Real Property, § 1507.

32. E. g., Mueller v. Jagerson Fuel Co., 1930, 203 Wis. 453, 233 N.W. 633, 72 A.L.R. 1059, noted, 1931, 15 Minn.L.Rev. 818, holding that it does not in a case where the mortgagor-maker paid the holder of the note and took an assignment of it after an assuming grantee had defaulted.

follow the same cleavage observed earlier in the case of defenses to a surety through extension of time to the principal.[33]

PAYMENT TO PROTECT AN INTEREST—CONTRIBUTION

279. One who pays to protect an interest which will be affected by enforcement of the obligation will be granted subrogation in order to obtain contribution from others who are benefited by the lifting of the common burden. The amount of contribution will be proportional to the value of the interests benefited.

Another group of cases in which the right of subrogation is not questioned is that in which a person, although not personally bound to pay, is compelled to do so in order to protect some interest of his own. Applied to the case of a mortgage, it may be laid down broadly that anyone who has an interest in a redemption right which may be adversely affected by the enforcement of a mortgage may pay off the mortgage and be subrogated to the position of the mortgagee. How far subrogation will be given depends on the extent to which his payment has lifted the mortgage burden from persons or property whose duty to pay it is primary. Thus a junior mortgagee may pay off a prior mortgage and be subrogated to all rights under it against the mortgagor.[34] And there is a large variety of other interests in property subject to a mortgage which possess a similar power.[35] The wife may have joined in the mortgage thus subjecting her dower interest to it. Having this interest to protect she may pay off the entire mortgage, since the mortgage creditor may refuse to accept a piecemeal or proportionate payment of the debt, and then keep the mortgage alive through subrogation

hold that as against the mortgagor, a mortgagee may pay taxes and be subrogated to the tax lien of the taxing power to obtain reimbursement. See 1929, 60 A.L.R. 425; 1929, 61 A.L.R. 587; 1933, 84 A.L.R. 1366; 1937, 106 A.L.R. 1212, 1217. This is true even though the mortgage has been outlawed by the statute of nonclaim. Federal Land Bank of Columbia v. Brooks, Fla.1939, 190 So. 737, commented on in, 1940, 17 N.Y.Univ.L.Q.Rev. 295. But cf., State-Planters Bank & Trust Co. v. Pollard & Bagby Investment Corp., 1947, 186 Va. 217, 42 S.E.2d 287, commented on in 1947, 60 Harv.L.Rev. 1355, 1948, 34 Va.L.Rev. 98, mortgagee not subrogated to tax claim in order to recover from a non-assuming grantee the amount of delinquent taxes collected by a sale of the mortgaged property; Citizens Sav. Bank v. Guaranty Loan Co., 1939, 62 R.I. 448, 6 A. 2d 688, noted 53 Harv.L.Rev. 1444; see 1939, 123 A.L.R. 1248. However, if a first mortgage contains an acceleration clause giving the mortgagee a right to foreclose if the mortgagor is in default on tax payments, a second mortgagee who pays the taxes will not be given subrogation to the priority of the tax lien of the taxing authority over the first mortgage. Laventall v. Pomerantz, 1933, 263 N.Y. 110, 188 N.E. 271, discussed in notes, 1934, 19 Cornell L. Q. 487; 1934, 11 N.Y.Univ.L.Q.Rev. 655; 1934, 1 U. of Chi.L.Rev. 813; 1934, 29 Ill.L.Rev. 123; 1934, 20 Va.L.Rev. 914. See also notes, 1933, 46 Harv.L.Rev. 1036; 1933, 42 Yale L.J. 971; 1937, 17 Tex.L.Rev. 352; Pearmain v. Massachusetts Hospital Life Ins. Co., 1910, 206 Mass. 377, 92 N.E. 497; Marks v. Baum Bldg. Co., 1918, 73 Okl. 264, 175 P. 818; Noeker v. Howry, 1899, 119 Mich. 626, 78 N.W. 669, contra.

On the question of the effect of a breach of duty to pay taxes upon acquisition of title, see § 177, supra. See §§ 173, 179, and 232, supra, on other aspects of the payment of taxes.

35. See Hope, Officiousness, 1930, 15 Corn.L.Q. 25, 205, 239, for a survey of such interests. See also 1934, 93 A.L.R. 89 for a collection of authorities on the right to compel an assignment by one who has an interest to protect and pays.

In In re Keil's Estate, 1958, 51 Del. (1 Storey) 351, 145 A.2d 563, 76 A.L.R.2d 996, reargument denied 51 Del. (1 Storey) 351, 146 A.2d 398, discussed in 1959, 58 Mich.L.Rev. 137, 1959, 73 Harv.L.Rev. 425, the surviving mortgagor of entireties property given to secure a joint debt, the proceeds of which were used to improve the property, was held entitled to contribution against the estate of the deceased tenant.

---

33. See § 271, supra.

34. Godfrey v. Watson, 1747, 3 Atk. 517; Hopkins Mfg. Co. v. Ketterer, 1912, 237 Pa. 285, 85 A. 421, Ann.Cas.1914B, 558; Frisbee v. Frisbee, 1894, 86 Me. 444, 29 A. 1115. That a mortgagor has a duty to a junior mortgagee to pay off a prior mortgage, see § 177, supra. See Note, The Rights of a Junior Lienholder in Wisconsin, 1959, 43 Marq.L.Rev. 89, 93.

It is clear that a mortgagee who pays taxes on the mortgaged property may add the amount of such payment to his mortgage debt, and the combined claims then constitute a single cause of action. Hillsborough Inv. Co. v. Tampa, 1941, 149 Fla. 7, 5 So.2d 256; Stone v. Tilley, 1907, 100 Tex. 487, 101 S.W. 201, 10 L.R.A.,N.S., 678, 123 Am.St.Rep. 819, 15 Ann.Cas. 524; but cf. Snyder v. Elkan, 1938, 187 Ga. 164, 199 S.E. 891, discussed in note, 1939, 48 Yale L.J. 1293. Recovery by an independent action for taxes so paid is thus barred. Vincent v. Moore, 1883, 51 Mich. 618, 17 N.W. 81; see 1940, 17 N.Y. Univ.L.Q.Rev. 295, 296. And the cases generally

as against the other owners who have been benefited by her payment.[36] A similar right is granted to a remainderman who pays where both the life interest and remainder were mortgaged.[37] A creditor of the mortgagor who has levied an attachment or execution on the redemption interest may also pay off the debt and have subrogation.[38] A cotenant of the mortgaged property whose cotenancy is subject to the mortgage is entitled to pay and be subrogated for the purpose of obtaining contribution from his fellow cotenant.[39]

Persons who have fractional interests in the property, when they pay off the mortgage upon the entire property will not be given subrogation to the entire claim of the mortgage creditor as against other parties on whom the burden of the mortgage also rests. The discharge of the mortgage benefited the payors as well as the others, and to the extent the payors were so benefited they have no claim to collect from anyone else. However, they are entitled to subrogation in order to recover from holders of other interests in the property ratable contribution from them for the benefit conferred by the payment. In other words the subrogation against others

is proportional to the value of the interests in the property from which the burden of the mortgage has been removed by the action of the claimant in paying it.[40]

The problem of evaluation of the respective interests of the claimant and others for the purpose of giving proportionate contribution is not always simple[41] but both the right to it and the principles governing the allocation are well recognized.

THE VOLUNTEER RULE

280. The frequently stated rule that a volunteer is not entitled to subrogation is so indefinite as to either rationale or scope as to be of dubious value as a guide for denying the relief and of no worth as a guide for granting it.

Legal as opposed to conventional subrogation includes, as has been seen, those who pay

---

36. Swaine v. Perine, N.Y., 1821, 5 Johns.Ch. 482, 9 Am.Dec. 318, Osborne, Cases Property Security, 2nd Ed., 546; cf. Gibson v. Crehore, 1827, 22 Mass. (5 Pick.) 146; Fitcher v. Griffiths, 1913, 216 Mass. 174, 103 N.E. 471.

37. See § 280 note 45, infra. Cf. Mosely v. Marshall, 1860, 22 N.Y. 545, life tenant; Wunderle v. Ellis, 1905, 212 Pa. 618, 62 A. 106, tenant for years pays; cf. also Federal Land Bank v. Newsom, 1936, 175 Miss. 114, 166 So. 346, discussed, 1937, 50 Harv.L. Rev. 534.

38. Wheeler v. Willard, 1871, 44 Vt. 640; Young v. Williams, 1845, 17 Conn. 393; Simpson v. Gardiner, 1881, 97 Ill. 237; Senft v. Vanek, 1904, 209 Ill. 361, 70 N.E. 720; Aiken v. Gale, 1859, 37 N.H. 501; Haverford Bldg. & Loan Ass'n v. Fire Ass'n, 1897, 180 Pa. 522, 37 A. 179, 57 Am.St.Rep. 657—accord.

39. Newbold v. Smart, 1880, 67 Ala. 326; Young v. Williams, 1845, 17 Conn. 393; see 1907, 8 L.R.A.,N. S., 559.
Generally one co-owner may not defeat other co-owner's right to redeem from a mortgage by purchasing the mortgaged premises at foreclosure sale. 1 Tiffany, Real Prop., 2d Ed., § 201.

40. "What rule should then govern the parties in adjusting the common burdens resting upon the property, in different parts of which they have respectively acquired an interest? We think the parties should contribute to the payment of the burden in proportion to the value of the property in which they are respectively interested." Tarbell v. Durant, 1889, 61 Vt. 516, 519, 17 A. 44, 45. See Carpenter v. Koons, 1852, 20 Pa. 222. Cf. McLaughlin v. Estate of Curtis, 1871, 27 Wis. 644.

41. E. G., The evaluation of a dower interest. See Swaine v. Perine, supra note 36. Similarly where the question arises between a life tenant and remainderman. "A tenant for life is bound to keep down the current interest, * * * but not to pay any part of the principal. Now if, for example, there is a tenant for life, and a remainderman in fee of an estate, subject to a mortgage which is due and must be paid at once to save foreclosure, and the remainderman, to save the estate, pays the mortgage, he is not obliged to take the share of the tenant for life in annual installments of interest to continue as long as he shall live. He is entitled, as equitable assignee of the mortgagee, to immediate payment; and the sum which he thus has a right to claim is whatever the present worth of an annuity equal to the amount of the annual interest would be, computed for the number of years which the tenant will live." 2 Washburn, Real Prop., 6th Ed., § 1142. See also Todd's Ex'r v. First Nat. Bank, 1917, 173 Ky. 60, 67, 190 S.W. 468; Damm v. Damm, 1896, 109 Mich. 619, 67 N.W. 984, 63 Am.St. Rep. 601; Tindall v. Peterson, 1904, 71 Neb. 160, 98 N.W. 688, 99 N.W. 659, 8 Ann.Cas. 721; Moore v. Simonson, 1895, 27 Or. 117, 39 P. 1105; Wilder's Ex'x v. Wilder, 1903, 75 Vt. 178, 53 A. 1072; 3 Pomeroy, Eq.Jur., 4th Ed., § 1223. Cf. Leach v. Hall, 1895, 95 Iowa, 611, 619, 64 N.W. 790.

as sureties[42] or to protect an interest of their own.[43] Conventional subrogation, in spite of statements or implications to the contrary, does not consist in enforcing the terms of an agreement.[44] However, the existence of certain kinds of agreements, express or implied in fact, is the important factor here in influencing equity to act,[45] just as the surety relation or an interest to protect so operates in legal subrogation. Since this is so, it is necessary to determine just what agreements will and what ones will not have that effect.[46] This inquiry at once encounters the rule which courts repeatedly state that a volunteer is not entitled to subrogation.[47] Persons who qualify for legal subrogation of the kinds just mentioned are never regarded as volunteers.[48] Where, however, the payment was not made in pursuance of an obligation as surety or to protect an interest, but only in accordance with an understanding or agreement with the debtor or creditor, subrogation is frequently denied on the ground that the payor is a volunteer unless the court decides that the particular agreement is one falling within the limits of the category "conventional subrogation" as recognized by courts in that jurisdiction.[49] Thus the determination of whether a person who pays off a debt in accordance with an agreement will be subrogated to the creditor's rights requires an investigation into the validity and scope of the volunteer rule.

The origin of the volunteer rule is doubtful[50] and both its rationale and limits are a

42. § 278, supra.

43. § 279, supra.

44. See § 277, supra.
"From our study we may draw the following conclusions: (1) That where a lender, in no way related to the property nor in any way required to protect an interest, advanced the money to pay off a lien, it could not be a case for legal subrogation, but must, if anything, come within the principles of conventional subrogation. (2) That in conventional subrogation there must be an agreement, express or implied, that the lender whose money pays off a lien will have the same status as the lien his money releases to the extent of the debt secured by that lien. (3) That equity applies the doctrine of subrogation in such cases, not in exacting a performance of the contract, but as a matter of doing justice under the circumstances; the so-called agreement only being of value showing such a situation where the doctrine should be applied in order to do justice and as evidence that the lender was not a volunteer." Martin v. Hickenlooper, 1936, 90 Utah, 150, 179, 59 P.2d 1139, 1152, 107 A.L.R. 762, rehearing denied 90 Utah 185, 61 P.2d 307.

45. The absence of an agreement has been deemed controlling to deny subrogation and denote the claimant a volunteer. Lentz v. Stoflet, 1937, 280 Mich. 446, 273 N.W. 763; Jackson v. Blackwell, 1931, 173 Ga. 614, 160 S.E. 772. See 1938, 24 Va.L. Rev. 774.

46. "(4) That the facts or circumstances from which the agreement will be implied vary in the different courts, some requiring evidence from which an actual understanding between the parties may be inferred, while others hold that payment under such circumstances as show that the lender "supposed" or "intended" to get security of the same dignity as that released by his payment is sufficient; and some go as far as holding that such intention may be inferred from the mere fact that the money was advanced for the purpose of paying off another lien." Martin v. Hickenlooper, 1936, 90 Utah, 150, 179, 59 P.2d 1139, 1152, 107 A.L.R. 762, rehearing denied 90 Utah 185, 61 P.2d 307.

47. In contrast to the Anglo-American attitude toward one who intermeddles in another's affairs is the encouragement accorded by the Roman Law. See Hope, Officiousness, 1929, 15 Cornell L.Q. 25. But cf. § 277, n. 14, supra.

48. Shinn v. Budd, 1862, 14 N.J.Eq. 234; Bingham v. Walker Bros., Bankers, 1929, 75 Utah 149, 283 P. 1055; see 1938, 24 Va.L.Rev. 771, 773.

49. "It is only in cases where the person advancing money to pay the debt of a third party, stands in the position of a surety, or is compelled to pay it to protect his own rights, that a court of equity substitutes him in the place of a creditor, as a matter of course, without any agreement to that effect. In other cases the demand of a creditor which is paid with the money of a third person, without any agreement that the security shall be assigned or kept on foot for the benefit of such third person, is absolutely extinguished." Watson v. Wilcox, 1876, 39 Wis. 643, 649, 20 Am.Rep. 63, quoting from Sandford v. McLean, N.Y.1832, 3 Paige 117, 23 Am.Dec. 773. Martin v. Martin, 1897, 164 Ill. 640, 45 N.E. 1007, 56 Am.St.Rep. 219; Desot v. Ross, 1883, 95 Mich. 81, 54 N.W. 694; Sandford v. McLean, N.Y.1832, 3 Paige 117, 23 Am.Dec. 773. See 1938, 24 Va.L.Rev. 773; 1941, 40 Mich.L.Rev. 133, 134. See also 1939, 48 Yale L.J. 683, 686, quoted note 54, infra.

50. See Subrogation and the Volunteer Rule, 1938, 24 Va.L.Rev. 771; Hope, Officiousness, 1929, 15 Corn. L.Q. 25, 29, suggesting that it developed out of (a) the English temperamental dislike for having anyone interfere in their affairs, and (b) the concept of privity of contract.

matter of dispute. It has been asserted that, whenever courts for any reason deny subrogation, they characterize the unsuccessful applicant as a volunteer.[51] Even when used with more discrimination, it still is frequently not clear whether it means that the plaintiff did not intend any legal consequences to flow from his act, e. g., he intended a gift, or that his intervention was unsolicited and therefore officious.[52] Usually it is the latter and this seems to be the present tendency.[53] But whether expressed in terms of volunteer or officious payor, there is an absence of precise content.[54] And a critical examination of the reasons[55] offered for using the rule to deny subrogation on payment of a creditor by a third person have revealed them to be so lacking in force as to make reasonable the suggestion that, in order for such a payment to be officious", it must be unnecessary and confer no benefit.[56] As a test of whether subrogation should be granted rather than as a criterion for denying it, the volunteer rule is obviously devoid of value.

The foregoing résumé indicates that, although the existence of the volunteer rule is a factor that must be reckoned with in determining whether subrogation will be granted, it is of dubious value as a guide for denying the relief and of no worth as a guide for granting it. Consequently, although it will be taken into account in dealing with the specific problems of mortgage law that is our concern, stress will be placed upon what is believed to be sounder and more rewarding criteria.

---

51. Pomeroy, Equity Juris, 4th ed., § 2348n.
"A good deal of the confusion concerning the volunteer rule has arisen because courts have carelessly termed the payor a volunteer in cases involving a situation where payment would ordinarily be considered not voluntary but subrogation is denied because of a superior intervening equity. It is submitted that these cases have misapplied the term and must be sharply distinguished." 1948, 32 Minn.L.Rev. 183, 185.

52. See 1933, 31 Mich.L.Rev. 826, 830.

53. " * * * a dissatisfaction with the word 'volunteer', and a belief that its use has had the effect of denying relief to many meritorious claimants has led to the suggestion that the granting of subrogation should depend upon whether or not a payment is 'officious'. Such shift in emphasis would seem more consonant with the true nature of subrogation, at least as tested by nonlegal reasoning. * * * Appreciation of the need of a definition of the word 'officious' is shown by the Restatement [of Restitution § 1626], which says expressly that a claimant is not officious where he makes the payment under a mistake, or where he is induced to make the payment by fraud or duress; or where under a duty to make the payment, as for example where he was a surety; or where he acts to protect an interest of his own; or where his property was used without his consent to discharge an obligation of another or a lien upon another's property." Subrogation and the Volunteer Rule, 1938, 24 Va.L.Rev. 771, 775. See Hope, Officiousness, 1930, 15 Cornell L.Q. 25, 205 (especially the doctrine of Neely v. Jones, 1880, 16 W.Va. 625, 37 Am.Rep. 794, expounded pp. 211 et seq.). See also note 1899, 13 Harv.L.Rev. 297; 1894, 23 L.R.A. 120.

54. "All courts subscribe to the rule that subrogation will not be permitted a mere 'volunteer'. But there is no general agreement as to the personification of the word. A minority of courts is prone to call everyone a volunteer who was not in the position of a surety or who did not have some previous interest to protect in the subject matter in question. At the other extreme, the liberal view leads to the result that the only volunteer would be one who, without invitation from any other party and purely as a philanthropist, relieved another from an obligation. * * * The label does not embrace one who pays another's debt under the erroneous belief that he is liable therefor, nor one who advances money to satisfy an obligation at the request of the debtor. It is, furthermore, possible to escape the rule by means of an agreement, implied in the payor's justifiable expectations as to his secured position. Beyond this it may only be added that the modern tendency is to use the label 'volunteer' in an ever narrowing sense." Note, 1939, 48 Yale L.J. 683, 686 (footnotes omitted).

55. The three basic reasons for not permitting subrogation on the ground that the person asking it is a volunteer are "(1) he is able to elect whether he is to pay or not, and knowing the facts he should protect himself by contract, (2) a debt paid without any agreement to keep it alive is extinguished, and (3) one cannot become a creditor of another against the other's will." 1948, 32 Minn.L.Rev. 183, citing Hope, Officiousness, 1929, 15 Corn.L.Q. 25, and note, 1938, 24 Va.L.Rev. 771, 776, enumerating and answering them.

56. Hope, Officiousness, 1929, 15 Cornell L.Q. 25, 205. A comment on this as a criterion stated, "Indeed, there would seem to be no great difference in principle in the case where a person theretofore unconnected with a transaction purchases a debt, which can obviously do against the express will of the debtor, and where he pays the debt absent any intention to make a gift." 1938, 24 Va.L.Rev. 771, 776.

LOANS TO PAY THE MORTGAGE

281. The basis for granting subrogation to one who loans for the purpose of paying off a mortgage and whose money is so used is a justified but defeated expectation of getting as security for his loan either the land free of the mortgage or the benefit of the mortgage itself. The extent to which courts go in granting subrogation in such cases depends both upon the terms of the lending agreement and the attitude of the court, strict or liberal, towards the doctrine of subrogation.

In mortgage law the problem of subrogation and the volunteer rule has occurred most frequently in the case of lenders whose money is used to pay off a mortgage. Whether such a person will be given subrogation against parties to the mortgage, or as against incumbrances and interest junior to the mortgage paid off, depends both upon the terms of the arrangement and the attitude of the particular court, strict or liberal, in granting subrogation.[57] Through the cases, however, runs the theme that subrogation is here based upon the general principle that one who advances money upon a justifiable but defeated expectation of receiving security upon faith of which he relied in making the payment is entitled to get it nonetheless. In all of these cases, the claimant's money is intended to be used, and is used, to pay off a specific encumbrance upon property. And the reliance of the lender, as evidenced by the agreement, is to get as security for his loan either the land free and clear of the encumbrance or else the benefit of the encumbrance itself.[58] It is quite clear that subro-

gation should not be given and is not given to one who loans on the general credit of the mortgagor.[59] On the other hand it is equally clear that if the loan was made on the understanding that the lender is to have the benefit of the existing mortgage, he will be given it by subrogation.[60] So, too, subrogation is given to one whose money was used to discharge a lien upon an agreement that the lender should receive a mortgage having at least equal rank with that which was paid.[61] Generally, too, a lender who lends money to pay off a prior encumbrance and receives a void or defective mortgage as security for his loan will be subrogated to the discharged encumbrance.[62] Subrogation has also been invoked

57. See Burgoon v. Lavezzo, 1937, 68 App.D.C. 20, 92 F.2d 726, 113 A.L.R. 944; Martin v. Hickenlooper, 1936, 90 Utah 150, 59 P.2d 1139, 107 A.L.R. 762, rehearing denied 90 Utah 185, 61 P.2d 307.

58. See 1921, 21 Col.L.Rev. 470, 471; 1933, 31 Mich. L.Rev. 826, 833. There are cases that depart from this principle, but it is a sound one and most decisions are in accord with it even though not recognizing it explicitly. Thus, for example, courts sometimes justify the granting of subrogation, not upon the principle suggested, but by holding that there is an implied agreement to be subrogated when clearly there is no sufficient foundation in fact for such an inference. See 1933, 31 Mich.L. Rev. 826, 836. See infra, note 62.

59. Kocher v. Kocher, 1898, 56 N.J.Eq. 545, 39 A. 535; Heiney v. Lontz, 1897, 147 Ind. 417, 46 N.E. 665; see 1921, 21 Col.L.Rev. 470, 471. Citizens State Bank v. Pittsburg County Broadcasting Co., Okl.1954, 271 P.2d 725, commented on by Updike, Mortgages, in 1954 Annual Survey of American Law, 1955, 30 N.Y.U.L.Rev. 805, 809, followed this test in a chattel mortgage case.

60. Tolman v. Smith, 1890, 85 Cal. 280, 24 P. 743; Heuser v. Sherman, 1893, 89 Iowa 355, 56 N.W. 525, 48 Am.St.Rep. 390; Emmert v. Thompson, 1892, 49 Minn. 386, 52 N.W. 31, 32 Am.St.Rep. 566; Contoocook Fire Precinct v. Hopkinton, 1902, 71 N.H. 574, 53 A. 797. Cf. Boley v. Daniel, 1916, 72 Fla. 121, 72 So. 644, L.R.A. 1917A, 734, denying recovery because lender did not stipulate for the original mortgage, only a "first lien."

61. Hughes Co. v. Callahan, 1930, 181 Ark. 733, 27 S.W.2d 509; Home Owners Loan Corporation v. Collins, 1936, 120 N.J.Eq. 266, 184 A. 621; Federal Union Life Ins. Co. v. Deitsch, 1933, 127 Ohio St. 505, 189 N.E. 440; Martin v. Hickenlooper, 1936, 90 Utah 150, 59 P.2d 1139, 107 A.L.R. 762, rehearing denied 90 Utah 185, 61 P.2d 307; discussed in notes, 1937, 36 Mich.L.Rev. 151; 1937, 6 Fordham L.Rev. 138; 1937, 107 A.L.R. 785; Federal Land Bank of Baltimore v. Joynes, 1942, 179 Va. 394, 18 S.E.2d 917; Home Owners Loan Corporation of Washington, D. C. v. Dougherty, 1937, 226 Wis. 8, 275 N.W. 363.

62. Davies v. Pugh, 1907, 81 Ark. 253, 99 S.W. 78, on the ground, difficult to support, that there was an implied agreement for subrogation; Kaminskas v. Cepaukis, 1938, 369 Ill. 566, 17 N.E.2d 558; Brannon v. Hills, 1933, 111 Fla. 491, 149 So. 556; Crippen v. Chappel, 1886, 35 Kan. 495, 11 P. 453, 57 Am. Rep. 187; Gans v. Thieme, 1883, 93 N.Y. 225; Landis v. State ex rel. Commissioners of Land Office, 1937, 179 Okl. 547, 66 P.2d 519; MacGreal v. Taylor, 1897, 167 U.S. 688, 17 S.Ct. 961, 42 L.Ed. 326; see Otis v. Gregory, 1887, 111 Ind. 504, 13 N.E. 39, saying that if one means of security fails, the courts

where the loan which pays off the old mortgage is on the faith of a promise of a new mortgage which the owner refuses to execute.[63] Going beyond these are cases in which the money is loaned for the express purpose of paying off an incumbrance and is so used but the expectation of security does not relate specifically to the particular property freed from the prior lien.[64] And finally there are cases in which the sole case for subrogation is that money is loaned for the

express purpose of paying off an incumbrance and is so used.[65] This last represents the extreme position of liberality.

LOANS TO PAY THE MORTGAGE—SUBROGATION AGAINST INTERVENING INTERESTS

282. Where a lender has advanced money for the purpose of discharging a prior encumbrance in reliance upon obtaining security equivalent to the discharged lien, and his money is so used, the majority and preferable rule is that if he did so in ignorance of junior liens or other interests he will be subrogated to the prior lien. Although stressed in some cases as an objection to relief, neither negligence nor constructive notice should be material.

When a mortgagor pays off a prior mortgage, the liens of later mortgages advance in priority.[66] Further, there is a recognized duty on the part of the mortgagor to pay off a senior mortgage so as to permit a junior mortgage to step into its place in priority ranking.[67] It follows that if a mortgagor pays off a prior mortgage he is not able to keep it alive against later mortgagees either by taking an assignment or by asking subrogation.[68] Will third persons who loaned at the request of the mortgagor for the purpose of paying off a prior mortgage, whose money

will grant it by any means at hand. See 1921, 21 Col.L.Rev. 471; 1933, 31 Mich.L.Rev. 855; 1938, 24 Va.L.Rev. 771, 774; 1939, 25 Va.L.R. 632. See also 1913, 46 L.R.A.,N.S., 1049; 1914, 50 L.R.A.,N.S., 489; 1926, 43 A.L.R. 1393. But occasionally subrogation is denied on such facts. Brown v. Rouse, 1899, 125 Cal. 645, 58 P. 267, noted 1899, 13 Harv. L.Rev. 297. And cf. Thompson v. Davis, 1921, 297 Ill. 11, 130 N.E. 455, criticized in note, 1922, 16 Ill. L.Rev. 379. A distinction suggested in 1926, 43 A. L.R. 1393, that subrogation should be granted when the plaintiff wanted *security* primarily but not if he intended to rely upon the particular mortgage he took appears to be impractical and not warranted by the authorities. See 1933, 31 Mich.L.Rev. 826, 833.

So, too, will the purchaser on a void foreclosure sale be subrogated to the rights of the foreclosing mortgagee. Muir v. Berkshire, 1875, 52 Ind. 149. See note, 10 Harv.L.Rev. 453.

63. Smith v. Sprague, 1928, 244 Mich. 577, 222 N.W. 207; Baker v. Baker, 1891, 2 S.Dak. 261, 49 N.W. 1064, 39 Am.St.Rep. 776; see 1921, 21 Col.L.Rev. 471; 1933, 31 Mich.L.Rev. 826, 835. On whether an oral agreement to give a mortgage on property subject to a mortgage, the borrowed money to be used to discharge the existing encumbrance, is taken out of the Statute of Frauds, see § 63, supra.

64. "It is at least questionable whether the defeated expectation of some security for the loan will justify subrogation to the lien that was in fact paid off with the lender's money." 1933, 31 Mich.L.Rev. 826, 833.

In Elmora & West End Bldg. & Loan Ass'n v. Dancy, 1931, 108 N.J.Eq. 542, 155 A. 796, commented on in, 1931, 45 Harv.L.Rev. 390, M loaned the widow of his mortgagor, A, money, part of which was used to pay off the mortgage held by him, taking as security a mortgage on her dower interest in the property. M marked the mortgage "paid" and sent it to his solicitor for cancellation but it was never cancelled of record. Before the new debt was paid the widow died, thus extinguishing the security. M sued to foreclose on his original mortgage, and the land was sold. A's heirs petitioned to open the decree and set aside the sale. Held, that M was entitled to foreclose the original mortgage to the extent that the money borrowed from him was applied thereto.

65. Chrisman v. Daniel, 1938, 134 Neb. 326, 278 N.W. 565; see Martin v. Hickenlooper, 1936, 90 Utah, 150, 170, 178, 59 P.2d 1139, 1148, 1152, 107 A.L.R. 762, rehearing denied 90 Utah 185, 61 P.2d 307; § 280, note 6, supra; 1937, 36 Mich.L.Rev. 151, 152.

66. See Boley v. Daniel, 1916, 72 Fla. 121, 125, 72 So. 644, 646, L.R.A. 1917A, 734.

67. See § 177, supra.

68. A mortgagor may be entitled to be subrogated as against an assuming grantee or one who takes subject to a mortgage which the mortgagor pays and yet he may not be entitled to subrogation as against his own second mortgagee. See Pomeroy, Equity Juris., 4th ed., § 1213; quotation from Note, 1937, 36 Mich.L.Rev. 151, 154, in the next footnote. However, a mortgagor who has conveyed to a purchaser subject to the mortgage and then pays off the mortgage when it falls due is entitled to be subrogated to the discharged mortgage, or to have the mortgage assigned to him on payment, as protection against a second mortgage on the property executed by his grantee. Howard v. Robbins, 1902, 170 N.Y. 498, 63 N.E. 530.

was used for that purpose, and who would be entitled to subrogation to the lien of the first mortgage as against the mortgagor under the decisions looked at in the preceding section, be entitled to subrogation as against such junior interests which otherwise would have jumped ahead in order of payment?[69]

A lender who knows of an encumbrance junior to the one his money is advanced to discharge is not subrogated to the position of the one he paid off as against the later lien. The reasoning is that he should have protected himself by getting an assignment or expressly stipulating for priority.[70] If he

did not do so he cannot defeat the effect of his payment by seeking to step into the priority position of the discharged mortgage through equitable subrogation. On the other hand, the majority of cases hold that one who advances money to discharge a prior lien in reliance upon getting a first mortgage, or one as good as that which was paid off, is entitled to subrogation to the prior lien as against the holder of an intervening lien of which he was ignorant.[70a] A variety of reasons are given for this result. It is pointed out that one who pays at the request of the mortgagor cannot be properly regarded as officious.[71] Permitting subrogation to the lender will not prejudice the junior lienor because he will occupy the same position by allowing subrogation as he occupied before the prior lien was paid and discharged.[72] Although this amounts only to saying that no obstacle to subrogation, otherwise proper, exists on account of the junior lienor,[73] affirmative ground for granting it is found in the lending in mistaken reliance upon getting security upon the property which would not be postponed to an incumbrance of which he was unaware.[74] Further, although a junior

---

69. See notes, 1921, 21 Col.L.Rev. 470; 1937, 6 Fordham L.Rev. 138; 1913, 26 Harv.L.Rev. 261; 1929, 42 Harv.L.Rev. 962; 1933, 31 Mich.L.Rev. 826, 833; 1937, 36 Mich.L.Rev. 151; 1932, 9 N.Y.Univ.L.Q.Rev. 378; 1931, 70 A.L.R. 1396; 1937, 107 A.L.R. 785. In spite of some confused opinions to the contrary, there is no difficulty in permitting subrogation as against a mortgagor and denying it against a second mortgagee of the mortgagor, or vice versa. The point is well made in a discussion of Martin v. Hickenlooper, 1936, 90 Utah 150, 59 P.2d 1139, 107 A.L.R. 762, rehearing denied 90 Utah 185, 61 P.2d 307, in Note, 1937, 36 Mich.L.Rev. 151, 154, "In the principal case * * * the real disagreement was over giving the lender subrogation as against the second mortgagee when it was denied as against the mortgagor. * * * This particular point was not fully discussed by either the majority or the dissenting justices, but there would seem to be no sound reason why only a portion of the security rights of the original first mortgagee should not be kept alive for the benefit of the lender if the equities of all parties point to that result; nor does a sound reason appear as to why the superior equity of the original mortgagor as to the lender should affect the relationship between the lender and the second mortgagee." See also §§ 273, 275, ante.

See McCrackin, Survey of South Carolina Law: Security Transactions, 1959, 12 S.C.L.Rev. 100, 141, noting Meaders Bros. v. Skelton, 1959, 234 S.C. 134, 107 S.E.2d 1, holding that a third mortgagee who loaned the mortgagor money to pay off an existing first mortgage was entitled to be subrogated so as to come in ahead of the second mortgagee.

70. An agreement for priority establishes the lender's anticipation of getting security instead of relying on the general credit of the mortgagor, the expectation of a preferred position, and that he was not officious. 1921, 21 Col.L.Rev. 472. See Home Sav. Bank of Chicago v. Bierstadt, 1897, 168 Ill. 618, 626, 48 N.E. 161, 61 Am.St.Rep. 146. See also Citizens State Bank v. Pittsburg County Broadcasting Co., Okl.1954, 271 P.2d 725, a chattel mortgage case commented on by Updike, Mortgages, in 1954 Annual Survey of American Law, 1955, 30 N.Y.U.L.Rev. 805, 809.

70a. See note 70, supra. In accord with the text statement is Potter v. United States, D.C.R.I., 1953, 111 F.Supp. 585.

71. See 1939, 48 Yale L.Jour. 683, 686; 1933, 31 Mich.L.Rev. 826, 830. The same is true of one who pays as part of the purchase price. Burgoon v. Lavezzo, 1937, 68 App.D.C. 20, 92 F.2d 726, 113 A.L.R. 944.

72. See 1931, 70 A.L.R. 1396, 1414.

73. "It should be noted, however, in the interest of clarity of reasoning in respect of the right of subrogation, that absence of injury to the junior lienor can hardly be regarded as a predicate for subrogation. Rather it is but a negative factor. That is to say, the right of subrogation in situations like that at bar, is founded on advance of money under mistake of fact and must rest on that affirmative foundation. It will not be recognized if innocent persons will be prejudiced. Therefore to say that the junior lienor is not harmed is but to say that no obstacle to subrogation, otherwise proper, exists on his account." Burgoon v. Lavezzo, 1937, 68 App.D.C. 20, 27, 92 F.2d 726, 733, 113 A.L.R. 944. See also 1933, 31 Mich.L.Rev. 826, 833.

74. See § 281, supra.

encumbrancer has a right to rise when the payment is made by his mortgagor, a lender of money to the mortgagor does not occupy the same position as the mortgagor in this respect.[75] The third party is not paying the mortgagor's debt but is making a loan to the mortgagor on the faith of getting security which would be superior to the junior claimant.[76] To permit the later encumbrancer to advance under these circumstances would give him a windfall advantage at the expense of the justifiable expectations of the lender, and this is properly regarded as unjust enrichment.[77]

Where the lender's ignorance is due to his own negligence there is divergence in the authorities as to whether subrogation will be granted.[78] The preferable view is that negligence should be disregarded.[79] This is so "because subsequent lienholders should not be permitted to gain by another's mishap or carelessness when thus gaining would be purely fortuitous and accidental."[80] There are expressions in some of the cases that if the negligence is inexcusable equity will not grant relief although it will if the negligence is only ordinary.[81] It is submitted that in these cases, where no one has been misled or injured thereby,[82] negligence of any sort is entirely immaterial. Negligence has proper significance when the question of subsequent intervening rights are involved.[83] And the

---

75. It has been pointed out that the objection to subrogation against a junior encumbrancer on the ground it would prevent him rising is "pure question begging; the junior encumbrancer has a right to advance only if the prior encumbrance was paid by one not entitled to subrogation." 1939, 48 Yale L.J. 683, 689. See Burgoon v. Lavezzo, 1937, 68 App.D.C. 20, 26, 92 F.2d 726, 732, 113 A.L.R. 944. "It cannot be argued that the junior incumbrancer has a right to become senior incumbrancer whenever the first mortgage is paid off, as he could then defeat subrogation in every case. His advancement to first mortgagee on extinguishment of the prior lien is a purely fortuitous benefit, to which he has no equitable or legal right." 1921, 21 Col.L.Rev. 471, 472 fn. 20.

76. Kaminskas v. Cepauskis, 1938, 369 Ill. 566, 17 N. E.2d 558, 25 Va.L.Rev. 632; see 1921, 21 Col.L.Rev. 471, 472; 1938, 24 Va.L.Rev. 771, 774.

77. "There is no reason for advancing [the junior lienor] to the position of a senior lienor, since all he ever contracted for was a junior encumbrance. Not only were his rights not prejudiced by the intervention of the new mortgagee, but they were saved from extinction. It would be grossly inequitable to deny the new mortgagee priority over rights which he has himself kept alive." 1921, 21 Col.L.Rev. 471, 472. See 1938, 24 Va.L.Rev. 771, 774. Cf. § 254, supra.

78. See Martin v. Hickenlooper, 1936, 90 Utah 150, 160 et seq., 59 P.2d 1139, 1142 et seq., 107 A.L.R. 762, rehearing denied 90 Utah 186, 61 P.2d 307, for a discussion of the significance of negligence and constructive notice with a thorough review of the authorities; 1939, 48 Yale L.J. 683, 688.

79. E. g., Federal Land Bank v. Joynes, 1942, 179 Va. 394, 18 S.E. 917. See also authorities in following footnotes.

80. Martin v. Hickenlooper, 1936, 90 Utah 150, 160, 59 P.2d 1139, 1142, 107 A.L.R. 762, rehearing denied 90 Utah 186, 61 P.2d 307.

81. E. G., "(5) That according to the modern view, indiligence in searching the record will not prevent equity from applying the doctrine unless it is culpable or unjustifiable negligence. * * * (6) That in many of the cases the doctrine of subrogation would not need to have been applied, because there were facts from which equity would have restored the released lien on the ground of mistake, accident, or fraud, but that in the application of such equitable doctrine, the mistake or accident cannot be the result of inexcusable negligence; that it is this rule that where the mistake or accident has been caused by inexcusable neglect or inertness, equity will not be moved to grant relief, which has caused much of the confusion in the cases where conventional subrogation was discussed and denied." Martin v. Hickenlooper, 1936, 90 Utah 150, 178, 59 P.2d 1139, 1152, 107 A.L.R. 762, rehearing denied 90 Utah 186, 61 P.2d 307. See also Banta v. Vreeland, 1862, 15 N.J.Eq. 103, 82 Am.Dec. 269.

82. See Seeley v. Bacon, N.J.Ch.1896, 34 A. 139, 141; Kent v. Bailey, 1917, 181 Iowa 489, 500, 164 N.W. 852, 856.

83. See Fed. Land Bank v. Joynes, 1942, 179 Va. 394, 18 S.E.2d 917, "the negligence should be chiefly of significance when there are subsequently intervening rights involved which would be prejudiced if subrogation were allowed."

"There seems to be, however, a distinct connection between the effect of such negligence and the presence or absence of an implied agreement between the lender and the mortgagor. Thus in a case where the court feels the negligence so culpable that the junior lienor should advance to the senior position in preference to the payer, it will refuse to imply an agreement for subrogation of the payer; but where no harm is done and the payer's negli-

principle of inexcusable or culpable negligence may have justification where the question is one of relieving against contracts entered into under a mistake.[84] But where, as here, the only consequence of the mistake is that junior mortgagees are getting an unbargained for and wholly adventitious enrichment at the expense of another who expected to have prior security to protect him,[85] negligence should not be a factor.

Constructive notice under recording statutes has been regarded as an obstacle to subrogation of the lender by some courts.[86] Again, the better view is that constructive notice should be disregarded.[87] "If it is true that negligence in searching the record or lack of due care is not a hindrance to subrogation, the doctrine of constructive notice would seem to be quite immaterial."[88] It can have no relevancy on the question whether the lender actually expected to get priority of security in the property because that can be inferred only from his actual knowledge.[89] Insofar as it implies that there is culpability in the lender, the answer is the same as was given above in respect to negligence. Fault of the person at whose expense another has been enriched fortuitously, provided that other has not been misled or harmed, should not bar restitution.[90] In passing it may be worth remark that if the basis for subrogation really is contractual it would be puzzling to understand why carelessness or notice should be thought to have any part whatsoever. "If subrogation depends upon an implied or express agreement to subrogate, what boots it whether or no the lender had notice of subsequent liens?"[91]

gence only 'ordinary,' the courts are prone to find an implied agreement. * * * That is, in a case involving no change of position by the junior lienor in reliance on the discharge of the original first lien, the courts will strain the concept of implied intent to the breaking point in order to prevent the junior lienor from claiming a windfall and advancing to the position of first encumbrancer, whereas their real reason for giving subrogation to the payer is that they feel he has superior equities on his side. Yet where the junior lienor has changed his position in reliance on the discharge of the original first lien, the courts will refuse the payer subrogation, though the same factors are present from which to imply an intent that he was to be subrogated. Thus, it appears preferable to approach these cases in terms of justice rather than intent and to invoke the doctrines of fraud and mistake or accident to reach the desired results." Note, 1937, 36 Mich.L.Rev. 151, 153.

84. See Banta v. Vreeland, 1862, 15 N.J.Eq. 103, 107, 82 Am.Dec. 269.

85. "Negligence has no bearing on the proof of his expectation * * * The junior encumbrancer is not prejudiced in any way * * * and should not be permitted to take an unearned advantage of the act of the new mortgagee." 1921, 21 Col.L.Rev. 471, 472. See quotations, ibid., notes 77, 79, supra. See Banta v. Vreeland, 1862, 15 N.J.Eq. 103, 107, 82 Am.Dec. 269, quoted with approval by Glenn, Mortgages, § 341 n. 7.

86. E. g., Stastny v. Pease, 1904, 124 Iowa 587, 100 N.W. 482; Kuhn v. Nat. Bank, 1906, 74 Kan. 456, 87 P. 551, 118 Am.St.Rep. 332.

87. Shaffer v. McCloskey, 1894, 101 Cal. 576, 36 P. 196; Louisville Joint Stock Land Bank v. Pembroke, 1928, 225 Ky. 375, 9 S.W.2d 113; Joyce v. Dauntz, 1896, 55 Ohio St. 538, 45 N.E. 900; see 1939, 48 Yale L.J. 683, 688; 1921, 21 Col.L.Rev. 471, 472, n. 18. But cf. 1933, 31 Mich.L.Rev. 826, 834. Potter v. United States, D.C.R.I.1953, 111 F.Supp. 585, follows the preferable view.

88. Martin v. Hickenlooper, 1936, 90 Utah 150, 160, 59 P.2d 1139, 1142, 107 A.L.R. 762, rehearing denied 90 Utah 186, 61 P.2d 307.

89. See 1921, 21 Col.L.Rev. 471, 472 n. 18, "Constructive notice, which is intended to protect the rights of an equitable lienor, cannot be invoked to increase those rights by imputing to the new mortgagee a knowledge of facts and a consequent expectation which he did not in fact possess."

90. "Equitable substitution is invoked in these cases simply as an appropriate means of preventing unjust enrichment. * * * The argument that the new mortgagee was negligent in not looking up the record * * * confuses the doctrine of bona fide purchase without notice with the doctrine of equitable substitution for the prevention of unjust enrichment." 1913, 26 Harv.L.Rev. 261.

91. Martin v. Hickenlooper, 1936, 90 Utah 150, 160, 59 P.2d 1139, 1142, 107 A.L.R. 762, rehearing denied 90 Utah 186, 61 P.2d 307. "He may be quite cognizant of the whole record, and yet if his right to be substituted for another depends upon an agreement to subrogate—which in equity is to be treated, upon his lending the money, as if an assignment of the creditor's lien had been made to him—his failure to look up the record would be no more material than if he had actually taken an assignment. The answer lies in the fact that even where there is an agreement to subrogate, the so-called right of subrogation is not one inherent in the contract, but arises in equity * * *." Idem.

GRANTEES—SUBROGATION AGAINST INTERVENING INTERESTS

283. Grantees who presently apply all or part of the purchase price to the payment of a prior incumbrance, or who assume it and pay it later, under mistake as to the existence of a junior or intervening lien, even though the latter is of record, should be subrogated to the position of the discharged lien as against the junior incumbrance. There is, however, a line of authorities denying it.

Where a grantee of the mortgagor assumes the payment of a prior mortgage in actual ignorance of the existence of a later incumbrance, even though it might be of record, the question arises as to whether, on paying the earlier lien he is entitled to be subrogated to it as against the later lienors.[92] A strong line of cases permits subrogation in such a case.[93] There are, however, a considerable number of authorities that refuse it.[94]

Those denying subrogation do so on several grounds.[95] One is that the assuming grantee has become primarily liable for the debt and the general rule applies that one paying his own debt is not entitled to subrogation. Coupled with this is the idea that by assuming the mortgagor's debt he must be regarded as having stepped into his grantor's shoes and therefore the payment has the same effect as if it had been made by the grantor before he parted with the property.[96] Where the grantee assumes any junior mortgages as well as a senior mortgage, as is the case when the assumption is of "all" encumbrances, no objection can be taken to this reasoning and the courts uniformly deny subrogation in such cases.[97] Since he has a duty to

---

92. See 1908, 16 L.R.A.,N.S., 470; 1914, 47 L.R.A.,N.S., 1190; 1925, 37 A.L.R. 384, 386; 1938, 113 A.L.R. 958, for collections of cases. See also authorities cited in following footnotes. For discussions of this and related problems, see 1915, 15 Col.L.Rev. 171; 1924, 38 Harv.L.Rev. 265; 1934, 19 Iowa L. Rev. 629; 1936, 14 N.Car.L.Rev. 295; 1939, 87 U. of Pa.L.Rev. 1012; 1939, 48 Yale L.Jour. 683. The same question is involved where the grantee, instead of assuming payment of the prior incumbrance, presently applies all or part of the agreed purchase price to the payment thereof, or causes it to be applied, provided, of course, that he acts under mistake as to the existence of the intervening incumbrance, even though the latter is of record. Burgoon v. Lavezzo, 1937, 68 App.D.C. 20, 92 F.2d 726, 113 A.L.R. 944.

93. E. g., Johnson v. Tootle, 1897, 14 Utah 482, 47 P. 1033, Campbell, Cases Property Security, 2d Ed., 446; Matzen v. Schaeffer, 1884, 65 Cal. 81, 3 P. 92; Capitol Nat. Bank v. Holmes, 1908, 43 Colo. 154, 95 P. 314, 16 L.R.A.,N.S., 470, 127 Am.St.Rep. 108; Young v. Morgan, 1878, 89 Ill. 199; Smith v. Dinsmore, 1887, 119 Ill. 656, 4 N.E. 648, recorded junior incumbrance; Federal Land Bank v. Smith, 1930, 129 Md. 233, 151 A. 420; Clute v. Emmerich, 1885, 99 N.Y. 342, 2 N.E. 6; Dixon v. Morgan, 1926, 154 Tenn. 389, 285 S.W. 558. See collections of cases in preceding footnote. See also cases cited in following footnotes.

94. Citizens' Mercantile Co. v. Easom, 1924, 158 Ga. 604, 123 S.E. 883, 37 A.L.R. 378, noted in 1924, 38 Harv.L.Rev. 266; Goodyear v. Goodyear, 1887, 72 Iowa 329, 33 N.W. 142; Kuhn v. National Bank, 1906, 74 Kan. 456, 87 P. 551, 118 Am.St.Rep. 332;

Smith v. Feltner, 1935, 259 Ky. 833, 83 S.W.2d 506; Conner v. Welch, 1881, 51 Wis. 431, 8 N.W. 260. See also collections of cases note 92, supra, and authorities cited in succeeding footnotes.

95. For a thorough survey of the reasons both for and against subrogation together with a comprehensive review of the authorities, see Burgoon v. Lavezzo, note 92, supra.

96. Kuhn v. National Bank, 1906, 74 Kan. 456, 87 P. 551, 118 Am.St.Rep. 332; Goodyear v. Goodyear, 1887, 72 Iowa 329, 33 N.W. 142; Poole v. Kelsey, 1900, 95 Ill.App. 233. See also a similar line of reasoning in 1939, 87 U. of Pa.L.Rev. 1012, "A possible rationale * * * may be found in the intention expressed between the grantee and the mortgagor-grantor that the grantee should pay the first mortgage and leave the land available for the payment of the second mortgage." If the mortgagor-grantor was bound to pay off the second mortgage for the benefit of his grantee such reasoning would seem fallacious. It would seem to have force if the grantee assumed or took subject to the second mortgage also.

97. E. g., Stastny v. Pease, 1904, 124 Iowa, 587, 100 N.W. 482; Martin v. C. Aultman & Co., 1891, 80 Wis. 150, 49 N.W. 749; Morris v. Twichell, 1933, 63 N.D. 747, 249 N.W. 905, commented on in, 1934, 19 Iowa L.Rev. 629, denied subrogation to a purchaser who assumed the first mortgage with knowledge of the second mortgage and who, when he paid the first mortgage, asked for and thought he had received an assignment instead of the cancellation which actually was executed. Although the purchaser did not expressly assume payment of the second mortgage the court stressed the fact that its amount had been deducted from the purchase price. The court said, "The rule is that when payment had been made by one primarily liable, it operates as an absolute satisfaction. * * * Neither by assignment nor by subrogation can he keep the mortgage alive as against other liens on the land."

pay the junior liens he cannot complain if his payment and discharge of the earlier mortgage advances them in priority. If the first mortgage only is assumed and the grantee has actual knowledge of the junior liens at the time of assumption, it is arguable that the same result is justified,[98] although there are authorities to the contrary.[1] In such a case he pays under no mistake, and the view that it would not be unfair for the same consequences to follow payment by him as would flow from payment by the mortgagor, namely elevation of the junior lienors, is not an unreasonable one. When, with his eyes open, he discharges the earlier mortgage without providing for it to accrue to him, or for other equally good security, the argument is persuasive that no justified expectation on his part of security in priority to the later mortgages has been defeated.

The same is not true when his assumption is of the first mortgage only and he pays and discharges it without knowledge of a junior lien. In such a case the grantee owes a duty to the mortgagor to pay off the first mortgage,[2] but he has entered into no agreement with the second mortgagee to discharge it for his benefit.[3] The only possible claim to rise that the second lienor may urge is through the duty of the mortgagor to pay off prior mortgages for his benefit.[4] But between the

mortgagor and the grantee the mortgagor has a duty to pay off the second mortgage entirely,[5] not to let it rise to a position of priority on the land now owned by the grantee. This being so, it would seem to follow clearly that the mortgagor could not claim that the grantee owed any duty to him, which could accrue derivatively to a second mortgagee, to pay off the first mortgage in order that the second mortgage, which he was bound to pay for the benefit of the grantee, might rise to a preferred position on the land. To permit the second mortgagee to rise to priority under these circumstances would give him an unwarranted enrichment at the expense of the grantee.[6]

Constructive notice [7] of the junior encumbrances, or negligence [8] in not discovering

5. If a grantee is ignorant of junior liens and does not, by his agreement of purchase, take their possible existence into account by assuming them or taking subject to them, it is clear that their amounts are not, as is that of the first mortgage which is assumed, deducted from the purchase price. Instead the amounts of the junior liens must have been included in what the grantee pays the mortgagor. If this is so, as to the junior liens the grantee would be surety only and the mortgagor would have the primary duty of discharging them, § 248. The result is that, while the mortgagor could compel the grantee to pay off the first mortgage, the grantee would have a similar right against the mortgagor as to the second mortgage.

6. Tibbitts v. Terrill, 1914, 26 Colo.App. 64, 140 P. 936, commented on in 1915, 15 Col.L.Rev. 171, in which an assuming grantee was subrogated to the lien of the first mortgage which he paid, although he had actual knowledge of the recordation of a lis pendens claim against the property at the time he bought it but bona fide, after legal advice, thought the claim invalid. The court made the point that to allow subrogation would work no hardship to the junior claimant. His security interest in the property when he acquired it was subject to this superior lien, and he should not reap the benefit of the other man's innocent mistake. See § 282, supra.

7. Ragan v. Standard Scale Co., 1907, 128 Ga. 544, 58 S.E. 31; Goodyear v. Goodyear, 1887, 72 Iowa 329, 33 N.W. 142; Kitchell v. Mudgett, 1877, 37 Mich. 81; see Stastny v. Pease, 1904, 124 Iowa 587, 591, 592, 100 N.W. 482, 483, 484.

In Duke v. Kilpatrick, 1935, 231 Ala. 51, 163 So. 640, criticized in note, 1936, 14 N.Car.L.Rev. 295, subrogation for the purpose of obtaining contribution

See 1925, 37 A.L.R. 384. The same should be true if the purchase was subject to the later as well as the earlier mortgages.

98. In some of the cases in which the courts stress the grantee's assumption as the basis of the decision the grantee had actual notice of the intervening liens. E. g., Lackawanna Trust & Safe Deposit Co. v. Gomeringer, 1912, 236 Pa. 179, 84 A. 757; De Roberts v. Stiles, 1901, 24 Wash. 611, 64 P. 795; Willson v. Burton, 1880, 52 Vt. 394; Cady v. Barnes, D.C.Ohio 1913, 208 F. 361, reversed 232 F. 318, 146 C.C.A. 366; cf. Kitchell v. Mudgett, 1877, 37 Mich. 81.

1. Joyce v. Dauntz, 1896, 55 Ohio St. 538, 45 N.E. 900; see Young v. Morgan, 1878, 89 Ill. 199, 202; cf. Stantons v. Thompson, 1870, 49 N.H. 272.

2. See § 259, supra.

3. Clute v. Emmerich, 1885, 99 N.Y. 342, 2 N.E. 6.

4. See §§ 177, 282, supra.

8. See Note 8 on page 576.

them is offered as other reasons for denying subrogation. What was said previously in connection with the same arguments when the right of a lender to subrogation was discussed is equally applicable here.[9] Only actual, not constructive notice, has relevancy on the question of what the expectations of the payor were.[10] Insofar as it implies culpability in not discovering the junior liens it stands on a footing with negligence.[11] And negligence which has not resulted in harm to anyone should not be invoked to permit unjust enrichment of the later lienors through their unearned and fortuitous advancement in priority by reason of the mistake of the grantee in paying and taking a discharge instead of an assignment.[12] Further, the function of constructive notice is to preserve an existing advantage and not to gain a new one.[13]

One court urged policy considerations in respect to the recording acts and certainty of transactions between the parties to a transfer of mortgaged property.[14] Whatev-er merit there may be to the suggestion, it is outweighed by the unfair result as between the payor and the junior lienors.

The suggestion that relief through subrogation should be refused on the ground that an assuming grantee is a volunteer [15] or officious when he pays the debt he agreed to pay flouts reality.[16] And only to a slightly less degree is this true where the first mortgage is paid off at the time of purchase rather than later.[17] In such cases, however, it is not always clear on the facts whether the purchase price included later mortgages or not. When the purchaser did not know of them this should be sufficient to indicate that it did not.

Where the conveyance is subject to the first mortgage, cases generally permit subrogation as against junior liens if the grantee paid off the prior incumbrance without actual knowledge of the subsequent ones.[18] In such cases the argument cannot be made that the grantee was merely paying off his own debt since he was not personally liable.

---

from his co-owner was denied to an assuming grantee who paid off the entire first mortgage on property which he had bought honestly thinking that he was getting full title when actually he was obtaining only a one-half interest in it. The fact of joint ownership of his grantor with another was on record and also appeared in the deed he received. Other courts allowing subrogation have expressly considered constructive notice as an obstacle and rejected it. E. g., see Prestridge v. Lazar, 1923, 132 Miss. 168, 177, 95 So. 837, 838; Burgoon v. Lavezzo, 1937, 68 App.D.C. 20, 24, 92 F.2d 726, 730, 113 A.L.R. 944. Look also at Smith v. Dinsmore, 1887, 119 Ill. 656, 4 N.E. 648; Neff v. Elder, 1907, 84 Ark. 277, 105 S.W. 260, 120 Am.St.Rep. 67.

8. Lamoille County Sav. Bank & Trust Co. v. Belden, 1916, 90 Vt. 535, 98 A. 1002; see Burgoon v. Lavezzo, 1937, 68 App.D.C. 20, 23, 92 F.2d 726, 729, 113 A.L.R. 944.

9. See § 282, supra.

10. Cf., § 282, note 89.

11. Cf., § 282, note-calls and notes 89, 90, supra.

12. Cf. § 282, supra, notes and note-calls, 81, 82, 83, 85.

13. See § 282, note 89, supra.

14. In Belcher v. Belcher, 1939, 161 Or. 340, 87 P.2d 762, 89 P.2d 893, commented on in note, 1939, 24 Minn.L.Rev. 121, the assuming grantee was denied

subrogation even though he paid off the first mortgage in ignorance of a recorded second mortgage. The court said, "Such a rule makes it incumbent upon a purchaser to consult available records in regard to contemplated real property transactions. It also minimizes, as to those transactions, the effect of any uncertainty of representation between vendor and vendee concerning existing incumbrances of record."

15. Kahn v. McConnell, 1913, 37 Okl. 219, 220, 131 P. 682, 47 L.R.A.,N.S., 1189.

16. Clute v. Emmerich, 1885, 99 N.Y. 342, 2 N.E. 6; cf. Weidner v. Thompson, 1886, 69 Iowa 36, 28 N.W. 422.

17. E. g., Burgoon v. Lavezzo, 1937, 68 App.D.C. 20, 92 F.2d 726, 113 A.L.R. 944, commented on, 1939, 48 Yale L.J. 683.

18. Darrough v. Herbert Kraft Company Bank, 1899, 125 Cal. 272, 57 P. 983, recorded junior encumbrance; Barnes v. Mott, 1876, 64 N.Y. 397, 21 Am. R. 625, recorded junior encumbrance; Ryer v. Gass, 1881, 130 Mass. 227; Hudson v. Dismukes, 1883, 77 Va. 242; see Burgoon v. Lavezzo, 1937, 68 App.D.C. 20, 23, 24; 92 F.2d, 726, 729, 730, 113 A.L.R. 944. See also 1936, 14 N.Car.L.Rev. 295, 297; 1915, 15 Col.L.Rev. 171. Contra: Hayden v. Huff, 1900, 60 Neb. 625, 83 N.W. 920, affirmed 63 Neb. 99, 88 N.W. 179, negligence in failure to examine records; cf. Storer v. Warren, 1934, 99 Ind.App. 616, 192 N.E. 325.

Apart from this, since the land is principal, it would seem that, up to the value of the land, there is little difference between the two groups of cases.

COMPELLING AN ASSIGNMENT

284. Generally one who is entitled to subrogation can compel the giving of an assignment.

In general subrogation is equivalent to an assignment of the mortgage creditor's rights.[19] It is not, however, identical with an assignment [20] and does not give as complete protection as does one. It is only an equitable right and consequently is subject to the greater hazards of such interests.[21] Frequently, therefore, one who has a right to be subrogated on payment of the mortgage creditor desires, instead, a formal assignment. Is he entitled to it?

The objection to compelling a mortgage creditor to execute an assignment under such circumstances is that on payment his only duty under his mortgage agreement is to cancel the debt and to discharge the mortgage on the land—not to keep the mortgage alive by assigning it. To compel the latter is to impose affirmative duties on him without his consent. To this there are answers. A technical one is that when a mortgage is entered into a relationship is created involving rights and duties not confined to those embodied in the agreement of the parties, express or implied in fact. A considerable number of legal incidents attach to the relationship regardless of the intention of the parties because equity courts have believed it desirable and fair, in view of the purposes of the transaction, that they should. Striking examples of equity adopting rules in respect to mortgages that operate actually to defeat expressed intentions are the creation of the equity of redemption itself and its protection once it has been created.[22] Other incidents, which may not frustrate intention but do not depend upon it are rights of exoneration [23] and the consequences of binding extensions of time by the mortgage creditor.[24] Consequently it would seem clear that, if the particular right or duty asserted by a party to a mortgage is one that courts of equity think is necessary or desirable and reasonable, it is not automatically barred either because it was not within the terms of the parties' agreement, or because it had not been recognized before as a staple of mortgage law.

Looking at the merits of the proposal it would seem an assignment should be compelled if the claimant shows any substantial need for it as opposed to subrogation. As contrasted with what the mortgagee must do on payment, execution of an assignment is not onerous. And to transfer the debt and mortgage without recourse imposes on him no additional risk.

The courts in passing on the question of compelling an assignment have given varying answers.[25] Most of the cases will grant it if the person paying the mortgage debt stands in the relation of surety for its payment.[26] Others go beyond this and grant it where the person paying did so to protect an interest,[27] and even in favor of lenders who

19. See § 277, supra.

20. "The most that can be said is that the subrogated creditor by operation of law represents the person to whose rights he is subrogated." City of New Orleans v. Whitney, 1890, 138 U.S. 595, 606, 11 S.Ct. 428, 431.

21. See §§ 182, 185, 277, supra. See also Pardee v. Van Anken, N.Y. 1848, 3 Barb. 534, 541.

22. See Chapter 4, supra.

23. See §§ 258, 259, supra, and § 285, infra.

24. See §§ 269, 270, supra.

25. For collections of authorities, see Ann.Cas.1914B, 562; 1919, 2 A.L.R. 242 (chattel mortgage); 1934, 93 A.L.R. 89.

26. E. g., Johnson v. Zink, 1873, 51 N.Y. 333. See 1934, 93 A.L.R. 89, 99.

27. E. g., Averill v. Taylor, 1853, 8 N.Y. 44. In Simonson v. Lauck, 1905, 105 App.Div. 82, 93 N.Y.S. 965, the mortgagor, owner of the fee simple as tenant-in-common with four others, demanded an assignment to a third person who had tendered payment of the entire mortgage at the request of the

are entitled to subrogation.[28] On the other hand some courts deny subrogation even though the payment was made to protect an interest in the property [29] or even when the payor was in the position of a surety.[30]

EXONERATION

285. One who personally stands surety, or whose interest in mortgaged property occupies that position, is entitled to exoneration against the person or property primarily bound to pay the debt. Such persons also, if it will not prejudice the rights of the mortgage creditor or third parties, may compel the mortgage creditor to enforce his claim first against the person or property primarily liable.

The right of a transferor of mortgaged property to exoneration where the grantee assumes or takes subject to the mortgage has been considered previously.[31] Similarly, the right of a mortgagor to demand that the

mortgagor. The mortgagor had brought an action for partition against his co-tenants and, apparently, wanted the assignment made both for the purpose of obtaining contribution against his co-tenants and, also, because it was the only way he could obtain a loan to pay off the debt and prevent foreclosure. The court ordered the assignment. Motes v. Roberson, 1902, 133 Ala. 630, 32 So. 225, accord. Cf. Fears v. Albea, 1887, 69 Tex. 437, 6 S.W. 286, 5 Am.St.Rep. 78. In Bayles v. Husted, N.Y., 1886, 40 Hun 376, the widow of a deceased mortgagor tendered to the mortgagee the amount of the secured debt and demanded that the mortgage be assigned to X. Held, the mortgagee should be compelled to make the assignment.

28. French v. Grand Beach Co., 1927, 239 Mich. 575, 215 N.W. 13, noted, 1927, 12 Minn.L.Rev. 189. Cf. Arant, Suretyship, 360–367; 1921, 34 Harv.L.Rev. 792; 1934, 20 Va.L.Rev. 917. Lackawanna Trust & Safe Deposit Co. v. Gomeringer, 1912, 236 Pa. 179, 84 A. 757, is contra.

29. Lamb v. Montague, 1873, 112 Mass. 352; Butler v. Taylor, 1855, 71 Mass. (5 Gray) 455; Hamilton v. Dobbs, 1868, 19 N.J.Eq. 227. Cf. Holland v. Citizens, etc., Bank, 1890, 16 R.I. 734, 19 A. 654, 8 L.R.A. 553.

See Updike, Mortgages, in 1954 Annual Survey of American Law, 1955, 30 N.Y.U.L. Rev. 805, 812, noting Marine View Sav. & Loan Ass'n v. Andrulonis, Ch. 1954, 31 N.J.Super. 378, 106 A.2d 559.

30. Fitcher v. Griffiths, 1913, 216 Mass. 174, 103 N.E. 471. Cf. Heighe v. Evans, 1933, 164 Md. 259, 164 A. 671, 93 A.L.R. 81.

31. See §§ 258, 259, supra. See also § 248. Marsh v. Pike, N.Y.1844, 10 Paige, 595, is the leading case

mortgagee foreclose the mortgage and consequences of a refusal was touched upon.[32] It was seen that such a right does not generally exist.[33] However, a party to the mortgage who is entitled to exoneration, e. g., because he stands in the position of surety as to the mortgaged property, or part of it, may compel a mortgagee who seeks to enforce the mortgage to resort first to that part of the property which is principal,[34] pro-

for exoneration. Look also at Fitcher v. Griffiths, 1913, 216 Mass. 174, 103 N.E. 471. As against a non-assuming grantee the exoneration is out of the land only; as against an assuming grantee the exoneration is available not only in respect to the land but as to the grantee personally.

On the right to exoneration in Mortgage Transactions, see also Storke and Sears, Transfer of Mortgaged Property, 1953, 38 Corn.L.Q. 185, 195–197.

32. Idem. See Marsh v. Pike, N.Y.1844, 10 Paige 595. Cf. Abell v. Coons, 1857, 7 Cal. 105, 68 Am.Dec. 229; Mowry v. Mowry, 1904, 137 Mich. 277, 100 N.W. 388.

33. Idem.

"The defendant Davies [mortgagor] having no right to compel the plaintiff to foreclose the mortgage, it is questionable whether a request to do so would have been of any avail. His request to collect the debt might have been answered by bringing an action against him on his bond; and the necessity of this he could have obviated by voluntarily paying it and being subrogated to the rights of the mortgagee. It is, to say the least, doubtful whether a mortgagor thus situated has any remedy except to protect himself by watching the security; and if he finds that it is becoming impaired by lapse of time and the accumulation of interest and taxes, to take the steps pointed out in Marsh v. Pike, supra [10 Paige, 595]." Marshall v. Davies, 1879, 78 N.Y. 414, 422.

Fish v. Glover, 1894, 154 Ill. 86, 39 N.E. 1081, accord. Cf. Gottschalk v. Jungmann, 1903, 78 App.Div. 171, 79 N.Y.S. 551. But cf., Hampe v. Manke, 1912, 28 S.D. 501, 134 N.W. 60, in which A mortgaged land to B to secure a debt. A requested B to have the mortgage recorded. Thereafter A transferred the land to C. C by an agreement not contained in the deed contracted to discharge the mortgage debt. B did not record the mortgage. Thereafter C for value conveyed the premises to D who had no notice of B's mortgage. Held, in a suit by B against A to recover the mortgage debt, that A was not liable.

34. A mortgaged land to B to secure his debt. Later A granted a portion of the mortgaged premises to C who took subject to the mortgage and assumed payment of the debt. Held, upon foreclosure, the land held by C should be first resorted to to satisfy the debt. Mead v. Peabody, 1899, 183 Ill. 126, 55 N.E. 719; Mowry v. Mowry, 1904, 137 Mich. 277, 100 N.W. 388; Scott v. Norris, 1917, 62 Okl. 292, 162 P.

vided this will not prejudice the mortgagee or third persons with superior rights. This principle is important when the doctrine of marshalling is involved and will be considered further when that subject is discussed.[35]

B. MARSHALLING

GENERAL PRINCIPLES

286. Where portions of a mortgaged property are later sold or mortgaged to different persons, the rights of such persons against each other, the mortgagor and the first mortgagee are adjusted by marshalling. The term covers two principles more accurately described as the "inverse order of alienation rule" and the "two funds" doctrine. Although marshalling must be invoked before foreclosure its results can be achieved in other ways. It will never be ordered to the prejudice of the first mortgagee.

Frequently a single tract of land consisting of several lots or parcels is mortgaged to secure one debt. Or it may be that two or more separate tracts are subject to a single mortgage debt. The various lots or tracts may then be sold or mortgaged to different parties either simultaneously or successively and one or more of the lots or tracts may be retained by the mortgagor. In such cases there are two or more pieces of property as security for the same debt and more than one person has an interest in the properties under the mortgage. For convenience in the following discussion the foregoing situation may be stated in hypothetical terms in which R is the mortgagor and E the mortgagee of the single tract, Blackacre, which is composed of three lots, X, Y and Z. T-1 and T-2 represent later purchasers or second mortgagees, as the case may be, of lots X and Y. Lot Z remains in the hands of R. If the transfers of X and Y are by sale, T-1 and T-2

may have bought upon any one of the three terms examined earlier. That is, they may have assumed the mortgage, taken subject to it, or paid the full value of the parcel with R bound to pay off the mortgage on it.[36] Or there may be agreements apportioning the debt in specified amounts or percentages among the various parcels transferred or retained by the mortgagor.[37] The transfer to T-1 may or may not have been recorded. T-2, whether he is purchaser or mortgagee, may have actual notice of the prior transfer to T-1.

The question is, what are the rights of these grantees or second mortgagees against not only each other and the mortgagor, but against the holder of the underlying first mortgage on the whole tract? The answer is found in the doctrine of marshalling.[38] If there were no principles of marshalling E could proceed against the three parcels in any order he wished. This would endow him with the power, to be exercised at his caprice, of wiping out the interest of T-1, T-2, or R in the parcel held by one or another of them by going against it rather than against another or all of them.[39] The purpose and effect of marshalling is to prevent this result.[40]

---

36. See § 248, supra.

37. See § 288, n. 94, infra.

38. Marshalling is "the ranking or ordering of several estates or parcels of land for the satisfaction of a judgment or mortgage to which all are liable." 1 Black, Judgments, § 440. For collections of authorities on various aspects of the problem of marshalling see, 1889, 5 L.R.A. 280; 1908, 12 L.R.A.,N.S. 965; 1912, id. 359; 1914, id. 302; Ann.Cas.1914A., 715; id. 1916D, 1119; 1925, 35 A.L.R. 1307; 1926, 44 id. 608; 1932, 77 id. 371; 1936, 101 id. 618; 1937, 106 id. 1102; 1937, 110 id. 65; 1939, 119 id. 1109; 1941, 131 A.L.R. 4. This last is a long and comprehensive survey of the inverse order of alienation rule.

39. See, e. g., the example stated in the text, infra, in illustration of the "two funds" doctrine. If T-1 or T-2 is a grantee from the mortgagor his interest could be destroyed in the same way by an uncontrolled action of the first mortgagee in foreclosing on his parcel rather than on another.

40. Cf. § 285, supra.

1085. Cf. Fitcher v. Griffiths, 1913, 216 Mass. 174, 103 N.E. 471.

On the right to exoneration in transfers of mortgaged property on death of the mortgagor, see Note, 1952, 40 Cal.L.Rev. 457.

35. See Chapter 10, Subdivision B, infra.

The term marshalling is used to cover two principles which are more accurately given the separate titles of the "inverse order of alienation" rule and the "two funds" doctrine.[41] The "inverse order of alienation" rule is "that a mortgagee or other lienor, where the land subject to lien has been aliened in separate parcels successively, shall satisfy his lien out of the land remaining in the grantor or original owner, if possible, and, if that be insufficient, that he shall resort to the parcels aliened in the inverse order of their alienation."[42] The rule has been traced back to Coke in England,[43] and was first enunciated in this country by Chancellor Kent[44] and later approved by the great weight of authority.[45]

The "two funds" rule applies where a senior encumbrancer has two funds and a junior only one out of which his debt may be made. For example, lots X and Y are mortgaged to E. T–1 then takes a second mortgage on lot X. Unless lot X is sufficient to pay both mortgages, if E should foreclose by taking payment out of it first there will be nothing left for T–1 and he will be reduced to the status of an unsecured creditor. On the other hand, if E takes his payment out of Y first before resorting to X, some or all of the latter is likely to be available for T–1. To prevent the caprice of the doubly secured creditor, E, from determining where the loss shall fall in such a case, the "two funds" rule may be invoked by T–1 to compel E to realize first on Y.[46]

Regardless of which of these two marshalling principles is applicable some things are clear. One is that all fractional interests remain bound by the first mortgage. The mortgagor can no more divest a portion of the mortgaged property by conveying it away or giving a second mortgage on it than he can free the entire property by the same means.[47] Provided, of course, the first mortgage is properly recorded, which it normally is. And it is equally fundamental that, although restrictions may be placed upon E's enforcement of his rights for the purpose of ordering or ranking the relative positions of T–1, T–2 and R, those restrictions must stop short of prejudicing E's paramount rights as first mortgagee.[48] This protection to the mortgagee can be accomplished by the de-

---

41. See Fidelity & Casualty Co. v. Massachusetts Mut. Life Ins. Co., 4th Cir. 1935, 74 F.2d 881.

For a criticism of the orthodox dichotomy stated in the text and a thesis that, instead, cases should be grouped under the two heads, "Suretyship Marshaling" and "Lien Marshaling," see Storke and Sears, Transfer of Mortgaged Property, 1953, 38 Corn. L. Q. 185, 201 et seq. For applications of the principles of marshaling in subdivision financing, see id. 211. See also Melli, Subdivision Control in Wisconsin, 1953, Wis.L.Rev. 389. See additionally, Green, Marshaling Assets in Texas, 1956, 34 Texas L.Rev. 1054. For a discussion of subdivision financing problems, see Storke and Sears, Subdivision Financing, 1956, 28 Rocky Mt. L. Rev. 1. See Note, The Rights of a Junior Lienholder in Wisconsin, 1959, 43 Marq.L.Rev. 89, 94.

42. Idem.

43. Harbert's Case, 1584, 3 Co.Rep. 11b. Cf. Lord Eldon in Aldrich v. Cooper, 1803, 8 Ves. 382, and Sugden, in Averall v. Wade, 1825, Ll. & G. 252, on the "two funds" doctrine. See Clowes v. Dickenson, N. Y. 1821, 5 Johns.Ch. 235. See also Sanford v. Hill, 1878, 46 Conn. 42; National Sav. Bank of District of Columbia v. Creswell, D.C. 1880, 100 U.S. 630, 25 L.Ed. 713.

44. In Clowes v. Dickenson, supra note 43.

45. Brown v. Simons, 1863, 44 N.H. 475; Cumming v. Cumming, 1847, 3 Ga. 460; Clowes v. Dickenson, note 43, supra; Sanford v. Hill, supra; National Sav. Bank v. Creswell, note 43, supra; see Iglehart v. Crane & Wesson, 1866, 42 Ill. 261, 265, 269. See 1889, 5 L.R.A. 276, 282; Ann.Cas.1916D, 1119.

46. See Cotton, L. J., in Webb v. Smith, 30 Ch.Div. 190. See also Lord Hardwicke in Lanoy v. Duke of Athol, 1741, 4 Atk. 444; Lord Eldon in Aldrich v. Cooper, 1803, 8 Ves. 382; 2 Story, Equity Juris., 14th ed., §§ 733, 758–781. Cf. Worth v. Hill, 1861, 14 Wis. 559. The rule goes back to Culpepper v. Aston, 1682, 2 Ch.Cas. 115, 117. As to the justice of this rule which operates to the prejudice of general creditors, see Langdell, A Brief Survey of Equity Jurisdiction, 15; note, 1930, 43 Harv.L.Rev. 501.

47. § 247, supra.

48. Hyde Park Thomson-Houston Light Co. v. Brown, 1898, 172 Ill. 329, 50 N.E. 127. The first mortgagee is entitled to sell all lots if necessary to satisfy his debt. Vanderspeck v. Federal Land Bank, 1936, 175 Miss. 759, 167 So. 782. The burden of establishing prejudice has been held to be on the mortgagee. Continental Oil Co. of Texas v. Graham, Tex.Civ. App. 1928, 8 S.W.2d 719. But see 19 Am. & Eng. Encyc.Law, 2d ed. 1901, 1266, n. 1.

cree itself.[49] After directing that the parcels shall be offered for sale in the inverse order of alienation, beginning with that part of the tract still in the hands of the mortgagor, it may then provide that " '[I]f the aggregate amount bid for the said lands so offered in severalty shall be insufficient to satisfy this decree, then the said master shall offer for sale said lots * * * together as one parcel * * *; and if the amount bid for the said lands so offered together shall exceed the aggregate of the amounts bid for said lands when offered in severalty * * * then said master shall sell said lands together' ".[50] It may be that such a procedure would add to the costs of the action. If so, it could be allocated to those for whose benefit the marshalling is ordered.[51]

It is generally held that one entitled to marshalling has a right only to require a certain order of realization out of the various parcels under the mortgage when foreclosure occurs. Consequently a grantee or junior encumbrancer who has such a right must properly assert his equity before sale or other foreclosure of his parcel takes place.[52] This he may do by bill in equity if the attempted foreclosure is under power of sale,[53] or by cross-bill, answer or the like, in case of judicial foreclosure.[54] Even where the mortgagee's suit is for strict foreclosure the same result can be obtained. In such an action an equity court will always order a sale if the equities of the junior parties in interest require it. And it has even been held that a grantee of one of two mortgaged tracts, in a proper case for marshalling, may require the mortgagee who is seeking strict foreclosure, to confine his remedy to the other tract where the net value of that tract is clearly equal to the mortgage debt.[55]

While the foregoing are the most usual ways in which principles of marshalling are worked out others should be mentioned. One is to utilize the right of subrogation. Instead of having the land sold on foreclosure by the mortgagee in the order to which a subsequent grantee or mortgagee is entitled, such a transferee may elect to pay off the underlying first mortgage and be subrogated to his rights.[56] Those rights are, however, subject to control according to the principles of marshalling just as they were in the hands of the first mortgagee. Another is by an action to redeem, in which the reciprocal rights of the parties may be adjusted by the decree.[57] Or, if the party wishes, he may permit the mortgagee to sell all of the mortgaged property and assert his priority right to the proceeds after the foreclosing mortgagee has been satisfied and before general creditors are paid.

With this much of the problem and principles of marshalling before us we may now turn to specific instances and applications in the following sections. In doing so we shall consider the problem as it arises where subsequent purchasers from the mortgagor are concerned, where junior encumbrancers

---

49. E. g., Hyde Park Thomson-Houston Light Co. v. Brown, 1898, 172 Ill. 329, 50 N.E. 127.

50. Idem.

51. See Glenn, Mortgages, § 292.

52. Vines v. Wilcutt, 1925, 212 Ala. 150, 102 So. 29, 35 A.L.R. 1301.

53. Idem.

54. Black v. Suydam, 1915, 81 Wash. 279, 142 P. 700, Ann.Cas.1916D, 1113. See 1924, 35 A.L.R. 1307, 1310. Control of all of the parcels by the foreclosing court is essential. Hence marshalling cannot be ordered if part of the mortgaged property is outside of the state. Drexler v. Commercial Sav. Bank, 1925, 5 F.2d 13, noted 1925, 25 Col.L.Rev. 974.

55. Markham v. Smith, 1935, 119 Conn. 355, 366, 367, 176 A. 880, 885; New England Mortgage Realty Co. v. Rossini, 1936, 121 Conn. 214, 183 A. 744. "On the other hand, the mortgagor, or a grantee or junior incumbrancer of *both* tracts, not being entitled to marshalling, is denied such relief on the ground that application should have been made to the court for an order of foreclosure by sale, in which event, by the usual practice, the tracts would have been sold separately, unless used as a whole." Campbell, Cases Mortgages, 2d ed., 620 n. 7, citing New Haven Bank N. B. A. v. Jackson, 1935, 119 Conn. 451, 453, 455, 177 A. 387, 388.

56. See §§ 278, 279, 283.

57. See Chapter 12, Subdivision A, infra.

are interested, where general creditors assert a claim, and the occasional case where the mortgagor himself is seeking protection, e. g., in a homestead subject to the mortgage.

GRANTEES—INVERSE ORDER RULE

287. By the weight of authority, the inverse order of alienation rule applies where there are successive purchasers of different fractions of mortgaged property, each one of whom takes with notice of prior sales of other fractions and, by paying the full value of his portion, acquires a right that the mortgagor and the residue of the mortgaged property in his hands shall have the primary duty to discharge the mortgage debt. A covenant against incumbrances in the conveyances is not essential to the rule in spite of statements to that effect. Recordation is sufficient to give notice to later grantees of other parcels. Failure to record has been held to reverse the order of marshalling as to subsequent purchasers without actual notice.

A minority rule pro rates the debt among the various parcels according to the value of each part.

The basis of the inverse order of alienation rule is that each of the successive purchasers has bought his parcel on terms which impose upon the mortgagor and the remaining property in his hands the primary obligation of paying the mortgage debt, the property in the hands of the grantee, although still liable, standing merely in the position of surety.[58] This situation occurs where the full price of the parcel is paid without deduction of the whole or any part of the debt secured by the blanket mortgage.[59] As has been

pointed out, persons who have notice of the underlying mortgage through searching the records or otherwise,[59a] would not enter into such a transaction if they possessed business experience or had consulted a competent lawyer.[60] But one having done so, he has a right to have the remaining property in the hands of the mortgagor exonerate the parcel he bought.[61]

It has sometimes been asserted that the right of grantee to have marshalling is dependent upon having received a deed with covenants of warranty.[62] Such is not the

---

parcel. The equity attaches when the consideration is paid. Libby v. Tufts, 1890, 121 N.Y. 172, 24 N.E. 12. This equity would be defeated, of course, if the purchaser of the second parcel did not have notice and could qualify as a bona fide purchaser in other respects.

59a. Their ignorance is as to the existence of the mortgage, not its legal consequences. It cannot, therefore, be urged against helping them that their plight is the result of a mistake of law. See note, 1937, 23 Va.L.Rev. 298.

60. Walsh and Simpson, Cas. Security Transactions, 369. Where sale of parcels of property subject to a single mortgage is contemplated at the time the mortgage is entered into, it is common practice to insert a provision for a partial release on payment of part of the debt. In the absence of such a provision the mortgagee is entitled to retain his lien upon every part of the land until the debt is entirely paid. See Graham v. Linden, 1872, 50 N.Y. 547, 550. The language of such provisions have not been standardized and in construing them there is a divergence of authority as to whether the partial release privilege is personal to the mortgagor or can be taken advantage of by purchasers of portions of the property. See 1931, 31 Col.L.Rev. 894, 895. For additional discussion of the matter, see under the subjects of Discharge, Chapter 11, infra, and Redemption Chapter 12, infra. A well advised purchaser of a portion of property covered by a single mortgage insists upon obtaining a release of the lot bought from the blanket mortgage on the application of the purchase price, or a part of it together with a purchase money mortgage on the plot sold, to the reduction of the underlying mortgage. See Walsh & Simpson, Cas. Security Transactions, 369.

61. See § 285, supra. Cf. §§ 258, 259, supra.

62. See, e.g., Pomeroy, Equity Juris., 5th ed., § 1225, "This relation * * * results from the form of the conveyance, which, being a warranty deed, or equivalent to a warranty, shows conclusively an intention between the two that the grantor is to assume the whole burden of the encumbrance as a

---

58. "In respect to that which the mortgagor still retains, the law is well settled, that it stands primarily liable for the payment of the whole debt; while that which he has sold is chargeable only for the deficiency after the other has been applied." Brown v. Simons, 1863, 44 N.H. 475, 478. Ventnor City Nat. Bank v. Troy Corp., 1930, 107 N.J.Eq. 187, 152 A. 921, affirming 1929, 7 N.J.Misc. 1083, 147 A. 862, accord. See § 248, supra.

See also Storke & Sears, Transfer of Mortgaged Property, 1953, 38 Cornell L. Q. 185, 202 n. 69.

59. Idem. This is true even though the purchaser does not receive a deed until after sale of a second

case.[63] The vital matter is whether, as between the grantee of a fractional interest and the mortgagor, the latter has the duty of paying the mortgage debt.[64] On that question, the presence or absence of covenants in the deed to him from the mortgagor has

> charge upon *his own* parcel, while the grantee is to take and hold his portion entirely free."

63. In Wadsworth v. Lyon, 1883, 93 N.Y. 201, 45 Am.Rep. 190, in spite of the absence of covenants of title, the grantee of mortgaged property who had paid the full value of the property was held entitled to exoneration. Look also at Howard v. Robbins, 1902, 170 N.Y. 498, 63 N.E. 530; Gray v. H. M. Loud & Sons Lumber Co., 1901, 128 Mich. 427, 87 N.W. 376, 54 L.R.A. 731. Cf. Atherton v. Toney, 1873, 43 Ind. 211; Bennett v. Bates, 1884, 94 N.Y. 354; Guernsey v. Kendall, 1882, 55 Vt. 201. In Wilcox v. Campbell, 1887, 106 N.Y. 325, 12 N.E. 823, although the grantee took a quitclaim deed he was held entitled to marshall against a prior grantee of another parcel who assumed the mortgage.

64. "It [the rule requiring sale in inverse order of alienation] rests chiefly, perhaps, upon the grounds that where one who is bound to pay a mortgage confers upon others rights in any portion of the property, retaining other portions himself, it is unjust that they should be deprived of their rights, so long as he has property covered by the mortgage, out of which the debt can be made. In other words, his debts should be paid out of his own estate, instead of being charged on the estates of his grantees. * * * The rule cannot, therefore, depend upon the existence or nonexistence of covenants of warranty. It depends simply on the fact whether he has or has not seen fit, in making a disposition of a part of his incumbered premises, to charge it primarily with the payment of the incumbrance. * * * It has, indeed, in several cases cited at the bar, been held that the covenant of warranty was very important, in determining the intent of the mortgagor not to charge the mortgage on the property sold. But there is no satisfactory authority holding that, in the absence of such a warranty, no such intent could be presumed. On the contrary, wherever the doctrine of priority is respected at all, it has been enforced unless an opposite intent was made out. And such appears to us the common sense inference; for a man owing a debt, for which his own property remains liable, must naturally be supposed to expect to have it paid out of his own means, unless he has bargained to the contrary." Cooper v. Bigley, 1865, 13 Mich. 463, 474.

Look at Hopper v. Smyser, 1900, 90 Md. 363, 45 A. 206; Howser v. Cruikshank, 1899, 122 Ala. 256, 25 So. 206, 82 Am.St.Rep. 76. See in addition, § 256, supra. See also Biswell v. Gladney, Tex.Civ.App. 1916, 182 S.W. 1168; Erlinger v. Boul, 1880, 7 Ill. App. 40; Woods v. Spalding, N.Y., 1866, 45 Barb. 602. But see Haskell v. State, 1876, 31 Ark. 91; Aderholt v. Henry, 1888, 87 Ala. 415, 6 So. 625, 6 L.R.A. 451. See 1941, 131 A.L.R. 103.

value as evidence in determining the question of fact, but otherwise it is immaterial.[65]

The agreement of purchase having created an equity of marshalling which attaches to the rest of the property under the mortgage remaining in the mortgagor's hands, that equity will follow it into the hands of anyone who has notice of it.[66] When T-2

65. See preceding footnote.

As to the effect of covenants of warranty or for title upon the right to exoneration of a grantee of the mortgaged property against his mortgagor-grantor, see Drury v. Holden, 1887, 121 Ill. 130, 13 N.E. 547; Brown v. South Boston Sav. Bank, 1889, 148 Mass. 300, 19 N.E. 382; Hopper v. Smyser, 1900, 90 Md. 363, 45 A. 206; Gerdine v. Menage, 1889, 41 Minn. 417, 43 N.W. 91; Bennett v. Keehn, 1886, 67 Wis. 154, 29 N.W. 207, 30 N.W. 112. See also Boice v. Coffeen, 1912, 158 Iowa, 705, 138 N.W. 857. Cf. Merritt v. Byers, 1891, 46 Minn. 74, 48 N.W. 417.

For a suggestion that the presence or absence of a covenant is immaterial if the transferor of part of the mortgaged property is personally liable for the debt but is of controlling importance where he is not, see Tiffany, Real Prop., 3d ed., § 1446. The distinction is without merit. It is based upon the erroneous notion that there must be a personal obligation upon the transferor in favor of the transferee that the portion retained shall be primarily liable, and that the presence or absence of a covenant is decisive on the question whether it exists.

66. "A man who purchases part of a tract covered by a mortgage, buying the title out and out, clear of encumbrances, and paying a full price for it, has a plain right to insist that his vendor shall allow the remainder of the mortgaged premises to be taken in satisfaction of the mortgage debt before the part sold is resorted to. This being the right of the vendee against the mortgagor himself, the latter cannot put the former in a worse condition by selling the remainder of the land to another person. The second purchaser sits in the seat of his grantor, and must pay the whole value of what he bought towards the extinguishment of the mortgage, before he can call on the first purchaser to pay anything. The first sale having thrown the whole burden on the part reserved, it cannot be thrown back again by the second sale. In other words the second purchaser takes the land he buys subject to all the liabilities under which the grantor held it." Carpenter v. Koons, 1852, 20 Pa. 222, 226.

Brown v. Simons, 1863, 44 N.H. 475. National Sav. Bank v. Creswell, D.C.1879, 100 U.S. 630, 637, 25 L. Ed. 713; Clowes v. Dickenson, N.Y.1821, 5 Johns. Ch. 235. See § 286, notes 43, 44, 45, supra. See also notes 67, 67a, infra.

"In the case of the sale by the mortgagor of all the mortgaged property to different purchasers at the same time, their equities must be regarded as equal, and each must contribute ratably to the discharge of the common burthen * * *." Brown v. Simons, 1863, 44 N.H. 475, 478.

buys Y with notice of T-1's equity he will, of course, take subject to it. Thus after T-1 bought parcel X, parcels Y and Z are subject in R's hands to T-1's equity that they shall be applied to E's debt before X is touched. But if T-2 bought on the same terms as T-1, he, in turn, has a similar equity against Z which stays in R's hands. Or, if R sells Z to T-3 who takes with notice, T-3 will take it subject to the prior equitable rights of T-1 and T-2. Thus when E seeks to foreclose, T-1 can compel him to proceed first against Y and Z before seeking to realize on X; and T-2 in turn can demand that, as between Y and Z, Z go first. Thus we have the rule of inverse order of alienation, which is, as was stated earlier, the great weight of authority in the United States.[67]

If T-2 and T-3 have actual notice there is no question but that the rule operates. If they do not have actual notice will they be charged with constructive notice by reason of the fact that T-1 recorded the conveyance to him? Most states say yes.[67a] The rule has been criticized, however, as placing an undue burden upon later purchasers, and as being contrary to the spirit of the recording acts.[68] And this objection raises some additional difficulties in the application of the majority rule. Even though the terms of the conveyance are not conclusive as to whether a grantee of a part of the mortgaged property is entitled to exoneration against the remainder when the only parties involved are the grantee and his mortgagor-grantor,[69] should a later purchaser of part or all of the rest of the property be put upon inquiry to find out, at his peril, what the real terms of the bargain are?[70] If so, and this is applied also to cases where notice of the prior conveyance is only constructive (because the prior conveyance is recorded), the objections stated above[71] become stronger.

In two states in the United States, Iowa and Kentucky, and possibly a third,[72] while

---

67. See § 286 note 45, supra. Farmers' Savings & Building & Loan Ass'n v. Kent, 1898, 117 Ala. 624, 23 So. 757; Wikoff v. Davis, 1842, 4 N.J.Eq. 224; Black v. Suydam, 1914, 81 Wash. 279, 142 P. 700, Ann.Cas.1916D, 1113—accord. See also National Savings Bank v. Creswell, 1879, 100 U.S. 630, 25 L. Ed. 713; Howser v. Cruikshank, 1899, 122 Ala. 256, 25 So. 206, 82 Am.St.Rep. 76; Fassett v. Medlock, 1880, 5 Colo. 466; Pomeroy, Eq.Jur., 4th Ed., § 1224 n. 2; Ann.Cas.1916D, 1119. Cf. Waters v. Hubbard, 1877, 44 Conn. 340. The majority rule has been held to govern in conveyances or "leases" of oil and gas. See Campbell, Cases Mortgages, 2d ed., 619 n. 6, citing, Continental Oil Co. of Texas v. Graham, Tex.Civ.App., 1928, 8 S.W.2d 719, 722; Arab Petroleum Corp. v. Maurer, Tex.Civ.App.1938, 115 S.W.2d 994, 996. But cf. Reed v. Tom, Tex.Civ.App., 1928, 2 S.W.2d 909. See Walker, Fee Simple Ownership of Oil and Gas in Texas, 6 Tex.L.Rev. 125, 140; and 7 id. 323.

For a criticism of the Inverse Order Rule, see Redden, Sale in the Inverse Order of Alienation; A Doctrine Both Fishy and Foul, 1958, 18 Md.L.Rev. 306.

67a. Brown v. Simons, 1863, 44 N.H. 475; see Iglehart v. Crane & Wesson, 1866, 42 Ill. 261, 265, 269; Ann.Cas.1916D, 1119.

68. "The court, in effect, is imposing upon C [the subsequent grantee from the mortgagor of a part of the mortgaged property] a duty of running back every chain of title connected with a blanket mortgage, to ascertain whether any latent equities exist. To impose such a duty is contrary to the spirit of our Recording Acts, the policy of which is to remove secret liens. To charge C with notice is to give B [the prior grantee from the mortgagor of a different part of the mortgaged property] a secret lien on a property, the existence of which lien is not discernible from the title to that property. * * * Prospective purchasers or mortgagees of real estate are rightly considered to be on notice of prior liens on the property concerned, but the equity to marshal is one that can only be uncovered after, what may be in some cases, a most exhaustive and unreasonable search." Note, 1931, 79 U. of Pa.L.Rev. 782, 787 n. 28.

69. See notes 63, 64, 65, supra.

70. Thus it might be important to consider whether, where the prior conveyance contained covenants of warranty, the later grantee should be permitted to go behind them; and, if so, under what circumstances? Look at Sternberger v. Hanna, 1884, 42 Ohio St. 305 (possession of part of a mortgaged tract under oral contract of purchase charges the purchaser of the rest of the tract with finding out, at his peril, the extent and nature of the interest of the prior purchaser); Aiken v. Gale, 1859, 37 N.H. 501 (separate bond from the mortgagor to the first grantee by quitclaim deed to save him harmless from the mortgage held no part of his title so as to put on notice a later grantee by quitclaim deed of another part. The court pro rated the mortgage between the two according to the value of the parts.)

71. See note 68.

72. See dictum in Continental Oil Co. v. Graham, Tex.Civ.App.1928, 8 S.W.2d 719. Since it was based

the rule of marshalling is accepted as between the grantee of one tract and the mortgagor or his heir, it is rejected as between the former and a subsequent grantee or mortgagee of the other tract, with the result that the two tracts or their respective proceeds must contribute ratably to the payment of the mortgage according to the value of each part.[73] Similar views were expressed by Story in his treatise on equity.[74] As stated in an early Iowa case, the argument in favor of the minority attitude is that "as between two grantees purchasing different parcels of the incumbered premises at different times, there is no more moral obligation on the one to pay than on the other. Both of them have purchased premises that are alike affected by a lien which neither created nor undertook to pay. The purchased premises are liable to be sold because of the failure of their grantor to discharge his undertaking, and not because of any failure on their part. In such cases, their interest is common, their

rights are equal, and there should be equality of burden." [75]

The argument is plausible but there are answers. A technical one is that a grantee, unless he can qualify as a bona fide purchaser, takes subject to the equities of third persons in the property that he buys.[76] Thus T-2 takes parcel Y subject to an existing equity in favor of T-1 which arose when T-1 bought X. Another is that, in actual practice, the weight of convenience is against it.[77] It enables a mortgagor, who has transferred a part of the land under the mortgage and so established an equity in that grantee to have the residue left in the mortgagor's hands first applied in satisfaction of the mortgage, to divest this equity at pleasure by transferring such residue to another.[78]

Going back to the majority view, what is the effect of a failure to record by a first grantee who otherwise would have a right to marshall against subsequent grantees? If there was no actual notice of T-1 by T-2, it is quite clear that T-1 could not have parcel Y taken before his own parcel X on foreclosure by E, although he could still insist upon Z in the hands of R going first. But will a court of equity under such circumstances adopt the minority rule and pro rate the debt between X and Y in accordance with their respective values? Or will it go to the opposite extreme and permit T-2 to have an equity of marshalling against X to the end that it be sold before Y is utilized? The latter has been held to be the rule.[79] And

on possible inconvenience to the mortgagee rather than the right of the purchaser, an untenable ground, it probably will have little weight. See § 286.

73. Bates v. Ruddick, 1856, 2 Iowa, 423, 2 Clarke 423, 65 Am.Dec. 774; Huff v. Farwell, 1885, 67 Iowa, 298, 301, 25 N.W. 252, 253, arguendo. Cf. Mickley v. Tomlinson, 1890, 79 Iowa 383, 41 N.W. 311, modified 79 Iowa 383, 44 N.W. 684. Dickey v. Thompson, 1848, 47 Ky. (8 B.Mon.) 312; see Bronaugh v. Burley Tobacco Co., 1926, 212 Ky. 680, 684, 280 S.W. 97, 98; Brown v. Simon, 1863, 44 N.H. 475, 479; Sanford v. Hill, 1878, 46 Conn. 42, 54. "Even in Kentucky marshalling is granted if the mortgagor agreed with the first grantee to confine the mortgage to the retained tract by procuring a release from its operation (Calhoun v. Federal Land Bank, 230 Ky. 460, 465, 20 S.W.2d 72, 74 [1929]), or, probably, if the mortgagor expressly agreed with him that he might have marshalling, and the subsequent grantee or mortgagee had knowledge of the agreement." Campbell, Cases Mortgages, 2d ed., 619 n. 6.

74. Story did not differentiate between "subsequent purchasers or incumbrancers." Of them he said, "each trusting to his own security upon the separate estate mortgaged to him, it is difficult to perceive that either has in consequence thereof any superiority of right or equity over the other." Story, Equity, 14th Ed., § 1640. See also idem, § 1233b, as quoted in National Sav. Bank of District of Columbia v. Creswell, D.C.1880, 100 U.S. 630, 637.

75. Bates v. Ruddick, 1856, 2 Iowa, 423, 430, 65 Am. Dec. 774, 779.

76. See §§ 182–184, supra.

77. See Glenn, Mortgages, § 291.

78. See Tiffany, Real Prop., 3d ed., § 1446. Cf. Shenkin, Marshaling of Securities, 1931, 79 U. of Pa.L.Rev. 785, n. 14.

79. In Gray v. H. M. Loud & Sons Lumber Co., 1901, 128 Mich. 427, 87 N.W. 376, 54 L.R.A. 731, the lower court had pro rated the mortgage between two tracts, each of which had been sold by warranty deed with each purchaser paying the full value of the property. The first grantee failed to record,

this seems correct if the rule of constructive notice by recordation is accepted. If T-1 is accorded the benefit of the recording act when he places his conveyance on record, T-2, reciprocally, should be able to take advantage of it and, if so, T-1 should be postponed to T-2 on failure to record. If, on the other hand, the recording acts do not apply to the record of T-1's conveyance so as to give T-2 notice, and T-2 has no actual notice, it would seem that the only proper result would be to pro rate the debt between the two parcels according to their respective values. The reasoning in the minority cases seems clearly applicable in such a case.[80] An example may be found in the case where, instead of all parcels being included in a single blanket mortgage deed, separate conveyances in mortgage of each parcel are given by the mortgagor and then each purchaser, when he buys and pays for his own lot has no actual notice that the first mortgage debt is secured by other property.[81]

EFFECT OF ASSUMPTION OR TAKING SUBJECT TO THE MORTGAGE

288. **A purchaser of a portion of mortgaged property who assumes the mortgage is not entitled to invoke the inverse order rule and, as to him, the rule is reversed. Where a purchaser of a fraction of such property takes subject to the mortgage, an explicit agreement or clear evidence that it is subject to a specified part or all of the debt will govern its liability. In the absence of such provision or evidence, the mortgage debt will be pro rated among successive purchasers of different parcels who take subject to the mortgage in accordance with the value of the various parcels.**

and the subsequent grantee had no actual notice of the first. The upper court reversed the decision and held that the entire mortgage should be paid out of the part first sold. Look also at LaFarge Fire Insurance Co. v. Bell, N.Y., 1856, 22 Barb. 54; Bode v. Rhodes, 1922, 119 Wash. 98, 204 P. 802.

80. See note-call 75, supra.

81. Cf. Green v. Ramage, 1848, 18 Ohio 428, 51 Am. Dec. 458, Osborne, Cases Property Security, 2d Ed., 574.

Where a mortgagor sells part of a mortgaged tract to a grantee who assumes the payment of the mortgage, the parcel conveyed becomes primarily liable for the payment of the mortgage and the part retained is only secondarily liable.[82] The grantee is also personally liable as principal for the payment of the debt and the mortgagor and the rest of the mortgaged land is surety only as to this personal obligation.[83] As a consequence, not only does the inverse order of alienation rule not apply [84] but the rule is reversed. Since not only the grantee but the parcel conveyed to him have the duty to exonerate the residue in the hands of the mortgagor, he can compel the mortgagee to foreclose first on the parcel transferred to the grantee.[85] Where the mortgagor afterwards sells the remainder of the tract to a third person who pays the full purchase price of the remaining portion, all of the mortgagor's rights with respect to the assuming grantee's duty in respect to this remaining part inure to the benefit of the second purchaser.[86]

82. Chancellor of New Jersey v. Towell, 1912, 80 N.J.Eq. 223, 82 A. 861, 39 L.R.A.,N.S., 359, Ann.Cas. 1914A, 710; Wilcox v. Campbell, 1887, 106 N.Y. 325, 12 N.E. 823; Reid v. Whisenant, 1926, 191 Ga. 503, 131 N.E. 904, 44 A.L.R. 599.

83. Idem. See §§ 248, 259, supra.

84. See 1941, 131 A.L.R. 4, 62. Where the first grantee of a portion of mortgaged land assumes or takes subject to the mortgage and other parcels are then sold to grantees who pay full value with an agreement that the mortgagor shall pay off the mortgage, although the parcel in the hands of the first grantee is subject to being sold first, the inverse order of alienation rule would apply to the other grantees. Moore v. Shurtleff, 1889, 128 Ill. 370, 21 N.E. 775.

85. Chancellor of New Jersey v. Towell, 1912, 80 N.J.Eq. 223, 82 A. 861, 39 L.R.A.,N.S., 359, Ann.Cas. 1914A, 710; Epperson v. Cappellino, 1931, 113 Cal. App. 473, 298 P. 533. Contra: Ewing v. Bay Minette Land Co., 1936, 232 Ala. 22, 26, 166 So. 409, 413, on ground marshalling cannot be invoked by a debtor. See § 291, post. This right of the mortgagor to marshalling will be available against subsequent transferees from the grantee if they are not bona fide purchasers. E. g., Costa v. Sardinha, 1928, 265 Mass. 319, 163 N.E. 887.

86. Reid v. Whisenant, note 82, supra. See 1926, 44 A.L.R. 608.

These rights give a choice of several courses. In a foreclosure action by the mortgagee he may have the parcel in the hands of the assuming grantee sold before that held by him.[87] If the proceeds of this sale are insufficient to pay the mortgage he may, at his option, either pay the balance due upon the mortgage in order to save his land, or let the land be sold.[88] In either event he has an action against the grantee for failing to perform his promise to pay the mortgage. His damages, depending upon which option he selected, would be the amount he paid,[89] or either the value of the parcel in his hands[90] or, at least, the amount of the proceeds from its sale that were applied in discharge of the mortgage foreclosure decree.[91]

Where the first purchaser of a portion of the mortgaged property purchases it subject to the mortgage, "the purchaser has no equity, as against the mortgagor, that the portion still held by the latter shall be first applied to the payment of the incumbrance, and, having

no equity against him, of course has none against his grantee."[92] If it were clear that the purchase of the part was subject to the *entire* amount of the mortgage which was deducted from its purchase price, the part sold would be primarily liable for the entire debt, and the rest of the tract in the hands of the mortgagor would be in the position of a surety only. In such a case the mortgagor and subsequent purchasers for full value of portions of the tract left in the hands of the mortgagor could insist that mortgagee, on foreclosing, resort first to the parcel sold subject to the mortgage.[93] Sometimes there is an explicit provision or clear evidence that the conveyance of a parcel is subject to a specified portion of the mortgage, and if so it will govern.[94] In most cases, however, there is no evidence that the grantee was intended to take subject to the entire debt and there is no allocation of a particular portion or amount of the mortgage debt to the parcel or parcels sold "subject to" the mortgage either by express agreement or otherwise. When such is the situation, where one parcel of a mortgaged tract is sold subject to the mortgage and a later portion is also sold subject to the mortgage, the weight of authority is that the debt will be pro rated between the two grantees in proportion to the value of

---

87. Wilcox v. Campbell, 1887, 106 N.Y. 325, 329, 12 N.E. 823, 826; Dieckman v. Walser, 1933, 114 N.J. Eq. 382, 386, 168 A. 582, 583; affirming 112 N.J.Eq. 46, 163 A. 284; Union Central Life Ins. Co. v. Cates, 1927, 193 N.C. 456, 463, 464, 137 S.E. 324, 327, 328; Welch v. Beers, 1864, 90 Mass. 151. Although the subsequent grantee may compel the mortgagee to foreclose first on the property held by the assuming grantee, in the event of a deficiency the mortgagee may sell the remainder of the tract in the hands of the mortgagor or subsequent grantee. Vanderspeck v. Federal Land Bank, 1936, 175 Miss. 759, 765, 167 So. 782, 783. See 1912, 39 L.R.A.,N.S., 359, 360.

88. See Wilcox v. Campbell, n. 87, supra. He might also pay off the entire mortgage before any of the property is sold. In that case he would be subrogated to the rights of the mortgagee and could enforce the mortgage against the assuming grantee and, if the property is insufficient, take a judgment for the deficiency. See § 279, supra.

89. See Cooley v. Murray, 1898, 11 Colo.App. 241, 52 P. 1108; Wilcox v. Campbell, 1887, 106 N.Y. 325, 12 N.E. 823.

90. Reid v. Whisenant, 1926, 161 Ga. 503, 131 N.E. 904, 44 A.L.R. 599.

91. Wilcox v. Campbell, 1887, 106 N.Y. 325, 12 N.E. 823. The various alternative remedies are not only set forth clearly but the underlying reasons for them are stated accurately by the court in its opinion.

92. Briscoe v. Power, 1868, 47 Ill. 447. See Carpenter v. Koons, 1852, 20 Pa. 222.

93. See 1912, 39 L.R.A.,N.S., 361; § 252, supra.

94. Mickle v. Maxfield, 1879, 42 Mich. 304, 3 N.W. 961; Engle v. Haines, 1845, 5 N.J.Eq. 186, 43 Am. Dec. 624, affirmed 5 N.J.Eq. 632; Moore v. Shurtleff, 1889, 128 Ill. 370, 21 N.E. 775; New England Loan & Trust Co. v. Stephens, 1898, 16 Utah 385, 52 P. 624.

It may be laid down as a general proposition that express agreements as to the order in which the mortgagee shall or may resort to various parts of the tract subject to his mortgage will control and prevent the application of the ordinary equitable rules as to marshalling. If such an agreement is put into the mortgage it clearly will be binding upon all later transferees of any part of the property. Mickle v. Maxfield, supra; Maurer v. Arab Petroleum Corp., 1940, 134 Tex. 256, 135 S.W.2d 87, 131 A. L.R. 1. See §§ 247, 286, note-call 47 supra. The same result can be accomplished by inserting a common provision in all deeds transferring fraction-

their respective lots.[95] And the same has been held where the mortgagor first conveyed one parcel of the mortgaged land to T-1 who assumed the payment of the mortgage and later conveyed another parcel to T-2 subject to it.[96]

GIFT CONVEYANCES

289. In a gift conveyance of a fraction of mortgaged property without covenant against the incumbrance, the mortgage debt will be prorated between the part conveyed and the residue of the property. If there is a covenant, the inverse rule applies.

Where the mortgagor makes a gift conveyance of a portion of a mortgaged tract and the conveyance does not contain covenants protecting the grantee against the mortgage it has been held that he will take it subject to a primary liability for a proportional part of the mortgage debt.[97] It has

been questioned whether this should be true where the grantor is personally liable for the debt.[98] In such cases, it is urged, the presumption should be that the transferor is to pay his own debt and, consequently, the land retained would be primarily liable.[99] If there is a covenant against encumbrances covering the mortgage, this has been held to be sufficient evidence of intention that the land under the gift conveyance shall not be liable for the debt as to throw the primary liability upon the residue in the hands of the grantor.[1]

SECOND MORTGAGES

290. Many American cases apply both the inverse alienation rule and the doctrine of constructive notice by recordation to successive second mortgages of different portions of mortgaged property, a situation to which the "two funds" rule properly applies. In England, the paramount mortgage is pro rated among the junior mortgages in proportion to the value of the mortgaged portions. In another line of cases in America, if a second mortgagee takes with notice of a proceeding to enforce a claim to marshalling by a prior junior lienor, the inverse order rule applies. Otherwise, on this view, at least if the later second mortgagees have parted with value, the debt is pro rated as in England regardless of recordation of prior junior mortgages on other parcels and, perhaps, even with actual knowledge of their existence.

The first line of American cases has been vigorously criticised and it also has been defended. If coupled with a flexible power to

al interests in the property. Moore v. Shurtleff, supra; New England Loan & Trust Co. v. Stephens, supra.

95. Briscoe v. Power, 1868, 47 Ill. 447; Carpenter v. Koons, 1852, 20 Pa. 222; Stephens v. Clay, 1892, 17 Colo. 489, 30 P. 43; Hooper v. Capitol Life Ins. Co., 1933, 92 Colo. 376, 384, 20 P.2d 1011, 1014; Markham v. Smith, 1935, 119 Conn. 355, 363, 176 A. 880, 884; Hall v. Morgan, 1883, 79 Mo. 47; Hog v. Bramhall, 19 N.J.Eq. 563, 97 Am.Dec. 687; Stuyvesant Security Co. v. Dreyer, 1929, 103 N.J.Eq. 457, 461, 143 A. 616, 617, affirmed 105 N.J.Eq. 585, 148 A. 920, values at time of conveyance taken; Dieckman v. Walser, 1932, 112 N.J.Eq. 46, 53, 55, 163 A. 284, 287, 288, affirmed 114 N.J.Eq. 382, 168 A. 582. Cf. Savings Investment & Trust Co. v. United Realty & Mortgage Co., 1915, 84 N.J.Eq. 472, 94 A. 588, Ann.Cas.1916D, 1134, "subject to" clause in second mortgage.

"Where all the purchasers from a mortgagor have bought subject to a mortgage, the obligation of each to pay the mortgage forming part of the consideration of his purchase, they all stand on equal footing, and the mortgagee has the right to sell any part he may think proper for the payment of his debt and the only remedy the party whose land is sold has, is a proceeding to compel contribution from the other purchasers." Burger v. Greif, 1881, 55 Md. 518, 529.

See 1929, 27 Mich.L.Rev. 709.

96. Pearson v. Bailey, 1901, 177 Mass. 318, 58 N.E. 1028.

97. Mills v. Kelley, 1901, 62 N.J.Eq. 213, 215, 50 A. 144, 145 ("Where the conveyance is voluntary, and there are no covenants, then equality is equity.

There is no reason why the voluntary grantee should not take the land with any charge that may rest upon it, except in so far as the parties themselves have otherwise stipulated."); Jackson v. Condict, 1898, 57 N.J.Eq. 522, 526, 41 A. 374. But see 1941, 131 A.L.R. 4, 88. Cf. § 250, supra, as to the effect of inter vivos gifts of the entire mortgaged property.

98. See Tiffany, Real Property, 3d ed., § 1446.

99. Idem. In re Darby's Estate [1907] 2 Ch. 465 (devisees of balance of mortgagor's property denied contribution against donee-grantee of mortgaged property by deed containing no reference to the mortgage and no covenants for title, express or implied).

1. Harrison v. Guerin, 1876, 27 N.J.Eq. 219. See Howser v. Cruikshank, 1898, 122 Ala. 256, 25 So. 206, 82 Am.St.Rep. 76.

deny marshalling in individual cases, it seems the preferable rule.

Reverting to our stock case,[2] if T-1 is a second mortgagee does he have the same right to marshall as against T-2, who may be a purchaser or another second mortgagee, that he would have if he had paid full value with an agreement throwing the duty of discharging the mortgage upon R and the residue of the mortgaged property retained by him? The situation suggested is one to which the "two funds" doctrine applies.[3] T-1 has but a single fund, X, on which to realize as a secured creditor. E not only has the paramount lien upon X but his security comprises, in addition, the rest of Blackacre, lots Y and Z. If R had not transferred a second parcel to T-2 it is clear that T-1 could force E to foreclose on Y and Z before seeking to realize on X.[4] But when the question involves a later transferee by way of mortgage or grant, two divergent lines of authority have developed.[5]

One group of courts holds that T-1 acquires a fixed and established right in equity at the time he takes his second mortgage on lot X to require E to look primarily to lots Y and Z when he forecloses and to sell them before he resorts to lot X held by T-1,[6] provided that E's rights will not be prejudiced by so doing.[7] This equity against the remaining property under the mortgage in R's hands is looked upon as being of the same quality, even though arising by operation of a rule of law rather than founded upon an agreement of the parties, as that accorded to a purchaser for full value under the inverse order of alienation rule. This being so, the inverse order of alienation rule of marshalling should

---

2. See § 286, supra.

3. Idem.

4. This was laid down by Lord Eldon in Aldrich v. Cooper, 1803, 8 Vesey 381, as unquestioned law. He said "that if a party has two funds * * * a person having an interest in one only has a right in equity to compel the former to resort to the other; if that is necessary for the satisfaction of both." See Newby v. Fox, 1913, 90 Kan. 317, 321, 133 P. 890, 892, 47 L.R.A.,N.S., 302, quoted n. 20, post. See also Miles v. National Bank of Kentucky, 1910, 140 Ky. 376, 131 S.W. 26; Ober & Sons Co. v. Keating, 1893, 77 Md. 100, 26 A. 501; Warren v. Warren, 1858, 30 Vt. 530; White v. Polleys, 1866, 20 Wis. 503, 91 Am.Dec. 432; Washburn, Real Prop., 6th Ed., § 1147; Pomeroy, Eq.Jur., 4th Ed., § 1414, note 6. And see § 286, supra, for additional authorities.

5. For an excellent collection of authorities, see 1937, 106 A.L.R. 1102. See Gest, Marshalling Assets with Reference to the Rights of Successive Part Purchasers and Incumbrancers, 1888, 27 Am. L.Reg.,N.S., 739; Strachan, The Marshalling of Mortgages, 1906, 22 L.Q.Rev. 307. See also notes, 1931, 79 U. of Pa.L.Rev. 782; 1905, 18 Harv.L.Rev. 453; 1939, 24 Iowa L.Rev. 328; 1937, 106 A.L.R. 1102; 1889, 5 L.R.A. 280; 1908, 12 L.R.A.,N.S., 965; 1939, 119 A.L.R. 1109.

Cal.Civ.Code § 2899 provides that "Where one has a lien upon several things, and other persons have subordinate liens upon, or interest in, some but not all of the same things, the person having the prior lien, if he can do so without risk of loss to himself, or of injustice to other persons, must resort to the

property in the following order, on the demand of any party interested:
"1. To the things upon which he has an exclusive lien;
"2. To the things which are subject to the fewest subordinate liens;
"3. In like manner inversely to the number of subordinate liens upon the same thing; and,
"4. When several things are within one of the foregoing classes, and subject to the same number of liens, resort must be had—
"(1) To the things which have not been transferred since the prior lien was created;
"(2) To the things which have been so transferred without a valuable consideration; and,
"(3) To the things which have been so transferred for a valuable consideration in the inverse order of the transfer."

6. See notes 8, 14, infra.

7. "While it is true the general rule is that, where a party has a lien or interest in two funds and another party has a lien in only one of the same funds, the party having the lien or interest in the two will be compelled by court of equity to first resort to the fund in which he has the sole interest, yet this rule will not be enforced, where it operates to the prejudice of the party holding the double interest." Friedlander v. Fenton, 1899, 180 Ill. 312, 316, 54 N. E. 329, 330, 72 Am.St.Rep. 207. See also Hyde Park Light Co. v. Brown, 1898, 172 Ill. 329, 50 N.E. 127; Newby v. Hope, 1913, 90 Kan. 317, 320, 133 P. 890, 891; Pope v. Baltimore Warehouse Co., 1906, 103 Md. 9, 62 A. 1119; Farwell v. Bigelow, 1897, 112 Mich. 285, 70 N.W. 579; Sternberger v. Sussman, 1905, 69 N.J.Eq. 199, 60 A. 195; Evertson v. Booth, N.Y.1822, 19 Johns. 486; Walker v. Covar, 1870, 2 S.C. 16; Sheldon, Subrogation, 2d Ed., § 63; 2 Story, Equity, 14th Ed., 232n. Cf. Willey v. St. Charles Hotel Co., 1899, 52 La.Ann. 1581, 28 So. 182; Goutzian & Co. v. Shakman, 1894, 89 Wis. 52, 61 N.W. 304, 46 Am.St.Rep. 820.

be applied.[8] Consequently any subsequent taker of lots X or Y by way of purchase for full value or as second mortgagee will take subject to T-1's prior equity unless he can qualify as a bona fide purchaser for value without notice.[9] Courts adopting this view also hold that T-1 can effectively guard against such a possibility by recording his second mortgage on X which will then give constructive notice of his equity to any later taker of Y or Z.[10] If the subsequent taker is not a bona fide purchaser, the priority of T-1

over him is said to rest upon the fact that his equity is not only prior in time but that the later equity is inferior to his either by reason of notice or lack of value being given for it.[11] If T-2, the subsequent purchaser or mortgagee of Y or Z, can qualify under the bona fide purchase rule, he would then stand on an equality with T-1 and the paramount mortgage would then be apportioned between them according to the value of their respective lots.[12]

The rule in England [13] and that followed by many cases in this country [14] is that the equi-

---

8. Sibley v. Baker, 1871, 23 Mich. 312; Hunt v. Townsend, N.Y.1847, 4 Sandf.Ch. 510; Riverside Apartment Corp. v. Capital Construction Co., 1930, 107 N.J.Eq. 405, 413, 152 A. 763, 769, affirmed 110 N.J. Eq. 67, 158 A. 740, probably constructive notice from recording; Fidelity & Casualty Co. v. Mass. Mut. Life Ins. Co., C.C.A.N.C.1935, 74 F.2d 881, paramount tax lien on the various parcels; Bank of Commerce of Evansville v. First Nat. Bank of Evansville, 1898, 150 Ind. 588, 594, 50 N.E. 566, 568, senior judgment lien on both properties; mortgage on one, followed by conveyance of other to trustee to pay creditors; Sanborn, McDuffee Co. v. Keefe, 1936, 88 N.H. 236, 187 A. 97, 106 A.L.R. 1097; Ingersoll v. Somers Land Co., 1913, 82 N.J.Eq. 476, 89 A. 288; Robeson's Appeal, 1888, 117 Pa. 628, 12 A. 51, senior judgment lien on both properties; recorded mortgage on one followed by mortgage on the other; later mortgagee charged with constructive notice of the earlier.

9. As to the rule where the transferees of other parcels have not parted with value cf. quotation from Newby v. Fox, n. 20, infra, decided in a jurisdiction following the second view in respect to marshalling by a junior mortgagee on the first parcel.

10. Harron v. Du Bois, 1903, 64 N.J.Eq. 657, 54 A. 857; Ingersoll v. Somers Land Co., note 8, supra; Appeal of Robeson, note 8, supra. If T-1 fails to record he cannot invoke the doctrine against one without actual notice. Birch River Boom & Lumber Co. v. Glendon Boom & Lumber Co., 1922, 71 W.Va. 139, 76 S.E. 167. It has been pointed out that in a considerable number of cases giving priority to T-1 in this situation it is not expressly stated that notice by T-2 of T-1's mortgage on X is a requisite of the rule or even mention the fact that there was notice. See 1937, 106 A.L.R. 1102, 1103.

If the paramount lien arises against each of the two or more parcels by separate instruments only most exhaustive search of all deeds or mortgages to or from the mortgagor could reveal to T-2 the prior junior mortgage on lot X to T-1. Although cases involving easements and equitable servitudes may lend some support to a view that T-2 should be charged with making such an exhaustive investigation, see 1937, 5 Duke B.A.J. 35, 39, such a burden is much too onerous to impose. Green v. Ramage, 1849, 18 Ohio, 428.

11. A mortgaged 360 acres of land to B to secure a debt. Thereafter A mortgaged the same land, with the exception of 75 acres thereof, to C to secure a debt. Still later A mortgaged the entire tract to secure a debt to D; D having notice of the two prior mortgages. Held, C, as against D, could require B to first resort for the satisfaction of his claim to the 75 acres not included in C's mortgage; that D's rights were inferior to C's. Conrad v. Harrison, Va.1882, 3 Leigh 532; Ingersoll v. Somers Land Co., 1913, 82 N.J.Eq. 476, 89 A. 288, constructive notice by record and later mortgage of other parcel was to secure pre-existing debt; Harron v. Du Bois, 1903, 64 N.J.Eq. 657, 54 A. 857, later encumbrance was judgment lien acquired with constructive notice of prior recorded mortgage. See Newby v. Fox, 1913, 90 Kan. 317, 319, 133 P. 890, 891; Bank of Commerce v. First Nat. Bank, note 8, supra, second parcel conveyed to trustee to pay creditors; Sanborn, McDuffie Co. v. Keefe, 1936, 88 N.H. 236, 187 A. 97, 106 A.L.R. 1097. See also 1937, 106 A.L.R. 1102, 1103. Cf. Sager v. Tupper, 1876, 35 Mich. 133; Reilly v. Mayer, 1858, 12 N.J.Eq. 55.

12. Cf. Green v. Ramage, 1849, 18 Ohio 428. Of course both T-1 and T-2 would have an equity to have lot Z in the hands of R sold before touching either X or Y. In such a case any deficiency would be prorated between the latter. See Newby v. Fox, quoted n. 20, infra.

13. "The source of much of the English law on marshaling of securities is Lord Eldon's opinion in Aldrich v. Cooper [1803, 8 Ves. 381], Lord Eldon was very careful to state that the general doctrine of marshaling is applicable 'if no third persons are concerned,' and in the later case of Barnes v. Racster, Vice-Chancellor Bruce, relying on Aldrich v. Cooper and on certain dicta in Averall v. Wade [1835, Lloyd & G.Temp.Sugden 252], decided that A [the first mortgagee of No. 1 and No. 2], must be paid ratably out of No. 1 and No. 2, and that B [second mortgagee of No. 1] and C [second mortgagee of No. 2] stood in pari passu, even though C took his mortgage with full knowledge of all prior incumbrances. The law as developed by this case, and by the later case of Bugden v. Bignold [1843, 2

14. See Note 14 on page 591.

ty of marshalling acquired by T-1 when he takes his second mortgage on X is not a fixed equitable right when T-1 acquires his lien, but remains inchoate until the right is invoked by actual proceedings to enforce it; and if at that time the rights of third persons are involved, it will not be enforced to their prejudice.[15] In some of the American

cases the result is supported also by denying that T-2 when he takes his interest in Y is charged with constructive notice of the inchoate equity of T-1 through his recorded second mortgage on X.[16] As a consequence, the paramount mortgage is prorated between the two junior mortgagees in proportion to the value of the parcel to which each has claim.[17] The English courts prorate even though the later second mortgagee of lot Y has actual notice of the prior junior lien on lot X.[18] There is American authority that T-1's prior equity, even though regarded as inchoate, will prevail over T-2 if the latter did not part with value for it.[19] However, if T-2

Y. & C.C.C. 377], has remained the law of England ever since, despite some doubts as to its logic expressed in Wellesley v. Lord Mornington [1869, 17 W.R. 355]. This disposition of the problem * * * is perhaps attributable to the absence of a recording system at the time the law crystallized. This fact kept the English courts from dealing with the question of presumed notice * * *." Shenkin, Marshaling of Securities, 1931, 79 U. of Pa.L.Rev. 782, 784.

See Kay, L.J., in Flint v. Howard, [1893] 2 Ch. 54, 73; Barnes v. Racster, 1842, 1 Younge & C.C.C. 401. See also 1937, 106 A.L.R. 1102, 1109. But cf. Falconbridge, Mortgages, 2d ed., 1931, § 139.

14. "The decided cases in this country are in conflict. Many jurisdictions adopt the English view, while equally as many courts * * * have reached a contrary result, and have practically accorded the equity to marshal the effect of a lien." Shenkin, op. cit. supra note 13. See cases in note 15 et seq., infra.

15. Bronaugh v. Burley Tobacco Co., 1926, 212 Ky. 680, 685, 280 S.W. 97, junior mortgage on one tract, followed by execution lien on other tract; Richards v. Cowles, 1898, 105 Iowa 734, 75 N.W. 648; Green v. Ramage, 1849, 18 Ohio 428, 430 alternative decision. See 1937, 106 A.L.R. 1102, 1109.

"The proposition contended for would amount to this: That, if at any time the situation of several subsequent mortgagees is such that as between themselves such a marshaling of securities could have been invoked, by proper application to a court of equity, as would result in the satisfaction of the senior mortgages out of a fund which the junior mortgagee could not reach, whereby the fund upon which he could only go should be left for his satisfaction, this inchoate equity cannot be disturbed, displaced, or defeated by any subsequent alienation or mortgage by the common debtor or mortgagor. This rule, if admitted, would result in elevating an inchoate equity to marshal assets or securities to the high plane of a lien. Yet it would be an incumbrance or lien of which a subsequent mortgagee would have no notice by record or otherwise. It would clearly be in antagonism to our registry laws. * * * It follows, therefore, from this view of the question, that the equity to marshal assets is not one which fastens itself upon the situation at the time the successive securities are taken, but, on the contrary, is one to be determined at the time the marshaling is invoked. The equity can only become a fixed right by taking proper steps to have it enforced; and until this is done it is sub-

ject to displacement and defeat by subsequently acquired liens upon the funds." Lurton, J., in Gilliam v. McCormack, 1887, 85 Tenn. 597, 606, 607, 4 S.W. 521, 524. The strong opinion of Lurton, J., in Gilliam v. McCormack, supra, has been impaired, however, by the later case of Meek v. Thompson, 1897, 99 Tenn. 732, 42 S.W. 685.

16. See Gilliam v. McCormack, note 15, supra; Bronaugh v. Burley Tobacco Co., note 15, supra; Cf. last sentence quoted from Shenkin, note 13, supra.

If T-1 has begun an action to assert his equity against lot Y at the time T-2 acquires his interest in it, T-1's equity is regarded as having become established as a firm right and T-2 is charged with notice of it through the action which directly involves it. See quotation from Newby v. Fox, note 20, infra.

17. E. g., Green v. Ramage, 1849, 18 Ohio, 428.

18. Barnes v. Racster, 1842, 1 Younge & C.C.C. 401. See n. 13, supra.

19. E. g., Ingersoll v. Somers Land Co., 1913, 82 N.J. Eq. 476, 89 A. 288, later mortgage of other parcel was to secure preexisting debt; Harron v. Du Bois, 1903, 64 N.J.Eq. 657, 54 A. 857, later encumbrance was judgment lien; Humphries v. Fitzpatrick, 1934, 253 Ky. 517, 69 S.W.2d 1058, attachment creditor as to second parcel; Bank of Commerce of Evansville v. First Nat. Bank of Evansville, 1898, 150 Ind. 588, 594, 50 N.E. 566, 568, later conveyance of second parcel to trustee to pay creditors. See quotation from Newby v. Fox, note 20, infra. General creditors of the mortgagor have been regarded as falling within this class, First Nat. Bank of Boston v. Proctor, 1930, 40 F.2d 841, in spite of a suggestion that this was unfair to them. See note 24, infra. However, in Langel v. Moore, 1928, 32 Ohio App. 352, 168 N.E. 57, affirmed 119 Ohio St. 299, 164 N.E. 118, commented on, 1930, 43 Harv.L.Rev. 501, where T-1 had a judgment lien on X (realty) which with Y (personalty) was subject to a paramount mortgage to E, and T-2 was an assignee for the benefit of R's creditors, the court not only denied

paid value, doubt has been expressed as to whether T-1 should prevail over him even if he actually knew of the existence of T-1's mortgage but had no reason to anticipate that T-1 would invoke the doctrine of marshalling.[20] Even if T-2 is a purchaser for value but has notice of a proceeding by T-1 to enforce his equity he will take subject to it.[21]

The doctrine of the first group of cases has been vigorously criticised as a mistaken and improper application of the doctrine of

sale in the inverse order of alienation.[22] It is said that a second mortgagee on X, unlike a purchaser of it for full value, does not pay to get the land free and clear of the first mortgage. He merely bargains for a security interest in it subordinate to the first mortgage.[23] So far as other portions of the tract are concerned, since he did not stipulate for any security interest in them, it even has been argued that as to them he should have no better right than general creditors and should come in, *pari passu,* with them.[24] And

T-1's request that E, as a doubly secured creditor should first exhaust Y before resorting to X which was T-2's single security, but ordered E to take his pay entirely out of X. The reason was that otherwise the general creditors, represented by T-2, would receive nothing. In other words, marshalling here seemed to have been granted in favor of general creditors as against a prior subordinate judgment lien on one parcel. Perhaps the case goes no further than this: T-1 was a general creditor before he fastened his judgment on X and the court merely refuses to let him come in ahead of other general creditors by reason of his getting a judgment lien on one portion of mortgaged property and then asking marshalling. It would appear however that he would revert to his former status as a general creditor and come in *pari passu* with other creditors under the assignment for their benefit. Cf. Shewmaker v. Yankey, 1902, 23 Ky.L.Rep. 1759, 66 S.W. 1, general creditors for whose benefit an assignment has been made; Bronaugh v. Burley Tobacco Co., 1926, 212 Ky. 680, 280 S.W. 97, judgment creditor.

20. "The rule that, as between the original parties, the mortgagee of a part of a tract may require the holder of a prior mortgage upon all of it to proceed first against that not covered by the second mortgage is manifestly fair. It does no injury to one creditor and confers a benefit on the other, while the common debtor cannot be heard to complain. Whether it should be applied against new parties depends upon their comparative equities. * * * One who acquires title through the debtor without parting with value (as a judgment creditor or a grantee in a voluntary conveyance) cannot thereby gain any superior standing. Even a purchaser for value who becomes such with notice of a proceeding to enforce the right to have the securities marshaled must be deemed to have acted at his peril. But it might unduly extend this merely equitable right to allow its enforcement against one who has bought and paid for the singly mortgaged land, knowing, to be sure, of the existence of the two mortgages, but having no particular reason to anticipate that the doctrine of marshaling securities will ever be invoked." Newby v. Fox, 1913, 90 Kan. 317, 323, 133 P. 890, 892. Cf. notecall 9, supra.

21. Ibid.

22. "The second mortgagee of each lot in cases of successive second mortgages on such lots is simply a lender of money acquiring a second lien on that lot subject to the lien of the first mortgage which applies pro rata to all of them. He is not a buyer who has paid the full price without deduction for the first mortgage on which the doctrine of sale in inverse order of alienation applies. If this doctrine is applied to successive second mortgages in these cases, and the second lot so mortgaged is sold first on foreclosure of the blanket mortgage to the exoneration of the second mortgage on the first lot, the result is almost surely to destroy altogether the second mortgage on that lot, as the proceeds will almost surely in every case be applied to pay the debt secured by the blanket mortgage leaving no surplus for the second mortgagee, and the second mortgage on the first lot will be increased proportionately, a result so unjust and so contrary to the actual liens created as to make almost incredible the acceptance of such a doctrine by respectable authorities. In Bernhardt v. Lymburner, 1881, 85 N.Y. 172 * * *, the injustice of applying the doctrine of marshalling to this situation is made clear, though the court says that the doctrine should be applied if it can be done without material injury to any of the parties. It should be clear that it never can be applied without such injury where the second parcel has been mortgaged instead of conveyed outright." Walsh & Simpson, Cas.Security Transactions, 376. See also Newby v. Fox, 1913, 90 Kan. 317, 325, 113 P. 890, 893.

23. Ibid.

24. "There is a class of cases in which the doctrine of subrogation seems to have been unwarrantably extended under the name of marshalling. For example, if the owner of houses A and B (worth, respectively, $10,000 and $5,000) mortgage them both to C for $5,000, and then mortgage A to D for $10,000, and then become insolvent, it is said that D may throw the whole of C's mortgage on B, and thus obtain payment in full of his own mortgage out of A, though the consequence be that unsecured creditors of the insolvent will receive nothing; and the principle upon which this is held is generalized by saying that when one of two creditors has the security of two funds, and the other has the security of only one of those funds, the latter creditor may throw the debt of the former creditor wholly

assuredly, it is contended, he should have no priority over T-2 who has acquired an interest in those other parcels without notice as purchaser for full value or as mortgagee.

In answer it is urged that "Second mortgages upon portions of mortgaged premises are rarely taken without considering and relying upon the equity which will arise in favor of the second mortgagee to have the first mortgage charged upon the residue of the property; * * *." [25] Furthermore, it has been pointed out that the English rule opens a door to the practice of fraud by the mortgagor-transferor. [26] And apart from this, it has been difficult for one scholar to understand how the right of a second mortgagee to marshalling, which at the time he takes his mortgage exists against his mortgagor and the owner of the paramount mortgage

of the whole tract [27] "can be lost by the intervention of a second mortgagee, over whom, and over the mortgagor, the second mortgagee has no control; nor is it easy to understand why a second mortgagee should be obliged to keep constant watch upon the registry of deeds and assert his equity by litigation against every casual purchaser who records a deed fixing a later lien upon the mortgaged land." [28]

For what it is worth, the present writer's views are as follows: The English rule of pro-ration even though the subsequent second mortgagee of Y had notice of the prior junior mortgage on X seems wrong. Very clearly T–1 did acquire an equity of marshalling against lots Y and Z at the time he took his second mortgage on X. [29] The equity he acquired at that time may well be regarded as "so weak that the rights of a bona fide purchaser for value without notice could displace it, but the equity should be sufficiently virile not to be defeated by the rights of a subsequent taker with notice of its existence." [30] On the other hand, the rule of pro-ration if T–2 takes without notice of any sort seems entirely fair and prevents the caprice of E from determining where any loss shall fall. If notice is only constructive through recordation of T–1's second mortgage, it is difficult to decide between the two results. The preferable solution would seem to be a compromise. Where the "two funds" rule of marshalling is proper it should not be regarded as creating in the first sub-mortgagee of a parcel a fixed indisplaceable equity as does the inverse order of alienation rule in favor of a first purchaser for full value. Rather it should be looked upon as a guide for a court of equity in adjusting the rights of par-

upon the fund which is not common to both (provided, of course, that fund be sufficient to pay it), in order that he may obtain payment of his own debt out of the fund which is common to both. This doctrine had its origin in efforts of courts of equity to prevent the harsh and unjust discriminations which the law formerly made between creditors of persons deceased, whose claims were in equity and justice equal; and it seems that the doctrine, as a general one, cannot be sustained upon any principle. For example, in the case just supposed, the doctrine of marshalling assumes that, in equity and justice, house B ought to exonerate house A from the first mortgage, whereas, in truth, they ought to bear the burden of the first mortgage equally. As between secured and unsecured creditors, equity clearly ought to favor the latter class, if either." Langdell, A Brief Survey of Equity Jurisdiction, 15.

25. La Farge Fire Insurance Co. v. Bell, N.Y., 1856, 22 Barb. 54, 65. Cf. as to the duty of a mortgagor to pay off a first mortgage for the benefit of a second mortgagee and the latter's justifiable expectation of advancement in that event see §§ 177, 282, supra.

26. "It should be noted that the English decisions leave the door open to the practice of fraud on the part of * * * the debtor. There is nothing to stop him from giving C, a friend, a mortgage on the second property, reducing to that extent the amount that B would otherwise get. Of course, if a court of equity even suspects the presence of fraud in the case, B and C will not be treated equally, but the possibility is still present, and it may be for this reason that a number of American jurisdictions have reached an opposite result." Shenkin, op. cit. supra note 13, 785 n. 14.

27. See n. 20, supra.

28. Keigwin, Cas.Morts., 583 n. 49.

29. See note 20, supra.

30. Shenkin, Marshaling of Securities, 1931, 79 U. of Pa.L.Rev. 782, 787.

ties having "jarring liens."[31] To this extent there is merit in the attitude of the courts in the second group of cases. So regarded, however, it seems desirable to accept the view of the first group to the extent that T–1's right to marshalling against the other parcels be recognized as the general rule but that relief will be refused in the particular case if it would work injustice.[32] This gives to the "two funds" doctrine to some extent the greater certainty of the inverse order rule and yet preserves to it sufficient flexibility to deal with the individual case, if this should be necessary, at the date the right is invoked by action. This flexibility, unimportant where the inverse rule is properly applicable, i. e., in case of successive purchases of portions of the mortgaged property for full value, is of consequence where sub-mortgages on different parcels are concerned. As has been pointed out, the reason is that the lienor on lot X may be amply secured whereas the lienor on lot Y is insufficiently margined.[33]

The last point has relevancy also where one of the sub-mortgagees of part of property subject to a paramount mortgage has taken, in addition, a piece of property not under that mortgage.[34] That is, lots X and Y only are mortgaged to E. T–1 takes a second mortgage on lot X and also takes a first mortgage on lot Z. T–2 then takes a second mortgage on lot Y with knowledge of the sit-

uation. T–1 as well as E is a doubly secured creditor and any equity of marshalling he may have as against E and Y would seem to be limited to the excess of his debt over the value of his outside security, Z. T–2, if T–1 is disregarded, has an equity to have E go first against X. The proper solution, therefore, would seem to be that T–2 should be able to have marshalling, limited only by T–1's superior claim to be able to reach X ahead of T–2 as to any deficiency he would have after applying the value of lot Z. If T–1 is amply secured by Z alone, there is authority for the indicated result.[35] Even if he is not, the principle suggested seems properly applicable and could be used without difficulty if T–1's debt was due at the time of E's foreclosure. Even if it was not, T–1 might be protected by requiring clear proof of the minimum amount Z would yield and reserving out of the sale of X an amount equal to the difference until T–1's debt matured.[36]

MARSHALLING BY MORTGAGOR— EXEMPTIONS

291. **A mortgagor, provided it will not prejudice the mortgagee, may restrict the method of enforcing foreclosure in various ways, one of which, if he is secondarily liable, is to compel the mortgagor to foreclose first on the mortgaged property primarily liable in the hands of grantees. He is also entitled to marshalling to preserve homestead or other exempt property which has been included in the mortgage along with other, non-exempt property, not only as against his first mortgagee, but, by the weight of authority, against junior mortgagees of non-exempt portions. The weight of authority refuses to apply the two funds doctrine in favor of junior lienors on non-exempt parts when the question arises between the secured creditors.**

On the general ground that a debtor is not entitled to invoke the doctrine of marshal-

---

31.   Shenkin, op. cit. supra note 30, at 785.

32.   E. g., Bernhardt v. Lymburner, 1881, 85 N.Y. 175, although recognizing the general rule of marshalling as being established, refused to apply it where it would work injustice. See also, Sternberger v. Sussman, 1905, 69 N.J.Eq. 199, 60 A. 195, affirmed 85 N.J.Eq. 593, 98 A. 1087. And see note 22, supra. Look also at Payne v. Avery, 1870, 21 Mich. 524; Milligan's Appeal, 1883, 104 Pa. 503.

33.   Glenn, Morts., § 298. The learned author adds: "The fact that one may have such a case in front of him does not require a general rule that there shall never be marshalling in the case of liens, but it will justify an exception in this case of hardship." Ibid.

34.   In general assets will not be marshalled where there are different funds, or the funds are not in the hands of a common debtor, but there are exceptions to this. See 1912, 8 L.R.A.,N.S., 965.

35.   Worth v. Hill, 1861, 14 Wis. 559. See Glenn, Morts., § 299.

36.   Cf. Worth v. Hill, 1861, 14 Wis. 559. The court said that where the adequacy of T–1's outside security could not be tested by sale, the court might nevertheless grant marshalling to T–2 upon testimony of witnesses provided that such testimony clearly established the entire adequacy of lot Z.

ling, it is said that a mortgagor cannot compel his doubly secured mortgagee to resort to one fund rather than to another.[37] Even where the mortgagor is primarily liable for the debt he can restrict the mortgagee to selling only so much of the property as is necessary to pay off the mortgage.[38] And he can compel the selling of the property by parcels or en masse as will be most advantageous to him.[39] If the mortgagor is only secondarily liable he can force the mortgagee to proceed against the person or property primarily liable if that will not prejudice the mortgagee.[40] Similarly, if the mortgagor in selling part of a mortgaged tract takes back a mortgage on the portion sold so that he now occupies the position of a singly secured creditor as well as being debtor-mortgagor of the doubly secured creditor, he is entitled to marshalling under the two funds doctrine.[41]

Perhaps the most frequent case where the question of a mortgagor's right to marshall has arisen is where one of the mortgaged parcels, X, is subject to a homestead exemption which was waived [42] in favor of E when R gave the mortgage on the entire tract of which X is a part.[43] Later R may have given a second mortgage on parcel Y on which R had no exemption. Where the question arises between the two creditors E and T-1, the weight of authority refuses to apply the usual two funds rule of marshalling in favor of T-1 even though the result may be that E will collect out of Y leaving T-1 unsecured.[44] The justification for this result is found in the policy of protecting homesteads from forced sales. And in some states legislation expressly protects the mortgagor and his family in such a situation.[45] There are, however, some cases which have held that T-1 may have marshalling against X, the homestead parcel, this being the fund to which he had no access.[46]

Where the question arises between the mortgagor and his creditors, E and T-1, the majority rule is that he may compel E on foreclosure to sell first the property to which the homestead exemption does not apply, i. e., that he may have marshalling against T-1.[47] And there are statutory provisions

---

37. See Dolphin v. Aylward, 4 Eng. & Irish.App.L. Rev. 486, 505; Newby v. Fox, 1913, 90 Kan. 317, 320, 133 P. 890, 891; Rogers v. Meyers, 1873, 68 Ill. 92, 97. See Schwartz, Marshaling Assets for Benefit of Mortgagor, 1930, 5 Not.D.Law. 208; 1914, 47 L.R.A.,N.S., 302.

38. Thomas v. Fewster, 1902, 95 Md. 446, 52 A. 750. See Quigley v. Beam's Adm'r, 1910, 137 Ky. 325, 125 S.W. 727. Cf. Miller v. Trudgeon, 1905, 16 Okl. 337, 86 P. 523, 8 Ann.Cas. 739.

39. Security Savings Bank v. King, 1924, 198 Iowa, 1151, 199 N.W. 166; McClintic-Marshall Co. v. Scandinavian-American Bldg. Co., C.C.A.Wash., 1924, 296 F. 601.

As to the right of the maker of a negotiable instrument to compel the marshaling of securities in his favor, look at Sowell v. Federal Reserve Bank of Dallas, 1925, 268 U.S. 449, 45 S.Ct. 528, 69 L.Ed. 1041, discussed in note, 1925, 39 Harv.L.Rev. 256. See also note, 1934, 34 Col.L.Rev. 779.

40. See § 285, supra. See also Newby v. Fox, note 37, supra.

41. Newby v. Fox, n. 37, supra.

42. A debtor may waive his homestead in property so far as the mortgage goes when he gives property on which he has declared it as security for a debt. See Thomas v. Wisner, 1919, 65 Colo. 243, 180 P.

744; Cleve v. Adams, 1942, 222 N.C. 211, 22 S.E.2d 567.

43. For discussions and collections of cases, see 1933, 46 Harv.L.Rev. 1035; 1934, 12 Tex.L.Rev. 514; 1939, 23 Minn.L.Rev. 692, reprinted, 1944, 23 Or.L. Rev. 204; 1926, 44 A.L.R. 758; 1932, 77 A.L.R. 371; 17 Ann.Cas. 1061; 1913, 47 L.R.A.,N.S., 302, 303.

44. McLaughlin v. Hart, 1873, 46 Cal. 638, approved on its special facts by Glenn, Mortgages, § 37.3; Bowers v. Norton, 1928, 175 Minn. 541, 222 N.W. 71, T-1 being an attaching creditor; McArthur v. Martin, 1876, 23 Minn. 74. See 1926, 44 A.L.R. 758; 1932, 77 A.L.R. 371.

45. E. g., Ill.Rev.Stat.1937, c. 52; Iowa Code of 1933, § 10155; S.C.Const., 1895, Art. 3, § 28; Wis.Stat., 1935, § 272.20. See 1926, 44 A.L.R. 758, 761; 1932, 77 A.L.R. 371, 372.

46. E. g., State Sav. Bank of Anderson v. Harbin, 1883, 18 S.C. 425; cf. Plain v. Roth, 1883, 107 Ill. 588. See 1926, 44 A.L.R. 758, 761, 762. Statutory enactments have overcome most of this authority. E. g., White v. Polleys, 1866, 20 Wis. 503, 91 Am. Dec. 432, later nullified by Wis.Stat.1935, § 272.20.

47. Boykin v. First State Bank, Tex.Civ.App. 1933, 61 S.W.2d 126, 129, T-1 being a second mortgagee; In re Tucker's Estate, 1938, 160 Or. 362, 85 P.2d 1025; Frick Co. v. Ketels, 1889, 42 Kan. 527, 22 P.

to the same effect.[48] There is, however, authority that the mortgagor cannot compel marshalling in such a case.[49]

Where the case arises only between R and E, the majority rule permitting R to save his homestead if E can get paid out of non-exempt property seems a desirable result.[50] Where exercise of the right to compel marshalling will result in saving the mortgaged homestead at the expense of a creditor whose hold is on non-exempt property the question moves into doubtful area. Perhaps T-1 should be granted marshalling against a homestead if he is a second mortgagee of Y but not if he acquired his lien by way of judgment or attachment lien.[51]

DUTY OF MORTGAGEE

292. **The owner of an underlying first mortgage with actual knowledge of the existence of subsequent sales or mortgages of portions of the mortgaged property is under a duty not to impair any right to marshalling that may have arisen, provided it will not prejudice his own rights to observe such a duty. Release of mortgaged property against which a right of marshalling runs, under circumstances constituting a violation of the duty, discharges the mortgage debt to the extent of the value of the property so released as against the person having the right.**

The paramount mortgagee of a tract, parcels of which have been transferred or mortgaged to persons under circumstances giving to them a right of marshalling against other portions of the property, must not do anything to defeat the rights of such persons if he knows of them.[52] The knowledge must be actual, not constructive through the recordation of subsequent conveyances or mortgages of portions of the mortgaged property.[53] However, if the paramount mortgagee does have actual notice of subsequent alienations or mortgages of parcels of the mortgaged property he acts at his peril in releasing from the mortgage any part of the property against which the marshalling equity runs.[54] Hence if he releases such a part, under such circumstances, he must deduct from the debt, before enforcing his lien against the property in the hands of these persons, the

---

580, 16 Am.St.Rep. 507. See 1926, 44 A.L.R. 758, 763; 1932, 77 A.L.R. 371, 373. Similarly a widow claiming dower may marshall against T-1. Bowen v. Brockenbrough, 1889, 119 Ind. 560, 20 N.E. 534; Stokes v. Stokes, 1934, 206 N.C. 108, 173 S.E. 18. Beneficiaries of life insurance policies may have the same right. Barbin v. Moore, 1932, 85 N.H. 362, 159 A. 409, 83 A.L.R. 62.

48. See note 45, supra. See 1926, 44 A.L.R. 758, 766; 1932, 77 A.L.R. 371, 374.

49. Booker v. Booker, 1932, 225 Ala. 626, 144 So. 870, discussed 1933, 46 Harv.L.Rev. 1034; Searle v. Chapman, 1876, 121 Mass. 19. See 1926, 44 A.L.R. 758, 766.

50. See 1933, 46 Harv.L.Rev. 1035; 1934, 12 Tex.L. Rev. 515.

51. E. g., in Merchants Nat. Bank v. Stanton, 1893, 55 Minn. 211, 56 N.W. 821, 43 Am.St.Rep. 491, a mortgagee was granted marshalling on the ground that his interest arose by contract and not *in invitum*. But cf. Boykin v. First State Bank, Tex. Civ.App.1933, 61 S.W.2d 126, 129.

52. That the equity of marshalling must be asserted before foreclosure by E, see § 286, supra. Also that it cannot be asserted if it would prejudice E's rights. Ibid.

53. "But the notice to the mortgagee must be actual, and not constructive. It would be unreasonable to require a mortgagee to take notice of the registry of deeds made subsequent to his own mortgage." Iglehart v. Crane & Wesson, 1866, 42 Ill. 261, 268; Woodward v. Brown, 1897, 119 Cal. 283, 51 P. 2, 63 Am.St.Rep. 108, modified 119 Cal. 283, 51 P. 542, 63 Am.St.Rep. 108; Ocean County Nat. Bank v. J. Edwin Ellor & Sons, Inc., 1934, 116 N.J.Eq. 287, 290, 173 A. 138, 139; Balen v. Lewis, 1902, 130 Mich. 567, 90 N.W. 416, 47 Am.St.Rep. 499; Bridgewater Roller Mills Co. v. Strough, 1900, 98 Va. 721, 37 S. E. 290; Clarke v. Cowan, 1910, 206 Mass. 252, 92 N.E. 474, 138 Am.St.Rep. 388, accord. See also Stuyvesant v. Hall, N.Y.1847, 2 Barb.Ch. 151, 158; 1937, 110 A.L.R. 65, 70; 1941, 131 A.L.R. 4, 109; Ann.Cas.1916D, 1119, 1133. Cf., Patty v. Pease & Seymour, N.Y.1846, 8 Paige, 277. Nor does knowledge of facts which would put a person on inquiry suffice to charge the mortgagee. Bridgewater Roller Mills v. Strough, supra. If the mortgagee had no notice of the later alienation by the mortgagor at the time he gave a release of other portions, it is clear that he may enforce his lien against the portion conveyed to the full amount of the debt. Bridgewater Roller Mills Co. v. Strough, supra; Bridgewater Roller Mills v. Receivers of Baltimore Building & Loan Ass'n, 1903, 124 F. 718. See 1937, 110 A.L.R. 65, 70, 75.

54. See Brooks v. Benham, 1897, 70 Conn. 92, 97, 38 A. 908, 910, 66 Am.St.Rep. 87, quoted in n. 57, infra. See also Green, Marshaling Assets in Texas, 1956, 34 Texas L.Rev. 1054.

value of the property released which they had a right to have him apply to the debt before resorting to the property held by them.[55] If the right was to have the entire parcel applied first, its entire value must be deducted.[56] On the other hand, if the right was only that the released lot should be used to satisfy its pro rata share of the debt, the mortgagee must abate the debt only to such a proportion of it as the value of released parcel bore to the value of the entire tract.[57]

If the property released is one against which there is no right of marshalling, e. g., if it is the parcel first aliened in cases where the inverse order of alienation rule applies, the mortgagee does not have to make any deduction of its value before he can enforce the mortgage against the other parcels.[58] Further, if in giving a release of a parcel the mortgagee received a consideration which he applied upon the mortgage debt, he may enforce the balance of the debt against the remaining property provided the amount received was equal to the fair value of the lot in question.[59] And if, as is provided in modern mortgages in which subdivisions are contemplated, the mortgagee is given permission to execute partial releases, he may release portions without further liability to other holders if he adheres to the terms of authorization.[60]

55. The discharge has been rested upon an impairment of the grantee or mortgagee's right of subrogation. Brooks v. Benham, n. 57, infra. Cf. §§ 269–271, supra, for the cognate problem where not just a portion, but the entire property has been sold. The doctrine of discharge here rests upon an application of the same basic principles applied, however, pro tanto.

56. A mortgaged lots 1 and 2 to B to secure a debt. Later A conveyed lot 1 to C with a covenant of warranty. Still later A conveyed lot 2 to D, and B at the same time released lot 2 from the mortgage lien. B had notice of A's prior conveyance. Held, if the value of lot 2 would have been sufficient to have satisfied the entire debt, B could not resort to lot 1; if the value of lot 2 would have been sufficient to have satisfied only part of the debt, B could then resort to lot 1, but only to procure a sum equal to the difference between the debt and the value of lot 2. Brown v. Simons, 1863, 44 N.H. 475; Hill v. Howell, 1882, 36 N.J.Eq. 25; Schrack v. Shriner, 1882, 100 Pa. 451; New South Bldg. & Loan Ass'n v. Reed, 1898, 96 Va. 345, 31 S.E. 514, 70 Am.St.Rep. 858; Schaad v. Robinson, 1908, 50 Wash. 283, 97 P. 104; Deuster v. McCamus, 1861, 14 Wis. 307—accord. See also Iglehart v. Crane & Wesson, 1866, 42 Ill. 261; Pomeroy, Eq.Jur., 4th Ed., § 1226, note 4; 1937, 110 A.L.R. 65, 67, 73; 1941, 131 A.L.R. 4, 108, 109. Cf. Gaskill v. Sine, 1861, 13 N.J.Eq. 400, 78 Am.Dec. 105; Snyder v. Crawford, 1881, 98 Pa. 414. Contra: McCoy v. Wynn, 1926, 215 Ala. 172, 174, 110 So. 129, 130.

57. E. g., where the parcels are subsequently sold by the mortgagor at the same time to different persons. In such a case "while the whole of the debt is secured by the whole of the land, each parcel of the land, as between the different proprietors, is equitably subject only to so much of the debt as corresponds to the proportion between its value and the value of all the land; and, if its owner should be compelled to redeem the mortgage, he can resort to the others for a ratable contribution, and for that purpose is entitled to the benefit of subroga-

tion to the mortgage title. To release any particular parcel from the mortgage incumbrance is to make, as respects that, any such subrogation impossible. The mortgagee therefore releases at his peril, if he had notice of the conveyances out of which the equities in question arise; and, if he does so without receiving from the releasee his proper contributory share of the debt, he is still equitably chargeable with the receipt of that share, in favor of the owners of the remaining parcels." Brooks v. Benham, 1897, 70 Conn. 92, 97, 38 A. 908, 910, 66 Am.St.Rep. 87. See Taylor v. Short's Adm'r, 1869, 27 Iowa 361, 1 Am.Rep. 280; Parkman v. Welch, 1837, 36 Mass. (19 Pick.) 231.

58. Clark v. Kraker, 1892, 51 Minn. 444, 53 N.W. 706; Lyman v. Lyman, 1859, 32 Vt. 79, 76 Am.Dec. 151. As to the effect the mortgagee's release of the mortgagor's personal liability by dealings with a purchaser of part of the mortgaged property who assumed the mortgage debt has upon the lien of the mortgage upon another part which has been conveyed by the mortgagor to a third person, see 1936, 101 A.L.R. 618.

59. Beardsley v. Empire Trust Co., 1924, 96 N.J.Eq. 212, 124 A. 457, noted 24 Col.L.Rev. 804. See Taylor v. Short's Adm'r, 1869, 27 Iowa 361, 362, 1 Am. Rep. 280.

60. Thompson v. Thomas, 1919, 43 Cal.App. 588, 185 P. 427. See 1937, 110 A.L.R. 65, 72, 77.

CHAPTER 11

DISCHARGE OF A MORTGAGE

PAYMENT

293. Payment made and accepted on or before the law day extinguishes the mortgage automatically. Payment after the law day in lien states extinguishes the mortgage lien; but in title states most courts hold that, although the mortgage is discharged in equity, it has vested indefeasibly in the mortgagee at law and can be ended only by a reconveyance which equity will compel him to execute. By statute a mortgagor may recover damages if a mortgagee mala fide refuses to release a mortgage which has been satisfied; it is doubtful whether he has such a common law right.

The authorities are unanimous that payment[1] of the mortgage debt on the law day will extinguish the mortgagee's security interest in the property and restore full legal ownership to the mortgagor without the necessity of any reconveyance, release or any other instrument being executed by the mortgagee.[2] And the same effect is given to guish it. Holman v. Bailey, 1841, 44 Mass. (3 Metc.) 55; In re Miller's Estate, 1915, 251 Pa. 201, 96 A. 473. However, it has already been seen that such conveyances by the mortgagor in satisfaction of the debt will be closely scrutinized and upset under certain circumstances. See §§ 100, 101, supra, Cf. §§ 272, 277, supra. However, the receipt by a mortgagee in possession of rents and profits equal to the amount of the mortgage debt does not amount to a legal satisfaction of the debt. Also, execution and acceptance of a promissory note does not constitute payment of an existing obligation in the absence of an agreement to that effect. E. K. Wood Lumber Co. v. Higgins, Cal.App. 1959, 1 Cal. Rptr. 348, affirmed 54 Cal.2d 91, 4 Cal.Rptr. 523, 351 P.2d 795. See note, 1910, 23 Harv.L.Rev. 301; § 167, supra. See §§ 102, 105, supra, as to the effect of changes in the form of the obligation and acts which end the remedy but do not affect the substantive obligation. The foregoing examples are merely illustrative. Just what acts will or will not have the effect of satisfying the mortgage obligation is a matter of the law of contracts generally. It is therefore, beyond the scope of this work to go into it in any detail.

As to the applicability of recording acts to and effect upon payment by the mortgagor and others, see §§ 236, 237, 238d, supra.

1. Payment is here used in a broad and generic sense to include not only the doing of the very act the mortgage was given to secure, whether that act be payment of money or rendering some other performance, but also any other act the operative effect of which is to satisfy the mortgage obligation. See e. g., Lit. § 344 "Also, in the case of feoffment in mortgage, if the feoffor payeth to the feoffee a horse, or a cup of silver, or a ring of gold, or any such other thing in full satisfaction of the money and the other receive it, this is good enough * * *." Neylan v. Green, 1889, 82 Cal. 128, 23 P. 42, accord. A conveyance of the mortgaged property by the mortgagor to the mortgagee in satisfaction of the mortgage debt will effectually extin-

2. In title states this is because the condition on which the conveyance was made is performed. "If the money is paid on the very day appointed for the payment of it, the condition is said to be performed, and the mortgagor, as in any other case where the grantee of land on condition performs the condition, may enter on the land and hold it, as of his former estate." Hargrave & Butler's Note to Coke upon Littleton, § 332. Munson v. Munson, 1862, 30 Conn. 425, 437, accord. In England, down to 1925, if the condition in the mortgage was for reconveyance on payment instead of voiding the mortgage there had to be a reconveyance to revest title in the mortgagor. See Coote, Mortgages, 9th

payment which is accepted before the law day.[3]

Where payment is made after the maturity of the obligation, there is some divergence in the cases as to its effect grounded, as is the more important similar difference as to the effect of tender after the law day,[4] upon the technical structure of the mortgage as giving legal title or only a lien to the mortgagee. In title and intermediate theory states[5] on failure of the mortgagor to perform the condition by performing on the law day, "at law the land is discharged of the condition; it becomes absolutely vested in the mortgagee; the mortgagor has no legal right to repossess himself of it by payment of the money; and the estates, for all legal purposes, remain in the mortgagee, and can only be revested in a mortgagor by a reconveyance from the mortgagee."[6] Payment

after default does not by itself operate to revest title in the mortgagor because the concept of the title theory is that only performance of the condition does that.[7] However payment does discharge all equitable interest of the mortgagee in the property regardless of whether it is made on, before, or after the law day.[8] Hence when the mortgagor pays after default the mortgagee becomes a holder of the bare legal title in trust[9] for the mortgagor who can require a reconveyance on application to a court of equity.[10] Some courts have departed from the logic of the title concept to permit the mortgagor to recover possession from the mortgagee in an action at law[11] and to deny a similar recovery by the

---

ed., 5, citing Re Ethel and Mitchell, [1901] 1 Ch. 945. Since the Law of Property Act of 1925, 15 Geo. V. C. 20, § 1(1), a receipt indorsed on, written at the foot of, or annexed to, a mortgage for all the money secured by it will operate as a discharge without reconveyance, surrender or release. Coote, Mortgages, 9th ed., 1413. In lien states since the mortgage lien is regarded as security only for the performance of an obligation, if the obligation is performed or satisfied in any way, the lien is automatically extinguished. Decker v. Decker, 1902, 64 Neb. 239, 89 N.W. 795; Bogert v. Bliss, 1896, 148 N.Y. 194, 42 N.E. 582, 51 Am.St.Rep. 684; Cumps v. Kiyo, 1899, 104 Wis. 656, 80 N.W. 937. See §§ 15, 127, supra.

In Twitty v. Harrison, 1956, 230 S.C. 174, 94 S.E.2d 879, noted in Karesh, Security Transactions, in Survey of South Carolina Law, 1957, 10 S.C.L.Rev. 114, 124, the court held that the burden was on the debtor to show payment and authority of the person paid, to receive payment. But, showing these, it was immaterial that the mortgagor, on making final payment, did not demand production of the mortgage papers and did not obtain and record a satisfaction of the mortgage.

3. Co.Litt. 212a; Burgaine v. Spurling, 1632, Cro. Car. 283; Holman v. Bailey, 1841, 44 Mass. (3 Metc.) 55; Cumps v. Kiyo, 1899, 104 Wis. 656, 80 N.W. 937, lien state, mortgage by deed absolute.

4. See § 294, infra.

5. See §§ 5, 14, 125, 126, supra.

6. Hargrave & Butler's Note to Coke upon Littleton, § 332.

7. Phelps v. Sage, Conn.1805, 2 Day 151; Smith v. Vincent, 1842, 15 Conn. 1, 14, 38 Am.Dec. 52; Cross v. Robinson, 1851, 21 Conn. 379, 387. See Moore v. Norman, 1890, 43 Minn. 428, 45 N.W. 857, 9 L.R.A. 55, 19 Am.St.Rep. 247; Farmers Fire Ins. & Loan Co. v. Edwards, N.Y.1841, 26 Wend. 541. Cf. Harrison v. Owen, 1738, 1 Atk. 520, in which the "Lord Chancellor said in this cause, that if a mortgagee cancels a mortgage, and it is found so in his possession, it is as much a release as cancelling a bond, but it does not convey or revest the estate in the mortgagor, for that must be done by some deed." See § 5 supra.

8. Palmer v. Uhl, 1930, 112 Conn. 125, 128, 151 A. 355, 356, alternative decision; see Desiderio v. Iadonisi, 1932, 115 Conn. 652, 655, 163 A. 254, 255, 88 A.L.R. 1349.

9. Cooper v. Cooper, 1912, 256 Ill. 160, 99 N.E. 871. See Stewart v. Crosby, 1863, 50 Me. 130, 134, approved in Hooper v. Bail, 1935, 133 Me. 412, 415, 179 A. 404, 405.

10. "But, in the view of a court of equity, the land, immediately on the payment of the mortgage-debt, becomes the absolute property of the mortgagor; and a court of equity will decree the mortgagee to reconvey it to him, and account to him for the intermediate profits." Hargrave & Butler's Note to Coke upon Littleton, § 332; Kelly v. Martin, 1894, 107 Ala. 479, 18 So. 132; Town of Clinton v. Town of Westbrook, 1871, 38 Conn. 9; Parsons v. Welles, 1821, 17 Mass. 419; Stewart v. Crosby, 1863, 50 Me. 130; Gardner v. Buckeye Savings & Loan Co., 1930, 108 W.Va. 673, 152 S.E. 530, 78 A.L.R. 1,—accord. And see Holman v. Bailey, 1841, 44 Mass. (3 Metc.) 55.

11. E. g., Perkins' Lessee v. Dibble, 1841, 10 Ohio, 433, 434, 440, 36 Am.Dec. 97, mortgagor's transferee allowed ejectment against one claiming under the mortgagee, the mortgage having been paid after maturity but no reconveyance having been made; Baker v. Gavitt, 1880, 128 Mass. 93, mortgagor who paid after the law day entitled to recover posses-

mortgagee from the mortgagor after the debt has been paid.[12] Statutes also have altered the rule as to revesting of title on late payment.[13]

In lien theory states it is held that payment of the mortgage debt, whether made on, before, or after default, extinguishes the mortgage lien at law as well as in equity.[14] This flows from the view that a lien is security only for the performance of an act and if the act has been performed there is nothing

for the lien to secure and it is, therefore, extinguished.[15]

However, even though payment may extinguish a mortgage, it usually has been recorded and it is necessary to have it discharged of record. This the mortgagor may compel the mortgagee to do by whatever means is required by the state where the property is.[16] Whether a mortgagor has a common law right to recover damages from the mortgagee for failure to cancel of record a satisfied mortgage is doubtful.[17] However in a very large number of states statutes give such a right and impose penalties upon a mortgagee who refuses to give a release, satisfaction piece, reconveyance, or whatever is necessary in that jurisdiction to clear up the record title.[18]

---

sion from his tenant who, after default, had attorned to the mortgagee, the court holding that the mortgagee, after such payment, held a bare legal title as trustee for the mortgagor and it would not defeat the latter's right to possession; McNair v. Picotte, 1862, 33 Mo. 57.

12. See Stewart v. Crosby, 1863, 50 Me. 130, 134; Baker v. Gavitt, 1880, 128 Mass. 93. Cf., Pollock v. Maison, 1866, 41 Ill. 516.

13. E. g., Alabama Code 1928, § 9026; N.H.Rev. Laws, 1942, c. 261, § 6; Miss. Code, 1930 Ann., § 2152; Hussey v. Fisher, 1900, 94 Me. 301, 47 A. 525. Cf. 7 Geo. II, c. 20 (1734), which gave the English law courts, under certain circumstances, an equitable power to compel the mortgagee to assign, surrender or convey the mortgaged premises to the mortgagor or his nominee upon payment into court of the debt. See Shields v. Lozear, 1869, 34 N.J. Law. 496. See also Note, Comparison of California Mortgages, Trust Deeds and Land Sale Contracts, 1960, 7 U.C.L.A.L.Rev. 83.

14. McMillan v. Richards, 1858, 9 Cal. 365, 70 Am. Dec. 655; Hendricks v. Hess, 1910, 112 Minn. 252, 127 N.W. 995; Tobin v. Tobin, 1909, 139 Wis. 494, 121 N.W. 144. Decker v. Decker, 1902, 64 Neb. 239, 89 N.W. 795; Wakefield v. Day, 1889, 41 Minn. 344, 43 N.W. 71; Cf. Ormsby v. Barr, 1870, 22 Mich. 80. See also note 2, supra.

"It is not now to be questioned that a mortgage being considered and treated merely as security for the payment of money * * * is simply a chose in action extinguishable by a parol release, which equity will execute as an agreement not to sue, or by turning the mortgagee into a trustee for the mortgagor." Ackla v. Ackla, 1847, 6 Pa. 228, 230. See also Wallis v. Long, 1849, 16 Ala. 738; Howard v. Gresham, 1859, 27 Ga. 347; Schweider v. Lang, 1882, 29 Minn. 254, 13 N.W. 33, 43 Am.Rep. 202; Hemmings v. Doss, 1899, 125 N.C. 400, 34 S.E. 511. Cf. Leavitt v. Pratt, 1865, 53 Me. 147.

Trust Deed Mortgages. "The provision for reconveyance, or any reconveyance actually made, had no legal effect beyond that of making the record title clear, since upon payment of the debt, the purpose of the trust ceased, and the property at once, without any reconveyance, revested in the party or parties who had owned it before." Nilson v. Sarment, 1908, 153 Cal. 524, 530, 96 P. 315, 317, 126 Am.St. Rep. 91. See Tyler v. Currier, 1905, 147 Cal. 31, 81

P. 319; McLeod v. Moran, 1908, 153 Cal. 97, 94 P. 604—accord. And see West's Ann.Cal.Civ.Code, §§ 871, 2279. See also notes 1931, 37 W.Va.L.Q. 223; 1939, 12 So.Cal.L.Rev. 485, 487.

15. "The debt, in the eye of the law, thus becomes the principal, and the landed security merely appurtenant and secondary; * * * Acceptance of payment of the amount due on a mortgage, at any time before foreclosure, has always been held to discharge the incumbrance on the land * * *" Kortright v. Cady, 1860, 21 N.Y. 343, 347, 78 Am. Dec. 145. See Caruthers v. Humphrey, 1864, 12 Mich. 270, accord. See also cases, note 14, supra.

16. See 1932, 78 A.L.R., 24, 101. A tender conditioned upon the execution of a release, etc., is a proper tender. Harding v. Home Invest. & Sav. Co., 1930, 49 Idaho 64, 286 P. 920, rehearing denied, 49 Idaho 75, 297 P. 1101; Wallowa Lake Amusement Co. v. Hamilton, 70 Or. 433, 142 P. 321. As to whether a tender so conditioned will discharge a mortgage, see § 294, infra; 1934, 93 A.L.R. 12, 74.

17. It has been held that he has such a right in Texas. Mickie v. McGehee, 1881, 27 Tex. 134; Knox v. Farmers State Bank of Merkel, Tex.Civ.App.1928, 7 S.W.2d 918, commented on in 1929, 7 Tex.L.Rev. 323. But Hasquet v. Big West Oil Co., C.C.A.Mont. 1928, 29 F.2d 78, is contra.

18. E. g., C.C.C. § 2941; Criminal penalties also may be imposed, C.C.C. § 2941.5. Mathieu v. Boston, 1927, 51 S.D. 619, 216 N.W. 361, 56 A.L.R. 332, honesty and good faith in refusing tender prevents recovery under such a statute. Richmond v. Lattin, 1884, 64 Cal. 273, 30 P. 818, a demand is a condition precedent. See Hasquet v. Big West Oil Co., C.C. A.Mont.1928, 29 F.2d 78, 80. Also see 1928, 56 A.L. R. 335, for a collection of authorities under such statutes.

The problem of release or discharge of a mortgage or deed of trust given to two or more obligees who are not joint tenants with right of survivorship to secure what appears to be a single debt causes some difficulty when one of the obligees purports to release or discharge it. "The obligation is usually described as a joint obligation and the mortgage as a joint mortgage. Whatever rights they may have as to one another, the obligees do not have separate rights to demand separate payment from the obligor as they would have if separate performances were stated to be owing to each of them individually. Only one performance or one payment is specified.

"If performance is rendered or payment is made to one joint obligee alone, the latter can give a complete release or discharge to the obligor. This was at one time rationalized by saying that the other obligee thereafter has no enforceable right because he could not sue without joining the releasing obligee; and because the latter had given a discharge, he had thereby deprived himself of any power to join in the action. Apart from this rationale, however, the rule has other support for it soundness. After the passage of time it is sometimes very difficult or impossible to locate each joint obligee and pay him his proportionate share of the joint debt, as the obligees may have agreed as among themselves to be their proportionate shares. As noted by one court, it is too much to expect an obligor of such a debt 'to hunt up each joint obligee and pay him his distributive share.'

"A substantial number of cases have held that one of two or more joint obligees may receive payment in full and release or discharge a mortgage or deed of trust given to them jointly. Moreover the discharge is effective even though the payee receiving payment does not account to the other; and it is nonetheless effective if made by a surviving joint obligee after the death of the other. This is true, not because of any right of survivorship, but because of the power of one joint obligee to receive payment of the entire debt and to execute a discharge of it at any time. Several statutes now declare the right of one joint obligee to receive payment in these cases and his power to give a complete release of the mortgage or deed of trust. This power is also recognized in a number of title standards." [18a]

TENDER—ON OR BEFORE MATURITY

294. Tender on the law day, although it does not affect the mortgage debt, discharges the mortgage and, if kept good, stops interest and liability for costs. Tender before the law day has no effect upon either mortgage or debt.

Proper tender [19] on the law day, though not accepted, discharges the mortgage in both

Esposito v. Satanella, Sup.Ct.1955, commented on by Million, Property Law, in 1955 Survey of New York Law, 1955, 30 N.Y.U.L.Rev. 1565, 1574, held that the statutory rule requiring a mortgagee to execute a satisfaction piece, or, if requested, an assignment, applies where the demanding owner was a tenant by the entireties, notwithstanding that his estranged wife, as the other co-owner, sought to require the mortgagee to issue only a satisfaction piece. In Cotofan v. Steiner, 1959, 170 Ohio St. 163, 163 N.E.2d 759, noted in 1960, 29 U. of Cin.L. Rev. 314, the plaintiff mortgagors were held entitled to recover compensation and exemplary damages from defendant's alleged malicious and wanton misconduct in refusing to accept full payment and execute a satisfaction of a mortgage debt required by plaintiffs to complete a transaction.

See Note, Mortgages: Penalty for Failure to Release, 1962, 15 Okl.L.R. 232.

18a. Basye, Clearance of Land Titles, 1970, § 353.

19. What constitutes a proper tender is, for the most part, a matter of general law not peculiar to mortgages. It is therefore, not covered in detail in this work. A few of the problems, e. g., whether it must be "kept good," and the effect of a tender by a non-assuming grantee, which have special significance in mortgage problems, are touched upon. For a good summary of the law of tender as applied in security transactions involving personal property, much of which is applicable where the security is land, at least in lien states, see Restatement of Security, Tentative Draft No. 2, pp. 168–174. See also Hunt, Law of Tender, 1903, c. 9.

Harpe v. Stone, 1956, 212 Ga. 341, 92 S.E.2d 522, noted by Loiseaux, Security Transactions, in Annual Survey of Georgia Law, June 1, 1955—June 1, 1956, 1956, 8 Mercer L.Rev. 144, 149, held that where the amount due on a debt is in dispute, the mortgagor must tender at least the amount admittedly due,

title and lien states [20] although it does not affect the obligation secured [21] except to stop the running of interest and prevent the debtor from being liable for costs, at least if the tender is kept good.[22] Although it is commonly said that such a tender constitutes performance of the condition,[23] this obviously is not so. A more careful and accurate statement would be that, the performance of the condition having been prevented by the mortgagee's refusal to accept payment, it will be excused.

Tender made before the due day, even if interest up to that date is added to the principal amount offered, is ineffectual to discharge the mortgage regardless of whether lien or title theory governs.[24] Unless there

even if the creditor is demanding more than that amount.

20. Co.Lit. §§ 338, 209a, 209b. Depon v. Shawye, 1928, 263 Mass. 206, 161 N.E. 243; see Security State Bank v. Waterloo Lodge, 1909, 85 Neb. 255, 122 N. W. 992; West's Ann.Cal.Civ.Code, §§ 1504, 2909. See also 1934, 93 A.L.R. 12, 25, 31. If the mortgagee waives payment at maturity it is not certain that a tender at a later date, in reliance on the waiver, will extinguish the mortgage although it will stop interest and costs on the debt. Wood v. Babb, 1882, 16 S.C. 427.

21. See Williston, Contracts, Rev. ed. 1938, § 1817; Co.Lit. 209a, 209b; Bacon's Abridgment, title Tender (f); Dixon v. Clark, 1848, 5 C.B. 365, 377.

22. Lutton v. Rodd, 1675, 2 Cas.Ch. 206, "the plaintiff ought to make oath that the money was kept, and no profit made of it"; Bank of New South Wales v. O'Connor, 1889, 14 App.Cas. 273; see Gyles v. Hall, 1726, 2 P.Wms. 378; Crain v. McGoon, 1877, 86 Ill. 431, 29 Am.Rep. 37. See also Note, Comparison of California Mortgages, Trust Deeds and Land Sale Contracts, 1960, 7 U.C.L.A.L.Rev. 83.

23. E. g., "Tender of the mortgage debt on the day named is performance of the condition, and, by force of the terms of the condition, determines the estate of the mortgagee, and the condition being complied with, the land reverts to the mortgagor by the simple operation of the condition." Shields v. Lozear, 1869, 34 N.J.L. 496, 504, 3 Am.St.Rep. 256.

24. Brown v. Cole, Ch.1845, 14 Sim. 427; Abbe v. Goodwin, 1829, 7 Conn. 377; Bowen v. Julius, 1895, 141 Ind. 310, 40 N.E. 700; Quyn v. Whetcroft, Md. 1793, 3 Harr. & McH. 136; Buchanan v. Selden, 1895, 43 Neb. 559, 61 N.W. 732; Pyross v. Fraser, 1909, 82 S.C. 498, 64 S.E. 407, 23 L.R.A.,N.S., 403, and 129 Am.St.Rep. 901, 17 Ann.Cas. 150. See West's Ann.Cal.Civ.Code, §§ 1490, 1491.

is a bargain to the contrary, the mortgagee is entitled to refuse to accept payment before the time set by the agreement. A tender before the law day, therefore, is neither performance of the mortgage condition nor an attempted performance that the mortgagee has a duty to accept at peril of losing his security.

TENDER—AFTER LAW DAY

295. **Tender after the law day in title states does not extinguish the mortgage. In lien states the majority view is that tender, even though not kept good, will discharge the mortgage lien. This doctrine is regarded as harsh and has been restricted in many ways, the most important of which is that tender, unless kept good, is not a basis for affirmative relief. Like tender on the law day, later tender does not affect the debt and must be kept good to stop interest and costs.**

No distinction should be drawn between tender on and after the law day; either should operate to discharge the mortgage and stop interest and costs if, but only if, kept good.

Where tender is made after maturity, in states following the common-law title theory of mortgages it does not extinguish the mortgage lien if the mortgagee refuses to accept it.[25] The courts in these states reason logically, if technically, from the legal structure and mechanics of the mortgage as they view it. The concept is that a mortgage is an absolute conveyance defeasible by performance of a condition subsequent in the manner and at the time stipulated for in the defeasance, i.e., the law day. In case of nonperformance as specified the mortgagee's estate becomes absolute, and it cannot thereafter be divested even by a full payment of the mortgage

On the right to prepay and the prepayment penalty, see Note, Secured Real Estate Loan Prepayment and the Prepayment Penalty, 1963, 51 Cal.L.Rev. 923–938.

25. Shields v. Lozear, 1869, 34 N.J.L. 496, is the leading case. Davis v. Ashburn, 1932, 224 Ala. 572, 574, 141 So. 226, 227; Stockton v. Dundee Mfg. Co., 1871, 22 N.J.Eq. 56; Sandler v. Green, 1934, 287 Mass. 404, 407, 192 N.E. 39, 41; Maynard v. Hunt, 1827, 22 Mass. (5 Pick.) 240, accord. See 1934, 94 A.L.R. 25–30.

debt. It follows as an obvious consequence that mere tender should not be given greater effect than actual payment. The mortgagor's only remedy, except insofar as he may have relief by statute, is in equity by a bill to redeem.[26] In a few states professing to accept the title theory a tender after maturity suspends the mortgagee's right to exercise a power of sale if the mortgage contains one, a result substantially impairing the mortgagee's security.[27]

In lien jurisdictions the weight of authority is that an unaccepted tender made after default does discharge the mortgage lien.[28] There are, however, several lien jurisdictions that hold such a tender does not affect it.[29] And in some states the rule is not settled.[30]

Reasons given for the majority rule that a belated, unaccepted tender will discharge the mortgage lien begin with the technical nature of the mortgage in lien states as contrasted with title states. Unlike a title theory mortgage, the technical situation of the lien mortgage remains the same after default as on or before the due day. Failure to perform at maturity does not vest indefeasibly any legal or other interest in the mortgagee as it does in title states. In contrast to a common law mortgage, payment after the law day extinguishes the mortgage just as does payment on the law day. This being so, there is no ground for not giving the same effect to tender made after default as is given to tender on the due day. If it is fair to deprive the mortgagee of his security when he refuses to accept a performance on the law day, it is equally fair to do so when he refuses a performance which would have that effect at a later time.[31]

It will be noted that the foregoing reasoning, while logical, does not get to the merits of the rule anymore than does the rule to the opposite effect in title jurisdictions. Both are grounded upon the technical legal structure of the mortgage. And an additional argument is in a similar category. A mortgage in a lien jurisdiction, it is urged, since it leaves legal title in the mortgagor and gives to the mortgagee only a chattel interest, should follow the analogy of pledges and possessory liens of tangible personal property in

---

26. For clear statements of the rationale of tender after the law day in title jurisdictions, see Moore v. Norman, 1890, 43 Minn. 428, 45 N.W. 857, 9 L.R.A. 55, 19 Am.St.Rep. 247; Shields v. Lozear, note 25, supra; Farmers' Fire Ins. & Loan Co. v. Edwards, N.Y.1841, 26 Wend. 541. See also 1934, 93 A.L.R. 12, 15, 25.

27. Garrett v. Cobb, 1918, 202 Ala. 241, 80 So. 79; Greer v. Turner, 1880, 36 Ark. 17; Wingert v. Brewer, 1911, 116 Md. 518, 82 A. 157; Tonkel v. Shields, 1921, 125 Miss. 461, 87 So. 646. See Wickhem, Tender in Security Transactions, 1942, 27 Iowa L.Rev. 579, 593; 1934, 93 A.L.R. 12, 30. Contra: Cranston v. Crane, 1867, 97 Mass. 459, 93 Am. Dec. 106; Debnam v. Watkins, 1919, 178 N.C. 238, 100 S.E. 336.

28. Kortright v. Cady, 1860, 21 N.Y. 343, is the leading case. Caruthers v. Humphrey, 1864, 12 Mich. 270, accord. See 1934, 93 A.L.R. 31.
Bowman v. Poole, 1956, 212 Ga. 261, 91 S.E.2d 770, noted by Loiseaux, Security Transactions, in Annual Survey of Georgia Law June 1, 1955—June 1, 1956, 1956, 8 Mercer L.Rev. 144, 150, held that a proper tender by a second mortgagee, which was refused, discharged the first mortgage and invalidated the deed executed by the first mortgagee to himself under a foreclosure sale.

29. E. g., Keese v. Parnell, 1925, 134 S.C. 207, 132 S.E. 620; but cf. Peoples Nat. Bank of Greenville v. Upchurch, 1937, 183 S.C. 147, 153, 190 S.E. 515, 518, holding mortgage lien discharged if mortgagor pays money into court. See 1934, 93 A.L.R. 12, 38–45.

30. E. g., Perre v. Castro, 1860, 14 Cal. 519, 76 Am. Dec. 444, and Himmelmann v. Fitzpatrick, 1875, 50 Cal. 650, hold that the mortgage is not discharged. Wiemeyer v. Southern Trust & Commerce Bank, 1930, 107 Cal.App. 165, 173, 290 P. 70, 73, holds that it is. And see Walker v. Houston, 1932, 215 Cal. 742, 746, 12 P.2d 952, 87 A.L.R. 937. See 1915, 3 Cal.L.Rev. 336. See also 1934, 93 A.L.R. 12, 46–49.

By West's Ann.Cal.Civ.Code, § 1500, a due offer of payment, immediately followed by a deposit of the amount of the debt in a bank within the state in the creditor's name and notice to him, operates as payment. Colton v. Oakland Bank of Savings, 1902, 137 Cal. 376, 70 P. 225. See also West's Ann.Cal. Civ.Code, §§ 1485, 1504. And see N.Y.Civ.Prac. Act, §§ 171–173.

For more recent discussions of the general problem see 1960, 7 U.C.L.A.L.Rev. 830 (discharge of mortgages and trust deed mortgages by offer of performance); Shapiro, Effect on a Mortgage of Tender: After Default, 1954, 32 Texas L.Rev. 595, with special reference to Texas law.

31. See Salinas v. Ellis, 1887, 26 S.C. 337, 2 S.E. 121; Kortright v. Cady, 1860, 21 N.Y. 343; 1934, 93 A.L. R. 12, 16 et seq.

which a proper tender destroys the security interest.[32] The fact that in such cases the creditor has actual possession of the debtor's chattel and, unless tender operated to destroy his security rights, would be able to deprive the debtor of any beneficial use of his property is not noted as a ground for distinguishing them from a land mortgage in a lien state. In the latter the mortgagor retains possession and beneficial use of his property until foreclosure. Consequently the hardship of failing to discharge the mortgage on tender boils down to two things: the marketability of his property is impaired by the cloud upon it of the continuing lien; he remains exposed to the danger of foreclosure action on the part of the mortgagee.

As to the first, the answer is that almost invariably a land mortgage is recorded and the record mortgage constitutes, practically, as much of a cloud on marketability as does the existence of the lien itself. And, to anticipate, no jurisdiction, even though holding that the substantive lien is gone, will give the mortgagor affirmative relief without payment to the mortgagee or into court in a proceeding which is equivalent to an action to redeem.[33] The mortgagor is always at liberty to bring such an action. Further, not only is the ordinary action in equity available for this purpose, but many states have enacted statutes giving summary relief so as to minimize hardship that might result from the slower equity action. These provide for a short form petition which will result in an order for cancellation of debt and mortgage on the mortgagor paying the money into court.[34] These statutes are in addition to the statutes mentioned earlier giving to the mortgagor a right to damages against a mortgagee who refuses to execute a release, etc., on payment.[35] The availability of such remedies which enable the mortgagor to end any possibility of foreclosure by the mort-

32. Coggs v. Bernard, 1703, 2 Ld.Raym. 909, 917. See Restatement of Security, §§ 39, 59, 78. Restatement of Security, Tentative Draft No. 2, pp. 168 et seq.; Wickhem, 1942, 27 Iowa L.Rev. 579, 586. Hunt, Law of Tender, 1903, C. 9.

In the case of an equitable mortgage by deposit of title deeds, a tender does not discharge the lien. In order to redeem the mortgagor must bring a bill for redemption or make a summary application on terms of substituting for the security a sum of money equal to the amount of the security with a proper margin. Bank of New South Wales v. O'Connor, 1889, 14 A.C. 273.

If the location of legal title is the criterion, it would seem that the same should be true in the case of chattel mortgages. Some courts where the lien theory of mortgages is followed as to land do assert that the fact that a chattel mortgagee has legal title changes the effect of the rule of tender after the law day. E. g., Noyes v. Wyckoff, 1889, 30 Hun 466, affirmed 114 N.Y. 204, 21 N.E. 158; See Edwards v. Farmers' Federal Ins. & Loan Co., N.Y. 1839, 21 Wend. 467, affirmed, 1841, 26 Wend. 541. But see 1934, 93 A.L.R. 12, 37. Other authorities that in the case of a chattel mortgage, tender after maturity will not revest title in the mortgagor are Darrow v. Wendelstadt, 1899, 43 App.Div. 426, 60 N.Y.S. 174; Gauche v. Milbrath, 1897, 94 Wis. 674, 69 N.W. 999. Cf. Gould v. Armagost, 1896, 46 Neb. 897, 65 N.W. 1064; Thomas v. Seattle Brewing & Malting Co., 1908, 48 Wash. 560, 94 P. 116, 15 L.R.A.,N.S., 1164, 125 Am.St.Rep. 945, 15 Ann.Cas. 494. See 1897, 33 L.R.A. 231, 235. On the other hand, other cases hold that tender after the law day will discharge a chattel mortgage. Moore v. Norman, 1890, 43 Minn. 428, 45 N.W. 857, 9 L.R.A. 55, 19 Am.St.Rep. 247. And see Wickhem, Tender in Security Transactions, 1942, 27 Iowa L.Rev. 579, 597.

33. Tender cannot be made the basis of an action to cancel a mortgage or for other affirmative relief in equity. Cowles v. Marble, 1877, 37 Mich. 158; Tuthill v. Morris, 1880, 81 N.Y. 94; Nelson v. Loder, 1892, 132 N.Y. 288, 30 N.E. 369; McClellan v. Coffin, 1883, 93 Ind. 456; Murray v. O'Brien, 1910, 56 Wash. 361, 105 P. 840, 28 L.R.A.,N.S., 998. See 1910, 10 Col.L.Rev. 252; 1934, 93 A.L.R. 12, 53; L.R.A.1918C, 186. See also the analogous situation as to the mortgagee in possession in lien states, § 161, supra. Cf. also § 296, infra.

34. E.g., New York Real Prop. Actions and Proceedings Law § 1921; McKinney's Consol.Laws of N.Y. Book. 49½; Geo. II, C. 20 (1874). See 1928, 56 A.L.R. 335. The remedy is not available against a mortgagee if the refusal is made in good faith under a claim that the tender is insufficient. Shelton v. Wilson, 1936, 274 Mich. 433, 264 N.W. 854. Cf. § 293, note 18, supra. Such statutes apply only to cases of refusal of tender and is not available to clear title on the basis of a prior payment or presumption of payment. Re Katzowitz, 1925, 214 App.Div. 429, 212 N.Y.S. 336; Turnbull v. Mann, 1897, 94 Va. 182, 26 S.E. 510. The Virginia statute was amended so as to cover such cases. See Va. Code of 1942, § 6456; Turnbull v. Mann, 1899, 99 Va. 41, 37 S.E. 288.

35. See § 293, note 18, supra.

gagee answers the second objection.[36] Additionally, if the foreclosure is by court action he always can end it by paying into court the amount of the debt.

The strongest argument in favor of the majority rule was advanced in the leading case for the doctrine. The court said, "It is not perceived how the mortgagee is to be embarrassed, or his security impaired by the adoption of this rule. * * * If the mortgagor does not tender the full amount due, the lien of the mortgage is not extinguished. The mortgagee runs no risk in accepting the tender. If it is the full amount due, his mortgage lien is extinguished. * * * His acceptance of the money tendered, if inadequate and less than the amount actually due, only extinguishes the lien pro tanto, and the mortgage remains intact for the residue." [37]

In general this statement is correct [38] and provides a sufficient answer to the claim that the rule is unfair in contrast to the rule of discharge by tender on the law day because at that time the mortgagee would "have anticipated payment and * * * have prepared himself to state the account accurately" [39] whereas at a later time he might be ready with an exact computation of the amount due at that particular moment.[40] However, this is not the only question. The real question is whether, even if the mortgagee will not be harmed by taking whatever payment is offered, the penalty for his failure to do so should be the harsh and drastic one of losing his substantive rights in the security.

Even courts in which the majority rule is thoroughly established have placed far-reaching restrictions upon the doctrine.[41] The most important of these has already been mentioned. It is the generally held rule that if the mortgagor is seeking affirmative relief, e. g., to remove the cloud of the mortgage on his title or to restrain the exercise of a power of sale, he must "do equity" by paying the principal and, at least, the interest and costs accruing up to the time of tender.[42] In addition, the mortgagee's refusal must be absolute and not in good faith; [43] the proof of a proper tender must be very clear and satisfactory; [44] and the tender must be unconditional, although on this last point there is a dispute.[45] Furthermore only the mortgagor or an assuming grantee can take advantage of the rule; a non-assuming grantee, even though he takes subject to the mortgage cannot.[46] Also, unless the tender

---

36. Such an action could stop a foreclosure under a power of sale and would forestall a court foreclosure action by the mortgagee.

37. Kortright v. Cady, 1860, 21 N.Y. 343, 354.

38. It has been pointed out that this is not so in a jurisdiction where tender is not invalidated by a demand for a receipt of payment in full. See 1934, 93 A.L.R. 12, 20. See note 45, infra.

39. Crain v. McGoon, 1877, 86 Ill. 431, 434, 29 Am. Rep. 37.

40. See Hudson Bros. Commission Co. v. Glencoe Sand & Gravel Co., 1897, 140 Mo. 103, 41 S.W. 450, 62 Am.St.Rep. 722; Crain v. McGoon, note 39, supra.

41. "This rule, though logical and well supported by authority, is a harsh one, penal in its nature, and courts have shown no disposition to extend it. * * * In order to discharge the lien of the mortgage, the proof must be clear that the refusal was palpably unreasonable, absolute, arbitrary and unaccompanied by any bona fide though mistaken claim of right." Easton v. Littooy, 1916, 91 Wash. 648, 654, 158 P. 531, 533. See Harris v. Jex, N.Y. 1873, 66 Barb. 232, affirmed 55 N.Y. 421, 14 Am. Rep. 285; 1934, 93 A.L.R. 13, 66—accord. See note 1910, 10 Col.L.Rev. 252; 1934, 93 A.L.R. 13, 19. See also notes, 1888, 27 Cent.L.J. 55; 1877, 3 So.L.Rev.,N.S., 767; 1903, 16 Harv.L.Rev. 526; 1896, 33 L.R.A. 231; 1908, 8 Ann.Cas. 363; 1910, 28 L.R.A.,N.S., 998. And see Wickhem, Tender in Security Transactions, 1942, 27 Iowa L.Rev. 579, 589 et seq., for an additional discussion of the doctrine.

42. Note 33, supra.

43. Myer v. Hart, 1879, 40 Mich. 517, 29 Am.Rep. 553; see Lanier v. Mandeville Mills, 1937, 183 Ga. 716, 720, 189 S.E. 532, 535. Cf. Easton v. Littooy, 1916, 91 Wash. 648, 654, 158 P. 531, 533. See 1934, 93 A.L.R. 12, 67.

44. See Engle v. Hall, 1880, 45 Mich. 57, 58, 7 N.W. 239; Hayward v. Chase, 1914, 181 Mich. 614, 618, 148 N.W. 214, 215–216.

45. There is some authority that a tender on condition that the mortgagee give a release or a receipt in full is effective to discharge the mortgage. E. g., Wallowa Lake Amusement Co. v. Hamilton, 1914, 70 Or. 433, 142 P. 321. See 1934, 93 A.L.R. 12, 74.

46. Harris v. Jex, N.Y.1873, 66 Barb. 232, affirmed 55 N.Y. 421, 14 Am.R. 285. See L.R.A.,1918C, 186,

is kept good, the mortgagor must pay interest accruing thereafter.[47]

Similar to the last requirement is the rule in some states that for a tender to discharge a mortgage when it is refused it must be kept good.[48] There is some authority that seems to limit this requirement to a tender after the law day[49] but the English law[50] and some American cases apply it to a tender on the law day.[51] It has been argued that such a requirement is in effect a negation of the rule that tender will operate to discharge a mortgage because until "some action has been brought arising out of the debt or the mortgage and it is shown that the tender has been kept good and the money has been paid into court"[52] the lien cannot be regarded as

discharged. The obvious answer is that the same could be said of the requirement of a tender *simpliciter*. Until the fact has been established by an action, it cannot be said with certainty that it has discharged the mortgage even if such was all that the law requires. Of greater validity is the observation that if this is made a requirement, so far as the mortgagor is concerned, the rule operates in substantially the same way as that in title states which says that the mortgage persists in spite of a tender after default until ended by an action to redeem in which he must tender payment.[53] There is one difference which the statement does not take into account. The tender and payment into court will operate to end all power of the mortgagee to foreclose the mortgage without the mortgagor taking any additional affirmative action. Under the other rule the mortgagor must actively bring an action to redeem or to clear his title. The difference is not, however, substantial.[54] If the mortgagor has to put up his money he will want to go ahead and finish the business which will necessitate bringing suit. And even though the act of tendering followed by payment into court may have destroyed a mortgagee's rights, court action is frequently necessary to prevent the attempted exercise of voided rights by persons who persist in asserting them notwithstanding.

What should be the rule as to the effect of tender which is refused upon the mortgage?

If the technical structure of the mortgage security is disregarded and only the substantial merits of the proposition[55] is looked at, it would be difficult to find any justification

As to the place of tender and party to whom it should be made, see Weyand v. Park Terrace Co., 1911, 202 N.Y. 231, 95 N.E. 723, 36 L.R.A.,N.S., 308, Ann.Cas.1912D, 1010; Hopkins Mfg. Co. v. Ketterer, 1912, 237 Pa. 285, 85 A. 421, Ann.Cas.1914B, 558.

Bowman v. Poole, 1956, 212 Ga. 261, 91 S.E.2d 770, noted by Loiseaux, Security Transactions, in Annual Survey of Georgia Law, June 1, 1955–June 1, 1956, 1956, 8 Mercer L.Rev. 144, 150, held that a second mortgagee by a proper tender which was refused could discharge a first mortgage.

47. Nelson v. Loder, 1892, 132 N.Y. 288, 30 N.E. 369. See 1934, 93 A.L.R. 12, 53; 1930, 39 Yale L.J. 434, 435.

48. Crain v. McGoon, 1877, 86 Ill. 431, 29 Am.Rep. 37; "In order that the tender may extinguish the mortgage lien, it must be kept up, * * * which is practically much the same thing as a bill in equity by the mortgagor or those holding under him to redeem." Knollenberg v. Nixon, 1902, 171 Mo. 445, 455, 72 S.W. 41, 44, 94 Am.St.Rep. 790. See Williston, Contracts, Rev.Ed., § 1816; 1921, 12 A.L.R. 938; 1934, 93 A.L.R. 12, 50. Cf., Nelson v. Loder, 1892, 132 N.Y. 288, 30 N.E. 369, tender must be kept good to prevent liability for subsequently accruing interest.

49. E.g., Crain v. McGoon, 1877, 86 Ill. 431, 29 Am. Rep. 37. See Wickhem, Tender in Security Transactions, 1942, 27 Iowa L.Rev. 579, 594; 1934, 93 A. L.R. 12, 52.

50. See cases § 294, note 22.

51. E.g., see White v. Eddy, 1919, 202 Ala. 672, 81 So. 628. But see, Mitchell v. Roberts, C.C.A.Ark. 1883, 17 F. 776, 5 McCrary 425; Balme v. Wambaugh, 1870, 16 Minn. 116, Gil. 106. See also Storke and Sears, Discharge of Security Transactions, 1954, 26 Rocky Mt.L.Rev. 115, 123.

52. 1934, 93 A.L.R. 12, 50.

53. Idem.

54. See quotation from Knollenberg v. Nixon, note 48, supra.

55. It is admitted that most of the cases base their conclusions not upon the substantive merits of the different rules, but on the location of title and the mechanics of the different technical legal structure of the security interests. See 1934, 93 A.L.R. 12, 15.

for differentiating between the effect of a tender on and tender after the law day. If tender on the law day, though refused, discharges the mortgage, tender afterwards should have the same effect. The argument that there would be no hardship on the mortgagee if tender is made at maturity because he would be ready with his accounts at that time but that a later tender should not have the same effect because he might not be prepared to accept or reject it then seems sufficiently answered by the quotation [56] from Kortwright v. Cady [57] above. However, tender on the law day, which even in title states extinguishes the mortgage,[58] should be effective to do so only if it is kept good by payment into court or deposit in such form that the mortgagee can always have it. There is no justification in depriving the mortgagee of security unless the mortgagor makes available to him the money which he is bound to pay as a substitute security paid into court.[59] That is the English rule going back to an early chancery case [60] and it is the rule also in some American states.[61] Indeed the English cases [62] and some American cases even in jurisdictions where a tender does not have to be kept good to destroy the mortgage lien,[63] hold that keeping the tender good is necessary in order to stop interest and costs. This rule clearly is justified. The mortgagor should not both be freed from the duty of paying interest on the debt to the mortgagee and at the same time be able to use the money [64] for investment, speculation or any other purpose he may please. It is equally difficult to see why, on the merits of the matter, any distinction should be drawn on this point between tender on and after the law day. The results to the parties are the same in either case.

On the other hand, the decisions denying any effect to a tender after the law day [65] seem equally wrong. Such tender should be valid if kept good, although only if kept good. It is almost universally recognized that it would constitute an unconscionable forfeiture of the mortgagee's rights and unjust enrichment of the mortgagor for a tender which was refused to extinguish the mortgagee's debt claim.[66] To deprive the mortgagee of his security in the land, frequently the only asset upon which he realizes,[67] at least ahead of other creditors as was his right by bargain, is only to a lesser degree a forfeiture.[68] It can be justified only on grounds of injustice to the mortgagor. Certainly there is no injustice in making the mortgagor put up the amount of the debt and interest to the time of his tender if he wishes to stop interest and costs and to have the right to have his property back free of the lien. He clearly owes that amount and, under the decisions of every state, he will have to pay that amount in order to free his land from the cloud of a record mortgage.[69] The only hardship on

56. Note-call 37, supra.

57. 1860, 21 N.Y. 354.

58. See § 294.

59. See Bank of New South Wales v. O'Connor, 1889, 14 A.C. 273, cited note 32, supra.

60. Lutton v. Rodd, 1675, 2 Cas.Ch. 206. See note 50, supra.

61. See notes 48, 49, 51, supra.

62. § 294, note 22, supra.

63. See note 47, supra.

64. See Crain v. McGoon, 1877, 86 Ill. 431, 29 Am. Rep. 37.

65. See note 25, supra.

66. See § 294, note 21.

67. "It is the security on the land, and not the responsibility of the debtor, to which men look in taking mortgages. The facility of transferring real estate and mortgages results, frequently, in ignoring the original mortgagor, and treating the lien on the land as the only thing of real value. To hold, then, that a mere tender, without actual payment, is a discharge of the lien, may sometimes operate very unjustly." Harris v. Jex., N.Y.1873, 66 Barb. 232, affirmed 1873, 55 N.Y. 421. Cf. dissenting opinion in Parker v. Beasley, 1895, 116 N.C. 1, 21 S.E. 955, 33 L.R.A. 231.

68. Shields v. Lozear, 1869, 34 N.J.L. 496, 3 Am.St. Rep. 256; Hudson Bros. Commission Co. v. Glencoe Sand & Gravel Co., 1897, 140 Mo. 103, 41 S.W. 450, 62 Am.St.Rep. 722. See 1934, 93 A.L.R. 23.

69. See notes 33, 42, supra.

him, therefore, is in having to post that money prior to the time when he may wish to bring an action to get back his title free and clear so as to be marketable—for when he brings such an action he must put it up.[70] He may have a legitimate grievance in the slowness of such proceedings and the necessity of having to resort to them. The remedy for this would seem to lie in more expeditious proceedings to clear up his title, and reasonable pressure on the mortgagee to make him accept tender and execute whatever instruments are necessary to that end. The former may be and, by many states, has been provided for by statute.[71] Deprivation of right to interest and costs after tender,[72] and subjecting the mortgagee to an action for damages for unreasonable or mala fide refusal of tender [73] should be sufficient for the latter without shearing away, in addition, the mortgagee's substantive security interest.

STATUTES OF LIMITATIONS

296. The general rule is that the barring of a remedy upon the mortgage debt does not affect the remedies upon the mortgage. A minority view, chiefly in lien jurisdictions, sometimes reinforced by or dependent upon statute, is contra. As in the analogous case of tender, no affirmative relief will be given to a mortgagor without payment of the debt.

The effect of lapse of time upon mortgages is complicated by the separate existence of the mortgage from the debt that it secures [73a] and the availability of separate remedies for the enforcement of each which, in most states, may be pursued independently.[74] The mortgage debt may take several forms. It may be a simple oral or written debt, it may

be in the form of a negotiable promissory note or bond, or it may be a covenant under seal either in the deed or apart from it. Quite commonly statutes of limitations provide longer or shorter periods of time depending upon the character of the obligation. And in this connection a point may be disposed of here. Where a mortgage executed to secure a note also contains a covenant in which the mortgagor agrees to pay the loan even though a shorter statute of limitations has run on the note the mortgagee may still enforce the covenant.[75] The rule illustrates and emphasizes the separate existence of remedies and the rule that barring one has no necessary effect upon another.

The concept of the interest of the mortgagee in the land as giving him legal title or a lien which is accessory to the debt plays another part; for the theory of the effect of the running of the statute of limitations upon a chose in action is quite different from that upon rights in real and personal property.[76] Again the mortgagee has different remedies to enforce his right in the land. He may bring an action at law to recover possession in title states; he may use a bill in equity to foreclose; or he may foreclose by exercising a power of sale contained in the mortgage.[77] The effect of the passage of time upon each one of these is a separate and distinct problem. The barring of the right to recover possession of the land is governed by statutes of limitations and doctrines quite

70. See note-calls and notes 33, 34, supra.

71. See preceding note.

72. Even if tender is kept good the mortgagee loses all interest on his money until he accepts it and puts it to work.

73. See § 293, note 18, supra.

73a. See §§ 102, 103, supra.

74. See Chapter 13, infra.

75. Dinniny v. Gavin, 1896, 4 App.Div. 298, 39 N.Y.S. 485, affirmed 159 N.Y. 556, 54 N.E. 1090; Empire Trust Co. v. Heinze, 1926, 242 N.Y. 475, 152 N.E. 266. See also Harris v. Mills, 1862, 28 Ill. 44, 81 Am.Dec. 259. The mortgagee may foreclose and get a deficiency judgment on the covenant. Holcomb v. Webley, 1946, 185 Va. 150, 37 S.E.2d 762, commented on, 1946, 32 Va.L.Rev. 1043; Guardian Depositors Corp. of Detroit v. Savage, 1938, 287 Mich. 193, 283 N.W. 26, 124 A.L.R. 635, discussed in notes, 1939, 87 U. of Pa.L.Rev. 741; 1939, 37 Mich.L.Rev. 1340.

See also 1911, 31 L.R.A.,N.S., 1013

76. See, e.g., Chapin v. Freeland, 1886, 142 Mass. 383, 8 N.E. 128, 56 Am.Rep. 701.

77. See Chapter 13, infra.

distinct from those covering the debt obligation whatever its form.[78] The former have led to a requirement insisted upon by some courts that, in order to bar a mortgagee's right to possession of the mortgaged property in title states there had to be some act by the mortgagor in the nature of a disseizin.[79] The conception behind the reasoning goes back to the early idea in the common law classical form mortgage that the mortgagor in possession was a tenant of some sort of the mortgagee.[80] The rule seems unfortunate. The time should begin to run on any remedy the mortgagee has to recover possession from the time he may exercise it without injecting into its barring ideas of disseizin or adverse possession.[81] The foreclosure action, being in equity, originally was not governed by statutes of limitations, which applied only to actions at law, but by the doctrine of laches. Even today the same is true in many jurisdictions.[82] And the exercise of a power of sale is a still different problem, as will be seen.

Taking up first the effect of the mortgage debt being barred by the running of a statute of limitations, common law title states must be differentiated from lien jurisdictions.[83] Title states almost unanimously hold that the running of the statute of limitations upon the mortgage debt has no effect upon the existence of or remedies upon the mortgage.[84] Having title, the mortgagee may take possession peaceably or maintain an action of ejectment or writ of entry.[85] This he may do even though not only action on the debt has been barred but an action to foreclose as well, provided the statute of limitations on the remedy of ejectment has not

---

78. Chapin v. Freeland, note 76, infra.

79. "The mortgagee may doubtless treat the possession of the mortgagor as a disseizin. * * * Until this power of election is exercised, the mortgagor is in with the privity and assent of the mortgagee. * * * This, it will at once be perceived, is wholly inconsistent with the idea of an adverse occupation. The mortgagor * * * may, however, give to his possession an adverse character by some unequivocal act, hostile to the title of the mortgagee, and distinctly brought to his knowledge. * * * But the act which is thus to change the character of the possession must be a clear, open, and explicit denial of the mortgagee's title, and a refusal to hold under it, * * * and until such actual disseizin by the mortgagor, or by the election of the mortgagee, the possession is not adverse, * * * and the statute of limitations does not begin to run." Tripe v. Marcy, 1859, 39 N.H. 439, 444. See note, 1931, 25 Ill.L.Rev. 563.

80. See § 5, supra. See also Turner, The Equity of Redemption, p. 97 et seq. And see § 297, infra, note-calls and notes 11, 12, 13.

81. A similar criticism applies to any requirement of adverse possession by the mortgagor in lien states as an ingredient in barring an action of a mortgagee to recover possession. It is, however, proper enough to hold that the statute will not begin to run until a mortgagee may bring his action, e.g., until the period of redemption has elapsed and the mortgagee has received a sheriff's deed. Comstock v. Finn, 1936, 13 Cal.App.2d 151, 56 P.2d 957. See comment, 1937, 25 Cal.L.Rev. 357.

82. The original Limitation Act, 1623, 21 James I, c. 16, did not in terms apply to suits in equity. Today fewer than two-thirds of the states have statutes of limitations for suits in equity. See Walsh, Equity, 474. See also notes, 1905, 49 Sol.J. 181, 201, 215, 233; 1930, 79 U. of Pa.L.Rev. 341; 1929, 77 U. of Pa.L.Rev. 701; 1930, 9 Tex.L.Rev. 93; 1931, 6 Wash.L.Rev. 91. But see Lord v. Morris, 1861, 18 Cal. 482.

83. See notes, 1903, 16 Harv.L.Rev. 445; 1913, 13 Col.L.Rev. 442; 1923, 32 Yale L.Jour. 611.

84. A collection of authorities in 1893 showed that twenty-six states, including both title and lien jurisdictions, held that the statute of limitations as to debts did not apply to remedies on the mortgage. Seven states, California, Illinois (title), Indiana, Iowa, Kansas, Kentucky, and Texas held the other way. All but Illinois were lien states. See 1893, 21 L.R.A. 550. In a similar collection in 1946, twenty-eight states are listed as holding that the running of the statute of limitations on the mortgage debt does not prevent foreclosure of the mortgage; fifteen that it does. Of the latter, nine are added to the original group, Arkansas, Colorado, Idaho, Louisiana, Mississippi, Missouri, Montana, Oklahoma and Washington. Of these only Arkansas is a title state. Indiana, originally in the minority list, is listed with the majority. 1946, 161 A.L.R. 886, 887, majority, and 890, minority.

See Note, The Statute of Limitations as a Defense to Foreclosure in Illinois, 1957, U. of Ill.L.Forum 469.

85. Bradfield v. Hale, 1902, 67 Ohio St. 316, 65 N.E. 1008; Taylor v. Quinn, 1941, 68 Ohio App. 164, 39 N.E.2d 627, noted 1942, 91 U. of Pa.L.Rev. 85; Thayer v. Mann, 1837, 36 Mass. (19 Pick.) 535, writ of entry.

run.[86] Or he may maintain an action to foreclose.[87] The reasoning usually is that the statute of limitations bars merely the remedy on the debt, not the right. And it does not purport to affect any other independent remedy on the mortgage or the mortgage itself. The debt remaining, the mortgage continues to secure it and is not extinguished indirectly upon any theory that a destruction of the obligation secured necessarily destroys the mortgage securing it.[88]

The lien states are in conflict. Probably the majority follows the reasoning of the courts in title states. There are independent rights and remedies on the debt and the mortgage lien. Barring of a remedy upon the debt does not affect the debt itself, nor does it have any operative effect upon either the lien or the remedy to enforce it. Consequently the mortgagee can foreclose his lien by court action [89] or by exercising a power of sale contained in the mortgage.[90] And, most strikingly, the same result has been reached in a jurisdiction in which the running of the statute on the debt is regarded as extinguishing it, not merely barring the remedy to enforce it.[91] A number of lien states, however, hold that when the remedy on the obligation is barred the remedy on the mortgage goes with it. The reason usually given is that the mortgage is merely an incident of the debt and should not be enforceable if the debt is not.[92] Where the debt itself is regarded as extinguished by the running of the statute the reason for such a rule is stronger and was persuasive in earlier decisions in a state holding this view.[93] The minority rule has been applied to mortgages by deeds absolute on their face but intended as mortgages.[94] This

86. Bradfield v. Hale, supra note 85; Taylor v. Quinn, supra note 85. As to the right of a mortgagee who has taken possession, see §§ 160–163, supra.

87. Belknap v. Gleason, 1836, 11 Conn. 160, 27 Am. Dec. 721; Elkins v. Edwards, 1850, 8 Ga. 325, and see Ga.Code of 1933, § 67–101; Norton v. Palmer, 1886, 142 Mass. 433, 8 N.E. 346. See 1946, 161 A. L.R. 886, 887. The rule is otherwise in Illinois, an intermediate state. Harris v. Mills, 1862, 28 Ill. 44, 81 Am.Dec. 259; Markus v. Chicago Title etc. Co., 1940, 373 Ill. 557, 27 N.E.2d 436, 128 A.L.R. 567. So too, in Arkansas. Johnson v. Lowman, 1936, 193 Ark. 8, 97 S.W.2d 86. Similarly, a mortgagor's discharge in bankruptcy does not deprive the mortgagee of his right to resort to the security to satisfy the debt. Harlow Realty Co. v. Cotter, 1933, 284 Mass. 68, 187 N.E. 118. See 1913, 42 L.R.A.,N.S., 292, 295.

88. See §§ 99, 102, 103, supra, on the dependence of a mortgage upon the existence of an obligation to secure. See also, 1923, 11 Cal.L.Rev. 429; 1934, 8 U. of Cin.L.Rev. 121, 123. Cf., § 293, supra, on the effect of payment of the debt upon the mortgage.

89. Hulbert v. Clark, 1891, 128 N.Y. 295, 28 N.E. 638, 14 L.R.A. 59; Mich. Ins. Co. of Detroit v. Brown, 1863, 11 Mich. 265; Slingerland v. Sherer, 1891, 46 Minn. 422, 49 N.W. 237.

90. House v. Carr, 1906, 185 N.Y. 453, 78 N.E. 171, 6 L.R.A.,N.S., 510, 7 Ann.Cas. 185; Menzel v. Hinton, 1903, 132 N.C. 660, 44 S.E. 385, 95 Am.St.Rep. 647, nullified by N.C.C.S. § 2589; Grant v. Burr, 1880, 54 Cal. 298. trust deed mortgage. Cf. Faxon v. All

Persons, etc., 1913, 166 Cal. 707, 137 P. 919, L.R.A. 1916B, 1209; Emory v. Keighan, 1878, 88 Ill. 482. See note, 1906, 6 Col.L.Rev. 528. See also 1907, 13 L. R.A.,N.S., 1210.

In Spain v. Hines, 1938, 214 N.C. 432, 200 S.E. 25, criticized in note, 1939, 17 N.Car.L.Rev. 448, under a statute of limitations expressly including the exercise of powers of sale in mortgages, the court held that not only the sale itself but the execution of the deed must take place within the statutory period in order for the purchaser to obtain title sufficient to maintain ejectment against the mortgagor.

91. First National Bank of Madison v. Kolbeck, 1945, 247 Wis. 462, 19 N.W.2d 908, 161 A.L.R. 882.

92. Allen v. Shepherd, 1915, 162 Ky. 756, 173 S.W. 135; see Prewitt v. Wortham, 1881, 79 Ky. 287, 288, 2 Ky.Law Rep. 282; 1943, 32 Ky.L.Rev. 78; Duty v. Graham, 1854, 12 Tex. 427, 62 Am.Dec. 534. See also note 83, 84, supra. And see 1946, 161 A.L.R. 886, 890. Tennant v. Hulet, 1917, 65 Ind.App. 24, 116 N.E. 748, reached the same result but is superseded by Yarlott v. Brown, 1923, 192 Ind. 648, 138 N.E. 17. Cf. 1922, 22 Col.L.Rev. 451. See 1941, 29 Col.L.Rev. 210, on the methods of pleading the statute of limitations as a bar.

93. Pierce v. Seymour, 1881, 52 Wis. 272, 9 N.W. 71, 38 Am.Rep. 737; Eingartner v. Illinois Steel Co., 1899, 103 Wis. 373, 79 N.W. 433, 74 Am.St.Rep. 871; see 1917, 2 Minn.L.Rev. 218, 219. But see note-call and note 91, supra.

94. Kern Valley Bank v. Koehn, 1910, 157 Cal. 237, 107 P. 111; Pratt v. Pratt, 1922, 121 Wash. 298, 209 P. 535, 28 A.L.R. 548, discussed in notes, 1923, 8 Cornell L.Q. 172; 1923, 71 U. of Pa.L.Rev. 284; 1923, 32 Yale L.J. 611. See also 1908, 11 L.R.A.,N. S., 825.

H. K. L. Realty Corp. v. Kirtly, Fla.1954, 74 So.2d 876, noted by Boyer, Real Property Law in Survey of Florida Law: 1953–1955, 1956, 10 Miami L.Q. 389, 391, 407, held that, although foreclosure of a

dependence of the remedy upon the mortgage upon that of the debt is provided for by statute in some jurisdictions which bar a remedy upon the mortgage when that on the debt is gone.[95] This view is accompanied by the rule that if the remedy on the debt is revived the mortgage also will again become enforceable.[96] A different type of statute provides that "a lien is extinguished by the lapse of time within which an action can be brought upon the principal obligation."[97] Under this, a mortgage is destroyed by the running of the statute so that it cannot be revived by any act of the mortgagor although the debt can be.[98]

The trust deed mortgage requires a separate word in connection with the running of the statute of limitations. Although the distinction between a mortgage in such a form and a regular form mortgage has been minimized it has not been obliterated.[99] One of the most important persisting notions is that it, like other trusts, continues until the performance of the trust purpose, viz., the payment of the debt for which the trust was created.[1] One result is that there is no time limit on it [2] except as so specifically provided by statute.[3] Barring of the remedy on the debt has no effect upon the trustee's power to sell the property and pay the debt with the proceeds.[4] And this is true under statutes extinguishing the "lien of a mortgage" when the remedy on the debt is barred, a trust deed mortgage not being a "lien" within the meaning of the provision.[5]

mortgage might be barred by the twenty-five year statute of limitations, the mortgagee could still recover for taxes paid on the mortgaged land. The rule was changed by statute. Fla.Laws 1955, c. 29977; Fla.Stat.Ann. § 95.28.

95. See, e. g., Ark.Dig.Stat., Pope, 1937, § 9465; Iowa Ann.Code, 1897, § 3447, par. 7; § 865, p. 1153, Mo.St.Ann.; Lord v. Morris, 1861, 18 Cal. 482, decided before enactment of C.C.C. § 2911.

96. Schmucker v. Sibert, 1877, 18 Kan. 104, 26 Am. Rep. 765; Schifferstein v. Allison, 1888, 123 Ill. 662, 15 N.E. 275. Cf., Clinton County v. Cox, 1873, 37 Iowa 570, extension. It will not revive to the prejudice of a subsequent grantee. New York Life Ins. Co. v. Covert, N.Y.1859, 29 Barb. 435; see Schmucker v. Sibert, supra.

97. West's Ann.Cal. Civ.Code § 2911. To the same effect are Okla.Stats., Harlow 1931, § 10957; Miss. Code Ann., 1930, § 2290.

For a discussion of the Colorado statute of limitations, see Storke and Sears, Discharge of Security Transactions, 1954, 26 Rocky Mt.L.Rev. 115, 127 et seq.

98. Wells v. Harter, 1880, 56 Cal. 342; Sanford v. Bergin, 1909, 156 Cal. 43, 103 P. 333; San Jose Safe Deposit Bank of Savings v. Bank of Madera, 1904, 144 Cal. 574, 78 P. 5. The destruction of the mortgage by the running of the statute of limitations also destroys any power of sale in the mortgage so that equity, at the request of the mortgagor will restrain an attempted exercise of it without requiring the mortgagor to tender payment to the mortgagee. Goldwater v. Hibernia Savings & Loan Soc., 1912, 19 Cal.App. 511, 126 P. 861, rehearing denied 19 Cal.App. 511, 126 P. 863. And the mortgagor can quiet title against a purchaser under the sale without paying his debt. Faxon v. All Persons, etc., 1913, 166 Cal. 707, 137 P. 919, L.R.A., 1916B, 1209.

99. See § 17, supra, for a brief résumé of the trust deed mortgage, together with references to additional authorities. See also Chapter 13, subdivision D, infra.

1. See Cunningham v. Williams, 1941, 178 Va. 542, 17 S.E.2d 355, "there was no time limit to these trust deeds * * *. They remained in effect until the debt was paid, payment to be established by evidence or by presumption unrebutted."

2. A common expression is "that the statute of limitations never runs against the power of sale in a deed of trust." Bank of Italy Nat. Trust & Sav. Ass'n v. Bentley, 1933, 217 Cal. 644, 20 P.2d 940. See note, 27 Cal.L.Rev. 66, 67. See also Note, Comparison of California Mortgages, Trust Deeds and Land Sale Contracts, 1960, 7 U.C.L.A.L.Rev. 83, 85.

3. There are now a good many statutes declaring that a deed of trust may not be foreclosed after the time that a mortgage, if it rather than a deed of trust had been given to secure the debt, could be foreclosed by action or after the debt it secures is barred by the statute. E. g., Va.Code of 1942, Michie, § 5827; N.C.Code Ann., Michie, 1939, § 2589. See 1943, 21 N.C.L.Rev. 223; 1939, 17 N.C.L.Rev. 448.

4. See Chapter 13, Subdivision D, infra. See also 1956, 58 W.Va.L.Q. 417, commenting on Kuhn v. Shreeve, 1955, 141 W.Va. 170, 89 S.E.2d 685.

5. Grant v. Burr, 1880, 54 Cal. 298; Travelli v. Bowman, 1907, 150 Cal. 587, 89 P. 347; Sacramento Bank v. Murphy, 1910, 158 Cal. 390, 115 P. 232. Cf. Hurley v. Estes, 1877, 6 Neb. 386. Illogically, however, the danger exists that an action to foreclose a trust deed mortgage, brought and prosecuted to judgment after the statute has run on the debt, may, if the debtor or even a grantee pleads the statute, result in the security interest being extinguished. Flack v. Boland, 1938, 11 Cal.2d 103, 77

By the weight of authority even in lien jurisdictions, a mortgagor may not maintain an action to cancel his mortgage or to quiet his title on the ground that the debt secured is barred by the statute of limitations, unless payment of the debt is tendered to the mortgagee.[6] The reason is that the debt is still due, morally and legally, and should be paid before equity will help him.[7] The reasoning

P.2d 1090, discussed in notes, 1938, 27 Cal.L.Rev. 66, 1939, 12 So.Cal.L.Rev. 485. For a discussion of the rule as to the time within which an action for a deficiency judgment must be brought on a trust deed mortgage in California, see Hamaker v. Williams, 1937, 22 Cal.App.2d 256, 70 P.2d 973, noted in 1938, 11 So.Cal.L.Rev. 528.

6. Tracy v. Wheeler, 1906, 15 N.D. 248, 107 N.W. 68, 6 L.R.A.,N.S., 516. Cf. Gibson v. Johnson, 1906, 73 Kan. 261, 84 P. 982; Mitchell v. Bickford, 1906, 192 Mass. 244, 78 N.E. 453. See notes, 1915, 15 Col.L. Rev. 720; 1922, 22 Col.L.Rev. 451 (also discussing the question whether a grantee of the mortgagor may have such relief). See 1946, 164 A.L.R. 1387. But cf., 1950, 7 Wash. & Lee L.Rev. 220. This is true even though the mortgage has been extinguished by the running of the statute. Booth v. Hoskins, 1888, 75 Cal. 271, 17 P. 225; see Faxon v. All Persons, etc., 1913, 166 Cal. 707, 720, 137 P. 919, 924, L.R.A.1916B, 1209. But cf. n. 98, supra. The same is true of deeds absolute on their face intended as mortgages. Sturdivant v. McCorley, 1907, 83 Ark. 278, 103 S.W. 732, 11 L.R.A.,N.S., 825; Doris v. Story, 1905, 122 Ga. 611, 50 S.E. 348; Gallagher v. Giddings, 1891, 33 Neb. 222, 49 N.W. 1126. Moreover, the mortgagor's right to quiet title or redeem may be lost by laches. Miller v. Smith, 1890, 44 Minn. 127, 46 N.W. 324; Green v. Capps, 1892, 142 Ill. 286, 31 N.E. 597. See 1923, 71 U. of Pa.L.Rev. 284. If, however, in an action by a mortgagor to clear the record of a barred mortgage the mortgagee cross complains for a foreclosure it will be denied, which will in effect remove the cloud from the title. Marshutz v. Seltzor, 1907, 5 Cal.App. 140, 89 P. 877; note, 1917, 5 Cal.L.Rev. 258.

For the right of a mortgagee in possession to hold onto it until the mortgage debt is paid although the statute of limitations has run, see §§ 160–162, ante; Stouffer v. Harlan, 1903, 68 Kan. 135, 74 P. 610, 64 L.R.A. 320, 104 Am.St.Rep. 396.

For an application in Idaho of the general rule, see Updike, Mortgages in 1953 Annual Survey of American Law, 1954, 29 N.Y.U.L.Rev. 729, 737, noting Trusty v. Ray, 1952, 73 Idaho 232, 249 P.2d 814.

7. "Common honesty requires a debtor to pay his just debts if he is able to do so, and courts, when called upon always enforce such payments if they can. The fact that the debt is barred by the statute of limitations in no way releases the debtor from his moral obligation to pay it. Moreover, one of the maxims which courts of equity should always act upon is * * * that 'he who seeks equity should do equity.'" Booth v. Hoskins, supra n. 6; Tracy

is the same as in the case previously examined where a tender is held to destroy the mortgage and the mortgagor seeks to clear up the record title.[8]

PRESUMPTION OF PAYMENT

297. Presumption of payment after twenty years lapse of time applies to debts secured by mortgage. Such a presumption may be the basis of affirmative relief to the mortgagor.

Antedating statutes of limitations as to debts was a common law presumption that a bond or judgment had been paid if twenty years passed without recognition of its existence by the debtor.[9] The concept that the mortgagor in possession was a tenant of some sort caused difficulty in applying the same presumption in the case of a mortgage.[10] Early cases [11] holding that it did not were repudiated by later authorities [12] and today it is firmly established that debts secured by mortgages are on the same footing with other demands.[13] There is, however, a

v. Wheeler, 1906, 15 N.D. 248, 249, 107 N.W. 68, 6 L.R.A.,N.S., 516, accord.

8. See § 295, n. 33, supra.

9. See 1919, 1 A.L.R. 781, for an extensive collection of cases on the presumption of payment generally; Wigmore, Evidence, 2d ed. § 2517.

That the presumption does not arise where the holder of a life interest in the mortgage becomes owner of the mortgaged premises during the twenty year period, see Updike, Mortgages, in 1953 Annual Survey of American Law, 1954, 29 N.Y.U.L.Rev. 829, 837, noting Warfield v. Christianson, 1953, 201 Md. 253, 93 A.2d 560.

10. See § 5, supra, note-calls and notes 85–90. See also the history of the doctrine in Howland v. Shurtleff, 1840, 43 Mass. (2 Metc.) 26.

11. Leman v. Newnham, 1747, 1 Ves.Sr. 51; Toplis v. Baker, 1787, 2 Cox, 119.

12. Lord Thurlow in Trash v. White, 1791, 3 Bro.C. C. 289; Christophers v. Sparke, 1820, 2 Jac. & W. 223; Cholmondeley v. Clinton, 1820, 2 Jac. & W. 1. See Turner, The Equity of Redemption, 97.

13. Howland v. Shurtleff, 1840, 43 Mass. (2 Metc.) 26; Spencer v. Hurd, 201 Ala. 269, 77 So. 683, 1 A. L.R. 761; Sheafer v. Woodside, 1917, 257 Pa. 276, 101 A. 753, 1 A.L.R. 775; Levensaler v. Batchelder, 1930, 84 N.H. 192, 150 A. 114; Baent v. Kennicutt, 1885, 57 Mich. 268, 23 N.W. 808; Jarvis v. Albro, 1877, 67 Me. 310; Smith v. Niagara Fire Ins. Co., 1888, 60 Vt. 682, 15 A. 353, 1 L.R.A. 216, 6 Am.St.

divergence of opinion as to whether it is merely a rebuttable presumption of fact with the burden of proof on the mortgagee to establish nonpayment [14] or whether, when the period has elapsed, it is an absolute bar that can be avoided only by a new promise.[15] The latter view is decidedly preferable. It would help to effectuate the policy behind not only the presumption rule but statutes of limitations.[16]

If the debt is paid, the mortgagor is entitled to have his title cleared by reconveyance or discharge on the record.[17] Tender of payment or the barring of the mortgagee's remedies on the debt and mortgage both affords no such basis for affirmative relief, and the same is true if the mortgage is ex-

tinguished but the record of it remains to impair marketability.[18] The reason, as was seen, is that a man should pay the money he justly owes before equity will relieve him. When there is a valid presumption that a man already has paid he should not be forced to make another payment before equity will help him.[19] Nevertheless, there are a number of cases that do not differentiate between the effect of the statute of limitations in this respect and a presumption of payment.[20]

STATUTES OF LIMITATIONS—EFFECT UPON JUNIOR INTERESTS OF TOLLING BY MORTGAGOR

298. Acts of a mortgagor which extend the period of the statute of limitations on the debt do so as to the mortgage on the property in his hands and as against subsequent junior interests by lien or conveyance. Such acts will not remove the bar of the statute as against junior interests acquired after the bar is complete, at least if acquired in reliance upon the bar. As to interests acquired before the mortgagor's act and before the bar is final, the authorities are divided: a majority of courts hold that the act will toll the statute; a minority that it will not.

It is thoroughly settled that any act of a mortgagor which extends the statute of limitations as to the mortgage obligation also extends it as to the mortgage provided he has retained the property unencumbered by junior liens.[21] Where third parties have ac-

Rep. 144; Bowie v. Poor School Soc. of Westmoreland, 1881, 75 Va. 300. For 1951 statutory changes in North Carolina, see 1951, 29 N.C.L.Rev. 408. The presumption cannot arise, obviously, until the end of the twenty year period. Coyle v. Wilkins, 1876, 57 Ala. 108.

14. Sheafer v. Woodside, 1917, 257 Pa. 276, 101 A. 753, 1 A.L.R. 775; Levensaler v. Batchelder, 1930, 84 N.H. 192, 150 A. 114.

Kuhn v. Shreeve, 1955, 141 W.Va. 170, 89 S.E.2d 685, commented on in 1956, 58 W.Va.L.Q. 417. Proof that no payment of principal or interest has been received by the mortgagee during more than twenty years after maturity, does not rebut the presumption of payment. Osborne Estate, 1955, 382 Pa. 306, 115 A.2d 201. See Note, Admissibility and weight of admissions and acknowledgments to rebut presumption of payment from lapse of time, 1956, 48 A.L.R.2d 868. See also Plowman, in Mortgages and Security Transactions, in 1956–1957 Survey of Pennsylvania Law, 1958, 19 U. of Pitt.L.Rev. 292, 294, noting Oaks Fire Co. v. Herbert, 1957, 389 Pa. 357, 132 A.2d 193; see, Secured Transactions, in 1957–1958 Survey of Pennsylvania Law, 1958, 20 U. of Pitt.L.Rev. 371, noting Sandman v. Old Delancy Bldg. & Loan Ass'n, 1957, 184 Pa.Super. 470, 135 A.2d 819.

15. Spencer v. Hurd, 1918, 201 Ala. 269, 77 So. 683, 1 A.L.R. 761; cf. Blue v. Everett, 1897, 55 N.J.Eq. 329, 36 A. 960, affirmed 56 N.J.Eq. 455, 39 A. 765. Bailey v. Blodgett, Del.Super.Ct.1955, 10 Terry 485, 119 A.2d 756, approved by Updike, Mortgages, in 1956 Annual Survey of American Law, 1957, 32 N.Y.U.L.Rev. 789, 791, granted the affirmative relief of compelling record of satisfaction of a mortgage, based upon the theory that the presumption of payment from lapse of time operates upon the obligation.

16. But see Glenn, Mortgages, § 56.

17. See § 293, supra.

18. See §§ 294, 296, supra.

19. Spencer v. Hurd, 1918, 201 Ala. 269, 77 So. 683, 1 A.L.R. 761; Kingman v. Sinclair, 80 Mich. 427, 45 N.W. 187, 20 Am.St.Rep. 522; Short v. Caldwell, 1891, 155 Mass. 57, 28 N.E. 1124; Downs v. Sooy, 1877, 28 N.J.Eq. 55; Gibbins v. Campbell, 1896, 148 N.Y. 410, 42 N.E. 1055.

20. See 1946, 164 A.L.R. 1385, 1388.

21. Colton v. Depew, 1900, 60 N.J.Eq. 454, 46 A. 728, 83 Am.St.Rep. 650; Hansen v. Branner, 1925, 52 N.D. 892, 204 N.W. 856, 41 A.L.R. 814. See Wood, Limitations, 4th ed., § 230; 1926, 41 A.L.R. 822.

On whether the recital "subject to" in a conveyance by a mortgagee-grantor tolls the statute, see Prunty, Review of New York Law, 1952 Mortgages, 1953, 27 N.Y.U.L.Rev. 1096, discussing Shohfi v. Shohfi, 1952, 303 N.Y. 370, 103 N.E.2d 330.

quired junior interests in the property as grantees or lienors, there is great confusion in the cases and lack of agreement as to rationale with the exception of certain propositions.[22] For one thing, the courts generally are in accord that when such persons acquire their rights after the mortgagor has done an act sufficient to extend the period of the statute as to the mortgage debt, it likewise extends the statute as to the mortgage both against the mortgagor and the third parties.[23] And the same is true of an act which revives a debt which had been barred.[24] Again, if the statute has run be-

fore the junior interest is acquired, the mortgagor cannot revive the mortgage as against the third party who may have acquired it on the faith of the bar,[25] even though his act may revive the debt and mortgage as to himself.[26] Further, in the great majority of cases, the courts do not attempt to differentiate between the effect upon the statute of the mortgagor's absence from the state and affirmative acts such as part payments of principal or interest or an acknowledgment of the indebtedness.[27] Beyond this harmony ceases.

Where a junior interest in the mortgaged property is acquired before the statute of limitations has run and before the mortgagor has done any act which extends the statute, and thereafter the mortgagor does such act there are two broad lines of authorities.[28] A minority of courts hold that after

---

In Niehaus v. Niehaus, 1954, 2 Ill.App.2d 434, 120 N. E.2d 66, noted, 1954, 33 Chi.Kent L.Rev. 82, it was held that the mortgagor having departed from the state, the mortgagee, who had taken and kept possession of the premises for over thirty years in an effort to remedy the defaults, was not barred from foreclosure by the Illinois statute of limitations on foreclosure actions. Ricci v. Perrini, 3d Dept. 1955, 285 App.Div. 502, 138 N.Y.S.2d 313, appeal denied 286 App.Div. 894, 143 N.Y.S.2d 654, held that a co-tenant's mortgage payment tolls the statute as to both co-tenants.

Winter v. Kram, Sup.Ct.1955, 140 N.Y.S.2d 126, reversed 3 App.Div.2d 175, 159 N.Y.S.2d 417, discussed by Million, Real Property, in 1955 Survey of New York Law, 1955, 30 N.Y.U.L.Rev. 1565, 1572, held that the bar of a statute of limitations on liens was waived by a conveyance by the mortgagor "subject to [described] mortgages, which are liens affecting the above premises," where the statute had completely run prior to the conveyance.

22. For discussions of the problem and collections of cases on it, see notes, 1936, 49 Harv.L.Rev. 639; 1938, 27 Cal.L.Rev. 66; 1938, 32 Ill.L.Rev. 750; 1909, 9 Col.L.Rev. 718; 1924, 9 Minn.L.Rev. 166. See also 1910, 28 L.R.A.,N.S., 169; 1910, 26 L.R.A., N.S., 898; 1925, 38 A.L.R. 833; 1926, 41 A.L.R. 822, 827, 828; 1936, 101 A.L.R. 337. See additionally Note, 1951, 51 Col.L.Rev. 1031.

23. Newhall v. Hatch, 1901, 134 Cal. 269, 66 P. 266, 55 L.R.A. 673; Palmer v. Butler, 1873, 36 Iowa, 576; First Nat. Bank of Sigourney v. Woodman, 1895, 93 Iowa 668, 62 N.W. 28, 57 Am.St.Rep. 287, modified 103 Iowa 421, 72 N.W. 651, only apparently barred, third party took as security for antecedent debt; Cook v. Union Trust Co., 1899, 106 Ky. 803, 51 S.W. 600, 45 L.R.A. 212. See 1938, 27 Cal. L.Rev. 66, 73. See also 1910, 28 L.R.A.,N.S., 169; 1926, 41 A.L.R. 822, 827; 1936, 101 A.L.R. 330, 338. See Storke and Sears, Discharge of Security Transactions, 1954, 26 Rocky Mt.L.Rev. 115, 131.

24. Clark v. Grant, 1910, 26 Okl. 398, 109 P. 234, 28 L.R.A.,N.S., 519, Ann.Cas.1912B, 505. Contra, by statute, Musser v. First Nat. Bank, 1933, 165 Miss. 873, 147 So. 783.

25. Lord v. Morris, 1861, 18 Cal. 482, decided before enactment of Cal.Civ.Code § 2911; Schmucker v. Sibert, 1877, 18 Kan. 104, 26 Am.Rep. 765; Cason v. Chambers, 1884, 62 Tex. 305; De Voe v. Rundle, 1903, 33 Wash. 604, 74 P. 836; see Kerndt v. Porterfield, 1881, 56 Iowa, 412, 9 N.W. 322. See also 1910, 28 L.R.A.,N.S., 169, 170; 1926, 41 A.L.R. 822, 828; 1936, 101 A.L.R. 330, 343.

"Since the subsequent interest holder may well have extended credit on the expectation that his lien would be the only one on the premises, or purchased the land with the belief that it was free from incumbrance because the senior mortgage appears to be completely barred, it would be unjust to defeat this expectation by allowing the mortgagor to revive the prior lien." Note, 1938, 32 Ill.L.Rev. 750, 751, n. 6.

26. Courts which hold that a mortgagor cannot extend the statute or revive the mortgage as to third parties, recognize that he may do so as to his own interest in the property. Brandenstein v. Johnson, 1903, 140 Cal. 29, 73 P. 744; Colonial & U. S. Mortgage Co. v. Flemington, 1905, 14 N.D. 181, 103 N.W. 929, 116 Am.St.Rep. 670; Cason v. Chambers, 1884, 62 Tex. 305. See 1909, 9 Col.L.Rev. 718, 719.

27. See Wood v. Goodfellow, 1872, 43 Cal. 185, 188. See also 1936, 49 Harv.L.Rev. 639, n. 2. As to the basis for extension because of the mortgagor's absence, see 1933, 46 Harv.L.Rev. 703.

28. In Smith v. Bush, 1935, 173 Okl. 172, 44 P.2d 921, 101 A.L.R. 330, the court listed Utah, Kentucky, North Dakota, California and Arkansas as subscribing to what is herein referred to as the minority view. It gave Kansas, Arizona, Iowa, Maryland, Texas, Nebraska, New York, Minnesota, Mississippi, Vermont, Oregon, and the Supreme Court of the

a third party acquires an interest in the mortgaged property the mortgagor cannot extend or revive the mortgage as to him.[29] The chief argument in favor of this is that it is unfair to allow the mortgagor, after he has conveyed away title or transferred a security interest in the property to another, to increase the burden on the transferred junior interest which he does not own, and an extension of time is an increase of the burden.[30] As applied to a grantee, the point has merit, and a few courts limit the doctrine to such a case.[31] A junior lienor, though, holds through the mortgagor and should be bound by the latter's conduct so far as it affects the first mortgage debt and mortgage.[32] In many cases, however, it is impossible to tell whether the court would distinguish between cases in which the mortgagor has divested himself of all property interest by a conveyance and those in which he has merely subjected the property to another lien.[33] Some cases clearly indicate

no such line of demarcation is drawn.[34] Nor is any distinction drawn between subsequent mortgage liens and any other valid lien (by judgment, attachment, etc.).[35] Additional considerations bolstering the rule are that it enables one taking a junior interest in the mortgaged property to know exactly the extent of the lien; and that there is no hardship on the mortgagee because it does not affect his right to foreclose during the normal period of the statute.[36]

Most minority courts hold that the mortgagee must be given notice of the intervention of the rights of the grantee or the latter will be bound by the acts of the mortgagor. However, the courts generally mention, without distinction, "actual or constructive" notice to the mortgagee [37] and hold that recordation of a subsequent change in the status of the mortgaged property acts as constructive notice.[38] And, occasionally, it is stated flatly that, regardless of notice of any sort to the mortgagee, the mortgagor cannot affect the running of the stat-

United States as adhering to the opposite, or majority doctrine. It cited extensive authorities from the foregoing jurisdictions. See also references in n. 22, ante. But see 1938, 32 Ill.L.Rev. 750, 752, stating that the latter is the minority view. The decisions do not turn upon any technical distinction as to the nature of the mortgage as lien or title. See 1936, 49 Harv.L.Rev. 639, 640.

29. See note 28, supra. See also Storke and Sears, Discharge of Security Transactions, 1954, 26 Rocky Mt.L.Rev. 115, 134.

30. See Lord v. Morris, 1861, 18 Cal. 482, 490; Wood v. Goodfellow, 1872, 43 Cal. 185, 189; Zoll v. Carnahan, 1884, 83 Mo. 35, 43–44; Consolidated Nat. Bank v. Van Slyke, 1925, 27 Ariz. 501, 234 P. 553, 38 A.L.R. 825. See also 1936, 47 Harv.L.Rev. 639, 641; 1938, 27 Cal.L.Rev. 66, 71.

31. E. g., Hess v. State Bank, 1924, 130 Wash. 147, 226 P. 257, 38 A.L.R. 829, discussed in notes, 1925, 9 Minn.L.Rev. 166; 1936, 49 Harv.L.Rev. 639, 642; 1938, 27 Cal.L.Rev. 66, 71, in which the court draws this distinction; George v. Butler, 1901, 26 Wash. 456, 67 P. 263, 57 L.R.A. 396, 90 Am.St.Rep. 756. Cf. Smith v. Bush, 1935, 173 Okl. 172, 44 P.2d 921, 101 A.L.R. 330. See 1938, 27 Cal.L.Rev. 66, 71; 1925, 38 A.L.R. 833.

32. Hess v. State Bank, note 31, supra.

33. See, e. g., 1938, 27 Cal.L.Rev. 69, 70, n. 24. See also 1938, 32 Ill.L.Rev. 750, 752.

34. E. g., see Lord v. Morris, 1861, 18 Cal. 482, 490.

35. Brandenstein v. Johnson, 1903, 140 Cal. 29, 73 P. 744; Watt v. Wright, 1884, 66 Cal. 202, 5 P. 91; De Voe v. Rundle, 1903, 33 Wash. 604, 74 P. 836.

36. See 1909, 9 Col.L.Rev. 718, 719.

37. See, e. g., Boucofski v. Jacobsen, 1909, 36 Utah, 165, 177, 104 P. 117, 121, 26 L.R.A.,N.S., 898.

38. E. g., Filipini v. Trobock, 1901, 134 Cal. 444, 66 P. 587.

"This peculiar extension of the policy and wording of recording statutes, which have usually affected only 'subsequent' purchasers, would seem to cast an unexpected burden upon the mortgagee." Note, 1936, 49 Harv.L.Rev. 639, 642. Where the subsequent mortgagee failed to record and no actual notice was shown, the court refused to allow tolling. Denny v. Palmer, 1901, 26 Wash. 469, 67 P. 268. The court in Redondo Improvement Co. v. O'Shaughnessy, 1914, 168 Cal. 323, 143 P. 538, held that unless a subsequent deed or mortgage is of record, the first mortgagee need take no notice of it or anyone claiming under it notwithstanding that he had actual knowledge of the later instrument, and that the rights of the subsequent party and anyone claiming under him arise only from recordation.

ute in favor of subsequently acquired interests.[39]

The majority view [40] is that any conduct by the mortgagor that keeps the debt enforceable as to him also keeps the mortgage alive as to grantees and junior lienors.[41] These courts argue, technically, that the mortgage is a mere incident of the debt and therefore anything that keeps the debt alive should likewise keep the mortgage alive.[42] The mortgage was not destroyed substantively any more than was the debt. It was

still there. If the remedy on the debt is now available, it is argued, so should be the remedy on the mortgage. In skepticism of the validity of this line of reasoning it is suggested that the remedy on the mortgage was available even though the remedy on the debt was barred. Also the remedy on the mortgage might be barred independently of the barring of the remedy on the debt. And if this be so, the question is asked whether the extension or revival of the remedy on the debt should have any effect upon the remedy on the mortgage.

In addition, the majority urged that any purchaser of a junior interest with notice of the paramount mortgage, actual or constructive, must be regarded as taking subject to the mortgage and all of its incidents including the possibility of extension of the debt by conduct of the mortgagor.[43] Further, the mortgagee should be free to deal with his debtor, the mortgagor, without having the burden of discovering and taking into account, until he is ready to foreclose, persons who might have acquired a junior interest in the property in between the taking of the mortgage and bringing an action to foreclose. And such a rule imposes no hardship on a transferee since it merely continues a claim on the land which was taken into account when he acquired his interest.[44]

STATUTES OF LIMITATIONS—TOLLING BY GRANTEE

299. By the majority, and better view, the statute of limitations cannot be tolled as to the mortgagor by acts of a grantee assuming or taking subject to the mortgage. An assuming grantee can extend it as to himself and the mortgaged property; and, similarly, one who takes subject to the mortgage can extend it as to remedies against the property.

39. See Benedict v. Griffith, 1909, 92 Ark. 195, 199, 122 S.W. 479, 480; Cook v. Union Trust Co., 1899, 106 Ky. 803, 809, 51 S.W. 600, 601–2, 45 L.R.A. 212.

40. See notes 22, 26, supra.

41. Consolidated Nat. Bank v. Van Slyke, 1925, 27 Ariz. 501, 234 P. 553, 38 A.L.R. 825; Smith v. Bush, 1935, 173 Okl. 172, 44 P.2d 921, 101 A.L.R. 330; Hess v. State Bank, 1924, 130 Wash. 147, 226 P. 257, 38 A.L.R. 829, as to junior mortgagee. In many of the decisions in which the junior interest was acquired before the mortgagor's conduct extending the time or reviving the debt occurred and also before the statute had run, the courts are not concerned with whether the mortgagor's act occurred before or after the statute had run. See 1936, 101 A.L.R. 330, 342. In some cases, however, the fact that the tolling occurred after the bar was complete was important in preventing recovery by the mortgagee. Cook v. Prindle, 1896, 97 Iowa 464, 66 N.W. 781, 59 Am.St.Rep. 424. See 1936, 101 A. L.R. 337, 343. Johnson v. Johnson, 1884, 81 Mo. 331, contra. Similarly, the fact that such tolling was made before the bar was complete has been a decisive factor in a few decisions refusing to permit the junior encumbrancer to plead the statute. Kaiser v. Idleman, 1910, 57 Or. 224, 108 P. 193, 28 L.R. A.,N.S., 169. See 1938, 32 Ill.L.Rev. 750, 752; 1925, 9 Minn.L.Rev. 166.

42. Schmucker v. Sibert, 1877, 18 Kan. 104, 26 Am. Rep. 765; Johnson v. Johnson, 1884, 81 Mo. 331; Smith v. Bush, 1935, 173 Okl. 172, 44 P.2d 921, 101 A.L.R. 330; see Clift v. Williams, 1899, 105 Ky. 559, 565, 49 S.W. 328, 329, rehearing denied 105 Ky. 559, 51 S.W. 821. But see Colonial & U. S. Mortgage Co. v. Northwest Thresher Co., 1905, 14 N.D. 147, 103 N.W. 915, 70 L.R.A. 814, 116 Am.St.Rep. 670, 8 Ann.Cas. 1160, criticizing the incident theory as applied to the statute of limitations. This reasoning has not been confined to lien jurisdictions where it is easiest to apply the incident theory. Richey v. Sinclair, 1897, 167 Ill. 184, 47 N.E. 364. See Harris v. Mills, 1862, 28 Ill. 44, 81 Am.Dec. 259. On the other hand the incident theory is not law in one leading lien jurisdiction. Hulbert v. Clark, 1891, 128 N.Y. 295, 28 N.E. 638, 14 L.R.A. 59. And see Colonial etc. Co. v. Northwest Thresher Co., supra.

43. See 1936, 49 Harv.L.Rev. 639, 643; 1909, 9 Col. L.Rev. 718, 719.

44. See Kerndt v. Porterfield, 1881, 56 Iowa 412, 415, 9 N.W. 322, 323. See also 1938, 27 Cal.L.Rev. 66, 71.

Turning around the question in the preceding section, can a grantee or junior lienor of mortgaged property extend the period of the statute of limitations as to the mortgagor by a new promise, acknowledgment of, or payment on the debt? In general, in order for such an act to interrupt or revive the running of the statute of limitations it must be made by the obligor or someone legally authorized to act for him.[45] On this test neither an assuming grantee nor one who takes subject to the mortgage should be able to affect the running of the statute as to the mortgagor. Their obligations, the former binding the grantee personally as well as the land in his hands,[46] the latter binding only the land,[47] are separate and independent and create no power to affect the remedies against their grantor, the mortgagor.[48] Many courts take this view both as to an assuming grantee[49] and one who takes subject to the mortgage.[50] Some courts, however, have held that where a grantee has assumed payment of the mortgage any payments by the grantee are made with the implied authority of the mortgagor and for the benefit of both. Hence these courts hold that interest payments toll the statute on the debt as well as the mortgage and so extends the running of the statute against the mortgagor.[51]

Although a grantee should not be able to bind the mortgagor by any acts that have the effect of extending or reviving the statute of limitations, he clearly should be able to and can bind himself or the property he acquired.[52] If he is an assuming grantee his act will affect his personal liability as well as the time within which the mortgage can be enforced against the property.[53] Indeed, the very act of assuming or of taking subject to the mortgage is one which starts a new period of limitations as to rights against the grantee.[54] A grantee who merely takes subject to the mortgage extends the statute only as to the mortgage on the land.[55]

45. Woodcock v. Putnam, 1907, 101 Minn. 1, 111 N. W. 639; cf., Brooklyn Bank v. Barnaby, 1910, 197 N.Y. 210, 90 N.E. 834, 27 L.R.A.,N.S., 843, reargument denied, 1910, 198 N.Y. 522, 92 N.E. 1079; Vaughan v. Mansfield, 1918, 229 Mass. 352, 118 N.E. 652. See Wood, Limitations, 4th ed., § 101. But cf., Innocenti v. Guisti, 1945, 71 R.I. 274, 43 A.2d 700, 165 A.L.R. 1394, criticized in 1946, 24 Tex.L.Rev. 390, holding application of proceeds of sale of mortgaged property to debt by mortgagee constituted acknowledgment of debt tolling the statute of limitations on the debt as to the unpaid balance.

46. §§ 248, 259, 260–265, supra.

47. §§ 248, 252, 258, supra.

48. See §§ 248, 252, 253, 258, 259, supra. See also cases in following footnotes.

49. Old Alms-House Farm of New Haven v. Smith, 1884, 52 Conn. 434; Trent v. Johnson, 1932, 185 Ark. 288, 47 S.W.2d 12, 80 A.L.R. 1431; Provident Inst. for Saving in Town of Boston v. Merrill, 311 Mass. 168, 40 N.E.2d 280; Regan v. Williams, 1904, 185 Mo. 620, 84 S.W. 959, 105 Am.St.Rep. 600; Frost v. Johnson, 1942, 140 Ohio St. 315, 43 N.E.2d 277, 142 A.L.R. 609; Cottrell v. Shepherd, 1894, 86 Wis. 649, 57 N.W. 983, 39 Am.St.Rep. 919. See 1922, 18 A.L.R. 1027, 1033; 1943, 142 A.L.R. 615, 621. See also 1932, 17 Minn.L.Rev. 97.

50. Home Life Ins. Co. v. Elwell, 1897, 111 Mich. 689, 70 N.W. 334; Fitzgerald v. Flanagan, 1912, 155 Iowa 217, 135 N.W. 738, Ann.Cas.1914C, 1104, noted, 1912, 26 Harv.L.Rev. 89; Turner v. Powell, 1929, 85 Mont. 241, 278 P. 512.

In accord is Winter v. Kram, 2d Dept.1957, 3 A.D.2d 175, 159 N.Y.S.2d 417, approved in Mortgages, in 1957 Survey of New York Law, 1957, 32 N.Y.U.L. Rev. 1426.

51. Biddle v. Pugh, 1900, 59 N.J.Eq. 480, 45 A. 626; Ramsey v. Hutchinson, 1936, 117 N.J.L. 222, 187 A. 650; Guardian Depositors Corp. v. Wagner, 1938, 287 Mich. 202, 283 N.W. 29; Levy v. Police Jury of Pointe Coupee, 1872, 24 La.Ann. 292, and Cucullu v. Hernandez, 1881, 103 U.S. 105, 26 L.Ed. 322, rule derived from Civil Law. See 1943, 143 A.L.R. 615, 623; 1922, 18 A.L.R. 1027, 1035.

52. See Schmucker v. Sibert, 1877, 18 Kan. 104, 112; Daniels v. Johnson, 1900, 129 Cal. 415, 61 P. 1107, 79 Am.St.Rep. 123; 1923, 11 Cal.L.Rev. 429, 431, 432. See also Fourth National Bank in Wichita v. Hill, 1957, 181 Kan. 683, 314 P.2d 312.

53. Daniels v. Johnson, 1900, 129 Cal. 415, 61 P. 1107, 79 Am.St.Rep. 123; Schmucker v. Sibert, 1877, 18 Kan. 104, 112.

54. Hendricks v. Brooks, 1909, 80 Kan. 1, 101 P. 622, 133 Am.St.Rep. 186; Bement v. Ohio Valley Banking Co., 1896, 99 Ky. 109, 35 S.W. 139, 59 Am.St. Rep. 445. See 1943, 142 A.L.R. 615, 616.

For the enactment of a uniform rule for the recording of mortgage discharges in New York, see Curtiss, The Commission and the Law of Real Property, 1955, 40 Cornell L.Q. 735.

55. Curtis v. Holee, 1921, 184 Cal. 726, 195 P. 395, 18 A.L.R. 1024; Fitzgerald v. Flanagan, 1912, 155

Regardless of what theory enables the mortgagee to reach an assuming grantee, the latter's liability [56] rests upon an agreement separate and independent from that of the mortgagor.[57] It arises at the time he enters into his contract of assumption and not before. If at that time the debt of the mortgagor which he assumed was not yet due, no cause of action would arise until maturity although his obligation became binding at the time of his agreement.[58] In such a case the statute of limitations would begin to run on the grantee's obligation at the same time as on the right of the mortgagee against the mortgagor, viz., at time of default at maturity.[59] This is not because there is only one obligation on which both are bound, but because the maturity date of each separate obligation is the same. If the assumption is after maturity, or even after the statute has run on the mortgagor's obligation, the grantee's obligation arises at that time and becomes enforceable at once because his promise is to pay a debt which is then owing. The statute, therefore, starts to run at once.[60]

Where a grantee takes subject to the mortgage instead of assuming it, his agreement confines his liability to the land he bought as a source of payment.[61] Apart from this more restricted coverage, the foregoing also applies to him.[62] Although the mortgagee's original mortgage rights in the land follow it into the hands of the grantee,[63] the latter's agreement that it shall be subject to the mortgage is a new promise in respect to the land which has an effect upon the period for enforcing the mortgage on the land similar to that of an assumption upon the debt period.[64]

MISCELLANEOUS

300. Several methods by which a mortgage may be discharged, besides those covered in the preceding sections, have been dealt with in other chapters. Additionally some courts hold that a levy on a mortgagor's redemption interest by the mortgagee under a judgment on the mortgage debt discharges the mortgage. Other courts, rejecting this result, have reached a variety of solutions.

In addition to discharge by payment,[65] actual or presumed, tender of payment [66] or the running of the statute of limitations,[67] there are various other methods by which the mortgage may be discharged. Several of these have already been sufficiently discussed in other connections, e. g., discharge

Iowa 217, 135 N.W. 738, Ann.Cas.1914C, 1104. See 1943, 142 A.L.R. 615, 619.

56. See §§ 260–264, supra.

57. Schmucker v. Sibert, 1877, 18 Kan. 104; Hendricks v. Brooks, 1909, 80 Kan. 1, 101 P. 622. See note 49, supra.

58. Carnahan v. Lloyd, 1896, 4 Kan.App. 605, 46 P. 323; Bogart v. Geo. K. Porter Co., 1924, 193 Cal. 197, 223 P. 959, 31 A.L.R. 1045.

59. See 1923, 11 Cal.L.Rev. 429, 431.

60. See 11 Cal.L.Rev. 429, 432. In a state like California where the running of the statute on the debt extinguishes the mortgage, a contract of assumption made after the statute is run, although it will be effective as to the debt will not revive the mortgage. Cf., Weinberger v. Weidner, 1901, 134 Cal. 599, 66 P. 869. Of course, if the agreement was one which satisfied the requirements for the creation of a new legal or equitable mortgage in the property it would be recognized as doing so. But it would be a new mortgage on the property and not a revival of the original one. See §§ 68, 124, supra. However, the mortgagee may be able to enforce the mortgage against such a purchaser upon a dubious application of the theory of estoppel or estoppel by deed. Davis v. Davis, 1912, 19 Cal.App. 797, 127 P.

1051; see 1923, 11 Cal.L.Rev. 429, 432. But see idem, 433.

61. Curtis v. Holee, 1921, 184 Cal. 726, 195 P. 395, 18 A.L.R. 1024. See §§ 252, 258, supra.

62. See Schmucker v. Sibert, 1877, 18 Kan. 104, 112

63. See § 248, supra.

64. Curtis v. Holee, 1921, 184 Cal. 726, 195 P. 395, 18 A.L.R. 1024; Fitzgerald v. Flanagan, 1912, 155 Iowa 217, 135 N.W. 738, Ann.Cas.1914C, 1104; see Schmucker v. Sibert, 1877, 18 Kan. 104, 112; cf., Daniels v. Johnson, 1900, 129 Cal. 412, 61 P. 1107, 79 Am.St.Rep. 123.

65. §§ 293, 297, supra.

66. §§ 294, 295, supra.

67. §§ 296, 297, 298, supra.

by extension of time;[68] merger,[69] including cases of conveyances by the mortgagor to the mortgagee [70] and assignments and transfers of the security interest by the mortgagee to the mortgagor or his transferee;[71] change in the form of the debt, including alteration;[72] and reconveyance, release [73] or satisfaction of the mortgage by the holder of the mortgage debt both as to substantive rights in the mortgaged property and on the record.[74] This last is peculiarly a matter of local law governed by the statutes in each state. Provisions for recordation of a reconveyance or release; the execution and recordation of a certificate of satisfaction, usually referred to as a "satisfaction piece" ; the discharge by an entry on the margin of the record signed by the mortgagee, personal representative or assignee; and redelivery of the mortgage documents are common.[75] The right to damages, imposition of criminal penalties and rights of action to compel the execution of acts effective to discharge

the mortgage have been referred to previously.[76]

One additional matter meriting attention here is the effect of levy on a mortgagor's redemption interest under a judgment on the mortgage debt [77] against the mortgagor by the mortgage creditor.[78] One view, and it provides the excuse for dealing with the problem at this point, is that such a levy discharges the mortgage altogether, the execution being regarded as a waiver by the mort-

68.   §§ 269–271, supra.

69.   §§ 272–276, supra.

70.   See § 238, Subdivision C, § 293 n. 1, in addition to §§ 272–276, supra. See also notes, 1947, 4 Wash. & Lee L.Rev. 206 ; 1940, 53 Harv.L.Rev. 502.

71.   §§ 237, 238, 239, supra. Cf. §§ 272–276, supra.

72.   See §§ 102, 105, 124, 293, n. 7, supra. Cf. Packard v. Kingman, 1860, 11 Iowa, 219. See 1903, 58 L.R.A. 788 ; 1924, 33 A.L.R. 149 ; 1935, 98 A.L.R. 843 ; note, 1934, 40 W.Va.L.Q. 280.

73.   See § 66, supra, as to the application of the Statute of Frauds to releases.

74.   See §§ 293–297, supra.

75.   E. g., West's Ann.Cal.Civ.Code § 2938 (see Code Civ.Proc. § 675), entry on margin of record ; § 2939, recordation of a certificate of discharge ; § 2939½, provision for satisfying mortgages by foreign executors ; § 2940, requirements as to recordation of a certificate of discharge ; § 2941, duty to execute certificate of discharge or request for reconveyance or to enter satisfaction of mortgage. Liability for refusal. Delivery of mortgage or deed of trust and note ; § 2941.5, Same. Criminal liability.

For a discussion of the most common methods of discharge of security transactions, with emphasis on Colorado law, see Storke and Sears, Discharge of Security Transactions, 1954, 26 Rocky Mt.L.Rev. 115.

76.   § 293, note 18 ; § 295, note-calls and notes 33, 34, 70–72, supra. See West's Ann.Cal.Civ.Code §§ 2941, 2941.5.

77.   A judgment on the mortgage debt has no effect upon the mortgage itself. E. g., Beckett v. Clark, 1938, 225 Iowa 1012, 282 N.W. 724, 121 A.L.R. 912. See note, 1939, 121 A.L.R. 912. See also §§ 102–105, supra.

78.   The ability of a creditor of the mortgagor to reach his interest in a title jurisdiction is affected by the theory of the mortgagor's interest. After default it is purely equitable and before default it was equitable plus a legal right of entry. Consequently, the ability of and means by which a creditor of a mortgagor could reach his redemption interest was influenced by the scope of the remedies available to reach such interests. For a good résumé of this problem, see Rowley, Execution on the Mortgagor's Interest After Judgment for a Debt Secured by a Realty Mortgage in Ohio, 1930, 8 U.Cin. L.Rev. 359. See McNair v. O'Fallon, 1843, 8 Mo. 188, 200 ; Carpenter v. Bowen, 1868, 42 Miss. 28, 46 et seq. Today, by some form of process, execution or equitable bill, the interest can be reached by a creditor, third party or mortgagee, on a debt other than the mortgage debt. See Wheeler and Durfee, Evasion of Mortgage Moratoria by Prosecution of Personal Remedies, 1935, 33 Mich.L.Rev. 1196, 1197. Cf., § 100, note 72, supra. The inquiry here is limited to the ability of a mortgage creditor to seize it under a judgment on the mortgage debt and, if he can, the effect of doing so. In England there were two difficulties confronting the mortgagee who got judgment on the mortgage debt. After all, he already had legal title and to levy on his own property by having the sheriff seize it on execution would seem most extraordinary. Further, only the writ of elegit was available to reach real property. It gave possession and only half of the income of the land, whereas if the mortgagee entered as mortgagee he got all of it. In America two developments altered this picture. One was the enactment of Stat. 5 Geo. II, c. 7, § 4 in 1732 making land in the colonies subject to execution. The other was the emergence of the lien theory under which the mortgagor retained title and possession, thus making it easier to fit it into ideas of what can be taken on a writ of execution. Cf., the similar problem in the case of a chattel mortgage. Note, 1934, 92 A.L.R. 1277. Cf. also the use of a statutory writ of *scire*

gagee of his lien on the property.[79] Sale under such a levy would, therefore, be free and clear of the mortgage lien and be equivalent to a foreclosure sale under the mortgage.[80] Apart from any objection on the ground that such a result "evades" usual rules of foreclosure procedure,[81] this is undesirable because there would seldom be any notice to purchasers that such would be the effect of the sale,[82] and there would be a consequent sacrifice of the mortgagor's interest greater than usually is the case.[83] This would occur in part because bidding without such notice would be on the assumption that the property was being sold subject to the mortgage.[84]

On the assumption that the levy and sale under it are valid,[85] two other results have been reached. Under both it is further assumed that the sale is of the mortgagor's interest subject to the mortgage. Under the first of these, the buyer takes the property subject to the entire mortgage debt, the proceeds going either to the mortgagor or, if they go to the mortgagee, the mortgagor being subrogated to the mortgage lien to that extent.[86] This solution has been characterized as "obviously absurd". In further criticism it is pointed out that "In working out this analysis, it may be thought necessary to differentiate between purchase by mortgagee, purchase by mortgagor, and purchase by third person, which complicates the absurdity. Further confusion is created by the employment of two sets of assumptions, one for common law and the other for equity."[87] The confusion and uncertainty in possible purchasers' minds tends to affect adversely bidding at such sales with resulting hardship on the mortgagor.[88] Under the other view, the proceeds of the sale are applied in reduction of the mortgage debt with the result that, as the bid increases, the amount

---

facias sur mortgage for the express purpose of foreclosure, discussed, § 316, infra.

See Note, Attachment, garnishment, execution, or similar process on note or bond, not resulting in sale of mortgaged property, as precluding foreclosure of real estate mortgage, 1954, 37 A.L.R.2d 959.

79. "But a mortgage by its very terms becomes extinguished by payment of the mortgage debt. * * * And, as a matter of course, if the land mortgaged be all appropriated on the mortgage debt, the mortgage would be extinguished, though the debt might not all be thereby paid. * * * Our opinion, therefore, is that the mortgage was extinguished by the levy and consequent appropriation of all land mortgaged on the mortgage debt. * * *" Lord v. Crowell, 1883, 75 Me. 399, 403.

See Whitmore v. Tatum, 1891, 54 Ark. 457, 16 S.W. 198, 26 Am.St.Rep. 56.

80. See Wheeler and Durfee, op. cit. supra, note 77, 1199.

81. See Atkins v. Sawyer, 1823, 18 Mass. (1 Pick.) 351, 356, 11 Am.Dec. 188; McNair v. O'Fallon, 1843, 8 Mo. 188, 203; Tice v. Annin, N.Y.1816, 2 Johns. Ch. 125, 129–130; Camp v. Coxe, 1834, 18 N.C. 52, 57.

82. But cf., Whitmore v. Tatum, 1891, 56 Ark. 457, 16 S.W. 198, 26 Am.St.Rep. 56.

83. See Tice v. Annin, N.Y.1816, 2 Johns.Ch. 125, 129; McNair v. O'Fallon, 1843, 8 Mo. 188, 202–203.

84. Wheeler and Durfee, op. cit. supra note 77, 1200.

85. See Whitmore v. Tatum, note 79, supra.

86. See Lumley v. Robinson, 1858, 26 Mo. 364, 368; Tice v. Annin, N.Y.1816, 2 Johns.Ch. 125, 128. See also Tiffany, Real Prop., 3d ed., § 1431.

87. Wheeler and Durfee, op. cit. supra note 77, 1198.

See Camp. v. Coxe, 1834, 18 N.C. 52, 56 et seq.; Tice v. Annin, note 81, supra; McNair v. O'Fallon, note 81, supra. See also Rowley, Execution on the Mortgagor's Interest after Judgment for a Debt Secured by a Realty Mortgage in Ohio, 1930, 4 U. of Cin.L.Rev. 359; note, 1910, 10 Col.L.Rev. 561; Tiffany, Real Prop., 3d ed., § 1431.

"Of course the creditor could not levy on the legal title, because that was his already; and he could not levy on the mere right to redeem, in order to pay the debt, because the right was, in reality, nothing but the privilege of reclaiming the land by paying the debt. The mortgagor's interest in the land was only the residue of his estate that would remain after payment of the debt. Hence to allow the mortgagee to sell it under an execution for that identical debt was tantamount to saying that he might enforce payment of the debt out of what would remain of the property after the debt was paid. The absurdity of such a proceeding is obvious." Editorial note, 11 Am.Dec. 197 et seq.

88. See Tice v. Annin, N.Y.1816, 2 Johns.Ch. 125, 129–130; McNair v. O'Fallon, 1843, 8 Mo. 188, 203. It has been suggested that the doctrine of merger might be invoked to discharge the personal obligation of the mortgagor and so mitigate hardship, "but why permit an irregular procedure which produces such complications?" Wheeler and Durfee, op. cit. supra note 77, at 1199. See Tiffany, Real Prop., 3d ed., § 1431. See also cases note 81, supra.

of the mortgage to which the property in the hands of the purchaser will be subject diminishes, and anything above the amount of the mortgage debt will be for the property free and clear of the mortgage.[89]

The objections to permitting such a levy and sale on any one of the proposed bases are strong and in some jurisdictions, either by statute [90] or decision,[91] they are forbidden or void. In others, although courts will restrain the sale if proceedings are initiated in time,[92] nevertheless if it is not enjoined, it will be valid.[93] The result of the sale, however, in view of the above conflicts and uncertainties, cannot produce a marketable title unless they have been definitely resolved by the highest court in the jurisdiction where the land is.[94]

STATUTORY TRENDS

301. Modern legislation has been enacted which makes the same period of time under statutes of limitations applicable to both debt

and mortgage, shortens the required period, and extends the bar to powers of sale under mortgages and deeds of trust. In addition one new type of statute bars completely for all purposes old mortgages undischarged of record after the lapse of a specified time from the date of maturity or last recorded actual extension. Another, less effective, creates a presumption of payment after the elapse of such a period as to subsequent purchasers and encumbrancers for value and without knowledge.

There are in every state a considerable number of old, recorded mortgages which have never been discharged of record by the formalities required for that purpose.[95] The doctrines examined in preceding sections dealing with the effect of the running of the statutes of limitations [96] and presumptions of payment after lapse of time [97] reveal that it is virtually impossible to tell from the record whether a mortgage is a valid subsisting lien, is barred by the statute of limitations, or has been paid but not discharged of record.[98] Part of this difficulty stems from the existence of separate periods of limitations for the debt and the mortgage and the independence of either in many cases of powers of sale, especially in trust deed mortgages.[99] One statutory trend to remedy this situation has been to enact statutes making the period of the statute the same as to both the debt and the lien so that the elapse of the same amount of time would bar both simul-

89. Tiffany, Real Prop., 3d ed., § 1431; Wheeler and Durfee, op. cit. supra note 77, 1198–1201.

90. See McKinney's Consol.Laws of N. Y., Civil Prac.Law & Rules, § 5236(b), applied by Delaplaine v. Hitchcock, N.Y., 1843, 6 Hill 14; see Palmer v. Foote, N.Y. 1839, 7 Paige 437; Mich.Comp. Laws, 1968, sec. 600.6060(1); Gale v. Hammond, 1881, 45 Mich. 147, 7 N.W. 761; see Preston v. Ryan, 1881, 45 Mich. 174, 7 N.W. 819; Linville v. Bell, 1874, 47 Ind. 547. But cf., Cottingham v. Springer, 1878, 88 Ill. 90.

91. Powell v. Williams, 1848, 14 Ala. 476, 48 Am.Dec. 105; Barker v. Bell, 1861, 37 Ala. 354. See Goring's Ex'r v. Shreve, 1838, 37 Ky. 64; Atkins v. Sawyer, Mass. 1823, 18 Mass. (1 Pick.) 351, 11 Am. Dec. 188; Carpenter v. Bowen, 1868, 42 Miss. 28; McNair v. O'Fallon, 1843, 8 Mo. 188; Lumley v. Robinson, 1858, 26 Mo. 364, when mortgage creditor buys; Camp v. Coxe, 1834, 18 N.C. 52; Simpson v. Simpson, 1885, 93 N.C. 373.

92. Carpenter v. Bowen, 1868, 42 Miss. 28; Van Mater v. Conover, 1866, 18 N.J.Eq. 38; see Lydecker v. Bogert, 1884, 38 N.J.Eq. 136, 140; Tice v. Annin, N.Y. 1816, 2 Johns.Ch. 125, 130.

93. Van Mater v. Conover, supra note 92; see Lydecker v. Bogert, supra note 92; Tice v. Annin, supra note 92.

94. Durfee and Wheeler, op. cit. supra note 78, 1201. "It seems clear, then, that no lawyer should advise such procedure." Ibid.

95. See § 300, note 75.

96. See §§ 296, 298, 299, supra.

97. See § 297, supra.

98. An excellent discussion of the effect of ancient, recorded mortgages upon marketable title and a state by state analysis of statutory provisions dealing with the problem, is contained in Basye, Clearance of Land Titles, Chapter 5. This painstaking work was published in 1953. A 1970 revision has all new and changed enactments. See supra § 293 note 18a. See also a brief survey of several types of remedial statutes, Note, 1951, 51 Col.L.Rev. 1031. As to whether a statutory conclusive presumption of payment applies to deeds of trust, see Hubbard, Deeds of Trust, and Article 66, Section 24, of the Maryland Code, 1953, 13 Md.L.Rev. 114.

99. See § 296, supra.

taneously.[1] And along with this development has gone a tendency to shorten the longer periods applicable in the older statutes to foreclosure actions.[2] However, doctrines of tolling statutes of limitations, or of reviving barred obligations together with the mortgages securing them [3] constitute hazards to title completely outside of the record and unaffected by such changes. Further equitable doctrines limit the employment of statutes of limitations and presumptions of payment to use as a shield and prevent them from being employed as an affirmative basis for clearing title. These added to the difficulties of perfecting a marketable title.[4] To remedy these defects many states have adopted additional legislation. In general the enactments follow one or the other of two main types. It may be in order, however, to utter a word of caution that the language of statutes of even the same type varies and interpretations are not uniform.[5]

One kind of statute, and by far the better, stems back to legislation in Minnesota [6] which was selected by the Commissioners on Uniform State Laws as a model in 1922 for a proposed Uniform Mortgage Act.[7] It provided for the barring of mortgages if they were neither discharged nor extended of record within a period of fifteen years from the date of maturity of the debt.[8] Although this draft was later changed, several states have passed statutes based upon it.[9] The purpose and effect of such statutes was to make the record plus reference to a calendar sufficient to determine whether any old mortgage, un-

---

1. See, e. g., as added by Laws of 1938, c. 499 and amended by Laws of 1941, c. 329, now McKinney's Consol. Laws of N. Y., Civil Prac.Law & Rules, § 213(4); Wis.Stat., 1935, § 330.16. See notes, 1941, 26 Cornell L.Q. 642; Mich.Comp.Laws of 1929, § 13975; 1947, 22 N.Y.Univ.L.Q.Rev. 730. See Campbell, Cases Mortgages, 2d ed., 394, n. 1. See also, Basye, op. cit. supra n. 98, Chapter 5, § 54. Look, too, at N.C.C.S. § 2589 for the North Carolina provision forbidding foreclosure by power of sale when a mortgage or deed of trust is barred. See 1939, 17 N.Car.L.Rev. 448; 1943, 21 N.Car.L.Rev. 223; § 296, supra.

2. E. g., a reduction to six years in New York and Wisconsin and four years in Arkansas, California and Texas. See preceding footnote and Ark.Stats., 1947, Ann., § 51.1103; Tex.Civ.Stats., Vernon, 1947, Art. 5520; Cal.Code Civ.Proc. §§ 337(1), 725a. This last is not applicable to foreclosure of deeds of trust by power of sale. See 1938, 27 Cal.L.Rev. 66, and § 296, supra. But cf. 1938, 11 So.Cal.L.Rev. 528, as to the time within which an action for a deficiency must be brought after such a sale. The six year period still applies to actions on "any mortgage, trust deed or other agreement pursuant to which * * * bonds, notes or debentures were issued" by any corporation. Cal.Code Civ.Proc. § 336a.

3. See §§ 298, 299, supra.

4. See §§ 296, 297, 298, 299, supra.

5. See, e. g., 1949, 174 A.L.R. 652, for the texts of statutes of one type together with decisions interpreting them.

6. Minn.Laws 1909, c. 181, § 1, 2.

7. See 1927, Handbook, Commissioners on Uniform State Laws, § 12, p. 680.
The Act was never adopted by any state and finally was withdrawn. See 1925, 38 Harv.L.Rev. 651, 653. The note contains numerous references to Handbooks of the Commissioners which give voluminous data on existing statutory provisions.

8. See note, 1936, 49 Harv.L.Rev. 639, 643.
Livingston v. Meyers, 1955, 6 Ill.2d 325, 129 N.E.2d 12, commented on in 1956, U. of Ill.L.Forum 143, held that Illinois Rev.Stat. (1953), c. 83, § 11b bars the mortgage lien itself regardless of whether the debt is barred, when twenty years have run after the due date of the last payment, provided that date appears on the face of the mortgage or trust deed mortgage or can be ascertained from its terms and no extension agreement or affidavit by the mortgagee had been recorded.

9. Basye, op. cit. supra, n. 98, lists Colorado, Florida, Georgia, Illinois, Indiana, Iowa, Kansas (in part), Minnesota, Missouri (probably), Nebraska, South Carolina, Tennessee and Virginia in this category.
See Florida's Marketable Title Act: Prospects and Problems, 1963, 18 U. of Miami L.Rev. 103. For New York legislation establishing a procedure for cancellation and discharge of record of outlawed mortgages, see Curtiss, The Commission and the Law of Real Property, 1955, 40 Cornell L.Q. 735, 737–741. See also Updike, Mortgages, in 1954 Annual Survey of American Law, 1955, 30 N.Y.U.L. Rev. 805, 810, noting the construction put on the Illinois statute in Zuks v. Bowne, 1953, 351 Ill.App. 491, 115 N.E.2d 577, and the contrasting attitude of the Florida statute in H.K.L. Realty Corp. v. Kirtly, Fla.1954, 70 So.2d 876. Compare Portnoy v. McFarland, Sup.Ct. 1954, 130 N.Y.S.2d 448, applying the New York statute permitting cancellation of a mortgage on which no payment has been made in six years. As to the 1953 Idaho statute covering the cancellation of mortgages, see Updike, Mortgages, in 1953 Annual Survey of American Law, 1954, 29 N.Y.U.L.Rev. 829, 837. See also Swenson, The Utah Land Title Standards, II, 1955, 4 Utah

discharged of record, constitutes a menace to title, and, also, to protect the mortgagor.[10]

The original draft of the Uniform Act was later watered down so that the mortgage should merely be "presumed to have been paid"; and even so, the presumption operated only in favor of "subsequent purchasers or encumbrancers for value who do not have actual knowledge that the mortgage has not been paid."[11] Statutes framed along the lines of this emasculated version have been enacted in quite a few states.[12] The object of this kind of statute is to permit subsequent purchasers and encumbrancers for value and without knowledge to ignore any mortgage of record after the specified time from its original maturity or recorded notice of some act which has in fact extended the period. They leave the protection of the mortgagor to the older type of statute and do not, even as to the parties they seek to protect, close the door to litigation.[13]

However, statutes of even the first mentioned type could not operate to bar a mortgage with a date of maturity which prevents compliance with the conditions of the statute.[14] The older mortgages are being barred in some states by enactment of stale claim statutes,[15] first in Iowa,[16] then in Illinois,[17] Indiana,[18] Wisconsin,[19] Minnesota,[20] Michigan,[21] Nebraska,[22] and South Dakota.[23] The general terms of these statutes are that to preserve his rights the claimant must file a designated instrument of record, usually a notice of claim, within a specified period, ranging from 30 years in Wisconsin to 75 years in Illinois; or specifying, in the acts of the last three named states, stale items, which, as between vendor and purchaser, shall not be deemed to affect marketability of the title.

L.Rev. 314, 316–321 (discharge of ancient mortgages by lapse of time); See Mass.Ann.Laws c. 260, § 33, added by Acts of 1957, c. 370.

10. "The passing of the statutory period expressly terminated the mortgagee's lien for all purposes. Such a simple and efficient provision ensures a title, the validity of which cannot be controverted after the period, and protects a paying mortgagor whose evidence has been impaired or destroyed." 1925, 38 Harv.L.Rev. 651, 653. See, also, 1936, 49 Harv.L.Rev. 639, 643; Basye, op. cit. supra, n. 98.

11. See 1925, 38 Harv.L.Rev. 651, 653.

12. Alabama, Alaska, Arkansas, Idaho, Kentucky, Louisiana, Michigan, Montana, Ohio, Oregon, South Dakota, and Texas are named by Basye, op. cit. supra, n. 98, as belonging in this group. See, also, 1940, 1 Mont.L.Rev. 74 for a discussion of the interpretation of M.R.C., 1921, § 8267 as amended in 1933; 1947, 25 N.Car.L.Rev. 407, for a statement as to the North Carolina law; 1948, 27 Or.L.Rev. 344, for a comment on the Oregon statute. See Updike, Mortgages, in 1953 Annual Survey of American Law, 1954, 29 N.Y.U.L.Rev. 829, 837, noting Trusty v. Ray, 1952, 73 Idaho 232, 249 P.2d 814, and calling attention to the new statute in Idaho, as to which see note 9 supra.

13. See 1925, 38 Harv.L.Rev. 651, 653; Basye, op. cit. supra, n. 98. The question of knowledge and whether value has been paid are ingredients in the validity of the subsequent taker's title—matters outside the record and subject to dispute. The objection on the score of providing a marketable title is enhanced if the burden of establishing these factors is on the subsequent purchaser or incumbrancer. 1925, 38 Harv.L.Rev. 151, 153.

14. Jentzen v. Pruter, 1921, 148 Minn. 8, 180 N.W. 1004; Kuhn v. Shreeve, 1955, 141 W.Va. 170, 89 S. E.2d 685, commented on in 1956, 58 W.Va.L.Q. 417.

15. Basye, op. cit. supra note 98; Basye, Streamlining Conveyancing Procedure, 1949, 47 Mich.L.Rev. 1097, 1110. See also, A.L.P. § 18.96, note 4 and § 18.96, notes 38–50 infra.

16. Iowa Acts 1919, c. 270, § 1, now, as amended, Iowa Code Ann. 1946, § 614.17, applied in Lane v. Travelers Ins. Co., 1941, 230 Iowa 973, 299 N.W. 553.

17. Ill.Laws 1941, c. 854, § 1, now Ill.Rev.Stat. 1967 (Smith-Hurd Supp.), c. 83, § 10a.

18. Ind.Acts. 1941, c. 141, as amended, Ind. Stat.Ann. (Burns Supp.1947), §§ 2–628 to 2–637. These provisions were repealed by Acts 1963, ch. 369, § 12. The present law, enacted in 1963 is Burns Ind.Stat. Ann., §§ 56–1101 to 56–1110.

19. Wis.Laws 1943, c. 109, now, as amended, Wis. Stat.Ann. § 330.15.

20. Minn.Laws 1943, c. 529; Laws 1945, c. 124; Laws 1945, c. 118, now Minn.Stat.Ann. § 541.023.

21. Mich.Comp.Laws 1948, § 565.106.

22. Neb.R.R.S.1943, §§ 76–288 to 76–298.

23. S.D.Laws 1947, c. 233, see SDC 43–30–1 through 43–30–15.

CHAPTER 12

REDEMPTION

A. FROM THE MORTGAGE

B. FROM FORECLOSURE SALE

A. FROM THE MORTGAGE

NATURE OF REDEMPTION

302. Redemption is the realization of a right to have the title of property restored free and clear of the mortgage, performance of the mortgage obligation being essential for that purpose. It is technically distinguishable from discharging the mortgage of record, recovering possession, etc. It is helpful to distinguish between redemption before and after the law day; and there are certain differences in lien as contrasted with title theory states.

Redemption of land from a mortgage has been defined as the payment of the mortgage debt.[1] Such a definition fails to bring out with sufficient clarity the central idea of the term. A right of redemption is a right to have title to the property which has been given as security restored free and clear of the mortgage lien; redemption is the realization of that right.[2] Performance of the mortgage obligation is essential to redemption [3] but performance alone may not be sufficient. Whether it is or not depends upon the time of performance [4] and the theory of the nature of a mortgage [5] in the particular jurisdiction in which the question arises. Although analytically distinguishable, it also depends upon the state of the record title. That is, the mortgagor may have been restored to his former ownership of the property with the mortgage lien discharged so far as substantive legal interest in the property is concerned.[6] However, the mortgage may still be of record and, until it is discharged

---

1. See Keigwin, Cas.Mortgages, 641.

2. Cf. West's Ann.Cal.Civ.Code, § 2903, "Every person, having an interest in property subject to a lien, has a right to redeem it from the lien, at any time after the claim is due, and before his right of redemption is foreclosed * * *." Idem § 2905, "Redemption from a lien is made by performing, or offering to perform, the act for the performance of which it is a security, and paying, or offering to pay, the damages, if any, to which the holder of the lien is entitled for delay."

3. See note 2, supra.

4. See § 293, supra.

5. See §§ 5, 13–16, supra.

6. See §§ 293, 300, supra.

of record, the mortgagor's former position in respect to his title to the land is not completely reestablished. Consequently, although it may be accurate to say that an action to clear the record title is not technically an action to redeem,[7] its purpose and effect is the same as one.

Pursuing the above analysis further, it seems helpful to differentiate between the right to redemption and what is necessary to realize it before and after breach of condition.[8] Before the law day his right consists in a legal right to have back the property by performance in strict accordance with the terms of his agreement.[9] If he does so perform, or if a performance before the time set is accepted by the mortgage creditor, the estate is automatically restored;[10] the only thing that may be left for the mortgagor to worry about is the state of the record title,[11] possibly some essential documents,[12] or the possession of the land itself.[13] Redemption, however, is complete in both lien and title states.

This right of redemption is in sharp contrast to the situation in title and intermediate states once the law day has passed. What the mortgagor now has is an "equity of redemption" which was created by chancery as was seen in an early section of this book.[14] All legal title is then vested indefeasibly in the mortgagee, and even full performance be-

lately made will not revest it in him.[15] In order for the equitable right of redemption to be realized there must be either voluntary or compelled action by the mortgagee in reconveying the title to the mortgagor and executing, if necessary, any additional writings required to clear the record. If the mortgagor will not act willingly, the mortgagor may bring a bill in equity to compel him to do so.[16] This equitable action to redeem is the one most commonly in mind when both the right to redeem and its enforcement are under discussion. And this is true in lien jurisdictions as well.[17] For, although the mortgagor retains title and payment or even a tender after the law day may wipe out the substantive mortgage lien,[18] in most instances there has not been payment and with great frequency, no tender. And, even if there has been, there is still the matter of the record mentioned above. And so he too resorts to the same sort of bill in equity to redeem or clear the record that the mortgagor in title states employs.[19] There are, it is true, statutory remedies to compel the mortgagee to act when the mortgage debt has actually been satisfied,[20] but even here, the equitable action is the staple remedy.

What, then are the general requirements for redemption? Who may redeem? And how may the right be ended? These ques-

---

7. E. g., Walsh, Mortgages, § 47.

8. See Hanna, Cas. Security, 3d ed., 1088.

9. See §§ 5, 6, 125, 126, supra. In some states this is referred to as a legal right of redemption. For example, it is so by statute in North Carolina. In some states this is called a "legal right of redemption" as contrasted with the "equity of redemption" after default. E. g., N.Car.Code, 1935, §§ 677, 679. Not retained in General Stats.N.C., 1966 and 1967.

10. See §§ 5, 293, supra.

11. See §§ 293, 300, supra.

12. E. g., the title deeds in the case of an equitable mortgage by deposit of title deeds. See §§ 34, 35, supra.

13. The mortgagee may be in possession of the property itself. See §§ 125, 126, 160–162, supra.

14. See §§ 6, 7, supra. See also note 9, supra.

15. See §§ 5, 293, 300, supra.

16. See Durfee and Doddridge, Redemption from Foreclosure Sale—The Uniform Act, 1925, 33 Mich. L.Rev. 825, 826; Coote, Mortgages, 9th ed., 753, 759.

17. E. g., Daubenspeck v. Platt, 1863, 22 Cal. 330.

18. See §§ 293–296, supra.

19. "There is no peculiarity in the laws of this state in reference to mortgages which takes from a mortgagor the right to redeem which exists in other states. * * * Although a redemption may not now be necessary after default in order to repurchase the legal title, it is still an important right in order to have the full beneficial enjoyment of the property." Daubenspeck v. Platt, 1863, 22 Cal. 330, 335.

"A bill to redeem has practically only been a proceeding to remove the incumbrance." Ibid.

20. See §§ 293, note 18; 295 notes 33, 34, 71, 73.

tions are taken up in the following sections. And following that, in a separate division of the chapter, attention will be devoted to the statutory right to redeem from foreclosure sale, a right which must be sharply distinguished from the right to redeem the mortgage itself which is now under consideration.

GENERAL REQUIREMENTS

303. **Apart from statute, a right to redeem is asserted through a bill in equity, the decree of which orders the mortgage creditor to do all acts necessary to discharge the mortgage provided that the redeeming party, within a short period set by the decree, shall pay the amount due. The determination of this sum frequently necessitates an accounting which will be ordered. If the redeeming party fails to pay, his bill will be dismissed and he will be foreclosed.**

The mortgagor is not entitled to redeem before the law day unless the mortgage specifies that he may do so.[21] The idea is that the mortgagee is entitled to keep his investment. And this same notion carries over into redemption after default, the mortgagee being generally entitled to notice before he can be compelled to accept payment. This is in order that he may have a reasonable opportunity to find new, secured placement of his money. In England this solicitude for the mortgagee has resulted in a settled rule that if the mortgagor defaults he must then, in order to redeem, give the mortgagee six months notice or interest for that period in lieu of notice.[22]

A person who desires to assert a right of redemption must do so by bringing a bill in equity.[23] In it first of all he must set forth

the mortgage. Then he must state the facts which show that he is one who is entitled to redeem.[24] Although there is some authority saying that prior to bringing the bill, he must have tendered full performance and so aver in his bill,[25] this is not necessary.[26] Nor is it essential that he make tender or payment into court at the time he brings his action.[26a] He may do so, of course, but it is sufficient that he assert that he stands ready and willing to pay the sum.[27] His prayer then is that, upon such payment, the mortgage creditor shall discharge the mortgage and do any other acts necessary to restore com-

---

21. Brown v. Cole, 1845, 14 Sim. 427; Bowen v. Julius, 1894, 141 Ind. 310, 40 N.E. 700, accord. Cf. Bovill v. Endle [1896] 1 Ch. 648. See note, 1868, 12 Sol.J. 872. See § 294, supra. See also Coote, op. cit. supra note 16, p. 730 et seq.

22. See Coote, Mortgages, 9th ed., p. 732.

23. See Hubbell v. Sibley, 1872, 50 N.Y. 468. See Coote, Mortgages, 9th ed., pp. 745–765. As to the right of a mortgagor to recover possession from a

mortgagee in possession by a legal action rather than a bill to redeem, see §§ 160–162, supra.

24. See Smith v. Austin, 1862, 9 Mich. 465, 474; Dawson v. Overmyer, 1895, 141 Ind. 438, 40 N.E. 1065; Coote, op. cit. supra note 16, p. 715 et seq. See also § 304, infra.

25. E. g., Lumsden v. Manson, 1902, 96 Me. 357, 52 A. 783; cf. Toole v. Weirick, 1909, 39 Mont. 359, 102 P. 590, 133 Am.St.Rep. 576.

26. Daubenspeck v. Platt, 1863, 22 Cal. 330, 334; Aust v. Rosenbaum, 1897, 74 Miss. 893, 21 So. 555; Casserly v. Witherbee, 1890, 119 N.Y. 522, 23 N.E. 1000; Nye v. Swan, 1892, 49 Minn. 431, 52 N.W. 39; Gerhardt v. Ellis, 1908, 134 Wis. 191, 114 N.W. 495; Beach v. Cooke, 1864, 28 N.Y. 508, 86 Am.Dec. 260. But see Higman v. Humes, 1901, 133 Ala. 617, 32 So. 574; Kopper v. Dyer, 1887, 59 Vt. 477, 489, 9 A. 4, 59 Am.Rep. 742; Hudkins v. Crim, 1911, 72 W.Va. 418, 427, 78 S.E. 1043. Tender is, of course, necessary to stop the running of interest. See §§ 294, 295, supra. See also Coote, op. cit. supra note 22, p. 735.

26a. Casserly v. Witherbee, 1890, 119 N.Y. 522, 23 N. E. 1000.

27. Perry v. Carr, 1860, 41 N.H. 371; Casserly v. Witherbee, 1890, 119 N.Y. 522, 23 N.E. 1000; Kopper v. Dyer, 1887, 59 Vt. 477, 9 A. 4, 59 Am.Dec. 742; Powell v. Woodbury, 1915, 85 Vt. 504, 83 A. 541, Ann.Cas.1914D, 606; Bishop of Winchester v. Paine, 1805, 11 Ves. 194.
"A bill to redeem does not proceed upon the ground that the complainant has an absolute right to a reconveyance or a cancellation of the mortgage, because the debt has been paid or extinguished by a tender, but it asks leave to pay it as still existing, and upon leave being granted, the complainant usually is charged with the costs of the action. In case any payments have been made, either directly or from the rents of the mortgaged premises, it is usual to ask that an account be taken, and for leave to redeem by paying any balance that may be found due." Daubenspeck v. Platt, 1863, 22 Cal. 330, 334. See Dawson v. Overmyer, 1895, 141 Ind. 438, 442, 40 N.E. 1065.

pletely the mortgagor's full interest in the property. It may be, and frequently is, the case that the amount due is uncertain and can only be ascertained by an accounting, in which case the bill will ask for one.[28]

Assuming that all of these allegations are established the court will then enter a decree for redemption "on terms." [29] That is, it will provide that the mortgagor may redeem by paying the amount found due plus costs,[30] and fixes a date in the future on or before which the specified payment must be made.[31] The time so allowed is usually six months, but it rests in discretion,[32] and may be more or less as determined by the circumstances of the particular case.[33] And it is further decreed that if the proper payment is made within the time specified the defendant shall discharge the mortgage, give over possession and do whatever else is necessary for a com-

plete redemption.[34] If the mortgagor fails to redeem within the specified time, his bill is dismissed and the mortgagor stands foreclosed.[35] Thus a bill to redeem may turn into a foreclosure and, although this is anticipating a later topic, the reverse also is true. If the mortgagee seeks to foreclose, his bill is granted "on terms", the chancellor again fixing a short day in the future within which the mortgagor may redeem and decreeing that, in default of such redemption, the mortgage be foreclosed.[36]

WHO MAY REDEEM

304. Persons who have an interest in the land as mortgagor, or in privity of title with him, may redeem provided his interest would be prejudiced by foreclosure of the mortgage.

"Any person who may have acquired any interest in the premises, legal or equitable, by operation of law or otherwise, in privity of title with the mortgagor, may redeem, and protect such interest in the land. * * * But it must be an interest in the land, and it must be derived in some way, mediate or im-

---

28. See Daubenspeck v. Platt, note 27, supra. Look at Frost v. Beekman, N.Y.1814, 1 Johns.Ch. 288. See §§ 164–176, supra.

29. See Coote, op. cit. supra note 22, p. 759. See Scott and Simpson, Cas.Jud.Rems. 741 for an old form of decree reprinted from the 7th ed., 1790, London, of Harrison, The Accomplished Practitioner in Chancery, 385. For more modern forms for American use see, 2 Abbott, Forms of Pleading, N. Y., 2d ed., 1918, p. 1843; see also 3 Daniels Ch. 6th Am. ed., 1918; Curtis, Equity Precedents, 1850, p. 87.

30. Ryer v. Morrison, 1899, 21 R.I. 127, 42 A. 509. See Daubenspeck v. Platt, note 27, supra.

31. Collins v. Gregg, 1899, 109 Iowa 506, 80 N.W. 562; Dennett v. Codman, 1893, 158 Mass. 371, 33 N.E. 574; Turner v. Turner, Va.1812, 3 Munf. 66. See also Durfee and Doddridge, Redemption for Foreclosure Sale—The Uniform Act, 1925, 23 Mich. L.Rev. 825, 826.

32. See Perine v. Dunn, N.Y.1819, 4 Johns.Ch. 140, 141; Clark v. Reyburn, 1869, 75 U.S. (8 Wall.) 318, 322, 324, 19 L.Ed. 354.

33. See Perine v. Dunn, supra, note 32. Murphy v. New Hampshire Sav. Bank, 1885, 63 N.H. 362, one year; Taylor v. Dillenburg, 1897, 168 Ill. 235, 48 N.E. 41, thirty days too short, ninety days allowed; Lindsey v. Delano, 1889, 78 Iowa 350, 43 N.W. 218, nine months.

For a description of the right of redemption in Nova Scotia, which is based on Irish practice, as compared with the right under English and Canadian law, see, 1954, 32 Can.B.Rev. 217.

34. See Chapter 11, supra, especially § 300.

35. Flanders v. Hall, 1893, 159 Mass. 95, 34 N.E. 178; Perine v. Dunn, N.Y.1819, 4 Johns.Ch. 140; Bolles v. Duff, 1871, 43 N.Y. 469; Smith v. Bailey, 1838, 10 Vt. 163; Martin v. Ratcliff, 1890, 101 Mo. 254, 13 S.W. 1051, 20 Am.St.Rep. 605; Sloane v. Lucas, 1905, 37 Wash. 348, 79 P. 949. Cf. Carpenter v. Plagge, 1901, 192 Ill. 82, 99, 61 N.E. 530; Stevens v. Miner, 1872, 110 Mass. 57; Cline v. Robbins, 1896, 112 Cal. 581, 44 P. 1023; Hollingsworth v. Campbell, 1881, 28 Minn. 18, 8 N.W. 873; see Turner v. Turner, Va.1812, 3 Munf. 66; Inman v. Wearing, 1850, 3 De G. & Sm. 729. As to the mortgagee's right to strict foreclosure, see Chapter 13, subdivision A, infra, and § 10, supra. The practice sometimes is to order a sale. Meigs v. McFarlan, 1888, 72 Mich. 194, 40 N.W. 246; Fosdick v. Van Husan, 1870, 21 Mich. 567; Ingram v. Smith, 1849, 41 N.C. 97; Turner v. Turner, Va., 1812, 3 Munf. 66. Cf. Odell v. Montross, 1877, 68 N.Y. 499.

36. "This is not a caprice of the chancellor, but is a natural consequence of the fact that either bill brought all the parties before the court and sought a solution of the mortgage relation, which is essentially a relation of suspense, looking toward further adjustments. That redemption has, in either case, the right of way over foreclosure, is a necessary consequence of the doctrine of redemption." Durfee and Doddridge, 1925, 23 Mich.L.Rev. 825, 827, n. 4.

mediate from or through, or in the right of the mortgagor; so as, in effect, to constitute a part of the mortgagor's original equity of redemption. Otherwise it cannot be affected by the mortgage, and needs no redemption." [37] This accurately states the general rule and is supported by numerous cases spelling it out in detail as to particular cases.[37a] Among those falling under the test, in addition to the mortgagor so long as he is living and has not completely divested himself of all interest,[38] are purchasers of the equity from the mortgagor,[39] an heir or devisee,[40] or any other person who succeeds to the mortgagor's interest in the mortgaged property, e.g., a purchaser at an execution or judicial sale.[41] Likewise an owner of a limited interest such as a tenant for life or years,[42] a remainderman or reversioner,[43] one who has dower even though it be inchoate only,[44] or the holder of an easement.[45] Similarly joint tenants and the like may redeem.[46] So too many persons who have become owners of fractional portions of land that are covered by the same underlying mortgage.[47] Junior lienors, whether by reason of a judgment or execution or because of a later mortgagee are also entitled to redemption.[48]

As among several persons who may be entitled to redeem the one whose interest is superior has priority, e. g., a second mortgagee comes ahead of a third mortgagee.[49] Further, "where there are successive mortgages, any subsequent mortgagee may redeem a prior mortgage and every redeeming party is

---

37. Christiancy, J., in Smith v. Austin, 1862, 9 Mich. 465, 474. See also, Dawson v. Overmyer, 1895, 141 Ind. 438, 431, 40 N.E. 1065, "A person can only redeem when he has an interest to protect, and where, without such redemption, he would be a loser."

37a. See text of rest of this section for many examples of the application of the general rule. On dower as a basis of a right to redeem, see Haskins, Dower in Mortgaged Property, 1951, 5 Miami L. Rev. 187, 194. Cf. Gay v. J. Exum & Co., 1951, 234 N.C. 378, 67 S.E.2d 290, noted in, 1952, 30 N.C.L. Rev. 340.

In Ward v. McGuire, 1951, 213 Ga. 563, 100 S.E.2d 276, noted in 1958, 10 Mercer L.Rev. 161, a lessee for a term of ten years with an option to purchase the leased property, which was subject to a mortgage by the lessor, was held to have such an interest in the property that he could make a tender of payment to the mortgagee and thus preclude the exercise of a power of sale.

38. See n. 51, infra.

39. Purcell v. Gann, 1914, 113 Ark. 332, 168 S.W. 1102; Loomis v. Knox, 1891, 60 Conn. 343, 22 A. 771; Dunlap v. Wilson, 1863, 32 Ill. 517; Watts v. Symes, 1849, 16 Sim. 640.

40. Hunter v. Dennis, 1884, 112 Ill. 568; Zaegel v. Kuster, 1881, 51 Wis. 31, 7 N.W. 781; Chew v. Hyman, C.C.Ill. 1881, 7 F. 7; Lewis v. Nangle, 1752, 2 Ves.Sr. 431.

41. Dalton v. Brown, 1917, 130 Ark. 200, 197 S.W. 32; Jackson v. Weaver, 1894, 138 Ind. 539, 38 N.E. 166; Millett v. Blake, 1889, 81 Me. 531, 18 A. 293, 10 Am.St.Rep. 275; Hayward v. Cain, 1872, 110 Mass. 273; Isam Mitchell & Co., Inc. v. Norwach, 1927, 26 Mass. 33.

42. Tarn v. Turner, 1888, L.R. 39 Ch. 456. See Bacon v. Bowdoin, 1839, 39 Mass. (22 Pick.) 401; Lamson v. Drake, 1870, 105 Mass. 564; Hamilton v. Dobbs & Robinson, 1868, 19 N.J.Eq. 227; Wunderle v. Ellis, 1905, 212 Pa. 618, 62 A. 106, 4 Ann.Cas. 806. See also 1925, 39 A.L.R. 1056.

43. Thielen v. Strong, 1931, 184 Minn. 333, 238 N.W. 678; see Coote, Mortgages 9th ed., p. 723.

44. Mackenna v. Fidelity Trust Co., 1906, 184 N.Y. 411, 77 N.E. 721, 3 L.R.A.,N.S. 1068.

45. Dundee Naval Stores Co. v. McDowell, 1913, 65 Fla. 15, 61 So. 108, Ann.Cas.1915A, 387, semble. Bacon v. Bowdoin, 1839, 39 Mass. (22 Pick.) 401, 405.

46. McQueen v. Whetstone, 1900, 127 Ala. 417, 30 So. 548; Titsworth v. Stout, 1868, 49 Ill. 78, 95 Am. Dec. 577; Merritt v. Hosmer, 1858, 77 Mass. (11 Gray) 276; Hubbard v. Ascutney Mill Dam Co., 1848, 20 Vt. 402, 50 Am.Dec. 41.

47. Howser v. Cruikshank, 1899, 122 Ala. 256, 25 So. 206, 82 Am.St.Rep. 76; Douglass v. Bishop, 1869, 27 Iowa 214.

48. See Lyon v. Sandford, 1825, 5 Conn. 544 (judgment creditor); Schuck v. Gerlach, 1882, 101 Ill. 338 (judgment creditor); Hasselman v. McKernan, 1875, 50 Ind. 441 (junior mortgagee); Wright v. Howell, 1872, 35 Iowa 288 (judgment creditor); Long v. Richards, 1898, 170 Mass. 120, 48 N.E. 1083, 64 Am.St.Rep. 281 (junior mortgagee). Cf. Kirkham & Woods v. Dupont, 1860, 14 Cal. 559; Bigelow v. Willson, 1823, 18 Mass. (1 Pick.) 485; Cardwell v. Virginia State Ins. Co., 1914, 186 Ala. 261, 65 So. 80.

49. Wiley v. Ewing, 1872, 47 Ala. 418; Loomis v. Knox, 1891, 60 Conn. 343, 22 A. 771; Moore v. Beasom, 1862, 44 N.H. 215; Wimpfheimer v. Prudential Ins. Co., 1898, 56 N.J.Eq. 585, 39 A. 916.

liable to be redeemed in his turn by those below him, and these latter are all liable to be redeemed by the mortgagor." [50]

As indicated above, only those with an interest in the property that will be prejudiced by foreclosure can redeem. Consequently a mortgagor who has conveyed away or otherwise lost all interest in the property cannot redeem.[51] The same is true of persons who, although they once had an interest giving them a right to redeem have lost it, e. g., a junior lienor which has been discharged.[52] The principle also excludes interests superior to the mortgage from which redemption is sought, e. g., a lien for taxes, a senior mortgage,[53] or the owner of a dower interest not subject to the mortgage.[54] Such interests cannot be affected by foreclosure and therefore give no right to redemption.

Although redemption from a mortgage operates to extinguish the mortgage so far as the mortgage creditor is concerned, it does not necessarily have that effect as regards the persons making the redemption. They may be entitled to keep the mortgage alive for certain purposes, and to accomplish this equity may subrogate them to the rights of the mortgage creditor, or, instead, may order him to assign the debt and mortgage to the one making payment rather than discharging the mortgage as in redemption strictly speaking. The principles governing such rights to subrogation or assignment were considered elsewhere.[55]

AMOUNT TO BE PAID

305. The general rule is that in order to redeem a party entitled to do so must pay the entire mortgage debt. To this there are exceptions.

The mortgagee is entitled to payment in full and to retain his lien on every part of the land until his debt is completely paid.[56] Therefore, in order to redeem, anyone seeking to do so must pay the entire amount to which the mortgagee is entitled even though the redeeming party owns only a fractional part of the property[57] or a limited interest in it as in some of the cases mentioned above.[58] This amount is the mortgage debt,

50. Snell's Equity, 18th ed., 290. "Where there are successive mortgages, the rule in an action of redemption or on foreclosure is that all persons must be made parties who will be affected by the accounts taken in the action. Hence in a redemption action by a puisne mortgagee, not only the mortgagee to be redeemed and the mortgagor, but also all incumbrancers subsequent to the plaintiff, are necessary parties. On the other hand, mortgagees antecedent to the earliest mortgagee whom the plaintiff seeks to redeem need not be joined; though later mortgagees, even if they precede the plaintiff's own mortgage must be joined. * * * These rules are expressed in the maxim, 'Redeem up; Foreclose down;'" Ibid. The foregoing maxim expresses accurately the general principles that one who seeks to redeem must pay off all incumbrances senior to his own and ignore those inferior to it, whereas, in order to foreclose, he must join all interests inferior to his own and, since his action cannot affect them, need not join senior interests. See Cheshire, Modern Real Prop. Law, 4 London ed., 1937, p. 601. Spence asserts that the right of successive mortgagees to redeem is derived from the Roman law. 1 Spence, Equity Juris. 600.

Though a junior mortgagee may redeem when a senior mortgagee is seeking foreclosure, he cannot do so if the senior mortgagee is not; that is, a junior mortgagee cannot, in effect, compel foreclosure by a senior mortgagee. Note, Rights of a Junior Lienholder in Wisconsin, 1959, 43 Marq.L.Rev. 89, 92.

51. Cardwell v. Virginia State Ins. Co., 1914, 186 Ala. 261, 65 So. 80; Phillips v. Leavitt, 1867, 54 Me. 405; Ingersoll v. Sawyer, 1824, 19 Mass. (2 Pick.) 276.

52. Colwell v. Warner, 1869, 36 Conn. 224; Thomas v. Stewart, 1888, 117 Ind. 50, 18 N.E. 505, 1 L.R.A. 715; McHenry v. Cooper, 1869, 27 Iowa 137.

53. See Dawson v. Overmyer, 1895, 141 Ind. 438, 441, 40 N.E. 1065, 1066, "The prior or senior lienholder has no right to redeem from the junior, because it does not protect any interest he has." See also Harwood v. Underwood, 1874, 28 Mich. 427.

54. Opdyke v. Bartles, 1856, 11 N.J.Eq. 133; Huston v. Seeley, 1869, 27 Iowa 183. Cf., Smith v. Austin, 1862, 9 Mich. 465, no interest shown.

55. See Chapter 10, Subdivision A, supra.

56. See Graham v. Linden, 1872, 50 N.Y. 547, 550.

57. E. g., Douglass v. Bishop, 1869, 27 Iowa 217; Street v. Beal, 1861, 16 Iowa, 68, 85 Am.Dec. 504; but cf., Coffin v. Parker, 1891, 127 N.Y. 117, 27 N.E. 814, 3 St.R. 143. See note 47, supra.

58. E. g., Dower: McGough v. Sweetser, 1893, 97 Ala. 361, 12 So. 162, 19 L.R.A. 470; Gibson v. Cre-

or so much of it as may be due, plus interest to the time of redemption, costs and such additional items as the mortgagee may be entitled to add onto his debt, e. g., taxes paid.[59] Nor can the owner of only a partial interest compel the owners of the rest of the property subject to the mortgage to contribute their shares of the obligation at the time of payment. He must advance the whole amount and recover from them later, being granted subrogation to the mortgage lien against them for that purpose as an effective remedy.[60]

The mortgage creditor may, of course, consent to a partial redemption.[61] And the rule goes beyond that, he may *insist* upon only a partial redemption, the right of election as to full redemption or redemption only to the extent of the redeeming party's interest in the

property subject to the mortgage resting with the mortgage creditor.[62] Where the mortgage creditor has become owner of the interest in that part or undivided share of the mortgaged property which is primarily or proportionately bound to discharge the mortgage, the rule that the owner of the other part or undivided interest must pay the whole debt is inapplicable. He may have redemption by paying only the amount that his interest in the property would have to contribute.[63]

As noted earlier,[64] when subdividing is contemplated at the time of the mortgage a section may be inserted in the mortgage providing for it. Some courts have held that the partial release privilege under such a clause is personal to the mortgagor.[65] Others hold

---

hore, 1827, 22 Mass. (5 Pick.) 146; and see note 44, supra. A junior mortgage: Smith v. Simpson, 1917, 129 Ark. 275, 195 S.W. 1067; see Titley v. Davis, 1739, 2 Eq.Cas.Abr. 604; and note 48, supra. But cf., Green v. Dixon, 1859, 9 Wis. 485, 489; and see 1931, 25 Ill.L.Rev. 720. Or an owner of a part interest in the right of redemption: Merritt v. Hosmer, 1858, 77 Mass. (11 Gray) 276, and note 46, supra.

59. See § 173, supra. For other things that the mortgagee may add, see generally, §§ 164–176. In the United States a mortgagor, in order to redeem, generally does not have to pay debts other than that for which the mortgage is given as security. Mackenna v. Fidelity Trust Co., 1906, 184 N.Y. 411, 77 N.E. 721, 3 L.R.A.,N.S., 1068, 12 Am.St.Rep. 620, 6 Ann.Cas. 471. See Mahoney v. Bostwick, 1892, 96 Cal. 53, 30 P. 1020, 31 Am.St.Rep. 175. Cf. Brown v. Coriell, 1893, 50 N.J.Eq. 753, 26 A. 915, 21 L.R.A. 321, 35 Am.St.Rep. 789. See also § 124, supra.

Where there has been an extension agreement, junior mortgagees may redeem according to the terms of the original mortgage. Meislin, Extension Agreements and the Rights of Junior Mortgagees, 1956, 42 Va.L.Rev. 939, 940, 951, 953.

Where the amount due is unascertained (the mortgagee having been in possession and being subject to an accounting), the mortgagor may bring an action for redemption and accounting without tender of payment. Gilbert v. Carson, 1957, 213 Ga. 387, 99 S.E.2d 105, noted in 1958, 10 Mercer L.Rev. 161.

60. See §§ 278, 279, 284, 285, supra.

61. Union Mut. Life Ins. Co. v. Kirchoff, 1890, 133 Ill. 368, 27 N.E. 91; Kerse v. Miller, 1896, 169 Mass. 44, 47 N.E. 504. See Quinn Plumbing Co. v. New Miami Shores Corp., 1930, 100 Fla. 413, 129 So. 690, 73 A.L.R. 600.

62. E. g., where the mortgagee has become owner of the redemption interest apart from that share of it belonging to the plaintiff. In such a case, if the plaintiff were required to pay the entire mortgage debt he would at once acquire a right of reimbursement against the mortgagee as owner of the other share of the redemption interest for the amount that share should contribute to the redemption and be subrogated to the mortgage in order to collect it. See § 279, supra; note 60 supra. As a short cut, the rule stated in the text applies. Robinson v. Fife, 1854, 3 Ohio St. 551; Simonton v. Gray, 1852, 34 Me. 50; Gibson v. Crehore, 1827, 22 Mass. (5 Pick.) 146. See Quinn Plumbing Co. v. New Miami Shores Corp., 1930, 100 Fla. 413, 129 So. 690, 73 A. L.R. 600. Cf. Barr v. Van Alstine, 1889, 120 Ind. 590, 22 N.E. 965. But cf. West's Ann.Cal.Code Civ. Proc. § 347.

The same principle has permitted the mortgage creditor a choice between requiring full redemption or releasing from the mortgage the part belonging to the party seeking to redeem or paying its value. Boqut v. Coburn, N.Y.1858, 27 Barb. 230; Wilson v. Tarter, 1892, 22 Or. 504, 30 P. 499. Cf. Mackenna v. Fidelity Trust Co., 1906, 184 N.Y. 411, 77 N.E. 721, 3 L.R.A.,N.S., 1068, 12 Am.St.Rep. 620, 6 Ann. Cas. 471.

Cooper v. Peak, 1952, 258 Ala. 167, 61 So.2d 62, certiorari denied 345 U.S. 957, 73 S.Ct. 939, 97 L.Ed. 1377, rehearing denied 346 U.S. 842, 74 S.Ct. 14, 98 L.Ed. 362, commented on in 1953, 52 Mich.L.Rev. 312, followed the general rule permitting the mortgagee to insist upon a partial redemption.

63. Bradley v. George, 1861, 84 Mass. (2 Allen) 392; Tillinghast v. Fry, 1847, 1 R.I. 53.

64. § 287, note 60, supra.

65. Gilman v. Forgione, 1930, 129 Me. 66, 149 A. 620, unless words "or his assigns" are included; Rugg

that it runs with the land.[66] The latter result is better "since the provision for partial release is made specifically with a view to the sale or further incumbrance of part of the property; and a rule limiting the privilege to the mortgagor will either diminish considerably the sale value of the property, or result merely in the release money changing hands twice." [67]

OMITTED PARTIES

305A. When a person entitled to redeem has been omitted as a party to the foreclosure action, his rights of redemption are the same as before the foreclosure.

Where a person entitled to redeem has been omitted as a party to the foreclosure action, his right to redeem is not cut off [68] as it would have been had he been named a defendant in the suit.[69] So far as he is concerned the foreclosure is void and his rights of redemption are the same as before the foreclosure. The purchaser on foreclosure sale succeeds to the rights of the mortgagee even though the sale is void as to an omitted party,[70] and he also succeeds to the rights of all owners of interests in the property subject to the mortgage who were joined in the foreclosure.[71] If the omitted party is owner of the entire redemption interest, the foreclosure sale is entirely void as to his interest, but the purchaser stands as assignee of the mortgage [72] and subject to an accounting as such.[73] If the omitted party was owner of less than the entire interest, the purchaser acquires the balance of the ownership in addition to the interest of the mortgage creditor.[74] Logically, therefore, he should be sub-

v. Record, 1926, 255 Mass. 247, 151 N.E. 95; Cf. Dimeo v. Ellenstein, 1930, 106 N.J.Eq. 298, 150 A. 675. As to the time within which partial release may be exercised when the covenant for it has no express limitation, see 1938, 24 Iowa L.Rev. 176. Also look at Rosenberg v. General Realty Service, Inc., 1931, 231 App.Div. 259, 247 N.Y.S. 461, commented on in 1931, 31 Col.L.Rev. 894; and 1936, 3 Pittsburgh L. Rev. 71.

66. Gammel v. Goode, 1897, 103 Iowa 301, 72 N.W. 531; Vawter v. Crafts, 1889, 41 Minn. 14, 42 N.W. 483; Rosenberg v. General Realty Service Co., 1931, 231 App.Div. 259, 274 N.Y.S. 461; Kerschensteiner v. Northern Mich. Land Co., 1928, 244 Mich. 403, 221 N.W. 322.

67. 1931, 31 Col.L.Rev. 894, 895. See also Storke and Sears, Transfer of Mortgaged Property, 1953, 38 Corn.L.Q. 185, 211.

68. Quinn Plumbing Co. v. New Miami Shores Corp., 1930, 100 Fla. 413, 129 So. 690, 73 A.L.R. 600; Decker v. Patton, 1887, 120 Ill. 464, 11 N.E. 897; Holmes v. Bybee, 1870, 34 Ind. 262; Arnold v. Haberstock, 1937, 213 Ind. 98, 10 N.E.2d 591, rehearing denied 213 Ind. 98, 11 N.E.2d 682; Peabody v. Roberts, N.Y., 1866, 47 Barb. 91; Mackenna v. Fidelity Trust Co., 1906, 184 N.Y. 411, 77 N.E. 721, 3 L.R.A.,N.S., 1068, 12 Am.St.Rep. 620, 6 Ann.Cas. 471; Monese v. Struve, 1936, 155 Or. 68, 62 P.2d 822; Milmo Nat. Bank v. Rich, 1897, 16 Tex.Civ. App. 363, 40 S.W. 1032; Godfrey v. Chadwell, 1707, 2 Vern. 601. See Haines v. Beach, 1818, 3 Johns. Ch. 459. See Note, Rights of Junior Lienholders in Wisconsin, 1959, 43 Marq.L.Rev. 89, 96.

69. Christ Protestant Episcopal Church v. Mack, 1883, 93 N.Y. 488, 45 Am.R. 260.

70. Robinson v. Ryan, 1862, 25 N.Y. 320; Quinn Plumbing Co. v. New Miami, etc. Corp., 1930, 100 Fla. 413, 129 So. 690, 73 A.L.R. 600. In spite of some authority in New York to the effect that the purchaser on foreclosure sale acquires the mortgagee's interest in the mortgage and the debt as well even though the price he paid was less than the amount of the debt, e. g., Brainard v. Cooper, 1852, 10 N.Y. 356, 359, and see Campbell, Cases on Mortgages, 2d ed., 284 n., the correct rule is, or should be, that the purchaser is entitled "to be subrogated to the place and rights of the mortgagee pro tanto, for the amount so paid to the mortgagee upon the mortgage debt. * * * The residue of the mortgage debt was * * * due to the holder of the bond mentioned in the mortgage." Childs v. Childs, 1859, 10 Ohio St. 339, 346, 75 Am.Dec. 512. Accord: Givins v. Carroll, 1894, 40 S.C. 413, 18 S.E. 1030, 42 Am.St.Rep. 889. See Wells v. Lincoln Co., 1883, 80 Mo. 424. Cf., Collins v. Riggs, 1871, 81 U. S. (14 Wall.) 491, 493, 20 L.Ed. 723. See also 1931, 73 A.L.R. 612, 630, 633, 635; Ann.Cas.1917D, 576.

71. Christ Protestant Episcopal Church v. Mack, 1883, 93 N.Y. 488, 45 Ab.R. 260; Smith v. Shay, 1883, 62 Iowa 119, 17 N.W. 444; Ferguson v. Cloon, 1913, 89 Kan. 202, 131 P. 144, Ann.Cas.1914D, 281; Renard v. Brown, 1878, 7 Neb. 449; Dorff v. Bornstein, 1938, 277 N.Y. 236, 14 N.E.2d 51, motion granted 278 N.Y. 566, 16 N.E.2d 105; Murphy v. Farwell, 1859, 9 Wis. 102. See 1931, 73 A.L.R. 612, 644. See also Chapter 13, Subdivision C, infra. Cf. Brainard v. Cooper, 1852, 10 N.Y. 356.

72. Robinson v. Ryan, 1862, 25 N.Y. 320.

73. See §§ 160–162, 164–176, supra. See also Updike, Mortgages, in 1953 Annual Survey of American Law, 1954, 29 N.Y.U.L.Rev. 829, 935.

74. Mackenna v. Fidelity Trust Co., 1906, 184 N.Y. 411, 77 N.E. 721, 3 L.R.A.,N.S., 1068, 12 Am.St.Rep. 620, 6 Ann.Cas. 471, "The foreclosure passed to the

ject only to a pro tanto accountability as mortgagee in possession. As was noted above, such an omitted party may have to pay the entire debt in order to redeem or he may be granted partial redemption.[75] In either case questions arise as to what proportion of the debt the redeeming party will have to stand out of his own pocket, involving, frequently, the problem of determining the value of his interest.[76] If partial redemption is given, the question arises at once. If the entire debt must be paid, it is postponed only; for the question of his right to contribution from the owner or owners of other portions of the redemption interest may then be raised through subrogation or otherwise.[77]

Where a junior lienor has not been made a party to the prior mortgagee's foreclosure he too has his equitable right to redeem from the purchaser on foreclosure sale. His relief differs, however, from that of an owner in whole or in part of the property itself. "The owner of a junior incumbrance redeems not the *premises*, strictly speaking, but the *senior incumbrance;* and then he is entitled not to a *conveyance* of the *premises,* but to an *assignment* of the security."[78] In order to so re-

deem he must pay the mortgage debt, and not the sale price, regardless of whether the latter be greater or less than the debt.[79] In New York, by reason of an unnecessarily technical interpretation of a statute, it was held in such a case that, although as to the mortgagor and all other parties to the suit the purchaser on foreclosure obtained the equivalent of a fee in the mortgaged property, as to the omitted junior lienor the foreclosure was entirely void and, therefore, the purchaser succeeded merely to the rights of the foreclosing mortgagee. As a consequence the redeeming second mortgagee was entitled to an accounting for profits from the purchaser.[80] The preferable view is that the purchaser acquires in respect to the junior lienor the interests of both mortgagor and mortgagee and so should not be bound to account for the profits during his possession in determining the amount that the junior lienor must pay to redeem.[81] Furthermore, the

---

defendant [purchaser on foreclosure sale] the title of all parties in interest, save that of the plaintiff [owner of inchoate dower, unjoined]"; Catterlin v. Armstrong, 1884, 101 Ind. 258, 263, "The purchaser at such a sale [i. e., foreclosure sale in which a junior mortgagee was not joined] has accomplished nothing more than to acquire and combine the rights and interests of the mortgagor and senior mortgagee. Thenceforth he stands to all intents and purposes in the shoes of both. * * * By his deed he acquired the legal title and right of redemption of the mortgagor. Superadded to these, equity maintains the senior mortgage on foot for his benefit. But neither the rights nor remedies of the junior mortgagee have been meanwhile affected or disturbed in the least degree." See 1931, 73 A. L.R. 612, 644.

75. See note-calls and notes, 57–66, supra.

76. See references to prior discussions in note 60. supra, especially, § 279, ante.

77. See note-call and note 60, supra.

78. Pardee v. Van Anken, N.Y., 1848, 3 Barb. 534, 537. "The owner of the *fee* of the equity of redemption redeems the *land itself*, and the decree in

such case directs the mortgagee to convey all his right and title to the redeeming party, and to deliver over all deeds, writings &c. relating to the same. * * * The difference in the nature of the relief granted, in the two cases, depends on the difference in the nature of the interest held by the redeeming party, which confers on him the right to redeem." Ibid. See Note, Rights of Junior Lienholders in Wisconsin, 1959, 43 Marq.L.Rev. 89, 96.

79. Smith v. Shay, 1883, 62 Iowa 119, 17 N.W. 444; see Collins v. Riggs, 1871, 81 U.S. (14 Wall.) 491, 493, 20 L.Ed. 723; see also Durfee and Doddridge, Redemption from Foreclosure Sale—The Uniform Act, 1925, 23 Mich.L.Rev. 825, 844 n. 58. And see note 58, supra. See also Hanna, Cas.Security, 3d ed., 1016, Note (8), as to whether an unjoined mortgagee should have to pay costs of the prior foreclosure in order to redeem. Compare Gage v. Brewster, 1864, 31 N.Y. 218 with Stanbrough v. Daniels, 1889, 77 Iowa 561. The latter case, representing the majority rule, requires the payment of costs. For a thorough survey of the rights and remedies of junior lienors omitted from prior foreclosure, see note, 1940, 88 U. of Pa.L.Rev. 994. See also Updike, Mortgages, in 1954 Annual Survey of American Law, 1954, 30 N.Y.U.L.Rev. 805, 811, noting Portland Mortgage Co. v. Creditors' Protective Ass'n, 1953, 199 Or. 432, 262 P.2d 918.

80. Brainard v. Cooper, 1852, 10 N.Y. 356.

81. Renard v. Brown, 1878, 7 Neb. 449. See Hanna, Rev. of Glenn, Mortgages, 1944, 53 Yale L.J. 590, 592. Cf., 1940, 88 U. of Pa.L.Rev. 994, 1004.

purchaser on foreclosure sale, whether he be the mortgage creditor or a third party, having succeeded to the rights of the owner of the redemption interest, may, if he wishes, redeem from the junior lienor by paying off his claim and thus get rid of him.[82] And, if the junior lienor does not act to redeem, the purchaser, as assignee of the senior mortgage, which is unforeclosed as to the omitted junior lienor, can foreclose against him.[83]

LOSS OF RIGHT TO REDEEM

306. A right to redeem may be barred in several ways: by foreclosure; by estoppel; or by passage of time provided it (a) constitutes laches, (b) fulfills the requirements of an applicable statute of limitations; or (c) is accepted by courts of equity as sufficient to end the right on analogy to some statute of limitation. The doctrine, given currency by some courts, that the remedies of redemption and foreclosure are reciprocal, is not properly applicable to the time period within which the rights may be enforced.

Foreclosure is the usual method by which a right of redemption is ended.[84] However it may be lost in other ways. Its exercise may be barred by estoppel in cases where its owner by conduct or words has induced some one to purchase or make expenditures upon the property in reliance upon representations that no right of redemption exists.[85] And it may be barred by such lapse of time as makes operative an applicable statute of limitations or a doctrine apart from statute the effect of which is to end the right to relief. As a general rule neither sort of bar will arise if the mortgagor is in possession.[86]

---

82. Smith v. Shay, 1883, 62 Iowa 119, 17 N.W. 444; Renard v. Brown, 1878, 7 Neb. 449; Murphy v. Farwell, 1859, 9 Wis. 102. See Durfee and Dodridge, op. cit. supra note 79. For limitations upon the remedies of an omitted junior lienor, see 1940, 88 U. of Pa.L.Rev. 994, 1005.

83. Quinn Plumbing Co. v. New Miami, etc., Corp., 1930, 100 Fla. 413, 129 So. 690, 73 A.L.R. 600, noted, 1931, 25 Ill.L.Rev. 720; Nelson v. First Nat. Bank, 1925, 199 Iowa 804, 202 N.W. 847; Sears Roebuck & Co. v. Camp, 1938, 124 N.J.Eq. 403, 1 A.2d 425, 118 A.L.R. 762, noted, 1939, 23 Minn.L.Rev. 388.
"If the junior mortgagee had been joined in the original foreclosure, an appropriate decree against it would have been to either redeem or be barred of its right of redemption. The same decree is sought in this bill. Such a decree would not be a decree of strict foreclosure which is unknown to our practice (Browne v. Browne, 17 Fla. 607, 623, 35 Am. Rep. 96), because its effect would be, *not* to divest the mortgagor of a right to redeem the legal title and to vest it indefeasibly in the mortgagee—that title being already in the complainant by reason of its purchase at the foreclosure sale which was valid as against the mortgagor—but its effect would be merely to extinguish a junior lien to which the legal title already in the complainant is subject. Manhattan Bank v. Wamego Bank, 103 Kan. 865, 176 P. 658. Any defense to which the junior mortgagee would have been entitled, had it been joined in the original foreclosure, is open to it here." Quinn Plumbing Co. v. New Miami, etc., Corp., supra.

In New York, before 1924, it was held that a foreclosure must, by reason of statutory provision, end in every case, including that against an omitted junior lienor, by a decree of sale. Moulton v. Cornish, 1893, 138 N.Y. 133, 33 N.E. 842, 20 L.R.A. 370; see Denton v. Ontario Co. Bank, 1896, 150 N.Y. 126, 44 N.E. 781. By an amendment, N.Y.Civ.Proc.Act, § 1082, amended by Laws of 1924, c. 510, now permits strict foreclosure against a second or subsequent lien which has "been matured for at least five years." But see Hanna Cas.Security, 3d ed., p. 996 n. 2. Hanna also cites cases from Indiana, Maryland, Massachusetts, Nebraska, New Jersey, Rhode Island, West Virginia. See further, as to strict foreclosure, Chapter 13, Subdivision A, infra. As to the right of an omitted junior lienor to foreclose his own mortgage, see § 324, infra.

84. See Chapter 13, infra.

85. Purcell v. Thornton, 1915, 128 Minn. 255, 150 N. W. 899; Ferguson v. Boyd, 1907, 169 Ind. 537, 81 N.E. 71. Cf. also Mackenna v. Fidelity Trust Co., 1906, 184 N.Y. 411, 77 N.E. 721, 3 L.R.A.,N.S., 1068, 12 Am.St.Rep. 620, 6 Ann.Cas. 471, where the estoppel idea was used to impose conditions upon the right of redemption by the holder of inchoate dower in the mortgaged property. A right of redemption is not, however, lost merely by abandonment alone. See Purcell v. Thornton, supra.

Munro v. Barton, 1903, 98 Me. 250, 56 A. 844; Kelly v. Hurt, 1875, 61 Mo. 463; Houston v. National Mut. Building & Loan Ass'n, 1902, 80 Miss. 31, 31 So. 540, 92 Am.St.Rep. 565; Ross v. Leavitt, 1900, 70 N.H. 602, 50 A. 110—accord. Cf. Mellish v. Robertson, 1853, 25 Vt. 603.

86. Miner v. Beekman, 1872, 50 N.Y. 337; Sumner v. Sumner, 1926, 217 App.Div. 163, 164, 216 N.Y.S. 389, 390; Knowlton v. Walker, 1860, 13 Wis. 264, 274; Waldo v. Rice, 1861, 14 Wis. 286. Cf. Bradley v. Norris, 1895, 63 Minn. 156, 167, 65 N.W. 357, 359, "If the land remains vacant and unoccupied, when the right of foreclosure is barred, the land remains the property of the mortgagor, for his legal title would draw to it the constructive possession. In that respect the result would be just the opposite

Falling within the latter group above is laches. Prior to the enactment of statutes of limitations applying to actions in equity laches alone affected the time within which such an action could be brought.[37] And laches still continues as a general equitable doctrine which is applicable also to the specific case of actions to redeem from a mortgage.[38] In applying it, a court is bound by no inflexible rules and, looking at the particular circumstances of each case, may deny relief even though the elapsed period is less than that allowed under an analogous statute of limitations, or may grant it even though it is longer.[39] To invoke it, the very staleness of the claim itself may persuade the court that it would be unjust to enforce it, but usually material changes in condition, such as altered value of the property, the state of the evidence or other circumstances must be shown in addition.

More generally equity courts have barred the right to redeem when the mortgagee is in possession by holding that the action must be brought within the time fixed by a statute of limitations which they regard as providing a good analogy. Statutes of limitations on actions at law to recover land or those fixing the time within which an action to foreclose may be brought are the ones usually chosen

for this purpose.[90] But more troublesome has been the character of the possession by the mortgagee required during the period in order for the mortgagor's claim to be ended.[91] On this, the cases divide into two main categories. In one, the mortgagee's possession must be actively adverse in the sense that his holding cannot be considered as being under the mortgage but is in pursuance of acts repudiating the existence of the mortgage relationship and in hostility to any claim to redeem by the other party,[92] and these facts are brought to his actual notice.[93] The bur-

from what it would be under the old common-law mortgage, for under the latter legal title and the right of possession were in the mortgagee."

87. See § 296, note 82, supra.

88. For cases dealing with the matter of laches, see Lucas v. Skinner, 1915, 194 Ala. 492, 70 So. 88; Askew v. Sanders, 1888, 84 Ala. 356, 4 So. 167; Walker v. Warner, 1899, 179 Ill. 16, 53 N.E. 594, 70 Am. St.Rep. 85; Deadman v. Yantis, 1907, 230 Ill. 243, 82 N.E. 592, 120 Am.St.Rep. 291; Chace v. Morse, 1905, 189 Mass. 559, 76 N.E. 142; Hoffman v. Harrington, 1876, 33 Mich. 392; Walker v. Schultz, 1913, 175 Mich. 280, 141 N.W. 543; Cassem v. Heustis, 1903, 201 Ill. 208, 66 N.E. 283, 94 Am.St.Rep. 160; Mahaffy v. Faris, 1909, 144 Iowa, 220, 122 N. W. 934, 24 L.R.A.,N.S., 840; Tukey v. Reinholdt, Iowa, 1911, 130 N.W. 727.

89. E. g., Askew v. Sanders, 1888, 84 Ala. 356, 4 So. 167; Chace v. Morse, 1905, 189 Mass. 559, 76 N.E. 142; see Kelley v. Boettcher, 1898, 85 F. 55, 62, 29 C. C.A. 14.

90. "It is said in 2 Story's Eq.Juris. § 1028(a), that, "in respect to the time within which a mortgage is redeemable, it may be remarked that the ordinary limitation is twenty years from the time when the mortgagee has entered into possession, after the breach, * * * by analogy to ordinary limitations of rights of entry and actions of ejectment.' " Roberts v. Littlefield, 1860, 48 Me. 61, 63.
See also Jarvis v. Woodruff, 1853, 22 Conn. 548. Clark v. Hannafeldt, 1907, 79 Neb. 566, 113 N.W. 135, accord. Bradley v. Norris, 1895, 63 Minn. 156, 65 N.W. 357, "The limitation upon the right to redeem, adopted by this court by analogy, is the statutory limitation on foreclosure by action."

91. See 1934, 20 Va.L.Rev. 464; 1922, 70 U. of Pa.L. Rev. 239; note, 1916, 52 Can.L.J. 414; note, 1917, 53 Can.L.J. 401; Pugh, Some Peculiarities of the Ohio Law of Mortgages, 1930, 4 U. of Cin.L.Rev. 297, 316. See also 1910, 23 L.R.A.,N.S., 754; 1949, 7 A.L.R.2d 1131; note, 1952, 30 N.C.L.Rev. 310.

92. "It is obviously the adverse character of the possession however, and not the mere fact of possession by the mortgagee, * * * that will operate to convert the mortgage title into an absolute one. * * * It is the nature of the mortgagee's occupancy which determines the question of the mortgagor's right to redeem. To constitute a bar to such a right, it must appear that the mortgagee's possession is unequivocally adverse to the mortgagor, or those claiming under him." Munro v. Barton, 1903, 98 Me. 250, 254, 56 A. 844, 846; Arrington v. Liscom, 1868, 34 Cal. 365, 94 Am.Dec. 722; see Grattan v. Wiggin, 1863, 23 Cal. 16, 34; Becker v. McCrea, 1908, 193 N.Y. 423, 86 N.E. 463, 23 L.R.A.,N.S., 754, under statute; Ham v. Flowers, 1949, 214 S.C. 212, 51 S.E.2d 753, 7 A.L.R.2d 1124. See 1949, 7 A.L.R.2d 1131, 1133; Knight v. Hilton, 1954, 224 S.C. 452, 79 S.E.2d 871, noted by Karesh, Survey of South Carolina Law: Security Transactions, 1954, 7 S.C.L.Q. 171.

93. Hurlburt v. Chrisman, 1921, 100 Or. 188, 197 P. 261; cf. Cohn v. Cohn, 1936, 7 Cal.2d 1, 59 P.2d 969. See 1949, 7 A.L.R.2d 1131, 1141.
In Dunham v. Davis, 1956, 229 S.C. 29, 91 S.E.2d 716, commented on by Karesh, Security Transactions, in Survey of South Carolina Law, 1956, 9 S.C.L.Q. 134,

den of proving both the fact of actual hostile holding and notice to the mortgagor are on the mortgagee.[94] In states where the mortgagee has no right to possession,[95] such possession may be initiated when it is taken without the consent of the mortgagor.[96] Where the mortgagee is in possession as a mortgagee, other unequivocal acts of repudiation of the mortgage relation are essential.[97]

The other line of authorities find the possession of the mortgagee for the required period to be sufficient to bar redemption, even though it be rightfully acquired under the mortgage and continued without active repudiation, provided that the mortgagee during that time has made no acknowledgment of the right to redeem.[98] The party seeking to redeem after the end of the period has the burden of showing such an acknowledgment.[99]

Because it has found recognition by some courts it is necessary to note one additional doctrine. It is that the right to foreclose and the right to redeem are reciprocal, and when one is barred, the other is also barred.[1] The mutuality idea is valid to the extent that " 'it shall not be competent for one party alone to consider it a mortgage.' "[2] Thus, if the mortgagee, through possession of the necessary kind, has been freed from an action to redeem by the mortgagor, and then, in order to clear up his title, brings an action to foreclose, this treatment of the mortgage as a subsisting relationship as to him, involves the consequence that it will be treated also as a mortgage in respect to the mortgagor.[3] If, however, a mortgagee or purchaser on foreclosure sale has thus barred the mortgagor's redemption interest, he is not precluded from clearing his title except at peril

---

135, it was held that a mortgagee who bought the mortgaged property at a tax sale got no title by adverse possession because his purchase would be deemed to be for the protection of his lien, and would not, therefore, be such an act by him as to give notice to the mortgagor that he was claiming as owner.

94. See 1949, 7 A.L.R.2d 1131, 1134.

95. See §§ 126, 127, supra.

96. Frady v. Ivester, 1924, 129 S.C. 536, 125 S.E. 134. See 1949, 7 A.L.R.2d 1131, 1137.

97. E. g., Cory v. Santa Ynez Land & Improvement Co., 1907, 151 Cal. 778, 91 P. 647. See 1949, 7 A.L. R.2d 1131, 1139.

Strictly speaking, in title states, since the mortgagee in possession already has legal title as well as possession it would seem to be technically inaccurate to describe his freeing the land of the mortgagor's right of redemption as acquiring title by adverse possession. What he has done, of course, is to bar the mortgagor's equity of redemption. Brown v. Berry, 1918, 89 N.J.Eq. 230, 108 A. 51.

In lien states, however, since the mortgagee has only a lien and the mortgagor has title, it is quite correct to talk in terms of acquiring title by adverse possession. However, in both cases the substantial question should be, and is, what sort of possession by the mortgagee is necessary to end the mortgagor's right to redeem, regardless of the technical nature of his interest in the property. Cf. § 16, supra.

98. Dexter v. Arnold, C.C.R.I.1837, 3 Sumner 152, F. Cas.No.3,859. See 1949, 7 A.L.R.2d 1131, 1142.

99. See 1949, 7 A.L.R.2d 1131, 1134.

1. "The right to foreclose and the right to redeem are reciprocal, and when one is barred, the other is barred. In Green v. Capps, 1892, 142 Ill. 286, we said (page 289 [31 N.E. 597]): 'Appellant concedes that the deed, regarded as a mortgage, could not have been foreclosed when this bill was filed, because the indebtedness it was given to secure was then barred by the statute of limitations. But if the statute * * * then barred foreclosure, it, for the same reason, barred a redemption from the deed, * * * for the right to redeem and the right to foreclose are reciprocal, and when the one is barred the other is barred.' * * * *" Fitch v. Miller, 1902, 200 Ill. 170, 183, 65 N.E. 650, 655. Locke v. Caldwell, 1879, 91 Ill. 417, 420; (but compare comment in Walker v. Warner, 1899, 179 Ill. 16, 27, 53 N.E. 594, 598, 70 Am.Dec. 85); Cunningham v. Hawkins, 1864, 24 Cal. 403, 85 Am.Dec. 73; Taylor v. McClain, 1882, 60 Cal. 651; and Allen v. Allen, 1892, 95 Cal. 184, 30 P. 213, 16 L.R.A. 646; (later abrogated by West's Ann.Code Civ.Proc. § 346; Allen v. Allen, supra. But see Raynor v. Drew, 1887, 72 Cal. 307, 312, 13 P. 866, for the possibility that the old reciprocity rule might still be applicable where the mortgagee is not in possession of the mortgaged premises); Crawford v. Taylor, 1875, 42 Iowa 260, 263; Adams v. Holden, 1900, 111 Iowa 54, 60, 82 N.W. 468, 470; (but cf. Tukey v. Reinholdt, Iowa, 1911, 130 N.W. 727); Leland v. Morrison, 1913, 92 S.C. 501, 75 S.E. 889, Ann.Cas. 1914B, 349; Gould v. McKillip, 1940, 55 Wyo. 251, 99 P.2d 67, 129 A.L.R. 1427. But cf. Bradley v. Norris, 1865, 63 Minn. 156, 165, 65 N.W. 357, 358.

2. Bradley v. Norris, 1895, 63 Minn. 156, 165, 65 N. W. 357, 358, quoting Coote, Mortgages, p. 26.

3. Calkins v. Isbell, 1859, 20 N.Y. 147, affirming Calkins v. Calkins, N.Y.1848, 3 Barb. 305.

of bringing to life the mortgagor's right. He may do so by an action designed for that purpose based, not upon a theory that the mortgage still subsists, as is a foreclosure suit, but upon the idea that the mortgage is gone and the plaintiff is now complete owner.[4]

However the doctrine never required that the rights of the parties should in every respect be on all fours. Certainly that is true as to the time within which the respective rights may be enforced, "for it is every day's practice, that one party may not be able to foreclose when the other may redeem."[5] And it would be objectionable to hold that they must be. For then "a person might one day be a mortgagee, having, in most jurisdictions, a lien merely on the premises, and the next day be their absolute owner,"[6] a result flowing from mere failure to enforce his rights.[7] Additionally "it would give to one claimant the benefit of disabilities to which his opponent is subject."[8]

The rule may correctly apply to redemption by a junior mortgagee; his right of redemption from the senior mortgage, in lien states at least, is dependent upon his right to foreclose his own mortgage and hence, when it is barred he also loses his right to redeem.[9] It has also been suggested that the statement means merely that, in fixing the equitable limitation upon suits to redeem, instead of

adopting the statutory period for bringing ejectment, a court will follow the time rule governing the bringing of an action to foreclose as more nearly analogous.[10]

In some states statutes have been enacted applying specifically to actions to redeem.[11] While these statutes set a definite time limit they do not necessarily dispose of the question of what kind of possession by the mortgagee is necessary for the period to run.[12] The history in New York provides an illustration.[13] There it was held that the suit to redeem, being equitable in nature, did not fall under the provision of the code limiting to twenty years an action to recover real property or its possession, but under the section covering actions not otherwise provided for with a ten year period.[14] A later enactment specifically provided that the right of a mortgagor, or those claiming under him, to redeem could be maintained unless the mortgagee, or those claiming under him, have

---

4. Arrington v. Liscom, 1868, 34 Cal. 365, 94 Am.Dec. 722; Chapin v. Wright, 1886, 41 N.J.Eq. 438, 5 A. 574.

5. Bradley v. Norris, 1895, 63 Minn. 156, 165, 65 N. W. 357, 358. " 'As in the instance cited in Talbot v. Braddel, 1 Vern. 395 [1685]. So, in a Welch Mortgage, the mortgagor may redeem at any time, but the mortgagee cannot foreclose, nor, without a covenant or bond, sue for the money.' " Ibid, The quotations by the court are from Coote, Mortgages, p. 26. See West's Ann.Cal.Code Civ.Proc. § 346.

6. Tiffany, Real. Prop., 3d ed., § 1501, citing Bradley v. Norris, 1895, 63 Minn. 156, 65 N.W. 357.

7. Idem.

8. Ibid.

9. Gower v. Winchester, 1871, 33 Iowa 303; Krutz v. Gardner, 1901, 25 Wash. 396, 65 P. 771.

10. Parsons v. Noggle, 1877, 23 Minn. 328. See Bradley v. Norris, 1895, 63 Minn. 156, 166, 65 N.W. 357, 359.

11. E. g., West's Ann.Cal.Code Civ.Proc., § 346 (5 years); Idaho Code, 1948, § 5–226 (5 years); N.Y. Civ.Prac. (Law & Rules) § 212(c), (McKinney Supp., 1969–70) (10 years). N.B. This appears in the 1963 permanent edition but was amended in 1964 to correct an error in punctuation and therefore appears in the 1969–70 Supplement to that Code. See Coote, Mortgages, 9th ed., pp. 766–773 (12 years in England). These statutes, although operating to bar the right of redemption and so, in a sense, might be classified as methods of foreclosure, are sufficiently different in operation and detail from those existing in four New England states as an explicit method of foreclosure, as to justify a different classification. For the latter, see §§ 314, 315, infra.

12. E. g., Peshine v. Ord, 1897, 119 Cal. 311, 51 P. 536, 63 Am.St.Rep. 131; Cory v. Santa Ynez Land and Improvement Co., 1907, 151 Cal. 778, 91 P. 647; Cohn v. Cohn, 1936, 7 Cal.2d 1, 59 P.2d 969. And see following discussion of the New York decisions.

13. See Campbell, Cases on Mortgages, 2d ed., 240 n. 4.

14. Hubbell v. Sibley, 1872, 50 N.Y. 468. Cf. Miner v. Beekman, 1872, 50 N.Y. 337, holding that the cause of action under this section accrued only upon entry by the mortgagee into possession; before then the action would be to remove a cloud on title resting upon a continuing right not affected by the statute of limitations.

maintained a continuous adverse possession for twenty years.[15] It was held that the term "adverse" was used in the ordinary sense [16] and therefore excluded a mortgagee who entered with the consent of the mortgagee and continued in possession as mortgagee.[17] In 1919, the word "adverse" was deleted.[18] The effect of this deletion has not been fully spelled out, but it has been held that if the mortgagee is not in possession, the statute is not applicable, and there is no limitation on a suit to redeem.[19]

B. FROM FORECLOSURE SALE

ORIGIN AND MAIN FEATURES

307. **Twenty-four states provide for redemption from foreclosure sale by statutes originating in time of economic depression in the 1820's and spread, to some extent at least, by imitative legislation motivated by desire for procedural simplicity and improvement. All specify the persons who may redeem, the amount to be paid, the time period for, and the order and effect of redemption. There are, however, endless variations in wording, details, and interpretations of the statutes.**

In an earlier section there is a short summary of the nature and objectives of statutory redemption from foreclosure sale together with criticisms of it and a list of references to discussions of the problem.[20] That ground will not be retraced. However, it is appropriate to make a brief survey of the origin of such legislation in this country, how prevalent it is, and the chief features that are common in states where it exists as well as some of its more important variations.

The early American statutes providing for redemption from sale coincided with periods of depression and may be associated with the general collapse of land values.[21] The first legislation in the 1820's was confined to redemption from execution sales, although in one state the statute was held to apply to mortgage foreclosure sales as well.[22] In the 1830's new redemption legislation following the panic of 1836 expressly included mortgage sales.[23] It has been suggested that the next development was more legalistic than economic in motivation, and came as a result of the spread through imitative legislation of the 1848 Field Code in New York [24] in many of the western states, one of the most important being California,[25] which in

15. N.Y.Civ.Prac., McKinney 1969–70, § 212(c), now provides for 10 years possession.

16. See note-calls and notes 92, 93, supra.

17. Becker v. McCrea, 1908, 193 N.Y. 423, 86 N.E. 463, 23 L.R.A.,N.S., 754.

18. Laws of N.Y., 1919, c. 281. The present statute, N.Y.Civ.Prac. McKinney 1969–70, § 212(c), continues this wording.

19. Sumner v. Sumner, 1926, 217 App.Div. 163, 164, 216 N.Y.S. 389, 390.

20. See § 8, supra.

21. Skilton, Government and the Mortgage Debtor, 1944, p. 20. See § 8, note 50, supra.

22. Henderson v. Lowry, 1833, 5 Yerg. (13 Tenn.) 198. See Skilton, op. cit. supra note 21, the first act was in New York in 1820. Laws N.Y.1819–1821, p. 167, interpreted as not applying to mortgage foreclosure sales in Tenbrook v. Lansing, N.Y.Ch.1820, 4 Johns. 601.

23. See Skilton, op. cit. supra note 21; Sutherland, Foreclosure and Sale, 1937, 22 Cornell L.Q. 216, 224 n. 35, as to the redemption statute of 1837, c. 410, in New York.

24. See Skilton, op. cit. supra note 21. N.Y.Code Civ.Proc., 1848, § 246 dealt with redemptions, reenacting the existing provisions.

25. Cal.Terr.Laws 1851, p. 88, held to apply to mortgage as well as other execution sales in Kent v. Laffan, 1852, 2 Cal. 595.

See Note, Statutory Right of Redemption from Execution and Foreclosure Sales in California, 1957, 45 Cal.L.Rev. 191, commenting on Salsbery v. Ritter, 1957, 48 Cal.2d 1, 306 P.2d 897, and Clark v. Cuin, 1956, 46 Cal.2d 386, 295 P.2d 401, 58 A.L.R.2d 460; Note, The Statutory Right of Redemption in California, 1964, 52 Cal.L.Rev. 846–875.

In City Bank of San Diego v. Ramage, 1968, 266 Cal. App.2d 570, 72 Cal.Rptr. 273, the amount to be paid on redemption by a mortgagor was stated to be the amount for which the property was sold on foreclosure under a trust deed and not the amount which the court determined to be the fair market value of the property at time of sale.

For the general scheme, the operation and an appraisal of the wisdom of the Colorado statutory redemption from foreclosure sale, see Storke and Sears, Colorado Security Law, 1952, 149–170.

turn served as a model for others.[26] The period provided by the California code was originally six months but in the last years of the nineteenth century this was changed to a year, and similar legislation in other states tended to establish or lengthen the previously existing period at a similar period.[27] No certain cause for either increase or decrease of the length of time for redemption can be stated with assurance; or for that matter, the settling upon a particular period in the first instance.[28] In the latest survey available,[29] the redemption period runs from six months in five states [30] to two years in one,

Alabama. The same survey shows that twenty-eight of the forty-eight states have statutory redemption periods, but in four the period is before foreclosure sale.[31] In the remaining nineteen states there is no statutory redemption period.[32] In twenty-four of the twenty-eight states the mortgagor is entitled to possession during the redemption period, the mortgagee in four.[33] The importance of this is minimized, however, by provisions which permit possession by a mortgagee or the appointment of a receiver.[34] In some states the redemption does not apply to sales under a power of sale.[35] However, it is usually immaterial whether the sale takes place under a power of sale or in a judicial proceeding.[36]

26. E. g., Idaho. Law Terr.Idaho, 1864, p. 129, § 237.

27. Skilton, op. cit. supra note 21, p. 22.

In 1957, Illinois shortened the period from fifteen to twelve months. See Prather, Foreclosure of the Security Interest, 1957 U. of Ill.L.Forum 420, 446–448. And see Wash.Laws 1961, c. 196, criticized as inadequate by Shattuck, Real Property Mortgage Foreclosure Redemption, 1961, 36 Wash.L.Rev. 309, reducing the period from one year to eight months for non-agricultural property in cases where the complaint in the foreclosure action waived any right to a deficiency. See also Brodkey, Current Changes in Illinois Real Property Law, 1960, 10 DePaul L.Rev. 566, 578–580, covering reduction in the period of redemption from foreclosure sale and other aspects of such redemption. Mount Moriss Sav. and Loan Ass'n v. Barber, 1961, 17 Ill.2d 723, 162 N.E.2d 347, held that a statutory amendment shortening the time limit for redemption by a judgment creditor of the mortgagor was procedural and should be applied retroactively.

28. See Skilton, op. cit. supra note 21, pp. 22, 23, speculating that the six months period was from the term commonly set in English equity decrees of foreclosure, and suggesting that in bad times the tendency is to extend the period in order to help the debtor while in good times it may be shortened to encourage investment. But cf. Glenn, Mortgages, § 228, not limiting his observation to the matter of redemption time in the statutes.

29. Bridewell, The Effects of Defective Mortgage Laws on Home Financing, 1938, 5 Law & Contemp.Problems, 544, 547–548, 558. See also Campbell, Cases on Mortgages, 2d ed., 1939, pp. 315–318 and 315 n. 1, reproducing the Minnesota statutes and giving references to seventeen other representative state enactments. For an earlier tabulated description of the situation in the different states, see 1922, Handbook of Com.Un.St.Laws, 280.

30. Arizona, Colorado, Oklahoma, Utah and Wyoming.

31. Bridewell, op. cit. supra note 29, pp. 547, 548. The four are Indiana, Nebraska, Oklahoma and Wisconsin. Skilton, op. cit. supra note 21, p. 24. The redemption period follows the sale in Washington, Oregon, California, Nevada, Montana, Idaho, Utah, Wyoming, Arizona, Colorado, New Mexico, North Dakota, South Dakota, Kansas, Minnesota, Iowa, Missouri, Arkansas, Illinois, Michigan, Indiana, Kentucky, Tennessee, Alabama, Vermont and Maine. Ibid.

32. Ibid.

33. Idem. p. 558.

34. See § 8, n. 51, supra.

35. E. g., in California this is so clear in the case of powers of sale in a trust deed mortgage that citation of primary authority is superfluous. See Kidd, Trust Deeds and Mortgages in California, 1916, 3 Cal.L.Rev. 381, 387; Cormack and Irsfeld, Jr., Mortgages and Trust Deeds in California, 1938, 26 Cal.L.Rev. 206, 216. The same rule probably applies to sales under powers of sales in a mortgage. See Cormack and Irsfeld, Jr., supra, 216 n. 59 and 219; Sacramento Bank v. Alcorn, 1898, 121 Cal. 379, 384, 53 P. 813; cf. Cormerais v. Genella, 1863, 22 Cal. 116; Kidd, supra, 388. See further, Note, Comparison of Mortgages, Trust Deeds and Land Sale Contracts, 1960, 7 U.C.L.A.L.Rev. 83, 88, 90.

36. See Campbell, Cases on Mortgages, 2d ed., 1939, p. 315 n. 1. In the proposed Model Power of Sale Mortgage Act § 9, a nine months redemption from foreclosure sale was provided. See 1940 Handbook, Com. on Un.St.Laws, 254; 1941, 27 Va.L.Rev. 926, 934. United States v. John Hancock Mut. Life Ins. Co., 1960, 364 U.S. 301, 81 S.Ct. 1, 5 L.Ed.2d 1 held that the United States, as second mortgagee of real estate, may redeem it after it has been judicially

Although the various statutes on redemption, in addition to the differences mentioned above, have widely varying phraseology and differ in a multitude of details, nevertheless there are certain main features that are common to all. These are (1) a specification of persons who may redeem, the owner of the equity of redemption being universally included, and most of them also including junior lienors and some others; (2) a specification of the sum which must be paid to redeem, the basic factor in which is the sale price to which is added interest and, in differing detail, usually other items; (3) a fixing of a time limit for redemption, which, in addition to the variations mentioned above often provides different periods for different classes of persons; and (4) provisions as to order and effect of redemption.[37] This last feature especially looms large in importance.

In the following discussion chief attention will be paid to the provisions and interpretations of the statutes of two states which probably come as close to being representative as any. They are Minnesota[38] and Iowa.[39]

WHO MAY REDEEM—NATURE OF INTEREST

308. Statutes usually divide those who may redeem from foreclosure sale into two groups: (1) Mortgagors and their successors in interest; (2) junior lienors. Traditional motions preventing restrictions on a mortgagor's equity of redemption have influenced the law as to the statutory right. Recognition that those ideas should not apply to corporate mortgages is found both in statutes eliminating the right of redemption altogether as to them and in decisions permitting waiver or extinction of it by agreement.

Statutes providing for redemption from foreclosure sale usually divide those who may exercise the right into two groups: first, the mortgagor, including by variously worded language, his successors in interest, in the whole or in any part of the premises, not including lienors;[40] and second, junior lienors whether by judgment or otherwise.[41] Al-

---

foreclosed and sold in a proceeding to which the United States was made a party under a federal statute authorizing it to be sued in such a proceeding and providing that it should have the right to redeem within one year from the date of sale, despite a conflicting state (Kansas) statute giving the mortgagor the exclusive right to redeem within that period. The decision is discussed and criticized in Note, 1961, 10 Kan.L.Rev. 99.

In United States v. Forest Glen Senior Residence, D.C.Or.1967, 278 F.Supp. 343, discussed 1968, 47 Or.L.Rev. 464, it was held (1) that federal, not state, law governs redemption procedures on an FHA mortgage, and (2) that where there is no existing federal rule on the precise point Oregon's redemption law should not be adopted. The reason given: (1) the right of redemption fails to protect the federal treasury, and (2) a uniform rule concerning the right of redemption is necessary under the National Housing Act.

37. See Durfee and Doddridge, Redemption from Foreclosure Sale—The Uniform Act, 1925, 23 Mich. L.Rev. 825, 835.

For a valuable general survey of the whole problem of redemption from foreclosure sale, see Durfee, Cases on Security, 1951, 287–304. He cites a few other valuable legal periodical writings on the subject. See also Note, Statutory Redemption: The Enemy of Home Financing, 1953, 28 Wash.L.Rev. 39.

38. The Minnesota legislation was a basis for the provisions incorporated into the 1927 proposed Uniform Real Estate Mortgage Act. See 1927, Handbook, Coms.Un.State Laws 654, 690–694. See Campbell, Cases on Mortgages, 2d ed., 315 et seq., and 315 n. 1; Durfee and Doddridge, op. cit. supra note 37.

39. See Blum, Iowa Statutory Redemption After Mortgage Foreclosure, 1949, 35 Iowa L.Rev. 72.

40. E. g., Minn.Stat.Ann. § 580.23, "the mortgagor, his personal representatives, or assigns"; Iowa Code Ann., §§ 628.3, 628.25, 1950; West's Ann.Cal.Code Civ.Proc. §§ 725a, 701, "the judgment debtor, or his successor in interest."

41. E. g., Minn.Stat.Ann. § 580.24; "creditor having a lien, legal or equitable"; Iowa Code, 1950, § 628.-5; West's Ann.Cal.Code Civ.Prov. § 701, "creditor having a lien by judgment or mortgage on the property sold * * * subsequent to that on which the property was sold." In some states, under certain circumstances, the process of redemption entails a public sale at which a redeeming creditor may have to bid against anyone who wishes to compete for the property. See 1938, 5 U. of Chi.L.Rev. 624, 628.

For a case holding that the Federal Housing Act prevails over a conflicting state act on who may redeem, see United States v. John Hancock Mut. Life Ins. Co., supra, § 307 n. 36.

though under some statutes a mortgagee is permitted to redeem from the sale ordered upon the foreclosure of his mortgage,[42] probably most jurisdictions hold that he cannot do so.[43] The latter is clearly preferable, the former diminishing to an important degree the pressure on the foreclosing creditor to bid more than the minimum necessary to obtain the property.[44] Although there is some divergence of opinion and reasoning in interpreting the language of different statutory provisions, both pre-foreclosure sale transferees[45] and post-foreclosure sale transferees[46] of the mortgagor have been included among those in the first group as ones who may exercise the right of redemption. The mortgagor's statutory right of redemption is usually regarded as alienable.[47] However, it probably cannot be levied on by the mortgagee on an execution under a deficiency judgment in the foreclosure action which resulted in the sale of the property.[48] Traditional ideas of protection of the mortgagor against restrictions on his equity of redemption present an objection to permitting the foreclosing mortgagee becoming an assignee of the statutory right to redeem from foreclosure sale by virtue of a contract to assign executed prior to foreclosure, and to some extent to an assignment after foreclosure.[49] In some states by statute waiver of the right is permitted in the case of a corporate mortgagor.[50] Redemption from foreclosure sale is incompatible with practical realities and necessities of corporate reorganization as worked out through foreclosure

---

42. See, e. g., the situation in Illinois under Smith-Hurd.Ill.Ann.Stat., 1966, c. 77, § 20. Crowder v. Scott State Bank, 1936, 365 Ill. 88, 5 N.E.2d 387, 108 A.L.R. 990; Strause v. Dutch, 1911, 250 Ill. 326, 95 N.E. 286, 35 L.R.A.,N.S., 413.

43. Hervey v. Krost, 1888, 116 Ind. 268, 19 N.E. 125; San Jose Water Co. v. Lyndon, 1899, 124 Cal. 518, 57 P. 481. See 1912, 35 L.R.A.,N.S., 413; 1937, 108 A.L.R. 993.

44. See Durfee and Doddridge, Redemption from Foreclosure Sale, 1925, 23 Mich.L.Rev. 825, 845, n. 59; 1937, 5 U. of Chi.L.Rev. 624, 629.

45. E. g., Pollard v. Harlow, 1903, 138 Cal. 390, 71 P. 648; Warner Bros. Co. v. Freud, 1903, 138 Cal. 651, 655, 72 P. 345; White v. Costigan, 1901, 134 Cal. 33, 66 P. 78; Willis v. Miller, 1893, 23 Or. 352, 31 P. 827; Cooper v. Maurer, 1904, 122 Iowa, 321, 98 N.W. 124. However, under statutes such as the California one, supra, n. 37, such a transfer does not prevent the mortgagor from redeeming, although when he does the redemption enures to the benefit of his prior grantee. Yoakum v. Bower, 1876, 51 Cal. 539; Huling v. Seccombe, 1928, 88 Cal.App. 238, 263 P. 362; Livingston v. Arnoux, 1874, 56 N.Y. 507. But look at Higgs v. McDuffie, 1916, 81 Or. 265, 158 P. 953 (statute involved revised later in 1917: see Olson, Oregon Laws §§ 245, 427). See note, 1928, 3 Wash.L.Rev. 177. See also 1928, 57 A.L.R. 1021; 1891, 21 Am.St.Rep. 245.

46. Big Sespe Oil Co. v. Cockran, C.C.A.Cal.1921, 276 F. 216, 264; Phillips v. Hagart, 1896, 113 Cal. 552, 45 P. 843, 54 Am.St.Rep. 369; Kaston v. Storey, 1905, 47 Or. 150, 80 P. 217, 114 Am.St.Rep. 912.

47. See cases in preceding footnote. But cf., Mixon v. Burelson, 1919, 203 Ala. 84, 82 So. 98; Smith v. Shaver, 1923, 112 Kan. 790, 212 P. 666; 1911, 29 L. R.A.,N.S., 508.

In Sayre v. Vander Voort, 1925, 200 Iowa, 990, 205 N. W. 760, 42 A.L.R. 880, discussed in notes, 1926, 26 Col.L.Rev. 363; 1926, 10 Minn.L.Rev. 440, the plaintiff obtained a judgment lien on land subject to a mortgage. The mortgage was foreclosed and the land sold. The next day the plaintiff levied execution on, sold, and bought in on the sale the debtor's right of possession during the year period within which the debtor might redeem from the foreclosure sale. In this action to clear the plaintiff's title, the court held, (1) this right of possession was not an interest in property subject to sale on execution, (2) if it was, the plaintiff took nothing under the sale of it for it in turn was subject to a year's right of possession in the debtor. See also Wheeler and Durfee, Evasion of Mortgage Moratoria by Prosecution of Personal Remedies, 1935, 33 Mich.L. Rev. 1196, 1202.

Complementary to the question of the nature and incidents of the mortgagor's interest in the mortgaged property during the statutory period allowed for redemption from foreclosure sale is that of the rights of the purchasers on the foreclosure sale during that same time. See Schweppe, Interest Acquired by Purchaser at Foreclosure Sale, 1930, 5 Wash.L. Rev. 105; note, 1935, 83 U. of Pa.L.Rev. 1032; note, 1919, 29 Yale L.J. 122. See also 1921, 11 A.L. R. 1308; 1890, 9 L.R.A. 676.

48. See Wheeler and Durfee, Evasion of Moratoria by Prosecution of Personal Remedies, 1935, 33 Mich.L.Rev. 1196, 1202. There seems no reason why execution should not be levied under the deficiency judgment after redemption from the sale. Idem, 1205.

49. See note, 1938, 5 U. of Chi.L.Rev. 625, 636.

50. E. g., Ill.Rev.Stats. (Smith-Hurd) 1966, c. 77, § 18a; Kansas Stat.Ann., 1964, §§ 60–2410(d), 60–2414(a).

proceedings and its elimination would not violate the purposes for which it is created.[51] Consequently, it is not surprising that courts, on some reasoning or other, find ways to uphold its waiver or termination apart from statute, although a legislative sanction for such a result is preferable.[52] And an individual mortgagor, by incorporating himself, may gain the same privilege.[53]

EFFECT OF REDEMPTION—BY MORT-GAGOR OR SUCCESSOR

309. Statutes providing for redemption from foreclosure sale universally permit mortgagors or their successors in interest to exercise the right. Redemption by either "nullifies" the sale in the sense that it ends the purchaser's title and restores that of the redemptioner as it existed before the sale. There are various views as to the effect of such "nullification" upon preexisting liens and the liens of judgments for any deficiency. Under the best existing statute a redemption by either revives no liens and neither is subject to any liability for any deficiency on the judgment under which the property is sold. Further, although judgment liens of other mortgagees or creditors may attach to the property on redemption by a mortgagor, they do not when his transferee redeems.

Redemption by the mortgagor or his successor is a universal feature of statutes providing for redemption from foreclosure sale. Statutes usually give them a priority in redemption over lienors for a certain period of time.[54] In several states concurrent per-

iods of redemption are provided for both mortgagors and lienors, with the latter subject to a redemption by the former if they should act first.[55] A redemption by the mortgagor is final.[56]

When a mortgagor or his transferee redeems, the effect is to "nullify" the foreclosure sale.[57] No court has gone to the length of treating the sale as avoided for all purposes.[58] On the other hand, it is probable that all courts would agree that the sale is avoided, at least for the purpose of ending the title of the purchaser; that the redeeming owner is restored to the title he had before foreclosure sale; and that he does not

51. See 1937, 4 U. of Chi.L.Rev. 675, 676. See also § 8, supra.

52. First Nat. Bank v. Bryn Mawr Beach Corp., 1937, 365 Ill. 409, 6 N.E.2d 654, 109 A.L.R. 1123, discussed 1937, 4 Chi.L.Rev. 675. See 1938, 5 Univ. of Chi.L.Rev. 625, 636. See also 1937, 31 Ill.L.Rev. 1114. Cf. note, 1934, 47 Harv.L.Rev. 530.

53. See Palcar Real Estate Co. v. Commissioner, C. C.A.Mo.1942, 131 F.2d 210. Cf. Jenkins v. Moyse, 1930, 254 N.Y. 319, 172 N.E. 521, 74 A.L.R. 205.

54. E. g., Minn.Stat.Ann., §§ 80.23, 580.24, 6 months generally but 12 months if prior to July 1, 1967, amt. due on date of notice of foreclosure is less than 66⅔% of original principal or the mort. premises exceed ten acres in size; Iowa Code Ann.1950, §§ 628.2–3, 628.5, mortgagor's right exclusive for 6 months and last 3 months of year.

55. E. g., West's Ann.Cal.Code Civ.Proc., §§ 702, 703. See 1937, 5 U. of Chi.L.Rev. 624, 630, for a description of the Illinois law under which redemption by a later judgment or decree creditor may be made during the primary period for redemption but has a different effect than when made later.

56. The same finality should attend a redemption by an assignee of the mortgagor. E. g., Iowa Code Ann.1950, § 628.5; Calkins v. Steinbach, 1884, 66 Cal. 117, 4 P. 1103. But see Tirrill v. Miller, 1928, 206 Iowa 426, 429, 218 N.W. 303, 304.

57. Most statutes so provide explicitly by clauses in which, although the language is not identical, the purport is the same. E. g., N.Y.Laws 1820, p. 167 (the pioneer statute) provided, "The said sale and certificate shall be null and void"; West's Ann. Cal.Code Civ.Proc. § 703, "the effect of the sale is terminated and he is restored to his estate"; Ill. Jones & Add., Ann.St.1913, § 6764, "Sale and certificate shall be null and void", the same language has been retained in Ill.Ann.Stat., Smith-Hurd, 1966, c. 77, § 18; Mich.Comp.St., 1915, §§ 12677, 14949, "Such deed [to the purchaser] shall be void and of no effect". Substantially the same language, "the deed of sale is void and of no effect", in Mich. Comp.Laws Ann., 1968, § 600, 3140, § 14949 was repealed and replaced by § 600.3201 but this is no longer in point; Gen.Stat.Minn. (1923) [Mason's Minn. Stat.1927] § 9630, "annuls the sale." Minn.Stat.Ann., § 580.27 retains the same. Even when the statute has no such express stipulation, courts have reached the same conclusion. E. g., Allen v. McGaughey, 1876, 31 Ark. 252, 260; Fields v. Danenhower, 1898, 65 Ark. 392, 46 S.W. 938, 43 L.R.A. 519. See Storke and Sears, Colorado Security Law, 1952, 1954–59, for Colorado law on redemption by the "owner" or "any person who might be liable on a deficiency."

58. See 1924, 9 Cornell L.Q. 208, 209. To do so would involve holding that the mortgage lien was restored to its original amount and require repayment by the mortgagee of any proceeds he might have received from the sale. See Durfee & Doddridge, Redemption from Foreclosure Sale—The Uniform Act, 1925, 23 Mich.L.Rev. 825, 850.

become a transferee of the title of the purchaser as does a lienor who redeems.[59] The important question, however, is whether nullification of the effect of the foreclosure sale will be carried to the extent that it will revive previously existing liens insofar as they have not been satisfied by the proceeds of the foreclosure sale.[60]

It is probably true today, as was hazarded over forty years ago,[61] that in no one state does a redeeming mortgagor take either subject to all the liens that would have existed had no sale occurred, save to the extent the purchase money satisfied them, or entirely free of them. Beyond that the situation is too complicated for helpful generalizations.[62] At one extreme are those authorities that hold even the lien of the mortgage under which the property was sold revives as to the unpaid deficiency.[63] At the other

extreme is a proposal, not adopted by any legislature, that a redemption by the mortgagor or his successor should be free of all encumbrances existing prior to the sale.[64] The scheme is designed to put pressure on the foreclosing mortgagee at the time of the sale to bid what he thinks the property is worth, up to the amount of his debt; and it puts pressure on a junior lienor during the period of his right to redeem to bid more than the price paid by the senior mortgagee.[65] Iowa at the present time comes closest to this suggested solution.[66] Under its statute the mortgagor's assignee on redemption clearly takes free of all liens against the mortgagor;[67] and since 1934 the mortgagor

---

59. See Durfee and Doddridge, supra note 58.

60. "The argument for revival of liens is exceedingly simple. The redemption statute suspends the operation of the sale and a redemption by the owner annuls the sale. The sale being suspended, the liens which would otherwise have been extinguished by the sale are not extinguished but merely suspended, and subsequent judgments which would have created liens had there been no sale will create inchoate liens; and then, when a redemption annuls the sale, these liens are revived, in the one case, or vivified in the other case. Not always fully expressed and not always consistently applied, this seems to be the reasoning underlying every case which holds liens to be revived. As a literal interpretation of the statute it is unimpeachable.

"Viewed, however, in the light of the purpose of the statute it does not seem so sound." Durfee and Doddridge, note 58, supra, p. 850.

61. Durfee & Doddridge, note 58, supra, p. 857.

62. See, 1914, 47 L.R.A.,N.S., 1048; 1920, 5 A.L.R. 145; 1940, 128 A.L.R. 796. See also discussions in authorities cited § 8, supra.

63. Although the cases holding that redemption revives the original lien under which the property was sold, except to the extent that the purchase price on the sale discharged it, are those involving judgment liens, no distinctions between them and mortgage liens can be upheld. New York is, perhaps, the leading jurisdiction for the doctrine. See note, 1924, 9 Cornell L.Q. 208; 1899, 67 Am.St.Rep. 510. See also Wheeler and Durfee, Evasion of Mortgage Moratoria by Prosecution of Personal Remedies, 1935, 33 Mich.L.Rev. 1196, 1205. Such seems to have been the early rule in Iowa. See

Harms v. Palmer, 1887, 73 Iowa 446, 449, 35 N.W. 515, 516, 5 Am.St.Rep. 691; Moody v. Funk, 1891, 82 Iowa 1, 3, 47 N.W. 1008, 31 Am.St.Rep. 455. Later decisions hold that on redemption, land in the hands of the redeeming mortgagor will from that moment become subject to the lien of prior judgments, but the original mortgage lien does not, apparently, revive. See Cooper v. Maurer, 1904, 122 Iowa 321, 327, 98 N.W. 124, 127; Durfee and Doddridge, op. cit. supra note 58, 856 n. 81 and 857, n. 84. But see Blum, Iowa Statutory Redemption after Mortgage Foreclosure, 1949, 35 Iowa L.Rev. 72, 77. The authorities cited go no farther than the proposition that a judgment lien will attach or reattach de novo at the time of redemption, not that the original lien will then revive. In 1934 an amendment to the redemption statute freed property redeemed by the mortgagor from any liability for any unpaid portion of the judgment under which the property was sold. Iowa Code, 1946, § 628.3.

64. This result would be accomplished by declaring that upon such a redemption the redeeming party shall acquire such title as would have gone to the purchaser if no redemption had taken place. To this is coupled a proposal that lienors shall be given priority in redemption, but with the owner having finally an opportunity to redeem from the purchaser or re-redeem from a lienor-redemptioner. See Durfee v. Doddridge, op. cit. supra note 58, 861, 852–3, 854 n. 78.

65. See idem, 862–863, for additional details and arguments for the proposal.

66. See Blum, op. cit. supra note 63, pp. 78–79.

67. Idem, p. 77, citing Tirrill v. Miller, 1928, 206 Iowa 426, 218 N.W. 303, prior judgment against mortgagor; Danforth v. Lindsey, 1916, 178 Iowa 834, 160 N.W. 318, deficiency judgment; see Cadd v. Snell, 1935, 219 Iowa 728, 734, 259 N.W. 590, 593; cf. Paulsen v. Jensen, 1929, 209 Iowa 453, 228 N.W. 357. See also Cooper v. Maurer, 1904, 122 Iowa

takes free of any liability for any deficiency on the judgment under which the property is sold.[68] Further a redeeming mortgagor takes free of any junior mortgage lien; although if its holder has obtained a judgment, the judgment lien will attach to the redeemed property just as it would to any other property acquired by the judgment debtor.[69] The statute does not, however, give a period of priority in redeeming to the junior lienor [70] and, consequently, the pressure is strong on him to bid high at the sale, at which time he is at a disadvantage in competing with the foreclosing mortgagee.[71] The latter may bid his debt up to its amount whereas the former must bid cash.[72]

A variety of additional distinctions have been drawn, only three of which will be mentioned. Some states differentiate between the effect of a redemption by the debtor-mortgagor and one by his transferee, the latter taking free of previously existing liens regardless of whether they might revive as against the former on redemption by him.[73]

The distinction has been criticised as violating the fundamental rule that a successor in interest, unless he be a bona fide purchaser for value without notice, "simply occupies the shoes of his predecessor." [74] However, the rule may be a most effective factor in forcing a foreclosing mortgagee to bid up for the property.[75] Some authority distinguishes between the restoration on redemption of the lien under which the property was sold and liens inferior to it, restoring the latter but not the former.[76] Finally, the restoration of prior liens constitutes a problem separate and distinct from that of the lien of a judg-

---

321, 98 N.W. 124. The above Iowa cases were before the 1934 amendment in that state. That enactment, however, changed the existing rule only as to redemption by the debtor-mortgagor.

68. See note 63, supra.

69. Anderson v. Renshaw, 1940, 229 Iowa 93, 294 N. W. 274. See Cooper v. Maurer, 1904, 122 Iowa 321, 327, 98 N.W. 124, 126; Paulsen v. Jensen, 1929, 209 Iowa 453, 458, 228 N.W. 357, 359.

70. Instead, the mortgagor-debtor has priority for six months and, if he exercises the right, the junior lienor will lose his chance. See Iowa Code Ann. 1950, §§ 628.2–.3, 628.5.

71. See Blum, op. cit. supra note 63, p. 79.

72. See 1938, 5 U. of Chi.L.Rev. 625, 626; Durfee and Doddridge, op. cit. supra note 58, 852, 854 n. 78. Although a junior lienor will have to pay cash to redeem, giving him a certain opportunity to do so for an extended period of time gives him a better chance to finance the deal. Idem, p. 863.

73. Simpson v. Castle, 1878, 52 Cal. 644; Sigler v. Phares, 1919, 105 Kan. 116, 181 P. 628, 5 A.L.R. 141, junior liens cut off as to grantee; see Iowa cases, n. 67, supra. See also 1913, 47 L.R.A.,N.S., 1048, 1050, as to liability for a deficiency on indebtedness for which it was originally sold; 1940, 128 A.L.R. 796; 1920, 5 A.L.R. 145, as to subordinate liens.

As to the position of a post-foreclosure grantee of the mortgagor who does not assume the mortgage debt under Illinois law, see note, 1938, 5 U. of Chi.L.Rev. 624, 632. But contrast Fletcher Ave. Savings Ass'n v. Zeller, 1940, 217 Ind. 244, 27 N.E.2d 351, 128 A. L.R. 793, under a statute with more specific language than most.

74. Flanders v. Aumack, 1897, 32 Or. 19, 25, 51 P. 447, 449, 67 Am.St.Rep. 504. While the criticism is valid insofar as it concerns liens existing, even though suspended against the property in the hands of the mortgagor before the transfer, the distinction would seem sound enough as to the lien of a judgment obtained against the mortgagor after the transfer and accruing for the first time, if at all, not before that date.

The question may be asked whether it would not be a fraudulent conveyance to permit an insolvent debtor to transfer his redemption right to one who, on redemption, takes the property free and clear of the debtor's creditors. The question would be even more acute if the debtor claimed exemption of the consideration received for the transfer. See note, 1928, 5 U. of Chi.L.Rev. 625, 234. And look at Kerr v. Miller, 1913, 259 Ill. 516, 102 N.E. 1050, commented on in, 1914, 9 Ill.L.Rev. 60. But see Glenn, Mortgages, § 234.

75. See 1938, 5 U. of Chi.L.Rev. 624, 633.

76. See Rist v. Anderson, 1945, 70 S.D. 579, 19 N.W. 2d 833, 161 A.L.R. 197. See also 1920, 5 A.L.R. 145, 149. But contrast Sigler v. Phares, 1919, 105 Kan. 116, 181 P. 628, 5 A.L.R. 141.

"Confining the inquiry to the restoration of liens, it is possible to distinguish between senior liens and junior liens, restoring the latter but not the former, and, with respect to each class, a further distinction is suggested,—as to senior liens, a distinction between mortgage liens and judgment liens, the latter being restored but the former not; as to junior liens, a diversity between a passive lienor and one who, as defendant in a suit to foreclose the senior lien, files a cross bill and obtains a decree enforcing his lien, the latter being classed with the senior lienor." Durfee and Doddridge, op. cit. supra note 58, p. 854.

ment obtained as a deficiency in the foreclosure action, or otherwise, attaching de novo to the property in the hands of the redeeming party at the time of redemption.[77] As to the latter, it may be argued that on redemption by the mortgagor the redeemed property should be treated like any other property and, therefore, subject to seizure to pay the judgment of any creditor, including the judgment for a deficiency by the foreclosing mortgagee.[78] A possible answer is that to permit a foreclosing mortgagee such a right would lessen the incentive for him to bid up to the full amount of his debt for the property on foreclosure sale and, by the same token, for the mortgagor to seek redemption.[79] If so, prime objects of the statute would be impaired.

EFFECT OF REDEMPTION—BY LIENORS

310. Holders of liens junior to that of the foreclosing mortgagee may redeem from foreclosure sale under terms, at times, and in order of priority specified in redemption statutes. Usually there may be a re-redemption from them by other specified lienors and the mortgagor and his successor in interest. The effect of redemption in most states is to transfer to

him the interest of the purchaser on foreclosure sale. There are divergent views as to the effect of redemption upon the mortgage debt; Iowa, of existing statutes, offers the best solution.

Holders of liens junior to that under which the property is sold on foreclosure are empowered to redeem,[80] although their right to do so is usually postponed to a time after that during which the right is exclusively reserved to the mortgagor and his successors in interest.[81] Where there are several junior lienors, although the provisions on the subject are not uniform, they usually are given the privilege of redemption at certain periods of time in accordance with their priority.[82] Further, when there is a redemption by one of the latter, there are provisions, again not uniform, providing for re-redemption by others within a specified period.[83] The terms of

---

77. See note, 1938, 5 U. of Chi.L.Rev. 625, 630. Where this is the effect of redemption, the further question arises whether, when the liens attach to the land at the moment of redemption, they do so as simultaneous liens or with priority. Cf. Hulbert v. Hulbert, 1916, 216 N.Y. 430, 111 N.E. 70, L.R.A. 1916D, 661, Ann.Cas.1917D, 180; Zink v. James River Nat. Bank, 1929, 58 N.D. 1, 224 N.W. 901, 67 A.L.R. 1294. Cf. also notes, 1916, 29 Harv.L.Rev. 755; 1916, 16 Col.L.Rev. 237; 1916, 14 Mich.L.Rev. 402; 1929, 17 Cal.L.Rev. 690; 1929, 78 U. of Pa.L. Rev. 246.

78. See Durfee v. Doddridge, op. cit. supra note 58, p. 853. If on such a redemption his judgment lien for the deficiency attaches to the redeemed property for the first time, he takes more risk that his priority in reaching the property will be gone.

79. Where on redemption by the mortgagor the original mortgage lien of the foreclosing lienor is revived such a mortgagee takes no risk in bidding as little as possible for the land at the foreclosure sale. See Durfee and Doddridge, op. cit. supra note 58, p. 851. But he does have another chance at it to collect his debt, and that fact will deter redemption by the mortgagor, making more probable his retention of the property at a bargain price.

80. See § 308, supra. As to the right to redeem of the creditor or mortgagee whose foreclosure resulted in the sale, see ibid., note-calls and notes 42–44.

As to the right and effect of redemption from a foreclosure sale by a junior lienor, see Note, The Rights of a Junior Lienholder in Wisconsin, 1959, 43 Marq.L.Rev. 89, 92. See also Storke and Sears, Colorado Security Law, 1952, 159–161.

81. See § 309, supra notes 55, 56.

82. E.g., Gen.Stats.Minn. (1923) [Mason's Minn.Stat. 1927] § 9628 and see Sprague v. Martin, 1882, 29 Minn. 226, 13 N.W. 34 Minn.Stat.Ann. § 580.24 retains substantially the same language; West's Ann. Cal.Code Civ.Proc. § 702. See Blum, Iowa Statutory Redemption After Mortgage Foreclosure, 35 Iowa L.Rev. 72, 75, for the Iowa law; 1937, 5 U. of Chi. L.Rev. 624, 630, for the law in Illinois.

83. See, e.g., Blum, op. cit. supra note 82, for Iowa law; Iowa Code Ann.1946, §§ 628.8, 628.9, 628.10, 628.14; Gen.Stat.Minn. (1923) [Mason's Minn.Stat. 1927] § language retained in Minn.Stat.Ann. 1970, § 580.24, West's Ann.Cal.Code Civ.Proc. §§ 702, 703. See Sprague v. Martin, 1882, 29 Minn. 226, 13 N.W. 34, for the Minnesota law and some aspects of the New York law. But cf. N.Y.Code Civ.Proc. §§ 1450, 1451, 1463 (Civil Practice Act [1920] §§ 728, 729, 741). These provisions have been omitted from the latest New York Civil Practice Law. Also cf. Benton v. Hatch, 1890, 122 N.Y. 322, 25 N.E. 486. The following questions are suggestive of the kinds of problems that may arise and cannot be answered except by an examination of the statutory provisions and their interpretation in any particular jurisdiction, together, perhaps, with a consideration of the policies underlying the statutes.

E–1, E–2, and E–3 designate the first, second and third mortgagees respectively.

such a re-redemption are usually what the prior redemptioner had paid and the amount of the encumbrance held by him, if senior to the re-redemptioner, plus certain other charges.[84]

Under most statutes the effect of redemption by a junior lienor is to transfer to him the rights of the purchaser on foreclosure sale which, if there is not a redemption from him by someone else, will ripen into the same title that the purchaser would have got if no one redeemed.[85] This solution has several advantages. It is fair to the owner;[86] it makes any further proceeding to enforce the rights so acquired unnecessary; and it is in accord with the policy of the statute in that, by providing an incentive to redeem, it increases probability of redemption and, therefore, puts pressure on the foreclosing mortgagee to bid up the price.[87]

1.) E–1, the first mortgagee, forecloses his mortgage, sells the property on the foreclosure sale for less than the amount of his debt, and gets a deficiency judgment which he records. May E–1 redeem from his own foreclosure sale? See 1912, 35 L.R.A.,N. S., 413; 1937, 108 A.L.R. 993. See § 308, supra.

a.) As to whether a junior mortgagee who has been joined in the foreclosure action of E–1, and has either brought a cross bill asking foreclosure of his own mortgage, or asked that any surplus remaining after payment of E–1's charge be applied to his mortgage, may redeem, see note, 1928, 3 Wash.L. Rev. 177, 185; note, 1938, 5 U. of Chi.L.Rev. 625, 633 and 634; § 309, ante note 63.

2.) E–2 forecloses and sells. May E–1 redeem?

3.) E–2 forecloses and sells. E–3 redeems. May E–1 redeem from E–3?

4.) E–1 forecloses and sells and E–3 redeems. May E–2 redeem from E–3? See 1923, 26 A.L.R. 435.

a.) If E–2 is permitted to redeem from E–3, may E–3 in turn re-redeem from E–2?

84. E.g., Iowa Code Ann., 1950, §§ 628.9, 628.10, 628.-14; West's Ann.Cal.Code Civ.Proc. § 703; Durfee and Doddridge, Redemption from Foreclosure Sale—The Uniform Act, 1925, 23 Mich.L.Rev. 825, 845; See also § 8, supra and references in preceding note.

85. E.g., Minn.Stat.Ann., [Mason's Minn.Stat.1927] § 580.27; Eldridge v. Wright, 1880, 55 Cal. 531. See 1941, 135 A.L.R. 196, 198.

86. The owner, being given a prior or subsequent opportunity to redeem, or both, cannot complain. See § 309, supra.

87. Durfee and Doddridge, op. cit. supra note 84, 847.

In some states, notably Illinois, the effect of redemption is not to transfer the title of the purchaser to the redeeming junior lienor, but merely to avoid it as in the case of a redeeming mortgagor. At the same time the junior lien, which may be considered to be suspended, is revived and to it is added the amount which had to be paid in order to redeem. The junior lienor then has to bring further proceedings to enforce his original mortgage augmented by the sum he has paid out in order to redeem.[88]

88. Ogle v. Koerner, 1892, 140 Ill. 170, 29 N.E. 563. See 1937, 5 U. of Chi.L.Rev. 624, 630; Durfee and Doddridge, op. cit. supra note 84, 846; 1941, 135 A. L.R. 196, 206. In Illinois priority of redemption rights of creditors rank in the order of their judgments or decrees. Ill.Ann.Stat., Smith-Hurd, 1966, c. 77, § 24. And a judgment or decree under which the property is sold is treated the same for this purpose as any other, such a creditor being permitted to redeem from his own enforcement sale. Crowder v. Scott State Bank, 1932, 365 Ill. 88, 5 N. E.2d 387, 108 A.L.R. 990. As has been pointed out in criticism, this has, in a large class of cases, a disastrous effect upon the policy of the statute of attempting to realize as much as possible from the sale by putting pressure on the foreclosing creditor. In the case of a mortgage, the deficiency decree would be thus ranked, and it might be, therefore, inferior to other judgments. In such a case the mortgagee would be forced to bid up at peril of an inadequate realization on his security. See 1937, 5 U. of Chi.L.Rev. 724, 729, 731.

In Note, Statutory Redemption, 1962, 34 Rocky Mt.L. Rev. 572, discussing Nelson v. Montgomery, 1961, 59 Wash.2d 268, 367 P.2d 621, which held that a second lienor, who brought an action to foreclose after a first lienor had taken a quit claim deed from the defaulting mortgagor and then gone into possession, was entitled to foreclose but not entitled to compel the prior lienor in possession to account for the rents, issues and profits accruing after a tender by the second lienor of the amount of the debt had been refused. The court, also, by implication denied to the first lienor the privilege of paying off the amount of the second lienor and retaining the property.

In 1959, Illinois, by statute provided a method for a purchaser at the foreclosure sale to pay, during the redemption period, principal, interest, and other amounts due under a prior mortgage and thus protect his interest. See Brodkey, Current Changes in Real Property Law, 1960, 10 DePaul L.Rev. 566, 582.

As to whether a purchaser at a foreclosure sale can prevent "statutory redemption" by a junior lien holder by tendering payment of the debt which the lien secures, see Note, Effect of Satisfying a Junior Lien on Statutory Right of Redemption, 1961, 15 Wyo.L.J. 223.

The effect of redemption by a junior lienor upon the mortgage debt has received varying answers. In jurisdictions where the effect of redemption is merely to continue or revive the subordinate lien, adding to it the amount paid to redeem, the original indebtedness remains unaffected.[89] Older cases in New York reached a similar result by holding that, though the redeeming junior encumbrancer got the purchaser's title, his own mortgage debt was not altered.[90] In Minnesota, however, the court likened the effect of the statute in this respect to a strict foreclosure. Then, proceeding upon the theory that the policy underlying the legislation, i. e., "to have the property of the debtor applied as it will go—as far as creditors will voluntarily apply it—in satisfaction of the debts of the mortgagor," would be furthered by such a construction, held that redemption extinguished the debt to the extent that the value of the land exceeded the redemption payment.[91] The argument in favor of no satisfaction is the incentive to redemption thus offered to a junior lienor, which in turn spurs bidding by the foreclosing mortgagee.[92] This last may offset the apparent injustice to the mortgagor of not having the real value of the property directly applied to the satisfaction of his mortgage debt by the junior lienor. The uncertain amount by which the redeeming junior encumbrancer's debt will be reduced, left to future litigation, which in itself is a deterrent to taking the action, are strong objections to the rule, minimizing as they do the policy of the statute.

The Iowa solution on this point, as in the case of redemption by the mortgagor or his successor,[93] seems the more desirable. It provides that, on redemption, the junior lienor may file a statement of the amount which he is willing to credit on his debt and if he does so, that amount only is credited. If he does not file such a statement, the whole debt is satisfied. And the land in his hands, whichever course he follows, is subject to re-redemption upon paying what he paid to redeem plus the amount credited on his debt.[94] This eliminates any litigation over the value of the property which would discourage redemption; permits the redemptioner to fix the amount he will credit on his debt; and safeguards against an undervaluation on this point by permitting redemption against him.[95]

89. See note-call and note 88, supra.

90. Van Horne v. McLaren, N.Y.1840, 8 Paige 285; Emmet's Admr. v. Bradstreet, N.Y.1838, 20 Wend. 50. Both the foregoing cases were cited as the New York law in Sprague v. Martin, 1882, 29 Minn. 226, 13 N.W. 34. But cf. N.Y.Civ.Prac.T.Act (1920) §§ 728, 729, 741. (These §§ have been omitted from the current Civil Prac. Law, see note 83, supra. Cf. also Benton v. Hatch, 1890, 122 N.Y. 322, 25 N. E. 486.

91. Sprague v. Martin, 1882, 29 Minn. 226, 13 N.W. 34. The decision was approved or followed in Northland Pine Co. v. Northern Insulating Co., 1920, 145 Minn. 395, 177 N.W. 635; Crown Iron Works Co. v. Melin, 1924, 159 Minn. 198, 198 N.W. 462; Work v. Braun, 1909, 19 S.D. 437, 103 N.W. 764, affirmed 23 S.D. 582, 122 N.W. 608. Miller v. Little, 1918, 37 N.D. 612, 164 N.W. 19, commented on in, 1918, 16 Mich.L.Rev. 204, reached a result similar to that in Sprague v. Martin, supra, by invoking the doctrine of merger. Look at Moore v. Penney, 1919, 141 Minn. 454, 170 N.W. 599, 3 A.L.R. 161. See Durfee and Doddridge, supra note 84, 847.

92. Durfee and Doddridge, op. cit. supra note 84, 848. See 1937, 5 U. of Chi.L.Rev. 624, 628.

93. See § 309, supra.

94. Iowa Code Ann.1950, §§ 628.13, 628.17, 628.19. See Durfee and Doddridge, op. cit. supra note 84, 849, 861; Blum, op. cit. supra note 82. See also Ala.Code, 1958, Tit. 7, §§ 729, 735ff.; Kan.Stat.Ann. 1964, § 60–2414.

95. See Durfee and Doddridge, op. cit. supra note 84, note 93, supra.

CHAPTER 13

FORECLOSURE

A. STRICT FORECLOSURE

Sec.
311. England.
312. United States—General Survey.
313. —— Use and Limitations.

B. FORECLOSURE BY STATUTORY SELF HELP AND ACTIONS AT LAW

314. Entry and Writs of Entry.
315. Advertisement or Notice.
316. Scire Facias.

C. BY JUDICIAL SALE

317. Development and General Character—England.
318. —— United States.
319. Parties Plaintiff.
320. Trust Indenture Mortgage Securing Bonds.
321. Parties Defendant.
322. Joinder—Effect of Recording Acts—Lis Pendens.
323. Senior Mortgages and Adverse Interests.
324. Omitted Junior Lienors.
325. Accrual of Rights to Foreclose—Interest, Installments.
326. —— Acceleration.
327. Conduct of Sale.
328. Position of Purchaser.
329. Adequacy of Sale Price—Ordinary Controls.
330. —— Depression Measures—Judicial.
331. —— Moratoria Legislation.
332. Deficiency Judgment—England.
333. Deficiency Judgment—United States.
334. The "One Action" Rule.
335. Anti-Deficiency Legislation.
336. —— Constitutionality and Other Problems.

D. POWER OF SALE

337. History and Nature.
338. Nature of Mortgagee's Power of Sale.
339. Trust Deed Mortgages.
340. Conduct of Sale.
341. Defective Sale.
342. Purchase by Mortgagee.
343. Disposition of Surplus.
344. Purchaser's Position.
345. Current Developments.

A. STRICT FORECLOSURE

ENGLAND

311. Foreclosure by equitable action in England purports to end the mortgagor's equity of redemption if the mortgagor does not perform the obligation within a "short day" set by a preliminary decree nisi. In operation it is slow, costly, and forecloses imperfectly. It has great potentialities of injustice to both parties.

Under the common law title theory of mortgages, failure of the mortgagor to perform on the law day ended, by the terms and operation of the transaction itself, all of his rights in the property so far as the law courts were concerned.[1] The only need that a mortgagee might have to resort to court help would be to obtain possession from a defiant mortgagor who refused to surrender the property to his creditor who had now become absolute owner. For this relief he had the remedy of ejectment. This was not predicated on any theory that by invoking it the erstwhile mortgagee was ending or foreclosing rights residing in the mortgage. Rather it was upon the idea that all rights were now in the mortgagee and that the mortgagor was violating them in refusing to let the mortgagee into possession.[2]

With the development of the equity of redemption,[3] unless the mortgage of land was to be reduced to the level of the common law possessory lien of a bailee of personal property with enforcement consisting only in a privilege to hold onto the property until the debtor performed,[4] some method of terminating it had to be devised. Chancery's solution was the bill in equity to foreclose.[5] Solicitude of the English court of equity for the protection of the equity of redemption extended to the proceeding in equity to foreclose it. Consequently, although the usual description of the first, or nisi, decree is that the chancellor fixed a "short day" within which the mortgagor must redeem or be finally foreclosed,[6] the actual time that would elapse was anything but short. The ordinary slowness and cost of any proceeding in chancery at the time insured that many months would pass before a decree would be entered at all.[7] This decree then ordered an accounting which consumed more time.[8] When the

---

1. See §§ 5, 14, 125, 126, 293, 295, 302, supra.

2. See §§ 5, 125, supra. See note 5, infra.

3. See §§ 6, 7, 301–306, supra.

4. Such a consequence "would not only prejudice the interests of the creditor-mortgagee class, but indirectly those of the debtor-mortgagor class, since the latter's borrowing power would be impaired if they could not under the law give an adequate security." Durfee and Doddridge, Redemption from Foreclosure Sale, 1925, 23 Mich.L.Rev. 824, 826.

5. "A strict foreclosure is a procedure designed to extinguish the equitable right of redemption, the creation of the English Court of Chancery in early times to mitigate the rigors of the common law conception of a mortgage as a conveyance of the legal title upon condition in the nature of a defeasance, i.e., the payment of the debt on the very day stipulated, in default of which the conveyance ipso facto became absolute and the mortgagee's estate ripened into an indefeasible legal title in consonance with the terms of the conveyance. Under the common law formalism, the mortgagee, upon the execution of the mortgage, became vested with the fee to the land, and, upon default in payment, the right of possession; and the mortgagor had no estate or interest therein, and no right of possession, after default in the payment of the mortgage money. The mortgagee's remedy was by ejectment, and in a court of law the mortgagor could not plead, after default, that he was willing and ready to pay the debt." Sears, Roebuck & Co. v. Camp, 1938, 124 N.J.Eq. 403, 406, 1 A.2d 425, 426, 118 A.L.R. 762, 764.

See §§ 10, 303, supra. See also 3 Dan.Ch.Practice, 6th Am. ed., pp. 1911–12; Maitland, Equity, 1936 ed., 182ff.; Tefft, The Myth of Strict Foreclosure, 1937, 4 U. of Chi.L.Rev. 575, 576; Note, 1939, 25 Va.L. Rev. 947. For a delightful as well as illuminating description of typical foreclosure bills, see Glenn, A Study on Strict Foreclosure, 1943, 29 Va.L.Rev. 519, 520. For modern English forms, see Fisher and Lightwood, Morts., 7th ed., 807ff.

For a scholarly and entertaining discussion of the equitable bill to foreclose in England, see Durfee, Cases on Security, 1951, pp. 21–25, 178–180.

6. See Seton, Forms and Orders in Equity, 1830. 139–144; 4 Kent, Comm., 14th ed. 1896, *181.

7. Jarndyce v. Jarndyce in Dickens' Bleak House portrays the picture with recognizable verisimilitude. For a more prosaic corroboration, see 9 Holdsworth, Hist. of Eng. Law, 335ff.

8. See §§ 164–176, 303, supra. See also Coote, Mortgages, 9th ed., § 1060; Fisher and Lightwood, Mortgages, 7th ed., 772.

accounting was concluded the mortgagor was granted, as a matter of course, a six months additional period within which to redeem,[9] and further extensions were common upon some showing of cause which might be very slender.[10] After the expiration of the redemption period the mortgagee was entitled to a second, or final decree,[11] up to the entry of which the mortgagor still might redeem. However, even after such a decree purporting to debar and foreclose a redemption absolutely and finally,[12] it might still be reopened either as a matter of indulgence or of right. The former lay in the discretion of the chancellor and its exercise was never precisely defined.[13] And it might be reopened not only against the mortgagee but against a purchaser from him.[14]

There neither was nor is such a thing as a decree for a deficiency in England.[15] However, the final decree of foreclosure does not prevent an action at law upon the mortgage obligation,[16] nor does it prevent the exercise of any power of sale that the mortgagee may have as mortgagee as distinct from his ability to dispose of the property as an incident of ownership. However, if the mortgagee sues the mortgagor on his personal obligation, the foreclosure is reopened as a matter of right

9. Coote, supra, 1061.

10. Edward v. Cunliffe, 1816, 1 Madd. 287, in which four extensions, totaling 24 months, were granted, is probably not typical in length, but it is in character. Look also at Ismoord v. Claypool, 1666–1667, 1 Rep.Ch. 262; Holford v. Yate, 1855, 1 K. § J. 677; Nanny v. Edwards, 1827, 4 Russ. 127. See Tefft, op. cit. supra note 5, supra, p. 578. For criticism, see Novosielski v. Wakefield, 1811, 17 Ves.Jr. 417, 418; and 2 Maddock, Ch.Prac., 4th Am. ed. 1832, p. 492. Under the older practice it was customary to give additional periods of redemption to each of any junior lienors. Spence, Equitable Jurisdiction, 1850, 687; Seton, Forms and Orders in Equity, 1830, 157, 161ff. The mortgagor then might have another three months beyond the last lienor's time for payment. Seton, Judgments and Orders, 7th ed., 1907. Modern English practice is to permit only one redemption period. Fisher and Lightwood, Mortgages, 7th ed., 779; Coote, Mortgages, 9th ed., 1061.

11. Seton, Judgments and Orders, 7th ed., 1825 et seq. For provisions in a foreclosure judgment, see Fisher and Lightwood, Mortgages, 7th ed. 772.

12. Since the mortgagee under the title theory already had complete legal ownership of the property the foreclosure decree created no new rights in him. If the mortgagor had retained possession, however, the mortgagee might need additional court help to enjoy his rights. And for this he would have to resort to an action at law. The equity foreclosure decree concerned itself only with the ending of the equitable right to redeem and the equity court refused to aid the mortgagee to get possession. See Tefft, op. cit. supra note 5, 578, 582; Turner, The English Mortgage of Land as Security, 1934, 20 Va. L.Rev. 729, 733, 735; Glenn, A Study of Strict Foreclosure, 1943, 29 Va.L.Rev. 519, 522, 529, 554. Today the decree may add an order for possession. Fisher and Lightwood, Mortgages, 7th ed., 801.

In the case of an equitable mortgage, foreclosure necessitated a conveyance of the legal title of the mortgagor to the mortgagee, and this equity would order the mortgagor to execute. Idem. 774. Cf. James v. James, 1873, L.R. 16 Eq. 153; York Union Banking Co. v. Artley, 1878, 11 Ch.D. 205; Marshall v. Shrewsbury, 1875, L.R. 10 Ch.App. 250.

13. See note-call and note 69, § 10, supra. See also Fisher and Lightwood, Mortgages, 7th ed., 784; Falconbridge, Mortgages., 2d ed., 418, Canadian law; Tefft, op. cit. supra note 5, 578. It might be granted years later. Burgh v. Langton, 1724, 5 Bro.P.C., 213, 15 Vin.Abr. 476, 2 Eq.Cas.Abr. 609 (16 years after final decree); Jones v. Creswicke, 1839, 9 Sim. 304.

14. Campbell v. Holyland, 1876, 7 Ch.D. 166; Maitland, Equity, rev. ed., 186–187; Tefft, note 5, supra, 578. This would not be true where the sale was a considerable time after the final order and without notice of facts which would lead to a reopening. Re Power and Carton's Contract, 1890, 25 L.R.Ir. 459, refusing to reopen; see Campbell v. Holyland, 1887, 7 Ch.D.; Fisher and Lightwood, Mortgages, 7th ed., 784.

15. "That is because foreclosure is regarded as cutting off the mortgagor's equity, and not a step in the collection of the debt due the mortgagee." Glenn, Rev. of Walsh, Mortgages, 1935, 21 Va.L. Rev. 595, 597. See Turner, op. cit. supra note 12, at 732, 735. Tefft, op. cit. supra note 5, supra, 586–7; 1939, 25 Va.L.Rev. 947, 948. However, in bankruptcy the mortgagee might prove only for the amount of his debt reduced by the value of the security, i. e., in effect for a deficiency. See Fisher and Lightwood, Mortgages, 7th ed., 442; Glenn, A Study on Strict Foreclosure, 1943, 29 Va.L.Rev. 519, 529; Turner, op. cit. supra note 12, 735.

16. See Turner, op. cit. supra note 12, 733, 735. There was some early opinion that it did operate as a complete bar to an action on the debt. See Perry v. Barker, 1806, 13 Ves. 198. Today under the Judicature Act, a mortgagee may obtain in the Chancery Division in his suit to foreclose not only foreclosure but a judgment on the mortgagor's covenant. Judicature Act, 1875, 38 & 39 Vict., c. 77; see Poulett v. Hill, [1893] 1 Ch.D. 277; Maitland, Equity, rev. ed., 185.

and the mortgagor is permitted to redeem.[17] If the mortgagee in his capacity as owner has sold the property to a third person so that he cannot restore it on redemption, his action may be enjoined.[18] If, after foreclosure, the mortgagee sells under a power of sale the purchaser gets title which cannot be disturbed,[19] but the foreclosure is reopened as to the purchase money for which he will have to account to the mortgagor.[20]

There is nothing to prevent the mortgagee first suing upon the debt, getting judgment, collecting what he can out of other assets of the mortgagor, and then foreclosing on the mortgaged property.[21] Normally a mortgagor against whom foreclosure is necessary would have no other assets of value at that time which could be reached under a judgment at law. And the price of the chance of reaching whatever there might be would be the costs of two suits and postponement of the time when the mortgagee can reach the rents and profits of the mortgaged property.[22]

The foregoing summary justifies the conclusion that strict foreclosure in England is unsatisfactory to mortgagees because it is slow, costly, and forecloses imperfectly.[23] If the property is of less value than the mortgage debt the mortgagee is likely to suffer because he has no convenient way of collecting the deficiency. On the other hand, if the land is worth more than the amount of the debt, there is injustice to the mortgagor.[24] As a consequence other methods of ending the mortgagor's right of redemption and realizing upon the security were developed[25] and resorted to.[26] These methods will be examined in later subdivisions of this chapter.[27]

UNITED STATES—GENERAL SURVEY

312. Strict foreclosure, although available under certain circumstances in at least nineteen states, is commonly used only in three. The different development of the process in America which made it harsh, summary and oppressive, the prevalence of the lien theory, and statutory provisions account for the little use made of it.

In the United States in a majority of states strict foreclosure of a mortgagor's interest by a mortgagee is not permitted.[28] However it

17. Dashwood v. Blythway, 1729, 1 Eq.Cas.Abr. 317; Aylet v. Hill, ch. 1779, Dick. 551; Tooke v. Hartley, 1784, 2 Dick.Ch. 785, s. c. 1786, 2 Bro.C.C. 125; see Lockhart v. Hardy, 1846, 9 Beav. 349, 357. See also Turner, op. cit. supra note 12, 733. Glenn, op. cit. supra note 5, 526. As a consequence Maitland observed that "One is not very safe in purchasing a foreclosed estate, and owing to this meddlesome equity foreclosure is not a procedure upon which prudent mortgagees will place much of their reliance." Maitland, Equity, rev. ed., 186.

18. Perry v. Barker, 1806, 13 Ves.Jr. 198. See Turner, op. cit. supra note 12, 733; Coote, Mortgages, 9th ed., 901; Fisher and Lightwood, Mortgages, 7th ed., 785.

19. Cf. Watson v. Marston, 1853, 4 De G. M. & G. 230; Stevens v. Theatres [1903], 1 Ch. 857, commented on, 1903, 47 Sol.J. 564.

20. See Fisher and Lockwood, Morts., 7th ed., 786; Turner, op. cit. supra note 12, 733.

21. See 2 Coote, Mortgages, 9th ed., 901.

22. See Tefft, op. cit. supra note 5, 582, 586.

23. Idem. 579.

24. See 1939, 25 Va.L.Rev. 947, 948.

25. The Chancery Improvement Act (1852), 15 & 16 Vict.Ch. 86, § 48, was the first of these enactments. This act gave the English courts discretionary power to order a sale, though neither party has an absolute right to require it. It was succeeded by the Conveyancing Act (1881) 44 & 45 Vict., c. 41, § 25. See Campbell, Cases on Mortgages, 2d ed., 247, n. 1. See also Moulton v. Cornish, 1893, 138 N.Y. 133, 33 N.E. 842, 20 L.R.A. 370, Campbell, Cases on Morts., 2d ed., 245; Sears Roebuck & Co. v. Camp, 1938, 124 N.J.Eq. 403, 1 A.2d 425, 118 A.L.R. 762, Osborne, Cases Property Security, 656. Lord Eldon, as early as 1813, ordered a sale without the aid of statute on the theory that an equity court has inherent power to decree a sale. Mondey v. Mondey, 1813, 1 V. & B. 223. The modern English mortgage usually contains an express power of sale. Turner, The English Mortgage of Land as a Security, 1934, 20 Va.L.Rev. 729.

26. Today, in England, the decree of sale or power of sale, especially the latter, has all but supplanted the action for foreclosure as the means of barring the mortgagor's interest. See Turner, An English View of Mortgage Deficiency Judgments, 1935, 21 Va.L.Rev. 601, 604.

27. Subdivisions C, D, infra.

28. 1893, 20 L.R.A. 370; 1939, 118 A.L.R. 769. See note, 1939, 25 Va.L.Rev. 947, 949; 1899, 18 Eng.

does exist in a good many jurisdictions. In Connecticut strict foreclosure was and still is the usual form [29] even though in 1886 a statute [30] provided for foreclosure sale on written notice by any party, the granting of which is subject to the court's discretion. In Vermont, also, strict foreclosure by bill and decree is the customary remedy.[31] Illinois is a third state in which strict foreclosure, hedged about by salutary restrictions,[32] remains in common use. Decisions in that state lay down three requirements for its employment, all of which must concur [33]: the

premises must not be worth more than the debt plus interest and costs; [34] the mortgagee must be willing to take the property in full satisfaction of the debt; [35] and the mortgagor must be insolvent.[36] In at least [37] sixteen additional states strict foreclosure is allowed under certain circumstances.[38]

There are several reasons for the prevailing view. Perhaps underlying all of them, and accounting as well for some other developments in American foreclosure law, is

Rul.Cas. 501. See Durfee, Cases on Security, 1951, p. 180.

29. Waters v. Hubbard, 1877, 44 Conn. 340.

30. Conn.Gen.Stat.1930, § 5112, retained in Conn. Gen.Stat.Ann.1960, § 49.24. See Bradford Realty Corp. v. Beetz, 1928, 108 Conn. 26, 31, 142 A. 395, 397; North End Bank & Trust Co. v. Mandell, 1931, 113 Conn. 241, 245; 155 A. 80, 81.

31. Vt.Stat.Ann., 1958, Tit. 12, §§ 4–521, 4–522, petition and decree and by bill. Devereaux v. Fairbanks, 1880, 52 Vt. 587; Paris v. Hulett, 1854, 26 Vt. 308; see Hill v. Hill, 1887, 59 Vt. 125, 7 A. 468, 471. An alternative, seldom used, is ejectment. Vt.Pub.Laws, 1923, §§ 1557–9, apparently no longer provided for.

32. So satisfactory is the working of the remedy in Illinois that its extension has been advocated. See Kircher, Some Suggestions Concerning Illinois Foreclosure Laws, 1937, 3 J. Marshall L.Q. 193, 300; Anderson, Proposed Mortgage Foreclosure Law in Illinois, 1936, 2 J. Marshall L.Q. 293, 297.

For the requirements of strict foreclosure in Illinois, see Prather, Foreclosure of the Security Interest, 1957 U. of Ill.L.Forum, 420, 446. See also Brodkey, Current Changes in Illinois Real Property Law, 1960, 10 DePaul L.Rev. 566, 580.

33. See Carpenter v. Plagge, 1901, 192 Ill. 82, 99, 61 N.E. 530, 536; Johnson v. Donnell, 1853, 15 Ill. 97, 99. See also Thomas, Strict Foreclosure in Illinois, 1910, 4 Ill.L.Rev. 572; Anderson, Proposed Mortgage Foreclosure Law in Illinois, 1936, 2 John Marshall L.Q. 293, 297; Carey, Brabner-Smith & Sullivan, Studies in Foreclosures in Cook County: II. Foreclosure Methods and Redemption, 1933, 27 Ill. L.Rev. 595, 609; idem, 870; MacChesney with Leesman, Collaborator, Mortgages, Foreclosures and Reorganizations, 31 Ill.L.Rev. 287, 300; note, 1939, 25 Va.L.Rev. 947, 950; Campbell, Cases on Mortgages, 2d ed., 247, n. 2. See also Leesman, Corporate Trusteeship and Receivership, 1933, 28 Ill.L. Rev. 238, 245 for the possibility of strict foreclosure in the case of a corporate mortgage by trust deed. A fourth requirement, that there be no junior lienors nor creditors, has practically disappeared. Rexroat v. Ford, 1916, 201 Ill.App. 342; Barnes v. Ward, 1914, 190 Ill.App. 392.

34. Carpenter v. Plagge, 1901, 192 Ill. 82, 61 N.E. 530; Barnes v. Ward, 1914, 190 Ill.App. 392, 395, 398, 399.

35. Griesbaum v. Baum, 1886, 18 Ill.App. 614; Miller v. Davis, 1879, 5 Ill.App. 474.

36. Rabbit v. First Nat. Bank, 1925, 237 Ill.App. 289. The Illinois law has been praised as eliminating the most serious objections to strict foreclosure in America by protecting the mortgager against paying a small debt with property worth much more, losing his property and being saddled besides with a deficiency judgment, or forfeiting his property when he might be able to pay a money judgment. See note, 1939, 25 Va.L.Rev. 947, 950.

37. Glenn, A Study on Strict Foreclosure, 1943, 29 Va.L.Rev. 519, suggests that under certain circumstances it may be available in all states. See also 1939, 118 A.L.R. 769, 770.

38. They are Alabama, California, Indiana, Iowa, Maryland, Massachusetts, Minnesota, Mississippi, Nebraska, New Jersey, New York, North Carolina, Oregon, Rhode Island, South Dakota, Utah. 1939, 25 Va.L.Rev. 947, 949 n. 32. See also 1893, 20 L.R. A. 370; 1939, 118 A.L.R. 769. West Virginia may be added to the list. Froidevaux v. Jordan, 1908, 64 W.Va. 388, 62 S.E. 686, 131 Am.St.Rep. 911. Among the scarce authorities to be found in these states are Jackson v. Weaver, 1894, 138 Ind. 539, 38 N.E. 166; Andrews v. Scotton, Md.1826, 2 Bland. 629; Shaw v. Norfolk R. Co., 1855, 71 Mass. (5 Gray) 162; Woods v. Shields, 1871, 1 Neb. 453; Pettingill v. Hubbell, 1895, 53 N.J.Eq. 584, 32 A. 76; Hazard v. Robinson, 1886, 15 R.I. 226, 2 A. 433.

For a discussion of the New York law, see Sutherland, Foreclosure and Sale—Some Suggested Changes in the New York Procedure, 1937, 22 Cornell L.Q. 216, 222; note, 1939, 25 Va.L.Rev. 947, 952 n. 67. In the note last cited is a good summary of the requirements for strict foreclosure in the other states which permit it.

In Hermann v. Churchill, 1963, 235 Or. 327, 385 P.2d 190, commented on in Note, 1964, 43 Or.L.Rev. 350, the court held that strict foreclosure may be decreed in a suit to have a deed absolute declared a mortgage, in spite of a statute providing for foreclosure of "all liens" by a foreclosure sale. The court said the statute did not apply to an action to redeem. See §§ 77 n. 67 and 78 n. 72a, supra.

a marked difference in the speed, severity, and finality of the proceeding in this country as compared with that in England. Extensions are not granted freely as in England; [39] in some jurisdictions no redemption is permitted after the lapse of time set in the first decree; [40] and the final decree is, as its language purports to be, really final and cuts off permanently all possibility of redemption.[41] It has been stated that an action on the debt after foreclosure does not reopen the foreclosure so as to permit redemption, but this may be doubted.[42] In such an action the judgment would be limited to the difference between the value of the security and the mortgage debt, i. e., in effect a deficiency judgment.[43] However, the mort-

gagor is not entitled to any surplus if the worth of the property exceeds that of the debt.[44] The severity to the mortgagor of these features has been accentuated by sudden and extreme fluctuations of land values.[45] As a result the process of foreclosure without sale in America may be justly described as operating "summarily, harshly, and oppressively." [46] The difference between it and its English prototype is indicated in the terminology in the two countries. The common and well-founded belief in the inequitable nature of such relief is reflected in America by the descriptive epithet "strict" which preceded "foreclosure" when this process was

---

39. See Tefft, The Myth of Strict Foreclosure, 1937, 4 U. of Chi.L.Rev. 577, 588, pointing out that in Jones, Mortgages, 8th ed., § 1994, the only American authority cited for the statement that the time for redemption may be enlarged for satisfactory reason is a dictum in Downing et al. v. Palmateer, Ky. 1824, 1 T.B.Mon. (17 Ky.) 64, 66, which was a case of foreclosure by sale. But in Vermont the redemption period itself is a long one. See Langdon v. Stiles, Vt.1827, 2 Aiken 184.

40. See Ellis v. Leek, 1889, 127 Ill. 60, 20 N.E. 218, 3 L.R.A. 259.

41. See Tefft, op. cit. supra note 39, 588. But cf. Doty v. Whitlesey, Conn.1791, 1 Root 310, lengthening the term because of accident preventing payment; Bostwick v. Stiles, 1868, 35 Conn. 195, payment not made because of sickness, term extended.

42. See Tefft, supra, citing Hatch v. White, C.C.N. H.1814, 2 Gall. 152. See contra, Lovell v. Leland, 1831, 3 Vt. 581, 588; Andrews v. Scotton, Md.1826, 2 Bland.Ch. 629, 665; Hazard v. Robinson, 1886, 15 R.I. 226, 2 A. 433.

43. Devereaux v. Fairbanks, 1880, 52 Vt. 587; Paris v. Hulett, 1854, 26 Vt. 308, decree operates as satisfaction in whole or in part; see Hill v. Hill, 1886, 59 Vt. 125, 130, 7 A. 468; Hazard v. Robinson, 1886, 15 R.I. 226, 2 A. 433. See Sears, Roebuck & Co. v. Camp, 1938, 124 N.J.Eq. 403, 1 A.2d 425, 118 A.L.R. 762, "A decree of strict foreclosure does not operate to extinguish the debt, unless the mortgaged lands are of sufficient value to satisfy it. The value of the property may be ascertained in the event of a suit at law upon the mortgage debt." Cf. Amory v. Fairbanks, 1793, 3 Mass. 562; Dooley v. Potter, 1884, 140 Mass. 49, 2 N.E. 935; Hatch v. White, C. C.N.H.1841, 2 Gall. 152. Before 1833 in Connecticut foreclosure extinguished the debt regardless of the value of the property. Derby Bank v. Landon, 1819, 3 Conn. 62. Legislation in that year, Conn. Pub.Acts 1833, c. 18, and later, Conn.Laws, 1878, ch.

129, § 2, provide for recovery of the difference between the mortgage debt and the value of the property as estimated at the end of the period set for redemption. See Windham Co. Sav. Bank v. Himes, 1887, 55 Conn. 433, 12 A. 517. In Illinois, because of the rule that in order to have strict foreclosure the mortgagee must accept the property in full satisfaction, there can be no deficiency judgment. See n. 35, ante. See also Carpenter v. Plagge, 1901, 192 Ill. 82, 61 N.E. 530. The early rule, however, was the other way. See Vansant v. Allmon, 1859, 23 Ill. 30.

A different fundamental attitude toward the purpose of foreclosure helps explain why American courts granted a deficiency judgment after a strict foreclosure. To them every kind of foreclosure was merely a means of applying the security to the satisfaction of the debt. See Sprague v. Martin, 1882, 29 Minn. 226, 229, 13 N.W. 34, 36. See also Glenn, A Study in Strict Foreclosure, 1943, 29 Va.L.Rev. 519, 529, 554. In England, foreclosure was concerned solely with disencumbering the property of any claim to it by the mortgagor; collection of the debt was left to a separate process.

See § 311, note 12, supra. See Glenn, A Study of Strict Foreclosure, 1943, 29 Va.L.Rev. 519, 554; Tefft, The Myth of Strict Foreclosure, 1937, 4 U. of Chi.L.Rev. 575, 594; 1939, 25 Va.L.Rev. 947, 949.

44. Andreas v. Hubbard, 1882, 50 Conn. 351; Perry v. Ward, 1909, 82 Vt. 1, 71 A. 721; cf. Flint v. Winter Harbor Land Co., 1896, 89 Me. 420, 36 A. 634.

45. Tefft, op. cit., supra note 43, 588.

46. Tefft, op. cit. supra note 43, 595. See also Perine v. Dunn, N.Y.1819, 4 Johns.Ch. 140, 143; Bolles v. Duff, 1871, 43 N.Y. 469, 474; Jefferson v. Coleman, 1886, 110 Ind. 515, 11 N.E. 465; Bradley v. The Chester Valley R. R. Co., 1860, 36 Pa. 141, 150; Hord v. James, 1805, 1 Tenn. 201. On the other hand it has the merit of saving the costs of a sale, which are considerable. See Barnes v. Ward, 1914, 190 Ill.App. 392, 399. See also Turner, An English view of Mortgage Deficiency Judgments, 1935, 21 Va.L.Rev. 601, 608.

meant as distinguished from "foreclosure by sale." [47]   In contrast the English usage is between "foreclosure" and "sale in lieu of foreclosure." [48]

Another technical reason why strict foreclosure did not flourish in the United States is the prevalence of the lien theory.   Strict foreclosure is thought of as not creating any new rights in the mortgagee, but as merely destroying all interest of the mortgagor in the property, leaving the mortgagee's title to it free and clear. [49]   A requirement, therefore, is that the mortgagee must have legal title. [50]   Where he has only a legal lien with legal title in the mortgagor, it obviously will

not work. [51]   This is true even though the mortgagor is owner of only a portion of the legal title. [52]

In several states absence of strict foreclosure is accounted for by statutes making a sale the exclusive remedy or forbidding any form of foreclosure not expressly provided for, with strict foreclosure not listed. [53]   This

47. See Chancellor Kent in Perine v. Dunn, N.Y.1819, 4 Johns.Ch. 140, 143, and 4 Kent, Comm., 14th ed., § 181. See also Tefft, op. cit. supra note 43, 577.

48. Coote, Mortgages, 9th ed., 1049.

49. See § 311, notes 5, 12, supra; Warner Bros. Co. v. Freud, 1903, 138 Cal. 651, 72 P. 345, "Strict foreclosure * * * is closely analogous to actions to quiet title where the plaintiff holds the legal title and seeks to remove some claim asserted against it." See also Bresnahan v. Bresnahan, 1879, 46 Wis. 385, 1 N.W. 39, 42.

50. "Generally speaking, in cases of strict foreclosure, the plaintiff must have title against which the defendant has or asserts some equity." Warner Bros. Co. v. Freud, 1903, 138 Cal. 651, 654, 72 P. 345, 346.
Accord: Jackson v. Weaver, 1894, 138 Ind. 539, 38 N. E. 166; Jefferson v. Coleman, 1887, 110 Ind. 515, 11 N.E. 465; Mickelson v. Anderson, 1932, 81 Utah 444, 19 P.2d 1033. See Moulton v. Cornish, 1893, 138 N.Y. 133, 141, 33 N.E. 842, 844, 20 L.R.A. 370. See note, 1939, 25 Va.L.Rev. 947, 950. See also § 77 note 67, supra.
"So strict foreclosure is often resorted to in cases of land contracts where the vendor has retained the title and the vendee has failed to perform his contract. In such case the court finds the amount unpaid, and decrees that it be paid on or before a day stated, and upon failure to make the payment that defendant's equity be foreclosed." Warner Bros. Co. v. Freud, 1903, 138 Cal. 651, 654, 72 P. 345, 346. See Vanneman, Strict Foreclosure on Land Contracts, 1930, 14 Minn.L.Rev. 342; Glenn, Book Review, 1935, 21 Va.L.Rev. 595, 596; note, 1938, 17 Or.L.Rev. 333. See also 1932, 77 A.L.R. 270. Cf. Arnold, The Mortgage in Essence, 1946, 19 Rocky Mt.L.Rev. 123.
For other discussions of the use of strict foreclosure by a vendor in land contracts, see Am.L.Prop., 1952, §§ 11.75, .76.

51. See Moulton v. Cornish, 1893, 138 N.Y. 133, 136, 33 N.E. 842, 844, 20 L.R.A. 370, "this proceeding has been termed a strict foreclosure, but it is apparent that it has no appropriate place in a system of laws and jurisprudence where it has been declared that the mortgage does not operate as a conveyance of the legal title, but is only a chose in action constituting a lien upon the land as security for the debt or other obligation of the mortgagor." But cf. § 311, note 12, supra. Equity found no difficulty in granting a strict foreclosure of an equitable mortgage by compelling the mortgagor, who had the legal title, to convey it to the mortgagee, who had only an equitable interest, and then barring any claim to get it back. The mechanics for working out a strict foreclosure in a lien jurisdiction could be the same. It may be urged that the basis for equitable intervention to force transfer of title from mortgagor to mortgagee is different in the case of an equitable mortgage than in the case of a legal lien; that equity is merely first giving to the mortgagee the title in mortgage to which his agreement entitles him, and then proceeding to foreclose the mortgagor's equity in the ordinary way. This breaks down, of course, where the equitable mortgage does not contemplate a legal mortgage at any time. See §§ 24, 29, supra. And it seems doubtful that the chancery court would have felt incapable of action because of such a distinction had it really felt it highly desirable to give such relief.

52. Silver v. Berger, 1930, 228 App.Div. 591, 240 N. Y.S. 468; South Omaha Sav. Bank v. Levy, Neb. 1901, 95 N.W. 603.
In Surety Bldg. & Loan Ass'n. of Newark v. Risack, 1935, 118 N.J.Eq. 425, 179 A. 680, commented on in, 1935, 22 Va.L.Rev. 227, one of the mortgagors who had title to an undivided one-half interest in the mortgaged property had not been served with process in the foreclosure proceedings. The mortgagee sought to cut off the rights of this omitted party by a proceeding of strict foreclosure. Held, that the remedy of strict foreclosure is not available against the owner of a fee or a part thereof, and that the omitted party must be proceeded against in an independent foreclosure action.

53. E. g., Ariz.Code Ann., 1939, 62–517, held unconstitutional in Tucson Manor v. Federal Nat. Mortgage Ass'n, 1952, 73 Ariz. 387, 241 P.2d 1126. Ariz. Rev.Stat.Ann.1956, § 33–725 deals with the matter but does not support the text. Ark.Stat.Ann.1947, 51–1108; Burns, Ind.Stats.1933, Ann. (Bobbs-Merrill, 1946 Replacement), 3–1801; Iowa Code, Ann. 1950, Ch. 6554.5 and Gamut v. Gregg, 1873, 37 Iowa

was true in New York[54] before an amendment in 1924 which permitted its use against a second or subsequent lien which has been matured for five years or more.[55]

UNITED STATES—USE AND LIMITATIONS

313. Strict foreclosure is permitted in lien states where the plaintiff has acquired legal title and the process is regarded by the court under the circumstances of the case as an equitable method of ending an outstanding right of redemption. Its most important use for this purpose, except in states allowing it in an original foreclosure action, is by bona fide purchasers on foreclosure sale against junior interests, chiefly subordinate liens, which were unintentionally omitted from the prior foreclosure proceeding.

The requirement of strict foreclosure that the plaintiff must have legal title[56] is met in lien states in certain situations. Where the mortgage is in the form of a deed absolute on its face it is held in some lien states that the grantee gets legal title rather than a lien and hence the condition is satisfied.[57]

The most frequent instance in which the remedy may be used is, however, where a mortgagee has foreclosed by sale but has failed to join some party who has an interest in the property subject to the mortgage.[58] The mortgagee, or a third person, may purchase at the foreclosure sale and thus unite in himself all interest in the property[59] save that of the unjoined party which is of course, unaffected by the action.[60] Where the prior foreclosure is defective because the mortgagor or owner of the property, or part of it, was not joined, strict foreclosure is not allowed, sale being required.[61] In such a case the legal title in whole or in part remains outstanding in the unjoined party; the mort-

57³. Also, Nevin v. Lulu & White Silver Mining Co., 1887, 10 Colo. 357, 15 P. 611.

54. N.Y.Code Civ.Proc. § 1626; Moulton v. Cornish, 1893, 138 N.Y. 133, 33 N.E. 842, 20 L.R.A 370.

55. Laws of 1925, c. 510 (N.Y.Civ.Pr.Act § 1082). N. Y. Real Prop.Actions & Proc.Law §§ 1351, 1354, 1355, 1362, 1352 has the present provisions. § 1352 is derived from § 1082, supra.

56. See § 312 note-calls and notes 50–52.

57. Blanchard v. Hoffman, 1923, 154 Minn. 525, 192 N.W. 352; Gallagher v. Giddings, 1891, 33 Neb. 222, 49 N.W. 1126; Hunt v. Lewin, Ala.1833, 4 Stew. & P. 138. See Sears, Roebuck & Co. v. Camp, 1938, 124 N.J.Eq. 403, 1 A.2d 425, 118 A.L.R. 762, saying that strict foreclosure has been recognized in such cases but observing that foreclosure by sale is preferable. But cf. § 77, supra. Contra: Murdock v. Clark, 1891, 90 Cal. 427, 442, 27 P. 275, 279, deed absolute mortgage gets only a lien; Sibel v. Pierce, 1934, 147 Or. 132, 31 P.2d 1106. But see § 77 n. 67 ante. And see McCaughey v. McDuffie, 1903, 7 Cal.Unrep. 175, 187, 74 P. 751, 754. See also Glenn, A Study in Strict Foreclosure, 1943, 29 Va. L.Rev. 519, 545.

58. Cf. § 305, supra. Apart from the three jurisdictions, see § 312, supra, in which foreclosure is commonly used by the mortgagee in the original foreclosure action, this statement applies in title as well as lien states.

59. E. g., Miles v. Stehle, 1888, 22 Neb. 740, 36 N.W. 142; Sears, Roebuck & Co. v. Camp, 1938, 124 N.J. Eq. 403, 1 A.2d 425, 118 A.L.R. 762; noted, 1939, 23 Minn.L.Rev. 388. See 1939, 118 A.L.R. 769; 1949, 88 U. of Pa.L.Rev. 994. See also note 63, infra; and § 324, infra. The same situation occurs where the mortgagee buys in the premises on an execution sale under a judgment against the mortgagor. Benedict v. Mortimer, N.J.Eq.1887, 8 A. 515; Eldridge v. Eldridge, 1862, 14 N.J.Ch. 195.

60. In the absence of statute, this is generally true even though the foreclosing mortgagee has no knowledge or notice of the subordinate interest of another person in the mortgaged property. See Haines v. Beach, N.Y.1818, 3 Johns.Ch. 459, 461; § 306, supra; Campbell, Cases on Mortgages, 2d ed., 273 n. 1. However, under recording acts, in accordance with their policy, if a purchaser on foreclosure sale has no actual notice of the existence of such an interest, and is not charged with constructive notice because its holder has failed to record, the latter will be bound by the foreclosure to the same extent as if he had been joined as a party. Sibell v. Weeks, 1903, 65 N.J.Eq. 714, 55 A. 244; Rogers v. Houston, 1901, 94 Tex. 403, 60 S.W. 869; Walker v. Schreiber, 1877, 47 Iowa 529, actual notice; Hoppin v. Doty, 1868, 22 Wis. 621, actual notice. See 1940, 88 U. of Pa.L.Rev. 994, 997. And if the unjoined party held only an equitable interest, it could be cut off by the foreclosure sale the purchaser under the doctrine of bona fide purchase if the buyer had no notice of its existence and paid value bona fide. See §§ 182, 185, supra.

61. Georgia Casualty Co. v. O'Donnell, 1933, 109 Fla. 290, 147 So. 267; Gamut v. Gregg, 1873, 37 Iowa 573; United States Sav. Bank v. Schnitzer, 1935, 118 N.J.Eq. 584, 180 A. 624; Surety Building & Loan Ass'n v. Risack, 1935, 118 N.J.Eq. 425, 179 A. 680, 22 Va.L.Rev. 227; Mickelson v. Anderson, 1933, 81 Utah 444, 19 P.2d 1033. See 1939, 118 A.L.R. 769, 779.

gagee or third party purchaser, who succeeds in such a case only to the interest of
the mortgagee and joined parties, is still only
a mortgagee and must foreclose by sale in
order to protect the title holder.[62]

Where the legal title has passed to the
purchaser on foreclosure sale, but is still subject to a redemptive right in some person
whose interest is subordinate to the mortgage and who was not joined as a party to
the foreclosure action strict foreclosure may
be ordered.[63] There is authority that in order to have strict foreclosure against such
omitted junior interests the plaintiff must establish both that he bought in good faith
without knowledge of the outstanding interest and that its holder knew of the sale

and permitted the plaintiff to buy without
disclosing his own interest.[64] And it is quite
clear that if the holder of the junior interest
is intentionally omitted from the foreclosure
action, the mortgagee cannot later have
strict foreclosure to cut off his redemption
right.[65] Other cases follow a flexible rule
that there must be equitable grounds for relief and, in general, require that the omission must be through inadvertence or mistake untinged with bad faith.[66] In addition,
the courts look at the amount the property
sold for at the prior foreclosure sale or the
value of the property.[67] If the premises are
worth no more than the encumbrances prior
to the one sought to be foreclosed, it is persuasive that strict foreclosure should be
granted.[68] However, the right of a junior
mortgagee to have a judicial sale at which its
holder may appear and protect the lien by

---

62. See note 61, supra; § 312, notes 50–52, supra; §
305, ante. See also, Glenn, A Study on Strict Foreclosure, 1943, 29 Va.L.Rev. 519, 547. "Conceivably
the interest of the omitted party, though he be not
a mere encumbrancer, may be so insignificant, remote, or contingent, or be so affected by his inequitable conduct, as to render the requirement of a
second foreclosure sale unnecessary, impractical, or
unjust." 1939, 118 A.L.R. 769. Kansas courts have
held that, in their discretion, they may permit
strict foreclosure against a mortgagor or other
owner to even a "mortgagee in possession." Bankers' Mortgage Co. of Topeka v. O'Donovan, 1933,
137 Kan. 309, 312, 20 P.2d 809, 811; Sutor v. First
Nat. Bank, 1937, 146 Kan. 52, 69 P.2d 315.

63. See 1940, 88 U. of Pa.L.Rev. 994, 1006; Glenn,
op. cit. supra note 62; 1939, 25 Va.L.Rev. 947, 951;
1939, 118 A.L.R. 769, 770; Campbell, Cases Mortgages, 248 n. 4. Cf. § 305, supra, for the related
problem of strict foreclosure on a bill to redeem.
Examples of such interests include: a junior mortgage, Leslie v. Smith, 1931, 58 S.D. 14, 234 N.W.
669; Quinn Plumbing Co. v. New Miami Shores
Corp., 1930, 100 Fla. 413, 129 So. 690, 73 A.L.R.
600; Evans v. Atkins, 1888, 75 Iowa 448, 39 N.W.
702; Miles v. Stehle, 1888, 22 Neb. 740, 36 N.W.
142; Shepard v. Barrett, 1915, 84 N.J.Eq. 408, 93 A.
852; Sears, Roebuck & Co. v. Camp, 1938, 124 N.J.
Eq. 403, 1 A.2d 425, 118 A.L.R. 762; a judgment
lien, Koerner v. Willamette Iron Works, 1899, 36
Or. 90, 58 P. 863; Lockard v. Hendrickson, N.J.Ch.
1892, 25 A. 512; a lease, Mesiavech v. Newman,
1936, 120 N.J.Eq. 192, 184 A. 538; an easement,
Hinners v. Birkevaag, 1933, 113 N.J.Eq. 413, 167 A.
209; but cf. Monese v. Struve, 1936, 155 Or. 68, 62
P.2d 822, noted, 1937, 50 Harv.L.Rev. 990; and dower, Northwestern Trust Co. v. Ryan, 1911, 115
Minn. 143, 132 N.W. 202; Loeb v. Tinkler, 1890, 124
Ind. 331, 24 N.E. 235; Eldridge v. Eldridge, 1862, 14
N.J.Eq. 195; Ross v. Boardman, N.Y.1880, 22 Hun.
527; see 1939, 118 A.L.R. 769, 782.

64. Moulton v. Cornish, 1893, 138 N.Y. 133, 33 N.E.
842, 20 L.R.A. 370. See note, 1940, 88 U. of Pa.L.
Rev. 994, 1007.

65. Indiana Invest. Co. v. Evens, 1936, 121 N.J.Eq.
72, 187 A. 158, denying even a later foreclosure by
sale, criticised on this point in 1938, 17 Chi-Kent
L.Rev. 148; Moulton v. Cornish, note 64, supra;
see 1939, 118 A.L.R. 769, 775. See also Surety
Building & Loan Ass'n v. Risack, 1935, 118 N.J.Eq.
425, 427, 179 A. 680, 681, party originally joined but
not served.

66. See Sears, Roebuck & Co. v. Camp, 1938, 124 N.
J.Eq. 403, 407, 1 A.2d 425, 428, 118 A.L.R. 762, constructive notice insufficient to prevent strict foreclosure even though search was careless; Mesiavich v. Newman, 1936, 120 N.J.Eq. 192, 184 A. 538;
Koerner v. Willamette Iron Works, 1899, 36 Or. 90,
58 P. 863, strict foreclosure against a junior lienor
although no showing of "good faith." See also
note, 1940, 88 U. of Pa.L.Rev. 994, 1007; 1939, 118
A.L.R. 769, 774. "Knowledge of and acquiescence"
in the foreclosure by the omitted party is not essential. See Campbell, Cases on Mortgages, 2d ed. 249
n. 4. But cf. Denton v. Ontario County Nat. Bank,
1896, 150 N.Y. 126, 44 N.E. 781.

67. See note, 1940, 88 U. of Pa.L.Rev. 994, 1007.

68. Mesiavich v. Newman, 1936, 120 N.J.Eq. 192, 184
A. 538; Miles v. Stehle, 1888, 22 Neb. 740, 36 N.W.
142; see 1939, 25 Va.L.Rev. 947, 953. But contra,
see Denton v. Ontario County Nat. Bank, 1896, 150
N.Y. 126, 44 N.E. 781. Of course if the foreclosure
sale produced an excess over the amount of the
mortgage debt, a mortgagee-purchaser cannot have
strict foreclosure to eliminate junior liens. Pettingill v. Hubbell, 53 N.J.Eq. 584, 32 A. 76.

bidding up the property so that it will bring a proper price is a fundamental one and should be denied only for good reason.[69]

B. FORECLOSURE BY STATUTORY SELF HELP AND ACTIONS AT LAW

ENTRY AND WRITS OF ENTRY

314. **Foreclosure by entry and continued possession, initiated by self help under certain specified conditions or by legal process, exists in four New England states by virtue of legislation originally enacted in Massachusetts in colonial times.**

Certain methods of foreclosure by forms of self help or by actions in courts of law developed in a relatively few states. The most important of these, going back to colonial origins,[70] is found in the four states of Massachusetts,[71] Maine,[72] New Hampshire,[73] and Rhode Island.[74] It was accomplished by providing for a very short period of time[75] at the end of which the mortgagor's equity of

redemption will be barred if he does not perform the mortgage obligation after an entry made under specified conditions without court help[76] or, in the alternative, by the aid of an action at law.[77]

Where the entry is without process of law it must be peaceable.[78] In addition there is required a memorandum or certification of the entry by the mortgagor, or witnesses, or publication of the time, manner and purposes of the entry and an affidavit of such publication by the mortgagee followed by a recordation of the required document, which constitutes evidence of the entry.[79] The entry and possession by the mortgagee may be constructive, it thus being possible to leave the mortgagor in occupancy provided he holds as

---

69. See note, 1940, 88 U. of Pa.L.Rev. 994, 998.

70. The method goes back to early legislation in Massachusetts. See Story, J., in Gordon v. Lewis, C.C.Me.1884, 1 Sumn. 525, Fed.Cas.No. 5612, citing a colonial act of 1698. See also Story, J., in Gray v. Jenks, C.C.Me, 1825, 3 Mason 520, Fed.Cas.No. 5, 720; Weston, C. J., in Boyd v. Shaw, 1836, 14 Me. 58; Gray, J., in Holbrook v. Bliss, 1864, 91 Mass. (9 Allen) 69.

71. Mass.Gen.Laws Ann., 1959, Supp.1969, c. 244, §§ 1, 2, 3, 5.

A good commentary on foreclosure of mortgages both generally and in Massachusetts, including the history and features of the methods available in that state is contained in an Introduction to c. 244, supra, pp. 240–252.

72. Me.Rev.Stat.Ann., 1964, Supp.1968–1969, Tit. 14, §§ 6201, 6203, 6251, 6252; Redemption in One Year, §§ 6202, 6204.

73. N.H.Rev.Stat., Ann., 1968, Ch. 479: § 19, I, II, III; §§ 20, 21.

74. Gen.Laws (R.I.) 1956, §§ 34–23–3, 34–23–4.

75. In Massachusetts and Rhode Island, it is three years. See statutes, supra notes 71, 74. In Maine and New Hampshire, it is one year. See statutes, supra notes 72, 73.

76. Cf. with this method, expressly designed for the purpose of *foreclosing* the mortgagor's equity of redemption, an analogous method of ending the redemption right of the mortgagor through adverse possession by the mortgagee. See § 306, supra, note-call and note 11.

77. In Massachusetts, Maine and New Hampshire the court remedy is a writ of entry. See statutes, notes 71, 72, 73, supra. In Rhode Island it is by ejectment. See statute, note 74, supra.

78. E. g., Mass.Gen.Laws, 1959, Supp.1969, c. 244, § 1, "open and peaceable entry;" Me.Rev.Stat.Ann., 1964, Supp.1968–1969, Tit. 14, § 6201, "enter * * * and hold by consent in writing of the mortgagor, or the person holding under him" or "enter peaceably and openly, if not opposed, in the presence of two witnesses;" N.H.Rev.Stat., Ann., ch. 479; § 19, II, "peaceable entry;" Gen.Laws (R.I.) 1956, § 34–23–3, "open entry in the presence of two witnesses." See Thompson v. Kenyon, 1968, 100 Mass. 108; Bennett v. Conant, 1852, 64 Mass. (10 Cush.) 163; Harlon Realty Co. v. Cotter, 1933, 284 Mass. 68, 187 N.E. 118. New Hampshire also specifically provides for the case of the mortgagee already in possession. Statute, supra, § 19, III. But it has been held without the aid of express statutory provision that foreclosure by entry is "not precluded by the fact that the mortgagee already has possession." See Carleton & Hovey Co. v. Burns, 1935, 285 Mass. 479, 485, 189 N.E. 612, 615.

79. Gen.Laws, Mass.Ann., 1959, Supp.1969, c. 244, § 2; N.H.Rev.Stat.Ann., 1968, ch. 479: § 19, II, III. Entry or Possession and Publication and § 21 recordation of affidavits; Gen.Laws (R.I.) 1956 § 34–23–4; Me.Rev.Stat., Ann., 1964, § 3, II, III. See Fitchburg Co-operative Bank v. Normandin, 1920, 236 Mass. 332, 128 N.E. 415; Bennett v. Conant, 1852, 64 Mass. (10 Cush.) 163.

tenant of the mortgagee.[80] However, if after entry, the mortgagee accepts a payment of interest or principal he is deemed to have waived the entry and cannot complete his foreclosure.[81]

The actions at law to foreclose by putting the mortgagee into possession are essentially equitable in nature,[82] being examples of the working out of equitable relief in the courts of law in states in which the establishment of full equitable jurisdiction was comparatively late.[83] In using them the mortgagee declares upon his title under the mortgage and alleges default in performance by the mortgagor.[84] An account is taken to determine the amount due and a judgment for recovery of the possession is given, conditional upon nonperformance by the mortgagor within a short period.[85] If the mortgagor fails to perform

within the time set, the mortgage creditor is put into possession. If the possession is maintained for the required period, the redemption right is extinguished and title is then held unconditionally by the foreclosing mortgagee.[86]

Foreclosure by entry and continued possession, whether under legal process or by self help, is strict foreclosure. As previously seen, American courts using the analogous method of strict foreclosure by equitable bill hold that the mortgage debt is discharged by the value of the land and permit the mortgagee to recover the balance due upon the claim.[87] So, too, in foreclosure by entry, the effect of the foreclosure is to extinguish the mortgage debt by the value of the land at the time when the foreclosure is completed.[88]

If a mortgage contains a power of sale, as ordinarily is the case,[89] entry for the purpose of foreclosure does not prevent the mort-

---

80. "The possession which the law contemplates may be constructive, and it will be presumed to continue after the open, peaceable entry which the law requires has been formally made, even if the mortgagor remain on the premises." Morse v. Bassett, 1882, 132 Mass. 502, 509.

See Swift v. Mendell, 1851, 62 Mass. (8 Cush.) 357; Thompson v. Ela, 1878, 58 N.H. 490; Bennett v. Conant, 1852, 64 Mass. (10 Cush.) 163; Tarbell v. Page, 1892, 155 Mass. 256, 29 N.E. 585.

81. Me.Rev.Stat., 1930, Ann., 1964, Supp. 1968–1969, Tit. 14, § 6204; Trow v. Berry, 1873, 113 Mass. 139, 147; Willard v. Kimball, 1931, 277 Mass. 350, 358, 178 N.E. 607, 610. But cf. Donovan v. Sweetser, 1938, 135 Me. 349, 196 A. 767, receipt of money as rent from mortgagor is not a waiver.

82. See Gray, J., in Holbrook v. Bliss, note 70, supra.

83. See Wilson, Courts of Chancery in the American Colonies, 2 Select Essays in Anglo-American Legal History, 79. Cf. Fisher, The Administration of Equity Through Common Law Forms in Pennsylvania, 1885, 1 Law Q.Rev. 455.

84. As to what statements are essential to render a certificate of entry valid, see Snow v. Pressey, 1890, 82 Me. 552, 20 A. 78; Hawkes v. Brigham, 1860, 82 Mass. (16 Gray) 561; Thompson v. Kenyon, 1868, 100 Mass. 108. Additionally as to the nature and requisites of the action, see Green v. Cross, 1864, 45 N.H. 574; Carpenter v. Carpenter, 1859, 6 R.I. 542; Fiedler v. Carpenter, C.C.Mass.1846, 2 Woodb. & M. 211, Fed.Cas.No. 4,759.

85. Mass.Gen.Laws Ann., 1959, Supp.1969, c. 244, § 5; Me.Rev.Stat.Ann.1964, Supp.1968–1969; Tit. 14, § 6252.

86. Mass.Gen.Laws Ann., 1959, Supp.1969, c. 241, § 1; Me.Rev.Stat.Ann., 1964, Supp.1968–1969, Tit. 14, §§ 6202, 6204; N.H.Rev.Stat., Ann., 1968, ch. 479; § 19; Gen.Laws (R.I.) 1956, § 34–23–3.

87. See § 312, supra.

88. Hatch v. White, C.C.N.H.1814, 2 Gall. 152, Fed. Cas.No.6,209; Morse v. Merritt, 1872, 110 Mass. 458 (with dictum that action for debt by mortgagee reopens the foreclosure, and that if the mortgagee has sold he cannot deny the sufficiency of the property as payment. But that suit for the debt does not reopen the foreclosure, see Newall v. Wright, 1807, 3 Mass. 138, 148, 3 Am.Dec. 98; Hunt v. Stiles, 1839, 10 N.H. 466; Stevens v. Fellows, 1899, 70 N.H. 148, 47 A. 135, "value is the amount for which the property could have been sold at a sale held at a reasonable time and place, after reasonable notice, and conducted with reasonable skill and diligence for the purpose of obtaining the highest price"; Flint v. Winter Harbor Land Co., 1896, 89 Me. 420, 36 A. 634. See also Dooley v. Potter, 1885, 140 Mass. 49, 59, 2 N.E. 935, 942. Cf. Hadley Falls Trust Co. v. United States, D.C.Mass.1938, 22 F. Supp. 346, 349. Look at McKeen v. Cook, 1905, 73 N.H. 410, 62 A. 729, 3 L.R.A.,N.S., 343 (no presumption that the value of the land is sufficient to pay the mortgage debt). But see Fitchburg Co-operative Bank v. Normandin, 1920, 236 Mass. 332, 128 N.E. 415; Glenn, A Study in Strict Foreclosure, 1943, 29 Va.L.Rev. 519, 550.

89. There is statutory recognition of powers of sale. E.g., N.H.Rev.Stat., Ann., 1968, ch. 479; §§ 22–27; Gen.Laws (R.I.) 1956, § 34–27–4.

gagee foreclosing under the power.[90] Indeed, it is common practice to make the required entry and recordation of memorandum or certificate before exercising the power in order to protect against possible defects in the foreclosure under the power of sale.[91] And by the same token, a defective foreclosure by entry may be cured by a valid exercise of the power of sale.[92] Furthermore, the mortgagee today may also resort to foreclosure and sale by an equitable action, which in some instances provides a more adequate relief.[93]

ADVERTISEMENT OR NOTICE

315. In Maine strict foreclosure may be accomplished by advertisement or service of notice of default and intention to foreclose followed by the passage of one year's time.

In Maine, an additional although similar type of strict foreclosure was developed—foreclosure by advertisement or service of notice. Entry and adverse possession by the mortgagee after default are dispensed with.[94] Instead, the mortgagee may give public notice of default and intention to foreclose by published advertisement and recordation of a certified copy of it; or he may serve an attested copy of such a notice on the mortgagor, or record holder of title, and record the

original notice.[95] At the end of one year from the first publication or service of notice, unless the mortgagor redeems, his right of redemption is forever foreclosed.[96]

SCIRE FACIAS

316. In Pennsylvania foreclosure through levy and sale by legal process under a statutory writ of *scire facias sur mortgage* was commonly used but is now suspended. It existed also in Delaware, Illinois and New Jersey but was seldom employed. A 1952 revision in New Jersey failed to reenact this procedure.

The same original lack of an equity court [97] which led to the types of foreclosure described in the two preceding sections in four New England states resulted in a different form of foreclosure by legal process in Pennsylvania. This was the action of *Scire Facias Sur Mortgage*, created by the colonial Act of January 12, 1705.[98] It was fashioned after the English writ of *scire facias*—a summary proceeding available on matters of court record—and is similar to the process open to an ordinary execution creditor.[99] It provid-

---

90. E.g., Fitchburg Co-operative Bank v. Normandin, 1920, 236 Mass. 332, 128 N.E. 415; Barry v. Dudley, 1933, 282 Mass. 258, 259, 184 N.E. 815, 816.

91. See Harlow Realty Co. v. Cotter, 1913, 284 Mass. 68, 187 N.E. 118.

92. Cases note 90, supra.

93. Gen.Laws (R.I.) 1956, § 34–27–1; Carleton & Hovey Co. v. Burns, 1935, 285 Mass. 479, 189 N.E. 612; Federal Trust Co. v. Bristol Co. St. Ry., 1914, 218 Mass. 367, 105 N.E. 1064. For Maine Law see notes 72, 77 supra.

94. This method is distinct from the procedure in New Hampshire. See § 314, note 79, supra. There an entry or an existing possession is essential and, in addition, publication of notice of the time the possession was taken or the character of the existing possession changed, together with recordation of the published notice.

95. Me.Rev.Stat.Ann., 1964, Supp.1968–1969, Tit. 14, §§ 6203, 6204.

96. Idem, § 6204.

97. See Fisher, The Administration of Equity Through Common Law Forms in Pennsylvania, 1885, 1 Law Q.Rev. 455; § 314, note 83, supra.

98. 2 Stats. at Large (Pa.) 244, § 3; id. 527; 1 Smith's Laws of Pa. 57. See Durfee, Cases on Security, 1951, pp. 173, 175–177, 241. See Lloyd, The Mortgage Theory of Pennsylvania, 1924, 73 U. of Pa.L.Rev. 43, 46; Skilton, Government and the Mortgage Debtor, 13.

The present law is in Purdon's Pa.Stats.Ann., Cum. Supp.1969, Tit. 21, §§ 791–820. It is now almost all suspended by Rules of Civil Procedure. See Rules 3232, 3241, 3244.

99. See Rowle, Some Contrasts in the Growth of Pennsylvania and English Law, Oct. 21, 1881, Phila.Legal Intelligencer, 380. A mortgage could be foreclosed by *scire facias* even though unrecorded. Tryon v. Munson, 1874, 77 Pa. 250. Execution under the judgment was limited to the mortgaged property. On the other hand, the purchaser acquired title free of encumbrances placed upon the property after giving the mortgage. Under ordinary process the creditor's execution lien was prior only to those creditors whose liens attached subsequent to his own judgment of execution lien.

ed that, after default, a writ of *scire facias* shall issue against the mortgagor, his heir, or personal representative requiring him to show cause why the mortgaged land should not be taken in execution to satisfy the defaulted mortgage obligation.[1] Upon a judgment, after inquest determining the amount, a writ of *levari facias* issued and the mortgaged premises were sold at public sale,[2] the proceeds being used to pay the mortgagee with any surplus over the mortgage debt and costs returned to the defendant.[3] The purchaser got the property "freed from all equity and benefit of redemption and all other encumbrances made or suffered by the mortgagors, their heirs, or assigns."[4] One drawback in the act, that it was not available until twelve months after the default, was remedied usually by a waiver of the requirement.[5]

Scire facias proceedings were available also in Delaware,[6] New Jersey[7] and Illinois.[8] In Pennsylvania it has been a common method of foreclosure,[9] although an action on the bond with judgment enforced by a writ of *fieri facias* levied upon the mortgaged property was also popular.[10] In the other three states it was seldom used. Although it had the advantages of a simplified, expeditious and inexpensive procedure with some of the characteristics of the modern foreclosure by power of sale,[11] it also had disadvantages. It is not thought to be as flexible nor as affording as secure a title as does the foreclosure in equity in which conflicting interests and the claims of various parties can be deter-

---

Cf. the effect of a levy upon the mortgagor's redemption interest under a judgment on the mortgage debt previously discussed, § 300, supra.

1. Purdon's Pa.Stat., Title 21, § 791, suspended, eff. 1950 by Rules of Civ.Proc., Rule 1460.

2. Ibid.

3. Idem, § 793. In New Jersey the overplus was applied toward discharging any junior judgments and liens before being returned to the defendant. N.J. Rev.Stat., 1937, § 2:65–33. In Pennsylvania, junior lienors were cut off by the sale, but could lay claim to the surplus. Priority among them was determined in proceedings with respect to the fund. Rosenberg v. Cupersmith, 1913, 240 Pa. 162, 87 A. 570, 47 L.R.A.,N.S., 706, Ann.Cas.1915A, 312.

4. Idem, § 791. The Delaware statute has the same language. Del.Code Ann., 1953, 10 §§ 5061–5067. The New Jersey statute added to substantially the same provision that the purchaser shall take the property "freed and discharged as aforesaid, in as good and perfect an estate as the mortgagor, at the time of executing such mortgage deed, was invested with." N.J.Rev.Stat. 2:65–34. In Illinois, the act does not specify what title the purchaser gets. Apparently it is no different from that of a purchaser under any other writ of execution, apart from the date as to which it takes effect. See MacChesney, with collaboration of Leesman, Mortgage Foreclosures and Reorganizations, 1931, 31 Ill.L.Rev. 287, 302.

5. See Lloyd, op. cit. supra note 98, 46.

6. Delaware Code Ann.1953, 10 §§ 5061–5067.

7. N.J.Rev.Stat., 1937, § 2:65–34. However, in the revision of this statute, effective in 1952, this procedure was not reenacted. See 1952, a A:1–14 N.J. S.A. p. 64. As a result *scire facias* may no longer be used.

8. Smith-Hurd, Ill.Ann.Stats., 1953, Cum.Supp. to 1969. See Carey et al., Studies of Foreclosures in Cook County: II. Foreclosure Methods and Redemption, 1933, 27 Ill.L.Rev. 595, 612; Leesman, Corporate Trusteeship and Receivership, 1933, 28 Ill.L. Rev. 238, 243. See MacChesney, op. cit. supra, n. 4, at 301. Apparently a similar sort of foreclosure was provided by early statutes in Ohio and South Carolina. See Reedy v. Burgert, 1823, 1 Ohio 157; Biggerstaff v. Loveland, 1837, 8 Ohio 44, stating that that the act providing for the process had been repealed; Doe ex dem. Heighway v. Pendleton, 1846, 15 Ohio 735, stating that the act establishing the process was the act of 1795. See 5 S.C.Stats., 1786–1814, p. 169. So, too, apparently in Kansas when a territory. Clark v. Reyburn, 1868, 75 U.S. (8 Wall.) 318, 19 L.Ed. 354.

9. See Skilton, Government and the Mortgage Debtor, 14; Campbell, Cases on Mortgages, 2d ed., 256 n. 1; Carey et al., op. cit. supra note 8, 613.

10. Purdon's Pa.Stats.Ann., 1955, Tit. 21 § 804. See Skilton, note 9, supra; note, 1940, 45 Dickinson L. Rev. 78, discussing Pennsylvania Co. v. Emmons, 1940, 338 Pa. 513, 13 A.2d 417, stating that this procedure had become the almost exclusive method of foreclosing mortgages by action in Pennsylvania, it being speedier and less expensive than foreclosure by *scire facias*.

11. See Lloyd, op. cit. supra note 98; Carey et al., op. cit. supra note 8; MacChesney, op. cit. supra note 4. One important advantage is that only the mortgagor, his heir, or personal representative need be joined as defendant, obviating an expensive title search for subsequent interests. See Carey, et. al., supra.

mined.[12] Even in Pennsylvania, corporate mortgages were usually foreclosed by action in equity.[13]

C. BY JUDICIAL SALE

DEVELOPMENT AND GENERAL CHARACTER—ENGLAND

317. Although sale under decree in an equitable action by a mortgagee was occasionally ordered in exceptional cases in early cases and discretionary power to order such sales in lieu of strict foreclosure was conferred on chancery courts by Parliament in 1852, it is not often resorted to in England. Unlike the process in America the mortgagee cannot purchase at the sale and there is no statutory right of redemption after sale.

Dissatisfaction with the workings of foreclosure without sale led to the development of different methods of realization and ending the redemption interest in both England and America.[14] In England the chief substitute worked out for a suit to foreclose is the exercise of a power of sale.[15] Recourse to sale under court action is infrequent.[16] Nevertheless, although the chancery court before 1852 exercised the power only in occasional cases of exceptional nature,[17] there are instances of its use going quite far back.[18] Apparently, however, there was some doubt whether it could be ordered in the ordinary

writing without application to the Court and a sale is usually made under a statutory power without recourse to the Court at all. The sale need not be by auction but must be bona fide to a stranger and at a reasonable price. The mortgagee may not become a purchaser, nor may his solicitor or agent or the secretary of a mortgagee building society. At an auction sale he may fix a reserve price. A subsequent mortgagee may buy from a first mortgagee and vice versa. * * * in most cases the mortgagee does not have recourse to the court at all to release his security. The Borrower vacates as a result of arrangement or threats in order to avoid expense and the security is realized by possession, receivership and sale. Action on the covenant is usually brought prior to sale, if at all, with a view to attaching by way of execution any other assets of the debtor. Judgment is obtained by a cheap and speedy method and the proceeds of any possession, sale or receivership must be credited to the amount of the judgment. Foreclosure or sale by the Court is comparatively rare, the mortgagee avoiding the expense of these proceedings, which he will probably never recover from the borrower preferring to rely on his powers of possession, leasing and sale, and ultimately acquiring title by limitation after 12 years unless a sale has meanwhile taken place. Foreclosure proper is only used where the mortgagee hopes he will ultimately obtain more from the property than the mortgage debt and costs and he wishes to bar the right of redemption. It is reopened by subsequent action on the covenant, which is not permitted if the property cannot be returned intact. Action on the covenant is permitted after sale, whether in or out of Court. It is usually the only legal proceeding necessary for a deficiency judgment to be obtained. A sale is always an out and out sale, whether effected by the mortgagee under his powers, or by order of the Court. There is no period for redemption after sale has been effected." Turner, An English View of Mortgage Deficiency Judgments, 1935, 21 Va.L.Rev. 600, 603. See also Maitland, supra, 191–203; Tefft, The Myth of Strict Foreclosure, 1934, 4 U. of Chi.L.Rev. 575–587.

16. See Turner, note 15, supra; Maitland, note 15, supra, 187–188. See also Turner, English Mortgage of Land as Security, 1934, 20 Va.L.Rev. 729, 733.

17. For a review of the earlier English cases, see Lansing v. Goelet, N.Y.1827, 9 Cowen 346, 371ff.

18. Ibid. See Turner, op.cit. supra, note 15, 606 fns. 5–7. See also Federal Title & Mortg. Guaranty Co. v. Loewenstein, 1933, 113 N.J.Eq. 200, 166 A. 538.

---

12. See Leesman, op. cit. supra note 8; MacChesney, op. cit. supra note 4; Carey et al., op. cit. supra note 8, discussing its lack of use by Illinois lawyers. Emphasized as disadvantageous where the property is income producing is the lack of provision for a receivership or putting the purchaser into possession. It is doubtful whether it would be available in Illinois to the trustee under a trust deed mortgage. MacChesney, supra.

13. See McElrath v. Pittsburgh & S. R. Co., 1867, 55 Pa. 189. Although it is suggested that the court has equity powers in such a case because a trust is involved, this seems dubious. See Crane, Soldiers' and Sailors' Relief Act of 1940, 12 Pa. Bar Ass'n Quar., 113, 119 n. But cf. Pennsylvania Co. v. Emmons, 1940, 338 Pa. 513, 13 A.2d 417.

14. See Turner, The English Mortgage of Land as a Security, 1934, 20 Va.L.Rev. 729; Turner, An English View of Mortgage Deficiency Judgments, 1935, 21 Va.L.Rev. 601, 603ff.; Tefft, The Myth of Strict Foreclosure, 1937, 4 U. of Chi.L.Rev. 575, 580ff.

15. See Maitland, Equity, rev. ed., 187ff.

The modern English practice has been summarized by an eminent authority: "In England the mortgagee's remedies, possession, sale, appointment of a receiver, action on the covenant, and foreclosure, can be pursued concurrently. The mortgagor may be ousted from possession by cheap and speedy summary proceedings without foreclosure, rents are attached by notice to the tenant, a receiver is appointed by

case [19] until the Chancery Amendment Act of 1852 clearly established the authority to do so.[20]

The English practice of court sale, when employed,[21] has two main features strikingly at variance from the similar procedure as developed in America. First, and most important, the mortgagee can never become a purchaser.[22] And there is no redemption from foreclosure sale.[23] The latter flows from the former because its primary purpose

is to force the mortgagee to bid the value of the property, at least up to the amount of the mortgage debt.[24] In England, since the mortgagee cannot buy in the property on sale, he will use his best efforts to see that it fetches a good price.[25] Indeed it is the mortgagee in England who occasionally needs and is given protection against an inadequate sale price.[26]

DEVELOPMENT AND GENERAL CHARACTER—UNITED STATES

318. Firmly established at an early date, foreclosure by sale in an equitable court action is today the exclusive or generally used process in a substantial majority of the United States and is available in all. Among its important features are permissible, and usual, purchase by the mortgagee, statutory redemption from the foreclosure sale, and, in most states, a decree for a deficiency with the sale price conclusively determining the value of the property. Although it is the best method for producing firm titles it is complicated, costly and time-consuming.

In the United States sale under court action in equity became firmly established at least as early as the first part of the nineteenth century,[27] and possibly earlier.[28] Today it is the exclusive [29] or generally used method of foreclosure in a substantial majori-

19. See Adams, Equity, 3d Am.ed., 120, 121; Coote, Mortgages, 3d ed., 1850, 493. In Ireland, however, it was general practice to decree public sale of the property in all cases. 4 Kent, Comm., 1st ed.1830, 174; Lansing v. Goelet, N.Y.1827, 9 Cowen 346, 373, 378.

20. Chancery Procedure Amendment Act, 1852, 15 & 16 Vict., c. 86, § 48 replaced by Conveyancing and Law of Property Act, 1881, 44 & 45 Vict., c. 41, § 25 (2) which, in turn, is now replaced by Law of Property Act, 1925, 15 Geo. V., c. 20, § 91(2).

21. The jurisdiction to order sale in lieu of foreclosure is discretionary and may be denied or ordered subject to restrictions. See Coote, Mortgages, 9th ed. 1069ff. For example, it "will not be exercised over the mortgagee's objection when the property is not likely to bring the full amount of the mortgage debt; * * * at least, not unless security is put up to protect the objecting mortgagee; * * * or a bidding reserved sufficient to cover the amount due the mortgagee * * *." Louisville Joint Stock Land Bank v. Radnor, 1935, 295 U.S. 555, 580 n. 8, 55 S.Ct. 854, 859, n. 8, 79 L. Ed. 1593, 97 A.L.R. 1106. See also Turner, The English Mortgage of Land as a Security, 1934, 20 Va.L.Rev. 719, 734.

22. See Turner, English Mortgage of Land as a Security, 1934, 20 Va.L.Rev. 729, 734. See also Turner, op.cit. supra note 15, 604, "This seems to be the main flaw in American practice, the allowing of the mortgagee to bid for the property on auction sale." Cf. the American attitude as expressed by Brandeis, J., in Louisville Joint Stock Land Bank v. Radford, 1935, 295 U.S. 555, 580, 55 S.Ct. 854, 859, 79 L.Ed. 1593, 97 A.L.R. 1106, "This right of the mortgagee to insist upon full payment before giving up his security has been deemed of the essence of a mortgage. His position in this respect was not changed when foreclosure by public sale superseded strict foreclosure or when the legislatures of many states created a right of redemption at the sale price. To protect his right to full payment on the mortgaged property, the mortgagee was allowed to bid at the judicial sale on foreclosure."

23. See Turner, op.cit. supra note 15, 606, "To an English mind this [redemption from foreclosure sale] must render the whole intention of a sale abortive."

24. See §§ 8, 307, supra.

25. See Turner, op.cit. supra note 15, 605. The sale need not be at public auction and, when made at the mortgagee's application, its conduct is usually given to the mortgagor. Turner, The English Mortgage of Land as a Security, 1934, 20 Va.L.Rev. 729, 734.

26. See note 21, supra.

27. Chancellor Kent in Mills v. Dennis, N.Y.1818, 3 Johns.Ch. 367 sustained the power, and nine years later, in a basic decision, it was recognized as both an inherent part of equity jurisdiction and also authorized by statute. Lansing v. Goelet, N.Y.1827, 9 Cowen, 346.

28. See Keigwin, Cas.Mortgages, 572, note 1, stating that the practice was established at or shortly after the time of the Revolution. Hanna, Cas. Security, 3d ed., 1012.

29. E. g., § 312, notes 53, 54, supra.

ty of states [30] and is available in all [31] by virtue of express statutory enactment, as an incident to the inherent jurisdiction of courts of equity, or both.[32]

As indicated above, the two most far-reaching innovations made by the American courts consisted in permitting the mortgagee to purchase at the foreclosure sale [33] and providing for redemption after sale from the purchaser.[34] A third development of importance was allowing the mortgagee a claim, in most states in the foreclosure proceeding itself in the form of a decree for a deficiency,[35] for the difference between the sale price and the original claim.[36] For this

30. See Bridewell, the Effects of Defective Mortgage Laws on Home Financing, 1938, 5 Law & Contemp. Probs. 545, 547, Map II, 555, Table I; Reeve, The New Proposal for a Uniform Real Estate Mortgage Act, 1938, 5 Law & Contemp.Probs., 564, 565 n. 9; Hanna, Cas.Security, 3d ed., 1012. See also Eaton, Deficiency Judgments and Decrees, 1934, 20 Va.L. Rev. 743, dealing chiefly with deficiencies. Bridewell lists twenty-nine states in which court foreclosure is used neither because required by statute, in 12, or as the customary method. However, in two of these, Vermont and Connecticut, the action is strict foreclosure. See § 313, supra. Another, Pennsylvania, it is by scire facias. See § 316, supra. With these excluded the states are New York, New Jersey, Delaware, South Carolina, Florida, Ohio, Indiana, Kentucky, Illinois, Wisconsin, Iowa, Arkansas, Louisiana, Oklahoma, Kansas, Nebraska, North Dakota, Montana, Wyoming, New Mexico, Arizona, Utah, Idaho, Washington, Oregon and Nevada. Hanna, supra, states that in 28 states foreclosure by action and sale is the exclusive or almost exclusive method; and in twenty more it is a concurrent remedy, usually resorted to, especially in contested cases. He does not list the states. Durfee, Cases on Security, 1951, 176, states that in 26 states judicial foreclosure is the usual method of foreclosure and in some of them it is the only one.

In 38 states the type of security instrument in general use is an ordinary mortgage; in 9 states a deed of trust; in one, an outright deed. Bridewell, supra, 546 fn. la.

31. See, e.g., § 314, note 93, and § 316, note 10, supra, for examples of court foreclosure by equitable action in states where another process is usually employed.

32. E.g., Lansing v. Goelet, note 27, supra; Belloc v. Rogers, 1858, 9 Cal. 123; Sprague, History of Chancery and Advertisement Foreclosures in Michigan, 1935, 5 Detroit L.Rev. 63, 64ff. That an action to foreclose by sale is equitable in nature is evidenced by holdings of federal courts that they have power to issue a decree of sale in such a proceeding as an incident of the equity jurisdiction derived from the constitution and laws of the United States, and also to enter a deficiency decree provided that a rule providing for it has been established by the Supreme Court. See Noonan v. Lea, 1863, 2 Black 499; Shepherd v. Pepper, 1890, 133 U.S. 626, 10 S.Ct. 438, 33 L.Ed. 706; Northwestern Mut. Life Ins. Co. v. Keith, C.C.A.Kan.1896, 77 F. 374, 23 C.C.A. 196. And it is also recognized by the general rule that issues in the foreclosure action are triable according to equity practice with no right of trial by jury. Stilwell v. Kellogg, 1861, 14 Wis. 461, including the cause of action on the debt; Frank v. Davis, 1892, 135 N.Y. 275, 31 N.E. 1100, 17 L.R.A. 306, by statute as to the deficiency judgment; Young v. Vail, 1924, 29 N.Mex. 324, 222 P. 912, 34 A.L.R. 980, as to deficiency as well as the

sale decree. In Jamaica Sav. Bank v. M. S. Investing Co., 1937, 274 N.Y. 215, 8 N.E.2d 493, 112 A. L.R. 1485, a mortgagor guarantor was held not entitled to a jury trial as to liability for a deficiency. See 1937, 32 Ill.L.Rev. 491; 1937, 23 Corn.L.Q.Rev. 194; 1937, 7 Brooklyn L.Rev. 109. There are conflicting opinions as to whether in a decree for a deficiency the defendant is entitled to a jury trial as a matter of right. The question will be reverted to later. For the present, see the foregoing citations. See also Friedman, The Enforcement of Personal Liability on Mortgage Debts in New York, 1942, 51 Yale L.J. 382, 383, 409ff.

See Boyer, Real Property Law, in Survey of Florida Law: 1953–1955, 1956, 10 Miami L.Q. 389, commenting on Florida Stat., 1955, § 702.02, amended by Fla.Laws 1955, c. 29700, which provides that foreclosure may be by clerk of court or in accordance with pre-existing procedures, i.e., chancery proceedings with the aid of masters.

33. See Louisville Joint Stock Bank v. Radford, quoted in note 22, supra. The court in fn. 8, cites a list of supporting authorities. Some states have gone so far as to enact statutes abrogating the general rule that a mortgagee cannot purchase at a foreclosure sale made in pursuance of a power of sale given to the mortgagee by the mortgage. Ibid., citing Heighe v. Sale of Real Estate, 1933, 164 Md. 259, 164 A. 671, 676, 93 A.L.R. 81; Ten Eyck v. Craig, 1875, 62 N.Y. 406, 421, when foreclosure is by advertisement; Galvin v. Newton, 1895, 19 R.I. 176, 178, 36 A. 3, at public auction sale on giving notice to mortgagor of intention to bid.

34. See §§ 8, 307–310, supra.

35. See note, 1929, 27 Mich.L.Rev. 797; 1925, 34 A. L.R. 1015. Durfee and Doddridge, Redemption from Foreclosure Sale, 1925, 23 Mich.L.Rev. 825, 830 n. 19; See also authorities in note 32, supra.

36. See Tefft, op. cit. supra § 317, note 15, 593; Turner, op. cit. supra § 317, note 15; Eaton, Deficiency Judgments and Decrees, 1934, 20 Va.L.Rev. 743; Perlman, Mortgage Deficiency Judgments During an Economic Depression, 1934, 20 Va.L.Rev. 771; Brabner-Smith, Economic Aspects of the Deficiency Judgment, 1934, 20 Va.L.Rev. 719; Skilton, Proposed Uniform Legislation, 1942, 9 Am.L.School Rev. 1128. See also Durfee, Cases on Security, 1951, 174, 180–182.

purpose the sale price was regarded as conclusively establishing the value of the property.

In spite of being the most popular method of foreclosure in America today, justified to an extent by the fact that it is the best method of determining conclusively the rights of all interested parties and, consequently, of producing the firmest and most marketable title,[37] it has serious disadvantages. It is complicated, costly, and time-consuming.[38] A typical action in equity to foreclose and sell involves a long series of steps: a preliminary title search to determine all parties in interest; filing of the foreclosure bill of complaint and lis pendens notice; service of process; a hearing, usually by a master in chancery who then reports to the court; the decree or judgment; notice of sale; actual sale and issuance of certificate of sale; report of the sale; proceedings for determination of the right to any surplus; possible redemptions from foreclosure sale; and the entry of a decree for a deficiency.[39] Although there is great diversity of procedure from state to state, in general it falls into three stages: first, the procedure that must be followed up to and including the decree of sale; second, the sale and its attendant consequences as to the property and the proceeds; and third, a judgment or decree for a deficiency. The most important problems connected with these three stages will be considered in the following sections.

PARTIES PLAINTIFF

319. In order to determine the ownership, existence and amount of the obligation and whether there has been a default in its performance all persons who have an interest in the ownership of the obligation secured by a mortgage must be parties to a foreclosure action. Similarly, all persons who have a share in security interest in the property given in mortgage must be parties.

The basic principles determining who should be parties to a foreclosure suit are relatively simple and flow from the fundamental concept of a mortgage as an interest in property held by one person as security for the performance of an act by some other person.[40] Although it is possible to have a mortgage without anyone being personally bound to perform the act, the usual situation is one in which there is such an obligation.[41] On the mortgagee side of the transaction, therefore, there will be two separate and distinct interests: the in personam claim, and the interest in the property which secures it.[42] In order to foreclose the mortgage it is essential that the owners of both of these interests be parties to the foreclosure action. This is so for good reasons that are so obvious it seems scarcely necessary to state them.

The purpose of a foreclosure action is to satisfy, out of the proceeds of a sale of the estate in the mortgaged property as it stood at the time the mortgage was executed, the claim of the holder of the obligation when there is a default in the performance of the act it is given to secure.[43] Consequently the person to whom the obligation runs must be a party to the proceedings in order to establish the existence and amount of the obli-

37. See Skilton, note 36, supra, 1130; Hanna, Cas. Security, 3d ed., 1012. Cf. Durfee and Fleming, Res Judicata and Recording Acts, 1930, 28 Mich.L.Rev. 811. But cf. the problem as to omitted parties, §§ 305–313, supra, and § 324, infra.

38. See Carey, et al., Studies in Foreclosures in Cook County: Foreclosure Methods and Redemption, 1933, 27 Ill.L.Rev. 595, 596–609; Bridewell, The Effects of Defective Mortgage Laws on Home Financing, 1938, 5 Law & Contemp. Probs. 545, 549ff, especially Table I, p. 555.

39. Ibid.
For a survey of the steps in foreclosure by action and sale in Colorado, see Storke and Sears, Enforcement of Security Interests in Colorado, 1952, 27 Rocky Mt.L.Rev. 1, 12–20.
For the rights of a joined junior lienholder's rights in a foreclosure, see Note, The Rights of a Junior Lienholder in Wisconsin, 1959, 43 Marq.L.Rev. 89, 95.

40. See § 102, supra.

41. See §§ 102–104, supra.

42. See §§ 223–226, supra.

43. See San Francisco, City & County of, v. Lawton, 1861, 18 Cal. 465, 79 Am.Dec. 187.

gation [44] and his ownership of it.[45] It is essential to determine the size of the obligation both for the purpose of establishing the amount of the proceeds of the sale which will go to the holder of the obligation and also to inform the mortgagor exactly how much he must pay in order to prevent the foreclosure action being completed.[46] Furthermore, all persons who participate in the ownership of the obligation must be parties.[47] If more than one person has an interest in the claim, he must either get all others to join with him as plaintiffs or, if they will not, join them as defendants so that their claims can be adjudicated in the same action with his.[48]

44. "It is obvious that the finding of the amount due, for non-payment of which, according to the terms of the decree, the mortgaged property is ordered to be sold, is the foundation of the right of the mortgagee further to proceed." Chicago, D. & V. R. Co. v. Fosdick, 1882, 106 U.S. 47, 71, 1 S.Ct. 10, 27 L.Ed. 47.

45. Thus where there has been a valid assignment of the entire debt, the assignee being the sole owner of it is the only one entitled to foreclose the mortgage. Adler v. Sargent, 1895, 109 Cal. 42, 41 P. 799. See Walsh and Simpson, Cases Security Transactions, 447, note. This requirement finds expression in the general rule that there can be no foreclosure of a mortgage without first producing or accounting for the note. Bennett v. Taylor, 1855, 5 Cal. 502.

See Ward v. Munson, 1895, 105 Mich. 647, 63 N.W. 498; Bergen v. Urbahn, 1880, 83 N.Y. 49. Cf. Roney v. Moss, 1883, 74 Ala. 390; Graham v. Anderson, 1867, 42 Ill. 514, 92 Am.Dec. 89. See also Locklair v. Raybourn, 1940, 193 S.C. 214, 8 S.E.2d 349. Cf. Whitfield v. Fausset, 1749, 1 Ves.Sr. 387; Reeves v. Morgan, 1891, 48 N.J.Eq. 415, 21 A. 1040.

46. "But as in cases of strict foreclosure, so in cases of sale, the equity of the mortgagor as against the mortgagee is not exhausted until sale actually confirmed; for if at any time prior he should bring into court, for the mortgagee, the amount of the debt, interest and costs, he will be allowed to redeem." Chicago, D. & V. R. Co. v. Fosdick, 1882, 106 U.S. 47, 71, 1 S.Ct. 10, 27 L.Ed. 47.

47. See Tyler v. Yreka Water Co., 1859, 14 Cal. 212, 219.

48. Goodall v. Mopley, 1873, 45 Ind. 355; Hopkins v. Ward, 1851, 51 Ky. (12 B.Mon.) 185; Christie v. Herrick & Clark, N.Y.1845, 1 Barb.Ch. 254; Pettibone v. Edwards, 1862, 15 Wis. 95; Mangels v. Donau Brew. Co., 1892, C.C.Wash., 53 F. 513; Lowe v. Morgan, 1784, 1 Bro.C.C. 368; Studebaker Bros. Mfg. Co. v. McCurgur, 1886, 20 Neb. 500, 30 N.W. 686; Woodruff v. Depue, 1862, 14 N.J.Eq. 168;

The rule against splitting a cause of action prevents an owner of a part interest in the obligation from bringing his own action and letting others do the same.[49] The mortgagor should not be harassed by several actions to foreclose when his property has been given to secure a single obligation; and other persons having an interest in the claim and its security should be parties in order that the decree may justly provide for the rights of all. The fact of ownership must be proved in order to establish any right to have any proceeds produced by the action, or paid to him if produced.[50] And, of course, default in the performance of the obligation must be established, since it is only by reason of a default that the right to foreclose accrues.[51]

And not only must the owner or owners of the obligation be parties to the foreclosure action but so, too, must the owner or owners of the security interest in the property. The purpose of the sale under the decree is to pass to a purchaser the entire title to the property, both that of the mortgagor and of the mortgagee as it was at the time the mortgage was given.[52] Consequently, any person

Pine v. Shannon, 1879, 30 N.J.Eq. 501, affirmed 31 N.J.Eq. 367.

49. Cf. Mascarel v. Raffour, 1876, 51 Cal. 242; Widman v. Hammack, 1920, 110 Wash. 77, 187 P. 1091, 42 A.L.R. 468. Cf., § 173, supra.

50. Adler v. Sargent, 1895, 109 Cal. 42, 41 P. 799.

51. "What is indispensable * * * is, that there should be declared the fact, nature and extent of the default which constituted the breach of the condition of the mortgage and which justified the complainant in filing his bill to foreclose it, and the amount due on account thereof, which, with any further sums subsequently accruing and having become due * * * the mortgagor is required to pay within a reasonable time, to be fixed by the court, and which if not paid, a sale of the mortgaged premises is directed." Chicago D. & V. R. Co. v. Fosdick, 1882, 106 U.S. 47, 70, 1 S.Ct. 10, 27 L.Ed. 47. See Ryan v. Holliday, 1895, 110 Cal. 335, 42 P. 891.

52. "The effect of the foreclosure deed * * * is to vest in the purchaser the entire interest and estate of mortgagor and mortgagee as it existed at the date of the mortgage." Rector etc., of Christ Protestant Episcopal Church v. Mack, 1883, 93 N.Y. 488, 45 Am.R. 260. See also Depue, J., in Champion v. Hinkle, 1889, 45 N.J.Eq. 162, 165, 16 A. 701, 703;

who has title to the security interest in the mortgaged property must be made a party in order to achieve this result.[53]

These are the general principles. And if a mortgage were always a simple transaction in which a single individual owner of land borrowed a sum of money from another individual to be repaid all at one time in the future, gave a single plot of land to secure the loan, and then both lived and held on to their respective interests until maturity, there would be little difficulty in application. That situation, however, seldom exists. It is not often that the obligation is the simple one supposed.[54] It frequently is split into fractions in the form of notes or bonds which become widely distributed.[55] And there are transfers of both the obligation or parts of it, and the security.[56] All of these have been discussed before in some detail which cannot be repeated here.[57] But when a foreclosure action is brought all of these matters must be kept in mind and applied for the purpose of determining who, because they are owners of all or a part of either the obligation or the security interest in the property, must be parties to a foreclosure action.

TRUST INDENTURE MORTGAGE SECURING BONDS

320. In a trust indenture mortgage securing a number of bonds or notes the trustee forecloses the mortgage. Except as his right is restricted by reasonable provisions in the trust indenture so drafted as to bind him, a bondholder has the right to enforce the obligation of the bond. To these general propositions there are some exceptions.

Although it would be impossible, short of an extensive treatise,[58] to examine or reexamine at this point all of the diverse and complex matters mentioned at the end of the preceding section, one matter needs some attention here, although it cannot be explored in detail. That is the case of a corporate mortgage in which the mortgage indebtedness takes the form of bonds or notes in the hands of the investing public while the security is vested in trustees under a trust indenture to which the bonds or other evidences of indebtedness usually refer.[59] Two questions of concern in the present connection are whether individual bondholders may foreclose or whether that right is vested exclusively in the trustee; and second, whether bondholders may bring individual actions on the bonds to enforce the money claim.[60]

Field, C. J., in Goodenow v. Ewer, 1860, 16 Cal. 461, 469, 76 Am.Dec. 540; N. Y. Real Prop. Actions & Proc. Law, McKinney 1963, § 1353. See § 305, notes 70, 71, supra. See additionally Survey of Illinois Law, 1954–1955, 34 Chi.-Kent L.Rev. 81, noting Kling v. Ghilarducci, 1954, 3 Ill.2d 454, 121 N.E.2d 752, 46 A.L.R.2d 1189.

53. E. g., the original mortgagee must be made a party in a title state where, although there has been an assignment of the note and mortgage, it does not appear that the legal title to the land was transferred to the assignee by the assignment. Flagg v. Florence Discount Co., 1933, 228 Ala. 153, 153 So. 177; Pratt City Sav. Bank v. Merchants Bank & Trust Co., 1933, 228 Ala. 251, 153 So. 185. See § 224, supra. For the same reason, as will be seen, all parties having an interest in the property subject to the mortgage must be joined if their interests are to be transferred to the purchaser. See § 320, infra.

54. See, e. g., §§ 113–124, supra.

55. See §§ 123, 243–246, supra.

56. See §§ 223–226, 243, supra.

57. See, especially, Chapters 5, 8, supra.

58. E. g., a standard treatise on the subject of foreclosure, Wiltsie, Mortgage Foreclosure, 5th ed., in Chs. XVIII, XIX, and XXII devotes a total of 80 pages directly to the problems dealt with in these two sections, as well as additional chapters devoted to the background matters which produce them.

59. See n. 74, infra, for the effect of such references in incorporating the terms of the indenture, into the bond or giving holders notice of it.

60. BONDHOLDERS AND CORPORATE REORGANIZATIONS. —Implicit in the problems raised here is the question of protecting the average investor in corporate bonds. So long as the bonds are not in default few questions arise. When they are in default usually a reorganization of the corporation ensues. In either case, the right of the individual bondholder to act by and for himself, either to sue on the bond or to foreclose on the mortgage, is illusory even if permitted. The practice has grown up of forming bondholders' protective committees to safeguard the rights of those bondholders who are willing to band together. Frequently there will be more than one such committee. And, also, there will always be some bondholders who do not

That the trustee must be a party to a fore-closure action is clear,[61] for in him is vested the sole title to the security. But is he the only one who may bring the action? In general, the answer is yes.[62] The trust indenture is the instrument that governs in determining the rights of the bondholder against the

join with any group. Even where the trustee is the one who has the power to sue, there exists the problem of protection to the minority bondholders as well as the question of the rights and duties of the trustee. Any complete treatment of these problems is beyond the possible scope of this work. They belong in the field of corporate reorganization rather than in that of security, simpliciter. However, since one of the common court methods of carrying through a reorganization, prior to the comparatively recent bankruptcy amendments, was by the inappropriate machinery of mortgage fore-closure, some notice of them is desirable.

Among the more important references, in addition to those cited in connection with the specific problems dealt with in the text are the following: Securities and Exchange Commission, Report on the Study and Investigation of the Work, Activities, Personnel and Functions of Protective and Reorganization Committees, Part III, Committees for the Holders of Real Estate Bonds, 1936; Report of the Select Committee on Investigations of Real Estate Bond-holders' Reorganizations, H.R.Rep.No. 35, 74th Cong., 1st Sess., 1935; A Functional Study of Bond-holders' Protective Committees in Realty Reorganizations, 1935, 35 Col.L.Rev. 905; Reorganization of Unguaranteed Mortgage Investments in the State Courts, 1934, 34 Col.L.Rev. 706; Rodgers, Rights and Duties of the Committee in Bondholders' Reorganizations, 1929, 42 Harv.L.Rev. 899; Rohrlich, Protective Committees, 1932, 80 U. of Pa.L.Rev. 670; Katz, The Protection of Minority Bondholders in Foreclosures and Receiverships, 1936, 3 U. of Chi.L.Rev. 517; Carey, Brabner-Smith & Sullivan, Studies in Realty Mortgage Foreclosures: IV. Reorganization, 1933, 27 Ill.L.Rev. 849; Carey and Brabner-Smith, Studies in Realty Mortgage Foreclosures: V. Reorganization, 1933, 28 Ill.L.Rev. 1; Lowenthal, The Stock Exchange and Protective Committee Securities, 1933, 33 Col.L.R. 1293; Sabel, Unauthorized Expenditures by Bondholders' Protective Committees, 1934, 18 Minn.L.Rev. 784; note, 1934, 47 Harv.L.Rev. 530; note, 1938, 17 N.Car.L.Rev. 36; note, 1937, 50 Harv.L.Rev. 525; note, 1935, 35 Col.L.Rev. 291; note, 1933, 42 Yale L.J. 984; Report on the Study and Investigation of the Work, Activities, Personnel, and Functions of Protective and Reorganization Committees, Part VIII, 1940, reviewed, 1941, 54 Harv.L.Rev. 1253.

61. Busch v. City Trust Co., 1931, 101 Fla. 392, 134 So. 226.

62. See Posner, The Trustee and the Trust Indenture, 1937, 46 Yale L.J. 737, 774; Note, 1927, 27 Col.L.Rev. 443, 445ff.; 1893, 20 L.R.A. 535; 1908, 16 L.R.A.,N.S., 1006.

security. Such indentures almost invariably contain express restrictions upon the right of action by individual holders of one or more of a series of corporate bonds or other obligations in what is generally referred to as a "no action clause." Its intention and effect is to vest in the trustee exclusively as representative of all the bondholders certain rights of action upon the security and the bonds themselves, and to prohibit or impose conditions on the right of action of individual bondholders. The purpose is to protect the interests of the bondholders as a class against unwise or improperly timed suits by minority or individual bondholders who might, if they had the power to do so, seize upon some critical moment in the financial affairs of the issuing mortgagor to bring action of foreclosure or suit that would impair the security and business health of the mortgagor to the detriment of the bondholders generally. And, too, there is the design to protect the mortgagor against a multiplicity of actions.[63] Such clauses so far as they relate to foreclosure are usually enforced if they are reasonable.[64]

The clauses are held not to prevent the intervention of an individual bondholder in

63. See 1927, 27 Col.L.Rev. 443.

64. Florida Nat. Bank v. Jefferson Standard Life Ins. Co., 1936, 123 Fla. 525, 167 So. 378, 108 A.L.R. 77, rehearing denied and adhered to 125 Fla. 386, 169 So. 729, 108 A.L.R. 87; Seibert v. Minneapolis & St. L. Ry. Co., 1893, 52 Minn. 148, 53 N.W. 1134, 20 L.R.A. 535, 38 Am.St.Rep. 530. Cf. First National Bank of Dallas v. Brown, Tex.Civ.App.1930, 34 S.W.2d 412. See note, 1932, 31 Mich.L.Rev. 86; note, 1931, 79 U. of Pa.L.Rev. 1144; Lobingier, Bondholders as Complainants in the Foreclosure of Corporate Mortgages, 1902, 54 Cent.L.J. 364. See also 1893, 20 L.R.A. 535; 1937, 108 A.L.R. 88, 90, 118; 174 A.L.R. 436, 439, 454; notes, 1927, 27 Col. L.Rev. 579; 1935, 33 Mich.L.Rev. 1082, 1086.

Where the prohibition against the bondholder enforcing the security is in terms absolute, it has been held invalid. First Nat. Bank of Dallas v. Brown, Tex.Civ.App. 1930, 34 S.W.2d 412, discussed 1931, 79 U. of Pa.L.Rev. 1144; 1933, 31 Mich.L.Rev. 86. Contra: Jones v. Atlantic & W. Ry., 1927, 193 N.C. 590, 137 S.E. 706. Both cases involved appointment of receivers. See note-call and note 67, infra.

a foreclosure action by the trustee.[65] Nor do they apply where, in special circumstances, the bondholder seeks to take action to prevent impairment of the common security by the conduct of the corporation or the trustee.[66] There is divergence of view as to whether it applies to prevent an action for the appointment of a receiver.[67] And, although in general the bondholder's remedy is to compel the trustee to act, in extreme cases of neglect, incompetency, or refusal to act on the part of the trustee, bondholders may bring an action to enforce the security for the benefit of all [68] in which other bondholders must be permitted to intervene and their rights protected.[69]

The answer to the second question, aside from the effect of restrictive clauses in the trust indenture, is clearly yes.[70] However,

---

65. Kitchen Bros. Hotel Co. v. Omaha Safe Deposit Co., 1934, 126 Neb. 744, 254 N.W. 507. See 1927, 27 Col.L.Rev. 443, 446; 1937, 108 A.L.R. 88, 119; 1948, 174 A.L.R. 436, 455.

66. E. g., Whitmore v. International Fruit & Sugar Co., 1913, 214 Mass. 525, 102 N.E. 59, enjoining issuance of additional bonds; Hoyt v. E. I. du Pont de Nemours Powder Co., 1917, 88 N.J.Eq. 196, 102 A. 666, enjoining disposal of assets; Fortney v. Carter, 1913, 203 F. 454, 121 C.C.A. 514, enjoining threatened damage to security; see Florida Nat. Bank v. Jefferson Standard Life Ins. Co., 1936, 123 Fla. 525, 167 So. 378, 108 A.L.R. 77, rehearing denied and adhered to 125 Fla. 386, 169 So. 729, 108 A.L.R. 87. See also Posner, The Trustee and the Trust Indenture: A Further Study, 1937, 46 Yale L.J. 737, 776; 1933, 31 Mich.L.Rev. 86, 87.

67. See note 64, supra. See also 1937, 108 A.L.R. 88, 120; 1948, 174 A.L.R. 436, 455.

68. Chicago, D. & V. R. Co. v. Fosdick, 1882, 106 U.S. 47, 1 S.Ct. 10, 27 L.Ed. 47; Martin v. Bankers' Trust Co., 1916, 18 Ariz. 55, 156 P. 87, Ann.Cas. 1918E, 1240; Manor Coal Co. v. Beckman, 1926, 151 Md. 102, 133 A. 893. See also 1908, 16 L.R.A.,N.S., 1006, 1014. In Ettlingeer v. Persian Rug & Carpet Co., 1894, 142 N.Y. 189, 36 N.E. 1055, 40 Am.St.Rep. 587, a bondholder was allowed to sue alone to foreclose where the trustee had left the jurisdiction and become insane. See 1927, 27 Col.L.Rev. 443, 446. But cf. the strict construction given to provisions allowing a specified majority of bondholders to control the foreclosure. Poage v. Co-operative Publishing Co., 1937, 57 Idaho 561, 66 P.2d 1119, 110 A.L.R. 1322 and note, 1937, 110 A.L.R. 1339, 1341, 1345. For a broader discussion of "majority clauses," see Billyou, Corporate Mortgage Bonds and Majority Clauses, 1948, 57 Yale L.J. 595. Particular provisions of the mortgage may give the bondholder a right to sue but if he does it must be for the benefit of all. E. g., Mason v. York & C. R. Co., 1861, 52 Me. 82.

There are may other problems that arise in connection with the trustee's powers and duties in relationship with the bondholders that are beyond the scope of this work, e. g., the scope and validity of clauses exculpating the trustee from liability for failure to act in case of default or notify bondholders of defaults as well as giving to the trustee discretionary powers to act in ways that might be prejudicial to the bondholders. Marshall & Isley Bank v. Guaranty Inv. Co., 1933, 213 Wis. 415, 250 N.W. 862, commented on, 1934, 47 Harv.L.Rev. 882, is an example. Cf. Marshall & Ilsley Bank v. Hackett, Hoff & Thiermann, 1933, 213 Wis. 426, 250 N.W. 866. Look at First Trust Co. v. Carlsen, 1935, 129 Neb. 118, 261 N.W. 333; Wells v. Carlsen, 1936, 130 Neb. 773, 266 N.W. 618; Starr v. Chase National Bank, Sept. 21, 1936, 96 N.Y.L.J. 771, noted, 1937, 37 Col.L.Rev. 130; 1937, 4 U. of Chi.L.Rev. 346; 1937, 46 Yale L.J. 866. See Securities and Exchange Commission, Report on the Study and Investigation of the Work, Activities, Personnel and Functions of Protective and Reorganization Committees, Part VI, Trustees Under Indentures, 1936. Appendix G of the foregoing report contains an excellent bibliography. In addition, see Posner, The Trustee and the Trust Indenture, 1937, 46 Yale L.J. 737 (especially at pp. 753, 763, and 780); note, 1938, 36 Mich.L.Rev. 996; note, 1937, 31 Ill.L.Rev. 1060; note, 1931, 29 Mich.L.Rev. 355; note, 1928, 28 Col. L.Rev. 829; 1928, 57 A.L.R. 468; 1931, 71 A.L.R. 1413. See also discussing the findings and recommendations of the Securities and Exchange Commission, McCollom, The Securities and Exchange Commission and Corporate Trustees, 1936, 36 Col. L.Rev. 1197; Posner, supra, 790 et seq.; Wham, Trustees Under Indentures, 1937, 23 A.B.A.J. 179, 181. For discussions of the legislation growing out of the recommendations of the Securities and Exchange Commission, see The Trust Indenture Act of 1939, 25 Cornell L.Q. 105; Banks, Jr., Indenture Securities and the Barkley Bill, 1939, 48 Yale L.J. 533; Posner, The Proposed Federal Measure to Regulate Trust Indentures, 1937, 71 U.S.L.Rev. 397; Palmer, Trusteeship Under the Trust Indenture, 1941, 41 Col.L.Rev. 193; McKeehan, The Duties of a Trustee of a Mortgage Given to Secure Bondholders, 1944, 49 Dickinson L.Rev. 1; Indenture Trustees and State Regulation of Foreign Corps., 1941, 41 Col.L.Rev. 475.

As to the extent a court of equity has power to alter provisions of corporate mortgage trust deeds, see note, by Hardin, in 1949, 3 Ark.L.Rev. 437.

69. Farmers' Loan & Trust Co. v. New York & N. R. Co., 1896, 150 N.Y. 410, 44 N.E. 1043, 34 L.R.A. 76, 55 Am.St.Rep. 689.

70. Brown v. Michigan R. Co., 1924, 124 Misc. 630, 207 N.Y.S. 630; Fleming v. Fairmont & Minnington R. R., 1913, 72 W.Va. 835, 79 S.E. 826, 49 L.R.A.,N. S., 155; See 1931, 41 Yale L.J. 312; Posner, The Trustee and the Trust Indenture; A Further Study, 1937, 46 Yale L.J. 737, 775; 1937, 35 Mich. L.Rev. 1200; 1927, 27 Col.L.Rev. 443, 444. Cf.

most trust indentures securing bond issues contain "no action" clauses broad enough to cover actions at law on the bonds as well as foreclosure proceedings.[71] If reasonable, their validity is generally upheld.[72] They are, however, strictly construed so that a clause which is ambiguous or does not expressly or by necessary implication deprive the bondholder of the right to sue will not have that effect.[73] Even when the provision is explicit on the point many courts have permitted suit nevertheless on the ground that the reference in the bond to the indenture did not incorporate the provisions of the latter into the bond or give notice of them to its holder.[74] And an unconditional

promise to pay contained in the bond and coupons has been held to prevail over the inconsistent provision in the indenture attempting to limit a holder's right to bring suit on default.[75]

PARTIES DEFENDANT

321. **Authorities commonly distinguish between "necessary" and "proper" parties to a foreclosure action without, however, reaching general agreement as to the meaning of either term. Since the purpose of foreclosure is to end the right to redeem of all persons having interests in the property subject to the mortgage and to vest in the mortgagee or purchaser at foreclosure sale the title as it was at the date of the mortgage, any person having an interest in the property essential to the accomplishment of this purpose should be regarded as essential in the sense that, if not joined, his interest will not be affected by the foreclosure. A proper party is one whose joinder is not necessary for the above purpose but is desirable for a full determination of the rights of the parties to the foreclosure.**

Guaranty Trust Co. of New York v. La Porte Oil & Refining Corp., C.C.A.N.Y.1926, 16 F.2d 22, noted in 1927, 40 Harv.L.Rev. 910, and in 1927, 36 Yale L.J. 885. Unless the indenture contains a clear authorization to the trustee to sue at law for the collection of the entire debt, that remedy is denied it, Maloney v. Home Bank & Trust Co., 1933, 97 Ind.App. 564, 186 N.E. 897, mod., 97 Ind.App. 564, 187 N.E. 682; In re Indiana Flooring Co., D.C.N.Y.1931, 53 F.2d 263, commented on 1933, 33 Col.L.Rev. 1249. An express clause in a trust indenture authorizing payment to the trustee and giving him power to present claims in bankruptcy has been held to be valid. In re International Match Corp., D.C.N.Y., 1932, 3 F.Supp. 445, commented on in 1933, 46 Harv.L.Rev. 309, and 1933, 33 Col.L.Rev. 1249.

71. See 1937, 108 A.L.R. 88; 1948, 174 A.L.R. 454. See also 1935, 33 Mich.L.Rev. 1082.

72. Central Hanover Bank & Trust Co. v. Siemens & Halske Aktiengesellschaft, D.C.N.Y.1936, 15 F.Supp. 927, affirmed C.C.A., 84 F.2d 993, commented on in 1937, 35 Mich.L.Rev. 1200. See Posner, The Trustee and the Trust Indenture, 1937, 46 Yale L.J. 737, 765. See also notes, 1932, 46 Harv.L.Rev. 309; 1927, 36 Yale L.J. 884; 1927, 40 Harv.L.Rev. 910; 1933, 33 Col.L.Rev. 1249; 1937, 108 A.L.R. 88, 90, 96; 1948, 174 A.L.R. 434, 439, 445.

73. Miller v. Corvallis General Hospital Ass'n, 1947, 182 Or. 18, 185 P.2d 549, 174 A.L.R. 424. See 1937, 108 A.L.R. 88, 94, 108, 117, 118; 1948, 174 A.L.R. 434, 439, 445, 454.

74. E. g., Guardian Depositor's Corp. v. David Stott Flour Mills, 1939, 291 Mich. 180, 289 N.W. 122, noted, 1940, 25 Wash.U.L.Q. 473.

On the question whether the clause in the bond referring to the provisions in the mortgage will incorporate them into the bond or put the holder of the bond or coupon on notice of them, see notes, 1935, 33 Mich.L.Rev. 604, 605; idem, 1082; 1937, 35 Mich.L.Rev. 1200; 1927, 27 Col.L.Rev. 443, 448. And see 1937, 108 A.L.R. 88, 95 et seq.; 1948, 174

A.L.R. 436, 439 et seq.; 1940, 8 Duke B.A.J. 93. See also § 232, note 81, supra.

In jurisdictions in which an action to foreclose must be brought on any obligation secured by a mortgage before any judgment on the obligation itself may be obtained, it would seem that the trustee must first foreclose provided the statute is held applicable to trust deed mortgages and that there is sufficient reference in the bond to the indenture for it to be held to be a secured obligation within the meaning of the statute. And since the foreclosure action is also the "one action" in which a judgment in personam for a deficiency on the bond is given, it would follow that the trustee would be the person to obtain it. Barker v. Utah-Idaho Cent. R. Co., 1921, 57 Utah 494, 195 P. 635. Cf. Westinghouse Electric & Mfg. Co. v. Idaho Ry., St. & Power Co., D.C.Idaho 1915, 228 F. 972. See 1927, 27 Col.L.Rev. 443, 445.

75. Berman v. Consolidated Nevada-Utah Corp., 1928, 132 Misc. 462, 230 N.Y.S. 421. Lidgerwood v. Hale & Kilburn Corporation, D.C.1930, 47 F.2d 318, contra. See note, 1932, 41 Yale L.J. 312. See also Posner, The Trustee and the Trust Indenture, 1937, 46 Yale L.J. 737, 773; note, 1927, 27 Col.L.Rev. 443; note, 1935, 33 Mich.L.Rev. 604, 608; 1937, 108 A.L.R. 88, 117; 1948, 174 A.L.R. 434, 454. In Verner v. McLarty, 1957, 243 Ga. 472, 99 S.E.2d 890, noted in 1958, 10 Mercer L.Rev. 160, it was held that the terms of the deed controlled where the provisions of the note are not incorporated by reference into the deed.

The list of classes of persons who qualify under these tests is a formidable one. In general, it includes the general owner of the proprety subject to the mortgage or any part of it, and all persons who have an interest in the mortgaged property acquired from, or through the owner of the property subject to the mortgage subsequent to its execution.

Persons are made parties defendant in a foreclosure action for one or the other of two purposes: one is to give the court jurisdiction to make a valid order to sell the person's interest in the mortgaged property at the foreclosure sale; the other is to obtain a decree against him on the mortgage obligation.[76] Strictly speaking, foreclosure is only concerned with the first objective. However, in jurisdictions where a decree for a deficiency may be had in the same equitable action after the property has been sold in the foreclosure suit,[77] it is a customary feature of the proceeding, even though the nature of that part of the action and decree which seeks to so bind the named defendant is fundamentally different from the foreclosure sale portion of it.[78]

In dealing with the question of who should or may be made parties defendant in a foreclosure action, it is common to draw a distinction between "necessary" and "proper" parties.[79] There is, however, no generally agreed on meaning for either term.[80]

The basic objective of an action to foreclose is to enable the mortgage creditor to get his debt paid out of the security. To accomplish this end it is the purpose of the foreclosure sale to end the right to redeem of all persons who have interests in the property subject to the mortgage and to vest in the purchaser on the sale the title to the property as it stood at the time of the execution of the mortgage.[81] Every person who has such an interest should be a "necessary" party in that his joinder in the action is essential to accomplish its purpose completely.

76. Cf. Jones v. Conde, N.Y.1822, 6 Johns. ch. 77.
Additional purposes of joinder of a junior lienor are to permit a judicial determination of his rights, e. g., to pay and be subrogated, to defend, and to share in any surplus. See Note, The Rights of a Junior Lienholder in Wisconsin, 1959, 43 Marq.L. Rev. 89.

77. E. g., West's Ann.Cal.Code.Civ.Proc., § 726. See §§ 332, 333, infra.

78. See Cook, Powers of Courts of Equity, 1915, 15 Col.L.Rev. 37, 48, 108, 133 (strict foreclosure), 135 (foreclosure by sale); Restatement, Conflict of Laws, §§ 101a(3) and 97c; § 429d; § 77. See also Jones v. Conde, note 76, supra.

79. E. g., Iowa County Board of Supervisors v. Mineral Point R. R. Co., 1869, 24 Wis. 93. See Terrell v. Allison, 1874, 88 U.S. (21 Wall.) 289, 22 L.Ed. 634; Gage v. Perry, 1879, 93 Ill. 176.

80. "The question as to who may or may not be necessary or proper parties * * * constitutes of itself a title in the law of equity jurisprudence, upon which great learning has been expended, without the ascertainment of any rule of general or universal application." Iowa County Board of Supervisors v. Mineral Point R. R. Co., 1869, 24 Wis. 93. See note, 1940, 88 U. of Pa.L.Rev. 994, 996, bringing out that the tests differ according to the stage at which the question is raised, this being especially true as between the period before and after sale. One author of a standard work takes the position that the term "necessary parties" is of relative signification, depending upon the purpose of the relief sought, e. g., "parties who are necessary in order to obtain title free of all subsequent encumbrances may not be necessary if the purpose of the action is merely to cut off the equity of redemption without affecting the subsequent liens and encumbrances." Wiltsie, Mortgages Foreclosure, 5th ed., § 329. See idem, § 330. Another writer defines a necessary party as "one whose presence before the court is indispensable to the rendering of a judgment which shall have any effect upon the property; without whom the court might properly refuse to proceed, because its decree would be practically nugatory." Jones, Mortgages, 8th ed., § 1780. This test clearly includes the present owner of the property since the general ownership of the property cannot be transferred unless he is made a party. Further, every person who has acquired any interest in the property subsequent to the mortgage falls within the test both logically and as a practical matter. The latter is true because if such persons are not joined a third party purchaser may refuse to accept title; and a mortgagee purchaser must bring another suit to rid his title of such interests. Ibid.

81. See San Francisco v. Lawton, 1861, 18 Cal. 465. See also § 319, note-call and note 43 and note 52; and § 305 notes 70, 71, supra.
In Rezak v. King's Trading & Holding Co., Sup.Ct. 1955, 154 N.Y.S.2d 298, noted in Mortgages, in 1957 Survey of New York Law, 1957, 32 N.Y.U.L.Rev. 1425, a judgment creditor having a lien subordinate to the mortgage being foreclosed was permitted to assert the defense of lack of consideration for the mortgage, although the original mortgagors were not parties to the action and their assuming grantees defaulted.

This does not mean that the failure to join such a person makes the entire action nugatory. It means that as to persons having such an interest the proceeding leaves it unaffected unless he is made a party.[82] It may be suggested that a "proper" party is one whose joinder is not essential to the accomplishment of the foregoing narrow purpose, but whose participation in the action is desirable for the full determination of the rights of the parties.[83]

A comprehensive catalogue of all the various classes of persons who would qualify under the foregoing principles as defendants in an action to foreclose a mortgage by sale is so formidable[84] that only a few of the more important instances can be given in brief compass.

First in any list comes one who has title to the general ownership of the property subject to the mortgage or any part of it. The mortgagor so long as he retains the property falls under this category and must be joined.[85] But the mortgagor frequently sells the property and in that case the purchaser of the entire property or any part of it must be made a party.[86] If the mortgagor has parted with all of the property he is no longer a necessary party for foreclosure purposes.[87] Since he is the obligor, and normally remains such,[88] he is usually joined in order that a personal decree may be entered against him in case of a deficiency.[89] A transferee who in turn has disposed of the property is likewise unnecessary for foreclosure.[90] If he has assumed the mortgage debt he may be joined so as to get a deficiency decree against him as in the similar case of a mortgagor who has divested himself of all interest in the property.[91] On the death of a mortgagor or person in whom the present ownership of the property subject to the mortgage is vested, the persons in whom the title then vests, the heirs or devisees, must be joined in the foreclosure.[92]

---

82. E. g., Iowa County Board of Supervisors v. Mineral Point R. R. Co., 1869, 24 Wis. 93; Spokane Sav. & Loan Soc. v. Liliopoulos, 1930, 160 Wash. 71, 294 P. 561. See 1940, 88 U. of Pa.L.Rev. 994. See also, §§ 305, 313, supra; and note 80, supra.

Hagan v. Gardner, C.A. 9th, 1960, 283 F.2d 643, held that an unjoined grantee of the mortgagor was not affected by a foreclosure to which he was not a party.

83. E. g., in a foreclosure by a junior mortgagee a prior mortgagee is not a necessary party within the test suggested. However, in order that a sale subject to it may be intelligently made and bring a maximum amount it is important that he be a party for the purpose of making clear and definite the nature and extent of the prior lien. See § 323, post, for a further discussion of prior lienors and adverse claimants as parties. See also Campbell, Cases Mortgages, 2d ed., 260 n. 4, 5, as to the meaning of "proper."

84. E. g., in Wiltsie, Mortgage Foreclosure, 5th ed., § 329, are listed 51 different classes of persons who, either normally or under certain circumstances or in certain states, may be joined as defendants. 103 pages are devoted to covering parties who are such by having an interest in the property subject to the mortgage. Chs. XX, XXI. An additional 15 pages is devoted to prior lienors and adverse claimants, Ch. XXIII. And another 20 pages to parties who are made defendants because personally liable. Ch. XXIV.

85. See Goodenow v. Ewer, 1860, 16 Cal. 461, 76 Am. Dec. 540.

86. Terrell v. Allison, 1874, 88 U.S. (21 Wall.) 289, 22 L.Ed. 634; Walker v. Warner, 1899, 179 Ill. 16, 53 N.E. 594, 70 Am.St.Rep. 85; Fowler v. Lilly, 1889, 122 Ind. 297, 23 N.E. 767; Winslow v. Clark, 1872, 47 N.Y. 261. See Slingluff, The Mortgagee's Right in the Event of a Deficiency, 1937, 1 Md.L.Rev. 128.

87. Thompson v. Menfee, 1928, 218 Ala. 332, 118 So. 587; Brockway v. McClun, 1909, 243 Ill. 196, 90 N. E. 374; Fitzgerald v. Flanagan, 1912, 155 Iowa 217, 135 N.W. 738, Ann.Cas.1914C, 1104; Delacroix v. Stanley, 1933, 113 N.J.Eq. 121, 165 A. 882; McNeal v. Moberly, 1931, 150 Okl. 253, 1 P.2d 707.

88. See § 247, supra.

89. See § 333, infra. See also 1937, 108 A.L.R. 1351.

90. Howell v. Baker, 1930, 106 N.J.Eq. 434, 151 A. 117; James v. Brainard-Jackson Co., 1911, 64 Wash. 175, 116 P. 633.

91. Scarry v. Eldridge, 1878, 63 Ind. 44; Vrooman v. Turner, 1877, 69 N.Y. 280, 25 Am.R. 195. See § 332, infra; §§ 260–265, supra.

92. White v. Rittenmyer, 1870, 30 Iowa 268; Abbott v. Godfroy's Heirs, 1849, 1 Mich. 178; Chadbourn v. Johnston, 1896, 119 N.C. 282, 25 S.E. 705; Chew v. Hyman, C.C.Ill.1881, 7 F. 7. Cf., Reedy v. Camfield, 1896, 159 Ill. 254, 42 N.E. 833. Statutes sometimes provide that the personal representative rather than the heir or devisee shall be made a party. See Tierney v. Spiva, 1888, 97 Mo. 98, 10 S.W. 433; Kelsey v. Welch, 1896, 8 S.D. 255, 66 N.W. 390.

Where a dower interest is made subject to a mortgage the wife or widow is an essential party to foreclosure.[93] Where there are future interests created in the property subject to the mortgage, there are many statements that contingent remaindermen need not be made parties to a foreclosure action, that it is sufficient to join the first person in being who has a vested estate of inheritance.[94] However, if contingent remaindermen are living and available, they should be joined.[95] Although the general rule is that both trustees and beneficiaries should be made parties,[96] there are important exceptions.[97] One of these, "as well established as the rule itself, * * * is, that whenever the parties in interest are, or, from the nature of the case, may be, so numerous that it would be difficult or impractical to bring them all before the court, and their rights are such as may be fairly and fully represented and tried without joining them, the application of the rule may be dispensed with." [98]

In addition to the foregoing, all persons who have an interest in the mortgaged premises acquired by or through the owner of the property subject to the mortgage subsequent to its execution must be made defendants.[99] Under this classification fall junior mortgagees and holders of other subordinate liens.[1] The owner of an easement or restrictive covenant falls within the same reasoning.[2] Although there is a minority of authority the other way,[3] the majority and preferable rule is that where a lease is executed by the mortgagor subsequent to the mortgagee the lessee must be joined in the foreclosure action in order to extinguish his lease.[4]

---

93. Bigoness v. Hibbard, 1915, 267 Ill. 301, 108 N.E. 294, commented on in, 1915, 10 Ill.L.Rev. 137; McArthur v. Franklin, 1865, 15 Ohio St. 485, 16 Ohio St. 193.

94. See Jones, Mortgages, 8th ed., § 1401; Wiltsie, Mortgage Foreclosure, 5th ed., § 362. See also Hanna, Cas.Security, 3d ed., 1019, note, citing, Shackley v. Homer, 1910, 87 Neb. 146, 127 N.W. 145, L.R.A. 1915C, 993; McCampbell v. Mason, 1894, 151 Ill. 500, 38 N.E. 672; see Clarke v. Cordis, 1862, 86 Mass. (4 Allen) 466, 478; Powell v. Wright, 1844, 7 Beav. 444.

95. See Hess v. Hess, 1922, 233 N.Y. 164, 135 N.E. 231; N.Y. Real Prop.Actions & Proc.Law, McKinney 1963, § 1311 and N. Y. Estates Powers & Trusts Law, McKinney 1967, § 6–5.1; Mass.Gen. Laws, Ann.1959, c. 244, § 13; Ohio Code, Throckmorton, 1936, § 11926.

96. Clark v. Reyburn, 1868, 75 U.S. 318, 8 Wall. 318, 19 L.Ed. 354. See Iowa County Board of Supervisors v. Mineral Point R. R. Co., 1869, 24 Wis. 93; White v. Macqueen, 1935, 360 Ill. 236, 195 N.E. 832, 93 A.L.R. 1115; Williamson v. Field's Ex'rs & Devisees, N.Y.1845, 2 Sandf.Ch. 533. First Nat. Bank v. Leslie, 1930, 106 N.J.Eq. 564, 151 A. 501.

97. See Wiltsie, Mortgage Foreclosure, 5th ed., § 360.

98. Iowa County Board of Supervisors v. Mineral Point R. R. Co., 1869, 24 Wis. 93. See State ex rel. Ashley v. Circuit Court, 1935, 219 Wis. 38, 47, 261 N.W. 737, 741. See also 1893, 20 L.R.A. 535; 1908, 16 L.R.A.,N.S., 1006; 1912, 35 L.R.A.,N.S., 196.

99. See Osborne, Cases Property Security, 671 n. 2.

1. Gould v. Wheeler, 1877, 28 N.J.Eq. 541, requiring stay of foreclosure action until subsequent mortgagee made a party—a decision unique in this respect; cf., Catterlin v. Armstrong, 1884, 101 Ind. 258, 263. See 1940, 88 U. of Pa.L.Rev. 994. As to redemption by an omitted junior lienor, see § 305, ante. As to the right of strict foreclosure against such an omitted party, see § 313, supra. See § 324, post, for the right of such an omitted party to foreclose his junior lien.

2. Rector of Christ Protestant Episcopal Church v. Mack, 1883, 93 N.Y. 488, 45 Am.R. 260; Krich v. Zemel, 1897, 99 N.J.L. 191, 122 A. 739.

3. Dolese v. Bellows-Claude Neon Co., 1932, 261 Mich. 57, 245 N.W. 569, discussed in note, 1933, 32 Mich.L.Rev. 119; McDermott v. Burke, 1860, 16 Cal. 580. See 1921, 14 A.L.R. 664, 668.
That this may be technically correct in a title state, see note, 1942, 17 Wash.L.Rev. 37, 42. See also, Gard, Lessee's Status After Foreclosure of a Prior Mortgage, 1933, 1 Kan.City L.Rev. 11.

4. Metropolitan Life Ins. Co. v. Childs, 1921, 230 N. Y. 285, 130 N.E. 295; 14 A.L.R. 658, reargument denied 231 N.Y. 551, 132 N.E. 885; Dundee Naval Stores Co. v. McDowell, 1913, 65 Fla. 15, 61 So. 108, Ann.Cas.1915A, 387. See 1942, 17 Wash.L.Rev. 37, 43; 1937, 21 Minn.L.Rev. 610; 1934, 8 Wash.L.Rev. 184. See also 1921, 14 A.L.R. 664, 672; L.R.A. 1915C, 190, 204. There is some divergence of opinion as to the effect of nonjoinder. The New York rule is that the purchaser on foreclosure sale takes the property subject to the lease just as though he were a purchaser of the reversion. Metropolitan Life Ins. Co. v. Childs, supra. See 1942, 17 Wash. L.Rev. 37, 44 et seq. Other states leave the status of an unjoined lessee somewhat in doubt. See 1937, 21 Minn.L.Rev. 611. It is well settled that a lease prior to a mortgage is unaffected by foreclosure and should not be joined, the purchaser on the sale

JOINDER—EFFECT OF RECORDING ACTS—LIS PENDENS

322. The general rule is that, regardless of lack of knowledge or notice by the foreclosing mortgage creditor, unless a person who holds a subordinate interest in the mortgaged property is made a party to the foreclosure action, his interest is not affected by the decree. The operation of the rule is limited by the bona fide purchase rule, by provisions of recording acts, and by the common law doctrine of lis pendens or statutes to the same end.

The general rule is that lack of knowledge or notice of the subordinate interest of another person in the mortgaged land does not excuse a foreclosing mortgagee from making such person a party to his suit. If he fails to do so, the subordinate interest, regardless of whether it be legal or equitable and one of ownership or lien, is not subject to the decree.[5] There are, however, limitations upon the operation of this rule. A purchaser on the foreclosure sale who acquires the legal title for which he pays value without notice of the unjoined interest qualifies as a *bona fide* purchaser and thus will take free of such an interest if it is equitable only.[6] Similarly, under the familiar type of statute

avoiding unrecorded conveyances as against subsequent purchasers, a purchaser on foreclosure sale who buys without knowledge or notice of an outstanding but unrecorded interest may take free and clear of it just as effectively as though its holder had been joined in the foreclosure action.[7] Other statutes, either explicitly or as interpreted, go beyond this and have the effect of concluding an unjoined party whose interest was not recorded as effectively as though he had been made a party to the suit.[8] Under the most extreme of these, this is true even though the mortgagee at the time he began his foreclosure action had actual knowledge of the unrecorded interest.[9] Under others, although notice

merely taking the interest of the mortgagor and becoming the landlord of the lessee. 1921, 14 A.L.R. 664, 678.

5. First National Bank v. Leslie, 1930, 106 N.J.Eq. 564, 151 A. 501, commented on, Campbell, Cases Mortgages, 2d ed. 274 n. 3; Pancoast v. Geishaker, 1899, 58 N.J.Eq. 537, 43 A. 883; White v. Melchert, 1929, 208 Iowa 1404, 1407, 227 N.W. 347, 348, 73 A. L.R. 595; Nelson v. First Nat. Bank, 1925, 199 Iowa 804, 202 N.W. 847; Holliger v. Bates, 1885, 43 Ohio St. 437, 2 N.E. 841; Mesiavich v. Newman, 1936, 120 N.J.Eq. 192, 184 A. 538; Morrett v. Westerne, 1710, 2 Vern. 663; Godfrey v. Chadwell, 1707, 6 Vern. 601; see Haines v. Beach, N.Y.1818, 3 Johns.Ch. 459.

6. See First Nat. Bank of Union City v. Leslie, 1930, 106 N.J.Eq. 654, 151 A. 501; Pancoast v. Geishaker, 1899, 58 N.J.Eq. 537, 43 A. 883. See §§ 294, 297, *ante.* "*Bona fide suit* in which the legal title is brought before the court is analogous to *bona fide purchase* of legal title, and it may well be asked why the suitor is not equally protected. * * * Yet we know of no case which has extended the equitable doctrine of bona fide purchase to the case of the suitor." Durfee and Fleming, Res Judicata and Recording Acts, 1930, 28 Mich.L.Rev. 811, 814, n. 6.

7. Pinney v. The Merchants' Nat. Bank, 1904, 71 Ohio St. 173, 72 N.E. 884; Duff v. Randall, 1897, 116 Cal. 226, 48 P. 66, 58 Am.St.Rep. 158; Shippen v. Kimball, 1891, 47 Kans. 173, 27 P. 813; Ehle v. Brown, 1872, 31 Wis. 405. Possession under some circumstances may give notice. See Ehle v. Brown, 1872, 31 Wis. 405, 413; Hodson v. Treat, 1858, 7 Wis. 263; Noyes v. Hall, C.C.Ill.1877, 97 U.S. 34, 24 L.Ed. 909. See 1934, 89 A.L.R. 171, 182. By the weight of authority, a foreclosing mortgagee, as such is not protected under this type of statute. See Durfee and Fleming, Res Judicata and Recording Acts, 1926, 28 Mich.L.Rev. 811, 819. But "[w]e have seen no case in which the court has applied to a chancery sale that curious notion, not infrequently applied to sheriff's sales under general execution, that a purchaser at judicial sale (at least if he is the judgment creditor) can not qualify as a bona fide purchaser. * * * Query, on what theory is the chancery sale distinguishable?" Idem, 822, n. 23. See note, 1937, 25 Cal.L.Rev. 480, 485.

8. For a thorough survey and analysis of the theory and operative effects of such statutes, together with a list of them as of the date of the article, see Durfee and Fleming, Res Judicata and Recording Acts: Does a Judgment Conclude Non-Parties of Whose Interests the Plaintiff Has No Notice? 1930, 28 Mich.L.Rev. 811. See also Campbell, Cases Mortgages, 2d ed., 277, n. 3; note, 1937, 25 Cal.L.Rev. 480; note 1940, 88 U. of Pa.L.Rev. 994, 997. See Curtis, The Commission and the Law of Real Property, 1955, 40 Cornell L.Q. 755.

9. West's Ann.Cal.Code Civ.Proc., § 726, "No person holding a conveyance from or under the mortgagor of the property mortgaged, or having a lien thereon, which conveyance or lien does not appear of record in the proper office at the time of the commencement of the action need be made a party to such action, and the judgment therein rendered, and the proceedings therein had, are as conclusive against the party holding such unrecorded conveyance or lien as if he had been a party to the ac-

before suit is begun will necessitate joinder,[10] neither notice by recordation, or outside of recordation, pending suit makes it necessary to join the holder of an interest that was acquired but not recorded prior to action.[11] And where there is no recordation or notice of any kind until after the foreclosure decree it has been held that the omitted party cannot object.[12] Under such holdings a purchaser at the foreclosure sale would be protected even though he had full knowledge of the facts.[13] Although there may be some argument as to the proper basis of the result,[14]

tion." Hager v. Astorg, 1904, 145 Cal. 548, 79 P. 68, 104 Am.St.Rep. 68; Collingwood v. Brown, 1890, 106 N.C. 362, 10 S.E. 868; cf. Holman v. Toten, 1942, 54 Cal.App.2d 309, 128 P.2d 808. Also cf. Idaho Code, 1932, § 9–101, referred to in Harding v. Harker, 1909, 17 Idaho 341, 105 P. 788, 134 Am.St. Rep. 259.

10. Scott v. Marquette Bank, 1928, 173 Minn. 225, 217 N.W. 136; Munger v. T. J. Beard & Bro., 1907, 79 Neb. 764, 113 N.W. 214, 126 Am.St.Rep. 688; Lamont v. Cheshire, 1875, 65 N.Y. 30; Martin v. Morris, 1885, 62 Wis. 418, 22 N.W. 525. See Durfee and Fleming, op. cit. supra note 8, 856; 1937, 25 Cal.L. Rev. 480, 481.

11. Van Gorder v. Hanna, 1887, 72 Iowa 572, 34 N. W. 332; Jones v. Fisher, 1911, 88 Neb. 627, 130 N. W. 269; Sibell v. Weeks, 1903, 65 N.J.Eq. 714, 55 A. 244; Pinney v. Merchants' Nat. Bank, 1904, 71 Ohio St. 173, 72 N.E. 884. See Durfee and Fleming, op. cit. supra note 8, 858. The strongest types of such statutes are those in New York and California. N. Y.C.P.A. § 121, "A person whose conveyance or incumbrance is subsequently executed or subsequently recorded is bound by all proceedings taken in the action after the filing of notice, to the same extent as if he was a party to the action." West's Ann. Cal.Civ.Code, § 1214, "Every conveyance of real property * * * is void * * * as against any judgment affecting title, unless such conveyance shall have been duly recorded prior to the record of notice of action." Cf. Conn.Gen.Stat., 1930, § 5746, giving the grantee of an unrecorded deed an opportunity to intervene and assert his claim; the plaintiff, however, not being required to take affirmative action. Bristol Lumber Co. v. Dery, 1931, 114 Conn. 88, 157 A. 640. See 1937, 25 Cal.L.Rev. 480.

12. Boice v. Mich. Mut. Life Ins. Co., 1888, 114 Ind. 480, 15 N.E. 825; Wolfenberger v. Hubbard, 1915, 184 Ind. 25, 27, 110 N.E. 198, 199, Ann.Cas.1918C, 81; Rev.Stat.1881, §§ 2926, 2931 (Burns' Ind.Stat. Ann.1961, §§ 56–118, 56–119).

13. Cf. Bristol Lumber Co. v. Dery, 1931, 114 Conn. 88, 157 A. 640.

14. See Durfee and Fleming, op. cit. supra, note 8.

it seems highly desirable to protect both the foreclosing mortgagee as well as a purchaser on foreclosure sale against interests that are acquired but remain unrecorded prior to the beginning of a foreclosure action. That protection should extend at least far enough to cut off all such interests of which there was no actual notice before suit, or actual knowledge during the pendency of the litigation.

Where the subordinate interest is acquired during the pendency of the foreclosure action it is uniformly held that the foreclosure sale will cut it off just as effectively as though its owner had been made a party. This result is reached either by virtue of the common law doctrine of lis pendens,[15] or under statutes to the same end but requiring notice of action to be recorded.[16]

SENIOR MORTGAGES AND ADVERSE INTERESTS

323. The general rule is that a prior encumbrancer cannot be made a party to a foreclosure action without his consent. Exceptions, in addition to active consent or acquiescence, include joinder to determine the amount of the superior lien, whether priority actually exists and, under certain circumstances, e. g., when

15. Stewart v. Wheeling and Lake Erie Ry. Co., 1895, 53 Ohio St. 151, 41 N.E. 247, 29 L.R.A. 438, noting that the rule was formulated by Lord Chancellor Bacon, and attributing its effect to constructive notice. See also, Worsley v. Scarborough, 1746, 3 Atk. 392. But cf. Lord Cranworth in Bellamy v. Sabine, 1857, 1 De G. & J. 566, 578, that lis pendens binds a person "not because it amounts to notice, but because the law does not allow litigant parties to give to others, pending the litigation, rights to the property in dispute, so as to prejudice the opposite party." Warford v. Sullivan, 1896, 147 Ind. 14, 46 N.E. 27; Provident Mut. Life Ins. Co. v. Vinton Co., 1937, 282 Mich. 84, 275 N.W. 776; Jones v. Williams, 1911, 155 N.C. 179, 71 S.E. 222, 36 L.R.A., N.S., 426.

16. E. g., N.Y.C.P.A., §§ 120, 122, 1080, 988; West's Ann.Cal.Civ.Code, § 1214, discussed in note, 1937, 25 Cal.L.Rev. 480; Va.Code Ann.1957, § 8–14. Cf. Fuller v. Scribner, 1879, 76 N.Y. 190; Coe v. Manseau, 1885, 62 Wis. 81, 91, 22 N.W. 155, 159; Huntington v. Meyer, 1896, 92 Wis. 557, 561, 66 N.W. 500, 501. See note, 1937, 25 Cal.L.Rev. 480. But see 1935, 23 Cal.L.Rev. 108.

the senior mortgage has matured, selling the entire property free and clear of all liens.

Like a senior lienor, the holder of an adverse claim to the property is, by the prevailing view, not a necessary or proper party to a foreclosure action although the rule has been criticised.

The general rule that the holder of a paramount encumbrance cannot be made a party to a foreclosure action without his consent finds expression in many cases.[17] The reasons given are both logical and practical in nature. The proper object of a foreclosure action is to sell the property given as security by the mortgagor and in doing so cut off the rights of redemption in that property of the mortgagor and everyone claiming under him.[18] A junior mortgagee's security is the property subject to prior encumbrances. That, therefore, is all that can be sold when he forecloses his lien, and only rights of redemption based upon it can be cut off by the sale.[19] Since a senior mortgagee's interest cannot be affected by an action to foreclose a junior lien, it follows that an attempt to join him as a party to such an action can be defeated through timely objection. Such is the logic of the rule. To it is added the practical reason that the prior mortgagee should be able to choose his own time for

selling and not be forced to realize in a market that in his judgment is unfavorable.[20] The argument is especially strong when the junior's foreclosure action is brought before the senior lien has matured, and it has force even if it is due.

There are, however, qualifications.[21] One of them is suggested by the rule as stated. There is no reason why, if the first mortgagee is willing to be a party to the action, he should not be. Consequently if he becomes a party on his own motion he will be bound by the decree.[22] Furthermore, if he is joined in an action in which the plaintiff alleges that the defendant's lien is a prior one and asks that the property be sold free of it, his failure to appear and object operates as consent and bars his mortgage.[23] In such a case the property is sold free of both liens, but the

---

17. Hudnit v. Nash, 1862, 16 N.J.Eq. 550, 560; Krause v. Hartung, 1931, 108 N.J.Eq. 507, 155 A. 621; Osage Oil & Refining Co. v. Muber Oil Co., C. C.A.Okl., 1930, 43 F.2d 306, 308; Jerome v. McCarter, 1876, 94 U.S. 734, 24 L.Ed. 136; Wickenden v. Rayson, 1855, 6 De G. M. & G. 210, 213; Langton v. Langton, 1855, 7 De G. M. & G. 30, 39. For a list of states, together with authorities, adhering to the general rule, see note 1941, 89 U. of Pa.L.Rev. 373, 378. Pennsylvania, however, goes to the opposite extreme and as a regular practice permits the divestiture of prior liens on forclosure by a junior encumbrancer. Idem, 373–377, 379–384.

18. "Strictly, a prior mortgagee is not a proper party to an action by a junior mortgagee, * * * because the proper object of the action is to bar the equities of the mortgagor and rights accruing subsequent to the mortgage." Foster v. Johnson, 1890, 44 Minn. 290, 292, 46 N.W. 350.

San Francisco v. Lawton, 1861, 18 Cal. 465. Cf. Pritchard v. Fruit, 1917, 208 Ill.App. 77, 82. See note 30, infra. See also, § 321, supra.

19. Fendley v. Smith, 1928, 217 Ala. 166, 115 So. 103.

20. "Lands which today are a slender security for money which may have been loaned by way of mortgage become amply sufficient tomorrow. But if the plaintiff's [subsequent lienor] theory be correct, the mortgagee, as against a subsequent incumbrancer by way of mortgage, cannot exercise his own judgment as to whether he will retain his lien until the security becomes good. * * * The rights of the parties could not thus be reversed, except with the express consent of the prior incumbrancer." McReynolds v. Munns, N.Y.1865, 41 N.Y. (2 Keyes) 214. See Campbell, Cases Mortgages, 2d ed., 261 n. 5a, for additional authorities. See also note 30 infra.

21. "But prior lienors may consent to become parties to such an action, or may be made such, where the object is to ascertain the extent of their claims, and to have the premises sold subject thereto, or absolutely to create a fund out of which the several incumbrances shall be paid in their order; but such purpose or object should clearly appear from the complaint." Foster v. Johnson, 1890, 44 Minn. 290, 292, 46 N.W. 350. Cf. Gargan v. Grimes, 1877, 47 Iowa, 180; Champlin v. Foster, 1846, 7 B.Mon., Ky., 104; Cochran v. Goodell, 1881, 131 Mass. 464; Roll v. Smalley, 1847, 6 N.J.Eq. 464; Western Ins. Co. v. Eagle Fire Ins. Co., 1828, 1 Paige, N.Y., 284; Vanderkemp v. Shelton, 1844, 11 Paige, N.Y., 28.

22. See Kraus v. Hartung, 1932, 111 N.J.Eq. 531, 533, 162 A. 724, 725; 1941, 89 U. of Pa.L.Rev. 373, 379. Cf. Palmer v. Guaranty Trust Co., C.C.A.N.Y.1940, 111 F.2d 115. But cf., McReynolds v. Munn, 1865, 41 N.Y.(2 Keyes) 214. See note 21, supra.

23. Jacobie v. Wickle, 1894, 144 N.Y. 237, 39 N.E. 66.

respective priorities persist as to the proceeds.[24]

The possibility of joinder, however, goes beyond active consent or acquiescence of a prior lienor. The junior mortgagee is seeking a sale, and in order to have one in which possible buyers will participate and pay a proper price for the property, the nature and extent of prior liens should be determined so that a prospective purchaser may know with certainty for what he is paying his money. Consequently, even though the senior lien is not yet due, the foreclosing junior mortgagee may join its owner for the purpose of such determination.[25] Under the English practice it has been possible to join a prior mortgagee for such a purpose and also to compel him to consent or refuse to permit a sale of the property free from both liens. If he consented, the property was sold and he was given priority of payment out of the proceeds. If he refused, the sale was made subject to the mortgage of the determined amount.[26] Later English practice permits the court to order a junior lienor to deposit in court the probable costs of a sale and then have the property sold free of prior liens fixing a reserve price sufficient to cover their claims.[27] Furthermore, there is au-

thority that the question of priority of encumbrances, i. e., whether another lien is prior or subsequent to the one being foreclosed, may be litigated in a foreclosure action.[28] Where a paramount mortgage debt is due and payable, or will be before decree and sale, such prior mortgagee may be joined and the property sold under what amounts to a joint foreclosure of both mortgages, the proceeds being used to pay off the mortgagees in the order of their priority.[29] This deprives an earlier mortgagee of the privilege of exercising his own judgment as to when he will foreclose and sell his security.[30] It is justified as being, in effect, the enforcement of the junior mortgagee's right to redeem in order to protect his own security; and to do so without the necessity of advancing out of his own funds the amount necessary to do so, a requirement which often makes the right, as a practical matter, illusory.[31] And there are other instances

The practice is possible under 44 & 45 Vict. c. 41, § 25.

28. Iowa County Board of Supervisors v. Mineral Point R. R. Co., 1869, 24 Wis. 93; see Whipple v. Edelstein, 1933, 148 Misc. 681, 684, 266 N.Y.S. 127, 131; cf. Ruyter v. Wickes, Sup.Ct.1889, 22 N.Y.S. 200, 4 N.Y.S. 743, affirmed 121 N.Y. 498, 24 N.E. 791, 31 St.R. 387. Contra, Krause v. Hartung, 1931, 108 N.J.Eq. 507, 155 A. 621, second mortgage expressly subject to first mortgage. And cf. Dawson v. Danbury Bank, 1867, 15 Mich. 489; Strobe v. Downer, 1860, 13 Wis. 11, 80 Am.Dec. 709. And see note 35, infra.

29. Hagan v. Walker, 1852, 55 U.S. (14 How.) 29, 37, 14 L.Ed. 312; Masters v. Templeton, 1883, 92 Ind. 447; see Emigrant, etc., Sav. Bank v. Goldman, 1878, 75 N.Y. 127, 132.

30. See note 20, supra. See also Three-foot v. Hillman, 1900, 130 Ala. 244, 30 So. 513, 89 Am.St.Rep. 39; Waters v. Bossel, 1881, 58 Miss. 602; cf., Bigelow v. Cassedy, 1875, 26 N.J.Eq. 557.

31. See Hefner v. Northwestern Life Ins. Co., 1887, 123 U.S. 747, 754, 8 S.Ct. 337, 31 L.Ed. 309, "the bill in such a case being in effect both a bill to foreclose the second mortgage and a bill to redeem from the first mortgage." See also Peabody v. Roberts, N.Y.1866, 47 Barb. 91, "And in Norton v. Warner (3 Edw.Ch. 106) it was held that there is no objection to a second mortgagee's filing a bill for a foreclosure and sale to pay off all the incumbrances according to their respective priorities, * * *. It is very important for the promotion of the interests of junior mortgagees that this right should be

24. See note 27, infra.

25. Missouri K. & T. Trust Co. v. Richardson, 1899, 57 Neb. 617, 78 N.W. 273; see Foster v. Johnson, 1890, 44 Minn. 290, 292, 46 N.W. 350, 351; Jerome v. McCarter, 1876, 94 U.S. 734, 736, 24 L.Ed. 136. But see Kraus v. Hartung, 1932, 111 N.J.Eq. 531, 533, 162 A. 724, 725.

26. Wickenden v. Rayson, n. 17, ante; Coote, Mortgages, 9th ed., 1072; Fisher, Mortgages, 7th ed., 425. Apparently the same sort of relief is possible in New York. Look at Metropolitan Trust Co. v. Tonawanda Valley & C. R. R. Co., 1887, 43 Hun 521, 524, affirmed, 106 N.Y. 673, 13 N.E. 937; cf. Tax Lien Co. v. Schultze, 1914, 213 N.Y. 9, 13, 106 N.E. 751, 753, L.R.A.1915D, 1115, Ann.Cas.1916E, 636; Whipple v. Edelstein, 1933, 148 Misc. 681, 684, 266 N.Y.S. 127, 131. For the same practice in Mississippi, look at Waters v. Bossel, 1881, 58 Miss. 602. See Campbell, Cases Mortgages, 2d ed., 262 n. 5c.

27. Woolley v. Colman, 1882, 21 Ch.D. 169; cf. Gordon v. Horsfall, 1846, 5 Moore's P.C.Cas. 393, 427.

where the interests of the mortgagor and encumbrancers require that a prior mortgagee be joined and the property be sold free and clear of both junior and senior liens.[32]

The holder of a claim in the property adverse to the title of the mortgagor is usually bracketed with senior lienors as one who is not a necessary or proper party to a foreclosure action.[32a] If his claim is a valid one, his interest cannot be sold in the foreclosure because it is not under the mortgage sued upon. And whether or not it is valid should not be determined incidentally in an action whose purpose is not to decide such an issue but merely to sell property that secures the plaintiff's claim.[33] Such is, at least, the argument and prevailing view. Yet if the claimant appears and litigates the question of his title he is bound by the decree, the court having power to decide the question if the claimant acquiesces.[34] And the same is true if he is properly joined and defaults in a case in which the foreclosing mortgagee sets forth facts from which he claims that the defendant's title is subordinate to his mortgage.[35]

carefully maintained; for where they do not possess the pecuniary ability of redeeming the senior mortgage, it is the only means afforded them through which the security can be applied to the payment of the debt it secures."

32. E. g., where the first mortgage extended only to a small part of the property covered by the second mortgage, a sale under foreclosure of the latter could not be made advantageously if a purchase had to take subject to a partial mortgage. Shepherd v. Pepper, 1890, 133 U.S. 626, 10 S.Ct. 438, 33 L.Ed. 706.

32a. Gage v. Perry, 1879, 93 Ill. 176; San Francisco v. Lawton, 1861, 18 Cal. 465; Dial v. Reynolds, 1877, 96 U.S. 340, 24 L.Ed. 644; Toucey v. New York Life Ins. Co., 1941, 314 U.S. 118, 62 S.Ct. 139, 86 L.Ed. 100, 137 A.L.R. 967, 137 footnote 8; Wells v. American Mortgage Co., 1895, 109 Ala. 430, 20 So. 136; Corning v. Smith, 1851, 6 N.Y. 82—accord. Provident Loan Trust Co. v. Marks, 1898, 59 Kan. 230, 52 P. 449, 68 Am.St.Rep. 349, contra. See also Masters v. Templeton, 1884, 92 Ind. 447; Bradley v. Parkhurst, 1878, 20 Kan. 462; note, 1878, 7 Cent.L. J. 473; note, 1885, 21 Cent.L.J. 223.

In Harrison v. Mary Bain Estates, Inc., 1956, 2 Misc. 2d 52, 152 N.Y.S.2d 239, affirmed without opinion, 1st Dept., 1956, 2 A.D.2d 670, 153 N.Y.S.2d 552, a former record holder of the title to the property subject to the mortgage was permitted to intervene in the foreclosure action for the purpose of showing that her deed to the mortgagor was a forgery and thus void.

33. The idea that disputes as to legal title are for the law courts and are not to be adjudicated in an equitable proceeding has been relied upon. E. g., Gage v. Perry, 1879, 93 Ill. 176, "It has always been supposed that a court of law was the proper forum in which to settle and determine adverse legal titles to real estate, where all questions of fact in relation thereto can be submitted to and determined by a jury under proper instructions from the court,

and we are aware of no authority holding that an ordinary bill of foreclosure forms an exception to this general rule of law. In a bill to foreclose a mortgage, not only the mortgagor, but all persons claiming by, through or under him, or under his chain of title, are proper and necessary parties to the bill, and when such parties are brought before the court their rights may be passed upon and settled by a decree, but we have not been referred to a single authority which sustains the right of a complainant, in such a case, to bring in a party who claims adversely, and have such adverse title passed upon and settled by decree."

34. See Beronio v. Ventura County Lumber Co., 1900, 129 Cal. 232, 61 P. 958, 79 Am.St.Rep. 118; Goebel v. Iffla, 1888, 111 N.Y. 170, 18 N.E. 649.

35. "* * * We think that * * * a default ought to be construed as an admission that, at the time he [the holder of a paramount title] failed to appear as required, he had no interest in the property in question, and hence as conclusive of any prior claim of interest or title adverse to the plaintiff." Barton v. Anderson, 1886, 104 Ind. 578, 581, 4 N.E. 420. Cf. note 23, supra.

It has been held that a purchaser at a tax sale held subsequent to the giving of a mortgage is a proper party to a foreclosure of the mortgage, and the validity of such purchaser's title may be settled in the foreclosure action. Hefner v. North Western Mut. Life Ins. Co., 1887, 123 U.S. 747, 754, 8 S.Ct. 337, 31 L.Ed. 309. See also Upjohn v. Moore, 1932, 45 Wyo. 96, 16 P.2d 40, 85 A.L.R. 1063, commented on in, 1933, 33 Col.L.Rev. 543. But cf., Erie County Sav. Bank v. Shuster, 1907, 187 N.Y. 111, 79 N.E. 843. It is difficult to see why the fact that the tax sale occurred subsequent to the giving of the mortgage should affect the question of joinder. Regardless of when the sale occurred its holder is asserting a claim paramount and adverse to the mortgagor's title held as security by the mortgagee and within the reasons given for excluding him as a party to a foreclosure action.

However, "[u]nder the usual allegation in a complaint for foreclosure that a defendant other than the mortgagor claims some interest in the premises, and that such interest is subsequent and subordinate to that created by the mortgage, any prior interest held by such defendant is not affected by the judgment therein." Beronio v. Ventura Lumber Co., 1900, 129 Cal. 232, 61 P. 958, 79 Am.St.Rep. 118; Summers v. Bromley, 1873, 28 Mich. 125. See

Furthermore, it has been urged that there is no good reason why the claimant should ever object to having the validity of his claim passed upon, whereas to exclude the question "has the unfortunate result of requiring a sale of a very uncertain quantity largely defeating the purpose of the change from strict foreclosure to that of sale." [36]

OMITTED JUNIOR LIENORS

324. **In general a junior mortgagee may pursue the same remedies after a foreclosure and sale to which he was not a party as he could have before. One of these is to bring an independent action to foreclose his own lien. To protect himself, the purchaser on foreclosure sale under the senior mortgage may pay off the junior lien, re-foreclose by sale, or, under certain circumstances, have strict foreclosure.**

There is a dispute as to whether, where a foreclosure sale has taken place and produced a surplus, a junior mortgagee who was not a party to the action may share in it.

That a junior mortgagee who is not made a party to a foreclosure action is not affected by it is thoroughly established.[37] And, it is said that in order "to ascertain what remedies a junior mortgagee may pursue after a foreclosure and sale on a senior mortgage to which he was not a party, it is only necessary to determine what he might have done be-

fore." [38] A good bit of this story has already been told. Thus the right of an omitted junior lienor to redeem from a purchaser on foreclosure sale was investigated earlier.[39] We saw, too, that a purchaser on such a foreclosure sale, acquires the title and right of redemption of the mortgagor and that, added to these, equity maintains the senior mortgage on foot for his benefit.[40] The availability to such a purchaser of strict foreclosure was also explored.[41] There remain some additional points.

An omitted junior lienor, even though he acquires his lien after the start of a foreclosure action by a senior mortgagee, may intervene in the latter's action.[42] Or he may bring his own independent action to foreclose subject to the senior mortgage.[43] However, such a suit should be consolidated into one action with all lienors made parties so that the foreclosure sale can be made free of all incumbrances.[44] In cases where a junior mortgagee is a party to foreclosure by a prior mortgagee, the lien of the former, cut off as to the land by the sale, is transferred to any surplus that may be derived from the foreclosure sale.[45]

---

38. Catterlin v. Armstrong, note 37, supra.

39. § 305, supra.

40. See § 305, note 74. See also on the prevention of merger by equity in such a case, §§ 272–277, supra, and the granting of subrogation, §§ 282, 283.

41. § 313, supra.

42. Some statutes expressly give the omitted party an opportunity to intervene and assert his claim. Conn.Gen.Stat., 1930, § 5746. See 1937, 25 Cal.L. Rev. 480. See § 321, note 1, supra.

43. Cronin v. Hazeltine, 1862, 85 Mass. (3 Allen) 324; Vanderkemp v. Shelton, N.Y.1844, 11 Paige 28; Peabody v. Roberts, N.Y.1866, 47 Barb. 91.

44. Farmers Loan & Trust Co. v. Lake St. El. Ry., 1900, 177 U.S. 51, 20 S.Ct. 564, 44 L.Ed. 667; Kewanee Lumber etc., Co. v. Guest Laundry Co., 1940, 306 Ill.App. 491, 29 N.E.2d 115.

45. Soles v. Sheppard, 1881, 99 Ill. 616. "The foreclosure of the prior mortgage affords relief to all subsequent encumbrances, as they have the right when parties defendant to participate in the distribution of the surplus."—and, this is true without the necessity of filing a cross-bill or even putting

---

Campbell, Cases Mortgages, 2d ed., 262 n. 5e, for additional cases. See also note 28, supra. But cf., Hefner v. North Western Mut. Life Ins. Co., supra.

36. Durfee, Cases Mortgages, 296 n. The learned author suggests that a court might solve any difficulty as to the propriety of trying title in an equitable proceeding to foreclose by directing an issue to be tried at law. Ibid. For a fuller discussion of the problem of the paramount mortgage and the adverse claim, see Durfee, Cases Security, 196–204.

For statutory amendments in New York dealing with the determination of adverse claims, see Curtiss, The Commission and the Law of Real Property, 1955, 40 Cornell L.Q. 735.

37. Catterlin v. Armstrong, 1884, 101 Ind. 258, 263, "That the rights of a junior mortgagee, who was not made a party, are in no manner affected by the foreclosure of and sale on a senior mortgage, has been so often determined that this much may now be accepted as settled."

See also Note, The Rights of a Junior Lienholder in Wisconsin 1959, 43 Marq.L.Rev. 89.

Our problem here, however, is with the case where the foreclosure process has been completed without the junior mortgagee having been made a party and the question is whether he may now maintain his own independent action to foreclose subject to the senior mortgage in the hands of the purchaser on foreclosure. In general the answer is yes, and without first offering to redeem.[46] A junior mortgagee's right to have the value of the land tested by a judicial sale at which he may appear and protect his interest by bidding up the property to an amount which will cover his lien is a fundamental one.[47] Where a sale under foreclosure by a senior mortgagee takes place under proceedings to which he was not made a party and in which he had no opportunity to intervene [48] a right to redeem from the purchaser [49] does not afford him the protection he is entitled to. He should be allowed to foreclose his own lien just the same as though there had been no prior foreclosure by the senior mortgagee.[50]

To protect himself against the exercise of the remedies of foreclosure or redemption by an omitted junior lienor, the purchaser may under certain circumstances have strict

foreclosure [51] or he may get rid of it by payment of the subordinate mortgage debt.[52] And it is well established that, on discovering the defect in his title, a purchaser on foreclosure under a senior mortgage may re-foreclose by sale against the omitted junior lienor.[53] This affords to the latter what he was denied on the previous foreclosure, namely, a sale at which he can appear and protect his interest.[54]

Where a foreclosure sale has taken place and produced a surplus, whether a junior mortgagee who was not a party to the action can share in the surplus is a matter of dispute. In some states no intervention by an omitted junior lienor is permitted.[55] The reasoning is that the purchaser bought the property subject to the omitted party's lien and therefore "what the purchaser obtained and paid his money for was the title of the mortgagor in the land, and a subrogation to the rights of the first mortgagee." [56] The surplus money should go, therefore, to the mortgagor, and not to the second mortgagee who still has his second mortgage on the land intact. An answer is that it is to the advantage of both purchaser and mortgagor to permit intervention. To deny it means that the purchaser will have to bring another action to free his title of the omitted lien or else

in an answer. See Powell v. Starr, 1901, 100 Ill. App. 105; Brown v. Crookston Agricultural Ass'n, 1886, 34 Minn. 545, 26 N.W. 907; Carpenter v. Dake, 1907, 144 N.C. 291, 56 S.E. 938; Markey v. Langley, 1875, 92 U.S. 142, 23 L.Ed. 701. Cf. Johnson v. Hambleton, 1879, 52 Md. 378; Moss v. Robertson, 1898, 56 Neb. 774, 77 N.W. 403; Lithauer v. Royle, 1864, 17 N.J.Eq. 40.

In some states the determination of relative rights as to surplus money is regarded as a "special proceeding" as distinct from a step in the foreclosure suit itself. Velleman v. Rohrig, 1908, 193 N.Y. 439, 86 N.E. 476; Walker v. Carroll, 1923, 123 Misc. 712, 205 N.Y.S. 805, affirmed 204 N.Y.S. 956.

46. Catterlin v. Armstrong, 1884, 101 Ind. 258, 263; see Peabody v. Roberts, N.Y.1866, 47 Barb. 91, 99. See 1940, 88 U. of Pa.L.Rev. 994, 998.

47. See note, 1940, 88 U. of Pa.L.Rev. 994, 998–999.

48. See § 322, supra.

49. See § 305, supra.

50. See note 43, 46, supra. See also § 323, supra. And see Durfee, Cases on Security, 1951, 221.

51. See § 313, supra.

52. See § 305, supra. The objection to this is, of course, that it forces the purchaser to pay out the amount of such junior mortgage debt in addition to the price that he had previously paid for the property at the sale when unaware of its existence. The chances of reimbursing himself by recovery from the mortgagor are, as a practical matter, usually remote.

53. Mortgage Com. Realty Corp. v. Columbia Hts. Garage Corp., 1938, 169 Misc. 618, 7 N.Y.S.2d 740. See note, 1940, 88 U. of Pa.L.Rev. 994, 1006. See 1931, 73 A.L.R. 612, 633.

54. Note, 1940, 88 U. of Pa.L.Rev. 994, 1006.

55. Milmo Nat. Bank v. Rich, 1897, 16 Tex.Civ.App. 363, 40 S.W. 1032; Horr v. Herrington, 1908, 22 Okl. 590, 98 P. 443, 20 L.R.A.,N.S., 47, 132 Am.St. Rep. 648. See also Greensburg Fuel Co. v. Irwin Nat. Gas Co., 1894, 162 Pa. 78, 29 A. 274.

56. Milmo Nat. Bank v. Rich, supra.

pay off the junior claim. If intervention is permitted it amounts to an election to give up the junior lien on the property in the hands of the purchaser in favor of sharing in the surplus of the proceeds, and that is clearly beneficial to the purchaser. Since it also reduces the amount of the junior claim against the mortgagor, it is desirable from his point of view. In New York, the omitted subordinate mortgagee may, if he wishes, take his share of the surplus and credit it on his claim against the mortgagor. His only alternative to this is to redeem—he cannot have an independent foreclosure of his own lien subject to the first mortgage leaving the surplus from the prior foreclosure stand.[57] In at least one state he is permitted to elect between the surplus and an action of foreclosure.[58]

ACCRUAL OF RIGHT TO FORECLOSE— INTEREST, INSTALLMENTS

325. Default is a fundamental condition to foreclosure. When it occurs the right to foreclose accrues at once, its creation being independent of any agreement by the parties. Defaults in payment of interest or installments also give a right to foreclose. When foreclosure is for such a partial default, several answers have been given as to how the security is to be applied.

Default in the performance of any act or acts that a mortgage is given to secure is a fundamental condition precedent to the bringing of an action to foreclose.[59] When default occurs the right to foreclose accrues at once, its creation being quite independent of any provision for it in the mortgage.[60] If

the mortgage is security for the performance of one single act such as the payment of a lump sum on a given day, the problem of accrual of the right to foreclose and what to do about it is a relatively simple matter. Difficulties arise where part only of the mortgage obligation goes into default.[61] For the most part these difficulties can be avoided by the insertion of an acceleration clause in the mortgage.[62] The most frequent instances of default in the performance of a part only of the entire obligation secured occur in connection with failure of the mortgagor to pay interest or installments of the principal.[63]

It is clear that non-payment of interest provided for in the mortgage obligation constitutes a default enabling a mortgagee to foreclose.[64] Similarly, where the principal is

57. Fliess v. Buckley, 1882, 90 N.Y. 286, lien transferred to fund; Denton v. Ontario County Bank, 1896, 150 N.Y. 126, 44 N.E. 781.

58. Harris v. Hooper, 1878, 50 Md. 537. Cf. Ducker, v. Belt, 1851, 3 Md.Ch. 13.

59. See § 319, note-call and note 51.

See also Storke and Sears, Enforcement of Security Interests in Colorado, 1952, 25 Rocky Mt.L.Rev. 1, 5–10.

60. "In order to give a court of equity the right to maintain an action to foreclose a mortgage it is not necessary that the mortgage itself should provide for such foreclosure. The right to maintain the action, * * * arises out of the fact that the mortgagor has failed to perform the conditions of the mortgage by paying the debt secured thereby in the manner and at the time or times agreed upon in the mortgage." Scheibe v. Kennedy, 1885, 64 Wis. 564, 25 N.W. 646.

61. "The rule is that the foreclosure of a mortgage may be commenced when any condition of the mortgage is broken by the non-payment of any part of the debt secured thereby, when the same becomes due and remains unpaid." Scheibe v. Kennedy, supra note 60.

See 1905, 37 L.R.A. 737, for analysis and discussion of proceedings to enforce a mortgage for a part of the mortgage debt.

62. For discussion of some of the problems that arise when such an acceleration clause is inserted, see §§ 173, 177, 179, 232, 279, supra. See also, § 326, infra.

63. It has been suggested that a default by the mortgagor in the payment of taxes which are then paid by the mortgagee should stand on the same footing as interest or an installment in permitting the mortgagee to have an action to foreclose for the taxes so paid independent of foreclosure for the principal. Glenn, Mortgages, § 91.1. The prevailing view, as was seen earlier, § 173 supra, is that the mortgagee may add the amount he has to pay out for taxes to his mortgage debt but can maintain no separate action for it.

64. Scheibe v. Kennedy, 1885, 64 Wis. 564, 25 N.W. 646; Gordon v. Donovan, 1930, 111 Conn. 106, 149 A. 397; Cross v. Hurlbut, 1935, 120 Fla. 85, 162 So. 148; see Pennsylvania Co. for Ins. on Lives &

repayable in installments, the right to foreclose arises on a default in any one installment.[65]

Where the action to foreclose is for a partial default several answers have been given as to how the security is to be applied.[66] Some courts take the view that the security is indivisible and that a foreclosure action must be of the entire security regardless of whether the default being sued for is of a portion or all of the debt.[67] The result of this harsh doctrine is that if a mortgagee forecloses for an installment or interest he will be barred later from foreclosing for the balance or any other portion of his obliga-

tion. But most courts, either by decision or under statutes, arrive at more equitable solutions. Thus, if it is possible, which it usually is not, to divide the property into parcels without injury to the whole a sale will be decreed of only so much of the premises as will be sufficient to satisfy the amount due, and the decree will stand as security on the unsold portion of the property for the balance of the debt as it comes due.[68] Where the property is not susceptible to piecemeal sale without injury to the whole, it may be sold as an entirety free and clear of the entire mortgage debt.[69] The surplus over the amount necessary to satisfy the partial default is then handled in various ways.[70] Even without the aid of statute, it has been held that the chancellor will direct its application to the liquidation of the balance of the debt, with a fair and equitable rebate of interest

Granting Annuities v. Broadway-Stevens Co., 1930, 105 N.J.Eq. 494, 499, 148 A. 575, 577.

"In a word, the interest is part of the substance of the mortgage debt. It belongs not to it by tacking; it is not an incident of the debt, but pro tanto, it is the debt itself." West Branch Bank v. Chester, 1849, 11 Pa. 282, 290, 51 Am.Dec. 547. See also Winchell v. Coney, 1886, 54 Conn. 24, 5 A. 354. Van Doren v. Dickerson, 1881, 33 N.J.Eq. 388; Howell v. Western R. Co., 1876, 94 U.S. 463, 24 L. Ed. 254—accord. Cf. Yoakam v. White, 1893, 97 Cal. 286, 32 P. 238; Van Loo v. Van Aken, 1894, 104 Cal. 269, 37 P. 925. See 1913, 42 L.R.A.,N.S., 108.

As to when the principal sum is paid where a mortgage calls for payment of interest until the whole of the principal sum and interest is paid, see Note, Termination of Interest Payments in Foreclosure Proceedings, 1960, 21 Md.L.Rev. 86, discussing Ex Parte Aurora Fed. Sav. & Loan Ass'n, 1960, 223 Md. 135, 162 A.2d 739.

65. Black v. Reno, C.C.Mo.1894, 59 F. 917.

66. Where the principal sum will come due in a short time it is possible to avoid the problem by starting a suit for partial foreclosure and then enlarging it by supplemental complaint to include the principal amount and any later partial defaults. Milo Manor v. Woodard, 1937, 67 App.D.C. 296, 92 F.2d 220; N. Y. Security & Trust Co. v. Lincoln St. Ry. Co., 1896, 74 F. 67, affirmed 77 F. 525; Gordon v. Donovan, 1930, 111 Conn. 106, 149 A. 397; Malcolm v. Allen, 1872, 49 N.Y. 448, semble.

67. Curtis v. Cutler, 1896, 76 F. 16, 22 C.C.A. 16, 37 L.R.A. 737, abrogated by Gen.Stat.Minn., Mason, 1927, § 9610. See Prideaux v. Des Moines Joint Stock Bank, D.C.Minn.1929, 34 F.2d 308, appeal dismissed 282 U.S. 800, 51 S.Ct. 40, 75 L.Ed. 720; Rains v. Mann, 1873, 68 Ill. 264; Cf., Wells v. Ordway, 1899, 108 Iowa 86, 78 N.W. 806, 75 Am.St.Rep. 209; Mascarel v. Raffour, 1876, 51 Cal. 242, foreclosing on only one parcel. But cf., Widman v. Hammack, 1920, 110 Wash. 77, 187 P. 1091, 42 A.L. R. 468. See §§ 173, 319, supra.

68. Blazey v. Delius, 1874, 74 Ill. 299; Griffin v. Reis, 1879, 68 Ind. 9; Caufman v. Sayre, Ky.1841, 2 B.Mon. 202. See Reno v. Black, supra note 65; 1905, 37 L.R.A. 737, 743. See also Minn.Stat.Ann., § 580.09, "Where a mortgage is given to secure the payment of money by instalments—each instalment, either for principal or interest may be taken and deemed to be a separate and independent mortgage, and such mortgage for each instalment may be foreclosed in the same manner as if a separate mortgage was given for each subsequent instalment"; West's Ann.Cal.Code Civ.Proc., § 728, "If the debt for which the mortgage, lien, or incumbrance is held is not all due, so soon as sufficient of the property has been sold to pay the amount due, with costs, the sale must cease; and afterwards, as often as more comes due, for principal or interest, the court may, on motion, order more to be sold." See note 67, supra.

69. A mortgagee foreclosed his mortgage upon the mortgagor's partial default. Held, the premises, when sold under the decree, passed to the purchaser discharged from the mortgage lien. Poweshiek County v. Dennison, 1873, 36 Iowa, 244, 14 Am.Rep. 521; Buford v. Smith, 1842, 7 Mo. 489; Reno v. Black, note 65, supra. But see Borden v. McNamara, 1910, 20 N.D. 225, 127 N.W. 104, Ann.Cas. 1912C, 841, 846; Edgar v. Beck, 1893, 96 Mich. 419, 56 N.W. 15.

70. For cases dealing with the disposition of surplus arising from a sale under foreclosure for partial default, see Hatcher v. Chancey, 1883, 71 Ga. 689; Peyton v. Ayres, 1849, 2 Md.Ch. 64; Fowler v. Johnson, 1880, 26 Minn. 338, 3 N.W. 986, 6 N.W. 486; Cox v. Wheeler, N.Y.1838, 7 Paige 248; Schreiber v. Carey, 1879, 48 Wis. 208, 4 N.W. 124.

on it.[71] And the same practice is authorized by statute in some jurisdictions.[72] Others direct that the surplus be held in trust to meet the unmatured portion of the debt.[73] But it has also been held proper to decree a sale of the mortgaged premises, subject to the continued lien of the mortgage for the balance of the debt.[74]

ACCRUAL OF RIGHT TO FORECLOSE— ACCELERATION

326. Acceleration clauses are commonly inserted in mortgages. They enable a mortgagee, if he so elects, to declare the entire mortgage obligation due on default on some part performance. Acceleration may be waived or prevented in various ways. However, the prevailing view is that it is neither a forfeiture nor a penalty. Hence the general rule is that no relief will be given against its enforcement for a default occurring by reason of the mortgagor's negligence or mistake, or by accident.

It is common practice to insert in mortgages an acceleration clause which enables the mortgagee, if he so elects,[75] on any specified default of part performance such as payment of interest, installments of principal, taxes and insurance, to declare the whole amount of the mortgage due and, on failure to pay to foreclose. Various problems in connection with such clauses have been dealt with elsewhere.[76] There are a few additional points that should be touched upon.

In most jurisdictions the bringing of a foreclosure action is a sufficient election unless the mortgage expressly requires the giving of notice before starting the action.[77] There is, however, some authority that bringing a foreclosure action is not a sufficient election; other notice must be given.[78]

71. E.g., Black v. Reno, note 65, supra; 1905, 37 L. R.A. 737.

72. N.J.Stat.Ann.1952, § 2A: 50:33, payment with rebate for interest, if mortgagee willing to receive it; Cal.Code Civ.Proc., § 728, rebate of interest where such rebate is proper; N.Y.C.P.A. § 1086, payment with rebate for interest, or investment; Banzer v. Richter, 1911, 68 Misc. 192, 123 N.Y.S. 678, affirmed 146 App.Div. 913, 131 N.Y.S. 1103; Wis.Stat.Ann. § 278.07–08, payment with rebate for interest, or investment.

73. Ga.Code, 1933, § 67–502. And see New York and Wisconsin statutes—in preceding note.

74. Light v. Federal Land Bank, 1928, 177 Ark. 846, 7 S.W.2d 975; Miami Mortgage & Guaranty Co. v. Drawdy, 1930, 99 Fla. 1092, 1097, 127 So. 323, 325; Hughes v. Frisbie, 1876, 81 Ill. 188, 193; Chicago Title & Trust Co. v. Prendergast, 1929, 335 Ill. 646, 167 N.E. 769; Fremont Joint Stock Bank v. Foster, 1933, 215 Iowa 1209, 247 N.W. 815; McCurdy v. Clark, 1873, 27 Mich. 445; Cary v. Met. Life Ins. Co., 1933, 141 Or. 388, 17 P.2d 1111; McDougal v. Downey, 1872, 45 Cal. 165; Burroughs v. Ellis, 1888, 76 Iowa, 649, 38 N.W. 141. See, generally, Leesman, The Effect of Foreclosure of Part Only of a Mortgage Debt, 1937, 31 Ill.L.Rev. 1056; note, 1930, 30 Col.L.Rev. 893. See also 1897, 37 L.R.A. 737. In New York, by an amendment in 1927, Laws of 1927, c. 683, N.Y.C.P.A. § 1086 was changed to permit this as an alternative practice. In the face of the statute it was held improper to decree a sale for the defaulted portion of a debt with a continuing lien for the unmatured balance. Bank of America Nat. Ass'n v. Dames, 1930, 135 Misc. 391, 239 N.Y.S. 558, 30 Col.L.Rev. 893. A later case, however, held the other way, giving effect to the clear language of the act. Prudence Co. v. Sussman, 1932, 143 Misc. 686, 258 N.Y.S. 241.

75. A self-operative acceleration clause is unusual. Cf. Seligman v. Burg, 1931, 233 App.Div. 221, 251 N.Y.S. 689.

In Bank of America National Association v. Dames, 1930, 135 Misc. 391, 239 N.Y.S. 558, commented on in, 1930, 30 Col.L.Rev. 893, the court held that an acceleration clause could not provide for partial maturity of the debt on default at the option of the mortgagee; acceleration must be for the entire debt.

See also 1925, 34 A.L.R. 897; 1908, 12 L.R.A.,N.S., 1190.

76. See §§ 173, 177, 179, 232, 279, supra.

77. Pizer v. Herzig, 1907, 120 App.Div. 102, 105 N.Y. S. 38; Swearingen v. Lahner, 1894, 93 Iowa 147, 61 N.W. 431, 26 L.R.A. 765, 57 Am.St.Rep. 261. As to what will constitute, for this purpose, the commencement of a foreclosure action, see Trowbridge v. Malex Realty Corp., 1920, 111 Misc. 211, 183 N. Y.S. 53, reversed on other grounds, 198 App.Div. 656, 191 N.Y.S. 97. See also Walsh v. Henel, 1929, 226 App.Div. 198, 235 N.Y.S. 34, noted 1929, 7 N.Y. Univ.L.Q.Rev. 214. See further Updike, Mortgages, in 1954 Annual Survey of American Law, 1955, 30 N.Y.U.L.Rev. 805, 812, noting Jacobson v. McClanahan, 1953, 43 Wash.2d 751, 264 P.2d 253.

78. Basse v. Gallegger, 1858, 7 Wis. 442, 76 Am.Dec. 225. Look at Albertina Realty Co. v. Rosbro Realty Corp., 1932, 258 N.Y. 472, 180 N.E. 176, affirmed 233 App.Div. 737, 250 N.Y.S. 841, and comment on it in Walsh & Simpson, Cases Security Transactions, 482, Note (2).

Statutes specifying that an election to sell on default under a trust deed mortgage shall contain a state-

Such notice, however, may be waived by the mortgagor.[79] Acceptance by the mortgagee of the amount in default before he has elected to enforce the acceleration operates as a waiver of the provision. And a payment or tender before election destroys the right to accelerate.[80] However, a failure to foreclose on the first default in payment does not operate as a waiver of the option to foreclose because of later defaults.[81] Further, he may take such payment after he has elected in favor of acceleration without waiving his right to foreclose the mortgage for the balance.[82]

The general rule is that an acceleration clause works neither a forfeiture nor a penalty but is simply a matter of contract determining when the debt is payable.[83] Conse-

quently it is enforced in both law and equity, and a mortgagor will not be relieved against its enforcement for a default occurring by his negligence, mistake or by accident in the absence of fraud, bad faith or other conduct on the part of the mortgagee rendering it unconscionable for him to avail himself of it.[84] There is some authority, however, that a mortgagor will be protected from defaults that are the result of an accident or a mistake while acting in good faith, or unusual circumstances beyond his control.[85]

ment of breach of secured obligation and its nature must be strictly followed. Bisno v. Sax, 1960, 175 Cal.App.2d 714, 346 P.2d 814.

79. Grootemaat v. Bertrand, 1927, 192 Wis. 519, 213 N.W. 294.

80. Trinity County Bank v. Haas, 1907, 151 Cal. 553, 91 P. 385; Van Vlissingen v. Lenz, 1897, 171 Ill. 162, 49 N.E. 422; Cresco Realty Co. v. Clark, 1908, 128 App.Div. 144, 112 N.Y.S. 550. See West's Ann. Cal.Civ.Code §§ 2924c, 2924d, providing that payment of arrearages and costs cures defaults, with certain exceptions.

In accord with the statement in the text is Bisno v. Sax, 1960, 175 Cal.App.2d 714, 346 P.2d 814.

81. Dunn v. Barry, 1917, 35 Cal.App. 325, 169 P. 910; Bower v. Stein, 1910, 177 F. 673, 101 C.C.A. 299.

82. La Plant v. Beechley, 1918, 182 Iowa 452, 165 N. W. 1019; Robinson v. Miller, 1925, 317 Ill. 501, 148 N.E. 319; Odell v. Hoyt, 1878, 73 N.Y. 343.

See, 1928, 53 A.L.R. 525; 1926, 41 A.L.R. 732; 1922, 19 A.L.R. 284; 1920, 5 A.L.R. 437.

See Mortgages in 1957 Survey of New York Law, 1957, 32 N.Y.U.L.Rev. 1426, noting Mayer v. Myers, Sup.Ct.1956, 155 N.Y.S.2d 129, and Clark-Robinson Corp. v. Jet Enterprises, Inc., Sup.Ct.1957, 159 N.Y. S.2d 214.

83. Graf v. Hope Bldg. Corp., 1930, 254 N.Y. 1, 171 N.E. 884, 70 A.L.R. 984. The case, because of an important dissenting opinion by Cardozo, J., was widely discussed. See notes: 1930, 40 Yale L.J. 141; 1930, 30 Col.L.Rev. 1064; 1930, 17 Va.L.Rev. 80; 1930, 16 Cornell L.Q. 106; 1930, 10 Boston U. L.Rev. 558; 1930, 29 Mich.L.Rev. 380; 1930, 8 N.Y. Univ.L.Q.Rev. 331; 1930, 79 U. of Pa.L.Rev. 229; 1930, 6 Wis.L.Rev. 45; 1931, 70 A.L.R. 993. See also notes, 1939, 88 U. of Pa.L.Rev. 94; 1922, 22

Col.L.Rev. 266; 1895, 40 Cent.L.J. 513; 1895, 41 Cent.L.J. 118. See also Trinity County Bank v. Haas, 1907, 151 Cal. 553, 91 P. 385; Collins v. Nagel, 1925, 200 Iowa 562, 203 N.W. 702. See further Updike, Mortgages, in 1954 Annual Survey of American Law, 1955, 30 N.Y.U.L.Rev. 812, noting Law v. Edgecliff Realty Co., Sup.Ct.1954, 133 N.Y.S.2d 418, and August Tobler, Inc. v. Goolsby, Fla.1953, 67 So. 2d 537. And see A–Z Servicenter v. Segall, 1956, 334 Mass. 672, 138 N.E.2d 266, 269, citing text.

84. Graf v. Hope Bldg. Corp., supra, note 83. See 1931, 70 A.L.R. 993. Jacobson v. McClanahan, 1953, 43 Wash.2d 751, 264 P.2d 253, discussed in 1953, 29 Wash.L.Rev. 101, places Washington in accord.

85. See Cardozo, J., dissenting in Graf v. Hope Bldg. Corp., supra note 83; 1931, 70 A.L.R. 993, 1000. And look at Lettieri v. Mistretta, 1927, 102 N.J.Eq. 1, 139 A. 514, approved in 1928, 37 Yale L.J. 672.

Updike, Mortgages, in 1956 Annual Survey of American Law, 1957, 32 N.Y.U.L.Rev. 789, 793, observes that, to ameliorate the strictness of the general rule, "courts often entertain more compassionate views in acceleration cases, and readily find waiver, lack of good faith on the part of the accelerator, or some other factual basis for relief." He also suggests that mortgagors "should insist upon provisions for written notice of default (at least in relation to covenants other than those for interest and instalments of principal) and some reasonable period of grace to make good." For relief from acceleration on the ground that, on the facts of the case, it was oppressive and unconscionable, look at Rockaway Park Series Corp. v. Hollis Automotive Corp., 1954, 206 Misc. 955, 135 N.Y.S.2d 588, affirmed 285 App.Div. 1140, 142 N.Y.S.2d 364, commented on by Million, Property Law, in 1955 Survey of New York Law, 1955, 30 N.Y.U.L.Rev. 1065, 1074. In Bisno v. Sax, 1960, 175 Cal.App.2d 714, 346 P.2d 814, the court relieved against an acceleration previously declared under a trust deed mortgage in which time was not made of the essence and where all payments of interest and principal payable before trial had been made and accepted so that the only basis for acceleration was the notice. For recent statutory relief from acceleration clauses, see Bradkey, Current Changes in Illinois Real Property Law, 1960, 10 DePaul L.Rev. 566, 582.

CONDUCT OF SALE

327. Foreclosure by sale under court direction is usually regulated by statutes which vary from state to state. Equity courts have power, apart from statute, to decree and control the process. Statutes or court decrees usually call for a public sale with requirements for giving notice of time, place, manner and terms of sale. Provision may be for other matters such as sales by parcels or as an entirety as is most advantageous, and also sale in accordance with priorities. Sales require court confirmation and may be set aside under certain circumstances.

The method of conducting a foreclosure sale is now largely regulated by statute and is, therefore, mostly a matter of local law which must be consulted in each jurisdiction. Such legislation ordinarily provides for a public sale under the direction of either the sheriff or an officer of the court appointed for that purpose.[86] In the absence of statutory provision, a court of equity has ample power to order a master to make a judicial sale.[87] The decree in such cases will commonly contain provisions specifying the giving of notice, the time, place, manner and terms of conducting the sale, and other matters that are generally covered by statutory regulation.[88] There seems to be no clear au-

thority in either England or America for a decree directing a private sale.[89]

Occasionally a mortgage covers two distinct parcels of real estate. Where this is the case, and one parcel, upon sale, will bring sufficient to satisfy the mortgage debt, the decree should direct the sale of such parcel only, and not of both.[90] This matter also is frequently regulated by statute.[91]

The purpose of notice is to inform the public as to the date, place, nature and condition of the property to be sold and terms of the sale.[92] Questions as to the sufficiency and definiteness of notice to accomplish these purposes sometimes are of importance.[93]

Although under statutory provision, or by provision of a chancery decree, the sale is to be conducted by the sheriff as in sales under execution,[94] it usually differs from such sales

86. Typical statutes are West's Ann.Cal.Code Civ. Proc., §§ 726, 729, incorporating by reference provisions governing the conduct of a sale under execution by a sheriff but authorizing court to appoint a commissioner or elisor to do the job; Thompson's Laws N.Y., 1939, N.Y.C.P.A., Rule 259, "Unless otherwise specially ordered by the court, the judgment shall direct that the mortgaged premises * * * be sold by or under the direction of the sheriff of the county or a referee."; Ga.Code Ann. 1967, § 67–401, "sold in the manner and under the same regulations which govern sheriff's sales under execution"; Minn.Stats.Ann., § 581.03. See State ex rel. Elliott v. Holliday, 1892, 35 Neb. 327, 53 N. W. 142. As to the practice in federal courts, see Blossom v. Milwaukee & C. R. Co., 1865, 70 U.S. (3 Wall.) 196, 18 L.Ed. 43, "by the marshal of the district where the decree was entered, or by the master appointed by the court, as directed in the decree."

87. 2 Daniell's Ch.Pl. & Pr., 5th ed., 1264.

88. See Leesman, Some Considerations Involving the Decretal Parts of the Decree of Sale in a Foreclosure Proceeding, 1941, 6 J.Marshall L.Q. 314.

89. Durfee and Doddridge, Redemption from Foreclosure Sale—The Uniform Mortgage Act, 1925, 23 Mich.L.Rev. 825, 832, n. 28. See Wright v. Vinton Branch of the Mountain Trust Bank of Roanoke, 1936, 300 U.S. 440, 457, 57 S.Ct. 556, 81 L.Ed. 736, 112 A.L.R. 1455, listing as one of the mortgagee's rights that of realization "upon the security by a judicial public sale."

90. See Dozier v. Farrior, 1914, 187 Ala. 181, 65 So. 364; Blazey v. Delius, 1874, 74 Ill. 299; Hughes v. Riggs, 1897, 84 Md. 502, 36 A. 269; Miller v. Kendrick, N.J.1888, 15 A. 259; Guarantee Trust & Safe Deposit Co. v. Jenkins, 1885, 40 N.J.Eq. 451, 2 A. 13. See also Leesman, op. cit. supra note 88; note, 1937, 25 Cal.L.Rev. 469; L.R.A.1917B, 517. Cf. also 1941, 15 S.Cal.L.Rev. 19.

91. See Security Sav. Bank of Cedar Rapids v. King, 1924, 198 Iowa, 1151, 199 N.W. 166; Clark v. Kraker, 1892, 51 Minn. 444, 53 N.W. 706; Thomas v. Thomas, 1911, 44 Mont. 102, 119 P. 283, Ann.Cas. 1913B, 616; Miller v. Trudgeon, 1905, 16 Okl. 337, 86 P. 523, 8 Ann.Cas. 739; Person v. Leathers, 1890, 67 Miss. 548, 7 So. 391. See also 1908, 8 Ann. Cas. 741; Ann.Cas.1913B, 619; West's Ann.Cal. Code Civ.Proc. § 726. On the right to maintain a single suit to foreclose separate mortgages of real property in different counties securing the same debt, see, note, 1937, 25 Cal.L.Rev. 469, 471; West's Ann.Cal.Code Civ.Proc., § 726. See also 1939, 120 A.L.R. 660.

92. See Leesman, op. cit. supra note 88.

93. See notes, 1918, 2 Minn.L.Rev. 157; 1921, 5 Minn.L.Rev. 325; 1931, 9 Tex.L.Rev. 454. See also 1939, 120 A.L.R. 660.

94. See, e. g., provisions in statutes, note 86, supra.

in important respects. The most fundamental is that "the whole business is * * * under the guidance and superintendence of the court [of chancery] itself."[95] One consequence of the sale being a judicial one under direction of the court is that the sale is equally for the benefit of all lienholders whose rights have been adjudicated by it.[96] And sale of the various parcels of property under the mortgage may be ordered in accordance with priorities determined by such doctrines as the inverse order of alienation rule.[97] So, too, the decree may fix a limit to the amount under which the property may not be sold at the sale.[98]

The fact that the sale on foreclosure is a judicial one also has a bearing upon when title passes under the sale. In a sheriff's sale usually it passes when the property is struck off at the sale and the successful bidder completes his purchase, there being no need for court approval of either the sale or the sheriff's deed.[99] A foreclosure sale, how-

---

95. Blossom v. Milwaukee & C. R. Co., 1865, 70 U.S. (3 Wall.) 196, 18 L.Ed. 43. "The whole proceeding, from the beginning to the final confirmation of the reported sale, and the passing of title to the vendee and the money to the persons entitled to it, was under the supervision and control of the court." Penn's Adm'r v. Tolleson, 1859, 20 Ark. 652, 661. Look at Jones v. Williams, 1911, 155 N.C. 179, 71 S.E. 222, 36 L.R.A.,N.S., 426. Nat. Reserve Life Ins. Co. v. Kemp, 1959, 184 Kan. 648, 339 P.2d 368.

96. "The decree being equally for the benefit of all lienholders whose rights have been adjudicated by it * * * the writ of fieri facias which is issued for the purpose of executing the decree, although usually sued out by the complainant, directs the sale of the mortgaged premises to be made, not for the purpose of satisfying the complainant's lien alone, but all the liens which have been established by the decree. A writ of fieri facias issued on a decree in foreclosure for the purpose of satisfying the claims of several encumbrancers, although single in its frame is multiform in substance, * * *." Welsh v. Lawler, 1907, 73 N.J.Eq. 371, 68 A. 218, 133 Am.St.Rep. 737. Look also at Laub v. Warren Guarantee etc., Co., 1936, 54 Ohio App. 457, 8 N.E.2d 258; Brant v. Lincoln Nat. Life Ins. Co. of Ft. Wayne, 1935, 209 Ind. 268, 198 N.E. 785.

97. "If lands are subject to mortgage * * * and are sold successively in different parcels to different persons, a court of equity, in decreeing a sale of them for the satisfaction of the mortgage, or the lien of the vendor, or in charging them with the incumbrance, will pursue the inverse order of alienation. * * * This is an equity of the several purchasers, and must be claimed and asserted by them. If not claimed and asserted, it is not obligatory upon the court. * * *" Prickett v. Sibert, 1883, 75 Ala. 315, 319.

Detroit Sav. Bank v. Truesdail, 1878, 38 Mich. 431, accord. See also De Haven v. Musselman, 1889, 123 Ind. 62, 24 N.E. 171; Drake v. Collins, Miss.1840, 5 How. 253; Appeal of Uniontown Building & Loan Ass'n, 1879, 92 Pa. 200. Cf., Gilbert v. Haire, 1880, 43 Mich. 283, 5 N.W. 321. See Chapter 10, supra, especially, §§ 286–292.

While a mortgagee, after notice, may not by agreement or release disturb the various equities of jun-

ior incumbrancers or owners of the land subject to his mortgage (see §§ 268–271, ante) he may foreclose his mortgage, and in such a proceeding no duty is imposed upon him to safeguard the rights of such persons, who are parties to the suit. See also Vines v. Wilcutt, 1924, 212 Ala. 150, 102 So. 29, 35 A.L.R. 1301.

98. "The court, in ordering a sale or a resale, may, in its discretion, take notice of the present emergency, and, after a proper hearing, fix a minimum or upset price at which the premises must be bid in if the sale is to be confirmed. This is a power that courts of equity ordinarily exercise in cases of foreclosure of corporate property which is of such size and character as to preclude the establishment of a fair price by competitive or cash bidding, Northern Pacific Railway Co. v. Boyd, 228 U.S. 482, 33 S.Ct. 554, 57 L.Ed. 931. We see no reason why the same power should not be exercised in cases where economic conditions are such as to preclude the element of competitive bidding, and to make ineffective the ordinary and usual manner of fixing the market value of the property." Suring State Bank v. Giese, 1933, 210 Wis. 489, 246 N.W. 556, 85 A.L.R. 1477. See Leesman, op.cit. supra note 88, 316.

Wilson v. Fouke, 1934, 188 Ark. 811, 67 S.W.2d 1030; Levy v. Broadway-Carmen Bldg. Corporation, 1937, 366 Ill. 279, 8 N.E.2d 671—accord.

"There is little or no difference between the equitable jurisdiction and power in a chancery court to refuse approval to a report of sale on foreclosure, and the power to fix, in advance, a reserved or upset price, as a minimum at which the property may be sold. * * * No reason appears why the chancellor cannot prevent a sale at a grossly inadequate price by fixing a reasonable sale price in advance. * * * It is common practice in both the State and Federal courts * * *. Cases wherein an upset price has been fixed are not confined to large properties for which, by reason of their great value, the market is limited or there is no market whatever." Idem, 1937, 366 Ill. 279, 289, 8 N.E.2d 671, 676.

See, further, §§ 329, 330, infra.

99. Coulter v. Blieden, C.C.A.Ark.1939, 104 F.2d 29, certiorari denied 308 U.S. 583, 60 S.Ct. 106, 84 L.Ed. 488; Glenn v. Hollums, C.C.A.Tex.1936, 80 F.2d 555; Shreiner v. Farmers Trust Co., C.C.A.3rd 1937, 91 F.2d 606, certiorari denied 58 S.Ct. 36, 302 U.S. 686, 82 L.Ed. 530; State Bank of Hardinsburg

ever, requires confirmation.[1] Even in states where the foreclosure takes place by way of execution, confirmation may be required by statute [2] or the court may reserve power to confirm the sale when made.[3] And there exists power to set aside a sale under certain circumstances and order a new one.[4] All of these powers of judicial control are important on the question of how far courts, without the aid of statute, are capable of protecting mortgagors from the hardship of inadequate sales prices on foreclosure, especially in times of depression, a matter dealt with in later sections.[5]

v. Brown, 1942, 317 U.S. 135, 63 S.Ct. 128, 87 L.Ed. 140, rehearing denied 317 U.S. 712, 63 S.Ct. 432, 87 L.Ed. 567; Leviston v. Swan, 1867, 33 Cal. 480; Pollard v. Harlow, 1903, 138 Cal. 390, 71 P. 648; Bateman v. Kellogg, 1922, 59 Cal.App. 464, 472, 474, 211 P. 46.

1. George v. Cone, 1905, 77 Ark. 216, 91 S.W. 557, 113 Am.St.Rep. 143, 7 Ann.Cas. 171.

See Mayhew v. West Virginia Oil & Oil Land Co., C. C.1885, 24 F. 205, 215; Blossom v. Milwaukee & C. R. Co., 1865, 70 U.S. (3 Wall.) 196, 207, 18 L.Ed. 43, 46.

A purchased a chattel under a foreclosure sale made pursuant to a decree. The sale was not confirmed by the court. Held, replevin for the chattel would not lie by A. Gowan v. Jones, Miss.1848, 10 Smedes & M. 164; Allen v. Elderkin, 1885, 62 Wis. 627, 22 N.W. 842. Cf. Fort v. Burch, N.Y.1849, 6 Barb. 60.

2. E.g., Minn.Stat.Ann. § 581.08. But cf. Leviston v. Swan, 1867, 33 Cal. 480, "There is, under our system, no Master in Chancery—no Master's report— and no confirmation of the sale by the Court. That mode of procedure is wholly foreign to our system." It would seem that the same is true in New York. Nat. City Bank v. Gelfert, 1940, 284 N. Y. 13, 29 N.E.2d 449, 130 A.L.R. 1472. However, see Thomas v. San Diego College Co., 1896, 111 Cal. 358, 366, 43 P. 965, trust deed mortgage; court has power to refuse to confirm a sale under the decree, and may set it aside and order a resale, where special circumstances have prevented competition, and assurance is given that upon a resale a better price can be obtained sufficient to justify the delay and additional expense.

3. E.g., Laub v. Warren Guar. etc. Co., 1936, 54 Ohio App. 457, 8 N.E.2d 258.

4. Van Senden v. O'Brien, 1932, 61 App.D.C. 137, 58 F.2d 689; Bank of America Nat. Trust & Savings Ass'n v. Reidy Lumber Co., 1940, 15 Cal.2d 243, 101 P.2d 77; Ellis v. Powell, Mo.1938, 117 S.W.2d 225; Kloepping v. Stellmacher, 1871, 21 N.J.Eq. 328. See §§ 329, 330, infra.

5. See §§ 329, 330, 331, 335, infra. Megliola v. Special Justice, etc., 1938, 299 Mass. 325, 12 N.E.2d 874.

POSITION OF PURCHASER

328. **The successful bid at a court foreclosure sale is subject to confirmation in the court's discretion, the discretion however being a judicial one. The bidder is bound from the moment his bid is accepted but he is entitled to a marketable title although the sale is without warranty, and he is given an opportunity to make a title search. After confirmation, the purchaser is invested with title of the mortgagor, subject to certain qualifications, as of the date of the mortgage. He is then entitled to possession, to obtain which several remedies are available.**

A bid at a foreclosure sale is only an offer to buy which is accepted and becomes binding upon the bidder when the officer in charge of the sale strikes it off to him.[6] An accepted bidder, it is usually said, "acquires no independent rights until the sale be confirmed by the court, and * * * the court may exercise a discretion in either confirming or rejecting the sale." [7] What this means is that the purchaser has no contract right to have the sale confirmed; and until it is confirmed, the sale agreement is not enforceable by him. Whether it shall or shall not be is to be determined according to whether the terms of the sale conform to certain requirements to be determined by the court in its discretion.[8] The discretion, however, is a judicial, not an arbitrary one, and must be exercised in accordance with legal rules governing it. Consequently, the purchaser may insist that "confirmation must follow unless there exist some reason recognized by law as warranting a refusal to confirm," [9] and, in this sense, he does have a vested right at once. And, for the purpose of encouraging

6. Blossom v. Milwaukee & C. R. Co., 1865, 70 U.S. (3 Wall.) 196, 18 L.Ed. 43.

7. George v. Cone, 1905, 77 Ark. 216, 91 S.W. 557, 113 Am.St.Rep. 143, 7 Ann.Cas. 171. See § 327, note 1, supra.

8. George v. Cone, note 7, supra; Blossom v. Milwaukee, etc., Ry., note 6, supra; Kable v. Mitchell, 1876, 9 W.Va. 492.

9. Allen v. Martin, 1883, 61 Miss. 78.

bidding, it is highly important that a bidder should have this degree of certainty of confirmation.[10]

On the purchaser's side, however, once his bid is accepted, "he submits himself to the jurisdiction of the court and becomes a party to the cause in which the sale has been decreed, and he may be compelled to stand by the offer he has made." [11]   The court, after confirmation, may compel the purchaser to take title and pay the bid price, or it may order a resale and hold the purchaser liable for any loss that may result.[12]   In this respect the purchaser's contract obligations are governed by substantially the same rules that apply to a vendee in the ordinary contract for the sale of land.[13]   Consequently he is entitled to a marketable title and has a reasonable time within which to make an examination and raise the question as to defects which he discovers.[14]   These are of two sorts: (a) defects in the title the mortgagor possessed at the execution of the mortgage; and (b) those that are the result of flaws in the foreclosure action.[15]   There is authority that the doctrine of *caveat emptor* applies to sales in foreclosure action.   However, even courts which accept the doctrine as a general proposition may refuse to apply it to irregularities in the foreclosure proceedings, such as the failure to join the mortgagor or his successors or a party holding a subsequent interest under the mortgagor, which result in the estate directed to be sold not passing, or passing subject to defects due to the irregularity.[16]   As to the first type of defect some

10.   See Morrisse v. Inglis, 1890, 46 N.J.Eq. 306, 19 A. 16, quoted with approval in George v. Cone, note 7, supra; Stump v. Martin, 1873, 72 Ky. 285, 292, "Considerations of public policy demand that some confidence be had in the stability of public sales, so as to invite competition in bidders by an assurance to men of fidelity and promptness in their business habits that the chancellor is at least bound by the same rules of fair dealing that such men are in their business transactions with each other."   Quigley v. Breckinridge, 1899, 180 Ill. 627, 54 N.E. 580; Page v. Kress, 1890, 80 Mich. 85, 44 N.W. 1052, 20 Am.St.Rep. 504.

11.   Allen v. Martin, supra note 9; Dills v. Jasper, 1864, 33 Ill. 262, 272; Travellers' Ins. Co. v. Thompson, 1941, 140 Neb. 109, 299 N.W. 329.

12.   Camden v. Mayhew, 1888, 129 U.S. 73, 9 S.Ct. 246, 32 L.Ed. 608; Fienhold v. Babcock, 1916, 275 Ill. 282, 113 N.E. 962.   See Thomas v. San Diego College Co., 1896, 111 Cal. 358, 366, 43 P. 965.

"After the court has approved of the bid, it may summarily require the bidder to pay the amount thereof, or it may order the property to be resold at the bidder's risk and expense, and if, upon a resale, it does not bring the amount of the bidder's liability, the court may summarily enforce the payment of the difference."   Dills v. Jasper, 1864, 33 Ill. 263, 273.   Cf., Riggs v. Pursell, 1878, 74 N.Y. 370; Whitehead v. Whitehurst, 1891, 108 N.C. 458, 13 S. E. 166; Ogilvie v. Richardson, 1860, 14 Wis. 157.

13.   "The Court, however, treats a contract made with one of its officers as being made with the court itself, and will deal with the contractee upon equitable principles,—the same principles, indeed, which govern in all cases of specific performance."   Boorum v. Tucker, 1893, 51 N.J.Eq. 135, 26 A. 456, 52 N.J.Eq. 587, 33 A. 50, per Pitney, V. C.

14.   E.g., Timmermann v. Cohn, 1912, 204 N.Y. 614, 97 N.E. 589; Raleigh & C. R. Co. v. Baltimore Nat. Bank, D.C.S.C.1941, 41 F.Supp. 599.

15.   See Boggs v. Fowler, 1860, 16 Cal. 559, 564, 76 Am.Dec. 561.

For New York legislation establishing procedure by which a purchaser in a defective foreclosure may perfect his title, see Curtiss, The Commission and the Law of Real Property, 1955, 40 Cornell L.Q. 735, 739.

16.   "The doctrine of *caveat emptor* * * * is usually invoked with reference to sales upon execution issued against the general property of a judgment debtor. * * * But a somewhat different rule prevails in cases where specific property is the subject of sale, by a specific adjudication: as where the interest of A in a certain tract is decreed to be sold. * * * A valid decree in a mortgage case operates upon such interest as the mortgagor possessed in the property at the execution of the mortgage.   That interest may not constitute a valid title; it may not, in fact, be of any value; and the purchaser takes that risk.   To that extent the doctrine of *caveat emptor* applies even in those cases * * * but no further.   The interest specifically subjected to sale, whatever it may be worth, a purchaser is entitled to receive; it is for that interest he makes his bid and pays his money. It has, therefore, in a multitude of instances, been held that a purchaser, under a decree of this character, may petition to be released from his purchase, or that the sale be set aside, where it has been subsequently discovered that the Court rendering the decree had not acquired jurisdiction of the subject matter, or of persons having interests in the property, or for other reasons that the estate directed to be sold would not pass."   Boggs v. Fowler, 1860, 16 Cal. 559, 564, 76 Am.Dec. 561.   See 1931, 73 A.L.R. 612, 620.

If a foreclosure sale is irregular, but not void, or caused by the fraud of any of the parties thereto,

courts proceed upon the theory that there is no warranty of title by anyone to a purchaser on a judicial foreclosure sale, that what is offered for sale is the interest of the mortgagor whatever it may be subject to all defects and that the buyer purchases this at his peril.[17] Coupled with this is the doctrine that the chancellor, if a defect of this sort is discovered and objected to before the sale is completed, will grant relief but that he will not act after the buyer has accepted the deed.[18] The objection to this view is that a would-be purchaser at a foreclosure sale must either make an intensive title search before bidding on property he has no assurance of acquiring or else forego bidding except at a figure that would take into account the hazard he runs. Usually the first course is impracticable, and the second is sure to dampen bidding and result in sacrificing the property at a price below that normally attendant upon a forced sale.[19] The better practice, therefore, is to purport to sell a clear title except as to paramount interests in the property which are definitely stated in the pleadings and notices of sale.[20]

When all the steps of the foreclosure sale, including confirmation, have been completed, the purchaser is invested with title, this being accomplished under the usual practice by a deed executed and delivered to him by the master or other officer under order of the court. The title so acquired, as has been seen in different connections previously, is the "entire interest and estate of mortgagor and mortgagee as it existed at the date of the mortgage."[21] This statement, of course, is subject to the qualifications as to defects in joinder of parties [22] and, of course, the immediately preceding discussion. Having title, he is entitled to enjoy it by getting possession if he does not already have it.[23]

---

objection to the irregularity must be made at or prior to confirmation. Watson v. Tromble, 1891, 33 Neb. 450, 50 N.W. 331, 29 Am.St.Rep. 492; Clement v. Ireland, 1905, 138 N.C. 136, 50 S.E. 570; Allison v. Allison, 1891, 88 Va. 328, 13 S.E. 549; Strand v. Griffith, 1911, 63 Wash. 334, 115 P. 512; Core v. Strickler, 1884, 24 W.Va. 689.

17. A purchased property under a foreclosure sale. The land was subject to a prior tax lien, of which A was ignorant. The sale was duly confirmed. Held, A was bound to complete the purchase and was entitled to no deduction from the purchase price. "There is no warranty of title by the chancellor or the creditor, and * * * where there is a judgment to enforce the mortgage, and a sale under it, the purchaser buys at his peril, and cannot complain of a want of title, unless he applies to the chancellor before the sale is completed by an order of confirmation. The chancellor is more lenient than the common-law judge, and if, before the sale is made complete, it is discovered that his vendee acquires no title, or some equitable reason is presented for canceling the bonds of the purchaser, the relief will be granted." Farmers' Bank of Ky. v. Peter, Ky.1878, 13 Bush 591, 594; Brown v. Gilmor's Ex'rs, 1855, 8 Md. 322, accord. Cf. Lawrence v. Cornell, N.Y.1820, 4 Johns.Ch. 542. See Boggs v. Fowler, note 16, supra.

18. See notes 16, 17, supra.

19. See Walsh, Mortgages, 310.

20. See Walsh & Simpson, Cases Security Trans., 503 Note (3).

21. Rector of Christ Protestant Episcopal Church v. Mack, 1883, 93 N.Y. 488, 45 Am.R. 260; Bateman v. Kellogg, 1922, 59 Cal.App. 464, 211 P. 46, accord.

See also Champion v. Hinkle, 1888, 45 N.J.Eq. 162, 16 A. 701; Coomes v. Frey, 1911, 141 Ky. 740, 133 S. W. 758.

A mortgagee may be estopped from setting up a reversionary interest of record unless, at the foreclosure sale, he specifies that the property is to be sold subject to it. Ferguson v. Cloon, 1913, 89 Kan. 202, 131 P. 144, Ann.Cas.1914D, 281. Cf. Young v. Brand, 1884, 15 Neb. 601, 19 N.W. 494. See §§ 319, n. 52, 324, supra.

See additionally Survey of Illinois Law, 1954–1955, 34 Chi.-Kent L.Rev. 81, commenting on Kling v. Ghilarducci, 1954, 3 Ill.2d 454, 121 N.E.2d 752, 46 A.L. R.2d 1189.

In Schwoyer v. Smith, 1957, 388 Pa. 637, 131 A.2d 385, commented on in Plowman, Mortgages and Secured Transactions, in 1956–1957 Survey of Pennsylvania Law, 1958, 19 U. of Pitt.L.Rev. 292, 293, it was held that the subsequent acquisition, by the mortgagor of the dominant tenement, of the servient tenement cannot affect by merger an easement of right of way so as to present the purchaser on foreclosure sale of the dominant tenement from asserting it against the purchaser on foreclosure sale of the servient tenement. United States v. Brosnan, C.C.A.3d, 1959, 264 F.2d 762, affirmed 363 U.S. 237, 80 S.Ct. 1108, 4 L.Ed.2d 1192, held that federal tax liens on certain realty were junior in point of time to a duly recorded mortgage and were divested on foreclosure sale of the latter, title on foreclosure sale relating back to the inception of the mortgage.

22. See §§ 284, 298, 303, 305, 319, 324, supra.

23. See §§ 125, 126, 147–149, 160–162, 314, supra.

Various remedies are available for this purpose. The writ of assistance [24] is common, but additionally ejectment,[25] writs of possession,[26] and statutory remedies [27] have been held to lie.

ADEQUACY OF SALE PRICE— ORDINARY CONTROLS

329. Acceptance of an advance bid, refusal to confirm or ordering a new sale because of inadequate price, and fixing an upset price, in some states after an appraisal, have been used for the purpose of obtaining an adequate price for property sold on mortgage foreclosure sale. Courts refuse to grant postponements of sale to achieve this end.

Much attention has been paid by both courts and legislatures to the problem of obtaining an adequate price on foreclosure sale of the property.[28] One American device to achieve that end, the statutory right of redemption from foreclosure sale, was discussed earlier.[29] Several other methods have been invoked. Among them are acceptance of an advance bid, refusal to confirm a bid because of inadequacy, ordering a new sale, fixing an upset price, and postponing the sale. The terrific strain of the depression years of the thirties, during which in great areas of the country a market for the sale

of real-estate was virtually non-existent, with a resultant breakdown in the normal functioning of foreclosure proceedings, caused both a wave of remedial legislation and a reexamination by courts of their own powers and doctrines.[30] For the sake of convenience, the discussion to follow will be divided into two parts. The balance of this section will cover what may be described as normal methods of control used to prevent an inadequate sale price. A following one will deal with changes wrought by the extraordinary conditions ushered in by the depression period.[31] Although the problem of an adequate price at the foreclosure sale is intimately bound up with the question of a deficiency judgment, it is, nevertheless, distinct. Hence the question of the price, or valuation, of the property on foreclosure sale in connection with denial of or restrictions upon a deficiency decree or judgment will be dealt with at a subsequent point when the whole matter of such relief is discussed.[32]

An early method of attempting to make the property on foreclosure sale produce as much as possible is the advance bid.

The old English rule in chancery sales was to reopen the bidding before confirmation of the sale if anyone could be found to offer an advance of at least ten per cent on the last highest bid. The practice was criticized in England, by Lord Eldon among others,[33] and was abolished by Parliament in 1867.[34] It has been generally rejected in the United States as a reason standing by itself for reopening the sale or refusing to confirm the highest bid at the auction.[35] More recently

24. Ludlow v. Lansing, N.Y.1824, 1 Hopk.Ch. 231; Sullivan v. Superior Court of Mendocino County, 1921, 185 Cal. 133, 195 P. 1061; State ex rel. Wyandotte Lodge No. 35 v. Evans, 1903, 176 Mo. 310, 75 S.W. 914; Pratt v. Engel, 1933, 112 N.J.Eq. 451, 164 A. 696, affirmed 115 N.J.Eq. 147, 169 A. 822; Richmond v. Robertson, 1915, 50 Okl. 635, 151 P. 203; Terrell v. Allison, 1874, 88 U.S. (21 Wall.) 289, 22 L. Ed. 634; Wright v. Union Central Life Ins. Co., 1937, 212 Ind. 563, 10 N.E.2d 726.

25. Hyde v. Boyle, 1894, 105 Cal. 102, 38 P. 643.

26. Sexton v. Harper & Mayfield, 1925, 213 Ala. 308, 104 So. 802; Kessinger v. Whittaker, 1876, 82 Ill. 22.

27. Conn.Gen.Stat.Ann.1960, § 49–22.

28. See Gelfert v. National City Bank, 1941, 313 U.S. 221, 231, 61 S.Ct. 898, 902, 133 A.L.R. 1467, "The control of judicial sales of realty by courts of equity and by legislatures to prevent sacrificial prices has a long history."

29. See §§ 8, 307–310, supra.

30. See § 8, note 56, supra, for a list of references. See also §§ 330, 331, 335, infra.

31. § 330, infra.

32. §§ 332, 335, infra.

33. See Morice v. Bishop of Durham, 1805, 11 Ves.Jr. 57; Gelfert v. National City Bank, n. 28, supra; Stump v. Martin, 1872, 72 Ky. 281, 285; Williams, Real Prop., 1872 ed., 164.

34. 1867, 30 & 31 Vict., c. 48, § 7.

35. George v. Cone, 1905, 77 Ark. 216, 91 S.W. 557, 113 Am.St.Rep. 143, 7 Ann.Cas. 171. See Campbell

there is some evidence of a tendency to recognize an advance bid, if substantial, as a reason for offering the property for sale again with the new, higher bid as an upset price, and the original high bidder permitted to participate.[36]

The American rule is equally well settled that, in normal times at least, a court of equity will not refuse to confirm a sale or set it aside "on account of mere inadequacy of price unless the inadequacy be so gross as to shock the conscience or raise a presumption of fraud or unfairness",[37] or there are additional circumstances against its fairness such as chilled bidding.[38] Nor will a court order a postponement of a foreclosure sale for the purpose of selling at a possibly more favorable time in the future.[39] And it has been held that the existence of a depression does not justify a court in enjoining a sale under a power in a trust deed or mortgage.[40]

---

v. Gardner, 1857, 11 N.J.Eq. 423, 69 Am.Dec. 598. See cases, § 328, notes 9, 10, supra. The strong objection to allowing advance bids in is that it tends to make judicial sales unstable and chills the bidding with the result that foreclosure sales will produce less, not more money. Ibid. See also Hardy v. Coley, 1913, 114 Va. 570, 77 S.E. 458; note, 1930, 8 N.Car.L.Rev. 313, 315.

In A. J. Straus Paying Agency, Inc. v. Jensen, 1938, 226 Wis. 462, 277 N.W. 105, noted in, 1938, 36 Mich.L.Rev. 1401, the court ordered confirmation over the objection of the trustee, who offered evidence to show that, on a resale, the property would bring a substantially larger price. On the original sale the purchaser had bid more than three times the amount of the upset price which had been fixed.

36. American Trading etc., Corp. v. Conner, C.C.A. Md.1940, 109 F.2d 871; Baltimore Trust Co. v. Interocean Oil Co., D.C.Md.1939, 29 F.Supp. 269; H. O. L. C. v. Braxtan, 1942, 220 Ind. 587, 44 N.E.2d 989. Cf. Shipe v. Consumers' Service Co., C.C.A. Ind.1928, 29 F.2d 321, certiorari denied 279 U.S. 850, 49 S.Ct. 347, 73 L.Ed. 993; Everett v. Forst, 1921, 269 F. 867, 50 App.D.C. 215. Also cf. Clayton Banking Co. v. Green, 1929, 197 N.C. 534, 149 S.E. 689, noted 1930, 8 N.Car.L.Rev. 313.

37. George v. Cone, supra note 35; Speers Sand & Clay Works, Inc., v. American Trust Co., C.C.A.Md. 1931, 52 F.2d 831, certiorari denied 286 U.S. 548, 52 S.Ct. 500, 76 L.Ed. 1284; Raleigh & C. R. Co. v. Baltimore Nat. Bank, D.C.S.C.1941, 41 F.Supp. 599; Detroit Trust Co. v. Hart, 1936, 277 Mich. 561, 269 N.W. 598; Graffam v. Burgess, 1886, 117 U.S. 180, 6 S.Ct. 686, 29 L.Ed. 839; see Gelfert v. National City Bank, note 28, supra. See also Durfee and Doddridge, Redemption from Foreclosure Sale—The Uniform Act, 1925, 23 Mich.L.Rev. 833; Vaughan, Reform of Mortgage Foreclosure Procedure, 1940, 88 U. of Pa.L.Rev. 957, 963.

The leading American case refusing confirmation because of inadequacy of price (property worth seven times the amount bid) is Ballentyne v. Smith, 1907, 205 U.S. 285, 27 S.Ct. 527, 51 L.Ed. 803. See note, 1927, 26 Mich.L.Rev. 87. Cf. Wells v. Lenox, 1912, 108 Ark. 366, 159 S.W. 1099, Ann.Cas.1914D, 11;

Wyandotte State Bank v. Murray, 1911, 84 Kan. 524, 114 P. 847; Farmers' Bank of Grass Lake v. Quick, 1888, 71 Mich. 534, 39 N.W. 752, 15 Am.St. Rep. 280; Allison v. Allison, 1891, 88 Va. 328, 13 S. E. 549. See Ann.Cas.1914D, 3; cf. 1942, 40 Mich.L. Rev. 1242. Admiral Co. v. Thomas, D.D.C.1958, 164 F.Supp. 569, reversed 106 U.S.App.D.C. 266, 271 F.2d 849, ($7,500 purchase price for property having agreed value between $12,000 and $12,800 did not render sale under trust deed defective).

In Handy v. Rogers, 1960, 143 Colo. 1, 351 P.2d 819, the court held that an equity court has inherent power to refuse confirmation of a foreclosure sale to safeguard the interests of the mortgagor so as to prevent inequitable and unconscionable results: and any sale at a price having no relationship to the value of the property should be disapproved.

38. See Gelfert v. National City Bank, note 28, supra; Graffam v. Burgess and other cases, note 37, supra.

See also Crofoot v. Tarman, 1957, 147 Cal.App.2d 443, 305 P.2d 56; Brown v. Busch, 1957, 152 Cal.App.2d 200, 313 P.2d 19.

39. This has generally been held to be true in court foreclosure cases. Kenly v. Huntingdon Building Ass'n, 1934, 166 Md. 182, 170 A. 526, 90 A.L.R. 1321; Kotler v. John Hancock Mut. Life Ins. Co., 1933, 113 N.J.Eq. 544, 168 A. 36; Marneil Realty Corporation v. Twin Brook Realty Corporation, 1935, 119 N.J.Eq. 205, 181 A. 882; Equitable Life Assurance Soc. v. Lickness, 1935, 63 S.D. 618, 262 N.W. 206. But cf. Columbia Theological Seminary v. Arnette, 1932, 168 S.C. 272, 167 S.E. 465; Brand v. Woolson, 1935, 120 Conn. 211, 180 A. 293. See note, 1935, 24 Geo.L.J. 200.

40. Bolich v. Prudential Ins. Co. of America, 1932, 202 N.C. 789, 164 S.E. 335, 82 A.L.R. 974, noted, 1932, 81 U. of Pa.L.Rev. 87; 1933, 19 Va.L.Rev. 420; 1933, 11 N.Car.L.Rev. 172; 1933, 36 Law Notes, 73. See also 1933, 82 A.L.R. 976. The court said, "Perhaps no court is wise enough to declare with absolute finality that no economic or financial stringency or distress would warrant the intervention of equitable principles in restraining the power of sale in instruments securing debts, but certainly the mere allegations of general depression before the property has been sold and an unconscionable purchase price established has not heretofore been deemed adequate to invoke equitable power." It also quoted with approval the statement by the court in Lipscomb v. New York Life Ins. Co., 1897, 138 Mo. 17, 39 S.W. 465 that "courts cannot and ought not to be made the instruments of specula-

In the foreclosure of corporate mortgages, the setting of an upset price in advance of foreclosure sale has been sanctioned.[41] The fact that in such mortgages the mortgage debt is split up into a large number of pieces in the form of bonds which are widely distributed, and the further fact in such mortgages that foreclosure machinery has been used for the purpose of effectuating a corporate reorganization[42] inject elements not

tion in the future values of property, even for the benefit of the unfortunate". But see lower New York court decisions in Friedman, Personal Liability on Mortgage Debts, 51 Yale L.J. 382, 386 n. 26.

A North Carolina statute empowering the court to enjoin the consummation of sales under powers of sale on the ground that the highest bid at the sale does not represent the reasonable value of the property was held constitutional in Woltz v. Asheville Safe Deposit Co., 1934, 206 N.C. 239, 173 S.E. 587, noted, 1934, 12 N.Car.L.Rev. 363.

41. Clinton Trust Co. v. 142–144 Joralmon St. Corp., 1933, 237 App.Div. 789, 263 N.Y.S. 359, Osborne, Cases Property Security, 2d ed., 716; Manhattan Ry. v. Central Hanover B. & T. Co., C.C.A.N.Y.1938, 99 F.2d 789, certiorari denied, 1939, 306 U.S. 641, 59 S.Ct. 582, 83 L.Ed. 1041; Straus v. Anderson, 1937, 366 Ill. 426, 9 N.E.2d 205, upset price on resale. See Gelfert v. National City Bank, note 28, supra; Vaughan, op. cit. supra note 37, 964. See also authorities cited in the following footnotes. It has been held that court, in the case of an inadequate bid, cannot merely raise the bid price as a condition to confirmation without ordering a resale as an alternative. Bovay v. Townsend, C.C.A.Ark.1935, 78 F.2d 343, noted, 1935, 45 Yale L.J. 377. See also 1936, 105 A.L.R. 366. But the contrary has been decided. Barnard v. First Nat. Bank of Miami, 1936, 176 Or. 326, 55 P.2d 972.

"It is much simpler to determine why the courts have fixed upset prices than to tell how they have fixed them. In view of the difficulties it is perhaps not surprising that few of the judges who have fixed such prices have given any indication of how the figure was arrived at. Even those that have are usually sparing in details. The possibilities are at least four:

"A. A mere nominal valuation; that is, a valuation sufficient to yield the amount of cash necessary to pay expenses and prior claims plus a merely nominal amount for minority bondholders. * * *

"B. Scrap value. * * *

"C. A valuation of the property made with the intent to equate the cash settlement that is made with the minority and the property settlement that is made with the majority. * * *

"D. The highest figure which in the opinion of the court will permit the reorganization to succeed. * * *" Weiner, Conflicting Functions of the Upset Price, 1927, 27 Col.L.Rev. 132, 138.

42. Clinton Trust Co. v. 142–144 Joralmon St. Corp. and other cases, note 41, supra. And see § 320, note 60, supra; § 123, supra.

First National Bank v. Bryn Mawr Beach Bldg. Corporation, 1937, 365 Ill. 409, 6 N.E.2d 654, 109 A.L.R. 1123, discussed in notes, 1937, 31 Ill.L.Rev. 1114; 1937, 4 U. of Chi.L.Rev. 675, is another case illustrative of the tendency of courts to consider directly the fairness of plans for reorganization in exercising their powers to fix upset prices, refuse confirmation of the sale, or permit or order trustee purchase.

Trustee Purchase. Another method of protection of minority bondholders in corporate mortgage foreclosures is to permit or order the trustee to purchase. See Clinton Trust Co. v. 142–144 Joralmon St. Corp., supra; First Nat. Bank v. Bryn Mawr Beach Bldg. Corp., supra.

"The familiar provision authorizing the trustee to bid for and purchase the property on foreclosure in behalf of all bondholders is in furtherance of the desire for unity and equality; not infrequently it affords protection against losses consequent upon sale in a depressed market. In these circumstances, courts have translated such power into a duty, often quoting with approval the statement of the Pennsylvania Supreme Court that a trustee empowered to buy in at foreclosure who nevertheless stands by and allows the property to be sold for a fraction of its value is guilty of 'supine negligence or wilful default.'

"There is a sharp division among the courts, however, where express authority to buy in at foreclosure is lacking." Posner, The Trustee and the Trust Indenture, 1937, 46 Yale L.J. 737, 768.

For other discussions canvassing the merits of trustee purchase as one of the methods of protecting minority bondholders in corporate mortgage foreclosures, see Katz, The Protection of Minority Bondholders in Foreclosures and Receiverships, 1936, 3 U. of Chi.L.Rev. 517, 548; Carey, Brabner-Smith & Sullivan, Studies in Realty Mortgage Foreclosures: IV. Reorganization, 1933, 27 Ill.L.Rev. 849, 865; Breidenbach, Right of a Trustee to Bid at Foreclosure Sale, 1937, 21 Marq.L.Rev. 61; Flamm, Extending the Use of Chancery Powers to End Deadlocks in Real Estate Bond Foreclosures, 1933, 12 Chicago-Kent L.Rev. 1; notes, 1934, 1 U. of Chi.L. Rev. 623; 1934, 28 Ill.L.Rev. 929, 1934, 29 Ill.L.Rev. 218; 1933, 47 Harv.L.Rev. 358; 1936, 49 Harv.L. Rev. 487; 1936, 30 Ill.L.Rev. 680; 1942, 26 Minn.L. Rev. 575; 1935, 7 Rocky Mt.L.Rev. 282; 1934, 88 A.L.R. 1260; 1935, 96 A.L.R. 1456; 1913 Ann.Cas. 1915A, 237. See, also, references cited in note, Osborne, Cas.Prop.Security, pp. 682, 689.

Granting the trustee's right to purchase at the sale, the method of payment by him may create an additional problem. Union Guardian Trust Co. v. Building Securities Corporation, 1937, 280 Mich. 717, 276 N.W. 697, noted, 1938, 23 Cornell L.Q. 430.

On the right of a trustee in a corporate bond mortgage foreclosure to make a "paper bid" over the objection of one of the bondholders, see note, 1938, 12 So.Cal.L.Rev. 94.

present in smaller mortgages held by individuals.[43] Hence decisions in these cases are not too reliable as precedents in the latter type of case and courts have been reluctant to apply them. There is, nevertheless, authority for doing so.[44] Further, there is older legislation providing for an appraisal of the property in advance of sale and requiring that the sale price equal a stated percentage of the appraised value.[45]

43. The upset price in corporate mortgage foreclosures, employed for the purposes suggested by the court in the case of Clinton Trust Co. v. 142–144 Joralmon St. Corp., n. 41, ante, as contrasted with the same device used for simpler objectives in ordinary, single-note mortgage cases such as Suring State Bank v. Giese, 1933, 210 Wis. 489, 246 N.W. 556, 85 A.L.R. 1477, Osborne, Cas. Property Security; Levy v. Broadway-Carmen Bldg. Corp., 1937, 366 Ill. 279, 8 N.E.2d 671, and similar cases, see § 327, n. 98, ante, has been discussed in Weiner, n. 41, supra; Spring, Upset Prices in Corporate Reorganization, 1919, 32 Harv.L.Rev. 489; Kearns, Upset Prices in Corporate Reorganizations, 1931, 26 Ill.L. Rev. 325; Carey and Brabner-Smith, Studies in Realty Mortgage Foreclosures: V. Reorganization, 1933, 28 Ill.L.Rev. 1, 11; Swaine, Reorganizations of Corporations: Certain Developments of the Last Decade, 1927, 27 Col.L.Rev. 901; Katz, The Protection of Minority Bondholders in Foreclosures and Receiverships, 1936, 3 U. of Chi.L.Rev. 517, 524; Colin, Why Upset Price? An Argument for Reorganization by Decree, 1933, 28 Ill.L.Rev. 225; Rosenberg, A New Scheme of Reorganization, 1917, 17 Col.L.Rev. 523; Rosenberg Reorganization—The Next Step, 1922, 22 Col.L.Rev. 14; Swaine, Reorganization—The Next Step: A Reply, 1922, 22 Col.L.Rev. 121; Cravath, Reorganization of Corporations in Some Legal Phases of Corporate Financing, Reorganization, and Regulation, 1922, 153; Dwelling, Financial Policy of Corporations, Rev. Ed.1926, Book V.

44. Bechtel v. Rocke, 1937, 288 Ill.App. 229, 5 N.E.2d 872; Farmers' and Mechanics' Sav. Bank v. Eagle Bldg. Co., 1934, 151 Misc. 249, 271 N.Y.S. 306. See, also, Vaughan, Reform of Mortgage Foreclosure Procedure, 1940, 88 U. of Pa.L.Rev. 957, 964. See § 327, note 96, supra. Depression inspired legislation in some states authorized courts to fix upset prices. 1948, 47 Mich.L.Rev. 254, 258.

45. See Gelfert v. National City Bank, note 28, supra; Van Senden v. Obrien, 1932, 58 F.2d 689, 61 App.D.C. 137; Vaughan, Reform of Mortgage Foreclosure Procedure, 1940, 88 U. of Pa.L.Rev. 957, 965; 1948, 47 Mich.L.Rev. 254, 257. Although there was an early Virginia statute, 12 Va.Stat., Hening, 1787, c. VII, § 5, these appraisal statutes seem to have their origin in Spanish Civil Law with Louisiana statutes as the model. La.Acts 1805, c. 25, § 9; c. 26, § 14. See Skilton, Government and the Mortgage Debtor, 24 ff. Among the states which

ADEQUACY OF SALE PRICE—DEPRESSION MEASURES—JUDICIAL

330. The depression of the thirties caused some courts to hold that, where it is impossible to establish the fair value of mortgaged property by judicial sale because, due to economic prostration, there is no market for real estate, equity courts have inherent power to give relief by such measures as refusing to confirm inadequate bids; ordering resales for the same reason; setting upset prices initially or on resale; and requiring the fair value of the property to be credited upon the foreclosure judgment as a condition to confirmation. Later decisions tended to limit the scope of such doctrines.

The economic prostration in the early thirties was of unprecedented magnitude. Among the factors affecting real property mortgages were a disastrous decline in cash income from lands, a precipitous drop in land values, the prevailing practice in the majority of cases of lending, not on a long run amortization basis, but on short term mortgages which were periodically refunded, and the collapse of thousands of banks and other lending institutions which necessitated liquidation of mortgages held by them and made refinancing impossible.[46] The normal functioning of foreclosure machinery proved to be wholly inadequate in this abnormal situation. Measures to alleviate or remedy it were of several kinds. One was by action of courts of equity without the aid of legislation. More generally resort was had to legislation. Moratory legislation, that is, legislation designed to delay foreclosure, was generally enacted. Statutes designed to protect a mortgagor against excessive deficiency decrees and judgments by placing restrictions on their amounts, or by denying them entirely and by making moratoria legislation applicable to them were passed. Spe-

adopted legislation of this type are Mississippi, Ohio, Kansas, Tennessee, Illinois, Indiana, Nebraska, Oklahoma, Arkansas, Michigan and Iowa. Ibid.

46. See Skilton, Government and the Mortgage Debtor, ch. IV; Cf., Wickens, Adjusting the Mortgagor's Obligation to Economic Cycles, 1938, 5 **Law** & Contemp.Probs. 617; Turner, English Mortgage of Land as Security, 1934, 21 Va.L.Rev. 729, **731**, 735.

cific attention was paid to the farm mortgage by amendment of the Bankruptcy Act.[47] And, on a variety of fronts, government sponsored methods and agencies for financ-

ing and refinancing mortgages were set up.[48] To these last measures, born of hard years, should be added the special purpose war housing provisions engrafted on one of them,[49] and the program of veterans' legislation enacted following World War II.[50] This last is projected on a scale so vast as to dwarf by comparison the earlier ventures.[51] The first two of these methods will be considered in this section and the next. The third will be taken up in connection with the question of deficiency judgments.[52] The others are beyond the scope of this work.[53]

47. The purpose of the legislation was to delay enforcement and to scale down the amount of the mortgage debt. The first attempt of the federal government to relieve the plight of the farmer mortgagor through bankruptcy legislation, the original Frazier-Lemke Act, was held unconstitutional in Louisville Joint Stock Land Bank v. Radford, 1935, 295 U.S. 555, 55 S.Ct. 854, 79 L.Ed 1593, 97 A. L.R. 1106, discussed in notes, 1935, 35 Col.L.Rev. 1136, 1935, 20 Minn.L.Rev. 85, 1936, 13 N.Y.Univ.L. Q.Rev. 465, 1935, 33 Mich.L.Rev. 1210, 1935, 15 Boston U.L.Rev. 818, 1936, 11 Ind.L.J. 381. See also Corwin, Relief of Distressed Farmers Under Frazier-Lemke Act, 1934, 3 Geo.Wash.L.Rev. 86; Britton, The Farm Moratorium Amendment to Section 75, 1934, 9 J.Nat.Ass'n.Ref.Bank. 41; Maltman, Validity of Frazier-Lemke Act, 1935, 29 Ill.L.Rev. 645; Roberts, Property, Mortgaged Land, and the Frazier-Lemke Act, 1935, 13 N.Car.L.Rev. 291; Hanna, Agriculture and the Bankruptcy Act, 1934, 19 Minn.L.Rev. 1; Hanna, Agricultural Compositions and Extensions Under the Bankruptcy Act, 1934, 20 A.B.A.J. 9; Hanna, Frazier-Lemke Amendments to Section 75, 1934, 20 A.B.A.J. 687; Hanna, Adjustment of Farmers' Debts in Bankruptcy, 1934, 12 Neb.L.Bull. 231; notes, 1934, 48 Harv.L.Rev. 332; 1935, 44 Yale L.J. 651; 1935, 83 U. of Pa.L.Rev. 375; 1935, 22 Va.L.Rev. 218; 1935, 21 Cornell L.Q. 171; 1935, 3 Geo.Wash.L.Rev. 105, 243, 388; 1936, 4 Geo.Wash.L.Rev. 525; 1934, 23 Geo.L.J. 124; 1936, 24 Geo.L.J. 686; 1935, 99 A.L.R. 1378. The amended Frazier-Lemke Act was upheld in Wright v. Vinton Branch of Mountain Trust Bank of Roanoke, Va., 1937, 300 U.S. 440, 57 S.Ct. 556, 81 L.Ed. 736, 112 A.L.R. 1455. See Diamond & Letzler, The New Frazier-Lemke Act: A Study, 1937, 37 Col.L.Rev. 1092; Hanna, New Frazier-Lemke Act, 1936, 1 Mo.L.Rev. 1, 19; Roberts, New Frazier-Lemke Act: Its Provisions, Its Constitutionality, 1936, 22 A.B.A.J. 15; Breihan, New Frazier-Lemke Amendment, 1936, 41 Comm.L.J. 152; Reynolds, New Frazier-Lemke Act Litigation, 1936, 5 Geo. Wash.L.Rev. 80; notes, 1937, 35 Mich.L.Rev. 1130; 1937, 25 Cal.L.Rev. 489; 1937, 10 So.Cal.L.Rev. 474; 1937, 23 Va.L.Rev. 944; 1937, 32 Ill.L.Rev. 239; 1936, 84 U. of Pa.L.Rev. 545; 1936, 13 N.Y.Univ. L.Q.Rev. 465; 1937, 22 Minn.L.Rev. 102; 1936, 30 Ill.L.Rev. 794; 1937, 43 W.Va.L.Q. 335. See also notes, 1940, 24 Minn.L.Rev. 981; 1941, 28 Va.L.Rev. 94; 1943, 29 Va.L.Rev. 655; 1946, 59 Harv.L.Rev. 1309. And see, additionally, Skilton, Government and the Mortgage Debtor, 137–143.

See Chapter XII of the Chandler Act of 1938, 11 U.S. C.A. § 801 et seq., for the latest provisions of the bankruptcy act dealing with the adjustment of the rights of secured creditors. A glance at the above bibliography is sufficient to understand why an exploration of the working of the Bankruptcy Act on this matter is beyond the possible scope of the present book.

48. Probably the best survey of these measures is found in Skilton, Government and the Mortgage Debtor, Chapters VIII–XI; Skilton, Government and the Mortgage Debtor 1940–1946, 1946, 95 U. of Pa.L.Rev. 119, 132. See also Tretter, Public Housing Finance, 1941, 54 Harv.L.Rev. 1325; Wallace, Survey of Federal Legislation Relating to Private Home Financing Since 1932, 1938, 5 Law & Contemp.Probs. 481; Bell, Shifts in Sources of Funds for Home Financing, 1930–1937, 1938, 5 Law & Contemp.Probs. 510; Brabner-Smith, The Financing of Large-Scale Rental Housing, 1938, 5 Law & Contemp.Probs. 608. As to the wisdom of governmental intervention in this field, see Hanna, rev. of Skilton, supra, 1945, 45 Col.L.Rev. 803.

49. See Skilton, Government and the Mortgage Debtor 1940–1946, 1946, 95 U. of Pa.L.Rev. 119, 134–138.

50. Servicemen's Readjustment Act of 1944, Title III, 58 Stat. 291, 38 U.S.C. § 694 et seq. (Supp.1946), revised, Dec. 28, 1945, Pub.L.No. 268, 79th Cong., 1st Sess., popularly known as the G.I. Bill of Rights law.

51. See Skilton, Government and the Mortgage Debtor 1940–1946, 1946, 95 U. of Pa.L.Rev. 119, 138 et seq. "The effects of these provisions, as they will operate over the next two decades, may well determine the course of real estate financing, government intervention in the field, and the land tenure system in the United States." Idem, 139.

52. See § 335, infra.

53. Legislative measures for the financing of mortgages under government sponsorship have a profound effect upon mortgage economics. They also have sufficient connection, direct and indirect, upon mortgage law, especially procedural aspects of it, to justify incorporating it into, or, at least, dealing with it in the same book alongside mortgage law as it is more usually confined. Nevertheless, because it is a subject of large scope, because its main incidence is economic and financial rather than legal, and because various practical considerations dictate the objective and the amount of space and time that can be devoted to the subject of mortgage law in this work, no further development of the subject

In cases arising during financial panics and economic depressions prior to the great one beginning in 1929, courts had uniformly held that distress conditions as to land values and the money market was insufficient reason for equity courts to depart from ordinary rules either to postpone foreclosure or to set aside a sale and order a resale.[54] In the cases that arose during the great depression, courts continued their earlier position that the absence of a market in which the property could be sold for an adequate price is no ground to grant postponement of or to enjoin foreclosure sales.[55] Courts were more receptive to the idea that they had inherent power, without the aid of any legislation, to take one or all of three steps to protect the parties against the inadequacy of a judicial sale to establish the fair value of the security because of the almost complete lack of a market for real estate due to the economic prostration. The three steps are (1) refuse to confirm the sale where the bid is substantially inadequate; (2) in ordering a sale or a resale, in the court's discretion and after a proper hearing, fix a minimum price at

which the land must be bid in if the sale is to be confirmed; and (3) in cases where no upset price has been fixed, establish the value of property at a hearing and require that its fair value be credited upon the foreclosure judgment as a condition to confirmation. Probably the best known decision stating these views is Suring State Bank v. Giese [56] in which the lower court had followed the third of these procedures but failed to give the plaintiff an option to accept or reject the option. It was decided that he should have such an option and, if he should reject the condition, a new sale should be ordered in accordance with the foregoing principles. Other courts accepted the theory of recognizing the depression as a basis for exercising inherent power in the court to prevent the property going at sacrifice prices by employing the type of controls set forth above.[57]

---

can be undertaken. The same is true of the Bankruptcy Act provisions, see n. 47, ante, as well as various other subjects which have been touched upon here and there throughout this work.

54. E. g., Miller v. Parker, 1875, 73 N.C. 58; Anderson v. White, 1894, 2 App.D.C. 408; Nebraska Loan & Trust Co. v. Hamer, 1894, 40 Neb. 281, 58 N.W. 695; Lipscomb v. New York Life Ins. Co., 1897, 138 Mo. 17, 39 S.W. 465. See 1938, 33 Ill.L.Rev. 299, 301.

55. Morris v. Waite, 1935, 119 Fla. 3, 160 So. 516; First Union Trust & Sav. Bank v. Division State Bank, 1934, 272 Ill.App. 487, noted, 1933, 33 Col.L. Rev. 744; Fed. Land Bank v. Wilmarth, 1934, 218 Iowa 339, 252 N.W. 507, 94 A.L.R. 1338; Loma Holding Corp. v. Cripple Bush Realty Corp., 1933, 147 Misc. 655, 265 N.Y.S. 125, affirmed 1934, 265 N. Y. 463, 193 N.E. 272; Equitable Life Assurance Soc. of U. S. v. Lickness, 1935, 63 S.D. 618, 262 N. W. 206; Williams v. Jones, 1935, 165 Va. 398, 182 S.E. 280. See notes, 1937, 24 Va.L.Rev. 44, 46; 1938, 33 Ill.L.Rev. 299, 302–305; 1933, 82 A.L.R. 976. See also § 329, notes 39, 40, supra. Requests to scale down the amount of the debt were also denied. Federal Land Bank v. Wilmarth, supra; Equitable Life Assurance Soc. v. Lickness, supra. See also Louisville Joint Stock Land Bank v. Radnor, 1935, 295 U.S. 555, 55 S.Ct. 854, 79 L.Ed. 1593, 97 A.L.R. 1106; note 47, supra.

56. Suring State Bank v. Giese, 1933, 210 Wis. 489, 246 N.W. 556, 85 A.L.R. 1477, commented on in, 1933, 33 Col.L.Rev. 744; 1933, 42 Yale L.J. 960; 1933, 81 U. of Pa.L.Rev. 883; 1933, 27 Ill.L.Rev. 950; 1933, 17 Minn.L.Rev. 821; 1933, 8 Wis.L.Rev. 286; 1933, 21 Cal.L.Rev. 522; 1933, 18 St.Louis L. Rev. 265; 1933, 17 Marq.L.Rev. 154; 1933, 85 A.L. R. 1480. See also Perlman, Mortgage Deficiency Judgments During an Economic Depression, 1934, 20 Va.L.Rev. 771, 806 et seq.; 1934, 47 Harv.L.Rev. 299, 307.

57. Among such cases are Federal Title and Mort. Guar. Co. v. Lowenstein, 1933, 113 N.J.Eq. 200, 166 A. 538, commented on, 1934, 19 Cornell L.Q. 316; Cal.Joint S. L. Bank v. Gore, 1936, 153 Or. 267, 55 P.2d 1118, noted 1936, 15 Or.L.Rev. 385, order of resale proper, but fixing upset price is not; Michigan Trust Co. v. Cody, 1933, 264 Mich. 258, 249 N.W. 844; see Michigan Trust Co. v. Dutmers, 1934, 265 Mich. 651, 252 N.W. 478; Monaghan v. May, 1934, 242 App.Div. 64, 273 N.Y.S. 475. In Home Owners' Loan Corporation v. Wood, 1937, 164 Misc. 215, 298 N.Y.S. 427, noted, 1938, 51 Harv.L.Rev. 749. In foreclosure proceedings under a mortgage given after July 1, 1932 (and to which, therefore, N.Y.Civ. Prac.Act § 1083(a) was inapplicable), the court of its own motion inserted a provision in the decree that the deficiency judgment was to be determined according to § 1083(a). Plaintiff applied to the court to have this provision stricken out. Held, that equity has inherent power to determine a deficiency judgment in any manner that it deems most just. Application denied. As to whether a court may deny a deficiency judgment after conformation of the foreclosure sale, look at Kremer v. Rule, 1934, 216 Wis. 331, 257 N.W. 166. Cf. Washington v. Young, 1931, 224 Ala. 232, 139 So. 92; Fidelity &

Later decisions in some jurisdictions operated to restrict the scope of the doctrines as originally laid down.[58] Difficulty was encountered in trying to establish, in the absence of a market, a proper test as to the value of the property.[59] Probably the total impact of

Columbia Trust Co. v. White Construction Co., 1935, 258 Ky. 475, 80 S.W.2d 550.

In Chemical Bank & Trust Co. v. Adam Schumann Associates, Inc., 1934, 150 Misc. 221, 268 N.Y.S. 674, noted in, 1934, 20 Iowa L.Rev. 163, gross inadequacy of the foreclosure sale price was held a sufficient basis for setting aside a deficiency judgment. See, Why Mortgagors Leave Home: Extent of Equitable Relief in Depression Foreclosures, 1938, 33 Ill.L.Rev. 299; Brabner-Smith, Economic Aspects of the Deficiency Judgment, 1934, 20 Va.L.Rev. 719; Perlman, Mortgage Deficiency Judgments During an Economic Depression, 1934, 20 Va.L.Rev. 771, 806; notes, 1937, 24 Va.L.Rev. 44; 1938, 51 Harv. L.Rev. 749; 1934, 47 Harv.L.Rev. 299, 307; 1934, 19 Cornell L.Q. 316, 317; 1936, 15 Or.L.Rev. 385; 1934, 9 Wash.L.Rev. 232; 1934, 14 Boston U. L.Rev. 460; 1935, 19 Marq.L.Rev. 141. See also 1934, 89 A.L.R. 1087; 1934, 90 A.L.R. 1330; 1935, 94 A.L.R. 1358; 1935, 96 A.L.R. 857; 1935, 97 A.L.R. 1127; 1936, 104 A.L.R. 375. For an additional list of references on the question of whether a court of equity may relieve a mortgagor in times of depression by denying or enjoining foreclosure, by fixing an upset price for sale, by setting aside the sale and requiring resale, by granting confirmation of the sale on terms, or the like, see Campbell, Cases Mortgages, 2d ed., 245 n. 1(1). Legislation in some states authorized courts to fix upset prices or to refuse confirmation if a fair price had not been received. See 1948, 47 Mich.L.Rev. 258.

58. For example, for limitations on the Suring case, look at Kremer v. Rule, 1934, 216 Wis. 331, 257 N. W. 166; Weimer v. Uthus, 1935, 217 Wis. 56, 258 N.W. 358; Buel v. Austin, 1935, 219 Wis. 397, 263 N.W. 82; Drach v. Hornig, 1936, 221 Wis. 575, 267 N.W. 291; Wahl v. H. W. & S. M. Tullgren, 1936, 222 Wis. 306, 267 N.W. 278; and in New Jersey, the Lowenstein case has been restricted. Young v. Weber, 1934, 117 N.J.Eq. 242, 175 A. 273; see Fidelity Union Trust Co. v. Pasternack, 1937, 122 N.J.Eq. 180, 181, 192 A. 837, 838, affirmed 1938, 123 N.J.Eq. 181, 196 A. 469. See 1937, 24 Va.L.Rev. 44, 46–47; 1938, 33 Ill.L.Rev. 299, 310–314. But cf. Fidelity Union Trust Co. v. Matthews, 1941, N.J.Ct.Errors & App., 128 N.J.Eq. 475, 17 A.2d 154, reducing the deficiency judgment by the fair value of the property in action against mortgagor after conveyance to assuming grantee, commented on, 1941, 89 U. of Pa.L. Rev. 1106.

59. "'Real value of the premises,' as used in the Suring Case, should approximate that price which a person willing and able to buy the property would reasonably pay for it, not for purposes of speculation, but for that use to which it has been or reasonably may be put." Kremer v. Rule, 1934, 216 Wis. 331, 339, 257 N.W. 166, 169.

emergency relief by court action was not great.[60] An important reason for this lies in the enactment in many states of legislation to which parties turned for relief.

ADEQUACY OF SALE PRICE—MORATORIA LEGISLATION

331. Moratoria statutes of many types and species were widely adopted as emergency measures during the great depression. Courts generally upheld their constitutionality. Most have now lapsed, been repealed, or their continuation held invalid on the ground that an emergency no longer existed. However, there is authority that a legislative pronouncement that an emergency still exists, made after deliberation and based upon an investigation and finding of facts, the legislature's opinion being

"* * * it is apparent that 'fair value,' as used in our cases and which we have held that a court, in the exercise of its equitable powers, may require a mortgagee to credit upon the mortgage indebtedness as a condition of immediate confirmation, is that amount which, under all of the circumstances of a given case, will not shock the conscience of the court. * * * 'Fair value' obviously does not mean 'market value,' as that term is generally understood, or that value which the property may probably have in the future under more favorable economic conditions, or that value which it may have if the property be remodeled and put to other or more extensive uses which possibly may prove more profitable. It is, of course, difficult to state a rule which may readily be applied to every possible situation. Trial courts, however, should have no great difficulty in applying the rules stated, if they will keep in mind their obligation to do justice between both mortgagors and mortgagees." Northwestern Loan & Trust Co. v. Bidinger, 1937, 226 Wis. 239, 245, 276 N.W. 645, 648.

See also note, 1938, 33 Ill.L.Rev. 299, 319; note, 1935, 84 U. of Pa.L.Rev. 223, 228; Bonbright, Valuation of Property, C. 25. For a similar problem of valuation under a deficiency judgment statute, see Fulton Trust Co. v. Kraft, 1935, 155 Misc. 769, 280 N. Y.S. 397, noted in, 1935, 35 Col.L.Rev. 1314; Heiman v. Bishop, 1936, 272 N.Y. 83, 4 N.E.2d 944, noted in, 1937, 23 Va.L.Rev. 718; Poteat, State Legislative Relief for the Mortgage Debtor During the Depression, 1938, 5 Law & Contemp. Probs. 517, 534; 1938, 33 Ill.L.Rev. 299, 319; Friedman, Personal Liability on Mortgage Debts, 51 Yale L.J. 382, 395. See, further, § 335, infra. Cf., § 329, note 41, supra. See also as to valuation under the G. I. Bill of Rights, Skilton, Government and the Mortgage Debtor 1940–1946, 1946, 95 U. of Pa.L.Rev. 119, 139–141. And see, 1940, 18 N.Y.Univ.L.Q.Rev. 102, which deals with problems of valuation of property for tax purposes.

60. See §§ 331, 335, infra.

concurred in by the governor of the state, will be accepted by the courts.

Moratoria legislation [61] is of venerable antiquity.[62] Its first significant use as a measure for the relief of mortgage debtors in the great depression was the enactment of the Iowa statute in February, 1933.[63] Within a month and a half, fourteen other states followed suit and by the end of eighteen months twelve more states took similar action.[64] The statutes passed included practically every type of moratorium and different species and variation in detail of each kind.[65]

There was the purely legislative moratorium which attempted to set forth in the statute itself all the criteria for granting relief.[66] Administration of this sort of law was inexpensive and parties could be certain of their rights. It had the weakness of many flat, general rules; it gave too much protection to some and too little to others.[67] A more usual kind gave authority to courts to grant postponement upon petition of mortgagors in individual cases. For the most part these acts gave broad discretion to the judiciary with both the circumstances which justified relief and the conditions upon which it was to be granted left pretty much at large.[68]

61. "The moratorium is a postponement of fulfillment of obligations decreed by the state through the medium of the courts or the legislature. Its essence is the application of the sovereign power." Feller, Moratory Legislation: A Comparative Study, 1933, 46 Harv.L.Rev. 1061.

62. An example is found in the Code of Hammurabi, King of Babylon, *circa* 2250 B.C. See The Code of Hammurabi, Harper's 2d ed. 1904, § 48, p. 27, quoted by Poteat, State Legislative Relief for the Mortgage Debtor During the Depression, 1938, 5 Law & Contemp. Problems, 517. See also Feller, Moratory Legislation: A Comparative Study, 1933, 46 Harv. L.Rev. 1061; Skilton, Government and the Mortgage Debtor, 1946, Ch. III.

63. Acts Reg.Sess.Iowa, 1933, p. 211 (February 8, 1933).

64. See Skilton Government and the Mortgage Debtor, 1946, p. 78.
Summaries of moratory legislation by states may be found in Bridewell, Digest of State Moratorium Legislation and Judicial Interpretation of the Same, U. S. Central Housing Comm., Spec.Rep.No. 1, app. I, 1936; Poteat, State Legislative Relief for the Mortgage Debtor During the Depression, 1938, 5 Law and Contemp.Probs. 517, 539; Feller, supra, note 61, 1081; Skilton, supra, Chaps. V, VI.

65. Moratory legislation has been much discussed in legal periodicals. See Feller, Moratory Legislation: A Comparative Study, 1933, 46 Harv.L.Rev. 1061; Jeffers, The Texas Moratorium Law, 1934, 12 Tex. L.Rev. 383; McCarthy & Rowley, Constitutionality and Retroactive Application of New Trust Deed and Power of Sale Mortgage Law, 1934, 22 Cal.L. Rev. 170; Allen, Mortgage Moratorium Legislation, 1933, 17 Marq.L.Rev. 200; Stone, Mortgage Moratoria, 1936, 11 Wis.L.Rev. 203; Poteat, State Legislative Relief for the Mortgage Debtor During the Depression, 1938, 5 Law & Contemp.Probs. 517, 520–529; Skilton, Government and the Mortgage Debtor 1940–1946, 1946, 95 U. of Pa.L.Rev. 119, 120–127; Wheeler & Durfee, Evasion of Mortgage Moratoria by Prosecution of Personal Remedies, 1935, 33 Mich.L.Rev. 1196; Mischler, After the Mortgage Moratorium—What? 1934, 19 Iowa L.Rev. 560;

notes, 1937, 24 Va.L.Rev. 44, 49; 1934, 20 Iowa L. Rev. 158; 1933, 19 Iowa L.Rev. 108; 1933, 47 Harv.L.Rev. 299; 1934, 48 Harv.L.Rev. 135; 1934, 19 Cornell L.Q. 316, 322; 1935, 33 Mich.L.Rev. 1261; 1933, 1 Geo.Wash.L.Rev. 500; 1934, 8 Wash. L.Rev. 179; 1934, 82 U. of Pa.L.Rev. 261, 265; 1934, 22 Cal.L.Rev. 350; 1934, 13 Tex.L.Rev. 78; 1939, 23 Minn.L.Rev. 371; 1936, 11 Temple L.Q. 63; 1940, 40 Col.L.Rev. 867; 1940, 25 Cornell L.Q. 401; 1941, 27 Va.L.Rev. 553; 1942, 30 Cal.L.Rev. 172; 1945, 20 N.Y.Univ.L.Q.Rev. 506; 1946, 44 Mich.L. Rev. 652; 1946, 32 Va.L.Rev. 416; 1947, 22 N.Y. Univ.L.Q.Rev. 732. See Skilton, Government and the Mortgage Debtor, 1946, pp. 73–114. And see Campbell, Cases Mortgages, 245, n. 1(2) for another list of references. See also § 8, supra. Cf. Soldiers' and Sailors' Civil Relief Act of 1940, Pub. L.No. 861, 76th Cong., 3d Sess., Oct. 17, 1940, 50 U. S.C.A.App. § 501 et seq., 1964. See 1941, 18 N.Y. Univ.L.Q.Rev. 302.

66. E. g., N.Y.Laws 1933, c. 793; Laws 1934, cc. 278, 357, 890; Laws 1935, cc. 1, 17, 318, 763; Laws 1936, cc. 86, 266, 611, 703; Laws 1937, cc. 82, 713, 714; Laws 1938, c. 500, applies where default is in payment of principal or instalments thereof. N.Y. Unconsol.Laws, McKinney 1949, is a codification of Laws 1936, c. 703, supra.

67. For a critique of its operation, see Report of Joint Legislative Committee on Mortgage Moratorium and Deficiency Judgments, State of New York Legislative Document No. 58 (1938).

68. E. g., Iowa, Laws 1933, c. 182, court directed to grant after a hearing unless "good cause is shown to the contrary."; Cal.Laws 1935, c. 7; Laws 1935, c. 348; Laws 1937, cc. 5, 167. See 1942, 30 Cal.L. Rev. 172. The first enactments, Cal.Laws 1933, cc. 30, 263, 1057; Laws 1933, c. 642, were the legislative variety. Cf. Miss.Laws 1934, c. 247; Tex.Gen. Laws, 1933, p. 37; Tex.Gen.Laws, 1933, p. 126. The courts themselves worked out criteria for the granting of relief upon such questions as the burden of proof, good faith of the debtor, right to rents, and good cause to refuse relief. See Poteat, op. cit. su-

Such legislation had the merit of elasticity and individualization of application, but also possessed the demerit of uncertainty of result and slowness in getting the matter settled. Other statutes provided for moratorium directed by an administrative officer,[69] and in Wisconsin a plan of compulsory mediation was set up.[70] Another type of emergency relief was statutory extension of the period of redemption from foreclosure sale.[71] Similar to this was a lengthening of the time before foreclosure sale could be had, either by giving courts power to stay proceedings,[72] or by stretching out the time for each step in the foreclosure action.[73]

The constitutionality of these moratoria laws was challenged in both federal and state courts. The lead of the United States Supreme Court in upholding the carefully drawn Minnesota act,[74] was followed in most of the state courts.[75]

Moratoria statutes purported to be of limited duration and depended for their validity upon the existence of an emergency. Nevertheless they were repeatedly extended.[76] By 1940 most legislatures had allowed their statutes to lapse or had repealed them.[77] Others have been invalidated by courts on the ground that the conditions warranting their original enactment no longer exist.[78] However in Wisconsin, the state supreme court refused to question a legislative recital in the

pra note 62, pp. 523–25; 1942, 30 Cal.L.Rev. 172, 174; Skilton, op. cit. supra note 62, pp. 98–108.

Iowa Code Ann., 1950, § 654.15 gives the court power to grant a continuance for one year to a foreclosure action where payment was not made because of depressions, floods, etc. The phrase, supra "good cause." is not in the section. For later California law, see note 77 infra. The Mississippi laws were temporary and have expired. The same is true of the Texas law.

69. La.Laws 1934, 2d Ex.Sess., No. 2; Laws 1935, 4th Ex.Sess., No. 13. Applies to all debts. Both laws were temporary and have since expired.

70. Wis.Laws, 1933, c. 15, 281.20, p. 171.

71. Twelve states passed this sort of statute. See Poteat, op. cit. supra note 62 pp. 525–529, 539 et seq.

72. Twenty-one states had provisions of this sort. See Poteat, supra note 71.

73. E. g., Ark.Laws, 1933, act 21; Laws 1935, act 49; Laws 1937, act 221 repealed one section of the 1933 Act. The rest are codified in Ark.Stat.Ann., 1947, §§ 51–1115, 51–1117 to 19.

74. The landmark case upholding the constitutionality of such legislation is Home Building & Loan Ass'n v. Blaisdell, 1934, 290 U.S. 398, 54 S.Ct. 231, 78 L.Ed. 413, 88 A.L.R. 1481. See Prosser, The Minnesota Mortgage Moratorium, 1934, 7 So.Cal.L. Rev. 353; Heffernan, The Minnesota Mortgage Moratorium Case, 1934, 9 Ind.L.J. 337; notes, 1934, 8 So.Cal.L.Rev. 30; 1934, 34 Col.L.Rev. 361; 1934, 18 Minn.L.Rev. 319; 1935, 19 Minn.L.Rev. 210; 1933, 9 Wis.L.Rev. 92; 1933, 32 Mich.L.Rev. 71;

1934, 12 Tex.L.Rev. 352; 1936, 21 Iowa L.Rev. 639. See also 1933, 86 A.L.R. 1539; 1934, 88 A.L.R. 1519; 1896, 31 L.R.A. 721.

75. E. g., Des Moines Joint Stock Land Bank v. Nordholm, 1934, 217 Iowa 1319, 253 N.W. 701; Russell v. Battle Creek Lumber Co., 1934, 265 Mich. 649, 252 N.W. 561; Metropolitan Life Ins. Co. v. Morris, 1935, 181 La. 277, 159 So. 388; Wilson Banking Co. Liquidating Corp. v. Colvard, 1935, 172 Miss. 804, 161 So. 123. See 1938, 33 Ill.L.Rev. 299, 315, stating that eight states had found their statutes constitutional and in five others there had been no attack upon their validity. See also Poteat, op. cit. supra note 62, pp. 521 and 539 et seq.; 1937, 24 Va.L.Rev. 44, 50–51; Skilton, op. cit. supra note 62, pp. 87–92. A few state courts invalidated their acts. E. g., Travellers Ins. Co. v. Marshall, 1934, 124 Tex. 45, 76 S.W.2d 1007, 96 A.L.R. 802.

76. See, e. g., the California legislation, in note 68, supra, and the New York legislation, in n. 66, supra. The last extension of the California act was in 1941. Cal.Stats.1941, p. 1263. See 1942, 30 Cal. L.Rev. 172. See also Skilton, op. cit. supra note 62, pp. 92–95; Poteat, op. cit. supra note 62, pp. 521– 522; Skilton, Government and the Mortgage Debtor 1940–1946, 1946, 95 U. of Pa.L.Rev. 119, 120–127.

77. See Skilton, Government and the Mortgage Debtor 1940–1946, 1946, 95 U. of Pa.L.Rev. 119, 120–127; Poteat, op. cit. supra note 76. See also Riesenfeld, California Legislation Curbing Deficiency Judgments, 1960, 48 Cal.L.Rev. 705, noting that in California all general moratoria were ended by the clean-up legislation of 1945, Cal.Stat.1945, ch. 294, pp. 752, 756, § 10.

78. E.g., First Trust Joint Stock Land Bank of Chicago v. Arp, 1939, 225 Iowa 1331, 283 N.W. 441, 120 A.L.R. 932, Osborne, Cases Property Security, 723, discussed in notes, 1939, 37 Mich.L.Rev. 1240; 1939, 24 Iowa L.Rev. 607. Jefferson Standard Life Ins. Co. v. Noble, 1939, 185 Miss. 360, 188 So. 289; Pouquette v. O'Brien, 1940, 55 Ariz. 248, 100 P.2d 979; H.O.L.C. of Washington, D.C. v. Oleson, 1942, 68 S. Dak. 435, 3 N.W.2d 880.

First Trust Co. of Lincoln v. Smith, 1938, 134 Neb. 84, 277 N.W. 762, noted in, 1938, 51 Harv.L.Rev. 1292; 1938, 36 Mich.L.Rev. 1379; 1938, 23 Iowa L. Rev. 652, accord.

statutes of alleged facts supporting a finding that an emergency still existed warranting an extension of the moratorium from 1939 to 1941.[79] Similarly, in East New York Savings Bank v. Hahn, both the New York Court of Appeals [80] and the United States Supreme Court [81] refused to go behind a legislative pronouncement that an emergency existed in 1943 warranting continuation of the law.[82]

DEFICIENCY JUDGMENT—ENGLAND

332. Before the invention of foreclosure by sale, English courts gave the mortgagee no effective method of both foreclosing the mortgage and getting a judgment on the secured claim. Today, after foreclosure by sale a mortgagee may obtain a judgment for a balance after applying the proceeds of the sale on the debt. Originally the judgment must be sued for in a court of law. Since the Judicature Acts, if foreclosure is by court action, it may be had in the foreclosure action. A mortgagee may not purchase at foreclosure sale, hence it still is impossible for a mortgagee as a result of a foreclosure to obtain both the property free and clear of the mortgage and a judgment for a deficiency.

The dual character of a mortgagee's rights is again [83] manifest when he undertakes to enforce them on default. The mortgage creditor has two fundamentally different methods of collecting his claim. One of them is to get it out of the mortgaged property by means of procedures based upon his existing security interest in it. The most important of these measures [84] is foreclosure by one or another of the various processes considered in this chapter. The other is by an action upon the personal obligation in which he may obtain a judgment [85] and then levy upon any and all of the mortgage debtor's property.[86] In England, an action to foreclose was and still is a purely equitable proceeding,[87] just as it is in most states in this country.[88] The action on the debt on the other hand, was exclusively one for the law courts.[89] Before the invention of foreclosure by sale either in an action to foreclose or by exercise of a power of sale outside of court, the English courts gave to the mortgagee no effective means of reaching unmortgaged assets even though the debt was not barred by foreclosure.[90] The chancellor refused to value the property and give a deficiency decree in the equitable action.[91] If the mortgagee brought an action at law upon his debt it reopened the foreclosure.[92] And while an action on the debt before foreclosure was theoretically possible it was not a practicable remedy.[93]

---

79. Onsrud v. Kenyon, 1941, 238 Wis. 496, 300 N.W. 359. There was a vigorous dissent by Justice Fowler. The legislation was extended to 1943 in 1941 but limited to mortgages on homes. Wis.Laws 1941, c. 31. It was not renewed in 1943. There have been no enactments of moratorium statutes since 1943.

80. 1944, 293 N.Y. 622, 59 N.E.2d 625, affirmed 326 U.S. 230, 66 S.Ct. 69, 90 L.Ed. 34, 160 A.L.R. 1279.

81. 1945, 326 U.S. 230, 66 S.Ct. 69, 90 L.Ed. 34, 160 A.L.R. 1279. Stress was laid upon the fact that there had been a legislative investigation and that the Governor had recommended the measure.

82. See 1946, 44 Mich.L.Rev. 652; Skilton, op.cit. supra note 77. There were a few other survivals of moratoria legislation in the late 1940's. See 1948, 47 Mich.L.Rev. 254, 255.

83. See §§ 102, 224–226, 247, 321, supra, for other instances.

84. Additional remedies, either to obtain possession or to have a receiver appointed, have the same foundation in the mortgagee's existing interest in the specific property. See §§ 125, 127, 147–149, 314, 328, supra. See also Turner, The English Mortgage of Land as Security, 1934, 20 Va.L.Rev. 719, 731–735; Turner, An English View of Mortgage Deficiency Judgments, 1935, 21 Va.L.Rev. 601, 603; Maitland, Equity, rev.ed., 186; Tefft, The Myth of Strict Foreclosure, 1937, 4 U. of Chi.L.Rev. 575, 582.

85. See Maitland, Equity, rev.ed., 181, Turner, ops. cit. supra note 84.

86. As to whether, under a judgment on the mortgage debt, the plaintiff may levy on the mortgaged property, see § 300, supra. See also § 333, infra.

87. See §§ 311, 317, supra.

88. See §§ 312, 318, supra.

89. See Perry v. Barker, 1806, 13 Ves. 198; Maitland, Equity, rev.ed., 181, 185.

90. See § 311, supra.

91. Ibid.

92. Ibid.

93. Ibid.

When realization by power of sale [94] and sale in lieu of foreclosure [95] developed in England in the last half of the nineteenth century it was possible for the mortgagee both to realize on the mortgaged property and to reach unmortgaged assets. The amount for which the property sold on either sort of sale fixed the value of the mortgaged land and the mortgagee could then get a judgment for the balance of his unsatisfied debt.[96] If he sold under a power of sale, by far the most popular method in England, it was clear that his action to collect the unpaid balance of his debt must be in a court of law.[97] Even when the sale was in an action in equity to sell in lieu of foreclosure, the same was true; the chancellor was steadfast in refusing to grant a deficiency decree in the equitable proceeding.[98] The Judicature Act changed this and today in such a foreclosure action the mortgagee can obtain not only foreclosure, but a judgment on the mortgagor's covenant for a deficiency.[99] Since a mortgagee is not permitted to purchase at foreclosure sales in England,[1] it still is not possible for him to obtain the property free from a right of redemption by the mortgagor, and, in addition, obtain a deficiency judgment for a balance over an amount to be credited on the debt.[2] If he wants the property free and clear, he must forego a deficiency judgment; if he wants a deficiency judgment, he must let the property be sold

to a third person and apply on his debt what that person is willing to pay for it.[3]

DEFICIENCY JUDGMENT—UNITED STATES

333. In the United States a mortgagee may obtain, without reopening the foreclosure, a judgment or decree for a deficiency measured by the difference between the debt and the foreclosure sale price, or, in cases of strict foreclosure, an appraisal value of the land. Today the deficiency may be by decree in the foreclosure action itself. Jurisdiction to do this, by majority view, rests on statute; a strong minority holds it to be an inherent power of a court of equity. The ability of a mortgagee to acquire the property on foreclosure coupled with the right to a deficiency decree creates a possibility of double satisfaction which does not exist in England.

In the United States, as in England, the mortgagee has the same two basic methods of collecting his debt; and in most states they may be pursued concurrently or successively.[4] He may sue and get judgment at

---

94. See, infra, § 336.

95. § 317, supra.

96. Rudge v. Richens, 1873, L.R. 8, C.P. 358; Gordon Grant & Co. v. Boos, [1926] A.C. 781.

97. See Tefft, op.cit. supra note 84, p. 587.

98. See Tefft, op.cit. supra note 84, p. 586. See also note 89, supra.

99. Judicature Act, 1875, 38 & 39 Vict., c. 77; Poulett v. Hill [1893] 1 Ch. 277. See Maitland, Equity, rev.ed., 184.

1. § 317, supra.

2. See articles by Turner, cited, note 84, supra.

3. See Tefft, op.cit. supra note 84, p. 587. See also articles by Turner, cited note 84, supra.

4. See Jones v. Conde, N.Y.1822, 6 Johns.Ch. 77, "THE CHANCELLOR [KENT]. The rule is settled, that a mortgagee may sue, at the same time, at law, upon his bond, and in this court upon his mortgage. The case of a mortgagee forms an exception to the general rule, that a party shall not be allowed to sue at law, and here, at the same time, for the same debt. The one remedy is in rem, and the other in personam; and the general rule to which this case is an exception, applies only to cases where the demand at law and in equity are equally personal, and not where the cumulative remedy is in personam, while the other remedy is upon the pledge."

See Rossiter v. Merriman, 1909, 80 Kan. 739, 104 P. 858, 24 L.R.A.,N.S., 1095; Jewett v. Hamlin, 1878, 68 Me. 172; Bateman v. Grand Rapids & I. R. Co., 1893, 96 Mich. 441, 56 N.W. 28; Gibson v. Green's Adm'r, 1893, 89 Va. 524, 16 S.E. 661, 37 Am.St.Rep. 888. Cf. Wahl v. Phillips, 1861, 12 Iowa 81.

In some states, the above stated rule is altered by statutes permitting only "one action" to enforce a mortgage or by other legislation. Kent's statement represents the early law in New York, later modified. See Friedman, The Enforcement of Personal Liability on Mortgage Debts in New York, 1942, 51 Yale L.J. 382, 386. Only in a minority of states, however, is it necessary for the mortgage creditor first to exhaust his security before reaching other property of his debtor. See § 334, infra.

law upon the personal obligation and enforce it by levy upon any property of the debtor.[5] Or he may foreclose upon the property. Regardless of the method of foreclosure, the mortgagee in most states can obtain a judgment for a deficiency. In states where the mortgagee may obtain a strict foreclosure, either by equitable action or by cutting off the mortgagor's rights through taking and holding possession, he can obtain a deficiency judgment for the difference between the value of the land as appraised, normally by the verdict of a jury in the action for the deficiency, and the amount of the debt plus interest and costs.[6] And such a judgment does not reopen the foreclosure so as to give the mortgagor another chance to redeem. This is, of course, in striking contrast to the English system.[7] Although foreclosure by *scire facias,* where allowed, is regarded as strictly in rem with satisfaction confined to the mortgaged property in that action, a separate action could be brought upon the bond for the balance not realized in the *scire facias* proceeding.[8] If he sells under a power of sale out of court the sale price conclusively determines the amount to be credited on the debt and, as in England, the mortgagee can then sue for the balance in an action at law.[9] Although the general rule is that a mortgagee cannot purchase at the sale made by him out of court under a power of sale in the mortgage there are exceptions which operate to nullify the rule.[10] Where foreclosure is by sale under judicial decree in a court action, the usual method in America and the one under chief consideration here, the amount realized on sale is an automatic determina-

tion of the amount to be applied upon the debt and the mortgage creditor, apart from statutes,[11] most of them depression-born, is entitled to recover the balance.[12] Today this ordinarily may be obtained by a deficiency decree given by the equity court in the foreclosure action itself.[13] There is, however, divergent opinion as to whether the power to do so rests solely upon statute or whether it is an inherent attribute of equity jurisdiction. The first view, traceable to Chancellor Kent [14] has been widely accepted.[15] How-

5. Subject to the caveat in § 332, note 86, supra. See § 300, supra.

6. See §§ 312, 314, supra. See Tefft, The Myth of Strict Foreclosure, 1937, 4 U. of Chi.L.Rev. 575, 594.

7. See § 332, supra.

8. See Lloyd, The Mortgage Theory of Pennsylvania, 1924, 73 U. of Pa.L.Rev. 43.

9. See §§ 337, 338, infra.

10. Osborne, Cases Property Security, 2d Ed., 761, footnote.

11. See § 335, infra.

12. Although the point was considered by Chancellor Kent in Dunkley v. Van Buren, N.Y.1818, 3 Johns. Ch. 330, and not definitely decided until Lansing v. Goelet, N.Y.1827, 9 Cow. 346, no case held that a foreclosure sale discharged the personal obligation beyond the amount it produced at the sale. In accord is McKnight v. United States, C.A.9th, 1958, 259 F.2d 540.

13. For an examination into the practice in seeking deficiency judgments, state by state, with a brief summary of the law of each, see Eaton, Deficiency Judgments and Decrees, 1934, 20 Va.L.Rev. 743. For the English law and a constructive criticism of the American practice in the light of English experience, see Turner, English Mortgage of Land as Security, 1934, 20 Va.L.Rev. 729; Turner, An English View of Mortgage Deficiency Judgments, 1935, 21 Va.L.Rev. 601; Tefft, The Myth of Strict Foreclosure, 1937, 4 U. of Chi.L.Rev. 575, 585.

See also 1937, 108 A.L.R. 1351.

See Herrick, Action to Recover a Deficiency, 1936, 2 Iowa Bar Rev. 27 for the Iowa rule that the mortgagee, if he brings an action to foreclose, must ask for a deficiency judgment, if he wants one, in the foreclosure action; he cannot later sue on the note. For a discussion of Maryland law, see Slingluff, The Mortgagee's Right in the Event of a Deficiency, 1937, 1 Md.L.Rev. 128.

14. In Dunkley v. Van Buren, N.Y.1818, 3 Johns.Ch. 330. This was, as was seen, § 332, ante, the law in England until the Judicature Act. Provision for a personal judgment for a deficiency in the foreclosure action was made in New York by statute in 1828. R.S. (New York) 6th ed., part 3, title 2, sec. 191. Similar statutory authority exists in a large number of states. E.g., West's Ann.Cal.Code Civ. Proc., § 726; Mich.Comp.Laws Ann.1968, § 600.-3150–60. See 1929, 27 Mich.L.Rev. 797.

15. E. g., Stellmacher v. Sampson, 1928, 195 Wis. 635, 219 N.W. 343; Michigan Ins. Co. of Detroit v. Brown, 1863, 11 Mich. 265; see Burgess v. Souther, 1885, 15 R.I. 202, 2 A. 441. And look at Union Trust Co. v. Detroit Trust Co., 1928, 243 Mich. 451, 220 N.W. 728, criticized in 1929, 27 Mich.L.Rev. 797. For an additional vigorous criticism of the views expressed in the Michigan decisions, see Sprague,

ever in an opinion exhaustively discussing the cases bearing upon the point, the New Mexico court came to the opposite conclusion.[16] When it comes to jury trial, the prevailing view even in jurisdictions adhering to the first view is that the mortgagor has no right to one on the demand for a deficiency judgment when made in the foreclosure action.[17]

The ability of a mortgagee in America to acquire the property on foreclosure free and clear of any right of the mortgagor to redeem from the mortgage and also to obtain a judgment for a deficiency for the difference between the sale price, or in the case of strict foreclosure, an appraised value of the property, has created an opportunity of "double" satisfaction which does not exist in England.[18] The methods aimed at preventing an inadequate price being paid for the property on foreclosure sale were for the most part a product of this system.[19] A still different method, that of directly limiting the amount of the deficiency judgment or denying it altogether, was adopted by a large number of states during the depression. It will be discussed in later sections.[20]

THE "ONE ACTION" RULE

334. In a few states a debt secured by a mortgage may be enforced only by an action to foreclose in which a judgment for a deficiency may be obtained. The requirement may not be waived by agreement at the time the mortgage is executed. However, it is an affirmative defense and if not pleaded to an action by the mortgagee on the debt a judgment will be given. Such a judgment, though, can be pleaded in bar of a later foreclosure action. After earlier doubts, it is settled in California at least that the rule applies to trust deed mortgages. There are limitations on the operation of the rule, e. g., security becomes valueless, land is in another state.

Legislation in some other states tends toward the same goal as the "one action" statutes.

Closely connected with the question whether a mortgage creditor may obtain a deficiency judgment in his foreclosure action is the rule in a few states that there can be only one action for the enforcement of an obligation secured by a mortgage, that action being a foreclosure in which the mortgagee may also get a deficiency judgment.[21] The purpose of

Hist. of Chancery and Advertisement Foreclosures in Michigan, 1935, 5 Detroit L.Rev. 63. See Glenn, Mortgages, § 77.1, who takes the position that the jurisdiction to render a deficiency decree must either be conferred by statute or be provided for by rule of court which the court must have inherent authority to make. As an example of the latter power he cites the rules adopted by the Federal courts which first provided for a deficiency judgment by Equity Rule 92, adopted in 1864. Under present Fed.Rules Civ.Proc., Rule 18b, the mortgagee has an option to take a deficiency in the foreclosure action or to sue for it later. 1 Moore's Fed.Pr. 175 (1938). The distinction, with due deference, is without merit. A court of equity may or may not have inherent power to grant a deficiency decree in a foreclosure action. This writer agrees with the New Mexico court on that. But whether it does or does not, has no connection with authority to establish the practice by rule of court.

16. Young v. Vail, 1924, 29 N.M. 324, 222 P. 912, 34 A.L.R. 980.

17. Although there was a right to jury trial as to a deficiency when the action was at law, New York held that there was no such right on this branch of the case in a foreclosure action. Carroll v. Diemel, 1884, 95 N.Y. 252; Frank v. Davis, 1892, 135 N.Y. 275, 31 N.E. 1100, 17 L.R.A. 306. And the same rule was extended in a foreclosure action to a demand for a deficiency against a guarantor of a mortgage. Jamaica Sav. Bank v. M. S. Investing Co., 1937, 274 N.Y. 215, 8 N.E.2d 493, commented on, 1937, 23 Cornell L.Q. 194; 1937, 32 Ill.L.Rev. 491; 1937, 7 Brooklyn L.Rev. 109. Other cases holding there is no right to a jury trial on this issue are Downing v. Le Du, 1890, 82 Cal. 471, 23 P. 202; Dover Lumber Co. v. Case, 1918, 31 Idaho 276, 170 P. 108; Young v. Vail, supra note 16; Escamilla v. Pingree, 1914, 49 Utah 421, 141 P. 103; Stilwell v. Kellogg, 1861, 14 Wis. 461. However, there are authorities the other way. They include Keller v. Wenzel, 1873, 23 Ohio 579; Jones v. Benson, 1932, 158 Okl. 25, 12 P.2d 202.

18. See § 332, supra. See also §§ 335, 336, infra.

19. See §§ 327, 329, 330, 331, and §§ 8, 307, supra.

20. §§ 335, 336, infra.

21. "There can be but one action for the recovery of any debt, or the enforcement of any right secured by mortgage upon real estate or personal property, * * *. In such action the court may, by its judgment, direct the sale of the encumbered property * * *." Section 726, West's Ann.Cal.Code Civ.Proc., 1931. In 1933 the wording was changed to "one form of action". See note, 1937, 25 Cal.L. Rev. 469, 470. For the legislative history of the

the statute is dual. One is to protect the mortgagor against multiplicity of actions when the separate actions, though theoretically distinct, are so closely connected that normally they can and should be decided in one suit.[22] The other is to compel a creditor who has taken a mortgage on land to exhaust his security before attempting to reach any unmortgaged property to satisfy his claim.[23] The mortgagee, under these provisions, cannot disregard his security even if he wishes to do so, and sue upon the note or debt.[24] Nor may the requirement of the statute be waived by the mortgagor through a provision in the mortgage.[25] However, a waiver subsequent to the execution may be effective.[26] There is authority that the requirement is an affirmative defense putting on the defendant the burden of showing the existence of the mortgage.[27] Consequently, if a mortgagee sues upon the note without stating that it is secured and the defendant does not plead the existence of the security, a valid judgment will be entered for the plaintiff.[28] However, the mortgagor can then plead the prior judgment in bar of a foreclosure action.[29] Further, the rule does not apply when the mortgaged land securing the debt lies in another jurisdiction [30] or when the security has become valueless.[31]

One of the important questions arising under these provisions is whether they apply to a mortgage in the form of a trust deed so as to compel the secured creditor first to exhaust the security before suing upon the note.[32] After a period of considerable doubt

section, see note, 1923, 11 Cal.L.Rev. 195, 196, n. 3; 1943, 31 Cal.L.Rev. 429. Four other states, Montana, Nevada, Utah, and Idaho, have a "one action" statute copied from California. Mont.Rev.Codes Ann., 1947, 93, 6001; Nev.Rev.Stat.1957, § 40.430; Utah, Code Ann., Supp.1969, § 78–37–1; Idaho Code Ann., Supp.1969, § 6–101. See also Note, Anti-Deficiency Judgment Legislation in California, 1956, 3 U.C.L.A.L.Rev. 192.

22. Toby v. Oregon Pac. R. Co., 1893, 98 Cal. 490, 33 P. 550; Felton v. West, 1894, 102 Cal. 266, 36 P. 676.
See note, 1943, 31 Cal.L.Rev. 429, 430–431, insisting that this was the sole intent of the section; that the other "purpose" of the statute really is an effect engrafted later. The same principle finds expression in the rules that all owners of the mortgage debt must be made parties to the action, § 320, supra, and the view of some courts that the security is indivisible, § 325, supra. Cf., the "no action" clause in bond issue mortgages, § 320, supra.

23. Bank of Italy v. Bentley, 1933, 217 Cal. 644, 20 P.2d 940, noted, 1932, 20 Cal.L.Rev. 318; 1932, 5 So.Cal.L.Rev. 227; 1932, 6 ibid. 7; 1934, 8 ibid. 35. But see 1943, 31 Cal.L.Rev. 429, 431.

24. Barbieri v. Ramelli, 1890, 84 Cal. 154, 23 P. 1086; Crescent Lumber Co. v. Larson, 1913, 166 Cal. 168, 135 P. 502; Clark v. Paddock, 1913, 24 Idaho 142, 132 P. 795, 46 L.R.A.,N.S., 475; Coburn v. Bartholomew, 1922, 50 Utah 566, 167 P. 1156; Cf., Barth v. Ely, 1929, 85 Mont. 310, 278 P. 1002. See note, 1937, 25 Cal.L.Rev. 469, 476.

25. Winklemen v. Sides, 1939, 31 Cal.App.2d 387, 88 P.2d 147, Sup.Ct. hearing den., May 8, 1939, commented on 1939, 27 Cal.L.Rev. 752. Cf., California Bank v. Stimson, 1949, 89 Cal.App. 552, 201 P.2d 39, commented on, 1949, 22 So.Cal.L.Rev. 502. In 1937 such a waiver was explicitly prohibited by code amendment. Cal.Civ.Code, § 2953. Before the Winkleman case there had been doubt on this waiver point on the law as it stood before 1937. See 1939, 27 Cal.L.Rev. 752.

26. Cf. Salter v. Ulrich, 1943, 22 Cal.2d 263, 138 P.2d 7, 146 A.L.R. 1344, commented on, 1943, 31 Cal.L. Rev. 431, in which the mortgagor's failure to plead the defense resulted in a judgment on the note under which the property was sold. Cf., also, cases in next two footnotes. And see § 336, notes 79–82, infra.

27. Bank of Paso Robles v. Blackburn, 1905, 2 Cal. App. 146, 83 P. 262; State Sav. Bank v. Albertson, 1909, 39 Mont. 414, 102 P. 692. See 1937, 25 Cal.L. Rev. 469, 477; 1943, 31 ibid. 433. As to the problem of setoffs and counterclaims when one claim is secured, see note, 1937, 25 Cal.L.Rev. 352.

28. Hibernia Sav. & Loan Soc. v. Thornton, 1897, 117 Cal. 481, 49 P. 573; Kempton v. Appellate Division of Superior Court in & for Los Angeles County, 1934, 3 Cal.App.2d 374, 39 P.2d 846; Salter v. Ulrich, supra note 26.

29. Campan v. Molle, 1899, 124 Cal. 415, 57 P. 208; Coburn v. Coburn, 1931, 89 Mont. 386, 388, 298 P. 349; cf., Ould v. Stoddard, 1880, 54 Cal. 613. See 1937, 25 Cal.L.Rev. 576, 585; 1943, 31 ibid. 434.

30. Denver Stockyards Bank v. Martin, 1918, 177 Cal. 223, 170 P. 428; McGue v. Rommel, 1906, 148 Cal. 539, 83 P. 1000. As to its effect upon the enforcement of the mortgage debt in a foreign jurisdiction, see note, 1937, 25 Cal.L.Rev. 576; note, 1921, 9 Cal.L.Rev. 503.

31. Hibernia Sav. & Loan Soc. v. Thornton, 1895, 109 Cal. 427, 42 P. 447, 50 Am.St.Rep. 52. See Barbieri v. Ramelli, 1890, 84 Cal. 154, 23 P. 1086; note, 1937, 25 Cal.L.Rev. 469, 473. See also 1937, 108 A. L.R. 397.

32. For early comments on the matter, see Kidd, Trust Deeds and Mortgages in California, 1915, **3**

it was finally settled in California, at least, that they do.[33]

There is legislation in some other states tending toward the same goal as the "one action" statutes.[34] New York is one of them, although its provisions are milder than those just considered. Following the passage of legislation permitting a deficiency decree in the equitable foreclosure action,[35] a series of statutes consolidated the mortgagee's remedies into two separate actions, one on the note and the other to foreclose.[36] The two remedies cannot, however, be pursued concurrently.[37] If the mortgagee sues upon the debt, he cannot later foreclose until execution has been returned wholly or partially unsatisfied.[38] Conversely, while a foreclosure action is pending or after final decree he cannot bring an action on the debt alone without permission of the court in which the foreclosure action was brought.[39]

ANTI-DEFICIENCY LEGISLATION

335. Depression-born relief to mortgagors included statutes, and to some extent judicial action, which (1) substituted the fair value of the property for the price at foreclosure sale as the amount to be deducted from the debt in order to fix the amount of a deficiency judgment, and (2) denied any deficiency judgment under certain circumstances. The legislation to accomplish these ends varied in methods and coverage.

Efforts of courts and legislatures to devise methods to make mortgaged property produce a fair price on foreclosure sale have been considered in earlier sections.[40] Much of the stimulus for these measures came from a solicitude for debtor classes that is centuries old.[41] More specifically it has been directed at mitigating the hardship that results from a forced sale which even in normal times does not reflect the reasonable market value of the property, and which in times of deep depression, when there is no market, results in stripping the debtor of his property in return for nominal amounts.[42] And, un-

Cal.L.Rev. 381, 391; note, 1913, 1 Cal.L.Rev. 297; note, 1924, 12 Cal.L.Rev. 307, 308.

33. Bank of Italy v. Bentley, 1933, 217 Cal. 644, 20 P.2d 940, commented on in, 1932, 20 Cal.L.Rev. 318, 1937, 25 ibid. 347; 1932, 5 So.Cal.L.Rev. 227; 1934, 8 ibid. 35; Cormack and Irsfeld, Applications of the Distinction Between Mortgages and Trust Deeds in California, 1938, 26 Cal.L.Rev. 206, 217. There are many types of secured obligations not subject to the section. See note, 1937, 25 Cal.L.Rev. 347, 349. Thus West's Ann.Cal.Code of Civ.Proc. § 726 is inapplicable to a note secured by an assignment in pledge of a note secured by a second trust deed mortgage of real property. Guyselman v. Ramsey, 1960, 179 Cal.App.2d 802, 4 Cal.Rptr. 133.

34. E. g., Wis.Stat.Ann.1957, § 269.59; Ind.Stat.Ann., Burns 1968, §§ 2–3909, 3–1801 to 3–1809.

In Hanauer v. Republic Bldg. Co., 1934, 216 Wis. 49, 255 N.W. 136, 256 N.W. 784, noted in, 1934, 48 Harv.L.Rev. 126, the statute, supra, applying to existing obligations, prohibiting an action upon an evidence of indebtedness secured by a mortgage of real property until after foreclosure of the mortgage, was held unconstitutional in an action brought by a bondholder, the deed of trust of which vested the sole power to foreclose in the trustee or a majority of the bondholders. Cf., § 320, supra. And look at H. O. L. C. v. Wise, 1939, 215 Ind. 445, 19 S.E.2d 737.

35. See § 333, n. 14, supra. Cf., § 333, note 4, supra.

36. See Friedman, Personal Liability on Mortgage Debts in New York, 1942, 51 Yale L.J. 382, 387.

37. Dudley v. Congregation of St. Francis, 1893, 138 N.Y. 451, 34 N.E. 281, 53 St.R. 19. See Friedman, op. cit. supra note 36.

38. N.Y.C.P.A., § 1077. Cf. also N.Y.C.P.A., §§ 1083a, 1083b. See Cooper v. Bresler, 1862, 9 Mich. 534; Bing v. Morse, 1897, 51 Neb. 842, 71 N.W. 712. To

the same effect is N.D.Cent.Code, 1960, § 32–19–05. This section must be read in connection with § 32–19–07 which abolishes a deficiency judgment in a foreclosure action. See § 335, infra, note 61.

39. N.Y.C.P.A., § 1078. See Honeyman v. Hanan, 1936, 275 N.Y. 382, 9 N.E.2d 970. See also Friedman, op. cit. supra note 36, 388–390. And see § 336, note 83–85, infra. But cf., 1941, 20 Neb.L.Rev. 70, for the decisions under a similar Nebraska provision.

40. See §§ 8, 307, 329–331.

41. See, e. g., the creation of the equity of redemption itself and its protection, § 6 and Chapter 4, supra.

42. See Gelfert v. National City Bank, 1940, 313 U.S. 221, 231, 61 S.Ct. 898, 85 L.Ed. 1299, 133 A.L.R. 1467, "The control of judicial sales of realty * * * in order to prevent sacrificial prices has a long history. * * * So far as mortgage foreclosures are concerned, numerous devices have been employed to safeguard mortgagors from sales which will, or may, result in mortgagees collecting

less he seeks relief in bankruptcy, he is still bound to pay the balance of his debt out of any future acquisitions. That spectacle by itself probably would have been sufficient to account for many of the measures that have been examined.[43] In the United States, however, there is an added feature to which attention has already been called.[44] That is the privilege of the mortgagee to purchase at foreclosure sale [45] and nevertheless get a deficiency judgment for the difference between the sale price and the amount of the mortgage debt. The mortgagee is not entitled to recover more than the full amount of his mortgage debt.[46] When the mortgagee buys in the property at less than its actual value and gets such a judgment he is getting something more than a full recovery and getting it at the expense of the mortgagor. His profit is the difference between the actual value of the property and the price at which it is bid in.[47] Such a profit usually accrues even in

ordinary times, and in a depression it becomes so great as to be shocking.[48] Taking into account the difficulties of boosting the amount that the property will fetch so as to close the gap,[49] it is not difficult to understand why legislatures in the thirties turned to a new technique.[50] Instead of measures

more than their due. The variety of formulae which has been employed to that end is ample evidence not only of the intrusion which advanced notions of fairness have made on the earlier concern for stability of judicial sales but also of the flexibility of the standards of fairness themselves. Underlying that change has been the realization that the price which property commands at a forced sale may be hardly even a rough measure of its value." For a description of a typical foreclosure sale, see Sutherland, Foreclosure and Sale, 1937, 22 Cornell L.Q. 216, 217, "the 'auction' is very often attended only by the referee and by the plaintiff's attorney, who patiently waits until the terms of sale are read and then buys in the property without competition."

43. E. g., see the reasoning in Kirkpatrick v. Stelling, 1940, 36 Cal.App. 658, 669, 98 P.2d 566.

44. See §§ 318, 332, 333.

45. The Supreme Court has even listed the bidding in the land at foreclosure sale as a property right of the mortgagee. See Louisville Joint Stock Land Bank v. Radford, 1935, 295 U.S. 555, 594, 55 S.Ct. 854, 79 L.Ed. 1593, 97 A.L.R. 1106. See quotation from Gelfert v. National City Bank, note 42, supra.

46. Gelfert v. National City Bank, n. 42, supra, p. 333, "Mortgagees are constitutionally entitled to no more than payment in full. Honeyman v. Jacobs [1938, 306 U.S. 539, 59 S.Ct. 702, 83 L.Ed. 972]. They cannot be heard to complain on constitutional grounds if the legislature takes steps to see to it that they get no more than that."

47. See 1941, 18 N.Y.Univ.L.Q.Rev. 299.

48. The reasoning is logical and the enrichment of the mortgagee through getting more than full payment would be shocking *provided* the deficiency judgment can be equated into payment. The fact is that the judgment is generally worthless. See Brabner-Smith, Economic Aspects of the Deficiency Judgment, 1934, 20 Va.L.Rev. 719, 722. Hence in fact the only payment the mortgagee usually gets is the land itself. This may help explain why the practice has been tolerated. When this is the result, any profit the mortgagee may make is only whatever excess value the land has over the amount of his debt, rather than over what he bid it in for. In such case, it falls, as a practical matter, into the same category as the strict foreclosure. If this last reasoning is accepted, the basis of which is the worthlessness of the deficiency judgment, it prompts the question, why should there be any strong objection to its abolition? Or at least to crediting on it the fair value of the property? Even if the judgment is regarded as the equivalent of payment. (See Holmes, J., in Miller v. Hyde, 1894, 161 Mass. 472, 37 N.E. 760, 25 L.R.A. 42, 42 Am.St.Rep. 425, "I am not informed of any statistics which establish that judgments for money usually give the judgment creditor only an empty right.") Objection to the latter may be met by the fact that the mortgagee is getting all the value to which he is entitled. Gelfert v. National City Bank, note 42, supra. But cf. note 57, infra, objection (1).

49. "The paralysis of real estate markets during periods of depression, the wide discrepancy between the money value of property to the mortgagee and the cash price which the property would receive at a forced sale, the fact that the price realized at such a sale may be a far cry from the price at which the property would be sold to a willing buyer by a willing seller, reflect the considerations which may have motivated departures from the theory that competitive bidding in this field amply protects the debtor." Gelfert v. National City Bank, note 42, supra, p. 233.

50. A similar end was achieved by judicial action without legislation in some instances by requiring, as a condition to confirmation of a sale on foreclosure, crediting the fair value of the property on the judgment, or refusing to grant any deficiency. E. g., Suring State Bank v. Giese, 1933, 210 Wis. 498, 246 N.W. 556, 85 A.L.R. 1477; Monaghan v. May, 1934, 242 App.Div. 64, 273 N.Y.Supp. 475. See 1938, 33 Iowa L.Rev. 299, 302 et seq.; Perlman, Mortgage Deficiency Judgments During an Economic Depression, 1934, 20 Va.L.Rev. 771, 806 et seq. See also, § 330, supra. However, the most important medium was by legislative action.

attempting to insure an adequate sale price for the property,[51] the price obtained through the sheriff's sale was abandoned as a test of the deficiency. For it was substituted the "fair value," or some similar standard, of the premises;[52] or they were prohibited altogether under some or all circumstances.[53]

The methods employed and the coverage of statutes enacted to cut down the amount of deficiency judgments have been diverse.[54] If the foreclosure is by court action, the court, depending upon the terms of the particular statute, either on the demand of a party, on its own motion,[55] or automatically upon application by the plaintiff for a deficiency,[56] must ascertain the fair value of the property and give a decree for the difference between it and the debt.[57] If fore-

---

51. See n. 40, supra.

For a carefully selected list of legal periodical articles dealing with legislative enactments affecting deficiency judgments, see Currie and Lieberman, Purchase Money Mortgages and State Lines: A Study in Conflict-of-Laws Method, 1960, Duke L. Jour. 1, 11 n. 31, 13 n. 48. And see infra, note 53.

52. In 1948 there were twelve states having statutes of this nature. They were Arizona, California, Idaho, New Jersey, New York, North Carolina, Oklahoma, Pennsylvania, South Carolina, South Dakota, Washington and Wisconsin. See 1948, 47 Mich.L. Rev. 254, 259 n. 34, for a list of statutory citations. Among the terms used, besides "fair value" are "fair market value," "true value," "actual value." See 1948, 47 Mich.L.Rev. 254, 259 n. 33. See also Harvey, Valuation of Mortgage Security, 1957 U. of Ill.L.Forum 412.

53. See 1948, 47 Mich.L.Rev. 254, 260.

Statutory restrictions upon deficiency judgments have received much attention from commentators, usually being discussed along with moratoria laws. See Perlman, Mortgage Deficiency Judgments During an Economic Depression, 1934, 20 Va.L.Rev. 771; Small, The Legality of State Legislation for Debtors' Relief, 1933, 11 N.Y.Univ.L.Q.Rev. 183; McCarthy & Rowley, Constitutionality and Retroactive Application of New Trust Deed and Power of Sale Mortgage Law, 1934, 22 Cal.L.Rev. 170, 180; Fiechter, Considerations Regarding the Late Deficiency Judgment Acts, 1937, 41 Dickinson L.Rev. 75 (discussing the consequences of decisions holding such acts unconstitutional); notes, 1935, 84 U. of Pa.L. Rev. 223, 231; 1932, 21 Cal.L.Rev. 471; 1934, 22 Cal.L.Rev. 170; 1939, 27 Cal.L.Rev. 532; 1942, 30 Cal.L.Rev. 172; 1949, 37 Cal.L.Rev. 690; 1936, 9 So.Cal.L.Rev. 354; 1935, 10 Tulane L.Rev. 142; 1934, 13 Tex.L.Rev. 78, 85; 1934, 8 Wash.L.Rev. 179, 182; 1934, 82 U. of Pa.L.Rev. 261, 267; 1935, 21 Va.L.Rev. 328 and 329; 1937, 24 Va.L.Rev. 44, 52. See Vaughan, Reform of Mortgage Foreclosure Procedure—Possibilities Suggested by Honeyman v. Jacobs, 1940, 88 U. of Pa.L.Rev. 957; Warm, A Study of Some of the Problems Concerning Foreclosure Sales and Deficiency Judgments, 1936, 6 Brooklyn L.Rev. 167; Skilton, Government and the Mortgage Debtor, Ch. VII; Skilton, Government and the Mortgage Debtor, 1940-46, 1946, 95 U. of Pa.L.Rev. 119, 127. See Campbell, Cases Mortgages, 2d ed., 246 n. 1(3) for another list of references. And see, in addition, references to cases and other authorities in the following footnotes and in § 336 infra.

54. For a summary, state by state, of legislation regulating deficiency judgments, see Poteat, State Legislative Relief for the Mortgage Debtor During the Depression, 1938, 5 Law and Contemp.Probs. 517, 539.

In United States v. Shimer, C.A.3d, 1960, 367 U.S. 374, 81 S.Ct. 1554, 6 L.Ed.2d 908, it was held that the Regulations of the Administrator under Servicemen's Readjustment Act displaced the local Deficiency Judgment Act of Pennsylvania which released a guarantor of a real property mortgage if the mortgagee failed to initiate judicial proceedings for determining the fair market value of the property purchased by it at a foreclosure sale and permitted recovery from the veteran mortgagor, by way of indemnity of the amount which the Veteran's Administration paid as guarantor of the loan on mortgaged property purchased by lender, upon the veteran's default, at a foreclosure sale, although under state law the guarantor had been released.

In addition to the references cited in notes 51 and 53, supra, and notes 58 and 59, infra, there are several important articles of more recent date. Although listed here, they will be referred to again in connection with particular problems, in § 336 infra. They are as follows: Note, Right of a Second Purchase Money Mortgagee When a Foreclosure of the First Mortgage Exhausts the Security, 1955, 6 Hastings L.Jour. 248; Riesenfeld, California Legislation Curbing Deficiency Judgments, 1960, 48 Cal.L.Rev. 705; Hetland, Deficiency Judgment Limitations—A New Judicial Approach, 1963, 51 Cal.L.Rev. 1; Hetland, Real Property and Real Property Security: The Well-Being of the Law, 1965, 53 Cal.L.Rev. 151, 159–165; Deficiency Judgment Granted Against Endorsing Assignor of Trust Deed, 1962, 15 Stan.L. Rev. 121; Exonerating the Surety: Implications of the California Antideficiency Scheme, 1969, 57 Cal. L.Rev. 218.

55. E. g., West's Ann.Cal.Code Civ.Proc., § 726.

56. E. g., N.Y.C.P.A. §§ 1083–a, 1083.

57. Objections to such statutes have been summarized as follows: "(1) they compel the creditor to take the security instead of cash, regardless of the ability of the particular debtor to pay the full amount in cash; (2) they provide for appraisal of property at a so-called fair value—not defined by the statutes, and not capable of exact definition— leaving ample room for abuse of discretion by the fact-finding body; (3) the debtor may have protec-

closure is by sale out of court under a trust deed or power of sale, then similarly the value is to be ascertained in an action at law on the debt with a judgment for the difference only.[58] Also to be found in them are provisions denying any deficiency where the debt secured is for the purchase price;[59] where it is asked following sale out of court under power of sale or trust deed mortgage;[60] and under any circumstances.[61] Generally

they provide for limiting the amount of the deficiency by the value of the property, the determination of this to be made, usually, by the court or jury.[62] Some purported to be emergency measures,[63] others permanent.[64] Most purported to apply to existing [65] as well as to future transactions.[66]

ANTI-DEFICIENCY LEGISLATION—CONSTITUTIONALITY AND OTHER PROBLEMS

336. Although many anti-deficiency statutes were invalidated by earlier state decisions, the trend was changed by Supreme Court decisions upholding them. What constitutes fair value

the personal credit of the debtor; (2) that a mortgage creditor should share in the loss occasioned by depressions—the debtor losing his equity, the creditor his personal claim; (3) that such legislation forces the creditor to loan exclusively on the security, and thus his loan will be made on a sounder and more conservative basis." Skilton, op. cit. supra, n. 57, at p. 108. There are strong objections to the first two. While there is merit in the third, basically whether it is valid depends upon the needs at different times of particular communities. Idem, pp. 128–130.

tion only by participating in a legal controversy; (4) waiver may destroy the value of the statutes." Skilton, Government and the Mortgage Debtor, 126. As to valuation difficulties, see § 336, note-calls and notes 73–77, infra. As to waiver, see § 336, notes 78–82, infra.

See also Note, Anti-Deficiency Judgment Legislation in California, 1956, 3 U.C.L.A.L.Rev. 192, 194.

58. E.g., West's Ann.Cal.Code Civ.Proc. § 580a. This section is probably superseded as to *notes* executed subsequent to March 6, 1941, by West's Ann.Cal. Code Civ.Proc. § 580d, which bars any deficiency after an out of court sale as to such instruments. § 580a, enacted in 1933, applies to *obligations.* See 1949, 37 Cal.L.Rev. 690, 691. As to whether the difference in language actually creates a difference, see § 336, infra. See also Note, Anti-Deficiency Judgment Legislation in California, 1956, 3 U.C.L. A.L.Rev. 192, 193.

59. E. g., West's Ann.Cal.Code Civ.Proc., § 580b. Held, invalid as to existing mortgages or trust deed mortgages. Hales v. Snowden, 1937, 19 Cal.App.2d 366, 65 P.2d 847; Mont.Rev.Code Ann., 1947, § 93–6008; N.C.Gen.Stat.1966, § 45–21.38.

See additionally Note, Anti-Deficiency Judgment Legislation in California, 1956, 3 U.C.L.A.L.Rev. 192, 195. See also Note, 1957, 35 N.C.L.Rev. 492, discussing Fleishel v. Jessup, 1956, 244 N.C. 451, 94 S.E.2d 308, and North Carolina case law under its deficiency judgment legislation. For a penetrating analysis of the purpose and operation of deficiency judgments in general and, in particular, their abolition entirely with respect to purchase money mortgages, see Currie and Lieberman, op. cit. supra, note 51, pp. 9–40. This latter examination is centered upon the North Carolina legislation.

60. E. g., West's Ann.Cal.Code Civ.Proc. § 580d; N. C.Gen.Stat., 1966, § 45–21.38. See also Model Power of Sale Mortgage Foreclosure Act, Handbook of the Nat.Conf.Com. on Un.St.Laws, 1940, pp. 254–264. See N.D.Cent.Code 1960 §§ 32–19–06, 32–19–07; note 1948, 47 Mich.L.Rev. 254, 260.

61. Ark.Laws 1933, act 57, held unconstitutional in Adams v. Spillyards, 1933, 187 Ark. 641, 61 S.W.2d 686, 86 A.L.R. 1493, noted in 1933, 20 Va.L.Rev. 122. See generally Skilton, Government and the Mortgage Debtor, 127. The arguments in favor of legislation eliminating the deficiency decree altogether have been summarized as three: "(1) that mortgage creditors loan money on the security, and not on

62. E. g., by the court: N.Y. Real Prop. Actions, McKinney 1963, § 1371; West's Ann.Cal.Code Civ. Proc., §§ 726, 580a. By the court or jury: Ariz. Laws 1933, c. 88. See § 32 note 53, supra as to later developments in Arizona. In South Carolina it was to be determined by three appraisers, one to be appointed by the debtor, one by the creditor, and one by the court. S.C.Code Ann.1962, § 45–91.

Ingerton v. First Nat. Bank & Trust Co. of Tulsa, C. A.10th, 1961, 291 F.2d 662, held that entry of a deficiency judgment is a judicial determination and the provision requiring a motion for deficiency judgment within ninety days after a foreclosure sale has the operative effect, if not complied with, of satisfying the debt and depriving the court of authority to render a deficiency judgment.

63. E. g., N.Y.C.P.A., § 1083–a. This section was omitted from the codification of the act. There is no language in the codes purporting to make this "emergency legislation."

64. E. g., N.Y.Real Prop. Actions, McKinney 1963, § 1371.

65. E. g., Ark.Laws 1933, act 57, so construed in Adams v. Spillyards, note 61, supra, to apply only to existing mortgages. See § 312 note 53. Not codified since being held unconstitutional.

66. E. g., N.Y.Real Prop. Actions, McKinney 1963, § 1371; S.C.Code, Supp.1934, § 8712–1, held unconstitutional in Federal Land Bank of Columbia v. Garrison, 1937, 185 S.C. 255, 193 S.E. 308. See discussion as to constitutionality, § 336 infra.

under them is left largely to fact finders under necessarily indefinite tests. There is authority that the benefit of the statutes cannot be waived, at least in the mortgage itself. Some states couple them with "one action" or similar restrictions. Transferees of mortgagees are bound by them. Under statutes applying to purchase money mortgages, lenders of purchase money as well as vendors are included. Whether mortgage guarantors are protected has received varying answers.

A variety of purposes have been attributed to legislatures in enacting anti-deficiency legislation. The curb on purchase money mortgage deficiency judgments has a different purpose and rationale than that on deficiency judgments after a non-judicial foreclosure by power of sale. And the same is true as to other legislative provisions. Important decisions and articles by legal scholars have clarified many of the problems but there remain unanswered questions.

1. *Constitutionality.*

That anti-deficiency statutes would raise a large number of questions was inevitable. Their constitutionality was challenged in both state and federal courts. Many were invalidated by state decisions,[67] before the Su-

preme Court, first, upon the limited ground that the statute applied to only one of alternative remedies leaving the other one unabridged,[68] and later, on the sweeping princi-

---

67. E. g., Kresos v. White, 1936, 47 Ariz. 175, 54 P.2d 800, invalid as to existing mortgages; but valid as to subsequent ones, Perkins v. First Nat. Bank, 1936, 47 Ariz. 376, 56 P.2d 639, certiorari denied 299 U.S. 540, 57 S.Ct. 20, 81 L.Ed. 397. See § 335, n. 59, 61, 65, 66, supra. In California the provisions, apart from their application to court foreclosure of a trust deed mortgage, see Miller v. Hart, note 68, infra, have been held unconstitutional as to or not intended to apply to existing mortgages and trust deed mortgages but constitutional as to future ones. Banta v. Rosasco, 1936, 12 Cal.App.2d 420, 55 P.2d 601, as to §§ 726, 580b; Hales v. Snowden, 1937, 19 Cal.App.2d 366, 65 P.2d 847, as to West's Ann.Code Civ.Proc. §§ 726, 580b; Central Bank of Oakland v. Proctor, 1936, 5 Cal.2d 237, 54 P.2d 718, as to West's Ann.Code Civ.Proc. § 580a; Bennett v. Superior Court of Los Angeles County, 1938, 5 Cal.App. 2d 13, 42 P.2d 80, § 580a; Kirkpatrick v. Stelling, 1940, 36 Cal.App.2d 658, 98 P.2d 566, as to § 580a; cf., Rosenberg v. Janssen, 1935, 11 Cal.App.2d 15, 52 P.2d 952, as to Civ.Code § 2924½ (§ 2924½ expired by its own terms as of Sept. 1, 1938. Cal.Stats. 1933, ch. 643, § 8 at 1674, as amended, Cal.Stats. 1935, ch. 669, § 1, at 1538.); Brown v. Ferdon, 5 Cal.2d 226, 54 P.2d 712, as to Civ.Code § 2924½. See 1934, 22 Cal.L.Rev. 170, 180; 1938, 26 Cal.L. Rev. 215; 1936, 9 So.Cal.L.Rev. 355; 1939, 13 So. Cal.L.Rev. 119.

For collections of cases in state courts passing upon the constitutionality of their deficiency judgment

statutes, see Poteat, op. cit. supra, § 335, note 49; note, 1941, 35 Ill.L.Rev. 594, 599 n. 5; 1937, 108 A.L. R. 891; 1938, 115 A.L.R. 435. Note, 1941, 36 Ill.L. Rev. 467, notes 14, 15, 16, found that of states having a "contract" clause and also deficiency judgment legislation, eight had held their statutes unconstitutional, at least in part; two had upheld them, and in eleven there had been no decision up to that date. See also Skilton, Government and the Mortgage Debtor 1940–1946, 1946, 95 U. of Pa.L.Rev. 119, 127. See note 71, infra as to later decisions in Pennsylvania and Oklahoma validating their enactments. For a careful survey of the constitutionality, or applicability, of the anti-deficiency legislation to pre-existing mortgages or trust deeds in California, see Riesenfeld, California Legislation Curbing Deficiency Judgments, 1960, 48 Cal.L.Rev. 705, 707. See also Comment: Anti-Deficiency Judgment Legislation in California, 1955, 3 U.C.L.A.L.Rev. 192, 200. Riesenfeld found that there was never any real doubt about the *prospective* application of the legislation. Further that § 580d by its terms applied only to mortgages or trust deeds executed in the future. Further § 580b has been held inapplicable in its entirety to mortgages and deeds of trust executed prior to its effective date. § 580a, insofar as it limits the amount of the deficiency judgment, could not be applied constitutionally to a pre-existing mortgage or deed of trust. The three-month limitation on actions for a deficiency under § 580a could be and was intended to have retrospective application. The limitation in § 726 as to the amount of the deficiency judgments applicable to deeds of trust executed before its effective date was held valid but on grounds that did not apply to a mortgage.

68. Richmond Mortgage Corp. v. Wachovia Bank, 1936, 300 U.S. 124, 57 S.Ct. 338, 81 L.Ed. 552, 108 A.L.R. 886.

For comments on this case, see, 1937, 15 N.Car.L.Rev. 273; 1937, 85 U. of Pa.L.Rev. 533; 1937, 108 A.L.R. 891. See also note, 1935, 84 U. of Pa.L.Rev. 223, 233.

On analogous reasoning, Miller v. Hart, 1938, 11 Cal. 2d 739, 81 P.2d 923, commented on in, 1939, 13 So. Cal.L.Rev. 119, held constitutional a statute applying to preexisting trust deed mortgages which permitted them to be foreclosed by judicial proceedings and limited deficiency judgments to the difference between the total indebtedness and the appraised valuation of the property.

Cf. Bennett v. Superior Court, 1935, 5 Cal.App.2d 13, 42 P.2d 80, holding that the limitation on the amount of deficiency judgments to a similar sum could not be retroactively applied to actions by the trustee after sales under the power contained in trust deed mortgages antedating the enactment of the statute (West's Ann.Cal.Code Civ.Proc. § 580a). See note 67, supra.

ple that legislation is constitutional even as to existing mortgages that limits mortgagees to payment in full, held valid both the emergency statute in New York,[69] and a permanent provision to the same effect applying to existing and future mortgages.[70] Since then two state statutes have been upheld and it seems likely that others will be if challenged.[71]

69. Honeyman v. Jacobs, 1939, 306 U.S. 539, 59 S.Ct. 702, 83 L.Ed. 972, discussed 1939, 52 Harv.L.Rev. 1367. See Vaughan, Reform of Mortgage Foreclosure Procedure Suggested by Honeyman v. Jacobs, 1940, 88 U. of Pa.L.Rev. 967.

70. Gelfert v. National City Bank, 1941, 313 U.S. 221, 61 S.Ct. 898, 85 L.Ed. 1299, 133 A.L.R. 1467, reversing the New York Court of Appeals, commented on, 1941, 36 Ill.L.Rev. 465; 1941, 30 Cal.L.Rev. 71; 1941, 27 Va.L.Rev. 1092; 1941, 16 Temple L.Q. 91; 1941, 16 St. John's L.Rev. 143; 1941, 11 Brooklyn L.Rev. 103. The decision of the Court of Appeals, sub nom., National City Bank v. Gelfert, 1940, 284 N.Y. 13, 29 N.E.2d 449, 130 A.L.R. 1472, is commented on, in notes, 1941, 35 Ill.L.Rev. 594; 1941, 18 N.Y.Univ.L.Q.Rev. 299; 1940, 10 Brooklyn L.Rev. 208; 1941, 4 U.Det.L.J. 116; 1941, 10 Ford.L.Rev. 315; 1940, 29 Georgetown L.J. 914. See § 335, note 46, supra, for quotation from the Supreme Court opinion.

71. Fidelity-Philadelphia Trust Co. v. Allen, 1941, 343 Pa. 428, 22 A.2d 896, commented on in 1942, 90 U. of Pa.L.Rev. 330; commented on, 1942, 8 U. of Pitt.L.Rev. 187; Alliance Trust Co. v. Hill, 1945, 196 Okl. 310, 164 P.2d 984, commented on, 1946, 15 Ford.L.Rev. 139.

The history of deficiency judgment legislation in Pennsylvania may be significant as indicating a trend. The Pennsylvania Supreme Court originally held unconstitutional a statute substantially like that of New York. Beaver County Bldg. & Loan Ass'n v. Winowich, 1936, 323 Pa. 483, 187 A. 481, 921, noted in, 1937, 35 Mich.L.Rev. 830, 1936, 85 U. of Pa.L.Rev. 114. See also Farage, Mortgage Deficiency Judgment Acts and Their Constitutionality, 1937, 41 Dickinson L.Rev. 67; notes, 1936, 2 U. of Pitt.L.Rev. 212; 1936, 3 U. of Pitt.L.Rev. 54; 1938, 4 U. of Pitt.L.Rev. 242. Legislative attempts in 1935 and 1937 to cure the constitutional objections to the act both failed. See notes, 1937, 85 U. of Pa.L.Rev. 321; 1938, 86 U. of Pa.L.Rev. 295; idem. 901. In 1941, the act was again passed and this time was upheld. Fidelity-Philadelphia Trust Co. v. Allen, supra. See Skilton, op.cit. supra note 67. Further, in subsequent decisions, the act was held to apply retroactively to a foreclosure sale and deficiency judgment antedating the effective date of the act. Pennsylvania Co. for Insurances on Lives and Granting Annuities v. Scott, 1942, 346 Pa. 13, 29 A.2d 328, 144 A.L.R. 849, noted, 1942, 90 U. of Pa.L.Rev. 746; Dearnley v. Survetnick, 1949, 360 Pa. 572, 63 A.2d 66, noted, 1949, 6 W. & L.L.Rev. 235.

The cases raising the question of constitutionality of the deficiency judgment statutes have been ones in which the mortgagee was the purchaser. Whether they are constitutional when a third person buys for cash and the mortgagee is nevertheless required to credit on his debt, not the amount of cash paid by the purchaser, but the fair value of the property, may still be open.[72]

2. *Fair Value.*

One of the difficult problems raised by those statutes which specify that the "fair value," or an amount arrived at under some similar test, be credited on the debt is that of applying the test laid down. None of them set up any standard by which it can be determined with any precision just what the value is that must be credited.[73] Market val-

72. In the Gelfert case, note 70, supra, the New York court based its holding that the statute was unconstitutional partly upon the fact that it would apply to such a case as well as to where the mortgagee bought it in. The Supreme Court did not refer to this argument. And the broad ground of its decision was that of single satisfaction by the mortgagee. This would not apply to the case where a third person bought. The mortgagee would not have both the land for which he paid less than its value and his debt claim besides. See 1940, 18 N.Y.Univ.L.Q.Rev. 299, 301. In a California case upholding West's Ann.Cal.Code Civ.Proc., § 580a, as to new transactions the court mentioned the point by way of dictum, saying, "The state has also declared that if the creditor either buys in the property himself or sells to a third person at a figure less than the fair market value, he has participated in a sale, to the detriment of the debtor, that is unfair and unconscionable, and he must bear the consequences." Kirkpatrick v. Stelling, 1940, 36 Cal.App.2d 658, 667, 98 P.2d 566, 572. Such a doctrine goes beyond the stated basis of the Gelfert case. The mortgagee must credit the fair value on his debt, not because he otherwise would be getting more than full payment, but because his failure to bid up the price at the sale has permitted a third person, against whom no one has a claim for anything, to acquire the mortgagor's property by paying less than it was worth, thus getting a bargain at the expense of the mortgagor. If the doctrine is accepted, the mortgagee is forced to bid up the property if he wishes to protect himself against having the third party get a bargain at his expense. North Carolina, Pennsylvania, and South Dakota make the procedure operative only when the property is bid in by the mortgagor directly or indirectly. See 1948, 47 Mich.L. Rev. 254, 259.

73. Cf. § 335, note 57, supra. Arizona fixed the value as of the time of the execution of the mortgage.

ue when there is no market, and the substitute test is set up because there is none, is ruled out. The New York statute stipulates that the "fair and reasonable market value" as of the sale date "or such nearest earlier date as there shall have been any market value thereof." [74] After three years, during which some lower courts went back to pre-depression values, it was held that the statute intended to set up a new "equitable standard" in lieu of market value, in which market transactions, if any, was only one item.[75] The values found on the new test have been said to approximate tax assessments.[76] In general, wide latitude seems to be accorded the finders of the fact.[77]

3. *Waiver.*

If a waiver of the benefit of the anti-deficiency statutes is permitted their effectiveness as a protection to mortgagors may be eroded away.[78] There is legislative recognition of such danger in some states in statutes enacted to prevent it.[79] And similar aware-

---

Ariz.Code Ann., 1939, § 62–517. This stat. was held unconstitutional in 1952. See § 312 note 53 supra. There has been no comparable legislation since then.

74. The same test appears in both the temporary section, N.Y.C.P.A., § 1083–a, and the permanent one, N.Y. Real Prop. Actions, McKinney 1963, § 1371(2).

75. See Heiman v. Bishop, 1936, 272 N.Y. 83, 4 N.E. 2d 944; notes, 1935, 35 Col.L.Rev. 1314; 1937, 23 Va.L.Rev. 718.

76. See Friedman, Personal Liability on Mortgage Debts in New York, 1942, 51 Yale L.J. 382, 396. In California the court may, on motion by any party or on its own initiative appoint an inheritance tax appraiser to appraise the value and submit his appraisal to the court where it shall be admissible as evidence. West's Ann.Cal.Code Civ.Proc. § 726; § 580a. See also 1940, 18 N.Y.Univ.L.Q.Rev. 102. For additional authorities and references, see § 330, note 59, supra. Cf., § 329, note 41, supra.

77. See Skilton, Government and the Mortgage Debtor, 124; Poteat, State Legislative Relief for the Mortgage Debtor, 1938, 5 Law & Contemp. Problems, 517, 534. See also Skilton, op. cit. supra note 67, p. 130, "In dealing with this mixed question of fact and law—fair value—where admittedly even the most expert of real estate appraisers must feel at times that they are not very far above the 'look-spit-and-guess' technique, it would not be surprising if occasionally lower court judges took some very original approaches."

One limitation, of course, is that the judgment may not exceed the actual deficiency, i. e., the difference between the indebtedness and the amount for which the property was sold. See Cal.Code Civ.Proc. §§ 726 and 580a. Also certain formalities are specified in the foregoing sections for proving "fair value" at the time of sale. Courts have insisted on faithful observance of these requirements, 1945, 68 Cal.App. 577, 157 P.2d 651. See Riesenfeld, California Legis-

lation Curbing Deficiency Judgments, 1960, 48 Cal. L.Rev. 705, 727.

78. See Skilton, Government and the Mortgage Debtor, 125. See also § 335, note 57, supra. Cf., Chapter 4, supra. Cf. also the similar problem of waiver of the "one action" rule, § 334, note 25, supra.

79. E. g., Pa.Stat.Ann.1967, tit. 12, § 2621.10; West's Ann.Cal.Civ.Code § 2953; Cf., N.Y.C.P.A. § 1077d. The New York statute was omitted from codification; no new statutes to this effect have been enacted

West's Ann.Cal.Civ.Code, § 2953 vitiates "any express agreement made or entered into at the time of or in connection with the making or renewing of any loan secured by a deed of trust, mortgage or other instrument creating a lien on real property, whereby the borrower agrees to waive the rights, or privileges conferred upon him by sections 2924, 2924b, 2924c of the Civil Code or by sections 580a or 726 of the Code of Civil Procedure." The omission from this catalogue of any mention of sections 580b and 580d raises the question whether their provisions could be waived. There is strong dicta that § 580b benefits may not be waived in advance at the time of execution of the mortgage or trust deed. See Riesenfeld, California Legislation Curbing Deficiency Judgments, 1960, 48 Cal.L.Rev. 705, 718, 724. Of course, the secured creditor cannot waive his security in order to avoid the bar of either section 580b or 580d. Whether a subsequent agreement between the mortgagor or trustor and the mortgagee, trustee, or beneficiary would be valid is still open. The answer depends on whether the policies behind sections 580b and 580d are so strong as to make even a subsequent waiver impermissible. Or, in the alternative, that the policies which permit subsequent waiver of the other sections named in section 2953 apply also to sections 580b and 580d. See Riesenfeld, op. cit. supra. See also notes and notecalls 81 and 82 infra.

In Engelman v. Bookasta, 1968, 264 Cal.App.2d 915, 71 Cal.Rptr. 120, the plaintiffs held as security for a note both a trust deed on real property and an assignment of rents. Defendant executed a guaranty by which he agreed to pay the note. By written agreement the defendant waived any right to require holder of instrument to proceed against the maker or any other person or to apply any security it might hold, or proceed to further exhaust any security it might hold, or to pursue any other remedy. The plaintiff sued the defendant and attacked defendant's property as an unsecured creditor. The court held that the waiver, which deprived plaintiff of the benefits of §§ 2845 and 2849 of the Civil Code, was valid and, consequently the plaintiff

ness is found in some court decisions.[80] However, a distinction between a waiver entered into at the time the mortgage is given and one subsequent in time has been drawn, the former being bad and the latter good.[81] This corresponds to the similar distinction broadly drawn by the courts when the question is one of protecting the mortgagor's right of redemption.[82]

4. *One Action Rule.*

In some states limitations on the amount of a deficiency have been coupled with restrictions on the bringing of an action on the debt alone under which unmortgaged assets can be reached. This is true, of course, in states already having the "one action" rule.[83] But other states have enacted legislation toward the same end, notably New York.[84]

It has been suggested that this is necessary if the object of the deficiency statute is to be accomplished.[85] If he may sue at law at the same time he brings his action to foreclose, he may obtain a judgment on the debt prior to his foreclosure decree, levy on any available unmortgaged assets, then get his foreclosure decree for the balance. The debt so reduced may be then so greatly oversecured that even though it is wiped out by crediting the real value of the property on it, he will have made a handsome profit at the expense of the debtor.

5. *Legislative Purposes: The Purchase Money Mortgage Deficiency Judgment Limitation.*

A variety of purposes have been attributed to legislatures in enacting anti-deficiency legislation, some by legal scholars, some by the courts. The same purposes that apply to the curb on purchase money mortgage deficiency judgments under California Code of Civil Procedure section 580b do not necessarily exist in respect to section 580d which denies any deficiency judgment after a non-judicial foreclosure by power of sale. And, of course, the same is true as to other legislative provisions, e.g., California Code of Civil Procedure sections 726 and 580a.

Turning first to the purchase money deficiency legislation, one of the most thorough and scholarly inquiries into the legislative aim in barring any deficiency judgment in such security transactions came to the conclusion that it was designed to discourage vendor financing because it might be, and probably was, irresponsible amateur financ-

could maintain his action and attachment under C. C.P. § 537(1).

80. Salter v. Ulrich, 1943, 22 Cal.2d 263, 266, 138 P. 2d 7, 146 A.L.R. 1344; Morello v. Metzenbaum, 1944, 25 Cal.2d 494, 154 P.2d 670. Cf., Winklemen v. Sides, 1939, 31 Cal.App.2d 387, 88 P.2d 147; Cf. also California Bank v. Stimson, 1949, 89 Cal.App. 2d 552, 201 P.2d 39, commented on, 1949, 22 So.Cal. L.Rev. 502. See Notes, 1939, 27 Cal.L.Rev. 752; 1943, 31 Cal.L.Rev. 429, 434; Cf., 1943, 31 Cal.L. Rev. 429.

81. West's Ann.Cal.Civ.Code, § 2953; Salter v. Ulrich, 1943, 22 Cal.2d 263, 266, 138 P.2d 7, 146 A.L.R. 1344; Morello v. Metzenbaum, 1944, 25 Cal.2d 494, 499, 154 P.2d 670. But in Pennsylvania a waiver or release is void regardless of whether before, after, or at the time the mortgage is given. Pa.Stat.Ann. 1967, tit. 12, § 2621.10.

82. See Chapter 4, supra.

83. See § 334, supra. See also Comment, Anti-Deficiency Judgment Legislation in California, 1955, 3 U.C.L.A.L.Rev. 192, 193.

84. Ibid. A statute requiring that the right to a deficiency judgment must be determined in the foreclosure action as against one who was a party to that action is not unconstitutional. Honeyman v. Hanan, 1937, 302 U.S. 375, 58 S.Ct. 273, 81 L.Ed. 476. The New York statute was held inapplicable to an action by a junior mortgagee brought after foreclosure of a prior mortgage. Weisel v. Hagdahl Realty Co., 1934, 241 App.Div. 314, 271 N.Y.S. 629, noted, 1934, 48 Harv.L.Rev. 126. See note, 1929, 8 Or.L.Rev. 289 (semble). To the same effect, Carr v. H. O. L. C., 1947, 148 Ohio St. 553, 76 N.E.2d 389. A mortgagee who failed to seek a deficiency judgment after foreclosure sale has been held not to be entitled to reach additional security without credit-

ing its fair value on the debt. Matter of Williams' Will, 1940, 258 App.Div. 592, 17 N.Y.S.2d 335, noted, 1940, 53 Harv.L.Rev. 1400. See also 1949, 37 Cal.L. Rev. 690, 695. And see § 334, note-calls and notes 36–39, supra.

85. See Skilton, op. cit. supra note 78, "To afford protection to the debtor, it was necessary that the deficiency judgment statutes be framed so as to compel the creditor to foreclose first upon the security, or to provide for appraisal of other assets attached in the event that the creditor pursued this remedy at law and attached other property first."

ing.[86] In the study, concentrating on the North Carolina statute passed in 1933,[87] the conclusion was summarized as follows: "The North Carolina legislature visualized the purchase-money mortgage as one given by an amateur lender, either to furnish all the necessary credit or to provide junior-lien financing; in either case the security was likely to be inadequate, the terms oppressive, and the consequences harsh." [88] Since the search for legislative motives in limiting purchase money anti-deficiency benefits was on the assumption that the secured creditor was the vendor, the conclusion reached, even if valid on its assumption,[89] would not apply to a statute that included third party lenders of the purchase money.[90]

86. See Currie and Lieberman, Purchase-Money Mortgages, 1960 Duke L.Jour. 1, 9–40.

87. N.C.Gen.Stat.1957, § 45–21.38. An amendment in 1967 deleted the 2d paragraph of the section that dealt with conditional sales contracts.

88. Id. 38.

89. The assumption was reasonable enough at the time. See Hetland, Deficiency Judgment Limitations in California—A New Judicial Approach, 1963, 51 Cal.L.Rev. 1, 3 n. 13. However, the validity of the conclusion, in spite of the scholarly work of the inquirers, is dubious. See Riesenfeld, California Legislation Curbing Deficiency Judgments, 1960, 48 Cal.L.Rev. 705, 715 n. 44: "Currie and Lieberman's careful study reveals that it is well-nigh impossible to ascertain a clearly defined statutory policy and that in the absence of clarification by the legislatures the courts must make the somewhat arbitrary choice of whether the vendee or third party financer should bear the risk of misjudgments, at the time of the real estate acquisition, as to present or future property values."

90. See Hetland, op. cit. supra note 89, 3, 15–17; Currie and Lieberman, op. cit., supra note 86, pp. 17, 18. Montana expressly limited the bar to purchase money mortgage deficiency judgments to vendors. Mont.Rev.Code Ann. § 93–6008 (1947). Oregon and South Dakota statutory restriction of their application to vendor purchase money mortgages was by judicial construction. Hetland, op. cit. supra 15 n. 61. In North Carolina, "informed opinion" was relied on for the conclusion that the legislation applied only to vendor mortgages. Currie and Lieberman, op. cit. supra 18. In California, although there was earlier authority that only vendor mortgagees fell within C.C.P. § 580b, the purchase money anti-deficiency provision, the landmark case of Bargioni v. Hill, 1963, 59 Cal.2d 121, 28 Cal.Rptr. 321, 378 P.2d 593, decided that the identity of the lender made no difference. See Hetland, op. cit. su-

Two landmark cases in California in 1963 gave authoritative clarification of the legislative purposes of C.C.P. § 580b as well as pointing out the significance of other sections limiting deficiency judgments: the first was Roseleaf Corporation v. Chierighino; [91] the other was Bargioni v. Hill.[92]

In the *Roseleaf* case the defendant bought a hotel from the plaintiff giving him in part payment four promissory notes. One note, not involved in the litigation, was secured by a purchase money trust deed on the hotel. The other three notes were secured by junior trust deeds on other property owned by the defendant, the senior encumbrances being held by third parties who were strangers to the action. The senior security holders had foreclosed by nonjudicial sales of the property covered by these three trust deeds leaving the three notes unsecured. Plaintiff action was to recover on the three notes. The court, opinion by Traynor, C. J., held that plaintiff's action was not barred nor limited by C.C.P. §§ 580a, 580d, or 726.

In the *Bargioni* case the plaintiff was a third party lender of purchase money who took as security for his note a junior trust deed on the purchased property. The senior encumbrancer exhausted the security by foreclosure sale. The plaintiff sued on the note. The court held that he was barred from recovery by the 580b deficiency provision.

In Brown v. Jensen,[93] several explanations were given as to the legislative purposes in enacting 580b. These were examined in Roseleaf and rejected. The possibilities so discarded were as follows: [94]

1. That it was designed to prevent creditors from buying in at a nominal sum, after

pra 17–19. See also Riesenfeld, op. cit. supra note 89, pp. 711–717.

91. 59 Cal.2d 35, 27 Cal.Rptr. 873, 378 P.2d 97.

92. 59 Cal.2d 121, 28 Cal.Rptr. 321, 378 P.2d 593.

93. 1953, 41 Cal.2d 193, 259 P.2d 425, certiorari denied 347 U.S. 905, 74 S.Ct. 430, 98 L.Ed. 1064.

94. See the opinion of Traynor in the Roseleaf case and also Hetland, op. cit. supra note 89, 10.

a debtor has defaulted, and then holding the debtor for the deficiency. In answer Traynor, C. J., pointed out that this purpose is accomplished by the fair value sections, and does not explain for what purpose purchase money mortgages were singled out for special treatment.

2. That it was to make certain that in the case of "a purchase money mortgage or deed of trust the security alone can be looked to for the recovery of the debt." This, however, is merely a statement of the effect of the statute after assuming that it applies, but offers no rationale for deciding whether or not it applies.

3. That it was to place the risk of the value of the security becoming inadequate on the one taking a purchase money mortgage or trust deed because he knows the value of his security. In answer, it might be true that the average vendor or financer in real estate transactions is more astute as to the value of his land than the average vendee or financer in real estate transactions but it is "doubtful" whether that was the reason for § 580b.[95]

The two purposes of § 580b as found by the court in *Roseleaf,* were summarized in *Bargioni* as follows: "To discourage land sales that are unsound because the land is overvalued and, in the event of a depression in land values to prevent the aggravation of the downturn that would result if default-

ing purchasers lost the land and were further burdened with personal liability." [96]

6. *Applicability of C.C.P. 580b.*

    A. Judgments Prohibited.

        1. The Nonforeclosing Creditor: *Brown v. Jensen.*

In California under C.C.P. § 726 a mortgagee or holder of a trust deed must proceed against the security before going against the mortgagor or trustor. It was well settled, however, that if the security has become valueless through no fault of the mortgagor or trustor, the secured creditor may then proceed directly against the mortgagor or trustor.[97] In Brown v. Jensen,[98] however, the California Supreme Court held that § 580b barred a junior purchase money lender, the vendor, from recovering a personal judgment from the vendee-borrower even though his security had been lost through foreclosure by the senior deed of trust also a security for a lender of part of the purchase money. To reach this result the court held that the exception mentioned above did not apply because the action was for a deficiency on a note secured by a purchase money trust deed, stating that "a deficiency is nothing more than the difference between the security and

---

95. See Currie and Lieberman, op. cit. supra note 89 at p. 31. See also Riesenfeld, op. cit. supra note 89, at p. 727. "It is hard to perceive why a vendor 'knows the value of his security' better than the skilled personnel of a lending institution. Even less valid is the assumption that a vendor means to rely only upon the security and 'assumes the risk that it may become worthless while a lending institution does not do so.3 * * * The main factor which rationally could be relied upon for that purpose is the proposition that vendors have the last word on the price for which they are willing to part with the property and, therefore, should be burdened with a risk from which mere financers remain free." See also Comment, Anti-Deficiency Judgment Legislation in California, 1955, 3 U.C.L. A.L.Rev. 192, 195, n. 14 and accompanying text.

96. According to one qualified writer (he was *amicus curiae* in the *Roseleaf* case) the second is the real purpose of the statute, the first being a subsidiary one. He writes: "Standing alone, the first purpose, preventing overvaluation, would lead to the opposite result under the Roseleaf facts; would compel that an unsecured note for part of the purchase price would be uncollectable under § 580b; would bar an action against a guarantor of a purchase money instrument; and would compel an inquiry into the total consideration rather than into the secured consideration. Yet the statute does none of this." Hetland, Deficiency Judgment Limitations in California—A New Judicial Approach, 1963, 51 Cal. L.Rev. 1, 4. Id.: text at notecalls 86–102 on separate unsecured note; and text at notecalls 103–127 on guarantor. For an amplification of Hetland's thesis that the main purpose of 580b is "standby or cycle leveling legislation," or "depression cushion," see id. 4–7.

97. See § 344 supra. See also Comment, 3 U.C.L.A. L.Rev. 192, 195.

98. 1953, 41 Cal.2d 193, 259 P.2d 425, certiorari denied, 1954, 347 U.S. 905, 74 S.Ct. 430, 98 L.Ed. 1064.

the debt" and therefore may consist of the whole debt.[99] The court said that the nature of the security transaction as a purchase money one is determined and fixed for all time at the time it is executed so that no deficiency judgment may be obtained regardless of whether the security becomes valueless. It also relied on the language of § 580b which states that in *no event* shall there be a deficiency judgment.

There was a vigorous dissent by Spence, J., in Brown v. Jensen and a strong contemporaneous criticism of it.[1] Additionally it has been argued that the repudiation by the later Roseleaf case of most of the legislative purposes relied on by Brown v. Jensen[2] results in an analytical, if not an actual, overruling of the latter case.[3]

Institutional lenders seldom can, or will, take a junior encumbrance.[4] Consequently the vast majority of junior purchase money lenders are individual sellers. Furthermore, the enormous increase in recent years of the use of subordination agreements by sellers who are nonprofessionals in the real property business has resulted in the junior encumbrancer being a seller, frequently a farmer or rancher, who has subordinated his purchase money lien to the construction loan mortgage of the buyer, a real estate pro-

moter or developer.[5] The application of Brown v. Jensen to this kind of a transaction results in a patent inequity.[6] "Since the construction loan typically is several times larger than the seller's land loan, the subordinated seller rarely has any hope of reinstating the construction loan in the event of the developer's default. If doing so is a prerequisite to his protection, as it is under Brown v. Jensen, he is without remedy. There is nothing in section 580b that expressly precludes the junior from recovering a judgment against the developer for the amount owing after the construction lender takes the security; only Brown v. Jensen's strained construction of section 580b prevents it." [7]

In 1963 an amendment to § 580b[8] allowed third party lenders of purchase money to recover against commercial as opposed to resi-

99. Brown v. Jensen, supra at 195, 198, 259 P.2d at 426, 427.

1. Note, Right of a Second Purchase Money Mortgagee When a Foreclosure of the First Mortgage Exhausts the Security, 1955, 6 Hastings L.Jour. 284. The writer pointed out that a deficiency judgment in California and other jurisdictions demands a prior sale under a power of sale in the trust deed or mortgage or a judicial foreclosure under the trust deed or mortgage *by the creditor seeking the foreclosure.* Further, the Ohio Court of Appeals case cited and relied on for its definition of what constitutes a deficiency was reversed by the Supreme Court of Ohio. Carr v. Home Owners Loan Corp., 1947, 148 Ohio St. 533, 76 N.E.2d 389.

2. See text and notes at notecalls 93–96 supra.

3. See Hetland, Real Property and Real Property Security: The Well Being of the Law, 1965, 53 Cal.L. Rev. 151, 159.

4. See § 44 at notecalls 10 and 11.

5. See text and notes, § 212, supra, at notecalls 11–29.

6. "With respect to the inequity of forcing the junior to make an additional investment to protect himself, Justice Traynor said in Roseleaf: 'Equitable considerations favor placing the burden on the debtor, not only because it is his default that provokes the senior sale, but also because he has the benefit of his bargain with the junior lienor who, unlike the selling senior, might end up with nothing.' 59 Cal.2d 35, 41, 378 P.2d 97, 100, 27 Cal.Rptr. 873, 876 (1963)." Hetland, op. cit. supra note 3 at p. 161 n. 59.

7. Hetland, op. cit. supra note 3, 161.

8. The italicized language was added to West's Ann. Cal.Code Civ.Proc. § 580b, last paragraph, in 1963: "No deficiency judgment shall lie in any event after any sale of real property for failure of the purchaser to complete his contract of sale, or under a deed of trust, or mortgage, given *to the vendor* to secure payment of the balance of the purchase price of real property, *or under a deed of trust, or mortgage, on a dwelling for not more than four families given to a lender to secure repayment of a loan which was in fact used to pay all or part of the purchase price of such dwelling occupied, entirely or in part, by the purchaser.*" Cal.Stats.1963, c. 2158, § 1, at 4–500.

In Kistler v. Vasi, 1969, —— Cal.2d ——, 78 Cal.Rptr. 170, 455 P.2d 106, it was held that plaintiffs, lenders of money for the purchase of real property other than the defined residential property covered by the 1963 amendment, could recover a deficiency judgment on a note given by defendant secured by second deed of trust on realty after security had been exhausted by sale under first deed of trust.

dential purchasers. The burden of Brown v. Jensen is thus placed even more heavily on the individual seller. "Now he is the only lender who remains barred against all buyers including the most likely deficiency judgment candidate, the property developer. To decide, therefore, whether a sold-out junior should be able to recover judgment on the note after a senior has taken all the security, one has to decide who the buyer and seller are likely to be and then compare their relative equities."[9] In view of the preceding considerations the equity of the sold out junior is superior and the results of Brown v. Jensen are unfortunate. Nevertheless Brown v. Jensen is still recognized as law.[10]

One other point should be noted. Section 580d does not apply to the sold-out junior. That is, it does not bar a junior creditor who has not himself had the nonjudicial sale which exhausted the security.[11]

2. Third Party Money.

Under statutes denying deficiency judgments to mortgages or trust deeds securing the balance of the purchase price of real property, it is obvious that the purchaser is protected as against a deficiency when the note and security is given directly by the vendee to the vendor.[12] Where the mortgagee is not the seller, but a lender of the money to finance the purchase, the money so advanced is not "purchase money" in other states having legislation similar to California's § 580b.[13] In California the question was not definitively settled until *Bargioni* in 1963 decided that the identity of the lender made no difference.[14]

The 1963 amendment to § 580b gave third party purchase money lenders a right to a deficiency judgment in some situations.[15] It left the residential purchaser protected from a deficiency judgment by a vendor or third party lender of the purchase money. It took away protection from the non-residential purchaser only, a result consistent with Traynor's opinion in the *Bargioni* and *Roseleaf* cases.[16]

3. The Assuming Grantee.

A buyer of property encumbered by a prior purchase money security device will get the 580b protection of the original mortgagor or trustor even though he expressly assumes the indebtedness. And the same result has been reached where the original purchase money mortgagor sells and, in carrying out the transaction, the mortgagee releases him and

---

9. Hetland, op. cit. supra note 3, 160.

10. Jackson v. Taylor, 1969, — Cal.App.2d —, 76 Cal.Rptr. 891, 895. The court said, "We recognize the manifest inequity of disallowing the *typical* junior purchase money lender from recovering a personal judgment against the borrower after a senior lienholder has exhausted the security by the sale under the senior lien. * * * 'But the Supreme Court has not overruled Brown v. Jensen. It stands as the expression of law on this subject.' Under the compulsion of Brown v. Jensen, *supra*, * * *, we must reverse the judgment."

11. See Hetland, Deficiency Judgment Limitations in California—A New Judicial Approach, 1963, 51 Cal. L.Rev. 1–31; Comment, Exonerating the Surety: Implications of the California Anti-Deficiency Scheme, 1969, 57 Cal.L.Rev. 218, 230.

12. Stockton Sav. & Loan Bank v. Massanet, 1941, 18 Cal.2d 200, 114 P.2d 592.

13. See note 90 supra.

14. See text at notecall 94 supra, and Hetland, Real Property and Real Property Security: The Well-Being of the Law, 1965, 53 Cal.L.Rev. 151, 162–163. See also 1949, 37 Cal.L.Rev. 690, 692; 30 Cal.L.Rev. 172, 178; 1939, 27 Cal.L.Rev. 532, 533.

15. See note 8 supra.

16. See Hetland, op. cit. supra note 3, 164. The author added: "Equally consistent and even better legislation would have been to withdraw the protection from the commercial purchaser entirely and to allow even the vendor to recover from him." Ibid.

In an action by vendors of real property against purchasers from original purchasers on promissory notes secured by second deed of trust given by defendants to plaintiffs the court held that the second deed of trust was one to secure payment of balance of the purchase price and thus within the protection of C.C.P. § 580b. Jackson v. Taylor, 1969, — Cal.App.2d —, 76 Cal.Rptr. 891. The court stated that "The 1963 amendment narrowed the statutory prohibition against deficiencies only insofar as *third party lenders* may now recover deficiencies from non-residential purchasers." — Cal.App.2d —, 76 Cal.Rptr. 891, 893.

takes a new note and mortgage from the transferee.[17]

Where the original encumbrance is not for purchase money a different question is raised as to a grantee of the mortgagor or trustor who, as part of his purchase price, assumed its payment, the mortgagee not being a party to the transaction. An early case suggested that § 580b protection would be denied.[18] "If the creditor consented to the assumption, or even if he had the right to call the loan upon sale and by failing to do so impliedly consented, it seems reasonable to consider him a third party purchase money lender, vis-a-vis the assuming grantee. In this event, his right to a personal judgment would be limited to his claim against the original grantee in the latter's new capacity as surety."[19]

Even where the creditor had no control over the assumption there is a good "chance that the assuming grantee of a non-purchase money encumbrance will be entitled to 580b protection and will be immune from a judgment in favor of either the creditor or the original debtor."[20] "In the abstract, the creditor seems not particularly prejudiced by the extension of 580b protection to the assuming grantee. The assuming grantee is a purchaser and nominally within the protected class; the security is upon the purchased property, and the creditor reserves the right to recover from the trustor upon whom he presumably relied, if personal credit was of importance to him. *Bargioni* re-

moved the possibility of his exclusion as a third party lender and *Roseleaf* suggested no policy that would exclude him on other grounds."[21]

4. The Land Contract.

In 1935 an amendment to § 580b extended it to prohibit deficiency judgments after "any sale of real property for failure of the purchaser to complete his contract of sale." Since the purpose of the amendment was to put land sale contracts under the section when they were used as a security substitute for purchase money mortgages or trust deeds it is understandable that the courts should conclude that it applied only to contracts of sale in which credit is involved and does not apply to sales for cash.[22]

The possibility that the doctrine of Brown v. Jensen, previously considered earlier in this section, 6A 1 supra, "calls for caution in not placing too much reliance upon the requirement of a previous sale in connection with the limitations on the vendor's rights under a land sale contract where he has re-

17. Stockton Sav. & Loan Bank v. Massanet, 1941, 18 Cal.2d 200, 114 P.2d 592. Jackson v. Taylor, 1969, — Cal.App.2d —, 76 Cal.Rptr. 891, accord. See especially, Hetland, op. cit. supra note 89, 14. See also Riesenfeld, op. cit. supra note 89 at 716. But in a transaction carried out in the same way, if the original mortgage is not for the purchase money, the substituted mortgagor may not be entitled to protection against the mortgagee on the ground that the mortgage is one for the purchase price.

18. Banta v. Rosasco, 1936, 12 Cal.App.2d 420, 55 P.2d 601. But see 1939, 27 Cal.L.Rev. 497, 505, n. 26, 532; 1936, 9 So.Cal.L.Rev. 355.

19. Hetland, op. cit. supra, note 89, 14–15.

20. Hetland, op. cit. supra note 89, 15.

21. Ibid. See also Comment, Anti-Deficiency Judgment Legislation in California, 1955, 3 U.C.L.A.L. Rev. 192, 202.

22. See Comment, Anti-Deficiency Judgment Legislation in California, 1955, 3 U.C.L.A.L.Rev. 192, 198–200: "* * * there is a large area of uncertainty where each case must be determined on the basis of whether or not the contract was essentially a security device intended as a substitute for a deed of trust or mortgage." See also Riesenfeld, California Legislation Curbing Deficiency Judgments, 1960, 48 Cal.L.Rev. 705, 720–722: "A deficiency judgment within the meaning of section 580b as applied to the enforcement of a land contract is a judgment for the balance of the purchase price or for damages flowing from the nonperformance of the contract of sale remaining after the seller has relied upon his title to make himself whole."

For a survey of the land contract in California, including the problem of the application of § 580b, see Hetland, The California Land Contract, 1960, 48 Cal.L.Rev. 729. Consideration of the vendor's remedies and the anti-deficiency legislation, including the relevance of Brown v. Jensen, is dealt with, id. 748–755, 769–770. See also Hetland, Deficiency Judgment Limitations in California—A New Judicial Approach, 1963, 51 Cal.L.Rev. 1, 12–13. For a brief treatment of the land sale contract compared with a mortgage see § 20 supra.

lied upon his title as his principal security. It is not unlikely that the courts will come to apply the bar of section 580b even in cases of foreclosure without sale by means of quiet title actions. Generally speaking all the principles governing the applicability of section 580b in the case of purchase-money mortgages and deeds of trust control similarly in case of land contracts serving as purchase money security." [23]

Applicability of C.C.P. 580b—(Continued)

B. Deficiency Judgments Permitted.

There are legitimate credit arrangements even for a purchase price that are not part of the secured transaction and are outside of the purpose of § 580b. Such transactions are not avoided by it.

1. The Separately Secured Note.

Before the *Roseleaf* decision there were cases holding that § 580b "does not prohibit the vendor's taking additional security for the purchase money on other property, whether owned by the vendee or third persons, and enforcing such security by judicial proceedings, as well as by sale under a power." [24]

In the *Roseleaf* case [25] in holding that the three notes on property other than the purchased hotel could be sued on after they were left unsecured by the extrajudicial sale of the senior encumbrancer, the court decided that § 580b did not bar recovery; nor did §§ 580a, 580b, 580d, or 726. The court said, "The purchaser will not lose the property he purchased yet remain liable for the purchase price. To apply section 580b here would mean that Chierighinos [the buyers] would acquire the hotel at less than the agreed price." The important point is that for the *Roseleaf* result to occur the separate notes must not be part of the secured transaction to which section 580b is limited by its language and they must be beyond the statute's purpose. In other words, the separate note must in no sense be secured by the purchased property. "Unlike the single-debt, multiple-security transaction, the creditor with two economically separate notes has no recourse to the purchased property as security for the note secured by other property. This note is not part of the security transaction.[26]

2. The Separate Unsecured Note.

It is entirely clear that a third party lender of purchase money who, in addition to a mortgage on the purchased property to secure the loan, takes a separate unsecured note for part of the purchase price, is not barred by § 580b from collecting on the unsecured note in addition to foreclosing the mortgage on the purchased property.[27] Where it is the vendor who takes a purchase money mortgage as security for one note and then purports to take a separate unsecured note for a part of the purchase price the answer is not so clear. The reason is that a vendor's lien is given by law on the purchased property as security for that part of the purchase price that is unpaid and not

---

23. Riesenfeld, op. cit. supra note 22 at p. 721. See also Hetland, op. cit. supra (both) note 22.

24. Riesenfeld, op. cit. supra note 22, 716 citing Mortgage Guarantee Co. v. Sampsell, 1942, 51 Cal.App.2d 180, 124 P.2d 353. See also Comment, 3 U.C.L.A.L. Rev. 192, 205, 235 n. 105. However, Freedland v. Greco, 1955, 45 Cal.2d 462, 289 P.2d 463, seems to hold that although an action to foreclose on additional security is not barred after the sale of real property under a power of sale, the creditor cannot get a deficiency judgment on foreclosing on the additional security. A dictum in Peterson v. Wilson, 1948, 88 Cal.App.2d 617, 632, 199 P.2d 757, 766, was disapproved in the Greco case. In 1949 a second paragraph was added to § 580b. It prohibited a deficiency judgment on either security interest where given to secure a combined purchase of both realty and personalty. See discussion of this amendment in Note, 1949, 37 Cal.L.Rev. 600, 696.

25. See text at notecall 91, supra.

26. Hetland, Deficiency Judgment Legislation in California—A New Judicial Approach, 1963, 51 Cal.L. Rev. 1, 19.

27. Christopherson v. Allen, 1961, 190 Cal.App.2d 848, 12 Cal.Rptr. 658, discussed in Hetland, op. cit. supra note 26, 21-23.

otherwise secured.[28] If the vendor's lien were an equivalent substitute for a mortgage or deed of trust, the separate "unsecured" note would obviously be part of the same "debt," "note," and "purchase price" specified in Cal. Code Civ.Proc. §§ 726, 580d, and 580b.[29] The vendor's lien, however, is not an equivalent or satisfactory substitute for a junior consensual encumbrance by way of mortgage or trust deed.[30]

A learned and acute scholar has further observed that "If the court were ultimately to hold the separate unsecured note to be barred by section 580b because of the 'security' of the vendor's lien, it would also have to hold the unsecured note for the total price to be within the statute for the same reason. The vendor's lien then would make the totally unsecured vendor a secured creditor, denying him the right to a judgment and forcing him to look only to the 'security.' This would be incredible."[31]

In spite of characterizing such a result incredible, the writer suggests that, since the lien's benefits are negligible the vendor should get rid of it by express waiver in the note or by separate agreement.[32]

3. The Guarantor and Surety.

Although not entirely free from doubt, recent cases pretty clearly indicate that a guarantor or surety of a purchase money debt secured by a mortgage or trust deed cannot invoke the bar of C.C.P. § 580b when sued for a deficiency.[33] Various rationales have been offered in support of this conclusion. One, expressed before the more recent decisions, after stating that the question was completely open at that time, 1955, suggested that "the defense afforded by the antideficiency legislation could be treated as analogous to the defense of infancy or incapacity. If this position is taken, the result would be that the surety would be liable for a deficiency and could not obtain reimbursement from the principal where the principal would have had the protection of the antideficiency legislation if sued by the creditor."[34]

Professor Hetland's reasoning was stated thus: "*Roseleaf* confined the scope of section 580b to the debtor's obligation secured by the purchased security. The guarantor's obligation is not within this delineation. It is not secured by the purchased security and it is not the debtor's obligation. It is simply ad-

28. In some states the vendor's lien is provided for by statute, e. g., West's Ann.Cal.Civ.Code § 3046. It is, however, an equitable lien which arises even though there is no legislative provision for it. See III A.L.P. § 11.73. See also § 19 supra. In the case put in the text, the vendor's lien would apparently attach to the unsecured note for part of the price even though another note for the balance is secured. See Hetland, op. cit. supra note 26, 20 n. 88, citing Mills v. Mills, 1956, 147 Cal.App.2d 107, 305 P.2d 61.

29. See Hetland, op. cit. supra note 26, 21.

30. See Hetland, op. cit. supra note 26, 22, pointing out that it cannot be expressed in written form; it cannot be recorded; and it may be cut off by a subsequent bona fide purchaser; and consequently "it is a singularly tenuous security interest."

31. Hetland, op. cit. supra note 26, 22.

32. Ibid.

33. Heckes v. Sapp, 1964, 229 Cal.App.2d 549, 40 Cal. Rptr. 485; Roberts v. Graves, 1969, —— Cal.App. 2d ——, 75 Cal.Rptr. 130. See Comment, Anti-Deficiency Judgment Legislation in California, 1955, 3 U.C.L.A.L.Rev. 192, 201, 202–205; Hetland, op. cit. supra, 26, 25–28; Comment, Exonerating the Surety: Implications of the California Anti-Deficiency Scheme, 1969, 57 Cal.L.Rev. 218, 235–336. But see Riesenfeld, op. cit. supra note 22, 719, suggesting that of three possible solutions to the problem, the "courts evince an inarticulate preference" for holding that the surety incurs no liability on his undertaking vis-à-vis the promisee if the principal obligation is one for purchase money secured by a mortgage or deed of trust." See also Note, 1962, 15 Stanford L.Rev. 121.

In New York a guarantor is held to be within the terms of the antideficiency judgment statute where the guaranty was made at the time of the execution of the note and mortgage. Klinke v. Samuels, 1934, 264 N.Y. 144, 190 N.E. 324. See note, 1939, 17 N.Car.L.Rev. 179. See also Friedman, op. cit. supra note 76, 403. As to whether guaranties executed later are under the statute, see Friedman, supra. In Pennsylvania, guarantors were expressly put under the protection of the act (limiting deficiency to amount over the fair value of the property). Pa. Laws 1941, No. 151 §§ 6, 2a; 12 Purdon, Penn. Stats.Ann., 1967, §§ 2621.1–11.

34. Comment, 1955, 3 U.C.L.A.L.Rev. 192, 204.

ditional security. It is not, therefore, part of the purchase money secured transaction."[35] He also stated: "The argument for guarantor deficiency protection does not lie in the possibility that the guarantor could enforce the obligation against the principal and thus obviate the anti-deficiency legislation; such a possibility does not exist. The courts consistently strike down schemes aimed at avoiding the deficiency legislation by illusory changes in form. A flimsy avoidance device based upon an intermediate surety would have no chance of success."[36] In support of this latter statement, upon which his first statement depends, he cites four cases, none of which involved a "true" guarantor or surety whose right to reimbursement, through direct action against the principal or by subrogation to the creditor's rights, could not be dismissed on the ground that it was "simply an illusory change in form."[37]

The most recent exploration of the problem of the anti-deficiency legislation's application to guarantors or sureties[38] concentrates mainly on section 580d but also deals with the effect of § 580b. It suggests two possible bases for denying the anti-deficiency bar to sureties: First, that the surety is exonerated by acts of the creditor which prejudice his, the surety's rights. Second, the statutory intent of the anti-deficiency legislation could give the surety a defense. The former invokes the general rule of suretyship law that a "material alteration of the contract governing the principal obligation where substantial rights of the parties thereto are changed, whether such alteration increases or decreases the obligation, or is otherwise prejudicial or beneficial to the surety.[39] The second considers the concept of a prohibited deficiency from the standpoint of the statutory purpose of section 580d and also as an exemption from its bar as additional security.[40] This latter approach is, of course, not applicable to the problem under § 580b.

There are several problems if the first theory is followed. One is that if the surety has consented to the prejudicial acts they do not exonerate him. And before finding that a surety has consented to remain liable in spite of changes in the original obligation that consent must be explicit.[41]

Another difficulty, where section 580b governs is that although its deficiency pro-

---

35. Hetland, op. cit. supra note 26, 27.

36. Ibid. 26.

37. See Union Bank v. Gradsky, 1968, 265 Cal.App.2d 40, 55 n. 8, 71 Cal.Rptr. 64, 69–70, n. 8, criticising Hetland's statement on the ground that he cites no authority for his "broad statement" and does not purport to deal with the situation in which the enforcement of a guaranty is not simply an "illusory" change in form. In defense of Hetland, a recent Comment refers to the four cases mentioned in the text to this notecall. It also quoted the court's language in reference to question before it which involved § 580d, not § 580b, to argue that the court actually did agree with Hetland's statement. The court said, "To permit a guarantor to recover reimbursement from the debtor would permit circumventing the purpose of section 580d." The result would "permit the recovery of a deficiency judgment following a nonjudicial sale of the security under a different label. It makes no difference to [the principal's] purse whether the recovery is by the original creditor in a direct action following nonjudicial sale of the security, or whether the recovery is in an action by the guarantor for the same sum." Id. at 54, 71 Cal.Rptr. at 69. Of course, the purpose of § 580d which the court refers to as being circumvented is different from that of § 580b, and therefore, as the court pointed out, "the cases interpreting section 580b of the Code of Civil Procedure are of limited use in deciding a case under section 580d because the legislative purposes were not identical * * * as the Supreme Court explained in the *Bargioni* and *Roseleaf* cases." Ibid.

38. Comment, Exonerating the Surety: Implications of the California Anti-Deficiency Scheme, 1969, 57 Cal.L.Rev. 218.

39. Id. at 220. See West's Ann.Cal.Civ.Code §§ 2819, 2845, 2848, 2849. See also Osborne, Cases on Secured Transactions, 1967, ch. 13.

40. Op. cit. supra note 38, 220–231, 231–238.

41. Id., 223–227. In Union Bank v. Gradsky, 1968, 265 Cal.App.2d 40, 71 Cal.Rptr. 64, a 580d case, the court said that it was undesirable "to strain the instrument to find that waiver [of the guarantor's defense] by implication." The writer of the Comment concludes that "the courts should require unequivocal proof of the surety's intention to remain bound" after the creditor's acts have given him a defense. Id.

hibition releases the principal from personal liability the surety remains liable.[42] The creditor in foreclosing to collect on a debt incurred to purchase the property merely activates an already existing deficiency prohibition. Where the transaction falls under section 580b the surety never had any right to reimbursement. He has not benefited the principal by paying a deficiency because the principal had no duty to pay it. And it would be practically impossible to spell out an implied in fact agreement by the principal debtor to reimburse the surety. As Hetland has pointed out, on entering into the agreement the "surety would know of the debtor's 580b defense in the same sense that he would know of the debtor's right to rely upon the statute of limitations or any other statutory defense." [43]

The argument that the surety's "continued liability in the purchase money situation governed by section 580b derives from the fact that the statutory purpose does not require his release. Section 580b was intended to protect the purchaser of property by preventing 'the aggravation of the downturn that would result if defaulting purchasers were burdened with large personal liability during depression periods." This legislative purpose is achieved by relieving the purchaser of personal liability to the seller or purchase money lender who takes a security interest in the property purchased. Since section 580b was intended to serve as a depression cushion for the benefit of defaulting purchasers, excluding the surety from its scope does not defeat its purpose. Section 580b's definition of a deficiency as a 'personal judgment on the debt against the debtor' derives from the statute's purchaser-protection purpose without which the definition fails. Once a statute turns from preoccupation with protecting the purchaser to remedying the creditor's unfair advantage it is no

longer necessary to exclude the surety from its scope merely because his is not the purchaser's liability." [44]

7. Rationale and Applicability of Statute Barring Deficiency Judgment After Nonjudicial Foreclosure Sale.

A creditor secured by a mortgage or trust deed with a power of sale has two alternative methods of realizing on the security. He may bring a judicial action to foreclose, or he can exercise his power of sale and foreclose nonjudicially. If he follows the first course, in a large number of states the mortgagor and others are given a right of redemption from the foreclosure sale.[45] If he utilizes the second method there will be no right to redeem. Under either procedure, in the absence of legislation barring or limiting such relief, the creditor may get a judgment for the deficiency, i. e., the difference between the amount of the debt and the sale price of the security.[46] However, in some states, notably in California by California Code of Civil Procedure section 580d, the principal debtor is released from liability for a personal judgment following a nonjudicial sale. The rationale and coverage of this legislation is distinct from that, just considered, of the purchase money secured transaction. California Code of Civil Procedure § 580d is chosen for the purpose of considering these matters.[47]

A. Statutory Purpose of C.C.P. Section 580d.

California Code of Civil Procedure § 580d was intended to equalize the advantages of

---

42. See note and text at notecall 33 supra.

43. Hetland, op. cit. supra note 26, at 26. See also Comment, op. cit. supra note 38, at 228.

44. Comment, op. cit. supra note 38, at 235.

45. See sections 307 et seq. supra.

46. See §§ 333, 335 supra, and § 337 infra.

47. For discussions of West's Ann.Cal.Code Civ.Proc. § 580d see Riesenfeld, op. cit. supra note 22, 722–725; Hetland, op. cit. supra note 26, 28–34; Comment, Exonerating the Surety: Implications of the California Anti-Deficiency Scheme, 1969, 57 Cal.L. Rev. 218, considering the liability of a surety under, chiefly, West's Ann.Code Civ.Proc. § 580d, but also under West's Ann.Code Civ.Proc. § 580b.

judicial and nonjudicial foreclosure by prohibiting a deficiency judgment after nonjudicial sale.[48] "This was accomplished by equalizing the sanctions which judicial and nonjudicial foreclosure offered as alternatives to the creditor. Before the enactment of section 580d 'it was to the creditor's advantage to exercise a power of sale rather than to foreclose by judicial action.' Creditors preferred private sale because it avoided a statutory period of redemption. By exercising the power instead of foreclosing judicially, the creditor could obtain a deficiency judgment as well as the enhanced proceeds of a redemption-free sale. This procedure allowed the creditor to bid in the property himself at unfairly low price—or offer that opportunity to someone else—secure in the knowledge that any deficiency would be recoverable in a personal judgment against the principal. The absence of a redemption right rendered the principal vulnerable to an unrealistically low sales price, and prevented * * * him * * * from protecting [himself] by redeeming for the property's true worth. The creditor had an opportunity for a 'double recovery' on the debt."[49] The prohibition against a deficiency judgment contained in section 580d "forces the creditor to assume the risk of receiving an unreasonably low bid at private sale. The realization that he will receive only the amount of the bid—in view of the statutory denial of recourse to a deficiency—provides the creditor with an incentive to insure the fairness of the sale and the economic reality of the purchase price. With the creditor bearing the burden of loss, the principal's position is protected; and his need for redemption right is alleviated."[50]

B. The Nonselling Creditor Under Section 580d.

Unlike the conclusion reached under section 580b by Brown v. Jensen considered earlier in this section (subsection 6–A–1), section 580d does not apply to a sold-out junior. In other words section 580d requires that there have been an actual sale by the mortgagee or trustee under the power, and to exclude situations in which the security is exhausted in some other fashion.[51]

C. Applicability of Section 580d to Obligations Other than "Upon a Note."

Section 580d prohibits only deficiency judgments upon notes.[52] It does not bar other judgments, such as judgments for the foreclosure of other security interests or the

---

48. Roscleaf Corp. v. Chierighino, 1963, 59 Cal.2d 35, 43, 378 P.2d 97, 102, 27 Cal.Rptr. 873, 878. See Hetland, op. cit. supra note 26, at 30.

49. Comment, op. cit. supra note 47, 232. The writer cites Kass v. Weber, 1968, 261 Cal.App.2d 417, 421, 67 Cal.Rptr. 876, 879 as authority that the creditor may obtain a deficiency judgment after a power of sale foreclosure.

50. Comment, op. cit. supra note 47, 233. On the legislative purpose of section 580d see Hetland, op. cit. supra note 26, 28–31: "By enacting section 580d in 1939, the legislature placed the remedies on a substantial par. To do so, it had the choice of affording the same statutory right of redemption after nonjudicial sale that he enjoyed with judicial foreclosure, or of denying the creditor a deficiency judgment following extrajudicial sale. * * * In selecting the latter alternative, in the form of section 380d, the legislature established a balance between the remedies without depriving the creditor of the opportunity to choose a remedy that could result in an immediate nonredeemable title."

51. See Riesenfeld, op. cit. supra note 22, 724; Hetland, op. cit. supra note 26, 31. Hetland states the matter as follows: "It [580d] does not bar a junior creditor * * * who has not himself had the nonjudicial sale which exhausted the security. A redemption statute substitute should bar no one other than a creditor whose lien is foreclosed; certainly it should not impair the remedy of one who himself would have the right to redeem. [Citing in a fn. C.C.P. § 701 and San Jose Water Co. v. Lyndon, 1899, 124 Cal. 518, 57 P. 481]. To have applied 580d to the nonselling junior would have distorted the symmetry of remedy which was the legislative motivation behind the parallel enforcement devices —a legislative purpose recognized in Roseleaf."

In id. p. 31 n. 43, Hetland spells out the reasons why the decision of Brown v. Jensen under 580b, even if correct, would not control a similar situation under 580d.

52. The language of West's Ann.Cal.Code Civ.Proc. § 580d is as follows: "No judgment shall be rendered for any deficiency upon a note secured by a deed of

assertion of rights as against other lien claimants [53] or a judgment for restitution of leased premises in an unlawful detainer action brought upon default of the tenant.[54]

Whether or no the section applies to obligations other than notes has not been definitely settled. It has been suggested that "The strongest possibility, because it most completely carries out the redemption-substitution purpose ascribed to section 580d by *Roseleaf* is that 580d's 'note' is as broad as the 'obligations' and 'debt' of the other sections except in the corporate and public utility context. It is clear, in any event, that there is not reason consistent with 580d's redemption-substitute purpose that would dictate artificially confining the prohibition to the *negotiable* note."[55]

D. Guarantor and Surety.

Whether a surety may invoke the bar against a deficiency judgment where the case is a purchase money transaction falling under C.C.P. § 580b has been previously considered in this section.[56] Although some of the reasoning discussed in the earlier treatment is applicable to the question of a surety's liability where the transaction falls under § 580d the problem is basically different because the legislative purposes of the two sections are not the same.[57]

In the two most recent California Appellate Court decisions the creditors were denied recovery from guarantors of the unpaid balance upon notes following the creditors' nonjudicial sale of the security.[58] The basis of decision in both cases was that the creditors, having destroyed the guarantors' subrogation rights against the principal debtors by electing the remedy of nonjudicial sale of the security, was estopped from recovering from the guarantors the unpaid balance upon the notes. The second of the two cases, expressly relying on the earlier one, stressed the facts that the defendants were "true" guarantors on their continuing guaranties and that there had not been an "explicit waiver" of their rights as is required under the doctrine laid down in the prior case. The result is that there is clear recognition in California that a secured non-purchase money creditor who provides the principal with antideficiency protection by foreclosing nonjudicially has exonerated the surety.

A recent competent student examination of a surety's defense under 580d concludes that a surety should be entitled to antideficiency protection under that section, and not merely afforded a waivable exoneration defense as in the two California Appellate Court decisions.[59] In exploring this thesis the writer, as was pointed out earlier, suggested two

trust or mortgage upon real property hereafter executed in any case in which the real property has been sold by the mortgagee or trustee under power of sale contained in such mortgage or deed of trust."

53. Bank of America Nat. Trust and Sav. Ass'n v. United States, S.D.Cal.1949, 84 F.Supp. 387; Freedland v. Greco, 1955, 45 Cal.2d 462, 289 P.2d 463.

54. See Riesenfeld, op. cit. supra note 22, 724.

55. Hetland, op. cit. supra note 26, 33. Willys of Marin Co. v. Pierce, 1956, 140 Cal.App.2d 826, 296 P.2d 25, had limited the coverage to negotiable notes. Hetland admits that it is arguable that the "note" limitation in 580d "represents legislative reluctance to interfere with the extraordinary and dissimilar, non-note secured transaction," e. g., an oral obligation, an open account, rent, as well as bonds and corporate evidences of debt. Hetland, supra, id.

56. Supra 6–B–3.

57. See note 37, supra.

58. Union Bank v. Gradsky, 1968, 265 Cal.App.2d 40, 71 Cal.Rptr. 64 (hearing denied by California Supreme Court); Union Bank v. Brummell, 1969, —— Cal.App.2d ——, 75 Cal.Rptr. 234.

59. Comment, Exonerating the Surety: Implications of the California Anti-Deficiency Scheme, 1969, 57 Cal.L.Rev. 218. The writer's conclusion: "The statutory purpose of section 580d requires that the surety be encompassed within its protection. Section 580d's equalizing role would be defeated if the creditor could obtain the advantage of nonredeemable private sale and at the same time be able to hold the surety personally for a deficiency. The inequities of the present untenable judicial position respecting additional security should not be extended to sureties. The creditor should be regarded as seeking a deficiency prohibited by section 580d rather than merely exhausting additional security when he attempts to resort to the surety following private sale. A creditor who elects to enforce his lien out of court should thereafter be barred from

possible bases.[60] Some overlapping of the prior and this consideration of the matters is difficult to avoid.

Invocation of the familiar suretyship doctrine that a material alteration of the principal's obligation releases the surety is the first approach dealt with. One of the important rights of a surety is reimbursement from the principal, either by direct action or through subrogation to the creditor's rights against the principal when he pays the obligation of the principal to the creditor. When a creditor chooses to foreclose nonjudicially his action in doing so deprives the surety of his right to reimbursement. In so prejudicing the surety's interests by his choice of remedy the creditor is estopped from recovering from him.[61]

Possible difficulties in applying this exoneration theory were reviewed. If the surety consents to the creditor's prejudicial acts he is not exonerated by them. Both of the decisions concerned with the matter rejected implied consent as adequate to waive the surety's defense and stressed the requirement that it must be "specifically waive[d]." The author of the Comment thought this judicial stance "reflect[ed] approval of the surety's publicly useful function and a desire to encourage its continuation.[62] He went even further, stating that "the courts should require unequivocal proof of the surety's intention to remain bound after loss of his right to reimbursement.[63]

Where § 580b governs the transaction the surety remains liable in spite of the principal's release.[64] This result, however, "should not compel similar liability in the section 580d, non-purchase money content. * * *

seeking the benefits associated with judicial enforcement of a personal judgment." Id. at 239.

60. See text and footnotes supra at notecalls 39–44.

61. See Comment, note 59 supra 220–223.

62. Id. 227.

63. Ibid.

64. See supra, this section 6–B–3.

Osborne Law of Mortgages 2d Ed. HB—46

In section 580b's purchase money context the surety never had any right to reimbursement; the character of the obligation itself precludes the surety from recovering from the principal. Therefore, the purchase money creditor has not prejudiced the surety's position by foreclosing nonjudicially. In contrast, in the section 580d non-purchase money situation, the creditor who chooses private sale has prejudiced the surety's right to reimbursement from the principal. The creditor, by his own action in electing nonjudicial foreclosure, has invoked the section 580d bar, releasing the principal from personal liability."[65]

In California, a doctrine similar to the old English rule enunciated by Lord Eldon in Copis v. Middleton,[66] goes back to Yule v. Bishop.[67] By this doctrine, payment by a surety extinguishes the right of the creditor against the principal so that there is nothing left to which the paying surety may be subrogated. Uniform Commercial Code § 3603 (2) has in one respect an even broader scope. By it "payment or satisfaction may be made with the consent of the holder by any person including any stranger to the instrument." However, the section also provides that "surrender of the instrument to such a person gives him the rights of a transferee." Of course, this latter provision applies only where there is a surrender of the instrument,

65. Comment, note 59, supra, 228.

66. 1 Turn. & Russ. 224.

67. 1901, 133 Cal. 574, 62 P. 68. See note, 1928, 17 Cal.L.Rev. 281. See also Osborne, Cases on Secured Transactions, 62–68.

The doctrine of Yule v. Bishop seems to be settled law in California in spite of holdings or statements to the contrary. See, e. g., the statement in Union Bank v. Gradsky, 1968, 265 Cal.App.2d 40, 71 Cal. Rptr. 64, 68, that the surety's payment of the principal's "debt evidenced by a negotiable note did not extinguish the note nor affect the security." The only authority cited by the court was Sanders v. Magill, 1938, 9 Cal.2d 145, 70 P.2d 159, which did not mention Yule v. Bishop or the later case of Wills v. Woolner, 1913, 21 Cal.App. 528, 132 P. 283. The statement in Gradsky about the security being unaffected is correct as the text and footnotes at notecalls 68 and 69, infra, bring out.

a fact not found in the Gradsky case. But see § 3415(5).

Even under the Copis v. Middleton rule in England any security interest in property held by the creditor continued to be available to the paying surety.[68] And the similar Yule v. Bishop rule in California reaches the same result as to security. It does so by virtue of statutory provisions.[69]

"By the majority view * * * the obligation of the principal to reimburse the surety arises at, and exists from, the time of making the contract of suretyship by which the surety becomes expressly bound to the surety.

"The rule has grown up in California, however, that no liability exists on the part of the principal to reimburse his surety by reason simply of the existence of the contract of suretyship between the surety and creditor; nor does any such liability come into existence until the surety actually makes payment for his principal."[70]

This theory of a separate and independent obligation arising after the extinguishment of the principal obligation, and having no anterior foundation, it has been pointed out, would prevent the section 580d defense being "available to prevent the surety from recovering the amount he has been forced to expend under the suretyship agreement from the principal. Given the result, there is no

need to relieve the surety of liability."[71] The nonjudicial foreclosure by the creditor could have no effect on the right of reimbursement of the surety which had no existence before payment by the surety of the principal's obligation. Nor could it have operative effect to destroy a right of subrogation to the creditor's in personam right against the principal since payment by the surety had extinguished that right.

"When a creditor who possesses a senior lien forecloses nonjudicially, section 580d does not release the principal from liability to the 'sold-out' junior creditor. Therefore, a surety on the junior debt is not barred from seeking reimbursement from the principal and is not exonerated."[72]

The second argument advanced to give the surety protection under § 580d,[73] i. e., that the purpose of the section directly prohibits a deficiency judgment against him after a nonjudicial foreclosure by the creditor, is more difficult to sustain because it is not sup-

---

68. See Osborne, Cases on Secured Transactions, Note, 73. Ibid. 66–72.

69. West's Ann.Cal.Civ.Code, § 2849.

70. Note, 1928, 17 Cal.L.Rev. 281, 282. The same doctrine was accepted in Berrington v. Williams, 1966, 244 Cal.App.2d 130, 52 Cal.Rptr. 772. See Comment supra, 229. In the Gradsky case, note 58, supra, the court said that statements in Berrington that payment by a surety extinguishes the principal obligation must be disregarded. Since both Yule v. Bishop and U.C.C. § 3603(2) are to the contrary (there being present no evidence of a surrender of the instrument to the payer so as to make him a transferee) the Gradsky observation would appear to be incorrect. See also note 67, supra. But see U.C.C. § 3415.5.

71. Comment, note 59, supra, 229. This result has been criticised: Upholding a separate obligation "for reimbursement between the surety and principal subverts the intent of section 580d by preserving the principal's personal liability after nonjudicial sale has defeated his statutory right of redemption. * * * the courts would be permitting the principal to waive, indirectly the protection afforded by section 580d * * *." Ibid. Since the surety's right of reimbursement, on this theory, is nonconsensual, arising by operation of law, it is difficult to argue that the *principal* is waiving his protection. Whether, notwithstanding this conclusion, the same result should be accorded to the non-consensual right of reimbursement is a different matter.

72. Comment, op. cit. supra note 59, 230. See this section 7–B supra.

In Roseleaf Corp. v. Chierighino, 1963, 59 Cal.2d 35, 78 Cal.Rptr. 104, 378 P.2d 35, the senior's nonjudicial foreclosure did not release the principal from liability to the junior. There is no reason, therefore, to give the endorsers antideficiency protection in a suit by sold-out junior lienors. Since the principal is still liable personally, the surety retains his right to reimbursement and has not been prejudiced.

On the related question of whether West's Ann.Cal. Civ.Code, § 726's "one form of action" provision applied to a junior lienholder whose security had been exhausted by a sale under the terms of a senior encumbrance, Comstock v. Fiorella, 1968, 260 Cal. App.2d 261, 67 Cal.Rptr. 104, held that it did not.

73. Comment, op. cit. supra note 59, 231.

ported by clear judicial authority [74] but rests upon (1) theories as to legislative purpose, and (2) differentiating it from judicially permitted "additional security."

As was stated previously,[75] section 580d was intended to equalize the advantages of judicial and nonjudicial foreclosure by prohibiting a deficiency judgment after a nonjudicial sale. Where there is no surety this purpose is substantially accomplished. Where there is a surety the situation is altered. "The curative function of section 580d is defeated by denying antideficiency protection to the surety. The creditor can bid in the property for a low price and recover the balance of the debt from the surety in a personal judgment unrestricted by the property's true value.[76] * * * Permitting such a result destroys the creditor's incentive to insure the fairness of the sale, and to promote maximum liquidation of the debt out of its proceeds. He obtains a double advantage by foreclosing nonjudicially. He can obtain a deficiency from the surety without reference to the property's actual value, and no redemption right exists to encourage a realistic price. This inequitable situation clearly parallels that which existed prior to the time the legislature prescribed the preventive medicine of section 580d in order to remedy the unfair advantage afforded the creditor as a consequence of his nonjudicial foreclosure. * * * The creditor should not be allowed to frustrate the statutory balancing scheme where the surety benefits from its enforcement. The statutory equalization of the creditor's alternatives should be enforced irrespective of who is thereby protected." [77]

Differentiating the surety's obligation to the creditor from "additional security" which the California Supreme Court has held the deficiency prohibition of section 580d does not prevent the creditor from realizing on by foreclosure,[78] presents difficulties. It would, of course, be possible to characterize as additional security anything the creditor is given by the principal in addition to his promise to repay, including a suretyship agreement. "The real issue is whether it would frustrate the objectives of the statute to allow the creditor to recover personal money judgment from the surety. If it would, the courts should regard the surety's obligation as a prohibited deficiency, rather than additional security." [79]

It has been argued that it should be regarded as a deficiency. "The value of an interest in real or other property is uncertain as contrasted with a personal judgment against a solvent surety. A personal judgment against a reputable person or business firm carries with it a moral compulsion that a property interest lacks. * * * Where additional real or personal property security is involved, the creditor does not enjoy the advantages of a personal judgment after private sale. * * * The courts' approach toward real or personal property should not be construed as authority for allowing the creditor to resort to the personal liability represented by a suretyship obligation." [80]

---

74. That the courts have not held that a surety is entitled to the deficiency protection of § 580d is admitted. Id. at 231 n. 81. And the Gradsky case, based upon the creditor's estoppel from resorting to the surety for recovery of a personal judgment by "electing to pursue a [nonjudicial] remedy which destroys both the security and the possibility of the surety's reimbursement from the principal debtor," was denied a hearing by the California Supreme Court. Union Bank v. Gradsky, 1968, 265 Cal.App. 2d 40, 55, 71 Cal.Rptr. 64, 69, hearing denied by California Supreme Court, see Union Bank v. Brummell, 1969, —— Cal.App.2d ——, 75 Cal.Rptr. 234, 235.

75. See this section, 7-A supra, at notecall 48, in discussing the statutory purpose of C.C.P. § 580d.

76. See Comment, op. cit. supra note 59, 233 n. 92 for this statement.

77. Comment, op. cit. supra note 59, 233–234.

78. See text and note at notecall 24 supra; Hatch v. Security-First Nat. Bank, 1942, 19 Cal.2d 254, 260, 120 P.2d 869, 873; Comment, op. cit. supra 59, 235 236–237.

79. Comment, op. cit. supra note 59, 236.

80. Id. 237.

"The most compelling reason why the concept of additional security should not be extended to include a personal money judgment from the surety is that it would subvert the equalizing purpose of section 580d. As the California Supreme Court has implemented the concept of additional security with respect to the principal, the creditor can resort to additional security after nonjudicial sale without first having to comply with section 580a of the California Code of Civil Procedure and obtain a judicial determination of the actual deficit remaining on the debt. This means that no 'fair value' limitation applies to restrict the creditor's recovery after nonjudicial sale. The creditor can continue to exhaust additional security regardless of the actual value of the property sold so long as the proceeds from prior sales do not satisfy the debt. This judicial position clearly weights nonjudicial sale in the creditor's favor and unfairly jeopardizes the principal's interests. A judicial determination that a surety's obligation also constitutes additional security under section 580d would magnify the unfair advantage to the creditor. A creditor with foresight and some acquaintance with the law would demand a surety bond as well as additional property security and thereby insure himself a succession of recoveries. Permitting the creditor this kind of windfall promotes depressed sales prices since it is to his interest to preserve as much of the outstanding debt as possible. The assurance of an ultimate personal judgment encourages the creditor to purchase the property for a deflated price at his own sale, unless someone else overbids him. He then stands to recover a money judgment from the surety which is far in excess of the actual amount remaining due, in terms of the true value of the property he has acquired or disposed of." [81]

81.   Comment, op. cit. supra note 59, 237–238.

8. Applicability of Bar of Section 580b to Transferees of Purchase Money Notes.

Cases have arisen in which it is necessary to decide whether the particular plaintiff is one to whom the limitations on deficiency judgments apply. If they apply to the original mortgagee, usually his transferee will be similarly bound.[82] When the note secured by the mortgage is a negotiable one which does not refer to the mortgage and is negotiated to a holder who takes without knowledge of the security, it would seem that he should be able to enforce the note free of any restriction. However, if he should learn of the mortgage and elect to go against it, the deficiency provisions should apply.[83]

D. POWER OF SALE

HISTORY AND NATURE

337. In spite of earlier doubts as to the validity of powers of sales it became customary to insert them in English mortgages. Today, by statute, there is an implied power of sale in all legal mortgages in the absence of an express provision to the contrary and out-of-court sale by its use is the common method of foreclosure in England.

In the United States powers of sale have been consistently held valid and their use was recog-

82.   E.g., Everts v. Matteson, 1942, 21 Cal.2d 437, 132 P.2d 476.

83.   See 1949, 37 Cal.L.Rev. 690, 693. Cf. §§ 232, 242, supra. See Riesenfeld, California Legislation Curbing Deficiency Judgments, 1960, 48 Cal.L.Rev. 705, 719–720.

There is California authority to the effect that principles of negotiability override the recording acts as those acts relate to mortgages and deeds of trust. Ross v. Title Guarantee & Trust Co., 1934, 136 Cal. App. 393, 29 P.2d 236. See Comments, 1949, 37 Cal.L.Rev. 690, 694; 1934, 22 Cal.L.Rev. 677, 680. See also Currie and Lieberman Purchase Money Mortgages and State Lines: A Study in Conflict-of-Law Method, 1960 Duke L.J. 1 at 15 nn. 51, 19 & 47. And see further § 242 supra. "It is doubtful whether this policy in favor of negotiability will be extended to the clash between the protection accorded a purchaser of real estate and that given to commerce in negotiable instruments. Such a result might appear too conducive to an easy circumvention of the social objectives of section 580b to be palatable to the courts." Riesenfeld, op. cit. supra 720.

nized earlier than in England. At present several states bar their employment by legislation and in only eighteen is foreclosure under them the prevailing practice. Where available it is a cumulative, not an exclusive remedy. Generally, although there is contrary authority, it cannot be employed pending a court action to foreclose.

In England, the mortgagee under a common law mortgage acquired complete legal title upon default by the mortgagor.[84] Because power to dispose of property by sale or otherwise is an incident of ownership,[85] it followed that, so far as the law courts were concerned, a mortgagee could sell and convey a good title to any one immediately after the law day without any provision in the mortgage authorizing him to do so.[86] But after equity created the equity of redemption, if the mortgagee tried to sell free and clear of it [1] without having first foreclosed, equity would stop him by injunction.[2] To enable a mortgagee to sell a title good in both law and equity against any claim of the mortgagor, express powers of sale in broad terms were inserted in the mortgage.[3] In spite of grave early doubts as to their validity,[4] it being the opinion of many that they would fall within the prohibition against fettering the

84. See §§ 5, 302, supra.

85. See Restatement, Property, § 10.

86. See Maitland, Equity, rev. ed., 188, "It has not been *said* that he can sell, but there is no good in saying that an absolute owner can sell; of course he may."

1. In contradistinction to merely selling the debt and security interest.

2. Maitland, supra note 86. And even if he sold after foreclosure, the foreclosure might be reopened to permit redemption from a purchaser. See § 311, supra. Of course, if the mortgagee sold to a bona fide purchaser, a most unlikely event because the deed to the mortgagee would disclose the fact of mortgage, the equity would be cut off.

3. See Maitland, note 86 supra p. 189, for a summary of the provisions in such a power of sale.

4. Croft v. Powell, 1738, 2 Com.Rep. 603; King v. Edington, 1801, 1 East 288.

equity of redemption,[5] they were regarded as valid in the early part of the nineteenth century,[6] and by the middle of the century were customarily included in mortgages.[7] This custom was confirmed by statute, first in 1860,[8] and then in 1881.[9] By the latter act, where the mortgage is by deed, there is an implied power of sale in the absence of express stipulation to the contrary. Today mortgagees generally rely upon the statutory power of sale, and out-of-court sale under a power of sale has all but supplanted an action for foreclosure in England.[10]

5. See Durfee, Cases Mortgages, 263 n., referring to Powell, Mortgages, 1785 ed., p. 12. The question was still considered doubtful in the 4th ed. of Powell in 1799, p. 13 ff. In the 6th ed., Coventry refers to the power of sale as a modern development. 2 Powell, Mortgages, 6th ed. 1828, 961, n. A. See also Corder v. Morgan, 1811, 18 Ves.Jr. 344. See, additionally, § 125, supra.

Although there are statements that the power of sale by a mortgagee existed in the Roman law, Jones, Mortgages, 8th ed., § 2286, citing Ricks v. Goodrich, 3 La.Ann. 212, there is some doubt as to this. Some writers have indicated that sale of security in the Roman system could be only under decretal order of court. 1 Coote, Mortgages, 8th ed., c. II, § ii, p. 8; Bacon's Abridgement, Mortgage [A]. Where the debtor could not be found and notice of the sale could not be given to him a decretal order clearly was necessary. 3 Story, Equity Juris., 14th ed., § 1352. Two notices were necessary, one a notice to pay the debt, and the other, notice of foreclosure sale. Markby, Elements of Law, 6th ed., § 456. Apparently if notice was given, a creditor could, by waiting two years, sell without court order. Mackeldey, Civil Law, § 350, footnote, p. 385.

6. Roberts v. Bozan, in a manuscript opinion by Lord Eldon in February, 1825, cited in Coventry's Prac.Mortgages, p. 150, and Powell, Mortgages, Am. ed., 9a, note, and quoted in Jones, Mortgages, 8th ed., § 2286, and Johnson v. Johnson, 1887, 27 S.C. 309, 3 S.E. 606, 13 Am.St.Rep. 636. See 1 Coote, Mortgages, 1st ed., 1821, p. 128; Turner, The English Mortgage of Land as Security, 1934, 20 Va.L. Rev. 729, 732. And see preceding note.

7. See Stevens v. Theatres, Ltd. [1903] 1 Ch. 857. But the practice was said to be not universal in 1857. See Clark v. Royal Panopticon, 1857, 4 Drew. 26, 30.

8. Lord Cranworth's Act, 1860, 23 & 24 Vict. c. 145.

9. Conveyancy Act, 1881, 44 & 45 Vict., c. 41, § 19(1), replaced by Law of Property Act, 1925, 15 Geo. V, c. 20, §§ 101(1) (i), 103. See Maitland, op. cit. supra note 3.

10. See Turner, An English View of Mortgage Deficiency Judgments, 1935, 21 Va.L.Rev. 601, 604;

In the United States courts have consistently recognized the validity of powers of sale in mortgages in the absence of statutes [11] to the contrary. Apparently they existed and were used at an early date,[12] a statute regulating them being enacted in New York in 1774,[13] long before they were considered good in England. The validity of the power does not depend upon statute, but its exercise has to follow any requirements laid down.[14] Although valid, their use was said to be rare in the early part of the nineteenth century.[15] And the practice did not go uncriticised by more modern decisions.[16]

Today there are a number of states in which the use of power of sale as a method of foreclosure is prevented by statute.[17] And in only eighteen jurisdictions are they generally used, judicial process being preferred.[18] Nor

Turner, The English Mortgage of Land as a Security, 1934, 20 Va.L.Rev. 729; Tefft, The Myth of Strict Foreclosure, 1937, 4 U. of Chi.L.Rev. 575, 580; Maitland, Equity, rev. ed., 191. See also §§ 10, 12, supra. As to the fiduciary character of the mortgagee under the English statute, see 1944, 31 Va.L.Rev. 215.

11. Professor Durfee could find only one state in which the power of sale is judicially nullified, Nebraska. See Durfee, Cases Mortgages, 355, n. 23, citing Cullen v. Casey, 1901, 1 Neb. 344, 95 N.W. 605; Kirkendall v. Weatherley, 1906, 77 Neb. 421, 109 N.W. 757, 9 L.R.A.,N.S., 515.

12. See Slee v. President, etc. Manhattan Co., N.Y. 1828, 1 Paige 48, "these powers and the sales under them, are as ancient as the formation of the English government in this state."

13. See Mowry v. Sanborn, 1877, 68 N.Y. 153, for early New York legislation; Wilson v. Troup, N.Y. 1823, 2 Cow. 195, 14 Am.Dec. 458. The use of the power of sale had arisen out of real or fancied incompetence of the colonial chancery court in that state. See Carey, et al., Studies in Foreclosure, 1933, 27 Ill.L.Rev. 595, 616.

14. Butterfield v. Farnham, 1872, 19 Minn. 85, Gil. 542; Webb v. Haeffer, 1879, 53 Md. 187; Very v. Russell, 1874, 65 N.H. 646, 23 A. 522; Slee v. Manhattan Co., supra n. 12; Mowry v. Sanborn, supra n. 13; Bell Silver & Copper Mining Co. v. First Nat. Bank, 1895, 156 U.S. 470, 15 S.Ct. 440, 39 L.Ed. 497; Blackshear v. First Nat. Bank of Dothan, C. C.A.Ala.1919, 261 F. 601. See Johnson v. Johnson, 1887, 27 S.C. 309, 3 S.E. 606, 13 Am.St.Rep. 636; Fogarty v. Sawyer, 1861, 17 Cal. 589; Bloom v. Van Rensselaer, 1854, 15 Ill. 503; In Michigan the power of sale, contrary to the general view, depends for its validity upon statute. Pierce v. Grimley, 1889, 77 Mich. 273, 43 N.W. 932. In California, because most of the code provisions dealing with powers in connection with real property were repealed, doubt has existed as to their status. However the doubt did not extend to power of sale in a mortgage because Cal.Civ.Code, § 3932, recognizing it, was left untouched.

A power to sell mortgaged lands for default in payment of the secured debt must be expressly given. See Gunn v. Brantley, 1852, 21 Ala. 633; Goodenow v. Ewer, 1860, 16 Cal. 461, 468, 76 Am.Dec. 540.

It is otherwise, however, in the case of a chattel mortgage. See Hart v. Ten Eyck, N.Y.1816, 2 Johns.Ch. 62; Bryant v. Carson River Lumber Co., 1867, 3 Nev. 313, 93 Am.Dec. 403; Freeman v. Freeman, 1864, 17 N.J.Eq. 44. Cf. Ex parte Official Receiver, 1886, L.R. 18 Q.B. 222.

15. Eaton v. Whiting, 1826, 20 Mass. (3 Pick.) 484.

16. E. g., Johnson v. Johnson, 1887, 27 S.C. 309, 313, 3 S.E. 606, 13 Am.St.Rep. 636.

17. E. g., Iowa Code Ann.1950, § 654.1, "No deed of trust or mortgage of real estate shall be foreclosed in any other manner than by action in court by equitable proceedings."; Todd v. Johnson, 1878, 51 Iowa 192, 1 N.W. 498. Other states have similar legislation: Ariz.Rev.Stat.Ann.1956, § 33–721. This section also provides that a trustee under a deed of trust may foreclose by sale in accordance with the term of the trust; Davis v. First Nat. Bank of Oakland, 1924, 26 Ariz. 621, 229 P. 391; Ill.Ann.Stat., Smith-Hurd 1950, c. 95, § 23; De Voigne v. Chicago Title & Trust Co., 1922, 304 Ill. 177, 136 N.E. 498; see Carey, et al. op. cit. supra, n. 13, at pp. 618–619; Kan.Stat.Ann.1964, § 58–2313; Okl.Stat.Ann.1960, § 686; Or.Code Ann.1930, § 6–501; Marquarm v. Ross, 1905, 47 Or. 374, 78 P. 698. Cf. S.C.Code Ann.1962, § 45–83.

"It is true that in the instrument it is provided that 'this instrument shall not be construed as a mere mortgage,' and that the grantors by the instrument constitute Fiske their attorney in fact 'to make sale of said premises and deed of conveyance of the same, vesting an indefeasible title in the purchaser thereto'; but this language cannot control the whole instrument. The decisive facts * * * are that the instrument was intended to convey the land as security for the payment of certain debts, and * * * under the rule in this state is a mortgage and must be foreclosed as one." Fiske v. Mayhew, 1911, 90 Neb. 196, 199, et seq., 133 N.W. 195, Ann.Cas.1913A, 1043.

For a discussion of the reasons advanced for such prohibition, see Carey, et al., op. cit. supra, p. 617ff.

Durfee, Cases on Security, 177 lists seventeen jurisdictions in which the power of sale foreclosure is "usual." His enumeration is taken from the 1922 Handbook of the Com'rs on Uniform State Laws. From the same source he lists twenty-six states in which the "usual" method is judicial action.

18. See Bridewell, The Effects of Defective Mortgage Laws on Home Financing, 1938, 5 Law & Contemp.Probs. 545, 547, 555; Reeve, The New Propos-

did a carefully drafted Model Power of Sale Act meet with legislative acceptance although it was available for many years.[19] Possibly the chief reason for the failure to gain greater acceptance by a method of foreclosure which is admittedly speedier, simpler, and less expensive [20] is the belief that it fails to provide as solidly marketable title as does a judicial process.[21]

al for a Uniform Mortgage Act, 1938, 5 Law & Contemp.Probs., 564, 572.

For an excellent analysis of the nature of a power of sale in a mortgage (agency or power coupled with an interest) see Durfee, Cases on Security, 1951, 253. For other aspects of the power of sale (history, number of states where it is usual, 17, or permissible, most) see idem. 23, 173, 248–278.

19. 1940 Handbook, Commissioners on Uniform State Laws, 254 (prefatory statement), 256. See Skilton, Proposed Uniform Legislation, 1942, 9 Am.Law School Rev. 1128; Reeve, n. 18, supra. See notes, 1938, 86 U. of Pa.L.Rev. 517; 1941, 27 Va.L.Rev. 926. A Uniform Mortgage Act containing provisions for power of sale foreclosure was originally proposed in 1927 and finally withdrawn in 1943 without having been enacted in any state other than the one whose legislation served as its model. See 1925 Handbook, Commissioners on Uniform State Laws, 303; 1927, ibid., 656; 1944, ibid., 389. See § 345, infra.

20. See Carey, Brabner-Smith, & Sullivan, Studies in Foreclosure in Cook County: Foreclosure Methods and Redemption, 1933, 27 Ill.L.Rev. 594, 616 for a general discussion of power of sale foreclosures. See, also, MacChesney and Leesman, Mortgages, Foreclosures and Reorganizations, 1936, 31 Ill.L.Rev. 287, 296; Sprague, History of Chancery and Advertisement Foreclosure in Michigan, 1934, 5 Detroit L.Rev. 63; Traynor, Real Estate Mortgage Foreclosures in North Dakota, 1930, 3 Dak. L.Rev. 25; Lauder, Power of Sale in Mortgages, 1940, 5 J.Marshall L.Q. 406; notes, 1930, 5 Ind.L.J. 293; 1939, 4 Mo.L.Rev. 186, Missouri law. See also references in note 19, supra; § 345, infra.

21. See, e. g., the experience in Wisconsin, where it is seldom used although available. 1949 Wis.L.Rev. 341. Cf. § 318, supra. But see Skilton, Government and the Mortgage Debtor, 17, 18. See also Carey, et al., supra, note 17. According to the Handbook of the Commissioners on Uniform State Laws, 1927, 656–657, of the states using judicial foreclosure, sixteen do so because there is no proper statute for power of sale foreclosure. See Cormack & Irsfeld, Mortgages and Trust Deeds in California, 1938, 26 Cal.L.Rev. 206, 219; Kidd, Trust Deeds and Mortgages in California, 1915, 3 Cal.L.Rev. 381, 388, as why foreclosure under powers of sale in mortgages have not been used in California. See also § 338, infra as to the California usage.

Where the power of sale is in use it is a cumulative, not an exclusive, remedy.[22] Cases generally hold that bringing an action in court prevents the exercise, during the pendency of the action, of sale out of court under the power.[23] However, there is authority that a mortgagee may exercise his power of sale notwithstanding the pendency of a suit to foreclose the same mortgage.[24] After selling under the power in these circumstances, it is also held that the mortgagee may obtain a deficiency decree in the foreclosure action.[25]

NATURE OF MORTGAGEE'S POWER OF SALE

338. **Powers of sale in mortgages are sui generis and should not be governed either by rules of agency or powers of appointment. Hence they are not ended by the death or insanity of the mortgagor and may be exercised by anyone entitled to enforce the security.**

22. See Cormerais v. Genella, 1863, 22 Cal. 116, 123; Harlow Realty Co. v. Cotter, 1933, 284 Mass. 68, 187 N.E. 118; McDonald v. Vinson, 1879, 56 Miss. 497. The same is true of a trust deed mortgage where the power to foreclose by court action exists. Flack v. Boland, 1938, 11 Cal.2d 103, 77 P.2d 1090, discussed in 1938, 27 Cal.L.Rev. 66; 1939, 12 So. Cal.L.Rev. 485; Carpenter v. Title Ins. & Trust Co., 1945, 71 Cal.App.2d 593, 163 P.2d 73. Giving notice of sale under a trust deed mortgage does not prevent a later court action to foreclose. Carpenter v. Title Ins. & Trust Co., supra. See West's Ann.Cal. Code Civ.Proc., § 725a. Cf., § 339, infra.

23. See 1937, 107 A.L.R. 721.

24. Commercial Centre Realty Co. v. Superior Court, 1936, 7 Cal.2d 121, 59 P.2d 978, 107 A.L.R. 714. See Harlow Realty Co. v. Cotter, 1933, 284 Mass. 68, 187 N.E. 118. Cf., Stevens v. Theatres, Ltd., [1903] 1 Ch. 857, power may be exercised by leave of court after bringing of action but before, although not after, decree *nisi* for foreclosure. See 1943, 31 Cal. L.Rev. 429, 432; 1937, 25 Cal.L.Rev. 469, 477. Cf. as to trust deed mortgage, California cases, note 22, supra. See § 339, infra.

25. Commercial Centre Realty Co. v. Superior Court, supra note 24. In the principal case the notes and mortgages were executed before the enactment of legislation limiting or denying a deficiency judgment after sale out of court under a power of sale in a mortgage or trust deed mortgage. West's Ann.Cal.Code Civ.Proc., §§ 580a, 580d. Presumably those sections would apply to a demand for a deficiency under the above practice as to mortgages executed after their effective dates.

The nature of a power of sale in a mortgage has come in for attention in two different connections: (1) whether it is ended by the death or insanity of the mortgagor; (2) whether it can be exercised by an assignee of the mortgage. One approach to the first problem is to treat a mortgagee's power of sale as governed by the principles applicable to powers conferred upon an agent. This view makes survival of the power upon death or insanity of the mortgagor depend upon whether it satisfies the murky test of "power coupled with an interest." [26] At the opposite extreme, they are likened to powers of appointment creating springing future interests or powers of sale or appointment given to a trustee by will.[27] Criticism of the agency theory by an exponent of this second view is sound.[28] However, it also is open to objection as being too narrow and resting upon the wrong foundation. The power conferred upon an agent and the power to appoint real property are merely specialized instances of the use of one of the fundamental conceptions of the law.[29] When employed in certain types of transactions, definite bodies of rules, principles and standards developed which governed its exercise in that particular field. Familiar instances of this are to be found in the law of agency regulating the powers given to an agent and quite different from it, the technical law of powers of appointment of real property. A power of sale given to a mortgagee is separate and distinct in its purpose and use from either of these examples. It is *sui generis* and should be so treated rather than assimilated into a category whose rules were formulated for other ends.[30] It is given to the mortgagee as an integral part of his security and should no more be lost to a mortgagee by reason of the death or insanity of the mortgagor than any other incident of it which is necessary to its realization. The better authorities reach this conclusion although the opinions tend to include some talk of "coupled with an interest" which is, on this analysis, irrelevant.[31]

The same ideas have appeared in assignment cases, although here there are, in title states, some technical problems not met in the preceding problem. In England, unless the contractual power of sale specifically said that it could be exercised by assigns it was held to be personal to the mortgagee.[32]

---

26. Johnson v. Johnson, 1887, 27 S.C. 309, 3 S.E. 606, 13 Am.St.Rep. 636; Wilkins v. McGehee, 1891, 86 Ga. 764, 13 S.E. 84. Cf., Baggett v. Edwards, 1906, 126 Ga. 463, 55 S.E. 250, not revoked when mortgagee is given legal title. See 1928, 56 A.L.R. 224.

27. See Walsh, Mortgages, § 81.

28. "Powers of sale and powers of appointment do not depend on any agency relation. When such powers are created by will they cannot come into existence until after the death of the donor of the power, and no court has suggested any agency relation in such cases. They are future executory gifts to a person or group of persons to be ascertained when the donee appoints the persons who are to take or sells the property in changing investments or otherwise under a power of sale, and it is quite immaterial whether he have title as trustee, mortgagee or life tenant, or be an entire stranger to the title otherwise than as donee of the power. When he exercises the power the person or persons and the event on which the future estate is to vest are determined and the estate then vests, not by conveyance from the donee but under the deed or will of the original donor of the power. The application of these elementary principles to powers of sale in mortgages eliminates all difficulty." Walsh, Mortgages, 343.

See also Durfee, op. cit. supra, § 337 note 18.

29. See Hohfeld, Fundamental Legal Conceptions, 1919, 50; idem, foreword by Cook, 7. "A power * * * is an ability on the part of a person to produce a change in a given legal relation by doing or not doing a given act." Restatement of Property, § 3.

30. For a similar instance of courts attempting to force a mortgage relation which is sui generis into the mold of another legal category see the effort to treat a mortgagor left in possession in a title state as some sort of tenant of the mortgagee. See §§ 5, 125, supra.

31. Grandin v. Emmons, 1901, 10 N.D. 223, 86 N.W. 723, 54 L.R.A. 610, 88 Am.St.Rep. 684; Reilly v. Phillips, 1894, 4 S.D. 604, 57 N.W. 780. See also 1907, 4 Ann.Cas. 58; 1906, 70 L.R.A. 135; 1928, 56 A.L.R. 224. Cf., Harlow Realty Co. v. Cotter, 1933, 284 Mass. 68, 187 N.E. 118.

32. In re Rumney and Smith, 1897, 2 Ch. 351. See 2 Coote, Mortgages, 9th ed., 911.

However, the statutory power of sale in all legal mortgages is made part of the security itself and may be exercised by any one entitled to the mortgage.[33] There is some American authority in accord with the English rule as to non-statutory powers.[34] The majority American rule, however, is that the assignee may exercise the power without reference to whether the power is given in terms to assigns.[35] In several states statutes provide that the power of sale may be exercised by any person, who, by assignment or otherwise, becomes entitled to the money secured.[36]

Even though an assignee may exercise the power of sale in a mortgage, a few additional problems arise. If the mortgagee transfers only the debt in a state where legal title would still remain in the mortgagee after the transfer it has been held that the transferee cannot exercise the power of sale. To do so he must have the legal estate in the proper-

ty.[37] However, after assigning either the debt or the mortgage, a mortgagee cannot thereafter exercise a power of sale contained in the mortgage.[38] Where the mortgage debt is assigned as collateral security for a loan to the mortgagee, it is held that the assignee, because of conflicting equities cannot exercise the power of sale.[39]

TRUST DEED MORTGAGES

339. The trust deed mortgage, used in a good many states, is normally enforced by out of court sale. In general foreclosure by court action is available only on a showing of special circumstances. The trustee is a fiduciary as to both debtor and creditor and hence is subject to various rules and court control applicable to trust fiduciaries generally. There is divergence of opinion as to whether title passes to the purchaser on foreclosure sale because legal title is in the trustee or by virtue of a power of sale vested in him. A distinction between trust deed and ordinary form mortgages in lien jurisdictions, frequently stated as fundamental, that the former confers legal title and the latter a lien only, is either non-existent or without important significance.

In a good many states the trust deed mortgage, in which the borrower conveys to a third party to hold in trust for the holder of the note,[40] or series of notes, is used either

33. Law of Property Act, 1925, 15 Geo. V. c. 20, § 205(1) (XVI), providing that it may be exercised by "any person from time to time deriving title under the original mortgagee." See 2 Coote, Mortgages, 9th ed., 913.

34. E. g., Dolbear v. Norduft, 1884, 84 Mo. 619.

35. Maslin v. Marshall, 1902, 94 Md. 480, 51 A. 85; Ramsey v. Sibert, 1915, 192 Ala. 176, 68 So. 349; Holmes v. Turner's Falls Co., 1890, 150 Mass. 535, 23 N.E. 305, 6 L.R.A. 283.

36. N.Y. Real Prop.Law, sec. 146; Mich.Comp.Laws Ann.1967, § 556.60, repealed and nothing comparable has been reenacted; Wis.Stat.Ann.1957, § 232.56; Ala.Code, 1958, tit. 47, § 164.

"Where a power to sell real property is given to a mortgagee, or other incumbrancer, by an instrument intended to secure the payment of money, the power is to be deemed a part of the security, and vests in any person who, by assignment, becomes entitled to the money so secured to be paid, and may be exercised whenever the assignment is duly acknowledged and recorded." West's Ann.Cal.Civ. Code § 858.

"The reason for this requirement [i. e., recordation] is to make certain that after foreclosure there will be a clear record title. These reasons are lacking in the case of a trust deed [mortgage] since no lien passes to the creditor to be assigned by him, and legal title remains at all time in the trustee." Cormack and Irsfeld, Jr., Applications of the Distinctions Between Mortgages and Trust Deeds in California, 1938, 26 Cal.L.Rev. 206, 210.

37. Dameron v. Eskridge, 1889, 104 N.C. 621, 10 S.E. 700; Hussey v. Hill, 1897, 120 N.C. 312, 26 S.E. 919, 58 Am.St.Rep. 789.

38. Hamilton v. Lubukee, 1869, 51 Ill. 415, 99 Am. Dec. 562; Cushing v. Ayer, 1845, 25 Me. 383; Cutler v. Clementson, C.C.Minn.1895, 67 F. 409.

39. Olcott v. Crittenden, 1888, 68 Mich. 230, 36 N.W. 41. Contra: Holmes v. Turner's Falls Lumber Co., 1890, 150 Mass. 535, 23 N.E. 305, 6 L.R.A. 283.

40. Martin v. Alter, 1884, 42 Ohio St. 94; cf., Spruill v. Ballard, 1932, 61 App.D.C. 112, 58 F.2d 517. The creditor himself, rather than a third party, may be the trustee in some jurisdictions. California Trust Co. v. Smead, 1935, 6 Cal.App.2d 432, 44 P.2d 624; Bank of America Nat. Trust & Savings Ass'n v. Century Land & Water Co., 1937, 19 Cal.App.2d 194, 65 P.2d 109. The fact that the security interest in the property is vested in a trustee and remains in him at all times, except as it may be transferred to a substituted trustee, has an effect upon assignments of the mortgage debt. In a jurisdiction requiring recordation of an assignment of a mortgage before the assignee may exercise a power of sale in

as the prevailing form of security or to some extent.[41] In twenty-five of the states in which they are available enforcement statutes make specific mention of trust deed mortgages.[42] The variety of provision in this connection, as well as the diversity of opinion in court decisions, underscores the fact that the nature and incidents of a trust deed mortgage is essentially local in character. Only after a careful examination of the statutes and decisions in each jurisdiction can an accurate statement be made as to them.[43]

Nevertheless, a few features peculiar to a trust deed mortgage may be mentioned. The normal method of foreclosure under a trust deed mortgage is by the trustee selling the property as is both his power and duty to do under the terms of the trust. Foreclosure by suit in equity is not usually available to either the trustee or note holder in the absence of some special reason for asking it. The idea is that a trustee for this purpose, as for others, should and does carry out the terms of the trust without going to court for either authority or directions.[44] There

---

the mortgage, in the case of a trust deed mortgage, "an assignee of the creditor can order the trustee to sell the property without having had his assignment recorded [citing Stockwell v. Barnum, 1908, 7 Cal.App. 413, 94 P. 400]. Under deed of trust [mortgage] the creditor's assignee cannot himself sell the property, because his assignor did not have a power of sale to transfer [it being vested in the trustee]. Cormack v. Irsfeld, Jr., Applications of the Distinctions Between Mortgages and Trust Deeds in California, 1938, 26 Cal.L.Rev. 206, 210.

41. See § 17 supra. For a valuable note on the characteristics of a trust deed mortgage and of the states in which it is available as a security device, see Hanna, Cas. Security, 2d ed., 612–614. In seventeen jurisdictions it is used little or not at all. They are Connecticut, Florida, Hawaii, Kansas, Louisiana, Maine, Massachusetts, Michigan, Minnesota, Nevada, New Jersey, Ohio, Oregon, Rhode Island, Utah, Vermont and Washington. Ibid. In ten states it is the preferred form and in some of them its use is almost universal. The ten are California, Colorado (public trustee provided for by statute, Colo.Rev.Stat.1963, § 118–3–1), District of Columbia, Delaware (for large corporate mortgages of entire assets), Mississippi, Missouri, Tennessee, Texas, Virginia and West Virginia. Ibid. See also Spruill v. Ballard, 1932, 61 App.D.C. 112, 58 F.2d 517, "nearly universal method in effect in the District of Columbia"; Va.Code 1950, §§ 55–58 to –66; W.Va.Code Ann.1966, §§ 38–1–2 to –8, providing for statutory forms of trust deeds and provisions as to sale by trustee on default. Mortgages and trust deeds are used without discrimination in the twenty-two remaining jurisdictions. Hanna, supra, 614.

For the Procedure in a foreclosure by statutory public trustee sale, see Morris, Foreclosure by Sale by Public Trustee of Deeds of Trust in Colorado, 1951, 28 Dicta 437; Storke and Sears, Enforcement of Security Interests in Colorado, 1952, 25 Rocky Mt. L.Rev. 1, 20–25.

42. See Hanna, note 41, supra, 614, with a list of citations to statutes.

43. E. g., contrast the result in the California case of Koch v. Briggs, note 44, infra, with the Idaho case of Brown v. Bryan, note 44, infra, both states having much the same legislation.

For a review of California mortgages and trust deeds, see Note, Comparison of California Mortgages, Trust Deeds and Land Sale Contracts, 1960, 7 U.C. L.A.L.Rev. 83–102.

44. There is old English authority for the proposition as well as modern American cases. Benham v. Newcomb, 1684, 1 Vern. 232; see Turner, Mortgage Deficiency Judgments, 1935, 21 Va.L.Rev. 601, 605.

"It is only when the aid of a court of equity is necessary that it ought to be applied for; and it is only in such a case that its aid will be extended. If there are no real impediments in the way of a fair execution of the trust, then its aid is not necessary, and the costs of a lawsuit ought not to be added to the ordinary cost of executing the trust." George v. Zinn, 1905, 57 W.Va. 15, 22, 49 S.E. 904, 110 Am. St.Rep. 721, contra. See also Clark v. Jones, 1894, 93 Tenn. 639, 27 S.W. 1009, 42 Am.St.Rep. 931; Taylor v. Stearns, 1868, 59 Va. (18 Grat.) 244.

In California, before the enactment in 1933 of Code Civ.Proc. § 725a expressly permitting foreclosure of a trust deed mortgage by regular foreclosure action, it was doubtful whether there existed any method of enforcing the security in such a mortgage other than by sale under the trustee's power. See Koch v. Briggs, 1859, 14 Cal. 256, 263, 73 Am.Dec. 651; Kidd, Trust Deeds and Mortgages in California, 1915, 3 Cal.L.Rev. 381, 389; notes, 1924, 12 Cal.L. Rev. 307 n. 4; 1932, 5 So.Cal.L.Rev. 227, 232; 1934, 8 So.Cal.L.Rev. 35; 1935, 9 So.Cal.L.Rev. 65; 1939, 12 So.Cal.L.Rev. 485; 1933, 21 Cal.L.Rev. 471; 1934, 22 Cal.L.Rev. 170, 184; 1940, 27 Cal.L.Rev. 66; Cormack and Irsfeld Jr., Applications of the Distinction Between Mortgages and Trust Deeds in California, 1938, 26 Cal.L.Rev. 206, 217. But cf., Brown v. Bryan, 1898, 6 Idaho 1, 51 P. 995, in which the Idaho court, although that state has adopted much of California's statute law, held that a trust deed mortgage was in substance a mortgage which must be foreclosed as such. Cf. also Bank of Italy v. Bentley, 1933, 217 Cal. 644, 20 P.2d 940, decided before the adoption of § 725a, supra.

For an older, general discussion of powers of sale in trust deed mortgages, see J. F. D., Sales and Titles Under Deeds of Trust, 1863, 2 Am.L.Reg.,N.S., 641, 705.

is, however, authority to the contrary, i. e., that no special ground for resorting to chancery for sale is necessary.[45] Further, an action in equity to foreclose a trust mortgage may be brought not only for the purpose of effectuating a proper exercise of the power of sale but in order to take an accounting to determine the amount due or to discover whether in fact there had been a default.[46] Another instance of exercise of the same sort of jurisdiction is when there are junior liens and it is desirable to decide the relative priorities.[47] When the trustee in cases like these invokes the jurisdiction of a court of equity, the court may properly order the resulting sale to be made by an officer of the court according to the usual foreclosure practice, instead of by the trustee.[48]

The death of the mortgagor under a trust deed mortgage does not revoke the power of sale in the trustee under the trust deed. But it has been held that a sale by the trustee after the death of the mortgagor and before an administrator has been appointed is voidable by the administrator. Pearce v. Stokes, 1956, 155 Tex. 564, 291 S.W.2d 309, noted in 1956, 35 Texas L.Rev. 151.

45. McDonald v. Vinson, 1879, 56 Miss. 497; Dupee v. Rose, 1894, 10 Utah, 305, 37 P. 567. See 1935, 98 A.L.R. 1132. Today in California, by reason of Cal.Code Civ.Proc. § 725a, a trust deed mortgage may be foreclosed by court action in the same way as an ordinary form mortgage. And cf., Bank of Italy v. Bentley, note 44, supra; Brown v. Bryan, note 44, supra.

46. " * * * There can be no doubt but that it is improper in a trustee to make a sale under a deed of trust, * * * so long as it remains uncertain what amount is due on account of said debt. And if it be uncertain what is the amount of the debt due, or what is the amount of the credits properly applicable thereto, but not so applied, it is the duty of the trustee, before making the sale, to ascertain the amount to be raised by the sale, and to bring a suit in chancery to procure a settlement * * * if necessary." Hogan v. Duke, Va.1871, 20 Grat. 244, 253.

47. Cleveland Trust Co. v. Capitol Theaters Co., 1936, 117 W.Va. 1, 183 S.E. 457, 103 A.L.R. 1435, noted 1937, 42 W.Va.L.Q.Rev. 250; Hudson v. Barham, 1903, 101 Va. 63, 43 S.E. 189, 99 Am.St.Rep. 849.

48. Battle v. Crystal Ice Co., 1940, 122 W.Va. 723, 12 S.E.2d 507; Morrissey v. Dean, 1897, 97 Wis. 302, 72 N.W. 873.

The trustee is a fiduciary as to both the creditor and the debtor.[49] Hence, if the trustee has an interest in the mortgage loan or in the mortgaged land he may not exercise the power of sale; foreclosure by suit in equity is the proper method.[50] The power of sale given to the trustee under a trust deed mortgage is personal to him and cannot be transferred or delegated except as to matters of detail.[51] In case of a trustee's disqualification, refusal to act, or death, a court of equity may appoint a new one if the trust deed itself does not make provision for such an event.[52] And, of course, a court of equity may remove a trustee under a trust deed mortgage for cause and appoint a successor.[53]

The trustee's sale transfers to a purchaser all the title that the mortgagor had at the time he executed the trust deed as security. There has been some divergence of opinion, however, as to whether that title comes to him by reason of a transfer to him by the

49. White v. Macqueen, 1935, 360 Ill. 236, 195 N.E. 832, 98 A.L.R. 1115. See Spruill v. Ballard, 1932, 61 App.D.C. 112, 58 F.2d 517.

50. Spruill v. Ballard, n. 47, supra; Morgan v. Glendy, 1895, 92 Va. 86, 22 S.E. 854; Spencer v. Lee, 1881, 19 W.Va. 179.

51. Greenfield v. Stout, 1905, 122 Ga. 303, 50 S.E. 111; Polliham v. Reveley, 1904, 181 Mo. 622, 81 S. W. 182; Fuller v. O'Neil, 1887, 69 Tex. 349, 6 S.W. 181, 5 Am.St.Rep. 59; Graham v. King, 1872, 50 Mo. 22, 11 Am.Rep. 401; Fuller v. O'Neil, 1887, 69 Tex. 349, 6 S.W. 181, 5 Am.St.Rep. 59. A creditor who has been given power to appoint a substitute trustee has been permitted to delegate the power. San Antonio Joint Stock Land Bank v. Taylor, 1937, 129 Tex. 335, 105 S.W.2d 650, noted 1938, 51 Harv.L.Rev. 360. But see Randolph v. Citizens Nat. Bank, Tex.Civ.App.1940, 141 S.W.2d 1030. See West's Ann.Cal.Civ.Code § 2924a, permitting the attorney for a trustee to conduct the sale and act as auctioneer. Statutory authority for substitution of trustees by concurrence of the beneficiaries may be given. See West's Ann.Cal.Civ.Code § 2934a.

52. See 1935, 98 A.L.R. 1132. Cf. Morrissey v. Dean, 1897, 97 Wis. 302, 72 N.W. 873, statute authorizes sheriff to act in such a case.

53. Caldwell v. Hill, 1934, 179 Ga. 417, 176 S.E. 381, 98 A.L.R. 1124; Flynn v. Brooks, 1939, 70 App.D.C. 243, 105 F.2d 766; Lunsford v. Davis, 1923, 300 Mo. 508, 254 S.W. 878. See 1935, 98 A.L.R. 1132.

trustee of legal title vested in him by the deed of trust, the sale operating to cut off the equitable beneficial interest left in the mortgagor; [54] or whether it comes from the mortgagor through the exercise of the power conferred upon the trustee.[55] The nature of the interest in the property under a trust deed given as security in a lien state bobs up in this connection. Many statements are made to the effect that one of the fundamental differences between trust deed and straight form mortgages in lien states is that the former confers legal title whereas the latter leaves the legal title in the mortgagor and gives the mortgagee only a lien.[56] The truth is that, for almost all purposes, the so-called fundamental distinction has no significance whatsoever.[57] And, for the purpose in hand,

the title acquired by the purchaser on trustee's sale could rest on either conception indifferently.[58] As an eminent scholar stated, "a court which holds that no legal title passes to the mortgagee will generally hold that no title passes when the conveyance is made to trustees." [59] If language having no necessary relation to the decision in cases is disregarded, the observation accurately sums up the authorities as a whole.

CONDUCT OF SALE

340. **The conduct of a sale under a power is determined by the provisions in the instrument creating it and the statutory regulations governing its exercise which have been enacted in many jurisdictions. In England the sale may be private. In the United States it is almost invariably by public auction preceded by notice, usually by advertisement although other methods are found, commonly specifying time, place, description of the property, and other terms of the sale. The sale must be conducted fairly so as to produce as good a price as such sales may. There is some disagreement whether sales may be by parcels in the absence of stipulation in the mortgage or statutory authority for it. Courts, impressed by the danger of oppression and unfairness to the mortgagor by the summary nature of the process, scrutinize every step and require strict adherence to all requirements in the exercise of the power.**

In England sale by a mortgagee under a power in the mortgage may be conducted privately, the mortgagor being thought to be sufficiently protected by the requirement that the sale must be "bona fide to a stranger and at a reasonable price." [60] In the United

---

54. Early Virginia cases reasoned along this line. E. g. Taylor v. King, 1819, 20 Va. (6 Munf.) 358, 8 Am.Dec. 746. Cf. Ruffners v. Lewis' Ex'rs, Va. 1836, 34 Va. (7 Leigh.) 720, 30 Am.Dec. 513.

Brown v. Busch, 1957, 152 Cal.App.2d 200, 313 P.2d 19, states that a trustee under a trust deed mortgage sells the title received by him and owes no duty to guarantee the title or to assure anyone that it is good and marketable, but must sell such title on proper demand, even if it is defective.

55. See Lile, Lien Theory of Mortgage or Deed of Trust, 1922, 8 Va.L.Rev. 224.

56. See § 127, note-call and note 46, supra.

57. For example, of the differences between a trust deed mortgage and straight mortgage in California listed in an excellent article by Cormack and Irsfeld, Jr., in 1938, 26 Cal.L.Rev. 206, only one has any dependence upon whether the trustee holds title or a lien. That one is the different procedures required to effect formal discharge. Another one, that a mortgagee may create a trust of the mortgage by parol whereas a trustee under a trust deed mortgage must do so by writing since he has title seems clearly fallacious. In either case the debt is the principal thing and the security interest in the property only an incident. And there is no prohibition upon declaring an oral trust of a debt. See Kidd, Trust Deeds and Mortgages in California, 1915, 3 Cal.L.Rev. 381, 399. And see the expressions in California cases, § 127, note 46, supra. But to the contrary is the reasoning in Tapia v. Demartini, 1888, 77 Cal. 383, 19 P. 641, 11 Am.St.Rep. 288. And see Cormack v. Irsfeld, Jr., supra, at 210.

For a survey of the similarities and differences between mortgages and trust deed mortgages, see Note, 1960, 7 U.C.L.A.L.Rev. 83, cited in note 43 supra.

58. E. g., some later Virginia cases, although the language of the decision was to the effect that the creditor got no title under a trust deed mortgage, did no more than hold that the purchaser acquired title, a result the earlier authority had rationalized as flowing from title in the trustee. See Runkle v. Runkle, 1900, 98 Va. 663, 37 S.E. 279; Augusta Nat. Bank v. Beard, 1902, 100 Va. 687, 694, 42 S.E. 694; Swann v. Young, 1892, 36 W.Va. 57, 14 S.E. 426. Cf. note 54, supra, for the early Virginia view.

59. Kidd, Trust Deeds and Mortgages in California, 1915, 3 Cal.L.Rev. 381.

60. Turner, English View of Mortgage Deficiency Judgment, 1935, 21 Va.L.Rev. 601, 603. The sale

States, either because statutes so provide or the stipulation in the mortgage is to that effect, sale is almost always at public auction.[61] These sales are generally controlled by statute, the scope and particularity of which varies from jurisdiction to jurisdiction.[62] These statutes are merely regulatory. In their absence the terms of the security instrument is the sole source of the authority; and those provisions prescribe the manner of its execution. However, regardless of whether it is a statute or the language of the mortgage itself that is looked to, the attitude of courts toward these powers has strongly influenced the law governing their exercise. And, it may be added, that the contents of the statutory regulations themselves bespeak a similar attitude on the part of legislatures.

The mortgagee on whom the power is conferred is not, of course, a trustee or fiduciary within an accurate use of those terms.[63] Nevertheless courts, although recognizing its advantages as a "cheap and expeditious method of foreclosing a mortgage without action," [64] are also impressed by the danger to the mortgagor in its very summary nature. They regard the mortgagor as being "in an important sense, completely in the power of the mortgagee", and not infrequently call him a trustee.[65] Consequently, whether the exercise of the power is governed by statutory regulation or is controlled entirely by the provisions in the security instrument, "courts regard such powers with suspicion and watchfulness." [66] They require that the power be "strictly and fairly pursued" and "if the execution of the power is tainted with fraud; or if any mistake is made in conducting the sale adapted to mislead those who might desire to purchase, so that the sale, if at auction, occurs under circumstances calculated to depreciate the value of the property sold, or prevent it bringing a fair auction price, the sale will be held invalid." [67]

This belief and attitude finds expression in many ways. Among the chief of these is the requirements of notice. These are of two sorts. One kind purports to give notice generally to everybody interested in the matter without attempting to see that it reaches any particular person. The other is design-

---

need not be for cash but may be on the basis of a purchase money mortgage. Belton v. Buss, etc. Co., 1922, 2 Ch. 449; Cheshire, Modern Real Property, 1937, 596–7. Although there must be notice of default given to the mortgagee, there seems to be no provision for giving the mortgagor time and opportunity to voice objections to a privately conducted sale. See Turner, supra, 607; Cheshire, supra, 599.

61. In the absence of statutory regulation, a power of sale may by express provision authorize private sale. See Durfee & Doddridge, 1925, 23 Mich.L.Rev. 815, 832, n. 28; Wiltsie, Mortgage Foreclosure, 5th ed., § 837; But see Glenn, Mortgages, § 100. Where the sale is conducted by a third party instead of by the mortgagee there is no objection to permitting such a sale, Brunswick & A. R. Co. v. Hughes, 1874, 52 Ga. 557; Etna Coal & Iron Co. v. Marting Iron, etc., Co., 1904, 127 F. 32, 61 C.C.A. 396.

62. Minnesota is typical of the several states in which the exercise of a power of sale in a mortgage in order to foreclose a mortgage is regulated comprehensively by legislation. Minn.Stat.Ann. 1947, § 580.01 et seq. Similar statutes exist in several other states. Mich.Comp.Laws Ann.1968, § 600, 3201 et seq.; N.D.Cent.Code, 1960, ch. 35–22, §§ 2201–2225; S.D.Comp.Laws, 1967, § 21–48–1 et seq., Wis.Stats., 1967, ch. 297; Wyo.Stat., Ann., 1957, §§ 34–68 et seq., 59–301 to 304, as to deeds of trust. A proposed Model Power of Sale Foreclosure Act also covers the process of such foreclosure in full detail. See § 345, infra, for references to it and discussions of it. For other varieties of legislation look at West's Ann.Cal.Civ.Code §§ 2924–2924b; Md.Ann.1957 Code Rule W 73–74; Gen.Laws Mass. 1959, c. 244, §§ 14–17; N.Y.Real Prop. Actions, 1963, § 1401 et seq.; Va.Code Ann.1950, §§ 55–59, 55–61 to 63.

63. See Warner v. Jacob, 1882, 51 L.J., Ch., 642, "a mortgagee is, strictly speaking, not a trustee of the power of sale. It is a power given to him for his own benefit to enable him the better to realize his mortgage debt."

64. See Gooch v. Vaughan, 1885, 92 N.C. 610.

65. Ibid. Cf., as to the fiduciary character of the mortgagee under the English statute. 1944, 31 Va. L.Rev. 215.

66. Ibid.

Thus a foreclosure sale pursuant to a power of sale in a trust deed mortgage may be attacked in an equitable proceeding and set aside on the ground that the note and trust deed were contingent upon delivery of them and there was no such delivery. Stirton v. Pastor, 1960, 177 Cal.App.2d 232, 2 Cal.Rptr. 135.

67. Fenner v. Tucker, 1860, 6 R.I. 551, 554. See 1941, 27 Va.L.Rev. 924, 929, et seq.

ed to give notice personally to certain designated individuals. The most common statutory requirement of notice is of the first type and is that it be by advertisement. This fact has caused the process to be described in many jurisdictions as "foreclosure by advertisement."[68] Sometimes additional or alternative methods of giving notice of one kind or another are sanctioned, e. g., by recordation,[69] posting of notice,[70] service on the party in possession of the premises,[71] or by registered letter.[72] Occasionally personal service in the same manner as is required in a judicial proceeding is demanded by statute.[73] When notice is of the personal variety, unless it is required by the terms of the power itself or by statute,[74] it does not have

to be given to any one other than the mortgagor. In other words, subsequent grantees or junior lienors may be ignored.[75] The notion is that it is incumbent upon such parties to keep themselves informed.[76]

The contents of the notice always must include the time and place of the sale.[77] A description of the property to be sold also is a usual requirement but the particularity and definiteness of the description insisted upon is not laid down with the precision it should be.[78] The fact of default is basic to the validity of the exercise of the power[79] and consequently a statement of it usually is put in the notice. However, failure to do so has

Armille v. Lovett, 1956, 100 N.H. 203, 122 A.2d 265, 267.

68. See Minn.Stat.Ann., 1947, §§ 580.1–.30; Md.Ann. Code, 1957, Rule W 74, § a(2) (this provision was moved into the Maryland Rules of Court); Mich. Comp.Laws Ann., 1968, § 600.3208; Mass.Gen.Laws Ann., 1959, c. 244, § 14; N.D.Cent.Code, 1960, § 35–22–01; Wis.Stat.Ann., 1958, § 297.01; Wyo.Stat. Ann., 1957, § 34–68.

69. West's Ann.Cal.Civ.Code, § 2924.

70. N.Y.Real Prop. Actions 1963, § 1402; Mich. Comp.Laws Ann.1968 § 600.3208.

71. Minn.Stat.Ann.1947, § 580.03.

72. See Moss v. Keary, 1925, 231 Mich. 295, 204 N.W. 93; Bailey v. Hendrickson, 1913, 25 N.D. 500, 143 N.W. 134, Ann.Cas.1913C, 739; Garrett v. Crawford, 1907, 128 Ga. 519, 57 S.E. 792, 119 Am.St.Rep. 398, 11 Ann.Cas. 167; Ritchie v. Judd, 1891, 137 Ill. 453, 27 N.E. 682; cf., Tracy v. Lawrence, 1854, 2 Drew. 403. Also cf. Cal.Civ.Code § 2924b, by registered letter to persons who have recorded request for notice. See Model Power of Sale Foreclosure Act, § 3; Skilton, Proposed Uniform Mortgage Legislation, 1942, 9 Am.L.School Rev. 1128, 1134. See also note 73, infra.

73. N.Y.Real Prop. Actions, 1963, § 1402; Wis.Stat. Ann., 1958, § 297.04; N.D.Cent.Code, 1960, § 35–22–03. Ketcham v. Deutsch, 1914, 211 N.Y. 85, 105 N.E. 85; Denton v. Ontario County Bank, 1896, 150 N.Y. 126, 44 N.E. 781. See 1949 Wis.L.Rev. 341.

74. Such occasionally is the case. See New York, North Dakota and Wisconsin statutes, note 73, supra. In California, any person desiring a notice of default and of notice of sale under a power of sale may become entitled to it by recording an acknowledged request for a copy; the mortgage or deed of trust may contain a request that copies of such notices shall be mailed to any person a party thereto. In lieu of such requests advertisement is sufficient notice. West's Ann.Cal.Civ.Code § 2924b.

75. Scott v. Paisley, 1926, 271 U.S. 632, 46 S.Ct. 591, 70 L.Ed. 1123. See Hardwicke v. Hamilton, 1894, 121 Mo. 465, 26 S.W. 342. See also 1941, 27 Va.L. Rev. 924, 932.

76. See Watkins v. Booth, 1913, 55 Colo. 91, 132 P. 1141.

77. For cases dealing with the sufficiency of statements as to the date and time of a proposed sale, see Burr v. Borden, 1871, 61 Ill. 389; Gray v. Shaw, 1851, 14 Mo. 341; Coxe v. Halsted, 1840, 2 N.J.Eq. 311; Mowry v. Sanborn, 1877, 68 N.Y. 153; Jensen v. Weinlander, 1870, 25 Wis. 477. See West's Ann.Cal.Civ.Code § 2924(c) as a typical requirement. See, also, statutory provisions in legislation cited, note 62, supra.

78. In Newman v. Jackson, 1827, 12 Wheat. 570, 6 L.Ed. 732, the published notice misdescribed the addition to the city of Georgetown in which the property was located, but gave the correct street number of the lot with an accurate description of its size and the type of structure on it. Held, the misdescription was not sufficiently material to invalidate the sale. See also Reeside v. Peter, 1870, 33 Md. 120; Model Lodging House Ass'n v. Boston, 1873, 114 Mass. 133; Jackson v. Harris, N.Y.1824, 3 Cow. 241; Hoffman v. Anthony, 1859, 6 R.I. 282, 75 Am.Dec. 701; Fenner v. Tucker, 1860, 6 R.I. 551; Austin v. Hatch, 1893, 159 Mass. 198, 34 N.E. 95; West's Ann.Cal.Civ.Code § 2924.

79. Rogers v. Barnes, 1897, 169 Mass. 179, 47 N.E. 602, 38 L.R.A. 145, "On principle * * * a mortgagee, when there has been no default or breach of the conditions of the mortgage, cannot sell the land mortgaged under the usual power of sale contained in a mortgage, so as to pass a good title to a bona fide purchaser for value, or to any subsequent purchase from him." And see Crowley v. Adams, 1917, 226 Mass. 582, 116 N.E. 241; Redmond v. Packenham, 1872, 66 Ill. 434; Huntington v. Crafton, 1890, 76 Tex. 497, 13 S.W. 542.

been held not to be fatal to the validity of the sale.[80] The amount for which the mortgage is being foreclosed is important to state, especially for the benefit of the mortgagors and others who may wish to exercise their right to redeem, as they may, up to the last moment before the sale.[81] It is important, also, for the purpose of applying the proceeds, first, to the mortgage debt, and, second, as to any surplus, to payment to the mortgagor.[82] If the amount is in dispute the exercise of the power will be restrained until the amount of the secured indebtedness is determined.[83]

The conduct of the sale itself is scrutinized to see that it is conducted fairly as an auction sale should be conducted so as to produce as good a price as such a sale can bring.[84] Consequently the mortgagee is bound not to "chill the bidding" by word or deed before or during the sale.[85] However, it is "a notorious fact that when land is sold, by auction, under a power contained in a mortgage, it seldom, if ever, brings a price which reaches its real value."[86] Hence the rule, previously encountered,[87] that a sale will not be set aside for mere inadequacy of price.[88] And if the mortgagor himself is the one who does something to discourage bidding he has no standing to object.[89]

Whether the mortgaged property should be sold as a whole or by parcels frequently is a matter of considerable importance and well drawn mortgages should cover the point. In foreclosure by judicial sale the matter can

---

80. Model Lounging House Ass'n v. Boston, 1873, 114 Mass. 133.

81. Pritchard v. Sanderson, 1880, 84 N.C. 299, the mortgagor "ought to know definitely what sum he is required to pay, and have an opportunity to redeem without sale." Cf., Crowley v. Adams, 1917, 226 Mass. 582, 116 N.E. 241; Shippen v. Whittier, 1886, 117 Ill. 282, 7 N.E. 642. See West's Ann.Cal. Civ.Code § 2924c.

82. See Webster v. Singley, 1875, 53 Ala. 208, 25 Am.Rep. 609; Mattel v. Conant, 1892, 156 Mass. 418, 31 N.E. 487; Eliason v. Sidle, 1895, 61 Minn. 285, 63 N.W. 730; Oldham v. First Nat. Bank, 1881, 84 N.C. 304. Cf. Price v. Blankenship, 1898, 144 Mo. 203, 45 S.W. 1123. See § 343, infra.

83. Gooch v. Vaughan, 1885, 92 N.C. 610. "* * * There can be no doubt but that it is improper in a trustee to make a sale under a deed of trust, * * * so long as it remains uncertain what amount is due on account of said debt. And if it be uncertain what is the amount of the debt due, or what is the amount of the credits properly applicable thereto, but not so applied, it is the duty of the trustee, before making the sale, to ascertain the amount to be raised by the sale, and to bring a suit in chancery to procure a settlement * * * if necessary." Hogan v. Duke, Va.1871, 20 Grat. 244, 253.
See also Wilkins v. Gordon, 1841, 38 Va. (11 Leigh) 547. Cf., Alston v. Lehman, 1896, 113 Ala. 506, 20 So. 950; More v. Calkins, 1890, 85 Cal. 177, 24 P. 729; Ryan v. Gilliam, 1881, 75 Mo. 132; Carey v. Fulmer, 1897, 74 Miss. 729, 21 So. 752. Cf. Dickerson v. Hayes, 1879, 26 Minn. 100, 1 N.W. 834. See S.C.Code, 1932, § 8708. As a rule an injunction will not be granted without payment or tender of an amount admitted to be due. See Sloan v. Coolbaugh, 1859, 10 Iowa, 31; Stanley v. Gadsby, 1836, 10 Pet. 521, 9 L.Ed. 518. Cf. Macleod v. Jones, 1883, L.R. 24 Ch.Div. 289.

84. Austin v. Hatch, 1893, 159 Mass. 198, 34 N.E. 95. See Richards v. Holmes, 1855, 18 How. 143, 15 L. Ed. 304; Thornton v. Boyden, 1863, 31 Ill. 200; Dexter v. Shepard, 1875, 117 Mass. 480; Mahoney v. Mackubin, 1879, 52 Md. 357; Dunton v. Sharpe, 1893, 70 Miss. 850, 12 So. 800; Dunn v. McCoy, 1899, 150 Mo. 548, 52 S.W. 21.
See also L.R.A.1915B, 640.
See also Horsey v. Hough, 1873, 38 Md. 130; Newman v. Meek, Miss.1843, 1 Freem.Ch. 441; Vail v. Jacobs, 1876, 62 Mo. 130; Bird v. Davis, 1862, 14 N.J.Eq. 467; Stacy v. Smith, 1896, 9 S.D. 137, 68 N.W. 198; Brown v. Busch, 1957, 152 Cal.App.2d 200, 313 P.2d 19.

85. Sullivan v. Federal Farm Mort. Corp., 1940, 62 Ga.App. 402, 8 S.E.2d 126; Aultman & Taylor Co. v. Meade, 1905, 121 Ky. 241, 89 S.W. 137, 123 Am. St.Rep. 193; Fenton v. Torrey, 1882, 133 Mass. 138.

86. Austin v. Hatch, supra note 84.

87. See §§ 329, 330, 331, supra.

88. See Cambridge Sav. Bank v. Cronin, 1935, 289 Mass. 379, 194 N.E. 289; Austin v. Hatch, 1893, 159 Mass. 198, 34 N.E. 95. Cf. note, 1927, 26 Mich.L. Rev. 87.
"Equity requires a foreclosure to be conducted with entire good faith, and with reasonable regard for the mortgagor's interests, it is true, but after a certain point it must respect bargains. It does not require the land to be sold for its value. It only requires reasonable efforts to be made to avoid a sacrifice, and to obtain the value of the land." Stevenson v. Dana, 1896, 166 Mass. 163, 170, 44 N.E. 128. But cf., Horsey v. Hough, 1873, 38 Md. 130; Vail v. Jacobs, 1876, 62 Mo. 130; Stacy v. Smith. 1896, 9 S.D. 137, 68 N.W. 198.

89. Realty Investment & Securities Co. v. H. L. Rust Co., 1939, 71 App.Div.D.C. 213, 109 F.2d 456.

be taken care of by the court where the mortgage is silent.[90] Where sale is under a power, there are divergent views as to whether a court of equity, if appealed to by one or other of the parties, will authorize or direct a sale by parcels or as a whole. One notion is that the property was mortgaged as a unit and must be so sold since the contract of the parties, which is the source of authority to sell under the power, does not specify that it may be broken up.[91] Other courts reason that realization of the security is put into the mortgagee's control, and therefore he not only has the authority to sell by parcels but must do so if that is the most favorable method of disposal.[92] The matter is settled by statute in several states.[93] Where there is such a statute and it is disregarded, unless the plaintiff can show that the sale as made damaged him, a court of equity will not act to set it aside.[94]

90. See § 327, supra.

91. Williams v. Jones, 1935, 165 Va. 398, 182 S.E. 280. Cf., 1941, 15 S.Cal.L.Rev. 19, as to Cal.Civ. Code Proc., § 694, being inapplicable to sales under trust deed powers.

92. "Where property is susceptible of division, and it will bring more by being divided and sold in separate parcels or lots than by being sold in a body, or where by a sale of a part of the premises a sufficient amount can be realized to pay off the secured debt, then it is the duty of the trustee to make the division and sell a portion accordingly, and if he fails in this the sale will be held invalid on application of the party aggrieved. There are instances in which the whole of a piece of property will sell for more than it would by being separated, and in all such cases the trustee must exercise a sound discretion." Tatum v. Holliday, 1875, 59 Mo. 422, 428. See also Hill v. Farmers & Mech. Bank, 1878, 97 U. S. 450, 24 L.Ed. 1051; Loveland v. Clark, 1888, 11 Colo. 265, 18 P. 544; Singleton v. Scott, 1859, 11 Iowa, 589; Patterson v. Miller, 1879, 52 Md. 388; Terry v. Fitzgerald, Va.1879, 32 Grat. 843; L.R.A. 1917B, 526.

93. See Mich.Comp.Laws Ann., 1968, § 600.3224; Minn.Stat.Ann., 1947, § 580.08; N.Y.Real Prop.Actions, 1963, § 1407; N.D.Cent.Code, 1960, § 35-22-09; Wyo.Stat.Ann., 1957, § 34-73. See also Walker v. Schultz, 1913, 175 Mich. 280, 141 N.W. 543. See note, 1913, 5 Detroit L.J. 134. Cf., Kelly v. Carmichael, 1928, 217 Ala. 534, 117 So. 67.

94. Petoskey v. H.O.L.C., 1942, 300 Mich. 391, 1 N. W.2d 584; see Meux v. Trezevant, 1901, 132 Cal. 487, 64 P. 848. If redemption from foreclosure sale

DEFECTIVE SALE

341. When a sale under a power is defective the mortgagor, under certain conditions, may have a right to damages which can be asserted either by affirmative action or as a defense to a claim for a deficiency. More commonly he may require, by one method or another, a resale.

The critical attitude of courts towards powers of sale[95] which makes them quick to grant relief against even slight irregularities and deviations from the terms of the powers or requirements makes for considerable uncertainty of title.[96] "Lawyers examining titles flowing from sales under powers are required to exercise an experienced and nice judgment in determining which departures from a perfect compliance with the law may be passed over and which must be viewed with alarm or be ratified by a court decree in which all interested parties are brought within the jurisdiction of the court."[97]

When the defect is such as to invalidate the sale several possibilities present themselves. Where the defect is discovered before the purchase price is paid or conveyance executed, the mortgagee may, and ordinarily should, hold a new sale in which the provisions of law and stipulations of the instrument under which he is acting are strictly complied with.[98] Or the mortgagor may

of this sort is permitted, the terms of the sale may protect the mortgagor by allowing him to redeem, at his option, by parcels or by the entirety. Petoskey v. H.O.L.C., supra.

95. See § 340, supra.

96. See 1941, 27 Va.L.Rev. 926, 930.

97. Reeve, The New Proposal for a Uniform Mortgage Act, 1938, 5 Law and Contemp.Probs. 564, 573. For a discussion of mere irregularity in foreclosure and the protection of a bona fide purchaser thereunder where the mortgagor is not prejudiced or does not make timely objection, see 1931, 73 A.L.R. 612, 615, 626, 627, 638.

98. Brett v. Davenport, 1909, 151 N.C. 56, 65 S.E. 611. And there is authority that a second sale may be made even after it has been completed if it should turn out to be void. See Polk v. Dale, 1908, 93 Miss. 664, 47 So. 386, 17 Ann.Cas. 754; Bottineau v. Aetna Life Ins. Co., 1883, 31 Minn. 125, 16

have the aid of a court of equity's injunctive relief to the same end.[99] When the invalid sale is completed the mortgagor may sue in equity to set the sale aside and restore the situation as it was before sale.[1] Or the equitable action may result in a decree providing for the cumulative remedy of a judicial foreclosure.[2] But this does not end the resources available to a mortgagor. A wrongful sale under the power may be a tort entitling him to recover damages in an action at law.[3] Or, if the sale does not bring enough to pay off the mortgage debt and he is sued for a deficiency, the mortgagor may use the improper sale as a defense to recovery to the extent that he has been damaged by it. This defense is available to a mortgagor who has parted with the property,[4] but it is doubtful whether it may be used by one who has retained ownership of the property and therefore still has a clear right to redeem if he wishes.[5]

From the mortgagor's point of view this last remedy has drawbacks. He has the burden of proving the misconduct which makes the sale invalid.[6] And the result of its use is merely to defeat or cut down recovery without giving affirmative relief to which the mortgagor may be entitled. Where the mortgagee is the purchaser and is suing for the deficiency, the preferable course would be, depending upon the practice in the particular jurisdiction, to present the defense to the deficiency action and at the same time

---

N.W. 849. But cf., Koester v. Burke, 1876, 81 Ill. 436.

"Trust deeds given as security and mortgages containing a power of sale vest the legal title in the trustee. * * * The legal title of the trustee is supplemented by a power which authorizes him * * * to advertise and sell the property; * * * He may divest himself of the legal title without compliance with the conditions of the trust. But a sale and deed, except in strict compliance with the power specified, is of no effect whatever, so far as the trustor's equitable estate is concerned. If the trustee, in disobedience of the trust conditions, by deed transfer the legal title, his grantee takes only the trustee's interest. He steps into the trustee's shoes, so to speak, and holds subject to all reserved rights of the trustor. Neither courts of law nor courts of equity regard the trustee's deed as absolutely void. Both recognize the fact that it conveys the legal title. The difference is, that the grantee's title or ownership cannot be challenged at law, while equity treats him as a successor to the trust and protects the trustor's estate. Equity does not vacate the trustee's deed and regard the title as remaining in him. Appropriate equitable relief is usually obtained in one of the following modes: The cumulative remedy of a regular judicial foreclosure and sale is allowed; or a decree is entered requiring the grantee to execute the power in accordance with the terms of the trust deed as the trustee should have done; or the execution of the power is, by decree, devolved upon a new trustee appointed for the purpose. Upon delivery of his deed, the original trustee ceases, both at law and in equity, to have any further interest in the property. The power of sale is extinguished, so far as he is concerned, leaving him in the same position as a total stranger; and an effort on his part to exercise the power originally vested in him, by an attempted resale or a second deed, is of no more force or effect than if the same proceedings were taken by one who had never been connected with the title." Stephens v. Clay, 1892, 17 Colo. 489, 30 P. 43, 44, 31 Am.St.Rep. 328.

99. Smith v. Clark & Smith, N.Y.1834, 4 Paige 368.

1. Peterson v. Kansas City Life Ins. Co., 1936, 339 Mo. 700, 98 S.W.2d 770, 108 A.L.R. 583; Cambridge Sav. Bank v. Cronin, 1935, 289 Mass. 379, 194 N.E. 289; Manning v. Liberty Trust Co., 1920, 234 Mass. 544, 125 N.E. 691, 8 A.L.R. 999.

2. E. g., Harriss v. Hughes, 1941, 220 N.C. 473, 17 S.E.2d 679.

3. Rogers v. Barnes, 1897, 169 Mass. 179, 47 N.E. 602, 38 L.R.A. 145, selling the premises in the absence of a default; Fenton v. Torrey, 1882, 133 Mass. 138, "chilling" the bidding; Mills v. Mutual B. & L. Ass'n, 1940, 216 N.C. 664, 6 S.E.2d 549, mortgagee making unauthorized purchase at own sale. See Cambridge Sav. Bank v. Cronin, 1935, 289 Mass. 379, 194 N.E. 289. Cf. 1932, 16 Minn.L.Rev. 716, mortgagor's damages for premature foreclosure in Minnesota. See also 1937, 108 A.L.R. 592, 594.

4. Dexter v. Aronson, 1933, 282 Mass. 124, 184 N.E. 455; Sullivan v. Federal Farm Mortg. Corp., 1940, 62 Ga.App. 402, 8 S.E.2d 126.

5. Cambridge Sav. Bank v. Cronin, 1935, 289 Mass. 379, 194 N.E. 289.

6. Gordon v. Harris, 1935, 290 Mass. 482, 485, 195 N.E. 744, 745; Cambridge Sav. Bank v. Cronin, 1935, 289 Mass. 379, 194 N.E. 289. Cf. Jefferson Standard Life Ins. Co. v. Boogher, 1944, 224 N.C. 563, 31 S.E.2d 771, commented on, 1945, 23 N.C.L.Rev. 261, involving proper advertisement of foreclosure when the trustee's deed contains a recital of advertisement duly made.

seek to set aside the sale and to stay the deficiency action meanwhile.[7]

PURCHASE BY MORTGAGEE

342. In England under no circumstances may the mortgagee purchase at a power of sale foreclosure. In the United States, in the absence of consent by the mortgagor, statutory sanction, or conduct of the sale by an authorized third person or public official, the mortgagee is not permitted to buy. These conditions are met in a great many jurisdictions. Even when they are not, the sale is voidable, not void.

In England under no circumstances may the mortgagee be a purchaser at his power of sale foreclosure.[8]

In the United States, a mortgagee who is armed with a valid power of sale is regarded as invested with so great an ability to do harm to the mortgagor that he is, for this purpose, treated like, and frequently called, a trustee.[9] Consequently, without the mortgagor's express consent or in the absence of unusual circumstances, the mortgagee may not bid in the mortgaged premises at an out of court sale under a power which he himself exercises.[10] Such a purchase renders the sale

voidable,[11] not void, so that a subsequent sale to a bona fide purchaser for value without notice will cut it off.[12] Where the terms of the mortgage permits the mortgagee to purchase, the sale is perfectly valid.[13] In such a case a delineation is drawn between the mortgagee's duty to see that the sale is fairly conducted and his self interest as a bidder at the sale.[14] The mortgagee's purchase will

---

7. Taylor v. Weingartner, 1916, 223 Mass. 243, 111 N.E. 909; Robinson v. Robinson, 1933, 112 W.Va. 39, 163 S.E. 633.

8. Robertson v. Norris, 1858, 1 Giff. 421; Martinson v. Clowes, 1882, 21 Ch.D. 857; 2 Coote, Mortgages, 9th Ed., 934; Turner, An English View of Mortgage Deficiency Judgments, 1935, 21 Va.L.Rev. 601, 605; Tefft, The Myth of Strict Foreclosure, 1937, 4 U. of Chi.L.Rev. 575, 581. In Roman law the creditor could not purchase at his own foreclosure sale, directly or indirectly, and a sale by the creditor "presupposed that the creditor had either obtained a judgment against the debtor, or at least had notified the latter of his intention to sell, and had waited two years after such notice." Mackeldey, Civil Law, § 350, footnote p. 385.

9. Cf. the analogous problem of the attitude of courts toward him in scrutinizing his conduct of the sale in other respects. § 340, supra. See also Horsey v. Hough, 1873, 38 Md. 130.

10. Mills v. Mut. B. & L. Ass'n, 1940, 216 N.C. 664, 6 S.E.2d 549; Jackson v. Blankenship, 1925, 213 Ala. 607, 105 So. 684; Imboden v. Hunter, 1861, 23 Ark. 622, 79 Am.Dec. 116; Dyer v. Shurtleff, 1873, 112 Mass. 165, 17 Am.Rep. 77; Martin v. McNeely, 1888, 101 N.C. 634, 8 S.E. 231; Blockley v. Fowler,

1863, 21 Cal. 326, 82 Am.Dec. 747. See 1941, 27 Va. L.Rev. 926, 931.

The trustee in a trust deed mortgage cannot purchase at his foreclosure sale without the consent of the debtor and creditor. Carter v. Thompson, 1867, 41 Ala. 375; Sypher v. McHenry, 1864, 18 Iowa 232; Jodd v. Lee, 1914, 256 Mo. 536, 165 S.W. 991. See § 329, note 42, for references on trustee purchase under corporate trust indenture foreclosures.

The rule invalidating any purchase by the trustee under a deed of trust at a foreclosure of such an instrument equally voids such foreclosure purchase by his wife. Lee v. Lee, 1959, 236 Miss. 260, 109 So.2d 870, commented on by Million, Lesar, and Martz, 1959 Annual Survey of American Law: Real and Personal Property, 1960, 35 N.Y.U.L.Rev. 427, 449. And see Admiral Co., Inc. v. Thomas, 1959, 106 U.S.App.D.C. 266, 271 F.2d 849 (semble).

The creditor secured by the trust deed mortgage has no such disability. Easton v. German-American Bank, 1888, 127 U.S. 532, 8 S.Ct. 1297, 32 L.Ed. 210; Sacramento Bank v. Copsey, 1901, 133 Cal. 663, 66 P. 8, 205, 85 Am.St.Rep. 242; Monroe Bros. v. Fuchtler, 1897, 121 N.C. 101, 28 S.E. 63. Admiral Co. v. Thomas, D.D.C.1958, 164 F.Supp. 569 (purchase by officer of corporate lender at trust deed sale did not render sale defective).

See, however, Hartman, Creditors' Rights and Security Transactions in Annual Survey of Tennessee Law, 1957, 10 Vand.L.Rev. 1058, 1061, discussing Jones v. Thomas, 1957, 41 Tenn.App. 503, 296 S.W. 2d 646, holding that a creditor, secured by a trust deed mortgage, "breached his trust relationship" toward the debtor by buying the property at the trustee's sale.

11. The mortgagor, therefore, may sue to redeem, Morris v. Carroll, 1916, 171 N.C. 761, 88 S.E. 511, or to have the sale set aside. Jackson v. Blankenship, 1925, 213 Ala. 607, 105 So. 684.

12. Very v. Russell, 1894, 65 N.H. 646, 23 A. 522. But cf. Cornelius v. Bishop, 1921, 205 Ala. 503, 88 So. 592.

13. Brown v. Eckhardt, 1940, 23 Tenn.App. 217, 129 S.W.2d 1122; Dexter v. Shepard, 1875, 117 Mass. 480; Cambridge Bank v. Cronin, 1935, 289 Mass. 379, 194 N.E. 289.

14. "When * * * a mortgagee is both seller and buyer, his position is one of great delicacy. Yet, when he has done his full duty to the mortgagor in his conduct of the sale under the power, and the bidding begins, in his capacity of bidder a mortga-

also be valid if the sale under the power is conducted by a public officer,[15] as is sometimes provided for by statute.[16]

There is controversy over whether the mortgagee ought to be permitted to bid at a power of sale foreclosure. An eminent English authority ascribes to the practice allowing him to do so most of the American difficulties in obtaining a fair price and preventing oppression of the mortgagor.[17] Some American writers and courts, on the other hand, take the view that it is necessary or desirable that a mortgagee be permitted to bid in order to protect his security and to benefit the mortgagor.[18] And the practice has been sanctioned by statutes.[19]

DISPOSITION OF SURPLUS

343. A variety of rules, some of them statutory, govern disposition by a mortgagee of a surplus yielded by a foreclosure sale under a power. Apart from simple cases, his safest course is to seek court determination of the matter.

Where the sale produces a surplus instead of a deficit a question frequently arises as to whether it should go to the mortgagor or to other parties, junior lienors, grantees, and like persons who have or claim an interest in the redemption right. Usually this is determined either in a bill of interpleader by the mortgagee, or in an action by one claimant joining others.[20]

Where the mortgagee distributes the surplus without the protection of a court decree it is clear that, insofar as he has knowledge or actual notice of junior encumbrancers and subsequent grantees, he must pay it to them in order of their priority.[21] There is a divergence in the authorities as to whether he must go beyond this and search the record to discover junior or subsequent interests so that they may participate.[22] There are

gee may buy as cheaply as he can, and owes no duty to bid the full value of the property as that value may subsequently be determined by a judge or a jury." Cambridge Savings Bank v. Cronin, 1935, 289 Mass. 379, 194 N.E. 289.

15. Ramsey v. Merriam, 1861, 6 Minn. 168.

16. E. g., Minn.Stat.Ann., 1947, § 580.06; Mich.Comp. Laws Ann., 1968, § 600.3216; Wis.Stat.Ann., 1958, § 297.06; Wyo.Stat.Ann., 1957, § 34–74. The proposed Model Power of Sale Foreclosure Act, under which sale is to be made by the sheriff, permits the "mortgagee, the record owner of the mortgage, or any party having an interest in the mortgage" to bid at the foreclosure sale, § 4(1) (2) of the Act. See also § 344, infra.

17. See Turner, An English View of Mortgage Deficiency Judgments, 1935, 21 Va.L.Rev. 601, 604.

18. See Walsh, Mortgages, § 83. Cf., Glenn, Mortgages, § 108, to the same effect, and suggesting that the fact sales under a power may be private ones in England may color an English observers opinion. Also that objections, which may be strong in such a sale are minimized or absent in America where sale is by public auction. Cf. also Howard v. Davis, 1851, 6 Tex. 174, 183: "A mortgagee is a trustee, but in a qualified sense. He does not hold for the benefit of others, but for himself. He has an interest in the property. It is pledged expressly to secure his claim, and, were he deprived of the power to purchase, he might suffer great loss by its sale at a low price. He has an interest that the bid shall amount to his incumbrance, and that the property be not sacrificed, to the injury as well of the mortgagor, * * * and it is the interest of the mortgagor that the mortgagee should enter into the competition at the sale." See, also, Taylor v. Weingartner, 1916, 223 Mass. 243, 111 N.E. 909. Cf., Clark v. Simmons, 1890, 150 Mass. 357, 23 N.E. 108. See 1909, 11 Ann.Cas. 170.

19. Mass.Gen.Laws Ann.1958, 1932, c. 183, § 25, mortgagee may purchase unless the mortgage provides

to the contrary; Minn.Stat.Ann., 1947, ch. 580.11; Mich.Comp.Laws Ann.1968, § 600.3228; N.Y.Real Prop.Actions, 1963, § 1408; N.D.Cent.Code, 1960, § 35–22–10; Wyo.Stat., Ann., 1957, § 34–74. See Hyndman v. Hyndman, 1845, 19 Vt. 9, 46 Am.Dec. 171, commenting on the New York provisions; Mowry v. Sanborn, 1877, 68 N.Y. 153, 162.

20. Wyant v. Crittenden, 1940, 72 App.D.C. 163, 113 F.2d 170. Cf., Smith v. Swormstedt, 1853, 57 U.S. 288, 16 How. 288, 14 L.Ed. 942. Pending such litigation the court should take charge of the money. Spruill v. Ballard, D.C.D.C.1941, 36 F.Supp. 729.

Dockrey v. Gray, 1959, 172 Cal.App.2d 388, 341 P.2d 746, held that liens of mortgages and mechanics' liens attached to the proceeds of the sales under a prior trust deed in the same manner and in the same order and with the same effect as they bound the premises before the sale.

21. Thomas v. Haines, 1934, 285 Mass. 90, 188 N.E. 621; Seward v. New York Life Ins. Co., 154 Va. 154, 152 S.E. 346.

22. W. A. H. Church v. Holmes, 1931, 60 App.D.C. 27, 46 F.2d 608, that search must be made; Wartell v. Novograd, 1927, 48 R.I. 296, 137 A. 776. 53 A.L.R. 365. The problem is similar to whether, as a prelude to exercising the power of sale, a title search for claimants of interests in the redemption should

statutory provisions on the point in some states.[23] Other statutes are silent or nearly so.[24] The mortgagee's safest course is to invoke the aid of a court with equitable jurisdiction instead of proceeding on his own.[25]

PURCHASER'S POSITION

344. The position of a purchaser under a power of sale foreclosure is, as to rights, substantially the same as that of a buyer at a judicial foreclosure sale. The latter's title, however, is stronger because it is founded upon a permanent court record in which the issues and the regularity of the proceedings have had a judicial determination binding upon the parties. Various measures to fortify and make more marketable the title of purchasers at power of sale foreclosures have been suggested. A good many states have enacted legislation to that end.

The power of sale given to a mortgagee authorizes him to transfer to a purchaser the mortgagor's title as it existed at the time the mortgage was made and that is what a purchaser at a sale under it gets.[26] In this respect he is like a purchaser under a judicial

foreclosure sale.[27] Of course, the sale under the power is intended to include the mortgagee's interest as well as the mortgagor's redemption so that a whole title will pass and the advertisement offer should make this clear.[28] One important consequence of this is that should the sale be defective so as to make it voidable as to the mortgagor, the purchaser may be regarded as having nevertheless succeeded to the position of the mortgagee to the extent that he will be accorded such equitable rights by way of subrogation or otherwise as are necessary to protect him if he has paid the purchase money in good faith.[29] Naturally, if there are prior liens, they must be mentioned in the notice so that a purchaser may know for just what he is bidding,[30] since the sale must be subject to them [31] although it cuts off interests in the property subsequent to the creation of the mortgage.[32]

Just as in the case of foreclosure by judicial sale, it is usually stated that the doctrine of *caveat emptor* applies to foreclosure sales

be made and personal notice of some sort be given to others than the mortgagor. See § 340, supra.

23. E. g., Mich.Comp.Laws Ann., 1968, § 600.3252; Md.Ann.Code Rule, 1957, W 75; N.Y.Real Prop.Action, 1963, §§ 1441–44; N.D.Cent.Code, 1960, § 35–22–22; Wis.Stat.Ann., 1958, § 297.15; Wyo.Stat. Ann., 1957, § 34–79; West's Ann.Cal.Civ.Code, § 2924b (Supp.1969). Cf. West's Ann.Cal.Civ.Code, § 2924b.

24. E. g., Mass.Gen.Laws Ann., 1959, ch. 244, § 14; Minn.Stat.Ann., 1947, § 580.10; Va.Code Ann., 1950, §§ 55–59.

25. There is authority that an action at law may be maintained against a mortgagee by subsequent lienors or grantees to recover their share in a surplus. Webster v. Singley, 1875, 53 Ala. 208, 25 Am.Rep. 609; Mattel v. Conant, 1892, 156 Mass. 418, 31 N.E. 487; Eliason v. Sidle, 1895, 61 Minn. 285, 63 N.W. 730. See § 340, note 82, supra.

26. See Comer v. John Hancock Ins. Co., C.C.A.Mo. 1935, 80 F.2d 413; Wharton v. Farmers & Merchants Bank of Green Ridge, C.C.A.Mo.1941, 119 F. 2d 487. See also Minn.Stat.Ann.1947, § 580.12. N. Dak.Cent.Code 1960, ch. 35–22, § 2221, with an especially sweeping provision as to the effect upon junior interests.

In United States v. Bank of America Nat. Trust & Savings Ass'n, C.A.Cal.1959, 265 F.2d 862, reversed

363 U.S. 237, 80 S.Ct. 1108, 4 L.Ed.2d 1192, the court held that, though the title of a purchase on nonjudicial trust deed foreclosure sale is the title at the time of execution of the trust deed, such a sale could not divest federal liens attaching to the property subsequent to that date; only a judicial foreclosure sale can do that. However, as to this, see § 221A, supra.

27. See § 328, supra.

28. See Fowle v. Merrill, 1866, 92 Mass. (10 Allen) 356; Varnum v. Meserve, 1864, 90 Mass. (8 Allen) 158.

29. See Brett v. Davenport, 1909, 151 N.C. 56, 65 S. E. 611. See Chapter 10, Subdivision A, supra.

30. See Brooks v. Bennett, 1931, 277 Mass. 8, 177 N. E. 685.

31. Cf., § 323, supra. If the prior liens are misstated, the sale is not void, but voidable by the purchaser. Russell v. Bon, 1915, 221 Mass. 370, 108 N. E. 1048.

32. Virginia-Carolina Chemical Co. v. Floyd, 1925, 159 Ga. 555, 126 S.E. 378; Metropolis Trust & Sav. Bank v. Barnet, 1913, 165 Cal. 449, 132 P. 833. See 1941, 27 Va.L.Rev. 924, 932. But cf., Denton v. Ontario County Nat. Bank, 1896, 150 N.Y. 126, 44 N.E. 781. And see 1949, Wis.L.Rev. 341. Cf. §§ 321, 322, supra.

under a power.[33] All this means is that the mortgagee in selling does not give, and has no authority to give, any warranty of title; he has power to sell only the title that has been given to him as security.[34] Hence the purchaser, as is the case in any ordinary contract of the sale of land, ordinarily must make his own investigation of title and find out what defects there may be in the title that is offered. However, if in the advertized terms of sale the mortgagee makes misrepresentations as to the extent of the property, a purchaser relying on that statement may recover damages from the mortgagee when the acreage turns out to be less by reason of a prior release by the mortgagee of some of it, even though the release was of record.[35] And an even clearer instance along the same line is the doctrine that a purchaser in good faith is entitled to rely upon the recitals in the deed given to him as to the conformity of the procedure of sale to the terms of the mortgage or requirements of statutes.[36]

One of the advantages of judicial foreclosure is that it offers a better marketable title through a permanent record which has the stamp of judicial approval.[37] By the same token, one of the objections to the similar method of out of court foreclosure is that it offers no similarly trustworthy muniment of title.[38] The only things the purchaser can rely on are the recitals in his deed,[39] and he is reluctant to back any faith in them by paying out substantial sums of money. Recognizing this defect there have been statutory remedies enacted and proposed. One method, exemplified by the Maryland legislation, is to bring the mortgagee into court both at the inception of the process and again at the end at which time he reports the sale to the court. The proceeding from then on is the same as if the sale had been completely under judicial process.[40] Other methods are to provide that the sale may,[41] as an alternative to the person appointed in the security instrument to execute the power, or must[42] be made by the sheriff. Much more important are provisions for a permanent memorial of the transaction. Legislation making affidavits as to proper giving of notice and conduct of the sale, executed at the

33. See Hayes v. Delzell, 1886, 21 Mo.App. 679; Brewer v. Christian, 1881, 9 Ill.App. 57; Barden v. Stickney, 1902, 130 N.C. 62, 40 S.E. 842.

34. Adams v. Boyd, 1933, 332 Mo. 484, 58 S.W.2d 704; H. Weill & Bros. v. Davis, 1915, 168 N.C. 298, 84 S.E. 395. Thus a second mortgagee can sell and convey only the redemption interest. Brett v. Davenport, 1909, 151 N.C. 56, 65 S.E. 611.

See Gassenheimer v. Molton, 1887, 80 Ala. 521, 2 So. 652; Bloom v. Van Rensselaer, 1854, 15 Ill. 503; Kinsley v. Ames, Mass.1840, 2 Metc. 29. See note, 1935, 22 Va.L.Rev. 107.

35. Hayes v. Delzell, 1886, 21 Mo.App. 679.

"By the advertisement and terms of sale, it was plainly the intention to sell the land, and not an equity of redemption. The purchaser must have so understood. The defendant is bound to give, but does not offer to give, a good title, * * * and the plaintiff is therefore entitled to recover the deposit of money she made." Callaghan v. O'Brien, 1884, 136 Mass. 378, 383. See also Dirks Trust & Title Co. v. Koch, 1913, 32 S.D. 551, 143 N.W. 952, 49 L. R.A.,N.S., 513.

36. See Randolph v. Citizens Nat. Bank, Tex.Civ. App.1940, 141 S.W.2d 1030; Nat. Valley Bank v. Kanawha Banking & Trust Co., 1928, 151 Va. 446, 145 S.E. 432. See also N.Y.Real Prop.Actions & Proc.Law, 1963, § 1411; Minn.Stat.Ann., 1947, § 580.19; N.D.Cent.Code, 1960, §§ 35–22–11, 35–22–16 to –18; Wis.Stat.Ann., 1958, § 297.17. Cf. West's

Ann.Cal.Civ.Code § 2924b, making recital in the deed of compliance with the law requiring mailing of copies of notices for which requests have been recorded prima facie evidence of compliance therewith, and conclusive evidence thereof in favor of bona fide purchasers and encumbrancers for value and without notice. This paragraph was deleted in 1968. Cf. also 1945, 23 N.C.L.Rev. 261.

37. See Reeve, The New Proposal for a Uniform Mortgage Act, 1938, 5 Law & Contemp. Probs., 564, 574.

38. Idem, 573. But cf., Carey, et al., Studies in Foreclosures in Cook County, 1933, 27 Ill.L.Rev. 595, 616 et seq.

39. See Vail v. Jacobs, 1876, 62 Mo. 130.

40. Md. Ann.Code of 1957, Rules 72–74. See Maslin v. Marshall, 1902, 94 Md. 480, 51 A. 85; Rouskulp v. Kershner, 1878, 49 Md. 516.

41. Mich. Comp.Laws Ann., 1968, § 600.3212; Wis. Stat., 1958, § 297.14; Wyo.Stat. 1959, § 34–74 (1959).

42. Minn.Stat.Ann., 580.03. Such also is the proposal in the Model Power of Sale Mortgage Foreclosure Act, § 4.

time, prima facie evidence of compliance with requirements is helpful.[43] Some states have gone beyond this and strengthened the purchaser's title by requiring proofs of regularity of the process to be recorded and making the record admissible as evidence of the fact.[44]

CURRENT DEVELOPMENTS

345. Dissatisfaction with existing foreclosure methods and mortgage law led to a proposal for a new Uniform Mortgage Act. The drafting of a Model Power of Sale Foreclosure Act, not yet adopted by any state, is the only tangible fruit of that proposal.

The final draft of a Uniform Real Estate Mortgage Act was approved by the Commissioners on Uniform State Laws in 1927.[45] This act, based chiefly upon existing Minnesota legislation as a model, failed to find legislative favor, and the difficulties of the depression years resulted in much critical reexamination of it and the law of mortgages, most of it centering around the problems of foreclosure.[46] The chief defects appear to lie

in costly time-consuming foreclosure procedures, cumbersome mortgage instruments, and the law relating to moratoria, deficiency judgments, redemption periods, right to rents and profits, and future advances.[47] A survey of legislation affecting home financing, made for the National Emergency Council in 1937, listed the following factors as favorable to home financing:[48] foreclosure by advertisement; short period required to foreclose (under four months); inexpensive foreclosures ($150 or under for average, small mortgage); no moratorium law; no period of redemption from foreclosure sale or one that may be waived; state, county, and local taxes collected by one collector; provision for notice to mortgagees of tax delinquencies prior to sale; savings and loan associations exempt from taxation or subject only to a light one; effective supervision of subdivision lot

---

43. See Mowry v. Sanborn, 1877, 68 N.Y. 153.

44. Mass.Gen.Laws Ann., 1959, ch. 244, § 15; Mich. Comp.Laws Ann., 1968, §§ 600.3256–68; N.Y. Real Prop. Actions, 1963, §§ 1421–24; Wis.Stat.Ann., 1958, §§ 297.16–.19. The same provision is included in the Model Power of Sale Mortgage Foreclosure Act, § 19. In Minnesota, the sheriff's certificate of sale, when recorded, is prima facie evidence. Minn. Stat.Ann., 1947, § 580.19. There is also a time limitation on the right to set it aside, § 580.21. See also Wis.Stat., 1947, supra. Look also at provisions such as N.Y. Real Prop. Actions, 1963, § 14.11 and N.D.Cent. Code, 1960, § 35–22–21, which strengthen the purchaser's position.

45. See, 1920, Handbook, 166; 1921, ibid. 245; 1925, ibid., 303. See also Pomeroy, The Uniform Mortgage Act, 1926, 34 J.Pol.Econ. 383; notes, 1927, 27 Col.L.Rev. 861; 1925, 38 Harv.L.Rev. 651; 1926, 15 Ky.L.J. 22; 1930, 17 Va.L.Rev. 179.

46. MacChesney & Leesman, 1936, Mortgages, Foreclosures, and Reorganizations, 1936, 31 Ill.L.Rev. 287; MacChesney & Leesman, The Mortgage Foreclosure Problem, 1937, 23 A.B.A.J. 41; Carey, Brabner-Smith & Lansden, Studies in Foreclosures in Cook County, 1933, 27 Ill.L.Rev. 475; Carey, Brabner-Smith & Sullivan, Studies in Foreclosures in Cook County, 1933, 27 Ill.L.Rev. 595; Carey, Brabner-Smith & Sullivan, Studies in Realty Mortgage Foreclosures, 1933, 27 Ill.L.Rev. 849; Carey and

Brabner-Smith, Studies in Realty Mortgage Foreclosures, 1933, 27 Ill.L.Rev. 717; ibid., 1933, 28 Ill.L. Rev. 1; Sutherland, Foreclosure and Sale: Some Suggested Changes in the New York Procedure, 1937, 22 Cornell L.Q. 216; Tefft, The Myth of Strict Foreclosure, 1937, 4 U. of Chi.L.Rev. 575, 596; Mischler, After the Mortgage Moratorium—What?, 1934, 19 Iowa L.Rev. 560; Symposium on Mortgage Deficiency Judgments, 1934, 20 Va.L.Rev. 719 et seq.; Turner, An English View of the Mortgage Deficiency Judgment, 1935, 21 Va.L.Rev. 601; Bridewell, The Effects of Defective Mortgage Laws on Home Financing, 1938, 5 Law & Contemp.Probs. 545; Special Report No. 1 on Social and Economic Effects of Existing Foreclosure Procedure and Emergency Moratorium Legislation, Central Housing Committee, April 2, 1936; Special Report No. 4 on the Administration of the Payment of Taxes on Real Estate, With Recommendations Concerning Improvements in the System, Central Housing Committee, April 15, 1936; Russell, Survey of Foreclosure Operations of H. O. L. C., August 27, 1937; Russell, Foreclosures, Address before U. S. Bldg. & Loan League, October 7, 1937; Warm, A Study of Some of the Problems Concerning Foreclosure Sale and Deficiency Judgments, 1936, 6 Brooklyn L.Rev. 167; Stanley, The Effect of Economic Depression Upon Foreclosure, 1939, 27 Ky.L.Rev. 365; de Funiak, Right to a Deficiency Judgment Where Mortgagee Purchasing at Foreclosure Sale Has Later Resold at a Profit, 1939, 27 Ky.L.J. 410.

47. Bridewell, note 46, supra.

48. Comprehensive Housing Legislation Chart, Prepared by the Central Housing Committee, Sub-Committee on Law and Legislation, Issued by National Emergency Council, 1937.

sales to prevent fraud and wild cat development; laws permitting mortgage loans up to eighty per cent of appraised valuation when insured by the Federal Housing Administrator. The unfavorable features were, for the most part, the opposites of the above. They included: foreclosure by court action only (either required by law or as a practical matter) with a somewhat extended period necessary to complete it; moratorium laws and laws limiting deficiency judgments; relatively expensive foreclosures; long periods of redemption (over four months) from foreclosure sale, frequently accompanied by a right in the mortgagor to possession during the period and difficulty in obtaining a receiver; increased cost to lender of maintaining tax records due to the fact that taxes are collected by more than one official; high taxes on savings and loan associations. In 1937, after a two year study of the experience gained in nation-wide lending and foreclosures during the depression, the Central Housing Committee prepared a new draft of a Uniform Real Estate Mortgage Act which, it hoped, would protect the borrower fully, and yet give better protection to the lender and thus increase the loanable value upon home properties.[49]

The Central Housing Committee proposal was submitted to the National Conference on Uniform State Laws in 1938.[50] That body decided that there are two, or perhaps three, fields of law concerning real property mortgages that might be embodied into separate acts.[51] They are: (1) a statutory short form mortgage act; (2) a power of sale foreclosure act; and (3) a codification of some of the substantive law of mortgages. A draft of a uniform act of the first type was presented to the 1939 Conference but no action was taken[52] and it has never been approved.[53] A Model Power of Sale Foreclosure Act was approved in 1940,[54] but it had not been adopted by any state up to 1967.[55]

A Model Real Property Lien Priority Act was considered in the early sixties but no action was ever taken. There the matter rests at this writing.

Although today the analogy is not as apt as when written, a quotation from an excellent study of developments in mortgage law may well end this book. "Possibly there will never be a complete satisfactory answer to the perennially disturbing relations between mortgagor and mortgagee. It has been said that if the Prime Ministers of England met in afterlife, they would have at least one problem in common to discuss: The Irish Problem, and the not completely satisfactory methods they used in dealing with it. In like manner, it is possible that if all the judges and legislators in the history of Anglo-American jurisprudence could convene together they would discuss the mortgage problem without end and without answer." [56]

---

49. See Reeve, The New Proposal for a Uniform Real Estate Mortgage Act, 1938, 5 Law & Contemp. Probs. 564; Russell and Bridewell, Mortgage Law and Mortgage Lending, 1938, 14 J. of Land & Pub. Util.Econ. 301; note, 1938, 86 U. of Pa.L.Rev. 517. See, also, the draft of the act submitted by Horace Russell, General Counsel, Federal Home Loan Bank Board, to the Section on Real Property, Probate, and Trust Law of the American Bar Association and to the Commissioners on Uniform State Laws, August 31, 1937. See further, 1938, Handbook, Commissioners on Uniform State Laws, 124; 1939, ibid., 255; 1940, ibid., 254. And see, Skilton, Government and the Mortgage Debtor, 201–206; Skilton, Proposed Uniform Mortgage Legislation, 1942, 9 Am.Law School Rev. 1128; 1941, 27 Va.L.Rev. 926.

50. See 1938, Handbook, Commissioners on Uniform State Laws, 124.

51. Ibid.

52. 1939, Handbook, 79, 255, 257.

53. It is not included in the 1967 list of uniform acts or model acts that have been approved or adopted. See 1967 Handbook, 163.

54. 1940 Handbook, 175, 254, 256.

55. See 1967 Handbook, 163.

For some proposals for foreclosure in federal courts in diversity cases, see Prather, Foreclosure of the Security Interest, 1957 U. of Ill.L. Forum 420, 448–461.

56. Skilton, Government and the Mortgage Debtor, 206.

TABLE OF CASES

References are to Pages

M

788   TABLE OF CASES
References are to Pages

INDEX